# THE GROWTH OF WORLD INDUSTRY, 1938-1961: NATIONAL TABLES

Presented in this publication are internationally comparable data on the industrial sector for almost 100 countries or territories of the world. The figures shown measure the growth in industrial output and employment from 1938 to 1961 and indicate the changes that took place in the mining, manufacturing, construction and electricity and gas industries. The data furnished also point to the existing relationships between industrial activity and other facets of the economy and to the links between the resources employed in and the output of the various industries.

In the chapter of the publication devoted to each of the countries or territories covered, the available data for the period, 1938-1961, are given on:

- Production and fixed capital formation in all sectors of the economy
- Index numbers of industrial production
- Index numbers of industrial employment
- Value added in industrial production
- Employment and wages and salaries paid in industrial activities
- Electricity and fuels consumed in industrial production
- The capacity of installed power equipment
- The number of industrial units

Also shown in each chapter are analytical measures such as:

- Average annual rates of growth in output and employment
- Value added per unit of labour employed
- Consumption of energy and capacity of installed power per unit of labour employed

All of the data presented are classified according to the International Standard Industrial Classification and have been compiled on as comparable a basis internationally as was feasible.

Each chapter of the publication starts with introductory notes on:

- The national publications and other documents furnishing the data
- The field of coverage, concepts and definitions for the data
- The comparability of the series of data

Department of Economic and Social Affairs
Statistical Office of the United Nations

Département des affaires économiques et sociales
Bureau de statistique de l'Organisation des Nations Unies

# THE GROWTH OF WORLD INDUSTRY
# LA CROISSANCE DE L'INDUSTRIE MONDIALE

## 1938-1961

## NATIONAL TABLES
## TABLEAUX PAR PAYS

UNITED NATIONS / NATIONS UNIES
New York, 1963

ST/STAT/SER.P/2

| UNITED NATIONS PUBLICATION | PUBLICATION DES NATIONS UNIES |
| --- | --- |
| Sales No.: 63. XVII. 5 | Numéro de vente : 63. XVII. 5 |

Price: $U.S. 10.00
(or equivalent in other currencies)

Prix: 10 dollars (USA)
(ou l'équivalent en monnaie du pays)

Inquiries should be directed to:

PUBLISHING SERVICE
UNITED NATIONS
NEW YORK, N.Y.

See also List of Sales Agents
on last page

Adressez toutes demandes de renseignements
au:

SERVICE DES PUBLICATIONS,
NATIONS UNIES
NEW YORK (N.Y.)

Voir aussi la liste des dépositaires
à la fin du volume

# TABLE OF CONTENTS—TABLE DES MATIERES

# TABLE OF CONTENTS (continued) — TABLE DES MATIERES (suite)

# INTRODUCTION

Internationally comparable data are presented in this publication on the industrial sector (the mining, manufacturing, construction, and electricity and gas industries) in relation to other aspects of the economy, for almost 100 countries or territories.[1] The series of statistics shown indicate the role of the industrial sector in the economy of these areas, delineate the character and structure of the sector, and measure the output resulting from and the key resources employed in industrial activities. Data are also furnished that are designed to reveal the relationships between the level of industrial output and other aspects of economic activity and the productivity with which key resources are utilized in the various industries. A separate chapter of the publication is devoted to each area or territory; and the statistical series presented therein refer to the period, 1938-1961, in so far as available figures permit.

The available data on the contribution of the branches of industrial activity to the gross product and on the growth in the output of these industries relative to that of other sectors of the economy, are furnished for the years, 1938, 1948 and 1950-1961. This is also the case for figures of gross fixed capital formation in the industrial, as well as other sectors of the economy, and for statistics on the major sources of demand (e.g., consumption, gross capital formation and exports) for the gross product. These figures have been derived from the national accounts of the areas covered and where available, are shown in Table 1 of each chapter. Index numbers for 1938 and each year of the period, 1948-1961, are given on the movement in the level of output and employment for each kind of mining and manufacturing, for construction, and for the electricity and gas industries. Where available, these indexes are set out in Tables 2 and 3, respectively, of each chapter. The other tables in each chapter are devoted to detailed statistics for individual industries, on value added, the employment of and payments to labour, the use of power equipment, and the consumption of electricity and other sources of energy. These figures refer to 1938, 1948, 1953, 1958 or years close to these dates and have been derived from industrial censuses or similar types of inquiries.

Set out in the tables of each chapter are not only basic data on the items mentioned above but also derived figures

La présente publication contient des données internationalement comparables sur le secteur industriel (industries extractives et manufacturières, bâtiment et travaux publics, industries de l'électricité et du gaz) de près de 100 pays ou territoires, considéré dans ses rapports avec d'autres éléments de l'économie[1]. Les séries statistiques présentées montrent le rôle du secteur industriel dans l'économie de ces régions, en font ressortir les caractéristiques et la structure et indiquent, pour les différentes activités industrielles, la production obtenue et les principales ressources utilisées. On trouvera également des données qui visent à mettre en évidence les rapports entre le niveau de la production industrielle et d'autres aspects de l'activité économique, et l'efficacité d'utilisation des ressources importantes dans les diverses industries. Un chapitre distinct est consacré à chaque région ou territoire; les séries statistiques présentées ont été établies pour la période 1938-1961, dans la mesure où les chiffres disponibles le permettaient.

Les données disponibles sur la contribution des différentes branches d'activité industrielle au produit brut et sur l'expansion de la production de ces industries par rapport à celle d'autres secteurs de l'économie sont fournies pour les années 1938, 1948 et 1950 à 1961. Il en est de même pour les chiffres de la formation brute de capital fixe dans le secteur industriel et dans d'autres secteurs de l'économie et pour les statistiques relatives aux sources principales de la demande du produit brut (par exemple, la consommation, la formation brute de capital et les exportations). Ces chiffres ont été tirés des comptabilités nationales des pays des régions considérées et, lorsqu'on a pu se les procurer, on les a reproduits, dans chaque chapitre, au tableau 1. Pour 1938 et pour chaque année comprise entre 1948 et 1961, on donne les indices de la variation du niveau de la production et de l'emploi dans chaque type d'industrie extractive et manufacturière, dans le bâtiment et les travaux publics et dans les industries de l'électricité et du gaz. Chaque fois que l'on a pu obtenir ces indices, on les a fait figurer, dans chaque chapitre, aux tableaux 2 et 3 respectivement. Les autres tableaux de chaque chapitre contiennent des renseignements détaillés sur différentes industries, sur la valeur ajoutée, l'emploi et la rémunération de la main-d'œuvre, l'utilisation de la puissance installée et la consommation d'électricité et d'autres formes d'énergie. Ces chiffres portent sur les années 1938, 1948, 1953 et 1958 ou sur des années proches de ces dates et sont tirés de recensements industriels ou d'enquêtes analogues.

Dans chaque chapitre, les tableaux présentent non seulement des données de base sur les rubriques mentionnées

---

[1] The industrial sector consists of units classified to the following parts of the International Standard Industrial Classification of all Economic Activity: Mining and quarrying (Division 1); Manufacturing (Divisions 2-3); Construction (Division 4); and Electricity, gas and steam (Major group 51). For definitions and descriptions of these categories see: *International Standard Industrial Classification of All Economic Activities*, Statistical Papers, Series M, No. 4, Rev. 1, Sales No: 58.XVII.7, Statistical Office of the United Nations, New York, 1958.

[1] Le secteur industriel comprend les unités classées dans les parties ci-après de la Classification internationale, par industrie, de toutes les branches d'activité économique : Industries extractives (Branche 1); Industries manufacturières (Branches 2 et 3); Bâtiment et travaux publics (Branche 4); Électricité, gaz et vapeur (Classe 51). Ces catégories sont définies et décrites dans la *Classification internationale type, par industrie, de toutes les branches d'activité économique*, Etudes statistiques, série M, No 4/Rev. 1, No de vente : 58.XVII.7, Bureau de statistique de l'Organisation des Nations Unies, New York, 1958.

designed to reveal some of the patterns implicit in the basic figures. These derived statistics consist of distributions in per cent of selected items of data, average annual rates of change in such aggregates as the gross domestic products at constant prices or index numbers of industrial production, and analytical ratios such as value added per unit of wages and salaries paid or consumption of energy per unit of labour employed. Some of the derived figures highlight, in the case of each country or territory, the place, nature and structure of the industrial sector at various points in time. Other analytical measures indicate the rates of growth in the output from and the resources employed in the various industrial activities, relative to one another and to the rates of change in other sectors of the national economy.

It is considered that the data presented in this publication for almost 100 countries or territories furnish valuable basic materials for analyses of the process of industrial growth and the role of the industrial sector in economic development. Statistical series are furnished for countries or territories at various stages of industrialization and with varying endowments in natural and other resources. These countries are also characterized by differing economic and social institutions and arrangements. Furthermore, the period, 1938-1961, witnessed very marked expansion in industrial activity in the case of most countries of the world. Associated with this growth were substantial changes in the characteristics and structure of the industrial sector and significant alterations in the coefficients relating the resources employed in industrial activities to output. The data shown in this volume should also be of considerable interest in inquiries into the economic characteristics and potentialities of each of the countries or territories covered, as well as studies of the distribution of industrial activities and resources over the world.

This publication is a more current and expanded version of Part II of *Patterns of Industrial Growth, 1938-1958*.[2] Statistical series are presented for later years than in Part II of the earlier publication, for many more countries and on a greater number of items. It is planned that another publication will be issued in order to revise and extend Part I of *Patterns of Industrial Growth, 1938-1958*.[2] In that publication basic data and estimates will be presented for the period, 1938 through 1961 or 1962, for regions of the world and for countries grouped according to stage of industrialization, as well as for the world as a whole. The publication will also contain analyses of the data set out there and in this volume. The studies will be designed to reveal the character of and strategic factors in the process of industrial growth and the degree of industrialization and the industrial strength of various parts of the world. Attention will also be devoted to the relationships between industrial activities and resources and other aspects of economies.

ci-dessus, mais encore d'autres chiffres qui en ont été tirés afin de mettre en relief certaines caractéristiques que ces données par elles-mêmes ne font pas apparaître. Les statistiques ainsi élaborées comprennent la répartition en pourcentage pour certaines catégories de données, les taux annuels moyens de variation d'agrégats tels que le produit intérieur brut aux prix constants ou les indices de la production industrielle, et des rapports de caractère analytique comme la valeur ajoutée par unité de traitements et salaires payés ou la consommation d'énergie par unité de main-d'œuvre employée. Certaines des données obtenues indirectement font ressortir, pour chaque pays ou territoire, le rôle, la nature et la structure du secteur industriel à différentes dates. D'autres données analytiques permettent de comparer les taux d'accroissement de la production de diverses industries et de la consommation de ressources de ces industries entre eux et avec les taux de variation correspondants d'autres secteurs de l'économie nationale.

Les données contenues dans le présent ouvrage, qui concernent près de cent pays ou territoires, constituent, estime-t-on, une documentation de base utile pour analyser le processus de l'expansion industrielle et le rôle du secteur industriel dans le développement économique. Les séries statistiques présentées se rapportent à des pays et territoires qui en sont à des degrés différents d'industrialisation et dont les ressources naturelles et autres ne sont pas les mêmes. Ces pays se caractérisent également par des systèmes et des mécanismes économiques et sociaux différents. De plus, la période comprise entre 1938 et 1961 a été marquée par un accroissement très prononcé de l'activité industrielle dans la plupart des pays du monde. Cette expansion s'est accompagnée de modifications appréciables des caractéristiques et de la structure du secteur industriel, ainsi que des coefficients qui expriment le rapport entre les ressources employées par l'industrie et la production industrielle. En outre, les données qui figurent dans le présent volume devraient être d'une grande utilité tant pour les enquêtes sur les caractéristiques et les possibilités économiques de chacun des pays ou territoires considérés que pour les études sur la répartition des activités industrielles et des ressources dans le monde.

La présente publication est une version mise à jour et augmentée de la deuxième partie de *Aperçu de l'expansion industrielle, 1938-1958*[2]. Elle contient des séries statistiques pour les années ultérieures à 1958 et pour un plus grand nombre de pays et de rubriques. On compte publier séparément une édition revisée et augmentée de la première partie de *Aperçu de l'expansion industrielle, 1938-1958*[2]. Cet ouvrage contiendra des données de base et des estimations se rapportant à la période comprise entre 1938 et 1961 ou 1962, aux régions du monde et aux pays groupés selon le degré d'industrialisation, ainsi qu'à l'ensemble du monde. On y trouvera également des analyses des données qui y seront présentées ainsi que de celles du présent volume. Ces études seront conçues de manière à faire ressortir les caractéristiques et les facteurs essentiels du processus d'expansion industrielle, ainsi que le degré d'industrialisation et la puissance industrielle de diverses parties du monde. Les rapports entre les activités industrielles et les ressources et d'autres éléments de l'économie y seront également examinés.

2 *Patterns of Industrial Growth, 1938-1958*, Sales No: 59.XVII.6, United Nations, New York, 1960.

2 *Aperçu de l'expansion industrielle, 1938-1958*, No de vente: 59.XVII.6, Nations Unies, New York, 1960.

## Sources and Comparability of Data

The Statistical Office of the United Nations has compiled the data set out in this publication from available national statistical publications and the annual national accounts questionnaires and other correspondence received from national statistical authorities. The sources utilized in putting together the various statistical series for each country or territory are enumerated in the introductory text to the chapter on the area. The data show in each chapter have been compiled on as comparable a basis internationally as was feasible. In classifying the figures according to kind of economic activity, the International Standard Industrial Classification was followed.[3] In gathering and compiling the series from national accounts, the United Nations system of national accounts was employed; and in compiling the data on the characteristics and structure of the industrial sector, the international recommendations on basic industrial statistics were utilized.[4] The definitions from these international recommendations utilized in compiling the data in the publication are summarized below. Significant deviations from the pertinent international recommendations in the definitions of the items of data set out in the tables of each chapter are indicated in the introductory text to the chapter or in the footnotes to the tables. Differences between the classification of the data according to kind of economic activity and the International Standard Classification are, in general, shown in the footnotes to the tables. In the case of index numbers of industrial production and employment, the introductory text to each chapter furnishes a brief description of the field covered in these series and the concepts and methods utilized by the national statistical authority in gathering and compiling them. The introductory text to each chapter also describes the field of coverage of the data shown in the tables on the characteristics and structure of industrial units and points to any significant lapses in comparability in the data for different periods of time.

## International Definitions of National Accounts Statistics

The various measures of production in the United Nations system of national accounts (e.g., gross domestic or national product or net national product) relate to the total output of final goods and non-factor services during a period. Final goods and non-factor services are those which have not been purchased and charged to current costs (i.e., consumed in production) by producers (enterprises) during the period. The scope of the goods and services to be included is broadly defined as follows:

In the case of units principally engaged in agriculture, forestry, hunting, fishing or mining, all production in these activities and all other goods and services produced and exchanged. In the case of units principally engaged in any other kind of economic activity listed in the International Standard Industrial Classification, the total of all their

---

[3] For this scheme of classification see *International Standard Industrial Classification of All Economic Activities*, op. cit.

[4] For the system of national accounts see *A System of National Accounts and Supporting Tables*, Studies in Methods, Series F, No. 2, Rev. 1, Sales No: 59.XVII.11, United Nations, New York, 1960. For the recommendations on basic industrial statistics see *International Recommendations in Basic Industrial Statistics*, Statistical Papers, Series M, No. 17, Rev. 1, Sales No: 60.XVII.8, United Nations, New York, 1960.

---

## Sources et comparabilité des données

Le Bureau de statistique de l'ONU a établi les données qui figurent dans le présent ouvrage à partir des publications des services de statistiques nationaux ainsi que des réponses aux questionnaires annuels sur la comptabilité nationale et autres communications que ces services lui envoient. Le chapitre relatif à chaque région comprend une introduction où sont indiquées les sources que l'on a utilisées pour construire les diverses séries statistiques concernant chaque pays ou territoire. Les données qui figurent dans chaque chapitre ont été rendues, dans la mesure du possible, internationalement comparables. Pour le classement des données selon le type d'activité économique, le Bureau de statistique a suivi la classification internationale type[3]. Pour rassembler et préparer les séries à partir des comptes nationaux, on s'est conformé au système de comptabilité nationale de l'ONU; pour établir les données sur les caractéristiques et la structure du secteur industriel, on a appliqué les recommandations internationales relatives aux statistiques industrielles de base[4]. On trouvera ci-après un bref résumé des définitions empruntées à ces recommandations internationales que l'on a utilisées pour établir les données reproduites dans la présente publication. Lorsque les définitions des catégories de données présentées dans les tableaux de chaque chapitre s'écartent sensiblement des recommandations internationales correspondantes, l'introduction au chapitre ou les notes des tableaux donnent des précisions à ce sujet. Les divergences entre la classification des données selon le type d'activité économique et la Classification internationale type sont généralement indiquées dans les notes des tableaux. Dans le cas des nombres-indices de la production industrielle et de l'emploi dans l'industrie, l'introduction à chaque chapitre donne une brève description du champ des séries ainsi que des concepts et méthodes que les services de statistique du pays considéré ont appliqués pour les recueillir et les construire. L'introduction au chapitre décrit également la portée des données qui figurent dans les tableaux sur les caractéristiques et la structure des unités industrielles et souligne, lorsqu'il y a lieu, les défauts de comparabilité importants entre les données pour différentes périodes.

## Définitions internationales des statistiques de la comptabilité nationale

Les diverses mesures de la production employées dans le système de comptabilité nationale de l'ONU (par exemple, le produit national ou intérieur brut ou le produit national net) se rapportent à la production totale de produits finaux et de services non facteurs de production pendant une période donnée. Les produits finals et les services non facteurs de production sont ceux qui n'ont été ni achetés, ni imputés aux dépenses courantes (c'est-à-dire consommés au cours de la production) par des producteurs (entreprises) pendant la période considérée. D'une manière générale, les biens et services à enregistrer peuvent être définis comme suit :

Dans le cas des unités occupées principalement dans l'agriculture, la sylviculture, la chasse, la pêche ou les industries extractives, toute la production qui résulte de ces activités et tous les autres biens et services produits et échangés. En ce qui concerne les unités occupées principalement dans tout autre type d'activité économique rémunéré dans la

---

[3] Voir *Classification internationale type, par industrie, de toutes les branches d'activité économique*, op. cit.

[4] Voir *Système de comptabilité nationale et tableaux connexes*, Etudes méthodologiques, série F, No 2/Rev. 1, No de vente : 59.XVII.11, Nations Unies, New York, 1960, et *Recommandations internationales relatives aux statistiques industrielles de base*, Etudes statistiques, série M, No 17/Rev. 1, No de vente : 60.XVII.8, Nations Unies, New York, 1960.

output of agricultural and mining products, of all production in their own industry and of other production that is exchanged.

Since home-ownership is regarded as an industry for national accounting purposes, production includes the services of owner-occupied dwellings. In the tables on data from national accounts, this activity has been designated as Division 9 of the International Standard Industrial Classification.

A major difference between the system of national accounts of the United Nations and the system of material product accounts of countries with centrally planned economies, is the breadth of the concept of production utilized. In the case of the system of material product accounts, the activities of units classified to certain portions of the International Standard Industrial Classification are not included in production. In general, this is the case for units that would be classified under the categories, Government, Community, Business or Personal services, of the International Classification and for the rental of dwellings or other buildings. Other activities which do not involve the production or handling of commodities—for example, communication services, transport of passengers—are also often excluded from the concept of production. Where such activities are included in given figures of the material product, this fact is indicated in the introductory text or footnotes to the tables of the pertinent chapter.

The measures of the value of production that are included in the United Nations system of national accounts and utilized in the statistics shown in chapters of this publication, are defined as follows:

1. *Gross domestic product at market prices* is the market value of the product, before deduction of provisions for the consumption of fixed capital, attributable to factor services rendered to resident producers of the given country. It is identically equal to the sum of consumption expenditure and gross domestic capital formation, private and public, and the net exports of goods and services of the given country.

2. *Gross domestic product at factor cost* is the value at factor cost of the product, before deduction of provisions for the consumption of fixed capital, attributable to factor services rendered to resident producers of the given country. It differs from the gross domestic product at market prices by the exclusion of the excess of indirect taxes over subsidies.

3. *Gross national product at market prices* is the market value of the product, before deduction of provisions for the consumption of fixed capital, attributable to the factors of production supplied by normal residents of the given country. It is identically equal to the sum of consumption expenditure and gross domestic capital formation, private and public, and the net exports of goods and services plus the net factor incomes received from abroad.

4. *Net national product at factor cost* is the value at factor cost of the product, after deduction of provisions for the consumption of fixed capital, attributable to the factors of production supplied by normal residents of the given country. It is identically equal to the national income. National income is the sum of the incomes accruing to factors of production supplied by normal residents of the given country before deduction of direct taxes.

In addition, figures of the net and gross material product are set out in chapters of the publication on countries utilizing the system of material product accounts. The net material

Classification internationale type, la somme de toute leur production de produits agricoles et miniers de toute la production de leur propre industrie et des autres produits qui sont échangés.

Etant donné que la comptabilité nationale considère que le propriétaire d'une maison d'habitation exerce une activité économique, les services rendus par les immeubles d'habitation occupés par leur propriétaire sont compris dans la production. Dans les tableaux qui reproduisent les données des comptabilités nationales, cette activité a été classée dans la branche 9 de la Classification internationale type.

Le système de comptabilité nationale de l'ONU et le système de comptabilité du produit matériel appliqué par les pays à économie planifiée présentent une différence primordiale qui tient à la portée même de la notion de production. Dans le système de comptabilité du produit matériel, on ne fait pas entrer dans la production les activités d'unités rangées dans certaines parties de la Classification internationale type. Il s'agit en général d'unités qui seraient classées dans les groupes "Services gouvernementaux", "Services fournis à la collectivité", "Services fournis aux entreprises" ou "Services personnels" de la Classification internationale, et de la location de maisons d'habitation ou autres bâtiments. Il arrive souvent aussi que d'autres activités qui ne comprennent pas la production ou la manutention de produits — par exemple, les services de communications, les transports de voyageurs — soient exclues du concept de production. Lorsque ces activités ont été comprises dans certaines données relatives au produit matériel, le fait est signalé dans l'introduction ou les notes des tableaux du chapitre pertinent.

Les mesures de la valeur de la production qui sont employées dans le système de comptabilité nationale de l'ONU et dans les statistiques présentées dans les chapitres de la présente publication sont définies comme suit :

1. Le *produit intérieur brut aux prix du marché* est la valeur commerciale, avant déduction des provisions pour consommation de capital fixe, du produit attribuable aux services facteurs de production fournis aux producteurs résidents du pays considéré. Il est identiquement égal à la somme des dépenses de consommation et de la formation brute de capital intérieur, privées et publiques, et des exportations nettes de biens et services du pays considéré.

2. Le *produit intérieur brut au coût des facteurs* est la valeur, au coût des facteurs, et avant déduction des provisions pour consommation de capital fixe, du produit attribuable aux services facteurs de production fournis aux producteurs résidant dans le pays considéré. Il diffère du produit intérieur brut au prix du marché en ce qu'il ne comprend pas l'excédent des impôts indirects sur les subventions.

3. Le *produit national brut aux prix du marché* est la valeur commerciale, avant déduction des provisions pour consommation de capital fixe, du produit attribuable aux facteurs de production fournis par les agents qui résident normalement dans le pays considéré. Il est identiquement égal à la somme des dépenses de consommation et de la formation brute de capital intérieur, privées et publiques, et des exportations nettes de biens et services, plus les rentrées nettes de revenus de facteurs reçus de l'étranger.

4. Le *produit national net au coût des facteurs* est la valeur, au coût des facteurs et après déduction des provisions pour consommation de capital fixe, du produit attribuable aux facteurs de production fournis par les personnes qui résident normalement dans le pays considéré. Il est identiquement égal au revenu national. Le revenu national est la somme des revenus correspondant aux facteurs de production fournis par les personnes qui résident normalement dans le pays considéré, avant déduction des impôts directs.

En outre, les chapitres relatifs aux pays qui utilisent le système de comptabilité du produit matériel contiennent des données sur le produit matériel net et le produit matériel

product is the value at market prices of the domestic (territorial) material product after deduction of provisions for consumption of fixed capital. The gross material product is the market value of this output before deduction of these provisions.

The definition in the United Nations system of national accounts of the other items for which figures are set out in the chapters of this volume are as follows:

1. *Consumpion expenditure* is the total of expenditures on private consumption and government consumption. The former type of expenditures consist of the value of final expenditure by households and private non-profit institutions on current goods and services less sales of similar goods (mainly second-hand) and services plus value of gifts in kind (net) received from the rest of the world. For households, all purchases of goods, irrespective of their durability, are entered with the exception of land and buildings. Government consumption expenditures consist of the compensation of employees and purchases by general government from enterprises and from the rest of the world less sales of goods and services (other than surplus stores which are treated as a decrease in government stocks) to enterprises and households. The general government sector covers all central, state or local government agencies other than those defined as public enterprises. Expenditure of a capital nature for national defence (excluding civil defence) is treated as consumption expenditure while all expenditure on capital formation for civil purposes is included in gross domestic fixed capital formation. Transfers in kind made by general government to the rest of the world are excluded, being included in exports of the donor country while transfers in kind received from abroad by general government form part of its consumption expenditure. Cash transfers are not included in any component of final expenditure. However, transfers of military equipment are entered in consumption expenditure rather than in exports and omitted in the accounts of the receiving country.

2. *Gross domestic capital formation* is the sum of gross fixed capital formation and increases in stocks. Increases in stocks are equivalent to the value of the physical change in raw materials, work in progress (other than work in progress on dwellings and non-residential buildings which is included in fixed capital formation) and finished goods held by enterprises. Changes in stocks of strategic materials or other emergency stocks held by general government are also included. Increases in natural resources due to growth, as with forests and standing crops, are excluded entirely. Changes in stocks of commodities owned by residents but located abroad are included while changes in stocks held in the country but owned by non-residents are excluded.

3. *Gross domestic fixed capital formation* is the value of purchases and own-account construction of fixed assets by enterprises (including households in their capacity as house owners), private non-profit institutions and general government. Expenditures on irrigation projects, flood control, forest clearance, land reclamation and improvement, etc., and on the development of plantations, orchards, vineyards, forests, etc., are included. The value of newly discovered mineral deposits and other natural resources is, on the other hand, excluded. In principle, expenditures on repairs over and above what is needed to keep the capital goods in the state of continuous good working condition are included but normal repairs and maintenance are treated as current expenditure. Transfer costs involved in the purchase of used domestic assets, including transportation costs, legal fees, installation expenses, etc., are part of fixed capital formation. Change in work in progress in construction are also included.

4. *Exports and imports of goods and services* consist of the value of the goods and services sold to the rest of the world and the value of the corresponding purchases, respectively. These goods and services comprise merchandise and transportation, insurance and other non-factor services. The value of gifts in kind and other exports and imports financed by means of international transfers is included but the

brut. Le produit matériel net est la valeur, aux prix du marché, du produit matériel intérieur (territorial) après déduction des provisions pour consommation de capital fixe. Le produit matériel brut est la valeur commerciale de cette production avant déduction de ces provisions.

Le système de comptabilité nationale des Nations Unies définit comme suit les autres rubriques sous lesquelles des données sont présentées dans les différents chapitres du présent ouvrage :

1. La *dépense de consommation* est la somme de la dépense de consommation privée et de la dépense de consommation de l'Etat. La dépense de consommation privée est égale à la valeur des dépenses terminales des ménages et organismes privés à but non lucratif en biens et services courants, moins les ventes de biens (principalement de biens de reprise) et services analogues, plus les dons en nature (montant net) reçus du reste du monde. Pour les ménages, on inclut les achats de tous biens, quelle que soit leur durée, sauf les terres et les bâtiments. La dépense de consommation de l'Etat est égale à la rémunération du personnel et aux achats effectués par l'Etat auprès d'entreprises et du reste du monde, moins les ventes de biens et services (autres que celles de surplus qui sont assimilées à une diminution des stocks de l'Etat) aux entreprises et aux ménages. Le secteur de l'Etat englobe tous les services publics relevant du pouvoir central, des Etats ou autorités locales, qui ne répondent pas à la définition des entreprises publiques. Les dépenses de capital faites pour la défense nationale (à l'exclusion de la défense passive) sont traitées comme des dépenses de consommation, tandis que toutes les dépenses concourant à la formation de capital à des fins civiles sont comprises dans la formation brute de capital fixe intérieur. Les transferts en nature effectués par l'Etat au profit du reste du monde figurent non sous cette rubrique mais parmi les exportations du pays donateur, tandis que les transferts en nature que l'Etat reçoit de l'étranger font partie de ses dépenses de consommation. Les transferts en espèces ne sont comptabilisés dans aucun élément de la dépense terminale. Les transferts de matériel militaire s'inscrivent dans les dépenses de consommation et non dans les exportations; le pays destinataire ne les fait donc pas figurer dans ses comptes.

2. La *formation brute de capital intérieur* est la somme de la formation brute de capital fixe et de l'accroissement des stocks. L'accroissement des stocks équivaut à la valeur du progrès des travaux en cours (autres que la construction de bâtiments résidentiels et non résidentiels, qui est comprise dans la formation de capital fixe), de la variation du volume des matières premières et des stocks de produits finis détenus par les entreprises. Les variations des stocks de l'Etat, qu'il s'agisse de produits stratégiques ou d'autres produits précieux en temps de crise, figurent également sous cette rubrique. L'accroissement des ressources naturelles dû à la croissance végétale des forêts et des récoltes sur pied est entièrement exclu. Il est tenu compte des variations des stocks de marchandises appartenant à des résidents, mais situés à l'étranger, mais non des modifications concernant les stocks détenus dans le pays par des personnes qui n'y résident pas.

3. La *formation brute de capital fixe intérieur* est la valeur des biens de capital fixe achetés ou construits pour leur propre compte par les entreprises, y compris les ménages agissant en tant que propriétaires d'habitations, les organismes privés à but non lucratif et l'Etat. Les dépenses relatives aux travaux d'irrigation, à la défense contre les inondations, au déboisement, à l'assèchement et à la bonification des terres, etc., ainsi qu'à la construction de plantations, de vergers, de vignobles, de forêts, etc., entrent en ligne de compte. Par contre, la valeur des gisements minéraux et autres ressources naturelles nouvellement découvertes est exclue. En principe, on inclut toutes les dépenses de réparation au-delà de celles qui sont nécessaires pour maintenir constamment les biens de capital en bon état de fonctionnement mais non les réparations et l'entretien normaux, qui sont traités comme des dépenses courantes. Les frais de transfert découlant de l'achat, dans le pays considéré, de biens usagés, y compris les frais de transport, les honoraires d'hommes de loi, les dépenses d'installation, etc., font partie de la formation de capital fixe. On peut inclure aussi le progrès des travaux de construction en cours.

4. Les *exportations et importations de biens et de services* représentent la valeur des biens et services achetés et vendus au reste du monde, respectivement. Ces biens et services comprennent le coût des marchandises et les frais de transport, d'assurance et autres services ne provenant pas des facteurs de production. On enregistre la valeur des dons en nature et d'autres exportations et importations financées par

value of military equipment transferred between governments is excluded. In the case of some countries with fluctuating or multiple exchange rates, the value in national currency of exports and imports of merchandise may be based on an official or similar fixed exchange rate rather than an average effective exchange rate.

The definitions of a number of the categories of expenditure in the system of material product accounts differ significantly from that in the United Nations system of national accounts. For example, consumption expenditures are the sum of individual (personal) consumption and collective consumption of goods and services included in the material product. Collective consumption includes the expenditures on such goods and services of a current nature by all organizations, agencies and institutions engaged in activities which are considered non-productive—i.e., do not contribute to the material product. Expenditures on goods by these organizations for capital formation are covered under net domestic fixed capital formation. The figures of fixed capital formation shown in material product accounts are after deduction of provisions for consumption of capital. Net domestic capital formation is the sum of the value of changes in stocks and net domestic fixed capital formation. Included in the data on changes in stocks are the stocks of productive enterprises only—i.e., units contributing to the material product. The scope and valuation of exports and imports in material product accounts also differ from that in the United Nations system of national accounts.

### Index Numbers of Industrial Production and Employment

Index numbers of industrial production indicate the trend over time in some measure of output, expressed in constant prices. These index numbers are essentially ratios by which quanta of output during two intervals of time (e.g., a current year and a base year) are compared to one another. As has been recommended internationally, many of the series of index numbers set out in the publication relate, in principle, to the value, in constant prices, of net output—in most instances, value added but, in some instances, contribution to the gross or net domestic product.[5] These measures of net output are usually priced at factor cost.

A number of series of indexes dealing, in principle, with net output, relate, in practice, to the value in constant prices, of a mixture of net output and gross production. This is due to the way in which these series of indexes are compiled. As may be noted from the introductory text to various chapters, much of the basic data for the series of index numbers consists of the quantity of gross output for important and representative products; and in combining the elementary series of relatives (ratios) based on these data into index numbers for detailed classes of activity, the weights that are frequently utilized are proportional to the value of gross output of

des transferts internationaux, mais non celle des cessions de matériel militaire entre Etats. Dans le cas de certains pays ayant des taux de change multiples ou variables, la valeur des exportations et des importations de marchandises en monnaie nationale peut être calculée d'après un taux de change officiel ou tout autre taux fixe analogue, plutôt que d'après la moyenne des cours de change effectifs.

Le système de comptabilité du produit matériel donne de plusieurs catégories de dépenses des définitions qui diffèrent sensiblement de celles du système de comptabilité nationale de l'ONU. Par exemple, les dépenses de consommation sont définies comme la somme de la consommation individuelle (personnelle) et de la consommation collective de biens et services qui entrent dans le produit matériel. La consommation collective comprend les dépenses faites en échange de tels biens et services de caractère courant par toutes les organisations, organismes et institutions dont les activités sont considérées comme non productives, en ce sens qu'elles ne contribuent pas au produit matériel. Les achats de biens effectués par ces organisations en vue de la formation de capital sont compris dans la formation nette de capital fixe intérieur. Les chiffres de la formation de capital fixe sont enregistrés, dans la comptabilité du produit matériel, après déduction des provisions pour consommation de capital. La formation nette de capital intérieur est la somme de la valeur des variations des stocks et de la formation nette de capital fixe intérieur. Les données relatives aux variations des stocks portent sur les stocks des entreprises productives seulement, c'est-à-dire des unités qui contribuent au produit matériel. Dans la comptabilité du produit matériel, la notion et la méthode d'évaluation des exportations et des importations diffèrent également de celles du système de comptabilité nationale de l'ONU.

### Nombres-indices de la production industrielle et de l'emploi dans l'industrie

Les nombres-indices de la production industrielle indiquent l'évolution dans le temps d'une mesure quelconque de la production, exprimée en prix constants. Ce sont essentiellement des rapports qui permettent de comparer le volume de la production pendant deux intervalles de temps (par exemple, l'année en cours et une année de base). Conformément aux recommandations internationales, un grand nombre des séries d'indices du présent ouvrage se rapportent en principe à la valeur en prix constants de la production nette, c'est-à-dire dans la plupart des cas la valeur ajoutée, et, parfois, la contribution au produit intérieur brut ou net[5]. La production nette est généralement calculée au coût des facteurs.

Plusieurs séries d'indices qui se rapportent, en principe, à la production nette ont trait, en pratique, à la valeur en prix constants d'une combinaison de la production nette et de la production brute. Cela tient à la façon dont ces séries sont établies. Comme il ressort de l'introduction aux divers chapitres, la majeure partie des données dont on extrait les séries de nombres-indices concernent le volume de la production brute de produits importants et caractéristiques; d'autre part, lorsque l'on combine les séries élémentaires de rapports fondés sur ces données en nombres-indices relatifs à divers types d'activité, on utilise fréquemment des poids

---

[5] For the international suggestions and recommendations see *Index Numbers of Industrial Production*, Series F, No. 1, Sales No: 50.XVII.4, Statistical Office of the United Nations, New York, 15 September 1960.

[5] Ces suggestions et recommandations internationales se trouvent dans *Nombres-indices de la production industrielle*, série F, No 1, No de vente : 50.XVII.4, Bureau de statistique de l'Organisation des Nations Unies, New York, 15 septembre 1960.

these commodities during the base year. However, the weights utilized in combining these index numbers into those for broader classes of industrial activity are determined from data on the value of net output. In the case of a number of countries with centrally planned economies, the series of index numbers of industrial production presented in this publication relate, in principle as well as in practice, to the value, in constant enterprise prices (i.e., excluding turnover taxes), of gross output. These series of index numbers are usually compiled from basic data on all elements of gross output.

Most series of indexes of industrial production shown in this publication are, in effect, compiled by use of a base-weighted (Laspeyres) formula and fixed weights for the base year. Many of these series are also compiled in successive stages. The first step in compilation usually is the combination of elementary series of relatives on quanta of output for industrial products into index numbers for detailed categories of industrial activity. The following steps consist of compiling index numbers for successively broader classes of activity from the indexes resulting from the immediately preceding step. These practices have been recommended internationally.

The field covered in the index numbers of employment given in this volume for various countries is as comparable as feasible to that covered in the indexes of production for the country. Where several series of employment indexes were available, the series chosen was the one that was most similar in coverage to the series of index numbers of production. Where the Statistical Office of the United Nations compiled series of employment indexes from absolute figures of employment, available data on employment was utilized that related to the field of industrial units which was most like that covered in the index numbers of production.

### International Definitions of Industrial Statistics

Three main types of statistical units are represented in the counts of units set out in the tables of this volume, and are basic to the classification and compilation of the other industrial statistics shown. These units are the establishment, the local unit and the enterprise; and are defined in the following manner:

The establishment is, ideally, an economic unit which engages, under a single ownership or control, in one or predominantly one kind of industrial activity at a single location—e.g., the individual mine, workshop, factory or generating station. The local unit comprises, ideally, all the industrial activities carried on at a single location under a single ownership or control. The concept of the enterprise utilized in the industrial inquiries dealt with in this publication is the legal entity. The legal entity is an individual proprietorship or any association of persons or organization owning and carrying on a business undertaking. In general, this unit is a legally recognized entity possessing the right to conduct business in its own name—for example, enter contractual agreements, own property, incur liability for debts and establish bank accounts. In countries where business enterprises are, for the most part, owned and controlled by the Government, the legal entity has a single administration with the right to conclude contracts, an independent production plan and current bank accounts, and a self-contained system of accounting.

proportionnels à la valeur de la production brute de ces produits pendant l'année de base. Cependant, les poids utilisés pour combiner ces indices en indices de catégories d'activité industrielle plus larges sont déterminés à partir de chiffres de la valeur de la production nette. Dans le cas de plusieurs pays à économie planifiée, les séries d'indices de la production industrielle présentées se rapportent, en pratique aussi bien qu'en théorie, à la valeur de la production brute en prix constants des entreprises (c'est-à-dire déduction faite de l'impôt sur le chiffre d'affaires). Ces séries de nombres-indices sont généralement construites à partir de données de base sur tous les éléments de la production brute.

La plupart des séries d'indices qui figurent dans la présente publication sont en fait établies au moyen d'une formule à pondération fixe (Laspeyres) et de poids fixes pour l'année de base. Un bon nombre de ces séries sont également construites par opérations successives. La première consiste en général à combiner les séries élémentaires de rapports quantitatifs de la production de produits industriels pour en extraire les nombres-indices relatifs à des catégories précises d'activité industrielle. Les étapes suivantes consistent à établir les nombres-indices de catégories d'activité de plus en plus larges en utilisant à chaque fois les indices obtenus par l'opération précédente. Ces méthodes ont fait l'objet de recommandations internationales.

La portée des nombres-indices de l'emploi qui sont donnés dans la présente publication pour divers pays a été rendue comparable, dans la mesure du possible, à celle des indices de la production du pays considéré. Lorsque l'on disposait de plusieurs séries d'indices de l'emploi, on a choisi celle qui se rapprochait le plus par sa portée de la série d'indices de la production. Dans les cas où le Bureau de statistique de l'Organisation des Nations Unies a établi des séries d'indices de l'emploi à partir de chiffres absolus, il s'est servi des données relatives au domaine d'activité industrielle se rapprochant le plus de celui auquel se rapportaient les indices de la production.

### Définitions internationales des statistiques industrielles

Parmi les unités statistiques énumérées dans les tableaux du présent volume, on retrouve trois types principaux d'unités qui servent de base pour classer et établir les autres statistiques industrielles présentées. Ce sont l'établissement industriel, l'unité locale et l'entreprise, que l'on définit comme suit :

L'établissement industriel est théoriquement une unité économique qui, sous un régime de propriété ou de contrôle unique, exerce, exclusivement ou principalement, un seul type d'activité industrielle en un lieu unique — mine, puits atelier, usine ou centrale électrique. L'unité locale comprend théoriquement toutes les activités industrielles exercées en un lieu unique sous un régime de propriété ou de contrôle unique. Dans les enquêtes industrielles analysées dans la présente publication, l'entreprise est définie comme l'entité juridique. L'entité juridique est tout propriétaire individuel, tout groupement de personnes ou toute organisation qui exerce une activité industrielle ou commerciale ou possède une entreprise ayant une telle activité. En général, cette unité est une entité juridiquement reconnue et possède le droit d'effectuer des transactions en son propre nom, par exemple passer des contrats, posséder des biens, contracter des dettes, avoir des comptes en banque. Dans les pays où le plus souvent, l'entreprise industrielle ou commerciale appartient à l'Etat et est placée sous son contrôle. l'entité juridique a une direction unique, le droit de passer des contrats, un plan de production et un compte en banque indépendants et un système autonome de comptabilité.

The distinction between the establishment and the local unit and between these and the legal entity is of interest where the legal entity engages in more than a single class of industrial activity and/or carries on its activities at more than one location. The extent to which and the way in which such a multi-unit legal entity may be subdivided into establishments or local units will depend, in practice, on the manner in which the legal entity organizes and keeps records which can provide the data required in industrial inquiries. Each of the establishments into which the legal entity is subdivided should be engaged in the production of as homogeneous a set of products and/or services and be confined to as limited a geographic area as is feasible in the light of the records that are maintained. When subdividing the legal entity into local units, the restrictions as to the homogeneity of the products and/or services produced is removed.

The application of these criteria results, in practice, in statistical units which are often wider in scope than the ideal definition of the establishment or local unit, especially in the case of units mainly engaged in mining. construction or the electricity and gas industries. In the case of mining, it is suggested in the international recommendations that the establishment embrace the collection of wells, shafts or pits of the legal entity that tap a single field. Any ore processing or beneficiating plants located at the mine site would be included as part of the establishment. In the case of construction, it is proposed that all the activities and resources of the legal entity involved in construction for the account of others should be included in the statistical unit. For the electricity, gas and steam industries, it is suggested that the statistical unit be defined to embrace the producing plan and its associated distribution system.

The concepts and definitions in the international recommendations for other items of industrial statistics dealt with in this publication are as follows:

1. *Value added, gross output, and gross receipts.* Value added is the total value of gross output during a period less the sum of the cost of all purchased goods (e.g., raw materials, supplies, fuels, electricity, goods sold in the same condition as purchased) utilized during the period and the cost of all services of an industrial nature (e.g., fabricating, assembling repairs or maintenance) provided by others. The total value of gross output during a period comprises the gross value of all products completed during the period for shipment or sale to others, and all services rendered to others, the algebraic change between the end and beginning of the period in the value of work in process, the value of goods shipped in the same condition as purchased, the value of fixed assets produced during the period by the unit for its own use. Gross output and value added may be valued at market prices (i.e., including indirect taxes such as excise, sales or turnover taxes and excluding direct subsidies received) or factor cost (i.e., excluding indirect taxes but including direct subsidies). Gross receipts usually relate to the part of gross output that has actually been provided or sold to others.

2. *Number of persons engaged, number of employees and number of operatives.* The number of persons engaged is the total number of persons who work in or for the statistical unit, including working proprietors and active business partners, unpaid family workers, possibly homeworkers and employees. Working proprietors and active business partners include all owners of the legal entity (individual proprietorship or partnership) who are actively engaged in its work. Unpaid family workers are all persons living in the household of the legal entity and working in the statistical unit without regular pay for at least one-third of the working time normal to that unit. Some countries find it convenient to specify an absolute minimum time a family member must work in the business (e.g., fifteen hours per week) before he is counted as an unpaid family worker. Homeworkers are all persons employed by the statistical unit (usually on a piece-work basis) who perform the work in their own homes. Employees include all persons who do work in the statistical unit for which they receive pay,

La distinction entre l'établissement industriel et l'unité locale et entre ces unités et l'entité juridique présente un intérêt lorsque l'entité juridique exerce plus d'un type d'activité industrielle ou exerce ces activités en plus d'un lieu ou lorsque ces deux situations se présentent en même temps. La manière dont une entité juridique complexe de ce genre peut être subdivisée en établissements ou unités locales, et la mesure dans laquelle cela est faisable, dépendent, dans la pratique, de la manière dont l'entité juridique organise et tient une comptabilité pouvant fournir les données recherchées dans les enquêtes industrielles. Chacun des établissements en lesquels l'entité juridique est subdivisée doit autant que possible produire un ensemble homogène de marchandises ou de services ou de marchandises et de services et son activité doit s'exercer dans une aire géographique aussi restreinte que possible eu égard à la comptabilité tenue. Lorsqu'on subdivise l'entité juridique en unités locales, la condition relative à l'homogénéité des marchandises ou des services produits ne s'impose pas.

L'application de ces critères fait que l'on aboutit en pratique à des unités statistiques souvent plus larges que celles de la définition idéale de l'établissement industriel ou de l'unité locale, surtout dans le cas des unités dont l'activité principale relève des branches "industries extractives", "construction" ou "industries de l'électricité et du gaz". Dans le cas des industries extractives, on suggère dans les recommandations internationales que la définition de l'établissement comprenne l'ensemble des puits de l'entité juridique qui exploitent un gîte unique. Toutes les installations de traitement ou d'enrichissement du minerai situées sur le carreau de la mine seraient considérées comme faisant partie de l'unité statistique. Dans le cas du bâtiment et des travaux publics, l'unité statistique devrait englober toutes les activités et ressources de l'entité juridique qui sont mises en œuvre dans les travaux effectués pour le compte d'autrui. Pour ce qui est des industries de l'électricité, du gaz et de la vapeur, il y aurait intérêt à ce que la définition de l'unité statistique englobe la centrale ou l'usine de production et son réseau de distribution.

Les concepts et définitions d'autres catégories de statistiques industrielles figurant dans le présent ouvrage sont énoncés comme suit dans les recommandations internationales :

1. *Valeur ajoutée, production brute et recettes brutes.* La valeur ajoutée est la valeur total de la production brute pendant une période donnée, moins le coût total de toutes les marchandises achetées (par exemple, matières premières, fournitures, combustibles, électricité, marchandises revendues en l'état) qui sont utilisées pendant la période considérée et le coût de tous les services de caractère industriel (par exemple, fabrication, montage, réparation ou entretien) fournis par d'autres unités statistiques. La valeur totale de la production brute pendant une période considérée comprend la valeur brute de tous les produits achevés pendant la periode en vue de leur expédition ou de leur vente et tous les services rendus à d'autres unités, la modification algébrique de la valeur des travaux en cours entre le début et la fin de la période, la valeur des marchandises réexpédiées en l'état, la valeur des capitaux fixes produits par l'unité pour sa propre consommation pendant ladite période. La production brute et la valeur ajoutée peuvent être évaluées aux prix du marché (c'est-à-dire y compris les impôts indirects tels que le droit de régie, la taxe sur les transactions ou l'impôt sur le chiffre d'affaires et non compris les subventions directes reçues) ou au coût des facteurs (non compris les impôts indirects mais y compris les subventions directes). Les recettes brutes correspondent généralement à la partie de la production brute qui a effectivement été fournie ou vendue à d'autres unités.

2. *Nombre de personnes employées, nombre de salariés et nombre d'ouvriers.* Le nombre de personnes occupées est le nombre total des personnes travaillant dans une unité statistique ou pour son compte, y compris les propriétaires qui travaillent et les associés actifs, les travailleurs familiaux non rémunérés et, éventuellement, les travailleurs à domicile et les employés. La catégorie des propriétaires qui travaillent et des associés actifs comprend tous les propriétaires d'entités juridiques (propriétaires individuels ou associés) qui participent effectivement à l'activité de ces entités. Les travailleurs familiaux non rémunérés sont toutes les personnes qui habitent au domicile de l'entité juridique et qui travaillent dans l'unité statistique sans percevoir de rémunération régulière pendant au moins un tiers de la durée du travail considérée comme normale dans cette unité. Certains pays jugent à propos de fixer le temps minimal qu'un membre de la famille doit consacrer à l'entreprise (par exemple, 15 heures par semaine) pour pouvoir être considéré comme travailleur familial non rétribué.

and persons working away from the unit when paid by and under the control of the unit. Operatives are all employees who are directly engaged in the production or related activities of the unit. Included are any clerical or working supervisory personnel whose function is to record or expedite any step in the production process and persons engaged in truck driving, repair and maintenance and similar occupations in activities ancillary to the main activity of the unit. The counts of the number of persons engaged, employees, etc., should relate to the number engaged during a specified period of time and should include persons on short-term leave such as sick leave, casual leave or paid vacation and persons on strike. Excluded from the counts should be persons on unlimited leave, military leave or on pension.

3. *Man-hours worked by operatives* is the total number of hours actually spent by operatives at work, including waiting time. Time spent on vacation, casual leave or sick leave should be excluded.

4. *Wages and salaries* paid cover all payments, whether in cash or in kind, made by the employer in connexion with the work done, to all persons included in the count of employees and, if counted as a part of the number of persons engaged, homeworkers. Included are bonuses: cost-of-living or dearness allowances; wages paid during periods of vacation and sick leave; lay-off payments or compensation for unemployment except where such payments are made from trust or other special funds set up expressly for this purpose; and taxes, social insurance contributions and the like payable by the employee and deducted by the employer. Excluded are social insurance contributions and the like payable by the employer as well as pension payments, family allowances and similar social benefits.

5. *Capacity of installed power equipment* is the sum of the capacity of installed prime movers not driving electric generators and the capacity of all installed electric motors, as of the reference date, or the sum of the capacity of all installed prime movers except those driving vehicles and the capacity of installed electric motors driven by purchased electricity, as of the reference date. Installed prime movers or electric motors consist of those in use or in reserve as of the reference date. Included are prime movers, whether mobile or stationary, and electric motors used in connexion with the production activities of the statistical unit. The capacity of prime movers and electric motors should be measured in terms of rated horsepower—i.e.. the horsepower indicated by the manufacturer.

## Energy Statistics

The data presented in a number of chapters of this publication on the consumption, in coal equivalents, of energy are designed to measure the use of fuels and electricity as a source of heat or motivating power, without the double counting which might result from the use of fuels to produce other fuels or electricity. In the case of the electricity industry however, the figures of energy consumed refer, in most instances, to the use of fuels to produce electricity. Similarly, for units classified to the gas industry, the data relate to the use of fuels, excepting manufactured gas, and of electricity to produce manufactured gas. It should be noted that in the tables shown on the quantity and value of individual fuels and electricity consumed, possible double counting between them has not been eliminated. For example, data are set out in these tables on electricity or manufactured gas produced on own account, using coal or other fuels.

In order to avoid double counting, the data on fuels and electricity that were utilized in computing the figures of

Les travailleurs à domicile sont toutes les personnes employées par l'unité statistique (et généralement payées aux pièces) qui exercent leur activité professionnelle à leur domicile propre. Les salariés sont toutes les personnes qui travaillent dans l'unité statistique considérée et qui reçoivent une rémunération pour ce travail, ainsi que les personnes qui travaillent hors de l'unité, relèvent de ladite unité et sont payées par elle. Les ouvriers sont tous les salariés qui participent directement à la production ou aux activités connexes de l'unité. Cette définition englobe le personnel de secrétariat ou de maîtrise qui est chargé d'enregistrer ou de faire exécuter toute opération intervenant dans le processus de production et les personnes affectées à la conduite des camions, à la réparation et à l'entretien et à des occupations analogues dans les activités auxiliaires de l'activité principale de l'unité. Le recensement du nombre de personnes occupées, de salariés, etc., doit porter sur le nombre de personnes occupées pendant une période déterminée et comprendre les personnes qui sont en congé pour une période de courte durée (congé de maladie, congé exceptionnel ou congé payé), ainsi que les personnes en grève. Il ne faut pas compter les personnes en congé de durée indéterminée, ni celles qui accomplissent leur service militaire, ni les retraités.

3. *Par heures effectuées par les ouvriers,* on entend le nombre total d'heures que les ouvriers consacrent effectivement à leur travail, y compris les périodes d'attente. Il faut exclure du décompte les congés payés, les congés exceptionnels ou les congés de maladie.

4. *Les traitements et salaires versés* comprennent toutes les sommes en espèces et prestations en nature versées par un employeur à toutes les personnes comptées au nombre des salariés et, s'ils sont inclus dans le nombre des personnes occupées, les travailleurs à domicile, en rémunération de leur travail. Sont comprises les gratifications, indemnités de cherté de vie, congés de maladie, congés payés, les indemnités de chômage sauf si elles proviennent d'un fonds ou d'une réserve spécialement constituée, les impôts, cotisations de sécurité sociale et autres paiements dus par les salariés et retenus par l'employeur. Ne sont pas comprises les cotisations de sécurité sociale et autres dues par l'employeur, ni les allocations familiales, pensions de retraite et autres prestations sociales analogues.

5. *La puissance installée* est la somme de la puissance des moteurs primaires n'entraînant pas de générateurs électriques et de la puissance de tous les moteurs électriques, à la date de référence, ou somme de la puissance de tous les moteurs primaires (à l'exception de ceux qui équipent des véhicules) et de la puissance des moteurs électriques actionnés par de l'électricité achetée, à la date de référence. Les moteurs primaires ou moteurs électriques installés sont ceux qui sont en service ou en réserve à la date de référence. Ils comprennent les moteurs primaires, mobiles ou fixes, et les moteurs électriques utilisés pour actionner l'outillage productif de l'unité statistique. La puissance des moteurs primaires et des moteurs électriques est la puissance nominale, c'est-à-dire le nombre de chevaux-vapeur indiqué par le constructeur.

## Statistiques de l'énergie

Les données relatives à la consommation d'énergie (exprimées en tonnes de charbon), que l'on trouvera dans certains chapitres du présent ouvrage, visent à mesurer l'utilisation des combustibles et de l'électricité comme sources de chaleur ou de puissance motrice, sans le double compte qui pourrait résulter de l'emploi de combustibles pour produire d'autres combustibles ou de l'électricité. Cependant, en ce qui concerne l'industrie de l'électricité, les chiffres de la consommation d'énergie se rapportent le plus souvent aux quantités de combustibles employées pour produire de l'électricité. De même, dans le cas des unités classées dans l'industrie du gaz, les données ont trait aux combustibles (exception faite du gaz d'usine) et à l'électricité utilisés pour produire du gaz d'usine. On remarquera qu'il n'a pas été possible d'éliminer tout double compte dans les tableaux où sont indiquées la quantité et la valeur des différents combustibles et de l'électricité consommés. Par exemple, on y trouve des données sur l'électricité ou le gaz d'usine produits pour compte propre à partir de charbon ou d'autres combustibles.

Afin d'éviter le double compte, on a calculé la consommation d'énergie, en général, sur la base de la consommation de

energy consumed relate, in general, to the quantities consumed of purchased fuels and electricity. However, in the case of coal mining and the extraction of crude petroleum and natural gas, the data utilized cover the use, on own account, of extracted coal or crude petroleum and natural gas respectively. In some instances, double counting was avoided by basing the data on energy consumption on the quantity of various fuels and electricity utilized directly as a source of heat or motivating power or by adjusting the data on the consumption of certain fuels for the quantities consumed in the production of electricity on own account. Where double counting could occur in the figures of energy consumed because it was not feasible to eliminate possible duplication between electricity produced and consumed on own account and the fuels used for this purpose, data were not compiled on the total amount of energy consumed. However, data on the total consumption of energy were computed in a few instances where slight duplication may have occured between gas manufactured and consumed on account and the coal or coke that was used primarily for this purpose but was recorded in the statistics of the consumption of fuels. Where the total amount of energy consumed may as a result have been overstated, the possibility is mentioned in the pertinent introductory text.

In order to compile the required data on the consumption of energy, the quantities of coal, coke, crude petroleum or other fuels utilized as raw materials—for example, to manufacture chemicals, dyes or refined petroleum products—were not included in computing these data. This practice was not followed in the case of coal or coke employed in blast furnaces or the like, where the gas manufactured as a by-product, was utilized in the same unit as a source of heat or motivating power but was not recorded in the statistics on the consumption of fuels. It was not always feasible to exclude coal, coke or gas utilized as a raw material from the data that were compiled on the consumption of energy. Where the amount of energy consumed may, as a result, have been overstated, this possibility is indicated in the relevant introductory text.

In converting the quantity of various fuels and electricity consumed to coal equivalents, the following coefficients were, in general, used:

| | Coal Equivalents (metric tons) |
|---|---|
| Coal or coal briquettes, anthracite or bituminous (metric tons) | 1.0 |
| Coke of anthracite or bituminous coal (metric tons) | 0.9 |
| Briquettes or coke of brown coal or of lignite or pitch coal (metric tons) | 0.67 |
| Lignite (metric tons) | 0.6 to 0.3, varying with country |
| Crude petroleum (metric tons) | 1.3 |
| Gasoline (incl. natural gasoline), kerosene or fuel oils (metric tons) | 1.5 |
| Liquified petroleum and refinery gases (metric tons) | 1.67 |
| Natural gas 1000 (cubic metres) | 1.33 |
| Manufactured and coke oven gases (1000 cubic metres) | 0.6 |
| Electricity (1000 kwh) | 0.125 |
| Peat (metric tons) | 0.5 |
| Fuel wood (per cubic metre solid measure) | 0.25 |

combustibles et d'électricité achetés. Toutefois, dans le cas de l'extraction du charbon et de la production de pétrole brut et de gaz naturel, l'utilisation pour compte propre d'une partie du charbon ou du pétrole brut et du gaz naturel produits entre dans les données recueillies. On a parfois évité le double compte en calculant la consommation d'énergie à partir des quantités de divers combustibles et d'électricité employés directement comme sources de chaleur ou de puissance motrice, ou bien en ajustant les chiffres relatifs à la consommation de certains combustibles pour tenir compte des quantités employées à produire de l'électricité pour compte propre. Lorsqu'en raison de l'impossibilité d'éliminer tout double compte entre l'électricité produite et consommée pour compte propre et les combustibles utilisés à cette fin, les chiffres de la consommation d'énergie risquaient d'être faussés par un double compte, on n'a pas présenté de statistiques de la consommation totale d'énergie. Cependant, on a calculé le volume total d'énergie consommée dans quelques cas où un léger chevauchement a pu se produire entre le gaz produit et consommé pour compte propre et le charbon ou le coke utilisé principalement à cette fin mais déjà compté dans la consommation de combustibles. Si pour cette raison la consommation totale d'énergie a pu être surestimée, cette possibilité est signalée dans l'introduction au chapitre pertinent.

Pour obtenir les données nécessaires sur la consommation de l'énergie, on a exclu les quantités de charbon, de coke, de pétrole brut ou d'autres combustibles utilisés comme matières premières, par exemple pour fabriquer des produits chimiques, des colorants ou des produits à base de pétrole raffiné. Cette méthode n'a pas été appliquée dans le cas du charbon ou du coke utilisé dans les hauts-fourneaux puisque le gaz fabriqué comme sous-produit est employé dans la même unité comme source de chaleur ou de puissance motrice mais n'est pas compté dans la consommation de combustibles. Il n'a pas toujours été possible d'exclure le charbon, le coke ou le gaz employé comme matière première des données qui ont été recueillies sur la consommation d'énergie. Si pour cette raison la consommation d'énergie a pu être surestimée, cette possibilité est signalée dans l'introduction au chapitre pertinent.

Pour obtenir l'équivalent en charbon des quantités de divers combustibles et d'électricité consommées, on a appliqué en général les coefficients suivants:

| | Equivalent en charbon (tonnes métriques) |
|---|---|
| Charbon ou briquettes de charbon, anthracite ou charbon bitumineux (tonnes métriques) | 1,0 |
| Coke d'anthracite ou de charbon bitumineux (tonnes métriques) | 0,9 |
| Briquettes ou coke de houille brune ou de lignite ou de houille bitumineuse (tonnes métriques) | 0,67 |
| Lignite (tonnes métriques) | 0,6 à 0,3 selon le pays |
| Pétrole brut (tonnes métriques) | 1,3 |
| Essence (y compris l'essence naturelle), kérosène ou huile lourde tonnes (métriques) | 1,5 |
| Gaz de pétrole et gaz de raffinerie liquéfiés (tonnes métriques) | 1,67 |
| Gaz naturel (1 000 mètres cubes) | 1,33 |
| Gaz d'usine et gaz de four à coke (1 000 mètres cubes) | 0,6 |
| Electricité (1 000 kWh) | 0,125 |
| Tourbe (tonnes métriques) | 0,5 |
| Bois de chauffage (par mètre cube) | 0,25 |

Where the only data available on the consumption of miscellaneous minor fuels related to the cost, on purchase, of these fuels, the conversion to coal equivalents was based on estimates of the cost, on purchase, of the equivalent of one metric ton of coal compiled for each industry from the available data on quantity and cost for each major type of fuel.

## Relations Between National Accounting and Industrial Statistics

The concepts utilized in the data on the contribution to the gross domestic product of the categories of industry that are shown in Table 1 for a number of countries and in the data on value added in these divisions of industrial activity shown in the tables on industrial statistics are, in most instances, similar but not identical. The data on the contribution to the gross domestic product are net of the cost of all the services employed in production which were purchased from others whereas the figures of value added are usually net of such services that are of an industrial nature only. For example, the costs of purchased transportation, communication or business services are excluded from the former figures but included in the latter data. It is interesting to note that in this regard the gross material product and value added are more similar to each other. The completeness with which industrial units are covered also often differs between the two series of data. For example, the data on the gross domestic product relate to all units principally engaged in industrial activities but the figures of value added may be restricted to the larger industrial units only. Furthermore, the gross domestic product relates to the output of resident producers whereas value added concerns the output of industrial units located within the political boundaries of a country. From this point of view, the gross material product and value added are the same in concept.

Differences such as those mentioned above may be reflected in differences between the movements in the gross domestic product in constant prices and in index numbers of industrial production which are, ideally, ratios between figures of value added in constant prices. Other factors contributing to these divergencies may be differences in the nature of the basic data utilized in computing the two series. For example, considerable use may be made of price index numbers in converting figures of the gross domestic product in current prices to those in constant prices but little use may be made of price indexes in compiling index numbers of industrial production. In the case of indexes of industrial production, much more use is likely to be made of measures of physical output. Also, the figures of the gross product in constant prices may be compiled from elementary series of data on gross output and raw materials and other gross inputs whereas the indexes of industrial production may be compiled from elementary series of data on gross output only. Significant differences may also occur in the scope and extent of the basic series utilized in compiling the two aggregates. Because of differences in concept, field of coverage and sources of basic data, in the case of certain countries, the average annual rates of change for the gross domestic product in constant prices

Lorsque les seules données disponibles sur la consommation de divers combustibles d'importance secondaire avaient trait au prix d'achat de ces combustibles, la conversion en équivalent en charbon a été basée sur le coût d'achat estimatif de l'équivalent d'une tonne métrique de charbon, calculé pour chaque industrie à partir des données disponibles sur la quantité et le coût de chaque type principal de combustible.

## Relations entre la comptabilité nationale et les statistiques industrielles

Pour établir les données sur la contribution au produit intérieur brut des catégories d'industries qui figurent au tableau I pour un certain nombre de pays et pour calculer les chiffres de la valeur ajoutée dans les branches d'activité industrielle qui figurent dans les tableaux de statistiques industrielles, on a appliqué des concepts qui sont le plus souvent analogues, sans toutefois être identiques. Les données relatives à la contribution au produit intérieur brut s'entendent déduction faite du coût de tous les services concourant à la production qui ont été achetés à d'autres sources, tandis que les chiffres de la valeur ajoutée s'entendent habituellement déduction faite de ceux de ces services qui ont un caractère industriel seulement. Par exemple, les dépenses relatives aux transports, aux communications et aux services commerciaux ne sont pas comptées dans le produit intérieur brut, mais elles le sont dans la valeur ajoutée. Il est intéressant de noter qu'à cet égard le produit matériel brut et la valeur ajoutée sont plus proches l'un de l'autre. Souvent aussi la mesure dans laquelle les unités industrielles sont intégralement couvertes diffère pour chaque série. Par exemple, les données relatives au produit intérieur brut se rapportent à toutes les unités qui exercent principalement une activité industrielle, alors que pour la valeur ajoutée elles peuvent être limitées aux unités industrielles les plus importantes seulement. De plus, le produit intérieur brut est basé sur la production des résidents du pays, tandis que la valeur ajoutée se rapporte à la production des unités industrielles situées à l'intérieur des frontières politiques du pays. De ce point de vue, le produit matériel brut et la valeur ajoutée correspondent à la même conception.

A cause de divergences comme celles qui viennent d'être mentionnées ci-dessus, des différences peuvent apparaître entre les variations du produit intérieur brut en prix constants et les mouvements des indices de la production industrielle, qui sont, en théorie, des rapports entre les chiffres de la valeur ajoutée évaluée en prix constants. Des différences de nature entre les données de base utilisées pour établir les deux séries peuvent également contribuer à ces divergences. Par exemple, on peut avoir recours dans une large mesure aux indices de prix pour convertir en prix constants les chiffres du produit intérieur brut en prix courants; il se peut, d'autre part, que l'on utilise relativement peu les indices des prix notamment, pour établir les indices de la production industrielle. Dans le cas des indices de la production industrielle, il est probable que l'on se servira beaucoup plus de mesures de la production matérielle. En outre, les chiffres du produit brut en prix constants peuvent être établis à partir de séries élémentaires de données relatives à la production brute et aux matières premières et autres entrées brutes, tandis que les indices de la production industrielle peuvent être établis à partir de séries élémentaires de données relatives à la production brute seulement. Il peut également y avoir des différences importantes dans le champ et l'étendue des séries de

that are shown in Table 1 differ from those for the indexes of industrial production set out in Table 2.

### Average Annual Rates of Change

Average annual rates of change are shown for various periods in the case of data in constant prices on the gross domestic product, the various kinds of expenditure on the gross domestic product and gross fixed capital formation according to sector of purchase and in the case of index numbers of industrial production and employment. In all instances, these rates of change have been computed as the geometric average of the year-to-year change between the terminal years of each of the periods indicated in the relevant tables.

### Conventions Used

The following conventions have been followed in making entries in the tables of this population:

1. Dash (—) signifies that the figure is nil or less than 1 in the last place to which the figures have been rounded —for example, less than 0.1 if figures have been rounded to this place.

2. Three dots (. . .) indicate that the figure is not available.

3. One dot (.) means that the figure is not applicable or has not been sought on the item of data in question.

4. A horizontal bar (——) across the column indicates a substantial discontinuity in the homogeneity of a series.

5. A broken bar (— —) on either side of an index number signifies that two series of index numbers have been linked at that point.

The description of countries and territories and the arrangement of material in this publication should not be considered to imply any endorsement or other judgement by the Secretariat of the United Nations regarding the legal status of any country or territory, or of its authorities, or in respect of the delineation of its boundaries.

base utilisées pour obtenir les deux agrégats. Dans le cas de certains pays, en raison de différences dans les conceptions, la couverture et les sources des données de base, les taux annuels moyens de variation du produit intérieur brut en prix constants indiqués au tableau 1 diffèrent des taux annuels moyens de variation des indices de la production industrielle présentés au tableau 2.

### Taux annuels moyens de variation

Les taux annuels moyens de variation sont indiqués pour diverses périodes dans le cas des données en prix constants relatives au produit intérieur brut, aux diverses dépenses imputées au produit intérieur brut et à la formation brute de capital fixe par secteur d'achat, ainsi que dans le cas des nombres-indices de la production industrielle et de l'emploi dans l'industrie. Dans tous les cas, ces taux de variation équivalent à la moyenne géométrique des changements survenus d'une année à l'autre entre les années terminales de chacune des périodes indiquées dans les tableaux pertinents.

### Signes employés

Les signes suivants sont employés dans les tableaux de la présente publication:

1. Le tiret (—) indique que le chiffre est égal à zéro ou inférieur à une unité du dernier rang auquel les chiffres ont été arrondis — par exemple: inférieur à 0,1 si les chiffres ont été arrondis au dixième.

2. Trois points (. . .) indiquent que l'on n'a pas de données.

3. Un point (.) indique que la rubrique ne s'applique pas à la colonne ou que le chiffre n'a pas été calculé pour la rubrique en question.

4. Un trait horizontal (——) en travers de la colonne indique un défaut important dans l'homogénéité de la série.

5. Deux tirets (— —) de chaque côté d'un nombre-indice indique que deux séries de nombres-indices ont été raccordées à ce point.

Les termes employés pour désigner les pays et territoires et la façon dont les renseignements sont disposés dans la présente publication ne doivent pas être considérés comme impliquant, de la part du Secrétariat de l'Organisation des Nations Unies, une approbation ou un jugement sur le statut légal de tel pays ou territoire et les autorités qui le gouvernent, ou en ce qui concerne la délimitation de ses frontières.

## Gross Domestic Product

The data on the gross domestic product given in Table 1 are from the reply of the Service de la statistique générale de l'Algérie, Alger, to the United Nations questionnaire on national accounts. Except that the military forces in Algeria were considered to be residents, the estimates shown in Table 1 are consistent, on the whole, with the concept and definition of the United Nations system of national accounts.

## Index Numbers of Industrial Production

The index numbers set out in Table 2 are in the main derived from indexes of industrial production computed by the Service de la statistique générale of the Délégation générale du Gouvernement en Algérie that were issued in *Bulletin de statistique générale, Statistiques trimestrielles* and supplied to the Statistical Office of the United Nations in correspondence. It should be noted that the Statistical Office of the United Nations computed the index numbers for each of the major groups of mining from data on the quantity of individual minerals extracted. Also, the indexes for the years, 1950-1953, in the case of a few of the major groups of manufacturing were compiled by the Office from figures of indexes of production and of quantities of individual commodities produced issued by the Service de la statistique générale.

All of the indexes of industrial production are computed as base-weighted arithmetic averages, starting mainly from figures of the quantity of individual commodities produced. The weighting base is 1950 for the index numbers for years prior to 1954 and 1954 for the index numbers for this year and thereafter. In combining series of relatives on the output of individual commodities into index numbers for detailed categories of industry, the weights are derived from gross value of production during the base year. However, in aggregating these indexes to index numbers for broader classes of industrial activity, the weights are based on contribution to the gross domestic product at market prices. The weights for the indexes based on 1954 were derived from the inquiry described below, but, unlike the data from this inquiry that are shown in Table 3, neither the weights nor the elementary series utilized in constructing the indexes relate to handicrafts and other small units or to business units engaged primarily in repairs or the extraction of petroleum.

Further details concerning the index numbers of industrial production may be found in "Les nouveaux indices de la production industrielle base 100 en 1954," *Bulletin de statistique générale,* 1958, *Statistiques trimestrielles,* No. 4, Service de la statistique générale, Alger.

## Produit intérieur brut

Les données du tableau 1 concernant le produit intérieur brut sont tirées de la réponse du Service de la statistique générale de l'Algérie, Alger, au questionnaire de l'ONU sur la comptabilité nationale. Si ce n'est que les militaires servant en Algérie ont été considérés comme résidents, les estimations du tableau 1 sont, dans l'ensemble, conformes aux concepts et définitions du système de comptabilité nationale de l'ONU.

## Indices de la production industrielle

Les indices du tableau 2 sont tirés principalement d'indices de la production industrielle établis par le Service de la statistique générale, Délégation générale du Gouvernement en Algérie et publiés dans le *Bulletin de statistique générale, Statistiques trimestrielles* ou communiqués par correspondance au Bureau de statistique de l'ONU. On notera que le Bureau de statistique de l'ONU a construit les indices de chacune des classes des industries extractives en partant de données quantitatives sur l'extraction des divers produits minéraux. Pour certaines des classes des industries manufacturières, le Bureau de statistique a établi les indices de 1950-1953 en partant des indices de la production et des chiffres concernant le volume de la production de chaque marchandise, qui sont publiés par le Service de la statistique générale.

Tous les indices de la production industrielle sont des moyennes arithmétiques à pondération fixe établies principalement à partir du volume de la production de chaque marchandise. La base de pondération est 1950 pour les indices des années antérieures à 1954, et 1954 pour les indices de cette année et des années suivantes. Pour combiner les séries de rapports sur la production de chaque marchandise en indices de catégorie détaillée, on a tiré les poids de la valeur brute de la production pendant l'année de base. En revanche, pour combiner ces indices en indices plus larges, on a pondéré en fonction de la contribution au produit intérieur brut, aux prix du marché. Pour les indices basés sur 1954, les poids ont été tirés des résultats de l'enquête dont il est question ci-après, mais, à l'opposé des données résultant de cette enquête qui sont fournies au tableau 3, ni les poids ni les séries élémentaires qui ont servi à construire les indices ne portent sur les unités artisanales et les autres petites unités ou sur les unités industrielles effectuant essentiellement des réparations ou s'occupant principalement de l'extraction du pétrole.

Pour plus de détails sur les indices de la production industrielle, voir "Les nouveaux indices de la production industrielle base 100 en 1954", *Bulletin de statistique générale,* 1958, *Statistiques trimestrielles,* No. 4, Service de la statistique générale, Alger.

### The Characteristics and Structure of Industrial Activity

The data presented in Table 3 relate to all enterprises irrespective of size including handicrafts—essentially those subject to the tax on industrial and commercial activity. The figures of value added were compiled from *Les Comptes Economiques de l'Algérie et du Sahara pour les années, 1957 et 1958* and the data on employment were abstracted from *Bulletin de statistique générale*, 1959, *Statistiques trimestrielles*, No. 4. Both publications were issued by the Service de Statistique générale of the Délégation générale du Gouvernement en Algérie. The data on value added and employment were estimated by the Service from figures gathered as parts of the administration of the tax on industrial and commercial activity as well as in annual industrial inquiries. The annual industrial inquiries covered all industrial enterprises but very limited information was gathered for handicrafts, other small businesses and units engaged in repairs and the extraction of petroleum. Differences therefore occur between the figures shown in Table 3 and the corresponding data from the annual industrial inquiries, issued in summary fashion in, for example, *Bulletin de statistique générale*, 1958, *Statistiques trimestrielles*, No. 4.

The estimates of value added shown in Table 3 refer to the contribution to the gross domestic product at market prices. The reason for the minor differences between these figures and the comparable estimates set out in Table 1, are not known. The data on the number of employees shown in Table 3 also cover working proprietors. Included, in addition, in the estimates of the number of persons engaged are unpaid family workers but not homeworkers.

The data shown in Table 4 cover enterprises which paid 400 thousand or more old francs in wages and salaries during the year and were therefore required to submit certain tax returns. The lower limit to the amount of wages and salaries paid is equivalent to having at least one full-time employee. The figures of number of employees were abstracted from *Bulletin de statistique générale*, 1959, *Statistiques trimestrielles*, No. 4; the data on wages and salaries for 1954 and 1957 come from *Perspectives décennales de développement économique de l'Algérie*, Ministère de l'Algérie and *Les Comptes Economiques de l'Algérie et du Sahara pour les années, 1957 et 1958*, respectively. The definitions utilized for the number of employees and wages and salaries paid to them are consistent with those of the International Standards in Basic Industrial Statistics.

### Caractéristiques et structure de l'activité industrielle

Les données du tableau 3 concernent toutes les entreprises, quelle que soit leur dimension, y compris les entreprises artisanales — notamment celles qui sont soumises à la taxe sur l'activité industrielle et commerciale (TAIC). Les chiffres de la valeur ajoutée sont tirés de *Les Comptes Economiques de l'Algérie et du Sahara pour les années 1957 et 1958* et les chiffres sur l'emploi du *Bulletin de statistique générale*, 1959, *Statistiques trimestrielles*, No. 4. Ces deux publications sont publiées par le Service de la statistique générale, Délégation générale du gouvernement en Algérie. Les données relatives à la valeur ajoutée et à l'emploi ont été établies par le Service de la statistique générale à partir de chiffres fournis par l'administration de la TAIC et par les enquêtes industrielles annuelles. Ces enquêtes portaient sur toutes les entreprises industrielles, mais elles n'ont permis d'obtenir que des renseignements très limités sur les unités artisanales, les autres petites entreprises et les unités s'occupant de réparations ou de l'extraction du pétrole. Il y a donc certaines différences entre les chiffres du tableau 3 et les données correspondantes fournies par les enquêtes industrielles annuelles, qui sont publiées sous une forme abrégée, par exemple dans le *Bulletin de statistique générale*, 1958 *Statistiques trimestrielles*, No. 4.

Les estimations de la valeur ajoutée reproduites au tableau 3 correspondent à la contribution au produit intérieur brut aux prix du marché. Il existe de légères différences entre ces chiffres et les estimations correspondantes du tableau 1; on en ignore la raison. Les données du tableau 3 relatives au nombre de salariés comprennent également les propriétaires qui travaillent. En outre, les estimations du nombre de personnes occupées comprennent les travailleurs familiaux non rémunérés, mais non les travailleurs à domicile.

Les données du tableau 4 portent sur les entreprises ayant payé au moins 400 000 anciens francs en traitements et salaires pendant l'année et qui étaient par conséquent tenues de présenter une déclaration servant de base à la détermination de certains impôts. La limite inférieure fixée pour les traitements et salaires versés correspond à l'emploi d'un salarié au moins à plein temps. Les chiffres indiquant le nombre de salariés ont été tirés du *Bulletin de statistique générale*, 1959, *Statistiques trimestrielles*, No. 4; les données sur les traitements et salaires pour 1954 et 1957 ont été tirées de *Perspectives décennales de développement économique de l'Algérie*, Ministère de l'Algérie et *Les Comptes Economiques de l'Algérie et du Sahara pour les années 1957 et 1958*, respectivement. Les définitions adoptées pour le nombre de salariés et les traitements et salaires qui leur sont versés sont conformes aux Normes internationales relatives aux statistiques industrielles de base.

## 1. THE GROSS DOMESTIC PRODUCT — PRODUIT INTERIEUR BRUT

Thousand million old Francs                                           Milliards d'anciens francs

### A. Expenditure on the Gross Domestic Product at Market Prices
### Dépenses relatives au produit intérieur brut aux prix du marché

| Item of data and year<br>Rubrique et année | Total | Consumption<br>Consommation | | Gross Domestic Capital Formation<br>Formation brute de capital intérieur | | Net exports of goods and services<br>Exportations nettes de biens et de services | |
|---|---|---|---|---|---|---|---|
| | | Total | Government<br>Etat | Total | Fixed<br>Fixe | Exports less imports<br>Exportations moins importations | Exports<br>Exportations |
| *a. At Current Prices — Aux prix courants* | | | | | | | |
| Absolute figures — Chiffres absolus | | | | | | | |
| 1950 | 457.8 | 350.0 | 57.9 | 137.9 | 123.5 | −30.1 | 127.1 |
| 1951 | 528.8 | 449.7 | 77.3 | 153.6 | 143.3 | −74.5 | 147.0 |
| 1952 | 624.8 | 531.9 | 94.5 | 162.3 | 157.6 | −69.4 | 159.8 |
| 1953 | 644.2 | 541.1 | 103.6 | 160.2 | 155.7 | −57.1 | 152.6 |
| 1954 | 685.5 | 582.0 | 114.2 | 172.0 | 159.0 | −68.5 | 156.4 |
| 1955 | 737.2 | 655.2 | 152.6 | 148.0 | 164.0 | −66.0 | 185.0 |
| 1956 | 908.0 | 819.0 | 273.1 | 199.5 | 181.0 | −110.5 | 171.0 |
| 1957 | 1 055.1 | 1 012.5 | 361.4 | 226.7 | 208.8 | −184.1 | 199.0 |
| 1958 | 1 224.6 | 1 213.4 | 435.5 | 287.2 | 302.2 | −276.0 | 227.0 |
| 1959 | 1 414.4 | 1 347.4 | 489.7 | 362.1 | ... | −295.1 | 277.0 |
| Percentage distribution of average annual expenditure — Distribution en pourcentage des dépenses annuelles moyennes | | | | | | | |
| 1950 − 1958 | 100.0 | 89.6 | 24.3 | 24.0 | 23.2 | −13.6 | 22.2 |
| 1950 | 100.0 | 76.5 | 12.6 | 30.1 | 27.0 | −6.6 | 27.8 |
| 1953 | 100.0 | 84.0 | 16.1 | 24.9 | 24.2 | −8.9 | 23.7 |
| 1954 | 100.0 | 84.9 | 16.6 | 25.1 | 23.2 | −10.0 | 22.8 |
| 1958 | 100.0 | 99.1 | 35.6 | 23.4 | 24.7 | −22.5 | 18.5 |
| *b. At Prices of 1957 — Aux prix de 1957* | | | | | | | |
| Absolute figures — Chiffres absolus | | | | | | | |
| 1950 | 628.0 | 483.0 | 78.0 | 194.0 | ... | −49.0 | 176.0 |
| 1951 | 643.0 | 552.0 | 93.0 | 175.0 | ... | −84.0 | 182.0 |
| 1952 | 681.0 | 581.0 | 103.0 | 171.0 | ... | −71.0 | 186.0 |
| 1953 | 703.0 | 590.0 | 111.0 | 176.0 | ... | −63.0 | 182.0 |
| 1954 | 725.0 | 619.0 | 121.0 | 184.0 | ... | −78.0 | 187.0 |
| 1955 | 790.0 | 691.0 | 163.0 | 156.0 | ... | −57.0 | 238.0 |
| 1956 | 932.0 | 849.0 | 287.0 | 203.0 | ... | −120.0 | 194.0 |
| 1957 | 1 055.1 | 1 012.5 | 361.4 | 226.7 | 208.8 | −184.1 | 199.0 |
| 1958 | 1 106.0 | 1 122.0 | 402.0 | 276.0 | 282.0 | −292.0 | 168.0 |
| Percentage distribution of average annual expenditure — Distribution en pourcentage des dépenses annuelles moyennes | | | | | | | |
| 1950 − 1958 | 100.0 | 89.4 | 23.7 | 24.3 | ... | −13.7 | 23.6 |
| 1950 | 100.0 | 76.9 | 12.4 | 30.9 | ... | −7.8 | 28.0 |
| 1953 | 100.0 | 83.9 | 15.8 | 25.0 | ... | −8.9 | 25.9 |
| 1954 | 100.0 | 85.4 | 16.7 | 25.4 | ... | −10.8 | 25.8 |
| 1958 | 100.0 | 101.4 | 36.3 | 25.0 | 25.5 | −26.4 | 15.2 |
| Average annual rate of growth — Taux annuel moyen d'accroissement | | | | | | | |
| 1950 − 1958 | 7.3 | 11.1 | 22.7 | 4.5 | ... | . | −0.6 |
| 1950 − 1953 | 3.8 | 6.9 | 12.5 | −3.2 | ... | . | 1.1 |
| 1954 − 1958 | 11.1 | 16.0 | 35.0 | 10.7 | ... | . | 2.6 |

## B.   The Gross Domestic Product at Market Prices According to Origin
### Origine par secteur d'activité du produit intérieur brut aux prix du marché

| Item of data and year / Rubrique et année | Total [1] | Agricultural sector [2] / Secteur agricole [2] | Industrial Sector — Secteur industriel | | | | | Transportation and communication / Transports et communications | Other sectors [3] / Autres secteurs [3] |
|---|---|---|---|---|---|---|---|---|---|
| | | | Total | Mining / Industries extractives | Manufacturing / Industries manufacturières | Construction / Bâtiment et travaux publics | Electricity and gas / Electricité et gaz | | |
| ISIC — CITI | 0–9 | 0, 521 | 1–51 | 1 | 2–3 | 4 | 51 | 7 | 522, 6, 8–9 |
| **a. At Current Prices — Aux prix courants** | | | | | | | | | |
| **Absolute figures — Chiffres absolus** | | | | | | | | | |
| 1950 | 454.0 | 153.0 | 109.7 | 10.0 | 63.0 | 28.7 | 8.0 | ... | 191.3 |
| 1951 | 524.4 | 168.5 | 130.2 | 13.0 | 71.1 | 36.8 | 9.3 | ... | 225.7 |
| 1952 | 619.1 | 184.0 | 149.4 | 16.0 | 82.4 | 41.0 | 10.0 | ... | 285.7 |
| 1953 | 638.4 | 187.0 | 155.8 | 19.0 | 85.8 | 40.3 | 10.7 | ... | 295.6 |
| 1954 | 678.8 | 199.3 | 161.8 | 19.5 | 86.2 | 44.6 | 11.5 | 34.0 | 283.7 |
| 1955 | 727.0 | 193.4 | 169.6 | 19.0 | 91.0 | 47.0 | 12.6 | ... | 364.0 |
| 1956 | 893.0 | 239.5 | 183.4 | 18.6 | 101.0 | 50.0 | 13.8 | ... | 470.1 |
| 1957 | 1 040.2 | 257.3 | 203.1 | 26.9 | 107.1 | 53.7 | 15.4 | 44.5 | 535.4 |
| 1958 | 1 209.7 | 250.3 | 253.6 | 33.6 | 129.0 | 72.8 | 18.2 | 55.0 | 650.8 |
| **Percentage distribution according to sector— Distribution en pourcentage par secteur** | | | | | | | | | |
| 1950 – 1958 | 100.0 | 27.0 | 22.3 | 2.5 | 12.1 | 6.1 | 1.6 | ... | 50.7 |
| 1950 | 100.0 | 33.7 | 24.1 | 2.2 | 13.8 | 6.4 | 1.7 | ... | 42.2 |
| 1953 | 100.0 | 29.2 | 24.4 | 3.0 | 13.5 | 6.3 | 1.6 | ... | 46.4 |
| 1954 | 100.0 | 29.3 | 23.8 | 2.9 | 12.7 | 6.6 | 1.6 | 5.1 | 41.8 |
| 1958 | 100.0 | 20.6 | 21.0 | 2.8 | 10.7 | 6.0 | 1.5 | 4.6 | 53.8 |
| **b. At Prices of 1957 — Aux prix de 1957** | | | | | | | | | |
| **Absolute figures — Chiffres absolus** | | | | | | | | | |
| 1950 | 623.0 | 199.0 | 140.0 | 15.0 | 80.0 | 37.0 | 8.0 | ... | 284.0 |
| 1951 | 638.0 | 207.0 | 138.0 | 16.0 | 73.0 | 40.0 | 9.0 | ... | 293.0 |
| 1952 | 676.0 | 207.0 | 149.0 | 17.0 | 82.0 | 40.0 | 10.0 | ... | 320.0 |
| 1953 | 692.0 | 205.0 | 164.0 | 20.0 | 89.0 | 44.0 | 11.0 | ... | 323.0 |
| 1954 | 738.0 | 227.0 | 170.0 | 21.0 | 90.0 | 47.0 | 12.0 | ... | 341.0 |
| 1955 | 779.0 | 220.0 | 175.0 | 20.0 | 94.0 | 48.0 | 13.0 | ... | 384.0 |
| 1956 | 919.0 | 251.0 | 188.0 | 20.0 | 103.0 | 51.0 | 14.0 | ... | 480.0 |
| 1957 | 1 040.3 | 257.3 | 203.1 | 26.9 | 107.1 | 53.7 | 15.4 | 44.5 | 535.4 |
| 1958 | 1 093.0 | 221.0 | 231.0 | 29.0 | 119.0 | 65.0 | 18.0 | ... | 641.0 |
| **Percentage distribution according to sector— Distribution en pourcentage par secteur** | | | | | | | | | |
| 1950 – 1958 | 100.0 | 27.7 | 21.6 | 2.5 | 11.7 | 5.9 | 1.5 | ... | 50.7 |
| 1950 | 100.0 | 31.9 | 22.5 | 2.4 | 12.8 | 6.0 | 1.3 | ... | 45.6 |
| 1953 | 100.0 | 29.6 | 23.7 | 2.9 | 12.8 | 6.4 | 1.6 | ... | 46.7 |
| 1954 | 100.0 | 30.7 | 23.0 | 2.9 | 12.1 | 6.4 | 1.6 | ... | 46.3 |
| 1958 | 100.0 | 20.2 | 21.1 | 2.6 | 10.9 | 6.0 | 1.6 | ... | 58.7 |
| **Average annual rate of growth—Taux annuel moyen d'accroissement** | | | | | | | | | |
| 1950 – 1958 | 7.3 | 1.3 | 6.5 | 8.6 | 5.1 | 7.3 | 10.7 | ... | 10.7 |
| 1950 – 1953 | 3.6 | 1.0 | 5.4 | 10.1 | 3.6 | 5.9 | 11.2 | ... | 4.4 |
| 1954 – 1958 | 10.3 | 0.6 | 8.0 | 8.4 | 7.2 | 8.4 | 10.7 | ... | 14.2 |

[1] The figures of the total gross domestic product in Table 1B are less than those in Table 1A because the figures of the total gross domestic product in Table 1A reflect the difference between expenditures by residents abroad and expenditures by non-residents in Algeria whereas those in Table 1B reflect expenditures by non-residents in Algeria only.
[2] Included is Water supply (ISIC group 521).
[3] In the case of 1950-1953 and 1955-1957 for the data in current prices and 1950-1956 and 1958 for the data in prices of 1957, Transportation and communication (ISIC division 7) is included in Other sectors. The percentages and average annual rates of growth shown for Other sectors involving any of these years are therefore computed to include Transportation and communication.

[1] Les chiffres du produit intérieur brut total présentés au tableau 1B sont inférieurs aux chiffres du produit intérieur brut total présentés au tableau 1A car ces derniers tiennent compte du solde des dépenses des résidents à l'étranger et des non-résidents en Algérie, tandis que le chiffres du tableau 1B ne tiennent compte que des dépenses effectuées en Algérie par les non-résidents.
[2] Y compris la Distribution d'eau (CITI groupe 521).
[3] Pour 1950-1953 et 1955-1957 dans le cas des données aux prix courants et pour 1950-1956 et 1958 dans le cas des données aux prix de 1957, les Transports et communications (CITI branche 7) sont compris dans Autres secteurs. Les pourcentages et taux annuels moyens d'accroissement indiqués sous Autres secteurs pour l'une quelconque de ces années sont donc calculés de manière qu'ils comprennent les Transports et communications.

## 2. INDEX NUMBERS OF INDUSTRIAL PRODUCTION — INDICES DE LA PRODUCTION INDUSTRIELLE

### A. The Divisions of Industrial Activity
### Les branches de l'activité industrielle

| Period / Période | Total [1,2] | Mining [1] Industries extractives [1] | Manufacturing [2] Industries manufacturières [2] | Construction Bâtiment et travaux publics | Electricity and gas Electricité et gaz |
|---|---|---|---|---|---|
| ISIC — CITI | 1-4, 511-512 | 1 | 2-3 | 4 | 511-512 |

#### a. Indexes — Indices (1958 = 100)

| Period | Total | Mining | Manuf. | Constr. | Elec. |
|---|---|---|---|---|---|
| 1948....... | 50 | 76 | 47 | 52 | 45 |
| 1949....... | 50 | 90 | 44 | 59 | 50 |
| 1950....... | 56 | 94 | 51 | 68 | 56 |
| 1951....... | 66 | 103 | 62 | 74 | 63 |
| 1952....... | 67 | 112 | 61 | 74 | 66 |
| 1953....... | 69 | 124 | 61 | 75 | 72 |
| 1954....... | −75− | −123− | −68− | −78− | −77− |
| 1955....... | 82 | 143 | 75 | 79 | 81 |
| 1956....... | 85 | 109 | 81 | 82 | 88 |
| 1957....... | 90 | 110 | 86 | 87 | 93 |
| 1958....... | 100 | 100 | 100 | 100 | 100 |
| 1959....... | 102 | 90 | 102 | 117 | 110 |
| 1960....... | 111 | 128 | 108 | 122 | 121 |
| 1961....... | 110 | 114 | 106 | ... | 127 |

#### b. Average Annual Rate of Change — Taux annuel moyen de variation

| Period | Total | Mining | Manuf. | Constr. | Elec. |
|---|---|---|---|---|---|
| 1950 − 1960. | 7.1 | 3.1 | 7.8 | 6.0 | 8.0 |
| 1948 − 1953. | 6.7 | 10.3 | 5.4 | 7.6 | 9.9 |
| 1954 − 1958. | 7.5 | −5.0 | 10.1 | 6.4 | 6.8 |
| 1958 − 1960. | 5.4 | 13.1 | 3.9 | 10.5 | 10.0 |

For footnotes see end of table.

Pour les notes, voir au bas du tableau.

### B. The Major Groups of Mining
### Les classes de la branche Industries extractives

| Period / Période | All mining [1] Toutes industries extractives [1] | Coal mining Extraction du charbon | Metal mining Extraction des minerais métalliques | Crude petroleum and natural gas Pétrole brut et gaz naturel | Other mining Autres industries extractives |
|---|---|---|---|---|---|
| ISIC — CITI | 1 | 11 | 12 | 13 | 14-19 |

#### a. Indexes — Indices (1958 = 100)

| Period | All mining | Coal | Metal | Crude pet. | Other |
|---|---|---|---|---|---|
| 1938....... | ... | 9 | 115 | — | 89 |
| 1948....... | 76 | −150− | 73 | — | 101 |
| 1949....... | 90 | 177 | 94 | — | 97 |
| 1950....... | 94 | 172 | 96 | 1 | 103 |
| 1951....... | 103 | 164 | 107 | 2 | 117 |
| 1952....... | 112 | 180 | 118 | 10 | 104 |
| 1953....... | 124 | 193 | 133 | 19 | 91 |
| 1954....... | −123− | −198− | −123− | 17 | −114− |
| 1955....... | 143 | 198 | 148 | 13 | 119 |
| 1956....... | 109 | 195 | 110 | 7 | 97 |
| 1957....... | 110 | 155 | 112 | 4 | 97 |
| 1958....... | 100 | 100 | 100 | 100 | 100 |
| 1959....... | 90 | 80 | 89 | 296 | 95 |
| 1960....... | 128 | 76 | 141 | 1 961 | 91 |
| 1961....... | 114 | 51 | 126 | 3 498 | 80 |

#### b. Average Annual Rate of Change — Taux annuel moyen de variation

| Period | All mining | Coal | Metal | Crude pet. | Other |
|---|---|---|---|---|---|
| 1938 − 1960. | ... | 10.2 | 0.9 | ... | 0.1 |
| 1938 − 1948. | ... | 32.5 | −4.4 | ... | 1.3 |
| 1950 − 1960. | 3.1 | −7.8 | 3.9 | . | −1.2 |
| 1948 − 1953. | 10.3 | 5.2 | 12.7 | ... | −0.2 |
| 1954 − 1958. | −5.0 | −15.7 | −5.0 | 55.7 | −3.2 |
| 1958 − 1960. | 13.1 | −12.8 | 18.7 | 40.0 | −4.6 |

For footnotes see end of table.

Pour les notes, voir au bas du tableau.

## C. Selected Major Groups of Manufacturing
### Quelques classes de la branche Industries manufacturières

| Period<br>Période | Manu-<br>facturing [2]<br><br>Industries<br>manufac-<br>turières [2] | Food,<br>beverages<br>and<br>tobacco<br><br>Industries<br>alimen-<br>taires,<br>boissons,<br>tabac | Textiles | Paper<br>and<br>paper<br>products<br><br>Papier<br>et<br>ouvrages<br>en<br>papier | Printing<br>and<br>publishing<br><br>Im-<br>primerie<br>et<br>édition | Chemicals<br>and<br>chemical<br>products<br><br>Produits<br>chi-<br>miques | Non-<br>metallic<br>mineral<br>products<br><br>Produits<br>minéraux<br>non<br>métal-<br>liques | Basic<br>metals<br><br>Métal-<br>lurgie<br>de base | Metal<br>products<br><br>Ouvrages<br>en<br>métaux |
|---|---|---|---|---|---|---|---|---|---|
| ISIC — CITI | 2–3 | 20–22 | 23 | 27 | 28 | 31 | 33 | 34 | 35–38 |

### a. Indexes — Indices (1958 = 100)

| | | | | | | | | | |
|---|---|---|---|---|---|---|---|---|---|
| 1950............. | 51 | 49 | 159 | 38 | 67 | 50 | 50 | 87 | 64 |
| 1951............. | 62 | 52 | 150 | 65 | 70 | 59 | 64 | 95 | 78 |
| 1952............. | 61 | 53 | 184 | 50 | 70 | 53 | 63 | 70 | 76 |
| 1953............. | 61 | 56 | 185 | 63 | 66 | 57 | 66 | 63 | 67 |
| 1954............. | – 68 – | – 60 – | – 164 – | – 74 – | – 65 – | – 67 – | – 78 – | – 67 – | – 68 – |
| 1955............. | 75 | 72 | 56 | 86 | 76 | 80 | 82 | 83 | 78 |
| 1956............. | 81 | 79 | 56 | 95 | 85 | 86 | 81 | 80 | 80 |
| 1957............. | 86 | 86 | 70 | 96 | 93 | 88 | 85 | 86 | 85 |
| 1958............. | 100 | 100 | 100 | 100 | 100 | 100 | 100 | 100 | 100 |
| 1959............. | 102 | 101 | 95 | 105 | 102 | 117 | 112 | 104 | 94 |
| 1960............. | 108 | 103 | 106 | 107 | 115 | 123 | 120 | 109 | 104 |
| 1961............. | 106 | 108 | 116 | 121 | 109 | 123 | 119 | 100 | 85 |

### b. Average Annual Rate of Change — Taux annuel moyen de variation

| | | | | | | | | | |
|---|---|---|---|---|---|---|---|---|---|
| 1950–1960....... | 7.8 | 7.7 | −4.0 | 10.9 | 5.5 | 9.4 | 9.2 | 2.3 | 5.0 |
| 1954–1958....... | 10.1 | 13.6 | −11.6 | 7.8 | 11.4 | 10.5 | 6.4 | 10.5 | 10.1 |
| 1958–1960....... | 3.9 | 1.5 | 3.0 | 3.4 | 7.2 | 10.9 | 9.5 | 4.4 | 2.0 |

[1] The index numbers for Mining (ISIC division 1) exclude crude petroleum and natural gas (ISIC major group 13) although separate indexes are shown for this major group.

[2] The index numbers for Manufacturing (ISIC division 2–3) for 1950-1953 do not cover Food and beverages (ISIC major groups 20–21) and glass hollow ware (part of ISIC group 332) although major group index numbers are shown covering these activities. In addition, the following kinds of manufacturing activities are excluded from the index numbers for all years: Clothing, footwear and made-up textiles (ISIC major group 24), Wood products and furniture (ISIC major groups 25–26), Leather and leather products (ISIC major group 29), Rubber products (ISIC major group 30), Petroleum and coal product (ISIC major group 32) and Miscellaneous manufacturing (ISIC major group 39).

[1] Les indices concernant les Industries extractives (CITI branche 1) ne comprennent pas Pétrole brut et gaz naturel (CITI classe 13), bien que des indices distincts soient présents pour cette classe.

[2] Les indices de 1950-1953 concernant les Industries manufac-turières (CITI branches 2-3) ne comprennent pas les Industries alimentaires et boissons (CITI classes 20–21) et la fabrication des récipients en verre (dans CITI groupe 332), bien que les indices de classe reproduits couvrent ces activités. En outre, les industries ci-après sont exclues pour toutes les années; Articles d'habillement, chaussures et ouvrages en tissu (CITI classe 24), Bois et meubles (CITI classes 25–26), Cuir et articles en cuir (CITI classe 29), Ouvrages en caoutchouc (CITI classe 30), Produits dérivés du charbon et du pétrole (CITI classe 32) et Industries manufacturières diverses (CITI classe 39).

## 3. CHARACTERISTICS OF ALL INDUSTRIAL ENTERPRISES

## CARACTERISTIQUES DE TOUTES LES ENTREPRISES INDUSTRIELLES

### 1954, 1957

Value added in thousand million old Francs; number of engaged and employees, including working proprietors, in thousands.

Valeur ajoutée en milliards d'anciens francs; nombre de personnes occupées et de salariés, y compris les propriétaires qui travaillent, en milliers.

### A. The Divisions of Industrial Activitiy — Les branches de l'activité industrielle

| Year and item of data | All industrial activity — Toutes industries | Mining [1] Industries extractives [1] | Manu- facturing[1] Industries manu- facturières[1] | Con- struction Bâtiment et travaux publics | Electricity and gas Electricité et gaz | Année et rubrique | Year and item of data | All industrial activity — Toutes industries | Mining [1] Industries extractives [1] | Manu- facturing[1] Industries manu- facturières[1] | Con- struction Bâtiment et travaux publics | Electricity and gas Electricité et gaz | Année et rubrique |
|---|---|---|---|---|---|---|---|---|---|---|---|---|---|
| ISIC | 1-4,511-512 | 11-13, 19 | 14, 2-3 | 4 | 511-512 | CITI | ISIC | 1-4,511-512 | 11-13, 19 | 14, 2-3 | 4 | 511-512 | CITI |
| | a. Absolute Figures — Chiffres absolus | | | | | | | b. Structure | | | | | |
| 1954 Value added....... | 163.3 | 19.2 | 88.0 | 44.6 | 11.5 | 1954 Valeur ajoutée Nombre de salariés, y compris les propriétaires qui travaillent | 1954 Distribution in percent of: Value added..... Number of employees....... | 100.0 100.0 | 11.7 7.3 | 53.9 51.8 | 27.4 38.9 | 7.0 2.0 | 1954 Distribution en pourcentage: Valeur ajoutée Nombre de salariés |
| Number of employees, including working proprietors...... | 264.8 | 19.4 | 137.1 | 102.9 | 5.4 | | | | | | | | |
| 1957 Value added....... | 203.3 | 26.9 | 107.3 | 53.7 | 15.4 | 1957 Valeur ajoutée Nombre de personnes occupées Nombre de salariés, y compris les propriétaires qui travaillent | 1957 Distribution in percent of: Value added..... Number of employees....... | 100.0 100.0 | 13.2 7.5 | 52.8 50.8 | 26.4 39.9 | 7.6 1.8 | 1957 Distribution en pourcentage: Valeur ajoutée Nombre de salariés |
| Number of engaged........ | 284.7 | 20.9 | 146.7 | 112.1 | 5.0 | | | | | | | | |
| Number of employees, including working proprietors...... | 278.0 | 20.9 | 141.3 | 110.8 | 5.0 | | | | | | | | |

For footnotes see end of table.                                 Pour les notes, voir au bas du tableau.

### B. The Major Groups of Mining — Les classes de la branche Industries extractives

| Year and item of data | Total [1] | Crude petroleum and natural gas Pétrole brut et gaz naturel | Other mining [1] Divers [1] | Année et rubrique | Year and item of data | Total [1] | Crude petroleum and natural gas Pétrole brut et gaz naturel | Other mining [1] Divers [1] | Année et rubrique |
|---|---|---|---|---|---|---|---|---|---|
| ISIC | 11-13, 19 | 13 | 11, 12, 19 | CITI | ISIC | 11-13, 19 | 13 | 11, 12, 19 | CITI |
| | a. Absolute Figures Chiffres absolus | | | | | b. Structure | | | |
| 1954 Value added................. | 19.2 | 5.5 | 13.7 | 1954 Valeur ajoutée | 1954 Distribution in percent of: Value added............... Number of employees........ | 100.0 100.0 | 28.7 14.4 | 71.3 85.6 | 1954 Distribution en pourcentage: Valeur ajoutée Nombre de salariés |
| Number of engaged............ | 19.4 | 2.8 | 16.6 | Nombre de personnes occupées | | | | | |
| Number of employees, including working proprietors.......... | 19.4 | 2.8 | 16.6 | Nombre de salariés, y compris les propriétaires qui travaillent | | | | | |
| 1957 Value added................. | 26.9 | 12.7 | 14.2 | 1957 Valeur ajoutée | 1957 Distribution in percent of: Value added............... Number of employees........ | 100.0 100.0 | 47.2 27.3 | 52.8 72.7 | 1957 Distribution en pourcentage: Valeur ajoutée Nombre de salariés |
| Number of engaged............ | 20.9 | 5.7 | 15.2 | Nombre de personnes occupées | | | | | |
| Number of employees, including working proprietors.......... | 20.9 | 5.7 | 15.2 | Nombre de salariés, y compris les propriétaires qui travaillent | | | | | |

For footnotes see end of table.                                 Pour les notes, voir au bas du tableau.

## C.  The Major Groups of Manufacturing — Les classes de la branche Industries manufacturières

| Year and item of data | Manufacturing [1]<br>Industries manufacturières [1] | Food beverages and tobacco [2]<br>Industries alimentaires, boissons, tabac [2] | Textiles and clothing [3]<br>Textiles et articles d'habillement [3] | Wood products and furniture<br>Bois et meubles | Paper and paper products<br>Papier et ouvrages en papier | Printing and publishing<br>Imprimerie et édition | Leather and leather products [3]<br>Cuir et articles en cuir [3] | Rubber products<br>Ouvrages en caoutchouc | Chemicals and chemical, petroleum and coal products [2]<br>Produits chimiques et dérivés du pétrole et du charbon [2] | Non-metallic mineral products [1]<br>Produits minéraux non métalliques [1] | Basic metals<br>Métallurgie de base | Metal products<br>Ouvrages en métaux | Other manufacturing<br>Autres industries manufacturières | Année et rubrique |
|---|---|---|---|---|---|---|---|---|---|---|---|---|---|---|
| ISIC | 14, 2–3 | 20–22 | 23, 243-244 | 25–26 | 27 | 28 | 241, 29 | 30 | 31–32 | 14, 33 | 34 | 35–38 | 39 | CITI |
| *a. Absolute Figures — Chiffres absolus* | | | | | | | | | | | | | | |
| **1954** Value added......... | 88.0 | 32.2 | 8.6 | 3.7 | 0.8 | 3.2 | 4.5 | 0.2 | 3.6 | 7.6 | 0.2 | 20.4 | 3.0 | **1954** Valeur ajoutée |
| Number of employees, including working proprietors.......... | 137.1 | 35.5 | 28.3 | 7.3 | 1.2 | 4.1 | 8.2 | 0.4 | 3.9 | 14.3 | 0.3 | 27.1 | 6.6 | Nombre de salariés, y compris les propriétaires qui travaillent |
| **1957** Value added......... | 107.3 | 43.0 | 7.8 | 4.4 | 1.4 | 4.2 | 4.2 | 0.5 | 6.1 | 9.1 | 0.5 | 23.6 | 2.5 | **1957** Valeur ajoutée |
| Number of engaged.... | 146.7 | 38.2 | 29.6 | 8.6 | 1.4 | 4.7 | 9.4 | 0.4 | 4.7 | 13.3 | 0.3 | 29.5 | 6.6 | Nombre de personnes occupées |
| Number of employees, including working proprietors.......... | 141.3 | 36.5 | 28.6 | 8.0 | 1.4 | 4.6 | 8.8 | 0.4 | 4.7 | 13.2 | 0.3 | 28.5 | 6.4 | Nombre de salariés, y compris les propriétaires qui travaillent |
| *b. Structure* | | | | | | | | | | | | | | |
| **1954** Distribution in percent of: | | | | | | | | | | | | | | **1954** Distribution en pourcentage: |
| Value added........ | 100.0 | 36.6 | 9.8 | 4.2 | 0.9 | 3.6 | 5.1 | 0.2 | 4.1 | 8.6 | 0.2 | 23.3 | 3.4 | Valeur ajoutée |
| Number of employees. | 100.0 | 25.9 | 20.6 | 5.3 | 0.9 | 3.0 | 6.0 | 0.3 | 2.8 | 10.4 | 0.2 | 19.8 | 4.8 | Nombre de salariés |
| **1957** Distribution in percent of: | | | | | | | | | | | | | | **1957** Distribution en pourcentage: |
| Value added........ | 100.0 | 40.0 | 7.3 | 4.1 | 1.3 | 3.9 | 3.9 | 0.5 | 5.7 | 8.5 | 0.5 | 22.0 | 2.3 | Valeur ajoutée |
| Number of employees. | 100.0 | 26.0 | 20.2 | 5.6 | 1.0 | 3.2 | 6.2 | 0.3 | 3.3 | 9.3 | 0.2 | 20.2 | 4.5 | Nombre de salariés |

[1] Stone quarrying (ISIC major group 14) is included in Manufacturing under Non-metallic mineral products (ISIC major group 33).
[2] The manufacture of matches (part of ISIC major group 31) is included in Tobacco manufacturing (ISIC major group 22).
[3] The Manufacture of footwear (ISIC group 241) is included under Leather and leather products (ISIC major group 29).

[1] L'Extraction de la pierre à bâtir (CITI classe 14) est comprise dans Industries manufacturières sous Produits minéraux non métalliques (CITI classe 33).
[2] La fabrication des allumettes (dans CITI classe 31) est comprise dans Industrie du tabac (CITI classe 22).
[3] La fabrication des chaussures (CITI groupe 241) est comprise dans Cuir et articles en cuir (CITI classe 29).

# 4. CHARACTERISTICS OF INDUSTRIAL ENTERPRISES WITH ONE OR MORE EMPLOYEE

## CARACTERISTIQUES DES ENTREPRISES INDUSTRIELLES OCCUPANT UN SALARIE OU PLUS

### 1954, 1957

Number of enterprises in units; wages and salaries in thousand million old Francs; and number of employees in thousands.

Nombre d'entreprises en unités; traitements et salaires en milliards d'anciens francs; nombre de salariés en milliers.

## A. The Divisions of Industrial Activity — Les branches de l'activité industrielle

| Year and item of data | All industrial activity<br>Toutes industries | Mining [1]<br>Industries ex-tractives [1] | Manu-facturing [1]<br>Industries manu-facturières[1] | Con-struction<br>Bâtiment et travaux publics | Electricity and gas<br>Electricité et gaz | Année et rubrique |
|---|---|---|---|---|---|---|
| ISIC | 1-4,511-512 | 1 | 2-3 | 4 | 511-512 | CITI |
| | a. Absolute Figures — Chiffres absolus | | | | | |
| **1954** | | | | | | **1954** |
| Number of employees....... | 213.5 | 19.4 | 92.4 | 96.3 | 5.4 | Nombre de salariés |
| Wages and salaries. | 56.0 | 6.2 | 25.3 | 21.0 | 3.5 | Traitements et salaires |
| **1957** | | | | | | **1957** |
| Number of enterprises...... | 7 583 | 75 | 5 312 | 2 181 | 15 | Nombre d'entreprises |
| Number of employees....... | 226.4 | 20.9 | 96.5 | 104.0 | 5.0 | Nombre de salariés |
| Wages and salaries. | 63.6 | 6.4 | 28.7 | 23.9 | 4.6 | Traitements et salaire |

For footnotes see end of table.

Pour les notes, voir au bas du tableau.

## B. The Major Groups of Mining — Les classes de la branche Industries extractives

| Year and item of data | Total [1] | Crude petroleum and natural gas<br>Pétrole brut et gaz naturel | Other mining [1]<br>Divers [1] | Année et rubrique |
|---|---|---|---|---|
| ISIC | 1 | 13 | 11, 12, 19 | CITI |
| | a. Absolute Figures<br>Chiffres absolus | | | |
| **1954** | | | | **1954** |
| Number of employees.......... | 19.4 | 2.8 | 16.6 | Nombre de salariés |
| Wages and salaries............. | 6.2 | 2.3 | 3.9 | Traitements et salaires |
| **1957** | | | | **1957** |
| Number of enterprises......... | 75 | 19 | 56 | Nombre d'entreprises |
| Number of employees.......... | 20.9 | 5.7 | 15.2 | Nombre de salariés |
| Wages and salaries............. | 6.4 | 2.6 | 3.8 | Traitements et salaires |

For footnotes see end of table.

Pour les notes, voir au bas du tableau.

## C. The Major Groups of Manufacturing — Les classes de la branche Industries manufacturières

| Year and item of data | Manufacturing[1] / Industries manufacturières[1] | Food beverages and tobacco[2] / Industries alimentaires, boissons, tabac[2] | Textiles and clothing / Textiles et articles d'habillement | Wood products and furniture / Bois et meubles | Paper and paper products / Papier et ouvrages en papier | Printing and publishing / Imprimerie et édition | Leather and leather products[3] / Cuir et articles en cuir[3] | Rubber products / Ouvrages en caoutchouc | Chemicals and chemical, petroleum and coal products[2] / Produits chimiques et dérivés du pétrole et du charbon[2] | Non-metallic mineral products[1] / Produits minéraux non métalliques[1] | Basic metals / Métallurgie de base | Metal products / Ouvrages en métaux | Other manufacturing / Autres industries manufacturières | Année et rubrique |
|---|---|---|---|---|---|---|---|---|---|---|---|---|---|---|
| ISIC | 14, 2-3 | 20-22 | 23, 243-244 | 25-26 | 27 | 28 | 241, 29 | 30 | 31-32 | 14, 33 | 34 | 35-38 | 39 | CITI |
| *a. Absolute Figures — Chiffres absolus* | | | | | | | | | | | | | | |
| **1954** | | | | | | | | | | | | | | **1954** |
| Number of employees... | 92.4 | 27.3 | 7.7 | 5.9 | 1.2 | 3.6 | 3.3 | 0.3 | 3.9 | 13.8 | 0.3 | 20.2 | 4.9 | Nombre de salariés |
| Wages and salaries..... | 25.3 | 6.9 | 2.0 | 1.3 | 0.4 | 1.6 | 0.7 | — | 1.4 | 3.6 | 0.1 | 6.5 | 0.8 | Traitements et salaires |
| **1957** | | | | | | | | | | | | | | **1957** |
| Number of enterprises... | 5 312 | 2 177 | 530 | 339 | 23 | 259 | 216 | 49 | 99 | 291 | 4 | 1 102 | 223 | Nombre d'entreprises |
| Number of employees... | 96.5 | 28.2 | 8.2 | 6.4 | 1.4 | 4.0 | 3.8 | 0.3 | 4.7 | 12.8 | 0.3 | 22.0 | 4.4 | Nombre de salariés |
| Wages and salaries..... | 28.7 | 8.8 | 1.2 | 1.5 | 0.5 | 1.8 | 0.6 | 0.1 | 1.7 | 3.3 | — | 8.3 | 0.9 | Traitements et salaires |

[1] Stone quarrying (ISIC major group 14) is included in Manufacturing under Non-metallic mineral products (ISIC major group 33).
[2] The manufacture of matches (part of ISIC major group 31) is included in Tobacco manufacturing (ISIC major group 22).
[3] The Manufacture of footwear (ISIC group 241) is included under Leather and leather products (ISIC major group 29).

[1] L'Extraction de la pierre à bâtir (CITI classe 14) est comprise dans Industries manufacturières sous Produits minéraux non métalliques (CITI classe 33).
[2] La fabrication des allumettes (dans CITI classe 31) est comprise dans Industrie du tabac (CITI classe 22).
[3] La fabrication des chaussures (CITI groupe 241) est comprise dans Cuir et articles en cuir (CITI classe 29).

# ARGENTINA — ARGENTINE

## The Gross Domestic Product

Estimates of expenditure on and the industrial origin of the gross domestic product are presented in Table 1. This table has been compiled from data supplied by the Banco Central de la República, Buenos Aires in response to the United Nations national accounts questionnaire. Official estimates are published by the Banco in its monthly publication *Boletín Estadístico*. Estimates up to 1954 have been published by the Secretaría de Asuntos Económicos in *Producto e Ingreso de la República Argentina en el período 1935-54*, which also gives details of the methods and sources used.

## Index Numbers of Industrial Production

The index numbers set out in Table 2 are derived from indexes of industrial production calculated by the Dirección Nacional de Estadística y Censos, Buenos Aires, and its predecessor agencies. The index numbers have been issued for earlier years in *La Actividad Industrial Argentina desde 1937 a 1949,* Dirección General del Servicio Estadístico Nacional, September 1950 and *Indices del Costo del Nivel de Vida, Actividad Industrial y Costo de la Construcción* and in recent years in *Boletín Mensual de Estadística.*

The index numbers of production are computed as base weighted arithmetic averages. The weighting base for the indexes is 1943 but the comparison base utilized by the Dirección in publishing the indexes is 1952. The indicators employed in compiling the indexes are series of relatives on the quantity of individual commodities produced, for the most part, but on the amount of individual raw materials consumed, the number of man-hours worked or even the number of employees, in some cases. The weights for combining quantity relatives into index numbers for detailed classes of industrial activity are based on the gross value of production of each of the individual commodities represented. However, weights for combining these indexes into index numbers for broader categories of industry are derived from value added in 1943 at market prices. Further details concerning the index numbers of industrial production may be found in *La Actividad Industrial Argentina desde 1937 a 1949.*

## Index Numbers of Industrial Employment

The index numbers of industrial employment presented in Table 3 have been obtained from index numbers based on the number of operatives employed compiled by the Dirección Nacional de Estadística y Censos and its predecessor agencies. The index numbers up to 1949 have been published in *La Actividad Industrial Argentina desde 1937 a 1949,* Dirección General del Servicio Estadístico Nacional, September 1950. The indexes

## Le produit intérieur brut

Des estimations du produit intérieur brut ainsi que celles de ses composantes, ventilées suivant le secteur industriel d'origine sont reproduites au tableau 1. Ce tableau a été construit à partir des données fournies par la Banco Central de la República, Buenos Aires en réponse au questionnaire de l'O.N.U. relatif aux comptes nationaux. Les estimations relatives aux années précédant 1954, 1954 incluse, ont été publiées par le Secretaría de Asuntos Económicos dans *Producto e Ingreso de la República Argentina en el período 1953-54*, publication qui fournit également les détails relatifs aux méthodes adoptées et aux sources utilisées.

## Indices de la production industrielle

Les indices du tableau 2 sont tirés d'indices de la production industrielle construits par la Dirección Nacional de Estadística y Censos, Buenos Aires, et par les organismes qui l'ont précédé. Les indices des premières années ont été publiés dans *La Actividad Industrial Argentina desde 1937 a 1949*, Dirección General del Servicio Estadístico Nacional, septembre 1950, et *Indices del Costo del Nivel de Vida, Actividad Industrial y Costo de la Construcción*, et ceux des années suivantes dans *Boletín Mensual de Estadística.*

Les indices de la production sont des moyennes arithmétiques à pondération fixe. La base de pondération est 1943, mais la base de comparaison utilisée par la Dirección pour les indices qu'elle publie est 1952. Les indicateurs utilisés pour construire ces indices sont en général des séries de rapports quantitatifs concernant la production de chaque marchandise, mais aussi, dans certains cas, le volume de la consommation de chaque matière première, le nombre d'heures de travail effectuées ou même le nombre de salariés. Pour combiner les rapports quantitatifs en indices de catégorie, on a pondéré en fonction de la valeur brute de la production de chaque marchandise. Toutefois, les poids utilisés pour combiner ces indices de catégorie en indices valables pour les subdivisions plus larges de l'activité économique sont tirés de la valeur ajoutée en 1943, calculée aux prix du marché. Pour plus amples détails sur les indices de la production industrielle, voir *La Actividad Industrial Argentina desde 1937 a 1949.*

## Indices de l'emploi industriel

Les indices de l'emploi industriel reproduits au tableau 3 ont été obtenus à partir d'indices fondés sur le nombre d'ouvriers occupés, calculés par la Dirección Nacional de Estadística y Censos et les bureaux qui en tenaient lieu avant sa création. Les indices relatifs aux années précédant 1949, 1949 incluse, ont été publiés par *La Actividad Industrial Argentina desde 1937 a 1949*, Dirección General del Servicio Estadístico Nacional, septembre 1950. Les

for the following years up to 1957 have been published in *Annuario Estadístico 1957* and for the most recent years in *Boletín Mensual de Estadística,* both issued by the Dirección Nacional de Estadística y Censos. The Statistical Office of the United Nations also received some extra details by correspondence.

The number of operatives employed, on which the indexes are based, are those employed full time by approximately 2,000 reporting establishments; the figures include persons absent because of illness, leave, accident or strike. The indexes are computed monthly and the weights used to combine the various series are the numbers employed, as shown by the 1943 Industrial Census. The indexes have been published up to 1958 with a comparison base of 1943; for the years 1958 onwards, the comparison base has been changed to 1952.

### The Characteristics and Structure of Industrial Activity

The data set out in Tables 4 and 5 are from the results of Censuses of Industry taken by the Dirección Nacional de Estadística y Censos and its predecessor agencies. The published sources of these data are: *Estadística Industrial de 1939* for the 1939 figures; *Anuario Estadístico, 1949-1950* for the 1948 figures; and both *Censo Industrial 1954* and *Boletín Mensual de Estadística,* January 1959 for the 1953 data. Although the Censuses for 1939, 1948 and 1953 were, in principle, comparable to one another with regard to the inclusion of industrial establishments irrespective of size, this was not so in fact. In the case of the 1948 census, establishments in some less important manufacturing industries which engaged fewer than five persons were omitted. Perhaps a more important factor contributing to incomparabilities between the three Censuses was the differences in the number of non-respondents among the establishments covered, for which, it should be noted, adjustments have not been made in the published results. The coverage of the data for 1953 seems to be much more complete than the data for 1939 or 1948.

It should be emphasized, however, that contributing to comparability between the data from the three Censuses was the use of the same definitions for items of data sought and of the same detailed scheme of classification according to kind of activity in compiling and publishing results. The counts of establishments relate to the number in business during the census year for which returns were received. The definitions of the other items of data sought are basically consistent with the International Standards in Basic Industrial Statistics. However, homeworkers are excluded from the number engaged, whilst payments to homeworkers are included in the figure of payments of wages and salaries to employees. Also, in 1953, the number of engaged and the number of employees are composed of figures of the number of operatives, which are the

indices relatifs aux années suivantes et jusqu'en 1957, inclusivement, ont été publiés dans *Annuario Estadístico 1957* et ceux relatifs aux années les plus récentes dans *Boletín Mensual de Estadística;* les deux publications ont été éditées par la Dirección Nacional de Estadística y Censos. Le Bureau de Statistique de l'O.N.U. reçoit également des détails complémentaires par voie de correspondance.

Le nombre d'ouvriers occupés, sur lequel sont basés les indices, couvre les ouvriers employés à plein temps par approximativement 2000 établissements enregistrés; ces chiffres couvrent les personnes absentes pour causes de maladie, congé, accident ou grève. Les indices sont calculés mensuellement et les coefficients de pondération utilisés pour combiner les différentes séries, sont basés sur le nombre de personnes occupées au recensement industriel de 1943. Ces indices ont été publiés pour les années précédant 1958 avec comme base de comparaison 1943; à partir de 1958, 1952 a été prise comme nouvelle base de comparaison.

### Caractéristiques et structure de l'activité industrielle

Les données des tableaux 4 et 5 sont tirées des résultats des recensements de l'industrie effectués tous les deux ans par la Dirección Nacional de Estadística y Censos et par les organismes qui l'ont précédée. Ces résultats sont publiés dans *Estadística Industrial de 1939* (source des chiffres de 1939), dans *Anuario Estadístico, 1949-1950* (source des chiffres de 1948) et dans *Censo Industrial 1954* et *Boletín Mensual de Estadística,* janvier 1959 (source des chiffres de 1953). Bien que les recensements de 1939, 1948 et 1953 soient théoriquement comparables du fait qu'ils devaient porter sur tous les établissements industriels, quelle que fût leur dimension, il n'en est pas en fait ainsi. Dans le cas du recensement de 1948, les établissements de certaines industries manufacturières secondaires, qui occupaient moins de cinq personnes ont été exclus. Un élément peut-être plus important encore qui a provoqué ces défauts de comparabilité entre les trois recensements est le fait que le nombre des établissements qui n'ont pas répondu au questionnaire n'était pas le même et qu'aucun ajustement n'a été fait pour en tenir compte dans les résultats publiés. La couverture des données de 1953 semble être bien plus complète que celle des données de 1939 ou 1948.

Il convient de souligner cependant que les données provenant des trois recensements restent comparables du fait qu'on a utilisé les mêmes définitions pour chaque rubrique et le même système de classement par type d'activité pour l'exploitation et la publication des résultats. Le nombre d'établissements est celui des établissements qui étaient en activité pendant l'année du recensement et qui ont répondu au questionnaire. Les définitions utilisées pour les autres rubriques sont fondamentalement compatibles avec les Normes internationales relatives aux statistiques industrielles de base. Cependant, le nombre de personnes occupées ne comprend pas les travailleurs à domicile, quoique les traitements et salaires payés aux salariés couvrent ceux payés aux travailleurs à domicile. De plus en 1953 le nombre de personnes occupées et le nombre de salariés sont calculés à partir d'un chiffre don-

monthly average for the year 1953, and figures of the other persons engaged or employed, which are the number as at the 30th July 1954. Value added is valued at market prices, ex-factory. The capacity of installed power equipment is the sum of the horsepowers of all prime movers and electric motors driven by purchased electricity that were in use and in reserve. The figures of energy consumed for 1953 relate to fuels and purchased electricity consumed. As the figures of fuels consumed are not restricted to purchased fuels, it is possible that the figures of energy consumed are overstated for certain industries where, for example, gas for own use is manufactured from coal or coke.

nant le nombre d'ouvriers qui est la moyenne mensuelle pour 1953, et d'un chiffre donnant le nombre de personnes engagées ou occupées, qui est le nombre relevé au 30 juillet 1954. La valeur ajoutée est calculée aux prix du marché, départ usine. La puissance installée représente la puissance de tous les moteurs primaires et des moteurs électriques actionnés avec de l'électricité achetée, qui étaient en service normal ou en réserve. Les chiffres relatifs à l'énergie consommée pour 1953 couvrent les combustibles consommés et l'électricité achetée et consommée. Comme les chiffres relatifs aux combustibles consommés ne se réduisent pas aux combustibles achetés seulement il est possible que les chiffres relatifs à l'énergie consommée soient surestimés pour les industries où, par exemple, le gaz autoconsommé est fabriqué à partir du charbon ou du coke.

## 1. THE GROSS DOMESTIC PRODUCT — PRODUIT INTERIEUR BRUT

Million Pesos                                                                 Millions de pesos

### A. Expenditure on the Gross Domestic Product at Market Prices
### Dépenses relatives au produit intérieur brut aux prix du marché

| Item of data and year<br>Rubrique et année | Total | Consumption<br>Consommation | | Gross Domestic Capital Formation<br>Formation brute de capital intérieur | | Net exports of goods and services<br>Exportations nettes de biens et de services |
|---|---|---|---|---|---|---|
| | | Total | Government [1]<br>Etat [1] | Total [2] | Fixed<br>Fixe | |
| *a. At Current Prices — Aux prix courants* | | | | | | |
| **Absolute figures — Chiffres absolus** | | | | | | |
| 1938 | 10 604 | 9 195 | 1 212 | 1 943 | 1 528 | −534 |
| 1948 | 43 800 | 31 527 | 5 684 | 11 961 | 10 324 | 312 |
| 1950 | 62 291 | 48 282 | 7 716 | 13 584 | 14 261 | 425 |
| 1951 | 87 792 | 69 224 | 10 541 | 21 032 | 19 298 | −2 464 |
| 1952 | 100 253 | 81 218 | 13 278 | 22 353 | 20 173 | −3 318 |
| 1953 | 112 099 | 92 334 | 15 067 | 17 965 | 19 176 | 1 800 |
| 1954 | 125 258 | 100 317 | 18 048 | 24 055 | 22 216 | 886 |
| 1955 | 146 718 | 121 504 | 20 438 | 26 996 | 26 466 | −1 782 |
| 1956 | 180 666 | 149 250 | 25 633 | 33 938 | 35 258 | −2 522 |
| 1957 | 232 075 | 188 524 | 28 096 | 51 168 | 52 863 | −7 617 |
| 1958 | 321 154 | 260 878 | 43 500 | 66 635 | 67 845 | −6 359 |
| 1959 | 610 056 | 495 526 | 78 660 | 110 600 | 112 905 | 3 930 |
| 1960 | 790 034 | 633 474 | 88 590 | 167 270 | 164 315 | −10 710 |
| 1961 | 932 000 | 782 725 | 122 734 | 189 675 | 196 012 | −40 400 |
| **Percentage distribution of average annual expenditure — Distribution en pourcentage des dépenses annuelles moyennes** | | | | | | |
| 1938 | 100.0 | 86.7 | 11.4 | 18.3 | 14.4 | −5.0 |
| 1948 | 100.0 | 72.0 | 13.0 | 27.3 | 23.6 | 0.7 |
| 1950 – 1960 | 100.0 | 80.9 | 12.6 | 20.1 | 20.0 | −1.0 |
| 1950 | 100.0 | 77.5 | 12.4 | 21.8 | 22.9 | 0.7 |
| 1953 | 100.0 | 82.4 | 13.4 | 16.0 | 17.1 | 1.6 |
| 1954 | 100.0 | 80.1 | 14.4 | 19.2 | 17.7 | 0.7 |
| 1958 | 100.0 | 81.2 | 13.5 | 20.8 | 21.1 | −2.0 |
| 1960 | 100.0 | 80.2 | 11.2 | 21.2 | 20.8 | −1.4 |
| *b. At Prices of 1950 [3] — Aux prix de 1950 [3]* | | | | | | |
| **Absolute figures — Chiffres absolus** | | | | | | [4] |
| 1938 | 39 408 | 29 972 | 4 082 | 11 932 | 10 925 | −2 496 |
| 1948 | 65 890 | 46 311 | 8 255 | 19 160 | 17 046 | 419 |
| 1950 | 62 249 | 48 282 | 7 716 | 13 584 | 14 261 | 383 |
| 1951 | 64 046 | 49 776 | 7 900 | 15 963 | 14 766 | −1 693 |
| 1952 | 59 715 | 46 919 | 8 044 | 14 479 | 13 297 | −1 683 |
| 1953 | 63 034 | 50 348 | 8 258 | 11 607 | 12 699 | 1 079 |
| 1954 | 65 226 | 50 761 | 8 704 | 13 918 | 13 214 | 547 |
| 1955 | 68 292 | 54 599 | 8 658 | 14 818 | 14 597 | −1 125 |
| 1956 | 67 703 | 54 566 | 8 963 | 13 851 | 14 295 | −714 |
| 1957 | 70 415 | 54 990 | 8 472 | 16 887 | 17 416 | −1 462 |
| 1958 | 72 350 | 56 803 | 8 300 | 16 780 | 17 040 | −1 233 |
| 1959 | 68 900 | 54 602 | 8 780 | 14 250 | 14 525 | 48 |
| 1960 | 71 933 | 54 920 | 8 562 | 17 920 | 17 805 | −907 |
| 1961 | 76 000 | 60 800 | 9 077 | 18 600 | 18 900 | −3 400 |
| **Percentage distribution of average annual expenditure — Distribution en pourcentage des dépenses annuelles moyennes** | | | | | | |
| 1938 | 100.0 | 76.0 | 10.4 | 30.3 | 27.7 | −6.3 |
| 1948 | 100.0 | 70.3 | 12.5 | 29.1 | 25.9 | 0.6 |
| 1950 – 1960 | 100.0 | 78.6 | 12.6 | 22.3 | 22.3 | −0.9 |
| 1950 | 100.0 | 77.6 | 12.4 | 21.8 | 22.9 | 0.6 |
| 1953 | 100.0 | 79.9 | 13.1 | 18.4 | 20.1 | 1.7 |
| 1954 | 100.0 | 77.8 | 13.3 | 21.4 | 20.3 | 0.8 |
| 1958 | 100.0 | 78.5 | 11.5 | 23.2 | 23.6 | −1.7 |
| 1960 | 100.0 | 76.4 | — | 24.9 | 24.8 | −1.3 |
| **Average annual rate of growth — Taux annuel moyen d'accroissement** | | | | | | |
| 1938 – 1960 | 2.8 | 2.8 | 3.4 | 1.9 | 2.2 | . |
| 1938 – 1948 | 5.3 | 4.5 | 7.3 | 4.9 | 4.6 | . |
| 1948 – 1953 | −0.9 | 1.7 | — | −9.5 | −5.7 | . |
| 1950 – 1960 | 1.5 | 1.3 | 1.0 | 2.8 | 2.2 | . |
| 1950 – 1953 | 0.4 | 1.4 | 2.3 | −5.1 | −3.7 | . |
| 1954 – 1958 | 2.6 | 2.9 | −1.2 | 4.8 | 6.6 | . |
| 1958 – 1960 | −0.3 | −1.7 | 1.6 | 3.3 | 2.2 | . |

For footnotes see end of table.                                   Pour les notes, voir au bas du tableau.

## B. The Gross Domestic Product at Factor Cost According to Origin
### Origine par secteur d'activité du produit intérieur brut au coût des facteurs

| Item of data and year<br>Rubrique et année | Total | Agricultural sector [5]<br>Secteur agricole [5] | Industrial Sector — Secteur industriel | | | | | Transportation and communication<br>Transports et communications | Other sectors [6]<br>Autres secteurs [6] |
|---|---|---|---|---|---|---|---|---|---|
| | | | Total | Mining<br>industries extractives | Manufacturing [5]<br>Industries manufacturières [5] | Construction<br>Bâtiment et travaux publics | Electricity, gas and water<br>Electricité, gaz et eau | | |
| ISIC — CITI | 0–9 | 0 | 1–5 | 1 | 2–3 | 4 | 5 | 7 | 6, 8–9 |
| *a. At Current Prices — Aux prix courants* | | | | | | | | | |
| **Absolute figures — Chiffres absolus** | | | | | | | | | |
| 1938 | 9 905 | 2 401 | ... | 131 | 1 596 | 303 | ... | ... | 5 479 |
| 1948 | 41 497 | 7 249 | ... | 363 | 9 440 | 2 464 | ... | ... | 21 981 |
| 1950 | 58 599 | 9 144 | ... | 565 | 13 700 | 4 330 | ... | ... | 30 860 |
| 1951 | 81 563 | 14 234 | ... | 736 | 18 500 | 5 158 | ... | ... | 42 935 |
| 1952 | 93 147 | 15 475 | ... | 996 | 20 725 | 5 437 | ... | ... | 50 514 |
| 1953 | 105 473 | 23 025 | ... | 1 127 | 20 818 | 5 249 | ... | ... | 55 254 |
| 1954 | 117 692 | 21 691 | ... | 1 306 | 25 417 | 6 358 | ... | ... | 62 920 |
| 1955 | 139 310 | 24 457 | ... | 1 575 | 32 223 | 7 062 | ... | ... | 73 993 |
| 1956 | 107 102 | 31 080 | 49 551 | 1 921 | 36 824 | 9 147 | 1 659 | 19 981 | 69 490 |
| 1957 | 215 823 | 41 064 | 62 420 | 2 243 | 46 570 | 11 547 | 2 060 | 23 904 | 88 435 |
| 1958 | 306 854 | 58 100 | 87 810 | 2 800 | 65 810 | 16 200 | 3 000 | 37 100 | 123 844 |
| 1959 | 566 800 | 130 389 | 153 038 | 4 782 | 115 283 | 26 258 | 6 715 | 61 462 | 221 911 |
| 1960 | 715 034 | 159 700 | 200 094 | 7 700 | 152 494 | 31 100 | 8 800 | 71 600 | 283 640 |
| 1961 | 847 000 | 170 800 | 246 500 | 11 400 | 185 000 | 40 100 | 10 000 | 83 300 | 346 400 |
| **Percentage distribution according to sector — Distribution en pourcentage par secteur** | | | | | | | | | |
| 1938 | 100.0 | 24.2 | ... | 1.3 | 16.1 | 3.1 | ... | ... | 55.3 |
| 1948 | 100.0 | 17.5 | ... | 0.9 | 22.7 | 5.9 | ... | ... | 53.0 |
| 1950–1960 | 100.0 | 20.6 | ... | 1.0 | 21.3 | 5.0 | ... | ... | ... |
| 1950 | 100.0 | 15.6 | ... | 1.0 | 23.4 | 7.4 | ... | ... | 52.6 |
| 1953 | 100.0 | 21.8 | ... | 1.1 | 19.7 | 5.0 | ... | ... | 52.4 |
| 1954 | 100.0 | 18.4 | ... | 1.1 | 21.6 | 5.4 | ... | ... | 53.5 |
| 1958 | 100.0 | 18.9 | 28.6 | 0.9 | 21.4 | 5.3 | 1.0 | 12.1 | 40.4 |
| 1960 | 100.0 | 22.3 | 28.0 | 1.1 | 21.3 | 4.3 | 1.3 | 10.0 | 39.7 |
| *b. At Prices of 1950 — Aux prix de 1950* | | | | | | | | | |
| **Absolute figures — Chiffres absolus** | | | | | | | | | |
| 1950 | 58 599 | 9 144 | ... | 565 | 13 700 | 4 330 | ... | ... | 30 860 |
| 1951 | 60 422 | 9 732 | ... | 628 | 14 043 | 4 253 | ... | ... | 31 766 |
| 1952 | 56 395 | 8 610 | ... | 617 | 13 015 | 3 620 | ... | ... | 30 533 |
| 1953 | 59 560 | 11 040 | ... | 650 | 12 741 | 3 438 | ... | ... | 31 691 |
| 1954 | 61 557 | 10 665 | ... | 673 | 13 837 | 3 748 | ... | ... | 32 634 |
| 1955 | 64 829 | 11 075 | ... | 700 | 15 097 | 3 915 | ... | ... | 34 042 |
| 1956 | 64 721 | 10 861 | 20 192 | 724 | 14 865 | 3 728 | 875 | 6 657 | 27 011 |
| 1957 | 67 752 | 11 048 | 21 671 | 757 | 15 608 | 4 422 | 884 | 6 876 | 28 157 |
| 1958 | 69 578 | 11 208 | 22 592 | 805 | 16 434 | 4 521 | 832 | 7 095 | 28 683 |
| 1959 | 65 910 | 11 063 | 19 831 | 924 | 14 307 | 3 802 | 798 | 7 197 | 27 819 |
| 1960 | 68 698 | 11 168 | 21 454 | 1 184 | 15 372 | 4 070 | 828 | 7 425 | 28 651 |
| 1961 | 72 604 | 11 398 | 23 712 | 1 602 | 17 002 | 4 269 | 839 | 7 792 | 29 702 |
| **Percentage distribution according to sector — Distribution en pourcentage par secteur** | | | | | | | | | |
| 1950–1960 | 100.0 | 16.6 | ... | 1.2 | 22.8 | 6.3 | ... | ... | ... |
| 1950 | 100.0 | 15.6 | ... | 1.0 | 23.4 | 7.4 | ... | ... | 52.6 |
| 1953 | 100.0 | 18.5 | ... | 1.1 | 21.4 | 5.8 | ... | ... | 53.2 |
| 1954 | 100.0 | 17.3 | ... | 1.1 | 22.5 | 6.1 | ... | ... | 53.0 |
| 1958 | 100.0 | 16.1 | 32.5 | 1.2 | 23.6 | 6.5 | 1.2 | 10.2 | 41.2 |
| 1960 | 100.0 | 16.2 | 31.2 | 1.7 | 22.4 | 5.9 | 1.2 | 10.8 | 41.8 |
| **Average annual rate of growth — Taux annuel moyen d'accroissement** | | | | | | | | | |
| 1950–1960 | 1.6 | 2.0 | ... | 7.7 | 1.2 | −0.6 | ... | ... | ... |
| 1950–1953 | 0.5 | 6.5 | ... | 4.8 | −2.4 | −7.4 | ... | ... | 1.9 |
| 1954–1958 | 3.1 | 1.2 | ... | 4.6 | 4.4 | 4.8 | ... | ... | — |
| 1958–1960 | −0.6 | −0.3 | −2.5 | 21.3 | −3.3 | −5.1 | −0.3 | 2.3 | — |

[1] Includes some purchases of capital equipment by general government.
[2] Prior to 1955 stock changes were limited mainly to certain of the more important stocks in agriculture and industry; beginning 1955, they are limited to stocks of agricultural commodities only.
[3] Gross national product.
[4] Includes net factor incomes from abroad and an adjustment for changes in the terms of trade.
[5] Forestry is included in manufacturing.
[6] For years, 1938–1955, includes Electricity, gas and water (ISIC major group 51 and group 521) and Transportation and communication (ISIC division 7).

[1] Y compris certains achats de bien d'équipement par l'Etat.
[2] Avant 1955 l'accroissement des stocks comprenait principalement certains des plus importants stocks de produits agricoles et industriels; àpartir de 1955, il a été limité aux stocks de produits agricoles seulement.
[3] Produit intérieur brut.
[4] Y compris le revenu net des facteurs reçu de l'étranger, ainsi que des ajustements pour compenser les fluctuations des termes de l'échange.
[5] La silviculture est comprise dans les industries manacturières.
[6] Pour les années 1938–1955, sont inclus: Electricité, gaz et eau (CITI 51 et 521) et Transports et communications (CITI 7).

ARGENTINA

## 2. INDEX NUMBERS OF INDUSTRIAL PRODUCTION
### INDICES DE LA PRODUCTION INDUSTRIELLE

### A. Selected Divisions of Industrial Activity
### Quelques branches de l'activité industrielle

| Period<br>Période | Total | Mining<br>Industries<br>extractives | Manu-<br>facturing<br>Industries<br>manu-<br>facturières | Electricity<br>and gas<br>Electricité<br>et gaz |
|---|---|---|---|---|
| ISIC — CITI | 1–3, 511–512 | 1 | 2–3 | 511–512 |
| *a.* Indexes — Indices (1958 = 100) | | | | |
| 1939 | 51 | 58 | 52 | 44 |
| 1948 | 84 | 64 | 86 | 72 |
| 1949 | 81 | 62 | 83 | 74 |
| 1950 | 84 | 63 | 85 | 80 |
| 1951 | 86 | 66 | 87 | 84 |
| 1952 | 81 | 69 | 81 | 83 |
| 1953 | 80 | 75 | 79 | 88 |
| 1954 | 86 | 78 | 86 | 95 |
| 1955 | 94 | 82 | 94 | 101 |
| 1956 | 94 | 85 | 92 | 108 |
| 1957 | 97 | 94 | 95 | 109 |
| 1958 | 100 | 100 | 100 | 100 |
| 1959 | 89 | 119 | 87 | 94 |
| 1960 | 92 | 164 | 88 | 99 |
| 1961 | 102 | 210 | 97 | 107 |
| *b.* Average Annual Rate of Change — Taux annuel moyen de variation | | | | |
| 1939–1960 | 2.8 | 5.1 | 2.5 | 3.9 |
| 1939–1948 | 5.7 | 1.1 | 5.8 | 5.6 |
| 1950–1960 | 0.9 | 10.0 | 0.3 | 2.2 |
| 1948–1953 | −1.0 | 3.2 | −1.7 | 4.1 |
| 1954–1958 | 3.8 | 6.4 | 3.8 | 1.3 |
| 1958–1960 | −4.1 | 28.1 | −6.2 | −0.5 |

### B. The Major Groups of Mining
### Les classes de la branche Industries extractives

| Period<br>Période | All mining<br>Toutes<br>industries<br>extractives | Coal<br>mining<br>Extraction<br>du charbon | Metal mining<br>Extraction<br>des minerais<br>métalliques | Crude petro-<br>leum and<br>natural gas<br>Pétrole brut<br>et gaz naturel | Other mining<br>Autres<br>industries<br>extractives |
|---|---|---|---|---|---|
| ISIC — CITI | 1 | 11 | 12 | 13 | 14–19 |
| *a.* Indexes — Indices (1958 = 100) | | | | | |
| 1939 | 58 | — | 152 | 52 | 23 |
| 1948 | 64 | 7 | 75 | 65 | 47 |
| 1949 | 62 | 7 | 62 | 63 | 52 |
| 1950 | 63 | 10 | 69 | 66 | 37 |
| 1951 | 66 | 15 | 78 | 68 | 43 |
| 1952 | 69 | 43 | 80 | 70 | 62 |
| 1953 | 75 | 32 | 68 | 80 | 40 |
| 1954 | 78 | 36 | 75 | 83 | 51 |
| 1955 | 82 | 51 | 92 | 86 | 50 |
| 1956 | 85 | 58 | 98 | 87 | 60 |
| 1957 | 94 | 79 | 107 | 95 | 69 |
| 1958 | 100 | 100 | 100 | 100 | 100 |
| 1959 | 119 | 115 | 100 | 125 | 90 |
| 1960 | 164 | 104 | 91 | 179 | 107 |
| 1961 | 210 | 130 | 106 | 236 | 94 |
| *b.* Average Annual Rate of Change — Taux annuel moyen de variation | | | | | |
| 1939–1960 | 5.1 | — | −2.5 | 6.1 | 7.6 |
| 1939–1948 | 1.1 | — | −7.6 | 2.5 | 8.3 |
| 1950–1960 | 10.0 | 26.4 | 2.8 | 10.5 | 11.2 |
| 1948–1953 | 3.2 | 35.5 | −1.9 | 4.2 | −3.2 |
| 1954–1958 | 6.4 | 29.1 | 7.5 | 4.8 | 18.3 |
| 1958–1960 | 28.1 | 2.0 | −4.6 | 33.8 | 3.4 |

*127171*

## C. The Major Groups of Manufacturing — Les classes de la branche Industries manufacturières

| Period / Période | Manufacturing / Industries manufacturières | Food, beverages and tobacco / Industries alimentaires, boissons, tabac | Textiles | Clothing, footwear and made-up textiles / Articles d'habillement, chaussures et ouvrages en tissu | Wood products and furniture / Bois et meubles | Paper and paper products / Papier et ouvrages en papier | Printing and publishing / Imprimerie et édition | Leather and leather products except wearing apparel / Cuir et articles en cuir, à l'exclusion des articles d'habillement | Rubber products / Ouvrages en caoutchouc | Chemicals and chemical, petroleum and coal products / Produits chimiques et dérivés du pétrole et du charbon | Non-metallic mineral products / Produits minéraux non métalliques | Basic metals / Métallurgie de base | Metal products [1] / Ouvrages en métaux [1] | Other manufacturing / Autres industries manufacturières |
|---|---|---|---|---|---|---|---|---|---|---|---|---|---|---|
| ISIC — CITI | 2–3 | 20–22 | 23 | 24 | 25–26 | 27 | 28 | 29 | 30 | 31–32 | 33 | 34 | 35–38 | 39 |
| *a.* Indexes — Indices (1958 = 100) | | | | | | | | | | | | | | |
| 1939 | 52 | 60 | 55 | 102 | 65 | 34 | 75 | 61 | 44 | 36 | 46 | 30 | 50 | 46 |
| 1948 | 86 | 74 | 120 | 170 | 124 | 54 | 89 | 120 | 66 | 61 | 75 | 56 | 92 | 96 |
| 1949 | 83 | 75 | 124 | 157 | 111 | 53 | 82 | 106 | 60 | 61 | 79 | 58 | 77 | 102 |
| 1950 | 85 | 77 | 121 | 137 | 114 | 61 | 94 | 114 | 55 | 70 | 83 | 65 | 74 | 118 |
| 1951 | 87 | 74 | 120 | 130 | 113 | 66 | 80 | 107 | 79 | 71 | 82 | 66 | 85 | 132 |
| 1952 | 81 | 76 | 98 | 111 | 98 | 57 | 57 | 91 | 81 | 68 | 74 | 50 | 88 | 133 |
| 1953 | 79 | 80 | 98 | 112 | 103 | 51 | 61 | 98 | 67 | 70 | 72 | 50 | 82 | 114 |
| 1954 | 86 | 80 | 103 | 116 | 105 | 66 | 69 | 94 | 83 | 77 | 77 | 63 | 88 | 131 |
| 1955 | 94 | 85 | 110 | 119 | 99 | 78 | 77 | 94 | 96 | 83 | 85 | 74 | 104 | 126 |
| 1956 | 92 | 96 | 112 | 116 | 98 | 86 | 80 | 96 | 93 | 85 | 91 | 71 | 87 | 115 |
| 1957 | 95 | 92 | 104 | 109 | 106 | 89 | 97 | 99 | 97 | 96 | 98 | 78 | 97 | 104 |
| 1958 | 100 | 100 | 100 | 100 | 100 | 100 | 100 | 100 | 100 | 100 | 100 | 100 | 100 | 100 |
| 1959 | 87 | 85 | 79 | 87 | 90 | 99 | 94 | 68 | 96 | 93 | 93 | 88 | 86 | 76 |
| 1960 | 88 | 83 | 84 | 84 | 100 | 84 | 99 | 67 | 117 | 90 | 93 | 91 | 94 | 57 |
| 1961 | 97 | 86 | 88 | 108 | 104 | 105 | 109 | 67 | 161 | 97 | 103 | 104 | 102 | 51 |
| *b.* Average Annual Rate of Change — Taux annuel moyen de variation | | | | | | | | | | | | | | |
| 1939–1960 | 2.5 | 1.5 | 2.0 | −0.9 | 2.1 | 4.4 | 1.3 | 0.4 | 4.8 | 4.4 | 3.4 | 5.4 | 3.1 | 1.0 |
| 1939–1948 | 5.8 | 2.3 | 9.1 | 5.8 | 7.4 | 5.3 | 1.9 | 7.8 | 4.6 | 6.0 | 5.6 | 7.2 | 7.0 | 8.5 |
| 1950–1960 | 0.3 | 0.8 | −3.6 | −4.8 | −1.3 | 3.3 | 0.5 | −1.3 | 7.8 | 2.5 | 1.1 | 3.4 | 2.4 | −7.0 |
| 1948–1953 | −1.7 | 1.6 | −4.0 | −8.0 | −3.6 | −1.1 | −7.3 | −4.0 | 0.3 | 2.8 | −0.8 | −2.2 | −2.3 | 3.5 |
| 1954–1958 | 3.8 | 5.7 | −0.7 | −3.6 | −1.2 | 10.9 | 9.7 | 1.6 | 4.8 | 6.8 | 6.8 | 12.2 | 3.2 | −6.5 |
| 1958–1960 | −6.2 | −8.9 | −8.3 | −8.3 | — | −8.3 | −0.5 | −18.1 | 8.2 | −5.1 | −3.6 | −4.6 | −3.0 | −24.5 |

[1] Metal furniture (part of ISIC major group 26) is included under Metal products (ISIC major groups 35-38).

[1] La fabrication des meubles métalliques (dans CITI 26) est comprise dans Ouvrages en métaux (CITI 35-38).

### 3. INDEX NUMBERS OF INDUSTRIAL EMPLOYMENT
### INDICES DE L'EMPLOI DANS L'INDUSTRIE

## A. Selected Divisions of Industrial Activity
## Quelques branches de l'activité industrielle

| Period Période | Total [1] | Mining [1] Industries extractives [1] | Manufacturing Industries manufacturières | Electricity and gas Electricité et gaz |
|---|---|---|---|---|
| ISIC — CITI | 1-3, 511-512 | 1 | 2-3 | 511-512 |
| *a.* Indexes — Indices (1958 = 100) | | | | |
| 1939.......... | 61 | 59 | 61 | 54 |
| 1948.......... | 110 | 87 | 111 | 64 |
| 1949.......... | 108 | 88 | 110 | 68 |
| 1950.......... | 107 | 82 | 108 | 76 |
| 1951.......... | 107 | 81 | 109 | 80 |
| 1952.......... | 104 | 90 | 104 | 84 |
| 1953.......... | 98 | 93 | 98 | 85 |
| 1954.......... | 99 | 94 | 99 | 86 |
| 1955.......... | 102 | 95 | 103 | 91 |
| 1956.......... | 102 | 98 | 102 | 95 |
| 1957.......... | 101 | 98 | 101 | 99 |
| 1958.......... | 100 | 100 | 100 | 100 |
| 1959.......... | 96 | 96 | 96 | 104 |
| 1960.......... | 89 | 93 | 88 | 101 |
| 1961.......... | 86 | 92 | 85 | 104 |
| *b.* Average Annual Rate of Change — Taux annuel moyen de variation | | | | |
| 1939 - 1960.... | 1.8 | 2.2 | 1.8 | 3.0 |
| 1939 - 1948.... | 6.8 | 4.4 | 6.9 | 1.9 |
| 1950 - 1960.... | -1.8 | 1.3 | -2.0 | 2.9 |
| 1948 - 1953.... | -2.3 | 1.3 | -2.5 | 5.8 |
| 1954 - 1958.... | 0.2 | 1.6 | 0.2 | 3.8 |
| 1958 - 1960.... | -5.7 | -3.6 | -6.2 | 0.5 |

For footnotes see end of table.

## B. Selected Major Groups of Mining
## Quelques classes de la branche Industries extractives

| Period Période | All mining [1] Toutes industries extractives [1] | Metal mining Extraction des minerais métalliques | Crude petroleum and natural gas Pétrole brut et gaz naturel | Other mining Autres industries extractives |
|---|---|---|---|---|
| ISIC — CITI | 1 | 12 | 13 | 14-19 |
| *a.* Indexes — Indices (1958 = 100) | | | | |
| 1939.......... | 59 | 162 | 44 | 44 |
| 1948.......... | 87 | 75 | 77 | 97 |
| 1949.......... | 88 | 61 | 82 | 84 |
| 1950.......... | 82 | 61 | 83 | 82 |
| 1951.......... | 81 | 80 | 81 | 78 |
| 1952.......... | 90 | 96 | 87 | 92 |
| 1953.......... | 93 | 100 | 92 | 88 |
| 1954.......... | 94 | 104 | 92 | 89 |
| 1955.......... | 95 | 113 | 93 | 87 |
| 1956.......... | 98 | 119 | 94 | 94 |
| 1957.......... | 98 | 104 | 98 | 90 |
| 1958.......... | 100 | 100 | 100 | 100 |
| 1959.......... | 96 | 73 | 100 | 95 |
| 1960.......... | 93 | 65 | 102 | 93 |
| 1961.......... | 92 | 68 | 99 | 77 |
| *b.* Average Annual Rate of Change — Taux annuel moyen de variation | | | | |
| 1939 - 1960.... | 2.2 | -4.2 | 4.1 | 3.6 |
| 1939 - 1948.... | 4.4 | -8.2 | 6.4 | 9.2 |
| 1950 - 1960.... | 1.3 | 0.6 | 2.1 | 1.3 |
| 1948 - 1953.... | 1.3 | 5.9 | 3.6 | -1.9 |
| 1954 - 1958.... | 1.6 | -1.0 | 2.1 | 3.0 |
| 1958 - 1960.... | -3.6 | -19.4 | 1.0 | -3.6 |

Pour les notes, voir au bas du tableau.

## C. The Major Groups of Manufacturing — Les classes de la branche Industries manufacturières

| Period / Période | Manu-facturing / Industries manufac-turières | Food, beverages and tobacco / Industries alimen-taires, boissons, tabac | Textiles | Clothing, footwear and made-up textiles / Articles d'habil-lement, chaussures et ouvrages en tissu | Wood products and furniture / Bois et meubles | Paper and paper products / Papier et ouvrages en papier | Printing and publishing / Im-primerie et édition | Leather and leather products except wearing apparel / Cuir et articles en cuir, à l'exclu-sion des articles d'habil-lement | Rubber products / Ouvrages en caout-chouc | Chemicals and chemical, petroleum and coal products / Produits chi-miques et dérivés du pétrole et du charbon | Non-metallic mineral products / Produits minéraux non métal-liques | Basic metals / Métal-lurgie de base | Metal products / Ouvrages en métaux | Other manu-facturing / Autres industries manufac-turières |
|---|---|---|---|---|---|---|---|---|---|---|---|---|---|---|
| ISIC — CITI | 2–3 | 20–22 | 23 | 24 | 25–26 | 27 | 28 | 29 | 30 | 31–32 | 33 | 34 | 35–38 | 39 |

### a. Indexes — Indices (1958 = 100)

| Period | 2–3 | 20–22 | 23 | 24 | 25–26 | 27 | 28 | 29 | 30 | 31–32 | 33 | 34 | 35–38 | 39 |
|---|---|---|---|---|---|---|---|---|---|---|---|---|---|---|
| 1939 | 61 | 64 | 64 | 70 | 86 | 38 | 84 | 63 | 30 | 42 | 49 | 52 | 57 | 78 |
| 1948 | 111 | 104 | 131 | 118 | 175 | 74 | 116 | 134 | 73 | 89 | 118 | 90 | 100 | 163 |
| 1949 | 110 | 101 | 134 | 125 | 161 | 73 | 110 | 126 | 72 | 93 | 120 | 90 | 98 | 159 |
| 1950 | 108 | 100 | 133 | 115 | 153 | 76 | 110 | 122 | 71 | 95 | 118 | 90 | 95 | 150 |
| 1951 | 109 | 99 | 135 | 111 | 150 | 78 | 104 | 125 | 88 | 98 | 118 | 94 | 98 | 150 |
| 1952 | 104 | 97 | 127 | 106 | 132 | 77 | 105 | 113 | 91 | 98 | 110 | 94 | 96 | 142 |
| 1953 | 98 | 96 | 114 | 101 | 120 | 74 | 102 | 110 | 82 | 95 | 97 | 85 | 90 | 130 |
| 1954 | 99 | 94 | 114 | 106 | 113 | 76 | 103 | 109 | 88 | 98 | 95 | 90 | 94 | 136 |
| 1955 | 103 | 98 | 114 | 110 | 110 | 82 | 108 | 104 | 97 | 100 | 100 | 97 | 102 | 128 |
| 1956 | 102 | 98 | 111 | 107 | 107 | 91 | 111 | 103 | 91 | 98 | 100 | 97 | 98 | 121 |
| 1957 | 101 | 98 | 108 | 108 | 105 | 95 | 111 | 102 | 92 | 98 | 101 | 95 | 97 | 117 |
| 1958 | 100 | 100 | 100 | 100 | 100 | 100 | 100 | 100 | 100 | 100 | 100 | 100 | 100 | 100 |
| 1959 | 96 | 93 | 97 | 91 | 93 | 106 | 96 | 88 | 108 | 100 | 98 | 100 | 98 | 78 |
| 1960 | 88 | 82 | 89 | 86 | 82 | 100 | 89 | 74 | 105 | 93 | 87 | 92 | 95 | 65 |
| 1961 | 85 | 79 | 86 | 97 | 74 | 100 | 88 | 65 | 108 | 87 | 82 | 86 | 92 | 53 |

### b. Average Annual Rate of Change — Taux annuel moyen de variation

| Period | 2–3 | 20–22 | 23 | 24 | 25–26 | 27 | 28 | 29 | 30 | 31–32 | 33 | 34 | 35–38 | 39 |
|---|---|---|---|---|---|---|---|---|---|---|---|---|---|---|
| 1939 – 1960 | 1.8 | 1.2 | 1.6 | 1.0 | −0.2 | 4.7 | 0.3 | 0.8 | 4.5 | 3.9 | 2.8 | 2.8 | 2.5 | −0.9 |
| 1939 – 1948 | 6.9 | 5.5 | 8.3 | 6.0 | 8.2 | 7.7 | 3.7 | 8.7 | 10.4 | 8.7 | 10.3 | 6.3 | 6.4 | 8.5 |
| 1950 – 1960 | −2.0 | −2.0 | −3.9 | −2.9 | −6.0 | 2.8 | −2.1 | −4.9 | 4.0 | −0.2 | −3.0 | 0.2 | — | −8.0 |
| 1948 – 1953 | −2.5 | −1.6 | −2.7 | −3.1 | −7.3 | — | −2.6 | −3.9 | 2.4 | 1.3 | −3.8 | −1.1 | −2.1 | −4.4 |
| 1954 – 1958 | 0.2 | 1.6 | −3.2 | −1.5 | −3.0 | 7.1 | −0.7 | −2.1 | 3.2 | 0.5 | 1.3 | 2.7 | 1.6 | −7.4 |
| 1958 – 1960 | −6.2 | −9.4 | −5.7 | −7.3 | −9.4 | — | −5.7 | −14.0 | 2.5 | −3.6 | −6.7 | −4.1 | −2.5 | −19.4 |

[1] Excludes Coal mining (ISIC Major group 11).

[1] Non compris l'Extraction du charbon (CITI 11).

# ARGENTINA

## 4. CHARACTERISTICS OF ALL INDUSTRIAL ESTABLISHMENTS
## CARACTERISTIQUES DE TOUS LES ETABLISSEMENTS INDUSTRIELS
### 1939, 1948, 1953

Number of establishments in units; value added ·and wages and salaries in million Pesos; number of engaged, employees and operatives in thousands; energy consumed in thousand metric tons of coal equivalents; capacity of installed power equipment in thousand horsepower; value added per engaged and wages and salaries per employee and per operative in thousand Pesos; energy consumed per engaged and per operative in metric tons of coal equivalents; capacity of installed power equipment per engaged and per operative in horsepower.

Nombre d'établissements en unités; valeur ajoutée et traitements et salaires en millions de pesos; nombre de personnes occupées, de salariés et d'ouvriers en milliers; énergie consommée en milliers de tonnes métriques d'équivalent charbon; puissance installée en milliers de chevaux-vapeur; valeur ajoutée par personne occupée et traitements et salaires par salarié et par ouvrier en milliers de pesos; énergie consommée par personne occupée et par ouvrier en tonnes métriques d'équivalent charbon; puissance installée par personne occupée et par ouvrier en chevaux-vapeur.

## A. Selected Divisions of Industrial Activity — Quelques branches de l'activité industrielle

### a. Absolute Figures — Chiffres absolus

| Year and item of data | Total | Mining Industries ex-tractives | Manu-facturing Industries manu-facturières | Electricity and gas Electricité et gaz | Année et rubrique |
|---|---|---|---|---|---|
| ISIC | 1-4,511-512 | 1 | 2-3 | 511-512 | CITI |
| **1939** | | | | | **1939** |
| Number of establishments | 49 629 | 309 | 48 368 | 952 | Nombre d'établissements |
| Value added | 1 688.6 | 74.8 | 1 402.1 | 211.7 | Valeur ajoutée |
| Number of engaged (As of 31.XII) | 669.2 | 17.8 | 630.8 | 20.6 | Nombre de personnes occupées (Au 31.XII) |
| Employees: | | | | | Salariés: |
| Number (As of 31.XII) | 593.1 | 17.6 | 555.6 | 19.9 | Nombre (au 31.XII) |
| Wages and salaries | 929.4 | 29.1 | 850.0 | 50.3 | Traitements et salaires |
| Capacity of installed power equipment (As of 31.XII) | . | 89.0 | 1 186.9 | 1 662.8 | Puissance installée (au 31.XII) |
| **1948** | | | | | **1948** |
| Number of establishments | 80 299 | 526 | 78 798 | 975 | Nombre d'établissements |
| Value added | 11 728.9 | 425.8 | 10 880.9 | 422.2 | Valeur ajoutée |
| Number of engaged (As of 31.XII) | 1 187.4 | 28.1 | 1 132.4 | 26.9 | Nombre de personnes occupées (au 31.XII) |
| Employees: | | | | | Salariés: |
| Number (As of 31.XII) | 1 046.7 | 27.4 | 993.2 | 26.1 | Nombre (au 31.XII) |
| Wages and salaries | 4 882.2 | 148.2 | 4 548.1 | 185.9 | Traitements et salaires |
| Capacity of installed power equipment (As of 31.XII) | . | 154.6 | 1 915.1 | 1 812.8 | Puissance installée (au 31.XII) |
| **1953** | | | | | **1953** |
| Number of establishments | 147 223 | 2 568 | 143 766 | 889 | Nombre d'établissements |
| Value added | 40 778.6 | 1 234.1 | 38 383.1 | 1 161.4 | Valeur ajoutée |
| Number of engaged | 1 469.9 | 38.2 | 1 411.0 | 20.7 | Nombre de personnes occupées |
| Employees: | | | | | Salariés: |
| Number | 1 204.1 | 34.4 | 1 149.5 | 20.2 | Nombre |
| Wages and salaries | 14 395.3 | 478.6 | 13 624.4 | 292.3 | Traitements et salaires |
| Number of operatives (Average for 1953) | 1 037.7 | 30.7 | 991.4 | 15.6 | Nombre d'ouvriers (moyenne pendant 1953) |
| Energy consumed | . | 374.0 | 5 616.7 | 2 888.8 | Energie consommée |
| Capacity of installed power equipment (As of 30.VII.1954) | . | 235.1 | 3 027.3 | 2 170.8 | Puissance installée (au 30.VII.1954) |

### b. Structure

| Year and item of data | Total | Mining Industries ex-tractives | Manu-facturing Industries manu-facturières | Electricity and gas Electricité et gaz | Année et rubrique |
|---|---|---|---|---|---|
| ISIC | 1-4,511-512 | 1 | 2-3 | 511-512 | CITI |
| **1939** | | | | | **1939** |
| Distribution in percent of: | | | | | Distribution en pourcentage: |
| Value added | 100.0 | 4.4 | 83.0 | 12.6 | Valeur ajoutée |
| Number of engaged | 100.0 | 2.7 | 94.2 | 3.1 | Nombre de personnes occupées |
| Per person engaged: | | | | | Par personne occupée: |
| Value added | 2.5 | 4.2 | 2.2 | 10.3 | Valeur ajoutée |
| Capacity of installed power equipment | . | 5.00 | 1.88 | 80.72 | Puissance installée |
| Employees as a percent of engaged | 88.6 | 98.9 | 88.1 | 96.6 | Salariés en pourcentage des personnes occupées |
| Value added per unit of wages and salaries | 1.82 | 2.57 | 1.65 | 4.21 | Valeur ajoutée par unité de traitements et salaires |
| Wages and salaries per employee | 1.6 | 1.6 | 1.5 | 2.5 | Traitements et salaires par salarié |
| **1948** | | | | | **1948** |
| Distribution in percent of: | | | | | Distribution en pourcentage: |
| Value added | 100.0 | 3.6 | 92.8 | 3.6 | Valeur ajoutée |
| Number of engaged | 100.0 | 2.3 | 95.4 | 2.3 | Nombre de personnes occupées |
| Per person engaged: | | | | | Par personne occupée: |
| Value added | 9.9 | 15.2 | 9.6 | 15.7 | Valeur ajoutée |
| Capacity of installed power equipment | . | 5.50 | 1.69 | 67.39 | Puissance installée |
| Employees as a percent of engaged | 88.2 | 97.5 | 87.7 | 97.0 | Salariés en pourcentage des personnes occupées |
| Value added per unit of wages and salaries | 2.40 | 2.87 | 2.39 | 2.27 | Valeur ajoutée par unité de traitements et salaires |
| Wages and salaries per employee | 4.7 | 5.4 | 4.6 | 7.1 | Traitements et salaires par salarié |
| **1953** | | | | | **1953** |
| Distribution in percent of: | | | | | Distribution en pourcentage: |
| Value added | 100.0 | 3.0 | 94.1 | 2.9 | Valeur ajoutée |
| Number of engaged | 100.0 | 2.6 | 96.0 | 1.4 | Nombre de personnes occupées |
| Per person engaged: | | | | | Par personne occupée: |
| Value added | 27.7 | 32.3 | 27.2 | 56.1 | Valeur ajoutée |
| Energy consumed | 6.06 | 9.79 | 3.98 | 139.56 | Energie consommée |
| Capacity of installed power equipment | . | 6.15 | 2.14 | 104.9 | Puissance installée |
| Employees as a percent of engaged | 81.9 | 90.0 | 81.5 | 97.6 | Salariés en pourcentage des personnes occupées |
| Value added per unit of wages and salaries | 2.83 | 2.58 | 2.82 | 3.97 | Valeur ajoutée par unité de traitements et salaires |
| Operatives as a percent of employees | 86.2 | 89.2 | 86.2 | 77.2 | Ouvriers en pourcentage des salariés |
| Wages and salaries per employee | 12.0 | 13.9 | 11.8 | 14.5 | Traitements et salaires par salarié |
| Per operative: | | | | | Par ouvrier: |
| Energy consumed | . | 12.18 | 5.66 | 185.18 | Energie consommée |
| Capacity of installed power equipment | . | 7.66 | 3.05 | 139.15 | Puissance installée |

## B. The Major Groups of Mining — Les classes de la branche Industries extractives

### a. Absolute Figures — Chiffres absolus

| Year and item of data | All mining — Toutes industries extractives | Coal mining — Extraction du charbon | Metal mining — Extraction des minerais métalliques | Crude petroleum and natural gas — Pétrole brut et gaz naturel | Other mining [1] — Divers [1] | Année et rubrique |
|---|---|---|---|---|---|---|
| ISIC | 1 | 11 | 12 | 13 | 14-19 | CITI |
| **1939** | | | | | | **1939** |
| Number of establishments... | 309 | ... | 47 | 11 | 251 | Nombre d'établissements |
| Value added...... | 74.8 | ... | 12.3 | 50.8 | 11.7 | Valeur ajoutée |
| Number of engaged (As of 31.XII).... | 17.8 | ... | 4.3 | 7.1 | 6.4 | Nombre de personnes occupées (au 31.XII) |
| Employees: Number (As of 31.XII)......... | 17.6 | ... | 4.3 | 7.1 | 6.2 | Salariés: Nombre (au 31.XII) |
| Wages and salaries........ | 29.1 | ... | 5.1 | 16.8 | 7.2 | Traitements et salaires |
| Capacity of installed power equipment (As of 31.XII).... | 89.0 | ... | 6.1 | 66.2 | 16.7 | Puissance installée au (31.XII) |
| **1948** | | | | | | **1948** |
| Number of establishments... | 526 | 11 | 32 | 11 | 472 | Nombre d'établissements |
| Value added...... | 425.8 | 9.2 | 25.3 | 288.4 | 102.9 | Valeur ajoutée |
| Number of engaged (As of 31.XII).... | 28.1 | 1.8 | 2.0 | 12.8 | 11.5 | Nombre de personnes occupées (au 31.XII) |
| Employees: Number (As of 31.XII)......... | 27.4 | 1.8 | 2.0 | 12.8 | 10.8 | Salariés: Nombre (au 31.XII) |
| Wages and salaries........ | 148.2 | 6.4 | 7.4 | 98.9 | 35.5 | Traitements et salaires |
| Capacity of installed power equipment (As of 31.XII).... | 154.6 | 2.5 | 7.6 | 120.1 | 24.4 | Puissance installée (au 31.XII) |
| **1953** | | | | | | **1953** |
| Number of establishments... | 2 568 | 11 | 550 | 17 | 1 990 | Nombre d'établissements |
| Value added...... | 1 234.1 | 12.6 | 174.8 | 761.0 | 285.7 | Valeur ajoutée |
| Number of engaged........ | 38.2 | 2.5 | 6.4 | 12.2 | 17.1 | Nombre de personnes occupées |
| Employees: Number........ | 34.4 | 2.5 | 5.5 | 12.2 | 14.2 | Salariés: Nombre |
| Wages and salaries........ | 478.6 | 37.6 | 52.4 | 260.7 | 127.9 | Traitements et salaires |
| Number of operatives (Average for 1953) | 30.7 | 2.3 | 5.1 | 10.1 | 13.2 | Nombre d'ouvriers (moyenne pendant 1953) |
| Energy consumed.. | 374.0 | 12.9 | 25.0 | 106.6 | 229.5 | Energie consommée |
| Capacity of installed power equipment (As of 30.VII.1954)..... | 235.1 | 6.3 | 15.8 | 159.7 | 53.3 | Puissance installée (au 30.VII.1954) |

### b. Structure

| Year and item of data | All mining — Toutes industries extractives | Coal mining — Extraction du charbon | Metal mining — Extraction des minerais métalliques | Crude petroleum and natural gas — Pétrole brut et gaz naturel | Other mining [1] — Divers [1] | Année et rubrique |
|---|---|---|---|---|---|---|
| ISIC | 1 | 11 | 12 | 13 | 14-19 | CITI |
| **1939** | | | | | | **1939** |
| Distribution in percent of: | | | | | | Distribution en pourcentage: |
| Value added..... | 100.0 | ... | 16.4 | 67.9 | 15.7 | Valeur ajoutée |
| Number of engaged........ | 100.0 | ... | 24.1 | 39.9 | 36.0 | Nombre de personnes occupées |
| Per person engaged: Value added..... | 4.2 | ... | 2.9 | 7.2 | 1.8 | Par personne occupée: Valeur ajoutée |
| Capacity of installed power equipment....... | 5.00 | ... | 1.42 | 9.32 | 2.61 | Puissance installée |
| Employees as a percent of engaged........ | 98.9 | ... | 100.0 | 100.0 | 96.9 | Salariés en pourcentage des personnes occupées |
| Value added per unit of wages and salaries..... | 2.57 | ... | 2.41 | 3.02 | 1.62 | Valeur ajoutée par unité de traitements et salaires |
| Wages and salaries per employee.... | 1.6 | ... | 1.2 | 2.4 | 1.2 | Traitements et salaires par salarié |
| **1948** | | | | | | **1948** |
| Distribution in percent of: | | | | | | Distribution en pourcentage: |
| Value added..... | 100.0 | 2.2 | 5.9 | 67.7 | 24.2 | Valeur ajoutée |
| Number of engaged........ | 100.0 | 6.4 | 7.1 | 45.6 | 40.9 | Nombre de personnes occupées |
| Per person engaged: Value added..... | 15.2 | 5.1 | 12.6 | 22.5 | 8.9 | Par personne occupée: Valeur ajoutée |
| Capacity of installed power equipment....... | 5.50 | 1.39 | 3.80 | 9.38 | 2.12 | Puissance installée |
| Employees as a percent of engaged........ | 97.5 | 100.0 | 100.0 | 100.0 | 93.9 | Salariés en pourcentage des personnes occupées |
| Value added per unit of wages and salaries..... | 2.87 | 1.44 | 3.42 | 2.92 | 2.90 | Valeur ajoutée par unité de traitements et salaires |
| Wages and salaries per employee.... | 5.4 | 3.6 | 3.7 | 7.7 | 3.3 | Traitements et salaires par salarié |
| **1953** | | | | | | **1953** |
| Distribution in percent of: | | | | | | Distribution en pourcentage: |
| Value added..... | 100.0 | 1.0 | 14.2 | 61.7 | 23.1 | Valeur ajoutée |
| Number of engaged........ | 100.0 | 6.5 | 16.8 | 31.9 | 44.8 | Nombre de personnes occupées |
| Per person engaged: Value added..... | 32.3 | 5.0 | 27.3 | 62.4 | 16.7 | Par personne occupée: Valeur ajoutée |
| Energy consumed....... | 9.79 | 5.16 | 3.91 | 8.74 | 13.42 | Energie consommée |
| Capacity of installed power equipment....... | 6.15 | 2.52 | 2.47 | 13.09 | 3.12 | Puissance installée |
| Employees as a percent of engaged........ | 90.0 | 100.0 | 85.9 | 100.0 | 83.0 | Salariés en pourcentage des personnes occupées |
| Value added per unit of wages and salaries..... | 2.58 | 0.34 | 3.34 | 2.92 | 2.23 | Valeur ajoutée par unité de traitements et salaires |
| Operatives as a percent of employees....... | 89.2 | 92.0 | 92.7 | 82.8 | 93.0 | Ouvriers en pourcentage des salariés |
| Wages and salaries per employee.... | 13.9 | 15.0 | 9.5 | 21.4 | 9.0 | Traitements et salaires par salarié |
| Per operative: Energy consumed. | 12.18 | 5.61 | 4.90 | 10.55 | 17.39 | Par ouvrier: Energie consommée |
| Capacity of installed power equipment....... | 7.66 | 2.74 | 3.10 | 15.81 | 4.04 | Puissance installée |

[1] Includes coal mining in 1939.

[1] Y compris l'extraction du charbon en 1939.

# ARGENTINA

## C. The Major Groups of Manufacturing — Les classes de la branche Industries manufacturières

| Year and item of data | Manufacturing / Industries manufacturières | Food, beverages and tobacco / Industries alimentaires, boissons, tabac | Textiles | Clothing, footwear and made-up textiles / Articles d'habillement, chaussures et ouvrages en tissu | Wood products and furniture / Bois et meubles | Paper and paper products / Papier et ouvrages en papier | Printing and publishing / Imprimerie et édition | Leather and leather products except wearing apparel / Cuir et articles en cuir, à l'exclusion des articles d'habillement | Rubber products / Ouvrages en caoutchouc | Chemicals and chemical, petroleum and coal products / Produits chimiques et dérivés du pétrole et du charbon | Non-metallic mineral products / Produits minéraux non métalliques | Basic metals / Métallurgie de base | Metal products / Ouvrages en métaux | Other manufacturing / Autres industries manufacturières | Année et rubrique |
|---|---|---|---|---|---|---|---|---|---|---|---|---|---|---|---|
| ISIC | 2–3 | 20–22 | 23 | 24 | 25–26 | 27 | 28 | 29 | 30 | 31–32 | 33 | 34 | 35–38 | 39 | CITI |
| | | | | | a. Absolute Figures — Chiffres absolus | | | | | | | | | | |
| **1939** | | | | | | | | | | | | | | | **1939** |
| Number of establishments | 48 368 | 13 802 | 1 066 | 6 655 | 5 138 | 264 | 2 496 | 749 | 44 | 1 354 | 2 993 | 240 | 12 045 | 1 522 | Nombre d'établissements |
| Value added | 1 402.1 | 379.9 | 133.5 | 145.1 | 78.2 | 19.4 | 128.7 | 19.5 | 10.3 | 91.5 | 59.1 | 46.5 | 262.5 | 27.9 | Valeur ajoutée |
| Number of engaged (As of 31.XII) | 630.8 | 165.0 | 70.6 | 63.6 | 48.5 | 10.5 | 34.8 | 9.3 | 4.0 | 32.4 | 32.9 | 17.4 | 125.0 | 16.8 | Nombre de personnes occupées (au 31.XII) |
| Number of employees (As of 31.XII) | 555.6 | 142.6 | 69.0 | 53.3 | 41.1 | 10.1 | 31.0 | 7.8 | 4.0 | 30.6 | 27.7 | 17.0 | 106.8 | 14.6 | Nombre de salariés (au 31.XII) |
| Wages and salaries paid | 850.0 | 216.0 | 84.3 | 105.7 | 48.8 | 12.3 | 61.1 | 11.8 | 6.1 | 47.4 | 35.8 | 29.1 | 171.3 | 20.3 | Traitements et salaires payés |
| Capacity of installed power equipment (As of 31.XII) | 1 186.9 | 494.3 | 95.0 | 20.8 | 76.4 | 51.7 | 28.6 | 16.2 | 13.7 | 96.3 | 92.7 | 34.5 | 149.2 | 17.5 | Puissance installée (au 31.XII) |
| **1948** | | | | | | | | | | | | | | | **1948** |
| Number of establishments | 78 798 | 16 810 | 2 554 | 12 153 | 9 210 | 543 | 2 883 | 1 652 | 121 | 2 419 | 5 360 | 557 | 21 158 | 3 378 | Nombre d'établissements |
| Value added | 10 880.9 | 2 554.4 | 1 662.8 | 1 037.2 | 579.0 | 226.5 | 425.3 | 162.8 | 125.4 | 1 268.6 | 510.2 | 344.1 | 1 724.6 | 260.0 | Valeur ajoutée |
| Number of engaged (As of 31.XII) | 1 132.4 | 248.4 | 159.8 | 110.4 | 94.2 | 19.7 | 45.1 | 19.2 | 7.3 | 67.6 | 70.6 | 31.0 | 226.8 | 32.3 | Nombre de personnes occupées (au 31.XII) |
| Number of employees (As of 31.XII) | 993.2 | 215.9 | 155.1 | 89.9 | 78.7 | 18.6 | 39.8 | 16.4 | 7.0 | 63.6 | 60.5 | 29.9 | 191.2 | 26.6 | Nombre de salariés (au 31.XII) |
| Wages and salaries paid | 4 548.1 | 976.6 | 663.6 | 518.6 | 267.5 | 74.7 | 202.7 | 71.2 | 34.4 | 308.2 | 240.7 | 155.3 | 929.1 | 105.5 | Traitements et salaires payés |
| Capacity of installed power equipment (As of 31.XII) | 1 915.1 | 626.2 | 200.3 | 29.2 | 138.7 | 56.2 | 54.1 | 29.0 | 26.0 | 214.0 | 140.4 | 82.7 | 292.5 | 25.8 | Puissance installée (au 31.XII) |
| **1953** | | | | | | | | | | | | | | | **1953** |
| Number of establishments | 143 766 | 23 447 | 6 085 | 20 381 | 19 082 | 952 | 3 691 | 2 581 | 525 | 2 755 | 12 281 | 1 728 | 43 646 | 6 612 | Nombre d'établissements |
| Value added | 38 383.1 | 9 069.4 | 5 158.1 | 3 000.6 | 1 790.8 | 702.0 | 1 235.6 | 485.9 | 546.6 | 4 525.1 | 1 767.4 | 1 384.4 | 7 924.3 | 792.9 | Valeur ajoutée |
| Number of engaged | 1 411.0 | 279.5 | 175.5 | 116.4 | 125.3 | 22.2 | 42.3 | 19.3 | 16.6 | 73.0 | 93.2 | 52.6 | 356.4 | 38.7 | Nombre de personnes occupées |
| Employees: Number | 1 149.5 | 232.0 | 163.9 | 80.8 | 93.7 | 20.2 | 35.7 | 14.8 | 15.5 | 68.1 | 68.1 | 49.1 | 280.9 | 26.7 | Salariés: Nombre |
| Wages and salaries | 13 624.4 | 2 754.7 | 2 071.4 | 1 147.4 | 699.0 | 240.2 | 454.4 | 168.5 | 163.7 | 962.7 | 676.7 | 619.7 | 3 415.7 | 250.3 | Traitements et salaires |
| Number of operatives (Average for 1953) | 991.4 | 195.2 | 146.3 | 69.7 | 87.9 | 17.9 | 25.6 | 13.2 | 13.8 | 50.5 | 62.9 | 41.4 | 243.8 | 23.2 | Nombre d'ouvriers (moyenne pendant 1953) |
| Energy consumed | 5 616.7 | 1 670.2 | 432.4 | 18.4 | 57.1 | 158.5 | 9.8 | 31.0 | 61.2 | 1 039.3 | 1 307.9 | 807.6 | | 23.3 | Énergie consommée |
| Capacity of installed power equipment (As of 30.VII.1954) | 3 027.3 | 797.8 | 299.4 | 35.2 | 264.2 | 139.3 | 43.5 | 39.2 | 51.7 | 298.0 | 223.1 | 210.1 | 583.9 | 41.9 | Puissance installée (au 30.VII.1954) |

## C. The Major Groups of Manufacturing (continued) — Les classes de la branche Industries manufacturières (suite)

| Year and item of data | Manu-facturing / Industries manufac-turières | Food, beverages and tobacco / Industries alimen-taires, boissons, tabac | Textiles | Clothing, footwear and made-up textiles / Articles d'habil-lement, chaussures et ouvrages en tissu | Wood products and furniture / Bois et meubles | Paper and paper products / Papier et ouvrages en papier | Printing and publish-ing / Im-primerie et édition | Leather and leather products except wearing apparel / Cuir et articles en cuir, à l'exclu-sion des articles d'habil-lement | Rubber products / Ouvrages en caout-chouc | Chemicals and chemical, petroleum and coal products / Produits chi-miques et dérivés du pétrole et du charbon | Non-metallic mineral products / Produits minéraux non métal-liques | Basic metals / Métal-lurgie de base | Metal products / Ouvrages en métaux | Other manu-factur-ing / Autres in-dustries manufac-turières | Année et rubrique |
|---|---|---|---|---|---|---|---|---|---|---|---|---|---|---|---|
| ISIC | 2–3 | 20–22 | 23 | 24 | 25–26 | 27 | 28 | 29 | 30 | 31–32 | 33 | 34 | 35–38 | 39 | CITI |

### b. Structure

| Year and item of data | Manu-facturing | Food, bev. and tobacco | Textiles | Clothing etc. | Wood prod. | Paper | Printing | Leather | Rubber | Chemicals | Non-met. min. | Basic metals | Metal prod. | Other manuf. | Année et rubrique |
|---|---|---|---|---|---|---|---|---|---|---|---|---|---|---|---|
| **1939** Distribution in percent of: | | | | | | | | | | | | | | | **1939** Distribution en pourcentage: |
| Value added | 100.0 | 27.0 | 9.6 | 10.3 | 5.6 | 1.4 | 9.2 | 1.3 | 0.8 | 6.5 | 4.2 | 3.3 | 18.8 | 2.0 | Valeur ajoutée |
| Number of engaged | 100.0 | 26.1 | 11.2 | 10.1 | 7.7 | 1.6 | 5.6 | 1.4 | 0.7 | 5.1 | 5.2 | 2.8 | 19.8 | 2.7 | Nombre de personnes occupées |
| Value added per person engaged | 2.2 | 2.3 | 1.9 | 2.3 | 1.6 | 1.8 | 3.7 | 2.1 | 2.6 | 2.8 | 1.8 | 2.7 | 2.1 | 1.7 | Valeur ajoutée par personne occupée |
| Employees as a percent of engaged | 88.1 | 86.4 | 97.7 | 83.8 | 84.7 | 96.2 | 89.1 | 83.9 | 100.0 | 94.4 | 84.2 | 97.7 | 85.4 | 86.9 | Salariés en pourcentage des personnes occupées |
| Wages and salaries per employee | 1.5 | 1.5 | 1.2 | 2.0 | 1.2 | 1.2 | 2.0 | 1.5 | 1.5 | 1.5 | 1.3 | 1.7 | 1.6 | 1.4 | Traitements et salaires par salarié |
| Value added per unit of wages and salaries | 1.65 | 1.76 | 1.58 | 1.37 | 1.60 | 1.58 | 2.11 | 1.65 | 1.69 | 1.93 | 1.65 | 1.60 | 1.53 | 1.37 | Valeur ajoutée par unité de traitements et salaires |
| Capacity of installed power equipment per person engaged | 1.88 | 3.00 | 1.35 | 0.33 | 1.58 | 4.92 | 0.82 | 1.74 | 3.42 | 2.97 | 2.82 | 1.98 | 1.19 | 1.04 | Puissance installée par personne occupée |
| **1948** Distribution in percent of: | | | | | | | | | | | | | | | **1948** Distribution en pourcentage: |
| Value added | 100.0 | 23.4 | 15.3 | 9.5 | 5.4 | 2.0 | 4.0 | 1.4 | 1.2 | 11.7 | 4.6 | 3.2 | 15.9 | 2.4 | Valeur ajoutée |
| Number of engaged | 100.0 | 21.9 | 14.1 | 9.7 | 8.4 | 1.7 | 4.0 | 1.7 | 0.6 | 6.0 | 6.2 | 2.8 | 20.0 | 2.9 | Nombre de personnes occupées |
| Value added per person engaged | 9.6 | 10.3 | 10.4 | 9.4 | 6.1 | 11.5 | 9.4 | 8.5 | 17.2 | 18.8 | 7.2 | 11.1 | 7.6 | 8.0 | Valeur ajoutée par personne occupée |
| Employees as a percent of engaged | 87.7 | 86.9 | 97.0 | 81.4 | 83.5 | 94.4 | 88.2 | 85.4 | 95.9 | 94.1 | 85.7 | 96.4 | 84.3 | 82.4 | Salariés en pourcentage des personnes occupées |
| Wages and salaries per employee | 4.6 | 4.5 | 4.3 | 5.8 | 3.4 | 4.0 | 5.1 | 4.3 | 4.9 | 4.8 | 4.0 | 5.2 | 4.8 | 4.0 | Traitements et salaires par salarié |
| Value added per unit of wages and salaries | 2.39 | 2.62 | 2.51 | 2.00 | 2.16 | 3.03 | 2.10 | 2.29 | 3.65 | 4.12 | 2.12 | 2.22 | 1.86 | 2.46 | Valeur ajoutée par unité de traitements et salaires |
| Capacity of installed power equipment per person engaged | 1.69 | 2.52 | 1.25 | 0.26 | 1.47 | 2.85 | 1.20 | 1.51 | 3.56 | 3.17 | 1.99 | 2.67 | 1.29 | 0.80 | Puissance installée par personne occupée |
| **1953** Distribution in percent of: | | | | | | | | | | | | | | | **1953** Distribution en pourcentage: |
| Value added | 100.0 | 23.6 | 13.4 | 7.8 | 4.7 | 1.8 | 3.2 | 1.3 | 1.4 | 11.8 | 4.6 | 3.6 | 20.7 | 2.1 | Valeur ajoutée |
| Number of engaged | 100.0 | 19.8 | 12.4 | 8.2 | 8.9 | 1.6 | 3.0 | 1.4 | 1.1 | 5.2 | 6.6 | 3.7 | 25.3 | 2.8 | Nombre de personnes occupées |
| Per person engaged: Value added | 27.2 | 32.4 | 29.4 | 25.8 | 14.3 | 31.6 | 29.2 | 25.2 | 32.9 | 62.0 | 19.0 | 26.3 | 22.2 | 20.5 | Par personne occupée: Valeur ajoutée |
| Energy consumed | 3.98 | 5.98 | 2.46 | 0.16 | 0.46 | 7.14 | 0.23 | 1.61 | 3.69 | 14.24 | 14.03 | 1.97 | | 0.60 | Energie consommée |
| Capacity of installed power equipment | 2.14 | 2.85 | 1.70 | 0.30 | 2.11 | 6.27 | 1.03 | 2.03 | 3.11 | 4.08 | 2.39 | 3.99 | 1.64 | 1.08 | Puissance installée |
| Employee as a percent of engaged | 81.5 | 83.0 | 93.4 | 69.4 | 74.8 | 91.0 | 84.4 | 76.7 | 93.4 | 93.3 | 73.1 | 93.3 | 78.8 | 69.0 | Salariés en pourcentage des personnes occupées |
| Value added per unit of wages and salaries | 2.82 | 3.29 | 2.49 | 2.62 | 2.56 | 2.92 | 2.72 | 2.88 | 3.34 | 4.70 | 2.61 | 2.23 | 2.32 | 3.17 | Valeur ajoutée par unité de traitements et salaires |
| Wages and salaries per employee | 11.8 | 11.9 | 12.6 | 14.2 | 7.4 | 11.9 | 12.7 | 11.4 | 10.6 | 14.1 | 9.9 | 12.6 | 12.2 | 9.4 | Traitements et salaires par salarié |
| Operatives as a percent of employees | 86.2 | 84.1 | 89.3 | 86.3 | 93.8 | 88.6 | 71.7 | 89.2 | 89.0 | 74.2 | 92.4 | 84.3 | 86.8 | 86.9 | Ouvriers en pourcentage des salariés |
| Per operative: Energy consumed | 5.66 | 8.56 | 2.96 | 0.26 | 0.65 | 8.85 | 0.38 | 2.35 | 4.43 | 20.58 | 20.79 | 2.83 | | 1.00 | Par ouvrier: Energie consommée |
| Capacity of installed power equipment | 3.05 | 4.09 | 2.05 | 0.50 | 3.00 | 7.78 | 1.70 | 2.97 | 3.75 | 5.90 | 3.55 | 5.07 | 2.39 | 1.81 | Puissance installée |

23

## 5. FUELS AND ELECTRICITY CONSUMED BY ALL INDUSTRIAL ESTABLISHMENTS
## COMBUSTIBLES ET ELECTRICITE CONSOMMES PAR L'ENSEMBLE DES ETABLISSEMENTS INDUSTRIELS
### 1953

### A. Percentage Distribution of Energy Consumed According to Source
### Répartition en pourcentage de l'énergie consommée suivant la source

Quantities in thousand metric tons of coal equivalents.    Quantités en milliers de tonnes métriques d'équivalent charbon.

| Item of data | Mining (Industries extractives) | Manu-facturing (Industries manufac-turières) | Food, beverages and tobacco (Industries alimentaires, boissons, tabac) | Textiles | Clothing, footwear and made-up textiles (Articles d'habillement, chaussures et ouvrages en tissu) | Wood products and furniture (Bois et meubles) | Paper and paper products (Papier et ouvrages en papier) | Printing and publishing (Imprimerie et édition) | Leather and leather products except wearing apparel (Cuir et articles en cuir, à l'exclusion des articles d'habillement) | Rubber products (Ouvrages en caoutchouc) | Chemicals and chemical, petroleum and coal products (Produits chimiques et dérivés du pétrole et du charbon) | Non-metallic mineral products (Produits minéraux non métalliques) | Basic metals and metal products (Métallurgie de base et ouvrages en métaux) | Other manu-facturing (Autres industries manufac-turières) | Electricity and gas (Electricité et gaz) |
|---|---|---|---|---|---|---|---|---|---|---|---|---|---|---|---|
| ISIC | 1 | 2–3 | 20–22 | 23 | 24 | 25–26 | 27 | 28 | 29 | 30 | 31–32 | 33 | 34–38 | 39 | 511-512 |
| Total energy consumed: Quantity | 374.0 | 5 616.7 | 1 670.2 | 432.4 | 18.4 | 57.1 | 158.5 | 9.8 | 31.0 | 61.2 | 1 039.3 | 1 307.9 | 807.6 | 23.3 | 2 888.8 |
| Percent of total in specified industry | . | 100.0 | 29.7 | 7.7 | 0.3 | 1.0 | 2.9 | 0.1 | 0.6 | 1.1 | 18.5 | 23.3 | 14.3 | 0.5 | . |
| Percent consumed as: Coal | 8.6 | 3.6 | 2.6 | 0.4 | 5.5 | 2.1 | 0.4 | 3.0 | 3.5 | 0.8 | 0.9 | 7.7 | 5.7 | 2.1 | 20.8 |
| Wood | 17.1 | 20.0 | 35.9 | 4.4 | 9.8 | 63.4 | 8.9 | 6.1 | 21.4 | 2.9 | 6.2 | 25.1 | 7.5 | 13.6 | 0.5 |
| Coke | 4.2 | 0.9 | 0.9 | — | — | — | 0.2 | — | — | — | 0.5 | 1.0 | 3.7 | — | 0.9 |
| Refined oil fuels | 30.8 | 61.8 | 45.9 | 85.0 | 53.3 | 22.2 | 83.5 | 43.9 | 65.6 | 84.1 | 77.5 | 64.0 | 53.5 | 76.0 | 77.6 |
| Gas | 38.5 | 2.7 | 0.4 | 0.1 | 5.6 | 1.4 | 1.0 | 8.2 | 0.3 | 0.2 | 9.6 | 0.7 | 3.2 | 4.0 | . |
| Electricity purchased | 0.2 | 3.3 | 3.0 | 8.0 | 24.0 | 8.9 | 5.9 | 36.8 | 6.3 | 10.0 | 1.3 | 0.9 | 5.2 | 3.9 | . |
| Other fuels | 0.6 | 7.7 | 12.2 | 2.1 | 1.8 | 1.8 | 0.3 | 2.0 | 2.9 | 2.0 | 4.0 | 0.6 | 21.2 | 0.4 | 0.2 |

Rubrique: Energie totale consommée: Quantité / Pourcentage du total par industrie indiquée / Pourcentage consommée sous forme de: Charbon / Bois / Coke / Pétrole raffiné / Gaz / Electricité achetée / Autres combustibles

### B. Quantity and Value of Fuels Consumed and Electricity Purchased and Produced
### Consommation de combustibles et électricité achetée et produite: quantités et valeur

Coal, coke, refined oil fuels and wood in thousand metric tons; gas in million cubic metres; electricity in million KWH; other fuels in thousand metric tons of coal equivalents; values in million Pesos.    Charbon, coke, pétrole raffiné et bois en milliers de tonnes métriques; gaz en millions de mètres cubes; électricité en millions de kWh; autres combustibles en milliers de tonnes métriques d'équivalent charbon; valeur en millions de pesos.

| Source of energy | Mining | Manu-facturing | Food, beverages and tobacco | Textiles | Clothing, footwear and made-up textiles | Wood products and furniture | Paper and paper products | Printing and publishing | Leather and leather products except wearing apparel | Rubber products | Chemicals and chemical, petroleum and coal products | Non-metallic mineral products | Basic metals and metal products | Other manu-facturing | Electricity and gas |
|---|---|---|---|---|---|---|---|---|---|---|---|---|---|---|---|
| ISIC | 1 | 2–3 | 20–22 | 23 | 24 | 25–26 | 27 | 28 | 29 | 30 | 31–32 | 33 | 34–38 | 39 | 511-512 |
| Coal — quantity | 32.5 | 209.2 | 42.9 | 2.0 | 0.9 | 1.2 | 0.7 | 0.3 | 1.2 | 0.5 | 9.7 | 101.3 | 46.5 | 2.0 | 602.8 |
| Coke — quantity | 17.6 | 54.3 | 1.1 | — | — | 0.1 | — | — | — | — | — | 5.4 | 14.1 | 33.6 | 27.3 |
| Refined oil fuels — quantity | 78.5 | 2347.8 | 507.1 | 245.1 | 5.9 | 8.9 | 88.3 | 3.1 | 14.9 | 34.4 | 539.7 | 559.2 | 294.3 | 46.9 | 1 496.2 |
| Manufactured gas — quantity | 239.7 | 252.0 | 10.7 | 1.1 | 1.5 | 1.3 | 2.9 | 1.3 | 0.2 | 0.2 | 167.2 | 15.4 | 44.0 | 6.2 | 49.0 |
| Electricity: Purchased: Quantity | 6.0 | 1 471.2 | 333.7 | 274.9 | 22.6 | 38.1 | 73.7 | 28.8 | 26.5 | 49.0 | 107.2 | 91.2 | 338.3 | 87.2 | ... |
| Value | 2.2 | 629.6 | 118.4 | 128.1 | 11.6 | 19.1 | 47.3 | 14.0 | 12.8 | 22.2 | 49.9 | 37.7 | 130.2 | 38.3 | ... |
| Produced — quantity | 54.0 | 1 028.0 | 243.9 | 92.6 | 0.7 | 6.9 | 75.1 | 0.5 | 3.3 | 10.9 | 278.0 | 210.8 | 99.6 | 5.7 | ... |
| Wood — quantity | 127.5 | 2 272.1 | 1 182.3 | 37.2 | 3.2 | 70.4 | 27.9 | 1.1 | 14.5 | 3.5 | 129.2 | 655.6 | 122.2 | 25.0 | 28.6 |
| Other fuels: Quantity | 2.2 | 437.2 | 201.3 | 9.1 | 0.3 | 1.0 | 0.6 | 0.2 | 1.0 | 1.2 | 41.1 | 7.7 | 173.3 | 0.4 | 2.9 |
| Value | 0.3 | 110.6 | 49.7 | 1.8 | 0.1 | 0.3 | 0.1 | 0.1 | 0.5 | 0.2 | 5.5 | 1.6 | 49.6 | 1.3 | 0.6 |

Source d'énergie: Charbon — quantité / Coke — quantité / Pétrole raffiné — quantité / Gaz manufacturé — quantité / Electricité: Achetée: Quantité / Valeur / Produite — quantité / Bois — quantité / Autres combustibles: Quantité / Valeur

# AUSTRALIA — AUSTRALIE

## Gross Domestic Product

The estimates of the gross domestic product according to source of expenditure in Table 1 are derived from the response of the Commonwealth Bureau of Census and Statistics, Canberra, to the United Nations questionnaire on national accounts. The official estimates and description are published in the annual paper, *National Income and Expenditure*, which accompanies the Commonwealth Budget, and in the semi-annual publication of the Bureau, *The Australian Balance of Payments*.

## Index Numbers of Industrial Employment

The index numbers set out in Table 2 are based on absolute figures of employment from the annual Censuses of Industries taken by the Commonwealth Bureau of Census and Statistics, Canberra, or from the interim estimates of the Commonwealth Bureau. The interim estimates are based on a combination of the latest available data from the annual Censuses and pay-roll tax returns. The index numbers shown in Table 2 for all years before 1960, except for mining, were compiled from the Census figures published by the Commonwealth Bureau in the annual issues of *Primary Industries, Part II—Non-Rural Industries and Value of Production, Secondary Industries* and *Yearbook of the Commonwealth of Australia*. In the case of mining, the annual Census was also the source of the data for 1960. The index numbers for 1960 and 1961 for the manufacturing and electricity and gas industries, were compiled from the interim estimates shown, in the publication, *Monthly Bulletin of Employment Statistics*. In compiling the indexes, the interim estimates were linked to the Census results at 1959 in view of the differences noted below between the two series.

The annual Census data from which the index numbers were compiled relate to the number of persons engaged (i.e. working proprietors, employees and home-workers) in the industrial pursuits of the covered units, expressed in full-year equivalents. Persons engaged in the selling and distributing activities of the covered establishments are excluded from the figures. In the case of mining, the figures cover, in principle, mines irrespective of size. In the case of the manufacturing and electricity and gas industries, the field of coverage consists of establishments in which four or more persons are engaged or which have installed power equipment.

## Produit intérieur brut

Les estimations du produit intérieur brut par poste de dépense qui figurent au tableau 1 sont tirées de la réponse du Commonwealth Bureau of Census and Statistics, Canberra, au questionnaire de l'ONU sur la comptabilité nationale. Les estimations officielles et les renseignements connexes sont publiés dans l'étude annuelle intitulée *National Income and Expenditure* qui accompagne le Commonwealth Budget, et dans la publication semestrielle du Bureau, *The Australian Balance of Payments*.

## Indices de l'emploi dans l'industrie

Les indices du tableau 2 sont fondés sur les chiffres absolus de l'emploi fournis par les recensements annuels des industries effectués par le Commonwealth Bureau of Census and Statistics, Canberra, ou sur les estimations provisoires du Commonwealth Bureau. Les estimations provisoires reposent sur une combinaison des données les plus récentes fournies par les recensements annuels et par l'état des retenues fiscales opérées sur les salaires. Les indices du tableau 2 pour toutes les années antérieures à 1960, à l'exception des indices relatifs aux industries extractives, ont été établis à partir des données de recensements publiées par le Commonwealth Bureau dans les numéros annuels de *Primary Industries, Part II — Non-Rural Industries and Value of Production, Secondary Industries* et *Yearbook of the Commonwealth of Australia*. Pour les industries extractives, les données de 1960 ont été tirées également des résultats du recensement annuel. Pour les industries manufacturières et les industries de l'électricité et du gaz, les indices de 1960 et 1961 ont été calculés à partir des estimations provisoires publiées dans le *Monthly Bulletin of Employment Statistics*. Lors du calcul des indices, les estimations provisoires ont été raccordées aux données de recensement au niveau de 1959, vu les différences signalées ci-dessous entre les deux séries.

Les indices ont été établis à partir des données que les recensements annuels fournissent sur le nombre des personnes occupées (propriétaires qui travaillent, salariés et travailleurs à domicile) qui participent aux activités industrielles des unités recensées, ce nombre étant exprimé en équivalent d'années de travail à plein temps. Les personnes participant aux activités de vente et de distribution des établissements recensés ne sont pas comprises dans les chiffres. Dans le cas des industries extractives, les chiffres concernent en principe toutes les unités minières, quelle que soit leur dimension. Pour les industries manufacturières et les industries de l'électricité et du gaz, ne sont compris que les établissements occupant au moins quatre personnes ou utilisant la force motrice.

The interim estimates of employment utilized in compiling the indexes concern the annual average of the number of employees and homeworkers on the payroll of covered establishments during the latter part of each month. For purposes of the interim estimates, employees and homeworkers are defined in the same fashion as in the annual Census, but working proprietors are not included; and the interim estimates are not expressed in full-time equivalents, as in the annual Censuses. The establishments required to make the monthly pay-roll tax returns on which the interim estimates are based are those paying more than £200 a week wages and salaries.

In view of the differences between mining, on the one hand, and manufacturing and electricity, on the other, in the field covered by the absolute figures of employment utilized in compiling the indexes, the Statistical Office of the United Nations computed the series of indexes for these three divisions of industrial activity, combined, as base-weighted arithmetic means of the indexes for each of the divisions. The weights utilized for this purpose were proportional to the estimated number of persons engaged in each division of industrial activity during the period, 1 July 1953 – 30 June 1954, in the case of the indexes for the years up to 1955 and during the period, 1 July 1958 – 30 June 1959 for 1955 and thereafter.

### Characteristics and Structure of Industrial Activity

The information shown in Tables 3 and 4 is derived from the results of annual Censuses of Industries published by the Commonwealth Bureau of Census and Statistics, Canberra, in *Production, 1938-39*, Bulletin No. 33; Part I—*Secondary Industries, Production, 1948-49*, Bulletin No. 43; *Primary Industries*, Part II, *1953-54* and *1958-1959*, Bulletin Nos. 48 and 53, respectively, and *Secondary Industries, 1953-54* and *1958-1959*, Bulletin Nos. 48 and 53, respectively. In general, the Censuses covered industrial establishments having four or more persons employed or using power other than manual. In the case of mining, the Commonwealth Bureau published data on number of mines and quarries, value added and number of persons engaged that related to all mines since estimates were made for the excluded units. It should be noted, however, that the statistics on mining are, to some extent, incomplete in the case of the quarrying of construction materials and the mining of a few other non-metallic minerals.

The definitions of the items of data are consistent with the International Standards in Basic Industrial Statistics except that the figures of employment and wages and salaries exclude persons not directly connected with the industrial activities of the covered establishment, such as salesmen, collectors and carters engaged solely on outward delivery of manufactured goods, and that homeworkers are included in the count of employees. As was noted above, the counts of number of employees are expressed

Les estimations provisoires de l'emploi utilisées pour le calcul des indices concernent la moyenne annuelle du nombre des salariés et des travailleurs à domicile figurant sur les états de paie des établissements intéressés pendant la dernière partie de chaque mois. Aux fins des estimations provisoires, salariés et travailleurs à domicile sont définis de la même façon que pour le recensement annuel, mais les propriétaires qui travaillent ne sont pas compris; en outre, les estimations provisoires ne sont pas exprimées en équivalent de travail à plein temps comme dans le cas des recensements annuels. Les établissements tenus de présenter un état mensuel des retenues fiscales opérées sur les salaires, lequel sert à établir les estimations, sont ceux qui payent plus de 200 livres par semaine en traitements et salaires.

En raison des différences existant entre, d'une part, les industries extractives et, d'autre part, les industries manufacturières et les industries de l'électricité quant à la portée des chiffres absolus de l'emploi utilisés pour le calcul des indices, le Bureau de statistique de l'ONU a calculé la série d'indices pour ces trois branches de l'activité industrielle combinées en faisant une moyenne arithmétique à pondération fixe des indices de chacune des branches. Les coefficients de pondération utilisés à cette fin sont proportionnels aux estimations du nombre de personnes occupées dans chaque branche entre le 1er juillet 1953 et le 30 juin 1954 pour les indices de 1954 et des années antérieures, et entre le 1er juillet 1958 et le 30 juin 1959 pour 1955 et les années suivantes.

### Caractéristiques et structure de l'activité industrielle

Les renseignements des tableaux 3 et 4 sont tirés des résultats des recensements annuels des industries; ces résultats ont été publiés par le Commonwealth Bureau of Census and Statistics, Canberra, dans *Production, 1938-39, Bulletin No 33; Part I — Secondary Industries, Production, 1948-49, Bulletin No 43; Primary Industries, Part II, 1953-54* et *1958-1959*, Bulletin Nos 48 et 53 respectivement. En général, ces recensements couvraient les établissements industriels employant au moins quatre personnes ou utilisant la force motrice. Dans le cas des industries extractives, les chiffres publiés par le Commonwealth Bureau au sujet des mines et carrières (nombre, valeur ajoutée et nombre de personnes occupées) concernaient toutes les mines et carrières, des estimations ayant été faites pour les unités non recensées. Il y a lieu de noter cependant que les statistiques des industries extractives sont, jusqu'à un certain point, incomplètes dans le cas de l'extraction des matériaux de construction et de quelques autres minéraux non métalliques.

Les définitions des rubriques sont conformes aux Normes internationales relatives aux statistiques industrielles de base, si ce n'est que les chiffres de l'emploi et des traitements et salaires ne tiennent pas compte des personnes qui ne participent pas directement à l'activité industrielle de l'établissement recensé, par exemple les vendeurs, les encaisseurs et les transporteurs chargés uniquement de livrer à l'extérieur les marchandises produites; d'autre part, les travailleurs à domicile sont com-

in full-year equivalents. Value added is based on the value of production at factor cost, ex mine or factory.

The capacity of installed power equipment is equivalent, in general, to the sum of the rated horsepower of all prime movers in use and of all electric motors in use that are driven by purchased electricity. In the case of the Electricity and Gas industries, the capacity of installed power equipment has been restricted to the rated horsepower of all prime movers in use. The data shown in Table 4 on purchased fuels and electricity consumed relate to the use of the various fuels as a source of heat or power only, including the production of electricity, but not gas. Coke charged to blast furnaces is also included.

pris parmi les salariés. Comme on l'a indiqué plus haut, le nombre de personnes occupées et de salariés est exprimé en années de travail à plein temps. La valeur ajoutée est calculée d'après la valeur de la production au coût des facteurs, au départ de l'usine ou de la mine.

La puissance installée équivaut en général à la puissance nominale de tous les moteurs primaires en service et de tous les moteurs électriques en service qui sont actionnés par de l'électricité achetée. Dans le cas de l'électricité et du gaz, la puissance installée représente uniquement la puissance nominale de tous les moteurs primaires en service. Les données du tableau 4 relatives aux combustibles achetés et à l'électricité consommée concernent l'utilisation des différents combustibles comme source de chaleur ou d'énergie seulement, y compris la production d'électricité mais à l'exclusion de celle du gaz. Le coke utilisé dans les hauts fourneaux est également inclus.

## 1. EXPENDITURE ON THE GROSS DOMESTIC PRODUCT AT MARKET PRICES
## DEPENSES RELATIVES AU PRODUIT INTERIEUR BRUT AUX PRIX DU MARCHE

Million Pounds Australian     Millions de livres australiennes

| Item of data and year / Rubrique et année | Total | Consumption [2] / Consommation [2] | | Gross Domestic Capital Formation [3] / Formation brute de capital intérieur [3] | | Net exports of goods and services / Exportations nettes de biens et de services | |
|---|---|---|---|---|---|---|---|
| | | Total | Government / Etat | Total | Fixed / Fixe | Exports less imports / Exportations moins importations | Exports / Exportations |
| *a. At Current Prices — Aux prix courants* | | | | | | | |
| Absolute figures — Chiffres absolus [1] | | | | | | | |
| 1948 | 2 283 | 1 673 | 175 | 530 | 442 | 80 | 579 |
| 1950 | 3 633 | 2 346 | 293 | 1 110 | 864 | 177 | 1 051 |
| 1951 | 3 869 | 2 809 | 402 | 1 546 | 1 126 | −486 | 749 |
| 1952 | 4 213 | 3 031 | 464 | 907 | 1 041 | 275 | 933 |
| 1953 | 4 562 | 3 272 | 441 | 1 201 | 1 137 | 89 | 901 |
| 1954 | 4 919 | 3 602 | 469 | 1 460 | 1 285 | −143 | 860 |
| 1955 | 5 315 | 3 873 | 524 | 1 549 | 1 380 | −107 | 881 |
| 1956 | 5 748 | 4 078 | 544 | 1 448 | 1 408 | 222 | 1 104 |
| 1957 | 5 828 | 4 336 | 567 | 1 544 | 1 522 | −52 | 933 |
| 1958 | 6 231 | 4 540 | 611 | 1 744 | 1 606 | −53 | 943 |
| 1959 | 6 894 | 5 038 | 671 | 1 940 | 1 823 | −84 | 1 085 |
| 1960 | 7 255 | 5 306 | 725 | 2 180 | 1 925 | −231 | 1 104 |
| 1961 | 7 327 | 5 437 | 772 | 1 764 | 1 887 | 126 | 1 256 |
| Percentage distribution of average annual expenditure — Distribution en pourcentage des dépenses annuelles moyennes | | | | | | | |
| 1948 | 100.0 | 73.3 | 7.7 | 23.2 | 19.4 | 3.5 | 25.4 |
| 1950-1960 | 100.0 | 72.2 | 9.8 | 28.5 | 25.8 | −0.7 | 18.0 |
| 1950 | 100.0 | 64.6 | 8.1 | 30.5 | 23.8 | 4.9 | 28.9 |
| 1953 | 100.0 | 71.7 | 9.7 | 26.3 | 24.9 | 2.0 | 19.8 |
| 1954 | 100.0 | 73.2 | 9.5 | 29.7 | 26.1 | −2.9 | 17.5 |
| 1958 | 100.0 | 72.9 | 9.8 | 28.0 | 25.8 | −0.9 | 15.1 |
| 1960 | 100.0 | 73.1 | 10.0 | 30.0 | 26.5 | −3.1 | 15.2 |

[1] Fiscal years beginning 1st July.
[2] Includes expenditures of financial enterprises, interest on consumers' debt and current transfers from households to general government other than direct taxes; and in the case of Government, contributions to international organizations and increases in stocks of strategic materials less sales of surplus stores. Excludes expenditures on motor vehicles for personal use.
[3] Includes, in the case of fixed capital formation, expenditure on motor vehicles for personal use and on maintenance of roads; excludes changes in stocks of livestock and of strategic materials held by Government. Changes in stocks determined at book value.

[1] Années fiscales commençant le 1er juillet.
[2] Y compris les dépenses des entreprises financières, l'intérêt de la dette des consommateurs et les transferts courants des ménages à l'Etat autres que les impots directs; dans le cas de l'Etat, y compris les contributions aux organisations internationales et l'accroissement des stocks de matières stratégiques, déduction faite des ventes de stocks excédentaires. Non compris les dépenses effectuées au titre des voitures particulières.
[3] Y compris, dans le cas de la formation de capital fixe, les dépenses relatives aux voitures particulières et à l'entretien des routes; non compris les variations du cheptel et des stocks de matières stratégiques détenus par l'Etat. Les variations de stocks sont déterminées en valeur comptable.

## 2. INDEX NUMBERS OF INDUSTRIAL EMPLOYMENT — INDICES DE L'EMPLOI DANS L'INDUSTRIE

### A. Selected Divisions of Industrial Activity
### Quelques branches de l'activité industrielle

| Period / Période | Total | Mining / Industries extractives | Manu-facturing / Industries manu-facturières | Electricity and gas / Electricité et gaz |
|---|---|---|---|---|
| ISIC — CITI | 1–3, 511–512 | 1 | 2–3 | 511–512 |

**a. Indexes — Indices (1958 = 100)**

| Period | Total | Mining | Manufacturing | Electricity and gas |
|---|---|---|---|---|
| 1938.......... | ... | ... | 52 | 56 |
| 1948.......... | ... | ... | 81 | 74 |
| 1949.......... | ... | ... | 84 | 78 |
| 1950.......... | ... | ... | 87 | 81 |
| 1951.......... | ... | ... | 90 | 85 |
| 1952.......... | 96 | 113 | 88 | 88 |
| 1953.......... | 97 | 113 | 89 | 91 |
| 1954.......... | 99 | 113 | 93 | 94 |
| 1955.......... | – 101 – | 112 | 97 | 96 |
| 1956.......... | 102 | 111 | 98 | 97 |
| 1957.......... | 102 | 108 | 99 | 99 |
| 1958.......... | 100 | 100 | 100 | 100 |
| 1959.......... | – 99 – | 95 | – 103 – | – 100 – |
| 1960.......... | 99 | 95 | 104 | 98 |
| 1961.......... | ... | ... | 101 | 96 |

**b. Average Annual Rate of Change — Taux annuel moyen de variation**

| Period | Total | Mining | Manufacturing | Electricity and gas |
|---|---|---|---|---|
| 1938 – 1960.... | ... | ... | 3.2 | 2.6 |
| 1938 – 1948.... | ... | ... | 4.5 | 2.8 |
| 1950 – 1960.... | ... | ... | 1.8 | 1.9 |
| 1948 – 1953.... | ... | ... | 1.9 | 4.2 |
| 1954 – 1958.... | 0.3 | –3.0 | 1.8 | 1.6 |
| 1958 – 1960.... | –0.5 | –2.5 | 2.0 | –1.0 |

### B. The Major Groups of Mining
### Les classes de la branche Industries extractives

| Period / Période | All mining / Toutes industries extractives | Coal mining / Extraction du charbon | Metal mining / Extraction des minerais métalliques | Other mining / Autres industries extractives |
|---|---|---|---|---|
| ISIC — CITI | 1 | 11 | 12 | 14–19 |

**a. Indexes — Indices (1958 = 100)**

| Period | All mining | Coal mining | Metal mining | Other mining |
|---|---|---|---|---|
| 1938.......... | ... | 94 | 203 | ... |
| 1948.......... | ... | 109 | 106 | ... |
| 1949.......... | ... | 112 | 106 | ... |
| 1950.......... | ... | 114 | 114 | ... |
| 1951.......... | ... | 116 | 116 | ... |
| 1952.......... | 113 | 127 | 105 | 96 |
| 1953.......... | 113 | 126 | 108 | 90 |
| 1954.......... | 113 | 126 | 104 | 94 |
| 1955.......... | 112 | 122 | 108 | 94 |
| 1956.......... | 111 | 114 | 114 | 96 |
| 1957.......... | 108 | 107 | 112 | 101 |
| 1958.......... | 100 | 100 | 100 | 100 |
| 1959.......... | 95 | 90 | 99 | 97 |
| 1960.......... | 95 | 89 | 97 | 109 |

**b. Average Annual Rate of Change — Taux annuel moyen de variation**

| Period | All mining | Coal mining | Metal mining | Other mining |
|---|---|---|---|---|
| 1938 – 1960.... | ... | –0.4 | –3.3 | ... |
| 1938 – 1948.... | ... | 1.5 | –6.3 | ... |
| 1950 – 1960.... | ... | –2.4 | –1.6 | ... |
| 1948 – 1953.... | ... | 2.9 | 0.4 | ... |
| 1954 – 1958.... | –3.0 | –5.6 | –1.4 | 1.6 |
| 1958 – 1960.... | –2.5 | –5.7 | –1.5 | 4.4 |

## C. The Major Groups of Manufacturing — Les classes de la branche Industries manufacturières

| Period / Période | Manufacturing / Industries manufacturières | Food, beverages and tobacco / Industries alimentaires, boissons, tabac | Textiles | Clothing, footwear and made-up textiles / Articles d'habillement, chaussures et ouvrages en tissu | Wood products and furniture [2] / Bois et meubles [2] | Paper and paper products / Papier et ouvrages en papier | Printing and publishing / Imprimerie et édition | Leather and leather products except wearing apparel / Cuir et articles en cuir, à l'exclusion des articles d'habillement | Rubber products / Ouvrages en caoutchouc | Chemicals and chemical, petroleum and coal products [1] / Produits chimiques et dérivés du pétrole et du charbon [1] | Non-metallic mineral products [1] / Produits minéraux non métalliques [1] | Basic metals / Métallurgie de base | Metal products [2] / Ouvrages en métaux [2] | Other manufacturing / Autres industries manufacturières |
|---|---|---|---|---|---|---|---|---|---|---|---|---|---|---|
| ISIC — CITI | 2–3 | 20–22 | 23 | 24 | 25–26 | 27 | 28 | 29 | 30 | 31–32 | 33 | 34 | 35–38 | 39 |

### a. Indexes — Indices (1958 = 100)

| Period / Période | 2–3 | 20–22 | 23 | 24 | 25–26 | 27 | 28 | 29 | 30 | 31–32 | 33 | 34 | 35–38 | 39 |
|---|---|---|---|---|---|---|---|---|---|---|---|---|---|---|
| 1938 | 52 | 66 | 67 | 87 | 56 | 42 | 69 | 106 | 41 | 39 | 58 | 46 | 37 | 40 |
| 1948 | 81 | 93 | 96 | 112 | 84 | 69 | 77 | 121 | 62 | 68 | 75 | 58 | 72 | 84 |
| 1949 | 84 | 97 | 98 | 115 | 88 | 74 | 80 | 122 | 66 | 71 | 80 | 63 | 75 | 87 |
| 1950 | 87 | 99 | 100 | 117 | 93 | 77 | 84 | 121 | 71 | 75 | 85 | 65 | 79 | 89 |
| 1951 | 90 | 99 | 98 | 116 | 98 | 82 | 85 | 114 | 75 | 80 | 90 | 69 | 84 | 88 |
| 1952 | 88 | 98 | 92 | 106 | 97 | 79 | 84 | 108 | 72 | 80 | 89 | 70 | 84 | 83 |
| 1953 | 89 | 98 | 96 | 103 | 96 | 78 | 84 | 108 | 74 | 80 | 89 | 70 | 86 | 85 |
| 1954 | 93 | 100 | 102 | 106 | 99 | 86 | 88 | 111 | 86 | 85 | 94 | 74 | 91 | 91 |
| 1955 | 97 | 101 | 102 | 105 | 102 | 90 | 92 | 109 | 92 | 91 | 99 | 80 | 96 | 95 |
| 1956 | 98 | 101 | 102 | 103 | 101 | 93 | 96 | 103 | 96 | 95 | 99 | 88 | 97 | 99 |
| 1957 | 99 | 100 | 102 | 101 | 99 | 96 | 98 | 101 | 98 | 98 | 98 | 95 | 98 | 101 |
| 1958 | 100 | 100 | 100 | 100 | 100 | 100 | 100 | 100 | 100 | 100 | 100 | 100 | 100 | 100 |
| 1959 | –103– | –101– | –102– | –100– | –102– | 105 | 103 | –99– | –102– | –101– | –103– | –105– | –104– | –102– |
| 1960 | 104 | 99 | 104 | 98 | 99 | ... | ... | 94 | 101 | 101 | 106 | 107 | | 103 |
| 1961 | 101 | 98 | 99 | 93 | 92 | ... | ... | 89 | 97 | 99 | 106 | 104 | | 100 |

### b. Average Annual Rate of Change — Taux annuel moyen de variation

| Period / Période | 2–3 | 20–22 | 23 | 24 | 25–26 | 27 | 28 | 29 | 30 | 31–32 | 33 | 34 | 35–38 | 39 |
|---|---|---|---|---|---|---|---|---|---|---|---|---|---|---|
| 1938 – 1960 | 3.2 | 1.9 | 2.0 | 0.5 | 2.6 | ... | ... | −0.5 | 4.2 | 4.4 | 2.8 | ... | ... | 4.4 |
| 1938 – 1948 | 4.5 | 3.5 | 3.7 | 2.6 | 4.1 | 5.1 | 1.1 | 1.3 | 4.2 | 5.7 | 2.6 | 2.3 | 6.9 | 7.7 |
| 1950 – 1960 | 1.8 | — | 0.4 | −1.8 | 0.6 | ... | ... | −2.5 | 3.6 | 3.0 | 2.2 | ... | ... | 1.5 |
| 1948 – 1953 | 1.9 | 1.1 | — | −1.7 | 2.7 | 2.5 | 1.8 | −2.3 | 3.6 | 3.3 | 3.5 | 3.8 | 3.6 | 0.2 |
| 1954 – 1958 | 1.8 | — | −0.5 | −1.4 | 0.2 | 3.8 | 3.2 | −2.6 | 3.8 | 4.1 | 1.6 | 7.8 | 2.4 | 2.4 |
| 1958 – 1960 | 2.0 | −0.5 | 2.0 | −1.0 | −0.5 | ... | ... | −3.0 | 0.5 | 0.5 | 3.0 | ... | ... | 1.5 |

[1] Briquetting and pulverizing coal (part of ISIC major group 32) is covered under Non-metallic mineral products (ISIC major group 33).
[2] Manufacture of metal furniture (part of ISIC major group 26) is covered under Metal products (ISIC major group 35).

[1] La fabrication des briquettes en charbon et la pulvérisation du charbon (dans CITI classe 32) sont comprises dans Produits minéraux non métalliques (CITI classe 33).
[2] La fabrication des meubles métalliques (dans CITI classe 26) est comprise dans Ouvrages en métaux (CITI classe 35).

# AUSTRALIA

## 3. THE CHARACTERISTICS OF INDUSTRIAL ESTABLISHMENTS ENGAGING FOUR OR MORE PERSONS OR USING POWER EQUIPMENT

### CARACTERISTIQUES DES ETABLISSEMENTS INDUSTRIELS OCCUPANT AU MOINS QUATRE PERSONNES OU UTILISANT LA FORCE MOTRICE

### 1.VII.1938-30.VI.1939, 1.VII.1948-30.VI.1949, 1.VII.1953-30.VI.1954, 1.VII.1958-30.VI.1959

Number of establishments in units; value added and wages and salaries in million Australian Pounds; number of engaged and employees in thousands; capacity of installed power equipment in thousand horsepower; value added per person engaged in thousand Australian Pounds; capacity of installed power equipment per person engaged in horsepower

Nombre d'établissements en unités; valeur ajoutée et traitements et salaires en millions de livres australiennes; nombre de personnes occupées et de salariés en milliers; puissance installée en milliers de chevaux-vapeur; valeur ajoutée par personne occupée en milliers de livres australiennes; puissance installée par personne occupée en chevaux-vapeur

## A. Selected Divisions of Industrial Activity — Quelques branches de l'activité industrielle

### a. Absolute Figures — Chiffres absolus

| Year and item of data | Total | Mining [1] Industries extractives [1] | Manufacturing Industries manufacturières | Electricity and gas Electricité et gaz | Année et rubrique |
|---|---|---|---|---|---|
| ISIC | 1-3,511-512 | 1 | 2-3 | 511-512 | CITI |
| **1.VII.1938 – 30.VI.1939** | | | | | **1.VII.1938 – 30.VI.1939** |
| Number of units | ... | ... | 26 299 | 502 | Nombre d'unités |
| Value added | ... | ... | 191.3 | 11.4 | Valeur ajoutée |
| Number of engaged | 627.9 | 66.0 | 552.5 | 9.4 | Nombre de personnes occupées |
| Employees: | | | | | Salariés: |
| Number | ... | ... | 531.3 | 9.3 | Nombre |
| Wages and salaries | ... | ... | 103.6 | 2.7 | Traitements et salaires |
| Capacity of installed power equipment | . | ... | 1 457.7 | 2 222.5 | Puissance installée |
| **1.VII.1948 – 30.VI.1949** | | | | | **1.VII.1948 – 30.VI.1949** |
| Number of units | ... | ... | 39 006 | 464 | Nombre d'unités |
| Value added | 612.3 | 48.4 | 548.1 | 15.8 | Valeur ajoutée |
| Number of engaged | 930.7 | 49.6 | 868.4 | 12.7 | Nombre de personnes occupées |
| Employees: | | | | | Salariés: |
| Number | ... | ... | 836.6 | 12.6 | Nombre |
| Wages and salaries | ... | ... | 329.4 | 6.6 | Traitements et salaires |
| Capacity of installed power equipment | . | ... | 2 706.1 | 3 152.6 | Puissance installée |
| **1.VII.1953 – 30.VI.1954** | | | | | **1.VII.1953 – 30.VI.1954** |
| Number of units | 51 375 | 2 766 | 48 160 | 449 | Nombre d'unités |
| Value added | 1 321.3 | 104.8 | 1 178.3 | 38.2 | Valeur ajoutée |
| Number of engaged | 1 037.1 | 58.8 | 962.8 | 15.5 | Nombre de personnes occupées |
| Employees: | | | | | Salariés: |
| Number | ... | ... | 923.8 | 15.4 | Nombre |
| Wages and salaries | 750.9 | 52.0 | 684.8 | 14.1 | Traitements et salaires |
| Capacity of installed power equipment | ... | ... | 3 727.4 | 4 764.2 | Puissance installée |
| **1.VII.1958 – 30.VI.1959** | | | | | **1.VII.1958 – 30.VI.1959** |
| Number of units | 56 057 | 2 333 | 53 331 | 393 | Nombre d'unités |
| Value added | 1 947.1 | 118.3 | 1 754.2 | 74.6 | Valeur ajoutée |
| Number of engaged | 1 128.2 | 51.7 | 1 059.5 | 17.0 | Nombre de personnes occupées |
| Employees: | | | | | Salariés: |
| Number | ... | ... | 1 019.4 | 17.0 | Nombre |
| Wages and salaries | 1 020.3 | 57.3 | 944.7 | 18.3 | Traitements et salaires |
| Capacity of installed power equipment | ... | ... | 4 931.4 | 7 585.0 | Puissance installée |

### b. Structure

| Year and item of data | Total | Mining [1] Industries extractives [1] | Manufacturing Industries manufacturières | Electricity and gas Electricité et gaz | Année et rubrique |
|---|---|---|---|---|---|
| ISIC | 1-3,511-512 | 1 | 2-3 | 511-512 | CITI |
| **1.VII.1938 – 30.VI.1939** | | | | | **1.VII.1938 – 30.VI.1939** |
| Distribution in percent of number of engaged | 100.0 | 10.5 | 88.0 | 1.5 | Distribution en pourcentage du nombre de personnes occupées |
| Per person engaged: | | | | | Par personne occupée: |
| Value added | ... | ... | 0.3 | 1.2 | Valeur ajoutée |
| Capacity of installed power equipment | ... | ... | 2.64 | 236.4 | Puissance installée |
| Employees as a percent of engaged | ... | ... | 96.2 | 98.9 | Salariés en pourcentage des personnes occupées |
| Value added per unit of wages and salaries | ... | ... | 1.85 | 4.22 | Valeur ajoutée par unité de traitements et salaires |
| Wages and salaries per employee | ... | ... | 0.19 | 0.29 | Traitements et salaires par salarié |
| **1.VII.1948 – 30.VI.1949** | | | | | **1.VII.1948 – 30.VI.1949** |
| Distribution in percent of: | | | | | Distribution en pourcentage: |
| Value added | 100.0 | 7.9 | 89.5 | 2.6 | Valeur ajoutée |
| Number of engaged | 100.0 | 5.3 | 93.3 | 1.4 | Nombre de personnes occupées |
| Per person engaged: | | | | | Par personne occupée: |
| Value added | 0.6 | 1.0 | 0.6 | 1.2 | Valeur ajoutée |
| Capacity of installed power equipment | ... | ... | 3.12 | 24.24 | Puissance installée |
| Employees as a percent of engaged | ... | ... | 96.3 | 99.2 | Salariés en pourcentage des personnes occupées |
| Value added per unit of wages and salaries | ... | ... | 1.66 | 2.39 | Valeur ajoutée par unité de traitements et salaires |
| Wages and salaries per employee | ... | ... | 0.39 | 0.52 | Traitements et salaires par salarié |
| **1.VII.1953 – 30.VI.1954** | | | | | **1.VII.1953 – 30.VI.1954** |
| Distribution in percent of: | | | | | Distribution en pourcentage: |
| Value added | 100.0 | 7.9 | 89.2 | 2.9 | Valeur ajoutée |
| Number of engaged | 100.0 | 5.6 | 92.9 | 1.5 | Nombre de personnes occupées |
| Per person engaged: | | | | | Par personne occupée: |
| Value added | 1.3 | 1.8 | 1.2 | 2.5 | Valeur ajoutée |
| Capacity of installed power equipment | ... | ... | 38.7 | 307.37 | Puissance installée |
| Employees as a percent of engaged | ... | ... | 95.9 | 99.4 | Salariés en pourcentage des personnes occupées |
| Value added per unit of wages and salaries | 1.76 | 2.02 | 1.72 | 2.71 | Valeur ajoutée par unité de traitements et salaires |
| Wages and salaries per employee | ... | ... | 0.74 | 0.92 | Traitements et salaires par salarié |
| **1.VII.1958 – 30.VI.1959** | | | | | **1.VII.1958 – 30.VI.1959** |
| Distribution in percent of: | | | | | Distribution en pourcentage: |
| Value added | 100.0 | 6.0 | 90.1 | 3.9 | Valeur ajoutée |
| Number of engaged | 100.0 | 4.5 | 93.9 | 1.6 | Nombre de personnes occupées |
| Per person engaged: | | | | | Par personne occupée: |
| Value added | 1.7 | 2.3 | 1.6 | 4.4 | Valeur ajoutée |
| Capacity of installed power equipment | ... | ... | 4.65 | 446.18 | Puissance installée |
| Employees as a percent of engaged | ... | ... | 96.2 | 100.0 | Salariés en pourcentage des personnes occupées |
| Value added per unit of wages and salaries | 1.91 | 2.06 | 1.86 | 4.08 | Valeur ajoutée par unité de traitements et salaires |
| Wages and salaries per employee | ... | ... | 0.93 | 1.08 | Traitements et salaires par salarié |

[1] Calendar year in the case of Mining. Also see footnote 1 to table 3B.

[1] Année civile dans le cas des Industries extractives. Voir également la note 1 du tableau 3B.

## B. The Major Groups of Mining[1] — Les classes de la branche Industries extractives[1]

| Year and item of data | All mining<br>Toutes industries extractives | Coal mining<br>Extraction du charbon | Metal mining<br>Extraction des minerais métalliques | Other mining[2]<br>Divers[2] | Année et rubrique | Year and item of data | All mining<br>Toutes industries extractives | Coal mining<br>Extraction du charbon | Metal mining<br>Extraction des minerais métalliques | Other mining[2]<br>Divers[2] | Année et rubrique |
|---|---|---|---|---|---|---|---|---|---|---|---|
| ISIC | 1 | 11 | 12 | 14-19 | CITI | ISIC | 1 | 11 | 12 | 14-19 | CITI |
| | a. Absolute Figures — Chiffres absolus | | | | | | b. Structure | | | | |
| **1953** | | | | | **1953** | **1953** | | | | | **1953** |
| Number of units.......... | 2 766 | 285 | 1 099 | 1 382 | Nombre d'unités | Distribution in percent of: | | | | | Distribution en pourcentage: |
| Value added.............. | 104.8 | 46.2 | 46.2 | 12.4 | Valeur ajoutée | Value added............ | 100.0 | 44.1 | 44.1 | 11.8 | Valeur ajoutée |
| Number of engaged....... | 58.8 | 23.2 | 28.2 | 7.4 | Nombre de personnes occupées | Number of engaged..... | 100.0 | 39.4 | 48.0 | 12.6 | Nombre de personnes occupées |
| Wages and salaries paid... | 52.0 | 25.6 | 22.7 | 3.7 | Traitements et salaires payés | Value added per person engaged......... | 1.8 | 2.0 | 1.6 | 1.7 | Valeur ajoutée par personne occupée |
| | | | | | | Value added per unit of wages and salaries...... | 2.02 | 1.80 | 2.04 | 3.35 | Valeur ajoutée par unité de traitements et salaires |
| **1958** | | | | | **1958** | **1958** | | | | | **1958** |
| Number of units.......... | 2 333 | 234 | 708 | 1 391 | Nombre d'unités | Distribution in percent of: | | | | | Distribution en pourcentage: |
| Value added.............. | 118.3 | 45.9 | 49.4 | 23.0 | Valeur ajoutée | Value added............ | 100.0 | 38.8 | 41.8 | 19.4 | Valeur ajoutée |
| Number of engaged....... | 51.7 | 22.6 | 21.0 | 8.1 | Nombre de personnes occupées | Number of engaged..... | 100.0 | 43.7 | 40.6 | 15.7 | Nombre de personnes occupées |
| Wages and salaries........ | 57.3 | 26.2 | 25.5 | 5.6 | Traitements et salaires | Value added per person engaged......... | 2.3 | 2.0 | 2.4 | 2.8 | Valeur ajoutée par personne occupée |
| | | | | | | Value added per unit of wages and salaries...... | 2.06 | 1.75 | 1.94 | 4.11 | Valeur ajoutée par unité de traitements et salaires |

[1] Relates to mines and quarries employing fewer than four persons (fewer than five persons in Western Australia) in the case of the items of data on number of units, value added and number of engaged but not in the case of number of employees or wages and salaries paid.
[2] Includes fuel extraction other than coal.

[1] Mines et carrières employant moins de quatre personnes (moins de cinq personnes en Australie occidentale) pour les rubriques Nombre d'unités, Valeur ajoutée et Nombre de personnes occupées, mais non pour les rubriques Nombre de salariés et Traitements et salaires payés.
[2] Y compris l'extraction des combustibles autres que le charbon.

# AUSTRALIA

## C. The Major Groups of Manufacturing — Les classes de la branche Industries manufacturières

| Year and item of data | Manufacturing — Industries manufacturières | Food, beverages and tobacco — Industries alimentaires, boissons, tabac | Textiles | Clothing, footwear and made-up textiles — Articles d'habillement, chaussures et ouvrages en tissu | Wood products and furniture [2] — Bois et meubles [2] | Paper and paper products — Papier et ouvrages en papier | Printing and publishing — Imprimerie et édition | Leather and leather products except wearing apparel — Cuir et articles en cuir, à l'exclusion des articles d'habillement | Rubber products — Ouvrages en caoutchouc | Chemicals and chemical, petroleum and coal products [1] — Produits chimiques et dérivés du Pétrole et du charbon [1] | Non-metallic mineral products [1] — Produits minéraux non métalliques [1] | Basic metals — Métallurgie de base | Metal products [2] — Ouvrages en métaux [2] | Other manufacturing — Autres industries manufacturières | Année et rubrique |
|---|---|---|---|---|---|---|---|---|---|---|---|---|---|---|---|
| ISIC | 2–3 | 20–22 | 23 | 24 | 25–26 | 27 | 28 | 29 | 30 | 31–32 | 33 | 34 | 35–38 | 39 | CITI |
| | | | | | | a. Absolute Figures — Chiffres absolus | | | | | | | | | |
| **1.VII.1938 — 30.VI.1939** | | | | | | | | | | | | | | | **1.VII.1938—30.VI.1939** |
| Number of establishments | 26 299 | 5 202 | 611 | 4 257 | 3 869 | 200 | 1 579 | 533 | 299 | 676 | 1 025 | 642 | 6 632 | 774 | Nombre d'établissements |
| Value added | 191.3 | 41.6 | 10.9 | 16.1 | 13.3 | 3.4 | 11.0 | 3.2 | 2.8 | 12.9 | 10.2 | 16.0 | 46.5 | 3.4 | Valeur ajoutée |
| Number of engaged | 552.5 | 83.8 | 46.1 | 84.2 | 44.5 | 9.3 | 30.1 | 10.8 | 7.5 | 20.7 | 25.1 | 30.0 | 148.0 | 12.4 | Nombre de personnes occupées |
| Employees: | | | | | | | | | | | | | | | Salariés: |
| Number | 531.3 | 80.4 | 45.6 | 80.2 | 41.1 | 9.2 | 28.5 | 9.2 | 7.3 | 20.5 | 24.5 | 29.4 | 143.6 | 11.8 | Nombre |
| Wages and salaries | 103.6 | 17.1 | 6.4 | 10.2 | 8.3 | 1.5 | 6.5 | 1.9 | 1.5 | 4.4 | 5.3 | 7.4 | 31.1 | 2.0 | Traitements et salaires |
| Capacity of installed power equipment | 1 457.7 | 338.1 | 70.6 | 19.9 | 151.4 | 38.5 | 41.3 | 20.8 | 41.8 | 79.2 | 132.5 | 268.5 | 240.7 | 14.4 | Puissance installée |
| **1.VII.1948 — 30.VI.1949** | | | | | | | | | | | | | | | **1.VII.1948—30.VI.1949** |
| Number of establishments | 39 006 | 6 659 | 1 140 | 6 055 | 6 088 | 286 | 1 586 | 661 | 391 | 1 028 | 1 561 | 898 | 10 949 | 1 704 | Nombre d'établissements |
| Value added | 548.1 | 89.8 | 37.6 | 48.1 | 39.6 | 12.0 | 22.5 | 7.6 | 7.7 | 35.8 | 21.0 | 43.0 | 168.0 | 15.4 | Valeur ajoutée |
| Number of engaged | 868.4 | 118.2 | 67.1 | 110.7 | 69.2 | 15.5 | 34.0 | 12.2 | 11.8 | 36.0 | 33.1 | 42.4 | 291.3 | 26.9 | Nombre de personnes occupées |
| Employees: | | | | | | | | | | | | | | | Salariés: |
| Number | 836.6 | 113.2 | 66.4 | 105.1 | 63.6 | 15.4 | 32.8 | 11.7 | 11.6 | 35.6 | 32.0 | 41.6 | 282.2 | 25.4 | Nombre |
| Wages and salaries | 329.4 | 44.5 | 23.2 | 31.1 | 23.8 | 6.0 | 13.4 | 4.6 | 5.2 | 15.1 | 13.4 | 20.6 | 119.0 | 9.5 | Traitements et salaires |
| Capacity of installed power equipment | 2 706.1 | 491.9 | 136.1 | 35.8 | 341.7 | 90.9 | 55.5 | 27.4 | 71.2 | 180.3 | 199.3 | 371.8 | 660.4 | 43.8 | Puissance installée |
| **1.VII.1953 — 30.VI.1954** | | | | | | | | | | | | | | | **1.VII.1953—30.VI.1954** |
| Number of establishments | 48 160 | 7 379 | 1 395 | 6 443 | 7 763 | 334 | 1 746 | 706 | 465 | 1 127 | 1 909 | 895 | 16 009 | 1 989 | Nombre d'établissements |
| Value added | 1 178.3 | 177.9 | 78.8 | 84.6 | 85.1 | 30.8 | 46.6 | 11.9 | 21.1 | 89.5 | 50.1 | 63.2 | 405.5 | 33.2 | Valeur ajoutée |
| Number of engaged | 962.8 | 123.1 | 70.2 | 102.8 | 78.0 | 17.6 | 37.1 | 11.1 | 15.0 | 42.7 | 38.6 | 47.0 | 351.1 | 28.5 | Nombre de personnes occupées |
| Employees: | | | | | | | | | | | | | | | Salariés: |
| Number | 923.8 | 117.2 | 69.1 | 96.5 | 71.2 | 17.5 | 35.8 | 10.5 | 14.7 | 42.3 | 37.3 | 46.2 | 338.6 | 26.9 | Nombre |
| Wages and salaries | 684.8 | 87.8 | 45.8 | 54.7 | 50.6 | 13.3 | 27.5 | 7.5 | 12.2 | 34.0 | 29.8 | 41.0 | 261.5 | 19.1 | Traitements et salaires |
| Capacity of installed power equipment | 3 727.4 | 655.5 | 174.0 | 47.2 | 519.9 | 160.4 | 71.2 | 35.3 | 100.1 | 250.9 | 252.8 | 470.4 | 929.6 | 60.1 | Puissance installée |
| **1.VII.1958 — 30.VI.1959** | | | | | | | | | | | | | | | **1.VII.1958—30.VI.1959** |
| Number of establishments | 53 331 | 7 580 | 1 403 | 6 186 | 7 672 | 361 | 2 100 | 668 | 606 | 1 259 | 1 997 | 982 | 20 305 | 2 212 | Nombre d'établissements |
| Value added | 1 754.2 | 234.6 | 96.4 | 99.1 | 115.8 | 52.4 | 73.1 | 13.1 | 32.8 | 164.7 | 82.8 | 150.6 | 585.7 | 53.1 | Valeur ajoutée |
| Number of engaged | 1 059.5 | 125.4 | 67.6 | 96.1 | 80.1 | 21.8 | 44.1 | 9.9 | 18.5 | 52.3 | 42.7 | 67.7 | 402.1 | 31.2 | Nombre de personnes occupées |
| Employees: | | | | | | | | | | | | | | | Salariés: |
| Number | 1 019.4 | 118.8 | 66.6 | 90.4 | 74.2 | 21.7 | 42.6 | 9.4 | 18.2 | 52.0 | 41.6 | 67.1 | 387.1 | 29.7 | Nombre |
| Wages and salaries | 944.7 | 108.6 | 52.9 | 61.0 | 65.9 | 22.1 | 41.7 | 8.1 | 18.2 | 53.6 | 41.5 | 74.4 | 370.1 | 26.6 | Traitements et salaires |
| Capacity of installed power equipment | 4 931.4 | 754.0 | 198.3 | 49.9 | 599.2 | 205.1 | 80.2 | 34.3 | 137.6 | 440.0 | 313.3 | 888.6 | 1 149.3 | 81.6 | Puissance installée |

For footnotes see end of table.     Pour les notes, voir au bas du tableau.

## C. The Major Groups of Manufacturing (continued) — Les classes de la branche Industries manufacturières (suite)

| Year and item of data | Manufacturing / Industries manufacturières | Food, beverages and tobacco / Industries alimentaires, boissons, tabac | Textiles | Clothing, footwear and made-up textiles / Articles d'habillement, chaussures et ouvrages en tissu | Wood products and furniture[2] / Bois et meubles[2] | Paper and paper products / Papier et ouvrages en papier | Printing and publishing / Imprimerie et édition | Leather and leather products except wearing apparel / Cuir et articles en cuir, à l'exclusion des arti cles d'habillement | Rubber products / Ouvrages en caoutchouc | Chemicals and chemical, petroleum and coal products[1] / Produits chimiques et dérivés du pétrole et du charbon[1] | Non-metallic mineral products[1] / Produits minéraux non métalliques[1] | Basic metals / Métallurgie de base | Metal products[2] / Ouvrages en métaux[2] | Other manufacturing / Autres industries manufacturières | Année et rubrique |
|---|---|---|---|---|---|---|---|---|---|---|---|---|---|---|---|
| ISIC | 2–3 | 20–22 | 23 | 24 | 25–26 | 27 | 28 | 29 | 30 | 31–32 | 33 | 34 | 35–38 | 39 | CITI |

### b. Structure

| Year and item of data | 2–3 | 20–22 | 23 | 24 | 25–26 | 27 | 28 | 29 | 30 | 31–32 | 33 | 34 | 35–38 | 39 | Année et rubrique |
|---|---|---|---|---|---|---|---|---|---|---|---|---|---|---|---|
| **1.VII.1938 — 30.VI.1939** | | | | | | | | | | | | | | | **1.VII.1938—30.VI.1939** |
| Distribution in percent of: | | | | | | | | | | | | | | | Distribution en pourcentage: |
| Value added....... | 100.0 | 21.7 | 5.7 | 8.4 | 7.0 | 1.7 | 5.8 | 1.7 | 1.4 | 6.8 | 5.3 | 8.4 | 24.3 | 1.8 | Valeur ajoutée |
| Number of engaged... | 100.0 | 15.1 | 8.4 | 15.2 | 8.1 | 1.6 | 5.5 | 1.9 | 1.4 | 3.7 | 4.6 | 5.4 | 26.8 | 2.3 | Nombre de personnes occupées |
| Per person engaged: | | | | | | | | | | | | | | | Par personne occupée: |
| Value added....... | 0.3 | 0.5 | 0.2 | 0.2 | 0.3 | 0.4 | 0.4 | 0.3 | 0.4 | 0.6 | 0.4 | 0.5 | 0.3 | 0.3 | Valeur ajoutée |
| Capacity of installed power equipment..... | 2.64 | 4.03 | 1.53 | 0.24 | 3.40 | 4.14 | 1.37 | 1.92 | 5.57 | 3.83 | 5.28 | 8.95 | 1.63 | 1.16 | Puissance installée |
| Employees as a percent of engaged........ | 96.2 | 95.9 | 98.9 | 95.2 | 92.4 | 98.9 | 94.7 | 85.2 | 97.3 | 99.0 | 97.6 | 98.0 | 97.0 | 95.2 | Salariés en pourcentage des personnes occupées |
| Value added per unit of wages and salaries....... | 1.85 | 2.43 | 1.70 | 1.58 | 1.60 | 2.27 | 1.69 | 1.68 | 1.87 | 2.93 | 1.92 | 2.16 | 1.50 | 1.70 | Valeur ajoutée par unité de traitements et salaires |
| Wages and salaries per employee........ | 0.19 | 0.21 | 0.14 | 0.13 | 0.20 | 0.16 | 0.23 | 0.21 | 0.21 | 0.21 | 0.22 | 0.25 | 0.22 | 0.17 | Traitements et salaires par salarié |
| **1.VII.1948 — 30.VI.1949** | | | | | | | | | | | | | | | **1.VII.1948—30.VI.1949** |
| Distribution in percent of: | | | | | | | | | | | | | | | Distribution en pourcentage: |
| Value added....... | 100.0 | 16.3 | 6.9 | 8.8 | 7.2 | 2.2 | 4.1 | 1.4 | 1.4 | 6.5 | 3.8 | 7.9 | 30.6 | 2.9 | Valeur ajoutée |
| Number of engaged... | 00.0 | 13.6 | 7.7 | 12.7 | 8.0 | 1.8 | 3.9 | 1.4 | 1.4 | 4.1 | 3.8 | 4.9 | 33.6 | 3.1 | Nombre de personnes occupées |
| Per person engaged: | | | | | | | | | | | | | | | Par personne occupée: |
| Value added....... | 0.6 | 0.8 | 0.6 | 0.4 | 0.6 | 0.8 | 0.7 | 0.6 | 0.6 | 1.0 | 0.6 | 1.0 | 0.6 | 0.6 | Valeur ajoutée |
| Capacity of installed power equipment..... | 3.12 | 4.16 | 2.03 | 0.32 | 4.94 | 5.86 | 1.63 | 2.24 | 6.03 | 5.01 | 6.02 | 8.77 | 2.27 | 1.63 | Puissance installée |
| Employees as a percent of engaged........ | 96.3 | 95.8 | 99.0 | 94.9 | 91.9 | 99.4 | 96.5 | 95.9 | 98.3 | 98.9 | 96.7 | 98.1 | 96.9 | 94.4 | Salariés en pourcentage des personnes occupées |
| Value added per unit of wages and salaries....... | 1.66 | 2.02 | 1.62 | 1.55 | 1.66 | 2.00 | 1.68 | 1.65 | 1.48 | 2.37 | 1.57 | 2.09 | 1.41 | 1.62 | Valeur ajoutée par unité de traitements et salaires |
| Wages and salaries per employee........ | 0.39 | 0.39 | 0.35 | 0.30 | 0.37 | 0.39 | 0.41 | 0.39 | 0.45 | 0.42 | 0.42 | 0.50 | 0.42 | 0.37 | Traitements et salaires par salarié |
| **1.VII.1953 — 30.VI.1954** | | | | | | | | | | | | | | | **1.VII.1953—30.VI.1954** |
| Distribution in percent of: | | | | | | | | | | | | | | | Distribution en pourcentage: |
| Value added....... | 100.0 | 15.0 | 6.7 | 7.2 | 7.2 | 2.7 | 3.9 | 1.0 | 1.8 | 7.6 | 4.3 | 5.3 | 34.4 | 2.9 | Valeur ajoutée |
| Number of engaged... | 100.0 | 12.7 | 7.3 | 10.7 | 8.1 | 1.8 | 3.9 | 1.1 | 1.6 | 4.4 | 4.0 | 4.9 | 36.5 | 3.0 | Nombre de personnes occupées |
| Per person engaged: | | | | | | | | | | | | | | | Par personne occupée: |
| Value added....... | 1.2 | 1.4 | 1.1 | 0.8 | 1.1 | 1.8 | 1.2 | 1.1 | 1.4 | 2.1 | 1.3 | 1.3 | 1.2 | 1.2 | Valeur ajoutée |
| Capacity of installed power equipment..... | 3.87 | 5.32 | 2.48 | 0.46 | 6.66 | 9.11 | 1.92 | 3.18 | 6.67 | 5.88 | 6.55 | 10.01 | 2.65 | 2.11 | Puissance installée |
| Employees as a percent of engaged........ | 95.9 | 95.2 | 98.4 | 93.9 | 91.3 | 99.4 | 96.5 | 94.6 | 98.0 | 99.1 | 96.6 | 98.3 | 96.4 | 94.4 | Salariés en pourcentage des personnes occupées |
| Value added per unit of wages and salaries....... | 1.72 | 2.03 | 1.72 | 1.55 | 1.68 | 2.32 | 1.69 | 1.59 | 1.73 | 2.63 | 1.68 | 1.54 | 1.55 | 1.74 | Valeur ajoutée par unité de traitements et salaires |
| Wages and salaries per employee........ | 0.74 | 0.75 | 0.66 | 0.57 | 0.71 | 0.76 | 0.77 | 0.71 | 0.83 | 0.80 | 0.80 | 0.89 | 0.77 | 0.71 | Traitements et salaires par salarié |
| **1.VII.1958 — 30.VI.1959** | | | | | | | | | | | | | | | **1.VII.1958—30.VI.1959** |
| Distribution in percent of: | | | | | | | | | | | | | | | Distribution en pourcentage: |
| Value added....... | 100.0 | 13.3 | 5.5 | 5.7 | 6.6 | 3.0 | 4.1 | 0.8 | 1.8 | 9.4 | 4.7 | 8.6 | 33.4 | 3.1 | Valeur ajoutée |
| Number of engaged... | 100.0 | 11.8 | 6.4 | 9.0 | 7.6 | 2.1 | 4.1 | 1.0 | 1.7 | 4.9 | 4.1 | 6.4 | 37.9 | 3.0 | Nombre de personnes occupées |
| Per person engaged: | | | | | | | | | | | | | | | Par personne occupée: |
| Value added....... | 1.6 | 1.9 | 1.4 | 1.0 | 1.4 | 2.4 | 1.6 | 1.3 | 1.8 | 3.1 | 1.9 | 2.2 | 1.4 | 1.7 | Valeur ajoutée |
| Capacity of installed power equipment..... | 4.65 | 6.01 | 2.93 | 0.52 | 7.48 | 9.41 | 1.82 | 3.46 | 7.44 | 8.41 | 7.34 | 13.12 | 2.86 | 2.62 | Puissance installée |
| Employees as a percent of engaged........ | 96.2 | 94.7 | 98.5 | 94.1 | 92.6 | 99.5 | 96.6 | 94.9 | 98.4 | 99.4 | 97.4 | 99.1 | 96.3 | 95.2 | Salariés en pourcentage des personnes occupées |
| Value added per unit of wages and salaries....... | 1.86 | 2.16 | 1.82 | 1.62 | 1.76 | 2.37 | 1.75 | 1.62 | 1.80 | 3.07 | 2.00 | 2.02 | 1.58 | 2.00 | Valeur ajoutée par unité de traitements et salaires |
| Wages and salaries per employee........ | 0.93 | 0.91 | 0.79 | 0.67 | 0.89 | 1.02 | 0.98 | 0.86 | 1.00 | 1.03 | 1.00 | 0.99 | 0.96 | 0.90 | Traitements et salaires par salarié |

[1] Briquetting and pulverizing coal (part of ISIC major group 32) is covered under Non-metallic mineral products (ISIC major group 33).
[2] Manufacture of metal furniture (part of ISIC major group 26) is covered under Metal products (ISIC major group 35).

[1] La fabrication des briquettes en charbon et la pulvérisation du charbon (dans CITI classe 32) sont comprises dans Produits minéraux non métalliques (CITI classe 33).
[2] La fabrication des meubles métalliques (dans CITI classe 26) est comprise dans Ouvrages en métaux (CITI classe 35).

### 4. QUANTITY AND VALUE OF PURCHASED FUELS AND ELECTRICITY CONSUMED, INDUSTRIAL ESTABLISHMENTS ENGAGING FOUR OR MORE PERSONS OR USING POWER EQUIPMENT

### CONSOMMATION DE COMBUSTIBLES ET D'ELECTRICITE ACHETES : QUANTITES ET VALEUR ; ETABLISSEMENTS INDUSTRIELS OCCUPANT AU MOINS QUATRE PERSONNES OU UTILISANT LA FORCE MOTRICE

### 1.VII.1938-30.VI.1939, 1.VII.1948-30.VI.1949, 1.VII.1953-30.VI.1954, 1.VII.1958-30.VI.1959

Coal, lignite, coke, refined oil fuels and wood in thousand metric tons; values in thousand Australian Pounds. | Charbon, lignite, coke, pétrole raffiné et bois en milliers de tonnes métriques; valeur en milliers de livres australiennes.

## A. Electricity and Gas — Electricité et gaz

| Source of energy | Total | Electricity / Electricité | Gas / Gaz | Total | Electricity / Electricité | Gas / Gaz | Source d'énergie |
|---|---|---|---|---|---|---|---|
| ISIC | 511-512 | 511 | 512 | 511-512 | 511 | 512 | CITI |
| | *a.* 1.VII.1938 — 30.VI.1939 | | | *c.* 1.VII.1953 — 30.VI.1954 | | | |
| Coal: | | | | | | | Charbon: |
|   Quantity | 1 959.8 | 1 958.2 | 1.6 | 5 939.0 | 5 930.0 | 9.0 | Quantité |
|   Value | 2 037.5 | 2 036.0 | 1.5 | 24 279.4 | 24 233.6 | 45.8 | Valeur |
| Lignite: | | | | | | | Lignite: |
|   Quantity | 2 213.6 | 2 213.6 | — | 5 826.0 | 5 826.0 | — | Quantité |
|   Value | 311.8 | 311.8 | — | 5 302.5 | 5 302.5 | — | Valeur |
| Coke: | | | | | | | Coke: |
|   Quantity | 157.8 | 18.8 | 139.0 | 283.7 | 12.4 | 271.3 | Quantité |
|   Value | 156.1 | 10.7 | 145.4 | 1 528.8 | 80.6 | 1 448.2 | Valeur |
| Refined oil fuels:[3] | | | | | | | Pétrole raffiné [3]: |
|   Quantity | 84.9 | 72.0 | 12.9 | 289.5 | 250.9 | 38.6 | Quantité |
|   Value | 543.4 | 498.0 | 45.4 | 4 766.6 | 4 580.4 | 186.2 | Valeur |
| Manufactured gas — value | 75.7 | 75.7 | — | 121.2 | 121.2 | — | Gaz manufacturé — valeur |
| Electricity — value | 17.6 | — | 17.6 | 175.3 | — | 175.3 | Electricité — valeur |
| Wood: | | | | | | | Bois: |
|   Quantity | 214.2 | 209.8 | 4.4 | 70.9 | 67.4 | 3.5 | Quantité |
|   Value | 171.0 | 168.6 | 2.4 | 176.5 | 170.1 | 6.4 | Valeur |
| Other fuels — value | 12.7 | 9.1 | 3.6 | 312.3 | 91.6 | 220.7 | Autres combustibles — valeur |
| | *b.* 1.VII.1948 — 30.VI.1949 | | | *d.* 1.VII.1958 — 30.VI.1959 | | | |
| Coal: | | | | | | | Charbon: |
|   Quantity | 3 950.5 | 3 947.8 | 2.7 | 7 252.0 | 7 245.9 | 6.1 | Quantité |
|   Value | 8 057.0 | 8 053.5 | 3.5 | 26 395.1 | 26 355.8 | 39.3 | Valeur |
| Lignite: | | | | | | | Lignite: |
|   Quantity | 4 654.0 | 4 654.0 | — | 8 772.4 | 8 717.4 | 55.0 | Quantité |
|   Value | 1 574.7 | 1 574.7 | — | 5 592.3 | 5 501.3 | 91.0 | Valeur |
| Coke: | | | | | | | Coke: |
|   Quantity | 322.4 | 40.6 | 281.8 | 257.0 | 5.3 | 251.7 | Quantité |
|   Value | 538.8 | 53.9 | 484.9 | 1 593.3 | 13.1 | 1 580.2 | Valeur |
| Refined oil fuels:[3] | | | | | | | Pétrole raffiné [3]: |
|   Quantity | 246.6 | 205.8 | 40.8 | 492.7 | 468.3 | 24.4 | Quantité |
|   Value | 2 473.7 | 2 374.4 | 99.3 | 6 370.3 | 6 129.6 | 240.7 | Valeur |
| Manufactured gas — value | 68.8 | 68.8 | — | 179.9 | 179.9 | — | Gaz manufacturé — valeur |
| Electricity — value | 47.2 | — | 47.2 | 419.2 | — | 419.2 | Electricité — valeur |
| Wood: | | | | | | | Bois: |
|   Quantity | 228.1 | 226.5 | 1.6 | 123.8 | 122.8 | 1.0 | Quantité |
|   Value | 401.3 | 399.2 | 2.1 | 162.1 | 159.7 | 2.4 | Valeur |
| Other fuels — value | 53.1 | 50.6 | 2.5 | 472.3 | 297.2 | 175.1 | Autres combustibles — valeur |

For footnotes see end of table.      Pour les notes, voir au bas du tableau.

## B. The Major Groups of Manufacturing — Les classes de la branche Industries manufacturières

| Year and source of energy | Manufacturing / Industries manufacturières | Food, beverages and tobacco / Industries alimentaires, boissons, tabac | Textiles | Clothing, footwear and made-up textiles / Articles d'habillement, chaussures et ouvrages en tissu | Wood products and furniture [2] / Bois et meubles [2] | Paper and paper products / Papier et ouvrages en papier | Printing and publishing / Imprimerie et édition | Leather and leather products except wearing apparel / Cuir et articles en cuir, à l'exclusion des articles d'habillement | Rubber products / Ouvrages en caoutchouc | Chemicals and chemical, petroleum and coal products [1] / Produits chimiques et dérivés du pétrole et du charbon [1] | Non-metallic mineral products [1] / Produits minéraux non métalliques [1] | Basic metals / Métallurgie de base | Metal products [2] / Ouvrages en métaux [2] | Other manufacturing / Autres industries manufacturières |
|---|---|---|---|---|---|---|---|---|---|---|---|---|---|---|
| ISIC / CITI | 2–3 | 20–22 | 23 | 24 | 25–26 | 27 | 28 | 29 | 30 | 31–32 | 33 | 34 | 35–38 | 39 |
| **1.VII.1938 — 30.VI.1939** | | | | | | | | | | | | | | |
| *Coal / Charbon:* | | | | | | | | | | | | | | |
| Quantity / Quantité | 2 244.8 | 469.2 | 94.6 | 6.2 | 8.1 | 88.2 | 0.7 | 33.4 | 44.9 | 130.8 | 869.4 | 358.4 | 132.0 | 8.9 |
| Value / Valeur | 2 624.9 | 630.9 | 133.0 | 8.6 | 9.6 | 139.3 | 1.2 | 46.4 | 62.4 | 162.7 | 951.3 | 336.3 | 133.2 | 10.0 |
| *Lignite:* | | | | | | | | | | | | | | |
| Quantity / Quantité | 678.6 | 63.0 | 22.3 | 3.7 | 0.2 | 1.6 | 0.8 | 4.4 | 1.1 | 21.3 | 548.3 | 1.5 | 4.2 | 6.2 |
| Value / Valeur | 244.9 | 80.3 | 27.1 | 5.2 | 0.3 | 2.3 | 1.2 | 4.8 | 1.8 | 26.8 | 80.7 | 2.1 | 5.3 | 7.0 |
| *Coke:* | | | | | | | | | | | | | | |
| Quantity / Quantité | 1 355.1 | 71.8 | 2.7 | 2.6 | 1.0 | 0.4 | 0.6 | 2.4 | 2.2 | 41.8 | 17.2 | 1 128.9 | 80.9 | 2.6 |
| Value / Valeur | 1 543.3 | 104.1 | 4.4 | 3.8 | 2.0 | 0.8 | 0.9 | 2.7 | 4.2 | 35.6 | 25.3 | 1 215.9 | 141.1 | 2.5 |
| *Refined oil fuels [3] / Pétrole raffiné [3]:* | | | | | | | | | | | | | | |
| Quantity / Quantité | 136.0 | 28.8 | 5.5 | 1.9 | 3.0 | 0.4 | 1.7 | 1.2 | 0.6 | 11.0 | 17.8 | 27.3 | 36.1 | 0.7 |
| Value / Valeur | 783.5 | 217.5 | 21.9 | 11.3 | 39.6 | 2.2 | 12.4 | 4.7 | 3.6 | 50.8 | 89.4 | 129.1 | 196.9 | 4.1 |
| Manufactured gas — value / Gaz manufacturé — valeur | 736.4 | 94.7 | 3.8 | 23.4 | 9.6 | 5.8 | 37.0 | 2.8 | 4.2 | 23.4 | 26.8 | 396.0 | 96.7 | 12.2 |
| Electricity — value / Électricité — valeur | 4 198.1 | 888.3 | 318.5 | 169.0 | 217.6 | 53.2 | 167.1 | 60.1 | 139.8 | 244.7 | 426.6 | 668.7 | 786.4 | 58.1 |
| *Wood / Bois:* | | | | | | | | | | | | | | |
| Quantity / Quantité | 1 207.1 | 610.4 | 38.6 | 1.3 | 190.5 | 28.7 | 1.3 | 29.6 | 6.2 | 44.2 | 181.9 | 28.7 | 44.0 | 1.7 |
| Value / Valeur | 628.3 | 364.8 | 15.5 | 1.1 | 47.3 | 19.5 | 1.2 | 15.2 | 5.0 | 13.6 | 104.7 | 18.7 | 20.1 | 1.6 |
| Other fuels — value / Autres combustibles — valeur | 206.0 | 43.3 | 11.8 | 0.7 | 3.4 | — | 0.2 | 3.2 | 0.1 | 17.7 | 1.4 | 112.5 | 11.3 | 0.4 |
| **1.VII.1948 — 30.VI.1949** | | | | | | | | | | | | | | |
| *Coal / Charbon:* | | | | | | | | | | | | | | |
| Quantity / Quantité | 2 556.6 | 634.6 | 131.0 | 5.6 | 38.5 | 85.2 | 0.6 | 11.2 | 38.3 | 242.6 | 945.5 | 253.0 | 154.2 | 16.3 |
| Value / Valeur | 5 629.2 | 1 541.2 | 287.7 | 13.6 | 80.8 | 216.4 | 1.8 | 27.8 | 95.2 | 601.5 | 1 933.5 | 491.0 | 296.6 | 42.1 |
| *Lignite:* | | | | | | | | | | | | | | |
| Quantity / Quantité | 1 456.1 | 172.7 | 108.2 | 2.5 | 0.2 | 213.7 | 0.5 | 16.4 | 28.7 | 111.5 | 770.8 | 1.9 | 21.0 | 8.0 |
| Value / Valeur | 978.6 | 261.5 | 126.4 | 3.9 | 0.2 | 192.0 | 1.1 | 18.7 | 39.9 | 140.3 | 150.5 | 3.5 | 28.1 | 12.5 |
| *Coke:* | | | | | | | | | | | | | | |
| Quantity / Quantité | 1 491.5 | 118.8 | 12.5 | 1.9 | 1.3 | 1.4 | 0.6 | 2.5 | 6.0 | 80.6 | 26.8 | 1 139.1 | 96.2 | 3.8 |
| Value / Valeur | 4 514.9 | 303.4 | 34.6 | 5.0 | 3.1 | 4.2 | 1.7 | 7.4 | 14.7 | 139.5 | 80.8 | 3 598.9 | 304.8 | 16.8 |
| *Refined oil fuels [3] / Pétrole raffiné [3]:* | | | | | | | | | | | | | | |
| Quantity / Quantité | 408.4 | 67.9 | 23.3 | 4.2 | 7.4 | 9.2 | 2.4 | 0.7 | 14.9 | 61.2 | 59.2 | 92.4 | 61.6 | 4.0 |
| Value / Valeur | 4 245.8 | 834.4 | 250.0 | 53.9 | 151.1 | 117.8 | 32.7 | 9.6 | 176.3 | 606.0 | 579.2 | 646.3 | 734.0 | 54.5 |
| Manufactured gas — value / Gaz manufacturé — valeur | 1 425.1 | 188.0 | 47.6 | 41.0 | 11.5 | 7.8 | 41.5 | 4.3 | 9.2 | 56.0 | 165.6 | 523.1 | 290.7 | 38.8 |
| Electricity — value / Électricité — valeur | 10 540.4 | 2 151.3 | 743 8 | 391.9 | 598.4 | 238.0 | 246.8 | 94.5 | 307.8 | 783.1 | 774.5 | 1 666.2 | 2 283.4 | 260.7 |
| *Wood / Bois:* | | | | | | | | | | | | | | |
| Quantity / Quantité | 1 597.2 | 711.3 | 129.4 | 6.0 | 192.6 | 157.6 | 1.5 | 15.0 | 11.3 | 114.4 | 192.0 | 17.9 | 46.0 | 2.2 |
| Value / Valeur | 1 793.7 | 890.9 | 151.4 | 10.1 | 83.6 | 210.8 | 3.0 | 19.2 | 16.4 | 94.0 | 223.9 | 28.6 | 57.1 | 4.7 |
| Other fuels — value / Autres combustibles — valeur | 544.6 | 88.0 | 53.8 | 3.9 | 50.0 | 2.0 | 2.7 | 2.8 | 1.1 | 74.5 | 61.7 | 156.6 | 33.8 | 13.7 |
| **1.VII.1953 — 30.VI.1954** | | | | | | | | | | | | | | |
| *Coal / Charbon:* | | | | | | | | | | | | | | |
| Quantity / Quantité | 3 402.7 | 713.1 | 134.3 | 6.0 | 25.4 | 179.8 | 0.6 | 11.3 | 65.4 | 340.1 | 1 373.2 | 356.7 | 185.4 | 11.4 |
| Value / Valeur | 15 355.1 | 3 581.5 | 649.3 | 31.5 | 99.1 | 784.4 | 4.2 | 56.2 | 356.8 | 1 645.9 | 5 843.2 | 1 437.8 | 808.2 | 57.0 |
| *Lignite:* | | | | | | | | | | | | | | |
| Quantity / Quantité | 1 852.3 | 306.5 | 105.2 | 2.2 | — | 314.7 | 0.3 | 24.0 | 15.1 | 193.4 | 829.9 | 1.0 | 52.7 | 7.3 |
| Value / Valeur | 2 730.1 | 858.3 | 271.9 | 7.9 | 0.2 | 465.9 | 1.8 | 60.3 | 29.4 | 475.7 | 417.1 | 5.0 | 123.8 | 12.8 |
| *Coke:* | | | | | | | | | | | | | | |
| Quantity / Quantité | 2 209.1 | 60.5 | 3.8 | 1.1 | 1.1 | 1.7 | 0.2 | 0.7 | 3.8 | 40.0 | 29.0 | 1 978.4 | 87.3 | 1.5 |
| Value / Valeur | 14 243.2 | 384.0 | 24.4 | 6.3 | 6.1 | 10.2 | 1.7 | 4.8 | 22.3 | 295.3 | 197.8 | 12 548.3 | 722.6 | 19.4 |
| *Refined oil fuels [3] / Pétrole raffiné [3]:* | | | | | | | | | | | | | | |
| Quantity / Quantité | 646.7 | 101.6 | 34.4 | 5.8 | 20.2 | 9.0 | 3.3 | 1.2 | 17.2 | 115.6 | 70.9 | 173.6 | 87.1 | 6.8 |
| Value / Valeur | 9 716.3 | 2 010.5 | 533.1 | 104.6 | 578.1 | 155.6 | 65.7 | 23.7 | 293.5 | 1 397.3 | 1 075.6 | 1 671.7 | 1 683.0 | 123.9 |
| Manufactured gas — value / Gaz manufacturé — valeur | 3 314.6 | 575.6 | 20.6 | 86.2 | 21.1 | 18.8 | 74.5 | 6.2 | 16.1 | 163.4 | 415.3 | 970.8 | 858.0 | 88.0 |
| Electricity — value / Électricité — valeur | 28 659.8 | 5 466.7 | 1 757.1 | 796.5 | 1 552.0 | 599.8 | 735.2 | 226.3 | 1 007.7 | 2 640.0 | 2 524.6 | 3 636.0 | 6 969.6 | 748.3 |
| *Wood / Bois:* | | | | | | | | | | | | | | |
| Quantity / Quantité | 1 410.6 | 581.0 | 73.3 | 1.9 | 222.7 | 79.7 | 1.1 | 10.8 | 14.2 | 92.6 | 290.9 | 11.9 | 29.0 | 1.5 |
| Value / Valeur | 2 231.4 | 1 099.4 | 126.9 | 4.3 | 117.1 | 172.2 | 3.5 | 19.9 | 30.0 | 101.0 | 550.5 | 42.0 | 60.6 | 4.0 |
| Other fuels — value / Autres combustibles — valeur | 1 182.1 | 206.9 | 219.5 | 3.6 | 228.9 | 14.1 | 2.4 | 6.0 | 0.6 | 111.3 | 60.3 | 278.6 | 35.7 | 14.0 |
| **1.VII.1958 — 30.VI.1959** | | | | | | | | | | | | | | |
| *Coal / Charbon:* | | | | | | | | | | | | | | |
| Quantity / Quantité | 3 159.4 | 534.9 | 96.2 | 5.2 | 36.3 | 261.8 | 0.1 | 9.1 | 42.5 | 357.1 | 1 495.1 | 232.7 | 74.0 | 14.4 |
| Value / Valeur | 13 357.3 | 2 528.2 | 417.0 | 23.8 | 125.1 | 1 177.4 | 0.5 | 44.0 | 190.8 | 1 546.3 | 5 903.5 | 1 015.5 | 319.0 | 66.2 |
| *Lignite:* | | | | | | | | | | | | | | |
| Quantity / Quantité | 2 277.5 | 319.9 | 107.8 | 1.8 | 0.1 | 602.1 | — | 9.9 | 51.0 | 219.4 | 884.5 | 1.5 | 70.9 | 8.6 |
| Value / Valeur | 3 408.3 | 881.6 | 332.1 | 9.7 | 0.3 | 752.5 | 0.3 | 31.8 | 108.9 | 617.3 | 472.2 | 8.2 | 167.2 | 26.2 |
| *Coke:* | | | | | | | | | | | | | | |
| Quantity / Quantité | 2 351.3 | 27.3 | 1.0 | 0.5 | 0.2 | 0.8 | 0.2 | 0.3 | 0.9 | 54.0 | 19.7 | 2 292.7 | 52.6 | 1.1 |
| Value / Valeur | 15 744.9 | 233.9 | 8.0 | 4.1 | 1.4 | 6.0 | 1.9 | 2.0 | 6.1 | 400.4 | 172.9 | 14 283.9 | 608.9 | 15.4 |
| *Refined oil fuels [3] / Pétrole raffiné [3]:* | | | | | | | | | | | | | | |
| Quantity / Quantité | 1 764.9 | 172.1 | 57.4 | 5.2 | 26.8 | 22.2 | 3.8 | 6.3 | 35.0 | 724.6 | 163.6 | 401.5 | 134.7 | 11.7 |
| Value / Valeur | 23 289.5 | 3 239.4 | 932.3 | 109.7 | 749.1 | 350.2 | 70.2 | 92.6 | 600.8 | 7 352.2 | 2 273.3 | 5 011.4 | 2 289.4 | 218.9 |
| Manufactured gas — value / Gaz manufacturé — valeur | 5 197.3 | 759.4 | 31.9 | 78.8 | 37.2 | 24.6 | 77.1 | 7.3 | 16.7 | 505.6 | 510.5 | 1 538.6 | 1 482.5 | 127.1 |
| Electricity — value / Électricité — valeur | 46 831.5 | 7 575.2 | 2 384.8 | 1 011.3 | 2 392.7 | 1 175.4 | 1 144.0 | 268.8 | 1 475.1 | 5 507.9 | 3 880.3 | 7 706.4 | 11 136.9 | 1 172.7 |
| *Wood / Bois:* | | | | | | | | | | | | | | |
| Quantity / Quantité | 1 101.3 | 427.4 | 54.3 | 1.7 | 157.2 | 35.8 | 0.9 | 9.9 | 11.6 | 74.2 | 295.8 | 10.1 | 20.1 | 2.3 |
| Value / Valeur | 2 074.8 | 905.4 | 119.4 | 4.6 | 128.3 | 91.4 | 3.6 | 25.1 | 26.4 | 90.8 | 588.2 | 41.4 | 46.1 | 4.1 |
| Other fuels — value / Autres combustibles — valeur | 3 628.2 | 411.6 | 147.3 | 3.1 | 339.0 | 11.5 | 7.0 | 9.3 | 3.2 | 893.2 | 119.7 | 1 628.9 | 47.2 | 7.2 |

[1] Briquetting and pulverizing of coal (part of ISIC major group 32) is covered under Non-metallic mineral products (ISIC major group 33).
[2] Manufacture of metal furniture (part of ISIC major group 26) is covered under Metal products (ISIC major group 35).
[3] Includes tar used as a fuel.

[1] La fabrication des briquettes en charbon et la pulvérisation du charbon (dans CITI classe 32) sont comprises dans Produits minéraux non métalliques (CITI classe 33).
[2] La fabrication des meubles métalliques (dans CITI classe 26) est comprise dans Ouvrages en métaux (CITI classe 35).
[3] Y compris le goudron utilisé comme combustible.

# AUSTRIA — AUTRICHE

## Gross National Product and Gross Domestic Fixed Capital Formation

Estimates of the expenditure on and industrial origin of the gross national product, and of the industrial composition of the gross fixed capital formation, are presented in Table 1. This table has been compiled from data supplied by the Central Statistical Office of Austria in response to the United Nations national accounts questionnaire. Official estimates, together with descriptions of the data, are published annually by the Austrian Central Statistical Office in a Supplement to its publication, *Statistische Nachrichten*.

## Index Numbers of Industrial Production

The index numbers of industrial production shown in Table 2 have been compiled by the Austrian Institute of Economic Research. They are published in the monthly reports of the Institute entitled *Statistische Übersichten zu den Monatsberichten des Österreichischen Institutes für Wirtschaftsforschung*.

The indexes relate to industrial establishments other than handicraft establishments and, generally, only to those in which six or more persons are engaged. The indexes have been computed as base-weighted arithmetic averages. First, indexes have been computed for detailed categories of industrial activity from relatives of the quantities of individual commodities produced. Secondly, the resulting indexes have been combined into indexes for broader classes of activity. The weighting coefficients that have been used to combine the relatives into indexes for detailed categories of industry, and these restricted indexes into broader ones, were the values added at market prices in 1937 or 1956. The former weights were applied for the period, 1937-1953, and the latter ones were used for the period 1954 onwards.

The estimates of value added in 1937 which were used as weights in combining the relatives and the resulting indexes for categories of industrial activity more detailed than Groups were derived by applying the appropriate ratios of value added to gross value of production in Germany during 1936 to the gross value of production in Austria during 1937. The weights used for combining the indexes for groups of industrial activity into broader classes were derived by applying the value added per employee in Germany in 1936 to the figures of employment in Austria in 1937.

The estimates of value added in 1956 have been compiled by applying the ratio of value added to gross value of production in 1953 to the figures of gross value of

## Produit national brut et formation de capital fixe intérieur brut

Le tableau 1 fournit des estimations de dépenses imputées au produit national brut, des composantes du produit national brut ventilées suivant le secteur d'activité, ainsi que des estimations des composantes du capital fixe intérieur brut formé, suivant le secteur d'activité. Ce tableau a été élaboré à partir de données fournies par le Bureau central autrichien de statistique en réponse au questionnaire de l'ONU relatif aux comptes nationaux. Le Bureau central autrichien de statistique publie annuellement en supplément au *Statistische Nachrichten* des estimations officielles, auxquelles sont jointes des précisions sur les données.

## Indices de la production industrielle

Les indices de la production industrielle reproduits au tableau 2 ont été établis par l'Institut autrichien de recherche économique. L'Institut les publie dans ses rapports mensuels sous le titre: *Statistische Übersichten zu den Monatsberichten des Österreichischen Institutes für Wirtschaftsforschung*.

Ces indices se rappportent aux établissements industriels autres que les unités artisanales, plus précisément aux unités employant six personnes ou plus. Ce sont des moyennes arithmétiques à pondération fixe. A un premier stade ces indices ont été calculés pour des catégories détaillées des activités industrielles à partir de rapports fondés sur le volume de chaque marchandise produite. A un second stade, les indices obtenus ont été combinés en indices pour des catégories plus larges de l'activité industrielle. Pour cela on a adopté comme coefficients de pondération la valeur ajoutée aux prix du marché en 1937 ou 1956. Les premiers poids ont été utilisés pour la période 1937-1953, et les derniers à partir de 1954.

Les estimations de la valeur ajoutée de 1937 utilisées comme coefficients de pondération dans la combinaison des rapports et des indices résultant pour les catégories d'activité industrielle plus détaillées que les groupes ont été obtenues en appliquant les rapports appropriés valeur ajoutée/valeur brute de la production pour l'Allemagne en 1936 à la valeur brute de la production autrichienne en 1937. Les coefficients de pondération utilisés pour combiner les indices de groupes des activités industrielles en indices de classes plus larges, ont été obtenus en appliquant la valeur ajoutée par ouvrier en Allemagne en 1936 aux chiffres de l'emploi en Autriche en 1937.

Les estimations de la valeur ajoutée en 1956 ont été élaborées en appliquant le ratio: valeur ajoutée/valeur brute de la production en 1956 aux chiffres de la valeur

production in 1956. The sources of both the 1953 and the 1956 data are described below.

The manufacturing index has been computed by the Statistical Office of the United Nations by excluding from the index of all industrial activity those movements which result from changes in mining (including magnesite) and electricity production. Index numbers are shown for the year 1937 since data are not available for 1938. Beginning with 1955, the indexes include those industries which were formerly administered by the U.S.S.R.

For further details concerning the character of the indexes see Supplements No. 9, November 1949, and No. 69, December 1961, to the *Monatsberichte des Österreichischen Institutes für Wirtschaftsforschung* (Vienna).

### Index Numbers of Industrial Employment

The index numbers of industrial employment given in Table 3 have been based on data derived from a number of sources.

The index numbers for mining were computed by the Statistical Office of the United Nations from absolute figures of the number of employees for all mining units given in the table, "Beschäftigte Personen", of the chapter "Bergbau und Salinenwesen", *Statistisches Handbuch für die Republik Österreich*, of the Austrian Central Statistical Office.

The indexes for the period 1948-1956, in the case of almost all major groups of manufacturing and for all years in the case of the construction and electricity industries were derived from the index numbers of employment (original base period, 1934) issued in *Statistische Übersichten zu den Monatsberichten des Österreichischen Institutes für Wirstchaftsforschung*, Vienna. These indexes are based on the average monthly number of employees for 1678 representative firms. The indexes for 1956 and subsequent years in the case of almost all major groups of manufacturing were computed by the Statistical Office of the United Nations from the absolute figures of the average monthly number of employees shown in the table, "Betriebe und Beschäftigte in der Industrie", of the last mentioned publication. These figures relate to the same units that are covered in the annual survey of industrial establishments described below.

The index numbers of employment for all manufacturing are the weighted arithmetic averages of the indexes for the various major groups of manufacturing that were compiled by the Statistical Office of the United Nations. The weights used for the period, 1948-1955, were the average number of employees during 1953 as given in Table 4 below. The weights used for 1956 and subsequent years were the average number of employees during 1956, as given in the results of the annual survey of industrial establishments described below.

brute de la production en 1956. Les sources des données pour 1953 et 1956 sont indiquées ci-dessous.

L'indice de la production manufacturière est construit par le Bureau de statistique de l'O.N.U. qui élimine de l'indice général de l'activité industrielle les fluctuations dues aux variations qui affectent la production des industries extractives (y compris l'extraction de la magnésite) et de la production d'électricité. Les indices du tableau 1 portent sur 1937 car on ne possède aucune donnée valable pour 1938. A partir de 1955 ces indices comprennent les industries qui étaient exploitées auparavant par l'U.R.S.S.

Pour plus amples détails sur ces indices, voir les suppléments No. 9 de novembre 1949, et No. 69 de décembre 1961 au *Monatsberichte des Österreichischen Institutes für Wirtschaftsforschung* (Vienne).

### Indices de l'emploi industriel

Les indices de l'emploi dans l'industrie présentés au tableau 3 ont été obtenus à partir de données émanant de plusieurs sources.

Les indices pour l'industrie extractive ont été élaborés par le Bureau de statistique de l'ONU à partir des chiffres absolus donnant le nombre de salariés dans toutes les unités extractives reproduits dans le tableau intitulé "Beschäftigte Personen" du chapitre "Bergbau und Salinenwesen", *Statistisches Handbuch für die Republik Österreich*, publié par le Bureau central autrichien de statistique.

Les indices pour la période 1948-1956, en ce qui concerne la presque totalité des classes de l'industrie manufacturière, et pour toutes les années dans le cas de la construction et des industries de l'électricité, sont obtenus à partir des indices de l'emploi (Année de base, 1934) publiés dans *Statistische Übersichten zu den Monatsberichten des Österreichischen Institutes für Wirtschaftsforschung*, Vienne. Ces indices sont basés sur le nombre mensuel moyen des salariés de 1678 firmes représentatives. Les indices pour 1956 et les années suivantes, dans le cas de la presque totalité des classes de l'industrie manufacturière, sont calculés par le Bureau de statistique de l'ONU à partir des chiffres absolus donnant le nombre mensuel moyen de salariés, reproduit dans le tableau intitulé "Betriebe und Beschäftigte in der Industrie" de la publication dernièrement mentionnée. Ces chiffres se rapportent aux mêmes unités que celles que couvre l'enquête annuelle sur les établissements industriels décrite ci-dessous.

Les indices de l'emploi pour toutes les industries manufacturières sont les moyennes arithmétiques pondérées des indices des différentes classes de l'industrie manufacturière; ces indices sont calculés par le Bureau de statistique de l'ONU. Les coefficients de pondération pour la période, 1948-1955, sont les nombres moyens de salariés durant l'année 1953 reproduits dans le tableau 4 ci-dessous. Les pondérations utilisées à partir de 1956 sont les nombres moyens de salariés durant 1956 comme reproduits dans les résultats de l'enquête annuelle sur les établissements industriels décrite ci-dessous.

The index numbers for industrial activity as a whole are the weighted arithmetic averages of the indexes for the various divisions of industrial activity which were compiled by the Statistical Office of the United Nations. The character and source of the weights utilized for the periods 1948-1955 are the same as in the case of all manufacturing. The weights for 1956 and subsequent years are the estimated average number of employees during 1956.

### The Characteristics and Structure of Industrial Activity

The information shown in Table 4 is derived from the results of Austria's first census of all non-agricultural establishments, including handicrafts, which were in existence on 1 September 1954 and for which records were available in the year 1953. Public power plants and establishments located in Austria but administered by Soviet occupation authorities were excluded. The establishments thus affected were engaged principally in the extraction and refining of crude petroleum (ISIC groups 13 and 32) and also in the following industries: Food, beverages and tobacco (ISIC 20-22), Wood products and furniture (ISIC 25-26), Leather and leather products (ISIC 29), Chemicals and chemical products (ISIC 31), Basic metals (ISIC 34) and Metal products (ISIC 35-38). The detailed results of the census have been published by the Austrian Central Statistical Office, Vienna, in three publications, *Nichtlandwirtschaftliche Betriebszählung vom. 1 September 1954,* (Wien 1957), *Nichtlandwirtschaftliche Betriebszählung vom. 1 September 1954,* (Wien 1959) and *Ergebnisse der Nichtlandwirtschaftlichen Betriebszählung vom. 1 September 1954,* (Wien 1958).

The definitions of the items of data conform to the International Standards in Basic Industrial Statistics except that homeworkers are included in the count of employees, and wages and salaries include employers' contributions to social security and other funds on behalf of their employees. The data on employees relate to the average number of persons employed at the beginning of February, May, August and November. Value added is valued at market prices.

The data shown in Tables 5 and 6 were compiled from the results of the annual surveys of mining and manufacturing units registered with Chambers of Commerce — usually those with six or more persons engaged. These surveys commenced in 1954 but the figures shown for 1954 do not include establishments located in Austria which were administered by the Soviet occupation authorities. The data were compiled from *Österreichs Industrie in den Jahren, 1954 bis 1958,* Central Statistical Office, Vienna, 1959.

The figures on gross value of production shown in Table 5 are valued at market prices and the data on the number of persons engaged are defined as in the International

Les indices de l'activité industrielle dans son ensemble sont les moyennes arithmétiques pondérées des indices des différentes branches de l'activité industrielle qui sont calculés par le Bureau de statistique de l'ONU. Les caractéristiques et les sources des coefficients de pondération utilisées pour la période 1948-1955, sont les mêmes que pour les industries manufacturières. Les coefficients de pondération pour 1956 et les années suivantes sont les moyennes estimées du nombre des salariés durant l'année 1956.

### Les caractéristiques et la structure de l'activité industrielle

Les chiffres du tableau 4 sont tirés des résultats du premier recensement de tous les établissements non agricoles d'Autriche y compris les unités artisanales qui existaient au 1er septembre 1954 et qui pouvaient fournir des renseignements pour l'année 1953. Les centrales électriques du secteur public et les établissements situés en Autriche mais exploités par les autorités d'occupation soviétique n'ont pas été recensés. Il s'agissait d'établissements s'employant principalement dans l'extraction et le raffinage du pétrole (CITI classes 13 et 32), ainsi qu'aux industries suivantes: Industries alimentaires, boissons et tabac (CITI 20-22), Industries du bois et des meubles (CITI 25-26), Cuir et articles en cuir (CITI 29), Produits chimiques (CITI 31), Métallurgie de base (CITI 34) et Ouvrages en métaux (CITI 35-38). Le Bureau central autrichien de statistique, Vienne, a publié les résultats détaillés du recensement dans trois publications *Nichtlandwirtschaftliche Betriebszählung vom. 1 September 1954,* (Vienne 1957), *Nichtlandwirtschaftliche Betriebszählung vom. 1 September 1954,* (Vienne 1959), et *Ergebnisse der Nichtlandwirtschaftlichen Betriebszählung vom. 1 September 1954,* (Vienne 1958).

Les définitions des rubriques sont conformes aux Normes internationales relatives aux statistiques industrielles de base, si ce n'est que les travailleurs à domicile sont compris parmi les salariés et que les traitements et salaires comprennent les cotisations que les employeurs versent à la sécurité sociale, et à d'autre caisses instituées au profit des salariés qu'ils emploient. Le nombre de salariés correspond à la moyenne du nombre de salariés au début de février, mai, août et novembre 1953. La valeur ajoutée est comptée aux prix du marché.

Les tableaux 5 et 6 reproduisent des données calculées à partir des résultats des enquêtes annuelles sur les unités se rattachant aux industries extractives et manufacturières enregistrées par les chambres de commerce — généralement, les unités employant six personnes ou plus. Ces enquêtes démarrèrent en 1954 mais les chiffres présentés pour 1954 ne comprennent pas les établissements se trouvant en Autriche mais administrés par les autorités soviétiques occupantes. Les données sont élaborées à partir du document intitulé *Österreichs Industrie in den Jahren, 1954 bis 1958,* publié par le Bureau central autrichien de statistique, Vienne, 1959.

Les chiffres se rapportant à la valeur brute de la production reproduits au tableau 5 sont évalués aux prix du marché et ceux du nombre de personnes occupées sont

Standards in Basic Industrial Statistics. The figures of energy consumed relate to fuels and purchased electricity consumed. Except for crude petroleum in the case of petroleum refining, some of the fuels consumed in other industries (e.g., Chemical products) may have been utilized as raw materials rather than as sources of heat or power. Furthermore, because the figures of fuels consumed are not restricted to purchased fuels, the figures of energy consumed are overstated for industries where, for example, gas for own use is manufactured from coal, lignite or coke.

définis conformément aux Normes internationales relatives aux statistiques industrielles de base. Les chiffres relatifs à l'énergie consommée se rapportent à la consommation de combustible et d'électricité effectivement achetés. Mis à part le pétrole brut absorbé par les raffineries, certains combustibles consommés dans d'autres industries (produits chimiques par exemple) peuvent avoir été utilisés comme matière première plutôt que comme source de chaleur ou d'énergie. Par ailleurs, comme les chiffres donnés pour les combustibles consommés ne se restreignent pas aux combustibles effectivement achetés, les chiffres par conséquent donnés pour l'énergie consommée sont surestimés pour les industries ou, par exemple, le gaz utilisé est produit à partir du charbon, du lignite ou du coke.

## 1. THE GROSS NATIONAL PRODUCT AND GROSS DOMESTIC FIXED CAPITAL FORMATION
### PRODUIT NATIONAL BRUT ET FORMATION BRUTE DE CAPITAL FIXE INTERIEUR

Thousand million Schillings        Milliards de schillings

### A. Expenditure on the Gross National Product at Market Prices
### Dépenses relatives au produit national brut aux prix du marché

| Item of data and year / Rubrique et année | Total | Consumption / Consommation | | Gross Domestic Capital Formation / Formation brute de capital intérieur | | Net exports of goods and services / Exportations nettes de biens et de services | |
|---|---|---|---|---|---|---|---|
| | | Total | Government [1] / Etat [1] | Total | Fixed / Fixe | Exports less imports / Exportations moins importations | Exports / Exportations |
| **a. At Current Prices — Aux prix courants** | | | | | | | |
| Absolute figures — Chiffres absolus | | | | | | | |
| 1950 | 52.31 | 41.31 | 6.27 | 13.62 | 8.84 | 2.62 | 7.57 |
| 1951 | 69.61 | 54.66 | 9.10 | 20.06 | 13.08 | −5.11 | 11.00 |
| 1952 | 80.65 | 63.56 | 10.77 | 17.67 | 15.02 | −0.58 | 12.46 |
| 1953 | 82.97 | 66.10 | 11.43 | 15.04 | 14.29 | 1.83 | 15.67 |
| 1954 | 93.24 | 72.83 | 12.44 | 20.36 | 18.02 | 0.05 | 19.15 |
| 1955 | 107.62 | 81.01 | 13.33 | 28.73 | 24.17 | −2.12 | 22.07 |
| 1956 | 118.01 | 88.18 | 14.99 | 27.96 | 24.60 | 1.87 | 28.32 |
| 1957 | 130.82 | 96.74 | 17.86 | 32.36 | 27.70 | 1.72 | 32.84 |
| 1958 | 136.19 | 101.75 | 18.77 | 31.84 | 28.79 | 2.60 | 32.37 |
| 1959 | 143.23 | 107.88 | 19.60 | 34.65 | 31.14 | 0.70 | 35.15 |
| 1960 | 161.35 | 116.73 | 20.84 | 45.73 | 36.63 | −1.11 | 40.19 |
| 1961 | 176.8 | 127.9 | 22.2 | 48.9 | 40.7 | — | 43.6 |
| Percentage distribution of average annual expenditure — Distribution en pourcentage des dépenses annuelles moyennes | | | | | | | |
| 1950–1960 | 100.0 | 75.7 | 13.2 | 24.5 | 20.6 | −0.2 | 21.8 |
| 1950 | 100.0 | 78.9 | 12.0 | 26.1 | 16.9 | −5.0 | 14.5 |
| 1953 | 100.0 | 79.6 | 13.8 | 18.1 | 17.2 | 2.3 | 18.9 |
| 1954 | 100.0 | 78.1 | 13.3 | 21.8 | 19.3 | 0.1 | 20.5 |
| 1958 | 100.0 | 74.7 | 13.8 | 23.3 | 21.1 | 2.0 | 23.8 |
| 1960 | 100.0 | 72.3 | 12.9 | 28.3 | 22.7 | −0.6 | 24.9 |
| **b. At Prices of 1954 — Aux prix de 1954** | | | | | | | |
| Absolute figures — Chiffres absolus | | | | | | | |
| 1950 | 77.06 | 60.74 | 10.94 | 20.50 | 13.96 | −4.18 | 10.91 |
| 1951 | 82.40 | 63.07 | 11.52 | 24.31 | 16.89 | −4.98 | 11.65 |
| 1952 | 82.64 | 64.41 | 11.62 | 19.71 | 16.54 | −1.48 | 11.99 |
| 1953 | 85.87 | 68.73 | 11.85 | 15.17 | 14.42 | 1.97 | 15.90 |
| 1954 | 93.24 | 72.83 | 12.44 | 20.36 | 18.02 | 0.05 | 19.15 |
| 1955 | 103.59 | 78.77 | 12.02 | 28.43 | 23.69 | −3.61 | 20.66 |
| 1956 | 108.88 | 82.84 | 12.00 | 25.82 | 22.86 | 0.22 | 25.62 |
| 1957 | 115.30 | 87.21 | 13.02 | 28.26 | 24.92 | −0.17 | 28.68 |
| 1958 | 119.46 | 90.86 | 13.59 | 29.22 | 25.63 | −0.62 | 28.86 |
| 1959 | 122.29 | 95.24 | 13.85 | 30.71 | 26.98 | −3.66 | 31.70 |
| 1960 | 133.24 | 100.63 | 13.93 | 38.92 | 30.72 | −6.31 | 35.26 |
| 1961 | 139.5 | 106.5 | 14.2 | 40.4 | 32.5 | −7.4 | 37.7 |
| Percentage distribution of average annual expenditure — Distribution en pourcentage des dépenses annuelles moyennes | | | | | | | |
| 1950–1960 | 100.0 | 76.9 | 12.2 | 25.1 | 20.9 | −2.0 | 21.4 |
| 1950 | 100.0 | 78.8 | 14.2 | 26.6 | 18.1 | −5.4 | 14.2 |
| 1953 | 100.0 | 80.0 | 13.8 | 17.7 | 16.8 | 2.3 | 18.5 |
| 1954 | 100.0 | 78.1 | 13.3 | 21.8 | 19.3 | 0.1 | 20.5 |
| 1958 | 100.0 | 76.0 | 11.4 | 24.5 | 21.4 | −0.5 | 24.2 |
| 1960 | 100.0 | 75.5 | 10.4 | 29.2 | 23.0 | −4.7 | 26.5 |
| Average annual rate of growth — Taux annuel moyen d'accroissement | | | | | | | |
| 1950–1960 | 5.6 | 5.2 | 2.4 | 6.6 | 8.2 | . | 12.4 |
| 1950–1953 | 3.7 | 4.2 | 2.7 | −9.5 | 1.1 | . | 13.4 |
| 1954–1958 | 6.4 | 5.7 | 2.2 | 9.4 | 9.2 | . | 10.8 |
| 1958–1960 | 5.6 | 5.3 | 1.2 | 15.4 | 9.5 | . | 10.5 |

[1] Includes "Chambers of Commerce" which are considered entities of public law in Austria.  [1] Y compris les "chambres de commerce", qui, en Autriche, appartiennent au secteur public.

## B. The Gross National Product at Market Prices According to Origin
### Origine par secteur d'activité du produit intérieur brut aux prix du marché

| Item of data and year / Rubrique et année | Total | Agricultural sector / Secteur agricole | Industrial Sector — Secteur Industriel | | | | Transportation and communication / Transports et communications | Other sectors / Autres secteurs |
|---|---|---|---|---|---|---|---|---|
| | | | Total | Mining and Manufacturing / Industries extractives et manufacturières | Construction / Bâtiment et travaux public | Electricity, gas and water / Electricité, gaz et eau | | |
| ISIC — CITI | 0–9 | 0 | 1–5 | 1–3 | 4 | 5 | 7 | 6, 8–9 |
| | | | | *a. At Current Prices — Aux prix courants* | | | | |
| **Absolute figures — Chiffres absolus** | | | | | | | | |
| 1950 | 47.58 | 8.44 | 23.61 | 19.24 | 3.38 | 0.99 | 2.91 | 12.62 |
| 1951 | 63.37 | 10.35 | 32.43 | 25.92 | 4.90 | 1.61 | 3.33 | 17.26 |
| 1952 | 72.36 | 11.48 | 36.76 | 29.43 | 5.23 | 2.10 | 4.33 | 19.79 |
| 1953 | 73.57 | 11.63 | 36.98 | 30.00 | 4.83 | 2.15 | 4.98 | 19.98 |
| 1954 | 82.56 | 13.77 | 41.21 | 33.01 | 5.90 | 2.30 | 5.56 | 22.02 |
| 1955 | 94.58 | 14.53 | 49.03 | 38.70 | 7.84 | 2.49 | 6.17 | 24.85 |
| 1956 | 103.94 | 14.76 | 53.98 | 42.75 | 8.61 | 2.62 | 6.64 | 28.56 |
| 1957 | 114.95 | 15.72 | 59.41 | 46.88 | 9.61 | 2.92 | 7.20 | 32.62 |
| 1958 | 119.69 | 15.54 | 61.71 | 48.04 | 10.19 | 3.48 | 7.24 | 35.20 |
| 1959 | 125.04 | 14.83 | 65.13 | 50.01 | 11.29 | 3.83 | 7.90 | 37.18 |
| 1960 | 140.96 | 16.00 | 74.88 | 57.78 | 12.86 | 4.24 | 9.10 | 40.98 |
| 1961 | 153.3 | 17.7 | 80.6 | 61.8 | 14.3 | 4.5 | 10.2 | 44.8 |
| **Percentage distribution according to sector— Distribution en pourcentage par secteur** | | | | | | | | |
| 1950–1960 | 100.0 | 14.1 | 51.5 | 40.6 | 8.2 | 2.7 | 6.3 | 28.1 |
| 1950 | 100.0 | 17.7 | 49.6 | 40.4 | 7.1 | 2.1 | 6.1 | 26.6 |
| 1953 | 100.0 | 15.8 | 50.2 | 40.7 | 6.6 | 2.9 | 6.8 | 27.2 |
| 1954 | 100.0 | 16.6 | 49.9 | 40.0 | 7.2 | 2.7 | 6.8 | 26.7 |
| 1958 | 100.0 | 12.9 | 51.6 | 40.2 | 8.5 | 2.9 | 6.0 | 29.5 |
| 1960 | 100.0 | 11.3 | 53.1 | 41.0 | 9.1 | 3.0 | 6.5 | 29.1 |
| | | | | *b. At Prices of 1954 — Aux prix de 1954* | | | | |
| **Absolute figures — Chiffres absolus** | | | | | | | | |
| 1950 | 68.83 | 11.72 | 33.00 | 26.14 | 5.34 | 1.52 | 4.61 | 19.50 |
| 1951 | 74.51 | 10.97 | 37.68 | 29.93 | 5.99 | 1.76 | 5.14 | 20.72 |
| 1952 | 73.69 | 12.06 | 36.47 | 28.89 | 5.64 | 1.94 | 4.85 | 20.31 |
| 1953 | 76.17 | 13.10 | 37.18 | 29.95 | 5.15 | 2.08 | 5.07 | 20.82 |
| 1954 | 82.56 | 13.77 | 41.21 | 33.01 | 5.90 | 2.30 | 5.56 | 22.02 |
| 1955 | 91.63 | 13.87 | 48.10 | 38.03 | 7.54 | 2.53 | 6.34 | 23.32 |
| 1956 | 97.33 | 13.34 | 52.12 | 41.81 | 7.46 | 2.85 | 6.77 | 25.10 |
| 1957 | 103.46 | 14.04 | 55.49 | 44.62 | 7.86 | 3.01 | 7.24 | 26.69 |
| 1958 | 107.26 | 15.61 | 56.59 | 45.12 | 8.03 | 3.44 | 7.24 | 27.82 |
| 1959 | 109.08 | 13.76 | 59.09 | 46.96 | 8.43 | 3.70 | 7.62 | 28.61 |
| 1960 | 119.09 | 14.92 | 64.50 | 51.56 | 8.93 | 4.01 | 8.69 | 30.98 |
| 1961 | 124.8 | 15.9 | 67.4 | 53.7 | 9.5 | 4.2 | 8.9 | 32.6 |
| **Percentage distribution according to sector— Distribution en pourcentage par secteur** | | | | | | | | |
| 1950–1960 | 100.0 | 14.6 | 52.0 | 41.5 | 7.6 | 2.9 | 6.9 | 26.5 |
| 1950 | 100.0 | 17.0 | 47.9 | 38.0 | 7.7 | 2.2 | 6.7 | 28.4 |
| 1953 | 100.0 | 17.1 | 48.9 | 39.4 | 6.7 | 2.8 | 6.6 | 27.4 |
| 1954 | 100.0 | 16.6 | 49.9 | 40.0 | 7.2 | 2.7 | 6.8 | 26.7 |
| 1958 | 100.0 | 14.5 | 52.8 | 42.1 | 7.5 | 3.2 | 6.7 | 26.0 |
| 1960 | 100.0 | 12.5 | 54.1 | 43.3 | 7.5 | 3.3 | 7.3 | 26.1 |
| **Average annual rate of growth — Taux annuel moyen d'accroissement** | | | | | | | | |
| 1950–1960 | 5.6 | 2.4 | 6.9 | 7.0 | 5.3 | 10.2 | 6.5 | 4.7 |
| 1950–1953 | 3.4 | 3.8 | 4.1 | 4.6 | −1.2 | 11.0 | 3.2 | 2.2 |
| 1954–1958 | 6.8 | 3.2 | 8.2 | 8.1 | 8.0 | 10.6 | 6.8 | 6.0 |
| 1958–1960 | 5.4 | −2.2 | 6.8 | 6.9 | 5.5 | 8.0 | 9.5 | 5.5 |

## C. Gross Domestic Fixed Capital Formation According to Purchasing Sector
### Formation brute de capital fixe intérieur par secteur d'acquisition

| Item of data and year / Rubrique et année | Total | Agricultural sector / Secteur agricole | Industrial Sector — Secteur industriel | | | Other sectors / Autres secteurs |
|---|---|---|---|---|---|---|
| | | | Total | Manufacturing, mining and construction / Industries manufacturières et extractives; bâtiment et travaux publics | Electricity, gas and water / Electricité, gaz et eau | |
| ISIC — CITI | 0–9 | 0 | 1–5 | 1-4 | 5 | 6-9 |
| *a. At Current Prices — Aux prix courants* | | | | | | |
| Absolute figures — Chiffres absolus | | | | | | |
| 1950 | 8.84 | ... | ... | ... | 1.09 | ... |
| 1951 | 13.08 | 1.50 | 5.39 | 3.82 | 1.57 | 6.19 |
| 1952 | 15.02 | 1.96 | 5.77 | 4.20 | 1.57 | 7.29 |
| 1953 | 14.29 | 2.03 | 4.85 | 3.34 | 1.51 | 7.41 |
| 1954 | 18.02 | 2.44 | 5.22 | 3.21 | 2.01 | 10.36 |
| 1955 | 24.17 | 3.08 | 7.07 | 4.38 | 2.69 | 14.02 |
| 1956 | 24.60 | 3.58 | 8.35 | 5.29 | 3.06 | 12.66 |
| 1957 | 27.70 | 3.93 | 9.65 | 6.32 | 3.33 | 14.12 |
| 1958 | 28.79 | 4.03 | 10.53 | 7.41 | 3.12 | 14.23 |
| 1959 | 31.14 | 4.09 | 10.54 | 7.66 | 2.88 | 16.51 |
| 1960 | 36.63 | 4.75 | 11.93 | 9.00 | 2.93 | 19.95 |
| 1961 | 40.7 | ... | ... | ... | ... | ... |
| Percentage distribution according to sector— Distribution en pourcentage par secteur | | | | | | |
| 1951–1960 | 100.0 | 13.4 | 34.0 | 23.4 | 10.6 | 52.6 |
| 1951 | 100.0 | 11.4 | 41.2 | 29.2 | 12.0 | 47.4 |
| 1953 | 100.0 | 14.2 | 33.9 | 23.3 | 10.6 | 51.9 |
| 1954 | 100.0 | 13.5 | 29.0 | 17.8 | 11.2 | 57.5 |
| 1958 | 100.0 | 13.9 | 36.6 | 25.8 | 10.8 | 49.5 |
| 1960 | 100.0 | 12.9 | 32.6 | 24.6 | 8.0 | 54.5 |
| *b. At Prices of 1954 — Aux prix de 1954* | | | | | | |
| Absolute figures — Chiffres absolus | | | | | | |
| 1950 | 13.96 | ... | ... | ... | 1.78 | ... |
| 1951 | 16.89 | 1.94 | 7.09 | 4.94 | 2.15 | 7.86 |
| 1952 | 16.54 | 2.16 | 6.46 | 4.63 | 1.83 | 7.92 |
| 1953 | 14.42 | 2.05 | 4.92 | 3.37 | 1.55 | 7.45 |
| 1954 | 18.02 | 2.44 | 5.22 | 3.21 | 2.01 | 10.36 |
| 1955 | 23.69 | 3.02 | 6.93 | 4.29 | 2.64 | 13.74 |
| 1956 | 22.86 | 3.33 | 7.79 | 4.92 | 2.87 | 11.74 |
| 1957 | 24.92 | 3.54 | 8.71 | 5.69 | 3.02 | 12.67 |
| 1958 | 25.63 | 3.59 | 9.40 | 6.60 | 2.80 | 12.64 |
| 1959 | 26.98 | 3.54 | 9.15 | 6.64 | 2.51 | 14.29 |
| 1960 | 30.72 | 3.98 | 9.99 | 7.54 | 2.45 | 16.75 |
| 1961 | 32.5 | ... | ... | ... | ... | ... |
| Percentage distribution according to sector— Distribution en pourcentage par secteur | | | | | | |
| 1951–1960 | 100.0 | 13.4 | 34.2 | 23.4 | 10.8 | 52.4 |
| 1951 | 100.0 | 11.4 | 42.0 | 29.3 | 12.7 | 46.6 |
| 1953 | 100.0 | 14.2 | 34.1 | 23.3 | 10.8 | 51.7 |
| 1954 | 100.0 | 13.5 | 29.0 | 17.8 | 11.2 | 57.5 |
| 1958 | 100.0 | 14.0 | 36.6 | 25.7 | 10.9 | 49.4 |
| 1960 | 100.0 | 12.9 | 32.5 | 24.6 | 7.9 | 54.6 |
| Average annual rate of growth—Taux annuel moyen d'accroissement | | | | | | |
| 1951–1960 | 6.9 | 8.3 | 3.9 | 4.7 | 1.5 | 8.8 |
| 1951–1953 | −7.6 | 2.8 | −16.7 | −17.4 | −15.1 | −2.6 |
| 1954–1958 | 9.2 | 10.1 | 15.8 | 19.7 | 8.6 | 5.1 |
| 1958–1960 | 9.5 | 5.3 | 3.1 | 6.9 | −6.4 | 15.1 |

## 2. INDEX NUMBERS OF INDUSTRIAL PRODUCTION
### INDICES DE LA PRODUCTION INDUSTRIELLE

### A. Selected Divisions of Industrial Activity
### Quelques branches de l'activité industrielle

| Period Période | Total [1] | Mining [2] Industries extractives [2] | Manufacturing [1,2] Industries manufacturières [1,2] | Electricity Electricité |
|---|---|---|---|---|
| ISIC — CITI | 1-3, 511 | 1 | 2-3 | 511 |

#### a. Indexes — Indices (1958 = 100)

| | | | | |
|---|---|---|---|---|
| 1937.......... | 39 | 27 | 41 | 16 |
| 1948.......... | 36 | 39 | 35 | 37 |
| 1949.......... | 48 | 47 | 48 | 38 |
| 1950.......... | 56 | 57 | 57 | 44 |
| 1951.......... | 64 | 71 | 65 | 52 |
| 1952.......... | 65 | 80 | 64 | 57 |
| 1953.......... | 66 | 89 | 64 | 62 |
| 1954.......... | 75 | -95- | 74 | -70- |
| 1955.......... | 88 | 102 | 88 | 76 |
| 1956.......... | 92 | 104 | 92 | 84 |
| 1957.......... | 98 | 105 | 98 | 90 |
| 1958.......... | 100 | 100 | 100 | 100 |
| 1959.......... | 106 | 94 | 106 | 111 |
| 1960.......... | 117 | 102 | 118 | 119 |
| 1961.......... | 122 | 102 | 124 | 125 |

#### b. Average Annual Rate of Change — Taux annuel moyen de variation

| | | | | |
|---|---|---|---|---|
| 1937 – 1960.... | ... | 5.9 | ... | 9.1 |
| 1938 – 1948.... | ... | 3.4 | ... | 7.9 |
| 1950 – 1960.... | ... | 6.0 | ... | 10.5 |
| 1948 – 1953.... | ... | 17.9 | ... | 10.9 |
| 1954 – 1958.... | 7.5 | 1.3 | 7.8 | 9.3 |
| 1958 – 1960.... | 8.2 | 1.0 | 8.6 | 9.1 |

### B. The Major Groups of Mining
### Les classes de la branche Industries extractives

| Period Période | All mining [1] Toutes industries extractives [1] | Coal mining Extraction du charbon | Metal mining Extraction des minerals métalliques | Crude petroleum and natural gas Pétrole brut et gaz naturel | Other mining Autres industries extractives |
|---|---|---|---|---|---|
| ISIC — CITI | 11-13, 19 | 11 | 12 | 13 | 19 |

#### a. Indexes — Indices (1958 = 100)

| | | | | | |
|---|---|---|---|---|---|
| 1937....... | 27 | 57 | 43 | 1 | 26 |
| 1948....... | 39 | 58 | 33 | 32 | 34 |
| 1949....... | 47 | 65 | 43 | 38 | 40 |
| 1950....... | 57 | 73 | 52 | 56 | 42 |
| 1951....... | 71 | 84 | 67 | 76 | 52 |
| 1952....... | 80 | 88 | 79 | 92 | 56 |
| 1953....... | 89 | 93 | 83 | 107 | 62 |
| 1954....... | -95- | -105- | -84- | -114- | -64- |
| 1955....... | 102 | 108 | 86 | 124 | 77 |
| 1956....... | 104 | 108 | 94 | 116 | 89 |
| 1957....... | 105 | 106 | 101 | 109 | 101 |
| 1958....... | 100 | 100 | 100 | 100 | 100 |
| 1959....... | 94 | 96 | 100 | 94 | 89 |
| 1960....... | 102 | 92 | 102 | 100 | 116 |
| 1961....... | 102 | 84 | 104 | 99 | 128 |

#### b. Average Annual Rate of Change — Taux annuel moyen de variation

| | | | | | |
|---|---|---|---|---|---|
| 1937 – 1960. | 5.9 | 2.1 | 3.8 | 22.2 | 6.7 |
| 1938 – 1948. | 3.4 | 0.2 | -2.4 | 37.0 | 2.5 |
| 1950 – 1960. | 6.0 | 2.3 | 7.0 | 6.0 | 10.7 |
| 1948 – 1953. | 17.9 | 9.9 | 20.3 | 27.3 | 12.8 |
| 1954 – 1958. | 1.3 | -1.2 | 4.4 | -3.2 | 11.8 |
| 1958 – 1960. | 1.0 | -4.1 | 1.0 | — | 7.7 |

[1] Excludes Sawmills (ISIC group 251), Printing and publishing (ISIC major group 28) and Miscellaneous manufacturing (ISIC major group 39) in the case of all years; and Clothing and footwear (ISIC major group 24), Wood products and furniture (ISIC major group 25-26), and Leather and leather products (ISIC major group 29) in the case of 1953 and earlier years.
[2] Stone quarrying, clay and sand pits (ISIC major group 14) included in manufacturing rather than mining.

[1] Non compris les Scieries (CITI 251), l'Imprimerie et l'édition (CITI 28), et les Industries manufacturières diverses (CITI 39) pour toutes les années. La Fabrication des chaussures et des articles d'habillement (CITI 24), les Industries du bois et du meuble (CITI 25-26) et les Industries du cuir et d'articles en cuir (CITI 29) que pour 1953 et les années antérieures.
[2] L'Extraction de la pierre à bâtir de l'argile et du sable (CITI 14) est comprise dans Industries manufacturières et non dans Industries minières.

[1] Excludes Stone quarrying, clay and sand pits (ISIC major group 14).

[1] Non compris l'Extraction de la pierre à bâtir, de l'argile et du sable (CITI 14).

## C. The Major Groups of Manufacturing — Les classes de la branche Industries manufacturières

| Period / Période | Manufacturing[1,3] Industries manufacturières[1,3] | Food, beverages and tobacco Industries alimentaires, boissons, tabac | Textiles | Clothing, footwear and made-up textiles Articles d'habillement, chaussures et ouvrages en tissu | Wood products and furniture[1] Bois et meubles[1] | Paper and paper products Papier et ouvrages en papier | Leather and leather products except wearing apparel Cuir et articles en cuir, à l'exclusion des articles d'habillement | Rubber products[2] Ouvrages en caoutchouc[2] | Chemicals and chemical, petroleum and coal products[2] Produits chimiques et dérivés du pétrole et du charbon[2] | Non-metallic mineral products[3] Produits minéraux non métalliques[3] | Basic metals Métallurgie de base | Metal products Ouvrages en métaux |
|---|---|---|---|---|---|---|---|---|---|---|---|---|
| ISIC — CITI | 2-3 | 20-22 | 23 | 24 | 25-26 | 27 | 29 | 30 | 31-32 | 33 | 34 | 35-38 |

### a. Indexes — Indices (1958 = 100)

| Period | | | | | | | | | | | | |
|---|---|---|---|---|---|---|---|---|---|---|---|---|
| 1937 | 41 | 56 | 78 | ... | ... | 59 | ... | ... | 29 | 33 | 23 | 27 |
| 1948 | 35 | 47 | 40 | ... | ... | 41 | ... | ... | 35 | 47 | 28 | 27 |
| 1949 | 48 | 56 | 60 | ... | ... | 51 | ... | ... | 45 | 63 | 35 | 42 |
| 1950 | 57 | 66 | 74 | ... | ... | 58 | ... | ... | 55 | 72 | 40 | 51 |
| 1951 | 65 | 70 | 86 | ... | ... | 64 | ... | ... | 59 | 82 | 48 | 61 |
| 1952 | 64 | 73 | 74 | ... | ... | 60 | ... | ... | 53 | 74 | 54 | 64 |
| 1953 | 64 | 75 | 79 | ... | ... | 69 | ... | ... | 59 | 68 | 59 | 56 |
| 1954 | 74 | −74− | −87− | 70 | 64 | −86− | 98 | 78 | 69 | −84− | −70− | −66− |
| 1955 | 88 | 81 | 94 | 85 | 77 | 94 | 103 | 93 | 84 | 95 | 84 | 89 |
| 1956 | 92 | 90 | 100 | 93 | 86 | 95 | 101 | 86 | 89 | 97 | 90 | 91 |
| 1957 | 98 | 95 | 106 | 101 | 91 | 101 | 101 | 93 | 96 | 104 | 100 | 93 |
| 1958 | 100 | 100 | 100 | 100 | 100 | 100 | 100 | 100 | 100 | 100 | 100 | 100 |
| 1959 | 106 | 103 | 105 | 109 | 112 | 105 | 110 | 110 | 112 | 111 | 106 | 104 |
| 1960 | 118 | 107 | 117 | 121 | 124 | 116 | 103 | 140 | 122 | 124 | 126 | 115 |
| 1961 | 124 | 105 | 122 | 134 | 148 | 118 | 105 | 155 | 130 | 134 | 130 | 118 |

### b. Average Annual Rate of Change — Taux annuel moyen de variation

| Period | | | | | | | | | | | | |
|---|---|---|---|---|---|---|---|---|---|---|---|---|
| 1937 − 1960 | ... | 2.9 | 1.7 | ... | ... | 3.0 | ... | ... | ... | 5.9 | 7.7 | 6.5 |
| 1938 − 1948 | ... | −1.6 | −5.9 | ... | ... | −3.2 | ... | ... | ... | 3.3 | 1.8 | — |
| 1950 − 1960 | ... | 5.0 | 4.5 | ... | ... | 7.2 | ... | ... | ... | 5.6 | 12.2 | 8.5 |
| 1948 − 1953 | ... | 9.8 | 14.6 | ... | ... | 11.0 | ... | ... | ... | 7.7 | 16.1 | 15.7 |
| 1954 − 1958 | 7.8 | 7.8 | 3.5 | 9.3 | 11.8 | 3.8 | 0.5 | 6.4 | 9.7 | 4.4 | 9.3 | 10.9 |
| 1958 − 1960 | 8.6 | 3.4 | 8.2 | 10.0 | 11.4 | 7.7 | 1.5 | 18.3 | 11.4 | 10.5 | 12.2 | 7.2 |

[1] Excludes Sawmills (ISIC group 251), Printing and publishing (ISIC major group 28) and Miscellaneous manufacturing (ISIC major group 39) in the case of all years; and Clothing and footwear (ISIC major group 24), Wood products and furniture (ISIC major groups 25-26) and Leather and leather products (ISIC major group 29) in the case of 1953 and earlier years.
[2] Rubber products (ISIC group 300) included in Chemicals and chemical, coal and petroleum products (ISIC major groups 31-32) in the case of 1953 and earlier years.
[3] Includes Stone quarrying, clay and sand pits (ISIC major group 14).

[1] Non compris les Scieries (CITI 251), l'Imprimerie et l'édition (CITI 28) et les Industries manufacturières diverses (CITI 39) pour toutes les années. La Fabrication des chaussures et des articles d'habillement (CITI 24), les Industries du bois et du meuble (CITI 25-26) et les Industries du cuir et des articles en cuir (CITI 29) que pour 1953 et les années antérieure.
[2] L'Industrie du caoutchouc (CITI 300) est comprise dans Produits Chimiques et dérivés du pétrole et du charbon (CITI 31-32) jusqu'en 1953.
[3] Y compris l'Extraction de la pierre à bâtir, de l'argile et du sable (CITI 14).

### 3. INDEX NUMBERS OF INDUSTRIAL EMPLOYMENT
### INDICES DE L'EMPLOI DANS L'INDUSTRIE

#### A. The Divisions of Industrial Activity
#### Les branches de l'activité industrielle

| Period / Période | Total [1] | Mining [1, 2] Industries extractives [1, 2] | Manu-facturing [1, 2] Industries manufac-turières [1, 2] | Construction Bâtiment et travaux publics | Electricity Electricité |
|---|---|---|---|---|---|
| ISIC — CITI | 1 –4, 511 | 1 | 2–3 | 4 | 511 |
| *a. Indexes — Indices (1958 = 100)* | | | | | |
| 1948....... | 76 | 69 | 73 | 92 | 64 |
| 1949....... | 81 | 68 | 82 | 83 | 68 |
| 1950....... | 85 | 69 | 87 | 85 | 70 |
| 1951....... | 89 | 78 | 91 | 85 | 72 |
| 1952....... | 86 | 78 | 89 | 75 | 74 |
| 1953....... | 84 | 76 | 87 | 75 | 77 |
| 1954....... | 87 | 76 | 90 | 77 | 80 |
| 1955....... | 93 | 95 | 96 | 82 | 86 |
| 1956....... | –96– | 98 | –99– | 80 | 92 |
| 1957....... | 100 | 100 | 100 | 100 | 100 |
| 1958....... | 100 | 100 | 100 | 100 | 100 |
| 1959....... | 100 | 95 | 100 | 100 | 101 |
| 1960....... | 102 | 90 | 104 | 98 | 103 |
| 1961....... | 105 | 85 | 106 | 101 | 103 |
| *b. Average Annual Rate of Change — Taux annuel moyen de variation* | | | | | |
| 1950 – 1960. | ... | ... | 1.8 | 1.4 | 3.9 |
| 1948 – 1953. | ... | ... | 3.6 | –4.0 | 3.8 |
| 1954 – 1958. | ... | ... | 2.7 | 6.8 | 5.7 |
| 1958 – 1960. | 1.0 | –5.1 | 2.0 | –1.0 | 1.5 |

[1] Excludes Petroleum extraction (ISIC group 130) and Petroleum refining (ISIC group 321) before 1955 and Sawmills (ISIC group 251) and Miscellaneous manufacturing (ISIC major group 39) for all years. For 1955 and subsequent years, petroleum refining is excluded.
[2] Stone and gravel quarrying (ISIC group 140) is included in Manufacturing instead of Mining.

[1] Non compris l'Extraction du pétrole (CITI 130) et le Raffinage du pétrole (CITI 321) avant 1955, non plus que les Scieries (CITI 251) et les Industries manufacturières diverses (CITI 39) pour toutes les années. A partir de 1955, non compris le Raffinage du pétrole.
[2] L'Extraction de la pierre à bâtir et du gravier (CITI 140) est comprise dans Industries manufac-turières et non dans Industries extractives.

#### B. The Major Groups of Mining
#### Les classes de la branche Industries extractives

| Period / Période | All mining [1] Toutes industries extractives [1] | Coal mining Extraction du charbon | Metal mining Extraction des minerais métalliques | Crude petro-leum and natural gas [1] Pétrole brut et gaz naturel [1] | Other mining [1] Autres industries extractives [1] |
|---|---|---|---|---|---|
| ISIC — CITI | 11–13, 19 | 11 | 12 | 13 | 19 |
| *a. Indexes — Indices (1958 = 100)* | | | | | |
| 1948....... | 69 | 94 | 84 | ... | 75 |
| 1949....... | 68 | 91 | 86 | ... | 78 |
| 1950....... | 69 | 91 | 88 | ... | 78 |
| 1951....... | 79 | 103 | 97 | ... | 83 |
| 1952....... | 78 | 100 | 100 | ... | 90 |
| 1953....... | 76 | 97 | 98 | ... | 90 |
| 1954....... | 76 | 96 | 98 | ... | 96 |
| 1955....... | 95 | 98 | 95 | 92 | 91 |
| 1956....... | 98 | 99 | 99 | 98 | 95 |
| 1957....... | 100 | 100 | 102 | 100 | 98 |
| 1958....... | 100 | 100 | 100 | 100 | 100 |
| 1959....... | 95 | 93 | 99 | 95 | 96 |
| 1960....... | 90 | 85 | 100 | 88 | 96 |
| 1961....... | 85 | 77 | 101 | 83 | 97 |
| *b. Average Annual Rate of Change — Taux annuel moyen de variation* | | | | | |
| 1950 – 1960. | ... | –0.7 | 1.3 | ... | 2.1 |
| 1948 – 1953. | ... | 0.6 | 3.1 | ... | 3.7 |
| 1954 – 1958. | ... | 1.0 | 0.5 | ... | 1.0 |
| 1958 – 1960. | –5.1 | –7.8 | — | –6.2 | –2.0 |

[1] Excludes Petroleum extraction (ISIC group 130) before 1955; excludes Stone and gravel quarry-ing (ISIC group 140).

[1] L'Extraction du pétrole (CITI 130) est exclue jusqu'en 1955. Non compris l'Extraction de la pierre à bâtir et du gravier (CITI 140).

45

## C. The Major Groups of Manufacturing — Les classes de la branche Industries manufacturières

| Period / Période | Manufacturing[1] / Industries manufacturières [1] | Food, beverages and tobacco / Industries alimentaires, boissons, tabac | Textiles | Clothing, footwear and made-up textiles / Articles d'habillement, chaussures et ouvrages en tissu | Wood products and furniture [1] / Bois et meubles [1] | Paper and paper products / Papier et ouvrages en papier | Printing and publishing / Imprimerie et édition | Leather and leather products except wearing apparel / Cuir et articles en cuir, à l'exclusion des articles d'habillement | Chemicals and chemical, petroleum, coal and rubber products [1] / Produits chimiques, dérivés du pétrole et du charbon et ouvrages en caoutchouc [1] | Non-metallic mineral products [1] / Produits minéraux non métalliques [1] | Metal products / Ouvrages en métaux |
|---|---|---|---|---|---|---|---|---|---|---|---|
| ISIC — CITI | 2–3 | 20–22 | 23 | 24 | 25–26 | 27 | 28 | 29 | 30–32 | 33 | 34–38 |

### a. Indexes — Indices (1958 = 100)

| | | | | | | | | | | | |
|---|---|---|---|---|---|---|---|---|---|---|---|
| 1948.............. | 73 | 72 | 70 | 54 | 76 | 74 | 93 | 98 | 67 | 84 | 72 |
| 1949.............. | 82 | 83 | 88 | 61 | 83 | 82 | 95 | 102 | 74 | 92 | 78 |
| 1950.............. | 87 | 86 | 100 | 61 | 87 | 87 | 96 | 106 | 79 | 96 | 82 |
| 1951.............. | 91 | 87 | 107 | 66 | 93 | 95 | 97 | 109 | 81 | 102 | 86 |
| 1952.............. | 89 | 87 | 98 | 63 | 87 | 95 | 96 | 97 | 78 | 99 | 87 |
| 1953.............. | 87 | 89 | 95 | 68 | 85 | 93 | 94 | 92 | 78 | 94 | 83 |
| 1954.............. | 90 | 91 | 97 | 78 | 87 | 97 | 97 | 98 | 83 | 99 | 87 |
| 1955.............. | 96 | 93 | 99 | 85 | 94 | 101 | 99 | 103 | 89 | 101 | 95 |
| 1956.............. | –99– | –96– | –102– | 94 | –95– | –101– | –99– | –104– | –92– | –104– | –99– |
| 1957.............. | 100 | 98 | 105 | 99 | 98 | 102 | 99 | 103 | 96 | 102 | 99 |
| 1958.............. | 100 | 100 | 100 | 100 | 100 | 100 | 100 | 100 | 100 | 100 | 100 |
| 1959.............. | 100 | 101 | 95 | 105 | 100 | 99 | 98 | 100 | 103 | 101 | 101 |
| 1960.............. | 104 | 101 | 97 | 110 | 103 | 102 | 99 | 99 | 108 | 104 | 106 |
| 1961.............. | 106 | 102 | 97 | 115 | 109 | 104 | 101 | 100 | 112 | 106 | 111 |

### b. Average Annual Rate of Change — Taux annuel moyen de variation

| | | | | | | | | | | | |
|---|---|---|---|---|---|---|---|---|---|---|---|
| 1950 – 1960........ | 1.8 | 1.5 | −0.3 | 6.1 | 1.7 | 1.6 | 0.3 | −0.7 | 3.2 | 0.8 | 2.6 |
| 1948 – 1953........ | 3.6 | 4.3 | 6.3 | 4.7 | 2.3 | 4.7 | 0.2 | −1.3 | 3.1 | 2.3 | 2.9 |
| 1954 – 1958........ | 2.7 | 2.4 | 0.8 | 6.4 | 3.5 | 0.8 | 0.8 | 0.5 | 4.8 | 0.2 | 3.5 |
| 1958 – 1960........ | 2.0 | 0.5 | −1.5 | 4.9 | 1.5 | 1.0 | −0.5 | −0.5 | 3.9 | 2.0 | 3.0 |

[1] Sawmills (ISIC group 251), Petroleum refining (ISIC group 321) and Miscellaneous manufacturing (ISIC major group 39) are excluded but Stone and gravel quarrying (ISIC group 140) is included in Non-metallic mineral products (ISIC major group 33).

[1] Les Scieries (CITI 251), le Raffinage du pétrole (CITI 321), et les Industries manufacturières diverses (CITI 39) sont exclus, mais l'Extraction de la pierre à bâtir et du gravier (CITI 140) est comprise dans Produits minéraux non métalliques (CITI 33)

# 4. THE CHARACTERISTICS OF ALL INDUSTRIAL ESTABLISHMENTS
## CARACTERISTIQUES DE TOUS LES ETABLISSEMENTS INDUSTRIELS
### 1953

Number of establishments in units; value added and wages and salaries in million Schillings; number of engaged, employees and operatives in thousands; man-hours worked in millions; capacity of installed power equipment in thousand horsepower; value added per engaged and wages and salaries per employee and per thousand operative man-hours in thousand Schillings; average annual man-hours per operative in thousands; capacity of installed power equipment per engaged and per thousand operative man-hours in horsepower.

Nombre d'établissements en unités; valeur ajoutée et traitements et salaires en millions de schillings; nombre de personnes occupées, de salariés et d'ouvriers en milliers; heures de travail effectuées en millions; puissance installée en milliers de chevaux-vapeur; valeur ajoutée par personne occupée et traitements et salaires par salarié et par millier d'heures-ouvrier en milliers de schillings; moyenne annuelle des heures de travail par ouvrier en milliers; puissance installée par personne occupée et par millier d'heures-ouvrier en chevaux-vapeur.

## A. The Divisions of Industrial Activity — Les branches de l'activité industrielle

### a. Absolute Figures — Chiffres absolus

| Item of data | Total[1] | Mining[1] Industries extractives[1] | Manufacturing[1] Industries manufacturières[1] | Construction Bâtiment et travaux publics | Gas and steam Gaz et vapeur | Rubrique |
|---|---|---|---|---|---|---|
| ISIC | 1-4,512-513 | 1 | 2-3 | 4 | 512-513 | CITI |
| Number of units (As at 1.IX.1954) | 106 252 | 1 060 | 89 083 | 16 085 | 24 | Nombre d'unités (au 1.IX.1954) |
| Value added | 38 417.9 | 1 780.8 | 30 660.0 | 5 717.1 | 260.0 | Valeur ajoutée |
| Number of engaged (As at 1.IX.1954) | 1 063.4 | 43.6 | 790.8 | 225.1 | 3.9 | Nombre de personnes occupées (au 1.IX.1954) |
| Employees: Number (Average for year) | 815.0 | 39.3 | 616.8 | 155.0 | 3.9 | Salariés: Nombre (moyenne pour l'année) |
| Wages and salaries | 14 150.9 | 825.0 | 10 688.9 | 2 561.1 | 75.9 | Traitements et salaires |
| Operatives: Number (Average for year) | 631.3 | 35.2 | 469.3 | 124.0 | 2.8 | Ouvriers: Nombre (moyenne pour l'année) |
| Man-hours worked | 1 501.9 | 80.6 | 1 113.2 | 301.5 | 6.6 | Heures de travail effectuées |
| Wages and salaries | 10 932.9 | 712.7 | 8 035.7 | 2 132.7 | 51.8 | Traitements et salaires |
| Capacity of installed power equipment | 3 491.4 | 299.3 | 2 908.2 | 245.6 | 38.3 | Puissance installée |

### b. Structure

| Item of data | Total[1] | Mining[1] Industries extractives[1] | Manufacturing[1] Industries manufacturières[1] | Construction Bâtiment et travaux publics | Gas and steam Gaz et vapeur | Rubrique |
|---|---|---|---|---|---|---|
| ISIC | 1-4,512-513 | 1 | 2-3 | 4 | 512-513 | CITI |
| Distribution in percent of: Value added | 100.0 | 4.6 | 79.8 | 14.9 | 0.7 | Distribution en pourcentage: Valeur ajoutée |
| Number of engaged | 100.0 | 4.1 | 74.3 | 21.2 | 0.4 | Nombre de personnes occupées |
| Per person engaged: Value added | 36.1 | 40.8 | 38.8 | 25.4 | 66.7 | Par personne occupée: Valeur ajoutée |
| Capacity of installed power equipment | 3.28 | 6.86 | 3.68 | 1.09 | 9.82 | Puissance installée |
| Employees as a percent of engaged | 76.6 | 90.1 | 78.0 | 68.8 | 100.0 | Salariés en pourcentage des personnes occupées |
| Wages and salaries per employee | 17.4 | 21.0 | 17.3 | 16.5 | 19.5 | Traitements et salaires par salarié |
| Value added per unit of wages and salaries | 2.71 | 2.16 | 2.87 | 2.23 | 3.42 | Valeur ajoutée par unité de traitements et salaires |
| Operatives as a percent of employees | 77.5 | 89.6 | 76.1 | 80.0 | 71.8 | Ouvriers en pourcentage des salariés |
| Average annual man-hours per operative | 2.38 | 2.29 | 2.37 | 2.43 | 2.36 | Moyenne annuelle des heures de travail par ouvrier |
| Per thousand operative man-hours: Wages and salaries | 7.28 | 8.84 | 7.22 | 7.07 | 7.85 | Par millier d'heures-ouvrier de travail: Traitements et salaires |
| Capacity of installed power equipment | 2.32 | 3.71 | 2.61 | 0.81 | 5.80 | Puissance installée |

[1] Excludes the extraction and refining of crude petroleum (ISIC groups 130 and 321) and the production and distribution of electricity (ISIC group 511).

[1] Non compris l'extraction et le raffinage du pétrole brut (CITI groupes 130 et 321) ni la production et distribution d'électricité (CITI groupe 511).

## B. The Major Groups of Mining — Les classes de la branche Industries extractives

### a. Absolute Figures — Chiffres absolus

| Item of data | Total[1] | Coal mining Extraction du charbon | Metal mining Extraction des minerais métalliques | Other mining Divers | Rubrique |
|---|---|---|---|---|---|
| ISIC | 1 | 11 | 12 | 14-19 | CITI |
| Number of units (As at 1.IX.1954) | 1 060 | 31 | 11 | 1 018 | Nombre d'unités (au 1.IX.1954) |
| Value added | 1 780.8 | 746.6 | 247.0 | 787.2 | Valeur ajoutée |
| Number of engaged (As at 1.IX.1954) | 43.6 | 17.0 | 6.8 | 19.8 | Nombre de personnes occupées (au 1.IX.1954) |
| Employees: Number (Average for year) | 39.3 | 16.7 | 6.8 | 15.8 | Salariés: Nombre (moyenne pour l'année) |
| Wages and salaries | 825.0 | 362.5 | 144.8 | 317.7 | Traitements et salaires |
| Operatives: Number (Average for year) | 35.2 | 15.1 | 5.8 | 14.3 | Ouvriers: Nombre (moyenne pour l'année) |
| Man-hours worked | 80.6 | 33.8 | 12.8 | 34.0 | Heures de travail effectuées |
| Wages and salaries | 712.7 | 319.2 | 120.6 | 272.9 | Traitements et salaires |
| Capacity of installed power equipment | 299.3 | 121.2 | 84.0 | 94.1 | Puissance installée |

### b. Structure

| Item of data | Total[1] | Coal mining Extraction du charbon | Metal mining Extraction des minerais métalliques | Other mining Divers | Rubrique |
|---|---|---|---|---|---|
| ISIC | 1 | 11 | 12 | 14-19 | CITI |
| Distribution in percent of: Value added | 100.0 | 41.9 | 13.8 | 44.3 | Distribution en pourcentage: Valeur ajoutée |
| Number of engaged | 100.0 | 38.9 | 15.6 | 45.5 | Nombre de personnes occupées |
| Per person engaged: Value added | 40.8 | 43.9 | 36.3 | 39.8 | Par personne occupée: Valeur ajoutée |
| Capacity of installed power equipment | 6.86 | 7.13 | 12.35 | 4.75 | Puissance installée |
| Employees as a percent of engaged | 90.1 | 98.2 | 100.0 | 79.8 | Salariés en pourcentage des personnes occupées |
| Wages and salaries per employee | 21.0 | 21.7 | 21.3 | 20.1 | Traitements et salaires par salarié |
| Value added per unit of wages and salaries | 2.16 | 2.06 | 1.70 | 2.48 | Valeur ajoutée par unité de traitements et salaires |
| Operatives as a percent of employees | 89.6 | 90.4 | 85.3 | 90.5 | Ouvriers en pourcentage des salariés |
| Average annual man-hours per operative | 2.29 | 2.24 | 2.21 | 2.38 | Moyenne annuelle des heures de travail par ouvrier |
| Per thousand operative man-hours: Wages and salaries | 8.84 | 9.44 | 9.42 | 8.03 | Par millier d'heures-ouvrier: Traitements et salaires |
| Capacity of installed power equipment | 3.71 | 3.58 | 6.56 | 2.77 | Puissance installée |

[1] Excludes the Extraction of crude petroleum (ISIC major group 13).

[1] Non compris l'extraction du pétrole brut (CITI classe 13).

## C.  The Major Groups of Manufacturing — Les classes de la branche Industries manufacturières

| Item of data | Manu-facturing [1] / Industries manufac-turières [1] | Food, beverages and tobacco / Industries alimen-taires, boissons, tabac | Textiles | Clothing, footwear and made-up textiles / Articles d'habil-lement, chaussures et ouvrages en tissu | Wood products and furniture / Bois et meubles | Paper and paper products / Papier et ouvrages en papier | Printing and publish-ing / Im-primerie et édition | Leather and leather products except wearing apparel / Cuir et articles en cuir, à l'exclu-sion des articles d'habil-lement | Rubber products / Ouvrages en caout-chouc | Chemicals and chemical, petroleum and coal products [1] / Produits chi-miques et dérivés du pétrole et du charbon [1] | Non-metallic mineral products / Produits minéraux non métal-liques | Basic metals / Métal-lurgie de base | Metal products / Ouvrages en métaux | Other manu-factur-ing / Autres in-dustries manufac-turières | Rubrique |
|---|---|---|---|---|---|---|---|---|---|---|---|---|---|---|---|
| ISIC | 2–3 | 20–22 | 23 | 24 | 25–26 | 27 | 28 | 29 | 30 | 31–32 | 33 | 34 | 35–38 | 39 | CITI |
| *a.  Absolute Figures — Chiffres absolus* | | | | | | | | | | | | | | | |
| Number of establishments (As at 1.IX.1954)..... | 89 083 | 15 419 | 3 151 | 29 131 | 14 961 | 448 | 1 058 | 2 360 | 251 | 1 192 | 2 020 | 207 | 15 290 | 3 595 | Nombre d'établissements (au 1.IX.1954) |
| Value added.......... | 30 660.0 | 6 920.0 | 3 257.5 | 2 064.0 | 2 225.9 | 1 240.8 | 749.2 | 377.0 | 376.9 | 1 868.8 | 1 586.7 | 2 165.5 | 7 237.5 | 590.2 | Valeur ajoutée |
| Number of engaged (As at 1.IX.1954)..... | 790.8 | 110.1 | 90.2 | 101.6 | 83.8 | 31.3 | 14.5 | 12.0 | 7.2 | 31.7 | 45.0 | 48.3 | 194.2 | 20.9 | Nombre de personnes occupées (au 1.IX.1954) |
| Employees: Number (Average for year).......... | 616.8 | 80.1 | 82.0 | 60.1 | 59.7 | 28.6 | 12.1 | 8.6 | 6.5 | 27.3 | 36.1 | 45.3 | 155.8 | 14.6 | Salariés: Nombre (moyenne pour l'année) |
| Wages and salaries... | 10 688.9 | 1 447.1 | 1 264.8 | 739.4 | 850.6 | 565.9 | 229.2 | 129.6 | 116.5 | 571.8 | 711.3 | 1 015.8 | 2 818.7 | 228.2 | Traitements et salaires |
| Operatives: Number (Average for year)............ | 469.3 | 58.4 | 66.7 | 41.5 | 48.3 | 24.4 | 9.1 | 6.8 | 5.6 | 18.4 | 30.8 | 36.5 | 112.8 | 10.0 | Ouvriers: Nombre (moyenne pour l'année) |
| Man-hours worked.... | 1 113.2 | 143.8 | 151.5 | 95.5 | 116.1 | 58.1 | 23.2 | 16.3 | 11.5 | 44.8 | 73.7 | 84.4 | 269.8 | 24.5 | Heures de travail effectuées |
| Wages and salaries... | 8 035.7 | 1 055.0 | 970.7 | 561.7 | 744.6 | 445.1 | 172.0 | 105.0 | 95.7 | 326.7 | 573.6 | 777.8 | 2 048.3 | 159.5 | Traitements et salaires |
| Capacity of installed power equipment..... | 2 908.2 | 335.8 | 176.8 | 26.3 | 310.9 | 282.7 | 14.2 | 28.9 | 35.7 | 229.5 | 195.7 | 632.7 | 619.4 | 19.6 | Puissance installée |
| *b.  Structure* | | | | | | | | | | | | | | | |
| Distribution in percent of: Value added........ | 100.0 | 22.5 | 10.6 | 6.8 | 7.2 | 4.1 | 2.4 | 1.3 | 1.2 | 6.1 | 5.2 | 7.0 | 23.6 | 2.0 | Distribution en pour-centage: Valeur ajoutée |
| Number of engaged... | 100.0 | 13.9 | 11.4 | 12.8 | 10.6 | 4.0 | 1.8 | 1.5 | 0.9 | 4.1 | 5.6 | 6.1 | 24.6 | 2.7 | Nombre de personnes occupées |
| Per person engaged: Value added........ | 38.8 | 62.8 | 36.1 | 20.3 | 26.6 | 39.6 | 51.7 | 31.4 | 52.3 | 59.0 | 35.3 | 44.8 | 37.3 | 28.2 | Par personne occupée: Valeur ajoutée |
| Capacity of installed power equipment..... | 3.68 | 3.05 | 1.96 | 0.26 | 3.71 | 9.03 | 0.98 | 2.41 | 4.96 | 7.24 | 4.35 | 13.10 | 3.19 | 0.94 | Puissance installée |
| Employees as a percent of engaged........ | 78.0 | 72.8 | 90.9 | 59.2 | 71.2 | 91.4 | 83.4 | 71.7 | 90.3 | 86.1 | 80.2 | 93.8 | 80.2 | 69.8 | Salariés en pourcentage des personnes occupées |
| Wages and salaries per employee........ | 17.3 | 18.1 | 15.4 | 12.3 | 14.2 | 19.8 | 18.9 | 15.1 | 17.9 | 20.9 | 19.7 | 22.4 | 18.1 | 15.6 | Traitements et salaires par salarié |
| Value added per unit of wages and salaries. | 2.87 | 4.78 | 2.58 | 2.79 | 2.62 | 2.19 | 3.27 | 2.91 | 3.24 | 3.27 | 2.23 | 2.13 | 2.57 | 2.59 | Valeur ajoutée par unité de traitements et salaires |
| Operatives as a percent of employees........ | 76.1 | 72.9 | 81.3 | 69.0 | 80.9 | 85.3 | 75.2 | 79.1 | 86.2 | 67.4 | 85.3 | 80.6 | 72.4 | 68.5 | Ouvriers en pourcentage des salariés |
| Average annual man-hours per operative.......... | 2.37 | 2.46 | 2.27 | 2.30 | 2.40 | 2.38 | 2.55 | 2.40 | 2.05 | 2.43 | 2.39 | 2.31 | 2.39 | 2.45 | Moyenne annuelle des heures de travail par ouvrier |
| Per thousand operative man-hours: Wages and salaries... | 7.22 | 7.34 | 6.41 | 5.88 | 6.41 | 7.66 | 7.41 | 6.44 | 8.32 | 7.29 | 7.78 | 9.22 | 7.59 | 6.51 | Par millier d'heures-ouvrier: Traitements et salaires |
| Capacity of installed power equipment..... | 2.61 | 2.34 | 1.17 | 0.28 | 2.68 | 4.86 | 0.61 | 1.77 | 3.10 | 5.12 | 2.66 | 7.50 | 2.30 | 0.80 | Puissance installée |

[1] Excludes the Refining of crude petroleum (ISIC group 321).

[1] Non compris le Raffinage du pétrole brut (CITI 321).

## 5. THE CHARACTERISTICS OF MINING AND MANUFACTURING ESTABLISHMENTS WITH SIX OR MORE PERSONS ENGAGED

## CARACTERISTIQUES DES ETABLISSEMENTS MINIERS ET MANUFACTURIERS OCCUPANT SIX PERSONNES OU PLUS

### 1954, 1958

Number of establishments in units; gross value of production in million Schillings; number of engaged in thousands; energy consumed in thousand metric tons of coal equivalent; electricity consumed in million KWH; energy consumed per engaged in metric tons of coal equivalent; electricity consumed per engaged in thousand KWH.

Nombre d'établissements en unités; valeur brute de production en millions de schillings; nombre de personnes occupées en milliers; énergie consommée en milliers de tonnes métriques d'équivalent charbon; électricité consommée en millions de kWh; énergie consommée par personne occupée en tonnes métriques d'équivalent charbon; électricité consommée par personne occupée en milliers de kWh.

| Year and item of data | Mining and manufacturing [1] — Industries extractives et manufacturières [1] | Coal and metal mining [2] — Extraction de charbon et de minerais métalliques [2] | Crude petroleum and natural gas [3] — Pétrole brut et gaz naturel [3] | Food, beverages and tobacco — Industries alimentaires, boissons, tabac | Textiles | Clothing, footwear and made-up textiles — Articles d'habillement, chaussures et ouvrages en tissu | Wood products and furniture [1,4] — Bois et meubles [1,4] | Paper and paper products [5] — Papier et ouvrages en papier [5] | Leather and leather products except wearing apparel — Cuir et articles en cuir, à l'exclusion des articles d'habillement | Chemicals and chemical, coal and rubber products [3] — Produits chimiques, dérivés du charbon et ouvrages en caoutchouc [3] | Non-metallic mineral products [6] — Produits minéraux non métalliques [6] | Basic metals [2] — Métallurgie de base [2] | Metal products [1,4] — Ouvrages en métaux [1,4] | Année et rubrique |
|---|---|---|---|---|---|---|---|---|---|---|---|---|---|---|
| ISIC | 1–3 | 11-12, 19 | 13 | 20–22 | 23 | 24 | 25–26 | 27 | 29 | 30–32 | 33, 14 | 34 | 35–39 | CITI |
| *a. Absolute Figures — Chiffres absolus* | | | | | | | | | | | | | | |
| **1954** | | | | | | | | | | | | | | **1954** |
| Number of establishments | 4 741 | 95 | 5 | 570 | 514 | 346 | 379 | 254 | 173 | 452 | 605 | 186 | 1 162 | Nombre d'établissements |
| Gross value of production | 52 632.0 | 2 152.2 | 172.6 | 7 928.0 | 7 355.0 | 1 454.4 | 1 194.8 | 4 796.3 | 1 431.1 | 4 993.4 | 2 871.1 | 7 110.8 | 11 172.3 | Valeur brute de la production |
| Energy consumed | 8 687.5 | 646.8 | 39.0 | 320.6 | 140.7 | 14.5 | 35.8 | 569.3 | 17.8 | 488.5 | 720.6 | 5 494.5 | 199.4 | Energie consommée |
| Electricity consumed | 4 612.1 | 210.7 | 9.0 | 146.6 | 225.2 | 9.8 | 51.6 | 659.2 | 10.9 | 707.7 | 324.9 | 1 940.5 | 316.0 | Electricité consommée |
| **1958** | | | | | | | | | | | | | | **1958** |
| Number of establishments | 5 411 | 100 | 21 | 597 | 595 | 448 | 443 | 264 | 188 | 564 | 628 | 202 | 1 361 | Nombre d'établissements |
| Gross value of production | 79 316.3 | 2 991.3 | 2 440.9 | 11 117.4 | 9 207.8 | 2 346.0 | 2 142.5 | 5 932.5 | 1 816.9 | 8 195.9 | 3 945.8 | 10 709.1 | 18 470.2 | Valeur brute de la production |
| Number of engaged (As at 30.XII) | 573.8 | 33.6 | 12.4 | 51.5 | 72.4 | 25.4 | 21.8 | 29.3 | 17.3 | 42.0 | 38.3 | 53.4 | 176.4 | Nombre de personnes occupées (au 30.XII) |
| Energy consumed | 10 549.2 | 791.7 | 212.4 | 379.2 | 177.5 | 14.6 | 42.7 | 586.0 | 21.0 | 664.5 | 797.0 | 6 586.4 | 276.2 | Energie consommée |
| Electricity consumed | 6 041.4 | 315.4 | 59.1 | 199.1 | 270.6 | 15.6 | 75.9 | 800.7 | 11.7 | 933.8 | 406.8 | 2 484.6 | 468.1 | Electricité consommée |
| *b. Structure* | | | | | | | | | | | | | | |
| **1954** | | | | | | | | | | | | | | **1954** |
| Distribution in percent of gross value of production | 100.0 | 4.0 | 0.4 | 15.0 | 14.0 | 2.8 | 2.2 | 9.2 | 2.7 | 9.5 | 5.4 | 13.5 | 21.3 | Distribution en pourcentage de la valeur brute de la production |
| **1958** Distribution in percent of: Gross value of production | 100.0 | 3.7 | 3.1 | 14.0 | 11.6 | 3.0 | 2.7 | 7.5 | 2.3 | 10.3 | 5.0 | 13.5 | 23.3 | **1958** Distribution en pourcentage: Valeur brute de la production |
| Number of engaged | 100.0 | 5.8 | 2.2 | 8.9 | 12.7 | 4.4 | 3.8 | 5.1 | 3.0 | 7.3 | 6.7 | 9.3 | 30.8 | Nombre de personnes occupées |
| Per person engaged: Energy consumed | 18.38 | 23.56 | 17.13 | 7.36 | 2.45 | 0.57 | 1.96 | 20.00 | 1.21 | 15.82 | 20.81 | 123.34 | 1.56 | Par personne occupée: Energie consommée |
| Electricity consumed | 10.5 | 9.4 | 4.8 | 3.9 | 3.7 | 0.6 | 3.5 | 27.3 | 0.7 | 22.2 | 10.6 | 46.5 | 2.6 | Electricité consommée |

[1] Excludes Sawmills (ISIC group 251) and Printing and publishing (ISIC major group 28) except for bookbinding. Includes selected constructions activities in Wood products and furniture (ISIC major group 25-26) and Metal products (ISIC major group 35-38).
[2] Iron ore mining (ISIC major group 12) is included in Basic metals (ISIC major group 34).
[3] Refining of crude petroleum ISIC group 321 is included in Crude petroleum and natural gas (ISIC major group 13).
[4] Manufacture of wooden boats (in ISIC group 381) and some Miscellaneous manufacturing (ISIC major group 39) are included in Wood products and furniture (ISIC major groups 25-26).
[5] Includes bookbinding (in ISIC major group 28).
[6] Includes Sand and stone quarrying (ISIC major group 14).

[1] Non compris les Scieries (CITI 251), ni l'Imprimerie et édition (CITI 28) à l'exceptions des industries de la reliure. Y compris certaines activités de construction d'Ouvrages en bois et de meubles (CITI 25-26) et d'Ouvrages en métaux (CITI 35-38).
[2] L'Extraction des minerais métalliques (CITI 12), est comprise dans les Industries métallurgiques de base (CITI 34).
[3] Le Raffinage du pétrole brut (CITI 321) est compris dans Pétrole brut et gaz naturel (CITI 13).
[4] La construction d'embarcations en bois (dans CITI 381) et quelques Industries manufacturières diverses (CITI 39) sont comprises dans les Industries des Ouvrages en bois et du meuble (CITI 25-26).
[5] Y compris les Industries de la reliure (dans CITI 28).
[6] Y compris l'Extraction de la pierre à bâtir et du sable (CITI 14).

## 6. FUELS AND ELECTRICITY CONSUMED BY MINING AND MANUFACTURING ESTABLISHMENTS WITH SIX OR MORE PERSONS ENGAGED

### CONSOMMATION DE COMBUSTIBLES ET D'ELECTRICITE PAR LES ETABLISSEMENTS MINIERS ET MANUFACTURIERS OCCUPANT SIX PERSONNES OU PLUS

### 1954, 1958

Quantities in thousand metric tons of coal equivalents          Quantités en milliers de tonnes métriques d'équivalent charbon

### A.  Percentage Distribution of Energy Consumed According to Source
### Distribution, en pourcentage, de l'énergie consommée suivant la source

| Year and item of data | Mining and manufacturing [1] / Industries extractives et manufacturières [1] | Coal and metal mining [2] / Extraction de charbon et de minerais métalliques [2] | Crude petroleum and natural gas [3] / Pétrole brut et gaz naturel [3] | Food, beverages and tobacco / Industries alimentaires, boissons, tabac | Textiles | Clothing, footwear and made-up textiles / Articles d'habillement, chaussures et ouvrages en tissu | Wood products and furniture [1,4] / Bois et meubles [1,4] | Paper and paper products [5] / Papier et ouvrages en papier [5] | Leather and leather products except wearing apparel / Cuir et articles en cuir, à l'exclusion des articles d'habillement | Chemicals and chemical, coal and rubber products [3] / Produits chimiques, dérivés du charbon et ouvrages en caoutchouc [3] | Non-metallic mineral products [6] / Produits minéraux non métalliques [6] | Basic metals [2] / Métallurgie de base [2] | Metal products [1,4] / Ouvrages en métaux [1,4] | Année et rubrique |
|---|---|---|---|---|---|---|---|---|---|---|---|---|---|---|
| ISIC | 1–3 | 11-12, 19 | 13 | 20–22 | 23 | 24 | 25–26 | 27 | 29 | 30–32 | 33, 14 | 34 | 35–39 | CITI |
| **1954** | | | | | | | | | | | | | | **1954** |
| Total energy consumed: | | | | | | | | | | | | | | Energie totale consommée: |
| Quantity | 8 687.5 | 646.8 | 39.0 | 320.6 | 140.7 | 14.5 | 35.8 | 569.3 | 17.8 | 488.5 | 720.6 | 5 494.5 | 199.4 | Quantité |
| Percent of total in specified industry | 100.0 | 7.4 | 0.4 | 3.7 | 1.7 | 0.1 | 0.4 | 6.6 | 0.2 | 5.6 | 8.3 | 63.3 | 2.3 | Pourcentage du total par industrie indiquée |
| Percent consumed as: | | | | | | | | | | | | | | Pourcentage consommé en: |
| Coal | 26.9 | 8.2 | 0.9 | 13.8 | 39.5 | 21.3 | 7.2 | 10.6 | 12.0 | 6.0 | 28.4 | 33.8 | 11.2 | Charbon |
| Lignite | 21.7 | 83.1 | — | 27.0 | 24.6 | 11.4 | 36.1 | 66.1 | 77.1 | 27.0 | 40.0 | 6.2 | 31.8 | Lignite |
| Coke | 15.2 | 0.8 | — | 3.1 | 3.2 | 13.1 | 2.6 | 0.2 | 1.1 | 4.3 | 11.8 | 21.1 | 13.3 | Coke |
| Refined oil fuels [7] | 9.8 | 4.7 | 69.4 | 49.7 | 22.6 | 43.2 | 38.5 | 18.1 | 5.0 | 17.9 | 15.6 | 4.5 | 16.7 | Pétrole raffiné [7] |
| Gas | 22.0 | — | 26.8 | 2.2 | 0.3 | 2.8 | — | 0.1 | — | 31.3 | 0.5 | 31.3 | 11.1 | Gaz |
| Electricity | 4.4 | 3.2 | 2.9 | 4.2 | 9.8 | 8.2 | 15.6 | 4.9 | 4.4 | 13.5 | 3.7 | 3.1 | 15.9 | Electricité |
| **1958** | | | | | | | | | | | | | | **1958** |
| Total energy consumed: | | | | | | | | | | | | | | Energie totale consommée: |
| Quantity | 10 549.2 | 791.7 | 212.4 | 379.2 | 177.5 | 14.6 | 42.7 | 586.0 | 21.0 | 664.5 | 797.0 | 6 586.4 | 276.2 | Quantité |
| Percent of total in specified industry | 100.0 | 7.5 | 2.0 | 3.6 | 1.6 | 0.2 | 0.4 | 5.5 | 0.2 | 6.3 | 7.6 | 62.4 | 2.7 | Pourcentage du total par industrie indiquée |
| Percent consumed as: | | | | | | | | | | | | | | Pourcentage consommé en: |
| Coal | 24.2 | 8.8 | — | 10.0 | 40.2 | 13.0 | 3.5 | 5.8 | 6.7 | 3.7 | 27.8 | 31.2 | 11.0 | Charbon |
| Lignite | 18.9 | 77.6 | — | 22.1 | 20.3 | 13.4 | 31.6 | 65.7 | 75.1 | 27.6 | 35.2 | 4.8 | 23.4 | Lignite |
| Coke | 15.6 | 0.6 | — | 2.9 | 2.5 | 13.4 | 2.0 | 0.2 | 1.4 | 3.7 | 14.5 | 22.2 | 8.5 | Coke |
| Refined oil fuels [7] | 12.7 | 9.0 | 71.9 | 52.8 | 25.5 | 40.4 | 43.2 | 22.5 | 12.3 | 19.8 | 12.8 | 6.1 | 28.4 | Pétrole raffiné [7] |
| Gas? | 23.7 | — | 24.9 | 7.4 | 1.9 | 6.9 | — | 0.1 | 0.1 | 31.8 | 5.0 | 32.2 | 11.0 | Gaz |
| Purchased electricity | 4.9 | 4.0 | 3.2 | 4.8 | 9.6 | 12.9 | 19.7 | 5.7 | 4.4 | 13.4 | 4.7 | 3.5 | 17.7 | Electricité achetée |

For notes see end of table.                                        Pour les notes, voir au bas du tableau.

## B.   Quantity of Various Fuels and Electricity Consumed
## Quantités des différents combustibles et d'électricité consommés

Coal, lignite, coke and refined fuel oils in thousand metric tons; natural and manufactured gas in million cubic metres; electricity in million KWH.

Charbon, lignite, coke et fuel-oil raffiné en milliers de tonnes métriques; gaz naturel et gaz manufacturé en millions de mètres cubes; électricité en millions de kWh.

| Year and source of energy | Mining and manufacturing [1] — Industries extractives et manufacturières [1] | Coal and metal mining [2] — Extraction de charbon et de minerais métalliques [2] | Crude petroleum and natural gas [3] — Pétrole brut et gaz naturel [3] | Food, beverages and tobacco — Industries alimentaires, boissons, tabac | Textiles | Clothing, footwear and made-up textiles — Articles d'habillement, chaussures et ouvrages en tissu | Wood products and furniture [1,4] — Bois et meubles [1,4] | Paper and paper products [5] — Papier et ouvrages en papier [5] | Leather and leather products except wearing apparel — Cuir et articles en cuir, à l'exclusion des articles d'habillement | Chemicals and chemical, coal and rubber products [3] — Produits chimiques, dérivés du charbon et ouvrages en caoutchouc [3] | Non-metallic mineral products [6] — Produits minéraux non métalliques [6] | Basic metals [2] — Métallurgie de base [2] | Metal products [1,4] — Ouvrages en métaux [1,4] | Année et source d'énergie |
|---|---|---|---|---|---|---|---|---|---|---|---|---|---|---|
| ISIC | 1–3 | 11-12, 19 | 13 | 20–22 | 23 | 24 | 25–26 | 27 | 29 | 30–32 | 33, 14 | 34 | 35–39 | CITI |
| **1954** | | | | | | | | | | | | | | **1954** |
| Coal | 2 339.7 | 53.3 | 0.4 | 44.5 | 55.7 | 3.1 | 2.6 | 60.6 | 2.1 | 29.3 | 204.9 | 1 860.8 | 22.4 | Charbon |
| Lignite | 3 776.9 | 1 075.3 | — | 172.7 | 69.2 | 3.3 | 25.9 | 752.5 | 27.4 | 264.0 | 576.7 | 682.9 | 127.0 | Lignite |
| Coke | 1 461.5 | 5.4 | — | 11.1 | 5.0 | 2.1 | 1.0 | 1.5 | 0.3 | 23.7 | 94.3 | 1 287.6 | 29.5 | Coke |
| Refined oil fuels [7] | 569.3 | 20.4 | 18.0 | 106.3 | 21.2 | 4.2 | 9.2 | 68.8 | 0.6 | 58.3 | 74.8 | 165.3 | 22.2 | Pétrole raffiné [7] |
| Natural and manufactured gas | 3 187.3 | — | 17.5 | 11.8 | 0.6 | 0.7 | — | 0.4 | — | 254.5 | 5.9 | 2 859.0 | 36.9 | Gaz naturel et gaz manufacturé |
| Electricity: Purchased | 3 020.4 | 163.2 | 8.8 | 105.7 | 109.9 | 9.4 | 44.5 | 221.4 | 6.2 | 525.6 | 212.8 | 1 360.3 | 252.6 | Electricité: Achetée |
| Produced for own use | 1 591.5 | 47.5 | 0.2 | 40.9 | 115.3 | 0.3 | 7.1 | 437.8 | 4.7 | 182.0 | 112.1 | 580.2 | 63.4 | Produite pour l'auto-consommation |
| **1958** | | | | | | | | | | | | | | **1958** |
| Coal | 2 555.5 | 70.1 | — | 38.0 | 71.5 | 1.9 | 1.5 | 34.2 | 1.4 | 25.0 | 221.8 | 2 059.6 | 30.5 | Charbon |
| Lignite | 3 985.9 | 1 228.1 | — | 167.7 | 71.9 | 3.9 | 27.0 | 769.9 | 31.6 | 366.5 | 560.8 | 629.5 | 129.0 | Lignite |
| Coke | 1 837.4 | 5.2 | — | 12.3 | 4.9 | 2.2 | 0.9 | 1.4 | 0.3 | 27.5 | 128.8 | 1 627.8 | 26.1 | Coke |
| Refined oil fuels [7] | 891.7 | 47.7 | 101.9 | 133.6 | 30.2 | 3.9 | 12.3 | 87.8 | 1.7 | 87.5 | 68.3 | 264.3 | 52.5 | Pétrole raffiné [7] |
| Natural and manufactured gas | 4 155.0 | — | 88.1 | 46.8 | 5.6 | 1.7 | — | 0.8 | — | 352.6 | 65.6 | 3 543.2 | 50.6 | Gaz naturel et gaz manufacturé |
| Electricity: Purchased | 4 132.3 | 249.7 | 54.1 | 143.2 | 135.6 | 15.1 | 67.0 | 267.8 | 7.4 | 709.3 | 297.5 | 1 796.2 | 389.4 | Electricité: Achetée |
| Produced for own use | 1 909.3 | 65.7 | 5.0 | 55.9 | 135.1 | 0.6 | 8.9 | 532.9 | 4.3 | 224.5 | 109.3 | 688.4 | 78.7 | Produite pour l'auto-consommation |

[1] Excludes Sawmills (ISIC group 251) and Printing and publishing (ISIC major group 28) except for bookbinding. Includes selected construction activities in Wood products and furniture (ISIC major group 25-26) and Metal products (ISIC major group 35-38).
[2] Iron ore mining (ISIC major group 12) is included in Basic metals (ISIC major group 34).
[3] Refining of crude petroleum (ISIC group 321) is included in Crude petroleum and natural gas (ISIC major group 13).
[4] Manufacture of wooden boats (in ISIC group 381) and some Miscellaneous manufacturing (ISIC major group 39) are included in Wood products and furniture (ISIC major group 25-26).
[5] Includes bookbinding (in ISIC major group 28).
[6] Includes Sand and stone quarrying (ISIC major group 14).
[7] Covers light and heavy fuels oils; excludes gasoline.

[1] Non compris les Scieries (CITI 251) ni l'Imprimerie et édition (CITI 28), à l'exception des industries de la reliure. Y compris certaines activités de construction d'Ouvrages en bois et de meubles (CITI 25-26) et d'Ouvrages en métaux (CITI 35-38).
[2] L'Extraction des minerais métalliques (CITI 12) est comprise dans les Industries métallurgiques de base (CITI 34).
[3] La Raffinage du pétrole brut (CITI 321) est compris dans Pétrole brut et gaz naturel (CITI 13).
[4] La construction d'embarcations en bois (dans CITI 381) et quelques Industries manufacturières diverses (CITI 39) sont comprises dans les industries des Ouvrages en bois et du meuble (CITI 25-26).
[5] Y compris les industries des reliure (dans CITI 28).
[6] Y compris l'Extraction de la pierre à bâtir et du sable (CITI 14).
[7] Y compris les fuel-oils légers et lourds; non compris la gazoline.

# BARBADOS — BARBADE

## The Gross Domestic Product

Estimates of expenditure on and the industrial origin of the gross domestic product are presented in Table 1. The figures are derived from data supplied by the Barbados Statistical Service, Garrison, St. Michael, in response to the United Nations national accounts questionnaires. The official estimates and descriptions of sources and methods are published by the Statistical Service in *The National Income of Barbados, 1956-1959*.

## Characteristics and Structure of Industrial Activity

The data presented in Table 2 are derived from a survey of manufacturing establishments for 1958, published by the Statistical Service in a *Report on a Survey of Secondary Manufacturing Establishments, 1957-1958*. The survey covered only those establishments employing 5 or more persons. Out of 102 questionnaires sent out, 68 establishments completed returns. Sugar milling, the largest single industry in Barbados, was excluded from the inquiry together with the manufacturing activity of all Government Departments.

Definitions of items of data correspond to the International Standards in Basic Industrial Statistics. Value added is at market prices and the number of employees is the average of persons employed as at the 15th February, 30th April, 15th August, 30th September and 15th December.

## Le produit intérieur brut

Les estimations des dépenses imputées au produit intérieur brut, et des composantes du produit intérieur brut, ventilées suivant le secteur d'activité industrielle, sont reproduites au tableau 1. Les chiffres ont été tirés des données fournies par le Service de Statistique de la Barbade, Garrison, St. Michael, en réponse au questionnaire de l'O.N.U. relatif aux comptes nationaux. Les estimations officielles et les détails concernant les sources et méthodes adoptées ont été publiés par le Service de Statistique dans *National Income of Barbados, 1956-1959*.

## Caractéristiques et structure de l'activité industrielle

Les données exposées au tableau 2 sont tirées d'une enquête auprès des établissements manufacturiers pour 1958, publiées par le Service de Statistique dans *Report on a Survey of Secondary Manufacturing Establishments, 1957-1958*. L'enquête couvrait seulement les établissements occupant 5 personnes ou plus. Sur 102 questionnaires envoyés, 68 établissements ont renvoyé le questionnaire rempli. Le broyage de sucre, industrie la plus importante de la Barbade, était exclu du champ de l'enquête ainsi que les activités manufacturières de tous les départements gouvernementaux.

Les définitions des rubriques sont conformes aux Normes internationales relatives aux statistiques industrielles de base. La valeur ajoutée est calculée aux prix du marché et le nombre de salariés correspond au nombre moyen de personnes occupées au 15 février, 30 avril, 15 août, 30 septembre et 15 décembre.

# 1. THE GROSS DOMESTIC PRODUCT — PRODUIT INTERIEUR BRUT

Million B.W.I. dollars　　　　　　　　　　　　　　　　　　Millions de dollars des Antilles britanniques

## A. Expenditure on the Gross Domestic Product at Market Prices
## Dépenses relatives au produit intérieur brut aux prix du marché

| Item of data and year<br>Rubrique et année | Total | Consumption<br>Consommation | | Gross Domestic Capital Formation<br>Formation brute de capital intérieur | | Net exports of goods and services<br>Exportations nettes de biens et de services | |
| --- | --- | --- | --- | --- | --- | --- | --- |
| | | Total | Government<br>Etat | Total | Fixed<br>Fixe | Exports less imports<br>Exportations moins importations | Exports<br>Exportations |
| a. At Current Prices — Aux prix courants | | | | | | | |
| **Absolute figures — Chiffres absolus** | | | | | | | |
| 1948 | 43.7 | 44.3 | 4.3 | 11.2 | 9.8 | −11.8 | 19.7 |
| 1950 | 60.5 | 55.1 | 5.9 | 11.8 | 12.6 | −6.4 | 33.5 |
| 1951 | 70.4 | 61.2 | 6.5 | 20.3 | 15.3 | −11.1 | 42.0 |
| 1952 | 73.1 | 63.5 | 7.4 | 18.3 | 14.3 | −8.7 | 46.8 |
| 1953 | 78.7 | 65.7 | 8.4 | 13.1 | 15.8 | −0.1 | 46.7 |
| 1954 | 80.9 | 67.2 | 8.0 | 19.0 | 19.2 | −5.3 | 46.5 |
| 1955 | 84.4 | 73.9 | 8.9 | 22.2 | 21.3 | −11.7 | 47.2 |
| 1956 | 93.5 | 86.0 | 9.6 | 26.0 | 25.6 | −18.5 | 46.0 |
| 1957 | 113.6 | 93.2 | 10.3 | 31.6 | 29.1 | −11.2 | 60.8 |
| 1958 | 109.0 | 96.0 | 10.9 | 38.1 | 33.1 | −25.1 | 52.6 |
| 1959 | 115.4 | 100.4 | 11.8 | 33.5 | 32.3 | −18.5 | 60.6 |
| 1960 | ... | ... | ... | ... | ... | −33.6 | 55.7 |
| **Percentage distribution of average annual expenditure — Distribution en pourcentage des dépenses annuelles moyennes** | | | | | | | |
| 1948 | 100.0 | 101.4 | 9.8 | 25.6 | 22.4 | −27.0 | 45.1 |
| 1950−1959 | 100.0 | 88.4 | 10.1 | 25.8 | 25.5 | −14.2 | 53.5 |
| 1950 | 100.0 | 91.1 | 9.8 | 19.5 | 20.8 | −10.6 | 55.4 |
| 1953 | 100.0 | 83.5 | 10.7 | 16.6 | 20.1 | −0.1 | 59.3 |
| 1954 | 100.0 | 83.1 | 9.9 | 23.5 | 23.7 | −6.6 | 57.5 |
| 1958 | 100.0 | 88.1 | 10.0 | 34.9 | 30.4 | −23.0 | 48.3 |

## B. The Gross Domestic Product at Factor Cost According to Origin
## Origine par secteur d'activité du produit intérieur brut au coût des facteurs

| Item of data and year<br>Rubrique et année | Total | Agricultural sector<br>Secteur agricole | Mining<br>Industries extractives | Manufacturing<br>Industries manufacturières | Construction<br>Bâtiment et travaux publics | Transportation and communication<br>Transports et communications | Other sectors [1]<br>Autres secteurs [1] |
| --- | --- | --- | --- | --- | --- | --- | --- |
| ISIC — CITI | 0–9 | 0 | 1 | 2–3 | 4 | 7 | 5–6, 8–9 |
| a. At Current Prices — Aux prix courants | | | | | | | |
| **Absolute figures — Chiffres absolus** | | | | | | | |
| 1955 | 74.9 | 25.9 | 0.5 | 12.7 | 5.4 | 4.6 | 25.8 |
| 1956 | 83.4 | 25.0 | 0.5 | 13.0 | 5.6 | 5.7 | 33.6 |
| 1957 | 102.3 | 35.3 | 0.5 | 16.1 | 6.7 | 6.0 | 37.8 |
| 1958 | 97.1 | 28.0 | 0.5 | 15.6 | 6.9 | 6.0 | 40.1 |
| 1959 | 102.4 | 32.0 | 0.5 | 16.5 | 7.0 | 6.0 | 40.4 |
| **Percentage distribution according to sector— Distribution en pourcentage par secteur** | | | | | | | |
| 1955 | 100.0 | 34.6 | 0.7 | 17.0 | 7.2 | 6.1 | 34.4 |
| 1958 | 100.0 | 28.8 | 0.5 | 16.1 | 7.1 | 6.2 | 41.3 |

[1] Includes Electricity, gas and water.　　　　　　　　　　[1] Y compris Electricité, gaz et eau.

## 2. CHARACTERISTICS OF MANUFACTURING ESTABLISHMENTS WITH 5 OR MORE EMPLOYEES
## CARACTERISTIQUES DES ETABLISSEMENTS MANUFACTURIERS COMPTANT 5 SALARIES OU PLUS
### 1958

Number of establishments in units; value added and wages and salaries in million B.W.I. Dollars; number of employees in thousands; value added per employee and wages and salaries per employee in thousand B.W.I. Dollars

Nombre d'établissements en unités; valeur ajoutée et traitements et salaires en millions de dollars des Antilles britanniques; nombre de salariés en milliers; valeur ajoutée par salarié et traitements et salaires par salarié en milliers de dollars des Antilles britanniques

| Item of data | Manu-facturing [1] Industries manufac-turières [1] | Food, beverages and tobacco [1] Industries alimen-taires, boissons, tabac [1] | Clothing, footwear, made-up textiles, leather and leather products Articles d'habil-lement, chaus-sures, ouvrages en tissu, cuir et articles en cuir | Wood products and furniture Bois et meubles | Printing and publish-ing Im-primerie et édition | Non-metallic mineral products Produits minéraux non métal-liques | Metal products Ouvrages en métaux | Other manu-factur-ing Autres in-dustries manufac-turières | Rubrique |
|---|---|---|---|---|---|---|---|---|---|
| ISIC | 2–3 | 20–22 | 24, 29 | 25–26 | 28 | 33 | 35–38 | 39 | CITI |
| *a. Absolute Figures — Chiffres absolus* | | | | | | | | | |
| Number of establishments. | 68 | 24 | 9 | 5 | 5 | 3 | 14 | 8 | Nombre d'établissements |
| Value added.......... | 8.1 | 4.9 | 0.5 | 0.1 | 0.8 | 0.1 | 0.7 | 1.0 | Valeur ajoutée |
| Employees: | | | | | | | | | Salariés: |
| Number (Average during the year)...... | 3.2 | 1.1 | 0.3 | 0.1 | 0.4 | 0.1 | 0.8 | 0.4 | Nombre (moyenne pendant l'année) |
| Wages and salaries... | 3.7 | 1.2 | 0.3 | 0.1 | 0.7 | 0.1 | 0.8 | 0.5 | Traitements et salaires |
| *b. Structure* | | | | | | | | | |
| Distribution in percent of: | | | | | | | | | Distribution en pour-centage: |
| Value added........ | 100 | 60.4 | 6.2 | 1.3 | 9.8 | 1.3 | 8.6 | 12.4 | Valeur ajoutée |
| Number of employees. | 100 | 34.3 | 9.4 | 3.1 | 12.5 | 3.2 | 25.0 | 12.5 | Nombre de salariés |
| Per employee: | | | | | | | | | Par salarié: |
| Value added........ | 2.5 | 4.4 | 1.7 | 1.0 | 2.0 | 1.0 | 0.9 | 2.5 | Valeur ajoutée |
| Wages and salaries... | 1.2 | 1.1 | 1.0 | 1.0 | 1.8 | 1.0 | 1.0 | 1.2 | Traitements et salaires |
| Value added per unit of wages and salaries............. | 2.19 | 4.08 | 1.67 | 1.00 | 1.14 | 1.00 | 0.88 | 2.00 | Valeur ajoutée par unité de traitements et salaires |

[1] Excludes sugar milling.

[1] Non compris le broyage du sucre.

# BELGIUM — BELGIQUE

## Gross Domestic Product

The estimates of expenditure on and origin of the gross domestic product, presented in Table 1, were contained in the reply by the Département d'Economie appliquée de l'Université libre de Bruxelles to the United Nations national accounts questionnaire. These estimates are published and described in *Les cahiers économiques de Bruxelles,* issued by that department.

## Index Numbers of Industrial Production

The index numbers of industrial production given in Table 2 are derived from indexes compiled by the Institut de Recherches Economiques et Sociales de l'Université Catholique de Louvain and published in the *Service Mensuel de Conjoncture* of the Institute.

The index numbers are base-weighted arithmetic averages, computed in successive stages. First, indexes are computed for groups of industrial activity from quantity relatives. The quantity relatives are generally based on quantities of individual commodities produced, though quantities of individual commodities shipped, man-hours worked or quantities of individual raw materials consumed are also utilized. Then, index numbers are compiled for successively wider classes of industrial activity, starting with the indexes for the Groups. The weights utilized at each stage of compilation are derived from contribution to gross domestic product at factor cost. The weights relate to 1936-1938 for the indexes for 1938 and 1948 and to 1953 for 1949 and subsequent years. Starting with 1953, the indexes are based on an expanded series of quantity relatives.

The indexes based on 1936-1938 are described in *Graphiques, Tableaux et Commentaires,* November 1948 and *Statistiques Rétrospectives,* March 1952 of *Service Mensuel de Conjoncture.* The indexes based on 1953 are described in *Statistiques Rétrospectives,* March 1956 of the same series of publications.

## Index Numbers of Industrial Employment

The index numbers of industrial employment given in Table 3 are derived from indexes of employment published by the Institut National de Statistique, Ministère des Affaires Economiques, in its *Bulletin de Statistique.*

The indexes are compiled by the Ministère du Travail from the results of a monthly enquiry into establishments carried out by the Institut National de Statistique. The indexes relate to all employees and are computed as base weighted arithmetic averages. The weights relate to the number of employees during 1953 in the case of the indexes for 1956 and 1957, and the number of employees during 1958 in the case of the indexes for 1958 and sub-

## Produit intérieur brut

Le tableau 1 fournit les estimations des dépenses imputées au produit national brut et des composantes du produit national brut, ventilées suivant le secteur d'activité. Ces estimations sont contenues dans la réponse du Département d'Economie appliquée de l'Université libre de Bruxelles, au questionnaire de l'O.N.U. relatif aux comptes nationaux. Elles sont également publiées et définies dans *Les cahiers économiques de Bruxelles* par les soins de ce même département.

## Indices de la production industrielle

Les indices de la production industrielle, reproduits au tableau 2, proviennent d'indices calculés par l'Institut de Recherches Economiques et Sociales de l'Université Catholique de Louvain et publiés dans le *Service Mensuel de Conjoncture* de cet Institut.

Ces indices sont des moyennes arithmétiques à coefficients de pondération fixes, calculés en plusieurs étapes. Au premier stade, les indices sont calculés pour les groupes d'activités industrielles en utilisant les rapports de volumes. Les rapports de volumes portent généralement sur le volume de la production de chaque marchandise ou parfois sur le volume des expéditions de chaque marchandise, le nombre d'heures de travail effectuées ou le volume de la consommation de chaque matière première. Ensuite, partant des indices de groupes, on calcule successivement les indices pour des classes plus larges de l'activité industrielle. Le système de pondération utilisé est fondé sur la contribution au produit intérieur brut au coût des facteurs, en 1936-1938 pour les indices de 1938 et de 1948, et en 1953 pour les années ultérieures. A partir de 1953 les indices sont basés sur des séries plus développées de rapports de volumes.

Les indices pour lesquels la période de base est 1936-1938 sont décrits dans *Graphiques, Tableaux et Commentaires,* novembre 1948 et *Statistiques Rétrospectives,* mars 1952, du *Service Mensuel de Conjoncture.* Les indices de base de 1953 sont décrits dans *Statistiques Rétrospectives,* mars 1956 de la même série de publications.

## Indices de l'emploi industriel

Les indices de l'emploi industriel reproduits dans le tableau 3 ont pour source les indices de l'emploi, publiés par l'Institut National de Statistique, Ministère des Affaires Economiques, dans son *Bulletin de Statistique.*

Les indices sont élaborés par le Ministère du Travail à partir des résultats d'enquêtes mensuelles exécutées par l'Institut National de Statistique auprès des établissements. Ces indices sont relatifs à tous les salariés. Ce sont des moyennes arithmétiques à coefficients de pondération fixes. Les coefficients de pondération sont fondés sur le nombre de salariés durant 1953 pour les indices de 1956 et 1957, le nombre de salariés durant 1958 pour les indi-

sequent years. The weights were derived from social security records.

Index numbers of employment have also been compiled by the Ministère du Travail and published by the Institut National de Statistique for the period, 1953-1956. This series of index numbers relates to wage-earners only.

### The Characteristics and Structure of Industrial Activity

The data shown in Table 4 are based on the results of decennial census covering all establishments in business at least four days prior to the date of the census. The data were compiled from *Recensement Economique et Social au 27 février 1937*, Vol. II, Office Central de Statistique, Bruxelles, 1937 and *Recensement Général de la Population, de l'Industrie et du Commerce au 31 décembre 1947*, Vols. X and XI, Institut National de Statistique, Ministère des Affaires Economiques, Bruxelles, 1952 and 1953, respectively.

The number of establishments is a count of the units which were in business for at least four days prior to the date of the census. Units under the same ownership which engaged in different kinds of activity or were located at different sites were, in general, considered to be separate establishments. However, in the case of construction, distinctions were not drawn according to location, while in the case of mining, underground and surface activities at the same site were treated as separate establishments.

The data for 1955 and 1958 shown in Tables 5 and 6 were compiled from various issues, from 1956 to 1961, of the monthly publication, *Bulletin de Statistique*, referred to above and *Annuaire Statistique de la Belgique et du Congo Belge, 1959*, Institut National de Statistique.

In general, the data relate to establishments with 5 or more operatives (wage-earners) in relatively important manufacturing industries. However, a lower limit of 10 operatives was utilized in the case of some classes of manufacturing—for example, weaving and the making of footwear in 1955 and 1958 and tanneries and the extracting and refining of animal and vegetable oils in 1958; and establishments engaged in refining non-ferrous metals were included in the enquiry for 1958 only if they employed 20 or more operatives. Further, the field covered in the data for 1955 and 1958 is not the same because some classes of manufacturing included in the 1958 enquiry were omitted from the 1955 enquiry.

The definitions for the items of data shown in Table 5 are similar to those in the International Standards in Basic Industrial Statistics except that homeworkers are included in the data on employees and operatives. Value added is at factor cost. The figures shown in Table 6 relate to purchased fuels consumed and to purchased electricity. The former kinds of commodities are included whether utilized as sources of heat or power or as raw materials.

ces de 1958 et les années ultérieures. Les coefficients de pondération proviennent de documents fournis par la sécurité sociale.

Les indices de l'emploi ont été également calculés par le Ministère du Travail et publiés par l'Institut National de Statistique pour la période 1953-1956. Ces indices sont relatifs aux ouvriers seulement.

### Caractéristiques et structures de l'activité industrielle

Les chiffres que fournit le tableau 4 proviennent d'une analyse des résultats de recensements décennaux portant sur tous les établissements qui exerçaient une activité industrielle ou commerçante depuis quatre jours au moins à la date du recensement. Les données ont été tirées du *Recensement Economique et Social au 27 février 1937*, Vol. II, Office Central de Statistique, Bruxelles, 1937 et du *Recensement Général de la Population, de l'Industrie et du Commerce au 31 décembre 1947*, Vols. X et XI, Institut National de Statistique, Ministère des Affaires Economiques, Bruxelles, 1952 et 1953, respectivement.

Le nombre d'établissements est celui des unités qui étaient en activité depuis quatre jours au moins à la date du recensement. Les unités ayant le même propriétaire et exerçant différents types d'activité ou implantées dans des endroits différents ont été en général considérées comme autant d'établissements. Toutefois, dans le cas du bâtiment et des travaux publics, il n'a pas été fait de distinction en fonction de l'emplacement et, dans le cas des industries extractives, les travaux de fond et les travaux à ciel ouvert, au même puits, ont été considérés comme relevant d'établissements distincts.

Les données pour 1955 et 1958 reproduites aux tableaux 5 et 6, proviennent de publications variées, celles de 1956 à 1961, sont issues de la publication mensuelle: *Bulletin de Statistique*, à laquelle on s'est référé ci-dessus et de l'*Annuaire Statistique de la Belgique et du Congo Belge, 1959*, Institut National de Statistique.

En général, les données sont relatives aux établissements employant 5 ouvriers ou plus parmi les industries manufacturières relativement importantes. Cependant, le seuil plus bas de 10 ouvriers a été adopté pour certaines classes d'industries manufacturières, par exemple, le tissage et la fabrication de chaussures en 1955 et 1958, les tanneries et l'extraction et raffinage d'huiles animales et végétales en 1958; il n'était tenu compte des établissements de raffinage des métaux non ferreux que s'ils employaient au moins 20 ouvriers, dans l'enquête de 1958. De plus, le champ couvert par les données pour les années 1955 et 1958 n'est pas le même, vu que certaines classes des industries manufacturières comprises dans l'enquête de 1958 étaient exclues de l'enquête de 1955.

Les définitions des rubriques reproduites au tableau 5 sont conformes aux normes internationales relatives aux statistiques industrielles de base, si ce n'est que les travailleurs à domicile sont compris parmi les salariés et les ouvriers. La valeur ajoutée est calculée au coût des facteurs. Les chiffres du tableau 6 sont relatifs aux combustibles achetés et consommés et à l'électricité achetée. Les combustibles sont compris dans le coût, qu'ils soient utilisés comme sources de chaleur, d'énergie ou comme matière première.

# 1. THE GROSS DOMESTIC PRODUCT
# LE PRODUIT INTERIEUR BRUT

Thousand Million Francs          Milliards de Francs

## A. Expenditure on the Gross Domestic Product at Market Prices —
## Dépenses relatives au produit intérieur brut aux prix du marché

| Item of data and year / Rubrique et année | Total | Consumption / Consommation | | Gross Domestic Capital Formation / Formation brute de capital intérieur | | Net exports of goods and services / Exportations nettes de biens et de services | |
|---|---|---|---|---|---|---|---|
| | | Total | Government / Etat | Total | Fixed / Fixe | Exports less imports / Exportations moins importations | Exports / Exportations |
| **a. At Current Prices — Aux prix courants** | | | | | | | |
| **Absolute figures — Chiffres absolus** | | | | | | | |
| 1948 | 331.1 | 287.8 | 29.6 | 55.9 | 51.3 | −12.6 | 78.0 |
| 1950 | 358.6 | 313.6 | 35.6 | 59.8 | 59.9 | −14.8 | 90.5 |
| 1951 | 413.6 | 343.6 | 44.2 | 63.8 | 57.8 | 6.2 | 139.1 |
| 1952 | 422.9 | 356.5 | 52.8 | 65.3 | 61.5 | 1.1 | 128.6 |
| 1953 | 431.4 | 366.9 | 54.9 | 66.8 | 65.0 | −2.3 | 122.8 |
| 1954 | 453.1 | 384.2 | 55.8 | 75.3 | 72.3 | −6.4 | 129.0 |
| 1955 | 476.1 | 397.2 | 53.2 | 74.3 | 74.7 | 4.6 | 153.5 |
| 1956 | 511.8 | 417.2 | 55.6 | 90.4 | 86.4 | 4.2 | 177.1 |
| 1957 | 545.4 | 442.3 | 58.2 | 101.9 | 95.2 | 1.2 | 183.8 |
| 1958 | 542.1 | 440.0 | 62.8 | 90.4 | 89.6 | 11.7 | 179.5 |
| 1959 | 564.7 | 468.0 | 67.0 | 97.2 | 98.5 | −0.5 | 183.8 |
| 1960 | 598.1 | 489.7 | 72.3 | 110.2 | 106.5 | −1.8 | 208.3 |
| **Percentage distribution of average annual expenditure — Distribution en pourcentage des dépenses annuelles moyennes** | | | | | | | |
| 1948 | 100.0 | 86.9 | 8.9 | 16.9 | 15.5 | −3.8 | 23.6 |
| 1950–1960 | 100.0 | 83.1 | 11.5 | 16.8 | 16.3 | 0.1 | 31.9 |
| 1950 | 100.0 | 87.4 | 9.9 | 16.7 | 16.7 | −4.1 | 25.2 |
| 1953 | 100.0 | 85.0 | 12.7 | 15.5 | 15.1 | −0.5 | 28.5 |
| 1954 | 100.0 | 84.8 | 12.3 | 16.6 | 16.0 | −1.4 | 28.5 |
| 1958 | 100.0 | 81.2 | 11.6 | 16.7 | 16.5 | 2.1 | 33.1 |
| 1960 | 100.0 | 81.9 | 12.1 | 18.4 | 17.8 | −0.3 | 34.8 |
| **b. At Prices of 1953 — Aux prix de 1953** | | | | | | | |
| **Absolute figures — Chiffres absolus** | | | | | | | |
| 1948 | 363.8 | 324.4 | 37.3 | 64.8 | 59.7 | −25.4 | 82.7 |
| 1950 | 394.6 | 345.8 | 40.7 | 69.5 | 69.8 | −20.7 | 100.5 |
| 1951 | 417.8 | 356.2 | 47.5 | 67.7 | 62.2 | −6.1 | 116.5 |
| 1952 | 414.4 | 360.9 | 52.8 | 64.8 | 61.2 | −11.3 | 109.4 |
| 1953 | 431.4 | 366.9 | 54.9 | 66.8 | 65.0 | −2.3 | 122.8 |
| 1954 | 451.8 | 379.1 | 57.9 | 76.3 | 73.3 | −3.6 | 136.9 |
| 1955 | 465.9 | 389.8 | 51.7 | 72.4 | 72.8 | 3.7 | 158.1 |
| 1956 | 482.5 | 399.0 | 52.0 | 84.2 | 80.5 | −0.7 | 173.6 |
| 1957 | 493.8 | 408.7 | 51.8 | 88.9 | 82.8 | −3.8 | 175.0 |
| 1958 | 484.3 | 402.1 | 52.5 | 78.0 | 77.6 | 4.2 | 179.8 |
| 1959 | 502.9 | 423.7 | 55.2 | 84.5 | 85.2 | −5.3 | 192.9 |
| 1960 | 524.6 | 438.2 | 55.7 | 94.1 | 90.5 | −7.7 | 216.2 |
| **Percentage distribution of average annual expenditure — Distribution en pourcentage des dépenses annuelles moyennes** | | | | | | | |
| 1948 | 100.0 | 89.2 | 10.2 | 17.8 | 16.4 | −7.0 | 22.7 |
| 1950–1960 | 100.0 | 84.3 | 11.3 | 16.7 | 16.2 | −1.0 | 33.2 |
| 1950 | 100.0 | 87.6 | 10.3 | 17.6 | 17.7 | −5.2 | 25.5 |
| 1953 | 100.0 | 85.0 | 12.7 | 15.5 | 15.1 | −0.5 | 28.5 |
| 1954 | 100.0 | 83.9 | 12.8 | 16.9 | 16.2 | −0.8 | 30.3 |
| 1958 | 100.0 | 83.0 | 10.8 | 16.1 | 16.0 | 0.9 | 37.1 |
| 1960 | 100.0 | 83.5 | 10.6 | 18.0 | 17.2 | −1.5 | 41.2 |
| **Average annual rate of growth — Taux annuel moyen d'accroissement** | | | | | | | |
| 1948–1953 | 3.5 | 2.5 | 8.0 | 0.6 | 1.7 | . | 8.2 |
| 1950–1960 | 2.9 | 2.4 | 3.2 | 3.1 | 2.6 | . | 8.0 |
| 1950–1953 | 3.0 | 2.0 | 10.5 | −1.3 | −2.4 | . | 6.9 |
| 1954–1958 | 1.8 | 1.5 | −2.4 | 0.5 | 1.4 | . | 7.0 |
| 1958–1960 | 4.1 | 4.4 | 3.0 | 9.8 | 8.0 | . | 9.6 |

## B. The Gross Domestic Product at Factor Cost According to Origin
### Origine par secteur d'activité du produit intérieur brut au coût des facteurs

| Item of data and year / Rubrique et année | Total | Agricultural sector / Secteur agricole | Industrial Sector — Secteur industriel | | | | | Transportation and communication / Transport et communication | Other sectors / Autres secteurs |
|---|---|---|---|---|---|---|---|---|---|
| | | | Total | Mining [1] / Industries extractives [1] | Manufacturing / Industries manufacturières | Construction / Bâtiments et travaux publics | Electricity, [2] gas and water / Electricité, gaz et eau [2] | | |
| ISIC — CITI | 0–9 | 0 | 1–5 | 1 | 2–3 | 4 | 5 | 7 | 6, 8, 9 |
| *a. At Current Prices — Aux prix courants* | | | | | | | | | |
| **Absolute figures — Chiffres absolus** | | | | | | | | | |
| 1948 | 307.2 | 32.2 | 147.8 | 13.6 | 107.6 | 20.7 | 5.9 | 21.2 | 106.0 |
| 1950 | 334.4 | 30.6 | 160.7 | 17.1 | 110.6 | 25.7 | 7.3 | 24.4 | 118.7 |
| 1951 | 382.4 | 33.4 | 189.7 | 18.9 | 136.6 | 25.7 | 8.5 | 28.3 | 131.0 |
| 1952 | 387.0 | 33.6 | 187.7 | 20.2 | 132.6 | 25.7 | 9.2 | 29.5 | 136.2 |
| 1953 | 396.4 | 35.3 | 186.9 | 19.6 | 130.2 | 27.7 | 9.4 | 30.0 | 144.2 |
| 1954 | 417.4 | 35.6 | 199.0 | 18.9 | 139.5 | 29.6 | 11.0 | 30.5 | 152.3 |
| 1955 | 438.4 | 35.5 | 211.4 | 20.0 | 150.7 | 29.3 | 11.4 | 33.0 | 158.5 |
| 1956 | 470.9 | 34.3 | 233.9 | 20.8 | 167.8 | 32.4 | 12.9 | 36.6 | 166.1 |
| 1957 | 499.1 | 37.2 | 248.4 | 23.8 | 174.3 | 37.9 | 12.4 | 37.8 | 175.7 |
| 1958 | 494.7 | 36.3 | 238.4 | 21.7 | 168.3 | 36.0 | 12.4 | 38.3 | 181.7 |
| 1959 | 515.2 | 38.7 | 247.9 | 16.9 | 179.8 | 38.2 | 13.0 | 40.2 | 188.4 |
| 1960 | 548.3 | 37.4 | 269.3 | 16.2 | 197.6 | 40.9 | 14.6 | 42.9 | 198.7 |
| **Percentage distribution according to sector— Distribution en pourcentage par secteur** | | | | | | | | | |
| 1948 | 100.0 | 10.5 | 48.1 | 4.4 | 35.0 | 6.8 | 1.9 | 6.9 | 34.5 |
| 1950 – 1960 | 100.0 | 7.9 | 48.6 | 4.4 | 34.6 | 7.1 | 2.5 | 7.6 | 35.9 |
| 1950 | 100.0 | 9.1 | 48.1 | 5.1 | 33.1 | 7.7 | 2.2 | 7.3 | 35.5 |
| 1953 | 100.0 | 8.9 | 47.1 | 4.9 | 32.8 | 7.0 | 2.4 | 7.6 | 36.4 |
| 1954 | 100.0 | 8.5 | 47.7 | 4.5 | 33.4 | 7.1 | 2.7 | 7.3 | 36.5 |
| 1958 | 100.0 | 7.4 | 48.2 | 4.4 | 34.0 | 7.3 | 2.5 | 7.7 | 36.7 |
| 1960 | 100.0 | 6.8 | 49.1 | 2.9 | 36.0 | 7.5 | 2.7 | 7.8 | 36.3 |
| *b. At Prices of 1953 — Aux prix de 1953* | | | | | | | | | |
| **Absolute figures — Chiffres absolus** | | | | | | | | | |
| 1948 | 334.0 | 25.4 | 156.7 | 17.3 | 122.8 | 8.5 | 8.1 | 26.3 | 125.6 |
| 1950 | 365.8 | 32.1 | 174.6 | 17.7 | 139.5 | 8.7 | 8.7 | 26.2 | 132.9 |
| 1951 | 387.3 | 30.9 | 187.6 | 19.3 | 147.9 | 10.4 | 10.0 | 29.5 | 139.3 |
| 1952 | 387.2 | 32.4 | 184.1 | 19.8 | 145.6 | 9.0 | 9.7 | 29.7 | 141.0 |
| 1953 | 396.4 | 35.3 | 186.9 | 19.6 | 148.4 | 9.5 | 9.4 | 30.0 | 144.2 |
| 1954 | 413.6 | 35.7 | 199.6 | 19.1 | 160.4 | 10.1 | 10.0 | 30.7 | 147.6 |
| 1955 | 430.9 | 34.9 | 210.6 | 19.8 | 169.0 | 11.0 | 10.8 | 33.2 | 152.2 |
| 1956 | 451.2 | 36.9 | 222.7 | 19.8 | 179.4 | 11.7 | 11.8 | 36.0 | 155.6 |
| 1957 | 463.4 | 40.1 | 227.7 | 19.6 | 183.9 | 11.9 | 12.3 | 36.7 | 158.9 |
| 1958 | 458.7 | 39.0 | 221.3 | 17.5 | 179.8 | 11.2 | 12.8 | 37.2 | 161.2 |
| 1959 | 470.9 | 37.7 | 230.8 | 14.9 | 190.4 | 12.2 | 13.3 | 37.7 | 164.7 |
| 1960 | 492.5 | 37.7 | 245.8 | 15.1 | 203.0 | 13.3 | 14.4 | 40.4 | 168.6 |
| **Percentage distribution according to sector— Distribution en pourcentage par secteur** | | | | | | | | | |
| 1948 | 100.0 | 7.6 | 46.9 | 5.2 | 36.8 | 2.5 | 2.4 | 7.9 | 37.6 |
| 1950 – 1960 | 100.0 | 8.3 | 48.6 | 4.3 | 39.2 | 2.5 | 2.6 | 7.8 | 35.3 |
| 1950 | 100.0 | 8.8 | 47.7 | 4.8 | 38.1 | 2.4 | 2.4 | 7.2 | 36.3 |
| 1953 | 100.0 | 8.9 | 47.1 | 4.9 | 37.4 | 2.4 | 2.4 | 7.6 | 36.4 |
| 1954 | 100.0 | 8.6 | 48.3 | 4.6 | 38.8 | 2.5 | 2.4 | 7.4 | 35.7 |
| 1958 | 100.0 | 8.5 | 48.2 | 3.8 | 39.2 | 2.4 | 2.8 | 8.1 | 35.2 |
| 1960 | 100.0 | 7.7 | 49.9 | 3.1 | 41.2 | 2.7 | 2.9 | 8.2 | 34.2 |
| **Average annual rate of growth—Taux annuel moyen d'accroissement** | | | | | | | | | |
| 1948 – 1953 | 3.5 | 6.8 | 3.6 | 2.5 | 3.9 | 2.3 | 3.0 | 2.7 | 2.8 |
| 1950 – 1960 | 3.0 | 1.6 | 3.5 | − 1.6 | 3.8 | 4.3 | 5.2 | 4.4 | 2.4 |
| 1950 – 1953 | 2.7 | 3.2 | 2.3 | 3.4 | 2.1 | 3.0 | 2.6 | 4.6 | 2.8 |
| 1954 – 1958 | 2.6 | 2.2 | 2.6 | − 2.2 | 2.9 | 2.6 | 6.4 | 4.9 | 2.2 |
| 1958 – 1960 | 3.6 | − 1.7 | 5.4 | − 7.1 | 6.3 | 9.0 | 6.1 | 4.2 | 2.3 |

[1] Coal mining only.
[2] Includes the production of coke.

[1] Il s'agit des charbonnages exclusivement.
[2] Y compris les cokeries.

## 2. INDEX NUMBERS OF INDUSTRIAL PRODUCTION
### INDICES DE LA PRODUCTION INDUSTRIELLE

### A. Selected Divisions of Industrial Activity
### Quelques branches de l'activité industrielle

| Period / Période | Total | Mining [1] Industries extractives [1] | Manufacturing [2] Industries manufacturières [2] | Electricity and gas Electricité et gaz |
|---|---|---|---|---|
| ISIC — CITI | 1-3; 511-512 | 1 | 2-3 | 511-512 |

*a. Indexes — Indices (1958 = 100)*

| | | | | |
|---|---|---|---|---|
| 1938............. | 64 | 109 | 59 | 42 |
| 1948............. | 78 | 97 | 75 | 63 |
| 1949............. | -78- | -101- | -75- | -64- |
| 1950............. | 80 | 100 | 77 | 66 |
| 1951............. | 91 | 109 | 88 | 74 |
| 1952............. | 87 | 110 | 83 | 74 |
| 1953............. | -86- | -109- | -82- | -77- |
| 1954............. | 91 | 106 | 88 | 83 |
| 1955............. | 100 | 109 | 98 | 88 |
| 1956............. | 106 | 109 | 106 | 95 |
| 1957............. | 106 | 107 | 106 | 100 |
| 1958............. | 100 | 100 | 100 | 100 |
| 1959............. | 104 | 86 | 107 | 105 |
| 1960............. | 111 | 86 | 115 | 111 |
| 1961............. | 116 | 84 | 121 | 118 |

*b. Average Annual Rate of Change — Taux annuel moyen de variation*

| | | | | |
|---|---|---|---|---|
| 1938-1960..... | 2.5 | -1.1 | 3.1 | 4.5 |
| 1938-1948..... | 2.0 | -1.2 | 2.4 | 4.1 |
| 1950-1960..... | 3.3 | -1.5 | 4.1 | 5.3 |
| 1948-1953..... | 2.0 | 2.4 | 1.8 | 4.1 |
| 1954-1958..... | 2.4 | -1.4 | 3.2 | 4.8 |
| 1958-1960..... | 5.4 | -7.3 | 7.2 | 5.4 |

[1] Production in Metal mining (ISIC major group 12), is not included.
[2] Production of wearing apparel and made-up textile goods (in ISIC major group 24) and in Wood products and furniture (ISIC major groups 25-26), Printing and publishing (ISIC major group 28) and Other manufacturing (ISIC major group 39) is not covered.

[1] Non compris l'Extraction des minerais métalliques (CITI 12).
[2] Non compris la production dans les classes suivantes: Articles d'habillement, chaussures et ouvrages en tissu (CITI 24), Bois et meubles (CITI 25-26), Imprimerie et édition (CITI 28) et Autres industries manufacturières (CITI 39).

### B. The Major Groups of Mining
### Les classes de la branche Industries extractives

| Period / Période | Mining [1] Industries extractives [1] | Coal mining Extraction du charbon | Other mining Autres industries extractives |
|---|---|---|---|
| ISIC — CITI | 1 | 11 | 14-19 |

*a. Indexes — Indices (1958 = 100)*

| | | | |
|---|---|---|---|
| 1938............. | 109 | ... | ... |
| 1948............. | 97 | 99 | 85 |
| 1949............. | -101- | -103- | -84- |
| 1950............. | 100 | 102 | 88 |
| 1951............. | 109 | 110 | 102 |
| 1952............. | 110 | 112 | 94 |
| 1953............. | -109- | -111- | -91- |
| 1954............. | 106 | 108 | 89 |
| 1955............. | 109 | 110 | 97 |
| 1956............. | 109 | 109 | 103 |
| 1957............. | 107 | 107 | 106 |
| 1958............. | 100 | 100 | 100 |
| 1959............. | 86 | 84 | 107 |
| 1960............. | 86 | 83 | 114 |
| 1961............. | 84 | 80 | 126 |

*b. Average Annual Rate of Change — Taux annuel moyen de variation*

| | | | |
|---|---|---|---|
| 1938-1960..... | -1.1 | ... | ... |
| 1938-1948..... | -1.2 | ... | ... |
| 1950-1960..... | -1.5 | -2.0 | 2.7 |
| 1948-1953..... | 2.4 | 2.3 | 1.4 |
| 1954-1958..... | -1.4 | -1.9 | 3.0 |
| 1958-1960..... | -7.3 | -8.9 | 6.8 |

[1] Production in Metal mining (ISIC major group 12) is not included.

[1] Non compris l'Extraction des minerais métalliques (CITI 12)

### C. The Major Groups of Manufacturing — Les classes de la branche Industries manufacturières

| Period / Période | Manufacturing [1] Industries manufacturières [1] | Food, beverages and tobacco Industries alimentaires, boissons, tabac | Textiles | Paper and paper products Papier et ouvrages en papier | Leather and leather products except wearing apparel Cuir et articles en cuir, à l'exclusion des articles d'habillement | Rubber products Ouvrages en caoutchouc | Chemicals and chemical, petroleum and coal products Produits chimiques et dérivés du pétrole et du charbon | Non-metallic mineral products Produits minéraux non métalliques | Basic metals Métallurgie de base | Metal products Ouvrages en métaux |
|---|---|---|---|---|---|---|---|---|---|---|
| ISIC — CITI | 2-3 | 20-22 | 23 | 27 | 29 | 30 | 31-32 | 33 | 34 | 35-38 |

*a. Indexes — Indices (1958 = 100)*

| | | | | | | | | | | |
|---|---|---|---|---|---|---|---|---|---|---|
| 1938...... | 59 | 76 | 75 | 51 | 139 | 43 | 42 | 71 | 48 | 50 |
| 1948...... | 75 | 72 | 85 | 66 | 132 | 63 | 61 | 94 | 68 | 79 |
| 1949...... | -75- | -76- | -88- | -68- | -132- | -60- | -62- | -73- | -71- | -76- |
| 1950...... | 77 | 79 | 107 | 78 | 140 | 61 | 61 | 79 | 69 | 73 |
| 1951...... | 88 | 82 | 106 | 84 | 134 | 91 | 78 | 95 | 90 | 86 |
| 1952...... | 83 | 85 | 89 | 64 | 118 | 89 | 74 | 75 | 87 | 83 |
| 1953...... | -82- | -87- | -99- | -72- | -108- | -99- | -73- | -83- | -79- | -79- |
| 1954...... | 88 | 90 | 105 | 77 | 110 | 105 | 82 | 91 | 86 | 84 |
| 1955...... | 98 | 94 | 108 | 83 | 114 | 126 | 88 | 101 | 101 | 99 |
| 1956...... | 106 | 97 | 116 | 95 | 117 | 114 | 97 | 106 | 108 | 107 |
| 1957...... | 106 | 99 | 121 | 105 | 116 | 112 | 98 | 103 | 104 | 107 |
| 1958...... | 100 | 100 | 100 | 100 | 100 | 100 | 100 | 100 | 100 | 100 |
| 1959...... | 107 | 101 | 113 | 106 | 104 | -115- | 114 | 113 | 108 | 104 |
| 1960...... | 115 | 106 | 121 | 118 | 92 | 120 | 123 | 124 | 118 | 110 |
| 1961...... | 121 | 110 | 130 | 126 | 106 | 137 | 132 | 122 | 117 | 118 |

*b. Average Annual Rate of Change — Taux annuel moyen de variation*

| | | | | | | | | | | |
|---|---|---|---|---|---|---|---|---|---|---|
| 1938-1960. | 3.1 | 1.5 | 2.2 | 3.9 | -1.8 | 4.8 | 5.0 | 2.6 | 4.2 | 3.6 |
| 1938-1948. | 2.4 | -0.5 | 1.3 | 2.6 | -0.5 | 3.9 | 3.8 | 2.8 | 3.5 | 4.7 |
| 1950-1960. | 4.1 | 3.0 | 1.2 | 4.2 | -4.1 | 7.0 | 7.3 | 4.6 | 5.5 | 4.2 |
| 1948-1953. | 1.8 | 3.9 | 3.1 | 1.8 | -3.9 | 9.5 | 3.7 | -2.5 | 3.0 | — |
| 1954-1958. | 3.2 | 2.7 | -1.2 | 6.8 | -2.4 | 1.2 | 5.1 | 2.4 | 3.8 | 4.4 |
| 1958-1960. | 7.2 | 3.0 | 10.0 | 8.6 | -4.1 | 9.5 | 10.9 | 11.4 | 8.6 | 4.9 |

[1] Production of wearing apparel and made-up textile goods (in ISIC major group 24) and in Wood products and furniture (ISIC major groups 25-26), Printing and publishing (ISIC major group 28) and Other manufacturing (ISIC major group 39) is not covered.

[1] Non compris la production dans les classes suivantes: Articles d'habillement, chaussures et ouvrages en tissu (CITI 24), Bois et meubles (CITI 25-26), Imprimerie et édition (CITI 28) et Autres industries manufacturières (CITI 39).

# 3. INDEX NUMBERS OF INDUSTRIAL EMPLOYMENT
## INDICES DE L'EMPLOI DANS L'INDUSTRIE

### A. The Divisions of Industrial Activity
### Les branches de l'activité industrielle

| Period<br>Période | Total [1, 2] | Mining [1]<br>Industries extractives [1] | Manu-facturing [2]<br>Industries manu-facturières [2] | Construction<br>Bâtiment et travaux publics | Electricity, gas and water<br>Electricité, gaz et eaux |
|---|---|---|---|---|---|
| ISIC — CITI | 1–4, 511–521 | 1 | 2–3 | 4 | 511–521 |

*a.* Indexes — Indices (1958 = 100)

| | | | | | |
|---|---|---|---|---|---|
| 1956....... | 104 | 100 | 102 | 117 | 98 |
| 1957....... | 105 | 101 | 104 | 120 | 100 |
| 1958....... | – 100 – | – 100 – | – 100 – | – 100 – | – 100 – |
| 1959....... | 97 | 90 | 98 | 98 | 100 |
| 1960....... | 98 | 77 | 101 | 100 | 100 |
| 1961....... | 101 | 68 | 105 | 101 | 100 |

[1] Does not include metal mining (ISIC major group 12).
[2] Commercial photographic studios (ISIC group 856) are included in manufacturing.

[1] Non compris l'Extraction des minerais métalliques (CITI classe 12).
[2] Y compris les studios photographiques commerciaux (CITI groupe 856).

### B. The Major Groups of Mining
### Les classes de la branche Industries extractives

| Period<br>Période | Mining [1]<br>Industries extractives [1] | Coal mining<br>Extraction du charbon | Other mining<br>Autres industries extractives |
|---|---|---|---|
| ISIC — CITI | 1 | 11 | 14–19 |

*a.* Indexes — Indices (1958 = 100)

| | | | |
|---|---|---|---|
| 1956............ | 100 | 99 | 108 |
| 1957............ | 101 | 100 | 109 |
| 1958............ | – 100 – | – 100 – | – 100 – |
| 1959............ | 90 | 89 | 93 |
| 1960............ | 77 | 76 | 93 |
| 1961............ | 68 | 66 | 95 |

[1] Does not include metal mining (ISIC major group 12).

[1] Non compris l'Extraction des minerais métalliques (CITI classe 12).

### C. The Major Groups of Manufacturing — Les classes de la branche Industries manufacturières

| Period<br>Période | Manu-facturing [1]<br>Industries manufac-turières [1] | Food, beverages and tobacco<br>Industries alimen-taires, boissons, tabac | Textiles | Clothing, footwear and made-up textiles<br>Articles d'habil-lement, chaussures et ouvrages en tissu | Wood products and furniture<br>Bois et meubles | Paper and paper products<br>Papier et ouvrages en papier | Printing and publishing<br>Imprimerie et édition | Leather and leather products except wearing apparel<br>Cuir et articles en cuir, à l'exclu-sion des articles d'habil-lement | Rubber products<br>Ouvrages en caout-chouc | Chemicals and chemical, petroleum and coal products<br>Produits chi-miques et dérivés du pétrole et du charbon | Non-metallic mineral products<br>Produits minéraux non métal-liques | Basic metals<br>Métal-lurgie de base | Metal products<br>Ouvrages en métaux | Other manu-facturing<br>Autres industries manufac-turières |
|---|---|---|---|---|---|---|---|---|---|---|---|---|---|---|
| ISIC — CITI | 2–3 | 20–22 | 23 | 24 | 25–26 | 27 | 28 | 29 | 30 | 31–32 | 33 | 34 | 35–38 | 39 |

*a.* Indexes — Indices (1958 = 100)

| | | | | | | | | | | | | | | |
|---|---|---|---|---|---|---|---|---|---|---|---|---|---|---|
| 1956.............. | 102 | 103 | 114 | 98 | 109 | 99 | 96 | 112 | 112 | 100 | 105 | 104 | 103 | 96 |
| 1957.............. | 104 | 102 | 114 | 100 | 108 | 102 | 98 | 105 | 107 | 101 | 107 | 104 | 107 | 97 |
| 1958.............. | – 100 – | – 100 – | – 100 – | – 100 – | – 100 – | – 100 – | – 100 – | – 100 – | – 100 – | – 100 – | – 100 – | – 100 – | – 100 – | – 100 – |
| 1959.............. | 98 | 100 | 98 | 97 | 94 | 99 | 98 | 100 | 95 | 100 | 102 | 100 | 94 | 105 |
| 1960.............. | 101 | 99 | 99 | 100 | 98 | 102 | 100 | 98 | 98 | 103 | 109 | 103 | 100 | 107 |
| 1961.............. | 105 | 104 | 99 | 102 | 103 | 105 | 100 | 99 | 102 | 105 | 111 | 107 | 107 | 109 |

[1] Commercial photographic studios (ISIC group 856) are included in Printing and publishing (ISIC major group 28).

[1] Les studios photographiques commerciaux sont rattachés à la rubrique: Imprimerie et éditions (CITI classe 28).

# 4. NUMBER OF AND EMPLOYMENT IN ALL INDUSTRIAL ESTABLISHMENTS
## 27 February 1937 and 31 December 1947

## NOMBRE D'ETABLISSEMENTS INDUSTRIELS ET EMPLOI DANS CES ETABLISSEMENTS
### 27 février 1937 et 31 décembre 1947

Number of establishments in units; number of engaged and employees in thousands

Nombre d'établissements en unités; nombre de personnes occupées et de salariés en milliers

## A. The Divisions of Industrial Activity — Les branches de l'activité industrielle

| Item of data | All industrial activity / Toutes industries | | Mining / Industries extractives | | Manufacturing / Industries manufacturières | | Construction / Bâtiment et travaux publics | | Electricity and gas / Electricité et gaz | | Rubrique |
|---|---|---|---|---|---|---|---|---|---|---|---|
| | 27.II.1937 | 31.XII.1947 | 27.II.1937 | 31.XII.1947 | 27.II.1937 | 31.XII.1947 | 27.II.1937 | 31.XII.1947 | 27.II.1937 | 31.XII.1947 | |
| ISIC | 1–4, 511–512 | | 1 | | 2–3 | | 4 | | 511–512 | | CITI |
| Number of establishments | 220 371 | 217 812 | 1 297 | 934 | 181 280 | 175 320 | 37 709 | 41 187 | 85 | 371 | Nombre d'établissements |
| Number of engaged (Pay period including specified date) | 1 120.7 | 1 412.9 | 169.2 | 170.5 | 843.2 | 1 063.7 | 101.9 | 153.0 | 6.4 | 25.7 | Nombre de personnes occupées (période de paie comprenant la date indiquée) |
| Number of employees (Pay period including specified date) | 1 076.5 | 1 264.1 | 160.2 | 169.6 | 813.0 | 941.2 | 96.9 | 128.0 | 6.4 | 25.3 | Nombre de salariés (période de paie comprenant la date indiquée) |

## B. The Major Groups of Mining — Les classes de la branche Industries extractives

| Item of data | 27.II.1937 | | | | 31.XII.1947 | | | | Rubrique |
|---|---|---|---|---|---|---|---|---|---|
| | All mining / Toutes industries extractives | Coal mining / Extraction du charbon | Metal mining / Extraction des minerais métalliques | Other mining / Divers | All mining / Toutes industries extractives | Coal mining / Extraction du charbon | Metal mining / Extraction des minerais métalliques | Other mining / Divers | |
| ISIC | 1 | 11 | 12 | 14–19 | 1 | 11 | 12 | 14–19 | CITI |
| Number of establishments | 1 297 | 434 | 17 | 846 | 934 | 380 | 7 | 547 | Nombre d'établissements |
| Number of engaged (Pay period including specified date) | 169.2 | 137.4 | 0.5 | 31.3 | 170.5 | 157.0 | 0.1 | 13.4 | Nombre de personnes occupées (période de paie comprenant la date indiquée) |
| Number of employees (Pay period including specified date) | 160.2 | 137.4 | 0.5 | 22.3 | 169.6 | 156.6 | 0.1 | 12.9 | Nombre de salariés (période de paie comprenant la date indiquée) |

## C. The Major Groups of Manufacturing — Les classes de la branche Industries manufacturières

| Year and item of data | Manufacturing / Industries manufacturières | Food, beverages and tobacco / Industries alimentaires, boissons, tabac | Textiles | Clothing, footwear and made-up textiles / Articles d'habillement, chaussures et ouvrages en tissu | Wood products and furniture / Bois et meubles | Paper and paper products / Papier et ouvrages en papier | Printing and publishing / Imprimerie et édition | Leather and leather products except wearing apparel / Cuir et articles en cuir, à l'exclusion des articles d'habillement | Rubber products / Ouvrages en caoutchouc | Chemicals and chemical, petroleum and coal products / Produits chimiques et dérivés du pétrole et du charbon | Non-metallic mineral products / Produits minéraux non métalliques | Basic metals / Métallurgie de base | Metal products / Ouvrages en métaux | Other manufacturing / Autres industries manufacturières | Année et rubrique |
|---|---|---|---|---|---|---|---|---|---|---|---|---|---|---|---|
| ISIC | 2–3 | 20–22 | 23 | 24 | 25–26 | 27 | 28 | 29 | 30 | 31–32 | 33 | 34 | 35–38 | 39 | CITI |
| 27.II.1937 Number of establishments | 181 280 | 31 710 | 8 567 | 66 137 | 25 650 | 563 | 3 561 | 2 549 | 318 | 1 706 | 2 161 | 789 | 26 389 | 11 180 | 27.II.1937 Nombre d'établissements |
| Number of engaged (Pay period including 27.II.1937) | 843.2 | 106.5 | 164.8 | 80.3 | 51.9 | 19.3 | 22.2 | 15.4 | 8.1 | 61.5 | 62.0 | 64.7 | 153.9 | 32.6 | Nombre de personnes occupées (période de paie comprenant la journée du 27.II.1937) |
| Number of employees (Pay period including 27.II.1937) | 813.0 | 95.5 | 162.2 | 71.8 | 47.5 | 19.2 | 21.6 | 15.1 | 8.1 | 61.3 | 61.7 | 64.5 | 153.1 | 31.4 | Nombre de salariés (période de paie comprenant la journée du 27.II.1937) |
| 31.XII.1947 Number of establishments | 175 320 | 47 630 | 7 480 | 44 703 | 19 807 | 646 | 6 023 | 3 403 | 371 | 1 658 | 3 892 | 1 128 | 30 495 | 8 084 | 31.XII.1947 Nombre d'établissements |
| Number of engaged (Pay period including 31.XII.1947) | 1 063.7 | 137.1 | 174.9 | 109.6 | 63.6 | 24.1 | 29.1 | 16.6 | 9.4 | 60.0 | 73.3 | 99.5 | 232.5 | 34.0 | Nombre de personnes occupées (période de paie comprenant la journée du 31.XII.1947) |
| Number of employees (Pay period including 31.XII.1947) | 941.2 | 107.3 | 164.4 | 76.8 | 49.7 | 23.2 | 25.4 | 14.1 | 9.0 | 58.2 | 69.6 | 98.1 | 214.9 | 30.5 | Nombre de salariés (période de paie comprenant la journée du 31.XII.1947) |

# BELGIUM

## 5. THE CHARACTERISTICS OF SELECTED KINDS OF MANUFACTURING ESTABLISHMENTS WITH FIVE OR MORE OPERATIVES

### CARACTERISTIQUES DE CERTAINS ETABLISSEMENTS MANUFACTURIERS SELECTIONNES, AVEC CINQ OUVRIERS OU PLUS.

Number of establishments in units; value added and wages and salaries in million Francs; number of employees and operatives in thousands; energy consumed in thousand metric tons of coal equivalents; value added per employee and wages and salaries per employee in thousand Francs; energy consumed per employee in metric tons of coal equivalents.

Nombre d'établissements en unités; valeur ajoutée et traitements et salaires en millions de francs; nombre de salariés et d'ouvriers en milliers; énergie consommée en milliers de tonnes métriques d'équivalent charbon; valeur ajoutée par salarié et traitements et salaires par salarié en milliers de francs; énergie consommée par salarié en tonnes métriques d'équivalent charbon.

| Year and item of data | Manufacturing [1] Industries manufacturières [1] | Food beverages and tobacco [1] Industries alimentaires, boissons, tabac [1] | Textiles [1] | Clothing, footwear and made-up textiles Articles d'habillement, chaussures et ouvrages en tissu | Wood products and furniture Bois et meubles | Paper and paper products Papier et ouvrages en papier | Leather and leather products except wearing apparel Cuir et articles en cuir, à l'exclusion des articles d'habillement | Rubber products Ouvrages en caoutchouc | Chemicals and chemical, petroleum and coal products Produits chimiques et dérivés du pétrole et du charbon | Non-metallic mineral products [1] Produits minéraux non métalliques [1] | Basic metals Métallurgie de base | Metal products Ouvrages en métaux | Année et rubrique |
|---|---|---|---|---|---|---|---|---|---|---|---|---|---|
| ISIC | 2–3 | 20–22 | 23 | 24 | 25–26 | 27 | 29 | 30 | 31–32 | 33 | 34 | 35–38 | CITI |
| *a. Absolute Figures — Chiffres absolus* | | | | | | | | | | | | | |
| **1955** | | | | | | | | | | | | | **1955** |
| Number of establishments. | 7 650 | 174 | 1 187 | 1 944 | 725 | 331 | 59 | 48 | 344 | 490 | 114 | 2 234 | Nombre d'établissements |
| Value added . . . . . . . . | ... | 2 242.3 | 8 836.4 | 3 768.5 | 2 101.2 | 2 540.9 | 436.2 | 907.9 | 8 285.0 | 2 143.5 | ... | 25 222.9 | Valeur ajoutée |
| Employees: | | | | | | | | | | | | | Salariés: |
| Number (Average during year) . . . . . . | 634.7 | 23.1 | 109.2 | 65.9 | 25.4 | 21.7 | 5.2 | 8.3 | 49.9 | 22.4 | 75.9 | 227.7 | Nombre (moyenne annuelle) |
| Wages and salaries . . . | 36 652.1 | 960.6 | 4 789.0 | 2 210.7 | 1 186.6 | 1 263.1 | 263.9 | 502.6 | 3 652.6 | 1 194.9 | 5 961.4 | 14 666.7 | Traitements et salaires |
| Operatives: | | | | | | | | | | | | | Ouvriers: |
| Number (Average during year) . . . . . . | 549.8 | 20.6 | 101.3 | 60.2 | 23.9 | 18.4 | 4.7 | 6.7 | 38.7 | 20.9 | 66.2 | 188.2 | Nombre (moyenne annuelle) |
| Wages and salaries . . . | 27 216.4 | 709.0 | 3 914.6 | 1 752.8 | 1 034.0 | 889.4 | 201.7 | 348.0 | 2 236.4 | 1 048.4 | 4 725.7 | 10 356.2 | Traitements et salaires |
| Energy consumed . . . . . . | 17 199.7 | 247.6 | 345.7 | 36.8 | 54.5 | 353.7 | 32.5 | 54.8 | 1 664.5 | 255.8 | 13 406.8 | 747.0 | Energie consommée |
| **1958** | | | | | | | | | | | | | **1958** |
| Number of establishments. | 7 849 | 185 | 1 181 | 1 820 | 974 | 327 | 47 | 44 | 311 | 686 | 112 | 2 162 | Nombre d'établissements |
| Value added . . . . . . . . | ... | 2 808.6 | 9 023.2 | 4 272.9 | 2 600.0 | 2 857.5 | 358.1 | 869.9 | 9 221.3 | 8 489.0 | ... | 30 131.9 | Valeur ajoutée |
| Employees: | | | | | | | | | | | | | Salariés: |
| Number (Average during year) . . . . . . | 650.1 | 23.2 | 103.8 | 64.0 | 26.8 | 22.2 | 4.0 | 7.4 | 50.4 | 50.2 | 77.4 | 220.7 | Nombre (moyenne annuelle) |
| Wages and salaries . . . | 44 436.9[2] | 1 134.3[2] | 5 220.9 | 2 534.2 | 1 541.9 | 1 465.9 | 231.3 | 552.4 | 4 349.6 | 3 330.6 | 6 853.7 | 17 222.1 | Traitements et salaires |
| Operatives: | | | | | | | | | | | | | Ouvriers: |
| Number (Average during year) . . . . . . | 555.1 | 20.4 | 95.0 | 57.4 | 24.9 | 18.6 | 3.5 | 5.8 | 38.8 | 45.0 | 66.9 | 178.8 | Nombre (moyenne annuelle) |
| Wages and salaries . . . | 32 657.9 | 838.7 | 4 132.1 | 2 004.0 | 1 342.7 | 1 029.6 | 172.9 | 354.4 | 2 700.3 | 2 752.0 | 5 416.0 | 11 915.2 | Traitements et salaires |
| Energy consumed . . . . . . | 17 089.5 | 294.3 | 418.3 | 31.5 | 55.2 | 376.9 | 22.1 | 48.6 | 1 817.8 | 863.8 | 12 312.9 | 848.1 | Energie consommée |
| *b. Structure* | | | | | | | | | | | | | |
| **1955** | | | | | | | | | | | | | **1955** |
| Distribution in percent of number of employees. | 100.0 | 3.6 | 17.2 | 10.4 | 4.0 | 3.4 | 0.8 | 1.3 | 7.9 | 3.5 | 12.0 | 35.9 | Distribution en pourcentage du nombre de salariés |
| Per employee: | | | | | | | | | | | | | Par salarié |
| Value added . . . . . . . | ... | 97.1 | 80.9 | 57.2 | 82.7 | 117.1 | 83.9 | 109.4 | 166.0 | 95.7 | ... | 110.8 | Valeur ajoutée |
| Energy consumed . . . . . | 27.10 | 10.72 | 3.16 | 0.56 | 2.14 | 16.30 | 6.25 | 6.60 | 33.36 | 11.42 | 176.64 | 3.28 | Energie consommée |
| Value added per unit of wages and salaries . . . | ... | 2.33 | 1.84 | 1.70 | 1.77 | 2.01 | 1.65 | 1.81 | 2.27 | 1.79 | ... | 1.72 | Valeur ajoutée par traitements et salaires unitaires |
| Wages and salaries per employee . . . . . . . . | 57.7 | 41.6 | 43.8 | 33.5 | 46.7 | 58.2 | 50.8 | 60.6 | 73.2 | 53.3 | 78.5 | 64.4 | Traitements et salaires par salarié |
| Operatives as a percent of employees . . . . . . . | 86.6 | 89.2 | 92.8 | 91.4 | 94.1 | 84.8 | 90.4 | 80.7 | 77.6 | 93.3 | 87.2 | 82.6 | Ouvriers en pourcentage des salariés |
| **1958** | | | | | | | | | | | | | **1958** |
| Distribution in percent of number of employees. | 100.0 | 3.5 | 16.0 | 9.8 | 4.2 | 3.4 | 0.6 | 1.1 | 7.8 | 7.7 | 11.9 | 34.0 | Distribution en pourcentage du nombre de salariés |
| Per employee: | | | | | | | | | | | | | Par salarié |
| Value added . . . . . . . | ... | 121.1 | 86.9 | 66.8 | 97.0 | 128.7 | 89.5 | 117.6 | 183.0 | 169.1 | ... | 136.5 | Valeur ajoutée |
| Energy consumed . . . . . | 26.29 | 12.68 | 4.03 | 0.49 | 2.06 | 16.98 | 5.52 | 6.57 | 36.07 | 17.21 | 159.08 | 3.84 | Energie consommée |
| Value added per unit of wages and salaries . . . | ... | ... | 1.73 | 1.69 | 1.69 | 1.95 | 1.55 | 1.57 | 2.12 | 2.55 | ... | 1.75 | Valeur ajoutée par unité de salaire et de traitement |
| Wages and salaries per employee . . . . . . . . . | ... | ... | 50.3 | 39.6 | 57.5 | 66.0 | 57.8 | 74.6 | 86.3 | 66.3 | 88.5 | 78.0 | Traitements et salaires par salarié |
| Operatives as a percent of employees . . . . . . . | 85.4 | 87.9 | 91.5 | 89.7 | 92.9 | 83.8 | 87.5 | 78.4 | 77.0 | 89.6 | 86.4 | 81.0 | Ouvriers en pourcentage des salariés |

[1] Excludes for both 1955 and 1958, Printing and publishing (ISIC major group 28), Miscellaneous manufacturing (ISIC group 39), and some relatively unimportant detailed classes of industry in other major groups of manufacturing. Excludes, in addition, for 1955, the Beverage industries (ISIC major group 21), the finishing of textiles on the account of others (in ISIC major group 23) and Glass and glass products and Pottery, china and earthenware (ISIC groups 332 and 333).
[2] Excludes the beverage industries (ISIC major group 21).

[1] Non compris pour 1955 et 1958 Les Imprimeries et éditions (CITI classe 28), les Industries manufacturières diverses (CITI classe 39) et quelques classes détaillées relativement peu importantes par rapport aux autres classes des industries manufacturières. Non compris pour 1955 seulement, La Fabrication de boissons (CITI classe 21), le finissage de textiles pour le compte d'autrui (dans la classe 23 de la CITI) la Fabrication du verre et de la verrerie, des grès, porcelaines et faïences (CITI groupes 332 et 333).
[2] Non compris la Fabrication des boissons (CITI classe 21).

# 6. PURCHASED FUELS AND ELECTRICITY CONSUMED BY SELECTED KINDS OF MANUFACTURING ESTABLISHMENTS WITH FIVE OR MORE OPERATIVES

## CONSOMMATION DE COMBUSTIBLES ET D'ELECTRICITE ACHETES PAR CERTAINS ETABLISSEMENTS MANUFACTURIERS SELECTIONNES, AVEC CINQ OUVRIERS OU PLUS.
### 1955, 1958

### A. Percentage Distribution of Energy Consumed According to Source
### Distribution en pourcentage de l'énergie consommée suivant la source.

Quantities in thousand metric tons of coal equivalents.　　　　Quantités en milliers de tonnes métriques d'équivalent charbon.

| Year and item of data | Manufacturing[1] Industries manufacturières [1] | Food, beverages and tobacco Industries alimentaires, boissons, tabac | Textiles | Clothing, footwear and made-up textiles Articles d'habillement, chaussures et ouvrages en tissu | Wood products and furniture Bois et meubles | Paper and paper products Papier et ouvrages en papier | Leather and leather products except wearing apparel Cuir et articles en cuir, à l'exclusion des articles d'habillement | Rubber products Ouvrages en caoutchouc | Chemicals and chemical, petroleum and coal products Produits chimiques et dérivés du pétrole et du charbon | Non-metallic mineral products Produits minéraux non métalliques | Basic metals Métallurgie de base | Metal products Ouvrages en métaux | Année et rubrique |
|---|---|---|---|---|---|---|---|---|---|---|---|---|---|
| ISIC | 2–3 | 20–22 | 23 | 24 | 25–26 | 27 | 29 | 30 | 31–32 | 33 | 34 | 35–38 | CITI |
| **1955** | | | | | | | | | | | | | **1955** Energie totale consommée: Quantité |
| Total energy consumed: Quantity | 17 199.7 | 247.6 | 345.7 | 36.8 | 54.5 | 353.7 | 32.5 | 54.8 | 1 664.5 | 255.8 | 13 406.8 | 747.0 | |
| Percent of total in specified industry | 100.0 | 1.4 | 2.0 | 0.2 | 0.3 | 2.1 | 0.2 | 0.3 | 9.7 | 1.5 | 77.9 | 4.4 | Pourcentage du total par industrie indiquée |
| Percent consumed as: | | | | | | | | | | | | | Pourcentage consommé comme: |
| Coal | 42.1 | 81.5 | 33.7 | 35.0 | 69.5 | 52.2 | 39.6 | 72.8 | 39.4 | 80.1 | 41.6 | 25.3 | Charbon |
| Coke | 3.0 | 4.9 | 0.6 | 5.4 | 2.0 | 0.6 | 2.5 | 0.2 | 6.5 | 3.9 | 1.8 | 19.6 | Coke |
| Refined oil fuels | 5.9 | 11.7 | 46.9 | 43.5 | 19.1 | 23.9 | 51.1 | 15.3 | 11.2 | 11.2 | 1.7 | 32.4 | Pétrole raffiné |
| Gas | 44.7 | 0.3 | 0.1 | 3.8 | 0.4 | 0.2 | — | 0.2 | 30.3 | — | 52.9 | 10.8 | Gaz |
| Electricity | 3.2 | 0.6 | 14.3 | 7.4 | 6.2 | 5.4 | 4.3 | 11.5 | 8.3 | 2.4 | 2.0 | 9.7 | Electricité |
| Other fuels | 1.1 | 1.0 | 4.4 | 4.9 | 2.8 | 17.7 | 2.5 | — | 4.3 | 2.4 | — | 2.2 | Autres combustibles |
| **1958** | | | | | | | | | | | | | **1958** Energie totale consommée: Quantité |
| Total energy consumed: Quantity | 17 089.5 | 294.3 | 418.3 | 31.5 | 55.2 | 376.9 | 22.1 | 48.6 | 1 817.8 | 863.8 | 12 312.9 | 848.1 | |
| Percent of total in specified industry | 100.0 | 1.7 | 2.4 | 0.2 | 0.3 | 2.2 | 0.2 | 0.2 | 10.7 | 5.0 | 72.1 | 5.0 | Pourcentage du total par industrie indiquée |
| Percent consumed as: | | | | | | | | | | | | | Pourcentage consommé en: |
| Coal | 42.4 | 74.6 | 18.2 | 26.6 | 61.0 | 53.6 | 31.6 | 66.8 | 28.6 | 45.5 | 45.6 | 16.7 | Charbon |
| Coke | 2.7 | 5.5 | 0.5 | 4.5 | 1.5 | 0.3 | 1.8 | — | 6.6 | 2.2 | 1.4 | 14.5 | Coke |
| Refined oil fuels | 10.2 | 16.7 | 62.7 | 55.5 | 20.8 | 27.9 | 59.8 | 21.6 | 19.2 | 41.0 | 2.6 | 30.0 | Pétrole raffiné |
| Gas | 39.7 | 0.2 | 0.2 | 3.5 | 0.5 | 0.2 | — | — | 31.9 | 5.0 | 48.2 | 26.1 | Gaz |
| Electricity | 3.8 | 0.7 | 12.9 | 8.9 | 7.5 | 7.3 | 5.8 | 11.6 | 9.9 | 3.8 | 2.2 | 9.1 | Electricité |
| Other fuels | 1.2 | 2.3 | 5.5 | 1.0 | 8.7 | 10.7 | 1.0 | — | 3.8 | 2.5 | — | 3.6 | Autres combustibles |

[1] For footnotes see end of table below.　　　　[1] Pour les N.B. voir le bas du tableau ci-dessous.

63

## B. Quantity of Various Fuels and Electricity Purchased

## Quantités des différents combustibles et d'électricité achetées.

Coal, coke and refined oil fuels in thousand metric tons; manufactured gas in million cubic metres; electricity in million KWH.

Charbon, coke et pétrole raffiné en milliers de tonnes métriques; gaz manufacturé en millions de métres cubes; électricité en millions de kWh.

| Year and source of energy | Manu-facturing [1] Industries manufac-turières [1] | Food beverages and tobacco Industries alimen-taires, boissons, tabac | Textiles | Clothing, footwear and made-up textiles Articles d'habil-lement, chaussures et ouvrages en tissu | Wood products and furniture Bois et meubles | Paper and paper products Papier et ouvrages en papier | Leather and leather products except wearing apparel Cuir et articles en cuir, à l'exclu-sion des articles d'habil-lement | Rubber products Ouvrages en caout-chouc | Chemicals and chemical, petroleum and coal products Produits chi-miques et dérivés du pétrole et du charbon | Non-metallic mineral products Produits minéraux non métal-liques | Basic metals Métal-lurgie de base | Metal products Ouvrages en métaux | Année et source d'énergie |
|---|---|---|---|---|---|---|---|---|---|---|---|---|---|
| ISIC | 2–3 | 20–22 | 23 | 24 | 25–26 | 27 | 29 | 30 | 31–32 | 33 | 34 | 35–38 | CITI |
| **1955** | | | | | | | | | | | | | **1955** |
| Coal | 7 246.6 | 201.8 | 116.7 | 12.9 | 37.9 | 184.9 | 12.9 | 39.9 | 657.4 | 205.1 | 5 587.7 | 189.4 | Charbon |
| Coke | 574.1 | 13.5 | 2.4 | 2.2 | 1.2 | 2.4 | 0.9 | 0.1 | 118.9 | 11.1 | 258.4 | 163.0 | Coke |
| Refined oil fuels | 674.9 | 19.3 | 107.9 | 10.7 | 6.9 | 56.3 | 11.1 | 5.6 | 124.7 | 19.0 | 152.1 | 161.3 | Pétrole raffiné |
| Manufactured gas | 12 807.4 | 1.1 | 0.7 | 2.4 | 0.3 | 1.3 | — | 0.2 | 840.5 | 0.1 | 11 826.8 | 134.0 | Gaz manufacturé |
| Electricity | 4 508.1 | 12.5 | 394.7 | 22.0 | 26.9 | 152.0 | 10.8 | 50.6 | 1 110.1 | 49.5 | 2 098.5 | 580.5 | Electricité |
| Other fuels | 175.9 | 2.3 | 15.2 | 1.8 | 1.5 | 62.5 | 0.8 | — | 70.0 | 5.9 | — | 15.9 | Autres combustibles |
| **1958** | | | | | | | | | | | | | **1958** |
| Coal | 7 257.0 | 219.6 | 76.4 | 8.4 | 33.7 | 202.2 | 7.0 | 32.5 | 520.0 | 393.7 | 5 621.7 | 141.8 | Charbon |
| Coke | 509.2 | 18.0 | 2.1 | 1.6 | 0.9 | 1.4 | 0.4 | 0.1 | 134.1 | 20.7 | 193.3 | 136.6 | Coke |
| Refined oil fuels | 1 166.1 | 32.9 | 175.0 | 11.6 | 7.7 | 70.1 | 8.8 | 7.0 | 233.3 | 235.9 | 214.3 | 169.5 | Pétrole raffiné |
| Manufactured gas | 11 299.2 | 1.2 | 1.1 | 1.8 | 0.5 | 1.4 | — | 0.1 | 963.6 | 72.0 | 9 887.8 | 369.7 | Gaz manufacturé |
| Electricity | 5 218.5 | 15.0 | 430.1 | 22.4 | 32.6 | 219.8 | 10.5 | 44.4 | 1 451.6 | 269.3 | 2 105.0 | 617.8 | Electricité |
| Other fuels | 193.6 | 6.7 | 23.0 | 0.3 | 4.8 | 40.2 | 0.2 | — | 67.6 | 20.8 | — | 30.0 | Autres combustibles |

[1] Excludes for both 1955 and 1958, Printing and publishing (ISIC major group 28), Miscellaneous manufacturing (ISIC group 39) and, some relatively unimportant detailed classes of industry in other major groups of manufacturing. Excluded, in addition, for 1955, the Beverage industries (ISIC major group 21), the finishing of textiles on the account of others (in ISIC major group 23) and Glass and glass products and Pottery, china and earthenware (ISIC groups 332 and 333).

[1] Non compris pour 1955 et 1958 Les Imprimeries et éditions (CITI classe 28), les Industries manufacturières diverses (CITI classe 39) et quelques classes détaillées relativement peu importantes par rapport aux autres classes des industries manufacturières. Non compris pour 1955 seulement La Fabrication de boissons (CITI classe 21), le finissage de textiles pour le compte d'autrui (dans la classe 23 de la CITI), la Fabrication du verre et de la verrerie, des grès, porcelaines et faïences (CITI groupes 332–333).

# BRAZIL — BRESIL

## The Domestic Product

Estimates of expenditure on the gross domestic product and the origin of the net domestic product are presented in Table 1. The data are derived from information supplied by the Instituto Brasileiro de Economia, Fundação Getúlio Vargas, Rio de Janeiro in response to the United Nations national accounts questionnaire. Official estimates are published in *Revista Brasileira de Economia,* Ano 15, Número 1, Março de 1961, Rio de Janeiro, which also contained a description of the methods and sources used.

## Index Numbers of Industrial Production

The index numbers of industrial production shown in Table 2 are compiled on an annual basis by the Instituto Brasileiro de Economia and furnished to the Statistical Office of the United Nations through correspondence.

These index numbers are computed as base weighted arithmetic averages, starting from elementary series of relatives of the quantity produced for individual commodities, except for construction, for which data from building permits are utilized. In combining the series of relatives into indexes for mining as a whole and into detailed groups of manufacturing, the gross value of production is utilized as weights. In aggregating these detailed group indexes into indexes for major groups of manufacturing activity, the weights are based on value added at factor cost. Values added at factor cost weights are also used when aggregating the indexes for the divisions of mining, manufacturing, construction and electricity into an index of industrial activity as a whole. The weighting base years are 1939 for years prior to 1948, 1949 for the years 1948 and 1954 and the average of 1955 to 1957 for the year 1955 onwards. For further details on the construction of the indexes up to 1953 see "O Desenvolvimento de Produção Real e dos Recursos Disponíveis no Brasil, 1939-1953" by Gustaaf F. Loeb and Pierre van der Meiren in *Revista Brasileira de Economia,* December 1954 (Rio de Janeiro).

## Index Numbers of Industrial Employment

The index numbers of employment in manufacturing industries presented in Table 3 are derived from absolute figures of the monthly average of the number of operatives engaged, published by the Conselho Nacional de Estatística (IBGE) Rio de Janeiro in *Produção Brasileiro* and in *Anuario Estatístico.* The figures of the number of operatives are part of the results of the annual

## Le produit intérieur

Les estimations des dépenses imputées au produit intérieur brut et des composantes du produit intérieur net ventilées suivant le secteur d'activité d'origine sont reproduites au tableau 1. Les données ont été fournies par l'Instituto Brasileiro de Economia, Fundação Getúlio Vargas, Rio de Janeiro en réponse au questionnaire de l'O.N.U. relatif aux comptes nationaux. Des estimations officielles ainsi que des descriptions des sources et méthodes adoptées sont publiées dans *Revista Brasileira de Economia,* Ano 15, Número 1, Março de 1961, Rio de Janeiro.

## Indices de la production industrielle

Les indices de la production industrielle reproduits au tableau 2 sont établis annuellement par l'Instituto Brasileiro de Economia et communiqués par correspondance au Bureau de statistique de l'Organisation des Nations Unies.

Ces indices sont des moyennes arithmétiques à pondération fixe calculées à partir de séries élémentaires de rapports concernant le volume de la production de chaque marchandise, sauf dans le cas du bâtiment et des travaux publics, auquel cas on se sert de données tirées des permis de construire. Pour combiner ces séries de rapports en indices valables pour l'ensemble des industries extractives et pour les divers groupes détaillés des industries manufacturières, on pondère en fonction de la valeur brute de la production. Pour obtenir les indices de classes des activités manufacturières à partir des indices de groupes détaillés, on pondère en fonction de la valeur ajoutée au coût des facteurs. Pour obtenir à partir des indices relatifs aux branches d'industries: Industries extractives, industries manufacturières, bâtiments et travaux publics et électricité les indices relatifs à l'ensemble de l'activité industrielle, les valeurs ajoutées au coût des facteurs sont également utilisées comme coefficients de pondération. Les années de pondération de base sont 1939 pour les années antérieures à 1948, 1949 pour les années 1948 à 1954 et la moyenne des années 1955 à 1957 à partir de 1955. Pour plus amples détails sur la construction de ces indices voir "O Desenvolvimento de Produção Real e dos Recursos Disponíveis no Brasil, 1939-1953" par Gustaaf F. Loeb et Pierre van der Meiren dans *Revista Brasileira de Economia,* décembre 1954 (Rio de Janeiro).

## Indices de l'emploi industriel

Les indices de l'emploi dans les industries manufacturières reproduits au tableau 3 ont été calculés à partir des chiffres absolus du nombre mensuel moyen d'ouvriers occupés, publiés par le Conselho Nacional de Estatística (IBGE) Rio de Janeiro dans *Produção Brasileiro* et dans *Anuario Estatístico.* Les chiffres relatifs au nombre d'ouvriers découlent des résultats de l'enquête annuelle auprès

survey of registered industrial establishments. The survey covers establishments that employed, in any month of the year, 5 or more persons, excluding repair establishments. The monthly figures on which each annual figure is based are the numbers as on the last work day of each month. Considerable reservations attach themselves to these indices as the number of reporting establishments, especially in the manufacture of foodstuffs (ISIC major group 20), fluctuated from year to year.

### The Characteristics and Structure of Industrial Activity

The information shown in Tables 4 and 5 is derived from the results of the 1940 and 1950 Industrial Censuses published by the Conselho Nacional de Estatística of the Instituto Brasileiro de Geografia e Estatístcia in *Recenseamento Geral do Brasil* (1º de setembro de 1940), *Censos Econômicos*, Vol. III (Rio de Janeiro, 1950) and in VI *Recenseamento Geral do Brasil*, 1950, *Censo Industrial* (Rio de Janeiro, 1957).

The two Censuses are not exactly comparable in coverage. The 1940 Census covered all establishments (enterprises in the case of construction) engaged in industrial activity which were registered and active during 1939. Although a number of rural industries, such as the processing of cotton, coffee, rice and sugar, were included in the Census, production in households of items, such as fruit preserves and lace, were not covered. On the other hand, the 1950 Census covered all industrial establishments which were active during 1949, excepting relatively small units engaged in certain industries, such as the production of butter and cheese, sugar, wine and spirits, flour and meat. The distribution of electricity and certain forms of mineral prospecting seem to have been entirely omitted.

On the whole, however, comparable definitions have been utilized in the two Censuses for the same items of data. The statistical unit is the establishment except that, in the case of construction, it is the enterprise in the 1940 Census and all projects of the same enterprise within the boundaries of each state in the 1950 Census. The data on value added from both Censuses are based on the value of output, at sales price, ex-factory and net of excise taxes, including their receipts from industrial services rendered but excluding the value of goods merchandised by industrial establishments. It should be noted that payments to homeworkers are included with the costs of raw materials, supplies, fuels and power consumed and of work given out that have been subtracted from the value of output in order to compute value added. Homeworkers are not covered in the count of number of engaged or in the figures of wages and salaries paid. Except for the electricity-producing industry, the capacity of installed power equipment, in the case of the 1940 Census, is the sum of the rated horsepowers of all prime movers in use connected directly to machinery except electric generators and of all electric motors in use and in reserve. However, in the case of the 1950 Census, the rated horsepowers of all installed prime movers, whether or not in use or connected to electric generators, and of installed electric mo-

des établissements industriels enregistrés. L'enquête couvre les établissements occupant, pendant un mois quelconque de l'année, 5 personnes ou plus, à l'exclusion des établissements de réparations. Les chiffres mensuels sur lesquels est basé chaque chiffre annuel sont les nombres relevés au dernier jour ouvrable de chaque mois. Ces indices sont cependant sujet à caution vu que le nombre d'établissements enregistrés, particulièrement dans les industries alimentaires (CITI classe 20), subit des fluctuations d'année en année.

### Les caractéristiques et la structure de l'activité industrielle

Les renseignements des tableaux 4 et 5 sont tirés des résultats des recensements industriels de 1940 et 1950 qui ont été publiés par le Conselho Nacional de Estatística de l'Instituto Brasileiro de Geografia e Estatística dans *Recenseamento Geral do Brasil* (1º de setembro de 1940), *Censos Econômicos* tome III (Rio de Janeiro, 1950) et dans VI *Recenseamento Geral do Brasil*, 1950, *Censo Industrial* (Rio de Janeiro, 1957).

Ces deux recensements ne sont pas exactement comparables au point de vue couverture. Le recensement de 1940 couvrait tous les établissements enregistrés (les entreprises dans le cas du bâtiment et des travaux publics) qui exerçaient une activité industrielle en 1939. S'il portait sur un certain nombre d'industries rurales — transformation du coton, du café, du riz et du sucre par exemple — il ne couvrait cependant pas la production, dans les ménages, de certains articles comme les conserves de fruits et la dentelle. Par contre, le recensement de 1950 couvrait tous les établissements industriels qui étaient en activité en 1949, à l'exception d'unités relativement peu importantes produisant certains articles comme le beurre et le fromage, le sucre, le vin et les spiritueux, la farine et la viande. La distribution d'électricité et certaines formes de prospection minérale semblent avoir été entièrement omises.

Dans l'ensemble cependant, des définitions comparables ont été utilisées dans les deux recensements pour les mêmes rubriques. L'unité statistique est l'établissement, si ce n'est que, dans le cas du bâtiment et des travaux publics, c'est l'entreprise qui a servi d'unité pour le recensement de 1940 et tous les chantiers de la même entreprise, sur le territoire de chaque état, pour le recensement de 1950. Les chiffres de la valeur ajoutée, calculés à partir des résultats de ces deux recensements, sont fondés sur la valeur de la production, au prix de vente départ usine et déduction faite des impôts indirects, y compris les recettes provenant de services industriels fournis, mais non compris la valeur des marchandises revendues en l'état par les établissements industriels. Noter à ce sujet qu'on a déduit également de la valeur de la production les paiements aux travailleurs à domicile, en plus du coût des matières premières, des fournitures, des combustibles et de l'énergie consommés, et du coût des travaux confiés à des sous-traitants. Les travailleurs à domicile ne sont pas compris dans le nombre de personnes occupées ni dans les chiffres concernant les traitements et salaires payés. Sauf pour ce qui est de l'industrie productrice d'électricité, la puissance installée, dans le cas du recensement de 1940, représente la puissance nominale de tous les moteurs primaires en service actionnant directement des machines autres que

tors driven by purchased electricity have been summed to determine the capacity of installed power equipment. In both Censuses the capacity of installed power equipment for the electricity-producing industry is the rated horsepower of all installed prime movers only.

The data shown in Table 6 are derived from the results of annual surveys of manufacturing establishments for 1953 and 1958 published by the Conselho Nacional de Estatística. The 1953 results are issued in *Anuario Estatístico, 1956* (Rio de Janeiro, 1956) and the 1958 results are published in *Produção Industrial Brasileira 1958* and in *Anuario Estatístico 1961*. The annual surveys are based on a register of mining and manufacturing establishments having five or more employees on the last working day of any month of the year surveyed. The definitions of the items of data are the same as for the two Censuses described above except that the figures of wages and salaries include withdrawals by working proprietors and partners.

des générateurs électriques, plus celle de tous les moteurs électriques en service et en réserve. Toutefois, dans le cas du recensement de 1950, on a fait la somme de la puissance nominale de tous les moteurs primaires installés, qu'ils fussent ou non en service ou reliés à des générateurs électriques, et des moteurs électriques installés qui étaient actionnés par de l'électricité achetée, pour déterminer la puissance installée totale. Dans les deux recensements, la puissance installée dans l'industrie productrice d'électricité représente exclusivement la puissance nominale de tous les moteurs primaires installés.

Les données du tableau 6 ont été tirées des résultats des enquêtes annuelles auprès des établissements manufacturiers, relatives à 1953 et 1958 publiés par le Conselho Nacional de Estatística. Les résultats de 1953 ont paru dans *Anuario Estatístico, 1956* (Rio de Janeiro, 1956) et ceux de 1958 ont paru dans *Produção Industrial Brasileiro 1958* et dans *Anuario Estatístico 1961*. Les enquêtes annuelles sont fondées sur un répertoire des établissements miniers ou manufacturiers comptant cinq salariés ou plus au dernier jour ouvrable d'un mois quelconque de l'année de l'enquête. Les définitions des rubriques sont les mêmes que pour les deux recensements dont il est question ci-dessus, si ce n'est que les traitements et salaires comprennent les sommes prélevées sur les recettes par les propriétaires qui travaillent et par leurs associés.

## 1. THE DOMESTIC PRODUCT — PRODUIT INTERIEUR

Thousand million cruzeiros
Milliards de cruzeiros

### A. Expenditure on the Gross Domestic Product at Market Prices
### Dépenses relatives au produit intérieur brut aux prix du marché

| Item of data and year<br>Rubrique et année | Total | Consumption [1]<br>Consommation [1] | | Gross Domestic Capital Formation<br>Formation brute de capital intérieur | | Net exports of goods and services<br>Exportations nettes de biens et de services | |
|---|---|---|---|---|---|---|---|
| | | Total [1] | Government<br>Etat | Total | Fixed<br>Fixe | Exports less imports<br>Exportations moins importations | Exports<br>Exportations |
| *a. At Current Prices — Aux prix courants* | | | | | | | |
| **Absolute figures — Chiffres absolus** | | | | | | | |
| 1948 | 186.5 | 156.1 | 21.8 | 29.3 | 30.0 | 1.1 | 23.2 |
| 1950 | 252.9 | 220.3 | 32.0 | 28.9 | 33.6 | 3.7 | 26.0 |
| 1951 | 305.6 | 254.9 | 38.1 | 57.8 | 49.2 | −7.1 | 33.9 |
| 1952 | 350.4 | 291.5 | 45.1 | 71.4 | 54.4 | −12.5 | 27.5 |
| 1953 | 428.6 | 365.9 | 65.0 | 58.5 | 55.8 | 4.2 | 33.0 |
| 1954 | 555.3 | 443.5 | 75.4 | 113.9 | 91.4 | −2.1 | 47.5 |
| 1955 | 691.7 | 574.2 | 94.0 | 112.7 | 99.2 | 4.8 | 61.1 |
| 1956 | 884.4 | 743.7 | 130.4 | 133.1 | 117.0 | 7.6 | 70.4 |
| 1957 | 1 056.5 | 893.7 | 152.7 | 170.4 | 137.9 | −7.6 | 74.2 |
| 1958 | 1 310.0 | 1 111.6 | 180.5 | 206.4 | 181.0 | −8.0 | 89.0 |
| 1959 | 1 789.0 | 1 453.5 | 242.8 | 354.1 | 288.0 | −18.6 | 134.1 |
| 1960 | 2 385.7 | 1 998.0 | 337.9 | 423.8 | 355.6 | −36.1 | 166.8 |
| 1961 | 3 522.0 | ... | ... | ... | ... | −22.0 | 278.0 |
| **Percentage distribution of average annual expenditure — Distribution en pourcentage des dépenses annuelles moyennes** | | | | | | | |
| 1948 | 100.0 | 83.7 | 11.7 | 15.7 | 16.1 | 0.6 | 12.4 |
| 1950 – 1960 | 100.0 | 83.5 | 13.8 | 17.2 | 14.5 | −0.7 | 7.6 |
| 1950 | 100.0 | 87.1 | 12.6 | 11.4 | 13.3 | 1.5 | 10.3 |
| 1953 | 100.0 | 85.4 | 15.2 | 13.6 | 13.0 | 1.0 | 7.7 |
| 1954 | 100.0 | 79.9 | 13.6 | 20.5 | 16.4 | −0.4 | 8.6 |
| 1958 | 100.0 | 84.8 | 13.8 | 15.8 | 13.8 | −0.6 | 6.8 |
| 1960 | 100.0 | 83.7 | 14.2 | 17.8 | 14.9 | −1.5 | 7.0 |

For footnotes see end of table.

Pour les notes, voir au bas du tableau.

## B.  The Domestic Product at Factor Cost According to Origin
## Origine par secteur d'activité du produit intérieur au coût des facteurs

| Item of data and year<br>Rubrique et année | Total | Agricultural sector<br><br>Secteur agricole | Industrial sector [2]<br><br>Secteur industriel [2] | Transportation and communication<br><br>Transports et communications | Other sectors<br><br>Autres secteurs |
|---|---|---|---|---|---|
| ISIC — CITI | 0–9 | 0 | 1–5 | 7 | 6, 8–9 |
| **a. Net Domestic Product at Current Prices — Produit intérieur net aux prix courants** | | | | | |
| Absolute figures<br>— Chiffres absolus | | | | | |
| 1948............ | 158.5 | 44.8 | 34.2 | 12.3 | 67.2 |
| 1950............ | 214.4 | 61.4 | 51.1 | 15.8 | 86.1 |
| 1951............ | 254.5 | 70.9 | 64.2 | 19.1 | 100.3 |
| 1952............ | 293.3 | 84.9 | 68.9 | 22.7 | 116.9 |
| 1953............ | 360.3 | 104.7 | 88.4 | 26.5 | 140.7 |
| 1954............ | 455.9 | 135.8 | 119.3 | 30.5 | 170.3 |
| 1955............ | 579.1 | 172.0 | 142.4 | 43.3 | 221.4 |
| 1956............ | 733.6 | 199.3 | 176.7 | 56.9 | 300.7 |
| 1957............ | 871.9 | 243.2 | 203.9 | 69.4 | 355.4 |
| 1958............ | 1 056.2 | 271.4 | 264.9 | 80.2 | 439.7 |
| 1959............ | 1 418.5 | 384.1 | 358.7 | 104.0 | 571.7 |
| 1960............ | 1 901.2 | 536.0 | 490.4 | 143.6 | 731.2 |
| Percentage distribution according to sector—<br>Distribution en pourcentage par secteur | | | | | |
| 1948............ | 100.0 | 28.3 | 21.6 | 7.7 | 42.4 |
| 1950 – 1960..... | 100.0 | 27.8 | 24.9 | 7.5 | 39.8 |
| 1950............ | 100.0 | 28.6 | 23.8 | 7.4 | 40.2 |
| 1953............ | 100.0 | 29.1 | 24.5 | 7.4 | 39.0 |
| 1954............ | 100.0 | 29.8 | 26.2 | 6.7 | 37.3 |
| 1958............ | 100.0 | 25.7 | 25.1 | 7.6 | 41.6 |
| 1960............ | 100.0 | 28.2 | 25.8 | 7.6 | 38.4 |
| **b. Gross Domestic Product at Prices of 1949<br>— Produit intérieur brut aux prix de 1949** | | | | | |
| Index number — Indices | | | | | |
| 1948............ | 94.7 | 95.7 | 90.6 | 92.3 | 97.2 |
| 1950............ | 105.0 | 101.5 | 111.4 | 108.0 | 102.9 |
| 1951............ | 110.4 | 102.2 | 118.5 | 118.8 | 105.9 |
| 1952............ | 116.6 | 111.5 | 124.4 | 126.4 | 109.0 |
| 1953............ | 120.3 | 111.7 | 135.2 | 137.8 | 112.2 |
| 1954............ | 129.6 | 120.5 | 146.7 | 147.7 | 115.5 |
| 1955............ | 138.4 | 129.8 | 162.3 | 152.4 | 118.9 |
| 1956............ | 141.0 | 126.7 | 173.5 | 157.5 | 122.4 |
| 1957............ | 150.7 | 138.5 | 183.2 | 166.9 | 126.0 |
| 1958............ | 160.7 | 141.3 | 213.2 | 176.7 | 129.7 |
| 1959............ | 172.5 | 148.8 | 240.7 | 188.7 | 133.6 |
| 1960............ | 183.4 | 154.0 | 266.3 | 219.1 | 137.5 |
| 1961............ | 197.5 | 167.0 | 295.0 | 240.0 | 141.5 |
| Average annual rate of growth—Taux annuel moyen d'accroissement | | | | | |
| 1948 – 1953..... | 4.9 | 3.1 | 8.3 | 8.3 | 2.9 |
| 1950 – 1960..... | 5.7 | 4.3 | 9.1 | 7.3 | 2.9 |
| 1950 – 1953..... | 4.6 | 3.2 | 6.7 | 8.5 | 2.9 |
| 1954 – 1958..... | 5.5 | 4.1 | 9.8 | 4.6 | 2.9 |
| 1958 – 1960..... | 6.8 | 4.4 | 11.8 | 11.4 | 3.0 |

[1] Private consumption expenditure is obtained as a residual by subtracting the other components of gross domestic product shown in the table, independently estimated, from the aggregate estimate of net domestic product (Table 1B) plus indirect taxes, net of subsidies, and depreciation.
[2] Includes mining, manufacturing, construction, electricity, gas and water.

[1] On obtient la dépense de consommation privée en retranchant du produit intérieur net (Tableau 1B), majoré des impôts indirects, moins les subventions, et de l'amortissement, les autres éléments du produit intérieur brut estimés séparément.
[2] Y compris Industries extractives, Industries manufacturières, bâtiment et travaux publics, électricité, gaz et eau.

## 2. INDEX NUMBERS OF INDUSTRIAL PRODUCTION
### INDICES DE LA PRODUCTION INDUSTRIELLE

### A. The Divisions of Industrial Activity
### Les branches de l'activité industrielle

| Period<br>Période | Total excluding construction<br>Total à l'exclusion du bâtiment et des travaux publics | Mining<br>Industries extractives | Manufacturing [1]<br>Industries manufacturières [1] | Construction<br>Bâtiment et travaux publics | Electricity<br>Electricité |
|---|---|---|---|---|---|
| ISIC — CITI | 1–3, 511 | 1 | 2–3 | 4 | 511 |

a. Indexes — Indices (1958 = 100)

| | | | | | |
|---|---|---|---|---|---|
| 1939....... | 24 | 44 | 23 | 32 | 24 |
| 1948....... | 42 | 58 | 41 | 51 | 51 |
| 1949....... | 47 | 57 | 46 | 54 | 54 |
| 1950....... | 52 | 55 | 52 | 55 | 57 |
| 1951....... | 56 | 67 | 55 | 63 | 60 |
| 1952....... | 58 | 65 | 58 | 68 | 56 |
| 1953....... | 63 | 70 | 63 | 73 | 54 |
| 1954....... | 69 | 69 | 69 | 71 | 61 |
| 1955....... | 76 | 74 | 76 | 75 | 70 |
| 1956....... | 81 | 82 | 81 | 85 | 79 |
| 1957....... | 86 | 85 | 86 | 88 | 90 |
| 1958....... | 100 | 100 | 100 | 100 | 100 |
| 1959....... | 113 | 125 | 113 | ... | 107 |
| 1960....... | 125 | 141 | 125 | ... | 112 |
| 1961....... | 139 | ... | ... | ... | ... |

b. Average Annual Rate of Change — Taux annuel moyen de variation

| | | | | | |
|---|---|---|---|---|---|
| 1939 – 1960. | 8.2 | 5.7 | 8.4 | ... | 7.6 |
| 1939 – 1948. | 6.4 | 3.1 | 6.6 | 5.3 | 8.7 |
| 1950 – 1960. | 9.2 | 9.9 | 9.2 | ... | 7.0 |
| 1948 – 1953. | 8.4 | 3.8 | 9.0 | 7.4 | 1.2 |
| 1954 – 1958. | 9.7 | 9.7 | 9.7 | 8.9 | 13.1 |
| 1958 – 1960. | 11.8 | 18.7 | 11.8 | ... | 5.8 |

For footnotes see end of table.

Pour les notes, voir au bas du tableau.

## B. The Major Groups of Manufacturing — Les classes de la branche Industries manufacturières

| Period / Période | Manufacturing [1] Industries manufacturières [1] | Food, beverages and tobacco Industries alimentaires, boissons, tabac | Textiles | Clothing and footwear Articles d'habillement et chaussures | Wood products and furniture Bois et meubles | Paper and paper products Papier et ouvrages en papier | Printing and publishing Imprimerie et édition | Leather and leather products except wearing apparel Cuir et articles en cuir, à l'exclusion des articles d'habillement | Rubber products Ouvrages en caoutchouc | Chemicals and chemical products Produits chimiques | Non-metallic mineral products Produits minéraux non métalliques | Basic metals [2] Métallurgie de base [2] | Metal products [2] Ouvrages en métaux [2] |
|---|---|---|---|---|---|---|---|---|---|---|---|---|---|
| ISIC — CITI | 2–3 | 20–22 | 23 | 24 | 25–26 | 27 | 28 | 29 | 30 | 31 | 33 | 34–35 | 36–38 |
| *a. Indexes — Indices (1958 = 100)* | | | | | | | | | | | | | |
| 1939 | 23 | 33 | 42 | 38 | ... | 27 | 29 | 64 | 6 | ... | 16 | 10 | ... |
| 1948 | 41 | 49 | 63 | 57 | ... | 45 | 40 | 72 | 34 | ... | 44 | 39 | ... |
| 1949 | 46 | 52 | 68 | 58 | ... | 52 | 41 | 74 | 43 | ... | 50 | 43 | ... |
| 1950 | 52 | 59 | 72 | 64 | ... | 60 | 49 | 75 | 50 | ... | 56 | 57 | ... |
| 1951 | 55 | 66 | 70 | 77 | ... | 63 | 57 | 80 | 54 | ... | 63 | 62 | ... |
| 1952 | 58 | 69 | 73 | 71 | ... | 63 | 64 | 76 | 60 | ... | 68 | 64 | ... |
| 1953 | 63 | 75 | 77 | 73 | ... | 70 | 66 | 81 | 67 | ... | 80 | 72 | ... |
| 1954 | 69 | 76 | 91 | 70 | ... | 75 | 75 | 81 | 80 | ... | 84 | 85 | ... |
| 1955 | 76 | 83 | 96 | 84 | 69 | 80 | 79 | 80 | 88 | 52 | 88 | 85 | 25 |
| 1956 | 81 | 85 | 100 | 91 | 91 | 91 | 86 | 88 | 86 | 62 | 98 | 98 | 38 |
| 1957 | 86 | 90 | 87 | 86 | 73 | 87 | 103 | 91 | 88 | 80 | 101 | 90 | 56 |
| 1958 | 100 | 100 | 100 | 100 | 100 | 100 | 100 | 100 | 100 | 100 | 100 | 100 | 100 |
| 1959 | 113 | 108 | 115 | 116 | 140 | 106 | 100 | 97 | 117 | 126 | 122 | 111 | 112 |
| *b. Average Annual Rate of Change — Taux annuel moyen de variation* | | | | | | | | | | | | | |
| 1939–1948 | 6.6 | 4.5 | 4.6 | 4.6 | ... | 5.8 | 3.6 | 1.3 | 21.3 | ... | 11.9 | 16.3 | ... |
| 1948–1953 | 9.0 | 8.9 | 4.1 | 5.1 | ... | 9.2 | 10.5 | 2.4 | 14.5 | ... | 12.7 | 13.0 | ... |
| 1954–1958 | 9.7 | 7.1 | 2.4 | 9.3 | ... | 7.5 | 7.5 | 5.4 | 5.7 | ... | 4.4 | 4.1 | ... |

[1] Excludes Made-up textiles (ISIC group 244), Petroleum and coal products (ISIC major group 32) and Miscellaneous manufacturing industries (ISIC major group 39).
[2] Manufacture of metal products, except machinery and transport equipment (ISIC major group 35) is included in Basic metals (ISIC major group 34).

[1] Non compris Ouvrages en tissu (CITI 244), Dérivés du pétrole et du charbon (CITI 32) et Industries manufacturières diverses (CITI 39).
[2] La fabrication des ouvrages en métaux, à l'exclusion des machines et du matériel de transport (CITI 35), est comprise dans Métallurgie de base (CITI 34).

## 3. INDEX NUMBERS OF MANUFACTURING EMPLOYMENT
## INDICES DE L'EMPLOI DANS LES INDUSTRIES MANUFACTURIERES

| Period / Période | Manufacturing [1] Industries manufacturières [1] | Food, beverages and tobacco Industries alimentaires, boissons, tabac | Textiles | Clothing, footwear and made-up textiles Articles d'habillement, chaussures et ouvrages en tissu | Wood products and furniture Bois et meubles | Paper and paper products Papier et ouvrages en papier | Printing and publishing Imprimerie et édition | Leather and leather products except wearing apparel Cuir et articles en cuir, à l'exclusion des articles d'habillement | Rubber products Ouvrages en caoutchouc | Chemicals and chemical products Produits chimiques | Non-metallic mineral products Produits minéraux non métalliques | Basic metals [2] Métallurgie de base [2] | Metal products [2] Ouvrages en métaux [2] | Other manufacturing [3] Autres industries manufacturières [3] |
|---|---|---|---|---|---|---|---|---|---|---|---|---|---|---|
| ISIC — CITI | 2–3 | 20–22 | 23 | 24 | 25–26 | 27 | 28 | 29 | 30 | 31 | 33 | 34–35 | 36–38 | 39 |
| *a. Indexes — Indices (1958 = 100)* | | | | | | | | | | | | | | |
| 1952 | 90 | 112 | 102 | 90 | 90 | 82 | 85 | 89 | 53 | 85 | 98 | 74 | 47 | 77 |
| 1953 | 95 | 119 | 104 | 100 | 102 | 86 | 90 | 92 | 73 | 80 | 103 | 82 | 54 | 82 |
| 1954 | 99 | 117 | 109 | 98 | 102 | 90 | 90 | 95 | 91 | 101 | 106 | 86 | 64 | 84 |
| 1955 | 103 | 126 | 113 | 96 | 108 | 98 | 95 | 94 | 91 | 101 | 104 | 91 | 66 | 85 |
| 1956 | 101 | 109 | 112 | 99 | 107 | 96 | 98 | 93 | 88 | 97 | 102 | 98 | 74 | 88 |
| 1957 | 96 | 100 | 100 | 93 | 99 | 96 | 98 | 91 | 89 | 92 | 103 | 94 | 82 | 88 |
| 1958 | 100 | 100 | 100 | 100 | 100 | 100 | 100 | 100 | 100 | 100 | 100 | 100 | 100 | 100 |
| *b. Average Annual Rate of Change — Taux annuel moyen de variation* | | | | | | | | | | | | | | |
| 1954–1958 | 0.2 | −3.8 | −2.1 | 0.5 | −0.5 | 2.7 | 2.7 | 1.3 | 2.4 | −0.3 | −1.4 | 3.8 | 11.8 | 4.4 |

[1] Excludes Petroleum refining (ISIC major group 32).
[2] Manufacture of metal products, except machinery and transport equipment (ISIC major group 35) is included in Basic metals (ISIC major group 34).
[3] Includes Manufacture of ice (part of ISIC major group 20).

[1] Non compris le Raffinage du pétrole (CITI 32).
[2] La Fabrication des ouvrages en métaux, à l'exclusion des machines et du matériel de transport (CITI 35), est comprise dans Métallurgie de base (CITI 34).
[3] Y compris la Fabrication de la glace hydrique (dans CITI 20).

# 4. THE CHARACTERISTICS OF ALL INDUSTRIAL ESTABLISHMENTS
## CARACTERISTIQUES DE TOUS LES ETABLISSEMENTS INDUSTRIELS
### 1939, 1949

Number of establishments in units; value added and wages and salaries in million Cruzeiros; number of engaged, employees and operatives in thousands; energy consumed in thousand metric tons of coal equivalents; electricity consumed in million KWH; capacity of installed power equipment in thousand horsepower; value added per engaged and wages and salaries per employee and per operative in thousand Cruzeiros; energy consumed per engaged and per operative in metric tons of coal equivalents; electricity consumed per engaged and per operative in thousand KWH; capacity of installed power equipment per engaged and per operative in horsepower.

Nombre d'établissements en unités; valeur ajoutée et traitements et salaires en millions de cruzeiros; nombre de personnes occupées, de salariés et d'ouvriers en milliers; énergie consommée en milliers de tonnes métriques d'équivalent charbon; électricité consommée en millions de kWh; puissance installée en milliers de chevaux-vapeur; valeur ajoutée par personne occupée et traitements et salaires par salarié et par ouvrier en milliers de cruzeiros; énergie consommée par personne occupée et par ouvrier en tonnes métriques d'équivalent charbon; électricité consommée par personne occupée et par ouvrier en milliers de kWh; puissance installée par personne occupée et par ouvrier en chevaux-vapeur.

## A. The Divisions of Industrial Activity — Les branches de l'activité industrielle

| Item of data | All industrial activity [1] Toutes industries [1] | | Mining Industries extractives | | Manufacturing Industries manufacturières | | Construction Bâtiment et travaux publics | | Electricity and gas [1] Electricité et gaz [1] | | Rubrique |
|---|---|---|---|---|---|---|---|---|---|---|---|
| | 1939 | 1949 | 1939 | 1949 | 1939 | 1949 | 1939 | 1949 | 1939 | 1949 | |
| ISIC | 1–4; 511–512 | | 1 | | 2–3 | | 4 | | 511–512 | | CITI |
| *a. Absolute Figures — Chiffres absolus* | | | | | | | | | | | |
| Number of units......... | 47 527 | 90 829 | 2 267 | 1 608 | 40 899 | 82 145 | 1 243 | 3 015 | 3 118 | 4 061 | Nombre d'unités |
| Value added............ | 7 654.0 | 54 428.4 | 163.4 | 892.6 | 6 419.9 | 47 575.2 | 603.3 | 3 571.3 | 467.4 | 2 389.3 | Valeur ajoutée |
| Number of engaged [4]..... | 939.5 | 1 495.4 | 35.5 | 37.7 | 814.5 | 1 309.7 | 61.1 | 118.0 | 28.4 | 30.0 | Nombre de personnes occupées [4] |
| Number of employees [4].... | 880.6 | ... | 33.0 | ... | 761.0 | ... | 59.2 | ... | 27.4 | ... | Nombre de salariés [4] |
| Wages and salaries paid............... | 2 219.0 | 15 723.2 | 58.4 | 337.1 | 1 847.6 | 13 485.1 | 188.0 | 1 393.1 | 125.0 | 507.9 | Traitements et salaires payés |
| Operatives: | | | | | | | | | | | Ouvriers: |
| Number.............. | 765.7 | ... | 27.9 | 33.3 | 669.1 | 1 142.1 | 53.7 | 99.1 | 15.0 | ... | Nombre |
| Wages and salaries..... | 1 673.1 | ... | 44.0 | 293.4 | 1 422.5 | 10 935.4 | 151.8 | 1 148.0 | 54.8 | ... | Traitements et salaires |
| Energy consumed......... | ... | 6 025.8 | ... | 28.9 | 2 710.9 | 5 420.1 | 21.3 | 54.9 | 705.3 | 521.9 | Energie consommée |
| Electricity consumed....... | ... | ... | 8.9 | 40.2 | 775.6 | 2 733.1 | 4.6 | 12.6 | ... | ... | Electricité consommée |
| Capacity of installed power equipment (As of 1.IX.1940 or 1.I.1950)........... | 2 385.9 | 4 910.8 | 25.9 | 52.0[3] | 1 117.5 | 2 630.6 | 19.1 | 54.4 | 1 223.4 [2] | 2 173.8 | Puissance installée (au 1.IX.1940 ou au 1.I.1950) |
| *b. Structure* | | | | | | | | | | | |
| Distribution in percent of: | | | | | | | | | | | Distribution en pourcentage: |
| Value added.......... | 100.0 | 100.0 | 2.1 | 1.6 | 83.9 | 87.4 | 7.9 | 6.6 | 6.1 | 4.4 | Valeur ajoutée |
| Number of engaged.... | 100.0 | 100.0 | 3.8 | 2.5 | 86.7 | 87.6 | 6.5 | 7.9 | 3.0 | 2.0 | Nombre de personnes occupées |
| Per person engaged: | | | | | | | | | | | Par personne occupée |
| Value added.......... | 8.1 | 36.4 | 4.6 | 23.7 | 7.9 | 36.3 | 9.9 | 30.3 | 16.4 | 79.6 | Valeur ajoutée |
| Energy consumed....... | ... | 4.03 | ... | 0.77 | 3.33 | 4.14 | 0.35 | 0.46 | 24.83 | 17.40 | Energie consommée |
| Electricity consumed..... | ... | ... | 0.2 | 1.1 | 1.0 | 2.1 | 0.1 | 0.1 | ... | ... | Electricité consommée |
| Capacity of installed power equipment..... | 2.54 | 3.28 | 0.73 | 1.38 | 1.37 | 2.01 | 0.31 | 0.46 | 43.08 | 72.46 | Puissance installée |
| Employees as a percent of engaged.............. | 93.7 | ... | 93.0 | ... | 93.4 | ... | 96.9 | ... | 96.5 | ... | Salariés en pourcentage des personnes occupées |
| Value added per unit of wages and salaries.... | 3.45 | 3.46 | 2.80 | 2.65 | 3.47 | 3.53 | 3.21 | 2.56 | 3.74 | 4.70 | Valeur ajoutée par unité de traitements et salaires |
| Wages and salaries per employee............. | 2.5 | ... | 1.8 | ... | 2.4 | ... | 3.2 | ... | 4.6 | ... | Traitements et salaires par salarié |
| Operatives as a percent of engaged............. | 81.5 | ... | 78.6 | 88.3 | 82.1 | 87.2 | 87.9 | 84.0 | 52.8 | ... | Ouvriers en pourcentage des personnes occupées |
| Per operative: | | | | | | | | | | | Par ouvrier |
| Wages and salaries..... | 2.18 | ... | 1.58 | 8.81 | 2.12 | 9.57 | 2.83 | 11.58 | 3.65 | ... | Traitements et salaires |
| Energy consumed....... | ... | ... | ... | 0.87 | 4.05 | 4.74 | 0.40 | 0.55 | 47.02 | ... | Energie consommée |
| Electricity consumed..... | ... | ... | 0.32 | 1.21 | 1.16 | 2.39 | 0.08 | 0.13 | ... | ... | Electricité consommée |
| Capacity of installed power equipment..... | 3.12 | ... | 0.93 | 1.56 | 1.67 | 2.30 | 0.36 | 0.55 | 81.56 | ... | Puissance installée |

[1] Includes water and sanitary services in 1939 and excludes the distribution of electricity in 1949.
[2] Excludes the prime movers of gas- and waterworks.
[3] Does not include the capacity of installed power equipment in Crude petroleum and natural gas (ISIC major group 13).
[4] Sum of the average of employment in each month during 1949 for operatives and of the employment on 1 January 1950 for other engaged persons. All employment figures in 1939 are as of 1.IX.1940.

[1] Y compris les services des eaux et les services sanitaires en 1939, et non compris la distribution d'électricité en 1949.
[2] Non compris les moteurs primaires des usines à gaz et des services des eaux.
[3] Non compris la puissance installée des industries de la classe 13 de la CITI (Pétrole brut et gaz naturel).
[4] Somme de la moyenne mensuelle pendant 1949 pour les ouvriers et de l'emploi au 1er janvier 1950 pour les autres personnes occupées. Tous les chiffres de l'emploi en 1939 ont été calculés au 1.IX.1940.

## B. The Major Groups of Mining — Les classes de la branche Industries extractives

| Item of data | 1939 | | | | 1949 | | | | | Rubrique |
|---|---|---|---|---|---|---|---|---|---|---|
| | All mining Toutes industries extractives | Coal mining Extraction du charbon | Metal mining Extraction des minerais métalliques | Other mining Autres industries extractives | All mining Toutes industries extractives | Coal mining Extraction du charbon | Metal mining Extraction des minerais métalliques | Crude petroleum and natural gas Pétrole brut et gaz naturel | Other mining Autres industries extractives | |
| ISIC | 1 | 11 | 12 | 14–19 | 1 | 11 | 12 | 13 | 14–19 | CITI |
| *a. Absolute Figures — Chiffres absolus* | | | | | | | | | | |
| Number of establishments... | 2 267 | 39 | 142 | 2 086 | 1 608 | 39 | 92 | 4 | 1 473 | Nombre d'établissements |
| Value added............ | 163.4 | 44.8 | 20.0 | 98.6 | 892.6 | 368.2 | 191.5 | 5.5 | 327.4 | Valeur ajoutée |
| Number of engaged [2]...... | 35.5 | 7.8 | 5.6 | 22.1 | 37.7 | 12.7 | 8.6 | 0.1 | 16.3 | Nombre de personnes occupées [2] |
| Number of employees [2].... | 33.0 | ... | ... | ... | ... | ... | ... | ... | ... | Nombre de salariés [2] |
| Wages and salaries paid................ | 58.4 | 20.0 | 8.1 | 30.3 | 337.1 | 167.3 | 75.7 | 0.4 | 93.7 | Traitements et salaires payés |
| Operatives: | | | | | | | | | | Ouvriers: |
| Number............ | 27.9 | ... | ... | ... | 33.3 | ... | ... | ... | ... | Nombre |
| Wages and salaries..... | 44.0 | ... | ... | ... | 293.4 | ... | ... | ... | ... | Traitements et salaires |
| Energy consumed.......... | ... | ... | ... | ... | 28.9 | ... | ... | ... | ... | Energie consommée |
| Electricity consumed....... | 8.9 | ... | ... | ... | 40.2 | ... | ... | ... | ... | Electricité consommée |
| Capacity of installed power equipment (As of 1.IX.1940 or 1.I.1950)............ | 25.9 | ... | ... | ... | 52.0 [1] | 17.5 | 14.3 | ... | 20.2 | Puissance installée (au 1.IX.1940 ou au 1.I.1950) |
| *b. Structure* | | | | | | | | | | |
| Distribution in percent of: | | | | | | | | | | Distribution en pourcentage: |
| Value added.......... | 100.0 | 27.4 | 12.2 | 60.4 | 100.0 | 41.2 | 21.5 | 0.6 | 36.7 | Valeur ajoutée |
| Number of engaged..... | 100.0 | 22.0 | 15.8 | 62.2 | 100.0 | 33.7 | 22.8 | 0.3 | 43.2 | Nombre de personnes occupées |
| Per person engaged: | | | | | | | | | | Par personne occupée: |
| Value added.......... | 4.6 | 5.7 | 3.6 | 4.5 | 23.7 | 29.0 | 22.3 | 55.0 | 20.1 | Valeur ajoutée |
| Energy consumed....... | ... | ... | ... | ... | 0.77 | ... | ... | ... | ... | Energie consommée |
| Electricity consumed..... | 0.2 | ... | ... | ... | 1.1 | ... | ... | ... | ... | Electricité consommée |
| Capacity of installed power equipment..... | 0.73 | ... | ... | ... | 1.38 | ... | ... | ... | ... | Puissance installée |
| Employees as a percent of engaged............ | 93.0 | ... | ... | ... | ... | ... | ... | ... | ... | Salariés en pourcentage des personnes occupées |
| Value added per unit of wages and salaries...... | 2.80 | 2.24 | 2.47 | 3.25 | 2.65 | 2.20 | 2.53 | 13.75 | 3.49 | Valeur ajoutée par unité de traitements et salaires |
| Wages and salaries per employee............. | 1.8 | ... | ... | ... | ... | ... | ... | ... | ... | Traitements et salaires par salarié |
| Operatives as a percent of engaged............ | 78.6 | ... | ... | ... | 88.3 | ... | ... | ... | ... | Ouvriers en pourcentage des personnes occupées |
| Per operative: | | | | | | | | | | Par ouvrier: |
| Wages and salaries..... | 1.58 | ... | ... | ... | 8.81 | ... | ... | ... | ... | Traitements et salaires |
| Energy consumed...... | ... | ... | ... | ... | 0.87 | ... | ... | ... | ... | Energie consommée |
| Electricity consumed.... | 0.32 | ... | ... | ... | 1.21 | ... | ... | ... | ... | Electricité consommée |
| Capacity of installed power equipment.... | 0.93 | ... | ... | ... | 1.56 | ... | ... | ... | ... | Puissance installée |

[1] The capacity of installed power equipment in Crude petroleum and natural gas (ISIC major group 13) is not included.
[2] Sum of the average of employment in each month during 1949 for operatives and of the employment on 1 January 1950 for other engaged persons. All employment figures in 1939 are as of 1.IX.1940.

[1] Non compris la puissance installée des industries de la classe 13 de la CITI (Pétrole brut et gaz naturel).
[2] Somme de la moyenne mensuelle pendant 1949 pour les ouvriers et de l'emploi au 1er janvier 1950 pour les autres personnes occupées. Tous les chiffres de l'emploi en 1939 ont été calculés au 1.IX.1940.

## C. The Major Groups of Manufacturing — Les classes de la branche Industries manufacturières

| Year and item of data | Manufacturing — Industries manufacturières | Food, beverages and tobacco — Industries alimentaires, boissons, tabac | Textiles | Clothing, footwear and made-up textiles — Articles d'habillement, chaussures et ouvrages en tissu | Wood products and furniture — Bois et meubles | Paper and paper products — Papier et ouvrages en papier | Printing and publishing — Imprimerie et édition | Leather and leather products except wearing apparel — Cuir et articles en cuir, à l'exclusion des articles d'habillement | Rubber products — Ouvrages en caoutchouc | Chemicals and chemical, petroleum and coal products — Produits chimiques et dérivés du pétrole et du charbon | Non-metallic mineral products — Produits minéraux non métalliques | Basic metals [2] — Métallurgie de base [2] | Metal products [2] — Ouvrages en métaux [2] | Other manufacturing — Autres industries manufacturières | Année et rubrique |
|---|---|---|---|---|---|---|---|---|---|---|---|---|---|---|---|
| ISIC | 2–3 | 20–22 | 23 | 24 | 25–26 | 27 | 28 | 29 | 30 | 31–32 | 33 | 34–35 | 36–38 | 39 | CITI |

### a. Absolute Figures — Chiffres absolus

| Year and item of data | | | | | | | | | | | | | | | Année et rubrique |
|---|---|---|---|---|---|---|---|---|---|---|---|---|---|---|---|
| **1939** | | | | | | | | | | | | | | | **1939** |
| Number of establishments | 40 899 | 16 606 | 2 212 | 3 218 | 5 614 | 228 | 2 207 | 1 315 | 65 | 1 784 | 4 861 | 1 460 | 694 | 635 | Nombre d'établissements |
| Value added | 6 419.9 | 1 936.0 | 1 412.6 | 310.2 | 342.8 | 94.0 | 229.5 | 110.2 | 41.3 | 691.2 | 340.4 | 488.6 | 352.9 | 70.2 | Valeur ajoutée |
| Number of engaged [1] | 814.5 | 203.5 | 233.4 | 49.3 | 66.1 | 12.3 | 31.6 | 14.9 | 4.5 | 43.9 | 57.4 | 61.3 | 25.6 | 10.7 | Nombre de personnes occupées [1] |
| Number of employees [1] | 761.0 | 183.2 | 230.1 | 45.2 | 58.3 | 11.9 | 28.8 | 13.2 | 4.4 | 41.0 | 51.7 | 59.0 | 24.4 | 9.8 | Nombre de salariés [1] |
| Wages and salaries paid | 1 847.6 | 396.8 | 482.9 | 109.7 | 140.3 | 30.9 | 102.7 | 31.6 | 10.8 | 116.9 | 117.1 | 187.3 | 95.4 | 25.2 | Traitements et salaires payés |
| Operatives: Number | 669.1 | 147.5 | 216.5 | 40.9 | 50.9 | 10.6 | 22.1 | 11.9 | 3.7 | 34.3 | 46.5 | 53.8 | 21.5 | 8.9 | Ouvriers: Nombre |
| Wages and salaries | 1 422.5 | 267.3 | 405.1 | 92.7 | 118.0 | 22.8 | 68.9 | 24.0 | 7.0 | 73.2 | 97.0 | 154.0 | 71.9 | 20.6 | Traitements et salaires |
| Energy consumed | 2 710.9 | 963.6 | 443.5 | 36.4 | 70.2 | 82.3 | 5.0 | 30.7 | 13.7 | 147.5 | 720.8 | 165.2 | 26.1 | 5.9 | Energie consommée |
| Electricity consumed | 775.6 | 174.3 | 261.1 | 13.6 | 33.2 | 33.4 | 15.8 | 8.5 | 9.4 | 74.1 | 48.8 | 69.0 | 23.1 | 11.3 | Electricité consommée |
| Capacity of installed power equipment (As of 1.IX.1940) | 1 117.5 | 327.0 | 323.9 | 12.8 | 103.6 | 41.5 | 16.5 | 17.9 | 15.1 | 67.8 | 56.7 | 86.9 | 42.0 | 5.8 | Puissance installée (au 1.IX.1940) |
| **1949** | | | | | | | | | | | | | | | **1949** |
| Number of establishments | 82 145 | 37 533 | 2 941 | 5 076 | 10 444 | 441 | 2 749 | 2 104 | 119 | 2 658 | 12 777 | 2 221 | 1 645 | 1 437 | Nombre d'établissements |
| Value added | 47 575.2 | 12 579.2 | 9 358.5 | 2 034.4 | 3 038.3 | 1 072.4 | 1 899.1 | 627.2 | 901.8 | 4 450.6 | 3 427.6 | 4 469.0 | 2 843.3 | 873.8 | Valeur ajoutée |
| Number of engaged [1] | 1 309.7 | 287.2 | 338.0 | 76.5 | 107.3 | 25.0 | 49.4 | 21.2 | 10.9 | 73.5 | 128.9 | 102.8 | 62.6 | 26.4 | Nombre de personnes occupées [1] |
| Wages and salaries paid | 13 485.1 | 2 298.1 | 3 319.5 | 734.5 | 998.2 | 274.2 | 742.5 | 178.3 | 175.2 | 908.4 | 1 076.4 | 1 481.8 | 1 013.6 | 284.4 | Traitements et salaires payés |
| Operatives: Number | 1 142.1 | 258.3 | 313.8 | 64.1 | 87.7 | 22.3 | 34.5 | 17.3 | 9.1 | 61.0 | 111.6 | 90.2 | 49.9 | 22.3 | Ouvriers: Nombre |
| Wages and salaries | 10 935.4 | 1 782.0 | 2 857.7 | 640.6 | 882.3 | 224.2 | 507.1 | 154.6 | 124.4 | 637.8 | 919.6 | 1 197.3 | 770.9 | 236.9 | Traitements et salaires |
| Energy consumed | 5 420.1 | 1 548.3 | 765.2 | 14.8 | 191.1 | 228.9 | 6.8 | 43.5 | 50.6 | 356.9 | 1 669.3 | 454.0 | 51.8 | 38.9 | Energie consommée |
| Electricity consumed | 2 733.1 | 463.4 | 617.6 | 20.6 | 68.6 | 272.4 | 30.5 | 17.4 | 60.2 | 319.0 | 259.4 | 496.8 | 78.2 | 28.8 | Electricité consommée |
| Capacity of installed power equipment (As of 1.I.1950) | 2 630.6 | 734.9 | 519.1 | 28.1 | 235.0 | 159.9 | 33.7 | 40.0 | 44.7 | 181.2 | 169.2 | 351.5 | 112.0 | 21.3 | Puissance installée (au 1.I.1950) |

### b. Structure

| Year and item of data | | | | | | | | | | | | | | | Année et rubrique |
|---|---|---|---|---|---|---|---|---|---|---|---|---|---|---|---|
| **1939** | | | | | | | | | | | | | | | **1939** |
| Distribution in percent of: Value added | 100.0 | 30.1 | 22.0 | 4.8 | 5.4 | 1.4 | 3.6 | 1.7 | 0.7 | 10.7 | 5.4 | 7.6 | 5.5 | 1.1 | Distribution en pourcentage: Valeur ajoutée |
| Number of engaged | 100.0 | 24.9 | 28.7 | 6.0 | 8.2 | 1.5 | 3.8 | 1.9 | 0.5 | 5.4 | 7.1 | 7.5 | 3.1 | 1.4 | Nombre de personnes occupées |
| Per person engaged: Value added | 7.9 | 9.5 | 6.0 | 6.3 | 5.2 | 7.6 | 7.3 | 7.4 | 9.2 | 15.7 | 5.9 | 8.0 | 13.8 | 6.6 | Par personne occupée: Valeur ajoutée |
| Energy consumed | 3.33 | 4.74 | 1.90 | 0.74 | 1.06 | 6.69 | 0.16 | 2.06 | 3.04 | 3.36 | 12.56 | 2.69 | 1.02 | 0.55 | Energie consommée |
| Electricity consumed | 1.0 | 0.8 | 1.1 | 0.3 | 0.5 | 2.7 | 0.5 | 0.6 | 2.1 | 1.7 | 0.8 | 1.1 | 0.9 | 1.0 | Electricité consommée |
| Capacity of installed power equipment | 1.37 | 1.61 | 1.39 | 0.26 | 1.57 | 3.37 | 0.52 | 1.20 | 3.36 | 1.54 | 0.99 | 1.42 | 1.64 | 0.54 | Puissance installée |
| Employees as a percent of engaged | 93.4 | 90.0 | 98.6 | 91.7 | 88.2 | 96.7 | 91.1 | 88.6 | 97.8 | 93.4 | 90.1 | 96.2 | 95.3 | 91.6 | Salariés en pourcentage des personnes occupées |
| Value added per unit of wages and salaries | 3.47 | 4.88 | 2.92 | 2.83 | 2.44 | 3.04 | 2.23 | 3.49 | 3.82 | 5.91 | 2.91 | 2.61 | 3.70 | 2.78 | Valeur ajoutée par unité de traitements et salaires |
| Wages and salaries per employee | 2.4 | 2.2 | 2.1 | 2.4 | 2.4 | 2.6 | 3.6 | 2.4 | 2.4 | 2.8 | 2.3 | 3.2 | 3.9 | 2.6 | Traitements et salaires par salarié |
| Operatives as a percent of engaged | 82.1 | 72.5 | 92.8 | 83.0 | 77.0 | 86.2 | 69.9 | 79.9 | 82.2 | 78.1 | 81.0 | 87.8 | 84.0 | 83.2 | Ouvriers en pourcentage des personnes occupées |
| Per operative: Wages and salaries | 2.12 | 1.81 | 1.87 | 2.27 | 2.32 | 2.15 | 3.12 | 2.02 | 1.89 | 2.13 | 2.09 | 2.86 | 3.34 | 2.31 | Par ouvrier: Traitements et salaires |
| Energy consumed | 4.05 | 6.53 | 2.05 | 0.89 | 1.38 | 7.76 | 0.23 | 2.58 | 3.70 | 4.30 | 15.50 | 3.07 | 1.21 | 0.66 | Energie consommée |
| Electricity consumed | 1.16 | 1.18 | 1.21 | 0.33 | 0.65 | 3.15 | 0.71 | 0.71 | 2.54 | 2.16 | 1.05 | 1.28 | 1.07 | 1.27 | Electricité consommée |
| Capacity of installed power equipment | 1.67 | 2.22 | 1.50 | 0.31 | 2.04 | 3.92 | 0.75 | 1.50 | 4.08 | 1.98 | 1.22 | 1.62 | 1.95 | 0.65 | Puissance installée |
| **1949** | | | | | | | | | | | | | | | **1949** |
| Distribution in percent of: Value added | 100.0 | 26.4 | 19.7 | 4.2 | 6.4 | 2.3 | 4.0 | 1.3 | 1.9 | 9.3 | 7.2 | 9.4 | 6.0 | 1.9 | Distribution en pourcentage: Valeur ajoutée |
| Number of engaged | 100.0 | 21.9 | 25.8 | 5.8 | 8.2 | 1.9 | 3.8 | 1.6 | 0.9 | 5.6 | 9.8 | 7.8 | 4.8 | 2.1 | Nombre de personnes occupées |
| Per person engaged: Value added | 36.3 | 43.8 | 27.7 | 26.6 | 28.3 | 42.9 | 38.4 | 29.6 | 82.7 | 60.6 | 26.6 | 43.5 | 45.4 | 33.1 | Par personne occupée: Valeur ajoutée |
| Energy consumed | 4.14 | 5.39 | 2.26 | 0.19 | 1.78 | 9.16 | 0.14 | 2.05 | 4.64 | 4.86 | 12.95 | 4.42 | 0.83 | 1.47 | Energie consommée |
| Electricity consumed | 2.1 | 1.6 | 1.8 | 0.3 | 0.6 | 10.9 | 0.6 | 0.8 | 5.5 | 4.3 | 2.0 | 4.8 | 1.2 | 1.1 | Electricité consommée |
| Capacity of installed power equipment | 2.01 | 2.56 | 1.54 | 0.37 | 2.19 | 6.40 | 0.68 | 1.89 | 4.10 | 2.46 | 1.31 | 3.42 | 1.79 | 0.81 | Puissance installée |
| Value added per unit of wages and salaries | 3.53 | 5.47 | 2.82 | 2.77 | 3.04 | 3.91 | 2.56 | 3.52 | 5.15 | 4.90 | 3.18 | 3.02 | 2.80 | 3.07 | Valeur ajoutée par unité de traitements et salaires |
| Operatives as a percent of engaged | 87.2 | 89.9 | 92.8 | 83.8 | 81.7 | 89.2 | 69.8 | 81.6 | 83.5 | 83.0 | 86.6 | 87.7 | 79.7 | 84.5 | Ouvriers en pourcentage des personnes occupées |
| Per operative: Wages and salaries | 9.57 | 6.90 | 9.11 | 9.99 | 10.06 | 10.05 | 14.70 | 8.94 | 13.67 | 10.46 | 8.24 | 13.27 | 15.45 | 10.62 | Par ouvrier: Traitements et salaires |
| Energy consumed | 4.74 | 5.99 | 2.44 | 0.23 | 2.18 | 10.26 | 0.20 | 2.51 | 5.56 | 5.85 | 14.96 | 5.03 | 1.04 | 1.74 | Energie consommée |
| Electricity consumed | 2.39 | 1.79 | 1.97 | 0.32 | 0.78 | 12.22 | 0.88 | 1.00 | 6.62 | 5.23 | 2.32 | 5.51 | 1.57 | 1.29 | Electricité consommée |
| Capacity of installed power equipment | 2.30 | 2.84 | 1.65 | 0.44 | 2.68 | 7.17 | 0.98 | 2.31 | 4.91 | 2.97 | 1.52 | 3.90 | 2.24 | 0.96 | Puissance installée |

[1] Sum of the average of employment in each month during 1949 for operatives and of the employment on 1 January 1950 for the other engaged persons. All employment figures in 1939 are as of 1.IX.1940.

[2] Metal products excluding machinery and transport equipment (ISIC major group 35) included with Basic metals (ISIC major group 34).

[1] Somme de la moyenne mensuelle pendant 1949 pour les ouvriers et de l'emploi au 1er janvier 1950 pour les autres personnes occupées. Tous les chiffres de l'emploi en 1939 ont été calculés au 1.IX.1940.

[2] Les Ouvrages en métaux, à l'exclusion des machines et du matériel de transport (CITI 35) sont compris dans Métallurgie de base (CITI 34).

## 5. FUELS AND ELECTRICITY CONSUMED BY ALL MINING AND MANUFACTURING ESTABLISHMENTS
## CONSOMMATION DE COMBUSTIBLES ET D'ELECTRICITE DE TOUS LES ETABLISSEMENTS MINIERS ET MANUFACTURIERS
### 1939, 1949

### A. Percentage Distribution of Purchased Energy Consumed According to Source
### Répartition en pourcentage de l'énergie achetée et consommée suivant la source

Quantities in thousand metric tons of coal equivalents.　　　　　　　　Quantités en milliers de tonnes métriques d'équivalent charbon.

### a. Mining, Construction, Electricity and Gas
### Industries extractives, Bâtiment et travaux publics, Electricité et gaz

| Year and item of data | Mining<br>Industries ex-tractives | Con-struction<br>Bâtiment et travaux publics | Electricity and gas[1]<br>Electricité et gaz [1] | Année et rubrique |
|---|---|---|---|---|
| ISIC | 1 | 4 | 511-512 | CITI |
| **1939** | | | | **1939** |
| | | | | Energie totale |
| Total energy consumed.. | ... | 21.3 | 705.3 | consommée |
| | | | | Pourcentage consommé |
| Percent consumed as: | | | | sous forme de: |
| Coal............. | ... | 7.3 | 6.0 | Charbon |
| Lignite............. | ... | 0.1 | 1.5 | Lignite |
| Coke............. | ... | 1.5 | 0.2 | Coke |
| Refined oil fuels...... | ... | 55.7 | 18.0 | Pétrole raffiné |
| Gas............. | ... | — | . | Gaz |
| Electricity........... | ... | 2.4 | . | Electricité |
| Wood.............. | ... | 33.0 | 74.3 | Bois |
| **1949** | | | | **1949** |
| | | | | Energie totale |
| Total energy consumed.. | 28.9 | 54.9 | 521.9 | consommée |
| | | | | Pourcentage consommé |
| Percent consumed as: | | | | sous forme de: |
| Coal............. | 10.7 | 14.4 | 23.2 | Charbon |
| Lignite............. | 5.2 | 0.2 | 0.7 | Lignite |
| Coke............. | 0.2 | 0.3 | 0.2 | Coke |
| Refined oil fuels...... | 22.0 | 73.1 | 40.2 | Pétrole raffiné |
| Gas............. | — | . | . | Gaz |
| Electricity........... | 10.9 | 2.8 | . | Electricité |
| Wood.............. | 51.0 | 9.2 | 35.7 | Bois |

For footnotes see end of table.

Pour les notes, voir au bas du tableau.

## b. The Major Groups of Manufacturing — Les classes de la branche Industries manufacturières

| Year and item of data | Manufacturing — Industries manufacturières | Food, beverages and tobacco — Industries alimentaires, boissons, tabac | Textiles | Clothing, footwear and made-up textiles — Articles d'habillement, chaussures et ouvrages en tissu | Wood products and furniture — Bois et meubles | Paper and paper products — Papier et ouvrages en papier | Printing and publishing — Imprimerie et édition | Leather and leather products except wearing apparel — Cuir et articles en cuir, à l'exclusion des articles d'habillement | Rubber products — Ouvrages en caoutchouc | Chemicals and chemical, petroleum and coal products — Produits chimiques et dérivés du pétrole et du charbon | Non-metallic mineral products — Produits minéraux non métalliques | Basic metals [2] — Métallurgie de base [2] | Metal products [2] — Ouvrages en métaux [2] | Other manufacturing — Autres industries manufacturières | Année et rubrique |
|---|---|---|---|---|---|---|---|---|---|---|---|---|---|---|---|
| ISIC | 2–3 | 20–22 | 23 | 24 | 25–26 | 27 | 28 | 29 | 30 | 31–32 | 33 | 34–35 | 36–38 | 39 | CITI |
| **1939** Total energy consumed | | | | | | | | | | | | | | | **1939** Energie totale consommée |
| Quantity | 2 710.9 | 963.6 | 443.5 | 36.4 | 70.2 | 82.3 | 5.0 | 30.7 | 13.7 | 147.5 | 720.8 | 165.2 | 26.1 | 5.9 | Quantité |
| Percent of total in specified industry | 100.0 | 35.5 | 16.4 | 1.3 | 2.6 | 3.0 | 0.2 | 1.1 | 0.5 | 5.5 | 26.6 | 6.1 | 0.9 | 0.3 | Pourcentage du total par industrie indiquée |
| Percent consumed as: | | | | | | | | | | | | | | | Pourcentage consommée sous forme de: |
| Coal | 3.9 | 4.1 | 1.6 | 0.3 | 0.3 | 1.0 | 2.2 | 0.2 | 0.3 | 1.3 | 6.3 | 2.7 | 28.8 | — | Charbon |
| Lignite | 1.0 | 0.1 | 0.1 | 0.1 | 0.1 | 0.1 | 0.2 | — | 0.1 | 0.1 | — | 13.4 | 0.7 | 0.9 | Lignite |
| Coke | 1.6 | 0.3 | 0.5 | 0.2 | 0.2 | 0.1 | 2.9 | 0.1 | 0.3 | 1.2 | 0.3 | 18.3 | 18.1 | 2.1 | Coke |
| Refined oil fuels | 26.1 | 12.2 | 27.6 | 76.2 | 13.1 | 32.7 | 20.9 | 11.0 | 46.8 | 34.7 | 35.9 | 45.4 | 22.4 | 35.3 | Pétrole raffiné |
| Gas | 0.4 | — | — | 0.2 | — | 0.1 | 6.9 | —' | | 0.2 | 1.4 | 0.2 | 0.4 | 0.8 | Gaz |
| Electricity | 3.3 | 2.0 | 7.1 | 4.6 | 5.2 | 4.8 | 39.9 | 3.3 | 8.6 | 6.0 | 0.7 | 4.7 | 11.0 | 24.0 | Electricité |
| Wood | 63.7 | 81.3 | 63.1 | 18.4 | 81.1 | 61.2 | 27.0 | 85.4 | 43.9 | 56.5 | 55.4 | 15.3 | 18.6 | 36.9 | Bois |
| **1949** Total energy consumed | | | | | | | | | | | | | | | **1949** Energie totale consommée |
| Quantity | 5 420.1 | 1 548.3 | 765.2 | 14.8 | 191.1 | 228.9 | 6.8 | 43.5 | 50.6 | 356.9 | 1 669.3 | 454.0 | 51.8 | 38.9 | Quantité |
| Percent of total in specified industry | 100.0 | 28.5 | 14.1 | 0.3 | 3.5 | 4.3 | 0.1 | 0.8 | 0.9 | 6.6 | 30.8 | 8.4 | 0.9 | 0.8 | Pourcentage du total par industrie indiquée |
| Percent consumed as: | | | | | | | | | | | | | | | Pourcentage consommé sous forme de: |
| Coal | 1.4 | 1.8 | 2.4 | 0.5 | 0.1 | 1.6 | — | — | — | 0.3 | 0.7 | 1.1 | 13.0 | — | Charbon |
| Lignite | 2.4 | 0.2 | 0.1 | 0.1 | 0.2 | — | 0.8 | 0.2 | 0.1 | 0.6 | 0.1 | 26.3 | 2.2 | 0.4 | Lignite |
| Coke | 0.8 | 0.2 | 0.1 | 0.1 | 0.1 | — | 1.0 | — | 0.1 | 0.5 | 0.2 | 5.8 | 16.6 | 0.4 | Coke |
| Refined oil fuels | 28.2 | 12.7 | 32.2 | 37.6 | 3.4 | 32.8 | 10.7 | 13.1 | 57.1 | 46.1 | 36.4 | 37.9 | 28.9 | 12.0 | Pétrole raffiné |
| Gas | 1.1 | — | — | 0.6 | — | — | 2.4 | | | 3.3 | — | 10.1 | 1.1 | 0.4 | Gaz |
| Electricity | 5.1 | 3.1 | 8.7 | 17.2 | 3.9 | 9.9 | 55.6 | 4.5 | 14.6 | 8.0 | 1.6 | 11.0 | 18.5 | 9.1 | Electricité |
| Wood | 61.0 | 82.0 | 56.5 | 43.9 | 92.3 | 55.7 | 29.5 | 82.2 | 28.1 | 41.2 | 61.0 | 7.8 | 19.7 | 77.7 | Bois |

For footnotes see end of table.     Pour les notes, voir au bas du tableau.

## B. Quantity and Value of Selected Purchased Fuels Consumed and Electricity Purchased and Produced

## Consommation de quelques combustibles achetés et électricité achetée et produite: quantités et valeur

Coal, lignite, coke and refined oil fuels in thousand metric tons; gas in million cubic metres; electricity in million KWH; wood in thousand cubic metres; values in million Cruzeiros

Charbon, lignite, coke et pétrole raffiné en milliers de tonnes métriques; gaz en millions de mètres cubes; électricité en millions de kWh; bois en milliers de mètres cubes; valeur en milliers de cruzeiros

### a. Mining, Construction and Electricity and Gas

### Industries extractives, Bâtiment et travaux publics et Electricité et gaz

| Year and source of energy | Mining<br>Industries ex-tractives | Con-struction<br>Bâtiment et travaux publics | Electricity and gas[1]<br>Electricité et gaz[1] | Année et source d'énergie |
|---|---|---|---|---|
| ISIC | 1 | 4 | 511-512 | CITI |
| 1939 | | | | 1939 |
| Coal: | | | | Charbon: |
| Quantity............ | 13.2 | 1.6 | 42.8 | Quantité |
| | | | | Valeur (y compris |
| Value (including coke). | 4.1 | 0.5 | 10.4 | le coke) |
| Lignite: | | | | Lignite: |
| Quantity............ | 4.0 | — | 3.7 | Quantité |
| Value.............. | 1.2 | — | 1.1 | Valeur |
| Coke — quantity....... | 1.8 | 0.4 | 11.9 | Coke — quantité |
| Refined oil fuels: | | | | Pétrole raffiné |
| Quantity............ | ... | 7.9 | 84.4 | Quantité |
| Value.............. | ... | 6.2 | 21.8 | Valeur |
| Manufactured gas: | | | | Gaz manufacturé: |
| Quantity............ | 60.5 | — | 0.1 | Quantité |
| Value.............. | ... | — | — | Valeur |
| Electricity: | | | | Electricité: |
| Purchased: | | | | Achetée: |
| Quantity............ | 5.1 | 4.1 | 9.3 | Quantité |
| Value.............. | 1.4 | 1.5 | 2.2 | Valeur |
| Produced — quantity.. | 3.8 | 0.5 | 12.2 | Produite — quantité |
| Wood: | | | | Bois: |
| Quantity............ | 689 | 42 | 3 134 | Quantité |
| Value.............. | 5.0 | 0.4 | 19.3 | Valeur |
| 1949 | | | | 1949 |
| Coal: | | | | Charbon: |
| Quantity............ | 3.1 | 7.9 | 121.4 | Quantité |
| Value.............. | 0.6 | 4.3 | 59.3 | Valeur |
| Lignite: | | | | Lignite: |
| Quantity............ | 5.0 | 0.3 | 4.4 | Quantité |
| Value.............. | 1.5 | 0.2 | 1.8 | Valeur |
| Coke: | | | | Coke: |
| Quantity............ | 0.1 | 0.2 | 3.7 | Quantité |
| Value.............. | 0.1 | 0.2 | 2.4 | Valeur |
| Refined oil fuels: | | | | Pétrole raffiné: |
| Quantity............ | 4.2 | 26.8 | 139.8 | Quantité |
| Value.............. | 6.4 | 29.7 | 89.8 | Valeur |
| Manufactured gas: | | | | Gaz manufacturé: |
| Quantity............ | — | — | — | Quantité |
| Value.............. | — | — | — | Valeur |
| Electricity: | | | | Electricité: |
| Purchased: | | | | Achetée: |
| Quantity.......... | 25.2 | 12.3 | 105.1 | Quantité |
| Value............. | 6.9 | 7.3 | 22.0 | Valeur |
| Produced — quantity.. | 14.9 | 0.3 | 0.3 | Produite — quantité |
| Wood: | | | | Bois: |
| Quantity............ | 88 | 30 | 1 114 | Quantité |
| Value............. | 2.8 | 1.1 | 35.5 | Valeur |

For footnotes see end of table.

Pour les notes, voir au bas du tableau.

## b. The Major Groups of Manufacturing — Les classes de la branche Industries manufacturières

| Year and source of energy | Manufacturing<br>Industries manufacturières | Food, beverages and tobacco<br>Industries alimentaires, boissons, tabac | Textiles | Clothing, footwear and made-up textiles<br>Articles d'habillement, chaussures et ouvrages en tissu | Wood products and furniture<br>Bois et meubles | Paper and paper products<br>Papier et ouvrages en papier | Printing and publishing<br>Imprimerie et édition | Leather and leather products except wearing apparel<br>Cuir et articles en cuir, à l'exclusion des articles d'habillement | Rubber products<br>Ouvrages en caoutchouc | Chemicals and chemical, petroleum and coal products<br>Produits chimiques et dérivés du pétrole et du charbon | Non-metallic mineral products<br>Produits minéraux non métalliques | Basic metals [2]<br>Métallurgie de base [2] | Metal products [2]<br>Ouvrages en métaux [2] | Other manufacturing<br>Autres industries manufacturières | Année et source d'énergie |
|---|---|---|---|---|---|---|---|---|---|---|---|---|---|---|---|
| ISIC | 2-3 | 20-22 | 23 | 24 | 25-26 | 27 | 28 | 29 | 30 | 31-32 | 33 | 34-35 | 36-38 | 39 | CITI |
| **1939** | | | | | | | | | | | | | | | **1939** |
| Coal | | | | | | | | | | | | | | | Charbon |
| Quantity | 108.3 | 39.9 | 7.3 | 0.1 | 0.3 | 0.9 | 0.1 | 0.1 | — | 1.9 | 45.6 | 4.6 | 7.5 | — | Quantité |
| Value (including coke) | 34.0 | 6.8 | 2.2 | 0.1 | 0.1 | 0.2 | 0.1 | — | — | 1.0 | 10.1 | 10.0 | 3.4 | — | Valeur (y compris le coke) |
| Lignite | | | | | | | | | | | | | | | Lignite |
| Quantity | 82.1 | 3.6 | 2.0 | — | 0.3 | 0.1 | — | — | — | 0.8 | 1.0 | 73.5 | 0.6 | 0.2 | Quantité |
| Value | 26.3 | 1.1 | 0.6 | — | 0.1 | — | — | — | — | 0.2 | 0.3 | 23.8 | 0.2 | — | Valeur |
| Coke | | | | | | | | | | | | | | | Coke |
| Quantity | 48.7 | 3.1 | 2.2 | 0.1 | 0.1 | — | 0.2 | — | — | 1.9 | 2.1 | 33.7 | 5.2 | 0.1 | Quantité |
| Refined oil fuels | | | | | | | | | | | | | | | Pétrole raffiné |
| Quantity | 472.0 | 78.4 | 81.6 | 18.5 | 6.1 | 18.0 | 0.7 | 2.2 | 4.3 | 34.1 | 172.8 | 50.0 | 3.9 | 1.4 | Quantité |
| Value | 150.8 | 33.8 | 24.4 | 5.0 | 8.0 | 5.3 | 0.7 | 1.2 | 1.2 | 9.2 | 44.8 | 14.6 | 2.1 | 0.5 | Valeur |
| Manufactured gas | | | | | | | | | | | | | | | Gaz manufacturé |
| Quantity | 19.6 | 1.0 | 0.1 | 0.1 | — | 0.1 | 0.6 | — | — | 0.4 | 16.6 | 0.5 | 0.1 | 0.1 | Quantité |
| Value | ... | 0.4 | 0.1 | 0.1 | — | — | 0.3 | — | — | 0.2 | ... | 0.3 | 0.1 | — | Valeur |
| Electricity | | | | | | | | | | | | | | | Electricité |
| Purchased | | | | | | | | | | | | | | | Achetée |
| Quantity | 714.3 | 149.0 | 251.2 | 13.5 | 29.4 | 32.1 | 15.8 | 8.1 | 9.4 | 70.8 | 38.6 | 62.1 | 23.0 | 11.3 | Quantité |
| Value | 182.3 | 41.0 | 61.7 | 3.6 | 7.3 | 9.6 | 5.0 | 1.8 | 1.6 | 14.6 | 10.9 | 18.7 | 4.8 | 1.7 | Valeur |
| Produced—quantity | 61.2 | 25.3 | 9.9 | 0.1 | 3.8 | 1.2 | — | 0.4 | — | 3.3 | 10.2 | 6.9 | 0.1 | — | Produite—quantité |
| Wood | | | | | | | | | | | | | | | Bois |
| Quantity | 10 328 | 4 689 | 1 675 | 40 | 341 | 301 | 8 | 157 | 36 | 499 | 2 389 | 151 | 29 | 13 | Quantité |
| Value | 91.0 | 39.2 | 16.6 | 0.4 | 2.6 | 3.4 | 0.1 | 1.3 | 0.3 | 4.9 | 20.2 | 1.5 | 0.3 | 0.2 | Valeur |
| **1949** | | | | | | | | | | | | | | | **1949** |
| Coal | | | | | | | | | | | | | | | Charbon |
| Quantity | 76.9 | 29.2 | 18.6 | 0.1 | 0.2 | 3.7 | — | — | — | 1.3 | 12.0 | 5.0 | 6.8 | — | Quantité |
| Value | 26.7 | 8.3 | 3.1 | — | 0.1 | 1.8 | — | — | — | 0.8 | 5.8 | 3.7 | 3.1 | — | Valeur |
| Lignite | | | | | | | | | | | | | | | Lignite |
| Quantity | 434.4 | 10.4 | 1.7 | 0.1 | 1.3 | 0.2 | 0.2 | 0.3 | 0.2 | 6.9 | 10.2 | 398.7 | 3.7 | 0.5 | Quantité |
| Value | 194.7 | 6.3 | 0.8 | 0.1 | 0.9 | 0.1 | 0.1 | 0.2 | 0.1 | 4.6 | 6.2 | 172.6 | 2.3 | 0.4 | Valeur |
| Coke | | | | | | | | | | | | | | | Coke |
| Quantity | 47.0 | 2.1 | 1.1 | — | 0.1 | 0.1 | 0.1 | — | 0.1 | 2.0 | 2.4 | 29.2 | 9.6 | 0.2 | Quantité |
| Value | 51.9 | 2.4 | 1.4 | — | 0.1 | 0.1 | 0.1 | — | 0.1 | 1.7 | 1.8 | 31.8 | 12.2 | 0.2 | Valeur |
| Refined oil fuels | | | | | | | | | | | | | | | Pétrole raffiné |
| Quantity | 1 019.8 | 131.3 | 164.4 | 3.7 | 4.4 | 50.0 | 0.5 | 3.8 | 19.2 | 109.8 | 404.9 | 114.7 | 10.0 | 3.1 | Quantité |
| Value | 644.7 | 93.0 | 98.0 | 2.4 | 6.0 | 31.8 | 0.7 | 3.5 | 11.5 | 66.0 | 243.2 | 78.4 | 7.6 | 2.6 | Valeur |
| Manufactured gas | | | | | | | | | | | | | | | Gaz manufacturé |
| Quantity | 100.9 | 1.3 | 0.3 | 0.2 | — | — | 0.3 | — | — | 19.3 | 1.6 | 76.8 | 0.9 | 0.2 | Quantité |
| Value | 35.8 | 1.5 | 0.3 | 0.2 | — | — | 0.3 | — | — | 6.5 | 1.8 | 24.1 | 0.9 | 0.2 | Valeur |
| Electricity | | | | | | | | | | | | | | | Electricité |
| Purchased | | | | | | | | | | | | | | | Achetée |
| Quantity | 2 217.2 | 381.0 | 532.1 | 20.5 | 59.7 | 180.6 | 30.3 | 15.5 | 58.9 | 229.6 | 205.0 | 398.8 | 76.7 | 28.5 | Quantité |
| Value | 648.4 | 144.7 | 140.7 | 11.2 | 30.7 | 36.3 | 16.9 | 6.6 | 12.1 | 59.0 | 47.6 | 99.2 | 32.5 | 10.9 | Valeur |
| Produced—quantity | 516.0 | 82.4 | 85.7 | 0.1 | 9.0 | 91.8 | 0.2 | 1.9 | 1.3 | 89.4 | 54.4 | 98.0 | 1.5 | 0.3 | Produite—quantité |
| Wood | | | | | | | | | | | | | | | Bois |
| Quantity | 19 780 | 7 597 | 2 586 | 39 | 1 056 | 763 | 12 | 214 | 85 | 879 | 6 097 | 210 | 61 | 181 | Quantité |
| Value | 6 35.8 | 227.0 | 100.7 | 1.8 | 17.3 | 22.0 | 0.5 | 6.5 | 3.2 | 35.0 | 201.1 | 8.4 | 2.4 | 9.9 | Valeur |

[1] Includes water and sanitary services in 1939 and excludes the distribution of electricity in 1949.
[2] Metal products excluding machinery and transport equipment (ISIC major group 35) included with Basic metals (ISIC major group 34).

[1] Y compris les services des eaux et les services sanitaires en 1939, et non compris la distribution d'électricité en 1949.
[2] Les Ouvrages en métaux, à l'exclusion des machines et du matériel de transport (CITI 35) sont compris dans Métallurgie de base (CITI 34).

## 6.  THE CHARACTERISTICS OF MANUFACTURING ESTABLISHMENTS WITH FIVE OR MORE EMPLOYEES
### CARACTERISTIQUES DES ETABLISSEMENTS MANUFACTURIERS COMPTANT CINQ SALARIES OU PLUS
#### 1953, 1958

Number of establishments in units; value added and wages and salaries in million Cruzeiros; number of engaged and operatives in thousands; value added per engaged and wages and salaries per operative in thousand Cruzeiros.

Nombre d'établissements en unités; valeur ajoutée et traitements et salaires en millions de cruzeiros; nombre de personnes occupées et d'ouvriers en milliers; valeur ajoutée par personne occupée et traitements et salaires par ouvrier en milliers de cruzeiros.

| Year and item of data | Manufacturing / Industries manufacturières | Food, beverages and tobacco / Industries alimentaires, boissons, tabac | Textiles | Clothing, footwear and made-up textiles / Articles d'habillement, chaussures et ouvrages en tissu | Wood products and furniture / Bois et meubles | Paper and paper products / Papier et ouvrages en papier | Printing and publishing / Imprimerie et édition | Leather and leather products except wearing apparel / Cuir et articles en cuir, à l'exclusion des articles d'habillement | Rubber products / Ouvrages en caoutchouc | Chemicals and chemical, petroleum and coal products / Produits chimiques et dérivés du pétrole et du charbon | Nonmetallic mineral products / Produits minéraux non métalliques | Basic metals [1] / Métallurgie de base [1] | Metal products [1] / Ouvrages en métaux [1] | Other manufacturing [2] / Autres industries manufacturières [2] | Année et rubrique |
|---|---|---|---|---|---|---|---|---|---|---|---|---|---|---|---|
| ISIC | 2–3 | 20–22 | 23 | 24 | 25–26 | 27 | 28 | 29 | 30 | 31–32 | 33 | 34–35 | 36–38 | 39 | CITI |
| **a. Absolute Figures — Chiffres absolus** | | | | | | | | | | | | | | | |
| **1953** | | | | | | | | | | | | | | | **1953** |
| Number of establishments | 38 845 | 12 077 | 3 084 | 2 951 | 6 732 | 514 | 1 462 | 650 | 108 | 1 720 | 4 808 | 2 171 | 1 461 | 1 107 | Nombre d'établissements |
| Value added | 89 897 | 19 954 | 16 254 | 4 233 | 5 936 | 2 726 | 3 081 | 1 198 | 1 917 | 10 121 | 6 462 | 5 472 | 10 424 | 2 119 | Valeur ajoutée |
| Number of engaged (As of 31.XII.1953) | 1 421.5 | 269.9 | 354.6 | 89.6 | 125.3 | 32.6 | 47.3 | 21.9 | 14.3 | 80.3 | 125.8 | 131.7 | 90.2 | 38.0 | Nombre de personnes occupées (au 31.XII.1953) |
| Wages and salaries paid | 28 678.9 | 4 690.7 | 5 963.0 | 1 679.8 | 2 323.3 | 723.6 | 1 407.9 | 390.3 | 434.5 | 1 967.5 | 2 310.5 | 3 294.5 | 2 635.2 | 858.1 | Traitements et salaires payés |
| Operatives: Number | 1 205.9 | 223.2 | 324.3 | 78.2 | 109.7 | 27.0 | 35.7 | 18.6 | 11.0 | 59.3 | 110.0 | 106.2 | 70.9 | 31.8 | Ouvriers: Nombre |
| Wages and salaries | 20 976.5 | 3 048.1 | 4 984.2 | 1 341.2 | 1 835.4 | 497.2 | 970.8 | 294.3 | 299.3 | 1 060.3 | 1 743.6 | 2 415.6 | 1 851.8 | 634.7 | Traitements et salaires |
| **1958** | | | | | | | | | | | | | | | **1958** |
| Number of establishments | 33 949 | 6 365 | 2 870 | 3 118 | 6 650 | 565 | 1 576 | 671 | 198 | 1 623 | 4 470 | 2 349 | 2 302 | 1 192 | Nombre d'établissements |
| Value added | 319 592.0 | 59 776.3 | 43 919.9 | 12 137.4 | 17 253.9 | 8 946.3 | 10 255.3 | 3 817.0 | 5 798.9 | 43 695.5 | 20 834.0 | 38 865.2 | 45 880.0 | 8 412.3 | Valeur ajoutée |
| Number of engaged | 1 547.0 | 238.3 | 335.3 | 89.5 | 125.6 | 38.9 | 55.2 | 23.8 | 19.2 | 107.2 | 124.9 | 163.8 | 178.7 | 46.6 | Nombre de personnes occupées |
| Wages and salaries | 95 224.1 | 13 367.2 | 16 941.4 | 4 592.5 | 6 239.6 | 2 429.9 | 4 455.2 | 1 262.4 | 1 512.1 | 8 639.6 | 6 500.0 | 12 101.0 | 14 263.7 | 2 919.5 | Traitements et salaires |
| Operatives: Number | 1 269.8 | 188.2 | 310.6 | 78.6 | 107.5 | 31.2 | 39.8 | 20.2 | 14.9 | 73.6 | 106.4 | 129.5 | 130.7 | 38.6 | Ouvriers: Nombre |
| Wages and salaries | 68 644.0 | 8 620.9 | 14 452.0 | 3 730.8 | 4 803.9 | 1 802.9 | 2 956.2 | 999.3 | 1 079.7 | 4 694.0 | 4 933.3 | 8 913.1 | 9 506.4 | 2 151.5 | Traitements et salaires |
| **b. Structure** | | | | | | | | | | | | | | | |
| **1953** Distribution in percent of: | | | | | | | | | | | | | | | **1953** Distribution en pourcentage: |
| Value added | 100.0 | 22.1 | 18.1 | 4.7 | 6.6 | 3.1 | 3.4 | 1.3 | 2.2 | 11.2 | 7.2 | 6.1 | 11.6 | 2.4 | Valeur ajoutée |
| Number of engaged | 100.0 | 18.9 | 25.0 | 6.3 | 8.8 | 2.3 | 3.3 | 1.6 | 1.0 | 5.6 | 8.9 | 9.2 | 6.4 | 2.7 | Nombre de personnes occupées |
| Value added per person engaged | 63.2 | 73.9 | 45.8 | 47.2 | 47.4 | 83.6 | 65.1 | 54.7 | 134.0 | 126.0 | 51.4 | 41.5 | 115.6 | 55.8 | Valeur ajoutée par personne occupée |
| Value added per unit of wages and salaries | 3.13 | 4.25 | 2.72 | 2.52 | 2.55 | 3.77 | 2.19 | 3.07 | 4.41 | 5.14 | 2.80 | 1.66 | 3.96 | 2.47 | Valeur ajoutée par unité de traitements et salaires |
| Operatives as a percent of engaged | 84.8 | 82.7 | 91.4 | 87.3 | 87.5 | 82.8 | 75.5 | 84.9 | 76.9 | 73.8 | 87.4 | 80.6 | 78.6 | 83.7 | Ouvriers en pourcentage des personnes occupées |
| Wages and salaries per operative | 17.39 | 13.66 | 15.37 | 17.15 | 16.73 | 18.41 | 27.19 | 15.82 | 27.21 | 17.88 | 15.85 | 22.74 | 26.12 | 19.96 | Traitements et salaires par ouvrier |
| **1958** Distribution in percent of: | | | | | | | | | | | | | | | **1958** Distribution en pourcentage: |
| Value added | 100.0 | 18.7 | 13.7 | 3.8 | 5.4 | 2.8 | 3.2 | 1.2 | 1.8 | 13.7 | 6.5 | 12.2 | 14.3 | 2.7 | Valeur ajoutée |
| Number of engaged | 100.0 | 15.4 | 21.6 | 5.8 | 8.1 | 2.5 | 3.6 | 1.6 | 1.2 | 6.9 | 8.1 | 10.6 | 11.5 | 3.1 | Nombre de personnes occupées |
| Value added per person engaged | 206.6 | 250.8 | 131.0 | 135.6 | 137.4 | 230.0 | 185.8 | 160.4 | 302.0 | 407.6 | 166.8 | 237.3 | 256.7 | 180.5 | Valeur ajoutée par personne occupée |
| Value added per unit of wages and salaries | 3.36 | 4.47 | 2.59 | 2.64 | 2.76 | 3.68 | 2.30 | 3.02 | 3.83 | 5.06 | 3.20 | 3.21 | 3.22 | 2.88 | Valeur ajoutée par unité de traitements et salaires |
| Operatives as a percent of engaged | 82.1 | 79.0 | 92.6 | 87.8 | 85.6 | 80.2 | 72.1 | 84.9 | 77.6 | 68.6 | 85.2 | 79.0 | 73.1 | 82.8 | Ouvriers en pourcentage des personnes occupées |
| Wages and salaries per operative | 54.06 | 45.81 | 46.53 | 47.46 | 44.69 | 57.78 | 74.28 | 49.47 | 72.46 | 63.78 | 46.36 | 68.83 | 72.73 | 55.74 | Traitements et salaires par ouvrier |

[1] Metal products excluding machinery and transport (ISIC major group 35) included with Basic metals (ISIC major group 34).
[2] Includes Manufacture of ice (part of ISIC major group 20).

[1] Les Ouvrages en métaux, à l'exclusion des machines et du matériel de transport (CITI 35) sont compris dans Métallurgie de base (CITI 34).
[2] Y compris la Fabrication de la glace hydrique (dans CITI 20).

# BULGARIA — BULGARIE

## Net Material Product

The figures of the net material product shown in Table 1 were compiled from data received from the Central Office of Statistics, Sofia, or issued by that Office in *Statisticheski Godishnik Na Narodna Republika Bulgaria, 1959*. The concepts and definitions governing these data are those associated with the system of material product accounts, which is briefly described in the introduction to this publication. This system of accounts differs in a number of important respects from the United Nations system of national accounts.

## Index Numbers of Industrial Production

The index numbers of industrial production set out in Table 2 were derived from two sources of information. The indexes for divisions of industrial activity shown in Table 2A, are based on data furnished by the Central Statistical Office, Sofia, in correspondence with the Statistical Office of the United Nations. The classification of this series of index numbers is quite similar to the International Standard Classification. The indexes for the sub-divisions of mining and manufacturing set out in Table 2B were mainly compiled from *Statisticheski Godishnik Na Narodna Republika Bulgaria, 1961* and extended to 1961 through correspondence with the Bulgarian Central Statistical Office. The grouping of this series of index numbers is based on the Bulgarian Industrial Classification and, as may be noted from Table 2B, differs, in a number of respects, from the International Standard Industrial Classification.

Both series of index numbers relate to the value of the gross industrial output in constant enterprise prices (i.e. excluding turnover taxes) of all publicly owned, co-operative and privately owned enterprises. Included is the gross industrial output of enterprises mainly engaged in activities other than mining, manufacturing and the production of electricity, gas and steam. The gross industrial output of an enterprise consists mainly of shipments of industrial products to other enterprises, the algebraic change in the stocks of such finished products, and the industrial services rendered to other enterprises. Included in addition in gross industrial output, are selected commodities which are produced and utilized as materials in further processing within the same enterprise and the algebraic changes in the work in process of certain kinds of enterprises. The selected commodities consist of coal, meat products, animal fats, vegetable oil, sugar, wheat flour, fish products, cellulose and paper pulp, cement, spare and repair parts and electricity. Previous to 1958, the algebraic changes in the work in process of enterprises mainly engaged in the construction or repair of machinery, in the making of other metal products and in the manufacture of leather products were included in

## Produit matériel net

Les chiffres du tableau 1 relatifs au produit matériel net ont été établis à partir de données fournies par l'Office central de statistique, Sofia, ou publiées par l'Office dans *Statisticheski Godishnik Na Narodna Republika Bulgaria, 1959*. Les concepts et définitions sur lesquels reposent ces données sont ceux du système de comptabilité relatif au produit matériel, qui est décrit, brièvement dans l'introduction de cette publication. Ce système de comptabilité diffère à plus d'un égard du système de comptabilité nationale de l'ONU.

## Indices de la production industrielle

Les indices de la production industrielle reproduits au tableau 2 sont tirés de deux sources de renseignements. Les indices du tableau 2A relatifs au branches de l'activité industrielle sont fondés sur des données fournies par l'Office central de statistique, Sofia, par voie de correspondance avec le Bureau de statistique de l'ONU. La classification de ces séries d'indices est très proche de la Classification internationale type. Les indices du tableau 2B relatifs aux subdivisions des branches des industries extractives et manufacturières sont fondés essentiellement sur la publication *Statisticheski Godishnik Na Narodna Republika Bulgaria, 1961;* on les a étendus à 1961 au moyen des données fournies par voie de correspondance par l'Office central de statistique de Bulgarie. Le regroupement de ces séries d'indices est fondé sur la nomenclature industrielle bulgare et, comme on peut le constater d'après le tableau 2B, il s'écarte à plus d'un égard de la Classification internationale type.

Les deux séries d'indices portent sur la valeur de la production industrielle brute en prix constants, départ entreprise (c'est-à-dire, non compris les impôts sur le chiffre d'affaires) de toutes les entreprises publiques, coopératives et entreprises privées. Elles comprennent la production industrielle brute des entreprises dont l'activité principale relève d'une catégorie autre que les industries extractives, les industries manufacturières ou la production d'électricité, de gaz et de vapeur. La production industrielle brute d'une entreprise comprend essentiellement l'expédition de produits vers d'autres entreprises, la valeur algébrique de la variation des stocks de produits finis et les services industriels rendus à d'autres entreprises. Sont comprises également dans la production brute quelques marchandises produites par l'entreprise et utilisées comme matières premières à un stade plus avancé de la production de la même entreprise, ainsi que la valeur algébrique des variations des travaux en cours pour certains types d'entreprises. Les marchandises en question sont les suivantes : charbon, préparations de viandes, graisses animales, huile végétale, sucre, farine de froment, produits comestibles à base de poisson, cellulose et pâte à papier, ciment, pièces de rechange et électricité.

the gross output of these enterprises. Since 1958, the enterprises for which changes in work in process are counted in gross output have been restricted to a very small number engaged in the construction or heavy repair of complex machinery or in other manufacturing with a very long production cycle.

The enterprise prices in which gross industrial output is valued for purposes of the series of index numbers are those prevailing on 1 April 1956. The original comparison base year utilized by the Central Statistical Office, Sofia, in compiling the indexes is 1939. The series of index numbers of that Office are therefore equivalent to indexes computed as base-weighted arithmetic averages of series of elementary relatives on quantities of output for each industrial product. The original weights for the series of indexes may be considered to be the gross output during 1939 of each industrial product valued at the enterprise prices prevailing on 1 April 1956.

### Index Numbers of Industrial Employment

The index numbers in Table 3 were compiled from absolute figures of employment published in *Statisticheski Godishnik Na Narodna Republika Bulgaria, 1961* and furnished by the Central Statistical Office, Sofia, in correspondence. These absolute figures relate to the average of the number of employees in each month of the year of all co-operatives and/or publicly owned enterprises mainly engaged in mining, manufacturing and the production of electricity, gas and steam. All employees of these enterprises, whether or not engaged in the industrial activities of the enterprises, are covered in the data. The count of employees includes persons on sick leave, vacation or other forms of temporary leave.

### Characteristics and Structure of Industrial Activity

The data shown in Table 4 were compiled from *Statisticheski Godishnik Na Narodna Republika Bulgaria, 1960* or *1961*. The figures, except for those on the cost of production, relate to all co-operative and/or publicly owned enterprises mainly engaged in mining, manufacturing and the production of electricity, gas and steam. In the case of the data on the costs of production, small publicly owned enterprises, engaged in mixed kinds of industrial activities, are excluded.

The figures of gross output during 1956 shown in Table 4 are valued at enterprise prices (i.e. at the enterprise and excluding turnover taxes) prevailing on 1 April 1956; and are defined and classified as was described above, in connexion with indexes of industrial production. As for gross output, the data on number of op-

Avant 1958, la valeur algébrique des variations des travaux en cours des entreprises dont l'activité principale est la construction ou la réparation de machines, la production d'autres articles métalliques et la fabrication des articles en cuir était comprise dans la production brute de ces entreprises. A partir de 1958, on n'a inclus les variations des travaux en cours dans la production brute que pour un très petit nombre d'entreprises s'occupant de la construction ou des grosses réparations de machines complexes ou exerçant d'autres activités manufacturières à long cycle de production.

Les prix départ entreprise qui ont permis d'évaluer la production afin de calculer les séries d'indices sont les prix en vigueur au 1er avril 1956. L'année de comparaison de base prise initialement par l'Office central de statistique, Sofia, pour construire les indices, est 1939. Les séries d'indices de cet Office sont donc équivalentes à des indices calculés comme moyennes arithmétiques à pondération fixe de séries élémentaires de rapports des quantités produites de chaque marchandise. Les coefficients de pondération utilisés initialement pour le calcul de ces séries d'indices peuvent être considérés comme étant la production brute de chaque marchandise en 1939, évaluée aux prix départ entreprise en vigueur au 1er avril 1956.

### Indices de l'emploi dans l'industrie

Les indices du tableau 3 ont été établis à partir de chiffres absolus de l'emploi publiés dans *Statisticheski Godishnik Na Narodna Republika Bulgaria, 1961* et fournis par l'Office central de statistique, Sofia, par voie de correspondance. Ces chiffres absolus concernent la moyenne pour chaque mois de l'année, du nombre des salariés employés dans toutes les coopératives et/ou les entreprises publiques dont l'activité principale relève des industries extractives, des industries manufacturières et de la production d'électricité, de gaz et de vapeur. Tous les salariés de ces entreprises, qu'ils soient affectés ou non aux activités industrielles, sont compris dans les données. Le nombre de salariés comprend les personnes en congé de maladie, en congé annuel ou temporairement absentes pour d'autres raisons.

### Caractéristiques et structure de l'activité industrielle

Les données du tableau 4 sont tirées de *Statisticheski Godishnik Na Narodna Republika Bulgaria, 1960* ou *1961*. Les chiffres, à l'exception de ceux qui ont trait au coût de la production, concernent toutes les coopératives et/ou les entreprises publiques dont l'activité principale relève des industries extractives, des industries manufacturières et de la production d'électricité, de gaz et de vapeur. Dans le cas des données relatives aux coûts de production, les petites entreprises publiques exerçant différents types d'activités sont exclues.

Les chiffres du tableau 4 relatifs à la production brute en 1956 sont évalués aux prix départ entreprise (c'est-à-dire non compris les impôts sur le chiffre d'affaires) en vigueur au 1er avril 1956; ils sont définis et classés comme décrit plus haut dans le cas des indices de la production industrielle. Comme pour la production brute, les don-

eratives, consumption of electricity and capacity of installed power equipment are limited to the industrial activities of the enterprises covered. However, the figures of the number of persons engaged and employees and probably the costs of production relate to all of the activities of these enterprises and are therefore not exactly comparable to the other items of data. The data on the number of employees shown in Table 4 are identical with the absolute figures utilized to compile the index numbers of employment set out in Table 3. In the case of the publicly owned enterprises, the number of persons engaged and the number of employees are identical. In the case of co-operatives, this is not the case since the figures of the number of persons engaged cover working members, as well as employees, of co-operatives. The figures of operatives relate to manual workers, including working members in the case of co-operatives, engaged in the industrial activities of enterprises. The capacity of installed power equipment covers the rated capacity (converted from kilowatts) of all prime movers connected directly to machinery other than electric generators plus that of all electric motors. The element of cost of production shown in Table 4, except for "Other" relate to costs incurred in the industrial activities of the enterprises covered; and except for this restriction, appear to be defined as in the International Standards in Basic Industrial Statistics. "Other" costs probably refer to costs of transportation and communication in addition to costs incurred in the non-industrial activities of the enterprises covered.

nées relatives au nombre d'ouvriers, à la consommation d'électricité et à la puissance installée ne concernent que les activités industrielles des entreprises recensées. Cependant, les chiffres relatifs au nombre de personnes occupées, au nombre de salariés et, probablement, aux coûts de production concernent toutes les activités de ces entreprises; ils ne sont donc pas tout à fait comparables aux données présentées sous les autres rubriques. Les données du tableau 4 relatives au nombre de salariés sont celles que l'on a utilisées pour calculer les indices de l'emploi reproduits au tableau 3. Dans le cas des entreprises publiques, le nombre des personnes occupées est le même que celui des salariés. Il n'en est pas ainsi pour les coopératives, car les chiffres relatifs au nombre de personnes occupées comprennent les membres actifs aussi bien que les salariés des coopératives. Les chiffres relatifs aux ouvriers concernent les travailleurs manuels, y compris les membres actifs dans le cas des coopératives, affectés aux activités industrielles des entreprises. La puissance installée représente la puissance nominale (originalement en kilowatts) de tous les moteurs primaires entraînant directement des machines, à l'exclusion des générateurs d'électricité, plus la puissance nominale de tous les moteurs électriques. Les éléments du coût de la production reproduits au tableau 4, à l'exception des coûts dus à "d'autres facteurs", concernent les coûts découlant des activités industrielles des entreprises retenues; à tous autres égards, ils semblent être conformes aux Normes internationales relatives aux statistiques industrielles de base. Les coûts dus à "d'autres facteurs" sont probablement les frais de transport et de communication, ainsi que les coûts engendrés par les activités non industrielles des entreprises considérées.

## 1. THE NET MATERIAL PRODUCT — LE PRODUIT MATERIEL NET

Million Leva

Millions de leva

### A. Expenditure on the Net Material Product
### Dépenses relatives au produit matériel net

| Item of data and year<br>Rubrique et année | Total | Consumption<br>Consommation | | Net Domestic Capital Formation<br>Formation nette de capital intérieur | | Net exports of goods of services [2]<br>Exportations nettes de biens et de services [2] |
|---|---|---|---|---|---|---|
| | | Total | Collective consumption [1]<br>Consommation collective [1] | Total | Fixed<br>Fixe | |
| | | | At Prices of 1957 — Aux prix de 1957 | | | |
| **Absolute figures — Chiffres absolus** | | | | | | |
| 1953 | 26 822 | 18 412 | 1 428 | 8 017 | 1 868 | 393 |
| 1954 | 26 628 | 20 393 | 1 511 | 5 197 | 3 379 | 1 038 |
| 1955 | 28 112 | 21 364 | 1 821 | 5 579 | 4 435 | 1 169 |
| 1956 | 28 361 | 23 676 | 1 957 | 3 953 | 3 633 | 732 |
| 1957 | 32 089 | 24 774 | 1 972 | 6 237 | 3 797 | 1 078 |
| 1958 | 34 283 | 27 253 | 2 052 | 6 579 | 3 720 | 451 |
| 1959 | 41 671 | 30 545 | 2 445 | 13 149 | 6 166 | −2 023 |
| 1960 | 44 570 | 32 531 | 2 938 | 12 355 | 6 922 | −316 |
| 1961 | 45 918 | 35 191 | 3 004 | 10 094 | 6 819 | 633 |
| **Percentage distribution of average annual expenditure — Distribution en pourcentage des dépenses annuelles moyennes** | | | | | | |
| 1953 – 1960 | 100.0 | 75.7 | 6.1 | 23.3 | 12.9 | 1.0 |
| 1953 | 100.0 | 68.6 | 5.3 | 29.9 | 7.0 | 1.5 |
| 1954 | 100.0 | 76.6 | 5.7 | 19.5 | 12.7 | 3.9 |
| 1958 | 100.0 | 79.5 | 6.0 | 19.2 | 10.9 | 1.3 |
| 1960 | 100.0 | 73.0 | 6.6 | 27.7 | 15.5 | −0.7 |
| **Average annual rate of growth — Taux annuel moyen d'accroissement** | | | | | | |
| 1953 – 1960 | 7.5 | 8.5 | 10.9 | 6.4 | 20.6 | . |
| 1954 – 1958 | 6.5 | 7.5 | 8.0 | 6.1 | 2.4 | . |
| 1958 – 1960 | 14.0 | 9.3 | 19.7 | 35.5 | 36.4 | . |

[1] Consumption of goods by organizations and institutions which do not contribute to the material product.
[2] Includes a statistical discrepancy.

[1] Consommation de biens par les organisations qui ne concourent pas à la formation du produit matériel.
[2] Y compris les écarts statistiques.

## B. The Net Material Product According to Origin
### Origine par secteur du produit matériel net
#### 1958

| Item of data and form of organization | Total | Agricultural sector<br><br>Secteur agricole | Mining, manufacturing and electricity<br><br>Industries extractives et manufacturières et électricité | Construction<br><br>Bâtiment et travaux publics | Transportation and communication<br><br>Transports et communications | Other sectors [1]<br><br>Autres secteurs [1] | Rubrique et type d'organisation |
|---|---|---|---|---|---|---|---|
| ISIC | 0–5, 611–612, 7, 841, 852 | 0 | 1–3, 511–512 | 4 | 7 | 611–612, 841, 852 | CITI |

*a. At Current Prices — Aux prix courants*

| | | | | | | | |
|---|---|---|---|---|---|---|---|
| **Absolute figures:** | | | | | | | **Chiffres absolus:** |
| Total..................... | 33 900 | 12 035 | 13 976 | 1 961 | 1.144 | 4 784 | Total |
| Publicly-owned enterprises........ | 17 647 | 306 | 11 932 | 1 678 | 796 | 2 935 | Entreprises publiques |
| Co-operatives ................. | 11 065 | 7 944 | 1 842 | 178 | 29 | 1 072 | Coopératives |
| Auxiliary activities of members of co-operatives and employees of publicly-owned enterprises...... | 3 661 | 2 959 | — | 97 | — | 605 | Activités secondaires des membres de coopératives et des salariés des entreprises publiques |
| Privately-owned enterprises........ | 1 527 | 826 | 202 | 8 | 319 | 172 | Entreprises privées |
| **Percentage distribution according to sector or form of organization:** | | | | | | | **Distribution en pourcentage par secteur ou type d'activité:** |
| Total..................... | 100.0 | 35.5 | 41.2 | 5.8 | 3.3 | 14.2 | Total |
| Publicly-owned enterprises........ | 52.0 | 1.7 | 67.6 | 9.5 | 4.5 | 16.7 | Entreprises publiques |
| Co-operatives ................. | 32.6 | 71.7 | 16.7 | 1.6 | 0.3 | 9.7 | Coopératives |
| Auxiliary activities of members of co-operatives and employees of publicly-owned enterprises...... | 10.8 | 80.8 | — | 2.6 | — | 16.6 | Activités secondaires des membres de coopératives et des salariés des entreprises publiques |
| Privately-owned enterprises....... | 4.6 | 54.0 | 13.3 | 0.5 | 20.9 | 11.3 | Entreprises privées |

[1] Includes material production not classified elsewhere such as publishing, wholesale and retail trade, motion picture production and individual arts and crafts.

[1] Y compris le produit matériel non classé ailleurs, tel que: édition, commerce de gros et de détail production de films cinématographiques et divers arts et métiers.

## 2. INDEX NUMBERS OF INDUSTRIAL PRODUCTION — INDICES DE LA PRODUCTION INDUSTRIELLE

### A. Selected Divisions of Industrial Activity
### Quelques branches de l'activité industrielle

| Period<br>Période | Total [1] | Mining<br><br>Industries extractives | Manufacturing [1]<br><br>Industries manufacturières [1] | Electricity and steam<br><br>Electricité et vapeur |
|---|---|---|---|---|
| ISIC — CITI | 1–3, 511–513 | 1 | 2–3, 512 | 511,513 |

*a. Indexes — Indices (1958 = 100)*

| | | | | |
|---|---|---|---|---|
| 1939.......... | 11 | ... | ... | 9 |
| 1948.......... | 22 | ... | ... | 18 |
| 1949.......... | 30 | ... | ... | 20 |
| 1950.......... | 35 | ... | ... | 24 |
| 1951.......... | 41 | ... | ... | 32 |
| 1952.......... | 48 | ... | ... | 43 |
| 1953.......... | 55 | 67 | 54 | 52 |
| 1954.......... | 61 | 80 | 59 | 59 |
| 1955.......... | 65 | 87 | 63 | 68 |
| 1956.......... | 75 | 90 | 74 | 78 |
| 1957.......... | 87 | 97 | 86 | 87 |
| 1958.......... | 100 | 100 | 100 | 100 |
| 1959.......... | 121 | 111 | 121 | 129 |
| 1960.......... | 137 | 130 | 136 | 157 |
| 1961.......... | 153 | 135 | 153 | 181 |

*b. Average Annual Rate of Change — Taux annuel moyen de variation*

| | | | | |
|---|---|---|---|---|
| 1939 – 1960.... | 12.8 | ... | ... | 14.6 |
| 1938 – 1948.... | 8.0 | ... | ... | 8.0 |
| 1950 – 1960.... | 14.6 | ... | ... | 20.7 |
| 1948 – 1953.... | 20.1 | ... | ... | 23.6 |
| 1954 – 1958.... | 13.1 | 5.7 | 14.1 | 14.1 |
| 1958 – 1960.... | 17.0 | 14.0 | 16.6 | 25.3 |

For footnotes see end of table.

Pour les notes, voir au bas du tableau.

## B. The Major Sub-divisions of Mining and Manufacturing
## Les principales subdivisions des Industries extractives et manufacturières

| Period / Période | Mining and manufacturing [1] / Industries extractives et manufacturières [1] | Food, beverages and tobacco [2] / Industries alimentaires, boissons, tobac [2] | Textiles and clothing [4] / Textiles et articles d'habillement [4] | Wood products and furniture [1,3] / Bois et meubles [1,3] | Paper and paper products / Papier et ouvrages en papier | Printing [1] / Imprimerie [1] | Leather and leather products [4] / Cuir et articles en cuir [4] | Chemicals, coal, crude petroleum and products [5] / Produits chimiques, charbon, pétrole brut et produits dérivés [5] | Non-metallic minerals and products / Minéraux non métalliques et produits dérivés | Metal mining and basic metals / Minerais métalliques et métallurgie de base | Metal products [6] / Ouvrages en métaux [6] | Other manufacturing / Autres industries manufacturières |
|---|---|---|---|---|---|---|---|---|---|---|---|---|
| ISIC — CITI | 1-3, 512 | 20-22 | 23, 243-244 | 25-26 | 27 | 28 | 241, 29 | 11, 13, 192, 30-32, 512 | 14, 199, 33 | 12, 34 | 35-38 | 39 |

### a. Indexes — Indices (1958 = 100)

| Period | | | | | | | | | | | | |
|---|---|---|---|---|---|---|---|---|---|---|---|---|
| 1939 | 11 | 18 | 12 | 19 | 14 | 26 | 9 | 10 | 7 | 1 | 2 | . |
| 1948 | 23 | 30 | 22 | 44 | 30 | 43 | 25 | 19 | 15 | 10 | 12 | 8 |
| 1949 | 30 | 40 | 29 | 56 | 36 | 60 | 36 | ... | 29 | 13 | 19 | ... |
| 1950 | 35 | 46 | 32 | 54 | 49 | 56 | 49 | 30 | 26 | 18 | 24 | 11 |
| 1951 | 41 | 56 | 37 | 62 | 45 | 50 | 67 | ... | 42 | 27 | 30 | ... |
| 1952 | 48 | 61 | 48 | 61 | 47 | 60 | 70 | 40 | 39 | 31 | 36 | 23 |
| 1953 | 55 | 66 | 55 | 66 | 57 | 65 | 72 | 47 | 53 | 39 | 44 | 35 |
| 1954 | 61 | 67 | 63 | 75 | 64 | 75 | 59 | 58 | 69 | 51 | 52 | 41 |
| 1955 | 65 | 66 | 66 | 84 | 81 | 81 | 60 | 68 | 78 | 56 | 58 | 55 |
| 1956 | 75 | 80 | 76 | 81 | 87 | 87 | 65 | 82 | 81 | 65 | 64 | 61 |
| 1957 | 87 | 87 | 91 | 94 | 92 | 91 | 91 | 90 | 96 | 83 | 80 | 80 |
| 1958 | 100 | 100 | 100 | 100 | 100 | 100 | 100 | 100 | 100 | 100 | 100 | 100 |
| 1959 | 120 | 108 | 118 | 115 | 121 | 115 | 118 | 132 | 141 | 130 | 142 | 114 |
| 1960 | 136 | 122 | 129 | 126 | 136 | 123 | 109 | 155 | 183 | 150 | 172 | 121 |
| 1961 | 152 | 141 | 129 | 138 | 146 | 122 | 118 | 175 | 253 | 167 | 196 | 136 |

### b. Average Annual Rate of Change — Taux annuel moyen de variation

| Period | | | | | | | | | | | | |
|---|---|---|---|---|---|---|---|---|---|---|---|---|
| 1939 – 1960 | 12.7 | 9.5 | 12.0 | 9.4 | 11.4 | 7.7 | 12.6 | 13.9 | 16.8 | 26.9 | 23.6 | ... |
| 1939 – 1948 | 8.5 | 5.8 | 7.0 | 9.8 | 8.8 | 5.8 | 12.0 | 7.4 | 8.8 | 29.2 | 22.0 | ... |
| 1950 – 1960 | 14.5 | 10.2 | 15.0 | 8.8 | 10.7 | 8.2 | 8.3 | 17.8 | 21.5 | 23.6 | 21.8 | 27.2 |
| 1948 – 1953 | 19.0 | 17.1 | 20.1 | 8.4 | 13.7 | 8.6 | 23.6 | 19.9 | 28.7 | 29.3 | 29.7 | 34.3 |
| 1954 – 1958 | 13.1 | 10.5 | 12.2 | 7.5 | 11.8 | 7.5 | 14.1 | 14.6 | 9.7 | 18.3 | 17.8 | 24.9 |
| 1958 – 1960 | 16.6 | 10.5 | 13.6 | 12.2 | 16.6 | 10.9 | 4.4 | 24.5 | 35.3 | 22.5 | 31.2 | 10.0 |

[1] Includes Logging (ISIC group 022) and Gas manufacturing (ISIC group 512) but excludes publishing part of ISIC major group 28).
[2] Includes Salt extraction (ISIC group 191), Vegetable and animal oils and fats (ISIC group 312) and Soap and perfume manufacturing (ISIC group 319).
[3] Includes match manufacturing (part of ISIC group 319).
[4] Includes the Manufacture of footwear and fur apparel (ISIC group 241 and parts of ISIC group 243, respectively).
[5] Includes the Manufacture of photographic goods (ISIC group 392).
[6] Includes Professional and scientific instruments (ISIC group 391) and Watches and clocks (ISIC group 393).

[1] Y compris l'Exploitation forestière (CITI groupe 022), l'Industrie du gaz (CITI groupe 512), mais non compris l'édition (dans CITI classe 28).
[2] Y compris l'Extraction du sel (CITI groupe 191), les Corps gras d'origine végétale ou animale (CITI groupe 312), ainsi que les savonneries et parfumeries (CITI groupe 319).
[3] Y compris la Fabrication des allumettes (dans CITI groupe 319).
[4] Y compris la Fabrication des chaussures (CITI groupe 241) et des articles d'habillement en fourrure (dans CITI groupe 243).
[5] Y compris la Fabrication du matériel photographique (CITI groupe 392).
[6] Comprend la Fabrication du matériel médico-chirurgical (CITI groupe 391) et la Fabrication des montres et horloges (CITI groupe 393).

### 3. INDEX NUMBERS OF INDUSTRIAL EMPLOYMENT — INDICES DE L'EMPLOI DANS L'INDUSTRIE

**A. Publicly-Owned Enterprises and Co-operatives; Mining, Manufacturing and Electricity, Gas and Steam**

**Entreprises publiques et coopératives; Industries extractives et manufacturières et Electricité, gaz et vapeur**

| Period<br>Période | Total [1] | Publicly-owned<br>enterprises [1]<br>Entreprises<br>publiques [1] | Co-operatives [1]<br>Coopératives [1] |
|---|---|---|---|
| ISCI — CITI | 1–3, 511–513 | 1–3, 511–513 | 1–3, 511–513 |

*a. Indexes — Indices (1958 = 100)*

| | | | |
|---|---|---|---|
| 1948............ | 43 | 44 | 41 |
| 1950............ | 59 | 60 | 52 |
| 1952............ | 66 | 67 | 58 |
| 1953............ | 68 | 70 | 60 |
| 1954............ | 74 | 75 | 66 |
| 1955............ | 76 | 78 | 67 |
| 1956............ | 80 | 82 | 71 |
| 1957............ | 93 | 93 | 94 |
| 1958............ | 100 | 100 | 100 |
| 1959............ | 118 | 120 | 110 |
| 1960............ | 132 | 135 | 115 |
| 1961............ | 134 | 138 | 114 |

*b. Average Annual Rate of Change — Taux annuel moyen de variation*

| | | | |
|---|---|---|---|
| 1950 – 1960...... | 8.4 | 8.4 | 8.3 |
| 1948 – 1953...... | 9.6 | 9.7 | 7.9 |
| 1954 – 1958...... | 7.8 | 7.5 | 10.9 |
| 1958 – 1960...... | 14.9 | 16.2 | 7.2 |

# BULGARIA

## B. Publicly-Owned Enterprises; Major Sub-Divisions of Mining and Manufacturing and Electricity and Steam

### Entreprises publiques; principales subdivisons des branches Industries extractives et manufacturières et Electricité et vapeur

| Period / Période | Mining and manufacturing [1] / Industries extractives et manufacturières [1] | Food, beverages and tobacco [2] / Industries alimentaires, boissons, tabac [2] | Textiles and clothing [4] / Textiles et articles d'habillement [4] | Wood products and furniture [1,3] / Bois et meubles [1,3] | Paper and paper products / Papier et ouvrages en papier | Printing [1] / Imprimerie [1] | Leather and leather products [4] / Cuir et articles en cuir [4] | Chemicals, coal, crude petroleum and products [5] / Produits chimiques, charbon, pétrole brut et produits dérivés [5] | Non-metallic minerals and products / Minéraux non métalliques et produits dérivés | Metal mining and basic metals / Minerais métalliques et métallurgie de base | Metal products [6] / Ouvrages en métaux [6] | Other manufacturing / Autres industries manufacturières | Electricity and steam / Electricité et vapeur |
|---|---|---|---|---|---|---|---|---|---|---|---|---|---|
| ISIC — CITI | 1-3 | 20–22 | 23, 243–244 | 25–26 | 27 | 28 | 241, 29 | 11,13,192, 30-32, 512 | 14, 199, 33 | 12, 34 | 35–38 | 39 | 511, 513 |

#### a. Indexes — Indices (1958 = 100)

| Period | | | | | | | | | | | | | |
|---|---|---|---|---|---|---|---|---|---|---|---|---|---|
| 1948 | 44 | 50 | 50 | 82 | 55 | 60 | 30 | 44 | 44 | 14 | 33 | 15 | 39 |
| 1950 | 61 | 63 | 65 | 104 | 57 | 102 | 52 | 61 | 59 | 20 | 62 | 23 | 48 |
| 1952 | 67 | 82 | 69 | 86 | 55 | 89 | 63 | 66 | 58 | 38 | 65 | 46 | 63 |
| 1953 | 70 | 74 | 72 | 86 | 68 | 86 | 63 | 71 | 65 | 50 | 68 | 55 | 74 |
| 1954 | 75 | 73 | 73 | 98 | 74 | 88 | 55 | 84 | 82 | 62 | 70 | 59 | 80 |
| 1955 | 78 | 72 | 74 | 104 | 85 | 86 | 58 | 94 | 80 | 67 | 72 | 66 | 86 |
| 1956 | 82 | 82 | 76 | 95 | 89 | 88 | 65 | 96 | 83 | 74 | 78 | 70 | 87 |
| 1957 | 93 | 96 | 90 | 98 | 93 | 92 | 86 | 100 | 91 | 88 | 88 | 90 | 92 |
| 1958 | 100 | 100 | 100 | 100 | 100 | 100 | 100 | 100 | 100 | 100 | 100 | 100 | 100 |
| 1959 | 120 | 119 | 125 | 116 | 107 | 108 | 115 | 111 | 119 | 109 | 132 | 119 | 104 |
| 1960 | 136 | 145 | 132 | 142 | 117 | 116 | 117 | 118 | 148 | 124 | 149 | 127 | 108 |
| 1961 | 138 | 148 | 126 | 146 | 119 | 114 | 114 | 119 | 169 | 138 | 155 | 120 | 113 |

#### b. Average Annual Rate of Change — Taux annuel moyen de variation

| Period | | | | | | | | | | | | | |
|---|---|---|---|---|---|---|---|---|---|---|---|---|---|
| 1950 – 1960 | 8.4 | 8.7 | 7.3 | 3.2 | 7.5 | 1.3 | 8.4 | 6.8 | 9.6 | 20.0 | 9.2 | 18.6 | 8.4 |
| 1948 – 1953 | 9.7 | 8.2 | 7.6 | 1.0 | 4.3 | 7.5 | 16.0 | 10.0 | 8.1 | 29.0 | 15.6 | 29.7 | 13.7 |
| 1954 – 1958 | 7.5 | 8.2 | 8.2 | 0.5 | 7.8 | 3.2 | 16.1 | 4.4 | 5.1 | 12.7 | 9.3 | 14.1 | 5.7 |
| 1958 – 1960 | 16.6 | 20.4 | 14.9 | 19.2 | 8.2 | 7.7 | 8.2 | 8.6 | 21.7 | 11.4 | 22.1 | 12.7 | 3.9 |

[1] Includes Logging (ISIC group 022) and Gas manufacturing (ISIC group 512) but excludes publishing (part of ISIC major group 28).
[2] Includes Salt extraction (ISIC group 191), Vegetable and animal oils and fats (ISIC group 312) and Soap and perfume manufacturing (ISIC group 319).
[3] Includes match manufacturing (parts of ISIC group 319).
[4] Includes the Manufacture of footwear and fur apparel (ISIC group 241 and parts of ISIC group 243, respectively).
[5] Includes the Manufacture of photographic goods (ISIC group 392).
[6] Includes Professional and scientific instruments (ISIC group 391) and Watches and clocks (ISIC group 393).

[1] Y compris l'Exploitation forestière (CITI groupe 022), l'Industrie du gaz (CITI groupe 512), mais non compris l'édition (dans CITI classe 28).
[2] Y compris l'Extraction du sel (CITI groupe 191), les Corps gras d'origine végétale ou animale (CITI groupe 312), ainsi que les savonneries et parfumeries (CITI groupe 319).
[3] Y compris la fabrication des allumettes (dans CITI groupe 319).
[4] Y compris la Fabrication des chaussures (CITI groupe 241) et des articles d'habillement en fourrure (dans CITI groupe 243).
[5] Y compris la Fabrication du matériel photographique (CITI groupe 392).
[6] Comprend la Fabrication du matériel médico-chirurgical (CITI groupe 391) et la Fabrication des montres et horloges (CITI groupe 393).

## 4. THE CHARACTERISTICS OF ALL PUBLICLY-OWNED AND CO-OPERATIVE INDUSTRIAL ENTERPRISES

### CARACTERISTIQUES DE TOUTES LES ENTREPRISES PUBLIQUES ET ENTREPRISES COOPERATIVES INDUSTRIELLES

#### 1948, 1953, 1956, 1958

Number of enterprises in units; value of gross output in million Leva; number of engaged, employees and operatives in thousands; electricity consumed in million KWH; capacity of installed power equipment in thousand horsepower; cost of production in million Leva; electricity consumed per operative in thousand KWH; capacity of installed power equipment per operative in horsepower.

Nombre d'entreprises en unités; valeur de la production en millions de leva; nombre de personnes occupées, de salariés et d'ouvriers en milliers; électricité consommée en millions de kWh; puissance installée en milliers de chevaux-vapeur; coût total de la production en millions de leva; électricité consommée par ouvrier en milliers de kWh; puissance installée par ouvrier en chevaux-vapeur.

### A. Mining, Manufacturing and Electricity, Gas and Steam
### Industries extractives et manufacturières et Electricité, gaz et vapeur

| | Number of enterprises<br>Nombre d'entreprises | | | Number of persons engaged (Average during year)<br>Nombre de personnes occupées (moyenne pendant l'année) | | | Distribution in percent of number of persons engaged<br>Répartition en pourcentage des personnes occupées | | |
| | Total | Publicly-owned enterprises<br>Entreprises publiques | Co-operatives<br>Coopératives | Total | Publicly-owned enterprises<br>Entreprises publiques | Co-operatives<br>Coopératives | Total | Publicly-owned enterprises<br>Entreprises publiques | Co-operatives<br>Coopératives |
|---|---|---|---|---|---|---|---|---|---|
| ISIC — CITI | 1–3, 511–513 | 1–3, 511–513 | 1–3, 511–513 | 1–3, 511–513 | 1–3, 511–513 | 1–3, 511–513 | 1–3, 511–513 | 1–3, 511–513 | 1–3, 511–513 |
| 1948............... | ... | ... | ... | 251.1 | 213.3 | 37.8 | 100.0 | 84.9 | 15.1 |
| 1953............... | 2 253 | 1 143 | 1 110 | 395.3 | 339.8 | 55.5 | 100.0 | 86.0 | 14.0 |
| 1956............... | 1 860 | 964 | 896 | 463.6 | 398.5 | 65.1 | 100.0 | 86.0 | 14.0 |
| 1958............... | 1 830 | 985 | 845 | 578.8 | 486.7 | 92.1 | 100.0 | 84.1 | 15.9 |

[1] For footnotes see end of table.

[1] Pour les notes, voir à la fin du tableau.

## B. The Major Sub-divisions of Mining and Manufacturing and Electricity and Steam
### Les principales subdivisions des Industries extractives et manufacturières et Electricité et vapeur

| Year and item of data | Mining and manufacturing [1] Industries extractives et manufacturières [1] | Food, beverages and tobacco [2] Industries alimentaires, boissons, tabac [2] | Textiles | Clothing, and made-up textiles Articles d'habillement, et ouvrages en tissu | Wood products and furniture [1,3] Bois et meubles [1,3] | Paper and paper products Papier et ouvrages en papier | Printing [1] Imprimerie [1] | Leather and leather products [4] Cuir et articles en cuir [4] | Chemicals, coal, crude petroleum and products Produits chimiques, charbon, pétrole brut et produits dérivés | Non-metallic minerals and products Minéraux non métalliques et produits dérivés | Metal mining and basic metals Minerais métalliques et métallurgie de base | Metal products [6] Ouvrages en métaux [6] | Other manufacturing Autres industries manufacturières | Electricity, and steam Electricité, et vapeur | Année et rubrique |
|---|---|---|---|---|---|---|---|---|---|---|---|---|---|---|---|
| ISIC | 1–3,512 | 20–22 | 23 | 243-244 | 25–26 | 27 | 28 | 241, 29 | 11,13,192 30–32, 512 | 14, 199, 33 | 12, 34 | 35–38 | 39 | 511, 513 | CITI |
| *a. Publicly-owned enterprises and co-operatives — Entreprises publiques et coopératives* | | | | | | | | | | | | | | | |
| **1948** **Operatives:** | | | | | | | | | | | | | | | **1948** **Ouvriers:** |
| Number (Average during year) | 199.5 | 34.4 | 35.2 | 11.3 | 40.3 | 2.1 | 2.4 | 10.6 | 19.4 | 13.1 | 3.5 | 21.7 | 5.5 | 2.1 | Nombre (moyenne pendant l'année) |
| Distribution in percent | 100.0 | 17.2 | 17.6 | 5.7 | 20.2 | 1.1 | 1.2 | 5.3 | 9.7 | 6.6 | 1.7 | 10.9 | 2.8 | . | Répartition en pourcentage |
| **1953** **Operatives:** | | | | | | | | | | | | | | | **1953** **Ouvriers:** |
| Number (Average during year) | 303.0 | 49.2 | 49.4 | 15.7 | 41.4 | 2.8 | 3.5 | 10.7 | 31.1 | 16.3 | 11.9 | 43.7 | 27.3 | 4.7 | Nombre (moyenne pendant l'année) |
| Distribution in percent | 100.0 | 16.2 | 16.3 | 5.2 | 13.6 | 1.0 | 1.1 | 3.5 | 10.3 | 5.4 | 3.9 | 14.4 | 9.1 | . | Répartition en pourcentage |
| **1956** Gross output | 22 572 | 7 074 | 3 696 | 1 014 | 1 499 | 353 | 220 | 545 | 2 141 | 743 | 1 282 | 2 563 | 1 442 | 653 | **1956** Production brute |
| Number of operatives (Average during year) | 368.7 | 59.0 | 54.2 | 19.5 | 44.7 | 4.1 | 3.8 | 10.4 | 43.8 | 20.8 | 17.5 | 53.5 | 37.4 | 5.7 | Nombre d'ouvriers (moyenne pendant l'année) |
| Distribution in percentage of: | | | | | | | | | | | | | | | Répartition en pourcentage: |
| Gross output | 100.0 | 31.3 | 16.4 | 4.5 | 6.6 | 1.6 | 0.9 | 2.5 | 9.4 | 3.3 | 5.7 | 11.4 | 6.4 | . | Du nombre d'ouvriers |
| Number of operatives | 100.0 | 16.0 | 14.7 | 5.2 | 12.2 | 1.1 | 1.0 | 2.8 | 11.9 | 5.6 | 4.8 | 14.5 | 10.2 | . | De la production brute |
| **1958** Number of operatives (Average during year) | 463.6 | 65.6 | 62.9 | 41.2 | 48.2 | 4.6 | 4.5 | 15.3 | 46.0 | 25.2 | 23.9 | 69.4 | 56.8 | 6.5 | **1958** Nombre d'ouvriers (moyenne pendant l'année) |
| Electricity consumed | 1 381.6 | 131.4 | 163.0 | 1.8 | 26.0 | 53.1 | 4.3 | 6.5 | 373.8 | 139.0 | 314.5 | 167.6 | 0.6 | ... | Electricité consommée |
| Capacity of installed power equipment | 1 084.3 | 160.9 | 96.6 | 1.5 | 51.9 | 28.5 | 5.6 | 13.7 | 206.3 | 96.7 | 186.7 | 234.0 | 1.9 | ... | Puissance installée |
| Distribution in percent of number of operatives | 100.0 | 14.1 | 13.6 | 8.9 | 10.4 | 0.9 | 1.0 | 3.3 | 9.9 | 5.5 | 5.1 | 15.0 | 12.3 | . | Répartition en pourcentage du nombre d'ouvriers |
| Per operative: | | | | | | | | | | | | | | | Par ouvrier: |
| Electricity consumed | 2.98 | 2.00 | 2.59 | 0.04 | 0.54 | 11.55 | 0.95 | 0.43 | 8.12 | 5.51 | 13.16 | 2.41 | 0.01 | ... | Electricité consommée |
| Capacity of installed power equipment | 2.34 | 2.45 | 1.54 | 0.04 | 1.08 | 6.20 | 1.24 | 0.90 | 4.48 | 3.84 | 7.81 | 3.37 | 0.03 | ... | Puissance installée |
| *b. Publicly-owned enterprises — Entreprises publiques* | | | | | | | | | | | | | | | |
| **1948** Number of employees (Average during year) | 208.9 | 42.6 | 39.9 | 2.2 | 41.3 | 2.7 | 3.3 | 3.1 | 24.6 | 12.7 | 4.5 | 25.8 | 6.2 | 4.4 | **1948** Nombre de salariés (moyenne pendant l'année) |
| Number of operatives (Average during year) | 166.6 | 34.2 | 32.1 | 2.0 | 33.4 | 2.0 | 2.4 | 2.5 | 19.2 | 11.7 | 3.5 | 18.8 | 4.8 | 2.1 | Nombre d'ouvriers (moyenne pendant l'année) |
| Distribution in percent of: | | | | | | | | | | | | | | | Répartition en pourcentage: |
| Number of employees | 100.0 | 20.3 | 19.1 | 1.1 | 19.8 | 1.3 | 1.5 | 1.5 | 11.8 | 6.1 | 2.1 | 12.4 | 3.0 | . | Du nombre de salariés |
| Number of operatives | 100.0 | 20.5 | 19.2 | 1.2 | 20.1 | 1.2 | 1.4 | 1.5 | 11.6 | 7.0 | 2.1 | 11.3 | 2.9 | . | Du nombre d'ouvriers |
| **1953** Number of enterprises | 1 065 | 356 | 161 | 32 | 135 | 15 | 29 | 24 | 66 | 63 | 17 | 115 | 52 | 78 | **1953** Nombre d'entreprises |
| Number of employees (Average during year) | 331.3 | 63.7 | 56.1 | 4.6 | 42.9 | 3.4 | 4.7 | 6.5 | 39.1 | 18.8 | 15.9 | 52.9 | 22.7 | 8.5 | Nombre de salariés (moyenne pendant l'année) |
| Number of operatives (Average during year) | 258.1 | 46.3 | 46.4 | 3.9 | 35.1 | 2.6 | 3.5 | 5.4 | 30.6 | 15.6 | 11.9 | 38.7 | 18.1 | 4.7 | Nombre d'ouvriers (moyenne pendant l'année) |
| Distribution in percent of: | | | | | | | | | | | | | | | Répartition en pourcentage: |
| Number of employees | 100.0 | 19.2 | 16.9 | 1.4 | 12.9 | 1.1 | 1.4 | 2.0 | 11.8 | 5.6 | 4.8 | 16.0 | 6.9 | . | Du nombre de salariés |
| Number of operatives | 100.0 | 17.9 | 18.0 | 1.5 | 13.6 | 1.0 | 1.3 | 2.1 | 11.9 | 6.0 | 4.6 | 15.0 | 7.1 | . | Du nombre d'ouvriers |
| Total cost of production | 12 378 | 4 097 | 2 378 | 362 | 1 002 | 207 | 172 | 462 | 1 145 | 434 | 503 | 1 591 | ... | 356 | Coût total de la production |
| Percentage of total cost of production due to: | | | | | | | | | | | | | | | Pourcentage du coût total de la production dû: |
| Materials, fuels and electricity | 73.2 | 87.1 | 79.0 | 88.8 | 43.1 | 78.3 | 70.2 | 85.6 | 52.7 | 56.0 | 58.9 | 64.2 | ... | 43.3 | Aux matières premières et auxiliaires, combustibles et électricité |
| Wages and salaries | 18.1 | 7.6 | 14.9 | 10.2 | 36.1 | 11.4 | 20.6 | 10.9 | 33.3 | 32.4 | 27.0 | 25.5 | ... | 18.1 | Aux traitements et salaires |
| Depreciation | 4.1 | 2.4 | 3.7 | 0.2 | 3.2 | 5.9 | 5.3 | 1.3 | 10.1 | 6.8 | 7.3 | 4.7 | ... | 34.0 | A l'amortissement |
| Other | 4.6 | 2.9 | 2.4 | 0.8 | 17.6 | 4.4 | 3.9 | 2.2 | 3.9 | 4.8 | 6.8 | 5.6 | ... | 4.6 | A d'autres facteurs |

For footnotes see end of table.　　　　Pour les notes, voir au bas du tableau.

**B. The Major Sub-divisions of Mining and Manufacturing and Electricity and Steam** (continued)

**Les principales subdivisions des Industries extractives et manufacturières et Electricité et vapeur** (suite)

| Year and item of data | Mining and manu-facturing [1] / Industries ex-tractives et manufac-turières [1] | Food, beverages and tobacco [2] / Industries alimen-taires, boissons, tabac [2] | Textiles | Clothing, and made-up textiles / Articles d'habil-lement, et ouvrages en tissu | Wood products and furniture [1,3] / Bois et meubles [1,3] | Paper and paper products / Papier et ouvrages en papier | Printing [1] / Im-primerie [1] | Leather and leather products [4] / Cuir et articles en cuir [4] | Chemicals, coal, crude petroleum and products / Produits chimiques charbon, pétrole brut et produits dérivés | Non-metallic minerals and products / Minéraux non métal-liques et produits dérivés | Metal mining and basic metals / Minerais métal-liques et métal-lurgie de base | Metal products [6] / Ouvrages en métaux [6] | Other manu-facturing / Autres in-dustries manufac-turières | Electricity, and steam / Electricité et vapeur | Année et rubrique |
|---|---|---|---|---|---|---|---|---|---|---|---|---|---|---|---|
| ISIC | 1–3,512 | 20–22 | 23 | 243-244 | 25–26 | 27 | 28 | 241, 29 | 11,13,192 30–32, 512 | 14, 199, 33 | 12, 34 | 35–38 | 39 | 511, 513 | CITI |

*b. Publicly-owned enterprises — Entreprises publiques*

| Year and item of data | 1–3,512 | 20–22 | 23 | 243-244 | 25–26 | 27 | 28 | 241, 29 | 11,13,192 30–32, 512 | 14, 199, 33 | 12, 34 | 35–38 | 39 | 511, 513 | Année et rubrique |
|---|---|---|---|---|---|---|---|---|---|---|---|---|---|---|---|
| **1956** | | | | | | | | | | | | | | | **1956** |
| Gross output | 20 612 | 6 798 | 3 590 | 422 | 1 346 | 333 | 220 | 402 | 2 106 | 720 | 1 282 | 2 349 | 1 044 | 653 | Production brute |
| Number of enterprises | 932 | 270 | 122 | 14 | 121 | 14 | 25 | 14 | 67 | 74 | 17 | 101 | 93 | 32 | Nombre d'entreprises |
| Number of employees (Average during year) | 388.5 | 70.4 | 58.7 | 6.1 | 47.2 | 4.4 | 4.7 | 6.8 | 53.5 | 24.0 | 23.8 | 60.2 | 28.7 | 10.0 | Nombre de salariés (moyenne pendant l'année) |
| Number of operatives (Average during year) | 313.0 | 56.1 | 49.8 | 5.4 | 38.7 | 3.6 | 3.8 | 5.7 | 42.9 | 20.1 | 17.5 | 46.6 | 22.8 | 5.7 | Nombre d'ouvriers (moyenne pendant l'année) |
| Distribution in percent of: | | | | | | | | | | | | | | | Répartition en pour-centage: |
| Gross output | 100.0 | 32.9 | 17.4 | 2.1 | 6.5 | 1.6 | 1.1 | 2.0 | 10.2 | 3.5 | 6.2 | 11.4 | 5.1 | . | De la production brute |
| Number of employees | 100.0 | 18.1 | 15.1 | 1.6 | 12.1 | 1.1 | 1.2 | 1.8 | 13.8 | 6.1 | 6.2 | 15.5 | 7.4 | . | Du nombre de salariés |
| Number of operatives | 100.0 | 17.9 | 15.9 | 1.7 | 12.4 | 1.1 | 1.2 | 1.9 | 13.7 | 6.4 | 5.6 | 14.9 | 7.3 | . | Du nombre d'ouvriers |
| Total cost of production | 17 095 | 5 440 | 3 556 | 290 | 1 200 | 263 | 175 | 344 | 1 883 | 666 | 1 281 | 1 997 | ... | 491 | Coût total de la production |
| Percentage of total cost of production due to: | | | | | | | | | | | | | | | Pourcentage du coût total de la production dû: |
| Materials, fuels and electricity | 72.6 | 86.5 | 83.5 | 88.5 | 44.2 | 76.3 | 65.2 | 80.1 | 53.4 | 51.5 | 66.2 | 62.2 | ... | 46.0 | Aux matières pre-mières et auxiliaires, combustibles et électricité |
| Wages and salaries | 18.5 | 9.3 | 13.4 | 9.8 | 36.6 | 13.2 | 25.0 | 15.1 | 29.5 | 33.2 | 20.4 | 27.2 | ... | 18.0 | Aux traitements et salaires |
| Depreciation | 5.4 | 2.5 | 3.6 | 0.4 | 4.6 | 7.9 | 7.3 | 2.4 | 12.6 | 10.1 | 9.3 | 6.5 | ... | 32.3 | A l'amortissement |
| Other | 3.5 | 1.7 | 1.5 | 1.3 | 14.6 | 2.6 | 2.5 | 2.4 | 4.5 | 5.2 | 4.1 | 4.1 | ... | 3.7 | A d'autres facteurs |
| **1958** | | | | | | | | | | | | | | | **1958** |
| Number of enterprises | 956 | 275 | 121 | 18 | 121 | 13 | 24 | 16 | 59 | 80 | 16 | 107 | 106 | 29 | Nombre d'entreprises |
| Number of employees (Average during year) | 475.2 | 86.1 | 68.3 | 15.5 | 49.6 | 5.0 | 5.4 | 10.4 | 55.4 | 29.0 | 32.1 | 77.7 | 40.7 | 11.5 | Nombre de salariés (moyenne pendant l'année) |
| Number of operatives (Average during year) | 382.0 | 62.2 | 58.8 | 14.3 | 40.9 | 4.1 | 4.5 | 9.0 | 44.6 | 24.6 | 23.9 | 60.7 | 34.4 | 6.5 | Nombre d'ouvriers (moyenne pendant l'année) |
| Distribution in percent of: | | | | | | | | | | | | | | | Répartition en pour-centage: |
| Number of employees | 100.0 | 18.1 | 14.3 | 3.3 | 10.4 | 1.1 | 1.1 | 2.2 | 11.7 | 6.1 | 6.7 | 16.4 | 8.6 | . | Du nombre de salariés |
| Number of operatives | 100.0 | 16.2 | 15.4 | 3.8 | 10.7 | 1.0 | 1.2 | 2.4 | 11.7 | 6.4 | 6.3 | 15.8 | 9.1 | . | Du nombre d'ouvriers |
| Total cost of production | 22 847 | 7 145 | 5 055 | 619 | 1 386 | 277 | 200 | 526 | 2 161 | 800 | 1 730 | 2 901 | ... | 594 | Coût total de la production |
| Percentage of total cost of production due to: | | | | | | | | | | | | | | | Pourcentage du coût de la production dû: |
| Materials, fuels and electricity | 74.7 | 87.0 | 85.2 | 85.4 | 45.9 | 76.6 | 65.3 | 79.8 | 55.1 | 51.2 | 61.1 | 66.2 | ... | 42.6 | Aux matières pre-mières et auxiliaires, combustibles et électricité |
| Wages and salaries | 17.3 | 9.1 | 11.1 | 13.6 | 35.8 | 14.8 | 25.7 | 17.1 | 27.5 | 33.6 | 20.8 | 25.6 | ... | 17.3 | Aux traitements et salaires |
| Depreciation | 4.6 | 1.8 | 2.8 | 0.3 | 3.8 | 6.8 | 5.8 | 1.5 | 13.8 | 8.8 | 12.0 | 4.3 | ... | 36.0 | A l'amortissement |
| Other | 3.4 | 2.1 | 0.9 | 0.7 | 14.5 | 1.8 | 3.2 | 1.6 | 3.6 | 6.4 | 6.1 | 3.9 | ... | 4.1 | A d'autres facteurs |

For footnotes see end of table.    Pour les notes, voir au bas du tableau.

# BULGARIA

## B.   The Major Sub-divisions of Mining and Manufacturing and Electricity and Steam (continued)
## Les principales subdivisions des Industries extractives et manufacturières et Electricité et vapeur (suite)

| Year and item of data | Mining and man-facturing [1] / Industries ex-tractives et manufac-turières [1] | Food, beverages and tobacco [2] / Industries alimen-taires, boissons, tabac [2] | Textiles | Clothing, and made-up textiles / Articles d'habil-lement, et ouvrages en tissu | Wood products and furniture[1,3] / Bois et meubles[1,3] | Paper and paper products / Papier et ouvrages en papier | Printing [1] / Im-primerie[1] | Leather and leather products[4] / Cuir et articles en cuir [4] | Chemicals coal, crude petroleum and products / Produits chimiques, charbon, pétrole brut et produits dérivés | Non-metallic minerals and products / Minéraux non métal-liques et produits dérivés | Metal mining and basic metals / Minerais métal-liques et métal-lurgie de base | Metal products [6] / Ouvrages en métaux [6] | Other manu-facturing / Autres in-dustries manufac-turières | Electricity, and steam / Electricité et vapeur | Année et rubrique |
|---|---|---|---|---|---|---|---|---|---|---|---|---|---|---|---|
| **ISIC** | 1–3, 512 | 20–22 | 23 | 243-244 | 25–26 | 27 | 28 | 241, 29 | 11,13,192 30–32, 512 | 14, 199, 33 | 12, 34 | 35–38 | 39 | 511, 513 | **CITI** |
| | | | | | *c. Co-operatives — Coopératives* | | | | | | | | | | |
| **1948** Operatives: Number (Average during year) | 32.9 | 0.2 | 3.1 | 9.3 | 6.9 | 0.1 | — | 8.1 | 0.2 | 1.4 | — | 2.9 | 0.7 | — | **1948** Ouvriers: Nombre (moyenne pendant l'année) |
| Distribution in percent | 100.0 | 0.6 | 9.4 | 28.2 | 21.0 | 0.3 | — | 24.6 | 0.7 | 4.2 | — | 8.8 | 2.2 | — | Répartition en pour-centage |
| **1953** Operatives: Number (Average during year) | 44.9 | 2.9 | 3.0 | 11.8 | 6.3 | 0.2 | — | 5.3 | 0.5 | 0.7 | — | 5.0 | 9.2 | — | **1953** Ouvriers: Nombre (moyenne pendant l'année) |
| Distribution in percent | 100.0 | 6.4 | 6.7 | 26.3 | 14.0 | 0.4 | — | 11.9 | 1.1 | 1.5 | — | 11.2 | 20.5 | — | Répartition en pour-centage |
| **1956** Gross output: Value | 1 960 | 276 | 106 | 592 | 153 | 20 | — | 143 | 35 | 23 | — | 214 | 398 | — | **1956** Production brute Valeur |
| Distribution in percent | 100.0 | 14.0 | 5.4 | 30.2 | 7.9 | 1.0 | — | 7.3 | 1.8 | 1.1 | — | 10.9 | 20.4 | — | Répartition en pour-centage |
| Operatives: Number (Average during year) | 55.7 | 2.9 | 4.4 | 14.1 | 6.0 | 0.5 | — | 4.7 | 0.9 | 0.7 | — | 6.9 | 14.6 | — | Ouvriers: Nombre (moyenne pendant l'année) |
| Distribution in percent | 100.0 | 5.2 | 7.9 | 25.3 | 10.7 | 0.9 | — | 8.5 | 1.6 | 1.3 | — | 12.3 | 26.3 | — | Répartition en pour-centage |
| **1958** Operatives: Number (Average during year) | 81.6 | 3.4 | 4.1 | 26.9 | 7.3 | 0.5 | — | 6.3 | 1.4 | 0.6 | — | 8.7 | 22.4 | — | **1958** Ouvriers: Nombre (moyenne pendant l'année) |
| Distribution in percent | 100.0 | 4.1 | 5.0 | 33.0 | 9.0 | 0.6 | — | 7.7 | 1.7 | 0.7 | — | 10.7 | 27.5 | — | Répartition en pour-centage |

[1] Includes Logging (ISIC group 022) but excludes publishing (part of ISIC major group 28).
[2] Includes Salt extraction (ISIC group 191), Vegetable and animal oils and fats (ISIC group 312) and Soap and perfume manufacturing (ISIC group 319).
[3] Includes match manufacturing (part of ISIC group 319).
[4] Includes the Manufacture of footwear and fur apparel (ISIC group 241 and parts of ISIC group 243, respectively).
[5] Includes the Manufacture of photographic goods (ISIC group 392).
[6] Includes Professional and scientific instruments (ISIC group 391) and Watches and clocks (ISIC group 393).

[1] Y compris l'Exploitation forestière (CITI groupe 022), l'Industrie du gaz (CITI groupe 512), mais non compris l'édition (dans CITI classe 28).
[2] Y compris l'Extraction du sel (CITI groupe 191), les Corps gras d'origine végétale ou animale (CITI groupe 312), ainsi que les savonneries et parfumeries (CITI groupe 319).
[3] Y compris la fabrication des allumettes (dans CITI groupe 319).
[4] Y compris la Fabrication des chaussures (CITI groupe 241) et des articles d'habillement en fourrure (CITI groupe 243).
[5] Y compris la Fabrication du matériel photographique (CITI groupe 392).
[6] Comprend la Fabrication du matériel médico-chirurgical (CITI groupe 391) et la Fabrication des montres et horloges (CITI groupe 393).

# BURMA — BIRMANIE

## Gross Domestic Product

Estimates of expenditure on and the origin of the gross domestic product are presented in Table 1. The data are derived from information received from the Central Statistical and Economics Department, Rangoon, in response to the United Nations national accounts questionnaire and the annual publication on national income. Official estimates and descriptions are published annually in *The National Income of Burma*, Ministry of National Planning, Rangoon.

## Characteristics and Structure of Industrial Activity

The data set out in Table 2 result from the First Industrial Census taken for the year, 1952-1953, by the Government and were abstracted from the *Advance Publications, 1953 Census Stage, Industry and Cottage Industry*, Series A, Advance Release No. 7, published by the Census Department, Rangoon, 28 February 1955. The Census covered all units engaged in manufacturing, including those in households, located in 252 cities and towns of Burma proper. The cities and towns included in the Census comprised practically all of the urban areas of the country although regions of the country such as the Shan States were not covered by the Census. The Census involved the collection of data from all manufacturing establishments engaging 10 or more and from a sample of smaller units.

The data in Table 3 are derived from that part of the results of the 1952-1953 Census mentioned above which covered establishments with 10 or more employees, and from the results of the 1958-1959 annual survey of manufactures, which also covered establishments in urban areas with 10 or more employees. In the case of this latter survey, data for about 10 per cent of the establishments included were estimated. The results of the 1952-1953 Census are published as mentioned above, the results of the 1958-1959 survey are published in *Annual Survey of Manufactures 1958-1959* by the Directorate of Industries and the Central Statistical and Economics Department.

The data shown in Table 4 are taken from that part of the results of the 1952-1953 Census mentioned above which covered establishments with 9 or fewer employees, and from the results of the sample survey of establishments with 9 or fewer employees in selected major groups in urban areas for the year 1957-1958. An area sampling technique was used to conduct the survey.

The restriction of all of the enquiries to urban areas resulted in incomplete data on a number of important kinds of industrial activity in Burma—namely, rice mill-

## Produit intérieur brut

Le tableau 1 contient des estimations des dépenses imputées au produit intérieur brut, ainsi que des estimations du produit intérieur brut par secteur d'activité d'origine. Les données sont tirées des renseignements communiqués par le Central Statistical and Economics Department, Rangoon, en réponse au questionnaire de l'ONU sur la comptabilité nationale et de la publication annuelle concernant le revenu national. Les estimations officielles et les renseignements connexes sont publiés chaque année dans *The National Income of Burma*, Ministry of National Planning, Rangoon.

## Caractéristiques et structure de l'activité industrielle

Les données du tableau 2 sont tirées du premier recensement industriel exécuté pour l'année 1952-1953 par le gouvernement et proviennent de *Advance Publications, 1953 Census Stage, Industry and Cottage Industry*, Series A, Advance Release No 7, publié par le Service de recensement, Rangoon, 28 février 1955. Le recensement couvrait toutes les unités exerçant une activité manufacturière, y compris les ménages, situées dans 252 villes de la Birmanie proprement dite. Les villes en question comprenaient pratiquement toutes les régions urbaines du pays; cependant, certaines régions comme les Etats Shan n'ont pas été comprises dans le recensement. Les unités recensées étaient tous les établissements manufacturiers occupant 10 personnes ou plus, et un échantillon d'unités plus petites.

Les données du tableau 3 sont tirées de la partie des résultats du recensement de 1952-1953 mentionné ci-dessus qui couvrait les établissements occupant 10 salariés ou plus et des résultats de l'enquête annuelle de 1958-1959 sur l'industrie manufacturière, qui couvrait également les établissements des régions urbaines occupant 10 salariés ou plus. Dans le cas de l'enquête, les données reposent sur des estimations pour 10 p. 100 environ des établissements retenus. Les résultats du recensement de 1952-1953 sont publiés dans l'ouvrage indiqué ci-dessus; ceux de l'enquête de 1958-1959 sont publiés dans *Annual Survey of Manufactures 1958-1959* par le Directorate of Industries et le Central Statistical and Economics Department.

Les données du tableau 4 sont tirées de la partie des résultats du recensement de 1952-1953 mentionné ci-dessus qui couvrait les établissements occupant 9 salariés ou moins et des résultats de l'enquête par sondage de 1957-1958 effectuée dans les régions urbaines, auprès des établissements de certaines classes occupant 9 salariés ou moins. Un sondage géographique a été utilisé dans le cas de cette enquête.

Etant donné que toutes les enquêtes ont été limitées aux régions urbaines, elles n'ont fourni que des renseignements incomplets sur un certain nombre d'activités indus-

ing (in ISIC major group 20) and saw milling and related activities (in ISIC major group 25). However, the considerable increase in the value added in ISIC major group 31-32 between 1952-53 and 1958-59 is the result of a change in the method of valuing production in the case of petroleum refining.

The definitions utilized for the items of data tabulated below are believed to conform to the International Standards in Basic Industrial Statistics. Value added is valued at market prices, but its definition in the case of the 1958-1959 survey covering establishments with 10 or more employees differs from that for value added in the other enquiries in that it excludes the value of repair and maintenance work.

trielles importantes en Birmanie, notamment le décorticage, etc., du riz (dans la classe 20 de la CITI), ainsi que les scieries et le travail mécanique du bois (dans la classe 25 de la CITI). Cependant, l'augmentation considérable de la valeur ajoutée dans les classes 31-32 de la CITI entre 1952-1953 et 1958-1959 vient de ce qu'on a modifié la méthode d'évaluation de la production dans le cas du raffinage du pétrole.

On pense que les définitions des rubriques qui apparaissent dans le tableau sont conformes aux Normes internationales relatives aux statistiques industrielles de base. La valeur joutée est comptée aux prix du marché, mais dans le cas de l'enquête de 1958-1959 sur les établissements occupant 10 salariés ou plus, elle n'est pas définie de la même manière que pour les autres enquêtes en ce sens qu'elle ne comprend pas la valeur des travaux de réparation et d'entretien.

## 1. THE GROSS DOMESTIC PRODUCT — PRODUIT INTERIEUR BRUT

Million kyats      Millions de kyats

### A. Expenditure on the Gross Domestic Product at Market Prices
### Dépenses relatives au produit intérieur brut aux prix du marché

| Item of data and year [1]<br>Rubrique et année [1] | Total | Consumption<br>Consommation | | Gross Domestic Capital Formation<br>Formation brute de capital intérieur | | Net exports of goods and services<br>Exportations nettes de biens et de services | |
|---|---|---|---|---|---|---|---|
| | | Total | Government<br>Etat | Total | Fixed<br>Fixe | Exports less imports<br>Exportations moins importations | Exports<br>Exportations |
| | | | *a. At Current Prices — Aux prix courants* | | | | |
| **Absolute figures —Chiffres absolus** | | | | | | | |
| 1939 | 1 458 | 1 029 | 114 | 178 | 147 | 251 | ... |
| 1948 | 3 557 | 3 173 | 280 | 602 | 525 | −218 | 744 |
| 1951 | 3 690 | 2 986 | 318 | 476 | 431 | 228 | 1 020 |
| 1952 | 4 084 | 3 119 | 395 | 743 | 610 | 222 | 1 154 |
| 1953 | 4 620 | 3 460 | 525 | 876 | 652 | 284 | 1 342 |
| 1954 | 4 589 | 3 673 | 698 | 1 011 | 833 | −95 | 1 113 |
| 1955 | 4 813 | 3 759 | 638 | 1 009 | 906 | 45 | 1 165 |
| 1956 | 5 162 | 4 071 | 688 | 930 | 952 | 161 | 1 232 |
| 1957 | 5 452 | 4 634 | 746 | 1 085 | 1 018 | −267 | 1 245 |
| 1958 | 5 373 | 4 529 | 848 | 1 183 | 1 135 | −339 | 984 |
| 1959 | 5 583 | 4 605 | 875 | 1 098 | 1 003 | −102 | 1 098 |
| 1960 | 5 991 | 5 065 | 969 | 1 119 | 976 | −193 | 1 267 |
| 1961 | 6 221 | 5 314 | 940 | 1 000 | 954 | −93 | 1 085 |
| **Percentage distribution of average annual expenditure — Distribution en pourcentage des dépenses annuelles moyennes** | | | | | | | |
| 1939 | 100.0 | 70.6 | 7.8 | 12.2 | 10.1 | 17.2 | ... |
| 1948 | 100.0 | 89.2 | 7.9 | 16.9 | 14.8 | −6.1 | 20.9 |
| 1951−1960 | 100.0 | 80.8 | 13.6 | 19.3 | 17.2 | −0.1 | 23.5 |
| 1951 | 100.0 | 80.9 | 8.6 | 12.9 | 11.7 | 6.2 | 27.6 |
| 1953 | 100.0 | 74.9 | 11.4 | 19.0 | 14.1 | 6.1 | 29.1 |
| 1954 | 100.0 | 80.0 | 15.2 | 22.0 | 18.2 | −2.0 | 24.3 |
| 1958 | 100.0 | 84.3 | 15.8 | 22.0 | 21.1 | −6.3 | 18.3 |
| 1960 | 100.0 | 84.2 | 16.2 | 19.1 | 16.7 | −3.3 | 21.2 |

For footnotes see end of table.      Pour les notes, voir au bas du tableau.

## B. The Gross Domestic Product at Market Prices According to Origin
### Origine par secteur d'activité du produit intérieur brut aux prix du marché

| Item of data and year[1]<br>Rubrique et année[1] | Total | Agricultural sector<br>Secteur agricole | Industrial Sector — Secteur industriel | | | | | Transportation and communication<br>Transports et communications | Other sectors<br>Autres secteurs |
|---|---|---|---|---|---|---|---|---|---|
| | | | Total | Mining<br>Industries extractives | Manufacturing<br>Industries manufacturières | Construction<br>Bâtiment et travaux publics | Electricity, gas and water<br>Electricité, gaz et eau | | |
| ISIC — CITI | 0–9 | 0 | 1–5 | 1 | 2–3 | 4 | 5 | 7 | 6, 8–9 |

### a. At Current Prices — Aux prix courants

| Item of data and year[1] | Total | Agricultural | Total | Mining | Manufacturing | Construction | Electricity | Transport | Other |
|---|---|---|---|---|---|---|---|---|---|
| **Absolute figures — Chiffres absolus** | | | | | | | | | |
| 1939 | 1 458 | 699 | ... | 128 | ... | ... | 8 | 31 | 592 [2] |
| 1951 | 3 690 | 1 713 | 552 | 58 | 380 | 95 | 19 | 53 | 1 372 |
| 1952 | 4 084 | 1 853 | 634 | 74 | 416 | 126 | 18 | 62 | 1 535 |
| 1953 | 4 620 | 1 990 | 683 | 63 | 470 | 132 | 18 | 71 | 1 876 |
| 1954 | 4 589 | 1 990 | 736 | 49 | 492 | 165 | 30 | 83 | 1 780 |
| 1955 | 4 813 | 2 026 | 804 | 73 | 523 | 172 | 36 | 96 | 1 887 |
| 1956 | 5 162 | 2 101 | 835 | 77 | 561 | 160 | 37 | 95 | 2 131 |
| 1957 | 5 452 | 2 269 | 966 | 82 | 678 | 165 | 41 | 90 | 2 127 |
| 1958 | 5 373 | 2 179 | 1 019 | 82 | 713 | 177 | 47 | 89 | 2 086 |
| 1959 | 5 583 | 2 374 | 1 083 | 95 | 787 | 164 | 37 | 99 | 2 027 |
| 1960 | 5 991 | 2 533 | 1 204 | 101 | 852 | 186 | 65 | 124 | 2 130 |
| 1961 | 6 221 | 2 688 | ... | 92 | ... | ... | 73 | 112 | 3 256 [2] |
| **Percentage distribution according to sector— Distribution en pourcentage par secteur** | | | | | | | | | |
| 1939 | 100.0 | 48.0 | ... | 8.8 | ... | ... | 0.5 | 2.1 | 40.6 [2] |
| 1951 – 1960 | 100.0 | 42.6 | 17.3 | 1.5 | 11.9 | 3.1 | 0.7 | 1.7 | 38.4 |
| 1951 | 100.0 | 46.4 | 15.0 | 1.6 | 10.3 | 2.6 | 0.5 | 1.4 | 37.2 |
| 1953 | 100.0 | 43.1 | 14.8 | 1.4 | 10.2 | 2.8 | 0.4 | 1.5 | 40.6 |
| 1954 | 100.0 | 43.4 | 16.0 | 1.1 | 10.7 | 3.6 | 0.6 | 1.8 | 38.8 |
| 1958 | 100.0 | 40.5 | 19.0 | 1.5 | 13.3 | 3.3 | 0.9 | 1.7 | 38.8 |
| 1960 | 100.0 | 42.2 | 20.1 | 1.7 | 14.2 | 3.1 | 1.1 | 2.1 | 35.6 |

### b. At Prices of 1948 — Aux prix de 1948

| Item of data and year[1] | Total | Agricultural | Total | Mining | Manufacturing | Construction | Electricity | Transport | Other |
|---|---|---|---|---|---|---|---|---|---|
| **Absolute figures — Chiffres absolus** | | | | | | | | | [2] |
| 1939 | 4 945 | 2 267 | ... | 273 | ... | ... | 31 | 117 | 2 257 |
| 1948 | 3 557 | 1 724 | ... | 29 | ... | ... | 14 | 63 | 1 727 |
| 1951 | 3 431 | 1 589 | ... | 30 | ... | ... | 11 | 43 | 1 758 |
| 1952 | 3 636 | 1 706 | ... | 34 | ... | ... | 10 | 48 | 1 838 |
| 1953 | 3 899 | 1 813 | ... | 36 | ... | ... | 11 | 56 | 1 983 |
| 1954 | 4 046 | 1 810 | ... | 49 | ... | ... | 22 | 68 | 2 097 |
| 1955 | 4 294 | 1 880 | ... | 60 | ... | ... | 26 | 79 | 2 249 |
| 1956 | 4 456 | 1 931 | ... | 66 | ... | ... | 28 | 78 | 2 353 |
| 1957 | 4 934 | 2 097 | ... | 84 | ... | ... | 31 | 76 | 2 646 |
| 1958 | 4 770 | 1 967 | ... | 102 | ... | ... | 37 | 74 | 2 590 |
| 1959 | 5 106 | 2 144 | ... | 117 | ... | ... | 29 | 82 | 2 734 |
| 1960 | 5 513 | 2 230 | ... | 116 | ... | ... | 50 | 88 | 3 029 |
| 1961 | 5 408 | 2 207 | ... | 112 | ... | ... | 58 | 86 | 2 945 |
| **Percentage distribution according to sector— Distribution en pourcentage par secteur** | | | | | | | | | |
| 1939 | 100.0 | 45.9 | ... | 5.5 | ... | ... | 0.6 | 2.4 | 45.6 |
| 1948 | 100.0 | 48.5 | ... | 0.8 | ... | ... | 0.4 | 1.7 | 48.6 |
| 1951 – 1960 | 100.0 | 43.4 | ... | 1.6 | ... | ... | 0.6 | 1.6 | 52.8 |
| 1951 | 100.0 | 46.3 | ... | 0.9 | ... | ... | 0.3 | 1.3 | 51.2 |
| 1953 | 100.0 | 46.5 | ... | 0.9 | ... | ... | 0.3 | 1.4 | 50.9 |
| 1954 | 100.0 | 44.7 | ... | 1.2 | ... | ... | 0.6 | 1.7 | 51.8 |
| 1958 | 100.0 | 41.2 | ... | 2.1 | ... | ... | 0.8 | 1.6 | 54.3 |
| 1960 | 100.0 | 41.0 | ... | 2.1 | ... | ... | 0.9 | 1.6 | 54.4 |
| **Average annual rate of growth—Taux annuel moyen d'accroissement** | | | | | | | | | |
| 1939 – 1960 | 0.5 | −0.1 | ... | −4.0 | ... | ... | 2.3 | −1.4 | 1.4 |
| 1939 – 1948 | −3.6 | −3.0 | ... | — | ... | ... | −8.4 | −6.6 | −2.9 |
| 1948 – 1953 | 1.9 | 1.0 | ... | 4.4 | ... | ... | −4.7 | −2.3 | 2.8 |
| 1951 – 1960 | 5.4 | 3.8 | ... | 16.2 | ... | ... | 18.4 | 8.3 | 6.2 |
| 1951 – 1953 | 6.6 | 6.8 | ... | 9.5 | ... | ... | — | 14.1 | 6.2 |
| 1954 – 1958 | 4.2 | 2.1 | ... | 20.1 | ... | ... | 13.9 | 2.1 | 5.4 |
| 1958 – 1960 | 7.5 | 6.5 | ... | 6.6 | ... | ... | 16.2 | 9.0 | 6.6 |

[1] Fiscal year ending 30 September.
[2] Includes Manufacturing and Construction (ISIC divisions 2-4).

[1] Année fiscale se terminant le 30 septembre.
[2] Y compris Industries manufacturières et Bâtiment et travaux publics (CITI branches 2-4).

# BURMA

## 2. CHARACTERISTICS OF ALL MANUFACTURING ESTABLISHMENTS IN URBAN AREAS ACCORDING TO MAJOR GROUP OF INDUSTRIAL ACTIVITY

### CARACTERISTIQUES DE TOUS LES ETABLISSEMENTS MANUFACTURIERS DES REGIONS URBAINES, PAR CLASSE D'ACTIVITE INDUSTRIELLE

### 1. X. 1952 — 30. IX. 1953

Number of establishments in units; value added and wages and salaries in million Kyats; number of engaged in thousands; and value added per person engaged in thousand Kyats

Nombre d'établissements en unités; valeur ajoutée et traitements et salaires en millions de kyats; nombre de personnes occupées en milliers; valeur ajoutée par personne occupée en milliers de kyats

| Item of data | Manufacturing — Industries manufacturières | Food, beverages and tobacco — Industries alimentaires, boissons, tabac | Textiles | Clothing, footwear and made-up textiles — Articles d'habillement, chaussures et ouvrages en tissu | Wood products and furniture — Bois et meubles | Paper and paper products — Papier et ouvrages en papier | Printing and publishing — Imprimerie et édition | Leather and leather products except wearing apparel — Cuir et articles en cuir, à l'exclusion des articles d'habillement | Rubber products — Ouvrages en caoutchouc | Chemicals and chemical, petroleum and coal products — Produits chimiques et dérivés du pétrole et du charbon | Non-metallic mineral products — Produits minéraux non métalliques | Basic metals — Métallurgie de base | Metal products — Ouvrages en métaux | Other manufacturing — Autres industries manufacturières | Rubrique |
|---|---|---|---|---|---|---|---|---|---|---|---|---|---|---|---|
| ISIC | 2–3 | 20–22 | 23 | 24 | 25–26 | 27 | 28 | 29 | 30 | 31–32 | 33 | 34 | 35–38 | 39 | CITI |
| *a. Absolute Figures — Chiffres absolus* | | | | | | | | | | | | | | | |
| Number of establishments | 33 128 | 6 366 | 4 833 | 6 191 | 5 606 | 158 | 276 | 212 | 66 | 2 487 | 816 | 55 | 3 027 | 3 035 | Nombre d'établissements |
| Value added | 228.7 | 107.1 | 32.1 | 22.2 | 17.1 | 0.3 | 6.1 | 1.7 | 0.7 | 17.2 | 2.2 | 0.3 | 12.4 | 9.3 | Valeur ajoutée |
| Number of engaged (Highest number during the year) | 183.1 | 74.5 | 21.7 | 20.5 | 21.2 | 0.7 | 2.7 | 0.9 | 1.0 | 13.1 | 3.4 | 0.3 | 13.8 | 9.3 | Nombre de personnes occupées (maximum de l'année) |
| Wages and salaries paid | 60.8 | 27.6 | 5.7 | 5.6 | 5.7 | 0.1 | 2.8 | 0.6 | 0.3 | 3.3 | 0.5 | 0.2 | 5.8 | 2.6 | Traitements et salaires payés |
| *b. Structure* | | | | | | | | | | | | | | | |
| Distribution in percent of: Value added | 100.0 | 46.8 | 14.0 | 9.7 | 7.5 | 0.1 | 2.7 | 0.8 | 0.3 | 7.5 | 1.0 | 0.1 | 5.4 | 4.1 | Distribution en pourcentage: Valeur ajoutée |
| Number of engaged | 100.0 | 40.6 | 11.9 | 11.2 | 11.6 | 0.3 | 1.5 | 0.5 | 0.6 | 7.1 | 1.9 | 0.1 | 7.6 | 5.1 | Nombre de personnes occupées |
| Value added per person engaged | 1.2 | 1.4 | 1.5 | 1.1 | 0.8 | 0.4 | 2.2 | 1.9 | 0.7 | 1.3 | 0.6 | 1.0 | 0.9 | 1.0 | Valeur ajoutée par personne occupée |
| Value added per unit of wages and salaries | 3.76 | 3.88 | 5.63 | 3.96 | 3.00 | 3.00 | 2.18 | 2.83 | 2.33 | 5.18 | 4.40 | 1.50 | 2.14 | 3.58 | Valeur ajoutée par unité de traitements et salaires |

## 3. CHARACTERISTICS OF ALL MANUFACTURING ESTABLISHMENTS IN URBAN AREAS WITH 10 OR MORE EMPLOYEES

### CARACTERISTIQUES DE TOUS LES ETABLISSEMENTS MANUFACTURIERS DES REGIONS URBAINES AYANT 10 SALARIES OU PLUS

#### 1.X.1952-30.IX.1953, 1.X.1958-30.IX.1959

Number of establishments in units; value added and wages and salaries in million kyats; number of engaged in thousands; value added per engaged in thousand kyats.

Nombre d'établissements en unités; valeur ajoutée et traitements et salaires en millions de kyats; nombre de personnes occupées en milliers; valeur ajoutée par personne occupée en milliers de kyats.

| Year and item of data | Manu-facturing / Industries manufac-turières | Food, beverages and tobacco / Industries alimen-taires, boissons, tabac | Textiles | Clothing, footwear and made-up textiles / Articles d'habil-lement, chaussures et ouvrages en tissu | Wood products and furniture / Bois et meubles | Paper and paper products / Papier et ouvrages en papier | Printing and publish-ing / Im-primerie et édition | Leather and leather products except wearing apparel / Cuir et articles en cuir, à l'exclu-sion des articles d'habil-lement | Rubber products / Ouvrages en caout-chouc | Chemicals and chemical, petroleum and coal products [1] / Produits chi-miques et dérivés du pétrole et du charbon [1] | Non-metallic mineral products / Produits minéraux non métal-liques | Basic metals / Métal-lurgie de base | Metal products / Ouvrages en métaux | Other manu-factur-ing / Autres in-dustries manufac-turières | Année et rubrique |
|---|---|---|---|---|---|---|---|---|---|---|---|---|---|---|---|
| ISIC | 2–3 | 20–22 | 23 | 24 | 25–26 | 27 | 28 | 29 | 30 | 31–32 | 33 | 34 | 35–38 | 39 | CITI |
| *a. Absolute Figures — Chiffres absolus* | | | | | | | | | | | | | | | |
| **1.X.1952 — 30.IX.1953** | | | | | | | | | | | | | | | **1.X.1952 — 30.IX.1953** |
| Number of establishments. | 1 982 | 1 068 | 229 | 197 | 204 | 8 | 42 | 14 | 9 | 74 | 22 | 4 | 74 | 37 | Nombre d'établissements |
| Value added.......... | 149.0 | 86.2 | 23.7 | 6.7 | 9.5 | 0.1 | 5.0 | 0.8 | 0.6 | 9.6 | 0.4 | 0.1 | 5.5 | 0.8 | Valeur ajoutée |
| Number of engaged.... | 90.8 | 53.8 | 9.6 | 4.1 | 7.2 | 0.2 | 1.8 | 0.3 | 0.9 | 5.5 | 1.0 | 0.1 | 5.3 | 1.0 | Nombre de personnes occupées |
| Wages and salaries..... | 43.1 | 23.7 | 3.8 | 2.0 | 4.0 | — | 2.3 | 0.3 | 0.3 | 2.2 | 0.2 | 0.1 | 3.8 | 0.4 | Traitements et salaires |
| **1.X.1958 — 30.IX.1959** | | | | | | | | | | | | | | | **1.X.1958 — 30.IX.1959** |
| Number of establishments. | 2 541 | 1 333 | 357 | 228 | 225 | 3 | 55 | 15 | 30 | 85 | 55 | 14 | 96 | 45 | Nombre d'établissements |
| Value added.......... | 419.6 | 129.7 | 23.1 | 7.4 | 24.3 | 0.3 | 9.7 | 1.6 | 13.7 | 188.4 | 6.0 | 1.9 | 11.7 | 1.8 | Valeur ajoutée |
| Number of engaged.... | 120.9 | 57.6 | 17.8 | 6.2 | 12.8 | 0.2 | 3.4 | 0.5 | 4.4 | 7.4 | 3.4 | 1.9 | 4.4 | 0.9 | Nombre de personnes occupées |
| Wages and salaries..... | 95.0 | 37.3 | 11.5 | 3.5 | 11.4 | 0.2 | 5.8 | 0.6 | 3.5 | 8.2 | 2.9 | 2.3 | 6.6 | 1.2 | Traitements et salaires |
| *b. Structure* | | | | | | | | | | | | | | | |
| **1.X.1952 — 30.IX.1953** Distribution in percent of: | | | | | | | | | | | | | | | **1.X.1952 — 30.IX.1953** Distribution en pour-centage: |
| Value added....... | 100.0 | 57.8 | 15.9 | 4.5 | 6.4 | — | 3.4 | 0.5 | 0.4 | 6.5 | 0.3 | — | 3.7 | 0.6 | Valeur ajoutée |
| Number of engaged.. | 100.0 | 59.2 | 10.6 | 4.5 | 7.9 | 0.2 | 2.0 | 0.4 | 0.9 | 6.1 | 1.1 | 0.1 | 5.8 | 1.2 | Nombre de personnes occupées |
| Value added per person engaged........... | 1.6 | 1.6 | 2.5 | 1.6 | 1.3 | 0.5 | 2.8 | 2.7 | 0.7 | 1.7 | 0.4 | 1.0 | 1.0 | 0.8 | Valeur ajoutée par personne occupée |
| Value added per unit of wages and salaries... | 3.46 | 3.64 | 6.24 | 3.35 | 2.38 | | 2.17 | 2.67 | 2.00 | 4.36 | 2.00 | 1.00 | 1.45 | 2.00 | Valeur ajoutée par unité de traitements et salaires |
| **1.X.1958 — 30.IX.1959** Distribution in percent of: | | | | | | | | | | | | | | | **1.X.1958 — 30.IX.1959** Distribution en pour-centage: |
| Value added....... | 100.0 | 30.9 | 5.5 | 1.7 | 5.8 | 0.1 | 2.3 | 0.4 | 3.3 | 44.8 | 1.5 | 0.4 | 2.8 | 0.5 | Valeur ajoutée |
| Number of engaged.. | 100.0 | 47.6 | 14.7 | 5.1 | 10.6 | 0.2 | 2.8 | 0.4 | 3.7 | 6.1 | 2.8 | 1.6 | 3.6 | 0.8 | Nombre de personnes occupées |
| Value added per person engaged........... | 3.5 | 2.2 | 1.3 | 1.2 | 1.9 | 1.5 | 2.8 | 3.2 | 3.1 | 25.4 | 1.8 | 1.0 | 2.6 | 2.0 | Valeur ajoutée par personne occupée |
| Value added per unit of wages and salaries... | 4.42 | 3.48 | 2.01 | 2.11 | 2.13 | 1.50 | 1.67 | 2.67 | 3.91 | 22.98 | 2.07 | 0.83 | 1.77 | 1.50 | Valeur ajoutée par unité de traitements et salaires |

[1] The marked amount of value added in 1958-59 is due to the way in which the gross output of petroleum refineries was priced. The method of pricing utilized in 1958-1959 differed radically from that utilized in 1952-53.

[1] Les montants indiqués de la valeur ajoutée pour 1958-1959 sont dus à la façon dont la production brute des raffineries de pétrole a été évaluée. La méthode d'évaluation utilisée en 1958-1959 diffère radicalement de celle qui avait été adoptée en 1952-1953.

# BURMA

## 4. CHARACTERISTICS OF ALL MANUFACTURING ESTABLISHMENTS IN URBAN AREAS WITH 9 OR FEWER EMPLOYEES

### CARACTERISTIQUES DE TOUS LES ETABLISSEMENTS MANUFACTURIERS DES REGIONS URBAINES AYANT 9 SALARIES OU MOINS

### 1.X.1952-30.IX.1953, 1.X.1957-30.IX.1958

Number of establishments in units; value added and wages and salaries in million kyats; number of engaged in thousands; value added per engaged in thousand kyats.

Nombre d'établissements en unités; valeur ajoutée et traitements et salaires en millions de kyats; nombre de personnes occupées en milliers; valeur ajoutée par personne occupée en milliers de kyats.

| Year and item of data | Manu-facturing / Industries manufac-turières | Food, beverages and tobacco / Industries alimen-taires, boissons, tabac | Textiles | Clothing, footwear and made-up textiles / Articles d'habil-lement, chaussures et ouvrages en tissu | Wood products and furniture / Bois et meubles | Paper and paper products / Papier et ouvrages en papier | Printing and publish-ing / Im-primerie et édition | Leather and leather products except wearing apparel / Cuir et articles en cuir, à l'exclu-sion des articles d'habil-lement | Rubber products / Ouvrages en caout-chouc | Chemicals and chemical, petroleum and coal products / Produits chi-miques et dérivés du pétrole et du charbon | Non-metallic mineral products / Produits minéraux non métal-liques | Basic metals / Métal-lurgie de base | Metal products / Ouvrages en métaux | Other manu-factur-ing [1] / Autres in-dustries manufac-turières [1] | Année et rubrique |
|---|---|---|---|---|---|---|---|---|---|---|---|---|---|---|---|
| ISIC | 2–3 | 20–22 | 23 | 24 | 25–26 | 27 | 28 | 29 | 30 | 31–32 | 33 | 34 | 35–38 | 39 | CITI |

*a. Absolute Figures — Chiffres absolus*

| | | | | | | | | | | | | | | | |
|---|---|---|---|---|---|---|---|---|---|---|---|---|---|---|---|
| **I.X.1952 — 30.IX.1953** | | | | | | | | | | | | | | | I.X.1952 — 30.IX.1953 |
| Number of establishments | 31 146 | 5 298 | 4 604 | 5 994 | 5 402 | 150 | 234 | 198 | 57 | 2 413 | 794 | 51 | 2 953 | 2 998 | Nombre d'établissements |
| Value added | 79.5 | 20.8 | 8.4 | 15.4 | 7.6 | 0.2 | 1.1 | 0.9 | 0.1 | 7.6 | 1.8 | 0.2 | 6.9 | 8.5 | Valeur ajoutée |
| Number of engaged | 92.3 | 20.7 | 12.1 | 16.4 | 14.0 | 0.6 | 0.9 | 0.6 | 0.1 | 7.6 | 2.4 | 0.2 | 8.5 | 8.2 | Nombre de personnes occupées |
| Wages and salaries | 17.6 | 4.0 | 1.8 | 3.6 | 1.7 | 0.1 | 0.5 | 0.3 | — | 1.1 | 0.3 | 0.1 | 1.9 | 2.2 | Traitements et salaires |
| **I.X.1957 — 30.IX.1958** | | | | | | | | | | | | | | | I.X.1957 — 30.IX.1958 |
| Number of establishments | 43 821 | 7 760 | 7 599 | 8 354 | 3 228 | ... | ... | ... | ... | 2 527 | ... | ... | 2 729 | 11 624 | Nombre d'établissements |
| Value added | 204.1 | 33.7 | 40.5 | 24.8 | 7.2 | ... | ... | ... | ... | 19.7 | ... | ... | 8.1 | 70.1 | Valeur ajoutée |
| Number of engaged | 112.9 | 22.4 | 18.3 | 17.2 | 8.0 | ... | ... | ... | ... | 6.2 | ... | ... | 8.1 | 32.7 | Nombre de personnes occupées |
| Wages and salaries | 37.9 | 6.2 | 6.4 | 6.6 | 1.7 | ... | ... | ... | ... | 2.5 | ... | ... | 2.0 | 12.5 | Traitements et salaires |

*b. Structure*

| | | | | | | | | | | | | | | | |
|---|---|---|---|---|---|---|---|---|---|---|---|---|---|---|---|
| **I.X.1952 — 30.IX.1953** Distribution in percent of: | | | | | | | | | | | | | | | I.X.1952 — 30.IX.1953 Distribution en pour-centage: |
| Value added | 100.0 | 26.1 | 10.6 | 19.4 | 9.5 | 0.3 | 1.3 | 1.2 | 0.1 | 9.6 | 2.2 | 0.3 | 8.7 | 10.7 | Valeur ajoutée |
| Number of engaged | 100.0 | 22.4 | 13.1 | 17.8 | 15.1 | 0.7 | 0.9 | 0.7 | 0.1 | 8.2 | 2.6 | 0.3 | 9.2 | 8.9 | Nombre de personnes occupées |
| Value added per person engaged | 0.9 | 1.0 | 0.7 | 0.9 | 0.5 | 0.3 | 1.2 | 1.5 | 1.0 | 1.0 | 0.8 | 1.0 | 0.8 | 1.0 | Valeur ajoutée par personne occupée |
| Value added per unit of wages and salaries | 4.52 | 5.20 | 4.67 | 4.28 | 4.47 | 2.00 | 2.20 | 3.00 | | 6.91 | 6.00 | 2.00 | 3.63 | 3.86 | Valeur ajoutée par unité de traitements et salaires |
| **I.X.1957 — 30.IX.1958** Distribution in percent of: | | | | | | | | | | | | | | | I.X.1957 — 30.IX.1958 Distribution en pour-centage: |
| Value added | 100.0 | 16.5 | 19.8 | 12.2 | 3.5 | ... | ... | ... | ... | 9.6 | ... | ... | 4.0 | 34.4 | Valeur ajoutée |
| Number of engaged | 100.0 | 19.8 | 16.2 | 15.2 | 7.1 | ... | ... | ... | ... | 5.5 | ... | ... | 7.2 | 29.0 | Nombre de personnes occupées |
| Value added per person engaged | 1.8 | 1.5 | 2.2 | 1.4 | 0.9 | ... | ... | ... | ... | 3.2 | ... | ... | 1.0 | 2.1 | Valeur ajoutée par personne occupée |
| Value added per unit of wages and salaries | 5.38 | 5.44 | 6.33 | 3.76 | 4.24 | ... | ... | ... | ... | 7.88 | ... | ... | 4.05 | 5.61 | Valeur ajoutée par unité de traitements et salaires |

[1] In 1957-58 includes Paper and Paper products (ISIC major group 27); Printing and publishing (ISIC major group 28); Leather and leather products except wearing apparel (ISIC major group 29); Rubber products (ISIC major group 30); Non-metallic mineral products (ISIC major group 33) and Basic metals (ISIC major group 34).

[1] En 1957-1958, y compris Papier et ouvrages en papier (CITI classe 27), Imprimerie et édition (CITI classe 28), Cuir et articles en cuir, à l'exclusion des articles d'habillement (CITI classe 29), Ouvrages en caoutchouc (CITI classe 30), Produits minéraux non métalliques (CITI classe 33) et Métallurgie de base (CITI classe 34).

# CAMEROON [1] — CAMEROUN [1]

## Gross Domestic Product

The data shown in Table 1 are abstracted from *Comptés économiques et modèles,* published by the Ministère de la Coopération, France, in April 1962. The figures shown in that publication were derived from estimates made by the statistical authorities of Cameroon. The figures for gross domestic product at factor cost, which is termed "Gross Domestic Production" in that publication, differs in certain respects from that for the gross domestic product at factor cost in the United Nations system of national accounts, mainly in that wages and salaries paid by government and private non-profit organizations are excluded.

## Produit intérieur brut

Les données du tableau 1 ont été tirées de *Comptes économiques et modèles,* publié par le Ministère de la Coopération, France, en avril 1962. Les chiffres reproduits ont été tirés d'estimations faites par les services de statistique du Cameroun. Les chiffres relatifs au produit intérieur brut au coût des facteurs appelé "Production intérieure brute" dans cette publication diffèrent à certains égards de ceux donnant le produit intérieur brut au coût des facteurs tel qu'il est défini dans le système de comptabilité nationale de l'ONU; notamment, les traitements et salaires payés par les organismes d'Etat et les organisations privées à but non lucratif en sont exclus.

## Characteristics of Industrial Enterprises

The data presented in Table 2 are derived from *Tableaux économiques 1957,* Haut Commissariat de la République en Afrique-Occidentale française and other sources.

## Caractéristiques des entreprises industrielles

Les données du tableau 2 ont été tirées de *Tableaux économiques 1957,* Haut Commissariat de la République en Afrique-Occidentale française et autres sources.

[1] The data shown in this chapter refer to East Cameroon.

[1] Les données de ce chapitre sont relatives au Cameroun oriental.

## 1. THE GROSS DOMESTIC PRODUCT ACCORDING TO ORIGIN
## ORIGINE PAR SECTEUR D'ACTIVITE DU PRODUIT INTERIEUR BRUT
### 1956

Billion Francs C.F.A.                                   Milliards de francs C.F.A.

| Item of data | Total | Agricultural sector<br><br>Secteur agricole | Mining, manufacturing, electricity, gas and water, and construction<br><br>Industries extractives, manufacturières, électricité, gaz et eau, et bâtiment et travaux publics | Commerce, transportation and communication, and other services<br><br>Commerce, transports et communications, et autres services | Government [1]<br><br>Etat [1] | Rubrique |
|---|---|---|---|---|---|---|
| ISIC | 0-9 | 0 | 1-5 | 61-64, 71-73, 83-9 | 81-82 | CITI |
| **At market prices** | | | | | | **Aux prix du marché** |
| Absolute figures.............. | 79.0 | 38.1 | 9.4 | 22.7 | 8.8 | Chiffres absolus |
| Percentage distribution......... | 100.0 | 48.2 | 11.9 | 28.7 | 11.2 | Distribution en pourcentage |
| **At factor cost** | | | | | | **Au coût des facteurs** |
| Absolute figures.............. | 63.7 | 38.1 | 9.1 | 16.5 | . | Chiffres absolus |
| Percentage distribution......... | 100.0 | 59.7 | 14.3 | 26.0 | . | Distribution en pourcentage |

[1] Includes public administration and defense, government agencies and organizations furnishing educational, health and similar services, and private non-profit organizations furnishing services to households except private schools and hospitals. Excludes government enterprises.

[1] Y compris les administrations publiques et la défense nationale, et les services de l'Etat et organisations tels que l'enseignement, la santé et les autres services similaires, et les institutions privées à but non lucratif fournissant des services aux ménages à l'exclusion des écoles et hopitaux privés. Non compris les entreprises de l'Etat.

# CAMEROON

## 2. THE CHARACTERISTICS OF MANUFACTURING ENTERPRISES HAVING FIXED ASSETS OF 30 MILLION FRANCS OR MORE, ACCORDING TO MAJOR GROUPS OF INDUSTRIAL ACTIVITY

### 31 December 1956

### CARACTERISTIQUES DES ENTREPRISES AYANT UN CAPITAL FIXE DE 30 MILLIONS DE FRANCS OU PLUS, PAR CLASSE DES INDUSTRIES MANUFACTURIERES

### 31 décembre 1956

Number of enterprises in units; number of employees in thousands; capacity of installed power equipment in thousand horsepower

Nombre d'entreprises en unités; nombre de salariés en milliers; puissance installée en milliers de chevaux-vapeur

| Item of data | Manufacturing / Industries manufacturières | Food, beverages and tobacco / Industries alimentaires, boissons, tabac | Textiles | Clothing, footwear and made-up textiles / Articles d'habillement, chaussures et ouvrages en tissu | Wood products and furniture / Bois et meubles | Chemicals and chemical, petroleum and coal products / Produits chimiques et dérivés du pétrole et du charbon | Basic metals / Métallurgie de base | Metal products / Ouvrages en métaux | Other manufacturing / Autres industries manufacturières | Rubrique |
|---|---|---|---|---|---|---|---|---|---|---|
| ISIC | 2–3 | 20–22 | 23 | 24 | 25–26 | 31–32 | 34 | 35–38 | 39 | CITI |
| Number of enterprises..... | 75 | 18 | 3 | 2 | 26 | 21 | 1 | 3 | 1 | Nombre d'entreprises |
| Number of employees...... | 7.4 | 1.7 | 0.4 | 0.1 | 4.4 | ... | 0.5 | 0.3 | — | Nombre de salariés |
| Capacity of installed power equipment............. | ... | 0.3 | — | — | 0.5 | ... | 6 866.0 | ... | ... | Puissance installée |

# CANADA

## Gross Domestic Product and Gross Domestic Fixed Capital Formation

The data in Table 1 on the gross domestic product according to sources of expenditure and industrial origin and gross fixed capital formation according to sector of acquisition are from the response of the Dominion Bureau of Statistics, Ottawa, to the United Nations questionnaire on national accounts. Official estimates for the national accounts are issued annually by the Dominion Bureau in *National Accounts, Income and Expenditure*. Descriptions of these estimates are also furnished in the annual publications. Detailed description of the concepts and definitions and the sources and methods utilized in making the estimates is available in *National Accounts, Income and Expenditure, 1926-1956*. In responding to the United Nations questionnaire, the Dominion Bureau has adjusted the official estimates to the United Nations system of national accounts insofar as possible.

## Index Numbers of Industrial Production

The index numbers shown in Table 2 are based on indexes of industrial production computed by the Dominion Bureau of Statistics, Ottawa; and published in *Revised Index of Industrial Production, 1935-1957, (1949 = 100)*, and monthly, in the *Canadian Statistical Review* and *Index of Industrial Production*.

The index numbers of industrial production are computed as base-weighted arithmetic averages. The indicators of output utilized in computing all of the index numbers for 1953 and prior years and some of the index numbers for 1954 and 1955 have been derived from the results of the annual censuses described below. These indicators consist mainly of quantity of production for individual commodities and sometimes of value of production adjusted for price changes for groups of commodities. For years subsequent to 1953 or 1955, the indicators have been derived from the results of monthly inquiries of the Dominion Bureau and consist of quantities of individual commodities produced or man-hours worked, in most cases, and quantities of individual commodities shipped or raw materials consumed or value of individual commodities produced adjusted for price changes, in some cases.

The weights utilized in combining the elementary series of relatives based on the indicators of output, into indexes for detailed categories of industrial activity are, in effect, figures of the value of gross production during the base year compiled from the annual Census of Industry. The weights for aggregating these indexes to index numbers of major groups or somewhat narrower classes of

## Produit intérieur brut et formation brute de capital fixe intérieur

Les chiffres du tableau 1 relatifs au produit intérieur brut par poste de dépenses et branche d'activité d'origine, ainsi qu'à la formation brute de capital fixe intérieur par secteur d'acquisition, sont tirés de la réponse du Bureau fédéral de la statistique, Ottawa, au questionnaire de l'ONU sur la comptabilité nationale. Les estimations officielles relatives à la comptabilité nationale sont publiées chaque année par le Bureau fédéral dans *National Accounts, Income and Expenditure*. Les renseignements complémentaires concernant ces estimations sont également données dans les publications annuelles. Un exposé détaillé des concepts et définitions, ainsi que des sources et méthodes utilisées pour établir les estimations, est présenté dans *National Accounts, Income and Expenditure, 1926-1956*. Dans ses réponses au questionnaire de l'ONU, le Bureau fédéral a, autant que possible, ajusté les estimations officielles de manière à les rendre conformes au système de comptabilité nationale de l'ONU.

## Indices de la production industrielle

Les indices du tableau 2 sont tirés d'indices de la production industrielle calculés par le Bureau fédéral de la statistique, Ottawa, et publiés dans *Revised Index of Industrial Production, 1935-1957 (1949 = 100)* et, mensuellement, dans *Canadian Statistical Review* et *Indices de la production industrielle*.

Les indices de la production industrielle sont des moyennes arithmétiques à pondération fixe. Les indicateurs de la production utilisés pour le calcul de tous les indices concernant 1953 et les années antérieures, et de certains des indices concernant 1954 et 1955, ont été tirés des résultats des recensements annuels décrits ci-après. Ces indicateurs portent essentiellement sur le volume de la production de chaque marchandise et parfois sur la valeur de la production ajustée en fonction des variations de prix pour les divers groupes de marchandises. Pour les années postérieures à 1953 ou 1955, les indicateurs ont été tirés des résultats d'enquêtes mensuelles du Bureau fédéral; il s'agit dans la plupart des cas du volume de la production de chaque marchandise ou du nombre d'heures de travail effectuées, et parfois du volume des expéditions de chaque marchandise ou de la consommation de chaque matière première, ou encore de la valeur de la production de chaque marchandise, ajustée en fonction des variations de prix.

Les pondérations utilisées pour combiner les séries élémentaires de rapports fondés sur les indicateurs de la production en indices de catégorie détaillée de l'activité industrielle sont en fait les chiffres de la valeur brute de la production pendant l'année de base, tirés des résultats des recensements annuels de l'industrie. Pour combiner ces indices en indices de classe ou de subdivision un peu

industrial activity are value added, at factor cost, computed from the same source, but the weights for combining major groups into index numbers for broader classes (e.g., divisions of industrial activity) are figures of the contribution to the gross domestic product, at factor cost, derived from an input-output study and similar sources. In view of the nature of the sources from which the weights and elementary series have been computed, the index numbers of industrial production relate to the activity of all industrial establishments, irrespective of size.

The weight and comparison base years are 1949 in the case of the index numbers for 1948 and thereafter and 1935-1939 for the indexes for 1938. The Dominion Bureau linked the earlier series of indexes to the later series at 1946.

A detailed description of the index numbers of industrial production may be found in *Revised Index of Industrial Production 1935-1957, (1949 = 100)*, Dominion Bureau of Statistics, Ottawa, 1959.

### Index Numbers of Industrial Employment

The indexes of employment set out in Table 3 were compiled from index numbers computed by the Dominion Bureau of Statistics, and are issued by the Bureau in the *Canadian Yearbook* and in the monthly publications, *Canadian Statistical Review* and *Employment and Payrolls*. The index numbers shown in Table 3 are annual averages of monthly indexes relating to the number of employees receiving pay during the last pay roll period of the month. Employees on strike or unpaid leaves are not counted. In general, the indexes cover the employment of establishments which customarily have 15 or more employees.

The Dominion Bureau compiles the monthly indexes by comparing employment in the current month with average monthly employment during 1949 for the same set of establishments. The base figures of average monthly employment during 1949 include the employment of establishments which have gone out of business since 1949. Newly founded establishments since 1949, for which figures of employment are included in the data for the current month, are assigned zero employment in 1949. The employment during 1949 is included in the base-year figures in the case of other establishments which were added since 1949. The figures of employment utilized in compiling the index numbers are gathered by the Dominion Bureau in a monthly survey of the establishments in the field covered by the indexes.

### Characteristics and Structure of Industrial Activity

The data set out in Tables 4 and 5 were compiled from the annual censuses of industrial activities taken by the Dominion Bureau of Statistics. The data were abstracted mainly from the following publications of the Dominion Bureau: *Annual Report on the Mineral Production of Canada during the Calendar Year 1938, Mineral Statistics*

plus étroite de l'activité industrielle, on a pondéré par la valeur ajoutée au coût des facteurs, calculée d'après la même source, mais, pour combiner les indices de classe en indices plus larges (par exemple, les branches de l'activité industrielle), on a utilisé la contribution au produit intérieur brut, au coût des facteurs, tirée d'une étude sur les entrées et les sorties (input-output) et de sources analogues. De même que les chiffres d'où l'on a tiré les poids et les séries élémentaires, les indices de la production industrielle portent sur l'activité de tous les établissements industriels, quelle que soit leur dimension.

La base de pondération et de comparaison est 1949 pour les indices de 1948 et des années suivantes, et 1935-1939 pour les indices de 1938. Le Bureau fédéral a raccordé la première série d'indices à la seconde au niveau de 1946.

Pour une description détaillée des indices de la production industrielle, voir *Revised Index of Industrial Production, 1935-1957, (1949 = 100)*, Bureau fédéral de la statistique, Ottawa, 1959.

### Indices de l'emploi dans l'industrie

Les indices de l'emploi reproduits au tableau 3 ont été tirés d'indices établis par le Bureau fédéral de la statistique, et sont publiés par le Bureau fédéral dans le *Canadian Yearbook* et dans les publications mensuelles, *Canadian Statistical Review* et *Employment and Payrolls*. Les indices du tableau 3 sont des moyennes annuelles d'indices mensuels portant sur le nombre de salariés qui ont été payés pendant la dernière période de paie du mois. Les salariés en grève ou en congé non payé ne sont pas inclus. En général, les indices concernent l'emploi dans les établissements comptant ordinairement 15 salariés ou plus.

Pour calculer les indices mensuels, le Bureau fédéral compare l'emploi dans le mois considéré à l'emploi mensuel moyen en 1949 dans le même ensemble d'établissements. Les chiffres de base qui ont servi au calcul de l'emploi mensuel moyen en 1949 comprennent l'emploi dans les établissements ayant cessé toute activité depuis 1949. D'autre part, les chiffres de l'emploi relatifs au mois considéré comprennent l'emploi dans les établissements créés après 1949, tandis que, dans les chiffres de 1949, on a compté un emploi nul pour ces établissements. L'emploi pendant 1949 est compris dans les chiffres de l'année de base en ce qui concerne les autres établissements rajoutés depuis 1949. Les chiffres de l'emploi utilisés pour le calcul des indices sont rassemblés par le Bureau fédéral au moyen d'une enquête mensuelle auprès des établissements appartenant au champ couvert par les indices.

### Caractéristiques et structure de l'activité industrielle

Les données des tableaux 4 et 5 sont tirées des résultats des recensements de l'industrie que le Bureau fédéral de la statistique effectue chaque année. Ces données ont été puisées dans les publications suivantes du Bureau fédéral : *Annual Report on the Mineral Production of Canada during the Calendar Year 1938, Mineral Statistics*

of Canada, 1947-1948 and General Review of the Mining Industry, 1953 or 1958; Manufacturing Industries of Canada, 1938 or 1948 and General Review of the Manufacturing Industries of Canada, 1953 or 1958; Report on the Construction Industry in Canada, 1938, The Construction Industry in Canada, 1948 and Construction in Canada, 1953-1955 or 1957-1959; Census of Industry, Central Electric Stations in Canada, 1938-1948 or 1953; and Electric Power Statistics, 1958; Coke and Gas Industry in Canada, 1938 and The Coke and Gas Industry, 1950-1953 or 1958. Some of the data was supplied by the Dominion Bureau of Statistics in correspondence with the Statistical Office of the United Nations.

The data presented in Tables 4 and 5 for each of the divisions of industrial activity are, in principle, comparable from year to year, except that Newfoundland, which was covered for 1953 and 1958 was not included for 1938 and 1948. This, it should be noted, does not have a significant effect on comparability, excepting the data for the paper industry. The data for each year relate to all units, irrespective of size, which are mainly engaged in the specified industrial activity. For example, governmental departments, as well as private firms, that are classified to the construction industry, are included in the data on construction, and electricity and gas producing and distributing units, whether publicly or privately owned, are covered in the data on this industry. However, there may be some incomparability in actual coverage between the data for the same kind of industrial activity for 1938, 1948, 1953 and 1958 because of differences in the proportions of covered units which completed and returned questionnaires. Excepting the data on construction for 1953 and 1958, adjustments to the data do not seem to have been made for non-respondents.

Minor differences also occur between 1938 and 1948, on the one hand, and 1953 and 1958, on the other, in the definition of value added in manufacturing. For 1938 and 1948, the figures of value added for manufacturing do not cover receipts from goods sold without transformation by establishments and relate, in the case of goods, to production during the year. For 1953 and 1958, however, the data on value added cover receipts from goods sold without transformation and relate mainly, in the case of goods, to shipments during the year. The definitions for each of the three years of value added in the case of the other kinds of industrial activity and of the other items of data in the case of all kinds of industrial activity are consistent with one another. Value added is priced at factor cost in all cases, including manufacturing establishments; and is based on value of shipments for mining, value of work put in place for construction and value of sales for the electricity and gas industries.

The establishment is, on the whole, the tabulating unit in the case of mining, manufacturing and the electricity

of Canada, 1947-1948 et General Review of the Mining Industry, 1953 ou 1958; Manufacturing Industries of Canada, 1938 ou 1948 et General Review of the Manufacturing Industries of Canada, 1953 ou 1958; Report on the Construction Industry in Canada, 1938, The Construction Industry in Canada, 1948 et Construction in Canada, 1953-1955 ou 1957-1959; Census of Industry, Central Electric Stations in Canada, 1938-1948 ou 1953, et Electric Power Statistics, 1958; Coke and Gas Industry in Canada, 1938 et The Coke and Gas Industry, 1950-1953 ou 1958. Certaines de ces données ont été communiquées par correspondance au Bureau de statistique de l'ONU par le Bureau fédéral de la statistique.

Les données des tableaux 4 et 5 pour chacune des branches de l'activité industrielle sont, en principe, comparables d'une année à l'autre, si ce n'est que Terre-Neuve, comprise dans les chiffres de 1953 et 1958, ne l'est pas dans ceux de 1938 et 1948. Cela n'a guère d'effet sur la comparabilité, sauf en ce qui concerne l'industrie du papier. Les données fournies pour chaque année portent sur toutes les unités, quelle que soit leur dimension, dont l'activité principale est l'activité mentionnée. Par exemple, les services de l'Etat, ainsi que les entreprises privées, qui sont classées dans Bâtiment et travaux publics, sont tous compris dans les données sur le bâtiment et les travaux publics; de même, les données concernant la production et la distribution d'électricité et de gaz portent sur toutes les unités, publiques et privées, qui exercent ces activités. Il peut cependant y avoir certains défauts de comparabilité dans la couverture effective des données fournies pour le même type d'activité industrielle pour 1938, 1948, 1953 et 1958, du fait que les unités recensées n'ont pas rempli et retourné les questionnaires dans la même proportion. Sauf pour le bâtiment et les travaux publics en 1953 et 1958, il ne semble pas que des ajustements aient été faits pour tenir compte des non-réponses.

Certaines différences peu importantes existent aussi entre 1938 et 1948, d'une part, et 1953 et 1958, de l'autre, touchant la définition de la valeur ajoutée dans les industries manufacturières. Pour 1938 et 1948, les chiffres de la valeur ajoutée dans l'industries manufacturière ne couvrent pas les recettes provenant des marchandises revendues en l'état et ils portent, pour ce qui est des marchandises, sur la production de l'année. Pour 1953 et 1958, au contraire, les chiffres de la valeur ajoutée comprennent les recettes provenant des marchandises revendues en l'état et portent surtout, en ce qui concerne les marchandises, sur les expéditions de l'année. Pour chacune des trois années, la définition de la valeur ajoutée, dans le cas des autres types d'activité industrielle, de même que les définitions des autres rubriques dans le cas de tous les types d'activité industrielle sont mutuellement compatibles. La valeur ajoutée est évaluée au coût des facteurs dans tous les cas, y compris dans celui des établissements manufacturiers, et elle est tirée de la valeur des expéditions dans le cas des industries extractives, de la valeur des ouvrages construits dans le cas du bâtiment et des travaux publics, et de la valeur des ventes dans le cas de l'industrie du gaz et de l'électricité.

L'unité statistique est généralement l'établissement dans les industries extractives, les industries manufacturières

and gas industries, but the firm in the case of construction; and the count of these units is the number actually covered in the data. In the case of unincorporated business, number of employees probably covers working proprietors; and the amount of wages and salaries seems to include their regular withdrawals during the course of the year. The distinctions made between operatives and other employees and the definitions of the items of data on labour, excepting the probable inclusion of working proprietors in the count of employees and wages and salaries, are similar to those in the International Standards in Basic Industrial Statistics.

The figures of capacity of installed (in use and in reserve) power equipment for years other than 1958 relate, excepting electricity production and distribution, to the sum of the rated horsepower of all prime movers and of electric motors driven by purchased electricity. In the case of 1958, these figures refer to the sum of the rated horsepower of prime movers connected to machinery other than electric generators and of all electric motors. In the case of the electricity industry, the rated capacity of all prime movers only is included in the figures of capacity of installed power equipment. The data for the mining and manufacturing industries on energy and fuels consumed that are shown in Tables 4 and 5, cover fuels consumed as a source of heat or power, whether purchased or produced on own account. Nevertheless, the figures of energy consumed do not contain duplication because fuels utilized to produce gas for own use are not included in figures of fuels consumed and only purchased electricity was taken into account in compiling the figures of energy consumed. In the case of the electricity industry, the data on fuels consumed relate primarily to fuels utilized to produce electricity.

et les industries du gaz et de l'électricité, mais c'est l'entreprise dans le cas du bâtiment et des travaux publics; le nombre d'unités indiqué est celui des unités effectivement comprises dans les données. Pour les entreprises non constituées en société, le nombre de salariés comprend probablement les propriétaires qui travaillent, et le chiffre des traitements et salaires paraît comprendre les sommes qu'ils prélèvent régulièrement sur les recettes dans le courant de l'année. Les distinctions faites entre ouvriers et autres salariés, et les définitions des rubriques relatives à la main-d'oeuvre, à l'exception de l'inclusion probable des propriétaires qui travaillent dans le nombre des salariés et dans les traitements et salaires, sont conformes aux Normes internationales relatives aux statistiques industrielles de base.

La puissance installée (en service et en réserve) pour les années autres que 1958, représente, sauf en ce qui concerne la production et la distribution d'électricité, la puissance nominale de tous les moteurs primaires et des moteurs électriques actionnés par de l'électricité achetée. Dans le cas de 1958, les chiffres représentent la puissance nominale de tous les moteurs primaires branchés sur des machines autres que des générateurs d'électricité et celle de tous les moteurs électriques. Dans le cas des industries de l'électricité, seule la puissance nominale de tous les moteurs primaires est comprise dans les chiffres relatifs à la puissance installée. Les données des tableaux 4 et 5 relatives à l'énergie et aux combustibles consommés par les industries extractives et manufacturières concernent les combustibles consommés comme source de chaleur ou d'énergie, qu'ils soient achetés ou auto-produits. Néammoins, les chiffres relatifs à l'énergie consommée ne comportent pas de doubles emplois car les combustibles utilisés pour produire du gaz en vue de l'auto-consommation ne sont pas compris dans les chiffres des combustibles consommés et l'on n'a tenu compte que de l'électricité achetée pour calculer les chiffres de l'énergie consommée. Dans le cas de l'industrie de l'électricité, les données concernant les combustibles consommés se rapportent principalement aux combustibles utilisés pour produire de l'électricité.

# 1. THE GROSS DOMESTIC PRODUCT AND GROSS DOMESTIC FIXED CAPITAL FORMATION
## PRODUIT INTERIEUR BRUT ET FORMATION BRUTE DE CAPITAL FIXE INTERIEUR

Millions of dollars                                             Millions de dollars

## A. Expenditure on the Gross Domestic Product at Market Prices
### Dépenses relatives au produit intérieur brut aux prix du marché

| Item of data and year / Rubrique et année | Total[1] | Consumption / Consommation | | Gross Domestic Capital Formation / Formation brute de capital intérieur | | Net exports of goods and services / Exportations nettes de biens et de services | |
| --- | --- | --- | --- | --- | --- | --- | --- |
| | | Total | Government / Etat | Total | Fixed / Fixe | Exports less imports / Exportations moins importations | Exports / Exportations |
| *a. At Current Prices — Aux prix courants* | | | | | | | |
| **Absolute figures — Chiffres absolus** | | | | | | | |
| 1948 | 15 398 | 11 457 | 1 375 | 3 131 | 3 050 | 721 | 3 971 |
| 1950 | 18 419 | 13 929 | 1 898 | 4 339 | 3 870 | 83 | 4 080 |
| 1951 | 21 538 | 16 278 | 2 816 | 5 319 | 4 564 | −149 | 4 961 |
| 1952 | 24 297 | 18 321 | 3 540 | 5 686 | 5 185 | 491 | 5 412 |
| 1953 | 25 296 | 19 352 | 3 760 | 6 228 | 5 731 | −142 | 5 217 |
| 1954 | 25 186 | 19 889 | 3 722 | 5 377 | 5 592 | −93 | 4 982 |
| 1955 | 27 498 | 21 308 | 3 927 | 6 362 | 6 108 | −281 | 5 584 |
| 1956 | 31 021 | 23 145 | 4 315 | 8 899 | 7 847 | −881 | 6 202 |
| 1957 | 32 403 | 24 521 | 4 452 | 8 796 | 8 586 | −885 | 6 216 |
| 1958 | 33 398 | 26 021 | 4 780 | 8 000 | 8 292 | −522 | 6 151 |
| 1959 | 35 341 | 27 381 | 4 892 | 8 729 | 8 316 | −813 | 6 480 |
| 1960 | 36 493 | 28 557 | 5 191 | 8 483 | 8 172 | −512 | 6 822 |
| 1961 | 37 498 | 29 854 | 5 599 | 7 785 | 8 014 | −203 | 7 361 |
| **Percentage distribution of average annual expenditure — Distribution en pourcentage des dépenses annuelles moyennes** | | | | | | | |
| 1948 | 100.0 | 74.8 | 9.0 | 20.5 | 19.9 | 4.7 | 25.9 |
| 1950–1960 | 100.0 | 76.6 | 13.9 | 24.5 | 23.2 | −1.1 | 20.0 |
| 1950 | 100.0 | 75.9 | 10.3 | 23.6 | 21.1 | 0.5 | 22.2 |
| 1953 | 100.0 | 76.1 | 14.8 | 24.5 | 22.5 | −0.6 | 20.5 |
| 1954 | 100.0 | 79.0 | 14.8 | 21.3 | 22.2 | −0.3 | 19.8 |
| 1958 | 100.0 | 77.7 | 14.3 | 23.9 | 24.8 | −1.6 | 18.4 |
| 1960 | 100.0 | 78.1 | 14.2 | 23.3 | 22.4 | −1.4 | 18.7 |
| *b. At Prices of 1957 — Aux prix de 1957* | | | | | | | |
| **Absolute figures — Chiffres absolus** [2] | | | | | | | |
| 1948 | 21 148 | 15 231 | 2 214 | 4 657 | 4 598 | 892 | 4 877 |
| 1950 | 23 620 | 17 295 | 2 756 | 5 784 | 5 252 | 217 | 4 632 |
| 1951 | 24 911 | 18 395 | 3 655 | 6 260 | 5 471 | 7 | 5 066 |
| 1952 | 26 791 | 20 165 | 4 396 | 6 533 | 6 001 | 265 | 5 579 |
| 1953 | 27 786 | 21 157 | 4 509 | 7 028 | 6 457 | −245 | 5 507 |
| 1954 | 27 029 | 21 312 | 4 282 | 5 941 | 6 252 | −136 | 5 297 |
| 1955 | 29 363 | 22 671 | 4 378 | 7 082 | 6 669 | −538 | 5 703 |
| 1956 | 31 939 | 24 017 | 4 544 | 9 109 | 8 137 | −1 122 | 6 167 |
| 1957 | 32 403 | 24 521 | 4 452 | 8 796 | 8 586 | −885 | 6 216 |
| 1958 | 32 797 | 25 301 | 4 598 | 7 977 | 8 261 | −382 | 6 179 |
| 1959 | 33 829 | 26 173 | 4 549 | 8 436 | 8 050 | −822 | 6 407 |
| 1960 | 34 459 | 26 885 | 4 674 | 8 086 | 7 800 | −479 | 6 688 |
| 1961 | 35 168 | 27 738 | 4 877 | 7 407 | 7 660 | −35 | 7 136 |
| **Percentage distribution of average annual expenditure — Distribution en pourcentage des dépenses annuelles moyennes** | | | | | | | |
| 1948 | 100.0 | 73.3 | 10.6 | 22.4 | 22.1 | 4.3 | 23.5 |
| 1950–1960 | 100.0 | 76.2 | 14.4 | 25.0 | 23.7 | −1.2 | 19.5 |
| 1950 | 100.0 | 74.3 | 11.8 | 24.8 | 22.5 | 0.9 | 19.9 |
| 1953 | 100.0 | 75.7 | 16.1 | 25.2 | 23.1 | −0.9 | 19.7 |
| 1954 | 100.0 | 78.6 | 15.8 | 21.9 | 23.0 | −0.5 | 19.5 |
| 1958 | 100.0 | 76.9 | 14.0 | 24.2 | 25.1 | −1.1 | 18.8 |
| 1960 | 100.0 | 77.9 | 13.6 | 23.4 | 22.6 | −1.3 | 19.4 |
| **Average annual rate of growth — Taux annuel moyen d'accroissement** | | | | | | | |
| 1948–1953 | 5.6 | 6.8 | 15.3 | 8.6 | 7.0 | . | 2.5 |
| 1950–1960 | 3.8 | 4.5 | 5.4 | 3.4 | 4.0 | . | 3.7 |
| 1950–1953 | 5.6 | 6.9 | 17.8 | 6.7 | 7.1 | . | 5.9 |
| 1954–1958 | 4.9 | 4.4 | 1.8 | 7.7 | 7.2 | . | 3.9 |
| 1958–1960 | 2.5 | 3.1 | 0.8 | 0.7 | −2.8 | . | 4.0 |

[1] The gross domestic product does not equal the sum of the sources of expenditure because of the inclusion of a residual error of estimate in the Total.

[2] The gross domestic product at constant prices for the years, 1948-1955, includes adjustments to compensate for residual differences between the results of deflating the data for 1956, the year of linkage, by price indexes based on 1949 and price indexes based on 1957.

[1] Le produit intérieur brut n'est pas égal à la somme des dépenses réparties, car le total contient une erreur résiduelle d'estimation.

[2] On a corrigé le produit intérieur brut en prix constants des années 1948-1955 pour tenir compte des écarts résiduels dus au raccordement, en 1956, de séries ajustées au moyen d'indices de prix ayant pour bases 1949 et 1957 respectivement.

# CANADA

## B. The Gross Domestic Product at Factor Cost According to Origin
### Origine par secteur d'activité du produit intérieur brut au coût des facteurs

| Item of data and year / Rubrique et année | Total | Agricultural sector / Secteur agricole | Industrial Sector — Secteur industriel | | | | | Transportation and communication / Transports et communications | Other sectors / Autres secteurs |
| | | | Total | Mining / Industries extractives | Manufacturing / Industries manufacturières | Construction / Bâtiment et travaux publics | Electricity, gas and water / Electricité, gaz et eau | | |
| ISIC — CITI | 0–9 | 0 | 1–5 | 1 | 2–3 | 4 | 5 | 7 | 6, 8–9 |
| *a. At Current Prices — Aux prix courants* | | | | | | | | | |
| **Absolute figures — Chiffres absolus** | | | | | | | | | |
| 1948 | 13 699 | 2 070 | 5 428 | 525 | 3 909 | 689 | 305 | 1 251 | 4 950 |
| 1950 | 16 458 | 2 168 | 6 633 | 653 | 4 714 | 874 | 392 | 1 421 | 6 236 |
| 1951 | 19 126 | 2 930 | 7 630 | 794 | 5 474 | 921 | 441 | 1 721 | 6 845 |
| 1952 | 21 344 | 2 878 | 8 551 | 777 | 6 150 | 1 134 | 490 | 1 860 | 8 055 |
| 1953 | 22 206 | 2 499 | 9 136 | 782 | 6 453 | 1 356 | 545 | 1 993 | 8 578 |
| 1954 | 22 213 | 1 977 | 9 097 | 887 | 6 291 | 1 325 | 594 | 1 981 | 9 158 |
| 1955 | 24 326 | 2 290 | 9 899 | 1 071 | 6 779 | 1 385 | 664 | 2 260 | 9 877 |
| 1956 | 27 189 | 2 533 | 11 321 | 1 196 | 7 605 | 1 752 | 768 | 2 594 | 10 741 |
| 1957 | 28 455 | 2 052 | 11 940 | 1 222 | 7 904 | 1 935 | 879 | 2 690 | 11 773 |
| 1958 | 29 354 | 2 176 | 11 813 | 1 151 | 7 753 | 1 974 | 935 | 2 643 | 12 722 |
| 1959 | 31 065 | 2 126 | 12 475 | 1 295 | 8 270 | 1 896 | 1 014 | 2 894 | 13 570 |
| 1960 | 31 938 | 2 253 | 12 551 | 1 347 | 8 316 | 1 813 | 1 075 | 2 901 | 14 233 |
| 1961 | 32 837 | 1 973 | 12 836 | 1 423 | 8 496 | 1 797 | 1 120 | 2 996 | 15 032 |
| **Percentage distribution according to sector— Distribution en pourcentage par secteur** | | | | | | | | | |
| 1948 | 100.0 | 15.1 | 39.6 | 3.8 | 28.5 | 5.1 | 2.2 | 9.1 | 36.2 |
| 1950–1960 | 100.0 | 9.4 | 40.6 | 4.1 | 27.7 | 5.9 | 2.9 | 9.1 | 40.9 |
| 1950 | 100.0 | 13.1 | 40.3 | 4.0 | 28.6 | 5.3 | 2.4 | 8.7 | 37.9 |
| 1953 | 100.0 | 11.2 | 41.1 | 3.5 | 29.1 | 6.1 | 2.4 | 9.0 | 38.7 |
| 1954 | 100.0 | 8.9 | 40.9 | 3.9 | 28.4 | 5.9 | 2.7 | 8.9 | 41.3 |
| 1958 | 100.0 | 7.4 | 40.2 | 3.9 | 26.4 | 6.7 | 3.2 | 9.0 | 43.4 |
| 1960 | 100.0 | 7.0 | 39.3 | 4.2 | 26.1 | 5.6 | 3.4 | 9.1 | 44.6 |

## C. Gross Domestic Fixed Capital Formation According to Purchasing Sector
### Formation brute de capital fixe intérieur par secteur d'acquisition

| Item of data and year / Rubrique et année | Total | Agricultural sector / Secteur agricole | Industrial Sector — Secteur industriel | | | | | Transportation and communication / Transports et communications | Other sectors / Autres secteurs |
| | | | Total | Mining / Industries extractives | Manufacturing / Industries manufacturières | Construction / Bâtiment et travaux publics | Electricity, gas and water / Electricité, gaz et eau | | |
| ISIC — CITI | 0–9 | 0 | 1–5 | 1 | 2–3 | 4 | 5 | 7 | 6, 8–9 |
| *a. At Current Prices — Aux prix courants* | | | | | | | | | |
| **Absolute figures — Chiffres absolus** | | | | | | | | | |
| 1948 | 3 050 | 380 | 953 | 70 | 573 | 59 | 251 | 519 | 1 198 |
| 1950 | 3 870 | 516 | 1 100 | 114 | 502 | 71 | 413 | 587 | 1 667 |
| 1951 | 4 564 | 583 | 1 526 | 164 | 793 | 66 | 503 | 717 | 1 738 |
| 1952 | 5 185 | 601 | 1 869 | 205 | 973 | 73 | 618 | 1 010 | 1 705 |
| 1953 | 5 731 | 591 | 1 907 | 253 | 969 | 91 | 594 | 1 057 | 2 176 |
| 1954 | 5 592 | 446 | 1 722 | 278 | 822 | 97 | 525 | 992 | 2 432 |
| 1955 | 6 108 | 489 | 1 975 | 336 | 947 | 174 | 518 | 1 010 | 2 634 |
| 1956 | 7 847 | 564 | 2 907 | 542 | 1 394 | 200 | 771 | 1 556 | 2 820 |
| 1957 | 8 586 | 482 | 3 192 | 606 | 1 479 | 158 | 949 | 2 002 | 2 910 |
| 1958 | 8 292 | 498 | 2 439 | 342 | 1 095 | 157 | 845 | 1 956 | 3 399 |
| 1959 | 8 316 | 587 | 2 392 | 342 | 1 144 | 145 | 761 | 1 827 | 3 510 |
| 1960 | 8 172 | 604 | 2 394 | 400 | 1 178 | 130 | 686 | 1 892 | 3 282 |
| 1961 | 8 014 | 570 | 2 284 | 451 | 1 024 | 132 | 677 | 1 785 | 3 375 |
| **Percentage distribution according to sector— Distribution en pourcentage par secteur** | | | | | | | | | |
| 1948 | 100.0 | 12.5 | 31.2 | 2.3 | 18.8 | 1.9 | 8.2 | 17.0 | 39.3 |
| 1950–1960 | 100.0 | 8.3 | 32.5 | 4.9 | 15.7 | 1.9 | 10.0 | 20.1 | 39.1 |
| 1950 | 100.0 | 13.3 | 28.4 | 2.9 | 13.0 | 1.8 | 10.7 | 15.2 | 43.1 |
| 1953 | 100.0 | 10.3 | 33.3 | 4.4 | 16.9 | 1.6 | 10.4 | 18.4 | 38.0 |
| 1954 | 100.0 | 8.0 | 30.8 | 5.0 | 14.7 | 1.7 | 9.4 | 17.7 | 43.5 |
| 1958 | 100.0 | 6.0 | 29.4 | 4.1 | 13.2 | 1.9 | 10.2 | 23.6 | 41.0 |
| 1960 | 100.0 | 7.3 | 29.3 | 4.9 | 14.5 | 1.5 | 8.4 | 23.2 | 40.2 |

## 2. INDEX NUMBERS OF INDUSTRIAL PRODUCTION — INDICES DE LA PRODUCTION INDUSTRIELLE

### A. Selected Divisions of Industrial Activity
### Quelques branches de l'activité industrielle

| Period / Période | Total | Mining / Industries extractives | Manu- facturing / Industries manu- facturières | Electricity and gas / Electricité et gaz |
|---|---|---|---|---|
| ISIC — CITI | 1-3, 511–512 | 1 | 2–3 | 511–512 |
| *a.* Indexes — Indices (1958 = 100) | | | | |
| 1938 | 32 | 37 | 32 | 19 |
| 1948 | 62 | 40 | 69 | 40 |
| 1949 | 65 | 44 | 71 | 42 |
| 1950 | 69 | 48 | 75 | 47 |
| 1951 | 76 | 54 | 82 | 54 |
| 1952 | 78 | 58 | 84 | 59 |
| 1953 | 84 | 62 | 90 | 62 |
| 1954 | 83 | 70 | 87 | 68 |
| 1955 | 92 | 82 | 96 | 77 |
| 1956 | 100 | 94 | 103 | 86 |
| 1957 | 101 | 100 | 102 | 92 |
| 1958 | 100 | 100 | 100 | 100 |
| 1959 | 108 | 111 | 106 | 112 |
| 1960 | 108 | 112 | 106 | 125 |
| 1961 | 112 | 118 | 109 | 133 |
| *b.* Average Annual Rate of Change — Taux annuel moyen de variation | | | | |
| 1938–1960 | 5.7 | 5.2 | 5.6 | 8.9 |
| 1938–1948 | 6.8 | 0.8 | 8.0 | 7.7 |
| 1950–1960 | 4.6 | 8.8 | 3.5 | 10.3 |
| 1948–1953 | 6.3 | 9.2 | 5.5 | 9.2 |
| 1954–1958 | 4.8 | 9.3 | 3.5 | 10.1 |
| 1958–1960 | 3.9 | 5.8 | 3.0 | 11.8 |

### B. The Major Groups of Mining
### Les classes de la branche Industries extractives

| Period / Période | All mining / Toutes industries extractives | Coal mining / Extraction du charbon | Metal mining / Extraction des minerais métalliques | Crude petroleum and natural gas / Pétrole brut et gaz naturel | Other mining / Autres industries extractives |
|---|---|---|---|---|---|
| ISIC — CITI | 1 | 11 | 12 | 13 | 14–19 |
| *a.* Indexes — Indices (1958 = 100) | | | | | |
| 1938 | 37 | 136 | 56 | 5 | 24 |
| 1948 | 40 | 171 | 49 | 8 | 52 |
| 1949 | 44 | 176 | 55 | 13 | 46 |
| 1950 | 48 | 174 | 57 | 18 | 61 |
| 1951 | 54 | 169 | 60 | 29 | 70 |
| 1952 | 58 | 160 | 61 | 37 | 71 |
| 1953 | 62 | 144 | 64 | 49 | 70 |
| 1954 | 70 | 133 | 72 | 58 | 78 |
| 1955 | 82 | 131 | 79 | 77 | 86 |
| 1956 | 94 | 132 | 84 | 101 | 94 |
| 1957 | 100 | 115 | 94 | 108 | 96 |
| 1958 | 100 | 100 | 100 | 100 | 100 |
| 1959 | 111 | 92 | 112 | 112 | 108 |
| 1960 | 112 | 94 | 110 | 118 | 105 |
| 1961 | 118 | 88 | 106 | 136 | 117 |
| *b.* Average Annual Rate of Change — Taux annuel moyen de variation | | | | | |
| 1938–1960 | 5.2 | -1.7 | 3.1 | 15.5 | 6.9 |
| 1938–1948 | 0.8 | 2.3 | -1.3 | 4.8 | 8.0 |
| 1950–1960 | 8.8 | -6.0 | 5.6 | 20.7 | 5.6 |
| 1948–1953 | 9.2 | -3.4 | 5.5 | 43.7 | 6.1 |
| 1954–1958 | 9.3 | -6.9 | 8.6 | 14.6 | 6.4 |
| 1958–1960 | 5.8 | -3.0 | 4.9 | 8.6 | 2.5 |

### C. The Major Groups of Manufacturing — Les classes de la branche Industries manufacturières

| Period / Période | Manufacturing / Industries manufacturières | Food, beverages and tobacco / Industries alimentaires, boissons, tabac | Textiles | Clothing, footwear and made-up textiles / Articles d'habillement, chaussures et ouvrages en tissu | Wood products and furniture / Bois et meubles | Paper and paper products / Papier et ouvrages en papier | Printing and publishing / Imprimerie et édition | Leather and leather products except wearing apparel / Cuir et articles en cuir, à l'exclusion des articles d'habillement | Rubber products / Ouvrages en caoutchouc | Chemicals and chemical, petroleum and coal products / Produits chimiques et dérivés du pétrole et du charbon | Non-metallic mineral products / Produits minéraux non métalliques | Basic metals / Métallurgie de base | Metal products / Ouvrages en métaux | Other manufacturing / Autres industries manufacturières |
|---|---|---|---|---|---|---|---|---|---|---|---|---|---|---|
| ISIC — CITI | 2–3 | 20–22 | 23 | 24 | 25–26 | 27 | 28 | 29 | 30 | 31–32 | 33 | 34 | 35–38 | 39 |
| **a. Indexes — Indices (1958 = 100)** | | | | | | | | | | | | | | |
| 1938 | 32 | 37 | 44 | 54 | 38 | 29 | 39 | 72 | 40 | 20 | 17 | 41 | 26 | 22 |
| 1948 | 69 | 68 | 88 | 84 | 76 | 70 | 69 | 100 | 85 | 46 | 45 | 75 | 72 | 49 |
| 1949 | 71 | 70 | 91 | 86 | 76 | 74 | 74 | 98 | 73 | 49 | 48 | 76 | 73 | 60 |
| 1950 | 75 | 72 | 102 | 87 | 82 | 81 | 76 | 96 | 85 | 54 | 54 | 82 | 77 | 63 |
| 1951 | 82 | 74 | 103 | 86 | 87 | 87 | 78 | 84 | 91 | 60 | 58 | 92 | 88 | 72 |
| 1952 | 84 | 79 | 94 | 96 | 88 | 84 | 80 | 91 | 87 | 63 | 60 | 92 | 93 | 73 |
| 1953 | 90 | 82 | 98 | 99 | 95 | 87 | 85 | 98 | 95 | 71 | 68 | 94 | 100 | 85 |
| 1954 | 87 | 84 | 86 | 94 | 94 | 92 | 90 | 93 | 87 | 76 | 71 | 86 | 91 | 81 |
| 1955 | 96 | 88 | 104 | 97 | 103 | 97 | 94 | 102 | 103 | 84 | 83 | 104 | 100 | 82 |
| 1956 | 103 | 93 | 107 | 102 | 105 | 102 | 102 | 108 | 112 | 92 | 93 | 115 | 112 | 88 |
| 1957 | 102 | 95 | 107 | 102 | 96 | 100 | 103 | 106 | 108 | 96 | 93 | 110 | 107 | 92 |
| 1958 | 100 | 100 | 100 | 100 | 100 | 100 | 100 | 100 | 100 | 100 | 100 | 100 | 100 | 100 |
| 1959 | 106 | 104 | 113 | 100 | 103 | 107 | 106 | 101 | 117 | 107 | 108 | 118 | 105 | 110 |
| 1960 | 106 | 106 | 111 | 95 | 103 | 109 | 109 | 92 | 104 | 112 | 102 | 126 | 100 | 115 |
| 1961 | 109 | 109 | 122 | 96 | 106 | 113 | 110 | 106 | 106 | 114 | 107 | 129 | 101 | 128 |
| **b. Average Annual Rate of Change — Taux annuel moyen de variation** | | | | | | | | | | | | | | |
| 1938 – 1960 | 5.6 | 4.9 | 4.3 | 2.6 | 4.6 | 6.2 | 4.8 | 1.1 | 4.4 | 8.1 | 8.5 | 5.2 | 6.3 | 7.8 |
| 1938 – 1948 | 8.0 | 6.3 | 7.2 | 4.5 | 7.2 | 9.2 | 5.9 | 3.3 | 7.8 | 8.7 | 10.2 | 6.2 | 10.7 | 8.3 |
| 1950 – 1960 | 3.5 | 3.9 | 0.8 | 0.9 | 2.3 | 3.0 | 3.7 | −0.4 | 2.0 | 7.6 | 6.6 | 4.4 | 2.7 | 6.2 |
| 1948 – 1953 | 5.5 | 3.8 | 2.2 | 3.3 | 4.6 | 4.4 | 4.3 | −0.4 | 2.3 | 9.1 | 8.6 | 4.6 | 6.8 | 18.6 |
| 1954 – 1958 | 3.5 | 4.4 | 3.8 | 1.6 | 1.6 | 2.1 | 2.7 | 1.8 | 3.5 | 7.1 | 8.9 | 3.8 | 2.4 | 5.4 |
| 1958 – 1960 | 3.0 | 3.0 | 5.4 | −2.5 | 1.5 | 5.4 | 4.4 | −4.1 | 2.0 | 5.8 | 1.0 | 12.2 | — | 7.2 |

## 3. INDEX NUMBERS OF INDUSTRIAL EMPLOYMENT
### INDICES DE L'EMPLOI DANS L'INDUSTRIE

### A. The Divisions of Industrial Activity
### Les branches de l'activité industrielle

| Period<br>Période | Total | Mining<br>Industries extractives | Manufacturing<br>Industries manufacturières | Construction<br>Bâtiment et travaux publics | Electricity<br>Electricité |
|---|---|---|---|---|---|
| ISIC — CITI | 1–3, 4, 511 | 1 | 2–3 | 4 | 511 |

*a. Indexes — Indices (1958 = 100)*

| | | | | | |
|---|---|---|---|---|---|
| 1938....... | 51 | 72 | 51 | 45 | ... |
| 1948....... | 87 | 79 | 91 | 76 | ... |
| 1949....... | 88 | 81 | 91 | 79 | 73 |
| 1950....... | 89 | 86 | 92 | 82 | 74 |
| 1951....... | 95 | 90 | 98 | 88 | 78 |
| 1952....... | 99 | 95 | 100 | 98 | 82 |
| 1953....... | 100 | 90 | 103 | 94 | 85 |
| 1954....... | 95 | 89 | 98 | 88 | 87 |
| 1955....... | 97 | 92 | 100 | 91 | 89 |
| 1956....... | 104 | 99 | 105 | 104 | 94 |
| 1957....... | 106 | 103 | 105 | 108 | 98 |
| 1958....... | 100 | 100 | 100 | 100 | 100 |
| 1959....... | 101 | 100 | 101 | 103 | 99 |
| 1960....... | 100 | 97 | 100 | 100 | 99 |
| 1961....... | 98 | 94 | 99 | 96 | 100 |

*b. Average Annual Rate of Change — Taux annuel moyen de variation*

| | | | | | |
|---|---|---|---|---|---|
| 1938–1960. | 3.1 | 1.4 | 3.1 | 3.7 | ... |
| 1938–1948. | 5.5 | 0.9 | 6.0 | 5.4 | ... |
| 1950–1960. | 1.2 | 1.2 | 0.8 | 2.0 | 3.0 |
| 1948–1953. | 2.8 | 2.6 | 2.5 | 4.3 | ... |
| 1954–1958. | 1.3 | 3.0 | 0.5 | 3.2 | 3.5 |
| 1958–1960. | — | −1.5 | — | — | −0.5 |

### B. The Major Groups of Mining
### Les classes de la branche Industries extractives

| Period<br>Période | All mining<br>Toutes industries extractives | Coal mining<br>Extraction du charbon | Metal mining<br>Extraction des minerais métalliques | Crude petroleum and natural gas<br>Pétrole brut et gaz naturel | Other mining<br>Autres industries extractives |
|---|---|---|---|---|---|
| ISIC — CITI | 1 | 11 | 12 | 13 | 14–19 |

*a. Indexes — Indices (1958 = 100)*

| | | | | | |
|---|---|---|---|---|---|
| 1938....... | 72 | 192 | 74 | 31 | 86 |
| 1948....... | 79 | 171 | 71 | 28 | 89 |
| 1949....... | 81 | 177 | 74 | 35 | 77 |
| 1950....... | 86 | 172 | 77 | 42 | 92 |
| 1951....... | 90 | 166 | 82 | 54 | 94 |
| 1952....... | 95 | 162 | 87 | 61 | 102 |
| 1953....... | 90 | 148 | 82 | 63 | 101 |
| 1954....... | 89 | 136 | 82 | 65 | 100 |
| 1955....... | 92 | 124 | 86 | 75 | 102 |
| 1956....... | 99 | 119 | 93 | 92 | 109 |
| 1957....... | 103 | 109 | 100 | 101 | 107 |
| 1958....... | 100 | 100 | 100 | 100 | 100 |
| 1959....... | 100 | 86 | 104 | 98 | 102 |
| 1960....... | 97 | 81 | 101 | 98 | 102 |
| 1961....... | 94 | 72 | 97 | 97 | 108 |

*b. Average Annual Rate of Change — Taux annuel moyen de variation*

| | | | | | |
|---|---|---|---|---|---|
| 1938–1960. | 1.4 | −3.8 | 1.4 | 5.4 | 0.8 |
| 1938–1948. | 0.9 | −1.1 | −0.4 | −1.0 | 0.3 |
| 1950–1960. | 1.2 | −7.3 | 2.8 | 8.8 | 1.0 |
| 1948–1953. | 2.6 | −2.9 | 2.9 | 17.6 | 2.6 |
| 1954–1958. | 3.0 | −7.4 | 5.1 | 11.4 | — |
| 1958–1960. | −1.5 | −10.0 | 0.5 | −1.0 | 1.0 |

## C. The Major Groups of Manufacturing — Les classes de la branche Industries manufacturières

| Period<br>Période | Manu-facturing<br>Industries manufac-turières | Food, beverages and tobacco<br>Industries alimen-taires, boissons, tabac | Textiles | Clothing, footwear and made-up textiles<br>Articles d'habil-lement, chaussures et ouvrages en tissu | Wood products and furniture<br>Bois et meubles | Paper and paper products<br>Papier et ouvrages en papier | Printing and Publishing<br>Im-primerie et édition | Leather and leather products except wearing apparel<br>Cuir et articles en cuir, à l'exclu-sion des articles d'habil-lement | Rubber products<br>Ouvrages en caout-chouc | Chemicals and chemical, petroleum and coal products<br>Produits chi-miques et dérivés du pétrole et du charbon | Non-metallic mineral products<br>Produits minéraux non métal-liques | Basic metals<br>Métal-lurgie de base | Metal products<br>Ouvrages en métaux | Other manu-facturing<br>Autres industries manufac-turières |
|---|---|---|---|---|---|---|---|---|---|---|---|---|---|---|
| ISIC — CITI | 2-3 | 20-22 | 23 | 24 | 25-26 | 27 | 28 | 29 | 30 | 31-32 | 33 | 34 | 35-38 | 39 |

### a. Indexes — Indices (1958 = 100)

| | | | | | | | | | | | | | | |
|---|---|---|---|---|---|---|---|---|---|---|---|---|---|---|
| 1938.............. | 51 | 60 | 124 | 54 | 48 | 48 | 54 | 95 | 65 | 42 | 38 | 45 | 37 | 44 |
| 1948.............. | 91 | 90 | 129 | 105 | 100 | 85 | 82 | 135 | 109 | 74 | 73 | 84 | 87 | 76 |
| 1949.............. | 91 | 90 | 129 | 110 | 97 | 82 | 84 | 131 | 100 | 75 | 75 | 89 | 86 | 83 |
| 1950.............. | 92 | 90 | 131 | 108 | 101 | 83 | 87 | 131 | 104 | 77 | 79 | 88 | 86 | 85 |
| 1951.............. | 98 | 91 | 136 | 110 | 106 | 89 | 88 | 123 | 110 | 83 | 85 | 101 | 97 | 85 |
| 1952.............. | 100 | 93 | 120 | 109 | 99 | 90 | 88 | 117 | 103 | 86 | 83 | 105 | 104 | 82 |
| 1953.............. | 103 | 93 | 122 | 111 | 103 | 91 | 90 | 124 | 110 | 88 | 85 | 104 | 111 | 89 |
| 1954.............. | 98 | 94 | 104 | 101 | 98 | 94 | 92 | 109 | 103 | 91 | 86 | 94 | 103 | 88 |
| 1955.............. | 100 | 95 | 110 | 101 | 104 | 98 | 94 | 107 | 110 | 92 | 93 | 104 | 102 | 86 |
| 1956.............. | 105 | 97 | 112 | 103 | 108 | 102 | 97 | 110 | 115 | 97 | 101 | 114 | 111 | 91 |
| 1957.............. | 105 | 99 | 109 | 104 | 103 | 102 | 100 | 106 | 111 | 101 | 99 | 112 | 111 | 95 |
| 1958.............. | 100 | 100 | 100 | 100 | 100 | 100 | 100 | 100 | 100 | 100 | 100 | 100 | 100 | 100 |
| 1959.............. | 101 | 102 | 102 | 102 | 101 | 102 | 102 | 100 | 107 | 99 | 107 | 107 | 99 | 106 |
| 1960.............. | 100 | 101 | 99 | 99 | 100 | 102 | 104 | 92 | 102 | 100 | 105 | 108 | 95 | 109 |
| 1961.............. | 99 | 101 | 101 | 100 | 100 | 102 | 104 | 98 | 99 | 100 | 104 | 104 | 94 | 115 |

### b. Average Annual Rate of Change — Taux annuel moyen de variation

| | | | | | | | | | | | | | | |
|---|---|---|---|---|---|---|---|---|---|---|---|---|---|---|
| 1938 - 1960........ | 3.1 | 2.4 | −1.0 | 2.8 | 3.4 | 3.5 | 3.0 | −0.1 | 2.1 | 4.0 | 4.7 | 4.1 | 4.4 | 4.2 |
| 1938 - 1948........ | 6.0 | 4.1 | 0.4 | 6.9 | 7.6 | 5.9 | 4.3 | 3.6 | 5.3 | 5.8 | 6.7 | 6.4 | 8.9 | 5.6 |
| 1950 - 1960........ | 0.8 | 1.2 | −2.8 | −0.9 | −0.1 | 2.1 | 1.8 | −3.5 | −0.2 | 2.7 | 2.9 | 2.1 | 1.0 | 2.5 |
| 1948 - 1953........ | 2.5 | 0.7 | −1.1 | 1.1 | 0.6 | 1.4 | 1.9 | −1.7 | 0.2 | 3.5 | 3.1 | 4.4 | 5.0 | 3.2 |
| 1954 - 1958........ | 0.5 | 1.6 | −1.0 | −0.3 | 0.5 | 1.6 | 2.1 | −2.1 | −0.7 | 2.4 | 3.8 | 1.6 | −0.7 | 3.2 |
| 1958 - 1960........ | — | 0.5 | −0.5 | −0.5 | — | 1.0 | 2.0 | −4.1 | 1.0 | — | 2.5 | 3.9 | −2.5 | 4.4 |

## 4. THE CHARACTERISTICS OF ALL INDUSTRIAL ESTABLISHMENTS
## CARACTERISTIQUES DE TOUS LES ETABLISSEMENTS INDUSTRIELS
### 1938, 1948, 1953, 1958

Number of establishments in units; value added and wages and salaries in million dollars; number of employees and operatives in thousands; man-hours worked in millions; energy consumed in thousand metric tons of coal equivalents; electricity consumed in million KWH; capacity of installed power equipment in thousand horsepower; value added per employee and wages and salaries per employee, per operative and per thousand operative man-hours in thousand dollars; average annual man-hours per operative in thousands; energy consumed per employee, per operative and per thousand operative man-hours in metric tons of coal equivalents; electricity consumed per employee, per operative and per thousand operative man-hours in thousand KWH; capacity of installed power equipment per employee, per operative and per thousand operative man-hours in horsepower.

Nombre d'établissements en unités; valeur ajoutée et traitements et salaires en millions de dollars; nombre de salariés et d'ouvriers en milliers; heures de travail effectuées en millions; énergie consommée en milliers de tonnes métriques d'équivalent charbon; électricité consommée en millions de kWh; puissance installée en milliers de chevaux-vapeur; valeur ajoutée par salarié et traitements et salaires par salarié, par ouvrier et par millier d'heures-ouvrier en milliers de dollars; moyenne annuelle des heures de travail par ouvrier en milliers; énergie consommée par salarié, par ouvrier et par millier d'heures-ouvrier en tonnes métriques d'équivalent charbon; électricité consommée par salarié, par ouvrier et par millier d'heures-ouvrier en milliers de kWh; puissance installée par salarié, par ouvrier et par millier d'heures-ouvrier en chevaux-vapeur.

### A. The Divisions of Industrial Activity — Les branches de l'activité industrielle

| Year and item of data | All industrial activity / Toutes industries | Mining / Industries extractives | Manufacturing / Industries manufacturières | Construction / Bâtiment et travaux publics | Electricity and gas / Electricité et gaz | Année et rubrique | Year and item of data | All industrial activity / Toutes industries | Mining / Industries extractives | Manufacturing / Industries manufacturières | Construction / Bâtiment et travaux publics | Electricity and gas / Electricité et gaz' | Année et rubrique |
|---|---|---|---|---|---|---|---|---|---|---|---|---|---|
| ISIC | 1-4,511-512 | 1 | 2-3 | 4 | 511-512 | CITI | ISIC | 1-4,511-512 | 1 | 2-3 | 4 | 511-512 | CITI |
| | **a. Absolute Figures — Chiffres absolus** | | | | | | **b. Structure** | | | | | | |
| **1938** | | | | | | **1938** | **1938** | | | | | | **1938** |
| Number of establishments... | ... | 13 895 | 25 180 | ... | 609 | Nombre d'établissements | Distribution in percent of: | | | | | | Distribution en pourcentage: |
| Value added...... | 2 020.9 | 273.7 | 1 421.3 | 176.7 | 149.2 | Valeur ajoutée | Value added..... | 100.0 | 13.5 | 70.3 | 8.8 | 7.4 | Valeur ajoutée |
| Employees: | | | | | | Salariés: | Number of employees....... | 100.0 | 10.0 | 71.4 | 16.4 | 2.2 | Nombre de salariés |
| Number (Average for year)....... | 896.9 | 89.8 | 640.3 | 147.2 | 19.6 | Nombre (moyenne pour l'année) | Per employee: | | | | | | Par salarié: |
| Wages and salaries...... | 1 001.3 | 121.1 | 703.3 | 147.4 | 29.5 | Traitements et salaires | Value added.... | 2.2 | 3.0 | 2.2 | 1.2 | 7.6 | Valeur ajoutée |
| Operatives: | | | | | | Ouvriers: | Wages and salaries........ | 1.1 | 1.3 | 1.1 | 1.0 | 1.5 | Traitements et salaires |
| Number (Average for year)....... | ... | 82.9 | 520.3 | ... | 11.9 | Nombre (moyenne pour l année) | Capacity of installed power equipment....... | . | 9.74 | 7.76 | ... | 394.44 | Puissance installée |
| Wages and salaries........ | ... | 107.0 | 496.7 | ... | ... | Traitements et salaires | Value added per unit of wages and salaries..... | 2.02 | 2.26 | 2.02 | 1.20 | 5.06 | Valeur ajoutée par unité de traitements et salaires |
| Capacity of installed power equipment....... | ... | 875 | 4 970 | ... | 7 731 | Puissance installée | Operatives as a percent of employees....... | ... | 92.3 | 81.2 | ... | 60.7 | Ouvriers en pourcentage des salariés |
| | | | | | | | Per operative: Wages and salaries........ | ... | 1.3 | 1.0 | ... | ... | Par ouvrier: Traitements et salaires |
| | | | | | | | Capacity of installed power equipment....... | . | 10.55 | 9.55 | ... | 649.66 | Puissance installée |
| **1948** | | | | | | **1948** | **1948** | | | | | | **1948** |
| Number of establishments... | ... | 14 121 | 33 428 | ... | 654 | Nombre d'établissements | Distribution in percent of: | | | | | | Distribution en pourcentage: |
| Value added...... | 6 557.7 | 538.7 | 4 932.0 | 829.6 | 257.4 | Valeur ajoutée | Value added..... | 100.0 | 8.2 | 75.2 | 12.6 | 4.0 | Valeur ajoutée |
| Employees: | | | | | | Salariés: | Number of employees....... | 100.0 | 5.5 | 74.2 | 18.2 | 2.1 | Nombre de salariés |
| Number (Average for year)....... | 1 555.3 | 85.9 | 1 154.2 | 284.0 | 31.2 | Nombre (moyenne pour l'année) | Per employee: | | | | | | Par salarié: |
| Wages and salaries........ | 3 298.1 | 214.0 | 2 405.5 | 605.5 | 73.1 | Traitements et salaires | Value added.... | 4.2 | 6.3 | 4.3 | 2.9 | 8.2 | Valeur ajoutée |
| Operatives: | | | | | | Ouvriers: | Wages and salaries........ | 2.1 | 2.5 | 2.1 | 2.1 | 2.3 | Traitements et salaires |
| Number (Average for year)....... | ... | 78.2 | 956.3 | ... | .. | Nombre (moyenne pour l'année) | Value added per unit of wages and salaries..... | 1.99 | 2.52 | 2.05 | 1.37 | 3.52 | Valeur ajoutée par unité de traitements et salaires |
| Wages and salaries........ | ... | 189.9 | 1 873.9 | ...· | ... | Traitements et salaires | Operatives as a percent of employees....... | ... | 91.0 | 82.8 | ... | ... | Ouvriers en pourcentage des salariés |
| | | | | | | | Per operative: Wages and salaries........ | | 2.4 | 2.0 | ... | ... | Par ouvrier: Traitements et salaires |

# CANADA

## A. The Divisions of Industrial Activity (continued) — Les branches de l'activité industrielle (suite)

### a. Absolute Figures — Chiffres absolus

| Year and item of data | All industrial activity / Toutes industries | Mining / Industries extractives | Manufacturing / Industries manufacturières | Construction / Bâtiment et travaux publics | Electricity and gas / Electricité et gaz | Année et rubrique |
|---|---|---|---|---|---|---|
| ISIC | 1-4,511-512 | 1 | 2-3 | 4 | 511-512 | CITI |
| **1953** | | | | | | **1953** |
| Number of establishments... | ... | 20 300 | 38 091 | .... | 540 | Nombre d'établissements |
| Value added...... | 11 189.9 | 790.6 | 7 981.0 | 1 957.1 | 461.2 | Valeur ajoutée |
| Employees: | | | | | | Salariés: |
| Number (Average for year)... | 1 847.5 | 96.9 | 1 326.0 | 374.0 | 50.6 | Nombre (moyenne pour l'année) |
| Wages and salaries........ | 5 639.8 | 333.2 | 3 952.4 | 1 233.9 | 120.3 | Traitements et salaires |
| Operatives: | | | | | | Ouvriers: |
| Number (Average for year)... | ... | 86.0 | 1 052.2 | ... | 34.2 | Nombre (moyenne pour l'année) |
| Wages and salaries........ | ... | 286.8 | 2 936.9 | ... | ... | Traitements et salaires |
| Capacity of installed power equipment....... | . | 1 683 | 10 396 | ... | 15 719 | Puissance installée |
| **1958** | | | | | | **1958** |
| Number of establishments... | ... | 29 361 | 36 734 | .... | .... | Nombre d'établissements |
| Value added...... | 14 941.7 | 1 311.2 | 9 791.1 | 3 155.0 | 684.4 | Valeur ajoutée |
| Employees: | | | | | | Salariés: |
| Number (Average for year)... | 1 892.6 | 103.3 | 1 289.4 | 460.4 | 39.5 | Nombre (moyenne pour l'année) |
| Wages and salaries........ | 7 282.1 | 441.0 | 4 801.9 | 1 868.4 | 170.8 | Traitements et salaires |
| Operatives: | | | | | | Ouvriers: |
| Number (Average for year)... | ... | 88.4 | 981.4 | ... | 22.7 | Nombre (moyenne pour l'année) |
| Wages and salaries........ | ... | 364.2 | 3 332.7 | ... | 95.5 | Traitements et salaires |
| Capacity of installed power equipment. | . | 2 002 | 12 047 | ... | 14 758 | Puissance installée |

### b. Structure

| Year and item of data | All industrial activity / Toutes industries | Mining / Industries extractives | Manufacturing / Industries manufacturières | Construction / Bâtiment et travaux publics | Electricity and gas / Electricité et gaz | Année et rubrique |
|---|---|---|---|---|---|---|
| ISIC | 1-4,511-512 | 1 | 2-3 | 4 | 511-512 | CITI |
| **1953** | | | | | | **1953** |
| Distribution in percent of: | | | | | | Distribution en pourcentage: |
| Value added..... | 100.0 | 7.0 | 71.3 | 17.5 | 4.2 | Valeur ajoutée |
| Number of employees....... | 100.0 | 5.2 | 71.8 | 20.2 | 2.8 | Nombre de salariés |
| Per employee: | | | | | | Par salarié: |
| Value added..... | 6.0 | 8.2 | 6.0 | 5.2 | 9.1 | Valeur ajoutée |
| Wages and salaries........ | 3.0 | 3.4 | 3.0 | 3.3 | 2.4 | Traitements et salaires |
| Capacity of installed power equipment....... | . | 17.37 | 7.84 | ... | 310.65 | Puissance installée |
| Value added per unit of wages and salaries..... | 1.98 | 2.37 | 2.02 | 1.59 | 3.83 | Valeur ajoutée par unité de traitements et salaires |
| Operatives as a percent of employees....... | ... | 88.8 | 79.4 | ... | 67.6 | Ouvriers en pourcentage des salariés |
| Per operative: | | | | | | Par ouvrier: |
| Wages and salaries........ | ... | 3.3 | 2.8 | ... | ... | Traitements et salaires |
| Capacity of installed power equipment....... | . | 19.57 | 9.88 | ... | 459.62 | Puissance installée |
| **1958** | | | | | | **1958** |
| Distribution in percent of: | | | | | | Distribution en pourcentage: |
| Value added..... | 100.0 | 8.7 | 65.6 | 21.1 | 4.6 | Valeur ajoutée |
| Number of employees....... | 100.0 | 5.4 | 68.1 | 24.4 | 2.1 | Nombre de salariés |
| Per employee: | | | | | | Par salarié: |
| Value added..... | 7.9 | 12.7 | 7.6 | 6.8 | 17.3 | Valeur ajoutée |
| Wages and salaries........ | 3.8 | 4.3 | 3.7 | 4.0 | 4.3 | Traitements et salaires |
| Capacity of installed power equipment....... | . | 19.38 | 9.34 | ... | 373.62 | Puissance installée |
| Value added per unit of wages and salaries..... | 2.05 | 2.97 | 2.04 | 1.69 | 4.01 | Valeur ajoutée par unité de traitements et salaires |
| Operatives as a percent of employees....... | ... | 85.6 | 76.1 | ... | 57.5 | Ouvriers en pourcentage des salariés |
| Per operative: | | | | | | Par ouvrier: |
| Wages and salaries........ | ... | 4.1 | 3.4 | ... | 4.2 | Traitements et salaires |
| Capacity of installed power equipment....... | . | 22.65 | 12.28 | ... | 650.13 | Puissance installée |

## B. The Major Groups of Mining — Les classes de la branche Industries extractives

### a. Absolute Figures — Chiffres absolus

| Year and item of data | All mining (1) | Coal mining (11) | Metal mining (12) | Crude petroleum and natural gas (13) | Other mining (14-19) | Année et rubrique |
|---|---|---|---|---|---|---|
| **1938** | | | | | | **1938** |
| Number of establishments | 13 895 | 498 | 870 | 5 725 | 6 802 | Nombre d'établissements |
| Value added | 273.7 | 34.2 | 191.3 | 18.7 | 29.5 | Valeur ajoutée |
| Employees: Number (Average for year) | 89.8 | 27.1 | 43.7 | 3.9 | 15.1 | Salariés: Nombre (moyenne pour l'année) |
| Wages and salaries | 121.1 | 28.7 | 74.9 | 5.2 | 12.3 | Traitements et salaires |
| Operatives: Number (Average for year) | 82.9 | 25.8 | 40.1 | 2.8 | 14.2 | Ouvriers: Nombre (moyenne pour l'année) |
| Wages and salaries | 107.0 | 26.0 | 66.6 | 3.5 | 10.9 | Traitements et salaires |
| Capacity of installed power equipment | 875 | 201 | 509 | 36 | 129 | Puissance installée |
| **1948** | | | | | | **1948** |
| Number of establishments | 14 121 | 351 | 508 | 6 414 | 6 848 | Nombre d'établissements |
| Value added | 538.7 | 85.6 | 310.3 | 50.0 | 92.8 | Valeur ajoutée |
| Employees: Number (Average for year) | 85.9 | 24.3 | 41.9 | 3.5 | 16.2 | Salariés: Nombre (moyenne pour l'année) |
| Wages and salaries | 214.0 | 58.5 | 115.2 | 7.3 | 33.0 | Traitements et salaires |
| Operatives: Number (Average for year) | 78.2 | 22.6 | 37.7 | 3.1 | 14.8 | Ouvriers: Nombre (moyenne pour l'année) |
| Wages and salaries | 189.9 | 53.6 | 100.2 | 6.6 | 29.5 | Traitements et salaires |
| Energy consumed | 1 517.4 | 515.2 | 461.1 | 301.3 | 239.8 | Energie consommée |
| Electricity consumed | 2 180.0 | 250.7 | 1 659.7 | 4.0 | 265.6 | Electricité consommée |
| Capacity of installed power equipment | 1 381 | 234 | 883 | 39 | 225 | Puissance installée |
| **1953** | | | | | | **1953** |
| Number of establishments | 20 300 | 241 | 556 | 11 194 | 8 309 | Nombre d'établissements |
| Value added | 790.6 | 84.6 | 333.4 | 205.5 | 167.1 | Valeur ajoutée |
| Employees: Number (Average for year) | 96.9 | 19.8 | 51.7 | 6.9 | 18.5 | Salariés: Nombre (moyenne pour l'année) |
| Wages and salaries | 333.2 | 59.3 | 191.4 | 24.5 | 58.0 | Traitements et salaires |
| Operatives: Number (Average for year) | 86.0 | 18.2 | 45.8 | 5.2 | 16.8 | Ouvriers: Nombre (moyenne pour l'année) |
| Wages and salaries | 286.8 | 53.6 | 163.6 | 18.5 | 51.1 | Traitements et salaires |
| Energy consumed | 1 231.3 | 279.5 | 598.9 | 82.9 | 270.0 | Energie consommée |
| Electricity consumed | 2 813 | 277 | 2 132 | 26 | 378 | Electricité consommée |
| Capacity of installed power equipment | 1 683 | 248 | 1 021 | 75 | 339 | Puissance installée |

### b. Structure

| Year and item of data | All mining (1) | Coal mining (11) | Metal mining (12) | Crude petroleum and natural gas (13) | Other mining (14-19) | Année et rubrique |
|---|---|---|---|---|---|---|
| **1938** Distribution in percent of: | | | | | | **1938** Distribution en pourcentage: |
| Value added | 100.0 | 12.4 | 69.9 | 6.9 | 10.8 | Valeur ajoutée |
| Number of employees | 100.0 | 30.1 | 48.7 | 4.3 | 16.9 | Nombre de salariés |
| Per employee: Value added | 3.0 | 1.3 | 4.4 | 4.8 | 2.0 | Par salarié: Valeur ajoutée |
| Wages and salaries | 1.3 | 1.0 | 1.7 | 1.3 | 0.8 | Traitements et salaires |
| Capacity of installed power equipment | 9.74 | 7.42 | 11.65 | 9.23 | 8.54 | Puissance installée |
| Value added per unit of wages and salaries | 2.26 | 1.19 | 2.55 | 3.60 | 2.40 | Valeur ajoutée par unité de traitements et salaires |
| Operatives as a percent of employees | 92.3 | 95.2 | 91.8 | 71.8 | 94.0 | Ouvriers en pourcentage des salariés |
| Per operative: Wages and salaries | 1.3 | 1.0 | 1.7 | 1.2 | 0.8 | Par ouvrier: Traitements et salaires |
| Capacity of installed power equipment | 10.55 | 7.79 | 12.69 | 12.86 | 9.08 | Puissance installée |
| **1948** Distribution in percent of: | | | | | | **1948** Distribution en pourcentage: |
| Value added | 100.0 | 15.8 | 57.6 | 9.3 | 17.3 | Valeur ajoutée |
| Number of employees | 100.0 | 28.2 | 48.8 | 4.1 | 18.9 | Nombre de salariés |
| Per employee: Value added | 6.3 | 3.5 | 7.4 | 14.3 | 5.7 | Par salarié: Valeur ajoutée |
| Wages and salaries | 2.5 | 2.4 | 2.7 | 2.1 | 2.0 | Traitements et salaires |
| Energy consumed | 17.66 | 21.20 | 11.00 | 86.08 | 14.80 | Energie consommée |
| Electricity consumed | 25.4 | 10.3 | 39.6 | 1.1 | 16.4 | Electricité consommée |
| Capacity of installed power equipment | 16.08 | 9.63 | 21.07 | 11.14 | 13.89 | Puissance installée |
| Value added per unit of wages and salaries | 2.52 | 1.46 | 2.69 | 6.85 | 2.81 | Valeur ajoutée par unité de traitements et salaires |
| Operatives as a percent of employees | 91.0 | 93.0 | 90.0 | 88.6 | 91.4 | Ouvriers en pourcentage des salariés |
| Per operative: Wages and salaries | 2.4 | 2.4 | 2.6 | 2.1 | 2.0 | Par ouvrier: Traitements et salaires |
| Energy consumed | 19.40 | 22.80 | 12.23 | 97.19 | 16.20 | Energie consommée |
| Electricity consumed | 27.9 | 11.1 | 44.0 | 1.3 | 17.9 | Electricité consommée |
| Capacity of installed power equipment | 17.66 | 10.35 | 23.42 | 12.58 | 15.20 | Puissance installée |
| **1953** Distribution in percent of: | | | | | | **1953** Distribution en pourcentage: |
| Value added | 100.0 | 10.7 | 42.1 | 26.0 | 21.2 | Valeur ajoutée |
| Number of employees | 100.0 | 20.4 | 53.3 | 7.2 | 19.1 | Nombre de salariés |
| Per employee: Value added | 8.2 | 4.3 | 6.4 | 29.8 | 9.0 | Par salarié: Valeur ajoutée |
| Wages and salaries | 3.4 | 3.0 | 3.7 | 3.6 | 3.1 | Traitements et salaires |
| Energy consumed | 12.71 | 14.12 | 11.58 | 12.01 | 14.59 | Energie consommée |
| Electricity consumed | 29.0 | 14.0 | 41.2 | 3.8 | 20.4 | Electricité consommée |
| Capacity of installed power equipment | 17.37 | 12.52 | 19.75 | 10.87 | 18.32 | Puissance installée |
| Value added per unit of wages and salaries | 2.37 | 1.43 | 1.74 | 8.39 | 2.88 | Valeur ajoutée par unité de traitements et salaires |
| Operatives as a percent of employees | 88.8 | 91.9 | 88.6 | 75.4 | 90.8 | Ouvriers en pourcentage des salariés |
| Per operative: Wages and salaries | 3.3 | 2.9 | 3.6 | 3.6 | 3.0 | Par ouvrier: Traitements et salaires |
| Energy consumed | 14.32 | 15.36 | 13.08 | 15.94 | 16.07 | Energie consommée |
| Electricity consumed | 32.7 | 15.2 | 46.6 | 5.0 | 22.5 | Electricité consommée |
| Capacity of installed power equipment | 19.57 | 13.63 | 22.29 | 14.42 | 20.18 | Puissance installée |

## B. The Major Groups of Mining (continued) — Les classes de la branche Industries extractives (suite)

### a. Absolute Figures — Chiffres absolus

| Year and item of data | All mining (Toutes industries extractives) | Coal mining (Extraction du charbon) | Metal mining (Extraction des minerais métalliques) | Crude petroleum and natural gas (Pétrole brut et gaz naturel) | Other mining (Divers) | Année et rubrique |
|---|---|---|---|---|---|---|
| ISIC | 1 | 11 | 12 | 13 | 14-19 | CITI |
| **1958** | | | | | | **1958** |
| Number of establishments... | 29 361 | 158 | 754 | 19 854 | 8 595 | Nombre d'établissements |
| Value added... | 1 311.2 | 64.2 | 601.2 | 407.1 | 238.7 | Valeur ajoutée |
| Employees: | | | | | | Salariés: |
| Number (Average for year)... | 103.3 | 13.2 | 62.0 | 7.1 | 21.0 | Nombre (moyenne pour l'année) |
| Wages and salaries... | 441.0 | 42.2 | 289.6 | 33.3 | 75.9 | Traitements et salaires |
| Operatives: | | | | | | Ouvriers: |
| Number (Average for year)... | 88.4 | 12.0 | 52.8 | 5.2 | 18.4 | Nombre (moyenne pour l'année) |
| Wages and salaries... | 364.2 | 38.2 | 239.3 | 23.0 | 63.7 | Traitements et salaires |
| Energy consumed... | 1 935.4 | 148.2 | 1 061.8 | 327.2 | 398.2 | Energie consommée |
| Electricity consumed | 5 961 | 247 | 5 005 | 98 | 611 | Electricité consommée |
| Capacity of installed power equipment. | 2 002 | 193 | 1 142 | 144 | 523 | Puissance installée |

### b. Structure

| Year and item of data | All mining (Toutes industries extractives) | Coal mining (Extraction du charbon) | Metal mining (Extraction des minerais métalliques) | Crude petroleum and natural gas (Pétrole brut et gaz naturel) | Other mining (Divers) | Année et rubrique |
|---|---|---|---|---|---|---|
| ISIC | 1 | 11 | 12 | 13 | 14-19 | CITI |
| **1958** | | | | | | **1958** |
| Distribution in percent of: | | | | | | Distribution en pourcentage: |
| Value added... | 100.0 | 4.8 | 45.9 | 31.0 | 18.3 | Valeur ajoutée |
| Number of employees... | 100.0 | 12.7 | 60.0 | 6.9 | 20.4 | Nombre de salariés |
| Per employee: | | | | | | Par salarié: |
| Value added... | 12.7 | 4.9 | 9.7 | 57.3 | 11.4 | Valeur ajoutée |
| Wages and salaries... | 4.3 | 3.2 | 4.7 | 4.7 | 3.6 | Traitements et salaires |
| Energy consumed | 18.74 | 11.23 | 17.12 | 46.08 | 18.96 | Energie consommée |
| Electricity consumed... | 57.7 | 18.7 | 80.7 | 13.8 | 29.1 | Electricité consommée |
| Capacity of installed power equipment... | 19.38 | 14.62 | 18.42 | 20.28 | 24.90 | Puissance installée |
| Value added per unit of wages and salaries... | 2.97 | 1.52 | 2.08 | 12.22 | 3.14 | Valeur ajoutée par unité de traitements et salaires |
| Operatives as a percent of employees... | 85.6 | 90.9 | 85.2 | 73.2 | 87.6 | Ouvriers en pourcentage des salariés |
| Per operative: | | | | | | Par ouvrier: |
| Wages and salaries... | 4.1 | 3.2 | 4.5 | 4.4 | 3.5 | Traitements et salaires |
| Energy consumed | 21.89 | 12.35 | 20.11 | 62.92 | 21.64 | Energie consommée |
| Electricity consumed... | 67.4 | 20.6 | 94.8 | 18.8 | 33.2 | Electricité consommée |
| Capacity of installed power equipment... | 22.65 | 16.08 | 21.63 | 27.69 | 28.42 | Puissance installée |

## C. The Major Groups of Manufacturing — Les classes de la branche Industries manufacturières

| Year and item of data | Manufacturing / Industries manufacturières | Food, beverages and tobacco / Industries alimentaires, boissons, tabac | Textiles | Clothing, footwear and made-up textiles / Articles d'habillement, chaussures et ouvrages en tissu | Wood products and furniture / Bois et meubles | Paper and paper products / Papier et ouvrages en papier | Printing and publishing / Imprimerie et édition | Leather and leather products except wearing apparel / Cuir et articles en cuir, à l'exclusion des articles d'habillement | Rubber products / Ouvrages en caoutchouc | Chemicals and chemical, petroleum and coal products / Produits chimiques et dérivés du pétrole et du charbon | Non-metallic mineral products / Produits minéraux non métalliques | Basic metals / Métallurgie de base | Metal products / Ouvrages en métaux | Other manufacturing / Autres industries manufacturières | Année et rubrique |
|---|---|---|---|---|---|---|---|---|---|---|---|---|---|---|---|
| ISIC | 2–3 | 20–22 | 23 | 24 | 25–26 | 27 | 28 | 29 | 30 | 31–32 | 33 | 34 | 35–38 | 39 | CITI |

*a. Absolute Figures — Chiffres absolus*

| Year and item of data | 2–3 | 20–22 | 23 | 24 | 25–26 | 27 | 28 | 29 | 30 | 31–32 | 33 | 34 | 35–38 | 39 | Année et rubrique |
|---|---|---|---|---|---|---|---|---|---|---|---|---|---|---|---|
| **1938** | | | | | | | | | | | | | | | **1938** |
| Number of establishments | 25 180 | 9 479 | 602 | 2 013 | 5 505 | 409 | 2 273 | 312 | 53 | 1 094 | 755 | 334 | 1 683 | 668 | Nombre d'établissements |
| Value added | 1 421.3 | 315.1 | 95.4 | 92.8 | 76.7 | 110.2 | 83.4 | 10.8 | 35.5 | 113.8 | 37.2 | 139.8 | 281.6 | 29.0 | Valeur ajoutée |
| Employees: | | | | | | | | | | | | | | | Salariés: |
| Number (Average for year) | 640.3 | 120.9 | 65.5 | 73.4 | 59.4 | 41.2 | 37.5 | 7.0 | 12.9 | 30.2 | 13.6 | 38.2 | 125.3 | 15.2 | Nombre (moyenne pour l'année) |
| Wages and salaries | 703.3 | 125.0 | 56.1 | 62.6 | 50.7 | 53.9 | 50.6 | 6.9 | 14.1 | 42.4 | 15.3 | 52.0 | 157.6 | 16.1 | Traitements et salaires |
| Operatives: | | | | | | | | | | | | | | | Ouvriers: |
| Number (Average for year) | 520.3 | 92.1 | 59.5 | 62.4 | 50.7 | 34.8 | 23.6 | 5.9 | 10.4 | 20.3 | 11.4 | 34.5 | 102.7 | 12.0 | Nombre (moyenne pour l'année) |
| Wages and salaries | 496.7 | 82.2 | 44.7 | 44.8 | 40.3 | 38.8 | 28.3 | 4.9 | 9.7 | 23.2 | 11.4 | 43.3 | 114.6 | 10.5 | Traitements et salaires |
| Capacity of installed power equipment | 4 970 | 497 | 217 | | | 2 530 | | | 152 | | 259 | 1 288 | | 27 | Puissance installée |
| **1948** | | | | | | | | | | | | | | | **1948** |
| Number of establishments | 33 428 | 8 837 | 1 011 | 3 233 | 10 495 | 499 | 2 496 | 360 | 56 | 1 118 | 923 | 344 | 3 144 | 912 | Nombre d'établissements |
| Value added | 4 932.0 | 832.4 | 338.5 | 323.0 | 401.4 | 495.2 | 208.2 | 31.8 | 107.0 | 373.5 | 131.1 | 357.1 | 1 244.0 | 88.8 | Valeur ajoutée |
| Employees: | | | | | | | | | | | | | | | Salariés: |
| Number (Average for year) | 1 154.2 | 180.9 | 103.0 | 112.0 | 124.3 | 73.4 | 54.5 | 10.0 | 21.7 | 54.2 | 26.6 | 71.8 | 295.0 | 26.8 | Nombre (moyenne pour l'année) |
| Wages and salaries | 2 405.5 | 333.9 | 182.2 | 186.7 | 214.7 | 192.2 | 119.0 | 18.5 | 48.3 | 125.4 | 57.4 | 183.1 | 694.1 | 50.0 | Traitements et salaires |
| Operatives: | | | | | | | | | | | | | | | Ouvriers: |
| Number (Average for year) | 956.3 | 147.5 | 92.0 | 96.8 | 104.4 | 61.4 | 37.1 | 8.6 | 18.1 | 39.2 | 23.0 | 63.2 | 243.2 | 21.8 | Nombre (moyenne pour l'année) |
| Man-hours worked | 2 169.1 | 336.9 | 212.5 | 201.8 | 238.9 | 150.6 | 78.9 | 18.3 | 40.8 | 88.7 | 55.4 | 146.4 | 552.0 | 47.9 | Heures de travail effectuées |
| Wages and salaries | 1 873.9 | 253.8 | 149.4 | 140.6 | 180.5 | 150.2 | 77.2 | 14.2 | 38.1 | 83.4 | 47.8 | 156.4 | 545.6 | 36.7 | Traitements et salaires |
| Energy consumed | 19 955.0 | 2 118.0 | 728.2 | 67.2 | 210.1 | 4 658.7 | 73.2 | 85.7 | 162.4 | 3 089.2 | 1 634.6 | 5 513.5 | 1 551.7 | 62.5 | Energie consommée |
| Electricity consumed | 29 090.7 | 825.6 | 557.4 | 59.7 | 252.1 | 10 405.6 | 89.8 | 28.8 | 177.4 | 3 276.5 | 1 262.4 | 10 812.0 | 1 284.7 | 58.7 | Electricité consommée |
| Capacity of installed power equipment | 8 160 | 833 | 342 | | | 3 776 | | | 714 | | 384 | 2 070 | | 41 | Puissance installée |
| **1953** | | | | | | | | | | | | | | | **1953** |
| Number of establishments | 38 091 | 8 273 | 1 253 | 3 191 | 12 462 | 529 | 4 157 | 300 | 72 | 1 229 | 1 082 | 337 | 3 748 | 1 458 | Nombre d'établissements |
| Value added | 7 981.0 | 1 232.1 | 380.5 | 406.3 | 577.4 | 745.5 | 364.4 | 31.4 | 172.7 | 671.1 | 234.2 | 631.8 | 2 362.0 | 171.6 | Valeur ajoutée |
| Employees: | | | | | | | | | | | | | | | Salariés: |
| Number (Average for year) | 1 326.0 | 187.8 | 97.6 | 120.1 | 134.3 | 81.9 | 66.5 | 8.9 | 22.6 | 68.6 | 33.6 | 79.0 | 388.5 | 36.6 | Nombre (moyenne pour l'année) |
| Wages and salaries | 3 952.4 | 486.9 | 237.0 | 251.4 | 325.6 | 302.3 | 205.6 | 21.9 | 71.0 | 234.9 | 105.0 | 288.2 | 1 325.6 | 97.0 | Traitements et salaires |
| Operatives: | | | | | | | | | | | | | | | Ouvriers: |
| Number (Average for year) | 1 052.2 | 151.1 | 83.2 | 104.3 | 109.1 | 68.2 | 40.7 | 7.5 | 17.0 | 45.0 | 27.7 | 67.4 | 302.7 | 28.3 | Nombre (moyenne pour l'année) |
| Man-hours worked | 2 287.9 | 333.8 | 177.8 | 207.5 | 248.4 | 154.5 | 84.7 | 15.0 | 36.7 | 98.6 | 64.1 | 146.8 | 658.1 | 61.9 | Heures de travail effectuées |
| Wages and salaries | 2 936.9 | 363.6 | 182.3 | 194.1 | 261.7 | 234.7 | 124.5 | 16.8 | 50.8 | 142.4 | 83.0 | 238.1 | 978.9 | 66.0 | Traitements et salaires |
| Energy consumed | 22 082.8 | 2 270.8 | 732.3 | 64.8 | 311.2 | 5 331.8 | 89.1 | 71.1 | 178.9 | 4 129.2 | 2 137.8 | 4 890.4 | 1 780.8 | 94.6 | Energie consommée |
| Electricity consumed | 40 918 | 1 120 | 718 | 84 | 564 | 14 804 | 126 | 31 | 258 | 4 186 | 1 737 | 15 081 | 2 068 | 141 | Electricité consommée |
| Capacity of installed power equipment | 10 396 | 818 | 430 | 42 | 1 253 | 3 564 | 80 | 29 | 142 | 838 | 335 | 1 222 | 1 591 | 52 | Puissance installée |
| **1958** | | | | | | | | | | | | | | | **1958** |
| Number of establishments | 36 734 | 8 518 | 1 224 | 2 807 | 9 848 | 540 | 4 433 | 259 | 89 | 1 294 | 1 235 | 328 | 4 416 | 1 743 | Nombre d'établissements |
| Value added | 9 791.1 | 1 651.0 | 406.5 | 438.6 | 605.7 | 889.3 | 509.1 | 36.0 | 174.8 | 1 202.1 | 356.8 | 816.8 | 2 464.6 | 239.8 | Valeur ajoutée |
| Employees: | | | | | | | | | | | | | | | Salariés: |
| Number (Average for year) | 1 289.4 | 202.1 | 84.4 | 110.2 | 120.9 | 90.4 | 72.2 | 7.8 | 19.9 | 74.6 | 39.9 | 75.2 | 351.8 | 40.0 | Nombre (moyenne pour l'année) |
| Wages and salaries | 4 801.9 | 665.3 | 243.1 | 273.9 | 369.6 | 399.2 | 288.0 | 23.1 | 76.4 | 333.9 | 158.2 | 350.9 | 1 487.8 | 132.5 | Traitements et salaires |
| Operatives: | | | | | | | | | | | | | | | Ouvriers: |
| Number (Average for year) | 981.4 | 161.0 | 68.8 | 95.9 | 98.1 | 73.3 | 43.2 | 6.6 | 14.7 | 46.1 | 31.9 | 60.8 | 251.4 | 29.6 | Nombre (moyenne pour l'année) |
| Man-hours worked | 2 098.5 | 347.5 | 147.3 | 195.0 | 219.0 | 158.2 | 89.0 | 13.8 | 32.1 | 98.7 | 73.2 | 128.6 | 532.0 | 64.1 | Heures de travail effectuées |
| Wages and salaries | 3 332.7 | 491.2 | 171.9 | 208.9 | 290.2 | 299.1 | 169.8 | 17.8 | 52.1 | 186.1 | 119.5 | 267.6 | 974.0 | 84.5 | Traitements et salaires |
| Energy consumed | 27 192.6 | 2 637.5 | 772.4 | 81.2 | 413.7 | 6 080.9 | 162.4 | 66.4 | 222.5 | 6 661.9 | 2 905.7 | 4 897.5 | 2 156.6 | 133.9 | Energie consommée |
| Electricity consumed | 52 746 | 1 820 | 869 | 116 | 951 | 18 752 | 282 | 37 | 323 | 6 635 | 2 134 | 18 098 | 2 525 | 204 | Electricité consommée |
| Capacity of installed power equipment | 12 047 | 862 | 321 | 27 | 1 020 | 4 116 | 108 | 44 | 152 | 1 278 | 568 | 1 867 | 1 620 | 64 | Puissance installée |

*b. Structure*

| Year and item of data | 2–3 | 20–22 | 23 | 24 | 25–26 | 27 | 28 | 29 | 30 | 31–32 | 33 | 34 | 35–38 | 39 | Année et rubrique |
|---|---|---|---|---|---|---|---|---|---|---|---|---|---|---|---|
| **1938** | | | | | | | | | | | | | | | **1938** |
| Distribution in percent of: | | | | | | | | | | | | | | | Distribution en pourcentage: |
| Value added | 100.0 | 22.1 | 6.7 | 6.6 | 5.4 | 7.7 | 5.9 | 0.7 | 2.5 | 8.0 | 2.7 | 9.8 | 19.8 | 2.1 | Valeur ajoutée |
| Number of employees | 100.0 | 18.8 | 10.3 | 11.4 | 9.3 | 6.4 | 5.9 | 1.1 | 2.0 | 4.7 | 2.1 | 6.0 | 19.6 | 2.4 | Nombre de salariés |
| Per employee: | | | | | | | | | | | | | | | Par salarié: |
| Value added | 2.2 | 2.6 | 1.4 | 1.3 | 1.3 | 2.7 | 2.2 | 1.5 | 2.8 | 3.8 | 2.7 | 3.6 | 2.2 | 1.9 | Valeur ajoutée |
| Wages and salaries | 1.1 | 1.0 | 0.8 | 0.8 | 0.8 | 1.3 | 1.3 | 1.0 | 1.1 | 1.4 | 1.1 | 1.4 | 1.2 | 1.0 | Traitements et salaires |
| Capacity of installed power equipment | 7.76 | 4.11 | 1.56 | | | 18.32 | | | 3.03 | | 19.04 | 7.88 | | 1.78 | Puissance installée |
| Value added per unit of wages and salaries | 2.02 | 2.52 | 1.70 | 1.48 | 1.51 | 2.04 | 1.65 | 1.57 | 2.52 | 2.68 | 2.43 | 2.69 | 1.79 | 1.80 | Valeur ajoutée par unité de traitements et salaires |

# CANADA

## C. The Major Groups of Manufacturing (continued) — Les classes de la branche Industries manufacturières (suite)

| Year and item of data | Manufacturing — Industries manufacturières | Food, beverages and tobacco — Industries alimentaires, boissons, tabac | Textiles | Clothing, footwear and made-up textiles — Articles d'habillement, chaussures et ouvrages en tissu | Wood products and furniture — Bois et meubles | Paper and paper products — Papier et ouvrages en papier | Printing and publishing — Imprimerie et édition | Leather and leather products except wearing apparel — Cuir et articles en cuir, à l'exclusion des articles d'habillement | Rubber products — Ouvrages en caoutchouc | Chemicals and chemical, petroleum and coal products — Produits chimiques et dérivés du pétrole et du charbon | Non-metallic mineral products — Produits minéraux non métalliques | Basic metals — Métallurgie de base | Metal products — Ouvrages en métaux | Other manufacturing — Autres industries manufacturières | Année et rubrique |
|---|---|---|---|---|---|---|---|---|---|---|---|---|---|---|---|
| ISIC | 2–3 | 20–22 | 23 | 24 | 25–26 | 27 | 28 | 29 | 30 | 31–32 | 33 | 34 | 35–38 | 39 | CIT |
| **b. Structure** | | | | | | | | | | | | | | | |
| Operatives as a percent of employees | 81.2 | 76.2 | 90.8 | 85.0 | 85.4 | 84.5 | 62.9 | 84.3 | 80.6 | 67.2 | 83.8 | 90.3 | 82.0 | 78.9 | Ouvriers en pourcentage des salariés |
| Per operative: Wages and salaries | 1.0 | 0.9 | 0.8 | 0.7 | 0.8 | 1.1 | 1.2 | 0.8 | 0.9 | 1.1 | 1.0 | 1.2 | 1.1 | 0.9 | Par ouvrier: Traitements et salaires |
| Capacity of installed power equipment | 9.55 | 5.40 | 1.78 | | 23.19 | | | 4.15 | | 22.72 | | 9.39 | | 2.25 | Puissance installée |
| **1948** | | | | | | | | | | | | | | | **1948** |
| Distribution in percent of: | | | | | | | | | | | | | | | Distribution en pourcentage: |
| Value added | 100.0 | 16.8 | 6.9 | 6.5 | 8.2 | 10.0 | 4.2 | 0.7 | 2.2 | 7.5 | 2.7 | 7.2 | 25.2 | 1.9 | Valeur ajoutée |
| Number of employees | 100.0 | 15.6 | 8.9 | 9.8 | 10.7 | 6.4 | 4.7 | 0.9 | 1.8 | 4.7 | 2.3 | 6.3 | 25.5 | 2.4 | Nombre de salariés |
| Per employee: | | | | | | | | | | | | | | | Par salarié: |
| Value added | 4.3 | 4.6 | 3.3 | 2.9 | 3.2 | 6.7 | 3.8 | 3.2 | 4.9 | 6.9 | 4.9 | 5.0 | 4.2 | 3.3 | Valeur ajoutée |
| Wages and salaries | 2.1 | 1.8 | 1.8 | 1.7 | 1.7 | 2.6 | 2.2 | 1.8 | 2.2 | 2.3 | 2.2 | 2.6 | 2.4 | 1.9 | Traitements et salaires |
| Energy consumed | 17.29 | 11.71 | 7.07 | 0.60 | 1.69 | 63.47 | 1.34 | 8.57 | 7.48 | 57.00 | 61.45 | 76.79 | 5.26 | 2.33 | Énergie consommée |
| Electricity consumed | 25.2 | 4.6 | 5.4 | 0.5 | 2.0 | 141.8 | 1.6 | 2.9 | 8.2 | 60.4 | 47.4 | 150.6 | 4.4 | 2.2 | Électricité consommée |
| Capacity of installed power equipment | 7.07 | 4.60 | 1.59 | | 14.97 | | | 8.31 | | 14.44 | | 5.64 | | 1.53 | Puissance installée |
| Value added per unit of wages and salaries | 2.05 | 2.49 | 1.86 | 1.75 | 1.87 | 2.58 | 1.75 | 1.72 | 2.22 | 2.98 | 2.28 | 1.95 | 1.79 | 1.78 | Valeur ajoutée par unité de traitements et salaires |
| Operatives as a percent of employees | 82.8 | 81.5 | 89.3 | 86.4 | 84.0 | 83.6 | 68.1 | 86.0 | 83.4 | 72.3 | 86.5 | 88.0 | 82.4 | 81.3 | Ouvriers en pourcentage des salariés |
| Average man-hours per operative | 2.27 | 2.28 | 2.31 | 2.08 | 2.29 | 2.45 | 2.13 | 2.13 | 2.25 | 2.26 | 2.41 | 2.32 | 2.27 | 2.20 | Heures de travail: moyenne par ouvrier |
| Per thousand operative man-hour: | | | | | | | | | | | | | | | Par millier d'heures-ouvrier: |
| Wages and salaries | 0.86 | 0.75 | 0.70 | 0.70 | 0.76 | 1.00 | 0.98 | 0.78 | 0.93 | 0.94 | 0.86 | 1.07 | 0.99 | 0.77 | Traitements et salaires |
| Energy consumed | 9.20 | 6.29 | 3.43 | 0.33 | 0.88 | 30.93 | 0.93 | 4.68 | 3.98 | 34.83 | 29.50 | 37.66 | 2.81 | 1.30 | Énergie consommée |
| Electricity consumed | 13.41 | 2.45 | 2.62 | 0.30 | 1.06 | 69.09 | 1.14 | 1.57 | 4.35 | 36.94 | 22.79 | 73.85 | 2.33 | 1.22 | Électricité consommée |
| Capacity of installed power equipment | 3.76 | 2.47 | 0.82 | | 8.06 | | | 4.83 | | 6.93 | | 2.96 | | 0.86 | Puissance installée |
| **1953** | | | | | | | | | | | | | | | **1954** |
| Distribution in percent of: | | | | | | | | | | | | | | | Distribution en pourcentage: |
| Value added | 100.0 | 15.4 | 4.8 | 5.0 | 7.3 | 9.3 | 4.6 | 0.4 | 2.1 | 8.5 | 2.9 | 7.9 | 29.6 | 2.2 | Valeur ajoutée |
| Number of employees | 100.0 | 14.1 | 7.4 | 9.0 | 10.2 | 6.1 | 5.1 | 0.6 | 1.7 | 5.2 | 2.5 | 6.0 | 29.3 | 2.8 | Nombre de salariés |
| Per employee: | | | | | | | | | | | | | | | Par salarié: |
| Value added | 6.0 | 6.6 | 3.9 | 3.4 | 4.3 | 9.1 | 5.5 | 3.5 | 7.6 | 9.8 | 7.0 | 8.0 | 6.1 | 4.7 | Valeur ajoutée |
| Wages and salaries | 3.0 | 2.6 | 2.4 | 2.1 | 2.4 | 3.7 | 3.1 | 2.5 | 3.1 | 3.4 | 3.1 | 3.6 | 3.4 | 2.6 | Traitements et salaires |
| Energy consumed | 16.65 | 12.09 | 7.50 | 0.54 | 2.32 | 65.10 | 1.34 | 7.99 | 7.92 | 60.19 | 63.62 | 61.90 | 4.58 | 2.58 | Énergie consommée |
| Electricity consumed | 30.8 | 6.0 | 7.4 | 0.7 | 4.2 | 180.8 | 1.9 | 3.5 | 11.4 | 61.0 | 51.7 | 190.9 | 5.3 | 3.8 | Électricité consommée |
| Capacity of installed power equipment | 7.84 | 4.36 | 4.40 | 0.35 | 9.33 | 43.52 | 1.20 | 3.26 | 6.28 | 12.22 | 9.97 | 15.47 | 4.10 | 1.42 | Puissance installée |
| Value added per unit of wages and salaries | 2.02 | 2.53 | 1.60 | 1.62 | 1.77 | 2.47 | 1.77 | 1.43 | 2.43 | 2.86 | 2.23 | 2.19 | 1.78 | 1.77 | Valeur ajoutée par unité de traitements et salaires |
| Operatives as a percent of employees | 79.4 | 80.4 | 85.2 | 86.8 | 81.2 | 83.3 | 61.2 | 84.3 | 75.2 | 65.6 | 82.4 | 85.3 | 77.9 | 77.3 | Ouvriers en pourcentage des salariés |
| Average man-hours per operative | 2.17 | 2.21 | 2.14 | 1.99 | 2.28 | 2.26 | 2.08 | 2.00 | 2.16 | 2.19 | 2.31 | 2.18 | 2.17 | 2.19 | Heures de travail: moyenne par ouvrier |
| Per thousand operative man-hour: | | | | | | | | | | | | | | | Par millier d'heures-ouvrier: |
| Wages and salaries | 1.28 | 1.09 | 1.02 | 0.94 | 1.05 | 1.52 | 1.47 | 1.12 | 1.38 | 1.44 | 1.29 | 1.62 | 1.49 | 1.07 | Traitements et salaires |
| Energy consumed | 9.65 | 6.80 | 4.12 | 0.31 | 1.25 | 34.51 | 1.05 | 4.74 | 4.87 | 41.88 | 33.35 | 33.31 | 2.70 | 1.53 | Énergie consommée |
| Electricity consumed | 17.88 | 3.36 | 4.04 | 0.40 | 2.27 | 95.82 | 1.49 | 2.07 | 7.03 | 424.5 | 27.10 | 102.73 | 3.14 | 2.28 | Électricité consommée |
| Capacity of installed power equipment | 4.54 | 2.45 | 2.42 | 0.20 | 5.04 | 23.07 | 0.94 | 1.93 | 3.87 | 8.50 | 5.23 | 8.32 | 2.42 | 0.84 | Puissance installée |
| **1958** | | | | | | | | | | | | | | | **1958** |
| Distribution in percent of: | | | | | | | | | | | | | | | Distribution en pourcentage: |
| Value added | 100.0 | 16.8 | 4.2 | 4.4 | 6.2 | 9.1 | 5.2 | 0.4 | 1.8 | 12.2 | 3.7 | 8.3 | 25.2 | 2.5 | Valeur ajoutée |
| Number of employees | 100.0 | 15.6 | 6.6 | 8.5 | 9.4 | 7.0 | 5.6 | 0.6 | 1.6 | 5.7 | 3.1 | 5.9 | 27.2 | 3.2 | Nombre de salariés |
| Per employee: | | | | | | | | | | | | | | | Par salarié: |
| Value added | 7.6 | 8.2 | 4.8 | 4.0 | 5.0 | 9.8 | 7.0 | 4.6 | 8.8 | 16.1 | 8.9 | 10.9 | 7.0 | 6.0 | Valeur ajoutée |
| Wages and salaries | 3.7 | 3.3 | 2.9 | 2.5 | 3.0 | 4.4 | 4.0 | 3.0 | 3.8 | 4.5 | 4.0 | 4.7 | 4.2 | 3.3 | Traitements et salaires |
| Energy consumed | 21.09 | 13.05 | 9.15 | 0.74 | 3.42 | 67.27 | 2.25 | 8.51 | 11.18 | 89.30 | 72.82 | 65.13 | 6.13 | 3.35 | Énergie consommée |
| Electricity consumed | 40.9 | 9.0 | 10.3 | 1.0 | 7.9 | 207.4 | 3.9 | 4.7 | 16.2 | 88.9 | 53.5 | 240.7 | 7.2 | 5.1 | Électricité consommée |
| Capacity of installed power equipment | 9.34 | 4.26 | 3.80 | 0.24 | 8.44 | 45.53 | 1.50 | 5.64 | 7.64 | 17.13 | 14.24 | 24.83 | 4.60 | 1.60 | Puissance installée |
| Value added per unit of wages and salaries | 2.04 | 2.48 | 1.67 | 1.60 | 1.64 | 2.23 | 1.78 | 1.56 | 2.29 | 3.60 | 2.26 | 2.33 | 1.66 | 1.81 | Valeur ajoutée par unité de traitements et salaires |
| Operatives as a percent of employees | 76.1 | 79.7 | 81.5 | 87.0 | 81.1 | 81.1 | 59.8 | 84.6 | 73.9 | 61.8 | 79.9 | 80.8 | 71.5 | 74.0 | Ouvriers en pourcentage des salariés |
| Average man-hours per operative | 2.14 | 2.16 | 2.14 | 2.03 | 2.23 | 2.16 | 2.06 | 2.09 | 2.18 | 2.14 | 2.29 | 2.12 | 2.12 | 2.16 | Heures de travail: moyenne par ouvrier |
| Per thousand operative man-hour: | | | | | | | | | | | | | | | Par millier d'heures-ouvrier: |
| Wages and salaries | 1.59 | 1.41 | 1.17 | 1.07 | 1.32 | 1.89 | 1.91 | 1.29 | 1.62 | 1.88 | 1.63 | 2.08 | 1.83 | 1.32 | Traitements et salaires |
| Energy consumed | 12.96 | 7.59 | 5.24 | 0.42 | 1.89 | 38.44 | 1.82 | 4.81 | 6.93 | 67.50 | 39.70 | 38.08 | 4.05 | 2.09 | Énergie consommée |
| Electricity consumed | 25.14 | 5.24 | 5.90 | 0.59 | 4.34 | 118.53 | 3.17 | 2.68 | 10.06 | 67.22 | 29.15 | 140.73 | 4.75 | 3.18 | Électricité consommée |
| Capacity of installed power equipment | 5.74 | 2.48 | 2.18 | 0.14 | 4.66 | 26.02 | 1.21 | 3.19 | 4.74 | 12.95 | 7.76 | 14.52 | 3.04 | 1.00 | Puissance installée |

## 5. FUELS AND ELECTRICITY CONSUMED, ALL INDUSTRIAL ESTABLISHMENTS
## COMBUSTIBLES ET ELECTRICITE CONSOMMES, TOUS LES ETABLISSEMENTS INDUSTRIELS
### 1948, 1953, 1958

### A. Percentage Distribution of Energy Consumed According to Source
### Répartition en pourcentage de l'énergie consommée suivant la source

Quantities in thousand metric tons of coal equivalents     Quantités en milliers de tonnes métriques d'équivalent charbon.

### a. The Major Groups of Mining and Electricity
### Les classes des industries extractives et l'électricité

| Year and item of data | Mining — Industries extractives | | | | | Electricity Electricité | Année et rubrique |
|---|---|---|---|---|---|---|---|
| | Total | Coal mining Extraction du charbon | Metal mining Extraction des minerais métal-liques | Crude petroleum and natural gas Pétrole brut et gaz naturel | Other mining Divers | | |
| ISIC | 1 | 11 | 12 | 13 | 14–19 | 511 | CITI |
| **1948** | | | | | | | **1948** Energie totale consommée |
| Total energy consumed.. | 1 571.4 | 515.2 | 461.1 | 301.3 | 239.8 | 1 321.2 | |
| Percent consumed as: | | | | | | | Pourcentage consommé sous forme de: |
| Coal............... | 48.3 | 91.8 | 32.3 | — | 46.7 | 60.5 | Charbon |
| Lignite............. | 2.4 | 1.3 | 4.3 | — | 3.9 | 1.6 | Lignite |
| Coke............... | 0.1 | — | — | — | 0.4 | — | Coke |
| Refined oil fuels...... | 10.8 | 2.0 | 15.6 | 0.8 | 33.1 | 14.2 | Pétrole raffiné |
| Gas................ | 20.0 | 0.1 | — | 99.0 | 1.8 | 23.3 | Gaz |
| Electricity purchased... | 15.7 | 4.7 | 39.4 | 0.2 | 13.3 | — | Electricité achetée |
| Wood............. | 2.5 | 0.1 | 7.8 | — | 0.8 | — | Bois |
| Other fuels [1]........ | 0.2 | — | 0.6 | — | — | 0.4 | Autres combustibles [1] |
| **1953** | | | | | | | **1953** Energie totale consommée |
| Total energy consumed... | 1 231.3 | 279.5 | 598.9 | 82.9 | 270.0 | 2 236.7 | |
| Percent consumed as: | | | | | | | Pourcentage consommé sous forme de: |
| Coal............... | 39.6 | 81.4 | 27.3 | 3.7 | 34.8 | 66.8 | Charbon |
| Lignite............. | 1.2 | 2.0 | — | — | 2.9 | 4.3 | Lignite |
| Coke............... | 3.9 | 0.1 | 8.0 | — | 0.1 | — | Coke |
| Refined oil fuels...... | 22.7 | 5.1 | 18.6 | 46.8 | 42.9 | 11.4 | Pétrole raffiné |
| Gas................ | 3.6 | 0.3 | 0.1 | 45.2 | 1.7 | 17.1 | Gaz |
| Electricity purchased... | 26.4 | 11.1 | 41.0 | 3.6 | 17.0 | — | Electricité achetée |
| Wood............. | 2.1 | — | 4.0 | 0.7 | 0.6 | — | Bois |
| Other fuels [1]........ | 0.5 | — | 1.0 | — | — | 0.4 | Autres combustibles [1] |
| **1958** | | | | | | | **1958** Energie totale consommée |
| Total energy consumed... | 1 935.4 | 148.2 | 1 061.8 | 327.2 | 398.2 | 2 587.5 | |
| Percent consumed as: | | | | | | | Pourcentage consommé sous forme de: |
| Coal............... | 17.8 | 68.2 | 17.9 | 0.4 | 12.8 | 41.3 | Charbon |
| Lignite............. | 0.9 | 3.6 | — | 0.4 | 2.8 | 5.5 | Lignite |
| Coke............... | 0.2 | 0.2 | 0.3 | — | 0.1 | — | Coke |
| Refined oil fuels...... | 29.2 | 7.5 | 26.1 | 17.6 | 55.0 | 12.5 | Pétrole raffiné |
| Gas................ | 15.5 | 0.1 | 0.5 | 78.1 | 9.7 | 40.7 | Gaz |
| Electricity purchased... | 35.2 | 20.3 | 53.3 | 3.5 | 18.6 | — | Electricité achetée |
| Wood............. | 0.9 | 0.1 | 1.3 | — | 1.0 | — | Bois |
| Other fuels [1]........ | 0.3 | — | 0.6 | — | — | — | Autres combustibles [1] |

For footnotes see end of table.     Pour les notes, voir au bas du tableau.

## b. The Major Groups of Manufacturing — Les classes de la branche Industries manufacturières

| Year and item of data | Manufacturing — Industries manufacturières | Food, beverages and tobacco — Industries alimentaires, boissons, tabac | Textiles | Clothing, footwear and made-up textiles — Articles d'habillement, chaussures et ouvrages en tissu | Wood products and furniture — Bois et meubles | Paper and paper products — Papier et ouvrages en papier | Printing and publishing — Imprimerie et édition | Leather and leather products except wearing apparel — Cuir et articles en cuir, à l'exclusion des articles d'habillement | Rubber products — Ouvrages en caoutchouc | Chemicals and chemical, petroleum and coal products — Produits chimiques et dérivés du pétrole et du charbon | Non-metallic mineral products — Produits minéraux non métalliques | Basic metals — Métallurgie de base | Metal products — Ouvrages en métaux | Other manufacturing — Autres industries manufacturières | Année et rubrique |
|---|---|---|---|---|---|---|---|---|---|---|---|---|---|---|---|
| ISIC | 2–3 | 20–22 | 23 | 24 | 25–26 | 27 | 28 | 29 | 30 | 31–32 | 33 | 34 | 35 | 39 | CITI |
| **1948** Total energy consumed: | | | | | | | | | | | | | | | **1948** Energie totale consommée: |
| Quantity | 19 955.0 | 2 118.0 | 728.2 | 67.2 | 210.1 | 4 658.7 | 73.2 | 85.7 | 162.4 | 3 089.2 | 1 634.6 | 5 513.5 | 1 551.7 | 62.5 | Quantité |
| Percent of total in specified industry | 100.0 | 10.6 | 3.6 | 0.3 | 1.1 | 23.3 | 0.4 | 0.4 | 0.9 | 15.4 | 8.2 | 27.7 | 7.7 | 0.4 | Pourcentage du total par industrie indiquée |
| Percent consumed as: | | | | | | | | | | | | | | | Pourcentage consommé sous forme de: |
| Coal | 48.1 | 56.9 | 78.0 | 58.0 | 40.2 | 68.8 | 48.2 | 81.3 | 75.6 | 28.6 | 62.3 | 25.8 | 57.3 | 68.3 | Charbon |
| Lignite | 0.6 | 3.0 | — | 0.2 | 0.2 | 0.2 | 0.7 | — | 0.2 | — | 0.5 | — | 2.0 | 0.2 | Lignite |
| Coke | 2.9 | 2.7 | 0.5 | 0.4 | 0.2 | — | 1.6 | 0.4 | — | 6.2 | 2.0 | 5.0 | 1.7 | 0.6 | Coke |
| Refined oil fuels | 16.3 | 19.5 | 8.5 | 18.3 | 35.9 | 7.9 | 23.1 | 6.3 | 6.2 | 28.4 | 17.2 | 14.2 | 22.9 | 13.6 | Pétrole raffiné |
| Gas | 13.9 | 6.0 | — | 3.3 | 2.3 | 0.1 | 7.6 | — | 0.3 | 22.7 | 5.7 | 31.6 | 4.9 | 3.8 | Gaz |
| Electricity purchased | 15.4 | 4.6 | 9.5 | 11.0 | 14.1 | 21.6 | 15.3 | 4.2 | 13.6 | 8.7 | 9.6 | 22.7 | 9.1 | 11.7 | Electricité achetée |
| Wood | 1.1 | 6.5 | — | 2.8 | 5.4 | 0.1 | 3.3 | 1.4 | — | 0.1 | 2.5 | 0.1 | 0.4 | 1.0 | Bois |
| Other fuels [1] | 1.7 | 0.8 | 3.5 | 6.0 | 1.7 | 1.3 | 0.2 | 6.4 | 4.1 | 5.3 | 0.2 | 0.6 | 1.7 | 0.8 | Autres combustibles [1] |
| **1953** Total energy consumed: | | | | | | | | | | | | | | | **1953** Energie totale consommée: |
| Quantity | 22 082.8 | 2 270.8 | 732.3 | 64.8 | 311.2 | 5 331.8 | 89.1 | 71.1 | 178.9 | 4 129.2 | 2 137.8 | 4 890.4 | 1 780.8 | 94.6 | Quantité |
| Percent of total in specified industry | 100.0 | 10.2 | 3.3 | 0.3 | 1.5 | 24.1 | 0.4 | 0.3 | 0.8 | 18.7 | 9.7 | 22.2 | 8.0 | 0.5 | Pourcentage du total par industrie indiquée |
| Percent consumed as: | | | | | | | | | | | | | | | Pourcentage consommé sous forme de: |
| Coal | 40.7 | 44.5 | 67.1 | 43.8 | 22.3 | 54.8 | 30.0 | 77.9 | 76.3 | 25.5 | 51.9 | 25.1 | 45.4 | 50.0 | Charbon |
| Lignite | 0.6 | 1.5 | 0.1 | — | 0.5 | 1.3 | 0.5 | 0.8 | — | — | 0.3 | — | 1.6 | — | Lignite |
| Coke | 2.4 | 2.0 | 0.5 | 0.3 | 0.7 | — | 2.0 | 0.4 | — | 5.5 | 1.7 | 4.2 | 0.7 | 0.2 | Coke |
| Refined oil fuels | 25.3 | 30.9 | 16.7 | 30.9 | 44.9 | 16.8 | 39.1 | 10.9 | 5.9 | 33.5 | 22.9 | 24.1 | 31.7 | 25.4 | Pétrole raffiné |
| Gas | 9.2 | 8.6 | 0.9 | 2.6 | 4.0 | — | 7.6 | 0.4 | 0.3 | 23.5 | 10.7 | 10.3 | 5.3 | 4.4 | Gaz |
| Electricity purchased | 19.2 | 5.8 | 10.9 | 16.2 | 16.3 | 24.7 | 17.7 | 5.5 | 17.5 | 8.9 | 10.2 | 36.2 | 13.4 | 18.6 | Electricité achetée |
| Wood | 1.1 | 4.7 | 0.5 | 1.6 | 9.9 | 0.6 | 2.7 | 0.9 | — | — | 0.2 | 1.6 | 0.3 | 1.3 | Bois |
| Other fuels [1] | 1.5 | 2.0 | 3.3 | 4.6 | 1.4 | 1.8 | 0.4 | 3.2 | — | 2.9 | 0.7 | — | 1.6 | 0.1 | Autres combustibles [1] |
| **1958** Total energy consumed: | | | | | | | | | | | | | | | **1958** Energie totale consommée: |
| Quantity | 27 192.6 | 2 637.5 | 772.4 | 81.2 | 413.7 | 6080.9 | 162.4 | 66.4 | 222.5 | 6 661.9 | 2 905.7 | 4 897.5 | 2 156.6 | 133.9 | Quantité |
| Percent of total in specified industry | 100.0 | 9.6 | 2.9 | 0.3 | 1.5 | 22.4 | 0.6 | 0.2 | 0.8 | 24.5 | 10.7 | 18.0 | 8.0 | 0.5 | Pourcentage du total par industrie indiquée |
| Percent consumed as: | | | | | | | | | | | | | | | Pourcentage consommé sous forme de: |
| Coal | 29.1 | 30.4 | 45.5 | 25.3 | 15.1 | 40.7 | 9.2 | 71.2 | 63.3 | 15.5 | 46.7 | 16.7 | 34.9 | 28.3 | Charbon |
| Lignite | 0.5 | 0.9 | — | — | 0.2 | 1.6 | 0.1 | 1.3 | — | — | 0.2 | — | 1.2 | 0.1 | Lignite |
| Coke | 2.1 | 0.4 | 0.4 | 0.1 | 0.2 | — | 0.2 | — | — | 4.5 | 1.0 | 4.4 | 0.4 | 0.2 | Coke |
| Refined oil fuels | 27.8 | 40.0 | 35.3 | 44.6 | 40.7 | 22.1 | 34.4 | 13.6 | 13.5 | 31.0 | 22.1 | 23.2 | 31.2 | 33.9 | Pétrole raffiné |
| Gas | 14.7 | 12.6 | 3.0 | 3.8 | 4.1 | 3.5 | 20.4 | 1.5 | 0.7 | 31.1 | 17.5 | 11.9 | 9.9 | 11.4 | Gaz |
| Electricity purchased | 21.2 | 8.2 | 13.1 | 18.0 | 22.7 | 28.8 | 21.7 | 7.1 | 17.6 | 11.9 | 9.1 | 43.3 | 13.9 | 18.7 | Electricité achetée |
| Wood | 0.4 | 1.4 | — | 0.3 | 3.0 | 0.1 | — | 1.3 | — | 0.1 | 1.0 | 0.1 | 0.3 | 0.3 | Bois |
| Other fuels [1] | 4.2 | 6.1 | 2.7 | 7.9 | 14.0 | 3.2 | 14.0 | 4.0 | 4.9 | 5.9 | 2.4 | 0.4 | 8.2 | 7.1 | Autres combustibles [1] |

For footnotes see end of table.                    Pour les notes, voir au bas du tableau.

**B.   The Quantity and Value of Fuels Consumed and of Electricity Purchased, Produced and Sold**

**Quantité et valeur de combustibles consommés et de l'électricité achetée, produite et vendue**

**1948, 1953, 1958**

Coal, lignite, coke and refined fuel oils in thousand metric tons; natural and manufactured gas in million cubic metres; electricity in million KWH; wood in thousand cords; other fuels in thousand metric tons of coal equivalent; values in thousand dollars.

Charbon, lignite, coke et pétrole raffiné en milliers de tonnes métriques; gaz naturel et manufacturé en millions de mètres cubes, électricité en millions de kWh; bois en milliers de cordes; autres combustibles en milliers de tonnes métriques d'équivalent charbon; valeur en milliers de dollars.

### a.   The Major Groups of Mining and Electricity
### Les classes des industries extractives et l'électricité

| Year and source of energy | Mining — Industries extractives | | | | | Electricity Electricité | Année et source d'énergie |
| | Total | Coal mining Extraction du charbon | Metal mining Extraction des minerais métalliques | Crude petroleum and natural gas Pétrole brut et gaz naturel | Other mining Divers | | |
| ISIC | 1 | 11 | 12 | 13 | 14–19 | 511 | CITI |
| **1948** | | | | | | | **1948** |
| Coal: | | | | | | | Charbon: |
| Quantity | 734.4 | 473.1 | 149.0 | 0.2 | 112.1 | 800.3 | Quantité |
| Value | 6 208.8 | 3 017.0 | 1 780.3 | 2.2 | 1 409.3 | 4 792.8 | Valeur |
| Lignite: | | | | | | | Lignite: |
| Quantity | 109.8 | 20.7 | 60.6 | — | 28.5 | 62.6 | Quantité |
| Value | 473.5 | 28.1 | 324.7 | — | 120.7 | 101.1 | Valeur |
| Coke: | | | | | | | Coke: |
| Quantity | 1.3 | — | 0.2 | — | 1.1 | — | Quantité |
| Value | 24.5 | — | 3.6 | — | 20.9 | — | Valeur |
| Refined oil fuels: | | | | | | | Pétrole raffiné: |
| Quantity | 109.3 | 6.9 | 47.8 | 1.7 | 52.9 | 125.4 | Quantité |
| Value | 5 359.5 | 490.3 | 2 610.9 | 113.5 | 2 144.8 | 3 034.5 | Valeur |
| Natural and manufactured gas: | | | | | | | Gaz naturel et manufacturé: |
| Quantity | 231.4 | 0.4 | — | 224.2 | 6.8 | 452.6 | Quantité |
| Value | 1 872.5 | 7.4 | — | 1 833.5 | 31.6 | 455.5 | Valeur |
| Natural gas | | | | | | | Gaz naturel: |
| Quantity | 224.4 | — | — | 224.2 | 0.2 | 49.3 | Quantité |
| Value | 1 835.6 | 0.1 | — | 1 833.5 | 2.0 | 137.7 | Valeur |
| Manufactured gas: | | | | | | | Gaz manufacturé: |
| Quantity | 7.0 | 0.4 | — | — | 6.6 | 403.3 | Quantité |
| Value | 36.9 | 7.3 | — | — | 29.6 | 317.8 | Valeur |
| Electricity: | | | | | | | Electricité: |
| Purchased | | | | | | | Achetée |
| Quantity | 1 909.5 | 196.7 | 1 454.6 | 3.0 | 255.2 | — | Quantité |
| Value | 11 763.5 | 2 309.4 | 7 117.6 | 52.8 | 2 283.7 | — | Valeur |
| Produced-quantity: | 311.5 | 77.1 | 223.0 | 1.0 | 10.4 | 4 239.0 | Produite-quantité: |
| Sold | | | | | | | Vendue |
| Quantity | 41.0 | 23.1 | 17.9 | — | — | ... | Quantité |
| Value | 373.6 | 275.9 | 97.7 | — | — | ... | Valeur |
| Wood: | | | | | | | Bois: |
| Quantity | 50.9 | 0.1 | 48.4 | 0.1 | 2.3 | — | Quantité |
| Value | 488.1 | 0.4 | 470.9 | 0.4 | 16.4 | — | Valeur |
| Other fuels: [1] | | | | | | | Autres combustibles [1]: |
| Quantity | 2.5 | — | 2.5 | — | — | 4.7 | Quantité |
| Value | 47.5 | — | 47.5 | — | — | 30.3 | Valeur |

For footnotes see end of table.

Pour les notes, voir au bas du tableau.

## a. The Major Groups of Mining and Electricity (continued)
## Les classes des industries extractives et l'électricité (suite)

| Year and source of energy | Mining — Industries extractives | | | | | Electricity Electricité | Année et source d'énergie |
|---|---|---|---|---|---|---|---|
| | Total | Coal mining Extraction du charbon | Metal mining Extraction des minerais métalliques | Crude petroleum and natural gas Pétrole brut et gaz naturel | Other mining Divers | | |
| ISIC | 1 | 11 | 12 | 13 | 14–19 | 511 | CITI |
| **1953** | | | | | | | **1953** |
| Coal: | | | | | | | Charbon: |
| Quantity | 488.6 | 227.6 | 163.7 | 3.1 | 94.2 | 1 495.6 | Quantité |
| Value | 5 518.3⁶ | 1 799.4 | 2 127.4 | 33.1 | 1 558.4 | 13 638.4 | Valeur |
| Lignite: | | | | | | | Lignite: |
| Quantity | 41.8 | 17.3 | 0.4 | 0.1 | 24.0 | 293.2 | Quantité |
| Value | 168.9 | 23.1 | 6.6 | 1.1 | 138.1 | 665.2 | Valeur |
| Coke: | | | | | | | Coke: |
| Quantity | 53.4 | 0.2 | 53.1 | — | 0.1 | — | Quantité |
| Value | 380.5 | 4.8 | 374.0 | — | 1.7 | — | Valeur |
| Refined oil fuels: | | | | | | | Pétrole raffiné: |
| Quantity | 186.6 | 9.4 | 74.4 | 25.7 | 77.1 | 169.0 | Quantité |
| Value | 11 040.9 | 605.2 | 4 292.1 | 1 680.2 | 4 463.4 | 4 313.9 | Valeur |
| Natural and manufactured gas: | | | | | | | Gaz naturel et manufacturé: |
| Quantity | 36.4 | 1.5 | 0.8 | 28.2 | 5.9 | 413.3 | Quantité |
| Value | 212.3 | 19.7 | 10.8 | 116.4 | 65.4 | 1 049.2 | Valeur |
| Natural gas: | | | | | | | Gaz naturel: |
| Quantity | 29.7 | — | — | 28.2 | 1.5 | 186.3 | Quantité |
| Value | 122.5 | — | — | 116.4 | 6.1 | 810.4 | Valeur |
| Manufactured gas: | | | | | | | Gaz manufacturé: |
| Quantity | 6.7 | 1.5 | 0.8 | — | 4.4 | 227.0 | Quantité |
| Value | 89.8 | 19.7 | 10.8 | — | 59.3 | 238.8 | Valeur |
| Electricity: | | | | | | | Electricité: |
| Purchased: | | | | | | | Achetée |
| Quantity | 2 598 | 246 | 1 960 | 24 | 368 | — | Quantité |
| Value | 20 127.5 | 3 516.8 | 12 147.9 | 903.0 | 3 559.8 | — | Valeur |
| Produced-Quantity | 224 | 37 | 173 | 4 | 10 | 62 861 | Produite-quantité |
| Sold: | | | | | | | Vendue: |
| Quantity | 9 | 6 | 1 | 2 | — | ... | Quantité |
| Value | 191.5 | 124.3 | 26.6 | 37.7 | 2.9 | ... | Valeur |
| Wood: | | | | | | | Bois: |
| Quantity | 34.4 | — | 31.7 | 0.6 | 2.1 | — | Quantité |
| Value | 404.8 | 0.2 | 378.4 | 4.6 | 21.6 | — | Valeur |
| Other fuels: [1] | | | | | | | Autres combustibles: |
| Quantity | 6.4 | — | 6.4 | — | — | 6.8 | Quantité |
| Value | 132.7 | — | 132.7 | — | — | 59.8 | Valeur |
| **1958** | | | | | | | **1958** |
| Coal: | | | | | | | Charbon: |
| Quantity | 345.0 | 101.2 | 191.1 | 1.6 | 51.1 | 1 069.2 | Quantité |
| Value | 5 117.3 | 930.1 | 3 344.7 | 13.5 | 829.0 | 9 536.5 | Valeur |
| Lignite: | | | | | | | Lignite: |
| Quantity | 54.0 | 16.2 | 0.4 | 3.6 | 33.8 | 432.1 | Quantité |
| Value | 227.5 | 22.6 | 9.3 | 21.0 | 174.6 | 1 101.2 | Valeur |
| Coke: | | | | | | | Coke: |
| Quantity | 4.1 | 0.2 | 3.3 | — | 0.6 | — | Quantité |
| Value | 49.4 | 3.8 | 34.7 | — | 10.9 | — | Valeur |
| Refined oil fuels: | | | | | | | Pétrole raffiné: |
| Quantity | 375.6 | 7.3 | 184.3 | 38.1 | 145.9 | 216.7 | Quantité |
| Value | 20 905.4 | 504.4 | 9 259.2 | 3 184.7 | 7 957.1 | 4 389.2 | Valeur |
| Natural and manufactured gas: | | | | | | | Gaz naturel et manufacturé: |
| Quantity | 228.8 | 0.2 | 4.5 | 192.2 | 31.9 | 789.9 | Quantité |
| Value | 945.4 | 2.2 | 31.4 | 672.9 | 238.9 | 4 618.5 | Valeur |
| Natural gas: | | | | | | | Gaz naturel: |
| Quantity | 223.3 | — | 4.1 | 192.2 | 27.0 | 789.9 | Quantité |
| Value | 895.7 | — | 24.2 | 672.9 | 198.6 | 4 618.5 | Valeur |
| Manufactured gas: | | | | | | | Gaz manufacturé: |
| Quantity | 5.6 | 0.2 | 0.4 | — | 5.0 | — | Quantité |
| Value | 49.7 | 2.2 | 7.2 | — | 40.3 | — | Valeur |
| Electricity: | | | | | | | Electricité: |
| Purchased: | | | | | | | Achetée |
| Quantity | 5 450 | 241 | 4 527 | 90 | 592 | — | Quantité |
| Value | 32 014.8 | 3 500.9 | 20 023.7 | 2 511.4 | 5 978.8 | — | Valeur |
| Produced-quantity | 527 | 6 | 494 | 8 | 19 | 75 953 | Produite-quantité |
| Sold: | | | | | | | Vendue: |
| Quantity | 16 | — | 16 | — | — | ... | Quantité |
| Value | 216.7 | — | 215.3 | — | 1.4 | ... | Valeur |
| Wood: | | | | | | | Bois: |
| Quantity | 23.3 | 0.1 | 18.2 | — | 5.0 | — | Quantité |
| Value | 317.9 | 3.0 | 254.5 | — | 60.4 | — | Valeur |
| Other fuels: [1] | | | | | | | Autres combustibles [1]: |
| Quantity | 5.8 | — | 5.8 | — | — | — | Quantité |
| Value | 153.1 | — | 152.6 | — | 0.5 | — | Valeur |

For footnotes see end of table.  Pour les notes, voir au bas du tableau.

## b.  The Major Groups of Manufacturing — Les classes de la branche Industries manufacturières

| Year and source of energy | Manufacturing — Industries manufacturières (2–3) | Food, beverages and tobacco — Industries alimentaires, boissons, tabac (20–22) | Textiles (23) | Clothing, footwear and made-up textiles — Articles d'habillement, chaussures et ouvrages en tissu (24) | Wood products and furniture — Bois et meubles (25–26) | Paper and paper products — Papier et ouvrages en papier (27) | Printing and publishing — Imprimerie et édition (28) | Leather and leather products except wearing apparel — Cuir et articles en cuir, à l'exclusion des articles d'habillement (29) | Rubber products — Ouvrages en caoutchouc (30) | Chemicals and chemical, petroleum and coal products — Produits chimiques et dérivés du pétrole et du charbon (31–32) | Non-metallic mineral products — Produits minéraux non métalliques (33) | Basic metals — Métallurgie de base (34) | Metal products — Ouvrages en métaux (35–38) | Other manufacturing — Autres industries manufacturières (39) | Année et source d'énergie |
|---|---|---|---|---|---|---|---|---|---|---|---|---|---|---|---|
| ISIC | 2–3 | 20–22 | 23 | 24 | 25–26 | 27 | 28 | 29 | 30 | 31–32 | 33 | 34 | 35–38 | 39 | CITI |
| **1948** | | | | | | | | | | | | | | | **1948** |
| Coal: | | | | | | | | | | | | | | | Charbon: |
| Quantity | 9 599.0 | 1 206.6 | 568.5 | 39.0 | 84.5 | 3 207.9 | 35.3 | 69.7 | 122.9 | 885.7 | 1 018.4 | 1 427.6 | 890.2 | 42.7 | Quantité |
| Value | 104 028.5 | 13 772.0 | 6 649.2 | 493.7 | 1 051.2 | 35 896.3 | 480.8 | 800.0 | 1 380.3 | 8 193.2 | 11 326.2 | 13 757.9 | 9 699.7 | 528.0 | Valeur |
| Lignite: | | | | | | | | | | | | | | | Lignite: |
| Quantity | 343.6 | 192.6 | 1.1 | 0.3 | 1.5 | 21.7 | 1.6 | — | — | 3.7 | 24.1 | 0.2 | 96.6 | 0.2 | Quantité |
| Value | 1 597.9 | 965.5 | 7.3 | 4.0 | 11.8 | 106.8 | 12.9 | 0.1 | — | 23.1 | 91.6 | 1.1 | 371.7 | 2.0 | Valeur |
| Coke: | | | | | | | | | | | | | | | Coke: |
| Quantity | 653.6 | 62.9 | 3.6 | 0.3 | 0.6 | 0.1 | 1.3 | 0.5 | 0.3 | 212.2 | 37.6 | 305.1 | 28.7 | 0.4 | Quantité |
| Value | 9 094.8 | 738.0 | 34.3 | 4.6 | 11.0 | 1.1 | 20.0 | 5.7 | 2.3 | 2 407.2 | 683.5 | 4 611.7 | 568.7 | 6.7 | Valeur |
| Refined oil fuels: | | | | | | | | | | | | | | | Pétrole raffiné: |
| Quantity | 2 178.5 | 275.7 | 41.0 | 8.2 | 50.3 | 247.2 | 11.3 | 3.6 | 6.7 | 584.5 | 187.3 | 520.1 | 236.9 | 5.7 | Quantité |
| Value | 66 260.6 | 12 456.4 | 1 282.0 | 357.5 | 3 656.6 | 5 791.4 | 613.0 | 138.9 | 211.0 | 11 446.0 | 6 067.5 | 14 757.8 | 9 182.4 | 300.1 | Valeur |
| Natural and manufactured gas: | | | | | | | | | | | | | | | Gaz naturel et manufacturé: |
| Quantity | 4 274.1 | 120.4 | — | 3.1 | 4.1 | 1.6 | 6.7 | 0.1 | 0.8 | 1 050.6 | 85.0 | 2 902.5 | 95.6 | 3.5 | Quantité |
| Value | 21 711.2 | 1 731.8 | — | 99.3 | 51.3 | 40.7 | 192.6 | 3.4 | 25.2 | 10 425.0 | 626.5 | 6 096.6 | 2 293.2 | 125.6 | Valeur |
| Natural gas: | | | | | | | | | | | | | | | Gaz naturel: |
| Quantity | 263.2 | 73.9 | — | 0.5 | 3.4 | 0.6 | 2.2 | — | — | 97.0 | 56.9 | 4.4 | 23.9 | 0.4 | Quantité |
| Value | 2 072.2 | 518.4 | — | 5.1 | 26.8 | 7.9 | 30.6 | — | 0.3 | 405.4 | 278.8 | 96.3 | 695.4 | 7.2 | Valeur |
| Manufactured gas: | | | | | | | | | | | | | | | Gaz manufacturé: |
| Quantity | 4 010.9 | 46.5 | — | 2.6 | 0.7 | 1.0 | 4.5 | 0.1 | 0.8 | 953.6 | 28.1 | 2 898.1 | 71.7 | 3.2 | Quantité |
| Value | 19 639.0 | 1 213.4 | — | 94.2 | 24.5 | 32.8 | 162.0 | 3.4 | 24.9 | 10 019.6 | 347.7 | 6 000.3 | 1 597.8 | 118.4 | Valeur |
| Electricity: | | | | | | | | | | | | | | | Electricité: |
| Purchased: | | | | | | | | | | | | | | | Achetée: |
| Quantity | 24 633.4 | 786.0 | 557.4 | 59.7 | 236.0 | 8 078.3 | 89.8 | 28.8 | 177.4 | 2 143.8 | 1 257.4 | 10 020.8 | 1 139.3 | 58.7 | Quantité |
| Value | 93 952.8 | 8 408.7 | 4 344.8 | 1 345.0 | 3 816.4 | 23 036.9 | 1 403.6 | 382.0 | 1 191.5 | 8 590.6 | 5 215.1 | 24 834.8 | 10 458.6 | 924.8 | Valeur |
| Produced — quantity | 4 468.1 | 40.1 | — | — | 16.1 | 2 327.3 | — | — | — | 1 132.7 | 5.0 | 801.5 | 145.4 | — | Produite — quantité |
| Sold: | | | | | | | | | | | | | | | Vendue: |
| Quantity | 10.8 | 0.5 | — | — | — | — | — | — | — | — | — | 10.3 | — | — | Quantité |
| Value | 38.9 | 3.3 | — | — | — | — | — | — | — | — | — | 35.6 | — | — | Valeur |
| Wood: | | | | | | | | | | | | | | | Bois: |
| Quantity | 292.5 | 186.4 | — | 2.6 | 15.4 | 6.2 | 3.2 | 1.6 | — | 5.7 | 55.8 | 7.2 | 7.6 | 0.8 | Quantité |
| Value | 1 831.3 | 1 030.6 | — | 19.2 | 99.0 | 40.3 | 28.5 | 9.5 | — | 33.6 | 426.6 | 71.7 | 64.3 | 8.0 | Valeur |
| Other fuels [1] | | | | | | | | | | | | | | | Autres combustibles [1]: |
| Quantity | 334.4 | 15.3 | 24.8 | 4.0 | 3.5 | 56.8 | 0.1 | 5.4 | 6.5 | 161.1 | 2.3 | 28.5 | 25.6 | 0.5 | Quantité |
| Value | 4 199.3 | 234.2 | 312.7 | 69.2 | 97.1 | 659.2 | 1.9 | 68.2 | 78.2 | 1 966.0 | 29.4 | 265.3 | 409.0 | 8.9 | Valeur |
| **1953** | | | | | | | | | | | | | | | **1953** |
| Coal: | | | | | | | | | | | | | | | Charbon: |
| Quantity | 8 997.3 | 1 011.5 | 491.8 | 28.4 | 69.6 | 2 923.5 | 26.8 | 55.4 | 136.6 | 1 054.4 | 1 110.7 | 1 231.1 | 810.2 | 47.3 | Quantité |
| Value | 106 253.6 | 11 879.1 | 6 240.2 | 414.2 | 949.9 | 35 167.2 | 403.0 | 706.6 | 1 605.6 | 10 325.4 | 13 267.9 | 15 053.4 | 9 598.5 | 642.6 | Valeur |
| Lignite: | | | | | | | | | | | | | | | Lignite: |
| Quantity | 423.7 | 103.4 | 1.0 | — | 5.3 | 207.6 | 1.2 | 1.7 | — | 3.1 | 17.1 | 0.2 | 82.9 | 0.2 | Quantité |
| Value | 2 241.5 | 630.6 | 7.8 | 0.3 | 35.3 | 1 233.0 | 15.4 | 10.6 | — | 21.0 | 102.6 | 1.2 | 181.0 | 2.7 | Valeur |
| Coke: | | | | | | | | | | | | | | | Coke: |
| Quantity | 590.2 | 50.2 | 4.4 | 0.2 | 2.3 | — | 2.0 | 0.3 | — | 251.4 | 40.3 | 225.6 | 13.3 | 0.2 | Quantité |
| Value | 9 347.7 | 614.4 | 52.8 | 4.9 | 45.0 | 0.1 | 34.2 | 0.7 | — | 2 876.7 | 836.1 | 4 542.4 | 336.2 | 4.2 | Valeur |
| Refined oil fuels: | | | | | | | | | | | | | | | Pétrole raffiné: |
| Quantity | 3 715.5 | 467.9 | 81.3 | 13.4 | 93.0 | 598.7 | 23.2 | 5.2 | 7.1 | 921.7 | 326.6 | 786.2 | 375.2 | 16.0 | Quantité |
| Value | 102 580.7 | 20 927.2 | 2 326.9 | 620.5 | 6 873.6 | 11 286.0 | 1 256.2 | 184.3 | 220.4 | 17 015.1 | 8 956.2 | 18 035.5 | 14 044.4 | 834.4 | Valeur |
| Natural and manufactured gas: | | | | | | | | | | | | | | | Gaz naturel et manufacturé: |
| Quantity | 2 637.7 | 176.8 | 5.8 | 2.2 | 10.1 | 2.2 | 8.0 | 0.4 | 0.7 | 1 316.2 | 180.9 | 821.8 | 107.4 | 5.2 | Quantité |
| Value | 31 929.2 | 2 325.7 | 48.5 | 82.0 | 110.2 | 61.4 | 233.1 | 11.5 | 29.0 | 17 035.1 | 1 323.4 | 7 587.8 | 2 867.4 | 214.4 | Valeur |
| Natural gas: | | | | | | | | | | | | | | | Gaz naturel: |
| Quantity | 609.3 | 121.7 | 4.2 | 0.6 | 9.0 | 1.0 | 2.7 | 0.1 | — | 248.4 | 166.1 | 12.5 | 41.7 | 1.3 | Quantité |
| Value | 4 671.7 | 902.8 | 19.0 | 8.6 | 89.6 | 11.7 | 44.7 | 1.0 | 0.9 | 1 163.0 | 967.9 | 436.5 | 989.8 | 36.2 | Valeur |
| Manufactured gas: | | | | | | | | | | | | | | | Gaz manufacturé: |
| Quantity | 2 028.8 | 55.2 | 1.6 | 1.6 | 1.2 | 1.2 | 5.4 | 0.3 | 0.7 | 1 067.8 | 14.8 | 809.3 | 65.8 | 3.9 | Quantité |
| Value | 27 257.8 | 1 422.9 | 29.5 | 73.4 | 20.6 | 49.7 | 188.4 | 10.5 | 28.1 | 15 872.1 | 355.5 | 7 151.3 | 1 877.6 | 178.2 | Valeur |
| Electricity: | | | | | | | | | | | | | | | Electricité: |
| Purchased: | | | | | | | | | | | | | | | Achetée: |
| Quantity | 34 017 | 1 056 | 638 | 84 | 405 | 10 531 | 126 | 31 | 250 | 2 951 | 1 732 | 14 167 | 1 905 | 141 | Quantité |
| Value | 152 507.3 | 12 694.2 | 5 937.2 | 1 866.6 | 6 559.0 | 33 886.8 | 2 187.5 | 428.5 | 1 869.6 | 15 773.6 | 8 953.0 | 40 932.9 | 19 685.3 | 1 733.1 | Valeur |
| Produced — quantity | 7 251 | 65 | 97 | — | 176 | 4 576 | — | — | 8 | 1 243 | 5 | 918 | 163 | — | Produite — quantité |
| Sold: | | | | | | | | | | | | | | | Vendue: |
| Quantity | 350 | 1 | 17 | — | 17 | 303 | — | — | — | 8 | — | 4 | — | — | Quantité |
| Value | 2 486.0 | 8.0 | 103.4 | — | 134.4 | 1 704.3 | — | — | — | 525.8 | — | 10.1 | — | — | Valeur |
| Wood: | | | | | | | | | | | | | | | Bois: |
| Quantity | 299.4 | 143.2 | 4.6 | 1.3 | 41.4 | 42.6 | 3.2 | 0.8 | — | 6.7 | 45.6 | 3.1 | 5.3 | 1.6 | Quantité |
| Value | 1 368.0 | 500.1 | 7.8 | 12.8 | 189.2 | 116.4 | 29.1 | 4.1 | — | 31.3 | 379.4 | 41.8 | 42.5 | 13.5 | Valeur |
| Other fuels [1] | | | | | | | | | | | | | | | Autres combustibles [1]: |
| Quantity | 335.7 | 44.1 | 24.4 | 3.0 | 4.4 | 91.6 | 0.3 | 2.3 | — | 119.6 | 15.1 | 1.4 | 29.4 | 0.1 | Quantité |
| Value | 4 776.8 | 775.9 | 336.6 | 67.3 | 139.6 | 1 117.1 | 7.9 | 33.1 | — | 1 554.5 | 195.9 | 19.6 | 526.8 | 2.5 | Valeur |

For footnotes see end of table.  Pour les notes, voir au bas du tableau.

## b.  The Major Groups of Manufacturing (continued) — Les classes de la branche Industries manufacturières (suite)

| Year and source of energy | Manufacturing Industries manufacturières | Food, beverages and tobacco Industries alimentaires, boissons, tabac | Textiles | Clothing, footwear and made-up textiles Articles d'habillement, chaussures et ouvrages en tissu | Wood products and furniture Bois et meubles | Paper and paper products Papier et ouvrages en papier | Printing and publishing Imprimerie et édition | Leather and leather products except wearing apparel Cuir et articles en cuir, à l'exclusion des articles d'habillement | Rubber products Ouvrages en caoutchouc | Chemicals and chemical, petroleum and coal products Produits chimiques et dérivés du pétrole et du charbon | Non-metallic mineral products Produits minéraux non métalliques | Basic metals Métallurgie de base | Metal products Ouvrages en métaux | Other manufacturing Autres industries manufacturières | Année et source d'énergie |
|---|---|---|---|---|---|---|---|---|---|---|---|---|---|---|---|
| ISIC | 2–3 | 20–22 | 23 | 24 | 25–26 | 27 | 28 | 29 | 30 | 31–32 | 33 | 34 | 35–38 | 39 | CITI |
| **1958** | | | | | | | | | | | | | | | **1958** |
| Coal: | | | | | | | | | | | | | | | Charbon: |
| Quantity | 7 927.2 | 804.2 | 352.0 | 20.6 | 62.6 | 2 479.1 | 15.0 | 47.3 | 140.9 | 1 034.7 | 1 359.6 | 820.4 | 752.9 | 37.9 | Quantité |
| Value | 99 507.9 | 10 399.3 | 4 775.3 | 318.4 | 938.9 | 31 182.7 | 245.7 | 627.0 | 1 683.9 | 10 458.0 | 17 335.7 | 11 857.8 | 9 170.8 | 514.4 | Valeur |
| Lignite: | | | | | | | | | | | | | | | Lignite: |
| Quantity | 475.2 | 78.8 | 0.2 | — | 3.3 | 284.8 | 0.2 | 2.8 | — | 1.1 | 19.4 | 1.9 | 82.4 | 0.3 | Quantité |
| Value | 2 561.3 | 489.8 | 1.4 | 0.3 | 31.1 | 1 683.9 | 2.0 | 22.1 | — | 7.8 | 117.6 | 27.3 | 174.5 | 3.5 | Valeur |
| Coke: | | | | | | | | | | | | | | | Coke: |
| Quantity | 624.0 | 9.3 | 3.1 | 0.1 | 0.8 | — | 0.4 | — | — | 333.1 | 29.9 | 236.8 | 10.1 | 0.4 | Quantité |
| Value | 10 734.6 | 214.4 | 34.2 | 2.3 | 20.7 | 1.3 | 6.7 | 0.8 | — | 4 064.9 | 659.5 | 5 407.6 | 317.1 | 5.1 | Valeur |
| Refined oil fuels: | | | | | | | | | | | | | | | Pétrole raffiné: |
| Quantity | 5 017.0 | 701.2 | 181.7 | 24.1 | 111.9 | 895.3 | 37.2 | 5.9 | 20.0 | 1 375 2 | 427.9 | 759.5 | 446.7 | 30.4 | Quantité |
| Value | 146 790.0 | 32 401.4 | 4 702.5 | 1 345.7 | 8 282.6 | 19 344.8 | 1 821 8 | 224.0 | 645.3 | 27 523.3 | 13 913.6 | 18 548.5 | 16 445.4 | 1 591.1 | Valeur |
| Natural and manufactured gas: | | | | | | | | | | | | | | | Gaz naturel et manufacturé: |
| Quantity | 4 411.3 | 253.7 | 18.3 | 2.5 | 13.0 | 173.9 | 43.3 | 0.8 | 1.2 | 2 498.6 | 396.2 | 817.9 | 177.5 | 14.3 | Quantité |
| Value | 54 379.2 | 3 642.0 | 183.9 | 79.8 | 170.3 | 2 333.1 | 247.2 | 23.5 | 47.2 | 29 156.0 | 4 363.5 | 9 263.8 | 4 610.1 | 258.8 | Valeur |
| Natural gas: | | | | | | | | | | | | | | | Gaz naturel: |
| Quantity | 1 876.5 | 248.2 | 17.0 | 2.2 | 12.7 | 154.0 | 9.8 | 0.8 | 0.9 | 780.7 | 369.5 | 125.9 | 145.7 | 9.1 | Quantité |
| Value | 20 374.5 | 3 467.8 | 150.0 | 69.0 | 162.7 | 2 203.3 | 210.3 | 21.4 | 40.8 | 4 064.2 | 4 038.9 | 1 862.7 | 3 838.1 | 245.3 | Valeur |
| Manufactured gas: | | | | | | | | | | | | | | | Gaz manufacturé: |
| Quantity | 2 534.7 | 5.5 | 1.3 | 0.3 | 0.3 | 19.9 | 33.6 | 0.1 | 0.3 | 1 717.9 | 26.6 | 692 0 | 31.8 | 5.1 | Quantité |
| Value | 34 004.7 | 174.2 | 33.9 | 10.8 | 7.6 | 129.8 | 36.9 | 2.1 | 6.4 | 25 091.8 | 324.6 | 7 401.1 | 772.0 | 13.5 | Valeur |
| Electricity: | | | | | | | | | | | | | | | Electricité: |
| Purchased: | | | | | | | | | | | | | | | Achetée: |
| Quantity | 46 122 | 1 722 | 807 | 116 | 751 | 14 007 | 282 | 37 | 315 | 6 369 | 2 129 | 16 974 | 2 413 | 200 | Quantité |
| Value | 215 323.7 | 18 008.2 | 6 800.4 | 2 075.2 | 9 154.5 | 52 453.4 | 2 992.1 | 482.9 | 2 505.3 | 28 636.9 | 13 407.6 | 52 393.1 | 24 057.3 | 2 356.8 | Valeur |
| Produced — quantity | 7 090 | 98 | 62 | — | 210 | 5 152 | — | — | 8 | 282 | 5 | 1 157 | 112 | 4 | Produite — quantité |
| Sold: | | | | | | | | | | | | | | | Vendue: |
| Quantity | 466 | — | — | — | 10 | 407 | — | — | — | 16 | — | 33 | — | — | Quantité |
| Value | 2 534.7 | 4.5 | — | — | 49.2 | 2 182.1 | — | — | — | 215.0 | — | 83.9 | — | — | Valeur |
| Wood: | | | | | | | | | | | | | | | Bois: |
| Quantity | 123.2 | 51.2 | 0.2 | 0.3 | 16.8 | 3.4 | — | 1.2 | — | 3.2 | 36.4 | 3.5 | 6.3 | 0.7 | Quantité |
| Value | 942.9 | 347.8 | 2.8 | 1.9 | 123.4 | 28.2 | — | 5.8 | 0.1 | 22.1 | 321.8 | 63.2 | 20.0 | 5.8 | Valeur |
| Other fuels: [1] | | | | | | | | | | | | | | | Autres combustibles [1]: |
| Quantity | 1 137.1 | 159.6 | 20.2 | 6.4 | 57.8 | 194.4 | 22.7 | 2.6 | 10.7 | 390.7 | 69.1 | 17.0 | 176.5 | 9.4 | Quantité |
| Value | 19 008.5 | 3 349.0 | 301.0 | 184.7 | 2 112.0 | 2 566.8 | 504.2 | 39.3 | 147.5 | 5 082.9 | 986.5 | 278.2 | 3 232.2 | 224.2 | Valeur |

[1] Includes steam and other materials other than those specified, used as fuels in the case of all years and all kinds of fuels for establishments with value of shipments of less than 100,000 dollars in the case of 1958.

[1] Y compris, pour toutes les années, la vapeur et les autres matières non mentionnées ici qui sont utilisées comme combustibles et, pour 1958, tous les types de combustibles consommés par les établissements ayant effectué des expéditions de marchandises d'une valeur inférieure à 100 000 dollars.

# CEYLON — CEYLAN

## Gross Domestic Product

Estimates of expenditure on and the origin of the gross domestic product are presented in Table 1. The data are derived from information supplied by the Department of Census and Statistics, Colombo, in response to the United Nations national accounts questionnaire.

## Index Numbers of Industrial Production

The index numbers of industrial production published in Table 2 are derived from index numbers provided by correspondence by the Department of Census and Statistics, Colombo.

The index numbers provided to the Statistical office of the United Nations are computed as base weighted arithmetic averages, starting from elementary series of relatives. The relatives, based on quantities of production for various individual commodities, are combined into indexes for major groups and these major group indexes are, in turn, combined into indexes for manufacturing and mining as a whole. The index numbers for these two divisions of industrial activity, combined, are computed from the indexes for each division. The weights utilized at each stage of the computations are proportional to average annual value added during the period, 1952-1956.

## Characteristics and Structure of Industrial Activity

The data appearing in Table 3 are taken from the *Census of Industry, 1952*, issued by the Department of Census and Statistics, Ceylon. The Census covered industrial establishments engaging five or more persons, having at least three thousand Rupees in total capital and utilizing mechanical power. It should be noted however that large tea factories and rubber mills on agricultural estates, which are important activities in Ceylon, were not included in the Census. Roughly 85 percent of the number of establishments within the scope of the Census made a return. The establishments accounted however, for a larger part of the production of establishments falling within the scope of the Census since nonresponse was concentrated among the smaller of the units covered.

The definitions utilized for the items of data shown in the tables below are consistent with the International Standards in Basic Industrial Statistics except that the figures of value added, at market prices ex-factory, do not include goods sold by establishments without transformation and the data on number of engaged may not cover unpaid family workers. The number of employees and the wages and salaries paid to employees include the number of and payments to homeworkers. All the employment data are the average of the number during the last week of each calendar month.

## Produit intérieur brut

Le tableau 1 contient des estimations des dépenses imputées au produit intérieur brut et des estimations du produit intérieur brut par secteur d'activité d'origine. Ces données ont été tirées des renseignements fournis par le Department of Census and Statistics, Colombo, en réponse au questionnaire de l'ONU sur la comptabilité nationale.

## Indices de la production industrielle

Les indices de la production industrielle présentés au tableau 2 ont été établis à partir d'indices fournis par voie de correspondance par le Department of Census and Statistics, Colombo.

Les indices communiqués au Bureau de statistique de l'ONU sont des moyennes arithmétiques à pondération fixe; ils ont été calculés à partir de séries élémentaires de rapports. Les rapports, fondés sur les quantités produites de différentes marchandises, sont combinés en indices de classe, qui sont à leur tour combinés en indices relatifs à l'ensemble des industries extractives et manufacturières. Les indices relatifs à ces deux branches de l'activité industrielle combinées sont calculés à partir des indices relatifs à chacune des branches. Les coefficients de pondération utilisés à chacune des étapes du calcul sont proportionnels à la moyenne des valeurs ajoutées annuelles pendant la période 1952-1956.

## Caractéristiques et structure de l'activité industrielle

Les chiffres du tableau 3 sont tirés de *Census of Industry, 1952*, publié par le Department of Census and Statistics de Ceylan. Le recensement portait sur tous les établissements industriels qui occupaient 5 personnes ou plus, qui avaient un capital d'au moins 3 000 roupies et qui utilisaient de la force motrice. On notera cependant que les grandes fabriques de thé et de caoutchouc installées dans les plantations — et qui constituent une activité importante à Ceylan — n'ont pas été comprises dans le recensement. Environ 85 p. 100 des établissements interrogés ont répondu. Leur part de la production est cependant proportionnellement plus grande, car la majorité des non-réponses a été le fait des petites unités.

Les définitions des rubriques qui apparaissent dans les tableaux ci-après sont conformes aux Normes internationales relatives aux statistiques industrielles de base, si ce n'est que les chiffres de la valeur ajoutée, aux prix du marché départ usine, ne comprennent pas les marchandises revendues en l'état et que le nombre des personnes occupées ne comprend peut-être pas les travailleurs familiaux non rémunérés. Le nombre de salariés et les traitements et salaires payés aux salariés concernent le nombre de travailleurs à domicile, ainsi que les paiements qui leur sont versés. Toutes les données sur l'emploi sont les moyennes des nombres relevés la dernière semaine de chaque mois civil.

## 1. THE GROSS DOMESTIC PRODUCT — LE PRODUIT INTERIEUR BRUT

Million rupees                                                                 Millions de roupies

### A. Expenditure on the Gross Domestic Product at Market Prices
### Dépenses relatives au produit intérieur brut aux prix du marché

| Item of data and year<br>Rubrique et année | Total | Consumption<br>Consommation | | Gross Domestic Capital Formation<br>Formation brute de capital intérieur | | Net exports of goods and services<br>Exportations nettes de biens et de services | |
| --- | --- | --- | --- | --- | --- | --- | --- |
| | | Total | Government<br>Etat | Total | Fixed<br>Fixe | Exports<br>less imports<br>Exportations<br>moins<br>importations | Exports<br>Exportations |
| **a. At Current Prices — Aux prix courants** | | | | | | | |
| **Absolute figures — Chiffres absolus** | | | | | | | |
| 1950 | 4 169.8 | 3 432.0 | 440.0 | 395.7 | 357.8 | 342.1 | 1 630.3 |
| 1951 | 4 817.1 | 4 062.4 | 501.4 | 505.5 | 448.2 | 249.2 | 1 951.2 |
| 1952 | 4 538.4 | 4 226.9 | 570.9 | 603.5 | 544.1 | −292.0 | 1 564.7 |
| 1953 | 4 717.0 | 4 291.3 | 619.3 | 502.3 | 475.0 | −76.6 | 1 698.2 |
| 1954 | 4 997.3 | 4 153.6 | 598.6 | 469.5 | 435.5 | 374.2 | 1 914.3 |
| 1955 | 5 608.0 | 4 597.6 | 628.6 | 598.7 | 548.7 | 411.7 | 2 070.5 |
| 1956 | 5 143.2 | 4 571.2 | 809.2 | 583.6 | 549.8 | −11.6 | 1 845.9 |
| 1957 | 5 382.0 | 4 983.0 | 856.0 | 661.0 | 661.0 | −262.0 | 1 795.5 |
| 1958 | 5 662.6 | 5 069.2 | 923.8 | 682.6 | 682.6 | −89.2 | 1 912.1 |
| 1959 | 6 332.0 | 5 488.3 | 1 065.5 | 1 003.4 | 960.0 | −159.7 | 2 016.0 |
| 1960 | 6 492.9 | 5 796.8 | 1 080.7 | 894.0 | 925.5 | −197.9 | 2 010.6 |
| 1961 | 6 582.6 | 5 684.8 | 1 086.9 | 953.8 | 941.7 | −56.0 | 1 912.9 |
| **Percentage distribution of average annual expenditure — Distribution en pourcentage des dépenses annuelles moyennes** | | | | | | | |
| 1950 – 1960 | 100.0 | 87.5 | 14.0 | 12.0 | 11.4 | 0.5 | 35.3 |
| 1950 | 100.0 | 82.3 | 10.6 | 9.5 | 8.6 | 8.2 | 39.1 |
| 1953 | 100.0 | 91.0 | 13.1 | 10.6 | 10.1 | −1.6 | 36.0 |
| 1954 | 100.0 | 83.1 | 12.0 | 9.4 | 8.7 | 7.5 | 38.3 |
| 1958 | 100.0 | 89.5 | 16.3 | 12.1 | 12.1 | −1.6 | 33.8 |
| 1960 | 100.0 | 89.3 | 16.6 | 13.8 | 14.2 | −3.1 | 31.0 |
| **b. At Prices of 1948 — Aux prix de 1948** | | | | | | | |
| **Absolute figures — Chiffres absolus** | | | | | | | |
| 1950 | 3 593.1 | 3 366.7 | 432.7 | 387.5 | 349.5 | −161.1 | 1 140.1 |
| 1951 | 3 895.2 | 3 738.9 | 458.9 | 458.7 | 408.6 | −302.4 | 1 127.8 |
| 1952 | 4 039.1 | 3 828.8 | 517.8 | 484.4 | 435.3 | −274.1 | 1 176.4 |
| 1953 | 3 998.3 | 3 830.7 | 524.7 | 423.0 | 398.7 | −255.4 | 1 248.6 |
| 1954 | 4 116.0 | 3 824.1 | 576.1 | 450.2 | 417.3 | −158.3 | 1 267.7 |
| 1955 | 4 371.4 | 4 123.9 | 591.2 | 563.3 | 506.8 | −315.8 | 1 310.4 |
| 1956 | 4 130.2 | 4 101.5 | 774.7 | 533.8 | 508.5 | −505.1 | 1 247.2 |
| 1957 | 4 398.0 | 4 482.9 | 749.7 | 487.9 | 487.9 | −572.8 | 1 264.7 |
| 1958 | 4 571.4 | 4 583.4 | 819.3 | 555.4 | 555.4 | −567.4 | 1 375.6 |
| 1959 | 6 268.6 | 5 481.5 | 1 061.6 | 981.9 | 942.5 | −194.8 | 1 938.5 |
| 1960 | 6 515.9 | 5 880.4 | 1 093.9 | 867.6 | 891.6 | −232.1 | 1 933.6 |
| 1961 | 6 760.2 | 5 746.1 | 1 087.4 | 949.9 | 938.7 | 64.2 | 2 013.7 |
| **Percentage distribution of average annual expenditure — Distribution en pourcentage des dépenes annuelles moyennes** | | | | | | | |
| 1950 – 1960 | 100.0 | 94.6 | 15.2 | 12.4 | 11.8 | −7.0 | 30.1 |
| 1950 | 100.0 | 93.7 | 12.1 | 10.8 | 9.7 | −4.5 | 31.7 |
| 1953 | 100.0 | 95.8 | 13.1 | 10.6 | 10.0 | −6.4 | 31.2 |
| 1954 | 100.0 | 92.9 | 14.0 | 10.9 | 10.1 | −3.8 | 30.8 |
| 1958 | 100.0 | 100.3 | 17.9 | 12.1 | 12.2 | −12.4 | 30.1 |
| 1960 | 100.0 | 90.2 | 16.8 | 13.3 | 13.7 | −3.5 | 29.7 |
| **Average annual rate of growth — Taux annuel moyen d'accroissement** | | | | | | | |
| 1950 – 1960 | 6.1 | 5.7 | 9.7 | 8.4 | 9.8 | . | 5.4 |
| 1950 – 1953 | 3.6 | 4.4 | 6.6 | 3.0 | 4.5 | . | 3.1 |
| 1954 – 1958 | 2.7 | 4.6 | 9.2 | 5.4 | 7.4 | . | 2.1 |
| 1958 – 1960 | 19.4 | 13.3 | 15.5 | 25.0 | 26.7 | . | 18.6 |

## B. The Gross Domestic Product at Factor Cost According to Origin
### Origine par secteur d'activité du produit intérieur brut au coût des facteurs

| Item of data and year / Rubrique et année | Total | Agricultural sector / Secteur agricole | Industrial Sector — Secteur Industriel | | | | | Transportation and communication / Transports et communications | Other sectors / Autres secteurs |
|---|---|---|---|---|---|---|---|---|---|
| | | | Total | Mining / Industries extractives | Manufacturing / Industries manufacturières | Construction / Bâtiment et travaux publics | Electricity, gas and water / Electricité, gaz et eau | | |
| ISIC — CITI | 0–9 | 0 | 1–5 | 1 | 2–3 | 4 | 5 | 7 | 6, 8–9 |
| *a.* At Current Prices — Aux prix courants | | | | | | | | | |
| Absolute figures — Chiffres absolus | | | | | | | | | |
| 1950 | 3 848.6 | 2 226.3 | 436.9 | 6.2 | 154.6 | 258.5 | 17.6 | 166.0 | 1 019.4 |
| 1951 | 4 542.7 | 2 587.3 | 606.3 | 8.1 | 188.3 | 390.0 | 19.9 | 180.0 | 1 169.1 |
| 1952 | 4 413.9 | 2 301.4 | 620.5 | 6.2 | 196.0 | 396.0 | 22.3 | 220.0 | 1 272.0 |
| 1953 | 4 484.9 | 2 425.5 | 612.5 | 4.1 | 216.1 | 368.3 | 24.0 | 222.6 | 1 224.3 |
| 1954 | 4 652.8 | 2 571.0 | 596.1 | 4.7 | 215.4 | 351.0 | 25.0 | 222.2 | 1 263.5 |
| 1955 | 5 246.1 | 2 810.4 | 790.4 | 7.2 | 311.7 | 443.0 | 28.5 | 250.5 | 1 394.8 |
| 1956 | 4 997.7 | 2 474.6 | 728.6 | 7.4 | 233.5 | 459.0 | 28.7 | 270.9 | 1 523.6 |
| 1957 | 5 175.4 | 2 552.3 | 731.8 | 6.6 | 217.6 | 479.0 | 28.6 | 290.3 | 1 601.0 |
| 1958 | 5 442.9 | 2 677.0 | 799.4 | 3.8 | 243.7 | 512.0 | 39.9 | 300.7 | 1 665.8 |
| 1959 | 5 830.3 | 2 702.8 | 838.8 | 5.2 | 282.2 | 509.8 | 41.6 | 387.7 | 1 901.0 |
| 1960 | 6 102.0 | 2 852.4 | 870.5 | 5.8 | 308.1 | 509.0 | 47.6 | 407.8 | 1 971.3 |
| 1961 | 6 186.7 | 2 854.0 | 947.8 | 5.7 | 327.4 | 563.7 | 51.0 | 413.7 | 1 971.2 |
| Percentage distribution according to sector- Distribution en pourcentage par secteur | | | | | | | | | |
| 1950–1960 | 100.0 | 51.4 | 14.0 | 0.2 | 4.6 | 8.6 | 0.6 | 5.3 | 29.3 |
| 1950 | 100.0 | 57.8 | 11.3 | 0.2 | 4.0 | 6.7 | 0.4 | 4.4 | 26.5 |
| 1953 | 100.0 | 54.1 | 13.6 | 0.1 | 4.8 | 8.2 | 0.5 | 5.0 | 27.3 |
| 1954 | 100.0 | 55.3 | 12.8 | 0.1 | 4.6 | 7.6 | 0.5 | 4.8 | 27.1 |
| 1958 | 100.0 | 49.1 | 14.7 | 0.1 | 4.5 | 9.4 | 0.7 | 5.5 | 30.7 |
| 1960 | 100.0 | 46.7 | 14.3 | 0.1 | 5.0 | 8.4 | 0.8 | 6.6 | 32.4 |

## 2. INDEX NUMBERS OF INDUSTRIAL PRODUCTION — INDICES DE LA PRODUCTION INDUSTRIELLE

### A. Selected Divisions of Industrial Activity
### Quelques branches de l'activité industrielle

| Period / Période | Total | Mining / Industries extractives | Manufacturing / Industries manufacturières | Electricity and gas / Electricité et gaz |
|---|---|---|---|---|
| ISIC — CITI | 1–3, 511–512 | 1 | 2–3 | 511–512 |
| Indexes — Indices (1958 = 100) | | | | |
| 1957 | 95 | 218 | 94 | 91 |
| 1958 | 100 | 100 | 100 | 100 |
| 1959 | 110 | 137 | 109 | 112 |
| 1960 | 118 | 190 | 117 | 124 |
| 1961 | 124 | 163 | 122 | 131 |

# CEYLON

## B. The Major Groups of Manufacturing — Les classes de la branche Industries manufacturières

| Period / Période | Manufacturing [1] / Industries manufacturières [1] | Food, beverages and tobacco / Industries alimentaires, boissons, tabac | Textiles | Clothing, footwear and made-up textiles / Articles d'habillement, chaussures et ouvrages en tissu | Wood products and furniture / Bois et meubles | Paper and paper products / Papier et ouvrages en papier | Printing and publishing / Imprimerie et édition | Leather and leather products except wearing apparel / Cuir et articles en cuir, à l'exclusion des articles d'habillement | Rubber products / Ouvrages en caoutchouc | Chemicals and chemical products / Produits chimiques | Non-metallic mineral products / Produits minéraux non métalliques | Basic metals / Métallurgie de base | Metal products [1] / Ouvrages en métaux [1] | Other manufacturing / Autres industries manufacturières |
|---|---|---|---|---|---|---|---|---|---|---|---|---|---|---|
| ISIC — CITI | 2–3 | 20–22 | 23 | 24 | 25–26 | 27 | 28 | 29 | 30 | 31 | 33 | 34 | 35 | 39 |

### Indexes — Indices (1958 = 100)

| | | | | | | | | | | | | | | |
|---|---|---|---|---|---|---|---|---|---|---|---|---|---|---|
| 1957 | 94 | 93 | 84 | 59 | 115 | 113 | 95 | 119 | 109 | 106 | 71 | 138 | 120 | 100 |
| 1958 | 100 | 100 | 100 | 100 | 100 | 100 | 100 | 100 | 100 | 100 | 100 | 100 | 100 | 100 |
| 1959 | 109 | 104 | 123 | 143 | 111 | 202 | 103 | 132 | 104 | 125 | 111 | 112 | 144 | 107 |
| 1960 | 117 | 110 | 110 | 143 | 352 | 209 | 106 | 142 | 111 | 118 | 107 | 95 | 496 | 168 |
| 1961 | 122 | 114 | 114 | 154 | 113 | 210 | 109 | 167 | 114 | 167 | 106 | 106 | 788 | 107 |

[1] Excludes Manufacture of machinery except electrical machinery (ISIC major group 36), Manufacture of electrical machinery and equipment (ISIC major group 37), and the Manufacture of transport equipment (ISIC major group 38).

[1] Non compris la Construction de machines, à l'exclusion des machines électriques (CITI classe 36), la Construction de machines, appareils et fournitures électriques (CITI classe 37) et la Construction de matériel de transport (CITI classe 38).

## 3. CHARACTERISTICS OF LARGE INDUSTRIAL ESTABLISHMENTS
## CARACTERISTIQUES DES GRANDS ETABLISSEMENTS INDUSTRIELS
### 1951

Number of establishments in units; value added and wages and salaries in million rupees; number of engaged, employees and operatives in thousands; value added per engaged and wages and salaries per employee and per operative in thousand rupees.

Nombre d'établissements en unités; valeur ajoutée et traitements et salaires en millions de roupies; nombre de personnes occupées, de salariés et d'ouvriers en milliers; valeur ajoutée par personne occupée et traitements et salaires par salarié et par ouvrier en milliers de roupies.

### A. The Divisions of Industrial Activity — Les branches de l'activité industrielle

| Item of data | Total | Mining [1] / Industries extractives [1] | Manufacturing [2] / Industries manufacturières [2] | Electricity and gas [3] / Electricité et gaz [3] | Rubrique |
|---|---|---|---|---|---|
| ISIC | 1–3; 511-512 | 1 | 2–3 | 511-512 | CITI |
| *a. Absolute Figures — Chiffres absolus* | | | | | |
| Number of units | 692 | 20 | 639 | 33 | Nombre d'unités |
| Value added | 224.6 | 6.8 | 202.4 | 15.4 | Valeur ajoutée |
| Number of engaged (Average for the year) | 53.5 | 2.2 | 49.9 | 1.4 | Nombre de personnes occupées (moyenne pour l'année) |
| Employees: Number (Average for the year) | 52.9 | 2.2 | 49.3 | 1.4 | Salariés: Nombre (moyenne pour l'année) |
| Wages and salaries | 65.1 | 2.0 | 61.1 | 2.0 | Traitements et salaires |
| Operatives: Number (Average for the year) | 47.4 | 1.9 | 44.3 | 1.2 | Ouvriers: Nombre (moyenne pour l'année) |
| Wages and salaries | 43.7 | 1.3 | 41.1 | 1.3 | Traitements et salaires |
| *b. Structure* | | | | | |
| Distribution in percent of: Value added | 100.0 | 3.0 | 90.1 | 6.9 | Distribution en pourcentage: Valeur ajoutée |
| Number of engaged | 100.0 | 4.1 | 93.2 | 2.7 | Nombre de personnes occupées |
| Value added per person engaged | 4.2 | 3.1 | 4.0 | 11.0 | Valeur ajoutée par personne occupée |
| Employees as a percent of engaged | 98.9 | 100.0 | 98.8 | 100.0 | Salariés en pourcentage des personnes occupées |
| Value added per unit of wages and salaries | 3.45 | 3.40 | 3.31 | 7.70 | Valeur ajoutée par unité de traitements et salaires |
| Wages and salaries per employee | 1.2 | 0.9 | 1.2 | 1.4 | Traitements et salaires par salarié |
| Operatives as a percent of employees | 89.6 | 86.4 | 89.8 | 85.7 | Ouvriers en pourcentage des salariés |
| Wages and salaries per operative | 0.9 | 0.7 | 0.9 | 1.1 | Traitements et salaires par ouvrier |

For footnotes see end of table.

Pour les notes, voir au bas du tableau.

## B. The Major Groups of Manufacturing — Les classes de la branche Industries manufacturières

| Item of data | Manufacturing [2]<br>Industries manufacturières [2]<br>2–3 | Food, beverages and tobacco [2]<br>Industries alimentaires, boissons, tabac [2]<br>20–22 | Textiles<br>23 | Footwear [2]<br>Chaussures [2]<br>241 | Wood products [2]<br>Bois [2]<br>25 | Printing and publishing<br>Imprimerie et édition<br>28 | Leather and leather products except wearing apparel<br>Cuir et articles en cuir, à l'exclusion des articles d'habillement<br>29 | Rubber products [1]<br>Ouvrages en caoutchouc [1]<br>30 | Chemicals and chemical products [2]<br>Produits chimiques [2]<br>31 | Non-metallic mineral products<br>Produits minéraux non métalliques<br>33 | Metal products<br>Ouvrages en métaux<br>34–38 | Other manufacturing<br>Autres industries manufacturières<br>39 | Rubrique |
|---|---|---|---|---|---|---|---|---|---|---|---|---|---|
| ISIC | 2–3 | 20–22 | 23 | 241 | 25 | 28 | 29 | 30 | 31 | 33 | 34–38 | 39 | CITI |
| *a. Absolute Figures — Chiffres absolus* | | | | | | | | | | | | | |
| Number of establishments. | 639 | 137 | 134 | 3 | 56 | 117 | 6 | 6 | 96 | 15 | 61 | 8 | Nombre d'établissements |
| Value added.......... | 202.4 | 26.3 | 27.9 | 0.3 | 3.7 | 19.8 | 0.5 | 2.7 | 63.6 | 8.3 | 47.8 | 1.5 | Valeur ajoutée |
| Number of engaged (Average for the year). | 49.9 | 5.0 | 7.2 | 0.2 | 1.6 | 5.5 | 0.2 | 0.6 | 9.4 | 1.9 | 18.0 | 0.3 | Nombre de personnes occupées (moyenne pour l'année) |
| Employees: | | | | | | | | | | | | | Salariés: |
| Number (Average for the year)......... | 49.3 | 4.9 | 7.1 | 0.2 | 1.5 | 5.4 | 0.2 | 0.6 | 9.3 | 1.9 | 17.9 | 0.3 | Nombre (moyenne pour l'année) |
| Wages and salaries... | 61.1 | 5.8 | 5.0 | 0.2 | 1.7 | 10.5 | 0.3 | 1.0 | 9.6 | 2.4 | 24.3 | 0.3 | Traitements et salaires |
| Operatives: | | | | | | | | | | | | | Ouvriers: |
| Number (Average for the year)........ | 44.3 | 4.3 | 6.8 | 0.2 | 1.4 | 4.4 | 0.2 | 0.5 | 8.4 | 1.8 | 16.1 | 0.2 | Nombre (moyenne pour l'année) |
| Wages and salaries... | 41.1 | 3.8 | 4.3 | 0.2 | 1.4 | 6.1 | 0.3 | 0.4 | 6.4 | 1.8 | 16.2 | 0.2 | Traitements et salaires |
| *b. Structure* | | | | | | | | | | | | | |
| Distribution in percent of: | | | | | | | | | | | | | Répartition en pourcentage: |
| Value added........ | 100.0 | 12.9 | 13.8 | 0.2 | 1.8 | 9.8 | 0.2 | 1.4 | 31.4 | 4.1 | 23.6 | 0.8 | De la valeur ajoutée |
| Number of engaged... | 100.0 | 10.0 | 14.4 | 0.4 | 3.2 | 11.0 | 0.4 | 1.2 | 18.9 | 3.8 | 36.0 | 0.7 | Du nombre de personnes occupées |
| Value added per person engaged...... | 4.0 | 5.3 | 3.9 | 1.5 | 2.3 | 3.6 | 2.5 | 4.5 | 6.8 | 4.4 | 2.6 | 5.0 | Valeur ajoutée par personne occupée |
| Employees as a percent of engaged........ | 98.8 | 98.0 | 98.6 | 100.0 | 93.8 | 98.2 | 100.0 | 100.0 | 98.9 | 100.0 | 99.4 | 100.0 | Salariés en pourcentage des personnes occupées |
| Value added per unit of wages and salaries............. | 3.31 | 4.53 | 5.58 | 1.50 | 2.18 | 1.88 | 1.67 | 2.70 | 6.62 | 3.46 | 1.97 | 5.00 | Valeur ajoutée par unité de traitements et salaires |
| Wages and salaries per employee........ | 1.2 | 1.2 | 0.7 | 1.0 | 1.1 | 1.9 | 1.5 | 1.7 | 1.0 | 1.3 | 1.4 | 1.0 | Traitements et salaires par salarié |
| Operatives as a percent of employees........ | 89.8 | 87.8 | 95.8 | 100.0 | 93.3 | 81.5 | 100.0 | 83.3 | 90.3 | 94.7 | 89.9 | 66.7 | Ouvriers en pourcentage des salariés |
| Wages and salaries per operative........ | 0.9 | 0.9 | 0.6 | 1.0 | 1.0 | 1.4 | 1.5 | 0.8 | 0.8 | 1.0 | 1.0 | 1.0 | Traitements et salaires par ouvrier |

[1] Entirely Other mining (ISIC major groups 14-19).
[2] Excludes tea factories (part of ISIC group 209), Clothing and made up textiles (ISIC groups 243 and 244), Manufacture of furniture and fixtures (ISIC major group 26), oxygen and carbon dioxide gas production (part of ISIC major group 31).
[3] Includes oxygen and carbon dioxide gas production (part of ISIC major group 31).

[1] Il s'agit exclusivement des Autres industries extractives (CITI classes 14-19).
[2] Non compris les fabriques de thé (dans CITI groupe 209), les Articles d'habillement et ouvrages en tissu (CITI groupes 243 et 244), l'Industrie du meuble (CITI classe 26), ainsi que la production d'oxygène et de gaz carbonique (dans CITI classe 31).
[3] Y compris la production d'oxygène et de gaz carbonique (dans CITI classe 31).

## Gross Domestic Product

Estimates of expenditure on and industrial origin of the gross domestic product are presented in Table 1. This table has been compiled from data supplied by the Corporación de Fomento de la Producción, Santiago, in response to the United Nations national accounts questionnaire. Official estimates and information concerning methods and sources used are published by the Corporación in *Cuentas Nacionales de Chile, 1950-1960*.

## Index Numbers of Industrial Production

The index numbers of industrial production shown in Table 2 are based on indexes compiled by the Dirección de Estadística y Censos and its predecessor agency the Servicio Nacional de Estadística y Censos. For manufacturing industries, two series of base-weighted index numbers have been compiled and published. The first, with a base of 1936-1938, covers the years up to 1958; the second, with a base of 1953, covers the years 1957 and onwards; and the two series have been linked at 1957. The remaining divisions of industrial activity are covered for all years by one series of indexes, with a base of 1936-1938.

The index numbers for mining cover the extraction of all the important minerals and are computed as a base weighted arithmetic averages of relatives of quantities produced. The Dirección de Estadística y Censos compiles indexes for individual minerals which it combines into an index for mining as a whole, using as weights the gross values of production in 1936-38. This total mining index is published in Table 2. The Statistical Office of the United Nations compiles indexes for major groups of mining from the published indexes of individual minerals, which are combined into indexes for major groups using as weights estimates of the gross values of production in 1952 for the years, 1938-1954, and the gross values of production in 1958, for the years 1955 onwards.

The index numbers for manufacturing are also compiled by the Dirección de Estadística. The index numbers up to 1958, with 1936-38 as a weighting base, are computed by combining series of production indicators into indexes for major groups and these major group indexes into manufacturing as a whole, using as weights at both stages the value added in 1936-38. The later series of index numbers for manufacturing industries beginning in 1957, with 1953 as the base period, have been compiled monthly, using elementary indicators of the volume of production derived from a sample of manufacturing establishments with 5 or more employees.

## Produit intérieur brut

Le tableau 1 contient des estimations des dépenses imputées au produit intérieur brut et des estimations du produit intérieur brut par secteur d'activité d'origine. Ce tableau a été établi à partir des données fournies par la Corporación de Fomento de la Producción, Santiago, en réponse au questionnaire de l'ONU sur la comptabilité nationale. Les estimations officielles et les renseignements concernant les méthodes et sources utilisées sont publiés par la Corporación dans *Cuentas Nacionales de Chile, 1950-1960*.

## Indices de la production industrielle

Les indices de la production industrielle reproduits au tableau 2 sont fondés sur des indices établis par la Dirección de Estadística y Censos et par son prédécesseur, le Servicio Nacional de Estadística y Censos. Pour les indices concernant les industries manufacturières, deux séries d'indices à pondération fixe ont été construites et publiées. La première, ayant pour période de base 1936-1938, porte sur toutes les années jusqu'à 1958 et la seconde, ayant pour base 1953, commence en 1957; les deux séries ont été raccordées au niveau de 1957. Les autres branches de l'activité industrielle sont couvertes, pour toutes les années, par une série d'indices ayant pour période de base 1936-1938.

Les indices relatifs aux industries extractives comprennent l'extraction de tous les minéraux importants et sont des moyennes arithmétiques à pondération fixe des rapports de quantités produites. La Dirección de Estadística y Censos construit des indices pour chaque substance minérale, qu'elle combine en indice relatif à l'ensemble des industries extractives en utilisant comme coefficients de pondération les valeurs brutes de la production en 1936-1938. Cet indice des industries extractives figure au tableau 2. Le Bureau de statistique de l'ONU établit des indices de classes des industries extractives à partir des indices publiés pour chaque substance minérale; à cette fin, il utilise comme coefficients de pondération des estimations des valeurs brutes de la production en 1952 pour les années 1938-1954, et les valeurs brutes de la production en 1958 pour 1955 et les années suivantes.

Les indices relatifs aux industries manufacturières sont également calculés par la Dirección de Estadística. Jusqu'en 1958, on a calculé les indices ayant 1936-1938 comme période de base en combinant des séries d'indicateurs de la production en indices de classes, puis en combinant ces indices de classes en indices relatifs à l'ensemble des industries manufacturières; pour ces deux opérations, on a utilisé comme coefficients de pondération la valeur ajoutée en 1936-1938. Les séries plus récentes d'indices des industries manufacturières, commençant en 1957 et ayant 1953 comme période de base, ont été calculées mensuellement à partir de séries élémen-

These indicators consist, in the main, of quantity of output for individual products, though value of production adjusted for changes in prices and quantity of consumption of individual raw materials are also utilized. The value added in 1953 of the establishments covered in the sample represents about 65 per cent of the value added of the establishments included in the 1953 industrial inquiry, which covered all registered establishments employing 5 or more persons. The results of this 1953 inquiry is also the source from which the weights are derived. The indexes of the indicators for detailed categories have been combined into indexes for groups, using as weights the value of production at market prices in 1953. The indexes for groups are combined into indexes for major groups and the major group indexes into indexes for manufacturing as a whole, using as weights the value added at market prices in 1953. The annual indexes are the arithmetic averages of the monthly figures.

The index numbers for electricity and construction have also been compiled by the Dirección de Estadística. In the case of electricity, the indicators used were quantity relatives but in the case of construction the indexes were the value of construction work deflated by using a price index for construction materials.

The indexes published in Table 2 for mining, manufacturing and electricity combined have been calculated by the Statistical Office of the United Nations, using as a basis the indexes published by the Dirección de Estadística and estimates of value added in 1953 as weights.

The indexes, 1936-1938 = 100, for the years 1950 to 1959, for all divisions of industrial activity, and the indexes, 1953 = 100, for the years 1957 to 1959 for manufacturing, are all shown in *Estadística Chilena, Sinopsis 1959,* December 1959, published by the Servicio Nacional de Estadística y Censos. The latest indexes covering the construction industry have been obtained from *Estadística Chilena,* September-October 1960, published by the Dirección de Estadística y Censos and through correspondence. The later series of manufacturing indexes, 1953 = 100, and the most recent mining indexes can be found in both the *Boletín* (the successor to *Estadística Chilena*) of the Dirección de Estadística y Censos and the *Boletín Mensual* of the Banco Central de Chile.

Further details of the methods used in compiling the 1936-38 = 100 indexes can be found in *Estadística Chilena,* September, October, December 1945 and January-February 1947, published by the Servicio Nacional de Estadística y Censos. Further details of the manufacturing industries index 1953 = 100 can be found in *Indice de Producción Manufacturera Industrial (Base 1953 = 100)* Estudios metodológicos No. 3, published by the Servicio Nacional de Estadística y Censos, October 1959.

taires d'indicateurs du volume de la production provenant d'un échantillon d'établissements manufacturiers occupant cinq salariés ou plus. Ces indicateurs sont fondés principalement sur les quantités produites de chaque marchandise, mais la valeur de la production corrigée en fonction des variations de prix et les quantités de matières premières consommées sont également utilisées. La valeur ajoutée en 1953 par les établissements de l'échantillon représente environ 65 p. 100 de la valeur ajoutée par les établissements retenus pour l'enquête industrielle de 1953, qui portait sur tous les établissements enregistrés occupant cinq personnes ou plus. Les résultats de l'enquête de 1953 ont également servi à déterminer les coefficients de pondération utilisés. On a combiné les indices relatifs aux indicateurs de catégories détaillées en indices de groupes en utilisant comme coefficients de pondération la valeur de la production aux prix du marché en 1953. Ces indices de groupes ont été combinés en indices de classes, et ceux-ci en indices relatifs à l'ensemble des industries manufacturières; les poids utilisés à cette fin sont la valeur ajoutée aux prix du marché en 1953. Les indices annuels sont les moyennes arithmétiques des chiffres mensuels.

Les indices relatifs à l'électricité, ainsi qu'au bâtiment et aux travaux publics, ont été également établis par la Dirección de Estadística. Dans le cas de l'électricité, les indicateurs utilisés étaient les rapports quantitatifs, mais, pour le bâtiment et les travaux publics, les indices ont été fondés sur la valeur des travaux de construction, corrigée à l'aide d'un indice de prix des matériaux de construction.

Les indices du tableau 2 relatifs aux industries extractives, aux industries manufacturières et à l'électricité combinées ont été calculés par le Bureau de statistique de l'ONU, qui a utilisé comme base les indices publiés par la Dirección de Estadística et, comme coefficients de pondération, des estimations de la valeur ajoutée en 1953.

Les indices (1936-1938 = 100) des années 1950 à 1959 relatifs à toutes les branches de l'activité industrielle et les indices (1953 = 100) des années 1957 à 1959 relatifs aux industries manufacturières sont tous reproduits dans *Estadística Chilena, Sinopsis 1959,* décembre 1959, publié par le Servicio Nacional de Estadística y Censos. Les derniers indices concernant le bâtiment et les travaux publics ont été tirés de *Estadística Chilena,* septembre-octobre 1960, publié par la Dirección de Estadística y Censos ou obtenus par correspondance. Les dernières séries d'indices des industries manufacturières (1953 = 100) et les indices des industries extractives les plus récents figurent dans le *Boletín* (publication remplaçant *Estadística Chilena*) de la Dirección de Estadística y Censos et dans le *Boletín Mensual* du Banco Central de Chile.

Pour plus de détails sur les méthodes de calcul des indices ayant pour base 1936-1938 = 100, voir *Estadística Chilena,* septembre, octobre, décembre 1945 et janvier-février 1947, publié par le Servicio Nacional de Estadística y Censos. Pour plus de détails sur les indices relatifs aux industries manufacturières (1953 = 100), voir *Indice de Producción Manufacturera Industrial (Base 1953 = 100)* Estudios metodológicos No. 3, publié par le Servicio Nacional de Estadística y Censos, octobre 1959.

### Index Numbers of Industrial Employment

The indexes of industrial employment presented in Table 3 for the years, 1938 to 1956, are based on absolute figures of the number of operatives in the case of mining and the number of employees in the case of manufacturing. The data are derived from annual inquiries conducted by the Servicio Nacional de Estadística y Censos covering large mining establishments and manufacturing establishments with 5 or more employees. The annual absolute figures in the case of mining are an average for the year, whilst for manufacturing these figures are the average of the number of employees during the last week of months of March, June, September and December.

The index numbers in Table 3 for 1957 onwards are based on indexes compiled by the Dirección de Estadística y Censos (previously the Servicio Nacional de Estadística y Censos). Two sets of index numbers are compiled, one covering operatives only, the other covering total employees. In the case of mining, the indexes for operatives only have been used in order to maintain comparability with the figures up to 1956. In the case of manufacturing, the indexes for total employees have been used. These indexes are compiled from data gathered from large mining establishments accounting for about 80 per cent of mining employment in 1953, and a stratified sample of manufacturing establishments with 5 or more employees. The sample covers 417 establishments which represented about 55 per cent of total employment in manufacturing industries in 1953.

The data from which the indexes are compiled are the number of operatives and other employees during the last pay periods of March, June, September and December for manufacturing and during the whole of the same months in the case of mining. Workers on sick leave or vacation are excluded from the figures. The indexes are calculated and published for the months of March, June, September and December and the annual index is the arithmetic average of these quarterly figures. The indexes for the major groups are combined into indexes for mining as a whole and for manufacturing as a whole using as weights the total number of operatives and employees respectively as indicated by the 1953 annual inquiry covering establishments with 5 or more employees. The total index for mining and manufacturing combined has been calculated by the Statistical Office of the United Nations utilizing as weights estimates of the total number of persons engaged in 1953.

The absolute figures for 1938-1957 have been issued for mining in *Estadística Chilena, Sinopsis 1957*, Noviembre-Diciembre de 1957, and for manufacturing in various editions of *Industrias;* all have been published by the Servicio Nacional de Estadística y Censos. The index numbers, 1953 = 100, for 1957 onwards have been published in *Estadística Chilena,* by the Dirección de Estadística y Censos and in *Boletín Mensual* by the Banco Central de Chile.

### Indices de l'emploi dans l'industrie

Les indices du tableau 3 relatifs à l'emploi dans l'industrie de 1938 à 1956 sont fondés sur des chiffres absolus indiquant le nombre d'ouvriers dans le cas des industries extractives et le nombre de salariés dans celui des industries manufacturières. Les données proviennent d'enquêtes annuelles exécutées par le Servicio Nacional de Estadística y Censos auprès des grands établissements miniers et des établissements manufacturiers occupant cinq salariés ou plus. Dans le cas des industries extractives, les chiffres absolus annuels sont des moyennes pour l'ensemble de l'année, tandis que, dans le cas des industries manufacturières, ce sont les moyennes du nombre de salariés pendant la dernière semaine des mois de mars, juin, septembre et décembre.

Les indices du tableau 3 pour 1957 et les années suivantes sont construits à partir d'indices calculés par la Dirección de Estadística y Censos (initialement le Servicio Nacional de Estadística y Censos). Deux séries d'indices ont été établies, l'une pour les ouvriers seulement, l'autre pour l'ensemble des salariés. Dans le cas des industries extractives, on a utilisé les indices relatifs aux ouvriers seulement afin de maintenir la comparabilité avec les chiffres de 1956 et des années antérieures. Pour les industries manufacturières, on s'est servi des indices relatifs à l'ensemble des salariés. Ces indices sont construits à partir des données fournies par les grands établissements miniers employant 80 p. 100 de la main-d'œuvre totale des mines en 1953 et par un échantillon stratifié d'établissements manufacturiers occupant cinq salariés ou plus. L'échantillon comprend 417 établissements, qui employaient environ 55 p. 100 de la main-d'œuvre totale des industries manufacturières en 1953.

Les données qui ont servi au calcul des indices sont les nombres d'ouvriers et autres salariés pendant la dernière période de paie de mars, juin, septembre et décembre pour les industries manufacturières et pendant la totalité de ces mois dans le cas des industries extractives. Les travailleurs en congé de maladie ou en vacances sont exclus des chiffres. Les indices sont calculés et publiés pour les mois de mars, juin, septembre et décembre, et l'indice annuel est la moyenne arithmétique de ces chiffres trimestriels. Les indices de classes ont été combinés en indices relatifs à l'ensemble des industries extractives et en indices relatifs à l'ensemble des industries manufacturières; à cette fin, on a utilisé comme poids le nombre total des ouvriers et des salariés respectivement fourni par l'enquête annuelle sur les établissements ayant cinq salariés ou plus. L'indice relatif à l'ensemble des industries extractives et manufacturières combinées a été construit par le Bureau de statistique de l'ONU, qui a utilisé comme poids des estimations du nombre total de personnes occupées en 1953.

Les chiffres absolus relatifs à 1938-1957 ont été publiés par le Servicio Nacional de Estadística y Censos dans *Estadística Chilena, Sinopsis 1957*, novembre-décembre 1957, pour les industries extractives et dans différents numéros de *Industrias* pour les industries manufacturières. Les indices (1953 = 100) pour 1957 et les années ultérieures ont été publiés dans *Estadística Chilena* par la Dirección de Estadística y Censos et dans *Boletín Mensual* par le Banco Central de Chile.

## Characteristics and Structure of Manufacturing Establishments

The data for 1937 shown in Table 4 are derived from the results of Chile's Second Economic Census, covering all industrial and commercial establishments, except handicrafts, regardless of size, published by the Servicio Nacional de Estadística y Censos in *Censo Industrial y Comercial 1937*. The data in Tables 5 and 6 for 1957 are based on the published results of part of the third census of manufactures conducted in 1958 by the Dirección de Estadística to cover the year 1957. All manufacturing establishments were covered but results have been published only for those engaging 5 or more persons. These results have been published in *III Censo Nacional de Manufacturas,* (Santiago de Chile 1960) by the Dirección de Estadística y Censos.

The data in Tables 7 and 8 for the years 1938, 1948 and 1953 are based on the results of the annual industrial inquiries covering establishments with five or more employees. The establishments included in these surveys are those which have been granted licenses to operate by the municipalities. These data are incomplete and not comparable from year to year, either because of the failure of establishments to obtain licenses or because of incomplete response. Adjustments have not been made in the data for either type of incompleteness. Details of these particular annual inquiries have been abstracted from the following publications of the Servicio Nacional de Estadística: *Minería e Industria 1938, Industrias Años 1948, Industrias Año 1953.*

The definitions of items of data utilized in the different inquiries that are shown in Tables 4 to 8 are consistent with one another and, on the whole, with the International Standards in Basic Industrial Statistics. The data on value added, in the case of the 1938, 1948 and 1953 inquiries, were compiled by the Statistical Office of the United Nations by deducting from the gross value of production, at market prices ex-factory, the costs of raw materials and fuel and power consumed. The capacity of installed power equipment was obtained by the addition of the horsepower of prime movers driving machinery other than electric generators and the horsepower of all electric motors.

## Caractéristiques et structure des établissements manufacturiers

Les données de 1937 reproduites au tableau 4 sont tirées des résultats du second recensement économique du Chili, qui portait sur tous les établissements industriels et commerciaux, quelle que fût leur dimension, à l'exclusion des unités artisanales; ces résultats ont été publiés par le Servicio Nacional de Estadística y Censos dans *Censo Industrial y Commercial 1937*. Les données de 1957 figurant dans les tableaux 5 et 6 sont fondées sur les résultats partiels publiés du troisième recensement des industries manufacturières en 1957 effectué par la Dirección de Estadística pendant l'année 1958. Tous les établissements manufacturiers ont été recensés mais les résultats n'ont été publiés que pour les établissements occupant cinq personnes ou plus. Ces résultats ont été publiés dans *III Censo Nacional de Manufacturas* (Santiago de Chile 1960) par la Dirección de Estadística y Censos.

Les donnés des tableaux 7 et 8 relatives aux années 1938, 1948 et 1953 sont tirées des résultats des enquêtes industrielles annuelles sur les établissements occupant cinq salariés ou plus et dotés d'une autorisation municipale. Ces données sont incomplètes et ne sont pas comparables d'une année à l'autre, du fait que certains établissements n'ont pu obtenir d'autorisation ou que les réponses ont été incomplètes. Aucun ajustement n'a été fait pour en tenir compte. Les détails concernant ces enquêtes annuelles particulières ont été tirés des publications suivantes du Servicio Nacional de Estadística : *Minería e Industria 1938, Industrias Años 1948, Industrias Años 1953.*

Les définitions des rubriques utilisées dans les diverses enquêtes dont les résultats sont reproduits aux tableaux 4 à 8 sont cohérentes les unes par rapport aux autres et sont, dans l'ensemble, conformes aux Normes internationales relatives aux statistiques industrielles de base. Pour les enquêtes de 1938, 1948 et 1953, les chiffres de la valeur ajoutée ont été calculés par le Bureau de statistique de l'ONU, qui a déduit de la valeur brute de la production, aux prix du marché départ usine, le coût des matières premières, des combustibles et de l'énergie consommés. La puissance installée représente la somme des chevaux-vapeur des moteurs primaires actionnant des machines autres que des générateurs électriques et des chevaux-vapeur de tous les moteurs électriques.

## 1. THE DOMESTIC PRODUCT — LE PRODUIT INTERIEUR

Million Escudos                                                    Millions d'escudos

### A. Expenditure on the Gross Domestic Product at Market Prices
### Dépenses relatives au produit intérieur brut aux prix du marché

| Item of data and year / Rubrique et année | Total [1] | Consumption — Consommation | | Gross Domestic Capital Formation — Formation brute de capital intérieur | | Net exports of goods and services — Exportations nettes de biens et de services | |
|---|---|---|---|---|---|---|---|
| | | Total | Government / Etat | Total | Fixed / Fixe | Exports less imports / Exportations moins importations | Exports / Exportations |
| **a. At Current Prices — Aux prix courants** | | | | | | | |
| Absolute figures — Chiffres absolus | | | | | | | |
| 1950 | 155.6 | 135.3 | 13.7 | 17.6 | 14.3 | 2.7 | 16.8 |
| 1951 | 190.7 | 169.0 | 17.3 | 20.5 | 19.2 | 1.1 | 24.6 |
| 1952 | 258.9 | 233.0 | 24.4 | 22.5 | 24.5 | 3.4 | 33.2 |
| 1953 | 351.3 | 307.7 | 36.0 | 44.1 | 32.2 | −0.5 | 29.9 |
| 1954 | 571.1 | 529.3 | 56.6 | 37.8 | 47.5 | 4.1 | 42.2 |
| 1955 | 1 041.5 | 939.2 | 106.8 | 84.8 | 86.8 | 17.4 | 94.4 |
| 1956 | 1 659.0 | 1 462.1 | 161.9 | 166.8 | 138.3 | 30.2 | 202.0 |
| 1957 | 2 252.7 | 2 077.4 | 222.4 | 229.0 | 247.0 | −53.8 | 296.5 |
| 1958 | 2 971.8 | 2 699.2 | 278.4 | 300.7 | 309.9 | −28.3 | 359.3 |
| 1959 | 4 163.0 | 3 689.0 | 365.0 | 426.0 | 405.0 | 48.0 | 565.0 |
| 1960 | 4 781.0 | 4 342.0 | 430.0 | 426.0 | 405.0 | 13.0 | 753.0 |
| Percentage distribution of average annual expenditure — Distribution en pourcentage des dépenses annuelles moyennes | | | | | | | |
| 1950 – 1960 | 100.0 | 90.2 | 9.3 | 9.6 | 9.4 | 0.2 | 13.1 |
| 1950 | 100.0 | 87.0 | 8.8 | 11.3 | 9.2 | 1.7 | 10.8 |
| 1953 | 100.0 | 87.6 | 10.2 | 12.5 | 9.2 | −0.1 | 8.5 |
| 1954 | 100.0 | 92.7 | 9.9 | 6.6 | 8.3 | 0.7 | 7.4 |
| 1958 | 100.0 | 90.8 | 9.4 | 10.1 | 10.4 | −0.9 | 12.1 |
| 1960 | 100.0 | 90.8 | 9.0 | 8.9 | 8.5 | 0.3 | 15.8 |
| **b. At Prices of 1960 — Aux prix de 1960** | | | | | | | |
| Absolute figures — Chiffres absolus | | | | | | | |
| 1950 | 3 535.1 | 2 940.2 | 297.0 | 428.5 | 356.0 | 166.4 | 509.7 |
| 1951 | 3 447.5 | 2 963.3 | 301.6 | 412.0 | 389.3 | 72.3 | 492.2 |
| 1952 | 3 833.7 | 3 374.1 | 350.4 | 392.2 | 419.1 | 67.4 | 519.2 |
| 1953 | 4 059.3 | 3 535.5 | 413.1 | 559.1 | 426.8 | −35.3 | 404.6 |
| 1954 | 4 305.1 | 3 891.3 | 415.8 | 351.9 | 420.2 | 61.9 | 485.4 |
| 1955 | 4 452.6 | 3 913.0 | 444.8 | 477.6 | 485.6 | 62.0 | 558.8 |
| 1956 | 4 147.2 | 3 675.4 | 408.6 | 493.4 | 423.9 | −21.5 | 486.7 |
| 1957 | 4 429.9 | 4 049.5 | 426.4 | 441.9 | 472.8 | −61.6 | 518.3 |
| 1958 | 4 656.6 | 4 181.5 | 422.4 | 423.6 | 436.2 | 51.5 | 561.4 |
| 1959 | 4 686.8 | 4 126.2 | 403.9 | 483.5 | 461.4 | 77.1 | 594.1 |
| 1960 | 4 781.0 | 4 342.0 | 430.0 | 426.0 | 405.0 | 13.0 | 753.0 |
| Percentage distribution of average annual expenditure — Distribution en pourcentage des dépenses annuelles moyennes | | | | | | | |
| 1950 – 1960 | 100.0 | 88.5 | 8.4 | 10.5 | 10.1 | 1.0 | 12.7 |
| 1950 | 100.0 | 83.2 | 8.4 | 12.1 | 10.1 | 4.7 | 14.4 |
| 1953 | 100.0 | 87.1 | 10.2 | 13.8 | 10.5 | −0.9 | 10.0 |
| 1954 | 100.0 | 90.4 | 9.7 | 8.2 | 9.8 | 1.4 | 11.3 |
| 1958 | 100.0 | 89.8 | 9.1 | 9.1 | 9.4 | 1.1 | 12.1 |
| 1960 | 100.0 | 90.8 | 9.0 | 8.9 | 8.5 | 0.3 | 15.8 |
| Average annual rate of growth — Taux annuel moyen d'accroissement | | | | | | | |
| 1950 – 1960 | 3.1 | 4.0 | 3.8 | −0.1 | 1.3 | . | 4.0 |
| 1950 – 1953 | 4.7 | 6.3 | 11.6 | 9.3 | 6.2 | . | −7.4 |
| 1954 – 1958 | 2.0 | 1.8 | 0.4 | 4.8 | 0.9 | . | 3.7 |
| 1958 – 1960 | 1.3 | 1.9 | 0.9 | 0.3 | −3.6 | . | 15.8 |

For footnotes see end of table.                               Pour les notes, voir au bas du tableau.

## B.   The Net Domestic Product at Factor Cost According to Origin
### Origine par secteur d'activité du produit intérieur net au coût des facteurs

| Item of data and year / Rubrique et année | Total | Agricultural sector / Secteur agricole | Industrial Sector — Secteur industriel | | | | | Transportation and communication / Transports et communications | Other sectors / Autres secteurs |
|---|---|---|---|---|---|---|---|---|---|
| | | | Total | Mining / Industries extractives | Manufacturing / Industries manufacturières | Construction / Bâtiment et travaux publics | Electricity, gas and water / Electricité, gaz et eau | | |
| ISIC — CITI | 0–9 | 0 | 1–5 | 1 | 2–3 | 4 | 5 | 7 | 6, 8–9 |

### a.  At Current Prices — Aux prix courants

| | | | | | | | | | |
|---|---|---|---|---|---|---|---|---|---|
| **Absolute figures — Chiffres absolus** | | | | | | | | | |
| 1950............ | 127.7 | 22.2 | 29.9 | 8.0 | 18.3 | 2.8 | 0.8 | 7.6 | 68.0 |
| 1951............ | 162.6 | 26.3 | 37.8 | 10.7 | 22.6 | 3.5 | 1.0 | 8.7 | 89.8 |
| 1952............ | 217.3 | 42.6 | 48.9 | 14.1 | 27.1 | 6.3 | 1.4 | 12.2 | 113.6 |
| 1953............ | 289.7 | 50.3 | 65.1 | 18.9 | 37.2 | 7.1 | 1.9 | 16.9 | 157.4 |
| 1954............ | 498.1 | 76.2 | 150.8 | 28.1 | 108.1 | 11.7 | 2.9 | 28.5 | 242.6 |
| 1955............ | 878.9 | 140.3 | 260.9 | 50.8 | 185.9 | 19.9 | 4.3 | 44.5 | 433.2 |
| 1956............ | 1 460.8 | 201.3 | 448.4 | 91.5 | 324.8 | 24.2 | 7.9 | 71.3 | 739·8 |
| 1957............ | 1 986.4 | 255.6 | 560.8 | 103.1 | 418.7 | 27.8 | 11.2 | 102.4 | 1 067.6 |
| 1958............ | 2 536.0 | 363.6 | 680.8 | 114.8 | 513.1 | 35.3 | 17.6 | 130.5 | 1 361.1 |
| 1959............ | 3 528.0 | 462.0 | 1 098.0 | 165.0 | 811.0 | 95.0 | 27.0 | 161.0 | 1 807.0 |
| 1960............ | 4 004.0 | 554.0 | 1 141.0 | 180.0 | 806.0 | 122.0 | 33.0 | 179.0 | 2 130.0 |
| **Percentage distribution according to sector— Distribution en pourcentage par secteur** | | | | | | | | | |
| 1950 – 1960..... | 100.0 | 14.0 | 28.8 | 5.0 | 20.8 | 2.3 | 0.7 | 4.9 | 52.3 |
| 1950............ | 100.0 | 17.4 | 23.4 | 6.3 | 14.3 | 2.2 | 0.6 | 6.0 | 53.2 |
| 1953............ | 100.0 | 17.4 | 22.5 | 6.5 | 12.8 | 2.5 | 0.7 | 5.8 | 54.3 |
| 1954............ | 100.0 | 15.3 | 30.3 | 5.6 | 21.7 | 2.4 | 0.6 | 5.7 | 48.7 |
| 1958............ | 100.0 | 14.3 | 26.8 | 4.5 | 20.2 | 1.4 | 0.7 | 5.2 | 53.7 |
| 1960............ | 100.0 | 13.8 | 28.5 | 4.5 | 20.1 | 3.1 | 0.8 | 4.5 | 53.2 |

### b.  At Prices of 1960 — Aux prix de 1960

| | | | | | | | | | |
|---|---|---|---|---|---|---|---|---|---|
| **Absolute figures — Chiffres absolus** | | | | | | | | | |
| 1950............ | 2 874.3 | 500.2 | 673.8 | 179.9 | 411.0 | 63.8 | 19.1 | 170.2 | 1 530.1 |
| 1951............ | 2 909.3 | 470.6 | 676.7 | 191.3 | 404.5 | 62.4 | 18.5 | 156.6 | 1 605.4 |
| 1952............ | 3 171.2 | 622.4 | 713.1 | 205.2 | 396.0 | 92.1 | 19.8 | 178.5 | 1 657.2 |
| 1953............ | 3 299.3 | 573.0 | 741.0 | 215.7 | 423.7 | 80.5 | 21.1 | 192.6 | 1 792.7 |
| 1954............ | 3 699.7 | 566.3 | 1 120.1 | 209.0 | 802.6 | 86.9 | 21.6 | 211.8 | 1 801.5 |
| 1955............ | 3 653.7 | 583.4 | 1 084.9 | 211.3 | 772.8 | 82.7 | 18.1 | 184.8 | 1 800.6 |
| 1956............ | 3 584.0 | 493.9 | 1 100.3 | 224.6 | 796.9 | 59.4 | 19.4 | 174.8 | 1 815.0 |
| 1957............ | 3 914.3 | 503.6 | 1 105.1 | 203.2 | 825.1 | 54.7 | 22.1 | 201.7 | 2 103.9 |
| 1958............ | 4 005.6 | 574.3 | 1 075.4 | 181.4 | 810.5 | 55.7 | 27.8 | 206.1 | 2 149.8 |
| 1959............ | 3 968.2 | 519.6 | 1 235.0 | 185.6 | 912.2 | 106.8 | 30.4 | 181.1 | 2 032.5 |
| 1960............ | 4 004.0 | 554.0 | 1 141.0 | 180.0 | 806.0 | 122.0 | 33.0 | 179.0 | 2 130.0 |
| **Percentage distribution according to sector— Distribution en pourcentage par secteur** | | | | | | | | | |
| 1950 – 1960..... | 100.0 | 15.3 | 27.3 | 5.6 | 18.8 | 2.2 | 0.7 | 5.2 | 52.2 |
| 1950............ | 100.0 | 17.4 | 23.5 | 6.3 | 14.3 | 2.2 | 0.7 | 5.9 | 53.2 |
| 1953............ | 100.0 | 17.4 | 22.5 | 6·6 | 12.9 | 2.4 | 0.6 | 5.8 | 54.3 |
| 1954............ | 100.0 | 15.3 | 30.3 | 5.7 | 21.7 | 2.3 | 0.6 | 5.7 | 48.7 |
| 1958............ | 100.0 | 14.3 | 26.8 | 4.5 | 20.2 | 1.4 | 0.7 | 5.2 | 53.7 |
| 1960............ | 100.0 | 13.8 | 28.5 | 4.5 | 20.1 | 3.1 | 0.8 | 4.5 | 53.2 |
| **Average annual rate of growth—Taux annuel moyen d'accroissement** | | | | | | | | | |
| 1950 – 1960..... | 3.4 | 1.0 | 5.4 | — | 7.0 | 6.7 | 5.6 | 0.5 | 3.4 |
| 1950 – 1953..... | 4.7 | 4.6 | 3.2 | 6.2 | 1.0 | 8.1 | 3.4 | 4.2 | 5.4 |
| 1954 – 1958..... | 2.0 | 0.3 | –1.0 | –3.5 | 0.2 | –10.5 | 6.5 | –0.7 | 4.5 |
| 1958 – 1960..... | — | –1.8 | 3.0 | –0.4 | –0.3 | 50.0 | 8.9 | –6.7 | –0.5 |

[1] Includes a statistical discrepancy.

[1] Y compris les écarts statistiques.

## 2. INDEX NUMBERS OF INDUSTRIAL PRODUCTION — INDICES DE LA PRODUCTION INDUSTRIELLE

### A. The Divisions of Industrial Activity
### Les branches de l'activité industrielle

| Period<br>Période | Total excluding construction<br>Total à l'exclusion du bâtiment et des travaux publics | Mining [1]<br>Industries extractives [1] | Manu-facturing [2]<br>Industries manu-facturières [2] | Construction<br>Bâtiment et travaux publics | Electricity<br>Electricité |
|---|---|---|---|---|---|
| ISIC — CITI | 1–3, 511-512 | 1 | 2–3 | 4 | 511 |

*a. Indexes — Indices (1958 = 100)*

| | | | | | |
|---|---|---|---|---|---|
| 1936–1938. | 49 | 83 | 42 | 116 | 18 |
| 1948....... | 72 | 103 | 66 | 188 | 45 |
| 1949....... | 72 | 90 | 68 | 184 | 50 |
| 1950....... | 69 | 88 | 66 | 186 | 59 |
| 1951....... | 82 | 94 | 80 | 171 | 65 |
| 1952....... | 87 | 94 | 87 | 169 | 73 |
| 1953....... | 91 | 85 | 94 | 226 | 77 |
| 1954....... | 94 | 88 | 97 | 221 | 84 |
| 1955....... | 93 | 97 | 92 | 220 | 89 |
| 1956....... | 98 | 100 | 98 | 136 | 93 |
| 1957....... | 98 | 103 | 97 | 99 | 96 |
| 1958....... | 100 | 100 | 100 | 100 | 100 |
| 1959....... | 113 | 112 | 114 | 230 | 109 |
| 1960....... | ... | 107 | 112 | 167 | ... |
| 1961....... | ... | 112 | 119 | ... | ... |

*b. Average Annual Rate of Change — Taux annuel moyen de variation*

| | | | | | |
|---|---|---|---|---|---|
| (1936–1938)-1960..... | ... | 1.2 | 4.6 | 1.7 | ... |
| (1936–1938)-1948..... | 20.8 | 2.2 | 4.6 | 5.0 | 9.6 |
| 1950–1960. | ... | 2.0 | 5.4 | -1.1 | ... |
| 1948–1953. | 4.8 | -3.8 | 7.3 | 3.7 | 11.3 |
| 1954–1958. | 1.6 | 3.2 | 0.8 | -18.0 | 4.4 |
| 1958–1960. | ... | 3.4 | 5.8 | 29.2 | ... |

For footnotes see end of table.

### B. The Major Groups of Mining
### Les classes de la branche Industries extractives

| Period<br>Période | All mining [1]<br>Toutes industries extractives [1] | Coal mining<br>Extraction du charbon | Metal mining<br>Extraction des minerals métalliques | Crude petro-leum and natural gas<br>Pétrole brut et gaz naturel | Other mining<br>Autres industries extractives |
|---|---|---|---|---|---|
| ISIC — CITI | 1 | 11 | 12 | 13 | 14–19 |

*a. Indexes — Indices (1958 = 100)*

| | | | | | |
|---|---|---|---|---|---|
| 1936–1938. | 83 | 98 | 73 | — | 105 |
| 1948....... | 103 | 114 | 93 | — | 154 |
| 1949....... | 90 | 107 | 79 | 1 | 112 |
| 1950....... | 88 | 111 | 79 | 11 | 109 |
| 1951....... | 94 | 111 | 82 | 14 | 131 |
| 1952....... | 94 | 122 | 86 | 16 | 106 |
| 1953....... | 85 | 117 | 78 | 23 | 91 |
| 1954....... | 88 | 113 | 76 | 31 | 122 |
| 1955....... | 97 | 115 | – 88 – | 46 | – 118 – |
| 1956....... | 100 | 114 | 102 | 64 | 88 |
| 1957....... | 103 | 105 | 101 | 78 | 102 |
| 1958....... | 100 | 100 | 100 | 100 | 100 |
| 1959....... | 112 | 94 | 115 | 115 | 99 |
| 1960....... | 107 | 71 | 116 | 130 | 75 |
| 1961....... | 112 | 90 | 120 | 166 | 91 |

*b. Average Annual Rate of Change — Taux annuel moyen de variation*

| | | | | | |
|---|---|---|---|---|---|
| (1936–1938)-1960..... | 1.2 | -1.5 | 2.1 | . | -1.5 |
| (1936–1938)-1948..... | 2.2 | 1.5 | 2.5 | . | 3.9 |
| 1950–1960. | 2.0 | -4.4 | 3.9 | 28.0 | -3.7 |
| 1948–1953. | -3.8 | 0.5 | -3.4 | . | -10.0 |
| 1954–1958. | 3.2 | -3.0 | 7.1 | 34.0 | -4.8 |
| 1958–1960. | 3.4 | -15.7 | 7.7 | 14.0 | -13.4 |

Pour les notes, voir au bas du tableau.

## C. The Major Groups of Manufacturing — Les classes de la branche Industries manufacturières

| Period / Période | Manufacturing [2] / Industries manufacturières [2] | Food, beverages and tobacco / Industries alimentaires, boissons, tabac | Textiles | Clothing, footwear and made-up textiles / Articles d'habillement, chaussures et ouvrages en tissu | Wood products and furniture / Bois et meubles | Paper and paper products / Papier et ouvrages en papier | Printing and publishing / Imprimerie et édition | Leather and leather products except wearing apparel / Cuir et articles en cuir, à l'exclusion des articles d'habillement | Rubber products / Ouvrages en caoutchouc | Chemicals and chemical, petroleum and coal products / Produits chimiques et dérivés du pétrole et du charbon | Non-metallic mineral products / Produits minéraux non métalliques | Basic metals / Métallurgie de base | Metal products / Ouvrages en métaux | Other manufacturing / Autres industries manufacturières |
|---|---|---|---|---|---|---|---|---|---|---|---|---|---|---|
| ISIC — CITI | 2-3 | 20-22 | 23 | 24 | 25-26 | 27 | 28 | 29 | 30 | 31-32 | 33 | 34 | 35-38 | 39 |

### a. Indexes — Indices (1958 = 100)

| Period | 2-3 | 20-22 | 23 | 24 | 25-26 | 27 | 28 | 29 | 30 | 31-32 | 33 | 34 | 35-38 | 39 |
|---|---|---|---|---|---|---|---|---|---|---|---|---|---|---|
| 1936-1938 | 42 | 48 | 65 | 72 | ... | 38 | ... | ... | ... | 60 | 67 | 73 | ... | ... |
| 1948 | 66 | 74 | 94 | 82 | ... | 54 | ... | ... | ... | 77 | 94 | 87 | ... | ... |
| 1949 | 68 | 77 | 96 | 73 | ... | 55 | ... | ... | ... | 77 | 88 | 74 | ... | ... |
| 1950 | 66 | 78 | 96 | 74 | ... | 55 | ... | ... | ... | 79 | 92 | 70 | ... | ... |
| 1951 | 80 | 80 | 105 | 72 | ... | 57 | ... | ... | ... | 84 | 99 | 86 | ... | ... |
| 1952 | 87 | 86 | 102 | 75 | ... | 59 | ... | ... | ... | 85 | 109 | 96 | ... | ... |
| 1953 | 94 | 99 | 109 | 82 | 89 | 64 | 108 | 97 | 101 | 83 | 102 | 88 | 85 | 81 |
| 1954 | 97 | 103 | 112 | 88 | ... | 70 | ... | ... | ... | 85 | 105 | 86 | ... | ... |
| 1955 | 92 | 106 | 111 | 95 | ... | 69 | ... | ... | ... | 82 | 106 | 90 | ... | ... |
| 1956 | 98 | 109 | 100 | 87 | ... | 67 | ... | ... | ... | 87 | 104 | 104 | ... | ... |
| 1957 | −97− | −103− | −100− | −95− | 94 | −76− | 98 | 100 | 94 | −91− | −94− | −101− | 98 | 93 |
| 1958 | 100 | 100 | 100 | 100 | 100 | 100 | 100 | 100 | 100 | 100 | 100 | 100 | 100 | 100 |
| 1959 | 114 | 108 | 115 | 111 | 124 | 121 | 94 | 100 | 135 | 101 | 124 | 133 | 119 | 128 |
| 1960 | 112 | 115 | 103 | 103 | 127 | 110 | 108 | 87 | 148 | 108 | 113 | 114 | 124 | 132 |
| 1961 | 119 | 118 | 112 | 121 | 127 | 141 | 118 | 98 | 163 | 117 | 124 | 107 | 137 | 132 |

### b. Average Annual Rate of Change — Taux annuel moyen de variation

| Period | 2-3 | 20-22 | 23 | 24 | 25-26 | 27 | 28 | 29 | 30 | 31-32 | 33 | 34 | 35-38 | 39 |
|---|---|---|---|---|---|---|---|---|---|---|---|---|---|---|
| (1936-1938)-1960 | 4.6 | 4.1 | 2.1 | 1.6 | ... | 5.0 | ... | ... | ... | 2.7 | 2.4 | 2.0 | ... | ... |
| (1936-1938)-1948 | 4.6 | 4.4 | 3.8 | 1.3 | ... | 3.6 | ... | ... | ... | 2.5 | 3.4 | 1.8 | ... | ... |
| 1950-1960 | 5.4 | 4.0 | 0.7 | 3.4 | ... | 7.2 | ... | ... | ... | 3.2 | 2.1 | 5.0 | ... | ... |
| 1948-1953 | 7.3 | 6.0 | 3.0 | — | ... | 3.5 | ... | ... | ... | 1.5 | 1.6 | 0.2 | ... | ... |
| 1954-1958 | 0.8 | −0.7 | −2.8 | 3.2 | ... | 9.3 | ... | ... | ... | 4.1 | −1.2 | 3.8 | ... | ... |
| 1958-1960 | 5.8 | 7.2 | 1.5 | 1.5 | 12.7 | 4.9 | 3.9 | −6.7 | 21.7 | 3.9 | 6.3 | 6.8 | 11.4 | 14.9 |

[1] Excludes Crude petroleum and natural gas (ISIC major group 13); includes Smelting and refining of copper (ISIC group 342).
[2] Excludes slaughtering of animals (part of ISIC group 201); Sawmilling (ISIC group 251) and smelting and refining of copper (part of ISIC group 342). Prior to 1957 includes Manufacture of gas (ISIC group 512) but excludes Wood products and furniture (ISIC major groups 25-26); Printing and publishing (ISIC major group 28); Leather and leather products except wearing apparel (ISIC major group 29); Rubber products (ISIC major group 30); Metal products (ISIC major groups 35-38) and Other manufacturing (ISIC major group 39).

[1] Non compris Pétrole brut et gaz naturel (CITI classe 13); y compris la Fonderie et l'affinage du cuivre (CITI groupe 342).
[2] Non compris l'abattage des animaux (dans CITI groupe 201), les Scieries (CITI groupe 251) et la Fonderie et l'affinage du cuivre (dans CITI groupe 342). Avant 1957, y compris la Fabrication du gaz (CITI groupe 512), mais non compris: Ouvrages en bois et meubles (CITI classes 25-26); Imprimerie et édition (CITI classe 28); Cuir et ouvrages en cuir, à l'exclusion des articles d'habillement (CITI classe 29); Ouvrages en caoutchouc (CITI classe 30); Ouvrages en métaux (CITI classes 35-38); Autres industries manufacturières (CITI classe 39).

## 3. INDEX NUMBERS OF INDUSTRIAL EMPLOYMENT — INDICES DE L'EMPLOI DANS L'INDUSTRIE

### A. Selected Divisions of Industrial Activity
### Quelques branches de l'activité industrielle

| Period / Période | Total | Mining [1] / Industries extractives [1] | Manu-facturing [2] / Industries manu-facturières [2] |
|---|---|---|---|
| ISIC — CITI | 1–3 | 1 | 2–3 |

a. Indexes — Indices (1958 = 100)

| Period / Période | Total | Mining [1] | Manufacturing [2] |
|---|---|---|---|
| 1938 | 63 | 100 | 55 |
| 1948 | 88 | 107 | 85 |
| 1949 | 90 | 105 | 87 |
| 1950 | 93 | 104 | 90 |
| 1951 | 94 | 107 | 91 |
| 1952 | 96 | 108 | 94 |
| 1953 | 96 | 107 | 93 |
| 1954 | 97 | 103 | 96 |
| 1955 | 98 | 104 | 96 |
| 1956 | 98 | 104 | 97 |
| 1957 | – 104 – | – 98 – | – 105 – |
| 1958 | 100 | 100 | 100 |
| 1959 | 100 | 95 | 102 |
| 1960 | 102 | 84 | 106 |
| 1961 | 107 | 81 | 112 |

b. Average Annual Rate of Change — Taux annuel moyen de variation

| Period / Période | Total | Mining [1] | Manufacturing [2] |
|---|---|---|---|
| 1938 – 1960 | 2.2 | −0.8 | 3.0 |
| 1938 – 1948 | 3.4 | 0.7 | 4.4 |
| 1950 – 1960 | 0.9 | −2.1 | 1.7 |
| 1948 – 1953 | 1.8 | — | 1.8 |
| 1954 – 1958 | 0.8 | −0.7 | 1.0 |
| 1958 – 1960 | 1.0 | −8.3 | 3.0 |

For footnotes see end of table.

### B. The Major Groups of Mining
### Les classes de la branche Industries extractives

| Period / Période | All mining [1] / Toutes industries extractives [1] | Coal mining / Extraction du charbon | Metal mining [1] / Extraction des minerais métalliques [1] | Crude petroleum and natural gas / Pétrole brut et gaz naturel | Other mining / Autres industries extractives |
|---|---|---|---|---|---|
| ISIC — CITI | 1 | 11 | 12 | 13 | 14–19 |

a. Indexes — Indices (1958 = 100)

| Period / Période | All mining [1] | Coal mining | Metal mining [1] | Crude petroleum and natural gas | Other mining |
|---|---|---|---|---|---|
| 1938 | 100 | 76 | 116 | ... | 133 |
| 1948 | 107 | 86 | 82 | 16 | 151 |
| 1949 | 105 | 80 | 74 | 30 | 155 |
| 1950 | 104 | 84 | 66 | 38 | 150 |
| 1951 | 107 | 90 | 65 | 63 | 148 |
| 1952 | 108 | 92 | 62 | 78 | 147 |
| 1953 | 107 | 91 | 59 | 71 | 148 |
| 1954 | 103 | 92 | 58 | 76 | 136 |
| 1955 | 104 | 93 | 65 | 81 | 134 |
| 1956 | 104 | 100 | 80 | 87 | 118 |
| 1957 | – 98 – | – 98 – | 98 | – 97 – | – 97 – |
| 1958 | 100 | 100 | 100 | 100 | 100 |
| 1959 | 95 | 94 | 99 | 96 | 92 |
| 1960 | 84 | 83 | 102 | 130 | 72 |
| 1961 | 81 | 77 | 113 | 123 | 66 |

b. Average Annual Rate of Change — Taux annuel moyen de variation

| Period / Période | All mining [1] | Coal mining | Metal mining [1] | Crude petroleum and natural gas | Other mining |
|---|---|---|---|---|---|
| 1938 – 1960 | −0.8 | 0.4 | −0.6 | ... | −2.8 |
| 1938 – 1948 | 0.7 | 1.2 | −3.4 | ... | 1.3 |
| 1950 – 1960 | −2.1 | −0.1 | 4.5 | 13.1 | −7.1 |
| 1948 – 1953 | — | 1.1 | −6.4 | 34.7 | −0.4 |
| 1954 – 1958 | −0.7 | 2.1 | 14.6 | 7.1 | −7.4 |
| 1958 – 1960 | −8.3 | −8.9 | 1.0 | 14.0 | −15.5 |

Pour les notes, voir au bas du tableau.

## C. The Major Groups of Manufacturing — Les classes de la branche Industries manufacturières

| Period / Période | Manufacturing[2] / Industries manufacturières[2] | Food, beverages and tobacco[3] / Industries alimentaires, boissons, tabac[3] | Textiles | Clothing, footwear and made-up textiles / Articles d'habillement, chaussures et ouvrages en tissu | Wood products and furniture[4] / Bois et meubles[4] | Paper and paper products / Papier et ouvrages en papier | Printing and publishing / Imprimerie et édition | Leather and leather products except wearing apparel / Cuir et articles en cuir, à l'exclusion des articles d'habillement | Rubber products / Ouvrages en caoutchouc | Chemicals and chemical, petroleum and coal products[5] / Produits chimiques et dérivés du pétrole et du charbon[5] | Non-metallic mineral products / Produits minéraux non métalliques | Basic metals / Métallurgie de base | Metal products / Ouvrages en métaux |
|---|---|---|---|---|---|---|---|---|---|---|---|---|---|
| ISIC — CITI | 2-3 | 20-22 | 23 | 24 | 25-26 | 27 | 28 | 29 | 30 | 31-32 | 33 | 34 | 35-38 |

### a. Indexes — Indices (1958 = 100)

| Period | 2-3 | 20-22 | 23 | 24 | 25-26 | 27 | 28 | 29 | 30 | 31-32 | 33 | 34 | 35-38 |
|---|---|---|---|---|---|---|---|---|---|---|---|---|---|
| 1938 | 55 | 59 | 44 | 52 | 53 | 72 | 86 | 89 | 78 | 41 | 80 | 107 | 26 |
| 1948 | 85 | 86 | 92 | 100 | 76 | 92 | 89 | 136 | 103 | 94 | 127 | 99 | 59 |
| 1949 | 87 | 86 | 100 | 111 | 80 | 86 | 89 | 138 | 108 | 96 | 130 | 92 | 63 |
| 1950 | 90 | 91 | 109 | 112 | 72 | 75 | 87 | 148 | 122 | 94 | 131 | 84 | 79 |
| 1951 | 91 | 88 | 112 | 115 | 78 | 94 | 82 | 130 | 99 | 83 | 133 | 96 | 70 |
| 1952 | 94 | 90 | 118 | 116 | 77 | 95 | 83 | 134 | 122 | 83 | 135 | 103 | 70 |
| 1953 | 93 | 88 | 112 | 114 | 76 | 98 | 84 | 133 | 124 | 86 | 132 | 105 | 75 |
| 1954 | 96 | 92 | 122 | 107 | 82 | 100 | 83 | 134 | 128 | 90 | 134 | 101 | 83 |
| 1955 | 96 | 92 | 123 | 108 | 80 | 93 | 85 | 127 | 129 | 95 | 137 | 94 | 85 |
| 1956 | 97 | 94 | 121 | 93 | 82 | 106 | 85 | 134 | 88 | 105 | 149 | 102 | 84 |
| 1957 | -105- | -100- | -106- | -112- | -109- | -104- | -97- | -105- | -112- | -99- | -113- | -101- | -102- |
| 1958 | 100 | 100 | 100 | 100 | 100 | 100 | 100 | 100 | 100 | 100 | 100 | 100 | 100 |
| 1959 | 102 | 100 | 102 | 99 | 123 | 105 | 107 | 89 | 102 | 102 | 103 | 102 | 102 |
| 1960 | 106 | 119 | 96 | 96 | 129 | 100 | 113 | 105 | 114 | 103 | 100 | 94 | 105 |
| 1961 | 112 | 135 | 102 | 103 | 127 | 100 | 118 | 88 | 115 | 105 | 105 | 98 | 112 |

### b. Average Annual Rate of Change — Taux annuel moyen de variation

| Period | 2-3 | 20-22 | 23 | 24 | 25-26 | 27 | 28 | 29 | 30 | 31-32 | 33 | 34 | 35-38 |
|---|---|---|---|---|---|---|---|---|---|---|---|---|---|
| 1938-1960 | 3.0 | 3.2 | 3.6 | 2.8 | 4.1 | 1.5 | 1.2 | 0.8 | 1.7 | 4.3 | 1.0 | -0.6 | 6.5 |
| 1938-1948 | 4.4 | 3.8 | 7.7 | 6.8 | 3.7 | 2.5 | 0.5 | 4.3 | 2.8 | 8.7 | 4.7 | -0.8 | 8.5 |
| 1950-1960 | 1.7 | 2.7 | -1.3 | -1.5 | 6.0 | 2.9 | 2.7 | -3.4 | -0.7 | 0.9 | -2.7 | 1.1 | 2.9 |
| 1948-1953 | 1.8 | 0.5 | 4.0 | 2.7 | — | 1.3 | -1.1 | -0.4 | 3.8 | -1.8 | 0.8 | 1.2 | 4.9 |
| 1954-1958 | 1.0 | 2.1 | -4.8 | -1.7 | 5.1 | — | 4.8 | -7.1 | -6.0 | 2.7 | -7.1 | -0.3 | 4.8 |
| 1958-1960 | 3.0 | 9.1 | -2.0 | -2.0 | 13.6 | — | 6.3 | 2.5 | 6.8 | 1.5 | — | -3.0 | 2.5 |

1 Excludes gold mining (part of ISIC group 122).
2 Excludes Other manufacturing (ISIC major group 39) in all years but includes cold storage plant operation (part of ISIC group 720) in 1938 and 1948-1950.
3 Includes extraction of vegetable oil (part of ISIC group 312) and cold storage plant operation (part of ISIC group 720), but excludes distillation of alcohol (part of ISIC group 211) in 1938 and 1948-1950.
4 Includes broom and brush manufacturing (part of ISIC group 399) in 1938 and 1948-1950.
5 Includes distilling of alcohol (part of ISIC group 211) but excludes extraction of vegetable oil (part of ISIC group 313) in 1938 and 1948-1950.

1 Non compris les industries extractives d'or (dans CITI groupe 122).
2 Non compris Autres industries manufacturières (CITI classe 39) pour toutes les années, mais y compris les entrepôts frigorifiques (dans CITI groupe 720) en 1938 et 1948-1950.
3 Y compris l'extraction des huiles végétales (dans CITI groupe 312) et les entrepôts frigorifiques (dans CITI groupe 720), mais non compris la distillation des alcools (dans CITI groupe 211) en 1938 et 1948-1950.
4 Y compris la fabrication des brosses et des balais (dans CITI groupe 399) en 1938 et 1948-1950.
5 Y compris la distillation des alcools (dans CITI groupe 211), mais non compris l'extraction des huiles végétales (dans CITI groupe 313) en 1938 et 1948-1950.

# CHILE

## 4. THE CHARACTERISTICS OF ALL MANUFACTURING ESTABLISHMENTS
### March–April 1937

## CARACTERISTIQUES DE TOUS LES ETABLISSEMENTS MANUFACTURIERS
### mars–avril 1937

Number of establishments in units; number of engaged, employees and operatives in thousands.

Nombre d'établissements en unités; nombre de personnes occupées, de salariés et d'ouvriers en milliers.

| tem of data | Manu-facturing Industries manufac-turières | Food beverages and tobacco Industries alimen-taires, boissons, tabac | Textiles | Clothing, footwear and made-up textiles Articles d'habil-lement, chaussures et ouvrages en tissu | Wood products and furniture Bois et meubles | Paper and paper products Papier et ouvrages en papier | Printing and publish-ing Im-primerie et édition | Leather and leather products except wearing apparel Cuir et articles en cuir, à l'exclu-sion des articles d'habil-lement | Rubber products Ouvrages en caout-chouc | Chemicals and chemical, petroleum and coal products Produits chi-miques et dérivés du pétrole et du charbon | Non-metallic mineral products Produits minéraux non métal-liques | Basic metals [1] Métal-lurgie de base [1] | Metal products Ouvrages en métaux | Other manu-factur-ing Autres in-dustries manufac-turières | Rubrique |
|---|---|---|---|---|---|---|---|---|---|---|---|---|---|---|---|
| ISIC | 2–3 | 20–22 | 23 | 24 | 25–26 | 27 | 28 | 29 | 30 | 31–32 | 33 | 34 | 35–38 | 39 | CITI |
| | | | | | | a. Absolute figures — Chiffres absolus | | | | | | | | | |
| Number of establishments. | 17 714 | 5 085 | 372 | 5 017 | 1 287 | 79 | 460 | 552 | 115 | 860 | 429 | 187 | 3 222 | 49 | Nombre d'établissements |
| Number of engaged.... | 136.0 | 34.7 | 15.4 | 22.4 | 8.2 | 3.1 | 7.2 | 3.4 | 0.4 | 9.5 | 9.0 | 10.6 | 11.6 | 0.5 | Nombre de personnes occupées |
| Number of employees... | 129.8 | 32.8 | 15.4 | 20.3 | 7.9 | 3.1 | 7.1 | 3.2 | 0.3 | 9.4 | 9.0 | 10.5 | 10.3 | 0.5 | Nombre de salariés |
| Number of operatives... | 116.4 | 29.1 | 14.4 | 18.7 | 7.4 | 2.9 | 5.2 | 2.8 | 0.3 | 7.9 | 8.4 | 9.8 | 9.2 | 0.3 | Nombre d'ouvriers |
| | | | | | | b. Structure | | | | | | | | | |
| Distribution in percent of number of engaged... | 100.0 | 25.5 | 11.3 | 16.5 | 6.0 | 2.3 | 5.3 | 2.5 | 0.3 | 6.9 | 6.7 | 7.8 | 8.5 | 0.4 | Répartition en pourcen-tage du nombre de personnes occupées |
| Employees as a percent of engaged......... | 95.4 | 94.5 | 100.0 | 90.6 | 96.3 | 100.0 | 98.6 | 94.1 | 75.0 | 98.9 | 100.0 | 99.0 | 88.8 | 100.0 | Salariés en pourcentage des personnes oc-cupées |
| Operatives as a percent of employees........ | 89.7 | 88.7 | 93.5 | 92.1 | 93.7 | 93.5 | 73.2 | 87.5 | 100.0 | 84.0 | 93.3 | 93.3 | 89.3 | 60.0 | Ouvriers en pourcentage des salariés |

[1] Excludes the smelting and refining of non-ferrous metals (ISIC major group 342).

[1] Non compris la fonderie et l'affinage des métaux non ferreux (CITI classe 342).

# 5. CHARACTERISTICS OF MANUFACTURING ESTABLISHMENTS ENGAGING FIVE OR MORE PERSONS

## CARACTERISTIQUES DES ETABLISSEMENTS MANUFACTURIERS OCCUPANT 5 PERSONNES OU PLUS

### 1957

Number of establishments in units; value added and wages and salaries in thousand million Pesos; number of engaged, employees and operatives in thousands; man-hours worked in millions; energy consumed in thousand metric tons of coal equivalents; electricity consumed in million KWH; capacity of installed power equipment in thousand horsepower; value added per engaged and wages and salaries per employee and per thousand operative man-hours in million Pesos; average annual man-hours per operative in thousands; energy consumed per engaged and per thousand operative man-hours in metric tons of coal equivalent; electricity consumed per engaged and per thousand operative man-hours in thousand KWH; capacity of installed power equipment per engaged and per thousand operative man-hours in horsepower.

Nombre d'établissements en unités; valeur ajoutée et traitements et salaires en milliards de pesos; nombre de personnes occupées, de salariés et d'ouvriers en milliers; heures de travail effectuées en millions; énergie consommée en milliers de tonnes métriques d'équivalent charbon; électricité consommée en millions de kWh; puissance installée en milliers de chevaux-vapeur; valeur ajoutée par personne occupée et traitements et salaires par salarié et par millier d'heures-ouvrier en millions de pesos; moyenne annuelle des heures de travail par ouvrier en milliers; énergie consommée par personne occupée et par millier d'heures-ouvrier en tonnes métriques d'équivalent charbon; électricité consommée par personne occupée et par millier d'heures-ouvrier en milliers de kWh; puissance installée par personne occupée et par millier d'heures-ouvrier en chevaux-vapeur.

| Item of data | Manufacturing Industries manufacturières | Food, beverages and tobacco Industries alimentaires, boissons, tabac | Textiles | Clothing, footwear and made-up textiles Articles d'habillement, chaussures et ouvrages en tissu | Wood products and furniture Bois et meubles | Paper and paper products Papier et ouvrages en papier | Printing and publishing Imprimerie et édition | Leather and leather products except wearing apparel Cuir et articles en cuir, à l'exclusion des articles d'habillement | Rubber products Ouvrages en caoutchouc | Chemicals and chemical, petroleum and coal products Produits chimiques et dérivés du pétrole et du charbon | Non-metallic mineral products Produits minéraux non métalliques | Basic metals [1] Métallurgie de base [1] | Metal products Ouvrages en métaux | Other manufacturing Autres industries manufacturières | Rubrique |
|---|---|---|---|---|---|---|---|---|---|---|---|---|---|---|---|
| ISIC | 2–3 | 20–22 | 23 | 24 | 25–26 | 27 | 28 | 29 | 30 | 31–32 | 33 | 34 | 35–38 | 39 | CITI |
| *a. Absolute Figures — Chiffres absolus* | | | | | | | | | | | | | | | |
| Number of establishments | 5 854 | 1 603 | 587 | 1 027 | 614 | 69 | 197 | 134 | 37 | 278 | 253 | 87 | 814 | 154 | Nombre d'établissements |
| Value added | 303.4 | 85.0 | 40.2 | 23.6 | 14.5 | 5.7 | 11.2 | 3.8 | 3.8 | 33.4 | 15.9 | 33.0 | 29.6 | 3.7 | Valeur ajoutée |
| Number of engaged (As of 15.XII.1957) | 216.5 | 44.3 | 38.3 | 29.4 | 16.9 | 3.5 | 8.2 | 3.4 | 2.1 | 13.5 | 12.9 | 11.5 | 28.8 | 3.7 | Nombre de personnes occupées (au 15.XII. 1957) |
| Employees: | | | | | | | | | | | | | | | Salariés: |
| Number (Average for year) | 206.6 | 41.5 | 37.6 | 26.7 | 15.7 | 3.4 | 8.0 | 3.2 | 1.9 | 13.2 | 12.7 | 11.4 | 27.8 | 3.5 | Nombre (Moyenne pour l'année) |
| Wages and salaries | 80.7 | 16.5 | 12.4 | 7.8 | 4.3 | 1.6 | 4.6 | 1.3 | 0.9 | 6.9 | 5.3 | 7.2 | 10.8 | 1.1 | Traitements et salaires |
| Operatives: | | | | | | | | | | | | | | | Ouvriers: |
| Number (As of 15.XII.1957) | 178.8 | 35.8 | 34.5 | 24.3 | 14.1 | 3.0 | 5.3 | 2.8 | 1.6 | 9.8 | 11.2 | 9.3 | 24.0 | 3.1 | Nombre (Au 15. XII. 1957) |
| Man-hours worked | 445.3 | 89.7 | 89.4 | 57.6 | 33.2 | 7.7 | 14.2 | 6.9 | 3.9 | 24.6 | 26.5 | 24.8 | 59.3 | 7.5 | Heures de travail effectuées |
| Wages and salaries | 55.5 | 11.5 | 9.5 | 5.9 | 3.2 | 1.2 | 2.6 | 0.9 | 0.6 | 3.6 | 3.7 | 4.6 | 7.4 | 0.8 | Traitements et salaires |
| Energy consumed | 888.1 | 214.6 | 127.6 | 10.3 | 8.6 | 19.8 | 3.2 | 8.7 | 10.6 | 92.5 | 257.1 | 97.0 | 35.0 | 4.6 | Energie consommée |
| Electricity consumed | 907.0 | 146.6 | 96.1 | 15.4 | 16.9 | 156.4 | 15.2 | 5.1 | 8.8 | 80.7 | 101.0 | 221.0 | 39.2 | 4.6 | Electricité consommée |
| Capacity of installed power equipment | 649.1 | 129.1 | 71.0 | 13.8 | 41.4 | 59.1 | 9.1 | 10.0 | 5.6 | 66.3 | 44.0 | 127.4 | 50.9 | 21.4 | Puissance installée |
| *b. Structure* | | | | | | | | | | | | | | | |
| Distribution in percent of: | | | | | | | | | | | | | | | Distribution en pourcentage: |
| Value added | 100.0 | 28.0 | 13.2 | 7.8 | 4.8 | 1.9 | 3.6 | 1.3 | 1.2 | 11.1 | 5.2 | 10.9 | 9.7 | 1.3 | Valeur ajoutée |
| Number of engaged | 100.0 | 20.4 | 17.7 | 13.6 | 7.8 | 1.6 | 3.7 | 1.6 | 0.9 | 6.3 | 5.9 | 5.3 | 13.3 | 1.8 | Nombre de personnes occupées |
| Per person engaged: | | | | | | | | | | | | | | | Par personne occupée: |
| Value added | 1.40 | 1.92 | 1.05 | 0.80 | 0.86 | 1.63 | 1.36 | 1.12 | 1.81 | 2.47 | 1.23 | 2.87 | 1.03 | 1.00 | Valeur ajoutée |
| Energy consumed | 4.10 | 4.84 | 3.33 | 0.35 | 0.51 | 5.66 | 0.39 | 2.56 | 5.05 | 6.85 | 19.93 | 8.43 | 1.22 | 0.84 | Energie consommée |
| Electricity consumed | 4.19 | 3.31 | 2.51 | 0.52 | 1.00 | 44.68 | 1.85 | 1.50 | 4.19 | 5.98 | 7.83 | 19.22 | 1.36 | 1.24 | Electricité consommée |
| Capacity of installed power equipment | 3.00 | 2.91 | 1.85 | 0.47 | 2.45 | 16.88 | 1.11 | 2.94 | 2.67 | 4.91 | 3.41 | 11.08 | 1.77 | 5.78 | Puissance installée |
| Employee as a percent of engaged | 95.4 | 93.7 | 98.2 | 90.8 | 92.9 | 97.1 | 97.6 | 94.1 | 90.5 | 97.8 | 98.4 | 99.1 | 96.5 | 94.6 | Salariés en pourcentage des personnes occupées |
| Value added per unit of wages and salaries | 3.76 | 5.15 | 3.24 | 3.02 | 3.37 | 3.56 | 2.43 | 2.92 | 4.22 | 4.84 | 3.00 | 4.58 | 2.74 | 3.36 | Valeur ajoutée par unité de traitements et salaires |
| Wages and salaries per employee | 0.39 | 0.40 | 0.33 | 0.29 | 0.27 | 0.47 | 0.58 | 0.41 | 0.47 | 0.52 | 0.42 | 0.63 | 0.39 | 0.31 | Traitements et salaires par salarié |
| Operatives as a percent of employees | 86.5 | 86.3 | 91.8 | 91.0 | 89.8 | 88.2 | 66.2 | 87.5 | 84.2 | 74.2 | 88.2 | 81.6 | 86.3 | 88.6 | Ouvriers en pourcentage des salariés |
| Average man-hours per operative | 2.49 | 2.50 | 2.59 | 2.37 | 2.35 | 2.57 | 2.68 | 2.46 | 2.44 | 2.51 | 2.37 | 2.67 | 2.47 | 2.42 | Heures de travail: moyenne par ouvrier |
| Per thousand operative man-hours: | | | | | | | | | | | | | | | Par millier d'heures-ouvrier: |
| Wages and salaries | 0.12 | 0.13 | 0.11 | 0.10 | 0.10 | 0.16 | 0.18 | 0.13 | 0.15 | 0.15 | 0.14 | 0.18 | 0.12 | 0.11 | Traitements et salaires |
| Energy consumed | 1.99 | 2.39 | 1.43 | 0.18 | 0.26 | 2.57 | 0.22 | 1.26 | 2.72 | 3.76 | 9.70 | 3.91 | 0.59 | 0.41 | Energie consommée |
| Electricity consumed | 2.04 | 1.63 | 1.07 | 0.27 | 0.51 | 20.31 | 1.07 | 0.74 | 2.26 | 3.28 | 3.81 | 8.91 | 0.66 | 0.61 | Electricité consommée |
| Capacity of installed power equipment | 1.46 | 1.44 | 0.79 | 0.24 | 1.25 | 7.68 | 0.64 | 1.45 | 1.44 | 2.70 | 1.66 | 5.14 | 0.86 | 2.85 | Puissance installée |

[1] Excludes the smelting and refining of copper (part of ISIC group 342).

[1] Non compris la fonderie et l'affinage du cuivre (dans CITI groupe 342).

# 6. FUELS AND ELECTRICITY CONSUMED BY MANUFACTURING ESTABLISHMENTS ENGAGING 5 OR MORE PERSONS
## COMBUSTIBLES ET ELECTRICITE CONSOMMES PAR LES ETABLISSEMENTS MANUFACTURIERS OCCUPANT 5 PERSONNES OU PLUS
### 1957

## A. Percentage Distribution of Purchased Energy Consumed According to Source
### Répartition en pourcentage de l'énergie achetée et consommée suivant la source

Quantities in thousand metric tons of coal equivalents.     Quantités en milliers de tonnes métriques d'équivalent charbon.

| Item of data | Manufacturing Industries manufacturières | Food, beverages and tobacco Industries alimentaires, boissons, tabac | Textiles | Clothing, footwear and made-up textiles Articles d'habillement, chaussures et ouvrages en tissu | Wood products and furniture Bois et meubles | Paper and paper products Papier et ouvrages en papier | Printing and publishing Imprimerie et édition | Leather and leather products except wearing apparel Cuir et articles en cuir, à l'exclusion des articles d'habillement | Rubber products Ouvrages en caoutchouc | Chemicals and chemical, petroleum and coal products Produits chimiques et dérivés du pétrole et du charbon | Non-metallic mineral products Produits minéraux non métalliques | Basic metals [1] Métallurgie de base [1] | Metal products Ouvrages en métaux | Other manufacturing Autres industries manufacturières | Rubrique |
|---|---|---|---|---|---|---|---|---|---|---|---|---|---|---|---|
| ISIC | 2–3 | 20–22 | 23 | 24 | 25–26 | 27 | 28 | 29 | 30 | 31–32 | 33 | 34 | 35 | 39 | CITI |
| **Total energy consumed:** | | | | | | | | | | | | | | | **Energie totale consomée:** |
| Quantity | 888.1 | 214.6 | 127.6 | 10.3 | 8.6 | 19.8 | 3.2 | 8.7 | 10.6 | 92.5 | 257.1 | 97.0 | 35.0 | 3.1 | Quantité |
| Percent of total in specified industry | 100.0 | 24.1 | 14.4 | 1.1 | 1.0 | 2.2 | 0.4 | 1.0 | 1.2 | 10.4 | 28.9 | 11.0 | 3.9 | 0.4 | Pourcentage du total par industrie indiquée |
| **Percent consumed as:** | | | | | | | | | | | | | | | **Pourcentage consommé sous forme de:** |
| Coal | 44.7 | 38.6 | 27.8 | 23.3 | 11.6 | 4.0 | 9.3 | 25.2 | 66.0 | 49.2 | 68.3 | 43.5 | 4.2 | 3.2 | Charbon |
| Coke | 1.1 | 1.1 | 0.5 | 0.9 | 1.1 | — | — | 1.2 | — | 1.0 | 0.3 | 1.0 | 10.0 | — | Coke |
| Refined oil fuels | 29.5 | 31.6 | 42.8 | 40.8 | 52.4 | 6.6 | 40.7 | 59.8 | 17.0 | 40.0 | 16.1 | 23.3 | 54.9 | 64.5 | Pétrole raffiné |
| Electricity purchased | 10.7 | 7.5 | 9.2 | 18.4 | 23.2 | 87.8 | 31.2 | 6.9 | 9.4 | 4.7 | 4.4 | 22.3 | 14.0 | 19.3 | Electricité achetée |
| Other fuels: [2] | 14.0 | 21.2 | 19.7 | 16.6 | 11.7 | 1.6 | 18.8 | 6.9 | 7.6 | 5.1 | 10.9 | 9.9 | 16.9 | 13.0 | Autres combustibles [2] |

For footnotes see end of table.     Pour les notes, voir au bas du tableau.

## B. Quantity and Value of Purchased Fuels Consumed and Electricity Purchased, Produced and Sold
### Quantité et valeur des combustibles achetés et consommés, et de l'électricité achetée, produite et vendue

Coal, coke and refined oil fuels in thousand metric tons; electricity in million KWH; other fuels in thousand metric tons of coal equivalent; values in million Pesos.     Charbon, coke et pétrole raffiné en milliers de tonnes métriques; électricité en millions de kWh; autres combustibles en milliers de tonnes métriques d'équivalent charbon; valeur en millions de pesos.

| Item of data | Manufacturing Industries manufacturières | Food, beverages and tobacco Industries alimentaires, boissons, tabac | Textiles | Clothing, footwear and made-up textiles Articles d'habillement, chaussures et ouvrages en tissu | Wood products and furniture Bois et meubles | Paper and paper products Papier et ouvrages en papier | Printing and publishing Imprimerie et édition | Leather and leather products except wearing apparel Cuir et articles en cuir, à l'exclusion des articles d'habillement | Rubber products Ouvrages en caoutchouc | Chemicals and chemical, petroleum and coal products Produits chimiques et dérivés du pétrole et du charbon | Non-metallic mineral products Produits minéraux non métalliques | Basic metals [1] Métallurgie de base [1] | Metal products Ouvrages en métaux | Other manufacturing Autres industries manufacturières | Rubrique |
|---|---|---|---|---|---|---|---|---|---|---|---|---|---|---|---|
| ISIC | 2–3 | 20–22 | 23 | 24 | 25–26 | 27 | 28 | 29 | 30 | 31–32 | 33 | 34 | 35–38 | 39 | CITI |
| **Coal:** | | | | | | | | | | | | | | | **Charbon:** |
| Quantity | 397.2 | 83.0 | 35.5 | 2.4 | 1.0 | 0.8 | 0.3 | 2.2 | 7.0 | 45.6 | 175.7 | 42.2 | 1.5 | — | Quantité |
| Value | 5 434 | 1 211 | 403 | 39 | 16 | 15 | 4 | 30 | 78 | 633 | 2 342 | 639 | 23 | 1 | Valeur |
| **Coke:** | | | | | | | | | | | | | | | **Coke:** |
| Quantity | 10.6 | 2.6 | 0.8 | 0.1 | 0.1 | — | — | 0.1 | — | 1.0 | 0.8 | 1.1 | 3.9 | 0.1 | Quantité |
| Value | 193 | 46 | 14 | 3 | 1 | — | — | 2 | — | 18 | 15 | 21 | 73 | — | Valeur |
| **Refined oil fuels:** | | | | | | | | | | | | | | | **Pétrole raffiné:** |
| Quantity | 175.3 | 45.2 | 36.4 | 2.8 | 3.0 | 0.9 | 0.8 | 3.5 | 1.2 | 24.7 | 27.6 | 15.1 | 12.8 | 1.3 | Quantité |
| Value | 6 581 | 1 781 | 1 168 | 120 | 154 | 40 | 49 | 135 | 53 | 867 | 1 041 | 590 | 532 | 51 | Valeur |
| **Electricity:** | | | | | | | | | | | | | | | **Electricité:** |
| Purchased: | | | | | | | | | | | | | | | Achetée: |
| Quantity | 757.2 | 129.6 | 94.0 | 15.4 | 15.8 | 138.9 | 7.8 | 5.1 | 8.0 | 34.4 | 91.7 | 172.9 | 39.0 | 4.6 | Quantité |
| Value | 7 727 | 1 211 | 1 012 | 230 | 228 | 997 | 108 | 76 | 81 | 468 | 934 | 1 757 | 553 | 72 | Valeur |
| Produced — quantity | 171.7 | 17.2 | 2.2 | — | 1.1 | 17.6 | 7.4 | — | 0.8 | 46.4 | 21.2 | 57.7 | 0.1 | — | Produite — quantité |
| Sold — quantity | 21.6 | 0.2 | — | — | — | — | — | — | — | — | 11.8 | 9.6 | — | — | Vendue — quantité |
| **Other fuels: [2]** | | | | | | | | | | | | | | | **Autres combustibles [2]:** |
| Quantity | 123.8 | 45.3 | 25.1 | 1.7 | 1.0 | 0.3 | 0.6 | 0.6 | 0.8 | 4.7 | 27.8 | 9.6 | 5.9 | 0.4 | Quantité |
| Value | 2 330 | 898 | 438 | 42 | 32 | 9 | 19 | 14 | 12 | 86 | 434 | 182 | 154 | 10 | Valeur |

[1] Excludes the smelting and refining of copper (part of ISIC group 342).
[2] Other fuels include wood.

[1] Non compris la fonderie et l'affinage du cuivre (dans CITI groupe 342).
[2] Les Autres combustibles comprennent le bois.

# 7. THE CHARACTERISTICS OF LARGE MANUFACTURING ESTABLISHMENTS
## CARACTERISTIQUES DES GRANDS ETABLISSEMENTS MANUFACTURIERS
### 1938, 1948, 1953

Number of establishments in units; value added and wages and salaries in million Pesos; number of employees and operatives in thousands; electricity consumed in million KWH; value added per employee and wages and salaries per employee and per operative in thousand Pesos; electricity consumed per employee and per operative in thousand KWH.

Nombre d'établissements en unités; valeur ajoutée et traitements et salaires en millions de pesos; nombre de salariés et d'ouvriers en milliers; électricité consommée en millions de kWh; valeur ajoutée par salarié et traitements et salaires par salarié et par ouvrier en milliers de pesos; électricité consommée par salarié et par ouvrier en milliers de kWh.

| Year and item of data | Manufacturing [1] Industries manufacturières [1] | Food, beverages and tobacco Industries alimentaires, boissons, tabac | Textiles | Clothing, footwear and made-up textiles Articles d'habillement, chaussures et ouvrages en tissu | Wood products and furniture Bois et meubles | Paper and paper products Papier et ouvrages en papier | Printing and publishing Imprimerie et édition | Leather and leather products except wearing apparel Cuir et articles en cuir, à l'exclusion des articles d'habillement | Rubber products Ouvrages en caoutchouc | Chemicals and chemical, petroleum and coal products Produits chimiques et dérivés du pétrole et du charbon | Non-metallic mineral products Produits minéraux non métalliques | Basic metals [1] Métallurgie de base [1] | Metal products Ouvrages en métaux | Other manufacturing Autres industries manufacturières | Année et rubrique |
|---|---|---|---|---|---|---|---|---|---|---|---|---|---|---|---|
| ISIC | 2–3 | 20–22 | 23 | 24 | 25–26 | 27 | 28 | 29 | 30 | 31–32 | 33 | 34 | 35–38 | 39 | CITI |
| a. Absolute Figures — Chiffres absolus | | | | | | | | | | | | | | | |
| **1938** | | | | | | | | | | | | | | | **1938** |
| Number of establishments | 3 539 | 1 374 | 256 | 208 | 380 | 326 | | 68 | 143 | 263 | 222 | 282 | | 17 | Nombre d'établissements |
| Value added | 1 648.7 | 702.8 | 195.3 | 91.9 | 90.0 | 138.5 | | 63.1 | | 137.4 | 90.0 | 130.6 | | 9.1 | Valeur ajoutée |
| Number of employees (Monthly average during year) | 97.8 | 24.8 | 15.5 | 10.6 | 7.9 | 9.3 | | 4.1 | | 5.4 | 8.4 | 11.2 | | 0.6 | Nombre de salariés (moyenne mensuelle pendant l'année) |
| Wages and salaries paid | 459.0 | 122.8 | 67.9 | 36.7 | 28.9 | 63.7 | | 10.6 | 3.6 | 28.7 | 40.1 | 52.5 | | 3.5 | Traitements et salaires payés |
| Operatives: Number (Monthly average during year) | 88.8 | 22.5 | 14.4 | 10.1 | 7.3 | 7.6 | | 3.8 | | 4.5 | 7.8 | 10.4 | | 0.4 | Ouvriers: Nombre (moyenne mensuelle pendant l'année) |
| Wages and salaries | 344.9 | 92.1 | 52.3 | 31.5 | 23.0 | 43.4 | | 11.5 | | 15.5 | 31.8 | 42.2 | | 1.6 | Traitements et salaires |
| Electricity consumed | 196.1 | 41.9 | 20.1 | 3.1 | 3.5 | 52.7 | | 2.5 | | 15.2 | 47.4 | 9.5 | | 0.2 | Electricité consommée |
| **1948** | | | | | | | | | | | | | | | **1948** |
| Number of establishments | 4 259 | 1 403 | 466 | 432 | 358 | 249 | | 339 | | 361 | 186 | 446 | | 19 | Nombre d'établissements |
| Value added | 12 627.6 | 3 282.1 | 2 647.6 | 948.0 | 572.7 | 261.2 | 498.1 | 473.1 | | 1 444.6 | 840.1 | 940.9 | 678.6 | 40.6 | Valeur ajoutée |
| Number of employees (Monthly average during year) | 168.6 | 36.2 | 32.5 | 20.3 | 11.2 | 3.2 | 7.0 | 3.8 | 2.1 | 12.2 | 13.3 | 26.5 | | 0.3 | Nombre de salariés (moyenne mensuelle pendant l'année) |
| Wages and salaries paid | 4 486.1 | 899.0 | 898.1 | 423.7 | 216.5 | 362.6 | | 88.0 | 63.0 | 390.1 | 336.9 | 803.9 | | 4.3 | Traitements et salaires payés |
| Operatives: Number (Monthly average during year) | 148.6 | 31.7 | 30.1 | 18.7 | 10.2 | 7.0 | | 5.3 | | 9.6 | 12.1 | 23.6 | | 0.3 | Ouvriers: Nombre (moyenne mensuelle pendant l'année) |
| Wages and salaries | 3 282.2 | 634.3 | 734.3 | 330.7 | 164.5 | 193.8 | | 112.6 | | 215.2 | 268.4 | 624.6 | | 3.8 | Traitements et salaires |
| Electricity consumed | 456.9 | 63.5 | 64.3 | 7.7 | 9.5 | 62.7 | | 9.5 | | 85.3 | 104.3 | 50.0 | | 0.1 | Electricité consommée |
| **1953** | | | | | | | | | | | | | | | **1953** |
| Number of establishments | 4 109 | 1 198 | 532 | 628 | 376 | 66 | 154 | 133 | 29 | 263 | 190 | 37 | 407 | 96 | Nombre d'établissements |
| Value added | 40 828.7 | 10 851.1 | 7 844.8 | 2 876.3 | 1 555.3 | 1 011.0 | 1 749.3 | 787.3 | 542.0 | 4 341.3 | 2 457.1 | 3 385.2 | 3 178.9 | 249.1 | Valeur ajoutée |
| Number of employees (Monthly average during year) | 186.6 | 37.4 | 39.6 | 23.2 | 11.2 | 3.2 | 6.8 | 4.0 | 2.2 | 11.2 | 13.8 | 11.7 | 20.5 | 1.8 | Nombre de salariés (moyenne mensuelle pendant l'année) |
| Wages and salaries paid | 14 062.6 | 2 891.6 | 2 823.1 | 1 174.4 | 578.3 | 290.6 | 820.2 | 284.6 | 154.8 | 1 013.2 | 939.0 | 1 383.9 | 1 630.5 | 78.4 | Traitements et salaires payés |
| Operatives: Number (Monthly average during year) | 164.1 | 32.6 | 36.6 | 21.5 | 10.1 | 2.8 | 3.9 | 3.6 | 2.0 | 8.7 | 12.5 | 9.8 | 18.4 | 1.6 | Ouvriers: Nombre (moyenne mensuelle pendant l'année) |
| Wages and salaries | 10 098.2 | 2 033.8 | 2 294.7 | 926.4 | 435.3 | 192.9 | 358.1 | 213.0 | 108.2 | 530.4 | 702.9 | 970.8 | 1 272.5 | 59.2 | Traitements et salaires |
| Electricity consumed | 758.1 | 93.1 | 117.0 | 8.6 | 13.6 | 75.9 | 5.0 | 5.8 | 7.5 | 34.8 | 167.5 | 202.5 | 23.4 | 3.4 | Electricité consommée |

For footnotes see end of table.

Pour les notes, voir au bas du tableau.

## 7. THE CHARACTERISTICS OF LARGE MANUFACTURING ESTABLISHMENTS (continued)
## CARACTERISTIQUES DES GRANDS ETABLISSEMENTS MANUFACTURIERS (suite)
### 1938, 1948, 1953

*b. Structure*

| Year and item of data | Manufacturing [1] / Industries manufacturières [1] | Food, beverages and tobacco / Industries alimentaires, boissons, tabac | Textiles | Clothing, footwear and made-up textiles / Articles d'habillement, chaussures et ouvrages en tissu | Wood products and furniture / Bois et meubles | Paper and paper products / Papier et ouvrages en papier | Printing and publishing / Imprimerie et édition | Leather and leather products except wearing apparel / Cuir et articles en cuir, à l'exclusion des articles d'habillement | Rubber products / Ouvrages en caoutchouc | Chemicals and chemical, petroleum and coal products / Produits chimiques et dérivés du pétrole et du charbon | Non-metallic mineral products / Produits minéraux non métalliques | Basic metals [1] / Métallurgie de base [1] | Metal products / Ouvrages en métaux | Other manufacturing / Autres industries manufacturières | Année et rubrique |
|---|---|---|---|---|---|---|---|---|---|---|---|---|---|---|---|
| ISIC | 2-3 | 20-22 | 23 | 24 | 25-26 | 27 | 28 | 29 | 30 | 31-32 | 33 | 34 | 35-38 | 39 | CITI |
| **1938** | | | | | | | | | | | | | | | **1938** |
| Distribution in percent of: | | | | | | | | | | | | | | | Distribution en pourcentage: |
|  Value added | 100.0 | 42.6 | 11.8 | 5.6 | 5.5 | 8.4 | | 3.8 | | 8.3 | 5.5 | 7.9 | | 0.6 | Valeur ajoutée |
|  Number of employees | 100.0 | 25.3 | 15.9 | 10.8 | 8.1 | 9.5 | | 4.2 | | 5.5 | 8.6 | 11.4 | | 0.7 | Nombre de salariés |
| Per employee: | | | | | | | | | | | | | | | Par salarié: |
|  Value added | 16.8 | 28.3 | 12.6 | 8.7 | 11.4 | 14.9 | | 15.4 | | 25.4 | 10.7 | 11.7 | | 15.2 | Valeur ajoutée |
|  Wages and salaries | 4.7 | 5.0 | 4.4 | 3.5 | 3.6 | 6.8 | | 3.5 | | 5.3 | 4.8 | 4.7 | | 5.8 | Traitements et salaires |
|  Electricity consumed | 2.0 | 1.7 | 1.3 | 0.3 | 0.4 | 5.7 | | 0.6 | | 2.8 | 5.6 | 0.8 | | 0.3 | Électricité consommée |
| Value added per unit of wages and salaries | 3.59 | 5.72 | 2.88 | 3.46 | 3.11 | 2.17 | | 3.46 | | 4.79 | 2.24 | 2.49 | | 2.60 | Valeur ajoutée par unité de traitements et salaires |
| Operatives as a percent of employees | 90.8 | 90.7 | 92.9 | 95.3 | 92.4 | 81.7 | | 92.7 | | 83.3 | 92.8 | 92.8 | | 66.7 | Ouvriers en pourcentage des salariés |
| Per operative: | | | | | | | | | | | | | | | Par ouvrier: |
|  Wages and salaries | 3.9 | 4.1 | 3.6 | 3.1 | 3.2 | 5.7 | | 3.0 | | 3.4 | 4.1 | 4.0 | | 4.0 | Traitements et salaires |
|  Electricity consumed | 2.2 | 1.9 | 1.4 | 0.3 | 0.5 | 6.9 | | 0.6 | | 3.4 | 6.1 | 0.9 | | 0.5 | Électricité consommée |
| **1948** | | | | | | | | | | | | | | | **1948** |
| Distribution in percent of: | | | | | | | | | | | | | | | Distribution en pourcentage: |
|  Value added | 100.0 | 25.9 | 21.0 | 7.5 | 4.6 | 2.0 | 4.0 | 3.7 | | 11.5 | 6.6 | 7.5 | 5.3 | 0.4 | Valeur ajoutée |
|  Number of employees | 100.0 | 21.4 | 19.3 | 12.0 | 6.7 | 1.9 | 4.1 | 2.3 | 1.2 | 7.3 | 7.9 | 15.7 | | 0.2 | Nombre de salariés |
| Per employee: | | | | | | | | | | | | | | | Par salarié: |
|  Value added | 74.9 | 90.7 | 81.5 | 46.7 | 51.1 | 81.6 | 71.2 | 80.2 | | 118.4 | 63.2 | 61.1 | | 135.3 | Valeur ajoutée |
|  Wages and salaries | 26.6 | 24.8 | 27.6 | 20.9 | 19.3 | 35.5 | | 23.2 | 30.0 | 32.0 | 25.3 | 30.3 | | 14.3 | Traitements et salaires |
|  Electricity consumed | 2.7 | 1.8 | 2.0 | 0.4 | 0.8 | 6.1 | | 1.6 | | 7.0 | 7.8 | 1.9 | | 0.3 | Électricité consommée |
| Value added per unit of wages and salaries | 2.81 | 3.65 | 2.95 | 2.24 | 2.64 | 2.09 | | 3.13 | | 3.70 | 2.49 | 2.01 | | 9.44 | Valeur ajoutée par unité de traitements et salaires |
| Operatives as a percent of employees | 88.1 | 87.6 | 92.6 | 92.1 | 91.1 | 68.6 | | 89.8 | | 78.7 | 91.0 | 89.0 | | 100.0 | Ouvriers en pourcentage des salariés |
| Per operative: | | | | | | | | | | | | | | | Par ouvrier: |
|  Wages and salaries | 22.1 | 20.0 | 24.4 | 17.7 | 16.1 | 27.7 | | 21.2 | | 22.4 | 22.2 | 26.5 | | 12.7 | Traitements et salaires |
|  Electricity consumed | 3.1 | 2.0 | 2.1 | 0.4 | 0.9 | 9.0 | | 1.8 | | 8.9 | 8.6 | 2.1 | | 0.3 | Électricité consommée |
| **1953** | | | | | | | | | | | | | | | **1953** |
| Distribution in percent of: | | | | | | | | | | | | | | | Distribution en pourcentage: |
|  Value added | 100.0 | 26.5 | 19.2 | 7.1 | 3.8 | 2.5 | 4.3 | 1.9 | 1.3 | 10.6 | 6.1 | 8.3 | 7.7 | 0.7 | Valeur ajoutée |
|  Number of employees | 100.0 | 20.0 | 21.2 | 12.4 | 6.0 | 1.8 | 3.6 | 2.2 | 1.1 | 6.0 | 7.4 | 6.3 | 11.0 | 1.0 | Nombre de salariés |
| Per employee: | | | | | | | | | | | | | | | Par salarié: |
|  Value added | 218.8 | 290.1 | 198.1 | 124.0 | 138.9 | 315.9 | 257.2 | 196.8 | 246.4 | 387.6 | 178.0 | 289.3 | 155.1 | 138.4 | Valeur ajoutée |
|  Wages and salaries | 75.4 | 77.3 | 71.3 | 50.6 | 51.6 | 90.8 | 120.6 | 71.2 | 70.4 | 90.5 | 68.0 | 118.3 | 79.5 | 43.6 | Traitements et salaires |
|  Electricity consumed | 4.1 | 2.5 | 3.0 | 0.4 | 1.2 | 23.7 | 0.7 | 1.4 | 3.4 | 3.1 | 12.1 | 17.3 | 1.1 | 1.9 | Électricité consommée |
| Value added per unit of wages and salaries | 2.90 | 3.75 | 2.78 | 2.45 | 2.69 | 3.48 | 2.13 | 2.77 | 3.50 | 4.28 | 2.62 | 2.45 | 1.95 | 3.18 | Valeur ajoutée par unité de traitements et salaires |
| Operatives as a percent of employees | 87.9 | 87.2 | 92.4 | 92.7 | 90.2 | 87.5 | 57.4 | 90.0 | 90.9 | 77.7 | 90.6 | 83.8 | 89.8 | 88.9 | Ouvriers en pourcentage des salariés |
| Per operative: | | | | | | | | | | | | | | | Par ouvrier: |
|  Wages and salaries | 61.5 | 62.4 | 62.7 | 43.1 | 43.1 | 68.9 | 91.8 | 59.2 | 54.1 | 61.0 | 56.2 | 99.1 | 69.2 | 37.0 | Traitements et salaires |
|  Electricity consumed | 4.6 | 2.8 | 3.2 | 0.4 | 1.3 | 27.1 | 1.3 | 1.6 | 3.8 | 4.0 | 13.4 | 20.7 | 1.3 | 2.1 | Électricité consommée |

[1] Excludes the smelting and refining of non-ferrous metals (part of ISIC group 342).

[1] Non compris la fonderie et l'affinage des métaux non ferreux (dans CITI groupe 342).

## 8. QUANTITY AND VALUE OF ELECTRICITY PURCHASED AND PRODUCED BY LARGE MANUFACTURING ESTABLISHMENTS

## QUANTITE ET VALEUR DE L'ELECTRICITE ACHETEE ET PRODUITE PAR LES GRANDS ETABLISSEMENTS MANUFACTURIERS

### 1938, 1948, 1953

Quantities in million KWH; values in million Pesos.　　　　　　　　　　Quantités en millions de kWh; valeur en millions de pesos.

| Year and source of energy | Manufacturing / Industries manufacturières | Food beverages and tobacco / Industries alimentaires, boissons, tabac | Textiles | Clothing, footwear and made-up textiles / Articles d'habillement, chaussures et ouvrages en tissu | Wood products and furniture / Bois et meubles | Paper and paper products / Papier et ouvrages en papier | Printing and publishing / Imprimerie et édition | Leather and leather products except wearing apparel / Cuir et articles en cuir, à l'exclusion des articles d'habillement | Rubber products / Ouvrages en caoutchouc | Chemicals and chemical, petroleum and coal products / Produits chimiques et dérivés du pétrole et du charbon | Non-metallic mineral products / Produits minéraux non métalliques | Basic metals [1] / Métallurgie de base [1] | Metal products / Ouvrages en métaux | Other manufacturing / Autres industries manufacturières | Année et source d'énergie |
|---|---|---|---|---|---|---|---|---|---|---|---|---|---|---|---|
| ISIC | 2–3 | 20–22 | 23 | 24 | 25–26 | 27 | 28 | 29 | 30 | 31–32 | 33 | 34 | 35–38 | 39 | CITI |
| **1938 Purchased:** | | | | | | | | | | | | | | | **1938 Achetée:** |
| Quantity | 115.0 | 25.1 | 19.7 | 2.7 | 2.1 | 2.7 | | 2.3 | | 7.7 | 46.7 | 5.8 | | 0.2 | Quantité |
| Value | 32.2 | 8.6 | 7.1 | 1.3 | 1.2 | 1.5 | | 1.3 | | 2.9 | 5.9 | 2.3 | | 0.1 | Valeur |
| Produced — quantity | 80.9 | 16.8 | 0.4 | 0.3 | 1.4 | 50.0 | | 0.2 | | 7.5 | 0.7 | 3.6 | | — | Produite — quantité |
| **1948 Purchased:** | | | | | | | | | | | | | | | **1948 Achetée:** |
| Quantity | 323.7 | 55.3 | 56.2 | 6.9 | 5.8 | 5.2 | | 9.5 | | 52.6 | 82.4 | 49.7 | | 0.1 | Quantité |
| Value | 216.6 | 44.2 | 39.8 | 7.7 | 6.0 | 5.4 | | 7.3 | | 24.4 | 44.5 | 37.2 | | 0.1 | Valeur |
| Produced — quantity | 133.0 | 8.2 | 8.0 | 0.8 | 3.7 | 57.4 | | 0.1 | | 32.7 | 21.8 | 0.3 | | — | Produite — quantité |
| **1953 Purchased:** | | | | | | | | | | | | | | | **1953 Achetée:** |
| Quantity | 669.3 | 82.1 | 110.3 | 8.2 | 10.4 | 75.8 | 5.0 | 5.8 | 7.5 | 33.0 | 133.9 | 171.1 | 22.9 | 3.3 | Quantité |
| Value | 862.0 | 175.1 | 217.7 | 17.1 | 23.6 | 48.3 | 10.2 | 11.4 | 11.4 | 45.4 | 118.5 | 135.7 | 41.9 | 5.7 | Valeur |
| Produced — quantity | 89.0 | 11.0 | 6.7 | 0.4 | 3.2 | 0.1 | 0.1 | 0.1 | — | 1.8 | 33.6 | 31.4 | 0.5 | 0.1 | Produite — quantité |

[1] Excludes the smelting and refining of copper (part of ISIC major group 342).

[1] Non compris la fonderie et l'affinage du cuivre (dans CITI group 342).

## CHINA (Taiwan) — CHINE (Taïwan)

### Gross Domestic Product and Fixed Capital Formation

The data shown in Table 1 on the gross domestic product and gross fixed capital formation are from the reply of the Directorate-General of Budgets, Accounts and Statistics, Executive Yuan, Taipei, Taiwan, Republic of China to the United Nations national accounts questionnaire. Official estimates are published annually by the Directorate in its *Statistical Abstract of the Republic of China*.

### Index Numbers of Industrial Production

The index numbers which appear in Table 2 have been derived mainly from indexes of industrial production that are issued in *Taiwan Production Statistics Monthly*, Ministry of Economic Affairs and Bank of Taiwan, Taipei, and that are supplied by the Directorate-General of Budgets, Accounts and Statistics in correspondence with the Statistical Office of the United Nations.

The index numbers are computed as base-weighted arithmetic averages, starting from series of relatives on quantity produced of individual commodities. The weighting pattern for constructing indexes for both detailed and broad classes of industrial activity is based on value added, at factor cost, during 1954, which was computed from the results of the 1954 Census described below.

Changes in the series of relatives utilized in compiling the index are made occasionally in order to exclude commodities no longer produced, or to include products which have been newly developed since 1954. As a result, the number of products for which relatives are included in the indexes has increased from 117 to 160. The weights for the relatives on new products, i.e. value added in the production of these commodities are calculated in terms of the output of the year after the commencement of production of these commodities. Indexes of wholesale prices are utilized to convert the value added into 1954 prices. Further details concerning the indexes may be found in any issue of *Taiwan Production Statistics Monthly*.

### Index Numbers of Industrial Employment

The index numbers of industrial employment presented in Table 3 were calculated from absolute figures of the number of employees published in *Industry of Free China*, Taipei, Taiwan. The data for 1952-1960 and for 1960-1961 were based on two different surveys. Figures based on each of the surveys are available for 1960. It was therefore possible to link, at 1960 the indexes of the new series to those of the old series which is based on 1958 as 100.

### Produit intérieur brut et formation brute de capital fixe

Les données du tableau 1, relatives au produit intérieur brut et à la formation brute de capital fixe intérieur, sont tirées de la réponse de la Direction générale du budget, de la comptabilité et de la statistique, Yuan exécutif, Taïpeh, Taïwan, République de Chine, au questionnaire de l'ONU sur la comptabilité nationale. Des estimations officielles sont publiées chaque année par la Direction générale dans son *Statistical Abstract of the Republic of China*.

### Indices de la production industrielle

Les indices du tableau 2 sont tirés en grande partie des indices de la production industrielle publiés dans *Taiwan Production Statistics Monthly*, Ministère des affaires économiques et Banque de Taïwan, Taïpeh; la Direction générale du budget, de la comptabilité et de la statistique les communique par correspondance au Bureau de statistique de l'ONU.

Ces indices sont des moyennes arithmétiques à pondération fixe établies à partir de séries de rapports fondés sur le volume de la production de chaque marchandise. Pour la pondération des indices détaillés et des indices plus larges de l'activité industrielle, on a pris la valeur ajoutée en 1954, au coût des facteurs, qui a été calculée d'après les résultats du recensement de 1954 dont il est question ci-après.

On a parfois apporté des modifications aux séries de rapports utilisées pour calculer les indices de manière à en exclure les marchandises qui ne sont plus produites ou à y inclure des articles dont la production n'a commencé qu'à partir de 1954. En conséquence, le nombre de produits pour lesquels des rapports ont été calculés est passé de 117 à 160. Les coefficients de pondération affectés aux rapports concernant les nouveaux produits, c'est-à-dire la valeur ajoutée découlant de la production de ces marchandises, sont calculés à partir des données obtenues pendant la deuxième année de production de ces marchandises. On a utilisé des indices de prix de gros pour convertir la valeur ajoutée aux prix de 1954. Pour plus de détails sur ces indices, voir n'importe quel numéro de *Taiwan Production Statistics Monthly*.

### Indices de l'emploi dans l'industrie

Les indices de l'emploi dans l'industrie, présentés au tableau 3, ont été calculés à partir de chiffres absolus indiquant le nombre de salariés et publiés dans *Industry of Free China*, Taïpeh, Taïwan. Les données pour 1952-1960 et 1960-1961 sont fondées sur deux enquêtes différentes. Comme on disposait, pour 1960, de chiffres fournis séparément par les deux enquêtes, on a pu raccorder la nouvelle série d'indices à l'ancienne série (1958 = 100) au niveau de 1960.

## Characteristics and Structure of Industrial Activity

The figures set out in Table 4 are derived from the results of a census taken for 1954 which were published in *General Report on Industry and Commerce, Census of Taiwan, 1954* by the Executive Group of ICCT, Taipei, May 1956. All industrial establishments were covered in the Census except co-operatives affiliated with the government or related agencies, work shops operated by relief organizations or in prisons, itinerant repair men and unidentified part-time household industries.

The definitions of the items of data for which figures are shown in Table 4 are consistent, on the whole, with the International Standards in Basic Industrial Statistics. The figures of value added were computed by the Statistical Office of the United Nations by subtracting the cost of raw materials, fuels and power consumed in production from the receipts from sales of all goods, adjusted for changes in the value of inventories of finished and unfinished products, and from services rendered. Only persons who worked at least ten days in December 1954 were counted in the number of engaged or employees. Except for the electricity-producing industry, capacity of installed power equipment is the sum of the rated horsepowers of prime movers and electric motors in use for operating machinery other than electric generators. In the case of the electricity-producing industry, prime movers motivating electric generators are included.

The figures relating to the year 1959 and given in Table 5 are obtained from *Report on Mining and Manufacturing Survey in Taiwan, Vol. 1.* The survey was taken jointly by the Statistics Office, Ministry of Economic Affairs and Comptroller's Office, Department of Reconstruction and covered all establishments of mining and public utilities and selected establishments of manufacturing comprising about 76 percent of all establishments engaged in that activity. Establishments engaged in printing, publishing and bookbinding, or the manufacture and repair of furniture or the manufacturing of clothing were excluded from the coverage of the survey. In addition, it is likely that the type of establishments excluded from the 1954 Census were also excluded from the 1959 survey. The number of persons engaged shown in the table relate to the end of December, 1959. The figures of value added were published in the *Report* and are given net of indirect taxes. The definitions of the items of data are consistent with those for the 1954 Census and with the International Standards in Basic Industrial Statistics.

## Caractéristiques et structure de l'activité industrielle

Les chiffres du tableau 4 sont tirés des résultats d'un recensement effectué en 1954, qui ont été publiés dans *General Report on Industry and Commerce, Census of Taiwan, 1954* (Executive Group of ICCT), Taïpeh, en mai 1956. Tous les établissements ont été recensés, sauf les coopératives contrôlées par le gouvernement ou par des organismes gouvernementaux, les ateliers exploités par des organisations de secours, les ateliers des prisons, les réparateurs ambulants et certaines industries familiales travaillant à temps partiel, non spécifiées.

Les définitions des rubriques pour lesquelles des chiffres sont fournis au tableau 4 sont conformes, dans l'ensemble, aux Normes internationales relatives aux statistiques industrielles de base. Les chiffres de la valeur ajoutée ont été calculés par le Bureau de statistique de l'ONU d'après la formule suivante : recettes provenant de toutes les ventes de marchandises, ajustées en fonction des variations de la valeur des stocks de produits finis et non finis, plus recettes provenant des services fournis, moins coût des matières premières, des combustibles et de l'énergie consommés pour la production. Seules les personnes qui ont travaillé 10 jours au moins en décembre 1954 ont été comprises parmi les personnes occupées ou les salariés. Sauf en ce qui concerne la production d'électricité, la puissance installée est la puissance nominale de tous les moteurs primaires et moteurs électriques en service qui actionnent des machines autres que des générateurs électriques. Dans le cas de l'industrie productrice d'électricité, on a compté la puissance des moteurs primaires actionnant des générateurs électriques.

Les chiffres du tableau 5 relatifs à 1959 sont tirés de *Report on Mining and Manufacturing Survey in Taiwan, Vol. 1.* L'enquête dont il y est question a été effectuée conjointement par le Bureau de statistique, Ministère des affaires économiques, et le Bureau du Contrôleur, Département de la Reconstruction; elle portait sur tous les établissements des industries extractives et des services d'utilité publique, ainsi que sur certains établissements des industries manufacturières représentant environ 76 p. 100 de l'ensemble des établissements de cette branche d'activité. Les établissements dont l'activité relève de l'imprimerie, de l'éditon ou de la reliure, de la fabrication ou de la réparation des meubles ou de la confection d'articles d'habillement, étaient exclus du champ de l'enquête. En outre, il est probable que les types d'établissements exclus du recensement de 1954 ont été exclus également de l'enquête de 1959. Le nombre de personnes occupées indiqué dans le tableau se rapporte à la fin de décembre 1959. Les chiffres de la valeur ajoutée ont été publiés dans le *Report;* ils ont été établis après déduction des impôts indirects. Les définitions des rubriques sont conformes à celles du recensement de 1954 et aux Normes internationales relatives aux statistiques industrielles de base.

## 1. THE GROSS DOMESTIC PRODUCT AND GROSS DOMESTIC FIXED CAPITAL FORMATION
## LE PRODUIT INTERIEUR BRUT ET LA FORMATION BRUTE DE CAPITAL FIXE INTERIEUR

Million New Taiwan dollars                                                    Millions de nouveaux dollars de Taïwan

### A. Expenditure on the Gross Domestic Product at Market Prices
### Dépenses relatives au produit intérieur brut aux prix du marché

| Item of data and year / Rubrique et année | Total [1] | Consumption / Consommation | | Gross Domestic Capital Formation / Formation brute de capital intérieur | | Net exports of goods and services / Exportations nettes de biens et de services | |
|---|---|---|---|---|---|---|---|
| | | Total | Government / Etat | Total | Fixed / Fixe | Exports less imports / Exportations moins importations | Exports / Exportations |
| *a. At Current Prices — Aux prix courants* | | | | | | | |
| **Absolute figures — Chiffres absolus** | | | | | | | |
| 1951 | 10 821 | 9 285 | 1 875 | 1 792 | 1 308 | −525 | 1 137 |
| 1952 | 15 750 | 13 647 | 2 693 | 2 887 | 2 019 | −773 | 1 432 |
| 1953 | 21 203 | 18 911 | 3 145 | 3 519 | 2 540 | −1 249 | 2 079 |
| 1954 | 23 158 | 21 254 | 3 935 | 3 923 | 2 737 | −2 107 | 1 631 |
| 1955 | 27 889 | 24 677 | 4 792 | 4 264 | 3 487 | −1 114 | 2 122 |
| 1956 | 32 302 | 29 164 | 6 132 | 4 858 | 4 007 | −1 667 | 2 189 |
| 1957 | 38 049 | 34 119 | 7 125 | 6 253 | 5 044 | −2 323 | 4 320 |
| 1958 | 41 673 | 37 114 | 8 296 | 7 574 | 6 381 | −3 074 | 4 603 |
| 1959 | 48 697 | 43 234 | 9 798 | 9 718 | 8 478 | −4 451 | 6 429 |
| 1960 | 59 934 | 51 544 | 10 856 | 12 989 | 10 598 | −4 693 | 7 033 |
| 1961 | 66 409 | 56 739 | 11 976 | 14 608 | 11 748 | −4 877 | 8 991 |
| **Percentage distribution of average annual expenditure — Distribution en pourcentage des dépenses annuelles moyennes** | | | | | | | |
| 1951 – 1960 | 100.0 | 88.8 | 18.4 | 18.1 | 14.6 | −6.9 | 10.3 |
| 1951 | 100.0 | 88.0 | 17.8 | 17.0 | 12.4 | −5.0 | 10.8 |
| 1953 | 100.0 | 89.3 | 14.8 | 16.6 | 12.0 | −5.9 | 9.8 |
| 1954 | 100.0 | 92.1 | 17.1 | 17.0 | 11.9 | −9.1 | 7.1 |
| 1958 | 100.0 | 89.2 | 19.9 | 18.2 | 15.3 | −7.4 | 11.1 |
| 1960 | 100.0 | 86.1 | 18.1 | 21.7 | 17.7 | −7.8 | 11.7 |
| *b. At Prices of 1952 — Aux prix de 1952* | | | | | | | |
| **Absolute figures — Chiffres absolus** | | | | | | | |
| 1951 | 14 025 | 12 133 | 2 297 | 2 207 | 1 611 | −646 | 1 400 |
| 1952 | 15 750 | 13 647 | 2 693 | 2 887 | 2 019 | −773 | 1 432 |
| 1953 | 17 437 | 15 270 | 2 753 | 3 477 | 2 577 | −1 334 | 2 344 |
| 1954 | 18 900 | 17 426 | 3 335 | 3 453 | 2 388 | −2 069 | 1 759 |
| 1955 | 20 318 | 18 466 | 3 637 | 2 845 | 2 233 | −1 055 | 2 165 |
| 1956 | 21 134 | 19 838 | 4 256 | 3 024 | 2 430 | −1 673 | 2 351 |
| 1957 | 22 659 | 21 579 | 4 581 | 3 540 | 2 752 | −2 460 | 4 215 |
| 1958 | 24 098 | 22 618 | 5 095 | 4 222 | 3 471 | −2 823 | 5 193 |
| 1959 | 25 881 | 24 620 | 5 683 | 5 113 | 4 465 | −3 966 | 4 896 |
| 1960 | 27 897 | 26 591 | 5 750 | 6 243 | 5 071 | −5 003 | 4 804 |
| 1961 | 30 148 | 28 503 | 6 065 | 7 400 | 5 979 | −5 725 | 4 948 |
| **Percentage distribution of average annual expenditure — Distribution en pourcentage des dépenses annuelles moyennes** | | | | | | | |
| 1951 – 1960 | 100.0 | 92.7 | 19.3 | 17.8 | 14.0 | −10.5 | 14.7 |
| 1951 | 100.0 | 88.6 | 16.8 | 16.1 | 11.8 | −4.7 | 10.2 |
| 1953 | 100.0 | 87.7 | 15.8 | 20.0 | 14.8 | −7.7 | 13.5 |
| 1954 | 100.0 | 92.6 | 17.7 | 18.4 | 12.7 | −11.0 | 9.4 |
| 1958 | 100.0 | 94.2 | 21.2 | 17.6 | 14.5 | −11.8 | 21.6 |
| 1960 | 100.0 | 95.6 | 20.7 | 22.4 | 18.2 | −18.0 | 17.3 |
| **Average annual rate of growth — Taux annuel moyen d'accroissement** | | | | | | | |
| 1951 – 1960 | 7.9 | 9.1 | 10.7 | 12.2 | 13.6 | . | 14.7 |
| 1951 – 1953 | 11.5 | 12.2 | 9.5 | 25.5 | 26.5 | . | 29.4 |
| 1954 – 1958 | 6.3 | 6.7 | 11.2 | 5.2 | 9.8 | . | 28.9 |
| 1958 – 1960 | 7.6 | 8.5 | 6.2 | 21.4 | 21.0 | . | −4.1 |

For footnotes see end of table.                                    Pour les notes, voir au bas du tableau.

## B. The Gross Domestic Product at Factor Cost According to Origin
### Origine par secteur d'activité du produit intérieur brut au coût des facteurs

| Item of data and year<br>Rubrique et année | Total | Agricultural sector<br>Secteur agricole | Industrial Sector — Secteur industriel | | | | | Transportation and communication<br>Transports et communications | Other sectors [2]<br>Autres secteurs [2] |
|---|---|---|---|---|---|---|---|---|---|
| | | | Total | Mining<br>Industries extractives | Manufacturing<br>Industries manufacturières | Construction<br>Bâtiment et travaux publics | Electricity, gas and water<br>Electricité, gaz et eau | | |
| ISIC — CITI | 0–9 | 0 | 1–5 | 1 | 2–3 | 4 | 5 | 7 | 6, 8–9 |
| *At Current Prices — Aux prix courants* | | | | | | | | | |
| Absolute figures —<br>Chiffres absolus | | | | | | | | | |
| 1951............ | 9 664 | 3 242 | 2 497 | 99 | 1 791 | 449 | 158 | 579 | 3 346 |
| 1952............ | 13 881 | 4 878 | 3 189 | 289 | 2 106 | 635 | 159 | 804 | 5 010 |
| 1953............ | 18 791 | 7 413 | 4 033 | 286 | 2 754 | 757 | 236 | 840 | 6 505 |
| 1954............ | 19 970 | 6 671 | 5 039 | 270 | 3 416 | 1 100 | 253 | 949 | 7 311 |
| 1955............ | 23 966 | 8 065 | 6 124 | 359 | 4 211 | 1 203 | 351 | 1 162 | 8 615 |
| 1956............ | 27 813 | 9 100 | 7 471 | 608 | 5 084 | 1 348 | 431 | 1 363 | 9 879 |
| 1957............ | 32 414 | 10 211 | 9 040 | 727 | 6 314 | 1 472 | 527 | 1 944 | 11 219 |
| 1958............ | 35 463 | 10 950 | 9 632 | 927 | 6 510 | 1 564 | 631 | 2 175 | 12 706 |
| 1959............ | 41 667 | 12 460 | 11 781 | 971 | 8 231 | 1 837 | 742 | 2 332 | 15 094 |
| 1960............ | 52 052 | 17 387 | 13 974 | 1 126 | 9 522 | 2 257 | 1 069 | 2 884 | 17 807 |
| 1961............ | 58 223 | 18 089 | 16 070 | 1 247 | 10 943 | 2 543 | 1 337 | 3 707 | 20 357 |
| Percentage distribution according to sector—<br>Distribution en pourcentage par secteur | | | | | | | | | |
| 1951–1960..... | 100.0 | 32.7 | 26.4 | 2.1 | 18.1 | 4.6 | 1.6 | 5.5 | 35.4 |
| 1951............ | 100.0 | 33.5 | 25.8 | 1.0 | 18.6 | 4.6 | 1.6 | 6.0 | 34.7 |
| 1953............ | 100.0 | 39.4 | 21.5 | 1.5 | 14.7 | 4.0 | 1.3 | 4.4 | 34.7 |
| 1954............ | 100.0 | 33.4 | 25.2 | 1.3 | 17.1 | 5.5 | 1.3 | 4.7 | 36.7 |
| 1958............ | 100.0 | 30.8 | 27.2 | 2.6 | 18.4 | 4.4 | 1.8 | 6.1 | 35.9 |
| 1960............ | 100.0 | 33.4 | 26.8 | 2.1 | 18.3 | 4.3 | 2.1 | 5.5 | 34.3 |

For footnotes see end of table.     Pour les notes, voir au bas du tableau.

## C. Gross Domestic Fixed Capital Formation According to Purchasing Sector
### La formation brute de capital fixe intérieur par secteur d'acquisition

| Item of data and year<br>Rubrique et année | Total | Agricultural sector<br>Secteur agricole | Industrial Sector — Secteur industriel | | | | | Transportation and communication<br>Transports et communications | Other sectors<br>Autres secteurs |
|---|---|---|---|---|---|---|---|---|---|
| | | | Total | Mining<br>Industries extractives | Manufacturing<br>Industries manufacturières | Construction<br>Bâtiment et travaux publics | Electricity, gas and water<br>Electricité, gaz et eau | | |
| ISIC — CITI | 0–9 | 0 | 1–5 | 1 | 2–3 | 4 | 5 | 7 | 6, 8–9 |
| *At Current Prices — Aux prix courants* | | | | | | | | | |
| Absolute figures —<br>Chiffres absolus | | | | | | | | | |
| 1951............ | 1 308 | 445 | 365 | 13 | 247 | 4 | 101 | 178 | 320 |
| 1952............ | 2 019 | 566 | 586 | 21 | 341 | 6 | 218 | 311 | 556 |
| 1953............ | 2 540 | 689 | 742 | 13 | 543 | 9 | 177 | 362 | 747 |
| 1954............ | 2 737 | 707 | 916 | 15 | 493 | 11 | 397 | 253 | 861 |
| 1955............ | 3 487 | 848 | 1 469 | 27 | 839 | 17 | 586 | 270 | 900 |
| 1956............ | 4 007 | 872 | 1 637 | 46 | 974 | 59 | 558 | 464 | 1 034 |
| 1957............ | 5 044 | 937 | 2 115 | 84 | 1 300 | 33 | 698 | 710 | 1 282 |
| 1958............ | 6 381 | 1 117 | 2 814 | 90 | 1 720 | 41 | 963 | 937 | 1 513 |
| 1959............ | 8 478 | 1 813 | 3 665 | 125 | 1 877 | 60 | 1 603 | 1 039 | 1 961 |
| 1960............ | 10 598 | 1 908 | 3 830 | 207 | 2 428 | 36 | 1 159 | 2 021 | 2 839 |
| 1961............ | 11 748 | 2 212 | 4 324 | 220 | 2 670 | 66 | 1 368 | 2 301 | 2 911 |
| Percentage distribution according to sector—<br>Distribution en pourcentage par secteur | | | | | | | | | |
| 1951–1960..... | 100.0 | 21.2 | 38.9 | 1.4 | 23.1 | 0.6 | 13.8 | 14.0 | 25.8 |
| 1951............ | 100.0 | 34.0 | 27.9 | 1.0 | 18.9 | 0.3 | 7.7 | 13.6 | 24.5 |
| 1953............ | 100.0 | 27.1 | 29.2 | 0.5 | 21.4 | 0.3 | 7.0 | 14.3 | 29.4 |
| 1954............ | 100.0 | 25.8 | 33.5 | 0.6 | 18.0 | 0.4 | 14.5 | 9.3 | 31.4 |
| 1958............ | 100.0 | 17.5 | 44.1 | 1.4 | 27.0 | 0.6 | 15.1 | 14.7 | 23.7 |
| 1960............ | 100.0 | 18.0 | 36.1 | 2.0 | 22.9 | 0.3 | 10.9 | 19.1 | 26.8 |

[1] Includes statistical discrepancy.
[2] No imputation is made for the ownership of dwellings.

[1] Y compris les écarts statistiques.
[2] La propriété des maisons d'habitation n'a pas été imputée.

# CHINA (Taiwan)

## 2. INDEX NUMBERS OF INDUSTRIAL PRODUCTION — INDICES DE LA PRODUCTION INDUSTRIELLE

### A. The Divisions of Industrial Activity — Les branches de l'activité industrielle

| Period / Période | Total | Mining<br>Industries extractives | Manufacturing<br>Industries manufacturières | Construction<br>Bâtiment et travaux publics | Electricity and gas<br>Electricité et gaz |
|---|---|---|---|---|---|
| ISIC — CITI | 1–3, 511–512 | 1 | 2–3 | 4 | 511–512 |

*a. Indexes — Indices (1958 = 100)*

| | | | | | |
|---|---|---|---|---|---|
| 1948 | 27 | 52 | 22 | ... | 29 |
| 1949 | 33 | 48 | 30 | ... | 30 |
| 1950 | 36 | 46 | 33 | ... | 36 |
| 1951 | 43 | 54 | 39 | ... | 45 |
| 1952 | 54 | 73 | 51 | ... | 49 |
| 1953 | 67 | 70 | 68 | 57 | 54 |
| 1954 | 72 | 70 | 72 | 60 | 63 |
| 1955 | 80 | 79 | 81 | 82 | 68 |
| 1956 | 84 | 84 | 84 | 59 | 78 |
| 1957 | 96 | 93 | 96 | 66 | 89 |
| 1958 | 100 | 100 | 100 | 100 | 100 |
| 1959 | 114 | 108 | 114 | 67 | 111 |
| 1960 | 129 | 121 | 130 | 76 | 126 |
| 1961 | 144 | 128 | 149 | 72 | 142 |

*b. Average Annual Rate of Change — Taux annuel moyen de variation*

| | | | | | |
|---|---|---|---|---|---|
| 1950–1960 | 13.6 | 10.2 | 14.7 | ... | 13.4 |
| 1948–1953 | 19.9 | 6.1 | 25.3 | ... | 13.2 |
| 1954–1958 | 8.6 | 9.3 | 8.6 | 13.6 | 12.2 |
| 1958–1961 | 12.9 | 8.6 | 14.2 | −10.4 | 12.4 |

### B. The Major Groups of Mining — Les classes de la branche Industries extractives

| Period / Période | All mining<br>Toutes industries extractives | Coal mining<br>Extraction du charbon | Metal mining<br>Extraction des minerais métalliques | Crude petroleum and natural gas<br>Pétrole brut et gaz naturel | Other mining<br>Autres industries extractives |
|---|---|---|---|---|---|
| ISIC — CITI | 1 | 11 | 12 | 13 | 14–19 |

*a. Indexes — Indices (1958 = 100)*

| | | | | | |
|---|---|---|---|---|---|
| 1938 | ... | 69 | 222 | 112 | 40 |
| 1948 | 52 | 52 | 42 | 101 | 58 |
| 1949 | 48 | 50 | 42 | 91 | 40 |
| 1950 | 46 | 44 | 79 | 142 | 33 |
| 1951 | 54 | 52 | 67 | 108 | 55 |
| 1952 | 73 | 72 | 94 | 98 | 65 |
| 1953 | 70 | 75 | 75 | 109 | 40 |
| 1954 | 70 | 66 | 76 | 108 | 81 |
| 1955 | 79 | 74 | 98 | 102 | 91 |
| 1956 | 84 | 80 | 117 | 106 | 83 |
| 1957 | 93 | 92 | 106 | 109 | 92 |
| 1958 | 100 | 100 | 100 | 100 | 100 |
| 1959 | 108 | 112 | 90 | 100 | 101 |
| 1960 | 121 | 125 | 116 | 96 | 112 |
| 1961 | 128 | 133 | 123 | 139 | 106 |

*b. Average Annual Rate of Change — Taux annuel moyen de variation*

| | | | | | |
|---|---|---|---|---|---|
| 1938–1961 | ... | 2.9 | −12.5 | 0.9 | 4.3 |
| 1938–1948 | ... | −2.8 | −15.3 | −1.0 | 3.8 |
| 1950–1960 | 10.2 | 11.0 | 3.9 | −3.8 | 13.0 |
| 1948–1953 | 6.1 | 7.6 | 12.3 | 1.5 | −7.2 |
| 1954–1958 | 9.3 | 10.9 | 7.1 | −1.9 | 5.4 |
| 1958–1961 | 8.6 | 10.0 | 7.1 | 11.6 | 2.0 |

### C. Selected Major Groups of Manufacturing — Quelques classes de la branche Industries manufacturières

| Period / Période | Manufacturing<br>Industries manufacturières | Food, beverages and tobacco<br>Industries alimentaires, boissons, tabac | Textiles | Wood products and furniture<br>Bois et meubles | Paper and paper products<br>Papier et ouvrages en papier | Printing and publishing<br>Imprimerie et édition | Leather and leather products except wearing apparel<br>Cuir et articles en cuir, à l'exclusion des articles d'habillement | Rubber products<br>Ouvrages en caoutchouc | Chemicals and chemical, petroleum and coal products<br>Produits chimiques et dérivés du pétrole et du charbon | Non-metallic mineral products<br>Produits minéraux non métalliques | Basic metals<br>Métallurgie de base | Metal products<br>Ouvrages en métaux | Other manufacturing<br>Autres industries manufacturières |
|---|---|---|---|---|---|---|---|---|---|---|---|---|---|
| ISIC — CITI | 2–3 | 20–22 | 23 | 25–26 | 27 | 28 | 29 | 30 | 31–32 | 33 | 34 | 35–38 | 39 |

*a. Indexes — Indices (1958 = 100)*

| | | | | | | | | | | | | | |
|---|---|---|---|---|---|---|---|---|---|---|---|---|---|
| 1938 | ... | 64 | 5 | 33 | 41 | 28 | 70 | 3 | 29 | 18 | 12 | 13 | 57 |
| 1948 | 22 | 24 | 8 | 36 | 16 | 14 | 23 | 21 | 30 | 28 | 12 | 12 | 53 |
| 1949 | 30 | 46 | 16 | 38 | 15 | 25 | 17 | 27 | 30 | 32 | 10 | 17 | 55 |
| 1950 | 33 | 46 | 23 | 41 | 24 | 34 | 32 | 37 | 30 | 34 | 16 | 22 | 74 |
| 1951 | 39 | 36 | 34 | 51 | 31 | 48 | 55 | 61 | 49 | 43 | 18 | 25 | 94 |
| 1952 | 51 | 54 | 54 | 54 | 39 | 54 | 70 | 64 | 53 | 49 | 26 | 29 | 103 |
| 1953 | 68 | 80 | 84 | 60 | 42 | 71 | 82 | 71 | 61 | 55 | 41 | 44 | 92 |
| 1954 | 72 | 70 | 97 | 68 | 52 | 84 | 54 | 88 | 68 | 58 | 68 | 62 | 106 |
| 1955 | 81 | 83 | 102 | 69 | 60 | 97 | 67 | 91 | 78 | 65 | 66 | 77 | 101 |
| 1956 | 84 | 86 | 97 | 69 | 74 | 95 | 84 | 84 | 84 | 75 | 78 | 78 | 111 |
| 1957 | 96 | 102 | 108 | 76 | 87 | 98 | 88 | 106 | 96 | 75 | 94 | 103 | 96 |
| 1958 | 100 | 100 | 100 | 100 | 100 | 100 | 100 | 100 | 100 | 100 | 100 | 100 | 100 |
| 1959 | 114 | 101 | 122 | 104 | 126 | 106 | 80 | 111 | 117 | 109 | 129 | 144 | 104 |
| 1960 | 130 | 110 | 137 | 116 | 144 | 107 | 91 | 138 | 138 | 137 | 157 | 155 | 104 |
| 1961 | 149 | 122 | 161 | 167 | 156 | 106 | 108 | 162 | 160 | 153 | 165 | 146 | 111 |

*b. Average Annual Rate of Change — Taux annuel moyen de variation*

| | | | | | | | | | | | | | |
|---|---|---|---|---|---|---|---|---|---|---|---|---|---|
| 1938–1961 | ... | 2.8 | 16.3 | 7.3 | 6.0 | 6.0 | 1.9 | 18.9 | 7.7 | 9.8 | 12.1 | 11.1 | 2.9 |
| 1938–1948 | ... | −9.3 | 4.8 | 0.9 | −9.0 | −6.7 | −10.6 | 21.5 | 0.4 | 4.5 | — | −0.8 | −0.7 |
| 1950–1960 | 14.7 | 9.1 | 19.5 | 11.0 | 19.6 | 12.1 | 11.0 | 14.1 | 16.5 | 15.0 | 25.6 | 21.6 | 3.5 |
| 1948–1953 | 25.3 | 27.3 | 60.0 | 10.8 | 21.3 | 38.4 | 28.9 | 27.6 | 15.2 | 14.5 | 27.8 | 29.4 | 11.7 |
| 1954–1958 | 8.6 | 9.3 | 0.8 | 10.1 | 17.8 | 4.4 | 16.6 | 3.2 | 10.1 | 14.6 | 10.1 | 12.7 | −1.4 |
| 1958–1961 | 14.2 | 6.9 | 17.2 | 18.6 | 16.0 | 2.0 | 2.6 | 17.4 | 16.9 | 15.2 | 18.2 | 13.4 | 3.5 |

## 3. INDEX NUMBERS OF INDUSTRIAL EMPLOYMENT — INDICES DE L'EMPLOI DANS L'INDUSTRIE

### A. Selected Divisions of Industrial Activity
### Quelques branches de l'activité industrielle

| Period / Période | Total | Mining — Industries extractives | Manufacturing — Industries manufacturières | Electricity and gas — Electricité et gaz |
|---|---|---|---|---|
| ISIC — CITI | 1–3, 511–512 | 1 | 2–3 | 511–512 |
| *a. Indexes — Indices (1958 = 100)* | | | | |
| 1952 | 79 | 76 | 80 | 72 |
| 1953 | 88 | 78 | 91 | 69 |
| 1954 | 92 | 71 | 98 | 74 |
| 1955 | 93 | 74 | 99 | 77 |
| 1956 | 97 | 90 | 99 | 80 |
| 1957 | 100 | 100 | 100 | 88 |
| 1958 | 100 | 100 | 100 | 100 |
| 1959 | 101 | 100 | 101 | 104 |
| 1960 | – 103 – | – 103 – | – 103 – | – 110 – |
| 1961 | 107 | 106 | 107 | 116 |
| *b. Average Annual Rate of Change — Taux annuel moyen de variation* | | | | |
| 1954 – 1958 | 2.1 | 8.9 | 0.5 | 7.8 |
| 1958 – 1960 | 1.5 | 1.5 | 1.5 | 4.9 |

### B. The Major Groups of Mining
### Les classes de la branche Industries extractives

| Period / Période | All mining — Toutes industries extractives | Coal mining — Extraction du charbon | Metal mining — Extraction des minerais métalliques | Crude petroleum and natural gas — Pétrole brut et gaz naturel | Other mining — Autres industries extractives |
|---|---|---|---|---|---|
| ISIC — CITI | 1 | 11 | 12 | 13 | 14–19 |
| *a. Indexes — Indices (1958 = 100)* | | | | | |
| 1952 | 76 | 69 | 130 | 84 | 92 |
| 1953 | 78 | 71 | 132 | 87 | 90 |
| 1954 | 71 | 63 | 129 | 91 | 92 |
| 1955 | 74 | 66 | 135 | 98 | 87 |
| 1956 | 90 | 86 | 126 | 88 | 95 |
| 1957 | 100 | 101 | 106 | 98 | 93 |
| 1958 | 100 | 100 | 100 | 100 | 100 |
| 1959 | 100 | 101 | 96 | 100 | 98 |
| 1960 | – 103 – | – 105 – | – 94 – | 104 | – 93 – |
| 1961 | 106 | 109 | 92 | 106 | 95 |
| *b. Average Annual Rate of Change — Taux annuel moyen de variation* | | | | | |
| 1954 – 1958 | 8.9 | 12.2 | −6.2 | 2.4 | 2.1 |
| 1958 – 1960 | 1.5 | 2.5 | −3.0 | 2.0 | −3.6 |

### C. Selected Major Groups of Manufacturing
### Quelques classes de la branche Industries manufacturières

| Period / Période | Manufacturing — Industries manufacturières | Food, beverages and tobacco — Industries alimentaires, boissons, tabac | Textiles | Wood products and furniture — Bois et meubles | Paper and paper products — Papier et ouvrages en papier | Printing and publishing — Imprimerie et édition | Leather and leather products except wearing apparel — Cuir et articles en cuir, à l'exclusion des articles d'habillement | Rubber products — Ouvrages en caoutchouc | Chemicals and chemical, petroleum and coal products — Produits chimiques et dérivés du pétrole et du charbon | Nonmetallic mineral products — Produits minéraux non métalliques | Basic metals — Métallurgie de base |
|---|---|---|---|---|---|---|---|---|---|---|---|
| ISIC — CITI | 2–3 | 20–22 | 23 | 25–26 | 27 | 28 | 29 | 30 | 31–32 | 33 | 34 |
| *a. Indexes — Indices (1958 = 100)* | | | | | | | | | | | |
| 1952 | 80 | 77 | 89 | 62 | ...[1] | 60 | ...[1] | ...[1] | 66 | 74 | 66 |
| 1953 | 91 | 88 | 102 | 80 | 103 | 88 | 178 | 100 | – 80 – | 92 | 86 |
| 1954 | 98 | 97 | 103 | 93 | 105 | 99 | 113 | 100 | 94 | 99 | 100 |
| 1955 | 99 | 100 | 102 | 92 | 104 | 99 | 106 | 100 | 94 | 99 | 99 |
| 1956 | 99 | 100 | 102 | 94 | 103 | 100 | 108 | 99 | 96 | 100 | 99 |
| 1957 | 100 | 100 | 101 | 97 | 102 | 100 | 99 | 100 | 99 | 100 | 100 |
| 1958 | 100 | 100 | 100 | 100 | 100 | 100 | 100 | 100 | 100 | 100 | 100 |
| 1959 | 101 | 100 | 113 | 101 | 97 | 100 | 97 | 102 | 103 | 101 | 100 |
| 1960 | – 103 – | – 100 – | – 113 – | – 111 – | – 95 – | – 100 – | – 88 – | – 102 – | – 106 – | – 103 – | – 105 – |
| 1961 | 107 | 104 | 117 | 124 | 105 | 100 | 82 | 107 | 113 | 114 | 106 |
| *b. Average Annual Rate of Change — Taux annuel moyen de variation* | | | | | | | | | | | |
| 1954 – 1958 | 0.5 | 0.8 | −0.7 | 1.8 | −1.2 | 0.2 | −3.0 | — | 1.6 | 0.2 | — |
| 1958 – 1960 | 1.5 | — | 6.3 | 5.4 | −2.5 | — | −6.2 | 1.0 | 3.0 | 1.5 | 2.5 |

[1] Included in Chemicals and chemical, petroleum and coal products (ISIC major groups 31–32).

[1] Inclus dans Produits chimiques et dérivés du pétrole et du charbon (CITI classes 31–32).

# CHINA (Taiwan)

## 4. CHARACTERISTICS OF ALL INDUSTRIAL ESTABLISHMENTS
## CARACTERISTIQUES DE TOUS LES ETABLISSEMENTS INDUSTRIELS
### 1954

Number of establishments in units; value added and wages and salaries in million New Taiwan dollars; number of engaged and employees in thousands; capacity of installed power equipment in thousand horsepower; value added per person engaged in thousand New Taiwan dollars; capacity of installed power equipment per person engaged in horsepower

Nombre d'établissements en unités; valeur ajoutée et traitements et salaires en millions de nouveaux dollars de Taïwan; nombre de personnes occupées et de salariés en milliers; puissance installée en milliers de chevaux-vapeur; valeur ajoutée par personne occupée en milliers de nouveaux dollars de Taïwan; puissance installée par personne occupée en chevaux-vapeur

### A. The Divisions of Industrial Activity — Les branches de l'activité industrielle

| Item of data | All industrial activity<br>Toutes industries | Mining<br>Industries extractives | Manufacturing<br>Industries manufacturières | Construction<br>Bâtiment et travaux publics | Electricity and gas<br>Electricité et gaz | Rubrique |
|---|---|---|---|---|---|---|
| ISIC | 1–4, 511–512 | 1 | 2–3 | 4 | 511–512 | CITI |
| **a. Absolute Figures — Chiffres absolus** | | | | | | |
| Number of establishments....... | 43 868 | 426 | 40 713 | 2 683 | 46 | Nombre d'établissements |
| Value added................. | . | 327.0 | 4 395.0 | . | . | Valeur ajoutée |
| Number of engaged (During at least 10 days in December 1954).......... | 380.6 | 55.4 | 310.1 | 9.1 | 6.0 | Nombre de personnes occupées (pendant au moins 10 jours en décembre 1954) |
| Number of employees (During at least 10 days in December 1954).......... | 306.8 | 55.2 | 240.4 | 5.4 | 5.8 | Nombre de salariés (pendant au moins 10 jours en décembre 1954) |
| Wages and salaries paid....... | . | 265.7 | 1 039.3 | 144.9 | . | Traitements et salaires payés |
| Capacity of installed power equipment (31.XII.1954)...... | . | 65.8 | 429.2 | . | 604.2 | Puissance installée (31.XII.1954) |
| **b. Structure** | | | | | | |
| Distribution in percent of number of engaged......... | 100.0 | 14.5 | 81.5 | 2.4 | 1.6 | Distribution en pourcentage du nombre de personnes occupées |
| Value added per person engaged................. | . | 5.9 | 14.2 | . | . | Valeur ajoutée par personne occupée |
| Value added per unit of wages and salaries......... | . | . | 4.24 | . | . | Valeur ajoutée par unité de traitements et salaires |
| Capacity of installed power equipment per person engaged................. | . | 1.19 | 1.38 | . | 100.70 | Puissance installée par personne occupée |
| Employees as a percent of engaged............... | 80.6 | 99.6 | 77.5 | 59.3 | 96.7 | Salariés en pourcentage des personnes occupées |
| Wages and salaries per employee............. | . | 4.8 | 4.3 | 26.8 | . | Traitements et salaires par salarié |

148

## B. The Major Groups of Mining — Les classes de la branche Industries extractives

| Item of data | All mining<br>Toutes industries extractives | Coal mining<br>Extraction du charbon | Metal mining<br>Extraction des minerais métalliques | Crude petroleum and natural gas<br>Pétrole brut et gaz naturel | Other mining<br>Divers | Rubrique |
|---|---|---|---|---|---|---|
| ISIC | 1 | 11 | 12 | 13 | 14–19 | CITI |
| **a. Absolute Figures — Chiffres absolus** | | | | | | |
| Number of establishments....... | 426 | 276 | 11 | 7 | 132 | Nombre d'établissements |
| Value added................. | 327.0 | 237.8 | 19.4 | 3.1 | 66.7 | Valeur ajoutée |
| Number of engaged (During at least 10 days in December 1954).......... | 55.4 | 36.1 | 6.6 | 1.6 | 11.1 | Nombre de personnes occupées (pendant au moins 10 jours en décembre 1954) |
| Number of employees (During at least 10 days in December 1954).......... | 55.2 | 36.0 | 6.6 | 1.6 | 11.0 | Nombre de salariés (pendant au moins 10 jours en décembre 1954) |
| Wages and salaries paid....... | 265.7 | 193.4 | 22.3 | 13.7 | 36.3 | Traitements et salaires payés |
| Capacity of installed power equipment (31.XII.1954)...... | 65.8 | 42.3 | 13.2 | 7.7 | 2.6 | Puissance installée (31.XII.1954) |
| **b. Structure** | | | | | | |
| Distribution in percent of: Value added............... | 100.0 | 72.7 | 5.9 | 1.0 | 20.4 | Distribution en pourcentage: Valeur ajoutée |
| Number of engaged......... | 100.0 | 65.1 | 11.9 | 2.9 | 20.1 | Nombre de personnes occupées |
| Value added per person engaged................. | 5.9 | 6.6 | 2.9 | 1.9 | 6.0 | Valeur ajoutée par personne occupée |
| Capacity of installed power equipment per person engaged................. | 1.19 | 1.17 | 2.00 | 4.81 | 0.23 | Puissance installée par personne occupée |
| Employees as a percent of engaged................. | 99.6 | 99.7 | 100.0 | 100.0 | 99.1 | Salariés en pourcentage des personnes occupées |
| Value added per unit of wages and salaries.......... | 4.8 | 5.4 | 3.4 | 8.6 | 3.3 | Valeur ajoutée par unité de traitements et salaires |

# CHINA (Taiwan)

## C. The Major Groups of Manufacturing — Les classes de la branche Industries manufacturières

| Item of data | Manufacturing — Industries manufacturières | Food, beverages and tobacco — Industries alimentaires, boissons, tabac | Textiles | Clothing, footwear and made-up textiles — Articles d'habillement, chaussures et ouvrages en tissu | Wood products and furniture — Bois et meubles | Paper and paper products — Papier et ouvrages en papier | Printing and publishing — Imprimerie et édition | Leather and leather products except wearing apparel — Cuir et articles en cuir, à l'exclusion des articles d'habillement | Rubber products — Ouvrages en caoutchouc | Chemicals and chemical, petroleum and coal products — Produits chimiques et dérivés du pétrole et du charbon | Non-metallic mineral products — Produits minéraux non métalliques | Basic metals — Métallurgie de base | Metal products — Ouvrages en métaux | Other manufacturing — Autres industries manufacturières | Rubrique |
|---|---|---|---|---|---|---|---|---|---|---|---|---|---|---|---|
| ISIC | 2–3 | 20–22 | 23 | 24 | 25–26 | 27 | 28 | 29 | 30 | 31–32 | 33 | 34 | 35–38 | 39 | CITI |
| | | | | | | *a.* Absolute Figures — Chiffres absolus | | | | | | | | | |
| Number of establishments | 40 713 | 12 095 | 2 148 | 5 078 | 5 071 | 231 | 764 | 208 | 334 | 1 583 | 1 982 | 80 | 8 362 | 2 777 | Nombre d'établissements |
| Value added | 4 395.0 | 1 839.0 | 612.7 | 94.4 | 181.2 | 88.9 | 158.0 | 9.5 | 40.9 | 519.1 | 259.1 | 76.2 | 459.3 | 56.7 | Valeur ajoutée |
| Number of engaged (During at least 10 days in December 1954) | 310.1 | 70.2 | 52.3 | 15.6 | 24.1 | 6.6 | 10.5 | 1.5 | 5.4 | 26.9 | 29.9 | 6.4 | 50.9 | 9.8 | Nombre de personnes occupées (pendant au moins 10 jours en déc. 1954) |
| Number of employees (During at least 10 days in December 1954) | 240.4 | 45.3 | 48.6 | 8.6 | 16.3 | 6.1 | 9.3 | 1.1 | 4.8 | 24.0 | 26.3 | 6.2 | 38.7 | 5.1 | Nombre de salariés (pendant au moins 10 jours en décembre 1954) |
| Wages and salaries paid | 1 039.3 | 216.8 | 181.4 | 30.4 | 67.0 | 33.9 | 54.1 | 5.3 | 14.4 | 130.7 | 79.8 | 31.7 | 179.5 | 14.3 | Traitements et salaires payés |
| Capacity of installed power equipment (31.XII.1954) | 429.2 | 166.5 | 35.6 | 0.4 | 21.1 | 29.8 | 2.1 | 0.6 | 7.1 | 48.1 | 46.1 | 27.6 | 43.2 | 1.0 | Puissance installée (31.XII.1954) |
| | | | | | | *b.* Structure | | | | | | | | | |
| Distribution in percent of: Value added | 100.0 | 41.8 | 13.9 | 2.2 | 4.1 | 2.0 | 3.6 | 0.2 | 1.0 | 11.8 | 5.9 | 1.7 | 10.5 | 1.3 | Distribution en pourcentage: Valeur ajoutée |
| Number of engaged | 100.0 | 22.6 | 16.9 | 5.0 | 7.8 | 2.1 | 3.4 | 0.5 | 1.7 | 8.8 | 9.6 | 2.1 | 16.4 | 3.1 | Nombre de personnes occupées |
| Value added per person engaged | 14.2 | 26.2 | 11.7 | 6.0 | 7.5 | 13.5 | 15.0 | 6.3 | 7.6 | 19.0 | 8.7 | 11.9 | 9.0 | 6.0 | Valeur ajoutée par personne occupée |
| Value added per unit of wages and salaries | 4.23 | 8.48 | 3.38 | 3.10 | 2.70 | 2.62 | 2.92 | 1.79 | 2.84 | 3.97 | 3.25 | 2.40 | 2.56 | 3.96 | Valeur ajoutée par unité de traitements et salaires |
| Capacity of installed power equipment per person engaged | 1.38 | 2.37 | 0.68 | 0.02 | 0.88 | 4.52 | 0.20 | 0.40 | 1.31 | 1.76 | 1.54 | 4.31 | 0.85 | 0.10 | Puissance installée par personne occupée |
| Employees as a percent of engaged | 77.5 | 64.5 | 92.9 | 55.1 | 67.6 | 92.4 | 88.6 | 73.3 | 88.9 | 87.9 | 88.0 | 96.9 | 76.0 | 54.2 | Salariés en pourcentage des personnes occupées |
| Wages and salaries per employee | 4.3 | 4.8 | 3.7 | 3.5 | 4.1 | 5.6 | 5.8 | 4.8 | 3.0 | 5.4 | 3.0 | 5.1 | 4.6 | 2.8 | Traitements et salaires par salarié |

## 5. CHARACTERISTICS OF ALL MINING AND PUBLIC UTILITY ESTABLISHMENTS AND OF SELECTED MANUFACTURING ESTABLISHMENTS

### CARACTERISTIQUES DE TOUS LES ETABLISSEMENTS MINIERS ET D'UTILITE PUBLIQUE ET DE QUELQUES ETABLISSEMENTS MANUFACTURIERS

### 1959

Number of establishments in units; value added in million New Taiwan dollars; number of engaged in thousands.

Nombre d'établissements en unités; valeur ajoutée en millions de nouveaux dollars de de Taïwan; nombre personnes occupées en milliers.

### A. Selected Divisions of Industrial Activity — Quelques branches de l'activité industrielle

| Item of data | Total | Mining Industries extractives | Manu-facturing[1] Industries manu-facturières[1] | Electricity[1] Electricité[1] | Rubrique | Item of data | Total | Mining Industries extractives | Manu-facturing[1] Industries manu-facturières[1] | Electricity, gas and water Electricité, gaz et eau | Rubrique |
|---|---|---|---|---|---|---|---|---|---|---|---|
| ISIC | 1-3, 5 | 1 | 2-3 | 5 | CITI | ISIC | 1-3, 5 | 1 | 2-3 | 5 | CITI |
| | a. Absolute Figures — Chiffres absolus | | | | | | b. Structure | | | | |
| Number of establishments. | 3 012 | 416 | 2 593 | 3 | Nombre d'établissements | | | | | | Distribution en pourcentage du nombre de personnes occupées |
| Value added. | ... | ... | 6 280.6 | 724.7 | Valeur ajoutée | Distribution in percent of number of engaged. | 100.0 | 28.8 | 67.6 | 3.6 | |
| Number of engaged. | 255.8 | 73.8 | 173.0 | 9.0 | Nombre de personnes occupées | Value added per person engaged. | ... | ... | 36.3 | 80.5 | Valeur ajoutée par personne occupée |

[1] For footnotes see end of table.

[1] Pour les notes, voir au bas du tableau.

### B. The Major Groups of Mining — Les classes de la branche Industries extractives

| Item of data | All mining Toutes industries extrac-tives | Coal mining Extraction du charbon | Metal mining Extraction des minerais métal-liques | Crude petroleum and natural gas Pétrole brut et gaz naturel | Other mining Divers | Rubrique | Item of data | All mining Toutes industries extrac-tives | Coal mining Extraction du charbon | Metal mining Extraction des minerais métal-liques | Crude petroleum and natural gas Pétrole brut et gaz naturel | Other mining Divers | Rubrique |
|---|---|---|---|---|---|---|---|---|---|---|---|---|---|
| ISIC | 1 | 11 | 12 | 13 | 14-19 | CITI | ISIC | 1 | 11 | 12 | 13 | 14-19 | CITI |
| | a. Absolute Figures — Chiffres absolus | | | | | | | b. Structure | | | | | |
| Number of establishments... | 416 | 371 | 5 | 5 | 35 | Nombre d'établissements | | | | | | | Distribution en pourcentage du nombre de personnes occupées |
| Value added... | ... | 801.7 | 41.7 | ... | 78.2 | Valeur ajoutée | Distribution in percent of number of engaged... | 100.0 | 80.0 | 6.4 | 2.2 | 11.4 | |
| Number of engaged... | 73.8 | 59.1 | 4.7 | 1.6 | 8.4 | Nombre de personnes occupées | Value added per person engaged.. | ... | 13.6 | 8.9 | ... | 9.3 | Valeur ajoutée par personne occupée |

# CHINA (Taiwan)

## C. Selected Major Groups of Manufacturing — Quelques classes de la branche Industries manufacturières

| Item of data | Manufacturing [1] Industries manufacturières [1] | Food beverages and tobacco Industries alimentaires, boissons, tabac | Textiles | Wood products Bois | Paper and paper products Papier et ouvrages en papier | Leather and leather products except wearing apparel Cuir et articles en cuir, à l'exclusion des articles d'habillement | Rubber products Ouvrages en caoutchouc | Chemicals and chemical, petroleum and coal products Produits chimiques et dérivés du pétrole et du charbon | Non-metallic mineral products Produits minéraux non métalliques | Basic metals Métallurgie de base | Metal products Ouvrages en métaux | Other manufacturing Autres industries manufacturières | Rubrique |
|---|---|---|---|---|---|---|---|---|---|---|---|---|---|
| ISIC | 2–3 | 20–22 | 23 | 25 | 27 | 29 | 30 | 31–32 | 33 | 34 | 35–38 | 39 | CITI |
| *a. Absolute Figures — Chiffres absolus* | | | | | | | | | | | | | |
| Number of establishments. | 2 593 | 538 | 300 | 531 | 52 | 66 | 56 | 205 | 559 | 52 | 226 | 8 | Nombre d'établissements |
| Value added.......... | 6 280.6 | 2 277.5 | 798.9 | 521.7 | 210.0 | 7.0 | 68.0 | 1 005.9 | 701.1 | 295.0 | 388.2 | 7.3 | Valeur ajoutée |
| Number of engaged.... | 173.0 | 37.5 | 40.6 | 15.8 | 8.2 | 0.7 | 5.3 | 17.6 | 17.7 | 12.6 | 14.1 | 2.9 | Nombre de personnes occupées |
| *b. Structure* | | | | | | | | | | | | | |
| Distribution in percent of: | | | | | | | | | | | | | Distribution en pourcentage: |
| Value added........ | 100.0 | 36.2 | 12.7 | 8.3 | 3.4 | 0.1 | 1.1 | 16.0 | 11.2 | 4.7 | 6.1 | 0.2 | Valeur ajoutée |
| Number of engaged... | 100.0 | 21.6 | 23.5 | 9.1 | 4.8 | 0.4 | 3.0 | 10.2 | 10.2 | 7.3 | 8.2 | 1.7 | Nombre de personnes occupées |
| Value added per person engaged...... | 36.3 | 60.7 | 19.7 | 33.0 | 25.6 | 10.0 | 12.8 | 57.2 | 39.6 | 23.4 | 27.5 | 2.5 | Valeur ajoutée par personne occupée |

[1] Excludes the manufacture of Clothing, footwear and made-up textiles (ISIC major group 24); Furniture (ISIC major group 26) and Printing and publishing (ISIC major group 28).

[1] Non compris la fabrication des Articles d'habillement, chaussures et ouvrages en tissu (CITI classe 24), l'Industrie du meuble (CITI classe 26) et Imprimerie et édition (CITI classe 28).

# COLOMBIA — COLOMBIE

## Gross Domestic Product

Estimates of expenditure on and the origin of the gross domestic product are presented in Table 1. The data are derived from information supplied by the Banco de la República, Departamento de Investigaciones Económicas, Bogotá in response to the United Nations national accounts questionnaire. Official estimates are published by the Banco in *Cuentas Nacionales*.

## Index of Industrial Production

The indexes of industrial production presented in Table 2 are compiled from data derived from two sources. The two sets of index numbers for manufacturing activity are linked at 1950 and shown as one series. The first set of index numbers which are for manufacturing activities only and are used for years up to 1950 have been calculated by the Economic Commission for Latin America and published, together with a description of methods and data used, in *Analyses and Projections of Economic development; III. The Economic Development of Colombia*. The indexes for all industrial activities for the years 1950 and later have been calculated by the Departamento de Investigaciones Económicas of the Banco de la República and published in *Cuentas Nacionales*.

In the case of manufacturing, both sets of index numbers relate essentially, as far as both weights and indicators are concerned, to establishments with 5 or more persons engaged or a gross value of production of 24,000 pesos or more. Both series of index numbers are also computed as base weighted arithmetic averages in successive stages. In the case of the indexes compiled by the Economic Commission for Latin America, the basic series were relatives based, in the majority of cases, upon the consumption of raw materials, though in a few cases, quantities of production were available and used. These indexes were combined into indexes for major groups and the indexes for major groups into indexes for manufacturing as a whole using as weights the values added at market prices from the 1953 industrial Census. For the manufacturing sector of the index numbers of industrial activity calculated by the Banco de la República, the indicators utilized were mainly quantities of production, though in some cases, raw materials consumed or employment were taken. The weights used in combining individual indicators into major groups and the latter into manufacturing as a whole were the values added resulting from the 1957 Annual Manufacturing Survey.

The index numbers for industrial activity as a whole have been calculated by the Statistical Office of the

## Produit intérieur brut

Le tableau 1 contient des estimations des dépenses imputées au produit intérieur brut et des estimations du produit intérieur brut par secteur d'activité d'origine. Ces données ont été fournies par la Banco de la República, Departamento de Investigaciones Económicas, Bogotá, en réponse au questionnaire de l'ONU sur la comptabilité nationale. Des estimations officielles sont publiées par la Banco de la República dans *Cuentas Nacionales*.

## Indices de la production industrielle

Les indices de la production industrielle reproduits au tableau 2 ont été construits à partir de données émanant de deux sources. Les deux ensembles d'indices relatifs aux activités manufacturières ont été raccordés au niveau de 1950 et présentés en une seule série. La première série d'indices, qui concerne les activités manufacturières seulement jusqu'en 1950, a été calculée par la Commission économique pour l'Amérique latine et publiée, ainsi qu'une description des méthodes et données utilisées, dans *Analyses and Projections of Economic Development; III. The Economic Development of Colombia*. Les indices relatifs à toutes les activités industrielles pour 1950 et les années suivantes ont été calculés par le Departamento de Investigaciones Económicas de la Banco de la República et publiés dans *Cuentas Nacionales*.

Dans le cas des industries manufacturières, les deux ensembles d'indices se rapportent essentiellement, en ce qui concerne les coefficients de pondération et les indicateurs, aux établissements occupant 5 personnes ou plus ou ayant une production d'une valeur brute de 24.000 pesos ou plus. Les deux séries d'indices sont des moyennes arithmétiques à pondération fixe calculés en plusieurs étapes successives. Dans le cas des indices calculés par la Commission économique pour l'Amérique latine, les séries de base sont des rapports fondés, le plus souvent, sur la consommation de matières premières, mais on a parfois utilisé le volume de la production lorsqu'on disposait de données à cet égard. Ces indices ont été combinés en indices de classes et ceux-ci en indices relatifs à l'ensemble des industries manufacturières, les coefficients de pondération utilisés étant les valeurs ajoutées aux prix du marché fournies par le recensement industriel de 1953. En ce qui concerne le secteur manufacturier des indices relatifs aux activités industrielles calculés par la Banco de la República, les indicateurs employés sont principalement les quantités produites, mais on a parfois utilisé les matières premières consommées ou l'emploi. Les coefficients de pondération utilisés pour combiner chaque indicateur en indicateur de classe et celui-ci en indicateur relatif à l'ensemble des industries manufacturières sont les valeurs ajoutées tirées des résultats de l'enquête annuelle de 1957 sur les industries manufacturières.

Les indices relatifs à l'ensemble de l'activité industrielle ont été calculés par le Bureau de statistique de l'ONU.

United Nations. The weights utilised were the contributions in 1958 to the gross domestic product at factor cost of each of the divisions of industrial activity.

Les coefficients de pondération utilisés sont les contributions de chacune des branches de l'activité industrielle au produit intérieur brut au coût des facteurs en 1958.

### Index of Industrial Employment

The index numbers of employment in manufacturing industries presented in Table 3 are derived from index numbers of employment published monthly in *Boletin Mensual de Estadística* and annually in *Anuario General de Estadística* by the Departamento Administrativo Nacional de Estadística. The index numbers are based on a monthly sample survey of employment in manufacturing industries.

Beginning in January 1955, this survey of employment has been taken, using a stratified random sample of establishments covered by the published results of the 1953 Industrial Census. The monthly sample survey enumerated all establishments with 50 or more employees, 25 to 30 per cent of establishments with 20-49 employees, and 5 to 10 per cent of establishments with 5 to 19 employees. In July 1956, the pattern of the sample was changed and establishments enumerated are all those with 50 or more employees, 25 per cent of establishments with 15-49 employees, and 5 per cent of establishments with 5-14 employees. Geographically the survey covered all Departments except Choco.

The monthly absolute figures of numbers employed, on which the annual indexes are based, are made up of the number of operatives, which is the average for the last pay-period of the month, and the number of other employees, which is the average during the month. The annual figures are the arithmetic averages of the monthly figures. All persons who received remuneration, except homeworkers, are classified as employees; this includes persons on paid vacations and sick-leave.

The index numbers for the basic series utilised were combined into indexes for detailed categories, then into indexes for major groups and finally into indexes for manufacturing as a whole, using as weights at each stage, the number of employees as shown by the results of the 1953 Industrial Census.

### Characteristics and Structure of Industrial Activity

The data set out in Tables 4 and 5 have been derived from the results of two Censuses and a Manufacturing Survey. The first Census for the period, 1 July 1944-30 June 1945, covered manufacturing establishments only; the second Census for the year 1953, covered mining and manufacturing units; and the Annual Manufacturing Survey used was for the year 1958. The data from the first Census of Manufactures were published by the Contraloría General de la República in *Primer Censo Industrial, Resumen General*. The data from the second Census were issued by the Departamento Administrativo Nacional de Estadística in the *Boletin Mensual de Estadística,* Nos. 67, October 1956 and 72, March 1957, and in *Anuario General de Estadística,* 1954. The results of the 1958 Annual Manufacturing Survey were published in *Cifras Estadísticas de la Industria Manufacturera Nacio-*

### Indices de l'emploi dans l'industrie

Les indices de l'emploi dans les industries manufacturières reproduits au tableau 3 ont été établis à partir des indices de l'emploi publiés mensuellement dans le *Boletin Mensual de Estadística* et annuellement dans *Anuario General de Estadística* par le Departamento Administrativo Nacional de Estadística. Ces indices sont tirés des résultats d'une enquête mensuelle par sondage sur l'emploi dans les industries manufacturières.

A partir de janvier 1955, on s'est servi, pour cette enquête sur l'emploi, d'un échantillon stratifié d'établissements compris dans les résultats publiés du recensement industriel de 1953. L'enquête mensuelle par sondage portait sur tous les établissements de 50 salariés ou plus, 25 à 30 p. 100 des établissements de 20 à 49 salariés, et 5 à 10 p. 100 des établissements de 5 à 19 salariés. En juillet 1956, on a modifié la structure de l'échantillon de manière à y inclure tous les établissements de 50 salariés ou plus, 25 p. 100 des établissements de 15 à 49 salariés et 5 p. 100 des établissements de 5 à 14 salariés. Géographiquement, l'enquête couvrait tous les départements, à l'exception de Choco.

Les chiffres absolus mensuels relatifs au nombre de personnes occupées, sur lesquels sont fondés les indices annuels, concernent l'effectif moyen des ouvriers pendant la dernière période de paie du mois et le nombre mensuel moyen des autres salariés. Les chiffres annuels sont les moyennes arithmétiques des chiffres mensuels. Toutes les personnes recevant une rémunération, à l'exclusion des travailleurs à domicile, sont comptées comme salariés même si elles sont en congé payé ou en congé de maladie.

Les indices des séries de base utilisés sont combinés en indices de catégories détaillées, puis en indices de classes et, enfin, en indices relatifs à l'ensemble des industries manufacturières, la base de pondération utilisée étant, à chaque fois, le nombre de salariés fourni par le recensement industriel de 1953.

### Caractéristiques et structure de l'activité industrielle

Les chiffres des tableaux 4 et 5 sont tirés des résultats de deux recensements et d'une enquête sur les industries manufacturières. Le premier recensement, pour la période 1er juillet 1944-30 juin 1945, ne portait que sur les établissements manufacturiers; le second recensement, pour l'année 1953, couvrait les unités des industries extractives et manufacturières; l'enquête annuelle sur les industries manufacturières utilisée était relative à 1958. Les résultats du premier recensement des industries manufacturières ont été publiés par la Contraloría General de la República dans *Primer Censo Industrial, Resumen General.* Ceux du second recensement ont été publiés par le Departamento Administrativo Nacional de Estadística dans *Boletin Mensual de Estadística,* No 67, octobre 1956, et No 72, mars 1957, ainsi que dans *Anuario General de Estadística,* 1954. Les résultats de l'enquête annuelle de

*nal, 1958;* (junio 1961) ; by the Departamento Administrativo Nacional de Estadística.

The Census for the period, 1 July 1944-30 June 1945, related to manufacturing establishments the annual gross production of which was valued at 6,000 pesos or more whereas the second Census related to all mining and manufacturing establishments. However, in the case of the second Census, complete and detailed tabulations were prepared only for mining and manufacturing units engaging five or more persons or producing goods the gross value of which was 24,000 pesos or more, and it is these data, together with data from the first Census, which are set out in Table 4. The distinction between large and small establishments utilized in the 1953 Census is roughly comparable to the lower limit of coverage in the first Census of Manufactures. In the case of the second Census, a sample of the smaller manufacturing establishments was also tabulated in order to issue figures of key items of data. These tabulations, plus the tables relating to the larger establishments, are the basis of the data in Table 5.

The manufacturing industry survey for 1958 related to all establishments engaging 5 or more persons or having a gross value of production during the year of 24,000 pesos or more. The survey utilized sampling techniques to cover a small section of the establishments included in the field of coverage. The enumeration covered all establishments engaging 10 or more persons, all establishments engaging 5 or more persons or having a gross value of production during the year of 24,000 pesos or more in 11 out of the country's 15 administrative departments but in all departments for ISIC major groups 34 to 38. A systematic sample was utilized to cover all other establishments which fell within the field of coverage of the Survey.

Generally the definitions of the items of data are consistent with the International Standards in Basic Industrial Statistics. However, there were two deviations in the 1953 Census, the statistical and tabulating unit in the case of mining was the enterprise, and in all enquiries the number of and wages and salaries of employees include the number of and payments to homeworkers. Value added is valued at market prices. The capacity of all (in use and in reserve) power equipment, in 1944-45 and 1953 is the sum of the horsepower of all prime movers plus electric motors driven by purchased electricity; in 1958 it is the sum of the horsepower of prime movers connected to machinery other than generators plus all electric motors.

1958 sur les industries manufacturières ont été publiés par le Departamento Administrativo Nacional de Estadística dans *Cifras Estadísticas de la Industria Manufacturera Nacional, 1958* (juin 1961) .

Le recensement pour la période 1er juillet 1944-30 juin 1945 portait sur les établissements manufacturiers ayant une production brute évaluée à 6.000 pesos ou plus par an, tandis que le second recensement couvrait tous les établissements miniers et manufacturiers. Toutefois, dans le cas de ce dernier recensement, un classement complet et détaillé des données n'a été fait que pour les unités minières et manufacturières occupant 5 personnes ou plus ou produisant des marchandises d'une valeur brute de 24.000 pesos ou plus, et ce sont ces données qui, avec celles du premier recensement, sont reproduites au tableau 4. La distinction entre grands et petits établissements utilisée dans le recensement de 1953 est à peu près comparable à la limite inférieure de couverture adoptée pour le premier recensement des industries manufacturières. Dans le cas du second recensement, on a également exploité les chiffres d'un échantillon de petits établissements manufacturiers afin de publier des données pour les principales rubriques. Ce sont les résultats de cette opération qui, avec les chiffres tabulés des grands établissements, ont servi de base aux données du tableau 5.

L'enquête de 1958 sur les industries manufacturières portait sur tous les établissements occupant 5 personnes ou plus ou ayant eu, pendant l'année de l'enquête, une production d'une valeur brute de 24.000 pesos ou plus. Les méthodes de sondage n'ont été utilisées que pour une faible partie des établissements compris dans le champ de couverture. Dans 11 des 15 départements du pays et, pour les classes 34 à 38 de la CITI, dans tous les départements sans exception, on a dénombré tous les établissements occupant au moins 10 personnes, ainsi que tous les établissements occupant au moins 5 personnes ou ayant eu, pendant l'année, une production d'une valeur brute de 24.000 pesos ou plus. Un échantillon systématique a été utilisé pour tous les autres établissements inclus dans le champ de couverture de l'enquête.

Généralement, les définitions des rubriques utilisées sont compatibles avec les Normes internationales relatives aux statistiques industrielles de base. Dans le recensement de 1953, cependant, elles s'en écartent sur deux points : d'une part, l'entreprise a été utilisée comme unité statistique et de classement dans le cas des industries extractives; d'autre part, dans toutes les enquêtes, le nombre de salariés comprend celui des travailleurs à domicile, et les traitements et salaires des salariés comprennent les paiements versés à ces travailleurs. La valeur ajoutée est comptée aux prix du marché. En 1944-1945 et 1953, la puissance installée (en service ou en réserve) est égale au nombre de chevaux-vapeur de tous les moteurs primaires et de tous les moteurs électriques actionnés par de l'électricité achetée; en 1958, c'est le nombre de chevaux-vapeur des moteurs primaires entraînant des machines autres que des générateurs plus celui de tous les moteurs électriques.

# COLOMBIA

## 1.  THE GROSS DOMESTIC PRODUCT — PRODUIT INTERIEUR BRUT

Million Pesos                                                                 Millions de pesos

### A.   Expenditure on the Gross Domestic Product at Market Prices
### Dépenses relatives au produit intérieur brut aux prix du marché

| Item of data and year / Rubrique et année | Total | Consumption / Consommation | | Gross Domestic Capital Formation / Formation brute de capital intérieur | | Net exports of goods and services / Exportations nettes de biens et de services | |
|---|---|---|---|---|---|---|---|
| | | Total | Government / Etat | Total | Fixed / Fixe | Exports less imports / Exportations moins importations | Exports / Exportations |
| **a. At Current Prices — Aux prix courants** | | | | | | | |
| Absolute figures — Chiffres absolus | | | | | | | |
| 1950 | 7 860.5 | 6 522.6 | 433.2 | 1 324.7 | 1 112.7 | 13.2 | 913.1 |
| 1951 | 8 940.9 | 7 559.0 | 520.8 | 1 360.3 | 1 189.3 | 21.6 | 1 170.2 |
| 1952 | 9 650.9 | 8 166.2 | 581.8 | 1 492.6 | 1 333.2 | −7.9 | 1 196.5 |
| 1953 | 10 734.7 | 9 071.9 | 724.1 | 1 640.1 | 1 785.6 | 22.7 | 1 611.7 |
| 1954 | 12 758.8 | 10 665.1 | 856.0 | 2 142.0 | 2 161.8 | −48.3 | 1 848.9 |
| 1955 | 13 249.8 | 11 048.3 | 937.9 | 2 381.1 | 2 383.0 | −179.6 | 1 801.3 |
| 1956 | 14 862.8 | 11 857.8 | 959.4 | 2 704.6 | 2 526.7 | 300.4 | 2 319.6 |
| 1957 | 17 810.6 | 13 824.4 | 1 021.6 | 3 533.0 | 2 643.3 | 453.2 | 2 962.9 |
| 1958 | 20 682.5 | 16 347.5 | 1 196.1 | 3 862.6 | 3 338.8 | 472.4 | 3 891.1 |
| 1959 | 23 472.1 | 18 386.5 | 1 369.5 | 4 395.6 | 3 907.9 | 690.0 | 4 158.9 |
| 1960 | 26 417.6 | 21 468.4 | 1 659.3 | 5 476.6 | 4 826.7 | −527.4 | 3 792.2 |
| Percentage distribution of average annual expenditure — Distribution en pourcentage des dépenses annuelles moyennes | | | | | | | |
| 1950–1960 | 100.0 | 81.1 | 6.2 | 18.2 | 16.3 | 0.7 | 15.4 |
| 1950 | 100.0 | 83.0 | 5.5 | 16.8 | 14.2 | 0.2 | 11.6 |
| 1953 | 100.0 | 84.5 | 6.7 | 15.3 | 16.6 | 0.2 | 15.0 |
| 1954 | 100.0 | 83.6 | 6.7 | 16.8 | 16.9 | −0.4 | 14.5 |
| 1958 | 100.0 | 79.0 | 5.8 | 18.7 | 16.1 | 2.3 | 18.8 |
| 1960 | 100.0 | 81.3 | 6.3 | 20.7 | 18.3 | −2.0 | 14.4 |
| **b. At Prices of 1958 — Aux prix de 1958** | | | | | | | |
| Absolute figures — Chiffres absolus | | | | | | | |
| 1950 | 14 688.8 | 11 999.7 | 856.0 | 3 219.4 | 2 771.8 | −530.3 | 2 774.4 |
| 1951 | 15 146.6 | 12 148.2 | 965.5 | 3 073.0 | 2 752.5 | −74.6 | 3 109.2 |
| 1952 | 16 102.0 | 12 940.1 | 1 026.7 | 3 252.8 | 2 965.4 | −90.9 | 3 144.4 |
| 1953 | 17 081.0 | 13 879.8 | 1 231.9 | 3 785.9 | 4 011.7 | −584.7 | 3 858.7 |
| 1954 | 18 262.3 | 15 055.7 | 1 277.3 | 4 651.0 | 4 670.0 | −1 444.4 | 3 471.3 |
| 1955 | 18 976.1 | 15 647.5 | 1 329.4 | 4 924.0 | 4 935.7 | −1 595.4 | 3 535.3 |
| 1956 | 19 745.7 | 15 871.3 | 1 285.1 | 4 924.9 | 4 683.7 | −1 050.5 | 3 653.1 |
| 1957 | 20 186.2 | 16 060.7 | 1 146.4 | 4 460.7 | 3 511.6 | −335.2 | 3 678.5 |
| 1958 | 20 682.5 | 16 347.5 | 1 196.1 | 3 862.6 | 3 338.8 | 472.4 | 3 891.1 |
| 1959 | 22 128.6 | 17 284.3 | 1 214.3 | 4 072.9 | 3 587.7 | 771.4 | 4 502.7 |
| 1960 | 23 041.8 | 18 470.3 | 1 339.6 | 4 756.2 | 4 209.6 | −184.7 | 4 129.8 |
| Percentage distribution of average annual expenditure — Distribution en pourcentage des dépenses annuelles moyennes | | | | | | | |
| 1950–1960 | 100.0 | 80.4 | 6.2 | 21.8 | 20.1 | −2.2 | 19.3 |
| 1950 | 100.0 | 81.7 | 5.8 | 21.9 | 18.9 | −3.6 | 18.9 |
| 1953 | 100.0 | 81.2 | 7.2 | 22.2 | 23.5 | −3.4 | 22.6 |
| 1954 | 100.0 | 82.4 | 7.0 | 25.5 | 25.6 | −7.9 | 19.0 |
| 1958 | 100.0 | 79.0 | 5.8 | 18.7 | 16.1 | 2.3 | 18.8 |
| 1960 | 100.0 | 80.2 | 5.8 | 20.6 | 18.3 | −0.8 | 17.9 |
| Average annual rate of growth — Taux annuel moyen d'accroissement | | | | | | | |
| 1950–1960 | 4.6 | 4.4 | 4.6 | 4.0 | 4.3 | . | 4.1 |
| 1950–1953 | 5.2 | 5.0 | 12.9 | 5.6 | 13.1 | . | 11.6 |
| 1954–1958 | 3.2 | 2.1 | −1.5 | −4.6 | −8.1 | . | 2.9 |
| 1958–1960 | 5.5 | 6.3 | 5.8 | 11.0 | 12.3 | . | 3.0 |

## B. The Gross Domestic Product at Factor Cost According to Origin
## Origine par secteur d'activité du produit intérieur brut au coût des facteurs

| Item of data and year / Rubrique et année | Total | Agricultural sector / Secteur agricole | Industrial Sector — Secteur industriel | | | | | Transportation and communication / Transports et communications | Other sectors[1] / Autres secteurs[1] |
| | | | Total | Mining / Industries extractives | Manufacturing / Industries manufacturières | Construction / Bâtiment et travaux publics | Electricity, gas and water / Electricité, gaz et eau | | |
| ISIC — CITI | 0–9 | 0 | 1–5 | 1 | 2–3 | 4 | 5 | 7 | 6, 8–9 |
| a. At Current Prices — Aux prix courants | | | | | | | | | |
| Absolute figures — Chiffres absolus | | | | | | | | | |
| 1950 | 7 400.5 | 2 848.8 | 1 611.5 | 158.2 | 1 209.5 | 203.5 | 40.3 | 535.8 | 2 404.4 |
| 1951 | 8 345.2 | 3 235.3 | 1 775.4 | 217.9 | 1 290.6 | 213.3 | 53.6 | 576.4 | 2 758.1 |
| 1952 | 9 003.4 | 3 498.8 | 1 879.7 | 238.5 | 1 351.4 | 235.0 | 54.8 | 676.3 | 2 948.6 |
| 1953 | 10 006.6 | 3 790.3 | 2 118.5 | 254.4 | 1 496.5 | 302.8 | 64.8 | 744.7 | 3 353.1 |
| 1954 | 11 808.4 | 4 661.8 | 2 435.4 | 262.6 | 1 686.8 | 411.5 | 74.5 | 837.2 | 3 874.0 |
| 1955 | 12 254.4 | 4 541.2 | 2 731.6 | 276.5 | 1 891.2 | 476.2 | 87.7 | 921.9 | 4 059.7 |
| 1956 | 13 875.5 | 5 244.3 | 3 102.5 | 325.8 | 2 121.1 | 548.1 | 107.5 | 1 070.2 | 4 458.5 |
| 1957 | 16 739.9 | 6 481.0 | 3 841.6 | 479.4 | 2 643.9 | 599.7 | 118.6 | 1 158.8 | 5 258.5 |
| 1958 | 19 311.0 | 7 196.9 | 4 667.8 | 736.5 | 3 127.0 | 659.8 | 144.5 | 1 237.3 | 6 209.0 |
| 1959 | 21 943.0 | 7 897.5 | 5 446.9 | 802.9 | 3 633.0 | 842.0 | 169.0 | 1 344.3 | 7 254.3 |
| 1960 | 24 744.2 | 8 553.0 | 6 336.9 | 985.6 | 4 211.1 | 909.4 | 230.8 | 1 589.1 | 8 265.2 |
| Percentage distribution according to sector— Distribution en pourcentage par secteur | | | | | | | | | |
| 1950 – 1960 | 100.0 | 37.3 | 23.1 | 3.0 | 15.9 | 3.5 | 0.7 | 6.9 | 32.7 |
| 1950 | 100.0 | 38.5 | 21.8 | 2.1 | 16.3 | 2.9 | 0.5 | 7.2 | 32.5 |
| 1953 | 100.0 | 37.9 | 21.2 | 2.6 | 15.0 | 3.0 | 0.6 | 7.4 | 33.5 |
| 1954 | 100.0 | 39.5 | 20.6 | 2.2 | 14.3 | 3.5 | 0.6 | 7.1 | 32.8 |
| 1958 | 100.0 | 37.3 | 24.1 | 3.8 | 16.2 | 3.4 | 0.7 | 6.4 | 32.2 |
| 1960 | 100.0 | 34.6 | 25.6 | 4.0 | 17.0 | 3.7 | 0.9 | 6.4 | 33.4 |
| b. At Prices of 1958 — Aux prix de 1958 | | | | | | | | | |
| Absolute figures — Chiffres absolus | | | | | | | | | |
| 1950 | 13 754.2 | 5 568.7 | 2 888.9 | 515.6 | 1 914.2 | 388.8 | 70.3 | 798.4 | 4 498.2 |
| 1951 | 14 177.3 | 5 637.5 | 2 993.8 | 574.5 | 1 974.1 | 370.1 | 75.1 | 873.6 | 4 672.4 |
| 1952 | 15 070.3 | 6 021.5 | 3 166.7 | 576.7 | 2 111.1 | 396.7 | 82.2 | 988.4 | 4 893.7 |
| 1953 | 15 940.8 | 6 041.4 | 3 489.7 | 603.2 | 2 298.5 | 496.0 | 92.0 | 1 075.5 | 5 334.2 |
| 1954 | 16 994.1 | 6 201.9 | 3 876.5 | 620.9 | 2 507.7 | 646.8 | 101.1 | 1 187.1 | 5 728.6 |
| 1955 | 17 675.6 | 6 358.3 | 4 118.0 | 637.1 | 2 673.5 | 696.2 | 111.2 | 1 314.9 | 5 884.4 |
| 1956 | 18 407.6 | 6 568.2 | 4 407.1 | 695.3 | 2 866.9 | 719.9 | 125.0 | 1 344.9 | 6 087.4 |
| 1957 | 18 842.2 | 6 976.7 | 4 528.8 | 718.1 | 2 996.0 | 680.5 | 134.2 | 1 313.0 | 6 023.7 |
| 1958 | 19 311.0 | 7 196.9 | 4 667.8 | 736.5 | 3 127.0 | 659.8 | 144.5 | 1 237.3 | 6 209.0 |
| 1959 | 20 627.6 | 7 552.8 | 5 135.1 | 855.1 | 3 381.6 | 733.5 | 164.9 | 1 327.1 | 6 612.6 |
| 1960 | 21 442.6 | 7 561.8 | 5 354.9 | 886.0 | 3 586.6 | 689.6 | 192.7 | 1 469.5 | 7 056.4 |
| Percentage distribution according to sector— Distribution en pourcentage par secteur | | | | | | | | | |
| 1950 – 1960 | 100.0 | 37.3 | 23.2 | 3.8 | 15.3 | 3.4 | 0.7 | 6.7 | 32.8 |
| 1950 | 100.0 | 40.5 | 21.0 | 3.8 | 13.9 | 2.8 | 0.5 | 5.8 | 32.7 |
| 1953 | 100.0 | 37.9 | 21.9 | 3.8 | 14.4 | 3.1 | 0.6 | 6.7 | 33.5 |
| 1954 | 100.0 | 36.5 | 22.8 | 3.6 | 14.8 | 3.8 | 0.6 | 7.0 | 33.7 |
| 1958 | 100.0 | 37.3 | 24.1 | 3.8 | 16.2 | 3.4 | 0.7 | 6.4 | 32.2 |
| 1960 | 100.0 | 35.3 | 25.0 | 4.2 | 16.7 | 3.2 | 0.9 | 6.8 | 32.9 |
| Average annual rate of growth—Taux annuel moyen d'accroissement | | | | | | | | | |
| 1950 – 1960 | 4.5 | 3.1 | 6.4 | 5.6 | 6.5 | 5.9 | 10.6 | 6.3 | 4.6 |
| 1950 – 1953 | 5.0 | 2.8 | 6.5 | 5.4 | 6.3 | 8.5 | 9.4 | 10.4 | 5.9 |
| 1954 – 1958 | 3.2 | 3.8 | 4.8 | 4.4 | 5.7 | 0.5 | 9.3 | 1.0 | 2.0 |
| 1958 – 1960 | 5.4 | 2.5 | 7.1 | 9.7 | 7.1 | 2.2 | 15.5 | 9.0 | 6.6 |

[1] Includes all services of general government.

[1] Y compris tous les services de l'Etat.

# COLOMBIA

## 2. INDEX NUMBERS OF INDUSTRIAL PRODUCTION
### INDICES DE LA PRODUCTION INDUSTRIELLE

### A. The Divisions of Industrial Activity
### Les branches de l'activité industrielle

| Period Période | Total | Mining [1] Industries extractives | Manu-facturing Industries manu-facturières | Construction Bâtiment et travaux publics | Electricity Electricité |
|---|---|---|---|---|---|
| ISIC — CITI | 1-4, 511 | 1 | 2-3 | 4 | 511 |

#### a. Indexes — Indices (1958 = 100)

| | | | | | |
|---|---|---|---|---|---|
| 1950....... | 61 | 70 | 56 | 59 | 49 |
| 1951....... | 64 | 78 | 58 | 56 | 52 |
| 1952....... | 67 | 78 | 63 | 60 | 57 |
| 1953....... | 74 | 82 | 70 | 75 | 64 |
| 1954....... | 83 | 84 | 78 | 98 | 70 |
| 1955....... | 87 | 86 | 84 | 106 | 77 |
| 1956....... | 94 | 94 | 91 | 109 | 87 |
| 1957....... | 97 | 98 | 95 | 103 | 93 |
| 1958....... | 100 | 100 | 100 | 100 | 100 |
| 1959....... | 110 | 116 | 110 | 111 | 114 |
| 1960....... | 115 | 120 | 117 | 104 | 133 |

#### b. Average Annual Rate of Change — Taux annuel moyen de variation

| | | | | | |
|---|---|---|---|---|---|
| 1950 - 1960. | 6.5 | 5.5 | 7.6 | 5.8 | 10.5 |
| 1954 - 1958. | 4.8 | 4.4 | 6.4 | 0.5 | 9.3 |
| 1958 - 1960. | 7.2 | 9.5 | 8.2 | 2.0 | 15.5 |

For footnotes see end of table.

Pour les notes, voir au bas du tableau.

### B. Selected Major Groups of Mining
### Quelques classes de la branche Industries extractives

| Period Période | All mining [1] Toutes industries extractives [1] | Metal mining Extraction des minerais métalliques | Crude petroleum and natural gas Pétrole brut et gaz naturel | Other mining [2] Autres industries extractives |
|---|---|---|---|---|
| ISIC — CITI | 1 | 12 | 13 | 11, 14-19 |

#### a. Indexes — Indices (1958 = 100)

| | | | | |
|---|---|---|---|---|
| 1950.......... | 70 | 93 | 73 | 49 |
| 1951.......... | 78 | 101 | 82 | 49 |
| 1952.......... | 78 | 100 | 82 | 57 |
| 1953.......... | 82 | 107 | 84 | 59 |
| 1954.......... | 84 | 95 | 85 | 70 |
| 1955.......... | 86 | 102 | 85 | 78 |
| 1956.......... | 94 | 115 | 94 | 86 |
| 1957.......... | 98 | 92 | 98 | 89 |
| 1958.......... | 100 | 100 | 100 | 100 |
| 1959.......... | 116 | 103 | 114 | 105 |
| 1960.......... | 120 | 110 | 119 | 109 |

#### b. Average Annual Rate of Change — Taux annuel moyen de variation

| | | | | |
|---|---|---|---|---|
| 1950 - 1960.... | 5.5 | 1.7 | 5.0 | 8.3 |
| 1954 - 1958.... | 4.4 | 1.3 | 4.1 | 9.3 |
| 1958 - 1960.... | 9.5 | 4.9 | 9.1 | 4.4 |

For footnotes see end of table.

Pour les notes, voir au bas du tableau.

### C. The Major Groups of Manufacturing — Les classes de la branche Industries manufacturières

| Period Période | Manu-facturing Industries manu-facturières | Food, beverages and tobacco Industries alimentaires, boissons, tabac | Textiles | Clothing, footwear and made-up textiles Articles d'habillement, chaussures et ouvrages en tissu | Wood products and furniture Bois et meubles | Paper and paper products Papier et ouvrages en papier | Printing and publishing Imprimerie et édition | Leather and leather products except wearing apparel Cuir et articles en cuir, à l'exclusion des articles d'habillement | Rubber products Ouvrages en caoutchouc | Chemicals and chemical, petroleum and coal products Produits chimiques et dérivés du pétrole et du charbon | Non-metallic mineral products Produits minéraux non métalliques | Basic metals Métallurgie de base | Metal products Ouvrages en métaux |
|---|---|---|---|---|---|---|---|---|---|---|---|---|---|
| ISIC — CITI | 2-3 | 20-22 | 23 | 24 | 25-26 | 27 | 28 | 29 | 30 | 31-32 | 33 | 34 | 35-38 |

#### a. Indexes — Indices (1958 = 100)

| | | | | | | | | | | | | | |
|---|---|---|---|---|---|---|---|---|---|---|---|---|---|
| 1938.............. | 45 | 26 | 20 | 28 | 30 | 10 | 21 | 15 | 1 | 12 | 19 | 2 | 7 |
| 1948.............. | 48 | 56 | 46 | 52 | 47 | 24 | 45 | 51 | 22 | 35 | 48 | 7 | 21 |
| 1949.............. | 53 | 63 | 47 | 54 | 50 | 27 | 42 | 67 | 23 | 39 | 53 | 8 | 23 |
| 1950.............. | – 56 – | – 69 – | – 58 – | – 59 – | – 53 – | – 42 – | – 49 – | – 71 – | – 39 – | – 44 – | – 64 – | – 10 – | – 28 – |
| 1951.............. | 58 | 74 | 53 | 54 | 56 | 47 | 56 | 64 | 40 | 47 | 58 | 10 | 31 |
| 1952.............. | 63 | 77 | 62 | 62 | 60 | 57 | 62 | 76 | 42 | 50 | 68 | 10 | 34 |
| 1953.............. | 70 | 83 | 69 | 67 | 64 | 68 | 76 | 82 | 57 | 58 | 81 | 9 | 41 |
| 1954.............. | 78 | 93 | 79 | 78 | 64 | 80 | 76 | 80 | 67 | 64 | 81 | 11 | 47 |
| 1955.............. | 84 | 91 | 90 | 85 | 65 | 87 | 95 | 84 | 80 | 75 | 89 | 59 | 53 |
| 1956.............. | 91 | 94 | 91 | 96 | 86 | 94 | 112 | 96 | 96 | 81 | 110 | 78 | 68 |
| 1957.............. | 95 | 96 | 94 | 100 | 97 | 101 | 108 | 105 | 99 | 91 | 102 | 96 | 84 |
| 1958.............. | 100 | 100 | 100 | 100 | 100 | 100 | 100 | 100 | 100 | 100 | 100 | 100 | 100 |
| 1959.............. | 110 | 108 | 109 | 113 | 102 | 118 | 104 | 92 | 105 | 113 | 122 | 91 | 120 |
| 1960.............. | 117 | 112 | 119 | 123 | 102 | 139 | 103 | 95 | 119 | 120 | 119 | 124 | 136 |

#### b. Average Annual Rate of Change — Taux annuel moyen de variation

| | | | | | | | | | | | | | |
|---|---|---|---|---|---|---|---|---|---|---|---|---|---|
| 1938 - 1960........ | 4.4 | 6.9 | 8.4 | 7.0 | 5.7 | 12.7 | 7.5 | 8.8 | 24.3 | 11.0 | 8.7 | 20.6 | 14.4 |
| 1938 - 1948........ | 0.7 | 8.0 | 8.7 | 6.4 | 4.6 | 9.2 | 7.9 | 13.0 | 36.2 | 11.3 | 9.7 | 13.3 | 11.6 |
| 1950 - 1960........ | 7.6 | 5.0 | 7.5 | 7.6 | 6.8 | 12.7 | 7.7 | 3.0 | 11.8 | 10.6 | 6.4 | 28.6 | 17.1 |
| 1948 - 1953........ | 7.8 | 8.2 | 8.4 | 5.2 | 6.4 | 23.2 | 11.1 | 10.0 | 21.0 | 10.6 | 11.0 | 5.2 | 14.3 |
| 1954 - 1958........ | 4.4 | 1.8 | 6.1 | 6.4 | 11.8 | 5.7 | 7.1 | 5.7 | 10.5 | 11.8 | 5.4 | 73.6 | 20.8 |
| 1958 - 1960........ | 8.2 | 5.8 | 9.1 | 10.9 | 1.0 | 17.9 | 1.5 | -2.5 | 9.1 | 9.5 | 9.1 | 11.4 | 16.6 |

[1] Includes construction on own account.
[2] Includes Coal mining (ISIC major group 11).

[1] Y compris construction pour compte propre.
[2] Y compris Extraction du charbon (CITI 11).

# 3. INDEX NUMBERS OF MANUFACTURING EMPLOYMENT

## INDICES DE L'EMPLOI DANS LES INDUSTRIES MANUFACTURIERES

| Period<br>Période | Manu-<br>facturing<br><br>Industries<br>manufac-<br>turières | Food,<br>beverages<br>and<br>tobacco<br><br>Industries<br>alimen-<br>taires,<br>boissons,<br>tabac | Textiles | Clothing,<br>footwear<br>and<br>made-up<br>textiles<br><br>Articles<br>d'habil-<br>lement,<br>chaussures<br>et<br>ouvrages<br>en tissu | Wood<br>products<br>and<br>furniture<br><br>Bois et<br>meubles | Paper<br>and<br>paper<br>products,<br>printing<br>and<br>publishing<br><br>Papier<br>et<br>ouvrages<br>en<br>papier,<br>imprimerie<br>et<br>édition | Leather<br>and<br>leather<br>products<br>except<br>wearing<br>apparel<br><br>Cuir et<br>articles<br>en cuir,<br>à l'exclu-<br>sion<br>des<br>articles<br>d'habil-<br>lement | Rubber<br>products<br><br>Ouvrages<br>en<br>caout-<br>chouc | Chemicals<br>and<br>chemical,<br>petroleum<br>and<br>coal<br>products<br><br>Produits<br>chi-<br>miques<br>et<br>dérivés<br>du<br>pétrole<br>et du<br>charbon | Non-<br>metallic<br>mineral<br>products<br><br>Produits<br>minéraux<br>non<br>métal-<br>liques | Basic<br>metals<br>and<br>metal<br>products<br><br>Métal-<br>lurgie<br>de base<br>et<br>ouvrages<br>en<br>métaux | Other<br>manu-<br>facturing<br><br>Autres<br>industries<br>manufac-<br>turières |
|---|---|---|---|---|---|---|---|---|---|---|---|---|
| ISIC — CITI | 2–3 | 20–22 | 23 | 24 | 25–26 | 27–28 | 29 | 30 | 31–32 | 33 | 34–38 | 39 |
| *a.* Indexes — Indices (1958 = 100) | | | | | | | | | | | | |
| 1953.............. | 83 | 95 | 81 | 87 | 77 | 82 | 72 | 54 | 73 | 76 | 80 | 88 |
| 1955.............. | 91 | 96 | 92 | 91 | 87 | 88 | 72 | 79 | 84 | 91 | 95 | 85 |
| 1956.............. | 98 | 98 | 95 | 106 | 98 | 99 | 95 | 98 | 90 | 100 | 98 | 96 |
| 1957.............. | 100 | 99 | 100 | 107 | 98 | 99 | 98 | 101 | 94 | 103 | 99 | 93 |
| 1958.............. | 100 | 100 | 100 | 100 | 100 | 100 | 100 | 100 | 100 | 100 | 100 | 100 |
| 1959.............. | 104 | 103 | 104 | 105 | 100 | 104 | 100 | 104 | 108 | 103 | 104 | 105 |
| 1960.............. | 107 | 105 | 110 | 106 | 99 | 111 | 100 | 117 | 110 | 105 | 111 | 102 |
| 1961.............. | 109 | 107 | 112 | 106 | 100 | 115 | 99 | 124 | 110 | 105 | 113 | 104 |
| *b.* Average Annual Rate of Change — Taux annuel moyen de variation | | | | | | | | | | | | |
| 1953 – 1958........ | 3.8 | 1.0 | 4.3 | 2.8 | 5.4 | 4.1 | 6.8 | 13.1 | 6.5 | 5.6 | 4.6 | 2.6 |
| 1958 – 1961........ | 2.9 | 2.3 | 3.8 | 2.0 | — | 4.8 | −0.3 | 7.4 | 3.2 | 1.6 | 4.2 | 1.3 |

## 4. CHARACTERISTICS OF LARGE INDUSTRIAL ESTABLISHMENTS

### 1 July 1944–30 June 1945, 1953, 1958

## CARACTERISTIQUES DES GRANDS ETABLISSEMENTS INDUSTRIELS

### 1er juillet 1944–30 juin 1945, 1953, 1958

Number of establishments in units; value added and wages and salaries in million Pesos; number of engaged and employees in thousands; capacity of installed power equipment in thousand horsepower; value added per employee or person engaged and wages and salaries per employee in thousand Pesos; and capacity of installed power equipment per person engaged in horsepower.

Nombre d'établissements en unités; valeur ajoutée et traitements et salaires en millions de pesos; nombre de personnes occupées et de salariés en milliers; puissance installée en milliers de chevaux-vapeur; valeur ajoutée par salarié ou par personne occupée et traitements et salaires par salarié en milliers de pesos; puissance installée par personne occupée en chevaux-vapeur.

### A. The Major Groups of Mining — Les classes de la branche Industries extractives

| Item of data | 1953 | | | | | Rubrique |
|---|---|---|---|---|---|---|
| | All mining<br><br>Toutes industries extractives | Coal mining<br><br>Extraction du charbon | Metal mining<br><br>Extraction des minerais métalliques | Crude petroleum and natural gas<br><br>Pétrole brut et gaz naturel | Other mining<br><br>Autres industries extractives | |
| ISIC | 1 | 11 | 12 | 13 | 14–19 | CITI |
| *a.* Absolute Figures — Chiffres absolus | | | | | | |
| Number of enterprises............... | 914 | 344 | 94 | 7 | 469 | Nombre d'entreprises |
| Value added...................... | 287.1 | 13.2 | 33.7 | 222.5 | 17.7 | Valeur ajoutée |
| Number of engaged<br>(Last pay period of November)....... | 19.9 | 4.9 | 4.3 | 7.7 | 3.0 | Nombre de personnes occupées (dernière période de paie de novembre) |
| Number of employees<br>(Last pay period of November)....... | 18.6 | 4.4 | 4.1 | 7.7 | 2.4 | Nombre de salariés (dernière période de paie de novembre) |
| Wages and salaries................. | 79.9 | 8.0 | 12.3 | 55.2 | 4.4 | Traitements et salaires payés |
| Capacity of installed power equipment (31.XII.1953)..................... | 150.6 | 5.7 | 47.5 | 92.9 | 4.5 | Puissance installée (31.XII.1953) |
| *b.* Structure | | | | | | |
| Distribution in percent of: | | | | | | Distribution en pourcentage: |
| Value added..................... | 100.0 | 4.6 | 11.7 | 77.5 | 6.2 | Valeur ajoutée |
| Number of engaged............... | 100.0 | 24.6 | 21.6 | 38.7 | 15.1 | Nombre de personnes occupées |
| Value added per person engaged...... | 14.4 | 2.7 | 7.8 | 28.9 | 5.9 | Valeur ajoutée par personne occupée |
| Value added per unit of wages and salaries.................... | 3.6 | 1.6 | 2.7 | 4.0 | 4.0 | Valeur ajoutée par unité de traitements et salaires |
| Wages and salaries per employee...... | 4.3 | 1.8 | 3.0 | 7.2 | 1.8 | Traitements et salaires par salarié |
| Employees as a percent of engaged..... | 93.5 | 89.8 | 95.3 | 100.0 | 80.0 | Salariés en pourcentage des personnes occupées |
| Capacity of installed power equipment per person engaged............... | 7.57 | 1.16 | 11.05 | 12.06 | 1.50 | Puissance installée par personne occupée |

## B. The Major Groups of Manufacturing — Les classes de la branche Industries manufacturières

| Year and item of data | Manufacturing — Industries manufacturières | Food, beverages and tobacco — Industries alimentaires, boissons, tabac | Textiles | Clothing, footwear and made-up textiles — Articles d'habillement, chaussures et ouvrages en tissu | Wood products and furniture — Bois et meubles | Paper and paper products — Papier et ouvrages en papier | Printing and publishing — Imprimerie et édition | Leather and leather products except wearing apparel — Cuir et articles en cuir, à l'exclusion des articles d'habillement | Rubber products — Ouvrages en caoutchouc | Chemicals and chemical, petroleum and coal products — Produits chimiques et dérivés du pétrole et du charbon | Non-metallic mineral products — Produits minéraux non métalliques | Basic metals — Métallurgie de base | Metal products — Ouvrages en métaux | Other manufacturing — Autres industries manufacturières | Année et rubrique |
|---|---|---|---|---|---|---|---|---|---|---|---|---|---|---|---|
| ISIC | 2-3 | 20-22 | 23 | 24 | 25-26 | 27 | 28 | 29 | 30 | 31-32 | 33 | 34 | 35-38 | 39 | CITI |

*a. Absolute Figures — Chiffres absolus*

| Year and item of data | | | | | | | | | | | | | | | |
|---|---|---|---|---|---|---|---|---|---|---|---|---|---|---|---|
| **1.VII.1944—30.VI.1945** | | | | | | | | | | | | | | | **1.VII.1944—30.VI.1945** |
| Number of establishments | 7 810 | 2 735 | 337 | 1 566 | 839 | 38 | 252 | 316 | 42 | 385 | 556 | 31 | 497 | 216 | Nombre d'établissements |
| Value added | 144.6 | 48.2 | 29.0 | 12.0 | 7.9 | 0.6 | 7.5 | 3.5 | 1.7 | 9.0 | 13.2 | 0.9 | 8.6 | 2.5 | Valeur ajoutée |
| Number of employees (Pay period ending 30.VI) | 135.0 | 44.5 | 28.7 | 15.2 | 8.8 | 0.6 | 5.0 | 3.3 | 1.0 | 6.5 | 11.2 | 0.8 | 7.2 | 2.2 | Nombre de salariés (période de paie se terminant le 30.VI) |
| Wages and salaries paid | 92.6 | 29.8 | 19.5 | 7.3 | 5.7 | 0.3 | 5.0 | 2.4 | 0.8 | 5.6 | 7.7 | 0.6 | 6.2 | 1.7 | Traitements et salaires payés |
| **1953** | | | | | | | | | | | | | | | **1953** |
| Number of establishments | 11 243 | 3 443 | 553 | 2 754 | 957 | 51 | 338 | 291 | 72 | 497 | 981 | 66 | 996 | 244 | Nombre d'établissements |
| Value added | 1 498.5 | 669.6 | 266.1 | 99.6 | 37.7 | 15.5 | 42.5 | 26.2 | 35.5 | 113.8 | 98.8 | 8.3 | 67.3 | 17.6 | Valeur ajoutée |
| Number of engaged (Last pay period of November) | 199.1 | 59.1 | 36.6 | 28.6 | 9.8 | 2.0 | 7.7 | 4.0 | 2.8 | 11.6 | 17.9 | 1.4 | 14.1 | 3.5 | Nombre de personnes occupées (dernière période de paie de novembre) |
| Number of employees (Last pay period of November) | 181.2 | 53.5 | 35.3 | 24.3 | 8.4 | 1.9 | 7.3 | 3.6 | 2.8 | 10.9 | 16.3 | 1.3 | 12.6 | 3.0 | Nombre de salariés (dernière période de paie de novembre) |
| Wages and salaries paid | 430.4 | 131.9 | 90.8 | 38.3 | 16.2 | 5.1 | 21.3 | 10.4 | 8.2 | 34.4 | 33.7 | 3.8 | 29.6 | 6.7 | Traitements et salaires payés |
| Capacity of installed power equipment (As of 31.XII.1953) | 398.1 | 130.9 | 90.7 | 7.7 | 15.1 | 8.8 | 7.0 | 11.1 | 10.4 | 20.9 | 63.5 | 4.9 | 24.3 | 2.8 | Puissance installée (au 31.XII.1953) |
| **1958** | | | | | | | | | | | | | | | **1958** |
| Number of establishments | 11 125 | 3 249 | 463 | 2 211 | 906 | 84 | 439 | 267 | 52 | 599 | 991 | 75 | 1 562 | 227 | Nombre d'établissements |
| Value added | 3 234.0 | 1 224.2 | 534.6 | 175.1 | 66.7 | 45.6 | 94.7 | 47.0 | 75.7 | 398.3 | 180.5 | 71.3 | 258.8 | 61.5 | Valeur ajoutée |
| Number of engaged (Last pay period of November) | 236.8 | 55.0 | 39.4 | 30.7 | 11.0 | 3.4 | 9.8 | 4.9 | 5.0 | 16.5 | 20.5 | 5.4 | 29.9 | 5.3 | Nombre de personnes occupées (dernière période de paie de novembre) |
| Employees: Number (Last pay period of November) | 225.7 | 51.5 | 38.9 | 28.2 | 10.1 | 3.3 | 9.4 | 4.7 | 5.0 | 16.0 | 19.6 | 5.3 | 28.6 | 5.1 | Salariés: Nombre (dernière période de paie de novembre) |
| Wages and salaries | 1 048.3 | 237.8 | 198.5 | 77.8 | 34.6 | 17.5 | 45.4 | 19.2 | 31.3 | 110.6 | 78.8 | 38.1 | 133.4 | 25.3 | Traitements et salaires |
| Capacity of installed power equipment (31.XII) | 652.3 | 162.4 | 113.4 | 9.1 | 24.2 | 13.7 | 9.5 | 13.8 | 21.8 | 74.7 | 116.7 | 35.4 | 52.1 | 5.5 | Puissance installée (31.XII) |

*b. Structure*

| Year and item of data | | | | | | | | | | | | | | | |
|---|---|---|---|---|---|---|---|---|---|---|---|---|---|---|---|
| **1945** | | | | | | | | | | | | | | | **1945** |
| Distribution in percent of: | | | | | | | | | | | | | | | Distribution en pourcentage: |
| Value added | 100.0 | 33.3 | 20.0 | 8.3 | 5.5 | 0.4 | 5.2 | 2.4 | 1.2 | 6.2 | 9.2 | 0.6 | 5.9 | 1.8 | Valeur ajoutée |
| Number of employees | 100.0 | 32.9 | 21.3 | 11.2 | 6.6 | 0.4 | 3.7 | 2.4 | 0.8 | 4.8 | 8.3 | 0.6 | 5.3 | 1.7 | Nombre de salariés |
| Value added per employee | 1.1 | 1.1 | 1.0 | 0.8 | 0.9 | 1.0 | 1.5 | 1.1 | 1.7 | 1.4 | 1.2 | 1.1 | 1.2 | 1.1 | Valeur ajoutée par salarié |
| Wages and salaries per employee | 0.7 | 0.7 | 0.7 | 0.5 | 0.6 | 0.5 | 1.0 | 0.7 | 0.8 | 0.9 | 0.7 | 0.8 | 0.9 | 0.8 | Traitements et salaires par salarié |
| Value added per unit of wages and salaries | 1.56 | 1.62 | 1.49 | 1.64 | 1.38 | 2.00 | 1.50 | 1.46 | 2.12 | 1.61 | 1.71 | 1.50 | 1.39 | 1.47 | Valeur ajoutée par unité de traitements et salaires |
| **1953** | | | | | | | | | | | | | | | **1953** |
| Distribution in percent of: | | | | | | | | | | | | | | | Distribution en pourcentage: |
| Value added | 100.0 | 44.6 | 17.8 | 6.6 | 2.6 | 1.0 | 2.8 | 1.8 | 2.3 | 7.6 | 6.6 | 0.6 | 4.5 | 1.2 | Valeur ajoutée |
| Number of engaged | 100.0 | 29.6 | 18.4 | 14.4 | 4.9 | 1.0 | 3.9 | 2.0 | 1.4 | 5.8 | 9.0 | 0.7 | 7.1 | 1.8 | Nombre de personnes occupées |
| Value added per person engaged | 7.5 | 11.3 | 7.3 | 3.5 | 3.8 | 7.8 | 5.5 | 6.6 | 12.7 | 9.8 | 5.5 | 5.9 | 4.8 | 5.0 | Valeur ajoutée par personne occupée |
| Capacity of installed power equipment per person engaged | 2.00 | 2.21 | 2.48 | 0.27 | 1.54 | 4.40 | 0.91 | 2.78 | 3.71 | 1.80 | 3.55 | 3.50 | 1.72 | 0.80 | Puissance installée par personne occupée |
| Employees as a percent of engaged | 91.0 | 90.5 | 96.4 | 85.0 | 85.7 | 95.0 | 94.8 | 90.0 | 100.0 | 94.0 | 91.1 | 92.8 | 89.4 | 85.7 | Salariés en pourcentage des personnes occupées |
| Value added per unit of wages and salaries | 3.5 | 5.1 | 2.9 | 2.6 | 2.3 | 3.0 | 2.0 | 2.5 | 4.3 | 3.3 | 2.9 | 2.2 | 2.3 | 2.6 | Valeur ajoutée par unité de traitements et salaires |
| Wages and salaries per employee | 2.4 | 2.5 | 2.6 | 1.6 | 1.9 | 2.7 | 2.9 | 2.9 | 2.9 | 3.2 | 2.1 | 2.9 | 2.3 | 2.2 | Traitements et salaires par salarié |
| **1958** | | | | | | | | | | | | | | | **1958** |
| Distribution in percent of: | | | | | | | | | | | | | | | Distribution en pourcentage: |
| Value added | 100.0 | 37.8 | 16.5 | 5.4 | 2.1 | 1.4 | 2.9 | 1.5 | 2.3 | 12.4 | 5.5 | 2.2 | 8.0 | 2.0 | Valeur ajoutée |
| Number of engaged | 100.0 | 23.2 | 16.6 | 13.0 | 4.6 | 1.5 | 4.1 | 2.1 | 2.1 | 6.9 | 8.7 | 2.3 | 12.6 | 2.3 | Nombre de personnes occupées |
| Per person engaged: Value added | 13.6 | 22.2 | 13.6 | 5.7 | 6.1 | 13.4 | 9.7 | 9.6 | 15.1 | 24.1 | 8.8 | 13.2 | 8.6 | 11.6 | Par personne occupée: Valeur ajoutée |
| Capacity of installed power equipment | 2.75 | 2.95 | 2.88 | 0.30 | 2.20 | 4.03 | 0.97 | 2.82 | 4.36 | 4.53 | 5.69 | 6.56 | 1.74 | 1.04 | Puissance installée |
| Employees as a percent of engaged | 95.3 | 93.6 | 98.7 | 91.8 | 91.8 | 97.0 | 95.9 | 95.9 | 100.0 | 97.0 | 95.6 | 98.1 | 95.6 | 96.2 | Salariés en pourcentage des personnes occupées |
| Value added per unit of wages and salaries | 3.08 | 5.15 | 2.69 | 2.25 | 1.93 | 2.60 | 2.08 | 2.45 | 2.42 | 3.60 | 2.29 | 1.87 | 1.94 | 2.43 | Valeur ajoutée par unité de traitements et salaires |
| Wages and salaries per employee | 4.6 | 4.6 | 5.1 | 2.8 | 3.4 | 5.3 | 4.8 | 4.1 | 6.3 | 6.9 | 4.0 | 7.2 | 4.7 | 5.0 | Traitements et salaires par salarié |

# COLOMBIA

## 5. CHARACTERISTICS OF ALL MANUFACTURING ESTABLISHMENTS
## CARACTERISTIQUES DE TOUS LES ETABLISSEMENTS MANUFACTURIERS
### 1953

Number of establishments in units; value added and wages and salaries in million Pesos; number of engaged and employees in thousands; and value added per person engaged in thousand Pesos

Nombre d'établissements en unités; valeur ajoutée et traitements et salaires en millions de pesos; nombre de personnes occupées et de salariés en milliers; valeur ajoutée par personne occupée en milliers de pesos

| Item of data | Manu-facturing / Industries manufac-turières | Food, beverages and tobacco / Industries alimen-taires, boissons, tabac | Textiles | Clothing, footwear and made-up textiles / Articles d'habil-lement, chaussures et ouvrages en tissu | Wood products and furniture / Bois et meubles | Paper and paper products / Papier et ouvrages en papier | Printing and publish-ing / Im-primerie et édition | Leather and leather products except wearing apparel / Cuir et articles en cuir, à l'exclu-sion des articles d'habil-lement | Rubber products / Ouvrages en caout-chouc | Chemicals and chemical, petroleum and coal products / Produits chi-miques et dérivés du pétrole et du charbon | Non-metallic mineral products / Produits minéraux non métal-liques | Basic metals / Métal-lurgie de base | Metal products / Ouvrages en métaux | Other manu-factur-ing / Autres in-dustries manufac-turières | Rubrique |
|---|---|---|---|---|---|---|---|---|---|---|---|---|---|---|---|
| ISIC | 2–3 | 20–22 | 23 | 24 | 25–26 | 27 | 28 | 29 | 30 | 31–32 | 33 | 34 | 35–38 | 39 | CITI |
| *a. Absolute Figures — Chiffres absolus* | | | | | | | | | | | | | | | |
| Number of establishments | 47 353 | 6 973 | 2 323 | 21 014 | 5 977 | 61 | 578 | 1 131 | 132 | 967 | 2 441 | 116 | 3 976 | 1 664 | Nombre d'établissements |
| Value added | 1 603.2 | 679.6 | 269.7 | 147.1 | 53.1 | 15.5 | 44.5 | 28.5 | 35.6 | 115.4 | 103.1 | 8.7 | 79.2 | 23.2 | Valeur ajoutée |
| Number of engaged (Last pay period of November) | 263.6 | 67.4 | 40.7 | 57.0 | 18.4 | 2.0 | 8.4 | 5.4 | 2.9 | 12.6 | 21.8 | 1.5 | 19.9 | 5.6 | Nombre de personnes occupées (dernière période de paie de novembre) |
| Number of employees (Last pay period of November) | 199.4 | 56.3 | 35.8 | 30.8 | 11.0 | 1.9 | 7.7 | 4.0 | 2.8 | 11.3 | 18.1 | 1.4 | 14.9 | 3.4 | Nombre de salariés (dernière période de paie de novembre) |
| Wages and salaries paid | 448.2 | 133.7 | 91.1 | 44.9 | 19.3 | 5.1 | 21.9 | 10.8 | 8.2 | 34.6 | 35.2 | 3.9 | 32.2 | 7.3 | Traitements et salaires payés |
| *b. Structure* | | | | | | | | | | | | | | | |
| Distribution in percent of: Value added | 100.0 | 42.4 | 16.8 | 9.2 | 3.3 | 1.0 | 2.8 | 1.8 | 2.2 | 7.2 | 6.4 | 0.5 | 4.9 | 1.4 | Distribution en pour-centage: Valeur ajoutée |
| Number of engaged | 100.0 | 25.6 | 15.4 | 21.6 | 7.0 | 0.8 | 3.2 | 2.0 | 1.1 | 4.8 | 8.3 | 0.6 | 7.5 | 2.1 | Nombre de personnes occupées |
| Value added per person engaged | 6.1 | 10.1 | 6.6 | 2.6 | 2.9 | 7.8 | 5.3 | 5.3 | 12.3 | 9.2 | 4.7 | 5.8 | 4.0 | 4.1 | Valeur ajoutée par per-sonne occupée |
| Employees as a pcercent of engaged | 75.6 | 83.5 | 88.0 | 54.0 | 59.8 | 95.0 | 91.7 | 74.1 | 96.6 | 89.7 | 83.0 | 93.3 | 74.9 | 60.7 | Salariés en pourcentage des personnes occupées |
| Value added per unit of wages and salaries | 3.6 | 5.1 | 3.0 | 3.3 | 2.8 | 3.0 | 2.0 | 2.6 | 4.3 | 3.3 | 2.9 | 2.2 | 2.5 | 3.2 | Valeur ajoutée par unité de traitements et salaires |
| Wages and salaries per employee | 2.2 | 2.4 | 2.5 | 1.4 | 1.8 | 2.7 | 2.8 | 2.7 | 2.9 | 3.1 | 1.9 | 2.8 | 2.2 | 2.1 | Traitements et salaires par salarié |

# CONGO (LEOPOLDVILLE)

## Gross Domestic Product

Estimates of expenditure on and the origin of the gross domestic product are presented in Table 1. This table has been compiled from data supplied by the Banque Centrale du Congo Belge et du Ruanda-Urundi, Brussels, in response to the United Nations national accounts questionnaire. Official estimates (later revised as shown in the table) and descriptions of sources and methods have been published by the Banque in various additions of its monthly publication, *Bulletin de la Banque Centrale du Congo Belge et du Ruanda-Urundi,* which ceased publication in July 1961.

## Index of Industrial Production

The indexes of production in mining and selected major groups of manufacturing are presented in Table 2.

The indexes for mining are based on quantity series of the production of individual minerals. The indexes of the individual quantity series are combined into indexes for major groups, using the gross value of production in 1953 as weights. The major group indexes are combined into indexes for mining as a whole by the Statistical Office of the United Nations, using as weights estimates of value added in 1948 for the years, 1938 to 1950, and in 1953 for the years 1951 onwards.

The indexes for manufacturing are derived, except in the case of Basic metals (ISIC major group 34), from indexes which have been compiled by the Direction des Etudes Economiques. These indexes, which are for major groups of manufacturing, have been calculated from series of relatives on quantity of output for individual products, using value added in 1951 as weights. In the case of Basic Metals (ISIC major group 34), relatives on the quantity of smelter production of individual metals are combined by the Statistical Office of the United Nations into indexes, using as weights the gross value of production during 1953. The indexes for manufacturing as a whole have been calculated by the Statistical Office of the United Nations, using as weights, estimates of value added in 1948 for the years, 1938 to 1950, and in 1953 for the years 1951 onwards.

The production data utilised in compiling the indexes for Mining and Basic metals are derived from the *Statistical Yearbook* of the United Nations and, for the years 1959 and later, from *Bulletin de Statistiques Générales,* published quarterly since January 1962 by the Direction de la Statistique, Ministère du Plan et de la Coordination

## Produit intérieur brut

Le tableau 1 contient des estimations des dépenses imputées au produit intérieur brut et des estimations du produit intérieur brut par secteur d'activité d'origine. Ces données ont été fournies par la Banque centrale du Congo belge et du Ruanda-Urundi, Bruxelles, en réponse au questionnaire de l'ONU sur la comptabilité nationale. Les estimations officielles (reproduites dans le tableau après révision) et la description des sources et méthodes utilisées ont été publiées par la Banque dans divers suppléments de sa publication mensuelle, *Bulletin de la Banque centrale du Congo belge et du Ruanda-Urundi,* qui a cessé de paraître en juillet 1961.

## Indices de la production industrielle

Les indices de la production dans les industries extractives et dans quelques classes des industries manufacturières sont présentés au tableau 2.

Les indices relatifs aux industries extractives ont été établis à partir de séries quantitatives concernant la production de chaque substance minérale. Les indices tirés de ces séries quantitatives ont été combinés en indices de classe, la base de pondération utilisée étant la valeur brute de la production en 1953. Les indices de classes ont été combinés en indices relatifs à l'ensemble des industries extractives par le Bureau de statistique de l'ONU, qui a utilisé comme coefficients de pondération des estimations de la valeur ajoutée en 1948 pour les années 1938 à 1950, et de la valeur ajoutée en 1953 à partir de 1951.

Les indices relatifs aux industries manufacturières, à l'exclusion de la Métallurgie de base (CITI classe 34), sont établis à partir d'indices calculés par la Direction des études économiques. Ces indices, qui portent sur les classes des industries manufacturières, ont été construits à partir de séries de rapports fondés sur la production de chaque marchandise, la base de pondération étant la valeur ajoutée en 1951. En ce qui concerne la Métallurgie de base (CITI classe 34), le Bureau de statistique de l'ONU a combiné en indices des rapports fondés sur les quantités de chaque métal produites par les fonderies en utilisant comme base de pondération la valeur brute de la production en 1953. Les indices relatifs à l'ensemble des industries manufacturières ont été calculés par le Bureau de statistique de l'ONU, qui a utilisé comme coefficients de pondération des estimations de la valeur ajoutée en 1948 pour les années 1938 à 1950, et de la valeur ajoutée en 1953 à partir de 1951.

Les données concernant la production utilisées pour le calcul des indices relatifs aux industries extractives et à la Métallurgie de base ont été tirées de l'*Annuaire statistique* de l'ONU et, pour 1959 et les années suivantes, du *Bulletin de statistiques générales,* publié trimestriellement depuis janvier 1962 par la Direction de la statis-

# CONGO (LEOPOLDVILLE)

Economique, Leopoldville. The indexes utilised for the major groups of manufacturing have been issued up to 1959, at which point it ceased publication, in various editions of *La Situation Economique du Congo Belge et du Ruanda-Urundi,* published by the Direction des Etudes Economiques of the Ministère du Congo Belge et du Ruanda-Urundi. These indexes have also been published in various editions of the *Bulletin de la Banque Centrale du Congo Belge et du Ruanda-Urundi,* which ceased publication in July 1961.

tique, Ministère du plan et de la coordination économique, Léopoldville. Les indices utilisés pour les classes des industries manufacturières ont été publiés jusqu'en 1959, date à laquelle la publication ci-après a cessé de paraître, dans divers numéros de la *Situation économique du Congo belge et du Ruanda-Urundi,* publiés par la Direction des études économiques du Ministère du Congo belge et du Ruanda-Urundi. Ces indices ont été également publiés dans divers numéros du *Bulletin de la Banque centrale du Congo belge et du Ruanda-Urundi,* qui a cessé de paraître en juillet 1961.

## 1. THE GROSS DOMESTIC PRODUCT — PRODUIT INTERIEUR BRUT

Million francs          Millions de francs

### A. Expenditure on the Gross Domestic Product at Market Prices
### Dépenses relatives au produit intérieur brut aux prix du marché

| Item of data and year<br>Rubrique et année | Total | Consumption<br>Consommation | | Gross Domestic Capital Formation<br>Formation brute de capital intérieur | | Net exports of goods and services<br>Exportations nettes de biens et de services | |
|---|---|---|---|---|---|---|---|
| | | Total | Government<br>Etat | Total | Fixed<br>Fixe | Exports less imports<br>Exportations moins importations | Exports [1]<br>Exportations [1] |
| *a. At Current Prices — Aux prix courants* | | | | | | | |
| Absolute figures — Chiffres absolus | | | | | | | |
| 1950 | 35 190 | 22 040 | 3 210 | 7 710 | 7 510 | 5 440 | 16 260 |
| 1951 | 46 360 | 28 670 | 3 910 | 13 300 | 11 120 | 4 390 | 20 960 |
| 1952 | 51 940 | 33 790 | 5 190 | 16 670 | 14 770 | 1 480 | 23 280 |
| 1953 | 53 660 | 36 750 | 5 820 | 15 700 | 16 270 | 1 210 | 21 610 |
| 1954 | 56 750 | 38 970 | 6 490 | 16 250 | 15 250 | 1 530 | 24 720 |
| 1955 | 61 230 | 42 130 | 7 020 | 17 090 | 15 690 | 2 010 | 26 670 |
| 1956 | 65 760 | 45 520 | 8 370 | 18 420 | 16 320 | 1 820 | 29 750 |
| 1957 | 64 020 | 47 290 | 9 000 | 18 920 | 16 420 | −2 190 | 27 470 |
| 1958 | 63 400 | 49 440 | 10 840 | 13 150 | 14 270 | 810 | 25 170 |
| 1959 | 65 065 | 49 730 | 11 270 | 10 965 | 11 080 | 4 370 | 27 970 |
| Percentage distribution of average annual expenditure — Distribution en pourcentage des dépenses annuelles moyennes | | | | | | | |
| 1950–1959 | 100.0 | 70.0 | 12.6 | 26.3 | 24.6 | 3.7 | 43.3 |
| 1950 | 100.0 | 62.6 | 9.1 | 21.9 | 21.3 | 15.5 | 46.2 |
| 1953 | 100.0 | 68.5 | 10.8 | 29.2 | 30.3 | 2.3 | 40.3 |
| 1954 | 100.0 | 68.7 | 11.4 | 28.6 | 26.9 | 2.7 | 43.6 |
| 1958 | 100.0 | 78.0 | 17.1 | 20.7 | 22.5 | 1.3 | 39.7 |
| *b. At Prices of 1950 — Aux prix de 1950* | | | | | | | |
| Absolute figures — Chiffres absolus | | | | | | | |
| 1950 | 35 190 | 22 040 | 3 210 | 7 710 | 7 510 | 5 440 | 16 260 |
| 1951 | 39 320 | 26 290 | 3 980 | 11 860 | 9 920 | 2 300 | 16 680 |
| 1952 | 42 910 | 27 770 | 4 170 | 14 350 | 12 680 | −730 | 17 710 |
| 1953 | 45 330 | 30 670 | 4 530 | 14 190 | 14 720 | 580 | 18 730 |
| 1954 | 48 080 | 32 460 | 4 750 | 15 280 | 14 320 | −1 270 | 19 250 |
| 1955 | 49 930 | 35 050 | 4 940 | 16 400 | 15 070 | −2 000 | 20 150 |
| 1956 | 53 330 | 36 850 | 5 200 | 17 350 | 15 350 | −3 560 | 21 690 |
| 1957 | 54 990 | 37 670 | 5 520 | 16 710 | 14 630 | −2 840 | 21 840 |
| 1958 | 53 420 | 37 670 | 5 780 | 11 280 | 12 200 | 760 | 21 380 |
| 1959 | 55 800 | 37 100 | 5 910 | 10 010 | 10 110 | 5 170 | 25 090 |
| Percentage distribution of average annual expenditure — Distribution en pourcentage des dépenses annuelles moyennes | | | | | | | |
| 1950–1959 | 100.0 | 70.0 | 10.4 | 29.2 | 27.3 | 0.8 | 43.0 |
| 1950 | 100.0 | 62.6 | 9.1 | 21.9 | 21.3 | 15.5 | 46.2 |
| 1953 | 100.0 | 67.5 | 10.0 | 31.2 | 32.4 | 1.3 | 41.2 |
| 1954 | 100.0 | 69.8 | 10.2 | 32.9 | 30.8 | −2.7 | 41.4 |
| 1958 | 100.0 | 75.8 | 11.6 | 22.7 | 24.5 | 1.5 | 43.0 |
| Average annual rate of growth — Taux annuel moyen d'accroissement | | | | | | | |
| 1950–1959 | 5.3 | 6.0 | 7.0 | 2.9 | 3.4 | . | 4.9 |
| 1950–1953 | 8.8 | 11.7 | 12.2 | 22.5 | 25.1 | . | 4.8 |
| 1954–1958 | 2.7 | 3.8 | 5.0 | −7.3 | −3.9 | . | 2.7 |

For footnotes see end of table.      Pour les notes, voir au bas du tableau.

### B. The Gross Domestic Product at Market Prices According to Origin
### Origine par secteur d'activité du produit intérieur brut aux prix du marché

| Item of data and year<br>Rubrique et année | Total [6] | Agricultural sector<br>Secteur agricole | Industrial Sector — Secteur industriel | | | | Transportation and communication<br>Transports et communications | Other sectors<br>Autres secteurs |
|---|---|---|---|---|---|---|---|---|
| | | | Total | Mining [3]<br>Industries extractives [3] | Manufacturing [4]<br>Industries manufacturières [4] | Construction [5]<br>Bâtiment et travaux publics [5] | | |
| ISIC — CITI | 0–9 | 0 | 1–5 | 1 | 2–3, 5 | 4 | 7 | 6, 8–9 |
| a. At Current Prices — Aux prix courants | | | | | | | | |
| Absolute figures —<br>Chiffres absolus | | | | | | | | |
| 1950............ | 32 860 | 12 270 | 10 260 | 6 730 | 1 850 | 1 680 | 2 460 | 8 970 |
| 1951............ | 42 060 | 16 100 | 13 780 | 8 760 | 2 560 | 2 460 | 3 680 | 11 100 |
| 1952............ | 47 220 | 16 630 | 17 730 | 11 520 | 3 010 | 3 200 | 4 130 | 12 790 |
| 1953............ | 49 030 | 16 420 | 17 960 | 11 410 | 3 250 | 3 300 | 4 320 | 13 710 |
| 1954............ | 51 890 | 16 920 | 19 250 | 12 140 | 3 570 | 3 540 | 4 760 | 14 810 |
| 1955............ | 55 960 | 18 250 | 21 170 | 13 440 | 3 870 | 3 860 | 5 350 | 15 830 |
| 1956............ | 59 870 | 18 690 | 22 810 | 14 370 | 4 560 | 3 880 | 6 240 | 17 380 |
| 1957............ | 58 570 | 18 940 | 20 290 | 11 690 | 4 800 | 3 800 | 6 370 | 18 430 |
| 1958............ | 58 250 | 19 340 | 18 630 | 10 310 | 4 830 | 3 490 | 5 680 | 19 220 |
| 1959............ | 59 425 | 16 630 | 22 430 | 11 320 | 7 990 | 3 120 | 6 010 | 19 185 |
| Percentage distribution according to sector—<br>Distribution en pourcentage par secteur | | | | | | | | |
| 1950–1959..... | 100.0 | 30.7 | 33.2 | 20.1 | 7.3 | 5.8 | 8.8 | 27.3 |
| 1950............ | 100.0 | 36.1 | 30.2 | 19.8 | 5.5 | 4.9 | 7.3 | 26.4 |
| 1953............ | 100.0 | 31.3 | 34·3 | 21.8 | 6.2 | 6.3 | 8.2 | 26.2 |
| 1954............ | 100.0 | 30.3 | 34.6 | 21.8 | 6.4 | 6.4 | 8.5 | 26.6 |
| 1958............ | 100.0 | 30.8 | 29.6 | 16.4 | 7.7 | 5.5 | 9.0 | 30.6 |

[1] Exports of goods only.
[2] Components do not add to the total shown because of an adjustment item which is included in the totals but could not be allocated among the components. Estimates of total domestic product have been obtained by extrapolating the base year values by an index of the quantum of production, while components have been deflated by available price indexes. For the percentage distribution table the actual total of the constituent items has been used.
[3] Includes the smelting and refining of non-ferrous metals (part of ISIC divisions 2-3).
[4] Includes Electricity, gas and water (ISIC division 5); excludes smelting and refining of non-ferrous metals and production of building materials.
[5] Includes the production of building materials (part of ISIC divisions 2-3).
[6] The total is smaller than the sum of its components as the value of imported inputs has been deducted from the total product but not from its components. For the percentage distribution table, the actual total of the constituent items has been used.

[1] Exportations de marchandises exclusivement.
[2] La somme des éléments ne correspond pas aux totaux indiqués parce que ces derniers comportent un ajustement qui n'a pu être ventilé entre les éléments. Les estimations du produit intérieur total ont été obtenues par extrapolation à partir de la valeur de l'année de base au moyen d'un indice du quantum de la production, tandis que, pour les éléments, la conversion en prix constants a été faite au moyen des indices de prix disponibles. Pour le tableau relatif à la répartition en pourcentage, on a utilisé le total effectif des éléments.
[3] Y compris la fonderie et l'affinage des métaux non ferreux (dans CITI branches 2-3).
[4] Y compris Electricité, gaz et eau (CITI branche 5); non compris la fonderie et l'affinage des métaux non ferreux, ni la production de matériaux de construction.
[5] Y compris la production de matériaux de construction (dans CITI branches 2-3).
[6] Le total est plus petit que la somme des éléments, vu que la valeur des intrants importés à été déduite du produit total et non de ses composantes. Pour le tableau relatif à la répartition en pourcentage, on a utilisé le total effectif des éléments.

## 2. INDEX NUMBERS OF INDUSTRIAL PRODUCTION — INDICES DE LA PRODUCTION INDUSTRIELLE

### A. The Major Groups of Mining
### Les classes de la branche Industries extractives

| Period<br><br>Période | All mining<br><br>Toutes<br>industries<br>extractives | Coal<br>mining<br><br>Extraction<br>du charbon | Metal mining<br><br>Extraction<br>des minerais<br>métalliques | Other mining<br><br>Autres<br>industries<br>extractives |
|---|---|---|---|---|
| ISIC — CITI | 1 | 11 | 12 | 14-19 |

a. Indexes — Indices (1958 = 100)

| | | | | |
|---|---|---|---|---|
| 1938........... | 50 | 14 | 51 | 43 |
| 1948........... | 62 | 40 | 65 | 35 |
| 1949........... | 65 | 52 | 65 | 58 |
| 1950........... | 73 | 54 | 74 | 61 |
| 1951........... | 80 | 74 | 81 | 63 |
| 1952........... | 88 | 86 | 89 | 70 |
| 1953........... | 97 | 107 | 98 | 75 |
| 1954........... | 102 | 129 | 103 | 76 |
| 1955........... | 106 | 163 | 107 | 78 |
| 1956........... | 109 | 143 | 110 | 84 |
| 1957........... | 106 | 147 | 106 | 94 |
| 1958........... | 100 | 100 | 100 | 100 |
| 1959........... | 109 | 91 | 111 | 89 |
| 1960........... | 113 | 55 | 116 | 81 |
| 1961........... | 109 | 25 | 108 | 109 |

b. Average Annual Rate of Change — Taux annuel moyen de variation

| | | | | |
|---|---|---|---|---|
| 1938 – 1960.... | 3.8 | 6.4 | 3.8 | 2.9 |
| 1938 – 1948.... | 2.2 | 11.1 | 2.5 | −2.0 |
| 1950 – 1960.... | 4.5 | 0.2 | 4.6 | 2.9 |
| 1948 – 1953.... | 9.4 | 21.7 | 8.6 | 16.5 |
| 1954 – 1958.... | −0.5 | −6.2 | −0.7 | 7.1 |
| 1958 – 1960.... | 6.3 | −25.8 | 7.7 | −10.0 |

## B. Selected Major Groups of Manufacturing

## Quelques classes de la branche Industries manufacturières

| Period<br><br>Période | Manu-factur-ing [1]<br><br>Industries manufac-turières [1] | Food, and bever-ages [2]<br><br>Industries alimen-taires et boissons [2] | Textiles and clothing<br><br>Textiles et articles d'habil-lement | Chemicals and chemical products [3]<br><br>Produits chimiques [3] | Non-metallic mineral products [4]<br><br>Produits minéraux non métal-liques [4] | Basic metals<br><br>Métal-lurgie de base |
|---|---|---|---|---|---|---|
| ISIC — CITI | 2–3 | 20–21 | 23, 243 | 31 | 33 | 34 |

### a. Indexes — Indices (1958 = 100)

| | | | | | | |
|---|---|---|---|---|---|---|
| 1938............. | ... | ... | ... | ... | ... | 50 |
| 1948............. | 34 | 35 | 16 | 16 | 26 | 63 |
| 1949............. | 36 | 39 | 18 | 29 | 26 | 57 |
| 1950............. | 47 | 43 | 25 | 31 | 50 | 71 |
| 1951............. | 57 | 52 | 52 | 33 | 61 | 78 |
| 1952............. | 64 | 56 | 62 | 42 | 71 | 83 |
| 1953............. | 73 | 66 | 71 | 66 | 84 | 87 |
| 1954............. | 83 | 75 | 83 | 71 | 103 | 92 |
| 1955............. | 91 | 84 | 96 | 89 | 108 | 97 |
| 1956............. | 105 | 103 | 111 | 96 | 116 | 104 |
| 1957............. | 105 | 104 | 98 | 102 | 123 | 101 |
| 1958............. | 100 | 100 | 100 | 100 | 100 | 100 |
| 1959............. | 108 | 111 | 118 | 89 | 86 | 118 |
| 1960............. | ... | ... | ... | ... | ... | 125 |
| 1961............. | ... | ... | ... | ... | ... | 123 |

### b. Average Annual Rate of Change — Taux annuel moyen de variation

| | | | | | | |
|---|---|---|---|---|---|---|
| 1938 – 1960........ | ... | ... | ... | ... | ... | 4.3 |
| 1938 – 1948........ | ... | ... | ... | ... | ... | 2.3 |
| 1950 – 1960........ | ... | ... | ... | ... | ... | 5.8 |
| 1948 – 1953........ | 16.5 | 13.5 | 34.7 | 32.8 | 26.4 | 6.7 |
| 1954 – 1958........ | 4.8 | 7.5 | 4.8 | 8.9 | −0.7 | 2.1 |
| 1958 – 1960........ | ... | ... | ... | ... | ... | 11.8 |

[1] Includes only those major groups shown in the table plus Leather and leather products except wearing apparel (ISIC major group 29).
[2] Includes the extraction of vegetable oils (part of ISIC major group 31).
[3] Includes the manufacture of bottles (part of ISIC major group 33) and the manufacture of plastic objects (part of ISIC major group 39); excludes the extraction of vegetable oils (included with ISIC major groups 20-21).
[4] Includes sawmilling and plywood and veneer manufacturing (part of ISIC major group 25); excludes the manufacture of bottles (included with ISIC major group 31).

[1] Cette rubrique ne comprend que les classes indiquées dans le tableau, plus Cuir et articles en cuir à l'exclusion des articles d'habillement (CITI classe 29).
[2] Y compris l'extraction des huiles végétales (dans CITI classe 31).
[3] Y compris la fabrication des bouteilles (dans CITI classe 33) et la fabrication des objets en matières, plastiques (dans CITI classe 39); non compris l'extraction des huiles végétales (incluse dans CITI classe 20-21).
[4] Y compris les scieries et la fabrication des placages et contreplaqués (dans CITI classe 25); non compris la fabrication des bouteilles (incluse dans CITI classe 31).

# COSTA RICA

## The Gross Domestic Product

Estimates of expenditure on and the industrial origin of the gross domestic product are presented in Table 1. The data on which the table is based are provided by the Seccion Ingreso Nacional, Departamento de Estudios Economicos, Banco Central de Costa Rica, San José, in response to the United Nations national accounts questionnaire. Official estimates up to 1958 and descriptions of the sources and methods utilized are published by the Banco in *Ingreso y Producto Nacionales de Costa Rica, 1950-1958*.

## Characteristics and Structure of Industrial Activity

The data shown in Table 2 are derived from the results of Costa Rica's first and second Industrial Censuses published by the Dirección General de Estadística y Censos in *Censo de Comercia e Industrias de 1952*, San José, 1954 and in *Il Censo de Industrias en Costa Rica 1958*, San José, 1962. The Censuses included, in principle, all industrial establishments, regardless of size, which were in existence during the year ending 30 September 1951 or 30 September 1957. The first census covered activities between 1 October 1950 and 30 September 1951, and the second census covered activities between 1 October 1956 and 30 September 1957. In 1950-1951, due to non-response, chiefly among small home industries, about 96 per cent of all establishments engaged in mining and manufacturing were actually included.

The data on value added are based on the gross value of production at market prices and were furnished to the Statistical Office of the United Nations by the Dirección General de Estadística. For both Censuses the figures on wages and salaries were obtained by multiplying by 12 the data on wages and salaries paid for the month of September 1951 or September 1957, except for seasonal industries, such as coffee beneficiaries and sugar refineries, in which cases the September remunerations were multiplied by the actual number of months worked.

## Le produit intérieur brut

Des estimations des dépenses imputées au produit intérieur brut ainsi que celles des composantes du produit intérieur brut ventilées suivant le secteur industriel d'origine sont reproduites au tableau 1. Les données à partir desquelles le tableau a été construit ont été fournies par La Seccion Ingreso Nacional, Departamento de Estudios Economicos, Banco Central de Costa Rica, San José en réponse au questionnaire de l'O.N.U. relatif aux comptes nationaux. Les estimations officielles pour toutes les années antérieures à 1959 et les descriptions des sources et méthodes adoptées sont publiées par le Banco dans *Ingreso y Producto Nacionales de Costa Rica, 1950-1958*.

## Caractéristiques et structure de l'activité industrielle

Les données du tableau 2 ont été tirées des résultats du premier et second recensement industriel de Costa Rica publiés par la Dirección General de Estadística y Censos dans *Censo de Comercio e Industrias de 1952*, San José, 1954 et dans *Il Censo de Industrias en Costa Rica 1958*, San José, 1962. Les recensements couvraient, en principe, tous les établissements industriels, compte non tenu de la taille, qui existaient durant l'année se terminant au 30 septembre 1951 ou au 30 septembre 1957. Le premier recensement couvrait les activités exercées entre le 1er octobre 1950 et le 30 septembre 1951; le second recensement couvrait les activités exercées entre le 1er octobre 1956 et le 30 septembre 1957. En 1950-1951, à cause des non-réponses principalement des petites industries à domicile, seulement 96 pour cent des établissements exerçant une activité dans le secteur des industries extractives et manufacturières ont été en fait recensés.

Les données relatives à la valeur ajoutée sont fondées sur la valeur brute de la production aux prix du marché et sont fournies au Bureau de statistique de l'O.N.U. par la Dirección General de Estadística. En ce qui concerne les deux recensements, les chiffres donnant les traitements et salaires ont été obtenus en multipliant par 12 le montant des traitements et salaires payés en septembre 1951 ou en septembre 1957, sauf pour les industries saisonnières — préparation du café et sucreries —, pour lesquelles on a multiplié le montant des traitements et salaires par le nombre effectif de mois de travail.

## 1. THE GROSS DOMESTIC PRODUCT — PRODUIT INTERIEUR BRUT

Million Colones                                                                 Millions de colons

### A. Expenditure on the Gross Domestic Product at Market Prices
### Dépenses relatives au produit intérieur brut aux prix du marché

| Item of data and year / Rubrique et année | Total | Consumption / Consommation | | Gross Domestic Capital Formation / Formation brute de capital intérieur | | Net exports of goods and services / Exportations nettes de biens et de services | |
| --- | --- | --- | --- | --- | --- | --- | --- |
| | | Total | Government / Etat | Total | Fixed / Fixe | Exports less imports / Exportations moins importations | Exports / Exportations |
| | | | | *a.* At Current Prices — Aux prix courants | | | |
| **Absolute figures — Chiffres absolus** | | | | | | | |
| 1950 | 1 334.1 | 1 099.8 | 93.3 | 239.3 | 220.2 | —5.0 | 348.1 |
| 1951 | 1 442.2 | 1 184.6 | 107.9 | 261.1 | 239.1 | —3.5 | 387.8 |
| 1952 | 1 576.0 | 1 260.9 | 125.1 | 309.9 | 279.1 | 5.2 | 467.0 |
| 1953 | 1 739.3 | 1 365.7 | 126.3 | 369.3 | 344.0 | 4.3 | 505.2 |
| 1954 | 1 879.4 | 1 491.8 | 158.4 | 388.9 | 359.2 | —1.3 | 537.4 |
| 1955 | 2 051.3 | 1 677.0 | 193.2 | 425.5 | 394.1 | —51.2 | 531.4 |
| 1956 | 2 112.8 | 1 794.0 | 251.7 | 455.4 | 417.8 | —136.6 | 476.9 |
| 1957 | 2 302.7 | 1 933.2 | 256.3 | 467.2 | 434.8 | —97.7 | 596.4 |
| 1958 | 2 465.0 | 2 047.3 | 296.7 | 437.4 | 404.0 | —19.7 | 658.4 |
| 1959 | 2 529.8 | 2 174.7 | 291.2 | 492.9 | 451.4 | —137.8 | 555.9 |
| 1960 | 2 647.6 | 2 280.2 | 331.4 | 526.4 | 474.1 | —159.0 | 589.9 |
| 1961 | 2 789.3 | 2 382.4 | 353.0 | 507.6 | 484.6 | —100.7 | 636.8 |
| **Percentage distribution of average annual expenditure — Distribution en pourcentage des dépenses annuelles moyennes** | | | | | | | |
| 1950 – 1960 | 100.0 | 82.9 | 10.1 | 19.8 | 18.2 | —2.7 | 25.6 |
| 1950 | 100.0 | 82.4 | 7.0 | 17.9 | 16.5 | —0.3 | 26.1 |
| 1953 | 100.0 | 78.5 | 7.3 | 21.2 | 19.8 | 0.3 | 29.1 |
| 1954 | 100.0 | 79.4 | 8.4 | 20.7 | 19.1 | —0.1 | 28.6 |
| 1958 | 100.0 | 83.1 | 12.0 | 17.7 | 16.4 | —0.8 | 26.7 |
| 1960 | 100.0 | 86.1 | 12.5 | 19.9 | 17.9 | —6.0 | 22.3 |

## B. The Gross Domestic Product at Factor Cost According to Origin
### Origine par secteur d'activité du produit intérieur brut au coût des facteurs

| Item of data and year<br>Rubrique et année | Total | Agricultural sector [1]<br>Secteur agricole [1] | Mining and manufacturing<br>Industries extractives et industries manufacturières | Construction<br>Bâtiment et travaux publics | Transportation and communication<br>Transports et communications | Other sectors [2]<br>Autres secteurs [2] |
|---|---|---|---|---|---|---|
| ISIC — CITI | 0–9 | 0 | 1–3 | 4 | 7 | 5–6, 8–9 |
| | | | *a.* At Current Prices — Aux prix courants | | | |
| Absolute figures —<br>Chiffres absolus | | | | | | |
| 1950............. | 1 206.2 | 549.8 | 137.8 | 39.3 | 41.1 | 438.2 |
| 1951............. | 1 305.9 | 589.6 | 148.5 | 42.1 | 45.8 | 479.9 |
| 1952............. | 1 438.1 | 650.0 | 162.2 | 46.1 | 50.6 | 529.2 |
| 1953............. | 1 568.4 | 704.2 | 175.8 | 50.0 | 55.3 | 583.1 |
| 1954............. | 1 676.5 | 732.8 | 186.5 | 53.2 | 58.4 | 645.6 |
| 1955............. | 1 830.3 | 789.9 | 201.1 | 57.3 | 63.4 | 718.6 |
| 1956............. | 1 886.2 | 712.5 | 220.1 | 62.8 | 68.6 | 822.2 |
| 1957............. | 2 031.4 | 799.4 | 233.8 | 67.1 | 74.2 | 856.9 |
| 1958............. | 2 180.8 | 873.0 | 244.5 | 71.8 | 79.8 | 911.7 |
| 1959............. | 2 223.5 | 807.5 | 260.4 | 75.6 | 90.1 | 989.9 |
| 1960............. | 2 320.6 | 860.9 | 279.9 | 73.9 | 80.9 | 1 025.0 |
| 1961............. | 2 480.4 | 940.3 | 313.2 | 75.2 | 89.3 | 1 062.4 |
| Percentage distribution according to sector—<br>Distribution en pourcentage par secteur | | | | | | |
| 1950 – 1960..... | 100.0 | 41.0 | 11.4 | 3.3 | 3.6 | 40.7 |
| 1950............. | 100.0 | 45.6 | 11.5 | 3.2 | 3.4 | 36.3 |
| 1953............. | 100.0 | 44.9 | 11.2 | 3.2 | 3.5 | 37.2 |
| 1954............. | 100.0 | 43.7 | 11.1 | 3.2 | 3.5 | 38.5 |
| 1958............. | 100.0 | 40.0 | 11.2 | 3.3 | 3.7 | 41.8 |
| 1960............. | 100.0 | 37.0 | 12.1 | 3.2 | 3.5 | 44.2 |

[1] Includes the ownership of dwellings in the agricultural sector (part of ISIC division 9).
[2] Includes all government activities.

[1] Y compris la propriété de maisons d'habitation dans le secteur agricole (dans CITI 9).
[2] Y compris toutes les fonctions de l'Etat.

# 2. CHARACTERISTICS OF ALL INDUSTRIAL ESTABLISHMENTS

## CARACTERISTIQUES DE TOUS LES ETABLISSEMENTS INDUSTRIELS
### I.X.1950-30.IX.1951, I.X.1956-30.IX.1957

Number of establishments in units; value added and wages and salaries in million Colones; number of engaged, employees and operatives in thousands; man-hours worked in millions; value added per engaged and wages and salaries per employee and per thousand operative man-hours in thousand Colones; average annual man-hours per operative in thousands.

Nombre d'établissements en unités; valeur ajoutée et traitements et salaires en millions de colons; nombre de personnes occupées, de salariés et d'ouvriers en milliers; heures de travail effectuées en millions; valeur ajoutée par personne occupée et traitements et salaires par salarié et par millier d'heures-ouvrier en milliers de colons; moyenne annuelle des heures de travail par ouvrier en milliers.

## A. The Major Groups of Mining — Les classes de la branche Industries extractives

### a. Absolute Figures / Chiffres absolus

| Year and item of data | All mining — Toutes industries extractives | Metal mining — Extraction des minerais métalliques | Other mining — Divers | Année et rubrique |
|---|---|---|---|---|
| ISIC | 1 | 12 | 14–19 | CITI |
| **I.X.1950 – 30.IX.1951** | | | | **I.X.1950 – 30.IX.1951** |
| Number of establishments...... | 31 | 3 | 28 | Nombre d'établissements |
| Value added................ | 0.8 | 0.1 | 0.7 | Valeur ajoutée |
| Number of engaged (During IX.1951).................. | 0.3 | — | 0.3 | Nombre de personnes occupées (en IX.1951) |
| Employees | | | | Salariés |
| Number (During IX.1951)..... | 0.3 | — | 0.3 | Nombre (en IX.1951) |
| Wages and salaries.......... | 0.7 | 0.1 | 0.6 | Traitements et salaires |
| Operatives | | | | Ouvriers |
| Number (During IX.1951)..... | 0.3 | — | 0.3 | Nombre (en IX.1951) |
| Man-hours worked........... | 0.7 | 0.1 | 0.6 | Heures de travail effectuées |
| **I.X.1956 – 30.IX.1957** | | | | **I.X.1956 – 30.IX.1957** |
| Number of establishments...... | 86 | — | 86 | Nombre d'établissements |
| Value added................ | 1.3 | — | 1.3 | Valeur ajoutée |
| Number of engaged (During IX.1957).................. | 0.4 | — | 0.4 | Nombre de personnes occupées (en IX.1957) |
| Employees | | | | Salariés |
| Number (During IX.1957)..... | 0.3 | — | 0.3 | Nombre (en IX.1957) |
| Wages and salaries.......... | 0.5 | — | 0.5 | Traitements et salaires |
| Operatives | | | | Ouvriers |
| Number (During IX.1957)..... | 0.2 | — | 0.2 | Nombre (en IX.1957) |
| Man-hours worked........... | 0.3 | — | 0.3 | Heures de travail effectuées |
| Wages and salaries.......... | 0.5 | — | 0.5 | Traitements et salaires |

### b. Structure

| Year and item of data | All mining — Toutes industries extractives | Metal mining — Extraction des minerais métalliques | Other mining — Divers | Année et rubrique |
|---|---|---|---|---|
| ISIC | 1 | 12 | 14–19 | CITI |
| **I.X.1950 – 30.IX.1951** | | | | **I.X.1950 – 30.IX.1951** |
| Distribution in percent of: | | | | Distribution en pourcentage: |
| Value added................ | 100.0 | 12.5 | 87.5 | Valeur ajoutée |
| Number of engaged......... | 100.0 | — | 100.0 | Nombre de personnes occupées |
| Value added per person engaged.................. | 2.7 | ... | 2.3 | Valeur ajoutée par personne occupée |
| Employees as a percent of engaged.................. | 100.0 | — | 100.0 | Salariés en pourcentage des personnes occupées |
| Value added per unit of wages and salaries.......... | 1.14 | 1.00 | 1.17 | Valeur ajoutée par unité de traitements et salaires |
| Wages and salaries per employee.................. | 2.3 | ... | 2.0 | Traitements et salaires par salarié |
| Operatives as a percent of employees................. | 100.0 | — | 100.0 | Ouvriers en pourcentage des salariés |
| Average man-hours per operative.................. | 2.33 | ... | 2.00 | Heures de travail: moyenne par ouvrier |
| **I.X.1956 – 30.IX.1957** | | | | **I.X.1956 – 30.IX.1957** |
| Distribution in percent of: | | | | Distribution en pourcentage: |
| Value added................ | 100.0 | — | 100.0 | Valeur ajoutée |
| Number of engaged......... | 100.0 | — | 100.0 | Nombre de personnes occupées |
| Value added per person engaged.................. | 3.2 | — | 3.2 | Valeur ajoutée par personne occupée |
| Employees as a percent of engaged.................. | 75.0 | — | 75.0 | Salariés en pourcentage des personnes occupées |
| Value added per unit of wages and salaries.......... | 2.60 | — | 2.60 | Valeur ajoutée par unité de traitements et salaires |
| Wages and salaries per employee.................. | 1.7 | — | 1.7 | Traitements et salaires par salarié |
| Operatives as a percent of employees................. | 66.7 | — | 66.7 | Ouvriers en pourcentage des salariés |
| Average man-hours per operative.................. | 1.5 | — | 1.5 | Heures de travail: moyenne par ouvrier |
| Wages and salaries per thousand operative man-hours.... | 1.67 | — | 1.67 | Traitements et salaires par millier d'heures-ouvrier |

# COSTA RICA

## B. The Major Groups of Manufacturing — Les classes de la branche Industries manufacturières

| Year and item of data | Manu-facturing / Industries manufac-turières | Food beverages and tobacco / Industries alimen-taires, boissons, tabac | Textiles | Clothing, footwear and made-up textiles / Articles d'habil-lement, chaussures et ouvrages en tissu | Wood products and furni-ture[2] / Bois et meubles[2] | Paper and paper products / Papier et ouvrages en papier | Printing and publish-ing / Im-primerie et édition | Leather and leather products except wearing apparel / Cuir et articles en cuir, à l'exclu-sion des articles d'habil-lement | Rubber products / Ouvrages en caout-chouc | Chemicals and chemical, petroleum and coal products / Produits chi-miques et dérivés du pétrole et du charbon | Non-metallic mineral products / Produits minéraux non métal-liques | Metal prod-ucts[1,2] / Ouvrages en métaux[1,2] | Other manu-factur-ing / Autres in-dustries manufac-turières | Année et rubrique |
|---|---|---|---|---|---|---|---|---|---|---|---|---|---|---|
| ISIC | 2–3 | 20–22 | 23 | 24 | 25–26 | 27 | 28 | 29 | 30 | 31–32 | 33 | 35–38 | 39 | CITI |

### a. Absolute Figures — Chiffres absolus

| | | | | | | | | | | | | | | |
|---|---|---|---|---|---|---|---|---|---|---|---|---|---|---|
| **1.X.1950 — 30.IX.1951** | | | | | | | | | | | | | | **1.X.1950 — 30.IX.1951** |
| Number of establishments. | 3 245 | 1 510 | 43 | 663 | 378 | 9 | 21 | 88 | 10 | 63 | 105 | 275 | 80 | Nombre d'établissements |
| Value added.......... | 147.6 | 98.3 | 4.4 | 12.1 | 11.8 | 0.1 | 1.9 | 3.6 | 1.1 | 6.4 | 2.2 | 4.5 | 1.2 | Valeur ajoutée |
| Number of engaged (during IX.1951)...... | 18.0 | 9.9 | 0.5 | 2.7 | 1.8 | — | 0.2 | 0.4 | 0.1 | 0.6 | 0.6 | 1.0 | 0.2 | Nombre de personnes occupées (en IX.1951) |
| Employees: | | | | | | | | | | | | | | Salariés: |
| Number (During IX.1951)........... | 14.2 | 8.0 | 0.4 | 1.9 | 1.3 | — | 0.2 | 0.3 | 0.1 | 0.5 | 0.5 | 0.9 | 0.1 | Nombre (en IX.1951) |
| Wages and salaries... | 27.1 | 11.8 | 1.1 | 4.4 | 3.5 | — | 0.8 | 0.8 | 0.2 | 1.3 | 1.2 | 1.7 | 0.3 | Traitements et salaires |
| Operatives: | | | | | | | | | | | | | | Ouvriers: |
| Number (During IX.1951)........... | 13.5 | 7.6 | 0.4 | 1.8 | 1.2 | — | 0.2 | 0.3 | 0.1 | 0.5 | 0.5 | 0.8 | 0.1 | Nombre (en IX.1951) |
| Man-hours worked.... | 23.7 | 10.1 | 0.8 | 4.2 | 3.0 | — | 0.6 | 0.8 | 0.2 | 1.0 | 1.1 | 1.6 | 0.3 | Heures de travail effectuées |
| **1.X.1956 — 30.IX.1957** | | | | | | | | | | | | | | **1.X.1956 — 30.IX.1957** |
| Number of establishments. | 5 784 | 3 039 | 70 | 1 085 | 552 | 18 | 41 | 108 | 19 | 74 | 122 | 497 | 159 | Nombre d'établissements |
| Value added.......... | 301.4 | 181.1 | 13.7 | 23.4 | 20.5 | 1.1 | 10.7 | 3.5 | 3.2 | 17.3 | 6.4 | 17.1 | 3.4 | Valeur ajoutée |
| Number of engaged (During IX.1957)...... | 31.3 | 16.8 | 1.4 | 4.0 | 2.6 | 0.2 | 1.0 | 0.4 | 0.2 | 1.0 | 0.8 | 2.4 | 0.5 | Nombre de personnes occupées (en IX.1957) |
| Employees: | | | | | | | | | | | | | | Salariés: |
| Number (During IX.1957)........... | 21.7 | 11.1 | 1.2 | 2.6 | 1.9 | 0.1 | 1.0 | 0.3 | 0.2 | 0.9 | 0.6 | 1.6 | 0.2 | Nombre (en IX.1957) |
| Wages and salaries... | 74.3 | 31.8 | 3.8 | 8.6 | 6.7 | 0.5 | 5.0 | 1.1 | 0.8 | 3.9 | 2.5 | 8.7 | 0.9 | Traitements et salaires |
| Operatives: | | | | | | | | | | | | | | Ouvriers: |
| Number (During IX.1957)........... | 20.3 | 10.3 | 1.1 | 2.6 | 1.8 | 0.1 | 0.8 | 0.3 | 0.2 | 0.8 | 0.6 | 1.5 | 0.2 | Nombre (en IX.1957) |
| Man-hours worked.... | 38.9 | 19.0 | 2.5 | 2.1 | 4.3 | 0.3 | 1.8 | 0.9 | 0.5 | 1.9 | 1.6 | 3.4 | 0.6 | Heures de travail effectuées |
| Wages and salaries... | 58.9 | 24.3 | 3.1 | 8.0 | 5.9 | 0.4 | 3.5 | 1.0 | 0.7 | 2.4 | 2.1 | 6.7 | 0.8 | Traitements et salaires |

### b. Structure

| | | | | | | | | | | | | | | |
|---|---|---|---|---|---|---|---|---|---|---|---|---|---|---|
| **1.X.1950 — 30.IX.1951** | | | | | | | | | | | | | | **1.X.1950 — 30.IX.1951** |
| Distribution in percent of: | | | | | | | | | | | | | | Distribution en pour-centage: |
| Value added........ | 100.0 | 66.5 | 3.0 | 8.2 | 8.0 | 0.1 | 1.3 | 2.4 | 0.8 | 4.3 | 1.5 | 3.0 | 0.9 | Valeur ajoutée |
| Number of engaged.. | 100.0 | 55.0 | 2.7 | 15.0 | 10.0 | — | 1.1 | 2.3 | 0.5 | 3.4 | 3.3 | 5.5 | 1.2 | Nombre de personnes occupées |
| Value added per person engaged...... | 8.2 | 9.9 | 8.8 | 4.5 | 6.6 | ... | 9.5 | 9.0 | 11.0 | 10.7 | 3.7 | 4.5 | 6.0 | Valeur ajoutée par personne occupée |
| Employees as a percent of engaged........ | 78.9 | 80.8 | 80.0 | 70.4 | 72.2 | ... | 100.0 | 75.0 | 100.0 | 83.3 | 83.3 | 90.0 | 50.0 | Salariés en pourcentage des personnes occupées |
| Value added per unit of wages and salaries........... | 5.45 | 8.33 | 4.00 | 2.75 | 3.37 | ... | 2.38 | 4.50 | 5.50 | 4.92 | 1.83 | 2.65 | 4.00 | Valeur ajoutée par unité de traitements et salaires |
| Wages and salaries per employee........ | 1.9 | 1.5 | 2.8 | 2.3 | 2.7 | ... | 4.0 | 2.7 | 2.0 | 2.6 | 2.4 | 1.9 | 3.0 | Traitements et salaires par salarié |
| Operatives as a percent of employees........ | 95.1 | 95.0 | 100.0 | 94.7 | 92.3 | ... | 100.0 | 100.0 | 100.0 | 100.0 | 100.0 | 88.9 | 100.0 | Ouvriers en pourcentage des salariés |
| Average man-hours per operative........ | 1.76 | 1.33 | 2.00 | 2.33 | 2.50 | ... | 3.00 | 2.67 | 2.00 | 2.00 | 2.20 | 2.00 | 3.00 | Heures de travail: moyenne par ouvrier |
| **1.X.1956 — 30.IX.1957** | | | | | | | | | | | | | | **1.X.1956 — 30.IX.1957** |
| Distribution in percent of: | | | | | | | | | | | | | | Distribution en pour-centage: |
| Value added........ | 100.0 | 60.0 | 4.6 | 7.7 | 6.8 | 0.4 | 3.6 | 1.1 | 1.1 | 5.7 | 2.1 | 5.7 | 1.2 | Valeur ajoutée |
| Number of engaged.. | 100.0 | 53.6 | 4.5 | 12.8 | 8.3 | 0.6 | 3.2 | 1.3 | 0.6 | 3.2 | 2.6 | 7.7 | 1.6 | Nombre de personnes occupées |
| Value added per engaged............ | 9.6 | 10.8 | 9.8 | 5.8 | 7.9 | 5.5 | 10.7 | 8.8 | 16.0 | 17.3 | 8.0 | 7.1 | 6.8 | Valeur ajoutée par personne occupée |
| Employees as a percent of engaged........ | 69.3 | 66.1 | 85.7 | 65.0 | 73.1 | 50.0 | 100.0 | 75.0 | 100.0 | 90.0 | 75.0 | 66.7 | 40.0 | Salariés en pourcentage des personnes occupées |
| Value added per unit of wages and salaries........... | 4.06 | 5.69 | 3.60 | 2.72 | 3.06 | 2.20 | 2.14 | 3.18 | 4.00 | 4.44 | 2.56 | 1.96 | 3.78 | Valeur ajoutée par unité de traitements et salaires |
| Wages and salaries per employee........ | 3.4 | 2.9 | 3.2 | 3.3 | 3.5 | 5.0 | 5.0 | 3.7 | 4.0 | 4.3 | 4.2 | 5.4 | 4.5 | Traitements et salaires par salarié |
| Operatives as a percent of employees........ | 93.5 | 92.8 | 91.7 | 100.0 | 94.7 | 100.0 | 80.0 | 100.0 | 100.0 | 88.9 | 100.0 | 93.8 | 100.0 | Ouvriers en pourcentage des salariés |
| Average man-hours per operative........ | 1.92 | 1.84 | 2.27 | 0.81 | 2.39 | 3.00 | 2.25 | 3.00 | 2.50 | 2.38 | 2.67 | 2.27 | 3.00 | Heures de travail: moyenne par ouvrier |
| Wages and salaries per thousand opera-tive man-hour........ | 1.51 | 1.28 | 1.24 | 3.81 | 1.37 | 1.33 | 1.94 | 1.11 | 1.40 | 1.26 | 1.31 | 1.97 | 1.33 | Traitements et salaires par millier d'heures-ouvrier |

[1] The 1950-1951 data exclude one establishment engaged in the repair of aeroplanes engaging 315 persons and one establishment manufacturing carts.
[2] In 1950-1951 the manufacture of metal beds (part of ISIC major group 26) is included in Metal Products (ISIC major group 35-38).

[1] Pour l'année 1950-1951, non compris un atelier de réparation d'avions (315 personnes occupées) et une fabrique de charrettes.
[2] Pour l'année 1950-1951 la fabrication des lits en métal (dans CITI 26) est comprise les Ouvrages en métaux (CITI 35-38).

## Gross Domestic Product

Estimates of expenditure on and the origin of the gross domestic product are presented in Table 1. This table is compiled from data supplied by the Statistics and Research Department of the Ministry of Finance in response to the United Nations national accounts questionnaire. Official estimates and a description of the methods and sources used have been published annually in *Economic Review* by the Statistics and Research Department, Ministry of Finance, Nicosia.

## Produit intérieur brut

Le tableau 1 contient des estimations des dépenses imputées au produit intérieur brut et des estimations du produit intérieur brut par secteur d'activité d'origine. Ce tableau a été établi à partir de données fournies par le *Statistics and Research Department* du Ministère des finances en réponse au questionnaire de l'ONU sur la comptabilité nationale. Les estimations officielles et la description des méthodes et sources utilisées sont publiées annuellement dans *Economic Review* par le *Statistics and Research Department*, Ministère des finances, Nicosia.

## Characteristics and Structure of Industrial Activity

The data presented in Table 2 are derived from the results of a Census of Industrial Production taken, using sampling techniques, in 1955 for the year 1954. The results have been published by the Statistics and Research Department in *Census of Industrial Production 1954*, Nicosia 1956. The Census, in principle, covers all establishments but in addition to the exclusions noted in the footnotes to the table certain types of homeworkers were also excluded (e.g. those engaged in the making of foodstuffs, wines and spirits, and spinning, weaving, and clothing manufacture).

The sample was drawn from a registration list of all establishments, with the above-mentioned exclusions, and was stratified by type of industry and by size, based on the number of persons engaged. The sampling ratio ranged from 14 percent of establishments with one person engaged to 73 percent of establishments with 100 or more persons engaged.

The definitions of the items of data shown are consistent with the International Standards in Basic Industrial Statistics. Unpaid family workers have been included in the number engaged if they worked more than half the normal hours. Although the employment figure is generally the average during the year, for the few industries with seasonal activities, such as the canning and preserving of fruit and vegetables, the average during the season has been taken.

## Caractéristiques et structure de l'activité industrielle

Les données du tableau 2 sont tirées des résultats d'un recensement de la production industrielle en 1954 effectué par sondage pendant l'année 1955. Les résultats ont été publiés par le *Statistics and Research Department* dans *Census of Industrial Production 1954*, Nicosia 1956. En principe, le recensement porte sur tous les établissements, mais, outre les activités indiquées dans les notes du tableau, certaines catégories de travailleurs à domicile ont été exclues (notamment ceux qui s'occupent de la préparation de vins et spiritueux, de la filature, du tissage et de la fabrication d'articles d'habillement).

L'échantillon a été tiré d'un registre où sont catalogués tous les établissements, compte tenu des exceptions mentionnées ci-dessus. Il a été stratifié suivant le type d'industrie et la dimension en fonction du nombre de personnes occupées. Les fractions sondées vont de 14 p. 100 pour les établissements occupant une personne, à 73 p. 100 pour les établissements occupant 100 personnes ou plus.

Les définitions des rubriques utilisées sont conformes aux normes internationales relatives aux statistiques industrielles de base. Les travailleurs familiaux non rémunérés ont été inclus dans le nombre de personnes occupées lorsqu'ils avaient travaillé plus de la moitié des heures normales. Les chiffres de l'emploi sont généralement les moyennes annuelles mais, pour les quelques industries ayant des activités saisonnières, telles que la mise en boîte et la conserve de fruits et de légumes, on a utilisé la moyenne pendant la saison.

# CYPRUS

## 1. THE GROSS DOMESTIC PRODUCT
## PRODUIT INTERIEUR BRUT

Million Pounds                                                                 Millions de livres

### A. Expenditure on the Gross Domestic Product at Market Prices
### Dépenses relatives au produit intérieur brut aux prix du marché

| Item of data and year / Rubrique et année | Total | Consumption / Consommation | | Gross Domestic Capital Formation / Formation brute de capital intérieur | | Net exports of goods and services / Exportations nettes de biens et de services | |
|---|---|---|---|---|---|---|---|
| | | Total | Government / Etat | Total | Fixed / Fixe | Exports less imports / Exportations moins importations | Exports / Exportations |
| **a. At Current Prices — Aux prix courants** | | | | | | | |
| **Absolute figures — Chiffres absolus** | | | | | | | |
| 1950 | 41.0 | 37.7 | 4.1 | 5.6 | 5.6 | −2.3 | 13.3 |
| 1951 | 49.5 | 46.9 | 4.3 | 6.5 | 6.5 | −3.9 | 19.4 |
| 1952 | 58.5 | 53.2 | 5.1 | 7.8 | 7.8 | −2.5 | 19.6 |
| 1953 | 64.3 | 59.6 | 5.7 | 8.7 | 8.7 | −4.0 | 18.8 |
| 1954 | 68.3 | 56.3 | 5.5 | 13.2 | 13.4 | −1.2 | 25.0 |
| 1955 | 72.9 | 61.4 | 6.8 | 17.7 | 16.8 | −6.2 | 25.5 |
| 1956 | 87.3 | 72.2 | 12.3 | 20.5 | 19.7 | −5.4 | 35.5 |
| 1957 | 92.5 | 85.0 | 19.2 | 21.3 | 19.8 | −13.8 | 34.2 |
| 1958 | 87.9 | 77.0 | 20.3 | 14.0 | 14.5 | −3.1 | 36.8 |
| 1959 | 86.2 | 79.3 | 22.0 | 16.1 | 13.6 | −9.2 | 37.9 |
| 1960 | 84.0 | 73.9 | 18.9 | 14.4 | 12.4 | −4.3 | 38.8 |
| 1961 | 89.8 | 80.5 | 21.8 | 15.5 | 13.0 | −6.2 | 39.2 |
| **Percentage distribution of average annual expenditure — Distribution en pourcentage des dépenses annuelles moyennes** | | | | | | | |
| 1950–1960 | 100.0 | 88.6 | 15.7 | 18.4 | 17.5 | −7.0 | 38.5 |
| 1950 | 100.0 | 92.0 | 10.0 | 13.6 | 13.6 | −5.6 | 32.4 |
| 1953 | 100.0 | 92.7 | 8.9 | 13.5 | 13.5 | −6.2 | 29.2 |
| 1954 | 100.0 | 82.4 | 8.1 | 19.3 | 19.6 | −1.7 | 36.6 |
| 1958 | 100.0 | 87.6 | 23.1 | 15.9 | 16.5 | −3.5 | 41.9 |
| 1960 | 100.0 | 88.0 | 22.5 | 17.1 | 14.8 | −5.1 | 46.2 |
| **b. At Prices of 1950 — Aux prix de 1950** | | | | | | | |
| **Absolute figures — Chiffres absolus** | | | | | | | |
| 1950 | 41.0 | 37.7 | 4.1 | 5.6 | 5.6 | −2.3 | 13.3 |
| 1951 | 41.3 | 41.4 | 3.8 | 6.3 | 6.3 | −6.4 | 11.9 |
| 1952 | 45.7 | 45.5 | 4.3 | 6.9 | 6.9 | −6.7 | 12.1 |
| 1953 | 49.9 | 50.7 | 4.7 | 8.5 | 8.5 | −9.3 | 12.6 |
| 1954 | 50.3 | 47.4 | 4.3 | 12.8 | 13.0 | −9.9 | 16.1 |
| 1955 | 51.3 | 50.9 | 5.1 | 15.3 | 14.5 | −14.9 | 15.4 |
| 1956 | 58.0 | 61.9 | 8.5 | 16.5 | 15.8 | −20.4 | 18.4 |
| 1957 | 62.3 | 65.0 | 12.4 | 17.1 | 15.8 | −19.8 | 21.5 |
| 1958 | 58.2 | 58.4 | 12.6 | 11.1 | 11.5 | −11.3 | 24.3 |
| 1959 | 56.9 | 60.8 | 13.6 | 13.0 | 11.0 | −16.9 | 25.0 |
| 1960 | 55.9 | 57.0 | 11.7 | 11.6 | 10.0 | −12.7 | 25.6 |
| 1961 | 60.5 | 62.9 | 13.7 | 12.6 | 10.5 | −15.0 | 25.8 |
| **Percentage distribution of average annual expenditure — Distribution en pourcentage des dépenses annuelles moyennes** | | | | | | | |
| 1950–1960 | 100.0 | 101.0 | 14.9 | 21.9 | 20.8 | −22.9 | 34.4 |
| 1950 | 100.0 | 92.0 | 10.0 | 13.6 | 13.6 | −5.6 | 32.4 |
| 1953 | 100.0 | 101.6 | 9.4 | 17.0 | 17.0 | −18.6 | 25.3 |
| 1954 | 100.0 | 94.2 | 8.5 | 25.5 | 25.8 | −19.7 | 32.0 |
| 1958 | 100.0 | 100.3 | 21.6 | 19.1 | 19.8 | −19.4 | 41.8 |
| 1960 | 100.0 | 102.0 | 20.9 | 20.7 | 17.9 | −22.7 | 45.8 |
| **Average annual rate of growth — Taux annuel moyen d'accroissement** | | | | | | | |
| 1950–1960 | 3.1 | 4.2 | 11.1 | 7.6 | 6.0 | . | 6.8 |
| 1950–1953 | 6.8 | 10.4 | 4.6 | 14.9 | 14.9 | . | −1.8 |
| 1954–1958 | 3.7 | 5.4 | 30.8 | −3.5 | −3.0 | . | 10.8 |
| 1958–1960 | −2.0 | −1.2 | −3.7 | 2.2 | −6.7 | . | 2.6 |

## B. The Gross Domestic Product at Factor Cost According to Origin
### Origine par secteur d'activité du produit intérieur brut au coût des facteurs

| Item of data and year / Rubrique et année | Total | Agricultural sector / Secteur agricole | Industrial Sector — Secteur Industriel | | | | | Transportation and communication / Transports et communications | Other sectors / Autres secteurs |
| --- | --- | --- | --- | --- | --- | --- | --- | --- | --- |
| | | | Total | Mining / Industries extractives | Manufacturing / Industries manufacturières | Construction / Bâtiment et travaux publics | Electricity, gas and water / Electricité, gaz et eau | | |
| ISIC — CITI | 0–9 | 0 | 1–5 | 1 | 2–3 | 4 | 5 | 7 | 6, 8–9 |

*a. At Current Prices — Aux prix courants*

| | | | | | | | | | |
| --- | --- | --- | --- | --- | --- | --- | --- | --- | --- |
| **Absolute figures — Chiffres absolus** | | | | | | | | | |
| 1950 | 38.7 | 10.6 | 12.2 | 4.8 | 5.9 | 1.3 | 0.2 | 1.5 | 14.4 |
| 1951 | 46.1 | 12.4 | 15.3 | 7.0 | 6.4 | 1.7 | 0.2 | 2.1 | 16.3 |
| 1952 | 54.5 | 15.6 | 18.1 | 9.1 | 6.5 | 2.3 | 0.2 | 2.6 | 18.2 |
| 1953 | 60.0 | 19.5 | 17.1 | 6.9 | 7.0 | 2.9 | 0.3 | 3.1 | 20.3 |
| 1954 | 63.1 | 17.5 | 19.8 | 8.5 | 6.8 | 3.9 | 0.6 | 3.7 | 22.1 |
| 1955 | 66.9 | 16.4 | 21.7 | 9.2 | 7.7 | 4.0 | 0.8 | 4.2 | 24.6 |
| 1956 | 80.8 | 19.7 | 25.2 | 11.4 | 8.3 | 4.3 | 1.2 | 5.0 | 30.9 |
| 1957 | 84.2 | 18.2 | 23.8 | 9.2 | 8.6 | 4.4 | 1.6 | 5.2 | 37.0 |
| 1958 | 80.3 | 17.9 | 21.8 | 8.0 | 8.0 | 4.0 | 1.8 | 4.8 | 35.8 |
| 1959 | 76.6 | 16.8 | 22.0 | 8.4 | 8.4 | 3.2 | 2.0 | 4.8 | 33.0 |
| 1960 | 75.0 | 15.5 | 22.6 | 8.7 | 8.6 | 3.0 | 2.3 | 4.6 | 32.3 |
| 1961 | 81.8 | 19.2 | 27.4 | 7.6 | 9.2 | 2.8 | 2.5 | 5.3 | 35.2 |
| **Percentage distribution according to sector— Distribution en pourcentage par secteur** | | | | | | | | | |
| 1950 – 1960 | 100.0 | 24.8 | 30.3 | 12.6 | 11.3 | 4.8 | 1.6 | 5.7 | 39.2 |
| 1950 | 100.0 | 27.4 | 31.5 | 12.4 | 15.2 | 3.4 | 0.5 | 3.9 | 37.2 |
| 1953 | 100.0 | 32.5 | 28.5 | 11.5 | 11.7 | 4.8 | 0.5 | 5.2 | 33.8 |
| 1954 | 100.0 | 27.7 | 31.4 | 13.5 | 10.8 | 6.2 | 0.9 | 5.9 | 35.0 |
| 1958 | 100.0 | 22.3 | 27.2 | 10.0 | 10.0 | 5.0 | 2.2 | 6.0 | 44.5 |
| 1960 | 100.0 | 20.7 | 30.1 | 11.6 | 11.5 | 4.0 | 3.0 | 6.1 | 43.1 |

*b. At Prices of 1950 — Aux prix de 1950*

| | | | | | | | | | |
| --- | --- | --- | --- | --- | --- | --- | --- | --- | --- |
| **Absolute figures — Chiffres absolus** | | | | | | | | | |
| 1950 | 38.7 | 10.6 | 12.2 | 4.8 | 5.9 | 1.3 | 0.2 | 1.5 | 14.4 |
| 1951 | 39.0 | 9.5 | 12.7 | 5.1 | 5.9 | 1.5 | 0.2 | 1.9 | 14.9 |
| 1952 | 43.1 | 11.4 | 13.8 | 5.8 | 6.0 | 1.8 | 0.2 | 2.4 | 15.5 |
| 1953 | 47.1 | 14.8 | 13.3 | 4.6 | 6.4 | 2.0 | 0.3 | 2.7 | 16.3 |
| 1954 | 47.5 | 13.4 | 14.2 | 5.2 | 6.4 | 2.0 | 0.6 | 3.1 | 16.8 |
| 1955 | 48.4 | 12.7 | 14.4 | 4.9 | 6.5 | 2.2 | 0.8 | 3.2 | 18.1 |
| 1956 | 54.8 | 13.8 | 16.3 | 6.0 | 6.8 | 2.3 | 1.2 | 3.4 | 21.3 |
| 1957 | 58.8 | 14.2 | 17.4 | 6.4 | 7.0 | 2.4 | 1.6 | 3.7 | 23.5 |
| 1958 | 55.7 | 12.5 | 16.9 | 6.3 | 6.6 | 2.2 | 1.8 | 3.5 | 22.8 |
| 1959 | 55.1 | 13.4 | 17.2 | 6.5 | 6.9 | 1.8 | 2.0 | 3.5 | 21.0 |
| 1960 | 52.8 | 11.8 | 17.8 | 6.7 | 7.1 | 1.7 | 2.3 | 2.6 | 20.6 |
| 1961 | 57.7 | 14.5 | 20.8 | 5.9 | 7.8 | 1.6 | 2.5 | 3.0 | 22.4 |
| **Percentage distribution according to sector— Distribution en pourcentage par secteur** | | | | | | | | | |
| 1950 – 1960 | 100.0 | 25.6 | 30.7 | 11.5 | 13.2 | 3.9 | 2.1 | 5.8 | 37.9 |
| 1950 | 100.0 | 27.4 | 31.5 | 12.4 | 15.2 | 3.4 | 0.5 | 3.9 | 37.2 |
| 1953 | 100.0 | 31.4 | 28.3 | 9.8 | 13.6 | 4.3 | 0.6 | 5.7 | 34.6 |
| 1954 | 100.0 | 28.2 | 29.9 | 10.9 | 13.5 | 4.2 | 1.3 | 6.5 | 35.4 |
| 1958 | 100.0 | 22.4 | 30.4 | 11.3 | 11.9 | 4.0 | 3.2 | 6.3 | 40.9 |
| 1960 | 100.0 | 22.4 | 33.7 | 12.7 | 13.4 | 3.2 | 4.4 | 4.9 | 39.0 |
| **Average annual rate of growth—Taux annuel moyen d'accroissement** | | | | | | | | | |
| 1950 – 1960 | 3.2 | 1.1 | 3.8 | 3.4 | 1.9 | 2.7 | 27.7 | 5.7 | 3.6 |
| 1950 – 1953 | 6.8 | 11.8 | 2.9 | −1.4 | 2.8 | 15.4 | 14.5 | 21.6 | 4.2 |
| 1954 – 1958 | 4.1 | −1.7 | 4.4 | 4.9 | 0.8 | 2.4 | 31.6 | 3.1 | 7.9 |
| 1958 – 1960 | −2.6 | −2.8 | 2.6 | 3.1 | 3.7 | −12.1 | 13.0 | −13.8 | −4.9 |

## 2. CHARACTERISTICS OF ALL INDUSTRIAL ESTABLISHMENTS
## CARACTERISTIQUES DE TOUS LES ETABLISSEMENTS INDUSTRIELS
### 1954

Number of establishments in units; value added and wages and salaries in thousand Pounds; number of engaged and employees in thousands; value added per engaged and wages and salaries per employee in thousand Pounds.

Nombre d'établissements en unités; valeur ajoutée et traitements et salaires en milliers de livres; nombre de personnes occupées et de salariés en milliers; valeur ajoutée par personne occupée et traitements et salaires par salarié en milliers de livres.

### A. The Divisions of Industrial Activity — Les branches de l'activité industrielle

| Item of data | All industrial activity Toutes industries | Mining [4] Industries extractives [4] | Manufacturing [1] Industries manufacturières [1] | Construction [2] Bâtiment et travaux publics [2] | Electricity gas and water [3] Electricité gaz et eau [3] | Rubrique | Item of data | All industrial activity Toutes industries | Mining [4] Industries extractives [4] | Manufacturing [1] Industries manufacturières [1] | Construction [2] Bâtiment et travaux publics [2] | Electricity gas and water [3] Electricité gaz et eau [3] | Rubrique |
|---|---|---|---|---|---|---|---|---|---|---|---|---|---|
| ISIC | 1-4,511-512, 512 | 1 | 2-3 | 4 | 511-512,521 | CITI | ISIC | 1-4,511-512, 521 | 1 | 2-3 | 4 | 511-512,521 | CITI |
| | a. Absolute Figures — Chiffres absolus | | | | | | | b. Structure | | | | | |
| Number of establishments | 13 700 | 354 | 11 328 | 2 006 | 12 | Nombre d'établissements | Distribution in percent of: | | | | | | Distribution en pourcentage: |
| Value added | 16 825 | 8 445 | 4 694 | 3 220 | 466 | Valeur ajoutée | Value added | 100.0 | 50.2 | 27.9 | 19.1 | 2.8 | Valeur ajoutée |
| Number of engaged (Average during the year) | 49.3 | 6.7 | 26.2 | 15.6 | 0.8 | Nombre de personnes occupées (moyenne pendant l'année) | Number of engaged | 100.0 | 13.6 | 53.1 | 31.7 | 1.6 | Nombre de personnes occupées |
| Employees: Number (Average during the year) | 34.4 | 6.3 | 13.8 | 13.5 | 0.8 | Salariés: Nombre (moyenne pendant l'année) | Value added per person engaged | 0.34 | 1.27 | 0.18 | 0.21 | 0.58 | Valeur ajoutée par personne occupée |
| Wages and salaries | 6 084 | 1 622 | 1 897 | 2 416 | 149 | Traitements et salaires | Employees as a percent of engaged | 69.8 | 94.0 | 52.7 | 86.5 | 100.0 | Salariés en pourcentage des personnes occupées |
| | | | | | | | Value added per unit of wages and salaries | 2.76 | 5.21 | 2.47 | 1.33 | 3.13 | Valeur ajoutée par unité de traitements et salaires |
| | | | | | | | Wages and salaries per employee | 0.18 | 0.26 | 0.14 | 0.18 | 0.19 | Traitements et salaires par salarié |

For footnotes see end of table.                         Pour les notes, voir au bas du tableau.

### B. The Major Groups of Mining — Les classes de la branche Industries extractives

| Item of data | All mining [4] Toutes industries extractives [4] | Metal mining Extraction des minerais métalliques | Other mining Divers | Rubrique | Item of data | All mining [4] Toutes industries extractives [4] | Metal mining Extraction des minerais métalliques | Other mining Divers | Rubrique |
|---|---|---|---|---|---|---|---|---|---|
| ISIC | 1 | 12 | 14-19 | CITI | ISIC | 1 | 12 | 14-19 | CITI |
| | a. Absolute Figures Chiffres absolus | | | | | b. Structure | | | |
| Number of establishments | 354 | 4 | 350 | Nombre d'établissements | Distribution in percent of: | | | | Distribution en pourcentage: |
| Value added | 8 445 | 7 557 | 888 | Valeur ajoutée | Value added | 100.0 | 89.5 | 10.5 | Valeur ajoutée |
| Number of engaged (Average during the year) | 6.7 | 4.1 | 2.6 | Nombre de personnes occupées (moyenne pendant l'année) | Number of engaged | 100.0 | 61.2 | 38.8 | Nombre de personnes occupées |
| Employees: Number (Average during the year) | 6.3 | 4.1 | 2.2 | Salariés: Nombre (moyenne pendant l'année) | Value added per person engaged | 1.26 | 1.84 | 0.34 | Valeur ajoutée par personne occupée |
| Wages and salaries | 1 622 | 1 171 | 451 | Traitements et salaires | Employees as a percent of engaged | 94.0 | 100.0 | 84.6 | Salariés en pourcentage des personnes occupées |
| | | | | | Value added per unit of wages and salaries | 5.21 | 6.45 | 1.97 | Valeur ajoutée par unité de traitements et salaires |
| | | | | | Wages and salaries per employee | 0.26 | 0.28 | 0.20 | Traitements et salaires par salarié |

## C. The Major Groups of Manufacturing — Les classes de la branche Industries manufacturières

| Item of data | Manufacturing[1] Industries manufacturières[1] (2-3) | Food, beverages and tobacco[5] Industries alimentaires, boissons, tabac[5] (20-22) | Textiles (23) | Clothing, footwear and made-up textiles Articles d'habillement, chaussures et ouvrages en tissu (24) | Wood products and furniture Bois et meubles (25-26) | Paper and paper products Papier et ouvrages en papier (27) | Printing and publishing Imprimerie et édition (28) | Leather and leather products except wearing apparel Cuir et articles en cuir, à l'exclusion des articles d'habillement (29) | Rubber products Ouvrages en caoutchouc (30) | Chemicals and chemical, petroleum and coal products[6] Produits chimiques et dérivés du pétrole et du charbon[6] (31-32) | Non-metallic mineral products Produits minéraux non métalliques (33) | Metal products Ouvrages en métaux (35-38) | Other manufacturing Autres industries manufacturières (39) | Rubrique |
|---|---|---|---|---|---|---|---|---|---|---|---|---|---|---|
| ISIC | 2-3 | 20-22 | 23 | 24 | 25-26 | 27 | 28 | 29 | 30 | 31-32 | 33 | 35-38 | 39 | CITI |
| *a. Absolute Figures — Chiffres absolus* | | | | | | | | | | | | | | |
| Number of establishments | 11 328 | 1 551 | 26 | 6 668 | 830 | 3 | 86 | 20 | 21 | 52 | 305 | 1 058 | 708 | Nombre d'établissements |
| Value added | 4 694 | 1 619 | 45 | 1 032 | 396 | 2 | 223 | 45 | 19 | 66 | 352 | 643 | 252 | Valeur ajoutée |
| Number of engaged (Average during the year) | 26.2 | 5.3 | 0.5 | 11.1 | 2.1 | — | 0.7 | 0.1 | 0.1 | 0.2 | 1.6 | 3.1 | 1.4 | Nombre de personnes occupées (moyenne pendant l'année) |
| Employees: Number (Average during the year) | 13.8 | 3.4 | 0.4 | 4.2 | 1.2 | — | 0.7 | 0.1 | — | 0.2 | 1.1 | 1.9 | 0.6 | Salariés: Nombre (moyenne pendant l'année) |
| Wages and salaries | 1 897 | 584 | 62 | 343 | 159 | 2 | 150 | 14 | 8 | 34 | 138 | 288 | 115 | Traitements et salaires |
| *b. Structure* | | | | | | | | | | | | | | |
| Distribution in percent of: Value added | 100.0 | 34.5 | 1.0 | 22.0 | 8.4 | — | 4.7 | 1.0 | 0.4 | 1.4 | 7.5 | 13.7 | 5.4 | Distribution en pourcentage: Valeur ajoutée |
| Number of engaged | 100.0 | 20.2 | 1.9 | 42.4 | 8.0 | — | 2.7 | 0.4 | 0.4 | 0.8 | 6.1 | 11.8 | 5.3 | Nombre de personnes occupées |
| Value added per person engaged | 0.18 | 0.30 | 0.09 | 0.09 | 0.19 | ... | 0.32 | 0.45 | 0.19 | 0.33 | 0.22 | 0.21 | 0.18 | Valeur ajoutée par personne occupée |
| Employees as a percent of engaged | 52.7 | 64.2 | 80.0 | 37.8 | 57.1 | ... | 100.0 | 100.0 | ... | 100.0 | 68.8 | 61.3 | 42.8 | Salariés en pourcentage des personnes occupées |
| Value added per unit of wages and salaries | 2.47 | 2.77 | 0.72 | 3.01 | 2.49 | 1.00 | 1.49 | 3.21 | 2.38 | 1.94 | 2.55 | 2.23 | 2.19 | Valeur ajoutée par unité de traitements et salaires |
| Wages and salaries per employee | 0.14 | 0.17 | 0.16 | 0.08 | 0.13 | ... | 0.21 | 0.14 | ... | 0.17 | 0.12 | 0.15 | 0.19 | Traitements et salaires par salarié |

[1] Excludes slaughtering of animals (part of ISIC group 201) and manufacture of pharmaceutical preparations (part of ISIC group 319).
[2] Excludes work done by U.K. Armed Services and large local contractors working for the U.K. Armed Services under contracts placed in the United Kingdom.
[3] Excludes water supply in rural areas (part of ISIC group 521).
[4] Excludes crude petroleum and natural gas (ISIC major group 13). In 1954 there was 1 establishment with 10 persons engaged and 9 employees.
[5] Excludes slaughtering of animals (part of ISIC group 201).
[6] Excludes manufacture of pharmaceutical preparations (part of ISIC group 319).

[1] Non compris l'abattage du bétail (dans CITI groupe 201) et la fabrication de préparations pharmaceutiques (dans CITI groupe 319).
[2] Non compris les travaux effectués par les Services de l'Armée du Royaume-Uni et les sous-traitants locaux importants travaillant pour les Services de l'Armée du Royaume-Uni aux termes de contrats établis au Royaume-Uni.
[3] Non compris les services de distribution d'eau dans les régions rurales (dans CITI groupe 521).
[4] Non compris pétrole brut et gaz naturel (CITI classe 13). En 1954 existait un établissement ayant 10 personnes occupées et 9 salariés.
[5] Non compris l'abattage du bétail (dans CITI groupe 201).
[6] Non compris la fabrication de préparations pharmaceutiques (dans CITI groupe 319).

# CZECHOSLOVAKIA — TCHECOSLOVAQUIE

## Net Material Product

The data on the net material product shown in Table 1 were derived from correspondence with the State Statistical Office of Czechoslovakia, Prague. The final estimates are issued annually by the same office in *Statistická Ročenka, ČSSR*. The concepts and definitions governing these data are from the system of material product accounts, which is briefly described in the introduction to this publication and which differs, in a number of important respects, from the United Nations system of national accounts.

## Index Numbers of Industrial Production

The index numbers of industrial production set out in Table 2 have been compiled by the State Statistical Office of Czechoslovakia and published in *Statistická Ročenka, ČSSR, 1961* or furnished to the Statistical Office of the United Nations through correspondence. The series of index numbers relate to the value of gross industrial output, expressed in enterprise prices (i.e., excluding turnover taxes) as of 1 July 1954, of all publicly-owned enterprise and co-operatives principally engaged in mining, manufacturing, the production of electricity and gas and water supply.

The series of index numbers are, in effect, computed as base-weighted arithmetic averages of series of relatives on quantities produced for practically all of gross industrial output. Gross output includes the production of all commodities shipped, or intended for shipment, by the enterprise and the fabrication or processing of goods for, as well as the rendering of other kinds of industrial services to, other enterprises. The bases of comparison utilized in the series of relatives consist of average monthly quantities produced during 1953 for each of the elements of gross output. The weights employed in combining the series of relatives into index numbers consist of the product of these quantities and the corresponding enterprise prices as of 1 July 1954.

Further information concerning the series of index numbers may be found in "Statisticka a Evidence Průmyslová Výroby" (Statistics and Registration of Industrial Production) by Ing. A. Červený in *Otázky Statistiky*, No. 7, 1954 and *Průmyslová Statisticka* (Industrial Statistics) by Messrs. Korda, Červený and Vávrovský. Both publications were issued by the State Statistical Office of Czechoslovakia, Prague.

## Index Numbers of Industrial Employment

The index numbers in Table 3 were compiled from absolute figures issued in *Statistická Ročenka, ČSSR, 1961* or furnished through correspondence by the State

## Produit matériel net

Les données du tableau 1, relatives au produit matériel net, ont été fournies par l'Office statistique d'Etat de Tchécoslovaquie, Prague, par voie de correspondance. Les estimations définitives sont publiées annuellement par le même Office dans *Statisticka Ročenka, ČSSR*. Les concepts et définitions régissant ces données sont conformes au système de comptabilité du produit matériel, qui est décrit brièvement dans l'introduction de cette publication et qui, à plus d'un égard, diffère du système de comptabilité nationale de l'ONU.

## Indices de la production industrielle

Les indices de la production industrielle reproduits dans le tableau 2 ont été établis par l'Office statistique d'Etat de Tchécoslovaquie et publiés dans *Statistická Ročenka, ČSSR, 1961,* ou fournis au Bureau de statistique de l'ONU par voie de correspondance. Les séries d'indices portent sur la valeur brute de la production industrielle, au prix départ entreprise (c'est-à-dire, non compris les taxes sur le chiffre d'affaires) en vigueur au 1er juillet 1954, ceci pour toutes les entreprises publiques et coopératives dont l'activité principale relève des industries extractives ou manufacturières, de la production d'électricité et de gaz ou de la distribution de l'eau.

Les séries d'indices sont, en fait, des moyennes arithmétiques à pondération fixe de séries de rapports de quantités produites portant sur pratiquement toute la production industrielle brute. La production brute comprend la production de toutes les marchandises expédiées, ou sur le point de l'être, par l'entreprise, la fabrication et le traitement de marchandises à façon, ainsi que d'autres types de services industriels rendus à d'autres entreprises. Les bases de comparaison adoptées pour construire les séries de rapports sont les quantités mensuelles moyennes produites en 1953 de chacune des composantes de la production brute. Les coefficients de pondération utilisés pour combiner les séries de rapports en indices sont les valeurs de ces quantités aux prix correspondants, départ entreprise, en vigueur au 1er juillet 1954.

Pour plus de détails sur les séries d'indices, voir "Statisticka a Evidence Průmyslová Výroby" (Statistiques et enregistrement de la production industrielle) par Ing. A. Červený dans *Otázky Statistiky*, No. 7, 1954, et *Průmyslová Statisticka* (Statistiques industrielles) par MM. Korda, Červený et Vávrovský. Ces deux publications sont publiées par l'Office statistique d'Etat de Tchécoslovaquie, Prague.

## Indices de l'emploi dans l'industrie

Les indices du tableau 3 ont été construits à partir de chiffres absolus publiés dans *Statistická Ročenka, ČSSR, 1961* ou fournis, par voie de correspondance, par l'Office

Statistical Office. The absolute figures relate to the average number of operatives ( manual workers) during each month of the year employed in the industrial activities of all publicly-owned enterprises and co-operatives primarily engaged in mining, manufacturing, the production of electricity and gas, water supply and construction. The figures therefore do not cover all manual workers in these kinds of enterprises. The definition of the count of operatives appears to correspond, in other respects, to that of the International Standards in Basic Industrial Statistics.

statistique d'Etat. Les chiffres absolus sont les nombres moyens, pour chaque mois de l'année, des ouvriers (travailleurs manuels) engagés dans les activités industrielles de toutes les entreprises publiques et coopératives dont l'activité principale relève des industries extractives, des industries manufacturières, de la production d'électricité et de gaz, de la distribution de l'eau ou du bâtiment et des travaux publics. Les chiffres ne comprennent donc pas tous les travailleurs manuels de ces types d'entreprises. A tous autres égards, la définition de l'ouvrier semble être conforme aux Normes internationales relatives aux statistiques industrielles de base.

## Characteristics and Structure of Industrial Activity

The data in Table 4 were compiled from *Statistická Ročenka, ČSSR, 1959* or *1960,* and relate to all publicly-owned enterprises and co-operatives principally engaged in industrial activity in the case of Table 4A but only such publicly-owned enterprises that are managed by the central authorities in the case of Table 4B. The figures of the number of engaged are averages of monthly employment during the year, and do not cover apprentices. The data on operatives shown in the table have been described above. The elements of cost of production listed in Table 4B, have been described above. The elements of cost of production listed in Table 4B, excepting the category, "Other," related to costs incurred in the industrial activities of the enterprises covered; and, except for this restriction, are defined as in the International Standards in Basic Industrial Statistics.

## Caractéristiques et structure de l'activité industrielle

Les données du tableau 4, sont tirées de *Statistická Ročenka, ČSSR, 1959* ou *1960;* dans la partie A, elles se rapportent à toutes les entreprises publiques et coopératives exerçant principalement une activité industrielle, mais, dans la partie B, elles ne portent que sur les entreprises publiques gérées par les autorités centrales. Les chiffres relatifs au nombre de personnes occupées sont des moyennes de l'emploi mensuel pendant l'année et ne comprennent pas les apprentis. Les données du tableau qui ont trait aux ouvriers ont été décrites plus haut. Les éléments du coût de la production indiqués dans le tableau 4B, à l'exception de la rubrique "Divers", se rapportent aux coûts découlant de l'exercice des activités industrielles par les entreprises retenues; à tous autres égards, leur définition est conforme aux Normes internationales relatives aux statistiques industrielles de base.

## 1. THE NET MATERIAL PRODUCT ACCORDING TO ORIGIN
## ORIGINE PAR SECTEUR D'ACTIVITE DU PRODUIT MATERIEL NET

| Item of data and year<br>Rubrique et année | Total | Agricultural sector<br>Secteur agricole | Mining, manufacturing and electricity, gas and water Industries<br>Extractives et manufacturières et électricité, gaz et eau | Construction<br>Bâtiment et travaux publics | Transportation and communication [1]<br>Transports et communications [1] | Other sectors<br>Autres secteurs |
|---|---|---|---|---|---|---|
| ISIC — CITI | 521, 611-612, 7, 841, 852 | 0 | 1-3, 511-521 | 4 | 7 | 611-612 841, 852 |
| **a. At Current Prices — Aux prix courants** | | | | | | |
| Percentage distribution according to sector— Distribution en pourcentage par secteur | | | | | | |
| 1954............ | 100 | 13 | 64 | 11 | 3 | 9 |
| 1955............ | 100 | 16 | 62 | 10 | 3 | 9 |
| 1956............ | 100 | 16 | 62 | 12 | 3 | 7 |
| 1957............ | 100 | 15 | 62 | 12 | 3 | 8 |
| 1958............ | 100 | 15 | 62 | 11 | 3 | 9 |
| 1959............ | 100 | 14 | 64 | 11 | 3 | 8 |
| 1960............ | 100 | 16 | 62 | 10 | 4 | 8 |
| 1961............ | 100 | 14 | 64 | 10 | 4 | 8 |
| **b. At Prices of 1955 — Aux prix de 1955** | | | | | | |
| Index numbers — Indices (1958 = 100) | | | | | | [2] |
| 1950............ | 56 | 108 | 50 | 36 | ... | 56 |
| 1954............ | 74 | 91 | 70 | 68 | ... | 87 |
| 1955............ | 82 | 101 | 78 | 78 | ... | 93 |
| 1956............ | 86 | 98 | 84 | 88 | ... | 85 |
| 1957............ | 92 | 97 | 91 | 93 | ... | 93 |
| 1958............ | 100 | 100 | 100 | 100 | ... | 100 |
| 1959............ | 107 | 88 | 108 | 118 | ... | 99 |
| 1960............ | 115 | 91 | 119 | 129 | ... | 100 |
| 1961 [3]......... | 123 | 88 | 130 | 136 | ... | 104 |
| Percentage distribution according to sector— Distribution en pourcentage par secteur | | | | | | |
| 1954............ | 100 | 13 | 64 | 10 | 3 | 10 |
| 1955............ | 100 | 13 | 64 | 10 | 3 | 10 |
| 1956............ | 100 | 12 | 66 | 11 | 3 | 8 |
| 1957............ | 100 | 11 | 67 | 11 | 3 | 8 |
| 1958............ | 100 | 10 | 68 | 11 | 3 | 8 |
| 1959............ | 100 | 9 | 69 | 12 | 3 | 7 |
| 1960............ | 100 | 8 | 70 | 12 | 4 | 6 |
| 1960 [3]......... | 100 | 14 | 62 | 11 | 4 | 9 |
| 1961 [3]......... | 100 | 13 | 64 | 11 | 4 | 8 |
| Average annual rate of growth—Taux annuel moyen d'accroissement | | | | | | |
| 1950 – 1960..... | 7.5 | −1.7 | 9.1 | 13.6 | ... | 6.0 |
| 1950 – 1954..... | 7.2 | −4.2 | 8.8 | 17.2 | ... | 11.7 |
| 1954 – 1958..... | 7.8 | 2.4 | 9.3 | 10.1 | ... | 3.5 |
| 1958 – 1960..... | 7.2 | −4.6 | 9.1 | 13.6 | ... | — |

[1] Relates only to transportation of goods and communications for enterprises contributing to the material products.
[2] Includes in the case of the index numbers and average annual rates of growth, transportation of goods and communications for enterprises contributing to the material product.
[3] Valued at prices of 1960 instead of prices of 1955. The index numbers for 1961 have been linked at 1960 to the index numbers for earlier years.

[1] Cette rubrique comprend seulement le transport de marchandises et les communications pour le compte des entreprises qui concourent à la formation du produit matériel.
[2] Y compris, dans le cas des indices et du taux annuel moyen d'accroissement, le transport de marchandises et les communications pour le compte des entreprises qui concourent à la formation du produit matériel.
[3] Aux prix de 1960 et non aux prix de 1955. Les indices de 1961 ont été raccordés à ceux des années précédentes au niveau de 1960.

## 2. INDEX NUMBERS OF INDUSTRIAL PRODUCTION, MAJOR SUB-DIVISIONS OF MINING AND MANUFACTURING AND ELECTRICITY, STEAM AND WATER

## INDICES DE LA PRODUCTION INDUSTRIELLE, PRINCIPALES SUBDIVISIONS DES INDUSTRIES EXTRACTIVES ET MANUFACTURIERES, ET ELECTRICITE, VAPEUR ET EAU

| Period / Période | Total [1] | Coal mining, crude petroleum and natural gas / Extraction de charbon, pétrole brut et gaz naturel | Food, beverages and tobacco / Industries alimentaires, boissons, tabac | Textiles | Clothing, and made-up textiles [2] / Articles d'habillement, et ouvrages en tissu [2] | Wood products and furniture [1,3] / Bois et meubles [1,3] | Paper and paper products / Papier et ouvrages en papier | Printing [1] / Imprimerie [1] | Leather and leather products [2] / Cuir et articles en cuir [2] | Rubber products [4] / Ouvrages en caoutchouc [4] | Chemicals and chemical, petroleum and coal products / Produits chimiques et dérivés du pétrole et du charbon | Non-metallic minerals and products [4] / Minéraux non métalliques et produits dérivés [4] | Metal mining and basic metals / Minerais métalliques et métallurgie de base | Metal products [5] / Ouvrages en métaux [5] | Other manufacturing [3,4] / Autres industries manufacturières [3,4] | Electricity, steam and water / Electricité, vapeur et eau |
|---|---|---|---|---|---|---|---|---|---|---|---|---|---|---|---|---|
| **ISIC — CITI** | 1-3, 511-521 | 11, 13 | 20-22 | 23 | 243-244 | 25-26 | 27 | 28 | 241, 29 | 30 | 192, 31-32, 512 | 14, 199, 33 | 12, 34 | 35-38, 391-393 | 394-399 | 511, 513-521 |
| *a. Indexes — Indices (1958 = 100)* | | | | | | | | | | | | | | | | |
| 1937 | 31 | ... | ... | ... | ... | ... | ... | ... | ... | ... | ... | ... | ... | ... | ... | ... |
| 1948 | 33 | 50 | 42 | 47 | 39 | 34 | 48 | 59 | 49 | 27 | 34 | 31 | 36 | 20 | 15 | 36 |
| 1949 | 38 | 52 | 51 | 54 | 46 | 38 | 51 | 56 | 51 | 33 | 38 | 34 | 37 | 24 | 18 | 39 |
| 1950 | 44 | 54 | 63 | 58 | 57 | 44 | 58 | 68 | 53 | 34 | 41 | 36 | 41 | 29 | 21 | 45 |
| 1951 | 50 | 57 | 68 | 61 | 65 | 53 | 63 | 72 | 57 | 38 | 50 | 41 | 47 | 37 | 22 | 50 |
| 1952 | 59 | 63 | 73 | 66 | 73 | 65 | 68 | 69 | 61 | 48 | 59 | 46 | 61 | 49 | 47 | 56 |
| 1953 | 64 | 66 | 76 | 66 | 71 | 64 | 72 | 73 | 60 | 54 | 64 | 49 | 70 | 59 | 56 | 59 |
| 1954 | 67 | 71 | 79 | 71 | 67 | 70 | 77 | 80 | 64 | 59 | 66 | 55 | 69 | 62 | 59 | 65 |
| 1955 | 74 | 76 | 83 | 81 | 80 | 79 | 80 | 85 | 72 | 66 | 74 | 63 | 76 | 68 | 68 | 74 |
| 1956 | 82 | 81 | 87 | 83 | 79 | 86 | 85 | 87 | 75 | 83 | 81 | 72 | 85 | 78 | 83 | 84 |
| 1957 | 90 | 90 | 95 | 91 | 88 | 93 | 90 | 92 | 88 | 94 | 90 | 86 | 92 | 86 | 90 | 91 |
| 1958 | 100 | 100 | 100 | 100 | 100 | 100 | 100 | 100 | 100 | 100 | 100 | 100 | 100 | 100 | 100 | 100 |
| 1959 | 111 | 100 | 105 | 106 | 106 | 108 | 106 | 107 | 100 | 107 | 110 | 114 | 115 | 116 | 108 | 112 |
| 1960 | 124 | 106 | 112 | 112 | 120 | 115 | 114 | 114 | 117 | 124 | 134 | 130 | 126 | 133 | 117 | 129 |
| 1961 | 135 | 112 | 118 | 120 | 134 | 122 | 118 | 119 | 125 | 145 | 151 | 140 | 136 | 148 | 126 | 143 |
| *b. Average Annual Rate of Change — Taux annuel moyen de variation* | | | | | | | | | | | | | | | | |
| 1950–1960 | 10.9 | 7.0 | 5.9 | 6.8 | 7.7 | 10.1 | 7.0 | 5.3 | 8.2 | 13.8 | 12.6 | 13.7 | 11.9 | 16.5 | 18.7 | 11.1 |
| 1948–1953 | 14.2 | 5.7 | 12.6 | 7.0 | 12.7 | 13.5 | 8.4 | 4.3 | 4.1 | 14.9 | 13.5 | 9.6 | 14.2 | 24.2 | 30.1 | 10.4 |
| 1954–1958 | 10.5 | 8.9 | 6.1 | 8.9 | 10.5 | 9.3 | 6.8 | 5.7 | 11.8 | 14.1 | 10.9 | 16.1 | 9.7 | 12.7 | 14.1 | 11.4 |
| 1958–1960 | 11.4 | 3.0 | 5.8 | 5.8 | 9.5 | 7.2 | 6.8 | 6.8 | 8.2 | 11.4 | 15.8 | 14.0 | 12.2 | 15.3 | 8.2 | 13.6 |

[1] Includes Logging (ISIC group 022) under Wood products (ISIC major group 25) and the recording of gramophone discs (part of ISIC group 842) under Printing (ISIC major group 28), but excludes publishing (part of ISIC major group 28).
[2] Manufacture of Leather footwear (ISIC group 241) and of fur apparel (part of ISIC group 243) is included under Leather and leather products (ISIC major group 29).
[3] Wooden toys and recreational and cultural articles are included under Wood products (ISIC major group 25) instead of Miscellaneous manufacturing (ISIC major group 39).
[4] The manufacturing of asbestos products (part of ISIC group 339) and of rubber toys and sports goods (part of ISIC group 399) is included under Rubber products (ISIC major group 39).
[5] Includes the following types of manufacturing: Professional and scientific instruments, Photographic and optical goods and Watches and clocks (ISIC groups 391-393).

[1] Y compris l'Exploitation forestière (CITI groupe 022) classée sous Ouvrages en bois (CITI groupe 25), l'enregistrement sur disques de phonographes (dans CITI groupe 842) classé sous Imprimerie (CITI classe 28), mais non compris édition (dans CITI classe 28).
[2] La fabrication des Chaussures en cuir (CITI groupe 241) et des articles d'habillement en fourrure (dans CITI groupe 243) est comprise dans Cuir et articles en cuir (CITI groupe 29).
[3] Les jouets et articles récréatifs et culturels en bois sont compris dans Ouvrages en bois (CITI classe 25) et non dans Industries manufacturières diverses (CITI classe 39).
[4] La fabrication des ouvrages en amiante (dans CITI groupe 339) et des jouets et articles de sport en caoutchouc (dans CITI groupe 399) est comprise dans Ouvrages en caoutchouc (CITI classe 30).
[5] Y compris les industries manufacturières suivantes: Matériel médico-chirurgical et instruments de précision, Matériel photographique et instruments d'optique et Montres et horloges (CITI groupes 391-393).

## 3. INDEX NUMBERS OF INDUSTRIAL EMPLOYMENT — INDICES DE L'EMPLOI DANS L'INDUSTRIE

### A. The Divisions of Industrial Activity
### Les branches de l'activité industrielle

| Period<br>Période | Total | Mining and manufacturing [1]<br>Industries extractives et manufacturières [1] | Construction<br>Bâtiment et travaux publics | Electricity, steam and water<br>Electricité, vapeur et eau |
|---|---|---|---|---|
| ISIC — CITI | 1–4, 511–521 | 1–3 | 4 | 511, 513–521 |

*a.* Indexes — Indices (1958 = 100)

| | | | | |
|---|---|---|---|---|
| 1948 | 77 | 79 | 66 | 74 |
| 1950 | 82 | 81 | 89 | 83 |
| 1952 | 90 | 88 | 100 | 87 |
| 1953 | 89 | 87 | 101 | 87 |
| 1954 | 90 | 89 | 99 | 96 |
| 1955 | 91 | 91 | 95 | 100 |
| 1956 | 94 | 93 | 99 | 100 |
| 1957 | 97 | 96 | 99 | 100 |
| 1958 | 100 | 100 | 100 | 100 |
| 1959 | 104 | 103 | 105 | 104 |
| 1960 | 107 | 107 | 106 | 109 |
| 1961 | 109 | 110 | 104 | 109 |

*b.* Average Annual Rate of Change — Taux annuel moyen de variation

| | | | | |
|---|---|---|---|---|
| 1950 – 1960 | 2.7 | 2.8 | 1.8 | 2.8 |
| 1948 – 1953 | 2.9 | 1.9 | 8.9 | 3.3 |
| 1954 – 1958 | 2.7 | 3.0 | 0.2 | 1.0 |
| 1958 – 1960 | 3.4 | 3.4 | 3.0 | 4.4 |

For footnotes see end of table.       [1] Pour les notes, voir à la fin du tableau.

### B. The Major Group of Manufacturing — Les classes de la branche Industries manufacturières

| Period<br>Période | Mining and manufacturing [1]<br>Industries extractives et manufacturières [1] | Coal mining, crude petroleum and natural gas<br>Extraction de charbon, pétrole brut et gaz naturel | Food, beverages and tobacco<br>Industries alimentaires, boissons, tabac | Textiles | Clothing, and made-up textiles [2]<br>Articles d'habillement, et ouvrages en tissu [2] | Wood products and furniture [1,3]<br>Bois et meubles [1,3] | Paper and paper products<br>Papier et ouvrages en papier | Printing [1]<br>Imprimerie [1] | Leather and leather products [2]<br>Cuir et articles en cuir [2] | Rubber products [4]<br>Ouvrages en caoutchouc [4] | Chemicals and chemical, petroleum and coal products<br>Produits chimiques et dérivés du pétrole et du charbon | Non-metallic minerals and products<br>Minéraux non métalliques et produits dérivés | Metal mining and basic metals<br>Minerais métalliques et métallurgie de base | Metal products [5]<br>Ouvrages en métaux [5] | Other manufacturing [3,4]<br>Autres industries manufacturières [3,4] |
|---|---|---|---|---|---|---|---|---|---|---|---|---|---|---|---|
| ISIC — CITI | 1-3 | 11-13 | 20–22 | 23 | 243-244 | 25–26 | 27 | 28 | 241, 29 | 30 | 192, 31-32, 512 | 14, 199, 33 | 12, 34 | 35–38, 391-393 | 394-399 |

*a.* Indexes — Indices (1958 = 100)

| | | | | | | | | | | | | | | | |
|---|---|---|---|---|---|---|---|---|---|---|---|---|---|---|---|
| 1948 | 79 | 75 | 91 | 106 | 96 | 87 | 76 | 106 | 105 | 67 | 79 | 84 | 67 | 59 | 46 |
| 1950 | 81 | 76 | 102 | 97 | 103 | 90 | 79 | 106 | 97 | 75 | 80 | 86 | 74 | 64 | 80 |
| 1952 | 88 | 79 | 99 | 89 | 101 | 104 | 83 | 94 | 88 | 83 | 84 | 86 | 90 | 80 | 69 |
| 1953 | 87 | 80 | 96 | 86 | 92 | 95 | 86 | 99 | 75 | 83 | 87 | 85 | 93 | 86 | 100 |
| 1954 | 89 | 87 | 97 | 87 | 90 | 96 | 86 | 94 | 77 | 83 | 90 | 86 | 93 | 87 | 80 |
| 1955 | 91 | 86 | 96 | 90 | 97 | 98 | 90 | 94 | 82 | 83 | 92 | 88 | 92 | 89 | 100 |
| 1956 | 93 | 92 | 96 | 91 | 95 | 99 | 93 | 94 | 83 | 92 | 93 | 93 | 92 | 93 | 100 |
| 1957 | 96 | 95 | 99 | 96 | 97 | 99 | 97 | 94 | 92 | 92 | 97 | 96 | 95 | 97 | 100 |
| 1958 | 100 | 100 | 100 | 100 | 100 | 100 | 100 | 100 | 100 | 100 | 100 | 100 | 100 | 100 | 100 |
| 1959 | 103 | 99 | 99 | 102 | 101 | 103 | 103 | 100 | 103 | 100 | 107 | 105 | 105 | 105 | 120 |
| 1960 | 107 | 98 | 102 | 103 | 107 | 106 | 103 | 106 | 109 | 108 | 113 | 109 | 111 | 111 | 120 |
| 1961 | 110 | 99 | 103 | 104 | 114 | 108 | 103 | 106 | 115 | 117 | 120 | 109 | 115 | 115 | 120 |

*b.* Average Annual Rate of Change — Taux annuel moyen de variation

| | | | | | | | | | | | | | | | |
|---|---|---|---|---|---|---|---|---|---|---|---|---|---|---|---|
| 1950 – 1960 | 2.8 | 2.6 | — | 0.6 | 0.4 | 1.7 | 2.7 | — | 1.2 | 3.7 | 3.5 | 2.4 | 4.1 | 5.7 | 4.1 |
| 1948 – 1953 | 1.9 | 1.3 | 1.1 | —4.1 | —0.9 | 1.8 | 2.5 | —1.4 | —6.5 | 4.4 | 1.9 | 0.2 | 6.8 | 7.8 | 16.8 |
| 1954 – 1958 | 3.0 | 3.5 | 0.8 | 3.5 | 2.7 | 1.0 | 3.8 | 1.6 | 6.8 | 4.8 | 2.7 | 3.8 | 1.8 | 3.5 | 5.7 |
| 1958 – 1960 | 3.4 | —1.0 | 1.0 | 1.5 | 3.4 | 3.0 | 1.5 | 3.0 | 4.4 | 3.9 | 6.3 | 4.4 | 5.4 | 5.4 | 9.5 |

[1] Includes Logging (ISIC group 022) under Wood products (ISIC major group 25) and the recording of gramophone discs (part of ISIC group 842) under Printing (ISIC major group 28), but excludes publishing (part of ISIC major group 28).
[2] Manufacture of Leather footwear (ISIC group 241) and of fur apparel (part of ISIC group 243) is included under Leather and leather products (ISIC major group 29).
[3] Wooden toys and recreational and cultural articles are included under Wood products (ISIC major group 25) instead of Miscellaneous manufacturing (ISIC major group 39).
[4] The manufacturing of asbestos products (part of ISIC group 339) and of rubber toys and sports goods (part of ISIC group 399) is included under Rubber products (ISIC major group 30).
[5] Includes the following types of manufacturing: Professional and scientific instruments, Photographic and optical goods and Watches and clocks (ISIC groups 391-393).

[1] Y compris l'Exploitation forestière (CITI groupe 022) classée sous Ouvrages en bois (CITI groupe 25), l'enregistrement sur disques de phonographes (dans CITI groupe 842) classé sous Imprimerie (CITI classe 28), mais non compris l'édition (dans CITI classe 28).
[2] La fabrication des Chaussures en cuir (CITI groupe 241) et des articles d'habillement en fourrure (dans CITI groupe 243) est comprise dans Cuir et articles en cuir (CITI classe 29).
[3] Les jouets et articles récréatifs et culturels en bois sont compris dans Ouvrages en bois (CITI classe 25) et non dans Industries manufacturières diverses (CITI classe 39).
[4] La fabrication des ouvrages en amiante (dans CITI groupe 339) et des jouets et articles de sport en caoutchouc (dans CITI groupe 399) est comprise dans Ouvrages en caoutchouc (CITI classe 30).
[5] Y compris les industries manufacturières suivantes: Matériel médico-chirurgical et instruments de précision, Matériel photographique et instruments d'optique et Montres et horloges (CITI groupes 391-393).

## 4. CHARACTERISTICS OF PUBLICLY-OWNED AND CO-OPERATIVE INDUSTRIAL ENTERPRISES
## CARACTERISTIQUES DES ENTREPRISES INDUSTRIELLES PUBLIQUES ET COOPERATIVES
### 1953, 1958

Number of enterprises in units; number of engaged and operatives in thousands; electricity consumed per operative in thousand KWH.

Nombre d'entreprises en unités; nombre de personnes occupées et d'ouvriers en milliers; électricité consommée par ouvrier en milliers de kWh.

### A. Publicly-Owned and Co-operative Enterprises — Entreprises publiques et coopératives

| Year and item of data | Total [1] | Coal mining, crude petroleum and natural gas / Extraction de charbon, pétrole brut et gaz | Food, beverages and tobacco / Industries alimentaires, boissons, tabac | Textiles | Clothing, and made-up textiles [2] / Articles d'habillement, et ouvrages en tissu [2] | Wood products and furniture [1,3] / Bois et meubles [1,3] | Paper and paper products / Papier et ouvrages en papier | Printing [1] / Imprimerie [1] | Leather and leather products [2] / Cuir et articles en cuir [2] | Rubber products [4] / Ouvrages en caoutchouc [4] | Chemicals and chemical, petroleum and coal products / Produits chimiques et dérivés du pétrole et du charbon | Non-metallic minerals and products [4] / Minéraux non métalliques et produits dérivés [4] | Metal mining and basic metals / Minerais métalliques et métallurgie de base | Metal products [5] / Ouvrages en métaux [5] | Other manufacturing [3,4] / Autres industries manufacturières [3,4] | Electricity, steam and water / Electricité, vapeur et eau | Année et rubrique |
|---|---|---|---|---|---|---|---|---|---|---|---|---|---|---|---|---|---|
| ISIC | 1-3, 511-521 | 11, 13 | 20-22 | 23 | 243-244 | 25-26 | 27 | 28 | 241, 29 | 30 | 192, 31-32, 512 | 14, 199, 33 | 12, 34 | 35-38, 391-393 | 394-399 | 511, 513-521 | CITI |
| **1953** Number of persons engaged (Average during year). | 1 855 | ... | ... | ... | ... | ... | ... | ... | ... | ... | ... | ... | ... | ... | ... | ... | **1953** Nombre de personnes occupées (moyenne pendant l'année) |
| Operatives: Number (Average during year) | 1 426 | 113 | 133 | 160 | 68 | 92 | 25 | 16 | 49 | 10 | 66 | 106 | 120 | 443 | 5 | 20 | Ouvriers: Nombre (moyenne pendant l'année) |
| Distribution in percent.. | 100.0 | 7.9 | 9.3 | 11.2 | 4.8 | 6.4 | 1.8 | 1.1 | 3.5 | 0.7 | 4.6 | 7.4 | 8.4 | 31.1 | 0.3 | 1.5 | Répartition en pourcentage |
| **1958** Number of enterprises... | 1 689 | 61 | 191 | 107 | 162 | 191 | 13 | 22 | 98 | 5 | 82 | 173 | 31 | 485 | 28 | 40 | **1958** Nombre d'entreprises |
| Persons engaged: Number (Average during year) | 2 102.8 | 162.1 | 174.4 | 217.7 | 92.3 | 120.4 | 37.0 | 21.5 | 79.6 | 14.5 | 100.0 | 156.5 | 162.3 | 720.3 | 9.2 | 35.0 | Personnes occupées: Nombre (moyenne pendant l'année) |
| Distribution in percent.. | 100.0 | 7.7 | 8.3 | 10.3 | 4.4 | 5.7 | 1.8 | 1.0 | 3.8 | 0.7 | 4.7 | 7.5 | 7.7 | 34.3 | 0.4 | 1.7 | Répartition en pourcentage |
| Operatives: Number (Average during year) | 1 635 | 141 | 138 | 187 | 74 | 97 | 29 | 18 | 65 | 12 | 76 | 125 | 129 | 516 | 5 | 23 | Ouvriers: Nombre (moyenne pendant l'année) |
| Distribution in percent.. | 100.0 | 8.6 | 8.4 | 11.5 | 4.5 | 5.9 | 1.8 | 1.1 | 4.0 | 0.7 | 4.6 | 7.7 | 7.9 | 31.5 | 0.3 | 1.5 | Répartition en pourcentage |

For footnotes see end of table.

Pour les notes, voir au bas du tableau.

## B. Centrally Managed, Publicly-Owned Enterprises
## Entreprises publiques gérées par le gouvernement central

| Class of industrial activity | Consumption of electricity per operative / Consommation d'électricité par ouvrier | | Percentage of total cost of production in 1958 due to: / Pourcentage du coût total de la production en 1958 dû à: | | | | Catégorie d'activité industrielle |
|---|---|---|---|---|---|---|---|
| | 1953 | 1958 | Materials, fuels and electricity / Matières premières et auxiliaires, combustibles et électricité | Wages and salaries / Traitements et salaires | Depreciation / Amortissement | Other / Divers | |
| Total [1] | 7.0 | 9.5 | 61.1 | 26.9 | 7.0 | 5.0 | Total [1] |
| Coal, crude petroleum, and natural gas | 16.3 [6] | 20.3 [6] | 28.8 | 52.9 | 12.2 | 6.1 | Charbon pétrole brut et gaz naturel |
| Food, beverages and tobacco | 3.3 | 4.1 | 83.6 | 10.3 | 3.2 | 2.9 | Industries alimentaires, boissons et tabac |
| Textiles | 3.2 | 3.8 | 60.1 | 29.6 | 6.5 | 3.8 | Textiles |
| Clothing and made-up textiles [2] | 0.3 | 0.4 | 65.5 | 30.3 | 1.5 | 2.7 | Articles d'habillement et ouvrages en tissu [2] |
| Wood products and furniture [1,3] | 1.9 | 2.6 | 62.0 | 29.9 | 3.4 | 4.7 | Ouvrages en bois et meubles [1,3] |
| Paper and paper products | 19.3 | 22.0 | 60.4 | 25.5 | 9.7 | 4.4 | Papier et articles en papier |
| Printing [1] | 1.1 | 1.5 | 42.5 | 45.1 | 6.2 | 6.2 | Imprimerie [1] |
| Leather and leather products [2] | 2.4 | 2.6 | 65.4 | 28.0 | 3.9 | 2.7 | Cuir et articles en cuir [2] |
| Chemicals and chemical and rubber products [4] | 24.0 | 28.7 | 65.4 | 21.3 | 9.7 | 3.6 | Produits chimiques et ouvrages en caoutchouc [4] |
| Petroleum and coal products | ... | ... | 70.7 | 12.2 | 13.3 | 3.8 | Produits dérivés du pétrole et du charbon |
| Non-metallic minerals and products: [4] | | | | | | | Minéraux non métalliques et produits dérivés [4]: |
| Building materials | 6.8 | 9.9 | 37.6 | 39.8 | 11.6 | 11.0 | Matériaux de construction |
| Glass and porcelain | 2.5 | 3.0 | 35.9 | 45.9 | 8.1 | 10.1 | Verre et porcelaine |
| Metal mining and basic metals: | | | | | | | Minerais métalliques et métallurgie de base: |
| Ferrous | 13.7 | 20.4 | 62.8 | 24.0 | 8.8 | 4.4 | Métaux ferreux |
| Non-ferrous | 18.1 | 61.1 | 70.4 | 17.9 | 8.8 | 2.9 | Métaux non ferreux |
| Metal products [5] | 3.0 | 3.9 | 54.3 | 34.3 | 4.8 | 6.6 | Produits métalliques [5] |
| Electricity steam and water | 32.6 | 48.0 | 38.2 | 20.0 | 33.1 | 8.7 | Electricité, vapeur et gaz |

[1] Includes Logging (ISIC group 022) under Wood products (ISIC major group 25) and the recording of gramophone discs (part of ISIC group 842) under Printing (ISIC major group 28), but excludes publishing (part of ISIC major group 28).
[2] Manufacture of Leather footwear (ISIC group 241) and of fur apparel (part of ISIC group 243) is included under Leather and leather products (ISIC major group 29).
[3] Wooden toys and recreational and cultural articles are included under Wood products (ISIC major group 25) instead of Miscellaneous manufacturing (ISIC major group 39).
[4] The manufacturing of asbestos products (part of ISIC group 339) and of rubber toys and sports goods (part of ISIC group 399) is included under Rubber products (ISIC major group 30).
[5] Includes the following types of manufacturing: Professional and scientific instruments, Photographic and optical goods and Watches and clocks (ISIC groups 391-393).
[6] Data on the consumption of electricity per operative for the Manufacture of petroleum and coal products (ISIC major group 32) is included with Coal and crude petroleum ISIC major groups 11 and 13).

[1] Y compris l'Exploitation forestière (CITI groupe 022) classée sous Ouvrages en bois (CITI groupe 25), l'enregistrement sur disques de phonographes (dans CITI groupe 842) classé sous Imprimerie (CITI classe 28), mais non compris l'édition (dans CITI classe 28).
[2] La fabrication des Chaussures en cuir (CITI groupe 241) et des articles d'habillement en fourrure (dans CITI groupe 243) est comprise dans Cuir et articles en cuir (CITI classe 29).
[3] Les jouets et articles récréatifs et culturels en bois sont compris dans Ouvrages en bois (CITI classe 25) et non dans Industries manufacturières diverses (CITI classe 39).
[4] La fabrication des ouvrages en amiante (dans CITI groupe 339) et des jouets et articles de sport en caoutchouc (dans CITI groupe 399) est comprise dans Ouvrages en caoutchouc (CITI classe 30).
[5] Y compris les industries manufacturières suivantes: Matériel médico-chirurgical et instruments de précision, Matériel photographique et instruments d'optique et Montres et horloges (CITI groupes 391-393).
[6] Les données concernant la consommation d'électricité par ouvrier dans la Fabrication des produits dérivés du pétrole et du charbon (CITI classe 32) sont comprises dans Charbon et pétrole brut CITI classes 11 et 13).

# DENMARK — DANEMARK

## Gross Domestic Product and Gross Domestic Fixed Capital Formation

Estimates of expenditure on and industrial origin of the gross domestic product and of the industrial composition of the gross fixed capital formation are shown in Table 1. These data were supplied by the Danish Statistical Department, in response to the United Nations questionnaire on national accounts. Official estimates, as well as descriptions of the data, are published annually in *Økonomisk Årsoversigt*, Økonomiske Sekretariat, Copenhagen.

## Index Numbers of Industrial Production

The index numbers set out in Table 2 are derived from indexes computed by the Statistics Department and published in *Industriel Produktionsstatistik*.

The index numbers are base-weighted arithmetic averages, compiled from the results of the annual Censuses of Production described below. Both the weights and indicators for the series of index numbers relate, on the whole, to establishments having six or more operatives. The weighting patterns for the indexes consist of the value added at factor cost during 1939 for the years, 1938-1939, during 1949 for the years, 1948-1954, and during 1955 for subsequent years. The indicators for the index numbers are, for the most part, quantities of individual commodities produced.

For further details concerning the index numbers see the following publications of the Statistics Department, Copenhagen: *Industriel Produktionsstatistik, 1948* with regard to the indexes for 1938-1939; *Industriel Produktionsstatistik, 1951* and *Statistiske Efterretninger*, No. 72, 30 December 1952 concerning the indexes based on 1949; and *Industriel Produktionsstatistik, 1956* and *Statistiske Efterretninger*, No. 12, 6 March 1958 with regard to the indexes based on 1955.

## Index Numbers of Industrial Employment

The index numbers of manufacturing employment in Table 3 were compiled by the Statistical Office of the United Nations from the results of the annual Census of Production published each year in *Industriel Produktionsstatistik*. The index numbers relate to the number of all employees of manufacturing establishments with six or more operatives.

## Produit intérieur brut et formation brute de capital intérieur fixe

Le tableau 1 fournit des estimations des dépenses imputées au produit intérieur brut, des composantes du produit intérieur brut ventilées suivant le secteur d'activité, ainsi que des estimations des composantes du capital fixe intérieur brut formé, suivant le secteur d'activité industrielle. Ces données ont été fournies par le Département Danois de Statistique en réponse au questionnaire de l'O.N.U. relatif aux comptes nationaux. Des estimations officielles ainsi que des précisions sur les données sont publiées annuellement dans *Økonomisk Årsoversigt*, Økonomiske Sekretariat, Copenhague.

## Indices de la production industrielle

Les indices de la production industrielle reproduits au tableau 2 proviennent des indices élaborés par le Département de Statistique et publiés dans *Industriel Produktionsstatistik*.

Ces indices sont des moyennes arithmétiques à pondérations fixes, calculés à partir des résultats des recensements annuels de la production décrits ci-dessous. Les coefficients de pondération et les indicateurs pour les séries d'indices se rapportent tous deux la plupart du temps aux établissements de six ouvriers ou plus. La pondération utilisée pour le calcul des indices est fondée sur la valeur ajoutée au coût des facteurs en 1939 pour les années 1938-1939, en 1949, pour les années 1948-1954, en 1955, pour les années ultérieures. Les indicateurs utilisés pour le calcul des indices sont, en grande partie, les volumes de la production de chaque marchandise.

Pour plus amples détails sur la nature de ces indices, consulter les publications suivantes du Département de Statistique, Copenhague; *Industriel Produktionsstatistik, 1948* en ce qui concerne les indices de 1938-1939; *Industriel Produktionsstatistik, 1951* et *Statistiske Efterretninger* No. 72, 30 décembre 1952 dans le cas des indices ayant pour année de base 1949; et *Industriel Produktionsstatistik, 1956* et *Statistiske Efterretninger*, No. 12 du 6 mars 1958 en ce qui concerne les indices ayant pour année de base 1955.

## Indices de l'emploi industriel

Les indices de l'emploi dans les industries manufacturières reproduits au tableau 3 ónt été élaborés par le Bureau de Statistique de l'O.N.U. d'après les résultats des recensements annuels de la production publiés pour chaque année dans *Industriel Produktionsstatistik*. Ces indices se rapportent au nombre total de salariés des industries manufacturières de six ouvriers ou plus.

# DENMARK

## The Characteristics and Structure of Industrial Activity

The data in Table 4 were compiled from the results of the decennial Censuses of Establishments of the Statistics Department, and the figures in Tables 5 and 6 were derived from the results of the Department's annual Censuses of Production. All units in mining, manufacturing, construction and the production and distribution of gas and electricity were covered in the Censuses of Establishments, whereas only larger units in manufacturing and gas and government electricity production were included in the annual Censuses of Production. Establishments with six or more operatives were, in general, considered to be large, although smaller units which were state-owned or which accounted for much of the output of a particular industry were also covered in the annual Censuses. The sources of the data set out below are as follows: Table 4, *Erhvervstaellingen, 1935* and *1948* and *Statistike Efterretninger*, No. 39, 4 September 1962; Tables 5 and 6, *Industriel Produktionsstatistik, 1939, 1948, 1952, 1953* and *1958*—all published by the Danish Statistics Department.

There is a lack of comparability between the data from the various Censuses of Establishments that are set out in Table 4. The technical unit was the statistical unit in the case of the Census of Establishments taken as of 28 May 1935 whereas the establishment was the statistical unit in the two later Censuses. Further, the system of industrial classification employed in the Census of Establishments taken as of 2 June 1958 differed from that utized in the two earlier Censuses. The Danish Statistical Department revised its scheme of industrial classification during the intervening period. Also, in the case of the Census taken in 1958, the criterion for classifying establishments to manufacturing was the ratio of value added in manufacturing to gross profit from sales whereas in the case of the Census taken in 1948, the criterion utilized for this purpose was whether establishments produced goods for sale, irrespective of the importance of this activity relative to the re-sale of goods in the same condition as purchased. The forementioned differences between the three Censuses of Establishments result in lack of comparability, between the Census as of 28 May 1935 and the other two Censuses, in the counts of number of units and, between each of the Censuses, in the classification of data according to kind of economic activity.

Incomparabilities also occur in the data from the annual Censuses of Production shown in Table 5, in particular, the figures of employment, man-hours worked and wages and salaries. For 1939, operatives such as drivers or messengers, operatives not actually at work or other employees such as sales representatives were not included in these items of data. The omitted operatives were covered in the data for 1948, 1953 and 1958, and the omitted sales representatives were included in the data for 1953 and 1958. Differences between the annual Censuses for 1939 and 1948 and the annual Censuses for later

## Les caractéristiques et la structure de l'activité industrielle

Les données du tableau 4 sont tirées des résultats des recensements décennaux des établissements, effectués par le Département de Statistique, et les chiffres des tableaux 5 et 6 ont été calculés d'après les résultats des recensements annuels de la production effectués par le même Département. Les recensements des établissements portent sur toutes les unités des industries extractives, des industries manufacturières, du bâtiment et des travaux publics et du secteur de la production et de la distribution de gaz et d'électricité, tandis que les recensements de la production ne couvrent que les grandes unités des industries manufacturières, des industries gazières et du secteur public producteur d'électricité. Les établissements de six ouvriers ou plus sont en général considérés comme de grandes unités, mais les recensements annuels portent aussi sur des petites unités appartenant à l'Etat ou assurant une grande partie de la production dans telle ou telle industrie. Les sources des données reproduites ci-dessous sont les suivantes: Tableau 4, *Erhvervstaellingen, 1935* et *1948* et *Statistiske Efterretninger* No. 39 du 4 septembre 1962; Tableaux 5 et 6, *Industriel Produktionsstatistik, 1939, 1948, 1952, 1953* et *1958*, tous publiés par le Département Danois de Statistique.

Il y a un manque de comparabilité entre les données résultant des différents recensements d'établissements reproduites au tableau 4. L'unité technique a été prise comme unité statistique dans les recensements des établissements du 28 mai 1935 tandis que dans les deux derniers recensements c'est l'établissement qui a été retenu comme unité statistique. De plus, le système de classification industrielle utilisé au recensement 1958 diffère de celui utilisé dans les deux recensements précédents; le Département Danois de Statistique ayant revisé son type de classification industrielle entre-temps. Il est également à noter que, dans le cas du recensement effectué en 1958, le critère de classification des établissements dans les industries manufacturières était le ratio valeur ajoutée par l'industrie manufacturière/bénéfices bruts sur ventes, tandis que dans le cas du recensement effectué en 1948, le critère de classification était la production de biens destinés à la vente, compte non tenu de l'importance de l'activité purement commerciale de ces établissements. Des différences ci-dessus mentionnées entre les trois recensements des établissements, découle un manque de comparabilité entre le recensement effectué en mai 1935 et les deux autres recensements, dans le dénombrement du nombre d'unité, et entre chacun des recensements, dans la classification des données selon la branche d'activité économique.

Il y a également quelques défauts de comparabilité entre les données tirées des recensements annuels de la production reproduites au tableau 5, en particulier les chiffres relatifs à l'emploi, aux heures de travail et aux salaires et traitements. Pour 1939, le nombre d'ouvriers ne comprenait pas certains ouvriers tels que les chauffeurs ou les plantons, les ouvriers qui n'étaient pas effectivement présents ou d'autres salariés comme les représentants de commerce. Les ouvriers omis ont été rajoutés aux données relatives à 1948, 1953 et 1958, et les représentants de commerce, omis, furent rajoutés aux données relatives à

years, both in the scheme of industrial classification utilized and in the manufacturing establishments covered, in practice, contribute to the lack of exact comparability between the data for these years on all items set out in Table 5.

Except for the omissions from the data on operatives and employees mentioned above, the definitions utilized for the figures on labour in Tables 4 and 5 were similar to those recommended by the Statistical Commission of the United Nations. The figures of value added shown in Table 5 are the difference between sales value, ex-factory and net of excise taxes, of production during a given year and the cost, at the factory, of the purchased commodities, energy and sub-contract work consumed in this production. The data on capacity of installed power shown in Tables 4 and 5 represent the sum of the rated horsepower of all prime movers and of electric motors driven by purchased electricity—both in use and in reserve at the end of the year. The statistics of energy consumed set out in Tables 5 and 6 relate to purchased fuels and electricity only. However, some of the fuels included may have been utilized as raw materials. The figures of electricity consumed cover electricity produced for own use as well as electricity purchased.

1953 et 1958. Les différences entre les recensements annuels de 1939 et 1948 et les recensements relatifs aux années ultérieures, tant en ce qui concerne le schéma de classification utilisé que les établissements manufacturiers couverts, en pratique, entraine le manque de comparabilité entre les données de ces années sur toutes les rubriques reproduites au tableau 5.

Mis à part les omissions des ouvriers et des salariés mentionnées précédemment, les définitions utilisées pour les chiffres relatifs à l'emploi des tableaux 4 et 5 sont conformes à celles recommandées par la Commission de Statistique de l'O.N.U. Les chiffres relatifs à la valeur ajoutée reproduits au tableau 5 sont les différences entre le prix de vente, départ usine et déduction faite des impôts indirects, de la production de l'année et le coût, à l'usine, des matières achetées, de l'énergie consommée et des travaux exécutés par des sous-traitants. Les données relatives à la puissance installée des tableaux 4 et 5, représentent la puissance nominale en fin d'année, de tous les moteurs primaires et des moteurs électriques actionnés par de l'électricité achetée — moteurs en service normal et moteurs en réserve. Les statistiques de l'énergie consommée reproduites aux tableaux 5 et 6 se rapportent aux combustibles et à l'électricité achetés exclusivement. Cependant, quelques combustibles inclus peuvent avoir été utilisés comme matière première. Les chiffres relatifs à l'électricité consommée comprennent l'électricité produite pour l'autoconsommation aussi bien que l'électricité achetée.

# DENMARK

## 1. THE GROSS DOMESTIC PRODUCT AND GROSS DOMESTIC FIXED CAPITAL FORMATION
## LE PRODUIT INTERIEUR BRUT ET LA FORMATION BRUTE DE CAPITAL FIXE INTERIEUR

Million Kroner                 Millions de couronnes

### A. Expenditure on the Gross Domestic Product at Market Prices —
### Dépenses relatives au produit intérieur brut aux prix du marché

| Item of data and year / Rubrique et année | Total | Consumption / Consommation | | Gross Domestic Capital Formation / Formation brute de capital intérieur | | Net exports of goods and services / Exportations nettes de biens et de services | |
|---|---|---|---|---|---|---|---|
| | | Total | Government [1] / Etat [1] | Total | Fixed / Fixe | Exports less imports / Exportations moins importations | Exports / Exportations |
| a | | | | *a. At current prices — Aux prix courants* | | | |
| **Absolute figures — Chiffres absolus** | | | | | | | |
| 1948 | 17 439 | 14 660 | 1 964 | 3 050 | 2 294 | −271 | 3 516 |
| 1950 | 21 398 | 17 989 | 2 203 | 4 151 | 3 216 | −742 | 5 840 |
| 1951 | 23 138 | 19 425 | 2 625 | 3 916 | 3 776 | −203 | 7 586 |
| 1952 | 24 676 | 20 268 | 2 959 | 4 183 | 4 201 | 225 | 7 764 |
| 1953 | 26 433 | 21 291 | 3 235 | 4 966 | 4 495 | 176 | 8 051 |
| 1954 | 27 706 | 22 939 | 3 541 | 5 200 | 4 812 | −433 | 8 609 |
| 1955 | 28 921 | 24 016 | 3 732 | 4 622 | 4 626 | 283 | 9 521 |
| 1956 | 30 939 | 25 458 | 3 986 | 5 510 | 5 044 | −29 | 10 274 |
| 1957 | 32 869 | 26 234 | 4 225 | 6 266 | 5 548 | 369 | 11 154 |
| 1958 | 34 322 | 27 636 | 4 500 | 5 761 | 5 922 | 925 | 11 607 |
| 1959 | 38 108 | 29 917 | 4 877 | 8 019 | 7 160 | 172 | 12 585 |
| 1960 | 41 194 | 32 140 | 5 215 | 9 458 | 8 045 | −404 | 13 468 |
| 1961 | 45 132 | 35 871 | 6 080 | 9 870 | 9 200 | −609 | 13 857 |
| **Percentage distribution of average annual expenditure — Distribution en pourcentage des dépenses annuelles moyennes** | | | | | | | |
| 1948 | 100.0 | 84.0 | 11.3 | 17.5 | 13.2 | −1.5 | 20.2 |
| 1950–1960 | 100.0 | 81.0 | 12.5 | 18.8 | 17.2 | 0.2 | 32.3 |
| 1950 | 100.0 | 84.0 | 10.3 | 19.4 | 15.0 | −3.4 | 27.3 |
| 1953 | 100.0 | 80.5 | 12.2 | 18.8 | 17.0 | 0.7 | 30.4 |
| 1954 | 100.0 | 82.7 | 12.8 | 18.8 | 17.4 | −1.5 | 31.1 |
| 1958 | 100.0 | 80.5 | 13.1 | 16.8 | 17.2 | 2.7 | 33.8 |
| 1960 | 100.0 | 78.0 | 12.6 | 22.9 | 19.5 | −0.9 | 32.7 |
| b | | | | *b. At Prices of 1955 — Aux prix de 1955* | | | |
| **Absolute figures — Chiffres absolus** | | | | | | | |
| 1948 | 23 175 | 19 705 | 2 857 | 4 029 | 2 928 | −559 | 4 009 |
| 1950 | 26 077 | 21 704 | 2 863 | 5 050 | 3 835 | −677 | 6 683 |
| 1951 | 26 142 | 21 400 | 3 104 | 4 075 | 3 906 | 667 | 7 577 |
| 1952 | 26 534 | 21 813 | 3 278 | 4 068 | 4 138 | 653 | 7 436 |
| 1953 | 28 093 | 22 598 | 3 525 | 5 065 | 4 548 | 430 | 8 198 |
| 1954 | 28 923 | 23 976 | 3 691 | 5 339 | 4 911 | −392 | 8 833 |
| 1955 | 28 921 | 24 016 | 3 732 | 4 622 | 4 626 | 283 | 9 521 |
| 1956 | 29 535 | 24 418 | 3 739 | 5 278 | 4 826 | −161 | 9 744 |
| 1957 | 31 075 | 24 640 | 3 856 | 5 880 | 5 150 | 555 | 10 708 |
| 1958 | 31 883 | 25 689 | 3 881 | 5 308 | 5 515 | 886 | 11 682 |
| 1959 | 34 026 | 27 160 | 4 135 | 7 478 | 6 656 | −612 | 12 398 |
| 1960 | 36 606 | 28 731 | 4 382 | 8 745 | 7 345 | −870 | 13 385 |
| 1961 | 38 302 | 30 521 | 4 654 | 8 662 | 8 000 | −881 | 14 010 |
| **Percentage distribution of average annual expenditure — Distribution en pourcentage des dépenses annuelles moyennes** | | | | | | | |
| 1948 | 100.0 | 85.0 | 12.3 | 17.4 | 12.6 | −2.4 | 17.3 |
| 1950–1960 | 100.0 | 81.1 | 12.2 | 18.6 | 16.9 | 0.3 | 32.4 |
| 1950 | 100.0 | 83.2 | 11.0 | 19.3 | 14.7 | −2.5 | 25.6 |
| 1953 | 100.0 | 80.4 | 12.5 | 18.0 | 16.2 | 1.6 | 29.2 |
| 1954 | 100.0 | 82.8 | 12.8 | 18.5 | 17.0 | −1.3 | 30.5 |
| 1958 | 100.0 | 80.5 | 12.2 | 16.7 | 17.3 | 2.8 | 36.6 |
| 1960 | 100.0 | 78.4 | 12.0 | 23.9 | 20.1 | −2.3 | 36.6 |
| **Average annual rate of growth — Taux annuel moyen d'accroissement** | | | | | | | |
| 1948–1953 | 3.9 | 2.8 | 4.3 | 4.7 | 9.2 | . | 15.4 |
| 1950–1960 | 3.5 | 2.8 | 4.3 | 5.6 | 6.7 | . | 7.2 |
| 1950–1953 | 2.5 | 1.3 | 7.2 | 0.1 | 5.9 | . | 7.1 |
| 1954–1958 | 2.5 | 1.7 | 1.3 | −0.2 | 2.9 | . | 7.2 |
| 1958–1960 | 7.1 | 5.7 | 6.3 | 28.4 | 15.4 | . | 7.1 |

[1] Fiscal year beginning 1 April.           [1] Année fiscale commençant le 1er avril.

## B.  The Gross Domestic Product at Factor Cost According to Origin [1]
### Origine par secteur d'activité du produit intérieur brut au coût des facteurs [1]

| Item of data and year / Rubrique et année | Total | Agricultural sector [2] / Secteur agricole [2] | Industrial Sector — Secteur industriel | | | | | Transportation and communication / Transport et communication | Other sectors / Autres secteurs |
|---|---|---|---|---|---|---|---|---|---|
| | | | Total | Mining / Industries extractives | Manufacturing / Industries manufacturières | Construction / Bâtiment et travaux publics | Electricity, gas and water / Electricité, gaz et eau | | |
| ISIC — CITI | 0–9 | 0 | 1–5 | 1 | 2–3 | 4 | 5 | 7 | 6, 8–9 |
| **a. At Current Prices — Aux prix courants** | | | | | | | | | |
| *Absolute figures — Chiffres absolus* | | | | | | | | | |
| 1948 | 17 662 | 3 534 | 6 325 | 159 | 4 834 | 1 064 | 268 | 1 573 | 6 230 |
| 1950 | 21 618 | 4 535 | 7 792 | 47 | 5 984 | 1 424 | 337 | 1 799 | 7 492 |
| 1951 | 23 403 | 4 666 | 8 413 | 103 | 6 354 | 1 605 | 351 | 2 235 | 8 089 |
| 1952 | 24 985 | 5 326 | 8 753 | 96 | 6 455 | 1 811 | 391 | 2 373 | 8 533 |
| 1953 | 26 536 | 5 518 | 9 499 | 46 | 7 026 | 1 989 | 438 | 2 383 | 9 136 |
| 1954 | 27 618 | 5 142 | 10 166 | 43 | 7 549 | 2 103 | 471 | 2 545 | 9 765 |
| 1955 | 28 707 | 5 279 | 10 374 | 54 | 7 758 | 2 061 | 501 | 2 809 | 10 245 |
| 1956 | 30 643 | 5 691 | 10 893 | 78 | 8 110 | 2 152 | 553 | 3 182 | 10 877 |
| 1957 | 32 666 | 5 553 | 11 888 | 93 | 8 870 | 2 313 | 612 | 3 537 | 11 688 |
| 1958 | 33 963 | 5 408 | 12 550 | 76 | 9 427 | 2 389 | 658 | 3 417 | 12 588 |
| 1959 | 37 458 | 5 755 | 14 288 | 73 | 10 778 | 2 743 | 694 | 3 669 | 13 746 |
| 1960 | 40 517 | 5 836 | 15 828 | 57 | 12 028 | 3 010 | 733 | 3 918 | 14 935 |
| 1961 | 44 697 | 6 171 | 17 492 | 53 | 13 295 | 3 480 | 664 | 4 095 | 16 939 |
| *Percentage distribution according to sector— Distribution en pourcentage par secteur* | | | | | | | | | |
| 1948 | 100.0 | 20.0 | 35.8 | 0.9 | 27.3 | 6.1 | 1.5 | 8.9 | 35.3 |
| 1950 – 1960 | 100.0 | 17.8 | 36.8 | 0.3 | 27.5 | 7.2 | 1.8 | 9.7 | 35.7 |
| 1950 | 100.0 | 20.9 | 36.1 | 0.2 | 27.7 | 6.6 | 1.6 | 8.3 | 34.7 |
| 1953 | 100.0 | 20.7 | 35.8 | 0.2 | 26.5 | 7.5 | 1.6 | 9.0 | 34.5 |
| 1954 | 100.0 | 18.6 | 36.8 | 0.1 | 27.4 | 7.6 | 1.7 | 9.2 | 35.4 |
| 1958 | 100.0 | 15.9 | 36.9 | 0.2 | 27.8 | 7.0 | 1.9 | 10.1 | 37.1 |
| 1960 | 100.0 | 14.4 | 39.0 | 0.1 | 29.7 | 7.4 | 1.8 | 9.7 | 36.9 |
| **b. At Prices of 1955 — Aux prix de 1955** | | | | | | | | | |
| *Absolute figures — Chiffres absolus* | | | | | | | | | |
| 1948 | 22 984 | 4 139 | 8 277 | 192 | 6 319 | 1 504 | 262 | 2 096 | 8 472 |
| 1950 | 25 849 | 5 132 | 9 391 | 59 | 7 195 | 1 834 | 303 | 2 257 | 9 069 |
| 1951 | 25 949 | 4 972 | 9 473 | 115 | 7 185 | 1 850 | 323 | 2 396 | 9 108 |
| 1952 | 26 273 | 5 296 | 9 272 | 104 | 6 925 | 1 884 | 359 | 2 483 | 9 222 |
| 1953 | 27 833 | 5 698 | 9 772 | 49 | 7 234 | 2 105 | 384 | 2 594 | 9 769 |
| 1954 | 28 530 | 5 281 | 10 345 | 46 | 7 716 | 2 147 | 436 | 2 721 | 10 183 |
| 1955 | 28 707 | 5 279 | 10 374 | 54 | 7 758 | 2 061 | 501 | 2 809 | 10 245 |
| 1956 | 29 255 | 5 511 | 10 480 | 75 | 7 801 | 2 073 | 531 | 2 926 | 10 338 |
| 1957 | 30 821 | 5 983 | 10 894 | 90 | 8 178 | 2 122 | 504 | 3 094 | 10 850 |
| 1958 | 31 542 | 5 841 | 11 235 | 73 | 8 495 | 2 181 | 486 | 3 174 | 11 292 |
| 1959 | 33 464 | 5 593 | 12 546 | 74 | 9 439 | 2 430 | 603 | 3 301 | 12 024 |
| 1960 | 35 816 | 5 994 | 13 518 | 64 | 10 181 | 2 575 | 698 | 3 465 | 12 839 |
| 1961 | 37 292 | 6 262 | 13 990 | 55 | 10 550 | 2 715 | 670 | 3 594 | 13 446 |
| *Percentage distribution according to sector— Distribution en pourcentage par secteur* | | | | | | | | | |
| 1948 | 100.0 | 18.0 | 36.0 | 0.8 | 27.5 | 6.5 | 1.2 | 9.1 | 36.9 |
| 1950 – 1960 | 100.0 | 18.6 | 36.2 | 0.3 | 27.2 | 7.2 | 1.5 | 9.7 | 35.5 |
| 1950 | 100.0 | 19.8 | 36.3 | 0.2 | 27.9 | 7.1 | 1.1 | 8.8 | 35.1 |
| 1953 | 100.0 | 20.4 | 35.1 | 0.2 | 26.0 | 7.6 | 1.3 | 9.4 | 35.1 |
| 1954 | 100.0 | 18.5 | 36.2 | 0.1 | 27.1 | 7.5 | 1.5 | 9.6 | 35.7 |
| 1958 | 100.0 | 18.5 | 35.6 | 0.2 | 26.9 | 6.9 | 1.6 | 10.1 | 35.8 |
| 1960 | 100.0 | 16.7 | 37.7 | 0.2 | 28.4 | 7.2 | 1.9 | 9.7 | 35.9 |
| *Average annual rate of growth—Taux annuel moyen d'accroissement* | | | | | | | | | |
| 1948 – 1953 | 3.9 | 6.6 | 3.4 | −23.9 | 2.7 | 7.0 | 8.0 | 4.4 | 2.9 |
| 1950 – 1960 | 3.3 | 1.6 | 3.7 | 0.8 | 3.5 | 3.5 | 8.7 | 4.4 | 3.5 |
| 1950 – 1953 | 2.5 | 3.5 | 1.3 | −6.0 | 0.5 | 4.7 | 8.2 | 4.7 | 2.5 |
| 1954 – 1958 | 2.6 | 2.6 | 2.1 | 12.2 | 2.4 | 0.4 | 2.8 | 3.9 | 2.6 |
| 1958 – 1960 | 6.6 | 1.3 | 9.7 | −6.3 | 9.5 | 8.7 | 19.8 | 4.5 | 6.6 |

[1] Includes repairs, maintenance, and taxes on land and buildings.
[2] Includes dairies and slaughter houses.

[1] Y compris les réparations et l'entretien ainsi que les impôts sur les terres et les bâtiments.
[2] Y compris les laiteries et les abattoirs.

## C. Gross Domestic Fixed Capital Formation According to Purchasing Sector
## La formation brute de capital fixe intérieur par secteur d'aquisition

| Item of data and year / Rubrique et année | Total | Agricultural sector [1] / Secteur agricole [1] | Industrial Sector — Secteur industriel | | | | Transportation and communication / Transport et communication | Other sectors [1,2] / Autres secteurs [1,2] |
|---|---|---|---|---|---|---|---|---|
| | | | Total | Mining / Industries extractives | Manufacturing [2] / Industries manufacturières [2] | Electricity, gas and water / Electricité, gaz et eau | | |
| ISIC — CITI | 0–9 | 01 | 1–3, 5 | 1 | 2–3 | 5 | 7 | 02–04, 6, 8–9 |
| *a. At Current Prices — Aux prix courants* | | | | | | | | |
| Absolute figures — Chiffres absolus | | | | | | | | |
| 1948 | 2 294 | 310 | 480 | — | 370 | 110 | 403 | 1 101 |
| 1950 | 3 216 | 310 | 675 | — | 440 | 235 | 586 | 1 645 |
| 1951 | 3 776 | 680 | 705 | — | 455 | 250 | 573 | 1 818 |
| 1952 | 4 201 | 715 | 735 | — | 475 | 260 | 724 | 2 027 |
| 1953 | 4 495 | 690 | 770 | — | 515 | 255 | 895 | 2 140 |
| 1954 | 4 812 | 620 | 830 | — | 600 | 230 | 916 | 2 446 |
| 1955 | 4 626 | 575 | 800 | — | 600 | 200 | 925 | 2 326 |
| 1956 | 5 044 | 625 | 730 | — | 530 | 200 | 1 102 | 2 587 |
| 1957 | 5 548 | 595 | 990 | — | 725 | 265 | 1 150 | 2 813 |
| 1958 | 5 922 | 575 | 1 045 | — | 765 | 280 | 1 305 | 2 997 |
| 1959 | 7 160 | 765 | 1 230 | — | 960 | 270 | 1 554 | 3 611 |
| 1960 | 8 045 | 940 | 1 630 | — | 1 310 | 320 | 1 520 | 3 955 |
| 1961 | 9 200 | ... | ... | — | ... | ... | ... | ... |
| Percentage distribution according to sector— Distribution en pourcentage par secteur | | | | | | | | |
| 1948 | 100.0 | 13.5 | 20.9 | — | 16.1 | 4.8 | 17.6 | 48.0 |
| 1950 – 1960 | 100.0 | 12.4 | 17.9 | — | 13.0 | 4.9 | 19.8 | 49.9 |
| 1950 | 100.0 | 9.6 | 21.0 | — | 13.7 | 7.3 | 18.2 | 51.2 |
| 1953 | 100.0 | 15.3 | 17.1 | — | 11.5 | 5.6 | 19.9 | 47.7 |
| 1954 | 100.0 | 12.8 | 17.3 | — | 12.5 | 4.8 | 19.0 | 50.9 |
| 1958 | 100.0 | 9.7 | 17.6 | — | 12.9 | 4.7 | 22.0 | 50.7 |
| 1960 | 100.0 | 11.6 | 20.3 | — | 16.3 | 4.0 | 18.9 | 49.2 |
| *b. At Prices of 1955 — Aux prix de 1955* | | | | | | | | |
| Absolute figures — Chiffres absolus | | | | | | | | |
| 1948 | 2 928 | 415 | 592 | — | 450 | 142 | 558 | 1 363 |
| 1950 | 3 835 | 355 | 800 | — | 515 | 285 | 734 | 1 946 |
| 1951 | 3 906 | 770 | 722 | — | 460 | 262 | 618 | 1 796 |
| 1952 | 4 138 | 770 | 707 | — | 455 | 252 | 729 | 1 932 |
| 1953 | 4 548 | 725 | 764 | — | 505 | 259 | 920 | 2 139 |
| 1954 | 4 911 | 630 | 845 | — | 610 | 235 | 942 | 2 494 |
| 1955 | 4 626 | 575 | 800 | — | 600 | 200 | 925 | 2 326 |
| 1956 | 4 826 | 600 | 700 | — | 510 | 190 | 1 048 | 2 478 |
| 1957 | 5 150 | 555 | 921 | — | 680 | 241 | 1 041 | 2 633 |
| 1958 | 5 515 | 520 | 988 | — | 730 | 258 | 1 168 | 2 839 |
| 1959 | 6 656 | 690 | 1 149 | — | 905 | 244 | 1 393 | 3 424 |
| 1960 | 7 345 | 830 | 1 480 | — | 1 195 | 285 | 1 375 | 3 660 |
| 1961 | 8 000 | ... | ... | — | ... | ... | ... | ... |
| Percentage distribution according to sector— Distribution en pourcentage par secteur | | | | | | | | |
| 1948 | 100.0 | 14.1 | 20.2 | — | 15.4 | 4.8 | 19.1 | 46.6 |
| 1950 – 1960 | 100.0 | 12.6 | 17.8 | — | 12.9 | 4.9 | 19.7 | 49.9 |
| 1950 | 100.0 | 9.2 | 20.9 | — | 13.4 | 7.5 | 19.1 | 50.8 |
| 1953 | 100.0 | 15.9 | 16.8 | — | 11.1 | 5.7 | 20.2 | 47.1 |
| 1954 | 100.0 | 12.8 | 17.2 | — | 12.4 | 4.8 | 19.2 | 50.8 |
| 1958 | 100.0 | 9.4 | 17.9 | — | 13.2 | 4.7 | 21.2 | 51.5 |
| 1960 | 100.0 | 11.3 | 20.1 | — | 16.2 | 3.9 | 18.7 | 49.9 |
| Average annual rate of growth—Taux annuel moyen d'accroissement | | | | | | | | |
| 1948 – 1953 | 9.2 | 11.8 | 5.2 | — | 2.3 | 12.8 | 10.5 | 9.4 |
| 1950 – 1960 | 6.7 | 8.9 | 6.3 | — | 8.8 | — | 6.5 | 6.5 |
| 1950 – 1953 | 5.9 | 26.9 | -1.5 | — | -0.7 | -3.1 | 7.8 | 3.2 |
| 1954 – 1958 | 2.9 | -4.7 | 4.0 | — | 4.6 | 2.4 | 5.5 | 3.3 |
| 1958 – 1960 | 15.4 | 26.3 | 22.4 | — | 27.9 | 5.1 | 8.5 | 13.5 |

[1] Forestry and fishing are included in "Other sectors" rather than in the Agricultural sector.
[2] Handicrafts are included in "Other sectors" instead of Manufacturing.

[1] La sylviculture et la pêche sont comprises dans "Autres secteurs" plutôt que dans le Secteur agricole.
[2] L'artisanat est inclus dans "Autres secteurs" plutôt que dans les Industries manufacturières.

## 2. INDEX NUMBERS OF INDUSTRIAL PRODUCTION, MANUFACTURING AND ELECTRICITY AND GAS
## INDICES DE LA PRODUCTION INDUSTRIELLE, INDUSTRIES MANUFACTURIERES ET ELECTRICITE ET GAZ

| Period / Période | Total[1] | Manufacturing[1] Industries manufacturières[1] | Food, beverages and tobacco[1] Industries alimentaires, boissons, tabac[1] | Textiles | Clothing, footwear and made-up textiles Articles d'habillement, chaussures et ouvrages en tissu | Wood products and furniture Bois et meubles | Paper and paper products and printing Papier et ouvrages en papier et imprimerie | Chemicals and chemical, petroleum, coal and rubber products Produits chimiques, dérivés du pétrole et du charbon et ouvrages en caoutchouc | Non-metallic mineral products Produits minéraux non métalliques | Basic metals and metal products Métallurgie de base et ouvrages en métaux | Other manufacturing including leather products Autres industries manufacturières, y compris les articles en cuir | Electricity and gas Electricité et gaz |
|---|---|---|---|---|---|---|---|---|---|---|---|---|
| ISIC — CITI | 2-3, 511-512 | 2-3 | 20-22 | 23 | 24 | 25-26 | 27-28 | 30, 31-32 | 33 | 34, 35-38 | 29, 39 | 511-512 |
| *a. Indexes — Indices (1958 = 100)* | | | | | | | | | | | | |
| 1938 | ... | 53 | 54 | 66 | 78 | 50 | 54 | 61 | 72 | 45 | 54 | ... |
| 1948 | 66 | -68- | -74- | -88- | -75- | -72- | -71- | -67- | -94- | -55- | -86- | 52 |
| 1949 | 70 | 72 | 77 | 100 | 88 | 76 | 76 | 72 | 94 | 58 | 88 | 54 |
| 1950 | 79 | 81 | 83 | 122 | 100 | 84 | 80 | 84 | 102 | 66 | 100 | 59 |
| 1951 | 80 | 82 | 83 | 110 | 94 | 84 | 78 | 85 | 106 | 70 | 88 | 66 |
| 1952 | 77 | 79 | 80 | 101 | 96 | 81 | 74 | 77 | 105 | 68 | 76 | 71 |
| 1953 | 80 | 81 | 82 | 108 | 98 | 85 | 80 | 82 | 108 | 70 | 78 | 71 |
| 1954 | 87 | 88 | 84 | 104 | 100 | 89 | 89 | 89 | 113 | 81 | 83 | 84 |
| 1955 | -90- | -89- | -88- | -98- | -94- | -92- | -93- | -90- | -108- | -84- | -86- | -98- |
| 1956 | 92 | 90 | 90 | 99 | 94 | 89 | 93 | 93 | 102 | 86 | 88 | 104 |
| 1957 | 97 | 96 | 95 | 107 | 100 | 96 | 97 | 95 | 103 | 93 | 92 | 97 |
| 1958 | 100 | 100 | 100 | 100 | 100 | 100 | 100 | 100 | 100 | 100 | 100 | 100 |
| 1959 | 111 | 111 | 109 | 111 | 109 | 104 | 104 | 111 | 120 | 117 | 104 | 111 |
| 1960 | 122 | 121 | 117 | 113 | 111 | 111 | 111 | 115 | 129 | 133 | 105 | 130 |
| *b. Average Annual Rate of Change — Taux annuel moyen de variation* | | | | | | | | | | | | |
| 1938-1960 | ... | 3.8 | 3.6 | 2.5 | 1.4 | 3.7 | 3.3 | 2.9 | 2.7 | 5.0 | 3.1 | ... |
| 1938-1948 | ... | 2.5 | 3.2 | 2.9 | -0.4 | 3.7 | 2.8 | 0.9 | 2.7 | 2.0 | 4.8 | ... |
| 1950-1960 | 4.4 | 4.1 | 3.5 | -0.8 | 1.0 | 2.8 | 3.3 | 3.2 | 2.4 | 7.3 | 0.5 | 8.2 |
| 1948-1953 | 3.9 | 3.6 | 2.1 | 4.2 | 5.5 | 3.4 | 2.4 | 4.1 | 2.8 | 5.0 | -1.9 | 6.4 |
| 1954-1958 | 3.5 | 3.2 | 4.5 | -1.0 | — | 3.0 | 3.0 | 3.0 | -3.0 | 5.4 | 4.8 | 4.4 |
| 1958-1960 | 10.5 | 10.0 | 8.2 | 6.3 | 5.4 | 5.4 | 5.4 | 7.2 | 13.6 | 15.3 | 2.5 | 14.0 |

[1] Excludes dairies (in ISIC group 202) and slaughter houses (in ISIC group 201).       [1] Non compris les laiteries (dans CITI groupe 202) et les abattoirs (dans CITI groupe 201).

## 3. INDEX NUMBERS OF INDUSTRIAL EMPLOYMENT, MAJOR GROUPS OF MANUFACTURING
## INDICES DE L'EMPLOI DANS L'INDUSTRIE, CLASSES DE LA BRANCHE MANUFACTURIERE

| Period / Période | Manufacturing[1] Industries manufacturières[1] | Food, beverages and tobacco[1] Industries alimentaires, boissons, tabac[1] | Textiles | Clothing, footwear and made-up textiles Articles d'habillement, chaussures et ouvrages en tissu | Wood products and furniture Bois et meubles | Paper and paper products Papier et ouvrages en papier | Printing and publishing Imprimerie et édition | Leather and leather products except wearing apparel Cuir et articles en cuir, à l'exclusion des articles d'habillement | Rubber products Ouvrages en caoutchouc | Chemicals and chemical, petroleum and coal products Produits chimiques et dérivés du pétrole et du charbon | Non-metallic mineral products Produits minéraux non métalliques | Basic metals Métallurgie de base | Metal products Ouvrages en métaux | Other manufacturing Autres industries manufacturières |
|---|---|---|---|---|---|---|---|---|---|---|---|---|---|---|
| ISIC — CITI | 2-3 | 20-22 | 23 | 24 | 25-26 | 27 | 28 | 29 | 30 | 31-32 | 33 | 34 | 35-38 | 39 |
| *a. Indexes — Indices (1958 = 100)* | | | | | | | | | | | | | | |
| 1953 | 94 | 94 | 128 | 114 | 92 | 85 | 88 | 105 | 99 | 90 | 109 | 85 | 83 | 84 |
| 1954 | 98 | 97 | 119 | 109 | 96 | 89 | 95 | 105 | 105 | 92 | 114 | 91 | 92 | 86 |
| 1955 | 97 | 96 | 108 | 102 | 96 | 94 | 98 | 96 | 100 | 92 | 109 | 97 | 93 | 87 |
| 1956 | 96 | 95 | 102 | 98 | 93 | 97 | 98 | 96 | 95 | 95 | 104 | 100 | 95 | 88 |
| 1957 | 99 | 97 | 106 | 101 | 98 | 97 | 99 | 102 | 94 | 97 | 103 | 103 | 98 | 94 |
| 1958 | 100 | 100 | 100 | 100 | 100 | 100 | 100 | 100 | 100 | 100 | 100 | 100 | 100 | 100 |
| 1959 | 108 | 106 | 104 | 105 | 109 | 107 | 105 | 109 | 108 | 106 | 113 | 105 | 109 | 108 |
| 1960 | 116 | 113 | 104 | 108 | 123 | 116 | 113 | 95 | 107 | 113 | 122 | 108 | 122 | 121 |
| 1961 | 119 | 115 | 104 | 109 | 126 | 120 | 116 | 96 | 103 | 117 | 126 | 111 | 126 | 126 |
| *b. Average Annual Rate of Change — Taux annuel moyen de variation* | | | | | | | | | | | | | | |
| 1953-1960 | 3.0 | 2.7 | -2.9 | -0.8 | 4.2 | 4.5 | 3.6 | -1.4 | 1.1 | 3.3 | 1.6 | 3.5 | 5.7 | 5.3 |
| 1954-1958 | 0.5 | 0.8 | -4.3 | -2.1 | 1.0 | 3.0 | 1.3 | -1.3 | -1.3 | 2.1 | -3.1 | 2.4 | 2.1 | 3.8 |
| 1958-1960 | 7.7 | 6.3 | 2.0 | 3.9 | 10.9 | 7.7 | 6.3 | -2.5 | 3.4 | 6.3 | 10.5 | 3.9 | 10.5 | 10.0 |

[1] Excludes dairies (in ISIC group 202) and slaughter houses (in ISIC group 201).       [1] Non compris les laiteries (dans CITI groupe 202) et les abattoirs (dans CITI groupe 201).

# DENMARK

## 4. CHARACTERISTICS OF ALL INDUSTRIAL ESTABLISHMENTS
### 28 May 1935, 1 June 1948 and 2 June 1958

## CARACTERISTIQUES DE TOUS LES ETABLISSEMENTS INDUSTRIELS
### 28 mai 1935, 1er juin 1948 et 2 juin 1958

Number of technical units and establishments in units; wages and salaries and gross receipts in million Kroner; number of engaged, employees and operatives in thousands; capacity of installed power equipment in thousand horsepower; wages and salaries per employee in thousand Kroner; capacity of installed power equipment per engaged in horsepower.

Nombre d'unités techniques et d'établissements en unités; traitements et salaires et recettes brutes en millions de couronnes; nombre de personnes occupées, de salariés et d'ouvriers en milliers; puissance installée en milliers de chevaux-vapeur; traitements et salaires par salarié en milliers de couronnes; puissance installée par personne occupée en chevaux-vapeur.

## A. The Divisions of Industrial Activity — Les branches de l'activité industrielle

### a. Absolute Figures — Chiffres absolus

| Year and item of data (ISIC) | All industrial activity / Toutes industries (1-4, 511-512) | Mining / Industries extractives (1) | Manufacturing / Industries manufacturières (2-3) | Construction / Bâtiment et travaux publics (4) | Electricity and gas / Electricité et gaz (511-512) | Année et rubrique (CITI) |
|---|---|---|---|---|---|---|
| **28.V.1935** | | | | | | **28.V.1935** |
| Number of technical units... | 88 997 | 1 170 | 69 648 | 17 541[1] | 638 | Nombre d'unités techniques |
| Number of engaged | 433.9 | 7.1 | 342.0 | 79.1 | 5.7 | Nombre de personnes occupées |
| Number of employees | 361.2 | 6.1 | 288.8 | 60.7 | 5.6 | Nombre de salariés |
| Number of operatives | 306.5 | 5.7 | 239.6 | 57.5 | 3.7 | Nombre d'ouvriers |
| Capacity of installed power equipment | | 18.0 | 586.0 | 46.0 | 596.0 | Puissance installée |
| **1.VI.1948** | | | | | | **1.VI.1948** |
| Number of establishments | 94 507 | 3 917 | 69 186 | 20 836 | 568 | Nombre d'établissements |
| Number of engaged | 693.6 | 40.5 | 530.5 | 112.9 | 9.7 | Nombre de personnes occupées |
| Employees: Number | 594.3 | 40.5 | 454.3 | 89.8 | 9.7 | Salariés: Nombre |
| Wages and salaries (during 1947) | 3 089.1 | 132.5 | 2 433.7 | 456.7 | 66.2 | Traitements et salaires (en 1947) |
| Number of operatives | ... | ... | 367.5 | 82.3 | 6.9 | Nombre d'ouvriers |
| Capacity of installed power equipment | | 84.0 | 1 103.0 | 93.0 | 935.0 | Puissance installée |
| **2.VI.1958** | | | | | | **2.VI.1958** |
| Number of establishments... | 65 702 | 524 | 43 329 | 21 409 | 440 | Nombre d'établissements |
| Gross receipts (during 1957) | 30 605.1 | 131.9 | 25 942.3 | 3 386.0 | 1 144.9 | Recettes brutes (en 1957) |
| Number of engaged | 615.3 | 4.5 | 473.2 | 126.9 | 10.7 | Nombre de personnes occupées |
| Wages and salaries (during 1957) | 5 763.6 | 39.2 | 4 560.6 | 1 002.0 | 161.8 | Traitements et salaires (en 1957) |

### b. Structure

| Year and item of data (ISIC) | All industrial activity / Toutes industries (1-4, 511-512) | Mining / Industries extractives (1) | Manufacturing / Industries manufacturières (2-3) | Construction / Bâtiment et travaux publics (4) | Electricity and gas / Electricité et gaz (511-512) | Année et rubrique (CITI) |
|---|---|---|---|---|---|---|
| **28.V.1935** | | | | | | **28.V.1935** |
| Distribution in percent of number of engaged | 100.0 | 1.6 | 78.8 | 18.2 | 1.4 | Distribution en pourcentage du nombre de personnes occupées |
| Capacity of installed power equipment per person engaged | . | 2.54 | 1.71 | 0.58 | 104.56 | Puissance installée par personne occupée |
| Employees as a percent of engaged | 83.2 | 86.2 | 84.4 | 76.7 | 98.2 | Salariés en pourcentage des personnes occupées |
| Operatives as a percent of employees | 84.8 | 93.4 | 83.0 | 94.7 | 66.1 | Ouvriers en pourcentage des salariés |
| **1.VI.1948** | | | | | | **1.VI.1948** |
| Distribution in percent of number of engaged | 100.0 | 5.8 | 76.5 | 16.3 | 1.4 | Distribution en pourcentage du nombre de personnes occupées |
| Capacity of installed power equipment per person engaged | . | 2.07 | 2.08 | 0.82 | 96.39 | Puissance installée par personne occupée |
| Employees as a percent of engaged | 85.7 | 100.0 | 85.6 | 79.5 | 100.0 | Salariés en pourcentage des personnes occupées |
| Wages and salaries per employee | 5.2 | 3.3 | 5.4 | 5.1 | 6.8 | Traitements et salaires par salarié |
| Operatives as a percent of employees | ... | ... | 80.9 | 91.6 | 71.1 | Ouvriers en pourcentage des salariés |
| **2.VI.1958** | | | | | | **2.VI.1958** |
| Distribution in percent of: | | | | | | Distribution en pourcentage: |
| Gross receipts | 100.0 | 0.4 | 84.7 | 11.1 | 3.8 | Recettes brutes |
| Number of engaged | 100.0 | 0.7 | 76.9 | 20.6 | 1.8 | Nombre de personnes occupées |

[1] Number of enterprises rather than technical units.

[1] Nombre d'entreprises et non d'unités techniques.

## B. The Major Groups of Manufacturing — Les classes de la branche Industries manufacturières

| Year and item of data | Manufacturing — Industries manufacturières | Food, beverages and tobacco — Industries alimentaires, boissons, tabac | Textiles | Clothing, footwear and made-up textiles — Articles d'habillement, chaussures et ouvrages en tissu | Wood products and furniture — Bois et meubles | Paper and paper products — Papier et ouvrages en papier | Printing and publishing — Imprimerie et édition | Leather and leather products except wearing apparel — Cuir et articles en cuir, à l'exclusion des articles d'habillement | Rubber products — Ouvrages en caoutchouc | Chemicals and chemical, petroleum and coal products — Produits chimiques et dérivés du pétrole et du charbon | Non-metallic mineral products — Produits minéraux non métalliques | Basic metals — Métallurgie de base | Metal products — Ouvrages en métaux | Other manufacturing — Autres industries manufacturières | Année et rubrique |
|---|---|---|---|---|---|---|---|---|---|---|---|---|---|---|---|
| ISIC | 2–3 | 20–22 | 23 | 24 | 25–26 | 27 | 28 | 29 | 30 | 31–32 | 33 | 34 | 35–38 | 39 | CITI |
| *a. Absolute Figures — Chiffres absolus* | | | | | | | | | | | | | | | |
| **28.V.1935** | | | | | | | | | | | | | | | **28.V.1935** |
| Number of technical units | 69 648 | 16 045 | 980 | 17 959 | 8 591 | 209 | 1 681 | 1 605 | 341 | 1 046 | 1 354 | 17 427 || 2 410 | Nombre d'unités techniques |
| Number of engaged | 342.0 | 73.7 | 20.1 | 63.0 | 27.2 | 5.7 | 13.6 | 4.0 | 2.8 | 14.3 | 17.1 | 94.5 || 6.0 | Nombre de personnes occupées |
| Number of employees | 288.8 | 65.7 | 19.2 | 47.4 | 20.0 | 5.5 | 12.1 | 2.6 | 2.5 | 13.5 | 16.0 | 79.9 || 4.4 | Nombre de salariés |
| Number of operatives | 239.6 | 55.6 | 17.2 | 28.6 | 18.3 | 4.8 | 10.8 | 2.3 | 2.2 | 10.0 | 14.9 | 71.1 || 3.8 | Nombre d'ouvriers |
| Capacity of installed power equipment | 586 | 201 | 25 | 12 | 53 | 21 | 13 | 4 | 4 | 45 | 65 | 140 || 3 | Puissance installée |
| **1.VI.1948** | | | | | | | | | | | | | | | **1.VI.1948** |
| Number of establishments | 69 186 | 14 174 | 1 130 | 16 937 | 8 632 | 299 | 1 936 | 1 242 | 426 | 1 368 | 2 216 | 7 | 17 645 | 3 174 | Nombre d'établissements |
| Number of engaged | 530.5 | 110.3 | 32.8 | 74.7 | 43.8 | 9.3 | 28.4 | 5.8 | 4.6 | 23.5 | 26.8 | 1.9 | 149.2 | 19.4 | Nombre de personnes occupées |
| Number of employees | 454.3 | 93.0 | 31.6 | 56.2 | 34.4 | 9.1 | 26.3 | 4.4 | 4.2 | 22.3 | 24.8 | 1.9 | 130.3 | 15.8 | Nombre de salariés |
| Wages and salaries paid (During 1947) | 2 433.7 | 489.0 | 142.9 | 248.5 | 174.9 | 49.3 | 152.5 | 28.6 | 25.0 | 135.8 | 125.8 | 13.6 | 761.6 | 86.2 | Traitements et salaires payés (en 1947) |
| Number of operatives | 367.5 | 71.5 | 27.4 | 47.2 | 30.0 | 7.2 | 17.9 | 3.7 | 3.6 | 15.5 | 22.3 | 1.6 | 107.6 | 12.0 | Nombre d'ouvriers |
| Capacity of installed power equipment | 1 103 | 288 | 50 | 20 | 118 | 38 | 22 | 9 | 12 | 96 | 132 | 74 | 219 | 25 | Puissance installée |
| **2.VI.1958** | | | | | | | | | | | | | | | **2.VI.1958** |
| Number of establishments | 43 329 | 7 838 | 824 | 9 100 | 5 340 | 274 | 1 893 | 259 | *315 | 783 | 1 457 | 67 | 13 017 | 2 162 | Nombre d'établissements |
| Gross receipts (During 1957) | 25 942.3 | 10 891.6 | 1 072.5 | 1 336.4 | 1 012.1 | 690.0 | 1 072.2 | 154.3 | 199.0 | 1 585.8 | 753.6 | 512.9 | 6 139.0 | 522.9 | Recettes brutes (en 1957) |
| Number of engaged | 473.2 | 103.4 | 23.5 | 46.1 | 32.2 | 11.3 | 29.8 | 3.3 | 5.7 | 19.7 | 21.7 | 6.1 | 154.4 | 16.0 | Nombre de personnes occupées |
| Wages and salaries (During 1957) | 4 560.6 | 907.0 | 249.6 | 330.9 | 241.2 | 120.2 | 350.7 | 33.0 | 51.4 | 239.4 | 225.0 | 80.2 | 1 588.4 | 143.6 | Traitements et salaires payés (en 1957) |
| *b. Structure* | | | | | | | | | | | | | | | |
| **28.V.1935** | | | | | | | | | | | | | | | **28.V.1935** |
| Distribution in percent of number of engaged | 100.0 | 21.5 | 5.9 | 18.4 | 8.0 | 1.6 | 4.0 | 1.2 | 0.8 | 4.2 | 5.0 | 27.6 || 1.8 | Répartition en pourcentage du nombre de personnes occupées |
| Capacity of installed power equipment per person engaged | 1.71 | 2.73 | 1.24 | 0.19 | 1.95 | 3.68 | 0.96 | 1.00 | 1.43 | 3.15 | 3.80 | 1.48 || 0.50 | Puissance installée par personne occupée |
| Employees as a percent of engaged | 84.4 | 89.1 | 95.5 | 75.2 | 73.5 | 96.5 | 89.0 | 65.0 | 89.3 | 94.4 | 93.6 | 84.6 || 73.3 | Salariés en pourcentage des personnes occupées |
| Operatives as a percent of employees | 83.0 | 84.6 | 89.6 | 60.3 | 91.5 | 87.3 | 89.2 | 88.5 | 88.0 | 74.1 | 93.1 | 89.0 || 86.4 | Ouvriers en pourcentage des salariés |
| **1.VI.1948** | | | | | | | | | | | | | | | **1.VI.1948** |
| Distribution in percent of: Number of engaged | 100.0 | 20.7 | 6.2 | 14.1 | 8.3 | 1.7 | 5.4 | 1.1 | 0.8 | 4.5 | 5.0 | 0.4 | 28.1 | 3.7 | Répartition en pourcentage du nombre de personnes occupées |
| Capacity of installed power equipment per person engaged | 2.08 | 2.61 | 1.52 | 0.27 | 2.69 | 4.09 | 0.77 | 1.55 | 2.61 | 4.08 | 4.92 | 38.95 | 1.47 | 1.29 | Puissance installée par personne occupée |
| Employees as a percent of engaged | 85.6 | 84.3 | 96.3 | 75.2 | 78.5 | 97.8 | 92.6 | 75.9 | 91.3 | 94.9 | 92.5 | 100.0 | 87.3 | 81.4 | Salariés en pourcentage des personnes occupées |
| Wages and salaries per employee | 5.4 | 5.2 | 4.5 | 4.4 | 5.1 | 5.4 | 5.8 | 6.5 | 6.0 | 6.1 | 5.1 | 7.2 | 5.8 | 5.4 | Traitements et salaires par salarié |
| Operatives as a percent of employees | 80.9 | 76.9 | 86.7 | 84.0 | 87.2 | 79.1 | 68.1 | 84.1 | 85.7 | 69.5 | 89.9 | 84.2 | 82.6 | 75.9 | Ouvriers en pourcentage des salariés |
| **2.VI.1958** | | | | | | | | | | | | | | | **2.VI.1958** |
| Distribution in percent of: Gross receipts | 100.0 | 41.9 | 4.2 | 5.1 | 3.9 | 2.7 | 4.1 | 0.6 | 0.8 | 6.1 | 2.9 | 2.0 | 23.6 | 2.1 | Répartition en pourcentage: Recettes brutes |
| Number of engaged | 100.0 | 21.8 | 5.0 | 9.7 | 6.8 | 2.4 | 6.3 | 0.7 | 1.2 | 4.2 | 4.6 | 1.2 | 32.7 | 3.4 | Nombre de personnes occupées |

# DENMARK

## 5. THE CHARACTERISTICS OF MANUFACTURING ESTABLISHMENTS WITH SIX OR MORE OPERATIVES
## CARACTERISTIQUES DES ETABLISSEMENTS MANUFACTURIERS COMPTANT AU MOINS SIX OUVRIERS
### 1939, 1948, 1952, 1953, 1958

Number of establishments in units; value added and wages and salaries in million Kroner; number of engaged, employees and operatives in thousands; man-hours worked in millions; energy consumed in thousand metric tons of coal equivalents; electricity consumed in million KWH; capacity of installed power equipment in thousand horsepower; value added per engaged, per employee and wages and salaries per employee and per thousand operative man-hours in thousand Kroner; average annual man-hours per operative in thousands; energy consumed per engaged, per employee and per thousand operative man-hours in metric tons of coal equivalents; electricity consumed per engaged, per employee and per thousand operative man-hours in thousand KWH; capacity of installed power equipment per thousand operative man-hours in horsepower.

Nombre d'établissements en unités; valeur ajoutée et traitements et salaires en millions de couronnes; nombre de personnes occupées, de salariés et d'ouvriers en milliers; heures de travail en millions; énergie consommée en milliers de tonnes métriques d'équivalent charbon; électricité consommée en millions de kWh; puissance installée en milliers de chevaux-vapeur; valeur ajoutée par personne occupée, par salarié et traitements et salaires par salarié et par millier d'heures-ouvrier en milliers de couronnes; moyenne annuelle des heures de travail par ouvrier en milliers; énergie consommée par personne occupée, par salarié et par millier d'heures-ouvrier en tonnes métriques d'équivalent charbon; électricité consommée par salarié et par millier d'heures-ouvrier en milliers de kWh; puissance installée par millier d'heures-ouvrier en chevaux-vapeur.

| Year and item of data | Manufacturing / Industries manufacturières | Food, beverages and tobacco[1] / Industries alimentaires, boissons, tabac[1] | Textiles | Clothing, footwear and made-up textiles / Articles d'habillement, chaussures et ouvrages en tissu | Wood products and furniture[2] / Bois et meubles[2] | Paper and paper products / Papier et ouvrages en papier | Printing and publishing / Imprimerie et édition | Leather and leather products except wearing apparel / Cuir et articles en cuir, à l'exclusion des articles d'habillement | Rubber products / Ouvrages en caoutchouc | Chemicals and chemical, petroleum and coal products[3] / Produits chimiques et dérivés du pétrole et du charbon[3] | Non-metallic mineral products[4] / Produits minéraux non métalliques[4] | Basic metals / Métallurgie de base | Metal products / Ouvrages en métaux | Other manufacturing / Autres industries manufacturières | Année et rubrique |
|---|---|---|---|---|---|---|---|---|---|---|---|---|---|---|---|
| ISIC | 2–3 | 20–22 | 23 | 24 | 25–26 | 27 | 28 | 29 | 30 | 31–32 | 33 | 34 | 35–38 | 39 | CITI |
| **a. Absolute Figures — Chiffres absolus** | | | | | | | | | | | | | | | |
| **1939** | | | | | | | | | | | | | | | **1939** |
| Number of establishments | 5 542 | 1 398 | 307 | 679 | 438 | 150 | 509 | 67 | 21 | 381 | 517 | | 914 | 161 | Nombre d'établissements |
| Value added | 1 340.1 | 308.7 | 104.7 | 109.0 | 38.3 | 39.7 | 66.1 | 13.3 | | 156.3 | 75.3 | | 411.0 | 17.7 | Valeur ajoutée |
| Number of employees (Average during year) | 209.7 | 39.6 | 19.6 | 25.1 | 8.0 | 6.5 | 11.6 | 1.8 | 2.7 | 11.5 | 13.4 | | 66.8 | 3.1 | Nombre de salariés (Moyenne pendant l'année) |
| Number of operatives (Average during year) | 179.0 | 33.2 | 17.6 | 21.8 | 7.3 | 5.7 | 9.4 | 1.5 | 2.4 | 8.5 | 12.2 | | 56.8 | 2.6 | Nombre d'ouvriers (Moyenne pendant l'année) |
| Energy consumed | 1 455.7 | 402.6 | 87.4 | 9.6 | 13.2 | 85.5 | 8.7 | 11.6 | | 170.1 | 475.8 | | 184.8 | 6.4 | Energie consommée |
| Electricity consumed | 449.5 | 86.2 | 34.7 | 7.2 | 9.0 | 51.0 | 8.4 | 3.2 | | 76.4 | 79.8 | | 91.5 | 2.1 | Electricité consommée |
| Capacity of installed power equipment (At end of year) | 510 | 126 | 32 | 9 | 27 | 32 | 16 | 5 | | 56 | 87 | | 113 | 7 | Puissance installée (à la fin de l'année) |
| **1948** | | | | | | | | | | | | | | | **1948** |
| Number of establishments | 7 406 | 1 444 | 424 | 903 | 698 | 186 | 535 | 137 | 110 | 488 | 701 | 9 | 1 417 | 354 | Nombre d'établissements |
| Value added | 3 350.8 | 682.6 | 318.4 | 257.7 | 153.9 | 102.3 | 153.2 | 45.1 | 44.5 | 274.5 | 206.8 | 36.7 | 982.3 | 92.8 | Valeur ajoutée |
| Employees: Number (Average during year) | 266.6 | 44.3 | 27.7 | 26.5 | 14.6 | 7.9 | 13.3 | 3.1 | 3.9 | 15.2 | 17.9 | 1.8 | 82.5 | 7.9 | Salariés: Nombre (Moyenne pendant l'année) |
| Wages and salaries | 1 816.4 | 298.5 | 158.8 | 167.6 | 98.3 | 46.9 | 96.8 | 23.7 | 26.0 | 116.2 | 125.0 | 15.3 | 589.2 | 54.1 | Traitements et salaires |
| Operatives: Number (Average during year) | 222.8 | 36.9 | 24.2 | 22.2 | 12.9 | 6.7 | 10.8 | 2.6 | 3.4 | 10.6 | 16.2 | 1.4 | 68.4 | 6.5 | Ouvriers: Nombre (Moyenne pendant l'année) |
| Man-hours worked | 493.0 | 82.9 | 49.9 | 46.2 | 29.4 | 15.0 | 24.9 | 5.8 | 7.5 | 24.9 | 36.4 | 3.3 | 152.1 | 14.7 | Heures de travail effectuées |
| Wages and salaries | 1 377.9 | 224.1 | 121.8 | 127.2 | 83.5 | 35.8 | 75.7 | 17.9 | 21.4 | 68.4 | 106.4 | 11.2 | 443.8 | 40.7 | Traitements et salaires |
| Energy consumed | 1 746.9 | 421.9 | 114.6 | 13.6 | 16.4 | 100.2 | 11.8 | 14.1 | 17.2 | 176.0 | 564.8 | 69.3 | 215.0 | 12.0 | Energie consommée |
| Electricity consumed | 597.1 | 110.4 | 62.9 | 8.6 | 18.0 | 53.9 | 12.2 | 4.8 | 13.9 | 71.2 | 97.8 | 22.3 | 109.3 | 11.8 | Electricité consommée |
| Capacity of installed power equipment (At end of year) | 755 | 150 | 51 | 12 | 58 | 38 | 17 | 9 | 13 | 69 | 119 | 19 | 182 | 18 | Puissance installée (à la fin de l'année) |
| **1952** | | | | | | | | | | | | | | | **1952** |
| Number of establishments | 7 207 | 1 040 | 442 | 885 | 878 | 192 | 488 | 127 | 49 | 472 | 658 | 10 | 1 621 | 345 | Nombre d'établissements |
| Value added | 4 623.9 | 817.3 | 368.5 | 351.4 | 210.4 | 114.0 | 278.8 | 40.0 | 60.2 | 369.9 | 331.2 | 100.7 | 1 470.4 | 111.1 | Valeur ajoutée |
| Employees: Number (Average during year) | 293.5 | 44.6 | 29.0 | 29.7 | 17.0 | 8.7 | 16.3 | 2.7 | 4.2 | 16.6 | 19.1 | 2.6 | 95.4 | 7.6 | Salariés: Nombre (Moyenne pendant l'année) |
| Wages and salaries | 2 649.2 | 393.4 | 225.6 | 228.3 | 140.1 | 72.5 | 174.9 | 25.0 | 35.4 | 170.6 | 177.3 | 28.0 | 911.0 | 67.1 | Traitements et salaire |
| Operatives: Number (Average during year) | 238.3 | 36.6 | 24.5 | 24.4 | 14.9 | 7.0 | 11.0 | 2.2 | 3.6 | 11.1 | 17.1 | 2.1 | 77.8 | 6.0 | Ouvriers: Nombre (Moyenne pendant l'année) |
| Man-hours worked | 523.6 | 82.2 | 49.8 | 50.3 | 33.2 | 15.5 | 24.8 | 4.8 | 8.0 | 25.4 | 38.6 | 4.8 | 172.8 | 13.4 | Heures de travail effectuées |
| Wages and salaries | 1 921.9 | 290.5 | 165.6 | 168.9 | 118.5 | 51.2 | 104.8 | 18.0 | 28.0 | 95.6 | 148.1 | 20.8 | 664.3 | 47.6 | Traitements et salaires |
| Energy consumed | 1 927.5 | 395.9 | 117.0 | 13.6 | 19.4 | | 114.7 | [5] | | 226.9 | 666.7 | | 348.2 | 25.1[5] | Energie consommée |
| Electricity consumed | 847.8 | 140.1 | 81.2 | 12.0 | 27.3 | | 97.4 | [5] | | 115.1 | 150.4 | | 201.5 | 22.8[5] | Electricité consommée |
| Capacity of installed power equipment (At end of year) | 1 015 | 174 | 63 | 16 | 74 | 50 | 23 | 10 | 17 | 103 | 137 | 31 | 294 | 23 | Puissance installée (à la fin de l'année) |

194

## 5. THE CHARACTERISTICS OF MANUFACTURING ESTABLISHMENTS WITH SIX OR MORE OPERATIVES (continued)
## CARACTERISTIQUES DES ETABLISSEMENTS MANUFACTURIERS COMPTANT AU MOINS SIX OUVRIERS (suite)
### 1939, 1948, 1952, 1953, 1958

| Year and item of data | Manu-facturing / Industries manufac-turières | Food, beverages and tobacco[1] / Industries alimen-taires, boissons, tabac[1] | Textiles | Clothing, footwear and made-up textiles / Articles d'habil-lement, chaussures et ouvrages en tissu | Wood products and furniture[2] / Bois et meubles[2] | Paper and paper products / Papier et ouvrages en papier | Printing and publish-ing / Im-primerie et édition | Leather and leather products except wearing apparel / Cuir et articles en cuir, à l'exclu-sion des articles d'habil-lement | Rubber products / Ouvrages en caout-chouc | Chemicals and chemical, petroleum and coal products[3] / Produits chi-miques et dérivés du pétrole et du charbon[3] | Non-metallic mineral products[4] / Produits minéraux non métal-liques[4] | Basic metals / Métal-lurgie de base | Metal products / Ouvrages en métaux | Other manu-factur-ing / Autres in-dustries manufac-turières | Année et rubrique |
|---|---|---|---|---|---|---|---|---|---|---|---|---|---|---|---|
| ISIC | 2-3 | 20-22 | 23 | 24 | 25-26 | 27 | 28 | 29 | 30 | 31-32 | 33 | 34 | 35-38 | 39 | CITI |
| *a. Absolute figures — Chiffres absolus* | | | | | | | | | | | | | | | |
| 1953 | | | | | | | | | | | | | | | 1953 |
| Number of establishments | 7 192 | 993 | 426 | 900 | 893 | 185 | 491 | 127 | 45 | 469 | 677 | 9 | 1 630 | 347 | Nombre d'établissements |
| Value added | 5 028.4 | 890.6 | 400.3 | 375.0 | 236.3 | 154.4 | 314.3 | 43.6 | 67.7 | 433.8 | 357.2 | 91.0 | 1 543.1 | 121.1 | Valeur ajoutée |
| Employees: Number | | | | | | | | | | | | | | | Salariés: Nombre |
| (Average during year) | 301.2 | 44.9 | 29.2 | 31.4 | 18.0 | 9.0 | 16.7 | 2.8 | 4.6 | 17.3 | 19.5 | 2.7 | 97.2 | 7.9 | (Moyenne pendant l'année) |
| Wages and salaries | 2 828.8 | 417.0 | 238.2 | 249.6 | 154.0 | 77.8 | 186.4 | 27.0 | 39.5 | 182.6 | 186.9 | 30.7 | 966.0 | 73.1 | Traitements et salaires |
| Operatives: Number | | | | | | | | | | | | | | | Ouvriers: Nombre |
| (Average during year) | 241.8 | ·36.1 | 24.7 | 25.6 | 15.8 | 7.3 | 11.4 | 2.3 | 3.9 | 11.3 | 17.2 | 2.2 | 77.9 | 6.1 | (Moyenne pendant l'année) |
| Man-hours worked | 527.6 | 80.4 | 51.0 | 52.6 | 35.0 | 15.9 | 25.8 | 5.0 | 8.7 | 25.5 | 38.7 | 4.8 | 170.8 | 13.4 | Heures de travail effectuées |
| Wages and salaries | 2 026.0 | 302.0 | 175.5 | 180.9 | 129.6 | 55.4 | 116.1 | 19.5 | 31.4 | 99.8 | 154.3 | 22.2 | 689.3 | 50.0 | Traitements et salaires |
| Energy consumed | 1 969.0 | 412.0 | 123.2 | 11.8 | 21.0 | 133.5 | | 5 | 237.9 | | 665.8 | 337.8 | | 26.0 5 | Energie consommée |
| Electricity consumed | 906.7 | 146.3 | 85.1 | 13.6 | 30.6 | 112.0 | | 5 | 127.6 | | 154.0 | 212.6 | | 24.9 5 | Electricité consommée |
| 1958 | | | | | | | | | | | | | | | 1958 |
| Number of establishments | 5 994 | 670 | 357 | 719 | 762 | 177 | 462 | 95 | 34 | 413 | 558 | 11 | 1 444 | 292 | Nombre d'établissements |
| Value added | 6 867.4 | 1 212.1 | 402.5 | 408.3 | 331.1 | 245.4 | 445.2 | 51.9 | 80.9 | 577.3 | 431.9 | 123.2 | 2 358.8 | 198.8 | Valeur ajoutée |
| Number of engaged | 324.5 | 47.8 | 22.9 | 28.3 | 20.1 | 10.8 | 19.2 | 2.8 | 4.6 | 19.3 | 18.3 | 3.2 | 117.6 | 9.6 | Nombre de personnes occupées |
| Employees: Number | | | | | | | | | | | | | | | Salariés: Nombre |
| (Average during year) | 320.5 | 47.5 | 22.7 | 27.7 | 19.5 | 10.6 | 18.9 | 2.7 | 4.6 | 19.2 | 18.0 | 3.2 | 116.5 | 9.4 | (Moyenne pendant l'année) |
| Wages and salaries | 3 878.7 | 573.0 | 233.4 | 269.3 | 213.5 | 124.0 | 272.4 | 30.8 | 49.7 | 265.8 | 219.3 | 45.0 | 1 470.4 | 112.1 | Traitements et salaires |
| Operatives: Number | | | | | | | | | | | | | | | Ouvriers: Nombre |
| (Average during year) | 252.5 | 37.8 | 18.7 | 22.3 | 16.9 | 8.4 | 12.8 | 2.2 | 3.8 | 12.2 | 15.4 | 2.5 | 92.4 | 7.1 | (Moyenne pendant l'année) |
| Man-hours worked | 542.5 | 83.2 | 37.6 | 44.9 | 37.4 | 18.5 | 28.2 | 4.6 | 8.3 | 27.2 | 34.2 | 5.4 | 197.4 | 15.6 | Heures de travail effectuées |
| Wages and salaries | 2 684.8 | 401.4 | 165.4 | 189.5 | 174.1 | 86.7 | 169.4 | 21.6 | 38.0 | 137.8 | 174.0 | 32.0 | 1 021.1 | 73.8 | Traitements et salaires |
| Energy consumed | 2 097.2 | 404.3 | 109.1 | 14.1 | 24.1 | 136.5 | | 5 | 302.2 | | 644.6 | 429.3 | | 33.0 5 | Energie consommée |
| Electricity consumed | 1 222.5 | 190.3 | 87.1 | 16.7 | 41.5 | 139.8 | | 5 | 181.9 | | 182.8 | 344.4 | | 38.0 5 | Electricité consommée |
| *b. Structure* | | | | | | | | | | | | | | | |
| 1939 | | | | | | | | | | | | | | | 1939 |
| Distribution in percent of: | | | | | | | | | | | | | | | Répartition en pourcentage: |
| Value added | 100.0 | 23.0 | 7.8 | 8.1 | 2.9 | 3.0 | 4.9 | 1.0 | 11.6 | | 5.7 | 30.6 | | 1.4 | De la valeur ajoutée |
| Number of employees | 100.0 | 18.8 | 9.4 | 12.0 | 3.8 | 3.1 | 5.5 | 0.9 | 1.2 | 5.5 | 6.4 | 31.9 | | 1.5 | Du nombre de salariés |
| Per employee: | | | | | | | | | | | | | | | Par salarié: |
| Value added | 6.4 | 7.8 | 5.3 | 4.3 | 4.8 | 6.1 | 5.7 | 7.4 | 11.0 | | 5.6 | 6.2 | | 5.7 | Valeur ajoutée |
| Energy consumed | 6.94 | 10.17 | 4.46 | 0.38 | 1.65 | 13.15 | 0.75 | 6.44 | 11.98 | | 35.51 | 2.77 | | 2.06 | Energie consommée |
| Electricity consumed | 2.1 | 2.2 | 1.8 | 0.3 | 1.1 | 7.8 | 0.7 | 1.8 | 5.4 | | 6.0 | 1.4 | | 0.7 | Electricité consommée |
| Capacity of installed power equipment | 2.43 | 3.18 | 1.63 | 0.36 | 3.38 | 4.92 | 1.38 | 2.78 | 3.94 | | 6.49 | 1.69 | | 2.26 | Puissance installée |
| Operatives as a percent of employees | 85.4 | 83.8 | 89.8 | 86.8 | 91.2 | 87.7 | 81.0 | 83.3 | 88.9 | 73.9 | 91.0 | 85.0 | | 83.9 | Ouvriers en pourcentage des salariés |
| 1948 | | | | | | | | | | | | | | | 1948 |
| Distribution in percent of: | | | | | | | | | | | | | | | Répartition en pourcentage: |
| Value added | 100.0 | 20.3 | 9.5 | 7.7 | 4.6 | 3.1 | 4.5 | 1.4 | 1.3 | 8.2 | 6.2 | 1.1 | 29.3 | 2.8 | De la valeur ajoutée |
| Number of employees | 100.0 | 16.6 | 10.4 | 9.9 | 5.5 | 2.9 | 5.0 | 1.2 | 1.5 | 5.7 | 6.7 | 0.6 | 31.0 | 3.0 | Du nombre de salariés |
| Per employee: | | | | | | | | | | | | | | | Par salarié: |
| Value added | 12.6 | 15.4 | 11.5 | 9.7 | 10.5 | 12.9 | 11.5 | 14.5 | 11.4 | 18.0 | 11.6 | 20.4 | 11.9 | 11.7 | Valeur ajoutée |
| Wages and salaries | 6.8 | 6.7 | 5.7 | 6.3 | 6.7 | 5.9 | 7.3 | 7.6 | 6.7 | 7.6 | 7.0 | 8.5 | 7.1 | 6.8 | Traitements et salaires |
| Energy consumed | 6.55 | 9.52 | 4.14 | 0.51 | 1.12 | 12.68 | 0.89 | 4.55 | 4.41 | 11.58 | 31.55 | 38.50 | 2.61 | 1.52 | Energie consommée |
| Electricity consumed | 2.2 | 2.5 | 2.3 | 0.3 | 1.2 | 6.8 | 0.9 | 1.5 | 3.6 | 4.7 | 5.5 | 12.4 | 1.3 | 1.5 | Electricité consommée |
| Capacity of installed power equipment | 2.83 | 3.39 | 1.84 | 0.45 | 3.97 | 4.81 | 1.28 | 2.90 | 3.33 | 4.54 | 6.65 | 10.56 | 2.21 | 2.28 | Puissance installée |
| Value added per unit of wages and salaries | 1.84 | 2.29 | 2.00 | 1.54 | 1.56 | 2.18 | 1.58 | 1.90 | 1.71 | 2.36 | 1.65 | 2.40 | 1.67 | 1.72 | Valeur ajoutée par unité de traitements et salaires |
| Operatives as a percent of employees | 83.6 | 83.3 | 87.4 | 83.8 | 88.4 | 84.8 | 81.2 | 83.9 | 87.2 | 69.7 | 90.5 | 77.8 | 82.9 | 82.3 | Ouvriers en pourcentage des salariés |
| Average man-hours per operative | 2.21 | 2.25 | 2.06 | 2.08 | 2.28 | 2.24 | 2.30 | 2.23 | 2.20 | 2.35 | 2.25 | 2.36 | 2.22 | 2.26 | Heures de travail: moyenne par ouvrier |
| Per thousand operative man-hours: | | | | | | | | | | | | | | | Par millier d'heures de travail d'ouvrier: |
| Wages and salaries | 2.79 | 2.70 | 2.44 | 2.75 | 2.84 | 2.39 | 3.04 | 3.09 | 2.85 | 2.75 | 2.92 | 3.39 | 2.92 | 2.77 | Traitements et salaires |
| Energy consumed | 3.54 | 5.09 | 2.30 | 0.29 | 0.56 | 6.68 | 0.47 | 2.43 | 2.29 | 7.07 | 15.52 | 21.00 | 1.41 | 0.82 | Energie consommée |
| Electricity consumed | 1.21 | 1.33 | 1.26 | 0.19 | 0.61 | 3.59 | 0.49 | 0.83 | 1.85 | 2.86 | 2.69 | 6.76 | 0.72 | 0.80 | Electricité consommée |
| Capacity of installed power equipment | 1.53 | 1.81 | 1.02 | 0.26 | 1.97 | 2.53 | 0.68 | 1.55 | 1.73 | 2.77 | 3.27 | 5.76 | 1.20 | 1.22 | Puissance installée |

# DENMARK

## 5. THE CHARACTERISTICS OF MANUFACTURING ESTABLISHMENTS WITH SIX OR MORE OPERATIVES (continued)
## CARACTERISTIQUES DES ETABLISSEMENTS MANUFACTURIERS COMPTANT AU MOINS SIX OUVRIERS (suite)
### 1939, 1948, 1952, 1953, 1958

b. Structure

| Year and item of data | Manufacturing / Industries manufacturières | Food, beverages and tobacco[1] / Industries alimentaires, boissons, tabac[1] | Textiles | Clothing, footwear and made-up textiles / Articles d'habillement, chaussures et ouvrages en tissu | Wood products and furniture[2] / Bois et meubles[2] | Paper and paper products / Papier et ouvrages en papier | Printing and publishing / Imprimerie et édition | Leather and leather products except wearing apparel / Cuir et articles en cuir, à l'exclusion des articles d'habillement | Rubber products / Ouvrages en caoutchouc | Chemicals and chemical, petroleum and coal products[3] / Produits chimiques et dérivés du pétrole et du charbon[3] | Nonmetallic mineral products[4] / Produits minéraux non métalliques[4] | Basic metals / Métallurgie de base | Metal products / Ouvrages en métaux | Other manufacturing / Autres industries manufacturières | Année et rubrique |
|---|---|---|---|---|---|---|---|---|---|---|---|---|---|---|---|
| **ISIC** | 2–3 | 20–22 | 23 | 24 | 25–26 | 27 | 28 | 29 | 30 | 31–32 | 33 | 34 | 35–38 | 39 | CITI |
| **1952** | | | | | | | | | | | | | | | **1952** |
| *Distribution in percent of:* | | | | | | | | | | | | | | | *Répartition en pourcentage:* |
| Value added | 100.0 | 17.6 | 8.0 | 7.6 | 4.5 | 2.5 | 6.0 | 0.9 | 1.3 | 8.0 | 7.2 | 2.1 | 31.8 | 2.5 | De la valeur ajoutée |
| Number of employees | 100.0 | 15.1 | 9.9 | 10.1 | 5.8 | 3.0 | 5.6 | 0.9 | 1.4 | 5.7 | 6.5 | 0.9 | 32.5 | 2.6 | Du nombre de salariés |
| *Per employee:* | | | | | | | | | | | | | | | *Par salarié:* |
| Value added | 15.8 | 18.3 | 12.7 | 11.8 | 12.4 | 13.1 | 17.1 | 14.8 | 14.3 | 22.3 | 17.3 | 38.7 | 15.4 | 14.6 | Valeur ajoutée |
| Wages and salaries | 9.0 | 8.8 | 7.8 | 7.7 | 8.2 | 8.3 | 10.7 | 9.2 | 8.4 | 10.3 | 9.3 | 10.8 | 9.5 | 8.8 | Traitements et salai… |
| Energy consumed | 6.57 | 8.88 | 4.03 | 0.46 | 1.14 | 4.59 | | [5] | 10.91 | | 34.90 | 3.55 | | 2.44[5] | Energie consommée |
| Electricity consumed | 2.9 | 3.1 | 2.8 | 0.4 | 1.6 | 3.9 | | [5] | 5.5 | | 7.9 | 2.0 | | 2.2[5] | Électricité consommé… |
| Capacity of installed power equipment | 3.46 | 3.90 | 2.17 | 0.54 | 4.35 | 5.75 | 1.41 | 3.70 | 4.05 | 6.20 | 7.17 | 11.92 | 3.08 | 3.03 | Puissance installée |
| Value added per unit of wages and salaries | 1.74 | 2.08 | 1.63 | 1.54 | 1.50 | 1.57 | 1.59 | 1.60 | 1.70 | 2.17 | 1.87 | 3.60 | 1.61 | 1.66 | Valeur ajoutée par unité de traitements et salaires |
| Operatives as a percent of employees | 81.2 | 82.1 | 84.5 | 82.2 | 87.6 | 80.4 | 67.5 | 81.5 | 85.7 | 66.9 | 89.5 | 80.8 | 81.6 | 78.9 | Ouvriers en pourcenta… des salariés |
| Average man-hours per operative | 2.20 | 2.24 | 2.03 | 2.06 | 2.23 | 2.21 | 2.25 | 2.18 | 2.22 | 2.29 | 2.26 | 2.28 | 2.22 | 2.23 | Heures de travail: moyenne par ouvrie… |
| *Per thousand operative man-hours:* | | | | | | | | | | | | | | | *Par millier d'heures de travail d'ouvrier:* |
| Wages and salaries | 3.67 | 3.53 | 3.32 | 3.36 | 3.57 | 3.30 | 4.22 | 3.75 | 3.50 | 3.76 | 3.84 | 4.33 | 3.84 | 3.55 | Traitements et salai… |
| Energy consumed | 3.68 | 4.82 | 2.35 | 0.27 | 0.58 | 2.85 | | [5] | 6.79 | | 17.27 | 1.96 | | 1.38[5] | Energie consommée |
| Electricity consumed | 1.62 | 1.70 | 1.63 | 0.24 | 0.82 | 2.42 | | [5] | 3.45 | | 3.90 | 1.13 | | 1.25[5] | Électricité consommé… |
| Capacity of installed power equipment | 1.94 | 2.12 | 1.26 | 0.32 | 2.23 | 3.22 | 0.93 | 2.08 | 2.12 | 4.06 | 3.55 | 6.46 | 1.70 | 1.72 | Puissance installée |
| **1953** | | | | | | | | | | | | | | | **1953** |
| *Distribution in percent of:* | | | | | | | | | | | | | | | *Répartition en pourcentage:* |
| Value added | 100.0 | 17.7 | 7.9 | 7.5 | 4.7 | 3.0 | 6.3 | 0.9 | 1.3 | 8.6 | 7.1 | 1.9 | 30.6 | 2.5 | De la valeur ajouté… |
| Number of employees | 100.0 | 14.9 | 9.7 | 10.4 | 6.0 | 2.9 | 5.6 | 0.9 | 1.5 | 5.8 | 6.5 | 0.9 | 32.2 | 2.7 | Du nombre de salar… |
| *Per employee:* | | | | | | | | | | | | | | | *Par salarié:* |
| Value added | 16.7 | 19.8 | 13.7 | 11.9 | 13.1 | 17.2 | 18.8 | 15.6 | 14.7 | 25.1 | 18.3 | 33.7 | 15.9 | 15.3 | Valeur ajoutée |
| Wages and salaries | 9.4 | 9.3 | 8.2 | 7.9 | 8.6 | 8.6 | 11.2 | 9.6 | 8.6 | 10.6 | 9.6 | 11.4 | 9.9 | 9.2 | Traitements et salai… |
| Energy consumed | 6.54 | 9.18 | 4.22 | 0.38 | 1.17 | 5.19 | | [5] | 10.86 | | 34.14 | 3.38 | | 2.43[5] | Energie consommée |
| Electricity consumed | 3.0 | 3.2 | 2.9 | 0.4 | 1.7 | 4.4 | | [5] | 5.8 | | 7.9 | 2.1 | | 2.3[5] | Électricité consommé… |
| Value added per unit of wages and salaries | 1.78 | 2.14 | 1.68 | 1.50 | 1.53 | 1.98 | 1.69 | 1.61 | 1.71 | 2.38 | 1.91 | 2.96 | 1.60 | 1.66 | Valeur ajoutée par unité de traitements et salaires |
| Operatives as a percent of employees | 80.3 | 80.4 | 84.6 | 81.5 | 87.8 | 81.1 | 68.3 | 82.1 | 84.8 | 65.3 | 88.2 | 81.5 | 80.1 | 77.2 | Ouvriers en pourcenta… des salariés |
| Average man-hours per operative | 2.18 | 2.23 | 2.06 | 2.05 | 2.22 | 2.18 | 2.26 | 2.17 | 2.23 | 2.26 | 2.25 | 2.18 | 2.19 | 2.20 | Heures de travail: moyenne par ouvrie… |
| *Per thousand operative man-hours:* | | | | | | | | | | | | | | | *Par millier d'heures de travail d'ouvrier:* |
| Wages and salaries | 3.84 | 3.76 | 3.44 | 3.44 | 3.70 | 3.48 | 4.50 | 3.90 | 3.61 | 3.91 | 3.99 | 4.62 | 4.04 | 3.73 | Traitements et salai… |
| Energy consumed | 3.73 | 5.12 | 2.42 | 0.22 | 0.60 | 3.20 | | [5] | 6.96 | | 17.20 | 1.92 | | 1.41[5] | Energie consommée |
| Electricity consumed | 1.72 | 1.82 | 1.67 | 0.26 | 0.87 | 2.68 | | [5] | 3.73 | | 3.98 | 1.21 | | 1.35[5] | Électricité consommé… |
| **1958** | | | | | | | | | | | | | | | **1958** |
| *Distribution in percent of:* | | | | | | | | | | | | | | | *Répartition en pourcentage:* |
| Value added | 100.0 | 17.6 | 5.9 | 5.9 | 4.8 | 3.6 | 6.5 | 0.7 | 1.2 | 8.4 | 6.3 | 1.8 | 34.4 | 2.9 | De la valeur ajouté… |
| Number of engaged | 100.0 | 14.7 | 7.0 | 8.8 | 6.2 | 3.3 | 5.9 | 0.9 | 1.4 | 5.9 | 5.7 | 1.0 | 36.2 | 3.0 | Nombre de personn… occupées |
| Employees as a percent of engaged | 98.8 | 99.4 | 99.1 | 97.9 | 97.0 | 98.1 | 98.4 | 96.4 | 100.0 | 99.5 | 98.4 | 100.0 | 99.1 | 97.9 | Salariés en pourcenta… des personnes occupées |
| *Per employee:* | | | | | | | | | | | | | | | *Par salarié:* |
| Value added | 21.4 | 25.5 | 17.7 | 14.7 | 17.0 | 23.2 | 23.6 | 19.2 | 17.6 | 30.1 | 24.0 | 38.5 | 20.2 | 21.1 | Valeur ajoutée |
| Wages and salaries | 12.1 | 12.1 | 10.3 | 9.7 | 10.9 | 11.7 | 14.4 | 11.4 | 10.8 | 13.8 | 12.2 | 14.1 | 12.6 | 11.9 | Traitements et salai… |
| Energy consumed | 6.54 | 8.51 | 4.81 | 0.51 | 1.24 | 4.63 | | [5] | 12.70 | | 35.81 | 3.59 | | 2.73[5] | Energie consommée |
| Electricity consumed | 3.8 | 4.0 | 3.8 | 0.6 | 2.1 | 4.7 | | [5] | 7.6 | | 10.2 | 2.9 | | 3.1[5] | Électricité consommé… |
| Value added per unit of wages and salaries | 1.77 | 2.12 | 1.72 | 1.52 | 1.55 | 1.98 | 1.63 | 1.68 | 1.63 | 2.17 | 1.97 | 2.74 | 1.60 | 1.77 | Valeur ajoutée par unité de traitements et salaires |
| Operatives as a percent of employees | 78.8 | 79.6 | 82.4 | 80.5 | 86.7 | 79.2 | 67.7 | 81.5 | 82.6 | 63.5 | 85.6 | 78.1 | 79.3 | 75.5 | Ouvriers en pourcenta… des salariés |
| Average man-hours per operative | 2.15 | 2.20 | 2.01 | 2.01 | 2.21 | 2.20 | 2.20 | 2.09 | 2.18 | 2.23 | 2.22 | 2.16 | 2.14 | 2.20 | Heures de travail: moyenne par ouvrie… |
| *Per thousand operative man-hours:* | | | | | | | | | | | | | | | *Par millier d'heures de travail d'ouvriers:* |
| Wages and salaries | 4.95 | 4.82 | 4.40 | 4.22 | 4.66 | 4.69 | 6.01 | 4.70 | 4.58 | 5.07 | 5.09 | 5.92 | 5.17 | 4.73 | Traitements et salai… |
| Energy consumed | 3.86 | 4.86 | 2.90 | 0.31 | 0.64 | 2.92 | | [5] | 8.51 | | 18.85 | 2.12 | | 1.63[5] | Energie consommée |
| Electricity consumed | 2.25 | 2.29 | 2.32 | 0.37 | 1.11 | 2.99 | | [5] | 5.12 | | 5.34 | 1.70 | | 1.88[5] | Électricité consomm… |

[1] Dairies (in ISIC group 202) and slaughter houses (in ISIC group 201) are not included.
[2] The manufacture of wooden furniture (in ISIC major group 26) is not covered for 1939; only establishments with 20 or more employees engaged in such activities are included for 1948.
[3] Lignite mining (in ISIC major group 11) is included.
[4] Stone quarries and clay pits (ISIC major group 14) are included.
[5] The data for Leather and leather products (ISIC major group 29) are included in the data for Other manufacturing (ISIC major group 39).

[1] Non compris les laiteries (dans CITI groupe 202) et les abattoirs (dans CITI groupe 201).
[2] Pour 1939, non compris la fabrication de Meubles en bois (dans CITI classe 26); pour 1948 compris seulement les établissements employant au moins 20 salariés pour cette activité.
[3] Y compris l'extraction du lignite (dans CITI classe 11).
[4] Y compris l'extraction de la pierre à bâtir et de l'argile (CITI classe 14).
[5] Les données relatives aux autres Industries manufacturières (CITI classe 39) comprennent celles relatives au Cuir et ouvrages en cuir (CITI classe 29).

## 6. FUELS AND ELECTRICITY CONSUMED BY MANUFACTURING ESTABLISHMENTS WITH SIX OR MORE OPERATIVES
### CONSOMMATION DE COMBUSTIBLES ET D'ELECTRICITE PAR LES ETABLISSEMENTS MANUFACTURIERS EMPLOYANT SIX OUVRIERS OU PLUS
#### 1939, 1948, 1952, 1953, 1958

### A. Percentage Distribution of Purchased Energy Consumed According to Source
### Distribution en pourcentage de l'énergie achetée et consommée suivant la source

Quantities in thousand metric tons of coal equivalents. — Quantitées en milliers de tonnes métriques d'equivalent houille.

| Year and item of data | Manufacturing [1] / Industries manufacturières [1] | Food, beverages and tobacco [1] / Industries alimentaires, boissons, tabac [1] | Textiles | Clothing, footwear and made-up textiles / Articles d'habillement, chaussures et ouvrages en tissu | Wood products and furniture [2] / Bois et meubles [2] | Paper and paper products / Papier et ouvrages en papier | Printing and publishing / Imprimerie et édition | Leather and leather products except wearing apparel / Cuir et articles en cuir, à l'exclusion des articles d'habillement | Rubber products / Ouvrages en caoutchouc | Chemicals and chemical, petroleum and coal products [3] / Produits chimiques et dérivés du pétrole et du charbon [3] | Non-metallic mineral products [4] / Produits minéraux non métalliques [4] | Basic metals / Métallurgie de base | Metal products / Ouvrages en métaux | Other manufacturing / Autres industries manufacturières | Année et rubrique |
|---|---|---|---|---|---|---|---|---|---|---|---|---|---|---|---|
| ISIC | 2–3 | 20–22 | 23 | 24 | 25–26 | 27 | 28 | 29 | 30 | 31–32 | 33 | 34 | 35–38 | 39 | CITI |
| **1939** | | | | | | | | | | | | | | | **1939** |
| Total energy consumed: | | | | | | | | | | | | | | | Energie totale consommée: |
| Quantity.......... | 1 455.7 | 402.6 | 87.4 | 9.6 | 13.2 | 85.5 | 8.7 | 11.6 | 170.1 | | 475.8 | 184.8 | | 6.4 | Quantité |
| Percent of total in specified industry... | 100.0 | 27.6 | 6.0 | 0.7 | 0.9 | 5.9 | 0.5 | 0.8 | 11.7 | | 32.7 | 12.7 | | 0.5 | Pourcentage du total par industrie indiquée |
| Percent consumed as: | | | | | | | | | | | | | | | Pourcentage consommé comme: |
| Coal.............. | 80.0 | 84.9 | 85.6 | 45.5 | 30.5 | 96.7 | 21.0 | 89.4 | 86.4 | | 87.0 | 43.4 | | 47.0 | Charbon |
| Coke.............. | 9.8 | 8.5 | 4.4 | 34.7 | 4.2 | 1.8 | 54.1 | 7.0 | 3.1 | | 7.4 | 27.6 | | 40.3 | Coke |
| Refined oil fuels...... | 6.5 | 3.6 | 6.8 | 6.4 | 14.1 | 0.8 | 3.9 | 0.8 | 7.3 | | 3.2 | 22.6 | | 4.3 | Pétrole raffiné |
| Gas.............. | 0.6 | 0.5 | 0.1 | 4.8 | 0.2 | 0.2 | 8.4 | 0.1 | 0.2 | | 0.4 | 1.9 | | 4.2 | Gaz |
| Electricity.......... | 1.8 | 1.3 | 2.6 | 7.9 | 5.9 | 0.5 | 12.2 | 2.6 | 2.6 | | 0.6 | 4.0 | | 4.0 | Electricité |
| Firewood and peat... | 1.3 | 1.2 | 0.5 | 0.7 | 45.1 | — | 0.4 | 0.1 | 0.4 | | 1.4 | 0.5 | | 0.2 | Bois de chauffage et tourbe |
| **1948** | | | | | | | | | | | | | | | **1948** |
| Total energy consumed: | | | | | | | | | | | | | | | Energie totale consommée: |
| Quantity.......... | 1 746.9 | 421.9 | 114.6 | 13.6 | 16.4 | 100.2 | 11.8 | 14.1 | 17.2 | 176.0 | 564.8 | 69.3 | 215.0 | 12.0 | Quantité |
| Percent of total in specified industry... | 100.0 | 24.1 | 6.6 | 0.7 | 1.0 | 5.7 | 0.7 | 0.8 | 1.0 | 10.1 | 32.3 | 4.0 | 12.3 | 0.7 | Pourcentage du total par industrie indiquée |
| Percent consumed as: | | | | | | | | | | | | | | | Pourcentage consommé comme: |
| Coal.............. | 41.8 | 53.0 | 14.7 | 35.2 | 18.3 | 34.9 | 27.0 | 30.0 | 11.6 | 39.0 | 53.8 | 18.5 | 22.5 | 27.5 | Charbon |
| Lignite........... | 14.7 | 20.7 | 21.8 | 16.7 | 21.6 | 32.0 | 17.8 | 20.6 | 7.4 | 11.4 | 11.0 | 0.2 | 8.6 | 7.4 | Lignite |
| Coke.............. | 9.5 | 3.6 | 2.6 | 12.3 | 5.2 | 2.4 | 13.9 | 3.6 | 2.4 | 3.3 | 9.1 | 27.7 | 28.6 | 6.2 | Coke |
| Refined oil fuels...... | 22.3 | 11.8 | 53.4 | 9.7 | 11.8 | 18.3 | 3.8 | 33.3 | 66.5 | 35.9 | 16.9 | 47.5 | 21.4 | 35.2 | Pétrole raffiné |
| Gas.............. | 1.7 | 2.0 | 0.2 | 7.8 | 0.4 | 0.2 | 7.2 | 0.4 | 1.4 | 0.8 | 1.0 | 1.0 | 4.7 | 5.2 | Gaz |
| Electricity.......... | 2.7 | 1.8 | 4.4 | 6.9 | 10.7 | 0.9 | 12.9 | 3.3 | 10.1 | 4.1 | 0.9 | 3.3 | 5.1 | 10.3 | Electricité |
| Firewood and peat... | 7.3 | 7.1 | 2.9 | 11.4 | 32.0 | 11.3 | 17.4 | 8.8 | 0.6 | 5.5 | 7.3 | 1.8 | 9.1 | 8.2 | Bois de chauffage et tourbe |
| **1952** | | | | | | | | | | | | | | | **1952** |
| Total energy consumed: | | | | | | | | | | | | | | | Energie totale consommée: |
| Quantity.......... | 1 927.5 | 395.9 | 117.0 | 13.6 | 19.4 | 114.7 | [5] | | 226.9 | | 666.7 | 348.2 | | 25.1 [5] | Quantité |
| Percent of total in specified industry... | 100.0 | 20.5 | 6.1 | 0.7 | 1.0 | 5.9 | [5] | | 11.8 | | 34.6 | 18.0 | | 1.4 [5] | Pourcentage du total par industrie indiquée |
| Percent consumed as: | | | | | | | | | | | | | | | Pourcentage consommé comme: |
| Coal.............. | 45.3 | 47.6 | 13.2 | 22.0 | 26.5 | 43.2 | [5] | | 36.2 | | 64.5 | 26.5 | | 28.2 [5] | Charbon |
| Lignite........... | 6.2 | 7.1 | 7.4 | 3.4 | 14.7 | 17.5 | [5] | | 5.7 | | 6.0 | 1.7 | | 4.5 [5] | Lignite |
| Coke.............. | 7.8 | 5.2 | 2.4 | 29.6 | 8.3 | 3.2 | [5] | | 3.2 | | 6.5 | 18.3 | | 12.3 [5] | Coke |
| Refined oil fuels...... | 33.7 | 33.9 | 69.5 | 23.4 | 20.9 | 28.1 | [5] | | 47.0 | | 19.2 | 42.9 | | 41.5 [5] | Pétrole raffiné |
| Gas.............. | 1.8 | 2.2 | 0.3 | 8.9 | 0.5 | 1.1 | [5] | | 0.6 | | 1.1 | 3.8 | | 2.6 [5] | Gaz |
| Electricity.......... | 3.7 | 2.8 | 6.8 | 11.0 | 13.3 | 3.1 | [5] | | 5.1 | | 1.4 | 6.2 | | 10.1 [5] | Electricité |
| Firewood and peat... | 1.5 | 1.2 | 0.4 | 1.7 | 15.8 | 3.8 | [5] | | 2.2 | | 1.3 | 0.6 | | 0.8 [5] | Bois de chauffage et tourbe |
| **1953** | | | | | | | | | | | | | | | **1953** |
| Total energy consumed: | | | | | | | | | | | | | | | Energie totale consommée: |
| Quantity.......... | 1 969.0 | 412.0 | 123.2 | 11.8 | 21.0 | 133.5 | [5] | | 237.9 | | 665.8 | 337.8 | | 26.0 [5] | Quantité |
| Percent of total in specified industry... | 100.0 | 20.9 | 6.2 | 0.6 | 1.1 | 6.8 | [5] | | 12.1 | | 33.8 | 17.1 | | 1.4 [5] | Pourcentage du total par industrie indiquée |
| Percent consumed as: | | | | | | | | | | | | | | | Pourcentage consommé comme: |
| Coal.............. | 48.0 | 54.3 | 20.7 | 17.5 | 26.2 | 77.3 | [5] | | 37.2 | | 61.4 | 24.6 | | 21.2 [5] | Charbon |
| Lignite........... | 3.0 | 2.0 | 3.4 | 1.0 | 5.8 | 0.7 | [5] | | 3.1 | | 5.5 | 0.1 | | 0.6 [5] | Lignite |
| Coke.............. | 7.5 | 5.3 | 1.6 | 24.9 | 7.2 | 2.7 | [5] | | 3.0 | | 6.5 | 18.0 | | 11.7 [5] | Coke |
| Refined oil fuels...... | 34.8 | 33.2 | 67.3 | 31.8 | 20.5 | 14.7 | [5] | | 48.7 | | 22.8 | 46.3 | | 52.8 [5] | Pétrole raffiné |
| Gas.............. | 1.7 | 2.0 | 0.2 | 9.7 | 2.1 | 1.0 | [5] | | 0.5 | | 1.2 | 3.8 | | 2.4 [5] | Gaz |
| Electricity.......... | 3.9 | 2.9 | 6.5 | 14.3 | 13.3 | 3.3 | [5] | | 5.3 | | 1.5 | 6.7 | | 10.7 | Electricité |
| Firewood and peat... | 1.1 | 0.3 | 0.3 | 0.8 | 24.9 | 0.3 | [5] | | 2.2 | | 1.1 | 0.5 | | 0.6 [5] | Bois de chauffage et tourbe |
| **1958** | | | | | | | | | | | | | | | **1958** |
| Total energy consumed: | | | | | | | | | | | | | | | Energie totale consommée: |
| Quantity.......... | 2 097.2 | 404.3 | 109.1 | 14.1 | 24.1 | 136.5 | [5] | | 302.2 | | 644.6 | 429.3 | | 33.0 [5] | Quantité |
| Percent of total in specified industry... | 100.0 | 19.2 | 5.2 | 0.7 | 1.2 | 6.5 | [5] | | 14.4 | | 30.7 | 20.5 | | 1.6 [5] | Pourcentage du total par industrie indiquée |
| Percent consumed as: | | | | | | | | | | | | | | | Pourcentage consommé comme: |
| Coal.............. | 25.2 | 25.3 | 13.8 | 6.0 | 20.2 | 27.6 | [5] | | 7.4 | | 48.5 | 6.7 | | 12.6 [5] | Charbon |
| Lignite........... | 3.3 | 1.0 | 4.5 | 1.3 | 3.4 | 0.1 | [5] | | 3.4 | | 7.1 | 0.5 | | 0.1 [5] | Lignite |
| Coke.............. | 6.6 | 5.2 | 2.4 | 12.8 | 5.1 | 1.8 | [5] | | 3.1 | | 5.1 | 15.3 | | 5.0 [5] | Coke |
| Refined oil fuels...... | 57.4 | 62.2 | 70.5 | 60.0 | 35.5 | 64.1 | [5] | | 79.6 | | 35.4 | 65.1 | | 66.5 [5] | Pétrole raffiné |
| Gas.............. | 1.6 | 2.2 | 0.2 | 4.8 | 2.0 | 0.6 | [5] | | 0.5 | | 1.4 | 2.9 | | 2.3 [5] | Gaz |
| Electricity.......... | 5.4 | 3.9 | 8.3 | 14.8 | 18.0 | 5.6 | [5] | | 5.5 | | 2.0 | 9.3 | | 13.3 [5] | Electricité |
| Firewood and peat.... | 0.5 | 0.2 | 0.3 | 0.3 | 15.8 | 0.2 | [5] | | 0.5 | | 0.5 | 0.2 | | 0.2 [5] | Bois de chauffage et tourbe |

For footnotes see end of table.     Pour les notes, voir au bas du tableau.

# DENMARK

## B.  Quantity of Various Purchased Fuels and Electricity Consumed
### Quantités consommées des différents combustibles achetés et d'électricité

Coal, coke, refined oil fuels and peat in thousand metric tons; manufactured gas in million cubic meters; electricity in million KWH; wood in thousand cubic metres piled.

Charbon, coke, pétrole raffiné et tourbe en milliers de tonnes métriques; gaz manufacturé en millions de mètres cubes; électricité en millions de kWh; bois en milliers de mètres cubes empilés.

| Year and source of energy | Manufacturing [1] (2–3) | Food, beverages and tobacco [1] (20–22) | Textiles (23) | Clothing, footwear and made-up textiles (24) | Wood products and furniture [2] (25–26) | Paper and paper products (27) | Printing and publishing (28) | Leather and leather products except wearing apparel (29) | Rubber products (30) | Chemicals and chemical, petroleum and coal products [3] (31–32) | Non-metallic mineral products [4] (33) | Basic metals (34) | Metal products (35–38) | Other manufacturing (39) |
|---|---|---|---|---|---|---|---|---|---|---|---|---|---|---|
| **1939** | | | | | | | | | | | | | | |
| Coal and briquettes | 1 165.0 | 342.0 | 74.9 | 4.4 | 4.0 | 82.8 | 1.8 | 10.4 | | 147.1 | 414.3 | | 80.3 | 3.0 |
| Coke | 158.7 | 38.2 | 4.3 | 3.7 | 0.6 | 1.6 | 5.2 | 0.9 | | 5.9 | 38.8 | | 56.6 | 2.9 |
| Refined oil fuels | 62.7 | 9.6 | 4.0 | 0.4 | 1.2 | 0.4 | 0.2 | 0.1 | | 8.4 | 10.4 | | 27.8 | 0.2 |
| Manufactured gas | 15.3 | 3.3 | 0.1 | 0.8 | — | 0.3 | 1.2 | — | | 0.5 | 2.7 | | 6.0 | 0.4 |
| Electricity — Purchased | 199.5 | 39.7 | 17.6 | 6.1 | 6.1 | 3.2 | 8.4 | 2.4 | | 34.4 | 21.7 | | 57.9 | 2.0 |
| Electricity — Produced for own use | 250.1 | 46.6 | 17.1 | 1.1 | 2.9 | 47.8 | — | 0.8 | | 42.0 | 58.1 | | 33.6 | 0.1 |
| Wood | 84.4 | 24.2 | 0.2 | 0.3 | 30.8 | — | 0.2 | — | | 2.8 | 21.2 | | 4.7 | — |
| Peat | 6.6 | 0.6 | 0.7 | — | — | — | — | — | | — | 5.1 | | 0.2 | — |
| **1948** | | | | | | | | | | | | | | |
| Coal and briquettes | 730.3 | 223.8 | 16.9 | 4.8 | 3.0 | 35.0 | 3.2 | 4.2 | 2.0 | 68.8 | 303.9 | 12.8 | 48.6 | 3.3 |
| Lignite | 783.0 | 265.3 | 75.8 | 6.9 | 10.7 | 96.9 | 6.4 | 8.8 | 3.9 | 60.8 | 188.5 | 0.5 | 55.8 | 2.7 |
| Coke | 182.5 | 16.7 | 3.2 | 1.8 | 1.0 | 2.8 | 1.8 | 0.6 | 0.4 | 6.4 | 57.3 | 21.3 | 68.4 | 0.8 |
| Refined oil fuels | 260.9 | 33.3 | 40.9 | 0.9 | 1.3 | 12.2 | 0.3 | 3.1 | 7.6 | 42.2 | 63.7 | 22.0 | 30.6 | 2.8 |
| Manufactured gas | 48.2 | 13.7 | 0.3 | 1.8 | 0.1 | 0.1 | 1.4 | 0.1 | 0.4 | 2.3 | 8.9 | 1.1 | 16.8 | 1.0 |
| Electricity — Purchased | 378.6 | 62.0 | 40.5 | 7.6 | 14.0 | 6.8 | 12.2 | 3.7 | 13.9 | 57.0 | 44.7 | 18.3 | 88.1 | 9.8 |
| Electricity — Produced for own use | 218.2 | 48.4 | 22.4 | 1.0 | 4.0 | 47.1 | — | 1.0 | — | 14.2 | 53.0 | 3.9 | 21.2 | 2.0 |
| Wood | 58.3 | 9.6 | 2.3 | 1.0 | 8.3 | 0.6 | 1.5 | 0.4 | 0.2 | 3.2 | 22.6 | — | 8.1 | 0.5 |
| Peat | 230.4 | 55.6 | 5.6 | 2.7 | 7.3 | 22.4 | 3.5 | 2.3 | 0.1 | 18.1 | 72.7 | 2.4 | 35.9 | 1.8 |
| **1952** | | | | | | | | | | | | | | |
| Coal and briquettes | 874.0 | 188.8 | 15.6 | 3.0 | 5.1 | 49.6 | | [5] | | 82.2 | 430.2 | | 92.4 | 7.1 [5] |
| Lignite | 363.4 | 84.3 | 26.1 | 1.4 | 8.7 | 60.7 | | [5] | | 39.4 | 120.8 | | 18.6 | 3.4 [5] |
| Coke | 166.6 | 22.8 | 3.1 | 4.5 | 1.8 | 4.0 | | [5] | | 8.1 | 48.5 | | 70.4 | 3.4 [5] |
| Refined oil fuels | 433.2 | 89.5 | 54.2 | 2.1 | 2.7 | 21.5 | | [5] | | 71.1 | 85.4 | | 99.8 | 6.9 [5] |
| Manufactured gas | 56.5 | 14.8 | 0.5 | 2.0 | 0.2 | 2.0 | | [5] | | 2.2 | 11.5 | | 22.2 | 1.1 [5] |
| Electricity — Purchased | 571.8 | 87.5 | 64.3 | 11.9 | 20.6 | 28.3 | | [5] | | 92.9 | 75.9 | | 170.2 | 20.2 [5] |
| Electricity — Produced for own use | 275.8 | 52.6 | 16.9 | — | 6.7 | 69.1 | | [5] | | 22.2 | 74.4 | | 31.3 | 2.6 [5] |
| Wood | 28.2 | 4.8 | 1.3 | 0.6 | 6.1 | 0.7 | | [5] | | 2.0 | 6.9 | | 5.1 | 0.7 [5] |
| Peat | 45.4 | 7.4 | 0.2 | 0.2 | 3.7 | 8.4 | | [5] | | 8.9 | 14.3 | | 2.2 | 0.1 [5] |
| **1953** | | | | | | | | | | | | | | |
| Coal and briquettes | 946.7 | 223.8 | 25.5 | 2.1 | 5.5 | 103.3 | | [5] | | 88.7 | 409.1 | | 83.2 | 5.5 [5] |
| Lignite | 178.9 | 25.6 | 12.8 | 0.4 | 3.7 | 2.6 | | [5] | | 22.1 | 110.2 | | 1.0 | 0.5 [5] |
| Coke | 163.0 | 24.1 | 2.1 | 3.3 | 1.7 | 4.1 | | [5] | | 7.9 | 48.8 | | 67.6 | 3.4 [5] |
| Refined oil fuels | 456.7 | 91.1 | 55.3 | 2.5 | 2.9 | 13.0 | | [5] | | 77.3 | 101.1 | | 104.3 | 9.2 [5] |
| Manufactured gas | 57.0 | 14.4 | 0.5 | 1.9 | 0.7 | 2.3 | | [5] | | 2.1 | 12.8 | | 21.3 | 1.0 [5] |
| Electricity — Purchased | 614.8 | 94.7 | 64.0 | 13.6 | 22.3 | 35.7 | | [5] | | 100.0 | 80.2 | | 182.0 | 22.3 [5] |
| Electricity — Produced for own use | 291.8 | 51.6 | 21.2 | — | 8.2 | 76.3 | | [5] | | 27.6 | 73.8 | | 30.5 | 2.6 [5] |
| Wood | 23.6 | 3.5 | 0.6 | 0.4 | 8.5 | 0.9 | | [5] | | 0.9 | 3.6 | | 4.6 | 0.6 [5] |
| Peat | 31.9 | 0.6 | 0.3 | — | 7.2 | 0.2 | | [5] | | 9.9 | 12.7 | | 1.0 | — [5] |
| **1958** | | | | | | | | | | | | | | |
| Coal and briquettes | 529.4 | 102.4 | 15.1 | 0.8 | 4.9 | 37.7 | | [5] | | 22.4 | 312.9 | | 29.0 | 4.2 [5] |
| Lignite | 207.4 | 12.6 | 14.8 | 0.5 | 2.5 | 0.6 | | [5] | | 31.3 | 138.2 | | 6.8 | 0.1 [5] |
| Coke | 154.2 | 23.3 | 3.0 | 2.0 | 1.4 | 2.6 | | [5] | | 10.4 | 36.5 | | 73.1 | 1.9 [5] |
| Refined oil fuels | 802.3 | 167.8 | 51.2 | 5.6 | 5.7 | 58.4 | | [5] | | 160.5 | 152.2 | | 186.3 | 14.6 [5] |
| Manufactured gas | 56.7 | 14.7 | 0.4 | 1.1 | 0.8 | 1.3 | | [5] | | 2.2 | 14.8 | | 20.2 | 1.2 [5] |
| Electricity — Purchased | 906.3 | 124.7 | 72.8 | 16.6 | 34.7 | 61.8 | | [5] | | 133.0 | 107.4 | | 320.1 | 35.2 [5] |
| Electricity — Produced for own use | 316.0 | 65.6 | 14.3 | — | 6.7 | 78.0 | | [5] | | 49.0 | 75.4 | | 24.2 | 2.8 [5] |
| Wood | 28.8 | 3.1 | 1.2 | 0.1 | 8.1 | 0.6 | | [5] | | 3.7 | 9.0 | | 2.7 | 0.3 [5] |
| Peat | 8.5 | 0.2 | — | — | 4.5 | 0.1 | | [5] | | 1.5 | 1.9 | | 0.3 | — [5] |

French column headings / source of energy: Année et source d'énergie — Industries manufacturières [1]; Industries alimentaires, boissons, tabac [1]; Textiles; Articles d'habillement, chaussures et ouvrages en tissu; Bois et meubles [2]; Papier et ouvrages en papier; Imprimerie et édition; Cuir et articles en cuir, à l'exclusion des articles d'habillement; Ouvrages en caoutchouc; Produits chimiques et dérivés du pétrole et du charbon [3]; Produits minéraux non métalliques [4]; Métallurgie de base; Ouvrages en métaux; Autres industries manufacturières. Sources: Charbon et briquettes; Lignite; Coke; Pétrole raffiné; Gaz manufacturé; Électricité Achetée / Produite pour l'autoconsommation; Bois; Tourbe.

[1] Dairies (in ISIC group 202) and slaughter houses (in ISIC group 201) are not included.
[2] The manufacture of wooden furniture (in ISIC major group 26) is not covered for 1939; only establishments with 20 or more employees engaged in such activities are included for 1948.
[3] Lignite mining (in ISIC major group 11) is included.
[4] Stone quarries and clay pits (ISIC major group 14) are included.
[5] The data for Leather and leather products (ISIC major group 29) are included in the data for Other manufacturing (ISIC major group 39).

[1] Non compris les laiteries (dans CITI groupe 202) et les abattoirs (dans CITI groupe 201).
[2] Pour 1939, non compris la fabrication de Meubles en bois (dans CITI classe 26); pour 1948, compris seulement les établissements employant au moins 20 salariés pour cette activité.
[3] Y compris l'extraction du lignite (dans CITI classe 11).
[4] Y compris l'extraction de la pierre à bâtir et de l'argile (CITI classe 14).
[5] Les données relatives aux Autres industries manufacturières (CITI classe 39) comprennent celles relatives au Cuir et ouvrages en cuir (CITI classe 29).

# DOMINICAN REPUBLIC — REPUBLIQUE DOMINICAINE

## Gross National Product

Estimates of the expenditure on the gross national product are presented in Table 1. The data are derived from information provided by the Sección de Publicaciones y Estadísticas Bancarias, Banco Central de la República Dominicana, Santo Domingo, in response to the United Nations national accounts questionnaire. A short official description of the methods of estimation used is given in *Producto ó Gasto Nacional de la República,* May 1952, issued by the same office.

## Characteristics and Structure of Industrial Activity

The data shown in Tables 2 and 3 are derived from the results of quarterly inquiries of all establishments, regardless of size, registered in the Industrial Directory. The results for 1948, 1953 and 1958 have been published by the Dirección General de Estadística in *Anuario Estadístico 1948-49, Estadística Industrial 1953* and *Estadística Industrial 1958,* respectively. In the case of manufacturing and electricity industries, establishments in rural areas are not included in the figures shown. These establishments are engaged principally in the manufacture of certain food products, lime, hats, baskets and brooms.

As far as is known the definitions of the items of data correspond to the International Standards in Basic Industrial Statistics. The data in Table 3 relate to the consumption, for all purposes, of fuels and electricity. As a consequence in the cases where, for example, an establishment produces its own electricity using fuel oil, double counting exists. The data therefore cannot be added together to compute energy consumption figures.

## Produit intérieur brut

Les estimations des dépenses imputées au produit intérieur brut sont reproduites au tableau 1. Ces données sont tirées des renseignements fournis par la Sección de Publicaciones y Estadísticas Bancarias, Banco Central de la República Dominicana, Santo Domingo, en réponse au questionnaire de l'ONU sur la comptabilité nationale. Une brève description officielle des méthodes d'estimation adoptées est donnée dans *Producto ó Gasto Nacional de la República,* mai 1952, publié par le même service.

## Caractéristiques et structure de l'activité industrielle

Les chiffres des tableaux 2 et 3 sont tirés des résultats d'enquêtes trimestrielles auprès de tous les établissements, quelle que soit leur dimension, qui sont inscrits au Registre des industries. Les résultats de 1948, 1953 et 1958 ont été publiés par la Dirección General de Estadística dans *Anuario Estadístico 1948-49, Estadística Industrial 1953* et *Estadística Industrial 1958,* respectivement. Dans le cas des industries manufacturières et des industries de l'électricité, les établissements des régions rurales ne sont pas compris dans les chiffres présentés. Ces établissements produisent surtout certaines denrées alimentaires, de la chaux, des chapeaux, des paniers et des balais.

Autant qu'on sache, les définitions des rubriques correspondent aux normes internationales relatives aux statistiques industrielles de base. Les données du tableau 3 concernent la consommation, à quelque fin que ce soit, des combustibles et de l'électricité. Des doubles emplois existent du fait que, dans certains établissements, par exemple, l'électricité autoconsommée est produite à partir du fuel-oil. On ne peut donc pas obtenir les chiffres de la consommation d'énergie en faisant la somme des données.

## 1. EXPENDITURE ON THE GROSS NATIONAL PRODUCT AT MARKET PRICES
## DEPENSES RELATIVES AU PRODUIT NATIONAL BRUT AUX PRIX DU MARCHE

Million pesos                                                                                                           Millions de pesos

| Item of data and year<br>Rubrique et année | Total | Consumption<br>Consommation | | Gross Domestic Capital Formation<br>Formation brute de capital intérieur | | Net exports of goods and services [1]<br>Exportations nettes de biens et de services [1] | |
|---|---|---|---|---|---|---|---|
| | | Total | Government<br>Etat | Total | Fixed<br>Fixe | Exports<br>less imports<br>Exportations<br>moins<br>importations | Exports<br>Exportations |
| a. At Current Prices — Aux prix courants | | | | | | | |
| **Absolute figures — Chiffres absolus** | | | | | | | |
| 1951.................................... | 380.9 | 315.4 | 40.8 | 46.4 | ... | 19.1 | ... |
| 1952.................................... | 424.8 | 345.9 | 50.3 | 83.4 | ... | −4.5 | ... |
| 1953.................................... | 437.4 | 368.7 | 49.7 | 67.5 | ... | 1.2 | ... |
| 1954.................................... | 483.6 | 382.4 | 50.9 | 79.8 | ... | 21.4 | ... |
| 1955.................................... | 518.3 | 415.0 | 63.3 | 112.1 | ... | −8.8 | ... |
| 1956.................................... | 566.8 | 462.6 | 81.6 | 108.7 | ... | −4.5 | ... |
| 1957.................................... | 631.4 | 499.7 | 96.6 | 111.6 | ... | 20.1 | ... |
| 1958.................................... | 644.6 | 539.3 | 108.8 | 119.0 | ... | −13.7 | ... |
| 1959.................................... | 659.8 | 561.4 | 113.5 | 104.5 | ... | −6.1 | ... |
| **Percentage distribution of average annual expenditure — Distribution en pourcentage des dépenses annuelles moyennes** | | | | | | | |
| 1951−1959......................... | 100.0 | 81.9 | 13.8 | 17.6 | ... | 0.5 | ... |
| 1951.................................... | 100.0 | 82.8 | 10.7 | 12.2 | ... | 5.0 | ... |
| 1953.................................... | 100.0 | 84.3 | 11.4 | 15.4 | ... | 0.3 | ... |
| 1954.................................... | 100.0 | 79.1 | 10.5 | 16.5 | ... | 4.4 | ... |
| 1959.................................... | 100.0 | 85.1 | 17.2 | 15.8 | ... | −0.9 | ... |

[1] Includes net factor income from the rest of the world.      [1] Y compris le revenu net des facteurs reçu de l'étranger.

## 2. CHARACTERISTICS OF ALL INDUSTRIAL ESTABLISHMENTS [1]
## CARACTERISTIQUES DE TOUS LES ETABLISSEMENTS INDUSTRIELS [1]
### 1948, 1953, 1958

Number of establishments in units; gross value of sales and wages and salaries in million pesos; number of employees and operatives in thousands; electricity consumed in thousand KWH; wages and salaries per employee in thousand pesos; electricity consumed per employee in KWH.

Nombre d'établissements en unités; valeur brute des ventes et traitements et salaires en millions de pesos; nombre de salariés et d'ouvriers en milliers; électricité consommée en milliers de kWh; traitements et salaires par salarié en milliers de pesos; électricité consommée par salarié en kWh.

### A. Selected Divisions of Industrial Activity — Quelques branches de l'activité industrielle

| Year and item of data | Total | Mining Industries ex-tractives | Manu-facturing Industries manu-facturières | Electricity Electricité | Année et rubrique | Year and item of data | Total | Mining Industries ex-tractives | Manu-facturing Industries manu-facturières | Electricity Electricité | Année et rubrique |
|---|---|---|---|---|---|---|---|---|---|---|---|
| ISIC | 1-3, 511 | 1 | 2-3 | 511 | CITI | ISIC | 1-3, 511 | 1 | 2-3 | 511 | CITI |
| | **a. Absolute Figures — Chiffres absolus** | | | | | | **b. Structure** | | | | |
| **1948** | | | | | **1948** | **1948** | | | | | **1948** |
| Number of establishments | 2 998 | 3 | 2 968 | 27 | Nombre d'établissements | Distribution in percent of number of employees | 100.0 | 0.4 | 98.7 | 0.9 | Distribution en pourcentage du nombre de salariés |
| Gross value of sales | 114.1 | 0.9 | 111.3 | 1.9 | Valeur brute des ventes | Wages and salaries per employee | 0.4 | 0.5 | 0.4 | 1.0 | Traitements et salaires par salarié |
| Employees: Number (Average of quarters) | 46.6 | 0.2 | 46.0 | 0.4 | Salariés: Nombre (moyenne trimestrielle) | Operatives as a percent of employees | 91.6 | 100.0 | 91.7 | 75.0 | Ouvriers en pourcentage des salariés |
| Wages and salaries | 21.3 | 0.1 | 20.8 | 0.4 | Traitements et salaires | | | | | | |
| Number of operatives (Average of quarters) | 42.7 | 0.2 | 42.2 | 0.3 | Nombre d'ouvriers (moyenne trimestrielle) | | | | | | |
| **1953** | | | | | **1953** | **1953** | | | | | **1953** |
| Number of establishments | 3 494 | 4 | 3 435 | 55 | Nombre d'établissements | Distribution in percent of number of employees | 100.0 | 1.7 | 96.9 | 1.4 | Distribution en pourcentage du nombre de salariés |
| Gross value of sales | 154.3 | 1.2 | 149.4 | 3.7 | Valeur brute des ventes | Per employee: Wages and salaries | 0.4 | 0.1 | 0.4 | 1.1 | Par salarié: Traitements et salaires |
| Employees: Number (Average of quarters) | 64.0 | 1.1 | 62.0 | 0.9 | Salariés: Nombre (moyenne trimestrielle) | Electricity consumed | ... | ... | 1 009 | ... | Electricité consommée |
| Wages and salaries | 29.2 | 0.1 | 28.1 | 1.0 | Traitements et salaires | Operatives as a percent of employees | 93.8 | 90.9 | 94.0 | 77.8 | Ouvriers en pourcentage des salariés |
| Number of operatives (Average of quarters) | 60.0 | 1.0 | 58.3 | 0.7 | Nombre d'ouvriers (moyenne trimestrielle) | | | | | | |
| Electricity consumed | ... | ... | 62 537 | ... | Electricité consommée | | | | | | |
| **1958** | | | | | **1958** | **1958** | | | | | **1958** |
| Number of establishments | 2 860 | 4 | 2 811 | 45 | Nombre d'établissements | Distribution in percent of number of employees | 100.0 | 1.0 | 97.5 | 1.5 | Distribution en pourcentage du nombre de salariés |
| Gross value of sales | 219.1 | 2.6 | 208.8 | 7.7 | Valeur brute des ventes | Per employee: Wages and salaries | 0.4 | 0.9 | 0.4 | 1.2 | Par salarié: Traitements et salaires |
| Employees: Number (Average of quarters) | 84.9 | 0.8 | 82.8 | 1.3 | Salariés: Nombre (moyenne trimestrielle) | Electricity consumed | ... | 342 | 1 788 | ... | Electricité consommée |
| Wages and salaries | 38.0 | 0.7 | 35.7 | 1.6 | Traitements et salaires | Operatives as a percent of employees | 93.4 | 87.5 | 93.7 | 76.9 | Ouvriers en pourcentage des salariés |
| Number of operatives (Average of quarters) | 79.3 | 0.7 | 77.6 | 1.0 | Nombre d'ouvriers (moyenne trimestrielle) | | | | | | |
| Electricity consumed | ... | 274 | 148 041 | ... | Electricité consommée | | | | | | |

For footnotes see end of table.

Pour les notes, voir au bas du tableau.

# DOMINICAN REPUBLIC

## B.  The Major Groups of Manufacturing — Les classes de la branche Industries manufacturières

| Year and item of data | Manufacturing  Industries manufacturières | Food, beverages and tobacco  Industries alimentaires, boissons, tabac | Textiles | Clothing, footwear and made-up textiles  Articles d'habillement, chaussures et ouvrages en tissu | Wood products and furniture  Bois et meubles | Paper and paper products  Papier et ouvrages en papier | Printing and publishing  Imprimerie et édition | Leather and leather products except wearing apparel  Cuir et articles en cuir, à l'exclusion des articles d'habillement | Rubber products  Ouvrages en caoutchouc | Chemicals and chemical, petroleum and coal products  Produits chimiques et dérivés du pétrole et du charbon | Nonmetallic mineral products  Produits minéraux non métalliques | Basic metals  Métallurgie de base | Metal products  Ouvrages en métaux | Other manufacturing  Autres industries manufacturières | Année et rubrique |
|---|---|---|---|---|---|---|---|---|---|---|---|---|---|---|---|
| ISIC | 2–3 | 20–22 | 23 | 24 | 25–26 | 27 | 28 | 29 | 30 | 31–32 | 33 | 34 | 35–38 | 39 | CITI |
| *a. Absolute Figures — Chiffres absolus* | | | | | | | | | | | | | | | |
| **1948** | | | | | | | | | | | | | | | **1948** |
| Number of establishments | 2 968 | 1 098 | 6 | 705 | 585 | 6 | 70 | 113 | 30 | 88 | 61 | 7 | 170 | 29 | Nombre d'établissements |
| Gross value of sales | 111.3 | 91.7 | 0.5 | 4.8 | 3.6 | 0.3 | 1.5 | 1.2 | 0.1 | 4.1 | 2.3 | 0.2 | 0.9 | 0.1 | Valeur brute des ventes |
| Employees: | | | | | | | | | | | | | | | Salariés: |
| Number (Average of the quarters) | 46.0 | 37.8 | 0.2 | 2.1 | 2.7 | 0.1 | 0.6 | 0.3 | 0.1 | 0.5 | 0.7 | 0.2 | 0.7 | — | Nombre (moyenne trimestrielle) |
| Wages and salaries | 20.8 | 17.0 | 0.1 | 0.8 | 1.0 | — | 0.5 | 0.2 | — | 0.2 | 0.5 | 0.1 | 0.4 | — | Traitements et salaires |
| Number of operatives (Average of the quarters) | 42.2 | 34.7 | 0.2 | 2.0 | 2.6 | 0.1 | 0.4 | 0.3 | — | 0.4 | 0.6 | 0.2 | 0.7 | — | Nombre d'ouvriers (moyenne trimestrielle) |
| **1953** | | | | | | | | | | | | | | | **1953** |
| Number of establishments | 3 435 | 1 219 | 10 | 791 | 666 | 14 | 81 | 83 | 61 | 107 | 84 | 6 | 273 | 40 | Nombre d'établissements |
| Gross value of sales | 149.4 | 121.6 | 1.6 | 5.9 | 4.5 | 0.6 | 2.0 | 1.1 | 0.4 | 4.6 | 5.4 | 0.1 | 1.5 | 0.1 | Valeur brute des ventes |
| Employees: | | | | | | | | | | | | | | | Salariés: |
| Number (Average of the quarters) | 62.0 | 53.1 | 0.7 | 1.9 | 2.5 | 0.1 | 0.6 | 0.2 | 0.1 | 0.6 | 1.2 | 0.1 | 0.9 | — | Nombre (moyenne trimestrielle) |
| Wages and salaries | 28.2 | 23.2 | 0.3 | 0.9 | 0.9 | 0.1 | 0.6 | 0.1 | 0.1 | 0.3 | 0.9 | 0.1 | 0.7 | — | Traitements et salaires |
| Number of operatives (Average of the quarters) | 58.3 | 50.1 | 0.7 | 1.8 | 2.3 | 0.1 | 0.5 | 0.2 | 0.1 | 0.5 | 1.0 | 0.1 | 0.9 | — | Nombre d'ouvriers (moyenne trimestrielle) |
| Electricity consumed | 62 537 | 44 556 | 875 | 279 | 602 | 59 | 553 | 359 | 228 | 301 | 13 975 | 43 | 701 | 6 | Electricité consommée |
| **1958** | | | | | | | | | | | | | | | **1958** |
| Number of establishments | 2 811 | 1 010 | 18 | 589 | 486 | 11 | 83 | 83 | 60 | 102 | 82 | 7 | 257 | 23 | Nombre d'établissements |
| Gross value of sales | 208.8 | 156.8 | 4.5 | 7.3 | 6.9 | 1.6 | 3.3 | 1.4 | 1.5 | 11.9 | 10.7 | — | 2.9 | | Valeur brute des ventes |
| Employees: | | | | | | | | | | | | | | | Salariés: |
| Number (Average of the quarters) | 82.8 | 70.8 | 1.2 | 2.5 | 2.7 | 0.2 | 0.8 | 0.3 | 0.2 | 1.3 | 1.6 | — | 1.2 | — | Nombre (moyenne trimestrielle) |
| Wages and salaries | 35.7 | 27.8 | 0.8 | 1.2 | 1.0 | 0.1 | 0.8 | 0.2 | 0.2 | 1.1 | 1.5 | — | 1.0 | — | Traitements et salaires |
| Number of operatives (Average of the quarters) | 77.6 | 66.6 | 1.2 | 2.4 | 2.4 | 0.2 | 0.6 | 0.3 | 0.2 | 1.2 | 1.4 | — | 1.1 | — | Nombre d'ouvriers (moyenne trimestrielle) |
| Electricity consumed | 148 041 | 108 415 | 2 713 | 506 | 984 | 85 | 812 | 576 | 730 | 4 675 | 27 409 | 5 | 1 123 | 8 | Electricité consommée |
| *b. Structure* | | | | | | | | | | | | | | | |
| **1948** | | | | | | | | | | | | | | | **1948** |
| Distribution in percent of number of employees | 100.0 | 82.1 | 0.5 | 4.5 | 5.9 | 0.2 | 1.3 | 0.7 | 0.2 | 1.1 | 1.5 | 0.4 | 1.6 | — | Distribution en pourcentage du nombre de salariés |
| Wages and salaries per employee | 0.4 | 0.4 | 0.5 | 0.4 | 0.4 | ... | 0.8 | 0.7 | ... | 0.4 | 0.7 | 0.5 | 0.6 | — | Traitements et salaires par salarié |
| Operatives as a percent of employees | 91.7 | 91.8 | 100.0 | 95.2 | 96.3 | 100.0 | 66.7 | 100.0 | ... | 80.0 | 85.7 | 100.0 | 100.0 | — | Ouvriers en pourcentage des salariés |
| **1953** | | | | | | | | | | | | | | | **1953** |
| Distribution in percent of number of employees | 100.0 | 85.6 | 1.1 | 3.1 | 4.0 | 0.2 | 1.0 | 0.3 | 0.1 | 1.0 | 1.9 | 0.2 | 1.5 | — | Distribution en pourcentage du nombre de salariés |
| Per employee: | | | | | | | | | | | | | | | Par salarié: |
| Wages and salaries | 0.4 | 0.4 | 0.4 | 0.5 | 0.4 | 1.0 | 1.0 | 0.5 | 1.0 | 0.5 | 0.8 | 1.0 | 0.8 | 0.4 | Traitements et salaires |
| Electricity consumed | 1 009 | 839 | 1 250 | 147 | 241 | 590 | 922 | 1 795 | 2 280 | 502 | 11 646 | 430 | 779 | ... | Electricité consommée |
| Operatives as a percent of employees | 94.0 | 94.4 | 100.0 | 94.7 | 92.0 | 100.0 | 83.3 | 100.0 | 100.0 | 83.3 | 83.3 | 100.0 | 100.0 | ... | Ouvriers en pourcentage des salariés |
| Electricity consumed per operative | 1 073 | 889 | 1 250 | 155 | 262 | 590 | 1 106 | 1 795 | 2 280 | 602 | 13 975 | 430 | 779 | ... | Electricité consommée par ouvrier |
| **1958** | | | | | | | | | | | | | | | **1958** |
| Distribution in percent of number of employees | 100.0 | 85.5 | 1.4 | 3.0 | 3.3 | 0.2 | 1.0 | 0.4 | 0.2 | 1.6 | 1.9 | — | 1.5 | — | Distribution en pourcentage du nombre de salariés |
| Per employee: | | | | | | | | | | | | | | | Par salarié: |
| Wages and salaries | 0.4 | 0.4 | 0.7 | 0.5 | 0.4 | 0.5 | 1.0 | 0.7 | 1.0 | 0.8 | 0.9 | — | 0.8 | — | Traitements et salaires |
| Electricity consumed | 1 788 | 1 531 | 2 261 | 202 | 364 | 425 | 1 015 | 1 920 | 3 650 | 3 596 | 17 131 | — | 936 | ... | Electricité consommée |
| Operatives as a percent of employees | 93.7 | 94.1 | 100.0 | 96.0 | 88.9 | 100.0 | 75.0 | 100.0 | 100.0 | 92.3 | 87.5 | 100.0 | 91.7 | ... | Ouvriers en pourcentage des salariés |
| Electricity consumed per operative | 1 907 | 1 627 | 2 261 | 211 | 410 | 425 | 1 353 | 1 920 | 3 650 | 3 896 | 19 578 | ... | 1 021 | ... | Electricité consommée par ouvrier |

[1] Includes all mining establishments, but manufacturing and electricity establishments in urban areas only.

[1] Couvre tous les établissements miniers, mais seulement les établissements manufacturiers et producteurs d'électricité des centres urbains.

# 3. QUANTITY AND VALUE OF SELECTED FUELS AND ELECTRICITY CONSUMED BY ALL INDUSTRIAL ESTABLISHMENTS[1]
## QUANTITE ET VALEUR DE QUELQUES COMBUSTIBLES ET DE L'ELECTRICITE CONSOMMES PAR TOUS LES ETABLISSEMENTS INDUSTRIELS[1]
### 1953, 1958

Liquid fuels, coal, charcoal and wood in metric tons; electricity consumed in thousand KWH; values in thousand Pesos

Combustibles liquides, charbon, charbon de bois et bois en tonnes métriques; électricité consommée en milliers de kWh; valeur en milliers de pesos

## A. The Major Groups of Mining and Electricity
### Les classes de la branche Industries extractives et l'Electricité

| Year and source of energy | Total | Metal mining — Extraction des minerais métalliques | Other mining — Divers | Electricity — Electricité | Année et source d'énergie |
|---|---|---|---|---|---|
| ISIC | 1 | 12 | 14–19 | 511 | CITI |
| **1953** Liquid fuels: | | | | | **1953** Combustibles liquides: |
| Quantity | 22 | — | 22 | 28 036 | Quantité |
| Value | 2 | — | 2 | 566 | Valeur |
| **1958** Liquid fuels: | | | | | **1958** Combustibles liquides: |
| Quantity | 1 193 | 370 | 823 | 92 771 | Quantité |
| Value | 57 | 12 | 45 | 2 733 | Valeur |
| Electricity: | | | | | Electricité: |
| Quantity | 274 | — | 274 | — | Quantité |
| Value | 6 | — | 6 | — | Valeur |

## B. The Major Groups of Manufacturing — Les classes de la branche Industries manufacturières

| Year and source of energy | Manufacturing — Industries manufacturières | Food, beverages and tobacco — Industries alimentaires, boissons, tabac | Textiles | Clothing, footwear and made-up textiles — Articles d'habillement, chaussures et ouvrages en tissu | Wood products and furniture — Bois et meubles | Paper and paper products — Papier et ouvrages en papier | Printing and publishing — Imprimerie et édition | Leather and leather products except wearing apparel — Cuir et articles en cuir, à l'exclusion des articles d'habillement | Rubber products — Ouvrages en caoutchouc | Chemicals and chemical, petroleum and coal products — Produits chimiques et dérivés du pétrole et du charbon | Non-metallic mineral products — Produits minéraux non métalliques | Basic metals — Métallurgie de base | Metal products — Ouvrages en métaux | Other manufacturing — Autres industries manufacturières | Année et source d'énergie |
|---|---|---|---|---|---|---|---|---|---|---|---|---|---|---|---|
| ISIC | 2–3 | 20–22 | 23 | 24 | 25–26 | 27 | 28 | 29 | 30 | 31–32 | 33 | 34 | 35–38 | 39 | CITI |
| **1953** Coal: | | | | | | | | | | | | | | | **1953** Charbon: |
| Quantity | 1 145 | 951 | — | — | 34 | — | — | — | — | — | 3 | 152 | 5 | — | Quantité |
| Value | 55 | 39 | — | — | 2 | — | — | — | — | — | — | 14 | — | — | Valeur |
| Charcoal: | | | | | | | | | | | | | | | Charbon de bois: |
| Quantity | 256 | 76 | — | 73 | 4 | 2 | 3 | — | 4 | 8 | 3 | 17 | 66 | — | Quantité |
| Value | 10 | 3 | — | 3 | — | — | — | — | — | — | — | 1 | 3 | — | Valeur |
| Liquid fuels: | | | | | | | | | | | | | | | Combustibles liquides: |
| Quantity | 47 102 | 14 893 | 384 | 4 | 1 050 | 9 | 70 | 16 | 140 | 19 | 30 318 | 8 | 191 | — | Quantité |
| Value | 1 624 | 941 | 10 | — | 122 | 1 | 6 | 3 | 10 | 3 | 502 | 1 | 25 | — | Valeur |
| Electricity: | | | | | | | | | | | | | | | Electricité: |
| Quantity | 62 537 | 44 556 | 875 | 279 | 602 | 59 | 553 | 359 | 228 | 301 | 13 975 | 43 | 701 | 6 | Quantité |
| Value | 1 177 | 740 | 24 | 16 | 27 | 3 | 20 | 14 | 8 | 12 | 291 | 2 | 20 | — | Valeur |
| Wood: | | | | | | | | | | | | | | | Bois: |
| Quantity | 95 964 | 87 306 | 783 | 713 | 2 145 | — | 29 | 523 | 573 | 1 585 | 2 299 | — | — | 8 | Quantité |
| Value | 349 | 300 | 4 | 4 | 8 | — | — | 4 | 4 | 9 | 16 | — | — | — | Valeur |
| **1958** Coal: | | | | | | | | | | | | | | | **1958** Charbon: |
| Quantity | 460 | 413 | — | — | — | — | — | — | — | — | 23 | 21 | 3 | — | Quantité |
| Value | 26 | 23 | — | — | — | — | — | — | — | — | 1 | 2 | — | — | Valeur |
| Charcoal: | | | | | | | | | | | | | | | Charbon de bois: |
| Quantity | 424 | 313 | 2 | 37 | — | 4 | 1 | 1 | 2 | 3 | — | 5 | 56 | — | Quantité |
| Value | 13 | 8 | — | 2 | — | — | — | — | — | — | — | — | 3 | — | Valeur |
| Liquid fuels: | | | | | | | | | | | | | | | Combustibles liquides: |
| Quantity | 124 215 | 64 363 | 609 | 38 | 1 642 | 23 | 147 | 24 | 332 | 11 346 | 45 603 | 12 | 76 | — | Quantité |
| Value | 3 684 | 2 260 | 17 | 3 | 183 | 2 | 18 | 4 | 30 | 194 | 963 | 1 | 9 | — | Valeur |
| Electricity: | | | | | | | | | | | | | | | Electricité: |
| Quantity | 148 041 | 108 415 | 2 713 | 506 | 984 | 85 | 812 | 576 | 730 | 4 675 | 27 409 | 5 | 1 123 | 8 | Quantité |
| Value | 2 144 | 1 332 | 68 | 24 | 39 | 4 | 30 | 21 | 24 | 40 | 527 | — | 34 | 1 | Valeur |
| Wood: | | | | | | | | | | | | | | | Bois: |
| Quantity | 96 205 | 86 679 | 375 | 674 | 748 | — | — | 1 119 | 1 540 | 3 796 | 1 261 | — | 13 | — | Quantité |
| Value | 334 | 285 | 2 | 3 | 4 | — | — | 6 | 8 | 20 | 6 | — | — | — | Valeur |

[1] Includes, all mining establishments, and manufacturing and electricity establishments in urban areas.

[1] Couvre tous les établissements miniers, ainsi que les établissements manufacturiers et producteurs d'électricité des centres urbains.

# ECUADOR — EQUATEUR

## The Gross Domestic Product

Estimations of the expenditure on and the origin of the gross domestic product are presented in Table 1. The data are derived from information provided by the Banco Central del Ecuador, Departamento de Investigaciones Económicas, Quito, in response to the United Nations national accounts questionnaire. Official estimates for the years prior to 1958 are published by the same Office in *Contabilidad Nacional del Ecuador, 1950-1956-1957*. A description of the methods and sources used has been published in *El Ingreso Nacional y las Cuentas Nacionales de la República del Ecuador, Años 1950-1953*, by Dr. H. Rijken Van Olst.

## Index of Industrial Production

The index numbers of manufacturing production presented in Table 2 are derived from the results of a series of industrial enquiries. These enquiries are the first industrial Census in 1955 described below, and the annual industrial enquiries for 1956 to 1959, all conducted by the Dirreción de Estadística y Censos, and the industrial enquiries carried out by the Banco Central in the years 1959 to 1961. The indexes are published for the years 1955 to 1960 by the Dirección de Estadística y Censos in *Sintesis Estadistica del Ecuador 1955-1960*, Quito, Ecuador 1962. Later data are provided in correspondence by the Banco Central. The indicators used were the gross values of production at 1955 prices of those establishments with a gross value of production of 300,000 Sucres or more in 1958. The indexes for the 34 sub-groups utilised initially were combined into indexes for major groups and the major group indexes combined into indexes for manufacturing as a whole by using as weights the values added resulting from the 1955 Industrial Census described below.

## Characteristics and Structure of Industrial Activity

The data shown in Table 3 are derived from the results of the first inquiry into mining and manufacturing of the Dirección General de Estadística y Censos that were published in *Primer Censo Industrial*, Comité Ejecutivo del Censo Industrial, 1955, Quito. It was intended that the Census should relate to industrial establishments with five or more persons engaged, or a gross value of production of one hundred thousand Sucres or more, or with fixed assets valued at two hundred thousand Sucres or more, excepting rural industries. However, many establishments did not return the Census questionnaires and adjustments were not made in the data that were published for incompleteness of coverage. Slightly more than 5 percent of the establishments included in the di-

## Le produit intérieur brut

Des estimations relatives aux dépenses imputées au produit intérieur brut, ainsi que celles des composantes du produit intérieur brut ventilées par branche d'activité sont reproduites au tableau 1. Les données ont été tirées d'informations fournies par la Banco Central del Ecuador, Departamento de Investigaciones Económicas, Quito, en réponse au questionnaire de l'O.N.U. relatif aux comptes nationaux. Les estimations officielles pour les années précédant 1958 sont publiées par le même bureau dans *Contabilidad Nacional del Ecuador, 1950-1956-1957*. Une description des sources et méthodes utilisées a été publiée dans *El Ingreso Nacional y las Cuentas Nacionales de la República del Ecuador, Años 1950-1953*, par Dr. H. Rijken Van Olst.

## Indices de la production industrielle

Les indices de la production manufacturière reproduits au tableau 2 ont été tirés à partir d'une série d'enquêtes industrielles. Ces enquêtes sont: le premier recensement industriel pour 1955 décrit ci-dessous, et les enquêtes industrielles annuelles pour les années 1956 à 1959 toutes dirigées par la Dirección de Estadística y Censos pendant les années 1959 à 1961. Les indices sont publiés pour les années 1955 à 1960 par la Dirección de Estadística y Censos dans *Sintesis Estadística del Ecuador 1955-1960*, Quito, Ecuador 1962. Les données plus récentes sont fournies par voie de correspondance par la Banco Central. Les indicateurs utilisés sont les valeurs brutes de la production aux prix de 1955 des établissements ayant atteint une valeur brute de production de 300.000 sucres ou plus en 1958. Les indices relatifs aux 34 sous-groupes initialement utilisés ont été combinés en indices de classes et ces indices de classes en indices relatifs à l'ensemble des industries manufacturières, les coefficients de pondération utilisés étant les valeurs ajoutées tirées du recensement industriel de 1955 décrit ci-dessous.

## Caractéristiques et structure de l'activité industrielle

Les données du tableau 3 sont tirées des résultats de la première enquête sur les industries extractives et manufacturières, exécutée par la Dirección General de Estadística y Censos. Ces résultats ont été publiés dans *Primer Censo Industrial*, Comité Ejecutivo del Censo Industrial, 1955, Quito. Il avait été décidé que le recensement couvrirait tous les établissements industriels occupant 5 personnes ou plus, ou dont la valeur brute de la production serait égale ou supérieure à 100.000 sucres, ou encore qui posséderaient des biens en capital fixe évalués à 200.000 sucres ou plus, à l'exclusion des industries rurales. Cependant, de nombreux établissements n'ont pas retourné les questionnaires de recensement et on n'a pas ajusté les données publiées pour en tenir compte. Un peu plus de

rectory, which was used as the basis for distributing the questionnaires, returned the questionnaires. However, it is estimated that these establishments accounted for 92 percent of the value of gross production of the establishments listed in the directory. The response to the questionnaire, as well as to individual items of the questionnaire, varied from industry to industry. In particular, the data shown in the tables below for the extraction and refining of petroleum are known to be rather incomplete and the figures of value added are not comparable to the figures of wages and salaries or employment for a number of industries, for example printing and metal products.

The data shown in Table 4 are derived from the results of the above mentioned Census for 1955, and the 1958 results of the annual industrial enquiry. The establishments for which data are shown in the table are restricted to those having a gross value of production of 300,000 Sucres or more in 1958. The data on which this table is based are published by the Banco Central del Ecuador in *Boletín*, Nos. 406 and 407, May and June of 1961, and in the *Memoria 1960*. Quito, Ecuador 1961.

The definitions of the items of data shown in Tables 3 and 4 correspond to the International Standards in Basic Industrial Statistics. Value added is valued at market prices and in the 1955 Census the capacity of installed (in use and in reserve) power equipment is the sum of the rated horsepower of prime movers connected to machinery other than electric generators and all electric motors.

5 pour 100 des établissements inscrits dans le répertoire sur la base duquel le questionnaire avait été distribué ont retourné ce questionnaire, mais on estime que ces établissements représentent 92 pour 100 de la valeur de la production brute des établissements inscrits dans le répertoire. Le pourcentage des réponses a varié d'une industrie à l'autre en ce qui concerne tant l'ensemble du questionnaire que les diverses rubriques. On sait en particulier que les chiffres donnés dans les tableaux ci-après au sujet de l'extraction et du raffinage du pétrole sont assez incomplets, et les chiffres de la valeur ajoutée ne sont pas comparables aux chiffres des traitements et salaires ou de l'emploi pour un certain nombre d'industries — par exemple l'imprimerie et les ouvrages en métaux.

Les données du tableau 4 ont été tirées des résultats du recensement de 1955 ci-dessus mentionné, et des résultats de 1958 de l'enquête industrielle annuelle. Les établissements pour lesquels des données sont reproduites au tableau se réduisent à ceux justifiant d'une valeur brute de la production de 300.000 sucres ou plus en 1958. Les données sur lesquelles ce tableau est fondé sont publiées par la Banco Central del Ecuador dans *Boletín*, Nos. 406 et 407, mai et juin 1961, et dans *Memoria 1960*, Quito, Ecuador 1961.

Les définitions des rubriques figurant dans les tableaux ci-après correspondent aux Normes internationales relatives aux statistiques industrielles de base. La valeur ajoutée est comptée aux prix du marché et la puissance installée (en service et en réserve) est égale à la puissance nominale en chevaux-vapeur des moteurs primaires entraînant des machines autres que des générateurs électriques, plus celle de tous les moteurs électriques.

## 1. THE GROSS DOMESTIC PRODUCT — PRODUIT INTERIEUR BRUT

Million Sucres                                                                 Millions de sucres

### A. Expenditure on the Gross Domestic Product at Market Prices
### Dépenses relatives au produit intérieur brut aux prix du marché

| Item of data and year / Rubrique et année | Total | Consumption / Consommation | | Gross Domestic Capital Formation / Formation brute de capital intérieur | | Net exports of goods and services / Exportations nettes de biens et de services | |
|---|---|---|---|---|---|---|---|
| | | Total | Government / Etat | Total | Fixed / Fixe | Exports less imports / Exportations moins importations | Exports / Exportations |
| *a.* At Current Prices — Aux prix courants | | | | | | | |
| Absolute figures — Chiffres absolus | | | | | | | |
| 1950 | 7 244 | 6 014 | 997 | 783 | 617 | 447 | 1 390 |
| 1951 | 7 761 | 6 722 | 1 050 | 1 004 | 855 | 35 | 1 229 |
| 1952 | 8 854 | 7 466 | 1 123 | 908 | 810 | 480 | 1 708 |
| 1953 | 9 349 | 7 908 | 1 254 | 1 263 | 1 002 | 178 | 1 716 |
| 1954 | 10 447 | 8 706 | 1 334 | 1 631 | 1 382 | 110 | 2 153 |
| 1955 | 11 049 | 9 224 | 1 374 | 1 806 | 1 538 | 19 | 2 070 |
| 1956 | 11 266 | 9 492 | 1 367 | 1 780 | 1 560 | −6 | 2 097 |
| 1957 | 12 007 | 9 944 | 1 407 | 1 811 | 1 561 | 252 | 2 377 |
| 1958 | 12 357 | 10 393 | 1 413 | 1 772 | 1 516 | 192 | 2 312 |
| 1959 | 13 009 | 10 803 | 1 533 | 1 921 | 1 734 | 285 | 2 454 |
| 1960 | 14 060 | 11 925 | 1 813 | 2 081 | 1 856 | 54 | 2 530 |
| 1961 | 15 076 | 12 985 | 2 057 | 2 255 | 1 946 | −164 | 2 513 |
| Percentage distribution of average annual expenditure — Distribution en pourcentage des dépenses annuelles moyennes | | | | | | | |
| 1950–1960 | 100.0 | 84.0 | 12.5 | 14.2 | 12.3 | 1.8 | 18.8 |
| 1950 | 100.0 | 83.0 | 13.8 | 10.8 | 8.5 | 6.2 | 19.2 |
| 1953 | 100.0 | 84.6 | 13.4 | 13.5 | 10.7 | 1.9 | 18.4 |
| 1954 | 100.0 | 83.3 | 12.8 | 15.6 | 13.2 | 1.1 | 20.6 |
| 1958 | 100.0 | 84.1 | 11.4 | 14.3 | 12.3 | 1.6 | 18.7 |
| 1960 | 100.0 | 84.8 | 12.9 | 14.8 | 13.2 | 0.4 | 18.0 |
| *b.* At Prices of 1950 — Aux prix de 1950 | | | | | | | |
| Absolute figures — Chiffres absolus | | | | | | | |
| 1950 | 7 244 | 6 014 | 997 | 783 | 617 | 447 | 1 390 |
| 1951 | 7 448 | 6 451 | 1 008 | 964 | 821 | 33 | 1 179 |
| 1952 | 8 229 | 6 939 | 1 044 | 844 | 753 | 446 | 1 587 |
| 1953 | 8 492 | 7 183 | 1 139 | 1 147 | 910 | 162 | 1 559 |
| 1954 | 9 180 | 7 650 | 1 172 | 1 433 | 1 214 | 97 | 1 892 |
| 1955 | 9 427 | 7 870 | 1 172 | 1 541 | 1 312 | 16 | 1 766 |
| 1956 | 9 764 | 8 226 | 1 185 | 1 543 | 1 352 | −5 | 1 817 |
| 1957 | 10 271 | 8 507 | 1 204 | 1 549 | 1 335 | 215 | 2 033 |
| 1958 | 10 508 | 8 838 | 1 202 | 1 507 | 1 289 | 163 | 1 966 |
| 1959 | 11 052 | 9 178 | 1 302 | 1 632 | 1 473 | 242 | 2 085 |
| 1960 | 11 717 | 9 938 | 1 511 | 1 734 | 1 547 | 45 | 2 108 |
| 1961 | 12 051 | 10 379 | 1 644 | 1 803 | 1 556 | −131 | 2 009 |
| Percentage distribution of average annual expenditure — Distribution en pourcentage des dépenses annuelles moyennes | | | | | | | |
| 1950–1960 | 100.0 | 84.0 | 12.5 | 14.2 | 12.2 | 1.8 | 18.8 |
| 1950 | 100.0 | 83.0 | 13.8 | 10.8 | 8.5 | 6.2 | 19.2 |
| 1953 | 100.0 | 84.6 | 13.4 | 13.5 | 10.7 | 1.9 | 18.4 |
| 1954 | 100.0 | 83.3 | 12.8 | 15.6 | 13.2 | 1.1 | 20.6 |
| 1958 | 100.0 | 84.1 | 11.4 | 14.3 | 12.3 | 1.6 | 18.7 |
| 1960 | 100.0 | 84.8 | 12.9 | 14.8 | 13.2 | 0.4 | 18.0 |
| Average annual rate of growth — Taux annuel moyen d'accroissement | | | | | | | |
| 1950–1960 | 4.9 | 5.2 | 4.3 | 8.3 | 9.6 | . | 4.3 |
| 1950–1953 | 5.4 | 6.1 | 4.5 | 13.6 | 13.8 | . | 3.9 |
| 1954–1958 | 3.4 | 3.7 | 0.6 | 1.3 | 1.5 | . | 1.0 |
| 1958–1960 | 5.6 | 6.0 | 12.1 | 7.2 | 9.5 | . | 3.5 |

## B. The Gross Domestic Product at Factor Cost According to Origin
### Origine par secteur d'activité du produit intérieur brut au coût des facteurs

| Item of data and year / Rubrique et année | Total | Agricultural sector / Secteur agricole | Industrial Sector — Secteur Industriel | | | | | Transportation and communication / Transports et communications | Other sectors / Autres secteurs |
|---|---|---|---|---|---|---|---|---|---|
| | | | Total | Mining / Industries extractives | Manufacturing / Industries manufacturières | Construction / Bâtiment et travaux publics | Electricity, gas and water / Electricité, gaz et eau | | |
| ISIC — CITI | 0–9 | 0 | 1–5 | 1 | 2–3 | 4 | 5 | 7 | 6, 8–9 |

**a. At Current Prices — Aux prix courants**

| | | | | | | | | | |
|---|---|---|---|---|---|---|---|---|---|
| **Absolute figures — Chiffres absolus** | | | | | | | | | |
| 1950 | 6 611 | 2 565 | 1 419 | 150 | 1 055 | 180 | 34 | 318 | 2 309 |
| 1951 | 6 963 | 2 704 | 1 507 | 149 | 1 137 | 181 | 40 | 365 | 2 387 |
| 1952 | 8 077 | 3 327 | 1 675 | 161 | 1 237 | 222 | 55 | 405 | 2 670 |
| 1953 | 8 437 | 3 388 | 1 805 | 162 | 1 324 | 248 | 71 | 426 | 2 818 |
| 1954 | 9 426 | 3 671 | 2 002 | 200 | 1 437 | 279 | 86 | 486 | 3 267 |
| 1955 | 9 971 | 3 598 | 2 162 | 243 | 1 499 | 311 | 109 | 508 | 3 703 |
| 1956 | 10 183 | 3 756 | 2 254 | 228 | 1 564 | 354 | 108 | 491 | 3 682 |
| 1957 | 10 775 | 3 936 | 2 357 | 232 | 1 625 | 380 | 120 | 522 | 3 960 |
| 1958 | 11 159 | 4 005 | 2 475 | 222 | 1 739 | 388 | 126 | 530 | 4 149 |
| 1959 | 11 769 | 4 250 | 2 663 | 233 | 1 830 | 462 | 138 | 546 | 4 310 |
| 1960 | 12 775 | 4 600 | 2 997 | 312 | 2 010 | 527 | 148 | 555 | 4 623 |
| 1961 | 13 769 | 5 100 | ... | 340 | 2 115 | 1 256 [1] | ... | ... | 4 958 |
| **Percentage distribution according to sector — Distribution en pourcentage par secteur** | | | | | | | | | |
| 1950–1960 | 100.0 | 37.5 | 22.0 | 2.2 | 15.5 | 3.3 | 1.0 | 4.8 | 35.7 |
| 1950 | 100.0 | 38.8 | 21.5 | 2.3 | 16.0 | 2.7 | 0.5 | 4.8 | 34.9 |
| 1953 | 100.0 | 40.2 | 21.4 | 1.9 | 15.7 | 3.0 | 0.8 | 5.0 | 33.4 |
| 1954 | 100.0 | 38.9 | 21.2 | 2.1 | 15.3 | 2.9 | 0.9 | 5.2 | 34.7 |
| 1958 | 100.0 | 35.9 | 22.2 | 2.0 | 15.6 | 3.5 | 1.1 | 4.7 | 37.2 |
| 1960 | 100.0 | 36.0 | 23.4 | 2.4 | 15.7 | 4.2 | 1.1 | 4.4 | 36.2 |

**b. At Prices of 1950 — Aux prix de 1950**

| | | | | | | | | | |
|---|---|---|---|---|---|---|---|---|---|
| **Absolute figures — Chiffres absolus** | | | | | | | | | |
| 1950 | 6 611 | 2 565 | 1 419 | 150 | 1 055 | 180 | 34 | 318 | 2 309 |
| 1951 | 6 681 | 2 595 | 1 446 | 143 | 1 091 | 174 | 38 | 350 | 2 290 |
| 1952 | 7 507 | 3 092 | 1 557 | 150 | 1 150 | 206 | 51 | 376 | 2 482 |
| 1953 | 7 663 | 3 077 | 1 639 | 147 | 1 203 | 225 | 64 | 387 | 2 560 |
| 1954 | 8 284 | 3 226 | 1 760 | 176 | 1 263 | 245 | 76 | 427 | 2 871 |
| 1955 | 8 507 | 3 070 | 1 844 | 207 | 1 279 | 265 | 93 | 433 | 3 160 |
| 1956 | 8 823 | 3 255 | 1 954 | 198 | 1 355 | 307 | 94 | 425 | 3 189 |
| 1957 | 9 218 | 3 367 | 2 016 | 198 | 1 390 | 325 | 103 | 447 | 3 388 |
| 1958 | 9 490 | 3 406 | 2 105 | 189 | 1 479 | 330 | 107 | 451 | 3 528 |
| 1959 | 9 999 | 3 611 | 2 263 | 198 | 1 555 | 393 | 117 | 464 | 3 661 |
| 1960 | 10 646 | 3 833 | 2 498 | 260 | 1 675 | 439 | 124 | 463 | 3 852 |
| 1961 | 11 006 | 4 077 | ... | 272 | 1 691 | 1 004 [1] | ... | ... | 3 962 |
| **Percentage distribution according to sector — Distribution en pourcentage par secteur** | | | | | | | | | |
| 1950–1960 | 100.0 | 37.5 | 22.0 | 2.2 | 15.5 | 3.3 | 1.0 | 4.8 | 35.7 |
| 1950 | 100.0 | 38.8 | 21.5 | 2.3 | 16.0 | 2.7 | 0.5 | 4.8 | 34.9 |
| 1953 | 100.0 | 40.2 | 21.4 | 1.9 | 15.7 | 3.0 | 0.8 | 5.0 | 33.4 |
| 1954 | 100.0 | 38.9 | 21.2 | 2.1 | 15.3 | 2.9 | 0.9 | 5.2 | 34.7 |
| 1958 | 100.0 | 35.9 | 22.2 | 2.0 | 15.6 | 3.5 | 1.1 | 4.7 | 37.2 |
| 1960 | 100.0 | 36.0 | 23.4 | 2.4 | 15.7 | 4.2 | 1.1 | 4.4 | 36.2 |
| **Average annual rate of growth — Taux annuel moyen d'accroissement** | | | | | | | | | |
| 1950–1960 | 4.9 | 4.1 | 5.8 | 5.7 | 4.7 | 9.3 | 13.8 | 3.8 | 5.3 |
| 1950–1953 | 5.0 | 6.2 | 4.9 | −0.7 | 4.5 | 7.7 | 23.5 | 6.8 | 3.5 |
| 1954–1958 | 3.5 | 1.4 | 4.6 | 1.8 | 4.0 | 7.7 | 8.9 | 1.4 | 5.3 |
| 1958–1960 | 5.9 | 6.1 | 8.9 | 17.3 | 6.4 | 15.3 | 7.7 | 1.3 | 4.5 |

[1] Includes Electricity, gas and water (ISIC division 5) and Transportation and communication (ISIC division 7).

[1] Y compris Electricité, gaz et eau (CITI 5) et Transports et communications (CITI 7).

## 2. INDEX NUMBERS OF INDUSTRIAL PRODUCTION
## INDICES DE LA PRODUCTION INDUSTRIELLE

| Period / Période | Manufacturing [1] / Industries manufacturières [1] | Food, beverages and tobacco / Industries alimentaires, boissons, tabac | Textiles | Footwear / Chaussures | Paper and paper products / Papier et ouvrages en papier | Leather and leather products except wearing apparel / Cuir et articles en cuir, à l'exclusion des articles d'habillement | Chemicals and chemical, petroleum and coal products / Produits chimiques et dérivés du pétrole et du charbon | Non-metallic mineral products / Produits minéraux non métalliques | Other manufacturing / Autres industries manufacturières |
|---|---|---|---|---|---|---|---|---|---|
| ISIC — CITI | 2–3 | 20–22 | 23 | 241 | 27 | 29 | 31–32 | 33 | 39 |

### a. Indexes — Indices (1958 = 100)

| | | | | | | | | | |
|---|---|---|---|---|---|---|---|---|---|
| 1955 | 81 | 78 | 76 | 108 | 69 | 117 | 90 | 91 | 78 |
| 1956 | 86 | 87 | 81 | 100 | 84 | 109 | 88 | 94 | 98 |
| 1957 | 94 | 92 | 103 | 98 | 78 | 108 | 89 | 96 | 97 |
| 1958 | 100 | 100 | 100 | 100 | 100 | 100 | 100 | 100 | 100 |
| 1959 | 109 | 104 | 106 | 80 | 116 | 106 | 121 | 97 | 144 |
| 1960 | 126 | 115 | 113 | 50 | 139 | 110 | 159 | 125 | 156 |
| 1961 | ... | 119 | 128 | 51 | 150 | 116 | 177 | 136 | 157 |

### b. Average Annual Rate of Change — Taux annuel moyen de variation

| | | | | | | | | | |
|---|---|---|---|---|---|---|---|---|---|
| 1955–1958 | 7.3 | 8.6 | 9.6 | −2.5 | 13.2 | −5.1 | 3.6 | 3.2 | 8.6 |
| 1958–1960 | 12.2 | 7.2 | 6.3 | −29.3 | 17.9 | 4.9 | 26.1 | 11.8 | 24.9 |

[1] Excludes Clothing and made-up textiles (ISIC groups 243 and 244), Wood products and furniture (ISIC major groups 25-26), Printing and publishing (ISIC major group 28), Rubber products (ISIC major group 30), Basic metals (ISIC major group 34) and Metal products (ISIC major groups 35-38).

[1] Non compris Articles d'habillement et ouvrages en tissu (CITI 243 et 244), Bois et meubles (CITI 25-26), Imprimerie et édition (CITI 28), Ouvrages en caoutchouc (CITI 30), Métallurgie de base (CITI 34) et Ouvrages en métaux (CITI 35-38).

## 3. CHARACTERISTICS OF LARGE INDUSTRIAL ESTABLISHMENTS
## CARACTERISTIQUES DES GRANDS ETABLISSEMENTS INDUSTRIELS
### 1955

Number of establishments in units; value added and wages and salaries in million Sucres; number of engaged, employees and operatives in thousands; man-hours worked in thousands; electricity consumed in million KWH; capacity of installed power equipment in thousand horsepower; value added per engaged, wages and salaries per employee and per thousand operative man-hours in thousand Sucres; electricity consumed per engaged and per thousand operative man-hours in thousand KWH; capacity of installed power equipment per engaged and per thousand operative man-hours in horsepower.

Nombre d'établissements en unités; valeur ajoutée et traitements et salaires en millions de sucres; nombre de personnes occupées, de salariés et d'ouvriers en milliers; heures de travail effectuées en milliers; électricité consommée en millions de kWh; puissance installée en milliers de chevaux-vapeur; valeur ajoutée par personne occupée et traitements et salaires par salarié et par milliers d'heures de travail d'ouvrier en millier de sucres; électricité consommée par personne occupée et par millier d'heures de travail d'ouvrier en milliers de kWh; puissance installée par personne occupée et par millier d'heures de travail d'ouvrier en chevaux-vapeur.

### A. The Major Groups of Mining — Les classes de la branche Industries extractives

| Item of data | Total | Crude petroleum and natural gas / Pétrole brut et gaz naturel | Other mining / Divers | Rubrique | Item of data | Total | Crude petroleum and natural gas / Pétrole brut et gaz naturel | Other mining / Divers | Rubrique |
|---|---|---|---|---|---|---|---|---|---|
| ISIC | 1 | 13 | 14–19 | CITI | ISIC | 1 | 13 | 14–19 | CITI |
| **a. Absolute Figures / Chiffres absolus** | | | | | **b. Structure** | | | | |
| Number of units | 8 | 3 | 5 | Nombre d'unités | Distribution in percent of: | | | | Distribution en pourcentage: |
| Value added | 33.4 | 32.3 | 1.1 | Valeur ajoutée | Value added | 100.0 | 96.7 | 3.3 | Valeur ajoutée |
| Number of engaged (As of last pay period in December) | 0.6 | 0.5 | 0.1 | Nombre de personnes occupées (dernière période de paie de décembre) | Number of engaged | 100.0 | 83.3 | 16.7 | Nombre de personnes occupées |
| Number of employees (As of last pay period of December) | 0.6 | 0.5 | 0.1 | Nombre de salariés (dernière période de paie de décembre) | Per person engaged: Value added | 55.7 | 64.6 | 11.0 | Par personne occupée: Valeur ajoutée |
| Wages and salaries paid for the year | 9.6 | 8.8 | 0.8 | Traitements et salaires payés pour l'année | Electricity consumed | 3.5 | 4.2 | — | Électricité consommée |
| Operatives: | | | | Ouvriers: | Capacity of installed power equipment | 9.17 | 9.40 | 8.00 | Puissance installée |
| Number | 0.5 | 0.4 | 0.1 | Nombre | Value added per unit of wages and salaries | 3.48 | 3.67 | 1.38 | Valeur ajoutée par unité de traitements et salaires |
| Man-hours worked | 1.3 | 1.1 | 0.2 | Heures de travail effectuées | Operatives as a percent of employees | 83.3 | 80.0 | 100.0 | Ouvriers en pourcentage des salariés |
| Wages and salaries | 6.4 | 5.9 | 0.5 | Traitements et salaires | Wages and salaries per employee | 16.0 | 17.6 | 8.0 | Traitements et salaires par salarié |
| Electricity consumed | 2.1 | 2.1 | — | Électricité consommée | Average man-hours per operative | 2.60 | 2.75 | 2.00 | Heures de travail: moyenne par ouvrier |
| Capacity of installed power equipment (As of 31.XII.1955) | 5.5 | 4.7 | 0.8 | Puissance installée (au 31.XII.1955) | Per thousand operative man-hour: | | | | Par millier d'heures de travail d'ouvrier |
| | | | | | Wages and salaries | 4.92 | 5.36 | 2.50 | Traitements et salaires |
| | | | | | Electricity consumed | 1.62 | 1.91 | — | Électricité consommée |
| | | | | | Capacity of installed power equipment | 4.23 | 4.27 | 4.00 | Puissance installée |

## B. The Major Groups of Manufacturing — Les classes de la branche Industries manufacturières

| Item of data | Manu-facturing[1] Industries manufac-turières[1] | Food, beverages and tobacco Industries alimen-taires, boissons, tabac | Textiles | Clothing, footwear and made-up textiles Articles d'habil-lement, chaussures et ouvrages en tissu | Wood products and furniture Bois et meubles | Paper and paper products Papier et ouvrages en papier | Printing and publish-ing[2] Im-primerie et édition[2] | Leather and leather products except wearing apparel Cuir et articles en cuir, à l'exclu-sion des articles d'habil-lement | Rubber products Ouvrages en caout-chouc | Chemicals and chemical, petroleum and coal products Produits chi-miques et dérivés du pétrole et du charbon | Non-metallic mineral products Produits minéraux non métal-liques | Metal prod-ucts[3] Ouvrages en métaux[3] | Other manu-factur-ing Autres in-dustries manufac-turières | Rubrique |
|---|---|---|---|---|---|---|---|---|---|---|---|---|---|---|
| ISIC | 2-3 | 20-22 | 23 | 24 | 25-26 | 27 | 28 | 29 | 30 | 31-32 | 33 | 35-38 | 39 | CITI |
| | | | | | | *a.* Absolute Figures — Chiffres absolus | | | | | | | | |
| Number of establishments. | 986 | 236 | 81 | 184 | 111 | 6 | 85 | 28 | 8 | 64 | 39 | 122 | 22 | Nombre d'établissements |
| Value added.......... | 786.8 | 363.5 | 125.0 | 25.2 | 19.5 | 2.5 | 14.7 | 9.7 | 4.7 | 178.7 | 19.3 | 18.4 | 5.6 | Valeur ajoutée |
| Number of engaged (As of last pay period of December)........ | 29.9 | 7.5 | 7.0 | 2.7 | 2.0 | 0.2 | 1.9 | 0.6 | 0.2 | 4.2 | 1.0 | 2.3 | 0.3 | Nombre de personnes occupées (dernière période de paie de décembre) |
| Number of employees (As of last pay period of December)........ | 28.6 | 7.3 | 6.8 | 2.5 | 1.9 | 0.2 | 1.9 | 0.5 | 0.2 | 4.0 | 0.9 | 2.2 | 0.2 | Nombre de salariés (dernière période de paie de décembre) |
| Wages and salaries paid.............. | 289.1 | 96.1 | 55.5 | 12.5 | 12.3 | 1.2 | 15.5 | 4.7 | 1.2 | 58.2 | 11.2 | 18.2 | 2.5 | Traitements et salaires payés |
| Operatives: Number............. | 24.1 | 5.8 | 6.2 | 1.9 | 1.7 | 0.2 | 1.2 | 0.5 | 0.2 | 3.4 | 0.8 | 2.0 | 0.2 | Ouvriers: Nombre |
| Man-hours worked.... | 59.3 | 17.3 | 13.8 | 4.1 | 4.0 | 0.4 | 2.5 | 0.9 | 0.4 | 8.7 | 2.1 | 4.7 | 0.4 | Heures de travail effectuées |
| Wages and salaries... | 210.1 | 63.9 | 44.4 | 10.4 | 9.9 | 0.8 | 9.3 | 3.6 | 1.3 | 41.5 | 7.8 | 16.1 | 1.1 | Traitements et salaires |
| Electricity consumed..... | 81.9 | 25.8 | 20.2 | 1.4 | 2.7 | 0.1 | 0.9 | 1.1 | 0.4 | 10.7 | 16.6 | 1.8 | 0.2 | Electricité consommée |
| Capacity of installed power equipment (As of 31.XII.1955)... | 71.2 | 24.8 | 10.3 | 0.8 | 5.9 | 0.2 | 1.0 | 1.4 | 0.7 | 17.9 | 5.6 | 2.3 | 0.3 | Puissance installée (au 31.XII.1955) |
| | | | | | | *b.* Structure | | | | | | | | |
| Distribution in percent of: Value added........ | 100.0 | 46.1 | 15.9 | 3.2 | 2.5 | 0.3 | 1.9 | 1.2 | 0.6 | 22.7 | 2.5 | 2.3 | 0.8 | Distribution en pour-centage: Valeur ajoutée |
| Number of engaged.. | 100.0 | 25.0 | 23.4 | 9.1 | 6.7 | 0.6 | 6.4 | 2.0 | 0.7 | 14.0 | 3.4 | 7.6 | 1.1 | Nombre de personnes occupées |
| Per person engaged: Value added........ | ... | 48.5 | 17.8 | 9.3 | 9.8 | 12.5 | ... | 16.2 | 23.5 | 42.5 | 19.3 | ... | 18.7 | Par personne occupée: Valeur ajoutée |
| Electricity consumed... | ... | 3.4 | 2.9 | 0.5 | 1.4 | 0.5 | 0.5 | 1.8 | 2.0 | 2.5 | 16.6 | ... | 0.7 | Electricité consommée |
| Capacity of installed power equipment..... | 2.38 | 3.31 | 1.47 | 0.30 | 2.95 | 1.00 | 0.53 | 2.33 | 3.50 | 4.26 | 5.60 | 1.00 | 1.00 | Puissance installée |
| Employees as a percent of engaged........ | 95.6 | 97.3 | 97.1 | 92.6 | 95.0 | 100.0 | 100.0 | 83.3 | 100.0 | 95.2 | 90.0 | 95.6 | 66.7 | Salariés en pourcentage des personnes occupées |
| Value added per unit of wages and salaries....... | ... | 3.78 | 2.25 | 2.02 | 1.58 | 2.08 | ... | 2.06 | 3.92 | 3.07 | 1.72 | ... | 2.24 | Valeur ajoutée par unité de traitements et salaires |
| Wages and salaries per employee....... | 10.1 | 13.2 | 8.2 | 5.0 | 6.5 | 6.0 | 8.2 | 9.4 | 6.0 | 14.6 | 12.4 | 8.3 | 12.5 | Traitements et salaires par salarié |
| Operatives as a percent of employees........ | 84.3 | 79.4 | 91.2 | 76.0 | 89.5 | 100.0 | 63.2 | 100.0 | 100.0 | 85.0 | 88.9 | 90.9 | 100.0 | Ouvriers en pourcentage des salariés |
| Average man-hours per operative....... | 2.46 | 2.98 | 2.22 | 2.16 | 2.35 | 2.00 | 2.08 | 1.80 | 2.00 | 2.56 | 2.62 | 2.35 | 2.00 | Heures de travail: moyenne par ouvrier |
| Per thousand operative man-hours: Wages and salaries... | 3.54 | 3.69 | 3.22 | 2.54 | 2.48 | 2.00 | 3.72 | 4.00 | 3.25 | 4.77 | 3.71 | 3.42 | 2.75 | Par millier d'heures-ouvrier Traitements et salaires |
| Electricity consumed... | ... | 1.49 | 1.46 | 0.34 | 0.68 | 0.25 | 0.36 | 1.22 | 1.00 | 1.23 | 7.90 | ... | 0.50 | Electricité consommée |
| Capacity of installed power equipment..... | 1.20 | 1.43 | 0.75 | 0.20 | 1.48 | 0.50 | 0.40 | 1.56 | 1.75 | 2.06 | 2.67 | 0.49 | 0.75 | Puissance installée |

[1] Excludes one establishment in basic metals (ISIC 34) for which no items of data could be shown.
[2] Value added excluded for four large establishments for which the other items of data appear.
[3] Value added excluded for six large establishments and electricity consumed excluded for two large establishments, for which the other items of data appear.

[1] Non compris un établissement de la classe Métallurgie de base (CITI 34) au sujet duquel aucune donnée n'a pu être fournie.
[2] Sont exclus du chiffre de la valeur ajoutée quatre grands établissements compris dans les autres rubriques.
[3] Sont exclus du chiffre de la valeur ajoutée six grands établissements et du chiffre de l'électricité consommée deux grands établissements compris dans les autres rubriques.

## 4. CHARACTERISTICS OF INDUSTRIAL ESTABLISHMENTS WITH A GROSS VALUE OF PRODUCTION OF 300,000 SUCRES OR MORE DURING 1958

### CARACTERISTIQUE DES ETABLISSEMENTS INDUSTRIELS AYANT UNE VALEUR BRUTE DE PRODUCTION DE 300,000 SUCRES OU PLUS PENDANT 1958

#### 1955, 1958

Number of establishments in units; value added and wages and salaries in million Sucres; number of engaged in thousands; value added per engaged in thousand Sucres.

Nombre d'établissements en unités; valeur ajoutée et traitements et salaires e millions de sucres; nombre de personnes occupées en milliers; valeur ajoutée pe personne occupée en milliers de sucres.

### A. The Major Groups of Mining — Les classes de la branche Industries extractives

| Year and item of data | Total | Metal mining — Extraction des minerais métalliques | Crude petroleum and natural gas — Pétrole brut et gaz naturel | Other mining — Divers | Année et rubrique | Year and item of data | Total | Metal mining — Extraction des minerais métalliques | Crude petroleum and natural gas — Pétrole brut et gaz naturel | Other mining — Divers | Année et rubrique |
|---|---|---|---|---|---|---|---|---|---|---|---|
| ISIC | 1 | 12 | 13 | 14-19 | CITI | ISIC | 1 | 12 | 13 | 14-19 | CITI |
| | **a. Absolute Figures — Chiffres absolus** | | | | | | **b. Structure** | | | | |
| **1955** | | | | | 1955 | **1955** | | | | | 1955 |
| Number of establishments. | 5 | 1 | 3 | 1 | Nombre d'établissements | Distribution in percent of: | | | | | Distribution en pourcentage: |
| Value added............. | 40.3 | 7.1 | 32.3 | 0.9 | Valeur ajoutée | Value added........... | 100.0 | 17.6 | 80.2 | 2.2 | Valeur ajoutée |
| Number of engaged....... | 1.17 | 0.62 | 0.51 | 0.04 | Nombre de personnes occupées | Number of engaged..... | 100.0 | 53.0 | 43.6 | 3.4 | Nombre de personnes occupées |
| Wages and salaries........ | 14.9 | 5.4 | 8.8 | 0.7 | Traitements et salaires | Value added per person engaged....... | 34.4 | 11.4 | 63.3 | 22.5 | Valeur ajoutée par personne occupée |
| | | | | | | Value added per unit of wages and salaries..... | 2.70 | 1.31 | 3.67 | 1.28 | Valeur ajoutée par unité d traitements et salaires |
| **1958** | | | | | 1958 | **1958** | | | | | 1958 |
| Number of establishments. | 5 | 1 | 3 | 1 | Nombre d'établissements | Distribution in percent of: | | | | | Distribution en pourcentage: |
| Value added............. | 35.4 | 9.2 | 25.2 | 1.0 | Valeur ajoutée | Value added........... | 100.0 | 26.0 | 71.2 | 2.8 | Valeur ajoutée |
| Number of engaged....... | 1.02 | 0.62 | 0.36 | 0.04 | Nombre de personnes occupées | Number of engaged..... | 100.0 | 60.8 | 35.3 | 3.9 | Nombre de personnes occupées |
| Wages and salaries........ | 11.6 | 5.7 | 5.2 | 0.7 | Traitements et salaires | Value added per person engaged....... | 34.7 | 14.8 | 70.0 | 25.0 | Valeur ajoutée par personne occupée |
| | | | | | | Value added per unit of wages and salaries..... | 3.05 | 1.61 | 4.85 | 1.43 | Valeur ajoutée par unité d traitements et salaires |

## B. The Major Groups of Manufacturing — Les classes de la branche Industries manufacturières

| Year and item of data | Manufacturing [1] — Industries manufacturières [1] | Food, beverages and tobacco — Industries alimentaires, boissons, tabac | Textiles | Clothing, footwear and made-up textiles — Articles d'habillement, chaussures et ouvrages en tissu | Wood products and furniture — Bois et meubles | Paper and paper products — Papier et ouvrages en papier | Printing and publishing — Imprimerie et édition | Leather and leather products except wearing apparel — Cuir et articles en cuir, à l'exclusion des articles d'habillement | Rubber products — Ouvrages en caoutchouc | Chemicals and chemical, petroleum and coal products — Produits chimiques et dérivés du pétrole et du charbon | Non-metallic mineral products — Produits minéraux non métalliques | Metal products — Ouvrages en métaux | Other manufacturing — Autres industries manufacturières | Année et rubrique |
|---|---|---|---|---|---|---|---|---|---|---|---|---|---|---|
| ISIC | 2–3 | 20–22 | 23 | 24 | 25–26 | 27 | 28 | 29 | 30 | 31–32 | 33 | 35–38 | 39 | CITI |
| *a. Absolute Figures — Chiffres absolus* | | | | | | | | | | | | | | |
| **1955** | | | | | | | | | | | | | | **1955** |
| Number of establishments. | 365 | 142 | 58 | 25 | 16 | 6 | 29 | 14 | 6 | 31 | 15 | 16 | 7 | Nombre d'établissements |
| Value added......... | 697.7 | 370.2 | 132.8 | 11.5 | 11.5 | 2.5 | 11.1 | 8.8 | 6.2 | 109.7 | 16.4 | 7.5 | 9.5 | Valeur ajoutée |
| Number of engaged.... | 24.1 | 7.7 | 7.2 | 1.0 | 1.1 | 0.2 | 1.4 | 0.5 | 0.2 | 3.4 | 0.8 | 0.4 | 0.2 | Nombre de personnes occupées |
| Wages and salaries..... | 262.1 | 102.3 | 57.0 | 6.6 | 8.7 | 1.1 | 12.5 | 4.4 | 1.7 | 50.9 | 10.4 | 3.4 | 3.1 | Traitements et salaires |
| **1958** | | | | | | | | | | | | | | **1958** |
| Number of establishments. | 398 | 149 | 70 | 27 | 16 | 6 | 31 | 15 | 7 | 32 | 16 | 20 | 9 | Nombre d'établissements |
| Value added......... | 853.6 | 478.2 | 159.5 | 10.5 | 14.3 | 3.7 | 11.1 | 9.6 | 6.3 | 105.5 | 29.1 | 12.2 | 13.6 | Valeur ajoutée |
| Number of engaged.... | 30.4 | 13.1 | 7.8 | 1.0 | 1.1 | 0.2 | 1.5 | 0.5 | 0.3 | 3.3 | 0.9 | 0.5 | 0.2 | Nombre de personnes occupées |
| Wages and salaries..... | 324.4 | 131.7 | 61.4 | 7.0 | 9.9 | 1.5 | 16.0 | 4.9 | 2.5 | 69.0 | 11.9 | 5.2 | 3.4 | Traitements et salaires |
| *b. Structure* | | | | | | | | | | | | | | |
| **1955** Distribution in percent of: | | | | | | | | | | | | | | **1955** Distribution en pourcentage: |
| Value added........ | 100.0 | 53.0 | 19.0 | 1.7 | 1.6 | 0.4 | 1.6 | 1.3 | 0.8 | 15.8 | 2.3 | 1.1 | 1.4 | Valeur ajoutée |
| Number of engaged.. | 100.0 | 31.9 | 29.9 | 4.1 | 4.6 | 0.8 | 5.8 | 2.1 | 0.8 | 14.1 | 3.4 | 1.6 | 0.9 | Nombre de personnes occupées |
| Value added per person engaged...... | 29.0 | 48.1 | 18.4 | 11.5 | 10.4 | 12.5 | 7.9 | 17.6 | 31.0 | 32.3 | 20.5 | 18.8 | 47.5 | Valeur ajoutée par personne occupée |
| Value added per unit of wages and salaries............ | 2.66 | 3.62 | 2.33 | 1.74 | 1.32 | 2.27 | 0.89 | 2.00 | 3.65 | 2.16 | 1.58 | 2.20 | 3.06 | Valeur ajoutée par unité de traitements et salaires |
| **1958** Distribution in percent of: | | | | | | | | | | | | | | **1958** Distribution en pourcentage: |
| Value added........ | 100.0 | 56.0 | 18.7 | 1.2 | 1.7 | 0.4 | 1.3 | 1.1 | 0.8 | 12.3 | 3.4 | 1.5 | 1.6 | Valeur ajoutée |
| Number of engaged.. | 100.0 | 43.0 | 25.7 | 3.3 | 3.6 | 0.7 | 4.9 | 1.6 | 1.0 | 10.9 | 2.9 | 1.7 | 0.7 | Nombre de personnes occupées |
| Value added per person engaged...... | 28.1 | 36.5 | 20.4 | 10.5 | 13.0 | 18.5 | 7.4 | 19.2 | 21.0 | 32.0 | 32.3 | 24.4 | 68.0 | Valeur ajoutée par personne occupée |
| Value added per unit of wages and salaries............ | 2.63 | 3.63 | 2.60 | 1.50 | 1.44 | 2.47 | 0.69 | 1.96 | 2.52 | 1.53 | 2.44 | 2.35 | 4.00 | Valeur ajoutée par unité de traitements et salaires |

[1] Excludes Basic metals (ISIC major group 34).

[1] Non compris Métallurgie de base (CITI 34).

# EL SALVADOR — SALVADOR

## Gross Domestic Product and The Gross Domestic Fixed Capital Formation

Estimates of the expenditure on and the origin of the gross domestic product and the expenditure on the gross domestic fixed capital formation are presented in Table 1. The data are derived from information supplied by the Dirección General de Estadística y Censos, Ministerio de Economía, San Salvador, in response to the United Nations national accounts questionnaire.

## Index Numbers of Industrial Production

Index numbers of production in selected manufacturing industries are presented in Table 2. The indexes have been compiled and published monthly by the Banco Central de Reserva in *Revista Mensual del Banco Central de Reserva de El Salvador;* further unpublished details are obtained by the Statistical Office of the United Nations through correspondence with the Banco.

The indexes are computed as base weighted arithmetic averages, starting from elementary series of relatives of the quantity produced for 78 individual commodities. These relatives are combined into indexes for 21 detailed categories, using as weights the value of gross output in 1956. The indexes for the 21 detailed categories are combined by the Statistical office of the United Nations into indexes for major groups, using as weights the values added in 1956. The index for manufacturing as a whole is computed by the Banco Central by combining the indexes for the 21 detailed categories into indexes for 5 broader categories and then these indexes into an index for manufacturing as a whole, using as weights at both stages the values added in 1956. All the weights used in these calculations are derived from the results of the annual survey of manufacturing for 1956 described below.

## Index of Industrial Employment

Index numbers of employment in selected major groups of manufacturing are presented in Table 3. The indexes are based on data derived from the results of an annual survey of the most important manufacturing activities in El Salvador. This enquiry was conducted for 1956 and later years, although employment data begins in 1957. The enquiry is described below.

Some reservations are attached to these indexes as no allowance is made for changes in the number of establishments covered in each survey. The results utilised from the annual survey are the absolute total numbers of

## Produit intérieur brut et formation brute de capital fixe intérieur

Le tableau 1 contient des estimations des dépenses imputées au produit intérieur brut, du produit intérieur brut par secteur d'activité d'origine et de la formation brute de capital fixe intérieur. Les données sont tirées des renseignements fournis par la Dirección General de Estadística y Censos, Ministerio de Economía, San Salvador, en réponse au questionnaire de l'ONU sur la comptabilité nationale.

## Indices de la production industrielle

Les indices de la production de quelques industries manufacturières sont reproduits au tableau 2. Ces indices sont construits et publiés mensuellement par le Banco Central de Reserva dans *Revista Mensual del Banco Central de Reserva de El Salvador;* le Banco Central a communiqué en outre au Bureau de statistique de l'ONU, par correspondance, d'autres renseignements non publiés.

Les indices sont des moyennes arithmétiques à pondération fixe; ils sont construits à partir de séries élémentaires de rapports fondés sur les quantités produites de 78 marchandises. Ces rapports sont combinés en indices relatifs à 21 catégories détaillées, les coefficients de pondération utilisés étant la valeur brute de la production en 1956. Les indices relatifs aux 21 catégories détaillées ont été combinés en indices de classes par le Bureau de statistique de l'ONU, qui a utilisé comme coefficents de pondération les valeurs ajoutées en 1956. L'indice relatif à l'ensemble des industries manufacturières est construit par le Banco Central, qui combine les indices relatifs aux 21 catégories en indices relatifs à 5 catégories plus larges, puis ces indices en un indice relatif à l'ensemble des industries manufacturières, en utilisant comme poids, dans les deux cas, les valeurs ajoutées en 1956. Tous les poids utilisés dans ces calculs sont tirés des résultats de l'enquête annuelle de 1956 sur les industries manufacturières, qui est décrite ci-dessous.

## Indices de l'emploi dans l'industrie

Les indices de l'emploi dans quelques classes des industries manufacturières sont présentés au tableau 3. Ces indices sont fondés sur les résultats d'une enquête annuelle sur les activités manufacturières les plus importantes du Salvador. Cette enquête a été exécutée pour 1956 et les années suivantes, mais les données sur l'emploi ne sont fournies qu'à partir de 1957. L'enquête est décrite ci-dessous.

Ces indices font l'objet de certaines réserves, car il n'est pas tenu compte des variations enregistrées, d'une enquête à l'autre, dans le nombre des établissements recensés. L'enquête annuelle a fourni les chiffres absolus

persons employed. The indexes for major groups are indexes of the absolute number of employees derived from the survey; the index for manufacturing as a whole is compiled using the major group indexes and weights of the number of persons engaged from the 1956 Census.

indiquant le nombre de personnes occupées. Les indices de classes sont établis à partir des chiffres absolus fournis par l'enquête sur le nombre de salariés; l'indice relatif à l'ensemble des industries manufacturières est calculé à partir des indices de classes, que l'on combine en utilisant comme coefficients de pondération le nombre de personnes occupées fourni par le recensement de 1956.

### Characteristics and Structure of Industrial Activity

The information shown in Table 4 is derived from the results of El Salvador's First and Second Industrial Census as published by the Dirección General de Estadística y Censos in *Primer Censos Industrial y Comercial, 1951* (San Salvador, March 1955) and in *Segundo Censo Industrial y Comercial, 1956* (San Salvador, November 1959). The first Census covered all establishments engaged in industrial activity during the calendar year 1951 or the 1951/52 season (e.g., coffee-peeling mills and sugar refineries) and whose gross value of sales or production amounted to 1000 Colones or more. The second Census covered industrial activities during 1956 or the 1956/1957 season for such activities as coffee peeling and sugar refining. The establishments included were all those with a gross value of production of 1000 Colones, or more during the year or new establishments with a gross value of production of 700 Colones or more during the last three months of 1956. However sugar refineries were included if they had a gross value of production of 500 Colones or more during the year.

The data shown in Table 5 are from the results of the annual surveys of manufacturing for 1951 and 1953 published by the Dirección General de Estadística y Censos in the *Anuario Estadístico, 1953* (San Salvador, March 1956). These annual surveys covered establishments in selected manufacturing industries that had six or more employees and used power equipment and were carried out for the years 1951 to 1954.

The data shown in Table 6 are derived from the results of the annual surveys of manufacturing for 1956 and 1958, published by the Dirección General de Estadística y Censos in *Anuario Estadístico 1957* (San Salvador, April 1959) and *Anuario Estadístico 1958* (San Salvador, January 1960). This newer series of annual surveys, which began in 1956, cover in principle the most important manufacturing activities in the country. The survey in 1956 covers, in terms of the gross value of production in the 1956 Census, establishments accounting for about 20 per cent of the gross value of manufacturing production. A number of the important industries were completely covered in terms of the 1956 Census; whilst some industries with a large number of small establishments were partly covered.

The establishment was used as the reporting unit except that in the case of the 1951 Census the enterprise was used for construction. Value added is valued at

### Caractéristiques et structure de l'activité industrielle

Les chiffres du tableau 4 sont tirés des résultats des premier et second recensements industriels du Salvador, publiés par la Dirección General de Estadística y Censos dans *Primer Censos Industrial y Comercial, 1951* (San Salvador, mars 1955) et dans *Segundo Censo Industrial y Comercial, 1956* (San Salvador, novembre 1959). Le premier recensement portait sur tous les établissements ayant exercé une activité industrielle pendant l'année civile 1951 ou pendant la campagne 1951/1952 (épluchage du café et raffinage du sucre) et dont la valeur brute des ventes ou de la production avait été au moins égale à 1000 colons. Le second recensement portait sur tous les établissements exerçant une activité industrielle en 1956 ou pendant la campagne 1956/1957 (épluchage du café et raffinage du sucre) et dont la valeur brute de la production avait été au moins égale à 1000 colons pendant l'année, ainsi que sur les nouveaux établissements ayant atteint une valeur brute de production de 700 colons ou plus pendant les trois derniers mois de 1956. Cependant, le recensement portait également sur les sucreries ayant eu, pendant l'année, une production d'une valeur brute de 500 colons ou plus.

Les chiffres du tableau 5 proviennent des résultats des enquêtes annuelles de 1951 et 1953 sur les industries manufacturières, publiés par la Dirección General de Estadística y Censos dans *Anuario Estadístico, 1953* (San Salvador, mars 1956). Ces enquêtes annuelles portaient sur les établissements appartenant à certaines industries manufacturières qui comptaient 6 salariés ou plus et qui utilisaient la force motrice; elles ont été effectuées pour les années 1951 à 1954.

Les données du tableau 6 ont été tirées des résultats des enquêtes annuelles de 1956 et 1958 sur les établissements manufacturiers, publiés par la Dirección General de Estadística y Censos dans *Anuario Estadístico 1957* (San Salvador, avril 1959) et *Anuario Estadístico 1958* (San Salvador, janvier 1960). Cette série plus récente d'enquêtes annuelles, qui a commencé en 1956, porte en principe sur les activités manufacturières les plus importantes du pays. L'enquête de 1956 porte sur les établissements dont le valeur brute de la production représente environ 20 p. 100 de celle de la production manufacturière telle qu'elle ressort du recensement de 1956. Un certain nombre d'industries importantes ont été comprises intégralement si l'on se réfère au recensement de 1956, mais quelques industries comptant un grand nombre de petits établissements n'on été comprises qu'en partie.

C'est l'établissement qui a servi d'unité statistique, sauf pour le recensement de 1951, où l'on a adopté l'entreprise dans le cas du bâtiment et des travaux publics. La valeur

market prices and in the case of the 1956 and 1958 surveys of larger establishments was calculated by the Statistical Office of the United Nations by deducting the the value of the consumption of raw material from the total value of production. The resulting value added figure differs from that for the other enquiries and from the definitions of items of data as recommended in the International Standards in Basic Industrial Statistics, as it includes the value of fuels and electricity consumed. The employment data exclude part-time workers and persons on sick-leave, maternity leave or vacation. The wages and salary figures shown in Table 5 include withdrawals by working proprietors and partners. The data on installed capacity relates to equipment in use and in reserve and is equivalent to the sum of the horsepower of prime movers connected directly to machinery other than generators and the horsepower of all electric motors.

ajoutée est comptée aux prix du marché; pour les enquêtes de 1956 et 1958 sur les grands établissements, elle a été calculée par le Bureau de statistique de l'ONU, qui a déduit de la valeur totale de la production la valeur de la consommation de matières premières. Les chiffres de la valeur ajoutée ainsi obtenus diffèrent des chiffres fournis par les autres enquêtes et ne sont pas conformes aux définitions de rubriques recommandées dans les Normes internationales relatives aux statistiques industrielles de base en ce sens qu'ils comprennent le coût des combustibles et de l'électricité consommés. Les chiffres de l'emploi ne comprennent ni les travailleurs à temps partiel, ni les personnes en congé de maladie, en congé de maternité ou en vacances. Les traitements et salaires indiqués au tableau 5 comprennent les sommes prélevées sur les recettes de l'entreprise par les propriétaires qui travaillent et les associés. La puissance installée est celle du matériel en service et en réserve; elle représente la puissance des moteurs primaires entraînant directement des machines autres que des générateurs et celle de tous les moteurs électriques.

## 1. THE GROSS DOMESTIC PRODUCT AND GROSS DOMESTIC FIXED CAPITAL FORMATION
## LE PRODUIT INTERIEUR BRUT ET LA FORMATION BRUTE DE CAPITAL FIXE INTERIEUR

Million Colones                                                                 Millions de colons

### A. Expenditure on the Gross Domestic Product at Market Prices
### Dépenses relatives au produit intérieur brut aux prix du marché

| Item of data and year / Rubrique et année | Total | Consumption / Consommation | | Gross Domestic Capital Formation / Formation brûte de capital intérieur | | Net exports of goods and services / Exportations nettes de biens et de services | |
|---|---|---|---|---|---|---|---|
| | | Total [1] | Government / Etat | Total | Fixed / Fixe | Exports less imports / Exportations moins importations | Exports / Exportations |
| *a. At Current Prices — Aux prix courants* | | | | | | | |
| Absolute figures — Chiffres absolus | | | | | | | |
| 1958 | 1 292 | 1 123 | 152 | ... | 157 | 12 | 320 |
| 1959 | 1 259 | 1 112 | 150 | ... | 138 | 8 | 309 |
| 1960 | 1 321 | 1 198 | 148 | ... | 185 | —62 | 294 |
| Percentage distribution of average annual expenditure — Distribution en pourcentage des dépenses annuelles moyennes | | | | | | | |
| 1958 | 100.0 | 86.9 | 11.8 | ... | 12.2 | 0.9 | 24.8 |
| 1960 | 100.0 | 90.7 | 11.2 | ... | 14.0 | —4.7 | 22.2 |

[1] Includes increase in stocks.                                                [1] Y compris l'accroissement des stocks.

## B.   The Gross Domestic Product at Factor Cost According to Origin
### Origine par secteur d'activité du produit intérieur brut au coût des facteurs

| Item of data and year<br>Rubrique et année | Total | Agricultural sector<br>Secteur agricole | Industrial Sector — Secteur industriel | | | | | Transportation and communication<br>Transports et communications | Other sectors [1]<br>Autres secteurs [1] |
|---|---|---|---|---|---|---|---|---|---|
| | | | Total | Mining<br>Industries extractives | Manufacturing<br>Industries manufacturières | Construction<br>Bâtiment et travaux publics | Electricity, gas and water<br>Electricité, gaz et eau | | |
| ISIC — CITI | 0–9 | 0 | 1–5 | 1 | 2–3 | 4 | 5 | 7 | 6, 8–9 |
| *a.  At Current Prices — Aux prix courants* | | | | | | | | | |
| Absolute figures — Chiffres absolus | | | | | | | | | |
| 1958............ | 1 163 | 439 | 151 | 7 | 96 | 38 | 10 | 44 | 529 |
| 1959............ | 1 142 | 429 | 154 | 6 | 98 | 39 | 11 | 45 | 514 |
| 1960............ | 1 189 | 411 | 158 | 5 | 101 | 39 | 13 | 48 | 572 |
| Percentage distribution according to sector— Distribution en pourcentage par secteur | | | | | | | | | |
| 1958............ | 100.0 | 37.7 | 13.0 | 0.6 | 8.3 | 3.3 | 0.8 | 3.8 | 45.5 |
| 1960............ | 100.0 | 34.5 | 13.3 | 0.4 | 8.5 | 3.3 | 1.1 | 4.0 | 48.2 |

[1] Includes water and sanitary services (ISIC groups 521-522) for data relating to 1958 and 1959 only.

[1] Y compris les services des eaux et les services sanitaires (CITI groupes 521-522) en 1958 et 1959 seulement.

## C.   Gross Domestic Fixed Capital Formation According to Purchasing Sector
### La formation brute de capital fixe intérieur par secteur d'activité

| Item of data and year<br>Rubrique et année | Total | Agricultural sector<br>Secteur agricole | Industrial Sector — Secteur industriel | | | | Transportation and communication<br>Transports et communications | Other sectors<br>Autres secteurs |
|---|---|---|---|---|---|---|---|---|
| | | | Total | Mining and manufacturing<br>Industries extractives et manufacturières | Construction<br>Bâtiment et travaux publics | Electricity, gas and water<br>Electricité, gaz et eau | | |
| ISIC — CITI | 0–9 | 0 | 1–5 | 1–3 | 4 | 5 | 7 | 6, 8–9 |
| *a.  At Current Prices — Aux prix courants* | | | | | | | | |
| Absolute figures — Chiffres absolus | | | | | | | | |
| 1958............ | 157 | 21 | 22 | 15 | 4 | 3 | 28 | 86 |
| 1959............ | 138 | 20 | 17 | 12 | 2 | 3 | 21 | 80 |
| 1960............ | 185 | 14 | ... | 27 | [1] | 4 | 30 | 109 |
| Percentage distribution according to sector— Distribution en pourcentage par secteur | | | | | | | | |
| 1958............ | 100.0 | 13.3 | 14.0 | 9.6 | 2.5 | 1.9 | 17.9 | 54.8 |
| 1960............ | 100.0 | 7.6 | ... | 14.6 | [1] | 2.2 | 16.3 | 59.3 |

[1] Included in Other sectors (ISIC divisions 6, 8-9).

[1] Compris dans Autres secteurs (CITI branches 6, 8-9).

## 2. INDEX NUMBERS OF MANUFACTURING PRODUCTION
## INDICES DE LA PRODUCTION DES INDUSTRIES MANUFACTURIERES

| Period<br><br>Période | Manu-facturing [1]<br><br>Industries manufac-turières [1] | Food, beverages and tobacco<br><br>Industries alimen-taires, boissons, tabac | Textiles | Clothing, footwear and made-up textiles<br><br>Articles d'habil-lement, chaussures et ouvrages en tissu | Leather and leather products except wearing apparel<br><br>Cuir et articles en cuir, à l'exclu-sion des articles d'habil-lement | Chemicals and chemical products<br><br>Produits chi-miques | Non-metallic mineral products<br><br>Produits minéraux non métal-liques |
|---|---|---|---|---|---|---|---|
| ISIC — CITI | 2–3 | 20–22 | 23 | 24 | 29 | 31 | 33 |

### a. Indexes — Indices (1958 = 100)

| | | | | | | | |
|---|---|---|---|---|---|---|---|
| 1954............... | 83 | 92 | 89 | 84 | 109 | 54 | 71 |
| 1955............... | 81 | 88 | 76 | 68 | 100 | 72 | 71 |
| 1956............... | 88 | 93 | 80 | 68 | 92 | 87 | 81 |
| 1957............... | 102 | 109 | 98 | 76 | 89 | 98 | 92 |
| 1958............... | 100 | 100 | 100 | 100 | 100 | 100 | 100 |
| 1959............... | 95 | 87 | 108 | 118 | 100 | 104 | 93 |
| 1960............... | 106 | 92 | 151 | 143 | 115 | 105 | 99 |
| 1961............... | 110 | 90 | 188 | 174 | 117 | 95 | 95 |

### b. Average Annual Rate of Change — Taux annuel moyen de variation

| | | | | | | | |
|---|---|---|---|---|---|---|---|
| 1954 – 1958........ | 4.8 | 2.1 | 3.0 | 4.4 | −2.1 | 16.7 | 8.9 |
| 1958 – 1960........ | 3.0 | −4.1 | 22.9 | 19.6 | 7.2 | 2.5 | −0.5 |

[1] The data for manufacturing excludes Wood products and furniture (ISIC major groups 25-26), Printing and publishing (ISIC major group 28), Basic metals (ISIC major group 34), Metal products (ISIC major groups 35-38) and Other manufacturing (ISIC major group 39).

[1] Non compris: Bois et meubles (CITI classes 25-26), Imprimerie et édition (CITI classe 28), Métallurgie de base (CITI classe 34), Ouvrages en métaux (CITI classes 35-38) et Autres industries manufacturières (CITI classe 39).

## 3. INDEX NUMBERS OF MANUFACTURING EMPLOYMENT
## INDICES DE L'EMPLOI DANS LES INDUSTRIES MANUFACTURIERES

| Period<br><br>Période | Manu-facturing [1]<br><br>Industries manufac-turières [1] | Food, beverages and tobacco<br><br>Industries alimen-taires, boissons, tabac | Textiles | Clothing, footwear and made-up textiles<br><br>Articles d'habil-lement, chaussures et ouvrages en tissu | Wood products and furniture<br><br>Bois et meubles | Leather and leather products except wearing apparel<br><br>Cuir et articles en cuir, à l'exclu-sion des articles d'habil-lement | Rubber products<br><br>Ouvrages en caout-chouc | Chemicals and chemical products<br><br>Produits chimiques | Non-metallic mineral products<br><br>Produits minéraux non métal-liques |
|---|---|---|---|---|---|---|---|---|---|
| ISIC — CITI | 2–3 | 20–22 | 23 | 24 | 25–26 | 29 | 30 | 31 | 33 |

### a. Indexes — Indices (1958 = 100)

| | | | | | | | | | |
|---|---|---|---|---|---|---|---|---|---|
| 1957............... | 95 | 94 | 107 | 93 | 89 | 108 | 95 | 108 | 92 |
| 1958............... | 100 | 100 | 100 | 100 | 100 | 100 | 100 | 100 | 100 |
| 1959............... | 96 | 96 | 111 | 97 | 78 | 98 | 105 | 98 | 90 |
| 1960............... | 96 | 92 | 139 | 96 | 86 | 101 | 115 | 90 | 92 |
| 1961............... | 106 | 107 | 155 | 88 | 108 | 98 | 192 | 106 | 88 |

[1] The data for manufacturing excludes Paper and paper products (ISIC major group 27), Printing and publishing (ISIC major group 28), Basic metals (ISIC major group 34), Metal products (ISIC major groups 35-38) and Other manufacturing (ISIC major group 39).

[1] Non compris: Papier et articles en papier (CITI classe 27), Imprimerie et édition (CITI classe 28), Métallurgie de base (CITI classe 34), Ouvrages en métaux (CITI classes 35-38) et Autres industries manufacturières (CITI classe 39).

# 4. CHARACTERISTICS OF INDUSTRIAL ESTABLISHMENTS WITH GROSS VALUE OF PRODUCTION OF 1,000 COLONES OR MORE[1]

## CARACTERISTIQUES DES ETABLISSEMENTS INDUSTRIELS AYANT UNE PRODUCTION D'UNE VALEUR BRUTE 1 000 COLONS OU PLUS[1]

### 1951, 1956

Number of establishments in units; value added and wages and salaries in million Colones; number of engaged, employees and operatives in thousands; electricity consumed in million KWH; capacity of installed power equipment in thousand horsepower; value added per engaged and wages and salaries per employee and per operative in thousand Colones; electricity consumed per engaged and per operative in thousand KWH; capacity of installed power equipment per engaged and per operative in horsepower.

Nombre d'établissements en unités; valeur ajoutée et traitements et salaires en millions de colons; nombre de personnes occupées, de salariés et d'ouvriers en milliers; électricité consommée en millions de kWh; puissance installée en milliers de chevaux-vapeur; valeur ajoutée par personne occupée et traitements et salaires par salarié en milliers de colons; électricité consommée par personne occupée et par ouvrier en milliers de kWh; puissance installée par personne occupée et par ouvrier en chevaux-vapeur.

## A. The Divisions of Industrial Activity — Les branches de l'activité industrielle

### a. Absolute Figures — Chiffres absolus

| Year and item of data | All industrial activity — Toutes industries | Mining — Industries extractives | Manufacturing — Industries manufacturières | Construction — Bâtiment et travaux publics | Electricity and gas[2] — Electricité et gaz[2] | Année et rubrique |
|---|---|---|---|---|---|---|
| ISIC / CITI | 1-4,511-512 | 1 | 2-3 | 4 | 511-512 | |
| **1951** | | | | | | **1951** |
| Number of establishments | 8 451 | 134 | 8 266 | 9 | 42 | Nombre d'établissements |
| Value added | 149.3 | 2.9 | 129.9 | 11.7 | 4.8 | Valeur ajoutée |
| Number of engaged (Second week of December) | 63.9 | 2.2 | 51.7 | 9.4 | 0.6 | Nombre de personnes occupées (deuxième semaine de décembre) |
| Employees: Number (Second week of December) | 52.9 | 2.1 | 40.8 | 9.4 | 0.6 | Salariés: Nombre (deuxième semaine de décembre) |
| Wages and salaries | 32.1 | 1.6 | 23.5 | 6.3 | 0.7 | Traitements et salaires |
| **1956** | | | | | | **1956** |
| Number of establishments | ... | 224 | 11 091 | ... | 70 | Nombre d'établissements |
| Value added | ... | 1.6 | 152.8 | ... | 9.3 | Valeur ajoutée |
| Number of engaged (Second week of December) | ... | 1.5 | 60.3 | ... | 0.5 | Nombre de personnes occupées (deuxième semaine de décembre) |
| Employees: Number (Second week of December) | ... | 1.3 | 46.3 | ... | 0.5 | Salariés: Nombre (deuxième semaine de décembre) |
| Wages and salaries | ... | 0.8 | 36.1 | ... | 1.2 | Traitements et salaires |
| Operatives: Number (Second week of December) | ... | 1.2 | 43.1 | ... | 0.5 | Ouvriers: Nombre (deuxième semaine de décembre) |
| Wages and salaries | ... | 0.8 | 27.1 | ... | 0.9 | Traitements et salaires |
| Electricity consumed | ... | 2.6 | 37.8 | ... | 0.2 | Electricité consommée |

### b. Structure

| Year and item of data | All industrial activity — Toutes industries | Mining — Industries extractives | Manufacturing — Industries manufacturières | Construction — Bâtiment et travaux publics | Electricity and gas[2] — Electricité et gaz[2] | Année et rubrique |
|---|---|---|---|---|---|---|
| ISIC / CITI | 1-4,511-512 | 1 | 2-3 | 4 | 511-512 | |
| **1951** Distribution in percent of: | | | | | | **1951** Distribution en pourcentage: |
| Value added | 100.0 | 1.9 | 87.0 | 7.8 | 3.3 | Valeur ajoutée |
| Number of engaged | 100.0 | 3.4 | 80.9 | 14.7 | 1.0 | Nombre de personnes occupées |
| Value added per person engaged | 2.3 | 1.3 | 2.5 | 1.2 | 8.0 | Valeur ajoutée par personne occupée |
| Employees as a percent of engaged | 82.8 | 95.4 | 78.9 | 100.0 | 100.0 | Salariés en pourcentage des personnes occupées |
| Value added per unit of wages and salaries | 4.65 | 1.81 | 5.53 | 1.86 | 6.86 | Valeur ajoutée par unité de traitements et salaires |
| Wages and salaries per employee | 0.6 | 0.8 | 0.6 | 0.7 | 1.2 | Traitements et salaires par salarié |
| **1956** Per person engaged: | | | | | | **1956** Par personne occupée: |
| Value added | ... | 1.1 | 2.5 | ... | 18.6 | Valeur ajoutée |
| Electricity consumed | ... | 1.7 | 0.6 | ... | 0.4 | Electricité consommée |
| Capacity of installed power equipment | ... | 1.47 | 1.01 | ... | ... | Puissance installée |
| Employees as a percent of engaged | ... | 86.7 | 76.8 | ... | 100.0 | Salariés en pourcentage des personnes occupées |
| Value added per unit of wages and salaries | ... | 2.00 | 4.23 | ... | 7.75 | Valeur ajoutée par unité de traitements et salaires |
| Wages and salaries per employee | ... | 0.6 | 0.8 | ... | 2.4 | Traitements et salaires par salarié |
| Operatives as a percent of employees | ... | 92.3 | 93.1 | ... | 100.0 | Ouvriers en pourcentage des salariés |
| Per operative: Wages and salaries | ... | 0.7 | 0.6 | ... | 1.8 | Par ouvrier: Traitements et salaires |
| Electricity consumed | ... | 2.2 | 0.9 | ... | 0.4 | Electricité consommée |

[1] Included in addition are sugar mills with gross value of production of at least 500 colones, and new establishments with a gross value of production of at least 700 colones during last three months of 1956.
[2] In 1951 electricity only.

[1] Y compris, en outre, les sucreries ayant eu une production d'une valeur brute d'au moins 500 colons et les nouveaux établissements ayant eu une production d'une valeur brute d'au moins 700 colons pendant les trois derniers mois de 1956.
[2] En 1951, électricité seulement.

# EL SALVADOR

## B. The Major Groups of Mining — Les classes de la branche Industries extractives

### a. Absolute Figures — Chiffres absolus

| Year and item of data | All mining Toutes industries extractives | Metal mining Extraction des minerais métalliques | Other mining Divers | Année et rubrique |
|---|---|---|---|---|
| ISIC | 1 | 12 | 14-19 | CITI |
| **1951** | | | | **1951** |
| Number of establishments | 134 | 3 | 131 | Nombre d'établissements |
| Value added | 2.9 | 2.2 | 0.7 | Valeur ajoutée |
| Number of engaged (Second week of December) | 2.2 | 1.2 | 1.0 | Nombre de personnes occupées (deuxième semaine de décembre) |
| Employees: | | | | Salariés: |
| Number (Second week of December) | 2.1 | 1.2 | 0.9 | Nombre (deuxième semaine de décembre) |
| Wages and salaries | 1.6 | 1.3 | 0.3 | Traitements et salaires |
| Electricity consumed | 7.4 | 7.3 | 0.1 | Electricité consommée |
| **1956** | | | | **1956** |
| Number of establishments | 224 | 1 | 223 | Nombre d'établissements |
| Value added | 1.6 | 0.4 | 1.2 | Valeur ajoutée |
| Number of engaged (Second week of December) | 1.5 | 0.4 | 1.1 | Nombre de personnes occupées (deuxième semaine de décembre) |
| Employees: | | | | Salariés: |
| Number (Second week of December) | 1.3 | 0.4 | 0.9 | Nombre (deuxième semaine de décembre) |
| Wages and salaries | 0.8 | 0.5 | 0.3 | Traitements et salaires |
| Operatives: | | | | Ouvriers: |
| Number (Second week of December) | 1.2 | 0.4 | 0.8 | Nombre (deuxième semaine de décembre) |
| Wages and salaries | 0.8 | 0.5 | 0.3 | Traitements et salaires |
| Electricity consumed | 2.6 | 2.6 | — | Electricité consommée |
| Capacity of installed power equipment | 2.2 | 1.1 | 1.1 | Puissance installée |

### b. Structure

| Year and item of data | All mining Toutes industries extractives | Metal mining Extraction des minerais métalliques | Other mining Divers | Année et rubrique |
|---|---|---|---|---|
| ISIC | 1 | 12 | 14-19 | CITI |
| **1951** | | | | **1951** |
| Distribution in percent of: | | | | Distribution en pourcentage: |
| Value added | 100.0 | 75.8 | 24.2 | Valeur ajoutée |
| Number of engaged | 100.0 | 54.5 | 45.5 | Nombre de personnes occupées |
| Per person engaged: | | | | Par personne occupée: |
| Value added | 1.3 | 1.8 | 0.7 | Valeur ajoutée |
| Electricity consumed | 3.4 | 6.1 | 0.1 | Electricité consommée |
| Employees as a percent of engaged | 95.4 | 100.0 | 90.0 | Salariés en pourcentage des personnes occupées |
| Value added per unit of wages and salaries | 1.81 | 1.69 | 2.33 | Valeur ajoutée par unité de traitements et salaires |
| Wages and salaries per employee | 0.8 | 1.1 | 0.3 | Traitements et salaires par salarié |
| **1956** | | | | **1956** |
| Distribution in percent of: | | | | Distribution en pourcentage: |
| Value added | 100.0 | 25.0 | 75.0 | Valeur ajoutée |
| Number of engaged | 100.0 | 26.6 | 73.4 | Nombre de personnes occupées |
| Per person engaged: | | | | Par personne occupée: |
| Value added | 1.1 | 1.0 | 1.1 | Valeur ajoutée |
| Electricity consumed | 1.7 | 6.5 | — | Electricité consommée |
| Capacity of installed power equipment | 1.47 | 2.75 | 1.00 | Puissance installée |
| Employees as a percent of engaged | 86.7 | 100.0 | 81.8 | Salariés en pourcentage des personnes occupées |
| Value added per unit of wages and salaries | 2.00 | 0.80 | 4.00 | Valeur ajoutée par unité de traitements et salaires |
| Wages and salaries per employee | 0.6 | 1.2 | 0.3 | Traitements et salaires par salarié |
| Operatives as a percent of employees | 92.3 | 100.0 | 88.9 | Ouvriers en pourcentage des salariés |
| Per operative: | | | | Par ouvrier: |
| Wages and salaries | 0.7 | 1.2 | 0.4 | Traitements et salaires |
| Electricity consumed | 2.2 | 6.5 | — | Electricité consommée |
| Capacity of installed power equipment | 1.83 | 2.75 | 1.38 | Puissance installée |

## C. The Major Groups of Manufacturing — Les classes de la branche Industries manufacturières

| Year and item of data | Manu-facturing<br><br>Industries manufac-turières | Food, beverages and tobacco<br><br>Industries alimen-taires, boissons, tabac | Textiles | Clothing, footwear and made-up textiles<br><br>Articles d'habil-lement, chaussures et ouvrages en tissu | Wood products and furniture<br><br>Bois et meubles | Paper and paper products<br><br>Papier et ouvrages en papier | Printing and publish-ing<br><br>Im-primerie et édition | Leather and leather products except wearing apparel<br><br>Cuir et articles en cuir, à l'exclu-sion des articles d'habil-lement | Rubber products<br><br>Ouvrages en caout-chouc | Chemicals and chemical, petroleum and coal products<br><br>Produits chi-miques et dérivés du pétrole et du charbon | Non-metallic mineral products<br><br>Produits minéraux non métal-liques | Basic metals<br><br>Métal-lurgie de base | Metal products<br><br>Ouvrages en métaux | Other manu-factur-ing<br><br>Autres in-dustries manufac-turières | Année et rubrique |
|---|---|---|---|---|---|---|---|---|---|---|---|---|---|---|---|
| ISIC | 2–3 | 20–22 | 23 | 24 | 25–26 | 27 | 28 | 29 | 30 | 31–32 | 33 | 34 | 35–38 | 39 | CITI |
| *a. Absolute Figures — Chiffres absolus* | | | | | | | | | | | | | | | |
| **1951** | | | | | | | | | | | | | | | **1951** |
| Number of establishments. | 8 266 | 3 688 | 700 | 2 109 | 436 | 2 | 73 | 109 | 8 | 126 | 349 | — | 458 | 208 | Nombre d'établissements |
| Value added.......... | 129.9 | 86.8 | 12.6 | 10.2 | 2.0 | 0.1 | 3.6 | 1.5 | 0.3 | 3.2 | 3.0 | — | 5.3 | 1.3 | Valeur ajoutée |
| Number of engaged (Second week of December).......... | 51.7 | 28.7 | 5.7 | 7.4 | 1.6 | 0.1 | 0.9 | 0.6 | 0.1 | 1.2 | 1.7 | — | 3.0 | 0.7 | Nombre de personnes occupées (deuxième semaine de décembre) |
| Employees: | | | | | | | | | | | | | | | Salariés: |
| Number (Second week of December)........ | 40.8 | 23.3 | 4.7 | 4.9 | 1.1 | 0.1 | 0.8 | 0.5 | 0.1 | 1.0 | 1.2 | — | 2.5 | 0.6 | Nombre (deuxième semaine de décembre) |
| Wages and salaries... | 23.5 | 9.1 | 3.8 | 3.5 | 0.8 | — | 1.2 | 0.4 | 0.1 | 0.8 | 1.0 | — | 2.4 | 0.4 | Traitements et salaires |
| Electricity consumed..... | 20.7 | 10.7 | 7.7 | 0.1 | 0.2 | — | 0.5 | 0.2 | 0.2 | 0.4 | — | — | 0.7 | | Électricité consommée |
| **1956** | | | | | | | | | | | | | | | **1956** |
| Number of establishments | 11 091 | 5 126 | 461 | 3 433 | 532 | 4 | 91 | 122 | 19 | 121 | 327 | 6 | 594 | 255 | Nombre d'établissements |
| Value added.......... | 152.8 | 101.2 | 9.8 | 14.2 | 2.7 | 0.2 | 3.5 | 1.9 | 0.7 | 3.7 | 7.1 | 0.1 | 6.3 | 1.4 | Valeur ajoutée |
| Number of engaged (Second week of December).......... | 60.3 | 36.7 | 4.1 | 9.6 | 1.6 | 0.1 | 0.9 | 0.7 | 0.1 | 1.1 | 2.2 | 0.1 | 2.3 | 0.8 | Nombre de personnes occupées (deuxième semaine de décembre) |
| Employees: | | | | | | | | | | | | | | | Salariés: |
| Number (Second week of December)........ | 46.3 | 29.5 | 3.4 | 5.5 | 1.0 | 0.1 | 0.8 | 0.6 | 0.1 | 1.0 | 2.0 | — | 1.8 | 0.5 | Nombre (deuxième semaine de décembre) |
| Wages and salaries... | 36.1 | 16.3 | 4.1 | 5.2 | 1.0 | 0.1 | 1.5 | 0.8 | 0.2 | 1.2 | 2.5 | — | 2.7 | 0.5 | Traitements et salaires |
| Operatives: | | | | | | | | | | | | | | | Ouvriers: |
| Number (Second week of December)........ | 43.1 | 27.6 | 3.2 | 5.3 | 0.9 | 0.1 | 0.6 | 0.5 | 0.1 | 0.9 | 1.7 | — | 1.7 | 0.5 | Nombre (deuxième semaine de décembre) |
| Wages and salaries... | 27.1 | 11.1 | 3.3 | 4.8 | 0.9 | — | 0.9 | 0.6 | 0.1 | 0.8 | 1.9 | — | 2.2 | 0.5 | Traitements et salaires |
| Electricity consumed..... | 37.8 | 16.8 | 6.3 | 0.5 | 0.3 | 0.2 | 0.9 | 0.2 | 0.4 | 1.2 | 10.2 | — | 0.8 | — | Électricité consommée |
| Capacity of installed power equipment..... | 60.7 | 41.5 | 8.1 | 0.4 | 0.4 | 0.3 | 0.5 | 1.0 | 0.6 | 1.6 | 5.6 | — | 0.7 | — | Puissance installée |
| *b. Structure* | | | | | | | | | | | | | | | |
| **1951** | | | | | | | | | | | | | | | **1951** |
| Distribution in percent of: | | | | | | | | | | | | | | | Distribution en pour-centage: |
| Value added........ | 100.0 | 66.8 | 9.7 | 7.8 | 1.6 | — | 2.8 | 1.2 | 0.2 | 2.5 | 2.3 | — | 4.0 | 1.1 | Valeur ajoutée |
| Number of engaged... | 100.0 | 55.5 | 11.0 | 14.3 | 3.1 | 0.2 | 1.7 | 1.2 | 0.2 | 2.3 | 3.3 | — | 5.8 | 1.4 | Nombre de personnes occupées |
| Per person engaged: | | | | | | | | | | | | | | | Par personne occupée: |
| Value added........ | 2.5 | 3.0 | 2.2 | 1.4 | 1.2 | 1.0 | 4.0 | 2.5 | 3.0 | 2.7 | 1.8 | ... | 1.8 | 1.8 | Valeur ajoutée |
| Electricity consumed... | 0.4 | 0.4 | 1.4 | — | 0.1 | ... | 0.6 | 0.3 | 2.0 | 0.3 | ... | ... | 0.2 | ... | Électricité consommée |
| Employees as a percent of engaged........ | 78.9 | 81.2 | 82.4 | 66.2 | 68.8 | 100.0 | 88.9 | 83.3 | 100.0 | 83.3 | 70.6 | ... | 83.3 | 85.7 | Salariés en pourcentage des personnes occupées |
| Value added per unit of wages and salaries............ | 5.53 | 9.54 | 3.32 | 2.91 | 2.50 | ... | 3.00 | 3.75 | 3.00 | 4.00 | 3.00 | ... | 2.21 | 3.25 | Valeur ajoutée par unité de traitements et salaires |
| Wages and salaries per employee....... | 0.6 | 0.4 | 0.8 | 0.7 | 0.7 | ... | 1.5 | 0.8 | 1.0 | 0.8 | 0.8 | ... | 1.0 | 0.7 | Traitements et salaires par salariés |
| **1956** | | | | | | | | | | | | | | | **1956** |
| Distribution in percent of: | | | | | | | | | | | | | | | Distribution en pour-centage: |
| Value added........ | 100.0 | 66.2 | 6.4 | 9.3 | 1.8 | 0.1 | 2.3 | 1.2 | 0.5 | 2.4 | 4.6 | 0.1 | 4.1 | 1.0 | Valeur ajoutée |
| Number of engaged... | 100.0 | 60.8 | 6.8 | 15.9 | 2.7 | 0.2 | 1.4 | 1.2 | 0.2 | 1.8 | 3.6 | 0.2 | 3.8 | 1.4 | Nombre de personnes occupées |
| Per person engaged: | | | | | | | | | | | | | | | Par personne occupée: |
| Value added........ | 2.5 | 2.8 | 2.4 | 1.5 | 1.7 | 2.0 | 3.9 | 2.7 | 7.0 | 3.4 | 3.2 | 1.0 | 2.7 | 1.8 | Valeur ajoutée |
| Electricity consumed... | 0.6 | 0.4 | 1.5 | 0.1 | 0.2 | 2.0 | 1.0 | 0.3 | 4.0 | 1.1 | 4.6 | ... | 0.3 | ... | Électricité consommée |
| Capacity of installed power equipment..... | 1.01 | 1.13 | 1.98 | 0.04 | 0.25 | 3.00 | 0.56 | 1.43 | 6.00 | 1.45 | 2.54 | ... | 0.30 | ... | Puissance installée |
| Employees as a percent of engaged........ | 76.8 | 80.4 | 82.9 | 57.3 | 62.5 | 100.0 | 88.9 | 85.7 | 100.0 | 90.9 | 90.9 | ... | 78.3 | 62.5 | Salariés en pourcentage des personnes occupées |
| Value added per unit of wages and salaries............ | 4.23 | 6.21 | 2.39 | 2.73 | 2.70 | 2.00 | 2.33 | 2.38 | 3.50 | 3.08 | 2.84 | ... | 2.33 | 2.80 | Valeur ajoutée par unité de traitements et salaires |
| Wages and salaries per employee....... | 0.8 | 0.6 | 1.2 | 0.9 | 1.0 | 1.0 | 1.9 | 1.3 | 2.0 | 1.2 | 1.2 | ... | 1.5 | 1.0 | Traitements et salaires par salarié |
| Operatives as a percent of employees........ | 93.1 | 93.6 | 94.1 | 96.4 | 90.0 | 100.0 | 75.0 | 83.3 | 100.0 | 90.0 | 85.0 | ... | 94.4 | 100.0 | Ouvriers en pourcentage des salariés |
| Per operative: | | | | | | | | | | | | | | | Par ouvrier: |
| Wages and salaries... | 0.6 | 0.4 | 1.0 | 0.9 | 1.0 | ... | 1.5 | 1.2 | 1.0 | 0.9 | 1.1 | ... | 1.3 | 1.0 | Traitements et salaires |
| Electricity consumed... | 0.9 | 0.6 | 2.0 | 0.1 | 0.3 | 2.0 | 1.5 | 0.4 | 4.0 | 1.3 | 6.0 | ... | 0.5 | ... | Électricité consommée |
| Capacity of installed power equipment..... | 1.41 | 1.50 | 2.53 | 0.08 | 0.44 | 3.00 | 0.83 | 2.00 | 6.00 | 1.78 | 3.29 | ... | 0.41 | ... | Puissance installée |

# EL SALVADOR

## 5. CHARACTERISTICS OF ESTABLISHMENTS WITH SIX OR MORE EMPLOYEES AND USING POWER EQUIPMENT
### SELECTED MAJOR GROUPS OF MANUFACTURING

### CARACTERISTIQUES DES ETABLISSEMENTS AYANT SIX SALARIES OU PLUS ET UTILISANT LA FORCE MOTRICE
### QUELQUES CLASSES DE LA BRANCHE INDUSTRIES MANUFACTURIERES

### 1951, 1953

Number of establishments in units; value added and wages and salaries in million Colones; number of persons engaged in thousands; value added per person engaged in thousand Colones

Nombre d'établissements en unités; valeur ajoutée et traitements et salaires en millions de colons; nombre de personnes occupées en milliers; valeur ajoutée par personne occupée en milliers de colons

| Year and item of data | Manufacturing [1] / Industries manufacturières [1] | Food, beverages and tobacco / Industries alimentaires, boissons, tabac | Textiles | Clothing, footwear and made-up textiles / Articles d'habillement, chaussures et ouvrages en tissu | Paper and paper products / Papier et ouvrages en papier | Leather and leather products except wearing apparel / Cuir et articles en cuir, à l'exclusion des articles d'habillement | Chemicals and chemical, petroleum and coal products / Produits chimiques et dérivés du pétrole et du charbon | Non-metallic mineral products / Produits minéraux non métalliques | Année et rubrique |
|---|---|---|---|---|---|---|---|---|---|
| ISIC | 2-3 | 20-22 | 23 | 24 | 27 | 29 | 31-32 | 33 | CITI |
| *a.   Absolute Figures — Chiffres absolus* | | | | | | | | | |
| **1951** | | | | | | | | | **1951** |
| Number of establishments........ | 292 | 243 | 17 | 1 | 1 | 12 | 10 | 8 | Nombre d'établissements |
| Value added.................. | 79.8 | 69.4 | 7.0 | 0.1 | 0.1 | 1.0 | 1.6 | 0.6 | Valeur ajoutée |
| Number of engaged........... | 17.5 | 13.7 | 2.7 | 0.1 | — | 0.3 | 0.4 | 0.3 | Nombre de personnes occupées |
| Wages and salaries paid........ | 11.3 | 7.1 | 3.0 | 0.1 | — | 0.3 | 0.4 | 0.4 | Traitements et salaires payés |
| **1953** | | | | | | | | | **1953** |
| Number of establishments........ | 319 | 229 | 16 | 5 | 1 | 26 | 15 | 27 | Nombre d'établissements |
| Value added.................. | 68.0 | 55.0 | 7.4 | 0.4 | 0.1 | 0.8 | 1.7 | 2.6 | Valeur ajoutée |
| Number of engaged........... | 27.9 | 22.6 | 2.9 | 0.4 | — | 0.5 | 0.7 | 0.8 | Nombre de personnes occupées |
| Wages and salaries paid........ | 15.3 | 8.1 | 3.9 | 0.4 | — | 0.9 | 0.9 | 1.1 | Traitements et salaires payés |
| *b.   Structure* | | | | | | | | | |
| **1951** | | | | | | | | | **1951** |
| Distribution in percent of: | | | | | | | | | Distribution en pourcentage: |
| Value added............... | 100.0 | 86.9 | 8.8 | 0.1 | 0.1 | 1.3 | 2.0 | 0.8 | Valeur ajoutée |
| Number of engaged.......... | 100.0 | 78.2 | 15.4 | 0.6 | — | 1.8 | 2.2 | 1.8 | Nombre de personnes occupées |
| Value added per person engaged.................. | 4.6 | 5.1 | 2.6 | 1.0 | ... | 3.3 | 4.0 | 2.0 | Valeur ajoutée par personne occupée |
| Value added per unit of wages and salaries.............. | 7.06 | 9.77 | 2.33 | 1.00 | ... | 3.33 | 4.00 | 1.50 | Valeur ajoutée par unité de traitements et salaires |
| **1953** | | | | | | | | | **1953** |
| Distribution in percent of: | | | | | | | | | Distribution en pourcentage: |
| Value added............... | 100.0 | 80.8 | 10.9 | 0.6 | 0.2 | 1.1 | 2.5 | 3.9 | Valeur ajoutée |
| Number of engaged.......... | 100.0 | 81.0 | 10.4 | 1.4 | — | 1.8 | 2.5 | 2.9 | Nombre de personnes occupées |
| Value added per person engaged.................. | 2.4 | 2.4 | 2.6 | 1.0 | ... | 1.6 | 2.4 | 3.2 | Valeur ajoutée par personne occupée |
| Value added per unit of wages and salaries.............. | 4.44 | 6.79 | 1.90 | 1.00 | ... | 0.89 | 1.89 | 2.36 | Valeur ajoutée par unité de traitements et salaires |

[1] Excluding Wood products and furniture (ISIC 25-26), Printing and publishing (ISIC 28), Rubber products (ISIC 30), Metal products (ISIC 35-38) and Miscellaneous manufacturing industries (ISIC 39).

[1] Non compris Bois et meubles (CITI classes 25-26), Imprimerie et édition (CITI classe 28), Ouvrages en caoutchouc (CITI classe 30), Ouvrages en métaux (CITI classes 35-38) et Industries manufacturières diverses (CITI classe 39).

# 6. CHARACTERISTICS OF THE LARGER ESTABLISHMENTS IN THE MOST IMPORTANT MANUFACTURING ACTIVITIES

## CARACTERISTIQUES DES GRANDS ETABLISSEMENTS APPARTENANT AUX INDUSTRIES MANUFACTURIERES LES PLUS IMPORTANTES

### 1956, 1958

Value added and wages and salaries in million Colones; number of employees and operatives in thousands, value added per employee and wages and salaries per employee in thousand Colones.

Valeur ajoutée et traitements et salaires en millions de colons; nombre de salariés et d'ouvriers en milliers; valeur ajoutée par salarié et traitements et salaires par salarié en milliers de colons.

| Year and item of data | Food beverages and tobacco[2] / Industries alimentaires, boissons, tabac[2] | Textiles | Clothing, footwear and made-up textiles[3] / Articles d'habillement, chaussures et ouvrages en tissu[3] | Furniture / Meubles | Paper and paper products / Papier et ouvrages en papier | Leather and leather products except wearing apparel / Cuir et articles en cuir, à l'exclusion des articles d'habillement | Rubber products / Ouvrages en caoutchouc | Chemicals and chemical petroleum products / Produits chimiques | Non-metallic mineral products / Produits minéraux non métalliques | Année et rubrique |
|---|---|---|---|---|---|---|---|---|---|---|
| ISIC | 20–22 | 23 | 24 | 26 | 27 | 29 | 30 | 31 | 33 | CITI |
| *a. Absolute Figures — Chiffres absolus* | | | | | | | | | | |
| **1956** Value added [1] | 37.6 | 7.2 | 1.0 | ... | 0.1 | 1.3 | 0.3 | 2.7 | 6.1 | **1956** Valeur ajoutée [1] |
| **1958** Value added [1] | 41.1 | 10.0 | 2.2 | 1.1 | ... | 1.4 | 0.3 | 2.5 | 7.0 | **1958** Valeur ajoutée [1] Salariés: |
| Employees: Number | 3.8 | 2.4 | 0.8 | 0.4 | ... | 0.4 | — | 0.6 | 0.9 | Nombre |
| Wages and salaries | 8.8 | 4.4 | 1.0 | 0.6 | ... | 0.6 | 0.1 | 0.9 | 1.7 | Traitements et salaires |
| Operatives: Number | 3.1 | 2.4 | 0.8 | 0.4 | ... | 0.4 | — | 0.5 | 0.7 | Ouvriers: Nombre |
| Wages and salaries | 4.4 | 3.4 | 0.8 | 0.5 | ... | 0.4 | 0.1 | 0.6 | 1.2 | Traitements et salaires |
| *b. Structure* | | | | | | | | | | |
| **1958** Per employee: Value added | 10.8 | 4.2 | 2.8 | 2.8 | ... | 3.5 | ... | 4.2 | 7.8 | **1958** Par salarié: Valeur ajoutée |
| Wages and salaries | 2.3 | 1.8 | 1.2 | 1.5 | ... | 1.5 | ... | 1.5 | 1.9 | Traitements et salaires |
| Value added per unit of wages and salaries | 4.67 | 2.27 | 2.20 | 1.83 | ... | 2.33 | 3.00 | 2.78 | 4.12 | Valeur ajoutée par unité de traitements et salaires |
| Wages and salaries per operative | 1.4 | 1.4 | 1.0 | 1.2 | ... | 1.0 | ... | 1.2 | 1.7 | Traitements et salaires par ouvrier |

[1] Includes the value of fuels and electricity consumed.
[2] Excludes production of wheat flour and rice polishing in 1956.
[3] Excludes manufacture of shirts in 1956.

[1] Y compris le valeur des combustibles et de l'électricité consommés.
[2] Non compris la fabrication de la farine de froment et le glaçage du riz en 1956.
[3] Non compris la fabrication des chemises en 1956.

# ETHIOPIA — ETHIOPIE

## Index of Industrial Employment

The indexes of employment in manufacturing industries presented in Table 1 are based on absolute figures of the number of employees. These absolute figures are derived from the results of the annual Censuses of Industrial Production described below. The absolute number of employees is the average for the year. The Censuses covered the 12 provinces of Ethiopia excluding Eritrea in the years 1953 and 1954; in 1955 and later years, Eritrea was included. In the case of the major groups of the International Standard Industrial Classification for which establishments existed in Eritrea, the indexes were linked in 1955. The total manufacturing index has been derived from the unweighted aggregated absolute figures of employment for the individual major groups.

## Characteristics and Structure of Industrial Activity

The data published in Table 2 are derived from the results of the 1955 and 1958 annual Censuses of Industrial Production which in principle covered all establishments employing an average of 5 persons or more during the year surveyed. The 1955 results have been published in *Bulletin*, No. 11 - July 1958, by the Ministry of Commerce and Industry, Addis Ababa; the 1958 results have been published in *Economic Review*, No. 2—June 1960, by the Ministry of Commerce, Industry and Planning, Addis Ababa. The data shown in the table covers the 12 provinces of Ethiopia and the Federal Territory of Eritrea.

The definitions of the items of data shown appear to coincide with the International Standards in Basic Industrial Statistics. The data on value added is at market prices.

## Indices de l'emploi dans l'industrie

Les indices du tableau 1 relatifs à l'emploi dans les industries manufacturières sont fondés sur des chiffres absolus indiquant le nombre de salariés. Ces chiffres absolus sont tirés des résultats des recensements annuels de la production industrielle décrits ci-dessous. Le nombre de salariés représente la moyenne pour l'année. Les recensements couvraient les 12 provinces de l'Ethiopie, à l'exclusion de l'Erythrée dans le cas de 1953 et 1954; l'Erythrée est comprise depuis 1955. Pour les classes de la Classification internationale type auxquelles appartenaient des établissements situés en Erythrée, les indices ont été raccordés au niveau de 1955. L'indice relatif à l'ensemble des industries manufacturières a été établi à partir du total des chiffres absolus de l'emploi non pondérés pour chaque classe de l'activité manufacturière.

## Caractéristiques et structure de l'activité industrielle

Les données du tableau 2 sont tirées des résultats des recensements annuels de la production industrielle de 1955 et 1958; ces recensements portaient, en principe, sur tous les établissements ayant occupé en moyenne 5 personnes ou plus pendant l'année de l'enquête. Les résultats du recensement de 1955 ont été publiés dans *Bulletin*, No 11 — juillet 1958, par le Ministère du commerce et de l'industrie, Addis-Abéba; ceux du recensement de 1958 ont été publiés dans *Economic Review*, No 2 — juin 1960, par le Ministère du commerce, de l'industrie et de la planification, Addis-Abéba. Les données indiquées dans le tableau concernent les 12 provinces de l'Ethiopie et le territoire fédéral de l'Erythrée.

Les définitions des rubriques présentées semblent conformes aux Normes internationales relatives aux statistiques industrielles de base. La valeur ajouté est comptée aux prix du marché.

# 1. INDEX NUMBERS OF INDUSTRIAL EMPLOYMENT[1]
## INDICES DE L'EMPLOI DANS L'INDUSTRIE[1]

| Period<br>Période | Manu-<br>facturing [2]<br><br>Industries<br>manufac-<br>turières [2] | Food,<br>beverages<br>and<br>tobacco [3]<br><br>Industries<br>alimen-<br>taires,<br>boissons,<br>tabac [3] | Textiles | Wood<br>products [4]<br><br>Bois [4] | Printing<br>and<br>publishing<br><br>Im-<br>primerie<br>et<br>édition | Leather<br>and<br>leather<br>products<br><br>Cuir et<br>articles<br>en cuir | Chemicals<br>and<br>chemical,<br>petroleum<br>and<br>coal<br>products<br><br>Produits<br>chi-<br>miques<br>et<br>dérivés<br>du<br>pétrole<br>et du<br>charbon | Non-<br>metallic<br>mineral<br>products<br><br>Produits<br>minéraux<br>non<br>métal-<br>liques | Other<br>manu-<br>facturing<br><br>Autres<br>industries<br>manufac-<br>turières |
|---|---|---|---|---|---|---|---|---|---|
| ISIC — CITI | 2–3 | 20–22 | 23 | 25 | 28 | 241, 29 | 31–32 | 33 | 39 |

### a. Indexes — Indices (1958 = 100)

| | | | | | | | | | |
|---|---|---|---|---|---|---|---|---|---|
| 1953............. | 69 | 68 | 44 | 65 | 104 | 86 | 97 | 83 | 176 |
| 1954............. | 73 | 72 | 45 | 75 | 106 | 95 | 96 | 92 | 136 |
| 1955............. | – 80 – | – 77 – | 54 | 78 | 93 | – 98 – | – 109 – | – 101 – | – 156 – |
| 1956............. | 97 | 81 | 90 | 114 | 94 | 96 | 110 | 81 | 237 |
| 1957............. | 96 | 96 | 96 | 102 | 92 | 106 | 96 | 92 | 130 |
| 1958............. | 100 | 100 | 100 | 100 | 100 | 100 | 100 | 100 | 100 |
| 1959............. | 115 | 122 | 116 | 109 | 114 | 97 | 112 | 134 | 73 |
| 1960............. | 130 | 133 | 163 | 92 | 114 | 93 | 124 | 142 | 90 |

### b. Average Annual Rate of Change — Taux annuel moyen de variation

| | | | | | | | | | |
|---|---|---|---|---|---|---|---|---|---|
| 1953 – 1960........ | 9.5 | 10.1 | 20.6 | 5.1 | 1.3 | 1.1 | 3.6 | 8.0 | −9.1 |
| 1954 – 1958........ | 8.2 | 8.6 | 22.1 | 7.5 | −1.4 | 1.3 | 1.0 | 2.1 | −7.4 |
| 1958 – 1960........ | 14.0 | 15.3 | 27.7 | −4.1 | 6.8 | −3.6 | 11.4 | 19.2 | −5.1 |

[1] Excludes Eritrea for the years 1953 and 1954.
[2] Excludes Metal products (ISIC major groups 35-38) but includes non-factory workers on sugar and tomato plantations (part of ISIC major groups 01) and logging (part of ISIC major group 02).
[3] Includes non-factory workers on sugar and tomato plantations (part of ISIC major group 01).
[4] Includes logging (part of ISIC major group 02).

[1] Non compris Erythrée en 1953 et 1954.
[2] Non compris Ouvrages en métaux (CITI classes 35-38); y compris les personnes travaillant non pas dans des usines mais dans des plantations de sucre ou de tomates (dans CITI classe 01) et l'exploitation forestière (dans CITI classe 02).
[3] Y compris les personnes travaillant non pas dans des usines mais dans des plantations de sucre ou de tomates (dans CITI classe 01).
[4] Y compris l'exploitation forestière (dans CITI classe 02).

# ETHIOPIA

## 2. CHARACTERISTICS OF SELECTED KINDS OF MANUFACTURING ESTABLISHMENTS EMPLOYING 5 PERSONS OR MORE
## CARACTERISTIQUES DE QUELQUES TYPES D'ETABLISSEMENTS MANUFACTURIERS EMPLOYANT 5 PERSONNES OU PLUS
### 1955, 1958

Number of establishments in units; value added and wages and salaries in million Ethiopian Dollars; number of employees in thousands; value added and wages and salaries per employee in thousand Ethiopian Dollars.

Nombre d'établissements en unités; valeur ajoutée et traitements et salaires en millions de dollars éthiopiens; nombre de salariés en milliers; valeur ajoutée et traitements et salaires par salarié en milliers de dollars éthiopiens.

| Year and item of data | Manufacturing[1,2] / Industries manufacturières[1,2] | Food, beverages and tobacco[1] / Industries alimentaires, boissons, tabac[1] | Textiles | Wood products[2] / Bois[2] | Printing and publishing / Imprimerie et édition | Leather and leather products / Cuir et articles en cuir | Chemicals and chemical, petroleum and coal products / Produits chimiques et dérivés du pétrole et du charbon | Non-metallic mineral products / Produits minéraux non métalliques | Metal products / Ouvrages en métaux | Other manufacturing / Autres industries manufacturière | Année et rubrique |
|---|---|---|---|---|---|---|---|---|---|---|---|
| ISIC | 2–3 | 20–22 | 23 | 25 | 28 | 241, 29 | 31–32 | 33 | 35–38 | 39 | CITI |
| *a. Absolute Figures — Chiffres absolus* | | | | | | | | | | | |
| **1955** | | | | | | | | | | | **1955** |
| Number of establishments. | 141 | 56 | 6 | 13 | 4 | 11 | 19 | 7 | 3 | 22 | Nombre d'établissements |
| Value added......... | 33.0 | 20.8 | 4.9 | 1.1 | 0.2 | 0.9 | 1.6 | 1.6 | 0.3 | 1.6 | Valeur ajoutée |
| Employees: | | | | | | | | | | | Salariés: |
| Number............. | 15.9 | 6.7 | 2.9 | 1.2 | 0.3 | 0.9 | 1.1 | 0.9 | 0.2 | 1.7 | Nombre |
| Wages and salaries... | 10.0 | 4.3 | 1.8 | 0.9 | 0.3 | 0.5 | 0.8 | 0.6 | 0.1 | 0.7 | Traitements et salaires |
| **1958** | | | | | | | | | | | **1958** |
| Number of establishments. | 133 | 56 | 8 | 8 | 4 | 7 | 18 | 9 | — | 23 | Nombre d'établissements |
| Value added........ | 39.9 | 23.0 | 7.8 | 1.3 | 0.2 | 1.4 | 1.0 | 2.7 | — | 2.5 | Valeur ajoutée |
| Employees: | | | | | | | | | | | Salariés: |
| Number............. | 20.0 | 8.8 | 5.3 | 1.6 | 0.3 | 1.0 | 1.0 | 0.9 | — | 1.1 | Nombre |
| Wages and salaries... | 12.5 | 5.6 | 2.7 | 0.9 | 0.4 | 0.7 | 0.5 | 0.8 | — | 0.9 | Traitements et salaires |
| *b. Structure* | | | | | | | | | | | |
| **1955** | | | | | | | | | | | **1955** |
| Distribution in percent of: | | | | | | | | | | | Distribution en pourcentage: |
| Value added........ | 100.0 | 63.0 | 14.8 | 3.3 | 0.6 | 2.7 | 4.9 | 4.9 | 0.9 | 4.9 | Valeur ajoutée |
| Number of employees. | 100.0 | 42.1 | 18.2 | 7.5 | 1.9 | 5.7 | 6.9 | 5.7 | 1.3 | 10.7 | Nombre de salariés |
| Per employee: | | | | | | | | | | | Par salarié: |
| Value added........ | 2.1 | 3.1 | 1.7 | 0.9 | 0.7 | 1.0 | 1.4 | 1.8 | 1.5 | 0.9 | Valeur ajoutée |
| Wages and salaries... | 0.6 | 0.6 | 0.6 | 0.8 | 1.0 | 0.6 | 0.7 | 0.7 | 0.5 | 0.4 | Traitements et salaires |
| Value added per unit of wages and salaries............. | 3.30 | 4.84 | 2.72 | 1.22 | 0.67 | 1.80 | 2.00 | 2.67 | 3.00 | 2.28 | Valeur ajoutée par unité de traitements et salaires |
| **1958** | | | | | | | | | | | **1958** |
| Distribution in percent of: | | | | | | | | | | | Distribution en pourcentage: |
| Value added........ | 100.0 | 57.6 | 19.5 | 3.3 | 0.5 | 3.5 | 2.5 | 6.8 | — | 6.3 | Valeur ajoutée |
| Number of employees. | 100.0 | 44.0 | 26.5 | 8.0 | 1.5 | 5.0 | 5.0 | 4.5 | — | 5.5 | Nombre de salariés |
| Per employee: | | | | | | | | | | | Par salarié: |
| Value added........ | 2.0 | 2.6 | 1.5 | 0.8 | 0.7 | 1.4 | 1.0 | 3.0 | . | 2.3 | Valeur ajoutée |
| Wages and salaries... | 0.6 | 0.6 | 0.5 | 0.6 | 1.3 | 0.7 | 0.5 | 0.9 | . | 0.8 | Traitements et salaires |
| Value added per unit of wages and salaries............. | 3.19 | 4.11 | 2.89 | 1.44 | 0.50 | 2.00 | 2.00 | 3.38 | . | 2.78 | Valeur ajoutée par unité de traitements et salaires |

[1] Includes non-factory workers on sugar and tomato plantations (part of ISIC major group 01).
[2] Includes logging (part of ISIC major group 02).

[1] Y compris les personnes travaillant non pas dans des usines mais dans des plantations de sucre ou de tomates (dans CITI classe 01).
[2] Y compris l'exploitation forestière (dans CITI classe 02).

# FEDERATION OF MALAYA—FEDERATION DE MALAISIE

## Gross Domestic Product

Estimates of the expenditure on and the origin of the gross domestic product are presented in Table 1. The data are based on information supplied by the Department of Statistics, Kuala Lumpur, in response to the United Nations national accounts questionnaire.

## Index Numbers of Industrial Employment

The index numbers of industrial employment shown in Table 2 are based on absolute figures of the number of employees. The mining data has been published in *Bulletin of Statistics Relating to the Mining Industry, 1955* and *1956 to 1960*, by the Department of Mines of the Ministry of Rural Development. The manufacturing industries data has been published annually in the *Annual Report of the Ministry of Labour*.

The basic mining data covering all mining establishments are mainly the absolute figures of the numbers of employees as on the 31st December of each year, but also includes the number of Dulang washers of Tin which is the total number of licence holders during each year. The basic data for the manufacturing industries are the number of employees as at the 31st of July of each year in establishments engaging 10 persons or more in selected major groups of manufacturing. The index numbers for mining as a whole and manufacturing as a whole are the unweighted aggregated totals of the absolute figures for the individual major groups; these index numbers are combined into an index for mining and manufacturing, using as weights, estimates of the total numbers engaged in 1958.

## The Characteristics and Structure of Industrial Activity

The data presented in Table 3 are derived from the results of the first Census of Manufacturing Industries in Malaya taken in 1960 by the Department of Statistics for the year 1959. The results have been taken from *Census of Manufacturing Industries in the Federation of Malaya, 1959;* with amendments to a part of these 1959 figures in *Survey of Manufacturing Industries Federation of Malaya, 1960;* both published by the Department of Statistics, Federation of Malaya, Kuala Lumpur.

The Census list covered all establishments having 5 or more employees or using machinery, and partially covered, but to an unknown extent, establishments with less than 5 employees and not using machinery. All establishments on this list did not respond and estimates to the extent

## Produit intérieur brut

Le tableau 1 contient des estimations des dépenses imputées au produit intérieur brut et des estimations du produit intérieur brut par branche d'activité d'origine. Les données sont fondées sur les renseignements fournis par le Department of Statistics, Kuala Lumpur, en réponse au questionnaire de l'ONU sur la comptabilité nationale.

## Indices de l'emploi dans l'industrie

Les indices de l'emploi dans l'industrie, reproduits au tableau 2, sont fondés sur des chiffres absolus indiquant le nombre de salariés. Les données relatives aux industries extractives ont été publiées dans *Bulletin of Statistics Relating to the Mining Industry 1955* et *1956 à 1960* par le Département des mines du Ministère du développement rural. Les données concernant les industries manufacturières sont publiées annuellement dans l'*Annual Report of the Ministry of Labour*.

Pour l'ensemble des établissements miniers, les données de base sont principalement les chiffres absolus indiquant le nombre de salariés au 31 décembre de chaque année, mais elles comprennent également le nombre de laveurs d'étain suivant la méthode Dulang, c'est-à-dire le nombre total de détenteurs de patentes pendant chaque année. Pour les industries manufacturières, les données de base sont le nombre de salariés au 31 juillet de chaque année dans les établissements occupant 10 personnes ou plus et appartenant à certaines classes des industries manufacturières. Les indices relatifs à l'ensemble des industries extractives et à l'ensemble des industries manufacturières sont les totaux non pondérés des chiffres absolus concernant les diverses classes; ces indices ont été combinés en indices pour l'ensembles des industries extractives et manufacturières, les coefficients de pondération utilisés étant des estimations du nombre total de personnes occupées en 1958.

## Caractéristiques et structure de l'activité industrielle

Les données du tableau 3 sont tirées des résultats du premier recensement des industries manufacturières de Malaisie en 1959 effectué par le *Department of Statistics* en 1960. Les résultats ont paru dans *Census of Manufacturing Industries in the Federation of Malaya 1959* et certains des chiffres de 1959 revisés dans *Survey of Manufacturing Industries Federation of Malaya 1960;* ces deux ouvrages ont été publiés par le *Department of Statistics, Federation of Malaya*, Kuala Lumpur.

Le recensement portait sur tous les établissements ayant au moins 5 salariés ou utilisant des machines et, dans une proportion indéterminée, sur certains établissements occupant moins de 5 salariés et n'utilisant pas de machines. Les établissements enregistrés n'ont pas tous

of 15 percent of the number of establishments and 7 percent of the value added were made for the missing establishments. These estimates are included in the results shown. However the data shown in Table 3 exclude firstly, the processing of agricultural products on estates and secondly, the processing of estate-type agricultural products in factories off estate with the exception of rubber remilling, latex processing (included in ISIC major group 30, Rubber products) and coconut oil mills and refineries (included in ISIC major group 31, Chemical products).

In general the definitions of the items of data correspond to the International Standards in Basic Industrial Statistics. Value added is valued at prices ex-factory. The number engaged and the number of employees are the number as at the 31st December 1959 and include part-time workers, whilst the wages and salaries are those paid during the whole of 1959.

répondu et l'on a fait des estimations pour 15 p. 100 du nombre d'établissements et 7 p. 100 de la valeur ajoutée afin de tenir compte de ces non-réponses. Ces estimations sont comprises dans les résultats présentés. Cependant, les données du tableau 9 ne comprennent ni la transformation des produits agricoles dans les plantations elles-mêmes, ni la transformation des produits agricoles provenant des plantations dans des usines extérieures, à l'exception de la récupération du caoutchouc et du traitement du latex (dans CITI classe 30, Ouvrages de caoutchouc), ainsi que des huileries et raffineries de noix de coco (dans CITI classe 31, Produits chimiques).

En général, les définitions des rubriques sont conformes aux Normes internationales relatives aux statistiques industrielles de base. La valeur ajoutée est comptée aux prix départ usine. Le nombre de personnes occupées et le nombre de salariés sont relevés au 31 décembre 1959 et comprennent les travailleurs à temps partiel, tandis que les traitements et salaires sont ceux qui ont été payés pendant la totalité de l'année 1959.

## 1.  THE GROSS DOMESTIC PRODUCT — PRODUIT INTERIEUR BRUT

Million Malayan dollars  ·  Millions de dollars malais

### A.  Expenditure on the Gross Domestic Product at Market Prices
### Dépenses relatives au produit intérieur brut aux prix de marché

| Item of data and year / Rubrique et année | Total[1] | Consumption / Consommation | | Gross Domestic Capital Formation / Formation brute de capital intérieur | | Net exports of goods and services / Exportations nettes de biens et de services | |
|---|---|---|---|---|---|---|---|
| | | Total | Government / Etat | Total | Fixed / Fixe | Exports less imports / Exportations moins importations | Exports / Exportations |
| a. At Current Prices — Aux prix courants | | | | | | | |
| **Absolute Figures — Chiffres absolus** | | | | | | | |
| 1955 | 4 931 | 3 660 | 549 | 374 | 361 | 908 | 2 488 |
| 1956 | 4 999 | 3 908 | 598 | 449 | 428 | 621 | 2 422 |
| 1957 | 5 046 | 4 034 | 626 | 517 | 491 | 481 | 2 351 |
| 1958 | 4 841 | 3 983 | 651 | 491 | 457 | 336 | 2 040 |
| 1959 | 5 411 | 4 184 | 656 | 367 | 427 | 848 | 2 638 |
| 1960 | 5 916 | 4 462 | 671 | 609 | 538 | 786 | 3 070 |
| **Percentage distribution of average annual expenditure — Distribution en pourcentage des dépenses annuelles moyennes** | | | | | | | |
| 1955 | 100.0 | 74.0 | 11.1 | 7.6 | 7.3 | 18.4 | 50.3 |
| 1958 | 100.0 | 82.8 | 13.5 | 10.2 | 9.5 | 7.0 | 42.4 |
| 1960 | 100.0 | 76.2 | 11.4 | 10.4 | 9.2 | 13.4 | 52.4 |

[1] Statistical discrepancy exists in that the constituents do not add up to the total shown. In the percentage distribution section of the table the actual total of the constituents has been used.

[1] Des écarts statistiques existent du fait que la somme des éléments ne donne pas le total indiqué. Pour la distribution en pourcentage on a utilisé le total effectif des éléments.

## B. The Gross Domestic Product at Factor Cost According to Origin
### Origine par secteur d'activité du produit intérieur brut au coût des facteurs

| Item of data and year<br>Rubrique et année | Total | Agricultural sector<br>Secteur agricole | Mining<br>Industries extractives | Manufacturing and construction<br>Industries manufacturières, bâtiment et travaux publics | Electricity, gas, water, transportation and communication<br>Electricité, gaz, eau, transports et communications | Other sectors<br>Autres secteurs |
|---|---|---|---|---|---|---|
| ISIC — CITI | 0–9 | 0 | 1 | 2–4 | 5, 7 | 6, 8–9 |

*a. At Prices of 1949 — Aux prix de 1959*

| | | | | | | |
|---|---|---|---|---|---|---|
| Absolute figures — Chiffres absolus | | | | | | |
| 1955............ | 4 281 | 1 990 | 235 | 225 | 170 | 1 661 |
| 1956............ | 4 414 | 1 996 | 255 | 233 | 187 | 1 743 |
| 1957............ | 4 538 | 2 047 | 251 | 239 | 195 | 1 806 |
| 1958............ | 4 578 | 2 121 | 177 | 245 | 189 | 1 846 |
| 1959............ | 4 760 | 2 170 | 190 | 260 | 210 | 1 930 |
| 1960............ | 5 191 | 2 305 | 267 | 300 | 243 | 2 076 |
| 1961............ | 5 458 | 2 403 | 295 | 325 | 264 | 2 171 |
| Percentage distribution according to sector— Distribution en pourcentage par secteur | | | | | | |
| 1955............ | 100.0 | 46.5 | 5.5 | 5.2 | 4.0 | 38.8 |
| 1958............ | 100.0 | 46.3 | 3.9 | 5.4 | 4.1 | 40.3 |
| 1960............ | 100.0 | 44.4 | 5.1 | 5.8 | 4.7 | 40.0 |
| Average annual rate of growth—Taux annuel moyen d'accroissement | | | | | | |
| 1955 – 1958..... | 2.2 | 2.2 | −9.0 | 2.9 | 3.6 | 3.6 |
| 1958 – 1960..... | 6.5 | 4.3 | 22.8 | 10.6 | 13.4 | 6.0 |

## 2. INDEX NUMBERS OF INDUSTRIAL EMPLOYMENT — INDICES DE L'EMPLOI DANS L'INDUSTRIE

### A. Selected Divisions of Industrial Activity
### Quelques branches de l'activité industrielle

| Period<br>Période | Total [1,2] | Mining [1]<br>Industries extractives [1] | Manufacturing [2]<br>Industries manufacturières [2] |
|---|---|---|---|
| ISIC — CITI | 1–3, 511-512 | 1 | 2–3 |

*a. Indexes — Indices (1958 = 100)*

| | | | |
|---|---|---|---|
| 1955............ | 92 | 146 | 78 |
| 1956............ | – 104 – | 146 | – 93 – |
| 1957............ | – 113 – | 140 | – 106 – |
| 1958............ | 100 | 100 | 100 |
| 1959............ | 102 | 104 | 102 |
| 1960............ | 114 | 125 | 111 |
| 1961............ | ... | – 133 – | ... |

*b. Average Annual Rate of Change — Taux annuel moyen de variation*

| | | | |
|---|---|---|---|
| 1955 – 1958...... | 2.8 | −11.8 | 8.6 |
| 1958 – 1960...... | 6.8 | 11.8 | 5.4 |

For footnotes see end of table.

Pour les notes, voir au bas du tableau.

### B. Selected Major Groups of Mining
### Quelques classes de la branche Industries extractives

| Period<br>Période | All mining [1]<br>Toutes industries extractives [1] | Coal mining<br>Extraction du charbon | Metal mining [1]<br>Extraction des minerais métalliques [1] |
|---|---|---|---|
| ISIC — CITI | 1 | 11 | 12 |

*a. Indexes — Indices (1958 = 100)*

| | | | |
|---|---|---|---|
| 1938............ | ... | 1 980 | ... |
| 1948............ | 213 | 1 060 | 208 |
| 1949............ | 215 | 1 260 | 210 |
| 1950............ | 215 | 1 320 | 208 |
| 1951............ | 173 | 1 280 | 166 |
| 1952............ | 173 | 1 290 | 166 |
| 1953............ | 149 | 1 000 | 143 |
| 1954............ | 143 | 658 | 138 |
| 1955............ | 146 | 415 | 145 |
| 1956............ | 146 | 407 | 144 |
| 1957............ | 140 | 333 | 139 |
| 1958............ | 100 | 100 | 100 |
| 1959............ | 104 | 96 | 105 |
| 1960............ | 125 | — | 126 |
| 1961............ | – 133 – | — | – 134 – |

*b. Average Annual Rate of Change — Taux annuel moyen de variation*

| | | | |
|---|---|---|---|
| 1955 – 1958...... | −11.8 | −37.8 | −11.6 |
| 1958 – 1960...... | 11.8 | ... | 12.2 |

For footnotes see end of table.

Pour les notes, voir au bas du tableau.

## C. Selected Major Groups of Manufacturing
### Quelques classes de la branche Industries manufacturières

| Period<br>Période | Manu-<br>facturing [2]<br><br>Industries<br>manufac-<br>turières [2] | Food,<br>beverages<br>and<br>tobacco [3]<br><br>Industries<br>alimen-<br>taires,<br>boissons,<br>tabac [3] | Wood<br>products<br><br>Bois | Printing<br>and<br>publishing<br><br>Im-<br>primerie<br>et<br>édition | Rubber<br>products<br><br>Ouvrages<br>en<br>caout-<br>chouc | Chemicals<br>and<br>chemical<br>products<br><br>Produits<br>chi-<br>miques | Basic<br>metals<br>and<br>metal<br>products<br><br>Métallurgie<br>de<br>base et<br>ouvrages<br>en<br>métaux |
|---|---|---|---|---|---|---|---|
| ISIC — CITI | 2–3 | 20–22 | 25 | 28 | 30 | 31 | 34–38 |

### a. Indexes — Indices (1958 = 100)

| | | | | | | | |
|---|---|---|---|---|---|---|---|
| 1955............. | 78 | 91 | 77 | 90 | ... | ... | 56 |
| 1956............. | – 93 – | 94 | 114 | 75 | 92 | 99 | 80 |
| 1957............. | – 106 – | – 104 – | 123 | 99 | 95 | 119 | 102 |
| 1958............. | 100 | 100 | 100 | 100 | 100 | 100 | 100 |
| 1959............. | 102 | 99 | 102 | 114 | 105 | 92 | 100 |
| 1960............. | 111 | 102 | 108 | 126 | 119 | 92 | 116 |

### b. Average Annual Rate of Change — Taux annuel moyen de variation

| | | | | | | | |
|---|---|---|---|---|---|---|---|
| 1955–1958........ | 8.6 | 3.2 | 9.1 | 3.6 | ... | ... | 21.3 |
| 1958–1960........ | 5.4 | 1.0 | 3.9 | 12.2 | 9.1 | —4.1 | 7.7 |

[1] Excludes Dulang washers of tin in 1961.
[2] Excludes Textiles (ISIC major group 23); Clothing, footwear and made-up textiles (ISIC major group 24); Furniture (ISIC major group 26); Paper and paper products (ISIC major group 27); Leather and leather products except wearing apparel (ISIC major group 29; and Other manufacturing (ISIC major group 39) in all years; Rubber products (ISIC major group 30) and Chemicals and Chemical Products (ISIC major group 31) in 1955; and pineapple canning (part of ISIC major group 20) in 1955 and 1956.
[3] Excludes pineapple canning (part of ISIC major group 20) in 1955 and 1956.

[1] Non compris en 1961, les personnes s'occupant du lavage de l'étain suivant la méthode Dulang.
[2] Non compris Textiles (CITI classe 23), Articles d'habillement, chaussures et ouvrages en tissu (CITI classe 24) Meubles (CITI classe 26), Papier et ouvrages en papier (CITI classe 27), Cuir et articles en cuir à l'exclusion des articles d'habillement (CITI classe 29) et Autres industries manufacturières (CITI classe 39) dans le cas de toutes les années; Ouvrages en caoutchouc (CITI classe 30) et Produits chimiques (CITI classe 31) en 1955 et la préparation des conserves d'ananas (dans CITI classe 20) en 1955 et 1956.
[3] Non compris la préparation des conserves d'ananas (dans CITI classe 20) en 1955 et 1956.

# 3. CHARACTERISTICS OF MANUFACTURING ESTABLISHMENTS WITH 5 OR MORE EMPLOYEES OR UTILISING MACHINERY

## CARACTERISTIQUES DES ETABLISSEMENTS MANUFACTURIERS OCCUPANT 5 SALARIES OU PLUS OU EQUIPES DE MACHINES

### 1959

Number of establishments in units; value added and wages and salaries in million Malay Dollars; number of engaged and employees in thousands; value added per engaged and wages and salaries per employee in thousand Malay Dollars.

Nombre d'établissements en unités; valeur ajoutée et traitements et salaires en millions de dollars malais; nombre de personnes occupées et de salariés en milliers; valeur ajoutée par personne occupée et traitements et salaires par salarié en milliers de dollars malais.

## The Major Groups of Manufacturing — Les classes de la branche Industries manufacturières

| Item of data | Manu-facturing / Industries manufac-turières | Food, beverages and tobacco / Industries alimen-taires, boissons, tabac | Textiles | Clothing, footwear and made-up textiles / Articles d'habil-lement, chaussures et ouvrages en tissu | Wood products and furniture / Bois et meubles | Printing and publish-ing / Im-primerie et édition | Rubber products / Ouvrages en caout-chouc | Chemicals and chemical, petroleum and coal products / Produits chi-miques et dérivés du pétrole et du charbon | Non-metallic mineral products / Produits minéraux non métal-liques | Metal products / Ouvrages en métaux | Other manu-factur-ing [1] / Autres in-dustries manufac-turières [1] | Rubrique |
|---|---|---|---|---|---|---|---|---|---|---|---|---|
| ISIC | 2–3 | 20–22 | 23 | 24 | 25–26 | 28 | 30 | 31–32 | 33 | 35–38 | 27, 29, 34, 39 | CITI |
| *a. Absolute Figures — Chiffres absolus* | | | | | | | | | | | | |
| Number of establishments. | 4 876 | 2 111 | 24 | 104 | 712 | 209 | 223 | 205 | 173 | 810 | 305 | Nombre d'établissements |
| Value added......... | 234.0 | 62.5 | 0.9 | 1.4 | 33.0 | 16.8 | 51.0 | 23.5 | 12.7 | 23.9 | 8.3 | Valeur ajoutée |
| Number of engaged (As at 31.XII)........ | 67.0 | 19.5 | 0.6 | 0.6 | 10.6 | 4.6 | 13.4 | 3.4 | 2.9 | 8.3 | 3.1 | Nombre de personnes occupées (au 31.XII) |
| Employees: | | | | | | | | | | | | Salariés: |
| Number (As at 31.XII).. | 60.5 | 16.4 | 0.6 | 0.5 | 9.6 | 4.3 | 13.1 | 3.2 | 2.7 | 7.3 | 2.8 | Nombre (au 31.XII) |
| Wages and salaries... | 89.3 | 21.9 | 0.7 | 0.5 | 15.1 | 7.2 | 20.1 | 5.4 | 3.9 | 10.9 | 3.6 | Traitements et salaires |
| *b. Structure* | | | | | | | | | | | | |
| Distribution in percent of: | | | | | | | | | | | | Distribution en pourcentage: |
| Value added........ | 100.0 | 26.7 | 0.4 | 0.6 | 14.1 | 7.2 | 21.8 | 10.0 | 5.4 | 10.2 | 3.6 | Valeur ajoutée |
| Number of engaged.. | 100.0 | 29.1 | 0.9 | 0.9 | 15.8 | 6.9 | 20.0 | 5.1 | 4.3 | 12.4 | 4.6 | Nombre de personnes occupées |
| Value added per person engaged...... | 3.5 | 3.2 | 1.5 | 2.3 | 3.1 | 3.6 | 3.8 | 6.9 | 4.4 | 2.9 | 2.7 | Valeur ajoutée par personne occupée |
| Employees as a percent of engaged......... | 90.3 | 84.1 | 100.0 | 83.3 | 90.6 | 93.5 | 97.8 | 94.1 | 93.1 | 88.0 | 90.3 | Salariés en pourcentage des personnes occupées |
| Value added per unit of wages and salaries... | 26.2 | 2.85 | 1.28 | 2.80 | 2.18 | 2.33 | 2.54 | 4.35 | 3.26 | 2.19 | 2.30 | Valeur ajoutée par unité de traitements et salaires |
| Wages and salaries per employee........ | 1.5 | 1.3 | 1.2 | 1.0 | 1.6 | 1.7 | 1.5 | 1.7 | 1.4 | 1.5 | 1.3 | Traitements et salaires par salarié |

[1] Includes Paper and paper products (ISIC major group 27); Leather and leather products except wearing apparel (ISIC major group 29); Basic metals (ISIC major group 34); and part of Metal Products (ISIC major groups 35–38).

[1] Y compris Papier et ouvrages en papier (CITI classe 27), Cuir et articles en cuir, à l'exclusion des articles d'habillement (CITI classe 29), Métallurgie de base (CITI classe 34) et une partie d'Ouvrages en métaux (CITI classes 35–38).

# FEDERATION OF RHODESIA AND NYASALAND
# FEDERATION DE RHODESIE ET NYASSALAND

## Gross Domestic Product and Gross Domestic Fixed Capital Formation

Estimates of expenditure on and the origin of the gross domestic product and the origin of the expenditure on the gross domestic fixed capital formation are presented in Table 1. The table is derived from data provided by the Central Statistical Office, Salisbury, in response to the United Nations national accounts questionnaire. Official estimates together with a description of the methods and sources used have been published in the *National Accounts of the Federation of Rhodesia and Nyasaland, 1954-1961,* by the Central Statistical Office, Salisbury.

## Index of Industrial Production

The index numbers of industrial production published in Table 2 are based, in the main, on indexes (1959 = 100) compiled and published monthly by the Central Statistical Office, Salisbury, in the *Monthly Digest of Statistics.* The separate indexes for Northern and Southern Rhodesia for major groups of mining and the indexes for Basic metals (ISIC major group 34) are however compiled by the Statistical Office of the United Nations from data on the quantity of minerals produced in each territory shown in the same publication.

The index numbers for manufacturing industries (except Basic metals) compiled by the Central Statistical Office, Salisbury, are built up from indicators supplied by 220 firms in the Federation. These indicators are mainly the quantities of individual commodities produced, but the quantity of raw materials or electricity used, or the number of man hours worked have also been utilized. The establishments for which indicators are used generally represent more than 75 percent of the value added in each major group recorded in the 1959 Census described below, under Table 4. The Census covered establishments engaging 6 or more persons or utilizing power equipment.

The indicators of the quantity of output are adjusted to represent production per working day and are utilized to compile series of relatives for each item. The relatives are then combined into indexes for groups of manufacturing activity. These indexes are, in turn, combined into indexes for major groups and the indexes for major groups are compiled into indexes for manufacturing as a whole. The weights used at each stage of compilation are based on the average annual value added during the period 1957-1959, derived from the results of the Censuses

## Produit intérieur brut et formation brute de capital fixe intérieur

Le tableau 1 contient des estimations des dépenses imputées au produit intérieur brut du produit intérieur brut par secteur d'activité d'origine et de la formation brute de capital fixe intérieur par secteur d'acquisition. Ce tableau a été établi à partir de données fournies par l'Office central de statistique, Salisbury, en réponse au questionnaire de l'ONU sur la comptabilité nationale. Les estimations officielles, ainsi que les renseignements connexes relatifs aux méthodes et sources adoptées, ont été publiés dans *National Accounts of the Federation of Rhodesia and Nyasaland, 1954-1961,* par l'Office central de statistique, Salisbury.

## Indices de la production industrielle

Les indices de la production industrielle présentés au tableau 2 sont fondés essentiellement sur des indices (1959 = 100) calculés et publiés chaque mois par l'Office central de statistique, Salisbury, dans le *Monthly Digest of Statistics.* Les indices relatifs aux classes des industries extractives présentés séparément pour la Rhodésie du Nord et la Rhodésie du Sud, ainsi que les indices concernant la Métallurgie de base (CITI classe 34) sont cependant calculés par le Bureau de statistique de l'ONU à partir de données sur les quantités extraites de minéraux dans chacun des territoires reproduites dans la même publication.

Les indices concernant les industries manufacturières (à l'exclusion de la Métallurgie de base) calculés par l'Office central de statistique, Salisbury, sont construits à partir d'indicateurs fournis par 220 entreprises de la Fédération. Ces indicateurs sont principalement le volume de la production de chaque marchandise, mais il s'agit parfois des quantités de matières premières ou d'électricité utilisées, ou du nombre d'heures de travail effectuées. Les établissements pour lesquels des indicateurs ont été utilisés représentent en général plus de 75 p. 100 de la valeur ajoutée dans chaque classe, telle qu'elle ressort du recensement de 1959, décrit ci-dessous dans le commentaire du tableau 4. Le recensement portait sur les établissements occupant au moins six personnes ou utilisant la force motrice.

Les indicateurs du volume de la production sont ajustés de manière à représenter la production par jour de travail et servent ensuite à calculer les séries de rapports quantitatifs pour chaque élément. Les rapports sont alors combinés en indices concernant les groupes de l'activité manufacturière. Ces indices sont, à leur tour, combinés en indices de classe et ceux-ci en indices relatifs à l'ensemble des industries manufacturières. Les poids utilisés à chacun des stades du calcul sont fondés sur la moyenne annuelle de la valeur ajoutée pendant la

of Industrial Production described below, under Table 4.

The indexes for the major groups of mining by territory and for Basic metals for the Federation have been built up from relatives of the quantity of the individual minerals extracted and of the smelted and refined ores produced. In combining the relatives for individual minerals into indexes for major groups, the gross values of production in 1958 have been used as weights. In the case of Basic metals (ISIC major group 34), the relatives of the items making up Non-ferrous metal basic industries (ISIC group 342) have been combined into an index using the gross values of production in 1958 as weights. This index has in turn been combined with the index for Iron and Steel Basic Industries (ISIC group 341) using as weights, values added derived from the 1958 Census of Industrial Production. The indexes for the Iron and Steel Basic Industries have been published by the Central Statistical Office, Salisbury, in the abovementioned publication.

### Index of Industrial Employment

The index numbers of industrial employment presented in Table 3 have been compiled by the Statistical Office of the United Nations from absolute figures of the numbers engaged and employed.

The absolute figures of the average number engaged for years 1955 to 1959 have been derived from the results of the Censuses of Industrial Production, described below under Table 4. These Censuses covered establishments engaging 6 persons or more or utilizing power equipment or steam boilers. The absolute figures utilized in the index numbers for the years, 1960 and 1961, for the divisions of industrial activity, have been derived from the results of the Quarterly Employment Enquiries (started in September 1959) and the Federal Census of Non-African Population and of all Employees (held for September 1961). The results of these enquiries and the Census have been published in the *Monthly Digest of Statistics*.

The Quarterly Employment enquiries covered all establishments. All establishments with 20 or more employees have been enumerated whilst a 20 percent sample has been taken of those establishments with fewer than 20 employees. The sample has been selected from a field stratified by type of activity. The annual absolute figure is the average of the number of employees as at the end of March, June, September and December.

The index numbers for the divisions of industrial activity for the years, 1959 and before, have been obtained from the unweighted aggregated absolute figures for the individual major groups. The index numbers for 1960 and 1961 for the divisions of industrial activity have been linked to these earlier indexes at 1959.

période 1957-1959, telle qu'elle ressort des résultats des recensements de la production industrielle décrits ci-dessous dans le commentaire du tableau 4.

Les indices concernant les classes des industries extractives de chaque territoire et la Métallurgie de base dans l'ensemble de la Fédération ont été construits à partir de rapports fondés sur les quantités extraites de chaque minéral et sur les quantités de minerais fondus et affinés. Les valeurs brutes de la production en 1958 ont été utilisées comme coefficients de pondération pour combiner les rapports relatifs aux divers minéraux en indices de classe. Dans le cas de la Métallurgie de base (CITI classe 34), les rapports concernant les éléments constitutifs du groupe Production et première transformation des métaux non ferreux (CITI groupe 342) ont été combinés en indices, les coefficients de pondération utilisés étant les valeurs brutes de la production en 1958. Ces indices ont été à leur tour combinés avec les indices relatifs à la Sidérurgie (CITI groupe 341); les poids utilisés à cette fin étaient les valeurs ajoutées fournies par le recensement de la production industrielle de 1958. Les indices concernant la sidérurgie ont été publiés par l'Office central de statistique, Salisbury, dans la publication ci-dessus mentionnée.

### Indices de l'emploi dans l'industrie

Les indices de l'emploi dans l'industrie présentés au tableau 3 ont été calculés par le Bureau de statistique de l'ONU à partir de chiffres absolus concernant le nombre de personnes occupées et de salariés.

Les chiffres absolus concernant le nombre moyen de personnes occupées pour les années 1955 à 1959 ont été tirés des résultats des recensements de la production industrielle décrits ci-dessous dans le commentaire du tableau 4. Ces recensements portaient sur tous les établissements occupant au moins 6 personnes ou utilisant soit la force motrice, soit des générateurs de vapeur. Les chiffres absolus utilisés pour calculer les indices de 1960 et 1961 relatifs aux branches de l'activité industrielle ont été tirés des résultats des enquêtes trimestrielles sur l'emploi (commencées en septembre 1959) et du recensement fédéral de la population non africaine et de tous les salariés (effectué pour septembre 1961). Les résultats de ces enquêtes et du recensement ont été publiés dans le *Monthly Digest of Statistics*.

Les enquêtes trimestrielles sur l'emploi portaient sur l'ensemble des établissements. Tous les établissements comptant 20 salariés ou plus ont été recensés, et un échantillon au cinquième a été choisi parmi les établissements ayant moins de 20 salariés. L'échantillon a été tiré d'une population stratifiée par type d'activité. Les chiffres absolus annuels représentent la moyenne du nombre de salariés à la fin de mars, juin, septembre et décembre.

Les indices de 1959 et des années antérieures concernant les branches de l'activité industrielle ont été obtenus à partir des totaux non pondérés des chiffres absolus relatifs aux classes de chaque branche. Les indices de 1960 et 1961 concernant les branches de l'activité industrielle ont été raccordés à ceux des années précédentes au niveau de 1959.

# FEDERATION OF RHODESIA AND NYASALAND

## The Characteristics and Structure of Industrial Activity

The data presented in Table 4, which result from the first and fourth Censuses of Industrial Production for the Federation as a whole, have been compiled from *The Censuses of Production of the Federation of Rhodesia and Nyasaland 1958-1959* (containing figures for 1955 to 1959), the Central Statistical Office, Salisbury, September 1961. The figures in Tables 5 and 6 give the results of earlier, separate annual Censuses of Industrial Production for Northern and Southern Rhodesia, and have been derived from *An Economic Survey of the Colonial Territories, 1951,* Colonial Office of the United Kingdom, London, 1952 and *Southern Rhodesia, Thirteenth Report on the Census of Industrial Production, 1938-1953,* Central African Statistical Office, respectively.

The results of the censuses for 1955 and 1958 in Table 4, for the Federation as a whole, although, in principle, confined for purposes of enumeration to establishments engaging 6 or more persons or utilizing motive power or steam boilers, contain estimates made by the Central Statistical Office, Salisbury, for establishments engaged in mining, construction and electricity which fell outside this field. Moreover it was felt that, though no estimates were made for manufacturing activity which fell outside the field enumerated, no establishments of any importance were excluded from the published results of the censuses. However, household and cottage industries such as dress-making and tailoring are excluded.

The coverage of the separate censuses for Northern and Southern Rhodesia shown in Tables 5 and 6, in fact as well as in principle, is confined to establishments engaging 6 or more persons or utilizing motive power or steam boilers. Household or cottage industries and craftsmen engaged in construction activities are thus excluded. In addition the completeness of coverage of the field to which the censuses were in principle restricted is open to some reservations. However, it should be noted that the scope of the data shown for Southern Rhodesia for 1938, 1948 and 1953 is identical, as estimates were made for delinquent establishments included on the census lists.

The definitions of items of data for which figures are shown in Tables 4, 5 and 6 are identical and are, on the whole, consistent with the International Standards in Basic Industrial Statistics. However, receipts from goods sold in the same condition as purchased were not included in value added, and persons engaged mainly in merchanting activities were not counted among the number of engaged. In addition, in the case of Table 4, employers contributions to pension and welfare funds are included in wages and salaries and in all Censuses, wages and salaries data include payments in kind valued at cost to the establishment.

## Caractéristiques et structure de l'activité industrielle

Les chiffres du tableau 4, tirés des résultats des premier et quatrième recensements de la production industrielle de l'ensemble de la Fédération, ont été établis à partir des données contenues dans *The Censuses of Production of the Federation of Rhodesia and Nyasaland 1958-1959* (comprennant des chiffres pour 1955 à 1959), Office central de statistique, Salisbury, septembre 1961. Les chiffres des tableaux 5 et 6 proviennent des résultats des recensements annuels antérieurs de la production industrielle effectués séparément dans la Rhodésie du Nord et dans la Rhodésie du Sud; ils sont tirés respectivement de *An Economic Survey of the Colonial Territories, 1951,* Colonial Office of the United Kingdom, Londres 1952, et *Southern Rhodesia, Thirteenth Report on the Census of Industrial Production, 1938-1953,* Central African Statistical Office.

Les recensements de 1955 et 1958 pour l'ensemble de la Fédération, dont les résultats sont présentés au tableau 4, ne portaient en principe que sur les établissements occupant au moins six personnes ou utilisant soit la force motrice, soit des générateurs de vapeur; cependant, les résultats indiqués contiennent des estimations établies par l'Office central de statistique, Salisbury, pour les établissements dont l'activité relevait des industries extractives, du bâtiment et des travaux publics, ainsi que de la production d'électricité, et qui se trouvaient hors du champ du recensement. En outre, bien qu'aucune estimation n'ait été faite pour les activités manufacturières qui se trouvaient hors du champ étudié, on pense qu'aucun établissement important n'a été exclu des résultats publiés des recensements. Toutefois, les activités familiales et artisanales telles que la couture ont été exclues.

Les recensements effectués séparément dans la Rhodésie du Nord et dans la Rhodésie du Sud, dont les résultats sont présentés aux tableaux 5 et 6, ne portaient, en fait comme en principe, que sur les établissements occupant au moins six personnes ou utilisant soit la force motrice, soit des générateurs de vapeur. Les industries familiales et les artisans s'occupant de travaux de construction ont donc été exclus. En outre, les établissements inclus en principe dans le champ des recensements n'ont peut-être pas tous été effectivement recensés. Cependant, il y a lieu de noter que les données de 1938, 1948 et 1953 concernant la Rhodésie du Sud ont la même portée, étant donné que des estimations ont été faites pour les établissements qui n'ont pas répondu parmi ceux qui figuraient sur la liste utilisée pour le recensement.

Les définitions des rubriques pour lesquelles des chiffres sont présentés aux tableaux 4, 5 et 6 sont identiques et conformes, dans l'ensemble, aux Normes internationales relatives aux statistiques industrielles de base. Toutefois, les recettes provenant des marchandises revendues en l'état ne sont pas comprises dans la valeur ajoutée, et les personnes exerçant une activité essentiellement commerciale sont exclues du nombres des personnes occupées. En outre, dans le tableau 4, les traitements et salaires comprennent les contributions des employeurs aux caisses de pension et de sécurité sociale et, dans tous les recensements, ils comprennent les paiements en nature, évalués au coût pour l'établissement.

## 1. THE GROSS DOMESTIC PRODUCT AND GROSS DOMESTIC FIXED CAPITAL FORMATION
## LE PRODUIT INTERIEUR BRUT ET LA FORMATION BRUTE DE CAPITAL FIXE INTERIEUR

Million Pounds                                          Millions de livres

### A. Expenditure on the Gross Domestic Product at Market Prices
### Dépenses relatives au produit intérieur brut aux prix du marché

| Item of data and year / Rubrique et année | Total[1] | Consumption / Consommation | | Gross Domestic Capital Formation / Formation brute de capital intérieur | | Net exports of goods and services / Exportations nettes de biens et de services | |
|---|---|---|---|---|---|---|---|
| | | Total | Government / Etat | Total | Fixed / Fixe | Exports less imports / Exportations moins importations | Exports / Exportations |
| **a. At Current Prices — Aux prix courants** | | | | | | | |
| Absolute figures — Chiffres absolus | | | | | | | |
| 1954 | 372.4 | 272.3 | 32.3 | 90.0 | 94.1 | 15.1 | 183.6 |
| 1955 | 426.8 | 294.9 | 35.1 | 106.7 | 107.9 | 17.1 | 202.5 |
| 1956 | 480.5 | 325.2 | 42.5 | 148.7 | 134.7 | .1.8 | 212.9 |
| 1957 | 478.6 | 360.0 | 48.8 | 155.6 | 148.9 | −40.8 | 194.3 |
| 1958 | 476.1 | 378.6 | 53.5 | 140.6 | 137.4 | −37.1 | 176.1 |
| 1959 | 547.8 | 400.6 | 60.8 | 131.5 | 126.2 | 17.4 | 227.8 |
| 1960 | 579.1 | 422.5 | 64.7 | 128.1 | 119.4 | 31.9 | 250.9 |
| 1961 | 590.3 | 442.0 | 74.7 | 127.9 | 112.3 | 30.0 | 250.0 |
| Percentage distribution of average annual expenditure — Distribution en pourcentage des dépenses annuelles moyennes | | | | | | | |
| 1954−1960 | 100.0 | 73.0 | 10.0 | 26.8 | 25.8 | 0.2 | 43.1 |
| 1954 | 100.0 | 72.2 | 8.6 | 23.8 | 24.9 | 4.0 | 48.6 |
| 1958 | 100.0 | 78.5 | 11.1 | 29.2 | 28.5 | −7.7 | 36.5 |
| 1960 | 100.0 | 72.5 | 11.1 | 22.0 | 20.5 | 5.5 | 43.1 |
| **b. At Prices of 1954 — Aux prix de 1954** | | | | | | | |
| Absolute figures — Chiffres absolus | | | | | | | |
| 1954 | 372.4 | 272.3 | 32.3 | 90.0 | 94.1 | 15.1 | 183.6 |
| 1955 | 376.9 | 289.7 | 32.2 | 104.4 | 104.9 | −24.2 | 157.6 |
| 1956 | 426.7 | 311.2 | 36.9 | 136.6 | 124.1 | −25.4 | 176.4 |
| 1957 | 458.5 | 333.8 | 39.5 | 138.9 | 132.5 | −17.8 | 203.0 |
| 1958 | 465.5 | 340.4 | 41.1 | 119.7 | 117.5 | 11.2 | 207.9 |
| 1959 | 507.9 | 352.0 | 45.3 | 113.7 | 108.0 | 43.5 | 243.1 |
| 1960 | 528.7 | 362.6 | 46.2 | 109.0 | 101.1 | 60.4 | 263.6 |
| 1961 | 546.6 | 370.4 | 50.3 | 109.0 | 91.9 | 75.8 | 272.9 |
| Percentage distribution of average annual expenditure — Distribution en pourcentage des dépenses annuelles moyennes | | | | | | | |
| 1954−1960 | 100.0 | 72.1 | 8.7 | 25.9 | 24.9 | 2.0 | 45.7 |
| 1954 | 100.0 | 72.2 | 8.6 | 23.8 | 24.9 | 4.0 | 48.6 |
| 1958 | 100.0 | 72.2 | 8.7 | 25.4 | 24.9 | 2.4 | 44.1 |
| 1960 | 100.0 | 68.2 | 8.7 | 20.5 | 19.0 | 11.3 | 49.5 |
| Average annual rate of growth — Taux annuel moyen d'accroissement | | | | | | | |
| 1954−1960 | 6.0 | 4.9 | 6.1 | 3.2 | 1.2 | . | 6.2 |
| 1954−1958 | 5.7 | 5.7 | 6.2 | 7.4 | 5.7 | . | 3.1 |
| 1958−1960 | 6.6 | 3.2 | 6.0 | −4.6 | −7.3 | . | 12.6 |

[1] Includes a statistical discrepancy.                [1] Y compris la divergence statistique.

## B. The Gross Domestic Product at Factor Cost According to Origin
### Origine par secteur d'activité du produit intérieur brut au coût des facteurs

| Item of data and year<br>Rubrique et année | Total | Agricultural sector [1]<br>Secteur agricole [1] | Industrial Sector — Secteur industriel | | | | | Transportation and communication<br>Transports et communications | Other sectors [2]<br>Autres secteurs [2] |
|---|---|---|---|---|---|---|---|---|---|
| | | | Total | Mining<br>Industries extractives | Manufacturing<br>Industries manufacturières | Construction<br>Bâtiment et travaux publics | Electricity, gas and water<br>Electricité, gaz et eau | | |
| ISIC — CITI | 0–9 | 0 | 1–5 | 1 | 2–3 | 4 | 511–521 | 7 | 522, 6, 8–9 |
| | | | | At Current Prices — Aux prix courants | | | | | |
| **Absolute figures — Chiffres absolus** | | | | | | | | | |
| 1954............ | 362.3 | 79.8 | 151.7 | 93.6 | 29.8 | 23.6 | 4.7 | 18.4 | 112.4 |
| 1955............ | 413.5 | 81.5 | 186.1 | 117.6 | 35.3 | 27.8 | 5.4 | 21.9 | 124.0 |
| 1956............ | 461.3 | 92.6 | 205.7 | 123.3 | 40.6 | 33.1 | 8.7 | 25.4 | 137.6 |
| 1957............ | 458.3 | 93.5 | 178.5 | 82.7 | 47.0 | 39.2 | 9.6 | 29.7 | 156.6 |
| 1958............ | 455.7 | 91.5 | 167.4 | 67.3 | 50.8 | 38.8 | 10.5 | 28.8 | 168.0 |
| 1959............ | 524.2 | 99.5 | 208.3 | 109.3 | 53.5 | 34.3 | 11.2 | 34.8 | 181.6 |
| 1960............ | 552.9 | 100.9 | 223.3 | 121.9 | 55.8 | 31.2 | 14.4 | 38.4 | 190.3 |
| 1961............ | 561.5 | 113.7 | 209.2 | 110.0 | 58.3 | 25.5 | 15.4 | 38.0 | 200.6 |
| **Percentage distribution according to sector— Distribution en pourcentage par secteur** | | | | | | | | | |
| 1954 – 1960..... | 100.0 | 19.8 | 41.0 | 22.2 | 9.7 | 7.1 | 2.0 | 6.1 | 33.1 |
| 1954............ | 100.0 | 22.0 | 41.9 | 25.9 | 8.2 | 6.5 | 1.3 | 5.1 | 31.0 |
| 1958............ | 100.0 | 20.1 | 36.7 | 14.8 | 11.1 | 8.5 | 2.3 | 6.3 | 36.9 |
| 1960............ | 100.0 | 18.2 | 40.4 | 22.1 | 10.1 | 5.6 | 2.6 | 7.0 | 34.4 |

[1] Includes the value of African rural household income at producer prices (including value of work done on rural housing and grain stores).
[2] Includes Sanitary Service (ISIC group 522) and African rural household services (defined as the difference between the value of African rural household consumption at retail market prices and at producer prices).

[1] Y compris les revenus des ménages africains ruraux, évalués aux prix à la production (compte tenu de la valeur des travaux effectués sur les logements ruraux et des stocks de céréales).
[2] Y compris les Services sanitaires (CITI groupe 522) et les services des ménages africains ruraux (définis comme la différence entre la valeur de la consommation de ces ménages aux prix de détail et la valeur de cette consommation aux prix à la production).

## C. Gross Domestic Fixed Capital Formation According to Purchasing Sector
## La formation brute de capital fixe intérieur par secteur d'acquisition

| Item of data and year / Rubrique et année | Total | Agricultural sector / Secteur agricole | Industrial Sector — Secteur industriel | | | | | Other sectors [1] / Autres secteurs [1] |
|---|---|---|---|---|---|---|---|---|
| | | | Total | Mining / Industries extractives | Manufacturing / Industries manufacturières | Construction / Bâtiment et travaux publics | Electricity, gas and water / Electricité, gaz et eau | |
| ISIC — CITI | 0–9 | 0 | 1–5 | 1 | 2–3 | 4 | 5 | 6-9 |

### a. At Current Prices — Aux prix courants

| Item of data and year | Total | Agricultural | Total | Mining | Manufacturing | Construction | Electricity | Other |
|---|---|---|---|---|---|---|---|---|
| **Absolute figures — Chiffres absolus** | | | | | | | | |
| 1954 | 94.1 | 7.1 | 38.6 | 19.3 | 6.3 | 2.2 | 10.8 | 48.4 |
| 1955 | 108.0 | 8.7 | 49.5 | 24.3 | 7.4 | 2.8 | 15.0 | 49.8 |
| 1956 | 134.7 | 9.6 | 56.2 | 24.8 | 9.7 | 4.5 | 17.2 | 68.9 |
| 1957 | 149.0 | 9.2 | 56.6 | 20.2 | 12.2 | 2.6 | 21.6 | 83.2 |
| 1958 | 137.4 | 10.0 | 66.1 | 17.9 | 14.4 | 1.2 | 32.6 | 61.3 |
| 1959 | 126.2 | 9.5 | 54.7 | 12.5 | 13.0 | 1.3 | 27.9 | 62.0 |
| 1960 | 119.3 | 13.0 | 51.8 | 16.4 | 15.3 | 1.3 | 18.8 | 54.5 |
| 1961 | 112.4 | 14.6 | 45.1 | 23.0 | 7.9 | 0.8 | 13.4 | 52.7 |
| **Percentage distribution according to sector— Distribution en pourcentage par secteur** | | | | | | | | |
| 1954–1960 | 100.0 | 7.7 | 43.0 | 15.6 | 9.0 | 1.8 | 16.6 | 49.3 |
| 1954 | 100.0 | 7.6 | 41.0 | 20.5 | 6.7 | 2.3 | 11.5 | 51.4 |
| 1958 | 100.0 | 7.3 | 48.1 | 13.0 | 10.5 | 0.9 | 23.7 | 44.6 |
| 1960 | 100.0 | 10.9 | 43.4 | 13.7 | 12.8 | 1.1 | 15.8 | 45.7 |

### b. At Prices of 1954 — Aux prix de 1954

| Item of data and year | Total | Agricultural | Total | Mining | Manufacturing | Construction | Electricity | Other |
|---|---|---|---|---|---|---|---|---|
| **Absolute figures — Chiffres absolus** | | | | | | | | |
| 1954 | 94.1 | 7.1 | 38.6 | 19.3 | 6.3 | 2.2 | 10.8 | 48.4 |
| 1955 | 104.8 | 8.6 | 48.6 | 23.9 | 7.3 | 2.8 | 14.6 | 47.6 |
| 1956 | 124.0 | 8.8 | 51.9 | 22.7 | 9.0 | 4.2 | 16.0 | 63.3 |
| 1957 | 132.2 | 8.1 | 50.3 | 17.8 | 10.9 | 2.3 | 19.3 | 73.8 |
| 1958 | 117.5 | 8.4 | 56.4 | 15.1 | 12.3 | 1.1 | 27.9 | 52.7 |
| 1959 | 108.1 | 8.1 | 46.8 | 10.3 | 11.2 | 1.2 | 24.1 | 53.2 |
| 1960 | 101.0 | 10.7 | 44.0 | 13.5 | 13.3 | 1.1 | 16.1 | 46.3 |
| 1961 | 91.9 | 11.3 | 36.7 | 18.4 | 6.5 | 0.6 | 11.2 | 43.9 |
| **Percentage distribution according to sector— Distribution en pourcentage par secteur** | | | | | | | | |
| 1954–1960 | 100.0 | 7.6 | 43.1 | 15.7 | 9.0 | 1.9 | 16.5 | 49.3 |
| 1954 | 100.0 | 7.6 | 41.0 | 20.5 | 6.7 | 2.3 | 11.5 | 51.4 |
| 1958 | 100.0 | 7.1 | 48.0 | 12.9 | 10.5 | 0.9 | 23.7 | 44.9 |
| 1960 | 100.0 | 10.6 | 43.6 | 13.4 | 13.2 | 1.1 | 15.9 | 45.8 |
| **Average annual rate of growth—Taux annuel moyen d'accroissement** | | | | | | | | |
| 1954–1960 | 1.2 | 7.1 | 2.2 | —5.8 | 13.3 | —10.9 | 6.9 | —0.7 |
| 1954–1958 | 5.7 | 4.3 | 9.9 | —6.0 | 18.2 | —15.9 | 26.8 | 2.2 |
| 1958–1960 | —7.3 | 12.9 | —11.7 | —5.4 | 4.0 | — | —24.0 | —6.3 |

[1] Includes Transportation and communication (ISIC division 7).

[1] Y compris Transports et communications (CITI branche 7).

## 2. INDEX NUMBERS OF INDUSTRIAL PRODUCTION — INDICES DE LA PRODUCTION INDUSTRIELLE

### A. The Divisions of Industrial Activity
### Les branches de l'activité industrielle

| Period<br>Période | Total | Mining [4]<br>Industries<br>extractives [4] | Manu-<br>facturing [3]<br>Industries<br>manu-<br>facturières [3] | Construction<br>Bâtiment<br>et travaux<br>publics | Electricity<br>Electricité |
|---|---|---|---|---|---|
| ISIC — CITI | 1-3, 511 | 1 | 2-3 | 4 | 511 |

#### a. Indexes — Indices (1958 = 100)

| | | | | | |
|---|---|---|---|---|---|
| 1955....... | 83 | 86 | 74 | 68 | 94 |
| 1956....... | 94 | 98 | 86 | 79 | 103 |
| 1957....... | 103 | 107 | 98 | 98 | 99 |
| 1958....... | 100 | 100 | 100 | 100 | 100 |
| 1959....... | 119 | 131 | 104 | 84 | 112 |
| 1960....... | 127 | 138 | 110 | 76 | 113 |
| 1961....... | 131 | 139 | 117 | 65 | 142 |

#### b. Average Annual Rate of Change — Taux annuel moyen de variation

| | | | | | |
|---|---|---|---|---|---|
| 1955 – 1958. | 6.4 | 5.2 | 10.5 | 13.7 | 2.1 |
| 1958 – 1960. | 12.7 | 17.5 | 4.9 | −12.8 | 6.3 |

For footnotes see end of table.

Pour les notes, voir au bas du tableau.

### B. The Major Groups of Mining
### Les classes de la branche Industries extractives

| Period<br>Période | Federation<br>of Rhodesia<br>and<br>Nyasaland<br>Fédération<br>de<br>la Rhodésie<br>et du<br>Nyassaland<br>All<br>mining [4]<br>Toutes<br>industries<br>extractives [4] | Northern Rhodesia —<br>Rhodésie du Nord | | Southern Rhodesia —<br>Rhodésie du Sud | |
|---|---|---|---|---|---|
| | | Metal<br>mining [4]<br>Extraction<br>des minerais<br>métalliques [4] | Other<br>mining [1]<br>Divers [1] | Coal<br>mining<br>Extraction<br>du<br>charbon | Metal<br>mining<br>Extraction<br>des minerais<br>métalliques | Other<br>mining [2]<br>Divers [2] |
| ISIC — CITI | 1 | 12 | 14-19 | 11 | 12 | 14-19 |

#### a. Indexes — Indices (1958 = 100)

| | | | | | | |
|---|---|---|---|---|---|---|
| 1949........ | 67 | 70 | 26 | 54 | 77 | 63 |
| 1950........ | 69 | 76 | 26 | 60 | 77 | 56 |
| 1951........ | 74 | 83 | 41 | 65 | 76 | 61 |
| 1952........ | 76 | 83 | 66 | 72 | 78 | 67 |
| 1953........ | 89 | 97 | 56 | 74 | 84 | 69 |
| 1954........ | 93 | 101 | 70 | 78 | 87 | 63 |
| 1955........ | 86 | 91 | 74 | 94 | 86 | 83 |
| 1956........ | 98 | 102 | 81 | 100 | 87 | 94 |
| 1957........ | 107 | 111 | 110 | 109 | 100 | 104 |
| 1958........ | 100 | 100 | 100 | 100 | 100 | 100 |
| 1959........ | 131 | 139 | 116 | 106 | 97 | 94 |
| 1960........ | 138 | 146 | 88 | 101 | 104 | 105 |
| 1961........ | 139 | 146 | 102 | 87 | 99 | 127 |

#### b. Average Annual Rate of Change — Taux annuel moyen de variation

| | | | | | | |
|---|---|---|---|---|---|---|
| 1950 – 1960 . | 7.2 | 6.7 | 13.0 | 5.3 | 3.1 | 6.5 |
| 1949 – 1953 . | 7.3 | 8.5 | 21.1 | 8.2 | 2.2 | 2.3 |
| 1954 – 1958 . | 1.8 | −0.2 | 9.3 | 6.4 | 3.5 | 12.2 |
| 1958 – 1960 . | 17.5 | 20.8 | −6.2 | 0.5 | 2.0 | 2.5 |

For footnotes see end of table.

Pour les notes, voir au bas du tableau.

## C. The Major Groups of Manufacturing — Les classes de la branche Industries manufacturières

| Period / Période | Manu-facturing [3] / Industries manufac-turières [3] | Food, beverages and tobacco / Industries alimen-taires, boissons, tabac | Textiles | Clothing, footwear and made-up textiles / Articles d'habil-lement, chaussures et ouvrages en tissu | Wood products and furniture / Bois et meubles | Paper and paper products / Papier et ouvrages en papier | Printing and publishing / Im-primerie et édition | Rubber products / Ouvrages en caout-chouc | Chemicals and chemical, petroleum and coal products / Produits chi-miques et dérivés du pétrole et du charbon | Non-metallic mineral products / Produits minéraux non métal-liques | Basic metals [5] / Métal-lurgie de base [5] | Metal products / Ouvrages en métaux | Other manu-facturing / Autres industries manufac-turières |
|---|---|---|---|---|---|---|---|---|---|---|---|---|---|
| ISIC — CITI | 2–3 | 20–22 | 23 | 24 | 25–26 | 27 | 28 | 30 | 31–32 | 33 | 34 | 35–38 | 39 |
| *a. Indexes — Indices (1958 = 100)* | | | | | | | | | | | | | |
| 1955 | 74 | 67 | 72 | 76 | 77 | 74 | 68 | 60 | 74 | 68 | 90 | 85 | 62 |
| 1956 | 86 | 82 | 97 | 88 | 89 | 73 | 75 | 84 | 75 | 77 | 102 | 96 | 77 |
| 1957 | 98 | 91 | 103 | 102 | 105 | 86 | 83 | 96 | 87 | 98 | 111 | 106 | 102 |
| 1958 | 100 | 100 | 100 | 100 | 100 | 100 | 100 | 100 | 100 | 100 | 100 | 100 | 100 |
| 1959 | 104 | 106 | 125 | 119 | 105 | 98 | 100 | 114 | 119 | 79 | 138 | 100 | 106 |
| 1960 | 110 | 110 | 109 | 121 | 110 | 100 | 103 | 134 | 147 | 86 | 147 | 109 | 98 |
| 1961 | 117 | 121 | 127 | 130 | 102 | 109 | 102 | 167 | 157 | 74 | 153 | 110 | 126 |
| *b. Average Annual Rate of Change — Taux annuel moyen de variation* | | | | | | | | | | | | | |
| 1955 – 1958 | 10.5 | 14.3 | 11.6 | 9.6 | 9.1 | 10.5 | 13.7 | 18.6 | 10.5 | 13.7 | 3.6 | 5.6 | 17.3 |
| 1958 – 1960 | 4.9 | 4.9 | 4.4 | 10.0 | 4.9 | — | 1.5 | 15.8 | 21.2 | −7.3 | 21.2 | 4.4 | −1.0 |

[1] Covers limestone extraction only.
[2] Covers asbestos mining only.
[3] Excludes Leather and leather products except wearing apparel (ISIC major group 29), Repair of motor vehicles (ISIC group 384), and the very important group Non-ferrous metal basic industries (ISIC group 342) which has however been included in the index shown for Basic metals (ISIC major group 34).
[4] Includes Non-ferrous metal basic industries (ISIC group 342).
[5] Includes the mining of non-ferrous metals (part of ISIC major group 12) in addition to Non-ferrous metal basic industries (ISIC group 342).

[1] Il s'agit exclusivement de l'extraction de pierre à chaux.
[2] Il s'agit exclusivement des industries extractives d'amiante.
[3] Non compris Cuir et articles en cuir à l'exclusion des articles d'habillement (CITI classe 29), Réparation des véhicules automobiles (CITI groupe 384) et Production et première transformation des métaux non ferreux (CITI groupe 342), groupe très important qui a été inclus dans les indices reproduits pour la Métallurgie de base (CITI classe 34).
[4] Y compris Production et première transformation des métaux non ferreux (CITI groupe 342).
[5] Y compris les industries extractives des métaux non ferreux (dans CITI classe 12), en plus de Production et première transformation des métaux non ferreux (CITI groupe 342).

## 3. INDEX NUMBERS OF INDUSTRIAL EMPLOYMENT — INDICES DE L'EMPLOI DANS L'INDUSTRIE

### A. The Divisions of Industrial Activity
### Les branches de l'activité industrielle

| Period / Période | Total [3] | Mining [1] / Industries extractives [1] | Manu-facturing [2] / Industries manu-facturières [2] | Construction / Bâtiment et travaux publics | Electricity [3] / Electricité [3] |
|---|---|---|---|---|---|
| ISIC — CITI | 1–3, 511 | 1 | 2–3 | 4 | 511 |
| *a. Indexes — Indices (1958 = 100)* | | | | | |
| 1955 | 92 | 102 | 83 | 90 | 83 |
| 1956 | 96 | 101 | 91 | 96 | 94 |
| 1957 | 102 | 102 | 102 | 107 | 94 |
| 1958 | 100 | 100 | 100 | 100 | 100 |
| 1959 | 100 | 97 | 103 | 91 | 106 |
| 1960 | – 103 – | 99 | 103 | 79 | – 111 – |
| 1961 | 102 | 96 | 102 | 65 | 104 |
| *b. Average Annual Rate of Change — Taux annuel moyen de variation* | | | | | |
| 1955 – 1958 | 2.8 | −0.7 | 6.4 | 3.6 | 6.4 |
| 1958 – 1960 | 1.5 | −0.5 | 1.5 | −11.1 | 5.4 |

For footnotes see end of table.

Pour les notes, voir au bas du tableau.

### B. The Major Groups of Mining
### Les classes de la branche Industries extractives

| Period / Période | All mining [1] / Toutes industries extractives [1] | Coal mining and other non-metallic mining and quarrying / Extraction du charbon et d'autres minéraux non métalliques | Metal mining [1] / Extraction des minerais métalliques [1] | Stone quarrying, clay and sandpits / Extraction de la pierre à bâtir, de l'argile et du sable |
|---|---|---|---|---|
| ISIC — CITI | 1 | 11, 19 | 12 | 14 |
| *a. Indexes — Indices (1958 = 100)* | | | | |
| 1955 | 102 | 104 | 102 | 74 |
| 1956 | 101 | 103 | 101 | 72 |
| 1957 | 102 | 100 | 103 | 93 |
| 1958 | 100 | 100 | 100 | 100 |
| 1959 | 97 | 93 | 98 | 92 |
| *b. Average Annual Rate of Change — Taux annuel moyen de variation* | | | | |
| 1955 – 1958 | −0.7 | −1.3 | −0.7 | 10.5 |

For footnotes see end of table.

Pour les notes, voir au bas du tableau.

## C. The Major Groups of Manufacturing — Les classes de la branche Industries manufacturières

| Period / Période | Manufacturing [2] / Industries manufacturières [2] | Food, beverages and tobacco / Industries alimentaires, boissons, tabac | Textiles | Clothing, footwear and made-up textiles / Articles d'habillement, chaussures et ouvrages en tissu | Wood products and furniture / Bois et meubles | Paper and paper products / Papier et ouvrages en papier | Printing and publishing / Imprimerie et édition | Rubber products / Ouvrages en caoutchouc | Chemicals and chemical, petroleum and coal products / Produits chimiques et dérivés du pétrole et du charbon | Non-metallic mineral products / Produits minéraux non métalliques | Basic metals [2] / Métallurgie de base [2] | Metal products / Ouvrages en métaux | Other manufacturing / Autres industries manufacturières |
|---|---|---|---|---|---|---|---|---|---|---|---|---|---|
| ISIC — CITI | 2–3 | 20–22 | 23 | 24 | 25–26 | 27 | 28 | 30 | 31–32 | 33 | 34 | 35–38 | 39 |

### a. Indexes — Indices (1958 = 100)

| | | | | | | | | | | | | | |
|---|---|---|---|---|---|---|---|---|---|---|---|---|---|
| 1955............. | 83 | 80 | 102 | 76 | 90 | 76 | 71 | 63 | 75 | 102 | 86 | 79 | 64 |
| 1956............. | 91 | 90 | 106 | 84 | 91 | 94 | 75 | 71 | 76 | 107 | 81 | 91 | 68 |
| 1957............. | 102 | 101 | 112 | 102 | 101 | 97 | 90 | 99 | 86 | 116 | 97 | 97 | 105 |
| 1958............. | 100 | 100 | 100 | 100 | 100 | 100 | 100 | 100 | 100 | 100 | 100 | 100 | 100 |
| 1959............. | 103 | 106 | 113 | 109 | 96 | 108 | 108 | 159 | 108 | 85 | 105 | 103 | 103 |

### b. Average Annual Rate of Change — Taux annuel moyen de variation

| | | | | | | | | | | | | | |
|---|---|---|---|---|---|---|---|---|---|---|---|---|---|
| 1955–1958....... | 6.4 | 7.7 | −0.7 | 9.6 | 3.6 | 9.6 | 12.1 | 16.6 | 10.1 | −0.7 | 5.2 | 8.2 | 16.0 |

[1] Includes Non-ferrous metals basic industries (ISIC group 342).
[2] Excludes Non-ferrous metals basic industries (ISIC group 342) in all years and Repair of motor vehicles (ISIC group 384— in 1960 and 1961.
[3] Includes Water and Sanitary Services (ISIC groups 521-522) in 1960 and 1961.

[1] Y compris Production et première transformation des métaux non ferreux (CITI groupe 342)
[2] Non compris Production et première transformation des métaux non ferreux (CITI groupe 342) pour toutes les années, et Réparation des véhicules automobiles (CITI groupe 384) en 1960 et 1961.
[3] Y compris Distribution publique de l'eau et Services sanitaires (CITI groupes 521-522) en 1960 et 1961.

## 4. CHARACTERISTICS OF INDUSTRIAL ESTABLISHMENTS
## CARACTERISTIQUES DES ETABLISSEMENTS INDUSTRIELS
### 1955, 1958

Number of establishments in units; value added and wages and salaries in million Rhodesian Pounds; number of engaged and operatives in thousands; value added per engaged and wages and salaries per operative in thousand Rhodesian Pounds.

Nombre d'établissements en unités; valeur ajoutée et traitements et salaires en millions de livres rhodésiennes; nombre de personnes occupées et d'ouvriers en milliers valeur ajoutée par personne occupée et traitements et salaires par ouvrier en milliers de livres rhodésiennes.

## A. The Divisions of Industrial Activity — Les branches de l'activité industrielle

| Year and item of data / ISIC | All industrial activity / Toutes industries / 1-4,511 | Mining [1] / Industries extractives [1] / 1 | Manufacturing [1,2] / Industries manufacturières [1,2] / 2-3 | Construction / Bâtiment et travaux publics / 4 | Electricity / Electricité / 511 | Année et rubrique / CITI | Year and item of data / ISIC | All industrial activity / Toutes industries / 1-4, 511 | Mining [1] / Industries extractives [1] / 1 | Manufacturing [1,2] / Industries manufacturières [1,2] / 2-3 | Construction / Bâtiment et travaux publics / 4 | Electricity / Electricité / 511 | Année et rubrique / CITI |
|---|---|---|---|---|---|---|---|---|---|---|---|---|---|
| | **a. Absolute Figures — Chiffres absolus** | | | | | | | **b. Structure** | | | | | |
| **1955** Number of establishments... | 185.9 | 113.5 | 103 | ... | 27 | **1955** Nombre d'établissements | **1955** Distribution in percent of: | | | | | | **1955** Distribution en pourcentage: |
| Value added....... | 185.9 | 113.5 | 39.9 | 26.9 | 5.6 | Valeur ajoutée | Value added..... | 100.0 | 61.0 | 21.5 | 14.4 | 3.1 | Valeur ajoutée |
| Number of engaged......... | 337.6 | 101.0 | 91.5 | 139.5 | 5.6 | Nombre de personnes occupées | Number of engaged......... | 100.0 | 29.9 | 27.1 | 41.3 | 1.7 | Nombre de personnes occupées |
| Wages and salaries. | 67.5 | 25.3 | 19.1 | 21.4 | 1.7 | Traitements et salaires | Value added per person engaged.. | 0.55 | 1.12 | 0.44 | 0.19 | 1.00 | Valeur ajoutée par personne occupée |
| Operatives: Number... | 318.9 | 94.1 | 84.9 | 134.8 | 5.1 | Ouvriers: Nombre | Value added per unit of wages and salaries | 2.75 | 4.49 | 2.09 | 1.26 | 3.29 | Valeur ajoutée par unité de traitements et salaires |
| Wages and salaries......... | 52.0 | 18.6 | 14.3 | 17.9 | 1.2 | Traitements et salaires | Operatives as a percent of engaged......... | 94.5 | 93.2 | 92.8 | 96.6 | 91.1 | Ouvriers en pourcentage des personnes occupées |
| | | | | | | | Wages and salaries per operative.... | 0.16 | 0.20 | 0.17 | 0.13 | 0.24 | Traitements et salaires par ouvrier |
| **1958** Number of establishments... | ... | ... | 1 321 | ... | 32 | **1958** Nombre d'établissements | **1958** Distribution in percent of: | | | | | | **1958** Distribution en pourcentage: |
| Value added....... | 183.2 | 72.2 | 56.4 | 44.7 | 9.9 | Valeur ajoutée | Value added..... | 100.0 | 39.4 | 30.7 | 24.4 | 5.5 | Valeur ajoutée |
| Number of engaged......... | 371.0 | 99.3 | 109.6 | 155.3 | 6.8 | Nombre de personnes occupées | Number of engaged......... | 100.0 | 26.7 | 29.6 | 41.8 | 1.9 | Nombre de personnes occupées |
| Wages and salaries. | 92.4 | 29.6 | 28.9 | 31.4 | 2.5 | Traitements et salaires | Value added per person engaged.. | 0.49 | 0.73 | 0.51 | 0.29 | 1.46 | Valeur ajoutée par personne occupée |
| Operatives: Number......... | 344.4 | 89.6 | 99.9 | 149.0 | 5.9 | Ouvriers: Nombre | Value added per unit of wages and salaries..... | 1.98 | 2.44 | 1.95 | 1.42 | 3.96 | Valeur ajoutée par unité de traitements et salaires |
| Wages and salaries......... | 69.8 | 21.3 | 21.1 | 25.6 | 1.8 | Traitements et salaires | Operatives as a percent of engaged......... | 92.8 | 90.2 | 91.1 | 95.9 | 86.8 | Ouvriers en pourcentage des personnes occupées |
| | | | | | | | Wages and salaries per operative.... | 0.20 | 0.24 | 0.21 | 0.17 | 0.30 | Traitements et salaires par ouvrier |

For footnotes see end of table.                   Pour les notes, voir au bas du tableau.

## B. The Major Groups of Mining — Les classes de la branche Industries extractives

### a. Absolute Figures — Chiffres absolus

| Year and item of data | All mining [1] Toutes industries extractives [1] | Metal mining [1] Extraction des minerais métalliques [1] | Other mining [3] Divers [3] | Année et rubrique |
|---|---|---|---|---|
| ISIC | 1 | 12 | 11, 14-19 | CITI |
| **1955** | | | | **1955** |
| Value added.................. | 113.5 | 104.3 | 9.2 | Valeur ajoutée |
| Number of engaged............ | 101.0 | 79.0 | 22.0 | Nombre de personnes occupées |
| Wages and salaries............ | 25.3 | 22.2 | 3.1 | Traitements et salaires |
| Operatives: | | | | Ouvriers: |
| Number.................... | 94.1 | 73.5 | 20.6 | Nombre |
| Wages and salaries.......... | 18.6 | 16.0 | 2.6 | Traitements et salaires |
| **1958** | | | | **1958** |
| Value added.................. | 72.2 | 63.4 | 8.8 | Valeur ajoutée |
| Number of engaged............ | 99.3 | 77.4 | 21.9 | Nombre de personnes occupées |
| Wages and salaries............ | 29.6 | 25.8 | 3.8 | Traitements et salaires |
| Operatives: | | | | Ouvriers: |
| Number.................... | 89.6 | 69.4 | 20.2 | Nombre |
| Wages and salaries.......... | 21.3 | 18.2 | 3.1 | Traitements et salaires |

### b. Structure

| Year and item of data | All mining [1] Toutes industries extractives [1] | Metal mining [1] Extraction des minerais métalliques [1] | Other mining [3] Divers [3] | Année et rubrique |
|---|---|---|---|---|
| ISIC | 1 | 12 | 11, 14-19 | CITI |
| **1955** | | | | **1955** |
| Distribution in percent of: | | | | Distribution en pourcentage: |
| Value added............... | 100.0 | 91.9 | 8.1 | Valeur ajoutée |
| Number of engaged......... | 100.0 | 78.2 | 21.8 | Nombre de personnes occupées |
| Value added per person engaged.................. | 1.12 | 1.32 | 0.42 | Valeur ajoutée par personne occupée |
| Value added per unit of wages and salaries.......... | 4.49 | 4.70 | 2.97 | Valeur ajoutée par unité de traitements et salaires |
| Operatives as a percent of engaged.................. | 93.2 | 93.0 | 93.6 | Ouvriers en pourcentage des personnes occupées |
| Wages and salaries per operative................. | 0.20 | 0.22 | 0.13 | Traitements et salaires par ouvrier |
| **1958** | | | | **1958** |
| Distribution in percent of: | | | | Distribution en pourcentage: |
| Value added............... | 100.0 | 87.8 | 12.2 | Valeur ajoutée |
| Number of engaged......... | 100.0 | 77.9 | 22.1 | Nombre de personnes occupées |
| Value added per person engaged.................. | 0.73 | 0.82 | 0.40 | Valeur ajoutée par personne occupée |
| Value added per unit of wages and salaries.......... | 2.44 | 2.46 | 2.32 | Valeur ajoutée par unité de traitements et salaires |
| Operatives as a percent of engaged.................. | 90.2 | 89.7 | 92.2 | Ouvriers en pourcentage des personnes occupées |
| Wages and salaries per operative................. | 0.24 | 0.26 | 0.15 | Traitements et salaires par ouvrier |

For footnotes see end of table.

Pour les notes voir, au bas du tableau.

# FEDERATION OF RHODESIA AND NYASALAND

## C.  The Major Groups of Manufacturing — Les classes de la branche Industries manufacturières

| Year and item of data | Manufacturing [1,2] Industries manufacturières [1,2] | Food, beverages and tobacco Industries alimentaires, boissons, tabac | Textiles | Clothing, footwear and made-up textiles Articles d'habillement, chaussures et ouvrages en tissu | Wood products and furniture Bois et meubles | Paper and paper products Papier et ouvrages en papier | Printing and publishing Imprimerie et édition | Rubber products Ouvrages en caoutchouc | Chemicals and chemical, petroleum and coal products Produits chimiques et dérivés du pétrole et du charbon | Non-metallic mineral products Produits minéraux non métalliques | Basic metals [1] Métallurgie de base[1] | Metal products [2] Ouvrages en métaux [2] | Other manufacturing Autres industries manufacturières | Année et rubrique |
|---|---|---|---|---|---|---|---|---|---|---|---|---|---|---|
| ISIC | 2–3 | 20–22 | 23 | 24 | 25–26 | 27 | 28 | 30 | 31–32 | 33 | 34 | 35–38 | 39 | CITI |

### a. Absolute Figures — Chiffres absolus

| | | | | | | | | | | | | | | |
|---|---|---|---|---|---|---|---|---|---|---|---|---|---|---|
| **1955** | | | | | | | | | | | | | | **1955** |
| Number of establishments. | 1 003 | 247 | 22 | 68 | 88 | 9 | 43 | 14 | 27 | 101 | 11 | 356 | 17 | Nombre d'établissements |
| Value added.......... | 39.9 | 11.6 | 2.0 | 2.4 | 2.5 | 0.5 | 2.0 | 0.3 | 1.8 | 4.3 | 2.0 | 9.9 | 0.6 | Valeur ajoutée |
| Number of engaged.... | 91.5 | 25.9 | 6.2 | 7.3 | 9.6 | 0.9 | 2.4 | 0.4 | 2.2 | 12.2 | 3.9 | 19.4 | 1.1 | Nombre de personnes occupées |
| Wages and salaries..... | 19.1 | 4.0 | 0.9 | 1.0 | 1.3 | 0.2 | 1.1 | 0.1 | 0.6 | 1.6 | 1.1 | 7.0 | 0.2 | Traitements et salaires |
| Operatives: | | | | | | | | | | | | | | Ouvriers: |
| Number............ | 84.9 | 24.1 | 6.0 | 6.7 | 9.3 | 0.8 | 1.9 | 0.3 | 1.8 | 11.8 | 3.4 | 17.8 | 1.0 | Nombre |
| Wages and salaries... | 14.3 | 2.7 | 0.7 | 0.7 | 1.1 | 0.1 | 0.7 | 0.1 | 0.3 | 1.2 | 1.0 | 5.6 | 0.1 | Traitements et salaires |
| **1958** | | | | | | | | | | | | | | **1958** |
| Number of establishments. | 1 321 | 314 | 26 | 106 | 128 | 11 | 60 | 22 | 49 | 113 | 18 | 445 | 29 | Nombre d'établissements |
| Value added.......... | 56.4 | 17.0 | 2.2 | 3.1 | 3.2 | 0.8 | 3.1 | 0.5 | 2.7 | 6.2 | 2.5 | 13.9 | 1.2 | Valeur ajoutée |
| Number of engaged.... | 109.6 | 32.5 | 6.0 | 9.5 | 10.7 | 1.2 | 3.4 | 0.6 | 2.9 | 11.9 | 4.6 | 24.6 | 1.7 | Nombre de personnes occupées |
| Wages and salaries..... | 28.9 | 6.1 | 1.1 | 1.6 | 1.9 | 0.4 | 1.9 | 0.2 | 1.0 | 2.3 | 1.7 | 10.4 | 0.3 | Traitements et salaires |
| Operatives: | | | | | | | | | | | | | | Ouvriers: |
| Number............ | 99.9 | 29.9 | 5.7 | 8.7 | 10.2 | 0.9 | 2.6 | 0.4 | 2.3 | 11.3 | 4.0 | 22.3 | 1.6 | Nombre |
| Wages and salaries... | 21.1 | 4.0 | 0.9 | 1.0 | 1.6 | 0.2 | 1.2 | 0.1 | 0.5 | 1.7 | 1.4 | 8.3 | 0.2 | Traitements et salaires |

### b. Structure

| | | | | | | | | | | | | | | |
|---|---|---|---|---|---|---|---|---|---|---|---|---|---|---|
| **1955** | | | | | | | | | | | | | | **1955** |
| Distribution in percent of: | | | | | | | | | | | | | | Distribution en pourcentage: |
| Value added....... | 100.0 | 29.0 | 5.0 | 6.1 | 6.2 | 1.3 | 5.0 | 0.7 | 4.5 | 10.8 | 5.0 | 24.8 | 1.6 | Valeur ajoutée |
| Number of engaged... | 100.0 | 28.3 | 6.7 | 8.0 | 10.5 | 1.0 | 2.6 | 0.4 | 2.5 | 13.3 | 4.2 | 21.2 | 1.3 | Nombre de personnes occupées |
| Value added per person engaged...... | 0.44 | 0.45 | 0.32 | 0.33 | 0.26 | 0.56 | 0.83 | 0.75 | 0.82 | 0.35 | 0.51 | 0.51 | 0.54 | Valeur ajoutée par personne occupée |
| Value added per unit of wages and salaries............ | 2.09 | 2.90 | 2.22 | 2.40 | 1.92 | 2.50 | 1.82 | 3.00 | 3.00 | 2.69 | 1.82 | 1.41 | 3.00 | Valeur ajoutée par unité de traitements et salaires |
| Operatives as a percent of engaged......... | 92.8 | 93.0 | 96.8 | 91.8 | 96.9 | 88.9 | 79.2 | 75.0 | 81.8 | 96.7 | 87.2 | 91.8 | 90.9 | Ouvriers en pourcentage des personnes occupées |
| Wages and salaries per operative....... | 0.17 | 0.11 | 0.12 | 0.10 | 0.12 | 0.12 | 0.37 | 0.33 | 0.17 | 0.10 | 0.29 | 0.31 | 0.10 | Traitements et salaires par ouvrier |
| **1958** | | | | | | | | | | | | | | **1958** |
| Distribution in percent of: | | | | | | | | | | | | | | Distribution en pourcentage: |
| Value added....... | 100.0 | 30.1 | 3.9 | 5.5 | 5.7 | 1.4 | 5.5 | 0.9 | 4.8 | 10.9 | 4.5 | 24.6 | 2.2 | Valeur ajoutée |
| Number of engaged... | 100.0 | 29.6 | 5.5 | 8.6 | 9.8 | 1.1 | 3.1 | 0.6 | 2.6 | 10.9 | 4.2 | 22.4 | 1.6 | Nombre de personnes occupées |
| Value added per person engaged...... | 0.51 | 0.52 | 0.37 | 0.33 | 0.30 | 0.67 | 0.91 | 0.83 | 0.93 | 0.52 | 0.54 | 0.56 | 0.70 | Valeur ajoutée par personne occupée |
| Value added per unit of wages and salaries............ | 1.95 | 2.79 | 2.00 | 1.94 | 1.68 | 2.00 | 1.63 | 2.50 | 2.70 | 2.70 | 1.47 | 1.34 | 4.00 | Valeur ajoutée par unité de traitements et salaires |
| Operatives as a percent of engaged......... | 91.1 | 92.0 | 95.0 | 91.6 | 95.3 | 75.0 | 76.5 | 66.7 | 79.3 | 95.0 | 87.0 | 90.6 | 94.1 | Ouvriers en pourcentage des personnes occupées |
| Wages and salaries per operative....... | 0.21 | 0.13 | 0.16 | 0.11 | 0.16 | 0.22 | 0.46 | 0.25 | 0.22 | 0.15 | 0.35 | 0.37 | 0.12 | Traitements et salaires par ouvrier |

[1] Non-ferrous metals basic industries (ISIC group 342) are included in Metal mining (ISIC major group 12).
[2] Excludes Repair of motor vehicles (ISIC group 384).
[3] Includes Coal mining (ISIC major group 11).

[1] Production et première transformation des métaux non ferreux (CITI groupe 342) est compris dans Extraction des minerais métalliques (CITI classe 12).
[2] Non compris Réparation des véhicules automobiles (CITI groupe 384).
[3] Y compris Extraction du charbon (CITI classe 11).

## 5. CHARACTERISTICS OF INDUSTRIAL ESTABLISHMENTS ENGAGING SIX OR MORE PERSONS OR UTILIZING POWER EQUIPMENT OR STEAM BOILERS, NORTHERN RHODESIA

## CARACTERISTIQUES DES ETABLISSEMENTS INDUSTRIELS OCCUPANT AU MOINS SIX PERSONNES OU UTILISANT LA FORCE MOTRICE OU DES GENERATEURS DE VAPEUR, RHODESIE DU NORD

### 1947

Number of establishments in units; value added and wages and salaries in thousand Rhodesian Pounds; number of engaged in thousands; and value added per person engaged in Rhodesian Pounds

Nombre d'établissements en unités; valeur ajoutée et traitements et salaires en milliers de livres rhodésiennes; nombre de personnes occupées en milliers; valeur ajoutée par personne occupée en livres rhodésiennes

### A. Selected Divisions of Industrial Activity
### Quelques branches de l'activité industrielle

| Item of data | Manufacturing and electricity producing [1]<br>Industries manufacturières et production d'électricité [1] | Construction<br>Bâtiment et travaux publics | Rubrique |
|---|---|---|---|
| ISIC | 2–3, 511 | 4 | CITI |
| *a.* Absolute Figures Chiffres absolus | | | |
| Number of establishments.......... | 82 | 14 | Nombre d'établissements |
| Value added.................... | 19 388.9 | 110.8 | Valeur ajoutée |
| Number of engaged.............. | | | Nombre de personnes occupées |
| (Average for year)............. | 42.5 | 1.7 | (moyenne pour l'année) |
| Wages and salaries paid.......... | 5 726.6 | 74.6 | Traitements et salaires payés |
| *b.* Structure | | | |
| Value added per person engaged... | 456 | 65 | Valeur ajoutée par personne occupée |
| Value added per unit of wages and salaries...................... | 3.39 | 1.49 | Valeur ajoutée par unité de traitements et salaires |

[1] Includes also the extraction of non-ferrous metal ores (in ISIC major group 12).

[1] Y compris aussi l'extraction des minerais de métaux non ferreux (partie de CITI classe 12).

### B. The Major Groups of Manufacturing and Electricity Producing
### Les classes de la branche Industries manufacturières et la production d'électricité

| Item of data | Manufacturing and electricity producing [1]<br>Industries manufacturières et production d'électricité [1] | Food, beverages and tobacco<br>Industries alimentaires, boissons, tabac | Textiles, clothing and footwear<br>Textiles, articles d'habillement et chaussures | Wood products and furniture<br>Bois et meubles | Printing and publishing<br>Imprimerie et édition | Non-metallic mineral products<br>Produits minéraux non métalliques | Basic metals [1]<br>Métallurgie de base [1] | Metal products<br>Ouvrages en métaux | Other manu-facturing<br>Autres industries manu-facturières | Rubrique |
|---|---|---|---|---|---|---|---|---|---|---|
| ISIC | 2–3, 511 | 20–22 | 23–24 | 25–26 | 28 | 33 | 34 | 35–38 | 39 | CITI |
| *a.* Absolute Figures — Chiffres absolus | | | | | | | | | | |
| Number of establishments... | 82 | 26 | 5 | 7 | 4 | 6 | 8 | 22 | 4 | Nombre d'établissements |
| Value added............. | 19 388.9 | 205.1 | 19.2 | 210.9 | 110.5 | 10.8 | 18 678.4 | 82.6 | 71.4 | Valeur ajoutée |
| Number of engaged (Average for year)...... | 42.5 | 1.3 | 0.2 | 3.5 | 0.2 | 0.4 | 36.2 | 0.4 | 0.3 | Nombre de personnes occupées (moyenne pour l'année) |
| Wages and salaries paid................. | 5 726.6 | 80.8 | 8.4 | 89.0 | 20.7 | 9.6 | 5 423.8 | 73.4 | 20.9 | Traitements et salaires payés |
| *b.* Structure | | | | | | | | | | |
| Distribution in percent of: Value added.......... | 100.0 | 1.1 | 0.1 | 1.1 | 0.6 | 0.1 | 96.3 | 0.4 | 0.3 | Répartition en pourcentage: De la valeur ajoutée |
| Number of engaged..... | 100.0 | 3.1 | 0.5 | 8.2 | 0.5 | 0.9 | 85.2 | 0.9 | 0.7 | Du nombre de personnes occupées |
| Value added per person engaged......... | 456.2 | 157.8 | 96.0 | 60.3 | 552.5 | 27.0 | 516.0 | 206.5 | 238.0 | Valeur ajoutée par personne occupée |
| Value added per unit of wages and salaries...... | 3.39 | 2.54 | 2.29 | 2.37 | 5.34 | 1.12 | 3.44 | 1.13 | 3.42 | Valeur ajoutée par unité de traitements et salaires |

[1] Includes the extraction of non-ferrous metal ores (in ISIC major group 12) and the Electricity producing industry (ISIC group 511).

[1] Y compris l'extraction des minerais de métaux non ferreux (partie de CITI classe 12) et la production d'électricité (CITI groupe 511).

## 6. THE CHARACTERISTICS OF INDUSTRIAL ESTABLISHMENTS ENGAGING SIX OR MORE PERSONS OR USING POWER EQUIPMENT OR STEAM BOILERS, SOUTHERN RHODESIA

### CARACTERISTIQUES DES ETABLISSEMENTS INDUSTRIELS OCCUPANT AU MOINS SIX PERSONNES OU UTILISANT LA FORCE MOTRICE OU DES GENERATEURS DE VAPEUR, RHODESIE DU SUD

#### 1938, 1948, 1953

Number of establishments in units; value added and wages and salaries in million Rhodesian Pounds; number of engaged in thousands; and value added per person engaged in thousand Rhodesian Pounds

Nombre d'établissements en unités; valeur ajoutée et traitements et salaires en millions de livres rhodésiennes; nombre de personnes occupées en milliers; valeur ajoutée par personne occupée en milliers de livres rhodésiennes

### A. Selected Divisions of Industrial Activity — Quelques branches de l'activité industrielle

| Item of data | Manufacturing Industries manufacturières | | | Construction Bâtiment et travaux publics | | | Electricity Electricité | | | Rubrique |
|---|---|---|---|---|---|---|---|---|---|---|
| | 1938 | 1948 | 1953 | 1938 | 1948 | 1953 | 1938 | 1948 | 1953 | |
| ISIC | 2-3 | | | 4 | | | 511 | | | CITI |
| a. Absolute Figures — Chiffres absolus | | | | | | | | | | |
| Number of establishments... | 299 | 473 | 714 | 70 | 251 | ... | 6 | 3 | 4 | Nombre d'établissements |
| Value added............ | 2.32 | 10.92 | 26.10 | 1.24 | 4.62 | ... | 0.30 | 0.86 | 1.46 | Valeur ajoutée |
| Number of engaged (Average for the year)... | 17.5 | 47.8 | 70.1 | 22.9 | 33.3 | ... | 1.4 | 3.2 | 4.9 | Nombre de personnes occupées (moyenne pour l'année) |
| Wages and salaries paid................ | 1.24 | 5.44 | 13.02 | 1.10 | 3.97 | ... | 0.10 | 0.44 | 1.18 | Traitements et salaires payés |
| Operatives: | | | | | | | | | | Ouvriers: |
| Number.............. | 16.6 | 45.6 | 66.5 | 22.6 | 32.4 | ... | 1.4 | 3.0 | 4.6 | Nombre |
| Wages and salaries..... | 0.89 | 4.00 | 9.75 | 0.97 | 3.42 | ... | 0.08 | 0.34 | 0.87 | Traitements et salaires |
| b. Structure | | | | | | | | | | |
| Value added per person engaged............. | 0.13 | 0.23 | 0.37 | 0.05 | 0.14 | ... | 0.21 | 0.27 | 0.30 | Valeur ajoutée par personne occupée |
| Value added per unit of wages and salaries...... | 1.87 | 2.01 | 2.00 | 1.13 | 1.16 | ... | 3.00 | 1.95 | 1.24 | Valeur ajoutée par unité de traitements et salaires |
| Operatives as a percent of engaged............ | 94.8 | 95.4 | 94.9 | 98.7 | 97.3 | ... | 100.0 | 93.8 | 93.9 | Ouvriers en pourcentage des personnes occupées |
| Wages and salaries per operative............. | 0.05 | 0.09 | 0.15 | 0.04 | 0.10 | ... | 0.06 | 0.11 | 0.19 | Traitements et salaires par ouvrier |

## B. The Major Groups of Manufacturing — Les classes de la branche Industries manufacturières

| Year and item of data | Manu-facturing Industries manu-facturières | Food, beverages and tobacco Industries alimen-taires, boissons, tabac | Textiles, clothing and footwear Textiles, articles d'habille-ment et chaussures | Wood products and furniture Bois et meubles | Paper and paper products and printing and publishing Papier, ouvrages en papier et imprimerie et édition | Rubber products Ouvrages en caoutchouc | Chemicals and chemical products Produits chimiques | Non-metallic mineral products Produits minéraux non métalliques | Basic metals and metal products Métallurgie de base et ouvrages en métaux | Other manu-facturing Autres industries manu-facturières | Année et rubrique |
|---|---|---|---|---|---|---|---|---|---|---|---|
| ISIC | 2-3 | 20-22 | 23-24 | 25-26 | 27-28 | 30 | 31 | 33 | 34-38 | 29, 32, 39 | CITI |
| *a.  Absolute Figures — Chiffres absolus* | | | | | | | | | | | |
| **1938** | | | | | | | | | | | **1938** |
| Number of establishments..... | 299 | 93 | 29 | 16 | 13 | 4 | 14 | 19 | 103 | 8 | Nombre d'établissements |
| Value added.............. | 2.32 | 0.90 | 0.05 | 0.12 | 0.25 | 0.01 | 0.12 | 0.16 | 0.64 | 0.07 | Valeur ajoutée |
| Number of engaged | | | | | | | | | | | Nombre de personnes occupées |
| (Average for the year)..... | 17.5 | 4.9 | 1.1 | 2.8 | 0.6 | — | 0.6 | 1.7 | 5.3 | 0.5 | (moyenne pour l'année) |
| Wages and salaries paid.... | 1.24 | 0.27 | 0.04 | 0.08 | 0.14 | — | 0.04 | 0.05 | 0.59 | 0.03 | Traitements et salaires payés |
| Operatives: | | | | | | | | | | | Ouvriers: |
| Number................ | 16.6 | 4.6 | 1.1 | 2.7 | 0.5 | — | 0.6 | 1.6 | 5.0 | 0.5 | Nombre |
| Wages and salaries....... | 0.89 | 0.16 | 0.03 | 0.06 | 0.09 | — | 0.02 | 0.04 | 0.47 | 0.02 | Traitements et salaires |
| **1948** | | | | | | | | | | | **1948** |
| Number of establishments..... | 473 | 115 | 52 | 40 | 15 | 8 | 15 | 57 | 157 | 14 | Nombre d'établissements |
| Value added.............. | 10.92 | 4.08 | 0.77 | 0.77 | 0.66 | 0.04 | 0.44 | 0.85 | 3.13 | 0.18 | Valeur ajoutée |
| Number of engaged | | | | | | | | | | | Nombre de personnes occupées |
| (Average for the year)..... | 47.8 | 13.2 | 5.3 | 5.1 | 1.0 | 0.1 | 0.9 | 6.7 | 14.6 | 0.9 | (moyenne pour l'année) |
| Wages and salaries paid..... | 5.44 | 1.11 | 0.41 | 0.37 | 0.36 | 0.02 | 0.13 | 0.42 | 2.54 | 0.08 | Traitements et salaires payés |
| Operatives: | | | | | | | | | | | Ouvriers: |
| Number................ | 45.6 | 12.6 | 5.1 | 5.0 | 0.8 | 0.1 | 0.7 | 6.6 | 13.8 | 0.9 | Nombre |
| Wages and salaries....... | 4.00 | 0.69 | 0.27 | 0.31 | 0.23 | 0.01 | 0.05 | 0.36 | 2.02 | 0.06 | Traitements et salaires |
| **1953** | | | | | | | | | | | **1953** |
| Number of establishments..... | 714 | 159 | 82 | 68 | 29 | 9 | 19 | 66 | 255 | 27 | Nombre d'établissements |
| Value added.............. | 26.10 | 8.02 | 3.11 | 1.64 | 1.57 | 0.12 | 1.36 | 2.34 | 7.30 | 0.64 | Valeur ajoutée |
| Number of engaged | | | | | | | | | | | Nombre de personnes occupées |
| (Average for the year)..... | 70.1 | 19.5 | 12.2 | 7.3 | 2.1 | 0.2 | 1.8 | 7.9 | 17.6 | 1.5 | (moyenne pour l'année) |
| Wages and salaries paid..... | 13.02 | 2.67 | 1.37 | 0.90 | 0.93 | 0.06 | 0.42 | 0.87 | 5.51 | 0.29 | Traitements et salaires payés |
| Operatives: | | | | | | | | | | | Ouvriers: |
| Number................ | 66.5 | 18.4 | 11.8 | 7.1 | 1.7 | 0.2 | 1.6 | 7.7 | 16.6 | 1.4 | Nombre |
| Wages and salaries....... | 9.75 | 1.75 | 1.03 | 0.70 | 0.63 | 0.03 | 0.22 | 0.66 | 4.53 | 0.20 | Traitements et salaires |
| *b.  Structure* | | | | | | | | | | | |
| **1938** | | | | | | | | | | | **1938** |
| Distribution in percent of: | | | | | | | | | | | Distribution en pourcentage: |
| Value added............. | 100.0 | 38.8 | 2.1 | 5.2 | 10.8 | 0.4 | 5.2 | 6.9 | 27.6 | 3.0 | Valeur ajoutée |
| Number of engaged....... | 100.0 | 28.0 | 6.3 | 16.0 | 3.4 | — | 3.4 | 9.7 | 30.3 | 2.9 | Nombre de personnes occupées |
| Value added per person engaged................ | 0.13 | 0.18 | 0.04 | 0.04 | 0.42 | — | 0.20 | 0.09 | 0.12 | 0.14 | Valeur ajoutée par personne occupée |
| Value added per unit of wages and salaries........ | 1.87 | 3.33 | 1.25 | 1.50 | 1.78 | — | 3.00 | 3.20 | 1.08 | 2.33 | Valeur ajoutée par unité de traitements et salaires |
| Operatives as a percent of engaged............. | 94.8 | 93.9 | 100.0 | 96.4 | 83.3 | — | 100.0 | 94.1 | 94.3 | 100.0 | Ouvriers en pourcentage des personnes occupées |
| Wages and salaries per operative........... | 0.05 | 0.03 | 0.03 | 0.02 | 0.18 | — | 0.03 | 0.02 | 0.09 | 0.04 | Traitements et salaires par ouvrier |
| **1948** | | | | | | | | | | | **1948** |
| Distribution in percent of: | | | | | | | | | | | Distribution en pourcentage: |
| Value added............. | 100.0 | 37.4 | 7.1 | 7.1 | 6.0 | 0.3 | 4.0 | 7.8 | 28.7 | 1.6 | Valeur ajoutée |
| Number of engaged....... | 100.0 | 27.6 | 11.1 | 10.7 | 2.1 | 0.2 | 1.9 | 14.0 | 30.5 | 1.9 | Nombre de personnes occupées |
| Value added per person engaged................ | 0.23 | 0.31 | 0.14 | 0.15 | 0.66 | 0.40 | 0.49 | 0.13 | 0.21 | 0.20 | Valeur ajoutée par personne occupée |
| Value added per unit of wages and salaries........ | 2.01 | 3.68 | 1.88 | 2.08 | 1.83 | 2.00 | 3.38 | 2.02 | 1.23 | 2.25 | Valeur ajoutée par unité de traitements et salaires |
| Operatives as a percent of engaged............. | 95.4 | 95.4 | 96.2 | 98.0 | 80.0 | 100.0 | 77.8 | 98.5 | 94.5 | 100.0 | Ouvriers en pourcentage des personnes occupées |
| Wages and salaries per operative........... | 0.09 | 0.05 | 0.05 | 0.06 | 0.29 | 0.10 | 0.07 | 0.05 | 0.15 | 0.07 | Traitements et salaires par ouvrier |
| **1953** | | | | | | | | | | | **1953** |
| Distribution in percent of: | | | | | | | | | | | Distribution en pourcentage: |
| Value added............. | 100.0 | 30.7 | 11.9 | 6.3 | 6.0 | 0.5 | 5.2 | 9.0 | 28.0 | 2.4 | Valeur ajoutée |
| Number of engaged....... | 100.0 | 27.8 | 17.4 | 10.4 | 3.0 | 0.3 | 2.6 | 11.3 | 25.1 | 2.1 | Nombre de personnes occupées |
| Value added per person engaged................ | 0.37 | 0.41 | 0.25 | 0.22 | 0.75 | 0.60 | 0.76 | 0.30 | 0.41 | 0.43 | Valeur ajoutée par personne occupée |
| Value added per unit of wages and salaries........ | 2.00 | 3.00 | 2.27 | 1.82 | 1.69 | 2.00 | 3.24 | 2.69 | 1.32 | 2.21 | Valeur ajoutée par unité de traitements et salaires |
| Operatives as a percent of engaged............. | 94.9 | 94.4 | 96.7 | 97.3 | 81.0 | 100.0 | 88.9 | 97.5 | 94.3 | 93.3 | Ouvriers en pourcentage des personnes occupées |
| Wages and salaries per operative........... | 0.15 | 0.10 | 0.09 | 0.10 | 0.37 | 0.15 | 0.14 | 0.08 | 0.27 | 0.14 | Traitements et salaires par ouvrier |

## Gross Domestic Product and Gross Domestic Fixed Capital Formation

The data set out in Table 1 on the gross domestic product and fixed capital formation were compiled from the response of the Central Statistical Office, Helsinki, to the United Nations national accounts questionnaire. The estimates are published annually in *Tilastokatsauksia* (Bulletin of Statistics) issued by that office.

## Index Numbers of Industrial Production

The index numbers of industrial production shown in Table 2 are published monthly in *Tilastokatsauksia*. In Number 10 of the issues of the publication for 1959, the Central Statistical Office of Finland furnished a series of these index numbers for the years, 1925-1958, which were classified, on as comparable a basis as possible, according to the latest industrial classification utilized by the Office. This industrial classification corresponds exactly to the International Standard Industrial Classification.

The series of index numbers relate to establishments covered in the annual Industrial Censuses described below—i.e., to establishments with five or more persons engaged or the equivalent in terms of a combination of capacity of installed power equipment and employment. The index numbers have been computed in successive steps, as base-weighted arithmetic averages. First, indexes have been compiled for detailed categories of industrial activity from quantity relatives. Secondly, the resulting indexes have been combined into indexes for broader classes of industrial activity. The weights utilized in the first stage of compilation are computed from gross value of production. The weighting patterns employed in the later stages of compilation are based on value added at factor cost.

The weight base year is 1938 in the case of the indexes for 1938, 1948 for the indexes for the years, 1948-1953, and 1954 for the indexes for the years, 1954-1961. Beginning with the indexes for 1962, the weight base year was shifted to 1959. The Central Statistical Office of Finland plans to utilize 1959 as the weight base for the indexes for 1961 as well. In each case the weighting pattern is based on the results of the pertinent annual Industrial Census. It should be noted that the figures of value added utilized in computing the 1938 and 1948 weights were not net of the cost of purchased fuels or electricity consumed.

The indicators utilized in the quantity relatives consist largely of the quantity of output of individual products. Man-hours worked and quantities of individual raw materials consumed are also utilized for this purpose. The indicators are derived annually from the Industrial

## Produit intérieur brut et formation brute de capital intérieur fixe

Les données du tableau 1 relatives au produit intérieur brut et à la formation de capital intérieur fixe ont été élaborées à partir de la réponse du Bureau central de Statistique, Helsinki, au questionnaire de l'ONU sur les comptes nationaux. Les estimations sont publiées annuellement dans *Tilastokatsauksia* (Bulletin de Statistique) par ce Bureau.

## Indices de la Production industrielle

Les indices de la production industrielle reproduits au tableau 2 sont publiés mensuellement dans *Tilastokatsauksia*. Dans le No 10 des publications relatives à 1959, le Bureau Central de Statistique de Finlande fournit des séries d'indices pour les années 1925-1958, qui sont classées sur une base aussi comparable que possible à celle adoptée dans la plus récente classification utilisée par le Bureau. Cette classification industrielle correspond exactement à la CITI.

Les séries d'indices sont relatives aux établissements couverts par les recensements industriels annuels décrits ci-dessous, c'est-à-dire les établissements occupant cinq personnes ou plus, ou d'importance égale, en fonction de la combinaison de la puissance installée et de l'emploi. Ces indices ont été calculés en plusieurs étapes, comme des moyennes arithmétiques à pondération fixe. Au premier stade, les indices ont été élaborés pour des catégories détaillées de l'activité industrielle à partir de rapports quantitatifs. A un second stade, les indices obtenus ont été combinés en indices relatifs à des classes plus larges de l'activité industrielle. Les coefficients de pondération utilisés au premier stade du calcul sont tirés de la valeur brute de la production. Les coefficients utilisés au second stade sont fondés sur la valeur ajoutée au coût des facteurs.

L'année de pondération de base étant 1938 dans le cas des indices pour 1938, 1948 pour les indices relatifs aux années 1948-1953, et 1954 pour les indices relatifs aux années 1954-1961, 1959 a été adoptée comme année de base à commencer par les indices de 1962. Le Bureau Central de Statistique de Finlande projette d'utiliser 1959 comme année de pondération de base pour les indices de 1961 également. Dans chaque cas les coefficients de pondération sont basés sur les résultats du Recensement industriel. Il est bon de noter que les chiffres relatifs à la valeur ajoutée, utilisés dans l'élaboration des coefficients de pondération, tiennent compte des combustibles achetés ou de l'électricité consommée.

Dans les rapports quantitatifs, l'indicateur utilisé est en grande partie le volume de la production de chaque marchandise, mais on s'est servi aussi du nombre d'heures de travail effectuées et du volume de la consommation de chaque matière première. Les indicateurs sont tirés des

Censuses, as the results of these Censuses become available. For recent years, for which the results of the annual Censuses are not yet available, the indicators are supplied by a monthly survey of a sample of establishments covered in these Censuses.

For further details concerning the character of the index numbers see: *Tilastokatsauksia,* Nos. 1-2, 1949 regarding the indexes based on 1938; *Tilastokatsauksia,* Nos. 11-12, 1950 and No. 4, 1959 in the case of the indexes based on 1948, and *Tilastokatsauksia,* Nos. 8 and 11, 1958 concerning the indexes based on 1954. Information on all of these series of index numbers is also presented in *Tilastokatsauksia,* No. 10, 1959.

### Index Numbers of Industrial Employment

The index numbers of industrial employment shown in Table 3 were compiled by the Statistical Office of the United Nations from the published results of the annual Industrial Censuses described below. The final data resulting from these Censuses are issued annually by the Central Statistical Office of Finland in its *Suomen Virallinen Tilasto* (Finland's Official Statistics) under the title, *Teollisuustilastoa* (Industrial Census). Preliminary data appear in various issues of *Tilastokatsauksia.*

The index numbers of industrial employment relate to the annual average number of engaged in establishments covered in the annual Industrial Censuses. As the footnotes to Table 3 indicate, certain incomparabilities in classification occur in the series of index numbers. This reflects the revision, as of 1954, of the scheme of industrial classification utilized by the Finnish Central Statistical Office in order to attain exact coincidence with the International Standard Industrial Classification.

### The Characteristics and Structure of Industrial Activity

The information given in Table 4 originates in a General Economic Census taken as of 22 May 1953. The Census covered all establishments in operation as of that date, irrespective of size, in mining, manufacturing, construction, and the electricity and gas industries, as well as in other business activities. It should be noted, however, that road building undertaken directly by government authorities was not covered. The results of the Census have been published by the Central Statistical Office of Finland in *Suomen Virallinen Tilasto,* XXXV, *Vuoden 1953, Liikeyrityslaskenta* (1953 General Economic Census), Volumes I-III.

The data shown in Tables 5 and 6 come from the annual Industrial Census taken by the Central Statistical Office of Finland. These figures were compiled from the publications of the Office, *Suomen Virallinen Tilasto, Teollisuustilastoa* (Industrial Census), *1938, 1948, 1953, 1954* and *1958,* respectively.

The annual Industrial Censuses cover establishments having five or more persons engaged or the equivalent in

résultats des recensements industriels exécutés annuellement par le Bureau Central de Statistique dès que ces résultats sont disponibles. En ce qui concerne les toutes dernières années pour lesquelles les résultats des recensements annuels ne sont pas encore disponibles, les indicateurs sont tirés d'une enquête mensuelle qui porte sur un échantillon des établissements couverts par le recensement.

Pour plus amples détails sur la nature de ces indices, voir *Tilastokatsauksia,* No 1-2, 1949, pour les indices pour lesquels la période de base est 1938, *Tilastokatsauksia,* No 11-12, 1950, et No 4, 1959, dans le cas des indices ayant pour période de base 1948, et *Tilastokatsauksia,* Nos 8 et 11, 1958, pour les indices ayant pour période de base 1954. Des renseignements sont également fournis dans *Tilastokatsauksia,* No 10, 1959.

### Indices de l'emploi industriel

Les indices de l'emploi industriel reproduits au tableau 3 ont été calculés par le Bureau de Statistique de l'ONU à partir des résultats publiés du recensement industriel annuel décrit ci-dessous. Les résultats définitifs de ces recensements sont reproduits annuellement par le Bureau Central de Statistique de Finlande dans sa publication *Suomen Virallinen Tilasto* (Statistiques Officielles Finlandaises) sous le titre, *Teollisuustilastoa* (recensement industriel). Des données provisoires sont également publiées dans différents numéros de *Tilastokatsauksia.*

Les indices de l'emploi sont relatifs au nombre moyen annuel de personnes occupées dans les établissements couverts par le recensement industriel annuel. Comme l'indiquent les notes au bas du tableau 3, certains défauts de comparabilité dans la classification se retrouvent dans les séries d'indices. Ceci est dû à la revision en 1954 du système de classification industrielle utilisé par le Bureau Central Finlandais de Statistique afin de le faire coïncider avec la Classification CITI.

### Les caractéristiques et la structure de l'activité industrielle

Les renseignements fournis au tableau 4 sont tirés d'un Recensement Economique Général au 22 mai 1953. Le recensement portait sur tous les établissements en activité à cette date, compte non tenu de leur dimension, dans les industries extractives, manufacturières, travaux publics et bâtiment, et dans les industries électriques et gazières, ainsi que dans les autres activités industrielles et commerciales. Les résultats de ce recensement ont été publiés dans *Suomen Virallinen Tilasto,* XXXV, *Vuoden 1953, Liikeyrityslaskenta* (Recensement Economique Général, 1953), vol. I-III, par le Bureau Central de Statistique de Finlande.

Les données reproduites aux tableaux 5 et 6 sont tirées des recensements industriels effectués annuellement par le Bureau Central de Statistique de Finlande. Ces chiffres ont été élaborés à partir des publications du Bureau, intitulées, *Suomen Virallinen Tilasto, Teollisuustilastoa* (recensement industriel) *1938, 1948, 1953, 1956* et *1958,* respectivement.

Ces recensements industriels annuels portaient sur les établissements industriels occupant cinq personnes ou

terms of a combination of installed power equipment and employment. Seven horsepower of installed power equipment is equated to one person engaged. The annual Industrial Censuses for 1948 and later years relate to a smaller territory than the Census for 1938. This has affected the comparability of the figures for 1938 with those for 1948 and later years. Further, the data for 1954 and 1958 are not precisely comparable with that for 1953 and earlier years because of the differences noted above in the schemes of industrial classification utilized.

The definitions of the items of data set out in Tables 4 and 5 are similar to those recommended in the International Standards in Basic Industrial Statistics. Value added is priced at factor cost. The figures of value added for 1953 and earlier years were estimated by the Statistical Office of the United Nations. This was done by subtracting published figures of the cost of raw materials consumed and estimates of the cost of purchased fuels and electricity consumed from published data on the gross value of production, ex-establishments and net of turnover and other indirect taxes. The estimates of the cost of fuels and electricity consumed were based on ratios of these costs to the gross value of production derived from the published results of the 1954 Industrial Census. The figures of installed power equipment relate to prime movers connected directly to machinery other than electric generators plus all electric motors except for the figures on the electricity producing industry for 1953, 1948 and 1938. In these instances, the data cover prime movers connected directly to electric generators plus all electric motors. The data on the installed power equipment in the electricity industry therefore relate essentially to the capacity to produce electricity in the case of 1953 and earlier years.

The figures of energy consumed set out in Tables 5 and 6 cover the consumption of fuels, steam, and purchased electricity except in the case of the electricity, gas and steam industries. The figures of energy consumed for these industries exclude the use of forms of energy, the production of which is their main business. The data for these industries therefore do not include double counting and relate primarily to the consumption of forms of energy to produce electricity, gas and/or steam. On the other hand, the data on energy consumed for mining or manufacturing industries deal primarily with the use of fuels and purchased steam and electricity as sources of heat and power though, in some instances, coal or certain other fuels may also be consumed as raw materials. There may also be some double counting included in these figures to the extent, for example, that coke and/or gas for own use are produced from coal by some manufacturing establishments.

plus, ou d'importance égale, en fonction de la combinaison de la puissance installée et de l'emploi. La puissance installée de sept chevaux-vapeur étant équivalente à une personne occupée. Les recensements annuels effectués pour 1948 et les années ultérieures couvrent un champ plus réduit que celui couvert par le recensement de 1938, ce qui entraîna un manque de comparabilité entre les chiffres de 1938 et ceux de 1948 et des années ultérieures. De plus, les données relatives aux années 1954 et 1958 ne sont pas précisément comparables avec celles de 1953 et des années antérieures, étant donné la différence mentionnée plus haut entre les systèmes de classification adoptés.

Les définitions de rubriques reproduites aux tableaux 4 et 5 sont similaires à celles des recommandations relatives aux statistiques industrielles de base. La valeur ajoutée est calculée au coût des facteurs. Les chiffres concernant la valeur ajoutée pour 1953 et les années antérieures sont des estimations du Bureau de Statistique de l'ONU, obtenues en soustrayant, pour chaque année, des chiffres publiés de la valeur brute de la production totale — départ établissement, déduction faite de l'impôt sur le chiffre d'affaires et autres impôts indirects — les chiffres publiés du coût des matières premières consommées et le coût estimatif des combustibles achetés et de l'électricité consommée. Les chiffres publiés du coût des combustibles et de l'électricité consommés sont fondés sur les rapports de ces coûts à la valeur brute de la production tirés des résultats publiés du recensement industriel de 1954. Les chiffres relatifs à la puissance installée concernent les moteurs primaires qui actionnent directement des machines autres que des générateurs d'électricité et tous les moteurs électriques, à l'exclusion des chiffres relatifs aux industries productrices d'électricité pour 1953, 1948 et 1938. Pour ces industries, les données couvrent les moteurs primaires reliés directement aux générateurs d'électricité plus tous les moteurs électriques. Les données relatives à la puissance installée dans les industries productrices d'électricité concernent, par conséquent, essentiellement la capacité de production d'électricité jusqu'en 1953 inclus.

Les chiffres relatifs à l'énergie consommée reproduits aux tableaux 5 et 6 comprennent la consommation de combustibles, de gaz, de vapeur et d'électricité achetée par les industries autres que les industries productrices d'électricité, de gaz et de vapeur. Les chiffres relatifs à l'énergie consommée par ces industries ne comprennent pas les formes d'énergie qu'elles produisent principalement. Les données qui se rapportent à ces industries par conséquent ne comportent pas de doubles emplois et concernent principalement la consommation du type d'énergie nécessaire à la production d'électricité, de gaz et de vapeur. D'autre part, les données relatives à l'énergie consommée par les industries extractives et manufacturières concernent en premier lieu les combustibles, la vapeur et l'électricité achetées, utilisés comme source de chaleur et de puissance, quoique, dans certains cas, le charbon ou certains autres combustibles puissent être utilisés comme matière première. Il peut également exister certains doubles emplois dans ces chiffres du fait que par exemple le coke et/ou le gaz autoconsommé sont produits à partir du charbon par certains établissements manufacturiers.

# 1. THE GROSS DOMESTIC PRODUCT AND GROSS DOMESTIC FIXED CAPITAL FORMATION
## LE PRODUIT INTERIEUR BRUT ET LA FORMATION BRUTE DE CAPITAL FIXE INTERIEUR

Thousand million markkaa                                     Milliards de markkaa

## A. Expenditure on the Gross Domestic Product at Market Prices
### Dépenses relatives au produit intérieur brut aux prix du marché

| Item of data and year<br>Rubrique et année | Total | Consumption<br>Consommation | | Gross Domestic Capital Formation<br>Formation brute de capital intérieur | | Net exports of goods and services<br>Exportations nettes de biens et de services | |
|---|---|---|---|---|---|---|---|
| | | Total | Government<br>Etat | Total | Fixed<br>Fixe | Exports<br>less imports<br>Exportations<br>moins<br>importations | Exports<br>Exportations |
| | | | | a. At Current Prices — Aux prix courants | | | |
| Absolute figures — Chiffres absolus | | | | | | | |
| 1948 | 370.2 | 283.3 [1] | 38.9 | [1] | 82.0 | +4.9 | 77.8 |
| 1950 | 499.0 | 377.9 [1] | 59.0 | [1] | 117.1 | +4.0 | 106.2 |
| 1951 | 729.3 | 508.1 [1] | 74.5 | [1] | 173.1 | +48.1 | 226.2 |
| 1952 | 743.1 | 555.5 [1] | 85.2 | [1] | 198.2 | —10.6 | 195.1 |
| 1953 | 753.0 | 555.4 [1] | 92.3 | [1] | 184.0 | +13.6 | 156.6 |
| 1954 | 823.4 | 596.2 [1] | 95.5 | [1] | 211.6 | +15.6 | 184.6 |
| 1955 | 911.2 | 658.3 [1] | 113.0 | [1] | 236.4 | +16.5 | 215.7 |
| 1956 | 1 030.4 | 752.7 [1] | 133.5 | [1] | 288.7 | —11.0 | 217.3 |
| 1957 | 1 112.0 | 817.0 | 145.4 | 294.5 | 279.1 | +0.5 | 258.8 |
| 1958 | 1 186.3 | 855.1 | 158.7 | 303.0 | 302.1 | +28.2 | 292.5 |
| 1959 | 1 257.6 | 916.9 | 177.6 | 330.3 | 331.4 | +10.4 | 315.4 |
| 1960 | 1 431.1 | 1 015.4 | 191.5 | 428.2 | 416.0 | —12.5 | 371.2 |
| 1961 | 1 585.6 | 1 122.2 | 218.2 | 482.5 | 463.8 | —19.1 | 399.5 |
| Percentage distribution of average annual expenditure — Distribution en pourcentage des dépenses annuelles moyennes | | | | | | | |
| 1948 | 100.0 | 76.5 [1] | 10.5 | [1] | 22.2 | +1.3 | 21.0 |
| 1950–1960 | 100.0 | 72.6 [1] | 12.6 | [1] | 26.0 | +1.0 | 24.2 |
| 1950 | 100.0 | 75.7 [1] | 11.8 | [1] | 23.5 | +0.8 | 21.3 |
| 1953 | 100.0 | 73.8 [1] | 12.2 | [1] | 24.4 | +1.8 | 20.8 |
| 1954 | 100.0 | 72.4 [1] | 11.6 | [1] | 25.7 | +1.9 | 22.4 |
| 1958 | 100.0 | 72.1 | 13.4 | 25.6 | 25.5 | +2.4 | 24.6 |
| 1960 | 100.0 | 70.9 | 13.4 | 29.9 | 29.1 | —0.8 | 25.9 |

[1] Changes in stocks are included in total consumption in the case of the data for the years, 1948-1956, and the average percentage for the period, 1950-1960.

[1] Les variations de stocks sont incluses dans la consommation totale, dans le cas des données relatives aux années, 1948-1956, et dans le cas des pourcentages moyens pour la période 1950-1960.

## B.   The Gross Domestic Product at Factor Cost According to Origin [1]
### Origine par secteur d'activité du produit intérieur brut au coût des facteurs [1]

| Item of data and year<br>Rubrique et année | Total | Agricultural sector<br><br>Secteur agricole | Industrial Sector — Secteur Industriel | | | Transportation and communication<br><br>Transport et communication | Other sectors<br><br>Autres secteurs |
|---|---|---|---|---|---|---|---|
| | | | Total | Mining, manufacturing, electricity gas and water<br><br>Industries extractives et manufacturières, électricité, gaz et eau | Construction<br><br>Bâtiments et travaux publics | | |
| ISIC — CITI | 0–9 | 0 | 1–5 | 1, 2–3, 5 | 4 | 7 | 6, 8–9 |

### a. At Current Prices — Aux prix courants

| | | | | | | | |
|---|---|---|---|---|---|---|---|
| Absolute figures — Chiffres absolus | | | | | | | |
| 1948............ | 317.1 | 100.3 | 123.9 | 100.1 | 23.8 | 20.7 | 72.2 |
| 1950............ | 431.6 | 106.0 | 176.5 | 138.7 | 37.8 | 31.6 | 117.5 |
| 1951............ | 637.7 | 175.8 | 263.7 | 211.9 | 51.8 | 44.3 | 153.9 |
| 1952............ | 639.4 | 162.0 | 261.1 | 204.5 | 56.6 | 45.6 | 170.7 |
| 1953............ | 653.7 | 155.5 | 269.3 | 208.8 | 60.5 | 46.5 | 182.4 |
| 1954............ | 721.2 | 171.4 | 301.6 | 235.6 | 66.0 | 50.6 | 197.6 |
| 1955............ | 814.8 | 192.2 | 336.6 | 265.9 | 70.7 | 61.9 | 224.1 |
| 1956............ | 922.2 | 204.3 | 379.0 | 293.9 | 85.1 | 74.8 | 264.1 |
| 1957............ | 974.4 | 197.5 | 405.0 | 316.3 | 88.7 | 83.2 | 288.7 |
| 1958............ | 1 042.1 | 215.0 | 435.3 | 339.1 | 96.2 | 86.7 | 310.1 |
| 1959............ | 1 107.8 | 222.7 | 456.1 | 352.0 | 104.1 | 91.5 | 337.5 |
| 1960............ | 1 260.9 | 262.3 | 526.4 | 412.0 | 114.4 | 102.0 | 370.2 |
| 1961............ | 1 403.1 | 291.6 | 587.6 | 462.2 | 125.4 | 112.9 | 411.0 |
| Percentage distribution according to sector— Distribution en pourcentage par secteur | | | | | | | |
| 1948............ | 100.0 | 31.6 | 39.1 | 31.6 | 7.5 | 6.5 | 22.8 |
| 1950 – 1960..... | 100.0 | 22.4 | 41.4 | 32.3 | 9.0 | 7.8 | 28.5 |
| 1950............ | 100.0 | 24.5 | 40.9 | 32.1 | 8.8 | 7.3 | 27.3 |
| 1953............ | 100.0 | 23.8 | 41.2 | 31.9 | 9.3 | 7.1 | 27.9 |
| 1954............ | 100.0 | 23.8 | 41.8 | 32.7 | 9.1 | 7.0 | 27.4 |
| 1958............ | 100.0 | 20.5 | 41.6 | 32.4 | 9.2 | 8.3 | 29.6 |
| 1960............ | 100.0 | 20.8 | 41.7 | 32.6 | 9.1 | 8.1 | 29.4 |

### b. At Prices of 1958 — Aux prix de 1958

| | | | | | | | |
|---|---|---|---|---|---|---|---|
| Absolute figures — Chiffres absolus | | | | | | | |
| 1948............ | 690.0 | 177.7 | 244.8 | 189.9 | 54.9 | 56.8 | 210.7 |
| 1950............ | 771.3 | 186.3 | 281.7 | 214.4 | 67.3 | 63.1 | 240.2 |
| 1951............ | 841.3 | 203.3 | 316.8 | 247.6 | 69.2 | 71.4 | 249.8 |
| 1952............ | 837.5 | 200.6 | 307.4 | 238.1 | 69.3 | 69.4 | 260.1 |
| 1953............ | 858.7 | 197.5 | 330.6 | 251.5 | 79.1 | 68.4 | 262.2 |
| 1954............ | 935.6 | 212.6 | 372.8 | 288.5 | 84.3 | 76.2 | 274.0 |
| 1955............ | 997.1 | 212.6 | 404.1 | 319.6 | 84.5 | 84.7 | 295.7 |
| 1956............ | 1 018.9 | 202.0 | 425.7 | 333.2 | 92.5 | 86.0 | 305.2 |
| 1957............ | 1 044.4 | 207.8 | 442.9 | 350.7 | 92.2 | 86.3 | 307.4 |
| 1958............ | 1 047.0 | 215.0 | 435.3 | 339.1 | 96.2 | 86.7 | 310.0 |
| 1959............ | 1 117.1 | 223.3 | 468.6 | 367.3 | 101.3 | 92.8 | 332.4 |
| 1960............ | 1 224.6 | 244.0 | 524.7 | 420.4 | 104.3 | 101.6 | 354.3 |
| 1961............ | 1 309.5 | 254.9 | 571.8 | 461.1 | 110.7 | 107.3 | 375.5 |
| Percentage distribution according to sector— Distribution en pourcentage par secteur | | | | | | | |
| 1948............ | 100.0 | 25.8 | 35.5 | 27.5 | 8.0 | 8.2 | 30.5 |
| 1950 – 1960..... | 100.0 | 21.5 | 40.3 | 31.5 | 8.8 | 8.3 | 29.9 |
| 1950............ | 100.0 | 24.2 | 36.5 | 27.8 | 8.7 | 8.2 | 31.1 |
| 1953............ | 100.0 | 22.9 | 38.5 | 29.3 | 9.2 | 8.0 | 30.6 |
| 1954............ | 100.0 | 22.7 | 39.8 | 30.8 | 9.0 | 8.2 | 29.3 |
| 1958............ | 100.0 | 20.5 | 41.6 | 32.4 | 9.2 | 8.2 | 29.7 |
| 1960............ | 100.0 | 19.9 | 42.8 | 34.3 | 8.5 | 8.3 | 29.0 |
| Average annual rate of growth—Taux annuel moyen d'accroissement | | | | | | | |
| 1948 – 1953..... | 4.5 | 2.1 | 6.2 | 5.8 | 7.6 | 3.8 | 4.5 |
| 1950 – 1960..... | 4.7 | 2.7 | 6.4 | 7.0 | 4.5 | 4.9 | 4.0 |
| 1950 – 1953..... | 3.6 | 2.0 | 5.5 | 5.5 | 5.5 | 2.7 | 3.0 |
| 1954 – 1958..... | 2.9 | 0.3 | 4.0 | 4.1 | 3.4 | 3.3 | 3.1 |
| 1958 – 1960..... | 8.2 | 6.5 | 9.8 | 11.4 | 4.1 | 8.3 | 6.9 |

[1] Includes export duties.                    [1] Y compris les droits à l'exportation.

## C. Gross Domestic Fixed Capital Formation According to Purchasing Sector[1]
### Formation brute de capital fixe intérieur par secteur d'acquisition [1]

| Item of data and year<br>Rubrique et année | Total | Agricultural sector<br>Secteur agricole | Mining, manufacturing, electricity, gas and water<br>Industries extractives et manufacturières, électricité, gaz et eau | Transportation and communication<br>Transport et communication | Other sectors<br>Autres secteurs |
|---|---|---|---|---|---|
| ISIC — CITI | 0–9 | 0 | 1, 2–3, 5 | 7 | 4, 6, 8–9 |
| | *a.* At Current Prices — Aux prix courants | | | | |
| Absolute figures —<br>Chiffres absolus | | | | | |
| 1948............ | 82.0 | 14.4 | 25.1 | 5.8 | 36.7 |
| 1950............ | 117.1 | 19.1 | 27.3 | 9.5 | 61.2 |
| 1951............ | 173.1 | 25.4 | 46.5 | 13.7 | 87.5 |
| 1952............ | 198.2 | 28.6 | 54.9 | 18.4 | 96.3 |
| 1953............ | 184.0 | 26.2 | 50.0 | 12.6 | 95.2 |
| 1954............ | 211.6 | 26.5 | 67.2 | 13.1 | 104.8 |
| 1955............ | 236.4 | 27.9 | 72.1 | 16.3 | 120.1 |
| 1956............ | 288.7 | 30.9 | 90.4 | 22.5 | 144.9 |
| 1957 [2]........ | 279.1 | 26.0 | 74.1 | 28.9 | 150.1 |
| 1958 [2]........ | 302.1 | 30.3 | 77.0 | 39.4 | 155.4 |
| 1959 [2]........ | 331.4 | 34.0 | 86.7 | 39.9 | 170.8 |
| 1960 [2]........ | 416.0 | 38.8 | 120.9 | 50.3 | 206.0 |
| 1961 [2]........ | 463.8 | 43.6 | 139.8 | 51.8 | 228.6 |
| Percentage distribution according to sector—<br>Distribution en pourcentage par secteur | | | | | |
| 1948............ | 100.0 | 17.6 | 30.6 | 7.1 | 44.7 |
| 1950 – 1960..... | ... | ... | ... | ... | ... |
| 1950............ | 100.0 | 16.3 | 23.3 | 8.1 | 52.3 |
| 1953............ | 100.0 | 14.2 | 27.2 | 6.8 | 51.8 |
| 1954............ | 100.0 | 12.5 | 31.8 | 6.2 | 49.5 |
| 1958 [2]........ | 100.0 | 10.0 | 25.5 | 13.1 | 51.4 |
| 1960 [2]........ | 100.0 | 9.3 | 29.0 | 12.1 | 49.6 |

[1] The fixed capital formation in the construction industry is distributed among other industries.
[2] The data for the years, 1957–1961, are not comparable to those for earlier years.

[1] La formation de capital fixe dans les industries de la construction est répartie entre les autres branches d'activité.
[2] Les données pour les années 1957–1961 ne sont pas comparables à celles des années postérieures.

# FINLAND

## 2. INDEX NUMBERS OF INDUSTRIAL PRODUCTION
## INDICES DE LA PRODUCTION INDUSTRIELLE

### A. Selected Divisions of Industrial Activity
### Quelques branches de l'activité industrielle

| Period<br>Période | Total | Mining<br>Industries extractives | Manu-facturing [1]<br>Industries manu-facturières [1] | Electricity and gas [2]<br>Electricité et gaz [2] |
|---|---|---|---|---|
| ISIC — CITI | 1-3, 511-512 | 1 | 2-3 | 511-512 |

*a. Indexes — Indices (1958 = 100)*

| | | | | |
|---|---|---|---|---|
| 1938.......... | 44 | 33 | 46 | 34 |
| 1948.......... | − 58 − | − 51 − | − 61 − | − 38 − |
| 1949.......... | 60 | 52 | 63 | 45 |
| 1950.......... | 64 | 53 | 67 | 52 |
| 1951.......... | 75 | 60 | 78 | 57 |
| 1952.......... | 72 | 63 | 74 | 60 |
| 1953.......... | 76 | 65 | 78 | 68 |
| 1954.......... | − 88 − | − 74 − | − 91 − | − 71 − |
| 1955.......... | 98 | 86 | 100 | 84 |
| 1956.......... | 101 | 91 | 103 | 86 |
| 1957.......... | 104 | 98 | 104 | 92 |
| 1958.......... | 100 | 100 | 100 | 100 |
| 1959.......... | 109 | 112 | 110 | 101 |
| 1960.......... | 124 | 121 | 125 | 112 |
| 1961.......... | 136 | 135 | 137 | 125 |

*b. Average Annual Rate of Change — Taux annuel moyen de variation*

| | | | | |
|---|---|---|---|---|
| 1938 − 1960.... | 4.8 | 6.1 | 4.6 | 5.6 |
| 1938 − 1948.... | 2.8 | 4.5 | 2.9 | 1.1 |
| 1950 − 1960.... | 6.8 | 8.6 | 6.4 | 8.0 |
| 1948 − 1953.... | 5.5 | 5.0 | 5.0 | 12.3 |
| 1954 − 1958.... | 3.2 | 7.8 | 2.4 | 8.9 |
| 1958 − 1960.... | 11.4 | 10.0 | 11.8 | .5.8 |

[1] Production in slaughtering and meat packing, dairies, repair of footwear and publishing are omitted and the quarrying of stone, clay and similar non-metallic minerals is included in years prior to 1954.
[2] Activity in the distribution of electricity is omitted prior to 1954

### B. The Major Groups of Mining
### Les classes de la branche Industries extractives

| Period<br>Période | All mining<br>Toutes industries extractives | Metal mining<br>Extraction des minerais métalliques | Other mining<br>Autres industries extractives |
|---|---|---|---|
| ISIC — CITI | 1 | 12 | 14-19 |

*a. Indexes — Indices (1958 = 100)*

| | | | |
|---|---|---|---|
| 1938........... | 33 | 31 | 41 |
| 1948........... | − 51 − | − 45 − | − 61 − |
| 1949........... | 52 | 46 | 62 |
| 1950........... | 53 | 39 | 70 |
| 1951........... | 60 | 49 | 76 |
| 1952........... | 63 | 53 | 77 |
| 1953........... | 65 | 54 | 81 |
| 1954........... | − 74 − | − 59 − | − 94 − |
| 1955........... | 86 | 73 | 104 |
| 1956........... | 91 | 78 | 110 |
| 1957........... | 98 | 93 | 106 |
| 1958........... | 100 | 100 | 100 |
| 1959........... | 112 | 108 | 118 |
| 1960........... | 121 | 114 | 130 |
| 1961........... | 135 | 124 | 150 |

*b. Average Annual Rate of Change — Taux annuel moyen de variation*

| | | | |
|---|---|---|---|
| 1938 − 1960...... | 6.1 | 6.1 | 5.4 |
| 1938 − 1948...... | 4.5 | 3.8 | 4.1 |
| 1950 − 1960...... | 8.6 | 11.3 | 6.4 |
| 1948 − 1953...... | 5.0 | 3.7 | 5.8 |
| 1954 − 1958...... | 7.8 | 14.1 | 1.6 |
| 1958 − 1960...... | 10.0 | 6.8 | 14.0 |

[1] Avant 1954, non compris l'abattage du bétail, la fabrication des préparations et conserves de viande, l'industrie du lait, la réparation des chaussures et l'édition, mais y compris l'extraction de la pierre à bâtir, de l'argile etc., et d'autres minéraux non métalliques.
[2] Avant 1954, non compris la distribution d'électricité.

## C. The Major Groups of Manufacturing — Les classes de la branche Industries manufacturières

| Period / Période | Manufacturing [4] / Industries manufacturières [4] | Food, beverages and tobacco [1] / Industries alimentaires, boissons, tabac [1] | Textiles | Clothing, footwear and made-up textiles [2] / Articles d'habillement, chaussures et ouvrages en tissu [2] | Wood products and furniture / Bois et meubles | Paper and paper products / Papier et ouvrages en papier | Printing and publishing [3] / Imprimerie et édition [3] | Leather and leather products except wearing apparel / Cuir et articles en cuir, à l'exclusion des articles d'habillement | Rubber products / Ouvrages en caoutchouc | Chemicals and chemical, petroleum and coal products / Produits chimiques et dérivés du pétrole et du charbon | Non-metallic mineral products [4] / Produits minéraux non métalliques [4] | Basic metals / Métallurgie de base | Metal products / Ouvrages en métaux | Other manufacturing / Autres industries manufacturières |
|---|---|---|---|---|---|---|---|---|---|---|---|---|---|---|
| ISIC — CITI | 2-3 | 20-22 | 23 | 24 | 25-26 | 27 | 28 | 29 | 30 | 31-32 | 33 | 34 | 35-38 | 39 |

### a. Indexes — Indices (1958 = 100)

| | | | | | | | | | | | | | | |
|---|---|---|---|---|---|---|---|---|---|---|---|---|---|---|
| 1938 | 46 | 39 | 66 | 53 | 75 | 53 | 40 | 78 | 43 | 17 | 57 | 34 | 34 | 29 |
| 1948 | −61− | −49− | −64− | −60− | −87− | −49− | −61− | −85− | −70− | −39− | −72− | −66− | −68− | −44− |
| 1949 | 63 | 53 | 73 | 63 | 87 | 46 | 63 | 90 | 74 | 41 | 79 | 65 | 73 | 43 |
| 1950 | 67 | 62 | 84 | 74 | 88 | 54 | 71 | 102 | 87 | 50 | 86 | 52 | 65 | 55 |
| 1951 | 78 | 69 | 91 | 76 | 106 | 64 | 74 | 102 | 97 | 55 | 94 | 73 | 82 | 61 |
| 1952 | 74 | 74 | 91 | 80 | 88 | 55 | 77 | 95 | 89 | 55 | 85 | 81 | 81 | 63 |
| 1953 | 78 | 78 | 94 | 83 | 96 | 60 | 78 | 106 | 92 | 65 | 94 | 76 | 80 | 70 |
| 1954 | −91− | −86− | −102− | −95− | −110− | −75− | −86− | −114− | −105− | −77− | −105− | −93− | −93− | −87− |
| 1955 | 100 | 93 | 118 | 111 | 111 | 86 | 93 | 120 | 122 | 82 | 113 | 98 | 105 | 96 |
| 1956 | 103 | 101 | 126 | 120 | 92 | 91 | 97 | 126 | 123 | 89 | 109 | 100 | 106 | 108 |
| 1957 | 104 | 99 | 124 | 108 | 97 | 100 | 101 | 114 | 113 | 100 | 113 | 108 | 107 | 106 |
| 1958 | 100 | 100 | 100 | 100 | 100 | 100 | 100 | 100 | 100 | 100 | 100 | 100 | 100 | 100 |
| 1959 | 110 | 105 | 119 | 113 | 112 | 107 | 104 | 95 | 107 | 105 | 117 | 120 | 111 | 119 |
| 1960 | 125 | 116 | 122 | 124 | 138 | 125 | 118 | 99 | 117 | 117 | 129 | 141 | 132 | 138 |
| 1961 | 137 | 124 | 128 | 136 | 142 | 145 | 124 | 108 | 126 | 125 | 147 | 156 | 150 | 175 |

### b. Average Annual Rate of Change — Taux annuel moyen de variation

| | | | | | | | | | | | | | | |
|---|---|---|---|---|---|---|---|---|---|---|---|---|---|---|
| 1938-1960 | 4.6 | 5.1 | 2.8 | 3.9 | 2.8 | 4.0 | 5.0 | 1.1 | 4.7 | 9.2 | 3.8 | 6.7 | 6.4 | 7.3 |
| 1938-1948 | 2.9 | 2.3 | −0.3 | 1.2 | 1.5 | −0.8 | 4.3 | 0.9 | 5.0 | 8.7 | 2.4 | 6.9 | 7.2 | 4.3 |
| 1950-1960 | 6.4 | 6.5 | 3.8 | 5.3 | 4.6 | 8.8 | 5.2 | −0.3 | 3.0 | 8.9 | 4.1 | 10.5 | 7.3 | 9.6 |
| 1948-1953 | 5.0 | 9.7 | 8.0 | 6.7 | 2.0 | 4.1 | 5.0 | 4.5 | 5.6 | 10.8 | 5.5 | 2.9 | 3.3 | 9.7 |
| 1954-1958 | 2.4 | 3.8 | −0.5 | 1.3 | −2.4 | 7.5 | 3.8 | −3.2 | −1.2 | 6.8 | −1.2 | 1.8 | 1.8 | 3.5 |
| 1958-1960 | 11.8 | 7.7 | 10.5 | 11.4 | 17.5 | 11.8 | 8.6 | −0.5 | 8.2 | 8.2 | 13.6 | 18.7 | 14.9 | 17.5 |

[1] Production in slaughtering and meat packing and dairies is omitted prior to 1954.
[2] Repair of footwear is omitted before 1954.
[3] Activity in publishing is not included before 1954.
[4] In addition to the preceding omissions, the quarrying of stone, clay and similar non-metallic minerals is included in the years prior to 1954.

[1] Avant 1954, non compris l'abattage du bétail, la fabrication des préparations et conserves de viande et l'industrie du lait.
[2] Avant 1954, non compris la réparation des chaussures.
[3] Avant 1954, non compris l'édition.
[4] Avant 1954, y compris l'extraction de la pierre à bâtir, de l'argile, etc., et d'autres minéraux non métalliques.

## 3. INDEX NUMBERS OF INDUSTRIAL EMPLOYMENT
### INDICES DE L'EMPLOI DANS L'INDUSTRIE

---

### A. Selected Divisions of Industrial Activity
### Quelques branches de l'activité industrielle

| Period<br>Période | Total [1] | Mining<br>Industries<br>extractives | Manu-<br>facturing [1]<br>Industries<br>manu-<br>facturières [1] | Electricity<br>and gas<br>Electricité<br>et gaz |
|---|---|---|---|---|
| ISIC — CITI | 1–3, 511–512 | 1 | 2–3 | 511–512 |

#### a. Indexes — Indices (1958 = 100)

| | | | | |
|---|---|---|---|---|
| 1938............ | 68 | 72 | 68 | 57 |
| 1948............ | 89 | 114 | 89 | 79 |
| 1949............ | 89 | 111 | 88 | 83 |
| 1950............ | 89 | 98 | 89 | 76 |
| 1951............ | 97 | 107 | 97 | 88 |
| 1952............ | 93 | 111 | 92 | 92 |
| 1953............ | 91 | 116 | 91 | 91 |
| 1954............ | – 98 – | – 107 – | – 98 – | – 88 – |
| 1955............ | 103 | 112 | 103 | 92 |
| 1956............ | 106 | 110 | 106 | 95 |
| 1957............ | 104 | 114 | 104 | 96 |
| 1958............ | 100 | 100 | 100 | 100 |
| 1959............ | 103 | 99 | 103 | 102 |
| 1960............ | 116 | 104 | 112 | 107 |
| 1961............ | 122 | 113 | 118 | 112 |

#### b. Average Annual Rate of Change — Taux annuel moyen de variation

| | | | | |
|---|---|---|---|---|
| 1938 – 1960.... | 2.5 | 1.7 | 2.3 | 2.9 |
| 1938 – 1948.... | 2.7 | 4.7 | 2.7 | 3.3 |
| 1950 – 1960.... | 2.7 | 0.6 | 2.3 | 3.5 |
| 1948 – 1953.... | 0.4 | 0.4 | 0.4 | 2.6 |
| 1954 – 1958.... | 0.5 | – 1.7 | 0.5 | 3.2 |
| 1958 – 1960.... | 7.7 | 2.0 | 5.8 | 3.4 |

For footnote see end of table.

Pour les notes, voir au bas du tableau.

---

### B. The Major Groups of Mining
### Les classes de la branche Industries extractives

| Period<br>Période | All mining<br>Toutes<br>industries<br>extractives | Metal mining<br>Extraction<br>des minerais<br>métalliques | Other mining<br>Autres<br>industries<br>extractives |
|---|---|---|---|
| ISIC — CITI | 1 | 12 | 14–19 |

#### a. Indexes — Indices (1958 = 100)

| | | | |
|---|---|---|---|
| 1938............ | 72 | 22 | 140 |
| 1948............ | 114 | 40 | 216 |
| 1949............ | 111 | 46 | 201 |
| 1950............ | 98 | 40 | 177 |
| 1951............ | 107 | 48 | 187 |
| 1952............ | 111 | 49 | 195 |
| 1953............ | 116 | 65 | 185 |
| 1954............ | – 107 – | – 87 – | – 132 – |
| 1955............ | 112 | 97 | 130 |
| 1956............ | 110 | 101 | 121 |
| 1957............ | 114 | 107 | 123 |
| 1958............ | 100 | 100 | 100 |
| 1959............ | 99 | 103 | 94 |
| 1960............ | 104 | 109 | 97 |
| 1961............ | 113 | 120 | 103 |

#### b. Average Annual Rate of Change — Taux annuel moyen de variation

| | | | |
|---|---|---|---|
| 1938 – 1960...... | 1.7 | 7.5 | – 1.6 |
| 1938 – 1948...... | 4.7 | 6.2 | 4.4 |
| 1950 – 1960...... | 0.6 | 10.5 | – 5.8 |
| 1948 – 1953...... | 0.4 | 10.2 | – 3.1 |
| 1954 – 1958...... | – 1.7 | 3.5 | – 6.7 |
| 1958 – 1960...... | 2.0 | 4.4 | – 1.5 |

## C. The Major Groups of Manufacturing — Les classes de la branche Industries manufacturières

| Period / Période | Manufacturing [1] Industries manufacturières [1] | Food, beverages and tobacco [1] Industries alimentaires, boissons, tabac [1] | Textiles | Clothing, footwear and made-up textiles Articles d'habillement, chaussures et ouvrages en tissu | Wood products and furniture Bois et meubles | Paper and paper products Papier et ouvrages en papier | Printing and publishing[1] Imprimerie et édition [1] | Leather and leather products except wearing apparel Cuir et articles en cuir, à l'exclusion des articles d'habillement | Rubber products Ouvrages en caoutchouc | Chemicals and chemical, petroleum and coal products Produits chimiques et dérivés du pétrole et du charbon | Non-metallic mineral products Produits minéraux non métalliques | Basic metals Métallurgie de base | Metal products [1] Ouvrages en métaux [1] | Other manufacturing Autres industries manufacturières |
|---|---|---|---|---|---|---|---|---|---|---|---|---|---|---|
| ISIC — CITI | 2–3 | 20–22 | 23 | 24 | 25–26 | 27 | 28 | 29 | 30 | 31–32 | 33 | 34 | 35–38 | 39 |
| *a.* Indexes — Indices (1958 = 100) | | | | | | | | | | | | | | |
| 1938 | 68 | 57 | 91 | 62 | 125 | 72 | 62 | 68 | 60 | 32 | 104 | 53 | 44 | 56 |
| 1948 | 89 | 67 | 83 | 65 | 120 | 78 | 78 | 98 | 84 | 79 | 111 | 99 | 92 | 84 |
| 1949 | 88 | 74 | 95 | 72 | 114 | 72 | 77 | 108 | 83 | 76 | 110 | 88 | 92 | 73 |
| 1950 | 89 | 80 | 103 | 80 | 117 | 74 | 77 | 118 | 88 | 82 | 113 | 72 | 84 | 82 |
| 1951 | 97 | 84 | 108 | 82 | 127 | 79 | 80 | 117 | 95 | 86 | 119 | 90 | 96 | 90 |
| 1952 | 92 | 85 | 106 | 82 | 105 | 75 | 82 | 106 | 91 | 82 | 105 | 90 | 96 | 86 |
| 1953 | 91 | 88 | 107 | 85 | 101 | 73 | 83 | 112 | 91 | 86 | 95 | 88 | 91 | 88 |
| 1954 | –98– | –94– | –110– | –92– | –113– | –88– | –87– | –113– | –100– | –94– | –110– | –94– | –95– | –98– |
| 1955 | 103 | 98 | 114 | 102 | 114 | 95 | 92 | 116 | 108 | 99 | 113 | 100 | 101 | 103 |
| 1956 | 106 | 102 | 122 | 115 | 103 | 100 | 96 | 122 | 114 | 100 | 113 | 103 | 106 | 106 |
| 1957 | 104 | 101 | 116 | 107 | 96 | 101 | 99 | 110 | 106 | 101 | 111 | 105 | 104 | 104 |
| 1958 | 100 | 100 | 100 | 100 | 100 | 100 | 100 | 100 | 100 | 100 | 100 | 100 | 100 | 100 |
| 1959 | 103 | 102 | 102 | 106 | 103 | 105 | 102 | 95 | 101 | 103 | 102 | 104 | 103 | 103 |
| 1960 | 112 | 108 | 104 | 112 | 119 | 117 | 107 | 94 | 106 | 109 | 108 | 118 | 114 | 116 |
| 1961 | 118 | 116 | 101 | 116 | 120 | 127 | 111 | 94 | 104 | 117 | 118 | 127 | 123 | 126 |
| *b.* Average Annual Rate of Change — Taux annuel moyen de variation | | | | | | | | | | | | | | |
| 1938–1960 | 2.3 | 2.9 | 0.6 | 2.7 | −0.2 | 2.2 | 2.5 | 1.5 | 2.6 | 5.7 | 0.2 | 3.7 | 4.4 | 3.4 |
| 1938–1948 | 2.7 | 1.6 | −0.9 | 0.5 | −0.4 | 0.8 | 2.3 | 3.7 | 3.4 | 9.5 | 0.7 | 6.5 | 7.7 | 4.1 |
| 1950–1960 | 2.3 | 3.0 | 0.1 | 3.4 | 0.2 | 4.7 | 3.3 | −2.2 | 1.9 | 2.9 | −0.4 | 5.1 | 3.1 | 3.5 |
| 1948–1953 | 0.4 | 5.6 | 5.2 | 5.5 | −3.4 | −1.3 | 1.2 | 2.7 | 1.6 | 1.7 | −3.1 | −2.3 | −0.2 | 0.9 |
| 1954–1958 | 0.5 | 1.6 | −2.4 | 2.1 | −3.0 | 3.2 | 3.5 | −3.0 | — | 1.6 | −2.4 | 1.6 | 1.3 | 0.5 |
| 1958–1960 | 5.8 | 3.9 | 2.0 | 5.8 | 9.1 | 8.2 | 3.4 | −3.0 | 2.5 | 4.4 | 3.9 | 8.6 | 6.8 | 7.7 |

[1] Slaughter houses, dairies, custom flour mills, and packing of spices, teas and similar products (all in ISIC major group 20), Repair of footwear (ISIC group 242) and publishing (in ISIC major group 28) excluded before 1954 but installation of electrical apparatus and iron work in buildings (in ISIC division 4) included in Metal products (ISIC major groups 35–38) before that year.

[1] Les abattoirs, les laiteries, les minoteries travaillant à façon, l'emballage des épices, le thé et les produits similaires (tous dans la classe 20 de la CITI), Réparation des chaussures (CITI groupe 242) et l'édition (dans CITI classe 28) sont exclus avant 1954, mais l'installation d'appareils électriques et le travail du fer dans la construction de bâtiments (dans CITI, division 4) sont compris dans les Ouvrages en métaux (CITI classe 35–38) avant cette année.

## 4. THE CHARACTERISTICS OF ALL INDUSTRIAL ESTABLISHMENTS
## CARACTERISTIQUES DE TOUS LES ETABLISSEMENTS INDUSTRIELS
### 1952

Number of establishments in units; number of engaged and employees in thousands; wages and salaries in million Markkaa

Nombre d'établissements en unités; nombre de personnes occupées et de salariés en milliers; traitements et salaires en millions de marks finlandais

### A. The Divisions of Industrial Activity — Les branches de l'activité industrielle

| Item of data | All industrial activity<br>Toutes industries | Mining<br>Industries extractives | Manufactur-ing<br>Industries manufac-turières | Construction [1]<br>Bâtiment et travaux publics [1] | Electricity and gas [2]<br>Electricité et gaz [2] | Rubrique |
|---|---|---|---|---|---|---|
| ISIC | 1–4, 511–512, 521 | 1 | 2–3 | 4 | 511–512, 521 | CITI |
| Number of establishments....... | 32 009 | 252 | 27 086 | 4 073 | 598 | Nombre d'établissements |
| Number of engaged (As of 22.V.1953)........... | 460.3 | 8.4 | 373.0 | 66.1 | 12.8 | Nombre de personnes occupées (au 22.V.1953) |
| Number of employees (Average during year)....... | 425.4 | 7.0 | 350.5 | 55.4 | 12.5 | Nombre de salariés (moyenne pendant l'année) |
| Wages and salaries paid....... | 142 745 | 2 218 | 113 814 | 21 995 | 4 718 | Traitements et salaires payés |

[1] Excludes roadbuilding undertaken directly by governmental authorities.
[2] Includes water supply stations.

[1] Non compris la construction de routes entreprise directement par les pouvoirs publics.
[2] Y compris les usines des eaux.

### B. The Major Groups of Mining — Les classes de la branche Industries extractives

| Item of data | All mining<br>Toutes industries extractives | Metal mining<br>Extraction des minerais métalliques | Other mining<br>Autres industries extractives | Rubrique |
|---|---|---|---|---|
| ISIC | 1 | 12 | 14–19 | CITI |
| Number of establishments...... | 252 | 6 | 246 | Nombre d'établissements |
| Number of engaged (As of 22.V.1953)......... | 8.4 | 2.1 | 6.3 | Nombre de personnes occupées (au 22.V.1953) |
| Number of employees (Average during year)...... | 7.0 | 2.1 | 4.9 | Nombre de salariés (moyenne pendant l'année) |
| Wages and salaries paid..... | 2 218 | 794 | 1 424 | Traitements et salaires payés |

### C. The Major Groups of Manufacturing — Les classes de la branche Industries manufacturières

| Item of data | Manu-facturing<br>Industries manufac-turières | Food, beverages and tobacco<br>Industries alimen-taires, boissons, tabac | Textiles | Clothing, footwear and made-up textiles<br>Articles d'habil-lement, chaussures et ouvrages en tissu | Wood products and furniture<br>Bois et meubles | Paper and paper products<br>Papier et ouvrages en papier | Printing and publish-ing<br>Im-primerie et édition | Leather and leather products except wearing apparel<br>Cuir et articles en cuir, à l'exclu-sion des articles d'habil-lement | Rubber products<br>Ouvrages en caout-chouc | Chemicals and chemical, petroleum and coal products<br>Produits chi-miques et dérivés du pétrole et du charbon | Non-metallic mineral products<br>Produits minéraux non métal-liques | Basic metals<br>Métal-lurgie de base | Metal products<br>Ouvrages en métaux | Other manu-factur-ing<br>Autres in-dustries manufac-turières | Rubrique |
|---|---|---|---|---|---|---|---|---|---|---|---|---|---|---|---|
| ISIC | 2–3 | 20–22 | 23 | 24 | 25–26 | 27 | 28 | 29 | 30 | 31–32 | 33 | 34 | 35–38 | 39 | CITI |
| Number of establishments. | 27 086 | 3 604 | 1 351 | 7 586 | 5 076 | 233 | 745 | 471 | 122 | 344 | 1 529 | 60 | 4 698 | 1 267 | Nombre d'établissements |
| Number of engaged (As of 22.V.1953).... | 373.0 | 42.8 | 38.3 | 38.7 | 62.9 | 32.3 | 19.9 | 4.2 | 4.8 | 10.6 | 19.4 | 6.5 | 86.0 | 6.6 | Nombre de personnes occupées (au 22.V.1953) |
| Number of employees (Average during year)............... | 350.5 | 39.3 | 36.7 | 29.9 | 56.3 | 34.5 | 19.3 | 3.7 | 4.7 | 10.4 | 17.3 | 7.0 | 85.9 | 5.5 | Nombre de salariés (moyenne pendant l'année) |
| Wages and salaries paid............. | 113 814 | 11 509 | 10 068 | 7 522 | 16 541 | 12 926 | 6 055 | 1 037 | 1 492 | 3 727 | 5 621 | 2 763 | 32 837 | 1 716 | Traitements et salaires payés |
| Distribution in percent of number engaged... | 100.0 | 11.4 | 10.3 | 10.4 | 16.8 | 8.7 | 5.3 | 1.2 | 1.2 | 2.9 | 5.2 | 1.7 | 23.1 | 1.8 | Répartition en pourcen-tage du nombre de personnes occupées |
| Employees as percent of engaged......... | 94.0 | 91.8 | 95.8 | 77.3 | 89.5 | 106.8 | 97.0 | 88.1 | 97.9 | 98.1 | 89.2 | 107.7 | 99.9 | 83.3 | Salariés en pourcentage des personnes occupées |
| Wages and salaries per employee........ | 324.7 | 292.8 | 274.3 | 251.6 | 293.8 | 374.7 | 313.7 | 280.3 | 317.4 | 358.4 | 324.9 | 394.7 | 382.3 | 312.0 | Traitements et salaires par salarié |

# 5. THE CHARACTERISTICS OF INDUSTRIAL ESTABLISHMENTS ENGAGING FIVE OR MORE PERSONS
## CARACTERISTIQUES DES ETABLISSEMENTS INDUSTRIELS OCCUPANT CINQ PERSONNES OU PLUS
### 1938, 1948, 1953, 1954, 1958

Number of establishments in units; value added and wages and salaries in million markkaa; number of engaged, employees and operatives in thousands; man-hours worked in millions; energy consumed in thousand metric tons of coal equivalents, electricity consumed in million KWH; capacity of installed power equipment in thousand horsepower; value added per engaged and wages and salaries per employee, per operative and per thousand operative man-hours in thousand markkaa; average annual man-hours per operative in thousands; energy consumed per engaged and per thousand operative man-hours in metric tons of coal equivalents; electricity consumed per engaged and per thousand operative man-hours in thousand KWH; capacity of installed power equipment per engaged, per operative and per thousand operative man-hours in horsepower.

Nombre d'établissements en unités; valeur ajoutée et traitements et salaires en millions de markkaa; nombre de personnes occupées, de salariés et d'ouvriers en milliers; heures de travail en millions; énergie consommée en milliers de tonnes métriques d'équivalent charbon; électricité consommée en millions de kWh; puissance installée en milliers de chevaux-vapeur; valeur ajoutée par personne occupée et traitements et salaires par salarié, par ouvrier, et par millier d'heures-ouvrier en milliers de markkaa; moyenne annuelle des heures de travail par ouvrier en milliers; énergie consommée par personne occupée et par millier d'heures-ouvrier en tonnes métriques d'équivalent charbon; électricité consommée par personne occupée et par millier d'heures-ouvrier en milliers de kWh; puissance installée par personne occupée, par ouvrier, et par millier d'heures-ouvrier en chevaux-vapeur.

## A. Selected Divisions of Industrial Activity — Quelques branches de l'activité industrielle

### a. Absolute Figures — Chiffres absolus

| Year and item of data | Total [1,2] | Mining Industries extractives | Manufacturing [1] Industries manufacturières [1] | Electricity, gas and steam [2] Electricité, gaz et vapeur [2] | Année et rubrique |
|---|---|---|---|---|---|
| ISIC | 1-3, 511-513 | 1 | 2-3 | 511-513 | CITI |
| **1938** | | | | | **1938** |
| Number of establishments | 4 357 | 72 | 4 019 | 266 | Nombre d'établissements |
| Value added | 6 930 | 169 | 6 523 | 238 | Valeur ajoutée |
| Number of employees (Average during year) | 226.4 | 3.3 | 219.3 | 3.8 | Nombre de salariés (moyenne pour l'année) |
| Operatives: | | | | | Ouvriers: |
| Number (Average during year) | 212.6 | 3.3 | 206.1 | 3.2 | Nombre (moyenne pour l'année) |
| Wages and salaries | 2 939.0 | 41.2 | 2 837.4 | 60.4 | Traitements et salaires |
| Capacity of installed power equipment | . | 14 | 1 050 | 1 072 [3] | Puissance installée |
| **1948** | | | | | **1948** |
| Number of establishments | 5 993 | 131 | 5 608 | 254 | Nombre d'établissements |
| Value added | 93 860 | 2 661 | 88 113 | 3 086 | Valeur ajoutée |
| Employees: | | | | | Salariés: |
| Number (Average during year) | 293.8 | 5.3 | 282.8 | 5.7 | Nombre (moyenne pour l'année) |
| Wages and salaries | 52 176.9 | 948.1 | 49 993.4 | 1 235.4 | Traitements et salaires |
| Operatives: | | | | | Ouvriers: |
| Number (Average during year) | 25.66 | 4.7 | 247.2 | 4.7 | Nombre (moyenne pour l'année) |
| Wages and salaries | 43 672.1 | 808.4 | 41 852.7 | 1 011.0 | Traitements et salaires |
| Capacity of installed power equipment | . | 37 | 1 260 | 1 201 [3] | Puissance installée |
| **1953** | | | | | **1953** |
| Number of establishments | 5 803 | 153 | 5 380 | 270 | Nombre d'établissements |
| Value added | 178 414 | 6 273 | 165 423 | 6 718 | Valeur ajoutée |
| Employees: | | | | | Salariés: |
| Number (Average during year) | 302.5 | 6.3 | 290.3 | 5.9 | Nombre (moyenne pour l'année) |
| Wages and salaries | 100 956.6 | 2 154.0 | 96 337.1 | 2 465.5 | Traitements et salaires |
| Operatives: | | | | | Ouvriers: |
| Number (Average during year) | 260.9 | 5.2 | 251.0 | 4.7 | Nombre (moyenne pour l'année) |
| Wages and salaries | 81 211.0 | 1 603.1 | 77 750.9 | 1 857.0 | Traitements et salaires |
| Capacity of installed power equipment | . | 76 | 1 740 | 1 999 [3] | Puissance installée |

### b. Structure

| Year and item of data | Total [1,2] | Mining Industries extractives | Manufacturing [1] Industries manufacturières [1] | Electricity, gas and steam [2] Electricité, gaz et vapeur [2] | Année et rubrique |
|---|---|---|---|---|---|
| ISIC | 1-3, 511-513 | 1 | 2-3 | 511-513 | CITI |
| **1938** | | | | | **1938** |
| Distribution in percent of: | | | | | Distribution en pourcentage: |
| Value added | 100.0 | 2.5 | 94.1 | 3.4 | Valeur ajoutée |
| Number of employees | 100.0 | 1.4 | 96.9 | 1.7 | Nombre de salariés |
| Per employee: | | | | | Par salarié: |
| Value added | 30.6 | 51.3 | 29.7 | 62.7 | Valeur ajoutée |
| Capacity of installed power equipment | . | 4.24 | 4.79 | 282.10 [3] | Puissance installée |
| Operatives as a percent of employees | 93.9 | 100.0 | 94.0 | 84.2 | Ouvriers en pourcentage des salariés |
| Per operative: | | | | | Par ouvrier: |
| Wages and salaries | 13.8 | 12.5 | 13.8 | 18.9 | Traitements et salaires |
| Capacity of installed power equipment | . | 4.24 | 5.09 | 335.00 [3] | Puissance installée |
| **1948** | | | | | **1948** |
| Distribution in percent of: | | | | | Distribution en pourcentage: |
| Value added | 100.0 | 2.8 | 93.9 | 3.3 | Valeur ajoutée |
| Number of employees | 100.0 | 1.8 | 96.3 | 1.9 | Nombre de salariés |
| Per employee: | | | | | Par salarié: |
| Value added | 319.5 | 502.1 | 311.6 | 541.4 | Valeur ajoutée |
| Capacity of installed power equipment | . | 6.98 | 4.46 | 210.70 [3] | Puissance installée |
| Wages and salaries | 177.61 | 178.9 | 176.8 | 216.7 | Traitements et salaires |
| Value added per unit of wages and salaries | 1.80 | 2.81 | 1.76 | 2.50 | Valeur ajoutée par traitements et salaires unitaires |
| Operatives as a percent of employees | 87.3 | 88.7 | 87.4 | 82.4 | Ouvriers en pourcentage des salariés |
| Per operative: | | | | | Par ouvrier: |
| Wages and salaries | 170.2 | 172.0 | 169.3 | 215.1 | Traitements et salaires |
| Capacity of installed power equipment | . | 7.87 | 5.10 | 255.53 [3] | Puissance installée |
| **1953** | | | | | **1953** |
| Distribution in percent of: | | | | | Distribution en pourcentage: |
| Value added | 100.0 | 3.5 | 92.7 | 3.8 | Valeur ajoutée |
| Number of employees | 100.0 | 2.1 | 96.0 | 1.9 | Nombre de salariés |
| Per employee: | | | | | Par salarié: |
| Value added | 589.8 | 995.7 | 569.8 | 1 138.6 | Valeur ajoutée |
| Capacity of installed power equipment | . | 12.06 | 5.99 | 338.87 [3] | Puissance installée |
| Wages and salaries | 333.7 | 341.9 | 331.8 | 417.9 | Traitements et salaires |
| Value added per unit of wages and salaries | 1.77 | 2.91 | 1.72 | 2.72 | Valeur ajoutée par traitements et salaires unitaires |
| Operatives as a percent of employees | 86.2 | 82.5 | 86.5 | 79.7 | Ouvriers en pourcentage des salariés |
| Per operative: | | | | | Par ouvrier: |
| Wages and salaries | 311.3 | 308.3 | 309.8 | 395.1 | Traitements et salaires |
| Capacity of installed power equipment | . | 14.62 | 6.93 | 425.32 [3] | Puissance installée |

For footnotes see end of table.

Pour les notes, voir au bas du tableau.

# FINLAND

## A. Selected Divisions of Industrial Activity (continued) — Quelques branches de l'activité industrielle (suite)

| Year and item of data | Total [1,2] | Mining / Industries extractives | Manufacturing [1] / Industries manufacturières[1] | Electricity gas and steam [2] / Electricité gaz et vapeur[2] | Année et rubrique |
|---|---|---|---|---|---|
| ISIC | 1-3,511-513 | 1 | 2-3 | 511-513 | CITI |

### a. Absolute Figures — Chiffres absolus

| Year and item of data | Total | Mining | Manufacturing | Electricity gas and steam | Année et rubrique |
|---|---|---|---|---|---|
| **1954** | | | | | **1954** |
| Number of establishments | 6 988 | 85 | 6 509 | 394 | Nombre d'établissements |
| Value added | 231 452.3 | 3 998.3 | 208 252.4 | 19 201.6 | Valeur ajoutée |
| Number of engaged (Average during year) | 345.7 | 5.4 | 328.7 | 11.6 | Nombre de personnes occupées (moyenne pour l'année) |
| Employees: | | | | | Salariés: |
| Number (Average during year) | 343.9 | 5.4 | 326.9 | 11.6 | Nombre (moyenne pour l'année) |
| Wages and salaries | 119 748.0 | 1 987.3 | 113 135.1 | 4 625.6 | Traitements et salaires |
| Operatives: | | | | | Ouvriers: |
| Number (Average during year) | 293.6 | 4.7 | 280.0 | 8.9 | Nombre (moyenne pour l'année) |
| Man-hours worked | 634.4 | 10.2 | 604.4 | 19.8 | Heures de travail effectuées |
| Wages and salaries | 94 408.2 | 1 634.1 | 89 369.5 | 3 404.6 | Traitements et salaires |
| Energy consumed | . | 26.4 | 3 520.6 | 1 947.6 [4] | Energie consommée |
| Electricity consumed | 4 042.4 | 99.6 | 3 600.7 | 342.1 | Electricité consommée |
| Capacity of installed power equipment | 2 183.7 | 74.1 | 2 012.6 | 97.0 [3] | Puissance installée |
| **1958** | | | | | **1958** |
| Number of establishments | 7 178 | 81 | 6 660 | 437 | Nombre d'établissements |
| Value added | 326 072.4 | 7 046.6 | 286 215.2 | 32 810.6 | Valeur ajoutée |
| Number of engaged (Average during year) | 353.4 | 5.1 | 335.1 | 13.2 | Nombre de personnes occupées (moyenne pour l'année) |
| Employees: | | | | | Salariés: |
| Number (Average during year) | 351.6 | 5.1 | 333.3 | 13.2 | Nombre (moyenne pour l'année) |
| Wages and salaries | 157 960.0 | 2 537.3 | 148 325.9 | 7 096.8 | Traitements et salaires |
| Operatives: | | | | | Ouvriers: |
| Number (Average during year) | 294.4 | 4.3 | 280.3 | 9.8 | Nombre (moyenne pour l'année) |
| Man-hours worked | 610.9 | 9.0 | 580.8 | 21.1 | Heures de travail effectuées |
| Wages and salaries | 118 578.1 | 1 946.7 | 111 817.4 | 4 814.0 | Traitements et salaires |
| Energy consumed | . | 42.2 | 4 078.7 | 2 459.4 [4] | Energie consommée |
| Electricity consumed | 5 571.9 | 131.1 | 4 860.5 | 580.3 | Electricité consommée |
| Capacity of installed power equipment | 2 782.8 | 95.6 | 2 530.1 | 157.1 [3] | Puissance installée |

### b. Structure

| Year and item of data | Total | Mining | Manufacturing | Electricity gas and steam | Année et rubrique |
|---|---|---|---|---|---|
| **1954** | | | | | **1954** |
| Distribution in percent of: | | | | | Distribution en pourcentage: |
| Value added | 100.0 | 1.7 | 90.0 | 8.3 | Valeur ajoutée |
| Number of engaged | 100.0 | 1.6 | 95.1 | 3.3 | Nombre de personnes occupées |
| Per person engaged: | | | | | Par personne occupée: |
| Value added | 669.5 | 740.4 | 633.6 | 1 655.3 | Valeur ajoutée |
| Energy consumed | . | 4.89 | 10.71 | . | Energie consommée |
| Electricity consumed | 11.7 | 18.4 | 11.0 | 29.5 | Electricité consommée |
| Capacity of installed power equipment | 6.32 | 13.72 | 6.12 | 8.36 [3] | Puissance installée |
| Employees as a percent of engaged | 99.5 | 100.0 | 99.4 | 100.0 | Salariés en pourcentage des personnes occupées |
| Value added per unit of wages and salaries | 1.93 | 2.01 | 1.84 | 4.15 | Valeur ajoutée par traitements et salaires unitaires |
| Wages and salaries per employee | 348.2 | 368.0 | 346.1 | 389.8 | Traitements et salaires par salarié |
| Operatives as a percent of employees | 85.4 | 87.0 | 85.6 | 76.7 | Ouvriers en pourcentage des salariés |
| Average man-hours per operative | 2.16 | 2.17 | 2.16 | 2.22 | Heures de travail: moyenne par ouvrier |
| Per thousand operative man-hour: | | | | | Par milliers d'heures-ouvrier de travail: |
| Wages and salaries | 148.81 | 160.20 | 147.86 | 171.95 | Traitements et salaires |
| Energy consumed | . | 2.59 | 5.82 | . | Energie consommée |
| Electricity consumed | 6.37 | 9.76 | 5.96 | 17.28 | Electricité consommée |
| Capacity of installed power equipment | 3.44 | 7.26 | 3.33 | 4.90 [3] | Puissance installée |
| **1958** | | | | | **1958** |
| Distribution in percent of: | | | | | Distribution en pourcentage: |
| Value added | 100.0 | 2.1 | 87.8 | 10.1 | Valeur ajoutée |
| Number of engaged | 100.0 | 1.4 | 94.8 | 3.8 | Nombre de personnes occupées |
| Per person engaged: | | | | | Par personne occupée: |
| Value added | 922.7 | 1 381.7 | 854.1 | 2 485.6 | Valeur ajoutée |
| Energy consumed | . | 8.27 | 12.17 | . | Energie consommée |
| Electricity consumed | 15.8 | 25.7 | 14.5 | 44.0 | Electricité consommée |
| Capacity of installed power equipment | 7.87 | 18.74 | 7.55 | 11.90 [3] | Puissance installée |
| Employees as a percent of engaged | 99.5 | 100.0 | 99.5 | 100.0 | Salariés en pourcentage des personnes occupées |
| Value added per unit of wages and salaries | 2.06 | 2.78 | 1.93 | 4.62 | Valeur ajoutée par traitements et salaires unitaires |
| Wages and salaries per employee | 449.3 | 497.5 | 445.0 | 537.6 | Traitements et salaires par salarié |
| Operatives as a percent of employees | 83.7 | 84.3 | 84.1 | 74.2 | Ouvriers en pourcentage des salariés |
| Average man-hours per operative | 2.08 | 2.09 | 2.07 | 2.15 | Heures de travail: moyenne par ouvrier |
| Per thousand operative man-hour: | | | | | Par milliers d'heures-ouvrier de travail: |
| Wages and salaries | 194.14 | 216.30 | 192.52 | 228.15 | Traitements et salaires |
| Energy consumed | . | 4.69 | 7.02 | . | Energie consommée |
| Electricity consumed | 9.12 | 14.57 | 8.37 | 27.50 | Electricité consommée |
| Capacity of installed power equipment | 4.56 | 10.62 | 4.36 | 7.44 [3] | Puissance installée |

[1] Excludes slaughtering and meat packing, dairies, repair of footwear and publishing before 1954.
[2] Excludes the distribution of electricity and the production and distribution of steam before 1954.
[3] In the case of the Electricity industry (ISIC group 511), the capacity of installed power equipment includes the capacity of installed prime movers connected to electric generators before 1954 but the capacity of installed prime movers attached to machinery other than electric generators in 1954 and thereafter.
[4] Covers consumption of fuels other than those produced by units classified to ISIC major group 51 — namely, electricity, gas and steam.

[1] Non compris l'abattage de bétail et la fabrication des préparations et conserves de viande, les laiteries la réparation des chaussures et l'édition avant 1954.
[2] Non compris la distribution d'électricité et la production et distribution de vapeur avant 1954.
[3] Dans le cas des industries de l'électricité (CITI groupe 511) la puissance installée comprend la puissance des moteurs primaires reliés aux générateurs électriques avant 1954, mais comprend seulement la puissance des moteurs primaires reliés à d'autres machines que les générateurs électriques à partir de 1954.
[4] Couvre la consommation de combustibles autres que ceux produits par les unités classées dans la classe 51 de la CITI, plus précisément l'électricité, le gaz et la vapeur.

## B.  The Major Groups of Mining — Les classes de la branche industries extractives

| Year and item of data | All mining<br>Toutes industries extractives | Metal mining<br>Extraction des minerais métalliques | Other mining<br>Divers | Année et rubrique | Year and item of data | All mining<br>Toutes industries extractives | Metal mining<br>Extraction des minerais métalliques | Other mining<br>Divers | Année et rubrique |
|---|---|---|---|---|---|---|---|---|---|
| SITC | 1 | 12 | 14-19 | CITI | SITC | 1 | 12 | 14-19 | CITI |
| | **a. Absolute Figures — Chiffres absolus** | | | | | **b. Structure** | | | |
| **1938** | | | | 1938 | **1938** | | | | 1938 |
| Number of establishments...... | 72 | 4 | 68 | Nombre d'établissements | Distribution in percent of: | | | | Distribution en pourcentage: |
| Value added................ | 169 | 90 | 79 | Valeur ajoutée | Value added............... | 100.0 | 53.2 | 46.8 | Valeur ajoutée |
| Number of employees | | | | Nombre de salariés | Number of employees........ | 100.0 | 18.2 | 81.8 | Nombre de salariés |
| (Average during year)....... | 3.3 | 0.6 | 2.7 | (moyenne pour l'année) | Per employee: | | | | Par salarié: |
| Operatives: | | | | Ouvriers: | Value added............... | 51.3 | 150.0 | 29.4 | Valeur ajoutée |
| Number (Average during year)................. | 3.3 | 0.6 | 2.7 | Nombre (moyenne pour l'année) | Capacity of installed power equipment................ | 4.24 | 10.00 | 2.96 | Puissance installée |
| Wages and salaries.......... | 41.2 | 10.8 | 30.4 | Traitements et salaires | Operatives as a percent of employees................ | 100.0 | 100.0 | 100.0 | Ouvriers en pourcentage des salariés |
| Capacity of installed power equipment................. | 14 | 6 | 8 | Puissance installée | Per operative: | | | | Par ouvrier: |
| | | | | | Wages and salaries.......... | 12.5 | 18.0 | 11.2 | Traitements et salaires |
| | | | | | Capacity of installed power equipment................ | 4.24 | 10.00 | 2.96 | Puissance installée |
| **1948** | | | | 1948 | **1948.** | | | | 1948 |
| Number of establishments...... | 131 | 8 | 123 | Nombre d'établissements | Distribution in percent of: | | | | Distribution en pourcentage: |
| Value added................ | 2 661 | 1 094 | 1 567 | Valeur ajoutée | Value added............... | 100.0 | 41.1 | 58.9 | Valeur ajoutée |
| Employees: | | | | Salariés: | Number of employees........ | 100.0 | 20.8 | 79.2 | Nombre de salariés |
| Number (Average during year)................. | 5.3 | 1.1 | 4.2 | Nombre (moyenne pour l'année) | Per employee: | | | | Par salarié: |
| Wages and salaries.......... | 948.1 | 272.2 | 675.9 | Traitements et salaires | Value added............... | 502.1 | 994.5 | 373.1 | Valeur ajoutée |
| Operatives: | | | | Ouvriers: | Wages and salaries.......... | 178.9 | 247.4 | 160.9 | Traitements et salaires |
| Number (Average during year)................. | 4.7 | 0.9 | 3.8 | Nombre (moyenne pour l'année) | Capacity of installed power equipment................ | 6.98 | 14.54 | 5.00 | Puissance installée |
| Wages and salaries.......... | 808.4 | 204.4 | 604.0 | Traitements et salaires | Value added per unit of wages and salaries.......... | 2.81 | 4.02 | 2.32 | Valeur ajoutée par traitements et salaires unitaires |
| Capacity of installed power equipment................. | 37 | 16 | 21 | Puissance installée | Operatives as a percent of employees................ | 88.7 | 81.8 | 90.5 | Ouvriers en pourcentage des salariés |
| | | | | | Per operative: | | | | Par ouvrier: |
| | | | | | Wages and salaries.......... | 172.0 | 227.1 | 158.9 | Traitements et salaires |
| | | | | | Capacity of installed power equipment................ | 7.87 | 17.78 | 5.53 | Puissance installée |
| **1953** | | | | 1953 | **1953** | | | | 1953 |
| Number of establishments...... | 153 | 15 | 138 | Nombre d'établissements | Distribution in percent of: | | | | Distribution en pourcentage: |
| Value added................ | 6 273 | 3 043 | 3 230 | Valeur ajoutée | Value added............... | 100.0 | 9.8 | 90.2 | Valeur ajoutée |
| Employees: | | | | Salariés: | Number of employees........ | 100.0 | 30.2 | 69.8 | Nombre de salariés |
| Number (Average during year)................. | 6.3 | 1.9 | 4.4 | Nombre (moyenne pour l'année) | Per employee: | | | | Par salarié: |
| Wages and salaries.......... | 2 154.0 | 739.6 | 1 414.4 | Traitements et salaires | Value added............... | 995.7 | 1 601.6 | 734.1 | Valeur ajoutée |
| Operatives: | | | | Ouvriers: | Wages and salaries.......... | 341.9 | 389.3 | 321.4 | Traitements et salaires |
| Number (Average during year)................. | 5.2 | 1.6 | 3.6 | Nombre (moyenne pour l'année) | Capacity of installed power equipment................ | 12.06 | 22.63 | 7.50 | Puissance installée |
| Wages and salaries.......... | 1 603.1 | 583.6 | 1 019.5 | Traitements et salaires | Value added per unit of wages and salaries.......... | 2.91 | 4.11 | 2.28 | Valeur ajoutée par traitements et salaires unitaires |
| Capacity of installed power equipment................. | 76 | 43 | 33 | Puissance installée | Operatives as a percent of employees................. | 82.5 | 84.2 | 81.8 | Ouvriers en pourcentage des salariés |
| | | | | | Per operative: | | | | Par ouvrier: |
| | | | | | Wages and salaries.......... | 308.3 | 364.8 | 283.2 | Traitements et salaires |
| | | | | | Capacity of installed power equipment................ | 14.62 | 26.88 | 9.17 | Puissance installée |
| **1954** | | | | 1954 | **1954** | | | | 1954 |
| Number of establishments...... | 85 | 8 | 77 | Nombre d'établissements | Distribution in percent of: | | | | Distribution en pourcentage: |
| Value added................ | 3 998.3 | 1 824.2 | 2 174.1 | Valeur ajoutée | Value added............... | 100.0 | 45.6 | 54.4 | Valeur ajoutée |
| Number of engaged | | | | Nombre de personnes occupées | Number of engaged.......... | 100.0 | 46.3 | 53.7 | Nombre de personnes occupées |
| (Average during year)....... | 5.4 | 2.5 | 2.9 | (moyenne pour l'année) | Per person engaged: | | | | Par personne occupée: |
| Employees: | | | | Salariés: | Value added............... | 740.4 | 729.7 | 749.7 | Valeur ajoutée |
| Number (Average during year)................. | 5.4 | 2.5 | 2.9 | Nombre (moyenne pour l'année) | Energy consumed............ | 4.89 | 7.64 | 2.52 | Energie consommée |
| Wages and salaries.......... | 1 987.3 | 1 089.7 | 897.6 | Traitements et salaires | Electricity consumed........ | 18.4 | 32.3 | 6.5 | Electricité consommée |
| Operatives: | | | | Ouvriers: | Capacity of installed power equipment................ | 13.72 | 17.48 | 10.48 | Puissance installée |
| Number (Average during year)................. | 4.7 | 2.0 | 2.7 | Nombre (moyenne pour l'année) | Employees as a percent of engaged................ | 100.0 | 100.0 | 100.0 | Salariés en pourcentage des personnes occupées |
| Man-hours worked.......... | 10.2 | 4.8 | 5.4 | Heures de travail effectuées | Value added per unit of wages and salaries.......... | 2.01 | 1.67 | 2.42 | Valeur ajoutée par traitements et salaires unitaires |
| Wages and salaries.......... | 1 634.1 | 846.9 | 787.2 | Traitements et salaires | Wages and salaries per employee................ | 368.0 | 435.9 | 309.5 | Traitements et salaires par salarié |
| Energy consumed............ | 26.4 | 19.1 | 7.3 | Energie consommée | Operatives as a percent of employees................ | 87.0 | 80.0 | 93.1 | Ouvriers en pourcentage des salariés |
| Electricity consumed......... | 99.6 | 80.7 | 18.9 | Electricité consommée | Average man-hours per operative................ | 2.17 | 2.40 | 2.00 | Heures de travail: moyenne par ouvrier |
| Capacity of installed power equipment................. | 74.1 | 43.7 | 30.4 | Puissance installée | Per thousand operative man-hour: | | | | Par milliers d'heures-ouvrier de travail: |
| | | | | | Wages and salaries.......... | 160.20 | 176.44 | 145.78 | Traitements et salaires |
| | | | | | Energy consumed........... | 2.59 | 3.98 | 1.35 | Energie consommée |
| | | | | | Electricity consumed | 9.76 | 16.81 | 3.50 | Electricité consommée |
| | | | | | Capacity of installed power equipment................ | 7.26 | 9.10 | 5.63 | Puissance installée |

## B. The Major Groups of Mining (continued) — Les classes de la branche industries extractives (suite)

| Year and item of data | All mining Toutes industries extrac- tives | Metal mining Extraction des minerais métal- liques | Other mining Divers | Année et rubrique | Year and item of data | All mining Toutes industries extrac- tives | Metal mining Extraction des minerais métal- liques | Other mining Divers | Année et rubrique |
|---|---|---|---|---|---|---|---|---|---|
| SITC | 1 | 12 | 14-19 | CITI | SITC | 1 | 12 | 14-19 | CITI |
| | a. Absolute Figures — Chiffres absolus | | | | | b. Structure | | | |
| **1958** | | | | **1958** | **1958** | | | | **1958** |
| Number of establishments...... | 81 | 6 | 75 | Nombre d'établissements | Distribution in percent of: | | | | Distribution en pourcentage: |
| Value added................. | 7 046.6 | 4 705.5 | 2 341.1 | Valeur ajoutée | Value added............... | 100.0 | 66.8 | 33.2 | Valeur ajoutée |
| Number of engaged | | | | Nombre de personnes occupées | Number of engaged.......... | 100.0 | 56.9 | 43.1 | Nombre de personnes occupées |
| (Average during year)........ | 5.1 | 2.9 | 2.2 | (moyenne pour l'année) | Per person engaged: | | | | Par personne occupée: |
| Employees: | | | | Salariés: | Value added............... | 1 381.7 | 1 622.6 | 1 064.1 | Valeur ajoutée |
| Number (Average during | | | | Nombre (moyenne pour | Energy consumed........... | 8.27 | 11.45 | 4.09 | Energie consommée |
| year)..................... | 5.1 | 2.9 | 2.2 | l'année) | Electricity consumed........ | 25.7 | 37.6 | 10.1 | Electricité consommée |
| Wages and salaries.......... | 2 537.3 | 1 628.3 | 909.0 | Traitements et salaires | Capacity of installed power | | | | Puissance installée |
| Operatives: | | | | Ouvriers: | equipment................ | 18.74 | 20.24 | 16.77 | |
| Number (Average during year) | 4.3 | 2.3 | 2.0 | Nombre (moyenne pour l'année) | Employees as a percent of | | | | Salariés en pourcentage des |
| Man-hours worked .......... | 9.0 | 5.1 | 3.9 | Heures de travail effectuées | engaged.................. | 100.0 | 100.0 | 100.0 | personnes occupées |
| Wages and salaries ....... | 1 946.7 | 1 189.1 | 757.6 | Traitements et salaires | Value added per unit of | | | | Valeur ajoutée par traitements et |
| Energy consumed ............. | 42.2 | 33.2 | 9.0 | Energie consommée | wages and salaries.......... | 2.78 | 2.89 | 2.58 | salaires unitaires |
| Electricity consumed........... | 131.1 | 108.9 | 22.2 | Electricité consommée | Wages and salaries per | | | | Traitements et salaires par |
| Capacity of installed | | | | | employee................. | 497.5 | 561.5 | 413.2 | salarié |
| power equipment........... | 95.6 | 58.7 | 36.9 | Puissance installée | Operatives as a percent of | | | | Ouvriers en pourcentage des |
| | | | | | employees................ | 84.3 | 79.3 | 90.9 | salariés |
| | | | | | Average man-hours per | | | | Heures de travail: moyenne |
| | | | | | operative................. | 2.09 | 2.22 | 1.95 | par ouvrier |
| | | | | | Per thousand operative | | | | Par milliers d'heures-ouvrier |
| | | | | | man-hour: | | | | de travail: |
| | | | | | Wages and salaries.......... | 216.30 | 233.16 | 194.26 | Traitements et salaires |
| | | | | | Energy consumed........... | 4.69 | 6.51 | 2.31 | Energie consommée |
| | | | | | Electricity consumed........ | 14.57 | 21.35 | 5.69 | Electricité consommée |
| | | | | | Capacity of installed power | | | | Puissance installée |
| | | | | | equipment................ | 10.62 | 11.51 | 9.46 | |

## C. The Major Groups of Manufacturing — Les classes de la branche Industries manufacturières

| Year and item of data | Manufacturing<br>Industries manufacturières | Food, beverages and tobacco[1]<br>Industries alimentaires, boissons, tabac[1] | Textiles | Clothing, footwear and made-up textiles[2]<br>Articles d'habillement, chaussures et ouvrages en tissu[2] | Wood products and furniture<br>Bois et meubles | Paper and paper products<br>Papier et ouvrages en papier | Printing and publishing[3]<br>Imprimerie et édition[3] | Leather and leather products except wearing apparel<br>Cuir et articles en cuir, à l'exclusion des articles d'habillement | Rubber products<br>Ouvrages en caoutchouc | Chemicals and chemical, petroleum and coal products<br>Produits chimiques et dérivés du pétrole et du charbon | Non-metallic mineral products<br>Produits minéraux non métalliques | Basic metals<br>Métallurgie de base | Metal products<br>Ouvrages en métaux | Other manufacturing<br>Autres industries manufacturières | Année et rubrique |
|---|---|---|---|---|---|---|---|---|---|---|---|---|---|---|---|
| ISIC | 2–3 | 20–22 | 23 | 24 | 25–26 | 27 | 28 | 29 | 30 | 31–32 | 33 | 34 | 35–38 | 39 | CITI |

*a. Absolute Figures — Chiffres absolus*

| Year and item of data | 2–3 | 20–22 | 23 | 24 | 25–26 | 27 | 28 | 29 | 30 | 31–32 | 33 | 34 | 35–38 | 39 | Année et rubrique |
|---|---|---|---|---|---|---|---|---|---|---|---|---|---|---|---|
| **1938** | | | | | | | | | | | | | | | **1938** |
| Number of establishments | 4 019 | 661 | 95 | 387 | 985 | 209[4] | 219 | 75 | 21 | 163 | 292 | 17 | 77 | 118 | Nombre d'établissements |
| Value added | 6 523 | 808 | 541 | 506 | 765 | 1 389[4] | 218 | 79 | 91 | 193 | 432 | 226 | 1 192 | 83 | Valeur ajoutée |
| Number of employees (Average during year) | 219.3 | 17.0 | 22.3 | 23.3 | 54.3 | 23.5[4] | 7.4 | 2.8 | 2.7 | 3.7 | 13.5 | 2.6 | 42.6 | 3.6 | Nombre de salariés (moyenne pour l'année) |
| Operatives: Number (Average during year) | 206.1 | 15.6 | 21.4 | 22.2 | 52.5 | 22.1[4] | 6.6 | 2.7 | 2.6 | 3.2 | 12.7 | 2.3 | 39.0 | 3.2 | Ouvriers: Nombre (moyenne pour l'année) |
| Wages and salaries | 2 837.4 | 217.7 | 236.3 | 255.9 | 566.1 | 332.5[4] | 126.0 | 33.9 | 33.5 | 43.9 | 179.3 | 42.6 | 724.9 | 44.8 | Traitements et salaires |
| Capacity of installed power equipment | 1 050 | 43 | 47 | 8 | 175 | 582[4] | 7 | 8 | 9 | 17 | 45 | 26 | 80 | 3 | Puissance installée |
| **1948** | | | | | | | | | | | | | | | **1948** |
| Number of establishments | 5 608 | 776 | 206 | 388 | 1 387 | 194 | 288 | 120 | 72 | 205 | 420 | 21 | 1 339 | 192 | Nombre d'établissements |
| Value added | 88 113 | 7 310 | 7 592 | 4 419 | 12 826 | 14 462 | 3 188 | 1 351 | 1 414 | 3 888[1] | 4 191 | 2 925 | 23 282 | 1 265 | Valeur ajoutée |
| Employees: Number (Average during year) | 282.8 | 20.0 | 26.4 | 18.0 | 52.3 | 24.0 | 11.4 | 4.1 | 3.8 | 8.8 | 14.4 | 4.8 | 90.2 | 4.6 | Salariés: Nombre (moyenne pour l'année) |
| Wages and salaries | 49 993.4 | 3 108.9 | 3 865.7 | 2 381.9 | 8 283.5 | 4 660.7 | 1 957.1 | 594.7 | 639.8 | 1 583.0 | 2 631.8 | 1 074.8 | 18 467.7 | 743.8 | Traitements et salaires |
| Operatives: Number (Average during year) | 247.2 | 17.3 | 24.6 | 16.1 | 47.5 | 21.1 | 9.9 | 3.6 | 3.3 | 7.0 | 12.5 | 3.8 | 76.6 | 3.9 | Ouvriers: Nombre (moyenne pour l'année) |
| Wages and salaries | 41 852.7 | 2 553.9 | 3 399.7 | 2 007.2 | 7 320.0 | 3 888.0 | 1 637.8 | 491.8 | 509.6 | 1 159.9 | 2 203.3 | 863.6 | 15 214.0 | 603.9 | Traitements et salaires |
| Capacity of installed power equipment | 1 260 | 52 | 59 | 7 | 216 | 531 | 9 | 11 | 13 | 33 | 66 | 49 | 208 | 7 | Puissance installée |
| **1953** | | | | | | | | | | | | | | | **1953** |
| Number of establishments | 5 380 | 880 | 251 | 441 | 1 154 | 208 | 278 | 94 | 55 | 224 | 364 | 84 | 1 228 | 119 | Nombre d'établissements |
| Value added | 165 423 | 18 286 | 18 113 | 10 191 | 18 008 | 18 261 | 6 390 | 1 886 | 2 807 | 10 641 | 7 916 | 4 989 | 46 230 | 1 705 | Valeur ajoutée |
| Employees: Number (Average during year) | 290.3 | 26.0 | 34.1 | 24.6 | 42.7 | 22.5 | 12.1 | 3.8 | 4.2 | 10.5 | 11.8 | 5.4 | 89.4 | 3.2 | Salariés: Nombre (moyenne pour l'année) |
| Wages and salaries | 96 337.1 | 7 744.5 | 9 426.5 | 6 453.0 | 12 579.2 | 8 271.4 | 4 289.4 | 1 071.1 | 1 307.8 | 3 766.3 | 3 997.5 | 2 152.4 | 34 251.0 | 1 027.0 | Traitements et salaires |
| Operatives: Number (Average during year) | 251.0 | 22.6 | 31.4 | 22.1 | 38.4 | 19.2 | 10.4 | 3.3 | 3.6 | 8.1 | 10.2 | 4.5 | 74.5 | 2.7 | Ouvriers: Nombre (moyenne pour l'année) |
| Wages and salaries | 77 750.9 | 6 261.1 | 7 995.2 | 5 314.9 | 10 819.0 | 6 520.5 | 3 541.1 | 843.8 | 1 017.0 | 2 558.0 | 3 256.2 | 1 762.7 | 27 045.5 | 815.9 | Traitements et salaires |
| Capacity of installed power equipment | 1 740 | 89 | 81 | 11 | 268 | 713 | 12 | 15 | 19 | 63 | 91 | 75 | 297 | 6 | Puissance installée |
| **1954** | | | | | | | | | | | | | | | **1954** |
| Number of establishments | 6 509 | 1 609 | 302 | 512 | 1 166 | 194 | 512 | 73 | 56 | 217 | 447 | 63 | 1 192 | 166 | Nombre d'établissements |
| Value added | 208 252.4 | 28 720.0 | 18 834.7 | 11 588.7 | 24 193.9 | 24 698.7 | 12 078.1 | 1 772.0 | 3 629.7 | 11 997.0 | 8 844.9 | 5 695.4 | 53 419.0 | 2 780.3 | Valeur ajoutée |
| Number of engaged (Average during year) | 328.7 | 37.8 | 36.4 | 26.9 | 48.5 | 29.4 | 18.3 | 3.6 | 5.0 | 11.4 | 15.1 | 6.8 | 84.8 | 4.7 | Nombre de personnes occupées (moyenne pour l'année) |
| Employees: Number (Average during year) | 326.9 | 37.4 | 36.3 | 26.7 | 48.2 | 29.4 | 18.2 | 3.5 | 4.9 | 11.4 | 14.9 | 6.8 | 84.5 | 4.7 | Salariés: Nombre (moyenne pour l'année) |
| Wages and salaries | 113 135.1 | 11 869.2 | 10 645.0 | 7 333.2 | 14 718.3 | 11 774.3 | 6 175.3 | 1 070.5 | 1 614.1 | 4 419.8 | 5 410.0 | 2 892.9 | 33 593.2 | 1 619.3 | Traitements et salaires |
| Operatives: Number (Average during year) | 280.0 | 32.1 | 33.3 | 23.9 | 43.6 | 24.8 | 13.5 | 3.2 | 4.2 | 8.9 | 12.6 | 5.6 | 70.3 | 4.0 | Ouvriers: Nombre (moyenne pour l'année) |
| Man-hours worked | 604.4 | 72.2 | 70.4 | 48.5 | 93.8 | 56.1 | 27.7 | 6.7 | 9.1 | 19.8 | 27.4 | 12.6 | 151.8 | 8.3 | Heures de travail effectuées |
| Wages and salaries | 89 369.5 | 9 398.5 | 8 900.9 | 5 969.2 | 12 610.4 | 9 132.9 | 4 134.7 | 856.9 | 1 198.0 | 3 049.2 | 4 238.5 | 2 260.3 | 26 360.1 | 1 259.9 | Traitements et salaires |
| Energy consumed | 3 520.6 | 293.3 | 121.3 | 17.2 | 319.5 | 1 698.1 | 11.4 | 20.0 | 34.2 | 175.7 | 450.0 | 154.2 | 220.0 | 5.7 | Energie consommée |
| Electricity consumed | 3 600.7 | 154.1 | 107.6 | 13.5 | 204.1 | 2 048.1 | 22.2 | 8.1 | 21.9 | 310.3 | 166.8 | 305.3 | 233.0 | 5.7 | Electricité consommée |
| Capacity of installed power equipment | 2 012.6 | 147.0 | 84.0 | 13.8 | 278.0 | 861.5 | 13.3 | 14.5 | 20.3 | 76.2 | 107.1 | 87.3 | 299.6 | 10.0 | Puissance installée |
| **1958** | | | | | | | | | | | | | | | **1958** |
| Number of establishments | 6 660 | 1 655 | 319 | 573 | 1 079 | 196 | 521 | 68 | 67 | 204 | 418 | 65 | 1 322 | 173 | Nombre d'établissements |
| Value added | 286 215.2 | 43 686.3 | 18 514.8 | 16 431.4 | 28 751.4 | 46 454.1 | 17 896.7 | 1 803.7 | 4 049.0 | 21 629.3 | 10 635.5 | 6 815.1 | 65 976.6 | 3 571.3 | Valeur ajoutée |
| Number of engaged (Average during year) | 335.1 | 40.2 | 33.2 | 29.3 | 43.0 | 33.2 | 21.0 | 3.2 | 4.9 | 12.1 | 13.7 | 7.2 | 89.3 | 4.8 | Nombre de personnes occupées (moyenne pour l'année) |
| Employees: Number (Average during year) | 333.3 | 39.7 | 33.1 | 29.2 | 42.6 | 33.2 | 20.9 | 3.1 | 4.9 | 12.1 | 13.5 | 7.2 | 89.0 | 4.8 | Salariés: Nombre (moyenne pour l'année) |
| Wages and salaries | 148 325.9 | 17 018.3 | 11 843.3 | 10 029.8 | 16 755.5 | 17 069.0 | 9 687.0 | 1 194.1 | 2 018.8 | 6 263.9 | 6 457.7 | 3 805.4 | 44 093.3 | 2 089.8 | Traitements et salaires |
| Operatives: Number (Average during year) | 280.3 | 33.6 | 29.5 | 25.9 | 38.3 | 28.0 | 15.6 | 2.7 | 4.0 | 9.1 | 11.1 | 5.8 | 72.7 | 4.0 | Ouvriers: Nombre (moyenne pour l'année) |
| Man-hours worked | 580.8 | 76.0 | 57.3 | 49.6 | 81.0 | 59.8 | 30.6 | 5.6 | 8.2 | 19.8 | 23.5 | 12.1 | 149.1 | 8.2 | Heures de travail effectuées |
| Wages and salaries | 111 817.4 | 13 053.9 | 9 207.3 | 7 867.1 | 14 108.4 | 12 931.2 | 6 509.7 | 879.7 | 1 392.0 | 3 976.5 | 4 676.3 | 2 772.1 | 32 870.8 | 1 572.4 | Traitements et salaires |
| Energy consumed | 4 078.7 | 338.9 | 113.4 | 22.1 | 330.1 | 2 165.2 | 14.8 | 17.7 | 31.0 | 266.2 | 390.2 | 139.2 | 242.6 | 7.3 | Energie consommée |
| Electricity consumed | 4 860.5 | 197.5 | 125.1 | 19.0 | 222.4 | 2 988.2 | 23.8 | 7.9 | 23.4 | 484.9 | 158.5 | 351.2 | 248.8 | 9.8 | Electricité consommée |
| Capacity of installed power equipment | 2 530.1 | 195.7 | 99.8 | 19.2 | 290.5 | 1 136.9 | 17.6 | 16.1 | 27.0 | 120.2 | 117.3 | 100.3 | 375.1 | 14.4 | Puissance installée |

For footnotes, see end of table.      Pour les notes, voir au bas du tableau.

# FINLAND

## C. The Major Groups of Manufacturing (continued)— Les classes de la branche Industries manufacturières (suite)

| Year and item of data | Manufacturing / Industries manufacturières | Food, beverages and tobacco [1] / Industries alimentaires, boissons, tabac [1] | Textiles | Clothing, footwear and made-up textiles [2] / Articles d'habillement, chaussures et ouvrages en tissu [2] | Wood products and furniture / Bois et meubles | Paper and paper products / Papier et ouvrages en papier | Printing and publishing [3] / Imprimerie et édition [3] | Leather and leather products except wearing apparel / Cuir et articles en cuir, à l'exclusion des articles d'habillement | Rubber products / Ouvrages en caoutchouc | Chemicals and chemical, petroleum and coal products / Produits chimiques et dérivés du pétrole et du charbon | Non-metallic mineral products / Produits minéraux non métalliques | Basic metals / Métallurgie de base | Metal products / Ouvrages en métaux | Other manufacturing / Autres industries manufacturières | Année et rubrique |
|---|---|---|---|---|---|---|---|---|---|---|---|---|---|---|---|
| ISIC | 2–3 | 20–22 | 23 | 24 | 25–26 | 27 | 28 | 29 | 30 | 31–32 | 33 | 34 | 35–38 | 39 | CITI |
| **b. Structure** | | | | | | | | | | | | | | | |
| **1938** | | | | | | | | | | | | | | | **1938** |
| Distribution in percent of: | | | | | | | | | | | | | | | Répartition en pourcentage: |
| Value added | 100.0 | 12.3 | 8.3 | 7.8 | 11.7 | 21.3 | 3.4 | 1.2 | 1.4 | 2.9 | 6.6 | 3.5 | 18.3 | 1.3 | De la valeur ajoutée |
| Number of employees | 100.0 | 7.7 | 10.2 | 10.6 | 24.8 | 10.7 | 3.3 | 1.3 | 1.3 | 1.6 | 6.2 | 1.2 | 19.4 | 1.7 | Du nombre de salariés |
| Value added per employee | 29.7 | 47.5 | 24.3 | 21.7 | 14.1 | 59.1 | 29.5 | 28.3 | 33.5 | 52.1 | 32.0 | 86.9 | 28.0 | 23.0 | Valeur ajoutée par salarié |
| Capacity of installed power equipment per employee | 4.79 | 2.53 | 2.11 | 0.34 | 3.22 | 24.77 | 0.9 | 2.86 | 3.33 | 4.59 | 3.33 | 10.00 | 1.88 | 0.83 | Puissance installée par salarié |
| Operatives as a percent of employees | 94.0 | 91.8 | 96.0 | 95.3 | 96.7 | 94.0 | 89.2 | 96.4 | 96.3 | 86.5 | 94.1 | 88.5 | 91.5 | 88.9 | Ouvriers en pourcentage des salariés |
| Per operative: | | | | | | | | | | | | | | | Par ouvrier: |
| Wages and salaries | 13.8 | 14.0 | 11.0 | 11.5 | 10.8 | 15.0 | 19.1 | 12.6 | 12.9 | 13.7 | 14.1 | 18.5 | 18.6 | 14.0 | Traitements et salaires |
| Capacity of installed power equipment | 5.09 | 2.76 | 2.20 | 0.36 | 3.33 | 26.33 | 1.06 | 2.96 | 3.46 | 5.31 | 3.54 | 11.30 | 2.05 | 0.94 | Puissance installée |
| **1948** | | | | | | | | | | | | | | | **1948** |
| Distribution in percent of: | | | | | | | | | | | | | | | Répartition en pourcentage: |
| Value added | 100.0 | 8.2 | 8.7 | 5.0 | 14.5 | 16.4 | 3.7 | 1.5 | 1.6 | 4.4 | 4.8 | 3.3 | 26.4 | 1.5 | De la valeur ajoutée |
| Number of employees | 100.0 | 7.0 | 9.4 | 6.3 | 18.5 | 8.5 | 4.0 | 1.5 | 1.4 | 3.1 | 5.1 | 1.7 | 31.9 | 1.7 | Du nombre de salariés |
| Per employee: | | | | | | | | | | | | | | | Par salarié: |
| Value added | 331.6 | 365.5 | 287.6 | 245.5 | 245.2 | 602.6 | 279.6 | 329.5 | 372.1 | 441.8 | 291.0 | 609.4 | 258.1 | 275.0 | Valeur ajoutée |
| Wages and salaries | 176.8 | 155.4 | 146.4 | 132.3 | 158.4 | 194.2 | 171.7 | 145.0 | 168.4 | 179.9 | 182.8 | 223.9 | 204.7 | 161.7 | Traitements et salaires |
| Capacity of installed power equipment | 4.46 | 2.60 | 2.23 | 0.39 | 4.13 | 22.12 | 0.79 | 2.68 | 3.42 | 3.75 | 4.58 | 10.21 | 2.30 | 1.30 | Puissance installée |
| Value added per unit of wages and salaries | 1.76 | 2.35 | 1.96 | 1.86 | 1.55 | 3.10 | 1.63 | 2.27 | 2.21 | 2.46 | 1.59 | 2.72 | 1.26 | 1.70 | Valeur ajoutée par unité de traitements et salaires |
| Operatives as a percent of employees | 87.4 | 86.5 | 93.2 | 89.4 | 90.8 | 87.9 | 86.8 | 87.8 | 86.8 | 79.5 | 86.8 | 79.2 | 84.9 | 84.8 | Ouvriers en pourcentage des salariés |
| Per operative: | | | | | | | | | | | | | | | Par ouvrier: |
| Wages and salaries | 169.3 | 147.6 | 138.2 | 124.7 | 154.1 | 184.3 | 165.4 | 136.6 | 154.4 | 165.7 | 176.3 | 227.3 | 198.6 | 154.8 | Traitements et salaires |
| Capacity of installed power equipment | 5.10 | 3.00 | 2.40 | 0.43 | 4.55 | 25.16 | 0.91 | 3.06 | 3.94 | 4.71 | 5.28 | 12.89 | 2.72 | 1.54 | Puissance installée |
| **1953** | | | | | | | | | | | | | | | **1953** |
| Distribution in percent of: | | | | | | | | | | | | | | | Répartition en pourcentage: |
| Value added | 100.0 | 11.0 | 11.0 | 6.1 | 10.9 | 11.0 | 3.9 | 1.1 | 1.7 | 6.5 | 4.8 | 3.0 | 27.9 | 1.1 | De la valeur ajoutée |
| Number of employees | 100.0 | 8.9 | 11.8 | 8.4 | 14.7 | 7.8 | 4.2 | 1.3 | 1.4 | 3.6 | 4.1 | 1.9 | 30.7 | 1.2 | Du nombre de salariés |
| Per employee: | | | | | | | | | | | | | | | Par salarié: |
| Value added | 569.8 | 703.3 | 531.2 | 414.3 | 421.7 | 811.6 | 528.1 | 496.3 | 668.3 | 1 013.4 | 670.8 | 923.9 | 517.1 | 532.8 | Valeur ajoutée |
| Wages and salaries | 331.8 | 297.9 | 276.4 | 262.3 | 294.6 | 376.6 | 354.5 | 281.9 | 311.4 | 358.7 | 338.8 | 398.6 | 383.1 | 320.9 | Traitements et salaires |
| Capacity of installed power equipment | 5.99 | 3.42 | 2.38 | 0.45 | 6.28 | 31.69 | 0.99 | 3.95 | 4.52 | 6.00 | 7.71 | 13.89 | 3.32 | 1.88 | Puissance installée |
| Value added per unit of wages and salaries | 1.72 | 2.36 | 1.92 | 1.58 | 1.43 | 2.21 | 1.49 | 1.76 | 2.15 | 2.82 | 1.98 | 2.32 | 1.35 | 1.66 | Valeur ajoutée par unité de traitements et salaires |
| Operatives as a percent of employees | 86.5 | 86.9 | 92.1 | 89.8 | 89.9 | 85.3 | 86.0 | 86.8 | 85.7 | 77.1 | 86.4 | 83.3 | 83.3 | 84.4 | Ouvriers en pourcentage des salariés |
| Per operative: | | | | | | | | | | | | | | | Par ouvrier: |
| Wages and salaries | 309.8 | 277.0 | 254.6 | 240.5 | 281.7 | 339.6 | 340.5 | 255.7 | 282.5 | 315.8 | 319.2 | 391.7 | 363.0 | 302.2 | Traitements et salaires |
| Capacity of installed power equipment | 6.93 | 3.94 | 2.58 | 0.50 | 6.98 | 37.14 | 1.15 | 4.54 | 5.28 | 7.78 | 8.92 | 16.67 | 3.99 | 2.22 | Puissance installée |
| **1954** | | | | | | | | | | | | | | | **1954** |
| Distribution in percent of: | | | | | | | | | | | | | | | Distribution en pourcentage: |
| Value added | 100.0 | 13.7 | 9.1 | 5.5 | 11.7 | 11.8 | 5.8 | 0.9 | 1.7 | 5.8 | 4.2 | 2.8 | 25.6 | 1.4 | Valeur ajoutée |
| Number of engaged | 100.0 | 11.4 | 11.1 | 8.2 | 14.8 | 8.9 | 5.6 | 1.1 | 1.5 | 3.5 | 4.6 | 2.0 | 25.8 | 1.5 | Nombre de personnes occupées |
| Per person engaged: | | | | | | | | | | | | | | | Par personne occupée: |
| Value added | 633.6 | 759.8 | 517.4 | 430.8 | 498.8 | 840.1 | 660.0 | 492.2 | 725.9 | 1 052.4 | 585.8 | 837.6 | 629.9 | 591.6 | Valeur ajoutée |
| Energy consumed | 10.71 | 7.76 | 3.33 | 0.64 | 6.59 | 57.76 | 0.62 | 5.56 | 6.84 | 15.41 | 29.80 | 22.68 | 2.59 | 1.21 | Energie consommée |
| Electricity consumed | 11.0 | 4.1 | 3.0 | 0.5 | 4.2 | 69.7 | 1.2 | 2.2 | 4.4 | 27.2 | 11.0 | 44.9 | 2.7 | 1.2 | Electricité consommée |
| Capacity of installed power equipment | 6.12 | 3.89 | 2.31 | 0.51 | 5.73 | 29.30 | 0.73 | 4.03 | 4.06 | 6.68 | 7.09 | 12.84 | 3.53 | 2.13 | Puissance installée |
| Employees as a percent of engaged | 99.4 | 98.9 | 99.7 | 99.2 | 99.4 | 100.0 | 99.4 | 97.2 | 98.0 | 100.0 | 98.7 | 100.0 | 99.6 | 100.0 | Salariés en pourcentage des personnes occupées |
| Value added per unit of wages and salaries | 1.84 | 2.42 | 1.77 | 1.58 | 1.64 | 2.10 | 1.96 | 1.66 | 2.25 | 2.71 | 1.63 | 1.97 | 1.59 | 1.72 | Valeur ajoutée par traitements et salaires unitaires |
| Wages and salaries per employee | 346.1 | 317.4 | 293.2 | 274.6 | 305.4 | 400.5 | 339.3 | 305.8 | 329.4 | 387.7 | 363.1 | 425.4 | 397.6 | 344.5 | Traitements et salaires par salarié |
| Operatives as a percent of employees | 85.6 | 85.8 | 91.7 | 89.5 | 90.4 | 84.4 | 74.2 | 91.4 | 85.7 | 78.1 | 84.6 | 82.4 | 83.2 | 85.1 | Ouvriers en pourcentage des salariés |
| Average man-hours per operative | 2.16 | 2.25 | 2.11 | 2.03 | 2.15 | 2.26 | 2.05 | 2.09 | 2.17 | 2.22 | 2.17 | 2.25 | 2.16 | 2.08 | Heures de travail: (moyenne par ouvrier) |
| Per thousand operative man-hour: | | | | | | | | | | | | | | | Par milliers d'heures-ouvrier de travail: |
| Wages and salaries | 147.86 | 130.17 | 126.43 | 123.08 | 134.44 | 162.80 | 149.27 | 127.90 | 131.65 | 154.00 | 154.69 | 179.39 | 173.65 | 151.80 | Traitements et salaires |
| Energy consumed | 5.82 | 4.06 | 1.72 | 0.35 | 3.41 | 30.27 | 0.41 | 2.98 | 3.76 | 8.87 | 16.42 | 12.24 | 1.45 | 0.69 | Energie consommée |
| Electricity consumed | 5.96 | 2.13 | 1.53 | 0.28 | 2.18 | 36.51 | 0.80 | 1.21 | 2.41 | 15.67 | 6.09 | 24.23 | 1.53 | 0.69 | Electricité consommée |
| Capacity of installed power equipment | 3.33 | 2.04 | 1.19 | 0.28 | 2.96 | 15.36 | 0.48 | 2.16 | 2.23 | 3.85 | 3.91 | 6.93 | 1.97 | 1.20 | Puissance installée |

For footnotes, see end of table.　　　　　　Pour les notes, voir au bas du tableau.

## C. The Major Groups of Manufacturing (continued) — Les classes de la branche Industries manufacturières (suite)

| Year and item of data | Manufacturing — Industries manufacturières | Food, beverages and tobacco[1] — Industries alimentaires, boissons, tabac[1] | Textiles | Clothing, footwear and made-up textiles[2] — Articles d'habillement, chaussures et ouvrages en tissu[2] | Wood products and furniture — Bois et meubles | Paper and paper products — Papier et ouvrages et papier | Printing and publishing[3] — Imprimerie et édition[3] | Leather and leather products except wearing apparel — Cuir et articles en cuir, à l'exclusion des articles d'habillement | Rubber products — Ouvrages en caoutchouc | Chemicals and chemical, petroleum and coal products — Produits chimiques et dérivés du pétrole et du charbon | Non-metallic mineral products — Produits minéraux non métalliques | Basic metals — Métallurgie de base | Metal products — Ouvrages en métaux | Other manufacturing — Autres industries manufacturières | Année et rubrique |
|---|---|---|---|---|---|---|---|---|---|---|---|---|---|---|---|
| ISIC | 2-3 | 20-22 | 23 | 24 | 25-26 | 27 | 28 | 29 | 30 | 31-32 | 33 | 34 | 35-38 | 39 | CITI |

b. Structure

| | 2-3 | 20-22 | 23 | 24 | 25-26 | 27 | 28 | 29 | 30 | 31-32 | 33 | 34 | 35-38 | 39 | |
|---|---|---|---|---|---|---|---|---|---|---|---|---|---|---|---|
| **1958** Distribution in percent of: | | | | | | | | | | | | | | | **1958** Distribution en pourcentage: |
| Value added........ | 100.0 | 15.2 | 6.5 | 5.7 | 10.1 | 16.2 | 6.3 | 0.6 | 1.4 | 7.6 | 3.7 | 2.4 | 23.0 | 1.3 | Valeur ajoutée |
| Number of engaged.. | 100.0 | 11.9 | 10.0 | 8.7 | 12.8 | 9.9 | 6.3 | 1.0 | 1.4 | 3.6 | 4.1 | 2.2 | 26.6 | 1.5 | Nombre de personnes occupées |
| Per person engaged: | | | | | | | | | | | | | | | Par personne occupée: |
| Value added........ | 854.1 | 1 086.7 | 557.7 | 560.8 | 668.6 | 1 399.2 | 852.2 | 563.6 | 826.3 | 1 787.5 | 776.3 | 946.5 | 738.8 | 744.0 | Valeur ajoutée |
| Energy consumed..... | 12.17 | 8.43 | 3.42 | 0.75 | 7.68 | 65.22 | 0.70 | 5.53 | 6.33 | 22.00 | 28.48 | 19.33 | 2.72 | 1.52 | Energie consommée |
| Electricity consumed... | 14.5 | 4.9 | 3.8 | 0.6 | 5.2 | 90.0 | 1.1 | 2.5 | 4.8 | 40.1 | 11.6 | 48.8 | 2.8 | 2.0 | Electricité consommée |
| Capacity of installed power equipment..... | 7.55 | 4.87 | 3.01 | 0.66 | 6.76 | 34.24 | 0.84 | 5.03 | 5.51 | 9.93 | 8.56 | 13.93 | 4.20 | 3.00 | Puissance installée |
| Employees as a percent of engaged......... | 99.5 | 98.8 | 99.7 | 99.6 | 99.1 | 100.0 | 99.5 | 96.9 | 100.0 | 100.0 | 98.5 | 100.0 | 99.7 | 100.0 | Salariés en pourcentage des personnes occupées |
| Value added per unit of wages and salaries. | 1.93 | 2.57 | 1.56 | 1.64 | 1.72 | 2.72 | 1.85 | 1.51 | 2.00 | 3.45 | 1.65 | 1.79 | 1.50 | 1.71 | Valeur ajoutée par traitements et salaires unitaires |
| Wages and salaries per employee........ | 445.0 | 428.7 | 357.8 | 343.5 | 393.3 | 514.1 | 463.5 | 385.2 | 412.0 | 517.7 | 478.3 | 528.5 | 495.4 | 435.4 | Traitements et salaires par salarié |
| Operatives as a percent of employees......... | 84.1 | 84.6 | 89.1 | 88.7 | 89.9 | 84.3 | 74.6 | 87.1 | 81.6 | 75.2 | 82.2 | 80.6 | 81.7 | 83.3 | Ouvriers en pourcentage des salariés |
| Average man-hours per operative........ | 2.07 | 2.26 | 1.94 | 1.92 | 2.11 | 2.14 | 1.96 | 2.07 | 2.05 | 2.18 | 2.12 | 2.09 | 2.05 | 2.05 | Heures de travail: moyenne par ouvrier |
| Per thousand operative man-hour: | | | | | | | | | | | | | | | Par milliers d'heures-ouvrier de travail: |
| Wages and salaries... | 192.52 | 171.76 | 160.68 | 158.61 | 174.18 | 216.24 | 212.74 | 157.09 | 169.76 | 200.83 | 198.99 | 229.10 | 220.46 | 191.76 | Traitements et salaires |
| Energy consumed..... | 7.02 | 4.46 | 1.98 | 0.44 | 4.08 | 36.21 | 0.48 | 3.16 | 3.78 | 13.44 | 16.60 | 11.50 | 1.63 | 0.89 | Energie consommée |
| Electricity consumed... | 8.37 | 2.60 | 2.18 | 0.38 | 2.74 | 49.97 | 0.78 | 1.41 | 2.85 | 24.49 | 6.74 | 29.02 | 1.67 | 1.20 | Electricité consommée |
| Capacity of installed power equipment..... | 4.36 | 2.58 | 1.74 | 0.39 | 3.59 | 19.01 | 0.58 | 2.88 | 3.29 | 6.07 | 4.99 | 8.29 | 2.52 | 1.76 | Puissance installée |

[1] Excludes slaughtering and meat packing and dairies before 1954.
[2] Excludes repair of footwear before 1954.
[3] Excludes publishing before 1954.
[4] Includes bookbinding.

[1] Non compris l'abattage du bétail et la fabrication des préparations et conserves de viande, et l'industrie du lait avant 1954.
[2] Non compris la réparation des chaussures avant 1954.
[3] Non compris l'édition avant 1954.
[4] Y compris la reliure.

## 6. FUELS AND ELECTRICITY CONSUMED BY INDUSTRIAL ESTABLISHMENTS ENGAGING FIVE OR MORE PERSONS

### CONSOMMATION DE COMBUSTIBLES ET D'ELECTRICITE PAR LES ETABLISSEMENTS INDUSTRIELS EMPLOYANT CINQ PERSONNES OU PLUS

### 1954, 1958

### A. Percentage Distribution of Energy Consumed According to Source

### Distribution en pourcentage de l'énergie consommée suivant la source

Quantities in thousand metric tons of coal equivalents.　　　　　Quantités en milliers de tonnes métriques d'équivalent houille.

### a. The Major Groups of Mining and the Groups of Electricity, Gas and Steam

### La classe des Industries extractives et les groupes de l'électricité, du gaz et de la vapeur

| Year and item of data | Mining — Industries extractives | | | Electricity, gas and steam — Electricité, gaz et vapeur | | | Année et rubrique |
| | Total | Metal mining Extraction des minerais métalliques | Other mining Divers | Total [2] | Electricity [2] Electricité [2] | Gas and steam [2] Gaz et vapeur [2] | |
|---|---|---|---|---|---|---|---|
| ISIC | 1 | 12 | 14–19 | 511-513 | 511 | 512-513 | CITI |
| **1954** | | | | | | | 1954 |
| Total energy consumed.. | 26.4 | 19.1 | 7.3 | 1 947.6 | 280.7 | 1 695.6 | Energie totale consommée |
| Percentage consumed as: | | | | | | | Pourcentage consommé comme: |
| Coal.............. | 0.8 | 0.7 | 1.1 | 28.3 | 30.4 | 27.5 | Charbon |
| Wood............. | 29.7 | 35.8 | 13.9 | 56.1 | 7.2 | 63.2 | Bois |
| Coke.............. | 1.0 | 0.8 | 1.2 | 0.7 | — | 0.8 | Coke |
| Refined oil fuels...... | 10.3 | 7.8 | 16.8 | 5.2 | 4.3 | 5.4 | Pétrole raffiné |
| Gas............... | — | — | — | . | — | . | Gaz |
| Electricity purchased.. | 48.6 | 54.7 | 32.6 | . | . | 1.7 | Electricité achetée |
| Other fuels......... | 9.6 | 0.2 | 34.4 | 9.7 | 58.1 | 1.4 | Autres combustibles |
| **1958** | | | | | | | 1958 |
| Total energy consumed.. | 42.2 | 33.2 | 9.0 | 2 459.4 | 344.1 | 2 174.1 | Energie totale consommée |
| Percentage consumed as: | | | | | | | Pourcentage consommé comme: |
| Coal.............. | 3.2 | 0.3 | 14.0 | 24.6 | 31.5 | 22.9 | Charbon |
| Wood............. | 12.3 | 14.4 | 4.7 | 55.1 | 3.4 | 61.7 | Bois |
| Coke.............. | 0.3 | 0.1 | 0.6 | 0.4 | 1.4 | 0.2 | Coke |
| Refined oil fuels...... | 40.2 | 42.9 | 30.5 | 10.1 | 2.4 | 11.1 | Pétrole raffiné |
| Gas............... | — | — | — | . | 0.1 | . | Gaz |
| Electricity purchased.. | 39.7 | 42.0 | 31.0 | . | . | 2.7 | Electricité achetée |
| Other fuels [1]........ | 4.3 | 0.3 | 19.2 | 9.8 | 61.2 | 1.4 | Autres combustibles [1] |

For footnotes, see end of table.　　　　　Pour les notes, voir au bas du tableau.

## b. The Major Groups of Manufacturing (continued) — Les classes de la branche Industries manufacturières (suite)

| Year and item of data | Manufacturing / Industries manufacturières | Food, beverages and tobacco / Industries alimentaires, boissons, tabac | Textiles | Clothing, footwear and made-up textiles / Articles d'habillement, chaussures et ouvrages en tissu | Wood products and furniture / Bois et meubles | Paper and paper products / Papier et ouvrages en papier | Printing and publishing / Imprimerie et édition | Leather and leather products except wearing apparel / Cuir et articles en cuir, à l'exclusion des articles d'habillement | Rubber products / Ouvrages en caoutchouc | Chemicals and chemical, petroleum and coal products / Produits chimiques et dérivés du pétrole et du charbon | Non-metallic mineral products / Produits minéraux non métalliques | Basic metals / Métallurgie de base | Metal products / Ouvrages en métaux | Other manufacturing / Autres industries manufacturières | Année et rubrique |
|---|---|---|---|---|---|---|---|---|---|---|---|---|---|---|---|
| ISIC | 2-3 | 20-22 | 23 | 24 | 25-26 | 27 | 28 | 29 | 30 | 31-32 | 33 | 34 | 35 | 39 | CITI |
| **1954** | | | | | | | | | | | | | | | **1954** |
| Total energy consumed: Quantity | 3 520.6 | 293.3 | 121.3 | 17.2 | 319.5 | 1 698.1 | 11.4 | 20.0 | 34.2 | 175.7 | 450.0 | 154.2 | 220.0 | 5.7 | Energie totale consommée: Quantité |
| Percent of total in specified industry | 100.0 | 8.3 | 3.4 | 0.5 | 9.1 | 48.2 | 0.3 | 0.6 | 1.0 | 5.0 | 12.8 | 4.3 | 6.3 | 0.2 | Pourcentage du total par industrie indiquée |
| *Percent consumed as: | | | | | | | | | | | | | | | Pourcentage consommé comme: |
| Coal | 18.3 | 22.7 | 55.0 | 19.8 | 0.6 | 3.7 | 16.5 | 73.3 | 20.2 | 10.9 | 64.4 | 29.8 | 28.3 | 27.9 | Charbon |
| Wood | 14.1 | 29.5 | 12.5 | 33.4 | 51.9 | 5.4 | 21.8 | 14.1 | 8.1 | 8.7 | 13.9 | 2.8 | 18.0 | 25.4 | Bois |
| Coke | 1.7 | 3 5 | 0.9 | 11.1 | 0.2 | — | 13.5 | 0.7 | 0.6 | 1.3 | 0.4 | 8.8 | 12.4 | 9.7 | Coke |
| Refined oil fuels | 10.3 | 22.0 | 16.0 | 14.9 | 3.0 | 2.7 | 22.1 | 2.5 | 23.7 | 31.7 | 14.5 | 27.7 | 20.0 | 22.1 | Pétrole raffiné |
| Gas | 0.2 | 0.6 | 0.1 | 0.5 | — | — | 1.5 | — | — | — | 0.1 | — | 0.6 | 1.1 | Gaz |
| Electricity purchased | 12.0 | 6.1 | 7.9 | 9.5 | 7.5 | 14.2 | 24.5 | 5.7 | 8.2 | 20.6 | 5.1 | 22.1 | 13.6 | 12.6 | Electricité achetée |
| Other fuels | 43.4 | 15.6 | 7.6 | 10.8 | 36.8 | 74.0 | 0.1 | 3.7 | 39.2 | 26.8 | 1.6 | 8.8 | 7.1 | 1.2 | Autres combustibles |
| **1958** | | | | | | | | | | | | | | | **1958** |
| Total energy consumed: Quantity | 4 078.7 | 338.9 | 113.4 | 22.1 | 330.1 | 2 165.2 | 14.8 | 17.7 | 31.0 | 266.2 | 390.2 | 139.2 | 242.6 | 7.3 | Energie totale consommée: Quantité |
| Percent of total in specified industry | 100.0 | 8.3 | 2.7 | 0.6 | 8.1 | 53.1 | 0.3 | 0.5 | 0.7 | 6.5 | 9.6 | 3.4 | 6.0 | 0.2 | Pourcentage du total par industrie indiquée |
| Percent consumed as: | | | | | | | | | | | | | | | Pourcentage consommé comme: |
| Coal | 11.5 | 14.8 | 39.2 | 13.7 | 0.3 | 2.0 | 16.2 | 50.8 | 10.2 | 8.4 | 57.2 | 9.2 | 20.9 | 21.8 | Charbon |
| Wood | 10.2 | 26.2 | 11.4 | 24.2 | 42.3 | 2.9 | 17.3 | 19.5 | 4.9 | 4.4 | 11.1 | 2.4 | 17.5 | 23.4 | Bois |
| Coke | 1.4 | 2.8 | 1.2 | 7.3 | 0.4 | — | 12.0 | 0.7 | 0.5 | 0.6 | 1.6 | 7.9 | 9.2 | 9.0 | Coke |
| Refined oil fuels | 14.3 | 31.8 | 31.8 | 33.6 | 3.4 | 3.6 | 32.1 | 21.7 | 18.6 | 41.8 | 22.5 | 39.5 | 29.2 | 27.8 | Pétrole raffiné |
| Gas | 0.2 | 0.7 | — | 0.5 | — | — | 1.1 | — | 0.2 | — | 0.1 | — | 0.7 | 1.2 | Gaz |
| Electricity purchased | 14.2 | 6.7 | 10.4 | 10.8 | 8.0 | 16.7 | 20.9 | 6.5 | 9.6 | 20.9 | 5.4 | 28.5 | 13.9 | 16.7 | Electricité achetée |
| Other fuels [1] | 48.2 | 17.0 | 6.0 | 9.9 | 45.6 | 74.8 | 0.4 | 0.8 | 56.0 | 23.9 | 2.1 | 12.5 | 8.6 | 0.1 | Autres combustibles [1] |

For footnotes, see end of table.    Pour les notes, voir au bas du tableau.

# FINLAND

## B. Quantity and Value of Fuels Consumed and of Electricity Purchased, Produced and Sold

### Quantité et valeur des combustibles consommés; quantité et valeur de l'électricité achetée, produite et vendue

Coal, coke and refined fuel oils in thousand metric tons; manufactured gas in thousand cubic meters; electricity purchased, produced and sold in million KWH; other fuels in thousand metric tons of coal equivalent; values in million Markkaa.

Charbon, coke et pétrole raffiné en milliers de tonnes métriques; gaz manufacturé en milliers de mètres cubes; électricité achetée, produite et vendue en millions de kWh; autres combustibles en milliers de tonnes métriques d'équivalent houille; valeurs en millions de markkaa.

#### a. The Major Groups of Mining and the Groups of Electricity, Gas and Steam

#### Les classes des industries extractives et les groupes de l'électricité, du gaz et de la vapeur

| Year and source of energy | Mining — Industries extractives | | | Electricity, gas and steam — Electricité, gaz et vapeur | | | Année et source d'énergie |
|---|---|---|---|---|---|---|---|
| | Total | Metal mining Extraction des minerais métalliques | Other mining Divers | Total | Electricity Electricité | Gas and steam Gaz et vapeur | |
| ISIC | 1 | 12 | 14–19 | 511-513 | 511 | 512, 513 | CITI |
| **1954** | | | | | | | **1954** |
| Coal: | | | | | | | Charbon: |
| Quantity | 0.3 | 0.2 | 0.1 | 553.0 | 85.2 | 467.8 | Quantité |
| Value | 1.4 | 1.0 | 0.4 | 2 512.7 | 405.7 | 2 107.0 | Valeur |
| Coke: | | | | | | | Coke: |
| Quantity | 0.3 | 0.2 | 0.1 | 14.2 | — | 14.2 | Quantité |
| Value | 2.2 | 1.4 | 0.8 | 66.7 | 0.2 | 66.5 | Valeur |
| Refined oil fuels: | | | | | | | Pétrole raffiné: |
| Quantity | 1.8 | 1.0 | 0.8 | 68.2 | 8.1 | 60.1 | Quantité |
| Value | 40.2 | 17.8 | 22.4 | 562.0 | 113.1 | 448.9 | Valeur |
| Manufactured gas: | | | | | | | Gaz manufacturé: |
| Quantity | — | — | — | 12 587 | 2 | 12 585 | Quantité |
| Value | — | — | — | 143.6 | 0.0 | 143.6 | Valeur |
| Electricity: | | | | | | | Electricité: |
| Purchased: | | | | | | | Achetée: |
| Quantity | 102.6 | 83.6 | 19.0 | ... | ... | 228.8 | Quantité |
| Value | 393.6 | 284.2 | 109.4 | 13 527.2 | 13 270.3 | 256.9 | Valeur |
| Produced: | | | | | | | Produite: |
| Quantity | 0.3 | 0.3 | — | 5 392.0 | 5 392.0 | — | Quantité |
| Value | 2.9 | 2.9 | — | 10 930.6 | 10 930.6 | — | Valeur |
| Sold: | | | | | | | Vendue: |
| Quantity | 3.3 | 3.2 | 0.1 | ... | ... | — | Quantité |
| Value | 11.4 | 11.0 | 0.4 | 23 950.7 | 23 950.7 | — | Valeur |
| Wood: | | | | | | | Bois: |
| Quantity | 47.0 | 40.9 | 6.1 | 6 541.2 | 120.3 | 6 420.9 | Quantité |
| Value | 49.9 | 42.6 | 7.3 | 3 051.2 | 93.3 | 2 957.9 | Valeur |
| Other fuels [1]: | | | | | | | Autres combustibles [1]: |
| Quantity | 2.5 | — | 2.5 | 195.5 | 163.2 | 32.3 | Quantité |
| Value | 11.6 | 0.3 | 11.3 | 736.2 | 571.0 | 165.2 | Valeur |
| **1958** | | | | | | | **1958** |
| Coal: | | | | | | | Charbon: |
| Quantity | 1.4 | 0.1 | 1.3 | 606.7 | 108.6 | 498.1 | Quantité |
| Value | 10.3 | 0.9 | 9.4 | 3 464.4 | 511.8 | 2 952.6 | Valeur |
| Coke: | | | | | | | Coke: |
| Quantity | 0.2 | 0.1 | 0.1 | 11.1 | 5.2 | 5.9 | Quantité |
| Value | 1.0 | 0.5 | 0.5 | 49.0 | 18.4 | 30.6 | Valeur |
| Refined oil fuels: | | | | | | | Pétrole raffiné: |
| Quantity | 11.3 | 9.5 | 1.8 | 165.9 | 5.6 | 160.3 | Quantité |
| Value | 198.8 | 142.8 | 56.0 | 1 859.7 | 111.1 | 1 748.6 | Valeur |
| Manufactured gas: | | | | | | | Gaz manufacturé: |
| Quantity | — | — | — | 29 569 | 487 | 29 082 | Quantité |
| Value | — | — | — | 243.2 | 3.9 | 239.3 | Valeur |
| Electricity: | | | | | | | Electricité: |
| Purchased: | | | | | | | Achetée: |
| Quantity | 133.8 | 111.5 | 22.3 | ... | ... | 467.8 | Quantité |
| Value | 621.5 | 464.3 | 157.2 | 25 615.9 | 25 044.9 | 571.0 | Valeur |
| Produced: | | | | | | | Produite: |
| Quantity | — | — | — | 7 649.9 | 7 649.9 | — | Quantité |
| Value | — | — | — | 19 796.1 | 19 796.1 | — | Valeur |
| Sold: | | | | | | | Vendue: |
| Quantity | 2.6 | 2.6 | — | ... | ... | — | Quantité |
| Value | 11.0 | 10.7 | 0.3 | 44 437.5 | 44 437.5 | — | Valeur |
| Wood: | | | | | | | Bois: |
| Quantity | 31.2 | 28.6 | 2.6 | 8 107.4 | 70.8 | 8 036.6 | Quantité |
| Value | 42.0 | 38.6 | 3.4 | 3 176.4 | 64.5 | 3 111.9 | Valeur |
| Other fuels [1]: | | | | | | | Autres combustibles [1]: |
| Quantity | 1.8 | 0.1 | 1.7 | 250.8 | 210.3 | 40.5 | Quantité |
| Value | 8.1 | 0.5 | 7.6 | 1 071.5 | 831.6 | 259.9 | Valeur |

For footnotes, see end of table.

Pour les notes, voir au bas du tableau.

## b. The Major Groups of Manufacturing — Les classes de la branche industries manufacturières

| Year and source of energy | Manufacturing — Industries manufacturières | Food, beverages and tobacco — Industries alimentaires, boissons, tabac | Textiles | Clothing, footwear and made-up textiles — Articles d'habillement, chaussures et ouvrages en tissu | Wood products and furniture — Bois et meubles | Paper and paper products — Papier et ouvrages en papier | Printing and publishing — Imprimerie et édition | Leather and leather products except wearing apparel — Cuir et articles en cuir, à l'exclusion des articles d'habillement | Rubber products — Ouvrages en caoutchouc | Chemicals and chemical, petroleum and coal products — Produits chimiques et dérivés du pétrole et du charbon | Non-metallic mineral products — Produits minéraux non métalliques | Basic metals — Métallurgie de base | Metal products — Ouvrages en métaux | Other manufacturing — Autres industries manufacturières | Année et source d'énergie |
|---|---|---|---|---|---|---|---|---|---|---|---|---|---|---|---|
| ISIC | 2–3 | 20–22 | 23 | 24 | 25–26 | 27 | 28 | 29 | 30 | 31–32 | 33 | 34 | 35–38 | 39 | CITI |
| **1954** | | | | | | | | | | | | | | | **1954** |
| Coal: | | | | | | | | | | | | | | | Charbon: |
| Quantity | 645.2 | 66.8 | 66.8 | 3.4 | 2.2 | 63.3 | 1.9 | 14.6 | 6.9 | 19.3 | 290.1 | 46.0 | 62.3 | 1.6 | Quantité |
| Value | 2 983.8 | 328.6 | 368.1 | 19.8 | 13.6 | 279.3 | 11.0 | 73.6 | 38.3 | 91.8 | 1 168.7 | 261.0 | 320.9 | 9.1 | Valeur |
| Coke: | | | | | | | | | | | | | | | Coke: |
| Quantity | 68.6 | 11.3 | 1.2 | 2.1 | 0.7 | 0.4 | 1.7 | 0.2 | 0.2 | 2.5 | 2.1 | 15.2 | 30.4 | 0.6 | Quantité |
| Value | 459.1 | 64.9 | 8.0 | 14.5 | 4.4 | 2.6 | 11.7 | 1.1 | 1.5 | 16.7 | 15.7 | 111.2 | 202.4 | 4.4 | Valeur |
| Refined oil fuels: | | | | | | | | | | | | | | | Pétrole raffiné: |
| Quantity | 241.0 | 43.1 | 13.0 | 1.7 | 6.5 | 30.0 | 1.7 | 0.3 | 5.4 | 37.2 | 43.5 | 28.4 | 29.4 | 0.8 | Quantité |
| Value | 3 053.4 | 713.8 | 134.4 | 38.1 | 245.0 | 320.6 | 30.8 | 12.3 | 50.6 | 314.2 | 436.9 | 263.5 | 479.3 | 13.9 | Valeur |
| Manufactured gas: | | | | | | | | | | | | | | | Gaz manufacturé: |
| Quantity | 6 243 | 2 757 | 143 | 136 | 2 | 7 | 282 | — | — | 12 | 670 | — | 2 134 | 100 | Quantité |
| Value | 74.1 | 33.2 | 1.8 | 1.9 | 0.1 | 0.1 | 3.4 | — | — | 0.2 | 8.1 | — | 24.1 | 1.2 | Valeur |
| Electricity: | | | | | | | | | | | | | | | Électricité: |
| Purchased: | | | | | | | | | | | | | | | Achetée: |
| Quantity | 3 392.4 | 142.1 | 76.9 | 13.1 | 191.7 | 1 928.6 | 22.5 | 9.1 | 22.2 | 288.5 | 181.5 | 272.3 | 238.2 | 5.7 | Quantité |
| Value | 10 112.4 | 947.0 | 457.7 | 121.1 | 1 000.5 | 3 785.8 | 188.7 | 57.7 | 79.2 | 691.6 | 846.4 | 554.4 | 1 336.8 | 45.5 | Valeur |
| Produced: | | | | | | | | | | | | | | | Produite: |
| Quantity | 313.6 | 14.4 | 41.3 | 0.4 | 27.4 | 142.2 | — | 0.5 | — | 24.4 | 0.1 | 42.8 | 20.1 | — | Quantité |
| Value | 909.4 | 65.4 | 118.5 | 1.7 | 207.8 | 254.2 | — | 1.9 | — | 45.9 | 0.6 | 104.0 | 109.4 | — | Valeur |
| Sold: | | | | | | | | | | | | | | | Vendue: |
| Quantity | 105.2 | 2.4 | 10.6 | — | 15.0 | 22.6 | 0.3 | 1.5 | 0.3 | 2.5 | 14.8 | 9.8 | 25.4 | — | Quantité |
| Value | 452.7 | 16.3 | 63.1 | — | 78.2 | 44.4 | 2.2 | 9.6 | 1.2 | 6.1 | 68.8 | 19.9 | 142.5 | 0.4 | Valeur |
| Wood: | | | | | | | | | | | | | | | Bois: |
| Quantity | 2 972.8 | 518.0 | 90.8 | 34.4 | 992.2 | 553.8 | 15.0 | 16.9 | 16.6 | 91.2 | 373.2 | 25.9 | 236.1 | 8.7 | Quantité |
| Value | 2 677.1 | 567.5 | 119.2 | 40.3 | 522.6 | 557.4 | 16.7 | 18.6 | 25.8 | 97.6 | 375.7 | 29.7 | 296.0 | 10.0 | Valeur |
| Other fuels: [1] | | | | | | | | | | | | | | | Autres combustibles [1]: |
| Quantity | 1 527.8 | 45.8 | 9.2 | 1.9 | 117.3 | 1 255.9 | — | 0.7 | 13.4 | 47.1 | 7.2 | 13.5 | 15.7 | 0.1 | Quantité |
| Value | 5 368.1 | 164.3 | 22.0 | 6.4 | 409.8 | 4 391.6 | — | 2.9 | 47.1 | 165.0 | 32.0 | 48.7 | 77.1 | 1.2 | Valeur |
| **1958** | | | | | | | | | | | | | | | **1958** |
| Coal: | | | | | | | | | | | | | | | Charbon: |
| Quantity | 469.0 | 50.4 | 44.5 | 3.0 | 1.0 | 44.3 | 2.4 | 9.0 | 3.2 | 22.5 | 223.5 | 12.8 | 50.8 | 1.6 | Quantité |
| Value | 2 613.1 | 370.8 | 305.0 | 22.5 | 8.6 | 279.5 | 18.8 | 55.8 | 22.8 | 120.5 | 963.1 | 87.6 | 346.8 | 11.3 | Valeur |
| Coke: | | | | | | | | | | | | | | | Coke: |
| Quantity | 63.7 | 10.5 | 1.4 | 1.8 | 1.4 | 0.1 | 0.1 | 0.1 | 0.2 | 1.6 | 6.7 | 12.3 | 24.9 | 0.7 | Quantité |
| Value | 665.2 | 96.5 | 16.0 | 16.8 | 11.8 | 1.3 | 20.0 | 1.1 | 2.1 | 15.6 | 50.2 | 136.3 | 291.1 | 6.4 | Valeur |
| Refined oil fuels: | | | | | | | | | | | | | | | Pétrole raffiné: |
| Quantity | 387.9 | 71.9 | 24.1 | 4.9 | 7.5 | 52.0 | 3.2 | 2.6 | 3.8 | 74.2 | 58.4 | 36.6 | 47.3 | 1.4 | Quantité |
| Value | 6 250.4 | 1 367.3 | 378.2 | 110.6 | 314.2 | 755.8 | 79.1 | 41.4 | 60.5 | 866.4 | 848.3 | 483.6 | 916.8 | 28.2 | Valeur |
| Manufactured gas: | | | | | | | | | | | | | | | Gaz manufacturé: |
| Quantity | 7 241 | 3 607 | 13 | 150 | — | 4 | 261 | — | 97 | 29 | 206 | 40 | 2 698 | 136 | Quantité |
| Value | 89.8 | 46.3 | 0.2 | 2.5 | — | 0.1 | 3.3 | — | 1.4 | 0.4 | 2.6 | 0.5 | 30.7 | 1.8 | Valeur |
| Electricity: | | | | | | | | | | | | | | | Électricité: |
| Purchased: | | | | | | | | | | | | | | | Achetée: |
| Quantity | 4 659.8 | 181.2 | 93.6 | 19.2 | 210.4 | 2 886.2 | 24.7 | 9.2 | 23.8 | 444.5 | 170.5 | 317.0 | 269.7 | 9.8 | Quantité |
| Value | 15 802.9 | 1 507.4 | 608.3 | 191.3 | 1 225.4 | 6 599.8 | 218.2 | 74.5 | 126.7 | 1 415.3 | 906.3 | 888.0 | 1 949.0 | 92.7 | Valeur |
| Produced: | | | | | | | | | | | | | | | Produite: |
| Quantity | 322.8 | 27.8 | 39.4 | 0.2 | 17.6 | 142.3 | — | 0.4 | — | 44.9 | — | 39.0 | 11.2 | — | Quantité |
| Value | 988.0 | 145.0 | 116.4 | 3.6 | 154.0 | 270.2 | — | 1.9 | — | 92.6 | 0.2 | 132.6 | 71.5 | — | Valeur |
| Sold: | | | | | | | | | | | | | | | Vendue: |
| Quantity | 122.2 | 11.5 | 7.9 | 0.4 | 5.6 | 40.3 | 0.9 | 1.6 | 0.4 | 4.6 | 12.0 | 4.8 | 32.2 | — | Quantité |
| Value | 625.3 | 95.9 | 51.3 | 4.5 | 32.5 | 92.1 | 8.5 | 13.3 | 2.3 | 14.6 | 64.0 | 13.5 | 232.4 | 0.4 | Valeur |
| Wood: | | | | | | | | | | | | | | | Bois: |
| Quantity | 2 510.3 | 531.7 | 77.7 | 32.0 | 837.5 | 370.9 | 15.4 | 20.7 | 9.0 | 70.8 | 260.5 | 20.1 | 253.7 | 10.3 | Quantité |
| Value | 2 583.2 | 661.4 | 98.1 | 35.5 | 477.9 | 484.1 | 21.5 | 28.2 | 15.4 | 91.8 | 291.6 | 27.9 | 340.8 | 9.0 | Valeur |
| Other fuels: [1] | | | | | | | | | | | | | | | Autres combustibles [1]: |
| Quantity | 1 964.1 | 57.6 | 6.8 | 2.2 | 150.4 | 1 619.9 | 0.1 | 0.1 | 17.3 | 63.4 | 8.1 | 17.4 | 20.8 | — | Quantité |
| Value | 7 819.2 | 239.4 | 27.0 | 8.8 | 596.5 | 6 410.1 | 0.6 | 0.4 | 68.6 | 256.5 | 39.2 | 69.4 | 102.4 | 0.3 | Valeur |

[1] Included in other fuels are steam, peat, charcoal and waste wooden containers, wood from wrecked buildings and similar items.
[2] Excluded from the data are consumption of electricity in the case of ISIC group 511, consumption of manufactured gas and steam in the case of ISIC groups 512-513 and consumption of all of these items in the case of ISIC major group 51.

[1] La vapeur, la tourbe, le charbon de bois, les caisses en bois démolies, les edifices en ruines, et les articles similaires sont compris dans autres combustibles.
[2] Sont exclues des données: la consommation d'électricité dans le cas du groupe 511 de la CITI, la consommation de gaz et de vapeur produits dans le cas des Groupes 512-513, et la consommation de tous ces articles dans le cas de la classe 51 de la CITI.

# FRANCE

## Gross Domestic Product and Gross Domestic Fixed Capital Formation

The data on the gross domestic product and gross domestic fixed capital formation were compiled from the response of the Institut national de la statistique et des études économiques, Paris to the United Nations national accounts questionnaire. The official estimates are published in the annual *Rapport sur les comptes de la nation,* Ministère des affaires économiques et financières, Service des études économiques et financières, Paris. The official estimates have been adjusted by the Institut national de la statistique et des études économiques to conform to the United Nations system of national accounts in so far as possible.

## Index Numbers of Industrial Production

The index numbers for 1949 and subsequent years that are set out in Table 2 are derived from those supplied by the Institut national de la statistique et des études économiques in *Etudes Statistiques,* the *Bulletin Mensuel de Statistique, Annuaire Statistique de la France,* and correspondence with the Statistical Office of the United Nations. It should be noted that the annual indexes shown in these tables for all industrial activity, excepting construction, and for manufacturing differ from the annual average of the monthly indexes for these categories that are set out in the publications of the Institut or in the *Monthly Bulletin of Statistics* of the Statistical Office of the United Nations because the manufacturing of food and beverages, clothing, and wood products and furniture is included in the former index numbers but not in the latter indexes. The indexes for earlier years were compiled from the *Supplément au Bulletin Hebdomadaire,* No. 429, of Saturday, 21 July 1956.

The series of index numbers relate, in principle, to all industrial units other than handicrafts. The indexes are base-weighted arithmetic averages of quantity relatives. The quantity relatives are, in most instances, derived from the output of individual products and, in a few cases, the consumption of individual raw materials or man-hours worked. The weights utilized in combining the index numbers for each detailed category of industrial activity, which are compiled from the gross-weighted quantity relatives, are contributions to the net domestic product at factor cost during 1952 for indexes for 1949 and subsequent years and during 1938 for 1948 and 1938.

The index numbers of volume of production for 1949 and subsequent years are described in *Etudes Statistiques* and the *Supplément Trimestriel du Bulletin Mensuel de*

## Produit intérieur brut et formation brute de capital fixe intérieur

Les données relatives au produit intérieur brut et à la formation brute de capital fixe intérieur ont été élaborées à partir de la réponse de l'Institut national de la statistique et des études économiques, Paris, au questionnaire de l'O.N.U. relatif aux comptes nationaux. Les estimations officielles sont publiées annuellement dans le *Rapport sur les comptes de la nation,* Ministère des affaires économiques et financières, Services des études économiques et financières, Paris. Ces estimations officielles ont été rajustées par les soins de l'Institut national de la statistique et des études économiques afin de les rendre aussi conformes que possible au système de comptes nationaux de l'O.N.U.

## Indices de la production industrielle

Les indices reproduits dans le tableau 2 pour 1949 et les années suivantes sont tirés des indices fournis par l'Institut national de la statistique et des études économiques, Paris, dans *Etudes Statistiques, Bulletin Mensuel de Statistique, Annuaire Statistique de la France,* et dans la correspondance de l'Institut avec le Bureau de statistique de l'O.N.U. On notera en l'occurrence que les indices annuels de toute l'activité industrielle — non compris le bâtiment et les travaux publics— et des industries manufacturières diffèrent de la moyenne annuelle des indices mensuels correspondants qui paraissent dans les publications de l'Institut ou dans le Bulletin Mensuel de Statistique du Bureau de Statistique de l'O.N.U., parce que les industries alimentaires, la fabrication des boissons, la fabrication des articles d'habillement et l'industrie du bois et du meuble sont comprises dans les indices reproduits ici et non dans les autres. Les indices relatifs aux années postérieures à 1949 ont été calculés d'après le *Supplément au Bulletin Hebdomadaire,* No. 429 du samedi 21 juillet 1956.

Les séries d'indices se rapportent, en principe, à toutes les unités industrielles autres que les unités artisanales. Ces indices sont des moyennes arithmétiques à pondération fixe de rapports quantitatifs. Les rapports quantitatifs sont le plus souvent tirés de la production de chaque marchandise et, dans certains cas, de la consommation de matière première ou du nombre d'heures de travail effectuées. Pour combiner les indices de chaque catégorie d'activité industrielle, qui sont construits d'après les rapports quantitatifs pondérés en fonction de la valeur brute de la production, on a pondéré par la contribution au produit intérieur net, au coût des facteurs, en 1952 pour les indices de 1949 et des années suivantes, et en 1938 pour les indices de 1948 et 1938.

Les indices du volume de la production pour 1949 et les années suivantes sont décrits dans *Etudes Statistiques* et dans le *Supplément Trimestriel du Bulletin Mensuel*

*Statistique*, No. 3, July-September 1958. For further details concerning the index numbers for earlier years see: *Bulletin de la Statistique Générale*, Supplement for January-March 1948, January-March 1949 and April-June 1950 of the Institut national de la statistique et des études économiques.

### Index Numbers of Industrial Employment

The index numbers shown in Table 3 are derived from index numbers of employment published in the *Bulletin mensuel de statistique* of the Institut national de la statistique et des études économiques. The series of index numbers relate to the average number of employees as of the end of each quarter of the year for industrial units with 10 or more employees. The count of employees covers all operatives and other employees 18 years of age or over, whether at work or temporarily absent.

The officially published index numbers are computed as base-weighted arithmetic averages in two stages. In the first step, index numbers for the various size groups of establishments in each detailed category of industrial activity are combined into indexes for the detailed categories. At the second stage, the resulting indexes are combined into indexes for broader categories of industrial activity. The weights utilized at each stage of compilation are derived from the average number of employees during the base year. The base year is 1954 for the indexes for 1954 and subsequent years and and 1938 for the indexes for 1953 and earlier years.

The index numbers shown in Table 3 for manufacturing as a whole and for industrial activity as a whole were calculated by the Statistical Office of the United Nations. The former series of indexes was computed from the officially published indexes for manufacturing and the petroleum industry. The latter series was compiled from the officially published indexes for mining, construction and electricity, gas and water and the indexes for manufacturing compiled by the Statistical Office of the United Nations. In each case, the weights utilized were based on data on employment from the 1954 Census of Population.

### Characteristics and Structure of Industrial Activity

Data from a register of private industrial and commercial establishments which were published in *Les établissements industriels et commerciaux en France en 1954* and *Les établissements industriels, artisanaux et commerciaux en France en 1958* by the Institut national de la statistique et des études économiques form the basis for the figures of Table 4. The register is maintained by the Institut in co-operation with several ministries of the Government from the administrative records of these organizations. The register relates to all establishments which are privately owned or operated. It should be noted that the figures of number of employees shown in the table may be understated since some five percent of the establishments included in the register did not indicate whether or not they had any employees.

*de Statistique*, No. 3, juillet-septembre 1958. Pour plus amples détails sur les indices des années antérieures voir: *Bulletin de la Statistique Générale*, Supplément pour janvier-mars 1949 et avril-juin 1950 de l'Institut national de la statistique et des études économiques.

### Indices de l'emploi industriel

Les indices de l'emploi reproduits au tableau 3 sont tirés des indices de l'emploi publiés dans le *Bulletin mensuel de statistique* de l'Institut national de la statistique et des études économiques. Les séries d'indices se rapportent au nombre moyen de salariés en fin de trimestre pour les unités industrielles de 10 salariés ou plus. Le nombre de salariés couvre tous les ouvriers et autres salariés de 18 ans ou plus, fussent-ils au travail ou temporairement absents.

Les indices publiés officiellement sont des moyennes arithmétiques à pondération fixe calculées en deux étapes. Au premier stade, les indices relatifs aux groupes de tailles différentes d'établissements dans chaque catégorie détaillée de l'activité industrielle ont été combinés pour donner les indices de catégories détaillées. Au second stade, les indices résultant sont combinés en indices pour des catégories plus larges de l'activité industrielle. Le nombre moyen de salariés durant l'année de base sert de coefficient de pondération pour le calcul de ces indices, l'année de base étant 1954 pour les indices de 1954 et des années suivantes, et 1938 pour 1953 et les années antérieures.

Les indices reproduits au tableau 3 pour l'ensemble des industries manufacturières et pour l'ensemble des activités industrielles ont été élaborés par le Bureau de Statistique de l'O.N.U. Les premières séries d'indices ont été calculées à partir des indices officiels publiés relatifs aux industries manufacturières et aux industries du pétrole. Les secondes séries ont été élaborées à partir des indices officiels publiés relatifs aux industries extractives, au bâtiment et travaux publics, à l'électricité, au gaz et eau, à partir des indices des industries manufacturières calculés par le Bureau de Statistique de l'O.N.U. Dans chaque cas, les coefficients de pondération utilisés sont basés sur les données sur l'emploi fournies par le recensement de 1954 de la population.

### Caractéristiques et structure de l'activité industrielle

Les chiffres du tableau 4 sont fondés sur des données tirées d'un répertoire *Les établissements industriels et commerciaux en France en 1954* et *Les établissements industriels, artisanaux et commerciaux en France en 1958*, publié par l'Institut national de la statistique et des études économiques. Ce répertoire est tenu par l'Institut en collaboration avec plusieurs ministères d'après la documentation administrative de ces organismes. Il porte sur tous les établissements du secteur privé. On notera que le nombre de salariés, dans les différents tableaux, peut être en dessous de la vérité, car quelque 5 pour cent des établissements inscrits au répertoire n'ont pas indiqué s'ils avaient ou non des salariés.

# FRANCE

The data on number of employees and wages and salaries shown in Table 5 for 1954 and 1958, are from *Etudes statistiques, supplément trimestriel du bulletin mensuel de statistique,* July-Sept., 1956 and Oct.-Dec., 1960. The figures are compiled by the Institut national de la statistique et des études économiques, from a sample of returns submitted each year to the Ministère des Finances by establishments with one or more employees. Covered are all such privately owned establishments and publicly or semi-publicly owned units engaged in practically all kinds of industrial activity. Except for the inclusion of pension payments in wages and salaries, the definition of the items of data shown in Table 5 correspond with the International Standards in Basic Industrial Statistics.

Les chiffres du tableau 5 concernant le nombre de salariés, les traitements et salaires pour 1954 et 1958, proviennent de *Etudes statistiques, supplément trimestriel du bulletin mensuel de statistique,* juillet-septembre 1956 et octobre-décembre 1960. Les chiffres sont élaborés par l'Institut national de la statistique et des études économiques à partir d'un échantillon de questionnaires remplis par les établissements occupant un salarié ou plus, et retournés au Ministère des Finances. Sont couverts, les établissements privés, les établissements publics ou semi-publics, engagés effectivement dans toutes les formes d'activité industrielle. A l'exclusion du paiement de pensions inclus dans les traitements et salaires, les définitions des rubriques reproduites au tableau 5 correspondent aux définitions types des Statistiques Industrielles de Base.

## 1. THE GROSS DOMESTIC PRODUCT AND GROSS DOMESTIC FIXED CAPITAL FORMATION
## LE PRODUIT INTERIEUR BRUT ET LA FORMATION BRUTE DE CAPITAL FIXE INTERIEUR

Thousand million new francs                                   Milliards de nouveaux francs

### A.  Expenditure on the Gross Domestic Product at Market Prices
### Dépenses relatives au produit intérieur brut aux prix du marché

| Item of data and year / Rubrique et année | Total | Consumption Consommation | | Gross Domestic Capital Formation Formation brute de capital intérieur | | Net exports of goods and services Exportations nettes de biens et de services | |
|---|---|---|---|---|---|---|---|
| | | Total | Government Etat | Total | Fixed Fixe | Exports less imports Exportations moins importations | Exports Exportations |
| *a. At Current Prices — Aux prix courants* | | | | | | | |
| **Absolute figures — Chiffres absolus** | | | | | | | |
| 1950 | 100.7 | 80.2 | 12.9 | 19.3 | 15.9 | 1.2 | 15.7 |
| 1951 | 123.6 | 100.5 | 16.7 | 23.3 | 20.8 | −0.2 | 20.4 |
| 1952 | 144.8 | 119.1 | 22.2 | 26.6 | 24.2 | −0.9 | 20.6 |
| 1953 | 151.1 | 125.2 | 23.7 | 25.4 | 24.1 | 0.5 | 20.8 |
| 1954 | 160.1 | 128.7 | 22.1 | 28.4 | 26.1 | 3.1 | 24.3 |
| 1955 | 171.3 | 136.3 | 22.2 | 31.6 | 29.9 | 3.4 | 25.6 |
| 1956 | 189.1 | 153.9 | 27.4 | 37.8 | 33.8 | −2.6 | 24.3 |
| 1957 | 211.5 | 171.4 | 31.1 | 43.6 | 39.8 | −3.4 | 26.6 |
| 1958 | 240.7 | 192.3 | 34.2 | 49.6 | 44.1 | −1.2 | 30.8 |
| 1959 | 261.1 | 208.6 | 38.9 | 48.5 | 46.2 | 4.0 | 37.4 |
| 1960 | 286.9 | 227.0 | 40.9 | 55.5 | 49.9 | 4.3 | 44.1 |
| 1961 | 310.1 | 247.9 | 45.0 | 58.0 | 55.1 | 4.1 | 46.7 |
| **Percentage distribution of average annual expenditure — Distribution en pourcentage des dépenses annuelles moyennes** | | | | | | | |
| 1950 – 1960 | 100.0 | 80.5 | 14.3 | 19.1 | 17.4 | 0.4 | 14.2 |
| 1950 | 100.0 | 79.6 | 12.8 | 19.2 | 15.8 | 1.2 | 15.6 |
| 1953 | 100.0 | 82.9 | 15.7 | 16.8 | 15.9 | 0.3 | 13.7 |
| 1954 | 100.0 | 80.4 | 13.8 | 17.7 | 16.3 | 1.9 | 15.2 |
| 1958 | 100.0 | 79.9 | 14.2 | 20.6 | 18.3 | −0.5 | 12.8 |
| 1960 | 100.0 | 79.1 | 14.3 | 19.4 | 17.4 | 1.5 | 15.4 |
| *b. At Prices of 1956 — Aux prix de 1956* | | | | | | | |
| **Absolute figures — Chiffres absolus** | | | | | | | |
| 1950 | 145.4 | 115.1 | 21.0 | 28.6 | 24.8 | 1.7 | 19.4 |
| 1951 | 154.2 | 123.5 | 22.2 | 28.7 | 26.2 | 2.0 | 22.1 |
| 1952 | 158.2 | 130.2 | 25.8 | 27.7 | 25.2 | 0.3 | 21.2 |
| 1953 | 162.7 | 135.5 | 26.6 | 26.5 | 25.4 | 0.7 | 21.4 |
| 1954 | 170.7 | 137.1 | 24.2 | 30.0 | 27.6 | 3.6 | 25.3 |
| 1955 | 180.2 | 143.4 | 24.1 | 32.9 | 31.1 | 3.9 | 26.8 |
| 1956 | 189.1 | 153.8 | 27.4 | 37.8 | 33.8 | −2.5 | 24.3 |
| 1957 | 200.3 | 162.1 | 28.8 | 41.1 | 37.2 | −2.9 | 25.6 |
| 1958 | 203.9 | 162.2 | 28.0 | 42.5 | 38.0 | −0.8 | 26.6 |
| 1959 | 208.8 | 165.8 | 29.2 | 40.0 | 38.2 | 2.9 | 30.4 |
| 1960 | 221.9 | 174.4 | 29.7 | 44.9 | 40.4 | 2.6 | 35.1 |
| 1961 | 231.6 | 183.6 | 31.1 | 45.8 | 43.6 | 2.2 | 37.0 |
| **Percentage distribution of average annual expenditure — Distribution en pourcentage des dépenses annuelles moyennes** | | | | | | | |
| 1950 – 1960 | 100.0 | 80.3 | 14.4 | 19.1 | 17.4 | 0.6 | 13.9 |
| 1950 | 100.0 | 79.1 | 14.4 | 19.7 | 17.0 | 1.2 | 13.3 |
| 1953 | 100.0 | 83.3 | 16.3 | 16.3 | 15.6 | 0.4 | 13.2 |
| 1954 | 100.0 | 80.3 | 14.2 | 17.6 | 16.2 | 2.1 | 14.8 |
| 1958 | 100.0 | 79.5 | 13.7 | 20.9 | 18.6 | −0.4 | 13.0 |
| 1960 | 100.0 | 78.6 | 13.4 | 20.3 | 18.2 | 1.1 | 15.8 |
| **Average annual rate of growth — Taux annuel moyen d'accroissement** | | | | | | | |
| 1950 – 1960 | 4.3 | 4.2 | 3.5 | 4.6 | 5.0 | . | 6.1 |
| 1950 – 1953 | 3.8 | 5.6 | 8.2 | −2.5 | 0.8 | . | 3.3 |
| 1954 – 1958 | 4.5 | 4.3 | 3.7 | 9.1 | 8.3 | . | 1.3 |
| 1958 – 1960 | 4.3 | 3.7 | 3.0 | 2.8 | 3.1 | . | 14.9 |

## B. The Gross Domestic Product at Market Prices According to Origin
### Origine par secteur d'activité du produit intérieur brut aux prix du marché

| Item of data and year / Rubrique et année | Total | Agricultural sector [1,2] / Secteur agricole [1,2] | Industrial Sector — Secteur Industriel | | | | | Transportation and communication / Transport et communication | Other sectors / Autres secteurs |
| --- | --- | --- | --- | --- | --- | --- | --- | --- | --- |
| | | | Total | Mining [3] / Industries extractives[3] | Manufacturing [1,2,3] / Industries manu-facturières [1,2,3] | Construction / Bâtiment et travaux publics | Electricity, gas and water / Electricité, gaz et eau | | |
| ISIC — CITI | 0–9 | 0 | 1–5 | 1 | 2–3 | 4 | 5 | 7 | 6, 8–9 |
| *a. At Current Prices — Aux prix courants* | | | | | | | | | |
| Absolute figures — Chiffres absolus | | | | | | | | | |
| 1950 | 100.8 | 14.8 | 47.7 | 2.2 | 38.6 | 5.6 | 1.3 | 5.5 | 32.8 |
| 1951 | 123.5 | 16.7 | 60.5 | 2.8 | 49.4 | 6.7 | 1.6 | 6.7 | 39.6 |
| 1952 | 144.8 | 18.3 | 69.5 | 3.4 | 55.2 | 8.8 | 2.1 | 8.5 | 48.5 |
| 1953 | 151.1 | 18.2 | 71.1 | 3.3 | 56.7 | 9.0 | 2.1 | 8.8 | 53.0 |
| 1954 | 160.1 | 19.1 | 74.6 | 3.5 | 58.9 | 9.9 | 2.3 | 9.2 | 57.2 |
| 1955 | 171.3 | 19.6 | 79.7 | 3.7 | 62.3 | 11.2 | 2.5 | 9.8 | 62.2 |
| 1956 | 189.1 | 19.3 | 90.1 | 3.9 | 70.9 | 12.6 | 2.7 | 10.6 | 69.1 |
| 1957 | 211.5 | 21.4 | 101.1 | 4.4 | 79.1 | 14.7 | 2.9 | 11.8 | 77.2 |
| 1958 | 240.7 | 26.1 | 113.3 | 5.0 | 89.1 | 15.7 | 3.5 | 13.7 | 87.6 |
| 1959 | 261.1 | 25.6 | 121.9 | 5.8 | 95.8 | 16.1 | 4.2 | 15.8 | 97.8 |
| 1960 | 286.9 | 28.6 | 132.3 | 6.2 | 105.2 | 16.3 | 4.6 | 16.9 | 109.1 |
| 1961 | 310.1 | 28.6 | 142.1 | 6.1 | 114.1 | 17.2 | 4.7 | 18.6 | 120.8 |
| Percentage distribution according to sector— Distribution en pourcentage par secteur | | | | | | | | | |
| 1950 – 1960 | 100.0 | 11.1 | 47.1 | 2.2 | 37.3 | 6.2 | 1.4 | 5.8 | 36.0 |
| 1950 | 100.0 | 14.7 | 47.3 | 2.1 | 38.3 | 5.6 | 1.3 | 5.5 | 32.5 |
| 1953 | 100.0 | 12.0 | 47.0 | 2.2 | 37.5 | 5.9 | 1.4 | 5.9 | 35.1 |
| 1954 | 100.0 | 11.9 | 46.7 | 2.2 | 36.8 | 6.2 | 1.5 | 5.8 | 35.6 |
| 1958 | 100.0 | 10.8 | 47.1 | 2.1 | 37.0 | 6.5 | 1.5 | 5.7 | 36.4 |
| 1960 | 100.0 | 9.9 | 46.1 | 2.2 | 36.6 | 5.7 | 1.6 | 5.9 | 38.1 |
| *b. At Prices of 1956 — Aux prix de 1956* | | | | | | | | | |
| Absolute figures— Chiffres absolus | | | | | | | | | |
| 1950 | 145.4 | 18.8 | 65.5 | 3.1 | 51.1 | 9.7 | 1.6 | 8.1 | 53.0 |
| 1951 | 154.2 | 18.3 | 71.2 | 3.3 | 55.9 | 10.1 | 1.9 | 8.8 | 55.9 |
| 1952 | 158.2 | 18.7 | 72.3 | 3.5 | 56.9 | 9.9 | 2.0 | 9.0 | 58.2 |
| 1953 | 162.7 | 20.1 | 74.0 | 3.4 | 58.5 | 10.0 | 2.1 | 8.8 | 59.8 |
| 1954 | 170.7 | 21.4 | 78.0 | 3.6 | 61.1 | 11.0 | 2.3 | 9.2 | 62.1 |
| 1955 | 180.2 | 21.4 | 83.2 | 3.8 | 64.8 | 12.2 | 2.4 | 9.9 | 65.7 |
| 1956 | 189.1 | 19.3 | 90.1 | 3.9 | 70.9 | 12.6 | 2.7 | 10.6 | 69.1 |
| 1957 | 200.3 | 20.9 | 95.2 | 4.1 | 75.0 | 13.2 | 2.9 | 11.5 | 72.7 |
| 1958 | 204.0 | 20.9 | 97.5 | 4.3 | 77.0 | 13.0 | 3.2 | 12.0 | 73.6 |
| 1959 | 208.8 | 22.1 | 99.5 | 4.5 | 78.4 | 13.3 | 3.3 | 12.3 | 74.9 |
| 1960 | 221.9 | 24.0 | 105.9 | 4.8 | 84.0 | 13.4 | 3.7 | 12.9 | 79.1 |
| 1961 | 231.6 | 23.5 | 110.9 | 4.9 | 88.2 | 13.9 | 3.9 | 13.7 | 83.5 |
| Percentage distribution according to sector— Distribution en pourcentage par secteur | | | | | | | | | |
| 1950 – 1960 | 100.0 | 11.3 | 46.7 | 2.1 | 36.8 | 6.4 | 1.4 | 5.7 | 36.3 |
| 1950 | 100.0 | 12.9 | 45.1 | 2.1 | 35.2 | 6.7 | 1.1 | 5.6 | 36.4 |
| 1953 | 100.0 | 12.3 | 45.5 | 2.1 | 35.9 | 6.2 | 1.3 | 5.4 | 36.8 |
| 1954 | 100.0 | 12.5 | 45.7 | 2.1 | 35.8 | 6.5 | 1.3 | 5.4 | 36.4 |
| 1958 | 100.0 | 10.2 | 47.8 | 2.1 | 37.8 | 6.4 | 1.5 | 5.9 | 36.1 |
| 1960 | 100.0 | 10.8 | 47.7 | 2.2 | 37.8 | 6.0 | 1.7 | 5.8 | 35.7 |
| Average annual rate of growth—Taux annuel moyen d'accroissement | | | | | | | | | |
| 1950 – 1960 | 4.3 | 2.5 | 4.9 | 4.5 | 5.1 | 3.2 | 8.5 | 4.8 | 4.1 |
| 1950 – 1953 | 3.8 | 2.2 | 4.1 | 3.3 | 4.6 | 1.1 | 8.1 | 2.8 | 4.2 |
| 1954 – 1958 | 4.6 | −0.6 | 5.7 | 4.7 | 5.9 | 4.2 | 9.0 | 6.7 | 4.4 |
| 1958 – 1960 | 4.3 | 7.3 | 4.2 | 6.3 | 4.4 | 1.5 | 7.2 | 3.8 | 3.7 |

For footnotes see end of table.

Pour les notes, voir au bas du tableau.

## C. Gross Domestic Fixed Capital Formation According to Purchasing Sector
## La formation brute de capital fixe intérieur par secteur d'acquisition

| Item of data and year<br>Rubrique et année | Total | Agricultural sector [1,2]<br><br>Secteur agricole [1,2] | Industrial sector — Secteur industriel | | | | Transportation and communication<br><br>Transport et communication | Other sectors<br><br>Autres secteurs |
|---|---|---|---|---|---|---|---|---|
| | | | Total | Mining [3]<br><br>Industries extractives [3] | Manufacturing and construction [1,2,3]<br><br>Industries manufacturières, bâtiment et travaux publiques [1,2,3] | Electricity, gas and water<br><br>Electricité, gaz et eau | | |
| ISIC — CITI | 0–9 | 0 | 1–5 | 1 | 2–3, 4 | 5 | 7 | 6, 8–9 |
| *a. At Current Prices — Aux prix courants* | | | | | | | | |
| Absolute figures — Chiffres absolus | | | | | | | | |
| 1950............ | 15.9 | ... | ... | ... | ... | ... | ... | ... |
| 1951............ | 20.8 | ... | ... | ... | ... | ... | ... | ... |
| 1952............ | 24.2 | ... | ... | ... | ... | ... | ... | ... |
| 1953............ | 24.1 | ... | ... | ... | ... | ... | ... | ... |
| 1954............ | 26.1 | ... | ... | ... | ... | ... | ... | ... |
| 1955............ | 29.9 | ... | ... | ... | ... | ... | ... | ... |
| 1956............ | 33.8 | 2.8 | 11.9 | 1.0 | 8.1 | 2.8 | 4.9 | 14.2 |
| 1957............ | 39.8 | 3.3 | 14.2 | 1.2 | 9.5 | 3.5 | 5.5 | 16.8 |
| 1958............ | 44.2 | 3.6 | 16.2 | 1.4 | 10.4 | 4.4 | 6.1 | 18.3 |
| 1959............ | 46.3 | 3.4 | 17.0 | 1.4 | 10.4 | 5.2 | 6.7 | 19.2 |
| 1960............ | 49.9 | 3.5 | 18.2 | 1.4 | 11.8 | 5.0 | 7.6 | 20.6 |
| 1961............ | 55.0 | 3.9 | 20.5 | 1.3 | 13.9 | 5.3 | 8.1 | 22.5 |
| Percentage distribution according to sector— Distribution en pourcentage par secteur | | | | | | | | |
| 1958............ | 100.0 | 8.0 | 36.6 | 3.1 | 23.6 | 9.9 | 13.8 | 41.6 |
| 1960............ | 100.0 | 7.0 | 36.3 | 2.7 | 23.7 | 9.9 | 15.3 | 41.4 |

[1] The production of wine is included in Agriculture rather than in Manufacturing.
[2] Fishing is included in Manufacturing instead of the Agricultural sector.
[3] Quarrying of building materials is included in Manufacturing rather than Mining.

[1] La production de vin est comprise dans le Secteur agricole plutôt que dans la branche des Industries manufacturières.
[2] La pêche est comprise dans la branche des Industries manufacturières au lieu d'être dans le Secteur agricole.
[3] L'extraction des matériaux de Construction est comprise dans la branche des Industries manufacturières plutôt que dans la branche des Industries extractives.

## 2. INDEX NUMBERS OF INDUSTRIAL PRODUCTION
## INDICES DE LA PRODUCTION INDUSTRIELLE

### A. The Divisions of Industrial Activity
### Les branches de l'activité industrielle

| Period<br>Période | All industrial activity excluding construction<br>Toutes industries à l'exclusion du bâtiment et des travaux publics | Mining [1]<br>Industries ex-tractives [1] | Manu-facturing [2]<br>Industries manu-facturières [2] | Construction<br>Bâtiment et travaux publics | Electricity and gas [3]<br>Electricité et gaz [3] |
|---|---|---|---|---|---|
| ISIC — CITI | 1–3, 511–512 | 1 | 2–3 | 4 | 511–512 |

a. Indexes — Indices (1958 = 100)

| | | | | | |
|---|---|---|---|---|---|
| 1938....... | 51 | 70 | 51 | 45 | 33 |
| 1948....... | 52 | 63 | 52 | 74 | 47 |
| 1949....... | – 57 – | – 74 – | – 56 – | – 74 – | – 50 – |
| 1950....... | 61 | 75 | 61 | 74 | 53 |
| 1951....... | 68 | 81 | 67 | 78 | 60 |
| 1952....... | 68 | 88 | 66 | 83 | 63 |
| 1953....... | 69 | 85 | 68 | 83 | 64 |
| 1954....... | 74 | 87 | 74 | 86 | 69 |
| 1955....... | 80 | 93 | 79 | 91 | 75 |
| 1956....... | 88 | 94 | 88 | 92 | 82 |
| 1957....... | 97 | 98 | 97 | 100 | 89 |
| 1958....... | 100 | 100 | 100 | 100 | 100 |
| 1959....... | 103 | 101 | 103 | 100 | 118 |
| 1960....... | 115 | 102 | 114 | 102 | 146 |
| 1961....... | 120 | 101 | 119 | 107 | 166 |

b. Average Annual Rate of Change — Taux annuel moyen de variation

| | | | | | |
|---|---|---|---|---|---|
| 1938 – 1960. | 3.8 | 1.7 | 3.7 | 3.8 | 7.0 |
| 1938 – 1948. | 0.2 | – 1.0 | 0.2 | 5.1 | 3.6 |
| 1950 – 1960. | 6.5 | 3.1 | 6.5 | 3.3 | 10.7 |
| 1948 – 1953. | 5.8 | 6.2 | 5.5 | 2.3 | 6.4 |
| 1954 – 1958. | 7.8 | 3.5 | 7.8 | 3.8 | 9.7 |
| 1958 – 1960. | 7.2 | 1.0 | 6.8 | 1.0 | 20.8 |

[1] Excludes production in ISIC major group 13 (Crude petroleum and natural gas).
[2] Includes the extraction of crude petroleum.
[3] Includes the extraction of natural gas.

[1] Non compris la classe 13 de la CITI (Pétrole brut et gaz naturel).
[2] Y compris l'extraction de pétrole brut.
[3] Y compris l'extraction de gaz naturel.

### B. The Major Groups of Mining
### Les classes de la branche Industries extractives

| Period<br>Période | All mining [1]<br>Toutes industries extractives [1] | Coal mining<br>Extraction du charbon | Metal mining<br>Extraction des minerais métalliques | Crude petro-leum and natural gas<br>Pétrole brut et gaz naturel | Other mining<br>Autres industries extractives |
|---|---|---|---|---|---|
| ISIC — CITI | 1 | 11 | 12 | 13 | 14–19 |

a. Indexes — Indices (1958 = 100)

| | | | | | |
|---|---|---|---|---|---|
| 1938....... | 70 | 79 | 53 | 4 | 48 |
| 1948....... | 63 | 75 | 40 | 9 | 46 |
| 1949....... | – 74 – | – 88 – | – 54 – | – 11 – | – 51 – |
| 1950....... | 75 | 88 | 52 | 14 | 55 |
| 1951....... | 81 | 91 | 61 | 23 | 64 |
| 1952....... | 88 | 95 | 70 | 26 | 77 |
| 1953....... | 85 | 90 | 72 | 25 | 77 |
| 1954....... | 87 | 93 | 73 | 32 | 78 |
| 1955....... | 93 | 95 | 84 | 48 | 89 |
| 1956....... | 94 | 95 | 87 | 68 | 94 |
| 1957....... | 98 | 98 | 96 | 83 | 100 |
| 1958....... | 100 | 100 | 100 | 100 | 100 |
| 1959....... | 101 | 99 | 102 | 168 | 105 |
| 1960....... | 102 | 97 | 112 | 251 | 108 |
| 1961....... | 101 | 91 | 112 | 318 | 118 |

b. Average Annual Rate of Change — Taux annuel moyen de variation

| | | | | | |
|---|---|---|---|---|---|
| 1938 – 1960. | 1.7 | 0.9 | 3.5 | 20.7 | 3.8 |
| 1938 – 1948. | – 1.0 | – 0.5 | – 2.8 | 8.4 | – 0.4 |
| 1950 – 1960. | 3.1 | 1.0 | 8.0 | 33.5 | 7.0 |
| 1948 – 1953. | 6.2 | 3.7 | 12.5 | 22.7 | 10.9 |
| 1954 – 1958. | 3.5 | 1.8 | 8.2 | 33.0 | 6.4 |
| 1958 – 1960. | 1.0 | – 1.5 | 5.8 | 58.4 | 3.9 |

[1] Although indexes for the extraction of crude petroleum and natural gas are shown separately in this table, the indexes presented for mining as a whole do not cover these activities.

[1] Bien que les indices concernant l'extraction du pétrole brut et du gaz naturel soient indiqués à part dans ce tableau, les indices relatifs à l'ensemble des industries extractives ne couvrent pas cette activité.

## C. The Major Groups of Manufacturing — Les classes de la branche Industries manufacturières

| Period<br>Période | Manu-facturing [1]<br>Industries manufac-turières [1] | Food, beverages and tobacco<br>Industries alimen-taires, boissons, tabac | Textiles | Clothing and made-up textiles<br>Articles d'habil-lement et ouvrages en tissu | Wood products and furniture<br>Bois et meubles | Paper and paper products<br>Papier et ouvrages en papier | Printing and publishing<br>Imprimerie et édition | Leather and leather products except wearing apparel<br>Cuir et articles en cuir, à l'exclu-sion des articles d'habil-lement | Rubber products<br>Ouvrages en caout-chouc | Chemicals and chemical, petroleum and coal products<br>Produits chi-miques et dérivés du pétrole et du charbon | Non-metallic mineral products<br>Produits minéraux non métal-liques | Basic metals<br>Métal-lurgie de base | Metal products<br>Ouvrages en métaux |
|---|---|---|---|---|---|---|---|---|---|---|---|---|---|
| ISIC — CITI | 2–3 | 20–22 | 23 | 243–244 | 25–26 | 27 | 28 | 29 | 30 | 31–32 | 33 | 34 | 35–38 |

### a. Indexes — Indices (1958 = 100)

| | | | | | | | | | | | | | |
|---|---|---|---|---|---|---|---|---|---|---|---|---|---|
| 1938............ | 51 | 82 | 85 | 89 | 51 | 52 | 51 | 115 | 38 | 32 | 46 | 45 | 32 |
| 1948............ | 52 | 64 | 78 | 84 | 60 | 52 | 48 | 100 | 51 | 41 | 60 | 50 | 42 |
| 1949............ | − 56 − | − 75 − | − 78 − | − 82 − | − 64 − | − 52 − | − 51 − | − 80 − | − 52 − | − 40 − | − 57 − | − 59 − | − 45 − |
| 1950............ | 61 | 83 | 88 | 90 | 66 | 59 | 50 | 92 | 58 | 45 | 58 | 57 | 49 |
| 1951............ | 67 | 84 | 89 | 95 | 70 | 69 | 61 | 90 | 68 | 54 | 68 | 68 | 57 |
| 1952............ | 66 | 78 | 83 | 87 | 70 | 56 | 58 | 94 | 65 | 51 | 65 | 71 | 60 |
| 1953............ | 68 | 85 | 86 | 88 | 71 | 64 | 58 | 94 | 66 | 55 | 64 | 63 | 60 |
| 1954............ | 74 | 85 | 92 | 94 | 76 | 74 | 68 | 101 | 74 | 63 | 71 | 72 | 66 |
| 1955............ | 79 | 90 | 88 | 90 | 80 | 81 | 77 | 97 | 80 | 73 | 78 | 84 | 74 |
| 1956............ | 88 | 91 | 95 | 95 | 84 | 88 | 90 | 97 | 88 | 80 | 85 | 89 | 87 |
| 1957............ | 97 | 98 | 105 | 105 | 92 | 96 | 96 | 108 | 95 | 88 | 95 | 96 | 93 |
| 1958............ | 100 | 100 | 100 | 100 | 100 | 100 | 100 | 100 | 100 | 100 | 100 | 100 | 100 |
| 1959............ | 103 | 98 | 95 | 95 | 106 | 109 | 101 | 99 | 104 | 112 | 101 | 100 | 102 |
| 1960............ | 114 | 109 | 102 | 102 | 112 | 123 | 111 | 97 | 112 | 141 | 106 | 112 | 109 |
| 1961............ | 119 | 111 | 104 | 106 | 116 | 129 | 118 | 105 | 114 | 154 | 113 | 118 | 112 |

### b. Average Annual Rate of Change — Taux annuel moyen de variation

| | | | | | | | | | | | | | |
|---|---|---|---|---|---|---|---|---|---|---|---|---|---|
| 1938–1960........ | 3.7 | 1.3 | 0.8 | 0.6 | 3.6 | 4.0 | 3.6 | −0.8 | 5.0 | 7.0 | 3.9 | 4.2 | 5.7 |
| 1938–1948........ | 0.2 | −2.4 | −0.9 | −0.6 | 1.6 | 0.0 | −0.6 | −1.4 | 3.0 | 2.5 | 2.7 | 1.1 | 2.8 |
| 1950–1960........ | 6.5 | 2.8 | 1.5 | 1.3 | 5.4 | 7.6 | 8.3 | 0.5 | 6.8 | 12.1 | 6.2 | 7.0 | 8.3 |
| 1948–1953........ | 5.5 | 5.8 | 2.0 | 0.9 | 3.4 | 4.2 | 3.9 | −1.2 | 5.3 | 6.0 | 1.3 | 4.7 | 7.4 |
| 1954–1958........ | 7.8 | 4.1 | 2.1 | 1.6 | 7.1 | 7.8 | 10.1 | −0.3 | 7.8 | 12.2 | 8.9 | 8.6 | 10.9 |
| 1958–1960........ | 6.8 | 4.4 | 1.0 | 1.0 | 5.8 | 10.9 | 5.4 | −1.5 | 5.8 | 18.7 | 3.0 | 5.8 | 4.4 |

[1] Although the extraction of petroleum is not included in the indexes set out in this table for ISIC major groups 31-32 (Chemicals and chemical, petroleum and coal products), the indexes for manufacturing as a whole include this activity.

[1] Bien que l'extraction du pétrole ne soit pas incluse dans les indices concernant les classes 31 et 32 de la CITI (Industrie chimique et Industrie des dérivés du pétrole et du charbon), les indices de l'ensemble des industries manufacturières comprennent ces activités.

## 3. INDEX NUMBERS OF INDUSTRIAL EMPLOYMENT — INDICES DE L'EMPLOI INDUSTRIEL

### A. The Divisions of Industrial Activity
### Les branches de l'activité industrielle

| Period<br>Période | Total | Mining [1]<br>Industries extractives [1] | Manu-facturing [1]<br>Industries manu-facturières [1] | Construction<br>Bâtiment et travaux publics | Electricity, gas and water [2]<br>Electricité, gaz et eau [2] |
|---|---|---|---|---|---|
| ISIC — CITI | 1–4, 511–521 | 1 | 2–3 | 4 | 511–521 |

*a. Indexes — Indices (1958 = 100)*

| | | | | | |
|---|---|---|---|---|---|
| 1938....... | 80 | 107 | 84 | 57 | 91 |
| 1948....... | 88 [3] | 134 | 90 | 68 | ... |
| 1949....... | 90 | 126 | 92 | 74 | 97 |
| 1950....... | 91 | 120 | 93 | 76 | 99 |
| 1951....... | 94 | 116 | 96 | 81 | 100 |
| 1952....... | 95 | 114 | 96 | 85 | 100 |
| 1953....... | 95 | 110 | 94 | 94 | 99 |
| 1954....... | −94− | −107− | −94− | −93− | −98− |
| 1955....... | 96 | 104 | 95 | 97 | 97 |
| 1956....... | 97 | 101 | 96 | 99 | 97 |
| 1957....... | 100 | 101 | 99 | 102 | 98 |
| 1958....... | 100 | 100 | 100 | 100 | 100 |
| 1959....... | 98 | 98 | 98 | 99 | 102 |
| 1960....... | 98 | 94 | 99 | 98 | 102 |
| 1961....... | 99 | 89 | 100 | 99 | 102 |

*b. Average Annual Rate of Change — Taux annuel moyen de variation*

| | | | | | |
|---|---|---|---|---|---|
| 1938 – 1960. | 0.9 | −0.6 | 0.7 | 2.5 | 0.5 |
| 1938 – 1948. | 1.0 | 2.3 | 0.7 | 1.8 | ... |
| 1950 – 1960. | 0.7 | −2.4 | 0.6 | 2.6 | 0.3 |
| 1948 – 1953. | 1.6 | −3.9 | 0.9 | 6.7 | ... |
| 1954 – 1958. | 1.6 | −1.7 | 1.6 | 1.8 | 0.5 |
| 1958 – 1960. | −1.0 | −3.0 | −0.5 | −1.0 | 1.0 |

[1] Extraction of petroleum and natural gas (ISIC major group 13) is in Manufacturing (ISIC Divisions 2–3) instead of Mining (ISIC Division 1).
[2] Electricity consists of urban distribution only.
[3] Excludes electricity and gas in 1948 only.

[1] L'extraction du pétrole et du gaz naturel (CITI classe 13) est comprise dans les Industries manu-facturières (CITI Branches 2–3) au lieu d'être dans les Industries extractives (CITI Branche 1).
[2] Dans l'électricité il n'est tenu compte que de la distribution urbaine.
[3] L'électricité et le gaz sont exclus pour 1948 seulement.

### B. The Major Groups of Mining
### Les classes de la branche Industries extractives

| Period<br>Période | All mining [1]<br>Toutes industries extractives [1] | Coal mining<br>Extraction du charbon | Metal and other mining<br>Extraction des minerais métalliques et autres industries extractives |
|---|---|---|---|
| ISIC — CITI | 1 | 11 | 12, 14–19 |

*a. Indexes — Indices (1958 = 100)*

| | | | |
|---|---|---|---|
| 1938............ | 107 | 110 | 99 |
| 1948............ | 134 | 145 | 107 |
| 1949............ | 126 | 133 | 108 |
| 1950............ | 120 | 125 | 108 |
| 1951............ | 116 | 119 | 108 |
| 1952............ | 114 | 117 | 107 |
| 1953............ | 110 | 112 | 105 |
| 1954............ | −107− | −108− | −106− |
| 1955............ | 104 | 104 | 105 |
| 1956............ | 101 | 101 | 103 |
| 1957............ | 101 | 101 | 102 |
| 1958............ | 100 | 100 | 100 |
| 1959............ | 98 | 98 | 97 |
| 1960............ | 94 | 93 | 95 |
| 1961............ | 89 | 87 | 92 |

*b. Average Annual Rate of Change — Taux annuel moyen de variation*

| | | | |
|---|---|---|---|
| 1938 – 1960...... | −0.6 | −0.8 | −0.2 |
| 1938 – 1948...... | 2.3 | 2.8 | 0.8 |
| 1950 – 1960...... | −2.4 | −2.9 | −1.3 |
| 1948 – 1953...... | −3.9 | −5.0 | −0.4 |
| 1954 – 1958...... | −1.7 | −1.9 | −1.4 |
| 1958 – 1960...... | −3.0 | −3.6 | −2.5 |

[1] Excludes Extraction of petroleum and natural gas (ISIC major group 13).

[1] Non compris l'Extraction du pétrole et du gaz naturel (CITI classe 13).

## C. The Major Groups of Manufacturing — Les classes de la branche Industries manufacturières

| Period<br>Période | Manufacturing [1]<br>Industries manufacturières [1] | Food and beverages [2]<br>Industries alimentaires et boissons [2] | Textiles [3] | Clothing and made-up textiles [4]<br>Articles d'habillement et ouvrages en tissu [4] | Wood products and furniture [6]<br>Bois et meubles [6] | Paper and paper products<br>Papier et ouvrages en papier | Printing and publishing<br>Imprimerie et édition | Leather and leather products except wearing apparel [4]<br>Cuir et articles en cuir, à l'exclusion des articles d'habillement [4] | Chemicals and tobacco, rubber, chemical, petroleum and coal products [1,2,3]<br>Produits chimiques, tabac, ouvrages en caoutchouc, dérivés du pétrole et du charbon [1,2,3] | Non-metallic mineral products<br>Produits minéraux non métalliques | Basic metals [5]<br>Métallurgie de base [5] | Metal products [5,6]<br>Ouvrages en métaux [5,6] | Other manufacturing [6]<br>Autres industries manufacturières [6] |
|---|---|---|---|---|---|---|---|---|---|---|---|---|---|
| ISIC — CITI | 2–3 | 20–21 | 23 | 243–244 | 25–26 | 27 | 28 | 241, 29 | 22, 30, 31–32 | 33 | 34 | 35–38 | 39 |

**a. Indexes — Indices (1958 = 100)**

| Period | | | | | | | | | | | | | |
|---|---|---|---|---|---|---|---|---|---|---|---|---|---|
| 1938 | 84 | 74 | 120 | 107 | 87 | 89 | 97 | 114 | 74 | 84 | 85 | 70 | 84 |
| 1948 | 90 | 67 | 115 | 96 | 100 | 88 | 91 | 114 | 85 | 92 | 92 | 84 | 93 |
| 1949 | 92 | 72 | 119 | 96 | 100 | 87 | 89 | 111 | 86 | 93 | 97 | 86 | 93 |
| 1950 | 93 | 77 | 120 | 97 | 101 | 88 | 92 | 113 | 88 | 92 | 96 | 86 | 97 |
| 1951 | 96 | 82 | 121 | 103 | 104 | 93 | 93 | 112 | 93 | 96 | 97 | 89 | 99 |
| 1952 | 96 | 83 | 114 | 102 | 104 | 93 | 92 | 109 | 92 | 95 | 99 | 90 | 97 |
| 1953 | 94 | 84 | 110 | 103 | 98 | 92 | 92 | 108 | 91 | 93 | 95 | 87 | 95 |
| 1954 | –94– | –86– | –108– | –101– | –97– | –94– | –94– | –104– | –94– | –94– | –91– | –89– | –96– |
| 1955 | 95 | 88 | 103 | 97 | 97 | 94 | 96 | 102 | 96 | 96 | 93 | 92 | 97 |
| 1956 | 96 | 91 | 101 | 97 | 97 | 96 | 96 | 100 | 97 | 97 | 96 | 95 | 98 |
| 1957 | 99 | 96 | 103 | 100 | 99 | 98 | 99 | 102 | 98 | 99 | 98 | 98 | 101 |
| 1958 | 100 | 100 | 100 | 100 | 100 | 100 | 100 | 100 | 100 | 100 | 100 | 100 | 100 |
| 1959 | 98 | 103 | 94 | 95 | 96 | 100 | 100 | 96 | 100 | 98 | 99 | 98 | 94 |
| 1960 | 99 | 104 | 95 | 96 | 93 | 102 | 101 | 96 | 102 | 98 | 102 | 99 | 93 |
| 1961 | 100 | 104 | 94 | 96 | 92 | 104 | 103 | 95 | 104 | 98 | 104 | 101 | 94 |

**b. Average Annual Rate of Change — Taux annuel moyen de variation**

| Period | | | | | | | | | | | | | |
|---|---|---|---|---|---|---|---|---|---|---|---|---|---|
| 1938–1960 | 0.7 | 1.6 | −1.0 | −0.5 | 0.3 | 0.6 | 0.2 | — | 1.5 | 0.7 | 0.8 | 1.6 | 0.5 |
| 1938–1948 | 0.7 | −1.0 | −0.4 | −1.1 | 1.4 | −0.1 | −0.6 | 0.1 | 1.4 | 0.9 | 0.8 | 1.8 | 1.0 |
| 1950–1960 | 0.6 | 3.1 | −2.3 | −0.1 | −0.8 | 1.5 | 0.9 | −1.6 | 1.5 | 0.6 | 0.6 | 1.4 | −0.4 |
| 1948–1953 | 0.9 | 4.6 | −0.9 | 1.4 | −0.4 | 0.9 | 0.2 | −1.1 | 1.4 | 0.2 | 0.7 | 0.7 | 0.4 |
| 1954–1958 | 1.6 | 3.8 | −1.9 | −0.2 | 0.8 | 1.6 | 1.6 | −1.0 | 1.6 | 1.6 | 2.4 | 3.0 | 1.0 |
| 1958–1960 | −0.5 | 2.0 | −2.5 | −2.0 | −3.6 | 1.0 | 0.5 | −2.0 | 1.0 | −1.0 | 1.0 | −0.5 | −3.6 |

[1] Includes Extraction of petroleum and natural gas (ISIC major group 13).
[2] Tobacco manufactures (ISIC major group 22) are in Chemicals and chemical products (ISIC major group 31), but manufacturing of soap and stearines (part of ISIC group 319) is in Food and beverages (ISIC major groups 20–21).
[3] The manufacture of synthetic fibres (part of ISIC group 311) is in textiles (ISIC major group 23).
[4] Footwear (ISIC group 241) is included with Leather and leather products (ISIC major group 29).
[5] Foundries and certain other primary working of refined metals are in Metal Products (ISIC major groups 35–38) instead of Basic metals (ISIC major group 34).
[6] Measuring instruments, optical glass and watches are in Metal products (ISIC major groups 35–38) instead of Other manufacturing (ISIC major group 39). Basket, straw and cork products are also included in the latter group, rather than in Wood products and furniture (ISIC major groups 25–26).

[1] Y compris l'Extraction du pétrole et du gaz naturel (CITI classe 13).
[2] Les Industries du tabac (CITI classe 22) sont comprises dans les Industries chimiques (CITI classe 31) mais la fabrication des savons et stéarines (partie de CITI groupe 319) est comprise dans les Industries alimentaires et la fabrication de boissons (CITI classes 20–21).
[3] La fabrication de fibres synthétiques (dans CITI groupe 311) est comprise dans les Industries textiles (CITI classe 23).
[4] La fabrication de chaussures (CITI groupe 241) est comprise dans Cuir et ouvrages en cuir (CITI classe 29).
[5] Les fonderies et certains autres travaux préliminaires de métaux affinés sont compris dans Ouvrages en métaux (CITI classes 35–38) au lieu d'être dans Industries métallurgiques de base (CITI classe 34).
[6] Les instruments de mesure, les lunettes de vue et les montres sont compris dans Ouvrages en métaux (CITI classes 35–38) au lieu d'être dans Autres industries manufacturières (CITI classe 39); les paniers, les ouvrages en liège et en paille sont également compris dans la classe dernièrement mentionnée plutôt que dans Ouvrages en bois et meubles (CITI classes 25–26).

## 4. THE NUMBER OF AND EMPLOYMENT IN PRIVATELY OWNED OR OPERATED INDUSTRIAL ESTABLISHMENTS
## NOMBRE D'ETABLISSEMENTS ET EMPLOI DANS L'INDUSTRIE PRIVEE
### 1954, 1958

Number of establishments in units; number of employees in thousands.          Nombre d'établissements en unités; nombre de salariés en milliers.

### A.   The Divisions of Industrial Activity — Les branches de l'activité industrielle

| Year and item of data | All industrial activity [1] — Toutes industries [1] | Mining — Industries extractives | Manufactur-ing — Industries manufac-turières | Construction — Bâtiment et travaux publics | Electricity, gas and water [1] — Electricité, gaz et eau [1] | Année et rubrique |
|---|---|---|---|---|---|---|
| ISIC | 1–4;511–521 | 1 | 2–3 | 4 | 511–521 | CITI |
| **1954** Number of establishments (As of 30.VI.1954).......... | 874 635 | 10 248 | 628 510 | 231 312 | 4 565 | **1954** Nombre d'établissements (au 30.VI.1954) |
| Number of employees (As of 1.I.1954) [2]........... | 5 914.9 | 380.2 | 4 397.8 | 1 003.7 | 133.2 | Nombre de salariés (au 1.I.1954) [2] |
| **1958** Number of establishments (As of 2.VII.1958).......... | 836 804 | 10 505 | 579 099 | 241 966 | 5 234 | **1958** Nombre d'établissements (au 2.VII.1958) |

[1] ISIC groups 513 (Steam heat and power) and 521 (Water supply) are included.
[2] For seasonal industries, peak number of employees during 1953.

[1] Y compris les groupes 513 (Vapeur pour le chauffage et la force motrice) et 521 (Distribution publique de l'eau) de la CITI.
[2] Pour les industries saisonnières, période de pointe en 1953.

### B.   The Major Groups of Mining — Les classes de la branche Industries extractives

| Year and item of data | All mining — Toutes industries extractives | Coal mining — Extraction du charbon | Metal mining — Extraction des minerais métalliques | Crude petroleum and natural gas — Pétrole brut et gaz naturel | Other mining — Divers | Année et rubrique |
|---|---|---|---|---|---|---|
| ISIC | 1 | 11 | 12 | 13 | 14–19 | CITI |
| **1954** Number of establishments (As of 30.VI.1954).......... | 10 248 | 540 | 328 | 51 | 9 329 | **1954** Nombre d'établissements (au 30.VI.1954) |
| Number of employees (As of 1.I.1954) [1]........... | 380.2 | 258.3 | 37.7 | 3.4 | 80.8 | Nombre de salariés (au 1.I.1954) [1] |
| **1958** Number of establishments (As of 2.VII.1958).......... | 10 505 | 549 | 349 | 149 | 9 458 | **1958** Nombre d'établissements (au 2.VII.1958) |

[1] For seasonal industries, peak employment during 1953.          [1] Pour les industries saisonnières, période de pointe en 1953.

### C.   The Major Groups of Manufacturing — Les classes de la branche Industries manufacturières

| Year and item of data | Manu-facturing — Industries manufac-turières | Food, beverages and tobacco — Industries alimen-taires, boissons, tabac | Textiles | Clothing, footwear and made-up textiles — Articles d'habil-lement, chaussures et ouvrages en tissu | Wood products and furniture — Bois et meubles | Paper and paper products — Papier et ouvrages en papier | Printing and publish-ing — Im-primerie et édition | Leather and leather products except wearing apparel — Cuir et articles en cuir, à l'exclu-sion des articles d'habil-lement | Rubber products — Ouvrages en caout-chouc | Chemicals and chemical, petroleum and coal products — Produits chi-miques et dérivés du pétrole et du charbon | Non-metallic mineral products — Produits minéraux non métal-liques | Basic metals — Métal-lurgie de base | Metal products — Ouvrages en métaux | Other manu-factur-ing — Autres in-dustries manufac-turières | Année et rubrique |
|---|---|---|---|---|---|---|---|---|---|---|---|---|---|---|---|
| ISIC | 2–3 | 20–22 | 23 | 24 | 25–26 | 27 | 28 | 29 | 30 | 31–32 | 33 | 34 | 35–38 | 39 | CITI |
| **1954** Number of establishments (As of 30.VI.1954).... | 628 510 | 99 390 | 29 244 | 150 540 | 60 863 | 3 222 | 22 258 | 22 036 | 2 466 | 10 942 | 13 416 | 1 327 | 178 071 | 34 735 | **1954** Nombre d'établissements (au 30.VI.1954) |
| Number of employees (As of 1.I.1954) [1]..... | 4 397.8 | 406.3 | 640.7 | 427.9 | 206.7 | 98.7 | 143.9 | 79.6 | 60.8 | 308.8 | 181.5 | 277.0 | 1 388.0 | 177.9 | Nombre de salariés (au 1.I.1954) [1] |
| **1958** Number of establishments (As of 2.VII.1958).... | 579 099 | 94 410 | 25 996 | 127 841 | 57 708 | 3 241 | 23 485 | 18 987 | 2 189 | 10 385 | 13 913 | 1 361 | 165 871 | 33 712 | **1958** Nombre d'établissements (au 2.VII.1958) |

[1] For seasonal industries, peak number of employees during 1953.          [1] Pour les industries saisonnières, période de pointe en 1953.

## 5. NUMBER OF EMPLOYEES AND WAGES AND SALARIES PAID IN INDUSTRIAL ESTABLISHMENTS WITH ONE OR MORE EMPLOYEES

## NOMBRE DE SALARIES ET TRAITEMENTS ET SALAIRES, ETABLISSEMENTS INDUSTRIELS COMPTANT AU MOINS UN SALARIE

### 1954, 1958

Number of employees in thousands; wages and salaries in million new francs; wages and salaries per employee in thousand new francs.

Nombre de salariés en milliers; traitements et salaires en milliards de nouveaux francs; traitements et salaires par salarié en milliers de nouveaux francs.

### A. The Divisions of Industrial Activity

### Les branches de l'activité industrielle

| Year and item of data | Total | Mining [1]<br>Industries ex-tractives [1] | Manu-facturing [1]<br>Industries manufac-turières [1] | Con-struction<br>Bâtiment et travaux publics | Electricity, gas and water [2]<br>Electricité, gaz et eau [2] | Année et rubrique |
|---|---|---|---|---|---|---|
| ISIC | 1-4, 511-521 | 1 | 2-3 | 4 | 511-521 | CITI |
| a. Absolute Figures — Chiffres absolus | | | | | | |
| **1954**<br>Employees:<br>Number (As at 31.XII. 1954)..... | 5 700.0 | 386.6 | 4 195.7 | 991.5 | 126.2 | **1954**<br>Salariés:<br>Nombre (Au 31.XII. 1954) |
| Wages and salaries (During 1954).... | 23 288 | 1 865 | 17 385 | 3 290 | 748 | Traitements et salaires (En 1954) |
| Wages and salaries per employee.... | 4.1 | 4.8 | 4.1 | 3.3 | 5.9 | Traitements et salaires par salarié |
| **1958**<br>Employees:<br>Number (As at 31.XII.1958)..... | 6 308.7 | 386.7 | 4 608.2 | 1 182.7 | 131.1 | **1958**<br>Salariés:<br>Nombre (Au 31.XII.1958) |
| Wages and salaries (During 1958).... | 40 153 | 2 963 | 29 620 | 6 529 | 1 041 | Traitements et salaires (En 1958) |
| Wages and salaries per employee.... | 6.4 | 7.7 | 6.4 | 5.5 | 7.9 | Traitements et salaires par salarié |

[1] Manufacture of petroleum products (part of ISIC major group 32) is included in Mining (ISIC Division 1) instead of in Manufacturing (ISIC Division 2-3).
[2] Urban areas only.

[1] La fabrication de produits dérivés du pétrole (dans CITI classe 32) est comprise dans les Industries extractives (CITI branche 1) au lieu d'être dans les Industries manufacturières (CITI branches 2-3).
[2] Régions urbaines seulement.

### B. The Major Groups of Mining — Les classes de la branche Industries extractives

| Year and item of data | All mining [1]<br>Toutes industries extrac-tives [1] | Coal mining [2]<br>Extraction du charbon [2] | Metal mining<br>Extraction des minerais métal-liques | Crude petroleum and natural gas [1]<br>Pétrole brut et gaz naturel [1] | Other mining [2]<br>Divers [2] | Année et rubrique | Year and item of data | All mining [1]<br>Toutes industries extrac-tives [1] | Coal mining [2]<br>Extraction du charbon [2] | Metal mining<br>Extraction des minerais métal-liques | Crude petroleum and natural gas [1]<br>Pétrole brut et gaz naturel [1] | Other mining [2]<br>Divers [2] | Année et rubrique |
|---|---|---|---|---|---|---|---|---|---|---|---|---|---|
| ISIC | 1 | 11, 19 | 12 | 13 | 14 | CITI | ISIC | 1 | 11, 19 | 12 | 13 | 14 | CITI |
| a. Absolute Figures — Chiffres absolus | | | | | | | b. Structure | | | | | | |
| **1954**<br>Employees:<br>Number (As at 31.XII.1954).... | 386.6 | 252.7 | 54.5 | 32.0 | 47.4 | **1954**<br>Salariés:<br>Nombre (Au 31.XII.1954)<br>Traitements et salaires (En 1954) | **1954**<br>Distribution in per-cent of number of employees....... | 100.0 | 65.3 | 14.1 | 8.3 | 12.3 | **1954**<br>Distribution en pour-centage du nombre de salariés<br>Traitements et salaires par salarié |
| Wages and salaries (During 1954).... | 1 865 | 1 188 | 303 | 214 | 160 | | Wages and salaries per employee.... | 4.8 | 4.7 | 5.6 | 6.7 | 3.4 | |
| **1958**<br>Employees:<br>Number (As at 31.XII.1958).... | 386.7 | 250.6 | 49.3 | 40.5 | 46.3 | **1958**<br>Salariés<br>Nombre (Au 31.XII.1958)<br>Traitements et salaires (En 1958) | **1958**<br>Distribution in per-cent of number of employees....... | 100.0 | 64.8 | 12.7 | 10.5 | 12.0 | **1958**<br>Distribution en pour-centage du nombre de salariés<br>Traitements et salaires par salarié |
| Wages and salaries (During 1958).... | 2 963 | 1 819 | 463 | 426 | 255 | | Wages and salaries per employee.... | 7.7 | 7.2 | 9.4 | 10.5 | 5.5 | |

[1] Manufacture of petroleum products (part of ISIC major group 32), is included in Crude petroleum and natural gas (ISIC major group 13).
[2] Extraction of non-metallic minerals is included with Coal mining (ISIC major group 12) rather than Other mining (ISIC major groups 14-19).

[1] La fabrication des produits dérivés du pétrole (dans CITI classe 32) est comprise dans Pétrole brut et gaz naturel (CITI classe 13).
[2] L'extraction des minerais non métalliques est comprise dans Extraction du charbon (CITI classe 12) plutôt que dans Autres industries extractives (CITI classes 14-19).

# FRANCE

## C. The Major Groups of Manufacturing — Les classes de la branche Industries manufacturières

| Year and item of data | Manu-facturing [1]  Industries manufac-turières [1] | Food, beverages and tobacco [2]  Industries alimen-taires, boissons, tabac [2] | Textiles  Textiles | Clothing, footwear and made-up textiles  Articles d'habil-lement, chaussures et ouvrages en tissu | Wood products and furniture  Bois et meubles | Paper and paper products  Papier et ouvrages en papier | Printing and publish-ing  Im-primerie et édition | Leather and leather products except wearing apparel  Cuir et articles en cuir, à l'exclu-sion des articles d'habil-lement | Rubber products [3]  Ouvrages en caout-chouc [3] | Chemicals and chemical, petroleum and coal products [1,2]  Produits chi-miques et dérivés du pétrole et du charbon [1,2] | Non-metallic mineral products [3]  Produits minéraux non métal-liques [3] | Basic metals  Métal-lurgie de base | Metal products  Ouvrages en métaux | Other manu-factur-ing  Autres in-dustries manufac-turières | Année et rubrique |
|---|---|---|---|---|---|---|---|---|---|---|---|---|---|---|---|
| ISIC | 2–3 | 20–22 | 23 | 24 | 25–26 | 27 | 28 | 29 | 30 | 31–32 | 33 | 34 | 35–38 | 39 | CITI |
| *a. Absolute figures — Chiffres absolus* | | | | | | | | | | | | | | | |
| 1954  Employees:  Number  (As at 31.XII.1954)... | 4 195.7 | 362.9 | 635.0 | 408.1 | 164.0 | 104.1 | 149.9 | 74.4 | 66.8 | 254.0 | 171.8 | 272.8 | 1 331.6 | 200.3 | 1954  Salariés:  Nombre  (Au 31.XII.1954) |
| Wages and salaries  (During 1954)........ | 17 385 | 1 348 | 2 146 | 1 072 | 512 | 424 | 757 | 223 | 289 | 1 332 | 684 | 1 268 | 6 521 | 809 | Traitements et salaires (En 1954) |
| 1958  Employees:  Number  (As at 31.XII.1958).... | 4 608.2 | 392.3 | 584.1 | 393.4 | 175.3 | 117.0 | 170.3 | 66.4 | 75.6 | 288.9 | 192.4 | 305.5 | 1 613.6 | 233.4 | 1958  Salariés:  Nombre  (Au 31.XII.1958) |
| Wages and salaries  During 1958)........ | 29 620 | 2 201 | 2 914 | 1 588 | 906 | 731 | 1 314 | 297 | 527 | 2 371 | 1 181 | 2 251 | 11 881 | 1 458 | Traitements et salaires (En 1958) |
| *b. Structure* | | | | | | | | | | | | | | | |
| 1954  Distribution in percent of number of employees.. | 100.0 | 8.6 | 15.1 | 9.8 | 3.9 | 2.5 | 3.5 | 1.8 | 1.6 | 6.0 | 4.1 | 6.5 | 31.8 | 4.8 | 1954  Distribution en pourcentage du nombre de salariés |
| Wages and salaries  per employee........ | 4.1 | 3.7 | 3.4 | 2.6 | 3.1 | 4.1 | 5.0 | 3.0 | 4.3 | 5.1 | 4.0 | 4.6 | 4.9 | 4.0 | Traitements et salaires par salarié |
| 1958  Distribution in percent of number of employees.. | 100.0 | 8.5 | 12.6 | 8.6 | 3.8 | 2.5 | 3.7 | 1.5 | 1.6 | 6.3 | 4.1 | 6.7 | 35.0 | 5.1 | 1958  Distribution en pourcentage du nombre de salariés |
| Wages and salaries  per employee........ | 6.4 | 5.6 | 5.0 | 4.0 | 5.2 | 6.2 | 7.7 | 4.5 | 7.0 | 8.2 | 6.1 | 7.4 | 7.4 | 6.2 | Traitements et salaires par salarié |

[1] Manufacture of petroleum products (part of ISIC major group 32) is excluded.
[2] Manufacture of matches are included in Food, beverages and tobacco (ISIC major groups 20–22) instead of Chemicals and chemical, petroleum and coal products (ISIC major groups 31–32).
[3] Asbestos products are included in Rubber products (ISIC major group 30) instead of Non-metallic minerals (ISIC major group 33).

[1] Non compris la fabrication de produits dérivés du pétrole (dans CITI classe 32).
[2] La fabrication des allumettes est comprise dans Industries alimentaires, fabrication de boissons et de tabac (CITI classes 20–22) au lieu d'être dans les Industries chimiques et industries des dérivés du pétrole et du charbon (CITI classe 31–32).
[3] Les produits en amiante sont compris dans Ouvrages en caoutchouc (CITI classe 30) au lieu d'être dans Minerais non métalliques (CITI classe 33).

# FORMER FRENCH EQUATORIAL AFRICA — ANCIENNE AFRIQUE-EQUATORIALE FRANÇAISE

### Gross Domestic Product

The data shown in the table below are abstracted from *Comptes économiques et modèles,* published by the Ministère de la Coopération, France, in April 1962. The figures shown in that publication were derived from estimates made by the statistical authorities of the former Federation of French Equatorial Africa. The figures for gross domestic product at factor cost, which is termed "Gross Domestic Production" in that publication, differs in certain respects from that for the gross domestic product at factor cost in the United Nations system of national accounts mainly in that wages and salaries paid by government and private non-profit organizations are excluded.

### Produit intérieur brut

Les données du tableau ci-dessous ont été tirées de *Comptes économiques et modèles,* publié par le Ministère de la Coopération, France, en avril 1962. Les chiffres reproduits ont été tirés d'estimations faites par le service de statistique de l'ancienne Fédération d'Afrique équatoriale française. Les chiffres relatifs au produit intérieur brut au coût des facteurs appelé "Production intérieure brute" dans cette publication diffèrent à certains égards de ceux donnant le produit intérieur brut au coût des facteurs tel qu'il est défini dans le système de comptabilité nationale de l'ONU; notamment, les traitements et salaires payés par les organismes d'Etat et les organisations privées à but non lucratif en sont exclus.

## THE GROSS DOMESTIC PRODUCT — LE PRODUIT INTERIEUR BRUT

### 1956

Billion Francs C.F.A.  Milliards de francs C.F.A.

### A. Expenditure on the Gross Domestic Product at Market Prices
### Dépenses relatives au produit intérieur brut aux prix du marché

| Item of data / Rubrique | Total | Consumption / Consommation | | Gross Domestic Capital Formation / Formation brute de capital intérieur | Net exports of goods and services / Exportations nettes de biens et de services | |
| --- | --- | --- | --- | --- | --- | --- |
| | | Total | Government [1] / Etat [1] | | Exports less imports / Exportations moins importations | Exports / Exportations |
| Absolute figures — Chiffres absolus............ | 95.0 | 88.3 | 10.3 | 12.3 | —5.6 | 15.0 |
| Percentage distribution — Distribution en pourcentage................................ | 100 | 93.0 | 10.8 | 12.9 | —5.9 | 15.8 |

For footnotes see end of table.  Pour les notes, voir au bas du tableau.

## B. The Gross Domestic Product According to Origin

### Origine par secteur d'activité du produit intérieur brut

| Item of data | Total | Agricultural sector<br><br>Secteur agricole | Mining, manufacturing, electricity, gas and water, and construction<br><br>Industries extractives, manufacturières, électricité, gaz et eau, et bâtiment et travaux publics | Commerce, transportation and communication, and other services<br><br>Commerce, transports et communications, et autres services | Government [1]<br><br>Etat [1] | Rubrique |
|---|---|---|---|---|---|---|
| ISIC | 0-9 | 0 | 1-5 | 61-64, 71-73, 83-9 | 81-82 | CITI |
| At market prices | | | | | | Aux prix du marché |
|   Absolute figures............... | 95.0 | 51.0 | 7.0 | 30.0 | 7.0 |   Chiffres absolus |
|   Percentage distribution........ | 100.0 | 53.7 | 7.4 | 31.5 | 7.4 |   Distribution en pourcentage |
| At factor cost | | | | | | Au coût des facteurs |
|   Absolute figures............... | 81.5 | 51.0 | 6.5 | 24.0 | . |   Chiffres absolus |
|   Percentage distribution........ | 100.0 | 62.6 | 8.0 | 29.4 | . |   Distribution en pourcentage |

[1] Includes public administrations and defense, government agencies and organizations furnishing educational, health and similar services, and private non-profit organizations furnishing services to households except private schools and hospitals. Excludes government enterprises.

[1] Y compris les administrations publiques et la défense nationale, et les services de l'Etat et organisations tels que l'enseignement, la santé et les autres services similaires, et les institutions privées à but non lucratif fournissant des services aux ménages à l'exclusion des écoles et hopitaux privés. Non compris les entreprises de l'Etat.

# FORMER FRENCH WEST AFRICA — ANCIENNE AFRIQUE-OCCIDENTALE FRANÇAISE

## Gross Domestic Product

The data shown in the table below are abstracted from *Comptés économiques et modèles,* published by the Ministère de la Coopération, France, in April 1962. The figures shown in that publication were derived from estimates made by the statistical authorities of the former Federation of French West Africa. The figures for gross domestic product at factor cost, which is termed "Gross Domestic Production" in that publication, differs in certain respects from that for the gross domestic product at factor cost in the United Nations system of national accounts, mainly in that wages and salaries paid by government and private non-profit organizations are excluded.

## Produit intérieur brut

Les données du tableau ci-dessous ont été tirées de *Comptes économiques et modèles,* publié par le Ministère de la Coopération, France, en avril 1962. Les chiffres reproduits ont été tirés d'estimations faites par le service de statistique de l'ancienne Fédération d'Afrique occidentale française. Les chiffres relatifs au produit intérieur brut au coût des facteurs appelé "Production intérieure brute" dans cette publication diffèrent à certains égards de ceux donnant le produit intérieur brut au coût des facteurs tel qu'il est défini dans le système de comptabilité nationale de l'ONU; notamment, les traitements et salaires payés par les organismes d'Etat et les organisations privées à but non lucratif en sont exclus.

## Characteristics and Structure of Manufacturing Activity

The data presented in Table 2 are derived from *Tableaux économiques, 1957,* Haut Commissariat de la République en Afrique-Occidentale française and other sources.

## Caractéristiques et structure de l'activité manufacturière

Les données du tableau 2 sont tirées de *Tableaux économiques,* 1957, Haut Commissariat de la République en Afrique Occidentale française, et de diverses autres sources.

## 1.  THE GROSS DOMESTIC PRODUCT ACCORDING TO ORIGIN
## ORIGINE PAR SECTEUR D'ACTIVITE DU PRODUIT INTERIEUR BRUT
### 1956

Billion Francs C.F.A. — Milliards de francs C.F.A.

| Item of data | Total | Agricultural sector<br><br>Secteur agricole | Mining, manufacturing, electricity, gas and water, and construction<br><br>Industries extractives, manufacturières, électricité, gaz et eau, et bâtiment et travaux publics | Commerce, transportation and communication, and other services<br><br>Commerce, transports et communications, et autres services | Government [1]<br><br>Etat [1] | Rubrique |
|---|---|---|---|---|---|---|
| ISIC | 0-9 | 0 | 1-5 | 61-64, 71-73, 83-9 | 81-82 | CITI |
| At market prices | | | | | | Aux prix du marché |
| Absolute figures............. | 460.5 | 266.4 | 39.5 | 112.5 | 42.1 | Chiffres absolus |
| Percentage distribution......... | 100.0 | 57.9 | 8.6 | 24.4 | 9.1 | Distribution en pourcentage |
| At factor cost | | | | | | Au coût des facteurs |
| Absolute figures............. | 382.8 | 266.0 | 35.5 | 81.3 | . | Chiffres absolus |
| Percentage distribution......... | 100.0 | 69.5 | 9.3 | 21.2 | . | Distribution en pourcentage |

[1] Includes public administration and defense, government agencies and organizations furnishing educational, health and similar services, and private non-profit organizations furnishing services to households except private schools and hospitals. Excludes government enterprises.

[1] Y compris les administrations publiques et la défense nationale, et les services de l'Etat et organisations tels que l'enseignement, la santé et les autres services similaires, et les institutions privées à but non lucratif fournissant des services aux ménages à l'exclusion des écoles et hopitaux privés. Non compris les entreprises de l'Etat.

## 2. THE CHARACTERISTICS OF MANUFACTURING ENTERPRISES HAVING FIXED ASSETS OF 30 MILLION FRANCS OR MORE, ACCORDING TO MAJOR GROUPS OF INDUSTRIAL ACTIVITY

### 31 December 1956

## CARACTERISTIQUES DES ENTREPRISES AYANT UN CAPITAL FIXE DE 30 MILLIONS DE FRANCS OU PLUS, PAR CLASSE D'INDUSTRIES MANUFACTURIERES

### 31 décembre 1956

Number of enterprises in units; number of employees in thousands; capacity of installed power equipment in thousand horsepower; and capacity of power equipment per employee in horsepower

Nombre d'entreprises en unités; nombre de salariés en milliers; puissance installée en milliers de chevaux-vapeur; puissance installée par salarié en chevaux-vapeur

| Item of data | Manufacturing [1] Industries manufacturières [1] | Food, beverages and tobacco Industries alimentaires, boissons, tabac | Textiles | Clothing, footwear and made-up textiles Articles d'habillement, chaussures et ouvrages en tissu | Wood products and furniture Bois et meubles | Paper and paper products Papier et ouvrages en papier | Printing and publishing Imprimerie et édition | Chemicals and chemical, petroleum and coal products Produits chimiques et dérivés du pétrole et du charbon | Non-metallic mineral products Produits minéraux non métalliques | Metal products Ouvrages en métaux | Rubrique |
|---|---|---|---|---|---|---|---|---|---|---|---|
| ISIC | 2–3 | 20–22 | 23 | 24 | 25–26 | 27 | 28 | 31–32 | 33 | 35–38 | CITI |
| *a. Absolute Figures — Chiffres absolus* | | | | | | | | | | | |
| Number of enterprises............ | 140 | 49 | 8 | 5 | 37 | 1 | 1 | 16 | 6 | 17 | Nombre d'entreprises |
| Number of employees............. | 14.4 | 6.6 | 1.5 | 0.4 | 2.4 | 0.3 | — | 0.9 | 0.5 | 1.8 | Nombre de salariés |
| Capacity of installed power equipment....................... | 28.2 | 18.6 | 2.4 | 0.3 | 0.3 | 0.1 | 0.4 | 1.7 | 3.2 | 1.2 | Puissance installée |
| *b. Structure* | | | | | | | | | | | |
| Distribution in percent of number of employees................. | 100.0 | 45.8 | 10.4 | 2.8 | 16.7 | 2.1 | — | 6.2 | 3.5 | 12.5 | Répartition en pourcentage du nombre de salariés |
| Capacity of installed power equipment per employee............. | 1.96 | 2.82 | 1.60 | 0.75 | 0.13 | 0.33 | 17.39 | 1.89 | 6.40 | 0.67 | Puissance installée par salarié |

[1] Enterprises engaged primarily in repairs, whether of automobiles or other items, are excluded.

[1] Non compris les entreprises s'occupant essentiellement de réparations, automobiles ou autres.

## GERMANY, Pre-War Territory, including the Saar
## ALLEMAGNE, territoire d'avant guerre, y compris la Sarre

A Census of Production for 1936, relating to the territory of the Weimar Republic plus the Saar and covering establishments engaging five or more persons, including important licensed handicraft units, and producing in 1936, is the source of the figures of Table 1. These data were published in 1939 by the Reichsamt für Wehrwirtschaftliche Planung, Berlin, in *Die Deutsche Industrie*. The figures of value added in these tables are priced at factor cost, ex-industrial establishment, and do not cover goods sold but not processed by the establishment. The data on number of engaged do not include homeworkers.

Les chiffres du tableau 1 sont tirés d'un recensement de la production, effectué en 1936, qui portait sur le territoire de la République de Weimar et de la Sarre et couvrait les établissements occupant au moins 5 personnes — y compris les grosses unités artisanales patentées — qui étaient en activité en 1936. Ces données ont été publiées en 1939 par le Reichsamt für Wehrwirtschaftliche Planung, Berlin dans *Die Deutsche Industrie*. Les chiffres de la valeur ajoutée, dans ces tableaux, sont évalués au coût des facteurs, départ établissement, et ne couvrent pas les marchandises revendues en l'état. Les données concernant le nombre de personnes occupées ne comprennent pas les travailleurs à domicile.

## 1. THE CHARACTERISTICS OF INDUSTRIAL ESTABLISHMENTS ENGAGING FIVE OR MORE PERSONS, PRE-WAR GERMANY, INCLUDING THE SAAR
## CARACTERISTIQUES DES ETABLISSEMENTS INDUSTRIELS OCCUPANT CINQ PERSONNES OU PLUS, ALLEMAGNE D'AVANT GUERRE, Y COMPRIS LA SARRE

### 1936

Value added and wages and salaries in million Reichsmarks; number of engaged and employees in thousands; and value added per person engaged in thousand Reichsmarks

Valeur ajoutée et traitements et salaires en millions de reichsmarks; nombre de personnes occupées et de salariés en milliers; valeur ajoutée par personne occupée en milliers de reichsmarks

### A. The Divisions of Industrial Activity — Les branches de l'activité industrielle

| Item of data | All industrial activity<br>Toutes industries | Mining<br>Industries extractives | Manufacturing<br>Industries manufacturières | Construction<br>Bâtiment et travaux publics | Electricity and gas<br>Electricité et gaz | Rubrique |
|---|---|---|---|---|---|---|
| ISIC | 1–4; 511–512 | 1 | 2–3 | 4 | 511–512 | CITI |
| *a. Absolute Figures — Chiffres absolus* | | | | | | |
| Value added.................... | 34 186.0 | 2 271.7 | 25 675.3 | 4 267.0 | 1 972.0 | Valeur ajoutée |
| Number of engaged (During VI.1936)............... | 7 950.2 | 657.1 | 5 909.3 | 1 220.0 | 163.8 | Nombre de personnes occupées (en VI.1936) |
| Number of employees (During VI.1936)............. | 7 794.9 | 652.8 | 5 786.8 | 1 192.0 | 163.3 | Nombre de salariés (en VI.1936) |
| Wages and salaries paid.......... | 13 261.5 | 1 291.5 | 10 352.7 | 1 192.0 | 425.3 | Traitements et salaires payés |
| *b. Structure* | | | | | | |
| Distribution in percent of: | | | | | | Répartition en pourcentage: |
| Value added.................... | 100.0 | 6.6 | 75.1 | 12.5 | 5.8 | De la valeur ajoutée |
| Number of engaged............. | 100.0 | 8.2 | 74.3 | 15.4 | 2.1 | Du nombre de personnes occupées |
| Value added per person engaged... | 4.3 | 3.4 | 4.3 | 3.5 | 12.0 | Valeur ajoutée par personne occupée |
| Value added per unit of wages and salaries.................... | 2.58 | 1.76 | 2.48 | 3.58 | 4.64 | Valeur ajoutée par unité de traitements et salaires |

## B. The Major Groups of Mining — Les classes de la branche Industries extractives

| Item of data | All mining<br>Toutes industries extractives | Coal mining<br>Extraction du charbon | Metal mining<br>Extraction des minerais métalliques | Crude petroleum and natural gas<br>Pétrole brut et gaz naturel | Other mining<br>Divers | Rubrique |
|---|---|---|---|---|---|---|
| ISIC | 1 | 11 | 12 | 13 | 14–19 | CITI |
| *a. Absolute Figures — Chiffres absolus* | | | | | | |
| Value added...................... | 2 271.7 | 1 614.5 | 52.9 | 39.1 | 565.2 | Valeur ajoutée |
| Number of engaged (VI.1936)................ | 657.1 | 447.8 | 34.3 | 3.7 | 171.3 | Nombre de personnes occupées (VI.1936) |
| Number of employees (VI.1936)................ | 652.8 | 447.8 | 34.3 | 3.7 | 167.0 | Nombre de salariés (VI.1936) |
| Wages and salaries paid............ | 1 291.5 | 971.1 | 59.9 | 7.7 | 252.8 | Traitements et salaires payés |
| *b. Structure* | | | | | | |
| Distribution in percent of: | | | | | | Répartition en pourcentage: |
| Value added.................. | 100.0 | 71.0 | 2.3 | 1.8 | 24.9 | De la valeur ajoutée |
| Number of engaged............. | 100.0 | 68.1 | 5.2 | 0.6 | 26.1 | Du nombre de personnes occupées |
| Value added per person engaged...... | 3.4 | 3.6 | 1.5 | 10.6 | 3.3 | Valeur ajoutée par personne occupée |
| Value added per unit of wages and salaries........................ | 1.76 | 1.66 | 0.88 | 5.08 | 2.24 | Valeur ajoutée par unité de traitements et salaires |

## C. The Major Groups of Manufacturing — Les classes de la branche Industries manufacturières

| Item of data | Manufacturing<br>Industries manufacturières | Food, beverages and tobacco<br>Industries alimentaires, boissons, tabac | Textiles | Clothing, footwear and made-up textiles<br>Articles d'habillement, chaussures et ouvrages en tissu | Wood products and furniture[1]<br>Bois et meubles[1] | Paper and paper products<br>Papier et ouvrages en papier | Printing and publishing<br>Imprimerie et édition | Leather and leather products except wearing apparel<br>Cuir et articles en cuir, à l'exclusion des articles d'habillement | Rubber products<br>Ouvrages en caoutchouc | Chemicals and chemical, petroleum and coal products<br>Produits chimiques et dérivés du pétrole et du charbon | Non-metallic mineral products<br>Produits minéraux non métalliques | Basic metals<br>Métallurgie de base | Metal products[1]<br>Ouvrages en métaux[1] | Other manufacturing<br>Autres industries manufacturières | Rubrique |
|---|---|---|---|---|---|---|---|---|---|---|---|---|---|---|---|
| ISIC | 2–3 | 20–22 | 23 | 24 | 25–26 | 27 | 28 | 29 | 30 | 31–32 | 33 | 34 | 35–38 | 39 | CITI |
| *a. Absolute Figures — Chiffres absolus* | | | | | | | | | | | | | | | |
| Value added......... | 25 675.3 | 3 399.6 | 2 673.6 | 1 052.2 | 1 004.4 | 742.0 | 721.0 | 348.8 | 242.1 | 3 241.9 | 1 355.1 | 2 421.0 | 7 893.7 | 579.9 | Valeur ajoutée |
| Number of engaged (VI.1936)........... | 5 909.3 | 595.5 | 876.3 | 339.9 | 351.4 | 184.4 | 199.1 | 85.8 | 52.4 | 415.2 | 423.1 | 450.0 | 1 762.1 | 174.1 | Nombre de personnes occupées (VI.1936) |
| Number of employees (VI.1936)........... | 5 786.8 | 577 5 | 862.5 | 326.2 | 345.9 | 181.6 | 194.2 | 82.1 | 52.2 | 408.7 | 414.4 | 447.9 | 1 738.6 | 155.0 | Nombre de salariés (VI.1936) |
| Wages and salaries paid.............. | 10 352.7 | 886.9 | 1 155.3 | 451.8 | 491.1 | 294.8 | 419.1 | 138.1 | 109.5 | 951.0 | 617.7 | 1 005.9 | 3 558.6 | 272.9 | Traitements et salaires payés |
| *b. Structure* | | | | | | | | | | | | | | | |
| Distribution in percent of: | | | | | | | | | | | | | | | Répartition en pourcentage: |
| Value added........ | 100.0 | 13.2 | 10.4 | 4.1 | 3.9 | 2.9 | 2.8 | 1.4 | 0.9 | 12.6 | 5.3 | 9.4 | 30.8 | 2.3 | De la valeur ajoutée |
| Number of engaged.. | 100.0 | 10.0 | 14.9 | 5.7 | 6.0 | 3.1 | 3.3 | 1.5 | 0.9 | 7.0 | 7.2 | 7.6 | 29.8 | 3.0 | Du nombre de personnes occupées |
| Value added per person engaged........... | 4.3 | 5.7 | 3.0 | 3.1 | 2.8 | 4.0 | 3.6 | 4.1 | 4.6 | 7.8 | 3.2 | 5.4 | 4.5 | 3.3 | Valeur ajoutée par personne occupée |
| Value added per unit of wages and salaries........... | 2.48 | 3.83 | 2.31 | 2.33 | 2.04 | 2.52 | 1.72 | 2.52 | 2.21 | 3.41 | 2.19 | 2.41 | 2.22 | 2.12 | Valeur ajoutée par unité de traitements et salaires |

[1] The manufacture of metal furniture is classified in Metal products (ISIC major groups 35–38) instead of Furniture (ISIC major group 26).

[1] La fabrication des meubles en métal est classée dans Ouvrages en métaux (CITI 35–38) et non dans Industrie du meuble (CITI 26).

## Net Material Product

The figures of the net material production classified according to kind of economic activity, shown in Table 1 were derived from the *Statistisches Jahrbuch der Deutschen Demokratischen Republik, 1962* issued by the State Central Statistical Office, East Berlin, and from a communication from the same office. The concepts and definitions utilized in compiling these data are those of the system of material product accounts, which differs, in a number of important respects, from the concepts and definitions of the United Nations system of national accounts.

## Index Numbers of Industrial Production

The index numbers set out in Table 2 are from series of indexes of industrial production compiled by the State Central Statistical Office and published in *Statistisches Jahrbuch der Deutschen Demokratischen Republik, 1962* and earlier issues or furnished to the Statistical Office of the United Nations through correspondence. The series of index numbers relate to the value of gross output at constant enterprise prices (i.e., ex-enterprise and excluding turnover and other indirect taxes) of all enterprises except licensed handicrafts which were principally engaged in mining, manufacturing, the production of electricity or gas or contract construction. Publicly-owned enterprises, co-operatives and privately-owned enterprises are all included.

The constant prices utilized in valuing gross output are the prices adopted for the Second Five-Year Plan in the case of the indexes for 1951 and thereafter and those adopted for the First Five-Year Plan in the case of the indexes for 1950 and earlier years. Most of the prices for the Second-Five Year Plan correspond to the actual enterprise prices charged by each enterprise as of 1 January 1955. The prices utilized in the First-Five Year Plan were established primarily from enterprise prices prevailing during 1944, for the most part, or during 1947-1948, in some instances.

In the case of mining, manufacturing or electricity or gas enterprises, the gross output dealt with in the series of indexes is the output of industrial products and services only. This output is restricted, in general, to products made by the enterprises on their own account and shipped to others, destined for such shipment, or utilized by the enterprises as capital goods or in capital repairs; goods processed or fabricated by the enterprises on the account of others; and repairs, installation and other industrial services rendered to others. Included, in addition, are changes in work-in-process in the case of enterprises engaged in industrial activities having a long production cycle; and the output and consumption in

## Produit matériel net

Les chiffres du tableau 1 relatifs au produit matériel net par type d'activité économique sont tirés du *Statistiches Jahrbuch der Deutschen Demokratischen Republik, 1962*, publié par l'Office statistique central d'Etat, Berlin-Est, ou ont été communiqués par cet office. Les concepts et définitions adoptés lors de l'élaboration des données sont ceux du système de comptabilité du produit matériel; ils différent à plus d'un égard des concepts et définitions utilisés dans le système de comptabilité nationale de l'ONU.

## Indices de la production industrielle

Les indices du tableau 2 ont été tirés de séries d'indices de la production industrielle établis par l'Office statistique central d'Etat et publiés dans *Statistisches Jahrbuch der Deutschen Demokratischen Republik, 1962* et dans les numéros précédents, ou communiqués par correspondance au Bureau de statistique de l'ONU. Les séries d'indices se rapportent à la valeur de la production brute en prix constants (c'est-à-dire, départ entreprise et non compris les impôts sur le chiffre d'affaires et autres impôts indirects) de toutes les entreprises, à l'exclusion des unités artisanales patentées dont l'activité principale relève des industries extractives, des industries manufacturières, de la production d'électricité et de gaz ou des travaux contractuels de construction. Les entreprises publiques, les entreprises privées et les coopératives sont toutes incluses.

Les prix constants utilisés pour évaluer la production brute sont les prix adoptés pour le deuxième plan quinquennal dans le cas des indices de 1951 et des années suivantes, et les prix adoptés pour le premier plan quinquennal dans le cas des indices de 1950 et des années antérieures. La plupart des prix adoptés pour le deuxième plan quinquennal correspondent aux prix effectifs de chaque entreprise au 1er janvier 1955. Les prix adoptés pour le premier plan quinquennal ont été établis essentiellement à partir des prix des entreprises en vigueur en 1944 et, dans certains cas, en 1947-1948.

Dans le cas des entreprises relevant des industries extractives et manufacturières, de l'électricité ou du gaz, la production brute utilisée pour établir les séries d'indices est la production de biens et services industriels seulement. Cette production se réduit, en général, aux produits fabriqués par l'entreprise par ses propres moyens et expédiés à des tiers, aux marchandises produites en vue de leur expédition, ou aux produits utilisés par les entreprises comme biens d'équipement ou destinés aux réparations considérées comme formation de capital, ainsi qu'aux produits préparés ou fabriqués à façon par les entreprises et aux réparations, installations et autres services industriels rendus à des tiers. Sont compris en

the same enterprise of coal, metal ores, pig iron, crude steel and fish catch in the case of the indexes for 1951 and thereafter. In the case of the indexes for 1950 and earlier years, a much larger number of intermediate industrial commodities were covered. In the case of enterprises principally engaged in contract construction, the gross output measured in the series of indexes relates to the work put in place on structures, harbors, roads and other forms of construction only.

The series of index numbers utilized for Table 2 are based on the classification of the data on gross output according to the main kind of activity of enterprises. The State Central Statistical Office also compiles a series of index numbers based on the classification of the data on gross output according to kind of industrial products. Both series of index numbers are compiled from complete data on the gross output of the enterprise included. The original comparison base of the series of index numbers is 1950 in the case of the indexes for 1951 and thereafter and 1936 in the case of the indexes for earlier years. The series of index numbers may be considered the equivalent of indices computed as base weighted arithmetic means of series of quantity relatives. In these elementary series of relatives, the quantity of gross output for each individual product during a period is compared to that during 1950 or 1936, respectively. The weighting utilized in combining the series of relatives into indexes for 1951 and thereafter is equivalent to the quantum of gross output during 1950 multiplied by the unit price for this gross output adopted in the Second Five-Year Plan. The weights in the case of the index numbers for 1950 and earlier years are equivalent to the product of the quantity of output for each industrial commodity during 1936 and the corresponding price adopted in the First-Five-Year Plan.

## Index Numbers of Industrial Employment

The index numbers in Table 3 are based on absolute figures of employment for all enterprises mainly engaged in mining, manufacturing, the production of electricity or gas or construction. Enterprises of all forms of legal organization—publicly-owned, co-operative and privately-owned—are covered in the figures. The absolute figures of employment relate to the average number of persons engaged in these enterprises during each month of the year; and the count of the number of persons engaged in defined similarly to that in the International Standards in Basic Industrial Statistics. The absolute figures of employment utilized in compiling the indexes were abstracted from various issues of *Statistisches Jahrbuch der Deutschen Demokratischen Republik.*

## Characteristics and Structure of Industrial Activity

The data set out in Tables 4 and 5 were compiled from data that the State Central Statistical Office, East Berlin, made available in *Statistisches Jahrbuch der*

outre, les variations enregistrées dans les travaux en cours des entreprises exerçant des activités industrielles ayant un long cycle de production, et, pour les indices de 1951 et des années suivantes, la production et la consommation dans les mêmes entreprises des produits suivants : charbon, minerais métalliques, fonte, acier brut et poisson pêché. Dans le cas des indices de 1950 et des années antérieures, on a inclus un plus grand nombre de produits industriels semi finis. Pour les entreprises qui effectuent principalement des travaux contractuels de construction, la production brute mesurée par les séries se rapporte aux travaux relatifs aux bâtiments, ports, routes et autres formes de construction seulement.

Les séries d'indices utilisées au tableau 2 sont fondées sur la classification des données relatives à la production suivant le principal type d'activité des entreprises. L'Office statistique central d'Etat établit également des séries d'indices fondées sur la classification des données concernant la production brute selon la nature du produit industriel. Les deux séries d'indices ont été construites à partir de données complètes sur la production brute des entreprises retenues. La base initiale de comparaison de la série d'indices est 1950 pour les indices de 1951 et des années suivantes, et 1936 pour les indices relatifs aux années antérieures. Les séries d'indices peuvent être considérées comme équivalant à des moyennes arithmétiques à pondération fixe de séries de rapports quantitatifs. Dans ces séries élémentaires de rapports, la production brute de chaque produit est comparée à celle de 1950 ou de 1936 respectivement. Pour combiner ces séries de rapports en indices relatifs à 1951 et aux années suivantes, on a pris comme base de pondération le produit du quantum de la production brute en 1950 par le prix unitaire correspondant adopté pour le deuxième plan quinquennal. Pour les indices de 1950 et des années antérieures, les coefficients de pondération utilisés sont les valeurs des quantités produites de chaque marchandise industrielle en 1936 aux prix adoptés pour le premier plan quinquennal.

## Indices de l'emploi dans l'industrie

Les indices du tableau 3 sont fondés sur les chiffres absolus de l'emploi dans toutes les entreprises dont l'activité principale relève des industries extractives, des industries manufacturières, de la production d'électricité ou de gaz ou du bâtiment et des travaux publics. Toutes les entreprises sont comprises, quelle que soit leur forme juridique — entreprises publiques, coopératives et entreprises privées. Les chiffres absolus de l'emploi représentent le nombre moyen de personnes occupées dans ces entreprises pendant chaque mois de l'année; le comptage du nombre de personnes occupées est défini conformément aux Normes internationales relatives aux statistiques industrielles de base. Les chiffres absolus de l'emploi utilisés pour le calcul des indices ont été tirés de différents numéros de *Statistisches Jahrbuch der Deutschen Demokratischen Republik.*

## Caractéristiques et structure de l'activité industrielle

Les données des tableaux 4 et 5 sont tirées de données que l'Office statistique central d'Etat, Berlin-Est, a publiées dans *Statistisches Jahrbuch der Deutschen Demo-*

*Deutschen Demokratischen Republik, 1958* and *1959* and in correspondence with the Statistical Office of the United Nations. Although the data of Table 4 relate, in principle, to industrial enterprises excepting licensed handicrafts, irrespective of size or type of ownership, figures of the Soviet-German Joint Stock Company, Wismut, and of enterprises managed by the Ministry of the Interior and the Office of Engineering of the Government are not covered in these data.

The data shown in Table 4 on the gross material product and in Table 5 on gross output are valued at current industry prices (*i.e.*, including turnover and other indirect taxes) and relate to all of the output of the enterprises covered, whether or not industrial in character. The figures of the number of persons engaged are defined as was indicated above in describing the index numbers of employment. The data on operatives in Table 4 relate to manual workers engaged in only the industrial activities of the enterprises covered. The scope of the figures of wages and salaries falls short of that recommended in the International Recommendations in Basic Industrial Statistics in that certain types of bonuses or dismissal payments are not included.

*kratischen Republik, 1958* et *1959* ou communiquées par correspondance au Bureau de statistique de l'ONU. Bien que les données du tableau 4 portent en principe sur toutes les entreprises industrielles, quelles que soient leur dimension ou leur forme juridique, à l'exclusion des unités artisanales patentées, elles ne couvrent cependant pas la Société anonyme germano-soviétique Wismut, ni les entreprises gérées par le Ministère de l'intérieur et la Direction du génie civil.

Les données du tableau 4 relatives au produit matériel net et celles du tableau 5 concernant la production brute ont été évaluées aux prix courants des industries (c'est-à-dire, y compris les impôts sur le chiffre d'affaires et autres impôts indirects) et se rapportent à la totalité de la production des entreprises considérées, qu'elle ait un caractère industriel ou non. Les chiffres relatifs au nombre de personnes occupées sont définis comme on l'a indiqué plus haut dans la description des indices de l'emploi. Les données du tableau 4 relatives aux ouvriers se rapportent aux travailleurs manuels affectés uniquement aux activités industrielles des entreprises retenues. Les chiffres relatifs aux traitements et salaires n'ont pas la portée recommandée dans les Recommandations internationales relatives aux statistiques industrielles de base en ce sens que certains types de primes ou d'indemnités de licenciement en sont exclus.

## 1. THE NET MATERIAL PRODUCT ACCORDING TO ORIGIN
## ORIGINE PAR SECTEUR D'ACTIVITE DU PRODUIT MATERIEL NET

Million Eastern D.M.          Millions de marks d'Allemagne orientale.

| Item of data and year<br>Rubrique et année | Total | Agricultural sector<br>Secteur agricole | Mining, manufacturing, electricity and gas<br>Industries extractives et manufacturières et électricité et gaz | Construction<br>Bâtiment et travaux publics | Transportation and communication<br>Transports et communications | Other sectors [1]<br>Autres secteurs [1] |
|---|---|---|---|---|---|---|
| ISIC — CITI | 0-4, 511-521, 61, 7, 841, 852 | 0 | 1-3, 511-513 | 4 | 7 | 521, 61, 841, 852 |
| *a. At Current Prices — Aux prix courants* | | | | | | |
| **Absolute figures — Chiffres absolus** | | | | | | |
| 1950............ | 30 291 | 4 589 | 16 969 | 1 518 | 1 835 | 5 380 |
| 1951............ | 36 934 | 4 659 | 21 210 | 2 118 | 2 169 | 6 778 |
| 1952............ | 42 181 | 5 472 | 24 521 | 2 338 | 2 403 | 7 447 |
| 1953............ | 44 419 | 5 134 | 25 617 | 2 539 | 2 851 | 8 278 |
| 1954............ | 48 328 | 5 875 | 30 566 | 2 625 | 2 920 | 6 342 |
| 1955............ | 52 552 | 6 455 | 33 549 | 3 057 | 3 000 | 6 491 |
| 1956............ | 54 713 | 6 095 | 35 256 | 3 386 | 3 119 | 6 857 |
| 1957............ | 58 504 | 7 280 | 37 204 | 3 805 | 3 296 | 6 919 |
| 1958............ | 64 899 | 8 355 | 42 897 | 3 778 | 3 405 | 6 464 |
| 1959............ | 70 428 | 8 541 | 47 834 | 4 457 | 3 460 | 6 136 |
| 1960............ | 73 641 | 8 672 | 50 703 | 4 640 | 3 560 | 6 066 |
| 1961............ | 76 678 | 8 381 | 53 836 | 4 928 | 3 693 | 5 840 |
| **Percentage distribution according to sector— Distribution en pourcentage par secteur** | | | | | | |
| 1950 – 1960..... | 100.0 | 12.3 | 63.5 | 5.9 | 5.6 | 12.7 |
| 1950............ | 100.0 | 15.1 | 56.0 | 5.0 | 6.1 | 17.8 |
| 1953............ | 100.0 | 11.6 | 57.7 | 5.7 | 6.4 | 18.6 |
| 1958............ | 100.0 | 12.9 | 66.1 | 5.8 | 5.2 | 10.0 |
| 1960............ | 100.0 | 11.8 | 68.9 | 6.3 | 4.8 | 8.2 |

[1] Includes publishing (part of ISIC major group 28).      Y compris l'édition (dans CITI classe 28)

## 2. INDEX NUMBERS OF INDUSTRIAL PRODUCTION — INDICES DE LA PRODUCTION INDUSTRIELLE

### A. The Divisions of Industrial Activity
### Les branches de l'activité industrielle

| Period<br>Période | Total excluding construction<br>Total à l'exclusion du bâtiment et des travaux publics | Mining [1]<br>Industries extractives [1] | Manu-facturing [1]<br>Industries manu-facturières [1] | Construction<br>Bâtiment et travaux publics | Electricity and gas<br>Electricité et gaz |
|---|---|---|---|---|---|
| ISIC — CITI | 1-3, 511-512 | 1 | 2–3 | 4 | 511-512 |

#### a. Indexes — Indices (1958 = 100)

| | | | | | |
|---|---|---|---|---|---|
| 1936....... | 38 | 42 | 37 | ... | 39 |
| 1948....... | 27 | 48 | 25 | ... | 53 |
| 1949....... | 33 | 54 | 31 | ... | 54 |
| 1950....... | 41 | 61 | 40 | 43 | 61 |
| 1951....... | −51− | −67− | −50− | −66− | −65− |
| 1952....... | 59 | 70 | 58 | 69 | 73 |
| 1953....... | 66 | 73 | 66 | 75 | 64 |
| 1954....... | 73 | 80 | 73 | 74 | 72 |
| 1955....... | 79 | 87 | 78 | 73 | 77 |
| 1956....... | 84 | 94 | 83 | 84 | 85 |
| 1957....... | 90 | 98 | 90 | 92 | 90 |
| 1958....... | 100 | 100 | 100 | 100 | 100 |
| 1959....... | 112 | 103 | 113 | 124 | 112 |
| 1960....... | 121 | 101 | 123 | 133 | 124 |
| 1961....... | 129 | 104 | 130 | 134 | 131 |

#### b. Average Annual Rate of Change — Taux annuel moyen de variation

| | | | | | |
|---|---|---|---|---|---|
| 1936 – 1960. | 4.9 | 3.7 | 5.1 | ... | 4.9 |
| 1936 – 1948. | −2.8 | 1.1 | −3.2 | ... | 2.6 |
| 1950 – 1960. | 11.4 | 5.2 | 11.9 | 11.9 | 7.4 |
| 1948 – 1953. | 19.6 | 8.7 | 21.4 | ... | 3.9 |
| 1954 – 1958. | 8.2 | 5.7 | 8.2 | 7.8 | 8.6 |
| 1958 – 1960. | 10.0 | 0.5 | 10.9 | 15.3 | 11.4 |

For footnotes see end of table.
Pour les notes, voir au bas du tableau.

## B. The Major Groups of Manufacturing — Les classes de la branche Industries manufacturières

| Period / Période | Manufacturing [1] / Industries manufacturières [1] | Food, beverages and tobacco [2] / Industries alimentaires, boissons, tabac [2] | Textiles | Clothing, footwear, leather and made-up textiles / Articles d'habillement, chaussures, cuir et ouvrages en tissu | Wood products and furniture [3] / Bois et meubles [3] | Paper and paper products [6] / Papier et ouvrages en papier [6] | Printing [1,6] / Imprimerie [1,6] | Chemicals and chemical, petroleum and rubber products [1,2,4] / Produits chimiques, dérivés du pétrole et ouvrages en caoutchouc [1,2,4] | Non-metallic mineral products [1,4] / Produits minéraux non métalliques [1,4] | Basic metals / Métallurgie de base | Metal products [5] / Ouvrages en métaux [5] | Other manufacturing [3,5] / Autres industries manufacturières [3,5] |
|---|---|---|---|---|---|---|---|---|---|---|---|---|
| ISIC — CITI | 14, 2-3 | 20–22 | 23 | 24-29 | 25–26 | 27 | 28 | 30–32 | 14, 33 | 34 | 35–38 | 39 |

### a. Indexes — Indices (1958 = 100)

| Period / Période | Manufacturing [1] | Food, beverages and tobacco [2] | Textiles | Clothing, footwear... | Wood products and furniture [3] | Paper and paper products [6] | Printing [1,6] | Chemicals... [1,2,4] | Non-metallic mineral products [1,4] | Basic metals | Metal products [5] | Other manufacturing [3,5] |
|---|---|---|---|---|---|---|---|---|---|---|---|---|
| 1936 | 37 | 48 | 48 | ... | 28 | 70 | 90 | 23 | 54 | 54 | 28 | 21 |
| 1948 | 25 | 25 | 31 | ... | 38 | 43 | 63 | 28 | 32 | 17 | 17 | 20 |
| 1949 | 31 | 30 | 35 | ... | 42 | 49 | 69 | 34 | 37 | 25 | 25 | 24 |
| 1950 | 40 | 38 | 47 | 43 | 50 | 63 | 77 | 41 | 48 | 32 | 34 | 38 |
| 1951 | −50− | −52− | −59− | −54− | −57− | −68− | −80− | −48− | −56− | −45− | −42− | −45− |
| 1952 | 58 | 63 | 64 | 61 | 62 | 75 | 85 | 56 | 62 | 56 | 52 | 50 |
| 1953 | 66 | 71 | 68 | 68 | 68 | 79 | 80 | 66 | 64 | 65 | 61 | 56 |
| 1954 | 73 | 76 | 79 | 75 | 74 | 79 | 83 | 72 | 69 | 74 | 68 | 63 |
| 1955 | 78 | 82 | 83 | 79 | 79 | 84 | 84 | 78 | 77 | 79 | 73 | 72 |
| 1956 | 83 | 86 | 86 | 76 | 83 | 87 | 88 | 84 | 82 | 85 | 80 | 76 |
| 1957 | 90 | 92 | 91 | 87 | 90 | 93 | 94 | 91 | 89 | 91 | 86 | 84 |
| 1958 | 100 | 100 | 100 | 100 | 100 | 100 | 100 | 100 | 100 | 100 | 100 | 100 |
| 1959 | 113 | 105 | 111 | 112 | 116 | 109 | 110 | 111 | 114 | 111 | 119 | 115 |
| 1960 | 123 | 114 | 116 | 116 | 128 | 114 | 118 | 119 | 124 | 123 | 131 | 123 |
| 1961 | 130 | 118 | 119 | 125 | 137 | 119 | 122 | 128 | 130 | 129 | 142 | 130 |

### b. Average Annual Rate of Change — Taux annuel moyen de variation

| Period / Période | Manufacturing [1] | Food, beverages and tobacco [2] | Textiles | Clothing, footwear... | Wood products and furniture [3] | Paper and paper products [6] | Printing [1,6] | Chemicals... [1,2,4] | Non-metallic mineral products [1,4] | Basic metals | Metal products [5] | Other manufacturing [3,5] |
|---|---|---|---|---|---|---|---|---|---|---|---|---|
| 1936–1960 | 5.1 | 3.7 | 3.7 | ... | 6.5 | 2.1 | 1.1 | 7.1 | 3.5 | 3.5 | 6.6 | 7.6 |
| 1936–1948 | −3.2 | −5.3 | −3.6 | ... | 2.6 | −4.0 | −2.9 | 1.7 | −4.3 | −9.2 | −4.1 | −0.4 |
| 1950–1960 | 11.9 | 11.6 | 9.5 | 10.4 | 9.9 | 6.1 | 4.4 | 11.2 | 10.0 | 14.4 | 14.4 | 12.5 |
| 1948–1953 | 21.4 | 23.2 | 17.0 | ... | 12.3 | 12.9 | 4.9 | 18.7 | 14.9 | 30.8 | 29.1 | 22.9 |
| 1954–1958 | 8.2 | 7.1 | 6.1 | 7.5 | 7.8 | 6.1 | 4.8 | 8.6 | 9.7 | 7.8 | 10.1 | 12.2 |
| 1958–1960 | 10.9 | 6.8 | 7.7 | 7.7 | 13.1 | 6.8 | 8.6 | 9.1 | 11.4 | 10.9 | 14.5 | 10.9 |

[1] Stone, clay and sand quarrying (ISIC major group 14) is included in Manufacturing (ISIC division 2-3) in Non-metallic mineral products (ISIC major group 33) whereas publishing (part of ISIC major group 28) is excluded, and coking and coal briquetting (part of ISIC major group 32) are included in Mining (ISIC division 1).
[2] The extraction of vegetable oil is covered in Food (ISIC major group 20) instead of in Chemicals and chemical products (ISIC major group 31).
[3] The production of musical instruments, toys, sporting goods and jewellery is covered in Wood products (ISIC major group 25) rather than in Miscellaneous manufacturing (ISIC major group 39).
[4] The manufacturing of asbestos products is covered in ISIC major groups 30-32 instead of in Non-metallic mineral products (ISIC major group 33).
[5] The production of office machinery is included in Other manufacturing (ISIC major group 39) instead of in Metal products (ISIC major groups 35-38).
[6] Bookbinding is included in Paper and paper products (ISIC major group 27) instead of in Printing (ISIC major group 28).

[1] L'Extraction de la pierre à bâtir, de l'argile et du sable (CITI classe 14) est comprise dans Industries manufacturières (CITI branches 2-3) sous Produits minéraux non métalliques (CITI classe 33), tandis que l'édition (dans CITI classe 28) est exclue; la fabrication du coke et des briquettes de charbon (dans CITI classe 32) est comprise dans Industries extractives (CITI branche 1).
[2] L'extraction des huiles végétales est comprise dans Industries alimentaires (CITI classe 20) et non dans Industrie chimique (CITI classe 31).
[3] La fabrication des instruments de musique, jouets, articles de sport et articles de bijouterie est comprise dans Ouvrages en bois (CITI classe 25) et non dans Industries manufacturières diverses (CITI classe 39).
[4] La fabrication des ouvrages en amiante est comprise dans les classes 30-32 de la CITI et non dans Produits minéraux non métalliques (CITI classe 33).
[5] La fabrication des machines de bureau est comprise dans Autres industries manufacturières (CITI classe 39) et non dans Ouvrages en métaux (CITI classes 35-38).
[6] La reliure est comprise dans Papier et ouvrages en papier (CITI classe 27) et non dans Imprimerie (CITI classe 28).

## 3. INDEX NUMBERS OF INDUSTRIAL EMPLOYMENT — INDICES DE L'EMPLOI DANS L'INDUSTRIE

### A. The Divisions of Industrial Activity
### Les branches de l'activité industrielle

| Period<br>Période | Total excluding construction<br>Total à l'exclusion du bâtiment et des travaux publics | Mining [1]<br>Industries extractives [1] | Manu-facturing [1]<br>Industries manu-facturières [1] | Construction<br>Bâtiment et travaux publics | Electricity and gas<br>Electricité et gaz |
|---|---|---|---|---|---|
| ISIC — CITI | 1-3, 511-512 | 1 | 2–3 | 4 | 511-512 |

*a.* Indexes — Indices (1958 = 100)

| | | | | | |
|---|---|---|---|---|---|
| 1950....... | 80 | 78 | 80 | ... | 80 |
| 1951....... | 86 | 83 | 86 | ... | 88 |
| 1952....... | 90 | 86 | 91 | ... | 90 |
| 1953....... | 93 | 89 | 93 | ... | 91 |
| 1954....... | 95 | 96 | 94 | ... | 97 |
| 1955....... | 95 | 95 | 95 | 96 | 96 |
| 1956....... | 95 | 96 | 94 | 94 | 96 |
| 1957....... | 98 | 98 | 98 | 100 | 99 |
| 1958....... | 100 | 100 | 100 | 100 | 100 |
| 1959....... | 103 | 101 | 103 | 109 | 102 |
| 1960....... | 103 | 93 | 104 | 111 | 106 |
| 1961....... | 102 | 91 | 103 | 108 | 107 |

*b.* Average Annual Rate of Change — Taux annuel moyen de variation

| | | | | | |
|---|---|---|---|---|---|
| 1950 – 1960. | 2.6 | 1.8 | 2.7 | ... | 2.9 |
| 1950 – 1953. | 5.1 | 4.5 | 5.1 | ... | 4.4 |
| 1954 – 1958. | 1.3 | 1.0 | 1.6 | ... | 0.8 |
| 1958 – 1960. | 1.5 | −3.6 | 2.0 | 5.4 | 3.0 |

For footnotes see end of table.

Pour les notes, voir au bas du tableau.

## B. The Major Groups of Manufacturing — Les classes de la branche Industries manufacturières

| Period / Période | Manufacturing [1] / Industries manufacturières [1] | Food, beverages and tobacco [2] / Industries alimentaires, boissons, tabac [2] | Textiles [7] | Clothing, footwear, leather and made-up textiles / Articles d'habillement, chaussures, cuir et ouvrages en tissu | Wood products and furniture [3] / Bois et meubles [3] | Paper and paper products [6] / Papier et ouvrages en papier [6] | Printing [1, 6] / Imprimerie [1, 6] | Chemicals and chemical, petroleum and rubber products [1,2,4,7] / Produits chimiques, dérivés du pétrole et ouvrages en caoutchouc [1,2,4,7] | Nonmetallic mineral products [1, 4] / Produits minéraux non métalliques [1, 4] | Basic metals / Métallurgie de base | Metal products [5] / Ouvrages en métaux [5] | Other manufacturing [3, 5] / Autres industries manufacturières [3, 5] |
|---|---|---|---|---|---|---|---|---|---|---|---|---|
| ISIC — CITI | 14, 2–3 | 20–22 | 23 | 24, 29 | 25–26 | 27 | 28 | 30–32 | 14, 33 | 34 | 35–38 | 39 |

### a. Indexes — Indices (1958 = 100)

| | | | | | | | | | | | | |
|---|---|---|---|---|---|---|---|---|---|---|---|---|
| 1950 | 80 | 82 | 91 | 72 | 96 | 93 | 124 | 78 | 85 | 74 | 72 | 73 |
| 1951 | 86 | 94 | 99 | 80 | 97 | 92 | 121 | 82 | 90 | 87 | 79 | 80 |
| 1952 | 91 | 104 | 97 | 82 | 94 | 94 | 122 | 86 | 91 | 100 | 86 | 83 |
| 1953 | 93 | 111 | 99 | 86 | 95 | 95 | 109 | 91 | 90 | 84 | 90 | 87 |
| 1954 | 94 | 111 | 101 | 89 | 94 | 92 | 108 | 94 | 94 | 90 | 91 | 91 |
| 1955 | 95 | 94 | 103 | 96 | 99 | 97 | 102 | 95 | 94 | 91 | 92 | 94 |
| 1956 | 94 | 94 | 100 | 91 | 98 | 96 | 102 | 96 | 96 | 92 | 92 | 94 |
| 1957 | 98 | 97 | 100 | 96 | 98 | 98 | 100 | 98 | 98 | 96 | 98 | 97 |
| 1958 | 100 | 100 | 100 | 100 | 100 | 100 | 100 | 100 | 100 | 100 | 100 | 100 |
| 1959 | 103 | 102 | 102 | 102 | 103 | 103 | 101 | 102 | 102 | 101 | 104 | 103 |
| 1960 | 104 | 104 | 101 | 101 | 102 | 102 | 99 | 104 | 102 | 120 | 104 | 102 |
| 1961 | 103 | 104 | 99 | 99 | 103 | 102 | 96 | 103 | 100 | 124 | 105 | 102 |

### b. Average Annual Rate of Change — Taux annuel moyen de variation

| | | | | | | | | | | | | |
|---|---|---|---|---|---|---|---|---|---|---|---|---|
| 1950 – 1960 | 2.7 | 2.4 | 1.0 | 3.4 | 0.6 | 0.9 | −2.2 | 2.9 | 1.8 | 5.0 | 3.7 | 3.4 |
| 1950 – 1953 | 5.1 | 10.6 | 2.9 | 6.1 | −0.3 | 0.7 | −4.2 | 5.3 | 1.9 | 4.3 | 7.7 | 6.0 |
| 1954 – 1958 | 1.6 | −2.6 | −0.2 | 3.0 | 1.6 | 2.1 | −1.9 | 1.6 | 1.6 | 2.7 | 2.4 | 2.4 |
| 1958 – 1960 | 2.0 | 2.0 | 0.5 | 0.5 | 1.6 | 1.0 | −0.5 | 2.0 | 1.0 | 9.5 | 2.0 | 1.0 |

[1] Stone, clay and sand quarrying (ISIC major group 14) is included in Manufacturing (ISIC division 2-3) in Non-metallic mineral products (ISIC major group 33) whereas publishing (part of ISIC major group 28) is excluded, and coking and coal briquetting (part of ISIC major group 32) are included in Mining (ISIC division 1).
[2] The extraction of vegetable oil is covered in Food (ISIC major group 20) instead of in Chemicals and chemical products (ISIC major group 31).
[3] The production of musical instruments, toys, sporting goods and jewelery is covered in Wood products (ISIC major group 25) rather than in Miscellaneous manufacturing (ISIC major group 39).
[4] The manufacturing of asbestos products is covered in ISIC major groups 30-32 instead of in Non-metallic mineral products (ISIC major group 33).
[5] The production of office machinery is included in Other manufacturing (ISIC major group 39) instead of in Metal products (ISIC major groups 35-38).
[6] Bookbinding is included in Paper and paper products (ISIC major group 27) instead of in Printing (ISIC major group 28).
[7] The manufacture of artificial fibers is included in Textiles (ISIC major group 28) instead of Chemicals and chemical products (ISIC major group 31).

[1] L'extraction de la pierre à bâtir, de l'argile et du sable (CITI classe 14) est comprise dans Industries manufacturières (CITI branches 2-3) sous Produits minéraux non métalliques (CITI classe 33), tandis que l'édition (dans CITI classe 28) est exclue; la fabrication du coke et des briquettes de charbon (dans CITI classe 32) est comprise dans Industries extractives (CITI branche 1).
[2] L'extraction des huiles végétales est comprise dans Industries alimentaires (CITI classe 20) et non dans Industrie chimique (CITI classe 31).
[3] La fabrication des instruments de musique, jouets, articles de sport et articles de bijouterie est comprise dans Ouvrages en bois (CITI classe 25) et non dans Industries manufacturières diverses (CITI classe 39).
[4] La fabrication des ouvrages en amiante est comprise dans les classes 30-32 de la CITI et non dans Produits minéraux non métalliques (CITI classe 33).
[5] La fabrication des machines de bureau est comprise dans Autres industries manufacturières (CITI classe 39) et non dans Ouvrages en métaux (CITI classes 35-38).
[6] La reliure est comprise dans Papier et ouvrages en papier (CITI classe 27) et non dans Imprimerie (CITI classe 28).
[7] La fabrication des fibres synthétiques est comprise dans Industrie textile (CITI classe 23) et non dans Industrie chimique (CITI classe 31).

## 4. THE CHARACTERISTICS OF ALL INDUSTRIAL ENTERPRISES EXCEPT LICENSED HANDICRAFT UNITS

### CARACTERISTIQUES DE TOUTES LES ENTREPRISES INDUSTRIELLES, A L'EXCLUSION DES UNITES ARTISANALES PATENTEES

**1958**

Number of enterprises in units; value added and wages and salaries paid in million Eastern D.M.; number of engaged and number of operatives in thousands; electricity consumed in million KWH; and electricity consumed per operative in thousand KWH.

Nombre d'entreprises en unités; valeur ajoutée et traitements et salaires en millions de marks d'Allemagne orientale; nombre de personnes occupées et d'ouvriers en milliers; électricité consommée en millions de kWh; électricité consommée par ouvrier en milliers de kWh.

## A. The Divisions of Industrial Activity, Publicly Owned, Co-operative and Privately Owned Enterprises

### Les branches de l'activité industrielle, entreprises publiques, coopératives et privées

| Item of data | All industrial activity [1] / Toutes industries [1] | Mining [1] / Industries extractives [1] | Manufacturing [1] / Industries manufacturières [1] | Construction / Bâtiment et travaux publics | Electricity and gas / Electricité et gaz | Rubrique |
|---|---|---|---|---|---|---|
| ISIC | 1–4, 511–512 | 1 | 2–3 | 4 | 511–512 | CITI |
| Number of enterprises (As of 31.XII) | 18 786 | 216 | 16 793 | 1 756 | 21 | Nombre d'entreprises (au 31.XII) |
| Gross material product | ... | 1 862 | 37 869 | ... | 905 | Produit matériel brut |
| Number of engaged (Average during the year) | 3 148.4 | 216.6 | 2 553.2 | 314.9 | 63.7 | Nombre de personnes occupées (moyenne pendant l'année) |
| Wages and salaries paid | 14 953.4 | 1 306.6 | 11 831.4 | 1 497.8 | 317.6 | Traitements et salaires payés |

For footnotes see end of table.                    Pour les notes, voir au bas du tableau.

## B. The Divisions of Industrial Activity, Publicly Owned and Co-operative Enterprises
### Les branches de l'activité industrielle, entreprises publiques et coopératives

| Item of data | All industrial activity [1] Toutes industries [1] | | | Mining [1] Industries extractives [1] | | | Manufacturing [1] Industries manufacturières [1] | | | Construction Bâtiment et travaux publics | | | Electricity and gas Electricité et gaz | | | Rubrique |
|---|---|---|---|---|---|---|---|---|---|---|---|---|---|---|---|---|
| | Total | Publicly owned Entreprises publiques | Co-operatives Coopératives | Total | Publicly owned Entreprises publiques | Co-operatives Coopératives | Total | Publicly owned Entreprises publiques | Co-operatives Coopératives | Total | Publicly owned Entreprises publiques | Co-operatives Coopératives | Total | Publicly owned Entreprises publiques | Co-operatives Coopératives | |
| ISIC | 1–4, 511–512 | | | 1 | | | 2–3 | | | 4 | | | 511–512 | | | CITI |
| Number of enterprises (As of 31.XII).... | 7 863 | 7 158 | 705 | 159 | 159 | — | 7 053 | 6 348 | 705 | 630 | 630 | — | 21 | 21 | — | Nombre d'entreprises (au 31.XII) |
| Number of engaged (Average during the year)..... | 2 766.1 | 2 734.3 | 31.8 | 215.9 | 215.9 | — | 2 222.5 | 2 190.7 | 31.8 | 264.0 | 264.0 | — | 63.7 | 63.7 | — | Nombre de personnes occupées (moyenne pendant l'année) |
| Wages and salaries paid.......... | 12 898.4 | ... | ... | 1 302.6 | ... | ... | 10 094.5 | ... | ... | 1 183.7 | 1 183.7 | — | 317.6 | 317.6 | — | Traitements et salaires payés |

For footnotes see end of table.                    Pour les notes, voir au bas du tableau.

## C. The Divisions of Industrial Activity, Privately Owned Enterprises — Les branches de l'activité industrielle, entreprises privées

| Item of data | All industrial activity [1] Toutes industries [1] | Mining [1] Industries extractives [1] | Manufacturing [1] Industries manufacturières [1] | Construction Bâtiment et travaux publics | Rubrique |
|---|---|---|---|---|---|
| ISIC | 1–4 | 1 | 2–3 | 4 | CITI |
| Number of enterprises (As of 31.XII)......................... | 10 923 | 57 | 9 740 | 1 126 | Nombre d'entreprises (au 31.XII) |
| Number of engaged (Average during the year)................. | 382.3 | 0.7 | 330.7 | 50.9 | Nombre de personnes occupées (moyenne pendant l'année) |
| Wages and salaries paid.................... | 2 055.0 | 4.0 | 1 736.9 | 314.1 | Traitements et salaires payés |

For footnotes see end of table.                    Pour les notes, voir au bas du tableau.

## D. The Major Groups of Mining, Publicly Owned Enterprises
### Les classes de la branche Industries extractives, entreprises publiques

| Item of data | All mining Toutes industries extractives | Coal mining [1] Extraction du charbon [1] | Metal mining Extraction des minerais métalliques | Other mining [1] Divers [1] | Rubrique |
|---|---|---|---|---|---|
| ISIC | 1 | 11 | 12 | 14–19 | CITI |
| Number of enterprises (As of 31.XII)................... | 159 | 60 | 15 | 84 | Nombre d'entreprises (au 31.XII) |
| Number of engaged (Average during the year)......... | 215.9 | 138.4 | 26.5 | 51.0 | Nombre de personnes occupées (moyenne pendant l'année) |
| Wages and salaries paid............ | 1 302.6 | 818.0 | 187.1 | 297.5 | Traitements et salaires payés |

For footnotes see end of table.                    Pour les notes, voir au bas du tableau.

## E.  The Major Groups of Manufacturing — Les classes de la branche Industries manufacturières

| Item of data | Manufacturing [1]  Industries manufacturières [1] | Food, beverages and tobacco [2]  Industries alimentaires, boissons, tabac [2] | Textiles [3] | Clothing, footwear, leather and made-up textiles  Articles d'habillement, chaussures, cuir et ouvrages en tissu | Wood products and furniture [4]  Bois et meubles [4] | Paper and paper products [7]  Papier et ouvrages en papier [7] | Printing [1,7]  Imprimerie [1,7] | Chemicals and chemical, petroleum and rubber products [1,2,3,5]  Produits chimiques, dérivés du pétrole et ouvrages en caoutchouc [1',2,3,5] | Non-metallic mineral products [1,5]  Produits minéraux non métalliques [1,5] | Basic metals  Métallurgie de base | Metal products [6]  Ouvrages en métaux [6] | Other manufacturing [4,6]  Autres industries manufacturières [4,6] | Rubrique |
|---|---|---|---|---|---|---|---|---|---|---|---|---|---|
| ISIC | 14, 2–3 | 20–22 | 23 | 24, 29 | 25–26 | 27 | 28 | 30–32 | 14, 33 | 34 | 35–38 | 39 | CITI |
| *a. All Enterprises — Toutes les entreprises* | | | | | | | | | | | | | |
| Number of enterprises (As of 31.XII) | 16 793 | 2 780 | 2 079 | 2 007 | 2 500 | 582 | 475 | 1 109 | 1 508 | 44 | 3 420 | 289 | Nombre d'entreprises (au 31.XII) |
| Gross material product | 37 869 | 11 316 | 4 443 | 2 305 | 1 334 | 577 | 366 | 4 834 | 1 309 | 891 | 9 520 | 974 | Produit matériel brut |
| Number of engaged (Average during year) | 2 553.2 | 207.7 | 357.3 | 191.1 | 150.9 | 61.9 | 41.3 | 251.0 | 160.8 | 90.5 | 943.2 | 97.5 | Nombre de personnes occupées (moyenne pour l'année) |
| Wages and salaries paid | 11 831.4 | 871.5 | 1 309.4 | 669.3 | 624.2 | 254.7 | 190.1 | 1 237.6 | 773.3 | 529.2 | 4 903.8 | 468.3 | Traitements et salaires payés |
| Number of operatives (Average during year) | 1 747.1 | 153.8 | 259.8 | 127.2 | 107.2 | 46.6 | 30.0 | 165.0 | 124.4 | 63.6 | 606.9 | 62.6 | Nombre d'ouvriers (moyenne pour l'année) |
| Electricity consumed | 18 469.3 | 709.8 | 1 130.9 | 106.2 | 205.7 | 804.6 | 48.3 | 11 155.6 | 584.4 | 2 070.1 | 1 541.0 | 112.7 | Electricité consommée |
| Distribution in percent of: | | | | | | | | | | | | | Distribution en pourcentage: |
| Gross material product | 100.0 | 29.9 | 11.7 | 6.1 | 3.5 | 1.5 | 1.0 | 12.8 | 3.4 | 2.4 | 25.1 | 2.6 | Produit matériel brut |
| Number of engaged | 100.0 | 8.1 | 14.0 | 7.5 | 5.9 | 2.4 | 1.6 | 9.8 | 6.3 | 3.6 | 37.0 | 3.8 | Nombre de personnes occupées |
| Per person engaged: | | | | | | | | | | | | | Par personne occupée: |
| Gross material product | 14.8 | 54.5 | 12.4 | 12.1 | 8.8 | 9.3 | 8.9 | 19.2 | 8.1 | 9.8 | 10.1 | 10.0 | Produit matériel brut |
| Electricity consumed | 7.2 | 3.4 | 3.2 | 0.6 | 1.4 | 13.0 | 1.2 | 44.4 | 3.6 | 22.9 | 1.6 | 1.2 | Electricité consommée |
| Operatives as a percentage of engaged | 68.4 | 74.0 | 72.7 | 66.6 | 71.0 | 75.3 | 72.6 | 65.7 | 77.4 | 70.3 | 64.3 | 64.2 | Ouvriers en pourcentage des personnes occupées |
| Electricity consumed per operative | 10.57 | 4.62 | 4.35 | 0.83 | 1.92 | 17.27 | 1.61 | 67.61 | 4.70 | 32.55 | 2.54 | 1.80 | Electricité consommée par ouvrier |
| *b. Publicly-Owned and Co-operative enterprises — Entreprises publiques et coopératives* | | | | | | | | | | | | | |
| Number of enterprises (As of 31.XII) | 7 053 | 1 638 | 588 | 524 | 748 | 198 | 212 | 475 | 789 | 37 | 1 712 | 132 | Nombre d'entreprises (au 31.XII) |
| Number of engaged (Average during year) | 2 222.5 | 176.4 | 295.6 | 131.6 | 102.5 | 47.3 | 34.0 | 230.7 | 140.2 | 90.3 | 881.5 | 92.4 | Nombre de personnes occupées (moyenne pour l'année) |
| Wages and salaries paid | 10 094.5 | 721.7 | 988.4 | 420.9 | 403.2 | 196.5 | 158.3 | 1 135.2 | 643.2 | 527.5 | 4 465.7 | 433.9 | Traitements et salaires payés |
| Operatives: Number | 1 339.2 | 120.7 | 189.5 | 77.5 | 64.2 | 34.1 | 23.8 | 147.5 | 58.6 | 63.3 | 503.4 | 56.6 | Ouvriers: Nombre |
| Wages and salaries paid | 6 541.4 | 512.9 | 720.3 | 298.1 | 294.7 | 147.6 | 117.9 | 740.7 | 299.6 | 387.5 | 2 751.0 | 271.1 | Traitements et salaires payés |
| Distribution in percent of number of engaged | 100.0 | 7.9 | 13.3 | 5.9 | 4.6 | 2.1 | 1.5 | 10.4 | 6.3 | 4.1 | 39.7 | 4.2 | Distribution en pourcentage du nombre de personnes occupées |
| Operatives as a percent of engaged | 60.2 | 68.4 | 64.1 | 58.9 | 62.6 | 72.1 | 70.0 | 63.9 | 41.8 | 70.1 | 57.1 | 61.2 | Ouvriers en pourcentage du nombre de personnes occupées |
| *Publicly owned enterprises:* | | | | | | | | | | | | | *Entreprises publiques:* |
| Number of enterprises (As of 31.XII) | 6 348 | 983 | 588 | 509 | 739 | 195 | 210 | 472 | 789 | 37 | 1 694 | 132 | Nombre d'entreprises (au 31.XII) |
| Number of engaged (Average during year) | 2 190.7 | 150.9 | 295.6 | 128.8 | 100.9 | 46.9 | 33.8 | 229.7 | 140.2 | 90.3 | 881.2 | 92.4 | Nombre de personnes occupées (moyenne pour l'année) |
| Distribution in percent of number of engaged | 100.0 | 6.9 | 13.5 | 5.9 | 4.6 | 2.2 | 1.5 | 10.5 | 6.4 | 4.1 | 40.2 | 4.2 | Distribution en pourcentage du nombre de personnes occupées |
| *Co-operatives:* | | | | | | | | | | | | | *Coopératives:* |
| Number of enterprises (As of 31.XII) | 705 | 655 | — | 15 | 9 | 3 | 2 | 3 | — | — | 18 | — | Nombre d'entreprises (au 31.XII) |
| Number of engaged (Average during year) | 31.8 | 25.5 | — | 2.8 | 1.6 | 0.4 | 0.2 | 1.0 | — | — | 0.3 | — | Nombre de personnes occupées (moyenne pour l'année) |
| Distribution in percent of number of engaged | 100.0 | 80.2 | — | 8.8 | 5.0 | 1.3 | 0.6 | 3.2 | — | — | 0.9 | — | Distribution en pourcentage du nombre de personnes occupées |

For footnotes see end of table.  Pour les notes, voir au bas du tableau.

## E. The Major Groups of Manufacturing (continued) — Les classes de la branche Industries manufacturières (suite)

| Item of data | Manufacturing [1]<br><br>Industries manufacturières [1] | Food, beverages and tobacco [2]<br><br>Industries alimentaires, boissons, tabac [2] | Textiles [3] | Clothing, footwear, leather and made-up textiles<br><br>Articles d'habillement, chaussures, cuir et ouvrages en tissu | Wood products and furniture [4]<br><br>Bois et meubles [4] | Paper and paper products [7]<br><br>Papier et ouvrages en papier [7] | Printing [1,7]<br><br>Imprimerie [1,7] | Chemicals and chemical, petroleum and rubber products [1,2,3,5]<br><br>Produits chimiques, dérivés du pétrole et ouvrages en caoutchouc [1,2,3,5] | Non-metallic mineral products [1,5]<br><br>Produits minéraux non métalliques [1,5] | Basic metals<br><br>Métallurgie de base | Metal products [6]<br><br>Ouvrages en métaux [6] | Other manufacturing [4,6]<br><br>Autres industries manufacturières [4,6] | Rubrique |
|---|---|---|---|---|---|---|---|---|---|---|---|---|---|
| ISIC | 14, 2–3 | 20–22 | 23 | 24, 29 | 25–26 | 27 | 28 | 30–32 | 14, 33 | 34 | 35–38 | 39 | CITI |
| | | | | | c. Privately-Owned Enterprises — Entreprises privées | | | | | | | | |
| Number of enterprises (As of 31.XII) | 9 740 | 1 142 | 1 491 | 1 483 | 1 752 | 384 | 263 | 634 | 719 | 7 | 1 708 | 157 | Nombre d'entreprises (au 31.XII) |
| Number of engaged (Average during year) | 330.7 | 31.3 | 61.7 | 59.5 | 48.4 | 14.6 | 7.3 | 20.3 | 20.6 | 0.2 | 61.7 | 5.1 | Nombre de personnes occupées (moyenne pour l'année) |
| Wages and salaries paid | 1 736.9 | 149.8 | 321.0 | 248.4 | 221.0 | 58.2 | 31.8 | 102.4 | 130.1 | 1.7 | 438.1 | 34.4 | Traitements et salaires payés |
| Distribution in percent of number of engaged | 100.0 | 9.5 | 18.7 | 18.0 | 14.6 | 4.4 | 2.2 | 6.1 | 6.2 | 0.1 | 18.7 | 1.5 | Distribution en pourcentage du nombre de personnes occupées |

[1] Stone, clay and sand quarrying (ISIC major group 14) is included in Manufacturing (ISIC division 2-3) in Non-metallic mineral products (ISIC major group 33) whereas publishing (part of ISIC major group 28) is excluded, and coking and coal briquetting (part of ISIC major group 32) is included in Mining (ISIC division 1).

[2] The extraction of vegetable oil is covered in Food (ISIC major group 20) instead of in Chemicals and chemical products (ISIC major group 31).

[3] The manufacturing of artificial textile fibres is included in Textiles (ISIC major group 23) instead of in Chemicals (ISIC major group 31).

[4] The production of musical instruments, toys, sporting goods and jewelery is covered in Wood products (ISIC major group 25) rather than in Other manufacturing (ISIC major group 39).

[5] The manufacturing of asbestos products is covered in ISIC major groups 30-32 instead of in Non-metallic mineral products (ISIC major group 33).

[6] The production of office machinery is included in Other manufacturing (ISIC major group 39) instead of in Metal products (ISIC major groups 35-38).

[7] Bookbinding is included in Paper and paper products (ISIC major group 27) instead of Printing (ISIC major group 28).

[1] L'extraction de la pierre à bâtir, de l'argile et du sable (CITI classe 14) est comprise dans Industries manufacturières (CITI branches 2-3) sous Produits minéraux non métalliques (CITI classe 33), tandis que l'édition (dans CITI classe 28) est exclue; la fabrication du coke et des briquettes de charbon (dans CITI classe 32) est comprise dans Industries extractives (CITI branche 1).

[2] L'extraction des huiles végétales est comprise dans Industries alimentaires (CITI 20) et non dans Industrie chimique (CITI classe 31).

[3] La fabrication des fibres textiles synthétiques est comprise dans Industrie textile (CITI classe 23) et non dans Industrie chimique (CITI classe 31).

[4] La fabrication des instruments de musique, jouets, articles de sport et articles de bijouterie est comprise dans Ouvrages en bois (CITI classe 25) et non dans Autres industries manufacturières (CITI classe 39).

[5] La fabrication des ouvrages en amiante est comprise dans les classes 30-32 de la CITI et non dans Produits minéraux non métalliques (CITI classe 33).

[6] La fabrication des machines de bureau est comprise dans Autres industries manufacturières (CITI classe 39) et non dans Ouvrages en métaux (CITI classes 35-38).

[7] La reliure est comprise dans Papier et ouvrages en papier (CITI classe 27) et non dans Imprimerie (CITI classe 28).

## 5. THE CHARACTERISTICS OF LICENSED HANDICRAFT ENTERPRISES
## CARACTERISTIQUES DES ENTREPRISES ARTISANALES PATENTEES
### 1958

Number of enterprises in units; gross value of output in million Eastern D.M. and number of engaged in thousands

Nombre d'entreprises en unités; valeur brute de la production en millions de marks d'Allemagne orientale; nombre de personnes occupées en milliers

### A. The Divisions of Industrial Activity — Les branches de l'activité industrielle

| Item of data | All industrial activity [1]  Toutes industries [1] | Mining [1]  Industries extractives [1] | Manufacturing [1]  Industries manufacturières [1] | Construction  Bâtiment et travaux publics | Rubrique |
|---|---|---|---|---|---|
| ISIC | 1–4, 511–512 | 1 | 2–3 | 4 | CITI |
| *a. All Enterprises — Toutes entreprises* | | | | | |
| Number of enterprises (As of 31.XII)......... | 189 727 | 20 | 161 248 | 28 459 | Nombre d'entreprises (au 31.XII) |
| Gross value of output..... | 8 282.2 | 0.7 | 6 671.4 | 1 610.1 | Valeur brute de la production |
| Number of engaged (As of 31.XII)......... | 665.4 | 0.1 | 516.5 | 148.8 | Nombre de personnes occupées (au 31.XII) |
| *b. Co-operatives — Coopératives* | | | | | |
| Number of enterprises (As of 31.XII)......... | 1 916 | — | 1 059 | 857 | Nombre d'entreprises (au 31.XII) |
| Gross value of output..... | 581.8 | — | 373.8 | 208.0 | Valeur brute de la production |
| Number of engaged (As of 31.XII)......... | 73.7 | — | 38.8 | 34.9 | Nombre de personnes occupées (au 31.XII) |
| *c. Privately Owned Enterprises — Entreprises privées* | | | | | |
| Number of enterprises (As of 31.XII)......... | 187 811 | 20 | 160 189 | 27 602 | Nombre d'entreprises (au 31.XII) |
| Gross value of output..... | 7 700.4 | 0.7 | 6 297.6 | 1 402.1 | Valeur brute de la production |
| Number of engaged (As of 31.XII)......... | 591.7 | 0.1 | 477.7 | 113.9 | Nombre de personnes occupées (au 31.XII) |

For footnotes see end of table.

Pour les notes, voir au bas du tableau.

## B. The Major Groups of Manufacturing — Les classes de la branche Industries manufacturières

| Item of data | Manufacturing[1] — Industries manufacturières[1] | Food, beverages and tobacco[2] — Industries alimentaires, boissons, tabac[2] | Textiles[3,5] — Textiles[3,5] | Clothing footwear and made-up textiles[5] — Articles d'habillement, chaussures et ouvrages en tissu[5] | Wood products and furniture[4] — Bois et meubles[4] | Paper and paper products — Papier et ouvrages en papier | Printing[1] — Imprimerie[1] | Leather and leather products[5] — Cuir et articles en cuir[5] | Chemicals and chemical, petroleum and rubber products 1, 2, 3, 6 — Produits chimiques, dérivés du pétrole et ouvrages en caoutchouc 1, 2, 3, 6 | Non-metallic mineral products 1, 6 — Produits minéraux non métalliques 1, 6 | Basic metals — Métallurgie de base | Metal products[7] — Ouvrages en métaux[7] | Other manufacturing 4, 7 — Autres industries manufacturières 4, 7 | Rubrique |
|---|---|---|---|---|---|---|---|---|---|---|---|---|---|---|
| **ISIC** | 14, 2–3 | 20–22 | 23 | 24 | 25–26 | 27 | 28 | 29 | 30–32 | 14, 33 | 34 | 35–38 | 39 | **CITI** |
| **a. All Enterprises — Toutes entreprises** | | | | | | | | | | | | | | |
| Number of enterprises (As of 31.XII) | 161 248 | 30 128 | 3 530 | 27 682 | 26 643 | 1 262 | 3 079 | 20 989 | 1 477 | 2 908 | — | 37 786 | 5 764 | Nombre d'entreprises (au 31.XII) |
| Gross value of output | 6 671.4 | 2 818.3 | 246.7 | 241.8 | 867.0 | 45.7 | 93.9 | 393.5 | 133.9 | 161.7 | — | 1 480.1 | 188.8 | Valeur brute de la production |
| Number of engaged (As of 31.XII) | 516.5 | 104.0 | 22.1 | 56.2 | 88.9 | 5.4 | 11.2 | 46.7 | 7.6 | 12.8 | — | 142.2 | 19.4 | Nombre de personnes occupée (au 31.XII) |
| Distribution in percent of number of engaged | 100.0 | 20.1 | 4.3 | 10.9 | 17.2 | 1.0 | 2.2 | 9.0 | 1.5 | 2.5 | — | 27.5 | 3.8 | Distribution en pourcentage du nombre de personnes occupées |
| **b. Co-operatives — Coopératives** | | | | | | | | | | | | | | |
| Number of enterprises (As of 31.XII) | 1 059 | 83 | 67 | 97 | 271 | 5 | 15 | 86 | 11 | 44 | — | 342 | 38 | Nombre d'entreprises (au 31.XII) |
| Gross value of output | 373.8 | 118.1 | 55.1 | 18.0 | 71.0 | 0.4 | 2.1 | 19.9 | 6.0 | 6.9 | — | 68.6 | 7.7 | Valeur brute de la production |
| Number of engaged (As of 31.XII) | 38.8 | 2.8 | 6.7 | 3.3 | 10.2 | 0.1 | 0.3 | 2.5 | 0.3 | 1.1 | — | 10.2 | 1.3 | Nombre de personnes occupées (au 31.XII) |
| Distribution in percent of number of engaged | 100.0 | 7.2 | 17.3 | 8.5 | 26.3 | 0.2 | 0.8 | 6.4 | 0.8 | 2.8 | — | 26.3 | 3.4 | Distribution en pourcentage du nombre de personnes occupées |
| **c. Privately Owned Enterprises — Entreprises privées** | | | | | | | | | | | | | | |
| Number of enterprises (As of 31.XII) | 160 189 | 30 045 | 3 463 | 27 585 | 26 372 | 1 257 | 3 064 | 20 903 | 1 466 | 2 864 | — | 37 444 | 5 726 | Nombre d'entreprises (au 31.XII) |
| Gross value of output | 6 297.6 | 2 700.2 | 191.6 | 223.8 | 796.0 | 45.3 | 91.8 | 373.6 | 127.9 | 154.8 | — | 1 411.5 | 181.1 | Valeur brute de la production |
| Number of engaged (As of 31.XII) | 477.7 | 101.2 | 15.4 | 52.9 | 78.7 | 5.3 | 10.9 | 44.2 | 7.3 | 11.7 | — | 132.0 | 18.1 | Nombre de personnes occupées (au 31.XII) |
| Distribution in percent of number of engaged | 100.0 | 21.2 | 3.2 | 11.1 | 16.5 | 1.1 | 2.3 | 9.3 | 1.5 | 2.4 | — | 27.6 | 3.8 | Distribution en pourcentage du nombre de personnes occupées |

[1] Stone, clay and sand quarrying (ISIC major group 14) is included in Manufacturing in Non-metallic mineral products (ISIC major group 33) whereas publishing (part of ISIC major group 28) is excluded, and coking and coal briquetting (part of ISIC major group 32) are covered in Mining.
[2] The extraction of vegetable oil is covered in Food (ISIC major group 20) instead of in Chemicals and chemical products (ISIC major group 31).
[3] The manufacturing of artificial textile fibres is included in Textiles (ISIC major group 23) instead of in Chemicals (ISIC major group 31).
[4] The production of musical instruments, toys, sporting goods and jewellery is covered in Wood products (ISIC major group 25) rather than in Other manufacturing (ISIC major group 39).
[5] The manufacture of leather and fur wearing apparel and felt and felt products is covered in Leather and leather products instead of in ISIC major groups 24 and 23, respectively.
[6] The manufacturing of asbestos products is covered in ISIC major groups 31-32 instead of in Non-metallic mineral products (ISIC major group 33).
[7] The production of office machinery is included in Other manufacturing (ISIC major group 39) instead of in Metal products (ISIC major groups 35-38).

[1] L'extraction de la pierre à bâtir, de l'argile et du sable (CITI classe 14) est comprise dans Industries manufacturières sous Produits minéraux non métalliques (CITI classe 33), tandis que l'édition (dans CITI classe 28) est exclue; la fabrication du coke et des briquettes de charbon (dans CITI classe 32) est comprise dans Industries extractives.
[2] L'extraction des huiles végétales est comprise dans Industries alimentaires (CITI classe 20) et non dans Industrie chimique (CITI classe 31).
[3] La fabrication des fibres textiles synthétiques est comprise dans Textiles (CITI classe 23) et non dans Industrie chimique (CITI classe 31).
[4] La fabrication des instruments de musique, jouets, articles de sport et articles de bijouterie est comprise dans Ouvrages en bois (CITI classe 25) et non dans Autres industries manufacturières (CITI classe 39).
[5] La fabrication des articles d'habillement en cuir et fourrure, ainsi que du feutre et des ouvrages en feutre, est comprise dans Cuir et articles en cuir (CITI classe 29) et non dans les classes 24 et 23 de la CITI respectivement.
[6] La fabrication des ouvrages en amiante est comprise dans les classes 31-32 de la CITI et non dans Produits minéraux non métalliques (CITI classe 33).
[7] La fabrication des machines de bureau est comprise dans Autres industries manufacturières CITI classe 39) et non dans Ouvrages en métaux (CITI classe 35-38).

## Gross Domestic Product

The data on the gross domestic product shown in Table I are derived from the replies of the Statistisches Bundesamt, Wiesbaden, to the United Nations national accounts questionnaire. The official estimates and descriptions of the estimates are published by that Office in *Wirtschaft und Statistik*. For purposes of the United Nations national accounts questionnaire, the Statistisches Bundesamt has adjusted these official estimates, insofar as possible, to the United Nations system of national accounts.

## Index Numbers of Industrial Production

The index numbers shown in Table 2 are derived principally from data supplied by the Statistisches Bundesamt, Wiesbaden, in *Produktion, Die Industrie der Bundesrepublik Deutschland*, Reihe 2, and in *Index of the Net Value of Industrial Production, Studies in Statistics*, No. 2. The indexes are base-weighted arithmetic averages of relatives computed chiefly from figures of the output of individual commodities. Some use is also made for this purpose of data on the value of output or of sales, deflated by price indexes, on man-hours worked, adjusted annually or quarterly by productivity indexes, or on the quantity of individual raw materials consumed. The weights utilized in combining the quantity relatives into indexes for detailed categories of industrial activity and the indexes into broader classes of activity are value added, at market price, during 1950. The weights, as well as the series of indexes, relate to all industrial units except licensed handicrafts. A detailed description of the index numbers may be found in *Index of the Net Value of Industrial Production, Studies in Statistics*, No. 2.

## Index Numbers of Industrial Employment

The index numbers of industrial employment set out in Table 3 were compiled by the Statistical Office of the United Nations from absolute figures of employment resulting from the same inquiries as the figures shown in Tables 6 and 7. These figures were abstracted from *Die Industrie der Bundesrepublik Deutschland*, Reihe 1, a monthly publication, and the *Statistisches Jahrbuch für die Bundesrepublik Deutschland*—both issued by the Statistisches Bundesamt.

## Produit intérieur brut

Les chiffres reproduits au tableau 1 relatifs au produit intérieur brut sont tirés de la réponse du Statistisches Bundesamt, Wiesbaden, au questionnaire de l'O.N.U. portant sur les comptes nationaux. Des estimations officielles et les explications relatives à ces estimations ont été publiées par ce bureau dans *Wirtschaft und Statistik*. Pour l'élaboration de la réponse au questionnaire de l'O.N.U. portant sur les comptes nationaux, le Statistisches Bundesamt a rajusté ces estimations officielles afin de les rendre aussi adéquates que possible avec le système de comptabilité nationale de l'O.N.U.

## Indices de la production industrielle

Les indices reproduits au tableau 2 sont tirés principalement des données fournies par le Statistisches Bundesamt, Wiesbaden, dans sa publication intitulée: *Produktion, Die Industrie der Bundesrepublik Deutschland*, Reihe 2, et dans *Indice de la valeur nette de la Production industrielle, Etudes Statistiques*, No 2. Ces indices sont des moyennes arithmétiques à pondération fixe de rapports calculés principalement à partir des chiffres de la production de chaque marchandise. A cette fin, on utilise quelquefois les données relatives à la valeur brute de la production ou des ventes, corrigées par l'indice des prix, ou les heures de travail effectuées corrigées annuellement ou trimestriellement par l'indice de la productivité, ou bien les volumes de chaque matière première consommée. La valeur ajoutée aux prix du marché en 1950 a été utilisée comme base de pondération pour combiner les rapports quantitatifs en indices pour les catégories détaillées de l'activité industrielle, et ces indices en d'autres relatifs à des classes plus larges de l'activité. Les coefficients de pondération, aussi bien que les séries d'indices, concernent toutes les unités industrielles à l'exclusion des unités artisanales. Une description détaillée de ces indices est fournie dans *Indice de la Valeur nette de la production industrielle, Etudes Statistiques*, No 2.

## Indices de l'emploi industriel

Les indices de l'emploi industriel reproduits au tableau 3 ont été calculés par le Bureau de Statistique de l'O.N.U. à partir des chiffres absolus de l'emploi résultant des mêmes enquêtes que celles utilisées pour les données des tableaux 6 et 7. Les chiffres ont été tirés de *Die Industrie der Bundesrepublik Deutschland*, Reihe 1, publication mensuelle, et du *Statistisches Jahrbuch für die Bundesrepublik Deutschland* — toutes deux publiées par le Statistisches Bundesamt.

---

[1] Unless otherwise indicated the data presented in this chapter relates to Federal Republic of Germany excluding the Saar.

[1] Sauf indication contraire, les données de ce chapitre concernent la République fédérale d'Allemagne à l'exclusion de la Sarre.

## GERMANY, Federal Republic of

The data on employment that the Statistical Office of the United Nations utilized in compiling the indexes, refer to the number of persons engaged, excepting homeworkers, during the year. Except for the electricity and gas industries, the number is the average of employment at the end of each month. For electricity and gas, it is the number of persons engaged as of the end of the year. In the case of mining and manufacturing, the data relate, in general, to local units with 10 or more persons engaged, except licensed handicrafts. For the construction industry, all units, including licensed handicrafts, are included in the data; and in the case of the electricity and gas industries, practically all public service units are covered.

### Characteristics and Structure of Industrial Activity

The data set out in Table 4 are derived from the results of Censuses of Establishments taken as of 17 May 1939 and 13 September 1950 which covered all local units engaged in industrial production as well as other kinds of activity. The results, for the territory of the Federal Republic of Germany, excluding the Saar, of the Censuses are set out in *Statistiches Jahrbuch, 1956* and *Statistik der Bundesrepublik Deutschland*, Band 45, Heft B, respectively, of the Statistisches Bundesamt. It should be noted that there are incomparabilities in the coverage and classification of data between the two Censuses of Establishments because in the early census activities ancillary to but physically separated from the main activity of the local unit were not included in the local unit.

The figures shown in Table 5 were compiled from the following publications of the Statistisches Bundesamt: *Brutto und Netto Produktionswerte der Industrie in Jahre 1950, and Brutto- und Netto Produktion, 1954, Die Industrie der Bundesrepublik Deutschland*, Sonderheft, No. 7 and Reihe 4, Heft 20, respectively; *Die Industrie der Bundesrepublik Deutschland*, Teil 1, No. 9, September 1951 and *Statistisches Jahrbuch, für die Bundesrepublik Deutschland, 1959*. Because of the difference between the data for 1954 and that for 1950 in the statistical unit utilized (the enterprise for the former data and the local unit for the latter), the two sets of data are not comparable. The definitions for items of data were, however, the same in both instances. The figures of gross receipts and value added are valued at market prices (i.e., including indirect taxes but excluding subsidies) and do not cover goods sold in the same condition as purchased. The data on number of persons engaged cover employees, working proprietors and unpaid family workers but not homeworkers.

The figures of Tables 6 and 7 were abstracted from the *Statistisches Jahrbuch für die Bundesrepublik Deutschland, 1956, 1957* or *1959*, and *Beschäftigung und Umsatz, Brennstoff- und Energieversorgung, 1955 bis 1958, Die Industrie der Bundesrepublik Deutschland*, Reihe 1. In the case of mining and manufacturing, these data originate in a monthly survey of mining and manufacturing units engaging ten or more persons and smaller units en-

Les chiffres relatifs à l'emploi qu'utilise le Bureau de Statistique de l'O.N.U. pour le calcul des indices sont ceux relatifs au nombre de personnes occupées pendant l'année à l'exclusion des travailleurs à domicile. Excepté en ce qui concerne les industries productrices d'électricité et de gaz, le nombre est la moyenne de l'emploi en fin de mois. En ce qui concerne l'électricité et le gaz, c'est le nombre de personnes occupées en fin d'année. En ce qui concerne les industries extractives et manufacturières les données se rapportent, en général, aux unités locales de 10 personnes occupées ou plus, à l'exclusion des unités artisanales patentées. Pour les industries du bâtiment et des travaux publics, toutes les unités, y compris les unités artisanales patentées sont comprises dans les données; dans le cas des industries d'électricité et de gaz, en pratique toutes les unités du service public sont couvertes.

### Caractéristiques et structure de l'activité industrielle

Les données du tableau proviennent des résultats des recensements des établissements au 17 mai 1939 et au 13 septembre 1950, couvrant toutes les unités locales dans la production industrielle ainsi que dans les autres types d'activité. Les résultats des recensements relatifs au territoire de la République Fédérale Allemande, non compris la Sarre, sont reproduits dans le *Statistisches Jahrbuch, 1956* et le *Statistik der Bundesrepublik Deutschland*, Band 45, Heft B, respectivement, du Statistisches Bundesamt. Il est bon de noter que dans le premier recensement les activités auxiliaires mais physiquement distinctes de l'activité principale d'une unité locale n'ont pas été rattachées à cette activité principale. Il en résulte un certain défaut de comparabilité entre les deux recensements pour ce qui est de la couverture et de la classification des données.

Les chiffres du tableau 5 sont calculés à partir des publications ci-après citées du Statistisches Bundesamt: *Brutto und Netto Produktionswerte der Industrie im Jahre 1950*, et *Brutto und Netto Produktion, 1954, Die Industrie der Bundesrepublik Deutschland*, Sonderheft, No 7 et Reihe 4, Heft 20, respectivement; *Die Industrie der Bundesrepublik Deutschland*, Teil 1, No 9, de septembre 1951 et *Statistisches Jahrbuch für die Bundesrepublik Deutschland, 1959*. Du fait de la différence entre les données de 1954 et celles de 1950 dans l'unité statistique adoptée (les entreprises pour les premières données et les unités locales pour les secondes) les deux ensembles de données ne sont pas comparables. Les définitions des rubriques sont, cependant, les mêmes dans les deux cas. Les chiffres relatifs aux recettes brutes et à la valeur ajoutée sont évalués aux prix du marché (c'est à dire comprenant les impôts indirects mais excluant les subventions) et ne couvrent pas les biens revendus en l'état. Les données relatives au nombre de personnes occupées couvrent les salariés, les propriétaires qui travaillent et les travailleurs familiaux non rémunérés.

Les chiffres des tableaux 6 et 7 sont tirés du *Statistisches Jahrbuch für die Bundesrepublik Deutschland, 1956, 1957* et *1959* et de *Beschäftigung und Umsatz, Brennstoff- und Energieversorgung, 1955 bis 1958, Die Industrie der Bundesrepublik Deutschland*, Reihe 1. Dans le cas des industries extractives et manufacturières ces données proviennent d'enquêtes mensuelles auprès des unités extractives et manufacturières occupant dix personnes ou plus et

gaged in classes of industrial activity where they account for a significant part of production. However, licensed handicrafts, irrespective of size, are not included in the survey. The local units covered in the survey account for about 97 percent of gross receipts and employment in mining and manufacturing, excepting licensed handicrafts. In the case of construction industry, the monthly survey relates to units engaging 20 or more persons. However, annually, data are gathered from all units, including licensed handicrafts; and the results of these two kinds of surveys are utilized to compile data covering all local units principally engaged in construction. The data on the electricity and gas industries result from an annual inquiry into public service electric power stations with installed capacity of more than 1,000 kwh. and all such gas works.

The data gathered in these inquiries on gross receipts and number of persons engaged are defined as indicated above. The definitions of the other items of data on labour are similar to those recommended by the Statistical Commission of the United Nations. The figures of selected fuels consumed shown in Table 7 refer to fuels utilized by local units as a source of heat or power, to produce electricity, or as raw materials. The figures of energy consumed set out in Table 6 exclude fuels used to produce electricity but include any fuels that may have been utilized by local units as raw material or to manufacture gas which these units themselves consume. The figures on consumption of energy for such industries as coal mining, which include coking and briquetting, chemical manufacturing or basic metals are probably overstated. It should be noted however, that the consumption of blast furnace gas is excluded from the data on energy consumption or on manufactured gas.

The figures of Table 8 came from Censuses of Licensed Handicrafts for 1949 and 1956. The data were compiled from *Handwerkszählung vom 30.9.1949* or *1956, Statistik der Bundesrepublik Deutschland*, Band 2 and 4 and 203, respectively. All licensed handicrafts in business as of the census date were covered in these Censuses. However, the data from the two Censuses lack comparability because of differences in licensing provisions between the two census dates and changes in the classification of the data according to kind of industrial activity. The definitions of the items of data gathered in the two Censuses were, however, the same. The figures of gross receipts covered all receipts, including those from the sale of goods sold in the same condition as purchased, and were valued at market prices. Unlike gross receipts, the items of data on labour gathered in the two Censuses were defined in the same way as in the other inquiries discussed above.

d'unités plus petites appartenant à des classes de l'activité industrielle dans lesquelles une part considérable de la production revient aux petites unités. Cependant les unités artisanales patentées, quelle que soit leur dimension, sont exclues de l'enquête. Les unités locales couvertes par l'enquête totalisent près de 97% des recettes brutes et de l'emploi dans les industries extractives et manufacturières, à l'exclusion des unités artisanales patentées. Dans le cas du bâtiment et travaux publics, l'enquête mensuelle concerne les unités occupant 20 personnes ou plus. Cependant on rassemble annuellement des données concernant toutes les unités, y compris les unités artisanales patentées, et les résultats de ces deux types d'enquêtes sont utilisés pour l'élaboration de données couvrant toutes les unités locales occupées dans le bâtiment et travaux publics. Les chiffres relatifs aux industries de l'électricité et du gaz proviennent d'une enquête auprès des centrales électriques du service public ayant une puissance installée de plus de 1 000 kwh. ainsi que toutes les usines de gaz du domaine public.

Les données rassemblées, à partir de ces enquêtes, se rapportant aux recettes brutes et au nombre de personnes occupées sont définies comme il a été indiqué plus haut. Les définitions de autres rubriques en ce qui concerne la main-d'œuvre, sont similaires à celles recommandées par la Commission de statistique de l'O.N.U. Les chiffres relatifs à certains combustibles consommés reproduits au tableau 7 concernent les combustibles consommés par les unités locales comme source de chaleur ou de puissance, pour la production de l'électricité, ou comme matière première. Les chiffres relatifs à l'énergie consommée reproduits au tableau 6 excluent les combustibles ayant servi à la production de l'électricité, mais comprennent tous les combustibles utilisés par l'unité locale, soit comme matière première, soit pour produire le gaz consommé par l'unité locale. Les chiffres concernant la consommation d'énergie pour les industries telles que l'industrie extractive de charbon, qui comprennent les cokeries et la fabrication de briquettes, les industries chimiques ou métallurgiques, sont probablement surestimés. Il est bon de noter, cependant, que la consommation de gaz de haut-fourneau est exclue des données relatives à l'énergie consommée ou de celles de la production gazière.

Les chiffres du tableau 8 proviennent des Recensements des unités artisanales effectués en 1949 et en 1956. Ces données ont été élaborées à partir de *Handwerkszählung vom 30.9.1949* ou *1956, Statistik der Bundesrepublik Deutschland*, Band 2 et 4 et 203 respectivement. Toutes les unités artisanales patentées en activité à la date du recensement ont été couvertes par ces recensements. Cependant, des différences dans les conditions d'attribution de patentes, et dans les classifications des données selon le type d'activité industrielle, entre les deux recensements, découle un manque de comparabilité entre les données obtenues à partir des deux recensements. Les définitions des rubriques rassemblées dans les deux recensements sont cependant identiques. Les chiffres relatifs aux recettes brutes sont évalués aux prix du marché et couvrent toutes les recettes y compris celles provenant de la vente de biens en l'état. A la différence des recettes brutes, les rubriques relatives à la main-d'œuvre, utilisées dans les deux recensements, ont été définies de la même façon que dans les autres enquêtes mentionnées plus haut.

# GERMANY, Federal Republic of

## 1. THE GROSS DOMESTIC PRODUCT
## LE PRODUIT INTERIEUR BRUT

Millions D.M.                                                                 Millions de D.M.

### A. Expenditure on the Gross Domestic Product at Market Prices
### Dépenses relatives au produit intérieur brut aux prix du marché

| Item of data and year / Rubrique et année | Total | Consumption / Consommation | | Gross Domestic Capital Formation / Formation brute de capital intérieur | | Net exports of goods and services / Exportations nettes de biens et de services | |
| --- | --- | --- | --- | --- | --- | --- | --- |
| | | Total | Government / Etat | Total | Fixed / Fixe | Exports less imports / Exportations moins importations | Exports / Exportations |
| *a. At Current Prices — Aux prix courants* | | | | | | | |
| **Absolute figures — Chiffres absolus** | | | | | | | |
| 1950 | 97 170 | 76 450 | 14 000 | 21 920 | 18 250 | −1 200 | 11 810 |
| 1951 | 118 600 | 89 950 | 17 440 | 26 380 | 22 450 | 2 270 | 19 250 |
| 1952 | 135 500 | 100 700 | 20 760 | 31 480 | 25 850 | 3 320 | 22 900 |
| 1953 | 145 450 | 108 690 | 21 050 | 31 350 | 29 300 | 5 410 | 25 960 |
| 1954 | 156 950 | 114 800 | 22 000 | 36 310 | 32 900 | 5 840 | 31 300 |
| 1955 | 179 060 | 127 170 | 23 750 | 46 950 | 40 950 | 4 940 | 36 850 |
| 1956 | 197 060 | 140 470 | 25 350 | 49 320 | 45 000 | 7 270 | 44 080 |
| 1957 | 214 200 | 152 910 | 27 300 | 51 960 | 46 650 | 9 330 | 52 320 |
| 1958 | 228 810 | 165 530 | 30 630 | 54 130 | 50 300 | 9 150 | 53 870 |
| 1959 | 248 420 | 177 790 | 33 630 | 61 650 | 57 100 | 8 980 | 59 980 |
| 1960 [1] | 282 820 | 198 950 | 38 430 | 75 700 | 67 700 | 8 170 | 68 380 |
| 1961 [1] | 311 360 | 220 400 | 43 650 | 83 200 | 77 900 | 7 760 | 71 650 |
| **Percentage distribution of average annual expenditure — Distribution en pourcentage des dépenses annuelles moyennes** | | | | | | | |
| 1950–1959 | 100.0 | 72.9 | 13.7 | 23.9 | 21.4 | 3.2 | 20.8 |
| 1950 | 100.0 | 78.7 | 14.7 | 22.5 | 18.8 | −1.2 | 12.2 |
| 1953 | 100.0 | 74.7 | 14.5 | 21.6 | 20.1 | 3.7 | 17.8 |
| 1954 | 100.0 | 73.2 | 14.0 | 23.1 | 21.0 | 3.7 | 19.9 |
| 1959 | 100.0 | 71.6 | 13.5 | 24.8 | 23.0 | 3.6 | 24.1 |
| 1960 [1] | 100.0 | 70.3 | 13.6 | 26.7 | 23.9 | 2.9 | 24.2 |
| *b. At Prices of 1954 — Aux prix de 1954* | | | | | | | |
| **Absolute figures — Chiffres absolus** | | | | | | | |
| 1950 | 113 070 | 86 640 | 17 400 | 25 450 | 21 550 | 980 | 14 230 |
| 1951 | 125 000 | 93 160 | 19 360 | 26 750 | 23 250 | 5 090 | 19 060 |
| 1952 | 135 300 | 100 720 | 21 450 | 30 100 | 24 800 | 4 480 | 21 840 |
| 1953 | 145 550 | 109 450 | 21 280 | 30 800 | 28 800 | 5 300 | 25 540 |
| 1954 | 156 950 | 114 800 | 22 000 | 36 310 | 32 900 | 5 840 | 31 300 |
| 1955 | 175 150 | 124 380 | 22 880 | 45 450 | 39 600 | 5 320 | 36 610 |
| 1956 | 187 030 | 133 650 | 23 150 | 46 200 | 42 100 | 7 180 | 42 580 |
| 1957 | 197 060 | 141 270 | 24 140 | 47 250 | 42 200 | 8 540 | 49 360 |
| 1958 | 203 180 | 148 720 | 26 110 | 48 300 | 44 720 | 6 160 | 51 070 |
| 1959 | 216 960 | 158 120 | 28 470 | 54 000 | 49 710 | 4 840 | 57 850 |
| 1960 [1] | 239 770 | 172 870 | 31 110 | 64 190 | 56 700 | 2 710 | 65 190 |
| 1961 [1] | 253 020 | 185 530 | 33 360 | 67 320 | 62 420 | 170 | 67 640 |
| **Percentage distribution of average annual expenditure — Distribution en pourcentage des dépenses annuelles moyennes** | | | | | | | |
| 1950–1959 | 100.0 | 73.1 | 13.7 | 23.6 | 21.1 | 3.3 | 21.1 |
| 1950 | 100.0 | 76.6 | 15.4 | 22.5 | 19.1 | 0.9 | 12.6 |
| 1953 | 100.0 | 75.2 | 14.6 | 21.2 | 19.8 | 3.6 | 17.5 |
| 1954 | 100.0 | 73.2 | 14.0 | 23.1 | 21.0 | 3.7 | 19.9 |
| 1959 | 100.0 | 72.8 | 13.1 | 24.9 | 22.9 | 2.3 | 26.7 |
| 1960 [1] | 100.0 | 72.1 | 13.0 | 26.8 | 23.6 | 1.1 | 27.2 |
| **Average annual rate of growth — Taux annuel moyen d'accroissement** | | | | | | | |
| 1950–1959 | 7.5 | 6.9 | 5.6 | 8.7 | 9.7 | . | 11.9 |
| 1950–1953 | 8.8 | 8.1 | 6.5 | 6.6 | 10.1 | . | 21.5 |
| 1954–1959 | 6.7 | 6.6 | 5.3 | 8.3 | 8.6 | . | 13.1 |

For footnotes, see end of table.                                        Pour les notes, voir au bas du tableau.

## B. The Gross Domestic Product at Market Prices According to Origin
### Origine par secteur d'activité du produit intérieur brut aux prix du marché

| Item of data and year / Rubrique et année | Total | Agricultural sector / Secteur agricole | Industrial Sector — Secteur Industriel | | | | | Transportation and communication / Transport et communication | Other sectors / Autres secteurs |
|---|---|---|---|---|---|---|---|---|---|
| | | | Total | Mining [2] / Industries extractives [2] | Manufacturing [2] / Industries manufacturières [2] | Construction / Bâtiments et travaux publics | Electricity, gas and water / Electricité, gaz et eau | | |
| ISIC — CITI | 0-9 | 0 | 1-5 | 1 | 2-3 | 4 | 5 | 7 | 6, 8-9 |
| **a. At Current Prices — Aux prix courants** | | | | | | | | | |
| **Absolute figures — Chiffres absolus** | | | | | | | | | |
| 1950 | 97 170 | 10 130 | 48 010 | 3 800 | 37 180 | 5 430 | 1 600 | 7 070 | 31 960 |
| 1951 | 118 600 | 12 220 | 60 960 | 4 610 | 48 370 | 6 220 | 1 760 | 8 220 | 37 200 |
| 1952 | 135 500 | 13 290 | 69 000 | 5 310 | 54 470 | 7 050 | 2 170 | 9 260 | 43 950 |
| 1953 | 145 450 | 13 390 | 75 500 | 6 170 | 58 510 | 8 410 | 2 410 | 9 610 | 46 950 |
| 1954 | 156 950 | 13 730 | 82 000 | 6 310 | 63 750 | 9 020 | 2 920 | 10 230 | 50 990 |
| 1955 | 179 060 | 14 520 | 95 280 | 6 630 | 74 220 | 11 110 | 3 320 | 11 990 | 57 270 |
| 1956 | 197 060 | 14 950 | 104 910 | 7 530 | 81 340 | 12 240 | 3 800 | 13 130 | 64 070 |
| 1957 | 214 200 | 15 590 | 113 270 | 8 180 | 88 460 | 12 750 | 3 880 | 14 180 | 71 160 |
| 1958 | 228 810 | 16 500 | 120 190 | 8 100 | 94 060 | 13 760 | 4 270 | 15 250 | 76 870 |
| 1959 | 248 420 | 16 850 | 131·500 | 7 820 | 102 730 | 16 190 | 4 760 | 16 710 | 83 360 |
| 1960 [1] | 282 820 | 17 580 | 152 570 | 8 780 | 119 600 | 18 940 | 5 250 | 18 640 | 94 030 |
| 1961 [1] | 311 360 | 17 860 | 170 200 | 14 500 [3] | 133 580 | 22 120 | ... | 19 700 | 103 600 |
| **Percentage distribution according to sector— Distribution en pourcentage par secteur** | | | | | | | | | |
| 1950-1959 | 100.0 | 8.2 | 52.3 | ... | 40.8 | 5.9 | ... | 6.7 | 32.8 |
| 1950 | 100.0 | 10.4 | 49.4 | 3.9 | 38.3 | 5.6 | 1.6 | 7.3 | 32.9 |
| 1953 | 100.0 | 9.2 | 51.9 | 4.2 | 40.2 | 5.8 | 1.7 | 6.6 | 32.3 |
| 1954 | 100.0 | 8.7 | 52.3 | 4.0 | 40.6 | 5.8 | 1.9 | 6.5 | 32.5 |
| 1959 | 100.0 | 6.7 | 53.0 | 3.2 | 41.3 | 6.6 | 1.9 | 7.5 | 33.6 |
| 1960 [1] | 100.0 | 6.2 | 53.9 | 3.1 | 42.3 | 6.7 | 1.8 | 6.6 | 33.3 |
| **b. At Prices of 1954 — Aux prix de 1954** | | | | | | | | | |
| **Absolute figures — Chiffres absolus** | | | | | | | | | |
| 1950 | 113 070 | 11 760 | 53 470 | 5 540 | 39 820 | 6 030 | 2 080 | 8 360 | 39 480 |
| 1951 | 125 000 | 13 390 | 60 870 | 6 270 | 45 830 | 6 450 | 2 320 | 9 010 | 41 730 |
| 1952 | 135 300 | 13 410 | 67 610 | 6 470 | 51 610 | 7 080 | 2 450 | 9 440 | 44 840 |
| 1953 | 145 550 | 13 450 | 74 840 | 6 280 | 57 560 | 8 490 | 2 510 | 9 630 | 47 630 |
| 1954 | 156 950 | 13 730 | 82 000 | 6 310 | 63 750 | 9 020 | 2 920 | 10 230 | 50 990 |
| 1955 | 175 150 | 13 550 | 94 670 | 6 890 | 73 960 | 10 500 | 3 320 | 11 720 | 55 210 |
| 1956 | 187 030 | 13 380 | 101 520 | 7 400 | 79 270 | 11 060 | 3 790 | 12 820 | 59 310 |
| 1957 | 197 060 | 13 780 | 106 720 | 7 450 | 84 360 | 10 970 | 3 940 | 13 450 | 63 110 |
| 1958 | 203 180 | 14 510 | 109 980 | 7 020 | 87 550 | 11 320 | 4 090 | 13 380 | 65 310 |
| 1959 | 216 960 | 14 970 | 118 130 | 6 820 | 94 360 | 12 570 | 4 380 | 14 370 | 69 490 |
| 1960 [1] | 239 770 | 15 810 | 132 930 | 7 620 | 106 950 | 13 550 | 4 810 | 15 600 | 75 430 |
| 1961 [1] | 253 020 | 15 890 | 141 880 | 13 050 [3] | 114 330 | 14 500 | ... | 16 270 | 78 980 |
| **Percentage distribution according to sector— Distribution en pourcentage par secteur** | | | | | | | | | |
| 1950-1959 | 100.3 | 8.2 | 52.5 | ... | 41.0 | 5.6 | ... | 6.8 | 32.5 |
| 1950 | 100.0 | 10.4 | 47.3 | 4.9 | 35.2 | 5.3 | 1.9 | 7.4 | 34.9 |
| 1953 | 100.0 | 9.3 | 51.4 | 4.3 | 39.6 | 5.8 | 1.7 | 6.6 | 32.7 |
| 1954 | 100.0 | 8.7 | 52.3 | 4.0 | 40.6 | 5.8 | 1.9 | 6.5 | 32.5 |
| 1959 | 100.0 | 6.8 | 54.5 | 3.2 | 43.5 | 5.8 | 2.0 | 6.6 | 32.1 |
| 1960 [1] | 100.0 | 6.5 | 55.5 | 3.2 | 44.6 | 5.7 | 2.0 | 6.5 | 31.5 |
| **Average annual rate of growth—Taux annuel moyen d'accroissement** | | | | | | | | | |
| 1950-1959 | 7.5 | 2.7 | 9.2 | 2.4 | 10.1 | 8.5 | 8.6 | 6.2 | 6.5 |
| 1950-1953 | 8.8 | 4.6 | 11.9 | 4.3 | 13.1 | 12.1 | 6.5 | 4.8 | 6.4 |
| 1954-1959 | 6.7 | 1.7 | 7.6 | 1.6 | 8.2 | 6.9 | 8.4 | 7.0 | 6.4 |

[1] The data for 1960 and 1961 include the Saar but the data for 1959 and earlier years exclude the Saar.
[2] Quarrying of sand and stone is included in Manufacturing (ISIC Divisions 2–3) and not in Mining (ISIC Division 1).
[3] The data on Electricity, gas, water and sanitary services (ISIC Division 5) are included in the data on Mining (ISIC Division 1).

[1] Les données pour 1960 et 1961 comprennent la Sarre. Elle en est exclue pour l'année 1959 et les années postérieures.
[2] L'extraction de la pierre à bâtir et du sable est incluse dans les Industries manufacturières (CITI Branche 2–3) et non pas dans les Industries extractives (CITI Branche 1).
[3] Les données relatives à L'électricité, le gaz, l'eau et les services sanitaires (CITI Branche 5) sont incluses dans celles des Industries extractives (CITI Branche 1).

## 2. INDEX NUMBERS OF INDUSTRIAL PRODUCTION — INDICES DE LA PRODUCTION INDUSTRIELLE

### A. The Divisions of Industrial Activity
### Les branches de l'activité industrielle

| Period / Période | All industrial activity, excluding construction / Toutes industries, à l'exclusion du bâtiment et des travaux publics | Mining [1] / Industries extractives [1] | Manufacturing [1] / Industries manufacturières [1] | Construction / Bâtiment et travaux publics | Electricity and gas / Electricité et gaz |
|---|---|---|---|---|---|
| ISIC — CITI | 1–3, 511–512 | 1 | 2–3 | 4 | 511–512 |

#### a. Indexes — Indices (1958 = 100)

| | | | | | |
|---|---|---|---|---|---|
| 1938....... | 51 | 83 | 49 | 76 | 34 |
| 1948....... | 26 | 52 | 24 | ... | 36 |
| 1949....... | 38 | 62 | 36 | 42 | 43 |
| 1950....... | 48 | 70 | 46 | 55 | 49 |
| 1951....... | 56 | 76 | 55 | 60 | 56 |
| 1952....... | 60 | 82 | 58 | 64 | 62 |
| 1953....... | 66 | 84 | 65 | 76 | 65 |
| 1954....... | 74 | 88 | 73 | 84 | 73 |
| 1955....... | 85 | 92 | 84 | 95 | 82 |
| 1956....... | 92 | 97 | 91 | 100 | 92 |
| 1957....... | 97 | 99 | 97 | 98 | 98 |
| 1958....... | 100 | 100 | 100 | 100 | 100 |
| 1959....... | 107 | 100 | 107 | 114 | 107 |
| 1960....... | 119 | 102 | 119 | 121 | 118 |
| 1961....... | 126 | 107 | 126 | 132 | 125 |

#### b. Average Annual Rate of Change — Taux annuel moyen de variation

| | | | | | |
|---|---|---|---|---|---|
| 1938 – 1960. | 3.9 | 0.9 | 4.1 | 2.1 | 5.8 |
| 1938 – 1948. | −6.5 | −4.6 | −6.9 | ... | 0.6 |
| 1950 – 1960. | 9.5 | 3.8 | 10.0 | 8.2 | 9.2 |
| 1948 – 1953. | 20.5 | 10.1 | 22.0 | ... | 12.5 |
| 1954 – 1958. | 7.8 | 3.2 | 8.2 | 4.4 | 8.2 |
| 1958 – 1960. | 9.1 | 1.0 | 9.1 | 10.0 | 8.6 |

[1] The manufacturing of coke and coal briquettes is included in Mining (ISIC division 1) and not in Manufacturing (ISIC division 2–3) whereas the quarrying of stone and sand is included in Manufacturing and not in Mining.

[1] La fabrication du coke et des briquettes est comprise dans Industries extractives (CITI branche 1) et non dans Industries manufacturières (CITI branches 2 et 3), tandis que l'extraction de la pierre et du sable est comprise dans Industries manufacturières et non dans Industries extractives.

### B. The Major Groups of Mining
### Les classes de la branche Industries extractives

| Period / Période | All mining [1] / Toutes industries extractives [1] | Coal mining / Extraction du charbon | Metal mining / Extraction des minerais métalliques | Crude petroleum and natural gas / Pétrole brut et gaz naturel | Other mining [2] / Autres industries extractives [2] |
|---|---|---|---|---|---|
| ISIC — CITI | 1 | 11 | 12 | 13 | 14–19 |

#### a. Indexes — Indices (1958 = 100)

| | | | | | |
|---|---|---|---|---|---|
| 1938....... | 83 | 103 | 81 | 12 | 55 |
| 1948....... | 52 | 66 | 43 | 14 | 34 |
| 1949....... | 62 | 78 | 58 | 18 | 45 |
| 1950....... | 70 | 84 | 69 | 24 | 56 |
| 1951....... | 76 | 90 | 79 | 30 | 66 |
| 1952....... | 82 | 93 | 88 | 38 | 75 |
| 1953....... | 84 | 94 | 90 | 48 | 78 |
| 1954....... | 88 | 96 | 90 | 58 | 93 |
| 1955....... | 92 | 99 | 96 | 71 | 98 |
| 1956....... | 97 | 101 | 100 | 81 | 97 |
| 1957....... | 99 | 100 | 106 | 90 | 99 |
| 1958....... | 100 | 100 | 100 | 100 | 100 |
| 1959....... | 100 | 95 | 97 | 115 | 106 |
| 1960....... | 102 | 95 | 100 | 125 | 113 |
| 1961....... | 107 | 96 | 101 | 140 | 117 |

#### b. Average Annual Rate of Change — Taux annuel moyen de variation

| | | | | | |
|---|---|---|---|---|---|
| 1938 – 1960. | 0.9 | −0.4 | 1.0 | 11.2 | 3.3 |
| 1938 – 1948. | −4.6 | −4.4 | −6.1 | 1.6 | −4.7 |
| 1950 – 1960. | 3.8 | 1.2 | 3.8 | 17.9 | 7.3 |
| 1948 – 1953. | 10.1 | 7.3 | 15.9 | 27.9 | 18.1 |
| 1954 – 1958. | 3.2 | 1.0 | 2.7 | 14.6 | 1.8 |
| 1958 – 1960. | 1.0 | −2.5 | — | 11.8 | 6.3 |

[1] Includes the production of coke and coal briquettes but not the quarrying of stone and sand. The indexes for coal mining (ISIC major group 11), however, do not cover the production of coke or coal briquets.
[2] Excludes the quarrying of stone and sand.

[1] Y compris la fabrication du coke et des briquettes, mais non l'extraction de la pierre et du sable. Toutefois les indices pour l'extraction du charbon (CITI 11) ne couvrent pas la fabrication du coke et des briquettes.
[2] Non compris l'extraction de la pierre et du sable.

## C. The Major Groups of Manufacturing — Les classes de la branche Industries manufacturières

| Period / Période | Manufacturing[1] / Industries manufacturières[1] | Food, beverages and tobacco / Industries alimentaires, boissons, tabac | Textiles | Clothing, footwear and made-up textiles / Articles d'habillement, chaussures et ouvrages en tissu | Wood products and furniture / Bois et meubles | Paper and paper products / Papier et ouvrages en papier | Printing and publishing / Imprimerie et édition | Leather and leather products except wearing apparel / Cuir et articles en cuir, à l'exclusion des articles d'habillement | Rubber products / Ouvrages en caoutchouc | Chemicals and chemical, petroleum and coal products / Produits chimiques et dérivés du pétrole et du charbon | Non-metallic mineral products[2] / Produits minéraux non métalliques[2] | Basic metals / Métallurgie de base | Metal products / Ouvrages en métaux | Other manufacturing / Autres industries manufacturières |
|---|---|---|---|---|---|---|---|---|---|---|---|---|---|---|
| ISIC — CITI | 2–3 | 20–22 | 23 | 24 | 25–26 | 27 | 28 | 29 | 30 | 31–32 | 33 | 34 | 35–38 | 39 |

### a. Indexes — Indices (1958 = 100)

| Period | | | | | | | | | | | | | | |
|---|---|---|---|---|---|---|---|---|---|---|---|---|---|---|
| 1938 | 49 | 51 | 59 | 41 | 69 | 60 | 48 | 90 | 54 | 42 | 57 | 74 | 43 | 38 |
| 1948 | 24 | 28 | 26 | 23 | 41 | 24 | 21 | 35 | 33 | 23 | 29 | 26 | 18 | 16 |
| 1949 | 36 | 42 | 48 | 36 | 56 | 41 | 36 | 49 | 43 | 24 | 45 | 41 | 28 | 23 |
| 1950 | 46 | 50 | 64 | 48 | 66 | 56 | 51 | 61 | 48 | 42 | 53 | 54 | 37 | 32 |
| 1951 | 55 | 56 | 72 | 55 | 75 | 62 | 53 | 62 | 53 | 51 | 63 | 63 | 48 | 43 |
| 1952 | 58 | 60 | 69 | 60 | 70 | 60 | 57 | 68 | 58 | 52 | 66 | 72 | 54 | 48 |
| 1953 | 65 | 70 | 83 | 69 | 74 | 69 | 67 | 76 | 67 | 60 | 72 | 67 | 56 | 57 |
| 1954 | 73 | 74 | 88 | 73 | 83 | 79 | 74 | 79 | 78 | 67 | 80 | 79 | 66 | 67 |
| 1955 | 84 | 82 | 96 | 86 | 90 | 87 | 79 | 91 | 94 | 77 | 91 | 97 | 82 | 80 |
| 1956 | 91 | 88 | 102 | 96 | 97 | 94 | 84 | 95 | 93 | 84 | 97 | 103 | 89 | 88 |
| 1957 | 97 | 96 | 106 | 105 | 99 | 99 | 91 | 104 | 97 | 93 | 97 | 106 | 93 | 94 |
| 1958 | 100 | 100 | 100 | 100 | 100 | 100 | 100 | 100 | 100 | 100 | 100 | 100 | 100 | 100 |
| 1959 | 107 | 102 | 104 | 106 | 106 | 108 | 105 | 102 | 116 | 114 | 111 | 109 | 108 | 114 |
| 1960 | 119 | 106 | 110 | 113 | 115 | 118 | 114 | 101 | 131 | 131 | 119 | 128 | 125 | 133 |
| 1961 | 126 | 110 | 110 | 121 | 120 | 120 | 124 | 107 | 135 | 142 | 127 | 128 | 135 | 145 |

### b. Average Annual Rate of Change — Taux annuel moyen de variation

| Period | | | | | | | | | | | | | | |
|---|---|---|---|---|---|---|---|---|---|---|---|---|---|---|
| 1938 – 1960 | 4.1 | 3.4 | 2.9 | 4.7 | 2.4 | 3.1 | 4.0 | 0.5 | 4.1 | 5.3 | 3.4 | 2.5 | 5.0 | 5.9 |
| 1938 – 1948 | −6.9 | −5.8 | −7.9 | −5.6 | −5.1 | −8.8 | −7.9 | −9.0 | −4.8 | −5.8 | −6.5 | −9.9 | −8.3 | −8.3 |
| 1950 – 1960 | 10.0 | 7.8 | 5.6 | 8.9 | 5.7 | 7.7 | 8.4 | 5.2 | 10.6 | 12.0 | 8.4 | 9.0 | 12.9 | 15.3 |
| 1948 – 1953 | 22.0 | 20.1 | 26.1 | 24.6 | 12.5 | 23.5 | 26.1 | 16.8 | 15.2 | 21.1 | 20.0 | 20.8 | 25.5 | 28.9 |
| 1954 – 1958 | 8.2 | 7.8 | 3.2 | 8.2 | 4.8 | 6.1 | 7.8 | 6.1 | 6.4 | 10.5 | 5.7 | 6.1 | 10.9 | 10.5 |
| 1958 – 1960 | 9.1 | 3.0 | 4.9 | 6.3 | 7.2 | 8.6 | 6.8 | 0.5 | 14.5 | 14.5 | 9.1 | 13.1 | 11.8 | 15.3 |

[1] Excludes the production of coke and coal briquettes although the indexes for Chemicals and chemical and coal products (ISIC major groups 31–32) cover this production.
[2] Covers, as well, the quarrying of stone and sand.

[1] Non compris la fabrication du coke et des briquettes; toutefois les indices pour l'industrie chimique et les dérivés du pétrole et du charbon (CITI 31–32) couvrent cette fabrication.
[2] Y compris, en outre, l'extraction de la pierre et du sable.

## 3. INDEX NUMBERS OF INDUSTRIAL EMPLOYMENT
## INDICES DE L'EMPLOI DANS L'INDUSTRIE

### A. The Divisions of Industrial Activity
### Les branches de l'activité industrielle

| Period / Période | Total | Mining[1,3] / Industries extractives[1,3] | Manufacturing[1,3] / Industries manufacturières[1,3] | Construction / Bâtiment et travaux publics | Electricity and gas / Electricité et gaz |
|---|---|---|---|---|---|
| ISIC — CITI | 1–4, 511–512 | 1 | 2–3 | 4 | 511–512 |

#### a. Indexes — Indices (1958 = 100)

| Period | | | | | |
|---|---|---|---|---|---|
| 1950 | 67 | 89 | 64 | 76 | 79 |
| 1951 | 74 | 92 | 71 | 76 | 82 |
| 1952 | 76 | 95 | 74 | 78 | *84 |
| 1953 | 80 | 98 | 77 | 87 | 87 |
| 1954 | 84 | 98 | 82 | 91 | 90 |
| 1955 | 92 | 98 | 89 | 100 | 93 |
| 1956 | 96 | 99 | 95 | 101 | 97 |
| 1957 | 99 | 102 | 99 | 100 | 99 |
| 1958 | 100 | 100 | 100 | 100 | 100 |
| 1959 | 101 | 93 | 101 | 107 | 100 |
| 1960 | 105 | 85 | 106 | 110 | 100 |
| 1961 | 108 | 81 | 110 | 114 | 101 |

#### b. Average Annual Rate of Change — Taux annuel moyen de variation

| Period | | | | | |
|---|---|---|---|---|---|
| 1950 – 1960 | 4.6 | −0.5 | 5.2 | 3.8 | 2.4 |
| 1950 – 1953 | 6.1 | 3.3 | 6.4 | 4.6 | 3.3 |
| 1954 – 1958 | 4.4 | 0.5 | 5.1 | 2.4 | 2.7 |
| 1958 – 1960 | 2.5 | −7.8 | 3.0 | 4.9 | — |

For footnotes, see end of table.
Pour les notes, voir au bas du tableau.

### B. The Major Groups of Mining
### Les classes de la branche Industries extractives

| Period / Période | All mining[1,3] / Toutes industries extractives[1,3] | Coal mining[3] / Extraction du charbon[3] | Metal mining / Extraction des minerais métalliques | Crude petroleum and natural gas / Pétrole brut et gaz naturel | Other mining[1] / Autres industries extractives[1] |
|---|---|---|---|---|---|
| ISIC — CITI | 1 | 11 | 12 | 13 | 14–19 |

#### a. Indexes — Indices (1958 = 100)

| Period | | | | | |
|---|---|---|---|---|---|
| 1950 | 89[2] | 89 | 97 | [2] | 75 |
| 1951 | 92[2] | 92 | 107 | [2] | 89 |
| 1952 | 95[2] | 94 | 115 | [2] | 94 |
| 1953 | 98 | 97 | 115 | 94 | 95 |
| 1954 | 98 | 97 | 104 | 100 | 97 |
| 1955 | 98 | 97 | 104 | 105 | 103 |
| 1956 | 99 | 99 | 106 | 108 | 104 |
| 1957 | 102 | 101 | 110 | 117 | 104 |
| 1958 | 100 | 100 | 100 | 100 | 100 |
| 1959 | 93 | 93 | 89 | 103 | 96 |
| 1960 | 85 | 85 | 83 | 98 | 94 |
| 1961 | 81 | 81 | 79 | 95 | 93 |

#### b. Average Annual Rate of Change — Taux annuel moyen de variation

| Period | | | | | |
|---|---|---|---|---|---|
| 1950 – 1960 | −0.5 | −0.5 | −1.5 | ... | 2.4 |
| 1950 – 1953 | 3.3 | 2.9 | 5.9 | ... | 8.2 |
| 1954 – 1958 | 0.5 | 0.8 | −1.0 | — | 0.8 |
| 1958 – 1960 | −7.8 | −7.8 | −8.9 | −1.0 | −3.0 |

For footnotes, see end of table.
Pour les notes, voir au bas du tableau.

# GERMANY, Federal Republic of

## C.  The Major Groups of Manufacturing — Les classes de la branche Industries manufacturières

| Period / Période | Manufacturing — Industries manufacturières | Food, beverages and tobacco — Industries alimentaires, boissons, tabac | Textiles | Clothing, footwear and made-up textiles [4] — Articles d'habillement, chaussures et ouvrages en tissu [4] | Wood products and furniture [6] — Bois et meubles [6] | Paper and paper products — Papier et ouvrages en papier | Printing and publishing — Imprimerie et édition | Leather and leather products except wearing apparel [4] — Cuir et articles en cuir, à l'exclusion des articles d'habillement [4] | Rubber products [5] — Ouvrages en caoutchouc [5] | Chemicals and chemical, petroleum and coal products [3] — Produits chimiques et dérivés du pétrole et du charbon [3] | Non-metallic mineral products [1,5] — Produits minéraux non métalliques [1,5] | Basic metals — Métallurgie de base | Metal products — Ouvrages en métaux | Other manufacturing [6] — Autres industries manufacturières [6] |
|---|---|---|---|---|---|---|---|---|---|---|---|---|---|---|
| ISIC — CITI | 2–3 | 20–22 | 23 | 24 | 25–26 | 27 | 28 | 29 | 30 | 31–32 | 33 | 34 | 35–38 | 39 |

### a.  Indexes — Indices (1958 = 100)

| Period / Période | 2–3 | 20–22 | 23 | 24 | 25–26 | 27 | 28 | 29 | 30 | 31–32 | 33 | 34 | 35–38 | 39 |
|---|---|---|---|---|---|---|---|---|---|---|---|---|---|---|
| 1950 | 64 [2] | 72 | 86 | 62 | 84 | 64 | 61 | 74 | 60 | 67 [2] | 71 | 65 | 53 | 50 |
| 1951 | 71 [2] | 76 | 95 | 71 | 90 | 72 | 67 | 80 | 64 | 72 [2] | 81 | 73 | 61 | 60 |
| 1952 | 74 [2] | 80 | 92 | 73 | 89 | 74 | 70 | 82 | 65 | 74 [2] | 84 | 78 | 65 | 66 |
| 1953 | 77 | 83 | 97 | 80 | 88 | 77 | 75 | 87 | 72 | 75 | 87 | 79 | 68 | 72 |
| 1954 | 82 | 86 | 98 | 82 | 93 | 83 | 79 | 90 | 80 | 80 | 92 | 82 | 74 | 79 |
| 1955 | 89 | 90 | 101 | 88 | 98 | 90 | 83 | 95 | 90 | 86 | 99 | 91 | 84 | 89 |
| 1956 | 95 | 95 | 104 | 96 | 101 | 96 | 88 | 100 | 94 | 92 | 103 | 97 | 92 | 95 |
| 1957 | 99 | 98 | 105 | 101 | 102 | 100 | 94 | 103 | 97 | 96 | 103 | 101 | 97 | 98 |
| 1958 | 100· | 100 | 100 | 100 | 100 | 100 | 100 | 100 | 100 | 100 | 100 | 100 | 100 | 100 |
| 1959 | 101 | 100 | 96 | 99 | 98 | 101 | 103 | 93 | 105 | 103 | 102 | 100 | 103 | 104 |
| 1960 | 106 | 101 | 99 | 103 | 98 | 108 | 102 | 93 | 116 | 109 | 105 | 106 | 110 | 110 |
| 1961 | 110 | 103 | 98 | 106 | 100 | 109 | 108 | 94 | 116 | 115 | 107 | 110 | 116 | 115 |

### b.  Average Annual Rate of Change — Taux annuel moyen de variation

| Period / Période | 2–3 | 20–22 | 23 | 24 | 25–26 | 27 | 28 | 29 | 30 | 31–32 | 33 | 34 | 35–38 | 39 |
|---|---|---|---|---|---|---|---|---|---|---|---|---|---|---|
| 1950–1960 | 5.2 | 3.4 | 1.4 | 5.2 | 1.6 | 5.4 | 5.3 | 2.3 | 6.8 | 5.0 | 4.0 | 5.0 | 7.6 | 8.2 |
| 1950–1953 | 6.4 | 4.9 | 4.1 | 8.9 | 1.6 | 6.4 | 7.1 | 5.6 | 6.3 | 3.8 | 7.0 | 6.7 | 8.7 | 12.9 |
| 1954–1958 | 5.1 | 3.8 | 0.5 | 5.1 | 1.8 | 4.8 | 6.1 | 2.7 | 5.7 | 5.7 | 2.1 | 5.1 | 7.8 | 6.1 |
| 1958–1960 | 3.0 | 0.5 | −0.5 | 1.5 | −1.0 | 3.9 | 1.0 | −3.6 | 7.7 | 4.4 | 2.5 | 3.0 | 4.9 | 4.9 |

[1] Stone and sand quarrying is included in the manufacture of Non-metallic mineral products (ISIC major group 33) rather than in Other mining (ISIC major groups 14–19).
[2] Crude petroleum and natural gas (ISIC major group 13) is included in Chemicals and petroleum and coal products (ISIC major groups 31–32) during the years, 1950–1952.
[3] The manufacture of coke and coal briquettes (part of ISIC major groups 31–32) is included in Coal mining (ISIC major group 11).
[4] The manufacture of leather gloves is covered in Leather and leather products (ISIC major group 29) instead of in Clothing (ISIC major group 24).
[5] Asbestos products are covered in Rubber products (ISIC 30) and not in Non-metallic mineral products (ISIC 33).
[6] Manufacturing of brushes and brooms is covered in Wood products (ISIC major groups 25–26) and not in Other manufacturing (ISIC major group 39).

[1] L'extraction de la pierre à bâtir et du sable est incluse dans Produits minéraux non métalliques (CITI classe 33) plutôt que dans Autres industries extractives (CITI classes 14–19).
[2] L'extraction du Pétrole brut et du gaz naturel (CITI classe 13) est incluse dans Industries chimiques et dérivés du pétrole et du charbon (CITI classes 31–32) pendant les années 1950–1952.
[3] Les cokeries et usines de briquettes de charbon (dans CITI classes 31–32) sont incluses dans les Industries extractives de charbon (CITI classe 11).
[4] La fabrication de gants en cuir est incluse dans Cuir et ouvrages en cuir (CITI classe 29) au lieu d'être dans Articles d'habillement (CITI classe 24).
[5] Les produits en amiante sont inclus dans Ouvrages en caoutchouc (CITI classe 30) plutôt que dans Produits minéraux non métalliques.
[6] La fabrication de brosses et de balais est couverte par Ouvrages en bois (CITI classes 25–26) non par Autres industries manufacturières (CITI classe 39).

## 4. NUMBER OF AND EMPLOYMENT IN ALL INDUSTRIAL LOCAL UNITS
### 17 May 1939 and 13 September 1950

## NOMBRE D'UNITES INDUSTRIELLES LOCALES ET EMPLOI DANS CES UNITES
### 17 mai 1939 et 13 septembre 1950

Number of local units in units; number of engaged and employees in thousands

Nombre d'unités locales en unités; nombre de personnes occupées et de salariés en milliers

### A. The Divisions of Industrial Activity — Les branches de l'activité industrielle

| Item of data | All industrial activity Toutes industries | | Mining [1] Industries extractives [1] | | Manufacturing [1] Industries manufacturières[1] | | Construction Bâtiment et travaux publics | | Electricity and gas Electricité et gaz | | Rubrique |
|---|---|---|---|---|---|---|---|---|---|---|---|
| | 17.V.1939 | 13.IX.1950 | 17.V.1939[2] | 13.IX.1950 | 17.V.1939[2,3] | 13.IX.1950 | 17.V.1939 | 13.IX.1950 | 17.V.1939 | 13.IX.1950 | |
| ISIC | 1–4, 511–512 | | 1 | | 2–3 | | 4 | | 511–512 | | CITI |
| Number of local units [4]... | 876 894 | 929 046 | 6 686 | 16 182 | 710 081 | 734 937 | 155 631 | 174 063 | 4 496 | 3 864 | Nombre d'unités locales [4] |
| Number of engaged (As of census date).... | 8 058 | 8 829.6 | 552 | 741.8 | 6 069 | 6 448.8 | 1 334 | 1 502.7 | 103 | 136.3 | Nombre de personnes occupées (à la date du recensement) |
| Number of employees (As of census date).... | ... | 7 598.5 | ... | 724.3 | ... | 5 456.4 | ... | 1 282.1 | ... | 135.7 | Nombre de salariés (à la date du recensement) |
| Distribution in percent of: Number of engaged... | 100.0 | 100.0 | 6.8 | 8.4 | 75.3 | 73.0 | 16.6 | 17.0 | 1.3 | 1.6 | Répartition en pourcentage: Du nombre de personnes occupées |

[1] The manufacturing of coke and coal briquettes is included in Mining (ISIC division 1) instead of manufacturing (ISIC division 2–3).
[2] Stone and sand quarrying is included in Manufacturing (ISIC division 2–3) instead of Mining (ISIC division 1), and petroleum refining is included in Mining instead of Manufacturing.
[3] Photostating services are included.
[4] In the 17 May 1939 census, activities ancillary to but physically separated from the main activity of the local unit were not covered in the local unit.

[1] La fabrication du coke et des briquettes est comprise dans Industries extractives (CITI branche 1) et non dans Industries manufacturières (CITI branche 2–3).
[2] L'extraction de la pierre et du sable est comprise dans Industries manufacturières (CITI branche 2–3) et non dans Industries extractives (CITI branche 1). Le raffinage du pétrole est compris dans Industries extractives et non dans Industries manufacturières.
[3] Y compris la préparation des photostats.
[4] Dans le recensement du 17 mai 1939, les activités auxiliaires — mais physiquement distinctes — de l'activité principale de l'unité locale n'ont pas été comprises dans l'unité locale.

### B. The Major Groups of Mining — Les classes de la branche Industries extractives

| Item of data | 17.V.1939 | | | | | 13.IX.1950 | | | | | Rubrique |
|---|---|---|---|---|---|---|---|---|---|---|---|
| | All mining Toutes Industries extractives | Coal mining [1] Extraction du charbon [1] | Metal mining Extraction des minerais métalliques | Crude petroleum and natural gas [2] Pétrole brut et gaz naturel [2] | Other mining [3] Divers [3] | All mining Toutes industries extractives | Coal mining [1] Extraction du charbon [1] | Metal mining Extraction des minerais métalliques | Crude petroleum and natural gas Pétrole brut et gaz naturel | Other mining Divers | |
| ISIC | 1 | 11 | 12 | 13 | 14–19 | 1 | 11 | 12 | 13 | 14–19 | CITI |
| Number of local units [4]......... | 6 686 | 294 | 203 | 68 | 6 121 | 16 182 | 552 | 153 | 105 | 15 372 | Nombre d'unités locales [4] |
| Number of engaged (As of census date)........... | 552 | 386 | 37 | 4 | 125 | 741.8 | 510.5 | 30.9 | 9.0 | 191.4 | Nombre de personnes occupées (à la date du recensement) |
| Number of employees (As of census date)........... | ... | ... | ... | ... | ... | 724.3 | 510.4 | 30.9 | 9.0 | 174.0 | Nombre de salariés (à la date du recensement) |
| Distribution in percent of number of engaged........ | 100.0 | 69.9 | 6.7 | 0.7 | 22.7 | 100.0 | 68.8 | 4.1 | 1.2 | 25.9 | Répartition en pourcentage du nombre de personnes occupées |
| Employees as a percent of engaged... | ... | ... | ... | ... | ... | 97.6 | 100.0 | 100.0 | 100.0 | 90.9 | Salariés en pourcentage des personnes occupées |

[1] Includes the manufacturing of coke and coal briquettes.
[2] Includes the refining of petroleum.
[3] Excludes stone and sand quarrying.
[4] In the 17.V.1939 census activities ancillary to but physically separated from the main activity of the local unit were not covered in the local unit.

[1] Y compris la fabrication du coke et des briquettes.
[2] Y compris le raffinage du pétrole.
[3] Non compris l'extraction de la pierre et du sable.
[4] Dans le recensement du 17.V.1939, les activités auxiliaires — mais physiquement distinctes — de l'activité principale de l'unité locale n'ont pas été comprises dans l'unité locale.

# GERMANY, Federal Republic of

## C. The Major Groups of Manufacturing — Les classes de la branche Industries manufacturières

| Year and item of data | Manu-facturing / Industries manufac-turières | Food, beverages and tobacco / Industries alimen-taires, boissons, tabac | Textiles | Clothing, footwear and made-up textiles / Articles d'habil-lement, chaussures et ouvrages en tissu | Wood products and furniture[7] / Bois et meubles[7] | Paper and paper products / Papier et ouvrages en papier | Printing and publish-ing / Im-primerie et édition | Leather and leather products except wearing apparel / Cuir et articles en cuir, à l'exclusion des articles d'habil-lement | Rubber products / Ouvrages en caout-chouc | Chemicals and chemical, petroleum and coal products[5] / Produits chi-miques et dérivés du pétrole et du charbon[5] | Non-metallic mineral products / Produits minéraux non métal-liques | Basic metals / Métal-lurgie de base | Metal products[7] / Ouvrages en métaux[7] | Other manu-factur-ing / Autres in-dustries manufac-turières | Année et rubrique |
|---|---|---|---|---|---|---|---|---|---|---|---|---|---|---|---|
| **ISIC** | 2–3 | 20–22 | 23 | 24 | 25–26 | 27 | 28 | 29 | 30 | 31–32 | 33 | 34 | 35–38 | 39 | **CITI** |
| *17.V.1939* Number of local units [9]... | 710 081 | 168 167 | 12 851[1] | 236 110 | 91 723 | 5 290[2] | 7 876[2,3] | 18 173 | 1 185 | 5 196[1,4] | 12 419[6] | 2 424 | 131 440[8] | 17 227[8] | *17.V.1939* Nombre d'unités locales[9] |
| Number of engaged (As of census date).... | 6 069 | 903 | 529[1] | 647 | 475 | 130[2] | 133[2,3] | 107 | 53 | 294[1,4] | 247[6] | 581 | 1 825[8] | 145[8] | Nombre de personnes occupées (à la date du recense-ment) |
| Distribution in percent of number of engaged.......... | 100.0 | 14.8 | 8.7[1] | 10.7 | 7.8 | 2.2[2] | 2.2[2,3] | 1.7 | 0.9 | 4.8[1,4] | 4.1[6] | 9.6 | 30.1[8] | 2.4[8] | Répartition en pourcen-tage du nombre de personnes occupées |
| *13.IX.1950* Number of local units.... | 734 937 | 145 993 | 20 910 | 246 240 | 107 126 | 2 991 | 9 384 | 18 982 | 1 732 | 7 189 | 8 157 | 2 966 | 135 033 | 28 234 | *13.IX.1950* Nombre d'unités locales |
| Number of engaged (As of census date).... | 6 448.8 | 903.1 | 612.6 | 757.8 | 610.4 | 122.0 | 155.2 | 103.1 | 61.4 | 332.8 | 252.0 | 415.3 | 1 896.5 | 226.6 | Nombre de personnes occupées (à la date du recense-ment) |
| Number of employees (As of census date).... | 5 456.4 | 630.7 | 583.8 | 480.6 | 471.8 | 117.3 | 141.5 | 78.3 | 59.3 | 324.3 | 240.8 | 412.0 | 1 723.5 | 192.5 | Nombre de salariés (à la date du recense-ment) |
| Distribution in percent of number of engaged.......... | 100.0 | 14.0 | 9.5 | 11.7 | 9.5 | 1.9 | 2.4 | 1.6 | 0.9 | 5.2 | 3.9 | 6.4 | 29.4 | 3.6 | Répartition en pourcen-tage du nombre de personnes occupées |
| Employees as a percent of engaged......... | 84.6 | 69.8 | 95.3 | 63.4 | 77.3 | 96.1 | 91.2 | 75.9 | 96.6 | 97.4 | 95.6 | 99.2 | 90.9 | 85.0 | Salariés en pourcentage des personnes occupées |

[1] The manufacture of synthetic fibres is included in Textiles (ISIC major group 23) instead of in Chemicals (ISIC major group 31).
[2] Bookbinding is covered in Paper and paper products (ISIC major group 27) rather than in Printing and publishing (ISIC major group 28).
[3] Includes photostating services.
[4] Excludes petroleum refining.
[5] Excludes the manufacture of coke and coal briquettes.
[6] Includes stone and sand quarrying.
[7] The manufacture of metal furniture is classified in Metal products (ISIC major groups 35–38) instead of in Furniture (ISIC major group 26).
[8] The manufacture of jewelry and the polishing of precious stones is covered in Metal products (ISIC groups 35–38) and not in Other manufacturing (ISIC major group 39).
[9] Activities ancillary to but physically separated from the main activity of the local unit were not included in the local unit.

[1] La fabrication des fibres synthétiques est comprise dans Textiles (CITI 23) et non dans Industrie chimique (CITI 31).
[2] La reliure est comprise dans Papier et ouvrages en papier (CITI 27) et non dans Imprimerie et édition (CITI 28).
[3] Y compris la préparation des photostats.
[4] Non compris le raffinage du pétrole.
[5] Non compris la fabrication du coke et des briquettes.
[6] Y compris l'extraction de la pierre et du sable.
[7] La fabrication des meubles en métal est classée dans Ouvrages en métaux (CITI 35–38) et non dans Industrie du meuble (CITI 26).
[8] La bijouterie et l'orfèvrerie ainsi que le polissage des pierres précieuses sont compris dans Ouvrages en métaux (CITI 35–38) et non dans Autres industries manufacturières (CITI 39).
[9] Les activités auxiliaires — mais physiquement distinctes — de l'activité principale de l'unité locale ne sont pas comprises dans l'unité locale.

## 5. THE CHARACTERISTICS OF ALL MINING AND MANUFACTURING UNITS, EXCEPTING LICENSED HANDICRAFTS ENGAGING LESS THAN TEN PERSONS

## CARACTERISTIQUES DE TOUTES LES UNITES MINIERES ET MANUFACTURIERES, A L'EXCLUSION DES UNITES ARTISANALES PATENTEES OCCUPANT MOINS DE 10 PERSONNES

### 1950, 1954

Number of local units and enterprises in units; gross receipts and value added in million D.M.; number of engaged in thousands; and value added per person engaged in thousand D.M.

Nombre d'unités locales et d'entreprises en unités; recettes brutes et valeur ajoutée en millions de D.M.; nombre de personnes occupées en milliers; valeur ajoutée par personne occupée en milliers de D.M.

### A. The Major Groups of Mining

### Les classes de la branche Industries extractives

| Year and item of data | All mining<br>Toutes industries extractives | Coal mining [1]<br>Extraction du charbon [1] | Metal mining<br>Extraction des minerais métalliques | Crude petroleum and natural gas<br>Pétrole brut et gaz naturel | Other mining [2]<br>Divers [2] | Année et rubrique |
|---|---|---|---|---|---|---|
| ISIC | 1 | 11 | 12 | 13 | 14-19 | CITI |
| a. Absolute Figures — Chiffres absolus | | | | | | |
| **1950**<br>Number of local units (During VIII.1950)...... | 957 | 391 | 108 | 176 | 282 | **1950**<br>Nombre d'unités locales (en VIII.1950) |
| Gross receipts...... | 5 245 | 4 503 | 276 | 148 | 318 | Recettes brutes |
| Value added...... | 3 948 | 3 375 | 197 | 133 | 243 | Valeur ajoutée |
| Number of engaged (During VIII.1950)...... | 585.6 | 518.0 | 30.2 | 9.0 | 28.4 | Nombre de personnes occupées (en VIII.1950) |
| **1954**<br>Number of Enterprises (During VIII.1954) | 297 | 98 | 17 | 12 | 170 | **1954**<br>Nombre d'entreprises (en VIII.1954) |
| Gross receipts...... | 9 989 | 8 141 | 276 | 1 110 | 462 | Recettes brutes |
| Value added...... | 7 202 | 6 030 | 168 | 665 | 339 | Valeur ajoutée |
| Number of engaged (During VIII.1954) | 632.8 | 554.9 | 21.9 | 30.4 | 25.6 | Nombre de personnes occupées (en VIII.1954) |
| b. Structure | | | | | | |
| **1950**<br>Distribution in percent of:<br>Value added..... | 100.0 | 85.4 | 5.0 | 3.4 | 6.2 | **1950**<br>Repartition en pourcentage:<br>De la valeur ajoutée |
| Number of engaged........ | 100.0 | 88.4 | 5.2 | 1.5 | 4.9 | Du nombre de personnes occupées |
| Value added per person engaged.. | 6.7 | 6.5 | 6.5 | 14.8 | 8.6 | Valeur ajoutée par personne occupée |
| **1954**<br>Distribution in percent of:<br>Value added.... | 100.0 | 83.7 | 2.3 | 9.2 | 4.8 | **1954**<br>Distribution en pourcentage:<br>Valeur ajoutée |
| Number of engaged........ | 100.0 | 87.7 | 3.5 | 4.8 | 4.0 | Nombre de personnes occupées |
| Value added per person engaged.. | 11.4 | 10.9 | 7.7 | 21.9 | 13.2 | Valeur ajoutée par personne occupée |

[1] Includes the manufacturing of coal and coke briquettes.
[2] Excludes the quarrying of stone and sand.

[1] Y compris la fabrication du coke et des briquettes.
[2] Non compris l'extraction de la pierre et du sable.

## B. The Major Groups of Manufacturing — Les classes de la branche Industries manufacturières

| Year and item of data | Manufacturing — Industries manufacturières | Food, beverages and tobacco — Industries alimentaires, boissons, tabac | Textiles | Clothing, footwear and made-up textiles [4] — Articles d'habillement, chaussures et ouvrages en tissu [4] | Wood products and furniture[1,2] — Bois et meubles[1,2] | Paper and paper products — Papier et ouvrages en papier | Printing and publishing [3] — Imprimerie et édition [3] | Leather and leather products except wearing apparel [4] — Cuir et articles en cuir, à l'exclusion des articles d'habillement [4] | Rubber products — Ouvrages en caoutchouc | Chemicals and chemical, petroleum and coal products — Produits chimiques et dérivés du pétrole et du charbon | Non-metallic mineral products[5,6] — Produits minéraux non métalliques[5,6] | Basic metals — Métallurgie de base | Metal products[2] — Ouvrages en métaux [2] | Other manufacturing [1] — Autres industries manufacturières [1] | Année et rubrique |
|---|---|---|---|---|---|---|---|---|---|---|---|---|---|---|---|
| ISIC / CITI | 2–3 | 20–22 | 23 | 24 | 25–26 | 27 | 28 | 29 | 30 | 31–32 | 33 | 34 | 35–38 | 39 | |
| *a. Absolute Figures — Chiffres absolus* | | | | | | | | | | | | | | | |
| **1950** | | | | | | | | | | | | | | | **1950** |
| Number of local units (During VIII.1950) | 103 075 | 19 399 | 7 557 | 7 227 | 13 523 | 2 230 | 6 121 | 2 012 | 430 | 5 539 | 11 897 | 2 213 | 19 681 | 5 246 | Nombre d'unités locales (en VIII.1950) |
| Gross receipts | 86 055 | 19 372 | 10 770 | 4 233 | 3 669 | 2 603 | 1 490 | 1 408 | 1 138 | 8 753 | 3 544 | 7 678 | 19 940 | 1 457 | Recettes brutes |
| Value added | 41 440 | 8 086 | 4 986 | 1 678 | 1 734 | 1 230 | 961 | 515 | 562 | 4 228 | 2 267 | 3 509 | 10 791 | 893 | Valeur ajoutée |
| Number of engaged (During VIII.1950) | 4 728.8 | 435.4 | 575.5 | 299.7 | 307.2 | 124.9 | 132.1 | 67.5 | 59.7 | 327.9 | 363.2 | 402.8 | 1 481.4 | 151.5 | Nombre de personnes occupées (en VIII.1950) |
| **1954** | | | | | | | | | | | | | | | **1954** |
| Number of enterprises (During VIII.1954) | 77 590 | 13 136 | 5 996 | 5 748 | 9 735 | 1 813 | 5 482 | 1 386 | 345 | 3 866 | 8 441 | 1 777 | 15 541 | 4 324 | Nombre d'entreprises (en VIII.1954) |
| Gross receipts | 143 966 | 25 074 | 12 661 | 5 804 | 5 735 | 4 397 | 2 502 | 1 536 | 1 906 | 16 920 | 6 286 | 17 125 | 40 758 | 3 262 | Recettes brutes |
| Value added | 64 377 | 9 628 | 5 112 | 2 379 | 2 497 | 1 963 | 1 517 | 585 | 929 | 7 512 | 3 857 | 6 661 | 19 909 | 1 828 | Valeur ajoutée |
| Number of engaged (During VIII.1954) | 5 739.6 | 440.4 | 615.2 | 350.9 | 301.2 | 152.3 | 151.7 | 69.9 | 79.0 | 392.0 | 380.6 | 501.4 | 2 089.1 | 215.9 | Nombre de personnes occupées (en VIII.1954) |
| *b. Structure* | | | | | | | | | | | | | | | |
| **1950** | | | | | | | | | | | | | | | **1950** |
| Distribution in percent of: Value added | 100.0 | 19.5 | 12.0 | 4.0 | 4.2 | 3.0 | 2.3 | 1.3 | 1.3 | 10.2 | 5.5 | 8.5 | 26.0 | 2.2 | Répartition en pourcentage: De la valeur ajoutée |
| Number of engaged | 100.0 | 9.2 | 12.2 | 6.3 | 6.5 | 2.6 | 2.8 | 1.4 | 1.3 | 6.9 | 7.7 | 8.5 | 31.3 | 3.3 | Du nombre de personnes occupées |
| Value added per person engaged | 8.8 | 18.6 | 8.7 | 5.6 | 5.6 | 9.8 | 7.3 | 7.6 | 9.4 | 12.9 | 6.2 | 8.7 | 7.3 | 5.9 | Valeur ajoutée par personne occupée |
| **1954** | | | | | | | | | | | | | | | **1954** |
| Distribution in percent of: Value added | 100.0 | 14.9 | 7.9 | 3.7 | 3.9 | 3.1 | 2.3 | 0.9 | 1.5 | 11.6 | 6.0 | 10.4 | 30.9 | 2.9 | Distribution en pourcentage: Valeur ajoutée |
| Number of engaged | 100.0 | 7.6 | 10.7 | 6.2 | 5.2 | 2.7 | 2.6 | 1.2 | 1.4 | 6.8 | 6.7 | 8.7 | 36.4 | 3.8 | Nombre de personnes occupées |
| Value added per person engaged | 11.2 | 21.9 | 8.3 | 6.8 | 8.3 | 12.9 | 10.0 | 8.4 | 11.8 | 19.2 | 10.1 | 13.3 | 9.5 | 8.5 | Valeur ajoutée par personne occupée |

[1] The manufacturing of brushes and brooms is classified in Wood products (ISIC major group 25) instead of in Other manufacturing (ISIC major group 39).
[2] The manufacturing of metal furniture is covered in Metal products (ISIC major group 35–38) instead of in Furniture (ISIC major group 26).
[3] Includes photostating services.
[4] The manufacture of leather gloves is included in Leather and leather products (ISIC major group 29) instead of Clothing (ISIC major group 24).
[5] The making of asbestos products is included in Rubber products (ISIC major group 30) instead of in Non-metallic products (ISIC major group 33).
[6] Stone and sand quarrying is also included.

[1] La brosserie est classée dans Industrie du bois (CITI 25) et non dans Autres industries manufacturières (CITI 39).
[2] La fabrication des meubles en métal est classée dans Ouvrages en métaux (CITI 35–38) et non dans Industrie du meuble (CITI 26).
[3] Y compris la préparation des photostats.
[4] La ganterie est comprise dans Industrie du cuir et articles en cuir (CITI 29) et non dans Articles d'habillement (CITI 24).
[5] La fabrication des ouvrages en amiante est comprise dans Ouvrages en caoutchouc (CITI 30) et non dans Produits minéraux non métalliques (CITI 33).
[6] Y compris, en outre, l'extraction de la pierre et du sable.

## 6. THE CHARACTERISTICS OF INDUSTRIAL LOCAL UNITS ENGAGING TEN OR MORE PERSONS, EXCEPTING LICENSED HANDICRAFTS
## LES CARACTERISTIQUES DES UNITES LOCALES INDUSTRIELLES OCCUPANT 10 PERSONNES OU PLUS, EXCEPTE L'ARTISANAT PATENTE
### 1950, 1953, 1958

Number of local units in units; gross receipts and wages and salaries in million D.M.; number of engaged, employees and operatives in thousands; man-hours worked in millions; energy consumed in thousand metric tons of coal equivalents, electricity consumed in million KWH; salaries per employee and per thousand operative man-hours in thousand D.M.; average annual man-hours per operative in thousands; energy consumed per engaged and per thousand operative man-hours in metric tons of coal equivalents; electricity consumed per engaged and per thousand operative man-hours in thousand KWH.

Nombre d'unités locales en unités; recettes brutes et traitements et salaires en millions de D.M.; nombre de personnes occupées, de salariés et d'ouvriers en milliers; heures de travail en millions; énergie consommée en milliers de tonnes métriques d'équivalent charbon; électricité consommée en millions de kWh; salaires par salarié et par millier d'heures-ouvrier en milliers de D.M.; moyenne annuelle des heures de travail par ouvrier en milliers; énergie consommée par personne occupée et par millier d'heures-ouvrier en tonnes métriques d'équivalent charbon; électricité consommée par personne occupée et par millier d'heures-ouvrier en milliers de kWh.

## A. The Divisions of Industrial Activity — Les branches de l'activité industrielle

### a. Absolute Figures — Chiffres absolus

| Year and item of data | All industrial activity — Toutes industries | Mining [1] — Industries extractives [1] | Manufacturing [1] — Industries manufacturières [1] | Construction [2] — Bâtiment et travaux publics [2] | Electricity and gas — Electricité et gaz | Année et rubrique |
|---|---|---|---|---|---|---|
| ISIC | 1-4, 511-512 | 1 | 2-3 | 4 | 511-512 | CITI |
| **1950** | | | | | | **1950** |
| Number of local units | ... | 545 | 46 145 | 64 343 | 2 213 | Nombre d'unités locales |
| Gross receipts | ... | 4 573 | 75 708 | ... | ... | Recettes brutes |
| Number of engaged (Average during year) | 5 813.3 | 571.4 | 4 206.1 | 912.8 | 123.0 | Nombre de personnes occupées (Moyenne pour l'année) |
| Employees: Number (Average during year) | 5 697.7 | 571.3 | 4 169.4 | 834.0 | 123.0 | Salariés: Nombre (Moyenne pour l'année) |
| Wages and salaries | 18 079 | 2 180 | 12 949 | 2 470 | 480 | Traitements et salaires |
| Operatives: Number (Average during year) | ... | ... | 3 755.9 | 793.6 | ... | Ouvriers: Nombre (Moyenne pour l'année) |
| Man-hours worked | 11 216.3 | 1 152.0 | 8 050.0 | 1 810.9 | 203.4 | Heures de travail effectuées |
| Wages and salaries | 14 359.0 | 1 893.0 | 9 882.0 | 2 297.3 | 286.7 | Traitements et salaires |
| Electricity consumed | ... | 5 528 | 23 314 | ... | ... | Electricité consommée |
| **1953** | | | | | | **1953** |
| Number of local units | ... | 696 | 49 570 | 64 682 | ... | Nombre d'unités locales |
| Gross receipts | ... | 7 321 | 118 687 | 10 690 | ... | Recettes brutes |
| Number of engaged (Average during year) | 6 917.6 | 643.2 | 5 087.2 | 1 051.3 | 135.9 | Nombre de personnes occupées (Moyenne pour l'année) |
| Employees: Number (Average during year) | 6 801.8 | 643.1 | 5 043.8 | 979.0 | 135.9 | Salariés: Nombre (Moyenne pour l'année) |
| Wages and salaries | 27 905 | 3 162 | 20 118 | 3 933 | 692 | Traitements et salaires |
| Operatives: Number (Average during year) | 5 811.9 | 591.3 | 4 204.2 | 928.1 | 88.3 | Ouvriers: Nombre (Moyenne pour l'année) |
| Man-hours worked | 13 240.8 | 1 258.0 | 9 585.0 | 2 179.5 | 218.3 | Heures de travail effectuées |
| Wages and salaries | 21 873.9 | 2 705.0 | 15 112.0 | 3 659.8 | 397.1 | Traitements et salaires |
| Electricity consumed | ... | 7 147 | 33 418 | ... | ... | Electricité consommée |
| **1958** | | | | | | **1958** |
| Number of local units | ... | 662 | 51 595 | 59 256 | ... | Nombre d'unités locales |
| Gross receipts | 229 919.0 | 9 577.0 | 195 495.0 | 17 172.0 | 7 675.0 | Recettes brutes |
| Number of engaged (Average during year) | 8 634.2 | 656.5 | 6 616.1 | 1 206.1 | 155.5 | Nombre de personnes occupées (Moyenne pour l'année) |
| Employees: Number (Average during year) | 8 513.4 | 656.4 | 6 561.6 | 1 139.9 | 155.5 | Salariés: Nombre (Moyenne pour l'année) |
| Wages and salaries | 46 254.5 | 4 376.0 | 34 602.0 | 6 199.5 | 1 077.0 | Traitements et salaires |
| Operatives: Number (Average during year) | 7 147.8 | 593.4 | 5 385.2 | 1 070.2 | 99.0 | Ouvriers: Nombre (Moyenne pour l'année) |
| Man-hours worked | 14 945.1 | 1 135.0 | 11 243.0 | 2 339.6 | 227.5 | Heures de travail effectuées |
| Wages and salaries | 35 243.8 | 3 654.0 | 25 305.0 | 5 691.8 | 593.0 | Traitements et salaires |
| Energy consumed | ... | 18 892 | 61 467 | ... | ... | Energie consommée |
| Electricity consumed | ... | 10 250 | 52 490 | ... | ... | Electricité consommée |

### b. Structure

| Year and item of data | All industrial activity — Toutes industries | Mining [1] — Industries extractives [1] | Manufacturing [1] — Industries manufacturières [1] | Construction [2] — Bâtiment et travaux publics [2] | Electricity and gas — Electricité et gaz | Année et rubrique |
|---|---|---|---|---|---|---|
| ISIC | 1-4, 511-512 | 1 | 2-3 | 4 | 511-512 | CITI |
| **1950** | | | | | | **1950** |
| Distribution in percent of number of engaged | 100.0 | 9.8 | 72.4 | 15.7 | 2.1 | Distribution en pourcentage du nombre de personnes occupées |
| Per person engaged: electricity consumed | ... | 9.7 | 5.5 | ... | 52.3 | Par personne occupée: électricité consommée |
| Employees as a percent of engaged | 98.0 | 100.0 | 99.1 | 91.4 | 100.0 | Salariés en pourcentage des personnes occupées |
| Wages and salaries per employee | 3.2 | 3.8 | 3.1 | 3.0 | 3.9 | Traitements et salaires par salarié |
| Operatives as a percent of employees | ... | ... | 90.1 | 95.2 | ... | Ouvriers en pourcentage des salariés |
| Average man-hours per operative | ... | ... | 2.14 | 2.28 | ... | Heures de travail: moyenne par ouvrier |
| Per thousand operative man-hour Wages and salaries | 1.28 | 1.64 | 1.23 | 1.27 | 1.41 | Par millier d'heures de travail d'ouvrier Traitements et salaires |
| Electricity consumed | ... | 4.80 | 2.90 | ... | ... | Electricité consommée |
| **1953** | | | | | | **1953** |
| Distribution in percent of number of engaged | 100.0 | 9.3 | 73.5 | 15.2 | 2.0 | Distribution en pourcentage du nombre de personnes occupées |
| Per person engaged: electricity consumed | ... | 11.1 | 6.6 | ... | 57.5 | Par personne engagée: électricité consommée |
| Employees as a percent of engaged | 98.3 | 100.0 | 99.1 | 93.1 | 100.0 | Salariés en pourcentage des personnes occupées |
| Wages and salaries per employee | 4.1 | 4.9 | 4.0 | 4.0 | 5.1 | Traitements et salaires par salarié |
| Operatives as a percent of employees | 85.4 | 91.9 | 83.4 | 94.8 | 65.0 | Ouvriers en pourcentage des salariés |
| Average man-hours per operative | 2.28 | 2.13 | 2.28 | 2.35 | 2.47 | Heures de travail: moyenne par ouvrier |
| Per thousand operative man-hour Wages and salaries | 1.65 | 2.15 | 1.58 | 1.68 | 1.82 | Par millier d'heures de travail d'ouvrier Traitements et salaires |
| Electricity consumed | | 5.68 | 3.49 | | | Electricité consommée |
| **1958** | | | | | | **1958** |
| Distribution in percent of number of engaged | 100.0 | 7.6 | 76.6 | 14.0 | 1.8 | Distribution en pourcentage du nombre de personnes occupées |
| Per person engaged: Energy consumed | ... | 28.78 | 9.29 | ... | ... | Par personne occupée: Energie consommée |
| Electricity consumed | ... | 15.6 | 7.9 | ... | 73.1 | Electricité consommée |
| Employees as a percent of engaged | 98.6 | 100.0 | 99.2 | 94.5 | 100.0 | Salariés en pourcentage des personnes occupées |
| Wages and salaries per employee | 5.4 | 6.7 | 5.3 | 5.4 | 6.9 | Traitements et salaires par salarié |
| Operatives as a percent of employees | 84.0 | 90.4 | 82.1 | 93.9 | 63.7 | Ouvriers en pourcentage des salariés |
| Average man-hours per operative | 2.09 | 1.91 | 2.09 | 2.19 | 2.30 | Heures de travail: moyenne par ouvrier |
| Per thousand operative man-hour Wages and salaries | 2.36 | 3.22 | 2.25 | 2.43 | 2.61 | Par millier d'heures-ouvrier Traitements et salaires |
| Energy consumed | ... | 16.64 | 5.47 | ... | ... | Energie consommée |
| Electricity consumed | ... | 9.03 | 4.67 | ... | ... | Electricité consommée |

[1] In the case of all the data shown, the manufacturing of coke and coal and coke briquettes (part of ISIC major group 32) is included in Mining (ISIC Division 1) and not in Manufacturing (ISIC Divisions 2-3) whereas the quarrying of sand and stone (in ISIC major group 14) is included in Manufacturing and not in Mining. In the case of data for 1950 the extraction of Crude petroleum and natural gas (ISIC major group 13) is included in Manufacturing and not in Mining.
[2] In the case of Construction (ISIC Division 4), all units, including licensed handicrafts, are covered.

[1] Dans le cas de toutes les données reproduites, les industries manufacturières de coke et de briquettes en coke (dans CITI classe 32) sont incluses dans les Industries extractives (CITI Branche 1) et non pas dans les Industries manufacturières (CITI Branches 2-3) tandis que l'extraction du sable et de la pierre à bâtir (dans CITI classe 14) est incluse dans les Industries manufacturières et non dans les Industries extractives. Dans le cas des données de 1950, l'extraction du Pétrole brut et du gas naturel (CITI classe 13) est incluse dans les Industries manufacturières et non pas dans les Industries extractives.
[2] Dans le cas des bâtiments et travaux publics (CITI Branche 4) toutes les unités, y compris les unités artisanales patentées, sont couvertes.

# GERMANY, Federal Republic of

## B. The Major Groups of Mining — Les classes de la branche Industries extractives

### a. Absolute Figures — Chiffres absolus

| Year and item of data | All mining 1 / Toutes industries extractives 1 | Coal mining 1 / Extraction du charbon 1 | Metal mining / Extraction des minerais métalliques | Crude petroleum and natural gas / Pétrole brut et gaz naturel | Other mining 3 / Divers 3 | Rubrique |
|---|---|---|---|---|---|---|
| ISIC / CITI | 1 | 11 | 12 | 13 | 14-19 | |
| **1950** | | | | | | **1950** |
| Number of local units | 545 [2] | 241 | 100 | ... | 204 | Nombre d'unités locales |
| Gross receipts | 4 573 [2] | 3 992 | 263 | ... | 318 | Recettes brutes |
| Number of engaged (Average during year) | 571.4 [2] | 516.5 | 29.6 | ... | 25.3 | Nombre de personnes occupées (moyenne pour l'année) |
| Employees: Number (Average during year) | 571.3 [2] | 516.5 | 29.6 | ... | 25.2 | Salariés: Nombre (moyenne pour l'année) |
| Wages and salaries | 2 180 [2] | 2 004 | 95 | ... | 81 | Traitements et salaires |
| Operatives: Man-hours worked | 1 152 [2] | 1 041 | 59 | ... | 52 | Ouvriers: Heures de travail effectuées |
| Wages and salaries | 1 893 [2] | 1 745 | 82 | ... | 66 | Traitements et salaires |
| Electricity consumed | 5 528 [2] | 4 916 | 328 | ... | 284 | Electricité consommée |
| **1953** | | | | | | **1953** |
| Number of local units | 696 | 329 | 106 | 42 | 219 | Nombre d'unités locales |
| Gross receipts | 7 321 | 6 109 | 335 | 380 | 497 | Recettes brutes |
| Number of engaged (Average during year) | 643.2 | 564.0 | 35.1 | 12.2 | 31.9 | Nombre de personnes occupées (moyenne pour l'année) |
| Employees: Number (Average during year) | 643.1 | 564.0 | 35.1 | 12.2 | 31.8 | Salariés: Nombre (moyenne pour l'année) |
| Wages and salaries | 3 162 | 2 832 | 147 | 55 | 128 | Traitements et salaires |
| Operatives: Number (Average during year) | 591.3 | 520.8 | 32.1 | 9.6 | 28.8 | Ouvriers: Nombre (moyenne pour l'année) |
| Man-hours worked | 1 258 | 1 102 | 68 | 23 | 65 | Heures de travail effectuées |
| Wages and salaries | 2 705 | 2 434 | 125 | 38 | 108 | Traitements et salaires |
| Electricity consumed | 7 147 | 6 248 | 436 | 71 | 392 | Electricité consommée |
| **1958** | | | | | | **1958** |
| Number of local units | 662 | 310 | 95 | 66 | 191 | Nombre d'unités locales |
| Gross receipts | 9 577 | 7 791 | 409 | 707 | 670 | Recettes brutes |
| Number of engaged (Average during year) | 656.5 | 579.0 | 30.6 | 13.0 | 33.9 | Nombre de personnes occupées (moyenne pour l'année) |
| Employees: Number (Average during year) | 656.4 | 579.0 | 30.6 | 13.0 | 33.8 | Salariés: Nombre (moyenne pour l'année) |
| Wages and salaries | 4 376 | 3 914 | 180 | 82 | 200 | Traitements et salaires |
| Operatives: Number (Average during year) | 593.4 | 526.4 | 27.3 | 9.6 | 30.1 | Ouvriers: Nombre (moyenne pour l'année) |
| Man-hours worked | 1 135 | 995 | 55 | 21 | 64 | Heures de travail effectuées |
| Wages and salaries | 3 654 | 3 297 | 147 | 50 | 160 | Traitements et salaires |
| Energy consumed | 18 892 | 17 958 | 439 | 41 | 454 | Energie consommée |
| Electricity consumed | 10 250 | 9 088 | 506 | 112 | 544 | Electricité consommé |

### b. Structure

| Year and item of data | All mining / Toutes industries extractives | Coal mining 1 / Extraction du charbon 1 | Metal mining / Extraction des minerais métalliques | Crude petroleum and natural gas / Pétrole brut et gaz naturel | Other Mining 3 / Divers 3 | Rubrique |
|---|---|---|---|---|---|---|
| ISIC / CITI | 1 | 11 | 12 | 13 | 14-19 | |
| **1950** | | | | | | **1950** |
| Distribution in percent of number of engaged | 100.0 | 90.4 | 5.2 | ... | 4.4 | Distribution en pourcentage du nombre de personnes occupées |
| Per person engaged: electricity consumed | 9.7 | 9.5 | 11.1 | ... | 11.2 | Par personne occupée: électricité consommée |
| Employees as a percent of engaged | 100.0 | 100.0 | 100.0 | ... | 99.6 | Salariés en pourcentage des personnes occupées |
| Wages and salaries per employee | 3.8 | 3.9 | 3.2 | ... | 3.2 | Traitements et salaires par salarié |
| Per thousand operative man-hours: Wages and salaries | 1.64 | 1.68 | 1.39 | ... | 1.27 | Par millier d'heures-ouvrier: Traitements et salaires |
| Electricity consumed | 4.80 | 4.72 | 5.56 | ... | 5.46 | Electricité consommée |
| **1953** | | | | | | **1953** |
| Distribution in percent of number of engaged | 100.0 | 87.7 | 5.4 | 1.9 | 5.0 | Distribution en pourcentage du nombre de personnes occupées |
| Per person engaged: electricity consumed | 11.1 | 11.1 | 12.4 | 5.8 | 12.3 | Par personne occupée: électricité consommée |
| Employees as a percent of engaged | 100.0 | 100.0 | 100.0 | 100.0 | 99.7 | Salariés en pourcentage des personnes occupées |
| Wages and salaries per employee | 4.9 | 5.0 | 4.2 | 4.5 | 4.0 | Traitements et salaires par salarié |
| Operatives as a percent of employees | 91.9 | 92.3 | 91.4 | 78.7 | 90.6 | Ouvriers en pourcentage des salariés |
| Average man-hours per operative | 2.13 | 2.12 | 2.12 | 2.40 | 2.26 | Heures de travail: moyenne par ouvrier |
| Per thousand operative man-hours: Wages and salaries | 2.15 | 2.21 | 1.84 | 1.65 | 1.66 | Par millier d'heures-ouvrier: Traitements et salaires |
| Electricity consumed | 5.68 | 5.67 | 6.41 | 3.09 | 6.03 | Electricité consommée |
| **1958** | | | | | | **1958** |
| Distribution in percent of number of engaged | 100.0 | 88.1 | 4.7 | 2.0 | 5.2 | Distribution en pourcentage du nombre de personnes occupées |
| Per person engaged: Energy consumed | 28.78 | 31.02 | 14.35 | 3.15 | 13.39 | Par personne occupée: Energie consommée |
| Electricity consumed | 15.6 | 15.7 | 16.5 | 8.6 | 16.0 | Electricité consommée |
| Employees as a percent of engaged | 100.0 | 100.0 | 100.0 | 100.0 | 99.7 | Salariés en pourcentage des personnes occupées |
| Wages and salaries per employee | 6.7 | 6.8 | 5.9 | 6.3 | 5.9 | Traitements et salaires par salarié |
| Operatives as a percent of employees | 90.4 | 90.9 | 89.2 | 73.8 | 89.0 | Ouvriers en pourcentage des salariés |
| Average man-hours per operative | 1.91 | 1.89 | 2.01 | 2.19 | 2.13 | Heures de travail: moyenne par ouvrier |
| Per thousand operative man-hours: Wages and salaries | 3.22 | 3.31 | 2.67 | 2.38 | 2.50 | Par millier d'heures-ouvrier: Traitements et salaires |
| Energy consumed | 16.64 | 18.05 | 7.98 | 1.95 | 7.09 | Energie consommé e |
| Electricity consumed | 9.03 | 9.13 | 9.20 | 5.33 | 8.50 | Electricité consommée |

[1] Includes the manufacturing of coke and coal briquettes.
[2] Excludes petroleum refining.
[3] Excludes stone and sand quarrying.

[1] Y compris la fabrication du coke et des briquettes.
[2] Non compris le raffinage du pétrole.
[3] Non compris l'extraction de la pierre et du sable.

## C. The Major Groups of Manufacturing — Les classes de la branche Industries manufacturières

| Year and item of data | Manufacturing [6] / Industries manufacturières [6] | Food, beverages and tobacco / Industries alimentaires, boissons, tabac | Textiles | Clothing, footwear and made-up textiles [3] / Articles d'habillement, chaussures et ouvrages en tissu [3] | Wood products and furniture [1] / Bois et meubles [1] | Paper and paper products / Papier et ouvrages en papier | Printing and publishing [2] / Imprimerie et édition [2] | Leather and leather products except wearing apparel [3] / Cuir et articles en cuir, à l'exclusion des articles d'habillement [3] | Rubber products [4] / Ouvrages en caoutchouc [4] | Chemicals and chemical, petroleum and coal products / Produits chimiques et dérivés du pétrole et du charbon | Non-metallic mineral products [4,6] / Produits minéraux non métalliques [4,6] | Basic metals / Métallurgie de base | Metal products / Ouvrages en métaux | Other manufacturing [1] / Autres industries manufacturières [1] | Année et rubrique |
|---|---|---|---|---|---|---|---|---|---|---|---|---|---|---|---|
| ISIC | 2-3 | 20-22 | 23 | 24 | 25-26 | 27 | 28 | 29 | 30 | 31-32 | 33 | 34 | 35-38 | 39 | CITI |

### a. Absolute Figures — Chiffres absolus

| Year and item of data | 2-3 | 20-22 | 23 | 24 | 25-26 | 27 | 28 | 29 | 30 | 31-32 | 33 | 34 | 35-38 | 39 | Année et rubrique |
|---|---|---|---|---|---|---|---|---|---|---|---|---|---|---|---|
| **1950** | | | | | | | | | | | | | | | **1950** |
| Number of local units... | 46 145[5] | 6 723 | 3 743 | 3 721 | 6 033 | 1 128 | 2 016 | 907 | 229 | 2 258[5] | 4 884 | 1 508 | 11 264 | 1 731 | Nombre d'unités locales |
| Gross receipts.......... | 75 708[5] | 14 875 | 9 863 | 3 709 | 3 005 | 2 432 | 1 186 | 1 268 | 1 092 | 7 915[5] | 3 106 | 8 396 | 17 636 | 1 225 | Recettes brutes |
| Number of engaged (Average for year)... | 4 206.1[5] | 337.8 | 530.6 | 260.1 | 253.5 | 113.2 | 102.8 | 57.5 | 56.4 | 310.8[5] | 291.5 | 385.5 | 1 376.3 | 130.1 | Nombre de personnes occupées (moyenne pour l'année) |
| Employees: Number (Average for year).......... | 4 169.4[5] | 333.7 | 526.2 | 256.7 | 247.5 | 112.2 | 100.8 | 56.6 | 56.3 | 309.3[5] | 287.6 | 384.7 | 1 369.3 | 128.5 | Salariés: Nombre (moyenne pour l'année) |
| Wages and salaries... | 12 949[5] | 932 | 1 389 | 572 | 669 | 338 | 361 | 167 | 192 | 1 154[5] | 894 | 1 423 | 4 498 | 360 | Traitements et salaires |
| Operatives: Number (Average for year).......... | 3 755.9[5] | 275.8 | 500.0 | 248.3 | 231.8 | 102.6 | 83.6 | 52.4 | 49.4 | 239.5[5] | 260.2 | 361.7 | 1 231.3 | 119.3 | Ouvriers: Nombre (moyenne pour l'année) |
| Man-hours worked.... | 8 050[5] | 624 | 1 045 | 475 | 510 | 233 | 198 | 112 | 98 | 535[5] | 611 | 792 | 2 576 | 241 | Heures de travail effectuées |
| Wages and salaries... | 9 882[5] | 644 | 1 126 | 459 | 565 | 265 | 268 | 135 | 142 | 725[5] | 767 | 1 170 | 3 345 | 271 | Traitements et salaires |
| Electricity consumed..... | 23 314[5] | 1 130 | 1 397 | 87 | 386 | 1 487 | 85 | 110 | 319 | 8 335[5] | 1 833 | 5 449 | 2 564 | 132 | Electricité consommée |
| **1953** | | | | | | | | | | | | | | | **1953** |
| Number of local units.... | 49 570 | 7 419 | 4 407 | 4 126 | 5 931 | 1 357 | 2 458 | 972 | 251 | 2 015 | 5 719 | 1 519 | 11 281 | 2 115 | Nombre d'unités locales |
| Gross receipts.......... | 118 687 | 20 658 | 11 907 | 5 196 | 4 314 | 3 543 | 1 929 | 1 458 | 1 616 | 12 396 | 5 329 | 15 121 | 32 757 | 2 463 | Recettes brutes |
| Number of engaged (Average for year)... | 5 087.2 | 389.1 | 599.5 | 333.9 | 267.3 | 136.2 | 126.2 | 67.2 | 68.2 | 337.4 | 354.4 | 466.2 | 1 755.1 | 186.5 | Nombre de personnes occupées (moyenne pour l'année) |
| Employees: Number (Average for year).......... | 5 043.8 | 384.4 | 594.6 | 329.5 | 261.0 | 135.0 | 123.8 | 66.2 | 68.1 | 335.8 | 349.7 | 465.2 | 1 746.2 | 184.3 | Salariés: Nombre (moyenne pour l'année) |
| Wages and salaries... | 20 118 | 1 383 | 1 970 | 893 | 875 | 515 | 563 | 230 | 294 | 1 656 | 1 390 | 2 281 | 7 413 | 655 | Traitements et salaires |
| Operatives: Number (Average for year).......... | 4 204.2 | 303.9 | 524.8 | 291.4 | 231.0 | 115.1 | 99.1 | 58.1 | 55.3 | 242.7 | 313.7 | 402.3 | 1 411.6 | 155.2 | Ouvriers: Nombre (moyenne pour l'année) |
| Man-hours worked.... | 9 585 | 721 | 1 147 | 608 | 538 | 276 | 245 | 131 | 120 | 554 | 747 | 921 | 3 229 | 348 | Heures de travail effectuées |
| Wages and salaries... | 15 112 | 957 | 1 564 | 721 | 735 | 396 | 422 | 187 | 217 | 1 000 | 1 188 | 1 838 | 5 392 | 495 | Traitements et salaires |
| Electricity consumed..... | 33 418 | 1 526 | 1 886 | 132 | 502 | 2 010 | 130 | 138 | 422 | 11 547 | 2 673 | 8 445 | 3 799 | 208 | Electricité consommée |
| **1958** | | | | | | | | | | | | | | | **1958** |
| Number of local units.... | 51 595 | 6 899 | 4 389 | 4 573 | 5 661 | 1 443 | 2 772 | 925 | 289 | 1 995 | 5 997 | 1 578 | 12 511 | 2 563 | Nombre d'unités locales |
| Gross receipts.......... | 195 495 | 31 523 | 14 128 | 7 648 | 6 611 | 5 579 | 3 253 | 1 864 | 2 608 | 22 041 | 8 476 | 24 082 | 63 187 | 4 495 | Recettes brutes |
| Number of engaged (Average for year)... | 6 616.1 | 466.7 | 618.8 | 419.7 | 303.7 | 176.0 | 168.3 | 77.3 | 94.3 | 447.0 | 408.5 | 593.1 | 2 582.6 | 260.1 | Nombre de personnes occupées (moyenne pour l'année) |
| Employees: Number (Average for year).......... | 6 561.6 | 461.1 | 613.7 | 414.2 | 296.5 | 174.5 | 165.1 | 76.1 | 94.1 | 444.9 | 403.1 | 591.8 | 2 569.5 | 257.0 | Salariés: Nombre (moyenne pour l'année) |
| Wages and salaries... | 34 602 | 2 305 | 2 645 | 1 522 | 1 370 | 869 | 936 | 333 | 517 | 2 903 | 2 152 | 3 808 | 14 070 | 1 172 | Traitements et salaires |
| Operatives: Number (Average for year).......... | 5 385.2 | 360.5 | 529.9 | 364.6 | 260.3 | 148.7 | 136.1 | 66.3 | 76.8 | 315.1 | 355.6 | 503.3 | 2 053.6 | 214.4 | Ouvriers: Nombre (moyenne pour l'année) |
| Man-hours worked.... | 11 243 | 801 | 1 041 | 706 | 560 | 325 | 296 | 137 | 151 | 652 | 783 | 1 038 | 4 313 | 440 | Heures de travail effectuées |
| Wages and salaries... | 25 305 | 1 570 | 2 033 | 1 224 | 1 135 | 659 | 710 | 265 | 379 | 1 708 | 1 786 | 3 000 | 9 971 | 865 | Traitements et salaires |
| Energy consumed...... | 61 467 | 3 942 | 2 306 | 209 | 395 | 2 224 | 135 | 240 | 440 | 11 745 | 9 606 | 25 128 | 4 844 | 253 | Energie consommée |
| Electricity consumed..... | 52 490 | 2 148 | 2 475 | 206 | 745 | 3 269 | 237 | 180 | 600 | 18 837 | 3 785 | 12 889 | 6 716 | 403 | Electricité consommée |

---

[1] The manufacturing of brushes and brooms is covered in Wood products (ISIC major group 25) instead of in Other manufacturing (ISIC major group 39).
[2] Includes photostating service.
[3] The manufacture of leather gloves is covered in Leather and leather products (ISIC major group 29) instead of Clothing (ISIC major group 24).
[4] The manufacturing of asbestos products is classified in Rubber products (ISIC major group 30) and not in Non-metallic mineral products (ISIC major group 33).
[5] Includes the extraction of crude petroleum.
[6] Includes stone and sand quarrying.

[1] La brosserie est classée dans Industrie du bois (CITI 25) et non dans Autres industries manufacturières (CITI 39).
[2] Y compris la préparation des photostats.
[3] La ganterie est comprise dans Industrie du cuir et des articles en cuir (CITI 29) et non dans Articles d'habillement (CITI 24).
[4] La fabrication des ouvrages en amiante est comprise dans Ouvrages en caoutchouc (CITI 30) et non dans Produits minéraux non métalliques (CITI 33).
[5] Y compris l'extraction du pétrole brut.
[6] Y compris l'extraction de la pierre et du sable.

# GERMANY, Federal Republic of

## C. The Major Groups of Manufacturing (continued) — Les classes de la branche Industries manufacturières (suite)

| Year and item of data | Manufacturing[6] / Industries manufacturières[6] | Food, beverages and tobacco / Industries alimentaires, boissons, tabac | Textiles | Clothing, footwear and made-up textiles[3] / Articles d'habillement, chaussures et ouvrages en tissu[3] | Wood products and furniture[1] / Bois et meubles[1] | Paper and paper products / Papier et ouvrages en papier | Printing and publishing[2] / Imprimerie et édition[2] | Leather and leather products except wearing apparel[3] / Cuir et articles en cuir, à l'exclusion des articles d'habillement[3] | Rubber products[4] / Ouvrages en caoutchouc[4] | Chemicals and chemical, petroleum and coal products / Produits chimiques et dérivés du pétrole et du charbon | Non-metallic mineral products[4,6] / Produits minéraux non métalliques[4,6] | Basic metals / Métallurgie de base | Metal products / Ouvrages en métaux | Other manufacturing[1] / Autres industries manufacturières[1] | Année et rubrique |
|---|---|---|---|---|---|---|---|---|---|---|---|---|---|---|---|
| ISIC | 2–3 | 20–22 | 23 | 24 | 25–26 | 27 | 28 | 29 | 30 | 31–32 | 33 | 34 | 35–38 | 39 | CITI |

b. Structure

| Year and item of data | 2–3 | 20–22 | 23 | 24 | 25–26 | 27 | 28 | 29 | 30 | 31–32 | 33 | 34 | 35–38 | 39 | Année et rubrique |
|---|---|---|---|---|---|---|---|---|---|---|---|---|---|---|---|
| **1950** | | | | | | | | | | | | | | | **1950** Distribution en pourcentage du nombre de personnes occupées |
| Distribution in percent of number of engaged... | 100.0 | 8.0 | 12.6 | 6.2 | 6.0 | 2.7 | 2.4 | 1.4 | 1.4 | 7.3 | 7.0 | 9.1 | 32.8 | 3.1 | |
| Per person engaged: Electricity consumed... | 5.5 | 3.3 | 2.6 | 0.3 | 1.5 | 13.1 | 0.8 | 1.9 | 5.6 | 26.8 | 6.3 | 14.1 | 1.9 | 1.0 | Par personne occupée: Electricité consommée |
| Employee as a percent of engaged......... | 99.1 | 98.8 | 99.2 | 98.7 | 97.6 | 99.1 | 98.0 | 98.4 | 99.8 | 99.5 | 98.7 | 99.8 | 99.5 | 98.8 | Salariés en pourcentage des personnes occupées |
| Wages and salaries per employee........ | 3.1 | 2.8 | 2.6 | 2.2 | 2.7 | 3.0 | 3.6 | 3.0 | 3.4 | 3.7 | 3.1 | 3.7 | 3.3 | 2.8 | Traitements et salaires par salarié |
| Operatives as a percent of employees........ | 90.1 | 82.6 | 95.0 | 96.7 | 93.6 | 91.4 | 82.9 | 92.6 | 87.7 | 77.4 | 90.5 | 94.0 | 89.9 | 92.8 | Ouvriers en pourcentage des salariés |
| Average man-hours: per operative........ | 2.14 | 2.26 | 2.09 | 1.91 | 2.20 | 2.27 | 2.37 | 2.14 | 1.98 | 2.23 | 2.35 | 2.19 | 2.09 | 2.02 | Heures de travail: moyenne par ouvrier |
| Per thousand operative man-hours: Wages and salaries... | 1.23 | 1.03 | 1.08 | 0.97 | 1.11 | 1.14 | 1.35 | 1.20 | 1.45 | 1.36 | 1.26 | 1.48 | 1.30 | 1.12 | Par millier d'heures-ouvrier Traitements et salaires |
| Electricity consumed... | 2.90 | 1.81 | 1.34 | 0.18 | 0.76 | 6.38 | 0.43 | 0.98 | 3.26 | 15.58 | 3.00 | 6.88 | 1.00 | 0.55 | Electricité consommée |
| **1953** | | | | | | | | | | | | | | | **1953** Distribution en pourcentage du nombre de personnes occupées |
| Distribution in percent of number of engaged... | 100.0 | 7.6 | 11.8 | 6.5 | 5.3 | 2.7 | 2.5 | 1.3 | 1.3 | 6.7 | 6.9 | 9.2 | 34.5 | 3.7 | |
| Per person engaged: Electricity consumed... | 6.6 | 3.9 | 3.1 | 0.4 | 1.9 | 14.8 | 1.0 | 2.0 | 6.2 | 34.2 | 7.5 | 18.1 | 2.2 | 1.1 | Par personne occupée: Electricité consommée |
| Employees as a percent of engaged......... | 99.1 | 98.8 | 99.2 | 98.7 | 97.6 | 99.1 | 98.1 | 98.5 | 99.8 | 99.5 | 98.7 | 99.8 | 99.5 | 98.8 | Salariés en pourcentage des personnes occupées |
| Wages and salaries per employee........ | 4.0 | 3.6 | 3.3 | 2.7 | 3.4 | 3.8 | 4.5 | 3.5 | 4.3 | 4.9 | 4.0 | 4.9 | 4.2 | 3.6 | Traitements et salaires par salarié |
| Operatives as a percent of employees........ | 83.4 | 79.0 | 88.3 | 88.4 | 88.5 | 85.2 | 80.0 | 87.8 | 81.2 | 72.3 | 89.7 | 86.5 | 80.8 | 84.2 | Ouvriers en pourcentage des salariés |
| Average man-hours per operative........ | 2.28 | 2.37 | 2.18 | 2.09 | 2.33 | 2.40 | 2.47 | 2.25 | 2.17 | 2.28 | 2.38 | 2.29 | 2.29 | 2.24 | Heures de travail: moyenne par ouvrier |
| Per thousand operative man-hours: Wages and salaries... | 1.58 | 1.33 | 1.36 | 1.18 | 1.37 | 1.43 | 1.72 | 1.43 | 1.81 | 1.80 | 1.59 | 2.00 | 1.67 | 1.42 | Par millier d'heures-ouvrier Traitements et salaires |
| Electricity consumed... | 3.49 | 2.12 | 1.64 | 0.22 | 0.93 | 7.28 | 0.53 | 1.05 | 3.52 | 20.84 | 3.58 | 9.17 | 1.18 | 0.60 | Electricité consommée |
| **1958** | | | | | | | | | | | | | | | **1958** Distribution en pourcentage du nombre de personnes occupées |
| Distribution in percent of number of engaged... | 100.0 | 7.0 | 9.4 | 6.3 | 4.6 | 2.7 | 2.5 | 1.2 | 1.4 | 6.7 | 6.2 | 9.0 | 39.0 | 4.0 | |
| Per person engaged: Energy consumed..... | 9.29 | 8.45 | 3.73 | 0.50 | 1.30 | 12.64 | 0.80 | 3.10 | 4.66 | 26.28 | 23.52 | 42.37 | 1.88 | 0.97 | Par personne occupée: Energie consommée |
| Electricity consumed... | 7.9 | 4.6 | 4.0 | 0.5 | 2.4 | 18.6 | 1.4 | 2.3 | 6.4 | 42.1 | 9.3 | 21.7 | 2.6 | 1.5 | Electricité consommée |
| Employee as a percent of engaged......... | 99.2 | 98.8 | 99.2 | 98.7 | 97.6 | 99.1 | 98.1 | 98.4 | 99.8 | 99.5 | 98.7 | 99.8 | 99.5 | 98.8 | Salariés en pourcentage des personnes occupées |
| Wages and salaries per employee........ | 5.3 | 5.0 | 4.3 | 3.7 | 4.6 | 5.0 | 5.7 | 4.4 | 5.5 | 6.5 | 5.3 | 6.4 | 5.5 | 4.6 | Traitements et salaires par salarié |
| Operatives as a percent of employees........ | 82.1 | 78.2 | 86.3 | 88.0 | 87.8 | 85.2 | 82.4 | 87.1 | 81.6 | 70.8 | 88.2 | 85.0 | 79.9 | 83.4 | Ouvriers en pourcentage des salariés |
| Average man-hours per operative........ | 2.09 | 2.22 | 1.96 | 1.94 | 2.15 | 2.18 | 2.17 | 2.07 | 1.97 | 2.07 | 2.20 | 2.06 | 2.10 | 2.05 | Heures de travail: moyenne par ouvrier |
| Per thousand operative man-hours: Wages and salaries... | 2.25 | 1.96 | 1.95 | 1.73 | 2.03 | 2.03 | 2.40 | 1.93 | 2.51 | 2.62 | 2.28 | 2.89 | 2.31 | 1.96 | Par millier d'heures-ouvrier Traitements et salaires |
| Energy consumed..... | 5.47 | 4.92 | 2.22 | 0.30 | 0.70 | 6.84 | 0.46 | 1.75 | 2.91 | 18.01 | 12.27 | 24.21 | 1.12 | 0.58 | Energie consommée |
| Electricity consumed... | 4.67 | 2.68 | 2.38 | 0.29 | 1.33 | 10.06 | 0.80 | 1.31 | 3.97 | 28.89 | 4.83 | 12.42 | 1.56 | 0.92 | Electricité consommée |

[1] The manufacturing of brushes and brooms is covered in Wood products (ISIC major group 25) instead of in Other manufacturing (ISIC major group 39).
[2] Includes photostating service.
[3] The manufacture of leather gloves is covered in Leather and leather products (ISIC major group 29) instead of Clothing (ISIC major group 24).
[4] The manufacturing of asbestos products is classified in Rubber products (ISIC major group 30) and not in Non-metallic mineral products (ISIC major group 33).
[5] Includes the extraction of crude petroleum.
[6] Includes stone and sand quarrying.

[1] La brosserie est classée dans Industrie du bois (CITI 25) et non dans Autres industries manufacturières (CITI 39).
[2] Y compris la préparation des photostats.
[3] La ganterie est comprise dans Industrie du cuir et des articles en cuir (CITI 29) et non dans Articles d'habillement (CITI 24).
[4] La fabrication des ouvrages en amiante est comprise dans Ouvrages en caoutchouc (CITI 30) et non dans Produits minéraux non métalliques (CITI 33).
[5] Y compris l'extraction du pétrole brut.
[6] Y compris l'extraction de la pierre et du sable.

# 7. QUANTITY OF SELECTED FUELS CONSUMED AND OF ELECTRICITY PURCHASED, PRODUCED AND SOLD, LOCAL UNITS ENGAGING TEN OR MORE PERSONS, EXCEPTING LICENSED HANDICRAFTS

## VOLUME DE QUELQUES COMBUSTIBLES CONSOMMES ET D'ELECTRICITE ACHETEE, PRODUITE ET VENDUE, UNITES LOCALES OCCUPANT DIX PERSONNES OU PLUS, EXCEPTE L'ARTISANAT PATENTE

### 1950, 1953, 1958

Coal and refined fuel oils in thousand metric tons; manufactured gas in million cubic meters; electricity in million KWH.

Charbon et pétrole raffiné en milliers de tonnes métriques; gaz manufacturé en millions de mètres cubes; électricité en millions de kWh.

## A. The Major Groups of Mining and Electricity
### Les classes des Industries extractives et de l'électricité

| Year and source of energy | Mining — Industries extractives | | | | | Electricity Electricité | Année et source d'énergie |
|---|---|---|---|---|---|---|---|
| | Total [1,3] | Coal mining [3] Extraction du charbon[3] | Metal mining Extraction des minerais métalliques | Crude petroleum and natural gas Pétrole brut et gaz naturel | Other mining [1] Divers [1] | | |
| ISIC | 1 | 11 | 12 | 13 | 14–19 | 511 | CITI |
| 1950 Coal [7] | 17 993 [2] | 17 324 | 194 | [2] | 475 | 13 430 | 1950 Charbon [7] |
| Refined oil fuels | ... | ... | ... | ... | ... | 65.3 | Pétrole raffiné |
| Manufactured gas | ... | ... | ... | ... | ... | 61.3 | Gaz manufacturé |
| 1953 Coal [7] | 17 729 | 16 920 | 258 | 44 | 507 | 16 356 | 1953 Charbon [7] |
| Refined oil fuels | ... | ... | ... | ... | ... | 105.6 | Pétrole raffiné |
| Manufactured gas | 6 303 | 6 302 | — | | 1 | ... | Gaz manufacturé |
| 1958 Coal [7] | 20 778 | 19 887 | 359 | 20 | 512 | 21 894 | 1958 Charbon [7] |
| Refined oil fuels | 81.7 | 43.4 | 11.1 | 4.8 | 22.4 | 157.3 | Pétrole raffiné |
| Manufactured gas | 7 123 | 7 122 | — | | 1 | 176 | Gaz manufacturé |
| Electricity: | | | | | | | Electricité: |
| Purchased | 4 112 | 3 320 | 482 | 106 | 204 | ... | Achetée |
| Produced | 17 693 | 17 269 | 48 | 5 | 371 | ... | Produite |
| Sold | 11 568 | 11 503 | 24 | — | 41 | ... | Vendue |

For footnotes see end of table. — Pour les notes, voir au bas du tableau.

## B. The Major Groups of Manufacturing — Les classes de la branche Industries manufacturières

| Year and source of energy | Manufacturing [1,3] Industries manufacturières [1,3] | Food, beverages and tobacco Industries alimentaires, boissons, tabac | Textiles | Clothing, footwear and made-up textiles [4] Articles d'habillement, chaussures et ouvrages en tissu [4] | Wood products and furniture [6] Bois et meubles [6] | Paper and paper products Papier et ouvrages en papier | Printing and publishing Imprimerie et édition | Leather and leather products except wearing apparel [4] Cuir et articles en cuir, à l'exclusion des articles d'habillement [4] | Rubber products [5] Ouvrages en caoutchouc [5] | Chemicals and chemical, petroleum and coal products Produits chimiques et dérivés du pétrole et du charbon | Non-metallic mineral products [1] Produits minéraux non métalliques [1] | Basic metals Métallurgie de base | Metal products Ouvrages en métaux | Other manufacturing [6] Autres industries manufacturières [6] | Année et source d'énergie |
|---|---|---|---|---|---|---|---|---|---|---|---|---|---|---|---|
| ISIC | 2–3 | 20–22 | 23 | 24 | 25–26 | 27 | 28 | 29 | 30 | 31–32 | 33 | 34 | 35–38 | 39 | CITI |
| 1950 Coal [7] | 37 269 [2] | 2 914 | 2 010 | 121 | 279 | 1 991 | 67 | 252 | 272 | 6 884 [2] | 6 414 | 13 532 | 2 406 | 127 | 1950 Charbon [7] |
| 1953 Coal | 44 156 | 3 406 | 2 308 | 142 | 319 | 2 246 | 73 | 252 | 305 | 7 875 | 7 678 | 16 899 [3] | 2 508 | 145 | 1953 Charbon [7] |
| Manufactured gas | 8 501 | 80 | 15 | 8 | 2 | 4 | 12 | 2 | 2 | 1 965 | 621 | 4 692 | 1 079 | 19 | Gaz manufacturé |
| 1958 Coal [7] | 48 572 | 3 332 | 2 111 | 118 | 323 | 2 477 | 65 | 241 | 305 | 9 230 | 7 357 | 20 316 [1] | 2 554 | 143 | 1958 Charbon [7] |
| Refined oil fuels | 4 755.4 | 358.4 | 131.2 | 40.1 | 49.2 | 295.8 | 20.8 | 15.9 | 59.5 | 1 239.2 | 951.5 | 944.0 | 608.6 | 41.2 | Pétrole raffiné |
| Manufactured gas | 10 857 | 115 | 16 | 8 | 3 | 6 | 14 | 2 | 3 | 2 684 | 765 | 5 762 | 1 458 | 21 | Gaz manufacturé |
| Electricity | | | | | | | | | | | | | | | Electricité |
| Purchased | 36 601 | 1 548 | 1 673 | 199 | 527 | 720 | 236 | 89 | 527 | 11 900 | 3 440 | 9 466 | 5 900 | 376 | Achetée |
| Produced | 18 981 | 683 | 973 | 8 | 255 | 2 627 | 2 | 95 | 73 | 8 281 | 367 | 4 571 | 1 014 | 32 | Produite |
| Sold | 3 094 | 84 | 171 | 1 | 38 | 79 | 1 | 5 | — | 1 342 | 21 | 1 149 | 199 | 4 | Vendue |

[1] Stone and sand quarrying is included in the manufacture of Non-metallic mineral products (ISIC major group 33) rather than in Other mining (ISIC major group 14–19).
[2] Crude petroleum and natural gas (ISIC major group 13) is included in Chemicals and petroleum and coal products (ISIC major groups 31–32) during 1950.
[3] The manufacture of coke and coal briquettes (part of ISIC major groups 31–32) is included in Coal mining (ISIC major group 11).
[4] The manufacture of leather gloves is covered in Leather and leather products (ISIC major group 29) instead of in Clothing (ISIC major group 24).
[5] Asbestos products are covered in Rubber products (ISIC 30) and not in Non-metallic mineral products (ISIC 33).
[6] Manufacturing of brushes and brooms is covered in Wood products (ISIC major groups 25–26) and not in Other manufacturing (ISIC major group 39).
[7] Includes the coal equivalent of lignite, coal and lignite briquettes and coke.

[1] L'extraction de la pierre à bâtir et du sable est incluse dans Produits minéraux non métalliques (CITI classe 32) plutôt que dans Autres industries extractives (CITI classes 14–19).
[2] L'extraction du Pétrole brut et du gaz naturel (CITI classe 13) est incluse dans Industries Chimiques et dérivés du pétrole et du charbon (CITI classes 31–32) pendant 1950.
[3] Les cokeries et usines de briquettes de charbon (Dans CITI classes 31–32) sont incluses dans les Industries extractives de charbon (CITI classe 11).
[4] La fabrication de gants en cuir est incluse dans Cuir et ouvrages en cuir (CITI classe 29) au lieu d'être dans Articles d'habillement (CITI classe 24).
[5] Les produits en amiante sont inclus dans Ouvrages en caoutchouc (CITI classe 30) plutôt que dans Produits minéraux non métalliques (CITI 33).
[6] La fabrication de brosses et de balais est couverte par Ouvrages en bois (CITI classes 25–26) non par Autres industries manufacturières (CITI classe 39).
[7] Y compris l'équivalent charbon de la lignite, du charbon, des briquettes en lignite et du coke.

# GERMANY, Federal Republic of

## 8. THE CHARACTERISTICS OF ALL LICENSED HANDICRAFT UNITS ENGAGED IN INDUSTRIAL ACTIVITY

### CARACTERISTIQUES DE TOUTES LES UNITES ARTISANALES PATENTEES EXERÇANT UNE ACTIVITE INDUSTRIELLE

#### 1949, 1956

Number of establishments in units; gross receipts in million D.M.; number of engaged and employees in thousands; wages and salaries per employee in thousand D.M.

Nombre d'établissements en unités; recettes brutes en millions de D.M.; nombre de personnes occupées et de salariés en milliers; traitements et salaires par salarié en milliers de D.M.

### A. The Divisions of Industrial Activity — Les branches de l'activité industrielle

| Year and item of data | All industrial activity<br>Toutes industries | Manufacturing<br>Industries manu-facturières | Construction<br>Bâtiment et travaux publics | Année et rubrique |
|---|---|---|---|---|
| ISIC | 2–3, 4 | 2–3 | 4 | CITI |
| **1949** | | | | **1949** |
| Number of local units......... | 796 845 | 622 454 | 174 391 | Nombre d'unités locales |
| Gross receipts (During 1.X.1948–30.IX.1949) | 19 073.5 | 13 522.2 | 5 551.3 | Recettes brutes (1.X.1948–30.IX.1949) |
| Number of engaged (As of 30.IX.1949)......... | 2 853.9 | 1 811.3 | 1 042.6 | Nombre de personnes occupées (au 30.IX.1949) |
| Number of employees (As of 30.IX.1949)......... | 1 810.5 | 984.5 | 826.0 | Nombre de salariés (au 30.IX.1949) |
| **1956** | | | | **1956** |
| Number of local units (31.V.1956).............. | 678 532 | 540 908 | 137 624 | Nombre d'unités locales (31.V.1956) |
| Gross receipts (during 1955) ... | 45 816.1 | 32 375.7 | 13 440.4 | Recettes brutes (en 1955) |
| Number of engaged (31.V.1956).............. | 3 334.8 | 1 954.0 | 1 380.8 | Nombre de personnes occupées (31.V.1956) |
| Employees: | | | | Salariés |
| Number (during 1955) ...... | 2 191.5 | 1 110.2 | 1 081.3 | Nombre (en 1955) |
| Wages and salaries (during 1955) ............. | 7 111.3 | 3 040.7 | 4 070.6 | Traitements et salaires (en 1955) |

### B. The Major Groups of Manufacturing — Les classes de la branche Industries manufacturières

| Year and item of data | Manu-facturing<br>Industries manufac-turières | Food, beverages and tobacco<br>Industries alimen-taires, boissons, tabac | Textiles | Clothing, footwear and made-up textiles<br>Articles d'habil-lement, chaussures et ouvrages en tissu | Wood products and furniture<br>Bois et meubles | Printing and publish-ing<br>Im-primerie et édition | Leather and leather products except wearing apparel<br>Cuir et articles en cuir, à l'exclu-sion des articles d'habil-lement | Rubber products<br>Ouvrages en caout-chouc | Non-metallic mineral products<br>Produits minéraux non métal-liques | Metal products<br>Ouvrages en métaux | Other manu-facturing<br>Autres industries manufac-turières | Année et rubrique |
|---|---|---|---|---|---|---|---|---|---|---|---|---|
| ISIC | 2–3 | 20–22 | 23 | 24 | 25–26 | 28 | 29 | 30 | 33 | 35–38 | 39 | CITI |
| **1949** | | | | | | | | | | | | **1949** |
| Number of local units........ | 622 454 | 116 198 | 7 617 | 235 257 | 124 081 | 3 498 | 7 994 | 1 507 | 3 528 | 102 092 | 20 682 | Nombre d'unités locales |
| Gross receipts (During 1.X.1948–30.IX.1949).............. | 13 522.2 | 5 575.3 | 123.6 | 1 560.5 | 2 031.8 | 86.0 | 84.3 | 166.9 | 71.6 | 3 416.1 | 406.1 | Recettes brutes (1.X.1948–30.IX.1949) |
| Number of engaged (30.IX.1949).............. | 1 811.3 | 404.1 | 24.7 | 479.1 | 409.5 | 12.3 | 9.9 | 7.2 | 10.9 | 409.5 | 44.1 | Nombre de personnes occupées (30.IX.1949) |
| Number of employees (30.IX.1949).............. | 984.5 | 185.8 | 9.9 | 216.0 | 251.5 | 7.6 | 4.3 | 5.6 | 6.1 | 277.0 | 20.7 | Nombre de salariés (30.IX.1949) |
| Distribution in percent of number of engaged....... | 100.0 | 22.3 | 1.3 | 26.5 | 22.6 | 0.7 | 0.5 | 0.4 | 0.6 | 22.6 | 2.5 | Répartition en pourcentage du nombre de personnes occu-pées |
| **1956** | | | | | | | | | | | | **1956** |
| Number of local units (31.V.1956).............. | 540 908 | 116 531 | 3 188 | 171 828 | 99 742 | 4 116 | 4 352 | 1 200 | 7 131 | 113 899 | 18 921 | Nombre d'unités locales (31.V.1956) |
| Gross receipts (during 1955).. | 32 375.7 | 13 536.9 | 124.2 | 2 289.8 | 4 165.5 | 223.5 | 163.1 | 287.3 | 418.6 | 10 388.8 | 778.0 | Recettes brutes (en 1955) |
| Number of engaged (31.V.1956).............. | 1 954.0 | 496.7 | 12.0 | 328.8 | 351.7 | 19.0 | 12.9 | 7.9 | 31.2 | 639.5 | 54.3 | Nombre de personnes occupées (31.V.1956) |
| Employees: | | | | | | | | | | | | Salariés: |
| Number (during 1955)..... | 1 110.2 | 261.6 | 7.5 | 126.9 | 209.3 | 12.5 | 7.2 | 6.2 | 20.4 | 430.2 | 28.4 | Nombre (en 1955) |
| Wages and salaries (during 1955)........... | 3 040.7 | 675.5 | 15.8 | 246.8 | 641.3 | 37.3 | 20.1 | 22.1 | 68.9 | 1 238.5 | 74.4 | Traitements et salaires (en 1955) |
| Distribution in percent of number of engaged....... | 100.0 | 25.4 | 0.6 | 16.8 | 18.0 | 1.0 | 0.6 | 0.4 | 1.6 | 32.8 | 2.8 | Répartition en pourcentage du nombre de personnes occu-pées |

# GERMANY, Federal Republic of, THE SAAR — ALLEMAGNE (République fédérale d'), SARRE

## Index Numbers of Industrial Production

The index numbers shown in Table 1 are derived from indexes issued in *Saarländische Bevölkerungs und Wirtschaftzahlen*, 1952, Heft 3/4, *Statistisches Handbuch Für Das Saarland*, 1958, and *Statistische Berichte* issued by the Statistischen Amt des Saarlandes and correspondence with the Office.

The series of index numbers relate to all industrial units except licensed handicrafts. The indexes are base-weighted arithmetic averages. The weights utilized in combining the index numbers are based on value added, at market prices. The base weight year is 1950 in the case of the indexes for the years, 1936-1957, and 1958 for the indexes for 1958 and subsequent years. The indicators utilized to compute indexes for detailed categories of industrial activity are principally quantities of individual commodities produced. In some instances, value of output, corrected for changes in prices, or man-hours or man-days worked are utilized as indicators.

## Index Numbers of Industrial Employment

The index numbers of employment for the years, 1950-1958, shown in Table 2 are based on absolute figures published in various issues of *Saarländische Bevölkerungs und Wirtschaftzahlen*. These data relate to the annual average number of employees, at the end of each month, among residents of the Saar; and are gathered through sickness insurance and manpower registration schemes. The index numbers for 1959 and subsequent years are derived from absolute figures published in *Die Saarländische Industrie im Jahre 1961, Saarland in Zahlen* of the Statistischen Amt des Saarlandes and *Statistisches Jahrbuch für die Bundesrepublik Deutschland 1961* or *1962* of the Statistisches Bundesamt, Wiesbaden. In the case of mining and manufacturing, these data relate to the annual average number of persons engaged, excepting homeworkers, at the end of each month; and are gathered through the same monthly survey from which the figures shown in Table 5 were derived. This monthly survey covers, in general, units other than licensed handicrafts engaging 10 or more persons. In order to compile a continuous series of index numbers of employment, the Statistical Office of the United Nations linked the two sets of index numbers to one another at 1958.

## The Characteristics and Structure of Industrial Activity

Censuses of all local units including those engaged in industrial activity which were taken as of 17 May, 1939 and 14 November, 1951 provided the data set out in

## Indices de la production industrielle

Les indices du tableau 1 proviennent d'indices publiés dans *Saarländische Bevölkerungs und Wirtschaftszahlen*, 1952, Heft 3/4, *Statistisches Handbuch Für Das Saarland*, 1958, et *Statistische Berichte* publiés par le Statistischen Amt des Saarlandes et de la correspondance avec le Bureau.

Les séries d'indices sont relatives à toutes les unités industrielles à l'exclusion des unités artisanales patentées. Ces indices sont des moyennes arithmétiques à pondération fixe. Pour les combiner on a pondéré par la valeur ajoutée aux prix du marché. L'année de pondération de base est 1950 en ce qui concerne les indices relatifs aux années 1936-1957, et 1958 en ce qui concerne les indices relatifs aux années 1958 et suivantes. L'indicateur choisi pour construire les indices relatifs aux catégories détaillées de l'activité industrielle est principalement le volume de la production de chaque marchandise, quelquefois, la valeur de la production brute corrigée des variations de prix, ou le nombre d'heures de travail ou de journées de travail effectuées.

## Indices de l'emploi industriel

Les indices de l'emploi industriel pour les années 1950-1958 reproduits au tableau 2 sont fondés sur des chiffres absolus publiés dans différents numéros de *Saarländische Bevölkerungs und Wirtschaftszahlen*. Ces données sont relatives au nombre moyen de salariés, à la fin de chaque mois, parmi les résidents de la Sarre. Elles ont été rassemblées à partir de documents fournis par l'assurance maladie et l'enregistrement de la main-d'œuvre. Les indices pour 1959 et les années suivantes proviennent de chiffres absolus publiés dans *Die Saarländische Industrie im Jahre 1961, Saarland in Zahlen* du Statistischen Amt des Saarlandes et *Statistisches Jahrbuch für die Bundesrepublik Deutschland 1961* ou *1962* du Statistisches Bundesamt, Wiesbaden. Dans le cas des industries extractives et des industries manufacturières ces données concernent le nombre moyen de personnes occupées, à l'exclusion des travailleurs à domicile, à la fin de chaque mois et sont issues des mêmes enquêtes mensuelles qui ont fourni les chiffres du tableau 5. Ces enquêtes mensuelles couvrent, en général, les unités autres que les unités artisanales patentées occupant 10 personnes ou plus. Afin d'élaborer une série continue d'indices de l'emploi, le Bureau de Statistique de l'O.N.U. a relié les deux ensembles d'indices au niveau de 1958.

## Caractéristiques et structures de l'activité industrielle

Les données du tableau 3 sont tirées des recensements, au 17 mai 1939 et au 14 novembre 1951, de toutes les unités locales, y compris celles qui exerçaient une activité

Table 3. The figures were published in the *Statistisches Handbuch für das Saarland,* 1950 and 1955, Saarbrücken.

A census of production for 1936 of pre-war Germany, including the Saar, is the source of the data set out in Table 4. The results of this census were issued in 1939 in *Die Deutsche Industrie, 1936* by the Reichsamt für Wehrwirtschaftliche Planung, Berlin. The census covered licensed handicrafts units in classes of industrial activity where they were important in addition to other establishments engaging five or more persons. It should be noted that the number of engaged does not include homeworkers. The figures of value added shown in the tables relate only to goods produced by establishments and are valued at factor cost.

The figures in Tables 5 and 6 were abstracted from *Die Saarländische Industrie im Jahre 1961 Saarland in Zahlen.* These data originate in a monthly survey of mining and manufacturing units engaging ten or more persons and smaller units engaged in classes of industrial activity when they account for a significant part of production. However, licensed handicrafts, irrespective of size, are not included in the inquiry.

The figures of gross receipts shown in Table 5 are valued at market prices and do not cover goods sold in the same condition as purchased. The data on number of persons engaged cover employees, working proprietors and unpaid family workers but not homeworkers. The definitions of the other items of data on labour shown in Table 5 are similar to those in the International Recommendations on Basic Industrial Statistics. The figures of energy consumed in Tables 5 and 6 relate to the consumption of the various fuels listed in Table 6 and of purchased electricity. Fuels utilized as raw materials and to produce gas, excepting blast furnace gas, and electricity, as well as sources of heat and power, are included in the data on the consumption of fuels. The figures of energy consumption are therefore overstated for such industries as coal mining, which includes coking and coal briquetting, or chemical or pig iron and steel manufacturing.

industrielle. Ces chiffres ont été publiés dans *Statistisches Handbuch für das Saarland,* 1950 et 1955, Sarrebruck.

Les données du tableau 4 proviennent d'un recensement, en 1936, de la production de l'Allemagne d'avant guerre, y compris la Sarre. Les résultats en ont été publiés en 1939 dans *Die Deutsche Industrie,* 1936 par le Reichsamt für Wehrwirtschaftliche Planung, Berlin. Ce recensement couvrait tous les établissements occupant au moins 5 personnes, y compris les unités artisanales patentées dans les secteurs où ces unités jouent un rôle important. Il y a lieu de noter que le nombre de personnes occupées ne comprend pas les travailleurs à domicile. Les chiffres de la valeur ajoutée ne concernent que les marchandises produites par les établissements et sont calculés ou coût des facteurs.

Les chiffres des tableaux 5 et 6 sont tirés de *Die Saarländische Industrie im Jahre 1961 Saarland in Zahlen.* Ces données proviennent d'une enquête mensuelle auprès des unités extractives et manufacturières occupant 10 personnes ou plus, et des unités plus petites appartenant à des classes de l'activité industrielle dans lesquelles elles assurent une part importante de la production. Cependant, les unités artisanales patentées, quelle que soit leur dimension, ne sont pas couvertes par l'enquête.

Les chiffres relatifs aux recettes brutes reproduits au tableau 5 sont évalués aux prix de marché et ne couvrent pas les biens revendus en l'état. Les données concernant le nombre de personnes occupées couvrent les salariés, les propriétaires qui travaillent et les travailleurs familiaux non rémunérés, mais ne couvrent pas les travailleurs à domicile. Les définitions des autres rubriques relatives à la main-d'œuvre, du tableau 5, sont similaires à celles des Recommandations Internationales relatives aux Statistiques Industrielles de Base. Les chiffres concernant l'énergie consommée des tableaux 5 et 6 se rapportent à la consommation de différents combustibles, figurant dans le tableau 6 et à l'électricité achetée. Les combustibles utilisés comme matières premières ou dans la production de gaz, à l'exclusion du gaz de fournaise, l'électricité utilisée aussi bien comme source de chaleur que de puissance, sont compris dans les données relatives à la consommation de combustibles. Les chiffres relatifs à la consommation sont par conséquent surestimés pour des industries telles que les industries extractives de charbon, qui comprennent les cokeries et la fabrication de briquettes en charbon, ou les industries chimiques ou les industries manufacturières de fonte et d'acier.

## 1. INDEX NUMBERS OF INDUSTRIAL PRODUCTION — INDICES DE LA PRODUCTION INDUSTRIELLE

| Period<br>Période | All industrial activity, excluding construction<br>Toutes industries à l'exclusion du bâtiment et des travaux publics | Mining [1]<br>Industries extractives [1] | Manufacturing [2]<br>Industries manufacturières [2] | Construction<br>Bâtiment et travaux publics | Electricity and gas<br>Electricité et gaz |
|---|---|---|---|---|---|
| ISIC — CITI | 1–3; 511–512 | 1 | 2–3 | 4 | 511–512 |

### a. Indexes — Indices (1958 = 100)

| | | | | | |
|---|---|---|---|---|---|
| 1936............. | 56 | 70 | 53 | 38 | 48 |
| 1948............. | 44 | 74 | 34 | 29 | 50 |
| 1949............. | 54 | 86 | 45 | 44 | 62 |
| 1950............. | 60 | 90 | 51 | 52 | 61 |
| 1951............. | 73 | 97 | 66 | 57 | 70 |
| 1952............. | 77 | 97 | 71 | 65 | 70 |
| 1953............. | 75 | 97 | 68 | 83 | 69 |
| 1954............. | 80 | 100 | 76 | 81 | 70 |
| 1955............. | 88 | 104 | 84 | 76 | 81 |
| 1956............. | 94 | 104 | 91 | 75 | 94 |
| 1957............. | 99 | 101 | 98 | 90 | 98 |
| 1958............. | – 100 – | – 100 – | – 100 – | – 100 – | – 100 – |
| 1959............. | 101 | 98 | 101 | 99 | 103 |
| 1960............. | 103 | 96 | 104 | 87 | 99 |
| 1961............. | 107 | 98 | 109 | 85 | 110 |

### b. Average Annual Rate of Change — Taux annuel moyen de variation

| | | | | | |
|---|---|---|---|---|---|
| 1936 – 1960....... | 2.6 | 1.3 | 2.8 | 3.5 | 3.1 |
| 1936 – 1948....... | −2.0 | 0.4 | −3.6 | −2.2 | 0.3 |
| 1950 – 1960....... | 5.6 | 0.7 | 7.4 | 5.3 | 5.0 |
| 1948 – 1953....... | 11.2 | 5.6 | 14.9 | 23.4 | 6.7 |
| 1954 – 1958....... | 5.7 | — | 7.1 | 5.4 | 9.3 |
| 1958 – 1960....... | 1.5 | −2.2 | 2.0 | −6.7 | −0.5 |

[1] The extraction of coal and the manufacture of coke and coal briquets are the only activities measured by the index numbers.
[2] Does not include the activities of cokeries or coal briquetting works.

[1] L'extraction du charbon et la fabrication du coke et des briquettes et agglomérés de charbon sont les seules activités couvertes par les indices.
[2] Non compris l'activité des cokeries et des fabriques de briquettes et agglomérés.

## 2. INDEX NUMBERS OF INDUSTRIAL EMPLOYMENT
## INDICES DE L'EMPLOI INDUSTRIEL

### A. The Divisions of Industrial Activity
### Les branches de l'activité industrielle

| Period<br>Période | Total | Coal mining [1]<br>Extraction du charbon [1] | Manufacturing [1, 2]<br>Industries manufacturières [1, 2] | Construction<br>Bâtiment et travaux publics | Electricity and gas<br>Electricité et gaz |
|---|---|---|---|---|---|
| ISIC — CITI | 11, 2–3, 4, 511–512 | 11 | 2–3 | 4 | 511–512 |

### a. Indexes — Indices (1958 = 100)

| | | | | | |
|---|---|---|---|---|---|
| 1950....... | 84 | 106 | 76 | – 82 – | 101 |
| 1951....... | 89 | 104 | 83 | 88 | 101 |
| 1952....... | 91 | 105 | 86 | 90 | 101 |
| 1953....... | 93 | 105 | 88 | 97 | 102 |
| 1954....... | 95 | 102 | 91 | 102 | 101 |
| 1955....... | 96 | 103 | 93 | 103 | 102 |
| 1956....... | 97 | 102 | 96 | 103 | 102 |
| 1957....... | 99 | 101 | 98 | 100 | 102 |
| 1958....... | 100 | – 100 – | – 100 – | 100 | 100 |
| 1959....... | ... | 96 | 99 | ... | ... |
| 1960....... | ... | 86 | 103 | ... | ... |
| 1961....... | ... | 79 | 108 | ... | ... |

### b. Average Annual Rate of Change — Taux annuel moyen de variation

| | | | | | |
|---|---|---|---|---|---|
| 1950 – 1960. | ... | −2.1 | 3.1 | ... | ... |
| 1950 – 1953. | 3.4 | −0.3 | 5.0 | 3.3 | 0.3 |
| 1954 – 1958. | 1.3 | −0.5 | 2.4 | −0.5 | −0.3 |
| 1958 – 1960. | ... | −7.3 | 1.5 | ... | ... |

For footnotes, see end of table.          Pour les voir notes, au bas du tableau.

## B. The Major Groups of Manufacturing — Les classes de la branche Industries manufacturières

| Period / Période | Manufacturing [1,2] / Industries manufacturières [1,2] | Food, beverages and tobacco / Industries alimentaires, boissons, tabac | Textiles | Clothing, footwear and made-up textiles [3] / Articles d'habillement, chaussures et ouvrages en tissu [3] | Wood products and furniture [4] / Bois et meubles [4] | Paper and paper products / Papier et ouvrages en papier | Printing and publishing / Imprimerie et édition | Leather and leather products except wearing apparel [3] / Cuir et articles en cuir, à l'exclusion des articles d'habillement [3] | Rubber products [5] / Ouvrages en caoutchouc [5] | Chemicals and chemical, petroleum and coal products / Produits chimiques et dérivés du pétrole et du charbon | Non-metallic mineral products [2] / Produits minéraux non métalliques [2] | Basic metals / Métallurgie de base | Metal products [5] / Ouvrages en métaux [5] |
|---|---|---|---|---|---|---|---|---|---|---|---|---|---|
| ISIC — CITI | 2–3 | 20–22 | 23 | 24 | 25–26 | 27 | 28 | 29 | 30 | 31–32 | 33 | 34 | 35–38 |

### a. Indexes — Indices (1958 = 100)

| | | | | | | | | | | | | | |
|---|---|---|---|---|---|---|---|---|---|---|---|---|---|
| 1950 | 76 | 65 | 102 | 81 | 95 | 67 | 82 | 171 | 56 | 62 | 70 | 82 | 71 |
| 1951 | 83 | 70 | 111 | 87 | 99 | 76 | 84 | 159 | 59 | 66 | 78 | 93 | 76 |
| 1952 | 86 | 72 | 104 | 90 | 101 | 76 | 84 | 146 | 55 | 69 | 81 | 97 | 82 |
| 1953 | 88 | 79 | 106 | 94 | 102 | 80 | 88 | 138 | 53 | 75 | 84 | 96 | 84 |
| 1954 | 91 | 85 | 112 | 92 | 105 | 85 | 93 | 125 | 58 | 84 | 89 | 97 | 86 |
| 1955 | 93 | 90 | 104 | 94 | 104 | 88 | 100 | 114 | 72 | 86 | 92 | 95 | 91 |
| 1956 | 96 | 93 | 104 | 97 | 103 | 93 | 105 | 118 | 93 | 91 | 97 | 98 | 94 |
| 1957 | 98 | 96 | 103 | 98 | 102 | 95 | 104 | 119 | 109 | 93 | 99 | 99 | 98 |
| 1958 | –100– | –100– | –100– | –100– | –100– | –100– | –100– | –100– | –100– | –100– | –100– | –100– | –100– |
| 1959 | 99 | 104 | 82 | 82 | 84 | ... | 104 | ... | 111 | ... | ... | 103 | 97 |
| 1960 | 103 | 106 | 113 | 93 | 80 | ... | 109 | ... | ... | ... | ... | 113 | 93 |
| 1961 | 108 | 113 | 122 | 96 | 75 | ... | 111 | ... | ... | ... | ... | 117 | 101 |

### b. Average Annual Rate of Change — Taux annuel moyen de variation

| | | | | | | | | | | | | | |
|---|---|---|---|---|---|---|---|---|---|---|---|---|---|
| 1950–1960 | 3.1 | 5.0 | 1.0 | 1.4 | −1.7 | ... | 2.9 | ... | ... | ... | ... | 3.3 | 2.7 |
| 1950–1953 | 5.0 | 6.7 | 1.3 | 5.1 | 2.4 | 6.1 | 2.4 | −6.9 | −1.9 | 6.6 | 6.3 | 5.4 | 5.8 |
| 1954–1958 | 2.4 | 4.1 | −2.8 | 2.1 | −1.2 | 4.1 | 1.8 | −5.4 | 14.6 | 4.4 | 3.0 | 0.8 | 3.8 |
| 1958–1960 | 1.5 | 3.0 | 6.3 | −3.6 | −10.6 | ... | 4.4 | ... | ... | ... | ... | 6.3 | −3.6 |

[1] The manufacture of coke and coal briquettes (part of ISIC major group 32) is included in Coal mining (ISIC major group 11).
[2] Stone and sand quarrying (part of ISIC major group 14) is included in Non-metallic mineral products (ISIC major group 33).
[3] The manufacture of leather gloves is covered in Leather and leather products (ISIC major group 29) instead of in Clothing (ISIC major group 24).
[4] Manufacturing of musical instruments, toys and brushes and brooms (part of ISIC major group 39) is included in Wood products (ISIC major group 25).
[5] Asbestos products are covered in Rubber products (ISIC major group 30) and not in Non-metallic mineral products (ISIC major group 33).
[6] The manufacture of optical instruments (part of ISIC major group 39) is covered under Metal products (ISIC major groups 35–38).

[1] La fabrication de coke et de briquettes en charbon (dans CITI classe 32) est comprise dans les industries extractives de charbon.
[2] L'extraction de la pierre à bâtir et du sable (dans CITI classe 14) est comprise dans Produits minéraux non-métalliques (CITI classe 33).
[3] La fabrication de gants en cuir est couverte par Cuir et articles en cuir (CITI classe 29) au lieu d'être dans Articles d'habillement (CITI classe 24).
[4] La fabrication d'instruments de musique, de jouets, et de brosses et balais (dans CITI classe 39) est comprise dans Ouvrages en bois (CITI classe 25).
[5] Les produits en amiante sont couverts par Ouvrages en Caoutchouc (CITI classe 30) et non par Produits minéraux non-métalliques (CITI classe 33).
[6] La fabrication d'instruments d'optique (dans CITI classe 39) est couverte par Produits métalliques (CITI classes 35–38).

## 3. NUMBER OF AND EMPLOYMENT IN ALL INDUSTRIAL LOCAL UNITS
### 17 May 1939 and 14 November 1951

## NOMBRE D'UNITES INDUSTRIELLES LOCALES ET EMPLOI DANS CES UNITES
### 17 mai 1939 et 14 novembre 1951

Number of local units in units; number of engaged and employees in thousands

Nombre d'unités locales en unités; nombre de personnes occupées et de salariés en milliers

### A. The Divisions of Industrial Activity — Les branches de l'activité industrielle

| Item of data | All industrial activity / Toutes industries | | Mining [1] / Industries extractives [1] | | Manufacturing [1] / Industries manufacturières [1] | | Construction / Bâtiment et travaux publics | | Electricity and gas / Electricité et gaz | | Rubrique |
|---|---|---|---|---|---|---|---|---|---|---|---|
| | 17.V.1939 | 14.XI.1951 | 17.V.1939 | 14.XI.1951 [2] | 17.V.1939 | 14.XI.1951 [2] | 17.V.1939 | 14.XI.1951 | 17.V.1939 | 14.XI.1951 | |
| ISIC | 1–4, 511–512 | | 1 | | 2–3 | | 4 | | 511–512 | | CITI |
| Number of local units | 10 785 | 13 114 | 121 | 185 | 8 846 | 9 988 | 1 743 | 2 819 | 75 | 122 | Nombre d'unités locales |
| Number of engaged (As of census date) | 198.0 | 224.2 | 48.5 | 64.4 | 102.1 | 124.5 | 44.9 | 32.3 | 2.5 | 3.0 | Nombre de personnes occupées (à la date du recensement) |
| Number of employees (As of census date) | . | 206.4 | . | 64.4 | . | 110.4 | . | 28.6 | . | 3.0 | Nombre de salariés (à la date du recensement) |

[1] The manufacture of coke is included in Mining (ISIC division 1) instead of manufacturing (ISIC division 2–3).
[2] Quarrying of stone and gravel is included in Manufacturing (ISIC division 2–3) instead of Mining (ISIC division 1).

[1] La fabrication du coke est comprise dans Industries extractives (CITI branche 1) et non dans Industries manufacturières (CITI branche 2–3).
[2] L'extraction de la pierre et du gravier est comprise dans Industries manufacturières (CITI branches 2–3) et non dans Industries extractives (CITI branche 1).

### B. The Major Groups of Mining — Les classes de la branche Industries extractives

| Item of data | 17.V.1939 | | | 14.XI.1951 | | | | Rubrique |
|---|---|---|---|---|---|---|---|---|
| | All mining — Toutes industries extractives | Coal mining [1] — Extraction du charbon [1] | Other mining — Divers | All mining — Toutes industries extractives | Coal mining [1] — Extraction du charbon [1] | Metal mining — Extraction des minerais métalliques | Other mining [2] — Divers [2] | |
| ISIC | 1 | 11 | 14–19 | 1 | 11 | 12 | 14–19 | CITI |
| Number of local units......... | 121 | 85 | 36 | 185 | 182 | 2 | 1 | Nombre d'unités locales |
| Number of engaged (As of census date)......... | 48.5 | 47.7 | 0.8 | 64.4 | 64.4 | — | — | Nombre de personnes occupées (à la date du recensement) |
| Number of employees (As of census date)......... | . | | . | 64.4 | 64.4 | — | — | Nombre de salariés (à la date du recensement) |

[1] The manufacture of coke is included.
[2] The quarrying of stone and gravel is excluded.

[1] Y compris la fabrication du coke.
[2] Non compris l'extraction de la pierre et du gravier.

### C. The Major Groups of Manufacturing — Les classes de la branche Industries manufacturières

| Year and item of data | Manufacturing — Industries manufacturières | Food, beverages and tobacco — Industries alimentaires, boissons, tabac | Textiles | Clothing, footwear and made-up textiles — Articles d'habillement, chaussures et ouvrages en tissu | Wood products and furniture — Bois et meubles | Paper and paper products — Papier et ouvrages en papier | Printing and publishing — Imprimerie et édition | Leather and leather products except wearing apparel — Cuir et articles en cuir, à l'exclusion des articles d'habillement | Rubber products — Ouvrages en caoutchouc | Chemicals and chemical, petroleum and coal products [1] — Produits chimiques et dérivés du pétrole et du charbon [1] | Non-metallic mineral products — Produits minéraux non métalliques | Basic metals — Métallurgie de base | Metal products — Ouvrages en métaux | Other manufacturing — Autres industries manufacturières | Année et rubrique |
|---|---|---|---|---|---|---|---|---|---|---|---|---|---|---|---|
| ISIC | 2–3 | 20–22 | 23 | 24 | 25–26 | 27 | 28 | 29 | 30 | 31–32 | 33 | 34 | 35–38 | 39 | CITI |
| *17.V.1939* Number of local units.... | 8 846 | 2 464 | 192 | 2 951 | 1 004 | 40 | 173 | 115 | 18 | 67 | 245 | 43 | 1 328 | 206 | *17.V.1939* Nombre d'unités locales |
| Number of engaged (As of census date).... | 102.1 | 12.0 | 1.1 | 7.9 | 5.2 | 0.7 | 1.5 | 0.5 | 0.1 | 1.0 | 8.5 | 42.0 | 21.0 | 0.6 | Nombre de personnes occupées (à la date du recensement) |
| Distribution in percent of number of engaged... | 100.0 | 11.7 | 1.1 | 7.7 | 5.1 | 0.7 | 1.5 | 0.5 | 0.1 | 0.9 | 8.4 | 41.1 | 20.6 | 0.6 | Répartition en pourcentage du nombre de personnes occupées |
| *14.XI.1951* Number of local units.... | 9 988 | 2 804 | 172 | 2 104 | 1 491 | 139 | | 907 | 25 | 92 | 407 [2] | 45 | 1 509 | 293 | *14.XI.1951* Nombre d'unités locales |
| Number of engaged (As of census date).... | 124.5 | 13.5 | 1.1 | 8.2 | 11.6 | 2.4 | | 2.7 | 0.4 | 1.7 | 10.5 [2] | 42.5 | 28.7 | 1.2 | Nombre de personnes occupées (à la date du recensement) |
| Number of employees (As of census date).... | 110.4 | 8.2 | 0.9 | 5.9 | 9.6 | 2.2 | | 1.6 | 0.4 | 1.6 | 10.0 [2] | 42.4 | 26.8 | 0.8 | Nombre de salariés (à la date du recensement) |
| Distribution in percent of number of engaged... | 100.0 | 10.8 | 0.9 | 6.6 | 9.3 | 1.9 | | 2.2 | 0.3 | 1.4 | 8.4 [2] | 34.1 | 23.1 | 1.0 | Répartition en pourcentage du nombre de personnes occupées |
| Employees as a percent of engaged......... | 88.7 | 60.7 | 81.8 | 72.0 | 82.8 | 91.7 | | 59.2 | 100.0 | 94.1 | 95.2 | 99.8 | 93.4 | 66.7 | Salariés en pourcentage des personnes occupées |

[1] The manufacture of coke is excluded.
[2] Quarrying of stone and gravel is included.

[1] Non compris la fabrication du coke.
[2] Y compris l'extraction de la pierre et du gravier.

## 4. THE CHARACTERISTICS OF INDUSTRIAL ESTABLISHMENTS ENGAGING FIVE OR MORE PERSONS
## CARACTERISTIQUES DES ETABLISSEMENTS INDUSTRIELS OCCUPANT CINQ PERSONNES OU PLUS

### 1936

Value added in million Reichsmarks; number of engaged in thousands; value added per person engaged in thousand Reichsmarks

Valeur ajoutée en millions de reichsmarks; nombre de personnes occupées en milliers; valeur ajoutée par personne occupée en milliers de reichsmarks

### A. The Divisions of Industrial Activity — Les branches de l'activité industrielle

| Item of data | All industrial activity Toutes industries | Mining Industries extractives | Manufacturing Industries manufacturières | Construction Bâtiment et travaux publics | Electricity and gas Electricité et gaz | Rubrique |
|---|---|---|---|---|---|---|
| ISIC | 1–4;511–512 | 1 | 2–3 | 4 | 511–512 | CITI |
| a. Absolute Figures — Chiffres absolus | | | | | | |
| Value added.............. | 454.2 | 111.4 | 292.5 | 33.9 | 16.4 | Valeur ajoutée |
| Number of engaged (VI.1936)................ | 116.3 | 45.6 | 58.8 | 10.1 | 1.8 | Nombre de personnes occupées (VI.1936) |
| b. Structure | | | | | | |
| Distribution in percent of: | | | | | | Répartition en pourcentage: |
| Value added.............. | 100.0 | 24.5 | 64.4 | 7.4 | 3.7 | De la valeur ajoutée |
| Number of engaged......... | 100.0 | 39.2 | 50.5 | 8.7 | 1.6 | Du nombre de personnes occupées |
| Value added per person engaged................. | 3.9 | 2.4 | 5.0 | 3.4 | 9.1 | Valeur ajoutée par personne occupée |

### B. The Major Groups of Mining — Les classes de la branche Industries extractives

| Item of data | All mining Toutes industries extractives | Coal mining Extraction du charbon | Other mining Divers | Rubrique |
|---|---|---|---|---|
| ISIC | 1 | 11 | 14–19 | CITI |
| a. Absolute Figures — Chiffres absolus | | | | |
| Value added............... | 111.4 | 107.8 | 3.6 | Valeur ajoutée |
| Number of engaged (VI.1936)................ | 45.6 | 44.8 | 0.8 | Nombre de personnes occupées (VI.1936) |
| b. Structure | | | | |
| Distribution in percent of: | | | | Répartition en pourcentage: |
| Value added............. | 100.0 | 96.8 | 3.2 | De la valeur ajoutée |
| Number of engaged........ | 100.0 | 98.2 | 1.8 | Du nombre de personnes occupées |
| Value added per person engaged................. | 2.4 | 2.4 | 4.5 | Valeur ajoutée par personne occupée |

## C.  The Major Groups of Manufacturing — Les classes de la branche Industries manufacturières

| Item of data | Manu-facturing<br><br>Industries manufac-turières | Food, beverages and tobacco<br><br>Industries alimen-taires, boissons, tabac | Textiles | Clothing, footwear and made-up textiles<br><br>Articles d'habil-lement, chaussures et ouvrages en tissu | Wood products and furniture[1]<br><br>Bois et meubles[1] | Paper and paper products<br><br>Papier et ouvrages en papier | Printing and publish-ing<br><br>Im-primerie et édition | Leather and leather products except wearing apparel<br><br>Cuir et articles en cuir, à l'exclu-sion des articles d'habil-lement | Rubber products<br><br>Ouvrages en caout-chouc | Chemicals and chemical, petroleum and coal products<br><br>Produits chi-miques et dérivés du pétrole et du charbon | Non-metallic mineral products<br><br>Produits minéraux non métal-liques | Basic metals<br><br>Métal-lurgie de base | Metal products[1]<br><br>Ouvrages en métaux[1] | Other manu-factur-ing<br><br>Autres in-dustries manufac-turières | Rubrique |
|---|---|---|---|---|---|---|---|---|---|---|---|---|---|---|---|
| ISIC | 2–3 | 20–22 | 23 | 24 | 25–26 | 27 | 28 | 29 | 30 | 31–32 | 33 | 34 | 35–38 | 39 | CITI |
| *a.  Absolute Figures — Chiffres absolus* | | | | | | | | | | | | | | | |
| Value added.......... | 292.5 | 28.1 | 0.5 | 2.8 | 1.8 | 1.1 | 3.1 | 1.2 | — | 30.0 | 24.6 | 153.7 | 45.4 | 0.2 | Valeur ajoutée |
| Number of engaged (VI.1936)........... | 58.8 | 3.6 | 0.3 | 1.7 | 0.9 | 0.3 | 1.3 | 0.1 | — | 4.0 | 8.4 | 26.2 | 11.9 | 0.1 | Nombre de personnes occupées (VI.1936) |
| *b.  Structure* | | | | | | | | | | | | | | | |
| Distribution in percent of:<br>Value added........ | 100.0 | 9.6 | 0.1 | 1.0 | 0.6 | 0.4 | 1.0 | 0.4 | — | 10.3 | 8.4 | 52.6 | 15.5 | 0.1 | Répartition en pour-centage:<br>De la valeur ajoutée |
| Number of engaged.. | 100.0 | 6.1 | 0.5 | 2.9 | 1.5 | 0.5 | 2.2 | 0.2 | — | 6.8 | 14.3 | 44.5 | 20.3 | 0.2 | Du nombre de person-nes occupées |
| Value added per person engaged........... | 5.0 | 7.8 | 1.7 | 1.6 | 2.0 | 3.7 | 2.4 | 12.0 | — | 7.5 | 2.9 | 5.9 | 3.8 | 2.0 | Valeur ajoutée par per-sonne occupée |

[1] The manufacture of metal furniture is classified in Metal products (ISIC major groups 35–38) instead of Furniture (ISIC major group 26).

[1] La fabrication des meubles en métal est classée dans Ouvrages en métaux (CITI 35–38) et non dans Industrie du meuble (CITI 26).

## 5. THE CHARACTERISTICS OF LOCAL UNITS ENGAGING TEN OR MORE PERSONS, EXCEPTING LICENSED HANDICRAFTS

### CARACTERISTIQUES DES UNITES LOCALES OCCUPANT 10 PERSONNES OU PLUS, A L'EXCLUSION DES UNITES ARTISANALES

### 1958

Number of local units in units; gross receipts and wages and salaries in million old Francs; number of engaged and operatives in thousands; man-hours worked in millions; energy consumed in thousand metric tons of coal equivalents; electricity consumed in million KWH; wages and salaries per thousand operative man-hours in thousand old Francs; average annual man-hours per operative in thousands; energy consumed per engaged and per thousand operative man-hours in metric tons of coal equivalents; electricity consumed per engaged and per thousand operative man-hours in thousand KWH.

Nombre d'unités locales en unités; recettes brutes et traitements et salaires en millions d'anciens francs; nombre de personnes occupées et d'ouvriers en milliers; heures de travail en millions; énergie consommée en milliers de tonnes métriques d'équivalent charbon; électricité consommée en millions de kWh; traitements et salaires par salarié et par millier d'heures-ouvrier en milliers d'anciens francs; moyenne annuelle des heures de travail par ouvrier en milliers; énergie consommée par personne occupée et par millier d'heures-ouvrier en tonnes métriques d'équivalent charbon; électricité consommée par personne occupée et par millier d'heures-ouvrier en milliers de kWh.

| Item of data | Mining [1] Industries extractives [1] | Manufacturing [2] Industries manufacturières [2] | Food, beverages and tobacco Industries alimentaires, boissons, tabac | Textiles | Clothing, footwear and made-up textiles [3] Articles d'habillement, chaussures et ouvrages en tissu [3] | Wood products and furniture [4] Bois et meubles [4] | Printing and publishing Imprimerie et édition | Leather and leather products except wearing apparel [3] Cuir et articles en cuir, à l'exclusion des articles d'habillement [3] | Chemicals and chemical, petroleum and coal products [1] Produits chimiques et dérivés du pétrole et du charbon [1] | Non-metallic mineral products [1,5] Produits minéraux non métalliques [1,5] | Basic metals [2] Métallurgie de base [2] | Metal products Ouvrages en métaux | Rubrique |
|---|---|---|---|---|---|---|---|---|---|---|---|---|---|
| ISIC | 1 | 2-3 | 20-22 | 23 | 24 | 25-26 | 28 | 29 | 31-32 | 33 | 34 | 35-38 | CITI |
| *a. Absolute Figures — Chiffres absolus* | | | | | | | | | | | | | |
| Number of local units.... | 27 | 719 | 130 | 13 | 50 | 92 | 35 | 19 | 43 | 91 | 29 | 189 | Nombre d'unités locales |
| Gross receipts.......... | 86 314 | 381 237 | 43 371 | 1 993 | 6 641 | 14 364 | 3 178 | 1 454 | 8 300 | 22 540 | 186 122 | 88 019 | Recettes brutes |
| Number of engaged.... | 64.5 | 115.7 | 7.4 | 0.8 | 4.4 | 5.8 | 1.6 | 0.8 | 1.8 | 12.6 | 44.6 | 33.8 | Nombre de personnes occupées |
| Wages and salaries..... | 54 884 | 77 493 | 4 373 | 362 | 1 576 | 3 147 | 1 221 | 335 | 1 153 | 7 457 | 35 309 | 21 545 | Traitements et salaires |
| Operatives: Number.............. | 58.1 | 97.7 | 5.8 | 0.7 | 3.7 | 5.0 | 1.2 | 0.7 | 1.2 | 11.5 | 38.7 | 27.4 | Ouvriers: Nombre |
| Man-hours worked.... | 111.4 | 216.2 | 13.5 | 1.5 | 6.7 | 10.9 | 2.6 | 1.3 | 2.5 | 24.4 | 87.8 | 61.6 | Heures de travail effectuées |
| Wages and salaries.......... | 45 744 | 58 364 | 2 994 | 258 | 1 102 | 2 462 | 791 | 248 | 603 | 6 330 | 26 458 | 15 123 | Traitements et salaires |
| Energy consumed...... | 2 348.9 | 4 257.8 | 45.8 | 2.3 | 2.2 | 17.2 | 1.7 | 1.1 | 9.9 | 184.7 | 3 899.9 | 83.0 | Energie consommée |
| Electricity consumed..... | 930.5 | 1 216.0 | 25.2 | 2.2 | 1.6 | 21.4 | 1.9 | 0.4 | 4.0 | 73.4 | 989.5 | 86.6 | Electricité consommée |
| Distribution in percent of: Gross receipts........ | . | 100.0 | 11.3 | 0.6 | 1.7 | 3.8 | 0.8 | 0.4 | 2.2 | 5.9 | 48.8 | 23.1 | Distribution en pourcentage: Recettes brutes |
| Number of engaged.. | . | 100.0 | 6.4 | 0.7 | 3.7 | 5.1 | 1.4 | 0.7 | 1.6 | 10.9 | 38.5 | 29.3 | Nombre de personnes occupées |
| Per person engaged: Energy consumed..... | 36.42 | 36.80 | 6.19 | 2.88 | 0.50 | 2.96 | 1.06 | 1.38 | 5.50 | 14.66 | 87.44 | 2.46 | Par personne occupée: Energie consommée |
| Electricity consumed... | 14.4 | 10.5 | 3.4 | 2.8 | 0.4 | 3.7 | 1.2 | 0.5 | 2.2 | 5.8 | 22.2 | 2.6 | Electricité consommée |
| Operatives as a percent of engaged... | 90.1 | 84.4 | 78.4 | 87.5 | 84.1 | 86.2 | 75.0 | 87.5 | 66.7 | 91.3 | 86.8 | 81.1 | Ouvriers en pourcentage des personnes occupées |
| Average man-hours per operative........ | 1.92 | 2.21 | 2.33 | 2.14 | 1.81 | 2.18 | 2.17 | 1.86 | 2.08 | 2.12 | 2.27 | 2.25 | Heures de travail: moyenne par ouvrier |
| Per thousand operative man-hours: Wages and salaries............. | 410.63 | 269.95 | 221.78 | 172.00 | 164.48 | 225.87 | 304.23 | 190.77 | 241.20 | 259.43 | 301.34 | 245.50 | Par millier d'heures-ouvrier: Traitements et salaires |
| Energy consumed..... | 21.08 | 19.69 | 3.39 | 1.53 | 0.33 | 1.57 | 0.65 | 0.85 | 3.96 | 7.57 | 44.42 | 1.35 | Energie consommée |
| Electricity consumed... | 8.35 | 5.62 | 1.87 | 1.47 | 0.24 | 1.96 | 0.73 | 0.31 | 1.60 | 3.01 | 11.27 | 1.40 | Electricité consommée |

[1] Coking and coal briquetting is covered in Mining (ISIC Division 1) and not in Petroleum and coal products (ISIC major group 32) but the quarrying of stone and sand is covered in Non-metallic mineral products (ISIC major group 33) and not in Mining (ISIC Division 1).

[2] The data for Manufacturing (ISIC Division 2-3) cover the following classes of manufacturing not shown in the classes into which Manufacturing is sub-divided: Paper and paper products (ISIC major group 27), Rubber products (ISIC major group 30), Non-ferrous basic metal industries (part of ISIC major group 34) and Other manufacturing (ISIC major group 39).

[3] The manufacture of shoes and leather gloves (part of ISIC major group 24) is included in Leather and leather products (ISIC major group 29).

[4] The manufacture of musical instruments, toys, brushes and brooms (part of ISIC major group 39) is included in Wood products (ISIC major group 25).

[5] The manufacture of asbestos products is not covered in Non-metallic mineral products (ISIC major group 33).

[1] La fabrication de coke et de briquettes en charbon est couverte par les Industries extractives (CITI Branche 1) non par les Produits dérivés du charbon et du pétrole (CITI classe 32) mais l'extraction de pierre à batir et de sable est couverte par Produits minéraux non par les Industries extractives (CITI Branche 1).

[2] Les données relatives aux Industries manufacturières (CITI Branche 2-3) couvrent les classes manufacturières suivantes non reproduites dans les classes qui composent les Industries manufacturières: Papiers et articles en papier (CITI classe 27), Ouvrages en Caoutchouc (CITI classe 30), Production et première transformation des métaux non ferreux (dans CITI classe 34) et Autres industries manufacturières (CITI classe 39).

[3] La fabrication des chaussures et des gants en cuir (dans CITI classe 24) est comprise dans Cuir et articles en cuir (CITI classe 29).

[4] La fabrication d'instruments de musique, de jouets, de brosses et balais (dans CITI classe 39) est comprise dans Ouvrages en bois (CITI classe 25).

[5] La fabrication d'ouvrages en amiante n'est pas couverte par Produits minéraux non métalliques (CITI classe 33).

# 6. SELECTED FUELS AND ELECTRICITY CONSUMED, LOCAL UNITS ENGAGING TEN OR MORE PERSONS EXCEPTING LICENSED HANDICRAFTS
## CONSOMMATION DE QUELQUES COMBUSTIBLES ET D'ELECTRICITE, UNITES LOCALES OCCUPANT DIX PERSONNES OU PLUS, EXCEPTE L'ARTISANAT PATENTE
### 1958

## A. Percentage Distribution of Energy Consumed According to Source
### Distribution en pourcentage de l'énergie consommée suivant la source

Quantities in thousand metric tons of coal equivalents.     Quantités en milliers de tonnes métriques d'équivalent houille.

| Item of data | Mining[1] Industries extractives[1] | Manufacturing[2] Industries manufacturières[2] | Food beverages and tobacco Industries alimentaires, boissons, tabac | Textiles | Clothing, footwear and made-up textiles[3] Articles d'habillement, chaussures et ouvrages en tissu[3] | Wood products and furniture[4] Bois et meubles[4] | Printing and publishing Imprimerie et édition | Leather and leather products except wearing apparel[3] Cuir et articles en cuir, à l'exclusion des articles d'habillement[3] | Chemicals and chemical, petroleum and coal products[1] Produits chimiques et dérivés du pétrole et du charbon[1] | Non-metallic mineral products[1,5] Produits minéraux non métalliques[1,5] | Basic metals[2] Métallurgie de base[2] | Metal products Ouvrages en métaux | Rubrique |
|---|---|---|---|---|---|---|---|---|---|---|---|---|---|
| ISIC | 1 | 2-3 | 20-22 | 23 | 24 | 25-26 | 28 | 29 | 31-32 | 33 | 34 | 35-38 | CITI |
| Total energy consumed: Quantity | 2 348.9 | 4 257.8 | 45.8 | 2.3 | 2.2 | 17.2 | 1.7 | 1.1 | 9.9 | 184.7 | 3 899.9 | 83.0 | Energie totale consommée: Quantité |
| Percent of total in specified industry | — | 100.0 | 1.1 | 0.1 | 0.1 | 0.4 | — | — | 0.2 | 4.4 | 91.6 | 1.9 | Pourcentage du total par industrie indiquée |
| Percent consumed as: Coal[6] | 92.9 | 10.3 | 77.5 | 23.7 | 23.0 | 76.9 | 13.5 | 42.8 | 83.1 | 57.7 | 6.4 | 22.3 | Pourcentage consommé comme: Charbon[6] |
| Lignite[6] | — | | 1.9 | | 0.1 | | — | 0.1 | 0.4 | | — | 0.2 | Lignite[6] |
| Coke | 1.0 | 71.8 | 7.2 | 8.5 | 27.1 | 6.5 | 59.3 | 38.6 | 8.0 | 16.9 | 76.9 | 21.1 | Coke |
| Refined oil fuels | 0.2 | 0.4 | 4.5 | 54.3 | 36.7 | 1.4 | 5.2 | 12.4 | 2.5 | 0.6 | 0.1 | 6.5 | Pétrole raffiné |
| Gas | 5.8 | 15.3 | 3.1 | 1.9 | 4.1 | 0.1 | 8.5 | 1.0 | 1.0 | 19.9 | 14.9 | 37.1 | Gaz |
| Electricity purchased | 0.1 | 2.2 | 5.8 | 11.6 | 9.0 | 15.1 | 13.5 | 5.1 | 5.0 | 4.9 | 1.7 | 12.8 | Electricité achetée |

For footnotes, see end of table.     Pour les notes, voir au bas du tableau.

## B. Quantity of Selected Fuels Consumed and of Electricity Purchased, Produced and Sold
### Volume de quelques combustibles consommés et d'électricité achetée, produite et vendue

Coal, lignite and refined fuel oils in thousand metric tons; manufactured gas in million cubic metres; electricity in million KWH.     Charbon, lignite et pétrole raffiné en milliers de tonnes métriques; gaz manufacturé en millions de mètres cubes; électricité en millions de kWh.

| Source of energy | Mining[1] Industries extractives[1] | Manufacturing[2] Industries manufacturières[2] | Food, beverages and tobacco Industries alimentaires, boissons, tabac | Textiles | Clothing, footwear and made-up textiles[3] Articles d'habillement, chaussures et ouvrages en tissu[3] | Wood products and furniture[4] Bois et meubles[4] | Printing and publishing Imprimerie et édition | Leather and leather products except wearing apparel[3] Cuir et articles en cuir, à l'exclusion des articles d'habillement[3] | Chemicals and chemical, petroleum and coal products[1] Produits chimiques et dérivés du pétrole et du charbon[1] | Non-metallic mineral products[1,5] Produits minéraux non métalliques[1,5] | Basic metals[2] Métallurgie de base[2] | Metal products Ouvrages en métaux | Source d'énergie |
|---|---|---|---|---|---|---|---|---|---|---|---|---|---|
| ISIC | 1 | 2-3 | 20-22 | 23 | 24 | 25-26 | 28 | 29 | 31-32 | 33 | 34 | 35-38 | CITI |
| Coal[6] | 2 183.2 | 441.5 | 35.5 | 0.6 | 0.5 | 13.2 | 0.2 | 0.5 | 8.3 | 106.6 | 250.5 | 18.6 | Charbon[6] |
| Lignite[6] | — | 2.0 | 1.3 | — | — | — | — | — | — | — | — | 0.3 | Lignite[6] |
| Coke | 25.4 | 3 396.3 | 3.7 | 0.2 | 0.7 | 1.2 | 1.1 | 0.5 | 0.9 | 34.8 | 3 332.9 | 19.4 | Coke |
| Refined oil fuels | 3.6 | 10.4 | 1.3 | 0.8 | 0.5 | 0.2 | 0.1 | 0.1 | 0.2 | 0.7 | 2.4 | 3.6 | Pétrole raffiné |
| Manufactured gas | 227.4 | 1 086.1 | 2.4 | 0.1 | 0.2 | | 0.2 | | 0.2 | 61.0 | 970.5 | 51.3 | Gaz manufacturé |
| Electricity: Purchased | 8.1 | 728.4 | 21.0 | 2.2 | 1.6 | 20.7 | 1.9 | 0.4 | 4.0 | 72.1 | 510.0 | 85.0 | Electricité: Achetée |
| Produced | 1 730.7 | 488.8 | 4.5 | — | 0.7 | — | — | — | 0.1 | 1.3 | 480.4 | 1.6 | Produite |
| Sold | 808.3 | 1.2 | 0.3 | — | — | — | — | — | — | — | 0.9 | — | Vendue |

[1] Coking and coal briquetting is covered in Mining (ISIC Division 1) and not in Petroleum and coal products (ISIC major group 32) but the quarrying of stone and sand is covered in Non-metallic mineral products (ISIC major group 33) and not in Mining (ISIC Division 1).
[2] The data for Manufacturing (ISIC Division 2-3) cover the following classes of manufacturing not shown in the classes into which Manufacturing is sub-divided: Paper and paper products (ISIC major group 27), Rubber products (ISIC major group 30), Non-ferrous basic metal industries (part of ISIC major group 34) and Other manufacturing (ISIC major group 39).
[3] The manufacture of shoes and leather gloves (part of ISIC major group 24) is included in Leather and leather products (ISIC major group 29).
[4] The manufacture of musical instruments, toys, brushes and brooms (part of ISIC major group 39) is included in Wood products (ISIC major group 25).
[5] The manufacture of asbestos products is not covered in Non-metallic mineral products (ISIC major group 33).
[6] The data on coal and lignite include briquettes of coal and lignite, respectively.

[1] La fabrication de coke et de briquettes en charbon est couverte par les Industries extractives (CITI Branche 1) non par les Produits dérivés du charbon et du pétrole (CITI classe 32) mais l'extraction de pierre à bâtir et de sable est couverte par Produits minéraux non par les Industries extractives (CITI Branche 1).
[2] Les données relatives aux Industries manufacturières (CITI Branche 2-3) couvrent les classes manufacturières suivantes non reproduites dans les classes qui composent les Industries manufacturières: Papiers et articles en papier (CITI classe 27), Ouvrages en Caoutchouc (CITI classe 30), Production et première transformation des métaux non ferreux (dans CITI classe 34) et Autres industries manufacturières (CITI classe 39).
[3] La fabrication des chaussures et des gants en cuir (dans CITI classe 24) est comprise dans Cuir et articles en cuir (CITI classe 29).
[4] La fabrication d'instruments de musique, de jouets, de brosses et balais (dans CITI classe 39) est comprise dans Ouvrages en bois (CITI classe 25).
[5] La fabrication d'ouvrages en amiante n'est pas couverte par Produits minéraux non métalliques (CITI classe 33).
[6] Les données relatives au charbon et au lignite couvrent les briquettes en charbon et en lignite, respectivement.

# GERMANY, WEST BERLIN — ALLEMAGNE, BERLIN-OUEST

## Index Numbers of Industrial Production

The index numbers for 1936 and 1950 and subsequent years shown in Table 1 are based on the indexes of the volume of production issued regularly by the Statistisches Landesamt, Berlin, in *Berliner Statistik, Monatsschrift.* The index numbers for the years 1948 and 1949 were compiled from an article, "Der Wiederaufbau der Industrie von Berlin West nach dem Zusammenbruch" in *Berliner Statistik,* January 1957.

The indexes compiled by the Statistisches Landesamt are arithmetic averages weighted by value added at market price during 1952 for each detailed class of manufacturing. The indicators of the volume of production for each of these classes of manufacturing are primarily the output of individual commodities. However, some of the indicators are value of output deflated by changes in price. The weights, as well as the indicators, for the indexes relate to industrial establishments other than licensed handicrafts. For further details concerning the index numbers of the volume of production see: *Berliner Statistik, Monatsschrift,* December 1953 and June 1956.

## Index Numbers of Industrial Employment

The index numbers of industrial employment set out in Table 2 were compiled by the Statistical Office of the United Nations resulting from the same inquiries as the figures shown in Table 4. The absolute figures were abstracted from the issues of *Berliner Statistik* devoted to annual summaries of the results of these inquiries—for example, Sonderhefte 38, 44, 64, 70 and 87. The data on employment that the Statistical Office of the United Nations utilized in compiling the index numbers refer to the average number of persons engaged, except homeworkers, at the end of each month of the year.

## Characteristics and Structure of Industrial Activity

Censuses of all business units taken as of 17 May 1939 and 13 September 1950 which covered the area of West Berlin yielded the data presented in Table 3. The figures as of 17 May 1939 come from *Berliner Statistik,* September-October, 1951 while those as of 13 September 1950 appear in *Statistik der Bundesrepublik Deutschland,* Band 46, Heft 7 and also the *Berliner Statistik,* Sonderheft 20, March 1952. The censuses covered, among other business enterprises, all units engaged in industrial activities, including licensed handicrafts. It should be noted that although, in both censuses, the local unit was utilized in gathering, classifying and compiling data, in the earlier census, activities which were ancillary to but physi-

## Indices de la production industrielle

Les indices reproduits dans le tableau 1 pour 1936 et pour 1950 et les années suivantes sont fondés sur des indices de la production publiés régulièrement par le Statistisches Landesamt, Berlin, dans *Berliner Statistik, Monatsschrift.* Les indices des années 1948 et 1949 ont été construits d'après les données d'un article paru dans le numéro de janvier 1957 de *Berliner Statistik* et intitulé "Der Wiederaufbau der Industrie von Berlin West nach dem Zusammenbruch".

Les indices établis par le Statistisches Landesamt sont des moyennes arithmétiques pondérées par la valeur ajoutée aux prix du marché en 1952 pour chaque catégorie d'industrie manufacturière. Pour chacune de ces catégories, l'indicateur du volume de la production est normalement le volume de la production des diverses marchandises, mais parfois l'indicateur est la valeur de la production corrigée des variations de prix. Les coefficients de pondération et les indicateurs, utilisés pour les indices, sont relatifs aux établissements industriels autres que les unités artisanales patentées. Pour plus amples détails concernant les indices du volume de la production, voir: *Berliner Statistik, Monatsschrift,* décembre 1953 et juin 1956.

## Indices de l'emploi industriel

Les indices de l'emploi industriel reproduits au tableau 2 ont été calculés par le Bureau de Statistique de l'O.N.U., à partir des résultats des mêmes enquêtes que celles qui ont servi à l'élaboration des données du tableau 4. Les chiffres absolus ont été tirés des publications du *Berliner Statistik* consacrées aux sommaires annuels des résultats de ces enquêtes — par exemple, Sonderhefte 38, 44, 64, 70 et 87. Les données de l'emploi que le Bureau de Statistique de l'O.N.U. utilisa pour calculer les indices sont celles relatives au nombre moyen de personnes occupées, à l'exclusion des travailleurs à domicile, à la fin de chaque mois.

## Caractéristiques et structure de l'activité industrielle

Les données du tableau 3 proviennent des recensements, au 17 mai 1939 et au 13 septembre 1950, de toutes les unités industrielles et commerciales du territoire actuel de Berlin-Ouest. Les chiffres au 17 mai 1939 sont tirés de *Berliner Statistik,* septembre-octobre 1951; les autres (13 septembre 1950) ont été publiés dans *Statistik der Bundesrepublik Deutschland,* Band 46, Heft 7, et aussi dans *Berliner Statistik,* Sonderheft 20, mars 1952. Ces recensements couvraient, entre autres entreprises, toutes les unités exerçant une activité industrielle, y compris les unités artisanales patentées. Il y a lieu de noter que si, dans les deux recensements, c'est l'unité locale qui a été prise comme base pour le rassemblement, le classement

cally separated from the main industrial activity were not combined with the main activity in the same local unit. This, of course, affects the comparability between the two censuses in the figures of number of units and of employment for each class of industrial activity.

Table 4 presents data for manufacturing units engaging ten or more persons, excepting licensed handicrafts. The data are derived from a monthly survey of these units and were abstracted from *Die Entwicklung der West-Berliner Industrie*, 1950 bis 1953 and *Die Entwicklung der Industrie in Berlin (West), 1959; Berliner Statistik*, Sonderhefte 38, March 1954 and 77, May 1960, respectively. The statistical unit employed in this survey was the local unit. The figures of number of engaged in Table 4 relate to all persons working for the unit, excepting homeworkers. The data on gross receipts cover the shipping value of goods, exclusive of consumption taxes, which had been processed—i.e., goods sold in the same form as purchased are not included in the value of gross receipts.

Censuses of licensed handicrafts provided the data shown in Table 5. The Censuses were taken as of 30 September 1949 and 31 May 1956 and covered all local units in operation on these two census days. The figures of number of engaged in the table relate to all persons working for the business unit except homeworkers. The data on gross receipts in this table cover the value of all goods sold, whether or not processed by the local unit. The sources of the data in Table 5 are, "Ergebnisse der Handwerkszählung in West Berlin am 30 September, 1949" in the *Berliner Statistik*, Sonderheft 10, issued by the Statistisches Landesamt, Berlin and *Handwerkszählung, Statistik der Bundesrepublik Deutschland*, Band 203, issued by the Statistisches Bundesamt, Wiesbaden.

et l'exploitation des données, dans le premier recensement en revanche les activités auxiliaires, mais physiquement distinctes, de l'activité principale d'une unité n'ont pas été rattachées à cette activité principale. Il en résulte naturellement un certain défaut de comparabilité entre les deux recensements pour ce qui est du nombre d'unités et de l'emploi dans chaque catégorie d'activité industrielle.

Le tableau 4 contient des données relatives aux unités manufacturières occupant au moins 10 personnes, à l'exclusion des unités artisanales patentées. Ces données sont le fruit d'une enquête mensuelle sur les dites unités et ont été tirées de *Die Entwicklung der West-Berliner Industrie*, 1950 bis 1953 et de *Die Entwicklung der Industrie in Berlin (Ouest), 1959*, paru dans *Berliner Statistik*, Sonderhefte 38, mars 1954 et 77, mai 1960 respectivement. L'unité statistique utilisée dans cette enquête était l'unité locale. Le nombre de personnes occupées (tableau 4) comprend toutes les personnes travaillant pour l'unité, à l'exclusion des travailleurs à domicile. Les recettes brutes correspondent à la valeur des expéditions de marchandises qui ont été transformées — non compris les droits de consommation — c'est-à-dire qu'il n'est pas tenu compte des marchandises revendues en l'état.

Les données du tableau 5 proviennent des recensements des unité artisanales patentées. Ces recensements ont été effectués au 30 septembre 1949 et au 31 mai 1956 et portaient sur toutes les unités locales en activité aux jours des recensements. Le nombre de personnes occupées comprend toutes les personnes travaillant pour l'unité visée, à l'exclusion des travailleurs à domicile. Les recettes brutes représentent la valeur de toutes les marchandises vendues, qu'elles aient été transformées ou non par l'unité locale. Les sources des données du tableau 5 sont "Ergebnisse der Handwerkszählung in West Berlin am 30 September, 1949" paru dans *Berliner Statistik*, Sonderheft 10, publié par le Statistisches Landesamt, Berlin, et *Handwerkszählung, Statistik der Bundesrepublik Deutschland*, Band 203, publié par Statistisches Bundesamt, Wiesbaden.

## 1. INDEX NUMBERS OF INDUSTRIAL PRODUCTION — INDICES DE LA PRODUCTION INDUSTRIELLE

| Period<br>Période | Manufac-<br>turing<br><br>Industries<br>manufac-<br>turières | Food,<br>beverages<br>and<br>tobacco<br><br>Industries<br>alimen-<br>taires,<br>boissons,<br>tabac | Clothing,<br>footwear<br>and<br>made-up<br>textiles<br><br>Articles<br>d'habil-<br>lement,<br>chaussures<br>et<br>ouvrages<br>en tissu | Wood<br>products<br><br>Bois | Paper<br>and<br>paper<br>products<br><br>Papier<br>et<br>ouvrages<br>en<br>papier | Printing<br>and<br>publishing<br><br>Imprimerie<br>et édition | Chemicals<br>and<br>chemical,<br>petroleum,<br>coal and<br>rubber<br>products<br><br>Produits<br>chimiques,<br>dérivés du<br>pétrole<br>et du<br>charbon et<br>ouvrages<br>en<br>caoutchouc | Non-<br>metallic<br>mineral<br>products [1]<br><br>Produits<br>minéraux<br>non<br>métal-<br>liques [1] | Basic<br>metals<br><br>Métal-<br>lurgie<br>de base | Metal<br>products<br><br>Ouvrages<br>en métaux | Other<br>manu-<br>facturing<br>including<br>textiles and<br>leather<br>products<br><br>Autres<br>industries<br>manu-<br>facturières,<br>y compris<br>textiles<br>et articles<br>en cuir |
|---|---|---|---|---|---|---|---|---|---|---|---|
| ISIC — CITI | 2–3 | 20–22 | 24 | 25 | 27 | 28 | 30–32 | 33 | 34 | 35–38 | 23, 29, 39 |
| a | | | | | *a. Indexes — Indices (1958 = 100)* | | | | | | |
| 1936........................ | 84 | 52 | 50 | 322 | 70 | 19 | 54 | 52 | 88 | 85 | 103 |
| 1950........................ | 27 | 34 | 24 | 326 | 29 | 37 | 26 | 25 | 13 | 26 | 30 |
| 1951........................ | 39 | 37 | 41 | 242 | 36 | 43 | 36 | 32 | 27 | 40 | 37 |
| 1952........................ | 43 | 38 | 52 | 84 | 36 | 49 | 37 | 40 | 39 | 43 | 41 |
| 1953........................ | 52 | 49 | 68 | 71 | 46 | 57 | 49 | 50 | 36 | 44 | 58 |
| 1954........................ | 64 | 55 | 83 | 119 | 67 | 69 | 57 | 61 | 46 | 62 | 71 |
| 1955........................ | 79 | 62 | 95 | 77 | 87 | 78 | 66 | 73 | 68 | 82 | 78 |
| 1956........................ | 90 | 73 | 104 | 81 | 98 | 90 | 79 | 74 | 97 | 92 | 89 |
| 1957........................ | 96 | 88 | 112 | 77 | 99 | 96 | 92 | 84 | 105 | 94 | 98 |
| 1958........................ | 100 | 100 | 100 | 100 | 100 | 100 | 100 | 100 | 100 | 100 | 100 |
| 1959........................ | 112 | 131 | 104 | 139 | 108 | 102 | 119 | 118 | 128 | 108 | 106 |
| 1960........................ | 128 | 168 | 111 | 184 | 120 | 110 | 133 | 132 | 160 | 123 | 118 |
| 1961........................ | 140 | 191 | 120 | 255 | 120 | 114 | 146 | 131 | 151 | 136 | 118 |
| b | | | | | *b. Average Annual Rate of Change — Taux annuel moyen de variation* | | | | | | |
| 1936 – 1960............... | 1.8 | 5.0 | 3.4 | −2.3 | 2.3 | −2.4 | 3.8 | 4.2 | 2.5 | 1.6 | 0.6 |
| 1950 – 1960............... | 16.8 | 17.3 | 16.6 | −5.6 | 15.3 | 11.5 | 17.7 | 18.1 | 28.5 | 16.8 | 14.7 |
| 1950 – 1953............... | 24.4 | 13.0 | 41.5 | −39.8 | 16.6 | 15.5 | 23.5 | 26.0 | 40.4 | 19.2 | 24.6 |
| 1954 – 1958............... | 11.8 | 16.1 | 4.8 | −4.3 | 10.5 | 9.7 | 15.1 | 13.1 | 21.4 | 12.7 | 8.9 |
| 1958 – 1960............... | 13.1 | 29.6 | 5.4 | 35.6 | 9.5 | 4.9 | 15.3 | 14.9 | 26.5 | 10.9 | 8.6 |

[1] Includes activity in Stone quarrying and clay and sand pits (ISIC major group 14).

[1] Y compris l'extraction de la pierre à bâtir, de l'argile et du sable (CITI 14).

## 2. INDEX NUMBERS OF INDUSTRIAL EMPLOYMENT — INDICES DE L'EMPLOI DANS L'INDUSTRIE

| Period / Période | Manufacturing [1] / Industries manufacturières [1] | Food, beverages and tobacco / Industries alimentaires, boissons, tabac | Textiles | Clothing, footwear and made-up textiles / Articles d'habillement, chaussures et ouvrages en tissu | Wood products and furniture [2] / Bois et meubles [2] | Paper and paper products / Papier et ouvrages en papier | Printing and publishing / Imprimerie et édition | Leather and leather products except wearing apparel / Cuir et articles en cuir, à l'exclusion des articles d'habillement | Rubber products / Ouvrages en caoutchouc | Chemicals and chemical, petroleum and coal products / Produits chimiques et dérivés du pétrole et du charbon | Non-metallic mineral products [1] / Produits minéraux non métalliques [1] | Basic metals / Métallurgie de base | Metal products [2,3] / Ouvrages en métaux [2,3] | Other manufacturing [2,3] / Autres industries manufacturières [2,3] | Electricity and gas / Électricité et gaz |
|---|---|---|---|---|---|---|---|---|---|---|---|---|---|---|---|
| ISIC — CITI | 2-3 | 20-22 | 23 | 24 | 25-26 | 27 | 28 | 29 | 30 | 31-32 | 33 | 34 | 35-38 | 39 | 511-512 |

*a.* Indexes — Indices (1958 = 100)

| | | | | | | | | | | | | | | | |
|---|---|---|---|---|---|---|---|---|---|---|---|---|---|---|---|
| 1950..... | 49 | 54 | 21 | 33 | 101 | 46 | 59 | 46 | 53 | 68 | 44 | 27 | 50 | 39 | 101 |
| 1951..... | 58 | 59 | 27 | 43 | 90 | 50 | 60 | 56 | 50 | 70 | 53 | 40 | 61 | 49 | 112 |
| 1952..... | 61 | 58 | 33 | 50 | 66 | 54 | 62 | 58 | 53 | 68 | 55 | 46 | 64 | 58 | 112 |
| 1953..... | 65 | 63 | 49 | 59 | 71 | 64 | 71 | 69 | 60 | 72 | 58 | 51 | 67 | 65 | 109 |
| 1954..... | 73 | 67 | 55 | 66 | 93 | 78 | 78 | 77 | 71 | 79 | 73 | 85 | 73 | 70 | 100 |
| 1955..... | 84 | 76 | 64 | 79 | 98 | 85 | 84 | 85 | 84 | 81 | 76 | 113 | 86 | 79 | 98 |
| 1956..... | 92 | 87 | 77 | 91 | 109 | 93 | 89 | 83 | 89 | 87 | 85 | 121 | 93 | 89 | 97 |
| 1957..... | 97 | 97 | 95 | 102 | 105 | 96 | 96 | 97 | 94 | 94 | 92 | 95 | 97 | 98 | 99 |
| 1958..... | 100 | 100 | 100 | 100 | 100 | 100 | 100 | 100 | 100 | 100 | 100 | 100 | 100 | 100 | 100 |
| 1959..... | 102 | 107 | 95 | 98 | 99 | 104 | 100 | 97 | 104 | 103 | 107 | 103 | 111 | 93 | 104 |
| 1960..... | 108 | 115 | 100 | 100 | 96 | 110 | 100 | 96 | 110 | 107 | 107 | 113 | 115 | 93 | 105 |
| 1961..... | 112 | 119 | 101 | 100 | 92 | 113 | 100 | 90 | 121 | 114 | 106 | 116 | 115 | 93 | 105 |

*b.* Average Annual Rate of Change — Taux annuel moyen de variation

| | | | | | | | | | | | | | | | |
|---|---|---|---|---|---|---|---|---|---|---|---|---|---|---|---|
| 1950-1960 | 8.2 | 7.9 | 16.9 | 11.7 | −0.5 | 9.1 | 5.4 | 7.6 | 7.6 | 4.6 | 9.3 | 15.5 | 8.2 | 9.1 | 0.3 |
| 1950-1953 | 9.9 | 5.3 | 32.6 | 21.4 | −11.1 | 11.6 | 6.4 | 14.5 | 4.2 | 1.9 | 9.6 | 23.8 | 10.2 | 18.6 | 2.6 |
| 1954-1958 | 8.2 | 10.5 | 16.1 | 10.9 | 1.8 | 6.4 | 6.4 | 6.8 | 8.9 | 6.1 | 8.2 | 4.1 | 8.2 | 9.3 | — |
| 1958-1960 | 3.9 | 7.2 | — | — | −2.0 | 4.9 | — | −2.0 | 4.9 | 3.4 | 3.4 | 6.3 | 5.4 | −3.6 | 2.0 |

[1] Stone quarrying and clay and sand pits (ISIC major group 14) is included in Non-metallic mineral products (ISIC major group 33).
[2] The manufacture of metal furniture (part of ISIC major group 26) is included in Metal products (ISIC major groups 35-38) but the manufacture of brooms and brushes (part of ISIC major group 39) is included in Wood products and furniture (ISIC major groups 25-26).
[3] The manufacturing of jewelry and the polishing of precious stones (part of ISIC major group 39) are covered in Metal products (ISIC major groups 35-38).

[1] L'extraction de la pierre à bâtir, de l'argile et de la tourbe (CITI classe 14) est comprise dans Produits minéraux non métalliques (CITI classe 33).
[2] La fabrication de meubles métalliques (dans CITI classe 26) est comprise dans Ouvrages en métaux (CITI classes 35-38) mais la fabrication de brosses et balais (dans CITI classe 39) est incluse dans Ouvrages en bois et meubles (CITI classes 25-26).
[3] La fabrication de bijoux et le polissage de pierres précieuses (dans CITI classe 39) sont couverts par Ouvrages en métaux (CITI classes 35-38).

## 3. THE NUMBER OF AND EMPLOYMENT IN ALL INDUSTRIAL LOCAL UNITS
### 17 May 1939, 13 September 1950

## NOMBRE D'UNITES INDUSTRIELLES LOCALES ET EMPLOI DANS CES UNITES
### 17 mai 1939, 13 septembre 1950

Number of local units in units; number of engaged and employees in thousands

Nombre d'unités locales en unités; nombre de personnes occupées et de salariés en milliers

### A. The Divisions of Industrial Activity — Les branches de l'activité industrielle

| Item of data | All industrial activity — Toutes industries | | Mining — Industries extractives | | Manufacturing — Industries manufacturières | | Construction — Bâtiment et travaux publics | | Electricity and gas — Electricité et gaz | | Rubrique |
|---|---|---|---|---|---|---|---|---|---|---|---|
| | 17.V.1939 | 13.IX.1950 | 17.V.1939 | 13.IX.1950 | 17.V.1939[1] | 13.IX.1950 | 17.V.1939[2] | 13.IX.1950 | 17.V.1939 | 13.IX.1950 | |
| ISIC | 1–4, 511–512 | | 1 | | 2–3 | | 4 | | 511–512 | | CITI |
| Number of local units[3]... | 67 198 | 35 633 | 16 | 8 | 58 031 | 27 698 | 9 010 | 7 803 | 141 | 124 | Nombre d'unités locales[3] |
| Number of engaged..... | 769.9 | 335.7 | 0.4 | 0.2 | 626.3 | 233.0 | 133.2 | 92.4 | 10.0 | 10.1 | Nombre de personnes occupées |
| Number of employees.... | ... | 291.2 | ... | 0.2 | ... | 197.7 | ... | 83.2 | ... | 10.1 | Nombre de salariés |

[1] Includes laundries and dry cleaning establishments and photostating services.
[2] Includes architects and chimney cleaning.
[3] In the Census as of 17.V.1939, activities ancillary to but physically separated from the main activity of the local unit were not covered in the local unit.

[1] Y compris la blanchisserie, la teinturerie et la préparation des photostats.
[2] Y compris les architectes et les ramoneurs.
[3] Dans le recensement du 17.V.1939, les activités auxiliaires — mais physiquement distinctes — de l'activité principale de l'unité locale n'ont pas été comprises dans l'unité locale.

### B. The Major Groups of Manufacturing — Les classes de la branche Industries manufacturières

| Year and item of data | Manufacturing Industries manufacturières | Food, beverages and tobacco Industries alimentaires, boissons, tabac | Textiles | Clothing, footwear and made-up textiles Articles d'habillement, chaussures et ouvrages en tissu | Wood products and furniture[7] Bois et meubles[7] | Paper and paper products[3] Papier et ouvrages en papier[3] | Printing and publishing[3] Imprimerie et édition[3] | Leather and leather products except wearing apparel Cuir et articles en cuir, à l'exclusion des articles d'habillement | Rubber products Ouvrages en caoutchouc | Chemicals and chemical, petroleum and coal products Produits chimiques et dérivés du pétrole et du charbon | Non-metallic mineral products Produits minéraux non métalliques | Basic metals Métallurgie de base | Metal products[7] Ouvrages en métaux[7] | Other manufacturing Autres industries manufacturières | Année et rubrique |
|---|---|---|---|---|---|---|---|---|---|---|---|---|---|---|---|
| ISIC | 2–3 | 20–22 | 23 | 24 | 25–26 | 27 | 28 | 29 | 30 | 31–32 | 33 | 34 | 35–38 | 39 | CITI |
| **17.V.1939** | | | | | | | | | | | | | | | **17.V.1939** |
| Number of local units[9]... | 58 031 | 5 975 | 3 916[1] | 27 933[5] | 3 455[2] | 895 | 2 456[4] | 701[5] | 209[6] | 968[1] | 531[6] | 197 | 9 058[8] | 1 737[2,8] | Nombre d'unités locales[9] |
| Number of engaged.... | 626.3 | 50.3 | 16.8[1] | 62.8[5] | 18.6[2] | 13.5 | 34.6[4] | 3.9[5] | 3.2[6] | 19.7[1] | 7.8[6] | 16.9 | 355.3[8] | 22.9[2,8] | Nombre de personnes occupées |
| Distribution in percent of number of engaged... | 100.0 | 8.0 | 2.7[1] | 10.0[5] | 3.0[2] | 2.1 | 5.5[4] | 0.7[5] | 0.5[6] | 3.1[1] | 1.3[6] | 2.7 | 56.7[8] | 3.7[2,8] | Répartition en pourcentage du nombre de personnes occupées |
| **13.IX.1950** | | | | | | | | | | | | | | | **13.IX.1950** |
| Number of local units.... | 27 698 | 4 745 | 518 | 9 634 | 2 993 | 161 | 862 | 392 | 159 | 665 | 373 | 147 | 5 217 | 1 832 | Nombre d'unités locales |
| Number of engaged.... | 233.0 | 35.0 | 2.9 | 34.3 | 14.8 | 2.8 | 11.0 | 1.5 | 1.0 | 9.1 | 4.6 | 2.6 | 104.4 | 9.0 | Nombre de personnes occupées |
| Number of employees... | 197.7 | 27.3 | 2.3 | 22.2 | 11.2 | 2.5 | 10.0 | 1.0 | 0.8 | 8.4 | 4.5 | 2.4 | 98.4 | 6.7 | Nombre de salariés |
| Distribution in percent of number of engaged... | 100.0 | 15.0 | 1.2 | 14.7 | 6.4 | 1.2 | 4.7 | 0.7 | 0.4 | 3.9 | 2.0 | 1.1 | 44.8 | 3.9 | Répartition en pourcentage du nombre de personnes occupées |

[1] Includes laundries and dry cleaning establishments and the manufacture of synthetic fibres, which should be classified in Chemicals (ISIC major group 31).
[2] Includes the making of brushes and brooms, which should be classified in Other manufacturing (ISIC major group 39).
[3] Includes bookbinding, which should be included in Printing and publishing (ISIC major group 28).
[4] Includes photostating service.
[5] Includes glove making, which should be included in Clothing (ISIC major group 24).
[6] Includes the manufacture of asbestos ware, which belongs in Non-metallic mineral products (ISIC major group 33).
[7] The manufacture of metal furniture is included in Metal products (ISIC major groups 35–38) rather than in Wood products and furniture (ISIC major groups 25–26).
[8] The manufacturing of jewelry and the polishing of precious stones is included in Metal products (ISIC major groups 35–38) instead of Other manufacturing (ISIC major group 39).
[9] Activities ancillary to but physically separated from the main activity of the local unit were not covered in the local unit.

[1] Y compris la blanchisserie et la teinturerie, ainsi que la fabrication des fibres synthétiques, qui devraient être classées dans Industrie chimique (CITI 31).
[2] Y compris la brosserie qui devrait être classée dans Autres industries manufacturières (CITI 39).
[3] Y compris la reliure qui devrait être classée dans Imprimerie et édition (CITI 28).
[4] Y compris la préparation des photostats.
[5] Y compris la ganterie qui devrait être classée dans Articles d'habillement (CITI 24).
[6] Y compris la fabrication des ouvrages en amiante, qui devrait être classée dans Industrie des produits minéraux non métalliques (CITI 33).
[7] La fabrication des meubles en métal est comprise dans Ouvrages en métaux (CITI 35–38) et non dans Industrie du bois et du meuble (CITI 25–26).
[8] La bijouterie et l'orfèvrerie ainsi que le polissage des pierres précieuses sont compris dans Ouvrages en métaux (CITI 35–38) et non dans Autres industries manufacturières (CITI 39).
[9] Les activités auxiliaires — mais physiquement distinctes — de l'activité principale de l'unité locale ne sont pas comprises dans l'unité locale.

## 4. CHARACTERISTICS OF MANUFACTURING ESTABLISHMENTS ENGAGING TEN OR MORE PERSONS, EXCEPTING LICENSED HANDICRAFTS

### CARACTERISTIQUES DES ETABLISSEMENTS MANUFACTURIERS OCCUPANT 10 PERSONS OU PLUS, A L'EXCLUSION DES UNITES ARTISANALES PATENTEES

### 1950, 1953, 1958

Gross receipts and wages and salaries in million D.M.; and number of engaged in thousands — Recettes brutes et traitements et salaires en millions de D.M.; nombre de personnes occupées en milliers

| Year and item of data | Manu-facturing Industries manufac-turières | Food, beverages and tobacco Industries alimen-taires, boissons, tabac | Textiles | Clothing, footwear and made-up textiles Articles d'habil-lement, chaussures et ouvrages en tissu | Wood products and furniture Bois et meubles | Paper and paper products[1] Papier et ouvrages en papier[1] | Printing and publish-ing[2] Im-primerie et édition[2] | Leather and leather products except wearing apparel Cuir et articles en cuir, à l'exclu-sion des articles d'habil-lement | Rubber products Ouvrages en caout-chouc | Chemicals and chemical, petroleum and coal products Produits chi-miques et dérivés du pétrole et du charbon | Non-metallic mineral products Produits minéraux non métal-liques | Basic metals Métal-lurgie de base | Metal products Ouvrages en métaux | Other manu-factur-ing Autres in-dustries manufac-turières | Année et rubrique |
|---|---|---|---|---|---|---|---|---|---|---|---|---|---|---|---|
| ISIC | 2–3 | 20–22 | 23 | 24 | 25–26 | 27 | 28 | 29 | 30 | 31–32 | 33 | 34 | 35–38 | 39 | CITI |
| *a. Absolute Figures — Chiffres absolus* | | | | | | | | | | | | | | | |
| **1950** Gross receipts | 1 598.5 | 319.2 | 10.8 | 213.9 | 29.7 | 26.5 | 60.7 | 7.1 | 5.0 | 97.4 | 33.5 | 23.5 | 739.0 | 32.2 | **1950** Recettes brutes |
| Number of engaged (Average for the year) | 137.0 | 11.7 | 1.2 | 7.8 | 3.7 | 2.6 | 7.1 | 0.6 | 0.7 | 7.5 | 3.2 | 1.9 | 84.7 | 4.3 | Nombre de personnes occupées (moyenne pour l'année) |
| Wages and salaries paid | 405.1 | 33.6 | 2.5 | 16.3 | 10.3 | 6.4 | 22.3 | 1.3 | 1.6 | 21.8 | 9.9 | 5.5 | 262.1 | 11.5 | Traitements et salaires payés |
| **1953** Gross receipts | 3 322.0 | 502.8 | 37.0 | 550.6 | 56.3 | 34.6 | 109.5 | 13.3 | 10.1 | 176.4 | 68.1 | 66.6 | 1 616.4 | 80.3 | **1953** Recettes brutes |
| Number of engaged (Average for the year) | 183.0 | 13.8 | 2.8 | 14.1 | 2.5 | 3.6 | 8.6 | 1.0 | 0.8 | 7.9 | 4.3 | 3.6 | 112.8 | 7.2 | Nombre de personnes occupées (moyenne pour l'année) |
| Wages and salaries paid | 684.6 | 50.6 | 8.0 | 40.2 | 8.7 | 11.4 | 35.8 | 2.4 | 2.5 | 29.4 | 17.7 | 13.9 | 439.8 | 24.2 | Traitements et salaires payés |
| **1958** Gross receipts | 6 951.3 | 1 433.5 | 105.0 | 849.7 | 69.2 | 121.1 | 209.4 | 22.2 | 22.8 | 347.8 | 148.7 | 179.8 | 3 267.4 | 174.7 | **1958** Recettes brutes |
| Number of engaged (Average for the year) | 280.9 | 21.9 | 5.8 | 24.0 | 3.7 | 5.7 | 12.1 | 1.4 | 1.2 | 11.0 | 7.4 | 7.1 | 168.7 | 10.9 | Nombre de personnes occupées (moyenne pour l'année) |
| Wages and salaries paid | 1 365.1 | 105.4 | 21.5 | 90.9 | 16.8 | 22.2 | 65.8 | 4.6 | 5.6 | 59.3 | 39.4 | 33.7 | 850.4 | 49.5 | Traitements et salaires payés |
| *b. Structure* | | | | | | | | | | | | | | | |
| **1950** Distribution in percent of: Gross receipts | 100.0 | 19.9 | 0.7 | 13.4 | 1.8 | 1.7 | 3.8 | 0.4 | 0.3 | 6.1 | 2.1 | 1.5 | 46.2 | 2.1 | **1950** Répartition en pour-centage du: Recettes brutes |
| Number of engaged | 100.0 | 8.5 | 0.9 | 5.7 | 2.7 | 1.9 | 5.1 | 0.5 | 0.5 | 5.5 | 2.3 | 1.4 | 61.8 | 3.2 | Nombre de personnes occupées |
| Wages and salaries per person engaged | 3.0 | 2.9 | 2.1 | 2.1 | 2.8 | 2.5 | 3.1 | 2.2 | 2.3 | 2.9 | 3.1 | 2.9 | 3.1 | 2.7 | Traitements et salaires par salarié |
| **1953** Distribution in percent of: Gross receipts | 100.0 | 15.1 | 1.1 | 16.6 | 1.7 | 1.0 | 3.3 | 0.4 | 0.3 | 5.3 | 2.1 | 2.0 | 48.6 | 2.5 | **1953** Répartition en pour-centage du: Recettes brutes |
| Number of engaged | 100.0 | 7.5 | 1.5 | 7.7 | 1.4 | 2.0 | 4.7 | 0.5 | 0.4 | 4.4 | 2.3 | 2.0 | 61.6 | 4.0 | Nombre de personnes occupées |
| **1958** Distribution in percent of: Gross receipts | 100.0 | 20.6 | 1.5 | 12.2 | 1.0 | 1.7 | 3.1 | 0.3 | 0.3 | 5.0 | 2.1 | 2.6 | 47.0 | 2.6 | **1958** Répartition en pour-centage du: Recettes brutes |
| Number of engaged | 100.0 | 7.7 | 2.1 | 8.6 | 1.3 | 2.0 | 4.3 | 0.5 | 0.4 | 4.0 | 2.6 | 2.5 | 60.1 | 3.9 | Nombre de personnes occupées |

[1] Includes bookbinding.
[2] Includes photostating service.

[1] Y compris la reliure.
[2] Y compris la préparation des photostats.

## 5. CHARACTERISTICS OF ALL LICENSED HANDICRAFT UNITS, MANUFACTURING AND CONSTRUCTION
## CARACTERISTIQUES DE TOUTES LES UNITES ARTISANALES PATENTEES, INDUSTRIES MANUFACTURIERES ET BATIMENT ET TRAVAUX PUBLICS

### 30.IX.1949, 31.V.1956

Number of local units in units; gross receipts and wages and salaries in million D.M.; number of persons engaged and employees in thousands; wages and salaries per employee in thousand D.M.

Nombre d'unités locales en unités; recettes brutes et traitements et salaires en millions de D.M.; nombre de personnes occupées et de salariés en milliers; traitements et salaires par salarié en milliers de D.M.

| Year and item of data | Manu-facturing / Industries manufac-turières | Food beverages and tobacco / Industries alimen-taires, boissons, tabac | Textiles | Clothing, footwear and made-up textiles / Articles d'habil-lement, chaussures et ouvrages en tissu | Wood products and furniture / Bois et meubles | Printing and publish-ing / Im-primerie et édition | Leather and leather products except wearing apparel [1] / Cuir et articles en cuir, à l'exclu-sion des articles d'habil-lement [1] | Rubber products / Ouvrages en caout-chouc | Non-metallic mineral products / Produits minéraux non métal-liques | Metal products / Ouvrages en métaux | Other manu-factur-ing / Autres in-dustries manufac-turières | Con-struction / Bâtiment et travaux publics | Année et rubrique |
|---|---|---|---|---|---|---|---|---|---|---|---|---|---|
| ISIC | 2–3 | 20–22 | 23 | 24 | 25–26 | 28 | 29 | 30 | 33 | 35–38 | 39 | 4 | CITI |
| a. Absolute Figures — Chiffres absolus | | | | | | | | | | | | | |
| 30.IX.1949 | | | | | | | | | | | | | 30.IX.1949 |
| Number of local units.... | 20 442 | 3 180 | 172 | 8 323 | 2 816 | 134 | 232 | — | 380 | 4 059 | 1 146 | 6 260 | Nombre d'unités locales |
| Gross receipts (1.X.1948-30.IX.1949). | 243.8 | 115.8 | 1.1 | 35.5 | 21.8 | 0.8 | 2.3 | — | 3.6 | 54.3 | 8.6 | 108.9 | Recettes brutes (1.X.1948-30.IX.1949) |
| Number of engaged (As of 30.IX.1949).... | 66.8 | 16.0 | 0.6 | 19.1 | 9.5 | 0.4 | 0.6 | — | 1.2 | 16.3 | 3.1 | 36.1 | Nombre de personnes occupées (au 30.IX.1949) |
| 31.V.1956 | | | | | | | | | | | | | 31.V.1956 |
| Number of local units.... | 15 803 | 2 978 | 96 | 5 131 | 2 074 | 409 | 138 | 77 | 474 | 3 404 | 1 022 | 3 768 | Nombre d'unités locales |
| Gross receipts (1955 calendar year). | 1 123.7 | 509.3 | 2.4 | 119.1 | 119.2 | 20.6 | 4.3 | 7.0 | 19.8 | 290.0 | 32.0 | 387.7 | Recettes brutes (année civile 1955) |
| Number of engaged (31.V.1956)........ | 78.9 | 20.7 | 0.4 | 17.0 | 10.6 | 2.0 | 0.3 | 0.3 | 1.7 | 23.4 | 2.5 | 42.3 | Nombre de personnes occupées (31.V.1956) |
| Employees: Number (31.V.1956)........ | 54.6 | 14.6 | 0.3 | 10.8 | 7.6 | 1.4 | 0.2 | 0.2 | 1.0 | 16.9 | 1.6 | 32.9 | Salariés: Nombre (31.V.1956) |
| Wages and salaries... | 153.0 | 37.1 | 0.6 | 25.3 | 25.3 | 4.6 | 0.3 | 0.5 | 3.1 | 52.0 | 4.2 | 137.7 | Traitements et salaires |
| b. Structure | | | | | | | | | | | | | |
| 30.IX.1949 Distribution in percent of: | | | | | | | | | | | | | 30.IX.1949 Répartition en pour-centage: |
| Gross receipts........ | 100.0 | 47.4 | 0.5 | 14.6 | 8.9 | 0.3 | 1.0 | — | 1.5 | 22.2 | ·3.6 | . | Des recettes brutes |
| Number of engaged.. | 100.0 | 23.9 | 0.9 | 28.6 | 14.2 | 0.6 | 0.9 | — | 1.8 | 24.4 | 4.7 | . | Du nombre de personnes occupées |
| 31.V.1956 Distribution in percent of: | | | | | | | | | | | | | 31.V.1956 Répartition en pour-centage: |
| Gross receipts........ | 100.0 | 45.3 | 0.2 | 10.6 | 10.6 | 1.8 | 0.4 | 0.6 | 1.8 | 25.8 | 2.9 | . | Des recettes brutes |
| Number of engaged.. | 100.0 | 26.2 | 0.5 | 21.5 | 13.5 | 2.5 | 0.4 | 0.4 | 2.1 | 29.7 | 3.2 | . | Du nombre de personnes occupées |
| Wages and salaries per employee....... | 2.8 | 2.5 | 2.0 | 2.3 | 3.3 | 3.3 | 1.5 | 2.5 | 3.1 | 3.1 | 2.6 | 4.2 | Traitements et salaires par salarié |

# GHANA

## Gross Domestic Product

Estimates of the expenditure on the gross domestic product are presented in Table 1. This table is based on data supplied by the Central Bureau of Statistics, Accra, in response to the United Nations national accounts questionnaire. Official estimates are published annually in *Economic Survey* by the Central Bureau of Statistics, Accra.

## Index Numbers of Industrial Production

The index numbers of industrial production presented in Table 2 have been compiled by the Central Bureau of Statistics, Accra and supplied to the Statistical Office of the United Nations by letter.

The indexes have been calculated monthly and are based on production figures for individual minerals and electricity. The annual indexes are the arithmetic average of the monthly figures. The indexes for mining as a whole have been calculated by combining indexes of the individual minerals using as weights the values of gross production in 1958. The major group indexes for mining have been calculated by the Statistical Office of the United Nations by combining the indexes of the individual product series using the values of gross production in 1958 as weights.

## Characteristics and Structure of Industrial Activity

The data presented in Table 3 are derived from the results of the annual industrial inquiry for the year 1959 covering all industrial establishments employing 6 persons or more. The results of this inquiry have been published by the Central Bureau of Statistics, Accra in *Industrial Statistics 1958 and 1959* (Statistical Reports, Series VII, No. 1). The establishments covered made returns for the calendar year 1959 and in the few cases where this was not possible estimates were made for the calendar year 1959 based on the two nearest financial years.

The definitions of the items of data shown in Table 3 conform to the International Standards in Basic Industrial Statistics. However in mining the value added figure is derived not from a figure of the gross value of the production but from the figure of the gross value of shipments from the mine during the year. The wages and salaries data include payments in kind valued at cost to the establishment. Value added is at market prices.

## Produit intérieur brut

Des estimations des dépenses imputées au produit intérieur brut sont reproduites au tableau 1. Ce tableau a été établi à partir de données fournies par le Central Bureau of Statistics, Accra, en réponse au questionnaire de l'ONU sur la comptabilité nationale. Des estimations officielles sont publiées annuellement dans *Economic Survey* par le Central Bureau of Statistics, Accra.

## Indices de la production industrielle

Les indices de la production industrielle reproduits au tableau 2 ont été calculés par le Central Bureau of Statistics, Accra, et communiqués par correspondance au Bureau de statistique de l'ONU.

Les indices ont été calculés mensuellement et sont fondés sur des chiffres de la production de chaque substance minérale et d'électricité. Les indices annuels sont les moyennes arithmétiques des indices mensuels. Les indices concernant l'ensemble des industries extractives ont été obtenus par combinaison des indices relatifs à chaque substance minérale, les coefficients de pondération utilisés étant les valeurs de la production brute en 1958. Les indices de classe des industries extractives ont été établis par le Bureau de statistique de l'ONU, qui a combiné les indices relatifs à chaque série de produits en utilisant comme coefficients de pondération les valeurs de la production brute en 1958.

## Caractéristiques et structure de l'activité industrielle

Les données du tableau 3 proviennent de l'enquête industrielle annuelle de 1959, qui portait sur tous les établissements occupant 6 personnes ou plus. Les résultats de cette enquête ont été publiés par le Central Bureau of Statistics, Accra, dans *Industrial Statistics 1958 and 1959* (Statistical Reports, Series VII, No 1). Les établissements recensés ont communiqué des renseignements pour l'année civile 1959 et, dans les quelques cas où cela n'était pas possible, on a fait des estimations pour l'année civile 1959 en se fondant sur les deux exercices financiers les plus rapprochés.

Les définitions des rubriques figurant au tableau 3 sont conformes aux Normes internationales relatives aux statistiques industrielles de base. Pour les industries extractives, cependant, les chiffres de la valeur ajoutée ne sont pas tirés des données concernant la valeur brute de la production, mais des chiffres relatifs à la valeur brute des expéditions, départ mine, pendant l'année. Les traitements et salaires comprennent les paiements en nature évalués au prix de revient pour l'établissement. La valeur ajoutée est comptée aux prix du marché.

## 1. EXPENDITURE ON THE GROSS DOMESTIC PRODUCT AT MARKET PRICES
## DEPENSES RELATIVES AU PRODUIT INTERIEUR BRUT AUX PRIX DU MARCHE

Million Ghanaian pounds          Millions de livres ghanéennes

| Item of data and year<br>Rubrique et année | Total | Consumption<br>Consommation | | Gross Domestic Capital Formation<br>Formation brute de capital intérieur | | Net exports of goods and services<br>Exportations nettes de biens et de services | |
| --- | --- | --- | --- | --- | --- | --- | --- |
| | | Total | Government<br>Etat | Total | Fixed<br>Fixe | Exports less imports<br>Exportations moins importations | Exports<br>Exportations |
| | | | | *a.* At Current Prices — Aux prix courants | | | |
| Absolute figures — Chiffres absolus | | | | | | | |
| 1955 | 334 | 278 | 26 | 52 | 52 | 4 | 101 |
| 1956 | 345 | 292 | 30 | 61 | 56 | −8 | 91 |
| 1957 | 363 | 324 | 33 | 50 | 56 | −11 | 96 |
| 1958 | 383 | 314 | 35 | 54 | 55 | 15 | 110 |
| 1959 | 435 | 356 | 39 | 85 | 75 | −6 | 120 |
| 1960 | 469 | 387 | 48 | 107 | 96 | −25 | 123 |
| 1961 | 499 | 450 | 55 | 90 | 104 | −41 | 122 |
| Percentage distribution of average annual expenditure — Distribution en pourcentage des dépense annuelles moyennes | | | | | | | |
| 1958 | 100.0 | 82.0 | 9.1 | 14.1 | 14.4 | 3.9 | 28.7 |
| 1960 | 100.0 | 82.5 | 10.2 | 22.8 | 20.5 | −5.3 | 26.2 |

## 2. INDEX NUMBERS OF INDUSTRIAL PRODUCTION — INDICES DE LA PRODUCTION INDUSTRIELLE

### A. Selected Divisions of Industrial Activity
### Quelques branches de l'activité industrielle

| Period<br>Période | Mining<br>Industries extractives | Electricity<br>Electricité |
| --- | --- | --- |
| ISIC — CITI | 1 | 511 |
| *a.* Indexes — Indices (1958 = 100) | | |
| 1955 | 82 | 55 |
| 1956 | 91 | 64 |
| 1957 | 104 | 82 |
| 1958 | 100 | 100 |
| 1959 | 101 | 116 |
| 1960 | 103 | 142 |
| 1961 | 94 | 167 |
| *b.* Average Annual Rate of Change — Taux annuel moyen de variation | | |
| 1955 – 1958 | 6.9 | 22.0 |
| 1958 – 1960 | 1.5 | 19.2 |

### B. The Major Groups of Mining
### Les classes de la branche Industries extractives

| Period<br>Période | All mining<br>Toutes industries extractives | Metal mining<br>Extraction des minerais métalliques | Other mining [1]<br>Autres industries extractives [1] |
| --- | --- | --- | --- |
| ISIC — CITI | 1 | 12 | 14–19 |
| *a.* Indexes — Indices (1958 = 100) | | | |
| 1955 | 82 | 86 | 72 |
| 1956 | 91 | 95 | 81 |
| 1957 | 104 | 106 | 100 |
| 1958 | 100 | 100 | 100 |
| 1959 | 101 | 103 | 98 |
| 1960 | 103 | 102 | 105 |
| 1961 | 94 | 90 | 103 |
| *b.* Average Annual Rate of Change — Taux annuel moyen de variation | | | |
| 1955 – 1958 | 6.9 | 5.2 | 11.6 |
| 1958 – 1960 | 1.5 | 1.0 | 2.5 |

[1] Diamond mining.
[1] Extraction de diamants.

## 3. CHARACTERISTICS OF INDUSTRIAL ESTABLISHMENTS EMPLOYING 6 PERSONS OR MORE
## CARACTERISTIQUES DES ETABLISSEMENTS INDUSTRIELS EMPLOYANT 6 PERSONNES OU PLUS
### 1959

Number of establishments in units; value added and wages and salaries in million Ghanaian pounds; number of engaged and employees in thousands; value added per engaged and wages and salaries per employee in thousand Ghanaian pounds.

Nombre d'établissements en unités; valeur ajoutée et traitements et salaires en millions de livres ghanéennes; nombre de personnes occupées et de salariés en millions; valeur ajoutée par personne occupée et traitements et salaires par salarié en milliers de livres ghanéénnes.

### A. The Divisions of Industrial Activity — Les branches de l'activité industrielle

| Item of data | All industrial activity Toutes industries | Mining Industries extractives | Manufacturing[1] Industries manufacturières[1] | Construction Bâtiment et travaux publics | Electricity Electricité | Rubrique | Item of data | All industrial activity Toutes industries | Mining Industries extractives | Manufacturing[1] Industries manufacturières[1] | Construction Bâtiment et travaux publics | Electricity Electricité | Rubrique |
|---|---|---|---|---|---|---|---|---|---|---|---|---|---|
| ISIC | 1-4, 511 | 1 | 2-3 | 4 | 511 | CITI | ISIC | 1-4, 511 | 1 | 2-3 | 4 | 511 | CITI |
| | a. Absolute Figures — Chiffres absolus | | | | | | | b. Structure | | | | | |
| Number of establishments... | 433 | 39 | 234 | 144 | 16 | Nombre d'établissements | Distribution in percent of: Value added..... | 100.0 | 35.3 | 27.7 | 34.7 | 2.3 | Distribution en pourcentage: Valeur ajoutée |
| Value added....... | 43.0 | 15.2 | 11.9 | 14.9 | 1.0 | Valeur ajoutée | Number of engaged........ | 100.0 | 28.4 | 21.9 | 46.4 | 3.3 | Nombre de personnes occupées |
| Number of engaged......... | 99.2 | 28.2 | 21.7 | 46.0 | 3.3 | Nombre de personnes occupées | Value added per person engaged.. | 0.4 | 0.5 | 0.5 | 0.3 | 0.3 | Valeur ajoutée par personne occupée |
| Employees: Number......... | 98.8 | 28.1 | 21.5 | 45.9 | 3.3 | Salariés: Nombre | Wages and salaries per employee.... | 0.2 | 0.2 | 0.2 | 0.2 | 0.2 | Traitements et salaires par salarié |
| Wages and salaries......... | 17.8 | 5.8 | 4.1 | 7.3 | 0.6 | Traitements et salaires | Value added per unit of wages and salaries..... | 2.42 | 2.62 | 2.90 | 2.04 | 1.67 | Valeur ajouté par unité de traitements et salaires |

For footnotes see end of table.

Pour les notes, voir au bas du tableau.

### B. The Major Groups of Mining — Les classes de la branche Industries extractives

| Item of data | All mining Toutes industries extractives | Metal mining Extraction des minerais métalliques | Other mining Divers | Rubrique | Item of data | All mining Toutes industries extractives | Metal mining Extraction des minerais métalliques | Other mining Divers | Rubrique |
|---|---|---|---|---|---|---|---|---|---|
| ISIC | 1 | 12 | 14-19 | CITI | ISIC | 1 | 12 | 14-19 | CITI |
| | a. Absolute Figures Chiffres absolus | | | | | b. Structure | | | |
| Number of establishments...... | 39 | 9 | 30 | Nombre d'établissements | Distribution in percent of: Value added................ | 100.0 | 80.3 | 19.7 | Distribution en pourcentage: Valeur ajoutée |
| Value added............ | 15.2 | 12.2 | 3.0 | Valeur ajoutée | Number of engaged......... | 100.0 | 84.4 | 15.6 | Nombre de personnes occupées |
| Number of engaged............ | 28.2 | 23.8 | 4.4 | Nombre de personnes occupées | Value added per person engaged............. | 0.5 | 0.5 | 0.7 | Valeur ajoutée par personne occupée |
| Employees: Number.................... | 28.1 | 23.8 | 4.3 | Salariés: Nombre | Wages and salaries per employee............... | 0.2 | 0.2 | 0.2 | Traitements et salaires par salarié |
| Wages and salaries .......... | 5.8 | 4.9 | 0.9 | Traitements et salaires | Value added per unit of wages and salaries........... | 2.62 | 2.49 | 3.33 | Valeur ajoutée par unité de traitements et salaires |

## C. The Major Groups of Manufacturing — Les classes de la branche Industries manufacturières

| Item of data | Manufacturing [1] / Industries manufacturières [1] | Food beverages and tobacco / Industries alimentaires, boissons, tabac | Textiles, clothing footwear and made-up textiles / Textiles, articles d'habillement, chaussures et ouvrages en tissu | Wood products and furniture [1] / Bois et meubles [1] | Printing and publishing / Imprimerie et édition | Leather and leather products except wearing apparel and rubber products / Cuir et articles en cuir, à l'exclusion des articles d'habillement, et ouvrages en caoutchouc | Chemicals and chemical products / Produits chimiques | Non-metallic mineral products / Produits minéraux non métalliques | Metal products / Ouvrages en métaux | Other manufacturing / Autres industries manufacturières | Rubrique |
|---|---|---|---|---|---|---|---|---|---|---|---|
| ISIC | 2–3 | 20–22 | 23–24 | 25–26 | 28 | 29–30 | 31 | 33 | 35–38 | 39 | CITI |
| *a. Absolute Figures — Chiffres absolus* | | | | | | | | | | | |
| Number of establishments. | 234 | 62 | 9 | 47 | 34 | 4 | 8 | 10 | 53 | 7 | Nombre d'établissements |
| Value added. . . . . . . . . | 11.9 | 4.5 | 0.1 | 5.0 | 0.4 | 0.1 | 0.4 | 0.2 | 1.1 | 0.1 | Valeur ajoutée |
| Number of engaged. . . . | 21.7 | 2.6 | 0.3 | 12.0 | 2.1 | 0.1 | 0.7 | 0.7 | 3.0 | 0.2 | Nombre de personnes occupées |
| Employees: | | | | | | | | | | | Salariés: |
| Number. . . . . . . . . . . | 21.5 | 2.6 | 0.3 | 12.0 | 2.1 | 0.1 | 0.7 | 0.6 | 3.0 | 0.1 | Nombre |
| Wages and salaries. . . | 4.1 | 0.4 | — | 2.2 | 0.6 | — | 0.1 | 0.1 | 0.7 | — | Traitements et salaires |
| *b. Structure* | | | | | | | | | | | |
| Distribution in percent of: | | | | | | | | | | | Distribution en pourcentage: |
| Value added. . . . . . . | 100.0 | 37.8 | 0.8 | 42.0 | 3.4 | 0.8 | 3.4 | 1.7 | 9.3 | 0.8 | Valeur ajoutée |
| Number of engaged. . . | 100.0 | 12.0 | 1.4 | 55.3 | 9.7 | 0.5 | 3.2 | 3.2 | 13.8 | 0.9 | Nombre de personnes occupées |
| Value added per person engaged. . . . . . | 0.5 | 1.7 | 0.3 | 0.4 | 0.2 | 1.0 | 0.6 | 0.3 | 0.4 | 0.5 | Valeur ajoutée par personne occupée |
| Wages and salaries per employee. . . . . . . | 0.2 | 0.2 | . . . | 0.2 | 0.3 | . . . | 0.1 | 0.2 | 0.2 | . . . | Traitements et salaires par salarié |
| Value added per unit of wages and salaries. . . . . . . . . . . | 2.90 | 11.25 | . . . | 2.27 | 0.67 | . . . | 4.00 | 2.00 | 1.57 | . . . | Valeur ajoutée par unité de traitements et salaires |

[1] Includes the Logging activities (part of ISIC major group 02) of sawmilling establishments.

[1] Y compris les activités exercées par les scieries dans le domaine de l'Exploitation forestière (dans CITI classe 02).

## GREECE — GRECE

### Gross Domestic Product and Gross Fixed Capital Formation

The data in Table 1 on the gross domestic product and gross fixed capital formation are from the response of the National Accounts Directorate, Ministry of Co-ordination, Athens to the United Nations national accounts questionnaire. The concepts, definitions and methods of estimation utilized in compiling the official estimates of national accounting data are described in *The National Accounts of Greece, 1946-53* published by the Directorate. In replying to the United Nations national accounts questionnaire, the official estimates have been adjusted by the Directorate, to the extent possible, to conform to the United Nations system of national accounts.

### Index Numbers of Industrial Production

The index numbers of industrial production shown in Table 2 are based on a number of different sources. The indexes for manufacturing for the years, 1939-1959, and the indexes for the electricity industry for all years are derived from index numbers compiled by the Federation of Greek Industries. The index numbers for practically all manufacturing industries and for manufacturing as a whole for the years, 1960-1961, are based on the provisional indexes of manufacturing production compiled by the National Statistical Service of Greece. The series of index numbers of both the Greek Federation of Industries and the National Statistical Service have been issued in the *Monthly Statistical Bulletin* of the Bank of Greece and the *Statistical Yearbook of Greece*. The latter organization has also published its series of provisional index numbers in its *Monthly Statistical Bulletin*. The index numbers for mining have been compiled by the Statistical Office of the United Nations.

All of the series of index numbers are computed as base-weighted arithmetic averages in successive stages, starting from elementary series of relatives.

In the case of the series of indexes of the Greek Federation of Industries, the weights utilized in combining elementary series into indexes for detailed categories of manufacturing and these index numbers into indexes for wider classes are derived from gross value of production during 1959. These weights presumably relate to all manufacturing units excepting handicrafts. The elementary series of relatives are based, for the most part, on quantities of output for individual products. For a more detailed description of the series of index numbers see *Supplement to the Monthly Bulletin of Statistics, 1954*, Statistical Office of the United Nations.

### Produit intérieur brut et formation brute de capital fixe

Les données reproduites au tableau 1, relatives au produit intérieur brut et à la formation brute de capital fixe, ont été obtenues à partir de la réponse de la Direction de la Comptabilité nationale, Ministère de la Coordination, Athènes, au questionnaire de l'O.N.U. relatif aux comptes nationaux. On peut trouver les concepts, définitions et méthodes d'estimation adoptés pour élaborer les estimations officielles des données relatives à la comptabilité nationale dans *The National Accounts of Greece, 1946-53*, publié par la Direction. Dans la réponse au questionnaire de l'O.N.U. relatif aux Comptes nationaux, les estimations officielles ont été ajustées par la Direction, afin de les rendre aussi cohérentes que possible avec le système de comptabilité nationale de l'O.N.U.

### Indices de la production industrielle

Les indices de la production industrielle reproduits au tableau 2 sont construits d'après des données de sources variées. Les indices relatifs aux industries manufacturières pour les années 1939-1959, et les indices relatifs aux industries productrices d'électricité pour toutes les années, proviennent d'indices calculés par la Fédération des industries grecques. Les indices relatifs à pratiquement toutes les industries manufacturières, et à l'ensemble de la production industrielle pour les années 1960-1961 sont fondés sur les indices provisoires de la production des industries manufacturières calculés par le Service national de Statistique de Grèce. Les séries d'indices, tant celles de la Fédération des industries grecques que celles du Service national de Statistique ont été publiées dans le *Monthly Statistical Bulletin* de la Banque de Grèce et dans le *Statistical Yearbook of Greece*. Le Service de Statistique a également publié des séries d'indices provisoires dans son *Monthly Statistical Bulletin*. Les indices relatifs aux industries extractives ont été élaborés par le Bureau de Statistique de l'O.N.U.

Toutes ces séries d'indices sont des moyennes arithmétiques à pondération fixe calculées à des stades successifs, à partir de séries élémentaires de rapports.

Les coefficients de pondération utilisés par la Fédération des industries grecques pour combiner les séries élémentaires en indices pour les catégories détaillées des industries manufacturières, et pour transformer ces indices en indices relatifs à des classes plus larges, sont fondés sur la valeur brute de la production durant 1959. Ces coefficients de pondération concernent probablement toutes les unités manufacturières, à l'exclusion des unités artisanales. Les séries élémentaires de rapports sont basées, pour la plupart, sur le volume de la production de chaque produit. Pour plus amples détails concernant les séries d'indices, voir *Supplement to the Monthly Bulletin of Statistics, 1954*, Bureau de Statistique de l'O.N.U.

In the case of the series of provisional index numbers of the National Statistical Service of Greece, the weights utilized to compile indexes for detailed categories of manufacturing from elementary series of relatives were gross value of production during 1957. However, the weights for combining these indexes into index numbers for broader classes of manufacturing were derived from contribution to the gross domestic product, at factor cost, during 1957. The elementary series of relatives were compiled principally from quantities of production for individual commodities. Man-days worked and quantity of individual raw materials consumed were also utilized for this purpose. The field of manufacturing to which the series of provisional index numbers relate consisted of establishments with 10 or more persons classified to kinds of manufacturing other than Clothing and wearing apparel (ISIC major group 24), Wood products and furniture (ISIC major groups 25-26), Printing and publishing (ISIC major group 28), and Petroleum and coal products (ISIC major group 32). For further details concerning the series of provisional indexes see *Provisional Index of Industrial Production,* National Statistical Service of Greece. It should also be noted that beginning with 1961, the National Statistical Service replaced the series of provisional indexes with a more comprehensive series of index numbers of manufacturing production.

The Statistical Office of the United Nations compiled the series of index numbers for the major groups of mining from relatives of quantities of output for individual minerals. The weights utilized in these calculations were value of gross output during 1953 in the case of the indexes for 1938-1955 and during 1958 for 1956-1961. Estimates of value added, at factor cost during 1953 and 1958, respectively, were utilized in combining the resulting index numbers into those for mining as a whole for corresponding years.

### Characteristics and Structure of Industrial Activity

The data in Table 3 come from the results of Censuses of Establishments taken as of 30 December 1950 and 15 November 1958. The figures relating to the first Census were compiled from *Statistical Summary of Greece, 1954* and *Yearbook of Greece, 1955,* both published by the National Statistical Service of Greece. The data from the second Census were compiled from *Recensement des établissements industriels et commerciaux effectué le 15 novembre 1958* issued by the same Service.

All establishments other than cottage industries were to be covered in the Census as of 30 December 1950, and cottage industries were added to the field to be covered in the Census as of 15 November 1958. However, there are some indications that the number of establishments enumerated fell short of the number that should have been covered in the case of each of the Censuses.

Dans le cas des séries d'indices provisoires fournies par le Service national de Statistique de Grèce, les coefficients de pondération adoptés pour combiner les séries élémentaires de rapports en indices relatifs aux catégories détaillées des industries manufacturières ont été fondés sur la valeur brute de la production en 1957. Cependant pour combiner ces indices en indices relatifs à des classes plus larges des industries manufacturières, la contribution au produit intérieur brut en 1957 a été utilisée comme base de pondération. Les séries élémentaires de rapports ont été construites à partir des volumes de la production de chaque marchandise. Les heures de travail effectuées, ainsi que les consommations de chaque matière première ont été utilisées à la même fin. Les industries manufacturières couvertes par les séries d'indices provisoires sont les établissements de dix personnes ou plus appartenant aux classes de l'activité manufacturière autres que celles des: Articles d'habillement (CITI classe 24). Ouvrages en bois et meubles (CITI classes 25-26), Imprimerie et édition (CITI classe 28), Produits dérivés du pétrole et du charbon (CITI classe 32). Pour plus amples détails concernant les séries d'indices provisoires consulter *Provisional Index of Industrial Production,* Service national de Statistique de Grèce. Il est bon de noter également qu'à partir de 1961, le Service national de Statistique a remplacé les séries d'indices provisoires par des séries plus étoffées d'indices de la production industrielle.

Le Bureau de Statistique de l'O.N.U. a calculé les séries d'indices relatifs aux classes des industries extractives à partir des rapports quantitatifs de la production de chaque substance minérale. Les coefficients de pondération adoptés dans les calculs sont la valeur de la production brute durant 1953 dans le cas des indices relatifs aux années 1938-1955 et durant 1958, dans le cas des indices relatifs aux années 1956-1961. Les estimations de la valeur ajoutée aux prix des facteurs pour 1953 et 1958, respectivement, ont été utilisées pour combiner les indices obtenus en indices pour l'ensemble des industries extractives pour les années correspondantes.

### Caractéristiques et structure de l'activité industrielle

Les données du tableau 3 proviennent des résultats des Recensements d'établissements exécutés au 30 décembre 1950 et au 15 novembre 1958. Les chiffres concernant le premier recensement ont été calculés à partir des données fournies dans *Statistical Summary of Greece, 1954* et *Yearbook of Greece, 1955,* tous deux publiés par le Service national de Statistique de Grèce. Les données concernant le deuxième recensement ont été calculées d'après les chiffres fournis dans *Recensement des établissements industriels et commerciaux effectué le 15 novembre 1958,* publié par le même Service.

Tous les établissements autres que les unités artisanales familiales devaient être couverts par le Recensement au 30 décembre 1950; les unités artisanales familiales ont été rajoutées au champ couvert par le recensement au 15 novembre 1958. Cependant il a été indiqué que le nombre d'établissements couverts semble être inférieur au nombre réel d'établissements entrant dans le champ du recensement, ceci dans chacun des deux recensements.

The data set out in Table 4 were compiled from *Results of the 1958 Annual Industrial Survey* published by the National Statistical Service of Greece. This survey is an annual sample inquiry relating to manufacturing establishments engaging an annual average of 10 or more persons.

The definitions utilized for the items on which data were gathered in the two Censuses and the 1958 Survey correspond to the International Recommendations in Basic Industrial Statistics. The number of persons engaged includes working proprietors, unpaid family workers and employees. The capacity of installed (in use and in reserve) power equipment is the sum of horsepower of all prime movers plus that of electric motors driven by purchased electricity. Value added is priced at factor cost.

Les données reproduites au tableau 4 ont été calculées d'après *Results of the 1958 Annual Industrial Survey*, publié par le Service national de Statistique de Grèce. Cette enquête est annuelle et est effectuée sur un échantillon d'établissements manufacturiers employant un nombre moyen annuel de 10 personnes ou plus.

Les définitions adoptées pour les rubriques pour lesquelles des données ont été rassemblées tant dans les deux recensements que dans l'enquête de 1958 correspondent aux Recommandations Internationales relatives aux Statistiques Industrielles de Base. Le nombre de personnes employées comprend les propriétaires qui travaillent, les travailleurs familiaux non rémunérés ainsi que les salariés. La puissance installée (en service normal ou en réserve) correspond à la puissance de tous les moteurs primaires augmentée de celle des moteurs électriques actionnés par de l'électricité achetée. La valeur ajoutée est évaluée au coût des facteurs.

# GREECE

## 1. THE GROSS DOMESTIC PRODUCT AND GROSS DOMESTIC FIXED CAPITAL FORMATION
## LE PRODUIT INTERIEUR BRUT ET LA FORMATION BRUTE DE CAPITAL FIXE INTERIEUR

Million drachmas            Millions de drachmes

### A. Expenditure on the Gross Domestic Product at Market Prices
### Dépenses relatives au produit intérieur brut aux prix du marché

| Item of data and year / Rubrique et année | Total | Consumption / Consommation | | Gross Domestic Capital Formation / Formation brute de capital intérieur | | Net exports of goods and services / Exportations nettes de biens et de services | |
|---|---|---|---|---|---|---|---|
| | | Total | Government / Etat | Total | Fixed / Fixe | Exports less imports / Exportations moins importations | Exports / Exportations |
| **a. At Current Prices — Aux prix courants** | | | | | | | |
| **Absolute figures — Chiffres absolus** | | | | | | | |
| 1948 | 19 178 | 20 202 | 2 601 | 1 844 | 2 137 | −2 868 | 1 153 |
| 1950 | 28 634 | 27 830 | 3 739 | 6 059 | 5 158 | −5 255 | 1 701 |
| 1951 | 35 539 | 33 614 | 5 062 | 6 578 | 4 810 | −4 653 | 1 845 |
| 1952 | 37 524 | 35 863 | 5 370 | 5 181 | 4 724 | −3 520 | 2 192 |
| 1953 | 49 751 | 45 517 | 5 806 | 7 557 | 5 895 | −3 323 | 4 486 |
| 1954 | 57 817 | 54 635 | 7 396 | 8 396 | 8 686 | −5 214 | 6 227 |
| 1955 | 65 619 | 59 528 | 8 048 | 10 534 | 9 757 | −4 443 | 8 220 |
| 1956 | 76 208 | 69 707 | 9 780 | 13 408 | 12 043 | −6 907 | 8 509 |
| 1957 | 81 737 | 74 220 | 10 356 | 15 242 | 12 443 | −7 725 | 9 861 |
| 1958 | 85 619 | 78 182 | 10 501 | 16 795 | 16 165 | −9 358 | 9 698 |
| 1959 | 89 003 | 80 160 | 11 633 | 19 345 | 18 745 | −10 502 | 9 154 |
| 1960 | 94 943 | 85 467 | 12 299 | 24 925 | 25 225 | −15 449 | 9 428 |
| 1961 | 106 757 | 93 630 | 13 172 | 27 220 | 25 570 | −14 093 | 10 774 |
| **Percentage distribution of average annual expenditure — Distribution en pourcentage des dépenses annuelles moyennes** | | | | | | | |
| 1948 | 100.0 | 105.4 | 13.6 | 9.6 | 11.2 | −15.0 | 6.0 |
| 1950−1960 | 100.0 | 91.7 | 12.8 | 19.1 | 17.6 | −10.8 | 10.2 |
| 1950 | 100.0 | 97.1 | 13.0 | 21.2 | 18.0 | −18.3 | 5.9 |
| 1953 | 100.0 | 91.5 | 11.7 | 15.2 | 11.9 | −6.7 | 9.0 |
| 1954 | 100.0 | 94.5 | 12.8 | 14.5 | 15.0 | −9.0 | 10.8 |
| 1958 | 100.0 | 91.3 | 12.3 | 19.6 | 18.9 | −10.9 | 11.3 |
| 1960 | 100.0 | 90.0 | 13.0 | 26.2 | 26.6 | −16.2 | 9.9 |
| **b. At Prices of 1954 — Aux prix de 1954** | | | | | | | |
| **Absolute figures — Chiffres absolus** | | | | | | | |
| 1948 | 37 735 | 39 786 | 7 011 | 5 121 | 5 460 | −7 172 | 2 645 |
| 1950 | 44 745 | 44 653 | 6 479 | 10 621 | 8 726 | −10 529 | 2 893 |
| 1951 | 48 812 | 47 150 | 7 060 | 10 161 | 7 543 | −8 499 | 3 175 |
| 1952 | 48 635 | 47 151 | 7 060 | 7 739 | 7 021 | −6 255 | 3 938 |
| 1953 | 55 933 | 51 036 | 6 855 | 8 751 | 7 181 | −3 854 | 5 401 |
| 1954 | 57 817 | 54 635 | 7 396 | 8 396 | 8 686 | −5 214 | 6 227 |
| 1955 | 62 366 | 56 870 | 7 297 | 10 083 | 9 336 | −4 587 | 7 731 |
| 1956 | 66 299 | 61 290 | 7 706 | 12 107 | 10 935 | −7 098 | 7 488 |
| 1957 | 71 962 | 65 785 | 8 234 | 13 450 | 11 283 | −7 273 | 8 759 |
| 1958 | 74 511 | 67 246 | 7 800 | 16 170 | 15 460 | −8 905 | 8 987 |
| 1959 | 77 333 | 68 965 | 8 380 | 18 690 | 17 940 | −10 322 | 9 156 |
| 1960 | 80 539 | 71 939 | 8 589 | 24 715 | 25 265 | −16 115 | 9 583 |
| 1961 | 89 456 | 76 988 | 8 810 | 26 130 | 24 730 | −13 662 | 11 054 |
| **Percentage distribution of average annual expenditure — Distribution en pourcentage des dépenses annuelles moyennes** | | | | | | | |
| 1948 | 100.0 | 105.4 | 18.6 | 13.6 | 14.5 | −19.0 | 7.0 |
| 1950−1960 | 100.0 | 92.4 | 12.0 | 20.4 | 18.8 | −12.8 | 10.6 |
| 1950 | 100.0 | 99.8 | 14.5 | 23.7 | 19.5 | −23.5 | 6.5 |
| 1953 | 100.0 | 91.3 | 12.3 | 15.6 | 12.8 | −6.9 | 9.7 |
| 1954 | 100.0 | 94.5 | 12.8 | 14.5 | 15.0 | −9.0 | 10.8 |
| 1958 | 100.0 | 90.2 | 10.5 | 21.7 | 20.7 | −11.9 | 12.1 |
| 1960 | 100.0 | 89.3 | 10.7 | 30.7 | 31.4 | −20.0 | 11.9 |
| **Average annual rate of growth — Taux annuel moyen d'accroissement** | | | | | | | |
| 1948−1953 | 8.2 | 5.1 | −0.4 | 11.3 | 5.6 | . | 15.3 |
| 1950−1960 | 6.1 | 4.9 | 2.9 | 8.8 | 11.2 | . | 12.7 |
| 1950−1953 | 7.7 | 4.6 | 1.9 | −6.2 | −6.3 | . | 23.1 |
| 1954−1958 | 6.6 | 5.3 | 1.3 | 17.8 | 15.5 | . | 9.6 |
| 1958−1960 | 4.0 | 3.4 | 4.9 | 23.6 | 27.8 | . | 3.2 |

## B. The Gross Domestic Product at Factor Cost According to Origin
## Origine par secteur d'activité du produit intérieur brut au coût des facteurs

| Item of data and year / Rubrique et année | Total [1] | Agricultural sector / Secteur agricole | Industrial Sector — Secteur Industriel | | | | | Transportation and communication [1] / Transport et communication[1] | Other sectors / Autres secteurs |
|---|---|---|---|---|---|---|---|---|---|
| | | | Total | Mining / Industries extractives | Manufacturing / Industries manufacturières | Construction / Bâtiment et travaux publics | Electricity, gas and water / Electricité, gaz et eau | | |
| ISIC — CITI | 0–9 | 0 | 1–5 | 1 | 2–3 | 4 | 5 | 7 | 6, 8–9 |

### a. At Current Prices — Aux prix courants

| | | | | | | | | | |
|---|---|---|---|---|---|---|---|---|---|
| **Absolute figures — Chiffres absolus** | | | | | | | | | |
| 1948 | 16 946 | 6 007 | 3 743 | 78 | 3 006 | 503 | 156 | 1 394 | 5 802 |
| 1950 | 25 937 | 8 824 | 6 488 | 166 | 4 977 | 1 133 | 212 | 2 257 | 8 368 |
| 1951 | 31 913 | 11 159 | 7 258 | 233 | 5 719 | 1 064 | 242 | 2 869 | 10 627 |
| 1952 | 33 583 | 11 375 | 7 274 | 280 | 5 584 | 1 106 | 304 | 3 210 | 11 724 |
| 1953 | 44 510 | 16 374 | 9 860 | 433 | 7 467 | 1 480 | 480 | 3 645 | 14 631 |
| 1954 | 51 611 | 17 729 | 12 415 | 534 | 9 342 | 1 938 | 601 | 4 127 | 17 340 |
| 1955 | 58 305 | 20 093 | 14 106 | 599 | 10 521 | 2 314 | 672 | 4 567 | 19 539 |
| 1956 | 67 627 | 22 758 | 16 605 | 781 | 12 134 | 2 804 | 886 | 5 106 | 23 158 |
| 1957 | 72 197 | 25 022 | 17 665 | 893 | 12 984 | 2 849 | 939 | 5 351 | 24 159 |
| 1958 | 75 234 | 23 731 | 19 732 | 933 | 14 186 | 3 547 | 1 066 | 5 579 | 26 192 |
| 1959 | 78 650 | 23 833 | 20 598 | 937 | 14 519 | 3 819 | 1 323 | 6 044 | 28 175 |
| 1960 | 83 537 | 23 700 | 23 014 | 1 023 | 15 859 | 4 738 | 1 394 | 6 666 | 30 157 |
| 1961 | 93 797 | 28 400 | 25 056 | 1 116 | 17 174 | 5 290 | 1 476 | 7 292 | 33 049 |
| **Percentage distribution according to sector— Distribution en pourcentage par secteur** | | | | | | | | | |
| 1948 | 100.0 | 35.5 | 22.1 | 0.5 | 17.7 | 3.0 | 0.9 | 8.2 | 34.2 |
| 1950 – 1960 | 100.0 | 32.8 | 24.9 | 1.1 | 18.2 | 4.3 | 1.3 | 7.9 | 34.4 |
| 1950 | 100.0 | 34.0 | 25.0 | 0.6 | 19.2 | 4.4 | 0.8 | 8.7 | 32.3 |
| 1953 | 100.0 | 36.8 | 22.1 | 1.0 | 16.7 | 3.3 | 1.1 | 8.2 | 32.9 |
| 1954 | 100.0 | 34.3 | 24.1 | 1.0 | 18.1 | 3.8 | 1.2 | 8.0 | 33.6 |
| 1958 | 100.0 | 31.5 | 26.2 | 1.2 | 18.9 | 4.7 | 1.4 | 7.4 | 34.9 |
| 1960 | 100.0 | 28.3 | 27.6 | 1.2 | 19.0 | 5.7 | 1.7 | 7.9 | 36.2 |

### b. At Prices of 1954 — Aux prix de 1954

| | | | | | | | | | |
|---|---|---|---|---|---|---|---|---|---|
| **Absolute figures — Chiffres absolus** | | | | | | | | | |
| 1948 | 33 640 | 10 557 | 6 342 | 124 | 4 929 | 958 | 331 | 2 765 | 13 976 |
| 1950 | 40 738 | 13 165 | 9 123 | 263 | 6 895 | 1 547 | 418 | 3 384 | 15 066 |
| 1951 | 44 028 | 15 201 | 9 439 | 359 | 7 348 | 1 260 | 472 | 3 708 | 15 680 |
| 1952 | 43 691 | 14 332 | 9 363 | 404 | 7 106 | 1 325 | 528 | 3 857 | 16 139 |
| 1953 | 49 902 | 18 071 | 10 932 | 468 | 8 276 | 1 606 | 582 | 3 807 | 17 092 |
| 1954 | 51 611 | 17 729 | 12 415 | 534 | 9 342 | 1 938 | 601 | 4 127 | 17 340 |
| 1955 | 55 453 | 19 304 | 13 525 | 632 | 10 087 | 2 077 | 729 | 4 401 | 18 223 |
| 1956 | 58 470 | 19 483 | 14 784 | 712 | 10 767 | 2 456 | 849 | 4 655 | 19 548 |
| 1957 | 63 452 | 22 499 | 15 666 | 829 | 11 438 | 2 442 | 957 | 4 802 | 20 485 |
| 1958 | 65 369 | 20 812 | 17 524 | 875 | 12 494 | 3 105 | 1 050 | 5 189 | 21 844 |
| 1959 | 68 431 | 21 840 | 18 215 | 889 | 12 823 | 3 289 | 1 214 | 5 451 | 22 925 |
| 1960 | 70 881 | 20 435 | 20 316 | 993 | 13 862 | 4 109 | 1 352 | 5 805 | 24 325 |
| 1961 | 78 674 | 24 153 | 22 117 | 1 061 | 14 952 | 4 608 | 1 496 | 6 249 | 26 155 |
| **Percentage distribution according to sector— Distribution en pourcentage par secteur** | | | | | | | | | |
| 1948 | 100.0 | 31.4 | 18.8 | 0.4 | 14.6 | 2.8 | 1.0 | 8.2 | 41.6 |
| 1950 – 1960 | 100.0 | 33.1 | 24.7 | 1.1 | 18.1 | 4.1 | 1.4 | 8.1 | 34.1 |
| 1950 | 100.0 | 32.3 | 22.4 | 0.7 | 16.9 | 3.8 | 1.0 | 8.3 | 37.0 |
| 1953 | 100.0 | 36.2 | 21.9 | 0.9 | 16.6 | 3.2 | 1.2 | 7.6 | 34.3 |
| 1954 | 100.0 | 34.3 | 24.1 | 1.0 | 18.1 | 3.8 | 1.2 | 8.0 | 33.6 |
| 1958 | 100.0 | 31.8 | 26.8 | 1.3 | 19.1 | 4.8 | 1.6 | 7.9 | 33.5 |
| 1960 | 100.0 | 28.8 | 28.6 | 1.4 | 19.5 | 5.8 | 1.9 | 8.2 | 34.4 |
| **Average annual rate of growth—Taux annuel moyen d'accroissement** | | | | | | | | | |
| 1948 – 1953 | 8.2 | 11.4 | 11.5 | 30.4 | 10.9 | 10.9 | 11.9 | 6.6 | 4.1 |
| 1950 – 1960 | 5.7 | 4.5 | 8.3 | 14.2 | 7.2 | 10.3 | 12.5 | 5.5 | 4.9 |
| 1950 – 1953 | 7.0 | 11.1 | 6.2 | 21.2 | 6.3 | 1.3 | 11.7 | 4.0 | 4.3 |
| 1954 – 1958 | 6.1 | 4.1 | 9.0 | 13.1 | 7.5 | 12.5 | 15.0 | 5.9 | 5.9 |
| 1958 – 1960 | 4.1 | −0.9 | 7.7 | 6.5 | 5.3 | 15.0 | 13.5 | 5.8 | 5.5 |

[1] Not included are the services rendered by ocean-going ships registered under the Greek flag or owned by Greek nationals.

[1] Non compris les services rendus par les navires de haute mer battant pavillon Grec, ou appartenant à des Grecs.

## C.   Gross Domestic Fixed Capital Formation According to Purchasing Sector
## La formation brute de capital fixe intérieur par secteur d'acquisition

| Item of data and year / Rubrique et année | Total | Agricultural sector / Secteur agricole | Industrial Sector — Secteur industriel | | | | Transportation and communication / Transport et communication | Other sectors [1] / Autres secteurs [1] |
|---|---|---|---|---|---|---|---|---|
| | | | Total | Mining / Industries extractives | Manufacturing / Industries manufacturières | Electricity, gas and water / Electricité, gaz et eau | | |
| ISIC — CITI | 0–9 | 0 | 1–3, 5 | 1 | 2–3 | 5 | 7 | 4, 6, 8–9 |

### a.   At Current Prices — Aux prix courants

| | | | | | | | | |
|---|---|---|---|---|---|---|---|---|
| **Absolute figures — Chiffres absolus** | | | | | | | | |
| 1948 | 2 137 | 166 | 359 | 16 | 309 | 34 | 713 | 899 |
| 1950 | 5 158 | 572 | 975 | 64 | 766 | 145 | 1 195 | 2 416 |
| 1951 | 4 810 | 657 | 1 446 | 187 | 736 | 523 | 682 | 2 025 |
| 1952 | 4 724 | 463 | 1 279 | 125 | 737 | 417 | 765 | 2 217 |
| 1953 | 5 895 | 460 | 1 525 | 90 | 706 | 729 | 633 | 3 277 |
| 1954 | 8 686 | 653 | 1 844 | 95 | 830 | 919 | 1 831 | 4 358 |
| 1955 | 9 757 | 679 | 1 998 | 76 | 941 | 981 | 1 570 | 5 510 |
| 1956 | 12 043 | 898 | 2 833 | 161 | 1 237 | 1 435 | 2 209 | 6 103 |
| 1957 | 12 443 | 1 488 | 2 552 | 219 | 1 513 | 820 | 2 816 | 5 587 |
| 1958 | 16 165 | 2 183 | 3 367 | 193 | 2 038 | 1 136 | 4 008 | 6 607 |
| 1959 | 18 745 | 2 322 | 3 323 | 90 | 1 731 | 1 502 | 6 362 | 6 738 |
| 1960 | 25 225 | 3 270 | 3 133 | 77 | 1 602 | 1 454 | 11 250 | 7 572 |
| 1961 | 25 570 | 3 550 | 3 674 | 125 | 2 142 | 1 407 | 9 683 | 8 663 |
| **Percentage distribution according to sector— Distribution en pourcentage par secteur** | | | | | | | | |
| 1948 | 100.0 | 7.8 | 16.8 | 0.7 | 14.5 | 1.6 | 33.3 | 42.1 |
| 1950 – 1960 | 100.0 | 11.0 | 19.6 | 1.1 | 10.4 | 8.1 | 27.0 | 42.4 |
| 1950 | 100.0 | 11.1 | 18.9 | 1.2 | 14.9 | 2.8 | 23.2 | 46.8 |
| 1953 | 100.0 | 7.8 | 25.9 | 1.5 | 12.0 | 12.4 | 10.7 | 55.6 |
| 1954 | 100.0 | 7.5 | 21.2 | 1.1 | 9.5 | 10.6 | 21.1 | 50.2 |
| 1958 | 100.0 | 13.5 | 20.8 | 1.1 | 12.7 | 7.0 | 24.8 | 40.9 |
| 1960 | 100.0 | 12.9 | 12.4 | 0.3 | 6.4 | 5.7 | 44.6 | 30.1 |

### b.   At Prices of 1954 — Aux prix de 1954

| | | | | | | | | |
|---|---|---|---|---|---|---|---|---|
| **Absolute figures — Chiffres absolus** | | | | | | | | |
| 1948 | 5 460 | 414 | 1 031 | 34 | 906 | 91 | 2 353 | 1 662 |
| 1950 | 8 726 | 1 018 | 1 989 | 97 | 1 592 | 300 | 2 188 | 3 531 |
| 1951 | 7 543 | 977 | 2 771 | 343 | 1 418 | 1 010 | 1 219 | 2 576 |
| 1952 | 7 021 | 655 | 2 138 | 199 | 1 305 | 634 | 1 375 | 2 853 |
| 1953 | 7 181 | 564 | 1 901 | 112 | 930 | 859 | 874 | 3 842 |
| 1954 | 8 686 | 653 | 1 844 | 95 | 830 | 919 | 1 831 | 4 358 |
| 1955 | 9 336 | 632 | 1 945 | 72 | 955 | 918 | 1 530 | 5 229 |
| 1956 | 10 935 | 799 | 2 634 | 148 | 1 166 | 1 320 | 1 969 | 5 533 |
| 1957 | 11 283 | 1 308 | 2 460 | 197 | 1 530 | 733 | 2 587 | 4 928 |
| 1958 | 15 460 | 2 044 | 3 139 | 170 | 1 964 | 1 005 | 4 528 | 5 749 |
| 1959 | 17 940 | 2 060 | 2 826 | 78 | 1 503 | 1 245 | 7 252 | 5 802 |
| 1960 | 25 265 | 2 858 | 2 626 | 67 | 1 295 | 1 264 | 13 230 | 6 551 |
| 1961 | 24 730 | 3 058 | 2 899 | 104 | 1 620 | 1 175 | 11 210 | 7 563 |
| **Percentage distribution according to sector— Distribution en pourcentage par secteur** | | | | | | | | |
| 1948 | 100.0 | 7.6 | 18.9 | 0.6 | 16.6 | 1.7 | 43.1 | 30.4 |
| 1950 – 1960 | 100.0 | 10.4 | 20.3 | 1.3 | 11.2 | 7.8 | 29.9 | 39.4 |
| 1950 | 100.0 | 11.7 | 22.8 | 1.1 | 18.3 | 3.4 | 25.1 | 40.4 |
| 1953 | 100.0 | 7.8 | 26.5 | 1.6 | 12.9 | 12.0 | 12.2 | 53.5 |
| 1954 | 100.0 | 7.5 | 21.2 | 1.1 | 9.5 | 10.6 | 21.1 | 50.2 |
| 1958 | 100.0 | 13.2 | 20.3 | 1.1 | 12.7 | 6.5 | 29.3 | 37.2 |
| 1960 | 100.0 | 11.3 | 10.4 | 0.2 | 5.2 | 5.0 | 52.3 | 26.0 |
| **Average annual rate of growth—Taux annuel moyen d'accroissement** | | | | | | | | |
| 1948 – 1953 | 5.6 | 6.4 | 13.0 | 26.9 | 0.5 | 56.7 | −18.0 | 18.3 |
| 1950 – 1960 | 11.2 | 10.9 | 2.8 | −3.6 | −2.0 | 15.5 | 19.7 | 6.4 |
| 1950 – 1953 | −6.3 | −17.9 | −1.4 | −4.9 | −16.4 | 42.0 | −26.4 | 2.9 |
| 1954 – 1958 | 15.5 | 33.0 | 14.2 | 15.7 | 24.0 | 2.3 | 25.4 | 7.2 |
| 1958 – 1960 | 27.8 | 18.2 | −8.6 | −37.2 | −18.8 | 12.2 | 70.9 | 6.8 |

[1] Includes the construction industry.       [1] Y compris le bâtiment et les travaux publics.

## 2. INDEX NUMBERS OF INDUSTRIAL PRODUCTION
## INDICES DE LA PRODUCTION INDUSTRIELLE

### A. Selected Divisions of Industrial Activity
### Quelques branches de l'activité industrielle

| Period<br>Période | Mining [1]<br>Industries<br>extractives [1] | Manufacturing [2]<br>Industries<br>manufacturières [2] | Electricity<br>Electricité |
|---|---|---|---|
| ISIC — CITI | 1 | 2-3 | 511 |
| *a.* Indexes — Indices (1958 = 100) | | | |
| 1939 [4]........... | 32 | 52 | 18 |
| 1948........... | 5 | 34 | 26 |
| 1949........... | 8 | 41 | 31 |
| 1950........... | 10 | 52 | 37 |
| 1951........... | 21 | 59 | 42 |
| 1952........... | 33 | 58 | 45 |
| 1953........... | 38 | 65 | 52 |
| 1954........... | 43 | 80 | 60 |
| 1955........... | 55 | 83 | 71 |
| 1956........... | 69 | 84 | 80 |
| 1957........... | 82 | 91 | 90 |
| 1958........... | 100 | 100 | 100 |
| 1959........... | 123 | – 101 – | 112 |
| 1960........... | 156 | 111 | 129 |
| 1961........... | 166 | 117 | 146 |
| *b.* Average Annual Rate of Change — Taux annuel moyen de variation | | | |
| 1939 – 1960 [4]..... | 7.8 | 3.7 | 9.8 |
| 1939 – 1948...... | —17.0 | —4.6 | 4.2 |
| 1950 – 1960...... | 31.6 | 7.9 | 13.3 |
| 1948 – 1953...... | 50.0 | 13.8 | 14.9 |
| 1954 – 1958...... | 23.5 | 5.7 | 13.6 |
| 1958 – 1960...... | 24.9 | 5.4 | 13.6 |

For footnotes, see end of table.

Pour les notes, voir au bas du tableau.

### B. Selected Major Groups of Mining
### Quelques classes de la branche Industries extractives

| Period<br>Période | Mining [1]<br>Industries<br>extractives [1] | Coal mining<br>Extraction<br>du charbon | Metal mining<br>Extraction des<br>minerais métalliques |
|---|---|---|---|
| ISIC — CITI | 1 | 11 | 12 |
| *a.* Indexes — Indices (1958 = 100) | | | |
| 1938........... | 32 | 9 | 40 |
| 1948........... | 5 | 11 | 3 |
| 1949........... | 8 | 15 | 3 |
| 1950........... | 10 | 15 | 8 |
| 1951........... | 21 | 15 | 22 |
| 1952........... | 33 | 21 | 35 |
| 1953........... | 38 | 37 | 34 |
| 1954........... | 43 | 59 | 32 |
| 1955........... | 55 | 66 | 45 |
| 1956........... | 69 | 67 | 70 |
| 1957........... | 82 | 84 | 81 |
| 1958........... | 100 | 100 | 100 |
| 1959........... | 123 | 135 | 112 |
| 1960........... | 156 | 212 | 107 |
| 1961........... | 166 | 211 | 128 |
| *b.* Average Annual Rate of Change — Taux annuel moyen de variation | | | |
| 1938 – 1960...... | 7.8 | 16.2 | 4.8 |
| 1938 – 1948...... | —17.0 | 2.0 | —22.8 |
| 1950 – 1960...... | 31.6 | 30.3 | 29.6 |
| 1948 – 1953...... | 50.0 | 27.5 | 62.5 |
| 1954 – 1958...... | 23.5 | 14.1 | 33.0 |
| 1958 – 1960...... | 24.9 | 45.6 | 3.4 |

For footnotes, see end of table.

Pour les notes, voir au bas du tableau.

## C. Selected Major Groups of Manufacturing — Quelques classes de la branche Industries manufacturières

| Period / Période | Manufacturing [2] / Industries manufacturières [2] | Food, beverages and tobacco / Industries alimentaires, boissons, tabac | Textiles | Wood products and furniture / Bois et meubles | Paper and paper products / Papier et ouvrages en papier | Leather and leather products except wearing apparel / Cuir et articles en cuir, à l'exclusion des articles d'habillement | Rubber products / Ouvrages en caoutchouc | Chemicals and chemical, petroleum and coal products / Produits chimiques et dérivés du pétrole et du charbon | Non-metallic mineral products / Produits minéraux non métalliques | Basic metals [3] / Métallurgie de base [3] | Metal products [3] / Ouvrages en métaux [3] |
|---|---|---|---|---|---|---|---|---|---|---|---|
| ISIC — CITI | 2–3 | 20–22 | 23 | 25–26 | 27 | 29 | 30 | 31–32 | 33 | 34 | 35–38 |

### a. Indexes — Indices (1958 = 100)

| Period | 2–3 | 20–22 | 23 | 25–26 | 27 | 29 | 30 | 31–32 | 33 | 34 | 35–38 |
|---|---|---|---|---|---|---|---|---|---|---|---|
| 1939 | 52 | 54 | 60 | 63 | 37 | 62 | 63 | | 29 | 40 | 39 |
| 1948 | 34 | 42 | 42 | 22 | 24 | 35 | 38 | | 21 | 23 | 21 |
| 1949 | 41 | 48 | 47 | 32 | 34 | 44 | 50 | | 24 | 27 | 26 |
| 1950 | 52 | 58 | 64 | 52 | 43 | 57 | 57 | | 29 | 32 | 34 |
| 1951 | 59 | 64 | 74 | 53 | 48 | 52 | 70 | | 37 | 56 | 40 |
| 1952 | 58 | 63 | 70 | 47 | 44 | 62 | 62 | | 45 | 68 | 41 |
| 1953 | 65 | 70 | 76 | 57 | 50 | 69 | 72 | | 56 | 76 | 48 |
| 1954 | 80 | 84 | 89 | 73 | 57 | 76 | 101 | | 68 | 78 | 68 |
| 1955 | 83 | 88 | 82 | 75 | 63 | 76 | 85 | 95 | 83 | 74 | 74 |
| 1956 | 84 | 90 | 83 | 88 | 76 | 86 | 89 | 81 | 92 | 77 | 74 |
| 1957 | 91 | 90 | 92 | 91 | 89 | 82 | 90 | 98 | 92 | 90 | 79 |
| 1958 | 100 | 100 | 100 | 100 | 100 | 100 | 100 | 100 | 100 | 100 | 100 |
| 1959 | –101– | –102– | –89– | 108 | –105– | –99– | –95– | –112– | –100– | –95– | –111– |
| 1960 | 111 | 106 | 101 | 110 | 114 | 103 | 80 | 130 | 99 | 122 | 124 |
| 1961 | 117 | 109 | 106 | 114 | 120 | 118 | 78 | 127 | 104 | 137 | 145 |

### b. Average Annual Rate of Change — Taux annuel moyen de variation

| Period | 2–3 | 20–22 | 23 | 25–26 | 27 | 29 | 30 | 31–32 | 33 | 34 | 35–38 |
|---|---|---|---|---|---|---|---|---|---|---|---|
| 1939–1960 | 3.7 | 3.3 | 2.5 | 2.7 | 5.5 | 2.4 | ... | | 6.0 | 5.5 | 5.7 |
| 1939–1948 | –4.6 | –2.8 | –3.9 | –11.0 | –4.7 | –6.2 | –5.4 | | –3.5 | –6.0 | –6.6 |
| 1950–1960 | 7.9 | 6.2 | 4.7 | 7.8 | 10.2 | 6.1 | ... | | 13.1 | 14.3 | 13.8 |
| 1948–1953 | 13.8 | 10.8 | 12.6 | 21.1 | 15.8 | 14.5 | 13.6 | | 21.7 | 27.0 | 18.0 |
| 1954–1958 | 5.7 | 4.4 | 3.0 | 8.2 | 15.1 | 7.1 | ... | | 10.1 | 6.4 | 10.1 |
| 1958–1960 | 5.4 | 3.0 | 0.5 | 4.9 | 6.8 | 1.5 | –10.6 | 14.0 | –0.5 | 10.5 | 11.4 |

[1] Excludes Other mining (ISIC major groups 14–19).
[2] Not including Clothing, footwear and made-up textiles (ISIC major group 24), Printing and publishing (ISIC major group 28), or Miscellaneous manufacturing industries (ISIC major group 39) in all years; and Wood products and furniture (ISIC major groups 25–26) and Petroleum and coal products (ISIC major group 32) in 1960–1961.
[3] The making and casting of iron and steel are included in Metal products (ISIC major groups 35–38) and not Basic metals (ISIC major group 34) for the years, 1939–1959.
[4] 1938 in case of Mining (ISIC Division 1).

[1] Non compris Autres industries manufacturières (CITI classes 14–19).
[2] Non compris Articles d'habillement, chaussures, et ouvrages en tissus (CITI classe 24), Imprimerie et édition (CITI classe 28) et les Industries manufacturières diverses (CITI classe 39) pour toutes les années, Ouvrages en bois et meubles (CITI classes 25–26) et Produits dérivés du pétrole et du charbon (CITI classe 32) pour 1960–1961.
[3] La fabrication et la fonderie de la fonte et de l'acier sont comprises dans Ouvrages en métaux (CITI classes 35–38) et non dans Métallurgie de base (CITI classe 34) pour les années 1939–1959.
[4] 1938 dans le cas des Industries extractives (CITI Branche 1).

# 3. THE CHARACTERISTICS OF ALL INDUSTRIAL ESTABLISHMENTS
## CARACTERISTIQUES DE TOUS LES ETABLISSEMENTS INDUSTRIELS
### 30.XII.1950 and 15.XI.1958

Number of establishments in units; number of persons engaged in thousands; capacity of installed power equipment in thousand horsepower; capacity of installed power equipment per person engaged in horsepower.

Nombre d'établissements en unités; nombre de personnes occupées en milliers; puissance installée en milliers de chevaux-vapeur; puissance installée par personne occupée en chevaux-vapeur.

## A. The Divisions of Industrial Activity — Les branches de l'activité industrielle

| Year and item of data | All industrial activity — Toutes industries | Mining — Industries extractives | Manufacturing — Industries manufacturières | Construction — Bâtiment et travaux publics | Electricity and gas — Electricité et gaz | Année et rubrique |
|---|---|---|---|---|---|---|
| ISIC | 1-4, 511-512 | 1 | 2-3 | 4 | 511-512 | CITI |
| **a. Absolute Figures — Chiffres absolus** | | | | | | |
| **30.XII.1950** | | | | | | **30.XII.1950** |
| Number of establishments... | 93 215 | 119 | 92 749 | 42 | 305 | Nombre d'établissements |
| Number of engaged... | ... | ... | 339.9 | ... | ... | Nombre de personnes occupées |
| Capacity of installed power equipment. | 673.5 | 18.4 | 349.3 | 4.0 | 301.8 | Puissance installée |
| **15.XI.1958** | | | | | | **15.XI.1958** |
| Number of establishments... | 121 258 | 1 348 | 109 236 | 10 117 | 557 | Nombre d'établissements |
| Number of engaged [1]... | 501.0 | 20.6 | 414.0 | 57.3 | 9.1 | Nombre de personnes occupées [1] |
| Number of employees... | 374.6 | 19.1 | 301.0 | 49.8 | 4.7 | Nombre de salariés |
| Capacity of installed power equipment. | . | 67.6 | 775.4 | ... | 687.2 | Puissance installée |

| Year and item of data | All industrial activity — Toutes industries | Mining — Industries extractives | Manufacturing — Industries manufacturières | Construction — Bâtiment et travaux publics | Electricity and gas — Electricité et gaz | Année et rubrique |
|---|---|---|---|---|---|---|
| ISIC | 1-4, 511-512 | 1 | 2-3 | 4 | 511-512 | CITI |
| **b. Structure** | | | | | | |
| **30.XII.1950** Capacity of installed power equipment per person engaged... | ... | ... | 1.03 | ... | ... | **30.XII.1950** Puissance installée par personne occupée |
| **15.XI.1958** Distribution in percent of number of engaged... | 100.0 | 4.1 | 82.6 | 11.4 | 1.9 | **15.XI.1958** Distribution en pourcentage du nombre de personnes occupées |
| Capacity of installed power equipment per person engaged... | . | 3.28 | 1.87 | ... | . | Puissance installée par personne occupée |
| Employees as a percent of engaged... | 74.8 | 92.7 | 72.7 | 86.9 | 51.6 | Salariés en pourcentage des personnes occupées |

For footnotes see end of table.

Pour les notes, voir au bas du tableau.

## B. The Major Groups of Mining — Les classes de la branche Industries extractives

| Year and item of data | All mining — Toutes industries extractives | Coal mining — Extraction du charbon | Metal mining — Extraction des minerais métalliques | Other mining — Divers | Année et rubrique |
|---|---|---|---|---|---|
| ISIC | 1 | 11 | 12 | 14-19 | CITI |
| **a. Absolute Figures — Chiffres absolus** | | | | | |
| **30.XII.1950** | | | | | **30.XII.1950** |
| Number of establishments. | 119 | 10 | 11 | 98 | Nombre d'établissements |
| Capacity of installed power equipment... | 18.4 | 1.6 | 6.9 | 9.9 | Puissance installée |
| **15.XI.1958** | | | | | **15.XI.1958** |
| Number of establishments. | 1 348 | 95 | 94 | 1 159 | Nombre d'établissements |
| Number of engaged [1]... | 20.6 | 5.4 | 5.8 | 9.4 | Nombre de personnes occupées [1] |
| Number of employees... | 19.1 | 5.8 | 4.7 | 8.6 | Nombre de salariés |
| Capacity of installed power equipment... | 67.6 | 13.2 | 15.7 | 38.7 | Puissance installée |

| Year and item of data | All mining — Toutes industries extractives | Coal mining — Extraction du charbon | Metal mining — Extraction des minerais métalliques | Other mining — Divers | Année et rubrique |
|---|---|---|---|---|---|
| ISIC | 1 | 11 | 12 | 14-19 | CITI |
| **b. Structure** | | | | | |
| **15.XI.1958** | | | | | **15.XI.1958** |
| Distribution in percent of number of engaged... | 100.0 | 26.2 | 28.1 | 45.7 | Distribution en pourcentage du nombre de personnes occupées |
| Capacity of installed power equipment per person engaged... | 3.28 | 2.44 | 2.71 | 4.12 | Puissance installée par personne occupée |
| Employees as a percent of engaged... | 92.7 | 107.4 | 81.0 | 91.5 | Salariés en pourcentage des personnes occupées |

For footnotes see end of table.

Pour les notes, voir au bas du tableau.

## C.  The Major Groups of Manufacturing — Les classes de la branche Industries manufacturières

| Year and item of data | Manufacturing<br>Industries manufacturières | Food, beverages and tobacco [2]<br>Industries alimentaires, boissons, tabac [2] | Textiles | Clothing, footwear and made-up textiles<br>Articles d'habillement, chaussures et ouvrages en tissu | Wood products and furniture<br>Bois et meubles | Paper and paper products<br>Papier et ouvrages en papier | Printing and publishing<br>Imprimerie et édition | Leather and leather products except wearing apparel<br>Cuir et articles en cuir, à l'exclusion des articles d'habillement | Rubber products<br>Ouvrages en caoutchouc | Chemicals and chemical, petroleum and coal products [2]<br>Produits chimiques et dérivés du pétrole et du charbon [2] | Non-metallic mineral products<br>Produits minéraux non métalliques | Basic metals<br>Métallurgie de base | Metal products<br>Ouvrages en métaux | Other manufacturing<br>Autres industries manufacturières | Année et rubrique |
|---|---|---|---|---|---|---|---|---|---|---|---|---|---|---|---|
| ISIC | 2–3 | 20–22 | 23 | 24 | 25–26 | 27 | 28 | 29 | 30 | 31–32 | 33 | 34 | 35–38 | 39 | CITI |
| *a. Absolute Figures — Chiffres absolus* | | | | | | | | | | | | | | | |
| 30.XII.1950<br>Number of establishments. | 92 749 | 17 069 | 7 161 | 39 746 | 8 364 | 201 | 811 | 2 280 | 38 | 833 | 1 333 | 10 | 12 959 | 1 944 | 30.XII.1950<br>Nombre d'établissements |
| Number of engaged.... | 339.9 | 67.1 | 71.3 | 80.2 | 22.2 | 3.6 | 6.7 | 5.6 | 2.5 | 15.0 | 11.7 | 0.9 | 46.5 | 6.6 | Nombre de personnes occupées |
| Capacity of installed power equipment..... | 349.3 | 142.4 | 45.3 | 1.7 | 22.5 | 8.8 | 3.2 | 7.2 | 3.2 | 19.7 | 24.7 | 5.8 | 45.0 | 19.8 | Puissance installée |
| 15.XI.1958<br>Number of establishments. | 109 236 | 18 743 | 3 570 | 32 819 | 16 734 | 242 | 1 400 | 1 441 | 323 | 7 991 | 3 595 | 56 | 20 242 | 2 080 | 15.XI.1958<br>Nombre d'établissements |
| Number of engaged [1]... | 414.0 | 92.0 | 53.3 | 67.5 | 45.2 | 4.8 | 9.6 | 6.0 | 3.9 | 26.6 | 22.4 | 3.0 | 73.4 | 6.3 | Nombre de personnes occupées [1] |
| Number of employees... | 301.0 | 57.4 | 51.2 | 35.3 | 27.4 | 4.6 | 8.2 | 4.5 | 3.7 | 34.2 | 16.5 | 2.8 | 51.1 | 4.1 | Nombre de salariés |
| Capacity of installed power equipment..... | 775.4 | 190.7 | 105.8 | 3.9 | 64.2 | 26.2 | 8.0 | 11.1 | 6.0 | 134.0 | 81.7 | 42.4 | 96.3 | 5.1 | Puissance installée |
| *b. Structure* | | | | | | | | | | | | | | | |
| 30.XII.1950<br>Distribution in percent of number of engaged.......... | 100.0 | 19.7 | 21.0 | 23.6 | 6.5 | 1.1 | 1.9 | 1.7 | 0.7 | 4.4 | 3.5 | 0.2 | 13.7 | 2.0 | 30.XII.1950<br>Répartition en pourcentage du nombre de personnes occupées |
| Capacity of installed power equipment per person engaged...... | 1.03 | 2.12 | 0.64 | 0.02 | 1.01 | 2.44 | 0.48 | 1.28 | 1.28 | 1.31 | 2.11 | 6.44 | 0.97 | 3.00 | Puissance installée par personne occupée |
| 15.XI.1958<br>Distribution in percent of number of engaged.......... | 100.0 | 22.2 | 12.8 | 16.4 | 10.9 | 1.1 | 2.3 | 1.5 | 0.9 | 6.5 | 5.4 | 0.7 | 17.7 | 1.6 | 15.XI.1958<br>Répartition en pourcentage du nombre de personnes occupées |
| Capacity of installed power equipment per person engaged...... | 1.87 | 2.07 | 1.98 | 0.06 | 1.42 | 5.46 | 0.83 | 1.85 | 1.54 | 5.04 | 3.65 | 14.13 | 1.31 | 0.81 | Puissance installée par personne occupée |
| Employees as a percent of engaged........ | 72.7 | 62.4 | 96.1 | 52.3 | 60.6 | 95.8 | 85.4 | 75.0 | 94.9 | 128.6 | 73.7 | 93.3 | 69.6 | 65.1 | Salariés en pourcentage des personnes occupées |

[1] Average of middle of February, May, August and November.
[2] Extraction and refining of olive oil is included in Chemicals and chemical products (ISIC major group 31) instead of Food (ISIC major group 20).

[1] Moyenne de mi-février, mai, août et novembre.
[2] L'extraction et le raffinage d'huile d'olive est comprise dans les Industries chimiques (CITI classe 31) au lieu d'être dans Industries alimentaires (CITI classe 20).

# 4. CHARACTERISTICS OF MANUFACTURING ESTABLISHMENTS WITH 10 OR MORE PERSONS ENGAGED

## CARACTERISTIQUES DES ETABLISSEMENTS MANUFACTURIERS OCCUPANT 10 PERSONNES OU PLUS

### 1958

Number of establishments in units; value added and wages and salaries in million drachmas; number of engaged, employees and operatives in thousands; value added per engaged and wages and salaries per employee in thousand drachmas.

Nombre d'établissements en unités; valeur ajoutée et traitements et salaires en millions de drachmas; nombre de personnes occupées, de salariés et d'ouvriers en milliers; valeur ajoutée par personne occupée et traitements et salaires par salarié en milliers de drachmas.

| Year and item of data | Manufacturing — Industries manufacturières | Food, beverages and tobacco[1] — Industries alimentaires, boissons, tabac[1] | Textiles | Clothing, footwear and made-up textiles — Articles d'habillement, chaussures et ouvrages en tissu | Wood products and furniture — Bois et meubles | Paper and paper products — Papier et ouvrages en papier | Printing and publishing — Imprimerie et édition | Leather and leather products except wearing apparel — Cuir et articles en cuir, à l'exclusion des articles d'habillement | Rubber products — Ouvrages en caoutchouc | Chemicals and chemical, petroleum and coal products[1] — Produits chimiques et dérivés du pétrole et du charbon[1] | Non-metallic mineral products — Produits minéraux non métalliques | Basic metals — Métallurgie de base | Metal products — Ouvrages en métaux | Other manufacturing — Autres industries manufacturières | Année et rubrique |
|---|---|---|---|---|---|---|---|---|---|---|---|---|---|---|---|
| ISIC | 2–3 | 20–22 | 23 | 24 | 25–26 | 27 | 28 | 29 | 30 | 31–32 | 33 | 34 | 35–38 | 39 | CITI |
| **a. Absolute Figures — Chiffres absolus** | | | | | | | | | | | | | | | |
| Number of establishments | 5 804 | 1 236 | 782 | 558 | 460 | 81 | 192 | 101 | 34 | 882 | 540 | 23 | 803 | 112 | Nombre d'établissements |
| Value added | 8 637 | 2 481 | 1 838 | 312 | 269 | 178 | 335 | 86 | 171 | 969 | 606 | 258 | 1 027 | 107 | Valeur ajoutée |
| Number of engaged (Average for the year) | 211.6 | 58.6 | 45.8 | 11.9 | 9.1 | 3.9 | 7.1 | 2.9 | 3.3 | 18.1 | 14.0 | 3.0 | 31.3 | 2.6 | Nombre de personnes occupées (moyenne pour l'année) |
| Employees: Number (Average for the year) | 203.2 | 56.3 | 44.7 | 10.9 | 8.3 | 3.8 | 6.9 | 2.8 | 3.3 | 17.4 | 13.1 | 3.0 | 30.2 | 2.5 | Salariés: Nombre (moyenne pour l'année) |
| Wages and salaries | 3 808 | 957 | 778 | 158 | 123 | 80 | 180 | 54 | 68 | 385 | 265 | 87 | 626 | 47 | Traitements et salaires |
| Operatives: Number (Average for the year) | 176.9 | 49.6 | 40.4 | 10.0 | 7.8 | 3.3 | 4.5 | 2.5 | 2.9 | 13.7 | 11.6 | 2.6 | 25.9 | 2.1 | Ouvriers: Nombre (moyenne pour l'année) |
| Wages and salaries | 2 835 | 715 | 596 | 140 | 110 | 60 | 104 | 43 | 56 | 238 | 208 | 62 | 469 | 34 | Traitements et salaires |
| **b. Structure** | | | | | | | | | | | | | | | |
| Distribution in percent of: Value added | 100.0 | 28.7 | 21.3 | 3.6 | 3.1 | 2.0 | 3.9 | 1.0 | 2.0 | 11.2 | 7.0 | 3.0 | 11.9 | 1.3 | Distribution en pourcentage: Valeur ajoutée |
| Number of engaged | 100.0 | 27.6 | 21.7 | 5.6 | 4.3 | 1.9 | 3.3 | 1.4 | 1.5 | 8.6 | 6.6 | 1.4 | 14.8 | 1.3 | Nombre de personnes occupées |
| Value added per person engaged | 40.8 | 42.3 | 40.1 | 26.2 | 29.6 | 45.6 | 47.2 | 29.6 | 51.8 | 53.5 | 43.3 | 86.0 | 32.8 | 41.2 | Valeur ajoutée par personne occupée |
| Employee as a percent of engaged | 96.0 | 96.1 | 97.6 | 91.6 | 91.2 | 97.4 | 97.2 | 96.6 | 100.0 | 96.1 | 93.6 | 100.0 | 96.5 | 96.2 | Salariés en pourcentage des personnes occupées |
| Value added per unit of wages and salaries | 2.27 | 2.59 | 2.36 | 1.97 | 2.19 | 2.22 | 1.86 | 1.59 | 2.51 | 2.52 | 2.29 | 2.96 | 1.64 | 2.28 | Valeur ajoutée par traitements et salaires unitaires |
| Wages and salaries per employee | 18.7 | 17.0 | 17.4 | 14.5 | 14.8 | 21.0 | 26.1 | 19.3 | 20.6 | 22.1 | 20.2 | 29.0 | 20.7 | 18.8 | Traitements et salaires par salarié |
| Operatives as a percent of employees | 87.0 | 88.1 | 90.4 | 91.7 | 94.0 | 86.8 | 65.2 | 89.3 | 87.9 | 78.7 | 88.5 | 86.7 | 85.8 | 84.0 | Ouvriers en pourcentage des salariés |

[1] Extraction and refining of olive oil is included in Chemicals and chemical products (ISIC major group 31) instead of Food (ISIC major group 20).

[1] L'extraction et le raffinage de huile d'olive est comprise dans les Industries chimiques (CITI classe 31) au lieu d'être dans Industries alimentaires (CITI classe 20).

# GUATEMALA

## Gross Domestic Product

Estimates of the expenditure on the gross domestic product and the industrial origin of the gross domestic product are presented in Table 1. This table has been compiled from data supplied by the Bank of Guatemala in response to the United Nations national accounts questionnaire. The official estimates are published by the Departamento de Estudios Económicos of the Banco de Guatemala in *Ingreso Nacional de Guatemala, 1950-1959*. A description of the sources and methods used in preparing the estimates can be found in *Ingreso Nacional 1956-1957*, a study prepared by the Departamento de Estudios Económicos.

## Index Numbers of Industrial Production

The index numbers of industrial production shown in Table 2 are compiled by the Dirección General de Estadística and published in the *Boletín Estadístico* of the Banco de Guatemala.

The indexes cover manufacturing industries and the production of electricity and are computed as base-weighted arithmetic averages of relatives based on quantities produced or raw materials consumed. The weighting coefficients used to combine industries relate to value added at market prices in 1946 obtained from the results of the 1946 industrial Census covering establishments employing five or more manual workers.

For further details concerning the character of the indexes see the *Boletín de la Dirección General de Estadística,* October 1950 (Guatemala City).

## Index Numbers of Industrial Employment

The index numbers of industrial employment shown in Table 3 are compiled by the Dirección General de Estadística and published in *Guatemala en Cifras*.

The indexes cover manufacturing industries and electricity establishments in Guatemala City only and are based on a sample of firms employing five or more manual workers. The data covers wage-earners (including foremen and apprentices but excluding persons on vacation and sick leave, etc.) who received pay during the reporting week, which usually included the fifteenth day of the month, irrespective of the time actually worked.

The indexes are computed monthly by major groups and are unweighted. The annual figures are the arithmetic averages of the monthly data.

For further details concerning the character of the indexes see the *Boletín Mensual*, 1957 No. 8.

## Produit intérieur brut

Le tableau 1 reproduit des estimations des dépenses imputées au produit intérieur brut ainsi qu'au produit intérieur brut ventilé suivant le secteur d'activité industrielle. Ce tableau a été construit à partir de données fournies par la Banque du Guatemala en réponse au questionnaire de l'O.N.U. relatif aux comptes nationaux. Les estimations officielles sont publiées par le Departamento de Estudios Económicos de la Banque du Guatemala dans *Ingreso Nacional de Guatemala, 1950-1959*. On peut trouver une description des sources et des méthodes utilisées dans l'élaboration de ces estimations dans *Ingreso Nacional 1956-1957*, étude préparée par le Departamento de Estudios Económicos.

## Indices de la production industrielle

Les indices de la production industrielle reproduits au tableau 2 sont établis par la Dirección General de Estadística et publiés dans le *Boletín Estadístico* de la Banque du Guatemala.

Ces indices couvrent les industries manufacturières et la production d'électricité; ce sont des moyennes arithmétiques à pondération fixe de rapports fondés sur les quantités produites ou les matières premières consommées. Les coefficients de pondération utilisés pour combiner les industries correspondent à la valeur ajoutée aux prix du marché en 1946, tirée des résultats du recensement industriel de 1946 qui couvrait les établissements employant au moins 5 travailleurs manuels.

Pour plus de détails sur ces indices, voir le *Boletín de la Dirección General de Estadística*, octobre 1950 (Guatemala).

## Indices de l'emploi industriel

Les indices de l'emploi industriel, reproduits au tableau 3, sont calculés par la Dirección General de Estadística et publiés dans *Guatemala en Cifras*.

Ces indices couvrent les industries manufacturières et les établissements producteurs et distributeurs d'électricité de la ville de Guatemala seulement et sont construits à partir d'un échantillon de firmes employant cinq travailleurs manuels ou plus. Les données couvrent les salariés (y compris les contremaîtres et les apprentis mais non compris les personnes en vacances ou en congé de maladie) rémunérés durant la semaine de l'enquête, qui, en général, couvre le quinzième jour du mois, compte non tenu de la durée de leur travail durant cette semaine.

Les indices sont calculés mensuellement par classes d'activité et ne sont pas pondérés. Les chiffres annuels sont les moyennes arithmétiques des données mensuelles.

Pour plus amples détails concernant ces indices consulter le *Boletín Mensual*, 1957 N° 8.

## Characteristics and Structure of Industrial Activity

The data shown for 1946 in Table 4 are derived from the results of Guatemala's First Industrial Census published by the Dirección General de Estadística in *Primer Censo Industrial, 1946* (Guatemala, October 1951). Although the Census covered all establishments with fixed assets valued at 500 Quetzales or more that were engaged in industrial activity during 1946, only those establishments employing five or more manual workers were included in the published results.

The definitions of the items of data appear to conform to the International Standards in Basic Industrial Statistics except that the figures on persons engaged exclude working proprietors. Data on wages and salaries are not shown since they were collected for one month only (December 1946). The data on value added are based on the value of production at market prices. The figures on installed power capacity relate to the horsepower of all prime movers in use connected directly to machinery (except generators) plus the horsepower of all electric motors in use.

The data shown for 1953 and 1958 in Table 5 are derived from the results of the Second and Third Industrial Censuses, respectively, both conducted by the Dirección General de Estadística. The results of the Second Industrial Census are published in *Segundo Censo Industrial 1953* (Guatemala 1957). The results of the Third Industrial Census 1958 were obtained by correspondence with the Dirección General de Estadística. All industrial establishments with three or more manual workers (including home workers and unpaid family workers) that were in operation during 1953 and 1958 and in existence at the end of the year were covered.

The definitions of the items of data conform to the International Standards in Basic Industrial Statistics. Data on wages and salaries are not shown for 1953 since they were collected for one month only (November 1953). The data on value added are based on the value of production at market prices. The figures on installed power capacity relate to the horsepower of all prime movers plus the horsepower of electric motors run on purchased electricity.

## Caractéristiques et structure de l'activité industrielle

Les chiffres pour 1946 du tableau 4 sont tirés des résultats du premier recensement industriel du Guatemala publiés par la Dirección General de Estadística dans *Primer Censo Industrial, 1946,* (Guatemala, octobre 1951). Le recensement couvrait tous les établissements qui possédaient des avoirs en capital fixe évalués à 500 quetzales ou plus et qui exerçaient une activité industrielle en 1946; cependant seuls les établissements employant 5 travailleurs manuels ou plus ont été compris dans les résultats publiés.

Les définitions des rubriques semblent conformes aux Normes internationales relatives aux statistiques industrielles de base, si ce n'est que les propriétaires qui travaillent ne sont pas compris parmi les personnes occupées. Aucun chiffre n'est donné sur les traitements et salaires car on n'en a recueilli que pour un mois seulement (décembre 1946). La valeur ajoutée est fondée sur la valeur de la production aux prix du marché. La puissance installée représente le nombre de chevaux-vapeur de tous les moteurs primaires en service entraînant directement des machines (à l'exception des générateurs), plus le nombre de chevaux-vapeur de tous les moteurs électriques en service.

Les données reproduites pour 1953 et 1958 au tableau 5 proviennent des résultats du deuxième et du troisième recensement industriel, respectivement, tous deux effectués par la Dirección General de Estadística. Les résultats du deuxième recensement industriel sont publiés dans *Segundo Censo Industrial 1953* (Guatemala 1957). Ceux du troisième recensement industriel effectué en 1958 ont été rassemblés à partir de la correspondance avec la Dirección General de Estadística. Tous les établissements industriels comptant 3 travailleurs manuels ou plus (y compris les travailleurs à domicile et les travailleurs familiaux non rémunérés) qui étaient en activité en 1953 et 1958 et qui existaient encore à la fin de l'année ont été recensés.

Les définitions des rubriques sont conformes aux Normes internationales relatives aux statistiques industrielles de base. Aucun chiffre n'est donné sur les traitements et salaires pour 1953 car on n'en a recueilli que pour un seul mois (novembre 1953). La valeur ajoutée est fondée sur la valeur de la production aux prix du marché. La puissance installée représente le nombre de chevaux-vapeur de tous les moteurs primaires, plus celui des moteurs électriques actionnés par de l'électricité achetée.

## 1. THE GROSS DOMESTIC PRODUCT
## LE PRODUIT INTÉRIEUR BRUT

Million quetzales                                                    Millions de quetzales

## A. Expenditure on the Gross Domestic Product at Market Prices —
### Dépenses relatives au produit intérieur brut aux prix du marché

| Item of data and year<br>Rubrique et année | Total | Consumption<br>Consommation | | Gross<br>Domestic Capital<br>Formation<br>Formation brute de<br>capital intérieur | Net exports of goods and services<br>Exportations nettes de biens et de services | |
|---|---|---|---|---|---|---|
| | | Total | Government<br>Etat | | Exports<br>less imports<br>Exportations<br>moins<br>importations | Exports<br>Exportations |
| *a. At Current Prices — Aux prix courants* | | | | | | |
| **Absolute figures — Chiffres absolus** | | | | | | |
| 1950 | 420.9 | 373.6 | 53.2 | 40.1 | 7.2 | 83.9 |
| 1951 | 443.4 | 398.4 | 41.9 | 45.5 | −0.5 | 89.2 |
| 1952 | 449.7 | 401.4 | 57.5 | 33.1 | 15.2 | 99.1 |
| 1953 | 471.6 | 408.6 | 53.7 | 41.4 | 21.6 | 112.3 |
| 1954 | 502.3 | 449.9 | 59.7 | 45.2 | 7.2 | 108.4 |
| 1955 | 568.8 | 507.9 | 61.1 | 60.0 | 0.9 | 112.5 |
| 1956 | 628.3 | 549.5 | 70.2 | 93.6 | −14.8 | 132.8 |
| 1957 | 652.5 | 588.6 | 81.7 | 97.5 | −33.6 | 126.3 |
| 1958 | 647.0 | 592.1 | 79.1 | 97.4 | −42.5 | 121.6 |
| 1959 | 659.1 | 600.6 | 89.0 | 84.1 | −25.6 | 122.5 |
| 1960 | 684.7 | 622.4 | 88.1 | 81.7 | −19.4 | 132.8 |
| 1961 | 690.9 | 633.7 | 97.2 | 74.7 | −17.5 | 128.7 |
| **Percentage distribution of average annual expenditure — Distribution en pourcentage des dépenses annuelles moyennes** | | | | | | |
| 1950−1960 | 100.0 | 89.6 | 12.0 | 11.7 | −1.3 | 20.2 |
| 1950 | 100.0 | 88.8 | 12.6 | 9.5 | 1.7 | 19.9 |
| 1953 | 100.0 | 86.6 | 11.4 | 8.8 | 4.6 | 23.8 |
| 1954 | 100.0 | 89.6 | 11.9 | 9.0 | 1.4 | 21.6 |
| 1958 | 100.0 | 91.5 | 12.2 | 15.1 | −6.6 | 18.8 |
| 1960 | 100.0 | 90.9 | 12.9 | 11.9 | −2.8 | 19.4 |
| *b. At Prices of 1950 — Aux prix de 1950* | | | | | | |
| **Absolute figures — Chiffres absolus** | | | | | | |
| 1950 | 420.9 | 373.6 | 53.2 | 40.1 | 7.2 | 83.9 |
| 1951 | 411.0 | 374.7 | 39.8 | 40.8 | −4.5 | 76.2 |
| 1952 | 440.4 | 402.2 | 55.1 | 29.7 | 8.5 | 85.9 |
| 1953 | 448.5 | 398.8 | 51.2 | 36.0 | 13.7 | 98.2 |
| 1954 | 433.1 | 409.1 | 54.3 | 39.0 | −15.0 | 78.5 |
| 1955 | 502.4 | 469.1 | 57.6 | 48.4 | −15.1 | 87.8 |
| 1956 | 542.9 | 513.1 | 66.3 | 69.6 | −39.8 | 91.6 |
| 1957 | 564.8 | 536.8 | 77.7 | 71.1 | −43.1 | 95.6 |
| 1958 | 596.2 | 548.8 | 74.4 | 71.5 | −24.1 | 116.1 |
| 1959 | 638.3 | 562.7 | 83.1 | 60.4 | 15.2 | 140.3 |
| 1960 | 667.3 | 588.6 | 83.2 | 58.6 | 20.1 | 148.2 |
| 1961 | 675.6 | 597.6 | 93.0 | 53.8 | 24.2 | 153.8 |
| **Percentage distribution of average annual expenditure — Distribution en pourcentage des dépenses annuelles moyennes** | | | | | | |
| 1950−1960 | 100.0 | 91.4 | 12.3 | 10.0 | −1.4 | 19.4 |
| 1950 | 100.0 | 88.8 | 12.6 | 9.5 | 1.7 | 19.9 |
| 1953 | 100.0 | 88.9 | 11.4 | 8.0 | 3.1 | 21.9 |
| 1954 | 100.0 | 94.4 | 12.5 | 9.0 | −3.4 | 18.1 |
| 1958 | 100.0 | 92.0 | 12.5 | 12.0 | −4.0 | 19.5 |
| 1960 | 100.0 | 88.2 | 12.5 | 8.8 | 3.0 | 22.2 |
| **Average annual rate of growth — Taux annuel moyen d'accroissement** | | | | | | |
| 1950−1960 | 4.7 | 4.6 | 4.6 | 3.9 | . | 5.9 |
| 1950−1953 | 2.2 | 2.2 | −1.3 | −3.5 | . | 5.4 |
| 1954−1958 | 8.3 | 7.6 | 8.2 | 16.4 | . | 10.3 |
| 1958−1960 | 5.8 | 3.5 | 5.7 | −9.4 | . | 13.0 |

## B. The Gross Domestic Product at Market Prices According to Origin
### Origine par secteur d'activité du produit intérieur brut aux prix du marché

Million quetzales                                                                                  Millions de quetzales

| Item of data and year Rubrique et année | Total | Agricultural sector Secteur agricole | Industrial Sector — Secteur Industriel | | | | Transportation and communication Transport et communication | Other sectors Autres secteurs |
|---|---|---|---|---|---|---|---|---|
| | | | Total | Mining and Manufacturing Industries extractives et manufacturières | Construction Bâtiments et travaux publics | Electricity, gas and water Electricité, gaz et eau | | |
| ISIC — CITI | 0–9 | 0 | 1–5 | 1–3 | 4 | 5 | 7 | 6, 8–9 |
| At Current Prices — Aux prix courants | | | | | | | | |
| Absolute figures — Chiffres absolus | | | | | | | | |
| 1956............ | 628.3 | 235.1 | 128.5 | 101.8 | 23.0 | 3.7 | 35.5 | 229.2 |
| 1957............ | 652.5 | 219.2 | 145.2 | 112.2 | 28.8 | 4.2 | 38.7 | 249.4 |
| 1958............ | 647.0 | 210.2 | 157.1 | 124.9 | 27.3 | 4.9 | 42.5 | 237.2 |
| 1959............ | 659.1 | 212.0 | 158.1 | 128.8 | 23.1 | 6.2 | 45.3 | 243.7 |
| 1960............ | 684.7 | 213.1 | 163.3 | 130.0 | 27.2 | 6.1 | 48.2 | 260.1 |
| 1961............ | 690.9 | 220.9 | 172.3 | 139.1 | 26.3 | 6.9 | 52.2 | 245.5 |
| Percentage distribution according to sector— Distribution en pourcentage per secteur | | | | | | | | |
| 1958............ | 100.0 | 32.5 | 24.2 | 19.3 | 4.2 | 0.7 | 6.6 | 36.7 |
| 1960............ | 100.0 | 31.1 | 23.8 | 19.0 | 3.9 | 0.9 | 7.1 | 38.0 |

## 2. INDEX NUMBERS OF INDUSTRIAL PRODUCTION
## INDICES DE LA PRODUCTION INDUSTRIELLE

### A. Selected Divisions of Industrial Activity
### Quelques branches de l'activité industrielle

| Period Période | Total | Manufacturing [1] Industries manufacturières [1] | Electricity Electricité |
|---|---|---|---|
| ISIC — CITI | 2–3, 511 | 2–3 | 511 |
| a. Indexes — Indices (1958 = 100) | | | |
| 1948............ | 65 | 68 | 45 |
| 1949............ | 66 | 69 | 41 |
| 1950............ | 69 | 72 | 46 |
| 1951............ | 68 | 70 | 52 |
| 1952............ | 72 | 74 | 56 |
| 1953............ | 71 | 73 | 61 |
| 1954............ | 72 | 73 | 64 |
| 1955............ | 76 | 76 | 70 |
| 1956............ | 82 | 83 | 76 |
| 1957............ | 92 | 92 | 87 |
| 1958............ | 100 | 100 | 100 |
| 1959............ | 106 | 103 | 128 |
| 1960............ | 106 | 103 | 124 |
| 1961............ | 112 | 108 | 141 |
| b. Average Annual Rate of Change — Taux annuel moyen de variation | | | |
| 1950–1960...... | 4.4 | 3.6 | 10.4 |
| 1948–1953...... | 1.8 | 1.4 | 6.3 |
| 1954–1958...... | 8.6 | 8.2 | 11.8 |
| 1958–1960...... | 3.0 | 1.5 | 11.4 |

[1] See footnotes at end of table.

[1] Voir les notes, au bas du tableau.

## B. The Major Groups of Manufacturing

## Les classes de la branche Industries manufacturières

| Period<br>Période | Manu-<br>facturing [1]<br><br>Industries<br>manufac-<br>turières [1] | Food,<br>beverages<br>and<br>tobacco<br><br>Industries<br>alimen-<br>taires,<br>boissons,<br>tabac | Textiles | Clothing,<br>footwear<br>and<br>made-up<br>textiles<br><br>Articles<br>d'habil-<br>lement,<br>chaussures<br>et<br>ouvrages<br>en tissu | Wood<br>products<br><br>Bois | Leather<br>and<br>leather<br>products<br>except<br>wearing<br>apparel<br><br>Cuir et<br>articles<br>en cuir,<br>à l'exclu-<br>sion<br>des<br>articles<br>d'habil-<br>lement | Chemicals<br>and<br>chemical<br>products<br><br>Produits<br>chi-<br>miques | Non-<br>metallic<br>mineral<br>products<br><br>Produits<br>minéraux<br>non<br>métal-<br>liques |
|---|---|---|---|---|---|---|---|---|
| ISIC— CITI | 2–3 | 20–22 | 23 | 24 | 25 | 29 | 31 | 33 |

### a. Indexes — Indices (1958 = 100)

| | | | | | | | | |
|---|---|---|---|---|---|---|---|---|
| 1948............... | 68 | 78 | − 86 − | − 41 − | − 67 − | − 92 − | − 38 − | 32 |
| 1949............... | 69 | 80 | 74 | 40 | 66 | 85 | 60 | 31 |
| 1950............... | 72 | 84 | 74 | 40 | 68 | 91 | 58 | 35 |
| 1951............... | 70 | 84 | 58 | 35 | 65 | 98 | 59 | 45 |
| 1952............... | 74 | 86 | 76 | 40 | 59 | 95 | 63 | 45 |
| 1953............... | 73 | 82 | 68 | 42 | 53 | 89 | 66 | 50 |
| 1954............... | 73 | 83 | 75 | 41 | 58 | 101 | 61 | 49 |
| 1955............... | 76 | 84 | 71 | 46 | 92 | 82 | 64 | 61 |
| 1956............... | 83 | 91 | 79 | 49 | 121 | 96 | 66 | 64 |
| 1957............... | 92 | 100 | 86 | 64 | 109 | 88 | 83 | 75 |
| 1958............... | 100 | 100 | 100 | 100 | 100 | 100 | 100 | 100 |
| 1959............... | 103 | 106 | 89 | 97 | 97 | 95 | 134 | 93 |
| 1960............... | 103 | 104 | 94 | 95 | 73 | 125 | 160 | 91 |
| 1961............... | 108 | 108 | 108 | 85 | 80 | 128 | 177 | 98 |

### b. Average Annual Rate of Change — Taux annuel moyen de variation

| | | | | | | | | |
|---|---|---|---|---|---|---|---|---|
| 1950–1960........ | 3.6 | 2.2 | 2.4 | 9.0 | 0.7 | 3.2 | 10.7 | 10.0 |
| 1948–1953........ | 1.4 | 1.0 | −4.6 | 0.5 | −4.6 | −0.7 | 11.7 | 9.3 |
| 1954–1958........ | 8.2 | 4.8 | 7.5 | 25.0 | 14.6 | −0.3 | 13.1 | 19.5 |
| 1958–1960........ | 1.5 | 2.0 | −3.0 | −2.5 | −14.6 | 11.8 | 26.5 | −4.6 |

[1] Excludes Furniture (ISIC major group 26), Paper and Paper Products (ISIC major group 27), Printing and Publishing (ISIC major group 28), Rubber Products (ISIC major group 30), Basic Metals (ISIC major group 34), Metal Products (ISIC major groups 35–38), and Other Manufacturing (ISIC major group 39).

[1] Non compris Industrie du meuble (CITI classe 26), Papier et articles en papier (CITI classe 27), Imprimerie et édition (CITI classe 28), Ouvrages en caoutchouc (CITI classe 30), Métallurgie de base (CITI classe 34), Ouvrages en métaux (CITI classes 35–38) et Autres industries manufacturières (CITI classe 39).

## 3. INDEX NUMBERS OF INDUSTRIAL EMPLOYMENT, MANUFACTURING AND ELECTRICITY; GUATEMALA CITY

### INDICES DE L'EMPLOI INDUSTRIEL, INDUSTRIES MANUFACTURIERES ET ELECTRICITE; LA VILLE DE GUATEMALA

| Period / Période | Manufacturing and electricity [1] / Industries manufacturières et électricité [1] | Food, beverages and tobacco / Industries alimentaires, boissons, tabac | Textiles | Clothing, footwear and made-up textiles / Articles d'habillement, chaussures et ouvrages en tissu | Wood products and furniture / Bois et meubles | Printing and publishing / Imprimerie et édition | Leather and leather products except wearing apparel / Cuir et articles en cuir, à l'exclusion des articles d'habillement | Chemicals and rubber and chemical products / Produits chimiques et ouvrages en caoutchouc | Non-metallic mineral products / Produits minéraux non métalliques | Basic metals and metal products / Métallurgie de base et ouvrages en métaux | Electricity / Electricité |
|---|---|---|---|---|---|---|---|---|---|---|---|
| ISIC — CITI | 2-3, 511 | 20-22 | 23 | 24 | 25-26 | 28 | 29 | 30-31 | 33 | 34-38 | 511 |

*a.* Indexes — Indices (1958 = 100)

| | | | | | | | | | | | |
|---|---|---|---|---|---|---|---|---|---|---|---|
| 1952 | 96 | 112 | 96 | 96 | 98 | 81 | 96 | 105 | 72 | 99 | 70 |
| 1953 | 93 | 100 | 107 | 86 | 96 | 78 | 66 | 111 | 79 | 87 | 69 |
| 1954 | 90 | 91 | 108 | 87 | 84 | 80 | 94 | 105 | 79 | 82 | 74 |
| 1955 | 89 | 91 | 97 | 87 | 86 | 84 | 94 | 99 | 84 | 81 | 80 |
| 1956 | 93 | 98 | 87 | 92 | 90 | 87 | 102 | 95 | 98 | 86 | 89 |
| 1957 | 100 | 100 | 92 | 99 | 102 | 102 | 102 | 106 | 104 | 94 | 87 |
| 1958 | 100 | 100 | 100 | 100 | 100 | 100 | 100 | 100 | 100 | 100 | 100 |
| 1959 | 102 | 111 | 105 | 98 | 95 | 102 | 104 | 100 | 98 | 104 | 107 |
| 1960 | 103 | 112 | 105 | 112 | 96 | 99 | 107 | 100 | 89 | 108 | 99 |
| 1961 | 105 | 110 | 119 | 115 | 92 | 104 | 102 | 111 | 85 | 101 | 98 |

*b.* Average Annual Rate of Change — Taux annuel moyen de variation

| | | | | | | | | | | | |
|---|---|---|---|---|---|---|---|---|---|---|---|
| 1954 – 1958 | 2.7 | 2.4 | −1.9 | 3.5 | 4.4 | 5.7 | 1.6 | −1.2 | 6.1 | 5.1 | 7.8 |
| 1958 – 1960 | 1.5 | 5.8 | 2.5 | 5.8 | −2.0 | −0.5 | 3.4 | — | −5.7 | 3.9 | −0.5 |

[1] Excludes Paper and Paper Products (ISIC Major Group 27) and Other Manufacturing (ISIC Major Group 39).

[1] Non compris Papier et articles en papier (CITI classe 27) et Autres industries manufacturières (CITI classe 39).

## 4. CHARACTERISTICS OF SELECTED INDUSTRIAL ESTABLISHMENTS WITH 5 OR MORE MANUAL WORKERS

### CARACTERISTIQUES DE QUELQUES ETABLISSEMENTS INDUSTRIELS COMPTANT CINQ TRAVAILLEURS MANUELS OU PLUS

**1946**

Number of establishments in units; value added in million Quetzales; number of engaged, employees and operatives in thousands; capacity of installed power equipment in thousand horsepower; value added per engaged in thousand Quetzales; capacity of installed power equipment per engaged in horsepower.

Nombre d'établissements en unités; valeur ajoutée en millions de quetzales; nombre de personnes occupées, de salariés et d'ouvriers en milliers; puissance installée en milliers de chevaux-vapeur; valeur ajoutée par personne occupée en milliers de quetzales; puissance installée par personne occupée en chevaux-vapeur.

### A. Selected Divisions of Industrial Activity — Quelques branches de l'activité industrielle

| Item of data | All industrial activity / Toutes industries | Mining / Industries extractives | Manufacturing [1] / Industries manufacturières [1] | Electricity and gas / Electricité et gaz | Rubrique | Item of data | All industrial activity / Toutes industries | Mining / Industries extractives | Manufacturing / Industries manufacturières | Electricity and gas / Electricité et gaz | Rubrique |
|---|---|---|---|---|---|---|---|---|---|---|---|
| ISIC | 1-3, 511-512 | 1 | 2-3 | 511-512 | CITI | ISIC | 1-3, 511-512 | 1 | 2-3 | 511-512 | CITI |
| | *a.* Absolute Figures — Chiffres absolus | | | | | | *b.* Structure | | | | |
| Number of establishments | 694 | 13 | 677 | 4 | Nombre d'établissements | Distribution in percent of: | | | | | Distribution en pourcentage: |
| Value added | 23.0 | 0.2 | 21.6 | 1.2 | Valeur ajoutée | Value added | 100.0 | 0.8 | 93.9 | 5.3 | Valeur ajoutée |
| Number of engaged (XII.1946) | 20.7 | 0.6 | 19.6 | 0.5 | Nombre de personnes occupées (XII.1946) | Number of engaged | 100.0 | 2.8 | 94.7 | 2.5 | Nombre de personnes occupées Par personne occupée: |
| Number of employees (XII.1946) | 19.7 | 0.6 | 18.6 | 0.5 | Nombre de salariés (XII.1946) | Per person engaged: Value added | 1.1 | 0.3 | 1.1 | 2.4 | Valeur ajoutée |
| Number of operatives (XII.1946) | 17.3 | 0.6 | 16.3 | 0.4 | Nombre d'ouvriers (XII.1946) | Capacity of installed power equipment | ... | 1.17 | 0.62 | ... | Puissance installée |
| Capacity of installed power equipment | ... | 0.7 | 12.2 | ... | Puissance installée | Employees as a percent of engaged | 95.2 | 100.0 | 94.9 | 100.0 | Salariés en pourcentage des personnes occupées |
| | | | | | | Operatives as a percent of employees | 87.8 | 100.0 | 87.6 | 80.0 | Ouvriers en pourcentage des salariés |

[1] Excludes sugar refineries.

[1] Non compris les sucreries.

# GUATEMALA

## B. The Major Groups of Mining — Les classes de la branche Industries extractives

| Item of data | All mining — Toutes industries extractives | Metal mining — Extraction des minerais métalliques | Other mining — Divers | Rubrique | Item of data | All mining — Toutes industries extractives | Metal mining — Extraction des minerais métalliques | Other mining — Divers | Rubrique |
|---|---|---|---|---|---|---|---|---|---|
| ISIC | 1 | 12 | 14-19 | CITI | ISIC | 1 | 12 | 14-19 | CITI |
| | **a. Absolute Figures — Chiffres absolus** | | | | | **b. Structure** | | | |
| Number of establishments | 13 | 3 | 10 | Nombre d'établissements | Distribution in percent of: Value added | 100.0 | — | 100.0 | Distribution en pourcentage: Valeur ajoutée |
| Value added | 0.2 | — | 0.2 | Valeur ajoutée | Number of engaged | 100.0 | 16.7 | 83.3 | Nombre de personnes occupées |
| Number of engaged (XII.1946) | 0.6 | 0.1 | 0.5 | Nombre de personnes occupées (XII.1946) | Per person engaged: Value added | 0.3 | — | 0.4 | Par personne occupée: Valeur ajoutée |
| Number of employees (XII.1946) | 0.6 | 0.1 | 0.5 | Nombre de salariés (XII.1946) | Capacity of installed power equipment | 1.17 | — | 1.40 | Puissance installée |
| Number of operatives (XII.1946) | 0.6 | 0.1 | 0.5 | Nombre d'ouvriers (XII.1946) | Employee as a percent of engaged | 100.0 | 100.0 | 100.0 | Salariés en pourcentage des personnes occupées |
| Capacity of installed power equipment | 0.7 | — | 0.7 | Puissance installée | Operatives as a percent of employees | 100.0 | 100.0 | 100.0 | Ouvriers en pourcentage des salariés |

## C. The Major Groups of Manufacturing — Les classes de la branche Industries manufacturières

| Item of data | Manufacturing — Industries manufacturières | Food beverages and tobacco[1] — Industries alimentaires, boissons, tabac[1] | Textiles | Clothing, footwear and made-up textiles — Articles d'habillement, chaussures et ouvrages en tissu | Wood products and furniture — Bois et meubles | Paper and paper products — Papier et ouvrages en papier | Printing and publishing — Imprimerie et édition | Leather and leather products except wearing apparel — Cuir et articles en cuir, à l'exclusion des articles d'habillement | Rubber products — Ouvrages en caoutchouc | Chemicals and chemical products — Produits chimiques | Non-metallic mineral products — Produits minéraux non métalliques | Basic metals — Métallurgie de base | Metal products — Ouvrages en métaux | Other manufacturing — Autres industries manufacturières | Rubrique |
|---|---|---|---|---|---|---|---|---|---|---|---|---|---|---|---|
| ISIC | 2-3 | 20-22 | 23 | 24 | 25-26 | 27 | 28 | 29 | 30 | 31 | 33 | 34 | 35-38 | 39 | CITI |
| **a. Absolute Figures — Chiffres absolus** | | | | | | | | | | | | | | | |
| Number of establishments | 677 | 167 | 74 | 177 | 76 | 4 | 21 | 35 | 2 | 24 | 44 | — | 42 | 11 | Nombre d'établissements |
| Value added | 21.6 | 13.0 | 2.8 | 1.1 | 1.3 | — | 0.7 | 0.3 | 0.2 | 0.8 | 0.9 | — | 0.4 | 0.1 | Valeur ajoutée |
| Number of engaged (XII.1946) | 19.6 | 5.3 | 4.3 | 3.0 | 2.2 | — | 0.8 | 0.5 | 0.2 | 0.9 | 1.5 | — | 0.7 | 0.2 | Nombre de personnes occupées (XII.1946) |
| Number of employees (XII.1946) | 18.6 | 5.2 | 4.2 | 2.3 | 2.1 | — | 0.8 | 0.5 | 0.2 | 0.9 | 1.5 | — | 0.7 | 0.2 | Nombre de salariés (XII.1946) |
| Number of operatives (XII.1946) | 16.3 | 4.3 | 4.0 | 2.0 | 1.8 | — | 0.7 | 0.4 | 0.2 | 0.8 | 1.3 | — | 0.7 | 0.1 | Nombre d'ouvriers (XII.1946) |
| Capacity of installed power equipment | 12.2 | 3.2 | 1.5 | 0.2 | 2.8 | — | 0.2 | 0.6 | 0.2 | 1.0 | 2.2 | — | 0.2 | 0.1 | Puissance installée |
| **b. Structure** | | | | | | | | | | | | | | | |
| Distribution in percent of: Value added | 100.0 | 60.1 | 13.0 | 5.1 | 6.0 | — | 3.3 | 1.3 | 1.0 | 3.7 | 4.1 | — | 1.9 | 0.5 | Répartition en pourcentage: De la valeur ajoutée |
| Number of engaged | 100.0 | 27.0 | 21.9 | 15.3 | 11.3 | — | 4.0 | 2.6 | 1.0 | 4.6 | 7.7 | — | 3.5 | 1.1 | Du nombre de personnes occupées |
| Value added per person engaged | 1.1 | 2.4 | 0.6 | 0.4 | 0.6 | — | 0.9 | 0.6 | 1.0 | 0.9 | 0.6 | — | 0.6 | 0.5 | Valeur ajoutée par personne occupée |
| Capacity of installed power equipment per person engaged | 0.62 | 0.60 | 0.35 | 0.07 | 1.27 | — | 0.25 | 1.20 | 1.00 | 1.11 | 1.47 | — | 0.28 | 0.50 | Puissance installée par personne occupée |
| Employees as a percent of engaged | 94.9 | 98.1 | 97.7 | 76.7 | 95.4 | — | 100.0 | 100.0 | 100.0 | 100.0 | 100.0 | — | 100.0 | 100.0 | Salariés en pourcentage des personnes occupées |
| Operatives as a percent of employees | 87.6 | 82.7 | 95.2 | 87.0 | 85.7 | — | 87.5 | 80.0 | 100.0 | 88.9 | 86.7 | — | 100.0 | 50.0 | Ouvriers en pourcentage des salariés |

[1] Excludes sugar refineries.

[1] Non compris les sucreries.

# 5. THE CHARACTERISTICS OF MANUFACTURING ESTABLISHMENTS WITH 3 OR MORE MANUAL WORKERS
## CARACTERISTIQUES DES ETABLISSEMENTS MANUFACTURIERS COMPTANT TROIS TRAVAILLEURS MANUELS OU PLUS
### 1953, 1958

Number of establishments in units; value added and wages and salaries in million Quetzales; number of engaged, employees and operatives in thousands; capacity of installed power equipment in thousand horsepower; value added per engaged in thousand Quetzales; capacity of installed power equipment per engaged in horsepower.

Nombre d'établissements en unités; valeur ajoutée et traitements et salaires en millions de quetzales; nombre de personnes occupées, de salariés et d'ouvriers en milliers; puissance installée en milliers de chevaux-vapeur; valeur ajoutée par personne occupée en milliers de quetzales; puissance installée par personne occupée en chevaux-vapeur.

| Year and item of data | Manu-facturing Industries manufac-turières | Food, beverages and tobacco[1] Industries alimen-taires, boissons, tabac[1] | Textiles | Clothing, footwear and made-up textiles Articles d'habil-lement, chaussures et ouvrages en tissu | Wood products and furniture Bois et meubles | Paper and paper products Papier et ouvrages en papier | Printing and publish-ing Imprimerie et édition | Leather and leather products except wearing apparel Cuir et articles en cuir, à l'exclu-sion des articles d'habil-lement | Rubber products Ouvrages en caout-chouc | Chemicals and chemical products Produits chi-miques | Non-metallic mineral products Produits minéraux non métal-liques | Basic metals Métal-lurgie de base | Metal products Ouvrages en métaux | Other manu-factur-ing Autres in-dustries manufac-turières | Année et rubrique |
|---|---|---|---|---|---|---|---|---|---|---|---|---|---|---|---|
| ISIC | 2–3 | 20–22 | 23 | 24 | 25–26 | 27 | 28 | 29 | 30 | 31 | 33 | 34 | 35–38 | 39 | CITI |

| | | | | | | | | *a. Absolute Figures — Chiffres absolus* | | | | | | | |
|---|---|---|---|---|---|---|---|---|---|---|---|---|---|---|---|
| **1953** | | | | | | | | | | | | | | | **1953** |
| Number of establishments | 1 032 | 313 | 45 | 218 | 124 | 3 | 32 | 53 | 5 | 54 | 76 | 9 | 89 | 11 | Nombre d'établissements |
| Value added | 25.5 | 11.4 | 2.5 | 2.6 | 1.6 | — | 1.1 | 0.4 | — | 2.5 | 1.4 | 0.9 | 1.0 | 0.1 | Valeur ajoutée |
| Number of engaged (As of 16.XI.1953) | 19.7 | 6.3 | 2.6 | 2.9 | 2.1 | — | 0.8 | 0.5 | — | 1.3 | 1.5 | 0.5 | 1.1 | 0.1 | Nombre de personnes occupées (au 16.XI.1953) |
| Number of employees (As of 16.XI.1953) | 18.6 | 6.0 | 2.5 | 2.3 | 2.0 | — | 0.8 | 0.5 | — | 1.3 | 1.5 | 0.5 | 1.1 | 0.1 | Nombre de salariés (au 16.XI.1953) |
| Number of operatives (As of 16.XI.1953) | 15.5 | 4.6 | 2.3 | 1.9 | 1.8 | — | 0.7 | 0.4 | — | 1.1 | 1.2 | 0.5 | 0.9 | 0.1 | Nombre d'ouvriers (au 16.XI.1953) |
| Capacity of installed power equipment (As of 31.XII.1953) | 31.1 | 11.7 | 3.6 | 0.5 | 4.4 | 1.9 | 0.7 | 0.8 | — | 1.9 | 4.1 | 0.5 | 1.0 | — | Puissance installée (au 31.XII.1953) |
| **1958** | | | | | | | | | | | | | | | **1958** |
| Number of establishments | 2 140 | 587 | 157 | 506 | 256 | 7 | 81 | 82 | 11 | 80 | 145 | 4 | 198 | 26 | Nombre d'établissements |
| Value added | 43.4 | 21.6 | 3.7 | 3.0 | 2.8 | 0.3 | 1.9 | 1.2 | 0.3 | 2.5 | 3.9 | — | 1.7 | 0.5 | Valeur ajoutée |
| Number of engaged (Average during the year) | 27.6 | 8.4 | 3.5 | 3.9 | 3.2 | 0.1 | 1.5 | 0.8 | 0.3 | 1.5 | 2.2 | — | 1.9 | 0.3 | Nombre de personnes occupées (moyenne pendant l'année) |
| Wages and salaries paid to employees | 16.7 | 5.7 | 1.8 | 1.8 | 1.6 | 0.1 | 1.2 | 0.4 | 0.2 | 1.2 | 1.6 | — | 1.0 | 0.1 | Traitements et salaires payés aux salariés |
| Operatives: Number (XI.1958) | 21.2 | 5.9 | 3.0 | 2.8 | 2.6 | 0.1 | 1.2 | 0.6 | 0.2 | 1.2 | 1.8 | — | 1.6 | 0.2 | Ouvriers: Nombre (XI.1958) |
| Wages and salaries | 11.8 | 3.3 | 1.5 | 1.3 | 1.3 | 0.1 | 1.0 | 0.3 | 0.1 | 0.7 | 1.2 | — | 0.9 | 0.1 | Traitements et salaires |

| | | | | | | | | *b. Structure* | | | | | | | |
|---|---|---|---|---|---|---|---|---|---|---|---|---|---|---|---|
| **1953** Distribution in percent of: | | | | | | | | | | | | | | | **1953** Répartition en pour-centage: |
| Value added | 100.0 | 44.7 | 9.8 | 10.2 | 6.2 | — | 4.3 | 1.6 | — | 9.8 | 5.5 | 3.5 | 4.0 | 0.4 | De la valeur ajoutée |
| Number of engaged | 100.0 | 31.9 | 13.2 | 14.7 | 10.7 | — | 4.1 | 2.5 | — | 6.6 | 7.6 | 2.6 | 5.5 | 0.6 | Du nombre de personnes occupées |
| Value added per person engaged | 1.3 | 1.8 | 1.0 | 0.9 | 0.8 | — | 1.4 | 0.8 | — | 1.9 | 0.9 | 1.8 | 0.9 | 1.0 | Valeur ajoutée par personne occupée |
| Capacity of installed power equipment per person engaged | 1.58 | 1.86 | 1.38 | 0.17 | 2.10 | — | 0.88 | 1.60 | — | 1.46 | 2.73 | 1.00 | 0.91 | — | Puissance installée par personne occupée |
| Employees as a percent of engaged | 94.4 | 95.2 | 96.2 | 79.3 | 95.2 | — | 100.0 | 100.0 | — | 100.0 | 100.0 | 100.0 | 100.0 | 100.0 | Salariés en pourcentage des personnes occupées |
| Operatives as a percent of employees | 83.3 | 76.7 | 92.0 | 82.6 | 90.0 | — | 87.5 | 80.0 | — | 84.6 | 80.0 | 100.0 | 81.8 | 100.0 | Ouvriers en pourcentage des salariés |
| **1958** Distribution in percent of: | | | | | | | | | | | | | | | **1958** Distribution en pour-centage de: |
| Value added | 100.0 | 49.7 | 8.5 | 7.0 | 6.4 | 0.7 | 4.4 | 2.7 | 0.7 | 5.8 | 9.0 | — | 3.9 | 1.2 | Valeur ajoutée |
| Number of engaged | 100.0 | 30.4 | 12.7 | 14.1 | 11.6 | 0.4 | 5.4 | 2.9 | 1.1 | 5.4 | 8.0 | — | 6.9 | 1.1 | Nombre de personnes occupées |
| Value added per person engaged | 1.6 | 2.6 | 1.0 | 0.8 | 0.9 | 3.0 | 1.3 | 1.5 | 1.0 | 1.7 | 1.8 | ... | 0.9 | 1.7 | Valeur ajoutée par personne occupée |
| Value added per unit of wages and salaries | 2.60 | 3.79 | 2.06 | 1.67 | 1.75 | 3.00 | 1.58 | 3.00 | 1.50 | 2.08 | 2.44 | ... | 1.70 | 5.00 | Valeur ajoutée par traitements et salaires unitaires |

[1] Excludes coffee beneficiaries.

[1] Non compris l'épluchage du café.

# HONDURAS

## Gross Domestic Product and the Gross Domestic Fixed Capital Formation

Estimates of the expenditure on and the industrial origin of the gross domestic product, and of the industrial composition of the gross fixed capital formation, are presented in Table 1. This table has been compiled from data supplied by the Departamento de Estudios Económicos, Banco Central de Honduras, Tegucigalpa D.C. in response to the United Nations national accounts questionnaire. The official estimates are published by the Banco Central in *Cuentas Nacionales 1948, 1950-1960*. Further information concerning methods and definitions may be found in *Cuentas Nacionales 1925-1955*.

## The Characteristics and Structure of Industrial Activity

The data shown in Table 2 are derived from industrial censuses carried out for the years 1950, 1953 and 1957. The figures for 1950 are from *Compendio Estadístico Centroamericano*, published by the Subcommittee on Statistical Co-ordination of the Committee on Economic Co-operation in Central America, Economic Commission for Latin America of the United Nations, Mexico, August 1957. The 1953 figures are taken from *Estadísticas Industriales, 1953* published by the Dirección General de Censos y Estadísticas, Tegucigalpa, September 1956. The figures for 1957 are from *Invesigación Industrial 1956-1957* published by the Dirección General de Censos y Estadísticas, Tegucigalpa, D.C.

The Censuses covered, by means of separate inquiries, establishments with five or more persons engaged and smaller establishments having at least one paid worker, using machinery or tools (in the case of the 1950 Census only) and producing goods for the market having a value of at least 2,000 Lempiras during the year. The data relating to the smaller establishments are based partly on estimates because of incomplete returns, particularly from establishments in rural areas. Even then data were not included on certain kinds of industry which are largely carried on in rural areas—for example, the manufacture of earthenware or rope.

The data are not strictly comparable between the Censuses due to a slight change in definition of the reporting unit and differences in the treatment of some industries—for example, coffee beneficiating on farms. As far as is known the definitions of the items of data are consistent between the Censuses and conform to the International Standards in Basic Industrial Statistics.

## Produit intérieur brut et formation brute de capital fixe intérieur

Les estimations des dépenses imputées au produit intérieur brut, des composantes du produit intérieur brut et du capital brut fixe formé, ventilées suivant le secteur d'activité industrielle, sont reproduites au tableau 1. Ce tableau a été construit à partir de données fournies par le Departamento de Estudios Económicos, Banco Central de Honduras, Tegucigalpa, D.C. en réponse au questionnaire de l'O.N.U. relatif aux comptes nationaux. Les estimations officielles ont été publiées par la Banco Central dans *Cuentas Nacionales 1948, 1950-1960*. Plus amples renseignements concernant les méthodes et définitions adoptées peuvent être trouvés dans *Cuentas Nacionales 1925-1955*.

## Caractéristiques et structure de l'activité industrielle

Les données du tableau 2 sont tirées des recensements industriels de 1950, 1953 et 1957. Les chiffres de 1950 proviennent du *Compendio Estadístico Centroamericano* publié par le Sous-Comité de coordination statistique du Comité de coopération économique de l'Amérique centrale (Commission économique de l'O.N.U. pour l'Amérique latine), Mexico, août 1957. Les chiffres de 1953 sont tirés des *Estadísticas Industriales, 1953*, publiées par la Dirección General de Censos y Estadísticas, Tegucigalpa, septembre 1956. Les chiffres de 1957 sont tirés des *Investigación Industrial 1956-1957* publiées par la Dirección General de Censos y Estadísticas, Tegucigalpa, D.C.

Les recensements couvraient, au moyen d'enquêtes séparées, les établissements ayant 5 personnes occupées ou plus et les petits établissements ayant au moins 1 ouvrier rémunéré, qui utilisaient des machines ou des outils (dans le cas du recensement de 1950 seulement) et qui avaient produit pour la vente, au cours de l'année, des marchandises ayant une valeur d'au moins 2.000 lempiras. Les données relatives aux petits établissements sont partiellement fondées sur des estimations parce que tous les établissements, notamment dans les régions rurales, n'ont pas répondu au questionnaire. Néanmoins, on n'a pas donné de chiffres sur certains types d'activités industrielles exercées surtout dans les régions rurales — par exemple, la poterie ou la corderie.

Les données ne sont pas strictement comparables d'un recensement à l'autre par suite d'une légère modification de la définition de l'unité recensée et des différences intervenues dans l'inclusion de certaines industries — par exemple l'épluchage du café dans les exploitations agricoles. Il semblerait que les définitions des rubriques soient comparables entre les recensements et conformes aux Normes internationales relatives aux statistiques industrielles de base.

The data shown in Table 3 are derived from the part of the 1953 Census mentioned above which covered establishments engaging 5 or more persons, and the results of an industrial inquiry for 1958, which was limited to establishments engaging 5 or more persons. The 1953 data are taken from *Estadísticas Industriales, 1953,* published by the Dirección General de Censos y Estadisticas, Tegucigalpa, September 1956. The 1958 data are taken from *Investigación Industrial, 1958* published by the Dirección General de Censos y Estadísticas, December 1960. Value added is at market prices and definitions of items of data are consistent between the two censuses and conform to the International Standards in Basic Industrial Statistics.

Les données reproduites au tableau 3 sont tirées de la partie du recensement de 1953 mentionnée ci-dessus qui couvre les établissements occupant 5 personnes ou plus et de l'enquête industrielle de 1958, qui était limitée aux établissements occupant 5 personnes ou plus. Les données de 1953 sont tirées de *Estadísticas Industriales, 1953* publié par la Dirección General de Censos y Estadísticas, Tegucigalpa, septembre 1956. Les données de 1958 sont tirées de *Investigación Industrial 1958* publié par la Dirección General de Censos y Estadísticas, décembre 1960. La valeur ajoutée est évaluée aux prix du marché et les définitions des rubriques sont conformes aux Normes internationales relatives aux statistiques industrielles de base.

# HONDURAS

## 1. THE GROSS DOMESTIC PRODUCT AND GROSS DOMESTIC FIXED CAPITAL FORMATION
## LE PRODUIT INTERIEUR BRUT ET LA FORMATION BRUTE DE CAPITAL FIXE INTERIEUR

Million Lempiras / Millions de lempiras

### A. Expenditure on the Gross Domestic Product at Market Prices —
### Dépenses relatives au produit intérieur brut aux prix du marché

| Item of data and year / Rubrique et année | Total | Consumption / Consommation | | Gross Domestic Capital Formation / Formation brute de capital intérieur | | Net exports of goods and services / Exportations nettes de biens et de services | |
|---|---|---|---|---|---|---|---|
| | | Total | Government / Etat | Total | Fixed / Fixe | Exports less imports / Exportations moins importations | Exports / Exportations |
| **a. At current prices — Aux prix courants** | | | | | | | |
| **Absolute figures — Chiffres absolus** | | | | | | | |
| 1948 | 383.6 | 296.5 | 22.7 | 48.3 | 42.1 | 38.8 | 116.1 |
| 1950 | 451.8 | 353.5 | 26.8 | 56.2 | 48.8 | 42.1 | 124.2 |
| 1951 | 502.4 | 392.1 | 31.7 | 76.1 | 62.2 | 34.2 | 142.9 |
| 1952 | 514.0 | 410.9 | 34.0 | 94.8 | 83.2 | 8.3 | 138.9 |
| 1953 | 595.1 | 480.7 | 38.7 | 96.6 | 95.0 | 17.8 | 148.7 |
| 1954 | 568.0 | 497.6 | 47.5 | 76.8 | 73.2 | −6.4 | 119.5 |
| 1955 | 623.6 | 552.1 | 47.2 | 88.4 | 82.8 | −16.9 | 113.0 |
| 1956 | 665.2 | 559.3 | 65.7 | 93.9 | 83.6 | 12.0 | 156.9 |
| 1957 | 688.3 | 610.3 | 63.2 | 103.9 | 94.1 | −25.9 | 139.0 |
| 1958 | 724.9 | 637.7 | 71.9 | 96.0 | 92.0 | −8.8 | 149.6 |
| 1959 | 751.1 | 657.2 | 70.4 | 94.5 | 89.4 | −0.6 | 147.7 |
| 1960 | 755.8 | 667.7 | 73.2 | 104.8 | 95.7 | −16.7 | 136.1 |
| **Percentage distribution of average annual expenditure — Distribution en pourcentage des dépenses annuelles moyennes** | | | | | | | |
| 1948 | 100.0 | 77.3 | 5.9 | 12.6 | 11.0 | 10.1 | 30.3 |
| 1950 − 1960 | 100.0 | 85.0 | 8.3 | 14.4 | 13.2 | 0.6 | 22.2 |
| 1950 | 100.0 | 78.2 | 5.9 | 12.4 | 10.8 | 9.4 | 27.5 |
| 1953 | 100.0 | 80.8 | 6.5 | 16.2 | 16.0 | 3.0 | 25.0 |
| 1954 | 100.0 | 87.6 | 8.4 | 13.5 | 12.9 | −1.1 | 21.0 |
| 1958 | 100.0 | 88.0 | 9.9 | 13.2 | 12.7 | −1.2 | 20.6 |
| 1960 | 100.0 | 88.3 | 9.7 | 13.9 | 12.7 | −2.2 | 18.0 |
| **b. At Prices of 1948 — Aux prix de 1948** | | | | | | | |
| **Absolute figures — Chiffres absolus** | | | | | | | |
| 1948 | 383.6 | 296.5 | 22.7 | 48.3 | 42.1 | 38.8 | 116.1 |
| 1950 | 403.4 | 323.2 | 23.5 | 54.4 | 46.9 | 25.8 | 108.1 |
| 1951 | 422.6 | 337.4 | 25.9 | 69.2 | 56.4 | 16.0 | 116.0 |
| 1952 | 435.9 | 362.5 | 26.6 | 84.4 | 73.3 | −11.0 | 110.7 |
| 1953 | 464.3 | 390.0 | 29.4 | 83.6 | 81.5 | −9.3 | 113.7 |
| 1954 | 434.8 | 401.7 | 32.7 | 63.7 | 60.1 | −30.6 | 86.3 |
| 1955 | 451.9 | 415.0 | 30.9 | 71.6 | 65.4 | −34.7 | 85.5 |
| 1956 | 493.4 | 431.8 | 43.7 | 75.3 | 66.5 | −13.7 | 109.0 |
| 1957 | 526.3 | 473.9 | 40.5 | 82.5 | 73.6 | −30.1 | 106.5 |
| 1958 | 539.1 | 483.1 | 46.1 | 69.8 | 66.3 | −13.8 | 116.0 |
| 1959 | 560.8 | 492.7 | 45.2 | 68.4 | 63.8 | −0.3 | 123.1 |
| 1960 | 570.6 | 506.2 | 47.9 | 75.8 | 67.9 | −11.4 | 113.6 |
| **Percentage distribution of average annual expenditure — Distribution en pourcentage des dépenses annuelles moyennes** | | | | | | | |
| 1948 | 100.0 | 77.3 | 5.9 | 12.6 | 11.0 | 10.1 | 30.3 |
| 1950 − 1960 | 100.0 | 87.0 | 7.4 | 15.1 | 13.6 | −2.1 | 22.4 |
| 1950 | 100.0 | 80.1 | 5.8 | 13.5 | 11.6 | 6.4 | 26.8 |
| 1953 | 100.0 | 84.0 | 6.3 | 18.0 | 17.6 | −2.0 | 24.5 |
| 1954 | 100.0 | 92.4 | 7.5 | 14.6 | 13.8 | −7.0 | 19.8 |
| 1958 | 100.0 | 89.6 | 8.6 | 13.0 | 12.3 | −2.6 | 21.5 |
| 1960 | 100.0 | 88.7 | 8.4 | 13.3 | 11.9 | −2.0 | 19.9 |
| **Average annual rate of growth — Taux annuel moyen d'accroissement** | | | | | | | |
| 1948 − 1953 | 3.9 | 5.6 | 5.3 | 11.6 | 14.1 | · | −0.4 |
| 1950 − 1960 | 3.5 | 4.6 | 7.4 | 3.4 | 3.8 | · | 0.5 |
| 1950 − 1953 | 4.8 | 6.5 | 7.8 | 15.4 | 20.2 | · | 1.7 |
| 1954 − 1958 | 5.5 | 4.7 | 9.0 | 2.3 | 2.5 | · | 7.7 |
| 1958 − 1960 | 2.9 | 2.4 | 1.9 | 4.2 | 1.2 | · | −1.0 |

## B. The Gross Domestic Product at Factor Cost According to Origin
### Origine par secteur d'activité du produit intérieur brut au coût des facteurs

| Item of data and year / Rubrique et année | Total | Agricultural sector / Secteur agricole | Industrial Sector — Secteur Industriel | | | | | Transportation and communication / Transport et communication | Other sectors [1] / Autres secteurs [1] |
|---|---|---|---|---|---|---|---|---|---|
| | | | Total | Mining / Industries extractives | Manufacturing / Industries manufacturières | Construction / Bâtiments et travaux publics | Electricity, gas and water / Electricité, gaz et eau | | |
| ISIC — CITI | 0–9 | 0 | 1–5 | 1 | 2–3 | 4 | 5 | 7 | 6, 8–9 |

### a. At Current Prices — Aux prix courants

| | | | | | | | | | |
|---|---|---|---|---|---|---|---|---|---|
| **Absolute figures — Chiffres absolus** | | | | | | | | | |
| 1948 | 358.4 | 201.8 | 45.9 | 5.4 | 25.9 | 14.3 | 0.3 | 21.1 | 89.6 |
| 1950 | 420.9 | 234.4 | 58.2 | 6.1 | 34.7 | 17.0 | 0.4 | 23.8 | 104.5 |
| 1951 | 467.1 | 264.0 | 68.0 | 6.8 | 39.0 | 21.6 | 0.6 | 25.4 | 109.7 |
| 1952 | 474.7 | 249.2 | 79.3 | 7.9 | 43.9 | 26.7 | 0.8 | 27.3 | 118.9 |
| 1953 | 553.5 | 275.5 | 94.6 | 13.2 | 48.6 | 31.8 | 1.0 | 28.5 | 154.9 |
| 1954 | 527.3 | 259.7 | 81.7 | 8.5 | 46.8 | 25.0 | 1.4 | 28.8 | 157.1 |
| 1955 | 573.1 | 295.3 | 87.2 | 6.1 | 51.5 | 28.0 | 1.6 | 30.4 | 160.2 |
| 1956 | 609.6 | 290.6 | 103.0 | 5.0 | 69.0 | 27.2 | 1.8 | 31.1 | 184.9 |
| 1957 | 626.6 | 305.8 | 106.6 | 5.3 | 71.3 | 27.9 | 2.1 | 32.0 | 182.2 |
| 1958 | 664.6 | 317.7 | 112.5 | 6.0 | 73.4 | 30.7 | 2.4 | 32.8 | 201.6 |
| 1959 | 690.1 | 323.6 | 114.1 | 5.6 | 80.6 | 25.1 | 2.8 | 36.1 | 216.3 |
| 1960 | 690.3 | 306.0 | 118.0 | 7.0 | 83.7 | 24.1 | 3.2 | 37.9 | 228.4 |
| **Percentage distribution according to sector— Distribution en pourcentage par secteur** | | | | | | | | | |
| 1948 | 100.0 | 56.3 | 12.8 | 1.5 | 7.2 | 4.0 | 0.1 | 5.9 | 25.0 |
| 1950 – 1960 | 100.0 | 49.6 | 16.2 | 1.2 | 10.2 | 4.5 | 0.3 | 5.3 | 28.9 |
| 1950 | 100.0 | 55.7 | 13.8 | 1.5 | 8.2 | 4.0 | 0.1 | 5.7 | 24.8 |
| 1953 | 100.0 | 49.8 | 17.1 | 2.4 | 8.8 | 5.7 | 0.2 | 5.1 | 28.0 |
| 1954 | 100.0 | 49.2 | 15.5 | 1.6 | 8.9 | 4.7 | 0.3 | 5.5 | 29.8 |
| 1958 | 100.0 | 47.8 | 16.9 | 0.9 | 11.0 | 4.6 | 0.4 | 4.9 | 30.4 |
| 1960 | 100.0 | 44.3 | 17.1 | 1.0 | 12.1 | 3.5 | 0.5 | 5.5 | 33.1 |

### b. At Prices of 1948 — Aux prix de 1948

| | | | | | | | | | |
|---|---|---|---|---|---|---|---|---|---|
| **Absolute figures — Chiffres absolus** | | | | | | | | | |
| 1948 | 358.4 | 201.8 | 45.9 | 5.4 | 25.9 | 14.3 | 0.3 | 21.1 | 89.6 |
| 1950 | 374.9 | 199.6 | 55.7 | 6.3 | 32.6 | 16.4 | 0.4 | 22.9 | 96.7 |
| 1951 | 391.9 | 205.7 | 62.6 | 6.4 | 36.4 | 19.3 | 0.5 | 24.4 | 99.2 |
| 1952 | 400.9 | 201.8 | 72.2 | 7.7 | 40.8 | 23.1 | 0.6 | 26.2 | 100.7 |
| 1953 | 430.1 | 209.4 | 84.6 | 10.2 | 47.0 | 26.7 | 0.7 | 27.4 | 108.7 |
| 1954 | 401.3 | 190.4 | 74.7 | 9.7 | 43.2 | 20.9 | 0.9 | 27.7 | 108.5 |
| 1955 | 413.3 | 193.4 | 76.7 | 5.7 | 48.4 | 21.6 | 1.0 | 29.2 | 114.0 |
| 1956 | 449.0 | 219.5 | 80.7 | 4.2 | 52.5 | 22.9 | 1.1 | 29.9 | 118.9 |
| 1957 | 476.9 | 225.1 | 84.3 | 4.9 | 55.0 | 23.1 | 1.3 | 30.8 | 136.7 |
| 1958 | 492.7 | 228.0 | 87.9 | 5.6 | 57.8 | 23.0 | 1.5 | 31.2 | 145.6 |
| 1959 | 513.6 | 244.9 | 84.9 | 4.8 | 60.4 | 18.0 | 1.7 | 34.7 | 149.1 |
| 1960 | 519.9 | 244.1 | 87.3 | 5.5 | 63.9 | 15.9 | 2.0 | 36.4 | 152.1 |
| **Percentage distribution according to sector— Distribution en pourcentage par secteur** | | | | | | | | | |
| 1948 | 100.0 | 56.3 | 12.8 | 1.5 | 7.2 | 4.0 | 0.1 | 5.9 | 25.0 |
| 1950 – 1960 | 100.0 | 48.5 | 17.5 | 1.5 | 11.0 | 4.8 | 0.2 | 6.6 | 27.4 |
| 1950 | 100.0 | 53.2 | 14.9 | 1.7 | 8.7 | 4.4 | 0.1 | 6.1 | 25.8 |
| 1953 | 100.0 | 48.6 | 19.7 | 2.4 | 10.9 | 6.2 | 0.2 | 6.4 | 25.3 |
| 1954 | 100.0 | 47.4 | 18.6 | 2.4 | 10.8 | 5.2 | 0.2 | 6.9 | 27.1 |
| 1958 | 100.0 | 46.3 | 17.8 | 1.1 | 11.7 | 4.7 | 0.3 | 6.3 | 29.6 |
| 1960 | 100.0 | 46.9 | 16.8 | 1.1 | 12.3 | 3.0 | 0.4 | 7.0 | 29.3 |
| **Average annual rate of growth—Taux annuel moyen d'accroissement** | | | | | | | | | |
| 1948 – 1953 | 3.7 | 0.7 | 13.0 | 13.6 | 12.7 | 13.3 | 18.5 | 5.4 | 3.9 |
| 1950 – 1960 | 3.3 | 2.0 | 4.6 | −1.3 | 7.0 | −0.3 | 17.5 | 4.7 | 4.6 |
| 1950 – 1953 | 4.7 | 1.6 | 14.9 | 17.4 | 13.0 | 17.6 | 20.5 | 6.1 | 4.0 |
| 1954 – 1958 | 5.3 | 4.6 | 4.2 | −12.8 | 7.6 | 2.4 | 13.6 | 3.0 | 7.6 |
| 1958 – 1960 | 2.7 | 3.5 | −0.4 | −0.9 | 5.2 | −16.9 | 15.5 | 8.0 | 2.2 |

[1] Includes an item "statistical discrepancy" which is the difference between the gross domestic product at factor cost obtained by subtracting indirect taxes net of subsidies from the aggregate gross domestic product at market prices and the sum of the above components of gross domestic product at factor cost.

[1] Y compris les "écarts statistiques": différence entre le produit intérieur brut au coût des facteurs obtenu par soustraction des impôts indirects et addition des subventions au produit intérieur brut aux prix du marché et la somme des composantes, ci-dessus mentionnées, du produit intérieur brut au coût des facteurs.

# HONDURAS

## C. Gross Domestic Fixed Capital Formation at Market Prices According to Purchasing Sector
### La formation brute de capital fixe intérieur aux prix du marché par secteur d'acquisition

| Item of data and year / Rubrique et année | Total | Agricultural sector / Secteur agricole | Industrial Sector — Secteur Industriel Total | Mining / Industries extractives | Manufacturing / Industries manufacturières | Construction / Bâtiment et travaux publics | Electricity, gas and water / Electricité, gaz et eau | Transportation and communication / Transports et communications | Other sectors / Autres secteurs |
|---|---|---|---|---|---|---|---|---|---|
| ISIC — CITI | 0–9 | 0 | 1–5 | 1 | 2–3 | 4 | 5 | 7 | 6, 8–9 |
| *a. At Current Prices — Aux prix courants* | | | | | | | | | |
| **Absolute figures — Chiffres absolus** | | | | | | | | | |
| 1950 | 48.8 | 15.1 | 6.3 | 0.4 | 4.1 | 0.7 | 1.1 | 3.7 | 23.7 |
| 1951 | 62.2 | 20.9 | 8.6 | 0.5 | 5.0 | 1.0 | 2.1 | 6.1 | 26.6 |
| 1952 | 83.2 | 28.5 | 10.8 | 0.9 | 6.5 | 1.4 | 2.0 | 11.2 | 32.7 |
| 1953 | 95.0 | 39.7 | 10.9 | 0.6 | 6.6 | 1.5 | 2.2 | 14.1 | 30.3 |
| 1954 | 73.3 | 21.6 | 10.3 | 0.2 | 7.4 | 1.2 | 1.5 | 12.5 | 28.9 |
| 1955 | 82.8 | 22.9 | 11.7 | 0.9 | 8.2 | 1.0 | 1.6 | 11.9 | 36.3 |
| **Percentage distribution according to sector — Distribution en pourcentage par secteur** | | | | | | | | | |
| 1950–1955 | 100.0 | 33.4 | 13.2 | 0.8 | 8.5 | 1.5 | 2.4 | 13.3 | 40.1 |
| 1950 | 100.0 | 30.9 | 12.9 | 0.8 | 8.4 | 1.4 | 2.3 | 7.6 | 48.6 |
| 1953 | 100.0 | 41.8 | 11.5 | 0.7 | 6.9 | 1.6 | 2.3 | 14.8 | 31.9 |
| 1954 | 100.0 | 29.5 | 14.1 | 0.3 | 10.1 | 1.6 | 2.1 | 17.0 | 39.4 |

## 2. CHARACTERISTICS OF INDUSTRIAL ESTABLISHMENTS — CARACTERISTIQUES DES ETABLISSEMENTS INDUSTRIELS

Number of establishments in units; value added and wages and salaries in million Lempiras; number of engaged and employees in thousands; capacity of installed power equipment in thousand horsepower; value added per engaged and wages and salaries per employee in thousand Lempiras; capacity of installed power equipment per engaged in horsepower.

Nombre d'établissements en unités; valeur ajoutée et traitements et salaires en millions de Lempiras; nombre de personnes occupées et de salariés en milliers; puissance installée en milliers de chevaux-vapeur; valeur ajoutée par personne occupée et traitements et salaires par salarié en milliers de Lempiras; puissance installée par personne occupée en chevaux-vapeur.

## A. Major Groups of Mining and Electricity — Les classes de la branche industries extractives et électricité
### 1950, 1953, 1957

### a. Absolute Figures — Chiffres absolus

| Year and item of data | All mining / Toutes industries extractives | Metal mining / Extraction des minerais métalliques | Other mining / Divers | Electricity / Electricité | Année et rubrique |
|---|---|---|---|---|---|
| ISIC | 1 | 12 | 14–19 | 511 | CITI |
| **1950** | | | | | **1950** |
| Number of establishments | 83 | 2 | 81 | 51 | Nombre d'établissements |
| Value added | 4.6 | 4.3 | 0.3 | ... | Valeur ajoutée |
| Number of engaged (As of end of 1950) | 2.0 | 1.7 | 0.3 | 0.7 | Nombre de personnes occupées (à la fin de 1950) |
| Wages and salaries paid | 2.1 | 2.0 | 0.1 | 0.8 | Traitements et salaires payés |
| Capacity of installed power equipment (As of end of 1950) | 10.9 | 10.9 | ... | ... | Puissance installée (à la fin de 1950) |
| **1953** | | | | | **1953** |
| Number of establishments | ... | 2 | ... | 64 | Nombre d'établissements |
| Value added | ... | 11.4 | ... | 2.8 | Valeur ajoutée |
| Number of engaged (Average for the year) | ... | 1.2 | ... | 0.4 | Nombre de personnes occupées (moyenne pendant l'année) |
| Employees: Number (Average for the year) | ... | 1.2 | ... | 0.4 | Salariés: Nombre (moyenne pendant l'année) |
| Wages and salaries | ... | 1.7 | ... | 0.6 | Traitements et salaires |
| **1957** | | | | | **1957** |
| Number of establishments | ... | 2 | ... | 51 | Nombre d'établissements |
| Value added | ... | 3.8 | ... | 4.6 | Valeur ajoutée |
| Number of engaged (Average for the year) | ... | 0.9 | ... | 1.1 | Nombre de personnes occupées (moyenne pendant l'année) |
| Employees: Number (Average for the year) | ... | 0.9 | ... | 1.1 | Salariés: Nombre (moyenne pendant l'année) |
| Wages and salaries | ... | 1.6 | ... | 1.7 | Traitements et salaires |

### b. Structure

| Year and item of data | All mining / Toutes industries extractives | Metal mining / Extraction des minerais métalliques | Other mining / Divers | Electricity / Electricité | Année et rubrique |
|---|---|---|---|---|---|
| ISIC | 1 | 12 | 14–19 | 511 | CITI |
| **1950** Distribution in percent of: | | | | | **1950** Répartition en pourcentage: |
| Value added | 100.0 | 93.5 | 6.5 | . | De la valeur ajoutée |
| Number of engaged | 100.0 | 85.0 | 15.0 | . | Du nombre de personnes occupées |
| Value added per person engaged | 2.3 | 2.5 | 1.0 | ... | Valeur ajoutée par personne occupée |
| Value added per unit of wages and salaries | 2.19 | 2.15 | 3.00 | ... | Valeur ajoutée par unité de traitements et salaires |
| Capacity of installed power equipment per person engaged | 5.45 | 5.45 | ... | ... | Puissance installée par personne occupée |
| **1953** | | | | | **1953** |
| Value added per person engaged | ... | 9.5 | ... | 7.0 | Valeur ajoutée par personne occupée |
| Wages and salaries per employee | ... | 1.4 | ... | 1.5 | Traitements et salaires par salarié |
| Employees as a percent of engaged | ... | 100.0 | ... | 100.0 | Salariés en pourcentage des personnes occupées |
| Value added per unit of wages and salaries | ... | 6.70 | ... | 4.67 | Valeur ajoutée par unité de traitements et salaires |
| **1957** | | | | | **1957** |
| Value added per person engaged | ... | 4.2 | ... | 4.2 | Valeur ajoutée par personne occupée |
| Wages and salaries per employee | ... | 1.8 | ... | 1.5 | Traitements et salaires par salarié |
| Employees as a percent of engaged | ... | 100.0 | ... | 100.0 | Salariés en pourcentage des personnes occupées |
| Value added per unit of wages and salaries | ... | 2.38 | ... | 2.70 | Valeur ajoutée par unité de traitements et salaires |

## B. The Major Groups of Manufacturing — Les classes de la branche Industries manufacturières
### 1950, 1953

| Year and item of data | Manu-facturing Industries manufac-turières | Food, beverages and tobacco[1] Industries alimen-taires, boissons, tabac[1] | Textiles | Clothing, footwear and made-up textiles Articles d'habil-lement, chaussures et ouvrages en tissu | Wood products and furniture Bois et meubles | Printing and publish-ing Im-primerie et édition | Leather and leather products except wearing apparel Cuir et articles en cuir, à l'exclu-sion des articles d'habil-lement | Rubber products Ouvrages en caout-chouc | Chemicals and chemical, petroleum and coal products Produits chi-miques et dérivés du pétrole et du charbon | Non-metallic mineral products[2] Produits minéraux non métal-liques[2] | Metal products Ouvrages en métaux | Other manu-factur-ing Autres in-dustries manufac-turières | Année et rubrique |
|---|---|---|---|---|---|---|---|---|---|---|---|---|---|
| ISIC | 2–3 | 20–22 | 23 | 24 | 25–26 | 28 | 29 | 30 | 31–32 | 33 | 35–38 | 39 | CITI |

*a. Absolute Figures — Chiffres absolus*

| Year and item of data | 2–3 | 20–22 | 23 | 24 | 25–26 | 28 | 29 | 30 | 31–32 | 33 | 35–38 | 39 | Année et rubrique |
|---|---|---|---|---|---|---|---|---|---|---|---|---|---|
| **1950** | | | | | | | | | | | | | **1950** |
| Number of establishments (As of end of year) | 3 667 | 794 | 2 | 1 039 | 434 | 73 | 223 | 1 | 52 | 450 | 381 | 218 | Nombre d'établissements (à la fin de l'année) |
| Value added | 32.9 | 13.4 | 0.5 | 4.0 | 4.8 | 1.0 | 1.0 | 0.1 | 3.7 | 1.5 | 2.5 | 0.4 | Valeur ajoutée |
| Number of engaged (As of end of year) | 17.6 | 5.0 | 0.2 | 3.3 | 3.5 | 0.7 | 0.5 | — | 0.8 | 1.5 | 1.7 | 0.4 | Nombre de personnes occupées (à la fin de l'année) |
| Wages and salaries paid | 13.2 | 3.0 | 0.1 | 2.2 | 3.3 | 0.7 | 0.2 | — | 0.9 | 0.6 | 2.0 | 0.2 | Traitements et salaires payés |
| Capacity of installed power equipment (As of end of year) | 8.5 | 2.8 | 0.1 | — | 3.3 | — | — | — | 0.8 | 0.1 | 0.8 | 0.6 | Puissance installée (à la fin de l'année) |
| **1953** | | | | | | | | | | | | | **1953** |
| Number of establishments | 3 683 | 566 | 3 | 1 077 | 624 | 44 | 176 | — | 43 | 457 | 557 | 136 | Nombre d'établissements |
| Value added | 40.9 | 19.8 | 1.5 | 4.3 | 5.5 | 0.7 | 0.5 | — | 3.2 | 0.7 | 3.6 | 1.1 | Valeur ajoutée |
| Number of engaged (Average for the year) | 19.8 | 5.8 | 0.5 | 3.7 | 4.3 | 0.4 | 0.5 | — | 0.6 | 1.2 | 2.3 | 0.5 | Nombre de personnes occupées (moyenne pendant l'année) |
| Number of employees (Average for the year) | 14.8 | 4.7 | 0.5 | 2.4 | 3.6 | 0.3 | 0.4 | — | 0.5 | 0.6 | 1.5 | 0.3 | Nombre de salariés (moyenne pendant l'année) |
| Wages and salaries paid | 13.8 | 4.2 | 0.4 | 1.9 | 2.6 | 0.3 | 0.2 | — | 0.8 | 0.3 | 2.7 | 0.4 | Traitements et salaires payés |

*b. Structure*

| Year and item of data | 2–3 | 20–22 | 23 | 24 | 25–26 | 28 | 29 | 30 | 31–32 | 33 | 35–38 | 39 | Année et rubrique |
|---|---|---|---|---|---|---|---|---|---|---|---|---|---|
| **1950** | | | | | | | | | | | | | **1950** |
| Distribution in percent of: | | | | | | | | | | | | | Répartition en pourcentage: |
| Value added | 100.0 | 40.7 | 1.5 | 12.2 | 14.5 | 3.1 | 3.0 | 0.3 | 11.3 | 4.5 | 7.6 | 1.3 | De la valeur ajoutée |
| Number of engaged | 100.0 | 28.4 | 1.1 | 18.7 | 19.9 | 4.0 | 2.9 | — | 4.5 | 8.5 | 9.7 | 2.3 | Du nombre de personnes occupées |
| Value added per person engaged | 1.9 | 2.7 | 2.5 | 1.2 | 1.4 | 1.4 | 2.0 | ... | 4.6 | 1.0 | 1.5 | 1.0 | Valeur ajoutée par personne occu-pée |
| Value added per unit of wages and salaries | 2.49 | 4.47 | 5.00 | 1.82 | 1.45 | 1.43 | 5.00 | ... | 4.11 | 2.50 | 1.25 | 2.00 | Puissance installée par personne occupée |
| Capacity of installed power equip-ment per person engaged | 0.48 | 0.56 | 0.50 | — | 0.94 | — | — | — | 1.00 | 0.07 | 0.47 | 1.50 | |
| **1953** | | | | | | | | | | | | | **1953** |
| Distribution in percent of: | | | | | | | | | | | | | Répartition en pourcentage: |
| Value added | 100.0 | 48.4 | 3.6 | 10.5 | 13.5 | 1.7 | 1.2 | — | 7.8 | 1.8 | 8.8 | 2.7 | De la valeur ajoutée |
| Number of engaged | 100.0 | 29.2 | 2.6 | 18.7 | 21.7 | 2.0 | 2.5 | — | 3.0 | 6.1 | 11.6 | 2.6 | Du nombre de personnes occupées |
| Value added per person engaged | 2.1 | 3.4 | 3.0 | 1.2 | 1.3 | 1.8 | 1.0 | . | 5.3 | 0.6 | 1.6 | 2.2 | Valeur ajoutée par personne occu-pée |
| Wages and salaries per employee | 0.9 | 0.9 | 0.8 | 0.8 | 0.7 | 1.0 | 0.5 | . | 1.6 | 0.5 | 1.8 | 1.3 | Traitements et salaires par salarié |
| Employees as a percent of engaged | 74.7 | 81.0 | 100.0 | 64.9 | 83.7 | 75.0 | 90.0 | . | 83.3 | 50.0 | 65.2 | 60.0 | Salariés en pourcentage des personnes occupées |
| Value added per unit of wages and salaries | 2.96 | 4.71 | 3.75 | 2.26 | 2.12 | 2.33 | 2.50 | . | 4.00 | 2.33 | 1.33 | 2.75 | Valeur ajoutée par unité de traite-ments et salaires |

[1] Excludes for both 1950 and 1953, small crude sugar mills and for 1953, municipal slaughter houses and coffee beneficiating conducted on farms.
[2] Excludes, for 1953, lime kilns and the manufacture of cement pipe in government establishments.

[1] Non compris en 1950 et en 1953, les petites fabriques de sucre brut et, en 1953, les abattoirs municipaux et l'épluchage du café dans les exploitations agricoles.
[2] Non compris en 1953 les fours à chaux et la fabrication des tuyaux en fibrociment dans les établissements d'Etat.

# HONDURAS

## 3. SELECTED INDUSTRIAL ESTABLISHMENTS ENGAGING 5 OR MORE PERSONS
### QUELQUES ETABLISSEMENTS INDUSTRIELS OCCUPANT 5 PERSONNES OU PLUS

Number of establishments in units; value added and wages and salaries in million Lempiras; number of engaged and employees in thousands; value added per engaged and wages and salaries per employee in thousand Lempiras.

Nombre d'établissements en unités; valeur ajoutée et traitements et salaires en millions de Lempiras; nombre de personnes occupées et de salariés en milliers; valeur ajoutée par personne occupée et traitements et salaires par salarié en milliers de Lempiras.

### A. Selected Divisions of Industrial Activity — Quelques branches de l'activité industrielle

#### a. Absolute Figures — Chiffres absolus

| Year and item of data | Mining¹ Industries extractives¹ | Manufacturing Industries manufacturières | Construction Bâtiment et travaux publics | Electricity Electricité | Année et rubrique |
|---|---|---|---|---|---|
| ISIC / CITI | 1 | 2-3 | 4 | 511 | |
| **1953** | | | | | **1953** |
| Number of establishments | 2 | 450 | ... | 64 | Nombre d'établissements |
| Value added | 11.4 | 34.9 | ... | 2.8 | Valeur ajoutée |
| Number of engaged (Average during the year) | 1.2 | 12.8 | ... | 0.4 | Nombre de personnes occupées (moyenne pendant l'année) |
| Employees: | | | | | Salariés: |
| Number (Average during the year) | 1.2 | 12.0 | ... | 0.4 | Nombre (moyenne pendant l'année) |
| Wages and salaries | 1.7 | 12.2 | ... | 0.6 | Traitements et salaires |
| **1958** | | | | | **1958** |
| Number of establishments | ... | 623 | 15 | 54 | Nombre d'établissements |
| Value added | ... | 46.0 | 3.7 | 3.0 | Valeur ajoutée |
| Number of engaged (Average during the year) | ... | 20.1 | 3.0 | 0.9 | Nombre de personnes occupées (moyenne pendant l'année) |
| Employees: | | | | | Salariés: |
| Number (Average during the year) | ... | 19.6 | 3.0 | 0.9 | Nombre (moyenne pendant l'année) |
| Wages and salaries | ... | 18.2 | 2.3 | 1.6 | Traitements et salaires |

#### b. Structure

| Year and item of data | Mining¹ Industries extractives¹ | Manufacturing Industries manufacturières | Construction Bâtiment et travaux publics | Electricity Electricité | Année et rubrique |
|---|---|---|---|---|---|
| ISIC / CITI | 1 | 2-3 | 4 | 511 | |
| **1953** | | | | | **1953** |
| Value added per engaged | 9.5 | 2.7 | ... | 7.0 | Valeur ajoutée par personne occupée |
| Wages and salaries per employee | 1.4 | 1.0 | ... | 1.5 | Traitements et salaires par salarié |
| Employees as a percentage of number engaged | 100.0 | 93.8 | ... | 100.0 | Salariés en pourcentage des personnes occupées |
| Value added per unit of wages and salaries | 6.70 | 2.86 | | 4.67 | Valeur ajoutée par traitements et salaires unitaires |
| **1958** | | | | | **1958** |
| Value added per engaged | ... | 2.3 | 1.2 | 3.3 | Valeur ajoutée par personne occupée |
| Wages and salaries per employee | ... | 0.9 | 0.8 | 1.8 | Traitements et salaires par salarié |
| Employees as a percentage of number engaged | ... | 97.5 | 100.0 | 100.0 | Salariés en pourcentage des personnes occupées |
| Value added per unit of wages and salaries | ... | 2.53 | 1.61 | 1.88 | Valeur ajoutée par unité de traitements et salaires |

¹ Metal Mining only.

¹ Extraction des minerais métalliques seulement.

## B. The Major Groups of Manufacturing — Les classes de la branche Industries manufacturières

| Year and item of data | Manufacturing / Industries manufacturières | Food, beverages and tobacco [1] / Industries alimentaires, boissons, tabac [1] | Textiles | Clothing, footwear and made-up textiles / Articles d'habillement, chaussures et ouvrages en tissu | Wood products and furniture / Bois et meubles | Printing and publishing / Imprimerie et édition | Leather and leather products except wearing apparel / Cuir et articles en cuir, à l'exclusion des articles d'habillement | Rubber products / Ouvrages en caoutchouc | Chemicals and chemical, petroleum and coal products / Produits chimiques et dérivés du pétrole et du charbon | Non-metallic mineral products [2] / Produits minéraux non métalliques [2] | Metal products [3] / Ouvrages en métaux [3] | Other manufacturing / Autres industries manufacturières | Année et rubrique |
|---|---|---|---|---|---|---|---|---|---|---|---|---|---|
| ISIC | 2-3 | 20-22 | 23 | 24 | 25-26 | 28 | 29 | 30 | 31-32 | 33 | 35-38 | 39 | CITI |

### a. Absolute Figures — Chiffres absolus

| | | | | | | | | | | | | | |
|---|---|---|---|---|---|---|---|---|---|---|---|---|---|
| **1953** | | | | | | | | | | | | | **1953** |
| Number of establishments. | 450 | 106 | 3 | 119 | 90 | 16 | 15 | — | 20 | 35 | 29 | 17 | Nombre d'établissements |
| Value added......... | 34.9 | 19.0 | 1.4 | 2.3 | 4.5 | 0.6 | 0.2 | — | 3.2 | 0.3 | 2.7 | 0.7 | Valeur ajoutée |
| Number of engaged (Average during the year)............. | 12.8 | 4.6 | 0.5 | 1.5 | 3.2 | 0.3 | 0.2 | — | 0.6 | 0.4 | 1.3 | 0.2 | Nombre de personnes occupées (moyenne pendant l'année) |
| Employees: Number (Average during the year)...... | 12.0 | 4.4 | 0.5 | 1.4 | 3.0 | 0.3 | 0.2 | — | 0.5 | 0.3 | 1.2 | 0.2 | Salariés: Nombre (moyenne pendant l'année) |
| Wages and salaries... | 12.2 | 4.1 | 0.4 | 1.2 | 2.2 | 0.3 | 0.2 | — | 0.8 | 0.2 | 2.5 | 0.3 | Traitements et salaires |
| **1958** | | | | | | | | | | | | | **1958** |
| Number of establishments. | 623 | 248 | 4 | 109 | 112 | 30 | 16 | 3 | 18 | 16 | 34 | 33 | Nombre d'établissements |
| Value added......... | 46.0 | 26.6 | 0.6 | 2.8 | 9.0 | 1.2 | 0.4 | 0.2 | 3.0 | 0.5 | 1.3 | 0.4 | Valeur ajoutée |
| Number of engaged (Average for the year)............. | 20.1 | 10.0 | 0.3 | 1.7 | 5.4 | 0.6 | 0.1 | | 0.8 | 0.4 | 0.6 | 0.2 | Nombre de personnes occupées (moyenne pendant l'année) |
| Employees: Number (Average for the year)........ | 19.6 | 9.7 | 0.3 | 1.6 | 5.3 | 0.6 | 0.1 | — | 0.8 | 0.4 | 0.6 | 0.2 | Salariés: Nombre (moyenne pendant l'année) |
| Wages and salaries... | 18.2 | 8.9 | 0.3 | 1.3 | 4.7 | 0.6 | 0.1 | 0.1 | 0.9 | 0.3 | 0.8 | 0.2 | Traitements et salaires |

### b. Structure

| | | | | | | | | | | | | | |
|---|---|---|---|---|---|---|---|---|---|---|---|---|---|
| **1953** | | | | | | | | | | | | | **1953** |
| Distribution in percent of: Value added........ | 100.0 | 54.4 | 4.0 | 6.6 | 12.9 | 1.7 | 0.6 | — | 9.1 | 0.9 | 7.7 | 2.1 | Distribution en pourcentage: Valeur ajoutée |
| Number of engaged.. | 100.0 | 35.9 | 3.9 | 11.7 | 25.0 | 2.4 | 1.5 | — | 4.7 | 3.1 | 10.2 | 1.6 | Nombre de personnes occupées |
| Value added per engaged............ | 2.7 | 4.1 | 2.8 | 1.5 | 1.4 | 2.0 | 1.0 | . | 5.3 | 0.8 | 2.1 | 3.5 | Valeur ajoutée par personne occupée |
| Wages and salaries per employee........ | 1.0 | 0.9 | 0.8 | 0.8 | 0.7 | 1.0 | 1.0 | . | 1.6 | 0.7 | 2.1 | 1.5 | Traitements et salaires par salarié |
| Employees as a percent of engaged......... | 93.8 | 95.6 | 100.0 | 93.3 | 93.8 | 100.0 | 100.0 | . | 83.3 | 75.0 | 92.3 | 100.0 | Salariés en pourcentage des personnes occupées |
| Value added per unit of wages and salaries. | 2.86 | 4.63 | 3.50 | 1.92 | 2.04 | 2.00 | 1.00 | . | 4.00 | 1.50 | 1.08 | 2.33 | Valeur ajoutée par traitements et salaires unitaires |
| **1958** | | | | | | | | | | | | | **1958** |
| Distribution in percent of: Value added........ | 100.0 | 57.8 | 1.3 | 6.1 | 19.5 | 2.6 | 0.9 | 0.4 | 6.6 | 1.1 | 2.8 | 0.9 | Distribution en pourcentage: Valeur ajoutée |
| Number of engaged.. | 100.0 | 49.7 | 1.5 | 8.5 | 26.8 | 3.0 | 0.5 | — | 4.0 | 2.0 | 3.0 | 1.0 | Nombre de personnes occupées |
| Value added per person engaged............ | 2.3 | 2.7 | 2.0 | 1.6 | 1.7 | 2.0 | 4.0 | ... | 3.8 | 1.2 | 2.2 | 2.0 | Valeur ajoutée par personne occupée |
| Wages and salaries per employee........ | 0.9 | 0.9 | 1.0 | 0.8 | 0.9 | 1.0 | 1.0 | ... | 1.1 | 0.8 | 1.3 | 1.0 | Traitements et salaires par salarié |
| Employees as a percent of engaged........ | 97.5 | 97.0 | 100.0 | 94.1 | 98.1 | 100.0 | 100.0 | ... | 100.0 | 100.0 | 100.0 | 100.0 | Salariés en pourcentage des personnes occupées |
| Value added per unit of wages and salaries. | 2.53 | 2.99 | 2.00 | 2.15 | 1.91 | 2.00 | 4.00 | 2.00 | 3.33 | 1.67 | 1.62 | 2.00 | Valeur ajoutée par unité de traitements et salaires |

[1] Excludes Slaughtering, Preparation and Preserving of Meat (ISIC group 201) and Manufacture of Dairy Products (ISIC group 202) in 1953.
[2] Excludes Manufacture of Glass and Glass Products (ISIC group 332) in 1958.
[3] Excludes repair of machinery (in ISIC group 360) and repair of electrical apparatus (in ISIC group 370) in 1958.

[1] Non compris Abattage du bétail; fabrication des préparations et conserves de viande (CITI groupe 201) et Industrie du lait (CITI groupe 202) en 1953.
[2] Non compris Industrie du verre (CITI groupe 332) en 1958.
[3] Non compris réparation de machines (dans CITI groupe 360) et réparation d'appareils électriques (dans CITI groupe 370) en 1958.

# HUNGARY — HONGRIE

## Net Material Product

The data on the net material product given in Table 1 were abstracted from correspondence with the Hungarian Central Statistical Office, Budapest and *Statisztikai Evkönyv, 1961,* published by that Office. The concepts, definitions and methods utilised in compiling the data are described in *A nemzeti jövedelem és a lakosság jövedelme 1958-ban* issued by the Central Statistical Office.

The concepts governing the official estimates of Hungary, and therefore the data shown in Table 1, are those of the system of material product accounts and are not comparable, in a number of respects, with the principles of the United Nations system of national accounts. The major features of the system of material product accounts are indicated in the introduction to this publication.

· It should also be noted that the data shown in Table 1 for 1960-1961, 1958-1959, and for earlier years are not strictly comparable with one another because of some differences in definitions and methodology. A number of these differences are noted in the footnotes to Table 1. Another change in methodology introduced in the data for 1960-1961 was the inclusion of the cost of work clothing utilised in "productive" activities in the net material product. Before, the cost of this item was considered part of material costs and thus excluded from the net material product.

## Index Numbers of Industrial Production

The indexes set out in Table 2 are based on index numbers of industrial production compiled monthly by the Central Statistical Office, Budapest, that are published in *Statisztikai Havi Közlemények.* It should be noted that this publication is not the source of the 1938 and 1948 indexes for total industrial production. These index numbers appear in *Statisztikai Evkönyv, 1957.* The series of index numbers cover publicly owned enterprises only.

All of the index numbers are compiled as base-weighted arithmetic averages of relatives of the quantity produced of individual commodities, in most cases, or of the quantity consumed of individual raw materials or the value, in constant enterprise prices, of gross output, in some cases. The weights utilized in combining the relatives, as well as the indexes resulting therefrom, are man-hours worked by operatives during the base year. The base year is 1954 for the index numbers for the period, 1949-1957, and 1958 for the index numbers for 1958 and later years.

## Produit matériel net

Les données du tableau 1 relatives au produit matériel net ont été communiquées, par correspondance, par l'Office central de statistique de Hongrie, Budapest, et tirées de *Statisztikai Evkönyv, 1961,* publié par cet Office. Les concepts, définitions et méthodes adoptés pour établir les données sont indiqués dans *A nemzeti jövedelem és a lakosság jövedelme 1958-ban,* publié par l'Office central de statistique.

Les concepts sur lesquels reposent les estimations officielles de la Hongrie et, par conséquent, les données du tableau 1 sont ceux du système de comptabilité du produit matériel; ces concepts diffèrent à plus d'un égard des principes adoptés dans le système de comptabilité nationale de l'ONU. Les caractéristiques principales du système de comptabilité du produit matériel sont indiquées dans l'introduction de la publication précitée.

Il y a lieu de noter également que les données du tableau 1 concernant 1960-1961, 1958-1959 et les années précédentes ne sont pas tout à fait comparables les unes aux autres en raison des différences existant quant aux définitions et méthodes adoptées. Certaines de ces différences sont indiquées en note au tableau 1. Les méthodes adoptées pour les données de 1960-1961 ont été modifiées en ce sens que l'on a inclus dans le produit matériel net le coût des survêtements de travail utilisés dans les activités qui contribuent à sa formation. Auparavant, le coût de cet article était considéré comme faisant partie des coûts matériels et était, par conséquent, exclu du produit matériel net.

## Indices de la production industrielle

Les indices du tableau 2 sont fondés sur les indices de la production industrielle établis chaque mois par l'Office central de statistique de Budapest et publiés dans *Statisztikai Havi Közlemények.* On notera que les indices de 1938 et de 1948 pour l'ensemble de la production industrielle sont tirés non pas de cette publication, mais de *Statisztikai Evkönyv, 1957.* Ces séries d'indices portent sur les entreprises publiques seulement.

Tous les indices sont des moyennes arithmétiques à pondération fixe de rapports quantitatifs du volume de la production de chaque marchandise, sauf quelques exceptions où il s'agit du volume de la consommation de chaque matière première ou de la valeur, en prix constants des entreprises, de la production brute. Les poids utilisés pour combiner ces rapports, ainsi que les indices qu'on en a tirés, sont fondés sur les heures de travail effectuées par les ouvriers pendant l'année de base. L'année de base est 1954 pour les indices de la période de 1949-1957, et 1958 pour les indices de 1958 et des années suivantes.

For details concerning the indexes of industrial production based on 1954 and 1958, respectively, see: *Az Ipar Termelési Indexe, 1949-1957* and *Az Ipar Termelési Indexének Felülvizsgálata, Statisztikai Szemle,* May 1959.

### Index Numbers of Industrial Employment

The index numbers appearing in Table 3 are based on absolute figures of the employment of publicly owned enterprises abstracted from various issues of *Statisztikai Evkönyv*. The absolute figures of employment are the average of the number of all persons engaged (employees), including apprentices, during each month of the year in these enterprises. The absolute figures are classified according to the main activity of the enterprises covered.

### The Characteristics and Structure of Industrial Activity

The figures appearing in Table 4 were compiled from *Magyar Statisztikai Evkönyv, 1938,* Central Statistical Office, Budapest, 1939. The data in Table 4 are not comparable to the data in Table 5 because of differences between the data in the field covered and the concepts and scheme of industrial classification utilised in gathering and compiling the figures as well as in the nature of the economy to which the figures refer.

The data set out in Table 5 were compiled from various publications of the Hungarian Central Statistical Office, Budapest and from figures furnished to the Statistical Office of the United Nations by that Office. Most of the data were abstracted from *Statisztikai Evkönyv, 1949-1955, 1958* and *1961* and from *A Magyar Ipar Statisztikai Adaptgyüjtemény,* published in 1961. In the case of the construction industry, many of the figures came from *Epitöipari Adaptok, 1949-1957* and *1958-1960.* Most of the data on privately owned enterprises were derived from *A Magyar Magánkisipar, Statisztikai Adaptgyüjtemény, 1938-1960.*

The figures in Table 5 for the same year—i.e., either 1955 or 1958—relating to various items of data are, with the exceptions of the few instances mentioned in the footnotes to the table, consistent with one another with regard to scope and industrial classification. This is also the case for the scope and definition of the data for the two years on the same item. However, because of some changes made between 1955 and 1958 in the structure and classification of industrial activity, some of the data for the two years relating to the same item may not be strictly comparable.

All of the figures of gross output shown in Table 5 are valued at current enterprise prices (i.e., actual transaction prices, excluding turnover and indirect taxes) and relate to the industrial activities only of the units covered. In other words, the definition of gross output is the same as that for gross industrial output in the International Standards in Basic Industrial Statistics. The gross material products shown in Table 5 was computed by the

### Indices de l'emploi dans l'industrie

Les indices du tableau 3 sont fondés sur des chiffres absolus de l'emploi dans les entreprises publiques, tirés de divers numéros du *Statisztikai Evkönyv*. Les chiffres absolus de l'emploi sont les moyennes, pour chaque mois de l'année, du nombre de personnes occupées (salariés), y compris les apprentis, dans ces entreprises. Les chiffres absolus sont classés d'après l'activité principale des entreprises considérées.

### Caractéristiques et structure de l'activité industrielle

Les chiffres du tableau 4 sont tirés du *Magyar Statisztikai Evkönyv, 1938,* Office central de statistique, Budapest, 1939. Les données du tableau 4 ne sont pas comparables aux données du tableau 5 en raison des différences existant entre les rubriques, les définitions et la structure de la nomenclature industrielle utilisée pour recueillir et élaborer les chiffres, ainsi que de la nature de l'économie à laquelle les chiffres se rapportent.

Les données du tableau 5 sont tirées de diverses publications de l'Office central de statistique de Hongrie, Budapest, et de chiffres fournis par cet Office au Bureau de statistique de l'ONU. La plupart des données ont été tirées de *Statisztikai Evkönyv, 1949-1955, 1958* et *1961* et de *A Magyar Ipar Statisztikai Adaptgyüjtemény,* publié en 1961. Dans le cas de l'industrie du bâtiment et des travaux publics, beaucoup de chiffres proviennent de *Epitöipari Adaptok, 1949-1957* et *1958-1960.* La plupart des données relatives aux entreprises privées ont été tirées de *A Magyar Magánkisipar, Statisztikai Adaptgyüjtemény, 1938-1960.*

Les chiffres du tableau 5 pour la même année, c'est-à-dire 1955 ou 1958, qui ont trait à diverses rubriques sont, à l'exclusion des quelques cas mentionnés en note au tableau, compatibles les uns avec les autres quant au champ couvert et à la nomenclature industrielle utilisée. C'est également le cas des données des deux années ayant trait aux mêmes rubriques en ce qui concerne leurs définitions et l'étendue du champ sur lequel elles portent. Cependant, en raison des changements intervenus entre 1955 et 1958 dans la structure et la classification des activités industrielles, certaines données concernant la même rubrique peuvent n'être pas tout à fait comparables d'une année à l'autre.

Tous les chiffres de la production brute présentés au tableau 5 sont évalués aux prix courants des entreprises (c'est-à-dire, prix réels des transactions, non compris l'impôt sur le chiffre d'affaires et autres impôts indirects) et ne portent que sur les activités industrielles des unités recensées. En d'autres termes, la définition de la production brute est la même que celle de la production industrielle brute donnée dans les Normes internationales rela-

Statistical Office of the United Nations by deducting from the value of this gross output, the cost of the raw-materials, fuels, electricity, supplies and subcontract work utilised in producing it. The gross material product is therefore equivalent to value added in industrial activities, priced at factor cost. However, the figures of the net material product in Table 5A are valued at industry prices (i.e., inclusive of turnover and indirect taxes) and relate to the "productive" non-industrial, as well as industrial, activities of the units covered.

The figures of persons engaged and wages and salaries paid to them cover all employees and homeworkers, irrespective of the activity in which they are engaged, in the case of publicly owned enterprises and these catagories plus all working members in the case of co-operatives. Operatives are however limited to the manual workers among the persons engaged who are employed in the industrial activities of the units covered. The figures of electricity consumed also appear to be restricted to the industrial activities of the units covered. The definition of the figures of wages and salaries seems to be like that in the International Standards in Basic Industrial Statistics. In the case of the data on privately owned enterprises, owners, employees and homeworkers, but not unpaid family workers, are included in the counts of persons engaged.

tives aux statistiques industrielles de base. Les chiffres du tableau 5 relatifs au produit matériel brut ont été calculés par le Bureau de statistique de l'ONU, qui a déduit de la valeur de la production brute le coût des matières premières, des combustibles, de l'électricité, des fournitures et des travaux confiés à des sous-traitants à des fins de production. Le produit matériel brut équivaut donc à la valeur ajoutée par les activités industrielles, comptée au coût des facteurs. Cependant, les chiffres du produit matériel net indiqués au tableau 5 A sont comptés aux prix des industries (c'est-à-dire y compris l'impôt sur le chiffre d'affaires et autres impôts indirects) et concernent toutes les activités, industrielles ou non, exercées par les unités recensées et contribuant à la formation du produit matériel.

Les chiffres relatifs au nombre de personnes occupées et aux traitements et salaires qui leur sont payés portent, dans le cas des entreprises publiques, sur tous les salariés et travailleurs à domicile, quelle que soit l'activité à laquelle ilss ont affectés, et, dans le cas des coopératives, sur ces catégories de travailleurs, ainsi que sur tous les membres qui travaillent. La catégorie des ouvriers est cependant limitée aux travailleurs manuels figurant parmi les personnes occupées qui sont affectées aux activités industrielles des unités recensées. La définition des traitements et salaires semble être conforme aux Normes internationales relatives aux statistiques industrielles de base. Dans le cas des données concernant les entreprises privées, les propriétaires, les salariés et les travailleurs à domicile sont inclus dans le nombre de personnes occupées, mais les travailleurs familiaux non rémunérés en sont exclus.

## 1. THE NET MATERIAL PRODUCT — PRODUIT MATERIEL NET

Million Forints                                         Millions de forints

### A.  Sources of Expenditure on the Net Material Product
### Dépenses relatives au produit matériel net

| Item of data and year [1]<br>Rubrique et année [1] | Total | Consumption<br>Consommation | | Net Domestic Capital Formation<br>Formation nette de capital intérieur | | Net exports of goods and services [4]<br>Exportations nettes de biens et de services [4] |
|---|---|---|---|---|---|---|
| | | Total [2] | Individual consumption<br>Consommation individuelle | Total | Fixed [3]<br>Fixe [3] | |
| *a. At Current Prices — Aux prix courants* | | | | | | |
| Absolute figures — Chiffres absolus | | | | | | |
| 1950........................... | 46 487 | 35 027 | 29 251 | 10 498 | 5 333 | 962 |
| 1951........................... | 65 315 | 47 161 | 40 101 | 17 531 | 7 647 | 623 |
| 1952........................... | 73 832 | 60 171 | 48 996 | 13 346 | 9 835 | 315 |
| 1953........................... | 82 975 | 63 958 | 50 806 | 18 467 | 11 405 | 550 |
| 1954........................... | 85 605 | 70 140 | 59 753 | 15 435 | 9 491 | 30 |
| 1955........................... | 94 292 | 73 301 | 64 408 | 19 091 | 10 159 | 1 900 |
| 1956........................... | 82 539 [5] | 77 626 | 69 508 | 3 413 | 8 962 | 300 |
| 1957........................... | 107 310 | 86 136 | 77 780 | 26 146 | 9 200 | −4 972 |
| 1958........................... | 109 980 | 91 313 | 83 143 | 16 430 | 11 500 | 2 237 |
| 1959........................... | 126 493 | 99 208 | 88 708 | 27 262 | 19 304 | 23 |
| 1960........................... | 141 649 | 108 057 | 101 563 | 37 104 | 27 504 | −3 512 |
| 1961........................... | 147 422 | 108 702 | 101 753 | 37 492 | 24 400 | 1 228 |
| Percentage distribution of average annual expenditure — Distribution en pourcentage des dépenses annuelles moyennes | | | | | | |
| 1950 – 1960..................... | 100.0 | 80.0 | 70.3 | 20.2 | 12.8 | −0.2 |
| 1950........................... | 100.0 | 75.3 | 62.9 | 22.6 | 11.5 | 2.1 |
| 1953........................... | 100.0 | 77.1 | 61.2 | 22.2 | 13.7 | 0.7 |
| 1954........................... | 100.0 | 82.0 | 69.8 | 18.0 | 11.1 | — |
| 1958........................... | 100.0 | 83.0 | 75.6 | 15.0 | 10.4 | 2.0 |
| 1960........................... | 100.0 | 76.3 | 71.7 | 26.2 | 19.4 | −2.5 |
| 1961........................... | 100.0 | 73.8 | 69.0 | 25.4 | 16.6 | 0.8 |
| *b. At Constant Prices [6] — En prix constants [6]* | | | | | | |
| Index numbers — Indices (1958 = 100) | | | | | | |
| 1950........................... | 63.1 | 59.6 | 60.8 | 74.0 | 45.6 | ... |
| 1951........................... | 73.8 | 63.7 | 63.4 | 109.7 | 70.1 | ... |
| 1952........................... | 72.4 | 68.7 | 60.9 | 89.9 | 84.1 | ... |
| 1953........................... | 82.0 | 74.2 | 62.8 | 112.8 | 91.6 | ... |
| 1954........................... | 78.6 | 78.8 | 75.4 | 85.6 | 74.7 | ... |
| 1955........................... | 85.6 | 82.0 | 80.7 | 101.9 | 79.7 | ... |
| 1956........................... | 76.4 | 87.8 | 88.0 | 18.6 | 70.2 | ... |
| 1957........................... | 94.1 | 95.2 | 95.9 | 127.2 | 64.5 | ... |
| 1958........................... | 100.0 | 100.0 | 100.0 | 100.0 | 100.0 | ... |
| 1959........................... | 106.9 | 108.1 | 107.8 | 117.7 | 110.4 | ... |
| 1960........................... | 117.7 | 116.1 | 115.1 | 157.8 | 152.8 | ... |
| 1961........................... | 124.5 | 118.0 | 116.6 | 164.8 | 140.7 | ... |
| Average annual rate of growth — Taux annuel moyen d'accroissement | | | | | | |
| 1950 – 1960..................... | 6.4 | 6.9 | 6.6 | 7.9 | 12.9 | ... |
| 1950 – 1953..................... | 9.1 | 7.6 | 1.1 | 15.2 | 26.2 | ... |
| 1954 – 1958..................... | 6.2 | 6.1 | 7.3 | 4.0 | 7.6 | ... |
| 1958 – 1960..................... | 8.5 | 7.7 | 7.3 | 25.6 | 23.6 | ... |

For footnotes see end of table.                        Pour les notes, voir au bas du tableau.

## B. The Net Material Product According to Origin
### Origine par secteur d'activité du produit matériel net

| Item of data and year [1]<br>Rubrique et année [1] | Total | Agricultural sector [7]<br>Secteur agricole [7] | Mining, manufacturing, electricity, gas and water [8]<br>Industries extractives et manufacturières, et électricité, gaz et eau [8] | Construction<br>Bâtiment et travaux publics | Transportation and communication [9]<br>Transports et communications [9] | Other sectors [10]<br>Autres secteurs [10] |
|---|---|---|---|---|---|---|
| ISIC — CITI | 0–852 | 0 | 1–3, 511–521 | 4 | 7 | 61, 841, 852 |
| *a. At Current Prices — Aux prix courants* | | | | | | |
| **Absolute figures — Chiffres absolus** | | | | | | |
| 1950 | 46 487 | 11 730 | 22 440 | 3 136 | 1 966 | 7 215 |
| 1951 | 65 315 | 22 185 | 25 284 | 4 273 | 2 487 | 11 086 |
| 1952 | 73 832 | 14 440 | 44 785 | 5 595 | 2 899 | 6 113 |
| 1953 | 82 975 | 20 541 | 46 928 | 6 015 | 3 497 | 5 994 |
| 1954 | 85 605 | 23 972 | 46 694 | 4 716 | 3 441 | 6 782 |
| 1955 | 94 292 | 31 535 | 50 465 | 5 543 | 3 439 | 3 310 |
| 1956 | 82 539 | 28 879 | 41 465 | 5 714 | 3 108 | 3 373 |
| 1957 | 107 310 | 38 620 | 52 738 | 7 026 | 3 519 | 5 407 |
| 1958 | 109 980 | 34 135 | 60 268 | 8 469 | 5 488 | 1 620 |
| 1959 | 126 493 | 34 642 | 68 833 | 12 849 | 5 116 | 5 053 |
| 1960 | 141 649 | 32 223 | 80 149 | 16 113 | 6 232 | 6 932 |
| 1961 | 147 422 | 30 143 | 88 525 | 14 978 | 7 127 | 6 649 |
| **Percentage distribution according to sector— Distribution en pourcentage par secteur** | | | | | | |
| 1950 – 1960 | 100.0 | 28.8 | 53.1 | 7.8 | 4.1 | 6.2 |
| 1950 | 100.0 | 25.2 | 48.3 | 6.8 | 4.2 | 15.5 |
| 1953 | 100.0 | 24.8 | 56.6 | 7.2 | 4.2 | 7.2 |
| 1954 | 100.0 | 28.0 | 54.6 | 5.5 | 4.0 | 7.9 |
| 1958 | 100.0 | 31.0 | 54.8 | 7.7 | 5.0 | 1.5 |
| 1960 | 100.0 | 22.7 | 56.6 | 11.4 | 4.4 | 4.9 |
| 1961 | 100.0 | 20.4 | 60.1 | 10.2 | 4.8 | 4.5 |
| *b. At Constant Prices [6] — En prix constants [6]* | | | | | | |
| **Indexes — Indices (1958 = 100)** | | | | | | |
| 1950 | 63.1 | 87.5 | 51.5 | 57.4 | ... | ... |
| 1951 | 73.8 | 104.2 | 60.6 | 78.1 | ... | ... |
| 1952 | 72.4 | 65.0 | 71.7 | 84.4 | ... | ... |
| 1953 | 82.0 | 90.2 | 79.7 | 89.9 | ... | ... |
| 1954 | 78.6 | 85.9 | 77.5 | 70.2 | ... | ... |
| 1955 | 85.6 | 99.2 | 86.4 | 78.9 | ... | ... |
| 1956 | 76.4 | 82.6 | 73.4 | 80.5 | ... | ... |
| 1957 | 94.1 | 97.2 | 88.9 | 90.4 | ... | ... |
| 1958 | 100.0 | 100.0 | 100.0 | 100.0 | ... | ... |
| 1959 | 106.9 | 104.1 | 108.2 | 112.4 | ... | ... |
| 1960 | 117.7 | 93.3 | 125.1 | 132.7 | ... | ... |
| 1961 | 124.5 | 88.9 | 138.1 | 130.2 | ... | ... |
| **Average annual rate of growth—Taux annuel moyen d'accroissement** | | | | | | |
| 1950 – 1960 | 6.4 | 0.6 | 9.3 | 8.7 | . | ... |
| 1950 – 1953 | 9.1 | 1.0 | 15.7 | 16.1 | . | ... |
| 1954 – 1958 | 6.2 | 3.9 | 6.6 | 9.2 | . | ... |
| 1958 – 1960 | 8.5 | —3.4 | 11.8 | 15.2 | . | ... |

[1] The data for the years, 1950-1957, 1958-1959 and 1960-1961, are not strictly comparable with one another, because of the differences that are indicated in the introduction to the chapter, in the scope of the net material products.

[2] Includes, in addition to "Individual consumption", all material consumption of non-productive institution in the case of the years, 1950-1959. Beginning with 1960, the material consumption of these institutions arising in connexion with services rendered to the population has been included under "Individual consumption".

[3] Includes changes in livestocks for the years, 1950-1957.

[4] Also includes transfers, reparations and a statistical discrepancy.

[5] Includes, in addition to the components shown, 1,200 million forints of unallocated expenditure.

[6] The constant prices utilized in compiling the data for the indexes are as of 1949 for the years 1950-1953, as of 1954 for the years, 1954-1957, and as of 1959 for 1958-1961. The series of data at different constant prices were linked to one another in compiling the indexes.

[7] In the case of 1961, a different method of pricing commodities produced and consumed in the Agricultural sector was utilized in estimating the net material products at current prices originating in this sector than in the case of earlier years. For 1961, these items were priced at state procurement prices, whereas for earlier years the commodities were valued at average producer prices. This difference in method has not affected the comparability of the indexes in constant prices.

[8] Includes laundries and dry cleaning and dyeing enterprises in the case of 1958 and later years.

[9] For the years, 1950-1957, transportation of goods and communication services for productive enterprises only; for 1958 and thereafter, all transportation and communication services.

[10] Also includes home and craft industries and a net adjustment, which has not been allocated according to sector, for the differences between prices at which commodities are imported and exported and the prevailing prices in internal markets.

[1] Les données de 1950-1957, de 1958-1959 et de 1960-1961 ne sont pas strictement comparables les unes aux autres en raison des différences indiquées dans l'introduction au présent chapitre en ce qui concerne le concept du produit matériel net.

[2] De 1950 à 1959, y compris, en plus de la "Consommation individuelle", la part du produit matériel consommé par les organismes qui ne contribuent pas à sa formation. A partir de 1960, le produit matériel consommé par ces organisimes au titre des services rendus à la population a été inclus dans "Consommation individuelle".

[3] Y compris les variations du cheptel dans le cas des années 1950-1957.

[4] Y compris les transferts, les réparations et les écarts statistiques.

[5] Y compris, en plus des composantes indiquées, 1 200 millions de forints correspondant aux dépenses non ventilées.

[6] Les prix constants adoptés lors de l'élaboration des données pour le calcul des indices ont été relevés en 1949 dans le cas des années 1950-1953, en 1954 pour les années 1954-1957 et en 1959 pour 1958-1961. Les séries de données en prix constants différents ont été raccordées les unes aux autres lors du calcul des indices.

[7] Dans le cas de 1961, on n'a pas utilisé la même méthode que dans le cas des années antérieures pour évaluer les marchandises produites et consommées dans le secteur agricole de manière à obtenir une estimation, aux prix courants, du produit matériel net provenant de ce secteur. Pour 1961, ces marchandises ont été évaluées aux prix de campagne fixés par l'Etat, tandis que pour les années précédentes, elles ont été évaluées aux prix moyen des producteurs. Cette différence dans la méthode appliquée n'a pas affecté la comparabilité des indices en prix constants.

[8] Y compris les entreprises de blanchissage de dégraissage et de teinturerie dans le cas de 1958 et des années suivantes.

[9] De 1950 à 1957, services de transports de marchandises et de communications desservant les entreprises productives seulement; à partir de 1958, tous les services de transports et communications.

[10] Y compris également les industries familiales et artisanales et un ajustement net, qui n'a pas été ventilé par secteur, pour tenir compte des différences existant entre les prix auxquels les marchandises sont importées et exportées et ceux qui sont en vigueur sur les marchés intérieurs.

## 2. INDEX NUMBERS OF INDUSTRIAL PRODUCTION — INDICES DE LA PRODUCTION INDUSTRIELLE

### A. Selected Divisions of Industrial Activity
### Quelques branches de l'activité industrielle

| Period<br>Période | Total | Mining [1]<br>Industries<br>extractives [1] | Manu-<br>facturing [1]<br>Industries<br>manu-<br>facturières [1] | Electricity<br>Electricité |
|---|---|---|---|---|
| ISIC — CITI | 1–3, 511–512 | 11–13, 19 | 14, 2–3, 512 | 511 |

*a.* Indexes — Indices (1958 = 100)

| | | | | |
|---|---|---|---|---|
| 1938........... | 28 | ... | ... | ... |
| 1948........... | 28 | ... | ... | ... |
| 1949........... | 38 | 55 | 36 | 38 |
| 1950........... | 48 | 60 | 47 | 45 |
| 1951........... | 62 | 68 | 61 | 53 |
| 1952........... | 74 | 79 | 74 | 63 |
| 1953........... | 82 | 86 | 82 | 69 |
| 1954........... | 80 | 88 | 79 | 73 |
| 1955........... | 86 | 92 | 85 | 82 |
| 1956........... | 78 | 84 | 77 | 79 |
| 1957........... | – 89 – | – 86 – | – 89 – | – 83 – |
| 1958........... | 100 | 100 | 100 | 100 |
| 1959........... | 111 | 105 | 111 | 112 |
| 1960........... | 125 | 110 | 127 | 122 |
| 1961........... | 139 | 117 | 142 | 129 |

*b.* Average Annual Rate of Change — Taux annuel moyen de variation

| | | | | |
|---|---|---|---|---|
| 1950–1960.... | 10.0 | 6.2 | 10.5 | 10.5 |
| 1950–1953.... | 19.5 | 12.7 | 20.4 | 15.3 |
| 1954–1958.... | 5.7 | 3.2 | 6.1 | 8.2 |
| 1958–1960.... | 11.8 | 4.9 | 12.7 | 10.5 |

For footnotes see end of table.

### B. The Major Groups of Mining
### Les classes de la branche Industries extractives

| Period<br>Période | All mining [1]<br>Toutes<br>industries<br>extractives [1] | Coal<br>mining [1]<br>Extraction<br>du charbon [1] | Metal mining<br>Extraction<br>des minerais<br>métalliques | Crude petro-<br>leum and<br>natural gas<br>Pétrole brut<br>et gaz naturel | Other mining [1]<br>Autres<br>industries<br>extractives [1] |
|---|---|---|---|---|---|
| ISIC — CITI | 11–13, 19 | 11 | 12 | 13 | 19 |

*a.* Indexes — Indices (1958 = 100)

| | | | | | |
|---|---|---|---|---|---|
| 1949....... | 55 | 57 | 41 | 69 | 22 |
| 1950....... | 60 | 62 | 44 | 70 | 35 |
| 1951....... | 68 | 71 | 50 | 72 | 51 |
| 1952....... | 79 | 81 | 60 | 90 | 66 |
| 1953....... | 86 | 89 | 62 | 115 | 83 |
| 1954....... | 88 | 90 | 65 | 146 | 83 |
| 1955....... | 92 | 93 | 67 | 176 | 91 |
| 1956....... | 84 | 86 | 56 | 134 | 78 |
| 1957....... | – 86 – | – 86 – | – 96 – | – 88 – | – 86 – |
| 1958....... | 100 | 100 | 100 | 100 | 100 |
| 1959....... | 105 | 104 | 125 | 112 | 118 |
| 1960....... | 110 | 109 | 151 | 119 | 133 |
| 1961....... | 117 | 114 | 160 | 130 | 148 |

*b.* Average Annual Rate of Change — Taux annuel moyen de variation

| | | | | | |
|---|---|---|---|---|---|
| 1950–1960. | 6.2 | 5.8 | 13.1 | 5.5 | 14.3 |
| 1950–1953. | 12.7 | 12.8 | 12.1 | 18.0 | 33.3 |
| 1954–1958. | 3.2 | 2.7 | 11.4 | –9.0 | 4.8 |
| 1958–1960. | 4.9 | 4.4 | 22.9 | 9.1 | 15.3 |

Pour les notes, voir au bas du tableau.

# HUNGARY

## C. The Major Groups of Manufacturing — Les classes de la branche Industries manufacturières

| Period / Période | Manufacturing [1] / Industries manufacturières [1] | Food, beverages and tobacco [1,2] / Industries alimentaires, boissons, tabac [1,2] | Textiles [3] | Clothing, footwear and made-up textiles [3] / Articles d'habillement, chaussures et ouvrages en tissu [3] | Wood products and furniture [4] / Bois et meubles [4] | Paper and paper products / Papier et ouvrages en papier | Printing [1] / Imprimerie [1] | Leather and leather products except wearing apparel / Cuir et articles en cuir, à l'exclusion des articles d'habillement | Rubber products [5] / Ouvrages en caoutchouc [5] | Chemicals and chemical, petroleum and coal products [1,2,4] / Produits chimiques et dérivés du pétrole et du charbon [1,2,4] | Non-metallic mineral products [1] / Produits minéraux non métalliques [1] | Basic metals / Métallurgie de base | Metal products [4,6] / Ouvrages en métaux [4,6] | Other manufacturing [5,6] / Autres industries manufacturières [5,6] |
|---|---|---|---|---|---|---|---|---|---|---|---|---|---|---|
| ISIC — CITI | 14, 2-3, 512 | 20–22 | 23 | 24 | 25–26 | 27 | 28 | 29 | 30 | 31–32, 512 | 14, 33 | 34 | 35–38 391-395 | 399 |

### a Indexes — Indices (1958 = 100)

| Period | | | | | | | | | | | | | | |
|---|---|---|---|---|---|---|---|---|---|---|---|---|---|---|
| 1949 | 36 | 39 | 58 | 20 | 27 | 52 | 52 | 60 | 30 | 26 | 36 | 49 | 31 | 7 |
| 1950 | 47 | 47 | 73 | 38 | 38 | 63 | 65 | 75 | 32 | 38 | 53 | 59 | 42 | 12 |
| 1951 | 61 | 59 | 85 | 65 | 64 | 76 | 69 | 74 | 40 | 49 | 61 | 72 | 56 | 22 |
| 1952 | 74 | 74 | 94 | 73 | 82 | 78 | 71 | 74 | 51 | 62 | 75 | 87 | 70 | 34 |
| 1953 | 82 | 87 | 89 | 71 | 83 | 80 | 78 | 86 | 61 | 63 | 86 | 97 | 80 | 51 |
| 1954 | 79 | 88 | 95 | 77 | 77 | 86 | 77 | 82 | 68 | 64 | 76 | 94 | 72 | 62 |
| 1955 | 85 | 94 | 100 | 86 | 81 | 88 | 80 | 87 | 69 | 70 | 85 | 98 | 78 | 68 |
| 1956 | 77 | 90 | 81 | 71 | 73 | 72 | 72 | 68 | 66 | 67 | 80 | 87 | 72 | 61 |
| 1957 | – 89 – | – 100 – | – 94 – | – 88 – | – 91 – | – 84 – | – 83 – | – 89 – | – 91 – | – 81 – | – 91 – | – 87 – | – 84 – | – 91 – |
| 1958 | 100 | 100 | 100 | 100 | 100 | 100 | 100 | 100 | 100 | 100 | 100 | 100 | 100 | 100 |
| 1959 | 111 | 108 | 103 | 107 | 113 | 110 | 111 | 99 | 111 | 119 | 117 | 109 | 115 | 111 |
| 1960 | 127 | 119 | 114 | 127 | 129 | 118 | 124 | 112 | 133 | 140 | 128 | 118 | 137 | 134 |
| 1961 | 142 | 134 | 123 | 137 | 143 | 133 | 137 | 126 | 168 | 171 | 132 | 129 | 156 | 160 |

### b. Average Annual Rate of Change — Taux annuel moyen de variation

| Period | | | | | | | | | | | | | | |
|---|---|---|---|---|---|---|---|---|---|---|---|---|---|---|
| 1950 – 1960 | 10.5 | 9.7 | 4.6 | 12.8 | 13.0 | 6.5 | 6.7 | 4.1 | 15.3 | 13.9 | 9.2 | 7.2 | 12.6 | 27.3 |
| 1950 – 1953 | 20.4 | 22.8 | 6.8 | 23.2 | 29.7 | 8.3 | 6.3 | 4.7 | 24.0 | 18.4 | 17.5 | 18.0 | 24.0 | 62.0 |
| 1954 – 1958 | 6.1 | 3.2 | 1.3 | 6.8 | 6.8 | 3.8 | 6.8 | 5.1 | 10.1 | 11.8 | 7.1 | 1.6 | 8.6 | 12.7 |
| 1958 – 1960 | 12.7 | 9.1 | 6.8 | 12.7 | 13.6 | 8.6 | 11.4 | 5.8 | 15.3 | 18.3 | 13.1 | 8.6 | 17.0 | 15.8 |

[1] Stone, clay and sand quarrying (ISIC major group 14), Gasworks (ISIC group 512), Water supply (ISIC group 521) and cold storage (part of ISIC major group 72) are included under Manufacturing (in ISIC major groups 33, 31-32 and 20-22, respectively) but publishing (part of ISID major group 28) is excluded and coal briquetting (part of ISIC major group 32) is included under Coal mining (ISIC major group 11).
[2] The manufacture of vegetable oils (part of ISIC major group 312) is covered under Food (ISIC major group 20) but the production of starch (part of ISIC major group 20) is covered under Chemical products (ISIC major group 31).
[3] Knitting mills are covered under Clothing (ISIC major group 24) instead of Textiles (ISIC major group 23).
[4] The manufacture of metal furniture (part of ISIC major group 26) is covered under Metal products (ISIC major group 35) but the production of matches (part of ISIC major group 31) is included in Wood products (ISIC major group 25).
[5] The making of plastic, products is covered in Rubber products (ISIC major group 30) instead of Other manufacturing (ISIC major group 39).
[6] Manufacturing of Professional and scientific equipment, Photographic and optical goods, Watches and clocks, Jewellery and Musical instruments (ISIC groups 391-395) and of metal office supplies (part of ISIC group 399) is covered under Metal products (ISIC major groups 35-38) instead of Other manufacturing (ISIC major group 39).

[1] Extraction de la pierre à bâtir, de l'argile et du sable (CITI classe 14), Production et distribution de gaz (CITI groupe 512), Distribution d'eau (CITI groupe 521) et entrepôts frigorifiques (dans CITI classe 72) sont inclus dans Industries manufacturières (dans CITI classes 33, 31-32 et 20-22 respectivement), mais l'édition (dans CITI classe 28) est exclue et la fabrication des briquettes en charbon (dans CITI classe 32) est comprise dans Industries extractives de charbon (CITI classe 11).
[2] La Fabrication des huiles végétales (dans CITI groupe 312) est comprise dans Industries alimentaires (CITI classe 20), mais la production d'amidon (dans CITI classe 20) est incluse dans Produits chimiques (CITI classe 31).
[3] La bonneterie est comprise dans Articles d'habillement (CITI classe 24) et non dans Industrie textile (CITI classe 23).
[4] La fabrication des meubles métalliques (dans CITI classe 26) est comprise dans ouvrages en métaux (dans CITI classe 35), mais la production des allumettes (dans CITI classe 31) est incluse dans Ouvrages en bois (CITI classe 25).
[5] La fabrication des produits en matière plastique est comprise dans Ouvrages en caoutchouc (CITI classe 30) et non dans Autres industries manufacturières (CITI classe 39).
[6] La fabrication du matériel médico-chirurgical et des instruments de précision, du matériel photographique et des instruments d'optique, des montres et horloges, des articles d'orfèvrerie et de bijouterie, des instruments de musique (CITI groupes 391-395) et des articles de bureau métalliques (dans CITI groupe 399) est comprise dans Ouvrages en métaux (CITI classes 35-38) et non dans Autres industries manufacturières (CITI classe 39).

## 3.  INDEX NUMBERS OF INDUSTRIAL EMPLOYMENT — INDICES DE L'EMPLOI DANS L'INDUSTRIE

### A.  The Divisions of Industrial Activity
### Les branches de l'activité industrielle

| Period<br>Période | Total | Mining [1]<br>Industries<br>extractives [1] | Manu-<br>facturing [1]<br>Industries<br>manu-<br>facturières [1] | Construction<br>Bâtiment<br>et travaux<br>publics | Electricity<br>Electricité |
|---|---|---|---|---|---|
| ISIC — CITI | 1–4, 511–512 | 11–13, 19 | 14, 2–3, 512 | 4 | 511 |

a. Indexes — Indices (1958 = 100)

| | | | | | |
|---|---|---|---|---|---|
| 1949 | 54 | 53 | 56 | 42 | 59 |
| 1950 | 72 | 56 | 67 | 108 | 61 |
| 1951 | 85 | 63 | 78 | 139 | 62 |
| 1952 | 97 | 73 | 89 | 156 | 67 |
| 1953 | 103 | 85 | 96 | 152 | 78 |
| 1954 | 99 | 90 | 98 | 113 | 82 |
| 1955 | 96 | 91 | 96 | 101 | 85 |
| 1956 | 99 | 93 | 98 | 108 | 92 |
| 1957 | 97 | 95 | 96 | 102 | 93 |
| 1958 | 100 | 100 | 100 | 100 | 100 |
| 1959 | 107 | 105 | 106 | 112 | 108 |
| 1960 | 113 | 107 | 113 | 117 | 115 |
| 1961 | 116 | 110 | 118 | 114 | 114 |

b. Average Annual Rate of Change — Taux annuel moyen de variation

| | | | | | |
|---|---|---|---|---|---|
| 1950–1960 | 4.6 | 6.7 | 5.4 | 0.8 | 6.5 |
| 1950–1953 | 12.7 | 14.9 | 12.7 | 12.1 | 8.5 |
| 1954–1958 | 0.2 | 2.7 | 0.5 | −3.0 | 5.1 |
| 1958–1960 | 6.3 | 3.4 | 6.3 | 8.2 | 7.2 |

For footnotes see end of table.

Pour les notes, voir au bas du tableau.

### B.  The Major Groups of Mining
### Les classes de la branche Industries extractives

| Period<br>Période | All mining [1]<br>Toutes<br>industries<br>extractives [1] | Coal<br>mining [1]<br>Extraction<br>du charbon [1] | Metal mining<br>Extraction<br>des minerais<br>métalliques | Crude petro-<br>leum and<br>natural gas<br>Pétrole brut<br>et gaz naturel | Other mining [1]<br>Autres<br>industries<br>extractives [1] |
|---|---|---|---|---|---|
| ISIC — CITI | 11–13, 19 | 11 | 12 | 13 | 19 |

a. Indexes — Indices (1958 = 100)

| | | | | | |
|---|---|---|---|---|---|
| 1949 | 53 | 56 | 43 | 33 | 43 |
| 1950 | 56 | 58 | 43 | 43 | 55 |
| 1951 | 63 | 65 | 46 | 57 | 80 |
| 1952 | 73 | 73 | 56 | 80 | 99 |
| 1953 | 85 | 85 | 67 | 93 | 111 |
| 1954 | 90 | 92 | 68 | 87 | 110 |
| 1955 | 91 | 93 | 66 | 84 | 107 |
| 1956 | 93 | 94 | 69 | 92 | 106 |
| 1957 | 95 | 96 | 95 | 92 | 97 |
| 1958 | 100 | 100 | 100 | 100 | 100 |
| 1959 | 105 | 104 | 103 | 108 | 108 |
| 1960 | 107 | 106 | 113 | 111 | 122 |
| 1961 | 110 | 109 | ... | ... | ... |

b. Average Annual Rate of Change — Taux annuel moyen de variation

| | | | | | |
|---|---|---|---|---|---|
| 1950–1960 | 6.7 | 6.2 | 10.1 | 9.9 | 8.3 |
| 1950–1953 | 14.9 | 13.6 | 15.9 | 29.3 | 26.4 |
| 1954–1958 | 2.7 | 2.1 | 10.1 | 3.5 | −2.4 |
| 1958–1960 | 3.4 | 3.0 | 6.3 | 5.4 | 10.5 |

For footnotes see end of table.

Pour les notes, voir au bas du tableau.

# HUNGARY

## C. The Major Groups of Manufacturing — Les classes de la branche Industries manufacturières

| Period / Période | Manufacturing [1] / Industries manufacturières [1] | Food, beverages and tobacco [1,2] / Industries alimentaires, boissons, tabac [1,2] | Textiles [3] | Clothing, footwear and made-up textiles [3] / Articles d'habillement, chaussures et ouvrages en tissu [3] | Wood products and furniture [4] / Bois et meubles [4] | Paper and paper products / Papier et ouvrages en papier | Printing [1] / Imprimerie [1] | Leather and leather products except wearing apparel / Cuir et articles en cuir, à l'exclusion des articles d'habillement | Rubber products [5] / Ouvrages en caoutchouc [5] | Chemicals and chemical, petroleum and coal products [1,2,4] / Produits chimiques et dérivés du pétrole et du charbon [1,2,4] | Non-metallic mineral products [1] / Produits minéraux non métalliques [1] | Basic metals / Métallurgie de base | Metal products [4,6] / Ouvrages en métaux [4,6] | Other manufacturing [4,6] / Autres industries manufacturières [4,6] |
|---|---|---|---|---|---|---|---|---|---|---|---|---|---|---|
| ISIC — CITI | 14, 2-3, 512 | 20-22 | 23 | 24 | 25-26 | 27 | 28 | 29 | 30 | 31-32, 512 | 14, 33 | 34 | 35-38 391-395 | 399 |

### a. Indexes — Indices (1958 = 100)

| Period | | | | | | | | | | | | | | |
|---|---|---|---|---|---|---|---|---|---|---|---|---|---|---|
| 1949 | 56 | 63 | 76 | 29 | 46 | 94 | 104 | 73 | 52 | 56 | 54 | 63 | 55 | 4 |
| 1950 | 67 | 65 | 87 | 44 | 58 | 94 | 125 | 79 | 50 | 64 | 75 | 71 | 69 | 6 |
| 1951 | 78 | 67 | 90 | 57 | 77 | 93 | 112 | 74 | 52 | 70 | 82 | 81 | 90 | 7 |
| 1952 | 89 | 79 | 94 | 66 | 86 | 92 | 95 | 73 | 65 | 78 | 94 | 91 | 105 | 11 |
| 1953 | 96 | 90 | 92 | 70 | 93 | 97 | 92 | 80 | 67 | 80 | 109 | 101 | 113 | 38 |
| 1954 | 98 | 100 | 95 | 80 | 96 | 100 | 96 | 84 | 72 | 82 | 102 | 107 | 107 | 71 |
| 1955 | 96 | 99 | 96 | 84 | 91 | 98 | 95 | 85 | 74 | 85 | 100 | 104 | 100 | 77 |
| 1956 | 98 | 100 | 94 | 84 | 91 | 99 | 96 | 84 | 89 | 91 | 106 | 104 | 103 | 72 |
| 1957 | 96 | 101 | 99 | 91 | 93 | 96 | 90 | 93 | 96 | 92 | 97 | 96 | 96 | 98 |
| 1958 | 100 | 100 | 100 | 100 | 100 | 100 | 100 | 100 | 100 | 100 | 100 | 100 | 100 | 100 |
| 1959 | 106 | 104 | 102 | 107 | 112 | 107 | 108 | 104 | 107 | 106 | 107 | 104 | 109 | 94 |
| 1960 | 113 | 108 | 106 | 114 | 125 | 113 | 116 | 112 | 120 | 114 | 111 | 109 | 119 | 98 |
| 1961 | 118 | 111 | 108 | 120 | 133 | 114 | 122 | 123 | 133 | 119 | 108 | 116 | 125 | 107 |

### b. Average Annual Rate of Change — Taux annuel moyen de variation

| Period | | | | | | | | | | | | | | |
|---|---|---|---|---|---|---|---|---|---|---|---|---|---|---|
| 1950–1960 | 5.4 | 5.2 | 2.0 | 10.0 | 8.0 | 1.9 | −0.7 | 3.6 | 9.2 | 5.9 | 4.0 | 4.4 | 5.6 | 32.2 |
| 1950–1953 | 12.7 | 11.5 | 1.9 | 16.7 | 17.0 | 1.1 | −9.7 | 0.4 | 10.2 | 7.7 | 13.3 | 12.5 | 17.9 | 85.0 |
| 1954–1958 | 0.5 | — | 1.3 | 5.7 | 1.0 | — | 1.0 | 4.4 | 8.6 | 5.1 | −0.5 | −1.7 | −1.7 | 8.9 |
| 1958–1960 | 6.3 | 3.9 | 3.0 | 6.8 | 11.8 | 6.3 | 7.7 | 5.8 | 9.5 | 6.8 | 5.4 | 4.4 | 9·1 | −1.0 |

[1] Stone, clay and sand quarrying (ISIC major group 14), Gasworks (ISIC group 512), Water supply (ISIC group 521) and cold storage (part of ISIC major group 72) are included under Manufacturing (in ISIC major groups 33, 31-32 and 20-22 respectively) but publishing (part of ISIC major group 28) is excluded and coal briquetting (part of ISIC major group 32) is included under Coal mining (ISIC major group 11).

[2] The manufacture of vegetable oils (part of ISIC group 312) is covered under Food (ISIC major group 20) but the production of starch (part of ISIC major group 20) is covered under Chemical products (ISIC major group 31).

[3] Knitting mills are covered under Clothing (ISIC major group 24) instead of Textiles (ISIC major group 23).

[4] The manufacture of metal furniture (part of ISIC major group 26) is covered under Metal products (ISIC major group 35) but the production of matches (part of ISIC major group 31) is included in Wood products (ISIC major group 25).

[5] The making of plastic products is covered in Rubber products (ISIC major group 30) instead of Other manufacturing (ISIC major group 39).

[6] Manufacturing of Professional and scientific equipment, Photographic and optical goods, Watches and clocks, Jewellery and Musical instruments (ISIC group 391–395) and of metal office supplies (part of ISIC group 399) is covered under Metal products (ISIC major groups 35-38) instead of Other manufacturing (ISIC major group 39).

[1] Extraction de la pierre à bâtir, de l'argile et du sable (CITI classe 14), Production et distribution de gaz (CITI groupe 512), Distribution d'eau (CITI groupe 521) et entrepôts frigorifiques (dans CITI classe 72) sont inclus dans Industries manufacturières (dans CITI classes 33, 31-32, 20-22 respectivement), mais l'édition (dans CITI classe 28) est exclue et la fabrication des briquettes en charbon (dans CITI classe 32) est comprise dans Industries extractives de charbon (CITI classe 11).

[2] La Fabrication des huiles végétales (dans CITI groupe 312) est comprise dans Industries alimentaires (CITI classe 20) mais la production d'amidon (dans CITI classe 20) est incluse dans Produits chimiques (CITI classe 31).

[3] La bonneterie est comprise dans Articles d'habillement (CITI classe 24) et non dans Industrie textile (CITI classe 23).

[4] La fabrication des meubles métalliques (dans CITI classe 26) est comprise dans Ouvrages en métaux (CITI classe 35), mais la production d'allumettes (dans CITI classe 31) est incluse dans Ouvrages en bois (CITI classe 25).

[5] La fabrication de produits en matière plastique est comprise dans Ouvrages en caoutchouc (CITI classe 30) et non dans Autres industries manufacturières (CITI classe 39).

[6] La Fabrication du matériel médico-chirurgical et des instruments de précision, du matériel photographique et des instruments d'optique, des montres et horloges, des articles d'orfèvrerie et de bijouterie, des instruments de musique (CITI groupes 391–395) et des articles de bureau métalliques (dans CITI groupe 399) est comprise dans Ouvrages en métaux (CITI classes 35-38) et non dans Autres industries manufacturières (CITI classe 39).

## 4. THE CHARACTERISTICS OF INDUSTRIAL ESTABLISHMENTS WITH 10 OR MORE OPERATIVES AND INSTALLED POWER EQUIPMENT
## CARACTERISTIQUES DES ETABLISSEMENTS INDUSTRIELS EMPLOYANT 10 OUVRIERS OU PLUS ET UTILISANT DE LA FORCE MOTRICE
### 1938

Number of establishments in units; gross value of output and wages and salaries paid in million Pengö and number of engaged and employees in thousands

Nombre d'établissements en unités; valeur brute de la production et traitements et salaires payés en millions de pengö; nombre de personnes occupées et de salariés en milliers

### A. Selected Divisions of Industrial Activity — Quelques branches de l'activité industrielle

| Item of data | Mining<br>Industries extractives | Manufacturing [1]<br>Industries manufacturières [1] | Electricity and gas<br>Electricité et gaz | Rubrique |
|---|---|---|---|---|
| ISIC | 1 | 2–3 | 511–512 | CITI |
| Number of establishments....... | 226 | 3 494 | 284 | Nombre d'établissements |
| Gross value of output.......... | 155.7 | 2 843.9 | 170.2 | Valeur brute de la production |
| Number of engaged (Average during the year).... | ... | 315.4 | 13.4 | Nombre de personnes occupées (moyenne pendant l'année) |
| Number of employees.......... (As of 1.X)................. | 51.3 | ... | ... | Nombre de salariés (au 1.X) |
| Wages and salaries paid....... | 64.6 | 508.8 [2] | 34.7 | Traitements et salaires payés |

[1] Does not include publishing (in ISIC major group 28).
[2] Excludes the wages and salaries paid by two iron smelting works with 1.2 thousand engaged and gross value of output of 34.9 million Pengö.

[1] Non compris l'édition (dans CITI classe 28).
[2] Non compris les traitements et salaires payés par deux fonderies de fonte (1 200 personnes occupées et valeur brute de la production: 34,9 millions de pengö).

### B. The Major Groups of Mining — Les classes de la branche Industries extractives

| Item of data | All mining<br>Toutes industries extractives | Coal mining<br>Extraction du charbon | Metal mining<br>Extraction des minerais métalliques | Crude petroleum and natural gas<br>Pétrole brut et gaz naturel | Other mining<br>Divers | Rubrique |
|---|---|---|---|---|---|---|
| ISIC | 1 | 11 | 12 | 13 | 14–19 | CITI |
| Number of establishments....... | 226 | 89 | 17 | 9 | 111 | Nombre d'établissements |
| Gross value of output.......... | 155.7 | 124.4 | 12.3 | 2.9 | 16.1 | Valeur brute de la production |
| Number of employees (As of 1.X)................. | 51.3 | 40.1 | 2.6 | 0.7 | 7.9 [1] | Nombre de salariés (au 1.X) |
| Wages and salaries paid....... | 64.6 | ... | ... | ... | ... | Traitements et salaires payés |
| Distribution in percent of number of employees............... | 100.0 | 78.1 | 5.1 | 1.4 | 15.4 | Répartition en pourcentage du nombre de salariés |

[1] Average during the year.

[1] Moyenne pendant l'année.

### C. The Major Groups of Manufacturing — Les classes de la branche Industries manufacturières

| Item of data | Manufacturing [1]<br>Industries manufacturières [1] | Food, beverages and tobacco<br>Industries alimentaires, boissons, tabac | Textiles | Clothing, footwear and made-up textiles<br>Articles d'habillement, chaussures et ouvrages en tissu | Wood products and furniture [3]<br>Bois et meubles [3] | Paper and paper products [2]<br>Papier et ouvrages en papier [2] | Printing [1, 2]<br>Imprimerie [1, 2] | Leather and leather products except wearing apparel<br>Cuir et articles en cuir, à l'exclusion des articles d'habillement | Rubber products<br>Ouvrages en caoutchouc | Chemicals and chemical, petroleum and coal products<br>Produits chimiques et dérivés du pétrole et du charbon | Non-metallic mineral products<br>Produits minéraux non métalliques | Basic metals<br>Métallurgie de base | Metal products [3]<br>Ouvrages en métaux [3] | Other manufacturing<br>Autres industries manufacturières | Rubrique |
|---|---|---|---|---|---|---|---|---|---|---|---|---|---|---|---|
| ISIC | 2–3 | 20–22 | 23 | 24 | 25–26 | 27 | 28 | 29 | 30 | 31–32 | 33 | 34 | 35–38 | 39 | CITI |
| Number of establishments. | 3 494 | 1 025 | 356 | 229 | 330 | 102 | 120 | 65 | 8 | 262 | 448 | 37 | 391 | 121 | Nombre d'établissements |
| Gross value of output.... | 2 843.9 | 900.6 | 464.0 | 90.2 | 74.3 | 56.1 | 50.5 | 73.8 | 28.1 | 254.1 | 94.9 | 226.6 | 501.3 | 29.4 | Valeur brute de la production |
| Number of engaged (Average during the year)......... | 315.4 | 42.7 | 71.1 | 13.0 | 13.5 | 6.7 | 9.3 | 6.4 | 3.4 | 18.6 | 24.9 | 22.6 | 77.6 | 5.6 | Nombre de personnes occupées (moyenne pendant l'année) |
| Wages and salaries paid............... | 508.8 | 66.1 | 94.5 | 22.4 | 17.1 | 10.5 | 23.3 | 11.9 | 5.9 | 38.0 | 30.8 | 35.8 [4] | 143.9 | 8.6 | Traitements et salaires payés |
| Distribution in percent of number of engaged........... | 100.0 | 13.5 | 22.6 | 4.1 | 4.3 | 2.1 | 2.9 | 2.0 | 1.1 | 5.9 | 7.9 | 7.2 | 24.6 | 1.8 | Répartition en pourcentage du nombre de personnes occupées |

[1] Excludes publishing (in ISIC major group 28).
[2] Bookbinding is classified in Paper and paper products (ISIC major group 27) instead of in Printing and publishing (ISIC major group 28).
[3] The manufacturing of metal furniture is included in Metal products (ISIC major groups 35–38) instead of in Furniture (ISIC major group 26).
[4] Excludes wages and salaries paid by two iron smelting works with 1.2 thousand engaged and gross value of output of 34.9 million Pengö.

[1] Non compris l'édition (dans CITI classe 28).
[2] La reliure est classée dans Papier et ouvrages en papier (CITI classe 27) et non dans Imprimerie et édition (CITI classe 28).
[3] La fabrication des meubles métalliques est classée dans Ouvrages en métaux (CITI classes 35–38 et non dans Industrie du meuble (CITI classe 26).
[4] Non compris les traitements et salaires payés par deux fonderies de fonte (1 200 de personnes occupées et valeur brute de la production: 34,9 millions de pengö)

# HUNGARY

## 5. THE CHARACTERISTICS OF ALL INDUSTRIAL ENTERPRISES
## CARACTERISTIQUES DE TOUTES LES ENTREPRISES INDUSTRIELLES
### 1955, 1958

Number of enterprises in units; value of gross output, net material product and wages and salaries in million Forints; number of engaged, employees and operatives in thousands; electricity consumed in million KWH; wages and salaries per engaged and per operative in thousand Forints; electricity consumed per engaged and per operative in thousand KWH.

Nombre d'entreprises en unités; valeur de la production brute, du produit matériel brut et net et traitements et salaires en millions de forints; nombre de personnes occupées de salariés et d'ouvriers en milliers; électricité consommée en millions de kWh traitements et salaires par personne occupée et par ouvrier en milliers de forints électricité consommée par personne occupée et par ouvrier en milliers de kWh.

### A. The Divisions of Industrial Activity — Les branches de l'activité industrielle

#### a. Publicly owned enterprises — Entreprises publiques

| Year and item of data (ISIC) | Total excluding construction (1–3, 511–512) | Mining[1] (11–13, 19) | Manufacturing[1] (14, 2–3, 512) | Construction (4) | Electricity and gas (511–512) | Année et rubrique (CITI) |
|---|---|---|---|---|---|---|
| **1955** | | | | | | **1955** |
| Value of gross output | 72 366.7 | 3 840.8 | 66 230.3 | 7 533.5 | 2 295.6 | Valeur de la production brute |
| Net material product | 45 795.1 | ... | ... | 4 580.4 | ... | Produit matériel net |
| Persons engaged: Number (Average during year) | 932.6 | 122.3 | 779.9 | 176.8 | 30.4 | Personnes occupées: Nombre (moyenne pendant l'année) |
| Wages and salaries | 13 537.5 | 2 302.8 | 10 784.8 | 2 428.0 | 449.9 | Traitements et salaires |
| Operatives: Number (Average during year) | 712.5 | 104.5 | 586.5 | 135.5 | 21.5 | Ouvriers: Nombre (moyenne pendant l'année) |
| Wages and salaries | 9 774.0 | 1 909.7 | 7 569.6 | ... | 294.7 | Traitements et salaires |
| Operatives as percent of engaged | 76.4 | 85.4 | 75.2 | 76.6 | 70.7 | Ouvriers en pourcentage des personnes occupées |
| Wages and salaries paid: Per person engaged | 14.5 | 18.8 | 13.8 | 13.7 | 14.8 | Traitements et salaires payés: Par personne occupée |
| Per operative | 13.7 | 18.3 | 12.9 | ... | 13.7 | Par ouvrier |
| **1958** | | | | | | **1958** |
| Number of establishments (As of end of year) | 7 455 | 306 | 7 045 | 175[2] | 104 | Nombre d'établissements (à la fin de l'année) |
| Value of gross output | 88 690.1 | 4 367.0 | 80 923.2 | 9 190.0 | 3 399.9 | Valeur de la production brute |
| Net material product | 52 755.0 | ... | ... | 5 353.0 | ... | Produit matériel net |
| Persons engaged: Number (Average during year) | 981.4 | 134.4 | 811.8 | 175.5 | 35.2 | Personnes occupées: Nombre (moyenne pendant l'année) |
| Wages and salaries | 18 046.2 | 3 407.4 | 13 980.1 | 3 195.0 | 658.7 | Traitements et salaires |
| Operatives: Number (Average during year) | 765.5 | 115.6 | 624.4 | 138.1 | 25.5 | Ouvriers: Nombre (moyenne pendant l'année) |
| Wages and salaries | 13 607.3 | 2 890.8 | 10 262.1 | ... | 454.4 | Traitements et salaires |
| Electricity consumed | 4 243.8 | 638.6 | 3 497.9 | ... | 107.3 | Electricité consommée |
| Operatives as percent of engaged | 78.0 | 86.0 | 76.9 | 78.7 | 72.4 | Ouvriers en pourcentage des personnes occupées |
| Wages and salaries paid: Per person engaged | 18.4 | 25.4 | 17.2 | 18.2 | 18.7 | Traitements et salaires payés: Par personne occupée |
| Per operative | 17.8 | 25.0 | 16.4 | ... | 17.8 | Par ouvrier |
| Electricity consumed: Per person engaged | 4.3 | 4.8 | 4.3 | ... | 3.0 | Electricité consommée: Par personne occupée |
| Per operative | 5.5 | 5.5 | 5.6 | ... | 4.2 | Par ouvrier |

#### b. Co-operatives — Coopératives

| Year and item of data (ISIC) | Total excluding construction (1–3, 511–512) | Mining[1] (11–13, 19) | Manufacturing[1] (14, 2–3, 512) | Construction (4) | Electricity and gas (511–512) | Année et rubrique (CITI) |
|---|---|---|---|---|---|---|
| **1955** | | | | | | **1955** |
| Number of enterprises (As of end of year) | 1 203 | — | 1 203 | 151 | — | Nombre d'entreprises (à la fin de l'année) |
| Value of gross output | 5 442.9 | — | 5 442.9 | 544.4 | — | Valeur de la production brute |
| Net material product | 2 492.9 | — | 2 492.9 | 282.1 | — | Produit matériel net |
| Persons engaged: Number (Average during year) | 117.5 | — | 117.5 | 13.2 | — | Personnes occupées: Nombre (moyenne pendant l'année) |
| Wages and salaries | 1 237.6 | — | 1 237.6 | 185.5 | — | Traitements et salaires |
| Operatives: Number (Average during year) | 98.8 | — | 98.8 | 10.1 | — | Ouvriers: Nombre (moyenne pendant l'année) |
| Wages and salaries | 1 019.8 | — | 1 019.8 | 147.4 | — | Traitements et salaires |
| Operatives as a percent of engaged | 84.1 | — | 84.1 | 76.5 | — | Ouvriers en pourcentage des personnes occupées |
| Wages and salaries paid: Per person engaged | 10.5 | — | 10.5 | 14.0 | — | Traitements et salaires payés: Par personne occupée |
| Per operative | 10.3 | — | 10.3 | 14.6 | — | Par ouvrier |
| **1958** | | | | | | **1958** |
| Number of enterprises (As of end of year) | 1 298 | — | 1 298 | 224 | — | Nombre d'entreprises (à la fin de l'année) |
| Value of gross output | 6 620.0 | — | 6 620.0 | 904.3 | — | Valeur de la production brute |
| Net material product | 3 342.0 | — | 3 342.0 | 714.0 | — | Produit matériel net |
| Persons engaged: Number (Average during year) | 144.6 | — | 144.6 | 18.1 | — | Personnes occupées: Nombre (moyenne pendant l'année) |
| Wages and salaries | 1 728.1 | — | 1 728.1 | 315.8 | — | Traitements et salaires |
| Operatives: Number (Average during year) | 124.6 | — | 124.6 | 13.6 | — | Ouvriers: Nombre (moyenne pendant l'année) |
| Wages and salaries | 1 407.4 | — | 1 407.4 | 246.2 | — | Traitements et salaires |
| Electricity consumed | 26.0 | — | 26.0 | ... | — | Electricité consommée |
| Operatives as a percent of engaged | 86.2 | — | 86.2 | 75.1 | — | Ouvriers en pourcentage des personnes occupées |
| Wages and salaries paid: Per person engaged | 12.0 | — | 12.0 | 17.4 | — | Traitements et salaires payés: Par personne occupée |
| Per operative | 11.3 | — | 11.3 | 18.1 | — | Par ouvrier |
| Electricity consumed: Per person engaged | 0.2 | — | 0.2 | ... | — | Electricité consommée: Par personne occupée |
| Per operative | 0.2 | — | 0.2 | ... | — | Par ouvrier |

For footnotes see end of table.

Pour les notes, voir au bas du tableau.

## A. The Divisions of Industrial Activity (continued)
### Les branches de l'activité industrielle (suite)

## B. The Major Groups of Mining
### Les classes de la branche Industries extractives

| Year and item of data | Total excluding construction — Total à l'exclusion du bâtiment et des travaux publics | Mining [1] — Industries extractives [1] | Manufacturing [1] — Industries manufacturières[1] | Construction — Bâtiment et travaux publics | Electricity and gas — Electricité et gaz | Année et rubrique |
|---|---|---|---|---|---|---|
| ISIC | 1–3, 511–512 | 11–13, 19 | 14, 2–3, 512 | 4 | 511–512 | CITI |
| | | c. Privately owned enterprises — Entreprises privées | | | | |
| 1955 | | | | | | 1955 |
| Number of enterprises [4] | 79.8 | — | 79.8 | 17.2 | — | Nombre d'entreprises [4] |
| Value of gross output | 4 295.3 | — | 4 295.3 | 1 440.8 | — | Valeur de la production brute |
| Net material product | 2 176.5 | — | 2 176.5 | 680.7 | — | Produit matériel net |
| Number of engaged (Average during year) | 90.0 | — | 90.0 | 20.6 | — | Nombre de personnes occupées (moyenne pendant l'année) |
| Number of employees (Average during year) | 10.2 | — | 10.2 | 3.5 | — | Nombre de salariés (moyenne pendant l'année) |
| 1958 | | | | | | 1958 |
| Number of enterprises [4] | 92.2 | — | 92.2 | 19.2 | — | Nombre d'entreprises [4] |
| Value of gross output | 6 621.2 | — | 6 621.2 | 4 098.0 | — | Valeur de la production brute |
| Net material product | 3 765.0 | — | 3 765.0 | 1 926.0 [5] | — | Produit matériel net |
| Number of engaged (Average during year) | 116.5 | — | 116.5 | 29.0 | — | Nombre de personnes occupées (moyenne pendant l'année) |
| Number of employees (Average during year) | 24.3 | — | 24.3 | 9.8 | — | Nombre de salariés (moyenne pendant l'année) |

For footnotes see end of table.

Pour les notes, voir au bas du tableau.

| Item of data | All mining — Toutes industries extractives | Coal mining [1] — Extraction du charbon [1] | Metal mining — Extraction des minerais métalliques | Crude petroleum and natural gas — Pétrole brut et gaz naturel | Other mining — Divers | Rubrique |
|---|---|---|---|---|---|---|
| ISIC | 11–13, 19 | 11 | 12 | 13 | 19 | CITI |
| 1955 | | | | | | 1955 |
| Value of gross output | 3 325.5 | 2 528.5 | 158.0 | 329.5 | 309.5 | Valeur de la production brute |
| Persons engaged: Number (Average during year) | 122.5 | 100.8 | 5.9 | 4.5 | 11.3 | Personnes occupées: Nombre (moyenne pendant l'année) |
| Wages and salaries | 2 280.3 | 1 951.9 | 98.2 | 73.0 | 157.2 | Traitements et salaires |
| Operatives: Number (Average during year) | 103.4 | 86.8 | 4.7 | 2.9 | 9.0 | Ouvriers: Nombre (moyenne pendant l'année) |
| Wages and salaries | 1 865.2 | 1 633.5 | 73.6 | 37.9 | 120.2 | Traitements et salaires |
| Distribution in percent of number of engaged | 100.0 | 82.2 | 4.9 | 3.6 | 9.3 | Distribution en pourcentage du nombre de personnes occupées |
| Operatives as a percent of engaged | 84.4 | 86.1 | 79.7 | 64.4 | 79.6 | Ouvriers en pourcentage des personnes occupées |
| Wages and salaries paid: Per person engaged | 18.6 | 19.4 | 16.6 | 16.2 | 13.9 | Traitements et salaires payés: Par personne occupée |
| Per operative | 18.0 | 18.8 | 15.6 | 13.1 | 13.4 | Par ouvrier |
| 1958 | | | | | | 1958 |
| Number of establishments (As of end of year) | 306 | 149 | 25 | 46 | 86 | Nombre d'établissements (à la fin de l'année) |
| Value of gross output | 4 367.0 | 3 047.5 | 321.9 | 854.7 | 142.9 | Valeur de la production brute |
| Persons engaged: Number (Average during year) | 134.4 | 112.7 | 9.6 | 8.7 | 3.4 | Personnes occupées: Nombre (moyenne pendant l'année) |
| Wages and salaries | 3 407.4 | 2 932.0 | 233.6 | 172.1 | 69.7 | Traitements et salaires |
| Operatives: Number (Average during year) | 115.6 | 98.3 | 7.8 | 6.8 | 2.7 | Ouvriers: Nombre (moyenne pendant l'année) |
| Wages and salaries | 2 890.9 | 2 521.1 | 187.3 | 128.6 | 53.9 | Traitements et salaires |
| Electricity consumed | 638.7 | 540.8 | 44.5 | 47.8 | 5.6 | Electricité consommée |
| Distribution in percent of number of engaged | 100.0 | 83.8 | 7.1 | 6.5 | 2.6 | Distribution en pourcentage du nombre de personnes occupées |
| Operatives as a percent of engaged | 86.0 | 87.2 | 81.2 | 78.2 | 79.4 | Ouvriers en pourcentage des personnes occupées |
| Wages and salaries paid: Per person engaged: | 25.4 | 26.0 | 24.3 | 19.8 | 20.5 | Traitements et salaires payés: Par personne occupée |
| Per operative | 25.0 | 25.6 | 24.0 | 18.9 | 20.0 | Par ouvrier |
| Electricity consumed: Per person engaged | 4.8 | 4.8 | 4.6 | 5.5 | 1.6 | Electricité consommée: Par personne occupée |
| Per operative | 5.5 | 5.5 | 5.7 | 7.0 | 2.1 | Par ouvrier |

For footnotes see end of table.

Pour les notes, voir au bas du tableau

# HUNGARY

## C. The Major Groups of Manufacturing — Les classes de la branche Industries manufacturières

| Year and item of data | Manufacturing[1] / Industries manufacturières[1] | Food, beverages and tobacco[1] / Industries alimentaires, boissons, tabac[1] | Textiles[6] | Clothing, footwear and made-up textiles[6] / Articles d'habillement, chaussures et ouvrages en tissu[6] | Wood products and furniture[7] / Bois et meubles[7] | Paper and paper products / Papier et ouvrages en papier | Printing[1] / Imprimerie[1] | Leather and leather products except wearing apparel / Cuir et articles en cuir, à l'exclusion des articles d'habillement | Rubber products[8] / Ouvrages en caoutchouc[8] | Chemicals and chemical, petroleum and coal products[1,7,8] / Produits chimiques et dérivés du pétrole et du charbon[1,7,8] | Non-metallic mineral products[1] / Produits minéraux non métalliques[1] | Basic metals / Métallurgie de base | Metal products[9] / Ouvrages en métaux[9] | Other manufacturing[7,8,9,10] / Autres industries manufacturières[7,8,9,10] | Année et rubrique |
|---|---|---|---|---|---|---|---|---|---|---|---|---|---|---|---|
| **ISIC** | 14, 2-3, 512 | 20–22 | 23 | 24 | 25–26 | 27 | 28 | 29 | 30 | 31-32, 512 | 14, 33 | 34 | 35–38 | 39 | **CITI** |
| a. Publicly owned enterprises — Entreprises publiques ||||||||||||||||
| **1955** | | | | | | | | | | | | | | | **1955** |
| Value of gross output.... | 66 291.5 | 22 447.5 | 6 941.6 | 4 769.6 | 1 324.8 | 656.5 | 517.8 | 1 134.8 | 741.2 | 3 164.7 | 2 009.7 | 5 498.7 | 16 552.6 | 532.1 | Valeur de la production brute |
| Persons engaged: | | | | | | | | | | | | | | | Personnes occupées: |
| Number (Average during year)........ | 759.7 | 97.3 | 107.9 | 37.5 | 24.7 | 6.7 | 11.1 | 7.6 | 5.2 | 30.6 | 54.8 | 66.4 | 294.3 | 15.6 | Nombre (moyenne pendant l'année) |
| Wages and salaries... | 10 577.1 | 1 171.4 | 1 301.8 | 451.6 | 319.4 | 91.4 | 150.7 | 100.2 | 73.9 | 446.0 | 731.6 | 1 090.6 | 4 479.2 | 169.3 | Traitements et salaires |
| Operatives: | | | | | | | | | | | | | | | Ouvriers: |
| Number (Average during year)........ | 568.9 | 67.4 | 86.9 | 30.5 | 18.6 | 5.2 | 8.3 | 5.7 | 4.0 | 21.4 | 44.9 | 51.7 | 211.4 | 12.9 | Nombre (moyenne pendant l'année) |
| Wages and salaries... | 7 404.6 | 761.8 | 965.6 | 355.7 | 226.0 | 67.1 | 109.0 | 71.9 | 51.9 | 280.4 | 578.9 | 809.9 | 2 994.1 | 132.3 | Traitements et salaires |
| Distribution in percent of number of engaged............ | 100.0 | 12.8 | 14.2 | 4.9 | 3.2 | 0.9 | 1.5 | 1.0 | 0.7 | 4.0 | 7.2 | 8.8 | 38.7 | 2.1 | Distribution en pourcentage du nombre de personnes occupées |
| Operatives as a percent of engaged........ | 74.9 | 69.3 | 80.5 | 81.3 | 75.3 | 77.6 | 74.8 | 75.0 | 76.9 | 69.9 | 81.9 | 77.9 | 71.8 | 82.7 | Ouvriers en pourcentage des personnes occupées |
| Wages and salaries paid: | | | | | | | | | | | | | | | Traitements et salaires payés: |
| Per person engaged.. | 13.9 | 12.0 | 12.1 | 12.0 | 12.9 | 13.6 | 13.6 | 13.2 | 14.2 | 14.6 | 13.4 | 16.4 | 15.2 | 10.8 | Par personne occupée |
| Per operative........ | 13.0 | 11.3 | 11.1 | 11.7 | 12.2 | 12.9 | 13.1 | 12.6 | 13.0 | 13.1 | 12.9 | 15.7 | 14.2 | 10.2 | Par ouvrier |
| **1958** | | | | | | | | | | | | | | | **1958** |
| Number of establishments. | 7 085 | 3 744 | 172 | 346 | 225 | 25 | 111 | 21 | 36 | 227 | 561 | 73 | 679 | 865 | Nombre d'établissements |
| Value of gross output.... | 31 346.6 | 25 764.2 | 6 579.5 | 7 280.4 | 1 908.1 | 752.2 | 670.9 | 1 072.7 | 1 116.2 | 5 680.0 | 2 725.4 | 6 731.3 | 18 609.8 | 2 455.9 | Valeur de la production brute |
| Gross material product.. | 24 463 | 3 927 | 2 280 | 1 606 | 748 | 241 | 314 | 258 | 343 | 1 663 | 1 478 | 1 855 | 8 501 | 1 249 | Produit matériel brut |
| Persons engaged: | | | | | | | | | | | | | | | Personnes occupées: |
| Number (Average during year)........ | 815.7 | 98.8 | 101.1 | 60.3 | 25.4 | 6.6 | 12.5 | 7.1 | 8.4 | 42.2 | 61.4 | 72.9 | 264.7 | 54.3 | Nombre (moyenne pendant l'année) |
| Wages and salaries... | 14 047.5 | 1 604.6 | 1 571.7 | 920.2 | 433.2 | 114.2 | 222.5 | 123.7 | 141.0 | 753.3 | 1 059.2 | 1 433.0 | 4 908.1 | 762.8 | Traitements et salaires |
| Operatives: | | | | | | | | | | | | | | | Ouvriers: |
| Number (Average during year)........ | 627.0 | 69.4 | 83.1 | 50.0 | 19.6 | 5.1 | 10.1 | 5.4 | 6.7 | 31.1 | 51.4 | 57.9 | 193.6 | 43.6 | Nombre (moyenne pendant l'année) |
| Wages and salaries... | 10 305.7 | 1 097.2 | 1 202.2 | 744.7 | 322.3 | 85.7 | 175.2 | 93.8 | 106.9 | 519.5 | 866.1 | 1 109.9 | 3 424.4 | 557.8 | Traitements et salaires |
| Electricity consumed..... | 3 510.0 | 344.5 | 293.9 | 30.0 | 23.2 | 84.0 | 10.3 | 15.2 | 34.1 | 384.2 | 217.8 | 1 590.8 | 462.4 | 19.6 | Électricité consommée |
| Distribution in percent of: | | | | | | | | | | | | | | | Distribution en pourcentage: |
| Gross material product. | 100.0 | 16.0 | 9.3 | 6.6 | 3.0 | 1.0 | 1.3 | 1.1 | 1.4 | 6.8 | 6.0 | 7.6 | 34.7 | 5.2 | Produit matériel brut |
| Number of engaged... | 100.0 | 12.1 | 12.4 | 7.3 | 3.2 | 0.8 | 1.5 | 0.9 | 1.0 | 5.2 | 7.5 | 8.9 | 32.5 | 6.7 | Nombre de personnes occupées |
| Operatives as a percent of engaged........ | 76.9 | 70.2 | 82.2 | 82.9 | 77.2 | 77.3 | 80.8 | 76.0 | 79.8 | 73.7 | 83.7 | 79.4 | 73.1 | 80.3 | Ouvriers en pourcentage des personnes occupées |
| Wages and salaries paid: | | | | | | | | | | | | | | | Traitements et salaires payés: |
| Per person engaged... | 17.2 | 16.2 | 15.5 | 15.3 | 17.0 | 17.3 | 17.8 | 17.4 | 16.8 | 17.8 | 17.2 | 19.6 | 18.5 | 14.0 | Par personne occupée |
| Per operative........ | 16.4 | 15.8 | 14.5 | 14.9 | 16.4 | 16.8 | 17.3 | 17.4 | 16.0 | 16.7 | 16.8 | 19.2 | 17.7 | 12.8 | Par ouvrier |
| Electricity consumed: | | | | | | | | | | | | | | | Électricité consommée: |
| Per person engaged... | 4.3 | 3.5 | 2.9 | 0.5 | 0.9 | 12.7 | 0.8 | 2.1 | 4.0 | 9.1 | 3.5 | 21.8 | 1.7 | 0.4 | Par personne occupée |
| Per operative........ | 5.6 | 5.0 | 3.5 | 0.6 | 1.2 | 16.5 | 1.0 | 2.8 | 5.1 | 12.4 | 4.2 | 27.5 | 2.4 | 0.4 | Par ouvrier |
| b. Co-operatives — Coopératives ||||||||||||||||
| **1955** | | | | | | | | | | | | | | | **1955** |
| Number of enterprises... | 1 209 | — | 131 | 283 | 110 | 6 | — | 17 | — | 14 | 4 | — | 252 | 392 | Nombre d'entreprises |
| Value of gross output.. | 5 188.1 | — | 736.1 | 2 277.5 | 391.6 | 64.8 | — | 147.3 | — | 135.9 | 45.6 | — | 902.8 | 486.5 | Valeur de la production brute |
| Persons engaged: | | | | | | | | | | | | | | | Personnes occupées: |
| Number (Average during year)........ | 113.8 | — | 40.2 | 27.9 | 7.6 | 0.9 | — | 1.7 | — | 1.5 | 0.8 | — | 19.0 | 14.1 | Nombre (moyenne pendant l'année) |
| Wages and salaries... | 1 194.3 | — | 206.8 | 355.1 | 112.2 | 12.4 | — | 25.2 | — | 25.0 | 12.6 | — | 291.0 | 154.0 | Traitements et salaires |
| Operatives: | | | | | | | | | | | | | | | Ouvriers: |
| Number (Average during year)........ | 95.4 | — | 38.4 | 22.3 | 5.7 | 0.8 | — | 1.3 | — | 1.3 | 0.6 | — | 14.0 | 11.0 | Nombre (moyenne pendant l'année) |
| Wages and salaries... | 978.8 | — | 182.4 | 293.8 | 89.8 | 10.2 | — | 20.5 | — | 18.7 | 9.6 | — | 230.8 | 123.0 | Traitements et salaires |
| Distribution in percent of number of engaged............ | 100.0 | — | 35.3 | 24.5 | 6.7 | 0.8 | — | 1.5 | — | 1.4 | 0.7 | — | 16.7 | 12.4 | Distribution en pourcentage des personnes occupées |

For footnotes see end of table.　　　　　　　　Pour les notes, voir au bas du tableau.

## C. The Major Groups of Manufacturing (continued) — Les classes de la branche Industries manufacturières (suite)

| Year and item of data | Manufacturing [1] / Industries manufacturières [1] | Food, beverages and tobacco [1] / Industries alimentaires, boissons, tabac [1] | Textiles [6] | Clothing, footwear and made-up textiles [6] / Articles d'habillement, chaussures et ouvrages en tissu [6] | Wood products and furniture [7] / Bois et meubles [7] | Paper and paper products / Papier et ouvrages en papier | Printing [1] / Imprimerie [1] | Leather and leather products except wearing apparel / Cuir et articles en cuir, à l'exclusion des articles d'habillement | Rubber products [8] / Ouvrages en caoutchouc [8] | Chemicals and chemical, petroleum and coal products [1,7,8] / Produits chimiques et dérivés du pétrole et du charbon [1,7,8] | Non-metallic mineral products [1] / Produits minéraux non métalliques [1] | Basic metals / Métallurgie de base | Metal products [9] / Ouvrages en métaux [9] | Other manufacturing [7,8,9,10] / Autres industries manufacturières [7,8,9,10] | Année et rubrique |
|---|---|---|---|---|---|---|---|---|---|---|---|---|---|---|---|
| ISIC | 14, 2-3, 512 | 20–22 | 23 | 24 | 25–26 | 27 | 28 | 29 | 30 | 31-32, 512 | 14, 33 | 34 | 35–38 | 39 | CITI |
| **b. Co-operatives — Coopératives** | | | | | | | | | | | | | | | |
| Operatives as a percent of engaged | 83.8 | — | 95.5 | 79.9 | 75.0 | 88.9 | — | 76.5 | — | 81.2 | 75.0 | — | 73.7 | 78.0 | Ouvriers en pourcentage des personnes occupées |
| Wages and salaries paid: | | | | | | | | | | | | | | | Traitements et salaires payés: |
| Per person engaged | 10.5 | — | 5.1 | 12.7 | 14.8 | 13.8 | — | 14.8 | — | 15.6 | 15.8 | — | 15.3 | 10.9 | Par personne occupée |
| Per operative | 10.2 | — | 4.8 | 13.2 | 15.8 | 12.8 | — | 15.8 | — | 14.4 | 16.0 | — | 16.5 | 11.2 | Par ouvrier |
| 1958 | | | | | | | | | | | | | | | 1958 |
| Number of enterprises | 472.0 | 6 | 449 | 1 399 | 350 | 21 | 6 | 69 | 72 | 43 | 38 | — | 555 | 1 712 | Nombre d'entreprises |
| Value of gross output | 6 555.8 | 15.6 | 1 115.7 | 2 762.2 | 489.9 | 53.9 | 11.5 | 146.1 | 125.8 | 114.8 | 57.9 | — | 863.5 | 798.9 | Valeur de la production brute |
| Persons engaged: | | | | | | | | | | | | | | | Personnes occupées: |
| Number (Average during year) | 143.6 | 0.2 | 63.7 | 31.8 | 8.5 | 1.0 | 0.2 | 2.1 | 2.1 | 0.8 | 1.0 | — | 14.9 | 17.3 | Nombre (moyenne pendant l'année) |
| Wages and salaries | 1 711.2 | 3.2 | 365.5 | 513.4 | 155.0 | 14.8 | 3.7 | 35.3 | 38.4 | 15.5 | 19.0 | — | 279.9 | 267.5 | Traitements et salaires |
| Operatives: | | | | | | | | | | | | | | | Ouvriers: |
| Number (Average during year) | 68.8 | 0.1 | 7.4 | 25.1 | 6.4 | 0.7 | 0.2 | 1.4 | 1.7 | 0.5 | 0.8 | — | 11.2 | 13.3 | Nombre (moyenne pendant l'année) |
| Wages and salaries | 1 162.6 | 2.0 | 95.5 | 413.1 | 124.3 | 10.5 | 2.9 | 26.2 | 28.4 | 10.0 | 14.6 | — | 219.4 | 215.7 | Traitements et salaires |
| Electricity consumed | 25.9 | 0.1 | 2.6 | 5.8 | 3.6 | 0.2 | — | 0.6 | 2.1 | 0.3 | 0.3 | — | 6.8 | 3.5 | Electricité consommée |
| Distribution in percent of number of engaged | 100.0 | 0.1 | 44.3 | 22.2 | 5.9 | 0.7 | 0.1 | 1.5 | 1.5 | 0.5 | 0.7 | — | 10.4 | 12.1 | Distribution en pourcentage du nombre de personnes occupées |
| Operatives as a percent of engaged | 47.9 | 50.0 | 11.6 | 78.9 | 75.3 | 70.0 | 100.0 | 66.7 | 81.0 | 62.5 | 80.0 | — | 75.2 | 76.9 | Ouvriers en pourcentage des personnes occupées |
| Wages and salaries paid: | | | | | | | | | | | | | | | Traitements et salaires payés: |
| Per person engaged | 11.9 | 16.0 | 5.7 | 16.1 | 18.2 | 14.8 | 18.5 | 16.8 | 18.3 | 19.4 | 19.0 | — | 18.8 | 15.5 | Par personne occupée |
| Per operative | 16.9 | 20.0 | 12.9 | 16.4 | 19.4 | 15.0 | 14.5 | 18.7 | 16.7 | 20.0 | 18.2 | — | 19.6 | 16.2 | Par ouvrier |
| Electricity consumed: | | | | | | | | | | | | | | | Electricité consommée: |
| Per person engaged | 0.2 | 0.5 | — | 0.2 | 0.4 | 0.2 | 0.2 | 0.3 | 1.0 | 0.4 | 0.3 | — | 0.4 | 0.2 | Par personne occupée |
| Per operative | 0.4 | 1.0 | 0.4 | 0.2 | 0.6 | 0.3 | 0.2 | 0.4 | 1.2 | 0.6 | 0.4 | — | 0.6 | 0.3 | Par ouvrier |
| **c. Privately owned enterprises — Entreprises privées** | | | | | | | | | | | | | | | |
| 1955 | | | | | | | | | | | | | | | 1955 |
| Number of enterprises [4] | 79 833 [11] | 2 176 | 3 573 | 34 163 | 14 309 | 336 | — | 1 046 | 702 | 174 | 1 065 | 75 | 11 961 | 9 132 | Nombre d'entreprises [4] |
| Number of engaged (in units) | 90 049 [11] | 2 408 | 3 638 | 36 344 | 17 672 | 376 | — | 1 158 | 766 | 181 | 1 215 | 87 | 14 837 | 10 246 | Nombre de personnes occupées (en unités) |
| Number of employees (in units) | 10 216 | 232 | 65 | 2 181 | 3 363 | 40 | — | 112 | 64 | 7 | 150 | 12 | 2 876 | 1 114 | Nombre de salariés (en unités) |
| 1958 | | | | | | | | | | | | | | | 1958 |
| Number of enterprises | 92 193 | 3 257 | 4 694 | 33 699 | 15 585 | 329 | — | 1 108 | 920 | 280 | 1 252 | 94 | 13 102 | 15 687 | Nombre d'entreprises |
| Number of engaged (in units) | 116 503 | 4 018 | 4 992 | 39 083 | 23 889 | 451 | — | 1 381 | 993 | 349 | 2 233 | 98 | 19 523 | 17 307 | Nombre de personnes occupées (en unités) |
| Number of employees (in units) | 24 310 | 761 | 298 | 5 384 | 8 304 | 122 | — | 273 | 73 | 69 | 981 | 4 | 6 421 | 1 620 | Nombre de salariés (en unités) |

[1] Included in Manufacturing in 1955 and 1958, are Stone, clay and sand quarrying (ISIC major group 14), Gasworks (ISIC group 512) and cold storage (part of ISIC major group 72) under ISIC major groups 33, 31-32 and 20-22, respectively; and, in 1958, are Waterworks (ISIC major group 521) under ISIC major group 20-22. Excluded from Manufacturing, in 1955 and 1958, are publishing (part of ISIC major group 28) and coal briquetting (part of ISIC major group 32, which is included under Coal mining (ISIC major group 11).

[2] Number of enterprises instead of number of establishments.

[3] The net material product contributed by the own-accounts construction of co-operatives is included in the data for publicly owned enterprises.

[4] The number of enterprises is the average number of private artisans having trade licenses during the year whether or not in business at the time of the census.

[5] Includes net material product in own-accounts construction of population as well as of privately owned construction enterprises. In 1958, Knitting mills (part of ISIC major group 23) are included under Clothing (ISIC major group 24).

[7] The manufacture of metal furniture (part of ISIC major group 26) is covered under Metal products (ISIC major group 35-38) but the production of matches (part of ISIC major group 31) and of wooden toys and office supplies (part of ISIC major group 39) are included under Wood products (ISIC major group 25).

[8] The manufacture of plastic production and of sensitized film, paper and plates (part of ISIC major group 39) are covered under Rubber products (ISIC major group 30) and Chemical products (ISIC major group 31), respectively.

[9] Included under Metal products (ISIC major group 35-38), in 1955 and 1958, are the manufacturing of Jewellery and related items, musical instruments, and metal office supplies (all part of ISIC major group 39); and in 1958, are Professional, scientific and measuring equipment (ISIC group 391).

[10] Includes enterprises with a mixture of different kinds of activity.

[11] Itinerant private artisans are included in the figures for Manufacturing as a whole but not the various major groups. Therefore, the total of the figures for the major groups does not equal the data shown for Manufacturing as a whole.

[1] Sont comprises dans Industries manufacturières en 1955 et 1958 l'Extraction de la pierre à bâtir, de l'argile et du sable (CITI classe 14), la Production et la distribution de gaz (CITI groupe 512) et les entrepôts frigorifiques (dans CITI classe 72) sous les classes 33, 31-32 et 20-22 de la CITI, respectivement; en 1958, la Distribution d'eau (CITI classe 521) est comprise dans CITI classes 20-22. Sont exclues des Industries manufacturières en 1955 et 1958, l'édition (dans CITI classe 28) et la fabrication des briquettes en charbon (dans CITI classe 32), laquelle est comprise dans Industries extractive de charbon (CITI classe 11).

[2] Nombre d'entreprises au lieu du nombre d'établissements.

[3] La part du produit matériel net provenant de la construction pour compte propre des coopératives est comprise dans les données relatives aux entreprises publiques.

[4] Le nombre d'entreprises est le nombre moyen des artisans privés possédant une patente de commerce pour l'année, qu'ils exercent une activité ou non à la date du recensement.

[5] Y compris la part du produit matériel net provenant de la construction pour compte propre de la population, ainsi que des entreprises privées de construction.

[6] En 1958, les Bonneteries (dans CITI classe 23) sont incluses dans Articles d'habillement (CITI classe 24).

[7] La fabrication des meubles métalliques (dans CITI classe 26) est comprise dans Ouvrages en métaux (CITI classe 35-38), mais la production d'allumettes (dans CITI classe 31), ainsi qui des jouets en bois et des fournitures de bureau (dans CITI classe 39) est comprise dans Ouvrages en bois (CITI classe 25).

[8] La fabrication des objets en matière plastique et des surfaces sensibles (pellicules, plaques et papier) (dans CITI classe 39) sont comprises dans Ouvrages en caoutchouc (CITI classe 30) et Produits chimiques (CITI classe 31) respectivement.

[9] Sont comprises dans Ouvrages en métaux (CITI classe 35-38), en 1955 et 1958, la fabrication des bijoux et articles analogues, des instruments de musique et des fournitures métalliques pour bureau (tous dans CITI classe 39) et, en 1958, la fabrication du Matériel médico-chirurgical, des instruments de précision et des appareils de mesure (CITI groupe 391).

[10] Y compris les entreprises exerçant plusieurs activités de types différents.

[11] Les artisans privés itinérants sont compris dans l'ensemble des Industries manufacturières, mais non dans les différentes classes. Le total des chiffres relatifs aux classes n'est donc pas égal au chiffre indiqué pour l'ensemble des Industries manufacturières.

### Gross National Product and Gross Domestic Fixed Capital Formation

Estimates of expenditure on the gross national product and on the gross domestic fixed capital formation according to sector are presented in Table 1. The table is based on data supplied by the Statistical Bureau of Iceland in response to the United Nations national accounts questionnaire. Official estimates have been published in *Úr Thjódar Búskapuum*, June 1962 by the Icelandic Development Bank.

### Characteristics and Structure of Industrial Activity

The data set out in Table 2 appear in the 1950 and 1953 issues of *Idnadarskýrslur Árid* (Industrial Production to the preceding type of figures for employees, the Iceland, Reykjavik. The data result from Censuses taken of establishments required to carry accident compensation. The figures of Table 1 include estimates for establishments subject to the Census which did not complete returns.

The number of employees shown in the table for 1950 is the sum of the average monthly number of wage earners and the number of other employees at the end of the year. The number engaged in 1953 includes, in addition to the preceding type of figures for employees, the number of working proprietors and unpaid family workers at the end of the year. Value added is valued at market price for 1950 but at factor cost for 1953 and apparently covers all proceeds of the establishments for 1953 but not for 1950, when sales of goods not processed by the establishments were excluded.

### Produit national brut et formation brute de capital fixe intérieur

Le tableau 1 contient des estimations des dépenses imputées au produit national brut et de la formation brute de capital fixe intérieur par secteur d'acquisition. Il a été établi à partir de données fournies par le Bureau islandais de statistique en réponse au questionnaire de l'ONU sur la comptabilité nationale. Des estimations officielles ont été publiées dans *Úr Thjódar Búskapuum*, juin 1962, par la Banque islandaise de développement.

### Caractéristiques et structure de l'activité industrielle

Les données du tableau 2 ont paru dans les numéros de 1950 et 1953 de *Idnadarskýrslur Árid* (Statistíques de la production industrielle), publié par le Bureau islandais de statistique, Reykjavik. Ces données proviennent de recensements portant sur les établissements assujettis à l'assurance-accidents. Les chiffres du tableau 1 comprennent de estimations touchant les établissements qui n'ont pas répondu aux questionnaires.

Le nombre de salariés indiqué dans le tableau pour 1950 est le nombre mensuel moyen d'ouvriers, augmenté du nombre des autres salariés en fin d'année. Le nombre de personnes occupées en 1953 comprend, outre le nombre de salariés calculé comme ci-dessus, le nombre de propriétaires qui travaillent et de travailleurs familiaux non rémunérés (en fin d'année). La valeur ajoutée a été calculée aux prix du marché pour 1950 et au coût des facteurs pour 1953; elle couvre apparemment toutes les recettes des établissements pour 1953, mais non pour 1950, année où les marchandises revendues en l'état ont été exclues.

# 1. THE GROSS NATIONAL PRODUCT AND GROSS DOMESTIC FIXED CAPITAL FORMATION
# LE PRODUIT NATIONAL BRUT ET LA FORMATION BRUTE DE CAPITAL FIXE INTERIEUR

Million Krónur                                        Millions de couronnes

## A. Expenditure on the Gross National Product at Market Prices
## Dépenses relatives au produit national brut aux prix du marché

| Item of data and year<br>Rubrique et année | Total | Consumption<br>Consommation | | Gross Domestic Capital Formation<br>Formation brute de capital intérieur | | Net exports of goods and services[2]<br>Exportations nettes de biens et de services[2] | |
| --- | --- | --- | --- | --- | --- | --- | --- |
| | | Total[1] | Government<br>Etat | Total[1] | Fixed<br>Fixe | Exports less imports<br>Exportations moins importations | Exports<br>Exportations |
| *a. At Current Prices — Aux prix courants* | | | | | | | |
| **Absolute figures — Chiffres absolus** | | | | | | | |
| 1948 | 1 731 | 1 452 | 155 | 326 | 397 | −47 | 511 |
| 1950 | 2 069 | 1 706 | 192 | 446 | 389 | −83 | 575 |
| 1951 | 2 535 | 2 158 | 237 | 514 | 513 | −137 | 893 |
| 1952 | 2 821 | 2 314 | 275 | 630 | 610 | −123 | 898 |
| 1953 | 3 376 | 2 690 | 296 | 790 | 730 | −104 | 1 159 |
| 1954 | 3 789 | 2 944 | 325 | 868 | 835 | −23 | 1 305 |
| 1955 | 4 403 | 3 326 | 379 | 1 219 | 1 091 | −142 | 1 349 |
| 1956 | 5 130 | 3 942 | 461 | 1 350 | 1 368 | −162 | 1 503 |
| 1957 | 5 395 | 4 057 | 517 | 1 504 | 1 515 | −166 | 1 386 |
| 1958 | 6 338 | 4 695 | 582 | 1 734 | 1 653 | −91 | 1 536 |
| 1959 | 7 066 | 5 389 | 631 | 1 898 | 1 889 | −221 | 1 556 |
| 1960 | 8 159 | 6 075 | 699 | 2 499 | 2 409 | −415 | 3 790 |
| 1961 | 9 151 | 6 646 | 710 | 2 280 | 2 075 | 225 | 4 599 |
| **Percentage distribution of average annual expenditure — Distribution en pourcentage des dépenses annuelles moyennes** | | | | | | | |
| 1948 | 100.0 | 83.9 | 9.0 | 18.8 | 22.9 | −2.7 | 29.5 |
| 1950–1960 | 100.0 | 76.9 | 9.0 | 26.3 | 25.4 | −3.2 | 31.2 |
| 1950 | 100.0 | 82.4 | 9.3 | 21.6 | 18.8 | −4.0 | 27.8 |
| 1953 | 100.0 | 79.7 | 8.8 | 23.4 | 21.6 | −3.1 | 34.3 |
| 1954 | 100.0 | 77.7 | 8.6 | 22.9 | 22.0 | −0.6 | 34.4 |
| 1958 | 100.0 | 74.1 | 9.2 | 27.4 | 26.1 | −1.5 | 24.2 |
| 1960 | 100.0 | 74.5 | 8.6 | 30.6 | 29.5 | −5.1 | 46.5 |
| *b. At Prices of 1954 — Aux prix de 1954* | | | | | | | |
| **Absolute figures — Chiffres absolus** | | | | | | | |
| 1948 | 3 284 | 2 738 | 281 | 747 | 836 | −201 | 880 |
| 1950 | 3 164 | 2 576 | 287 | 639 | 602 | −51 | 717 |
| 1951 | 3 067 | 2 483 | 282 | 609 | 627 | −25 | 906 |
| 1952 | 3 008 | 2 351 | 288 | 674 | 643 | −17 | 886 |
| 1953 | 3 481 | 2 734 | 299 | 804 | 754 | −57 | 1 157 |
| 1954 | 3 789 | 2 944 | 325 | 868 | 835 | −23 | 1 305 |
| 1955 | 4 117 | 3 150 | 349 | 1 145 | 1 020 | −178 | 1 324 |
| 1956 | 4 297 | 3 343 | 379 | 1 110 | 1 133 | −156 | 1 468 |
| 1957 | 4 292 | 3 275 | 410 | 1 128 | 1 153 | −111 | 1 344 |
| 1958 | 4 602 | 3 516 | 426 | 1 216 | 1 140 | −130 | 1 490 |
| 1959 | 4 739 | 3 718 | 436 | 1 308 | 1 215 | −287 | 1 479 |
| 1960 | 4 727 | 3 763 | 465 | 1 217 | 1 256 | −253 | 1 678 |
| **Percentage distribution of average annual expenditure — Distribution en pourcentage des dépenses annuelles moyennes** | | | | | | | |
| 1948 | 100.0 | 83.4 | 8.6 | 22.7 | 25.5 | −6.1 | 26.8 |
| 1950–1960 | 100.0 | 78.2 | 9.1 | 24.8 | 24.0 | −3.0 | 31.8 |
| 1950 | 100.0 | 81.4 | 9.1 | 20.2 | 19.0 | −1.6 | 22.7 |
| 1953 | 100.0 | 78.5 | 8.6 | 23.1 | 21.7 | −1.6 | 33.2 |
| 1954 | 100.0 | 77.7 | 8.6 | 22.9 | 22.0 | −0.6 | 34.4 |
| 1958 | 100.0 | 76.4 | 9.2 | 26.4 | 24.8 | −2.8 | 32.4 |
| 1960 | 100.0 | 79.6 | 9.8 | 25.7 | 26.6 | −5.3 | 35.5 |
| **Average annual rate of growth — Taux annuel moyen d'accroissement** | | | | | | | |
| 1948–1953 | 1.2 | — | 1.2 | 1.5 | −2.0 | . | 5.6 |
| 1950–1960 | 4.1 | 3.9 | 5.0 | 6.7 | 7.6 | . | 8.9 |
| 1950–1953 | 3.2 | 2.0 | 1.4 | 8.0 | 7.8 | . | 17.3 |
| 1954–1958 | 5.0 | 4.5 | 7.0 | 8.8 | 8.1 | . | 3.4 |
| 1958–1960 | 1.3 | 3.4 | 4.5 | — | 5.0 | . | 6.1 |

[1] Changes in the value of stocks of consumption goods are included in "Total, Consumption" instead of "Total, Gross Domestic Capital Formation."
[2] Includes factor incomes paid to and received from abroad.

[1] Les variations de la valeur des stocks de biens de consommation sont comprises dans "Consommation, Total" et non dans "Formation brute de capital intérieur, Total".
[2] Y compris les revenus de facteurs payés à l'étranger et reçus de l'étranger.

# ICELAND

## B. Gross Domestic Fixed Capital Formation According to Purchasing Sector
### La formation brute de capital fixe intérieur par secteur d'acquisition

| Item of data and year / Rubrique et année | Total | Agricultural sector / Secteur agricole | Industrial Sector — Secteur industriel / Total | Mining and manufacturing / Industries extractives et manufacturières | Construction / Bâtiment et travaux publics | Electricity, gas and water / Electricité, gaz et eau | Transportation and communication / Transports et communications | Other sectors / Autres secteurs |
|---|---|---|---|---|---|---|---|---|
| ISIC — CITI | 0–9 | 0 | 1–5 | 1–3 | 4 | 5 | 7 | 6, 8–9 |
| *a. At Current Prices — Aux prix courants* | | | | | | | | |
| **Absolute figures — Chiffres absolus** | | | | | | | | |
| 1948 | 397.0 | 71.8 | 76.1 | 51.3 | 3.6 | 21.2 | 37.0 | 212.1 |
| 1950 | 388.6 | 50.7 | 96.0 | 51.5 | 6.4 | 38.1 | 29.5 | 212.4 |
| 1951 | 513.3 | 125.2 | 145.9 | 71.5 | 7.7 | 66.7 | 40.4 | 201.8 |
| 1952 | 609.8 | 101.4 | 223.9 | 74.7 | 6.0 | 143.2 | 5.5 | 279.0 |
| 1953 | 729.8 | 79.4 | 273.6 | 137.6 | 7.7 | 128.3 | 39.1 | 337.7 |
| 1954 | 835.3 | 123.5 | 174.2 | 93.6 | 14.8 | 65.8 | 80.6 | 457.0 |
| 1955 | 1 091.4 | 156.0 | 189.5 | 107.0 | 19.3 | 63.2 | 130.9 | 615.0 |
| 1956 | 1 367.7 | 193.1 | 266.5 | 144.5 | 25.3 | 96.7 | 95.7 | 812.4 |
| 1957 | 1 514.9 | 211.7 | 352.6 | 192.8 | 22.6 | 137.2 | 98.5 | 852.1 |
| 1958 | 1 653.3 | 272.9 | 500.0 | 253.9 | 18.1 | 228.0 | 85.6 | 794.8 |
| 1959 | 1 889.2 | 322.1 | 458.5 | 199.8 | 40.1 | 218.6 | 145.8 | 962.8 |
| 1960 | 2 409.0 | 678.2 | 476.7 | 252.2 | 36.4 | 188.1 | 236.8 | 1 017.3 |
| 1961 | 2 075.3 | 335.1 | 437.2 | 257.4 | 41.7 | 138.1 | 244.0 | 1 059.0 |
| **Percentage distribution according to sector— Distribution en pourcentage par secteur** | | | | | | | | |
| 1948 | 100.0 | 18.1 | 19.2 | 12.9 | 0.9 | 5.4 | 9.3 | 53.4 |
| 1950–1960 | 100.0 | 17.8 | 24.3 | 12.1 | 1.6 | 10.6 | 7.6 | 50.3 |
| 1950 | 100.0 | 13.0 | 24.7 | 13.3 | 1.6 | 9.8 | 7.6 | 54.7 |
| 1953 | 100.0 | 10.9 | 37.4 | 18.8 | 1.0 | 17.6 | 5.4 | 46.3 |
| 1954 | 100.0 | 14.8 | 20.9 | 11.2 | 1.8 | 7.9 | 9.6 | 54.7 |
| 1958 | 100.0 | 16.5 | 30.2 | 15.3 | 1.1 | 13.8 | 5.2 | 48.1 |
| 1960 | 100.0 | 28.2 | 19.8 | 10.5 | 1.5 | 7.8 | 9.8 | 42.2 |
| *b. At Prices of 1954 — Aux prix de 1954* | | | | | | | | |
| **Absolute figures — Chiffres absolus** | | | | | | | | |
| 1948 | 835.8 | 176.2 | 157.8 | 108.0 | 10.9 | 38.9 | 109.5 | 392.3 |
| 1950 | 602.2 | 74.0 | 144.2 | 76.5 | 8.1 | 59.6 | 50.3 | 333.7 |
| 1951 | 627.1 | 148.9 | 177.6 | 86.8 | 8.1 | 82.7 | 49.5 | 251.1 |
| 1952 | 643.0 | 105.6 | 237.9 | 80.9 | 6.2 | 150.8 | 5.7 | 293.8 |
| 1953 | 754.4 | 79.9 | 284.4 | 143.4 | 7.8 | 133.2 | 39.5 | 350.6 |
| 1954 | 835.3 | 123.5 | 174.2 | 93.6 | 14.8 | 65.8 | 80.6 | 457.0 |
| 1955 | 1 020.5 | 144.6 | 177.5 | 100.6 | 18.8 | 58.1 | 130.0 | 568.4 |
| 1956 | 1 132.6 | 162.5 | 218.0 | 119.0 | 20.5 | 78.5 | 90.5 | 661.6 |
| 1957 | 1 152.7 | 166.4 | 264.6 | 143.5 | 16.8 | 104.3 | 85.4 | 636.3 |
| 1958 | 1 139.7 | 179.0 | 352.4 | 176.7 | 11.1 | 164.6 | 53.5 | 554.8 |
| 1959 | 1 215.4 | 203.8 | 302.4 | 128.0 | 22.3 | 152.1 | 85.6 | 623.6 |
| 1960 | 1 255.6 | 301.1 | 254.7 | 130.8 | 12.8 | 111.1 | 94.3 | 605.5 |
| **Percentage distribution according to sector— Distribution en pourcentage par secteur** | | | | | | | | |
| 1948 | 100.0 | 21.1 | 18.9 | 12.9 | 1.3 | 4.7 | 13.1 | 46.9 |
| 1950–1960 | 100.0 | 16.3 | 24.9 | 12.3 | 1.4 | 11.2 | 7.4 | 51.4 |
| 1950 | 100.0 | 12.3 | 23.9 | 12.7 | 1.3 | 9.9 | 8.4 | 55.4 |
| 1953 | 100.0 | 10.6 | 37.7 | 19.0 | 1.0 | 17.7 | 5.2 | 46.5 |
| 1954 | 100.0 | 14.8 | 20.9 | 11.2 | 1.8 | 7.9 | 9.6 | 54.7 |
| 1958 | 100.0 | 15.7 | 30.9 | 15.5 | 1.0 | 14.4 | 4.7 | 48.7 |
| 1960 | 100.0 | 24.0 | 20.3 | 10.4 | 1.0 | 8.9 | 7.5 | 48.2 |
| **Average annual rate of growth—Taux annuel moyen d'accroissement** | | | | | | | | |
| 1948–1953 | −2.0 | −14.6 | 12.5 | 5.8 | −6.5 | 27.9 | −18.4 | −2.2 |
| 1950–1960 | 7.6 | 15.1 | 5.9 | 5.5 | 4.7 | 6.4 | 6.5 | 6.1 |
| 1950–1953 | 7.8 | 2.6 | 25.4 | 23.3 | −1.2 | 30.7 | −7.8 | 1.7 |
| 1954–1958 | 8.1 | 9.7 | 19.3 | 17.2 | −6.9 | 25.8 | −9.7 | 5.0 |
| 1958–1960 | 5.0 | 29.7 | −15.0 | −14.0 | 7.4 | −17.8 | 32.8 | 4.5 |

## 2. CHARACTERISTICS OF MANUFACTURING ESTABLISHMENTS SUBJECT TO ACCIDENT COMPENSATING INSURANCE
## CARACTERISTIQUES DES ETABLISSEMENTS MANUFACTURIERS ASSUJETTIS A L'ASSURANCE-ACCIDENTS
### 1950, 1953

Number of establishments and of engaged and employees in units; value added and wages and salaries in million Krónur; and value added per employee or engaged and wages and salaries per employee in thousand Krónur.

Nombre d'établissements, de personnes occupées et de salariés en unités; valeur ajoutée et traitements et salaires en millions de couronnes islandaises; valeur ajoutée par salarié ou par personne occupée et traitements et salaires par salarié en milliers de couronnes islandaises.

| Year and item of data | Manu-facturing / Industries manufac-turières | Food, beverages and tobacco / Industries alimen-taires, boissons, tabac | Textiles | Clothing, footwear and made-up textiles / Articles d'habil-lement, chaussures et ouvrages en tissu | Wood products and furniture / Bois et meubles | Paper and paper products / Papier et ouvrages en papier | Printing and publish-ing / Im-primerie et édition | Leather and leather products except wearing apparel / Cuir et articles en cuir, à l'exclu-sion des articles d'habil-lement | Rubber products / Ouvrages en caout-chouc | Chemicals and chemical, petroleum and coal products / Produits chi-miques et dérivés du pétrole et du charbon | Non-metallic mineral products / Produits minéraux non métal-liques | Metal products / Ouvrages en métaux | Other manu-factur-ing / Autres in-dustries manufac-turières | Année et rubrique |
|---|---|---|---|---|---|---|---|---|---|---|---|---|---|---|
| ISIC | 2–3 | 20–22 | 23 | 24 | 25–26 | 27 | 28 | 29 | 30 | 31–32 | 33 | 35–38 | 39 | CITI |
| a. Absolute Figures — Chiffres absolus | | | | | | | | | | | | | | |
| **1950** | | | | | | | | | | | | | | **1950** |
| Number of establishments..... | 1 246 | 369 | 65 | 187 | 160 | 6 | 47 | 15 | 8 | 57 | 47 | 236 | 49 | Nombre d'établissements |
| Value added............... | 426.0 | 149.6 | 24.0 | 34.2 | 26.0 | 2.3 | 20.4 | 4.6 | 1.9 | 58.6 | 7.3 | 90.9 | 6.2 | Valeur ajoutée |
| Number of employees | | | | | | | | | | | | | | Nombre de salariés |
| (Average during year)..... | 12 272 | 4 744 | 782 | 1 357 | 785 | 60 | 664 | 110 | 44 | 625 | 180 | 2 730 | 191 | (moyenne pendant l'année) |
| Wages and salaries paid..... | 265.5 | 81.4 | 15.4 | 24.2 | 19.0 | 1.4 | 16.8 | 2.5 | 1.2 | 21.7 | 4.7 | 72.7 | 4.5 | Traitements et salaires payés |
| **1953** | | | | | | | | | | | | | | **1953** |
| Number of establishments..... | 1 082 | 347 | 51 | 134 | 149 | 6 | 41 | 10 | 7 | 58 | 48 | 199 | 32 | Nombre d'établissements |
| Value added............... | 612.0 | 269.6 | 25.5 | 38.5 | 31.5 | 4.0 | 24.0 | 2.7 | 1.9 | 52.6 | 16.1 | 140.5 | 5.1 | Valeur ajoutée |
| Number of engaged | | | | | | | | | | | | | | Nombre de personnes occupées |
| (Average during year)..... | 12 708 | 5 972 | 652 | 1 148 | 641 | 67 | 464 | 51 | 39 | 516 | 199 | 2 821 | 138 | (moyenne pendant l'année) |
| Wages and salaries paid..... | 390.2 | 155.4 | 16.6 | 27.4 | 22.5 | 2.4 | 17.2 | 1.7 | 1.1 | 22.6 | 8.3 | 112.0 | 3.0 | Traitements et salaires payés |
| b. Structure | | | | | | | | | | | | | | |
| **1950** | | | | | | | | | | | | | | **1950** |
| Distribution in percent of: | | | | | | | | | | | | | | Distribution en pourcentage: |
| Value added............ | 100.0 | 35.1 | 5.6 | 8.0 | 6.1 | 0.6 | 4.8 | 1.0 | 0.5 | 13.7 | 1.8 | 21.3 | 1.5 | Valeur ajoutée |
| Number of employees...... | 100.0 | 38.6 | 6.4 | 11.0 | 6.4 | 0.5 | 5.4 | 0.9 | 0.4 | 5.1 | 1.4 | 22.3 | 1.6 | Nombre de salariés |
| Value added per employee... | 34.7 | 31.5 | 30.7 | 25.2 | 33.1 | 38.3 | 30.7 | 41.8 | 43.2 | 93.8 | 40.6 | 33.3 | 32.5 | Valeur ajoutée par salarié |
| Wages and salaries per employee............. | 21.6 | 17.2 | 19.7 | 17.8 | 24.2 | 23.3 | 25.3 | 22.7 | 27.3 | 34.7 | 26.1 | 26.6 | 23.6 | Traitements et salaires par salarié |
| Value added per unit of wages and salaries........ | 1.60 | 1.84 | 1.56 | 1.41 | 1.37 | 1.64 | 1.21 | 1.84 | 1.58 | 2.70 | 1.55 | 1.25 | 1.38 | Valeur ajoutée par unité de traitements et salaires |
| **1953** | | | | | | | | | | | | | | **1953** |
| Distribution in percent of: | | | | | | | | | | | | | | Distribution en pourcentage: |
| Value added............ | 100.0 | 44.0 | 4.2 | 6.3 | 5.1 | 0.7 | 3.9 | 0.4 | 0.3 | 8.6 | 2.7 | 22.9 | 0.9 | Valeur ajoutée |
| Number of engaged....... | 100.0 | 46.9 | 5.2 | 9.0 | 5.1 | 0.5 | 3.6 | 0.4 | 0.3 | 4.1 | 1.6 | 22.2 | 1.1 | Nombre de personnes occupées |
| Value added per person engaged................. | 48.2 | 45.1 | 39.1 | 33.5 | 49.1 | 59.7 | 51.7 | 52.9 | 48.7 | 101.9 | 80.9 | 49.8 | 37.0 | Valeur ajoutée par personne occupée |
| Value added per unit of wages and salaries........ | 1.57 | 1.73 | 1.54 | 1.40 | 1.40 | 1.67 | 1.40 | 1.59 | 1.73 | 2.33 | 1.94 | 1.25 | 1.70 | Valeur ajoutée par unité de traitements et salaires |

## Net Domestic Product

The origin of the net domestic product at factor cost is presented in Table 1. The table is based on data derived from information supplied by the Central Statistical Organization, New Delhi, in response to the United Nations national accounts questionnaire. Officials estimates are published in *Estimates of National Income 1948/1949 to 1960/1961,* by the same Office.

## Index Numbers of Industrial Production

The index numbers set out in Table 2 are based mainly on the indexes of industrial production that are compiled by the Central Statistical Organisation, New Delhi, and published in the *Statistical Abstract, India* and *Monthly Statistics of the Production of Selected Industries of India.* However the index numbers for some of the groups of mining for all years; and for some of the other groups of mining as a whole, for some of the major groups of manufacturing, and for electricity, for the years up to 1951; have been calculated by the Statistical Office of the United Nations from data on the output of individual commodities. These data appear primarily in the *Statistical Abstract, India,* the *Geological Survey of India* and *Monthly Statistics of the Production of Selected Industries of India* for 1953-1954, and earlier years.

The Interim Index of Industrial Production (1946 = 100) calculated by the Ministry of Industry and Supply has been utilised for the years 1948 to 1950 for coal mining, manufacturing as a whole and for some of the major groups of manufacturing. This index has been built up from indexes of the quantities produced for 35 individual items. The weights utilised in combining, where necessary, the indexes for individual items into broader categories was the value of gross output in 1946. These broader categories were combined into a total index for manufacturing and into a total mining and manufacturing index, using as weights the values added in 1946. The major group indexes have been calculated by the Statistical Office of the United Nations by combining the indexes for the broader categories and using values added in 1946 as weights.

The index numbers (1951 = 100) calculated by the Central Statistical Organisation, are utilised in Table 2 for the years 1951 to 1954. This series of index numbers are built up from indexes of the production of 88 individual items. The latest indexes (1956 = 100) calculated by the same Organisation, are utilised in Table 2 for the

## Produit intérieur net

Le tableau 1 indique l'origine par secteur d'activité du produit intérieur net au coût des facteurs. Ce tableau est fondé sur des données tirées des renseignements fournis par l'Organisation centrale de statistique, New Delhi, en réponse au questionnaire de l'ONU sur la comptabilité nationale. Des estimations officielles sont publiées par le même service dans *Estimates of National Income 1948/1949 to 1960/1961.*

## Indices de la production industrielle

Les indices du tableau 2 sont fondés essentiellement sur les indices de la production industrielle construits par l'Organisation centrale de statistique, New Delhi, et publiés dans *Statistical Abstract, India* et *Monthly Statistics of the Production of Selected Industries of India.* Cependant, les indices relatifs à quelques groupes des industries extractives pour toutes les années, ainsi que les indices concernant quelques autres groupes des industries extractives, l'ensemble des industries extractives, quelques classes des industries manufacturières et l'électricité pour 1951 et les années précédentes, ont été calculés par le Bureau de statistique de l'ONU à partir de données sur la production de chaque marchandise. Ces données ont paru principalement dans les numéros de *Statistical Abstract, India, Geological Survey of India* et *Monthly Statistics of the Production of Selected Industries of India* de 1953-1954 et des années antérieures.

Les indices provisoires de la production industrielle (1946 = 100) calculés par le Ministère de l'industrie et des approvisionnements ont été utilisés pour les années 1948 à 1950 dans le cas des industries extractives de charbon, de l'ensemble des industries manufacturières et de quelques-unes des classes des industries manufacturières. Cet indice a été construit à partir d'indices des quantités produites de 35 articles. La valeur brute de la production en 1946 a servi de base de pondération chaque fois que l'on a dû combiner des indices relatifs à des articles distincts en indices de catégories plus larges. Pour combiner ces indices de grandes catégories en indices relatifs à l'ensemble des industries manufacturières et à l'ensemble des industries extractives et manufacturières, on a pondéré par les valeurs ajoutées en 1946. Les indices de classes ont été calculés par le Bureau de statistique de l'ONU, qui a combiné les indices de grandes catégories en utilisant les valeurs ajoutées en 1946 comme coefficients de pondération.

Les indices (1951 = 100) calculés par l'Organisation centrale de statistique sont présentés dans le tableau 2 pour les années 1951 à 1954. Ces séries d'indices ont été construites à partir d'indices de la production de 88 articles. Les indices les plus récents (1956 = 100), calculés par la même organisation, sont présentés dans le tableau 2

years 1955 onwards. This series of index numbers are built up from indexes of the production of 201 individual items. The increase in the number of individual items covered is not all due to the inclusion of new items; some items included in the previous index have been subdivided.

In both these series the indexes for the most detailed categories are combined into indexes for sub-groups, using gross value of output in the base year as weights. The sub-group indexes are combined into indexes for groups and these group indexes into indexes for major groups using, whenever available, the values added at factor cost in the base year as weights; if values added were unavailable, the values of gross output have been used as weights. The major group indexes have been combined into indexes for mining as a whole and manufacturing as a whole and the division indexes combined into indexes for mining, manufacturing and electricity as a whole using values added at factor cost in the base year as weights. The weights have been derived mainly from the results of the annual Censuses of Manufacturing described below under Tables 5 and 6 and from a variety of other sources, ranging from the results of the Sample Surveys of Manufacturing Industries described below under Table 4 to data supplied by producers of individual commodities.

Further details may be found in *Monthly Statistics of the Production of Selected Industries of India,* any recent issue, for the index numbers based on 1951 and 1956; and the May 1955 edition for the Interim Index of Industrial Production (1946 = 100).

## Index of Industrial Employment

The index numbers of industrial employment presented in Table 3 have been calculated by the Statistical Office of the United Nations based on absolute figures of employment derived from a number of sources.

The mining indexes have been derived from absolute figures of the average daily number of employees. These figures have been collected by the Department of Mines of the Ministry of Labour and Employment. The figures up to 1951 have been collected under authority of the Indian Mines Act 1923 and relate to pre-Partition British India areas of the Indian Union, i.e. the nine Part 'A' States and three Part 'C' States (Delhi, Ajmer and Coorg), the industrially significant areas. The figures for 1952 onwards have been collected under authority of the Mines Act and relate to all the States of the Indian Union except Jammu and Kashmir. The two series have not been linked but the effects of this change in coverage are thought to be slight. The annual figures are published by the Central Statistical Organisation in the various editions of the *Statistical Abstract of the Indian Union* and in certain editions of the *Monthly Abstract of Statistics.* The figures relate to employees both above ground and

pour 1955 et les années suivantes. Ces séries d'indices ont été établies à partir des indices de la production de 201 articles. L'augmentation du nombre d'articles inclus n'est pas entièrement due à l'addition de nouveaux éléments; elle résulte également de la subdivision de certains éléments compris dans les indices antérieurs.

Dans ces deux séries, les indices de catégories élémentaires ont été combinés en indices de sous-groupes, les coefficients de pondération utilisés étant les valeurs brutes de la production pendant l'année de base. Les indices de sous-groupes ont été combinés en indices de groupes et ceux-ci en indices de classes; les coefficients utilisés à cette fin étaient les valeurs ajoutées au coût des facteurs pendant l'année de base ou, à défaut, la valeur brute de la production. Les indices de classes ont été combinés en indices relatifs à l'ensemble des industries extractives et à l'ensemble des industries manufacturières, et ces indices de branches en indices relatifs à l'ensemble des industries extractives, manufacturières et productrices d'électricité, la base de pondération adoptée étant la valeur ajoutée au coût des facteurs pendant l'année de base. Les coefficients de pondération utilisés ont été tirés principalement des résultats des recensements annuels de l'industrie manufacturière décrits plus loin (commentaire des tableaux 5 et 6), ainsi que de sources diverses allant des résultats des enquêtes par sondage sur les industries manufacturières décrites ci-dessous (commentaire du tableau 4) aux données fournies par les producteurs des diverses marchandises.

Pour plus de détails, voir n'importe quel numéro récent de *Monthly Statistics of the Production of Selected Industries of India* en ce qui concerne les indices basés sur 1951 et 1956, et le numéro de mai 1955 en ce qui concerne les indices provisoires de la production industrielle (1946 = 100).

## Indices de l'emploi dans l'industrie

Les indices de l'emploi dans l'industrie présentés au tableau 5 ont été calculés par le Bureau de statistique de l'ONU à partir de chiffres absolus de l'emploi tirés de diverses sources.

Les indices relatifs aux industries extractives ont été calculés à partir de chiffres absolus indiquant le nombre moyen de salariés par jour. Ces chiffres ont été rassemblés par la section des mines du Ministère du travail et de l'emploi. Les chiffres relatifs à 1951 et aux années précédentes ont été recueillis en application de l'Indian Mines Act, 1923, et ont trait aux régions de l'Union indienne qui faisaient partie des Indes britanniques avant le partage, c'est-à-dire aux neuf Etats du secteur A et aux trois Etats du secteur C (Delhi, Ajmer et Courg), régions importantes du point de vue industriel. Les chiffres relatifs à 1952 et aux années suivantes ont été rassemblés en vertu du Mines Act et portent sur tous les Etats de l'Union indienne, à l'exception de Jammu et Cachemire. Les deux séries n'ont pas été raccordées car on a jugé que la différence de couverture n'avait que peu d'effet sur l'indice. Les chiffres annuels sont publiés par l'Organisation centrale de statistique dans les divers numéros

underground. The total mining indexes are the un-weighted aggregated totals of the absolute figures for the individual major groups.

The manufacturing and electricity and gas indexes have also been derived from absolute figures of the number of employees. Up to 1950 the indexes are based on figures derived from the results of the annual Censuses of Manufactures which cover registered establishments with 20 or more employees and utilising power in 29 selected industries and which are described below under Tables 5 and 6. These indexes are linked at 1950 with a series of indexes derived from absolute figures of the average daily number of workers employed in establishments registering under the Factories Act, 1948. All establishments with 20 or more employees or with 10 to 19 employees and utilising power are required to register. The figures are collected by the Labour Bureau of the Ministry of Labour and Employment. The annual absolute figures of average daily employment are published annually by the Labour Bureau in *Indian Labour Statistics* (which commenced publication for the year 1959). The data are also published in the *Statistical Abstract of the Indian Union* and, in summary form, in the *Monthly Abstract of Statistics*, both issued by the Central Statistical Organisation.

The indexes for manufacturing as a whole are based on the unweighted aggregated absolute figures of the individual major groups. The total combined indexes for mining, manufacturing and electricity and gas are calculated by combining the individual division indexes, using as weights estimates of the total number of engaged in 1958.

### The Characteristics and Structure of Manufacturing Activity

The data in Table 4 result from an annual sample survey that was started in 1951 and are derived from *Report on Sample Survey of Manufacturing Industries, 1953*, and *1957(1)*; Indian Statistical Institute, Calcutta. These data relate to the whole of India except the Andaman and Nicobar Islands and to all registered manufacturing establishments having 20 or more employees or 10 through 19 employees and utilising power. The sample of these units from which questionnaires were gathered was selected from strata of the registered establishments that were classified according to category of manufacturing and size.

The data set out in Tables 5 and 6 are compiled from the results of the annual Censuses of Manufactures taken by the Directorate of Industrial Statistics, Ministry of Commerce and Industry, Calcutta, that have been published in *Third Census of Manufactures, 1948; Report of*

du *Statistical Abstract of the Indian Union* et dans certains numéros du *Monthly Abstract of Statistics*. Les chiffres concernent les salariés de fond et de jour. Les indices relatifs à l'ensemble des industries extractives sont les totaux non pondérés des chiffres absolus se rapportant aux différentes classes.

Les indices des industries manufacturières et de l'électricité et du gaz ont été calculés également à partir de chiffres absolus indiquant le nombre de salariés. Jusqu'en 1950, les indices sont fondés sur des chiffres tirés des résultats des recensements annuels des industries manufacturières, qui portent sur les établissements enregistrés occupant 20 salariés et utilisant la force motrice, ceci dans 29 industries déterminées; ces recensements sont décrits plus loin dans le commentaire des tableaux 5 et 6. Ces indices sont raccordés au niveau de 1950 à des séries d'indices calculées à partir de chiffres absolus indiquant le nombre journalier moyen de travailleurs employés dans les établissements enregistrés en vertu du Factories Act, 1948. Tous les établissements comptant au moins 20 salariés, ou occupant de 10 à 19 salariés et utilisant la force motrice, sont tenus de se faire enregistrer. Les chiffres ont été recueillis par le Bureau du travail du Ministère du travail et de l'emploi. Les chiffres absolus annuels indiquant l'emploi journalier moyen sont publiés annuellement par le Bureau du travail dans *Indian Labour Statistics* (qui a commencé à paraître en 1959). Les données paraissent également dans le *Statistical Abstract of the Indian Union* et, sous une forme sommaire, dans le *Monthly Abstract of Statistics*, tous deux publiés par l'Organisation centrale de statistique.

Les indices relatifs à l'ensemble des industries manufacturières sont construits à partir les totaux non pondérés des chiffres absolus concernant les différentes classes. Les indices relatifs à l'ensemble des industries extractives, manufacturières et productrices d'électricité et de gaz ont été obtenus par combinaison des indices relatifs aux diverses branches, les coefficients de pondération utilisés étant des estimations du nombre total de personnes occupées en 1958.

### Caractéristiques et structure de l'activité industrielle

Les chiffres du tableau 4 proviennent d'une enquête annuelle par sondage commencée en 1951 et sont tirés de *Report on Sample Survey of Manufacturing Industries, 1953* et *1957 (1)*, Institut indien de statistique, Calcutta. Ces chiffres concernent l'ensemble du territoire de l'Inde, à l'exclusion des îles Andaman et Nicobar, et se rapportent à tous les établissements manufacturiers enregistrés comptant au moins 20 salariés ou occupant de 10 à 19 salariés et utilisant la force motrice. L'échantillon d'unités auxquelles des questionnaires ont été envoyés a été choisi parmi les établissements enregistrés que l'on a stratifiés selon la dimension et le type d'activité manufacturière.

Les données des tableaux 5 et 6 sont tirées des résultats des recensements annuels des industries manufacturières effectués par la Direction des statistiques industrielles, Ministère du commerce et de l'industrie, Calcutta; ces résultats ont été publiés dans *Third Census of Manu-*

the Eighth Census of Indian Manufactures, 1953; and in Thirteenth Census of Indian Manufactures, 1958. These Censuses are of limited scope; only registered manufacturing units, in 29 selected industries, which had 20 or more employees and utilised power were covered. In addition, some parts of India (some class B and C States and Territories), which are not important industrially, were omitted from all the Censuses, whilst establishments under the control of the Defense Ministry have also been excluded in all years.

The figures from the Censuses shown in Tables 5 and 6 are not precisely comparable. This lack of comparability stems from two factors; firstly differences in the proportion of covered establishments which returned questionnaires (no adjustments were made for non-response) and secondly differences in the geographic area included in the inquiries. Cochin was included in the 1948 Census but excluded in 1953 and 1958. Ajmer and Vindya Pradesh were included in 1948 and 1953 but excluded in 1958. In 1948 Patiala and the East Punjab States Union, Rajasthan and Saurashtra were partially covered; in 1953 they were completely covered, whilst in 1958 all except Rajasthan were entirely excluded. In 1958, Mysore and Kerala, excluded in the two earlier years, were covered.

The definitions of the items of data that are shown in Tables 4, 5 and 6 are consistent with one another except for value added. In the case of the three Censuses, value added is net of charges for depreciation, whereas in the case of the Sample Surveys, value added is gross of the charges for depreciation. The definitions of the items of data in both the Censuses and the Sample Surveys are also generally consistent with the International Standards in Basic Industrial Statistics. However value added does not cover receipts from goods merchandised by manufacturing establishments and is net of non-industrial costs, whilst wages and salaries excludes gratuities payable to employees on discharge. Value added is valued ex-factory and is net of indirect taxes.

factures, 1948, Report of the Eighth Census of Indian Manufactures, 1953, et Thirteenth Census of Indian Manufactures, 1958. Les recensements de 1948, 1953 et 1958 avaient une portée limitée; ils portaient uniquement sur les unités manufacturières enregistrées, appartenant à 29 industries déterminées, qui comptaient 20 salariés ou plus et qui utilisaient la force motrice. En outre, certaines parties de l'Inde industriellement peu importantes (certains Etats et territoires des secteurs B et C) n'ont pas été comprises dans le recensement, et les établissements dépendant du Ministère de la défense nationale ont été exclus pour toutes les années.

Les chiffres des tableaux 5 et 6 ne sont pas tout à fait comparables parce que, d'une part, la proportion des établissements recensés qui ont retourné les questionnaires n'est pas la même (aucune correction n'a été faite pour tenir compte des non-réponses) et, que, d'autre part, les régions géographiques recensées étaient différentes. Le Cochin faisait partie de la zone recensée en 1948, mais non en 1953 et 1958. L'Ajmer et le Vindya Pradesh étaient inclus en 1948 et 1953, mais non en 1958. Seules certaines parties du Rajasthan, du Saurashtra et de l'Union des Etats du Pendjab oriental et du Patiala ont été comprises dans le recensement de 1948; en 1953, ces Etats étaient compris en totalité, tandis qu'en 1958, ils étaient tous exclus, à l'exception du Rajasthan. En 1958, le Mysore et le Kerala, exclus des deux recensements précédents, ont été recensés.

Les définitions des rubriques des tableaux 4, 5 et 6 sont compatibles entre elles, sauf en ce qui concerne la valeur ajoutée. Dans les trois recensements, la valeur ajoutée s'entend déduction faite des charges pour amortissement, alors que ces charges ne sont pas déduites dans le cas des enquêtes par sondage. Les définitions des rubrique utilisées dans le recensements et les enquêtes par sondage sont généralement conformes aux Normes internationales relatives aux statistiques industrielles de base. Cependant, la valeur ajoutée ne comprend pas les recettes provenant des marchandises revendues en l'état par les établissements manufacturiers, et elle est calculée déduction faite des coûts non industriels; en outre, les indemnités versées aux salariés licenciés ne sont pas comprises dans les traitements et salaires payés. La valeur ajoutée est calculée départ usine et déduction faite des impôts indirects.

# 1. THE NET DOMESTIC PRODUCT AT FACTOR COST ACCORDING TO ORIGIN
## ORIGINE PAR SECTEUR D'ACTIVITE DU PRODUIT INTERIEUR NET AU COUT DES FACTEURS

Thousand million Rupees          Millards de roupies

| Item of data and year [2] / Rubrique et année [2] | Total | Agricultural sector / Secteur agricole | Industrial sector — Secteur industriel | | | Transportation and communication [1] / Transports et communications [1] | Other sectors / Autres secteurs |
|---|---|---|---|---|---|---|---|
| | | | Total | Mining / Industries extractives | Manufacturing, construction and electricity, gas and water / Industries manufacturières, bâtiment et travaux publics et électricité, gaz et eau | | |
| ISIC — CITI | 0-9 | 0 | 1-5 | 1 | 2-5 | 61, 7 | 62-64, 8-9 |
| **a. At Current Prices — Aux prix courants** | | | | | | | |
| **Absolute figures — Chiffres absolus** | | | | | | | |
| 1948 | 86.7 | 42.5 | 14.8 | 0.6 | 14.2 | 15.5 | 13.9 |
| 1950 | 95.5 | 48.9 | 15.3 | 0.7 | 14.6 | 16.2 | 15.1 |
| 1951 | 99.9 | 50.2 | 16.8 | 0.9 | 15.9 | 17.1 | 15.8 |
| 1952 | 98.3 | 48.1 | 17.0 | 0.9 | 16.1 | 17.1 | 16.1 |
| 1953 | 104.8 | 53.1 | 17.7 | 1.0 | 16.7 | 17.2 | 16.8 |
| 1954 | 96.1 | 43.5 | 18.0 | 0.9 | 17.1 | 17.3 | 17.3 |
| 1955 | 99.8 | 45.2 | 18.5 | 1.0 | 17.5 | 17.9 | 18.2 |
| 1956 | 113.0 | 55.2 | 20.0 | 1.2 | 18.8 | 18.5 | 19.3 |
| 1957 | 114.0 | 52.8 | 21.2 | 1.4 | 19.8 | 19.5 | 20.5 |
| 1958 | 126.2 | 62.4 | 21.7 | 1.4 | 20.3 | 20.2 | 21.9 |
| 1959 | 129.7 | 62.1 | 23.3 | 1.4 | 21.9 | 21.0 | 23.3 |
| 1960 | 142.4 | 68.6 | 26.4 | 1.6 | 24.8 | 22.1 | 25.3 |
| **Percentage distribution according to sector— Distribution en pourcentage par secteur** | | | | | | | |
| 1948 | 100.0 | 49.0 | 17.1 | 0.7 | 16.4 | 17.9 | 16.0 |
| 1950-1960 | 100.0 | 48.4 | 17.7 | 1.0 | 16.7 | 16.7 | 17.2 |
| 1950 | 100.0 | 51.2 | 16.0 | 0.7 | 15.3 | 17.0 | 15.8 |
| 1953 | 100.0 | 50.7 | 16.9 | 1.0 | 15.9 | 16.4 | 16.0 |
| 1954 | 100.0 | 45.3 | 18.7 | 0.9 | 17.8 | 18.0 | 18.0 |
| 1958 | 100.0 | 49.4 | 17.2 | 1.1 | 16.1 | 16.0 | 17.4 |
| 1960 | 100.0 | 48.2 | 18.5 | 1.1 | 17.4 | 15.5 | 17.8 |
| **b. At Prices of 1948 — Aux prix de 1948** | | | | | | | |
| **Absolute figures — Chiffres absolus** | | | | | [3] | [4] | |
| 1948 | 86.7 | 42.5 | 14.8 | ... | 14.8 | 16.0 | 13.4 |
| 1950 | 88.7 | 43.4 | 14.8 | ... | 14.8 | 16.6 | 13.9 |
| 1951 | 91.2 | 44.4 | 15.2 | ... | 15.2 | 17.3 | 14.3 |
| 1952 | 94.7 | 46.0 | 15.8 | ... | 15.8 | 17.9 | 15.0 |
| 1953 | 100.3 | 49.8 | 16.5 | ... | 16.5 | 18.3 | 15.7 |
| 1954 | 102.8 | 50.3 | 17.0 | ... | 17.0 | 19.1 | 16.4 |
| 1955 | 104.8 | 50.2 | 17.6 | ... | 17.6 | 19.7 | 17.3 |
| 1956 | 109.9 | 52.5 | 18.4 | ... | 18.4 | 20.8 | 18.2 |
| 1957 | 109.0 | 50.1 | 18.6 | ... | 18.6 | 21.1 | 19.2 |
| 1958 | 116.7 | 55.6 | 18.8 | ... | 18.8 | 21.9 | 20.4 |
| 1959 | 118.8 | 55.0 | 19.7 | ... | 19.7 | 22.7 | 21.4 |
| 1960 | 127.3 | 58.6 | 21.1 | ... | 21.1 | 24.5 | 23.1 |
| **Percentage distribution according to sector— Distribution en pourcentage par secteur** | | | | | | | |
| 1948 | 100.0 | 49.0 | 17.1 | — | 17.1 | 18.4 | 15.5 |
| 1950-1960 | 100.0 | 47.7 | 16.6 | — | 16.6 | 18.9 | 16.8 |
| 1950 | 100.0 | 48.9 | 16.7 | — | 16.7 | 18.7 | 15.7 |
| 1953 | 100.0 | 49.7 | 16.5 | — | 16.5 | 18.2 | 15.6 |
| 1954 | 100.0 | 48.9 | 16.5 | — | 16.5 | 18.6 | 16.0 |
| 1958 | 100.0 | 47.6 | 16.1 | — | 16.1 | 18.8 | 17.5 |
| 1960 | 100.0 | 46.0 | 16.6 | — | 16.6 | 19.2 | 18.2 |
| **Average annual rate of growth—Taux annuel moyen d'accroissement** | | | | | | | |
| 1948-1953 | 3.0 | 3.2 | 2.2 | . | 2.2 | 2.7 | 3.2 |
| 1950-1960 | 3.7 | 3.0 | 3.6 | . | 3.6 | 4.0 | 5.2 |
| 1950-1953 | 4.2 | 4.7 | 3.7 | . | 3.7 | 3.3 | 4.1 |
| 1954-1958 | 3.2 | 2.5 | 2.6 | . | 2.6 | 3.5 | 5.6 |
| 1958-1960 | 4.5 | 2.7 | 5.9 | . | 5.9 | 5.8 | 6.4 |

[1] Transportation and communication (ISIC division 7) includes Wholesale and retail trade (ISIC major group 61).
[2] Fiscal year beginning 1 April.
[3] Includes Mining (ISIC division 1).
[4] Includes Banking, Insurance and Real estate (ISIC major groups 62-64).

[1] Transports et communications (CITI branche 7) comprend Commerce de gros et de détail (CITI classe 61).
[2] Exercice financier commençant le 1er avril.
[3] Y compris Industries extractives (CITI branche 1).
[4] Y compris Banques, Assurances et Affaires immobilières (CITI classes 62-64).

## 2. INDEX NUMBERS OF INDUSTRIAL PRODUCTION — INDICES DE LA PRODUCTION INDUSTRIELLE

### A. Selected Divisions of Industrial Activity
### Quelques branches de l'activité industrielle

| Period<br>Période | Total [1, 2] | Mining [1]<br>Industries extractives [1] | Manu-facturing [2]<br>Industries manu-facturières [2] | Electricity<br>Electricité |
|---|---|---|---|---|
| ISIC — CITI | 1–3, 511 | 1 | 2–3 | 511 |

#### a. Indexes — Indices (1958 = 100)

| | | | | |
|---|---|---|---|---|
| 1939.......... | 56 | 60 | 57 | ... |
| 1948.......... | 64 | 64 | 66 | 37 |
| 1949.......... | 63 | 68 | 63 | 40 |
| 1950.......... | 62 | 70 | 62 | 42 |
| 1951.......... | –70– | –75– | –70– | –48– |
| 1952.......... | 72 | 79 | 73 | 50 |
| 1953.......... | 74 | 78 | 74 | 54 |
| 1954.......... | 79 | 80 | 79 | 61 |
| 1955.......... | –85– | –84– | –86– | 69 |
| 1956.......... | 92 | 86 | 94 | 78 |
| 1957.......... | 96 | 94 | 97 | 88 |
| 1958.......... | 100 | 100 | 100 | 100 |
| 1959.......... | 108 | 106 | 108 | 119 |
| 1960.......... | 120 | 118 | 120 | 134 |
| 1961.......... | 128 | 123 | 128 | 156 |

#### b. Average Annual Rate of Change — Taux annuel moyen de variation

| | | | | |
|---|---|---|---|---|
| 1939–1960.... | 3.7 | 3.3 | 3.6 | ... |
| 1939–1948.... | 1.5 | 0.7 | 1.6 | ... |
| 1950–1960.... | 6.8 | 5.4 | 6.8 | 12.3 |
| 1948–1953.... | 2.9 | 4.0 | 2.3 | 7.8 |
| 1954–1958.... | 6.1 | 5.7 | 6.1 | 13.1 |
| 1958–1960.... | 9.5 | 8.6 | 9.5 | 15.8 |

For footnotes see end of table.
Pour les notes, voir au bas du tableau.

### B. The Major Groups of Mining
### Les classes de la branche Industries extractives

| Period<br>Période | All mining [1]<br>Toutes industries extractives [1] | Coal mining<br>Extraction du charbon | Metal mining [3]<br>Extraction des minerals métalliques [3] | Crude petro-leum and natural gas<br>Pétrole brut et gaz naturel | Other mining [4]<br>Autres industries extractives [4] |
|---|---|---|---|---|---|
| ISIC — CITI | 1 | 11 | 12 | 13 | 14–19 |

#### a. Indexes — Indices (1958 = 100)

| | | | | | |
|---|---|---|---|---|---|
| 1939....... | 60 | ... | ... | ... | ... |
| 1948....... | 64 | 66 | 48 | 59 | 55 |
| 1949....... | 68 | 70 | 54 | 60 | 45 |
| 1950....... | 70 | 71 | 70 | 59 | 56 |
| 1951....... | –75– | –76– | –94– | 62 | –70– |
| 1952....... | 79 | 80 | 104 | 60 | 63 |
| 1953....... | 78 | 79 | 109 | 62 | 71 |
| 1954....... | 80 | 81 | 107 | 70 | 69 |
| 1955....... | –84– | –84– | 110 | 79 | 78 |
| 1956....... | 86 | 87 | 114 | 90 | 82 |
| 1957....... | 94 | 96 | 107 | 101 | 87 |
| 1958....... | 100 | 100 | 100 | 100 | 100 |
| 1959....... | 106 | 104 | 100 | 104 | 86 |
| 1960....... | 118 | 114 | 102 | 105 | 91 |
| 1961....... | 123 | 122 | 103 | 104 | 93 |

#### b. Average Annual Rate of Change — Taux annuel moyen de variation

| | | | | | |
|---|---|---|---|---|---|
| 1939–1960. | 3.3 | ... | ... | ... | ... |
| 1939–1948. | 0.7 | ... | ... | ... | ... |
| 1950–1960. | 5.4 | 4.9 | 3.8 | 5.9 | 5.0 |
| 1948–1953. | 4.0 | 3.7 | 17.8 | 1.0 | 5.2 |
| 1954–1958. | 5.7 | 5.4 | –1.7 | 9.3 | 9.7 |
| 1958–1960. | 8.6 | 6.8 | 1.0 | 2.5 | –4.6 |

For footnotes see end of table.
Pour les notes, voir au bas du tableau.

## C. The Major Groups of Manufacturing — Les classes de la branche Industries manufacturières

| Period Période | Manufacturing [2] Industries manufacturières [2] | Food, beverages and tobacco [5] Industries alimentaires, boissons, tabac [5] | Textiles | Footwear Chaussures | Wood products Bois | Paper and paper products Papier et ouvrages en papier | Leather and leather products except wearing apparel Cuir et articles en cuir, à l'exclusion des articles d'habillement | Rubber products Ouvrages en caoutchouc | Chemicals and chemical, petroleum and coal products [2] Produits chimiques et dérivés du pétrole et du charbon [2] | Non-metallic mineral products Produits minéraux non métalliques | Basic metals Métallurgie de base | Metal products Ouvrages en métaux |
|---|---|---|---|---|---|---|---|---|---|---|---|---|
| ISIC — CITI | 2–3 | 20–22 | 23 | 24 | 25 | 27 | 29 | 30 | 31–32 | 33 | 34 | 35–38 |

### a. Indexes — Indices (1958 = 100)

| Period | 2–3 | 20–22 | 23 | 24 | 25 | 27 | 29 | 30 | 31–32 | 33 | 34 | 35–38 |
|---|---|---|---|---|---|---|---|---|---|---|---|---|
| 1939 | 57 | 53 | 88 | ... | ... | ... | ... | ... | 34 | 27 | 69 | ... |
| 1948 | 66 | 67 | 91 | 72 | ... | 40 | 129 | 51 | 43 | 30 | 59 | 28 |
| 1949 | 63 | 67 | 82 | 67 | ... | 42 | 103 | 48 | 42 | 35 | 62 | 34 |
| 1950 | 62 | 74 | 74 | 66 | ... | 44 | 85 | 48 | 42 | 42 | 80 | 31 |
| 1951 | −70− | −72− | −82− | −78− | ... | −54− | −110− | −61− | −47− | −50− | −80− | −42− |
| 1952 | 73 | 80 | 85 | 70 | ... | 56 | 90 | 61 | 55 | 54 | 80 | 36 |
| 1953 | 74 | 74 | 87 | 76 | ... | 57 | 85 | 66 | 60 | 55 | 76 | 40 |
| 1954 | 79 | 72 | 90 | 72 | ... | 63 | 87 | 78 | 66 | 63 | 92 | 53 |
| 1955 | −86− | −86− | −93− | −76− | 83 | −75− | −98− | −85− | −74− | −68− | −90− | −68− |
| 1956 | 94 | 92 | 99 | 87 | 95 | 78 | 106 | 92 | 85 | 78 | 94 | 88 |
| 1957 | 97 | 99 | 99 | 101 | 99 | 86 | 98 | 96 | 91 | 89 | 93 | 99 |
| 1958 | 100 | 100 | 100 | 100 | 100 | 100 | 100 | 100 | 100 | 100 | 100 | 100 |
| 1959 | 108 | 102 | 102 | 105 | 130 | 114 | 107 | 109 | 111 | 113 | 130 | 108 |
| 1960 | 120 | 111 | 104 | 126 | 140 | 136 | 176 | 131 | 122 | 131 | 169 | 135 |
| 1961 | 128 | 122 | 108 | 145 | 157 | 143 | 120 | 146 | 142 | 137 | 172 | 152 |

### b. Average Annual Rate of Change — Taux annuel moyen de variation

| Period | 2–3 | 20–22 | 23 | 24 | 25 | 27 | 29 | 30 | 31–32 | 33 | 34 | 35–38 |
|---|---|---|---|---|---|---|---|---|---|---|---|---|
| 1939–1960 | 3.6 | 3.5 | 0.8 | ... | ... | ... | ... | ... | 6.3 | 7.8 | 4.4 | ... |
| 1939–1948 | 1.6 | 2.6 | 0.4 | ... | ... | ... | ... | ... | 2.6 | 1.2 | −1.7 | ... |
| 1950–1960 | 6.8 | 4.1 | 3.5 | 6.7 | ... | 11.9 | 7.5 | 10.6 | 11.3 | 12.0 | 7.8 | 15.9 |
| 1948–1953 | 2.3 | 2.0 | −0.9 | 1.1 | ... | 7.3 | −8.0 | 5.3 | 6.9 | 12.9 | 5.2 | 7.4 |
| 1954–1958 | 6.1 | 8.6 | 2.7 | 8.6 | ... | 12.2 | 3.5 | 6.4 | 10.9 | 12.2 | 2.1 | 17.2 |
| 1958–1960 | 9.5 | 5.4 | 2.0 | 12.2 | 18.3 | 16.6 | 32.7 | 14.5 | 10.5 | 14.5 | 30.0 | 16.2 |

[1] Includes only Coal mining (ISIC major group 11) and iron ore mining (part of ISIC major group 12).
[2] Excludes Clothing and made-up textiles (ISIC groups 243-244); Wood products (ISIC major group 25) except plywood up to and including 1954, Furniture (ISIC major group 26); Printing and publishing (ISIC major group 28); Petroleum and coal products (ISIC major group 32) up to and including 1954; and Other manufacturing (ISIC major group 39).
[3] Includes iron ore mining and the mining of other important metallic ores.
[4] Includes only the extraction of mica and salt.
[5] Includes extraction of vegetable oil (part of ISIC major group 31) for years 1955 and later.

[1] Comprend seulement Extraction du charbon (CITI classe 11) et extraction du minerai de fer (dans CITI classe 12).
[2] Non compris: Articles d'habillement et ouvrages en tissu (CITI groupes 243-244); Industrie du bois (CITI classes 25) à l'exclusion des contreplaqués jusqu'à 1954 inclusivement; Meubles (CITI classe 26); Imprimerie et édition (CITI classe 28); Industrie des dérivés du pétrole et du charbon (CITI classe 32) jusqu'en 1954 inclusivement, et Autres industries manufacturières (CITI classe 39).
[3] Y compris l'extraction du minerai de fer, ainsi que l'extraction d'autres minerais métalliques importants.
[4] Comprend seulement l'extraction du mica et du sel.
[5] Y compris l'extraction des huiles végétales (dans CITI classe 31) à partir de 1955.

## 3. INDEX NUMBERS OF INDUSTRIAL EMPLOYMENT — INDICES DE L'EMPLOI DANS L'INDUSTRIE

### A. Selected Divisions of Industrial Activity
### Quelques branches de l'activité industrielle

| Period<br>Période | Total [1,2,3] | Mining [1]<br>Industries extractives [1] | Manu-facturing [2]<br>Industries manu-facturières [2] | Electricity and gas [3]<br>Electricité et gaz [3] |
|---|---|---|---|---|
| ISIC — CITI | 1–3, 511–512 | 1 | 2–3 | 511–512 |

#### a. Indexes — Indices (1958 = 100)

| | | | | |
|---|---|---|---|---|
| 1948 | ... | 81 | 88 | ... |
| 1949 | ... | 78 | 87 | ... |
| 1950 | –84– | 81 | –84– | 72 |
| 1951 | –86– | –88– | –86– | –73– |
| 1952 | 87 | 88 | 87 | 72 |
| 1953 | 86 | 93 | 86 | 70 |
| 1954 | 88 | 87 | 88 | 73 |
| 1955 | 90 | 91 | 90 | 80 |
| 1956 | –99– | –96– | 99 | 88 |
| 1957 | 102 | 99 | 102 | 98 |
| 1958 | 100 | 100 | 100 | 100 |
| 1959 | –106– | –93– | 107 | 113 |
| 1960 | 110 | 97 | 111 | 124 |

#### b. Average Annual Rate of Change — Taux annuel moyen de variation

| | | | | |
|---|---|---|---|---|
| 1950–1960 | 2.7 | 1.8 | 2.8 | 5.6 |
| 1954–1958 | 3.2 | 3.5 | 3.2 | 8.2 |
| 1958–1960 | 4.9 | –1.5 | 5.4 | 11.4 |

For footnotes see end of table.
Pour les notes, voir au bas du tableau.

### B. Selected Major Groups of Mining
### Quelques classes de la branche Industries extractives

| Period<br>Période | All mining [1]<br>Toutes industries extractives [1] | Coal mining<br>Extraction du charbon | Metal mining [4]<br>Extraction des minerals métalliques [4] | Other mining [5]<br>Autres industries extractives [5] |
|---|---|---|---|---|
| ISIC — CITI | 1 | 11 | 12 | 14–19 |

#### a. Indexes — Indices (1958 = 100)

| | | | | |
|---|---|---|---|---|
| 1948 | 81 | 91 | 39 | 98 |
| 1949 | 78 | 90 | 46 | 77 |
| 1950 | 81 | 85 | 55 | 79 |
| 1951 | –88– | 92 | 68 | –95– |
| 1952 | 88 | 91 | 89 | 77 |
| 1953 | 93 | 89 | 116 | 79 |
| 1954 | 87 | 89 | 91 | 78 |
| 1955 | 90 | 91 | 97 | 82 |
| 1956 | –96– | 92 | 112 | 90 |
| 1957 | 99 | 97 | 114 | 91 |
| 1958 | 100 | 100 | 100 | 100 |
| 1959 | –93– | 100 | –81– | –86– |
| 1960 | 97 | 104 | 85 | 93 |

#### b. Average Annual Rate of Change — Taux annuel moyen de variation

| | | | | |
|---|---|---|---|---|
| 1950–1960 | 1.8 | 2.0 | 4.5 | 1.6 |
| 1954–1958 | 3.5 | 3.0 | 2.4 | 6.4 |
| 1958–1960 | –1.5 | 2.0 | –7.8 | –3.6 |

For footnotes see end of table.
Pour les notes, voir au bas du tableau.

## C. The Major Groups of Manufacturing — Les classes de la branche Industries manufacturières

| Period / Période | Manu-facturing [2] / Industries manufac-turières [2] | Food, beverages and tobacco [6] / Industries alimen-taires, boissons, tabac [6] | Textiles | Clothing, footwear and made-up textiles / Articles d'habil-lement, chaussures et ouvrages en tissu | Wood products and furniture / Bois et meubles | Paper and paper products / Papier et ouvrages en papier | Printing and publishing / Im-primerie et édition | Leather and leather products except wearing apparel / Cuir et articles en cuir, à l'exclu-sion des articles d'habil-lement | Rubber products / Ouvrages en caout-chouc | Chemicals and chemical, petroleum and coal products / Produits chi-miques et dérivés du pétrole et du charbon | Non-metallic mineral products / Produits minéraux non métal-liques | Basic metals / Métal-lurgie de base | Metal products / Ouvrages en métaux | Other manu-facturing / Autres industries manufac-turières |
|---|---|---|---|---|---|---|---|---|---|---|---|---|---|---|
| ISIC — CITI | 2–3 | 20–22 | 23 | 24 | 25–26 | 27 | 28 | 29 | 30 | 31–32 | 33 | 34 | 35–38 | 39 |

### a. Indexes — Indices (1958 = 100)

| Period / Période | 2–3 | 20–22 | 23 | 24 | 25–26 | 27 | 28 | 29 | 30 | 31–32 | 33 | 34 | 35–38 | 39 |
|---|---|---|---|---|---|---|---|---|---|---|---|---|---|---|
| 1948 | 88 | 72 | 110 | ... | 50 | 73 | ... | 88 | ... | 74 | 83 | 74 | 62 | ... |
| 1949 | 87 | 75 | 106 | ... | 50 | 74 | ... | 86 | ... | 76 | 86 | 75 | 62 | ... |
| 1950 | −84− | −80− | 99 | ... | 52 | 80 | 81 | 81 | ... | 74 | 87 | 77 | 65 | ... |
| 1951 | −86− | −86− | −99− | 63 | −65− | −78− | −84− | −89− | 76 | −74− | −95− | −77− | −68− | 70 |
| 1952 | 87 | 79 | 103 | 80 | 72 | 79 | 83 | 90 | 78 | 74 | 93 | 76 | 70 | 135 |
| 1953 | 86 | 78 | 103 | 76 | 65 | 75 | 79 | 108 | 78 | 74 | 90 | 69 | 69 | 133 |
| 1954 | 88 | 83 | 104 | 80 | 68 | 82 | 85 | 100 | 82 | 78 | 76 | 71 | 72 | 130 |
| 1955 | 90 | 86 | 105 | 73 | 74 | 85 | 87 | 103 | 87 | 84 | 80 | 78 | 76 | 132 |
| 1956 | 99 | 96 | 110 | 92 | 91 | 88 | 94 | 108 | 94 | 89 | 87 | 85 | 90 | 139 |
| 1957 | 102 | 98 | 110 | 98 | 94 | 96 | 97 | 107 | 100 | 90 | 96 | 90 | 96 | 137 |
| 1958 | 100 | 100 | 100 | 100 | 100 | 100 | 100 | 100 | 100 | 100 | 100 | 100 | 100 | 100 |
| 1959 | 107 | 102 | 106 | 100 | 116 | 111 | 106 | 102 | 110 | 109 | 113 | 115 | 111 | 110 |
| 1960 | 111 | 105 | 105 | 105 | 119 | 114 | 111 | 102 | 122 | 115 | 119 | 119 | 124 | 116 |

### b. Average Annual Rate of Change — Taux annuel moyen de variation

| Period / Période | 2–3 | 20–22 | 23 | 24 | 25–26 | 27 | 28 | 29 | 30 | 31–32 | 33 | 34 | 35–38 | 39 |
|---|---|---|---|---|---|---|---|---|---|---|---|---|---|---|
| 1948–1953 | −0.5 | 1.6 | −1.3 | ... | 5.4 | 0.5 | ... | 4.2 | ... | — | 1.6 | −1.4 | 2.2 | ... |
| 1954–1958 | 3.2 | 4.8 | −1.0 | 5.7 | 10.1 | 5.1 | 4.1 | — | 5.1 | 6.4 | 7.1 | 8.9 | 8.6 | −6.4 |
| 1958–1960 | 5.4 | 2.5 | 2.5 | 2.5 | 9.1 | 6.8 | 5.4 | 1.0 | 10.5 | 7.2 | 9.1 | 9.1 | 11.4 | 7.7 |

[1] Excludes part of Other mining (ISIC major groups 14-19) for the years 1948 to 1950. Crude petroleum and natural gas (ISIC major group 13) is excluded for the years, 1957 and later, but included in earlier years. Excludes in 1960 gold and chromite mining (part of ISIC major group 12), and all Other mining (ISIC major groups 14-19) except mica and salt mining.
[2] Excludes Tobacco manufactures (ISIC major group 22) and Printing and publishing (ISIC major group 28) for the years 1948 and 1949. Excludes Clothing, footwear and made-up textiles (ISIC major group 24), Rubber products (ISIC major group 30) and Other manufacturing (ISIC major group 39) for the years 1948 to 1950.
[3] Includes employment in the electricity producing plants of private factories.
[4] Excludes gold and chromite mining in 1960.
[5] Excludes certain minor items for the years 1948 to 1951, and for the year 1960 covers salt and mica mining only.
[6] Excludes Tobacco manufactures (ISIC major group 22) for the years 1948 and 1949.

[1] Non compris une partie de Autres industries extractives (CITI classes 14-19) de 1948 à 1950 Pétrole brut et gaz naturel (CITI classe 13) est exclu à partir de 1957, mais est compris les années précédentes. Non compris en 1960 l'extraction de l'or et du chrome (dans CITI classe 12) et Autres industries extractives (CITI classes 14-19), à l'exclusion de l'extraction du mica et du sel.
[2] Non compris Industrie du tabac (CITI classe 22) et Imprimerie et édition (CITI classe 28) en 1948 et 1949. Non compris Articles d'habillement, chaussures et ouvrages en tissu (CITI classe 24), Ouvrages en caoutchouc (CITI classe 30) et Autres industries manufacturières (CITI classe 39) de 1948 à 1950.
[3] Y compris l'emploi dans les unités productrices d'électricité des usines privées.
[4] Non compris l'extraction de l'or et du chrome en 1960.
[5] Non compris certaines activités peu importantes de 1948 à 1951; en 1960, ne comprend que l'extraction du mica et du sel.
[6] Non compris Industrie du tabac (CITI classe 22) en 1948 et 1949.

## 4. THE CHARACTERISTICS OF MANUFACTURING ESTABLISHMENTS EMPLOYING 20 OR MORE PERSONS OR 10–19 PERSONS AND USING POWER

### CARACTERISTIQUES DES ETABLISSEMENTS EMPLOYANT AU MOINS 20 PERSONNES OU 10 A 19 PERSONNES ET UTILISANT LA FORCE MOTRICE

### 1953, 1957

Number of establishments in units; value added and wages and salaries in million Rupees; number of employees in thousands; and value added and wages and salaries per employee in thousand Rupees.

Nombre d'établissements en unités; valeur ajoutée et traitements et salaires en millions de roupies; nombre de salariés en milliers; valeur ajoutée et traitements et salaires par salarié en milliers de roupies.

| Year and item of data | Manufacturing / Industries manufacturières | Food, beverages and tobacco / Industries alimentaires, boissons, tabac | Textiles | Clothing, footwear and made-up textiles / Articles d'habillement, chaussures et ouvrages en tissu | Wood products and furniture / Bois et meubles | Paper and paper products / Papier et ouvrages en papier | Printing and publishing / Imprimerie et édition | Leather and leather products except wearing apparel / Cuir et articles en cuir, à l'exclusion des articles d'habillement | Rubber products / Ouvrages en caoutchouc | Chemicals and chemical, petroleum and coal products / Produits chimiques et dérivés du pétrole et du charbon | Non-metallic mineral products / Produits minéraux non métalliques | Basic metals / Métallurgie de base | Metal products [1] / Ouvrages en métaux [1] | Other manufacturing / Autres industries manufacturières | Année et rubrique |
|---|---|---|---|---|---|---|---|---|---|---|---|---|---|---|---|
| ISIC | 2–3 | 20–22 | 23 | 24 | 25–26 | 27 | 28 | 29 | 30 | 31–32 | 33 | 34 | 35–38 | 39 | CITI |
| *a. Absolute Figures — Chiffres absolus* | | | | | | | | | | | | | | | |
| **1953** | | | | | | | | | | | | | | | **1953** |
| Number of establishments | 29 239 | 8 008 | 4 941 | 443 | 900 | 85 | 1 703 | 445 | 198 | 2 829 | 1 372 | 1 577 | 3 203 | 3 535 | Nombre d'établissements |
| Value added | 6 472.6 | 1 273.8 | 2 263.2 | 42.9 | 41.0 | 83.6 | 159.3 | 42.1 | 83.4 | 734.1 | 225.5 | 572.2 | 497.3 | 454.2 | Valeur ajoutée |
| Number of employees (Average during year) | 2 924.8 | 559.1 | 1 308.6 | 17.8 | 25.8 | 25.3 | 85.9 | 22.1 | 21.3 | 178.4 | 101.2 | 143.7 | 206.0 | 229.6 | Nombre de salariés (moyenne pendant l'année) |
| Wages and salaries paid | 3 255.0 | 369.1 | 1 528.6 | 25.7 | 21.9 | 33.7 | 112.7 | 23.5 | 29.8 | 209.2 | 106.0 | 254.8 | 303.7 | 236.3 | Traitements et salaires payés |
| **1957** | | | | | | | | | | | | | | | **1957** |
| Number of establishments | 35 680 | 9 790 | 6 815 | 653 | 1 189 | 112 | 2 165 | 463 | 257 | 3 054 | 772 | 1 910 | 4 433 | 4 067 | Nombre d'établissements |
| Value added | 8 310 | 1 660 | 2 374 | 49 | 97 | 134 | 220 | 46 | 184 | 831 | 297 | 1 012 | 992 | 414 | Valeur ajoutée |
| Employees: Number | 3 490 | 687 | 1 394 | 27 | 46 | 35 | 104 | 24 | 33 | 209 | 130 | 225 | 386 | 190 | Salariés: Nombre |
| Wages and salaries | 3 938 | 438 | 1 668 | 24 | 44 | 49 | 139 | 24 | 60 | 239 | 122 | 393 | 556 | 182 | Traitements et salaires |
| *b. Structure* | | | | | | | | | | | | | | | |
| **1953** | | | | | | | | | | | | | | | **1953** |
| Distribution in percent of: | | | | | | | | | | | | | | | Distribution en pourcentage: |
| Value added | 100.0 | 19.6 | 35.0 | 0.7 | 0.6 | 1.3 | 2.4 | 0.7 | 1.3 | 11.3 | 3.5 | 8.8 | 7.7 | 7.1 | Valeur ajoutée |
| Number of employees | 100.0 | 19.1 | 44.7 | 0.6 | 0.9 | 0.9 | 2.9 | 0.8 | 0.7 | 6.1 | 3.4 | 5.0 | 7.0 | 7.9 | Nombre de salariés |
| Value added per employee | 2.2 | 2.3 | 1.7 | 2.4 | 1.6 | 3.3 | 1.8 | 1.9 | 3.9 | 4.1 | 2.2 | 4.0 | 2.4 | 2.0 | Valeur ajoutée par salarié |
| Value added per unit of wages and salaries | 1.99 | 3.45 | 1.48 | 1.67 | 1.87 | 2.48 | 1.41 | 1.79 | 2.80 | 3.51 | 2.13 | 2.24 | 1.64 | 1.92 | Valeur ajoutée par unité de traitements et salaires |
| Wages and salaries per employee | 1.1 | 0.7 | 1.2 | 1.4 | 0.8 | 1.3 | 1.3 | 1.1 | 1.4 | 1.2 | 1.0 | 1.8 | 1.5 | 1.0 | Traitements et salaires par salarié |
| **1957** | | | | | | | | | | | | | | | **1957** |
| Distribution in percent of: | | | | | | | | | | | | | | | Distribution en pourcentage: |
| Value added | 100.0 | 19.9 | 28.6 | 0.6 | 1.2 | 1.6 | 2.6 | 0.6 | 2.2 | 10.0 | 3.6 | 12.1 | 12.0 | 5.0 | Valeur ajoutée |
| Number of employees | 100.0 | 19.6 | 40.0 | 0.8 | 1.3 | 1.0 | 3.0 | 0.6 | 1.0 | 6.0 | 3.7 | 6.4 | 11.1 | 5.5 | Nombre de salariés |
| Per employee: Value added | 2.4 | 2.4 | 1.7 | 1.8 | 2.1 | 3.8 | 2.1 | 1.9 | 5.6 | 4.0 | 2.3 | 4.5 | 2.6 | 2.2 | Par salarié: Valeur ajoutée |
| Wages and salaries | 1.1 | 0.6 | 1.2 | 0.9 | 1.0 | 1.4 | 1.3 | 1.0 | 1.8 | 1.1 | 0.9 | 1.7 | 1.4 | 1.0 | Traitements et salaires |
| Value added per unit of wages and salaries | 2.11 | 3.79 | 1.42 | 2.04 | 2.20 | 2.73 | 1.58 | 1.92 | 3.07 | 3.48 | 2.43 | 2.58 | 1.78 | 2.27 | Valeur ajoutée par unité de traitements et salaires |

[1] Excludes ordnance manufacturing by the Ministry of Defence and railway repair and locomotive workshops under the Ministry of Railways.

[1] Non compris la fabrication des armes à feu assurée par le Ministère de la défense, ainsi que les ateliers de réparation des wagons de chemins de fer et locomotives dépendant du Ministère des transports ferroviaires.

## 5. CHARACTERISTICS OF ESTABLISHMENTS IN SELECTED MAJOR GROUPS OF MANUFACTURING EMPLOYING 20 OR MORE PERSONS AND USING POWER

## CARACTERISTIQUES DES ETABLISSEMENTS EMPLOYANT 20 PERSONNES OU PLUS ET UTILISANT LA FORCE MOTRICE, DANS CERTAINES CLASSES DES INDUSTRIES MANUFACTURIERES

### 1948, 1953, 1958

Number of establishments in units; value added and wages and salaries in million Rupees; number of employees and operatives in thousands; man-hours worked in millions; energy consumed in thousand metric tons of coal equivalents; electricity purchased in million KWH; value added per employee and wages and salaries per employee and per thousand operative man-hours in thousand Rupees; average annual man-hours per operative in thousands; energy consumed per employee and per thousand operative man-hours in metric tons of coal equivalents; electricity purchased per employee and per thousand operative man-hours in thousand KWH.

Nombre d'établissements en unités; valeur ajoutée et traitements et salaires en millions de roupies; nombre de salariés et d'ouvriers en milliers; heures de travail effectuées en millions; énergie consommée en milliers de tonnes métriques d'équivalent charbon; électricité achetée en millions de kWh; valeur ajoutée par salarié et traitements et salaires par salarié et par millier d'heures-ouvrier en milliers de roupies; moyenne annuelle des heures de travail par ouvrier en milliers; énergie consommée par salarié et par millier d'heures-ouvrier en tonnes métriques d'équivalent charbon; électricité achetée par salarié et par millier d'heures-ouvrier en milliers de kWh.

| Year and item of data | Manu-facturing³ Industries manufac-turières³ | Food and beverages¹ Industries alimen-taires et boissons¹ | Textiles | Plywood and tea chests Contre-plaqué et caisses à thé | Paper and paper products Papier et ouvrages en papier | Leather Cuir | Chemicals and chemical products Produits chi-miques | Non-metallic mineral products² Produits minéraux non métal-liques² | Basic metals Métal-lurgie de base | Machinery and transport equip-ment Machines et matériel de transport | Année et rubrique |
|---|---|---|---|---|---|---|---|---|---|---|---|
| ISIC | 2–3 | 20–21 | 23 | Part of 25 Partie de 25 | 27 | 291 | 31 | 33 | 34 | 36–38 | CITI |

a. Absolute Figures — Chiffres absolus

| Year and item of data | Manu-facturing³ | Food and beverages¹ | Textiles | Contre-plaqué et caisses à thé | Paper et ouvrages en papier | Leather | Chemicals | Non-metallic mineral products² | Basic metals | Machinery and transport | Année et rubrique |
|---|---|---|---|---|---|---|---|---|---|---|---|
| **1948** | | | | | | | | | | | **1948** |
| Number of establishments. | 6 141 | 1 857 | 710 | 35 | 39 | 78 | 1 322 | 239 | 317 | 1 544 | Nombre d'établissements |
| Value added.......... | 3 312.1 | 262.9 | 2 125.7 | 7.0 | 41.2 | 12.3 | 277.0 | 71.6 | 269.1 | 245.3 | Valeur ajoutée |
| Number of employees (Average during year). | 1 704.2 | 177.8 | 1 070.3 | 3.4 | 20.4 | 9.5 | 116.2 | 54.7 | 99.8 | 152.1 | Nombre de salariés (moyenne pendant l'année) |
| Wages and salaries paid.............. | 1 607.8 | 96.8 | 1 078.6 | 2.3 | 19.4 | 6.8 | 90.4 | 36.3 | 131.3 | 145.9 | Traitements et salaires payés |
| Operatives: Number (Average during year)........ | 1 545.5 | 143.5 | 1 012.8 | 3.0 | 18.1 | 8.4 | 95.2 | 49.6 | 83.2 | 131.7 | Ouvriers: Nombre (moyenne pendant l'année) |
| Man-hours worked.... | 3 477.3 | 231.3 | 2 352.2 | 7.2 | 45.6 | 20.1 | 196.1 | 114.7 | 214.1 | 296.0 | Heures de travail effectuées |
| Wages and salaries... | 1 346.6 | 68.0 | 965.1 | 1.6 | 13.9 | 5.4 | 61.2 | 28.8 | 94.5 | 108.1 | Traitements et salaires |
| Energy consumed....... | 8 211.2 | 397.1 | 2 608.5 | 10.2 | 355.2 | 8.2 | 485.8 | 835.4 | 3 315.9 | 194.9 | Energie consommée |
| Electricity purchased..... | 1 509.1 | 29.5 | 1 134.0 | 0.2 | 33.1 | 2.0 | 103.5 | 44.1 | 111.3 | 51.4 | Electricité achetée |
| **1953** | | | | | | | | | | | **1953** |
| Number of establishments. | 6 400 | 1 982 | 613 | 41 | 45 | 96 | 1 313 | 190 | 329 | 1 791 | Nombre d'établissements |
| Value added.......... | 3 567.6 | 317.8 | 1 842.5 | 7.7 | 79.3 | 13.7 | 419.5 | 146.7 | 417.9 | 322.5 | Valeur ajoutée |
| Number of employees (Average during year). | 1 627.9 | 188.0 | 980.0 | 3.9 | 22.0 | 8.7 | 114.8 | 60.1 | 98.2 | 152.2 | Nombre de salariés (moyenne pendant l'année) |
| Wages and salaries paid.............. | 2 052.2 | 127.5 | 1 288.8 | 3.5 | 29.0 | 7.7 | 138.7 | 64.3 | 191.2 | 201.5 | Traitements et salaires payés |
| Operatives: Number (Average during year)........ | 1 470.8 | 157.4 | 925.6 | 3.2 | 19.4 | 7.4 | 94.2 | 53.0 | 81.6 | 129.0 | Ouvriers: Nombre (moyenne pendant l'année) |
| Man-hours worked.... | 3 347.9 | 231.2 | 2 231.6 | 7.2 | 47.0 | 17.8 | 196.9 | 127.7 | 196.7 | 291.8 | Heures de travail effectuées |
| Wages and salaries... | 1 647.3 | 83.5 | 1 126.7 | 1.9 | 19.6 | 5.7 | 87.9 | 46.5 | 134.1 | 141.4 | Traitements et salaires |
| Energy consumed....... | 9 920.3 | 372.5 | 2 465.6 | 11.2 | 474.2 | 5.3 | 1 041.0 | 1 684.0 | 3 666.4 | 200.1 | Energie consommée |
| Electricity purchased..... | 2 172.3 | 48.6 | 1 486.1 | 0.6 | 58.2 | 2.4 | 185.8 | 139.9 | 168.4 | 82.3 | Electricité achetée |
| **1958** | | | | | | | | | | | **1958** |
| Number of establishments. | 6 617 | 1 903 | 650 | 55 | 54 | 88 | 1 365 | 183 | 353 | 1 966 | Nombre d'établissements |
| Value added.......... | 5 375.2 | 545.8 | 2 077.6 | 17.7 | 186.4 | 14.7 | 756.0 | 261.8 | 736.6 | 778.6 | Valeur ajoutée |
| Employees: Number (Average during year)........ | 1 820.5 | 216.0 | 983.1 | 6.7 | 35.9 | 8.3 | 139.5 | 79.6 | 118.1 | 233.3 | Salariés: Nombre (moyenne pendant l'année) |
| Wages and salaries... | 2 681.1 | 189.2 | 1 450.9 | 6.9 | 55.6 | 8.3 | 216.3 | 106.9 | 271.8 | 375.2 | Traitements et salaires |
| Operatives: Number (Average during year)........ | 1 599.9 | 177.2 | 908.9 | 5.6 | 30.4 | 7.0 | 110.2 | 70.0 | 96.5 | 194.1 | Ouvriers: Nombre (moyenne pendant l'année) |
| Man-hours worked.... | 3 590.7 | 242.7 | 2 157.7 | 13.0 | 76.2 | 16.6 | 234.3 | 170.6 | 224.4 | 455.2 | Heures de travail effectuées |
| Wages and salaries... | 1 949.9 | 118.9 | 1 166.3 | 4.2 | 36.0 | 5.8 | 124.4 | 72.6 | 171.4 | 250.3 | Traitements et salaires |
| Energy consumed....... | 11 394.0 | 548.6 | 2 411.5 | 16.5 | 815.1 | 7.7 | 1 043.0 | 2 805.2 | 3 390.8 | 355.6 | Energie consommée |
| Electricity purchased..... | 4 294.7 | 115.9 | 2 117.8 | 4.7 | 224.4 | 4.4 | 493.5 | 361.6 | 766.4 | 206.0 | Electricité achetée |

For footnotes see end of table.

Pour les notes, voir au bas du tableau.

## 5. CHARACTERISTICS OF ESTABLISHMENTS IN SELECTED MAJOR GROUPS OF MANUFACTURING EMPLOYING 20 OR MORE PERSONS AND USING POWER (continued)

## CARACTERISTIQUES DES ETABLISSEMENTS EMPLOYANT 20 PERSONNES OU PLUS ET UTILISANT LA FORCE MOTRICE, DANS CERTAINES CLASSES DES INDUSTRIES MANUFACTURIERES (suite)

### 1948, 1953, 1958

| Year and item of data | Manufacturing[3] Industries manufacturières[3] | Food and beverages[1] Industries alimentaires et boissons[1] | Textiles | Plywood and tea chests Contre-plaqué et caisses à thé | Paper and paper products Papier et ouvrages en papier | Leather Cuir | Chemicals and chemical products Produits chimiques | Non-metallic mineral products[2] Produits minéraux non métalliques[2] | Basic metals Métallurgie de base | Machinery and transport equipment Machines et matériel de transport | Année et rubrique |
|---|---|---|---|---|---|---|---|---|---|---|---|
| ISIC | 2–3 | 20–21 | 23 | Part of 25 Partie de 25 | 27 | 291 | 31 | 33 | 34 | 36–38 | CITI |
| | | | | | *b. Structure* | | | | | | |
| **1948** | | | | | | | | | | | **1948** |
| Distribution in percent of: | | | | | | | | | | | Distribution en pourcentage: |
| Value added | 100.0 | 7.9 | 64.2 | 0.2 | 1.2 | 0.4 | 8.4 | 2.1 | 8.1 | 7.5 | Valeur ajoutée |
| Number of employees | 100.0 | 10.4 | 62.8 | 0.2 | 1.2 | 0.5 | 6.9 | 3.2 | 5.8 | 9.0 | Nombre de salariés |
| Per employee: | | | | | | | | | | | Par salarié: |
| Value added | 1.9 | 1.5 | 2.0 | 2.0 | 2.0 | 1.3 | 2.4 | 1.3 | 2.7 | 1.6 | Valeur ajoutée |
| Wages and salaries | 0.9 | 0.5 | 1.0 | 0.7 | 1.0 | 0.7 | 0.8 | 0.7 | 1.3 | 1.0 | Traitements et salaires |
| Energy consumed | 4.82 | 2.23 | 2.44 | 3.00 | 17.41 | 0.86 | 4.18 | 15.27 | 33.22 | 1.28 | Energie consommée |
| Electricity purchased | 0.9 | 0.2 | 1.0 | 0.1 | 1.6 | 0.2 | 0.9 | 0.8 | 1.1 | 0.3 | Electricité achetée |
| Value added per unit of wages and salaries | 2.06 | 2.72 | 1.97 | 3.04 | 2.12 | 1.81 | 3.06 | 1.97 | 2.05 | 1.68 | Valeur ajoutée par unité de traitements et salaires |
| Operatives as a percent of employees | 90.7 | 80.7 | 94.6 | 88.2 | 88.7 | 88.4 | 81.9 | 90.7 | 83.4 | 86.6 | Ouvriers en pourcentage des salariés |
| Average man-hours per operative | 2.25 | 1.61 | 2.32 | 2.40 | 2.52 | 2.39 | 2.06 | 2.31 | 2.57 | 2.25 | Heures de travail: moyenne par ouvrier |
| Per thousand operative man-hours: | | | | | | | | | | | Par millier d'heures-ouvrier: |
| Wages and salaries | 0.39 | 0.29 | 0.41 | 0.22 | 0.30 | 0.27 | 0.31 | 0.25 | 0.44 | 0.36 | Traitements et salaires |
| Energy consumed | 2.36 | 1.72 | 1.11 | 1.42 | 7.79 | 0.41 | 2.48 | 7.28 | 15.49 | 0.66 | Energie consommée |
| Electricity purchased | 0.43 | 0.13 | 0.48 | 0.03 | 0.72 | 0.10 | 0.53 | 0.38 | 0.52 | 0.17 | Electricité achetée |
| **1953** | | | | | | | | | | | **1953** |
| Distribution in percent of: | | | | | | | | | | | Distribution en pourcentage: |
| Value added | 100.0 | 8.9 | 51.6 | 0.2 | 2.2 | 0.4 | 11.8 | 4.1 | 11.7 | 9.1 | Valeur ajoutée |
| Number of employees | 100.0 | 11.5 | 60.2 | 0.2 | 1.4 | 0.5 | 7.1 | 3.7 | 6.0 | 9.4 | Nombre de salariés |
| Per employee: | | | | | | | | | | | Par salarié: |
| Value added | 2.2 | 1.7 | 1.9 | 2.0 | 3.6 | 1.6 | 3.6 | 2.4 | 4.2 | 2.1 | Valeur ajoutée |
| Wages and salaries | 1.3 | 0.7 | 1.3 | 0.9 | 1.3 | 0.9 | 1.2 | 1.1 | 1.9 | 1.3 | Traitements et salaires |
| Energy consumed | 6.09 | 1.98 | 2.52 | 2.87 | 21.55 | 0.61 | 9.07 | 28.02 | 37.34 | 1.31 | Energie consommée |
| Electricity purchased | 1.3 | 0.2 | 1.5 | 0.2 | 2.6 | 0.3 | 1.6 | 2.3 | 1.7 | 0.5 | Electricité achetée |
| Value added per unit of wages and salaries | 1.74 | 2.49 | 1.43 | 2.20 | 2.73 | 1.78 | 3.02 | 2.28 | 2.18 | 1.60 | Valeur ajoutée par unité de traitements et salaires |
| Operatives as a percent of employees | 90.3 | 83.7 | 94.4 | 82.0 | 88.2 | 85.0 | 82.0 | 88.2 | 83.1 | 84.8 | Ouvriers en pourcentage des salariés |
| Average man-hours per operative | 2.28 | 1.47 | 2.41 | 2.25 | 2.42 | 2.40 | 2.09 | 2.41 | 2.41 | 2.26 | Heures de travail: moyenne par ouvrier |
| Per thousand operative man-hours: | | | | | | | | | | | Par millier d'heures-ouvrier: |
| Wages and salaries | 0.49 | 0.36 | 0.50 | 0.26 | 0.42 | 0.32 | 0.45 | 0.36 | 0.68 | 0.48 | Traitements et salaires |
| Energy consumed | 2.96 | 1.61 | 1.10 | 1.56 | 10.09 | 0.30 | 5.29 | 13.19 | 18.64 | 0.68 | Energie consommée |
| Electricity purchased | 0.65 | 0.21 | 0.66 | 0.08 | 1.24 | 0.13 | 0.94 | 1.10 | 0.86 | 0.17 | Electricité achetée |
| **1958** | | | | | | | | | | | **1958** |
| Distribution in percent of: | | | | | | | | | | | Distribution en pourcentage: |
| Value added | 100.0 | 10.1 | 38.7 | 0.3 | 3.5 | 0.2 | 14.1 | 4.9 | 13.7 | 14.5 | Valeur ajoutée |
| Number of employees | 100.0 | 11.8 | 54.0 | 0.4 | 2.0 | 0.4 | 7.7 | 4.3 | 6.5 | 12.9 | Nombre de salariés |
| Per employee: | | | | | | | | | | | Par salarié: |
| Value added | 3.0 | 2.5 | 2.1 | 2.6 | 5.2 | 1.8 | 5.4 | 3.3 | 6.2 | 3.3 | Valeur ajoutée |
| Wages and salaries | 1.5 | 0.9 | 1.5 | 1.0 | 1.5 | 1.0 | 1.6 | 1.3 | 2.3 | 1.6 | Traitements et salaires |
| Energy consumed | 6.26 | 2.54 | 2.45 | 2.46 | 22.70 | 0.93 | 7.48 | 35.24 | 28.71 | 1.52 | Energie consommée |
| Electricity purchased | 2.4 | 0.5 | 2.2 | 0.7 | 6.2 | 0.5 | 3.5 | 4.5 | 6.5 | 0.9 | Electricité achetée |
| Value added per unit of wages and salaries | 2.00 | 2.88 | 1.43 | 2.56 | 3.35 | 1.77 | 3.50 | 2.45 | 2.71 | 2.08 | Valeur ajoutée par unité de traitements et salaires |
| Operatives as a percent of employees | 87.9 | 82.0 | 92.4 | 83.6 | 84.7 | 84.3 | 79.0 | 87.9 | 81.7 | 83.2 | Ouvriers en pourcentage des salariés |
| Average man-hours per operative | 2.24 | 1.37 | 2.37 | 2.32 | 2.51 | 2.37 | 2.13 | 2.44 | 2.32 | 2.34 | Heures de travail: moyenne par ouvrier |
| Per thousand operative man-hours: | | | | | | | | | | | Par millier d'heures-ouvrier: |
| Wages and salaries | 0.54 | 0.49 | 0.54 | 0.32 | 0.47 | 0.35 | 0.53 | 0.42 | 0.76 | 0.55 | Traitements et salaires |
| Energy consumed | 3.17 | 2.26 | 1.12 | 1.27 | 10.70 | 0.46 | 4.45 | 16.44 | 15.11 | 0.78 | Energie consommée |
| Electricity purchased | 1.20 | 0.48 | 0.98 | 0.36 | 2.94 | 0.36 | 2.11 | 2.12 | 3.42 | 0.45 | Electricité a chetée |

[1] Does not include Slaughtering and preserving of meat (ISIC group 201), Manufacture of dairy products (ISIC group 202), Canning and preserving of fish (ISIC group 204), Manufacture of bakery products (ISIC group 206), Manufacture of confectionery (in ISIC group 208) or most of Manufacture of miscellaneous food preparations (ISIC group 209).

[2] Does not include Manufacture of structural clay products (ISIC group 331).

[3] In addition to the exclusions noted above, Tobacco manufactures (ISIC major group 22), Clothing and footwear (ISIC major group 24), most of Wood products and furniture (ISIC major groups 25-26), Printing and publishing (ISIC major group 28), Manufacture of leather products (ISIC major group 293), Rubber products (ISIC major group 30), Petroleum and coal products (ISIC major group 32), Manufacture of metal products (ISIC major group 35) and Other manufacturing (ISIC major group 39) are not covered.

[1] Non compris Abattage du bétail et fabrication des conserves de viande (CITI groupe 201), Industrie du lait (CITI groupe 202), Fabrication des conserves de poissons (CITI groupe 204), Boulangerie et pâtisserie (CITI groupe 206), la confiserie (dans CITI groupe 208), et la majeure partie des Industries alimentaires diverses (CITI groupe 209).

[2] Non compris la Fabrication des matériaux de construction en terre cuite (CITI groupe 331).

[3] Non compris, en plus des industries mentionnées ci-dessus, Industrie du tabac (classe 22), Articles d'habillement et chaussures (CITI classe 24), la majeure partie des industries classées dans Bois et meubles (CITI classes 25-26), Imprimerie et édition (CITI classe 28), Fabrication des articles en cuir (CITI groupe 293), Ouvrages en caoutchouc (CITI classe 30), Dérivés du pétrole et du charbon (CITI classe 32), Fabrication des ouvrages en métaux (CITI classe 35), et Autres industries manufacturières (CITI classe 39).

## 6. PURCHASED FUELS AND ELECTRICITY CONSUMED BY ESTABLISHMENTS IN SELECTED MAJOR GROUPS OF MANUFACTURING EMPLOYING 20 OR MORE PERSONS AND USING POWER

### COMBUSTIBLES ET ELECTRICITE ACHETES ET CONSOMMES PAR LES ETABLISSEMENTS EMPLOYANT 20 PERSONNES OU PLUS ET UTILISANT LA FORCE MOTRICE DANS CERTAINES CLASSES DES INDUSTRIES MANUFACTURIERES

### 1948, 1953, 1958

#### A.   Percentage Distribution of Purchased Energy Consumed According to Source
#### Répartition en pourcentage de l'énergie achetée et consommée suivant la source.

Quantities in thousand metric tons of coal equivalents.              Quantités en milliers de tonnes métriques d'équivalent charbon

| Year and item of data | Manufacturing [3] / Industries manufacturières [3] | Food and beverages [1] / Industries alimentaires et boissons[1] | Textiles | Wood products and furniture / Bois et meubles | Paper and paper products / Papier et ouvrages en papier | Leather / Cuir | Chemicals and chemical, products / Produits chimiques | Nonmetallic mineral products [2] / Produits minéraux non métalliques [2] | Basic metals / Métallurgie de base | Machinery and transport equipment / Machines et matériel de transport | Année et rubrique |
|---|---|---|---|---|---|---|---|---|---|---|---|
| ISIC | 2–3 | 20–21 | 23 | Part of 25 Partie de 25 | 27 | 291 | 31 | 33 | 34 | 36–38 | CITI |
| **1948** | | | | | | | | | | | **1948** |
| Total energy consumed: | | | | | | | | | | | Energie totale consommée: |
| Quantity............ | 8 211.2 | 397.1 | 2 608.5 | 10.2 | 355.2 | 8.2 | 485.8 | 835.4 | 3 315.9 | 194.9 | Quantité |
| Percent of total in specified industry..... | 100.0 | 4.8 | 31.8 | 0.1 | 4.3 | 0.1 | 5.9 | 10.2 | 40.4 | 2.4 | Pourcentage du total par industrie indiquée |
| Percent consumed as: | | | | | | | | | | | Pourcentage consommé sous forme de: |
| Coal............... | 84.0 | 62.7 | 82.0 | 47.0 | 91.6 | 78.0 | 68.1 | 86.8 | 91.2 | 48.4 | Charbon |
| Charcoal and wood... | 2.5 | 28.0 | 0.7 | 45.1 | 0.2 | 1.2 | 7.7 | 1.6 | 0.5 | 3.1 | Charbon de bois et bois |
| Coke............... | 2.8 | 2.1 | 0.3 | — | 0.1 | — | 2.4 | 1.4 | 3.6 | 34.5 | Coke |
| Refined oil fuels...... | 6.1 | 2.9 | 11.4 | 1.0 | 1.7 | 7.3 | 15.0 | 8.9 | 0.7 | 8.1 | Pétrole raffiné |
| Gas................ | 0.4 | 0.2 | — | — | — | — | — | 0.2 | 0.8 | 0.7 | Gaz |
| Electricity.......... | 2.3 | 0.9 | 5.4 | — | 1.1 | 2.5 | 2.6 | 0.7 | 0.4 | 3.3 | Electricité |
| Other fuels.......... | 1.9 | 3.2 | 0.2 | 6.9 | 5.3 | 11.0 | 4.0 | 0.6 | 2.8 | 1.9 | Autres combustibles |
| **1953** | | | | | | | | | | | **1953** |
| Total energy consumed: | | | | | | | | | | | Energie totale consommée: |
| Quantity............ | 9 920.3 | 372.5 | 2 465.6 | 11.2 | 474.2 | 5.3 | 1 041.0 | 1 684.0 | 3 666.4 | 200.1 | Quantité |
| Percent of total in specified industry..... | 100.0 | 3.7 | 24.9 | 0.1 | 4.8 | — | 10.5 | 17.0 | 36.9 | 2.1 | Pourcentage du total par industrie indiquée |
| Percent consumed as: | | | | | | | | | | | Pourcentage consommé sous forme de: |
| Coal............... | 85.3 | 70.6 | 80.0 | 86.6 | 97.2 | 77.3 | 70.4 | 94.0 | 91.8 | 36.1 | Charbon |
| Charcoal and wood... | 1.0 | 14.8 | 0.2 | 8.9 | 0.1 | — | 1.5 | 0.3 | 0.3 | 3.0 | Charbon de bois et bois |
| Coke............... | 4.3 | 3.9 | 0.3 | — | 0.1 | — | 15.9 | 1.0 | 3.9 | 38.9 | Coke |
| Refined oil fuels...... | 5.0 | 5.1 | 11.6 | 2.7 | 0.7 | 11.3 | 7.5 | 3.2 | 0.7 | 13.5 | Pétrole raffiné |
| Gas................ | 0.4 | 0.2 | — | — | — | — | 0.2 | — | 0.9 | 0.8 | Gaz |
| Electricity.......... | 2.7 | 1.6 | 7.6 | — | 1.6 | 5.7 | 2.2 | 1.0 | 0.6 | 5.2 | Electricité |
| Other fuels.......... | 1.3 | 3.8 | 0.3 | 1.8 | 0.3 | 5.7 | 2.3 | 0.5 | 1.8 | 2.5 | Autres combustibles |
| **1958** | | | | | | | | | | | **1958** |
| Total energy consumed: | | | | | | | | | | | Energie totale consommée: |
| Quantity............ | 11 394.0 | 548.6 | 2 411.5 | 16.5 | 815.1 | 7.7 | 1 043.0 | 2 805.2 | 3 390.8 | 355.6 | Quantité |
| Percent of total in specified industry..... | 100.0 | 4.8 | 21.1 | 0.2 | 7.1 | 0.1 | 9.1 | 24.7 | 29.7 | 3.2 | Pourcentage du total par industrie indiquée |
| Percent consumed as: | | | | | | | | | | | Pourcentage consommé sous forme de: |
| Coal............... | 79.9 | 62.5 | 75.4 | 73.9 | 93.9 | 79.2 | 70.0 | 94.0 | 79.2 | 28.4 | Charbon |
| Charcoal and wood... | 2.2 | 20.7 | 0.2 | 17.0 | 0.2 | 2.6 | 5.3 | 0.3 | 1.7 | 2.7 | Charbon de bois et bois |
| Coke............... | 4.5 | 4.1 | 1.0 | — | 0.1 | 1.3 | 1.7 | 1.0 | 8.2 | 42.0 | Coke |
| Refined oil fuels...... | 6.7 | 6.9 | 12.0 | 3.0 | 1.7 | 5.2 | 13.7 | 2.6 | 4.2 | 15.2 | Pétrole raffiné |
| Gas................ | — | 0.2 | — | — | — | — | 0.1 | — | — | 0.9 | Gaz |
| Electricity.......... | 4.7 | 2.6 | 11.0 | 3.6 | 3.5 | 6.5 | 5.9 | 1.6 | 2.8 | 7.2 | Electricité |
| Other fuels.......... | 2.0 | 3.0 | 0.4 | 2.5 | 0.6 | 5.2 | 3.3 | 0.5 | 3.9 | 3.6 | Autres combustibles |

For footnotes see end of table.                              Pour les notes, voir au bas du tableau.

## B. Quantity and Value of Purchased Fuels Consumed and Electricity Purchased

### Quantité et valeur des combustibles achetés et consommés et de l'électricité achetée

Coal, charcoal, coke, refined oil fuels and wood in thousand metric tons; gas in million cubic metres; electricity in million KWH; other fuels in thousand metric tons of coal equivalents; values in thousand Rupees.

Charbon, charbon de bois, coke, pétrole raffiné et bois en milliers de tonnes métriques; gaz en millions de mètres cubes; électricité en millions de kWh; autres combustibles en milliers de tonnes métriques d'équivalent charbon; valeur en milliers de roupies.

| Year and source of energy | Manufacturing [3] / Industries manufacturières [3] | Food and beverages [1] / Industries alimentaires et boissons [1] | Textiles | Wood products and furniture / Bois et meubles | Paper and paper products / Papier et ouvrages en papier | Leather and leather products except wearing apparel / Cuir et articles en cuir, à l'exclusion des articles d'habillement | Chemicals and chemical products / Produits chimiques | Non-metallic mineral products [2] / Produits minéraux non métalliques [2] | Basic metals / Métallurgie de base | Machinery and transport equipment / Machines et matériel de transport | Année et source d'énergie |
|---|---|---|---|---|---|---|---|---|---|---|---|
| ISIC | 2–3 | 20–21 | 23 | Part of 25 / Partie de 25 | 27 | 29 | 31 | 33 | 34 | 36–38 | CITI |
| **1948** | | | | | | | | | | | **1948** |
| Coal: | | | | | | | | | | | Charbon: |
| Quantity | 6 903.0 | 249.3 | 2 140.1 | 4.8 | 325.5 | 6.4 | 331.2 | 725.5 | 3 025.7 | 94.5 | Quantité |
| Value | 171 625.5 | 7 049.6 | 65 509.7 | 116.0 | 7 480.0 | 178.0 | 10 293.1 | 17 735.6 | 50 922.1 | 2 341.4 | Valeur |
| Charcoal: | | | | | | | | | | | Charbon de bois: |
| Quantity | 11.2 | 3.1 | 1.0 | — | 0.1 | 0.2 | 1.5 | 0.5 | 2.3 | 2.5 | Quantité |
| Value | 1 306.3 | 230.7 | 149.6 | 1.3 | 13.2 | 21.6 | 229.2 | 70.0 | 246.0 | 344.7 | Valeur |
| Coke: | | | | | | | | | | | Coke: |
| Quantity | 252.6 | 9.3 | 9.0 | — | 0.5 | — | 12.7 | 12.7 | 133.7 | 74.7 | Quantité |
| Value | 10 945.4 | 443.9 | 461.6 | 1.3 | 22.1 | 2.4 | 731.3 | 268.2 | 4 969.0 | 4 045.6 | Valeur |
| Refined oil fuels: | | | | | | | | | | | Pétrole raffiné: |
| Quantity | 334.5 | 7.5 | 198.4 | 0.1 | 3.9 | 0.4 | 48.5 | 49.5 | 15.7 | 10.5 | Quantité |
| Value | 34 178.2 | 1 864.8 | 17 709.8 | 33.3 | 526.7 | 87.0 | 5 656.4 | 4 977.1 | 1 728.4 | 1 594.7 | Valeur |
| Manufactured gas: | | | | | | | | | | | Gaz manufacturé: |
| Quantity | 48.2 | 1.1 | 0.5 | — | — | — | 1.8 | 0.2 | 42.2 | 2.4 | Quantité |
| Value | 1 371.1 | 141.6 | 68.0 | — | — | 1.7 | 198.9 | 26.2 | 625.7 | 309.0 | Valeur |
| Electricity: | | | | | | | | | | | Electricité: |
| Purchased: | | | | | | | | | | | Achetée: |
| Quantity | 1 509.1 | 29.5 | 1 134.0 | 0.2 | 33.1 | 2.0 | 103.5 | 44.1 | 111.3 | 51.4 | Quantité |
| Value | 56 331.0 | 2 187.3 | 37 335.2 | 17.7 | 1 402.5 | 175.2 | 5 259.8 | 1 852.7 | 4 469.1 | 3 631.5 | Valeur |
| Wood: | | | | | | | | | | | Bois: |
| Quantity | 400.0 | 218.1 | 34.1 | 9.3 | 1.1 | 0.1 | 72.8 | 26.5 | 29.2 | 8.8 | Quantité |
| Value | 13 136.9 | 6 376.0 | 1 337.8 | 184.9 | 44.3 | 4.5 | 2 384.8 | 1 100.0 | 1 246.4 | 458.2 | Valeur |
| Other fuels: | | | | | | | | | | | Autres combustibles: |
| Quantity | 154.2 | 12.5 | 3.0 | 0.7 | 18.6 | 0.9 | 19.0 | 5.0 | 90.9 | 3.6 | Quantité |
| Value | 4 260.0 | 528.7 | 105.4 | 24.7 | 451.4 | 38.0 | 814.8 | 146.9 | 1 974.4 | 175.7 | Valeur |
| **1953** | | | | | | | | | | | **1953** |
| Coal: | | | | | | | | | | | Charbon: |
| Quantity | 8 468.2 | 263.0 | 1 972.7 | 9.7 | 461.0 | 4.1 | 732.9 | 1 584.6 | 3 367.8 | 72.4 | Quantité |
| Value | 218 233.1 | 7 556.3 | 60 617.0 | 315.7 | 11 392.4 | 131.8 | 18 600.6 | 46 962.3 | 70 547.2 | 2 109.8 | Valeur |
| Charcoal: | | | | | | | | | | | Charbon de bois: |
| Quantity | 4.6 | 0.4 | 0.4 | — | — | 0.1 | 0.6 | 0.1 | 1.6 | 1.4 | Quantité |
| Value | 581.7 | 54.3 | 55.5 | 1.0 | — | 12.7 | 68.2 | 15.4 | 168.4 | 206.2 | Valeur |
| Coke: | | | | | | | | | | | Coke: |
| Quantity | 471.7 | 16.2 | 9.3 | — | 0.6 | — | 184.5 | 17.9 | 156.8 | 86.4 | Quantité |
| Value | 19 594.4 | 856.5 | 514.2 | — | 25.9 | 0.2 | 7 591.3 | 494.5 | 5 739.8 | 4 372.0 | Valeur |
| Refined oil fuels: | | | | | | | | | | | Pétrole raffiné: |
| Quantity | 330.7 | 12.8 | 191.4 | 0.2 | 2.3 | 0.4 | 52.2 | 35.3 | 18.1 | 18.0 | Quantité |
| Value | 57 664.0 | 3 785.7 | 29 939.6 | 71.7 | 553.9 | 116.3 | 10 181.9 | 6 072.0 | 3 190.2 | 3 752.7 | Valeur |
| Manufactured gas: | | | | | | | | | | | Gaz manufacturé: |
| Quantity | 59.4 | 1.0 | 0.7 | — | — | — | 2.0 | 0.1 | 52.9 | 2.7 | Quantité |
| Value | 1 458.5 | 145.7 | 102.1 | — | — | 0.2 | 150.7 | 15.4 | 642.1 | 402.3 | Valeur |
| Electricity: | | | | | | | | | | | Electricité: |
| Purchased: | | | | | | | | | | | Achetée: |
| Quantity | 2 172.3 | 48.6 | 1 486.1 | 0.6 | 58.2 | 2.4 | 185.8 | 139.9 | 168.4 | 82.3 | Quantité |
| Value | 108 670.0 | 4 053.6 | 68 915.7 | 102.2 | 2 842.7 | 286.7 | 10 818.0 | 7 955.2 | 7 562.1 | 6 133.8 | Valeur |
| Wood: | | | | | | | | | | | Bois: |
| Quantity | 193.6 | 109.6 | 7.9 | 2.0 | 0.9 | — | 30.7 | 10.5 | 22.3 | 9.7 | Quantité |
| Value | 5 914.1 | 3 170.0 | 231.3 | 45.7 | 26.3 | 1.0 | 936.7 | 326.0 | 732.8 | 444.3 | Valeur |
| Other fuels: | | | | | | | | | | | Autres combustibles: |
| Quantity | 124.2 | 13.9 | 7.0 | 0.2 | 1.4 | 0.3 | 23.6 | 7.6 | 65.2 | 5.0 | Quantité |
| Value | 3 876.2 | 613.9 | 281.6 | 9.9 | 36.5 | 14.7 | 891.6 | 247.5 | 1 476.8 | 303.7 | Valeur |

For footnotes see end of table.    Pour les notes, voir au bas du tableau.

## B. Quantity and value of Purchased Fuels Consumed and Electricity Purchased (continued)
### Quantité et valeur des combustibles achetés et consommés et de l'électricité achetée (suite)

| Year and source of energy | Manu-facturing [3]<br>Industries manufac-turières [3] | Food and bever-ages [1]<br>Industries alimen-taires et boissons [1] | Textiles | Wood products and furniture<br>Bois et meubles | Paper and paper products<br>Papier et ouvrages en papier | Leather and leather products except wearing apparel<br>Cuir et articles en cuir, à l'exclu-sion des articles d'habil-lement | Chemicals and chemical products<br>Produits chi-miques | Non-metallic mineral products [2]<br>Produits minéraux non métal-liques [2] | Basic metals<br>Métal-lurgie de base | Machinery and transport equipment<br>Machines et maté-riel de transport | Année et source d'énergie |
|---|---|---|---|---|---|---|---|---|---|---|---|
| ISIC | 2–3 | 20–21 | 23 | Part of 25<br>Partie de 25 | 27 | 29 | 31 | 33 | 34 | 36–38 | CITI |
| **1958** | | | | | | | | | | | **1958** |
| **Coal:** | | | | | | | | | | | **Charbon:** |
| Quantity | 9 105.2 | 342.9 | 1 820.3 | 12.2 | 765.4 | 6.1 | 730.7 | 2 638.6 | 2 687.8 | 101.2 | Quantité |
| Value | 316 619.3 | 12 518.2 | 71 246.8 | 424.2 | 24 119.2 | 237.6 | 24 254.6 | 98 284.4 | 81 890.3 | 3 644.0 | Valeur |
| **Charcoal:** | | | | | | | | | | | **Charbon de bois:** |
| Quantity | 37.5 | 0.4 | 0.6 | — | — | — | 0.7 | 0.2 | 32.5 | 3.1 | Quantité |
| Value | 3 990.5 | 46.1 | 83.4 | 1.2 | 1.4 | 1.6 | 93.1 | 22.4 | 3 325.6 | 415.7 | Valeur |
| **Coke:** | | | | | | | | | | | **Coke:** |
| Quantity | 571.9 | 25.2 | 25.6 | — | 0.5 | 0.1 | 19.3 | 29.2 | 305.9 | 166.1 | Quantité |
| Value | 31 169.1 | 1 682.9 | 1 264.5 | — | 27.8 | 5.0 | 1 375.2 | 1 130.1 | 15 599.8 | 10 083.8 | Valeur |
| **Refined oil fuels:** | | | | | | | | | | | **Pétrole raffiné:** |
| Quantity | 503.9 | 25.1 | 192.0 | 0.3 | 9.5 | 0.2 | 95.4 | 49.6 | 95.9 | 35.9 | Quantité |
| Value | 93 143.1 | 6 932.9 | 31 323.3 | 157.3 | 1 834.5 | 91.6 | 17 136.4 | 10 143.3 | 16 750.2 | 8 773.6 | Valeur |
| **Manufactured gas:** | | | | | | | | | | | **Gaz manufacturé:** |
| Quantity | 9.4 | 2.0 | 0.8 | — | — | — | 1.2 | 0.2 | — | 5.2 | Quantité |
| Value | 1 470.1 | 300.0 | 126.1 | — | — | — | 190.7 | 31.1 | 6.4 | 815.8 | Valeur |
| **Electricity:** | | | | | | | | | | | **Électricité:** |
| **Purchased:** | | | | | | | | | | | **Achetée:** |
| Quantity | 4 294.7 | 115.9 | 2 117.8 | 4.7 | 224.4 | 4.4 | 493.5 | 361.6 | 766.4 | 206.0 | Quantité |
| Value | 236 224.6 | 10 264.2 | 121 488.9 | 419.8 | 13 783.7 | 502.4 | 26 675.6 | 20 315.5 | 27 811.6 | 14 962.9 | Valeur |
| **Wood:** | | | | | | | | | | | **Bois:** |
| Quantity | 465.4 | 226.9 | 10.9 | 5.7 | 4.5 | 0.4 | 110.4 | 17.7 | 73.8 | 15.1 | Quantité |
| Value | 14 942.5 | 7 894.5 | 382.4 | 113.5 | 153.0 | 23.1 | 2 941.1 | 564.5 | 2 109.0 | 761.4 | Valeur |
| **Other fuels:** | | | | | | | | | | | **Autres combustibles:** |
| Quantity | 218.1 | 16.0 | 9.2 | 0.4 | 4.7 | 0.4 | 33.7 | 11.7 | 129.4 | 12.6 | Quantité |
| Value | 9 522.3 | 909.1 | 451.9 | 17.8 | 157.4 | 20.9 | 1 635.0 | 468.6 | 4 890.8 | 970.8 | Valeur |

[1] Does not include Slaughtering and preserving of meat (ISIC group 201), Manufacture of dairy products (ISIC group 202), Canning and preserving of fish (ISIC group 204), Manufacture of bakery products (ISIC group 206), Manufacture of confectionery (in ISIC group 208) or most of Manufacture of Miscellaneous food preparations (ISIC group 209).
[2] Does not include Manufacture of structural clay products (ISIC group 331).
[3] In addition to the exclusions noted above, Tobacco manufactures (ISIC major group 22), Clothing and footwear (ISIC major group 24), most of Wood products and furniture (ISIC major groups 25-26), Printing and publishing (ISIC major group 28), Manufacture of leather products (ISIC group 293), Rubber products (ISIC major group 30), Petroleum and coal products (ISIC major group 32), Manufacture of metal products (ISIC major group 35) and Other manufacturing (ISIC major group 39) are not covered.

[1] Non compris Abattage du bétail et fabrication des conserves de viande (CITI groupe 201), Industrie du lait (CITI groupe 202), Fabrication des con-serves de poissons (CITI groupe 204), Boulangerie et pâtisserie (CITI groupe 206), la confiserie (dans CITI groupe 208), et la majeure partie des Industries alimentaires diverses (CITI groupe 209).
[2] Non compris la Fabrication des matériaux de construction en terre cuite (CITI groupe 331).
[3] Non compris, en plus des industries mentionnées ci-dessus, Industrie du tabac (CITI classe 22), Articles d'habillement et chaussures (CITI classe 24), la majeure partie des industries classées dans Bois et meubles (CITI classes 25-26), Imprimerie et édition (CITI classe 28), Fabrication des articles en cuir (CITI groupe 293), Ouvrages en caoutchouc (CITI classe 30), Dérivés du pétrole et du charbon (CITI classe 32), Fabrication des ouvrages en métaux (CITI classe 35) et Autres industries manufacturières (CITI classe 39).

# INDONESIA — INDONESIE

## Net Domestic Product

Estimates of the origin of the net domestic product are presented in Table 1. The data are derived from information supplied by the Biro Ekonomi dan Kenangan (Bureau of Economics and Finance), Djakarta, in response to the United Nations national accounts questionnaire. Official estimates for the years 1951-1955 and descriptions of the methods used are given in an article in *Economics and Finance in Indonesia,* Vol. XIII, No. ¾, Djakarta, March/April 1960.

## Characteristics and Structure of Industrial Activities

The figures presented in Tables 2 through 4 result from annual Censuses of large and medium-sized manufacturing units and were abstracted from *Parusahaan Industri, 1954,* Djakarta, 1956 and *Parusahaan Industri, 1958,* Djakarta, 1960. In the case of the 1954 Census, 85 percent of the large establishments and 77 per cent of the medium-sized units which were covered by the inquiry completed questionnaires and are included in the figures set out below. In the case of the 1958 Census, about 72 percent of all establishments covered by the inquiry completed questionnaires and are included in the tables below. The dividing line between large and medium-sized units was drawn at 50 employees or capacity of installed power equipment of five horsepower. Establishments with fewer than 10 employees or having no installed power equipment, were not included in the Censuses.

For 1958, value added has been calculated by the Statistical Office of the United Nations by deducting the value of raw materials and fuel used from the value of gross output at sales price ex-factory. However, because the value of the fuels consumed was not available for medium-sized establishments (i.e. those with 10-49 employees or having installed power equipment of less than 5 horsepower), this element of costs is included in the figures of value added in Table 2. The total capacity of installed power equipment has been obtained by adding the horsepower of prime movers connected to machinery other than generators and the horsepower of all electric motors. The data on fuels shown in Table 4 and utilized in computing data on energy consumed relate to selected fuels which were utilized as a source of heat and power only. Since figures were available for manufactured gas and electricity purchased, it was possible to compile data on energy consumed that did not reflect double counting.

## Produit intérieur net

Des estimations du produit intérieur net par secteur d'activité d'origine sont reproduites au tableau 1. Les données sont tirées des renseignements fournis par le Biro Ekonomi dan Kenangan (Bureau de l'économie et des finances), Djakarta, en réponse au questionnaire de l'ONU sur la comptabilité nationale. Des estimations officielles pour 1951-1955 et un exposé des méthodes adoptées sont présentés dans un article de *Economics and Finance in Indonesia,* vol. XIII, No 3/4, Djakarta, mars/avril 1960.

## Caractéristiques et structure des activités industrielles

Les chiffres des tableaux 2 à 4 proviennent des recensements annuels des grandes et moyennes unités manufacturières; ils sont tirés de *Parusahaan Industri, 1954,* Djakarta, 1956 et *Parusahaan Industri, 1958,* Djakarta, 1960. Dans le cas du recensement de 1954, 85 p. 100 des grands établissements et 77 p. 100 des unités moyennes visés par l'enquête ont répondu aux questionnaires et c'est sur eux que portent les chiffres des tableaux. Dans le cas du recensement de 1958, 72 p. 100 environ des établissements couverts par l'enquête ont répondu aux questionnaires et sont compris dans les tableaux. La ligne de démarcation entre grandes et moyennes unités a été fixée à 50 salariés ou à 5 chevaux-vapeur de puissance installée. Les établissements occupant moins de 10 personnes ou n'ayant aucune puissance installée n'ont pas été recensés.

Pour 1958, le Bureau de statistique de l'ONU a calculé la valeur ajoutée en déduisant la valeur des matières premières et du combustible utilisés de la valeur brute de la production aux prix de vente, départ usine. Cependant, comme on ne dispose pas de données sur la valeur des combustibles consommés par les établissements de taille moyenne (c'est-à-dire occupant de 10 à 49 salariés ou ayant une puissance installée de moins de 5 chevaux-vapeur), ces coûts sont inclus dans les chiffres du tableau 2 concernant la valeur ajoutée. On a obtenu la puissance installée totale en ajoutant le nombre de chevaux-vapeur des moteurs primaires reliés à des machines autres que des générateurs au nombre de chevaux-vapeur de tous les moteurs électriques. Les données du tableau 4 relatives aux combustibles, qui ont servi à calculer les chiffres de l'énergie consommée, concernent quelques combustibles utilisés comme source de chaleur ou d'énergie seulement. Comme on disposait de données sur le gaz manufacturé et l'électricité achetée, on a pu obtenir, pour l'énergie consommée, des chiffres ne comportant pas de doubles emplois.

## 1. THE NET DOMESTIC PRODUCT AT FACTOR COST ACCORDING TO ORIGIN
## ORIGINE PAR SECTEUR D'ACTIVITE DU PRODUIT INTERIEUR NET AU COUT DES FACTEURS

Thousand million rupiah                                                      Milliards de rupiahs

| Item of data and year<br>Rubrique et année | Total | Agricultural sector<br>Secteur agricole | Mining<br>Industries extractives | Manufacturing [1]<br>Industries manufacturières [1] | Other sectors [2]<br>Autres secteurs [2] |
|---|---|---|---|---|---|
| ISIC — CITI | 0–9 | 0 | 1 | 2–3 | 4–9 |
| **a. At Current Prices — Aux prix courants** | | | | | |
| Absolute figures — Chiffres absolus | | | | | |
| 1951............ | 64.1 | 34.4 | 1.5 | 6.1 | 22.1 |
| 1952............ | 79.2 | 45.6 | 1.8 | 6.7 | 25.1 |
| 1953............ | 83.9 | 47.2 | 1.9 | 7.2 | 27.6 |
| 1954............ | 91.9 | 52.2 | 2.0 | 7.6 | 30.1 |
| 1955............ | 121.5 | 67.6 | 2.8 | 13.7 | 37.4 |
| 1956............ | 141.0 | 76.1 | 5.6 | 14.9 | 44.4 |
| 1957............ | 165.6 | 84.7 | 8.3 | 18.3 | 54.3 |
| 1958............ | 175.0 | 105.5 | 5.3 | 14.1 | 50.1 |
| 1959............ | 204.0 | 114.2 | 5.1 | 16.3 | 68.4 |
| Percentage distribution according to sector— Distribution en pourcentage par secteur | | | | | |
| 1951–1959..... | 100.0 | 55.6 | 3.1 | . | . |
| 1953............ | 100.0 | 56.2 | 2.3 | 8.6 | 32.9 |
| 1954............ | 100.0 | 56.8 | 2.1 | 8.3 | 32.8 |
| 1958............ | 100.0 | 60.2 | 3.1 | 8.0 | 28.7 |
| **b. At Prices of 1955 — Aux prix de 1955** | | | | | |
| Absolute figures — Chiffres absolus | | | | | |
| 1951............ | 99.1 | 54.0 | 2.3 | 9.4 | 33.4 |
| 1952............ | 102.1 | 57.8 | 2.4 | 8.5 | 33.4 |
| 1953............ | 109.0 | 62.0 | 2.5 | 9.3 | 35.2 |
| 1954............ | 116.8 | 67.7 | 2.7 | 10.2 | 36.2 |
| 1955............ | 121.5 | 67.6 | 2.8 | 13.7 | 37.4 |
| 1956............ | 124.5 | 68.5 | 4.9 | 12.5 | 38.6 |
| 1957............ | 134.5 | 70.7 | 5.8 | 16.1 | 41.9 |
| 1958............ | 130.0 | 77.9 | 3.6 | 9.8 | 38.7 |
| 1959............ | 132.0 | 74.0 | 3.4 | 10.4 | 44.2 |
| Percentage distribution according to sector— Distribution en pourcentage par secteur | | | | | |
| 1951–1959..... | 100.0 | 56.1 | 2.8 | . | . |
| 1953............ | 100.0 | 56.9 | 2.3 | 8.5 | 32.3 |
| 1954............ | 100.0 | 58.0 | 2.3 | 8.7 | 31.0 |
| 1958............ | 100.0 | 59.9 | 2.8 | 7.5 | 29.8 |
| Average annual rate of growth—Taux annuel moyen d'accroissement | | | | | |
| 1951–1959..... | 3.6 | 4.0 | 5.0 | . | . |
| 1951–1954..... | 5.6 | 7.8 | 5.5 | 2.8 | 2.7 |

[1] Includes Electricity, gas and water (ISIC division 5) for years 1951-1955.
[2] Includes Construction (ISIC division 4) and Transportation and Communication (ISIC division 6) for all years and Electricity, gas and water (ISIC division 5) for the years 1956 onwards.

[1] Y compris Electricité, gaz et eau (CITI branche 5) pour les années 1951-1955.
[2] Y compris Bâtiment et travaux publics (CITI branche 4) et Transports et communications (CITI branche 6) pour toutes les années, et Electricité, gaz et eau (CITI branche 5) à partir de 1956.

## 2. CHARACTERISTICS OF MANUFACTURING ESTABLISHMENTS WITH 10 OR MORE EMPLOYEES OR POWER EQUIPMENT

### CARACTERISTIQUES DES ETABLISSEMENTS MANUFACTURIERS OCCUPANT AU MOINS 10 SALARIES OU UTILISANT LA FORCE MOTRICE
#### 1954, 1958

Number of establishments in units; value added and wages and salaries in million rupiahs; number of employees in thousands; capacity of installed power equipment in thousand horsepower; value added per employee in thousand rupiah; capacity of installed power equipment per employee in horsepower.

Nombre d'établissements en unités; valeur ajoutée et traitements et salaires en millions de rupiahs; nombre de salariés en milliers; puissance installée en milliers de chevaux-vapeur; valeur ajoutée par salarié en milliers de rupiahs; puissance installée par salarié en chevaux-vapeur.

| Year and item of data | Manufacturing [1] Industries manufacturières [1] | Food, beverages and tobacco [1] Industries alimentaires, boissons, tabac [1] | Textiles [1] | Clothing, and made-up textiles [2] Articles d'habillement et ouvrages en tissu [2] | Wood products and furniture Bois et meubles | Paper and paper products Papier et ouvrages en papier | Printing and publishing Imprimerie et édition | Leather and leather products [2] Cuir et articles en cuir [2] | Rubber products Ouvrages en caoutchouc | Chemicals and chemical, petroleum and coal products [1] Produits chimiques et dérivés du pétrole et du charbon [1] | Non-metallic mineral products Produits minéraux non métalliques | Metal products Ouvrages en métaux | Other manufacturing Autres industries manufacturières | Année et rubrique |
|---|---|---|---|---|---|---|---|---|---|---|---|---|---|---|
| ISIC | 2–3 | 20–22 | 23 | 24 | 25–26 | 27 | 28 | 29 | 30 | 31–32 | 33 | 35–38 | 39 | CITI |
| *a. Absolute Figures — Chiffres absolus* | | | | | | | | | | | | | | |
| 1954 | | | | | | | | | | | | | | 1954 |
| Number of establishments | 9 732 | 2 595 | 536 | 3 698 | 799 | 46 | 429 | 93 | 176 | 369 | 340 | 472 | 179 | Nombre d'établissements |
| Number of employees (At end of year) | 443.0 | 125.4 | 63.1 | 91.2 | 23.7 | 3.2 | 23.8 | 3.7 | 16.5 | 23.9 | 18.2 | 42.3 | 8.0 | Nombre de salariés (en fin d'année) |
| Capacity of installed power equipment (At end of year) | 213.8 | 74.6 | 11.0 | 1.6 | 26.3 | 2.4 | 6.7 | 3.3 | 26.1 | 24.4 | 10.1 | 26.3 | 1.0 | Puissance installée (en fin d'année) |
| 1958 | | | | | | | | | | | | | | 1958 |
| Number of establishments | 10 175 | 3 030 | 821 | 2 209 | 668 | 69 | 558 | 403 | 348 | 531 | 324 | 979 | 235 | Nombre d'établissements |
| Value added | 8 480.1 | 3 224.6 | 585.5 | 69.0 | 146.6 | 119.6 | 504.1 | 233.9 | 1 257.2 | 1 022.4 | 312.4 | 924.0 | 80.8 | Valeur ajoutée |
| Number of employees (At end of year) | 447.2 | 151.2 | 72.9 | 40.2 | 17.6 | 3.7 | 24.1 | 11.4 | 22.5 | 30.2 | 17.6 | 46.2 | 9.6 | Nombre de salariés (en fin d'année) |
| Wages and salaries | 2 012.3 | 458.3 | 252.8 | 23.8 | 92.6 | 17.1 | 217.9 | 68.4 | 172.6 | 252.2 | 80.8 | 352.0 | 23.8 | Traitements et salaires |
| Capacity of installed power equipment (At end of year) | 275.9 | 86.2 | 18.3 | 0.3 | 22.6 | 4.1 | 18.9 | 7.3 | 42.0 | 28.7 | 14.9 | 30.2 | 2.4 | Puissance installée (en fin d'année) |
| *b. Structure* | | | | | | | | | | | | | | |
| 1954 | | | | | | | | | | | | | | 1954 |
| Distribution in percent of number of employees | 100.0 | 28.3 | 14.2 | 20.6 | 5.3 | 0.8 | 5.3 | 0.9 | 3.7 | 5.4 | 4.1 | 9.5 | 1.9 | Distribution en pourcentage du nombre de salariés |
| Capacity of installed power equipment per employee | 0.48 | 0.59 | 0.17 | 0.02 | 1.11 | 0.75 | 0.28 | 0.89 | 1.58 | 1.02 | 0.55 | 0.62 | 0.12 | Puissance installée par salarié |
| 1958 | | | | | | | | | | | | | | 1958 |
| Distribution in percent of: | | | | | | | | | | | | | | Distribution en pourcentage: |
| Value added | 100.0 | 38.0 | 6.9 | 0.8 | 1.7 | 1.4 | 6.0 | 2.7 | 14.9 | 12.0 | 3.7 | 10.9 | 1.0 | Valeur ajoutée |
| Number of employees | 100.0 | 33.8 | 16.3 | 9.0 | 3.9 | 0.8 | 5.4 | 2.6 | 5.0 | 6.7 | 4.0 | 10.3 | 2.2 | Nombre de salariés |
| Per employee: Value added | 19.0 | 21.3 | 8.0 | 1.7 | 8.3 | 32.3 | 20.9 | 20.5 | 55.9 | 33.8 | 17.8 | 20.0 | 8.4 | Par salarié: Valeur ajoutée |
| Capacity of installed power equipment | 0.62 | 0.57 | 0.25 | 0.01 | 1.28 | 1.11 | 0.78 | 0.64 | 1.87 | 0.95 | 0.85 | 0.65 | 0.25 | Puissance installée |
| Value added per unit of wages and salaries | 4.21 | 7.04 | 2.32 | 2.90 | 1.58 | 6.99 | 2.31 | 3.42 | 7.28 | 4.05 | 3.87 | 2.62 | 3.39 | Valeur ajoutée par unité de traitements et salaires |

[1] Sugar mills on estates, batik mills and petroleum refineries, irrespective of size, are excluded.
[2] Leather, footwear and wearing apparel manufacturing is included in Leather and leather products (ISIC major group 29) instead of Clothing (ISIC major group 24).

[1] Non compris les sucreries installées dans les plantations, les fabriques de batik et les raffineries de pétrole, quelle que soit leur dimension.
[2] Le cuir, les chaussures et les articles d'habillement en cuir sont compris dans Cuir et articles en cuir (CITI classe 29) et non dans Articles d'habillement (CITI classe 24).

## 3. CHARACTERISTICS OF MANUFACTURING ESTABLISHMENTS WITH 50 OR MORE EMPLOYEES OR POWER EQUIPMENT OF 5 HORSEPOWER OR MORE

## CARACTERISTIQUES DES ETABLISSEMENTS MANUFACTURIERS COMPTANT AU MOINS 50 SALARIES OU AYANT UNE PUISSANCE INSTALLEE D'AU MOINS 5 CHEVAUX-VAPEUR

### 1954, 1958

Number of establishments in units; value added and wages and salaries in million rupiah; number of employees and operatives in thousands; energy consumed in thousand metric tons of coal equivalent; electricity consumed in million KWH; capacity of installed power equipment in thousand horsepower; value added per employee and wages and salaries per operative in thousand rupiah; energy consumed per employee and per operative in metric tons of coal equivalents; electricity consumed per employee and per operative in thousand KWH; capacity of installed power equipment per employee and per operative in horsepower.

Nombre d'établissements en unités; valeur ajoutée et traitements et salaires en millions de rupiahs; nombre de salariés et d'ouvriers en milliers; énergie consommée en milliers de tonnes métriques d'équivalent charbon; électricité consommée en millions de kWh; puissance installée en milliers de chevaux-vapeur; valeur ajoutée par salarié et traitements et salaires par ouvrier en milliers de rupiahs; énergie consommée par salarié et par ouvrier en tonnes métriques d'équivalent charbon; électricité consommée par salarié et par ouvrier en milliers de kWh; puissance installée par salarié et par ouvrier en chevaux-vapeur.

| Year and item of data | Manufacturing [1] — Industries manufacturières [1] | Food, beverages and tobacco [1] — Industries alimentaires, boissons, tabac [1] | Textiles [1] | Clothing, and made-up textiles [2] — Articles d'habillement, et ouvrages en tissu [2] | Wood products and furniture — Bois et meubles | Paper and paper products — Papier et ouvrages en papier | Printing and publishing — Imprimerie et édition | Leather and leather products [2] — Cuir et articles en cuir [2] | Rubber products — Ouvrages en caoutchouc | Chemicals and chemical, petroleum and coal products [1] — Produits chimiques et dérivés du pétrole et du charbon [1] | Non-metallic mineral products — Produits minéraux non métalliques | Metal products — Ouvrages en métaux | Other manufacturing — Autres industries manufacturières | Année et rubrique |
|---|---|---|---|---|---|---|---|---|---|---|---|---|---|---|
| ISIC | 2–3 | 20–22 | 23 | 24 | 25–26 | 27 | 28 | 29 | 30 | 31–32 | 33 | 35–38 | 39 | CITI |
| *a. Absolute figures — Chiffres absolus* | | | | | | | | | | | | | | |
| **1954** | | | | | | | | | | | | | | **1954** |
| Number of establishments | 1 820 | 599 | 360 | 55 | 67 | 17 | 189 | 27 | 94 | 129 | 68 | 172 | 43 | Nombre d'établissements |
| Number of employees (At end of year) | 263.4 | 83.0 | 56.7 | 7.6 | 7.9 | 2.5 | 19.0 | 2.3 | 14.4 | 19.1 | 11.4 | 34.6 | 4.9 | Nombre de salariés (en fin d'année) |
| Wages and salaries | 882.8 | 192.8 | 123.3 | 29.3 | 33.9 | 8.0 | 106.2 | 8.0 | 60.8 | 110.5 | 33.1 | 171.2 | 5.7 | Traitements et salaires |
| Operatives: Number (At end of year) | 226.0 | 74.5 | 52.2 | 6.6 | 6.0 | 2.2 | 12.1 | 1.8 | 12.0 | 14.7 | 10.4 | 29.1 | 4.4 | Ouvriers: Nombre (en fin d'année) |
| Wages and salaries | 546.0 | 134.7 | 95.2 | 20.4 | 22.2 | 4.9 | 46.2 | 4.8 | 38.3 | 51.7 | 25.2 | 99.0 | 4.4 | Traitements et salaires |
| Energy consumed | 211.7 | 27.4 | 15.6 | 1.4 | 1.5 | 7.9 | 1.7 | 1.2 | 43.4 | 32.8 | 66.1 | 12.6 | 3.4 | Energie consommée |
| Electricity consumed | 138.9 | 21.2 | 23.1 | 2.7 | 3.8 | 7.1 | 6.2 | 1.7 | 18.0 | 25.4 | 18.8 | 10.7 | 0.1 | Electricité consommée |
| Capacity of installed power equipment (At end of year) | 140.8 | 30.5 | 10.8 | 1.4 | 8.5 | 2.4 | 5.7 | 2.1 | 23.2 | 21.5 | 9.6 | 24.3 | 0.8 | Puissance installée (en fin d'année) |
| **1958** | | | | | | | | | | | | | | **1958** |
| Number of establishments | 3 121 | 1 064 | 410 | 46 | 224 | 28 | 253 | 92 | 183 | 212 | 111 | 421 | 77 | Nombre d'établissements |
| Value added | 7 874.5 | 3 055.7 | 574.8 | 39.9 | 102.3 | 114.5 | 467.6 | 207.8 | 1 160.5 | 958.5 | 277.9 | 853.0 | 62.0 | Valeur ajoutée |
| Number of employees (At end of year) | 334.5 | 122.2 | 62.4 | 3.3 | 10.4 | 3.1 | 19.8 | 8.4 | 19.7 | 25.8 | 13.4 | 38.9 | 7.1 | Nombre de salariés (en fin d'année) |
| Wages and salaries | 1 805.0 | 398.7 | 251.0 | 14.8 | 63.4 | 15.9 | 195.9 | 58.4 | 160.1 | 237.2 | 69.0 | 322.5 | 18.1 | Traitements et salaires |
| Operatives: Number (At end of year) | 279.6 | 108.6 | 56.0 | 2.5 | 7.6 | 2.7 | 12.2 | 6.8 | 15.7 | 19.8 | 11.6 | 29.9 | 6.2 | Ouvriers: Nombre (en fin d'année) |
| Wages and salaries | 1 053.2 | 260.4 | 174.8 | 8.6 | 37.4 | 10.5 | 85.2 | 31.3 | 97.8 | 110.3 | 47.2 | 180.9 | 8.8 | Traitements et salaires |
| Energy consumed | 362.0 | 41.7 | 30.0 | 0.1 | 5.8 | 7.4 | 2.4 | 3.5 | 79.3 | 33.7 | 137.8 | 19.4 | 8.8 | Energie consommée |
| Electricity consumed | 225.3 | 35.6 | 37.2 | 0.2 | 7.6 | 8.3 | 7.6 | 4.9 | 30.8 | 25.3 | 47.0 | 19.0 | 0.9 | Electricité consommée |
| Capacity of installed power equipment (At end of year) | 231.3 | 57.8 | 17.7 | 0.2 | 16.0 | 4.1 | 17.7 | 6.8 | 40.5 | 27.3 | 14.5 | 26.8 | 1.9 | Puissance installée (en fin d'année) |

For footnotes see end of table.

Pour les notes, voir au bas du tableau.

### 3. CHARACTERISTICS OF MANUFACTURING ESTABLISHMENTS WITH 50 OR MORE EMPLOYEES OR POWER EQUIPMENT OF 5 HORSEPOWER OR MORE (continued)

### CARACTERISTIQUES DES ETABLISSEMENTS MANUFACTURIERS COMPTANT AU MOINS 50 SALARIES OU AYANT UNE PUISSANCE INSTALLEE D'AU MOINS 5 CHEVAUX-VAPEUR (suite)

### 1954, 1958

| Year and item of data | Manufacturing [1] / Industries manufacturières [1] | Food, beverages and tobacco [1] / Industries alimentaires, boissons, tobac [1] | Textiles [1] | Clothing, and made-up textiles [2] / Articles d'habillement, et ouvrages en tissu [2] | Wood products and furniture / Bois et meubles | Paper and paper products / Papier et ouvrages en papier | Printing and publishing / Imprimerie et édition | Leather and leather products [2] / Cuir et articles en cuir [2] | Rubber products / Ouvrages en caoutchouc | Chemicals and chemical, petroleum and coal products [1] / Produits chimiques et dérivés du pétrole et du charbon [1] | Non-metallic mineral products / Produits minéraux non métalliques | Metal products / Ouvrages en métaux | Other manufacturing / Autres industries manufacturières | Année et rubrique |
|---|---|---|---|---|---|---|---|---|---|---|---|---|---|---|
| ISIC | 2–3 | 20–22 | 23 | 24 | 25–26 | 27 | 28 | 29 | 30 | 31–32 | 33 | 35–38 | 39 | CITI |
| **b. Structure** | | | | | | | | | | | | | | |
| **1954** | | | | | | | | | | | | | | **1954** Distribution en pourcentage du nombre de salariés |
| Distribution in percent of number of employees.. | 100.0 | 31.5 | 21.5 | 2.9 | 3.0 | 0.9 | 7.2 | 0.9 | 5.5 | 7.2 | 4.4 | 13.1 | 1.9 | Par salarié: |
| Per employee: | | | | | | | | | | | | | | |
| Energy consumed..... | 0.80 | 0.33 | 0.28 | 0.18 | 0.19 | 3.16 | 0.09 | 0.52 | 3.01 | 1.72 | 5.80 | 0.36 | 0.02 | Energie consommée |
| Electricity consumed... | 0.5 | 0.2 | 0.4 | 0.4 | 0.5 | 2.8 | 0.3 | 0.7 | 1.2 | 1.3 | 1.6 | 0.3 | — | Electricité consommée |
| Capacity of installed power equipment... | 0.53 | 0.37 | 0.19 | 0.18 | 1.08 | 0.96 | 0.30 | 0.91 | 1.61 | 1.12 | 0.84 | 0.70 | 0.16 | Puissance installée |
| Operatives as a percent of employees....... | 85.8 | 89.8 | 92.1 | 86.8 | 75.9 | 88.0 | 63.7 | 78.3 | 83.3 | 77.0 | 91.2 | 84.1 | 89.8 | Ouvriers en pourcentage des salariés |
| Per operative: | | | | | | | | | | | | | | Par ouvrier: |
| Wages and salaries... | 2.42 | 1.81 | 1.82 | 3.09 | 3.70 | 2.23 | 3.82 | 2.67 | 3.19 | 3.52 | 2.42 | 3.40 | 0.77 | Traitements et salaires |
| Energy consumed..... | 0.94 | 0.37 | 0.30 | 0.21 | 0.25 | 3.59 | 0.14 | 0.67 | 3.62 | 2.23 | 6.36 | 0.43 | 0.02 | Energie consommée |
| Electricity consumed... | 0.61 | 0.28 | 0.44 | 0.41 | 0.63 | 3.23 | 0.51 | 0.94 | 1.50 | 1.73 | 1.81 | 0.37 | 0.04 | Electricité consommée |
| Capacity of installed power equipment | 0.62 | 0.41 | 0.21 | 0.21 | 1.42 | 1.09 | 0.47 | 1.17 | 1.93 | 1.46 | 0.92 | 0.84 | 0.18 | Puissance installée |
| **1958** | | | | | | | | | | | | | | **1958** Distribution en pourcentage: |
| Distribution in percent of: | | | | | | | | | | | | | | |
| Value added........ | 100.0 | 38.8 | 7.3 | 0.5 | 1.3 | 1.4 | 6.0 | 2.6 | 14.7 | 12.2 | 3.5 | 10.9 | 0.8 | Valeur ajoutée |
| Number of employees. | 100.0 | 36.5 | 18.6 | 1.0 | 3.1 | 1.0 | 5.9 | 2.5 | 5.9 | 7.7 | 4.0 | 11.6 | 2.2 | Nombre de salariés |
| Per employee: | | | | | | | | | | | | | | Par salarié: |
| Value added........ | 23.5 | 25.0 | 9.2 | 12.1 | 9.8 | 36.9 | 23.6 | 24.7 | 58.9 | 37.2 | 20.7 | 21.9 | 8.7 | Valeur ajoutée |
| Energy consumed..... | 1.08 | 0.34 | 0.48 | 0.03 | 0.56 | 2.39 | 0.12 | 0.42 | 4.02 | 1.31 | 10.28 | 0.50 | 0.13 | Energie consommée |
| Electricity consumed... | 0.7 | 0.3 | 0.6 | 0.1 | 0.7 | 2.7 | 0.4 | 0.6 | 1.6 | 1.0 | 3.5 | 0.5 | 0.2 | Electricité consommée |
| Capacity of installed power equipment... | 0.69 | 0.47 | 0.28 | 0.06 | 1.54 | 1.32 | 0.89 | 0.81 | 2.06 | 1.06 | 1.08 | 0.69 | 0.27 | Puissance installée |
| Value added per unit of wages and salaries... | 4.36 | 7.66 | 2.29 | 2.70 | 1.61 | 7.20 | 2.39 | 3.56 | 7.25 | 4.04 | 4.03 | 2.64 | 3.42 | Valeur ajoutée par unité de traitements et salaires |
| Operatives as a percent of employees....... | 83.6 | 88.9 | 89.7 | 75.8 | 73.1 | 87.1 | 61.6 | 81.0 | 79.7 | 76.7 | 86.6 | 76.9 | 87.3 | Ouvriers en pourcentage des salariés |
| Per operative: | | | | | | | | | | | | | | Par ouvrier: |
| Wages and salaries... | 3.77 | 2.40 | 3.12 | 3.44 | 4.92 | 3.89 | 6.98 | 4.60 | 6.23 | 5.57 | 4.07 | 6.05 | 1.42 | Traitements et salaires |
| Energy consumed..... | 1.29 | 0.38 | 0.54 | 0.04 | 0.76 | 2.74 | 0.20 | 0.51 | 5.05 | 1.70 | 11.88 | 0.65 | 0.14 | Energie consommée |
| Electricity consumed... | 0.80 | 0.33 | 0.66 | 0.08 | 1.00 | 3.07 | 0.62 | 0.72 | 1.96 | 1.28 | 4.05 | 0.64 | 0.29 | Electricité consommée |
| Capacity of installed power equipment... | 0.83 | 0.53 | 0.32 | 0.08 | 2.10 | 1.52 | 1.45 | 1.00 | 2.58 | 1.38 | 1.25 | 0.90 | 0.31 | Puissance installée |

[1] Sugar mills on estates, batik mills and petroleum refineries, irrespective of size are excluded.
[2] Leather footwear and wearing apparel manufacturing is included under Leather and leather products (ISIC major group 29) instead of Clothing (ISIC major group 24).

[1] Non compris les sucreries installées dans les plantations, les fabriques de batik et les raffineries de pétrole, quelle que soit leur dimension.
[2] Le cuir, les chaussures et les articles d'habillement en cuir sont compris dans Cuir et articles en cuir (CITI classe 29) et non dans Articles d'habillement (CITI classe 24).

## 4. SELECTED FUELS AND ELECTRICITY CONSUMED, MANUFACTURING ESTABLISHMENTS WITH 50 OR MORE EMPLOYEES OR POWER EQUIPMENT OF 5 HORSEPOWER OR MORE

### QUELQUES COMBUSTIBLES ET ELECTRICITE CONSOMMES, ETABLISSEMENTS MANUFACTURIERS COMPTANT AU MOINS 50 SALARIES OU AYANT UNE PUISSANCE INSTALLEE D'AU MOINS 5 CHEVAUX-VAPEUR

### 1954, 1958

## A. Percentage Distribution of Purchased Energy Consumed According to Source

### Répartition en pourcentage de l'énergie achetée et consommée suivant la source

Quantities in thousand metric tons of coal equivalents      Quantités en milliers de tonnes métriques d'équivalent charbon

| Year and item of data | Manufactur-ing [1]<br>Industries manufac-turières [1] | Food, beverages and tobacco [1]<br>Industries alimen-taires, boissons, tabac [1] | Textiles [1] | Clothing, and made-up textiles [2]<br>Articles d'habil-lement, et ouvrages en tissu [2] | Wood products and furniture<br>Bois et meubles | Paper and paper products<br>Papier et ouvrages en papier | Printing and publish-ing<br>Im-primerie et édition | Leather and leather products [2]<br>Cuir et articles en cuir [2] | Rubber products<br>Ouvrages en caout-chouc | Chemicals and chemical, petroleum and coal products [1]<br>Produits chi-miques et dérivés du pétrole et du charbon [1] | Non-metallic mineral products<br>Produits minéraux non métal-liques | Metal products<br>Ouvrages en métaux | Other manu-factur-ing<br>Autres in-dustries manufac-turières | Année et rubrique |
|---|---|---|---|---|---|---|---|---|---|---|---|---|---|---|
| **ISIC** | 2–3 | 20–22 | 23 | 24 | 25–26 | 27 | 28 | 29 | 30 | 31–32 | 33 | 35–38 | 39 | **CITI** |
| **1954** | | | | | | | | | | | | | | **1954** |
| Total energy consumed: | | | | | | | | | | | | | | Energie totale consommée: |
| Quantity............ | 211.7 | 27.4 | 15.6 | 1.4 | 1.5 | 7.9 | 1.7 | 1.2 | 43.4 | 32.8 | 66.1 | 12.6 | 0.1 | Quantité |
| Percent of total in specified industry..... | 100.0 | 12.9 | 7.4 | 0.6 | 0.7 | 3.8 | 0.8 | 0.5 | 20.5 | 15.5 | 31.3 | 5.9 | 0.1 | Pourcentage du total par industrie indiqué |
| Percent consumed as: | | | | | | | | | | | | | | Pourcentage consommé sous forme de: |
| Coal.............. | 26.9 | 0.2 | 0.1 | — | — | — | — | — | 22.2 | 10.2 | 65.0 | 7.9 | — | Charbon |
| Coke.............. | 2.2 | 0.1 | 0.1 | — | — | — | — | — | 0.1 | 0.1 | 0.1 | 35.5 | — | Coke |
| Refined oil fuels...... | 64.3 | 88.4 | 83.5 | 86.0 | 91.7 | 96.3 | 55.1 | 85.9 | 72.5 | 81.0 | 34.6 | 45.5 | 94.1 | Pétrole raffiné |
| Gas purchased....... | 1.0 | 4.0 | — | — | — | — | 8.8 | — | 0.6 | 0.3 | — | 3.3 | 0.7 | Gaz acheté |
| Electricity purchased... | 5.6 | 7.3 | 16.3 | 14.0 | 8.3 | 3.7 | 36.1 | 14.1 | 4.6 | 8.4 | 0.3 | 7.8 | 5.2 | Electricité achetée |
| **1958** | | | | | | | | | | | | | | **1958** |
| Total energy consumed: | | | | | | | | | | | | | | Energie totale consommée: |
| Quantity............ | 362.0 | 41.7 | 30.0 | 0.1 | 5.8 | 7.4 | 2.4 | 3.5 | 79.3 | 33.7 | 137.8 | 19.4 | 0.9 | Quantité |
| Percent of total in specified industry..... | 100.0 | 11.5 | 8.3 | — | 1.6 | 2.0 | 0.7 | 1.0 | 21.9 | 9.3 | 38.0 | 5.4 | 0.3 | Pourcentage du total par industrie indiquée |
| Percent consumed as: | | | | | | | | | | | | | | Pourcentage consommé sous forme de: |
| Coal.............. | 9.5 | — | 0.2 | — | 8.6 | — | 0.1 | — | 20.1 | 0.8 | 12.1 | 4.4 | 0.2 | Charbon |
| Coke.............. | 0.9 | — | 0.3 | — | 0.5 | — | — | — | — | — | — | 16.4 | 0.2 | Coke |
| Refined oil fuels...... | 85.5 | 92.1 | 90.2 | 69.4 | 81.1 | 95.1 | 67.7 | 87.7 | 76.8 | 92.9 | 87.6 | 71.4 | 89.9 | Pétrole raffiné |
| Gas purchased....... | 0.5 | 1.6 | 0.1 | 19.0 | — | 0.1 | 7.7 | — | 0.3 | 0.4 | 0.1 | 1.9 | 2.6 | Gaz acheté |
| Electricity purchased... | 3.6 | 6.3 | 9.2 | 11.6 | 9.8 | 4.8 | 24.5 | 12.3 | 2.8 | 5.9 | 0.2 | 5.9 | 7.1 | Electricité achetée |

For footnotes see end of table.      Pour les notes, voir au bas du tableau.

## B. QUANTITY AND VALUE OF SELECTED FUELS CONSUMED AND ELECTRICITY PURCHASED AND PRODUCED
## QUANTITE ET VALEUR DE QUELQUES COMBUSTIBLES CONSOMMES ET DE L'ELECTRICITE ACHETEE ET PRODUITE

Coal, coke and refined oil fuels in metric tons; gas in thousand cubic metres; electricity in million KWH; values in thousand rupiah.

Charbon, coke et pétrole raffiné en tonnes métriques; gaz en milliers de mètres cubes; électricité en millions de kWh; valeur en milliers de rupiahs.

| Year and source of energy | Manufacturing¹ / Industries manufacturières¹ | Food, beverages and tobacco¹ / Industries alimentaires, boissons, tabac¹ | Textiles¹ | Clothing, and made-up textiles² / Articles d'habillement, et ouvrages en tissu² | Wood products and furniture / Bois et meubles | Paper and paper products / Papier et ouvrages en papier | Printing and publishing / Imprimerie et édition | Leather and leather products² / Cuir et articles en cuir² | Rubber products / Ouvrages en caoutchouc | Chemicals and chemical, petroleum and coal products¹ / Produits chimiques et dérivés du pétrole et du charbon¹ | Non-metallic mineral products / Produits minéraux non métalliques | Metal products / Ouvrages en métaux | Other manufacturing / Autres industries manufacturières | Année et source d'énergie |
|---|---|---|---|---|---|---|---|---|---|---|---|---|---|---|
| ISIC | 2–3 | 20–22 | 23 | 24 | 25–26 | 27 | 28 | 29 | 30 | 31–32 | 33 | 35–38 | 39 | CITI |
| **1954** | | | | | | | | | | | | | | **1954** |
| Coal — quantity | 57 144 | 71 | 31 | 1 | — | — | — | — | 9 666 | 3 345 | 43 026 | 1 004 | — | Charbon — quantité |
| Coke — quantity | 5 092 | 37 | 14 | — | 1 | — | — | — | 7 | 41 | 11 | 4 981 | — | Coke — quantité |
| Refined oil fuels — quantity | 90 783 | 16 176 | 8 656 | 808 | 902 | 5 081 | 613 | 682 | 20 978 | 17 715 | 15 262 | 3 824 | 86 | Pétrole raffiné — quantité |
| Manufactured gas purchased — quantity | 3 351 | 1 806 | — | — | — | — | 244 | — | 448 | 143 | 9 | 699 | 2 | Gaz manufacturé acheté — quantité |
| Electricity: | | | | | | | | | | | | | | Electricité: |
| Purchased — quantity | 94.4 | 16.0 | 20.3 | 1.6 | 1.0 | 2.3 | 4.8 | 1.3 | 15.7 | 21.9 | 1.6 | 7.8 | 0.1 | Achetée — quantité |
| Produced — quantity | 44.6 | 5.3 | 2.8 | 1.1 | 2.8 | 4.8 | 1.4 | 0.3 | 2.4 | 3.5 | 17.2 | 2.9 | 0.1 | Produite — quantité |
| **1958** | | | | | | | | | | | | | | **1958** |
| Coal: | | | | | | | | | | | | | | Charbon: |
| Quantity | 34 519 | 9 | 78 | — | 501 | — | 3 | — | 15 977 | 272 | 16 811 | 866 | 2 | Quantité |
| Value | 13 985 | 4 | 25 | — | 53 | — | 2 | 2 | 5 372 | 241 | 7 541 | 742 | 3 | Valeur |
| Coke: | | | | | | | | | | | | | | Coke: |
| Quantity | 3 729 | 16 | 111 | — | 33 | — | — | — | 3 | 12 | 3 | 3 549 | 2 | Quantité |
| Value | 10 874 | 51 | 40 | — | 118 | — | — | — | 8 | 35 | 10 | 10 606 | 6 | Valeur |
| Refined oil fuels: | | | | | | | | | | | | | | Pétrole raffiné: |
| Quantity | 206 513 | 25 633 | 18 064 | 56 | 3 133 | 4 728 | 1 108 | 2 046 | 40 611 | 20 862 | 80 502 | 9 239 | 531 | Quantité |
| Value | 78 687 | 11 700 | 8 433 | 28 | 2 255 | 1 345 | 662 | 932 | 17 150 | 7 388 | 23 339 | 5 056 | 399 | Valeur |
| Manufactured gas purchased: | | | | | | | | | | | | | | Gaz manufacturé acheté: |
| Quantity | 2 885 | 1 079 | 57 | 38 | 2 | 7 | 315 | — | 479 | 223 | 13 | 633 | 39 | Quantité |
| Value | 4 633 | 1 548 | 64 | 51 | 2 | 10 | 444 | — | 630 | 754 | 18 | 997 | 115 | Valeur |
| Electricity: | | | | | | | | | | | | | | Electricité: |
| Purchased: | | | | | | | | | | | | | | Achetée: |
| Quantity | 103.0 | 20.9 | 22.0 | 0.1 | 4.5 | 2.8 | 4.8 | 3.4 | 17.3 | 15.8 | 1.9 | 9.0 | 0.5 | Quantité |
| Value | 52 158 | 9 791 | 11 061 | 104 | 2 358 | 1 044 | 4 241 | 1 488 | 6 250 | 8 222 | 1 412 | 5 931 | 256 | Valeur |
| Produced — quantity | 122.3 | 14.7 | 15.2 | 0.1 | 3.1 | 5.4 | 2.8 | 1.5 | 13.6 | 9.5 | 45.1 | 10.0 | 1.3 | Produite — quantité |

[1] Sugar mills on estates, batik mills and petroleum refineries, irrespective of size, are excluded.
[2] Leather footwear and wearing apparel manufacturing is included under Leather and leather products (ISIC major group 29) instead of Clothing (ISIC major group 24).

[1] Non compris les sucreries installées dans les plantations, les fabriques de batik et les raffineries de pétrole, quelle que soit leur dimension.
[2] Le cuir, les chaussures et les articles d'habillement en cuir sont compris dans Cuir et articles en cuir (CITI classe 29) et non dans Articles d'habillement (CITI classe 24).

### Gross Domestic Product

The figures for sources of expenditure on the gross domestic product shown in Table 1 were compiled from estimates prepared by Dr. K. G. Fenelon, expert in statistics to the Government of Iraq, Baghdad, in his study, *Iraq National Income and Expenditure, 1950-1956.*

### The Characteristics and Structure of Industrial Activity

The data presented in Table 2 have been compiled from the *Report on the Industrial Census of Iraq, 1954*, Principal Bureau of Statistics, Baghdad, 1956. This Census resulted in comparable data for all industrial establishments, irrespective of size, excepting those engaged in the extraction and refining of petroleum or units not having a fixed location. The counts shown in the table of establishments and of persons engaged and employees were taken at the time the establishment was enumerated, which was sometime between January and April, 1954.

The figures shown in Table 3 were compiled from the data of a monthly industrial survey which covered the whole of the year 1958. This survey was taken by the Central Bureau of Statistics, Ministry of Planning, Baghdad, and the results were published by the Bureau in *The Monthly Industrial Statistics, 1958*. The survey covered all establishments employing 20 or more persons engaged in the fields of manufacturing, construction, electricity and water supply. Information was obtained from the establishments for each month of 1958. The number of establishments was not constant but changed from month to month. A factory which was out of production during a month of 1958 was not covered for that month, but when it resumed production in another month it was then covered by the survey if eligible. Moreover, when a small establishment increased its employees to 20 or more persons, it was included in the survey for that month; similarly when a large establishment decreased its employees to less than 20 persons it was excluded from that month's survey.

The survey covered all the establishments engaged in production or repair work, but it did not cover service industries or industrial establishments belonging to some governmental authorities such as the Ministry of Defence, Directorate General of Police, Directorate General of Prisons, Directorate General of Post, Telegram and Telephone and Directorate General of Railroads. The number of establishments given in Table 3 represents the monthly average for the year 1958 of establishments employing 20 or more persons.

### Produit intérieur brut

Les chiffres du tableau 1 concernant les dépenses imputées au produit intérieur brut par branche d'activité d'origine ont été calculés à partir des estimations présentées par M. K. G. Fenelon, expert statisticien auprès du Gouvernement irakien, dans son étude intitulée *Iraq National Income and Expenditure, 1950-1956.*

### Caractéristiques et structure de l'activité industrielle

Les données du tableau 2 sont tirées de *Report on the Industrial Census of Iraq, 1954*, Direction de la statistique, Bagdad, 1956. Le recensement industriel de 1954 a donnée des résultats comparables pour tous les établissements industriels de toute dimension, à l'exception des établissements s'occupant de l'extraction et du raffinage du pétrole ou des unités sans emplacement fixe. Pour le nombre des établissements, des personnes occupées et des salariés, les chiffres indiqués sont ceux du jour où l'établissement a été recensé, à une date quelconque entre janvier et avril 1954.

Les chiffres du tableau 3 sont tirés des résultats d'enquêtes mensuelles sur l'industrie concernant toute l'année 1958. Cette enquête a été effectuée par le Bureau central de statistique, Ministère de la planification, Bagdad; les résultats ont été publiés par le Bureau de statistique dans *The Monthly Industrial Statistics, 1958*. L'enquête a porté sur tous les établissements occupant 20 personnes ou plus et appartenant aux industries manufacturières, au bâtiment et aux travaux publics, aux industries de l'électricité et aux services de distribution d'eau. Des renseignements ont été recueillis auprès des établissements pour chaque mois de 1958. Le nombre d'établissements enquêtés variait d'un mois à l'autre. Une usine ayant cessé toute activité de production pendant un mois de 1958 était exclue du champ de l'enquête pendant ce mois; par contre, si elle reprenait ses activités pendant un autre mois, elle était alors recensée pourvu qu'elle remplît les conditions requises. En outre, lorsqu'un petit établissement augmentait sa main-d'œuvre au point d'atteindre 20 salariés ou plus, il était inclus dans le champ de l'enquête pendant le mois considéré; en revanche, lorsque l'effectif de la main-d'œuvre d'un grand établissement descendait au-dessous de 20 salariés, cet établissement n'était pas recensé pendant le mois en question.

L'enquête portait sur tous les établissements exerçant des activités de production ou effectuant des travaux de réparation, à l'exclusion des services ou des établissements industriels appartenant à l'Etat et relevant, par exemple, du Ministère de la défense, de la Direction générale de la police, de la Direction générale des prisons, de la Direction générale des postes, télégrammes et téléphones et de la Direction générale des chemins de fer. Les chiffres du tableau 3 relatifs au nombre d'établissements sont les moyennes mensuelles en 1958 du nombre d'établissements occupant 20 personnes ou plus.

In both the 1954 and 1958 Censuses, the figures of value added during the year were computed by subtracting the cost of raw materials, electricity and oil consumed from the receipts from the sale of products and other goods and from repair work and other services. It should be noted that no adjustments in the data on gross receipts could be made for changes in the value of inventories of finished and semi-finished goods and that the costs subtracted from gross receipts did not cover work contracted out by the industrial establishments.

Dans les recensements de 1954 et 1958, la valeur ajoutée pendant l'année est égale aux recettes tirées de la vente de produits et autres marchandises et des travaux de réparation et autres services fournis, moins le coût des matières premières, de l'électricité et du fuel-oil consommés. Il a été impossible d'ajuster le chiffre des recettes brutes pour tenir compte des changements intervenus dans la valeur des stocks de produits finis et semi-finis; d'autre part, le coût des travaux contractuels confiés à des sous-traitants par les établissements industriels n'a pas été déduit de ce chiffre.

## 1. EXPENDITURE ON THE GROSS DOMESTIC PRODUCT AT MARKET PRICES
## DEPENSES RELATIVES AU PRODUIT INTERIEUR BRUT AUX PRIX DU MARCHE

Million Iraqi Dinars                                                      Millions de dinars irakiens

| Item of data and year Rubrique et année | Total | Consumption Consommation | | Gross Domestic Capital Formation Formation brute de capital intérieur | | Net exports of goods and services Exportations nettes de biens et de services |
|---|---|---|---|---|---|---|
| | | Total | Government Etat | Total | Fixed Fixe | |
| a. At Current Prices — Aux prix courants | | | | | | |
| Absolute figures — Chiffres absolus | | | | | | |
| 1950............................... | 197 | 165 | 28 | 18 | 17 | 14 |
| 1951............................... | 221 | 187 | 30 | 22 | 21 | 12 |
| 1952............................... | 289 | 200 | 38 | 35 | 34 | 54 |
| 1953............................... | 345 | 218 | 51 | 48 | 46 | 79 |
| 1954............................... | 373 | 235 | 57 | 42 | 43 | 96 |
| 1955............................... | 402 | 251 | 62 | 71 | 67 | 80 |
| 1956............................... | 407 | 267 | 68 | 94 | 89 | 46 |
| Percentage distribution of average annual expenditure — Distribution en pourcentage des dépenses annuelles moyennes | | | | | | |
| 1950 – 1956......................... | 100.0 | 68.1 | 15.0 | 14.8 | 14.2 | 17.1 |
| 1950............................... | 100.0 | 83.7 | 14.2 | 9.1 | 8.6 | 7.2 |
| 1953............................... | 100.0 | 63.1 | 14.8 | 14.0 | 22.9 | 22.9 |
| 1954............................... | 100.0 | 63.0 | 15.3 | 11.2 | 11.5 | 25.8 |
| 1956............................... | 100.0 | 65.6 | 16.7 | 23.0 | 21.9 | 11.4 |

## 2. CHARACTERISTICS OF ALL INDUSTRIAL ESTABLISHMENTS
## CARACTERISTIQUES DE TOUS LES ETABLISSEMENTS INDUSTRIELS
### 1953

Number of establishments in units; value added and wages and salaries paid in million Dinars; number of engaged and employees in thousands; and value added per person engaged in thousand Dinars

Nombre d'établissements en unités; valeur ajoutée et traitements et salaires payés en millions de dinars; nombre de personnes occupées et de salariés en milliers, valeur ajoutée par personne occupée en milliers de dinars

### A.  The Divisions of Industrial Activity — Les branches de l'activité industrielle

| Item of data | All industrial activity<br>Toutes industries | Mining [1]<br>Industries extractives [1] | Manufacturing [2]<br>Industries manufacturières [2] | Construction<br>Bâtiment et travaux publics | Electricity, gas and water<br>Electricité, gaz et eau | Rubrique |
|---|---|---|---|---|---|---|
| ISIC | 1–4,511–521 | 1 | 2–3 | 4 | 511–521 | CITI |
| | | a. Absolute Figures — Chiffres absolus | | | | |
| Number of units............... | 22 423 | 60 | 22 253 | 39 | 71 | Nombre d'unités |
| Value added................. | 23.8 | 0.1 | 18.1 | 3.9 | 1.7 | Valeur ajoutée |
| Number of engaged (As of time of enumeration).... | 89.5 | 0.4 | 81.7 | 4.7 | 2.7 | Nombre de personnes occupées (au moment du dénombrement) |
| Number of employees (As of time of enumeration).... | 81.1 | 0.3 | 73.4 | 4.7 | 2.7 | Nombre de salariés (au moment du dénombrement) |
| Wages and salaries paid....... | 5.66 | 0.02 | 4.59 | 0.55 | 0.50 | Traitements et salaires payés |
| | | b.  Structure | | | | |
| Distribution in percent of: | | | | | | Distribution en pourcentage: |
| Value added............... | 100.0 | 0.4 | 76.0 | 16.4 | 7.2 | Valeur ajoutée |
| Number of engaged......... | 100.0 | 0.4 | 91.3 | 5.3 | 3.0 | Nombre de personnes occupées |
| Value added per person engaged................. | 0.3 | 0.2 | 0.2 | 0.8 | 0.6 | Valeur ajoutée par personne occupée |
| Value added per unit of wages and salaries............... | 4.20 | 5.00 | 3.94 | 7.09 | 3.40 | Valeur ajoutée par unité de traitements et salaires |

[1] Only Other mining (major groups 14–19). Does not include the extraction of Petroleum and natural gas (ISIC major group 13).
[2] Does not include Petroleum and coal products (ISIC major group 32) and 3 small unclassified establishments.

[1] Autres industries extractives exclusivement (CITI classes 14–19). Non compris Extraction du pétrole et du gaz naturel (CITI classe 13).
[2] Non compris Dérivés du pétrole et du charbon (CITI classe 32) et trois petits établissements exerçant une activité économique non déterminée.

### B.  The Major Groups of Manufacturing — Les classes de la branche Industries manufacturières

| Item of data | Manufacturing [1]<br>Industries manufacturières [1] | Food, beverages and tobacco<br>Industries alimentaires, boissons, tabac | Textiles | Clothing, footwear and made-up textiles<br>Articles d'habillement, chaussures et ouvrages en tissu | Wood products and furniture<br>Bois et meubles | Printing and publishing<br>Imprimerie et édition | Leather and leather products except wearing apparel<br>Cuir et articles en cuir, à l'exclusion des articles d'habillement | Chemicals and chemical products<br>Produits chimiques | Non-metallic mineral products<br>Produits minéraux non métalliques | Basic metals<br>Métallurgie de base | Metal products<br>Ouvrages en métaux | Other manufacturing [2]<br>Autres industries manufacturières [2] | Rubrique |
|---|---|---|---|---|---|---|---|---|---|---|---|---|---|
| ISIC | 2–3 | 20–22 | 23 | 24 | 25–26 | 28 | 29 | 31 | 33 | 34 | 35–38 | 27,30,39 | CITI |
| | | | | a. Absolute Figures — Chiffres absolus | | | | | | | | | |
| Number of establishments........ | 22 253 | 4 178 | 2 891 | 6 825 | 2 098 | 132 | 217 | 69 | 618 | 68 | 3 755 | 1 402 | Nombre d'établissements |
| Value added................. | 18.1 | 6.3 | 2.2 | 2.4 | 0.7 | 0.6 | 0.3 | 0.8 | 2.4 | 0.1 | 1.7 | 0.6 | Valeur ajoutée |
| Number of engaged (As of time of enumeration)...... | 81.7 | 23.8 | 12.0 | 12.7 | 4.0 | 1.0 | 0.9 | 1.2 | 10.2 | 0.3 | 12.7 | 2.9 | Nombre de personnes occupées (au moment du dénombrement) |
| Number of employees (As of time of enumeration)...... | 73.4 | 21.7 | 9.9 | 11.4 | 3.5 | 0.9 | 0.8 | 1.1 | 9.8 | 0.3 | 11.5 | 2.5 | Nombre de salariés (au moment du dénombrement) |
| Wages and salaries paid......... | 4.59 | 1.22 | 0.74 | 0.37 | 0.14 | 0.12 | 0.07 | 0.12 | 0.77 | 0.03 | 0.91 | 0.10 | Traitements et salaires payés |
| | | | | b.  Structure | | | | | | | | | |
| Distribution in percent of: | | | | | | | | | | | | | Distribution en pourcentage: |
| Value added............... | 100.0 | 34.8 | 12.2 | 13.3 | 3.9 | 3.3 | 1.6 | 4.4 | 13.2 | 0.6 | 9.4 | 3.3 | De la valeur ajoutée |
| Number of engaged........... | 100.0 | 29.1 | 14.7 | 15.5 | 4.9 | 1.2 | 1.1 | 1.5 | 12.5 | 0.4 | 15.6 | 3.5 | Du nombre de personnes occupées |
| Value added per person engaged................. | 0.2 | 0.3 | 0.2 | 0.2 | 0.2 | 0.6 | 0.3 | 0.7 | 0.2 | 0.3 | 0.1 | 0.2 | Valeur ajoutée par personne occupée |
| Value added per unit of wages and salaries............... | 3.94 | 5.16 | 2.97 | 6.49 | 5.00 | 5.00 | 4.28 | 6.67 | 3.12 | 3.33 | 1.87 | 6.00 | Valeur ajoutée par unité de traitements et salaires |

[1] Excludes Petroleum and coal products (ISIC major group 32) and 3 small establishments unclassified as to kind of economic activity.
[2] Includes Paper and paper products (ISIC major group 27) and Rubber products (ISIC major group 30).

[1] Non compris Dérivés du pétrole et du charbon (CITI classe 32) et trois petits établissements exerçant une activité économique non déterminée.
[2] Y compris Papier et ouvrages en papier (CITI classe 27) et Ouvrages en caoutchouc (CITI classe 30).

## 3. CHARACTERISTICS OF INDUSTRIAL ESTABLISHMENTS EMPLOYING 20 OR MORE PERSONS
## CARACTERISTIQUES DES ETABLISSEMENTS INDUSTRIELS OCCUPANT 20 PERSONNES OU PLUS
### 1958

Number of establishments in units; value added and wages and salaries in thousand Iraqi Dinars; number of employees in units; value added and wages and salaries per employee in Iraqi Dinars.

Nombre d'établissements en unités; valeur ajoutée et traitements et salaires en milliers de dinars irakiens; nombre de salariés en unités; valeur ajoutée et traitements et salaires par salarié en dinars irakiens.

### A. Selected Divisions of Industrial Activity
### Quelques branches de l'activité industrielle

| Item of data | Total | Manu-facturing<br>Industries manufac-turières | Construc-tion<br>Bâtiment et travaux publics | Electricity and water<br>Electricité et eau | Rubrique |
|---|---|---|---|---|---|
| ISIC | 2-4,511,521 | 2-3 | 4 | 511, 521 | CITI |
| Number of establishments. | 294 | 204 | 72 | 18 | Nombre d'établissements |
| Value added............. | ... | 15 853 | ... | 2 497 | Valeur ajoutée |
| Employees: | | | | | Salariés: |
| Number............... | 40 277 | 25 626 | 10 881 | 3 770 | Nombre |
| Wages and salaries...... | 9 577.5 | 5 435.5 | 3 102.0 | 1 040.0 | Traitements et salaires |
| Distribution in percent of number of employees.... | 100.0 | 63.6 | 27.0 | 9.4 | Distribution en pourcentage du nombre de salariés |
| Wages and salaries per employee.......... | 237.8 | 212.1 | 285.1 | 275.9 | Traitements et salaires par salarié |

### B. The Major Groups of Manufacturing — Les classes de la branche Industries manufacturières

| Item of data | Manu-facturing<br>Industries manufac-turières | Food, beverages and tobacco<br>Industries alimen-taires, boissons, tabac | Textiles | Clothing, footwear and made-up textiles<br>Articles d'habil-lement, chaussures et ouvrages en tissu | Wood products and furniture<br>Bois et meubles | Printing and publish-ing<br>Im-primerie et édition | Leather and leather products except wearing apparel<br>Cuir et articles en cuir, à l'exclu-sion des articles d'habil-lement | Chemicals and chemical, petroleum and coal products<br>Produits chi-miques et dérivés du pétrole et du charbon | Non-metallic mineral products<br>Produits minéraux non métal-liques | Metal products<br>Ouvrages en métaux | Other manu-factur-ing<br>Autres in-dustries manufac-turières | Rubrique |
|---|---|---|---|---|---|---|---|---|---|---|---|---|
| ISIC | 2–3 | 20–22 | 23 | 24 | 25–26 | 28 | 29 | 31–32 | 33 | 35–38 | 39 | CITI |
| Number of establishments. | 204 | 43 | 24 | 8 | 7 | 7 | 2 | 5 | 78 | 17 | 13 | Nombre d'établissements |
| Value added.......... | 15 853 | 3 182 | 1 558 | 577 | 139 | 189 | 123 | 5 394 | 3 888 | 270 | 533 | Valeur ajoutée |
| Employees: | | | | | | | | | | | | Salariés: |
| Number............ | 25 626 | 5 041 | 6 884 | 853 | 336 | 559 | 196 | 2 537 | 7 342 | 895 | 983 | Nombre |
| Wages and salaries... | 5 435.5 | 1 140.8 | 1 237.6 | 265.4 | 78.3 | 179.5 | 51.9 | 866.5 | 1 222.0 | 221.9 | 171.6 | Traitements et salaires |
| Distribution in percent of: | | | | | | | | | | | | Distribution en pour-centage: |
| Value added........ | 100.0 | 20.1 | 9.8 | 3.6 | 0.9 | 1.2 | 0.8 | 34.0 | 24.5 | 1.7 | 3.4 | Valeur ajoutée |
| Number of employees. | 100.0 | 19.6 | 26.9 | 3.3 | 1.3 | 2.2 | 0.8 | 9.9 | 28.6 | 3.5 | 3.9 | Nombre de personnes occupées |
| Wages and salaries per employee........ | 212.1 | 226.3 | 179.8 | 311.1 | 233.0 | 321.1 | 264.8 | 341.5 | 166.4 | 247.9 | 174.6 | Traitements et salaires par salarié |

# IRELAND — IRLANDE

## Gross Domestic Product and Fixed Capital Formation

The data shown in Table 1 on the gross domestic product and gross fixed capital formation are from the reply of the Central Statistical Office, Dublin, to the United Nations national accounts questionnaire. The official estimates for the national accounts and descriptions of the concepts and methods utilized in making the estimates are issued annually in *National Income and Expenditure* by the Central Statistical Office.

## Index Numbers of Industrial Production

The index numbers of industrial production set out in Table 2 are derived from indexes issued by the Central Statistical Office, Dublin, in its *Statistical Abstracts* and *Irish Trade Journal and Statistical Bulletin*. Excepting the figures for 1961, the index numbers are based on the results of the annual Censuses of Industrial Production of the Office and relate to all industrial establishments engaging three or more persons. The indexes for 1961 are preliminary and derived from the results of a quarterly survey of a sample of mining and manufacturing establishments, which accounts for roughly 80 percent of production in these fields.

The index numbers based on the results of the annual Censuses are chained cross-weighted geometric averages. The cross weights for combining quantity relatives for a specific year and class of activity into indexes consist of the gross value during that year and the preceding year of the products covered by the relatives. The cross weights for combining the index numbers for each of these classes of industrial activity into broader categories consist of value added, at factor cost, during the two years. In computing index numbers from the results of the quarterly survey, cross weights are not utilized. Instead the weights consist of figures of gross value and value added from the last available census—for example, in the case of the indexes for 1961 shown in Table 2, the 1960 Census. The quantity relatives are computed, in practically all instances, from quantities of individual commodities produced but, in a few instances, from quantities of industrial raw materials consumed or deflated wages and salaries.

The index numbers resulting from the computations described above are chained back to 1953 in the case of 1953 and subsequent years. In the case of years preceding 1953, the indexes were chained back to 1936. The two series of index numbers were linked to one another at

## Produit intérieur brut et formation de capital fixe

Les données du tableau 1, relatives au produit intérieur brut et à la formation de capital fixe, proviennent de la réponse de l'Office central de statistique, Dublin, au questionnaire de l'O.N.U. relatif aux comptes nationaux. Les estimations officielles des comptes nationaux ainsi que les descriptions des concepts et méthodes adoptés dans l'élaboration de ces estimations sont publiés annuellement dans *National Income and Expenditure* par l'Office central de statistique.

## Indices de la production industrielle

Les indices de la production industrielle reproduits au tableau 2 sont tirés des indices publiés par l'Office central de statistique, Dublin, dans *Statistical Abstracts* et dans *Irish Trade Journal and Statistical Bulletin*. A l'exception des chiffres de 1961, les indices sont fondés sur les résultats des recensements annuels de la production industrielle exécutés par l'Office et ils portent sur tous les établissements industriels occupant 3 personnes ou plus. Les indices de 1961 sont des indices préliminaires, calculés à partir des résultats d'une enquête trimestrielle portant sur un échantillon d'établissements miniers et manufacturiers, qui représente quelque 80 pour 100 de la production de ces branches d'activité.

Les indices fondés sur les résultats des recensements annuels sont des chaînes de moyennes géométriques (pondération croisée). Pour combiner en indices les rapports quantitatifs d'une année donnée et d'une catégorie d'activité donnée, on a employé, aux fins de la pondération croisée, la valeur brute — pendant l'année dont il s'agit et pendant l'année précédente — des marchandises comprises dans les rapports quantitatifs. Pour combiner les indices de chacune de ces catégories d'activité industrielle en indices plus larges, on a fait une pondération croisée d'après la valeur ajoutée, au coût des facteurs, pendant les deux années. La méthode de la pondération croisée n'a pas été utilisée pour les indices calculés à partir des résultats des enquêtes trimestrielles. Dans ce cas, au contraire, on a pondéré d'après les chiffres de la valeur brute et de la valeur ajoutée tirés du dernier recensement dont les résultats sont connus — il s'agit, par exemple, du recensement de 1960 dans le cas des indices de 1961 (tableau 2). Les rapports quantitatifs ont été calculés, dans presque tous les cas, à partir du volume de la production de chaque marchandise mais parfois on s'est fondé sur la consommation de matières premières industrielles ou sur les traitements et salaires en prix constants.

Les indices résultant des calculs décrits ci-dessus sont des indices-chaînes rapportés à 1953 pour 1953 et les années suivantes, rapportés à 1936 pour les années précédant 1953. Les deux séries d'indices ont été rattachés l'une à l'autre au niveau de 1953. On notera aussi qu'il existe

1953. It should also be noted that some minor incomparabilities between the index numbers for the years before 1953, on the one hand, and 1953 and the following years, on the other, result from changes in the system of classification according to kind of industrial activity.

Fuller descriptions of the index numbers of industrial production may be found in the *Report on Industrial Production, 1936* and *Irish Trade Journal and Statistical Bulletin,* June 1958, Central Statistical Office, Dublin.

### Index Numbers of Industrial Employment

The index numbers of industrial employment presented in Table 3 were derived by the Statistical Office of the United Nations from absolute figures of the number of persons engaged resulting from the annual Censuses of Production and estimated from a quarterly survey of industrial establishments. The estimates from the quarterly survey were utilized for 1961 only, in the case of the indexes shown in Table 3, since the Census results for 1961 were not yet available. The absolute figures from which the index numbers were computed are issued by the Central Statistical Office, Dublin, in its *Irish Trade Journal and Statistical Bulletin* and *Statistical Abstracts.*

The absolute figures from the annual Censuses and the estimates from the quarterly surveys relate to the number of persons engaged, excluding homeworkers, by establishments with 3 or more persons engaged. The annual Census figures are the sum of the average monthly number of operatives employed during the year plus the number of working proprietors and employees other than operatives engaged at mid-October. The estimates from the quarterly surveys are for the number of persons engaged during the middle of the last month of each quarter.

Because of differences in the scheme of industrial classification utilized, there are some incomparabilities in the absolute figures of the number of persons engaged in individual industries that were published for years after and before 1953. Since data were issued for 1953 according to both schemes of classification, it was feasible for the Statistical Office of the United Nations to compile a comparable series of index numbers by means of linking the two sets of data at 1953.

### Characteristics and Structure of Industrial Activity

The data set out in Table 4 are based on annual Censuses of Industrial Production. Although, in these Censuses, reports are requested from all establishments, excepting very small units of a quasi-industrial character, the detailed data issued by the Central Statistical Office of the Government and presented in Table 4 relate to establishments engaging three or more persons. The data in Table 4 were compiled from the *Census of Industrial Production, 1938,* Department of Industry and Commerce, Dublin, and the *Statistical Abstract, 1951, 1956* or *1960,* Central Statistical Office.

### Indices de l'emploi industriel

Les indices de l'emploi industriel reproduits au tableau 3 ont été calculés par l'Office de statistique de l'O.N.U. à partir de chiffres absolus du nombre de personnes engagées résultant des Recensements annuels de la production et des estimations faites à partir d'enquêtes trimestrielles auprès des établissements industriels. Les estimations provenant des enquêtes trimestrielles ont servi pour 1961 seulement, au calcul des indices reproduits au tableau 3, étant donné que les résultats du Recensement de 1961 n'étaient pas encore disponibles. Les chiffres absolus à partir desquels les indices sont calculés sont publiés par le Bureau central de statistique, Dublin dans *Irish Trade Journal and Statistical Bulletin* et *Statistical Abstracts.*

Les chiffres absolus tirés des Recensements annuels, et les estimations tirées des enquêtes trimestrielles concernent le nombre de personnes occupées, non compris les travailleurs familiaux, dans les établissements occupant 3 personnes ou plus. Les chiffres du Recensement annuel représentent la somme des nombres mensuels moyens d'ouvriers employés durant l'année, plus le nombre des propriétaires qui travaillent et des salariés autres que les ouvriers engagés à la mi-octobre. Les estimations tirées des enquêtes trimestrielles concernent le nombre de personnes occupées pendant le milieu du dernier mois de chaque trimestre.

La différence dans le type de classification industrielle adopté, entraine des défauts de comparabilité entre les chiffres absolus du nombre de personnes occupées dans chaque industrie, qui ont été publiés pour les années précédant et suivant 1953. Du fait que les données relatives à 1953 ont été publiées suivant les deux types de classification, il a été possible au Bureau de statistique de l'O.N.U. d'élaborer des séries comparables d'indices en reliant les deux ensembles d'indices au niveau de 1953.

### Les caractéristiques et la structure de l'activité industrielle

Les données du tableau 4 sont fondées sur les recensements annuels de la production industrielle. Bien que, dans ces recensements, on interroge tous les établissements, à l'exception des très petites unités de caractère quasi industriel, les chiffres publiés par l'Office central de statistique et reproduits au tableau 4 ne portent que sur les établissements occupant 3 personnes ou plus. Les chiffres du tableau 4 sont tirés de *Census of Industrial Production, 1938,* Department of Industry and Commerce, Dublin, et de *Statistical Abstract, 1951, 1956* ou *1960,* Office central de statistique, Dublin.

It should be noted that there are some minor incomparabilities between years in the data set out in Table 4. The figures have not been adjusted for variation between the years in the number of establishments which did not submit returns and certain differences occur between 1953 and later years, on the one hand, and 1948 and 1938 on the other, in the character of the figures. The data for 1953 and later years, but not for 1938 and 1948, for mining cover the working and development of peat bogs; and the figures of value added in the production of electricity during 1953 and subsequent years, but not during 1938 and 1948, include the value of own-account construction by this industry. In all years, however, value added covers all the output of the reporting establishments and is priced at factor cost; the number of engaged excludes homeworkers although the value of wages and salaries includes payments to homeworkers; and the number of engaged is the sum of the number of operatives averaged over twelve periods of the year and of the number of other employees, proprietors and unpaid family workers during the week ending in mid-October.

On notera qu'il y a quelques défauts de comparabilité entre années dans les chiffres du tableau 2. Ces chiffres n'ont pas été ajustés pour tenir compte du nombre variable selon les années des établissements qui n'ont pas répondu au questionnaire; de plus, il existe certaines différences, pour ce qui est de leur nature, entre les chiffres de 1953 et des années postérieures d'une part et ceux de 1948 et 1938 d'autre part. Dans le cas des industries extractives, les chiffres de 1953 et des années suivantes, mais non ceux de 1938 et 1948, comprennent l'exploitation des tourbières; dans le cas de la production d'électricité, les chiffres de la valeur ajoutée de 1953 et des années suivantes, mais non ceux de 1938 et 1948, comprennent la valeur des travaux de construction pour compte propre exécutés par cette industrie. En revanche, pendant toutes les années, la valeur ajoutée couvre la totalité de la production de tous les établissements ayant répondu au questionnaire et est chiffrée au coût des facteurs; le nombre de personnes occupées ne comprend pas les travailleurs à domicile, bien que la valeur des traitements et salaires comprenne les paiements aux travailleurs à domicile; enfin, le nombre des personnes occupées est la moyenne du nombre des ouvriers pendant douze périodes de l'année, plus le nombre des autres salariés, propriétaires et travailleurs familiaux non rémunérés, pendant la semaine se terminant à la mi-octobre.

## 1. THE GROSS DOMESTIC PRODUCT AND GROSS DOMESTIC FIXED CAPITAL FORMATION
## LE PRODUIT INTERIEUR BRUT ET LA FORMATION BRUTE DE CAPITAL FIXE INTERIEUR

Million £                                        Millions de £

### A. Expenditure on the Gross Domestic Product at Market Prices
### Dépenses relatives au produit intérieur brut aux prix du marché

| Item of data and year Rubrique et année | Total | Consumption Consommation | | Gross Domestic Capital Formation Formation brute de capital intérieur | | Net exports of goods and services Exportations nettes de biens et de services | |
|---|---|---|---|---|---|---|---|
| | | Total | Government Etat | Total | Fixed Fixe | Exports less imports Exportations moins importations | Exports Exportations |
| *a. At Current Prices — Aux prix courants* | | | | | | | |
| Absolute figures — Chiffres absolus | | | | | | | |
| 1948 | 337.5 | 331.8 | 42.8 | 49.7 | 40.6 | −44.0 | 100.6 |
| 1951 | 391.4 | 393.5 | 54.3 | 87.1 | 76.5 | −89.2 | 125.5 |
| 1952 | 450.3 | 410.7 | 57.1 | 75.5 | 79.7 | −35.9 | 146.7 |
| 1953 | 495.7 | 444.5 | 62.6 | 86.7 | 80.0 | −35.5 | 155.9 |
| 1954 | 498.4 | 453.6 | 64.0 | 79.8 | 85.2 | −35.0 | 154.2 |
| 1955 | 522.7 | 485.8 | 66.1 | 100.8 | 91.1 | −63.9 | 152.2 |
| 1956 | 531.7 | 492.6 | 70.2 | 82.0 | 89.9 | −42.9 | 148.5 |
| 1957 | 549.4 | 499.9 | 69.0 | 85.2 | 78.6 | −22.5 | 170.4 |
| 1958 | 564.6 | 526.9 | 72.0 | 70.9 | 78.6 | −33.2 | 172.7 |
| 1959 | 602.6 | 539.8 | 75.4 | 102.9 | 79.9 | −40.1 | 179.8 |
| 1960 | 635.1 | 573.1 | 78.8 | 96.6 | 85.1 | −34.6 | 201.6 |
| 1961 | 673.0 | 606.0 | 85.0 | 104.0 | 101.0 | −37.0 | 235.0 |
| Percentage distribution of average annual expenditure — Distribution en pourcentage des dépenses annuelles moyennes | | | | | | | |
| 1948 | 100.0 | 98.3 | 12.7 | 14.7 | 12.0 | −13.0 | 29.8 |
| 1951−1960 | 100.0 | 91.9 | 12.8 | 16.4 | 15.7 | −8.3 | 27.4 |
| 1951 | 100.0 | 100.5 | 13.9 | 22.3 | 19.5 | −22.8 | 32.1 |
| 1953 | 100.0 | 89.7 | 12.6 | 17.5 | 16.1 | −7.2 | 31.4 |
| 1954 | 100.0 | 91.0 | 12.8 | 16.0 | 17.1 | −7.0 | 30.9 |
| 1958 | 100.0 | 93.3 | 12.8 | 12.6 | 13.9 | −5.9 | 30.6 |
| 1960 | 100.0 | 90.2 | 12.4 | 15.2 | 13.4 | −5.4 | 31.7 |
| 1961 | 100.0 | 90.0 | 12.6 | 15.5 | 15.0 | −5.5 | 34.9 |
| *b. At Prices of 1958 — Aux prix de 1958* | | | | | | | |
| Absolute figures — Chiffres absolus | | | | | | | |
| 1948 | 487.7 | 480.8 | 63.3 | 64.6 | 51.7 | −57.7 | 131.8 |
| 1951 | 536.3 | 514.4 | 67.5 | 104.6 | 92.5 | −82.7 | 139.2 |
| 1952 | 561.6 | 498.5 | 67.7 | 92.9 | 88.3 | −29.8 | 156.1 |
| 1953 | 571.4 | 516.5 | 72.3 | 98.6 | 91.1 | −43.7 | 162.5 |
| 1954 | 579.3 | 527.0 | 74.4 | 92.3 | 98.1 | −40.0 | 162.6 |
| 1955 | 593.4 | 549.5 | 74.3 | 112.0 | 102.0 | −68.1 | 155.7 |
| 1956 | 584.0 | 535.8 | 75.8 | 86.2 | 95.1 | −38.0 | 156.0 |
| 1957 | 585.7 | 522.8 | 72.3 | 72.3 | 79.8 | −9.4 | 176.1 |
| 1958 | 564.6 | 526.9 | 72.0 | 70.9 | 78.6 | −33.2 | 172.7 |
| 1959 | 594.7 | 540.6 | 74.7 | 104.3 | 80.6 | −50.2 | 174.4 |
| 1960 | 628.6 | 570.8 | 76.2 | 95.8 | 84.4 | −38.0 | 199.1 |
| 1961 | 649.0 | 586.0 | 81.0 | 100.0 | 97.0 | −37.0 | 232.0 |
| Percentage distribution of average annual expenditure — Distribution en pourcentage des dépenses annuelles moyennes | | | | | | | |
| 1948 | 100.0 | 98.6 | 13.0 | 13.2 | 10.6 | −11.8 | 27.0 |
| 1951−1960 | 100.0 | 91.4 | 12.5 | 16.0 | 15.4 | −7.4 | 28.5 |
| 1951 | 100.0 | 95.9 | 12.6 | 19.5 | 17.2 | −15.4 | 26.0 |
| 1953 | 100.0 | 90.4 | 12.6 | 17.2 | 15.9 | −7.6 | 28.4 |
| 1954 | 100.0 | 91.0 | 12.8 | 15.9 | 16.9 | −6.9 | 28.1 |
| 1958 | 100.0 | 93.3 | 12.8 | 12.6 | 13.9 | −5.9 | 30.6 |
| 1960 | 100.0 | 90.8 | 12.1 | 15.2 | 13.4 | −6.0 | 31.7 |
| 1961 | 100.0 | 90.3 | 12.5 | 15.4 | 14.9 | −5.7 | 35.7 |
| Average annual rate of growth — Taux annuel moyen d'accroissement | | | | | | | |
| 1948−1953 | 3.2 | 1.4 | 2.7 | 8.8 | 12.0 | . | 4.3 |
| 1951−1960 | 1.8 | 1.2 | 1.4 | −1.0 | −1.0 | . | 4.1 |
| 1951−1953 | 3.2 | 0.2 | 3.5 | −2.9 | −0.8 | . | 8.0 |
| 1954−1958 | −0.6 | — | −0.8 | −6.4 | −5.4 | . | 1.5 |
| 1958−1960 | 5.5 | 4.1 | 2.9 | 16.2 | 3.6 | . | 7.4 |

## B. The Gross Domestic Product at Factor Cost According to Origin
## Origine par secteur d'activité du produit intérieur brut au coût des facteurs

| Item of data and year<br>Rubrique et année | Total | Agricultural sector<br><br>Secteur agricole | Industrial sector<br><br>Secteur industriel | Trade, transportation and communication<br><br>Commerce, transport et communication | Other sectors [1]<br><br>Autres secteurs [1] |
|---|---|---|---|---|---|
| ISIC — CITI | 0–9 | 0 | 1–5 | 61, 7 | 62–64, 8–9 |
| At Current Prices — Aux prix courants | | | | | |
| Absolute figures<br>— Chiffres absolus | | | | | |
| 1948............ | 304.7 | 96.3 | 71.5 | 51.8 | 85.1 |
| 1951............ | 352.3 | 105.7 | 99.8 | 62.2 | 84.6 |
| 1952............ | 394.2 | 122.2 | 103.8 | 61.7 | 106.5 |
| 1953............ | 430.8 | 132.2 | 117.6 | 63.2 | 117.8 |
| 1954............ | 434.3 | 124.7 | 125.2 | 65.7 | 118.7 |
| 1955............ | 456.3 | 136.7 | 130.9 | 68.2 | 120.5 |
| 1956............ | 457.6 | 124.9 | 136.5 | 71.3 | 124.9 |
| 1957............ | 470.1 | 137.2 | 133.6 | 70.2 | 129.1 |
| 1958............ | 481.2 | 126.3 | 138.5 | 72.5 | 143.9 |
| 1959............ | 515.4 | 137.0 | 150.7 | 77.2 | 150.5 |
| 1960............ | 549.0 | 139.9 | 164.1 | 85.3 | 159.7 |
| 1961............ | 586.0 | 147.0 | 178.0 | 91.0 | 170.0 |
| Percentage distribution according to sector—<br>Distribution en pourcentage par secteur | | | | | |
| 1948............ | 100.0 | 31.6 | 23.5 | 17.0 | 27.9 |
| 1951 – 1960..... | 100.0 | 28.3 | 28.6 | 15.4 | 27.7 |
| 1951............ | 100.0 | 30.0 | 28.3 | 17.7 | 24.0 |
| 1953............ | 100.0 | 30.7 | 27.3 | 14.7 | 27.3 |
| 1954............ | 100.0 | 28.7 | 28.8 | 15.1 | 27.4 |
| 1958............ | 100.0 | 26.2 | 28.8 | 15.1 | 29.9 |
| 1960............ | 100.0 | 25.5 | 29.9 | 15.5 | 29.1 |
| 1961............ | 100.0 | 25.1 | 30.4 | 15.5 | 29.0 |

[1] Adjustments for changes in the value of stocks are not included in the figures for each sector; the total of such adjustments is included in the figures for Other sectors.

[1] Les ajustements faits pour corriger les variations de la valeur des stocks ne sont pas inclus dans les chiffres relatifs à chaque secteur; le total de ces ajustements est compris dans les chiffres relatifs à Autres secteurs.

## C. Gross Domestic Fixed Capital Formation According to Purchasing Sector
## La formation brute de capital fixe intérieur par secteur d'acquisition

| Item of data and year / Rubrique et année | Total | Agricultural sector / Secteur agricole | Industrial Sector — Secteur Industriel | | | | | Transportation and communication / Transport et communication | Other sectors / Autres secteurs |
| | | | Total | Mining / Industries extractives | Manufacturing / Industries manufacturières | Construction / Bâtiment et travaux publics | Electricity, gas and water / Electricité, gaz et eau | | |
| ISIC — CITI | 0–9 | 0 | 1–5 | 1 | 2–3 | 4 | 5 | 7 | 6, 8–9 |

### a. At Current Prices — Aux prix courants

| | | | | | | | | | |
|---|---|---|---|---|---|---|---|---|---|
| **Absolute figures — Chiffres absolus** | | | | | | | | | |
| 1948 | 40.6 | 3.7 | 13.5 | 0.2 | 9.7 | 0.9 | 2.7 | 5.9 | 17.5 |
| 1951 | 76.5 | 8.1 | 26.2 | 0.1 | 13.7 | 2.3 | 10.1 | 10.5 | 31.7 |
| 1952 | 79.7 | 9.5 | 21.3 | 0.3 | 13.6 | 1.9 | 5.5 | 11.6 | 37.3 |
| 1953 | 80.0 | 12.4 | 21.4 | 1.4 | 11.0 | 2.0 | 7.0 | 13.6 | 32.6 |
| 1954 | 85.2 | 15.8 | 24.7 | 1.9 | 11.5 | 2.0 | 9.3 | 14.1 | 30.6 |
| 1955 | 91.1 | 16.1 | 28.4 | 1.9 | 12.2 | 2.2 | 12.1 | 13.9 | 32.7 |
| 1956 | 89.9 | 13.3 | 26.7 | 1.2 | 11.4 | 1.8 | 12.3 | 17.3 | 32.6 |
| 1957 | 78.6 | 14.8 | 24.6 | 1.1 | 11.5 | 0.9 | 11.1 | 14.7 | 24.5 |
| 1958 | 78.6 | 15.2 | 19.9 | 1.5 | 12.2 | 1.1 | 5.1 | 16.2 | 27.3 |
| 1959 | 79.9 | 16.1 | 22.0 | 1.8 | 12.1 | 1.6 | 6.5 | 14.9 | 26.9 |
| **Percentage distribution according to sector— Distribution en pourcentage par secteur** | | | | | | | | | |
| 1948 | 100.0 | 9.1 | 33.3 | 0.5 | 23.9 | 2.2 | 6.7 | 14.5 | 43.1 |
| 1951 | 100.0 | 10.6 | 34.2 | 0.1 | 17.9 | 3.0 | 13.2 | 13.7 | 41.5 |
| 1953 | 100.0 | 15.5 | 26.8 | 1.7 | 13.8 | 2.5 | 8.8 | 17.0 | 40.7 |
| 1954 | 100.0 | 18.6 | 29.0 | 2.2 | 13.5 | 2.4 | 10.9 | 16.5 | 35.9 |
| 1958 | 100.0 | 19.3 | 25.3 | 1.9 | 15.5 | 1.4 | 6.5 | 20.6 | 34.8 |

### b. At Prices of 1958 — Aux prix de 1958

| | | | | | | | | | |
|---|---|---|---|---|---|---|---|---|---|
| **Absolute figures — Chiffres absolus** | | | | | | | | | |
| 1948 | 51.7 | 5.5 | 17.7 | 0.2 | 13.0 | 1.4 | 3.1 | 6.9 | 21.6 |
| 1951 | 92.5 | 10.5 | 31.8 | 0.2 | 17.0 | 2.8 | 11.8 | 12.5 | 37.7 |
| 1952 | 88.3 | 11.1 | 24.6 | 0.3 | 16.0 | 2.1 | 6.2 | 13.1 | 39.5 |
| 1953 | 91.1 | 14.5 | 24.2 | 1.6 | 12.5 | 2.2 | 7.9 | 15.3 | 37.1 |
| 1954 | 98.1 | 18.4 | 28.4 | 2.3 | 13.1 | 2.2 | 10.8 | 16.1 | 35.2 |
| 1955 | 102.0 | 18.4 | 31.4 | 2.1 | 13.3 | 2.3 | 13.7 | 15.5 | 36.7 |
| 1956 | 95.1 | 14.3 | 28.0 | 1.3 | 11.8 | 1.9 | 13.0 | 18.1 | 34.7 |
| 1957 | 79.8 | 15.1 | 25.0 | 1.2 | 11.6 | 0.9 | 11.3 | 14.8 | 24.9 |
| 1958 | 78.6 | 15.2 | 19.9 | 1.5 | 12.2 | 1.1 | 5.1 | 16.2 | 27.3 |
| 1959 | 80.6 | 16.1 | 22.0 | 1.8 | 12.1 | 1.5 | 6.6 | 15.0 | 27.5 |
| **Percentage distribution according to sector— Distribution en pourcentage par secteur** | | | | | | | | | |
| 1948 | 100.0 | 10.6 | 34.2 | 0.4 | 25.1 | 2.7 | 6.0 | 13.4 | 41.8 |
| 1951 | 100.0 | 11.3 | 34.4 | 0.2 | 18.4 | 3.0 | 12.8 | 13.5 | 40.8 |
| 1953 | 100.0 | 15.9 | 26.6 | 1.8 | 13.7 | 2.4 | 8.7 | 16.8 | 40.7 |
| 1954 | 100.0 | 18.8 | 28.9 | 2.3 | 13.4 | 2.2 | 11.0 | 16.4 | 35.9 |
| 1958 | 100.0 | 19.3 | 25.3 | 1.9 | 15.5 | 1.4 | 6.5 | 20.6 | 34.8 |
| **Average annual rate of growth—Taux annuel moyen d'accroissement** | | | | | | | | | |
| 1948–1953 | 12.0 | 21.4 | 6.5 | 51.6 | −0.8 | 9.5 | 20.6 | 17.3 | 11.4 |
| 1951–1953 | −0.8 | 17.5 | −12.8 | 82.8 | −14.3 | 11.3 | −18.2 | 10.6 | −0.8 |
| 1954–1958 | −5.4 | −4.7 | −8.5 | −10.1 | −1.8 | −15.9 | −17.1 | 0.1 | −6.1 |

## 2. INDEX NUMBERS OF INDUSTRIAL PRODUCTION
## INDICES DE LA PRODUCTION INDUSTRIELLE

### A. The Divisions of Industrial Activity
### Les branches de l'activité industrielle

| Period<br>Période | Mining and Manufacturing<br>Industries extractives et manufacturières | Mining [1]<br>Industries extractives[1] | Manu-facturing<br>Industries manu-facturières | Construction<br>Bâtiment et travaux publics | Electricity and gas<br>Electricité et gaz |
|---|---|---|---|---|---|
| ISIC — CITI | 1–3 | 1 | 2–3 | 4 | 511–512 |

a. Indexes — Indices (1958 = 100)

| | | | | | |
|---|---|---|---|---|---|
| 1938....... | 50 | 29 | 51 | ... | 28 |
| 1948....... | 67 | 42 | 68 | 102 | 43 |
| 1949....... | 76 | 45 | 77 | 124 | 47 |
| 1950....... | 86 | 54 | 87 | 150 | 54 |
| 1951....... | 88 | 68 | 89 | 134 | 60 |
| 1952....... | 86 | 80 | 86 | 147 | 66 |
| 1953....... | – 94 – | – 87 – | – 94 – | – 138 – | – 71 – |
| 1954....... | 97 | 99 | 97 | 155 | 79 |
| 1955....... | 101 | 115 | 100 | 145 | 86 |
| 1956....... | 99 | 124 | 98 | 126 | 91 |
| 1957....... | 98 | 130 | 97 | 87 | 94 |
| 1958....... | 100 | 100 | 100 | 100 | 100 |
| 1959....... | 110 | 158 | 108 | 107 | 108 |
| 1960....... | 118 | 137 | 117 | 120 | 119 |
| 1961....... | 129 | 165 | 128 | ... | 124 |

b. Average Annual Rate of Change — Taux annuel moyen de variation

| | | | | | |
|---|---|---|---|---|---|
| 1938 – 1960. | 4.0 | 7.3 | 3.8 | ... | 6.8 |
| 1938 – 1948. | 3.0 | 3.8 | 2.9 | ... | 4.4 |
| 1950 – 1960. | 3.2 | 9.8 | 3.0 | – 2.2 | 8.2 |
| 1948 – 1953. | 7.0 | 15.7 | 6.7 | 6.2 | 10.5 |
| 1954 – 1958. | 0.7 | 0.2 | 0.7 | – 10.4 | 24.5 |
| 1958 – 1960. | 8.6 | 17.0 | 8.2 | 9.5 | 9.1 |

[1] Almost all of the activities covered fall in Other mining (ISIC major groups 14–19).

[1] Il s'agit presque exclusivement d'activités rentrant dans Autres industries extractives (CITI 14–19).

## B. The Major Groups of Manufacturing — Les classes de la branche Industries manufacturières

| Period / Période | Manufacturing [1] / Industries manufacturières [1] | Food, beverages and tobacco / Industries alimentaires, boissons, tabac | Textiles | Clothing, footwear and made-up textiles / Articles d'habillement, chaussures et ouvrages en tissu | Wood products and furniture / Bois et meubles | Paper and paper products / Papier et ouvrages en papier | Printing and publishing / Imprimerie et édition | Leather and leather products except wearing apparel / Cuir et articles en cuir, à l'exclusion des articles d'habillement | Chemicals and chemical, petroleum and coal products / Produits chimiques et dérivés du pétrole et du charbon | Non-metallic mineral products / Produits minéraux non métalliques | Metal products / Ouvrages en métaux |
|---|---|---|---|---|---|---|---|---|---|---|---|
| ISIC — CITI | 2–3 | 20–22 | 23 | 24 | 25–26 | 27 | 28 | 29 | 31–32 | 33 | 35–38 |

### a. Indexes — Indices (1958 = 100)

| Period | | | | | | | | | | | |
|---|---|---|---|---|---|---|---|---|---|---|---|
| 1938 | 51 | 68 | 38 | 91 | 99 | 30 | 70 | 44 | 57 | 32 | 47 |
| 1948 | 68 | 75 | 55 | 89 | 91 | 44 | 69 | 73 | 54 | 59 | 65 |
| 1949 | 77 | 86 | 59 | 96 | 106 | 52 | 72 | 75 | 66 | 73 | 76 |
| 1950 | 87 | 97 | 69 | 108 | 120 | 62 | 78 | 82 | 72 | 82 | 85 |
| 1951 | 89 | 98 | 70 | 97 | 131 | 65 | 80 | 84 | 73 | 91 | 88 |
| 1952 | 86 | 104 | 58 | 89 | 113 | 59 | 76 | 78 | 71 | 93 | 73 |
| 1953 | – 94 – | – 108 – | – 78 – | – 102 – | – 107 – | – 67 – | – 85 – | – 97 – | – 76 – | – 95 – | – 81 – |
| 1954 | 97 | 104 | 85 | 98 | 114 | 83 | 90 | 93 | 84 | 108 | 103 |
| 1955 | 100 | 102 | 89 | 101 | 116 | 92 | 96 | 88 | 89 | 116 | 105 |
| 1956 | 98 | 100 | 95 | 102 | 110 | 89 | 99 | 92 | 90 | 117 | 91 |
| 1957 | 97 | 99 | 98 | 98 | 97 | 92 | 96 | 96 | 99 | 98 | 92 |
| 1958 | 100 | 100 | 100 | 100 | 100 | 100 | 100 | 100 | 100 | 100 | 100 |
| 1959 | 108 | 104 | 108 | 105 | 102 | 110 | 106 | 107 | 115 | 111 | 115 |
| 1960 | 117 | 108 | 126 | 115 | 106 | 122 | 108 | 102 | 127 | 127 | 131 |
| 1961 | 128 | 116 | 133 | 125 | 108 | 132 | 117 | 111 | 153 | 140 | 146 |

### b. Average Annual Rate of Change — Taux annuel moyen de variation

| Period | | | | | | | | | | | |
|---|---|---|---|---|---|---|---|---|---|---|---|
| 1938–1960 | 3.8 | 2.1 | 5.6 | 1.1 | 0.3 | 6.6 | 2.0 | 3.9 | 3.7 | 6.5 | 4.8 |
| 1938–1948 | 2.9 | 1.0 | 3.8 | −0.2 | −0.8 | 3.9 | −0.1 | 5.2 | −0.5 | 6.3 | 3.3 |
| 1950–1960 | 3.0 | 1.1 | 6.2 | 0.6 | −1.2 | 7.0 | 3.3 | 2.2 | 5.8 | 4.5 | 4.4 |
| 1948–1953 | 6.7 | 7.6 | 7.2 | 2.8 | 3.3 | 8.8 | 4.3 | 5.9 | 7.1 | 10.0 | 4.5 |
| 1954–1958 | 0.7 | −1.0 | 4.1 | 0.5 | −3.2 | 4.8 | 2.7 | 1.8 | 4.4 | −1.9 | −0.7 |
| 1958–1960 | 8.2 | 3.9 | 12.2 | 7.2 | 3.0 | 10.5 | 3.9 | 1.0 | 12.7 | 12.7 | 14.5 |

[1] Excludes production in Other manufacturing (ISIC group 39).

[1] Non compris la production des Autres industries manufacturières (CITI 39).

## 3. INDEX NUMBERS OF INDUSTRIAL EMPLOYMENT
### INDICES DE L'EMPLOI DANS L'INDUSTRIE

### A. The Divisions of Industrial Activity
### Les branches de l'activité industrielle

| Period<br>Période | Total | Mining [1]<br><br>Industries<br>extractives [1] | Manu-<br>facturing [2]<br><br>Industries<br>manu-<br>facturières [2] | Construction<br><br>Bâtiment<br>et travaux<br>publics | Electricity<br>and gas<br><br>Electricité<br>et gaz |
|---|---|---|---|---|---|
| ISIC — CITI | 1–4, 511–512 | 1 | 2–3 | 4 | 511–512 |

a. Indexes — Indices (1958 = 100)

| | | | | | |
|---|---|---|---|---|---|
| 1938....... | 82 | 65 | 71 | 123 | 61 |
| 1948....... | –97– | 86 | –86– | 137 | 81 |
| 1949....... | 101 | 76 | 91 | 140 | 87 |
| 1950....... | 108 | 85 | 97 | 150 | 92 |
| 1951....... | 110 | 97 | 99 | 150 | 96 |
| 1952....... | 107 | 98 | 96 | 147 | 99 |
| 1953....... | –109– | –91– | –101– | 138 | 106 |
| 1954....... | 111 | 98 | 103 | 140 | 112 |
| 1955....... | 112 | 104 | 104 | 137 | 120 |
| 1956....... | 108 | 107 | 102 | 126 | 113 |
| 1957....... | 101 | 104 | 100 | 104 | 104 |
| 1958....... | 100 | 100 | 100 | 100 | 100 |
| 1959....... | 102 | 103 | 102 | 101 | 102 |
| 1960....... | 106 | 110 | 106 | 103 | 103 |
| 1961....... | ... | 119 | 111 | ... | ... |

b. Average Annual Rate of Change — Taux annuel moyen de variation

| | | | | | |
|---|---|---|---|---|---|
| 1938–1960. | 1.2 | 2.4 | 1.8 | –0.8 | 2.4 |
| 1938–1948. | 1.7 | 2.8 | 1.9 | 1.1 | 2.9 |
| 1950–1960. | –0.2 | 2.6 | 0.9 | –3.7 | 1.1 |
| 1948–1953. | 2.4 | 1.1 | 3.3 | 0.1 | 5.5 |
| 1954–1958. | –2.6 | 0.5 | –0.7 | –8.1 | –2.8 |
| 1958–1960. | 3.0 | 4.9 | 3.0 | 1.5 | 1.5 |

For footnotes see end of table.

Pour les notes, voir au bas du tableau.

## B. The Major Groups of Manufacturing — Les classes de la branche Industries manufacturières

| Period / Période | Manufacturing [2] / Industries manufacturières [2] | Food, beverages and tobacco [2] / Industries alimentaires, boissons, tabac [2] | Textiles | Clothing, footwear and made-up textiles / Articles d'habillement, chaussures et ouvrages en tissu | Wood products and furniture / Bois et meubles | Paper and paper products / Papier et ouvrages en papier | Printing and publishing / Imprimerie et édition | Leather and leather products except wearing apparel / Cuir et articles en cuir, à l'exclusion des articles d'habillement | Chemicals and chemical, petroleum and coal products / Produits chimiques et dérivés du pétrole et du charbon | Non-metallic mineral products / Produits minéraux non métalliques | Metal products [2] / Ouvrages en métaux [2] | Other manufacturing / Autres industries manufacturières |
|---|---|---|---|---|---|---|---|---|---|---|---|---|
| ISIC — CITI | 2-3 | 20-22 | 23 | 24 | 25-26 | 27 | 28 | 29 | 31-32 | 33 | 35-38 | 39 |

### a. Indexes — Indices (1958 = 100)

| | | | | | | | | | | | | |
|---|---|---|---|---|---|---|---|---|---|---|---|---|
| 1938 | 71 | 76 | 55 | 79 | 89 | 50 | 78 | 59 | 67 | 61 | 66 | ... |
| 1948 | −86− | −88− | 74 | 95 | 102 | 70 | 85 | 91 | −81− | 74 | 88 | ... |
| 1949 | 91 | 93 | 77 | 101 | 104 | 74 | 87 | 90 | 86 | 84 | 93 | ... |
| 1950 | 97 | 98 | 82 | 108 | 115 | 82 | 90 | 97 | 88 | 94 | 98 | ... |
| 1951 | 99 | 100 | 85 | 105 | 122 | 84 | 93 | 90 | 89 | 101 | 103 | ... |
| 1952 | 96 | 104 | 78 | 96 | 116 | 81 | 89 | 92 | 86 | 105 | 94 | ... |
| 1953 | −101− | −106− | −94− | −104− | −119− | −88− | −95− | −101− | −88− | −108− | −95− | 96 |
| 1954 | 103 | 103 | 97 | 103 | 117 | 98 | 98 | 104 | 93 | 116 | 104 | 100 |
| 1955 | 104 | 104 | 100 | 104 | 119 | 102 | 101 | 98 | 96 | 120 | 106 | 101 |
| 1956 | 102 | 100 | 102 | 104 | 114 | 103 | 102 | 101 | 97 | 116 | 100 | 98 |
| 1957 | 100 | 99 | 100 | 100 | 102 | 103 | 102 | 100 | 98 | 104 | 96 | 96 |
| 1958 | 100 | 100 | 100 | 100 | 100 | 100 | 100 | 100 | 100 | 100 | 100 | 100 |
| 1959 | 102 | 101 | 101 | 101 | 94 | 105 | 101 | 102 | 105 | 103 | 104 | 113 |
| 1960 | 106 | 102 | 109 | 103 | 93 | 111 | 102 | 101 | 114 | 113 | 114 | 122 |
| 1961 | 111 | 105 | 110 | 106 | 94 | 114 | 104 | 104 | 123 | 120 | 125 | 127 |

### b. Average Annual Rate of Change — Taux annuel moyen de variation

| | | | | | | | | | | | | |
|---|---|---|---|---|---|---|---|---|---|---|---|---|
| 1938-1960 | 1.8 | 1.4 | 3.2 | 1.2 | 0.2 | 3.7 | 1.2 | 2.5 | 2.4 | 2.8 | 2.5 | ... |
| 1938-1948 | 1.9 | 1.5 | 3.0 | 1.9 | 1.4 | 3.4 | 0.9 | 4.4 | 1.9 | 1.9 | 2.9 | ... |
| 1950-1960 | 0.9 | 0.4 | 2.9 | −0.5 | −2.1 | 3.1 | 1.3 | 0.4 | 2.6 | 1.9 | 1.5 | ... |
| 1948-1953 | 3.3 | 3.8 | 4.9 | 1.8 | 3.1 | 4.7 | 2.3 | 2.1 | 1.7 | 7.8 | 1.6 | ... |
| 1954-1958 | −0.7 | −0.7 | 0.8 | −0.7 | −3.8 | 0.5 | 0.5 | −1.0 | 1.8 | −3.6 | −1.0 | — |
| 1958-1960 | 3.0 | 1.0 | 4.4 | 1.5 | −3.6 | 5.4 | 1.0 | 0.5 | 6.8 | 6.3 | 6.8 | 10.5 |

[1] Consists almost entirely of Other mining (ISIC major groups 14–19). From 1938 to 1952, excludes bog development.
[2] From 1938 to 1952, excludes abattoirs and meat packing plants (part of ISIC major group 20) but includes non-manufacturing activities of railroads and tramways (in ISIC major groups 35–38).

[1] Il s'agit presque exclusivement de Autres industries extractives (CITI 14–19). De 1938 à 1952, non compris l'exploitation des tourbières.
[2] De 1938 à 1952, non compris les abattoirs et fabriques de préparations et conserves de viande (dans CITI classe 20) mais y compris les activités non industrielles des chemins de fer et des tramways (dans CITI classes 35–38).

## 4. CHARACTERISTICS OF INDUSTRIAL ESTABLISHMENTS ENGAGING THREE OR MORE PERSONS
## CARACTERISTIQUES DES ETABLISSEMENTS INDUSTRIELS OCCUPANT TROIS PERSONNES OU PLUS
### 1938, 1948, 1953, 1958

Number of establishments in units; value added and wages and salaries in million Pounds; number of engaged and operatives in thousands; value added per engaged and wages and salaries per employee and per operative in thousand Pounds.

Nombre d'établissements en unités; valeur ajoutée et traitements et salaires en millions de livres; nombre de personnes occupées et d'ouvriers en milliers; valeur ajoutée par personne occupée et traitements et salaires par salarié et par ouvrier en milliers de livres.

### A. The Divisions of Industrial Activity — Les branches de l'activité industrielle

| Year and item of data | All industrial activity Toutes industries | Mining [1] Industries extractives [1] | Manufacturing Industries manufacturières | Construction Bâtiment et travaux publics | Electricity and gas Electricité et gaz | Année et rubrique | Year and item of data | All industrial activity Toutes industries | Mining [1] Industries extractives [1] | Manufacturing Industries manufacturières | Construction Bâtiment et travaux publics | Electricity and gas Electricité et gaz | Année et rubrique |
|---|---|---|---|---|---|---|---|---|---|---|---|---|---|
| ISIC | 1-4, 511-512 | 1 | 2-3 | 4 | 511-512 | CITI | ISIC | 1-4, 511-512 | 1 | 2-3 | 4 | 511-512 | CITI |
| | **a. Absolute Figures — Chiffres absolus** | | | | | | | **b. Structure** | | | | | |
| **1938** | | | | | | **1938** | **1938** | | | | | | **1938** |
| Number of establishments... | 4 161 | 133 | 3 151 | 779 [3] | 98 | Nombre d'établissements | Distribution in percent of: Value added..... | 100.0 | 0.9 | 70.1 | 22.8 | 6.2 | Distribution en pourcentage: Valeur ajoutée |
| Value added....... | 34.73 [2] | 0.33 | 24.34 | 7.94 | 2.12 [2] | Valeur ajoutée | Number of engaged........ | 100.0 | 1.5 | 60.7 | 34.2 | 3.6 | Nombre de personnes occupées |
| Number of engaged (Average during year).......... | 162.8 | 2.5 | 98.8 | 55.8 | 5.7 | Nombre de personnes occupées | Value added per person engaged.. | 0.22 [2] | 0.13 | 0.25 | 0.14 | 0.37 [2] | Valeur ajoutée par personne occupée |
| Employees: Number (Average during year)..... | 160.1 | 2.4 | 96.9 | 55.1 | 5.7 | Salariés: Nombre (moyenne pour l'année) | Employees as a percent of engaged........ | 98.3 | 96.0 | 98.1 | 98.7 | 100.0 | Salariés en pourcentage des personnes occupées |
| Wages and salaries......... | ... | 0.22 | 12.40 | ... | 1.13 | Traitements et salaires | Value added per unit of wages and salaries..... | ... | 1.50 | 1.96 | ... | 1.88 [2] | Valeur ajoutée par traitements et salaires unitaires |
| Operatives: Number (Average during year)..... | 142.6 | 2.3 | 83.3 | 52.9 | 4.1 | Ouvriers: Nombre (moyenne pour l'année) | Operatives as a percent of employees........ | 89.1 | 92.0 | 84.3 | 96.0 | 71.9 | Ouvriers en pourcentage des salariés |
| Wages and salaries......... | 16.50 | 0.20 | 9.22 | 6.37 | 0.71 | Traitements et salaires | Wages and salaries per employee.... | ... | 0.09 | 0.13 | ... | 0.20 | Traitements et salaires par salarié |
| | | | | | | | Wages and salaries per operative.... | 0.12 | 0.09 | 0.11 | 0.12 | 0.17 | Traitements et salaires par ouvrier |
| **1948** | | | | | | **1948** | **1948** | | | | | | **1948** |
| Number of establishments... | | 95 | 3 130 | .... | .... | Nombre d'établissements | Distribution in percent of: Value added..... | 100.0 | 1.1 | 71.3 | 23.7 | 3.9 | Distribution en pourcentage: Valeur ajoutée |
| Value added....... | 73.43 [2] | 0.86 | 52.32 | 17.44 | 2.81 [2] | Valeur ajoutée | Number of engaged........ | 100.0 | 1.6 | 62.6 | 31.8 | 4.0 | Nombre de personnes occupées |
| Number of engaged (Average during year).......... | 194.5 | 3.3 | 121.6 | 62.0 | 7.6 | Nombre de personnes occupées | Value added per person engaged.. | 0.38 [2] | 0.26 | 0.43 | 0.28 | 0.37 [2] | Valeur ajoutée par personne occupée |
| Employees: Number (Average during year)..... | 191.8 | 3.2 | 120.0 | 61.0 | 7.6 | Salariés: Nombre (moyenne pour l'année) | Employees as a percent of engaged........ | 98.6 | 97.0 | 98.7 | 98.4 | 100.0 | Salariés en pourcentage des personnes occupées |
| Wages and salaries......... | 45.15 | 0.66 | 27.76 | 14.07 | 2.66 | Traitements et salaires | Value added per unit of wages and salaries..... | 1.63 [2] | 1.30 | 1.88 | 1.24 | 1.06 [2] | Valeur ajoutée par traitements et salaires unitaires |
| Operatives: Number (Average during year)..... | 170.8 | 3.0 | 101.8 | 60.4 | 5.6 | Ouvriers: Nombre (moyenne pour l'année) | Operatives as a percent of employees........ | 89.0 | 93.8 | 84.8 | 99.0 | 73.7 | Ouvriers en pourcentage des salariés |
| Wages and salaries......... | 36.28 | 0.61 | 21.02 | 12.98 | 1.67 | Traitements et salaires | Wages and salaries per employee.... | 0.24 | 0.21 | 0.23 | 0.23 | 0.35 | Traitements et salaires par salarié |
| | | | | | | | Wages and salaries per operative.... | 0.21 | 0.20 | 0.21 | 0.21 | 0.30 | Traitements et salaires par ouvrier |
| **1953** | | | | | | **1953** | **1953** | | | | | | **1953** |
| Number of establishments... | .... | 85 | 3 327 | 1 074 [3] | .... | Nombre d'établissements | Distribution in percent of: Value added..... | 100.0 | 3.1 | 69.6 | 19.9 | 7.4 | Distribution en pourcentage: Valeur ajoutée |
| Value added....... | 122.61 [2] | 3.84 | 85.35 | 24.41 | 9.01 [2] | Valeur ajoutée | Number of engaged........ | 100.0 | 3.4 | 64.5 | 27.7 | 4.4 | Nombre de personnes occupées |
| Number of engaged (Average during year)..... | 225.6 | 7.7 | 145.7 | 62.3 | 9.9 | Nombre de personnes occupées (moyenne pour l'année) | Value added per person engaged.. | 0.54 [2] | 0.50 | 0.58 | 0.39 | 0.91 [2] | Valeur ajoutée par personne occupée |
| Employees: Number (Average during year)..... | 223.1 | 7.7 | 144.2 | 61.3 | 9.9 | Salariés: Nombre (moyenne pour l'année) | Employees as a percent of engaged........ | 98.9 | 100.0 | 99.0 | 98.4 | 100.0 | Salariés en pourcentage des personnes occupées |
| Wages and salaries......... | 71.84 | 2.52 | 44.61 | 20.29 | 4.42 | Traitements et salaires | Value added per unit of wages and salaries..... | 1.71 [2] | 1.52 | 1.91 | 1.20 | 2.04 [2] | Valeur ajoutée par traitements et salaires unitaires |
| Operatives: Number (Average during year)..... | 196.2 | 6.9 | 123.7 | 58.1 | 7.5 | Ouvriers: Nombre (moyenne pour l'année) | Operatives as a percent of employees........ | 87.9 | 89.6 | 85.8 | 94.8 | 75.8 | Ouvriers en pourcentage des salariés |
| Wages and salaries......... | 57.85 | 2.19 | 34.48 | 18.37 | 2.81 | Traitements et salaires | Wages and salaries per employee.... | 0.32 | 0.33 | 0.31 | 0.33 | 0.45 | Traitements et salaires par salarié |
| | | | | | | | Wages and salaries per operative.... | 0.29 | 0.32 | 0.28 | 0.32 | 0.37 | Traitements et salaires par ouvrier |
| **1958** | | | | | | **1958** | **1958** | | | | | | **1958** |
| Number of establishments... | .... | 78 | 3 045 | 876 [3] | .... | Nombre d'établissements | Distribution in percent of: Value added..... | 100.0 | 3.0 | 71.7 | 15.5 | 9.8 | Distribution en pourcentage: Valeur ajoutée |
| Value added....... | 144.20 [2] | 4.44 | 103.42 | 22.32 | 14.02 [2] | Valeur ajoutée | Number of engaged........ | 100.0 | 4.0 | 69.6 | 21.8 | 4.6 | Nombre de personnes occupées |
| Number of engaged (Average during year)..... | 207.4 | 8.4 | 144.4 | 45.2 | 9.4 | Nombre de personnes occupées (moyenne pour l'année) | Value added per person engaged.. | 0.70 [2] | 0.53 | 0.72 | 0.49 | 1.49 [2] | Valeur ajoutée par personne occupée |
| Wages and salaries | 82.23 | 3.64 | 55.09 | 18.33 | 5.17 | Traitements et salaires | Value added per unit of wages and salaries..... | 1.75 [2] | 1.22 | 1.88 | 1.22 | 2.71 [2] | Valeur ajoutée par traitements et salaires unitaires |
| Operatives: Number (Average during year)..... | 177.0 | 7.6 | 121.8 | 40.8 | 6.8 | Ouvriers: Nombre (moyenne pour l'année) | Wages and salaries per operative.... | ... | 0.41 | 0.35 | 0.39 | ... | Traitements et salaires par ouvrier |
| Wages and salaries......... | ... | 3.15 | 42.23 | 16.06 | ... | Traitements et salaires | | | | | | | |

[1] Consists almost entirely of Other mining (ISIC major groups 14-19). Turf and bog production and development was not covered in the data for 1938 and 1948.

[2] The figures of value added and of value added per person engaged and value added per unit of wages and salaries paid for 1953 and 1958 on the one hand, and for 1938 and 1948, on the other, are not comparable because of the inclusion in value added for 1953, but not for the earlier years, of the value of own-account construction by the electricity producing establishments.

[3] The count of establishments excludes local governmental authorities primarily engaged in construction. These authorities are covered in the other items of data for the Construction (ISIC Division 4).

[1] Il s'agit presque exclusivement des Autres industries extractives (CITI 14-19). L'exploitation des tourbières n'était pas comprise dans les chiffres de 1938 et 1948.

[2] Les chiffres de la valeur ajoutée, de la valeur ajoutée par personne occupée et de la valeur ajoutée par unité de traitements et salaires versés, pour 1953 et 1958 d'une part, et pour 1938 et 1948 d'autre part, ne sont pas comparables attendu que la valeur ajoutée de 1953, mais non celle des années antérieures, comprend la valeur des travaux de construction exécutés pour compte propre par les établissements producteurs d'électricité.

[3] Le nombre d'établissements ne comprend pas les autorités gouvernementales locales ayant pour activité principale la construction. Ces autorités sont couvertes par la rubrique relative aux données du Bâtiment et travaux publics (CITI Branche 4).

## B. The Major Groups of Manufacturing — Les classes de la branche Industries manufacturières

| Year and item of data | Manufacturing<br>Industries manufacturières | Food, beverages and tobacco<br>Industries alimentaires, boissons, tabac | Textiles | Clothing, footwear and made-up textiles<br>Articles d'habillement, chaussures et ouvrages en tissu | Wood products and furniture[2]<br>Bois et meubles[2] | Paper and paper products<br>Papier et ouvrages en papier | Printing and publishing<br>Imprimerie et édition | Leather and leather products except wearing apparel<br>Cuir et articles en cuir, à l'exclusion des articles d'habillement | Chemicals and chemical, petroleum and coal products<br>Produits chimiques et dérivés du pétrole et du charbon | Non-metallic mineral products<br>Produits minéraux non métalliques | Metal products<br>Ouvrages en métaux | Other manufacturing[2]<br>Autres industries manufacturières[2] | Année et rubrique |
|---|---|---|---|---|---|---|---|---|---|---|---|---|---|
| ISIC | 2–3 | 20–22 | 23 | 24 | 25–26 | 27 | 28 | 29 | 31–32 | 33 | 35–38 | 39 | CITI |

*a. Absolute Figures — Chiffres absolus*

| Year and item of data | Manufacturing | Food, beverages and tobacco | Textiles | Clothing, footwear and made-up textiles | Wood products and furniture[2] | Paper and paper products | Printing and publishing | Leather products | Chemicals | Non-metallic mineral products | Metal products | Other manufacturing[2] | Année et rubrique |
|---|---|---|---|---|---|---|---|---|---|---|---|---|---|
| **1938** | | | | | | | | | | | | | **1938** |
| Number of establishments | 3 151 | 1 081[3] | 167 | 311[1] | 334 | 49 | 195 | 70 | 141[3] | 148 | 418 | 237 | Nombre d'établissements |
| Value added | 24.34 | 12.10[3] | 1.36 | 2.31[1] | 1.16 | 0.42 | 1.90 | 0.24 | 0.97[3] | 0.61 | 2.41 | 0.86 | Valeur ajoutée |
| Number of engaged (Average during year) | 98.8 | 31.9[3] | 10.7 | 17.6[1] | 6.4 | 2.3 | 7.0 | 1.2 | 3.3[3] | 3.0 | 11.5 | 3.9 | Nombre de personnes occupées (moyenne pour l'année) |
| Employees: | | | | | | | | | | | | | Salariés: |
| Number (Average during year) | 96.9 | 31.3[3] | 10.6 | 17.4[1] | 6.1 | 2.3 | 6.9 | 1.2 | 3.3[3] | 2.9 | 11.2 | 3.7 | Nombre (moyenne pour l'année) |
| Wages and salaries | 12.40 | 4.95[3] | 0.83 | 1.50[1] | 0.81 | 0.25 | 1.11 | 0.13 | 0.52[3] | 0.35 | 1.51 | 0.44 | Traitements et salaires |
| Operatives: | | | | | | | | | | | | | Ouvriers: |
| Number (Average during year) | 83.3 | 25.1[3] | 9.7 | 16.2[1] | 5.5 | 2.1 | 5.4 | 1.0 | 2.7[3] | 2.6 | 9.8 | 3.2 | Nombre (moyenne pour l'année) |
| Wages and salaries | 9.22 | 3.36[3] | 0.66 | 1.25[1] | 0.70 | 0.20 | 0.79 | 0.10 | 0.33[3] | 0.29 | 1.21 | 0.33 | Traitements et salaires |
| **1948** | | | | | | | | | | | | | **1948** |
| Number of establishments | 3 130 | 1 162 | 93 | 390 | 322 | 55 | 189 | 72 | 121 | 110 | 379 | 237 | Nombre d'établissements |
| Value added | 52.32 | 20.85 | 4.26 | 5.77 | 2.93 | 1.34 | 3.70 | 0.80 | 1.62 | 1.64 | 6.45 | 2.96 | Valeur ajoutée |
| Number of engaged (Average during year) | 121.6 | 36.8 | 14.5 | 21.0 | 7.3 | 3.2 | 7.7 | 1.8 | 3.1 | 3.7 | 15.3 | 7.2 | Nombre de personnes occupées (moyenne pour l'année) |
| Employees: | | | | | | | | | | | | | Salariés: |
| Number (Average during year) | 120.0 | 36.2 | 14.4 | 20.9 | 7.1 | 3.2 | 7.6 | 1.7 | 3.1 | 3.6 | 15.1 | 7.1 | Nombre (moyenne pour l'année) |
| Wages and salaries | 27.76 | 9.50 | 2.45 | 3.72 | 1.63 | 0.67 | 2.10 | 0.42 | 0.73 | 0.93 | 3.96 | 1.65 | Traitements et salaires |
| Operatives: | | | | | | | | | | | | | Ouvriers: |
| Number (Average during year) | 101.8 | 29.1 | 13.3 | 18.8 | 6.3 | 2.8 | 5.8 | 1.6 | 3.1 | 3.2 | 11.7 | 6.1 | Nombre (moyenne pour l'année) |
| Wages and salaries | 21.02 | 6.74 | 1.97 | 3.06 | 1.38 | 0.56 | 1.48 | 0.35 | 0.67 | 0.78 | 2.74 | 1.29 | Traitements et salaires |
| **1953** | | | | | | | | | | | | | **1953** |
| Number of establishments | 3 327 | 1 173 | 97 | 468 | 382 | 54 | 191 | 60 | 125 | 121 | 384 | 272 | Nombre d'établissements |
| Value added | 85.35 | 36.87 | 8.48 | 7.94 | 3.85 | 2.42 | 4.93 | 1.30 | 3.16 | 3.20 | 10.74 | 2.46 | Valeur ajoutée |
| Number of engaged (Average during year) | 145.7 | 46.1 | 19.0 | 22.6 | 8.7 | 4.1 | 8.8 | 2.2 | 4.1 | 5.4 | 20.1 | 4.6 | Nombre de personnes occupées (moyenne pour l'année) |
| Employees: | | | | | | | | | | | | | Salariés: |
| Number (Average during year) | 144.2 | 45.6 | 19.0 | 22.5 | 8.4 | 4.1 | 8.7 | 2.2 | 4.1 | 5.3 | 19.8 | 4.5 | Nombre (moyenne pour l'année) |
| Wages and salaries | 44.61 | 15.66 | 4.37 | 5.13 | 2.59 | 1.17 | 3.14 | 0.68 | 1.47 | 1.77 | 7.26 | 1.37 | Traitements et salaires |
| Operatives: | | | | | | | | | | | | | Ouvriers: |
| Number (Average during year) | 123.7 | 37.4 | 17.3 | 20.6 | 7.4 | 3.6 | 6.6 | 1.9 | 3.0 | 4.7 | 17.4 | 3.8 | Nombre (moyenne pour l'année) |
| Wages and salaries | 34.48 | 11.41 | 3.47 | 4.34 | 2.13 | 0.97 | 2.14 | 0.57 | 0.96 | 1.47 | 5.96 | 1.06 | Traitements et salaires |
| **1958** | | | | | | | | | | | | | **1958** |
| Number of establishments | 3 045 | 1 060 | 111 | 466 | 349 | 54 | 184 | 59 | 136 | 120 | 338 | 168 | Nombre d'établissements |
| Value added | 103.42 | 41.02 | 10.31 | 9.45 | 3.57 | 3.66 | 6.52 | 1.55 | 4.49 | 4.27 | 14.77 | 3.81 | Valeur ajoutée |
| Number of engaged (Average during year) | 144.4 | 43.7 | 19.9 | 21.9 | 7.3 | 4.6 | 9.2 | 2.1 | 4.7 | 5.0 | 21.1 | 4.9 | Nombre de personnes occupées (moyenne pour l'année) |
| Wages and salaries | 55.09 | 18.38 | 5.85 | 6.14 | 2.54 | 1.81 | 4.12 | 0.86 | 2.04 | 2.07 | 9.31 | 1.97 | Traitements et salaires |
| Operatives: | | | | | | | | | | | | | Ouvriers: |
| Number (Average during year) | 121.8 | 35.2 | 18.1 | 20.0 | 6.2 | 4.1 | 6.7 | 1.9 | 3.4 | 4.3 | 18.0 | 3.9 | Nombre (moyenne pour l'année) |
| Wages and salaries | 42.23 | 13.18 | 5.10 | 5.04 | 2.05 | 1.45 | 2.77 | 0.72 | 1.26 | 1.70 | 7.45 | 1.51 | Traitements et salaires |

417

# IRELAND

## B. The Major Groups of Manufacturing (continued) — Les classes de la branche Industries manufacturières (suite)

| Year and item of data | Manufacturing Industries [manufac-turières] | Food, beverages and tobacco Industries alimen-taires, boissons, tabac | Textiles | Clothing, footwear and made-up textiles Articles d'habil-lement, chaussures et ouvrages en tissu | Wood products and furniture Bois et meubles | Paper and paper products Papier et ouvrages en papier | Printing and publish-ing[1] Im-primerie et édition[1] | Leather and leather products except wearing apparel Cuir et articles en cuir, à l'exclu-sion des articles d'habil-lement | Chemicals and chemical, petroleum and coal products Produits chi-miques et dérivés du pétrole et du charbon | Non-metallic mineral products Produits minéraux non métal-liques | Metal products Ouvrages en métaux | Other manu-factur-ing Autres in-dustries manufac-turières | Année et rubrique |
|---|---|---|---|---|---|---|---|---|---|---|---|---|---|
| ISIC | 2–3 | 20–22 | 23 | 24 | 25–26 | 27 | 28 | 29 | 31–32 | 33 | 35–38 | 39 | CITI |

### b. Structure

| | | | | | | | | | | | | | |
|---|---|---|---|---|---|---|---|---|---|---|---|---|---|
| **1938** Distribution in percent of: | | | | | | | | | | | | | **1938** Distribution en pour-centage: |
| Value added | 100.0 | 49.7 | 5.5 | 9.5 | 4.8 | 1.7 | 7.8 | 1.0 | 4.0 | 2.5 | 9.9 | 3.6 | Valeur ajoutée |
| Number of engaged | 100.0 | 32.2 | 10.9 | 17.8 | 6.5 | 2.3 | 7.1 | 1.2 | 3.4 | 3.0 | 11.6 | 4.0 | Nombre de personnes occupées |
| Value added per person engaged | 0.25 | 0.38 | 0.13 | 0.13 | 0.18 | 0.18 | 0.27 | 0.20 | 0.29 | 0.20 | 0.21 | 0.22 | Valeur ajoutée par personne occupée |
| Employees as a percent of engaged | 98.1 | 98.1 | 99.1 | 98.9 | 95.3 | 100.0 | 98.6 | 100.0 | 100.0 | 96.7 | 97.4 | 94.9 | Salariés en pourcentage des personnes occupées |
| Value added per unit of wages and salaries | 1.96 | 2.44 | 1.64 | 1.54 | 1.43 | 1.68 | 1.71 | 1.85 | 1.86 | 1.74 | 1.60 | 1.95 | Valeur ajoutée par traitements et salaires unitaires |
| Operatives as a percent of employees | 86.0 | 80.2 | 91.5 | 93.1 | 90.2 | 91.3 | 78.3 | 83.3 | 81.8 | 89.6 | 87.5 | 86.5 | Ouvriers en pourcentage des salariés |
| Wages and salaries per employee | 0.13 | 0.16 | 0.08 | 0.09 | 0.13 | 0.11 | 0.16 | 0.11 | 0.16 | 0.12 | 0.13 | 0.12 | Traitements et salaires par salarié |
| Wages and salaries per operative | 0.11 | 0.13 | 0.07 | 0.08 | 0.13 | 0.10 | 0.15 | 0.10 | 0.12 | 0.11 | 0.12 | 0.10 | Traitements et salaires par ouvrier |
| **1948** Distribution in percent of: | | | | | | | | | | | | | **1948** Distribution en pour-centage: |
| Value added | 100.0 | 39.8 | 8.1 | 11.1 | 5.6 | 2.5 | 7.1 | 1.5 | 3.1 | 3.2 | 12.3 | 5.7 | Valeur ajoutée |
| Number of engaged | 100.0 | 30.2 | 11.9 | 17.3 | 6.0 | 2.6 | 6.4 | 1.5 | 2.5 | 3.0 | 12.6 | 6.0 | Nombre de personnes occupées |
| Value added per person engaged | 0.43 | 0.57 | 0.29 | 0.27 | 0.40 | 0.42 | 0.48 | 0.44 | 0.52 | 0.44 | 0.42 | 0.41 | Valeur ajoutée par personne occupée |
| Employees as a percent of engaged | 98.7 | 98.4 | 99.3 | 99.5 | 97.3 | 100.0 | 98.7 | 94.4 | 100.0 | 97.3 | 98.7 | 98.6 | Salariés en pourcentage des personnes occupées |
| Value added per unit of wages and salaries | 1.88 | 2.19 | 1.74 | 1.55 | 1.80 | 2.00 | 1.76 | 1.90 | 2.22 | 1.76 | 1.63 | 1.79 | Valeur ajoutée par traitements et salaires unitaires |
| Operatives as a percent of employees | 84.8 | 80.4 | 92.4 | 90.0 | 88.7 | 87.5 | 76.3 | 94.1 | 100.0 | 88.9 | 77.5 | 85.9 | Ouvriers en pourcentage des salariés |
| Wages and salaries per employee | 0.23 | 0.26 | 0.17 | 0.18 | 0.23 | 0.21 | 0.28 | 0.25 | 0.24 | 0.26 | 0.26 | 0.23 | Traitements et salaires par salarié |
| Wages and salaries per operative | 0.21 | 0.23 | 0.15 | 0.16 | 0.22 | 0.20 | 0.26 | 0.22 | 0.22 | 0.24 | 0.23 | 0.21 | Traitements et salaires par ouvrier |
| **1953** Distribution in percent of: | | | | | | | | | | | | | **1953** Distribution en pour-centage: |
| Value added | 100.0 | 43.1 | 10.0 | 9.3 | 4.5 | 2.8 | 5.8 | 1.5 | 3.7 | 3.8 | 12.6 | 2.9 | Valeur ajoutée |
| Number of engaged | 100.0 | 31.6 | 13.0 | 15.5 | 6.0 | 2.8 | 6.1 | 1.5 | 2.8 | 3.7 | 13.8 | 3.2 | Nombre de personnes occupées |
| Value added per person engaged | 0.58 | 0.80 | 0.45 | 0.35 | 0.44 | 0.59 | 0.56 | 0.59 | 0.77 | 0.59 | 0.53 | 0.53 | Valeur ajoutée par personne occupée |
| Employees as a percent of engaged | 99.0 | 98.9 | 100.0 | 99.6 | 96.6 | 100.0 | 98.9 | 100.0 | 100.0 | 98.1 | 98.5 | 97.8 | Salariés en pourcentage des personnes occupées |
| Value added per unit of wages and salaries | 1.91 | 2.35 | 1.94 | 1.55 | 1.49 | 2.07 | 1.57 | 1.91 | 2.15 | 1.81 | 1.48 | 1.80 | Valeur ajoutée par traitements et salaires unitaires |
| Operatives as a percent of employees | 85.8 | 82.0 | 91.0 | 91.6 | 88.1 | 87.8 | 75.9 | 86.4 | 73.2 | 88.7 | 87.9 | 84.4 | Ouvriers en pourcentage des salariés |
| Wages and salaries per employee | 0.31 | 0.34 | 0.23 | 0.23 | 0.31 | 0.28 | 0.36 | 0.31 | 0.36 | 0.33 | 0.37 | 0.30 | Traitements et salaires par salarié |
| Wages and salaries per operative | 0.28 | 0.30 | 0.20 | 0.21 | 0.29 | 0.27 | 0.32 | 0.30 | 0.32 | 0.31 | 0.34 | 0.28 | Traitements et salaires par ouvrier |
| **1958** Distribution in percent of: | | | | | | | | | | | | | **1958** Distribution en pour-centage: |
| Value added | 100.0 | 39.6 | 10.0 | 9.1 | 3.5 | 3.5 | 6.3 | 1.5 | 4.4 | 4.1 | 14.3 | 3.7 | Valeur ajoutée |
| Number of engaged | 100.0 | 30.2 | 13.8 | 15.2 | 5.0 | 3.2 | 6.4 | 1.4 | 3.3 | 3.4 | 14.7 | 3.4 | Nombre de personnes occupées |
| Value added per person engaged | 0.72 | 0.94 | 0.52 | 0.43 | 0.49 | 0.80 | 0.71 | 0.74 | 0.96 | 0.85 | 0.70 | 0.78 | Valeur ajoutée par personne occupée |
| Value added per unit of wages and salaries | 1.88 | 2.23 | 1.76 | 1.54 | 1.40 | 2.02 | 1.58 | 1.80 | 2.20 | 2.06 | 1.59 | 1.93 | Valeur ajoutée par traitements et salaires unitaires |
| Wages and salaries per operative | 0.35 | 0.37 | 0.28 | 0.25 | 0.33 | 0.35 | 0.41 | 0.38 | 0.37 | 0.40 | 0.41 | 0.39 | Traitements et salaires par ouvrier |

[1] The manufacturing of hosiery is included in Clothing (ISIC major group 24) instead of Textiles (ISIC major group 23).

[2] The manufacture of brushes and brooms is excluded from Other manufacturing (ISIC major group 39); it is included in the manufacture of Wood products (ISIC major group 25).

[3] The manufacture of animal feeds is included in Chemicals and chemical products (ISIC major group 31) and not in Food (ISIC major group 20).

[1] La bonneterie est comprise dans Articles d'habillement (CITI 24) et non dans Textiles (CITI 23).

[2] La brosserie est comprise dans Industrie du bois (CITI 25) et non dans Autres industries manufacturières (CITI 39).

[3] La fabrication de produits pour l'alimentation des animaux est comprise dans Industrie chimique (CITI 31) et non dans Industries alimentaires (CITI 20).

# ISRAEL

## Domestic Product and Gross Domestic Fixed Capital Formation

The estimates of the gross domestic product according to source of expenditure, of the net domestic product according to origin and of the gross domestic fixed capital formation according to purchasing industry, shown in Table 1 are from the replies of the Central Bureau of Statistics, Jerusalem, to the United Nations national account questionnaires. Official estimates are issued and published annually by the Bureau in the *Statistical Abstract of Israel*.

## Index Numbers of Industrial Production

The index numbers set out in Table 2 are derived from two series of index numbers calculated by the Central Bureau of Statistics, Jerusalem, and issued in the *Statistical Bulletin of Israel* and the *Statistical Abstract of Israel*. The indexes for the years, 1955-58, are obtained from the series for which the weighting base is 1 April 1951-31 March 1952. The indexes for the years, 1958-1961, were secured from a new series for which the weight base is 1958, started by the Bureau as from January 1959. The two series of indexes have been linked to one another at 1958.

The first series of index numbers relate to establishments engaging 15 or more persons. It is computed as base weighted arithmetic averages, starting from 120 series of relatives based on the quantity produced for individual commodities, for the most part, or on quantity consumed for individual raw materials or man-days worked, to some extent. The weights used in combining these relatives into indexes for detailed categories of industrial activity and the resulting index numbers into indexes for broader categories are derived primarily from the value added by establishments engaging 15 or more persons during the period, 1 April 1951-31 March 1952. The summarised results of the Census utilized for this purpose are shown in Table 5. Further details on this series of index numbers of industrial production may be found in the *Statistical Abstract of Israel, 1955/1956*.

The latter series of index numbers relate to mining and manufacturing establishments which engaged at least one employee for a month or longer in 1958. Members of co-operative societies and collective settlements were defined for this purpose as employees. However, the following kinds of industries were excluded from the scope of the indexes: Mineral exploration, exploration and experimental extraction of crude oil and natural gas, manufacture of explosives, military industries, shoe repair, metal workshops, repair to motor cars and motorcycles (in-

## Produit intérieur et formation brute de capital fixe intérieur

Le tableau 1 contient des estimations du produit intérieur brut par poste de dépense, du produit intérieur net par secteur d'activité d'origine et de la formation brute de capital fixe intérieur par secteur d'acquisition; ces chiffres sont tirés des réponses du Bureau central de statistique, Jérusalem, aux questionnaires de l'QNU sur la comptabilité nationale. Les estimations officielles sont publiées annuellement par le Bureau dans *Statistical Abstract of Israel*.

## Indice de la production industrielle

Les indices du tableau 2 sont obtenus à partir de deux séries d'indices calculées par le Bureau central de statistique, Jérusalem, et publiées dans le *Statistical Bulletin of Israel* et le *Statistical Abstract of Israel*. Les indices de 1955-1958 ont été établis à partir des séries ayant pour base de pondération la période 1er avril 1951-31 mars 1952. Les indices de 1958-1961 ont été obtenus à partir de nouvelles séries pour lesquelles la base de pondération est 1958; ces séries ont été commencées par le Bureau en janvier 1959. Les deux séries d'indices ont été raccordées l'une à l'autre au niveau de 1958.

La première série d'indices se rapporte aux établissements occupant 15 personnes ou plus. Ce sont des moyennes arithmétiques à pondération fixe, construites à partir de 120 séries de rapports fondés, le plus souvent, sur les quantités produites de chaque marchandise, et, parfois, sur le volume de la consommation de chaque matière première ou encore sur le nombre de journées de travail effectuées. Pour combiner les rapports en indices de catégories détaillées de l'activité industrielle et les indices ainsi obtenus en indices plus larges, on a adopté des coefficients de pondération fondés essentiellement sur la valeur ajoutée par les établissements qui occupaient 15 personnes ou plus pendant la période s'étendant du 1er avril 1951 au 31 mars 1952. Les résultats condensés du recensement que l'on a utilisés à cette fin sont reproduits au tableau 5. Pour plus de détails sur ces séries d'indices de la production industrielle, voir *Statistical Abstract of Israel, 1955/1956*.

Les dernières séries d'indices citées concernent les établissements miniers et manufacturiers ayant occupé au moins un salarié pendant un mois ou plus en 1958. Les membres des sociétés coopératives et des exploitations collectives sont comptés dans ce cas comme salariés. Cependant, les types d'industries ci-après ont été exclus du champ de l'indice: Prospection des minéraux, prospection et extraction expérimentale du pétrole brut et du gaz naturel, fabrication des explosifs, industries militaires, réparation des chaussures, ateliers de réparation métal-

cluding repairs to outer tyres and inner tubes) and repair and manufacture of clocks and watches.

This series of indexes are also computed as base weighted arithmetic averages, starting from 176 series of elementary relatives. The data for purpose of computing these relatives are gathered from a representative sample of 1,200 establishments drawn from the population of establishments covered by the indexes. Large establishments with 30 or more employees are invariably included in the sample, whereas in the cases of smaller and middle sized establishments, a representative sample is drawn every three months. The statistics gathered from the sample establishments utilized in computing the relatives consist in 104 instances, of quantities of individual major products produced; in 38 instances, of changes in the value of sales; in one case, of the changes in the value of exports; in 6 instances, of changes in the quantities of raw materials used; and in 27 instances, of the number of man-days worked by workers. The series of relatives are combined into indexes for detailed categories of industrial activity and the resulting index numbers are combined into indexes for broader categories, using weights which are proportional to the data on value added during 1958, derived from the results of the 1958 Survey of Industries shown in Table 6.

### Index Numbers of Industrial Employment

The index numbers shown in Table 3 are derived from two series of index numbers calculated by the Central Bureau of Statistics, Jerusalem, and published by the Bureau in the *Statistical Abstract of Israel*. The two series of index numbers were linked to one another at 1958.

The indexes for the years, 1955-1958, were obtained from a series of indexes with original comparison base, 1955. The indexes related to the employment of establishments with 15 or more employees. The weights used in the calculation of these indexes were derived from figures of the number of employees as of one day in 1951 obtained from the 1952 Census of Industry. Further details on this series is found in the 1955/56 issue of the *Statistical Abstract of Israel*.

The indexes for the years, 1958-1961, are obtained from a new series in which the weight base is 1958. This series of indexes were started in January, 1959, together with the indexes of industrial production. Both kinds of index numbers cover the same field of establishments and are calculated from the same survey of establishments. The index numbers of employment are based on the average of the number of employees as of a month during each quarter of the year. The weights used in calculating the indexes are derived from data on the average number of employees during 1958 as obtained from establishments surveyed for purposes of the index. For further details reference may be made to the 1959/60 issue of the *Statistical Abstract of Israel*.

liques, réparation des automobiles et des motocycles (y compris la réparation des pneumatiques et des chambres à air), réparation et fabrication des montres et des horloges.

Ces séries d'indices sont également des moyennes arithmétiques à pondération fixe, construite à partir de 176 séries de rapports élémentaires. Les données utilisées pour le calcul de ces rapports ont été recueillies auprès d'un échantillon représentatif de 1 200 établissements choisis parmi l'ensemble des établissements sur lesquels portent les indices. Les grands établissements occupant 30 salariés ou plus sont toujours compris dans l'échantillon, mais, pour les petites et moyennes unités, un échantillon représentatif est tiré tous les trois mois. Les données recueillies auprès des établissements échantillon et utilisées pour calculer les rapports concernent les éléments suivants : dans 104 cas, les quantités produites de chacune des principales marchandises; dans 38 cas, les variations du montant des ventes; dans un cas, les variations de la valeur des exportations; dans 6 cas, les variations enregistrées dans les quantités de matières premières consommées; dans 27 cas, le nombre de journées de travail effectuées. Les séries de rapports sont combinées en indices de catégories détaillées de l'activité industrielle et les indices ainsi obtenus en indices de catégories plus larges; les poids utilisés à cette fin sont proportionnels aux valeurs ajoutées en 1958 telles qu'elles ressortent des résultats de l'enquête de 1958 sur les industries reproduits au tableau 6.

### Indices de l'emploi dans l'industrie

Les indices du tableau 3 ont été établis à partir de deux séries d'indices calculés par le Bureau central de statistique, Jérusalem, et publiés par le Bureau dans le *Statistical Abstract of Israel*. Les deux séries d'indices ont été raccordées l'une à l'autre au niveau de 1958.

Les indices de 1955-1958 ont été obtenus à partir de séries d'indices ayant pour année de base 1955. Ces indices concernent l'emploi dans les établissements occupant 15 salariés ou plus. Les coefficients de pondération utilisés pour calculer ces indices sont fondés sur le nombre de salariés indiqué, pour un jour de 1951, par le recensement des industries de 1952. Pour plus de détails sur ces séries voir le numéro du *Statistical Abstract of Israel* de 1955/1956.

Les indices de 1958-1961 ont été obtenus à partir de nouvelles séries dont la base de pondération est 1958. Ces séries d'indices ont été commencées en janvier 1959, en même temps que les indices de la production industrielle. Les deux types d'indices couvrent le même champ d'établissements et sont calculés à partir des résultats de la même enquête sur les établissements. Les indices de l'emploi sont fondés sur la moyenne du nombre de salariés pendant un mois de chaque trimestre de l'année. Les coefficients de pondération utilisés sont obtenus à partir de données sur le nombre moyen de salariés en 1958 recueillies auprès des établissements enquêtés en vue de l'établissement des indices. Pour plus de détails, voir *Statistical Abstract of Israel*, numéro de 1959/1960.

## The Characteristics and Structure of Industrial Activity

The data shown in Tables 4 and 5 were compiled from the results of a census of all licensed mining and manufacturing establishments and electricity power stations taken by the Central Bureau of Statistics in 1952 and issued by the Bureau in *Census of Industry, 1952*, Parts A and B. Small manufacturing units located in households or in some isolated rural areas were not covered in the Census.

The figures set out in Table 4 relate to all licensed establishments whereas the data presented in Table 5 relate to the large licensed units. The dividing line between large and small units was drawn at 10 persons engaged as of 15 September 1951. The figures of value added do not cover goods sold by manufacturing establishments in the same condition as purchased and are probably valued at market price ex-factory. The data on wages and salaries paid probably include payments to homeworkers. The definitions of the items of data for which figures are shown in Tables 4 and 5 seem to be consistent in all other respects with the International Standards in Basic Industrial Statistics.

The data set out in Table 6 are derived from the results of the surveys of industries taken for 1956 and 1958 by the Central Bureau of Statistics, Jerusalem that were published respectively in the 1958/59 and 1959/60 editions of the *Statistical Abstract of Israel* issued by the Bureau. These surveys are part of a series of annual industrial sample surveys covering the fields of mining and manufacturing, which started with the Survey for 1955. The 1956 and 1958 Surveys covered establishments engaged in mining and manufacturing activities which employed at least one employee for a month or longer in 1956 or 1958. Manufacturing establishments organized in the form of cooperatives and those in collective settlements were included in the surveys whether or not they engaged workers other than their own members. Both surveys excluded establishments working on a non-profit basis and establishments engaged in the manufacture and repair of watches, abattoirs, defence industry, prospecting for and production of metals, and prospecting for and experimental production of non-ferrous metals. Moreover, the 1956 Survey excluded certain industries which were included in the 1958 Survey. These industries were production of crude oil, shoe repair, repair of tyres and inner tubes, refining of crude oil and the repair of vehicles and motor bikes. Another factor which should be taken into consideration when comparing the two surveys was that the lists of establishments available to the Bureau in respect of 1956 was found deficient and omitted a number of establishments which were in existence during that year.

For purposes of selecting the samples for the surveys, the registers of establishments were stratified according to kind of industrial activity and the probability of selection for each establishment in a stratum was proportional to its size—ie. number of employees. However, all establishments employing 25 employees or more were in-

## Caractéristiques et structure de l'activité industrielle

Les données des tableaux 4 et 5 sont tirées des résultats d'un recensement de tous les établissements miniers et manufacturiers patentés et des centrales électriques, effectué en 1952 par le Bureau central de statistique; le Bureau a publié ces résultats dans *Census of Industry, 1952*, parties A et B. Ce recensement ne couvrait pas certaines petites unités manufacturières constituées par des ménages ou installées dans des régions rurales isolées.

Les chiffres du tableau 4 portent sur tous les établissements patentés, tandis que les chiffres du tableau 5 ne concernent que les grandes unités patentées. On a considéré comme grandes unités celles qui comptaient 10 personnes occupées ou plus au 15 septembre 1951. Les chiffres de la valeur ajoutée ne comprennent pas les marchandises revendues en l'état par les établissements manufacturiers, et ils sont probablement calculés aux prix du marché, départ usine. Les traitements et salaires payés comprennent probablement les sommes versées aux travailleurs à domicile. A tous autres égards, les définitions des rubriques des tableaux 4 et 5 paraissent conformes aux Normes internationales relatives aux statistiques industrielles de base.

Les données du tableau 6 sont tirées des résultats des enquêtes sur les industries pour 1956 et 1958 exécutées par le Bureau central de statistique, Jérusalem; ces résultats ont paru respectivement dans les numéros de 1958/1959 et 1959/1960 du *Statistical Abstract of Israel*, publié par le Bureau. Ces enquêtes font partie de la série des enquêtes industrielles annuelles par sondage sur les industries minières et manufacturières, qui a commencé en 1955. Les enquêtes de 1956 et 1958 portaient sur les établissements exerçant des activités minières et manufacturières et ayant occupé au moins un salarié pendant un mois ou plus de 1956 ou 1958. Les établissements manufacturiers organisés en coopératives ou en exploitations collectives étaient compris dans le champ des enquêtes, qu'ils emploient ou non des travailleurs autres que leurs membres actifs. Les deux enquêtes ne portaient ni sur les établissements à caractère non lucratif ni sur les établissements relevant des activités ou industries suivantes : fabrication et réparation des horloges, abattoirs, industries de la défense nationale, prospection et production des métaux, prospection et production expérimentale des métaux non-ferreux. En outre, contrairement à l'enquête de 1958, l'enquête de 1956 ne portait pas sur les industries ci-après; production du pétrole brut, réparation des chaussures, réparation des pneumatiques et chambres à air, raffinage du pétrole brut et réparation des véhicules automobiles et des motocycles. Lorsqu'on compare les deux enquêtes, il faut aussi tenir compte du fait que les listes d'établissements dont le Bureau disposait pour 1956 se sont révélées incomplètes et ne comportaient pas tous les établissements existant alors.

Pour déterminer les échantillons relatifs à chaque enquête, on a stratifié les listes d'établissements suivant le type d'activité industrielle; dans chaque strate, les établissements ont été tirés avec une probabilité proportionnelle à leur dimension, c'est-à-dire au nombre de salariés qu'ils occupaient. Cependant, tous les établissements

cluded in the sample drawn for the 1956 survey and, in general, all establishments employing 15 or more employees were included in the sample drawn for 1958. The sample for 1956 comprised about 2,000 establishments while the number of establishments included in the 1958 survey was about 4,000.

Wages and salaries were not computed for members of collective settlements. Data for wages and salaries shown in Table 6 represent wages and salaries and fringe payments as reported in the results for the 1956 and 1958 Censuses. These payments include the employer's contribution to social benefit fund. The figures for value added do not cover goods sold by manufacturing establishments in the same condition as purchased. The definition of all other items of data in Table 6 is consistent with the recommendations in the International Standards in Basic Industrial Statistics.

occupant 25 salariés ou plus étaient compris dans l'échantillon prélevé pour l'enquête de 1956 et, en général, tous les établissments occupant 15 salariés ou plus étaient inclus dans l'échantillon de l'enquête de 1958. L'échantillon de 1956 comprenait environ 2 000 établissements, tandis que celui de 1958 en comprenait quelque 4 000.

Les traitements et salaires versés aux membres des exploitations collectives n'ont pas été inclus. Les données du tableau 6 relatives aux traitements et salaires représentent les traitements, salaires et paiements marginaux indiqués dans les résultats des recensements de 1956 et 1958. Ces paiements comprennent la contribution des employeurs aux caisses d'assurance sociale. Les chiffres de la valeur ajoutée ne comprennent pas les marchandises revendues en l'état par les établissements manufacturiers. Les définitions de toutes les autres rubriques du tableau 6 sont conformes aux Normes internationales relatives aux statistiques industrielles de base.

## 1. THE DOMESTIC PRODUCT AND GROSS DOMESTIC FIXED CAPITAL FORMATION
## LE PRODUIT INTERIEUR ET LA FORMATION BRUTE DE CAPITAL FIXE INTERIEUR

Million Israeli Pounds     Millions de livres israéliennes

### A. Expenditure on the Gross Domestic Product at Market Prices
### Dépenses relatives au produit intérieur brut aux prix du marché

| Item of data and year / Rubrique et année | Total | Consumption / Consommation | | Gross Domestic Capital Formation / Formation brute de capital intérieur | | Net exports of goods and services / Exportations nettes de biens et de services | |
|---|---|---|---|---|---|---|---|
| | | Total | Government / Etat | Total | Fixed / Fixe | Exports less imports / Exportations moins importations | Exports / Exportations |
| **a. At Current Prices — Aux prix courants** | | | | | | | |
| **Absolute figures — Chiffres absolus** | | | | | | | |
| 1950 | 474.4 | 434.5 | 91.9 | 143.4 | 139.1 | −103.5 | 13.8 |
| 1951 | 717.1 | 615.0 | 131.0 | 230.7 | 226.0 | −128.6 | 21.3 |
| 1952 | 1 094.3 | 992.0 | 198.0 | 355.1 | 325.9 | −252.8 | 72.8 |
| 1953 | 1 382.6 | 1 279.6 | 251.2 | 397.8 | 372.9 | −294.8 | 127.5 |
| 1954 | 1 819.6 | 1 655.7 | 322.9 | 506.4 | 470.5 | −342.5 | 233.6 |
| 1955 | 2 214.0 | 2 015.1 | 429.5 | 687.1 | 616.3 | −488.2 | 253.4 |
| 1956 | 2 652.1 | 2 559.4 | 677.0 | 715.6 | 676.3 | −622.9 | 306.3 |
| 1957 | 3 105.6 | 2 793.0 | 623.3 | 885.9 | 846.3 | −573.3 | 382.9 |
| 1958 | 3 558.7 | 3 149.9 | 677.2 | 969.2 | 905.8 | −560.4 | 407.8 |
| 1959 | 4 085.2 | 3 531.8 | 754.6 | 1 068.3 | 990.4 | −514.9 | 500.4 |
| 1960 | 4 560.5 | 3 963.0 | 858.8 | 1 128.4 | 1 042.7 | −530.9 | 620.9 |
| 1961 | 5 415.7 | 4 647.6 | 1 001.2 | 1 400.1 | 1 317.0 | −632.0 | 716.0 |
| **Percentage distribution of average annual expenditure — Distribution en pourcentage des dépenses annuelles moyennes** | | | | | | | |
| 1950–1960 | 100.0 | 89.6 | 19.5 | 27.6 | 25.8 | −17.2 | 11.5 |
| 1950 | 100.0 | 91.6 | 19.4 | 30.2 | 29.3 | −21.8 | 2.9 |
| 1953 | 100.0 | 92.6 | 18.2 | 28.8 | 27.0 | −21.4 | 9.2 |
| 1954 | 100.0 | 91.0 | 17.7 | 27.8 | 25.9 | −18.8 | 12.8 |
| 1958 | 100.0 | 88.5 | 19.0 | 27.2 | 25.5 | −15.7 | 11.5 |
| 1960 | 100.0 | 86.9 | 18.8 | 24.7 | 22.9 | −11.6 | 13.6 |
| **b. At Prices of 1955 — Aux prix de 1955** | | | | | | | |
| **Absolute figures — Chiffres absolus** | | | | | | | |
| 1950 | 1 247.3 | 1 209.6 | 275.0 | 605.6 | 593.3 | −567.9 | 72.2 |
| 1951 | 1 610.7 | 1 472.6 | 326.3 | 715.5 | 703.8 | −577.4 | 100.8 |
| 1952 | 1 679.5 | 1 539.8 | 308.9 | 613.0 | 566.8 | −473.3 | 141.8 |
| 1953 | 1 654.8 | 1 597.3 | 324.0 | 509.2 | 478.5 | −451.7 | 176.0 |
| 1954 | 1 963.0 | 1 843.8 | 379.1 | 561.5 | 523.1 | −442.3 | 250.0 |
| 1955 | 2 214.1 | 2 015.2 | 429.5 | 687.1 | 616.3 | −488.2 | 253.4 |
| 1956 | 2 412.2 | 2 349.5 | 617.4 | 647.6 | 612.2 | −584.9 | 287.6 |
| 1957 | 2 631.4 | 2 380.2 | 527.1 | 763.5 | 730.2 | −512.3 | 343.7 |
| 1958 | 2 825.3 | 2 580.4 | 542.1 | 811.6 | 758.4 | −566.7 | 384.4 |
| 1959 | 3 159.8 | 2 797.0 | 563.0 | 881.4 | 819.6 | −518.6 | 508.0 |
| 1960 | 3 425.3 | 3 042.4 | 618.7 | 902.9 | 832.8 | −520.0 | 638.8 |
| 1961 | 3 741.8 | 3 355.7 | 683.1 | 1 033.0 | 969.9 | −646.9 | 731.4 |
| **Percentage distribution of average annual expenditure — Distribution en pourcentage des dépenses annuelles moyennes** | | | | | | | |
| 1950–1960 | 100.0 | 92.0 | 19.8 | 31.0 | 29.1 | −23.0 | 12.7 |
| 1950 | 100.0 | 97.0 | 22.0 | 48.6 | 47.6 | −45.6 | 5.8 |
| 1953 | 100.0 | 96.5 | 19.6 | 30.8 | 28.9 | −27.3 | 10.6 |
| 1954 | 100.0 | 93.9 | 19.3 | 28.6 | 26.6 | −22.5 | 12.7 |
| 1958 | 100.0 | 91.3 | 19.2 | 28.7 | 26.8 | −20.0 | 13.6 |
| 1960 | 100.0 | 88.8 | 18.1 | 26.4 | 24.3 | −15.2 | 18.6 |
| **Average annual rate of growth — Taux annuel moyen d'accroissement** | | | | | | | |
| 1950–1960 | 10.6 | 9.7 | 8.4 | 4.1 | 3.5 | . | 24.4 |
| 1950–1953 | 9.9 | 9.7 | 5.6 | −5.6 | −6.9 | . | 34.6 |
| 1954–1958 | 9.5 | 8.8 | 9.4 | 9.6 | 9.7 | . | 11.4 |
| 1958–1960 | 10.1 | 8.6 | 6.8 | 5.5 | 4.8 | . | 28.9 |

## B. The Net Domestic Product at Factor Cost According to Origin

### Origine par secteur d'activité du produit intérieur net au coût des facteurs

| Item of data and year<br>Rubrique et année | Total [1] | Agricultural sector<br>Secteur agricole | Industrial Sector — Secteur industriel | | | | Transportation and communication<br>Transports et communications | Other sectors<br>Autres secteurs |
| --- | --- | --- | --- | --- | --- | --- | --- | --- |
| | | | Total | Mining and manufacturing<br>Industries extractives et manufacturières | Construction<br>Bâtiment et travaux publics | Electricity, gas and water<br>Electricité, gaz et eau | | |
| ISIC — CITI | 0–9 | 0 | 1–5 | 1–3 | 4 | 5 | 7 | 6, 8–9 |
| At Current Prices — Aux prix courants | | | | | | | | |
| **Absolute figures — Chiffres absolus** | | | | | | | | |
| 1952............ | 840.8 | 97.0 | 273.6 | 184.0 | 75.6 | 14.0 | 59.4 | 413.5 |
| 1953............ | 1 105.3 | 127.8 | 364.3 | 255.2 | 84.8 | 24.3 | 76.3 | 551.2 |
| 1954............ | 1 436.2 | 176.1 | 461.9 | 324.1 | 110.5 | 27.3 | 104.5 | 712.5 |
| 1955............ | 1 734.5 | 200.0 | 572.5 | 398.5 | 144.7 | 29.3 | 122.9 | 888.7 |
| 1956............ | 2 064.7 | 244.0 | 659.2 | 465.4 | 155.6 | 38.2 | 150.0 | 1 076.0 |
| 1957............ | 2 403.0 | 315.7 | 771.6 | 533.6 | 191.4 | 46.6 | 178.5 | 1 223.0 |
| 1958............ | 2 782.2 | 370.5 | 889.9 | 615.2 | 220.8 | 53.9 | 203.4 | 1 383.9 |
| 1959............ | 3 159.0 | 384.9 | 1 021.6 | 719.8 | 234.8 | 67.0 | 237.6 | 1 577.4 |
| 1960............ | 3 541.9 | 410.1 | 1 157.1 | 835.0 | 247.6 | 74.5 | 266.0 | 1 768.4 |
| 1961............ | 4 202.2 | 474.6 | 1 411.1 | 1 006.5 | 312.7 | 91.9 | 314.8 | 2 095.3 |
| **Percentage distribution according to sector— Distribution en pourcentage par secteur** | | | | | | | | |
| 1952 – 1960..... | 100.0 | 11.9 | 31.7 | 22.2 | 7.5 | 2.0 | 7.2 | 49.2 |
| 1953............ | 100.0 | 11.4 | 33.0 | 22.8 | 7.6 | 2.2 | 6.8 | 49.2 |
| 1954............ | 100.0 | 12.1 | 31.7 | 22.3 | 7.6 | 1.8 | 7.2 | 49.0 |
| 1958............ | 100.0 | 13.0 | 31.3 | 21.6 | 7.8 | 1.9 | 7.1 | 48.6 |
| 1960............ | 100.0 | 11.4 | 32.7 | 23.1 | 6.9 | 2.1 | 7.4 | 49.1 |

[1] The "Total" includes an adjustment which is not included in the figures for the various sectors. It includes net interest of central government and national institutions less an inventory and depreciation adjustment. The percentages however were computed on the basis of the total of the component items.

[1] Le "Total" comprend une correction qui n'a pas été apportée aux différentes composantes par secteur origine. Il comprend l'intérêt net de l'Etat et des organismes d'Etat, déduction faite de la valeur des stocks et de l'amortissement. Toutefois, les pourcentages sont fondés sur le total des différentes composantes.

### C. Gross Domestic Fixed Capital Formation According to Purchasing Sector
### La formation brute de capital fixe intérieur par secteur d'acquisition

| Item of data and year<br>Rubrique et année | Total | Agricultural sector<br>Secteur agricole | Mining, manufacturing, construction, electricity, gas and water<br>Industries extractives, industries manufacturières, bâtiment et travaux publics et électricité, gaz et eau | Transportation and communication<br>Transports et communications | Other sectors<br>Autres secteurs |
|---|---|---|---|---|---|
| ISIC — CITI | 0–9 | 0 | 1-5 | 7 | 6, 8–9 |
| | At Current Prices — Aux prix courants | | | | |
| **Absolute figures — Chiffres absolus** | | | | | |
| 1950............ | 139.1 | 24.5 | 19.7 | 17.5 | 77.4 |
| 1951............ | 226.0 | 37.4 | 33.0 | 20.6 | 135.0 |
| 1952............ | 325.9 | 58.4 | 67.4 | 37.6 | 162.5 |
| 1953............ | 372.9 | 88.0 | 77.1 | 35.7 | 172.1 |
| 1954............ | 470.5 | 109.3 | 103.3 | 41.9 | 216.0 |
| 1955............ | 616.3 | 128.6 | 123.9 | 67.5 | 296.3 |
| 1956............ | 676.3 | 137.4 | 165.6 | 74.3 | 299.0 |
| 1957............ | 846.3 | 153.7 | 155.5 | 143.6 | 393.5 |
| 1958............ | 905.8 | 183.4 | 211.2 | 110.2 | 401.0 |
| 1959............ | 990.4 | 180.2 | 242.3 | 121.0 | 446.9 |
| 1960............ | 1 042.7 | 176.6 | 235.3 | 154.6 | 476.2 |
| 1961............ | 1 317.0 | 188.5 | 303.2 | 228.9 | 596.4 |
| **Percentage distribution according to sector— Distribution en pourcentage par secteur** | | | | | |
| 1950 – 1960..... | 100.0 | 19.3 | 21.7 | 12.5 | 46.5 |
| 1950............ | 100.0 | 17.6 | 14.2 | 12.6 | 55.6 |
| 1953............ | 100.0 | 23.6 | 20.7 | 9.6 | 46.1 |
| 1954............ | 100.0 | 23.2 | 22.0 | 8.9 | 45.9 |
| 1958............ | 100.0 | 20.2 | 23.3 | 12.2 | 44.3 |
| 1960............ | 100.0 | 16.9 | 22.6 | 14.8 | 45.7 |

## 2. INDEX NUMBERS OF INDUSTRIAL PRODUCTION — INDICES DE LA PRODUCTION INDUSTRIELLE

### A. Selected Divisions of Industrial Activity
### Quelques branches de l'activité industrielle

| Period<br>Période | Total | Mining [1]<br>Industries extractives [1] | Manufacturing<br>Industries manufacturières |
|---|---|---|---|
| ISIC — CITI | 1–3 | 1 | 2-3 |
| *a.* Indexes — Indices (1958 = 100) | | | |
| 1955............ | 81 | 36 | 85 |
| 1956............ | 81 | 52 | 83 |
| 1957............ | 91 | 78 | 92 |
| 1958............ | – 100 – | – 100 – | – 100 – |
| 1959............ | 114 | 132 | 113 |
| 1960............ | 129 | 156 | 128 |
| 1961............ | 150 | 172 | 149 |
| *b.* Average Annual Rate of Change — Taux annuel moyen de variation | | | |
| 1955 – 1958..... | 7.3 | 40.6 | 5.6 |
| 1958 – 1961..... | 13.6 | 24.9 | 13.1 |

For footnotes see end of table.

Pour les notes, voir au bas du tableau.

# ISRAEL

## B. The Major Groups of Manufacturing — Les classes de la branche Industries manufacturières

| Period / Période | Manufacturing / Industries manufacturières | Food, beverages and tobacco / Industries alimentaires, boissons, tabac | Textiles | Clothing, footwear and made-up textiles [2] / Articles d'habillement, chaussures et ouvrages en tissu [2] | Wood products and furniture / Bois et meubles | Paper and paper products / Papier et ouvrages en papier | Printing and publishing / Imprimerie et édition | Leather and leather products except wearing apparel [2] / Cuir et articles en cuir, à l'exclusion des articles d'habillement [2] | Rubber products [3] / Ouvrages en caoutchouc [3] | Chemicals and chemical, petroleum and coal products [4] / Produits chimiques et dérivés du pétrole et du charbon [4] | Non-metallic mineral products / Produits minéraux non métalliques | Basic metals / Métallurgie de base | Metal products [5] / Ouvrages en métaux [5] | Other manufacturing [3, 6] / Autres industries manufacturières [3, 6] |
|---|---|---|---|---|---|---|---|---|---|---|---|---|---|---|
| ISIC — CITI | 2–3 | 20–22 | 23 | 24 | 25–26 | 27 | 28 | 29 | 30 | 31–32 | 33 | 34 | 35–38 | 39 |

### a. Indexes — Indices (1958 = 100)

| Period / Période | 2–3 | 20–22 | 23 | 24 | 25–26 | 27 | 28 | 29 | 30 | 31–32 | 33 | 34 | 35–38 | 39 |
|---|---|---|---|---|---|---|---|---|---|---|---|---|---|---|
| 1955 | 85 | 84 | 80 | 98 | 91 | 93 | | 189 | 76 | 86 | 85 | 81 | | .79 |
| 1956 | 83 | 84 | 81 | 90 | 87 | 88 | | 204 | 68 | 87 | 79 | 83 | | 80 |
| 1957 | 92 | 88 | 94 | 86 | 99 | 90 | | 213 | 89 | 97 | 91 | 92 | | 105 |
| 1958 | –100– | –100– | –100– | –100– | –100– | –100– | –100– | –100– | –100– | –100– | –100– | –100– | –100– | –100– |
| 1959 | 113 | 105 | 109 | 117 | 119 | 105 | 118 | 110 | 121 | 112 | 116 | 125 | 115 | 126 |
| 1960 | 128 | 112 | 128 | 129 | 121 | 131 | 134 | 118 | 133 | 131 | 123 | 146 | 130 | 169 |
| 1961 | 149 | 125 | 160 | 149 | 144 | 153 | 150 | 130 | 160 | 153 | 137 | 175 | 151 | 192 |

### b. Average Annual Rate of Change — Taux annuel moyen de variation

| Period / Période | 2–3 | 20–22 | 23 | 24 | 25–26 | 27 | 28 | 29 | 30 | 31–32 | 33 | 34 | 35–38 | 39 |
|---|---|---|---|---|---|---|---|---|---|---|---|---|---|---|
| 1955–1958 | 5.6 | 6.0 | 7.7 | 0.7 | 3.2 | 2.4 | | −19.1 | 9.6 | 5.2 | 5.6 | 7.3 | | 8.2 |
| 1958–1961 | 13.1 | 5.8 | 13.1 | 13.6 | 10.0 | 14.5 | 15.8 | 8.6 | 15.3 | 14.5 | 10.9 | 20.8 | 14.0 | 30.0 |

[1] Covers activities in Other mining (ISIC major groups 14-19) only.
[2] During the years, 1958-1961, footwear was classified with Leather and leather products except wearing apparel (ISIC major group 29) instead of Clothing, footwear and made-up textiles (ISIC major group 24).
[3] During the years, 1958-1961, plastic products (in ISIC group 399) were included with Rubber Products (ISIC major group 30).
[4] Figures for 1958-1961 exclude explosives.
[5] 1958-1961 figures exclude metal workshops and car and cycle repair.
[6] Figures for 1958-1961 exclude watches and clocks (ISIC group 393).

[1] Il s'agit exclusivement de Autres industries extractives (CITI classes 14-19).
[2] De 1958 à 1961 inclus, les chaussures sont classées dans Cuir et articles en cuir à l'exclusion des articles d'habillement (CITI classe 29) et non dans Articles d'habillement, chaussures et ouvrages en tissu (CITI classe 24).
[3] De 1958 à 1961 inclus, les articles en matière plastique (dans CITI groupe 399) sont classés dans Ouvrages en caoutchouc (CITI classe 30).
[4] Les chiffres de 1958-1961 ne couvrent pas les explosifs.
[5] Les chiffres de 1958-1961 ne couvrent ni les ateliers de réparation métallique ni les réparations des véhicules automobiles et des cycles.
[6] Les chiffres de 1958-1961 ne couvrent pas les montres et horloges (CITI groupe 393).

## 3. INDEX NUMBERS OF INDUSTRIAL EMPLOYMENT — INDICES DE L'EMPLOI DANS L'INDUSTRIE

### A. Selected Divisions of Industrial Activity
### Quelques branches de l'activité industrielle

| Period / Période | Total | Mining [1] / Industries extractives [1] | Manufacturing / Industries manufacturières |
|---|---|---|---|
| ISIC — CITI | 1–3 | 1 | 2–3 |

#### a. Indexes — Indices (1958 = 100)

| Period / Période | Total | Mining [1] | Manufacturing |
|---|---|---|---|
| 1955 | 92 | 101 | 92 |
| 1956 | 93 | 99 | 93 |
| 1957 | 96 | 105 | 95 |
| 1958 | –100– | –100– | –100– |
| 1959 | 108 | 111 | 108 |
| 1960 | 115 | 121 | 115 |
| 1961 | 130 | 120 | 130 |

#### b. Average Annual Rate of Change — Taux annuel moyen de variation

| Period / Période | Total | Mining [1] | Manufacturing |
|---|---|---|---|
| 1955–1960 | 4.6 | 3.7 | 4.6 |
| 1955–1958 | 2.8 | −0.3 | 2.8 |
| 1958–1960 | 7.2 | 10.0 | 7.2 |

For footnotes see end of table.

Pour les notes, voir au bas du tableau.

## B.  The Major Groups of Manufacturing — Les classes de la branche Industries manufacturières

| Period / Période | Manufacturing / Industries manufacturières | Food, beverages and tobacco / Industries alimentaires, boissons, tabac | Textiles | Clothing, footwear and made-up textiles [2] / Articles d'habillement, chaussures et ouvrages en tissu [2] | Wood products and furniture / Bois et meubles | Paper and paper products / Papier et ouvrages en papier | Printing and publishing / Imprimerie et édition | Leather and leather products except wearing apparel [2] / Cuir et articles en cuir, à l'exclusion des articles d'habillement [2] | Rubber products [3] / Ouvrages en caoutchouc [3] | Chemicals and chemical, petroleum and coal products [4] / Produits chimiques et dérivés du pétrole et du charbon [4] | Non-metallic mineral products / Produits minéraux non métalliques | Basic metals / Métallurgie de base | Metal products [5] / Ouvrages en métaux [5] | Other manufacturing [3,6] / Autres industries manufacturières [3,6] |
|---|---|---|---|---|---|---|---|---|---|---|---|---|---|---|
| ISIC — CITI | 2–3 | 20–22 | 23 | 24 | 25–26 | 27 | 28 | 29 | 30 | 31–32 | 33 | 34 | 35–38 | 39 |
| **a. Indexes — Indices (1958 = 100)** | | | | | | | | | | | | | | |
| 1955 | 92 | 84 | 89 | 106 | 90 | 95 | | 147 | 97 | 92 | 106 | 83 | | 85 |
| 1956 | 93 | 88 | 89 | 98 | 84 | 92 | | 129 | 80 | 95 | 99 | 84 | | 85 |
| 1957 | 95 | 91 | 93 | 95 | 91 | 93 | | 134 | 91 | 96 | 100 | 93 | | 107 |
| 1958 | 100 | 100 | 100 | 100 | 100 | 100 | 100 | 100 | 100 | 100 | 100 | 100 | 100 | 100 |
| 1959 | 108 | 103 | 105 | 108 | 114 | 106 | 107 | 103 | 109 | 112 | 108 | 116 | 111 | 111 |
| 1960 | 115 | 108 | 112 | 117 | 114 | 117 | 110 | 104 | 119 | 114 | 113 | 125 | 122 | 133 |
| 1961 | 130 | 120 | 144 | 136 | 133 | 129 | 118 | 115 | 137 | 120 | 124 | 138 | 134 | 148 |
| **b. Average Annual Rate of Change — Taux annuel moyen de variation** | | | | | | | | | | | | | | |
| 1955–1960 | 4.6 | 5.2 | 4.7 | 2.0 | 4.8 | ... | | −7.2 | 4.2 | 4.4 | 1.3 | ... | | 9.4 |
| 1955–1958 | 2.8 | 6.0 | 4.0 | −1.9 | 3.6 | 1.7 | | −13.7 | 1.0 | 2.8 | −1.9 | 6.4 | | 5.6 |
| 1958–1960 | 7.2 | 3.9 | 5.8 | 8.2 | 6.8 | 8.2 | 4.9 | 2.0 | 9.1 | 6.8 | 6.3 | 11.8 | 10.5 | 15.3 |

[1] Covers activities in Other mining (ISIC major groups 14-19) only.
[2] During the years, 1958-1961, footwear was classified with Leather and leather products except wearing apparel (ISIC major group 29) instead of Clothing, footwear and made-up textiles (ISIC major group 24).
[3] During the years, 1958-1961, plastic products (in ISIC group 399) were included with Rubber Products (ISIC major group 30).
[4] Figures for 1958-1961 exclude explosives.
[5] 1958-1961 figures exclude metal workshops and car and cycle repair.
[6] Figures for 1958-1961 exclude Watches and clocks (ISIC group 393).

[1] Il s'agit exclusivement de Autres industries extractives (CITI classes 14-19).
[2] De 1958 à 1951 inclus, les chaussures sont classées dans Cuir et articles en cuir à l'exclusion des articles d'habillement (CITI classe 29) et non dans Articles d'habillement, chaussures et ouvrages en tissu (CITI classe 24).
[3] De 1958 à 1961 inclus, les articles en matière plastique (dans CITI groupe 399) sont classés dans Ouvrages en caoutchouc (CITI classe 30).
[4] Les chiffres de 1958-1961 ne couvrent pas les explosifs.
[5] Les chiffres de 1958-1961 ne couvrent ni les ateliers de réparation métallique ni les réparations des véhicules automobiles et des cycles.
[6] Les chiffres de 1958-1961 ne couvrent pas les montres et horloges (CITI groupe 393).

## 4. CHARACTERISTICS OF LICENSED INDUSTRIAL ESTABLISHMENTS
### 1 April 1951–31 March 1952

## CARACTERISTIQUES DES ETABLISSEMENTS INDUSTRIELS PATENTES
### 1er avril 1951–31 mars 1952

Number of establishments in units; number of engaged and employees in thousands; wages and salaries paid in million Israeli Pounds; and wages and salaries per employee in thousand Israeli Pounds.

Nombre d'établissements en unités; nombre de personnes occupées et de salariés en milliers; traitements et salaires payés en millions de livres israéliennes; traitements et salaires par salarié en milliers de livres israéliennes.

### A. Selected Divisions of Industrial Activity — Quelques branches de l'activité industrielle

| Item of data | Total [2] | Mining [1] Industries extractives [1] | Manu-facturing [2] Industries manu-facturières [2] | Rubrique |
|---|---|---|---|---|
| ISIC | 1-3 | 1 | 2-3 | CITI |
| | a. Absolute Figures Chiffres absolus | | | |
| Number of establishments | 20 302 | 48 | 20 254 | Nombre d'établissements |
| Number of engaged (As of 15.IX.1951) | 100.9 | 0.8 | 100.1 | Nombre de personnes occupées (au 15.IX.1951) |
| Number of employees (As of 15.IX.1951) | 75.6 | 0.7 | 74.9 | Nombre de salariés (au 15.IX.1951) |
| Wages and salaries paid | 57.5 | 0.5 | 57.0 | Traitements et salaires payés |

| Item of data | Total [2] | Mining [1] Industries extractives [1] | Manu-facturing [2] Industries manu-facturières [2] | Rubrique |
|---|---|---|---|---|
| ISIC | 1-3 | 1 | 2-3 | CITI |
| | b. Structure | | | |
| Distribution in percent of number of engaged | 100.0 | 0.8 | 99.2 | Distribution en pourcentage du nombre de personnes occupées |
| Employees as a percent of engaged | 74.9 | 87.5 | 74.8 | Salariés en pourcentage des personnes occupées |
| Wages and salaries per employee | 0.8 | 0.7 | 0.8 | Traitements et salaires par salarié |

[1] Only Other mining (ISIC major groups 14-19).
[2] Includes Electricity power stations (in ISIC group 511).

[1] Exclusivement Autres industries extractives (CITI classes 14-19).
[2] Y compris les centrales électriques (dans CITI groupe 511).

### B. The Major Groups of Manufacturing — Les classes de la branche Industries manufacturières

| Item of data | Manu-facturing [1] Industries manufac-turières [1] | Food, beverages and tobacco Industries alimen-taires, boissons, tabac | Textiles | Clothing, footwear and made-up textiles Articles d'habil-lement, chaussures et ouvrages en tissu | Wood products and furniture Bois et meubles | Paper and paper products Papier et ouvrages en papier | Printing and publish-ing Imprimerie et édition | Leather and leather products except wearing apparel Cuir et articles en cuir, à l'exclu-sion des articles d'habil-lement | Rubber products Ouvrages en caout-chouc | Chemicals and chemical, petroleum and coal products Produits chimiques et dérivés du pétrole et du charbon | Non-metallic mineral products Produits minéraux non métal-liques | Basic metals Métal-lurgie de base | Metal products Ouvrages en métaux | Other manu-factur-ing [1] Autres in-dustries manufac-turières [1] | Rubrique |
|---|---|---|---|---|---|---|---|---|---|---|---|---|---|---|---|
| ISIC | 2-3 | 20–22 | 23 | 24 | 25–26 | 27 | 28 | 29 | 30 | 31–32 | 33 | 34 | 35–38 | 39 | CITI |
| | a. Absolute Figures — Chiffres absolus | | | | | | | | | | | | | | |
| Number of establishments | 20 254 | 1 759 | 1 264 | 5 928 | 3 590 | 189 | 568 | 582 | 91 | 393 | 667 | 117 | 3 777 | 1329 | Nombre d'établissements |
| Number of engaged (As of 15.IX.1951) | 100.1 | 18.9 | 9.2 | 13.6 | 10.6 | 1.2 | 3.4 | 1.5 | 1.0 | 4.2 | 9.2 | 1.7 | 18.1 | 7.5 | Nombre de personnes occupées (au 15.IX.1951) |
| Number of employees (As of 15.IX.1951) | 74.9 | 16.7 | 7.5 | 6.6 | 6.0 | 0.9 | 2.7 | 0.8 | 0.9 | 3.7 | 8.3 | 1.5 | 13.4 | 5.9 | Nombre de salariés (au 15.IX.1951) |
| Wages and salaries paid | 57.0 | 14.1 | 5.9 | 3.5 | 4.2 | 0.6 | 2.1 | 0.5 | 0.5 | 2.7 | 6.4 | 1.3 | 9.4 | 5.8 | Traitements et salaires payés |
| | b. Structure | | | | | | | | | | | | | | |
| Distribution in percent of number of engaged | 100.0 | 18.8 | 9.2 | 13.6 | 10.6 | 1.2 | 3.4 | 1.5 | 1.0 | 4.2 | 9.2 | 1.7 | 18.1 | 7.5 | Distribution en pourcentage du nombre de personnes occupées |
| Employees as a percent of engaged | 74.8 | 88.4 | 81.5 | 48.5 | 56.6 | 75.0 | 79.4 | 53.3 | 90.0 | 88.1 | 90.2 | 88.2 | 74.0 | 78.7 | Salariés en pourcentage des personnes occupées |
| Wages and salaries per employee | 0.8 | 0.8 | 0.8 | 0.5 | 0.7 | 0.7 | 0.8 | 0.6 | 0.6 | 0.7 | 0.8 | 0.9 | 0.7 | 1.0 | Traitements et salaires par salarié |

[1] Includes Electricity power stations (in ISIC group 511).

[1] Y compris les centrales électriques (dans CITI groupe 511).

# 5. CHARACTERISTICS OF LICENSED INDUSTRIAL ESTABLISHMENTS ENGAGING 10 OR MORE PERSONS
## 1 April 1951–31 March 1952

# CARACTERISTIQUES DES ETABLISSEMENTS INDUSTRIELS PATENTES OCCUPANT 10 PERSONNES OU PLUS
## 1er avril 1951–31 mars 1952

Number of establishments in units; value added and wages and salaries in million Israeli Pounds; number of engaged and employees in thousands; value added per person engaged in thousand Israeli Pounds; wages and salaries per employee in thousand Israeli Pounds.

Nombre d'établissements en unités; valeur ajoutée et traitements et salaires en millions de livres israéliennes; nombre de personnes occupées et de salariés en milliers; valeur ajoutée par personne occupée en milliers de livres israéliennes; traitements et salaires par salarié en milliers de livres israéliennes.

## A. Selected Divisions of Industrial Activity
## Quelques branches de l'activité industrielle

| Item of data | Total [2] | Mining [1, 2]<br><br>Industries extractives [1, 2] | Manufacturing [2]<br><br>Industries manu-facturières [2] | Rubrique |
|---|---|---|---|---|
| ISIC | 1–3 | 1 | 2–3 | CITI |
| *a. Absolute Figures — Chiffres absolus* | | | | |
| Number of units.............. | 1 700 | 32 | 1 668 | Nombre d'unités |
| Value added............... | 95.3 | 2.4 | 92.9 | Valeur ajoutée |
| Number of engaged (As of 15.IX.1951)......... | 52.9 | 1.5 | 51.4 | Nombre de personnes occupées (au 15.IX.1951) |
| Number of employees (As of 15.IX.1951)......... | 51.2 | 1.5 | 49.7 | Nombre de salariés (au 15.IX.1951) |
| Wages and salaries paid..... | 45.4 | 1.2 | 44.2 | Traitements et salaires payés |
| *b. Structure* | | | | |
| Distribution in percent of: | | | | Distribution en pourcentage: |
| Value added............. | 100.0 | 2.5 | 97.5 | De la valeur ajoutée |
| Number of engaged....... | 100.0 | 2.8 | 97.2 | Du nombre de personnes occupées |
| Value added per person engaged................ | 1.8 | 1.6 | 1.8 | Valeur ajoutée par personne occupée |
| Value added per unit of wages and salaries........ | 2.10 | 2.00 | 2.10 | Valeur ajoutée par unité de traitements et salaires |
| Employees as a percent of engaged.............. | 96.8 | 100.0 | 96.7 | Salariés en pourcentage des personnes occupées |
| Wages and salaries per employee................ | 0.9 | 0.8 | 0.9 | Traitements et salaires par salarié |

[1] Only Other mining (ISIC major groups 14–19).
[2] The figures for number of establishments and value added, number of engaged and employees and wages and salaries paid are not strictly comparable to one another because of differences in the number of establishments responding.

[1] Exclusivement Autres industries extractives (CITI classes 14-19).
[2] Les chiffres du nombre d'établissements et de la valeur ajoutée, du nombre de personnes occupées et de salariés, et des traitements et salaires payés ne sont pas strictement comparables entre eux en raison des différences qui existent dans le nombre des établissements ayant répondu.

## B. The Major Groups of Manufacturing — Les classes de la branche Industries manufacturières

| Item of data | Manu-facturing[1]<br>Industries manufac-turières[1] | Food, beverages and tobacco<br>Industries alimen-taires, boissons, tabac | Textiles | Clothing, footwear and made-up textiles<br>Articles d'habil-lement, chaussures et ouvrages en tissu | Wood products and furniture<br>Bois et meubles | Paper and paper products<br>Papier et ouvrages en papier | Printing and publish-ing<br>Im-primerie et édition | Leather and leather products except wearing apparel<br>Cuir et articles en cuir, à l'exclu-sion des articles d'habil-lement | Rubber products<br>Ouvrages en caout-chouc | Chemicals and chemical, petroleum and coal products<br>Produits chi-miques et dérivés du pétrole et du charbon | Non-metallic mineral products<br>Produits minéraux non métal-liques | Basic metals<br>Métal-lurgie de base | Metal products<br>Ouvrages en métaux | Other manu-factur-ing<br>Autres in-dustries manufac-turières | Rubrique |
|---|---|---|---|---|---|---|---|---|---|---|---|---|---|---|---|
| ISIC | 2-3 | 20-22 | 23 | 24 | 25-26 | 27 | 28 | 29 | 30 | 31-32 | 33 | 34 | 35-38 | 39 | CITI |
| *a. Absolute Figures — Chiffres absolus* | | | | | | | | | | | | | | | |
| Number of establishments. | 1 668 | 395 | 168 | 175 | 135 | 36 | 75 | 24 | 10 | 74 | 181 | 16 | 340 | 39 | Nombre d'établissements |
| Value added.......... | 92.9 | 23.6 | 12.1 | 6.0 | 7.5 | 0.8 | 3.0 | 0.8 | 1.0 | 4.8 | 11.6 | 1.7 | 18.4 | 1.6 | Valeur ajoutée |
| Number of engaged (As of 15.IX.1951).... | 51.4 | 12.0 | 6.0 | 3.9 | 3.7 | 0.6 | 2.1 | 0.4 | 0.4 | 3.0 | 7.4 | 1.2 | 9.9 | 0.8 | Nombre de personnes occupées (au 15.IX.1951) |
| Number of employees (As of 15.IX.1951).... | 49.7 | 11.5 | 5.8 | 3.6 | 3.5 | 0.6 | 2.0 | 0.4 | 0.4 | 3.0 | 7.3 | 1.2 | 9.6 | 0.8 | Nombre de salariés (au 15.IX.1951) |
| Wages and salaries paid.............. | 44.2 | 10.7 | 5.1 | 2.7 | 2.9 | 0.5 | 2.0 | 0.4 | 0.4 | 2.6 | 6.9 | 0.9 | 8.4 | 0.7 | Traitements et salaires payés |
| *b. Structure* | | | | | | | | | | | | | | | |
| Distribution in percent of: | | | | | | | | | | | | | | | Distribution en pour-centage: |
| Value added........ | 100.0 | 25.4 | 13.0 | 6.4 | 8.1 | 0.9 | 3.2 | 0.9 | 1.0 | 5.2 | 12.5 | 1.8 | 19.8 | 1.8 | De la valeur ajoutée |
| Number of engaged.. | 100.0 | 23.3 | 11.7 | 7.6 | 7.2 | 1.1 | 4.1 | 0.8 | 0.8 | 5.8 | 14.4 | 2.3 | 19.3 | 1.6 | Du nombre de per-sonnes occupées |
| Value added per person engaged........... | 1.8 | 2.0 | 2.0 | 1.5 | 2.0 | 1.3 | 1.4 | 2.0 | 2.5 | 1.6 | 1.6 | 1.4 | 1.8 | 2.0 | Valeur ajoutée par per-sonne occupée |
| Value added per unit of wages and salaries............ | 2.10 | 2.20 | 2.37 | 2.22 | 2.59 | 1.60 | 1.50 | 2.00 | 2.50 | 1.85 | 1.68 | 1.89 | 2.19 | 2.28 | Valeur ajoutée par unité de traitements et salaires |
| Employees as a percent of engaged... | 96.7 | 95.8 | 96.7 | 92.3 | 94.6 | 100.0 | 95.2 | 100.0 | 100.0 | 100.0 | 98.6 | 100.0 | 97.0 | 100.0 | Salariés en pourcentage des personnes occupées |
| Wages and salaries per employee........ | 0.9 | 0.9 | 0.9 | 0.8 | 0.8 | 0.8 | 1.0 | 1.0 | 1.0 | 0.9 | 0.9 | 0.8 | 0.9 | 0.9 | Traitements et salaires par salarié |

[1] For many of the major groups of manufacturing the figures for number of establishments and value added, number of engaged and employees and wages and salaries paid are not strictly comparable to one another because of differences in the number of establishments responding.

[1] Pour plusieurs classes des industries manufacturières les chiffres du nombre d'établissements et de la valeur ajoutée, du nombre de personnes occupées et de salariés, et des traitements et salaires payés ne sont pas strictement comparables entre eux en raison des différences qui existent dans le nombre des établissements ayant répondu.

## 6. CHARACTERISTICS OF INDUSTRIAL ESTABLISHMENTS EMPLOYING AT LEAST ONE PERSON
## CARACTERISTIQUES DES ETABLISSEMENTS INDUSTRIELS OCCUPANT UNE PERSONNE OU PLUS
### 1956, 1958

Number of establishments in units; value added and wages and salaries in million Israeli pounds; number of engaged and employees in thousands; electricity consumed in million KWH; value added per engaged and wages and salaries per employee in thousand Israeli pounds; and electricity consumed per engaged in thousand KWH.

Nombre d'établissements en unités; valeur ajoutée et traitements et salaires en millions de livres israéliennes; nombre de personnes occupées et de salariés en milliers; électricité consommée en millions de kWh; valeur ajoutée par personne occupée et traitements et salaires par salarié en milliers de livres israéliennes; électricité consommée par personne occupée en milliers de kWh.

### A. Selected Divisions of Industrial Activity — Quelques branches de l'activité industrielle

| Year and item of data | Total | Mining Industries ex-tractives | Manu-facturing Industries manu-facturières | Année et rubrique | Year and item of data | All industrial activity Toutes industries | Mining Industries ex-tractives | Manu-facturing Industries manu-facturières | Année et rubrique |
|---|---|---|---|---|---|---|---|---|---|
| ISIC | 1–3 | 1 | 2–3 | CITI | ISIC | 1–3 | 1 | 2–3 | CITI |
| | a. Absolute Figures Chiffres absolus | | | | | b. Structure | | | |
| **1956** | | | | **1956** | **1956** | | | | **1956** |
| Number of establishments...... | 7 502 | 97 | 7 405 | Nombre d'établissements | Distribution in percent of: | | | | Distribution en pourcentage: |
| Value added................. | 404.0 | 10.9 | 393.1 | Valeur ajoutée | Value added............... | 100.0 | 2.7 | 97.3 | Valeur ajoutée |
| Number of engaged | | | | Nombre de personnes occupées | Number of engaged.......... | 100.0 | 2.3 | 97.7 | Nombre de personnes occupées |
| (Average during year)........ | 93.8 | 2.2 | 91.6 | (moyenne pendant l'année) | Value added per person | | | | Valeur ajoutée par personne occupées |
| Employees: | | | | Salariés: | engaged................... | 4.3 | 5.0 | 4.3 | |
| Number (Average during | | | | Nombre (moyenne pendant. | Employees as a percent | | | | Salariés en pourcentage des personnes occupées |
| year)..................... | 85.0 | 2.1 | 82.9 | l'année) | of engaged................ | 90.6 | 95.4 | 90.5 | Valeur ajoutée par unité de traitements et salaires |
| Wages and salaries.......... | 239.7 | 8.7 | 231.0 | Traitements et salaires | Value added per unit of | | | | |
| | | | | | wages and salaries.......... | 1.68 | 1.25 | 1.70 | Traitements et salaires par salarié |
| | | | | | Wages and salaries | | | | |
| | | | | | per employee.............. | 2.8 | 4.1 | 2.8 | |
| **1958** | | | | **1958** | **1958** | | | | **1958** |
| Number of establishments...... | 9 271 | 75 | 9 196 | Nombre d'établissements | Distribution in percent of: | | | | Distribution en pourcentage: |
| Value added................. | 624.1 | 20.5 | 603.6 | Valeur ajoutée | Value added............... | 100.0 | 3.3 | 96.7 | Valeur ajoutée |
| Number of engaged | | | | Nombre de personnes occupées | Number of engaged.......... | 100.0 | 1.9 | 98.1 | Nombre de personnes occupées |
| (Average during year)........ | 118.4 | 2.3 | 116.1 | (moyenne pendant l'année) | Per person engaged: | | | | Par personne occupée: |
| Employees: | | | | Salariés: | Value added............... | 5.3 | 8.9 | 5.2 | Valeur ajoutée |
| Number (Average during | | | | Nombre (moyenne pendant | Electricity consumed........ | 4.5 | | 4.5 | Electricité consommée |
| year)..................... | 107.5 | 2.2 | 105.3 | l'année) | Employees as a percent | | | | Salariés en pourcentage des personnes occupées |
| Wages and salaries.......... | 346.9 | 10.2 | 336.7 | Traitements et salaires | of engaged................ | 90.8 | 95.6 | 90.7 | Valeur ajoutée par unité de traitements et salaires |
| Electricity consumed.......... | 532.2 | 532.2 | | Electricité consommée | Value added per unit of | | | | |
| | | | | | wages and salaries.......... | 1.80 | 2.01 | 1.79 | Traitements et salaires par salarié |
| | | | | | Wages and salaries | | | | |
| | | | | | per employee.............. | 3.2 | 4.6 | 3.2 | |

# ISRAEL

## B. The Major Groups of Manufacturing — Les classes de la branche Industries manufacturières

| Year and item of data | Manufacturing — Industries manufacturières | Food, beverages and tobacco — Industries alimentaires, boissons, tabac | Textiles | Clothing, footwear and made-up textiles[1] — Articles d'habillement, chaussures et ouvrages en tissu[1] | Wood products and furniture — Bois et meubles | Paper, paper products and printing and publishing — Papier et ouvrages en papier et imprimerie et édition | Leather and leather products except wearing apparel[1] — Cuir et articles en cuir, à l'exclusion des articles d'habillement[1] | Rubber products — Ouvrages en caoutchouc | Chemicals and chemical, petroleum and coal products[3] — Produits chimiques et dérivés du pétrole et du charbon[3] | Non-metallic mineral products — Produits minéraux non métalliques | Basic metals and metal products[4] — Métallurgie de base et ouvrages en métaux[4] | Other manufacturing — Autres industries manufacturières | Année et rubrique |
|---|---|---|---|---|---|---|---|---|---|---|---|---|---|
| ISIC | 2–3 | 20–22 | 23 | 24 | 25–26 | 27–28 | 29 | 30 | 31–32 | 33 | 34–38 | 39 | CITI |
| *a. Absolute Figures — Chiffres absolus* | | | | | | | | | | | | | |
| **1956** | | | | | | | | | | | | | **1956** |
| Number of establishments | 7 405 | 1 309 | 639 | 715 | 1 012 | 552 | 427 | 168 | 232 | 410 | 1 528 | 413 | Nombre d'établissements |
| Value added | 393.1 | 70.9 | 55.1 | 15.3 | 22.7 | 22.4 | 9.5 | 18.4 | 31.9 | 38.3 | 89.2 | 19.4 | Valeur ajoutée |
| Number of engaged (Average during year) | 91.6 | 17.1 | 11.6 | 4.8 | 6.9 | 5.4 | 3.0 | 2.9 | 5.2 | 7.9 | 21.8 | 5.2 | Nombre de personnes occupées (moyenne pendant l'année) |
| Employees: Number (Average during year) | 82.9 | 15.5 | 10.9 | 3.8 | 5.6 | 4.7 | 2.4 | 2.8 | 5.0 | 7.5 | 19.9 | 4.8 | Salariés: Nombre (moyenne pendant l'année) |
| Wages and salaries | 231.0 | 41.8 | 30.6 | 7.0 | 13.5 | 14.2 | 5.7 | 7.7 | 18.4 | 23.7 | 56.6 | 11.8 | Traitements et salaires |
| **1958** | | | | | | | | | | | | | **1958** |
| Number of establishments | 9 196 | 1 218 | 649 | 822 | 1 385 | 551 | 558 | 123 | 256 | 455 | 2 708 | 471 | Nombre d'établissements |
| Value added | 603.6 | 99.9 | 77.0 | 18.3 | 36.9 | 45.7 | 13.8 | 21.1 | 57.1 | 53.1 | 158.7 | 22.0 | Valeur ajoutée |
| Number of engaged (Average during year) | 116.1 | 18.9 | 13.6 | 5.3 | 9.5 | 8.2 | 3.8 | 2.9 | 7.3 | 8.5 | 32.3 | 5.8 | Nombre de personnes occupées (moyenne pendant l'année) |
| Employees: Number (Average during year) | 105.3 | 17.4 | 13.0 | 4.1 | 7.7 | 7.6 | 3.1 | 2.8 | 7.1 | 8.0 | 29.2 | 5.3 | Salariés: Nombre (moyenne pendant l'année) |
| Wages and salaries | 336.7 | 52.6 | 41.6 | 8.3 | 21.2 | 27.1 | 7.9 | 10.0 | 29.3 | 31.4 | 93.5 | 13.8 | Traitements et salaires |
| Electricity consumed | 532.2 [2] | 121.6 | 46.1 | 0.9 | 14.6 | 20.1 | 3.4 | — | 112.8 | 132.9 [2] | 50.4 | 29.4 | Electricité consommée |
| *b. Structure* | | | | | | | | | | | | | |
| **1956** | | | | | | | | | | | | | **1956** |
| Distribution in percent of: Value added | 100.0 | 18.0 | 14.0 | 3.9 | 5.8 | 5.7 | 2.4 | 4.7 | 8.1 | 9.7 | 22.7 | 5.0 | Distribution en pourcentage: Valeur ajoutée |
| Number of engaged | 100.0 | 18.6 | 12.7 | 5.2 | 7.6 | 5.9 | 3.2 | 3.2 | 5.7 | 8.6 | 23.6 | 5.7 | Nombre de personnes occupées |
| Value added per person engaged | 4.3 | 4.1 | 4.8 | 3.2 | 3.3 | 4.1 | 3.2 | 6.3 | 6.1 | 4.8 | 4.1 | 3.7 | Valeur ajoutée par personne occupée |
| Employees as a percent of engaged | 90.5 | 90.6 | 94.0 | 79.2 | 81.2 | 87.0 | 80.0 | 96.6 | 96.2 | 94.9 | 92.1 | 92.3 | Salariés en pourcentage des personnes occupées |
| Value added per unit of wages and salaries | 1.70 | 1.70 | 1.80 | 2.18 | 1.68 | 1.58 | 1.67 | 2.39 | 1.73 | 1.62 | 1.58 | 1.64 | Valeur ajoutée par unité de traitements et salaires |
| Wages and salaries per employee | 2.8 | 2.7 | 2.8 | 1.8 | 2.4 | 3.0 | 2.4 | 2.8 | 3.7 | 3.2 | 2.8 | 2.4 | Traitements et salaires par salarié |
| **1958** | | | | | | | | | | | | | **1958** |
| Distribution in percent of: Value added | 100.0 | 16.5 | 12.8 | 3.0 | 6.1 | 7.6 | 2.3 | 3.5 | 9.4 | 8.8 | 26.3 | 3.7 | Distribution en pourcentage: Valeur ajoutée |
| Number of engaged | 100.0 | 16.2 | 11.7 | 4.6 | 8.2 | 7.1 | 3.2 | 2.5 | 6.3 | 7.3 | 27.9 | 5.0 | Nombre de personnes occupées |
| Per person engaged: Value added | 5.2 | 5.3 | 5.7 | 3.4 | 3.9 | 5.6 | 3.6 | 7.3 | 7.8 | 6.2 | 4.9 | 3.8 | Par personne occupée: Valeur ajoutée |
| Electricity consumed | ... | 6.4 | 3.4 | 0.2 | 1.5 | 2.4 | 0.9 | — | 15.4 | ... | 1.6 | 5.1 | Electricité consommée |
| Employees as a percent of engaged | 90.7 | 92.1 | 95.6 | 77.4 | 81.0 | 92.7 | 81.6 | 96.6 | 97.3 | 94.1 | 90.4 | 91.4 | Salariés en pourcentage des personnes occupées |
| Value added per unit of wages and salaries | 1.79 | 1.90 | 1.85 | 2.20 | 1.74 | 1.69 | 1.75 | 2.11 | 1.95 | 1.69 | 1.70 | 1.59 | Valeur ajoutée par unité de traitements et salaires |
| Wages and salaries per employee | 3.2 | 3.0 | 3.2 | 2.0 | 2.8 | 3.6 | 2.5 | 3.6 | 4.1 | 3.9 | 3.2 | 2.6 | Traitements et salaires par salarié |

[1] Footwear classified with Leather products (ISIC major group 29) instead of Clothing, footwear and made-up textiles (ISIC major group 24).
[2] Includes electricity consumed by mines and quarries.
[3] Excludes Petroleum refineries (ISIC group 321).
[4] Excludes Motor vehicle repair (ISIC group 384).

[1] Les chaussures sont classés dans Ouvrages en cuir (CITI classe 29) et non dans Articles d'habillement, chaussures et ouvrages en tissu (CITI classe 24).
[2] Y compris l'électricité consommée dans les mines et carrières.
[3] Non compris les Raffineries de pétrole (CITI groupe 321).
[4] Y compris la Réparation des véhicules automobiles (CITI groupe 384).

## Gross Domestic Product and Gross Fixed Capital Formation

The estimates of gross domestic product and gross fixed capital formation shown in Table 1 are from the reply to the United Nations national accounts questionnaire by the Istituto Centrale di Statistica, Rome. Official estimates are published in *Annuario Statistico* and other publications of that Office. The Istituto Centrale di Statistica has adjusted the official estimates to the extent possible, to conform to the United Nations system of national accounts in replying to the United Nations questionnaire.

## Index Numbers of Industrial Production

The index numbers set out in Table 2 were compiled from various issues of the *Annuario Statistico*, the *Boletino Mensile di Statistica* and the *Compendio Statistico*, of the Istituto Centrale di Statistica, Rome. The index numbers in these tables for the years, 1938-60, are the annual indexes of the Istituto which are based on a greater number of indicators of output (e.g. the addition of data on the output of sugar, butter and cheese, beer, artificial silk, etc.) than its monthly indexes. The index numbers shown in Table 2 for 1961 are annual averages of these monthly series.

All the index numbers of volume of production are base-weighted arithmetic averages. The weighting bases are 1938 for the index numbers for 1938-52 and 1953 for those for later years. In each case, the weights utilized consist of gross value of output during the base year in combining indicators of the output of individual commodities into index numbers for detailed categories of industrial activity and of value added, at factor cost, in combining index numbers for the detailed categories into indexes for sub-groups and then for groups of industrial activity. However, in aggregating the group indexes into index numbers for the broader classes (major groups and divisions) of industrial activity, the contribution to the net domestic product, at factor cost, serves as weights. The indicators of outputs are quantities produced except that for diesel engine and electrical machinery manufacturing, man-hours worked are employed and for construction and repair of ships, the weight of the materials assembled and installed is utilized.

Detailed description of the index numbers of production may be found in the following publications: Indexes based on 1938, *Supplement to the Monthly Bulletin of Statistics,* Statistical Office of the United Nations, 1954; indexes based on 1953, *Numeri Indici della Produzione Industriale,* Series A, No. 1, October 1957 and *Annuario Statistico, 1955,* Istituto Centrale di Statistica, Rome.

## Produit intérieur brut et formation brute de capital fixe

Les estimations du produit intérieur brut et de la formation brute de capital fixe reproduites au tableau 1 ont été tirées de la réponse de l'Istituto Centrale di Statistica, Rome, au questionnaire de l'O.N.U. relatif aux comptes nationaux. Des estimations officielles ont paru dans *Annuario Statistico* et dans d'autres publications du même Bureau. Pour remplir le questionnaire, l'Istituto a ajusté les estimations officielles afin de les rendre aussi conformes que possible au système de comptabilité nationale de l'O.N.U.

## Indices de la production industrielle

Les indices du tableau 2 sont tirés de différents numéros de l'*Annuario Statistico*, du *Bolletino Mensile di Statistica* et du *Compendio Statistico*, publiés par l'Istituto Centrale di Statistica, Rome. Les indices annuels du tableau 2 pour 1938-60 sont les indices annuels de l'Istituto, qui sont fondés sur un plus grand nombre d'indicateurs de la production (par exemple, par addition de données sur la production du sucre, du beurre et du fromage, de la bière, de la soie artificielle) que ses indices mensuels. Les indices du tableau 2 pour 1961 sont des moyennes annuelles de ces séries mensuelles.

Tous les indices du volume de la production sont des moyennes arithmétiques à pondération fixe. Les bases de pondération sont 1938 pour les indices de 1938-52 et 1953 pour les années suivantes. Dans tous les cas, on a pris comme poids: a) la valeur brute de la production pendant l'année de référence pour combiner les indicateurs du volume de la production de chaque marchandise en indices de catégorie; b) la valeur ajoutée, au coût des facteurs, pour combiner ces indices de catégorie en indices de sous-groupe, puis ces indices de sous-groupe en indices de groupe. Cependant, pour passer des indices de groupe aux indices de subdivisions plus larges de l'activité économique (classes et branches), on a pondéré d'après la contribution au produit intérieur net, au coût des facteurs. Les indicateurs de la production sont les quantités produites, sauf pour la construction des moteurs diesel et la construction électrique où l'on a utilisé le nombre d'heures de travail effectuées, et pour la construction navale et la réparation des navires où l'on s'est servi du poids des pièces et des éléments montés ou installés.

Pour une description détaillée des indices de la production, se reporter aux publications suivantes: Indices base 1938, *Supplément au Bulletin mensuel de statistique,* Bureau de statistique de l'O.N.U., 1954; Indices base 1953, *Numeri Indici della Produzione Industriale,* Série A, No 1, octobre 1957, et *Annuario Statistico,* 1955, Istituto Centrale di Statistica, Rome.

### Index Numbers of Industrial Employment

The index numbers of industrial employment set out in Table 3, were compiled by the Statistical Office of the United Nations from absolute figures of employment. These absolute figures are published in *Statistica delle Miniere, Cave e Torbiere*, Direzione Generale della Miniere in the case of mining industries and *Rassegna di Statistiche del Lavoro*, Ministero del Lavoro e della Providenza Sociale in the case of other industrial activities.

All of the absolute figures utilized in compiling the indexes relate to the monthly average number of operatives (wage-earners) employed. In the case of the mining industries, the figures relate to the employment of operatives by mining units irrespective of size. In the case of most kinds of manufacturing and the electricity industry, the employment of local units with 10 or more operatives are covered in the figures. In the case of a few kinds of manufacturing, the employments of local units irrespective of size is included.

In view of the differences between the employment data for various kinds of manufacturing in the field of coverage, the Statistical Office of the United Nations computed indexes for manufacturing as a whole which are base-weighted arithmetic averages of the indexes for the individual categories of manufacturing. The weights for this purpose consisted of estimates of average employments during 1953, in the case of the index numbers for the period, 1948-55, and during 1958 in the case of the indexes for 1955 and later years. The two sets of indexes were linked to one another at 1955. For similar reasons, the Statistical Office of the United Nations employed the same procedure in combining the index numbers for mining, manufacturing and electricity into indexes for the total of these activities.

### The Characteristics and Structure of Industrial Activity

Censuses of all industrial and other kinds of units in business—one spread over the period 1937 through 1939, and the others taken as of 5 November 1951 and 16 October 1961—are the bases of the data set out in Table 4. The results of these three Censuses were published by the Istituto Centrale di Statistica, Rome, in *Censimento Industriale e Commerciale, 1937-40, Censimento Generale dell'Industria e del Commercio, 5 Novembre 1951* or *16 Ottobre 1961*, respectively. In the case of the last census, only Vol. 1, *Imprese unita locali, addetti* was available. Incomparabilities in data gathered occur not only between the first census and the last two censuses, but also between the different classes of industrial activity in the first census. Significant incomparabilities between the 1937-1940 Census and the two later censuses in the number of statistical units and the classification of data for these units result from the use of different statistical units—technical and ancillary units in the 1937-40 Census and the local units in the other censuses. Less significant incomparabilities are due to the change in the territory of Italy after World War II.

### Indices de l'emploi industriel

Les indices de l'emploi industriel reproduits au tableau 3, ont été calculés par le Bureau de Statistique de l'O.N.U. à partir de chiffres absolus de l'emploi. Ces chiffres absolus ont paru dans *Statistica delle Miniere, Cave e Torbiere*, Direzione Generale della Miniere en ce qui concerne les industries extractives et dans *Rassegna di Statistiche del Lavoro*, Ministero del Lavoro e della Providenza Sociale dans le cas des autres activités industrielles.

Tous les chiffres absolus qui ont servi au calcul de ces indices portent sur le nombre moyen mensuel d'ouvriers (salariés) employés. En ce qui concerne les industries extractives, les chiffres sont relatifs à l'emploi dans les unités extractives, quelle que soit leur dimension. Dans le cas de la plupart des industries manufacturières et de l'industrie de l'électricité, les chiffres absolus couvrent seulement l'emploi dans les unités locales de dix ouvriers ou plus. Dans le cas d'un nombre restreint de types d'activités manufacturières ils couvrent l'emploi dans toutes les unités quelle que soit leur dimension.

Vu les différences entre les données relatives à l'emploi pour diverses industries manufacturières, quant au champ couvert, le Bureau de Statistique de l'O.N.U. a calculé les indices de l'ensemble des industries manufacturières. Ces indices sont des moyennes arithmétiques à pondération fixe des indices de chaque catégorie manufacturière. Les coefficients de pondération utilisés sont les estimations des chiffres moyens de l'emploi en 1953, pour combiner les indices relatifs aux années 1948-55, et ceux en 1958 pour combiner les indices relatifs à 1955 et aux années suivantes. Les deux ensembles d'indices ont été reliés au niveau de 1955. Aux mêmes fins, le Bureau de Statistique de l'O.N.U. a employé les mêmes procédés pour combiner les indices pour les industries extractives, les industries manufacturières et les industries de l'électricité, en indices relatifs à l'ensemble de ces activités.

### Caractéristiques et la structure de l'activité industrielle

Les chiffres du tableau 4 sont tirés de recensements de tous les établissements, industriels et autres, en activité — le premier recensement s'étendant sur la période 1937-1939, et le second ayant été exécuté au 5 novembre 1951 et au 16 octobre 1961. Les résultats de ces deux recensements ont été publiés par l'Istituto Centrale di Statistica, Rome, dans *Censimento Industriale e Commerciale, 1937-40, Censimento Generale dell'Industria e del Commercio, 5 Novembre 1951* ou *16 Ottobre 1961*, respectivement. Dans le cas du dernier recensement, seulement Vol. I, *Imprese unita locali, addetti* était disponible. Des défauts de comparabilité apparaissent non seulement entre le premier recensement et les deux derniers recensements, mais aussi entre les différentes catégories de l'activité industrielle dans le premier recensement. Des défauts de comparabilité importants existent entre le recensement de 1937-40 et les deux derniers recensements en ce qui concerne le nombre des unités statistiques et le classement des données relatives à ces unités; ces défauts tiennent à ce que l'on a employé des unités statistiques différentes: unités techniques et auxiliaires pour le recensement de

Comparability between classes of industrial activity in data from the 1937-40 Census is limited by the fact that census days were spread over the years, 1937 through 1939. Despite this the Italian authorities felt that considerable biases would not be introduced by summing the data for different classes of industry.

However, the use of the same coverage and definitions for identical items of data preserves some degree of comparability between the last two censuses and the 1937-1940 Census. These definitions are consistent with the International Standards in Basic Industrial Statistics except for the exclusion of homeworkers from the count of persons engaged. The figures of the capacity of installed power equipment shown in Table 4, except for the electricity producing industry, are the sums of the rated horsepower of prime movers driving machinery other than electric generators and all electric motors that were in use and in reserve as of the census days. For electricity producing enterprises, these figures measure the capacity of all installed prime movers.

The figures of value added in all industrial enterprises that are set out in Table 5 were compiled from estimates of the Istituto Centrale di Statistica obtained from the following sources: *Indagine Statistica sullo sviluppo del reddito nazionale dell'Italia dal 1861 al 1956* and *Annuario di Statistiche Industriali, 1956* or *1959* and correspondence with the Istituto. The data on value added relate to industrial enterprises and not to industrial local units or technical and ancillary units and therefore are not comparable with any of the figures of Table 4. The figures of value added represent the contribution of each class of industrial activity to the gross domestic product at factor cost.

1937-40 et unités locales pour les autres recensements. Les modifications apportées aux frontières italiennes après la deuxième guerre mondiale ont, de leur côté, entraîné des défauts de comparabilité moins sensibles. La comparabilité entre catégories d'activité industrielle dans le recensement de 1937-40 est limitée du fait que les jours de recensement ont été étalés sur trois ans (de 1937 à 1939). Quoi qu'il en soit, les autorités italiennes ont estimé que l'on ne risquerait pas de graves erreurs à ajouter les données des différentes catégories.

Cependant, l'identité de couverture et de définition des rubriques des questionnaires assure en tout état de cause une certaine comparabilité entre les deux derniers recensements et le recensement de 1937-1940. Ces définitions sont compatibles avec les Normes internationales relatives aux statistiques industrielles de base, sauf que les travailleurs à domicile ne sont pas comptés parmi les personnes occupées. La puissance installée indiquée au tableau 4 — à l'exception de la production d'électricité — est égale à la puissance nominale des moteurs primaires entraînant des machines autres que des générateurs électriques, plus celle de tous les moteurs électriques en service ou en réserve au jour du recensement. Pour le secteur de la production d'électricité, la puissance installée est la puissance de tous les moteurs primaires installés.

Les chiffres de la valeur ajoutée de toutes les entreprises industrielles, donnés au tableau 5 sont tirés des estimations de l'Istituto Centrale di Statistica et proviennent des sources suivantes: *Indagine Statistica sullo sviluppo del reddito nazionale dell'Italia dal 1861 al 1956* et *Annuario di Statistiche Industriali, 1956* ou *1959*, ainsi que d'un échange de correspondance avec l'Istituto. Les chiffres de la valeur ajoutée se rapportent aux entreprises industrielles et non aux unités locales ou aux unités techniques ou auxiliaires et ils ne sont donc pas comparables aux chiffres du tableau 4. Ils représentent la contribution de chaque catégorie d'activité industrielle au produit intérieur brut, au coût des facteurs.

## 1. THE GROSS DOMESTIC PRODUCT AND GROSS DOMESTIC FIXED CAPITAL FORMATION
## LE PRODUIT INTERIEUR BRUT ET LA FORMATION BRUTE DE CAPITAL FIXE INTERIEUR

Thousand million Lire                                  Milliards de lires

### A. Expenditure on the Gross Domestic Product at Market Prices
### Dépenses relatives au produit intérieur brut aux prix du marché

| Item of data and year / Rubrique et année | Total | Consumption / Consommation | | Gross Domestic Capital Formation / Formation brute de capital intérieur | | Net exports of goods and services / Exportations nettes de biens et de services | |
|---|---|---|---|---|---|---|---|
| | | Total | Government / Etat | Total | Fixed / Fixe | Exports less imports / Exportations moins importations | Exports / Exportations |
| *a. At Current Prices — Aux prix courants* | | | | | | | |
| **Absolute figures — Chiffres absolus** | | | | | | | |
| 1948 | 7 470 | 6 350 | 1 003 | 1 342 | 1 378 | −222 | 717 |
| 1950 | 8 756 | 7 188 | 982 | 1 650 | 1 527 | −82 | 941 |
| 1951 | 10 150 | 8 238 | 1 191 | 2 083 | 1 860 | −171 | 1 248 |
| 1952 | 10 771 | 9 108 | 1 457 | 2 091 | 2 101 | −428 | 1 122 |
| 1953 | 11 802 | 9 887 | 1 544 | 2 284 | 2 254 | −369 | 1 289 |
| 1954 | 12 596 | 10 372 | 1 717 | 2 489 | 2 454 | −265 | 1 391 |
| 1955 | 13 790 | 11 100 | 1 887 | 2 940 | 2 750 | −250 | 1 576 |
| 1956 | 14 857 | 11 984 | 2 099 | 3 151 | 3 046 | −278 | 1 850 |
| 1957 | 15 942 | 12 661 | 2 233 | 3 518 | 3 434 | −237 | 2 263 |
| 1958 | 17 059 | 13 409 | 2 501 | 3 576 | 3 481 | 74 | 2 348 |
| 1959 | 18 213 | 14 051 | 2 695 | 3 935 | 3 786 | 227 | 2 605 |
| 1960 | 19 861 | 15 185 | 2 950 | 4 746 | 4 441 | −70 | 3 197 |
| 1961 | 21 806 | 16 419 | 3 225 | 5 358 | 5 058 | 29 | 3 677 |
| **Percentage distribution of average annual expenditure — Distribution en pourcentage des dépenses annuelles moyennes** | | | | | | | |
| 1948 | 100.0 | 85.0 | 13.4 | 18.0 | 18.4 | −3.0 | 9.6 |
| 1950−1960 | 100.0 | 80.1 | 13.8 | 21.1 | 20.2 | −1.2 | 12.9 |
| 1950 | 100.0 | 82.1 | 11.2 | 18.8 | 17.4 | −0.9 | 10.7 |
| 1953 | 100.0 | 83.8 | 13.1 | 19.3 | 19.1 | −3.1 | 10.9 |
| 1954 | 100.0 | 82.3 | 13.6 | 19.8 | 19.5 | −2.1 | 11.0 |
| 1958 | 100.0 | 78.6 | 14.7 | 21.0 | 20.4 | 0.4 | 13.8 |
| 1960 | 100.0 | 76.4 | 14.8 | 23.9 | 22.4 | −0.3 | 16.3 |
| *b. At Prices of 1954 — Aux prix de 1954* | | | | | | | |
| **Absolute figures — Chiffres absolus** | | | | | | | |
| 1948 | 8 918 | 7 630 | 1 207 | 1 524 | 1 559 | −236 | 695 |
| 1950 | 10 065 | 8 360 | 1 137 | 1 862 | 1 729 | −157 | 992 |
| 1951 | 10 833 | 8 841 | 1 278 | 2 102 | 1 890 | −110 | 1 108 |
| 1952 | 11 139 | 9 366 | 1 501 | 2 085 | 2 095 | −312 | 1 066 |
| 1953 | 11 977 | 10 019 | 1 550 | 2 295 | 2 265 | −337 | 1 281 |
| 1954 | 12 596 | 10 372 | 1 717 | 2 489 | 2 454 | −265 | 1 391 |
| 1955 | 13 445 | 10 743 | 1 761 | 2 895 | 2 706 | −193 | 1 594 |
| 1956 | 13 995 | 11 175 | 1 842 | 3 030 | 2 927 | −210 | 1 805 |
| 1957 | 14 850 | 11 623 | 1 916 | 3 277 | 3 196 | −50 | 2 206 |
| 1958 | 15 504 | 12 080 | 2 127 | 3 336 | 3 241 | 88 | 2 311 |
| 1959 | 16 671 | 12 690 | 2 198 | 3 726 | 3 568 | 255 | 2 691 |
| 1960 | 17 863 | 13 547 | 2 336 | 4 441 | 4 122 | −125 | 3 226 |
| 1961 | 19 268 | 14 440 | 2 448 | 4 910 | 4 598 | −82 | 3 768 |
| **Percentage distribution of average annual expenditure — Distribution en pourcentage des dépenses annuelles moyennes** | | | | | | | |
| 1948 | 100.0 | 85.5 | 13.5 | 17.1 | 17.5 | −2.6 | 78 |
| 1950−1960 | 100.0 | 79.7 | 13.0 | 21.2 | 20.3 | −0.9 | 13.2 |
| 1950 | 100.0 | 83.1 | 11.3 | 18.5 | 17.2 | −1.6 | 9.9 |
| 1953 | 100.0 | 83.6 | 12.9 | 19.2 | 18.9 | −2.8 | 10.7 |
| 1954 | 100.0 | 82.3 | 13.6 | 19.8 | 19.5 | −2.1 | 11.1 |
| 1958 | 100.0 | 77.9 | 13.7 | 21.5 | 20.9 | 0.6 | 14.9 |
| 1960 | 100.0 | 75.8 | 13.0 | 24.9 | 23.0 | −0.7 | 18.2 |
| **Average annual rate of growth — Taux annuel moyen d'accroissement** | | | | | | | |
| 1948−1953 | 6.1 | 5.6 | 5.1 | 8.5 | 7.8 | . | 13.0 |
| 1950−1960 | 5.9 | 5.0 | 7.5 | 9.1 | 9.1 | . | 12.5 |
| 1950−1953 | 6.0 | 6.2 | 10.9 | 7.2 | 9.4 | . | 8.9 |
| 1954−1958 | 5.3 | 3.9 | 5.5 | 7.6 | 7.2 | . | 13.5 |
| 1958−1960 | 7.3 | 5.9 | 4.8 | 15.4 | 12.8 | . | 18.2 |

## B. The Gross Domestic Product at Factor Cost According to Origin
### Originie par secteur d'activité du produit intérieur brut au coût des facteurs

| Item of data and year / Rubrique et année | Total | Agricultural sector / Secteur agricole | Industrial Sector — Secteur Industriel | | | | | Transportation and communication / Transport et communication | Other sectors [1] / Autres secteurs [1] |
|---|---|---|---|---|---|---|---|---|---|
| | | | Total | Mining / Industries extractives | Manufacturing / Industries manufacturières | Construction / Bâtiments et travaux publics | Electricity, gas and water / Electricité, gaz et eau | | |
| ISIC — CITI | 0–9 | 0 | 1–5 | 1 | 2–3 | 4 | 5 | 7 | 6, 8–9 |

### a. At Current Prices — Aux prix courants

| Item of data and year | Total | Agric. | Total | Mining | Manuf. | Constr. | Elec. | Transp. | Other |
|---|---|---|---|---|---|---|---|---|---|
| **Absolute figures – Chiffres absolus** | | | | | | | | | |
| 1948 | 6 755 | 2 248 | 2 427 | 56 | 2 030 | 198 | 143 | 393 | 1 687 |
| 1950 | 7 728 | 2 234 | 2 946 | 84 | 2 428 | 240 | 194 | 479 | 2 069 |
| 1951 | 8 928 | 2 332 | 3 748 | 101 | 3 114 | 306 | 227 | 534 | 2 314 |
| 1952 | 9 439 | 2 352 | 3 889 | 112 | 3 113 | 399 | 265 | 596 | 2 602 |
| 1953 | 10 496 | 2 678 | 4 249 | 116 | 3 305 | 534 | 294 | 665 | 2 904 |
| 1954 | 11 090 | 2 666 | 4 587 | 132 | 3 503 | 632 | 320 | 713 | 3 124 |
| 1955 | 12 134 | 2 820 | 5 068 | 154 | 3 816 | 756 | 342 | 799 | 3 447 |
| 1956 | 12 997 | 2 736 | 5 443 | 181 | 4 064 | 837 | 361 | 899 | 3 919 |
| 1957 | 14 002 | 2 837 | 5 912 | 195 | 4 362 | 978 | 377 | 962 | 4 291 |
| 1958 | 15 013 | 3 011 | 6 258 | 184 | 4 602 | 1 072 | 400 | 1 013 | 4 731 |
| 1959 | 15 961 | 3 033 | 6 791 | 189 | 4 987 | 1 177 | 438 | 1 075 | 5 062 |
| 1960 | 17 497 | 2 993 | 7 634 | 195 | 5 668 | 1 276 | 495 | 1 222 | 5 648 |
| 1961 | 19 115 | 3 297 | 8 467 | 208 | 6 327 | 1 405 | 527 | 1 331 | 6 020 |
| **Percentage distribution according to sector— Distribution en pourcentage par secteur** | | | | | | | | | |
| 1948 | 100.0 | 33.3 | 35.9 | 0.8 | 30.1 | 2.9 | 2.1 | 5.8 | 25.0 |
| 1950 – 1960 | 100.0 | 21.9 | 41.8 | 1.2 | 31.8 | 6.1 | 2.7 | 6.6 | 29.7 |
| 1950 | 100.0 | 28.9 | 38.1 | 1.1 | 31.4 | 3.1 | 2.5 | 6.2 | 26.8 |
| 1953 | 100.0 | 25.5 | 40.5 | 1.1 | 31.5 | 5.1 | 2.8 | 6.3 | 27.7 |
| 1954 | 100.0 | 24.0 | 41.4 | 1.2 | 31.6 | 5.7 | 2.9 | 6.4 | 28.2 |
| 1958 | 100.0 | 20.0 | 41.7 | 1.2 | 30.7 | 7.1 | 2.7 | 6.8 | 31.5 |
| 1960 | 100.0 | 17.1 | 43.6 | 1.1 | 32.6 | 7.1 | 2.8 | 7.0 | 32.3 |

### b. At Prices of 1954 — Aux prix de 1954

| Item of data and year | Total | Agric. | Total | Mining | Manuf. | Constr. | Elec. | Transp. | Other |
|---|---|---|---|---|---|---|---|---|---|
| **Absolute figures – Chiffres absolus** | | | | | | | | | |
| 1948 | 7 574 | 2 071 | 2 405 | 54 | 1 927 | 213 | 211 | 501 | 2 597 |
| 1950 | 8 724 | 2 391 | 3 033 | 67 | 2 452 | 284 | 230 | 546 | 2 754 |
| 1951 | 9 471 | 2 502 | 3 506 | 82 | 2 802 | 353 | 269 | 598 | 2 865 |
| 1952 | 9 758 | 2 551 | 3 704 | 99 | 2 872 | 451 | 282 | 628 | 2 875 |
| 1953 | 10 712 | 2 848 | 4 124 | 117 | 3 153 | 556 | 298 | 676 | 3 064 |
| 1954 | 11 090 | 2 666 | 4 587 | 132 | 3 503 | 632 | 320 | 713 | 3 124 |
| 1955 | 11 847 | 2 830 | 5 015 | 158 | 3 818 | 700 | 339 | 768 | 3 234 |
| 1956 | 12 315 | 2 782 | 5 355 | 206 | 4 063 | 731 | 355 | 814 | 3 364 |
| 1957 | 12 882 | 2 774 | 5 765 | 231 | 4 344 | 822 | 368 | 851 | 3 492 |
| 1958 | 13 671 | 3 134 | 6 028 | 237 | 4 508 | 882 | 401 | 878 | 3 631 |
| 1959 | 14 635 | 3 217 | 6 692 | 253 | 5 041 | 968 | 430 | 913 | 3 813 |
| 1960 | 15 718 | 3 055 | 7 518 | 267 | 5 755 | 1 012 | 484 | 1 002 | 4 143 |
| 1961 | 16 897 | 3 278 | 8 219 | 286 | 6 328 | 1 088 | 517 | 1 065 | 4 335 |
| **Percentage distribution according to sector— Distribution en pourcentage par secteur** | | | | | | | | | |
| 1948 | 100.0 | 27.3 | 31.8 | 0.7 | 25.5 | 2.8 | 2.8 | 6.6 | 34.3 |
| 1950 – 1960 | 100.0 | 23.5 | 42.3 | 1.4 | 32.4 | 5.6 | 2.9 | 6.4 | 27.8 |
| 1950 | 100.0 | 27.4 | 34.8 | 0.8 | 28.1 | 3.3 | 2.6 | 6.2 | 31.6 |
| 1953 | 100.0 | 26.6 | 38.5 | 1.1 | 29.4 | 5.2 | 2.8 | 6.3 | 28.6 |
| 1954 | 100.0 | 24.0 | 41.4 | 1.2 | 31.6 | 5.7 | 2.9 | 6.4 | 28.2 |
| 1958 | 100.0 | 22.9 | 44.1 | 1.7 | 33.0 | 6.5 | 2.9 | 6.4 | 26.6 |
| 1960 | 100.0 | 19.4 | 47.9 | 1.7 | 36.8 | 6.3 | 3.1 | 6.4 | 26.3 |
| **Average annual rate of growth—Taux annuel moyen d'accroissement** | | | | | | | | | |
| 1948 – 1953 | 7.2 | 6.5 | 11.4 | 16.7 | 10.3 | 21.1 | 7.1 | 6.2 | 3.4 |
| 1950 – 1960 | 6.1 | 2.5 | 9.5 | 14.8 | 8.9 | 13.6 | 7.7 | 6.3 | 4.2 |
| 1950 – 1953 | 7.1 | 6.0 | 10.8 | 20.4 | 8.7 | 25.1 | 9.0 | 7.4 | 3.6 |
| 1954 – 1958 | 5.4 | 4.1 | 7.1 | 15.7 | 6.5 | 8.7 | 5.8 | 5.3 | 3.8 |
| 1958 – 1960 | 7.2 | −1.0 | 11.7 | 6.1 | 13.0 | 7.1 | 9.9 | 6.8 | 6.8 |

[1] Includes total subsidies, less total banking and insurance service charges, each of which are not distributed according to sector.

[1] Y compris la totalité des subventions, moins le coût des services des banques et des assurances lesquels ne sont pas distribués suivant le secteur d'activité.

### C.  Gross Domestic Fixed Capital Formation According to Purchasing Sector

### La formation brute de capital fixe intérieur par secteur d'acquisition

| Item of data and year<br>Rubrique et année | Total | Agricultural sector<br>Secteur agricole | Industrial sector— Secteur industriel | | | | Transportation and communication<br>Transport et communication | Other sectors<br>Autres secteurs |
| --- | --- | --- | --- | --- | --- | --- | --- | --- |
| | | | Total | Mining<br>Industries extractives | Manufacturing and construction<br>Industries manufacturières et bâtiment et travaux publics | Electricity, gas and water<br>Electricité, gaz et eau | | |
| ISIC — CITI | 0–9 | 0 | 1–5 | 1 | 2–3, 4 | 5 | 7 | 6, 8–9 |
| | | | | | | | | |
| | | | | *a.* At Current Prices — Aux prix courants | | | | |
| Absolute figures — Chiffres absolus | | | | | | | | |
| 1948............ | 1 378 | ... | ... | ... | ... | ... | ... | ... |
| 1950............ | 1 527 | 180 | 585 | 36 | 395 | 154 | 270 | 492 |
| 1951............ | 1 860 | 265 | 717 | 51 | 497 | 169 | 270 | 608 |
| 1952............ | 2 101 | 270 | 791 | 61 | 568 | 162 | 310 | 730 |
| 1953............ | 2 254 | 310 | 740 | 55 | 535 | 150 | 358 | 846 |
| 1954............ | 2 454 | 337 | 750 | 50 | 550 | 150 | 414 | 953 |
| 1955............ | 2 750 | 372 | 847 | 60 | 630 | 157 | 424 | 1 107 |
| 1956............ | 3 046 | 373 | 945 | 70 | 705 | 170 | 498 | 1 230 |
| 1957............ | 3 434 | 404 | 1 068 | 65 | 836 | 167 | 494 | 1 468 |
| 1958............ | 3 481 | 414 | 1 027 | 62 | 742 | 223 | 477 | 1 563 |
| 1959............ | 3 786 | 450 | 1 086 | 86 | 772 | 228 | 561 | 1 689 |
| 1960............ | 4 441 | 538 | 1 309 | 105 | 978 | 226 | 747 | 1 847 |
| 1961............ | 5 058 | 539 | 1 590 | 122 | 1 241 | 227 | 892 | 2 037 |
| Percentage distribution according to sector— Distribution en pourcentage par secteur | | | | | | | | |
| 1950 – 1960..... | 100.0 | 12.5 | 31.8 | 2.3 | 23.2 | 6.3 | 15.5 | 40.2 |
| 1950............ | 100.0 | 11.8 | 38.3 | 2.3 | 25.9 | 10.1 | 17.7 | 32.2 |
| 1953............ | 100.0 | 13.8 | 32.8 | 2.5 | 23.7 | 6.6 | 15.9 | 37.5 |
| 1954............ | 100.0 | 13.7 | 30.6 | 2.1 | 22.4 | 6.1 | 16.9 | 38.8 |
| 1958............ | 100.0 | 11.9 | 29.5 | 1.8 | 21.3 | 6.4 | 13.7 | 44.9 |
| 1960............ | 100.0 | 12.1 | 29.5 | 2.4 | 22.0 | 5.1 | 16.8 | 41.6 |
| | | | | | | | | |
| | | | | *b.* At Prices of 1954 — Aux prix de 1954 | | | | |
| Absolute figures — Chiffres absolus | | | | | | | | |
| 1950............ | 1 729 | 207 | 633 | 39 | 427 | 167 | 291 | 598 |
| 1951............ | 1 890 | 277 | 701 | 50 | 486 | 165 | 264 | 648 |
| 1952............ | 2 095 | 271 | 770 | 59 | 553 | 158 | 303 | 751 |
| 1953............ | 2 265 | 305 | 735 | 54 | 531 | 150 | 359 | 866 |
| 1954............ | 2 456 | 337 | 750 | 50 | 550 | 150 | 414 | 955 |
| 1955............ | 2 706 | 361 | 832 | 59 | 618 | 155 | 433 | 1 080 |
| 1956............ | 2 927 | 354 | 904 | 67 | 676 | 161 | 499 | 1 170 |
| 1957............ | 3 196 | 373 | 987 | 60 | 776 | 151 | 487 | 1 349 |
| 1958............ | 3 241 | 379 | 949 | 58 | 690 | 201 | 478 | 1 435 |
| 1959............ | 3 568 | 415 | 1 013 | 81 | 725 | 207 | 577 | 1 563 |
| 1960............ | 4 122 | 491 | 1 202 | 97 | 906 | 199 | 770 | 1 659 |
| 1961............ | 4 598 | 482 | 1 411 | 109 | 1 109 | 193 | 925 | 1 780 |
| Percentage distribution according to sector— Distribution en pourcentage par secteur | | | | | | | | |
| 1950 – 1960..... | 100.0 | 12.5 | 31.4 | 2.2 | 23.0 | 6.2 | 16.1 | 40.0 |
| 1950............ | 100.0 | 12.0 | 36.6 | 2.3 | 24.7 | 9.6 | 16.8 | 34.6 |
| 1953............ | 100.0 | 13.5 | 32.4 | 2.4 | 23.4 | 6.6 | 15.9 | 38.2 |
| 1954............ | 100.0 | 13.7 | 30.5 | 2.0 | 22.4 | 6.1 | 16.9 | 38.9 |
| 1958............ | 100.0 | 11.7 | 29.3 | 1.8 | 21.3 | 6.2 | 14.7 | 44.3 |
| 1960............ | 100.0 | 11.9 | 29.2 | 2.4 | 22.0 | 4.8 | 18.7 | 40.2 |
| Average annual rate of growth—Taux annuel moyen d'accroissement | | | | | | | | |
| 1950 – 1960..... | 9.1 | 9.0 | 6.6 | 9.5 | 7.8 | 1.8 | 10.2 | 10.7 |
| 1950 – 1953..... | 9.4 | 13.8 | 5.1 | 11.5 | 7.5 | −3.5 | 7.3 | 13.1 |
| 1954 – 1958..... | 7.2 | 3.0 | 6.1 | 3.8 | 5.8 | 7.6 | 3.6 | 10.7 |
| 1958 – 1960..... | 12.8 | 13.8 | 12.5 | 29.3 | 14.6 | −0.5 | 27.1 | 7.5 |

# 2. INDEX NUMBERS OF INDUSTRIAL PRODUCTION
## INDICES DE LA PRODUCTION INDUSTRIELLE

## A. Selected Divisions of Industrial Activity
### Quelques branches de l'activité industrielle

| Period<br>Période | Total | Mining<br>Industries extractives | Manufacturing [1]<br>Industries manufacturières [1] | Electricity and gas<br>Electricité et gaz |
|---|---|---|---|---|
| ISIC — CITI | 1–3, 511–512 | 1 | 2–3 | 511–512 |
| *a. Indexes — Indices (1958 = 100)* | | | | |
| 1938......... | 43 | 35 | 44 | 37 |
| 1948......... | 44 | 29 | 43 | 54 |
| 1949......... | 47 | 32 | 47 | 50 |
| 1950......... | 54 | 36 | 54 | 58 |
| 1951......... | 62 | 43 | 62 | 68 |
| 1952......... | 64 | 52 | 64 | 72 |
| 1953......... | –70– | –62– | –70– | –75– |
| 1954......... | 77 | 68 | 77 | 81 |
| 1955......... | 84 | 76 | 84 | 86 |
| 1956......... | 90 | 87 | 90 | 91 |
| 1957......... | 96 | 98 | 96 | 95 |
| 1958......... | 100 | 100 | 100 | 100 |
| 1959......... | 111 | 106 | 112 | 106 |
| 1960......... | 128 | 112 | 129 | 121 |
| 1961......... | 140 | 120 | 142 | 129 |
| *b. Average Annual Rate of Change — Taux annuel moyen de variation* | | | | |
| 1938–1960.... | 5.1 | 5.4 | 5.0 | 5.5 |
| 1938–1948.... | 0.2 | –1.9 | –0.2 | 3.8 |
| 1950–1960.... | 9.0 | 12.0 | 9.1 | 7.6 |
| 1948–1953.... | 9.7 | 16.4 | 10.2 | 6.8 |
| 1954–1958.... | 6.8 | 10.1 | 6.8 | 5.4 |
| 1958–1960.... | 13.1 | 5.8 | 13.6 | 10.0 |

## B. The Major Groups of Mining
### Les classes de la branche Industries extractives

| Period<br>Période | All mining<br>Toutes industries extractives | Coal mining<br>Extraction du charbon | Metal mining<br>Extraction des minerals métalliques | Crude petroleum and natural gas<br>Pétrole brut et gaz naturel | Other mining<br>Autres industries extractives |
|---|---|---|---|---|---|
| ISIC — CITI | 1 | 11 | 12 | 13 | 14–19 |
| *a. Indexes — Indices (1958 = 100)* | | | | | |
| 1938....... | 35 | 102 | 68 | 1 | 75 |
| 1948....... | 29 | 130 | 46 | 2 | 58 |
| 1949....... | 32 | 137 | 50 | 4 | 60 |
| 1950....... | 36 | 127 | 54 | 7 | 67 |
| 1951....... | 43 | 144 | 60 | 13 | 72 |
| 1952....... | 52 | 135 | 68 | 22 | 81 |
| 1953....... | –62– | –132– | –72– | –34– | –87– |
| 1954....... | 68 | 120 | 80 | 43 | 90 |
| 1955....... | 76 | 112 | 88 | 55 | 96 |
| 1956....... | 87 | 108 | 97 | 73 | 98 |
| 1957....... | 98 | 104 | 102 | 92 | 102 |
| 1958....... | 100 | 100 | 100 | 100 | 100 |
| 1959....... | 106 | 117 | 92 | 116 | 101 |
| 1960....... | 112 | 94 | 93 | 126 | 106 |
| 1961....... | 120 | 128 | 92 | 131 | 122 |
| *b. Average Annual Rate of Change — Taux annuel moyen de variation* | | | | | |
| 1938–1960. | 5.4 | –0.4 | 1.4 | 24.6 | 1.6 |
| 1938–1948. | –1.9 | 2.5 | –3.8 | 7.2 | –2.5 |
| 1950–1960. | 12.0 | –3.0 | 5.6 | 33.5 | 4.7 |
| 1948–1953. | 16.4 | 0.3 | 9.4 | 76.2 | 8.4 |
| 1954–1958. | 10.1 | –4.5 | 5.7 | 23.5 | 2.7 |
| 1958–1960. | 5.8 | –3.0 | –3.6 | 12.2 | 3.0 |

[1] Does not cover production in the following classes of industrial activity: Clothing and made-up textiles (ISIC groups 243–244), Printing and publishing (ISIC major group 28) and Other manufacturing (ISIC major group 39).

[1] Ne comprend pas la production des industries suivantes: Articles d'habillement et ouvrages en tissu (CITI 243–244), Imprimerie et édition (CITI 28) et Autres industries manufacturières (CITI 39).

## C.  The Major Groups of Manufacturing — Les classes de la branche Industries manufacturières

| Period<br>Période | Manu-facturing [1]<br>Industries manufac-turières [1] | Food, beverages and tobacco<br>Industries alimen-taires, boissons, tabac | Textiles | Wood products and furniture<br>Bois et meubles | Paper and paper products<br>Papier et ouvrages en papier | Leather and leather products except wearing apparel<br>Cuir et articles en cuir, à l'exclusion des articles d'habillement | Rubber products<br>Ouvrages en caoutchouc | Chemicals and chemical, petroleum and coal products<br>Produits chimiques et dérivés du pétrole et du charbon | Non-metallic mineral products<br>Produits minéraux non métalliques | Basic metals<br>Métallurgie de base | Metal products<br>Ouvrages en métaux |
|---|---|---|---|---|---|---|---|---|---|---|---|
| ISIC — CITI | 2–3 | 20–22 | 23 | 25–26 | 27 | 29 | 30 | 31–32 | 33 | 34 | 35–38 |

### a.  Indexes — Indices (1958 = 100)

| | | | | | | | | | | | |
|---|---|---|---|---|---|---|---|---|---|---|---|
| 1938 | 44 | 52 | 82 | 53 | 56 | 90 | 54 | 25 | 38 | 39 | 41 |
| 1948 | 43 | 50 | 82 | 50 | 40 | 72 | 55 | 25 | 35 | 34 | 43 |
| 1949 | 47 | 59 | 84 | 55 | 51 | 74 | 62 | 29 | 37 | 33 | 48 |
| 1950 | 54 | 71 | 90 | 65 | 59 | 81 | 71 | 35 | 46 | 41 | 52 |
| 1951 | 62 | 73 | 95 | 74 | 64 | 73 | 81 | 46 | 50 | 53 | 58 |
| 1952 | 64 | 76 | 89 | 85 | 63 | 83 | 76 | 46 | 53 | 59 | 63 |
| 1953 | –70– | –78– | –95– | –88– | –71– | –81– | –86– | –56– | –62– | –58– | –70– |
| 1954 | 77 | 84 | 98 | 89 | 74 | 86 | 100 | 69 | 67 | 69 | 71 |
| 1955 | 84 | 93 | 90 | 94 | 81 | 82 | 104 | 76 | 81 | 86 | 81 |
| 1956 | 90 | 93 | 96 | 93 | 90 | 86 | 97 | 84 | 88 | 95 | 88 |
| 1957 | 96 | 95 | 104 | 97 | 98 | 95 | 102 | 89 | 95 | 106 | 97 |
| 1958 | 100 | 100 | 100 | 100 | 100 | 100 | 100 | 100 | 100 | 100 | 100 |
| 1959 | 112 | 110 | 110 | 114 | 112 | 114 | 115 | 119 | 111 | 108 | 108 |
| 1960 | 129 | 110 | 121 | 122 | 125 | 120 | 148 | 138 | 129 | 133 | 130 |
| 1961 | 142 | 110 | 121 | 132 | 137 | 132 | 164 | 155 | 140 | 145 | 148 |

### b.  Average Annual Rate of Change — Taux annuel moyen de variation

| | | | | | | | | | | | |
|---|---|---|---|---|---|---|---|---|---|---|---|
| 1938–1960 | 5.0 | 3.5 | 1.8 | 3.9 | 3.7 | 1.3 | 4.7 | 8.1 | 5.7 | 5.7 | 5.4 |
| 1938–1948 | –0.2 | –0.4 | 0.0 | –0.6 | –3.3 | –2.2 | 0.2 | — | –0.8 | –1.4 | 0.5 |
| 1950–1960 | 9.1 | 4.5 | 3.0 | 6.5 | 7.8 | 4.0 | 7.6 | 14.7 | 10.9 | 12.5 | 9.6 |
| 1948–1953 | 10.2 | 9.3 | 3.0 | 12.0 | 12.2 | 2.4 | 9.4 | 17.6 | 12.1 | 11.3 | 10.2 |
| 1954–1958 | 6.8 | 4.4 | 0.5 | 3.0 | 7.8 | 3.8 | — | 9.7 | 10.5 | 9.7 | 8.9 |
| 1958–1960 | 13.6 | 4.9 | 10.0 | 10.5 | 11.8 | 9.5 | 21.7 | 17.5 | 13.6 | 15.3 | 14.0 |

[1] Does not cover production in the following classes of industrial activity: Clothing and made-up textiles (ISIC groups 243-244), Printing and publishing (ISIC major group 28) and Other manufacturing (ISIC major group 39).

[1] Ne comprend pas la production des industries suivantes: Articles d'habillement et ouvrages en tissu (CITI 243-244), Imprimerie et édition (CITI 28) et Autres industries manufacturières (CITI 39).

## 3.  INDEX NUMBERS OF INDUSTRIAL EMPLOYMENT
## INDICES DE L'EMPLOI DANS L'INDUSTRIE

### A.  Selected Divisions of Industrial Activity
### Quelques branches de l'activité industrielle

| Period<br>Période | Total [1] | Mining<br>Industries extractives | Manufacturing [1]<br>Industries manufacturières [1] | Electricity and gas<br>Electricité et gaz |
|---|---|---|---|---|
| ISIC — CITI | 1–3, 511 | 1 | 2–3 | 511 |

#### a.  Indexes — Indices (1958 = 100)

| | | | | |
|---|---|---|---|---|
| 1948 | ... | ... | 90 | 88 |
| 1949 | ... | ... | 89 | 87 |
| 1950 | 90 | 95 | 90 | 88 |
| 1951 | 90 | 98 | 90 | 89 |
| 1952 | 91 | 108 | 91 | 90 |
| 1953 | 92 | 107 | 92 | 91 |
| 1954 | 95 | 105 | 95 | 95 |
| 1955 | 97 | 105 | 97 | 96 |
| 1956 | 99 | 104 | 99 | 98 |
| 1957 | 101 | 103 | 101 | 100 |
| 1958 | 100 | 100 | 100 | 100 |
| 1959 | 101 | 100 | 101 | 101 |
| 1960 | 108 | 103 | 108 | 102 |
| 1961 | ... | ... | 115 | 105 |

#### b. Average Annual Rate of Change — Taux annuel moyen de variation

| | | | | |
|---|---|---|---|---|
| 1950–1960 | 1.8 | 0.8 | 1.8 | 1.5 |
| 1948–1953 | ... | ... | 0.4 | 0.7 |
| 1954–1958 | 1.3 | –1.2 | 1.3 | 1.3 |
| 1958–1960 | 3.9 | 1.5 | 3.9 | 1.0 |

### B.  The Major Groups of Mining
### Les classes de la branche Industries extractives

| Period<br>Période | All mining<br>Toutes industries extractives | Coal mining<br>Extraction du charbon | Metal mining<br>Extraction des minerais métalliques | Crude petroleum and natural gas<br>Pétrole brut et gaz naturel | Other mining<br>Autres industries extractives |
|---|---|---|---|---|---|
| ISIC — CITI | 1 | 11 | 12 | 13 | 14–19 |

#### a.  Indexes — Indices (1958 = 100)

| | | | | | |
|---|---|---|---|---|---|
| 1950 | 95 | 257 | 104 | 46 | 81 |
| 1951 | 98 | 232 | 112 | 51 | 86 |
| 1952 | 108 | 236 | 126 | 64 | 96 |
| 1953 | 107 | 201 | 116 | 66 | 100 |
| 1954 | 105 | 178 | 104 | 74 | 102 |
| 1955 | 105 | 147 | 108 | 83 | 102 |
| 1956 | 104 | 114 | 108 | 125 | 98 |
| 1957 | 103 | 123 | 104 | 114 | 100 |
| 1958 | 100 | 100 | 100 | 100 | 100 |
| 1959 | 100 | 75 | 92 | 96 | 103 |
| 1960 | 103 | 60 | 87 | 91 | 110 |

#### b.  Average Annual Rate of Change — Taux annuel moyen de variation

| | | | | | |
|---|---|---|---|---|---|
| 1950–1960 | 0.8 | –13.6 | –1.8 | 7.1 | 3.1 |
| 1954–1958 | –1.2 | –13.4 | –1.0 | 7.8 | –0.5 |
| 1958–1960 | 1.5 | 22.5 | –6.7 | –4.6 | 4.9 |

For footnotes see end of table.
Pour les notes, voir au bas du tableau.

## C. The Major Groups of Manufacturing — Les classes de la branche Industries manufacturières

| Period / Période | Manu-facturing [1] / Industries manufac-turières [1] | Food / Industries alimen-taires | Textiles | Clothing, footwear and made-up textiles / Articles d'habil-lement, chaussures et ouvrages en tissu | Wood products / Bois | Paper and paper products / Papier et ouvrages en papier | Printing and publishing / Imprimerie et édition | Leather and leather products except wearing apparel / Cuir et articles en cuir, à l'exclu-sion des articles d'habil-lement | Rubber products / Ouvrages en caout-chouc | Chemicals and chemical products / Produits chi-miques | Non-metallic mineral products / Produits minéraux non métal-liques | Basic metals / Métal-lurgie de base | Metal products / Ouvrages en métaux |
|---|---|---|---|---|---|---|---|---|---|---|---|---|---|
| ISIC — CITI | 2–3 | 20 | 23 | 24 | 25 | 27 | 28 | 29 | 30 | 31 | 33 | 34 | 35–38 |

### a. Indexes — Indices (1958 = 100)

| | | | | | | | | | | | | | |
|---|---|---|---|---|---|---|---|---|---|---|---|---|---|
| 1948 | 90 | 73 | 135 | 79 | 69 | 98 | 71 | 142 | 116 | 84 | 78 | 102 | 86 |
| 1949 | 89 | 78 | 133 | 78 | 69 | 97 | 73 | 140 | 113 | 83 | 77 | 98 | 84 |
| 1950 | 90 | 83 | 129 | 78 | 75 | 97 | 76 | 130 | 112 | 82 | 80 | 94 | 85 |
| 1951 | 90 | 84 | 129 | 76 | 78 | 100 | 77 | 125 | 109 | 84 | 84 | 96 | 85 |
| 1952 | 91 | 85 | 124 | 77 | 84 | 103 | 78 | 122 | 106 | 85 | 88 | 96 | 85 |
| 1953 | 92 | 85 | 120 | 80 | 88 | 102 | 83 | 121 | 106 | 87 | 91 | 94 | 87 |
| 1954 | 95 | 88 | 117 | 83 | 98 | 103 | 86 | 117 | 109 | 91 | 96 | 92 | 90 |
| 1955 | 97 | 96 | 110 | 84 | 102 | 102 | 88 | 112 | 111 | 95 | 101 | 94 | 94 |
| 1956 | 99 | 97 | 106 | 88 | 104 | 102 | 93 | 106 | 111 | 98 | 100 | 100 | 99 |
| 1957 | 101 | 97 | 105 | 96 | 98 | 103 | 97 | 104 | 108 | 103 | 102 | 100 | 102 |
| 1958 | 100 | 100 | 100 | 100 | 100 | 100 | 100 | 100 | 100 | 100 | 100 | 100 | 100 |
| 1959 | 101 | 101 | 100 | 106 | 102 | 100 | 101 | 101 | 94 | 101 | 101 | 97 | 100 |
| 1960 | 108 | 104 | 105 | 116 | 106 | 102 | 106 | 109 | 104 | 107 | 104 | 102 | 110 |
| 1961 | 115 | 110 | 106 | 128 | 114 | 104 | 112 | 113 | 113 | 113 | 112 | 110 | 121 |

### b. Average Annual Rate of Change — Taux annuel moyen de variation

| | | | | | | | | | | | | | |
|---|---|---|---|---|---|---|---|---|---|---|---|---|---|
| 1950–1960 | 1.8 | 2.3 | −2.0 | 4.1 | 3.5 | 0.5 | 3.4 | −1.8 | −0.7 | 2.7 | 2.7 | 0.8 | 2.6 |
| 1948–1953 | 0.4 | 3.1 | −2.3 | 0.3 | 5.0 | 0.8 | 3.2 | −3.2 | −1.8 | 0.7 | 3.1 | −1.6 | 0.3 |
| 1954–1958 | 1.3 | 3.2 | −3.8 | 4.8 | 0.5 | −0.7 | 3.8 | −3.8 | −2.1 | 2.4 | 1.0 | 2.1 | 2.7 |
| 1958–1960 | 3.9 | 2.0 | 2.5 | 7.7 | 3.0 | 1.0 | 3.0 | 4.4 | 2.0 | 3.4 | 2.0 | 1.0 | 4.9 |

[1] Excludes Beverages (ISIC major group 21), Tobacco (ISIC major group 22), Furniture (ISIC major group 26), Petroleum and coal products (ISIC major group 32) and Miscellaneous manufactures (ISIC major group 39).

[1] Non compris les Industries des boissons (CITI 21), Tabac (CITI 22), Meubles (CITI 26), Dérivés du pétrole et du charbon (CITI 32) et Autres industries manufacturières (CITI 39).

## 4. CHARACTERISTICS OF ALL INDUSTRIAL UNITS
### Census days, 1937-1939, 5 November 1951 and 16 October 1961

## CARACTERISTIQUES DE TOUTES LES UNITES INDUSTRIELLES
### Journées de recensement 1937-1939, 5 novembre 1951 et 16 octobre 1961

Number of local units and other units in units; number of engaged and employees in thousands; wages and salaries paid in million Lire; capacity of installed power equipment in thousand horsepower; capacity of installed power equipment per person engaged in horsepower; wages and salaries per employee in thousand lire.

Nombre d'unités locales et autres unités en unités; nombre de personnes occupées et de salariés en milliers; traitements et salaires en millions de lires; puissance installée en milliers de chevaux-vapeur et puissance installée par personne occupée en chevaux-vapeur; traitements et salaires par salarié en milliers de lires.

### A. The Divisions of Industrial Activity — Les branches de l'activité industrielle

| Year and item of data | All industrial activity Toutes industries | Mining Industries ex-tractives | Manu-facturing[2] Industries manu-facturières[2] | Con-struction Bâtiment et travaux publics | Electricity and gas Electricité et gaz | Année et rubrique | Year and item of data | All industrial activity Toutes industries | Mining Industries ex-tractives | Manu-facturing Industries manu-facturières | Con-struction Bâtiment et travaux publics | Electricity and gas Electricité et gaz | Année et rubrique |
|---|---|---|---|---|---|---|---|---|---|---|---|---|---|
| ISIC | 1-4, 511-512 | 1 | 2-3 | 4 | 511-512 | CITI | ISIC | 1-4, 511-512 | 1 | 2-3 | 4 | 511-512 | CITI |
| | | a. Absolute Figures — Chiffres absolus | | | | | | | b. Structure | | | | |
| **1937 – 1939 [1]** Number of technical and ancillary units (as of census day)[3] | 788 172 | 11 353 | 705 160 | 68 699 | 2 960 | **1937 – 1939 [1]** Nombre des unités techniques et auxiliaires (au jour du recensement)[3] | **1937 – 1939** Distribution in percent of number of engaged | 100.0 | 3.3 | 81.0 | 14.8 | 0.9 | **1937 – 1939** Distribution en pourcentage du nombre de personnes occupées |
| Number of engaged (As of census day) | 4 083.8 | 138.5 | 3 306.4 | 605.1 | 33.8 | Nombre de personnes occupées (au jour du recensement) | Capacity of installed power equipment per person engaged | | 1.61 | 1.78 | 0.32 | 220.86 | Puissance installée par personne occupée |
| Number of employees (As of census day) | 3 324.8 | 126.8 | 2 634.6 | 529.6 | 33.8 | Nombre de salariés (au jour du recensement) | Employees as a percent of engaged | 81.4 | 91.6 | 79.7 | 87.5 | 100.0 | Salariés en pourcentage des personnes occupées |
| Wages and salaries (Calendar year preceding census day) | 10 780.2 | 386.6 | 8 455.4 | 1 704.4 | 233.8 | Traitements et salaires (l'année civile précédant le jour du recensement) | Wages and salaries per employee | 3.24 | 3.05 | 3.21 | 3.22 | 6.92 | Traitements et salaires par salarié |
| Capacity of installed power equipment (As of census day) | | 223 | 5 891 | 195 | 7 465 | Puissance installée (au jour du recensement) | | | | | | | |
| **5.XI.1951** Number of local units | 683 094 | 8 632 | 624 793 | 44 321 | 5 348 | **5.XI.1951** Nombre unités locales | **5.XI.1951** Distribution in percent of number of engaged | 100.0 | 2.8 | 82.2 | 13.1 | 1.9 | **5.XI.1951** Distribution en pourcentage du nombre de personnes occupées |
| Number of engaged | 4 216.7 | 121.1 | 3 463.5 | 553.0 | 79.1 | Nombre de personnes occupées | Capacity of installed power equipment per person engaged | | 3.58 | 2.89 | 0.69 | 142.86 | Puissance installée par personne occupée |
| Employees: Number | 3 307.6 | 109.4 | 2 625.0 | 496.0 | 77.2 | Salariés: Nombre | Employees as a percent of engaged | 78.4 | 90.3 | 75.8 | 89.7 | 97.6 | Salariés en pourcentage des personnes occupées |
| Wages and salaries (Calendar year preceding census day) | 1 020 417 | 34 691 | 843 399 | 96 266 | 46 061 | Traitements et salaires (l'année civile précédant le jour du recensement) | Wages and salaries per employee | 308.5 | 317.1 | 321.3 | 194.1 | 596.6 | Traitements et salaires par salarié |
| Capacity of installed power equipment | | 434 | 9 995 | 380 | 11 300 | Puissance installée | | | | | | | |
| **16.X.1961** Number of local units | 698 178 | 7 218 | 604 793 | 81 494 | 4 673 | **16.X.1961** Nombre d'unités locales | **16.X.1961** Distribution in percent of number of engaged | | | | | | **16.X.1961** Distribution en pourcentage du nombre de personnes occupées |
| Number of engaged | 5 596.3 | 103.8 | 4 484.0 | 918.9 | 89.6 | Nombre de personnes occupées | | 100.0 | 1.0 | 86.6 | 11.8 | 0.6 | |

[1] See Table 4B below for census day for mining and footnote 1, Table 4C below for census days for manufacturing. The census days were 31.XII.1938 for electricity production and distribution and 31.X.1938 for gasworks.
[2] Excluded are publishing and some very small units (e.g., those without employees) engaged in printing and in food, beverage and tobacco manufacturing.
[3] The statistical unit was the enterprise in the case of Construction (ISIC Division 4) and Electricity (ISIC group 511).

[1] Voir le tableau 4B ci-dessous pour la date du recensement des industries extractives et la note 1 du tableau 4C ci-dessous pour les dates du recensement des industries manufacturières. Le recensement des industries productrices et distributrices de l'électricité ayant été exécuté le 31.XII.1938, celui relatif aux industries du gaz le 31.X.1938.
[2] Non compris édition et quelques très petites unités (par exemple, celles sans salariés) engagées dans les industries de l'imprimerie de l'alimentation, des boissons et du tabac.
[3] Dans le cas du Bâtiment et travaux publics (CITI Branche 4) et de l'Electricité (CITI groupe 511) l'unité statistique adoptée était l'entreprise.

## B.  The Major Groups of Mining — Les classes de la branche Industries extractives

### a. Absolute Figures — Chiffres absolus

| Year and item of data | All mining — Toutes industries extractives | Coal mining — Extraction du charbon | Metal mining — Extraction des minerais métalliques | Crude petroleum and natural gas — Pétrole brut et gaz naturel | Other mining — Divers | Année et rubrique |
|---|---|---|---|---|---|---|
| SITC / ISIC | 1 | 11 | 12 | 13 | 14-19 | CITI |
| **30.VI.1938** | | | | | | **30.VI.1938** |
| Number of local units | 11 353 | 71 | 562 | 15 | 10 705 | Nombre d'unités locales |
| Number of engaged (as of census day) | 139.9 [1] | 22.8 | 30.9 | 0.6 | 84.2 | Nombre de personnes occupées (au jour du recensement) |
| Employees: Number (As of census day) | 126.8 [1] | 22.8 | 30.8 | 0.6 | 71.2 | Salariés: Nombre (au jour du recensement) |
| Wages and salaries (Calendar year preceding census day) | 386.6 [1] | 76.5 | 98.4 | 2.9 | 203.1 | Traitements et salaires (année civile précédant le jour du recensement) |
| Capacity of installed power equipment | 244 [1] | 43 | 64 | 5 | 111 | Puissance installée |
| **5.XI.1951** | | | | | | **5.XI.1951** |
| Number of local units | 8 632 | 95 | 227 | 211 | 8 099 | Nombre d'unités locales |
| Number of engaged | 121.1 | 20.0 | 23.8 | 4.3 | 73.0 | Nombre de personnes occupées |
| Employees: Number | 109.4 | 20.0 | 23.7 | 4.2 | 61.5 | Salariés: Nombre |
| Wages and salaries (Calendar year preceding census day) | 34 691 | 7 464 | 9 551 | 1 466 | 16 210 | Traitements et salaires (année civile précédant le jour du recensement) |
| Capacity of installed power equipment | 434 | 77 | 104 | 69 | 184 | Puissance installée |
| **16.X.1961** | | | | | | **16.X.1961** |
| Number of local units | 7 218 | 48 | 201 | 207 | 6 762 | Nombre d'unités locales |
| Number of engaged | 103.8 | 4.2 | 20.5 | 6.4 | 72.7 | Nombre de personnes occupées |

### b. Structure

| Year and item of data | All mining — Toutes industries extractives | Coal mining — Extraction du charbon | Metal mining — Extraction des minerais métalliques | Crude petroleum and natural gas — Pétrole brut et gaz naturel | Other mining — Divers | Année et rubrique |
|---|---|---|---|---|---|---|
| ISIC | 1 | 11 | 12 | 13 | 14-19 | CITI |
| **30.VI.1938** | | | | | | **30.VI.1938** |
| Distribution in percent of number of engaged | 100.0 | 16.4 | 22.3 | 0.5 | 60.8 | Distribution en pourcentage du nombre de personnes occupées |
| Capacity of installed power equipment per person engaged | 1.74 | 1.89 | 2.07 | 8.33 | 1.32 | Puissance installée par personne occupée |
| Employees as a percent of engaged | 90.6 | 100.0 | 99.7 | 100.0 | 84.6 | Salariés en pourcentage des personnes occupées |
| Wages and salaries per employee | 3.05 | 3.36 | 3.19 | 4.83 | 2.85 | Traitements et salaires par salarié |
| **5.XI.1951** | | | | | | **5.XI.1951** |
| Distribution in percent of number of engaged | 100.0 | 16.5 | 19.6 | 3.6 | 60.3 | Distribution en pourcentage du nombre de personnes occupées |
| Capacity of installed power equipment per person engaged | 3.58 | 3.85 | 4.37 | 16.05 | 2.52 | Puissance installée par personne occupée |
| Employees as a percent of engaged | 90.3 | 100.0 | 99.6 | 97.7 | 84.2 | Salariés en pourcentage des personnes occupées |
| Wages and salaries per employee | 317.1 | 373.2 | 403.0 | 349.0 | 263.6 | Traitements et salaires par salarié |
| **16.X.1961** | | | | | | **16.X.1961** |
| Distribution in percent of number of engaged | 100.0 | 0.6 | 2.9 | 2.8 | 93.7 | Distribution en pourcentage du nombre de personnes occupées |

[1] These figures do not equal the sum of the corresponding figures for each major group of mining because of the inclusion of the employment, wages and salaries paid and installed power capacity of ancillary mining units which were not allocated to a specific major group of mining

[1] Ces chiffres diffèrent de la somme des chiffres correspondants indiqués pour chacune des classes de la branche Industries extractives, du fait qu'on a inclus dans le total pour chaque rubrique—nombre de personnes occupées et de salariés, traitements et salaires payés et puissance installée—les unités extractives auxiliaires qui n'ont pas été rangées dans une classe déterminée de cette branche.

## C. The Major Groups of Manufacturing — Les classes de la branche Industries manufacturières

| Year and item of data | Manufacturing [2] Industries manufacturières [2] | Food beverages and tobacco [3] Industries alimentaires, boissons, tabac [3] | Textiles | Clothing, footwear and made-up textiles Articles d'habillement, chaussures et ouvrages en tissu | Wood products and furniture Bois et meubles | Paper and paper products Papier et ouvrages en papier | Printing [2] Imprimerie [2] | Leather and leather products except wearing apparel Cuir et articles en cuir, à l'exclusion des articles d'habillement | Rubber products Ouvrages en caoutchouc | Chemicals and chemical, petroleum and coal products Produits chimiques et dérivés du pétrole et du charbon | Non-metallic mineral products Produits minéraux non métalliques | Basic metals Métallurgie de base | Metal products Ouvrages en métaux | Other manufacturing Autres industries manufacturières | Année et rubrique |
|---|---|---|---|---|---|---|---|---|---|---|---|---|---|---|---|
| ISIC | 2–3 | 20–22 | 23 | 24 | 25–26 | 27 | 28 | 29 | 30 | 31–32 | 33 | 34 | 35–38 | 39 | CITI |

*a. Absolute Figures — Chiffres absolus*

| Year and item of data | | | | | | | | | | | | | | | Année et rubrique |
|---|---|---|---|---|---|---|---|---|---|---|---|---|---|---|---|
| **Census days, 1937–1939** [1] | | | | | | | | | | | | | | | **Journées de recensement, 1937–1939** [1] |
| Number of technical and ancillary units | 705 160 | 133 484 | 36 251 | 267 169 | 112 127 | 1 992 | 9 281 | 6 417 | 817 | 7 010 | 19 096 | 549 | 103 178 | 7 789 | Nombre d'unités techniques et auxiliaires |
| Number of engaged (As of census day) | 3 306.4 | 499.8 | 619.7 | 456.2 | 253.1 | 56.1 | 70.1 | 33.9 | 26.1 | 135.5 | 204.2 | 103.6 | 770.4 | 77.7 | Nombre de personnes occupées (au jour du recensement) |
| Number of employees (As of census day) | 2 634.6 | 397.0 | 579.6 | 159.3 | 114.3 | 54.0 | 61.5 | 26.4 | 25.1 | 128.2 | 177.6 | 103.4 | 738.7 | 69.5 | Nombre de salariés (au jour du recensement) |
| Wages and salaries paid (Calendar year preceding census day) | 8 455.4 | 785.1 | 1 615.4 | 255.8 | 266.5 | 178.1 | 272.0 | 92.4 | 95.8 | 555.1 | 538.5 | 575.2 | 2 974.3 | 251.2 | Traitements et salaires payés (année civile précédant le jour du recensement) |
| Capacity of installed power equipment (As of census day) | 5 891 | 905 | 1 040 | 31 | 196 | 261 | 42 | 52 | 78 | 620 | 382 | 1 074 | 1 128 | 82 | Puissance installée (au jour du recensement) |
| **5.XI.1951** | | | | | | | | | | | | | | | **5.XI.1951** |
| Number of local units | 624 793 | 78 676 | 38 519 | 212 652 | 109 661 | 2 127 | 7 411 | 6 600 | 1 751 | 6 835 | 17 517 | 1 005 | 131 478 | 10 561 | Nombre d'unités locales |
| Number of engaged | 3 463.5 | 412.6 | 650.0 | 395.1 | 290.8 | 63.4 | 74.5 | 38.6 | 40.1 | 199.8 | 202.4 | 145.1 | 856.3 | 94.8 | Nombre de personnes occupées |
| Number of employees | 2 625.0 | 285.7 | 609.9 | 139.7 | 137.3 | 60.0 | 63.0 | 28.9 | 37.8 | 190.6 | 175.0 | 143.9 | 674.5 | 78.7 | Nombre de salariés |
| Wages and salaries paid (Calander year preceding census day) | 843 399 | 81 071 | 165 120 | 21 809 | 26 948 | 18 945 | 25 018 | 8 558 | 18 388 | 80 851 | 49 976 | 67 428 | 257 624 | 21 663 | Traitements et salaires payés (année civile précédant le jour du recensement) |
| Capacity of installed power equipment | 9 995 | 1 508 | 1 211 | 66 | 522 | 420 | 76 | 110 | 198 | 1 259 | 714 | 1 792 | 2 011 | 108 | Puissance installée |
| **16.X.1961** | | | | | | | | | | | | | | | **16.X.1961** |
| Number of local units | 597 575 | 60 924 | 41 133 | 181 287 | 102 333 | 2 870 | 9 496 | 5 858 | 3 056 | 7 433 | 19 506 | 2 469 | 149 093 | 12 117 | Nombre d'unités locales |
| Number of engaged | 4 462.6 | 432.9 | 592.2 | 527.1 | 378.2 | 81.7 | 111.7 | 49.6 | 49.8 | 278.8 | 311.5 | 191.7 | 1 277.9 | 179.5 | Nombre de personnes occupées |

*b. Structure*

| Year and item of data | | | | | | | | | | | | | | | Année et rubrique |
|---|---|---|---|---|---|---|---|---|---|---|---|---|---|---|---|
| **Census days, 1937–1939** [1] | | | | | | | | | | | | | | | **Journées de recensement, 1937–1939** [1] |
| Distribution in percent of number of engaged | 100.0 | 15.1 | 18.7 | 13.8 | 7.7 | 1.7 | 2.1 | 1.0 | 0.8 | 4.1 | 6.2 | 3.1 | 23.3 | 2.4 | Répartition en pourcentage du nombre de personnes occupées |
| Capacity of installed power equipment per person engaged | 1.78 | 1.81 | 1.68 | 0.07 | 0.77 | 4.65 | 0.60 | 1.53 | 2.99 | 4.58 | 1.87 | 10.37 | 1.46 | 1.06 | Puissance installée par personne occupée |
| Employees as a percent of engaged | 79.7 | 79.4 | 93.5 | 34.9 | 45.2 | 96.3 | 87.7 | 77.9 | 96.2 | 94.6 | 87.0 | 99.8 | 95.9 | 89.4 | Salariés en pourcentage des personnes occupées |
| Wages and salaries per employee | 3.21 | 1.98 | 2.79 | 1.61 | 2.33 | 3.30 | 4.42 | 3.50 | 3.82 | 4.33 | 3.03 | 5.56 | 4.03 | 3.61 | Traitements et salaires par salarié |
| **5.XI.1951** | | | | | | | | | | | | | | | **5.XI.1951** |
| Distribution in percent of number of engaged | 100.0 | 11.9 | 18.7 | 11.4 | 8.4 | 1.9 | 2.1 | 1.1 | 1.2 | 5.8 | 5.8 | 4.2 | 24.7 | 2.8 | Répartition en pourcentage du nombre de personnes occupées |
| Capacity of installed power equipment per person engaged | 2.89 | 3.65 | 1.86 | 0.17 | 1.80 | 6.62 | 1.02 | 2.85 | 4.94 | 6.30 | 3.53 | 12.35 | 2.35 | 1.14 | Puissance installée par personne occupée |
| Employees as a percent of engaged | 75.8 | 69.2 | 93.8 | 35.3 | 47.2 | 94.6 | 84.6 | 74.9 | 94.3 | 95.4 | 86.5 | 99.2 | 78.8 | 83.0 | Salariés en pourcentage des personnes occupées |
| Wages and salaries per employee | 321.3 | 283.8 | 270.7 | 156.1 | 196.3 | 315.8 | 397.1 | 296.1 | 486.4 | 424.2 | 285.6 | 468.6 | 381.9 | 275.3 | Traitements et salaires par salarié |
| **16.X.1961** | | | | | | | | | | | | | | | **16.X.1961** |
| Distribution in percent of number engaged | 100.0 | 9.7 | 13.3 | 11.8 | 8.5 | 1.8 | 2.5 | 1.1 | 1.1 | 6.3 | 7.0 | 4.3 | 28.6 | 4.0 | Distribution en pourcentage du nombre de personnes occupées |

[1] Census days are as follows: 25.V, 30.VI, 1 or 25.VIII, or 15.X.1937 for ISIC major groups 20–22; 30.VI, 30.IX or 31.X.1938 for ISIC major group 23; 31.XII.1938 for ISIC major group 24; 30.XI or 31.XII.1938 for ISIC major groups 25–26; 31.X.1938 for ISIC major group 27; 31.X.1938 for ISIC major groups 28, 29 and 30; 31.V, 30.VI, 31.VIII or 31.X.1938 for ISIC major groups 31–32; 30.VI.1938 for ISIC major groups 33 and 34; 31.X.1938 or 30.IX.1939 for ISIC major groups 35–38, and 31.X or 31.XII.1938 for ISIC major group 39.

[2] Excluded are publishing and very small units (e.g. those without employees) in printing and in the manufacturing of food, beverages and tobacco.

[1] Le recensement a été effectué aux dates suivantes: 25.V, 30.VI, 1er ou 25.VIII, ou 15.X.1937 pour les classes 20–22 de la CITI; 30.VI, 30.IX ou 31.X.1938 pour la classe 23; 31.XII.1938 pour la classe 24; 30.XI ou 31.XII.1938 pour les classes 25–26; 31.X.1938 pour la classe 27; 31.X.1938 pour les classes 28, 29 et 30; 31.V, 30.VI, 31.VIII ou 31.X.1938 pour les classes 31–32; 30.VI.1938 pour les classes 33 et 34; 31.X.1938 ou 30.IX.1939 pour les classes 35–38, et 31.X ou 31.XII.1938 pour la classe 39.

[2] Non compris l'édition et les très petites unités (par exemple celles qui n'ont pas de salariés) dont l'activité rentre dans les classes Imprimerie et Industries alimentaires, boissons, tabac.

## 5. VALUE ADDED IN ALL INDUSTRIAL ENTERPRISES
## VALEUR AJOUTEE DANS TOUTES LES ENTREPRISES INDUSTRIELLES
### 1938, 1948, 1953, 1958

Value added in thousand million Lire　　　　　　　　　　　　　Valeur ajoutée en milliards de lires

### A.　The Divisions of Industrial Activity
### Les branches de l'activité industrielle

| Year and item of data | All industrial activity Toutes industries | Mining Industries ex-tractives | Manu-facturing Industries manu-facturières | Con-struction Bâtiment et travaux publics | Electricity and gas Electricité et gaz | Année et rubrique |
|---|---|---|---|---|---|---|
| ISIC | 1-4, 511-512 | 1 | 2-3 | 4 | 511-512 | CITI |
| Value added | | | | | | Valeur ajoutée |
| 1938............. | 46.0 | 1.2 | 38.0 | 3.2 | 3.6 | 1938 |
| 1948............. | 2 400 | 48 | 2 020 | 198 | 134 | 1948 |
| 1953............. | 4 161 | 116 | 3 237 | 531 | 277 | 1953 |
| 1958............. | 6 235 | 184 | 4 602 | 1 072 | 377 | 1958 |
| Distribution in per-cent of value added | | | | | | Répartition en pour-centage de la valeur ajoutée |
| 1938............. | 100.0 | 2.6 | 82.6 | 7.0 | 7.8 | 1938 |
| 1948............. | 100.0 | 2.0 | 84.2 | 8.2 | 5.6 | 1948 |
| 1953............. | 100.0 | 2.8 | 77.8 | 12.8 | 6.6 | 1953 |
| 1958............. | 100.0 | 2.9 | 73.8 | 17.2 | 6.1 | 1958 |

### B.　The Major Groups of Manufacturing — Les classes de la branche Industries manufacturières

| Year and item of data | Manu-facturing Industries manufac-turières | Food, beverages and tobacco Industries alimen-taires, boissons, tabac | Textiles Textiles | Clothing, footwear and made-up textiles Articles d'habil-lement, chaussures et ouvrages en tissu | Wood products and furniture Bois et meubles | Paper and paper products Papier et ouvrages en papier | Printing and publish-ing Im-primerie et édition | Leather and leather products except wearing apparel Cuir et articles en cuir, à l'exclu-sion des articles d'habil-lement | Rubber products Ouvrages en caout-chouc | Chemicals and chemical, petroleum and coal products Produits chi-miques et dérivés du pétrole et du charbon | Non-metallic mineral products Produits minéraux non métal-liques | Basic metals Métal-lurgie de base | Metal products Ouvrages en métaux | Other manu-factur-ing Autres in-dustries manufac-turières | Année et rubrique |
|---|---|---|---|---|---|---|---|---|---|---|---|---|---|---|---|
| ISIC | 2-3 | 20-22 | 23 | 24 | 25-26 | 27 | 28 | 29 | 30 | 31-32 | 33 | 34 | 35-38 | 39 | CITI |
| Value added | | | | | | | | | | | | | | | Valeur ajoutée |
| 1938............. | 38.0 | 8.2 | 6.0 | 3.4 [1] | | 1.3 [2] | 0.8 | [1] | [2] | 3.9 | 1.3 | 2.7 | 9.9 | 0.5 | 1938 |
| 1948............. | 2 020 | 412 | 337 | 108 [1] | 70 | 33 | 32 | [1] | 33 | 213 | 70 | 155 | 525 | 32 | 1948 |
| 1953............. | 3 237 | 632 | 335 | 119 | 172 | 53 | 114 | 18 | 55 | 488 | 141 | 288 | 775 | 47 | 1953 |
| 1958............. | 4 602 | 795 | 428 | 145 | 199 | 79 | 174 | 18 | 61 | 714 | 202 | 428 | 1 255 | 104 | 1958 |
| Distribution in percent of value added | | | | | | | | | | | | | | | Répartition en pourcen-tage de la valeur ajoutée |
| 1938............. | 100.0 | 21.6 | 15.8 | 8.9 [1] | | 3.4 [2] | 2.1 | [1] | [2] | 10.3 | 3.4 | 7.1 | 26.1 | 1.3 | 1938 |
| 1948............. | 100.0 | 20.4 | 16.7 | 5.3 [1] | 3.5 | 1.6 | 1.6 | [1] | 1.6 | 10.5 | 3.5 | 7.7 | 26.0 | 1.6 | 1948 |
| 1953............. | 100.0 | 19.5 | 10.3 | 3.7 | 5.3 | 1.6 | 3.5 | 0.6 | 1.7 | 15.1 | 4.4 | 8.9 | 23.9 | 1.5 | 1953 |
| 1958............. | 100.0 | 17.2 | 9.3 | 3.2 | 4.3 | 1.7 | 3.8 | 0.4 | 1.3 | 15.5 | 4.4 | 9.3 | 27.3 | 2.3 | 1958 |

[1] Value added in Leather and leather products (ISIC major group 29) is included with value added in Clothing, footwear and made-up textiles (ISIC major group 24).
[2] Value added in Rubber products (ISIC major group 30) is included in value added in Paper and paper products (ISIC major group 27).

[1] La valeur ajoutée dans les industries de la classe 29 de la CITI (Cuir et articles en cuir) est com-prise dans celle de la classe 24 (Articles d'habillement, chaussures et ouvrages en tissu).
[2] La valeur ajoutée dans les industries de la classe 30 (Ouvrages en caoutchouc) est comprise dans celle de la classe 27 (Papier et ouvrages en papier).

# JAMAICA — JAMAÏQUE

## Gross Domestic Product and the Gross Domestic Fixed Capital Formation

Estimates of expenditure on and the industrial origin of the gross domestic product and of the industrial composition of the gross fixed capital formation, are presented in Table 1. The figures are derived from data supplied by the Department of Statistics, Kingston in response to the United Nations national accounts questionnaire. Official estimates and descriptions of methods and sources are available in the series *National Accounts — Income and Expenditure,* published by the Department of Statistics, Kingston.

## Characteristics and Structure of Industrial Activity

The information shown in Table 2 is derived from the results of Jamaica's first Survey of Business Establishments for the year 1953. The survey attempted to cover nearly all non-agricultural activities by use of sampling techniques, utilising a list sample of the large and an area sample of the small business establishments. Government activities were excluded from the field of coverage of the survey and data on small private builders is felt to be incomplete, whilst the sugar industry, although included in the survey, was omitted from the published results. The results are published by the Department of Statistics in *Bulletin of Statistics, Survey of Business Establishments in Jamaica 1954,* (March 1956).

In general, the definitions of the items of data correspond to the International Standards in Basic Industrial Statistics. The number of engaged and the number of employees are the average of the number of persons during the week preceding the survey and the week six months previous. However, the figures for the number of employees included homeworkers; and it is also thought that apprentices were sometimes omitted from the employment data. Value added is based on the value of sales after the deduction of excise duty (i.e., at factor cost, if subsidies are non-existent) less the cost of the purchases of raw materials, fuels and electricity.

## Produit intérieur brut et la formation brute de capital fixe intérieur

Les estimations des dépenses imputées au produit intérieur brut, des composantes du produit intérieur brut ventilées par secteur industriel d'origine, et des composantes du capital fixe formé ventilées suivant le secteur d'activité industrielle sont reproduites au tableau 1. Les chiffres sont tirés des données fournies par le Département de Statistique, Kingston, en réponse au questionnaire de l'O.N.U. sur la comptabilité nationale. Les estimations officielles et les notes qui s'y rapportent relatives aux sources et méthodes adoptées peuvent être trouvées dans la série *National Accounts, Income and Expenditure,* publiée par le Département de Statistique, Kingston.

## Caractéristiques et structure de l'activité industrielle

Les renseignements fournis dans le tableau 2 sont tirés des résultats de la première enquête effectuée en Jamaïque auprès des établissements exerçant une activité industrielle ou commerciale, pour l'année 1953. L'enquête devait couvrir la presque totalité des activités non agricoles par recours aux techniques d'échantillonnage, utilisant un échantillon liste des grands établissements, et un échantillon aréolaire de petits établissements commerciaux et industriels. Les activités de l'État sont exclues du champ de l'enquête et les données relatives aux petits entrepreneurs privés de construction paraissent plutôt incomplètes, tandis que les industries du sucre quoique couvertès par l'enquête, les données s'y rapportant étaient omises des résultats publiés. Les résultats sont publiés par le Département de Statistique dans *Bulletin of Statistics, Survey of Business Establishments in Jamaica, 1954,* (mars 1956).

En général, les définitions des rubriques correspondent aux Normes internationales relatives aux statistiques industrielles de base. Le nombre de personnes occupées et le nombre de salariés sont les moyennes des nombres de personnes occupées durant la semaine précédant immédiatement l'enquête et la semaine précédant de six mois l'enquête. Cependant, les chiffres relatifs au nombre de salariés couvrent les travailleurs à domicile, et l'on pense également que les apprentis sont quelquefois omis des données relatives à l'emploi. La valeur ajoutée est fondée sur la valeur des ventes après déduction des impôts (c'est-à-dire au coût des facteurs s'il n'existe pas de subventions allouées) moins le prix d'achat des matières premières, des combustibles et de l'électricité.

# 1. THE GROSS DOMESTIC PRODUCT AND GROSS DOMESTIC FIXED CAPITAL FORMATION
## PRODUIT INTERIEUR BRUT ET FORMATION BRUTE DE CAPITAL FIXE INTERIEUR

Million Pounds             Millions de livres

## A. Expenditure on the Gross Domestic Product at Market Prices
### Dépenses relatives au produit intérieur brut aux prix du marché

| Item of data and year Rubrique et année | Total | Consumption Consommation | | Gross Domestic Capital Formation Formation brute de capital intérieur | | Net exports of goods and services Exportations nettes de biens et de services | |
|---|---|---|---|---|---|---|---|
| | | Total | Government [1] Etat [1] | Total | Fixed Fixe | Exports less imports Exportations moins importations | Exports Exportations |
| **a. At Current Prices — Aux prix courants** | | | | | | | |
| **Absolute figures — Chiffres absolus** | | | | | | | |
| 1950 | 77.3 | 74.5 | 6.7 | 7.9 | 6.9 | −5.1 | 18.6 |
| 1951 | 89.9 | 85.7 | 8.8 | 12.7 | 12.2 | −8.4 | 20.6 |
| 1952 | 103.2 | 98.2 | 9.0 | 14.5 | 13.7 | −9.5 | 24.5 |
| 1953 | 115.5 | 107.9 | 10.6 | 15.2 | 14.2 | −7.6 | 31.4 |
| 1954 | 129.0 | 117.8 | 11.2 | 18.8 | 17.3 | −7.6 | 37.0 |
| 1955 | 147.2 | 134.1 | 13.1 | 24.6 | 21.5 | −11.5 | 41.0 |
| 1956 | 171.4 | 147.5 | 16.2 | 41.6 | 38.8 | −17.7 | 45.9 |
| 1957 | 206.4 | 163.9 | 18.0 | 57.3 | 52.1 | −14.8 | 60.2 |
| 1958 | 213.5 | 174.7 | 19.1 | 50.9 | 47.4 | −12.1 | 61.2 |
| 1959 | 228.3 | 191.1 | 21.9 | 51.1 | 46.1 | −13.9 | 64.4 |
| 1960 | 249.1 | 209.0 | 24.9 | 53.7 | 50.7 | −13.6 | 75.5 |
| 1961 | 263.5 | 218.2 | 26.1 | 51.8 | 48.3 | −6.5 | 89.4 |
| **Percentage distribution of average annual expenditure — Distribution en pourcentage des dépenses annuelles moyennes** | | | | | | | |
| 1950–1960 | 100.0 | 86.8 | 9.2 | 20.2 | 18.6 | −7.0 | 27.7 |
| 1950 | 100.0 | 96.4 | 8.7 | 10.2 | 8.9 | −6.6 | 24.1 |
| 1953 | 100.0 | 93.4 | 9.2 | 13.2 | 12.3 | −6.6 | 27.2 |
| 1954 | 100.0 | 91.3 | 8.7 | 14.6 | 13.4 | −5.9 | 28.7 |
| 1958 | 100.0 | 81.8 | 8.9 | 23.9 | 22.2 | −5.7 | 28.7 |
| 1960 | 100.0 | 83.4 | 9.9 | 22.1 | 20.7 | −5.5 | 30.3 |
| **b. At Prices of 1956 — Aux prix de 1956** | | | | | | | |
| **Absolute figures — Chiffres absolus** | | | | | | | |
| 1953 | 127.0 | 109.8 | 12.3 | 29.3 | 28.1 | −12.1 | 33.9 |
| 1954 | 141.0 | 121.9 | 13.3 | 34.2 | 32.6 | −15.1 | 37.2 |
| 1955 | 155.0 | 135.3 | 13.8 | 36.7 | 33.4 | −17.0 | 39.8 |
| 1956 | 171.4 | 147.5 | 16.2 | 41.6 | 38.8 | −17.7 | 45.9 |
| 1957 | 192.1 | 159.5 | 17.4 | 52.9 | 48.2 | −20.3 | 52.4 |
| 1958 | 197.9 | 162.0 | 18.2 | 51.1 | 47.6 | −15.2 | 56.0 |
| 1959 | 205.3 | 172.4 | 20.0 | 46.7 | 41.9 | −13.8 | 60.7 |
| 1960 | 219.3 | 181.4 | 21.8 | 49.3 | 46.3 | −11.4 | 73.1 |
| **Percentage distribution of average annual expenditure — Distribution en pourcentage des dépenses annuelles moyennes** | | | | | | | |
| 1953 | 100.0 | 86.4 | 9.7 | 23.1 | 22.1 | −9.5 | 26.7 |
| 1954 | 100.0 | 86.4 | 9.4 | 24.3 | 23.1 | −10.7 | 26.4 |
| 1958 | 100.0 | 81.9 | 9.2 | 25.8 | 24.1 | −7.7 | 28.3 |
| 1960 | 100.0 | 82.7 | 9.9 | 22.5 | 21.1 | −5.2 | 33.3 |
| **Average annual rate of growth — Taux annuel moyen d'accroissement** | | | | | | | |
| 1954–1958 | 8.9 | 7.4 | 8.1 | 10.6 | 9.9 | | 10.8 |
| 1958–1960 | 5.3 | 5.8 | 9.5 | −1.6 | −1.3 | . | 14.2 |

For footnotes see end of table.       Pour les notes, voir au bas du tableau.

# JAMAICA

## B. The Gross Domestic Product at Factor Cost According to Origin
### Origine par secteur d'activité du produit intérieur brut au coût des facteurs

| Item of data and year<br>Rubrique et année | Total | Agricultural sector<br>Secteur agricole | Industrial Sector — Secteur Industriel | | | | | Transportation and communication<br>Transports et communications | Other sectors<br>Autres secteurs |
|---|---|---|---|---|---|---|---|---|---|
| | | | Total | Mining<br>Industries extractives | Manufacturing<br>Industries manufacturières | Construction<br>Bâtiment et travaux publics | Electricity, gas and water<br>Electricité, gaz et eau | | |
| ISIC — CITI | 0–9 | 0 | 1–5 | 1 | 2–3 | 4 | 5 | 7 | 6, 8–9 |

### a. At Current Prices — Aux prix courants

| | | | | | | | | | |
|---|---|---|---|---|---|---|---|---|---|
| **Absolute figures — Chiffres absolus** | | | | | | | | | |
| 1938 | 18.5 | 6.7 [2] | ... | ... | 1.2 | 0.6 | 0.2 | 4.5 [3] | 5.3 [3] |
| 1950 | 70.1 | 21.6 [2] | ... | ... | 7.9 | 5.3 | 0.8 | 5.0 | 29.6 |
| 1951 | 81.7 | 22.1 [2] | ... | ... | 9.2 | 8.9 | 0.8 | 5.4 | 35.3 |
| 1952 | 95.0 | 25.8 [2] | ... | ... | 11.6 | 10.3 | 0.9 | 5.6 | 40.7 |
| 1953 | 106.7 | 22.6 | 28.4 | 2.6 | 14.7 | 10.3 | 0.8 | 7.0 | 48.7 |
| 1954 | 119.7 | 24.0 | 32.9 | 4.8 | 16.8 | 10.4 | 0.9 | 8.3 | 54.5 |
| 1955 | 136.4 | 26.2 | 38.7 | 6.5 | 18.3 | 12.9 | 1.0 | 9.6 | 61.9 |
| 1956 | 158.5 | 25.7 | 50.8 | 8.7 | 20.7 | 20.2 | 1.2 | 10.5 | 71.5 |
| 1957 | 191.9 | 26.6 | 69.1 | 16.9 | 24.4 | 26.1 | 1.7 | 12.3 | 83.9 |
| 1958 | 198.7 | 26.8 | 68.8 | 17.5 | 24.9 | 24.5 | 1.9 | 12.8 | 90.3 |
| 1959 | 211.5 | 28.2 | 71.6 | 16.6 | 27.9 | 24.9 | 2.2 | 13.9 | 97.8 |
| 1960 | 230.7 | 28.6 | 79.2 | 19.9 | 30.8 | 26.2 | 2.3 | 15.1 | 107.8 |
| 1961 | 244.3 | 31.0 | 83.6 | 21.0 | 32.6 | 27.4 | 2.6 | 16.9 | 112.8 |
| **Percentage distribution according to sector — Distribution en pourcentage par secteur** | | | | | | | | | |
| 1938 | 100.0 | 36.2 [2] | ... | ... | 6.5 | 3.2 | 1.1 | 24.3 | 28.6 |
| 1953–1960 | 100.0 | 15.2 | 31.8 | 6.7 | 13.5 | 10.8 | 0.9 | 6.6 | 46.4 |
| 1950 | 100.0 | 30.8 [2] | ... | ... | 11.3 | 7.6 | 1.1 | 7.1 | 42.1 |
| 1953 | 100.0 | 21.2 | 26.6 | 2.4 | 13.8 | 9.7 | 0.7 | 6.6 | 45.6 |
| 1954 | 100.0 | 20.1 | 27.5 | 4.0 | 14.0 | 8.7 | 0.8 | 6.9 | 45.5 |
| 1958 | 100.0 | 13.5 | 34.6 | 8.8 | 12.5 | 12.3 | 1.0 | 6.5 | 45.4 |
| 1960 | 100.0 | 12.6 | 34.4 | 8.9 | 13.2 | 11.3 | 1.0 | 6.5 | 46.5 |

### b. At Prices of 1956 — Aux prix de 1956

| | | | | | | | | | |
|---|---|---|---|---|---|---|---|---|---|
| **Absolute figures — Chiffres absolus** | | | | | | | | | |
| 1950 | 87.7 | 20.8 | 19.6 | 0.2 | 11.9 | 6.8 | 0.7 | 7.6 | 39.7 |
| 1951 | 94.8 | 20.4 | 22.4 | 0.3 | 12.3 | 9.0 | 0.8 | 7.5 | 44.5 |
| 1952 | 102.6 | 20.5 | 25.7 | 1.4 | 13.2 | 10.2 | 0.9 | 7.5 | 48.9 |
| 1953 | 117.3 | 23.6 | 30.0 | 3.1 | 15.4 | 10.6 | 0.9 | 8.2 | 55.5 |
| 1954 | 130.3 | 25.3 | 34.8 | 5.9 | 16.8 | 11.1 | 1.0 | 8.7 | 61.5 |
| 1955 | 144.1 | 26.5 | 41.9 | 7.6 | 18.9 | 14.3 | 1.1 | 9.8 | 65.9 |
| 1956 | 158.4 | 25.7 | 50.7 | 8.7 | 20.7 | 20.1 | 1.2 | 10.6 | 71.4 |
| 1957 | 181.4 | 26.4 | 62.5 | 14.3 | 23.7 | 23.1 | 1.4 | 12.4 | 80.1 |
| 1958 | 184.0 | 26.8 | 61.8 | 14.7 | 23.7 | 21.9 | 1.5 | 12.3 | 83.1 |
| 1959 | 194.5 | 29.4 | 65.0 | 14.4 | 26.6 | 22.2 | 1.8 | 12.7 | 87.4 |
| 1960 | 207.0 | 28.3 | 71.3 | 17.7 | 28.3 | 23.5 | 1.8 | 13.8 | 93.6 |
| **Percentage distribution according to sector — Distribution en pourcentage par secteur** | | | | | | | | | |
| 1950–1960 | 100.0 | 16.7 | 30.8 | 6.1 | 13.6 | 10.3 | 0.8 | 7.3 | 45.2 |
| 1950 | 100.0 | 23.7 | 22.3 | 0.2 | 13.6 | 7.7 | 0.8 | 8.7 | 45.3 |
| 1953 | 100.0 | 20.1 | 25.6 | 2.6 | 13.1 | 9.1 | 0.8 | 7.0 | 47.3 |
| 1954 | 100.0 | 19.4 | 26.7 | 4.5 | 12.9 | 8.5 | 0.8 | 6.7 | 47.2 |
| 1958 | 100.0 | 14.6 | 33.6 | 8.0 | 12.9 | 11.9 | 0.8 | 6.7 | 45.1 |
| 1960 | 100.0 | 13.7 | 34.4 | 8.5 | 13.7 | 11.4 | 0.8 | 6.7 | 45.2 |
| **Average annual rate of growth — Taux annuel moyen d'accroissement** | | | | | | | | | |
| 1950–1960 | 9.0 | 3.1 | 13.8 | −1.2 | 9.1 | 13.2 | 9.9 | 6.2 | 9.0 |
| 1950–1953 | 10.2 | 4.3 | 12.0 | 149.4 | 9.0 | 16.0 | 8.7 | 2.6 | 11.8 |
| 1954–1958 | 9.0 | 1.4 | 14.2 | 25.6 | 9.0 | 18.5 | 10.7 | 9.0 | 7.8 |
| 1958–1960 | 6.1 | 2.8 | 7.4 | 9.7 | 9.3 | 3.6 | 9.5 | 5.9 | 6.1 |

For footnotes see end of table.                    Pour les notes, voir au bas du tableau.

## C. Gross Domestic Fixed Capital Formation According to the Purchasing Industry

### Formation brute de capital fixe intérieur par secteur d'acquisition

| Item of data and year<br>Rubrique et année | Total | Agricultural sector<br><br>Secteur agricole | Mining<br><br>Industries extractives | Manufacturing<br><br>Industries manufacturières | Electricity, gas and water<br><br>Electricité, gaz et eau | Other sectors [4]<br><br>Autres secteurs [4] |
|---|---|---|---|---|---|---|
| ISIC — CITI | 0–9 | 0 | 1 | 2–3 | 5 | 4, 6–9 |
| | | | a. At Current Prices — Aux prix courants | | | |
| Absolute figures — Chiffres absolus | | | | | | |
| 1956............ | 38.8 | 3.5 | 11.6 | 4.1 | 0.6 | 19.0 |
| 1957............ | 52.1 | 4.9 | 10.7 | 4.5 | 0.7 | 31.3 |
| 1958............ | 47.4 | 4.2 | 4.6 | 5.5 | 1.4 | 31.7 |
| 1959............ | 46.1 | 4.6 | 1.6 | 5.0 | 1.8 | 33.1 |
| 1960............ | 50.7 | 5.0 | 1.8 | 5.3 | 1.7 | 36.9 |
| 1961............ | 48.3 | 5.1 | 1.3 | 5.2 | 2.4 | 34.3 |
| Percentage distribution according to sector— Distribution en pourcentage par secteur | | | | | | |
| 1958............ | 100.0 | 8.9 | 9.7 | 11.6 | 2.9 | 66.9 |
| 1960............ | 100.0 | 9.9 | 3.5 | 10.6 | 3.3 | 72.7 |

[1] Allowances and grants by the government to the armed forces of the United Kingdom stationed in Jamaica are treated as transfers to the rest of the world. The government printing office is treated as a general government agency, not as an enterprise, and its expenditures are accordingly considered as consumption of final goods and services. No estimate of imputed rent for general government buildings is included.
[2] Includes Mining.
[3] Wholesale and retail trade is included in Transportation and communication rather than in Other sectors in the case of 1938.
[4] Includes Construction and Transportation and communication.

[1] Les transferts (indemnités et autres versements) de l'Etat aux forces armées du Royaume-Uni stationnées à la Jamaïque sont considérés comme des transferts au reste du monde. L'imprimerie nationale étant assimilée à un service de l'Etat et non à une entreprise, ses dépenses sont considérées comme des dépenses de consommation de biens et services terminaux. Il n'est pas fait d'imputation pour le loyer des bâtiments de l'Etat.
[2] Y compris Industries extractives.
[3] Pour 1938, le commerce de gros et de détail est compris dans Transports et communications au lieu de figurer sous Autres secteurs.
[4] Y compris Bâtiment et travaux publics, et Transports et communications.

## 2. CHARACTERISTICS OF ALL INDUSTRIAL ESTABLISHMENTS

### CARACTERISTIQUES DE TOUS LES ETABLISSEMENTS INDUSTRIELS
### 1953

Number of establishments in units; value added and wages and salaries in million Pounds Sterling; number of engaged and employee in thousands; value added per engaged and wages and salaries per employee in thousand Pounds Sterling.

Nombre d'établissements en unités; valeur ajoutée et traitements et salaires en millions de livres sterling; nombre de personnes occupées et de salariés en milliers; valeur ajoutée par personne occupée et traitements et salaires par salarié en milliers de livres sterling.

### A. The Divisions of Industrial Activity — Les branches de l'activité industrielle

| Item of data | All industrial activity<br>Toutes industries | Mining [1]<br>Industries extractives [1] | Manufacturing<br>Industries manufacturières | Construction<br>Bâtiment et travaux publics | Electricity and gas<br>Electricité et gaz | Rubrique | Item of data | All industrial activity<br>Toutes industries | Mining [1]<br>Industries extractives | Manufacturing<br>Industries manufacturières | Construction<br>Bâtiment et travaux publics | Electricity and gas<br>Electricité et gaz | Rubrique |
|---|---|---|---|---|---|---|---|---|---|---|---|---|---|
| ISIC | 1-4,511-512 | 1 | 2-3 | 4 | 511-512 | CITI | ISIC | 1-4,511-512 | 1 | 2-3 | 4 | 511-512 | CITI |
| | a. Absolute Figures — Chiffres absolus | | | | | | | b. Structure | | | | | |
| Number of establishments... | 5 833 | 4 | 5 705 | 120 | 4 | Nombre d'établissements | Distribution in percent of number of engaged...... | 100.0 | 3.7 | 88.1 | 6.9 | 1.3 | Distribution en pourcentage du nombre de personnes occupées |
| Value added....... | ... | ... | 9.9 | 1.1 | 0.8 | Valeur ajoutée | Value added per person engaged.. | ... | ... | 0.23 | 0.33 | 1.33 | Valeur ajoutée par personne occupée |
| Number of engaged (Average during the year)....... | 47.9 | 1.8 | 42.2 | 3.3 | 0.6 | Nombre de personnes occupées (moyenne pendant l'année) | Wages and salaries per employee.... | 0.12 | 0.33 | 0.10 | 0.19 | 0.50 | Traitements et salaires par salarié |
| Employees Number (Average during the year).. | 41.5 | 1.8 | 36.0 | 3.1 | 0.6 | Salariés Nombre (moyenne pendant l'année) | Employees as a percent of engaged........ | 86.6 | 100.0 | 85.3 | 93.9 | 100.0 | Salariés en pourcentage des personnes occupées |
| Wages and salaries......... | 5.2 | 0.6 | 3.7 | 0.6 | 0.3 | Traitements et salaires | Value added per unit of wages and salaries..... | ... | ... | 2.68 | 1.83 | 2.67 | Valeur ajoutée par unité de traitements et salaires |

[1] Includes Metal mining (ISIC major group 12) and Stone quarrying, clay and sandpits (ISIC major group 14), the breakdown of which is not available.

[1] Y compris Extraction des minerais métalliques (CITI classe 12) et Extraction de la pierre à bâtir, de l'argile et du sable (CITI classe 14), dont les données détaillées ne sont pas disponibles.

# JAMAICA

## B. The Major Groups of Manufacturing — Les classes de la branche Industries manufacturières

| Item of data | Manu-facturing<br><br>Industries manufac-turières | Food, beverages and tobacco<br><br>Industries alimen-taires, boissons, tabac | Textiles, clothing, footwear and made-up textiles<br><br>Textiles, articles d'habil-lement, chaussures et ouvrages en tissu | Wood products and furniture<br><br>Bois et meubles | Printing and publish-ing<br><br>Im-primerie et édition | Paper, leather and rubber products<br><br>Ouvrages en papier, cuir et caout-chouc | Chemicals and chemical products<br><br>Produits chimiques | Non-metallic mineral products<br><br>Produits minéraux non métal-liques | Metal products<br><br>Ouvrages en métaux | Other manu-factur-ing<br><br>Autres in-dustries manufac-turières | Rubrique |
|---|---|---|---|---|---|---|---|---|---|---|---|
| ISIC | 2–3 | 20–22 | 23–24 | 25–26 | 28 | 27, 29–30 | 31 | 33 | 35–38 | 39 | CITI |
| *a. Absolute Figures — Chiffres absolus* | | | | | | | | | | | |
| Number of establishments........ | 5 705 | 397 | 3 495 | 602 | 71 | 45 | 22 | 75 | 763 | 235 | Nombre d'établisse-ments |
| Value added......... | 9.9 | 4.3 | 1.8 | 0.5 | 0.6 | 0.2 | 0.9 | 0.6 | 0.7 | 0.3 | Valeur ajoutée |
| Number of engaged (Average during the year).............. | 42.2 | 9.2 | 11.0 | 3.0 | 11.4 | 0.3 | 1.4 | 1.3 | 3.5 | 1.1 | Nombre de personnes occupées (moyenne pendant l'année |
| Employees:<br>Number (Average during the year).... | 36.0 | 8.7 | 7.1 | 2.4 | 11.3 | 0.3 | 1.4 | 1.2 | 2.8 | 0.8 | Salariés:<br>Nombre (moyenne pendant l'année) |
| Wages and salaries... | 3.7 | 1.2 | 0.7 | 0.2 | 0.4 | 0.1 | 0.3 | 0.3 | 0.4 | 0.1 | Traitements et salaires |
| *b. Structure* | | | | | | | | | | | |
| Distribution in percent of:<br>Value added........ | 100.0 | 43.4 | 18.2 | 5.0 | 6.1 | 2.0 | 9.1 | 6.0 | 7.1 | 3.1 | Distribution en pourcentage:<br>Valeur ajoutée |
| Number of engaged........... | 100.0 | 21.8 | 26.0 | 7.1 | 27.0 | 0.8 | 3.3 | 3.0 | 8.3 | 2.7 | Nombre de personnes occupées |
| Value added per person engaged...... | 0.23 | 0.47 | 0.16 | 0.17 | 0.05 | 0.67 | 0.64 | 0.46 | 0.20 | 0.27 | Valeur ajoutée par personne accupée |
| Wages and salaries per employee........ | 0.10 | 0.14 | 0.10 | 0.08 | 0.04 | 0.33 | 0.21 | 0.25 | 0.14 | 0.12 | Traitements et salaires par salarié |
| Employees as a percent of engaged........ | 85.3 | 94.6 | 64.5 | 80.0 | 99.1 | 100.0 | 100.0 | 92.3 | 80.0 | 72.7 | Salariés en pourcentage des personnes occupées |
| Value added per unit of wages and salaries... | 2.68 | 3.58 | 2.57 | 2.50 | 1.50 | 2.00 | 3.00 | 2.00 | 1.75 | 3.00 | Valeur ajoutée par unité de traitements et sa-laires |

# JAPAN — JAPON

## Gross and Net Product

The data shown in Table 1 on the gross and net domestic product in current prices and the gross national product in constant prices are from the reply of the Economic Research Institute, Economic Planning Agency, Tokyo, to the United Nations national accounts questionnaire. The official estimates and descriptions are issued by the Agency in annual publications on national income accounts which are variously entitled, for example, *White Paper on National Income* or *National Income Accounts*. In reply to the United Nations questionnaire, the Economic Planning Agency has adjusted the official estimates to the United Nations system of national accounts insofar as the available data would permit.

## Index Numbers of Industrial Production

The index numbers set out in Table 2 are derived from indexes of industrial production compiled by the Ministry of International Trade and Industry since 1955 and by the Economic Planning Agency for years prior to 1955. The index numbers are now published monthly in *Monthly Statistics of Trade and Industry*, Ministry of International Trade and Industry, *Japanese Economic Statistics*, Economic Planning Agency, and annually in *Economic Statistics of Japan*, the Bank of Japan, and *Japanese Statistical Yearbook*, Bureau of Statistics, office of the Prime Minister.

The series of index numbers cover, in principle, privately-owned establishments irrespective of size. The orignal comparison and weight base years for the series are 1934-1936 for the indexes referring to 1938-1949, 1950 for the index numbers relating to 1950-1954, 1955 for the indexes for 1955-1959, and 1960 for the index numbers referring to 1960 and later years. The successive series of index numbers were linked to one another at 1949, December 1954 and 1960, respectively.

Each of the series of index numbers have been computed as base-weighted arithmetic averages, starting from series of relatives based on quantity produced for individual commodities. In combining these relatives into indexes for detailed categories of industrial activity, the weights utilized have been based on gross value of production or value added at factor cost during the base period, but in aggregating these indexes to index numbers for broader classes of industry, the weights have been derived only from value added at factor cost during the base period. It should be noted that many more elementary series of relatives have been utilized in computing the index numbers based on the year 1955 than in compiling the earlier set of index numbers. The number of elementary series of relatives utilized in compiling the

## Produit brut et net

Les·données du tableau 1, relatives au produit intérieur brut et net aux prix courants et au produit national brut en prix constants, sont tirées de la réponse de l'Institut de recherche économique, Office de planification économique, Tokyo, au questionnaire de l'ONU sur la comptabilité nationale. Les estimations officielles et les renseignements connexes sont publiés par cet Office dans les diverses publications annuelles sur la comptabilité du revenu national, notamment dans *White Paper on National Income* et dans *National Income Accounts*. En répondant au questionnaire de l'ONU et dans la mesure où les données existantes s'y prêtaient, l'Office de planification économique a ajusté les estimations officielles en fonction du système de comptabilité nationale de l'ONU.

## Indices de la production industrielle

Les indices du tableau 2 sont fondés sur les indices de la production industrielle calculés par le Ministère du commerce international et de l'industrie pour 1955 et les années suivantes, et par l'Office de planification économique pour les années antérieures à 1955. Ces indices sont maintenant publiés tous les mois dans *Monthly Statistics of Trade and Industry* (Ministère du commerce international et de l'industrie), *Japanese Economic Statistics* (Office de planification économique), et tous les ans dans *Economic Statistics of Japan* (Banque du Japon) et *Japanese Statistical Yearbook* (Bureau de statistique, Cabinet du Premier Ministre).

Les séries d'indices portent, en principe, sur les établissements privés, quelle que soit leur taille. Les années adoptées comme bases initiales de comparaison et de pondération des séries sont les suivantes : 1934-1936 pour les indices de 1938-1949; 1950 pour les indices de 1950-1954; 1955 pour les indices de 1955-1959; et 1960 pour les indices de 1960 et des années suivantes. Les séries successives d'indices ont été raccordées les unes aux autres au niveau de 1949, de décembre 1954 et de 1960 respectivement.

Ces indices sont des moyennes aritmétique à pondération fixe établies à partir de séries de rapports quantitatifs de la production de chaque marchandise. Pour combiner ces rapports en indices de catégories détaillées de l'activité industrielle, on a pondéré en fonction de la valeur brute de la production ou de la valeur ajoutée, au coût des facteurs, pendant la période de base, mais, pour la construction des indices plus larges, les poids ont été tirés uniquement de la valeur ajoutée, au coût des facteurs, pendant la période de base. En outre, il convient de noter qu'on a utilisé beaucoup plus de séries élémentaires de rapports pour calculer les indices basés sur 1955 que pour les séries antérieures. Le nombre de séries élémentaires de rapports utilisées pour calculer les indices basés sur 1960 est légèrement plus grand que le

indexes based on 1960 is somewhat larger than the number employed in computing the index numbers based on 1955.

For further details regarding the indexes see the latest available version of the *Japanese Statistical Yearbook* and the *Supplement to the Monthly Bulletin of Statistics,* 1950 and 1959 and the *Monthly Statistical Bulletin,* February 1963, Statistical Office of the United Nations.

### Index Numbers of Industrial Employment

The index numbers shown in Table 3 were compiled almost entirely from the index numbers of employment computed in the Ministry of Labor of Japan. The only exceptions are the index numbers for 1938, which were compiled by the Statistical Office of the United Nations from absolute figures of employment for 1938 and 1948 and linked to the indexes of the Ministry of Labor at 1948, and the series of index numbers for the mining, manufacturing and electricity and gas industries, combined. The index numbers of the Ministry of Labor are published monthly in the *Monthly Labor Statistics and Research Bulletin,* Ministerial Secretariat of Labor Ministry, Tokyo and annually in the *Japanese Statistical Yearbook,* Bureau of Statistics, Office of the Prime Minister, and *Yearbook of Labor Statistics,* Ministry of Labor.

The absolute figures of employment utilized by the Statistical Office in compiling the indexes for 1938 consisted of the number of operatives employed as of the end of 1938 and of 1948. These figures covered all mining and electricity producing establishments and manufacturing establishments engaging five or more operatives. The figures were abstracted from the *Japanese Statistical Yearbook, 1949, 1952, 1954* and *1955.*

The series of index numbers of the Ministry of Labor are based on the average monthly number of regular employees in establishments with 30 or more such employees. The count of regular employees excludes those employed on less than a 30-day basis or on a daily basis and who worked less than 60 days during the preceding six months. The comparison and weight base years for the series of index numbers are 1947 for the indexes referring to 1948-1950, 1955 for the indexes relating to 1951-1959, and 1960 for the index numbers for 1960 and later years.

The Statistical Office of the United Nations computed the index numbers for industrial activity as a whole, excluding construction, as base-weighted arithmetic averages of the indexes for each of the divisions of industrial activity. The weights utilized for this purpose were derived from the figures of the number of employees resulting from the 1954 Census of Establishments described below.

### The Characteristics and Structure of Industrial Activity

The data in Table 4 comes from the results of the three-year Establishment Censuses taken by the Bureau of Statistics, Office of the Prime Minister. These Censuses cover all privately and publicly-owned establishments,

nombre de séries employées pour calculer les indices basés sur 1955.

Pour plus de détails sur ces indices, voir les plus récents numéros disponibles de *Japanese Statistical Yearbook,* ainsi que le *Supplément au Bulletin mensuel de statistique,* 1950 et 1954, et le *Bulletin mensuel de statistique,* février 1963, Bureau de statistique de l'ONU.

### Indices de l'emploi dans l'industrie

Les indices du tableau 3 ont été établis presque entièrement à partir des indices de l'emploi calculés par le Ministère du travail du Japon. Seuls font exception les indices de 1938, qui ont été calculés par le Bureau de statistique de l'ONU à partir de chiffres absolus de l'emploi pour 1938 et 1948 et raccordés aux indices du Ministère du travail au niveau de 1948, et les séries d'indices relatives à l'ensemble des industries extractives, manufacturières et productrices d'électricité et de gaz. Les indices du Ministère du travail sont publiés chaque moins dans le *Monthly Labour Statistics and Research Bulletin* (Secrétariat ministériel du Ministère du travail, Tokyo) et chaque année dans le *Japanese Statistical Yearbook* (Bureau de statistique, Cabinet du Premier Ministre) et *Yearbook of Labour Statistics* (Ministère du travail).

Les chiffres absolus de l'emploi utilisés par le Bureau de statistique de l'ONU pour calculer les indices de 1938 concernent le nombre d'ouvriers à la fin de 1938 et de 1948. Ces chiffres portent sur tous les établissements miniers et producteurs d'électricité, ainsi que sur les établissements manufacturiers occupant cinq ouvriers ou plus. Les chiffres sont tirés du *Japanese Statistical Yearbook, 1949, 1952, 1954* et *1955.*

Les séries d'indices du Ministère du travail sont fondées sur le nombre mensuel moyen de salariés permanents dans les établissements qui en occupent 30 ou plus. Ce nombre ne comprend pas les salariés engagés pour moins de 30 jours ou les journaliers qui ont travaillé moins de 60 jours pendant les six mois précédant le jour de l'enquête. Les années adoptées comme bases de comparaison et de pondération des séries d'indices sont les suivantes : 1947 pour les indices de 1948-1950, 1955 pour les indices de 1951-1959, et 1960 pour les indices de 1960 et des années suivantes.

Les indices calculés par le Bureau de statistique de l'ONU pour l'ensemble de l'activité industrielle, à l'exclusion du bâtiment et des travaux publics, sont des moyennes arithmétiques à pondération fixe des indices de chacune des branches de l'activité industrielle. Les coefficients de pondération utilisés à cet égard ont été tirés des chiffres concernant le nombre de salariés fournis par le recensement des établissements de 1954, décrit ci-dessous.

### Caractéristiques et structure de l'activité industrielle

Les données du tableau 4 proviennent des résultats des recensements triennaux des établissements effectués par le Bureau de statistique, Cabinet du Premier Ministre. Ces recensements portent sur tous les établissements pu-

irrespective of size. The figures in Table 4 were abstracted from the following publications: *Report on the Establishment Census, 1947, Japanese Statistical Yearbook, 1957* — "Establishment Census, 1954," *1957 Establishment Census of Japan;* all published by the Bureau of Statistics, Office of the Prime Minister.

Although all industrial establishments were covered in each of the Establishment Censuses shown in Table 4, the field covered in the 1947 Census is not comparable to that covered in the later Censuses. This is due to the differences between the 1947 and the other Censuses in the scheme of classification utilized. In the case of the 1947 Census, for example, establishments engaging in both retail trade and manufacturing were classified to manufacturing, whereas in the case of the 1954 and 1957 Censuses, most of these establishments were classified to retail trade. Furthermore, a number of establishments which could not be properly classified were included in the category for Miscellaneous manufacturing. The results of the three Establishment Censuses shown in Table 4 are comparable to one another in all other respects. The counts of persons engaged cover working proprietors, unpaid family workers, homeworkers and employees, regular, temporary and daily. The establishment (local unit) was also defined in the same way in all the Censuses.

The figures set out in Table 5 come from the surveys of smaller manufacturing establishments taken by the Research and Statistics Division, Ministry of International Trade and Industry as part of annual Censuses of Manufacturing. The data on the large manufacturing establishments appearing in Tables 6 and 7 result from the same Censuses. It should be noted that the dividing line between small and large establishments in the case of the 1953 and 1958 Censuses of Manufacturing differed somewhat from that in the 1938 and 1948 Censuses. In the 1953 and 1958 Censuses, the dividing line was set at four persons engaged but in the 1938 and 1948 Censuses, it was set at five operatives employed. All of the figures set out in Tables 5, 6 and 7 relate to privately-owned establishments only.

The data on manufacturing shown in Tables 5, 6 and 7 were abstracted from the following publications: *History of the Censuses of Manufacturing for 1909-1958* and *Census of Manufacturing, 1948, 1953* and *1958;* all published by the Research and Statistics Division, Ministry of International Trade and Industry.

The data on mining shown in Tables 6 and 7 were derived from the results of the annual Censuses of Mining taken by the Research and Statistics Division, Ministry of International Trade and Industry. These results have been published by that Division in *Mining Yearbook of Japan, 1953* and *1958.*

blics et privés, quelle que soit leur dimension. Les chiffres du tableau 4 ont été tirés des publications suivantes : *Report on the establishment Census, 1947, Japanese Statistical Yearbook, 1957* — *"Establishment Census, 1954"* et *1957 Establishment Census of Japan,* toutes publiées par le Bureau de statistique, Cabinet du Premier Ministre.

Chacun des recensements des établissements dont les résultats sont reproduits au tableau 4 portait sur tous les établissements industriels; cependant, le champ du recensement de 1947 n'est pas comparable à celui des recensements suivants. Ce manque de comparabilité est dû au fait que l'on n'a pas utilisé le même système de classification dans le recensement de 1947 que dans les autres recensements. C'est ainsi que, pour le recensement de 1947, les établissements s'occupant à la fois de commerce de détail et d'activités manufacturières ont été classés dans la branche des industries manufacturières, tandis que, pour les recensements de 1954 et 1957, la plupart de ces établissements ont été classés dans la catégorie du commerce de détail. De plus, un grand nombre d'établissements qui ne pouvaient être classés dans une catégorie déterminée ont été rassemblés dans Industries manufacturières diverses. Les résultats des trois recensements des établissements, reproduits au tableau 4, sont comparables le uns aux autres à tous autres égards. Les personnes occupées comprennent les propriétaires qui travaillent, les travailleurs familiaux non rémunérés, les travailleurs à domicile et les salariés, permanents, temporaires ou journaliers. L'établissement (unité locale) a été défini de la même façon dans tous les recensements.

Les chiffres du tableau 5 proviennent d'enquêtes sur les petits établissements manufacturiers effectuées par la Division de la recherche et de la statistique, Ministère du commerce international et de l'industrie, dans le cadre des recensements annuels des industries manufacturières. Les données des tableaux 6 et 7 relatives aux grands établissements manufacturiers proviennent des mêmes recensements. Il y a lieu de noter que la distinction établie entre les grands et les petits établissements n'est pas exactement la même pour les recensements des industries manufacturières de 1953 et 1958 que pour ceux de 1938 et 1948. Dans les recensements de 1953 et 1958, la limite a été fixée à quatre personnes occupées, alors que, dans les recensements de 1938 et 1948, elle a été fixée à cinq ouvriers. Tous les chiffres des tableaux 5, 6 et 7 se rapportent aux établissements privées seulement.

Les données des tableaux 5, 6 et 7 relatives aux industries manufacturières sont tirées des publications suivants : *History of the Censuses of Manufacturing for 1909-1958* et *Census of Manufacturing, 1948, 1953* et *1958,* toutes publiées par la Division de la recherche et de la statistique, Ministère du commerce international et de l'industrie.

Les données des tableaux 6 et 7 relatives aux industries extractives sont tirées des résultats des recensements annuels des industries extractives effectués par la Division de la recherche et de la statistique, Ministère du commerce international et de l'industrie. Ces résultats ont été publiés par la Division dans *Mining Yearbook of Japan, 1953* et *1958.*

In the case of manufacturing or mining, the data for the different years on the same item shown in Tables 5, 6 and 7 are, on the whole, defined in the same fashion. This is not always the case for the same item of data for the two divisions of industrial activity.

The establishment is delineated in a manner consistent with the recommendations of the International Standards in Basic Industrial Statistics, both for mining and manufacturing. However, for large manufacturing units, but not for mining, the data on value added do not take account of changes in stocks of finished or semi-finished products. In both cases, receipts from industrial services rendered or non-industrial activities and the value of goods produced on own-account seem to be unaccounted for in value added. On the other hand, in the case of the small manufacturing establishments, the data on gross receipts refer to receipts from industrial and non-industrial activity. In all instances, value added is net of the cost of raw materials, fuels, electricity and supplies and sub-contract work utilized in production and is priced at factor cost.

Excluded in the case of manufacturing from the data on the number of, as well as on wages and salaries paid to, employees and operatives are workers hired on a less than 30-day basis — temporary workers — or on a daily basis who were employed less than 60 days during the preceding six months. Furthermore, unpaid family workers seem to be included in the counts of employees and operatives and in wages and salaries paid. Though temporary workers are included in these counts and in the data on wages and salaries paid in the case of mining, operatives employed through labour contractors are excluded. The figures of wages and salaries do not include payments in kind. However, the definitions of the items of data on labour appear to be consistent with those of the International Standards in Basic Industrial Statistics in all other respects.

The capacity of installed power equipment is the sum of the rated horsepowers of prime movers in use that are connected to machinery other than electric generators and of all electric motors in use and in reserve. The data on fuels consumed relate to purchased fuels which may have been utilized as raw materials, as well as sources of heat and power. This may result in over estimation of the energy consumed in industries such as the manufacturing of chemical products, where coal might be utilized as a raw material.

Dans le cas des industries manufacturières et des industries extractives, les rubriques des tableaux 5, 6 et 7 sont dans l'ensemble définies de la même façon pour toutes les années. En revanche, leur définition varie parfois d'une branche de l'activité industrielle à l'autre.

L'établissement est défini d'une manière conforme aux Normes internationales relatives aux statistiques industrielles de base, tant pour les industries extractives que pour les industries manufacturières. Cependant, pour les grandes unités manufacturières, mais non pour les unités minières, les données sur la valeur ajoutée ne tiennent pas compte des variations de stocks des produits finis ou semi-finis. Dans les deux cas, les recettes provenant des services industriels rendus ou des activités non industrielles et la valeur des biens produits pour compte propre ne semblent pas entrer en ligne de compte dans le calcul de la valeur ajoutée. Pour les petits établissements manufacturiers, en revanche, les données sur les recettes brutes concernent les recettes provenant de toutes les activités, industrielles et non industrielles. Dans tous les cas, la valeur ajoutée est comptée au coût des facteurs et déduction faite des éléments utilisés pour la production, c'est-à-dire des matières premières, des combustibles, de l'électricité, des fournitures et des travaux confiés à des sous-traitants.

Pour les industries manufacturières, les données concernant le nombre de salariés et d'ouvriers ainsi que les traitements et salaires qui leur sont payés, ne tiennent pas compte des travailleurs temporaires (c'est-à-dire engagés pour une période inférieure à 30 jours) ou journaliers qui ont été occupés moins de 60 jours pendant les six mois précédant l'enquête. En outre, le nombre de salariés et d'ouvriers, ainsi que les traitements et salaires versés, semblent comprendre les travailleurs familiaux non rémunérés. Bien que, dans le cas des industries extractives, les travailleurs temporaires soient compris dans ces diverses données, les ouvriers embauchés par l'intermédiaires d'entrepreneurs chargés de fournir de la main d'œuvre sont exclus. Les traitements et salaires ne comprennent pas les paiements en nature. A tous autres égards, cependant, les définitions des rubriques relatives à l'emploi semblent être conformes aux Normes internationales relatives aux statistiques industrielles de base.

La puissance installée est la puissance nominale de tous les moteurs primaires en service qui actionnent des machines autres que des générateurs d'électricité, plus celle de tous les moteurs électriques en service et en réserve. Les données sur les combustibles consommés se rapportent aux combustibles achetés qui peuvent avoir été utilisés comme matières premières ou comme source de chaleur ou d'énergie. Il peut en résulter une surestimation de l'énergie consommée par des industries telles que les industries chimiques, où le charbon peut être utilisé comme matière première.

## 1. THE GROSS AND NET PRODUCT — LE PRODUIT BRUT ET NET

Thousand million Yen             Milliards de yens

### A. Expenditure on the Gross Product at Market Prices — Dépenses relatives au produit brut aux prix du marché

| Item of data and year / Rubrique et année | Total | Consumption / Consommation | | Gross Domestic Capital Formation / Formation brute de capital intérieur | | Net exports of goods and services / Exportations nettes de biens et de services | |
|---|---|---|---|---|---|---|---|
| | | Total | Government [5] / Etat [5] | Total [4] | Fixed [1] / Fixe [1] | Exports less imports / Exportations moins importations | Exports / Exportations |
| **a. Gross Domestic Product at Current Prices — Produit intérieur brut aux prix courants** | | | | | | | |
| **Absolute figures — Chiffres absolus** | | | | | | | |
| 1948 | 2 666.7 | 2 023.4 | 282.3 | 752.2 | 443.1 | −108.9 | 81.1 |
| 1950 | 3 948.9 | 2 834.6 | 437.3 | 1 007.3 | 693.7 | 107.0 | 469.1 |
| 1951 | 5 105.9 | 3 328.6 | 465.4 | 1 620.7 | 1 006.3 | 156.6 | 867.9 |
| 1952 | 5 891.5 | 4 152.5 | 641.1 | 1 597.1 | 1 163.5 | 141.9 | 852.2 |
| 1953 | 6 871.0 | 4 900.3 | 683.4 | 1 939.5 | 1 505.1 | 31.2 | 880.3 |
| 1954 | 7 403.8 | 5 492.9 | 825.2 | 1 814.7 | 1 507.6 | 96.2 | 950.7 |
| 1955 | 8 197.3 | 5 903.2 | 892.1 | 2 133.0 | 1 469.0 | 161.1 | 1 041.6 |
| 1956 | 9 026.7 | 6 301.2 | 874.0 | 2 675.2 | 2 044.9 | 50.3 | 1 218.1 |
| 1957 | 10 160.9 | 6 873.7 | 987.1 | 3 424.8 | 2 684.3 | −137.6 | 1 361.1 |
| 1958 | 10 007.8 | 7 303.2 | 1 106.9 | 2 469.7 | 2 665.3 | 234.9 | 1 339.5 |
| 1959 | 12 076.5 | 7 839.2 | 1 134.3 | 4 042.0 | 3 263.2 | 195.3 | 1 529.4 |
| 1960 | 14 029.1 | 8 728.8 | 1 214.2 | 5 179.1 | 4 394.1 | 121.2 | 1 772.0 |
| 1961 | 17 195.2 | 10 002.8 | 1 417.4 | 7 466.5 | 5 990.5 | −274.1 | 1 824.3 |
| **Percentage distribution of average annual expenditure — Distribution en pourcentage des dépenses annuelles moyennes** | | | | | | | |
| 1948 | 100.0 | 75.9 | 10.6 | 28.2 | 16.6 | −4.1 | 3.0 |
| 1950–1960 | 100.0 | 68.7 | 10.0 | 30.0 | 24.9 | 1.3 | 13.3 |
| 1950 | 100.0 | 71.8 | 11.1 | 25.5 | 17.6 | 2.7 | 11.9 |
| 1953 | 100.0 | 71.3 | 9.9 | 28.2 | 21.9 | 0.5 | 12.8 |
| 1954 | 100.0 | 74.2 | 11.1 | 24.5 | 20.4 | 1.3 | 12.8 |
| 1958 | 100.0 | 73.0 | 11.1 | 24.7 | 26.6 | 2.3 | 13.4 |
| 1960 | 100.0 | 62.2 | 8.6 | 36.9 | 31.3 | 0.9 | 12.6 |
| 1961 | 100.0 | 58.2 | 8.2 | 43.4 | 34.8 | −1.6 | 10.6 |
| **b. Gross National Product at Prices of 1955 — Produit national brut aux prix de 1955** | | | | | | | |
| | | | | | | [2] | [3] |
| **Absolute figures — Chiffres absolus** | | | | | | | |
| 1953 | 7 138.3 | 5 263.4 | 734.0 | 1 881.4 | 1 441.7 | −6.5 | 812.4 |
| 1954 | 7 364.6 | 5 509.4 | 827.7 | 1 800.6 | 1 494.1 | 54.6 | 912.9 |
| 1955 | 8 188.9 | 5 891.4 | 890.3 | 2 148.4 | 1 482.4 | 149.1 | 1 060.6 |
| 1956 | 8 787.3 | 6 263.6 | 868.8 | 2 501.9 | 1 897.0 | 21.8 | 1 194.6 |
| 1957 | 9 614.6 | 6 641.2 | 953.7 | 3 083.5 | 2 396.6 | −110.1 | 1 303.3 |
| 1958 | 9 608.6 | 7 083.6 | 1 073.6 | 2 424.8 | 2 615.6 | 100.2 | 1 318.2 |
| 1959 | 11 371.2 | 7 523.2 | 1 088.6 | 3 922.8 | 3 171.2 | −74.8 | 1 492.2 |
| 1960 | 12 846.3 | 8 150.1 | 1 133.7 | 4 977.3 | 4 233.2 | −281.1 | 1 683.0 |
| 1961 | 14 915.3 | 8 875.6 | 1 257.7 | 6 799.3 | 5 470.8 | −759.6 | 1 780.1 |
| **Percentage distribution of average annual expenditure — Distribution en pourcentage des dépenses annuelles moyennes** | | | | | | | |
| 1953–1960 | 100.0 | 69.8 | 10.1 | 30.3 | 25.0 | −0.1 | 13.0 |
| 1954 | 100.0 | 74.8 | 11.2 | 24.4 | 20.3 | 0.8 | 12.4 |
| 1958 | 100.0 | 73.7 | 11.2 | 25.2 | 27.2 | 1.1 | 13.7 |
| 1960 | 100.0 | 63.5 | 8.8 | 38.7 | 33.0 | −2.2 | 13'1 |
| 1961 | 100.0 | 59.5 | 8.4 | 45.6 | 36.7 | −5.1 | 11.9 |
| **Average annual rate of growth — Taux annuel moyen d'accroissement** | | | | | | | |
| 1953–1960 | 8.8 | 6.4 | 6.4 | 14.9 | 16.6 | . | 11.0 |
| 1954–1958 | 6.9 | 6.5 | 6.7 | 7.7 | 15.0 | . | 9.6 |
| 1958–1960 | 15.6 | 7.2 | 2.8 | 43.3 | 27.2 | . | 13.0 |

For footnotes see end of table.      Pour les notes, voir au bas du tableau.

## B. The Net Domestic Product at Factor Cost According to Origin
### Origine par secteur d'activité du produit intérieur net au coût des facteurs

| Item of data and year / Rubrique et année | Total | Agricultural sector / Secteur agricole | Industrial Sector — Secteur industriel | | | | Electricity, gas and water, and transportation and communication / Electricité, gaz et eau, et transports et communications | Other sectors[5] / Autres secteurs[5] |
| | | | Total | Mining / Industries extractives | Manufacturing / Industries manufacturières | Construction / Bâtiment et travaux publics | | |
| ISIC — CITI | 0–9 | 0 | 1–4 | 1 | 2–3 | 4 | 5, 7 | 6, 8–9 |
| | | | | | *a.* Current Prices — Aux prix courants | | | |
| **Absolute figures — Chiffres absolus** | | | | | | | | |
| 1948 | 1 962.2 | 624.8 | 604.3 | 66.9 | 454.4 | 83.0 | 104.5 | 628.6 |
| 1950 | 3 383.7 | 879.4 | 1 074.8 | 98.7 | 839.5 | 136.6 | 250.1 | 1 179.4 |
| 1951 | 4 349.4 | 1 095.2 | 1 416.0 | 152.0 | 1 111.2 | 152.8 | 312.1 | 1 526.1 |
| 1952 | 4 967.1 | 1 233.4 | 1 556.1 | 200.7 | 1 146.8 | 208.6 | 392.4 | 1 785.2 |
| 1953 | 5 663.9 | 1 253.3 | 1 799.8 | 177.8 | 1 361.5 | 260.5 | 483.6 | 2 127.2 |
| 1954 | 6 008.9 | 1 315.5 | 1 890.3 | 151.5 | 1 444.9 | 293.9 | 532.1 | 2 271.0 |
| 1955 | 6 561.3 | 1 507.9 | 1 954.3 | 141.5 | 1 494.2 | 318.6 | 611.3 | 2 487.8 |
| 1956 | 7 416.5 | 1 456.7 | 2 448.7 | 159.1 | 1 918.7 | 370.9 | 696.7 | 2 814.4 |
| 1957 | 8 307.2 | 1 531.1 | 2 878.1 | 219.4 | 2 236.1 | 422.6 | 804.6 | 3 093.4 |
| 1958 | 8 394.0 | 1 552.4 | 2 799.4 | 187.3 | 2 155.0 | 457.1 | 845.8 | 3 196.3 |
| 1959 | 9 703.8 | 1 649.1 | 3 404.0 | 192.9 | 2 666.2 | 544.9 | 979.0 | 3 671.7 |
| 1960 | 11 519.3 | 1 778.7 | 4 310.0 | 201.7 | 3 434.6 | 673.7 | 1 134.8 | 4 295.8 |
| 1961 | 13,758.8 | 1 985.2 | 5 313.7 | 214.8 | 4 215.9 | 883.0 | 1 370.1 | 5 089.8 |
| **Percentage distribution according to sector— Distribution en pourcentage par secteur** | | | | | | | | |
| 1948 | 100.0 | 31.8 | 30.8 | 3.4 | 23.2 | 4.2 | 5.3 | 32.1 |
| 1950 – 1960 | 100.0 | 20.0 | 33.4 | 2.5 | 25.9 | 5.0 | 9.2 | 37.4 |
| 1950 | 100.0 | 26.0 | 31.7 | 2.9 | 24.8 | 4.0 | 7.4 | 34.9 |
| 1953 | 100.0 | 22.1 | 31.7 | 3.1 | 24.0 | 4.6 | 8.6 | 37.6 |
| 1954 | 100.0 | 21.9 | 31.4 | 2.5 | 24.0 | 4.9 | 8.9 | 37.8 |
| 1958 | 100.0 | 18.5 | 33.3 | 2.2 | 25.7 | 5.4 | 10.1 | 38.1 |
| 1960 | 100.0 | 15.5 | 37.4 | 1.8 | 29.8 | 5.8 | 9.9 | 37.2 |
| 1961 | 100.0 | 14.4 | 38.6 | 1.6 | 30.6 | 6.4 | 10.0 | 37.0 |

[1] Included are the changes in stocks of local government enterprises.
[2] Includes the difference between factor incomes received from abroad and factor income paid to abroad.
[3] Includes factor incomes received from abroad.
[4] Includes changes in the value of stocks without adjustments for changes in prices.
[5] Does not include computed rentals for government office buildings.

[1] Y compris les variations des stocks des entreprises des collectivités locales.
[2] Y compris la différence entre le revenu de facteurs reçu de l'étranger et celui qui a été payé à l'étranger
[3] Y compris le revenu de facteurs reçu de l'étranger.
[4] Y compris les variations de la valeur des stocks, compte non tenu des variations de prix.
[5] Non compris les valeurs locatives imputées aux bâtiments appartenant à l'Etat.

## 2. INDEX NUMBERS OF INDUSTRIAL PRODUCTION — INDICES DE LA PRODUCTION INDUSTRIELLE

### A. Selected Divisions of Industrial Activity
### Quelques branches de l'activité industrielle

| Period<br>Période | Total [1] | Mining<br>Industries<br>extractives | Manu-<br>facturing [1]<br>Industries<br>manu-<br>facturières [1] | Electricity<br>and gas<br>Electricité<br>et gaz |
|---|---|---|---|---|
| ISIC — CITI | 1–3, 511–512 | 1 | 2–3 | 511–512 |

**a. Indexes — Indices (1958 = 100)**

| Period | Total | Mining | Manufacturing | Electricity |
|---|---|---|---|---|
| 1938 | 57 | 90 | 57 | 39 |
| 1948 | 22 | 57 | 18 | 43 |
| 1949 | − 28 − | − 65 − | − 24 − | − 49 − |
| 1950 | 34 | 69 | 30 | 52 |
| 1951 | 46 | 79 | 43 | 56 |
| 1952 | 49 | 82 | 46 | 60 |
| 1953 | 60 | 87 | 57 | 65 |
| 1954 | − 64 − | − 84 − | − 63 − | − 69 − |
| 1955 | 69 | 85 | 68 | 74 |
| 1956 | 86 | 94 | 84 | 84 |
| 1957 | 99 | 103 | 100 | 94 |
| 1958 | 100 | 100 | 100 | 100 |
| 1959 | 124 | 99 | 126 | 115 |
| 1960 | − 156 − | − 108 − | − 161 − | − 135 − |
| 1961 | 186 | 116 | 193 | 157 |

**b. Average Annual Rate of Change — Taux annuel moyen de variation**

| Period | Total | Mining | Manufacturing | Electricity |
|---|---|---|---|---|
| 1938 − 1960 | 4.7 | 0.8 | 4.8 | 5.8 |
| 1938 − 1948 | −9.1 | −4.5 | −10.9 | 1.0 |
| 1950 − 1960 | 16.5 | 4.6 | 18.3 | 10.0 |
| 1948 − 1953 | 22.2 | 8.8 | 25.9 | 8.6 |
| 1954 − 1958 | 11.8 | 4.4 | 12.2 | 9.7 |
| 1958 − 1960 | 24.9 | 3.9 | 26.9 | 16.2 |

For footnotes see end of table.

### B. The Major Groups of Mining
### Les classes de la branche Industries extractives

| Period<br>Période | All mining<br>Toutes<br>industries<br>extractives | Coal<br>mining<br>Extraction<br>du charbon | Metal mining<br>Extraction<br>des minerais<br>métalliques | Crude petro-<br>leum and<br>natural gas<br>Pétrole brut<br>et gaz naturel | Other mining<br>Autres<br>industries<br>extractives |
|---|---|---|---|---|---|
| ISIC — CITI | 1 | 11 | 12 | 13 | 14–19 |

**a. Indexes — Indices (1958 = 100)**

| Period | All mining | Coal | Metal | Crude petroleum | Other |
|---|---|---|---|---|---|
| 1938 | 90 | 96 | 83 | 62 | 58 |
| 1948 | 57 | 69 | 31 | 31 | 25 |
| 1949 | − 65 − | − 77 − | − 41 − | − 37 − | − 33 − |
| 1950 | 69 | 78 | 50 | 51 | 42 |
| 1951 | 79 | 87 | 58 | 59 | 62 |
| 1952 | 82 | 87 | 71 | 57 | 65 |
| 1953 | 87 | 94 | 74 | 60 | 73 |
| 1954 | − 84 − | − 86 − | − 81 − | − 64 − | − 82 − |
| 1955 | 85 | 85 | 84 | 68 | 84 |
| 1956 | 94 | 94 | 93 | 70 | 99 |
| 1957 | 103 | 104 | 99 | 79 | 112 |
| 1958 | 100 | 100 | 100 | 100 | 100 |
| 1959 | 99 | 95 | 103 | 122 | 116 |
| 1960 | − 108 − | − 103 − | − 109 − | − 167 − | − 142 − |
| 1961 | 116 | 109 | 115 | 212 | 154 |

**b. Average Annual Rate of Change — Taux annuel moyen de variation**

| Period | All mining | Coal | Metal | Crude petroleum | Other |
|---|---|---|---|---|---|
| 1938 − 1960 | 0.8 | 0.3 | 1.2 | 4.6 | 4.2 |
| 1938 − 1948 | −4.5 | −3.2 | −9.4 | −6.7 | −8.1 |
| 1950 − 1960 | 4.6 | 2.8 | 8.1 | 12.6 | 13.0 |
| 1948 − 1953 | 8.8 | 6.4 | 19.0 | 14.1 | 23.9 |
| 1954 − 1958 | 4.4 | 3.8 | 5.4 | 11.8 | 5.1 |
| 1958 − 1960 | 3.9 | 1.5 | 4.4 | 29.2 | 19.2 |

Pour les notes, voir au bas du tableau.

## C. The Major Groups of Manufacturing — Les classes de la branche Industries manufacturières

| Period / Période | Manufacturing [1] / Industries manufacturières [1] | Food, beverages and tobacco / Industries alimentaires, boissons, tabac | Textiles | Wood products and furniture / Bois et meubles | Paper and paper products / Papier et ouvrages en papier | Leather and leather products except wearing apparel / Cuir et articles en cuir, à l'exclusion des articles d'habillement | Rubber products / Ouvrages en caoutchouc | Chemicals and chemical, petroleum and coal products / Produits chimiques et dérivés du pétrole et du charbon | Non-metallic mineral products / Produits minéraux non métalliques | Basic metals / Métallurgie de base | Metal products / Ouvrages en métaux | Other manufacturing / Autres industries manufacturières |
|---|---|---|---|---|---|---|---|---|---|---|---|---|
| ISIC — CITI | 2–3 | 20–22 | 23 | 25–26 | 27 | 29 | 30 | 31–32 | 33 | 34 | 35–38 | 39 |

### a. Indexes — Indices (1958 = 100)

| Period | | | | | | | | | | | | |
|---|---|---|---|---|---|---|---|---|---|---|---|---|
| 1938 | 57 | 71 | 96 | 44 | 34 | 70 | 40 | 45 | 56 | 52 | 27 | 32 |
| 1948 | 18 | 24 | 19 | 56 | 16 | 3 | 16 | 14 | 24 | 21 | 15 | 19 |
| 1949 | – 24 – | – 35 – | – 25 – | – 56 – | – 23 – | – 4 – | – 22 – | – 19 – | – 32 – | – 31 – | – 18 – | – 22 – |
| 1950 | 30 | 39 | 36 | 59 | 31 | 22 | 44 | 27 | 38 | 41 | 19 | 23 |
| 1951 | 43 | 49 | 51 | 88 | 43 | 53 | 46 | 36 | 52 | 54 | 32 | 28 |
| 1952 | 46 | 51 | 58 | 94 | 49 | 56 | 47 | 41 | 54 | 56 | 32 | 32 |
| 1953 | 57 | 75 | 70 | 90 | 62 | 84 | 60 | 51 | 64 | 64 | 40 | 41 |
| 1954 | – 63 – | – 81 – | – 76 – | – 88 – | – 68 – | – 76 – | – 65 – | – 58 – | – 73 – | – 69 – | – 45 – | – 49 – |
| 1955 | 68 | 86 | 85 | 88 | 78 | 88 | 68 | 67 | 74 | 77 | 45 | 57 |
| 1956 | 84 | 90 | 101 | 98 | 90 | 98 | 80 | 82 | 90 | 93 | 67 | 75 |
| 1957 | 100 | 95 | 112 | 104 | 102 | 112 | 102 | 96 | 106 | 105 | 93 | 96 |
| 1958 | 100 | 100 | 100 | 100 | 100 | 100 | 100 | 100 | 100 | 100 | 100 | 100 |
| 1959 | 126 | 105 | 117 | 106 | 126 | 108 | 130 | 116 | 117 | 132 | 144 | 136 |
| 1960 | – 161 – | – 112 – | – 138 – | – 118 – | – 147 – | – 112 – | – 166 – | – 140 – | – 148 – | – 170 – | – 207 – | – 170 – |
| 1961 | 193 | 121 | 149 | 125 | 173 | 148 | 189 | 162 | 170 | 211 | 267 | 210 |

### b. Average Annual Rate of Change — Taux annuel moyen de variation

| Period | | | | | | | | | | | | |
|---|---|---|---|---|---|---|---|---|---|---|---|---|
| 1938 – 1960 | 4.8 | 2.1 | 1.7 | 4.6 | 6.9 | 2.2 | 6.7 | 5.3 | 4.5 | 5.5 | 9.7 | 7.9 |
| 1938 – 1948 | –10.9 | –10.3 | –15.3 | 2.4 | –7.3 | –27.0 | –8.8 | –11.0 | –8.1 | –8.7 | –5.7 | –5.1 |
| 1950 – 1960 | 18.3 | 11.1 | 14.4 | 7.2 | 16.8 | 17.7 | 14.2 | 17.9 | 14.6 | 15.3 | 27.0 | 22.1 |
| 1948 – 1953 | 25.9 | 25.6 | 29.8 | 10.0 | 31.1 | 94.7 | 30.3 | 29.5 | 21.7 | 25.0 | 21.7 | 16.6 |
| 1954 – 1958 | 12.2 | 5.4 | 7.1 | 3.2 | 10.1 | 7.1 | 11.4 | 14.6 | 8.2 | 9.7 | 22.1 | 19.5 |
| 1958 – 1960 | 26.9 | 5.8 | 17.5 | 8.6 | 21.2 | 5.8 | 28.8 | 18.3 | 21.7 | 30.4 | 43.9 | 30.4 |

[1] Clothing and made-up textiles (ISIC groups 243–244) and Printing and publishing (ISIC major group 28) are not covered in the indexes for Manufacturing (ISIC divisions 2–3).

[1] Articles d'habillement et ouvrages en tissu (CITI groupes 243–244) et Imprimerie et édition (CITI classe 28) ne sont pas compris dans les indices des Industries manufacturières (CITI branche 2–3).

**3. INDEX NUMBERS OF INDUSTRIAL EMPLOYMENT — INDICES DE L'EMPLOI DANS L'INDUSTRIE**

### A. The Divisions of Industrial Activity

### Les branches de l'activité industrielle

| Period<br>Période | Total excluding construction<br>Total à l'exclusion du bâtiment et des travaux publics | Mining<br>Industries extractives | Manu-facturing<br>Industries manu-facturières | Construction<br>Bâtiment et travaux publics | Electricity and gas<br>Electricité et gaz |
|---|---|---|---|---|---|
| ISIC — CITI | 1-3, 511-512 | 1 | 2-3 | 4 | 511-512 |

*a.* Indexes — Indices (1958 = 100)

| | | | | | |
|---|---|---|---|---|---|
| 1938....... | 68 | 109 | 66 | ... | 72 |
| 1948....... | −71− | −130− | −67− | ... | −73− |
| 1949....... | 71 | 127 | 67 | ... | 81 |
| 1950....... | 67 | 116 | 63 | ... | 79 |
| 1951....... | −69− | −112− | −66− | ... | −79− |
| 1952....... | 71 | 115 | 68 | 52 | 84 |
| 1953....... | 74 | 104 | 72 | 66 | 92 |
| 1954....... | 77 | 92 | 76 | 74 | 99 |
| 1955....... | 79 | 89 | 78 | 78 | 97 |
| 1956....... | 86 | 93 | 85 | 78 | 97 |
| 1957....... | 96 | 98 | 96 | 86 | 97 |
| 1958....... | 100 | 100 | 100 | 100 | 100 |
| 1959....... | 110 | 100 | 111 | 122 | 103 |
| 1960....... | −126− | −96− | −128− | −152− | −105− |
| 1961....... | 138 | 90 | 142 | 181 | 108 |

*b.* Average Annual Rate of Change — Taux annuel moyen de variation

| | | | | | |
|---|---|---|---|---|---|
| 1938−1960. | 2.8 | −0.6 | 3.1 | ... | 1.7 |
| 1938−1948. | 0.4 | 1.8 | 0.1 | ... | 0.1 |
| 1950−1960. | 6.5 | −1.9 | 7.3 | ... | 2.9 |
| 1948−1953. | 0.8 | −4.4 | 1.5 | ... | 4.7 |
| 1954−1958. | 6.8 | 2.1 | 7.1 | 7.8 | 0.2 |
| 1958−1960. | 12.2 | −2.0 | 13.1 | 23.3 | 2.5 |

# JAPAN

## B. The Major Groups of Manufacturing — Les classes de la branche Industries manufacturières

| Period / Période | Manufacturing — Industries manufacturières | Food, beverages and tobacco [1] — Industries alimentaires, boissons, tabac [1] | Textiles | Clothing, and made-up textiles [2] — Articles d'habillement, et ouvrages en tissu [2] | Wood products and furniture [2,3] — Bois et meubles [2,3] | Paper and paper products — Papier et ouvrages en papier | Printing and publishing — Imprimerie et édition | Leather and leather products [2] — Cuir et articles en cuir [2] | Rubber products — Ouvrages en caoutchouc | Chemicals and chemical, petroleum and coal products [1] — Produits chimiques et dérivés du pétrole et du charbon [1] | Non-metallic mineral products — Produits minéraux non métalliques | Basic metals [4] — Métallurgie de base [4] | Metal products [4] — Ouvrages en métaux [4] | Other manufacturing [3] — Autres industries manufacturières [3] |
|---|---|---|---|---|---|---|---|---|---|---|---|---|---|---|
| ISIC — CITI | 2-3 | 20-22 | 23 | 243-244 | 25-26 | 27 | 28 | 29 | 30 | 31-32 | 33 | 34 | 35-38 | 39 |

### a. Indexes — Indices (1958 = 100)

| Period | | | | | | | | | | | | | | |
|---|---|---|---|---|---|---|---|---|---|---|---|---|---|---|
| 1951 | 66 | 47 | 95 | 51 | 56 | 53 | 60 | 60 | 69 | 75 | 59 | 69 | 59 | 35 |
| 1952 | 68 | 54 | 92 | 54 | 54 | 61 | 67 | 52 | 65 | 78 | 62 | 72 | 61 | 37 |
| 1953 | 72 | 60 | 90 | 54 | 57 | 66 | 75 | 56 | 72 | 80 | 65 | 75 | 66 | 44 |
| 1954 | 76 | 66 | 92 | 60 | 63 | 71 | 80 | 61 | 75 | 84 | 69 | 78 | 71 | 51 |
| 1955 | 78 | 73 | 93 | 68 | 68 | 75 | 83 | 67 | 78 | 86 | 73 | 79 | 71 | 59 |
| 1956 | 85 | 80 | 99 | 81 | 76 | 84 | 88 | 76 | 84 | 91 | 83 | 86 | 79 | 73 |
| 1957 | 96 | 90 | 106 | 93 | 89 | 95 | 93 | 90 | 95 | 96 | 95 | 97 | 93 | 90 |
| 1958 | 100 | 100 | 100 | 100 | 100 | 100 | 100 | 100 | 100 | 100 | 100 | 100 | 100 | 100 |
| 1959 | 111 | 111 | 100 | 110 | 119 | 109 | 108 | 109 | 118 | 109 | 111 | 112 | 116 | 120 |
| 1960 | –128– | –126– | –109– | –126– | –129– | –122– | –114– | –116– | –141– | –120– | –130– | –128– | –144– | –136– |
| 1961 | 142 | 146 | 112 | 132 | 138 | 132 | 120 | 129 | 149 | 131 | 142 | 145 | 166 | ... |

### b. Average Annual Rate of Change — Taux annuel moyen de variation

| Period | | | | | | | | | | | | | | |
|---|---|---|---|---|---|---|---|---|---|---|---|---|---|---|
| 1951–1960 | 7.6 | 11.6 | 1.5 | 10.6 | 9.7 | 9.7 | 7.2 | 7.6 | 8.3 | 5.4 | 9.2 | 7.1 | 10.4 | 16.3 |
| 1951–1953 | 4.5 | 13.0 | –2.7 | 2.9 | 0.9 | 11.6 | 11.8 | –3.4 | 2.1 | 3.3 | 5.0 | 4.3 | 5.8 | 12.1 |
| 1954–1958 | 7.1 | 10.9 | 2.1 | 13.6 | 12.2 | 8.9 | 5.7 | 13.1 | 7.5 | 4.4 | 9.7 | 6.4 | 8.9 | 18.3 |
| 1958–1960 | 13.1 | 12.2 | 4.4 | 12.2 | 13.6 | 10.5 | 6.8 | 7.7 | 18.7 | 9.5 | 14.0 | 13.1 | 20.0 | 16.6 |

[1] Salt refining (part of ISIC major group 20) is included in Chemicals and chemical products (ISIC major group 31).
[2] Manufacture of footwear (ISIC group 241) is included under Leather and leather products (ISIC major group 29) if made of leather or under Wood products (ISIC major group 25) if made of wood.
[3] The manufacture of cork products (part of ISIC major group 25) is covered under Other manufacturing (ISIC major group 39).
[4] The manufacturing of electrical wire and cable (part of major group 37) is included under Basic metals (ISIC major group 34).

[1] Le raffinage du sel (dans CITI classe 20) est compris dans Produits chimiques (CITI classe 31).
[2] La Fabrication des chaussures (CITI groupe 241) est comprise dans Cuir et articles en cuir (CITI classe 29) si la matière première est le cuir et dans Ouvrages en bois (CITI classe 25) si la matière première est le bois.
[3] La fabrication des ouvrages en liège (dans CITI classe 25) est comprise dans Autres industries manufacturières (CITI classe 39).
[4] La fabrication des fils et câbles électriques (dans CITI classe 37) est comprise dans Métallurgie de base (CITI classe 34).

# 4. THE CHARACTERISTICS OF ALL INDUSTRIAL ESTABLISHMENTS
## CARACTERISTIQUES DE TOUS LES ETABLISSEMENTS INDUSTRIELS
### 1.X.1947, 1.VII.1954, 1.VII.1957

Number of establishments in units; number of persons engaged and employees in thousands.

Nombre d'établissements en unités; nombre de personnes occupées et de salariés milliers.

## A. The Divisions of Industrial Activity — Les branches de l'activité industrielle

### a. Absolute Figures — Chiffres absolus

| Year and item of data | All industrial activity Toutes industries | Mining Industries extractives | Manufacturing Industries manufacturières | Construction Bâtiment et travaux publics | Electricity and gas Electricité et gaz | Année et rubrique |
|---|---|---|---|---|---|---|
| ISIC | 1-4,511-512 | 1 | 2-3 | 4 | 511-512 | CITI |
| I.X.1947 Number of establishments... | 1 307 864 | 11 625 | 1 031 280 | 257 260 | 7 699 | I.X.1947 Nombre d'établissements |
| Number of engaged........ | 8 623.9 | 661.4 | 6 332.9 | 1 492.3 | 137.3 | Nombre de personnes occupées |
| Number of employees...... | 6 834.7 | 649.3 | 4 864.4 | 1 183.7 | 137.3 | Nombre de salariés |
| I.VII.1954 Number of establishments... | 723 115 | 8 330 | 527 976 | 186 563 | 246 | I.VII.1954 Nombre d'établissements |
| Number of engaged........ | 8 068.9 | 473.2 | 6 195.0 | 1 245.3 | 155.4 | Nombre de personnes occupées |
| Number of employees...... | 7 155.9 | 464.9 | 5 495.7 | 1 039.9 | 155.4 | Nombre de salariés |
| I.VII.1957 Number of establishments... | 740 546 | 10 193 | 544 746 | 179 203 | 6 404 | I.VII.1957 Nombre d'établissements |
| Number of engaged........ | 9 622.5 | 530.7 | 7 488.5 | 1 445.8 | 157.5 | Nombre de personnes occupées |
| Number of employees...... | 8 250.4 | 514.2 | 6 390.4 | 1 189.8 | 156.0 | Nombre de salariés |

### b. Structure

| Year and item of data | All industrial activity Toutes industries | Mining Industries extractives | Manufacturing Industries manufacturières | Construction Bâtiment et travaux publics | Electricity and gas Electricité et gaz | Année et rubrique |
|---|---|---|---|---|---|---|
| ISIC | 1-4,511-512 | 1 | 2-3 | 4 | 511-512 | CITI |
| I.X.1947 Distribution in percent of number of engaged........ | 100.0 | 7.7 | 73.4 | 17.3 | 1.6 | I.X.1947 Distribution en pourcentage du nombre de personnes occupées |
| Employees as a percent of engaged........ | 79.2 | 98.2 | 76.8 | 79.3 | 100.0 | Salariés en pourcentage des personnes occupées |
| I.VII.1954 Distribution in percent of number of engaged........ | 100.0 | 5.9 | 76.8 | 15.4 | 1.9 | I.VII.1954 Distribution en pourcentage du nombre de personnes occupées |
| Employees as a percent of engaged........ | 88.7 | 98.2 | 88.7 | 83.5 | 100.0 | Salariés en pourcentage des personnes occupées |
| I.VII.1957 Distribution in percent of number of engaged........ | 100.0 | 5.5 | 77.8 | 15.0 | 1.7 | I.VII.1957 Distribution en pourcentage du nombre de personnes occupées |
| Employees as a percent of engaged........ | 85.7 | 96.9 | 85.3 | 82.3 | 99.0 | Salariés en pourcentage des personnes occupées |

## B. The Major Groups of Mining — Les classes de la branche Industries extractives

### a. Absolute Figures — Chiffres absolus

| Year and item of data | All mining Toutes industries extractives | Coal mining Extraction du charbon | Metal mining Extraction des minerais métalliques | Crude petroleum and natural gas Pétrole brut et gaz naturel | Other mining Divers | Année et rubrique |
|---|---|---|---|---|---|---|
| ISIC | 1 | 11 | 12 | 13 | 14-19 | CITI |
| I.X.1947 Number of establishments... | 11 625 | 3 321 | 1 369 | 164 | 6 771 | I.X.1947 Nombre d'établissements |
| Number of engaged........ | 661.4 | 504.1 | 75.7 | 12.0 | 69.6 | Nombre de personnes occupées |
| Number of employees....... | 649.3 | 501.6 | 74.1 | 12.0 | 61.6 | Nombre de salariés |
| I.VII.1954 Number of establishments... | 8 330 | 1 493 | 660 | 99 | 6 078 | I.VII.1954 Nombre d'établissements |
| Number of engaged........ | 473.2 | 330.7 | 60.5 | 5.3 | 76.7 | Nombre de personnes occupées |
| Number of employees...... | 464.9 | 329.8 | 60.3 | 5.3 | 69.5 | Nombre de salariés |
| I.VII.1957 Number of establishments... | 10 193 | 1 826 | 904 | 127 | 7 336 | I.VII.1957 Nombre d'établissements |
| Number of engaged........ | 530.7 | 358.3 | 83.6 | 6.5 | 82.3 | Nombre de personnes occupées |
| Number of employees....... | 514.2 | 354.8 | 82.4 | 6.4 | 70.6 | Nombre de salariés |

### b. Structure

| Item of data | All mining Toutes industries extractives | Coal mining Extraction du charbon | Metal mining Extraction des minerais métalliques | Crude petroleum and natural gas Pétrole brut et gaz naturel | Other mining Divers | Année et rubrique |
|---|---|---|---|---|---|---|
| ISIC | 1 | 11 | 12 | 13 | 14-19 | CITI |
| I.X.1947 Distribution in percent of number of engaged........ | 100.0 | 76.2 | 11.5 | 1.8 | 10.5 | I.X.1947 Distribution en pourcentage du nombre de personnes occupées |
| Employees as a percent of engaged........ | 98.2 | 99.5 | 97.9 | 100.0 | 88.5 | Salariés en pourcentage des personnes occupées |
| I.VII.1954 Distribution in percent of number of engaged........ | 100.0 | 69.9 | 12.8 | 1.1 | 16.2 | I.VII.1954 Distribution en pourcentage du nombre de personnes occupées |
| Employees as a percent of engaged........ | 98.2 | 99.7 | 99.7 | 100.0 | 90.6 | Salariés en pourcentage des personnes occupées |
| I.VII.1957 Distribution in percent of number of engaged........ | 100.0 | 67.5 | 15.8 | 1.2 | 15.5 | I.VII.1957 Distribution en pourcentage du nombre de personnes occupées |
| Employees as a percent of engaged........ | 96.9 | 99.0 | 98.6 | 98.5 | 85.8 | Salariés en pourcentage des personnes occupées |

461

# JAPAN

## C. The Major Groups of Manufacturing — Les classes de la branche Industries manufacturières

| Year and item of data | Manufacturing — Industries manufacturières | Food, beverages and tobacco [1] — Industries alimentaires, boissons, tabac [1] | Textiles | Clothing, footwear and made-up textiles [2] — Articles d'habillement, chaussures et ouvrages en tissu [2] | Wood products and furniture [2,3] — Bois et meubles [2,3] | Paper and paper products — Papier et ouvrages en papier | Printing and publishing — Imprimerie et édition | Leather and leather products except wearing apparel [2] — Cuir et articles en cuir, à l'exclusion des articles d'habillement [2] | Rubber products — Ouvrages en caoutchouc | Chemicals and chemical, petroleum and coal products [1,4] — Produits chimiques et dérivés du pétrole et du charbon [1,4] | Non-metallic mineral products — Produits minéraux non métalliques | Basic metals — Métallurgie de base | Metal products — Ouvrages en métaux | Other manufacturing [2,3,4] — Autres industries manufacturières [2,3,4] | Année et rubrique |
|---|---|---|---|---|---|---|---|---|---|---|---|---|---|---|---|
| **ISIC** | 2–3 | 20–22 | 23 | 24 | 25–26 | 27 | 28 | 29 | 30 | 31–32 | 33 | 34 | 35–38 | 39 | **CITI** |
| *a. Absolute Figures — Chiffres absolus* | | | | | | | | | | | | | | | |
| **1.X.1947** Number of establishments | 1 031 280 | 152 022 | 188 884 | | 168 599 | ... | 10 769 | | | 53 757 [5] | 28 028 | 134 427 | | 294 794 | **1.X.1947** Nombre d'établissements |
| Number of engaged | 6 332.9 | 623.8 | 1 056.6 | | 865.9 | ... | 108.3 | | | 690.6 [5] | 256.8 | 1 873.1 | | 857.8 | Nombre de personnes occupées |
| Number of employees | 4 864.4 | 365.4 | 785.3 | | 652.2 | ... | 93.3 | | | 603.8 [5] | 210.1 | 1 693.8 | | 460.5 | Nombre de salariés |
| **1.VII.1954** Number of establishments | 527 976 | 112 356 | 92 277 | 23 565 | 90 996 | 13 764 | 20 289 | 8 272 | 1 666 | 12 998 | 28 922 | 6 389 | 76 495 | 39 987 | **1.VII.1954** Nombre d'établissements |
| Number of engaged | 6 195.0 | 809.3 | 1 147.2 | 182.7 | 574.3 | 189.8 | 288.5 | 48.5 | 79.6 | 431.6 | 318.8 | 364.0 | 1 450.1 | 310.6 | Nombre de personnes occupées |
| Number of employees | 5 495.7 | 627.3 | 1 003.6 | 151.0 | 465.1 | 168.2 | 271.9 | 38.4 | 78.3 | 420.0 | 275.7 | 360.4 | 1 378.2 | 257.6 | Nombre des salarié |
| **1.VII.1957** Number of establishments | 544 746 | 110 871 | 85 505 | 37 071 | 86 412 | 15 829 | 20 915 | 4 326 | 1 985 | 10 814 | 28 383 | 7 712 | 80 965 | 53 958 | **1.VII.1957** Nombre d'établissements |
| Number of engaged | 7 488.5 | 907.0 | 1 291.8 | 304.7 | 628.9 | 246.8 | 324.7 | 34.1 | 110.4 | 488.0 | 379.4 | 470.4 | 1 811.1 | 491.2 | Nombre de personnes occupées |
| Number of employees | 6 390.4 | 661.9 | 1 108.2 | 234.7 | 480.8 | 212.1 | 282.4 | 25.6 | 105.9 | 464.2 | 320.5 | 453.0 | 1 653.9 | 387.2 | Nombre de salariés |
| *b. Structure* | | | | | | | | | | | | | | | |
| **1.X.1947** Distribution in per cent of number of engaged | 100.0 | 9.9 | 16.7 | | 13.7 | ... | 1.7 | | | 10.9 [5] | 4.0 | 29.6 | | 13.5 | **1.X.1947** Distribution en pourcentage du nombre de personnes occupées |
| Employees as a percent of engaged | 76.8 | 58.6 | 74.3 | | 75.3 | ... | 86.1 | | | 87.4 [5] | 81.8 | 90.4 | | 53.7 | Salariés en pourcentage des personnes occupées |
| **1.VII.1954** Distribution in percent of number of engaged | 100.0 | 13.1 | 18.5 | 2.9 | 9.3 | 3.1 | 4.6 | 0.8 | 1.3 | 7.0 | 5.1 | 5.9 | 23.4 | 5.0 | **1.VII.1954** Distribution en pourcentage du nombre de personnes occupées |
| Employees as a percent of engaged | 88.7 | 77.5 | 87.5 | 82.6 | 81.0 | 88.6 | 94.2 | 79.2 | 98.4 | 97.3 | 86.5 | 99.0 | 95.0 | 82.9 | Salariés en pourcentage des personnes occupées |
| **1.VII.1957** Distribution in percent of number of engaged | 100.0 | 12.1 | 17.2 | 4.1 | 8.4 | 3.3 | 4.3 | 0.4 | 1.5 | 6.5 | 5.1 | 6.3 | 24.2 | 6.6 | **1.VII.1957** Distribution en pourcentage du nombre de personnes occupées |
| Employees as a percent of engaged | 85.3 | 73.0 | 85.8 | 77.0 | 76.4 | 85.9 | 87.0 | 75.1 | 95.9 | 95.1 | 84.5 | 96.3 | 91.3 | 78.8 | Salariés en pourcentage des personnes occupées |

[1] Salt refining (part of ISIC major group 20) is included in Chemicals and chemical products (ISIC major group 31).
[2] The manufacturing of leather footwear and gloves; of wooden footwear; and of dressed and dyed furs and umbrellas (all part of ISIC major group 24) are included under Leather and leather products (ISIC major group 29), Wood products (ISIC major group 25) and Other manufacturing (ISIC major group 39), respectively.
[3] The manufacture of cork products and morticians goods (part of ISIC major group 25) is included under Other manufacturing (ISIC major group 39).
[4] The manufacturing of matches and fireworks (part of ISIC major group 31) is included under Other manufacturing (ISIC major group 39).
[5] The data as of 1.X.1947 for Paper and paper products (ISIC major group 27) are included with the data for ISIC major groups 29-32.

[1] Le raffinage du sel (dans CITI classe 20) est compris dans Produits chimiques (CITI classe 31).
[2] La fabrication des chaussures et gants en cuir, celle des chaussures en bois, ainsi que la préparation et la teinture des fourrures et la fabrication des parapluies (tous dans CITI classe 24) sont comprises dans Cuir et articles en cuir (CITI classe 29), Ouvrages en bois (CITI classe 25) et Autres industries manufacturières (CITI classe 39) respectivement.
[3] La fabrication des ouvrages en liège et des articles mortuaires (dans CITI classe 25) est comprise dans Autres industries manufacturières (CITI classe 39).
[4] La fabrication des allumettes et des explosifs d'artifice (dans CITI classe 31) est comprise dans Autres industries manufacturières (CITI classe 39).
[5] Les données au 1.X.1947 relatives à la rubrique Papier et articles en papier (CITI classe 27) sont comprises dans les données relatives aux classes 29-32 de la CITI.

## 5. CHARACTERISTICS OF MANUFACTURING ESTABLISHMENTS, HAVING LESS THAN FIVE OPERATIVES, 1948, AND HAVING LESS THAN FOUR PERSONS ENGAGED, 1953 and 1958

## CARACTERISTIQUES DES ETABLISSEMENTS MANUFACTURIERS COMPTANT MOINS DE CINQ OUVRIERS EN 1948 ET MOINS DE QUATRE PERSONNES OCCUPEES EN 1953 et 1958

Number of establishments in units; gross receipts in million Yen, and number of engaged and employees in thousands.

Nombre d'établissements en unités; recettes brutes en millions de yens; nombre de personnes occupées et de salariés en milliers.

| Year and item of data | Manu-facturing Industries manufac-turières | Food, beverages and tobacco Industries alimen-taires, boissons, tabac | Textiles | Clothing, footwear and made-up textiles Articles d'habil-lement, chaussures et ouvrages en tissu | Wood products and furniture Bois et meubles | Paper and paper products Papier et ouvrages en papier | Printing and publish-ing Im-primerie et édition | Leather and leather products except wearing apparel Cuir et articles en cuir, à l'exclu-sion des articles d'habil-lement | Rubber products Ouvrages en caout-chouc | Chemicals and chemical, petroleum and coal products Produits chi-miques et dérivés du pétrole et du charbon | Non-metallic mineral products Produits minéraux non métal-liques | Basic metals Métal-lurgie de base | Metal products Ouvrages en métaux | Other manu-factur-ing Autres in-dustries manufac-turières | Année et rubrique |
|---|---|---|---|---|---|---|---|---|---|---|---|---|---|---|---|
| ISIC | 2–3 | 20–22 | 23 | 24 | 25–26 | 27 | 28 | 29 | 30 | 31–32 | 33 | 34 | 35–38 | 39 | CITI |
| *a. Absolute Figures — Chiffres absolus* | | | | | | | | | | | | | | | |
| **1948** Number of establishments. | 119 772 | 25 334 | 21 601 | 1 911 | 24 285 | 3 984 | 2 376 | 914 | 473 | 3 860 | 6 260 | 874 | 17 262 | 10 638 | **1948** Nombre d'établissements |
| Gross receipts. | 49 748.4 | 13 111.1 | 8 721.3 | 602.0 | 7 378.7 | 990.1 | 4 234.3 | 305.0 | 207.6 | 2 379.7 | 2 811.2 | 554.8 | 5 624.7 | 2 827.9 | Recettes brutes |
| Number of engaged (As of 31.XII). | 372.3 | 84.8 | 65.2 | 5.5 | 68.1 | 12.8 | 12.8 | 2.2 | 1.5 | 14.2 | 23.2 | 3.0 | 52.8 | 26.2 | Nombre de personnes occupées (au 31.XII) |
| **1953** Number of establishments. | 233 176 | 59 645 | 47 449 | 16 424 | 40 095 | 6 187 | 3 946 | 1 603 | 411 | 3 743 | 12 637 | 1 068 | 26 130 | 13 838 | **1953** Nombre d'établissements |
| Gross receipts. | 168 660.2 | 63 506.6 | 29 290.1 | 8 171.4 | 24 178.3 | 3 169.3 | 2 763.7 | 2 039.7 | 407.5 | 3 758.9 | 6 970.5 | 1 540.1 | 15 343.0 | 7 521.1 | Recettes brutes |
| Number of engaged (As of 31.XII). | 512.4 | 132.9 | 109.0 | 33.5 | 83.6 | 14.8 | 9.1 | 3.6 | 0.9 | 8.5 | 29.6 | 2.5 | 56.4 | 28.0 | Nombre de personnes occupées (au 31.XII) |
| Number of employees (As of 31.XII). | 150.5 | 33.7 | 26.9 | 8.6 | 29.5 | 2.6 | 3.9 | 1.3 | 0.4 | 3.4 | 10.1 | 1.2 | 20.9 | 8.0 | Nombre de salariés (au 31.XII) |
| **1958** Number of establishments. | 242 647 | 61 355 | 42 169 | 14 282 | 41 180 | 6 421 | 4 820 | 1 660 | 532 | 2 904 | 12 258 | 1 087 | 28 061 | 25 918 | **1958** Nombre d'établissements |
| Gross receipts. | 231 350.7 | 86 800.3 | 28 169.4 | 10 621.5 | 35 742.8 | 4 938.2 | 4 492.8 | 3 072.5 | 615.8 | 4 995.0 | 8 819.7 | 2 472.2 | 22 710.0 | 17 900.5 | Recettes brutes |
| Number of engaged (As of 31.XII). | 552.7 | 146.3 | 96.8 | 31.0 | 88.9 | 15.6 | 11.8 | 3.9 | 1.3 | 7.1 | 29.4 | 2.6 | 61.9 | 56.1 | Nombre de personnes occupées (au 31.XII) |
| Number of employees (As of 31.XII). | 171.7 | 39.1 | 25.1 | 9.5 | 32.8 | 3.8 | 5.0 | 1.5 | 0.5 | 3.1 | 10.4 | 1.3 | 24.5 | 15.1 | Nombre de salariés (au 31.XII) |
| *b. Structure* | | | | | | | | | | | | | | | |
| **1948** Distribution in percent of number of engaged | 100.0 | 22.8 | 17.5 | 1.5 | 18.3 | 3.4 | 3.4 | 0.6 | 0.4 | 3.8 | 6.2 | 0.8 | 14.2 | 7.1 | **1948** Distribution en pour-centage du nombre de personnes occupées |
| **1953** Distribution in percent of number of engaged | 100.0 | 25.9 | 21.3 | 6.5 | 16.3 | 2.9 | 1.8 | 0.7 | 0.2 | 1.6 | 5.8 | 0.5 | 11.0 | 5.5 | **1953** Distribution en pour-centage du nombre de personnes occupées |
| Employees as a percent of engaged | 29.4 | 25.4 | 24.7 | 25.7 | 35.3 | 17.6 | 42.8 | 36.1 | 44.4 | 40.0 | 34.1 | 48.0 | 37.0 | 28.6 | Salariés en pourcentage des personnes occupées |
| **1958** Distribution in percent of number of engaged | 100.0 | 26.5 | 17.5 | 5.6 | 16.1 | 2.8 | 2.1 | 0.7 | 0.2 | 1.3 | 5.3 | 0.5 | 11.2 | 10.2 | **1958** Distribution en pour-centage du nombre de personnes occupées |
| Employees as a percent of engaged | 31.1 | 26.7 | 25.9 | 30.6 | 36.9 | 24.4 | 42.4 | 38.5 | 38.5 | 43.7 | 35.4 | 50.0 | 39.6 | 26.9 | Salariés en pourcentage des personnes occupées |

## 6. CHARACTERISTICS OF PRIVATELY-OWNED INDUSTRIAL ESTABLISHMENTS; HAVING FIVE OR MORE OPERATIVES, 1938 and 1948; AND HAVING FOUR OR MORE PERSONS ENGAGED, 1953 and 1958

### CARACTERISTIQUES DES ETABLISSEMENTS INDUSTRIELS PRIVES COMPTANT CINQ OUVRIERS OU PLUS EN 1938 et 1948, ET QUATRE PERSONNES OCCUPEES OU PLUS EN 1953 et 1958

Number of establishments in units; value added and wages and salaries in million Yen; number of engaged employees and operatives in thousands; energy consumed in thousand metric tons of coal equivalents; electricity consumed in million KWH; capacity of installed power equipment in thousand horsepower; value added per engaged and per employee and wages and salaries per employee and per operative in thousand Yen; energy consumed per engaged and per operative in metric tons of coal equivalents; electricity consumed per engaged, per employee and per operative in thousand KWH; capacity of installed power equipment per employee and per operative in horsepower.

Nombre d'établissements en unités; valeur ajoutée et traitements et salaires en millions de yens; nombre de personnes occupées, de salariés et d'ouvriers en milliers; énergie consommée en milliers de tonnes métriques d'équivalent charbon; électricité consommée en millions de kWh; puissance installée en milliers de chevaux-vapeur; valeur ajoutée par personne occupée et par salarié et traitements et salaires par salarié et par ouvrier en milliers de yens; énergie consommée par personne occupée et par ouvrier en tonnes métriques d'équivalent charbon; électricité consommée par personne occupée, par salarié et par ouvrier en milliers de kWh; puissance installée par personne occupée, par salarié et par ouvrier en chevaux-vapeur.

## A. The Major Groups of Mining — Les classes de la branche Industries extractives

### a. Absolute Figures – Chiffres absolus

| Year and item of data | All mining (Toutes industries extractives) | Coal mining (Extraction du charbon) | Metal mining (Extraction des minerais métalliques) | Crude petroleum and natural gas (Pétrole brut et gaz naturel) | Other mining (Divers) | Année et rubrique |
|---|---|---|---|---|---|---|
| ISIC | 1 | 11 | 12 | 13 | 14-19 | CITI |
| **1953** | | | | | | **1953** |
| Value added | 222 353.0 | 178 740.9 | 28 838.9 | 3 381.8 | 11 391.4 | Valeur ajoutée |
| Employees: Number (As of 31.XII) | 518.1 | 400.4 | 77.4 | 5.1 | 35.2 | Salariés: Nombre (au 31.XII) |
| Wages and salaries | ... | ... | 14 127.3 | 1 849.8 | 5 565.7 | Traitements et salaires |
| Operatives: Number (As of 31.XII) | 458.8 | 355.1 | 68.3 | 4.2 | 31.2 | Ouvriers: Nombre (au 31.XII) |
| Wages and salaries | ... | ... | 11 187.4 | 805.9 | 4 674.6 | Traitements et salaires |
| Energy consumed | ... | ... | 166.7 | 9.7 | 201.0 | Energie consommée |
| Electricity consumed | ... | ... | 664.7 | 45.9 | 85.5 | Electricité consommée |
| **1958** | | | | | | **1958** |
| Number of establishments | 8 262 | 1 066 | 740 | 5 316 | 1 140 | Nombre d'établissements |
| Value added | 230 119.0 | 169 523.2 | 40 442.1 | 4 820.5 | 15 333.2 | Valeur ajoutée |
| Employees: Number (As of 31.XII) | 467.7 | 355.5 | 69.0 | 5.9 | 37.3 | Salariés: Nombre (au 31.XII) |
| Wages and salaries | 123 359.5 | 99 761.7 | 15 567.3 | 1 630.1 | 6 400.4 | Traitements et salaires |
| Operatives: Number (As of 31.XII) | 413.9 | 317.0 | 60.1 | 4.5 | 32.3 | Ouvriers: Nombre (au 31.XII) |
| Wages and salaries | 100 449.2 | 81 554.9 | 12 435.2 | 1 227.4 | 5 231.7 | Traitements et salaires |
| Energy consumed | 2 177.3 | 1 750.1 | 234.6 | 42.8 | 149.8 | Energie consommée |
| Electricity consumed | 3 012.3 | 2 028.6 | 769.5 | 96.0 | 118.2 | Electricité consommée |

### b. Structure

| Year and item of data | All mining (Toutes industries extractives) | Coal mining (Extraction du charbon) | Metal mining (Extraction des minerais métalliques) | Crude petroleum and natural gas (Pétrole brut et gaz naturel) | Other mining (Divers) | Année et rubrique |
|---|---|---|---|---|---|---|
| ISIC | 1 | 11 | 12 | 13 | 14-19 | CITI |
| **1953** | | | | | | **1953** |
| Distribution in percent of: | | | | | | Distribution en pourcentage: |
| Value added | 100.0 | 80.4 | 13.0 | 1.5 | 5.1 | Valeur ajoutée |
| Number of employees | 100.0 | 77.3 | 14.9 | 1.0 | 6.8 | Nombre de salariés |
| Per employee: | | | | | | Par salarié: |
| Value added | 429.2 | 446.4 | 372.6 | 663.1 | 323.6 | Valeur ajoutée |
| Wages and salaries | ... | ... | 182.5 | 362.7 | 158.1 | Traitements et salaires |
| Energy consumed | 1.67 | 1.22 | 2.15 | 1.90 | 5.71 | Energie consommée |
| Electricity consumed | ... | ... | 8.6 | 9.0 | 2.4 | Electricité consommée |
| Value added per unit of wages and salaries | ... | ... | 2.04 | 1.83 | 2.05 | Valeur ajoutée par unité de traitements et salaires |
| Operatives as a percent of employees | 88.6 | 88.7 | 88.2 | 82.4 | 88.6 | Ouvriers en pourcentage des salariés |
| Per operative: | | | | | | Par ouvrier: |
| Wages and salaries | ... | ... | 163.80 | 191.88 | 149.83 | Traitements et salaires |
| Energy consumed | ... | ... | 2.44 | 2.31 | 6.44 | Energie consommée |
| Electricity consumed | ... | ... | 9.73 | 10.93 | 2.74 | Electricité consommée |
| **1958** | | | | | | **1958** |
| Distribution in percent of: | | | | | | Distribution en pourcentage: |
| Value added | 100.0 | 73.7 | 17.6 | 2.1 | 6.6 | Valeur ajoutée |
| Number of employees | 100.0 | 76.0 | 14.7 | 1.3 | 8.0 | Nombre de salariés |
| Per employee: | | | | | | Par salarié: |
| Value added | 492.0 | 476.8 | 586.1 | 817.0 | 411.1 | Valeur ajoutée |
| Wages and salaries | 263.8 | 280.6 | 225.6 | 276.3 | 171.6 | Traitements et salaires |
| Energy consumed | 4.66 | 4.92 | 2.40 | 7.25 | 4.02 | Energie consommée |
| Electricity consumed | 6.4 | 5.7 | 11.2 | 16.3 | 3.2 | Electricité consommée |
| Value added per unit of wages and salaries | 1.86 | 1.70 | 2.60 | 2.96 | 2.40 | Valeur ajoutée par unité de traitements et salaires |
| Operatives as a percent of employees | 88.5 | 89.2 | 87.1 | 76.3 | 86.6 | Ouvriers en pourcentage des salariés |
| Per operative: | | | | | | Par ouvrier: |
| Wages and salaries | 242.7 | 257.3 | 206.9 | 272.8 | 162.0 | Traitements et salaires |
| Energy consumed | 5.26 | 5.52 | 3.90 | 9.51 | 4.64 | Energie consommée |
| Electricity consumed | 7.28 | 6.40 | 12.80 | 21.33 | 3.66 | Electricité consommée |

## B. The Major Groups of Manufacturing — Les classes de la branche Industries manufacturières

| Year and item of data | Manufacturing / Industries manufacturières | Food, beverages and tobacco / Industries alimentaires boissons, tabac | Textiles | Clothing, footwear and made-up textiles / Articles d'habillement, chaussures et ouvrages en tissu | Wood products and furniture / Bois et meubles | Paper and paper products / Papier et ouvrages en papier | Printing and publishing / Imprimerie et édition | Leather and leather products except wearing apparel / Cuir et articles en cuir, à l'exclusion des articles d'habillement | Rubber products / Ouvrages en caoutchouc | Chemicals and chemical, petroleum and coal products / Produits chimiques et dérivés du pétrole et du charbon | Non-metallic mineral products / Produits minéraux non métalliques | Basic metals / Métallurgie de base | Metal products / Ouvrages en métaux | Other manufacturing / Autres industries manufacturières | Année et rubrique |
|---|---|---|---|---|---|---|---|---|---|---|---|---|---|---|---|
| ISIC | 2–3 | 20–22 | 23 | 24 | 25–26 | 27 | 28 | 29 | 30 | 31–32 | 33 | 34 | 35–38 | 39 | CITI |
| *a. Absolute Figures — Chiffres absolus* | | | | | | | | | | | | | | | |
| **1938** | | | | | | | | | | | | | | | **1938** |
| Number of establishments.... | 111 663 | 16 944 | 28 716 | 5 327 | 11 067 | 2 596 | 3 932 | 616 | 842 | 3 983 | 5 352 | 3 915 | 23 645 | 4 728 | Nombre d'établissements |
| Value added........ | 7 065.1 | 640.7 | 1 278.3 | 79.4 | 148.3 | 194.9 | 146.7 | 48.9 | 70.8 | 1 015.9 | 236.2 | 1 052.1 | 2 014.5 | 138.4 | Valeur ajoutée |
| Employees: Number (As of 31.XII).... | 3 479.7 | 212.2 | 1 038.7 | 86.4 | 133.6 | 73.7 | 72.7 | 14.9 | 34.2 | 269.0 | 127.2 | 279.0 | 1 040.4 | 97.7 | Salariés: Nombre (au 31.XII) |
| Operatives: Number (As of 31.XII).... | 3 204.8 | 190.7 | 996.4 | 81.7 | 122.0 | 67.6 | 63.6 | 13.6 | 31.0 | 241.5 | 116.8 | 255.4 | 934.3 | 90.2 | Ouvriers: Nombre (au 31.XII) |
| Wages and salaries......... | 1 432.6 | 62.1 | 272.0 | 25.2 | 54.7 | 26.6 | 37.6 | 8.9 | 14.8 | 111.3 | 55.8 | 183.9 | 541.5 | 38.2 | Traitements et salaires |
| Electricity consumed....... | 14 531.4 | 461.3 | 2 186.1 | 36.3 | 222.6 | 874.0 | 50.9 | 17.3 | 104.9 | 4 552.4 | 479.0 | 4 105.8 | 1 372.4 | 68.4 | Électricité consommée |
| Capacity of installed power equipment (As of 31.XII).... | 8 356.4 | 316.3 | 1 459.6 | 24.5 | 235.0 | 441.0 | 44.6 | 15.3 | 99.1 | 2 022.6 | 780.0 | 1 650.5 | 1 212.7 | 55.2 | Puissance installée (au 31.XII) |
| **1948** | | | | | | | | | | | | | | | **1948** |
| Number of establishments.... | 100 304 | 16 480 | 15 000 | 5 167 | 17 759 | 1 815 | 2 363 | 312 | 851 | 5 745 | 5 230 | 3 430 | 22 582 | 3 570 | Nombre d'établissements |
| Value added........ | 353 304 | 31 090 | 48 973 | 7 650 | 22 464 | 12 741 | 11 632 | 1 494 | 6 302 | 48 166 | 15 683 | 36 589 | 101 637 | 8 883 | Valeur ajoutée |
| Number of engaged........ | 3 678 | 265 | 651 | 132 | 319 | 90 | 101 | 9 | 62 | 360 | 167 | 293 | 1 124 | 105 | Nombre de personnes occupées |
| Employees: Number (As of 31.XII).... | 3 606 | 250 | 635 | 129 | 308 | 89 | 100 | 9 | 61 | 356 | 163 | 291 | 1 112 | 103 | Salariés: Nombre (au 31.XII) |
| Wages and salaries......... | 161 878 | 8 900 | 17 922 | 3 368 | 9 742 | 4 606 | 5 433 | 393 | 2 834 | 19 555 | 7 246 | 18 527 | 59 242 | 4 110 | Traitements et salaires |
| Operatives: Number (As of 31.XII).... | 2 939.7 | 195.8 | 572.2 | 109.5 | 244.0 | 72.0 | 68.2 | 6.3 | 49.3 | 282.2 | 136.9 | 241.7 | 878.8 | 82.8 | Ouvriers: Nombre (au 31.XII) |
| Wages and salaries......... | 125 753.1 | 6 744.3 | 14 665.4 | 2 690.7 | 7 938.7 | 3 578.7 | 3 635.1 | 288.4 | 2 050.0 | 14 606.7 | 5 940.8 | 15 001.5 | 45 473.5 | 3 139.3 | Traitements et salaires |
| Energy consumed ... | 16 130.2 | 1 269.7 | 1 298.6 | 52.9 | 140.2 | 1 114.6 | 26.9 | 19.3 | 235.9 | 5 138.5 | 2 161.8 | 2 681.3 | 1 897.3 | 93.2 | Énergie consommée |
| Electricity consumed....... | 12 853.8 | 689.9 | 776.8 | 36.4 | 252.3 | 931.4 | 45.2 | 8.6 | 125.2 | 5 271.8 | 505.5 | 2 572.8 | 1 582.6 | 55.3 | Électricité consommée |
| Capacity of installed power equipment (As of 31.XII).... | 10 117 | 498 | 823 | 55 | 529 | 473 | 45 | 19 | 347 | 1 904 | 582 | 2 321 | 2 451 | 70 | Puissance installée (au 31.XII) |
| **1953** | | | | | | | | | | | | | | | **1953** |
| Number of establishments.... | 172 612 | 30 146 | 31 666 | 8 727 | 28 423 | 4 217 | 7 396 | 920 | 805 | 5 111 | 11 049 | 5 416 | 30 965 | 7 771 | Nombre d'établissements |
| Value added........ | 1 686 402 | 162 139 | 238 756 | 26 888 | 74 598 | 77 862 | 86 096 | 4 216 | 28 996 | 244 792 | 92 009 | 203 656 | 403 703 | 42 691 | Valeur ajoutée |
| Number of engaged (As of 31.XII).... | 4 655 | 472 | 947 | 150 | 377 | 142 | 202 | 14 | 72 | 361 | 237 | 382 | 1 124 | 175 | Nombre de personnes occupées (au 31.XII) |
| Employees: Number (As of 31.XII).... | 4 518 | 443 | 913 | 141 | 358 | 138 | 198 | 14 | 72 | 360 | 225 | 380 | 1 107 | 169 | Salariés: Nombre (au 31.XII) |
| Wages and salaries......... | 667 323 | 49 512 | 90 751 | 12 183 | 36 782 | 25 592 | 33 650 | 2 054 | 10 383 | 68 601 | 33 036 | 87 739 | 195 683 | 21 357 | Traitements et salaires |
| Operatives: Number (As of 31.XII).... | 3 774.8 | 369.3 | 827.4 | 124.1 | 299.9 | 115.3 | 130.1 | 12.4 | 62.4 | 284.7 | 196.5 | 314.3 | 896.1 | 142.3 | Ouvriers: Nombre (au 31.XII) |
| Wages and salaries......... | 471 657.7 | 33 012.9 | 68 972.8 | 8 992.0 | 26 835.5 | 17 315.8 | 1 841.5 | 7 467.8 | 7467.8 | 44 157.3 | 25 084.1 | 65 786.3 | 138 177.2 | 15 423.1 | Traitements et salaires |
| Energy consumed ... | 38 033.0 | 2 720.0 | 2 525.3 | 43.3 | 140.6 | 2 313.3 | 112.8 | 32.1 | 346.1 | 11 856.8 | 5 331.8 | 10 666.0 | 1 767.0 | 177.9 | Énergie consommée |
| Electricity consumed....... | 30 513.2 | 1 287.4 | 2 115.9 | 60.6 | 336.5 | 2 333.4 | 118.2 | 14.8 | 236.6 | 14 177.2 | 1 228.3 | 6 309.0 | 2 172.8 | 122.5 | Électricité consommée |
| **1958** | | | | | | | | | | | | | | | **1958** |
| Number of establishments.... | 212 725 | 36 613 | 34 996 | 10 082 | 32 311 | 6 686 | 9 897 | 1 348 | 1 224 | 5 422 | 12 534 | 6 034 | 41 568 | 14 010 | Nombre d'établissements |
| Value added........ | 3 174 836.3 | 322 312.9 | 324 245.3 | 43 069.1 | 139 049.0 | 124 213.2 | 164 291.5 | 8 930.0 | 54 367.9 | 397 810.5 | 153 967.7 | 318 259.7 | 998 598.6 | 125 720.9 | Valeur ajoutée |
| Number of engaged (As of 31.XII).... | 6 111.7 | 657.2 | 1 032.4 | 185.0 | 484.0 | 212.8 | 267.7 | 22.0 | 103.8 | 411.1 | 315.5 | 441.4 | 1 632.2 | 346.6 | Nombre de personnes occupées (au 31.XII) |
| Employees: Number (As of 31.XII).... | 5 936.8 | 623.7 | 991.4 | 174.2 | 459.7 | 206.6 | 262.0 | 21.1 | 103.1 | 409.2 | 301.5 | 439.2 | 1 610.1 | 335.0 | Salariés: Nombre (au 31.XII) |
| Wages and salaries......... | 1 171 366.2 | 89 790.6 | 131 703.6 | 19 484.0 | 63 410.3 | 44 129.9 | 63 459.0 | 3 726.4 | 17 776.7 | 114 325.7 | 57 190.5 | 139 361.8 | 371 222.5 | 55 787.2 | Traitements et salaires |
| Operatives: Number (As of 31.XII).... | 4 892.5 | 514.5 | 890.6 | 153.0 | 388.7 | 171.0 | 175.3 | 17.5 | 89.3 | 312.4 | 259.7 | 359.1 | 1 281.3 | 280.1 | Ouvriers: Nombre (au 31.XII) |
| Wages and salaries......... | 802 187.7 | 58 163.1 | 98 890.9 | 14 491.6 | 46 625.8 | 30 304.4 | 33 141.1 | 2 613.0 | 12 742.5 | 71 386.1 | 42 396.8 | 100 634.1 | 252 319.1 | 38 479.2 | Traitements et salaires |

# JAPAN

## B. The Major Groups of Manufacturing (continued) — Les classes de la branche Industries manufacturières (suite)

| Year and item of data | Manufacturing<br>Industries manufacturières | Food, beverages and tobacco<br>Industries alimentaires, boissons, tabac | Textiles | Clothing, footwear and made-up textiles<br>Articles d'habillement, chaussures et ouvrages en tissu | Wood products and furniture<br>Bois et meubles | Paper and paper products<br>Papier et ouvrages en papier | Printing and publishing<br>Imprimerie et édition | Leather and leather products except wearing apparel<br>Cuir et articles en cuir, à l'exclusion des articles d'habillement | Rubber products<br>Ouvrages en caoutchouc | Chemicals and chemical, petroleum and coal products<br>Produits chimiques et dérivés du pétrole et du charbon | Non-metallic mineral products<br>Produits minéraux non métalliques | Basic metals<br>Métallurgie de base | Metal products<br>Ouvrages en métaux | Other manufacturing<br>Autres industries manufacturières | Année et rubrique |
|---|---|---|---|---|---|---|---|---|---|---|---|---|---|---|---|
| ISIC | 2–3 | 20–22 | 23 | 24 | 25–26 | 27 | 28 | 29 | 30 | 31–32 | 33 | 34 | 35–38 | 39 | CITI |
| **b. Structure** | | | | | | | | | | | | | | | |
| **1938** <br> Distribution in percent of: | | | | | | | | | | | | | | | **1938** <br> Distribution en pourcentage: |
| Value added | 100.0 | 9.1 | 18.1 | 1.1 | 2.1 | 2.8 | 2.1 | 0.7 | 1.0 | 14.4 | 3.3 | 14.9 | 28.5 | 1.9 | Valeur ajoutée |
| Number of employees | 100.0 | 6.1 | 29.9 | 2.5 | 3.8 | 2.1 | 2.1 | 0.4 | 1.0 | 7.7 | 3.7 | 8.0 | 29.9 | 2.8 | Nombre de salariés |
| Per employee: <br> Value added | 2.0 | 3.0 | 1.2 | 0.9 | 1.1 | 2.6 | 2.0 | 3.3 | 2.1 | 3.8 | 1.8 | 3.8 | 1.9 | 1.4 | Par salarié: <br> Valeur ajoutée |
| Electricity consumed | 4.2 | 2.2 | 2.1 | 0.4 | 1.7 | 11.8 | 0.7 | 1.2 | 3.1 | 16.9 | 3.8 | 14.7 | 1.3 | 0.7 | Électricité consommée |
| Capacity of installed power equipment | 2.40 | 1.49 | 1.40 | 0.28 | 1.76 | 5.98 | 0.61 | 1.03 | 2.90 | 7.52 | 6.13 | 5.92 | 1.16 | 0.56 | Puissance installée |
| Operatives as a percent of employees | 92.1 | 89.9 | 95.9 | 94.6 | 91.3 | 91.7 | 87.5 | 91.3 | 90.6 | 89.8 | 91.8 | 91.5 | 89.8 | 92.3 | Ouvriers en pourcentage des salariés |
| Per operative: <br> Wages and salaries | 0.45 | 0.32 | 0.27 | 0.31 | 0.45 | 0.39 | 0.59 | 0.65 | 0.48 | 0.46 | 0.48 | 0.72 | 0.58 | 0.42 | Par ouvrier: <br> Traitements et salaires |
| Electricity consumed | 4.53 | 2.42 | 2.19 | 0.44 | 1.82 | 12.93 | 0.80 | 1.27 | 3.38 | 18.85 | 4.10 | 16.08 | 1.47 | 0.76 | Électricité consommée |
| Capacity of installed power equipment | 2.61 | 1.66 | 1.46 | 0.30 | 1.93 | 6.52 | 0.70 | 1.12 | 3.20 | 8.38 | 6.68 | 6.46 | 1.30 | 0.61 | Puissance installée |
| **1948** <br> Distribution in percent of: | | | | | | | | | | | | | | | **1948** <br> Distribution en pourcentage: |
| Value added | 100.0 | 8.8 | 13.9 | 2.2 | 6.3 | 3.6 | 3.3 | 0.4 | 1.8 | 13.6 | 4.4 | 10.4 | 28.8 | 2.5 | Valeur ajoutée |
| Number of engaged | 100.0 | 7.2 | 17.7 | 3.6 | 8.7 | 2.4 | 2.7 | 0.2 | 1.7 | 9.8 | 4.5 | 8.0 | 30.6 | 2.9 | Nombre de personnes occupées |
| Per person engaged: <br> Value added | 96.0 | 117.3 | 75.2 | 58.0 | 70.4 | 141.6 | 115.2 | 166.0 | 101.6 | 133.8 | 93.9 | 124.9 | 90.4 | 84.6 | Par personne occupée: <br> Valeur ajoutée |
| Energy consumed | 4.38 | 4.79 | 1.99 | 0.40 | 0.44 | 12.38 | 0.27 | 2.14 | 3.80 | 14.27 | 12.94 | 9.15 | 1.69 | 0.89 | Énergie consommée |
| Electricity consumed | 3.5 | 2.6 | 1.2 | 0.3 | 0.8 | 10.3 | 0.4 | 1.0 | 2.0 | 14.6 | 3.0 | 8.8 | 1.4 | 0.5 | Électricité consommée |
| Capacity of installed power equipment | 2.75 | 1.88 | 1.26 | 0.42 | 1.66 | 5.26 | 0.44 | 2.11 | 5.60 | 5.29 | 3.48 | 7.92 | 2.18 | 0.67 | Puissance installée |
| Employees as a percent of engaged | 98.0 | 94.3 | 97.5 | 97.7 | 96.6 | 98.9 | 99.0 | 100.0 | 98.4 | 98.9 | 97.6 | 99.3 | 98.9 | 98.1 | Salariés en pourcentage des personnes occupées |
| Value added per unit of wages and salaries | 2.18 | 3.49 | 2.73 | 2.27 | 2.30 | 2.77 | 2.14 | 3.80 | 2.22 | 2.46 | 2.16 | 1.97 | 1.72 | 2.16 | Valeur ajoutée par unité de traitements et salaires |
| Operatives as a percent of employees | 81.5 | 78.3 | 90.1 | 84.9 | 79.2 | 80.9 | 68.2 | 70.0 | 80.8 | 79.3 | 84.0 | 83.0 | 79.0 | 80.4 | Ouvriers en pourcentage des salariés |
| Wages and salaries employee | 44.9 | 35.6 | 28.2 | 26.1 | 31.6 | 51.8 | 54.3 | 43.7 | 46.4 | 54.9 | 44.4 | 63.7 | 53.3 | 39.9 | Traitements et salaires par salarié |
| Per operative: <br> Wages and salaries | 42.78 | 34.44 | 25.63 | 24.57 | 32.54 | 49.70 | 53.30 | 45.78 | 41.58 | 51.76 | 43.40 | 62.07 | 51.74 | 37.91 | Par ouvrier: <br> Traitements et salaires |
| Energy consumed | 5.49 | 6.48 | 2.27 | 0.48 | 0.57 | 15.48 | 0.39 | 3.06 | 4.78 | 18.21 | 15.79 | 11.09 | 2.16 | 1.12 | Énergie consommée |
| Electricity consumed | 4.37 | 3.52 | 1.36 | 0.33 | 1.03 | 12 94 | 0.66 | 1.36 | 2.54 | 18.68 | 3.69 | 10.64 | 1.80 | 0.67 | Électricité consommée |
| Capacity of installed power equipment | 3.44 | 2.54 | 1.44 | 0.50 | 2.17 | 6.57 | 0.66 | 3.02 | 7.04 | 6.75 | 4.25 | 9.60 | 2.79 | 0.84 | Puissance installée |

**B.   The Major Groups of Manufacturing** (continued) **— Les classes de la branche Industries manufacturières** (suite)

| Year and item of data | Manufacturing — Industries manufacturières | Food, beverages and tobacco — Industries alimentaires, boissons, tabac | Textiles | Clothing, footwear and made-up textiles — Articles d'habillement, chaussures et ouvrages en tissu | Wood products and furniture — Bois et meubles | Paper and paper products — Papier et ouvrages en papier | Printing and publishing — Imprimerie et édition | Leather and leather products except wearing apparel — Cuir et articles en cuir, à l'exclusion des articles d'habillement | Rubber products — Ouvrages en caoutchouc | Chemicals and chemical, petroleum and coal products — Produits chimiques et dérivés du pétrole et du charbon | Nonmetallic mineral products — Produits minéraux non métalliques | Basic metals — Métallurgie de base | Metal products — Ouvrages en métaux | Other manufacturing — Autres industries manufacturières | Année et rubrique |
|---|---|---|---|---|---|---|---|---|---|---|---|---|---|---|---|
| ISIC | 2–3 | 20–22 | 23 | 24 | 25–26 | 27 | 28 | 29 | 30 | 31–32 | 33 | 34 | 35–38 | 39 | CITI |
| | | | | | | *b. Structure* | | | | | | | | | | |
| **1953** Distribution in percent of: Value added...... | 100.0 | 9.6 | 14.2 | 1.6 | 4.4 | 4.6 | 5.1 | 0.3 | 1.7 | 14.5 | 5.5 | 12.1 | 23.9 | 2.5 | **1953** Distribution en pourcentage: Valeur ajoutée: |
| Number of engaged......... | 100.0 | 10.1 | 20.3 | 3.2 | 8.1 | 3.1 | 4.3 | 0.3 | 1.5 | 7.8 | 5.1 | 8.2 | 24.2 | 3.8 | Nombre de personnes occupées |
| Per person engaged: Value added...... | 362.3 | 343.5 | 252.1 | 179.2 | 197.9 | 548.3 | 426.2 | 301.1 | 402.7 | 678.1 | 388.2 | 533.1 | 359.2 | 243.9 | Par personne occupée: Valeur ajoutée |
| Energy consumed. | 8.17 | 5.76 | 2.67 | 0.29 | 0.37 | 16.29 | 0.56 | 2.29 | 4.81 | 32.84 | 22.50 | 27.92 | 1.57 | 1.02 | Energie consommée |
| Electricity consumed........ | 6.6 | 2.7 | 2.2 | 0.4 | 0.9 | 16.4 | 0.6 | 1.0 | 3.3 | 39.3 | 5.2 | 16.5 | 1.9 | 0.7 | Electricité consommée |
| Employees as a percent of engaged......... | 97.0 | 93.8 | 96.4 | 94.0 | 95.0 | 97.2 | 98.0 | 100.0 | 100.0 | 99.7 | 94.9 | 99.5 | 98.5 | 96.6 | Salariés en pourcentage des personnes occupées |
| Value added per unit of wages and salaries...... | 2.53 | 3.27 | 2.63 | 2.21 | 2.03 | 3.04 | 2.56 | 2.05 | 2.79 | 3.57 | 2.78 | 2.32 | 2.06 | 2.00 | Valeur ajoutée par unité de traitements et salaires |
| Operatives as a percent of employees...... | 83.6 | 83.4 | 90.6 | 88.0 | 83.8 | 83.6 | 65.7 | 88.6 | 86.7 | 79.1 | 87.3 | 82.7 | 80.9 | 84.2 | Ouvriers en pourcentage des salariés |
| Wages and salaries per employee.... | 147.7 | 111.8 | 99.4 | 86.4 | 102.7 | 185.4 | 169.9 | 146.7 | 144.2 | 190.6 | 146.8 | 230.9 | 176.8 | 126.4 | Traitements et salaires par salarié |
| Per operative: Wages and salaries......... | 124.95 | 89.39 | 83.36 | 72.46 | 89.48 | 150.18 | 141.82 | 119.47 | 119.67 | 155.10 | 127.65 | 209.31 | 154.76 | 108.38 | Par ouvrier: Traitements et salaires |
| Energy consumed. | 10.08 | 7.36 | 3.05 | 0.35 | 0.47 | 20.06 | 0.87 | 2.59 | 5.55 | 41.65 | 27.13 | 33.94 | 1.97 | 1.25 | Energie consommée |
| Electricity consumed........ | 8.08 | 3.49 | 2.56 | 0.49 | 1.12 | 20.24 | 0.91 | 1.19 | 3.79 | 49.80 | 6.25 | 20.07 | 2.42 | 0.86 | Electricité consommée |
| **1958** Distribution in percent of: Value added...... | 100.0 | 10.1 | 10.2 | 1.4 | 4.4 | 3.9 | 5.2 | 0.3 | 1.7 | 12.5 | 4.8 | 10.0 | 31.5 | 4.0 | **1958** Distribution en pourcentage: Valeur ajoutée |
| Number of engaged......... | 100.0 | 10.7 | 16.9 | 3.0 | 7.9 | 3.5 | 4.4 | 0.4 | 1.7 | 6.7 | 5.2 | 7.2 | 26.7 | 5.7 | Nombre de personnes occupées |
| Value added per person engaged... | 51.95 | 490.4 | 314.1 | 232.8 | 287.3 | 583.7 | 613.7 | 405.9 | 523.8 | 967.7 | 488.0 | 721.0 | 611.8 | 362.7 | Valeur ajoutée par personne occupée |
| Employees as a percent of engaged......... | 97.1 | 94.9 | 96.0 | 94.2 | 95.0 | 97.1 | 97.9 | 95.9 | 99.3 | 99.5 | 95.6 | 99.5 | 98.6 | 96.6 | Salariés en pourcentage des personnes occupées |
| Value added per unit of wages and salaries...... | 2.71 | 3.59 | 2.46 | 2.21 | 2.19 | 2.81 | 2.59 | 2.40 | 3.06 | 3.48 | 2.69 | 2.28 | 2.69 | 2.25 | Valeur ajoutée par unité de traitements et salaires |
| Operatives as a percent of employees....... | 82.4 | 82.5 | 89.8 | 87.8 | 84.6 | 82.8 | 66.9 | 82.9 | 86.6 | 76.3 | 86.1 | 81.8 | 79.6 | 83.6 | Ouvriers en pourcentage des salariés |
| Wages and salaries per employee..... | 197.3 | 144.0 | 132.8 | 111.8 | 137.9 | 213.6 | 242.2 | 176.6 | 172.4 | 279.4 | 189.7 | 317.3 | 230.6 | 166.5 | Traitements et salaires par salarié |
| Wages and salaries per operative..... | 163.96 | 113.05 | 111.04 | 94.72 | 119.95 | 177.22 | 189.05 | 149.31 | 142.69 | 228.51 | 163.25 | 280.24 | 196.92 | 137.38 | Traitements et salaires par ouvrier |

## 7. FUELS AND ELECTRICITY CONSUMED BY PRIVATELY-OWNED INDUSTRIAL ESTABLISHMENTS; HAVING FIVE OR MORE OPERATIVES, 1948, AND HAVING FOUR OR MORE PERSONS ENGAGED, 1953 and 1958

### COMBUSTIBLES ET ELECTRICITE CONSOMMES PAR LES ETABLISSEMENTS INDUSTRIELS PRIVES COMPTANT CINQ OUVRIERS OU PLUS EN 1948 ET QUATRE PERSONNES OCCUPEES OU PLUS EN 1953 et 1958

### A. Percentage Distribution of Purchased Energy Consumed According to Source
### Répartition en pourcentage de l'energie achetée et consommée suivant la source

Quantities in thousand metric tons of coal equivalents.     Quantités en milliers de tonnes métriques d'équivalent charbon.

### a. The Major Groups of Mining
### Les classes de la branche Industries extractives

#### 1958

| Item of data | Total | Coal mining Extraction du charbon | Metal mining Extraction des minerais métalliques | Crude petroleum and natural gas Pétrole brut et gaz naturel | Other mining Divers | Rubrique |
|---|---|---|---|---|---|---|
| ISIC | 1 | 11 | 12 | 13 | 14-19 | CITI |
| Total energy consumed....... | 2 177.3 | 1 750.1 | 234.6 | 42.8 | 149.8 | Energie totale consommée |
| Percent initially consumed as: | | | | | | Pourcentage consommé sous forme de: |
| Coal............. | 74.2 | 83.1 | 24.8 | 2.6 | 68.0 | Charbon |
| Lignite.......... | 0.5 | 0.4 | 0.4 | 0.2 | 1.8 | Lignite |
| Coke............ | 0.6 | 0.1 | 2.0 | — | 4.1 | Coke |
| Refined oil fuels.. | 4.5 | 2.8 | 7.7 | 31.5 | 11.8 | Pétrole raffiné |
| Gas............. | 2.2 | 1.8 | 0.1 | 36.5 | — | Gaz |
| Electricity...... | 14.2 | 11.8 | 33.0 | 28.3 | 9.1 | Electricité |
| Other fuels...... | 3.8 | — | 32.0 | 0.9 | 5.2 | Autres combustibles |

### b. The Major Groups of Manufacturing — Les classes de la branche Industries manufacturières

| Year and item of data | Manu-facturing Industries manufac-turières | Food, beverages and tobacco Industries alimen-taires, boissons, tabac | Textiles | Clothing, footwear and made-up textiles Articles d'habil-lement, chaussures et ouvrages en tissu | Wood products and furniture Bois et meubles | Paper and paper products Papier et ouvrages en papier | Printing and publish-ing Im-primerie et édition | Leather and leather products except wearing apparel Cuir et articles en cuir, à l'exclu-sion des articles d'habil-lement | Rubber products Ouvrages en caout-chouc | Chemicals and chemical, petroleum and coal products Produits chi-miques et dérivés du pétrole et du charbon | Non-metallic mineral-products Produits minéraux non métal-liques | Basic metals Métal-lurgie de base | Metal products Ouvrages en métaux | Other manu-factur-ing Autres in-dustries manufac-turières | Année et rubrique |
|---|---|---|---|---|---|---|---|---|---|---|---|---|---|---|---|
| ISIC | 2-3 | 20-22 | 23 | 24 | 25-26 | 27 | 28 | 29 | 30 | 31-32 | 33 | 34 | 35-38 | 39 | CITI |
| **1948** | | | | | | | | | | | | | | | **1948** |
| Total energy consumed: | | | | | | | | | | | | | | | Energie totale consommée: |
| Quantity........... | 16 130.2 | 1 269.7 | 1 298.6 | 52.9 | 140.2 | 1 114.6 | 26.9 | 19.3 | 235.9 | 5 138.5 | 2 161.8 | 2 681.3 | 1 897.3 | 93.2 | Quantité |
| Percent of total in specified industry..... | 100.0 | 7.9 | 8.0 | 0.3 | 0.9 | 6.9 | 0.2 | 0.1 | 1.5 | 31.8 | 13.4 | 16.6 | 11.8 | 0.6 | Pourcentage du total par industrie indiquée |
| Percent consumed as: | | | | | | | | | | | | | | | Pourcentage consommé sous forme de: |
| Coal.............. | 64.3 | 51.9 | 55.4 | 27.2 | 32.9 | 60.7 | 35.3 | 68.9 | 76.8 | 74.2 | 76.9 | 61.6 | 46.0 | 53.4 | Charbon |
| Lignite............ | 3.8 | 6.0 | 16.4 | 10.0 | 7.9 | 7.0 | 7.4 | 9.3 | 9.8 | 1.5 | 3.0 | 0.8 | 2.0 | 7.9 | Lignite |
| Coke.............. | 8.3 | 0.8 | 1.2 | 4.2 | 3.5 | 0.5 | 2.2 | 2.1 | 0.3 | 6.3 | 2.3 | 13.7 | 28.8 | 11.6 | Coke |
| Refined oil fuels...... | 2.6 | 0.2 | 0.3 | 1.5 | 1.9 | 0.1 | 7.8 | 1.0 | 1.3 | 0.8 | 1.8 | 10.3 | 2.3 | 1.7 | Pétrole raffiné |
| Gas.............. | 1.6 | 0.1 | 0.1 | 1.0 | 0.1 | 0.1 | 10.1 | — | 0.1 | 3.1 | 1.0 | 0.8 | 2.4 | 2.4 | Gaz |
| Electricity.......... | 8.0 | 6.7 | 7.5 | 8.5 | 22.5 | 7.2 | 20.8 | 5.2 | 6.6 | 9.5 | 1.8 | 8.8 | 10.3 | 7.4 | Electricité |
| Other fuels.......... | 11.4 | 34.3 | 19.1 | 47.6 | 31.2 | 24.4 | 16.4 | 13.5 | 5.1 | 4.6 | 13.2 | 4.0 | 8.2 | 15.6 | Autres combustibles |
| **1953** | | | | | | | | | | | | | | | **1953** |
| Total energy consumed: | | | | | | | | | | | | | | | Energie totale consommée: |
| Quantity........... | 38 033.0 | 2 720.0 | 2 525.3 | 43.3 | 140.6 | 2 313.3 | 112.8 | 32.1 | 346.1 | 11 856.8 | 5 331.8 | 10 666.0 | 1 767.0 | 177.9 | Quantité |
| Percent of total in specified industry..... | 100.0 | 7.2 | 6.6 | 0.1 | 0.4 | 6.1 | 0.3 | 0.1 | 0.9 | 31.2 | 14.0 | 28.0 | 4.6 | 0.5 | Pourcentage du total par industrie indiquée |
| Percent consumed as: | | | | | | | | | | | | | | | Pourcentage consommé sous forme de: |
| Coal.............. | 66.1 | 62.3 | 58.4 | 29.1 | 13.6 | 74.8 | 25.2 | 62.0 | 61.6 | 69.8 | 75.8 | 64.4 | 37.5 | 43.8 | Charbon |
| Lignite............ | 1.1 | 2.3 | 6.2 | 1.1 | 0.6 | 1.8 | 0.7 | 1.5 | 2.5 | 0.4 | 1.6 | 0.1 | 0.7 | 2.9 | Lignite |
| Coke.............. | 7.0 | 0.8 | 0.3 | 2.5 | 1.1 | 0.1 | 0.5 | 0.3 | 0.1 | 7.0 | 3.0 | 12.4 | 17.2 | 5.1 | Coke |
| Refined oil fuels...... | 10.2 | 12.8 | 14.9 | 18.7 | 40.3 | 9.0 | 17.3 | 21.5 | 24.1 | 6.1 | 9.2 | 12.0 | 14.4 | 12.9 | Pétrole raffiné |
| Gas.............. | 4.8 | 2.6 | 0.8 | 11.8 | 1.3 | 1.9 | 31.3 | 1.9 | 0.4 | 7.9 | 3.1 | 3.3 | 8.9 | 14.4 | Gaz |
| Electricity.......... | 6.3 | 5.8 | 10.3 | 17.6 | 29.9 | 9.0 | 13.1 | 5.6 | 8.6 | 6.4 | 1.4 | 5.5 | 14.1 | 8.6 | Electricité |
| Other fuels.......... | 4.5 | 12.9 | 9.1 | 19.2 | 13.2 | 3.4 | 11.9 | 7.2 | 2.7 | 2.4 | 5.9 | 2.3 | 7.2 | 12.3 | Autres combustibles |

**B.   Quantity and Value of Purchased Fuels Consumed and Electricity Purchased, and Produced for Own Use**

### Quantité et valeur des combustibles achetés et consommés et de l'électricité achetée et produite pour l'autoconsommation

Coal, lignite, coke, refined oil fuels in thousand metric tons; gas in million cubic metres; electricity in million KWH; other fuels in thousand metric tons of coal equivalents; value in million Yen.

Charbon, lignite, coke, pétrole raffiné en milliers de tonnes métriques; gaz en millions de mètres cubes; électricité en millions de kWh; autres combustibles en milliers de tonnes métriques d'équivalent charbon; valeur en millions de yen.

### a.   The Major Groups of Mining

### Les classes de la branche Industries extractives

### 1958

| Source of energy | Total | Coal mining Extraction du charbon | Metal mining Extraction des minerais métalliques | Crude petroleum and natural gas Pétrole brut et gaz naturel | Other mining Divers | Source d'énergie |
|---|---|---|---|---|---|---|
| ISIC | 1 | 11 | 12 | 13 | 14-19 | CITI |
| Coal: | | | | | | Charbon: |
| Quantity | 1 614.8 | 1 453.7 | 58.2 | 1.1 | 101.8 | Quantité |
| Value | 4 370.5 | 3 360.9 | 340.7 | 8.9 | 660.0 | Valeur |
| Lignite: | | | | | | Lignite: |
| Quantity | 32.4 | 21.0 | 3.0 | 0.3 | 8.1 | Quantité |
| Value | 72.3 | 34.9 | 8.7 | 1.0 | 27.7 | Valeur |
| Coke: | | | | | | Coke: |
| Quantity | 13.7 | 1.6 | 5.2 | — | 6.9 | Quantité |
| Value | 152.8 | 23.1 | 60.4 | 0.2 | 69.1 | Valeur |
| Refined oil fuels: | | | | | | Pétrole raffiné: |
| Quantity | 66.3 | 33.5 | 12.0 | 9.1 | 11.7 | Quantité |
| Value | 1 327.1 | 664.8 | 289.8 | 113.4 | 259.1 | Valeur |
| Natural and manufactured gas: | | | | | | Gaz naturel et manufacturé: |
| Quantity | 36.0 | 23.8 | 0.4 | 11.8 | — | Quantité |
| Value | 108.4 | 25.6 | 7.0 | 75.3 | 0.5 | Valeur |
| Natural gas: | | | | | | Gaz naturel: |
| Quantity | 35.3 | 23.6 | — | 11.7 | — | Quantité |
| Value | 96.8 | 23.2 | — | 73.6 | — | Valeur |
| Manufactured gas: | | | | | | Gaz manufacturé: |
| Quantity | 0.7 | 0.2 | 0.4 | 0.1 | — | Quantité |
| Value | 11.6 | 2.4 | 7.0 | 1.7 | 0.5 | Valeur |
| Electricity: | | | | | | Electricité: |
| Purchased: | | | | | | Achetée: |
| Quantity | 2 445.3 | 1 623.9 | 618.2 | 95.6 | 107.6 | Quantité |
| Value | 12 640.9 | 8 706.1 | 2 820.1 | 440.4 | 674.3 | Valeur |
| Produced for own use— quantity | 566.9 | 404.7 | 151.3 | 0.3 | 10.6 | Produite pour l'auto-consommation— quantité |
| Other fuels: | | | | | | Autres combustibles: |
| Quantity | 83.9 | 0.6 | 75.1 | 0.4 | 7.8 | Quantité |
| Value | 190.8 | 14.8 | 113.8 | 3.7 | 58.5 | Valeur |

# JAPAN

## b.  The Major Groups of Manufacturing — Les classes de la branche Industries manufacturières

| Year and source of energy | Manufacturing / Industries manufacturières | Food, beverages and tobacco / Industries alimentaires, boissons, tabac | Textiles | Clothing, footwear and made-up textiles / Articles d'habillement, chaussures et ouvrages en tissu | Wood products and furniture / Bois et meubles | Paper and paper products / Papier et ouvrages en papier | Printing and publishing / Imprimerie et édition | Leather and leather products except wearing apparel / Cuir et articles en cuir, à l'exclusion des articles d'habillement | Rubber products / Ouvrages en caoutchouc | Chemicals and chemical, petroleum and coal products / Produits chimiques et dérivés du pétrole et du charbon | Non-metallic mineral products / Produits minéraux non métalliques | Basic metals / Métallurgie de base | Metal products / Ouvrages en métaux | Other manufacturing / Autres industries manufacturières | Année et source d'énergie |
|---|---|---|---|---|---|---|---|---|---|---|---|---|---|---|---|
| ISIC | 2–3 | 20–22 | 23 | 24 | 25–26 | 27 | 28 | 29 | 30 | 31–32 | 33 | 34 | 35–38 | 39 | CITI |
| **1948** | | | | | | | | | | | | | | | **1948** |
| Coal: | | | | | | | | | | | | | | | Charbon: |
| Quantity | 10 372.6 | 658.6 | 719.8 | 14.4 | 46.1 | 676.8 | 9.5 | 13.3 | 181.2 | 3 815.0 | 1 663.1 | 1 651.4 | 873.6 | 49.8 | Quantité |
| Value | 22 654.7 | 1 487.1 | 1 490.5 | 38.6 | 130.1 | 1 604.5 | 29.5 | 26.8 | 475.4 | 5 617.2 | 4 546.4 | 4 772.2 | 2 310.1 | 126.3 | Valeur |
| Lignite: | | | | | | | | | | | | | | | Lignite: |
| Quantity | 1 880.7 | 229.9 | .645.2 | 16.2 | 33.6 | 237.1 | 6.2 | 5.4 | 70.4 | 238.9 | 195.4 | 67.6 | 112.4 | 22.4 | Quantité |
| Value | 2 730.1 | 329.1 | 901.2 | 23.5 | 77.7 | 361.1 | 10.3 | 5.4 | 103.2 | 381.8 | 250.6 | 104.1 | 150.0 | 32.1 | Valeur |
| Coke: | | | | | | | | | | | | | | | Coke: |
| Quantity | 1 484.6 | 10.6 | 17.6 | 2.4 | 5.4 | 5.6 | 0.7 | 0.5 | 0.9 | 358.5 | 54.3 | 408.4 | 607.7 | 12.0 | Quantité |
| Value | 6 535.1 | 42.3 | 39.8 | 11.6 | 22.5 | 4.6 | 2.0 | 1.2 | 4.4 | 1 425.5 | 208.6 | 1 994.7 | 2 721.1 | 56.8 | Valeur |
| Refined oil fuels: | | | | | | | | | | | | | | | Pétrole raffiné: |
| Quantity | 276.0 | 1.9 | 2.7 | 0.5 | 1.8 | 0.5 | 1.4 | 0.1 | 2.0 | 25.6 | 25.2 | 184.4 | 28.8 | 1.1 | Quantité |
| Value | 3 580.0 | 67.1 | 70.2 | 21.7 | 117.6 | 9.0 | 34.9 | 2.2 | 44.6 | 330.2 | 195.1 | 2 024.1 | 635.4 | 27.9 | Valeur |
| Natural and manufactured gas: | | | | | | | | | | | | | | | Gaz naturel et manufacturé: |
| Quantity | 425.7 | 2.7 | 1.6 | 0.9 | 0.2 | 1.5 | 4.6 | — | 0.2 | 262.4 | 36.6 | 36.2 | 75.1 | 3.7 | Quantité |
| Value | 2 028.3 | 12.7 | 4.5 | 1.2 | 2.1 | 19.5 | 20.4 | — | 3.3 | 1 076.7 | 488.0 | 77.2 | 304.2 | 18.5 | Valeur |
| Electricity: Purchased: | | | | | | | | | | | | | | | Electricité: Achetée: |
| Quantity | 10 320.7 | 682.9 | 776.2 | 36.4 | 252.2 | 646.7 | 45.1 | 8.6 | 125.0 | 3 921.5 | 318.6 | 1 888.2 | 1 564.0 | 55.3 | Quantité |
| Value | 12 981.1 | 1 135.7 | 1 170.9 | 133.8 | 866.0 | 565.5 | 106.7 | 16.4 | 229.1 | 2 571.4 | -433.6 | 1 906.8 | 3 697.8 | 147.4 | Valeur |
| Produced for own use—quantity | 2 533.1 | 7.0 | 0.6 | — | 0.1 | 284.7 | 0.1 | — | 0.2 | 1 350.3 | 186.9 | 684.6 | 18.6 | — | Produite pour l'auto-consommation—quantité |
| Other fuels: | | | | | | | | | | | | | | | Autres combustibles: |
| Quantity | 1 842.1 | 435.9 | 248.2 | 25.2 | 43.8 | 272.1 | 4.4 | 2.6 | 12.0 | 236.1 | 285.7 | 105.7 | 155.9 | 14.5 | Quantité |
| Value | 5 337.3 | 1 129.1 | 652.1 | 104.9 | 236.2 | 714.1 | 25.5 | 5.9 | 36.5 | 472.6 | 884.9 | 405.5 | 617.3 | 52.7 | Valeur |
| **1953** | | | | | | | | | | | | | | | **1953** |
| Coal: | | | | | | | | | | | | | | | Charbon: |
| Quantity | 25 114.0 | 1 694.4 | 1 473.3 | 12.6 | 19.1 | 1 729.6 | 28.4 | 19.9 | 213.3 | 8 275.4 | 4 038.5 | 6 868.2 | 663.4 | 77.9 | Quantité |
| Value | 152 152.0 | 9 292.5 | 8 762.5 | 78.9 | 116.6 | 10 264.5 | 194.9 | 132.0 | 1 189.7 | 44 053.1 | 26 696.3 | 46 149.3 | 4 676.4 | 545.3 | Valeur |
| Lignite: | | | | | | | | | | | | | | | Lignite: |
| Quantity | 1 294.4 | 193.1 | 477.5 | 1.4 | 2.8 | 129.5 | 2.4 | 1.6 | 26.6 | 126.3 | 258.3 | 20.4 | 38.7 | 15.8 | Quantité |
| Value | 3 014.5 | 468.9 | 1 089.6 | 2.3 | 6.2 | 257.1 | 6.3 | 4.3 | 51.2 | 303.8 | 632.7 | 60.0 | 98.1 | 34.0 | Valeur |
| Coke: | | | | | | | | | | | | | | | Coke: |
| Quantity | 2 980.4 | 40.0 | 9.2 | 1.2 | 1.8 | 3.2 | 0.7 | 0.1 | 0.4 | 924.5 | 178.0 | 1 473.8 | 337.5 | 10.0 | Quantité |
| Value | 31 796.9 | 416.8 | 89.9 | 11.5 | 15.7 | 31.2 | 5.5 | 0.8 | 2.4 | 8 766.0 | 1 223.6 | 16 475.1 | 4 620.6 | 137.8 | Valeur |
| Refined oil fuels: | | | | | | | | | | | | | | | Pétrole raffiné: |
| Quantity | 2 587.0 | 232.0 | 250.2 | 5.4 | 37.7 | 138.3 | 13.0 | 4.6 | 55.6 | 484.8 | 328.3 | 852.6 | 169.2 | 15.3 | Quantité |
| Value | 37 687.4 | 3 442.4 | 3 929.3 | 137.3 | 1 465.3 | 2 074.1 | 404.3 | 71.2 | 1 237.0 | 5 460.4 | 4 879.7 | 10 514.1 | 3 724.0 | 348.3 | Valeur |
| Natural and manufactured gas: | | | | | | | | | | | | | | | Gaz naturel et manufacturé: |
| Quantity | 1 366.9 | 52.5 | 16.0 | 3.8 | 1.4 | 32.6 | 26.6 | 0.4 | 1.0 | 704.4 | 125.0 | 265.5 | 118.4 | 19.3 | Quantité |
| Value | 8 308.4 | 756.2 | 259.3 | 56.6 | 21.8 | 249.0 | 381.0 | 7.4 | 15.6 | 2 316.3 | 618.1 | 1 484.7 | 1 849.6 | 292.8 | Valeur |
| Electricity: Purchased: | | | | | | | | | | | | | | | Electricité: Achetée: |
| Quantity | 19 258.0 | 1 263.7 | 2 076.9 | 60.5 | 336.4 | 1 662.8 | 118.2 | 14.8 | 236.6 | 6 107.4 | 607.8 | 4 658.8 | 1 991.8 | 122.3 | Quantité |
| Value | 71 467.8 | 6 619.0 | 9 613.9 | 539.1 | 3 263.9 | 6 390.5 | 795.4 | 116.8 | 1 288.4 | 13 175.4 | 2 636.2 | 15 461.9 | 10 703.5 | 863.8 | Valeur |
| Produced for own use—quantity | 11 255.5 | 23.7 | 39.0 | 0.1 | 0.1 | 670.6 | — | — | — | 8 069.8 | 620.5 | 1 650.2 | 181.0 | 0.2 | Produite pour l'auto-consommation—quantité |
| Other fuels: | | | | | | | | | | | | | | | Autres combustibles: |
| Quantity | 1 703.0 | 349.6 | 229.9 | 8.3 | 18.5 | 79.5 | 13.4 | 2.3 | 9.3 | 280.2 | 313.2 | 250.3 | 126.7 | 21.8 | Quantité |
| Value | 12 295.8 | 2 271.7 | 1 595.8 | 87.0 | 375.5 | 505.3 | 157.2 | 17.8 | 75.3 | 1 578.0 | 2 157.6 | 1 900.7 | 1 363.2 | 210.7 | Valeur |

# JORDAN — JORDANIE

## Gross Domestic Product

The figures of the gross domestic product shown in Table 1 were obtained from the following publications: *Economic Trends in Jordan, 1954-1959*, prepared by Mr. R. S. Porter and published by the Middle East Development Division, British Embassy, Beirut; and the *National Income of Jordan, 1959-1960* prepared and published by the Department of Statistics, Ministry of Economy, Amman. Mr. R. S. Porter acted as adviser in the preparation of the second report.

## Characteristics and Structure of Industrial Activity

The 1954 figures shown in Table 2 were taken from the *Census of Mining and Manufacturing Industries in Jordan, 1954*, the Economic Planning Division of the Ministry of Economy, Amman, 1955. The Census related to mining and manufacturing establishments engaging five or more adult persons except those which were engaged primarily in repairs, custom manufacturing, such as tailoring to order, pressing olive oil, gold and silver smithing, and stone and sand quarrying.

However, the number of engaged shown in Table 2 includes children as well as adults working for the covered establishments as proprietors, unpaid family workers, homeworkers, or employees. The gross value of production is the sales value, ex-factory and net of excise and other indirect taxes, of all goods manufactured during the year of the Census and of services rendered during this period in the form of repairs and contract work done for other establishments. The capacity of installed power equipment is the sum of the rated horsepowers of all prime movers and of electric motors driven by purchased electricity.

The statistics for 1957 shown in Tables 2 and 3 were compiled from the results of the Labour and Industrial survey of 1957 published in *Annual Statistical Yearbook, 1957/58*, Department of Statistics, Ministry of Economy, Amman. The survey was taken by the Department and covered establishments irrespective of size. The figures for 1957 set out in Table 3 relate to all mining and manufacturing establishments whereas those given in Table 2 refer to establishments engaging five or more persons. The latter figures are comparable in field of coverage and definitions with data for 1954 given in Table 2.

The figures for 1959 given in Table 3 are based on the results of the 1959 Census of Manufacturing Industries taken by the Department of Statistics, Ministry of Econ-

## Produit intérieur brut

Les chiffres du tableau 1 relatifs au produit intérieur brut sont tirés des publications suivantes : *Economic Trends in Jordan, 1954-1959*, préparés par M. R. S. Porter et publiés par la Division du développement du Moyen-Orient, Ambassade britannique, Beyrouth, et le *National Income of Jordan, 1959-1960*, préparé et publié par le Département de la statistique, Ministère de l'économie, Amman. M. R. S. Porter a joué le rôle de conseiller technique pour l'établissement du second rapport.

## Caractéristiques et structure de l'activité industrielle

Les chiffres de 1954 reproduits au tableau 2 sont tirés de *Census of Mining and Manufacturing Industries in Jordan, 1954*, publié par la Division de la planification économique du Ministère des affaires économiques, Amman (1955). Le recensement de 1954 portait sur les établissements miniers et manufacturiers occupant au moins cinq adultes, à l'exception de ceux qui étaient surtout spécialisés dans les travaux de réparation, les travaux à façon (par exemple confection de vêtements sur mesure), l'extraction de l'huile d'olive, les travaux d'orfèvrerie et l'extraction de la pierre et du sable.

Toutefois, dans le tableau 2, le nombre de personnes occupées comprend les enfants et les adultes travaillant pour les établissements recensés en tant que propriétaires, travailleurs familiaux non rémunérés, travailleurs à domicile ou salariés. La valeur brute de la production est la valeur des ventes — départ usine et déduction faite des droits de consommation et autres impôts indirects — de toutes les marchandises produites pendant l'année du recensement et des services fournis pendant cette période sous forme de réparations et de travaux contractuels effectués pour d'autres établissements. La puissance installée représente la puissance nominale de tous les moteurs primaires et des moteurs électriques actionnés par de l'électricité achetée.

Les chiffres des tableaux 2 et 3 relatifs à 1957 ont été calculés à partir des résultats de l'enquête de 1957 sur l'industrie et la main-d'œuvre, publiés dans *Annual Statistical Yearbook, 1957/58*, Département de la statistique, Ministère de l'économie, Amman. L'enquête a été exécutée par le Département et portait sur tous les établissements, quelle que soit leur dimension. Les chiffres de 1957 reproduits au tableau 3 se rapportent à tous les établissements miniers et manufacturiers, tandis que ceux du tableau 2 se rapportent aux établissements occupant cinq personnes ou plus. Ces derniers chiffres sont comparables, quant à la couverture et aux définitions, aux données de 1954 présentées au tableau 2.

Les chiffres de 1959 reproduits au tableau 3 sont fondés sur les résultats du recensement des industries manufacturières de 1959 exécuté par le Département de la sta-

omy, Amman, and published by the same Department in *Report on the Industrial Census of 1959*. The census was limited to manufacturing industries and covered establishments of all sizes operating in that field of activity. In contrast to the previous censuses, more details were gathered from establishments in the 1959 census.

The definitions of the establishment and the items of data on labour (number of persons engaged, number of employees and wages and salaries) utilized in the 1959 Census are consistent with those utilized in the earlier Censuses and the recommendations in the International Standards in Basic Industrial Statistics. Wages and salaries paid include estimates of payments in kind. The data on value added shown from the 1959 Census are valued at market prices and are net of the cost of only the materials, fuels, electricity and industrial services from other establishments consumed in production.

tistique, Ministère de l'économie, Amman; ces résultats ont été publiés par le même Département dans *Report on the Industrial Census of 1959*. Le recensement était limité aux industries manufacturières et portait sur tous les établissements de cette branche d'activité, quelle que fût leur dimension. Contrairement aux recensements précédents, le recensement de 1959 a permis de recueillir plus de renseignements auprès des établissements.

Les définitions des établissements et des rubriques relatives à l'emploi (nombre de personnes occupées, nombre de salariés et traitements et salaires) adoptées pour le recensement de 1959 sont conformes aux définitions utilisées lors des recensements antérieurs et aux recommandations présentées dans les Normes internationales relatives aux statistiques indutrielles de base. Les traitements et salaires payés comprennent la valeur estimative des paiements en nature. Les chiffres de la valeur ajoutée provenant du recensement de 1959 sont évalués aux prix du marché; en sont exclus uniquement le coût des matières premières et auxiliaires, des combustibles et de l'électricité utilisés pour la production, ainsi que le coût des services industriels fournis aux mêmes fins par d'autres établissements.

## 1. THE GROSS DOMESTIC PRODUCT — PRODUIT INTERIEUR BRUT

Million Dinars          Millions de dinars

### A. Expenditure on the Gross Domestic Product at Market Prices
### Dépenses relatives au produit intérieur brut aux prix du marché

| Item of data and year / Rubrique et année | Total | Consumption / Consommation | | Gross Domestic Capital Formation / Formation brute de capital intérieur | | Net exports of goods and services / Exportations nettes de biens et de services | |
|---|---|---|---|---|---|---|---|
| | | Total | Government / Etat | Total | Fixed / Fixe | Exports less imports / Exportations moins importations | Exports / Exportations |
| **At Current Prices — Aux prix courants** | | | | | | | |
| **Absolute figures — Chiffres absolus** | | | | | | | |
| 1954 | 51.3 | 59.1 | 13.7 | 5.9 | 4.8 | −13.7 | 6.1 |
| 1955 | 47.3 | 61.7 | 14.6 | 5.1 | 8.0 | −19.5 | 7.3 |
| 1956 | 66.6 | 69.7 | 16.8 | 13.7 | 8.0 | −16.8 | 9.4 |
| 1957 | 67.4 | 79.8 | 19.7 | 9.3 | 8.3 | −21.7 | 10.7 |
| 1958 | 75.2 | 92.8 | 25.7 | 9.2 | 10.9 | −26.8 | 9.9 |
| 1959 | 85.8 | 106.3 | 27.7 | 10.6 | 13.7 | −31.1 | 11.5 |
| 1960 | 92.7 | 112.2 | 27.7 | 13.8 | 13.3 | −33.3 | 12.4 |
| **Percentage distribution of average annual expenditure — Distribution en pourcentage des dépenses annuelles moyennes** | | | | | | | |
| 1954–1960 | 100.0 | 119.5 | 30.0 | 13.9 | 13.8 | −33.4 | 13.8 |
| 1954 | 100.0 | 115.2 | 26.7 | 11.5 | 9.4 | −26.7 | 11.9 |
| 1958 | 100.0 | 123.4 | 34.2 | 12.2 | 14.5 | −35.6 | 13.2 |
| 1960 | 100.0 | 121.0 | 29.9 | 14.9 | 14.3 | −35.9 | 13.4 |

## B. The Gross Domestic Product at Factor Cost According to Origin
## Origine par secteur d'activité du produit intérieur brut au coût des facteurs

| Item of data and year / Rubrique et année | Total | Agricultural sector / Secteur agricole | Industrial Sector — Secteur Industriel | | | Transportation and communication / Transports et communications | Other sectors / Autres secteurs |
|---|---|---|---|---|---|---|---|
| | | | Total | Mining, manufacturing and electricity / Industries extractives, manufacturières et électricité | Construction / Bâtiment et travaux publics | | |
| ISIC — CITI | 0–9 | 0 | 1–511 | 1–3, 511 | 4 | 7 | 512–522, 6, 8–9 |
| | a. At Current Prices — Aux prix courants | | | | | | |
| Absolute figures — Chiffres absolus | | | | | | | |
| 1954............ | 47.7 | 14.2 | 5.4 | 4.2 | 1.2 | 4.4 | 23.7 |
| 1955............ | 43.0 | 6.2 | 6.7 | 5.2 | 1.5 | 5.5 | 24.6 |
| 1956............ | 61.4 | 19.0 | 8.0 | 6.3 | 1.7 | 6.8 | 27.6 |
| 1957............ | 61.9 | 12.8 | 8.7 | 6.8 | 1.9 | 8.3 | 32.1 |
| 1958............ | 69.1 | 12.9 | 10.0 | 7.6 | 2.4 | 9.0 | 37.2 |
| 1959............ | 77.9 | 11.4 | 11.7 | 8.0 | 3.7 | 9.7 | 45.1 |
| 1960............ | 84.3 | 13.0 | 11.4 | 8.4 | 3.0 | 10.1 | 49.8 |
| Percentage distribution according to sector— Distribution en pourcentage par secteur | | | | | | | |
| 1954 – 1960..... | 100.0 | 20.0 | 13.9 | 10.5 | 3.4 | 12.1 | 54.0 |
| 1954............ | 100.0 | 29.7 | 11.3 | 8.8 | 2.5 | 9.3 | 49.7 |
| 1958............ | 100.0 | 18.6 | 14.5 | 11.0 | 3.5 | 13.0 | 53.9 |
| 1960............ | 100.0 | 15.4 | 13.5 | 9.9 | 3.6 | 12.0 | 59.1 |

## 2. CHARACTERISTICS OF MINING AND MANUFACTURING ESTABLISHMENTS WITH FIVE OR MORE PERSONS ENGAGED
## CARACTERISTIQUES DES ETABLISSEMENTS MINIERS ET MANUFACTURIERS OCCUPANT CINQ PERSONNES OU PLUS
## 1954, 1957

Number of establishments in units; gross value of production and wages and salaries in thousand Dinars; number of engaged and employees in units; capacity of installed power equipment in horsepower; and capacity of installed power equipment per person engaged in horsepower.

Nombre d'établissements en unités; valeur brute de la production et traitements et salaires en milliers de dinars; nombre de personnes occupées et de salariés en unités; puissance installée en chevaux-vapeur; puissance installée par personne occupée en chevaux-vapeur.

### A. Selected Divisions of Industrial Activity — Quelques branches de l'activité industrielle

| Year and item of data | Total | Mining / Industries extractives | Manufacturing [1] / Industries manufacturières [1] | Année et rubrique | Year and item of data | Total | Mining / Industries extractives | Manufacturing [1] / Industries manufacturières [1] | Année et rubrique |
|---|---|---|---|---|---|---|---|---|---|
| ISIC | 1–3 | 1 | 2–3 | CITI | ISIC | 1–3 | 1 | 2–3 | CITI |
| | a. Absolute Figures Chiffres absolus | | | | | b. Structure | | | |
| 1954 | | | | 1954 | 1954 | | | | 1954 |
| Number of establishments...... | 425 | 3 | 422 | Nombre d'établissements | Distribution in percent of number of engaged.......... | 100.0 | 8.7 | 91.3 | Répartition en pourcentage du nombre de personnes occupées |
| Gross value of production....... | 6 929.2 | 174.0 | 6 755.2 | Valeur brute de la production | Capacity of installed power equipment per person engaged | 1.29 | 0.23 | 1.39 | Puissance installée par personne occupée |
| Number of engaged............ | 8 003 | 699 | 7 304 | Nombre de personnes occupées | Wages and salaries per employee | 99.8 | 92.8 | 100.5 | Traitements et salaires par salarié |
| Employees: | | | | Salariés: | Employees as a percent of engaged.................. | 90.6 | 97.1 | 90.0 | Salariés en pourcentage des personnes occupées |
| Number................... | 7 251 | 679 | 6 572 | Nombre | | | | | |
| Wages and salaries....... | 723.4 | 63.0 | 660.4 | Traitements et salaires | | | | | |
| Capacity of installed power equipment............... | 10 324 | 158 | 10 166 | Puissance installée | | | | | |
| 1957 | | | | 1957 | 1957 | | | | 1957 |
| Number of establishments...... | 1 038 | 13 | 1 025 | Nombre d'établissements | Distribution in percent of number of engaged.......... | 100.0 | 15.2 | 84.8 | Répartition en pourcentage du nombre de personnes occupées |
| Number of engaged............ | 13 453 | 2 040 | 11 413 | Nombre de personnes occupées | Employees as a percent of engaged.................. | 88.3 | 94.6 | 87.1 | Salariés en pourcentage des personnes occupées |
| Number of employees.......... | 11 877 | 1 931 | 9 946 | Nombre de salariés | | | | | |

For footnotes see end of table.

Pour les notes, voir au bas du tableau.

# JORDAN

## B. The Major Groups of Manufacturing — Les classes de la branche Industries manufacturières

| Year and item of data | Manufactur-ing [1] / Industries manufac-turières [1] | Food, beverages and tobacco / Industries alimen-taires, boissons, tabac | Textiles | Clothing, footwear and made-up textiles / Articles d'habil-lement, chaussures et ouvrages en tissu | Wood products and furniture / Bois et meubles | Paper and paper products / Papier et ouvrages en papier | Printing and publish-ing / Im-primerie et édition | Leather and leather products except wearing apparel / Cuir et articles en cuir, à l'exclu-sion des articles d'habil-lement | Rubber and chemical products / Caout-chouc et produits chi-miques | Non-metallic mineral products / Produits minéraux non métal-liques | Basic metals / Métal-lurgie de base | Metal products / Ouvrages en métaux | Other manufac-turing / Autres in-dustries manufac-turières | Année et rubrique |
|---|---|---|---|---|---|---|---|---|---|---|---|---|---|---|
| ISIC | 2–3 | 20–22 | 23 | 24 | 25–26 | 27 | 28 | 29 | 30–31 | 33 | 34 | 35–38 | 39 | CITI |

### a. Absolute Figures — Chiffres absolus

| | | | | | | | | | | | | | | |
|---|---|---|---|---|---|---|---|---|---|---|---|---|---|---|
| **1954** | | | | | | | | | | | | | | **1954** |
| Number of establishments. | 422 | 96 | 26 | 57 | 50 | 8 | 14 | 11 | 30 | 38 | — | 60 | 32 | Nombre d'établissements |
| Gross value of production | 6 755.2 | 3 645.4 | 171.7 | 348.7 | 290.5 | 156.0 | 176.4 | 55.1 | 381.6 | 942.2 | — | 521.4 | 66.2 | Valeur brute de la production |
| Number of engaged | 7 304 | 1 848 | 388 | 906 | 767 | 179 | 351 | 71 | 472 | 947 | — | 1 144 | 231 | Nombre de personnes occupées |
| Employees: | | | | | | | | | | | | | | Salariés: |
| Number | 6 572 | 1 637 | 343 | 833 | 670 | 172 | 314 | 35 | 426 | 901 | — | 1 055 | 186 | Nombre |
| Wages and salaries | 660.4 | 170.0 | 22.7 | 77.2 | 67.9 | 13.0 | 34.5 | 3.5 | 32.1 | 91.7 | — | 132.8 | 15.0 | Traitements et salaires |
| Capacity of installed power equipment | 10 166 | 2 896 | 161 | 104 | 960 | 75 | 145 | 53 | 124 | 4 476 | — | 1 139 | 33 | Puissance installée |
| **1957** | | | | | | | | | | | | | | **1957** |
| Number of establishments. | 1 025 | 186 | 54 | 292 | 172 | 12 | 21 | 4 | 29 | 88 | 1 | 159 | 7 | Nombre d'établissements |
| Number of engaged | 11 413 | 2 588 | 540 | 2 467 | 1 528 | 294 | 370 | 46 | 514 | 1 121 | 86 | 1 811 | 48 | Nombre de personnes occupées |
| Number of employees | 9 946 | 2 325 | 504 | 1 914 | 1 326 | 283 | 351 | 30 | 477 | 1 029 | 85 | 1 594 | 28 | Nombre de salariés |

### b. Structure

| | | | | | | | | | | | | | | |
|---|---|---|---|---|---|---|---|---|---|---|---|---|---|---|
| **1954** | | | | | | | | | | | | | | **1954** |
| Distribution in percent of number of engaged | 100.0 | 25.3 | 5.3 | 12.4 | 10.5 | 2.4 | 4.8 | 1.0 | 6.5 | 12.9 | — | 15.7 | 3.2 | Répartition en pourcentage du nombre de personnes occupées |
| Capacity of installed power equipment per person engaged | 1.39 | 1.57 | 0.41 | 0.11 | 1.25 | 0.42 | 0.41 | 0.75 | 0.26 | 4.73 | — | 1.00 | 0.14 | Puissance installée par personne occupée |
| Wages and salaries per employee | 100.5 | 103.8 | 66.2 | 92.7 | 101.3 | 75.6 | 109.9 | 100.0 | 75.4 | 101.8 | — | 125.9 | 80.6 | Traitements et salaires par salarié |
| Employees as a percent of engaged | 90.0 | 88.6 | 88.4 | 91.9 | 87.4 | 96.1 | 89.4 | 49.3 | 90.2 | 95.1 | — | 92.2 | 80.5 | Salariés en pourcentage des personnes occupées |
| **1957** | | | | | | | | | | | | | | **1957** |
| Distribution in percent of number of engaged | 100.0 | 22.6 | 4.8 | 21.6 | 13.4 | 2.5 | 3.3 | 0.4 | 4.5 | 9.8 | 0.8 | 15.8 | 0.5 | Répartition en pourcentage du nombre de personnes occupées |
| Employees as a percent of engaged | 87.1 | 89.8 | 93.3 | 77.6 | 86.8 | 96.2 | 94.9 | 65.2 | 92.8 | 91.8 | 98.8 | 88.0 | 58.3 | Salariés en pourcentage des personnes occupées |

[1] The 1954 figures exclude olive oil extraction (in ISIC major group 31), gold and silver smithing (in ISIC major group 34) and all establishments engaged entirely in repair or custom work.

[1] En 1954, non compris l'extraction de l'huile d'olive (dans CITI classe 31), l'orfèvrerie (dans CITI classe 34) et tous les établissements effectuant exclusivement des travaux de réparation ou des travaux à façon.

## 3. CHARACTERISTICS OF ALL MINING AND MANUFACTURING ESTABLISHMENTS
## CARACTERISTIQUES DE TOUS LES ETABLISSEMENTS MINIERS ET MANUFACTURIERS
### 1957, 1959

Number of establishments and number of engaged, employees and operatives in units; value added and wages and salaries in thousand Dinars; value added per engaged, and wages and salaries per employee in Dinars.

Nombre d'établissements et nombre de personnes occupées, de salariés et d'ouvriers en unités; valeur ajoutée et traitements et salaires en milliers de dinars; valeur ajoutée par personne occupée et traitements et salaires par salarié en dinars.

### A. Selected Divisions of Industrial Activity — Quelques branches de l'activité industrielle

| Year and item of data | Total | Mining / Industries ex-tractives | Manu-facturing / Industries manu-facturières | Année et rubrique | Year and item of data | Total | Mining / Industries ex-tractives | Manu-facturing / Industries manu-facturières | Année et rubrique |
|---|---|---|---|---|---|---|---|---|---|
| ISIC | 1-3 | 1 | 2-3 | CITI | ISIC | 1-3 | 1 | 2-3 | CITI |
| | **a. Absolute Figures — Chiffres absolus** | | | | | **b. Structure** | | | |
| **1957** | | | | 1957 | **1957** | | | | 1957 |
| Number of establishments | 5 138 | 365 | 4 773 | Nombre d'établissements | Distribution in percent of number of engaged | 100.0 | 13.9 | 86.1 | Répartition en pourcentage du nombre de personnes occupées |
| Number of engaged | 23 271 | 3 225 | 20 046 | Nombre de personnes occupées | Employees as a percent of engaged | 74.4 | 90.8 | 71.8 | Salariés en pourcentage des personnes occupées |
| Number of employees | 17 322 | 2 927 | 14 395 | Nombre de salariés | | | | | |

474

## B. The Major Groups of Manufacturing — Les classes de la branche Industries manufacturières

| Year and item of data | Manufacturing — Industries manufacturières | Food, beverages and tobacco — Industries alimentaires, boissons, tabac | Textiles — Textiles | Clothing, footwear and made-up textiles — Articles d'habillement, chaussures et ouvrages en tissu | Wood products and furniture — Bois et meubles | Paper and paper products — Papier et ouvrages en papier | Printing and publishing — Imprimerie et édition | Leather and leather products except wearing apparel — Cuir et articles en cuir, à l'exclusion des articles d'habillement | Rubber products — Ouvrages en caoutchouc | Chemicals and chemical, petroleum and coal products — Produits chimiques et dérivés du pétrole et du charbon | Non-metallic mineral products — Produits minéraux non métalliques | Basic metals — Métallurgie de base | Metal products — Ouvrages en métaux | Other manufacturing — Autres industries manufacturières | Année et rubrique |
|---|---|---|---|---|---|---|---|---|---|---|---|---|---|---|---|
| ISIC | 2–3 | 20–22 | 23 | 24 | 25–26 | 27 | 28 | 29 | 30 | 31–32 | 33 | 34 | 35–38 | 39 | CITI |
| *a. Absolute Figures — Chiffres absolus* | | | | | | | | | | | | | | | |
| **1957** | | | | | | | | | | | | | | | **1957** |
| Number of establishments. | 4 773 | 721 | 45 | 1 718 | 763 | 32 | 31 | 59 | 3 | 28 | 107 | 1 | 1 024 | 241 | Nombre d'établissements |
| Number of engaged.... | 20 046 | 4 047 | 330 | 5 272 | 2 941 | 325 | 399 | 148 | 151 | 705 | 912 | 86 | 3 894 | 836 | Nombre de personnes occupées |
| Number of employees... | 14 395 | 3 145 | 296 | 3 333 | 1 982 | 312 | 375 | 66 | 145 | 677 | 783 | 85 | 2 655 | 541 | Nombre de salariés |
| **1959** | | | | | | | | | | | | | | | **1959** |
| Number of establishments. | 6 887 | 1 303 | 103 | 3 204 | 840 | 14 | 39 | 35 | 14 | 25 | 129 | — | 961 | 220 | Nombre d'établissements |
| Value added.......... | 6 453.3 | 2 469.3 | 224.4 | 1 003.3 | 605.6 | 22.5 | 174.1 | 62.7 | 16.5 | 73.5 | 884.3 | — | 627.7 | 289.4 | Valeur ajoutée |
| Number of engaged.... | 23 068 | 6 126 | 1 345 | 6 416 | 2 562 | 84 | 710 | 122 | 51 | 224 | 1 359 | — | 3 331 | 738 | Nombre de personnes occupées |
| Number of employees... | 13 504 | 4 524 | 409 | 2 692 | 1 409 | 60 | 643 | 59 | 31 | 181 | 1 161 | — | 1 978 | 357 | Nombre de salariés |
| Wages and salaries..... | 1 309.6 | 425.5 | 39.6 | 204.5 | 142.7 | 2.8 | 62.5 | 12.3 | 3.7 | 11.2 | 175.4 | — | 191.8 | 37.6 | Traitements et salaires |
| Number of operatives... | 12 357 | 3 969 | 386 | 2 314 | 1 364 | 59 | 616 | 59 | 29 | 173 | 1 101 | — | 1 936 | 351 | Nombre d'ouvriers |
| *b. Structure* | | | | | | | | | | | | | | | |
| **1957** | | | | | | | | | | | | | | | **1957** |
| Distribution in percent of number of engaged... | 100.0 | 20.1 | 1.7 | 26.3 | 14.7 | 1.6 | 2.0 | 0.7 | 0.8 | 3.5 | 4.5 | 0.5 | 19.4 | 4.2 | Répartition en pourcentage du nombre de personnes occupées |
| Employees as a percent of engaged........ | 71.3 | 77.7 | 89.7 | 63.2 | 67.4 | 96.0 | 94.0 | 44.6 | 96.0 | 96.0 | 85.8 | 98.8 | 68.2 | 64.7 | Salariés en pourcentage des personnes occupées |
| **1959** | | | | | | | | | | | | | | | **1959** |
| Distribution in percent of: | | | | | | | | | | | | | | | Distribution en pourcentage: |
| Value added....... | 100.0 | 38.2 | 3.5 | 15.5 | 9.4 | 0.4 | 2.7 | 0.9 | 0.3 | 1.1 | 13.7 | — | 9.8 | 4.5 | Valeur ajoutée |
| Number of engaged.. | 100.0 | 26.5 | 5.8 | 27.9 | 11.1 | 0.3 | 3.1 | 0.5 | 0.2 | 1.0 | 5.9 | — | 14.5 | 3.2 | Nombre de personnes occupées |
| Value added per person engaged............. | 279.8 | 403.1 | 166.8 | 156.4 | 236.4 | 267.8 | 245.2 | 513.9 | 323.5 | 328.1 | 650.7 | — | 188.4 | 392.1 | Valeur ajoutée par personne occupée |
| Employees as a percent of engaged........ | 58.5 | 73.8 | 30.4 | 42.0 | 55.0 | 71.4 | 90.6 | 48.4 | 60.8 | 80.8 | 85.4 | — | 59.4 | 48.4 | Salariés en pourcentage des personnes occupées |
| Value added per unit of wages and salaries... | 4.93 | 5.80 | 5.67 | 4.91 | 4.24 | 8.04 | 2.78 | 5.10 | 4.46 | 6.56 | 5.04 | — | 3.27 | 7.70 | Valeur ajoutée par unité de traitements et salaires |
| Operatives as a percent of employees........ | 91.5 | 87.7 | 94.4 | 86.0 | 96.8 | 98.3 | 95.8 | 100.0 | 93.5 | 95.6 | 94.8 | — | 97.9 | 98.3 | Ouvriers en pourcentage des salariés |
| Wages and salaries per employee.......... | 97.0 | 94.0 | 96.8 | 75.2 | 101.3 | 46.7 | 97.2 | 208.5 | 119.4 | 61.9 | 151.1 | — | 97.0 | 105.3 | Traitements et salaires par salarié |

# KENYA

## Gross Domestic Product

Estimates of the origin of the gross domestic product are presented in Table 1. The table has been derived from information supplied by the Economics and Statistics Division of the Treasury, Nairobi, in response to the United Nations national accounts questionnaire. Official estimates have been published annually by the East African Statistical Department, Kenya Unit, in *Statistical Abstract*. Descriptions of the methods and sources used can be found in *Domestic Income and Product in Kenya* and in *Capital Formation in Kenya, 1954-1960*.

## Index of Industrial Employment

The index numbers of industrial employment are based on absolute figures of the number of persons engaged derived from the results of two separate enquiries. The data on the numbers engaged in 1956 and 1957 have been obtained from the results of the Surveys of Industrial Production which cover establishments engaging 5 or more persons and are described below under Table 3. Indexes based on these data have been linked in 1957 to indexes based on figures of the number engaged obtained from the Annual Enumeration of Employees carried out jointly by the East African Statistical Department and the Kenya Labour Department. This enumeration covered in principle all establishments, but it is thought that establishments engaging less than 10 persons are far from being completely covered. The data utilised as a basis for the index covers private establishments as the public sector is not available in major group detail.

In 1956 and 1957 the absolute figure is the average of the number engaged as at the final working day of the year surveyed and of the previous year. For 1957 and all the following years, the absolute figure used is the number engaged as at the end of June in each year. The indexes for total manufacturing, total mining and for mining, manufacturing, construction and electricity and gas as a whole, are derived from the unweighted aggregated absolute figures of their constituents.

The results of the Surveys of Industrial Production have been published in various editions of the *Survey of Industrial Production*. The results of the Annual Enumeration have been published annually, in summary form in the *Statistical Abstract* by the East African Statistical Department, Kenya Unit; and in detail in *Reported Employment and Earnings in Kenya* by the Economics and Statistics Division of the Treasury, Nairobi, Kenya.

## Produit intérieur brut

Le tableau 1 contient des estimations du produit intérieur brut par branche d'activité d'origine. Ce tableau a été établi à partir de renseignements fournis par l'*Economics and Statistics Division of the Treasury*, Nairobi, en réponse au questionnaire de l'ONU sur la comptabilité nationale. Les estimations officielles sont publiées chaque année par la Division du Kenya de l'*East African Statistical Department* dans *Statistical Abstract*. Les méthodes et sources utilisées sont indiquées dans *Domestic Income and Product in Kenya* et dans *Capital Formation in Kenya, 1954-1960*.

## Indices de l'emploi dans l'industrie

Les indices de l'emploi dans l'industrie sont fondés sur les chiffres absolus de l'emploi tirés des résultats de deux séries d'enquêtes. Les données concernant le nombre de personnes occupées en 1956 et 1957 ont été tirées des résultats des enquêtes sur la production industrielle dans les établissements occupant cinq personnes ou plus; ces enquêtes sont décrites plus loin dans le commentaire du tableau 3. Les indices fondés sur ces données ont été raccordés, au niveau de 1958, aux indices établis à partir du nombre de personnes occupées fourni par l'*Annual Enumeration of Employees* (Dénombrement annuel des salariés) effectué par l'*East African Statistical Department* et le *Kenya Labour Department*. Cette enquête porte, en principe, sur tous les établissements, mais il semble que les établissements occupant moins de 10 personnes sont loin d'être tous recensés. Les données utilisées pour le calcul de l'indice se rapportent aux établissements privés, car on ne dispose pas de données distinctes sur les diverses classes du secteur public.

En 1956 et 1957, le chiffre absolu représente la moyenne du nombre de personnes occupées au dernier jour ouvré de l'année de l'enquête et des années précédentes. Pour 1957 et les années suivantes, le chiffre absolu utilisé est le nombre de personnes occupées à la fin du mois de juin de chaque année. Les indices relatifs à l'ensemble des industries manufacturières, à l'ensemble des industries extractives et à l'ensemble constitué par les industries manufacturières, les industries extractives, le bâtiment et les travaux publics, et l'électricité et le gaz sont fondés sur les totaux non pondérés des chiffres absolus concernant les éléments de chaque ensemble.

Les résultats des enquêtes sur la production industrielle ont été publiés dans différents numéros de *Survey of Industrial Production*. Les résultats de l'*Annual Enumeration* sont publiés annuellement, sous une forme sommaire, dans *Statistical Abstract* par la Division du Kenya de l'*East African Statistical Department* et, sous une forme détaillée, dans *Reported Employment and Earnings in Kenya* par l'*Economics and Statistics Division of the Treasury*, Nairobi, Kenya.

**The Characteristics and Structure of Industrial Activity**

The data presented in Table 3 have been derived from the results of the first and third Surveys of Industrial Production covering the years 1954 and 1957, carried out by the Kenya Unit of the East African Statistical Department. The surveys have been published in *Kenya Survey of Industrial Production, 1954* and *1957* by the East African Statistical Department, Nairobi. The surveys covered all industrial establishments engaging 5 or more persons during the year surveyed, but in 1954 manufacturing and construction activities of the Public Works Department, local government authorities and the East African Railway workshops were excluded from the Survey altogether. Although returns were not received for all establishments which were covered in principle by the survey, estimates have been made for the missing establishments and are included in the data shown in Table 3.

In general the definitions of the items of data appear to coincide with the International Standards in Basic Industrial Statistics. However the number of engaged does not seem to include homeworkers or unpaid family workers. In 1954, the number of persons engaged is the average of the number as at the last working day of each of the four quarters of 1954. In 1957, it is the average of the number as at the 31 December 1956 and the 31 December 1957. The wages and salaries data shown include payments in kind valued at cost to the establishments. In 1954, the value added has been based on the gross value of production valued at market prices ex-factory, but in 1956, the value added has been based on the gross value of production priced at the point of delivery within the country.

**Caractéristiques et structure de l'activité industrielle**

Les données du tableau 3 sont tirées des résultats des première et troisième enquêtes sur la production industrielle, relatives aux années 1954 et 1957, effectuées par la Division du Kenya de l'*East African Statistical Department*. Les résultats des enquêtes ont été publiés dans *Kenya Survey of Industrial Production,* 1954 et 1957 par l'*East African Statistical Department*, Nairobi. Les enquêtes portaient sur tous les établissements industriels ayant occupé cinq personnes ou plus pendant l'année considérée; en 1954, cependant, ont été exclus du champ de l'enquête les activités manufacturières et les travaux de construction du Département des travaux publics, les services de l'administration locale et les ateliers de réparation de l'*East African Railway*. Les établissements enquêtés n'ont pas tous répondu, mais on a fait des estimations pour tenir compte des non-réponses; ces estimations sont incluses dans les données du tableau 3.

En général, les définitions des rubriques semblent être conformes aux Normes internationales relatives aux statistiques industrielles de base. Cependant, le nombre de personnes occupées ne semble pas comprendre les travailleurs à domicile ni les travailleurs familiaux non rémunérés. En 1954, le nombre de personnes occupées est la moyenne du nombre effectif au dernier jour ouvré de chacun des quatre trimestres de 1954. En 1957, c'est la moyenne du nombre effectif au 31 décembre 1956 et au 31 décembre 1957. Les traitements et salaires comprennent les paiements en nature évalués au coût pour l'établissement. En 1954, la valeur ajoutée est fondée sur la valeur brute de la production aux prix du marché départ usine, mais, en 1956, elle est fondée sur la valeur brute de la production calculée au lieu de livraison à l'intérieur du pays.

## 1. THE GROSS DOMESTIC PRODUCT AT FACTOR COST ACCORDING TO ORIGIN
## ORIGINE PAR SECTEUR D'ACTIVITE DU PRODUIT INTERIEUR BRUT AU COUT DES FACTEURS

Million Pounds           Millions de livres

| Item of data and year / Rubrique et année | Total | Agricultural sector / Secteur agricole | Industrial Sector — Secteur industriel | | | | | Transportation and communication / Transports et communications | Other sectors / Autres secteurs |
|---|---|---|---|---|---|---|---|---|---|
| | | | Total | Mining / Industries extractives | Manufacturing / Industries manufacturières | Construction / Bâtiment et travaux publics | Electricity gas and water / Electricité, gaz et eau | | |
| ISIC — CITI | 0–9 | 0 | 1–5 | 1 | 2–3 | 4 | 5 | 7 | 6, 8–9 |
| *a. At Current Prices — Aux prix courants* | | | | | | | | | |
| **Absolute figures— Chiffres absolus** | | | | | | | | | |
| 1954............. | 157.9 | 74.0 | 22.5 | 0.9 | 14.1 | 6.3 | 1.2 | 11.8 | 49.6 |
| 1955............. | 181.0 | 75.5 | 28.1 | 1.3 | 17.4 | 8.0 | 1.4 | 15.2 | 62.2 |
| 1956............. | 193.4 | 83.3 | 30.7 | 1.4 | 18.2 | 9.3 | 1.8 | 15.8 | 63.6 |
| 1957............. | 205.9 | 85.2 | 32.8 | 1.3 | 19.8 | 9.6 | 2.1 | 18.6 | 69.3 |
| 1958............. | 207.8 | 86.8 | 32.5 | 1.2 | 20.5 | 8.4 | 2.4 | 17.7 | 70.8 |
| 1959............. | 214.0 | 87.8 | 31.8 | 1.1 | 20.2 | 7.9 | 2.6 | 19.0 | 75.4 |
| 1960............. | 224.4 | 89.1 | 33.4 | 1.1 | 21.6 | 7.9 | 2.8 | 20.3 | 81.6 |
| 1961............. | 224.7 | 85.8 | 34.3 | 0.9 | 22.7 | 7.8 | 2.9 | 21.1 | 83.5 |
| **Percentage distribution according to sector— Distribution en pourcentage par secteur** | | | | | | | | | |
| 1954–1960..... | 100.0 | 42.0 | 15.3 | 0.6 | 9.5 | 4.2 | 1.0 | 8.6 | 34.1 |
| 1954............. | 100.0 | 46.9 | 14.2 | 0.6 | 8.9 | 4.0 | 0.7 | 7.5 | 31.4 |
| 1958............. | 100.0 | 41.8 | 15.6 | 0.6 | 9.9 | 4.0 | 1.1 | 8.5 | 34.1 |
| 1960............. | 100.0 | 39.7 | 14.9 | 0.5 | 9.6 | 3.5 | 1.3 | 9.0 | 36.4 |

## 2. INDEX NUMBERS OF INDUSTRIAL EMPLOYMENT — INDICES DE L'EMPLOI DANS L'INDUSTRIE

### A. The Divisions of Industrial Activity
### Les branches de l'activité industrielle

| Period<br>Période | Total | Mining<br>Industries<br>extractives | Manu-<br>facturing [2]<br>Industries<br>manu-<br>facturières [2] | Construction [1]<br>Bâtiment<br>et travaux<br>publics [1] | Electricity<br>and gas<br>Electricité<br>et gaz |
|---|---|---|---|---|---|
| ISIC — CITI | 1-4,<br>511-512 | 1 | 2-3 | 4 | 511-512 |
| *a.* Indexes — Indices (1958 = 100) | | | | | |
| 1956....... | 107 | 139 | 95 | 122 | 96 |
| 1957....... | -107- | -123- | -103- | -116- | -99- |
| 1958....... | 100 | 100 | 100 | 100 | 100 |
| 1959....... | 94 | 85 | 97 | 90 | 99 |
| 1960....... | 95 | 79 | 94 | 101 | -100- |
| 1961....... | ... | 59 | ... | 86 | 98 |
| *b.* Average Annual Rate of Change — Taux annuel moyen de variation | | | | | |
| 1956-1958. | -3.4 | -15.2 | 2.6 | -9.4 | 2.1 |
| 1958-1960. | -2.5 | -11.1 | -3.0 | 0.5 | — |

For footnotes see end of table.

### B. The Major Groups of Mining
### Les classes de la branche Industries extractives

| Period<br>Période | All mining<br>Toutes<br>industries<br>extractives | Metal mining<br>Extraction<br>des minerais<br>métalliques | Other mining<br>Autres<br>industries<br>extractives |
|---|---|---|---|
| ISIC — CITI | 1 | 12 | 14-19 |
| *a.* Indexes — Indices (1958 = 100) | | | |
| 1956............ | 139 | 241 | 124 |
| 1957............ | -123- | -186- | -115- |
| 1958............ | 100 | 100 | 100 |
| 1959............ | 85 | 121 | 80 |
| 1960............ | 79 | 133 | 72 |
| 1961............ | 59 | 135 | 68 |
| *b.* Average Annual Rate of Change — Taux annuel moyen de variation | | | |
| 1956-1958...... | -15.2 | -35.6 | -10.2 |
| 1958-1960...... | -11.1 | 15.3 | -15.1 |

Pour les notes, voir au bas du tableau.

### C. The Major Groups of Manufacturing — Les classes de la branche Industries manufacturières

| Period<br>Période | Manu-<br>facturing [2]<br>Industries<br>manufac-<br>turières [2] | Food,<br>beverages<br>and<br>tobacco<br>Industries<br>alimen-<br>taires,<br>boissons,<br>tabac | Textiles | Clothing,<br>footwear<br>and<br>made-up<br>textiles<br>Articles<br>d'habil-<br>lement,<br>chaussures<br>et<br>ouvrages<br>en tissu | Wood<br>products<br>and<br>furniture<br>Bois et<br>meubles | Paper<br>and<br>paper<br>products<br>Papier<br>et<br>ouvrages<br>en<br>papier | Printing<br>and<br>publishing<br>Im-<br>primerie<br>et<br>édition | Leather<br>and<br>leather<br>products<br>except<br>wearing<br>apparel<br>Cuir et<br>articles<br>en cuir,<br>à l'exclu-<br>sion<br>des<br>articles<br>d'habil-<br>lement | Chemicals<br>and<br>chemical,<br>petroleum<br>and<br>coal<br>products<br>Produits<br>chi-<br>miques<br>et<br>dérivés<br>du<br>pétrole<br>et du<br>charbon | Non-<br>metallic<br>mineral<br>products<br>Produits<br>minéraux<br>non<br>métal-<br>liques | Metal<br>products<br>Ouvrages<br>en<br>métaux | Other<br>manu-<br>facturing<br>Autres<br>industries<br>manufac-<br>turières |
|---|---|---|---|---|---|---|---|---|---|---|---|---|
| ISIC — CITI | 2-3 | 20-22 | 23 | 24 | 25-26 | 27 | 28 | 29 | 31-32 | 33 | 35-38 | 39 |
| *a.* Indexes — Indices (1958 = 100) | | | | | | | | | | | | |
| 1956............ | 95 | 83 | 97 | 107 | 117 | 61 | 93 | 66 | 120 | 80 | 92 | 78 |
| 1957............ | -103- | -90- | -93- | -103- | -118- | -66- | -96- | -103- | -115- | -102- | -108- | 108 |
| 1958............ | 100 | 100 | 100 | 100 | 100 | 100 | 100 | 100 | 100 | 100 | 100 | 100 |
| 1959............ | 97 | 89 | 118 | 104 | 96 | 108 | 100 | 116 | 96 | 89 | 102 | 116 |
| 1960............ | 94 | 74 | 119 | 112 | 100 | 134 | 119 | 128 | 99 | 88 | 101 | 114 |
| 1961............ | ... | 70 | 143 | ... | 73 | 127 | 125 | 165 | 101 | 71 | ... | ... |
| *b.* Average Annual Rate of Change — Taux annuel moyen de variation | | | | | | | | | | | | |
| 1956-1958........ | 2.6 | 9.8 | 1.5 | -3.4 | -7.5 | 28.0 | 3.7 | 23.1 | -8.7 | 11.8 | 4.3 | 13.2 |
| 1958-1960........ | -3.0 | -14.0 | 9.1 | 5.8 | — | 15.8 | 9.1 | 13.1 | -0.5 | -6.2 | 0.5 | 6.8 |

[1] Covers construction undertaken by private contractors only.
[2] Excludes Rubber products (ISIC major group 30).

[1] Il s'agit uniquement des travaux de construction effectués par des entrepreneurs privés.
[2] Non compris Ouvrages en caoutchouc (CITI classe 30).

## 3. CHARACTERISTICS OF INDUSTRIAL ESTABLISHMENTS ENGAGING 5 OR MORE PERSONS
## CARACTERISTIQUES DES ETABLISSEMENTS INDUSTRIELS OCCUPANT 5 PERSONNES OU PLUS
### 1954, 1957

Number of establishments in units; value added and wages and salaries in thousand Pounds; number of engaged in thousands; value added per engaged in Pounds.

Nombre d'établissements en unités; valeur ajoutée et traitements et salaires en milliers de livres; nombre de personnes occupées en milliers; valeur ajoutée par personne occupée en livres.

### A. The Divisions of Industrial Activity — Les branches de l'activité industrielle

| Year and item of data | All industrial activity Toutes industries | Mining Industries ex-tractives | Manu-facturing [1] Industries manufac-turières [1] | Con-struction Bâtiment et travaux publics | Electricity Electricité | Année et rubrique | Year and item of data | All industrial activity Toutes industries | Mining Industries ex-tractives | Manu-facturing [1] Industries manufac-turières [1] | Con-struction Bâtiment et travaux publics | Electricity Electricité | Année et rubrique |
|---|---|---|---|---|---|---|---|---|---|---|---|---|---|
| ISIC | 1-4, 511 | 1 | 2-3 | 4 | 511 | CITI | ISIC | 1-4, 511 | 1 | 2-3 | 4 | 511 | CITI |
| | **a. Absolute Figures — Chiffres absolus** | | | | | | | **b. Structure** | | | | | |
| **1954** | | | | | | **1954** | **1954** | | | | | | **1954** |
| Number of establishments... | ... | 102 | 941 | 348 | ... | Nombre d'établissements | Value added per person engaged.. | ... | 128 | 306 | 216 | ... | Valeur ajoutée par personne occupée |
| Value added...... | ... | 887 | 13 152 | 5 183 | ... | Valeur ajoutée | Value added per unit of wages and salaries..... | ... | 1.64 | 2.38 | 1.71 | ... | Valeur ajoutée par unité de traitements et salaires |
| Number of engaged......... | ... | 6.9 | 42.9 | 24.0 | ... | Nombre de personnes occupées | | | | | | | |
| Wages and salaries. | ... | 540 | 5 525 | 3 037 | ... | Traitements et salaires | | | | | | | |
| **1957** | | | | | | **1957** | **1957** | | | | | | **1957** |
| Number of establishments... | 1 695 | 139 | 1 037 | 509 | 10 | Nombre d'établissements | Distribution in percent of: Value added..... | 100.0 | 3.0 | 55.9 | 35.3 | 5.8 | Distribution en pourcentage: Valeur ajoutée |
| Value added...... | 37 083 | 1 110 | 20 739 | 13 080 | 2 154 | Valeur ajoutée | Number of engaged......... | 100.0 | 6.6 | 44.1 | 47.3 | 2.0 | Nombre de personnes occupées |
| Number of engaged......... | 118.9 | 7.9 | 52.4 | 56.2 | 2.4 | Nombre de personnes occupées | Value added per person engaged..... | 312 | 140 | 396 | 233 | 898 | Valeur ajoutée par personne occupée |
| Wages and salaries. | 20 499 | 730 | 9 028 | 10 093 | 647 | Traitements et salaires | Value added per unit of wages and salaries..... | 1.81 | 1.52 | 2.30 | 1.30 | 3.33 | Valeur ajoutée par unité de traitements et salaires |

For footnotes see end of table.

Pour les notes, voir au bas du tableau.

### B. The Major Groups of Mining — Les classes de la branche Industries extractives

| Year and item of data | All mining Toutes industries extrac-tives | Metal mining Extraction des minerais métal-liques | Other mining Divers | Année et rubrique | Year and item of data | All mining Toutes industries extrac-tives | Metal mining Extraction des minerais métal-liques | Other mining Divers | Année et rubrique |
|---|---|---|---|---|---|---|---|---|---|
| ISIC | 1 | 12 | 14–19 | CITI | ISIC | 1 | 12 | 14–19 | CITI |
| | **a. Absolute Figures Chiffres absolus** | | | | | **b. Structure** | | | |
| **1954** | | | | **1954** | **1954** | | | | **1954** |
| Number of establishments...... | 102 | 34 | 68 | Nombre d'établissements | Distribution in percent of: Value added............... | 100.0 | 30.1 | 69.9 | Distribution en pourcentage: Valeur ajoutée |
| Value added.................. | 887 | 267 | 620 | Valeur ajoutée | Number of engaged.......... | 100.0 | 31.9 | 68.1 | Nombre de personnes occupées |
| Number of engaged........... | 6.9 | 2.2 | 4.7 | Nombre de personnes occupées | Value added per person engaged................... | 128 | 121 | 132 | Valeur ajoutée par personne occupée |
| Wages and salaries........... | 540 | 214 | 326 | Traitements et salaires | Value added per unit of wages and salaries.......... | 1.64 | 1.25 | 1.90 | Valeur ajoutée par unité de traitements et salaires |
| **1957** | | | | **1957** | **1957** | | | | **1957** |
| Number of establishments...... | 139 | 20 | 119 | Nombre d'établissements | Distribution in percent of: Value added............... | 100.0 | 20.6 | 79.4 | Distribution en pourcentage: Valeur ajoutée |
| Value added.................. | 1 110 | 229 | 881 | Valeur ajoutée | Number of engaged.......... | 100.0 | 22.8 | 77.2 | Nombre de personnes occupées |
| Number of engaged........... | 7.9 | 1.8 | 6.1 | Nombre de personnes occupées | Value added per person engaged................... | 140 | 127 | 144 | Valeur ajoutée per personne occupée |
| Wages and salaries........... | 730 | 185 | 545 | Traitements et salaires | Value added per unit of wages and salaries.......... | 1.52 | 1.24 | 1.62 | Valeur ajoutée par unité de traitements et salaires |

## C. The Major Groups of Manufacturing — Les classes de la branche Industries manufacturières

| Year and item of data | Manufacturing [1] / Industries manufacturières [1] (2–3) | Food, beverages and tobacco [1] / Industries alimentaires, boissons, tabac [1] (20–22) | Textiles (23) | Clothing, footwear and made-up textiles / Articles d'habillement, chaussures et ouvrages en tissu (24) | Wood products and furniture / Bois et meubles (25–26) | Paper and paper products / Papier et ouvrages en papier (27) | Printing and publishing / Imprimerie et édition (28) | Leather and leather products except wearing apparel / Cuir et articles en cuir, à l'exclusion des articles d'habillement (29) | Rubber products / Ouvrages en caoutchouc (30) | Chemicals and chemical, petroleum and coal products / Produits chimiques et dérivés du pétrole et du charbon (31–32) | Non-metallic mineral products / Produits minéraux non métalliques (33) | Metal products / Ouvrages en métaux (35–38) | Other manufacturing / Autres industries manufacturières (39) | Année et rubrique |
|---|---|---|---|---|---|---|---|---|---|---|---|---|---|---|
| ISIC | 2–3 | 20–22 | 23 | 24 | 25–26 | 27 | 28 | 29 | 30 | 31–32 | 33 | 35–38 | 39 | CITI |
| *a. Absolute Figures — Chiffres absolus* | | | | | | | | | | | | | | |
| **1954** | | | | | | | | | | | | | | **1954** |
| Number of establishments. | 941 | 181 | 146 | | 205 | 57 | | 31 [2] | | 48 | 26 | 247 | ... | Nombre d'établissements |
| Value added.......... | 13 152 | 4 194 | 827 | | 1 602 | 1 021 | | 272 [2] | | 2 042 | 1 159 | 2 035 | ... | Valeur ajoutée |
| Number of engaged.... | 42.9 | 10.9 | 3:5 | | 11.6 | 1.9 | | 0.6 [2] | | 4.0 | 3.4 | 7.0 | ... | Nombre de personnes occupées |
| Wages and salaries..... | 5 525 | 1 271 | 429 | | 872 | 468 | | 106 [2] | | 608 | 376 | 1 395 | ... | Traitements et salaires |
| **1957** | | | | | | | | | | | | | | **1957** |
| Number of establishments. | 1 037 | 205 | 8 | 124 | 215 | 6 | 60 | 7 | 7 | 50 | 39 | 294 | 22 | Nombre d'établissements |
| Value added.......... | 20 739 | 7 052 | 347 | 840 | 1 728 | 242 | 1 507 | 84 | 151 | 2 275 | 1 902 | 4 464 | 147 | Valeur ajoutée |
| Number of engaged.... | 52.4 | 12.8 | 1.6 | 2.3 | 10.3 | 0.3 | 2.1 | 0.3 | 0.2 | 3.5 | 3.6 | 15.1 | 0.3 | Nombre de personnes occupées |
| Wages and salaries..... | 9 028 | 2 108 | 190 | 396 | 945 | 44 | 681 | 53 | 53 | 694 | 508 | 3 298 | 58 | Traitements et salaires |
| *b. Structure* | | | | | | | | | | | | | | |
| **1954** | | | | | | | | | | | | | | **1954** |
| Distribution in percent of: | | | | | | | | | | | | | | Distribution en pourcentage: |
| Value added........ | 100.0 | 31.9 | 6.3 | | 12.2 | 7.8 | | 2.1 | | 15.5 | 8.8 | 15.4 | — | Valeur ajoutée |
| Number of engaged... | 100.0 | 25.4 | 8.2 | | 27.0 | 4.4 | | 1.4 | | 9.3 | 7.9 | 16.4 | — | Nombre de personnes occupées |
| Value added per person engaged | 306 | 385 | 236 | | 138 | 537 | | 453 | | 510 | 341 | 291 | ... | Valeur ajoutée par personne occupée |
| Value added per unit of wages and salaries............ | 2.38 | 3.30 | 1.93 | | 1.84 | 2.18 | | 2.57 | | 3.36 | 3.08 | 1.46 | ... | Valeur ajoutée par unité de traitements et salaires |
| **1957** | | | | | | | | | | | | | | **1957** |
| Distribution in percent of: | | | | | | | | | | | | | | Distribution en pourcentage: |
| Value added....... | 100.0 | 34.0 | 1.7 | 4.0 | 8.3 | 1.2 | 7.3 | 0.4 | 0.7 | 11.0 | 9.2 | 21.5 | 0.7 | Valeur ajoutée |
| Number of engaged... | 100.0 | 24.4 | 3.0 | 4.4 | 19.6 | 0.6 | 4.0 | 0.6 | 0.4 | 6.7 | 6.9 | 28.8 | 0.6 | Nombre de personnes occupées |
| Value added per person engaged...... | 396 | 551 | 217 | 365 | 168 | 807 | 718 | 280 | 755 | 650 | 528 | 296 | 490 | Valeur ajoutée par personne occupée |
| Value added per unit of wages and salaries......... | 2.30 | 3.34 | 1.83 | 2.12 | 1.83 | 5.50 | 2.21 | 1.58 | 2.85 | 3.28 | 3.74 | 1.35 | 2.53 | Valeur ajoutée par unité de traitements et salaires |

[1] Excluded in 1957 is one establishment engaged in Tobacco manufactures (ISIC major group 22) with a gross value of production of 6 438 thousand Pounds, number engaged of 1.1 thousand and wages and salaries paid of 315 thousand Pounds.
[2] Includes Other manufacturing (ISIC major group 39).

[1] Non compris, en 1957, un établissement de l'Industrie du Tabac (CITI classe 22) pour lequel les chiffres sont les suivants: valeur brute de la production 6 438 milliers de livres; nombre de personnes occupées 1,1 millier; traitements et salaires payés 315 milliers de livres.
[2] Y compris Autres industries manufacturières (CITI classe 39).

## Gross Domestic Product and Gross Domestic Fixed Capital Formation

Estimates of the expenditure on and the origin of the gross domestic product and the origin of the expenditure on the gross domestic fixed capital formation are presented in Table 1. The table is derived from data supplied by the Research Department of the Bank of Korea in response to the United Nations national accounts questionnaire. Official estimates have been published in *Economic Statistics Yearbook, 1962,* by the Research Department of the Bank of Korea, Seoul, and in *Korea Statistical Yearbook,* by the Economic Planning Board, Seoul, Republic of Korea. Information on the methods and sources used has been published by the Bank of Korea in the *National Income and Gross National Product of Korea, (1953-1958).*

## Index Numbers of Industrial Production

The index numbers of industrial production presented in Table 2 are based on indexes compiled and published monthly by the Research Department of the Bank of Korea in the *Monthly Statistical Review.* Both series of index numbers (1958 = 100 and 1960 = 100) have been built up from series of quantity relatives on the production of 149 and 168 individual commodities, respectively. However in a few instances (grain mills, saw mills and printing and publishing), the quantity of electricity purchased was used as the basic indicator. The quantity relatives have been combined into indexes for major groups, using the value of shipments in the base year as weights. The major group indexes are combined into division indexes and these into an index for mining, manufacturing and electricity as a whole, using as weights, value added at factor cost in the base year. The values added used as weights have been derived from the results of the Censuses of Mining and Manufacturing in 1958 and 1960. The 1958 Census is described more fully below under Table 3 but, in principle, covered all establishments with 5 or more persons engaged whereas the 1960 Census differed in that it covered all establishments engaging 3 or more persons. The values added at market prices as published in the Census results have been changed to factor cost and adjusted for changes in stocks for the purposes of the index. The two series of index numbers have been linked at 1960.

Further details of the methods used in computing the indexes can be found in the *Monthly Statistical Review, June 1960, and July 1962,* published by the Bank of Korea.

## Produit intérieur brut et formation brute de capital fixe intérieur

Le tableau 1 contient des estimations des dépenses imputées au produit intérieur brut, du produit intérieur brut par secteur d'activité d'origine et de la formation brute de capital fixe intérieur par secteur d'acquisition. Ce tableau a été établi à partir de données fournies par la Division de la recherche de la Banque de Corée en réponse au questionnaire de l'ONU sur la comptabilité nationale. Des estimations officielles ont été publiées dans *Economic Statistics Yearbook, 1962* par la Division de la recherche de la Banque de Corée, Séoul, et dans *Korea Statistical Yearbook* par le Bureau de la planification économique, Séoul, République de Corée. Des renseignements sur les sources et méthodes adoptées ont été publiés par la Banque de Corée dans *National Income and Gross National Product of Korea (1953-1958).*

## Indices de la production industrielle

Les indices de la production industrielle présentés dans le tableau 2 sont fondés sur des indices calculés par la Division de la recherche de la Banque de Corée et publiés chaque mois dans *Monthly Statistical Review.* Les deux séries d'indices (1958 = 100 et 1960 = 100) ont été établies à partir de séries de rapports quantitatifs portant respectivement sur 149 et 168 marchandises différentes. Cependant, dans certains cas (minoteries, scieries, imprimerie et édition), c'est la quantité d'électricité achetée qui a été prise comme indicateur principal. Les rapports quantitatifs ont été combinés en indices de classes, les coefficients de pondération utilisés étant la valeur des expéditions pendant l'année de base. Les indices de classes ont ensuite été combinés en indices de branches d'activité et ceux-ci en indices relatifs à l'ensemble des industries extractives, manufacturières et productrices d'électricité; les coefficients de pondération utilisés à cette fin sont les valeurs ajoutées au coût des facteurs pendant l'année de base. Les valeurs ajoutées utilisées comme poids ont été tirées des résultats des recensements des industries extractives et manufacturières en 1958 et 1960. Le recensement de 1958 est décrit plus en détail ci-dessous dans le commentaire du tableau 3 mais, en principe, il portait sur tous les établissements occupant 5 personnes ou plus, tandis que le recensement de 1960 portait sur les établissements occupant 3 personnes ou plus. Les valeurs ajoutées qui sont indiquées dans les résultats du recensement sont comptées aux prix du marché; aux fins de l'indice, on les a exprimées au coût des facteurs et on les a corrigées pour tenir compte des variations de stocks. Les deux séries d'indices ont été raccordées au niveau de 1960.

Pour plus de détails sur les méthodes ayant servi à calculer les indices, voir *Monthly Statistical Review, juin 1960 et juillet 1962,* publié par la Banque de Corée.

## The Characteristics and Structure of Industrial Activity

The data shown in Table 3 are derived from the results of the First and Second Censuses of Mining and Manufacturing. The results of the first Census, covering the period between the 1st November 1954 and the 31st October 1955, have been shown in *Summary Report on Mining and Manufacturing Establishment Census, 1955,* published by the Research Department of the Bank of Korea; and the results of the second Census, covering the period between the 1st April 1958 and the 31st March 1959, have been shown in *Final Report—Census of Mining and Manufacturing, 1958,* published by the Korean Reconstruction Bank.

The two censuses covered all establishments which engaged 5 or more persons during October 1955 and March 1959 respectively, and also those establishments not operating during October 1955 or March 1959 but which engaged 5 or more persons during 3 months of the reporting year. However all establishments directly operated by the Central Government (such as tobacco manufacturing, salt extraction and railway workshops) or by the Armed Forces of the Republic of Korea, by the United Nations and by diplomatic missions in Korea have been excluded.

The definitions of the items of data shown are generally consistent with the International Standards in Basic Industrial Statistics except that value added in 1958 is derived from the gross value of shipments with no adjustment for stock changes. Value added is valued at market prices ex-factory. In the first Census, data of numbers engaged includes those working proprietors and unpaid family workers who worked more than one third of the normal working hours as at 31st October 1955, whilst in the second Census, all working proprietors were included together with those family workers who worked without payment for more than 16 hours a week. Wages and salaries data in both censuses included payments in kind, valued at cost to the establishment if purchased and at market prices ex-factory if produced by the establishment. The capacity of the installed power equipment is obtained by adding the horsepower of prime movers connected to machinery other than generators and the horsepower of all electric motors.

It should be noted that the figures in the table indicating value are given in Won although in the publications referred to they are given in Hwan. Ten Hwan equals 1 Won. Korea made this currency change on June 10th 1962.

## Caractéristiques et structure de l'activité industrielle

Les donnees du tableau 3 sont tirées des résultats des premier et deuxième recensements des industries extractives et manufacturières. Les résultats du premier recensement, qui portait sur la période allant du 1er novembre 1954 au 31 octobre 1955, ont été reproduits dans *Summary Report on Mining and Manufacturing Establishments Census, 1955,* publié par la Division de la recherche de la Banque de Corée; les résultats du deuxième recensement, qui portait sur la période allant du 1er avril 1958 au 31 mars 1959, ont été présentés dans *Final Report — Census of Mining and Manufacturing, 1958* publié par la Banque coréenne pour la reconstruction.

Les deux recensements portaient sur tous les établissements ayant occupé 5 personnes ou plus pendant octobre 1955 et mars 1959 respectivement, ainsi que sur les établissements n'ayant exercé aucune activité en octobre 1955 ou mars 1959 mais ayant occupé 5 personnes ou plus pendant trois mois de l'année du recensement. Cependant, tous les établissements gérés directement par l'Etat (notamment ceux qui relèvent de l'industrie du tabac et de l'extraction du sel et les ateliers de la compagnie de chemins de fer), par les Forces armées de la République de Corée, par les Nations Unies ou par les missions diplomatiques en Corée ont été exclus.

Les définitions des rubriques utilisées sont, en général, conformes aux Normes internationales relatives aux statistiques industrielles de base, si ce n'est que la valeur ajoutée en 1958 est tirée de la valeur brute des expéditions compte non tenu des variations de stocks. La valeur ajoutée est calculée aux prix du marché et départ usine. Dans le cas du premier recensement, les données relatives au nombre de personnes occupées comprennent les propriétaires qui travaillent et les travailleurs familiaux non rémunérés ayant travaillé plus du tiers des heures normales de travail au 31 octobre 1955, tandis que, dans le deuxième recensement, tous les propriétaires qui travaillent ont été inclus, ainsi que les travailleurs familiaux qui ont travaillé sans rémunération plus de 16 heures par semaine. Dans le cas des deux recensements, les données relatives aux traitements et salaires comprennent les paiements en nature, évalués au coût pour l'établissement si le produit est acheté et aux prix du marché, départ usine, s'il est produit par l'établissement. La puissance installée représente la puissance en chevaux-vapeur des moteurs électriques reliés à des machines autres que des générateurs et celle de tous les moteurs électriques.

Il y a lieu de noter que, dans le tableau, les valeurs sont exprimées en wons, tandis que, dans les publications mentionnées, elles sont exprimées en hwans. Un won équivaut à 10 hwans. La Corée a établi cette nouvelle monnaie le 10 juin 1962.

# 1. THE GROSS DOMESTIC PRODUCT AND GROSS DOMESTIC CAPITAL FORMATION
# LE PRODUIT INTERIEUR BRUT ET LA FORMATION BRUTE DE CAPITAL FIXE INTERIEUR

Thousand million Won                                                                          Milliards de wons

## A. Expenditure on the Gross Domestic Product at Market Prices
## Dépenses relatives au produit intérieur brut aux prix du marché

| Item of data and year / Rubrique et année | Total | Consumption[1] / Consommation[1] | | Gross Domestic Capital Formation[2] / Formation brute de capital intérieur[2] | | Net exports of goods and services / Exportations nettes de biens et de services | |
|---|---|---|---|---|---|---|---|
| | | Total | Government / Etat | Total | Fixed / Fixe | Exports less imports / Exportations moins importations | Exports / Exportations |
| **a. At Current Prices — Aux prix courants** | | | | | | | |
| Absolute figures — Chiffres absolus | | | | | | | |
| 1953 | 38.37 | 37.47 | 3.68 | 4.59 | 2.86 | −3.69 | 0.97 |
| 1954 | 56.05 | 52.36 | 6.63 | 7.47 | 6.20 | −3.78 | 0.98 |
| 1955 | 93.66 | 90.51 | 9.79 | 12.33 | 10.72 | −9.18 | 1.99 |
| 1956 | 120.61 | 128.76 | 13.34 | 9.72 | 12.85 | −17.87 | 1.96 |
| 1957 | 161.57 | 157.61 | 20.46 | 24.64 | 20.09 | −20.68 | 3.13 |
| 1958 | 170.68 | 164.53 | 25.06 | 22.98 | 21.94 | −168.3 | 4.12 |
| 1959 | 184.00 | 173.20 | 29.43 | 23.51 | 26.50 | −12.71 | 5.15 |
| 1960 | 209.00 | 199.82 | 33.51 | 26.23 | 24.70 | −17.05 | 8.16 |
| 1961 | 238.65 | 226.98 | 37.91 | 37.30 | 29.74 | −25.63 | 15.28 |
| Percentage distribution of average annual expenditure — Distribution en pourcentage des dépenses annuelles moyennes | | | | | | | |
| 1953 | 100.0 | 97.6 | 9.6 | 12.0 | 7.4 | −9.6 | 2.5 |
| 1954 | 100.0 | 93.4 | 11.8 | 13.3 | 11.1 | −6.7 | 1.8 |
| 1958 | 100.0 | 96.4 | 14.7 | 13.5 | 12.9 | −9.9 | 2.4 |
| 1960 | 100.0 | 95.6 | 16.0 | 12.6 | 11.8 | −8.2 | 3.9 |
| **b. At Prices of 1955 — Aux prix de 1955** | | | | | | | |
| Absolute figures — Chiffres absolus | | | | | | | |
| 1953 | 85.16 | 81.03 | 10.00 | 12.96 | 9.30 | −8.83 | 2.73 |
| 1954 | 90.01 | 83.21 | 9.71 | 13.45 | 11.60 | −6.65 | 1.89 |
| 1955 | 93.66 | 90.51 | 9.79 | 12.33 | 10.72 | −9.18 | 1.99 |
| 1956 | 93.99 | 96.50 | 11.06 | 7.87 | 9.65 | −10.38 | 1.82 |
| 1957 | 102.22 | 98.33 | 11.39 | 15.85 | 13.19 | −11.96 | 2.29 |
| 1958 | 109.39 | 104.14 | 13.48 | 14.92 | 14.33 | −9.67 | 2.90 |
| 1959 | 115.15 | 108.51 | 12.99 | 14.18 | 16.35 | −7.54 | 3.36 |
| 1960 | 117.55 | 112.16 | 13.61 | 13.92 | 13.60 | −8.53 | 3.93 |
| 1961 | 121.61 | 109.75 | 13.54 | 18.51 | 14.33 | −6.65 | 5.12 |
| Percentage distribution of average annual expenditure — Distribution en pourcentage des dépenses annuelles moyennes | | | | | | | |
| 1953 | 100.0 | 95.2 | 11.7 | 15.2 | 10.9 | −10.4 | 3.2 |
| 1954 | 100.0 | 92.5 | 10.8 | 14.9 | 12.9 | −7.4 | 2.1 |
| 1958 | 100.0 | 95.2 | 12.3 | 13.6 | 13.1 | −8.8 | 2.7 |
| 1960 | 100.0 | 95.4 | 11.6 | 11.9 | 11.6 | −7.3 | 3.3 |
| Average annual rate of growth — Taux annuel moyen d'accroissement | | | | | | | |
| 1954 – 1958 | 5.0 | 5.8 | 8.5 | 2.6 | 5.4 | . | 11.3 |
| 1958 – 1960 | 3.6 | 3.8 | 0.5 | −3.4 | −2.6 | . | 16.4 |

[1] Private consumption expenditure has been obtained as a residual.
[2] Stock changes are those for principal commodities only.

[1] La dépense de consommation privée à été obtenue par différence.
[2] On n'a tenu compte des variations de stocks que pour les principaux produits.

## B. The Gross Domestic Product at Factor Cost According to Origin
### Origine par secteur d'activité du produit intérieur brut au coût des facteurs

| Item of data and year — Rubrique et année | Total | Agricultural sector — Secteur agricole | Industrial Sector — Secteur industriel — Total | Mining — Industries extractives | Manufacturing — Industries manufacturières | Construction — Bâtiment et travaux publics | Electricity, gas and water — Electricité, gaz et eau | Transportation and communication — Transports et communications | Other sectors[1] — Autres secteurs[1] |
|---|---|---|---|---|---|---|---|---|---|
| ISIC — CITI | 0–9 | 0 | 1–5 | 1 | 2–3 | 4 | 5 | 7 | 6, 8–9 |

*a. At Current Prices — Aux prix courants*

| Item | Total | Agr. | Ind. Total | Mining | Manuf. | Constr. | Elec. | Transp. | Other |
|---|---|---|---|---|---|---|---|---|---|
| **Absolute figures — Chiffres absolus** | | | | | | | | | |
| 1948 | 0.85 | 0.42 | 0.11 | — | 0.07 | 0.01 | 0.03 | 0.01 | 0.31 |
| 1950 | 2.16 | 0.94 | 0.20 | 0.01 | 0.13 | 0.02 | 0.04 | 0.04 | 0.98 |
| 1951 | 9.13 | 4.81 | 0.72 | 0.03 | 0.53 | 0.12 | 0.04 | 0.18 | 3.42 |
| 1952 | 23.28 | 14.00 | 1.44 | 0.13 | 0.95 | 0.34 | 0.02 | 0.45 | 7.39 |
| 1953 | 36.69 | 17.30 | 4.25 | 0.40 | 2.75 | 0.92 | 0.18 | 0.82 | 14.32 |
| 1954 | 52.79 | 20.75 | 7.33 | 0.50 | 4.64 | 1.94 | 0.25 | 1.36 | 23.35 |
| 1955 | 89.20 | 39.95 | 12.70 | 0.75 | 8.15 | 3.30 | 0.50 | 2.89 | 33.66 |
| 1956 | 115.24 | 53.18 | 15.94 | 1.14 | 10.78 | 3.70 | 0·32 | 3.84 | 42.28 |
| 1957 | 152.69 | 66.24 | 22.17 | 1.68 | 13.42 | 6.08 | 0.99 | 6.11 | 58.17 |
| 1958 | 157.43 | 64.50 | 24.54 | 1.92 | 14.72 | 6.71 | 1.19 | 7.49 | 60.90 |
| 1959 | 164.71 | 59.58 | 28.87 | 2.60 | 16.87 | 8.16 | 1.24 | 8.19 | 68.07 |
| 1960 | 186.43 | 70.47 | 32.16 | 3.49 | 19.37 | 8.05 | 1.25 | 10.30 | 73.50 |
| 1961 | 220.22 | 90.78 | 37.86 | 4.94 | 20.99 | 9.15 | 2.78 | 11.63 | 79.95 |
| **Percentage distribution according to sector — Distribution en pourcentage par secteur** | | | | | | | | | |
| 1948 | 100.0 | 49.4 | 12.9 | — | 8.2 | 1.2 | 3.5 | 1.2 | 36.5 |
| 1950 – 1960 | 100.0 | 41.6 | 15.2 | 1.3 | 9.3 | 4.0 | 0.6 | 4.2 | 39.0 |
| 1950 | 100.0 | 43.5 | 9.3 | 0.5 | 6.0 | 0.9 | 1.9 | 1.8 | 45.4 |
| 1953 | 100.0 | 47.2 | 11.6 | 1.1 | 7.5 | 2.5 | 0.5 | 2.2 | 39.0 |
| 1954 | 100.0 | 39.3 | 13.9 | 0.9 | 8.8 | 3.7 | 0.5 | 2.6 | 44.2 |
| 1958 | 100.0 | 41.0 | 15.6 | 1.2 | 9.3 | 4.3 | 0.8 | 4.7 | 38.7 |
| 1960 | 100.0 | 37.8 | 17.3 | 1.9 | 10.4 | 4.3 | 0.7 | 5.5 | 39.4 |

*b. At Prices of 1955 — Aux prix de 1955*

| Item | Total | Agr. | Ind. Total | Mining | Manuf. | Constr. | Elec. | Transp. | Other |
|---|---|---|---|---|---|---|---|---|---|
| **Absolute figures — Chiffres absolus** | | | | | | | | | |
| 1948 | 69.60 | 37.98 | 3.99 | 0.33 | 2.20 | 1.17 | 0.29 | 1.25 | 26.38 |
| 1950 | 63.96 | 35.17 | 3.98 | 0.28 | 2.28 | 1.38 | 0.04 | 1.19 | 23.62 |
| 1951 | 59.06 | 29.86 | 3.53 | 0.13 | 2.27 | 1.06 | 0.07 | 1.35 | 24.32 |
| 1952 | 62.85 | 28.06 | 5.51 | 0.45 | 3.19 | 1.58 | 0.29 | 1.63 | 27.65 |
| 1953 | 81.08 | 36.54 | 9.42 | 0.76 | 5.08 | 3.12 | 0.46 | 2.37 | 32.75 |
| 1954 | 85.72 | 38.79 | 11.19 | 0.63 | 6.24 | 3.75 | 0.57 | 2.68 | 33.06 |
| 1955 | 89.20 | 39.95 | 12.70 | 0.75 | 8.15 | 3.30 | 0.50 | 2.89 | 33.66 |
| 1956 | 89.52 | 37.59 | 14.45 | 0.99 | 10.09 | 2.88 | 0.49 | 3.63 | 33.85 |
| 1957 | 97.36 | 40.88 | 17.04 | 1.19 | 11.36 | 3.97 | 0.52 | 3.87 | 35.57 |
| 1958 | 104.19 | 43.92 | 18.72 | 1.35 | 12.24 | 4.44 | 0.69 | 4.36 | 37.19 |
| 1959 | 109.68 | 44.53 | 21.45 | 1.71 | 13.45 | 5.47 | 0.82 | 4.92 | 38.78 |
| 1960 | 111.97 | 44.92 | 22.28 | 2.20 | 14.32 | 4.92 | 0.84 | 5.59 | 39.18 |
| 1961 | 115.83 | 49.09 | 23.28 | 2.58 | 14.35 | 5.48 | 0.87 | 5.65 | 37.81 |
| **Percentage distribution according to sector — Distribution en pourcentage par secteur** | | | | | | | | | |
| 1948 | 100.0 | 54.6 | 5.7 | 0.5 | 3.1 | 1.7 | 0.4 | 1.8 | 37.9 |
| 1950 – 1960 | 100.0 | 44.0 | 14.6 | 1.1 | 9.3 | 3.7 | 0.5 | 3.6 | 37.8 |
| 1950 | 100.0 | 55.0 | 6.2 | 0.4 | 3.6 | 2.1 | 0.1 | 1.9 | 36.9 |
| 1953 | 100.0 | 45.1 | 11.6 | 0.9 | 6.3 | 3.8 | 0.6 | 2.9 | 40.4 |
| 1954 | 100.0 | 45.2 | 13.1 | 0.7 | 7.3 | 4.4 | 0.7 | 3.1 | 38.6 |
| 1958 | 100.0 | 42.1 | 18.0 | 1.3 | 11.7 | 4.3 | 0.7 | 4.2 | 35.7 |
| 1960 | 100.0 | 40.1 | 19.9 | 2.0 | 12.8 | 4.4 | 0.7 | 5.0 | 35.0 |
| **Average annual rate of growth — Taux annuel moyen d'accroissement** | | | | | | | | | |
| 1948 – 1953 | 3.1 | −0.8 | 18.7 | 18.2 | 18.2 | 21.7 | 9.7 | 13.6 | 4.4 |
| 1950 – 1960 | 5.8 | 2.5 | 18.8 | 22.9 | 20.2 | 13.6 | 35.6 | 16.7 | 5.2 |
| 1950 – 1953 | 8.2 | 1.3 | 33.3 | 39.5 | 30.6 | 31.3 | 125.7 | 25.8 | 11.5 |
| 1954 – 1958 | 5.0 | 3.1 | 13.7 | 21.0 | 18.4 | 4.3 | 4.9 | 12.9 | 3.0 |
| 1958 – 1960 | 3.7 | 1.1 | 9.1 | 27.7 | 8.2 | 5.3 | 10.3 | 13.2 | 2.7 |

[1] No imputation has been made for rent of general government buildings.

[1] Il n'est pas fait d'imputation pour le loyer des bâtiments de l'Etat.

## C. Gross Domestic Fixed Capital Formation According to Purchasing Sector
## La formation brute de capital fixe interieur par secteur d'acquisition

| Item of data and year Rubrique et année | Total | Agricultural sector Secteur agricole | Industrial Sector — Secteur industriel | | | | | Transportation and communication Transports et communications | Other sectors Autres secteurs |
|---|---|---|---|---|---|---|---|---|---|
| | | | Total | Mining Industries extractives | Manufacturing Industries manufacturières | Construction Bâtiment et travaux publics | Electricity, gas and water Electricité, gaz et eau | | |
| ISIC — CITI | 0–9 | 0 | 1–5 | 1 | 2–3 | 4 | 5 | 7 | 6, 8–9 |
| *a. At Current Prices — Aux prix courants* | | | | | | | | | |
| Absolute figures — Chiffres absolus | | | | | | | | | |
| 1953............ | 2.86 | 0.44 | 0.59 | 0.08 | 0.39 | — | 0.12 | 0.45 | 1.38 |
| 1954............ | 6.20 | 0.63 | 1.26 | 0.14 | 0.86 | 0.01 | 0.25 | 1.27 | 3.04 |
| 1955............ | 10.72 | 1.16 | 2.84 | 0.22 | 1.59 | 0.01 | 1.02 | 2.31 | 4.41 |
| 1956............ | 12.85 | 1.74 | 3.44 | 0.54 | 1.86 | 0.01 | 1.03 | 3.06 | 4.61 |
| 1957............ | 20.09 | 2.59 | 4.51 | 0.65 | 2.50 | 0.02 | 1.34 | 7.55 | 5.44 |
| 1958............ | 21.94 | 2.17 | 6.61 | 0.48 | 4.04 | 0.04 | 2.05 | 5.85 | 7.31 |
| 1959............ | 26.50 | 2.80 | 7.90 | 0.80 | 5.08 | 0.11 | 1.91 | 6.06 | 9.74 |
| 1960............ | 24.70 | 3.24 | 5.68 | 1.01 | 3.71 | 0.08 | 0.88 | 5.41 | 10.37 |
| 1961............ | 29.74 | 4.95 | 8.42 | 1.01 | 4.21 | 0.19 | 3.01 | 7.00 | 9.37 |
| Percentage distribution according to sector— Distribution en pourcentage par secteur | | | | | | | | | |
| 1953............ | 100.0 | 15.4 | 20.6 | 2.8 | 13.6 | — | 4.2 | 15.7 | 48.3 |
| 1954............ | 100.0 | 10.2 | 20.3 | 2.2 | 13.9 | 0.2 | 4.0 | 20.5 | 49.0 |
| 1958............ | 100.0 | 9.9 | 30.1 | 2.2 | 18.4 | 0.2 | 9.3 | 26.7 | 33.3 |
| 1960............ | 100.0 | 13.1 | 23.0 | 4.1 | 15.0 | 0.3 | 3.6 | 21.9 | 42.0 |
| *b. At Prices of 1955 — Aux prix de 1955* | | | | | | | | | |
| Absolute figures — Chiffres absolus | | | | | | | | | |
| 1953............ | 9.30 | 1.39 | 1.86 | 0.19 | 1.31 | 0.02 | 0.34 | 1.46 | 4.59 |
| 1954............ | 11.60 | 1.13 | 2.21 | 0.22 | 1.53 | 0.02 | 0.44 | 2.27 | 5.99 |
| 1955............ | 10.72 | 1.16 | 2.84 | 0.22 | 1.59 | 0.01 | 1.02 | 2.31 | 4.41 |
| 1956............ | 9.65 | 1.33 | 2.45 | 0.40 | 1.36 | 0.01 | 0.68 | 2.32 | 3.55 |
| 1957............ | 13.19 | 1.73 | 2.89 | 0.42 | 1.67 | 0.01 | 0.79 | 4.94 | 3.63 |
| 1958............ | 14.33 | 1.46 | 4.20 | 0.32 | 2.61 | 0.02 | 1.25 | 3.87 | 4.80 |
| 1959............ | 16.35 | 1.82 | 4.70 | 0.51 | 3.06 | 0.07 | 1.06 | 3.73 | 6.10 |
| 1960............ | 13.60 | 1.91 | 3.00 | 0.57 | 1.92 | 0.04 | 0.47 | 2.98 | 5.71 |
| 1961............ | 14.33 | 2.70 | 3.50 | 0.46 | 1.70 | 0.06 | 1.28 | 3.40 | 4.73 |
| Percentage distribution according to sector— Distribution en pourcentage par secteur | | | | | | | | | |
| 1953............ | 100.0 | 14.9 | 20.0 | 2.0 | 14.1 | 0.2 | 3.7 | 15.7 | 49.4 |
| 1954............ | 100.0 | 9.7 | 19.1 | 1.9 | 13.2 | 0.2 | 3.8 | 19.6 | 51.6 |
| 1958............ | 100.0 | 10.2 | 29.3 | 2.3 | 18.2 | 0.1 | 8.7 | 27.0 | 33.5 |
| 1960............ | 100.0 | 14.0 | 22.1 | 4.2 | 14.1 | 0.3 | 3.5 | 21.9 | 42.0 |
| Average annual rate of growth—Taux annuel moyen d'accroissement | | | | | | | | | |
| 1954–1958..... | 5.4 | 6.6 | 17.4 | 9.8 | 14.3 | — | 29.8 | 14.3 | −5.4 |
| 1958–1960..... | −2.6 | 14.4 | −15.5 | 33.5 | −14.2 | 41.4 | −38.7 | −12.2 | 9.1 |

## 2. INDEX NUMBERS OF INDUSTRIAL PRODUCTION — INDICES DE LA PRODUCTION INDUSTRIELLE

### A. Selected Divisions of Industrial Activity
### Quelques branches de l'activité industrielle

| Period<br>Période | Total[1,2] | Mining [1]<br>Industries extractives [1] | Manu-facturing [2]<br>Industries manu-facturières [2] | Electricity and gas<br>Electricité et gaz |
|---|---|---|---|---|
| ISIC — CITI | 1–3, 511–512 | 1 | 2–3 | 511–512 |

#### a. Indexes — Indices (1958 = 100)

| | | | | |
|---|---|---|---|---|
| 1954 | 54 | 44 | 55 | 60 |
| 1955 | 64 | 54 | 66 | 58 |
| 1956 | 79 | 71 | 80 | 74 |
| 1957 | 91 | 95 | 90 | 88 |
| 1958 | 100 | 100 | 100 | 100 |
| 1959 | 115 | 139 | 111 | 112 |
| 1960 | – 125 – | – 183 – | – 117 – | – 112 – |
| 1961 | 132 | 207 | 122 | 117 |

#### b. Average Annual Rate of Change — Taux annuel moyen de variation

| | | | | |
|---|---|---|---|---|
| 1954 – 1958 | 16.7 | 22.8 | 16.1 | 13.6 |
| 1958 – 1960 | 11.8 | 35.3 | 8.2 | 5.8 |

For footnotes see end of table.

Pour les notes, voir au bas du tableau.

### B. The Major Groups of Mining
### Les classes de la branche Industries extractives

| Period<br>Période | All mining [1]<br>Toutes industries extractives [1] | Coal mining<br>Extraction du charbon | Metal mining<br>Extraction des minerais métalliques | Other mining<br>Autres industries extractives |
|---|---|---|---|---|
| ISIC — CITI | 1 | 11 | 12 | 14–19 |

#### a. Indexes — Indices (1958 = 100)

| | | | | |
|---|---|---|---|---|
| 1954 | 44 | 33 | 78 | 61 |
| 1955 | 54 | 49 | 66 | 93 |
| 1956 | 71 | 68 | 79 | 66 |
| 1957 | 95 | 91 | 100 | 102 |
| 1958 | 100 | 100 | 100 | 100 |
| 1959 | 139 | 155 | 98 | 104 |
| 1960 | – 183 – | – 200 – | – 140 – | – 124 – |
| 1961 | 207 | 220 | 174 | 76 |

#### b. Average Annual Rate of Change — Taux annuel moyen de variation

| | | | | |
|---|---|---|---|---|
| 1954 – 1958 | 22.8 | 31.9 | 6.4 | 13.1 |
| 1958 – 1960 | 35.3 | 41.4 | 18.3 | 11.4 |

For footnotes see end of table.

Pour les notes, voir au bas du tableau.

### C. Selected Major Groups of Manufacturing — Quelques classes de la branche Industries manufacturières

| Period<br>Période | Manu-facturing [2]<br>Industries manufac-turières [2] | Food, beverages and tobacco<br>Industries alimen-taires, boissons, tabac | Textiles | Wood products<br>Ouvrages en bois | Paper and paper products<br>Papier et ouvrages en papier | Printing and publishing<br>Im-primerie et édition | Leather and leather products except wearing apparel<br>Cuir et articles en cuir, à l'exclusion des articles d'habil-lement | Rubber products<br>Ouvrages en caout-chouc | Chemicals and chemical, petroleum and coal products [3]<br>Produits chi-miques et dérivés du pétrole et du charbon [3] | Non-metallic mineral products<br>Produits minéraux non métal-liques | Basic metals<br>Métal-lurgie de base | Metal products<br>Ouvrages en métaux | Other manu-facturing [4]<br>Autres industries manufac-turières [4] |
|---|---|---|---|---|---|---|---|---|---|---|---|---|---|
| ISIC — CITI | 2–3 | 20–22 | 23 | 25 | 27 | 28 | 29 | 30 | 31–32 | 33 | 34 | 35–38 | 39 |

#### a. Indexes — Indices (1958 = 100)

| | | | | | | | | | | | | | |
|---|---|---|---|---|---|---|---|---|---|---|---|---|---|
| 1954 | 55 | 48 | 56 | 95 | 69 | 51 | 61 | 77 | 54 | 41 | 38 | 57 | 86 |
| 1955 | 66 | 68 | 68 | 75 | 72 | 61 | 66 | 68 | 74 | 50 | 45 | 69 | 90 |
| 1956 | 80 | 86 | 80 | 83 | 82 | 68 | 86 | 68 | 84 | 67 | 69 | 93 | 99 |
| 1957 | 90 | 86 | 97 | 93 | 87 | 72 | 82 | 92 | 81 | 76 | 82 | 106 | 103 |
| 1958 | 100 | 100 | 100 | 100 | 100 | 100 | 100 | 100 | 100 | 100 | 100 | 100 | 100 |
| 1959 | 111 | 102 | 104 | 104 | 135 | 108 | 73 | 156 | 156 | 111 | 136 | 94 | 106 |
| 1960 | – 117 – | – 107 – | – 100 – | – 104 – | – 176 – | – 124 – | – 64 – | – 150 – | – 209 – | – 113 – | – 152 – | – 94 – | – 101 – |
| 1961 | 122 | 116 | 91 | 97 | 215 | 101 | 79 | 142 | 263 | 113 | 130 | 125 | 102 |

#### b. Average Annual Rate of Change — Taux annuel moyen de variation

| | | | | | | | | | | | | | |
|---|---|---|---|---|---|---|---|---|---|---|---|---|---|
| 1954–1958 | 16.1 | 20.1 | 15.6 | 1.3 | 9.7 | 18.3 | 13.1 | 6.8 | 16.7 | 25.0 | 27.4 | 15.1 | 3.8 |
| 1958–1960 | 8.2 | 3.4 | — | 2.0 | 32.7 | 11.4 | −20.0 | 22.5 | 44.6 | 6.3 | 23.3 | −3.0 | 0.5 |

[1] Excludes salt mining (part of major group 19).
[2] Excludes Clothing, footwear and made-up textiles (ISIC major group 24) and Manufacture of furniture and fixtures (ISIC major group 26) in all years and Petroleum and coal products (ISIC major group 32) up to 1960.
[3] Excludes Petroleum and coal products (ISIC major group 32) up to 1960.
[4] Includes manufacture of ice (part of ISIC major group 20).

[1] Non compris l'extraction du sel (dans CITI classe 19).
[2] Non compris Articles d'habillement, chaussures et ouvrages en tissu (CITI classe 24) et In-dustrie du meuble (CITI classe 26) pour toutes les années, et Produits dérivés du pétrole et du charbon (CITI classe 32) jusqu'en 1960.
[3] Non compris Produits dérivés du pétrole et du charbon (CITI classe 32) jusqu'en 1960.
[4] Y compris la fabrication de la glace (dans CITI classe 20).

# 3. CHARACTERISTICS OF MINING AND MANUFACTURING ESTABLISHMENTS ENGAGING 5 OR MORE PERSONS

## CARACTERISTIQUES DES ETABLISSEMENTS MINIERS ET MANUFACTURIERS OCCUPANT 5 PERSONNES OU PLUS

### 1955, 1958

Number of establishments in units; gross value of production, value added and wages and salaries in million Won; number of engaged, employees and operatives in thousands; capacity of installed power equipment in thousand horsepower; value added per engaged and wages and salaries per employee and per operative in thousand Won; capacity of installed power equipment per engaged and per operative in horsepower.

Nombre d'établissements en unités; valeur brute de la production, valeur ajoutée et traitements et salaires en millions de wons; nombre de personnes occupées, de salariés et d'ouvriers en milliers; puissance installée en milliers de chevaux-vapeur; valeur ajoutée par personne occupée et traitements et salaires par salarié et par ouvrier en milliers de wons; puissance installée par personne occupée et par ouvrier en chevaux-vapeur.

## A. The Major Groups of Mining — Les classes de la branche Industries extractives

| Year and item of data | All mining [1] Toutes industries extractives [1] | Coal mining Extraction du charbon | Metal mining Extraction des minerais métalliques | Other mining [1] Divers [1] | Année et rubrique |
|---|---|---|---|---|---|
| ISIC | 1 | 11 | 12 | 14-19 | CITI |
| **a. Absolute Figures — Chiffres absolus** | | | | | |
| **1955** | | | | | **1955** |
| Number of establishments | 283 | 64 | 155 | 64 | Nombre d'établissements |
| Gross value of production | 1 050.4 | 546.0 | 415.9 | 88.5 | Valeur brute de la production |
| Number of engaged (As of 31.IX.1955) | 29.8 | 12.7 | 14.2 | 2.9 | Nombre de personnes occupées (au 31.IX.1955) |
| Number of employees (As of 31.IX.1955) | 29.4 | 12.6 | 14.0 | 2.8 | Nombre de salariés (au 31.IX.1955) |
| **1958** | | | | | **1958** |
| Number of establishments | 363 | 85 | 140 | 138 | Nombre d'établissements |
| Value added | 2 289.2 | 1 509.1 | 535.2 | 244.9 | Valeur ajoutée |
| Number of engaged (As of III.1959) | 37.2 | 17.5 | 10.8 | 8.9 | Nombre de personnes occupées (au III.1959) |
| Employees: Number (As of III.1959) | 37.0 | 17.5 | 10.7 | 8.8 | Salariés: Nombre (au III.1959) |
| Wages and salaries | 1 182.4 | 758.2 | 276.0 | 148.2 | Traitements et salaires |
| Operatives: Number (As of III.1959) | 32.7 | 15.0 | 9.4 | 8.3 | Ouvriers: Nombre (au III.1959) |
| Wages and salaries | 959.2 | 615.2 | 218.2 | 125.8 | Traitements et salaires |
| Capacity of installed power equipment (As of III.1959) | 68.5 | 26.6 | 38.0 | 3.9 | Puissance installée (au III.1959) |

| Year and item of data | All mining [1] Toutes industries extractives [1] | Coal mining Extraction du charbon | Metal mining Extraction des minerais métalliques | Other mining [1] Divers [1] | Année et rubrique |
|---|---|---|---|---|---|
| ISIC | 1 | 11 | 12 | 14-19 | CITI |
| **b. Structure** | | | | | |
| **1955** | | | | | **1955** |
| Distribution in percent of number of engaged | 100.0 | 42.6 | 47.7 | 9.7 | Distribution en pourcentage du nombre de personnes occupées |
| Employees as a percent of engaged | 98.6 | 99.2 | 98.6 | 96.6 | Salariés en pourcentage des personnes occupées |
| **1958** | | | | | **1958** |
| Distribution in percent of: | | | | | Distribution en pourcentage: |
| Value added | 100.0 | 65.9 | 23.4 | 10.7 | Valeur ajoutée |
| Number of engaged | 100.0 | 47.1 | 29.0 | 23.9 | Nombre de personnes occupées |
| Per person engaged: | | | | | Par personne occupée: |
| Value added | 61.5 | 86.2 | 49.6 | 27.5 | Valeur ajoutée |
| Capacity of installed power equipment | 1.84 | 1.52 | 3.52 | 0.44 | Puissance installée |
| Employees as a percent of engaged | 99.5 | 100.0 | 99.1 | 98.9 | Salariés en pourcentage des personnes occupées |
| Value added per unit of wages and salaries | 1.94 | 1.99 | 1.94 | 1.65 | Valeur ajoutée par unité de traitements et salaires |
| Operatives as a percent of employees | 88.4 | 85.7 | 87.8 | 94.3 | Ouvriers en pourcentage des salariés |
| Wages and salaries per employee | 32.0 | 43.3 | 25.8 | 16.8 | Traitements et salaires par salarié |
| Per operative: | | | | | Par ouvrier |
| Wages and salaries | 29.3 | 41.0 | 23.2 | 15.2 | Traitements et salaires |
| Capacity of installed power equipment | 2.09 | 1.77 | 4.04 | 0.47 | Puissance installée |

For footnotes see end of table.

Pour les notes, voir au bas du tableau.

## B. The Major Groups of Manufacturing — Les classes de la branche Industries manufacturières

| Year and item of data | Manufacturing [1,2] / Industries manufacturières[1,2] | Food and beverages / Industries alimentaires et boissons | Textiles | Clothing, footwear and made-up textiles / Articles d'habillement, chaussures et ouvrages en tissu | Wood products and furniture / Bois et meubles | Paper and paper products / Papier et ouvrages en papier | Printing and publishing / Imprimerie et édition | Leather and leather products except wearing apparel / Cuir et articles en cuir, à l'exclusion des articles d'habillement | Rubber products / Ouvrages en caoutchouc | Chemicals and chemical, petroleum and coal products [1] / Produits chimiques et dérivés du pétrole et du charbon [1] | Non-metallic mineral products / Produits minéraux non métalliques | Basic metals / Métallurgie de base | Metal products / Ouvrages en métaux | Other manufacturing / Autres industries manufacturières | Année et rubrique |
|---|---|---|---|---|---|---|---|---|---|---|---|---|---|---|---|
| ISIC | 2–3 | 20–21 | 23 | 24 | 25–26 | 27 | 28 | 29 | 30 | 31–32 | 33 | 34 | 35–38 | 39 | CITI |
| *a. Absolute Figures — Chiffres absolus* | | | | | | | | | | | | | | | |
| **1955** | | | | | | | | | | | | | | | **1955** |
| Number of establishments | 8 810 | 2 009 | 2 908 | 309 | 745 | 162 | 321 | 59 | 135 | 375 | 595 | 201 | 873 | 118 | Nombre d'établissements |
| Gross value of production | 25 307.5 | 6 665.8 | 7 437.8 | 1 247.4 | 1 682.0 | 381.0 | 1 120.6 | 279.4 | 1 390.1 | 1 267.8 | 785.0 | 598.8 | 1 909.3 | 542.5 | Valeur brute de la production |
| Number of engaged (As of 31.IX.1955) | 222.2 | 36.7 | 86.4 | 6.1 | 10.9 | 4.6 | 9.7 | 0.9 | 13.8 | 9.7 | 15.7 | 5.5 | 19.0 | 3.2 | Nombre de personnes occupées (au 31.IX.1955) |
| Number of employees (As of 31.IX.1955) | 205.7 | 33.3 | 80.0 | 5.6 | 9.6 | 4.3 | 9.2 | 0.8 | 13.6 | 9.0 | 14.6 | 5.1 | 17.7 | 2.9 | Nombre de salariés (au 31.IX.1955) |
| **1958** | | | | | | | | | | | | | | | **1958** |
| Number of establishments | 12 971 | 2 813 | 2 801 | 1 102 | 1 292 | 274 | 535 | 58 | 120 | 909 | 1 008 | 249 | 1 513 | 297 | Nombre d'établissements |
| Value added | 15 754.9 | 3 175.0 | 4 314.6 | 632.5 | 758.7 | 296.3 | 795.4 | 96.5 | 630.8 | 1 161.5 | 1 342.5 | 656.4 | 1 565.6 | 329.1 | Valeur ajoutée |
| Number of engaged (As of III.1959) | 260.6 | 40.4 | 86.6 | 11.3 | 14.7 | 5.2 | 13.2 | 0.9 | 10.8 | 17.3 | 19.1 | 7.8 | 26.9 | 6.4 | Nombre de personnes occupées (au III.1959) |
| Employees: | | | | | | | | | | | | | | | Salariés: |
| Number (As of III.1959) | 243.1 | 36.9 | 81.7 | 9.8 | 13.1 | 4.8 | 12.6 | 0.8 | 10.7 | 16.3 | 17.8 | 7.5 | 25.1 | 6.0 | Nombre (au III.1959) |
| Wages and salaries | 5 765.3 | 819.3 | 1 625.0 | 273.7 | 345.9 | 105.5 | 427.6 | 34.1 | 226.9 | 380.8 | 433.2 | 267.4 | 701.9 | 124.0 | Traitements et salaires |
| Operatives: | | | | | | | | | | | | | | | Ouvriers: |
| Number (As of III.1959) | 219.8 | 31.5 | 78.3 | 9.1 | 11.7 | 4.4 | 8.7 | 0.7 | 10.1 | 14.1 | 16.6 | 6.3 | 22.9 | 5.4 | Nombre (au III.1959) |
| Wages and salaries | 4 744.7 | 625.3 | 1 458.2 | 248.3 | 290.2 | 91.2 | 263.0 | 33.8 | 197.4 | 286.4 | 370.4 | 195.8 | 583.7 | 101.0 | Traitements et salaires |
| Capacity of installed power equipment (As of III.1959) | 384.3 | 91.7 | 79.4 | 1.5 | 26.0 | 14.3 | 5.9 | 1.6 | 23.9 | 21.8 | 41.7 | 28.4 | 34.9 | 13.2 | Puissance installée (au III.1959) |
| *b. Structure* | | | | | | | | | | | | | | | |
| **1955** | | | | | | | | | | | | | | | **1955** |
| Distribution in percent of number of engaged | 100.0 | 16.5 | 38.9 | 2.7 | 4.9 | 2.1 | 4.4 | 0.4 | 6.2 | 4.4 | 7.1 | 2.5 | 8.5 | 1.4 | Distribution en pourcentage du nombre de personnes occupées |
| Employees as a percent of engaged | 92.6 | 90.7 | 92.6 | 91.8 | 88.1 | 93.5 | 94.8 | 88.9 | 98.6 | 92.8 | 93.0 | 92.7 | 93.2 | 90.6 | Salariés en pourcentage des personnes occupées |
| **1958** | | | | | | | | | | | | | | | **1958** |
| Distribution in percent of: Value added | 100.0 | 20.2 | 27.4 | 4.0 | 4.8 | 1.9 | 5.0 | 0.6 | 4.0 | 7.4 | 8.5 | 4.2 | 9.9 | 2.1 | Distribution en pourcentage: Valeur ajoutée |
| Number of engaged | 100.0 | 15.5 | 33.2 | 4.3 | 5.6 | 2.0 | 5.1 | 0.3 | 4.2 | 6.6 | 7.4 | 3.0 | 10.3 | 2.5 | Nombre de personnes occupées |
| Per person engaged: Value added | 60.4 | 78.6 | 49.8 | 56.0 | 51.6 | 57.0 | 60.2 | 107.2 | 58.4 | 67.1 | 70.3 | 84.2 | 58.2 | 51.4 | Par personne occupée: Valeur ajoutée |
| Capacity of installed power equipment | 1.47 | 2.27 | 0.92 | 0.13 | 1.77 | 2.75 | 0.45 | 1.78 | 2.21 | 1.26 | 2.18 | 3.64 | 1.30 | 2.06 | Puissance installée |
| Employees as a percent of engaged | 93.3 | 91.3 | 94.3 | 86.7 | 89.1 | 92.3 | 95.4 | 88.9 | 99.1 | 94.2 | 93.2 | 96.2 | 93.3 | 93.8 | Salariés en pourcentage des personnes occupées |
| Value added per unit of wages and salaries | 2.73 | 3.88 | 2.66 | 2.31 | 2.19 | 2.81 | 1.86 | 2.83 | 2.78 | 3.05 | 3.10 | 2.45 | 2.23 | 2.65 | Valeur ajoutée par unité de traitements et salaires |
| Operatives as a percent of employees | 90.4 | 85.4 | 95.8 | 92.8 | 89.3 | 91.7 | 69.0 | 87.5 | 94.4 | 86.5 | 93.2 | 84.0 | 91.2 | 90.0 | Ouvriers en pourcentage des salariés |
| Wages and salaries per employee | 23.7 | 22.2 | 19.9 | 27.9 | 26.4 | 22.0 | 33.9 | 42.6 | 21.2 | 23.4 | 24.3 | 35.6 | 28.0 | 20.7 | Traitements et salaires par salarié |
| Per operative: Wages and salaries | 21.6 | 19.8 | 18.6 | 27.3 | 24.8 | 20.7 | 30.2 | 48.3 | 19.5 | 20.3 | 22.3 | 31.1 | 25.5 | 18.7 | Par ouvrier: Traitements et salaires |
| Capacity of installed power equipment | 1.75 | 2.91 | 1.01 | 0.16 | 2.22 | 3.25 | 0.68 | 2.28 | 2.37 | 1.55 | 2.51 | 4.51 | 1.52 | 2.44 | Puissance installée |

[1] Salt mining (part of ISIC major group 19) is included in Chemicals and chemical, petroleum and coal products (ISIC major groups 31–32).
[2] Excludes Tobacco manufactures (ISIC major group 22).

[1] Extraction du sel (dans CITI classe 19) est inclus dans Produits chimiques et dérivés du pétrole et du charbon (CITI classes 31–32).
[2] Non compris Industries du tabac (CITI classe 22).

# LEBANON — LIBAN

## Net Domestic Product

The figures for the net domestic product according to origin, shown in Table 1 were obtained from estimates prepared by Dr. A. Y. Badre, Economic Research Institute, American University of Beirut. The estimates represent the latest revision of the data previously issued by the author on this subject.

## The Characteristics and Structure of Industrial Activity

The data presented in Table 2 are derived from the results of a census taken jointly by the General Statistical Service and The Economic Research Institute, Beirut, and published in *Industrial Census, 1955* by the Ministry of National Economy, Beirut, 1957. The Census covered all mining, manufacturing and public utility establishments engaging five or more persons except that establishments specializing in repairs and in the assembly and installation of machinery were excluded. Also, because the year of the Census was an unusually bad year for the production of olives, the production of olive oil was not covered in the Census.

The definitions of the items for which data are shown in the table below seem to be consistent with the recommendations in the International Standards in Basic Industrial Statistics.

## Produit intérieur net

Les chiffres du tableau 1 relatifs au produit intérieur net par branche d'activité d'origine proviennent d'estimations établies par M. A. Y. Badre, *Economic Research Institute, American University of Beyrut.* Ces estimations représentent les revisions les plus récentes des données déjà publiées par l'auteur sur ce sujet.

## Caractéristiques et structure de l'activité industrielle

Les données du tableau 2 sont tirées des résultats d'un recensement effectué conjointement par le Service général de la statistique et l'Institut de recherche économique, Beyrouth; ces résultats ont été publiés dans *Industrial Census, 1955* par le Ministère de l'économie nationale, Beyrouth, 1957. Le recensement portait sur tous les établissements des industries extractives, des industries manufacturières et des services d'utilité publique occupant cinq personnes ou plus, à l'exclusion des établissements spécialisés dans les travaux de réparation et dans le montage et l'installation des machines. En outre, comme l'année du recensement était une année exceptionnellement mauvaise pour la récolte d'olives, la production de l'huile d'olive a été omise.

Les définitions des rubriques pour lesquelles des chiffres sont fournis dans le tableau ci-après paraissent compatibles avec les Normes internationales relatives aux statistiques industrielles de base.

# LEBANON

## 1. THE NET DOMESTIC PRODUCT AT FACTOR COST ACCORDING TO ORIGIN
## ORIGINE PAR SECTEUR D'ACTIVITE DU PRODUIT INTERIEUR NET AU COUT DES FACTEURS

Million Lebanese pounds                                                                  Millions de livres libanaises

| Item of data and year<br>Rubrique et année | Total | Agricultural sector<br>Secteur agricole | Industrial Sector — Secteur industriel | | | Transportation and communications [1]<br>Transport et communications [1] | Other sectors<br>Autres secteurs |
|---|---|---|---|---|---|---|---|
| | | | Total | Mining, manufacturing, electricity, gas and water<br>Industries extractives et manufacturières et électricité gaz et eau | Construction<br>Bâtiments et travaux publics | | |
| ISIC — CITI | 0–9 | 0 | 1–5 | 1–3, 5 | 4 | 7 | 6, 8–9 |

At Current Prices — Aux prix courants

| | | | | | | | |
|---|---|---|---|---|---|---|---|
| Absolute figures —Chiffres absolus | | | | | | | |
| 1952............ | 1 115 | 216 | 203 | 155 | 48 | 45 | 651 |
| 1953............ | 1 168 | 221 | 208 | 161 | 47 | 50 | 689 |
| 1954............ | 1 256 | 226 | 226 | 166 | 60 | 60 | 744 |
| 1955............ | 1 374 | 223 | 235 | 175 | 60 | 75 | 841 |
| 1956............ | 1 417 | 231 | 233 | 183 | 50 | 78 | 875 |
| 1957............ | 1 503 | 238 | 230 | 189 | 41 | 80 | 955 |
| 1958............ | 1 325 | 219 | 219 | 181 | 38 | 57 | 830 |
| Percentage distribution according to sector— Distribution en pourcentage par secteur | | | | | | | |
| 1952 – 1958..... | 100.0 | 17.2 | 17.0 | 13.2 | 3.8 | 4.8 | 61.0 |
| 1953............ | 100.0 | 18.9 | 17.8 | 13.8 | 4.0 | 4.3 | 59.0 |
| 1954............ | 100.0 | 18.0 | 18.0 | 13.2 | 4.8 | 4.8 | 59.2 |
| 1958............ | 100.0 | 16.5 | 16.5 | 13.7 | 2.8 | 4.3 | 62.7 |

[1] Communication services rendered by government are included with ISIC division 8 in "Other sectors".

[1] Les services de communications rendus par l'Etat font partie de la branche 8 de la CITI et sont inclus dans "Autres secteurs".

## 2. CHARACTERISTICS OF ESTABLISHMENTS WITH FIVE OR MORE PERSONS ENGAGED IN MANUFACTURING EXCEPT ASSEMBLING OR REPAIRING

## CARACTERISTIQUES DES ETABLISSEMENTS MANUFACTURIERS OCCUPANT CINQ PERSONNES OU PLUS, A L'EXCLUSION DES ETABLISSEMENTS SPECIALISES DANS LE MONTAGE OU LA REPARATION

### 1955

Number of establishments in units; value added and wages and salaries in million Lebanese Pounds; number of engaged and employees in thousands; and value added per person engaged in thousand Lebanese Pounds

Nombre d'établissements en unités; valeur ajoutée et traitements et salaires en millions de livres libanaises; nombre de personnes occupées et de salariés en milliers; valeur ajoutée par personne occupée en milliers de livres libanaises

| Item of data | Manufacturing[1] Industries manufacturières[1] | Food, beverages and tobacco[1,2] Industries alimentaires, boissons, tabac[1,2] | Textiles | Clothing, footwear and made-up textiles Articles d'habillement, chaussures et ouvrages en tissu | Wood products and furniture Bois et meubles | Paper and paper products Papier et ouvrages en papier | Printing and publishing Imprimerie et édition | Leather and leather products except wearing apparel Cuir et articles en cuir, à l'exclusion des articles d'habillement | Rubber products Ouvrages en caoutchouc | Chemicals and chemical products Produits chimiques | Petroleum, coal, non-metallic mineral and metal products Dérivés du pétrole et du charbon, produits minéraux non métalliques et ouvrages en métaux | Other manufacturing[2] Autres industries manufacturières[2] | Rubrique |
|---|---|---|---|---|---|---|---|---|---|---|---|---|---|
| ISIC | 2–3 | 20–22 | 23 | 24 | 25–26 | 27 | 28 | 29 | 30 | 31 | 32–38 | 39 | CITI |
| *a. Absolute Figures — Chiffres absolus* | | | | | | | | | | | | | |
| Number of establishments........ | 1 793 | 631 | 113 | 245 | 239 | 16 | 108 | 45 | 15 | 37 | 301 | 43 | Nombre d'établissements |
| Value added.................. | 153.2 | 63.8 | 15.6 | 9.2 | 9.0 | 0.8 | 5.6 | 3.0 | 1.4 | 3.6 | 38.7 | 2.5 | Valeur ajoutée |
| Number of engaged (Average during the year)....... | 34.2 | 9.3 | 6.1 | 3.6 | 3.4 | 0.2 | 1.7 | 0.9 | 0.5 | 0.6 | 7.2 | 0.7 | Nombre de personnes occupées (moyenne pendant l'année) |
| Number of employees (Average during the year)....... | 31.0 | 8.0 | 5.8 | 3.2 | 3.0 | 0.2 | 1.5 | 0.9 | 0.5 | 0.6 | 6.7 | 0.6 | Nombre de salariés (moyenne pendant l'année) |
| Wages and salaries paid......... | 48.2 | 14.3 | 5.7 | 3.8 | 4.0 | 0.2 | 3.7 | 1.1 | 0.6 | 1.0 | 12.8 | 1.0 | Traitements et salaires payés |
| *b. Structure* | | | | | | | | | | | | | |
| Distribution in percent of: | | | | | | | | | | | | | Distribution en pourcentage: |
| Value added............... | 100.0 | 41.7 | 10.2 | 6.0 | 5.9 | 0.5 | 3.6 | 2.0 | 0.9 | 2.3 | 25.3 | 1.6 | De la valeur ajoutée |
| Number of engaged........... | 100.0 | 27.2 | 17.8 | 10.5 | 9.9 | 0.6 | 5.0 | 2.6 | 1.5 | 1.8 | 21.0 | 2.1 | Du nombre de personnes occupées |
| Value added per person engaged... | 4.5 | 6.9 | 2.6 | 2.6 | 2.6 | 4.0 | 3.3 | 3.3 | 2.8 | 6.0 | 5.4 | 3.6 | Valeur ajoutée par personne occupée |
| Value added per unit of wages and salaries.............. | 3.2 | 4.5 | 2.7 | 2.4 | 2.2 | 4.0 | 1.5 | 2.7 | 2.3 | 3.6 | 3.0 | 2.5 | Valeur ajoutée par unité de traitements et salaires |

[1] Excludes the extraction of olive oil.
[2] The manufacture of ice is classified in Other manufacturing (ISIC major group 39) instead of Food, beverages and tobacco (ISIC major groups 20–22).

[1] Non compris l'extraction de l'huile d'olive.
[2] La fabrication de la glace est classée dans Autres industries manufacturières (CITI classe 39) et non dans Industries alimentaires, boissons et tabac (CITI classes 20–22).

# LIBYA — LIBYE

## Gross Domestic Product

The figures for the gross domestic product at factor cost set out in Table 1 were obtained from the following publications issued by the Central Statistics Office, Ministry of National Economy, Tripoli; *National Income Estimates, 1958* and *Statistical Abstract of Libya, 1962.* The figures have been estimated by that Office.

## The Characteristics and Structure of Industrial Activity

The figures for the year 1956 shown in Table 2 were obtained from the publication, *Census of Employment and Production in Urban Areas, 1956—Part 1* prepared and issued by the Central Statistics Office. This Census was carried out during the period, July-November 1956, and was confined to urban areas. The number of persons engaged and of employees refer to those as found at the time of enumeration.

The figures for the year 1958 shown in Table 3 were obtained from the publication, *National Income Estimates, 1958* referred to in the first paragraph. The number of persons engaged shown in the table refer to the average for the month of November 1958.

## Produit intérieur brut

Les chiffres du tableau 1 concernant le produit intérieur brut au coût des facteurs sont tirés des publications ci-après du Bureau central de statistique, Ministère de l'économie nationale, Tripoli : *National Income Estimates, 1958* et *Statistical Abstract of Libya, 1962.* Les chiffres ont été établis par ce bureau.

## Caractéristiques et structure de l'activité industrielle

Les chiffres de 1956 reproduits au tableau 2 sont tirés de la publication intitulée *Census of Employment and Production in Urban Areas, 1956 — Part 1,* préparée et publiée par le Bureau central de statistique. Le recensement en question a été effectué de juillet à novembre 1956; il concernait les régions urbaines seulement. Le nombre de personnes occupées et le nombre de salariés sont ceux qui ont été relevés lors du recensement.

Les chiffres de 1958 reproduits au tableau 3 sont tirés de *National Income Estimates, 1958,* publication déjà mentionnée au premier paragraphe. Le nombre de personnes occupées indiqué dans le tableau représente la moyenne pendant le mois de novembre 1958.

## 1. THE GROSS DOMESTIC PRODUCT AT FACTOR COST ACCORDING TO ORIGIN
## ORIGINE PAR SECTEUR D'ACTIVITE DU PRODUIT INTERIEUR BRUT AU COUT DES FACTEURS

Thousand Libyan pounds — Milliers de livres libyennes

| Item of data and year / Rubrique et année | Total | Agricultural sector / Secteur agricole | Industrial Sector — Secteur industriel | | | | | Transportation and communication / Transports et communications | Other sectors / Autres secteurs |
|---|---|---|---|---|---|---|---|---|---|
| | | | Total | Mining / Industries extractives | Manufacturing / Industries manufacturières | Construction / Bâtiment et travaux publics | Electricity, gas and water / Electricité, gaz et eau | | |
| ISIC — CITI | 0–9 | 0 | 1–5 | 1 | 2–3 | 4 | 5 | 7 | 6, 8–9 |
| *a.* At Current Prices — Aux prix courants | | | | | | | | | |
| 1958............ | 52 110 | 13 560 | 12 126 | 3 569 | 5 988 | 1 808 | 761 | 2 909 | 23 515 |
| 1959............ | 56 116 | 13 750 | 13 543 | 4 300 | 6 406 | 2 000 | 837 | 4 072 | 24 751 |

## 2. NUMBER OF ESTABLISHMENTS AND EMPLOYMENT IN THE DIVISIONS OF INDUSTRIAL ACTIVITY
### NOMBRE D'ETABLISSEMENTS ET EMPLOI DANS LES BRANCHES DE L'ACTIVITE INDUSTRIELLE
### 1956

Number of establishments, persons engaged and employees in units.　　　　　Nombre d'établissements, de personnes occupées et de salariés en unités.

| Item of data | All industrial activity<br>Toutes industries | Mining<br>Industries ex-tractives | Manu-facturing<br>Industries manu-facturières | Con-struction<br>Bâtiment et travaux publics | Electricity gas and water<br>Electricité gaz et eau | Rubrique |
|---|---|---|---|---|---|---|
| ISIC | 1-5 | 1 | 2-3 | 4 | 5 | CITI |
| Number of establishments... | 3 244 | 17 | 3 121 | 89 | 17 | Nombre d'établissements |
| Number of engaged........ | 19 076 | 703 | 14 504 | 2 751 | 1 118 | Nombre de personnes occupées |
| Number of employees...... | 15 403 | 703 | 10 940 | 2 648 | 1 112 | Nombre de salariés |
| Distribution in percent of: | | | | | | Distribution en pourcentage: |
| Number of engaged........ | 100.0 | 3.7 | 76.0 | 14.4 | 5.9 | Nombre de personnes occupées |
| Number of employees...... | 100.0 | 4.6 | 71.0 | 17.2 | 7.2 | Nombre de salariés |

## 3. VALUE ADDED AND NUMBERS OF PERSONS ENGAGED IN INDUSTRIAL ACTIVITY
### VALEUR AJOUTEE ET NOMBRE DE PERSONNES EXERÇANT UNE ACTIVITE INDUSTRIELLE
### 1958

Value added in thousand Libyan pounds; number of engaged in units and value added per person engaged in Libyan pounds　　　Valeur ajoutée en milliers de livres libyennes; nombre de personnes occupées en unités; valeur ajoutée par personne occupée en livres libyennes

### A. The Divisions of Industrial Activity
### Les branches de l'activité industrielle

| Item of data | All industrial activity<br>Toutes industries | Mining<br>Industries ex-tractives | Manu-facturing<br>Industries manu-facturières | Con-struction<br>Bâtiment et travaux publics | Electricity and gas<br>Electricité et gaz | Rubrique |
|---|---|---|---|---|---|---|
| ISIC | 1-4,511-512 | 1 | 2-3 | 4 | 511-512 | CITI |
| Value added....... | 12 126 | 3 569 | 5 988 | 1 808 | 761 | Valeur ajoutée |
| Number of engaged........ | 22 938 | 3 654 | 13 032 | 5 244 | 1 008 | Nombre de personnes occupées |
| Distribution in percent of: | | | | | | Distribution en pourcentage: |
| Value added..... | 100.0 | 29.4 | 49.4 | 14.9 | 6.3 | Valeur ajoutée |
| Number of engaged........ | 100.0 | 15.9 | 56.8 | 22.9 | 4.4 | Nombre de personnes occupées |
| Value added per person engaged.. | 529 | 977 | 459 | 345 | 755 | Valeur ajoutée par personne occupée |

### B. The Major Groups of Mining
### Les classes de la branche Industries extractives

| Item of data | All mining<br>Toutes industries extrac-tives | Crude petroleum and natural gas<br>Pétrole brut et gaz naturel | Other mining<br>Divers | Rubrique |
|---|---|---|---|---|
| ISIC | 1 | 13 | 14-19 | CITI |
| Value added.................. | 3 569 | 3 449 | 120 | Valeur ajoutée |
| Number of engaged............ | 3 654 | 3 254 | 400 | Nombre de personnes occupées |
| Distribution in percent of: | | | | Distribution en pourcentage: |
| Value added............... | 100.0 | 96.6 | 3.4 | Valeur ajoutée |
| Number of engaged.......... | 100.0 | 89.1 | 10.9 | Nombre de personnes occupées |
| Value added per person engaged.................. | 977 | 1 060 | 300 | Valeur ajoutée par personne occupée |

### C. The Major Groups of Manufacturing — Les classes de la branche Industries manufacturières

| Item of data | Manu-facturing<br>Industries manufac-turières | Food, beverages and tobacco<br>Industries alimen-taires, boissons, tabac | Textiles | Clothing, footwear and made-up textiles<br>Articles d'habil-lement, chaussures et ouvrages en tissu | Wood products and furniture<br>Bois et meubles | Paper and paper products<br>Papier et ouvrages en papier | Printing and publish-ing<br>Im-primerie et édition | Leather and leather products except wearing apparel<br>Cuir et articles en cuir, à l'exclu-sion des articles d'habil-lement | Rubber products<br>Ouvrages en caout-chouc | Chemicals and chemical, petroleum and coal products<br>Produits chi-miques et dérivés du pétrole et du charbon | Non-metallic mineral products<br>Produits minéraux non métal-liques | Basic metals and metal products<br>Métal-lurgie de base et ouvrages en métaux | Other manu-factur-ing<br>Autres in-dustries manufac-turières | Rubrique |
|---|---|---|---|---|---|---|---|---|---|---|---|---|---|---|
| ISIC | 2-3 | 20-22 | 23 | 24 | 25-26 | 27 | 28 | 29 | 30 | 31-32 | 33 | 34-38 | 39 | CITI |
| Value added......... | 5 988 | 2 932 | 214 | 440 | 283 | 15 | 217 | 54 | 25 | 4 | 174 | 1 150 | 480 | Valeur ajoutée |
| Number of engaged.... | 13 032 | 4 272 | 968 | 1 287 | 899 | 30 | 343 | 82 | 108 | 16 | 510 | 4 173 | 344 | Nombre de personnes occupées |
| Distribution in percent of: | | | | | | | | | | | | | | Distribution en pour-centage: |
| Value added........ | 100.0 | 48.9 | 3.6 | 7.3 | 4.7 | 0.3 | 3.6 | 0.9 | 0.4 | 0.1 | 2.9 | 19.2 | 8.0 | Valeur ajoutée |
| Number of engaged... | 100.0 | 32.9 | 7.4 | 9.9 | 6.9 | 0.2 | 2.6 | 0.6 | 0.8 | 0.1 | 3.9 | 32.1 | 2.6 | Nombre de personnes occupées |
| Value added per person engaged...... | 459 | 686 | 221 | 342 | 315 | 500 | 633 | 659 | 231 | 250 | 341 | 276 | 1 395 | Valeur ajoutée par personne occupée |

# LUXEMBOURG

## Gross Domestic Product and Gross Domestic Fixed Capital Formation

The estimates of gross domestic product and gross domestic fixed capital formation shown in Table 1 are from the reply of the Service d'études et de documentation, Ministère des affaires économiques, Luxembourg to the United Nations national accounts questionnaire. The official estimates and descriptions are published by the Service in issues of *La comptabilité nationale du Grand-Duché de Luxembourg*. In replying to the United Nations questionnaire, the official estimates have been adjusted by the Service, to the extent possible, to conform to the United Nations system of national accounts.

## Index Numbers of Industrial Production

The index numbers in Table 2 are derived from indexes of industrial production published in the *Bulletin statistique* by the Office de la Statistique Générale, Luxembourg. The series of index numbers relate to industrial units having one or more employees and are computed as base-weighted arithmetic averages.

The weight base year is 1937-1938 in the case of the indexes for the years, 1937-1938 and 1948, and 1947 in the case of the indexes for 1949 and later years. The weighting diagram for combining the indexes for detailed categories of industrial activity into indexes for broader classes is based on the contribution to the net domestic product, at factor cost. The indexes for each of the detailed categories of industrial activity are computed from relatives of quantities of output for individual products, in most instances, but of man-hours worked, in some cases. In combining the relatives into indexes for detailed categories of industrial activity, use is made of weights derived from gross value of output.

Further details concerning the indexes may be found in *Bulletin du Service d'Etudes et de Documentation Economiques et de l'Office de la Statistique Générale*, Vol. I, Nos. 1-2, 1950.

## Index Numbers of Industrial Employment

The index numbers of industrial employment shown in Table 3 are based on absolute figures of employment published in various issues of *Economie Industrielle du Luxembourg, Cahiers économiques du Service d'Etudes* and *Annuaire Statistique, Office de la Statistique Generale*. These figures result from the annual Industrial Census dealt with in Table 4. The absolute figures relate to the average monthly employment of working proprietors and employees by industrial establishments having one or more employees.

## Produit intérieur brut et formation brute de capital fixe intérieur

Les estimations relatives au produit intérieur brut et à la formation brute de capital fixe intérieur, reproduites au tableau 1, proviennent de la réponse du Service d'études et de documentation, Ministère des affaires économiques, Luxembourg, au questionnaire de l'O.N.U. relatif aux comptes nationaux. Les estimations officielles ainsi que les descriptions des méthodes adoptées ont paru dans les publications du Service, intitulées *La comptabilité nationale du Grand-Duché de Luxembourg*. Pour remplir le questionnaire de l'O.N.U., le Service a ajusté ses estimations officielles afin de les rendre aussi conformes que possible au système de comptabilité nationale de l'O.N.U.

## Indices de la production industrielle

Les indices du tableau 2 sont tirés des indices de la production industrielle publiés dans le *Bulletin statistique* de l'Office de la statistique générale, Luxembourg. Les séries d'indices sont relatives aux unités industrielles ayant un salarié ou plus et sont des moyennes arithmétiques à pondération fixe.

L'année de pondération de base est 1937-1938 pour les indices relatifs aux années 1937-1938 et 1948, et 1947 pour les indices relatifs à 1949 et aux années suivantes. Le diagramme de pondération utilisé pour combiner les indices de chaque catégorie d'activité industrielle est fondé sur la contribution au produit intérieur net, au coût des facteurs. Les indices de catégorie sont construits à partir des rapports quantitatifs pour chaque marchandise, dans la plupart des cas, mais parfois aussi d'après le nombre d'heures de travail effectuées, la pondération se faisant en fonction de la valeur brute de la production. Pour combiner les rapports en indices relatifs à des catégories détaillées de l'activité industrielle, la valeur brute de la production a été utilisée comme base de pondération.

Pour plus amples détails en ce qui concerne ces indices, voir le *Bulletin du Service d'Etudes et de Documentation Economiques et de l'Office de la Statistique Générale*, tome 1, Nos 1-2, 1950.

## Indices de l'emploi industriel

Les indices de l'emploi industriel reproduits au tableau 3 ont été élaborés à partir de chiffres absolus de l'emploi, publiés dans différents numéros de l'*Economie Industrielle du Luxembourg, Cahiers économiques du Service d'Etudes* et *Annuaire Statistique, Office de la Statistique Générale*. Ces chiffres sont tirés du recensement industriel annuel auquel on s'est déjà référé pour le tableau 4. Ces chiffres absolus sont relatifs à l'emploi mensuel moyen des propriétaires qui travaillent et des salariés dans les établissements industriels ayant un salarié ou plus.

## The Characteristics and Structure of Industrial Activity

The data shown in Table 4 result from an annual Industrial Census of establishments with one or more employees that were in operation during the year. The sources of these figures are *Annuaire statistique,* 1955 or 1959 of the Office de la Statistique Générale, Luxembourg, and the *Economie industrielle du Luxembourg, Cahiers économiques du Service d'Etudes,* No. 18, 1957 or No. 25, 1959.

Although the statistical unit in the annual Censuses is, in general, the establishment, the enterprise is also utilized for such industrial activities as mining, construction and the production of electricity and gas. The figures of number of engaged cover only working proprietors and employees. Value added is computed at market prices ex-industrial establishment and relates to all the production of these units.

## Les caractéristiques et la structure de l'activité industrielle

Les données du tableau 4 proviennent d'un recensement annuel des établissements industriels qui comptaient au moins un salarié et qui étaient en activité pendant l'année. Les sources sont l'*Annuaire statistique, 1955 et 1959* de l'Office de la statistique générale, Luxembourg, et l'*Economie industrielle du Luxembourg, Cahiers économiques du Service d'études,* No 18, 1957 ou No 25, 1959.

Bien que l'unité statistique utilisée dans les recensements annuels soit en général l'établissement, c'est parfois aussi l'entreprise qui sert d'unité pour certains secteurs de l'activité industrielle (industries extractives, bâtiment et travaux publics, production de gaz et d'électricité). Les personnes occupées comprennent exclusivement les propriétaires qui travaillent et les salariés. La valeur ajoutée est calculée aux prix du marché, départ établissement, et elle englobe l'ensemble de la production des unités recensées.

# LUXEMBOURG

## 1. THE GROSS DOMESTIC PRODUCT AND GROSS DOMESTIC FIXED CAPITAL FORMATION
### PRODUIT INTERIEUR BRUT ET FORMATION BRUTE DE CAPITAL FIXE INTERIEUR

Million Francs                                                                           Millions de francs

### A. Expenditure on the Gross Domestic Product at Market Prices
### Dépenses relatives au produit intérieur brut aux prix du marché

| Item of data and year / Rubrique et année | Total | Consumption / Consommation | | Gross Domestic Capital Formation / Formation brute de capital intérieur | | Net exports of goods and services / Exportations nettes de biens et de services | |
|---|---|---|---|---|---|---|---|
| | | Total | Government / Etat | Total | Fixed / Fixe | Exports less imports / Exportations moins importations | Exports / Exportations |
| *a. At Current Prices — Aux prix courants* | | | | | | | |
| **Absolute figures — Chiffres absolus** | | | | | | | |
| 1952 | 18 380 | 11 702 | 2 227 | 2 961 | 3 141 | 3 717 | 17 348 |
| 1953 | 16 908 | 12 062 | 2 342 | 4 289 | 4 009 | 557 | 12 667 |
| 1954 | 17 341 | 12 430 | 2 352 | 4 198 | 3 952 | 713 | 12 629 |
| 1955 | 19 023 | 13 182 | 2 423 | 4 594 | 4 124 | 1 247 | 15 359 |
| 1956 | 20 841 | 13 941 | 2 297 | 4 380 | 4 030 | 2 520 | 18 355 |
| 1957 | 22 535 | 15 177 | 2 477 | 5 530 | 5 230 | 1 828 | 19 247 |
| 1958 | 22 270 | 15 933 | 2 797 | 5 627 | 5 227 | 710 | 17 218 |
| 1959 | 22 889 | 16 295 | 2 608 | 5 697 | 5 247 | 897 | 18 088 |
| 1960 | 24 572 | 16 667 | 2 534 | 4 849 | 5 125 | 3 056 | 21 686 |
| **Percentage distribution of average annual expenditure — Distribution en pourcentage des dépenses annuelles moyennes** | | | | | | | |
| 1953 | 100.0 | 71.3 | 13.8 | 25.4 | 23.7 | 3.3 | 74.9 |
| 1954 | 100.0 | 71.7 | 13.6 | 24.2 | 22.8 | 4.1 | 72.8 |
| 1958 | 100.0 | 71.5 | 12.6 | 25.3 | 23.5 | 3.2 | 77.3 |
| 1960 | 100.0 | 67.8 | 10.3 | 19.7 | 20.8 | 12.5 | 88.2 |
| *b. At Prices of 1954 — Aux prix de 1954* | | | | | | | |
| **Absolute figures — Chiffres absolus** | | | | | | | |
| 1952 | 17 166 | 11 780 | 2 249 | 3 630 | 3 043 | 1 756 | 13 194 |
| 1953 | 17 491 | 12 178 | 2 366 | 4 424 | 4 095 | 889 | 11 996 |
| 1954 | 17 341 | 12 430 | 2 352 | 4 198 | 3 952 | 713 | 12 629 |
| 1955 | 18 297 | 13 165 | 2 423 | 4 060 | 4 035 | 1 072 | 13 970 |
| 1956 | 19 210 | 13 760 | 2 274 | 4 253 | 3 870 | 1 197 | 15 235 |
| 1957 | 20 169 | 14 286 | 2 337 | 4 949 | 4 793 | 934 | 15 256 |
| 1958 | 20 338 | 14 901 | 2 614 | 4 955 | 4 802 | 482 | 15 102 |
| 1959 | 20 587 | 15 203 | 2 437 | 4 691 | 4 884 | 693 | 16 055 |
| **Percentage distribution of average annual expenditure — Distribution en pourcentage des dépenses annuelles moyennes** | | | | | | | |
| 1953 | 100.0 | 69.6 | 13.5 | 25.3 | 23.4 | 5.1 | 68.6 |
| 1954 | 100.0 | 71.7 | 13.6 | 24.2 | 22.8 | 4.1 | 72.8 |
| 1958 | 100.0 | 73.3 | 12.8 | 24.3 | 23.6 | 2.4 | 74.2 |
| **Average annual rate of growth — Taux annuel moyen d'accroissement** | | | | | | | |
| 1954–1958 | 4.1 | 4.6 | 2.7 | 4.2 | 5.0 | . | 4.6 |

## B. The Gross Domestic Product at Factor Cost According to Origin
### Origine par secteur d'activité du produit intérieur brut au coût des facteurs

| Item of data and year<br>Rubrique et année | Total | Agricultural sector<br>Secteur agricole | Industrial Sector — Secteur Industriel | | | | | Transportation<br>Transports | Other sectors [1]<br>Autres secteurs [1] |
|---|---|---|---|---|---|---|---|---|---|
| | | | Total | Mining<br>Industries extractives | Manufacturing<br>Industries manufacturières | Construction<br>Bâtiment et travaux publics | Electricity, gas and water<br>Electricité, gaz et eau | | |
| ISIC — CITI | 0–9 | 0 | 1–5 | 1 | 2–3 | 4 | 5 | 71–72 | 73, 6, 8–9 |
| *a.* At Current Prices — Aux prix courants | | | | | | | | | |
| Absolute figures — Chiffres absolus | | | | | | | | | |
| 1952............... | 17 007 | 1 574 | 9 575 | 720 | 7 833 | 906 | 116 | 1 118 | 4 740 |
| 1953............... | 15 542 | 1 586 | 7 461 | 683 | 5 557 | 1 089 | 132 | 1 124 | 5 371 |
| 1954............... | 16 150 | 1 549 | 7 849 | 540 | 5 982 | 1 161 | 166 | 1 298 | 5 454 |
| 1955............... | 17 810 | 1 657 | 9 495 | 550 | 7 512 | 1 259 | 174 | 1 482 | 5 176 |
| 1956............... | 19 288 | 1 735 | 10 602 | 594 | 8 507 | 1 316 | 185 | 1 419 | 5 532 |
| 1957............... | 20 886 | 1 744 | 11 362 | 640 | 9 058 | 1 482 | 182 | 1 475 | 6 305 |
| 1958............... | 20 663 | 1 809 | 10 641 | 614 | 8 240 | 1 613 | 174 | 1 445 | 6 768 |
| 1959............... | 21 447 | 1 847 | 11 213 | 596 | 8 784 | 1 642 | 191 | 1 545 | 6 842 |
| 1960............... | 22 783 | 1 769 | 12 515 | 601 | 10 018 | 1 706 | 190 | 1 623 | 6 876 |
| Percentage distribution according to sector — Distribution en pourcentage par secteur | | | | | | | | | |
| 1953............... | 100.0 | 10.2 | 48.0 | 4.4 | 35.8 | 7.0 | 0.8 | 7.2 | 34.6 |
| 1954............... | 100.0 | 9.6 | 48.6 | 3.4 | 37.0 | 7.2 | 1.0 | 8.0 | 33.8 |
| 1958............... | 100.0 | 8.8 | 51.5 | 3.0 | 39.9 | 7.8 | 0.8 | 7.0 | 32.7 |
| 1960............... | 100.0 | 7.7 | 54.9 | 2.7 | 43.9 | 7.5 | 0.8 | 7.2 | 30.2 |
| *b.* At Prices of 1954 — Aux prix de 1954 | | | | | | | | | |
| Absolute figures — Chiffres absolus | | | | | | | | | |
| 1952............... | 15 870 | 1 484 | 8 101 | 659 | 6 279 | 1 022 | 141 | 1 497 | 4 788 |
| 1953............... | 16 076 | 1 504 | 7 777 | 648 | 5 738 | 1 242 | 149 | 1 370 | 5 425 |
| 1954............... | 16 150 | 1 549 | 7 849 | 540 | 5 982 | 1 161 | 166 | 1 298 | 5 454 |
| 1955............... | 16 966 | 1 641 | 8 636 | 643 | 6 591 | 1 219 | 183 | 1 513 | 5 176 |
| 1956............... | 17 715 | 1 622 | 9 025 | 670 | 6 966 | 1 196 | 193 | 1 591 | 5 477 |
| 1957............... | 18 590 | 1 601 | 9 460 | 697 | 7 078 | 1 486 | 199 | 1 581 | 5 948 |
| 1958............... | 18 854 | 1 647 | 9 395 | 599 | 6 921 | 1 672 | 203 | 1 487 | 6 325 |
| 1959............... | 19 327 | 1 641 | 9 773 | 578 | 7 263 | 1 718 | 214 | 1 519 | 6 394 |
| Percentage distribution according to sector — Distribution en pourcentage par secteur | | | | | | | | | |
| 1953............... | 100.0 | 9.4 | 48.4 | 4.1 | 35.7 | 7.7 | 0.9 | 8.5 | 33.7 |
| 1954............... | 100.0 | 9.6 | 48.6 | 3.4 | 37.0 | 7.2 | 1.0 | 8.0 | 33.8 |
| 1958............... | 100.0 | 8.7 | 49.9 | 3.2 | 36.7 | 8.9 | 1.1 | 7.9 | 33.5 |
| Average annual rate of growth — Taux annuel moyen d'accroissement | | | | | | | | | |
| 1954 – 1958............. | 3.9 | 1.5 | 4.6 | 2.6 | 3.7 | 9.5 | 5.2 | 3.5 | 3.8 |

[1] Includes a statistical discrepancy.

[1] Y compris les écarts statistiques.

## C. Gross Domestic Fixed Capital Formation According to Purchasing Sector
### Formation brute de capital fixe intérieur par secteur d'acquisition

| Item of data and year | Total | Agriculture, commerce and services | Industrial Sector — Secteur industriel | | | Transportation | Other sectors |
| Rubrique et année | | Agriculture, commerce et services | Total | Manufacturing, mining and construction Industries manufacturières et extractives; bâtiment et travaux publics | Electricity, gas and water Electricité, gaz et eau | Transports | Autres secteurs |
|---|---|---|---|---|---|---|---|
| ISIC — CITI | 0–9 | 0, 6, 82–85 | 1–5 | 1, 2–3, 4 | 5 | 71–72 | 73, 81, 9 |
| | At Current Prices — Aux prix courants | | | | | | |
| **Absolute figures — Chiffres absolus** | | | | | | | |
| 1952 | 3 141 | 280 | 1 313 | 1 288 | 25 | 164 | 1 384 |
| 1953 | 4 157 | 237 | 1 762 | 1 726 | 36 | 403 | 1 755 |
| 1954 | 3 952 | 337 | 1 678 | 1 641 | 37 | 135 | 1 802 |
| 1955 | 4 124 | 289 | 1 677 | 1 639 | 38 | 246 | 1 912 |
| 1956 | 4 030 | 312 | 1 643 | 1 594 | 49 | 260 | 1 815 |
| 1957 | 5 230 | 417 | 2 407 | 2 353 | 54 | 331 | 2 075 |
| 1958 | 5 227 | 400 | 2 014 | 1 943 | 71 | 376 | 2 437 |
| 1959 | 5 247 | 382 | 2 098 | 2 046 | 52 | 254 | 2 513 |
| 1960 | 5 125 | 413 | 2 605 [1] | ... | ... | ... [1] | 2 107 |
| **Percentage distribution according to sector— Distribution en pourcentage par secteur** | | | | | | | |
| 1953 | 100.0 | 5.7 | 42.4 | 41.5 | 0.9 | 9.7 | 42.2 |
| 1954 | 100.0 | 8.5 | 42.5 | 41.5 | 1.0 | 3.4 | 45.6 |
| 1958 | 100.0 | 7.7 | 38.5 | 37.2 | 1.3 | 7.2 | 46.6 |
| 1960 | 100.0 | 8.0 | 50.9 [1] | ... | ... | ... [1] | 41.1 |

[1] Includes the Transportation industries (ISIC major groups 71-72).   [1] Y compris les Transports (CITI 71-72).

## 2. INDEX NUMBERS OF INDUSTRIAL PRODUCTION
## INDICES DE LA PRODUCTION INDUSTRIELLE

### A. The Divisions of Industrial Activity
### Les branches de l'activité industrielle

| Year Année | Total | Mining Industries extractives | Manufacturing [1] Industries manufacturières [1] | Electricity and gas Electricité et gaz |
|---|---|---|---|---|
| ISIC — CITI | 1–3, 511–512 | 1 | 2–3 | 511–512 |
| a. Indexes — Indices (1958 = 100) | | | | |
| 1937 – 1938 | 66 | 101 | 63 | 46 |
| 1948 | 74 | 57 | 77 | 51 |
| 1949 | – 70 – | – 69 – | – 72 – | – 54 – |
| 1950 | 74 | 67 | 75 | 60 |
| 1951 | 90 | 90 | 91 | 68 |
| 1952 | 90 | 110 | 89 | 70 |
| 1953 | 83 | 109 | 80 | 73 |
| 1954 | 86 | 90 | 85 | 82 |
| 1955 | 96 | 107 | 95 | 90 |
| 1956 | 102 | 112 | 102 | 95 |
| 1957 | 104 | 116 | 103 | 98 |
| 1958 | 100 | 100 | 100 | 100 |
| 1959 | 105 | 97 | 106 | 106 |
| 1960 | 115 | 102 | 116 | 115 |
| 1961 | 117 | 107 | 118 | 119 |
| b. Average Annual Rate of Change — Taux annuel moyen de variation | | | | |
| 1938 – 1960 | 2.6 | — | 2.8 | 4.3 |
| 1938 – 1948 | 1.1 | –5.6 | 2.0 | 1.0 |
| 1950 – 1960 | 4.5 | 4.3 | 4.5 | 6.7 |
| 1948 – 1953 | 2.3 | 13.8 | 0.8 | 7.4 |
| 1954 – 1958 | 3.8 | 2.7 | 4.1 | 5.1 |
| 1958 – 1960 | 7.2 | 1.0 | 7.7 | 7.2 |

[1] Production in Other manufacturing (ISIC major group 39) is not covered.

### B. The Major Groups of Mining
### Les classes de la branche Industries extractives

| Year Année | All mining Toutes industries extractives | Metal mining Extraction des minerais métalliques | Other mining Autres industries extractives |
|---|---|---|---|
| ISIC — CITI | 1 | 12 | 14–19 |
| a. Indexes — Indices (1958 = 100) | | | |
| 1937 – 1938 | 101 | 98 | 130 |
| 1948 | 57 | 52 | 112 |
| 1949 | – 69 – | – 62 – | – 125 – |
| 1950 | 67 | 58 | 145 |
| 1951 | 90 | 85 | 147 |
| 1952 | 110 | 109 | 114 |
| 1953 | 109 | 108 | 113 |
| 1954 | 90 | 88 | 104 |
| 1955 | 107 | 109 | 100 |
| 1956 | 112 | 114 | 90 |
| 1957 | 116 | 118 | 104 |
| 1958 | 100 | 100 | 100 |
| 1959 | 97 | 98 | 82 |
| 1960 | 102 | 105 | 80 |
| 1961 | 107 | 112 | 71 |
| b. Average Annual Rate of Change — Taux annuel moyen de variation | | | |
| 1938 – 1960 | — | 0.3 | –2.2 |
| 1938 – 1948 | –5.6 | –6.1 | –1.5 |
| 1950 – 1960 | 4.3 | 6.1 | –5.8 |
| 1948 – 1953 | 13.8 | 15.7 | 0.2 |
| 1954 – 1958 | 2.7 | 3.2 | –1.0 |
| 1958 – 1960 | 1.0 | 2.5 | –10.6 |

[1] Non compris Autres industries manufacturières (CITI 39).

## C. The Major Groups of Manufacturing — Les classes de la branche Industries manufacturières

| Year / Année | Manufacturing [1] Industries manufacturières [1] | Food, beverages and tobacco Industries alimentaires, boissons, tabac | Textiles | Clothing, footwear and made-up textiles Articles d'habillement, chaussures et ouvrages en tissu | Wood products and furniture Bois et meubles | Printing and publishing Imprimerie et édition | Leather and leather products except wearing apparel Cuir et articles en cuir, à l'exclusion des articles d'habillement | Chemicals and chemical, rubber, petroleum and coal products Produits chimiques, ouvrages en caoutchouc, et dérivés du pétrole et du charbon | Non-metallic mineral products Produits minéraux non métalliques | Basic metals Métallurgie de base | Metal products Ouvrages en métaux |
|---|---|---|---|---|---|---|---|---|---|---|---|
| ISIC — CITI | 2–3 | 20–22 | 23 | 24 | 25–26 | 28 | 29 | 30–32 | 33 | 34 | 35–38 |

### a. Indexes — Indices (1958 = 100)

| Year | | | | | | | | | | | |
|---|---|---|---|---|---|---|---|---|---|---|---|
| 1937–1938 | 63 | 57 | 154 | 162 | 104 | 75 | 261 | 59 | 50 | 60 | 75 |
| 1948 | 77 | 58 | 139 | 154 | 145 | 78 | 152 | 70 | 55 | 75 | 111 |
| 1949 | –72– | –58– | –131– | –151– | –145– | –77– | –141– | –64– | –59– | –69– | –114– |
| 1950 | 75 | 58 | 152 | 136 | 117 | 75 | 148 | 61 | 66 | 75 | 113 |
| 1951 | 91 | 66 | 133 | 111 | 123 | 76 | 131 | 81 | 71 | 94 | 100 |
| 1952 | 89 | 64 | 115 | 110 | 122 | 78 | 111 | 78 | 66 | 92 | 101 |
| 1953 | 80 | 66 | 136 | 110 | 120 | 77 | 124 | 75 | 75 | 80 | 100 |
| 1954 | 85 | 66 | 123 | 106 | 120 | 88 | 124 | 82 | 82 | 85 | 96 |
| 1955 | 95 | 73 | 118 | 103 | 126 | 91 | 124 | 98 | 92 | 96 | 96 |
| 1956 | 102 | 80 | 102 | 106 | 112 | 97 | 105 | 109 | 98 | 103 | 99 |
| 1957 | 103 | 93 | 108 | 110 | 103 | 96 | 123 | 108 | 100 | 104 | 100 |
| 1958 | 100 | 100 | 100 | 100 | 100 | 100 | 100 | 100 | 100 | 100 | 100 |
| 1959 | 106 | 112 | 82 | 94 | 86 | 101 | 105 | 90 | 98 | 108 | 97 |
| 1960 | 116 | 118 | 77 | 94 | 78 | 101 | 84 | 103 | 112 | 120 | 97 |
| 1961 | 118 | 126 | 70 | 105 | 77 | 101 | 69 | 106 | 121 | 121 | 98 |

### b. Average Annual Rate of Change — Taux annuel moyen de variation

| | | | | | | | | | | | |
|---|---|---|---|---|---|---|---|---|---|---|---|
| 1938–1960 | 2.8 | 3.4 | –3.1 | –2.4 | –1.3 | 1.4 | –5.0 | 2.6 | 3.7 | 3.2 | 1.2 |
| 1938–1948 | 2.0 | 0.2 | –1.0 | –0.5 | 3.4 | 0.4 | –5.3 | 1.7 | 1.0 | 2.3 | 4.0 |
| 1950–1960 | 4.5 | 7.4 | –6.6 | –3.6 | –4.0 | 3.0 | –5.5 | 5.4 | 5.4 | 4.8 | –1.5 |
| 1948–1953 | 0.8 | 2.6 | –0.4 | –6.5 | –3.7 | –0.3 | –4.0 | 1.4 | 6.4 | 1.3 | –2.1 |
| 1954–1958 | 4.1 | 10.9 | –5.0 | –1.5 | –4.5 | 3.2 | –5.2 | 5.1 | 5.1 | 4.1 | 1.0 |
| 1958–1960 | 7.7 | 8.6 | –12.2 | –3.0 | –11.7 | 0.5 | –8.3 | 1.5 | 5.8 | 9.5 | –1.5 |

[1] Production in Other manufacturing (ISIC major group 39) is not covered.  [1] Non compris Autres industries manufacturières (CITI 39).

## 3. INDEX NUMBERS OF INDUSTRIAL EMPLOYMENT
### INDICES DE L'EMPLOI DANS L'INDUSTRIE

### A. The Divisions of Industrial Activity
### Les branches de l'activité industrielle

| Period / Période | Total [1] | Mining Industries extractives | Manufacturing [1] Industries manufacturières [1] | Construction Bâtiment et travaux publics | Electricity, gas and water Électricité, gaz et eau |
|---|---|---|---|---|---|
| ISIC — CITI | 1–3, 511–512, 521 | 1 | 2–3 | 4 | 511–512, 521 |

#### a. Indexes — Indices (1958 = 100)

| | | | | | |
|---|---|---|---|---|---|
| 1948 | 81 | 106 | 86 | 51 | 93 |
| 1949 | 82 | 116 | 87 | 51 | 92 |
| 1950 | 82 | 106 | 84 | 65 | 91 |
| 1951 | 87 | 116 | 88 | 72 | 91 |
| 1952 | 86 | 123 | 88 | 65 | 90 |
| 1953 | 88 | 120 | 88 | 73 | 93 |
| 1954 | 87 | 107 | 90 | 69 | 92 |
| 1955 | 91 | 107 | 94 | 73 | 94 |
| 1956 | 93 | 108 | 96 | 73 | 94 |
| 1957 | 98 | 106 | 99 | 88 | 98 |
| 1958 | 100 | 100 | 100 | 100 | 100 |
| 1959 | 101 | 94 | 102 | 103 | 101 |
| 1960 | 103 | 89 | 104 | 105 | 102 |
| 1961 | 102 | 84 | 104 | 103 | 103 |

#### b. Average Annual Rate of Change — Taux annuel moyen de variation

| | | | | | |
|---|---|---|---|---|---|
| 1950–1960 | 2.3 | –1.7 | 2.2 | 4.9 | 1.1 |
| 1948–1953 | 1.7 | 2.5 | 0.5 | 7.4 | — |
| 1954–1958 | 3.5 | –1.7 | 2.7 | 9.7 | 2.1 |
| 1958–1960 | 1.5 | –5.7 | 2.0 | 2.5 | 1.0 |

### B. The Major Groups of Mining
### Les classes de la branche Industries extractives

| Period / Période | Total | Metal mining Extraction des minerais métalliques | Other mining Autres Industries extractives |
|---|---|---|---|
| ISIC — CITI | 1 | 12 | 14–19 |

#### a. Indexes — Indices (1958 = 100)

| | | | |
|---|---|---|---|
| 1948 | 106 | 109 | 102 |
| 1949 | 116 | 117 | 113 |
| 1950 | 106 | 99 | 122 |
| 1951 | 116 | 115 | 116 |
| 1952 | 123 | 127 | 114 |
| 1953 | 120 | 121 | 120 |
| 1954 | 107 | 102 | 117 |
| 1955 | 107 | 104 | 114 |
| 1956 | 108 | 107 | 111 |
| 1957 | 106 | 103 | 111 |
| 1958 | 100 | 100 | 100 |
| 1959 | 94 | 93 | 95 |
| 1960 | 89 | 91 | 84 |
| 1961 | 84 | 87 | 75 |

#### b. Average Annual Rate of Change — Taux annuel moyen de variation

| | | | |
|---|---|---|---|
| 1950–1960 | –1.7 | –0.8 | –3.7 |
| 1948–1953 | 2.5 | 2.1 | 3.3 |
| 1954–1958 | –1.7 | –0.5 | –3.8 |
| 1958–1960 | –5.7 | –4.6 | –8.3 |

For footnotes see end of table.
Pour les notes, voir au bas du tableau.

## C.   The Major Groups of Manufacturing — Les classes de la branche Industries manufacturières

| Period<br>Période | Manu-<br>facturing [1]<br><br>Industries<br>manufac-<br>turières [1] | Food,<br>beverages<br>and<br>tobacco<br><br>Industries<br>alimen-<br>taires,<br>boissons,<br>tabac | Textiles,<br>clothing<br>and<br>made-up<br>textiles<br><br>Textiles,<br>articles<br>d'habil-<br>lement<br>et ouvrages<br>en tissus | Wood<br>products<br>and<br>furniture<br><br>Bois et<br>meubles | Printing<br>and<br>publishing<br><br>Im-<br>primerie<br>et<br>édition | Leather<br>and<br>leather<br>products<br><br>Cuir et<br>articles<br>en cuir | Chemicals<br>and<br>chemical,<br>rubber,<br>petroleum<br>and coal<br>products<br><br>Produits<br>chimiques,<br>ouvrages en<br>caoutchouc,<br>et dérivés<br>du pétrole<br>et du<br>charbon | Non-<br>metallic<br>mineral<br>products<br><br>Produits<br>minéraux<br>non<br>métal-<br>liques | Basic<br>metals<br><br>Métal-<br>lurgie<br>de base | Metal<br>products [2]<br><br>Ouvrages<br>en<br>métaux [2] |
|---|---|---|---|---|---|---|---|---|---|---|
| ISIC — CITI | 2–3 | 20–22 | 23,243-244 | 25–26 | 28 | 242, 29 | 30–32 | 33 | 34 | 35–38 |

### a.  Indexes — Indices (1958 = 100)

| Period | | | | | | | | | | |
|---|---|---|---|---|---|---|---|---|---|---|
| 1948............. | 86 | 90 | 113 | 138 | 85 | 199 | 44 | 80 | 82 | 102 |
| 1949............. | 87 | 90 | 100 | 127 | 81 | 183 | 36 | 79 | 84 | 101 |
| 1950............. | 84 | 91 | 82 | 117 | 81 | 181 | 42 | 84 | 81 | 96 |
| 1951............. | 88 | 94 | 86 | 116 | 82 | 178 | 78 | 85 | 85 | 92 |
| 1952............. | 88 | 92 | 86 | 124 | 82 | 155 | 80 | 84 | 86 | 93 |
| 1953............. | 88 | 90 | 87 | 115 | 86 | 133 | 88 | 87 | 86 | 95 |
| 1954............. | 90 | 94 | 92 | 102 | 87 | 131 | 94 | 92 | 87 | 95 |
| 1955............. | 94 | 95 | 95 | 103 | 98 | 125 | 96 | 101 | 92 | 92 |
| 1956............. | 96 | 96 | 92 | 101 | 92 | 116 | 98 | 108 | 95 | 96 |
| 1957............. | 99 | 99 | 94 | 112 | 98 | 118 | 99 | 104 | 98 | 101 |
| 1958............. | 100 | 100 | 100 | 100 | 100 | 100 | 100 | 100 | 100 | 100 |
| 1959............. | 102 | 103 | 116 | 97 | 101 | 92 | 98 | 97 | 102 | 101 |
| 1960............. | 104 | 108 | 115 | 98 | 105 | 86 | 107 | 97 | 104 | 104 |
| 1961............. | 104 | 113 | ... | 96 | 104 | ... | 112 | 95 | 104 | 111 |

### b.  Average Annual Rate of Change — Taux annuel moyen de variation

| Period | | | | | | | | | | |
|---|---|---|---|---|---|---|---|---|---|---|
| 1950 – 1960........ | 2.2 | 1.7 | 3.4 | −1.8 | 2.6 | −7.2 | 9.8 | 1.5 | 2.5 | 0.8 |
| 1948 – 1953........ | 0.5 | — | −5.1 | −3.6 | 0.2 | −7.8 | 14.9 | 1.7 | 1.0 | −1.4 |
| 1954 – 1958........ | 2.7 | 1.6 | 2.1 | −0.5 | 3.5 | −6.5 | 1.6 | 2.1 | 3.5 | 1.3 |
| 1958 – 1960........ | 2.0 | 3.9 | 7.2 | −1.0 | 2.5 | −7.3 | 3.4 | −1.5 | 2.0 | 2.0 |

[1] Other manufacturing (ISIC major group 39) is not included.
[2] Certain non-ferrous foundries (part of ISIC major group 34) are included in Metal products (ISIC major groups 35-38).

[1] Non compris Autres industries manufacturières (CITI 39).
[2] Certaines fonderies de métaux non ferreux (dans CITI 34) sont comprises dans Ouvrages en métaux (CITI 35-38).

## 4. CHARACTERISTICS OF INDUSTRIAL ESTABLISHMENTS WITH ONE OR MORE EMPLOYEES
### CARACTERISTIQUES DES ETABLISSEMENTS INDUSTRIELS AYANT AU MOINS UN SALARIE
### 1948, 1953, 1958

Number of establishments in units; value added and wages and salaries in million Francs; number of engaged, employees and operatives in thousands; man-hours worked in millions; value added per engaged and wages and salaries per employee and per thousand operative man-hours in thousand Francs; average annual man-hours per operative in thousands.

Nombre d'établissements en unités; valeur ajoutée et traitements et salaires en millions de francs; nombre de personnes occupées, de salariés et d'ouvriers en milliers; heures de travail effectuées en millions; valeur ajoutée par personne occupée et traitements et salaires par salarié et par millier d'heures-ouvrier en milliers de francs; moyenne annuelle des heures de travail par ouvrier en milliers.

### A. The Divisions of Industrial Activity — Les branches de l'activité industrielle

#### a. Absolute Figures — Chiffres absolus

| Year and item of data — ISIC | All industrial activity / Toutes industries (1-4,511-521) | Mining / Industries extractives (1) | Manufacturing[1] / Industries manufacturières[1] (2-3) | Construction / Bâtiment et travaux publics (4) | Electricity and gas[2] / Electricité et gaz[2] (511-521) | Année et rubrique — CITI |
|---|---|---|---|---|---|---|
| **1948** | | | | | | **1948** |
| Number of establishments... | ... | 298 | 247 | 412 | ... | Nombre d'établissements |
| Value added | 5 477.3 | 395.8 | 4 589.5 | 386.0 | 106.0 | Valeur ajoutée |
| Number of engaged (Average during year) | 39.0 | 4.0 | 29.2 | 4.8 | 1.0 | Nombre de personnes occupées (moyenne pour l'année) |
| Employees: Number (Average year) | 38.5 | 3.8 | 29.0 | 4.7 | 1.0 | Salariés: Nombre (moyenne pour l'année) |
| Wages and salaries | 2 467.6 | 271.7 | 1 900.6 | 220.5 | 74.8 | Traitements et salaires |
| Operatives: Number (Average during year) | 34.4 | 3.5 | 25.8 | 4.5 | 0.6 | Ouvriers: Nombre (moyenne pour l'année) |
| Man-hours worked | 80.0 | 7.6 | 61.2 | 9.7 | 1.5 | Heures de travail effectuées |
| Wages and salaries | 2 035.9 | 242.1 | 1 547.1 | 208.2 | 38.5 | Traitements et salaires |
| **1953** | | | | | | **1953** |
| Number of establishments... | ... | 277 | ... | 240 | ... | Nombre d'établissements |
| Value added | 6 673.0 | 724.3 | 5 078.1 | 694.6 | 176.0 | Valeur ajoutée |
| Number of engaged (Average during year) | 42.3 | 4.5 | 29.9 | 6.9 | 1.0 | Nombre de personnes occupées (moyenne pour l'année) |
| Employees: Number (during year) | 41.5 | 4.3 | 29.5 | 6.7 | 1.0 | Salariés: Nombre (moyenne pour l'année) |
| Wages and salaries | 3 635.0 | 411.0 | 2 693.0 | 434.1 | 96.9 | Traitements et salaires |
| Operatives: Number (Average during year) | 37.2 | 4.1 | 26.1 | 6.5 | 0.5 | Ouvriers: Nombre (moyenne pour l'année) |
| Man-hours worked | 89.8 | 9.0 | 63.8 | 15.8 | 1.2 | Heures de travail effectuées |
| Wages and salaries | 2 926.1 | 365.0 | 2 109.5 | 413.0 | 38.6 | Traitements et salaires |
| **1958** | | | | | | **1958** |
| Value added | 10 357.4 | 680.5 | 8 176.1 | 1 251.7 | 249.1 | Valeur ajoutée |
| Number of engaged (Average during year) | 48.1 | 3.8 | 33.8 | 9.5 | 1.0 | Nombre de personnes occupées (moyenne pour l'année) |
| Employees: Number (during year) | 47.5 | 3.6 | 33.6 | 9.3 | 1.0 | Salariés: Nombre (moyenne pour l'année) |
| Wages and salaries | 4 799.5 | 400.0 | 3 637.8 | 635.5 | 126.2 | Traitements et salaires |
| Operatives: Number (Average during year) | 42.3 | 3.2 | 29.6 | 9.0 | 0.5 | Ouvriers: Nombre (moyenne pour l'année) |
| Man-hours worked | 101.0 | 6.9 | 71.7 | 21.3 | 1.1 | Heures de travail effectuées |
| Wages and salaries | 3 842.9 | 345.0 | 2 851.5 | 599.3 | 47.1 | Traitements et salaires |

#### b. Structure

| Year and item of data — ISIC | All industrial activity / Toutes industries (1-4,511-521) | Mining / Industries extractives (1) | Manufacturing[1] / Industries manufacturières[1] (2-3) | Construction / Bâtiment et travaux publics (4) | Electricity and gas[2] / Electricité et gaz[2] (511-521) | Année et rubrique — CITI |
|---|---|---|---|---|---|---|
| **1948** Distribution in percent of: | | | | | | **1948** Distribution en pourcentage: |
| Value added | 100.0 | 7.2 | 83.8 | 7.0 | 2.0 | Valeur ajoutée |
| Number of engaged | 100.0 | 10.2 | 74.9 | 12.3 | 2.6 | Nombre de personnes occupées |
| Value added per person engaged | 140.4 | 99.0 | 157.2 | 80.4 | 106.0 | Valeur ajoutée par personne occupée |
| Employees as a percent of engaged | 98.7 | 95.0 | 99.3 | 97.9 | 100.0 | Salariés en pourcentage des personnes occupées |
| Value added per unit of wages and salaries | 2.22 | 1.46 | 2.41 | 1.75 | 1.42 | Valeur ajoutée par unité de traitements et salaires |
| Wages and salaries per employee | 64.1 | 71.5 | 65.5 | 46.9 | 74.8 | Traitements et salaires par salarié |
| Operatives as a percent of employees | 89.4 | 92.1 | 89.0 | 95.7 | 60.0 | Ouvriers en pourcentage des salariés |
| Average man-hours per operative | 2.32 | 2.17 | 2.37 | 2.16 | 2.50 | Heures de travail: moyenne par ouvrier |
| Wages and salaries per thousand operative man-hours | 25.45 | 31.86 | 25.28 | 21.46 | 25.67 | Traitements et salaires par millier d'heures-ouvrier |
| **1953** Distribution in percent of: | | | | | | **1953** Distribution en pourcentage: |
| Value added | 100.0 | 10.8 | 76.1 | 10.4 | 2.7 | Valeur ajoutée |
| Number of engaged | 100.0 | 10.6 | 70.7 | 16.3 | 2.4 | Nombre de personnes occupées |
| Value added per person engaged | 157.8 | 161.0 | 169.8 | 100.7 | 176.0 | Valeur ajoutée par personne occupée |
| Employees as a percent of engaged | 98.1 | 95.6 | 98.7 | 97.1 | 100.0 | Salariés en pourcentage des personnes occupées |
| Value added per unit of wages and salaries | 1.84 | 1.76 | 1.88 | 1.60 | 1.82 | Valeur ajoutée par unité de traitements et salaires |
| Wages and salaries per employee | 87.6 | 95.6 | 91.3 | 64.8 | 96.9 | Traitements et salaires par salarié |
| Operatives as a percent of employees | 89.6 | 95.3 | 88.5 | 97.0 | 50.0 | Ouvriers en pourcentage des salariés |
| Average man-hours per operative | 2.41 | 2.20 | 2.44 | 2.43 | 2.40 | Heures de travail: moyenne par ouvrier |
| Wages and salaries per thousand operative man-hours | 32.58 | 40.56 | 33.06 | 26.14 | 32.17 | Traitements et salaires par millier d'heures-ouvrier |
| **1958** Distribution in percent of: | | | | | | **1958** Distribution en pourcentage: |
| Value added | 100.0 | 6.5 | 79.0 | 12.0 | 2.5 | Valeur ajoutée |
| Number of engaged | 100.0 | 7.9 | 70.2 | 19.8 | 2.1 | Nombre de personnes occupées |
| Value added per person engaged | 215.3 | 179.1 | 241.9 | 131.8 | 249.1 | Valeur ajoutée par personne occupée |
| Employees as a percent of engaged | 98.8 | 94.7 | 99.4 | 97.9 | 100.0 | Salariés en pourcentage des personnes occupées |
| Value added per unit of wages and salaries | 2.16 | 1.70 | 2.25 | 1.97 | 1.97 | Valeur ajoutée par unité de traitements et salaires |
| Wages and salaries per employee | 101.0 | 111.1 | 108.3 | 68.3 | 126.2 | Traitements et salaires par salarié |
| Operatives as a percent of employees | 89.0 | 88.9 | 88.1 | 96.8 | 50.0 | Ouvriers en pourcentage des salariés |
| Average man-hours per operative | 2.39 | 2.16 | 2.42 | 2.37 | 2.20 | Heures de travail: moyenne par ouvrier |
| Wages and salaries per thousand operative man-hours | 38.05 | 50.00 | 39.77 | 28.14 | 42.82 | Traitements et salaires par millier d'heures-ouvrier |

[1] Other manufacturing (ISIC Major group 39) is not included.
[2] Includes Water supply services (ISIC group 521).

[1] Non compris Autres industries manufacturières (CITI classe 39).
[2] Y compris les Services de distribution publique d'eau (CITI groupe 521).

## B. The Major Groups of Mining — Les classes de la branche Industries extractives

### a. Absolute Figures / Chiffres absolus

| Year and item of data | All mining — Toutes industries extractives | Metal mining — Extraction des minerais métalliques | Other mining — Divers | Année et rubrique |
|---|---|---|---|---|
| ISIC | 1 | 12 | 14–19 | CITI |
| **1948** | | | | **1948** |
| Number of establishments | 298 | 42 | 256 | Nombre d'établissements |
| Value added | 395.8 | 322.2 | 73.6 | Valeur ajoutée |
| Number of engaged (Average during year) | 4.0 | 2.8 | 1.2 | Nombre de personnes occupées (moyenne pour l'année) |
| Employees | | | | Salariés |
| Number (Average during year) | 3.8 | 2.8 | 1.0 | Nombre (moyenne pour l'année) |
| Wages and salaries | 271.7 | 227.7 | 44.0 | Traitements et salaires |
| Operatives | | | | Ouvriers |
| Number (Average during year) | 3.5 | 2.6 | 0.9 | Nombre (moyenne pour l'année) |
| Man-hours worked | 7.6 | 5.8 | 1.8 | Heures de travail effectuées |
| Wages and salaries | 242.1 | 201.5 | 40.6 | Traitements et salaires |
| **1953** | | | | **1953** |
| Number of establishments | 277 | 59 | 218 | Nombre d'établissements |
| Value added | 724.3 | 603.6 | 120.7 | Valeur ajoutée |
| Number of engaged (Average during year) | 4.5 | 3.1 | 1.4 | Nombre de personnes occupées (moyenne pour l'année) |
| Employees | | | | Salariés |
| Number (Average during year) | 4.3 | 3.1 | 1.2 | Nombre (moyenne pour l'année) |
| Wages and salaries | 411.0 | 332.3 | 78.7 | Traitements et salaires |
| Operatives | | | | Ouvriers |
| Number (Average during year) | 4.1 | 2.9 | 1.2 | Nombre (moyenne pour l'année) |
| Man-hours worked | 9.0 | 6.4 | 2.6 | Heures de travail effectuées |
| Wages and salaries | 365.0 | 292.7 | 72.3 | Traitements et salaires |
| **1958** | | | | **1958** |
| Number of establishments | | | | Nombre d'établissements |
| Value added | 680.5 | 524.3 | 156.2 | Valeur ajoutée |
| Number of engaged (Average during year) | 3.8 | 2.6 | 1.2 | Nombre de personnes occupées (moyenne pour l'année) |
| Employees | | | | Salariés |
| Number (Average during year) | 3.6 | 2.6 | 1.0 | Nombre (moyenne pour l'année) |
| Wages and salaries | 400.0 | 326.0 | 74.0 | Traitements et salaires |
| Operatives | | | | Ouvriers |
| Number (Average during year) | 3.2 | 2.3 | 0.9 | Nombre (moyenne pour l'année) |
| Man-hours worked | 6.9 | 4.9 | 2.0 | Heures de travail effectuées |
| Wages and salaries | 345.0 | 277.4 | 67.6 | Traitements et salaires |

### b. Structure

| Year and item of data | All mining — Toutes industries extractives | Metal mining — Extraction des minerais métalliques | Other mining — Divers | Année et rubrique |
|---|---|---|---|---|
| ISIC | 1 | 12 | 14–19 | CITI |
| **1948** | | | | **1948** |
| Distribution in percent of: | | | | Distribution en pourcentage: |
| Value added | 100.0 | 81.4 | 18.6 | Valeur ajoutée |
| Number of engaged | 100.0 | 70.0 | 30.0 | Nombre de personnes occupées |
| Value added per person engaged | 99.0 | 115.1 | 61.3 | Valeur ajoutée par personne occupée |
| Employees as a percent of engaged | 95.0 | 100.0 | 83.3 | Salariés en pourcentage des personnes occupées |
| Value added per unit of wages and salaries | 1.46 | 1.42 | 1.67 | Valeur ajoutée par unité de traitements et salaires |
| Wages and salaries per employee | 71.5 | 81.3 | 44.0 | Traitements et salaires par salarié |
| Operatives as a percent of employees | 92.1 | 92.8 | 90.0 | Ouvriers en pourcentage des salariés |
| Average man-hours per operative | 2.17 | 2.23 | 2.00 | Heures de travail: moyenne par ouvrier |
| Wages and salaries per thousand operative man-hours | 31.86 | 34.74 | 22.56 | Traitements et salaires par millier d'heures-ouvrier |
| **1953** | | | | **1953** |
| Distribution in percent of: | | | | Distribution en pourcentage: |
| Value added | 100.0 | 83.3 | 16.7 | Valeur ajoutée |
| Number of engaged | 100.0 | 68.9 | 31.1 | Nombre de personnes occupées |
| Value added per person engaged | 161.0 | 194.7 | 86.2 | Valeur ajoutée par personne occupée |
| Employees as a percent of engaged | 95.6 | 100.0 | 85.7 | Salariés en pourcentage des personnes occupées |
| Value added per unit of wages and salaries | 1.76 | 1.82 | 1.53 | Valeur ajoutée par unité de traitements et salaires |
| Wages and salaries per employee | 95.6 | 107.2 | 65.6 | Traitements et salaires par salarié |
| Operatives as a percent of employees | 95.3 | 93.5 | 100.0 | Ouvriers en pourcentage des salariés |
| Average man-hours per operative | 2.20 | 2.21 | 2.17 | Heures de travail: moyenne par ouvrier |
| Wages and salaries per thousand operative man-hours | 40.56 | 45.73 | 27.81 | Traitements et salaires par millier d'heures-ouvrier |
| **1958** | | | | **1958** |
| Distribution in percent of: | | | | Distribution en pourcentage: |
| Value added | 100.0 | 77.0 | 23.0 | Valeur ajoutée |
| Number of engaged | 100.0 | 68.4 | 31.6 | Nombre de personne occupées |
| Value added per person engaged | 179.1 | 201.6 | 130.2 | Valeur ajoutée par personne occupée |
| Employees as a percent of engaged | 94.7 | 100.0 | 83.3 | Salariés en pourcentage des personnes occupées |
| Value added per unit of wages and salaries | 1.70 | 1.61 | 2.11 | Valeur ajoutée par unité de traitements et salaires |
| Wages and salaries per employee | 111.1 | 125.4 | 74.0 | Traitements et salaires par salarié |
| Operatives as a percent of employees | 88.9 | 88.5 | 90.0 | Ouvriers en pourcentage des salariés |
| Average man-hours per operative | 2.16 | 2.13 | 2.22 | Heures de travail: moyenne par ouvrier |
| Wages and salaries per thousand operative man-hours | 50.00 | 56.61 | 33.80 | Traitements et salaires par millier d'heures-ouvrier |

**C. The Major Groups of Manufacturing — Les classes de la branche Industries manufacturières**

| Year and item of data | Manufacturing [3] — Industries manufacturières [3] | Food, beverages and tobacco — Industries alimentaires, boissons, tabac | Textiles and clothing [1] — Textiles et articles d'habillement [1] | Wood products and furniture — Bois et meubles | Printing and publishing [1] — Imprimerie et édition [1] | Leather and leather products except wearing apparel — Cuir et articles en cuir, à l'exclusion des articles d'habillement | Chemicals and chemical, petroleum, coal and rubber products — Produits chimiques, dérivés du pétrole et du charbon et ouvrages en caoutchouc | Non-metallic mineral products — Produits minéraux non métalliques | Basic metals [2] — Métallurgie de base [2] | Metal products [2] — Ouvrages en métaux [2] | Année et rubrique |
|---|---|---|---|---|---|---|---|---|---|---|---|
| ISIC | 1–2 | 20–22 | 23–24 | 25–26 | 28 | 29 | 30–32 | 33 | 34 | 35–38 | CITI |

*a.* Absolute Figures — Chiffres absolus

| Year and item of data | 1–2 | 20–22 | 23–24 | 25–26 | 28 | 29 | 30–32 | 33 | 34 | 35–38 | Année et rubrique |
|---|---|---|---|---|---|---|---|---|---|---|---|
| **1948** | | | | | | | | | | | **1948** |
| Number of establishments | 247 | 77 | 14 | 44 | 12 | 11 | 25 | 27 | 7 | 30 | Nombre d'établissements |
| Value added | 4 589.5 | 290.1 | 42.2 | 57.2 | 52.4 | 67.4 | 37.0 | 163.6 | 3 532.0 | 347.6 | Valeur ajoutée |
| Number of engaged (Average during year) | 29.2 | 1.9 | 0.8 | 0.8 | 0.4 | 0.8 | 0.5 | 1.5 | 19.0 | 3.5 | Nombre de personnes occupées (moyenne pour l'année) |
| Employees: | | | | | | | | | | | Salariés: |
| Number (Average during year) | 29.0 | 1.8 | 0.8 | 0.8 | 0.4 | 0.8 | 0.5 | 1.5 | 19.0 | 3.4 | Nombre (moyenne pour l'année) |
| Wages and salaries | 1 900.6 | 96.1 | 22.4 | 35.8 | 28.4 | 46.5 | 22.1 | 86.8 | 1 372.7 | 189.8 | Traitements et salaires |
| Operatives: | | | | | | | | | | | Ouvriers: |
| Number (Average during year) | 25.8 | 1.5 | 0.7 | 0.8 | 0.3 | 0.8 | 0.4 | 1.4 | 17.1 | 2.8 | Nombre (moyenne pour l'année) |
| Manhours worked | 61.2 | 3.6 | 1.2 | 1.8 | 0.7 | 1.9 | 0.7 | 3.3 | 41.7 | 6.3 | Heures de travail effectuées |
| Wages and salaries | 1 547.1 | 69.5 | 17.7 | 31.6 | 19.9 | 37.9 | 13.7 | 71.9 | 1 137.5 | 147.4 | Traitements et salaires |
| **1953** | | | | | | | | | | | **1953** |
| Number of establishments | ... | 75 | 16 | 35 | ... | 9 | 20 | 33 | 7 | 40 | Nombre d'établissements |
| Value added | 5 078.1 | 389.8 | 45.6 | 63.2 | 73.6 | 65.8 | 194.3 | 234.3 | 3 508.3 | 503.2 | Valeur ajoutée |
| Number of engaged (Average during year) | 29.9 | 1.9 | 0.6 | 0.7 | 0.4 | 0.6 | 1.0 | 1.6 | 19.9 | 3.2 | Nombre de personnes occupées (moyenne pour l'année) |
| Employees: | | | | | | | | | | | Salariés: |
| Number (Average during year) | 29.5 | 1.7 | 0.6 | 0.6 | 0.4 | 0.6 | 1.0 | 1.6 | 19.9 | 3.1 | Nombre (moyenne pour l'année) |
| Wages and salaries | 2 693.0 | 131.2 | 23.9 | 37.2 | 37.2 | 38.6 | 77.2 | 122.7 | 1 977.8 | 247.2 | Traitements et salaires |
| Operatives: | | | | | | | | | | | Ouvriers: |
| Number (Average during year) | 26.1 | 1.5 | 0.5 | 0.6 | 0.3 | 0.5 | 0.8 | 1.5 | 17.7 | 2.7 | Nombre (moyenne pour l'année) |
| Manhours worked | 63.8 | 3.9 | 1.0 | 1.4 | 0.7 | 1.2 | 1.8 | 3.5 | 43.9 | 6.4 | Heures de travail effectuées |
| Wages and salaries | 2 109.5 | 93.9 | 18.2 | 31.0 | 24.4 | 28.5 | 47.5 | 100.9 | 1 577.6 | 187.5 | Traitements et salaires |
| **1958** | | | | | | | | | | | **1958** |
| Value added | 8 176.1 | 595.8 | 70.0 | 97.0 | 99.9 | 44.7 | 333.3 | 288.4 | 5 858.7 | 788.3 | Valeur ajoutée |
| Number of engaged (Average during year) | 33.8 | 2.1 | 0.7 | 0.6 | 0.5 | 0.4 | 1.1 | 1.9 | 23.1 | 3.4 | Nombre de personnes occupées (moyenne pour l'année) |
| Employees: | | | | | | | | | | | Salariés: |
| Number (Average during year) | 33.6 | 2.0 | 0.7 | 0.6 | 0.5 | 0.4 | 1.1 | 1.9 | 23.1 | 3.3 | Nombre (moyenne pour l'année) |
| Wages and salaries | 3 637.8 | 175.1 | 33.7 | 42.4 | 52.4 | 32.8 | 118.5 | 169.3 | 2 677.8 | 335.8 | Traitements et salaires |
| Operatives: | | | | | | | | | | | Ouvriers: |
| Number (Average during year) | 29.6 | 1.7 | 0.6 | 0.5 | 0.4 | 0.4 | 0.8 | 1.7 | 20.6 | 2.9 | Nombre (moyenne pour l'année) |
| Manhours worked | 71.7 | 4.3 | 1.3 | 1.1 | 1.0 | 0.9 | 1.9 | 4.0 | 50.2 | 7.0 | Heures de travail effectuées |
| Wages and salaries | 2 851.5 | 120.5 | 25.4 | 35.3 | 33.5 | 24.4 | 72.3 | 139.0 | 2 148.1 | 253.0 | Traitements et salaires |

## C. The Major Groups of Manufacturing (continued)
## Les classes de la branche Industries manufacturières (suite)

| Year and item of data | Manu-facturing [3] Industries manufac-turières [3] | Food, beverages and tobacco Industries alimen-taires, boissons, tabac | Textiles and clothing [1] Textiles et articles d'habil-lement [1] | Wood products and furniture Bois et meubles | Printing and publish-ing [1] Im-primerie et édition [1] | Leather and leather products except wearing apparel Cuir et articles en cuir, à l'exclu-sion des articles d'habil-lement | Chemicals and chemical, petroleum, coal and rubber products Produits chimiques, dérivés du pétrole et du charbon et ouvrages en caout-chouc | Non-metallic mineral products Produits minéraux non métal-liques | Basic metals [2] Métal-lurgie de base[2] | Metal products[2] Ouvrages en métaux [2] | Année et rubrique |
|---|---|---|---|---|---|---|---|---|---|---|---|
| ISIC | 1–2 | 20–22 | 23–24 | 25–26 | 28 | 29 | 30–32 | 33 | 34 | 35–38 | CITI |
| | | | | | | b. Structure | | | | | |
| **1948** Distribution in percent of: | | | | | | | | | | | **1948** Distribution en pour-centage: |
| Value added....... | 100.0 | 6.3 | 0.9 | 1.2 | 1.2 | 1.4 | 0.9 | 3.5 | 77.0 | 7.6 | Valeur ajoutée |
| Number of engaged... | 100.0 | 6.5 | 2.7 | 2.7 | 1.4 | 2.7 | 1.8 | 5.1 | 65.1 | 12.0 | Nombre de personnes occupées |
| Value added per person engaged...... | 157.2 | 152.7 | 52.8 | 71.5 | 131.0 | 84.2 | 74.0 | 109.1 | 185.9 | 99.3 | Valeur ajoutée par personne occupée |
| Employees as a percent of engaged........ | 99.3 | 94.7 | 100.0 | 100.0 | 100.0 | 100.0 | 100.0 | 100.0 | 100.0 | 97.1 | Salariés en pourcentage des personnes occupées |
| Value added per unit of wages and salaries............ | 2.41 | 3.02 | 1.88 | 1.60 | 1.84 | 1.45 | 1.67 | 1.88 | 2.57 | 1.83 | Valeur ajoutée par unité de traitements et salaires |
| Wages and salaries per employee........ | 65.5 | 53.4 | 28.0 | 44.8 | 71.0 | 58.1 | 44.2 | 57.9 | 72.2 | 55.8 | Traitements et salaires par salarié |
| Operatives as a percent of employees........ | 89.0 | 83.3 | 87.5 | 100.0 | 75.0 | 100.0 | 80.0 | 93.3 | 90.0 | 82.4 | Ouvriers en pourcentage des salariés |
| Average man-hours per operative....... | 2.37 | 2.40 | 1.71 | 2.25 | 2.33 | 2.38 | 1.75 | 2.36 | 2.44 | 2.25 | Heures de travail: moyenne par ouvrier |
| Wages and salaries per thousand operative man-hours.. | 25.28 | 19.30 | 14.75 | 17.56 | 28.43 | 19.95 | 19.57 | 21.79 | 27.28 | 23.40 | Traitements et salaires par millier d'heures-ouvrier |
| **1953** Distribution in percent of: | | | | | | | | | | | **1953** Distribution en pourcentage: |
| Value added........ | 100.0 | 7.6 | 0.9 | 1.3 | 1.4 | 1.3 | 3.8 | 4.7 | 69.0 | 10.0 | Valeur ajoutée |
| Number of engaged.. | 100.0 | 6.3 | 2.0 | 2.4 | 1.3 | 2.0 | 3.3 | 5.4 | 66.5 | 10.8 | Nombre de personnes occupées |
| Value added per person engaged...... | 169.8 | 205.2 | 76.0 | 90.3 | 184.0 | 109.7 | 194.3 | 146.4 | 176.3 | 157.2 | Valeur ajoutée par personne occupée |
| Employees as a percent of engaged........ | 98.7 | 89.5 | 100.0 | 85.7 | 100.0 | 100.0 | 100.0 | 100.0 | 100.0 | 96.9 | Salariés en pourcentage des personnes occupées |
| Value added per unit of wages and salaries... | 1.88 | 2.97 | 1.91 | 1.70 | 1.98 | 1.70 | 2.52 | 1.91 | 1.77 | 2.04 | Valeur ajoutée par unité de traitements et sa-laires |
| Wages and salaries per employee.......... | 91.3 | 77.2 | 39.8 | 62.0 | 93.0 | 64.3 | 77.2 | 76.7 | 99.4 | 79.7 | Traitements et salaires par salarié |
| Operatives as a percent of employees........ | 88.5 | 88.2 | 83.3 | 100.0 | 75.0 | 83.3 | 80.0 | 93.8 | 88.9 | 87.1 | Ouvriers en pourcentage des salariés |
| Average man-hours per operative........... | 2.44 | 2.60 | 2.00 | 2.33 | 2.33 | 2.40 | 2.25 | 2.33 | 2.48 | 2.37 | Heures de travail: moyenne par ouvrier |
| Wages and salaries per thousand operative man-hours........... | 33.06 | 24.08 | 18.20 | 22.14 | 3.48 | 23.75 | 26.39 | 28.83 | 35.94 | 29.30 | Traitements et salaires par millier d'heures-ouvrier |
| **1958** Distribution in percent of: | | | | | | | | | | | **1958** Distribution en pourcentage: |
| Value added........ | 100.0 | 7.2 | 0.9 | 1.2 | 1.2 | 0.5 | 4.1 | 3.6 | 71.6 | 9.7 | Valeur ajoutée |
| Number of engaged.......... | 100.0 | 6.2 | 2.0 | 1.8 | 1.5 | 1.2 | 3.2 | 5.6 | 68.4 | 10.1 | Nombre de personnes occupées |
| Value added per person engaged...... | 241.9 | 283.7 | 100.0 | 161.7 | 199.8 | 111.8 | 303.0 | 151.8 | 253.6 | 231.8 | Valeur ajoutée par personne occupée |
| Employees as a percent of engaged........ | 99.4 | 95.2 | 100.0 | 100.0 | 100.0 | 100.0 | 100.0 | 100.0 | 100.0 | 97.0 | Salariés en pourcentage des personnes occupées |
| Value added per unit of wages and salaries.. | 2.25 | 3.40 | 2.08 | 2.29 | 1.91 | 1.36 | 2.81 | 1.70 | 2.19 | 2.35 | Valeur ajoutée par unité de traitements et sa-laires |
| Wages and salaries per employee.......... | 108.3 | 87.6 | 48.1 | 70.7 | 104.8 | 82.0 | 107.7 | 89.1 | 115.9 | 101.8 | Traitements et salaires par salarié |
| Operatives as a percent of employees........ | 88.1 | 85.0 | 85.7 | 83.3 | 80.0 | 100.0 | 72.7 | 89.5 | 89.2 | 87.9 | Ouvriers en pourcentage des salariés |
| Average man-hours per operative........... | 2.42 | 2.53 | 2.17 | 2.20 | 2.50 | 2.25 | 2.38 | 2.35 | 2.44 | 2.41 | Heures de travail: moyenne par ouvrier |
| Wages and salaries per thousand operative man-hours.......... | 39.77 | 28.02 | 19.54 | 32.09 | 33.50 | 27.11 | 38.05 | 34.75 | 42.79 | 36.14 | Traitements et salaires par millier d'heures-ouvrier |

[1] Footwear excluded from Textiles and clothing (ISIC major groups 23-24); included in Leather and leather products (ISIC major group 29).
[2] The smelting and other processing of non-ferrous metals is included in Metal products (ISIC major groups 35-38) rather than in Basic metals (ISIC major group 34).
[3] The activities of Other manufacturing (ISIC major group 39) are not included.

[1] La fabrication des chaussures n'est pas comprise dans Textiles et articles d'habillement (CITI 23-24), mais dans Cuir et articles en cuir (CITI 29).
[2] La fonderie et les autres opérations de transformation des métaux non ferreux sont comprises dans Ouvrages en métaux (CITI 35-38) plutot que dans Industrie métallurgique de base (CITI 34).
[3] Non compris Autres industries manufacturières (CITI 39).

# MADAGASCAR

## The Characteristics and Structure of Industrial Activity

The data presented in Table 1 are derived from the results of the third Recensement des entreprises agricoles et industrielles taken for 1950 and published in *Annuaire Statistique de Madagascar*, Volume 1, 1938-1951 by the Service de statistique générale, Direction des services économiques, Haut Commissariat de la République française à Madagascar et dépendances.

The data shown in the table cover all enterprises with 5 or more employees and which paid profit taxes in 1948 of 150,000 francs (C.F.A.) or more.

## Caractéristiques et structure de l'activité industrielle

Les données du tableau 1 sont tirées des résultats du troisième recensement des entreprises agricoles et industrielles (1950) effectué par le Service de statistique générale, Direction des services économiques, Haut Commissariat de la République française à Madagascar et dépendances; ces résultats ont été publiés par le Service de statistique générale dans *Annuaire statistique de Madagascar*, volume 1, 1938-1951.

Les données du tableau concernent toutes les entreprises occupant 5 salariés ou plus et ayant payé au moins 150 000 francs CFA d'impôt sur les bénéfices.

## 1. CHARACTERISTICS OF INDUSTRIAL ENTERPRISES WITH FIVE OR MORE EMPLOYEES
## CARACTERISTIQUES DES ENTREPRISES INDUSTRIELLES AYANT CINQ SALARIES OU PLUS

### 1950

Number of establishments in units; number of engaged, employees and operatives in units.

Nombre d'établissements en unités; nombre de personnes occupées, de salariés et d'ouvriers en unités.

### A. Selected Divisions of Industrial Activity — Quelques branches de l'activité industrielle

| Item of data | Total | Mining Industries ex-tractives | Manu-facturing Industries manu-facturières | Con-struction Bâtiment et travaux publics | Rubrique | Item of data | Total | Mining Industries ex-tractives | Manu-facturing Industries manu-facturières | Con-struction Bâtiment et travaux publics | Rubrique |
|---|---|---|---|---|---|---|---|---|---|---|---|
| ISIC | 1-4 | 1 | 2-3 | 4 | CITI | ISIC | 1-4 | 1 | 2-3 | 4 | CITI |
| | a. Absolute Figures — Chiffres absolus | | | | | | b. Structure | | | | |
| Number of establishments. | 1 363 | 338 | 901 | 124 | Nombre d'établissements | | | | | | |
| Number of engaged. . . . . . | 43 433 | 19 967 | 15 944 | 7 522 | Nombre de personnes occupées | Distribution in percent of number of engaged. . . . . | 100.0 | 46.0 | 36.7 | 17.3 | Distribution en pourcentage du nombre de personnes occupées |
| Number of employees. . . . . | 41 807 | 19 404 | 15 086 | 7 317 | Nombre de salariés | Employees as a percent of engaged. . . . . . . . . . . | 96.2 | 97.2 | 94.6 | 97.3 | Salariés en pourcentage des personnes occupées |
| Number of operatives. . . . . . | 40 820 | 19 221 | 14 414 | 7 185 | Nombre d'ouvriers | Operatives as a percent of employees. . . . . . . . . . | 97.6 | 99.0 | 95.5 | 98.2 | Ouvriers en pourcentage des salariés |

# MADAGASCAR

## B. The Major Groups of Mining — Les classes de la branche Industries extractives

| Item of data | All mining / Toutes industries extractives | Crude petroleum and natural gas / Pétrole brut et gaz naturel | Other mining / Divers | Rubrique | Item of data | All mining / Toutes industries extractives | Crude petroleum and natural gas / Pétrole brut et gaz naturel | Other mining / Divers | Rubrique |
|---|---|---|---|---|---|---|---|---|---|
| ISIC | 1 | 13 | 14–19 | CITI | ISIC | 1 | 13 | 14–19 | CITI |
| | a. Absolute Figures Chiffres absolus | | | | | b. Structure | | | |
| Number of establishments...... | 338 | 4 | 334 | Nombre d'établissements | Distribution in percent of number of engaged......... | 100.0 | 2.0 | 98.0 | Distribution en pourcentage du nombre de personnes occupées |
| Number of engaged............ | 19 967 | 395 | 19 572 | Nombre de personnes occupées | Employees as a percent of engaged................. | 97.2 | 96.4 | 97.2 | Salariés en pourcentage des personnes occupées |
| Number of employees.......... | 19 404 | 381 | 19 023 | Nombre de salariés | Operatives as a percent of employees............... | 99.0 | 97.1 | 99.1 | Ouvriers en pourcentage des salariés |
| Number of operatives.......... | 19 221 | 370 | 18 851 | Nombre d'ouvriers | | | | | |

## C. The Major Groups of Manufacturing — Les classes de la branche Industries manufacturières

| Item of data | Manufacturing / Industries manufacturières | Food, beverages and tobacco / Industries alimentaires, boissons, tabac | Textiles | Clothing, footwear and made-up textiles / Articles d'habillement, chaussures et ouvrages en tissu | Wood products and furniture / Bois et meubles | Paper and paper products / Papier et ouvrages en papier | Printing and publishing / Imprimerie et édition | Leather and leather products except wearing apparel / Cuir et articles en cuir, à l'exclusion des articles d'habillement | Chemicals and chemical, petroleum and coal products / Produits chimiques et dérivés du pétrole et du charbon | Non-metallic mineral products / Produits minéraux non métalliques | Basic metals / Métallurgie de base | Metal products / Ouvrages en métaux | Other manufacturing / Autres industries manufacturières | Rubrique |
|---|---|---|---|---|---|---|---|---|---|---|---|---|---|---|
| ISIC | 2–3 | 20–22 | 23 | 24 | 25–26 | 27 | 28 | 29 | 31–32 | 33 | 34 | 35–38 | 39 | CITI |
| a. Absolute Figures — Chiffres absolus | | | | | | | | | | | | | | |
| Number of establishments. | 901 | 592 | 14 | 8 | 52 | 2 | 34 | 16 | 11 | 30 | — | 78 | 64 | Nombre d'établissements |
| Number of engaged.... | 15 944 | 10 497 | 569 | 161 | 849 | 43 | 461 | 547 | 289 | 613 | — | 1 190 | 725 | Nombre de personnes occupées |
| Number of employees... | 15 086 | 9 917 | 557 | 156 | 792 | 41 | 434 | 522 | 278 | 587 | — | 1 112 | 690 | Nombre de salariés |
| Number of operatives... | 14 414 | 9 459 | 551 | 151 | 763 | 40 | 392 | 506 | 266 | 575 | — | 1 046 | 665 | Nombre d'ouvriers |
| b. Structure | | | | | | | | | | | | | | |
| Distribution in percent of number of engaged............ | 100.0 | 65.8 | 3.6 | 1.0 | 5.3 | 0.3 | 2.9 | 3.4 | 1.8 | 3.8 | — | 7.5 | 4.6 | Distribution en pourcentage du nombre de personnes occupées |
| Employees as a percent of engaged........ | 94.6 | 94.5 | 97.9 | 96.9 | 93.3 | 95.3 | 94.1 | 95.4 | 96.2 | 95.8 | — | 93.4 | 95.2 | Salariés en pourcentage des personnes occupées |
| Operatives as a percent of employees........ | 95.5 | 95.4 | 98.9 | 96.8 | 96.3 | 97.6 | 90.3 | 96.9 | 95.7 | 98.0 | — | 94.1 | 96.4 | Ouvriers en pourcentage des salariés |

# MALTA — MALTE

## Gross Domestic Product

Estimates of the expenditure on and the industrial origin of the gross domestic product are presented in Table 1. They were obtained from data supplied by the Central Office of Statistics, Valetta, Malta, in response to the United Nations national accounts questionnaire. Official estimates are made annually by that Office and published in *National Accounts of the Maltese Islands*. For further details on concepts and definitions reference may be made to this publication.

## The Characteristics and Structure of Industrial Activity

The figures shown in Tables 2, 3 and 4 are compiled from the results of Censuses of Production taken by the Central Office of Statistics that were published in *Census of Production for 1955, Final Report* and *Census of Production, Report for 1958*. The first Census of Production was taken for 1955 by that Office and was continued annually thereafter.

The Censuses relate to mining, manufacturing and construction units which were not owned or managed by the Government. However, the size of establishments covered varied between the various Censuses. The coverage of the 1955 Census was for all units which engaged 5 or more persons; while in the 1958 Census, the coverage was extended to 3 or more persons. In all the Censuses, fewer items of data were sought from smaller establishments than from larger establishments. Small establishments were regarded as those units which engaged on the average 5-9 persons in the case of the 1955 Census, and 3-10 persons in the case of the 1958 Census. Larger establishments were regarded as those units engaging in excess of 10 and 11 persons, respectively.

Tables 2 and 3 refer to all establishments covered by the 1955 and 1958 Censuses respectively. Table 4, on the other hand, gives data for the larger establishments covered in these two Censuses.

Roughly eight per cent of the establishments which fell within the scope of the 1955 Census did not submit questionnaires; and the data in Tables 2 and 3 do not cover these units. These non-respondents accounted however for less than eight per cent of employment and production. The overall response was better in the 1958 Census.

The definitions utilized for the items of data shown in Tables 2, 3 and 4 conform to the International Standards in Basic Industrial Statistics, except that the value added in 1955 was gross of work sub-contracted out and in both 1955 and 1958, receipts from goods sold by establish-

## Produit intérieur brut

Le tableau 1 contient des estimations des dépenses imputées au produit intérieur brut et des estimations du produit intérieur brut par branche d'activité d'origine. Ces estimations proviennent de données fournies par l'Office central de statistique, Valette, Malte, en réponse au questionnaire de l'ONU sur la comptabilité nationale. Des estimations officielles sont établies chaque année par cet Office publiées dans *National Accounts of the Maltese Islands*. Pour plus de détails sur les concepts et définitions adoptés, voir cette publication.

## Caractéristiques et structure de l'activité industrielle

Les chiffres des tableaux 2, 3, et 4 sont tirés des résultats des recensements de la production effectués par l'Office central de statistique, qui ont été publiés dans *Census of Production for 1955, Final Report* et *Census of Production, Report for 1958*. Ces recensements sont effectués tous les ans depuis 1955.

Les recensements portent sur toutes les unités appartenant aux branches Industries extractives, Industries manufacturières et Bâtiment et travaux publics qui ne faisaient pas partie du secteur public. Cependant, la taille des établissements recensés varie d'un recensement à l'autre. Le recensement de 1955 portait sur toutes les unités occupant 5 personnes ou plus, tandis que, dans le recensement de 1958, le champ a été étendu aux établissements occupant 3 personnes ou plus. Dans tous les recensements, on a demandé des renseignements moins détaillés aux petits établissements qu'aux grands. Les petits établissements étaient ceux qui occupaient en moyenne de 5 à 9 personnes dans le cas du recensement de 1955, et 3 à 10 personnes dans le cas du recensement de 1958. Les grands établissements étaient ceux qui occupaient plus de 10 personnes en 1955 et plus de 11 personnes en 1958.

Les tableaux 2 et 3 concernent tous les établissements dénombrés lors des recensements de 1955 et 1958 respectivement. Le tableau 4 contient, d'autre part, les données sur les grands établissements fournies par ces deux recensements.

Environ 8 p. 100 des établissements recensés en 1955 n'ont pas répondu au questionnaire et ne sont pas compris dans les chiffres des tableaux 2 et 3. Ces établissements représentaient cependant moins de 8 p. 100 de l'emploi et de la production. Le taux de réponse a été, dans l'ensemble, meilleur lors du recensement de 1958.

Les définitions utilisées pour les rubriques des tableaux 2, 3 et 4 sont conformes aux Normes internationales relatives aux statistiques industrielles de base; toutefois, les chiffres de la valeur ajoutée en 1955 ont été calculés sans déduction du coût des travaux confiés à des sous-

ments in the same condition as purchased were not included. Wages and salaries in each Census did not include payments in kind of employees.

traitants et, dans les deux recensements, ne couvrent pas les marchandises revendues en l'état par les établissements recensés. Les traitements et salaires ne comprennent pas les paiements en nature aux salariés.

## 1. THE GROSS DOMESTIC PRODUCT — PRODUIT INTERIEUR BRUT

Million Pounds                                                                      Millions de livres

### A. Expenditure on the Gross Domestic Product at Market Prices
### Dépenses relatives au produit intérieur brut au prix du marché

| Item of data and year Rubrique et année | Total | Consumption Consommation | | Gross Domestic Capital Formation Formation brute de capital intérieur | | Net exports of goods and services Exportations nettes de biens et de services | |
| --- | --- | --- | --- | --- | --- | --- | --- |
| | | Total | Government Etat | Total | Fixed Fixe | Exports less imports Exportations moins importations | Exports Exportations |
| | | At Current Prices — Aux prix courants | | | | | |
| Absolute figures — Chiffres absolus | | | | | | | |
| 1954 | 33.7 | 29.8 | 4.5 | 5.3 | 5.3 | −1.4 | 20.6 |
| 1955 | 34.2 | 30.5 | 5.2 | 6.1 | 6.0 | −2.4 | 20.8 |
| 1956 | 38.3 | 35.0 | 5.8 | 8.7 | 7.4 | −5.4 | 22.8 |
| 1957 | 40.0 | 36.9 | 6.4 | 9.6 | 8.9 | −6.5 | 23.2 |
| 1958 | 42.8 | 37.8 | 6.5 | 11.4 | 10.7 | −6.4 | 24.6 |
| 1959 | 44.3 | 39.6 | 6.3 | 9.6 | 9.3 | −4.9 | 25.5 |
| 1960 | 48.5 | 42.7 | 8.2 | 11.3 | 10.2 | −5.5 | 28.3 |
| 1961 | 51.5 | 44.2 | 8.3 | 10.7 | 9.5 | −3.4 | 29.0 |
| Percentage distribution of average annual expenditure — Distribution en pourcentage des dépenses annuelles moyennes | | | | | | | |
| 1954–1960 | 100.0 | 89.5 | 15.2 | 22.0 | 20.5 | −11.5 | 58.8 |
| 1954 | 100.0 | 88.4 | 13.4 | 15.7 | 15.7 | −4.1 | 61.1 |
| 1958 | 100.0 | 88.3 | 15.2 | 26.6 | 25.0 | −14.9 | 57.5 |
| 1960 | 100.0 | 88.0 | 16.9 | 23.3 | 21.0 | −11.3 | 58.4 |
| 1961 | 100.0 | 85.8 | 16.1 | 20.8 | 18.4 | −6.6 | 56.3 |

## B. The Gross Domestic Product at Factor Cost According to Origin
## Origine par secteur d'activité du produit intérieur brut au coût des facteurs

| Item of data and year<br>Rubrique et année | Total | Agricultural sector<br>Secteur agricole | Industrial Sector — Secteur industriel | | | | Transportation and communication<br>Transports et communications | Other sectors<br>Autres secteurs |
|---|---|---|---|---|---|---|---|---|
| | | | Total | Mining and construction<br>Industries extractives et bâtiment et travaux publics | Manufacturing<br>Industries manufacturières | Electricity, gas and water<br>Electricité, gaz et eau | | |
| ISIC — CITI | 0–9 | 0 | 1–5 | 1, 4 | 2–3 | 5 | 7 | 6, 8–9 |
| At Current Prices — Aux prix courants | | | | | | | | |
| Absolute figures<br>— Chiffres absolus | | | | | | | | |
| 1955............ | 30.4 | 2.6 | 5.7 | 2.6 | 2.5 | 0.6 | 1.1 | 21.0 |
| 1956............ | 34.4 | 3.1 | 6.6 | 3.1 | 2.9 | 0.6 | 1.6 | 23.1 |
| 1957............ | 36.1 | 2.9 | 7.3 | 3.5 | 3.2 | 0.6 | 1.6 | 24.3 |
| 1958............ | 38.0 | 3.0 | 7.7 | 3.7 | 3.3 | 0.7 | 1.7 | 25.6 |
| 1959............ | 39.3 | 2.9 | 8.8 | 3.5 | 4.6 | 0.7 | 1.5 | 26.1 |
| 1960............ | 43.2 | 3.2 | 10.6 | 4.1 | 5.5 | 1.0 | 1.7 | 27.7 |
| 1961............ | 45.1 | 3.4 | 10.9 | 4.0 | 5.7 | 1.2 | 2.1 | 28.7 |
| Percentage distribution according to sector—<br>Distribution en pourcentage par secteur | | | | | | | | |
| 1955–1960..... | 100.0 | 7.9 | 21.1 | 9.3 | 9.9 | 1.9 | 4.2 | 66.8 |
| 1955............ | 100.0 | 8.5 | 18.8 | 8.6 | 8.2 | 2.0 | 3.6 | 69.1 |
| 1958............ | 100.0 | 7.9 | 20.2 | 9.7 | 8.7 | 1.8 | 4.5 | 67.4 |
| 1960............ | 100.0 | 7.4 | 24.5 | 9.5 | 12.7 | 2.3 | 4.0 | 64.1 |
| 1961............ | 100.0 | 7.5 | 24.2 | 8.9 | 12.6 | 2.7 | 4.6 | 63.7 |

## 2. CHARACTERISTICS OF INDUSTRIAL ESTABLISHMENTS ENGAGING FIVE OR MORE PERSONS
## CARACTERISTIQUES DES ETABLISSEMENTS INDUSTRIELS OCCUPANT CINQ PERSONNES OU PLUS
### 1955

Number of establishments in units; value added in thousand Pounds; number of engaged in units; and value added per person engaged in Pounds

Nombre d'établissements en unités; valeur ajoutée en milliers de livres; nombre de personnes occupées en unités; valeur ajoutée par personne occupée en livres

## A. Selected Divisions of Industrial Activity — Quelques branches de l'activité industrielle

| Item of data | Total | Mining[2]<br>Industries extractives[2] | Manufacturing[1]<br>Industries manufacturières[1] | Construction[1]<br>Bâtiment et travaux publics[1] | Rubrique |
|---|---|---|---|---|---|
| ISIC | 1–4 | 1 | 2–3 | 4 | CITI |
| a. Absolute Figures — Chiffres absolus | | | | | |
| Number of establishments........ | 283 | 27 | 182 | 74 | Nombre d'établissements |
| Value added................. | . | . | 1 929.0 | 543.6 | Valeur ajoutée |
| Number of engaged (Average during year)........ | 7 213 | 260 | 4 920 | 2 033 | Nombre de personnes occupées (moyenne pendant l'année) |
| b. Structure | | | | | |
| Distribution in percent of number of engaged................. | 100.0 | 3.6 | 68.2 | 28.1 | Répartition en pourcentage du nombre de personnes occupées |
| Value added per person engaged................. | . | . | 392.1 | 267.4 | Valeur ajoutée par personne occupée |

For footnotes see end of table.                    Pour les notes, voir au bas du tableau.

## B. The Major Groups of Manufacturing — Les classes de la branche Industries manufacturières

| Item of data | Manu-facturing[1]<br><br>Industries manufac-turières[1] | Food and beverages<br><br>Industries alimen-taires et boissons | Textiles and wearing apparel<br><br>Textiles et articles d'habille-ment | Wood products and furniture<br><br>Bois et meubles | Paper products, printing and publishing<br><br>Ouvrages en papier, imprimerie et édition | Chemicals and chemical, petroleum and coal products<br><br>Produits chi-miques et dérivés du pétrole et du charbon | Non-metallic mineral products[1]<br><br>Produits minéraux non métalliques[1] | Metal products<br><br>Ouvrages en métaux | Other manu-factur-ing<br><br>Autres in-dustries manufac-turières | Rubrique |
|---|---|---|---|---|---|---|---|---|---|---|
| ISIC | 2–3 | 20–21 | 23–24 | 25–26 | 27–28 | 31–32 | 33 | 35–38 | 22,29–30,39 | CITI |
| | | | | a. Absolute Figures — Chiffres absolus | | | | | | |
| Number of establishments... | 182 | 65 | 20 | 34 | 9 | 5 | 7 | 28 | 14 | Nombre d'établissements |
| Value added............ | 1 929.0 | 886.1 | 181.3 | 127.1 | 152.9 | 83.0 | 27.6 | 84.3 | 386.7 | Valeur ajoutée |
| Number of engaged (Average during the year)............. | 4 920 | 1 703 | 643 | 547 | 518 | 116 | 341 | 480 | 572 | Nombre de personnes occupées (moyenne pendant l'année) |
| | | | | b. Structure | | | | | | |
| Distribution in percent of: | | | | | | | | | | Distribution en pourcentage: |
| Value added.......... | 100.0 | 45.9 | 9.4 | 6.6 | 7.9 | 4.3 | 1.4 | 4.4 | 20.1 | Valeur ajoutée |
| Number of engaged..... | 100.0 | 34.6 | 13.1 | 11.1 | 10.5 | 2.4 | 6.9 | 9.8 | 11.6 | Nombre de personnes occupées |
| Value added per person engaged.............. | 392.1 | 520.3 | 282.0 | 232.4 | 295.2 | 715.5 | 80.9 | 175.6 | 676.0 | Valeur ajoutée par personne occupée |

[1] The manufacturing of cement blocks, precast concrete and bricks and marble and stone works are included in Construction (ISIC division 4) instead of in Manufacturing (ISIC division 2–3).
[2] Entirely Other mining (ISIC major groups 14–19).

[1] La fabrication des parpaings en ciment, des éléments moulés en béton, des briques et des ouvrages en marbre et en pierre est comprise dans Bâtiment et travaux publics (CITI branche 4) et non dans Industries manufacturières (CITI branches 2–3).
[2] Il s'agit exclusivement des Autres industries extractives (CITI branches 14–19).

# 3. CHARACTERISTICS OF INDUSTRIAL ESTABLISHMENTS ENGAGING THREE OR MORE PERSONS
## CARACTERISTIQUES DES ETABLISSEMENTS INDUSTRIELS OCCUPANT TROIS PERSONNES OU PLUS
### 1958

Number of establishments in units; value added and wages and salaries in thousand Pounds; number of engaged and of employees in units and value added per engaged and wages and salaries per employee in Pounds.

Nombre d'établissements en unités; valeur ajoutée et traitements et salaires en milliers delivres; nombre de personnes occupées et de salariés en unités; valeur ajoutée par personne occupée et traitements et salaires par salarié en livres.

## A. Selected Divisions of Industrial Activity — Quelques branches de l'activité industrielle

| Item of data | Total | Mining<br>Industries ex-tractives | Manu-facturing<br>Industries manu-facturières | Con-struction<br>Bâtiment et travaux publics | Rubrique | Item of data | Total | Mining<br>Industries ex-tractives | Manu-facturing<br>Industries manu-facturières | Con-struction<br>Bâtiment et travaux publics | Rubrique |
|---|---|---|---|---|---|---|---|---|---|---|---|
| ISIC | 1–4 | 1 | 2–3 | 4 | CITI | ISIC | 1–4 | 1 | 2–3 | 4 | CITI |
| | a. Absolute Figures — Chiffres absolus | | | | | | b. Structure | | | | |
| Number of establishments. | 655 | 66 | 467 | 122 | Nombre d'établissements | Distribution in percent of: | | | | | Distribution en pourcentage: |
| Value added............. | 4 587.5 | 176.3 | 2 937.1 | 1 474.1 | Valeur ajoutée | Value added........... | 100.0 | 3.9 | 64.0 | 32.1 | Valeur ajoutée |
| Number of engaged (Average during the year)................ | 9 469 | 484 | 6 602 | 2 383 | Nombre de personnes occupées (moyenne pendant l'année) | Number of engaged..... | 100.0 | 5.1 | 69.7 | 25.2 | Nombre de personnes occupées |
| Number of employees (Average during the year)................ | 8 629 | 388 | 6 025 | 2 216 | Nombre de salariés (moyenne pendant l'année) | Value added per person engaged.............. | 484.5 | 364.3 | 444.9 | 618.6 | Valeur ajoutée par personne occupée |
| Wages and salaries........ | 2 261.6 | 104.1 | 1 373.1 | 784.4 | Traitements et salaires | Employees as a percent of engaged............ | 91.1 | 80.2 | 91.3 | 93.0 | Salariés en pourcentage des personnes occupées |
| | | | | | | Wages and salaries per employee............. | 262.1 | 268.3 | 227.9 | 354.0 | Traitements et salaires par salarié |
| | | | | | | Value added per unit of wages and salaries...... | 2.0 | 1.7 | 2.1 | 1.9 | Valeur ajoutée par unité de traitements et salaires |

## B. The Major Groups of Manufacturing — Les classes de la branche Industries manufacturières

| Item of data | Manufacturing — Industries manufacturières | Food beverages and tobacco — Industries alimentaires, boissons, tabac | Textiles | Clothing, footwear and made-up textiles — Articles d'habillement, chaussures et ouvrages en tissu | Wood products and furniture — Bois et meubles | Paper, paper products, printing and publishing — Papier et ouvrages en papier, imprimerie et édition | Leather and leather products except wearing apparel — Cuir et articles en cuir, à l'exclusion des articles d'habillement | Chemicals and chemical, petroleum and coal products — Produits chimiques et dérivés du pétrole et du charbon | Non-metallic mineral products — Produits minéraux non métalliques | Metal products — Ouvrages en métaux | Other manufacturing — Autres industries manufacturières | Rubrique |
|---|---|---|---|---|---|---|---|---|---|---|---|---|
| ISIC | 2–3 | 20–22 | 23 | 24 | 25–26 | 27–28 | 29 | 31–32 | 33 | 35–38 | 39 | CITI |
| *a. Absolute Figures — Chiffres absolus* | | | | | | | | | | | | |
| Number of establishments | 467 | 126 | 10 | 54 | 104 | 15 | 5 | 7 | 46 | 77 | 23 | Nombre d'établissements |
| Value added | 2 937.1 | 1 434.0 | 103.1 | 181.1 | 282.8 | 220.5 | 11.8 | 135.9 | 150.4 | 338.7 | 78.8 | Valeur ajoutée |
| Number of engaged (Average during the year) | 6 602 | 2 196 | 278 | 812 | 953 | 478 | 81 | 153 | 456 | 901 | 294 | Nombre de personnes occupées (moyenne pendant l'année) |
| Number of employees (Average during the year) | 6 025 | 1 986 | 267 | 763 | 831 | 473 | 76 | 147 | 400 | 815 | 267 | Nombre de salariés (moyenne pendant l'année) |
| Wages and salaries | 1 373.1 | 475.8 | 43.6 | 114.6 | 188.1 | 142.0 | 9.2 | 26.9 | 104.5 | 225.0 | 43.4 | Traitements et salaires |
| *b. Structure* | | | | | | | | | | | | |
| Distribution in percent of: Value added | 100.0 | 48.8 | 3.5 | 6.2 | 9.6 | 7.5 | 0.4 | 4.6 | 5.1 | 11.6 | 2.7 | Distribution en pourcentage: Valeur ajoutée |
| Number of engaged | 100.0 | 33.3 | 4.2 | 12.3 | 14.4 | 7.2 | 1.2 | 2.3 | 6.9 | 13.7 | 4.5 | Nombre de personnes occupées |
| Value added per person engaged | 444.9 | 653.0 | 370.9 | 223.0 | 296.7 | 461.3 | 145.7 | 888.2 | 329.8 | 375.9 | 268.0 | Valeur ajoutée par personne occupée |
| Employees as a percent of engaged | 91.3 | 90.4 | 96.0 | 94.0 | 87.2 | 99.0 | 93.8 | 96.1 | 87.7 | 90.5 | 90.8 | Salariés en pourcentage des personnes occupées |
| Wages and salaries per employee | 227.9 | 239.6 | 163.3 | 150.2 | 226.4 | 300.2 | 121.1 | 183.0 | 261.3 | 276.1 | 162.5 | Traitements et salaires par salarié |
| Value added per unit of wages and salaries | 2.1 | 3.0 | 2.4 | 1.6 | 1.5 | 1.6 | 1.3 | 5.1 | 1.4 | 1.5 | 1.8 | Valeur ajoutée par unité de traitements et salaires |

## 4. CHARACTERISTICS OF LARGER INDUSTRIAL ESTABLISHMENTS [1]
## CARACTERISTIQUES DES GRANDS ETABLISSEMENTS INDUSTRIELS [1]
### 1955, 1958

Number of establishments in units; value added and wages and salaries in thousand Pounds; number of engaged and employees in units; and value added per person engaged in Pounds.

Nombre d'établissements en unités; valeur ajoutée et traitements et salaires en milliers de livres; nombre de personnes occupées et de salariés en unités; valeur ajoutée par personne occupée en livres.

### A. Selected Divisions of Industrial Activity — Quelques branches de l'activité industrielle

| Year and item of data | Total | Mining [2] — Industries extractives [2] | Manufacturing [3] — Industries manufacturières [3] | Construction [3] — Bâtiment et travaux publics [3] | Rubrique et année | Year and item of data | Total | Mining [2] — Industries extractives [2] | Manufacturing [3] — Industries manufacturières [3] | Construction [3] — Bâtiment et travaux publics [3] | Rubrique et année |
|---|---|---|---|---|---|---|---|---|---|---|---|
| ISIC | 1–4 | 1 | 2–3 | 4 | CITI | ISIC | 1–4 | 1 | 2–3 | 4 | CITI |
| *a. Absolute Figures — Chiffres absolus* | | | | | | *b. Structure* | | | | | |
| **1955** | | | | | 1955 | **1955** | | | | | 1955 |
| Number of establishments | 160 | 6 | 107 | 47 | Nombre d'établissements | | | | | | |
| Value added | 2 432.7 | 87.2 | 1 802.0 | 543.5 | Valeur ajoutée | Distribution in percent of: Value added | 100.0 | 3.6 | 74.1 | 22.3 | Distribution en pourcentage: Valeur ajoutée |
| Number of engaged (Average during the year) | 6 331 | 132 | 4 379 | 1 820 | Nombre de personnes occupées (moyenne pendant l'année) | Number of engaged | 100.0 | 2.1 | 69.2 | 28.7 | Nombre de personnes occupées |
| Number of employees (Average during the year) | 6 119 | 117 | 4 218 | 1 784 | Nombre de salariés (moyenne pendant l'année) | Value added per person engaged | 384.3 | 660.6 | 411.5 | 298.6 | Valeur ajoutée par personne occupée |
| Wages and salaries paid | 1 281.5 | 32.3 | 770.2 | 479.0 | Traitements et salaires payés | Value added per unit of wages and salaries | 1.90 | 2.70 | 2.34 | 1.13 | Valeur ajoutée par unité de traitements et salaires |
| **1958** | | | | | 1958 | **1958** | | | | | 1958 |
| Number of establishments | 203 | 11 | 144 | 48 | Nombre d'établissements | | | | | | |
| Value added | 3 792.5 | 79.6 | 2 408.9 | 1 304.0 | Valeur ajoutée | Distribution in percent of: Value added | 100.0 | 2.1 | 63.5 | 34.4 | Distribution en pourcentage: Valeur ajoutée |
| Number of engaged (Average during the year) | 6 976 | 198 | 4 830 | 1 948 | Nombre de personnes occupées (moyenne pendant l'année) | Number engaged | 100.0 | 2.9 | 69.2 | 27.9 | Nombre de personnes occupées |
| Number of employees (Average during the year) | 6 716 | 184 | 4 663 | 1 869 | Nombre de salariés (moyenne pendant l'année) | Value added per person engaged | 543.6 | 402.0 | 498.7 | 669.4 | Valeur ajoutée par personne occupée |
| Wages and salaries paid | 1 815.0 | 50.3 | 1 080.2 | 684.5 | Traitements et salaires payés | Value added per unit of wages and salaries | 2.09 | 1.58 | 2.23 | 1.90 | Valeur ajoutée par unité de traitements et salaires |

For footnotes see end of table.    Pour les notes, voir au bas du tableau.

## B. The Major Groups of Manufacturing — Les classes de la branche Industries manufacturières

| Year and item of data | Manufacturing [3] Industries manufacturières [3] | Food beverages and tobacco Industries alimentaires, boissons, tabac | Textiles | Clothing, footwear and made-up textiles Articles d'habillement, chaussures et ouvrages en tissu | Wood products and furniture Bois et meubles | Paper products, printing and publishing Ouvrages en papier, imprimerie et édition | Leather and leather products except wearing apparel [4] Cuir et articles en cuir, à l'exclusion des articles d'habillement [4] | Chemicals and chemical, petroleum and coal products Produits chimiques et dérivés du pétrole et du charbon | Non-metallic mineral products [3] Produits minéraux non métalliques [3] | Metal products [5] Ouvrages en métaux [5] | Other manufacturing [6] Autres industries manufacturières [6] | Année et rubrique |
|---|---|---|---|---|---|---|---|---|---|---|---|---|
| ISIC | 2-3 | 20-22 | 23 | 24 | 25-26 | 27-28 | 29 | 31-32 | 33 | 35-38 | 39 | CITI |
| *a. Absolute Figures — Chiffres absolus* | | | | | | | | | | | | |
| **1955** | | | | | | | | | | | | 1955 |
| Number of establishments | 107 | 39 | 5 | 11 | 14 | 4 | ... | 5 | 7 | 13 | 9 | Nombre d'établissements |
| Value added | 1 802.0 | 835.9 | 71.4 | 107.5 | 96.8 | 145.9 | ... | 83.0 | 27.6 | 62.5 | 371.4 | Valeur ajoutée |
| Number of engaged (Average during the year) | 4 379 | 1 513 | 160 | 453 | 410 | 484 | ... | 116 | 341 | 373 | 529 | Nombre de personnes occupées (moyenne pendant l'année) |
| Number of employees (Average during the year) | 4 218 | 1 442 | 154 | 429 | 394 | 475 | ... | 110 | 333 | 360 | 521 | Nombre de salariés (moyenne pendant l'année) |
| Wages and salaries paid | 773.2 | 325.4 | 26.5 | 54.6 | 76.7 | 94.6 | ... | 21.3 | 22.4 | 58.9 | 92.8 | Traitements et salaires payés |
| **1958** | | | | | | | | | | | | 1958 |
| Number of establishments | 144 | 36 | 6 | 22 | 24 | 5 | 5 | 4 | 14 | 24 | 4 | Nombre d'établissements |
| Value added | 2 408.8 | 1 280.8 | 100.3 | 142.0 | 158.5 | 202.2 | 11.8 | 133.0 | 74.2 | 261.1 | 44.9 | Valeur ajoutée |
| Number engaged (Average during the year) | 4 830 | 1 655 | 260 | 657 | 524 | 420 | 81 | 132 | 252 | 648 | 201 | Nombre de personnes occupées (moyenne pendant l'année) |
| Number of employees (Average during the year) | 4 663 | 1 616 | 255 | 635 | 485 | 420 | 76 | 127 | 230 | 624 | 195 | Nombre de salariés (moyenne pendant l'année) |
| Wages and salaries paid | 1 080.3 | 404.7 | 42.3 | 90.7 | 114.1 | 130.8 | 9.2 | 24.9 | 56.6 | 179.0 | 28.0 | Traitements et salaires payés |
| *b. Structure* | | | | | | | | | | | | |
| **1955** | | | | | | | | | | | | 1955 |
| Distribution in percent of: Value added | 100.0 | 46.3 | 4.0 | 6.0 | 5.3 | 8.1 | ... | 4.6 | 1.6 | 3.4 | 20.7 | Distribution en pourcentage: Valeur ajoutée |
| Number of engaged | 100.0 | 34.6 | 3.7 | 10.3 | 9.4 | 11.0 | ... | 2.6 | 7.8 | 8.5 | 12.1 | Nombre de personnes occupées |
| Value added per person engaged | 411.5 | 552.5 | 446.3 | 237.3 | 236.1 | 301.4 | ... | 715.5 | 80.9 | 167.6 | 702.1 | Valeur ajoutée par personne occupée |
| Value added per unit of wages and salaries | 2.33 | 2.57 | 2.69 | 1.97 | 1.26 | 1.54 | ... | 3.99 | 1.23 | 1.06 | 4.00 | Valeur ajoutée par unité de traitements et salaires |
| **1958** | | | | | | | | | | | | 1958 |
| Distribution in percent of: Value added | 100.0 | 53.1 | 4.2 | 5.9 | 6.6 | 8.4 | 0.4 | 5.6 | 3.0 | 10.9 | 1.9 | Distribution en pourcentage: Valeur ajoutée |
| Number of engaged | 100.0 | 34.3 | 5.4 | 13.6 | 10.8 | 8.7 | 1.7 | 2.7 | 5.2 | 13.4 | 4.2 | Nombre de personnes occupées |
| Value added per person engaged | 498.7 | 773.8 | 385.8 | 216.1 | 302.5 | 481.4 | 145.7 | 1 007.6 | 294.4 | 402.9 | 223.4 | Valeur ajoutée par personne occupée |
| Value added per unit of wages and salaries | 2.23 | 3.16 | 2.37 | 1.56 | 1.39 | 1.54 | 1.28 | 5.34 | 1.31 | 1.46 | 1.60 | Valeur ajoutée par unité de traitements et salaires |

[1] Larger establishments are those engaging ten or more persons in the 1955 Census and eleven or more persons in the 1958 Census.
[2] Entirely Other mining (ISIC major groups 14-19).
[3] In 1955 the manufacturing of cement blocks, precast concrete and blocks and marble and stone works are included in construction (ISIC division 4) instead of in Manufacturing (ISIC divisions 2-3).
[4] The 1955 figures are included with Other manufacturing (ISIC major group 39).
[5] The 1958 figures include rebuilding and retreading of rubber tires.
[6] The 1955 figures include Tobacco (ISIC major group 22), Leather, and leather and fur products (ISIC major group 29), and Rubber products (ISIC major group 30).

[1] Les grands établissements sont ceux qui occupent 10 personnes ou plus dans le cas du recensement de 1955 et 11 personnes ou plus dans le cas du recensement de 1958.
[2] Il s'agit exclusivement des Autres industries extractives (CITI classes 14-19).
[3] En 1955, la fabrication des parpaings en ciment, des éléments moulés en béton, des briques et des ouvrages en marbre et en pierre est comprise dans Bâtiment et travaux publics (CITI branche 4) et non dans Industries manufacturières (CITI branches 2-3).
[4] Les chiffres de 1955 sont compris dans Autres industries manufacturières (CITI classe 39).
[5] Les chiffres de 1958 comprennent le rechappage des pneumatiques et chambres à air en caoutchouc.
[6] Les chiffres de 1955 comprennent Tabac (CITI classe 22), Cuir et articles en cuir et en fourrure (CITI classe 29) et Ouvrages en caoutchouc (CITI classe 30).

# MEXICO — MEXIQUE

## Gross National Product

Estimates of expenditure on the gross national product are presented in Table 1. This table has been compiled from data supplied by Banco de México, Departamento de Estudios Económicos in response to the United Nations national accounts questionnaire. The official estimates are published annually in *Informe Anual,* Nacional Financiera, S.A., Mexico, D.F.

## Index Numbers of Industrial Production

The index numbers of industrial production shown in Table 2 are compiled mainly by the Banco de México, Mexico City, and are made available to the Statistical Office of the United Nations through correspondence.

The indexes are computed as base-weighted arithmetic averages of product relatives. The weighting pattern used to combine indexes for detailed categories of industry is based on value added at market prices in 1944 derived from the results of Mexico's Fourth Industrial Census (Cuarto Censo Industrial de los Estados Unidos Mexicanos), covering industrial establishments with a value of production during the census year exceeding 10,000 pesos.

Since official indexes for some groups are not available or do not correspond to the ISIC, the Statistical Office of the United Nations compiled, in some cases, indexes for major groups of mining and manufacturing based on available information on the output of individual products. In the case of Metal mining (ISIC Major group 12), for example, output series for five metals are combined by using gross value of production during 1958 as weights. For Chemicals and chemical, petroleum and coal products (ISIC Major groups 31-32), annual series on the production of synthetic fibres and a number of basic industrial chemicals were added to the indexes of the Banco for soap, matches and petroleum refining. In the case of Basic metals, series on the smelter production of three non-ferrous metals are combined with the index of the Banco for the Iron and steel basic industries (ISIC group 341). The series for these major groups of manufacturing are combined by using weights based on value added during 1950 derived from the results of the 1950 Industrial Census.

It should also be noted that the Statistical Office of the United Nations computes the indexes for mining as a whole by combining the indexes of the Banco for the

## Produit national brut

Des estimations des dépenses imputées au produit national brut sont reproduites au tableau 1. Ce tableau a été établi à partir des données fournies par le Banco de México, Departamento de Estudios Económicos en réponse au questionnaire de l'ONU sur la comptabilité nationale. Les estimations officielles sont publiées chaque année dans *Informe Anual,* Nacional Financiera, S.A., Mexico, D.F.

## Indices de la production industrielle

Les indices de la production industrielle reproduits au tableau 2 sont établis en grande partie par le Banco de México (Mexico) et sont communiqués par correspondance au Bureau de statistique de l'ONU.

Ces indices sont des moyennes arithmétiques à pondération fixe de rapports quantitatifs de la production. Le système de pondération utilisé pour combiner les indices des catégories détaillées de l'activité industrielle est fondé sur la valeur ajoutée aux prix du marché en 1944, qui est tirée des résultats du quatrième recensement industriel du Mexique (Cuarto Censo Industrial de los Estados Unidos Mexicanos), lequel porte sur tous les établissements industriels dont la valeur de la production durant l'année de recensement dépasse 10 000 pesos.

Etant donné qu'il n'y a pas d'indices officiels pour certaines classes ou que ces indices ne correspondent pas à la CITI, le Bureau de statistique de l'ONU a construit dans certains cas des indices pour les classes des industries extractives et manufacturières en se fondant sur les renseignements dont il disposait au sujet de la production de chaque marchandise. Dans le cas de l'extraction des minerais métalliques par exemple (classe 12 de la CITI), il a combiné des séries concernant la production de cinq métaux en pondérant par la valeur brute de la production en 1958. Pour les produits chimiques et les dérivés du pétrole et du charbon (CITI classes 31-32), il a ajouté des séries annuelles sur la production de fibres synthétiques et d'un certain nombre de produits chimiques de base aux indices du Banco de México concernant la production de savon et d'allumettes et le raffinage du pétrole. Dans le cas de la métallurgie de base, des séries sur la production de trois métaux non ferreux au stade de la fonderie sont combinées avec l'indice établi par le Banco de México pour la sidérurgie et la première transformation de la fonte, du fer et de l'acier (CITI groupe 341). Pour ces classes des industries manufacturières, les séries sont combinées par pondération fondée sur la valeur ajoutée en 1950, qui est calculée d'après les résultats du recensement industriel de 1950.

On notera aussi que le Bureau de statistique de l'ONU calcule les indices pour l'ensemble des industries extractives en combinant les indices établis par le Banco de

extraction of crude petroleum and for metallic mining and metallurgy and the indexes for manufacturing as a whole by combining the indexes of the Banco for petroleum refining and for manufacturing.

### Index Numbers of Industrial Employment

The index numbers of manufacturing employment set out in Table 3 are based on absolute figures of the average number of employees during each quarter of the year gathered by the Dirección General de Estadística in a quarterly survey of selected larger establishments engaged in the most important kinds of manufacturing activity. The results of the quarterly surveys are published by the Dirección in the *Revista de Estadística*. The Statistical Office of the United Nations computed the index numbers for the summation of the manufacturing covered in the quarterly surveys as base-weighted arithmetic averages of the component indexes. The weights utilized in these computations were proportional to the average quarterly number of employees in the establishments covered in the survey during 1953 for the years, 1948-1954, and during 1958 for 1955 and thereafter. It should be noted that some of the index numbers shown in Table 3 may have been distorted by some variation, from time to time, in the number of completed returns received in the quarterly survey, despite the adjustments made in order to eliminate such distortion.

### Characteristics and Structure of Industrial Activity

The information shown in Table 4 is derived from the results of Mexico's Third and Fourth Industrial Censuses taken by the Dirección General de Estadística and published in *Tercer Censo Industrial de los Estados Unidos Mexicanos, 1940* (Mexico, 1952) and in *Cuarto Censo Industrial de los Estados Unidos Mexicanos, 1945* (Mexico, 1953). The two Censuses covered industrial establishments whose value of production during the census year exceeded 10,000 Pesos. The production of manufactured gas, construction (except road building) and repair and similar units serving industrial establishments were excluded.

The items of data appear to conform generally to the International Standards in Basic Industrial Statistics. Value added is based on value of production at market prices and does not cover receipts from work done for others. The figures on installed capacity relate to equipment in use and in reserve and are obtained by combining the horsepower of all prime movers with that of electric motors driven by purchased electricity.

The data shown in Table 5 are derived from the results of Mexico's Fifth and Sixth Industrial Censuses.

México pour l'extraction du pétrole brut et pour l'extraction de minerais métalliques et la métallurgie; de même, il construit les indices pour l'ensemble des industries manufacturières en combinant les indices du Banco de México concernant le raffinage du pétrole et les industries manufacturières.

### Indices de l'emploi dans l'industrie

Les indices du tableau 3 relatifs à l'emploi dans les industries manufacturières sont fondés sur des chiffres absolus indiquant le nombre moyen de salariés pendant chaque semestre de l'année; ces chiffres ont été rassemblés par la Dirección General de Estadística au moyen d'une enquête trimestrielle auprès de quelques grands établissements manufacturiers exerçant les types d'activité manufacturières en combinant les indices du Banco de enquêtes trimestrielles sont publiés par la Dirección dans *Revista de Estadística*. Les indices établis par le Bureau de statistique de l'ONU pour l'ensemble des industries manufacturières visées par les enquêtes trimestrielles sont des moyennes arithmétiques à pondération fixe des divers indices utilisés. Les coefficients de pondération adoptés à cet effet sont proportionnels au nombre trimestriel moyen de salariés dans les établissements couverts par l'enquête en 1953 pour les années 1948-1954, et en 1958 à partir de 1955. Il y a lieu de noter que certains des indices du tableau 3 ont pu être affectés par les variations enregistrées de temps à autre, dans le nombre des réponses reçues au titre de l'enquête trimestrielle, malgré les ajustements opérés pour éliminer l'effet de ces variations.

### Caractéristiques et structure de l'activité industrielle

Les renseignements du tableau 4 sont tirés des résultats des troisième et quatrième recensements industriels effectués par la Dirección General de Estadística; ces résultats sont publiés dans *Tercer Censo Industrial de los Estados Unidos Mexicanos, 1940* (Mexico, 1952) et dans *Cuarto Censo Industrial de los Estados Unidos Mexicanos, 1945* (Mexico, 1953). Ces deux recensements couvraient les établissements industriels dont la valeur de la production, pendant l'année du recensement, dépassait 10 000 pesos. La production de gaz d'usine, le bâtiment et les travaux publics (à l'exception de la construction de routes) et les ateliers de réparation et unités analogues travaillant pour des établissements industriels n'ont pas été compris dans le recensement.

Les rubriques paraissent conformes, dans l'ensemble, aux Normes internationales relatives aux statistiques industrielles de base. La valeur ajoutée est calculée d'après la valeur de la production aux prix du marché, et elle ne comprend pas les recettes provenant de travaux effectués pour des tiers. Les chiffres de la puissance installée concernent le matériel en service et en réserve; ils représentent la puissance de tous les moteurs primaires, plus celle des moteurs électriques actionnés par de l'électricité achetée.

Les données du tableau 5 proviennent des résultats des cinquième et sixième recensements industriels du Me-

These were conducted by the Dirección General de Estadística and published in *Estados Unidos, Quinto Censo Industrial y Tercer Censo de Transportes, 1950* (Mexico 1957) and in *Censo Industrial 1956 (Información Censal 1955)* (Mexico 1959) (Three Volumes), respectively. In principle the fifth and sixth Censuses covered all establishments regardless of size, that were engaged in industrial activity during 1950 and 1955 respectively. However, in practice, as is apparent from a comparison of results, there are differences in coverage between the two censuses.

The data on value added is based on the value of production at market prices, ex-factory. In 1950 value added includes the cost of containers utilized in production, in 1955 the cost of containers is excluded from value added. In both 1950 and 1955 wages and salary figures include payments to working proprietors.

The change in classification between 1950 and 1955 of metal mining and petroleum refining should be noted when utilizing the data.

xique. Ces recensements ont été effectués par la Dirección General de Estadística et publiés dans *Estados Unidos, Quinto Censo Industrial y Tercer Censo de Transportes, 1950* (Mexico 1957) et dans *Censo Industrial 1956 (Información Censal 1955)* (Mexico 1959; trois volumes) respectivement. En principe, les cinquième et sixième recensements portaient sur tous les établissements, quelle que fût leur dimension, qui exerçaient une activité industrielle en 1950 et 1955 respectivement. Cependant, en pratique, comme il apparaît quand on compare les résultats, il y a des différences entre les champs couverts par chacun des recensements.

La valeur ajoutée est calculée d'après la valeur de la production aux prix du marché, départ usine. En 1950, on a tenu compte du coût de l'emballage dans le calcul de la valeur ajoutée; en 1955, il en a été exclu. Tant en 1950 qu'en 1955, les traitements et salaires comprennent les versements aux propriétaires qui travaillent.

Lorsqu'on utilise les données, il faut tenir compte des différences existant entre 1950 et 1955 quant au mode de classification adopté pour les industries extractives de minerais métalliques et les raffineries de pétrole.

## 1. THE GROSS NATIONAL PRODUCT — PRODUIT NATIONAL BRUT

### Expenditure on the Gross National Product at Market Prices
### Dépenses relatives au produit national brut aux prix du marché

Million Pesos / Millions de pesos

| Item of data and year / Rubrique et année | Total | Consumption / Consommation | | Gross Domestic Capital Formation / Formation brute de capital intérieur | | Net exports of goods and services [1] / Exportations nettes de biens et de services[1] | |
|---|---|---|---|---|---|---|---|
| | | Total | Government / Etat | Total | Fixed / Fixe | Exports less imports / Exportations moins importations | Exports / Exportations |
| | | | | *a. At Current Prices — Aux prix courants* | | | |
| Absolute figures — Chiffres absolus | | | | | | | |
| 1952 | 58 300 | 50 970 | 3 027 | 8 169 | 8 166 | −839 | 8 493 |
| 1953 | 56 300 | 49 453 | 2 708 | 7 637 | 7 854 | −790 | 8 435 |
| 1954 | 66 478 | 54 243 | 3 328 | 12 624 | 9 765 | −389 | 11 873 |
| 1955 | 84 000 | 68 314 | 3 572 | 14 705 | 12 260 | 981 | 15 861 |
| 1956 | 94 000 | 78 418 | 4 472 | 16 183 | 13 720 | −601 | 17 598 |
| 1957 | 103 000 | 87 835 | 5 568 | 17 652 | 15 057 | −2 487 | 17 018 |
| 1958 | 114 000 | 96 017 | 6 374 | 20 252 | 17 346 | −2 269 | 17 014 |
| 1959 | 122 000 | 101 569 | 6 576 | 20 827 | 17 816 | −396 | 18 212 |
| 1960 | 134 400 | 112 581 | 8 136 | 23 995 | 21 051 | −2 176 | 19 004 |
| 1961 | 141 000 | ... | ... | ... | 21 367 | −884 | 20 152 |
| Percentage distribution of average annual expenditure — Distribution en pourcentage des dépenses annuelles moyennes | | | | | | | |
| 1953 | 100.0 | 87.8 | 4.8 | 13.6 | 14.0 | −1.4 | 15.0 |
| 1954 | 100.0 | 81.6 | 5.0 | 19.0 | 14.7 | −0.6 | 17.9 |
| 1958 | 100.0 | 84.2 | 5.6 | 17.8 | 15.2 | −2.0 | 14.9 |
| 1960 | 100.0 | 83.7 | 6.1 | 17.9 | 15.7 | −1.6 | 14.1 |

[1] Includes factor income.

[1] Y compris le revenu des facteurs.

## 2. INDEX NUMBERS OF INDUSTRIAL PRODUCTION — INDICES DE LA PRODUCTION INDUSTRIELLE

### A. Selected Divisions of Industrial Activity
### Quelques branches de l'activité industrielle

| Period / Période | Total excluding construction / Total à l'exclusion du bâtiment et des travaux publics | Mining [1] / Industries extractives [1] | Manufacturing [2] / Industries manufacturières [2] | Construction / Bâtiment et travaux publics | Électricity / Electricité |
|---|---|---|---|---|---|
| ISIC — CITI | 1-3, 511 | 1 | 2-3 | 4 | 511 |

*a.* Indexes — Indices (1958 = 100)

| | | | | | |
|---|---|---|---|---|---|
| 1948....... | 57 | 82 | 55 | 41 | 44 |
| 1949....... | 59 | 83 | 57 | 50 | 48 |
| 1950....... | 64 | 91 | 62 | 60 | 49 |
| 1951....... | 68 | 88 | 66 | 68 | 54 |
| 1952....... | 68 | 94 | 66 | 74 | 59 |
| 1953....... | 68 | 90 | 66 | 70 | 63 |
| 1954....... | 73 | 86 | 72 | 73 | 69 |
| 1955....... | 81 | 93 | 80 | 81 | 77 |
| 1956....... | 89 | 99 | 88 | 91 | 86 |
| 1957....... | 95 | 102 | 94 | 102 | 93 |
| 1958....... | 100 | 100 | 100 | 100 | 100 |
| 1959....... | 108 | 102 | 109 | 104 | 107 |
| 1960....... | 117 | 105 | 118 | 118 | 188 |
| 1961....... | 122 | 103 | 124 | ... | 129 |

*b.* Average Annual Rate of Change — Taux annuel moyen de variation

| | | | | | |
|---|---|---|---|---|---|
| 1950 - 1960. | 6.2 | 1.4 | 6.6 | 7.0 | 9.2 |
| 1948 - 1953. | 3.6 | 1.9 | 3.7 | 11.3 | 7.4 |
| 1954 - 1958. | 8.2 | 3.8 | 8.6 | 8.2 | 9.7 |
| 1958 - 1960. | 8.2 | 2.5 | 8.6 | 8.6 | 8.6 |

For footnotes see end of table.

### B. Selected Major Groups of Mining
### Quelques classes de la branche Industries extractives

| Period / Période | All mining [1] / Toutes industries extractives [1] | Coal mining / Extraction du charbon | Metal mining / Extraction des minerais métalliques | Crude petroleum and natural gas / Pétrole brut et gaz naturel |
|---|---|---|---|---|
| ISIC — CITI | 1 | 11 | 12 | 13 |

*a.* Indexes — Indices (1958 = 100)

| | | | | |
|---|---|---|---|---|
| 1948.......... | 82 | 72 | 98 | 62 |
| 1949.......... | 83 | 73 | 98 | 58 |
| 1950.......... | 91 | 62 | 108 | 76 |
| 1951.......... | 88 | 76 | 101 | 82 |
| 1952.......... | 94 | 89 | 110 | 82 |
| 1953.......... | 90 | 97 | 106 | 76 |
| 1954.......... | 86 | 89 | 98 | 88 |
| 1955.......... | 93 | 91 | 107 | 94 |
| 1956.......... | 99 | 95 | 101 | 96 |
| 1957.......... | 102 | 96 | 104 | 94 |
| 1958.......... | 100 | 100 | 100 | 100 |
| 1959.......... | 102 | 107 | 101 | 103 |
| 1960.......... | 105 | 120 | 102 | 106 |
| 1961.......... | 103 | 122 | 100 | 123 |

*b.* Average Annual Rate of Change — Taux annuel moyen de variation

| | | | | |
|---|---|---|---|---|
| 1950 - 1960.... | 1.4 | 6.8 | -0.6 | 3.4 |
| 1948 - 1953.... | 1.9 | 6.1 | 1.6 | 4.2 |
| 1954 - 1958.... | 3.8 | 3.0 | 0.5 | 3.2 |
| 1958 - 1960.... | 2.5 | 9.5 | 1.0 | 3.0 |

Pour les notes, voir au bas du tableau.

## C.   Selected Major Groups of Manufacturing

## Quelques classes de la branche Industries manufacturières

| Period<br><br>Période | Manu-<br>facturing [2]<br><br>Industries<br>manufac-<br>turières [2] | Food,<br>beverages<br>and<br>tobacco<br><br>Industries<br>alimen-<br>taires,<br>boissons,<br>tabac | Textiles | Paper<br>and<br>paper<br>products<br><br>Papier<br>et<br>ouvrages<br>en<br>papier | Rubber<br>products<br><br>Ouvrages<br>en<br>caout-<br>chouc | Chemicals<br>and<br>chemical,<br>petroleum<br>and<br>coal<br>products<br><br>Produits<br>chi-<br>miques<br>et<br>dérivés<br>du<br>pétrole<br>et du<br>charbon | Non-<br>metallic<br>mineral<br>products<br><br>Produits<br>minéraux<br>non<br>métal-<br>liques | Basic<br>metals<br><br>Métal-<br>lurgie<br>de base |
|---|---|---|---|---|---|---|---|---|
| ISIC — CITI | 2–3 | 20–22 | 23 | 27 | 30 | 31–32 | 33 | 34 |

### a.  Indexes — Indices (1958 = 100)

| | | | | | | | | |
|---|---|---|---|---|---|---|---|---|
| 1948............... | 55 | 50 | 91 | 52 | 62 | 40 | 36 | 55 |
| 1949............... | 57 | 54 | 86 | 53 | 54 | 45 | 47 | 64 |
| 1950............... | 62 | 62 | 90 | 59 | 59 | 51 | 57 | 66 |
| 1951............... | 66 | 70 | 87 | 65 | 74 | 54 | 64 | 73 |
| 1952............... | 66 | 66 | 83 | 63 | 73 | 59 | 63 | 72 |
| 1953............... | 66 | 69 | 80 | 72 | 68 | 60 | 67 | 74 |
| 1954............... | 72 | 74 | 90 | 70 | 78 | 66 | 72 | 76 |
| 1955............... | 80 | 82 | 97 | 75 | 89 | 75 | 84 | 82 |
| 1956............... | 88 | 85 | 101 | 86 | 91 | 84 | 94 | 89 |
| 1957............... | 94 | 94 | 102 | 101 | 89 | 89 | 101 | 98 |
| 1958............... | 100 | 100 | 100 | 100 | 100 | 100 | 100 | 100 |
| 1959............... | 109 | 103 | 111 | 104 | 110 | 117 | 107 | 106 |
| 1960............... | 118 | 113 | 124 | 114 | 118 | 124 | 120 | 115 |
| 1961............... | 124 | 112 | 116 | 122 | 120 | 137 | 117 | 116 |

### b.  Average Annual Rate of Change — Taux annuel moyen de variation

| | | | | | | | | |
|---|---|---|---|---|---|---|---|---|
| 1950 – 1960........ | 6.6 | 6.2 | 3.3 | 6.8 | 7.2 | 9.3 | 7.7 | 5.7 |
| 1948 – 1953........ | 3.7 | 6.7 | −2·6 | 6.7 | 1.9 | 8.4 | 13.2 | 6.1 |
| 1954 – 1958........ | 8.6 | 7.8 | 2.7 | 9.3 | 6.4 | 10.9 | 8.6 | 7.1 |
| 1958 – 1960........ | 8.6 | 6.3 | 11.4 | 6.8 | 8.6 | 11.4 | 9.5 | 7.2 |

[1] Excludes Coal mining (ISIC major group 11) and Other mining (ISIC major groups 14-19) but includes the Smelting of iron ferrous metals (ISIC group 342).

[2] Excludes Clothing, Footwear and Made-up Textiles (ISIC major group 24), Wood Products and Furniture (ISIC major groups 25-26), Printing and Publishing (ISIC major group 28), Leather Products (ISIC major group 29), Chemical Products (ISIC major group 31) except matches, soap and candles, Smelting of non-ferrous metals (ISIC group 342), Metal Products (ISIC major groups 35-38) and Other manufacturing (ISIC major group 39).

[1] Non compris Extraction du charbon (CITI classe 11) et Autres industries extractives (CITI classes 14-19), mais y compris les Fonderies des métaux non ferreux (CITI groupe 342).

[2] Non compris Articles d'habillement, chaussures et ouvrages en tissu (CITI classe 24), Bois et meubles (CITI classes 25-26), Imprimerie et édition (CITI classe 28), Cuir et articles en cuir (CITI classe 29), Produits chimiques (CITI classe 31), à l'exclusion des allumettes, savons et bougies, Fonderies des métaux non ferreux (CITI groupe 342), Ouvrages en métaux (CITI classes 35-38) et Autres industries manufacturières (CITI classe 39).

## 3. INDEX NUMBERS OF MANUFACTURING EMPLOYMENT
### INDICES DE L'EMPLOI DANS LES INDUSTRIES MANUFACTURIERES

| Period<br>Période | Manu-facturing [1]<br>Industries manufac-turières [1] | Food, beverages and tobacco<br>Industries alimen-taires, boissons, tabac | Textiles | Paper and paper products<br>Papier et ouvrages en papier | Rubber products<br>Ouvrages en caout-chouc | Chemicals and chemical, products<br>Produits chi-miques | Non-metallic mineral products<br>Produits minéraux non métal-liques | Basic metals<br>Métal-lurgie de base |
|---|---|---|---|---|---|---|---|---|
| ISIC — CITI | 2–3 | 20–22 | 23 | 27 | 30 | 31 | 33 | 34 |

*a.* Indexes — Indices (1958 = 100)

| | | | | | | | | |
|---|---|---|---|---|---|---|---|---|
| 1948............ | 93 | 68 | 120 | 68 | 63 | 64 | 50 | 91 |
| 1949............ | 96 | 84 | 117 | 69 | 63 | 68 | 58 | 96 |
| 1950............ | 97 | 82 | 117 | 69 | 63 | 79 | 61 | 98 |
| 1951............ | 98 | 88 | 114 | 72 | 67 | 80 | 65 | 103 |
| 1952............ | 92 | 65 | 108 | 86 | 48 | 86 | 65 | 110 |
| 1953............ | 96 | 91 | 105 | 97 | 71 | 85 | 68 | 109 |
| 1954............ | 96 | 95 | 96 | 103 | 77 | 94 | 78 | 112 |
| 1955............ | – 100 – | 98 | 100 | 118 | 85 | 98 | 86 | 112 |
| 1956............ | 100 | 105 | 97 | 101 | 92 | 104 | 100 | 104 |
| 1957............ | 101 | 104 | 98 | 101 | 96 | 100 | 98 | 106 |
| 1958............ | 100 | 100 | 100 | 100 | 100 | 100 | 100 | 100 |
| 1959............ | 98 | 99 | 97 | 101 | 103 | 100 | 104 | 96 |
| 1960............ | 100 | 98 | 98 | 119 | 98 | 100 | 108 | 100 |
| 1961............ | 97 | 100 | 90 | 127 | 102 | 94 | 109 | 94 |

*b.* Average Annual Rate of Change — Taux annuel moyen de variation

| | | | | | | | | |
|---|---|---|---|---|---|---|---|---|
| 1950 – 1960........ | 0.3 | 1.8 | –1.8 | 5.6 | 4.5 | 2.4 | 5.9 | 0.2 |
| 1948 – 1953........ | 0.6 | 6.0 | –2.6 | 7.4 | 2.4 | 5.8 | 6.3 | 3.7 |
| 1954 – 1958........ | 1.0 | 1.3 | 1.0 | –0.7 | 6.8 | 1.6 | 6.4 | –2.8 |
| 1958 – 1960........ | — | –1.0 | –1.0 | 9.1 | –1.0 | — | 3.9 | |

[1] Excludes employment in Clothing and made-up textiles (ISIC groups 243-244), Wood products and furniture (ISIC major group 25-26), Leather and leather products (ISIC major group 29), Petroleum and coal products (ISIC major group 32), Non-ferrous metal basic industries (ISIC group 342), Metal products (ISIC major groups 35-38) and Miscellaneous manufactures (ISIC major group 39).

[1] Non compris l'emploi dans les classes ci-après: Articles d'habillement et ouvrages en tissu (CITI classes 243-244), Bois et meubles (CITI classes 25-26), Cuir et articles en cuir (CITI classe 29), Produits dérivés du pétrole et du charbon (CITI classe 32), Métallurgie des métaux non-ferreux (CITI classe 342), Ouvrages en métaux (CITI classes 35-38) et Industries manufacturières diverses (CITI classe 39).

## 4. THE CHARACTERISTICS OF INDUSTRIAL ESTABLISHMENTS WITH VALUE OF PRODUCTION EXCEEDING 10,000 PESOS DURING YEAR
### CARACTERISTIQUES DES ETABLISSEMENTS INDUSTRIELS DONT LA VALEUR DE LA PRODUCTION DEPASSAIT 10 000 PESOS AU COURS DE L'ANNEE CONSIDEREE

### 1939, 1944

Number of establishments in units; value added and wages and salaries in million Pesos; number of engaged in thousands; capacity of installed power equipment in thousand horsepower; value added per person engaged in thousand Pesos; capacity of installed power equipment per person engaged in horsepower

Nombre d'établissements en unités; valeur ajoutée et traitements et salaires en millions de pesos; nombre de personnes occupées en milliers; puissance installée en milliers de chevaux-vapeur; valeur ajoutée par personne occupée en milliers de pesos; puissance installée par personne occupée en chevaux-vapeur

### A. The Divisions of Industrial Activity — Les branches de l'activité industrielle

| Item of data | Total | | Mining<br>Industries extractives | | Manufacturing [1]<br>Industries manufacturières [1] | | Construction [2]<br>Bâtiment et travaux publics [2] | | Electricity<br>Electricité | | Rubrique |
|---|---|---|---|---|---|---|---|---|---|---|---|
| | 1939 | 1944 | 1939 | 1944 | 1939 | 1944 | 1939 | 1944 | 1939 | 1944 | |
| ISIC | 1–4, 511 | | 1 | | 2–3 | | 4 | | 511 | | CITI |
| Number of establishments..... | 13 340 | 30 483 | 281 | 368 | 12 796 | 29 581 | 7 | 210 | 256 | 324 | Nombre d'établissements |
| Value added.............. | ... | ... | ... | ... | 1 000.1 | 3 029.0 | ... | ... | ... | ... | Valeur ajoutée |
| Number of engaged (Last week in XII.1939 and 12–18.XI.1945)........ | 382.9 | 534.7 | 59.4 | 62.3 | 309.0 | 451.3 | 4.0 | 7.6 | 10.5 | 13.5 | Nombre de personnes occupées (dernière semaine de XII.1939 et 12–18.XI.1945) |
| Wages and salaries paid..... | 557.8 | 1 111.4 | 111.5 | 141.2 | 418.5 | 912.4 | 5.0 | 14.6 | 22.8 | 43.2 | Traitements et salaires payés |
| Capacity of installed power equipment (31.XII.1939)............. | . | | 163.3 | | 657.3 | ... | 0.3 | ... | 836.2 | ... | Puissance installée (31.XII.1939) |
| Distribution in percent of number of engaged....... | 100.0 | 100.0 | 15.5 | 11.6 | 80.7 | 84.4 | 1.0 | 1.4 | 2.8 | 2.6 | Distribution en pourcentage du nombre de personnes occupées |

[1] Excludes repair and similar units serving industrial establishments
[2] Road building only.

[1] Non compris les ateliers de réparation et unités analogues travaillant pour des établissements industriels.
[2] Construction de routes seulement.

## B. The Major Groups of Mining — Les classes de la branche Industries extractives

| Item of data | 1939 | | | | | 1944 | | | | | Rubrique |
|---|---|---|---|---|---|---|---|---|---|---|---|
| | All mining Toutes industries extractives | Coal mining Extraction du charbon | Metal mining Extraction des minerais métalliques | Crude petroleum and natural gas Pétrole brut et gaz naturel | Other mining Divers | All mining Toutes industries extractives | Coal mining Extraction du charbon | Metal mining Extraction des minerais métalliques | Crude petroleum and natural gas Pétrole brut et gaz naturel | Other mining Divers | |
| ISIC | 1 | 11 | 12 | 13 | 14–19 | 1 | 11 | 12 | 13 | 14–19 | CITI |
| _a. Absolute Figures — Chiffres absolus_ | | | | | | | | | | | |
| Number of establishments. | 281 | 7 | 189 | 27 | 58 | 368 | 3 | 141 | 25 | 199 | Nombre d'établissements |
| Value added.......... | ... | 11.8 | ... | 70.7 | 5.6 | ... | 18.0 | ... | 71.1 | 20.3 | Valeur ajoutée |
| Number of engaged (Last week in XII.1939 and 12–18.XI.1945) | 59.4 | 2.9 | 44.6 | 8.4 | 3.5 | 62.3 | 3.5 | 43.3 | 8.0 | 7.5 | Nombre de personnes occupées (dernière semaine de XII.1939 et 12–18.XI.1945) |
| Wages and salaries paid.............. | 111.5 | 5.6 | 76.9 | 26.6 | 2.4 | 141.2 | 9.9 | 83.5 | 41.0 | 6.8 | Traitements et salaires payés |
| Capacity of installed power equipment (31.XII.1939)......... | 163.3 | 1.7 | 121.4 | 38.7 | 1.5 | ... | ... | ... | ... | ... | Puissance installée (31.XII.1939) |
| _b. Structure_ | | | | | | | | | | | |
| Distribution in percent of number of engaged.......... | 100.0 | 4.8 | 75.1 | 14.2 | 5.9 | 100.0 | 5.6 | 69.5 | 12.8 | 12.1 | Distribution en pourcentage du nombre de personnes occupées |
| Value added per person engaged............. | ... | 4.1 | ... | 8.4 | 1.6 | ... | 5.1 | ... | 8.9 | 2.7 | Valeur ajoutée par personne occupée |
| Value added per unit of wages and salaries............. | ... | 2.11 | ... | 2.66 | 2.33 | ... | 1.82 | ... | 1.73 | 2.98 | Valeur ajoutée par unité de traitements et salaires |
| Capacity of installed power equipment per person engaged...... | 2.75 | 0.59 | 2.72 | 4.61 | 0.43 | ... | ... | ... | ... | ... | Puissance installée par personne occupée |

## C. The Major Groups of Manufacturing — Les classes de la branche Industries manufacturières

| Year and item of data | Manufacturing[1] Industries manufacturières[1] | Food, beverages and tobacco Industries alimentaires, boissons, tabac | Textiles | Clothing, footwear and made-up textiles Articles d'habillement, chaussures et ouvrages en tissu | Wood products and furniture Bois et meubles | Paper and paper products Papier et ouvrages en papier | Printing and publishing Imprimerie et édition | Leather and leather products except wearing apparel Cuir et articles en cuir, à l'exclusion des articles d'habillement | Rubber products Ouvrages en caoutchouc | Chemicals and chemical, petroleum and coal products Produits chimiques et dérivés du pétrole et du charbon | Non-metallic mineral products Produits minéraux non métalliques | Basic metals Métallurgie de base | Metal products[1] Ouvrages en métaux[1] | Other manufacturing Autres industries manufacturières | Année et rubrique |
|---|---|---|---|---|---|---|---|---|---|---|---|---|---|---|---|
| ISIC | 2–3 | 20–22 | 23 | 24 | 25–26 | 27 | 28 | 29 | 30 | 31–32 | 33 | 34 | 35–38 | 39 | CITI |
| _a. Absolute Figures — Chiffres absolus_ | | | | | | | | | | | | | | | |
| **1939** | | | | | | | | | | | | | | | **1939** |
| Number of establishments. | 12 796 | 8 648 | 1 060 | 828 | 394 | 73 | 308 | 174 | 21 | 388 | 236 | 210 | 389 | 67 | Nombre d'établissements |
| Value added.......... | 1 000.1 | 300.0 | 216.4 | 36.0 | 21.5 | 19.7 | 23.6 | 8.6 | 17.6 | 130.2 | 33.0 | 131.3 | 55.7 | 6.5 | Valeur ajoutée |
| Number of engaged (Last week in XII.1939). | 309.0 | 80.2 | 84.1 | 17.9 | 12.3 | 5.0 | 8.0 | 3.1 | 3.0 | 26.1 | 10.3 | 25.4 | 31.1 | 2.5 | Nombre de personnes occupées (dernière semaine de XII.1939) |
| Wages and salaries paid.............. | 418.5 | 74.0 | 108.1 | 16.8 | 11.1 | 7.4 | 15.6 | 3.7 | 5.2 | 59.0 | 14.4 | 51.0 | 48.7 | 3.5 | Traitements et salaires payés |
| Capacity of installed power equipment (31.XII.1939).......... | 657.3 | 200.3 | 127.3 | 3.8 | 14.5 | 51.7 | 4.0 | 4.5 | 11.1 | 53.1 | 10.7 | 160.1 | 14.8 | 1.4 | Puissance installée (31.XII.1939) |
| **1944** | | | | | | | | | | | | | | | **1944** |
| Number of establishments. | 29 581 | 15 178 | 2 013 | 3 867 | 1 749 | 154 | 778 | 727 | 313 | 725 | 1 062 | 264 | 2 276 | 475 | Nombre d'établissements |
| Value added.......... | 3 029.0 | 835.0 | 740.9 | 152.3 | 100.1 | 54.8 | 47.5 | 32.7 | 37.3 | 463.3 | 113.9 | 318.3 | 72.3 | 60.6 | Valeur ajoutée |
| Number of engaged (12–18.XI.1945)...... | 451.3 | 131.0 | 115.7 | 32.5 | 28.7 | 7.0 | 11.0 | 5.9 | 5.0 | 31.3 | 22.0 | 28.4 | 24.8 | 8.0 | Nombre de personnes occupées (12–18.XI.1945) |
| Wages and salaries paid.............. | 912.4 | 215.9 | 227.5 | 60.8 | 47.4 | 16.1 | 27.1 | 11.3 | 14.0 | 107.7 | 41.5 | 73.8 | 52.2 | 17.1 | Traitements et salaires payés |

519

## C. The Major Groups of Manufacturing (continued) — Les classes de la branche Industries manufacturières (suite)

| Year and item of data | Manufacturing[1] Industries manufacturières[1] | Food, beverages and tobacco Industries alimentaires, boissons, tabac | Textiles | Clothing, footwear and made-up textiles Articles d'habillement, chaussures et ouvrages en tissu | Wood products and furniture Bois et meubles | Paper and paper products Papier et ouvrages en papier | Printing and publishing Imprimerie et édition | Leather and leather products except wearing apparel Cuir et articles en cuir, à l'exclusion des articles d'habillement | Rubber products Ouvrages en caoutchouc | Chemicals and chemical, petroleum and coal products Produits chimiques et dérivés du pétrole et du charbon | Non-metallic mineral products Produits minéraux non métalliques | Basic metals Métallurgie de base | Metal products[1] Ouvrages en métaux[1] | Other manufacturing Autres industries manufacturières | Année et rubrique |
|---|---|---|---|---|---|---|---|---|---|---|---|---|---|---|---|
| ISIC | 2-3 | 20-22 | 23 | 24 | 25-26 | 27 | 28 | 29 | 30 | 31-32 | 33 | 34 | 35-38 | 39 | CITI |
| | | | | | | | _b. Structure_ | | | | | | | | | |
| **1939** Distribution in percent of: | | | | | | | | | | | | | | | **1939** Distribution en pourcentage: |
| Value added........ | 100.0 | 29.9 | 21.7 | 3.6 | 2.1 | 2.0 | 2.4 | 0.8 | 1.8 | 13.0 | 3.3 | 13.1 | 5.6 | 0.7 | Valeur ajoutée |
| Number of engaged.. | 100.0 | 25.9 | 27.2 | 5.8 | 4.0 | 1.6 | 2.6 | 1.0 | 1.0 | 8.4 | 3.4 | 8.2 | 10.0 | 0.9 | Nombre de personnes occupées |
| Value added per person engaged............ | 3.2 | 3.7 | 2.6 | 2.0 | 1.7 | 3.9 | 3.0 | 2.8 | 5.9 | 5.0 | 3.2 | 5.2 | 1.8 | 2.6 | Valeur ajoutée par personne occupée |
| Value added per unit of wages and salaries............ | 2.39 | 4.05 | 2.00 | 2.14 | 1.94 | 2.66 | 1.51 | 2.32 | 3.38 | 2.21 | 2.29 | 2.57 | 1.14 | 1.86 | Valeur ajoutée par unité de traitements et salaires |
| Capacity of installed power equipment per person engaged...... | 2.13 | 2.50 | 1.51 | 0.21 | 1.18 | 10.34 | 0.50 | 1.45 | 3.70 | 2.03 | 1.04 | 6.30 | 0.48 | 0.56 | Puissance installée par personne occupée |
| **1944** Distribution in percent of: | | | | | | | | | | | | | | | **1944** Distribution en pourcentage: |
| Value added........ | 100.0 | 27.5 | 24.5 | 5.0 | 3.3 | 1.8 | 1.6 | 1.1 | 1.2 | 15.3 | 3.8 | 10.5 | 2.3 | 2.1 | Valeur ajoutée |
| Number of engaged.. | 100.0 | 29.0 | 25.6 | 7.2 | 6.4 | 1.5 | 2.5 | 1.3 | 1.1 | 6.9 | 4.9 | 6.3 | 5.5 | 1.8 | Nombre de personnes occupées |
| Value added per person engaged............ | 6.7 | 6.4 | 6.4 | 4.7 | 3.5 | 7.8 | 4.3 | 5.5 | 7.5 | 14.8 | 5.2 | 11.2 | 2.9 | 7.6 | Valeur ajoutée par personne occupée |
| Value added per unit of wages and salaries............ | 3.32 | 3.87 | 3.26 | 2.50 | 2.11 | 3.40 | 1.75 | 2.89 | 2.66 | 4.30 | 2.74 | 4.31 | 1.38 | 3.54 | Valeur ajoutée par unité de traitements et salaires |

[1] Excludes repairs and similar units serving industrial establishments.

[1] Non compris les ateliers de réparation et unités analogues travaillant pour des établissements industriels.

## 5. THE CHARACTERISTICS OF ALL INDUSTRIAL ESTABLISHMENTS
### CARACTERISTIQUES DE TOUS LES ETABLISSEMENTS INDUSTRIELS
### 1950, 1955

Number of establishments in units; value added and wages and salaries in million Pesos; number of engaged and operatives in thousands; value added per person engaged in thousand Pesos.

Nombre d'établissements en unités; valeur ajoutée et traitements et salaires en millions de pesos; nombre de personnes occupées et d'ouvriers en milliers; valeur ajoutée par personne occupée en milliers de pesos.

### A. The Divisions of Industrial Activity — Les branches de l'activité industrielle

| Year and item of data | All industrial activity Toutes industries | Mining[3] Industries extractives[3] | Manufacturing[4] Industries manufacturières[4] | Construction Bâtiment et travaux publics | Electricity and gas Electricité et gaz | Année et rubrique |
|---|---|---|---|---|---|---|
| ISIC | 1-4,511-512 | 1 | 2-3 | 4 | 511-512 | CITI |
| | a. Absolute Figures — Chiffres absolus | | | | | |
| **1950** | | | | | | 1950 |
| Number of establishments... | 73 287 | 783 | 71 311 | 279 | 914 | Nombre d'établissements |
| Value added...... | 10 582.5 | 909.6 [1] | 8 793.8 [2] | 510.3 | 368.8 | Valeur ajoutée |
| Number of engaged...... | 784.6 | 71.7 | 631.6 | 64.1 | 17.2 | Nombre de personnes occupées |
| Wages and salaries. | 3 426.8 | 399.0 | 2 721.2 | 200.6 | 106.0 | Traitements et salaires |
| **1955** | | | | | | 1955 |
| Number of establishments... | 74 866 | 764 | 70 755 | 1 214 | 2 133 | Nombre d'établissements |
| Value added...... | 32 573.5 | 1 621.7 | 24 798.4 | 5 389.6 | 763.8 | Valeur ajoutée |
| Number of engaged...... | 2 138.9 | 76.3 | 1 478.0 | 554.8 | 29.8 | Nombre de personnes occupées |
| Wages and salaries. | 10 864.3 | 504.8 | 8 045.5 | 2 026.4 | 287.6 | Traitements et salaires |
| Operatives: Number......... | 1 734.4 | 68.4 | 1 122.5 | 521.4 | 22.1 | Ouvriers: Nombre |
| Wages and salaries......... | 6 937.3 | 394.9 | 4 749.1 | 1 590.7 | 202.6 | Traitements et salaires |

| Year and item of data | All industrial activity Toutes industries | Mining[3] Industries extractives[3] | Manufacturing[4] Industries manufacturières[4] | Construction Bâtiment et travaux publics | Electricity and gas Electricité et gaz | Année et rubrique |
|---|---|---|---|---|---|---|
| ISIC | 1-4,511-512 | 1 | 2-3 | 4 | 511-512 | CITI |
| | b. Structure | | | | | |
| **1950** Distribution in percent of: | | | | | | 1950 Distribution en pourcentage: |
| Value added..... | 100.0 | 8.5 | 83.1 | 4.9 | 3.5 | Valeur ajoutée |
| Number of engaged......... | 100.0 | 9.1 | 80.5 | 8.2 | 2.2 | Nombre de personnes occupées |
| Value added per person engaged.. | 13.5 | ... | ... | 8.0 | 21.4 | Valeur ajoutée par personne occupée |
| Value added per unit of wages and salaries..... | 3.09 | ... | ... | 2.54 | 3.48 | Valeur ajoutée par unité de traitements et salaires |
| **1955** Distribution in percent of: | | | | | | 1955 Distribution en pourcentage: |
| Value added..... | 100.0 | 4.9 | 76.2 | 16.5 | 2.4 | Valeur ajoutée |
| Number of engaged......... | 100.0 | 3.5 | 69.1 | 26.0 | 1.4 | Nombre de personnes occupées |
| Value added per person engaged.. | 15.2 | 21.2 | 16.8 | 9.7 | 25.6 | Valeur ajoutée par personne occupée |
| Operatives as a percent of engaged......... | 81.1 | 89.6 | 75.9 | 94.0 | 74.2 | Ouvriers en pourcentage des personnes occupées |
| Value added per unit of wages and salaries..... | 3.00 | 3.21 | 3.08 | 2.66 | 2.66 | Valeur ajoutée par unité de traitements et salaires |

[1] Excludes Metal mining (ISIC group 12).
[2] Includes Metal mining (ISIC group 12).
[3] Includes petroleum refining in 1950.
[4] Excludes petroleum refining in 1950.

[1] Non compris l'Extraction des minerais métalliques (CITI classe 12).
[2] Y compris l'Extraction des minerais métalliques (CITI classe 12).
[3] Y compris le raffinage du pétrole en 1950.
[4] Non compris le raffinage du pétrole en 1950.

## B. The Major Groups of Mining — Les classes de la branche Industries extractives

| Year and item of data | All mining Toutes industries extractives | Coal mining Extraction du charbon | Metal mining Extraction des minerais métalliques | Crude petroleum and natural gas[1] Pétrole brut et gaz naturel[1] | Other mining Divers | Année et rubrique | Year and item of data | All mining Toutes industries extractives | Coal mining Extraction du charbon | Metal mining Extraction des minerais métalliques | Crude petroleum and natural gas[1] Pétrole brut et gaz naturel[1] | Other mining Divers | Année et rubrique |
|---|---|---|---|---|---|---|---|---|---|---|---|---|---|
| ISIC | 1 | 11 | 12 | 13 | 14-19 | CITI | ISIC | 1 | 11 | 12 | 13 | 14-19 | CITI |
| | a. Absolute Figures — Chiffres absolus | | | | | | | b. Structure | | | | | |
| **1950** Number of establishments... | 783 | 9 | 367 | 48 | 359 | **1950** Nombre d'établissements | **1950** Distribution in percent of: number of engaged........ | | | | | | **1950** Distribution en pourcentage du nombre de personnes occupées |
| Value added...... | 909.6[2] | 41.8 | ... | 828.5 | 39.3 | Valeur ajoutée | | 100.0 | 5.1 | 39.2 | 48.4 | 7.3 | |
| Number of engaged (Average of two weeks)........ | 71.7 | 3.7 | 28.1 | 34.7 | 5.2 | Nombre de personnes occupées (moyenne de deux semaines) | Value added per person occupied.. | ... | 11.3 | ... | 23.9 | 7.6 | Valeur ajoutée par personne occupée |
| Wages and salaries. | 399.0 | 19.4 | 109.8 | 255.5 | 14.3 | Traitements et salaires | Value added per unit of wages and salaries..... | ... | 2.15 | ... | 3.24 | 2.75 | Valeur ajoutée par unité de traitements et salaires |
| **1955** Number of establishments... | 764 | 12 | 320 | 46 | 386 | **1955** Nombre d'établissements | **1955** Distribution in percent of: Value added..... | 100.0 | 5.8 | 55.6 | 24.2 | 14.4 | **1955** Distribution en pourcentage: Valeur ajoutée |
| Value added...... | 1 621.7 | 94.6 | 902.6 | 392.3 | 232.2 | Valeur ajoutée | Number of engaged........ | 100.0 | 9.8 | 43.2 | 10.1 | 36.9 | Nombre de personnes occupées |
| Number of engaged........ | 76.3 | 7.5 | 33.0 | 7.7 | 28.1 | Nombre de personnes occupées | Value added per person engaged.. | 21.2 | 12.6 | 27.4 | 50.9 | 8.3 | Valeur ajoutée par personne occupée |
| Wages and salaries. | 504.8 | 44.2 | 252.2 | 100.1 | 108.3 | Traitements et salaires | Operatives as a percent of engaged........ | 89.6 | 86.7 | 88.2 | 96.1 | 90.4 | Ouvriers en pourcentage des personnes occupées |
| Operatives: Number........ | 68.4 | 6.5 | 29.1 | 7.4 | 25.4 | Ouvriers: Nombre | Value added per unit of wages and salaries..... | 3.21 | 2.14 | 3.58 | 3.92 | 2.14 | Valeur ajoutée par unité de traitements et salaires |
| Wages and salaries........ | 394.9 | 29.3 | 186.8 | 92.9 | 85.9 | Traitements et salaires | | | | | | | |

[1] Includes petroleum refining in 1950.
[2] Excludes Metal mining (ISIC major group 12).

[1] Y compris le raffinage du pétrole en 1950.
[2] Non compris l'Extraction des minerais métalliques (CITI classe 12).

## C. The Major Groups of Manufacturing — Les classes de la branche Industries manufacturières

| Year and item of data | Manufacturing [1] / Industries manufacturières [1] | Food, beverages and tobacco / Industries alimentaires, boissons, tabac | Textiles | Clothing, footwear and made-up textiles / Articles d'habillement, chaussures et ouvrages en tissu | Wood products and furniture / Bois et meubles | Paper and paper products / Papier et ouvrages en papier | Printing and publishing / Imprimerie et édition | Leather and leather products except wearing apparel / Cuir et articles en cuir, à l'exclusion des articles d'habillement | Rubber products / Ouvrages en caoutchouc | Chemicals and chemical, petroleum and coal products [1] / Produits chimiques et dérivés du pétrole et du charbon [1] | Non-metallic mineral products / Produits minéraux non métalliques | Basic metals / Métallurgie de base | Metal products / Ouvrages en métaux | Other manufacturing / Autres industries manufacturières | Année et rubrique |
|---|---|---|---|---|---|---|---|---|---|---|---|---|---|---|---|
| ISIC | 2–3 | 20–22 | 23 | 24 | 25–26 | 27 | 28 | 29 | 30 | 31–32 | 33 | 34 | 35–38 | 39 | CITI |
| *a. Absolute Figures — Chiffres absolus* | | | | | | | | | | | | | | | |
| **1950** | | | | | | | | | | | | | | | **1950** |
| Number of establishments. | 71 311 | 29 553 | 4 432 | 11 236 | 5 618 | 262 | 1 405 | 1 590 | 452 | 1 729 | 3 341 | 243 | 9 046 | 2 404 | Nombre d'établissements |
| Value added.......... | 8 793.8[2] | 2 594.6 | 1 175.5 | 369.1 | 417.3 | 169.9 | 172.6 | 78.2 | 182.7 | 815.3 | 369.9 | 1 545.7[2] | 826.5 | 76.5 | Valeur ajoutée |
| | | | | | | | | | | | | | | | Nombre de personnes occupées |
| Number of engaged.... | 631.6 | 166.7 | 137.7 | 51.3 | 44.5 | 10.3 | 16.4 | 8.3 | 5.6 | 36.2 | 34.5 | 47.3 | 63.6 | 9.2 | |
| Wages and salaries..... | 2 721.2 | 700.7 | 529.5 | 189.1 | 162.2 | 53.6 | 85.1 | 31.4 | 37.6 | 228.0 | 130.6 | 248.8 | 288.5 | 36.1 | Traitements et salaires |
| **1955** | | | | | | | | | | | | | | | **1955** |
| Number of establishments. | 70 755 | 28 604 | 4 302 | 11 078 | 4 688 | 398 | 2 175 | 1 398 | 560 | 1 972 | 2 527 | 401 | 10 280 | 2 372 | Nombre d'établissements |
| Value added.......... | 24 798.4 | 5 344.8 | 3 208.1 | 1 086.8 | 777.9 | 625.7 | 520.9 | 291.2 | 989.2 | 3 574.2 | 801.7 | 3 658.3 | 3 535.2 | 384.4 | Valeur ajoutée |
| | | | | | | | | | | | | | | | Nombre de personnes occupées |
| Number of engaged.... | 1 478.0 | 337.4 | 283.7 | 115.6 | 83.5 | 34.4 | 45.0 | 20.0 | 50.4 | 137.2 | 58.3 | 80.4 | 203.8 | 28.3 | |
| Wages and salaries..... | 8 045.5 | 1 571.4 | 1 303.0 | 500.2 | 336.2 | 193.2 | 254.4 | 97.8 | 299.3 | 945.6 | 282.0 | 1 037.2 | 1 009.5 | 215.7 | Traitements et salaires |
| Operatives: | | | | | | | | | | | | | | | Ouvriers: |
| Number............. | 1 122.5 | 246.9 | 249.4 | 84.6 | 65.2 | 28.3 | 32.6 | 14.7 | 29.4 | 97.7 | 44.0 | 63.7 | 146.2 | 19.8 | Nombre |
| Wages and salaries... | 4 749.1 | 907.7 | 993.9 | 306.8 | 240.4 | 125.0 | 134.5 | 52.3 | 136.8 | 443.0 | 180.9 | 653.9 | 505.7 | 68.2 | Traitements et salaires |
| *b. Structure* | | | | | | | | | | | | | | | |
| **1950** | | | | | | | | | | | | | | | **1950** |
| Distribution in percent of: | | | | | | | | | | | | | | | Distribution en pourcentage: |
| Value added........ | 100.0 | 29.5 | 13.3 | 4.2 | 4.8 | 1.9 | 2.0 | 0.8 | 2.1 | 9.3 | 4.2 | 17.6 | 9.4 | 0.9 | Valeur ajoutée |
| | | | | | | | | | | | | | | | Nombre de personnes occupées |
| Number of engaged... | 100.0 | 26.3 | 21.8 | 8.2 | 7.0 | 1.6 | 2.6 | 1.4 | 0.8 | 5.8 | 5.4 | 7.5 | 10.1 | 1.5 | |
| Value added per person engaged...... | ... | 15.6 | 8.5 | 7.2 | 9.4 | 16.5 | 10.5 | 9.4 | 32.6 | 22.5 | 10.7 | ... | 13.0 | 8.3 | Valeur ajoutée par personne occupée |
| Value added per unit of wages and salaries............. | ... | 3.70 | 2.22 | 1.95 | 2.57 | 3.17 | 2.03 | 2.49 | 4.86 | 3.58 | 2.83 | ... | 2.86 | 2.12 | Valeur ajoutée par unité de traitements et salaires |
| **1955** | | | | | | | | | | | | | | | **1955** |
| Distribution in percent of: | | | | | | | | | | | | | | | Distribution en pourcentage: |
| Value added........ | 100.0 | 21.5 | 12.9 | 4.4 | 3.2 | 2.5 | 2.1 | 1.2 | 3.9 | 14.5 | 3.2 | 14.7 | 14.3 | 1.6 | Valeur ajoutée |
| | | | | | | | | | | | | | | | Nombre de personnes occupées |
| Number of engaged... | 100.0 | 22.8 | 19.2 | 7.8 | 5.6 | 2.4 | 3.0 | 1.4 | 3.4 | 9.3 | 3.9 | 5.4 | 13.8 | 2.0 | |
| Value added per person engaged...... | 16.8 | 15.8 | 11.3 | 9.4 | 9.3 | 18.2 | 11.6 | 14.6 | 19.6 | 26.0 | 13.8 | 45.5 | 17.3 | 13.6 | Valeur ajoutée par personne occupée |
| Operatives as a percent of engaged........ | 75.9 | 73.2 | 87.9 | 73.2 | 78.1 | 82.3 | 72.4 | 73.5 | 58.3 | 71.2 | 75.5 | 79.2 | 71.7 | 70.0 | Ouvriers en pourcentage des personnes occupées |
| Value added per unit of wages and salaries............. | 3.08 | 3.40 | 2.46 | 2.17 | 2.31 | 3.24 | 2.05 | 2.98 | 3.30 | 3.78 | 2.84 | 3.53 | 3.50 | 1.78 | Valeur ajoutée par unité de traitements et salaires |

[1] Excludes petroleum refining in 1950.
[2] Includes Metal mining (ISIC major group 12).

[1] Non compris le raffinage du pétrole en 1950.
[2] Y compris l'Extraction des minerais métalliques (CITI classe 12).

# MOROCCO — MAROC

## Gross Domestic Product

Table 1 gives estimates of gross domestic production obtained from replies by the Service central des statistiques, Division de la coordination économique et du plan, Ministère de l'économie nationale, Rabat, to the United Nations national accounts questionnaire. The estimates for gross domestic production differ in certain respects from that for the gross domestic product in the United Nations system of national accounts, mainly in that wages and salaries and depreciation for general government and non-profit institutions are excluded.

## Index Numbers of Industrial Production

The index numbers shown in Table 2 are derived from two series of index numbers calculated by the Service central des statistiques, and published in *Annuaire statistique du Maroc* and in *La situation économique du Maroc*. The indexes for the years prior to 1958 are obtained from the series for which the weighting base is 1952 and which related to the "Sud du Maroc". The indexes for the years 1958-1961 are obtained from the new series for which the weighting base is 1958 and which covers the whole of Morocco. The two series of index numbers have been linked to one another at 1958.

Both series relate to mining, manufacturing and electricity, but the coverage of establishments differs. The coverage of the series based on 1952 is, generally speaking, limited to those establishments employing more than 10 persons and equipped with machinery operated by motors of a capacity of more than a couple of horsepower. Those establishments for which, for practical reasons, it was not possible to obtain adequate statistics were also omitted from the series. The result is that the indexes covered about 90 percent of all establishments which fulfilled the size and equipment criteria. The main exclusions due to the forementioned reasons were handicrafts of traditional type, establishments entirely engaged on repair work, quarrying and extraction of materials of construction, tailoring, furs and fur products, wood and wooden furniture, jewelry, brushes, games and toys and certain miscellaneous industries.

The coverage of the new series was more extensive than the old series. The whole of Morocco was included and the coverage of establishments engaged in industrial activities greatly extended.

The index numbers of the first series were computed as a base-weighted arithmetic average of 82 quantity relatives of output for individual products and are based on

## Production intérieure brute

Le tableau 1 contient des estimations de la production intérieure brute fournies par le Service central des statistiques, Division de la coordination économique et du plan, Ministère de l'économie nationale, Rabat, en réponse au questionnaire de l'ONU sur la comptabilité nationale. Les estimations de la production intérieure brute diffèrent à certains égards de celles du produit intérieur brut tel qu'il est défini dans le système de comptabilité nationale de l'ONU, notamment en ce sens que les traitements et salaires et l'amortissement des organismes d'Etat et des organisations à but non lucratif en sont exclus.

## Indices de la production industrielle

Les indices du tableau 2 proviennent de deux séries d'indices établies par le Service central des statistiques et publiées dans *l'Annuaire statistique du Maroc* et *La situation économique du Maroc*. Les indices des années antérieures à 1958 ont été obtenus à partir des séries ayant comme année de pondération de base 1952 et portant sur le "Sud du Maroc". Les indices de 1958-1961 ont été obtenus à partir des nouvelles séries ayant pour année de pondération de base 1958 et portant sur l'ensemble du Maroc. Les deux séries d'indices ont été raccordées l'une à l'autre au niveau de 1958.

Les deux séries concernent les industries extractives, manufacturières et productrices d'électricité, mais elles ne portent pas sur le même ensemble d'établissements. Les séries ayant 1952 comme année de base ne portent en général que sur les établissements occupant plus de 10 personnes et utilisant un moteur d'une puissance supérieure à quelques chevaux-vapeur. Les établissements pour lesquels on n'a pu, pour des raisons d'ordre pratique, obtenir de statistiques satisfaisantes ont été également exclus du champ de l'indice. En conséquence, les indices portent sur 90 p. 100 environ des établissements remplissant les conditions requises de taille et d'équipement. Les unités exclues pour les raisons susmentionnées sont principalement les unités artisanales de type traditionnel, les établissements s'occupant des travaux de réparation, de l'extraction des matériaux de construction, du travail des étoffes, de la pelleterie et des articles en fourrure, du bois et de l'ameublement, de la bijouterie, de la brosserie, des jeux et jouets, ainsi que les établissements de certaines autres industries diverses.

Les nouvelles séries ont un champ plus étendu que les anciennes. Elles concernent l'ensemble du Maroc et portent sur un ensemble plus vaste d'établissements exerçant des activités industrielles.

Les indices de la première série sont les moyennes arithmétiques à pondération fixe de 82 rapports quantitatifs fondés sur la production des différentes marchan-

the year 1952. The weights utilized in combining the relatives into indexes for 8 broader categories of industrial activities are the value added during 1952 by the respective industries covered by the index. For further details reference is made to *Bulletin mensuel de statistique, Supplément trimestriel No. 2 Août 1958,* issued by the Service central des statistiques.

The later series of index numbers for 1958-1961 were also computed as base-weighted arithmetic averages starting from 88 quantity relatives of output for individual products based on the year 1958. The weights utilized for combining the relatives into indexes for 11 broader categories of industrial activity were the value added during 1958 by the respective industries covered by the index. For further details on this subject reference is made to *La situation économique du Maroc en 1960* or *en 1961* issued by the Service central des statistiques.

### Index Numbers of Employment in Mining

The index numbers of employment in mining shown in Table 3 were computed from absolute figures of the annual average number of operatives employed in the "Zone Sud" for the mining division as a whole, and for selected major groups. The data were obtained from the *Annuaire statistique du Maroc, 1952-1957* published by the Service central des statistiques.

### Value Added by Industrial Enterprises

The data for value added shown in Table 4 are based on estimates prepared and published by the Service central des statistiques in *Bulletin mensuel de statistique, Supplément trimestriel No. 2 Août 1958* and in a mimeographed study entitled *Tableau économique du Maroc 1958* and *Notes au sujet du tableau.* The coverage of data for 1952 is the same as was mentioned in the previous paragraph on index numbers of industrial production. In fact, these figures furnished the basis of the weights for the series of indexes. The coverage of the 1958 data is probably complete since the data agree with the corresponding figures for gross domestic production. In both cases the figures of value added shown in Table 4 are defined in the same way as the contribution to the gross domestic product.

dises et ont pour année de base 1952. Pour combiner ces rapports en indices relatifs à huit grandes catégories de l'activité industrielle, on a utilisé comme base de pondération la valeur ajoutée en 1952 par les diverses industries sur lesquelles porte l'indice. Pour plus de détails, voir le *Bulletin mensuel de statistique, Supplément trimestriel No. 2, août 1958,* publié par le Service central des statistiques.

Les séries d'indices relatives à 1958-1961 sont également des moyennes arithmétiques à pondération fixe de 88 rapports quantitatifs fondés sur la production des différentes marchandises et ont pour année de base 1958. Les coefficients de pondération adoptés pour combiner ces rapports en indices relatifs à 11 grandes catégories de l'activité industrielle sont les valeurs ajoutées en 1958 par les diverses industries sur lesquelles porte l'indice. Pour plus de détails, voir *La situation économique du Maroc en 1960* ou *en 1961,* publié par le Service central des statistiques.

### Indices de l'emploi dans les industries extractives

Les indices du tableau 3, relatifs à l'emploi, dans les industries extractives, ont été établis à partir de chiffres absolus indiquant la moyenne annuelle du nombre d'ouvriers occupés dans la "Zone sud" pour l'ensemble des industries extractives et pour quelques classes de cette branche. Les données ont été tirées de l'*Annuaire statistique du Maroc, 1952-1957,* publié par le Service central des statistiques.

### Valeur ajoutée par les entreprises industrielles

Les données sur la valeur ajoutée, reproduites au tableau 4, sont fondées sur des estimations établies par le Service central des statistiques et publiées par ce Service dans le *Bulletin mensuel de statistique, Supplément trimestriel No 2, août 1958* et dans une étude miméographiée intitulée *Tableau économique du Maroc, 1958,* et *Notes au sujet du tableau.* Le champ des données de 1952 est le même que pour les indices de la production industrielle (voir plus haut). En fait, ces chiffres ont servi de base de pondération pour les séries d'indices. Le champ des données de 1958 englobe probablement l'ensemble des activités industrielles car les données coïncident avec les chiffres correspondants de la production intérieure brute. Dans les deux cas, la valeur ajoutée indiquée au tableau 4 est définie comme étant la contribution à la formation de la production intérieure brute.

# MOROCCO

## 1. THE GROSS DOMESTIC PRODUCTION AT MARKET PRICES ACCORDING TO ORIGIN
## ORIGINE PAR SECTEUR D'ACTIVITE DE LA PRODUCTION INTERIEURE BRUTE AUX PRIX DU MARCHE

Thousand million Moroccan Francs          Millards de francs marocains

| Item of data and year / Rubrique et année | Total | Agricultural sector / Secteur agricole | Industrial Sector — Secteur industriel | | | | | Transportation and communication / Transports et communications | Other sectors / Autres secteurs |
|---|---|---|---|---|---|---|---|---|---|
| | | | Total | Mining / Industries extractives | Manufacturing / Industries manufacturières | Construction / Bâtiment et travaux publics | Electricity, gas and water / Electricité, gaz et eau | | |
| ISIC — CITI | 0–9 | 0 | 1–5 | 1 | 2–3 | 4 | 5 | 7 | 6, 8–9 |
| At Prices of 1958 — Aux prix de 1958 | | | | | | | | | |
| Absolute figures — Chiffres absolus | | | | | | | | | |
| 1951 | 635 | 199 | 173 | 28 | 74 | 60 | 11 | 103 | 160 |
| 1952 | 672 | 200 | 194 | 29 | 79 | 75 | 11 | 112 | 166 |
| 1953 | 727 | 228 | 204 | 30 | 86 | 75 | 13 | 118 | 177 |
| 1954 | 757 | 247 | 202 | 32 | 88 | 67 | 15 | 125 | 183 |
| 1955 | 728 | 216 | 200 | 34 | 88 | 63 | 15 | 131 | 181 |
| 1956 | 714 | 224 | 191 | 34 | 91 | 49 | 17 | 133 | 166 |
| 1957 | 658 | 189 | 184 | 37 | 93 | 37 | 17 | 138 | 147 |
| 1958 | 739 | 247 | 186 | 39 | 97 | 33 | 17 | 140 | 166 |
| 1959 | 720 | 230 | 192 | 42 | 98 | 35 | 17 | 142 | 156 |
| 1960 | 746 | 227 | 201 | 45 | 105 | 34 | 17 | 146 | 172 |
| 1961 | 716 | 191 | 211 | 46 | 110 | 37 | 18 | 148 | 166 |
| Percentage distribution according to sector— Distribution en pourcentage par secteur | | | | | | | | | |
| 1951–1960 | 100.0 | 31.1 | 27.1 | 4.9 | 12.7 | 7.4 | 2.1 | 18.2 | 23.6 |
| 1951 | 100.0 | 31.3 | 27.2 | 4.4 | 11.7 | 9.4 | 1.7 | 16.3 | 25.2 |
| 1953 | 100.0 | 31.3 | 28.1 | 4.1 | 11.9 | 10.3 | 1.8 | 16.2 | 24.4 |
| 1954 | 100.0 | 32.6 | 26.7 | 4.2 | 11.6 | 8.9 | 2.0 | 16.5 | 24.2 |
| 1958 | 100.0 | 33.4 | 25.1 | 5.3 | 13.1 | 4.4 | 2.3 | 19.0 | 22.5 |
| 1960 | 100.0 | 30.4 | 26.9 | 6.0 | 14.1 | 4.5 | 2.3 | 19.6 | 23.1 |
| Average annual rate of growth—Taux annuel moyen d'accroissement | | | | | | | | | |
| 1951–1960 | 1.8 | 1.5 | 1.7 | 5.4 | 4.0 | −6.1 | 5.0 | 3.9 | 0.8 |
| 1951–1953 | 7.0 | 7.1 | 8.6 | 3.5 | 7.8 | 11.8 | 8.7 | 7.1 | 5.2 |
| 1954–1958 | −0.6 | — | −2.0 | 5.1 | 2.5 | −16.2 | 3.2 | 2.9 | −2.4 |
| 1958–1960 | 0.4 | −4.2 | 4.0 | 7.4 | 4.0 | 1.5 | — | 2.1 | 1.8 |

## 2. INDEX NUMBERS OF INDUSTRIAL PRODUCTION — INDICES DE LA PRODUCTION INDUSTRIELLE

### A. Selected Divisions of Industrial Activity
### Quelques branches de l'activité industrielle

| Period<br>Période | Total | Mining [1]<br>Industries extractives [1] | Manu-facturing [2]<br>Industries manu-facturières [2] | Electricity and gas<br>Electricité et gaz |
|---|---|---|---|---|
| ISIC — CITI | 1–3, 511–512 | 1 | 2–3 | 511–512 |

#### a. Indexes — Indices (1958 = 100)

| | | | | |
|---|---|---|---|---|
| 1938.......... | 30 | 23 | 36 | 14 |
| 1948.......... | 52 | 44 | 58 | 40 |
| 1949.......... | 54 | 50 | 58 | 46 |
| 1950.......... | 64 | 58 | 68 | 51 |
| 1951.......... | 76 | 74 | 78 | 64 |
| 1952.......... | 79 | 73 | 83 | 72 |
| 1953.......... | 86 | 75 | 92 | 79 |
| 1954.......... | 90 | 83 | 95 | 87 |
| 1955.......... | 94 | 88 | 98 | 93 |
| 1956.......... | 95 | 90 | 99 | 98 |
| 1957.......... | 95 | 93 | 98 | 99 |
| 1958.......... | −100− | −100− | −100− | −100− |
| 1959.......... | 100 | 107 | 95 | 99 |
| 1960.......... | 110 | 112 | 110 | 104 |
| 1961.......... | ... | ... | 115 | 109 |

#### b. Average Annual Rate of Change — Taux annuel moyen de variation

| | | | | |
|---|---|---|---|---|
| 1938–1960.... | 6.1 | 7.5 | 5.2 | 9.5 |
| 1938–1948.... | 5.7 | 6.7 | 4.9 | 11.1 |
| 1950–1960.... | 5.6 | 6.8 | 4.9 | 7.4 |
| 1948–1953.... | 10.6 | 11.3 | 9.7 | 14.6 |
| 1954–1958.... | 2.7 | 4.8 | 1.3 | 3.5 |
| 1958–1960.... | 4.9 | 5.8 | 4.9 | 2.0 |

For footnotes see end of table.

Pour les notes, voir au bas du tableau.

### B. The Major Groups of Mining
### Les classes de la branche Industries extractives

| Period<br>Période | All mining [1]<br>Toutes industries extractives [1] | Coal mining<br>Extraction du charbon | Metal mining<br>Extraction des minerais métalliques | Crude petro-leum and natural gas<br>Pétrole brut et gaz naturel | Other mining<br>Autres industries extractives |
|---|---|---|---|---|---|
| ISIC — CITI | 1 | 11 | 12 | 13 | 14–19 |

#### a. Indexes — Indices (1958 = 100)

| | | | | | |
|---|---|---|---|---|---|
| 1938....... | 23 | 28 | 18 | 4 | 23 |
| 1948....... | 44 | 57 | 36 | 17 | 51 |
| 1949....... | 50 | 67 | 45 | 24 | 58 |
| 1950....... | 58 | 72 | 55 | 53 | 61 |
| 1951....... | 74 | 77 | 76 | 102 | 74 |
| 1952....... | 73 | 90 | 92 | 136 | 62 |
| 1953....... | 75 | 111 | 88 | 138 | 66 |
| 1954....... | 83 | 95 | 87 | 158 | 79 |
| 1955....... | 88 | 92 | 92 | 138 | 84 |
| 1956....... | 90 | 94 | 93 | 131 | 87 |
| 1957....... | 93 | 102 | 99 | 101 | 88 |
| 1958....... | −100− | −100− | −100− | −100− | −100− |
| 1959....... | 107 | 91 | 100 | 127 | 113 |
| 1960....... | 112 | 81 | 102 | 124 | 118 |
| 1961....... | ... | 80 | 101 | 108 | 125 |

#### b. Average Annual Rate of Change — Taux annuel moyen de variation

| | | | | | |
|---|---|---|---|---|---|
| 1938–1960. | 7.5 | 4.9 | 8.0 | 17.2 | 7.8 |
| 1938–1948. | 6.7 | 7.4 | 7.2 | 15.6 | 8.3 |
| 1950–1960. | 6.8 | 1.2 | 6.4 | 8.9 | 6.8 |
| 1948–1953. | 11.3 | 14.3 | 19.6 | 52.2 | 5.3 |
| 1954–1958. | 4.8 | 1.3 | 3.6 | −10.8 | 6.1 |
| 1958–1960. | 5.8 | −10.0 | 1.0 | 11.4 | 8.6 |

For footnotes see end of table.

Pour les notes, voir au bas du tableau.

## C. The Major Groups of Manufacturing — Les classes de la branche Industries manufacturières

| Period<br><br>Période | Manu-facturing [2]<br>Industries manufac-turières [2] | Food, beverages and tobacco<br>Industries alimen-taires, boissons, tabac | Textiles | Clothing, footwear and made-up textiles [3]<br>Articles d'habil-lement, chaussures et ouvrages en tissu [3] | Paper and paper products<br>Papier et ouvrages en papier | Printing and publishing<br>Im-primerie et édition | Leather and leather products except wearing apparel [4]<br>Cuir et articles en cuir, à l'exclu-sion des articles d'habil-lement [4] | Rubber products and chemicals and chemical products<br>Ouvrages en caoutchouc et produits chimiques | Non-metallic mineral products<br>Produits minéraux non métal-liques | Basic metals<br>Métal-lurgie de base | Metal products [6]<br>Ouvrages en métaux [6] |
|---|---|---|---|---|---|---|---|---|---|---|---|
| ISIC — CITI | 2–3 | 20–22 | 23 | 24 | 27 | 28 | 29 | 30–31 | 33 | 34 | 35–38 |

### a. Indexes — Indices (1958 = 100)

| | | | | | | | | | | | |
|---|---|---|---|---|---|---|---|---|---|---|---|
| 1938 | 36 | 41 | 34 | 4 | ... | 81 | 18 | 28 | 29 | 35 | 15 |
| 1948 | 58 | 62 | 62 | 27 | ... | 25 | 56 | 45 | 63 | 40 | 43 |
| 1949 | 58 | 66 | 45 | 29 | ... | 37 | 42 | 46 | 68 | 52 | 45 |
| 1950 | 68 | 73 | 54 | 35 | ... | 72 | 50 | 57 | 76 | 68 | 64 |
| 1951 | 78 | 73 | 78 | 33 | 52 | 94 | 46 | 73 | 90 | 80 | 63 |
| 1952 | 83 | 77 | 83 | 37 | 54 | 65 | 83 | 74 | 105 | 94 | 73 |
| 1953 | 92 | 79 | 85 | 51 | 82 | 133 | 76 | 73 | 129 | 102 | 92 |
| 1954 | 95 | 78 | 81 | 57 | 98 | 157 | 75 | 80 | 124 | 103 | 89 |
| 1955 | 98 | 79 | 97 | 71 | 80 | 158 | 76 | 84 | 122 | 100 | 95 |
| 1956 | 99 | 92 | 78 | 64 | 86 | 152 | 72 | 84 | 116 | 101 | 85 |
| 1957 | 98 | 95 | 91 | 76 | 89 | 128 | 87 | 87 | 97 | 105 | 90 |
| 1958 | –100– | –100– | –100– | –100– | –100– | –100– | –100– | –100– | –100– | –100– | –100– |
| 1959 | 95 | 94 | 105 | 114 | 98 | 94 | 102 | 91 | 98 | 92 | 86 |
| 1960 | 110 | 107 | 119 | 147 | 121 | 96 | 99 | 102 | 113 | 101 | 106 |
| 1961 | 115 | 115 | 125 | 168 | 120 | 103 | 73 | 112 | 122 | 88 | 110 |

### b. Average Annual Rate of Change — Taux annuel moyen de variation

| | | | | | | | | | | | |
|---|---|---|---|---|---|---|---|---|---|---|---|
| 1938 – 1960 | 5.2 | 4.5 | 5.9 | 17.8 | ... | 0.8 | 18.6 | 6.1 | 6.4 | 4.9 | 21.6 |
| 1938 – 1948 | 4.9 | 4.2 | 6.2 | 21.0 | ... | –11.1 | 12.0 | 4.9 | 8.1 | 1.3 | 11.1 |
| 1950 – 1960 | 4.9 | 3.9 | 8.2 | 15.4 | ... | 2.9 | 7.1 | 6.0 | 4.1 | 4.0 | 5.2 |
| 1948 – 1953 | 9.7 | 5.0 | 6.5 | 13.6 | ... | 39.7 | 6.3 | 10.2 | 15.4 | 20.5 | 16.4 |
| 1954 – 1958 | 1.3 | 6.4 | 5.4 | 15.1 | 0.5 | –10.5 | 7.5 | 5.7 | –5.2 | –0.5 | 3.0 |
| 1958 – 1960 | 4.9 | 3.4 | 9.1 | 21.2 | 10.0 | –2.0 | –0.5 | 1.0 | 6.3 | 0.5 | 3.0 |

[1] Excludes quarrying.
[2] The indexes for the years prior to 1958 exclude establishments employing less than 10 persons and equipped with machinery operated with motors with a capacity of less than a couple of horsepower. This is besides other exclusions designated under the various major groups.
[3] Excludes tailoring.
[4] The indexes for the years prior to 1958 exclude Furs and fur products (ISIC group 292).
[5] Indexes for 1958 and subsequent years include margarine belonging to (ISIC group 209.)
[6] The indexes for the years prior to 1958 exclude establishments engaged entirely on repair work.

[1] Non compris les carrières.
[2] Les indices relatifs aux années antérieures à 1958 ne comprennent pas les établissements occupant moins de 10 personnes et utilisant des moteurs d'une puissance inférieure à quelques chevaux-vapeur. Cette réserve vient s'ajouter aux exclusions indiquées pour les différentes classes.
[3] Non compris le travail des étoffes.
[4] Les indices relatifs aux années antérieures à 1958 ne comprennent pas Pelleterie et articles en fourrure (CITI groupe 292).
[5] Les indices de 1958 et des années suivantes comprennent la fabrication de la margarine (dans CITI groupe 209).
[6] Les indices relatifs aux années antérieures à 1958 ne comprennent pas les établissements s'occupant uniquement de travaux de réparation.

## 3. INDEX NUMBERS OF MINING EMPLOYMENT — INDICES DE L'EMPLOI DANS LES INDUSTRIES EXTRACTIVES

| Period<br>Période | All mining<br>Toutes industries extractives | Coal mining<br>Extraction du charbon | Metal mining<br>Extraction des minerais métalliques | Other mining<br>Autres industries extractives |
|---|---|---|---|---|
| ISIC — CITI | 1 | 11 | 12 | 192 |

### a. Indexes — Indices (1957 = 100)

| | | | | |
|---|---|---|---|---|
| 1952 | 116 | 120 | 131 | 89 |
| 1953 | 104 | 127 | 114 | 81 |
| 1954 | 106 | 120 | 105 | 90 |
| 1955 | 96 | 100 | 100 | 88 |
| 1956 | 100 | 110 | 101 | 96 |
| 1957 | 100 | 100 | 100 | 100 |

### b. Average Annual Rate of Change — Taux annuel moyen de variation

| | | | | |
|---|---|---|---|---|
| 1952 – 1957 | –2.9 | –3.6 | –5.3 | 2.4 |
| 1954 – 1957 | –1.9 | –2.9 | –1.6 | 3.6 |

## 4. VALUE ADDED BY INDUSTRIAL ENTERPRISES — VALEUR AJOUTEE PAR LES ENTERPRISES INDUSTRIELLES
### 1952, 1958

Million Moroccan Francs.  Millions de francs marocains.

### A. The Divisions of Industrial Activity
### Les branches de l'activité industrielle

| Year and item of data | All industrial activity — Toutes industries | Mining[1] — Industries extractives[1] | Manufacturing — Industries manufacturières | Construction — Bâtiment et travaux publics | Electricity[8] — Electricité[8] | Année et rubrique |
|---|---|---|---|---|---|---|
| ISIC | 1-4, 511 | 1 | 2-3 | 4 | 511 | CITI |
| Value added (absolute figures): | | | | | | Valeur ajoutée (chiffres absolus): |
| 1952 | ... | 28 945 | 44 000 | ... | 3 100 | 1952 |
| 1958 | 186 106 | 39 569 | 97 388 | 32 404 | 16 745 | 1958 |
| Percentage Distribution: | | | | | | Distribution en pourcentage: |
| 1958 | 100.0 | 21.3 | 52.3 | 17.4 | 9.0 | 1958 |

For footnotes see end of table.
Pour les notes, voir au bas du tableau.

### B. The Major Groups of Mining
### Les classes de la branche Industries extractives

| Year and item of data | All mining — Toutes industries extractives | Coal mining — Extraction du charbon | Metal mining — Extraction des minerais métalliques | Crude petroleum and natural gas — Pétrole brut et gaz naturel | Other mining — Divers | Année et rubrique |
|---|---|---|---|---|---|---|
| ISIC | 1 | 11 | 12 | 13 | 14-19 | CITI |
| Value added (absolute figures): | | | | | | Valeur ajoutée (chiffres absolus): |
| 1952 | 28 945 | 1 865 | 11 670 | 180 | 15 230 | 1952 |
| 1958 | 39 569 | ...[8] | 17 211 | ...[8] | 22 358 | 1958 |
| Percentage Distribution: | | | | | | Distribution en pourcentage: |
| 1952 | 100.0 | 6.5 | 40.3 | 0.6 | 52.6 | 1952 |
| 1958 | 100.0 | ... | 43.5 | ... | 56.5 | 1958 |

For footnotes see end of table.
Pour les notes, voir au bas du tableau.

### C. The Major Groups of Manufacturing — Les classes de la branche Industries manufacturières

| Year and item of data | Manufacturing[2] — Industries manufacturières[2] | Food beverages and tobacco — Industries alimentaires, boissons, tabac | Textiles | Clothing, footwear and made-up textiles — Articles d'habillement, chaussures et ouvrages en tissu | Wood products and furniture[4] — Bois et meubles[4] | Paper and paper products, printing and publishing — Papier et ouvrages en papier, imprimerie et édition | Leather and leather products except wearing apparel[5] — Cuir et articles en cuir, à l'exclusion des articles d'habillement[5] | Rubber products — Ouvrages en caoutchouc | Chemicals and chemical, petroleum and coal products[8] — Produits chimiques et dérivés du pétrole et du charbon[8] | Non-metallic mineral products — Produits minéraux non métalliques | Basic metals — Métallurgie de base | Metal products[5] — Ouvrages en métaux[6] | Other manufacturing[7] — Autres industries manufacturières[7] | Année et rubrique |
|---|---|---|---|---|---|---|---|---|---|---|---|---|---|---|
| ISIC | 2-3 | 20-22 | 23 | 24 | 26 | 27-28 | 29 | 30 | 31-32 | 33 | 34 | 35-38 | 39 | CITI |
| Value added (absolute figures): | | | | | | | | | | | | | | Valeur ajoutée (chiffres absolus): |
| 1952 | 44 000 | 20 880 | 2 715 | 740 | 390 | 2 250 | 500 | 100 | 4 815 | 3 240 | 1 620 | 6 630 | 120 | 1952 |
| 1958 | 97 388 | 37 180 | 13 440 | 6 174 | 4 087 | 3 377 | 3 191 | 125 | 4 611 | 5 354 | 1 309 | 18 540 | ... | 1958 |
| Percentage distribution: | | | | | | | | | | | | | | Distribution en pourcentage: |
| 1952 | 100.0 | 47.4 | 6.2 | 1.7 | 0.9 | 5.1 | 1.1 | 0.2 | 10.9 | 7.4 | 3.7 | 15.1 | 0.3 | 1952 |
| 1958 | 100.0 | 38.2 | 13.8 | 6.3 | 4.2 | 3.5 | 3.3 | 0.1 | 4.7 | 5.5 | 1.4 | 19.0 | ... | 1958 |

[1] Excludes quarrying.
[2] The 1952 figures exclude establishments employing less than 10 persons and equipped with machinery operated with motors of less than a couple of horsepower capacity. This is besides other exclusions designated under the various major groups.
[3] Excludes tailoring.
[4] Limited to metal furniture in 1952.
[5] The 1952 figures exclude Furs and fur products (ISIC group 292).
[6] The 1952 figures exclude establishments engaged entirely on repair work.
[7] The 1952 figures exclude Manufacture of Jewelry (ISIC group 394); brush manufacturing; games and toys, and other miscellaneous manufacturing industries belonging to ISIC group 399.
[8] The 1958 figures for Electricity (ISIC group 511) include Extraction of coal (ISIC major group 11) and Extraction and refining of crude petroleum (ISIC major group 13 and group 321 respectively).

[1] Non compris les carrières.
[2] Les chiffres de 1952 ne comprennent pas les établissements occupant moins de 10 personnes et utilisant des moteurs d'une puissance inférieure à quelques chevaux vapeur. Cette réserve vient s'ajouter aux exclusions indiquées pour les différentes classes.
[3] Non compris le travail des étoffes.
[4] Il s'agit exclusivement des meubles métalliques en 1952.
[5] Les chiffres de 1952 ne comprennent pas Pelleterie et articles en fourrure (CITI groupe 292).
[6] Les chiffres de 1952 ne comprennent pas les établissements s'occupant uniquement de travaux de réparation.
[7] Les chiffres de 1952 ne comprennent pas les bijouteries (CITI groupe 394), les brosseries, les jeux et jouets et d'autres industries manufacturières diverses appartenant au groupe 399 de la CITI.
[8] Les chiffres de 1958 relatifs à l'électricité (CITI groupe 511) comprennent l'Extraction du charbon (CITI classe 11) et l'Extraction et le raffinage du pétrole brut (CITI classe 13 et groupe 321 respectivement).

# MOZAMBIQUE

The data set out in the tables below are derived from the results of the annual industrial inquiries taken by the Repartição Técnica de Estatística, Lourenço Marques, and published in *Estatística Industrial, 1948, 1953* or *1958*. All the three inquiries related to business units engaged in the fields of mining, manufacturing and electricity, they however included agricultural employment on tea and sisal plantations.

The coverage of the 1948 and 1953 censuses, the results of which are shown in Table 1, was limited to establishments with five or more persons, and industrial units such as sawmills or printing or machine shops were probably excluded. The coverage of the 1958 census, the results of which are shown in Table 2, probably extends to units of all sizes.

The definitions utilized for data presented in Tables 2 and 3 are the same for 1948, 1953 and 1958 and seem to be consistent with the International Standards in Basic Industrial Statistics. The figures of capacity of power equipment relate to the sum of the rated horsepower of installed (in use and in reserve) prime movers and electric motors driven by purchased electricity.

Les données des tableaux ci-après sont tirées des résultats des enquêtes industrielles annuelles effectuées par le Repartição Técnica de Estatística, Lourenço Marques; ces résultats sont publiés dans *Estatística Industrial, 1948, 1953* et *1958*. Les trois enquêtes portent sur les unités des industries extractives, manufacturières et productrices d'électricité, ainsi que sur la main-d'œuvre agricole des plantations de thé et de sisal.

Les recensements de 1948 et 1953, dont les résultats sont présentés au tableau 1, ne portaient que sur les établissements occupant cinq personnes ou plus, à l'exclusion, probablement, d'unités industrielles telles que les scieries, imprimeries et ateliers de construction mécanique. Le recensement de 1958, dont les résultats sont présentés au tableau 2, portait probablement sur les établissements de toutes dimensions.

Les définitions utilisées pour les données des tableaux 2 et 3 sont les mêmes pour 1948, 1953 et 1958, et elles semblent conformes aux Normes internationales relatives aux statistiques industrielles de base. La puissance installée représente la puissance nominale des moteurs primaires installés (en service et en réserve), plus celle des moteurs électriques actionnés par de l'électricité achetée.

## 1. CHARACTERISTICS OF ESTABLISHMENTS WITH FIVE OR MORE EMPLOYEES
## CARACTERISTIQUES DES ETABLISSEMENTS COMPTANT CINQ SALARIES OU PLUS

### 1948, 1953

Number of establishments in units; number of employees in thousands; wages and salaries in million Escudos; capacity of installed power equipment in thousand horsepower; and capacity of installed power equipment per employee in horsepower

Nombre d'établissements en unités; nombre de salariés en milliers; traitements et salaires en millions d'escudos; puissance installée en milliers de chevaux-vapeur; puissance installée par salarié en chevaux-vapeur

### A. Selected Divisions of Industrial Activity — Quelques branches de l'activité industrielle

| Item of data | All industrial activity Toutes industries | | Mining Industries extractives | | Manufacturing Industries manufacturières | | Electricity Electricité | | Rubrique |
|---|---|---|---|---|---|---|---|---|---|
| | 1948 | 1953 | 1948 | 1953 | 1948 | 1953 | 1948 | 1953 | |
| ISIC | 1–3, 511 | | 1 | | 2–3 | | 511 | | CITI |
| Number of units................. | ... | ... | 102 | 133 | 237 | 271 | ... | ... | Nombre d'unités |
| Number of employees (As of 31.XII)................. | 32.8 | 37.3 | 2.5 | 5.1 | 29.6 | 31.7 | 0.7 | 0.5 | Nombre de salariés (au 31.XII) |
| Wages and salaries paid.......... | 114.7 | 168.1 | 7.1 | 13.5 | 95.2 | 148.7 | 12.4 | 5.9 | Traitements et salaires payés |
| Capacity of installed power equipment (As of 31.XII)................. | . | . | 3.1 | 3.9 | 17.7 | 41.2 | . | . | Puissance installée (au 31.XII) |
| Capacity of installed power equipment per employee................. | . | . | 1.2 | 0.8 | 0.6 | 1.3 | . | . | Puissance installée par salarié |

**B.  The Major Groups of Mining — Les classes de la branche Industries extractives**

| Item of data | 1948 | | | 1953 | | | Rubrique |
|---|---|---|---|---|---|---|---|
| | All mining<br><br>Toutes industries extractives | Metal mining<br><br>Extraction des minerais métalliques | Other mining<br><br>Divers | All mining<br><br>Toutes industries extractives | Metal mining<br><br>Extraction des minerais métalliques | Other mining<br><br>Divers | |
| ISIC | 1 | 12 | 14–19 | 1 | 12 | 14–19 | CITI |
| Number of units............. | 102 | 59 | 43 | 133 | 40 | 93 | Nombre d'unités |
| Number of employees (As of 31.XII)............. | 2.5 | 1.3 | 1.2 | 5.1 | 3.1 | 2.0 | Nombre de salariés (au 31.XII) |
| Wages and salaries paid...... | 7.1 | 4.3 | 2.8 | 13.5 | 8.5 | 5.0 | Traitements et salaires payés |
| Capacity of installed power equipment (As of 31.XII)............. | 3.1 | 2.4 | 0.7 | 3.9 | 2.6 | 1.3 | Puissance installée (au 31.XII) |
| Capacity of installed power equipment per employee..... | 1.2 | 1.8 | 0.6 | 0.8 | 0.8 | 0.6 | Puissance installée par salarié |

**C.  Selected Major Groups of Manufacturing — Quelques classes de la branche Industries manufacturières**

| Year and item of data | Manufacturing<br><br>Industries manufacturières | Food, beverages and tobacco<br><br>Industries alimentaires, boissons, tabac | Textiles<br><br>Textiles | Leather and leather products except wearing apparel<br><br>Cuir et articles en cuir, à l'exclusion des articles d'habillement | Rubber products<br><br>Ouvrages en caoutchouc | Chemicals and chemical, petroleum and coal products<br><br>Produits chimiques et dérivés du pétrole et du charbon | Non-metallic mineral products<br><br>Produits minéraux non métalliques | Année et rubrique |
|---|---|---|---|---|---|---|---|---|
| ISIC | 2–3 | 20–22 | 23 | 29 | 30 | 31–32 | 33 | CITI |
| **1948** | | | | | | | | **1948** |
| Number of establishments............ | 237 | 100 | 70 | 3 | 1 | 42 | 21 | Nombre d'établissements |
| Number of employees (As of 31.XII)..................... | 29.6 | 11.5 | 14.9 | 0.1 | 0.1 | 1.4 | 1.6 | Nombre de salariés (au 31.XII) |
| Wages and salaries paid............. | 95.2 | 41.1 | 33.6 | 0.6 | 0.8 | 11.7 | 7.4 | Traitements et salaires payés |
| Capacity of installed power equipment (As of 31.XII)..................... | 17.7 | 7.1 | 6.9 | — | — | 2.5 | 1.2 | Puissance installée (au 31.XII) |
| Capacity of installed power equipment per employee.................... | 0.6 | 0.6 | 0.5 | 0.4 | — | 1.8 | 0.8 | Puissance installée par salarié |
| **1953** | | | | | | | | **1953** |
| Number of establishments............ | 271 | 134 | 64 | 4 | 2 | 38 | 29 | Nombre d'établissements |
| Number of employees (As of 31.XII)..................... | 31.7 | 14.7 | 13.0 | 0.1 | 0.1 | 1.6 | 2.2 | Nombre de salariés (au 31.XII) |
| Wages and salaries paid............. | 148.7 | 67.1 | 48.4 | 0.8 | 1.4 | 15.7 | 15.3 | Traitements et salaires payés |
| Capacity of installed power equipment (As of 31.XII)..................... | 41.2 | 16.2 | 12.9 | 0.1 | 0.3 | 4.7 | 7.0 | Puissance installée (au 31.XII) |
| Capacity of installed power equipment per employee.................... | 1.3 | 1.1 | 1.0 | 1.0 | 3.0 | 2.9 | 3.2 | Puissance installée par salarié |

# MOZAMBIQUE

## 2. CHARACTERISTICS OF INDUSTRIAL ESTABLISHMENTS
## CARACTERISTIQUES DES ETABLISSEMENTS INDUSTRIELS
### 1958

Number of establishments in units; value added and wages and salaries in million Escudos; number of engaged and employees in thousands; capacity of installed power equipment in thousand horsepower; value added per engaged and wages and salaries per employee in thousand Escudos; capacity of installed power equipment per engaged in horsepower.

Nombre d'établissements en unités; valeur ajoutée et traitements et salaires en millions d'escudos; nombre de personnes occupées et de salariés en milliers; puissance installée en milliers de chevaux-vapeur; valeur ajoutée par personne occupée et traitements et salaires par salarié en milliers d'escudos; puissance installée par personne occupée en chevaux-vapeur.

### A. Selected Divisions of Industrial Activity — Quelques branches de l'activité industrielle

| Item of data | Total | Mining Industries extractives | Manu-facturing Industries manu-facturières | Electricity Electricité | Rubrique | Item of data | Total | Mining Industries extractives | Manu-facturing Industries manu-facturières | Electricity Electricité | Rubrique |
|---|---|---|---|---|---|---|---|---|---|---|---|
| ISIC | 1-3, 511 | 1 | 2-3 | 511 | CITI | ISIC | 1-3, 511 | 1 | 2-3 | 511 | CITI |
| | **a. Absolute Figures — Chiffres absolus** | | | | | | **b. Structure** | | | | |
| Number of establishments. | 1 291 | 144 | 1 084 | 63 | Nombre d'établissements | | | | | | Distribution en pourcentage du nombre de personnes occupées |
| Value added (As of 31.XII). | ... | ... | 1 509.7 | ... | Valeur ajoutée (au 31.XII) | Distribution in percent of number of engaged ..... | 100.0 | 8.3 | 91.0 | 0.7 | |
| Number of engaged (As of 31.XII) ......... | 96.0 | 8.0 | 87.4 | 0.6 | Nombre de personnes occupées (au 31.XII) | Per person engaged: | | | | | Par personne occupée: |
| Employees: | | | | | Salariés: | Value added............ | ... | ... | 17.3 | ... | Valeur ajoutée |
| Number (As of 31.XII)... | 95.8 | 7.9 | 87.3 | 0.6 | Nombre (au 31.XII) | Capacity of installed power equipment....... | ... | 0.70 | 0.92 | ... | Puissance installée |
| Wages and salaries...... | 547.0 | 26.6 | 509.8 | 10.6 | Traitements et salaires | Employees as a percent of engaged............ | 99.8 | 98.8 | 99.9 | 100.0 | Salariés en pourcentage des personnes occupées |
| Capacity of installed power equipment (As of 31.XII)......... | ... | 5.6 | 80.2 | ... | Puissance installée (au 31.XII) | Value added per unit of wages and salaries...... | ... | ... | 2.96 | ... | Valeur ajoutée par unité de traitements et salaires |
| | | | | | | Wages and salaries per employee.............. | 5.7 | 3.4 | 5.8 | 17.7 | Traitements et salaires par salarié |

### B. The Major Groups of Mining — Les classes de la branche Industries extractives

| Item of data | All mining Toutes industries extrac-tives | Coal mining Extraction du charbon | Metal mining Extraction des minerais métal-liques | Other mining Divers | Rubrique | Item of data | All mining Toutes industries extrac-tives | Coal mining Extraction du charbon | Metal mining Extraction des minerais métal-liques | Other mining Divers | Rubrique |
|---|---|---|---|---|---|---|---|---|---|---|---|
| ISIC | 1 | 11 | 12 | 14-19 | CITI | ISIC | 1 | 11 | 12 | 14-19 | CITI |
| | **a. Absolute Figures — Chiffres absolus** | | | | | | **b. Structure** | | | | |
| Number of establishments. | 144 | 1 | 40 | 103 | Nombre d'établissements | | | | | | Distribution en pourcentage du nombre de personnes occupées |
| Number of engaged (As of 31.XII)........... | 8.0 | 1.1 | 3.0 | 3.9 | Nombre de personnes occupées (au 31.XII) | Distribution in percent of the number of engaged.............. | 100.0 | 13.7 | 37.5 | 48.8 | |
| Employees: | | | | | Salariés: | Capacity of installed power equipment per engaged.. | 0.70 | 1.36 | 0.53 | 0.64 | Puissance installée par personne occupée |
| Number (As of 31.XII)... | 7.9 | 1.1 | 3.0 | 3.8 | Nombre (au 31.XII) | Employees as a percent of engaged............. | 98.8 | 100.0 | 100.0 | 97.4 | Salariés en pourcentage des personnes occupées |
| Wages and salaries...... | 26.6 | 6.9 | 7.8 | 11.9 | Traitements et salaires | Wages and salaries per employee............. | 3.4 | 6.3 | 2.6 | 3.1 | Traitements et salaires par salarié |
| Capacity of installed power equipment (As of 31.XII)........., | 5.6 | 1.5 | 1.6 | 2.5 | Puissance installée (au 31.XII) | | | | | | |

## C. The Major Groups of Manufacturing — Les classes de la branche Industries manufacturières

| Item of data | Manufacturing / Industries manufacturières | Food, beverages and tobacco / Industries alimentaires, boissons, tabac | Textiles | Clothing, footwear and made-up textiles / Articles d'habillement, chaussures et ouvrages en tissu | Wood products and furniture / Bois et meubles | Paper and paper products / Papier et ouvrages en papier | Printing and publishing / Imprimerie et édition | Leather and leather products except wearing apparel / Cuir et articles en cuir, à l'exclusion des articles d'habillement | Rubber products / Ouvrages en caoutchouc | Chemicals and chemical, petroleum and coal products / Produits chimiques et dérivés du pétrole et du charbon | Non-metallic mineral products / Produits minéraux non métalliques | Metal products / Ouvrages en métaux | Other manufacturing / Autres industries manufacturières | Rubrique |
|---|---|---|---|---|---|---|---|---|---|---|---|---|---|---|
| ISIC | 2–3 | 20–22 | 23 | 24 | 25–26 | 27 | 28 | 29 | 30 | 31–32 | 33 | 35–38 | 39 | CITI |
| *a. Absolute Figures — Chiffres absolus* | | | | | | | | | | | | | | |
| Number of establishments. | 1 084 | 336 | 49 | 98 | 185 | 21 | 38 | 5 | 8 | 58 | 53 | 198 | 35 | Nombre d'établissements |
| Value added | 1 509.7 | 653.2 | 386.2 | 10.4 | 115.0 | 5.9 | 34.6 | 1.6 | 7.2 | 54.7 | 132.8 | 98.9 | 9.2 | Valeur ajoutée |
| Number of engaged (As of 31.XII) | 87.4 | 33.5 | 27.6 | 0.8 | 14.1 | — | 1.2 | 0.1 | 0.4 | 2.0 | 3.6 | 3.7 | 0.4 | Nombre de personnes occupées (au 31.XII) |
| Employees: Number (As of 31.XII). | 87.3 | 33.5 | 27.6 | 0.7 | 14.1 | — | 1.2 | 0.1 | 0.4 | 2.0 | 3.6 | 3.7 | 0.4 | Salariés: Nombre (au 31.XII) |
| Wages and salaries | 509.8 | 164.9 | 90.2 | 6.3 | 75.3 | 0.6 | 28.5 | 0.7 | 4.5 | 27.5 | 32.9 | 73.6 | 4.8 | Traitements et salaires |
| Capacity of installed power equipment (As of 31.XII) | 80.2 | 28.6 | 16.5 | 0.1 | 15.9 | — | — | 0.1 | 0.3 | 7.0 | 8.1 | 3.2 | 0.4 | Puissance installée (au 31.XII) |
| *b. Structure* | | | | | | | | | | | | | | |
| Distribution in percent of: Value added | 100.0 | 43.2 | 25.6 | 0.7 | 7.6 | 0.4 | 2.3 | 0.1 | 0.5 | 3.6 | 8.8 | 6.5 | 0.7 | Distribution en pourcentage: Valeur ajoutée |
| Number of engaged | 100.0 | 38.3 | 31.6 | 0.9 | 16.1 | — | 1.4 | 0.1 | 0.5 | 2.2 | 4.2 | 4.2 | 0.5 | Nombre de personnes occupées |
| Per person engaged: Value added | 17.3 | 19.5 | 14.0 | 13.0 | 8.2 | — | 28.8 | 16.0 | 18.0 | 27.4 | 36.9 | 26.7 | 23.0 | Par personne occupée: Valeur ajoutée |
| Capacity of installed power equipment | 0.92 | 0.85 | 0.60 | 0.12 | 1.13 | — | — | 1.00 | 0.75 | 3.50 | 2.25 | 0.86 | 1.00 | Puissance installée |
| Employees as a percent of engaged | 99.9 | 100.0 | 100.0 | 87.5 | 100.0 | — | 100.0 | 100.0 | 100.0 | 100.0 | 100.0 | 100.0 | 100.0 | Salariés en pourcentage des personnes occupées |
| Value added per unit of wages and salaries | 2.96 | 3.96 | 4.28 | 1.65 | 1.53 | 9.83 | 1.21 | 2.28 | 1.60 | 1.99 | 4.04 | 1.34 | 1.92 | Valeur ajoutée par unité de traitements et salaires |
| Wages and salaries per employee | 5.8 | 4.9 | 3.3 | 9.0 | 5.3 | — | 23.8 | 7.0 | 11.2 | 13.8 | 9.1 | 19.9 | 12.0 | Traitements et salaires par salarié |

## NETHERLANDS — PAYS-BAS

### Gross Domestic Product and Gross Fixed Capital Formation

The data set out in Table 1 concerning the gross domestic product and gross domestic fixed capital formation are derived from the reply of the Central Bureau of Statistics, the Hague, to the United Nations national accounts questionnaire. Official estimates and descriptions of national accounts data are issued annually by the Bureau in *Nationale rekeningen*. These official estimates have been adjusted by the Bureau, insofar as feasible, to the United Nations system of national accounts.

### Index Numbers of Industrial Production

The index numbers of industrial production shown in Table 2 are derived from indexes compiled by the Central Bureau of Statistics and published in *Maandstatistiek van de Nijverheid* (Monthly Statistical Bulletin of Manufacturing and Construction), or supplied to the Statistical Office of the United Nations through correspondence. The index numbers relate, in principle, to the production of establishments irrespective of size.

The series of index numbers have been computed as base-weighted arithmetic averages in successive stages. First, elementary series of quantity relatives are combined into index numbers for detailed categories of industrial activity. Secondly, the resulting indexes are combined into index numbers for broader classes of industrial activity. The elementary series of quantity relatives are based, in most cases, on the quantity of individual commodities produced. Where suitable measures of this type are not feasible, the quantity of individual raw materials consumed or man-hours worked are utilized.

The weight base years for the series of index numbers are 1938 in the case of 1938 and 1948 and 1949 for later years. In the case of the 1938 weight base, the weights have been derived from employment for purposes of combining elementary series of quantity relatives into indexes and from value added for purposes of combining the resulting indexes into index numbers for broader classes of industrial activity. The corresponding weights for the series of index numbers based on 1949 are contribution to the net domestic product, at market prices, in 1949. Where such figures were not available concerning the elementary series of relatives for a detailed category of industrial activity, the weights have been derived from gross value of output.

### Produit intérieur brut et formation brute de capital fixe

Les données reproduites au tableau 1 relatives au produit intérieur brut et à la formation brute de capital fixe intérieur ont été tirées de la réponse du Bureau central de statistique, La Haye, au questionnaire de l'O.N.U. relatif aux comptes nationaux. Des estimations officielles ainsi que la description des données relatives aux comptes nationaux sont publiées annuellement par le Bureau dans *Nationale rekeningen*. Ces estimations officielles ont été ajustées par le Bureau, de façon à les faire coincider autant que possible avec le système de comptabilité nationale de l'O.N.U.

### Indices de la production industrielle

Les indices de la production industrielle reproduits au tableau 2 sont tirés d'indices établis par le Bureau central de statistique des Pays-Bas et publiés dans *Maandstatistiek van de Nijverheid* (Bulletin statistique mensuel des industries manufacturières et du bâtiment), ou fournis au Bureau de l'O.N.U. par échange de correspondances. Ces indices concernent, en principe, la production des établissements, quelle que soit leur taille.

Les séries d'indices sont des moyennes arithmétiques à pondération fixe, calculées en plusieurs étapes. A un premier stade, à partir de séries élémentaires de rapports quantitatifs que l'on combine, on obtient des indices pour les catégories détaillées de l'activité industrielle. Au second stade, les indices résultants sont combinés en indices relatifs aux classes plus larges de l'activité industrielle. Les séries élémentaires de rapports quantitatifs sont construites, généralement, à partir du volume de chaque marchandise produite. A défaut de mesures convenables de ce type, on utilise le volume de matière première consommée par chaque industrie ou du nombre d'heures de travail effectuées.

L'année de pondération de base pour les séries d'indices est 1938 pour les indices de 1938 et 1948, 1949 pour les années ultérieures; dans le cas de la base de pondération de 1938, on a utilisé les chiffres de l'emploi comme coefficients de pondération pour combiner les séries élémentaires de rapports quantitatifs en indices, et la valeur ajoutée pour combiner les indices obtenus en indices relatifs à des classes plus étendues de l'activité industrielle. Les coefficients de pondération appliqués aux séries d'indices ayant 1949 comme année de base consistent en la contribution au produit intérieur net, aux prix du marché, en 1949. Chaque fois que de tels chiffres ne sont pas disponibles, pour calculer les séries élémentaires de rapports relatifs à une catégorie détaillée de l'activité industrielle, les coefficients de pondération ont été tirés de la valeur brute de la production.

For further details see the following publications of the Central Bureau of Statistics, the Hague: *Maandschrift* (Monthly Bulletin), Vol. 41, 1946 and *Statistische en Econometrische Onderzoekingen* (Statistical and Econometric Studies), No. 3, 1946 concerning the indexes for 1938 and 1948; and *Statistiche en Econometrische Onderzoekingen*, first quarter 1955, concerning the indexes beginning 1949.

Pour plus amples détails, voir les publications suivantes du Bureau central de statistique des Pays-Bas, La Haye: *Maandschrift* (Bulletin mensuel), vol. 41, 1946, et *Statistische en Econometrische Onderzoekingen* (Etudes statistiques et économétriques), tome 3, 1946, pour les indices de 1938 et 1948, et *Statistische en Econometrische Onderzoekingen*, premier trimestre 1955, pour les indices de 1949 et années suivantes.

### Index Numbers of Industrial Employment

The index numbers of industrial employment in Table 3 were compiled from absolute figures of the number of man years worked, published by the Central Bureau of Statistics, the Hague, in various issues of *Nationale Rekeningen*. These absolute figures relate to the employment in full-year equivalents of the employees of all industrial units, and are shown in Table 5 for 1948, 1953 and 1958.

### Indices de l'emploi industriel

Les indices de l'emploi industriel reproduits au tableau 3 sont calculés à partir des chiffres absolus donnant le nombre d'années de travail effectuées, publiés par le Bureau central de statistique, La Haye, dans différents numéros du *Nationale Rekeningen*. Les chiffres absolus se rapportent à l'emploi, exprimés en années de travail à plein temps, et aux salariés de toutes les unités industrielles, sont reproduits au tableau 5 pour 1948, 1953 et 1958.

### The Characteristics and Structure of Industrial Activity

The data shown in Table 4 were compiled from the results of the 1950 General Economic Census published by the Netherlands Central Bureau of Statistics in *2e Algemene Bedrijfstelling*, 16 October 1950 (Census of Industries, 16 October 1950). The census covered all local units engaged in mining, manufacturing, construction and the production of electricity, gas and steam. The items of data on employment are defined as in the International Standards in Basic Industrial Statistics. Installed capacity of power equipment relates to all prime movers in use together with electric motors in use driven by purchased electricity.

### Caractéristiques et structure de l'activité industrielle

Les données du tableau 4 sont tirées des résultats du recensement économique général de 1950, qui ont été publiés par le Bureau central de statistique des Pays-Bas dans *2e Algemene Bedrijfstelling* (Recensement des industries), 16 octobre 1950. Ce recensement portait sur toutes les unités locales des industries extractives et manufacturières, du bâtiment et des travaux publics, et du secteur de la production d'électricité, de gaz et de vapeur. Les définitions des rubriques relatives à l'emploi sont conformes à celles des Recommandations Internationales relatives aux Statistiques industrielles de base. La puissance installée comporte tous les moteurs primaires en service normal ainsi que tous les moteurs électriques en service normal actionnés par de l'électricité achetée.

The figures of value added and labour shown in Table 5 are from various issues of the two publications of the Central Bureau of Statistics, *Nationale rekeningen* and *De produktie-structuur van de Nederlandse volkshuishouding*, and from correspondence with the Bureau. The data on fuels, electricity and energy consumed set out in Tables 5 and 6 were compiled from *De Nederlandse energiehuishouding, Uitkomsten van maand- en kwartaaltellingen*, No. 1-2: *1946-1960* issued by the Central Bureau.

Les chiffres relatifs à la valeur ajoutée et à la main-d'œuvre reproduits au tableau 5 sont tirés de différents numéros des deux publications du Bureau central de statistique, *Nationale rekeningen et De produktie-structuur van de Nederlandse volkshuishouding*, et à partir d'un échange de lettres avec le Bureau. Les données concernant les combustibles, l'électricité et l'énergie consommés, reproduites aux tableaux 5 et 6, ont été tirées de *De Nederlandse energiehuishouding, Uitkomsten van maand- en kwartaaltellingen*, No. 1-2 : *1946-1960* publiés par le Bureau central.

The data shown in Tables 5 and 6 cover industrial units, irrespective of size. The figures of value added relate to the contribution to the gross domestic product at factor cost. The definitions of the items on the number of persons engaged and of employees and on wages and salaries paid are consistent with the recommendations of the Statistical Commission on basic industrial statistics. The data on energy consumed cover the consumption of fuels and electricity used as a source of heat and power only, and are free of any double counting between solid or liquid fuels, on the one hand, and electricity or gas, on the other.

Les données des tableaux 5 et 6 couvrent toutes les unités industrielles, quelle que soit leur taille. Les chiffres relatifs à la valeur ajoutée se rapportent à la contribution au produit intérieur brut au coût des facteurs, les définitions des rubriques relatives au nombre de personnes occupées au nombre de salariés et aux traitements et salaires payés sont conformes aux recommandations de la Commission de statistique, relatives aux statistique industrielles de base. Les données relatives à l'énergie consommé couvrent la consommation de combustibles et d'électricité utilisés comme sources de chaleur et de puissance seulement, et ne comportent pas de doubles comptes, tant entre les combustibles liquides ou solides, qu'entre l'électricité ou le gaz.

# NETHERLANDS

## 1. THE GROSS NATIONAL PRODUCT AND GROSS DOMESTIC FIXED CAPITAL FORMATION
### PRODUIT INTERIEUR BRUT ET FORMATION BRUTE DE CAPITAL FIXE INTERIEUR
Million Guilders      Millions de florins

### A. Expenditure on the Gross Domestic Product at Market Prices
### Dépenses relatives au produit intérieur brut aux prix du marché

| Item of data and year / Rubrique et année | Total | Consumption / Consommation | | Gross Domestic Capital Formation / Formation brute de capital intérieur | | Net exports of goods and services / Exportations nettes de biens et de services | |
|---|---|---|---|---|---|---|---|
| | | Total | Government / Etat | Total | Fixed / Fixe | Exports less imports / Exportations moins importations | Exports / Exportations |
| *a. At Current Prices — Aux prix courants* | | | | | | | |
| **Absolute figures — Chiffres absolus** | | | | | | | |
| 1948 | 15 013 | 12 700 | 2 114 | 3 930 | 3 151 | −1 617 | 4 268 |
| 1950 | 18 811 | 15 172 | 2 380 | 5 003 | 3 804 | −1 364 | 7 725 |
| 1951 | 21 475 | 16 726 | 2 856 | 5 271 | 4 183 | −522 | 10 302 |
| 1952 | 22 416 | 17 103 | 3 133 | 3 910 | 4 226 | 1 403 | 11 271 |
| 1953 | 23 849 | 18 060 | 3 414 | 4 850 | 5 046 | 939 | 11 506 |
| 1954 | 26 638 | 20 137 | 3 879 | 6 678 | 5 679 | −177 | 12 576 |
| 1955 | 29 741 | 22 046 | 4 337 | 7 446 | 6 798 | 249 | 14 239 |
| 1956 | 32 292 | 24 450 | 4 913 | 8 842 | 8 119 | −1 000 | 15 443 |
| 1957 | 35 120 | 25 923 | 5 282 | 9 954 | 9 044 | −757 | 17 029 |
| 1958 | 35 446 | 26 229 | 5 197 | 8 149 | 8 060 | 1 068 | 17 117 |
| 1959 | 37 827 | 27 421 | 5 184 | 9 181 | 8 913 | 225 | 18 745 |
| 1960 | 42 190 | 29 900 | 5 750 | 11 370 | 9 970 | 920 | 21 320 |
| 1961 | 43 880 | 31 760 | 6 160 | 12 100 | 10 800 | 20 | 21 520 |
| **Percentage distribution of average annual expenditure — Distribution en pourcentage des dépenses annuelles moyennes** | | | | | | | |
| 1948 | 100.0 | 84.6 | 14.1 | 26.2 | 21.0 | −10.8 | 28.4 |
| 1950–1960 | 100.0 | 74.6 | 14.2 | 24.7 | 22.7 | 0.7 | 48.3 |
| 1950 | 100.0 | 80.7 | 12.7 | 26.6 | 20.2 | −7.3 | 41.0 |
| 1953 | 100.0 | 75.7 | 14.3 | 20.3 | 21.2 | 4.0 | 48.2 |
| 1954 | 100.0 | 75.6 | 14.6 | 25.1 | 21.3 | −0.7 | 47.2 |
| 1958 | 100.0 | 74.0 | 14.7 | 23.0 | 22.7 | 3.0 | 48.3 |
| 1960 | 100.0 | 70.8 | 13.6 | 27.0 | 23.6 | 2.2 | 50.5 |
| *b. At Prices of 1958 — Aux prix de 1958* | | | | | | | |
| **Absolute figures — Chiffres absolus** | | | | | | | |
| 1948 | 23 290 | 19 690 | 4 080 | 6 220 | 5 140 | −2 620 | 4 620 |
| 1950 | 25 700 | 20 300 | 3 900 | 7 210 | 5 790 | −1 810 | 8 510 |
| 1951 | 26 360 | 20 030 | 3 940 | 6 680 | 5 600 | −350 | 9 420 |
| 1952 | 26 810 | 20 510 | 4 320 | 4 930 | 5 160 | 1 370 | 10 380 |
| 1953 | 29 050 | 21 810 | 4 750 | 6 230 | 6 380 | 1 010 | 11 740 |
| 1954 | 31 040 | 23 250 | 5 080 | 7 990 | 6 920 | −200 | 13 070 |
| 1955 | 33 200 | 24 660 | 5 260 | 8 570 | 7 900 | −30 | 14 310 |
| 1956 | 34 660 | 26 490 | 5 510 | 9 530 | 8 800 | −1 360 | 14 920 |
| 1957 | 35 780 | 26 420 | 5 410 | 10 140 | 9 270 | −780 | 16 010 |
| 1958 | 35 450 | 26 230 | 5 200 | 8 150 | 8 060 | 1 070 | 17 120 |
| 1959 | 37 180 | 27 120 | 5 130 | 9 290 | 9 030 | 770 | 18 850 |
| 1960 | 40 590 | 28 750 | 5 380 | 11 380 | 9 970 | 460 | 21 570 |
| 1961 | 41 440 | 29 930 | 5 540 | 11 960 | 10 640 | −450 | 22 130 |
| **Percentage distribution of average annual expenditure — Distribution en pourcentage des dépenses annuelles moyennes** | | | | | | | |
| 1948 | 100.0 | 84.5 | 17.5 | 26.7 | 22.1 | −11.2 | 19.8 |
| 1950–1960 | 100.0 | 74.6 | 15.1 | 25.3 | 23.3 | 0.1 | 43.8 |
| 1950 | 100.0 | 79.0 | 15.2 | 28.0 | 22.5 | −7.0 | 33.1 |
| 1953 | 100.0 | 75.0 | 16.4 | 21.5 | 22.0 | 3.5 | 40.4 |
| 1954 | 100.0 | 74.9 | 16.4 | 25.7 | 22.3 | −0.6 | 42.1 |
| 1958 | 100.0 | 74.0 | 14.7 | 23.0 | 22.7 | 3.0 | 48.3 |
| 1960 | 100.0 | 70.8 | 13.2 | 28.0 | 24.6 | 1.2 | 53.1 |
| **Average annual rate of growth — Taux annuel moyen d'accroissement** | | | | | | | |
| 1948–1953 | 4.5 | 2.1 | 3.1 | — | 4.4 | . | 20.5 |
| 1950–1960 | 4.7 | 3.5 | 3.3 | 4.7 | 5.6 | . | 9.7 |
| 1950–1953 | 4.2 | 2.4 | 6.8 | −4.8 | 3.3 | . | 11.3 |
| 1954–1958 | 3.4 | 3.1 | 0.6 | 0.5 | 3.9 | . | 7.0 |
| 1958–1960 | 7.0 | 4.7 | 1.7 | 18.2 | 11.2 | . | 12.2 |

## B. The Gross Domestic Product at Factor Cost According to Origin
### Origine par secteur d'activité du produit intérieur brut au coût des facteurs

| Item of data and year / Rubrique et année | Total | Agricultural sector / Secteur agricole | Industrial Sector — Secteur Industriel | | | | | Transportation and communication / Transports et communications | Other sectors / Autres secteurs |
|---|---|---|---|---|---|---|---|---|---|
| | | | Total | Mining / Industries extractives | Manufacturing / Industries manufacturières | Construction / Bâtiment et travaux publics | Electricity, gas and water / Electricité, gaz et eau | | |
| ISIC — CITI | 0–9 | 0 | 1–5 | 1 | 2–3 | 4 | 5 | 7 | 6, 8–9 |
| *a. At Current Prices — Aux prix courants* | | | | | | | | | |
| **Absolute figures — Chiffres absolus** | | | | | | | | | |
| 1948 | 13 644 | 1 875 | 5 438 | 226 | 4 090 | 875 | 247 | 1 199 | 5 132 |
| 1950 | 16 680 | 2 370 | 6 619 | 355 | 4 993 | 975 | 296 | 1 455 | 6 236 |
| 1951 | 18 931 | 2 597 | 7 486 | 426 | 5 638 | 1 087 | 335 | 1 813 | 7 035 |
| 1952 | 19 820 | 2 905 | 7 649 | 463 | 5 674 | 1 094 | 418 | 1 922 | 7 344 |
| 1953 | 21 159 | 2 621 | 8 787 | 506 | 6 332 | 1 479 | 470 | 1 934 | 7 817 |
| 1954 | 23 687 | 2 875 | 9 874 | 555 | 7 319 | 1 464 | 536 | 2 153 | 8 785 |
| 1955 | 26 738 | 3 053 | 11 008 | 592 | 8 193 | 1 674 | 549 | 2 511 | 10 166 |
| 1956 | 29 198 | 3 115 | 12 083 | 633 | 8 880 | 1 980 | 590 | 2 801 | 11 199 |
| 1957 | 32 129 | 3 526 | 13 349 | 699 | 9 735 | 2 266 | 649 | 3 170 | 12 084 |
| 1958 | 32 599 | 3 660 | 13 466 | 764 | 9 555 | 2 434 | 713 | 2 917 | 12 556 |
| 1959 | 34 536 | 3 435 | 14 683 | 765 | 10 585 | 2 540 | 793 | 3 108 | 13 310 |
| 1960 | 38 470 | 4 020 | 16 240 | ... | ... | ... | ... | 3 480 | 14 750 |
| 1961 | 39 910 | 3 950 | 16 880 | ... | ... | ... | ... | 3 510 | 15 570 |
| **Percentage distribution according to sector — Distribution en pourcentage par secteur** | | | | | | | | | |
| 1948 | 100.0 | 13.7 | 39.9 | 1.7 | 30.0 | 6.4 | 1.8 | 8.8 | 37.6 |
| 1950–1960 | 100.0 | 11.6 | 41.2 | ... | ... | ... | ... | 9.3 | 37.9 |
| 1950 | 100.0 | 14.2 | 39.7 | 2.1 | 29.9 | 5.9 | 1.8 | 8.7 | 37.4 |
| 1953 | 100.0 | 12.4 | 41.5 | 2.4 | 29.9 | 7.0 | 2.2 | 9.1 | 37.0 |
| 1954 | 100.0 | 12.1 | 41.7 | 2.3 | 30.9 | 6.2 | 2.3 | 9.1 | 37.1 |
| 1958 | 100.0 | 11.2 | 41.3 | 2.3 | 29.3 | 7.5 | 2.2 | 8.9 | 38.6 |
| 1960 | 100.0 | 10.4 | 42.2 | ... | ... | ... | ... | 9.0 | 38.4 |
| *b. At Prices of 1958 — Aux prix de 1958* | | | | | | | | | |
| **Indexes — Indices (1958 = 100)** | | | | | | | | | |
| 1950 | 72 | 82 | 69 | ... | ... | ... | ... | 61 | 76 |
| 1951 | 74 | 87 | 72 | ... | ... | ... | ... | 66 | 75 |
| 1952 | 75 | 90 | 72 | ... | ... | ... | ... | 72 | 76 |
| 1953 | 81 | 87 | 80 | ... | ... | ... | ... | 77 | 81 |
| 1954 | 87 | 90 | 86 | ... | ... | ... | ... | 84 | 87 |
| 1955 | 93 | 95 | 92 | ... | ... | ... | ... | 89 | 95 |
| 1956 | 97 | 88 | 98 | ... | ... | ... | ... | 95 | 98 |
| 1957 | 100 | 94 | 101 | ... | ... | ... | ... | 101 | 99 |
| 1958 | 100 | 100 | 100 | ... | ... | ... | ... | 100 | 100 |
| 1959 | 105 | 90 | 109 | ... | ... | ... | ... | 104 | 105 |
| 1960 | 116 | 114 | 120 | ... | ... | ... | ... | 116 | 110 |
| 1961 | 118 | 107 | 124 | ... | ... | ... | ... | 115 | 114 |
| **Average annual rate of growth — Taux annuel moyen d'accroissement** | | | | | | | | | |
| 1950–1960 | 4.9 | 3.3 | 5.7 | ... | ... | ... | ... | 6.6 | 3.8 |
| 1950–1953 | 4.0 | 2.0 | 5.0 | ... | ... | ... | ... | 8.1 | 2.2 |
| 1954–1958 | 3.5 | 2.7 | 3.8 | ... | ... | ... | ... | 4.4 | 3.5 |
| 1958–1960 | 7.7 | 6.8 | 9.5 | ... | ... | ... | ... | 7.7 | 4.9 |

### C. Gross Domestic Fixed Capital Formation According to Purchasing Sector
### Formation brute de capital fixe intérieur par secteur d'acquisition

| Item of data and year<br>Rubrique et année | Total | Agricultural sector<br><br>Secteur agricole | Industrial sector<br><br>Secteur industriel | Transportation and communication<br><br>Transports et communications | Other sectors<br><br>Autres secteurs |
|---|---|---|---|---|---|
| ISIC — CITI | 0–9 | 0 | 1–5 | 7 | 6, 8–9 |
| | | | *a. At Current Prices — Aux prix courants* | | |
| **Absolute figures**<br>— **Chiffres absolus** | | | | | |
| 1948............ | 3 151 | 210 | 912 | 588 | 1 441 |
| 1950............ | 3 804 | 236 | 1 292 | 578 | 1 698 |
| 1951............ | 4 183 | 248 | 1 467 | 584 | 1 884 |
| 1952............ | 4 226 | 219 | 1 419 | 644 | 1 944 |
| 1953............ | 5 046 | 244 | 1 479 | 710 | 2 613 |
| 1954............ | 5 679 | 302 | 1 759 | 905 | 2 713 |
| 1955............ | 6 798 | 334 | 2 180 | 1 208 | 3 076 |
| 1956............ | 8 119 | 332 | 2 652 | 1 475 | 3 660 |
| 1957............ | 9 044 | 310 | 2 698 | 1 850 | 4 186 |
| 1958............ | 8 060 | 288 | 2 249 | 1 525 | 3 998 |
| 1959............ | 8 913 | 361 | 2 482 | 1 587 | 4 483 |
| 1960............ | 9 970 | 390 | 2 860 | 1 920 | 4 800 |
| 1961............ | 10 800 | 460 | 3 280 | 1 870 | 5 190 |
| **Percentage distribution according to sector—**<br>**Distribution en pourcentage par secteur** | | | | | |
| 1948............ | 100.0 | 6.6 | 29.0 | 18.6 | 45.8 |
| 1950 – 1960..... | 100.0 | 4.4 | 30.5 | 17.6 | 47.5 |
| 1950............ | 100.0 | 6.2 | 33.9 | 15.2 | 44.7 |
| 1953............ | 100.0 | 4.8 | 29.3 | 14.1 | 51.8 |
| 1954............ | 100.0 | 5.3 | 30.9 | 16.0 | 47.8 |
| 1958............ | 100.0 | 3.5 | 27.9 | 18.9 | 49.7 |
| 1960............ | 100.0 | 3.9 | 28.6 | 19.3 | 48.2 |
| | | | *b. At Prices of 1958 — Aux prix de 1958* | | |
| **Absolute figures**<br>— **Chiffres absolus** | | | | | |
| 1948............ | 5 140 | 350 | 1 430 | 880 | 2 480 |
| 1950............ | 5 790 | 360 | 1 880 | 820 | 2 730 |
| 1951............ | 5 600 | 340 | 1 900 | 710 | 2 650 |
| 1952............ | 5 160 | 280 | 1 640 | 720 | 2 520 |
| 1953............ | 6 380 | 310 | 1 740 | 810 | 3 520 |
| 1954............ | 6 920 | 370 | 2 070 | 1 040 | 3 440 |
| 1955............ | 7 900 | 390 | 2 500 | 1 330 | 3 680 |
| 1956............ | 8 800 | 360 | 2 860 | 1 550 | 4 030 |
| 1957............ | 9 270 | 320 | 2 790 | 1 870 | 4 290 |
| 1958............ | 8 060 | 290 | 2 250 | 1 530 | 3 990 |
| 1959............ | 9 030 | 370 | 2 510 | 1 600 | 4 550 |
| 1960............ | 9 970 | 400 | 2 880 | 1 910 | 4 780 |
| 1961............ | 10 640 | 460 | 3 250 | 1 850 | 5 080 |
| **Percentage distribution according to sector—**<br>**Distribution en pourcentage par secteur** | | | | | |
| 1948............ | 100.0 | 6.8 | 27.8 | 17.1 | 48.3 |
| 1950 – 1960..... | 100.0 | 4.5 | 30.2 | 16.8 | 48.5 |
| 1950............ | 100.0 | 6.2 | 32.5 | 14.1 | 47.2 |
| 1953............ | 100.0 | 4.8 | 27.3 | 12.7 | 55.2 |
| 1954............ | 100.0 | 5.3 | 29.9 | 15.0 | 49.8 |
| 1958............ | 100.0 | 3.5 | 28.0 | 18.9 | 49.6 |
| 1960............ | 100.0 | 4.0 | 28.8 | 19.2 | 48.0 |
| **Average annual rate of growth—Taux annuel moyen d'accroissement** | | | | | |
| 1948 – 1953..... | 4.4 | −2.4 | 4.0 | −1.7 | 7.2 |
| 1950 – 1960..... | 5.6 | 1.1 | 4.4 | 8.8 | 5.8 |
| 1950 – 1953..... | 3.3 | −4.9 | −2.5 | −0.4 | 8.8 |
| 1954 – 1958..... | 3.9 | −5.9 | 2.1 | 10.1 | 3.8 |
| 1958 – 1960..... | 11.2 | 17.4 | 13.1 | 11.7 | 9.5 |

## 2. INDEX NUMBERS OF INDUSTRIAL PRODUCTION
### INDICES DE LA PRODUCTION INDUSTRIELLE

### A. Selected Divisions of Industrial Activity
### Quelques branches de l'activité industrielle

| Year<br>Année | Total | Mining<br>Industries<br>extractives | Manu-<br>facturing [1]<br>Industries<br>manu-<br>facturières [1] | Electricity<br>and gas [2]<br>Electricité<br>et gaz [2] |
|---|---|---|---|---|
| ISIC — CITI | 1–3, 511–521 | 1 | 2–3 | 511–521 |
| *a.* Indexes — Indices (1958 = 100) | | | | |
| 1938.......... | 49 [3] | ... | 49 | 31 |
| 1948.......... | 56 [3] | ... | 54 | 47 |
| 1949.......... | – 62 – | – 84 – | – 61 – | – 50 – |
| 1950.......... | 69 | 89 | 68 | 57 |
| 1951.......... | 72 | 91 | 72 | 60 |
| 1952.......... | 72 | 91 | 72 | 64 |
| 1953.......... | 79 | 91 | 79 | 71 |
| 1954.......... | 87 | 91 | 87 | 79 |
| 1955.......... | 93 | 92 | 94 | 84 |
| 1956.......... | 98 | 93 | 98 | 92 |
| 1957.......... | 100 | 95 | 100 | 98 |
| 1958.......... | 100 | 100 | 100 | 100 |
| 1959.......... | 109 | 103 | 109 | 107 |
| 1960.......... | 124 | 109 | 124 | 117 |
| 1961.......... | 125 | 112 | 126 | 124 |
| *b.* Average Annual Rate of Change — Taux annuel moyen de variation | | | | |
| 1938 – 1960.... | 4.3 | ... | 4.3 | 6.2 |
| 1938 – 1948.... | 1.3 | ... | 1.0 | 4.3 |
| 1950 – 1960.... | 6.0 | 2.0 | 6.2 | 7.5 |
| 1948 – 1953.... | 7.1 | ... | 7.9 | 8.6 |
| 1954 – 1958.... | 3.5 | 2.4 | 3.5 | 6.1 |
| 1958 – 1960.... | 11.4 | 4.4 | 11.4 | 8.2 |

### B. The Major Groups of Mining
### Les classes de la branche Industries extractives

| Year<br>Année | All mining<br>Toutes<br>industries<br>extractives | Coal<br>mining<br>Extraction<br>du charbon | Crude petro-<br>leum and<br>natural gas<br>Pétrole brut<br>et gaz naturel | Other mining<br>Autres<br>industries<br>extractives |
|---|---|---|---|---|
| ISIC — CITI | 1 | 11 | 13 | 14–19 |
| *a.* Indexes — Indices (1958 = 100) | | | | |
| 1938.......... | ... | 114 | — | ... |
| 1948.......... | ... | 93 | 30 | ... |
| 1949.......... | – 84 – | – 98 – | – 38 – | 46 |
| 1950.......... | 89 | 103 | 43 | 53 |
| 1951.......... | 91 | 104 | 44 | 60 |
| 1952.......... | 91 | 105 | 44 | 54 |
| 1953.......... | 91 | 104 | 50 | 60 |
| 1954.......... | 91 | 102 | 58 | 65 |
| 1955.......... | 92 | 100 | 63 | 72 |
| 1956.......... | 93 | 100 | 68 | 80 |
| 1957.......... | 95 | 96 | 94 | 99 |
| 1958.......... | 100 | 100 | 100 | 100 |
| 1959.......... | 103 | 101 | 109 | 111 |
| 1960.......... | 109 | 105 | 118 | 122 |
| 1961.......... | 112 | 106 | 126 | 130 |
| *b.* Average Annual Rate of Change — Taux annuel moyen de variation | | | | |
| 1950 – 1960.... | 2.0 | 0.2 | 10.6 | 8.7 |
| 1948 – 1953.... | ... | 2.3 | 10.8 | ... |
| 1954 – 1958.... | 2.4 | –0.5 | 14.6 | 11.4 |
| 1958 – 1960.... | 4.4 | 2.5 | 8.6 | 10.5 |

[1] Other manufacturing (ISIC major group 39) is not covered.
[2] Including water supply.
[3] The mining component covers coal mining only.

[1] Non compris les Autres industries manufacturières (CITI 39).
[2] Y compris la distribution publique de l'eau.
[3] Extraction du charbon seulement pour la branche Industries extractives.

# NETHERLANDS

## C. The Major Groups of Manufacturing — Les classes de la branche Industries manufacturières

| Period / Période | Manufacturing [1] / Industries manufacturières [1] | Food, beverages and tobacco / Industries alimentaires, boissons, tabac | Textiles | Clothing, footwear and made-up textiles / Articles d'habillement, chaussures et ouvrages en tissu | Wood products and furniture / Bois et meubles | Paper and paper products / Papier et ouvrages en papier | Printing and publishing / Imprimerie et édition | Leather and leather products except wearing apparel [2] / Cuir et articles en cuir, à l'exclusion des articles d'habillement [2] | Chemicals and chemical, petroleum and coal products / Produits chimiques et dérivés du pétrole et du charbon | Non-metallic mineral products / Produits minéraux non métalliques | Metal products [3] / Ouvrages en métaux [3] |
|---|---|---|---|---|---|---|---|---|---|---|---|
| ISIC — CITI | 2–3 | 20–22 | 23 | 24 | 25–26 | 27 | 28 | 29–30 | 31–32 | 33 | 34–38 |

### a. Indexes — Indices (1958 = 100)

| Period | | | | | | | | | | | |
|---|---|---|---|---|---|---|---|---|---|---|---|
| 1938 | 49 | 66 | 59 | 82 | 33 | 47 | 58 | 40 | 33 | 66 | 36 |
| 1948 | 54 | 64 | 62 | 66 | 56 | 52 | 64 | 82 | 37 | 63 | 44 |
| 1949 | −61− | −71− | −72− | −74− | −58− | −54− | −67− | −74− | −42− | −72− | −51− |
| 1950 | 68 | 78 | 78 | 78 | 69 | 63 | 72 | 79 | 56 | 79 | 59 |
| 1951 | 72 | 78 | 82 | 72 | 74 | 72 | 72 | 72 | 61 | 88 | 63 |
| 1952 | 72 | 80 | 82 | 69 | 68 | 66 | 75 | 74 | 61 | 88 | 64 |
| 1953 | 79 | 85 | 92 | 78 | 80 | 78 | 82 | 83 | 66 | 88 | 72 |
| 1954 | 87 | 87 | 99 | 84 | 91 | 85 | 90 | 89 | 77 | 93 | 86 |
| 1955 | 94 | 92 | 101 | 94 | 94 | 90 | 93 | 95 | 82 | 97 | 96 |
| 1956 | 98 | 96 | 104 | 103 | 100 | 91 | 98 | 90 | 87 | 101 | 101 |
| 1957 | 100 | 98 | 104 | 102 | 107 | 101 | 98 | 103 | 97 | 107 | 99 |
| 1958 | 100 | 100 | 100 | 100 | 100 | 100 | 100 | 100 | 100 | 100 | 100 |
| 1959 | 109 | 102 | 104 | 112 | 110 | 112 | 106 | 113 | 104 | 107 | 119 |
| 1960 | 124 | 110 | 110 | 118 | 122 | 122 | 117 | 119 | 116 | 113 | 145 |
| 1961 | 126 | 112 | 114 | 126 | 121 | 126 | 111 | 125 | 118 | 115 | 145 |

### b. Average Annual Rate of Change — Taux annuel moyen de variation

| Period | | | | | | | | | | | |
|---|---|---|---|---|---|---|---|---|---|---|---|
| 1938 – 1960 | 4.3 | 2.4 | 2.9 | 1.3 | 6.1 | 4.4 | 3.2 | 5.1 | 5.9 | 2.5 | 6.5 |
| 1938 – 1948 | 1.0 | −0.3 | 0.5 | −2.2 | 5.4 | 1.0 | 1.0 | 7.4 | 1.1 | −0.5 | 2.0 |
| 1950 – 1960 | 6.2 | 3.5 | 3.5 | 4.2 | 5.9 | 5.9 | 5.0 | 4.2 | 7.6 | 3.6 | 9.4 |
| 1948 – 1953 | 7.5 | 5.8 | 8.2 | 3.4 | 7.4 | 8.4 | 5.1 | 0.2 | 12.3 | 6.9 | 10.3 |
| 1954 – 1958 | 3.5 | 3.5 | 0.2 | 4.4 | 2.4 | 4.1 | 2.7 | 3.0 | 6.8 | 1.8 | 3.8 |
| 1958 – 1960 | 11.4 | 5.1 | 5.1 | 8.6 | 10.5 | 10.5 | 8.2 | 9.1 | 7.7 | 6.3 | 20.4 |

[1] Other manufacturing (ISIC major group 39) is not covered.
[2] Including rubber products manufacturing.
[3] Including the manufacture of basic metals.

[1] Non compris les Autres industries manufacturières.
[2] Y compris la fabrication des ouvrages en caoutchouc.
[3] Y compris la métallurgie de base.

## 3. INDEX NUMBERS OF INDUSTRIAL EMPLOYMENT
### INDICES DE L'EMPLOI DANS L'INDUSTRIE

### A. The Divisions of Industrial Activity
### Les branches de l'activité industrielle

| Period<br>Période | Total | Mining [1]<br><br>Industries<br>extractives [1] | Manu-<br>facturing<br><br>Industries<br>manu-<br>facturières | Construction<br><br>Bâtiment<br>et travaux<br>publics | Electricity,<br>gas and water<br><br>Electricité,<br>gaz et eau |
|---|---|---|---|---|---|
| ISIC — CITI | 1, 4, 511–521 | 1 | 2–3 | 4 | 511–521 |

a. Indexes — Indices (1958 = 100)

| | | | | | |
|---|---|---|---|---|---|
| 1948....... | 81 | 80 | 82 | 75 | 84 |
| 1949....... | 84 | 80 | 86 | 77 | 89 |
| 1950....... | 89 | 84 | 90 | 83 | 92 |
| 1951....... | 90 | 88 | 92 | 86 | 92 |
| 1952....... | 88 | 93 | 89 | 80 | 92 |
| 1953....... | 92 | 97 | 91 | 92 | 94 |
| 1954....... | 96 | 98 | 96 | 94 | 97 |
| 1955....... | 99 | 98 | 99 | 100 | 97 |
| 1956....... | 102 | 98 | 101 | 104 | 100 |
| 1957....... | 103 | 98 | 102 | 106 | 100 |
| 1958....... | 100 | 100 | 100 | 100 | 100 |
| 1959....... | 102 | 98 | 102 | 105 | 100 |
| 1960....... | 105 | 93 | 105 | 108 | 97 |
| 1961....... | 108 | 90 | 108 | 112 | 97 |

b. Average Annual Rate of Change — Taux annuel moyen de variation

| | | | | | |
|---|---|---|---|---|---|
| 1950 – 1960. | 1.7 | 1.0 | 1.6 | 2.7 | 0.5 |
| 1948 – 1953. | 2.6 | 3.9 | 2.1 | 4.2 | 2.3 |
| 1954 – 1958. | 1.0 | 0.5 | 1.0 | 1.6 | 0.8 |
| 1958 – 1960. | 2.5 | −3.6 | 2.5 | 3.9 | −1.5 |

[1] Coal mining is the major component of mining.

[1] L'Extraction du charbon est la composante principale de la branche Industries extractives.

### B. The Major Groups of Manufacturing — Les classes de la branche Industries manufacturières

| Period<br>Période | Manu-<br>facturing<br><br>Industries<br>manufac-<br>turières | Food,<br>beverages<br>and<br>tobacco<br><br>Industries<br>alimen-<br>taires,<br>boissons,<br>tabac | Textiles | Clothing,<br>footwear<br>and<br>made-up<br>textiles<br><br>Articles<br>d'habil-<br>lement,<br>chaussures<br>et<br>ouvrages<br>en tissu | Wood<br>products<br>and<br>furniture<br><br>Bois et<br>meubles | Paper<br>and<br>paper<br>products<br><br>Papier<br>et<br>ouvrages<br>en<br>papier | Printing<br>and<br>publishing<br><br>Im-<br>primerie<br>et<br>édition | Leather<br>and<br>leather<br>products<br>except<br>wearing<br>apparel [1]<br><br>Cuir et<br>articles<br>en cuir,<br>à l'exclu-<br>sion<br>des<br>articles<br>d'habil-<br>lement [1] | Chemicals<br>and<br>chemical,<br>petroleum<br>and<br>coal<br>products<br><br>Produits<br>chi-<br>miques<br>et<br>dérivés<br>du<br>pétrole<br>et du<br>charbon | Non-<br>metallic<br>mineral<br>products<br><br>Produits<br>minéraux<br>non<br>métal-<br>liques | Basic<br>metals<br><br>Métal-<br>lurgie<br>de base | Metal<br>products<br><br>Ouvrages<br>en<br>métaux | Other<br>manu-<br>facturing<br><br>Autres<br>industries<br>manufac-<br>turières |
|---|---|---|---|---|---|---|---|---|---|---|---|---|---|
| ISIC — CITI | 2–3 | 20–22 | 23 | 24 | 25–26 | 27 | 28 | 29–30 | 31–32 | 33 | 34 | 35–38 | 39 |

a. Indexes — Indices (1958 = 100)

| | | | | | | | | | | | | | |
|---|---|---|---|---|---|---|---|---|---|---|---|---|---|
| 1948.............. | 82 | 93 | 89 | 99 | 108 | 80 | 73 | 95 | 60 | 87 | 71 | 69 | 95 |
| 1949.............. | 86 | 98 | 98 | 107 | 104 | 84 | 75 | 86 | 63 | 96 | 75 | 73 | 98 |
| 1950.............. | 90 | 100 | 106 | 112 | 104 | 88 | 80 | 86 | 72 | 100 | 79 | 78 | 89 |
| 1951.............. | 92 | 99 | 106 | 105 | 106 | 88 | 82 | 86 | 77 | 102 | 88 | 82 | 91 |
| 1952.............. | 89 | 98 | 101 | 93 | 96 | 84 | 82 | 86 | 78 | 98 | 88 | 82 | 100 |
| 1953.............. | 91 | 98 | 106 | 97 | 94 | 88 | 83 | 95 | 78 | 98 | 92 | 85 | 84 |
| 1954.............. | 96 | 99 | 109 | 99 | 102 | 92 | 90 | 100 | 89 | 102 | 96 | 91 | 89 |
| 1955.............. | 99 | 99 | 107 | 103 | 104 | 92 | 93 | 104 | 93 | 104 | 96 | 97 | 84 |
| 1956.............. | 101 | 99 | 106 | 105 | 104 | 96 | 95 | 100 | 95 | 106 | 100 | 101 | 100 |
| 1957.............. | 102 | 99 | 106 | 108 | 104 | 100 | 97 | 100 | 100 | 106 | 104 | 102 | 102 |
| 1958.............. | 100 | 100 | 100 | 100 | 100 | 100 | 100 | 100 | 100 | 100 | 100 | 100 | 100 |
| 1959.............. | 102 | 102 | 100 | 102 | 102 | 100 | 103 | 100 | 102 | 102 | 108 | 102 | 102 |
| 1960.............. | 105 | 104 | 102 | 104 | 104 | 104 | 107 | 101 | 107 | 104 | ... | 106 | ... |

b. Average Annual Rate of Change — Taux annuel moyen de variation

| | | | | | | | | | | | | | |
|---|---|---|---|---|---|---|---|---|---|---|---|---|---|
| 1950 – 1960....... | 1.6 | 0.4 | −0.4 | −0.7 | — | 1.7 | 3.0 | 1.6 | 4.0 | 0.4 | ... | 3.1 | ... |
| 1948 – 1953....... | 2.1 | 1.1 | 3.6 | −0.4 | −2.7 | 1.9 | 2.6 | — | 5.4 | 2.4 | 5.3 | 4.3 | −2.4 |
| 1954 – 1958....... | 1.0 | 0.2 | −2.1 | 0.2 | −0.5 | 2.1 | 2.7 | — | 3.0 | −0.5 | 1.0 | 2.4 | 3.0 |
| 1958 – 1960....... | 2.5 | 2.0 | 1.0 | 2.0 | 2.0 | 2.0 | 3.4 | 0.5 | 3.4 | 2.0 | ... | 3.0 | ... |

[1] Includes Rubber products (ISIC major group 30).     [1] Y compris Ouvrages en Caoutchouc (CITI 30).

## 4. THE CHARACTERISTICS OF ALL INDUSTRIAL LOCAL UNITS
## CARACTERISTIQUES DE TOUTES LES UNITES INDUSTRIELLES LOCALES
### 16 October 1950 — 16 octobre 1950

Number of local units in units; number of engaged and employees in thousands; capacity of installed power equipment in thousand horsepower; capacity of installed power equipment per person engaged in horsepower.

Nombre d'unités locales en unités; nombre de personnes occupées et de salariés en milliers; puissance installée en milliers de chevaux-vapeur; puissance installée par personne occupée en chevaux-vapeur.

### A. The Divisions of Industrial Activity — Les branches de l'activité industrielle

| Item of data | All industrial activity<br>Toutes industries | Mining<br>Industries extractives | Manufacturing<br>Industries manufacturières | Construction<br>Bâtiment et travaux publics | Electricity and gas[1]<br>Electricité et gaz[1] | Rubrique |
|---|---|---|---|---|---|---|
| ISIC | 1–4, 511–521 | 1 | 2–3 | 4 | 511–521 | CITI |
| *a. Absolute Figures — Chiffres absolus* | | | | | | |
| Number of local units.............. | 150 114 | 879 | 100 644 | 48 042 | 549 | Nombre d'unités locales |
| Number of engaged............... | 1 564.8 | 52.4 | 1 160.4 | 323.3 | 28.7 | Nombre de personnes occupées |
| Number of employees.............. | 1 336.0 | 51.1 | 1 005.3 | 251.5 | 28.1 | Nombre de salariés |
| Capacity of installed power equipment. | . | 584.0 | 2 785.8 | 415.7 | 2 388.3 | Puissance installée |
| *b. Structure* | | | | | | |
| Distribution in percent of number of engaged................... | 100.0 | 3.3 | 74.2 | 20.6 | 1.9 | Distribution en pourcentage du nombre de personnes occupées |
| Capacity of installed power equipment per person engaged........ | . | 11.14 | 2.40 | 1.28 | 83.22 | Puissance installée par personne occupée |

[1] Water supply is included.　　　　　　　　　　　　　　[1] Y compris la distribution publique de l'eau.

### B. The Major Groups of Mining — Les classes de la branche Industries extractives

| Item of data | All mining<br>Toutes industries extractives | Coal mining<br>Extraction du charbon | Crude petroleum and natural gas<br>Pétrole brut et gaz naturel | Other mining<br>Divers | Rubrique |
|---|---|---|---|---|---|
| ISIC | 1 | 11 | 13 | 14–19 | CITI |
| *a. Absolute Figures — Chiffres absolus* | | | | | |
| Number of local units................ | 879 | 15 | 2 | 862 | Nombre d'unités locales |
| Number of engaged................ | 52.4 | 45.7 | 0.9 | 5.8 | Nombre de personnes occupées |
| Number of employees............... | 51.1 | 45.7 | 0.9 | 4.5 | Nombre de salariés |
| Capacity of installed power equipment.. | 584.0 | 533.3 | 12.6 | 38.1 | Puissance installée |
| *b. Structure* | | | | | |
| Distribution in percent of number of engaged...................... | 100.0 | 87.2 | 1.7 | 11.1 | Distribution en pourcentage du nombre de personnes occupées |
| Capacity of installed power equipment per person engaged.............. | 11.14 | 11.67 | 14.00 | 6.57 | Puissance installée par personne occupée |

## C.   The Major Groups of Manufacturing — Les classes de la branche Industries manufacturières

| Item of data | Manufacturing — Industries manufacturières | Food, beverages and tobacco — Industries alimentaires, boissons, tabac | Textiles | Clothing, footwear and made-up textiles — Articles d'habillement, chaussures et ouvrages en tissu | Wood products and furniture — Bois et meubles | Paper and paper products — Papier et ouvrages en papier | Printing and publishing — Imprimerie et édition | Leather and leather products except wearing apparel — Cuir et articles en cuir, à l'exclusion des articles d'habillement | Rubber products — Ouvrages en caoutchouc | Chemicals and chemical, petroleum and coal products — Produits chimiques et dérivés du pétrole et du charbon | Non-metallic mineral products — Produits minéraux non métalliques | Basic metals — Métallurgie de base | Metal products — Ouvrages en métaux | Other manufacturing — Autres industries manufacturières | Rubrique |
|---|---|---|---|---|---|---|---|---|---|---|---|---|---|---|---|
| ISIC | 2-3 | 20-22 | 23 | 24 | 25-26 | 27 | 28 | 29 | 30 | 31-32 | 33 | 34 | 35-38 | 39 | CITI |
| *a. Absolute Figures — Chiffres absolus* | | | | | | | | | | | | | | | |
| Number of local units.... | 100 644 | 23 162 | 2 145 | 26 986 | 7 026 | 455 | 3 205 | 1 362 | 260 | 1 303 | 2 258 | 102 | 27 046 | 5 334 | Nombre d'unités locales |
| Number of engaged.... | 1 160.4 | 227.5 | 122.4 | 156.4 | 59.9 | 23.6 | 51.0 | 12.8 | 7.9 | 58.0 | 53.5 | 21.2 | 339.2 | 27.0 | Nombre de personnes occupées |
| Number of employees... | 1 005.3 | 182.7 | 118.7 | 120.4 | 49.8 | 22.9 | 46.1 | 10.7 | 7.5 | 56.1 | 50.1 | 21.0 | 299.8 | 19.5 | Nombre de salariés |
| Capacity of installed power equipment..... | 2 785.8 | 568.8 | 288.4 | 52.6 | 156.8 | 154.5 | 47.4 | 27.4 | 27.9 | 419.3 | 146.2 | 121.1 | 753.4 | 22.0 | Puissance installée |
| *b. Structure* | | | | | | | | | | | | | | | |
| Distribution in percent of number of engaged... | 100.0 | 19.6 | 10.5 | 13.5 | 5.1 | 2.1 | 4.4 | 1.1 | 0.7 | 5.0 | 4.6 | 1.8 | 29.2 | 2.4 | Distribution en pourcentage du nombre de personnes occupées |
| Capacity of installed power equipment per person engaged...... | 2.40 | 2.50 | 2.36 | 0.34 | 2.62 | 6.55 | 0.93 | 2.14 | 3.53 | 7.23 | 2.73 | 5.71 | 2.22 | 0.81 | Puissance installée par personne occupée |

## 5. THE CHARACTERISTICS OF ALL INDUSTRIAL UNITS
## CARACTERISTIQUES DE TOUTES LES UNITES INDUSTRIELLES
### 1948, 1953, 1958

Value added and wages and salaries in million Guilder; number of man-years worked in thousands; energy consumed in thousand metric tons of coal equivalents; electricity consumed in million KWH; value added and wages and salaries per man-year worked in thousand Guilder; energy consumed per man-year in metric tons of coal equivalent; electricity consumed per man-year in thousand KWH.

Valeur ajoutée et traitements et salaires en millions de florins; nombre d'années de travail en milliers; énergie consommée en milliers de tonnes métriques d'équivalent charbon; électricité consommée en millions de kWh; valeur ajoutée et traitements et salaires par année de travail en milliers de florins; énergie consommée par année de travail en tonnes métriques d'équivalent charbon; électricité consommée par année de travail en milliers de kWh.

## A.  The Divisions of Industrial Activity — Les branches de l'activité industrielle

### a. Absolute Figures — Chiffres absolus

| Year and item of data / Année et rubrique | All industrial activity / Toutes industries (1-4,511-521) | Mining / Industries extractives (1) | Manufacturing / Industries manufacturières (2-3) | Construction / Bâtiment et travaux publics (4) | Electricity, gas and water / Electricité, gaz et eau (511-521) |
|---|---|---|---|---|---|
| **1948** | | | | | |
| Value added / Valeur ajoutée | 5 438 | 226 | 4 090 | 875 | 247 |
| Employees / Salariés: Man-years worked[1] / Années de travail[1] | 1 212 | 49 | 914 | 218 | 31 |
| Wages and salaries / Traitements et salaires | 2 740 | 176 | 1 993 | 499 | 72 |
| **1953** | | | | | |
| Value added / Valeur ajoutée | 8 787 | 506 | 6 332 | 1 479 | 470 |
| Man-years worked[1] / Années de travail[1] | 1 378 | 59 | 1 015 | 269 | 35 |
| Wages and salaries / Traitements et salaires | 4 083 | 254 | 2 907 | 814 | 108 |
| **1958** | | | | | |
| Value added / Valeur ajoutée | 13 466 | 764 | 9 555 | 2 434 | 713 |
| Man-years worked[1] / Années de travail[1] | 1 503 | 61 | 1 114 | 291 | 37 |
| Wages and salaries / Traitements et salaires | 6 782 | 398 | 4 920 | 1 245 | 219 |

### b. Structure

| Year and item of data / Année et rubrique | All industrial activity / Toutes industries (1-4,51-52) | Mining / Industries extractives (1) | Manufacturing / Industries manufacturières (2-3) | Construction / Bâtiment et travaux publics (4) | Electricity, gas and water / Electricité, gaz et eau (511-521) |
|---|---|---|---|---|---|
| **1948** Distribution in percent of: / Distribution en pourcentage: | | | | | |
| Value added / Valeur ajoutée | 100.0 | 4.1 | 75.2 | 16.1 | 4.6 |
| Employee man-years worked / Années de salarié | 100.0 | 4.0 | 75.4 | 18.0 | 2.6 |
| Per employee man-year worked: / Par année de travail de salarié: | | | | | |
| Value added / Valeur ajoutée | 4.5 | 4.6 | 4.5 | 4.0 | 8.0 |
| Wages and salaries / Traitements et salaires | 2.3 | 3.6 | 2.2 | 2.3 | 2.3 |
| Value added per unit of wages and salaries / Valeur ajoutée par unité de traitements et salaires | 1.98 | 1.28 | 2.05 | 1.75 | 3.43 |
| **1953** Distribution in percent of: / Distribution en pourcentage: | | | | | |
| Value added / Valeur ajoutée | 100.0 | 5.7 | 72.1 | 16.8 | 5.4 |
| Employee man-years worked / Années de travail de salarié | 100.0 | 4.2 | 73.7 | 19.5 | 2.6 |
| Per employee man-year worked: / Par année de travail de salarié: | | | | | |
| Value added / Valeur ajoutée | 6.4 | 8.6 | 6.2 | 5.5 | 13.4 |
| Wages and salaries / Traitements et salaires | 3.0 | 4.3 | 2.9 | 3.0 | 3.1 |
| **1958** Distribution in percent of: / Distribution en pourcentage: | | | | | |
| Value added / Valeur ajoutée | 100.0 | 5.6 | 71.0 | 18.1 | 5.3 |
| Employee man-years worked / Années de travail de salarié | 100.0 | 4.0 | 74.1 | 19.4 | 2.5 |
| Per employee man-year worked: / Par année de travail de salarié: | | | | | |
| Value added / Valeur ajoutée | 9.0 | 12.5 | 8.6 | 8.4 | 19.3 |
| Wages and salaries / Traitements et salaires | 4.5 | 6.5 | 4.4 | 4.3 | 5.9 |
| Value added per unit of wages and salaries / Valeur ajoutée par unité de traitements et salaires | 1.98 | 1.92 | 1.94 | 1.96 | 3.26 |

For footnote see end of table.

Pour la note, voir au bas du tableau.

## B. The Major Groups of Mining — Les classes de la branche Industries extractives

| Year and item of data | All mining Toutes industries extrac-tives | Coal mining Extraction du charbon | Other mining, including crude petroleum Autres industries extractives, y compris l'extraction du pétrole brut | Année et rubrique | Year and item of data | All mining Toutes industries extrac-tives | Coal mining Extraction du charbon | Other mining, including crude petroleum Autres industries extractives, y compris l'extraction du pétrole brut | Année et rubrique |
|---|---|---|---|---|---|---|---|---|---|
| ISIC | 1 | 11 | 13, 14–19 | CITI | ISIC | 1 | 11 | 13, 14–19 | CITI |
| | a. Absolute Figures Chiffres absolus | | | | | b. Structure | | | |
| 1948 | | | | 1948 | 1948 | | | | 1948 |
| Value added................. | 226 | 166 | 60 | Valeur ajoutée | Distribution in percent of: | | | | Distribution en pourcentage: |
| Employees | | | | Salariés | Value added................ | 100.0 | 73.5 | 26.5 | Valeur ajoutée |
| Man-years worked [1]......... | 49 | 42 | 7 | Années de travail [1] | Employee man-years worked. | 100.0 | 85.7 | 14.3 | Années de travail de salarié |
| Wages and salaries.......... | 176 | 153 | 23 | Traitements et salaires | Per employee man-year worked | | | | Par année de travail de salarié |
| | | | | | Value added................ | 4.6 | 4.0 | 8.6 | Valeur ajoutée |
| | | | | | Wages and salaries.......... | 3.6 | 3.6 | 3.3 | Traitements et salaires |
| | | | | | Value added per unit of | | | | Valeur ajoutée par unité de |
| | | | | | wages and salaries.......... | 1.28 | 1.08 | 2.61 | traitements et salaires |
| 1953 | | | | 1953 | 1953 | | | | 1953 |
| Value added................. | 506 | 401 | 105 | Valeur ajoutée | Distribution in percent of: | | | | Distribution en pourcentage: |
| Employees | | | | Salariés | Value added................ | 100.0 | 79.2 | 20.8 | Valeur ajoutée |
| Man-years worked [1]......... | 59 | 53 | 6 | Années de travail [1] | Employee man-years worked. | 100.0 | 89.8 | 10.2 | Années de travail de salarié |
| Wages and salaries.......... | 254 | 229 | 25 | Traitements et salaires | Per employee man-year worked | | | | Par année de travail de salarié |
| | | | | | Value added................ | 8.6 | 7.6 | 17.5 | Valeur ajoutée |
| | | | | | Wages and salaries.......... | 4.3 | 4.3 | 4.2 | Traitements et salaires |
| | | | | | Value added per unit of | | | | Valeur ajoutée par unité de |
| | | | | | wages and salaries.......... | 1.99 | 1.75 | 4.20 | traitements et salaires |
| 1958 | | | | 1958 | 1958 | | | | 1958 |
| Value added................. | 764 | 571 | 193 | Valeur ajoutée | Distribution in percent of: | | | | Distribution en pourcentage: |
| Employees | | | | Salariés | Value added................ | 100.0 | 74.7 | 25.3 | Valeur ajoutée |
| Man-years worked [1]......... | 61 | 56 | 5 | Années de travail [1] | Employee man-years worked. | 100.0 | 91.8 | 8.2 | Années de travail de salarié |
| Wages and salaries.......... | 398 | 359 | 39 | Traitements et salaires | Per employee man-year worked | | | | Par année de travail de salarié |
| | | | | | Value added................ | 12.5 | 10.2 | 38.6 | Valeur ajoutée |
| | | | | | Wages and salaries.......... | 6.5 | 6.4 | 7.8 | Traitements et salaires |
| | | | | | Value added per unit of | | | | Valeur ajoutée par unité de |
| | | | | | wages and salaries.......... | 1.92 | 1.59 | 4.95 | traitements et salaires |

For footnote see end of table

Pour la note, voir au bas du tableau.

# NETHERLANDS

## C. The Major Groups of Manufacturing — Les classes de la branche Industries manufacturières

| Year and item of data | Manu-facturing / Industries manufac-turières | Food, beverages and tobacco / Industries alimen-taires, boissons, tabac | Textiles | Clothing, footwear and made-up textiles / Articles d'habil-lement, chaussures et ouvrages en tissu | Wood products and furniture / Bois et meubles | Paper and paper products / Papier et ouvrages en papier | Printing and publish-ing / Im-primerie et édition | Leather and leather products except wearing apparel and rubber products / Cuir et articles en cuir, à l'exclu-sion des articles d'habil-lement, et ouvrages en caout-chouc | Chemicals and chemical, petroleum and coal products / Produits chi-miques et dérivés du pétrole et du charbon | Non-metallic mineral products / Produits minéraux non métal-liques | Basic metals / Métal-lurgie de base | Metal products / Ouvrages en métaux | Other manu-factur-ing / Autres in-dustries manufac-turières | Année et rubrique |
|---|---|---|---|---|---|---|---|---|---|---|---|---|---|---|
| ISIC | 2–3 | 20–22 | 23 | 24 | 25–26 | 27 | 28 | 29–30 | 31–32 | 33 | 34 | 35–38 | 39 | CITI |

### a. Absolute Figures — Chiffres absolus

| Year and item of data | 2–3 | 20–22 | 23 | 24 | 25–26 | 27 | 28 | 29–30 | 31–32 | 33 | 34 | 35–38 | 39 | |
|---|---|---|---|---|---|---|---|---|---|---|---|---|---|---|
| **1948** | | | | | | | | | | | | | | **1948** |
| Value added | 4 090 | 830 | 464 | 358 | 222 | 94 | 213 | 88 | 367 | 148 | 93 | 1 035 | 178 | Valeur ajoutée |
| Employees: | | | | | | | | | | | | | | Salariés: |
| Man-years worked [1] | 914 | 171 | 98 | 117 | 52 | 20 | 44 | 21 | 49 | 40 | 17 | 243 | 42 | Années travail [1] |
| Wages and salaries | 1 993 | 359 | 212 | 160 | 115 | 43 | 107 | 44 | 113 | 87 | 45 | 613 | 95 | Traitements et salaires |
| **1953** | | | | | | | | | | | | | | **1953** |
| Value added | 6 332 | 1 263 | 590 | 401 | 237 | 176 | 317 | 136 | 701 | 241 | 192 | 1 850 | 228 | Valeur ajoutée |
| Employees: | | | | | | | | | | | | | | Salariés: |
| Man-years worked [1] | 1 015 | 180 | 117 | 114 | 45 | 22 | 50 | 21 | 64 | 45 | 22 | 298 | 37 | Années de travail [1] |
| Wages and salaries | 2 907 | 471 | 306 | 211 | 129 | 67 | 156 | 54 | 206 | 121 | 76 | 982 | 128 | Traitements et salaires |
| **1958** | | | | | | | | | | | | | | **1958** |
| Value added | 9 555 | 1 761 | 721 | 602 | 343 | 314 | 538 | 158 | 1 036 | 368 | 430 | 2 955 | 329 | Valeur ajoutée |
| Employees: | | | | | | | | | | | | | | Salariés: |
| Man-years worked [1] | 1 114 | †84 | 110 | 118 | 48 | 25 | 60 | 22 | 82 | 46 | 24 | 351 | 44 | Années de travail [1] |
| Wages and salaries | 4 920 | 755 | 441 | 352 | 195 | 131 | 273 | 96 | 427 | 198 | 134 | 1 714 | 204 | Traitements et salaires |
| Energy consumed | 6 861.1 [2] | 1 415.2 | 540.4 | ... | ... | 565.2 | ... | ... | 1 492.4 | 692.4 | 1 807.5 | | ... | Energie consommée |
| Electricity consumed | 4 026.7 [2] | 469.2 | 354.2 | ... | ... | 220.9 | ... | ... | 1 265.0 | 261.8 | 1 194.0 | | ... | Electricité consommée |

### b. Structure

| Year and item of data | 2–3 | 20–22 | 23 | 24 | 25–26 | 27 | 28 | 29–30 | 31–32 | 33 | 34 | 35–38 | 39 | |
|---|---|---|---|---|---|---|---|---|---|---|---|---|---|---|
| **1948** | | | | | | | | | | | | | | **1948** |
| Distribution in percent of: | | | | | | | | | | | | | | Distribution en pourcentage: |
| Value added | 100.0 | 20.2 | 11.4 | 8.7 | 5.5 | 2.3 | 5.2 | 2.1 | 9.0 | 3.6 | 2.3 | 25.3 | 4.4 | Valeur ajoutée |
| Employees man-years worked | 100.0 | 18.7 | 10.7 | 12.8 | 5.7 | 2.2 | 4.8 | 2.3 | 5.3 | 4.4 | 1.9 | 26.6 | 4.6 | Années de travail de salarié |
| Per employee man-year worked: | | | | | | | | | | | | | | Par année de travail de salarié |
| Value added | 4.5 | 4.8 | 4.7 | 3.0 | 4.3 | 4.7 | 4.8 | 4.2 | 7.5 | 3.7 | 5.5 | 4.2 | 4.2 | Valeur ajoutée |
| Wages and salaries | 2.2 | 2.1 | 2.2 | 1.4 | 2.2 | 2.2 | 2.4 | 2.1 | 2.3 | 2.2 | 2.6 | 2.5 | 2.3 | Traitements et salaires |
| Value added per unit of wages and salaries | 2.05 | 2.31 | 2.19 | 2.24 | 1.93 | 2.19 | 1.99 | 2.00 | 3.25 | 1.70 | 2.07 | 1.69 | 1.87 | Valeur ajoutée par unité de traitements et salaires |
| **1953** | | | | | | | | | | | | | | **1953** |
| Distribution in percent of: | | | | | | | | | | | | | | Distribution en pourcentage: |
| Value added | 100.0 | 19.9 | 9.3 | 6.3 | 3.8 | 2.8 | 5.0 | 2.1 | 11.1 | 3.8 | 3.0 | 29.2 | 3.7 | Valeur ajoutée |
| Employees man-years worked | 100.0 | 17.7 | 11.5 | 11.2 | 4.5 | 2.1 | 5.0 | 2.0 | 6.3 | 4.5 | 2.1 | 29.4 | 3.7 | Années de travail de salarié |
| Per employee man-year worked: | | | | | | | | | | | | | | Par année de travail de salarié |
| Value added | 6.2 | 7.0 | 5.0 | 3.5 | 5.3 | 8.0 | 6.3 | 6.5 | 11.0 | 5.4 | 8.7 | 6.2 | 6.2 | Valeur ajoutée |
| Wages and salaries | 2.9 | 2.6 | 2.6 | 1.8 | 2.9 | 3.0 | 3.1 | 2.6 | 3.2 | 2.7 | 3.4 | 3.3 | 3.4 | Traitements et salaires |
| Value added per unit of wages and salaries | 2.18 | 2.68 | 1.93 | 1.90 | 1.84 | 2.63 | 2.03 | 2.52 | 3.40 | 1.99 | 2.53 | 1.88 | 1.78 | Valeur ajoutée par unité de traitements et salaires |
| **1958** | | | | | | | | | | | | | | **1958** |
| Distribution in percent of: | | | | | | | | | | | | | | Distribution en pourcentage: |
| Value added | 100.0 | 18.4 | 7.5 | 6.3 | 3.6 | 3.3 | 5.6 | 1.7 | 10.8 | 3.9 | 4.5 | 30.9 | 3.5 | Valeur ajoutée |
| Employees man-years worked | 100.0 | 16.5 | 9.8 | 10.6 | 4.3 | 2.3 | 5.4 | 1.9 | 7.4 | 4.1 | 2.2 | 31.5 | 4.0 | Années de travail de salarié |
| Per employee man-year worked: | | | | | | | | | | | | | | Par année de travail de salarié |
| Value added | 8.6 | 9.6 | 6.6 | 5.1 | 7.1 | 12.6 | 9.0 | 7.2 | 12.6 | 8.0 | 17.9 | 8.4 | 7.5 | Valeur ajoutée |
| Wages and salaries | 4.4 | 4.1 | 4.0 | 3.0 | 4.1 | 5.2 | 4.6 | 4.4 | 5.2 | 4.3 | 5.6 | 4.9 | 4.6 | Traitements et salaires |
| Energy consumed | 6.16 [2] | 7.69 | 4.91 | ... | ... | 22.61 | ... | ... | 18.20 | 15.05 | 4.82 | | ... | Energie consommée |
| Electricity consumed | 3.6 [2] | 2.6 | 3.2 | ... | ... | 8.8 | ... | ... | 15.4 | 5.7 | 3.2 | | ... | Electricité consommée |
| Value added per unit of wages and salaries | 1.94 | 2.33 | 1.63 | 1.71 | 1.76 | 2.40 | 1.97 | 1.64 | 2.43 | 1.86 | 3.21 | 1.72 | 1.61 | Valeur ajoutée par unité de traitements et salaires |

[1] One man-year is equivalent of 300 full days of employment.
[2] Covers all of the major groups of Manufacturing, including those for which separate data are not available.

[1] Une année de travail équivaut à trois cents jours d'emploi à plein temps.
[2] Sont incluses toutes les classes des Industries manufacturières, y compris celles pour lesquelles on ne dispose pas de données distinctes.

## 6. FUELS AND ELECTRICITY CONSUMED, ALL MANUFACTURING UNITS
### COMBUSTIBLES ET ELECTRICITE CONSOMMES PAR L'ENSEMBLE DES UNITES MANUFACTURIERES
### 1958

### A. Percentage Distribution of Energy Consumed According to Source
### Répartition en pourcentage de l'énergie consommée suivant la source

Quantities in thousand metric tons of coal equivalents.                    Quantités en milliers de tonnes métriques d'équivalent charbon.

| Item of data | Manu-facturing [1] Industries manufac-turières [1] | Food, beverages and tobacco Industries alimen-taires, boissons, tabac | Textiles | Paper and paper products Papier et ouvrages en papier | Chemicals and chemical, petroleum and coal products Produits chi-miques et dérivés du pétrole et du charbon | Non-metallic mineral products Produits minéraux non métal-liques | Basic metals and metal products Métal-lurgie de base et ouvrages en métaux | Rubrique |
|---|---|---|---|---|---|---|---|---|
| ISIC | 2–3 | 20–22 | 23 | 27 | 31–32 | 33 | 34–38 | CITI |
| Total energy consumed | | | | | | | | Energie totale consommée |
| Quantity | 6 861.1 | 1 415.2 | 540.4 | 565.2 | 1 492.4 | 692.4 | 1 807.5 | Quantité |
| Percent of total in specified industry | 100.0 | 20.6 | 7.9 | 8.2 | 21.8 | 10.1 | 26.3 | Pourcentage du total par industrie indiquée |
| Percent consumed as: | | | | | | | | Pourcentage consommé sous forme de: |
| Coal | 26.3 | 34.1 | 37.1 | 55.9 | 15.3 | 48.8 | 6.9 | Charbon |
| Coke | 19.2 | 3.9 | 0.2 | 0.4 | 24.8 | 3.1 | 47.6 | Coke |
| Refined oil fuels | 46.6 | 57.5 | 54.4 | 38.8 | 49.2 | 41.6 | 37.0 | Pétrole raffiné |
| Electricity | 7.4 | 4.2 | 8.2 | 4.9 | 10.6 | 4.8 | 8.3 | Electricité |
| Other solid fuels | 0.5 | 0.3 | 0.1 | — | 0.1 | 1.7 | 0.2 | Autres combustibles |

### B. Quantity of Fuels and Electricity Consumed
### Quantités de combustibles et d'électricité consommés

Coal, coke, refined oil fuels and other solid fuels in thousand metric tons; and electricity in million KWH.                    Charbon, coke, pétrole raffiné et autres combustibles solides en milliers de tonnes métriques; électricité en millions de kWh.

| Source of energy | Manu-facturing [1] Industries manufac-turières [1] | Food, beverages and tobacco Industries alimen-taires, boissons, tabac | Textiles | Paper and paper products Papier et ouvrages en papier | Chemicals and chemical, petroleum and coal products Produits chi-miques et dérivés du pétrole et du charbon | Non-metallic mineral products Produits minéraux non métal-liques | Basic metals and metal products Métal-lurgie de base et ouvrages en métaux | Source d'énergie |
|---|---|---|---|---|---|---|---|---|
| ISIC | 2–3 | 20–22 | 23 | 27 | 31–32 | 33 | 34–38 | CITI |
| Coal | 1 810.4 | 483.7 | 200.5 | 316.0 | 228.4 | 338.0 | 125.5 | Charbon |
| Coke | 1 463.2 | 60.8 | 1.4 | 2.8 | 412.1 | 23.9 | 957.0 | Coke |
| Refined oil fuels | 2 133.2 | 542.4 | 195.8 | 146.0 | 488.7 | 192.3 | 446.0 | Pétrole raffiné |
| Electricity consumed | 4 026.7 | 469.2 | 354.2 | 220.9 | 1 265.0 | 261.8 | 1 194.0 | Electricité consommée |
| Other solid fuels | 61.8 | 9.2 | 1.2 | 0.1 | 4.0 | 23.7 | 5.0 | Autres combustibles solides |

[1] Covers all of the major groups of Manufacturing, including those which are not shown in the table

[1] Sont incluses toutes les classes des Industries manufac-turières, y compris celles qui ne figurent pas dans le tableau.

# NEW ZEALAND — NOUVELLE-ZELANDE

## Gross Domestic Product and Gross Domestic Fixed Capital Formation

The estimates of the gross domestic product and gross domestic fixed capital formation presented in Table 1 are from the response of the Department of Statistics, Wellington, to the United Nations national accounts questionnaire. The official estimates and description of the concepts and methods utilized in making them are published annually in *Report on the Official Estimates of National Income*. The estimates for the fiscal years, 1952-1953 and 1954-1955, of the gross domestic product according to industrial origin and gross domestic fixed capital formation according to sector of purchase are given and described in *Report on the Inter-Industry Study of the New Zealand Economy for the year 1954-1955*.

## Index Numbers of Manufacturing Production

The index numbers shown in Table 2 are based on index numbers of manufacturing production compiled on an annual basis by the Department of Statistics, Wellington, and published in the *New Zealand Yearbook* and in *Industrial Production Statistics*. The series of index numbers relate, in general, to manufacturing establishments with at least two or more persons engaged.

The indexes are computed as base-weighted arithmetic averages in successive stages. The elementary series of relatives for the indexes are based, in most cases, on quantities produced but, in some instances, on raw materials consumed or hours worked. The weighting base years were 1 April 1938-31 March 1939 for the indexes for the periods, 1938-39 through 1948-49; 1 April 1949-31 March 1950 for the years, 1949-50 through 1955-56; and 1 April 1956-31 March 1957 for the periods, 1956-57 and thereafter. The elementary series of relatives are weighted by value of gross production during the base year when combined into index numbers for detailed categories of manufacturing. These index numbers are weighted by figures of value added, at factor cost, during the base year resulting from the Censuses described below, when combined into indexes for broader categories of industrial activity. It should be noted that quantity indicators for the elementary series of relatives are also derived from the results of these Censuses.

## Index Numbers of Industrial Employment

The index numbers shown in Table 3 are based, in practically all cases, on absolute figures of employment

## Produit intérieur brut et formation brute de capital fixe intérieur

Les estimations du produit intérieur brut et de la formation brute de capital fixe intérieur reproduites au tableau 1 ont été fournies par le Département de la statistique, Wellington, en réponse au questionnaire de l'ONU sur la comptabilité nationale. Les estimations officielles, ainsi que la description des concepts et méthodes adoptés pour les établir, sont publiées annuellement dans *Report on the Official Estimates of National Income*. Les estimations pour les exercices financiers 1952-1953 et 1954-1955 du produit intérieur brut par branche d'activité d'origine et de la formation brute de capital fixe intérieur par secteur d'acquisition sont présentées et décrites dans *Report on the Inter-Industry Study of the New Zealand Economy for the year 1954-1955*.

## Indices de la production manufacturière

Les indices du tableau 2 sont fondés sur les indices de la production manufacturière établis annuellement par le Département de la statistique, Wellington, et publiés dans le *New Zealand Yearbook* et dans *Industrial Production Statistics*. Les séries d'indices se rapportent, en général, aux établissements manufacturiers occupant deux personnes ou plus.

Ces indices sont des moyennes arithmétiques à pondération fixe. Les séries élémentaires de rapports servant au calcul des indices sont fondées, dans la plupart des cas, sur les quantités produites, mais parfois sur les quantités de matières premières consommées ou le nombre d'heures de travail effectuées. Pour la pondération, les années de base sont : 1er avril 1938-31 mars 1939 pour les indices 1938-1939 à 1948-1949; 1er avril 1949-31 mars 1950 pour les indices 1949-1950 à 1955-1956; et 1er avril 1956-31 mars 1957 pour les indices des années 1956-1957 et suivantes. Les séries élémentaires de rapports sont pondérées en fonction de la valeur brute de la production pendant l'année de base lorsqu'on les combine en indices de catégories détaillées de l'activité manufacturière. Pour passer de ces indices aux indices plus larges de l'activité industrielle, on pondère par la valeur ajoutée au coût des facteurs pendant l'année de base, qui est calculée d'après les résultats des recensements décrits ci-dessous. Il convient de noter que les indicateurs quantitatifs des séries élémentaires de rapports sont également tirés des résultats de ces recensements.

## Indices de l'emploi dans l'industrie

Les indices du tableau 3 sont fondés, dans pratiquement tous les cas, sur les chiffres absolus de l'emploi

from the annual Censuses of Production taken by the Department of Statistics. In the case of the period, 1961-62, for which the results of the annual Censuses were not yet available, use was made of absolute figures from the half-yearly Survey of Employment carried out by the Department of Labour, Wellington. Linkage between the two sets of absolute figures of employment was effected for the fiscal year, 1960-61. The data on employment from the annual Censuses were abstracted from the *Reports on the Industrial Statistics of New Zealand* and earlier versions of this publication and issues of the *New Zealand Official Yearbook*, all published by the Department of Statistics, Wellington. The figures from the half-yearly Surveys of Employment were compiled from *Labour and Employment Gazette*, Department of Labour and correspondence with this Department.

The absolute figures on employment utilized from the annual Censuses relate to the annual average number of persons engaged (i.e., employees, homeworkers and working proprietors) in the establishments covered, excepting persons engaged in selling and distribution. In the case of the mining industries, establishments engaging one or more persons are included in the annual Censuses figures. In the case of the manufacturing and electricity and gas industries, establishments are covered if they have at least two persons engaged. The data compiled from the half-yearly Surveys refer to the average monthly number of employees of units with two or more persons engaged.

Because of the differences between Mining and the two other divisions of industrial activity in the field of establishments covered, the Statistical Office of the United Nations computed the indexes for the three divisions, combined, as base-weighted arithmetic means of the indexes for each division. The weighting utilized in these computations was proportional to the average number of persons engaged during 1 April 1953-31 March 1954 for the indexes relating to 1954-55 and earlier fiscal years and during 1 April 1958-31 March 1959 in the case of 1955-56 and later periods.

## Characteristics and Structure of Industrial Activity

The information shown in Table 4 is derived from the results of the annual Censuses carried out by the Department of Statistics, Wellington, and published in *Statistical Report on The Factory and Building Production of the Dominion of New Zealand for the Year 1938-39, Statistical Report on the Factory Production of New Zealand for the Years 1946-47 and 1947-48,* and *Report on the Industrial Production Statistics of New Zealand for the Year 1953-54* or *1958-59,* as well as in various issues of the *New Zealand Official Yearbook.* Some of the data shown in Table 4 are from correspondence with the Department of Statistics.

Because of a change in coverage and classification in 1951-52, in the case of Manufacturing, the data for 1938-39

provenant des recensements annuels de la production exécutés par le Département de la statistique. Dans le cas de la période 1961-1962, pour laquelle les résultats des recensements annuels n'étaient pas encore disponibles, on a utilisé des chiffres absolus provenant de l'enquête semestrielle sur l'emploi effectuée par le Department of Labour, Wellington. Les deux ensembles de chiffres absolus portant sur l'emploi ont été raccordés au niveau de l'année financière 1960-1961. Les données sur l'emploi fournies par les recensements annuels ont été tirées de *Reports on the Industrial Statistics of New Zealand* et des versions précédentes de cette publication, ainsi que de quelques numéros du *New Zealand Official Yearbook,* tous publiés par le Département de statistique, Wellington. Les chiffres provenant des enquêtes semestrielles sur l'emploi ont été tirés de *Labour and Employment Gazette,* Department of Labour, et de la correspondance avec ce département.

Les chiffres absolus de l'emploi tirés des résultats des recensements annuels portent sur le nombre annuel moyen de personnes occupées (c'est-à-dire : salariés, travailleurs à domicile et propriétaires qui travaillent) dans les établissements recensés, à l'exception des personnes appartenant aux services de vente et de distribution. Dans le cas des industries extractives, les établissements occupant une personne ou plus sont couverts par les chiffres des recensements annuels. Dans le cas des industries manufacturières, de l'électricité et du gaz, les établissements sont compris s'ils ont au moins deux personnes occupées. Les données provenant des enquêtes semestrielles portent sur le nombre mensuel moyen de salariés des unités occupant deux personnes ou plus.

En raison des différences existant entre les industries extractives et les deux autres branches de l'activité industrielle quant au champ couvert, le Bureau de statistique de l'ONU a calculé les indices relatifs aux trois branches combinées comme moyennes arithmétiques à pondération fixe des indices relatifs à chaque branche. Le système de pondération adopté pour combiner ces indices est fondé sur le nombre moyen de personnes occupées entre le 1er avril 1953 et le 31 mars 1954 pour les indices de 1954-1955 et des exercices financiers antérieurs, et entre le 1er avril 1958 et le 31 mars 1959 pour 1955-1956 et les années suivantes.

## Caractéristiques et structure de l'activité industrielle

Les renseignements du tableau 4 sont tirés des résultats des recensements annuels effectués par le Département de la statistique, Wellington, ces résultats sont publiés dans *Statistical Report on the Factory and Building Production of the Dominion of New Zealand for the year 1938-39, Statistical Report on the Factory Production of New Zealand for the years 1946-47 and 1947-48,* et *Report on the Industrial Production Statistics of New Zealand for the year 1953-54* ou *1958-59,* ainsi que dans divers numéros du *New Zealand Official Yearbook.* Certaines données du tableau 4 ont été fournies par le Département de la statistique par voie de correspondance.

La couverture et le système de classement ayant été modifiés en 1951-1952 dans le cas des industries manu-

and 1947-48 are not comparable with those for 1953-54 and 1958-59. In the former Censuses all factories were covered which had at least two persons engaged or which used motive power, and butcheries, bakeries and smithies were entirely excluded. However, the following factories were included even though they engaged fewer than two persons or did not use motive power: bacon, butter, cheese, soap and candle factories, tanneries, brickyards and limeworks. In the 1953-54 and 1958-58 Censuses, all registered factories engaging at least two persons were covered except for the following: bakeries, butcheries, boot and watch repairers; bespoke tailors, dressmakers and milliners; railway and tramway workshops; and the naval dockyard. The logging operations of sawmills, which were included in 1938-39 and 1947-48, were excluded in 1953-54 and 1958-59.

The data shown in Table 4 for Mining, Construction and Electricity and gas are comparable from one period to another. In the case of the first two divisions of industrial activity, units having at least one person engaged are covered. In the case of the third division all establishments are, in effect, covered.

The figures of employment shown in Table 4 exclude all persons engaged in selling or distribution for the covered establishments, such as salesmen, carters engaged solely in the outward delivery of goods, sales office staff and warehousemen. The data on wages and salaries include amounts drawn by working proprietors in lieu of salaries. Value added is computed as the difference between the value of production, at factor cost ex-factory, and the cost of raw materials and containers consumed in this production. It therefore includes the cost of fuel and power consumed and of work sub-contracted but excludes the receipts from merchandised goods by the covered establishments. In other respects the definitions of the items of data appear to be consistent with the International Standards in Basic Industrial Statistics.

facturières, les données pour 1938-1939 et 1947-1948 ne sont pas comparables avec celles de 1953-1954 et 1958-1959. Les premiers recensements portaient sur tous les établissements qui occupaient au moins deux personnes ou qui utilisaient la force motrice, à l'exclusion des boucheries, boulangeries et ateliers de forgerons. Toutefois, les établissements suivants ont été recensés même s'ils occupaient moins de deux personnes ou s'ils n'utilisaient pas la force motrice : charcuteries, beurreries, fromageries, savonneries, fabriques de bougies, tanneries, briqueteries et fours à chaux. Dans les recensements de 1953-1954 et 1958-1959, tous les établissements enregistrés occupant au moins deux personnes ont été recensés, à l'exception des catégories suivantes : boulangeries, boucheries, cordonneries et horlogeries; tailleurs, couturières et modistes travaillant à façon; ateliers des chemins de fer et tramways, et arsenaux. Les opérations d'abattage effectuées par les scieries ont été comprises dans les recensements de 1938-1939 et 1947-1948, mais non dans ceux de 1953-1954 et 1958-1959.

Les données du tableau 4 relatives aux industries extractives, au bâtiment et aux travaux publics, ainsi qu'à l'électricité et au gaz sont comparables d'une période à l'autre. Dans le cas des deux premières branches de l'activité industrielle, les unités occupant au moins une personne sont comprises. Dans le cas de la troisième branche, tous les établissements sont effectivement inclus.

Les chiffres de l'emploi du tableau 4 ne comprennent pas les personnes s'occupant de la vente ou de la distribution pour le compte des établissements recensés, par exemple les vendeurs, les transporteurs chargés uniquement de livrer les produits à l'extérieur, le personnel des services de vente et les magasiniers. Les traitements et salaires comprennent les sommes prélevées en guise de traitements par les propriétaires qui travaillent. La valeur ajoutée est la différence entre la valeur de la production au coût des facteurs, départ usine, et le coût des matières premières et des emballages consommés pour la production. Elle comprend donc le coût des combustibles et de l'énergie consommés et des travaux confiés à des sous-traitants, mais non les recettes provenant des marchandises revendues en l'état par les établissements recensés. A tous autres égards, les définitions des rubriques paraissent conformes aux Normes internationales relatives aux statistiques industrielles de base.

# 1. THE GROSS NATIONAL PRODUCT AND GROSS DOMESTIC FIXED CAPITAL FORMATION
## LE PRODUIT INTERIEUR BRUT ET LA FORMATION BRUTE DE CAPITAL FIXE INTERIEUR

Million Pounds, New Zealand                    Millions de livres, Nouvelle-Zélande

## A. Expenditure on the Gross Domestic Product at Market Prices
### Dépenses relatives au produit intérieur brut aux prix du marché

| Item of data and year / Rubrique et année | Total | Consumption [2] / Consommation [2] | | Gross Domestic Capital Formation [3] / Formation brute de capital intérieur [3] | | Net exports of goods and services [3] / Exportations nettes de biens et de services [3] | |
| | | Total | Government / Etat | Total | Fixed / Fixe | Exports less imports / Exportations moins importations | Exports / Exportations |
|---|---|---|---|---|---|---|---|
| | | | | *a. At Current Prices — Aux prix courants* | | | |
| Absolute figures — Chiffres absolus [1] | | | | | | | |
| 1948............................... | 494 | 410 | 56 | 71 | 90 | 13 | 154 |
| 1951............................... | 730 | 566 | 85 | 184 | 147 | −21 | 262 |
| 1952............................... | 767 | 576 | 96 | 187 | 174 | 3 | 258 |
| 1953............................... | 846 | 639 | 103 | 166 | 187 | 40 | 260 |
| 1954............................... | 939 | 713 | 102 | 250 | 221 | −24 | 253 |
| 1955............................... | 990 | 767 | 110 | 245 | 226 | −22 | 281 |
| 1956............................... | 1 040 | 802 | 120 | 240 | 230 | −4 | 294 |
| 1957............................... | 1 101 | 871 | 126 | 267 | 251 | −37 | 294 |
| 1958............................... | 1 150 | 886 | 132 | 267 | 251 | −4 | 284 |
| 1959............................... | 1 233 | 906 | 141 | 267 | 261 | 60 | 333 |
| 1960............................... | 1 325 | 1 036 | 151 | 319 | 293 | −29 | 312 |
| 1961............................... | 1 362 | 1 077 | 157 | 314 | 302 | −28 | 312 |
| Percentage distribution of average annual expenditure — Distribution en pourcentage des dépenses annuelles moyennes | | | | | | | |
| 1948............................... | 100.0 | 83.0 | 11.3 | 14.4 | 18.2 | 2.6 | 31.2 |
| 1951 – 1960....................... | 100.0 | 76.7 | 11.5 | 23.6 | 22.2 | −0.3 | 28.0 |
| 1953............................... | 100.0 | 75.6 | 12.2 | 19.7 | 22.1 | 4.7 | 30.8 |
| 1954............................... | 100.0 | 75.9 | 10.9 | 26.6 | 23.5 | −2.5 | 26.9 |
| 1958............................... | 100.0 | 77.1 | 11.5 | 23.2 | 21.8 | −0.3 | 24.7 |
| 1960............................... | 100.0 | 78.2 | 11.4 | 24.1 | 22.1 | −2.3 | 23.5 |

For footnotes see end of table.                    Pour les notes, voir au bas du tableau.

## B. The Gross Domestic Product at Factor Cost According to Origin
### Origine par secteur d'activité du produit intérieur brut au coût des facteurs

| Item of data and year / Rubrique et année | Total | Agricultural sector / Secteur agricole | Industrial Sector — Secteur industriel | | | | | Transportation and communication / Transports et communications | Other sectors / Autres secteurs |
| | | | Total | Mining / Industries extractives | Manufacturing / Industries manufacturières | Construction / Bâtiment et travaux publics | Electricity, gas and water / Electricité, gaz et eau | | |
|---|---|---|---|---|---|---|---|---|---|
| ISIC — CITI | 0–9 | 0 | 1–5 | 1 | 2–3 | 4 | 5 | 7 | 6, 8–9 |
| | | | *a. At Current Prices — Aux prix courants* | | | | | | |
| Absolute figures — Chiffres absolus [1] | | | | | | | | | |
| 1952............ | 740 | 174 | 226 | 7 | 155 | 51 | 13 | 67 | 273 |
| 1954............ | 899 | 198 | 288 | 9 | 195 | 64 | 20 | 82 | 331 |
| Percentage distribution according to sector — Distribution en pourcentage par secteur | | | | | | | | | |
| 1954............ | 100.0 | 22.0 | 32.1 | 1.0 | 21.7 | 7.1 | 2.3 | 9.1 | 36.8 |

For footnotes see end of table.                    Pour les notes, voir au bas du tableau.

## C. Gross Domestic Fixed Capital Formation According to Purchasing Sector
### La formation brute de capital fixe intérieur par secteur d'acquisition

| Item of data and year<br>Rubrique et année | Total | Agricultural sector<br><br>Secteur agricole | Industrial Sector — Secteur industriel | | | | | Transportation and communication<br><br>Transports et communications | Other sectors<br><br>Autres secteurs |
| | | | Total | Mining<br><br>Industries extractives | Manufacturing<br><br>Industries manufacturières | Construction<br><br>Bâtiment et travaux publics | Electricity, gas and water<br><br>Electricité, gaz et eau | | |
|---|---|---|---|---|---|---|---|---|---|
| ISIC — CITI | 0-9 | 0 | 1-5 | 1 | 2-3 | 4 | 5 | 7 | 6, 8-9 |
| | *a. At Current Prices — Aux prix courants* | | | | | | | | |
| Absolute figures — Chiffres absolus [1] | | | | | | | | | |
| 1952............ | 167 | 22 | 54 | 1 | 30 | 4 | 19 | 19 | 72 |
| 1954............ | 207 | 22 | 61 | 1 | 33 | 6 | 21 | 20 | 104 |
| Percentage distribution according to sector— Distribution en pourcentage par secteur | | | | | | | | | |
| 1954............ | 100.0 | 10.6 | 29.5 | 0.5 | 15.9 | 2.9 | 10.2 | 9.7 | 50.2 |

[1] Fiscal Years beginning 1 April.
[2] Current transfers, other than direct taxes, from households to General Government and non-monetary social security benefits are included in "Consumption, Total". Government consumption expenditures are net of these items.
[3] Changes in stocks are not adjusted for changes in valuation.

[1] Exercices financiers commençant le 1er avril.
[2] Les transferts courants, autres que les impôts indirects, effectués par les ménages et allant à l'Etat, et les prestations non monétaires de la sécurité sociale sont compris dans "Consommation, Total". Ces éléments sont exclus des dépenses de consommation de l'Etat.
[3] Les variations des stocks ne tiennent pas compte des variations en valeur.

## 2. INDEX NUMBERS OF MANUFACTURING PRODUCTION — INDICES DE LA PRODUCTION MANUFACTURIERE

| Period [1]<br>Période [1] | Manufacturing [3]<br>Industries manufacturières [3] | Food, beverages and tobacco<br>Industries alimentaires, boissons, tabac | Textiles | Clothing, footwear and made-up textiles<br>Articles d'habillement, chaussures et ouvrages en tissu | Wood products<br>Bois | Paper and paper products<br>Papier et ouvrages en papier | Printing and publishing<br>Imprimerie et édition | Leather and leather products except wearing apparel<br>Cuir et articles en cuir, à l'exclusion des articles d'habillement | Rubber products<br>Ouvrages en caoutchouc | Chemicals and chemical, products<br>Produits chimiques | Non-metallic mineral products<br>Produits minéraux non métalliques | Metal products<br>Ouvrages en métaux |
|---|---|---|---|---|---|---|---|---|---|---|---|---|
| ISIC — CITI | 2-3 | 20-22 | 23 | 24 | 25 | 27 | 28 | 29 | 30 | 31 | 33 | 35-38 |
| | *a. Indexes — Indices (1958 = 100)* | | | | | | | | | | | |
| 1938.............. | 39 [2] | 40 | 26 | 32 | 55 | 8 | 54 | 51 | ... | 44 | 52 | 25 |
| 1948.............. | 60 [2] | 74 | 62 | 75 | 74 | 23 | 58 | 115 | ... | 63 | 60 | 50 |
| 1949.............. | -64- | -78- | -67- | -77- | -75- | -22- | -59- | -106- | 37 | -64- | -65- | -55- |
| 1950.............. | 67 | 76 | 69 | 86 | 84 | 27 | 61 | 109 | 50 | 69 | 65 | 58 |
| 1951.............. | 71 | 81 | 70 | 86 | 88 | 29 | 63 | 109 | 66 | 75 | 69 | 65 |
| 1952.............. | 71 | 81 | 66 | 78 | 88 | 29 | 66 | 103 | 49 | 74 | 73 | 66 |
| 1953.............. | 75 | 83 | 79 | 81 | 90 | 36 | 69 | 104 | 59 | 80 | 75 | 76 |
| 1954.............. | 83 | 87 | 82 | 89 | 94 | 45 | 80 | 101 | 80 | 91 | 86 | 87 |
| 1955.............. | 88 | 89 | 78 | 90 | 96 | 65 | 87 | 94 | 88 | 96 | 92 | 97 |
| 1956.............. | -88- | -90- | -78- | -87- | -95- | -76- | -91- | -85- | -87- | -96- | -89- | -93- |
| 1957.............. | 95 | 96 | 86 | 92 | 94 | 93 | 97 | 87 | 96 | 101 | 96 | 102 |
| 1958.............. | 100 | 100 | 100 | 100 | 100 | 100 | 100 | 100 | 100 | 100 | 100 | 100 |
| 1959.............. | 104 | 103 | 109 | 96 | 105 | 107 | 113 | 96 | 99 | 112 | 111 | 103 |
| 1960.............. | 114 | 106 | 116 | 101 | 113 | 117 | 127 | 107 | 109 | 124 | 120 | 122 |
| | *b. Average Annual Rate of Change — Taux annuel moyen de variation* | | | | | | | | | | | |
| 1938-1960........ | 5.0 | 4.5 | 7.0 | 5.4 | 3.3 | 13.0 | 4.0 | 3.4 | ... | 4.8 | 3.9 | 7.5 |
| 1938-1948........ | 4.4 | 6.3 | 9.1 | 8.9 | 3.0 | 11.1 | 0.7 | 8.5 | ... | 3.7 | 1.4 | 7.2 |
| 1950-1960........ | 5.5 | 3.4 | 5.3 | 1.6 | 3.0 | 15.8 | 7.6 | -0.2 | 8.1 | 6.0 | 6.3 | 7.7 |
| 1948-1953........ | 4.6 | 2.3 | 5.0 | 1.6 | 4.0 | 9.4 | 3.5 | -2.0 | ... | 4.9 | 4.6 | 8.7 |
| 1954-1958........ | 4.8 | 3.5 | 5.1 | 3.0 | 1.6 | 22.1 | 5.7 | -0.3 | 5.7 | 2.4 | 3.8 | 3.5 |
| 1958-1960........ | 6.8 | 3.0 | 7.7 | 0.5 | 6.3 | 8.2 | 12.7 | 3.4 | 4.4 | 11.4 | 9.5 | 10.5 |

[1] Years beginning 1 April and ending 31 March of each set of years stated.
[2] Includes logging operations of sawmillers and the production and distribution of electricity and gas.
[3] Although individual indexes are not shown for a number of the major groups of manufacturing, production in all of these major groups is covered in the indexes for manufacturing as a whole.

[1] Du 1er avril de la première année au 31 mars de la deuxième année.
[2] Y compris les opérations d'abattage effectuées par les scieries, ainsi que la production et la distribution d'électricité et de gaz.
[3] Bien qu'aucun indice ne soit fourni pour certaines classes de la branche Industries manufacturières, la production de toutes ces classes est comprise dans les indices concernant l'ensemble des industries manufacturières.

## 3. INDEX NUMBERS OF INDUSTRIAL EMPLOYMENT — INDICES DE L'EMPLOI DANS L'INDUSTRIE

### A. Selected Divisions of Industrial Activity
### Quelques branches de l'activité industrielle

| Period [1]<br>Période [1] | Total [2] | Mining<br>Industries<br>extractives | Manu-<br>facturing [2]<br>Industries<br>manu-<br>facturières [2] | Electricity<br>and gas<br>Electricité<br>et gaz |
|---|---|---|---|---|
| ISIC — CITI | 1–3, 511–512 | 1 | 2–3 | 511–512 |

#### a. Indexes — Indices (1958 = 100)

| | | | | |
|---|---|---|---|---|
| 1949 | 80 | 114 | 79 | 74 |
| 1950 | 83 | 111 | 82 | 77 |
| 1951 | 86 | 100 | 86 | 74 |
| 1952 | 85 | 100 | 85 | 79 |
| 1953 | 87 | 98 | 87 | 82 |
| 1954 | 91 | 98 | 91 | 84 |
| 1955 | –94– | 96 | 94 | 86 |
| 1956 | 93 | 96 | 93 | 90 |
| 1957 | 97 | 100 | 97 | 97 |
| 1958 | 100 | 100 | 100 | 100 |
| 1959 | 102 | 99 | 102 | 108 |
| 1960 | –107– | –97– | –108– | –108– |
| 1961 | 110 | 95 | 111 | 109 |

#### b. Average Annual Rate of Change — Taux annuel moyen de variation

| | | | | |
|---|---|---|---|---|
| 1950–1960 | 2.6 | –1.3 | 2.8 | 3.4 |
| 1954–1958 | 2.4 | 0.5 | 2.4 | 4.4 |
| 1958–1960 | 3.4 | –1.5 | 3.9 | 3.9 |

For footnotes see end of table.
Pour les notes, voir au bas du tableau.

### B. The Major Groups of Mining
### Les classes de la branche Industries extractives

| Period [1]<br>Période [1] | All mining<br>Toutes<br>industries<br>extractives | Coal<br>mining<br>Extraction<br>du charbon | Metal mining<br>Extraction<br>des minerals<br>métalliques | Other mining<br>Autres<br>industries<br>extractives |
|---|---|---|---|---|
| ISIC — CITI | 1 | 11 | 12 | 14–19 |

#### a. Indexes — Indices (1958 = 100)

| | | | | |
|---|---|---|---|---|
| 1938 | ... | 112 | ... | ... |
| 1943 | ... | 120 | ... | ... |
| 1949 | 114 | 124 | 398 | 52 |
| 1950 | 111 | 118 | 408 | 55 |
| 1951 | 100 | 107 | 395 | 44 |
| 1952 | 100 | 107 | 231 | 62 |
| 1953 | 98 | 104 | 184 | 68 |
| 1954 | 98 | 101 | 137 | 84 |
| 1955 | 96 | 95 | 119 | 94 |
| 1956 | 96 | 96 | 99 | 97 |
| 1957 | 100 | 98 | 93 | 105 |
| 1958 | 100 | 100 | 100 | 100 |
| 1959 | 99 | 96 | 107 | 108 |
| 1960 | –97– | –91– | –128– | –113– |
| 1961 | 95 | 86 | 135 | 119 |

#### b. Average Annual Rate of Change — Taux annuel moyen de variation

| | | | | |
|---|---|---|---|---|
| 1938–1960 | ... | –0.9 | ... | ... |
| 1938–1948 | ... | 0.7 | ... | ... |
| 1950–1960 | –0.3 | –2.6 | –11.0 | 7.5 |
| 1948–1953 | ... | –2.8 | ... | ... |
| 1954–1958 | 0.5 | –0.3 | –7.6 | 4.4 |
| 1958–1960 | –1.5 | –4.6 | 13.1 | 6.3 |

## C. The Major Groups of Manufacturing — Les classes de la branche Industries manufacturières

| Period [1] / Période [1] | Manu-[2] facturing / Industries manufac-turières [2] | Food, beverages and tobacco [2] / Industries alimen-taires, boissons, tabac [2] | Textiles | Clothing, footwear and made-up textiles [2] / Articles d'habil-lement, chaussures et ouvrages en tissu [2] | Wood products and furniture / Bois et meubles | Paper and paper products / Papier et ouvrages en papier | Printing and publishing / Im-primerie et édition | Leather and leather products except wearing apparel / Cuir et articles en cuir, à l'exclu-sion des articles d'habil-lement | Rubber products / Ouvrages en caout-chouc | Chemicals and chemical, petroleum and coal products / Produits chi-miques et dérivés du pétrole et du charbon | Non-metallic mineral products / Produits minéraux non métal-liques | Basic metals / Métal-lurgie de base | Metal products [2] / Ouvrages en métaux [2] | Other manu-facturing [2] / Autres industries manufac-turières [2] |
|---|---|---|---|---|---|---|---|---|---|---|---|---|---|---|
| ISIC — CITI | 2–3 | 20–22 | 23 | 24 | 25–26 | 27 | 28 | 29 | 30 | 31–32 | 33 | 34 | 35–38 | 39 |
| **a. Indexes — Indices (1958 = 100)** | | | | | | | | | | | | | | |
| 1938 | 71 | 76 | 68 | 68 | 75 | 23 | 81 | 93 | 24 | 84 | 80 | 108 | 74 | 23 |
| 1948 | 96 | 96 | 88 | 94 | 96 | 46 | 80 | 143 | 60 | 99 | 105 | 97 | 108 | 90 |
| 1949 | 79 | 80 | 81 | 92 | 81 | 50 | 76 | 114 | 61 | 82 | 79 | 74 | 72 | 79 |
| 1950 | 82 | 81 | 83 | 98 | 84 | 54 | 80 | 114 | 77 | 85 | 82 | 80 | 75 | 85 |
| 1951 | 86 | 84 | 80 | 100 | 96 | 55 | 81 | 108 | 85 | 87 | 86 | 88 | 79 | 83 |
| 1952 | 85 | 86 | 81 | 93 | 97 | 53 | 81 | 98 | 71 | 86 | 86 | 89 | 81 | 75 |
| 1953 | 87 | 86 | 86 | 95 | 97 | 61 | 83 | 103 | 78 | 87 | 86 | 81 | 83 | 77 |
| 1954 | 91 | 89 | 90 | 98 | 98 | 65 | 86 | 104 | 91 | 90 | 91 | 94 | 90 | 79 |
| 1955 | 94 | 93 | 87 | 98 | 100 | 84 | 91 | 100 | 98 | 92 | 93 | 93 | 93 | 79 |
| 1956 | 93 | 93 | 86 | 93 | 98 | 89 | 93 | 93 | 97 | 94 | 91 | 91 | 93 | 80 |
| 1957 | 97 | 97 | 91 | 98 | 98 | 94 | 97 | 91 | 96 | 97 | 96 | 92 | 97 | 86 |
| 1958 | 100 | 100 | 100 | 100 | 100 | 100 | 100 | 100 | 100 | 100 | 100 | 100 | 100 | 100 |
| 1959 | 102 | 101 | 104 | 96 | 102 | 103 | 104 | 97 | 99 | 107 | 105 | 110 | 103 | 111 |
| 1960 | – 108 – | – 102 – | – 112 – | – 100 – | – 107 – | – 113 – | – 110 – | – 106 – | – 106 – | – 111 – | – 112 – | – 116 – | – 112 – | – 125 – |
| 1961 | 111 | 106 | 119 | 99 | 109 | 118 | 115 | 106 | 112 | 110 | 115 | 121 | 117 | 128 |
| **b. Average Annual Rate of Change — Taux annuel moyen de variation** | | | | | | | | | | | | | | |
| 1938–1960 | 1.9 | 1.3 | 2.3 | 1.8 | 1.6 | 7.5 | 1.4 | 0.6 | 7.0 | 1.3 | 1.5 | 0.3 | 1.9 | 8.0 |
| 1938–1948 | 3.1 | 2.4 | 2.6 | 3.3 | 2.5 | 7.2 | −0.1 | 4.4 | 9.6 | 1.7 | 2.8 | −1.1 | 3.8 | 14.6 |
| 1950–1960 | 2.8 | 2.3 | 3.0 | 0.2 | 2.5 | 7.7 | 3.2 | −0.7 | 3.3 | 2·7 | 3.2 | 3.8 | 4.1 | 3.9 |
| 1948–1953 | −2.0 | −2.2 | −0.5 | 0.2 | 0.2 | 5.8 | 0.7 | −6.4 | 5.4 | −2.6 | −3.9 | −3.5 | −5.1 | −3.1 |
| 1954–1958 | 2.4 | 3.0 | 2.7 | 0.5 | 0.5 | 11.4 | 3.8 | −1.0 | 2.4 | 2.7 | 2.4 | 1.6 | 2.7 | 6.1 |
| 1958–1960 | 3.9 | 1.0 | 5.8 | — | 3.4 | 6.3 | 4.9 | 3.0 | 3.0 | 5.4 | 5.8 | 7.7 | 5.8 | 11.8 |

[1] Fiscal years beginning 1 April.
[2] Excludes abattoirs and bakeries (part of ISIC major group 20) and smithies (part of ISIC major group 35) in the case of all periods except 1961-1962 and boot and shoe repair, custom tailors, dressmakers and milliners (part of ISIC major group 24), railway and tramway workshops and naval dockyards (part of ISIC major group 38) and watch repairmen (part of ISIC major group 39) from 1951-1952 through 1960-1961.

[1] Exercices financiers commençant le 1er avril.
[2] Non compris les abattoirs et les boulangeries (dans CITI classe 20) et les ateliers de forgerons (dans CITI classe 35) dans le cas de toutes les périodes, à l'exception de 1961-1962; les cordon-niers et les tailleurs, couturières et modistes (dans CITI classe 24), les ateliers de réparation de chemins de fer et tramways et les arsenaux (dans CITI classe 38), ainsi que les horlogers (dans CITI classe 39) de 1951-1952 à 1960-1961.

# 4. THE CHARACTERISTICS OF INDUSTRIAL ESTABLISHMENTS [4]

## CARACTERISTIQUES DES ETABLISSEMENTS INDUSTRIELS [4]

### 1.IV.1938-31.III.1939, 1.IV.1947-31.III.1948
### 1.IV.1953-31.III.1954, 1.IV.1958-31.III.1959

Number of establishments and other units in units; value added and wages and salaries in million pounds (N.Z.); number of engaged, employees and operatives in thousands; capacity of installed power equipment in thousand horsepower; value added per engaged and wages and salaries per employee and per operative in thousand pounds (N.Z.); capacity of installed power equipment per engaged and per operative in horsepower.

Nombre d'établissements en unités; valeur ajoutée et traitements et salaires en millions de livres (N.Z.); nombre de personnes occupées, de salariés et d'ouvriers en milliers; puissance installée en milliers de chevaux-vapeur; valeur ajoutée par personne occupée et traitements et salaires par salarié et par ouvrier en milliers de livres (N.Z.); puissance installée par personne occupée et par ouvrier en chevaux-vapeur.

## A. The Divisions of Industrial Activity — Les branches de l'activité industrielle

### a. Absolute Figures — Chiffres absolus

| Year and item of data | All industrial activity — Toutes industries | Mining — Industries extractives | Manufacturing [2] — Industries manufacturières [2] | Construction [3] — Bâtiment et travaux publics [3] | Electricity and gas — Electricité et gaz | Année et rubrique |
|---|---|---|---|---|---|---|
| ISIC | 1-4,511-512 | 1 | 2-3 | 4 | 511-512 | CITI |
| **1.IV.1938 – 31.III.1939** | | | | | | **1.IV.1938 – 31.III.1939** |
| Number of units.... | ... | ... | 6 002 | 1 579 | 144 | Nombre d'unités |
| Value added....... | ... | ... | 36.8 | ... | 4.8 | Valeur ajoutée |
| Number of engaged (Annual average). | ... | ... | 96.8 | 14.0 | 5.7 | Nombre d'ouvriers (moyenne annuelle) |
| Employees: Number (Annual average)....... | ... | ... | 94.1 | 12.4 | 5.7 | Salariés: Nombre (moyenne annuelle) |
| Wages and salaries........ | ... | ... | 20.7 | 3.5 | 1.6 | Traitements et salaires |
| Capacity of installed power equipment. | . | ... | 263.4 | 9.7 | 584.4 | Puissance installée |
| **1.IV.1947 – 31.III.1948** | | | | | | **1.IV.1947 – 31.III.1948** |
| Number of units... | ... | ... | 7 823 | 2 344 | 140 | Nombre d'unités |
| Value added....... | ... | ... | 86.9 | 8.4 | 8.8 | Valeur ajoutée |
| Number of engaged (Annual average) | ... | ... | 134.1 | 15.2 | 6.2 | Nombre de personnes occupées (moyenne annuelle) |
| Employees: Number (Annual average)....... | ... | ... | 130.9 | 12.7 | 6.2 | Salariés: Nombre (moyenne annuelle) |
| Wages and salaries........ | ... | ... | 49.5 | 5.9 | 2.8 | Traitements et salaires |
| Number of operatives (Annual average) | ... | ... | 112.4 | ... | 4.3 | Nombre d'ouvriers (moyenne annuelle) |
| Capacity of installed power equipment | . | ... | 425.6 | 17.2 | 894.3 | Puissance installée |
| **1.IV.1953 – 31.III.1954** | | | | | | **1.IV.1953 – 31.III.1954** |
| Number of units.... | 13 475 | 245 | 8 377 | 4 716 | 137 | Nombre d'unités |
| Value added....... | ... | ... | 162.5 | ... | 14.4 | Valeur ajoutée |
| Number of engaged (Annual average). | 210.5 | 6.4 | 146.4 | 50.7 | 7.0 | Nombre de personnes occupées (moyenne annuelle) |
| Employees: Number (Annual average)....... | 202.8 | 6.2 | 144.0 | 45.6 | 7.0 | Salariés: Nombre (moyenne annuelle) |
| Wages and salaries........ | ... | ... | 86.6 | ... | 4.7 | Traitements et salaires |
| Capacity of installed power equipment. | . | ... | 583.9 | ... | 1 191.3 | Puissance installée |

### b. Structure

| Year and item of data | All industrial activity — Toutes industries | Mining — Industries extractives | Manufacturing [2] — Industries manufacturières [2] | Construction [3] — Bâtiment et travaux publics [3] | Electricity and gas — Electricité et gaz | Année et rubrique |
|---|---|---|---|---|---|---|
| ISIC | 1-4,511-512 | 1 | 2-3 | 4 | 511-512 | CITI |
| **1.IV.1938 – 31.III.1939** Per person engaged: | | | | | | **1.IV.1938 – 31.III.1939** Par personne occupée: |
| Value added | ... | ... | 0.38 | ... | 0.84 | Valeur ajoutée |
| Capacity of installed power equipment | . | ... | 2.72 | 0.69 | 102.53 | Puissance installée |
| Employees as a percent of engaged | ... | ... | 97.2 | 88.6 | 100.0 | Salariés en pourcentage des personnes occupées |
| Value added per unit of wages and salaries | ... | ... | 1.78 | ... | 3.00 | Valeur ajoutée par unité de traitements et salaires |
| Wages and salaries per employee | ... | ... | 0.22 | 0.28 | 0.28 | Traitements et salaires par salarié |
| **1.IV.1947 – 31.III.1948** Per person engaged: | | | | | | **1.IV.1947 – 31.III.1948** Par personne occupée: |
| Value added | ... | ... | 0.65 | 0.55 | 1.42 | Valeur ajoutée |
| Capacity of installed power equipment | . | ... | 3.17 | 1.13 | 144.24 | Puissance installée |
| Employees as a percent of engaged | ... | ... | 97.6 | 83.6 | 100.0 | Salariés en pourcentage des personnes occupées |
| Value added per unit of wages and salaries | ... | ... | 1.76 | 1.42 | 3.14 | Valeur ajoutée par unité de traitements et salaires |
| Operatives as a percent of employees | ... | ... | 85.9 | ... | 69.4 | Ouvriers en pourcentage des salariés |
| Wages and salaries per employee | ... | ... | 0.38 | 0.46 | 0.45 | Traitements et salaires par salarié |
| Capacity of installed power equipment per operative | . | ... | 3.79 | ... | 207.98 | Puissance installée par ouvrier |
| **1.IV.1953 – 31.III.1954** Distribution in percent of number of engaged | 100.0 | 3.1 | 69.5 | 24.1 | 3.3 | **1.IV.1953 – 31.III.1954** Distribution en pourcentage du nombre de personnes occupées |
| Per person engaged: Value added | ... | ... | 1.11 | ... | 2.06 | Par personne occupée: Valeur ajoutée |
| Capacity of installed power equipment | ... | ... | 3.99 | ... | 170.1 | Puissance installée |
| Employees as a percent of engaged | 96.3 | 96.9 | 98.4 | 89.9 | 100.0 | Salariés en pourcentage des personnes occupées |
| Value added per unit of wages and salaries | ... | ... | 1.88 | ... | 3.06 | Valeur ajoutée par unité de traitements et salaires |
| Wages and salaries per employee | ... | ... | 0.60 | ... | 0.67 | Traitements et salaires par salarié |

For footnotes see end of table.

Pour les notes, voir au bas fin du tableau.

# NEW ZEALAND

## A. The Divisions of Industrial Activity (continued) — Les branches de l'activité industrielle (suite)

### a. Absolute Figures — Chiffres absolus

| Year and item of data / ISIC | All industrial activity / Toutes industries (1-4,511-512) | Mining / Industries extractives (1) | Manufacturing [2] / Industries manufacturières [2] (2-3) | Construction [3] / Bâtiment et travaux publics [3] (4) | Electricity and gas / Electricité et gaz (511-512) | Année et rubrique / CITI |
|---|---|---|---|---|---|---|
| 1.IV.1958 31.III.1959 | | | | | | 1.IV.1958 31.III.1959 |
| Number of units | 15 578 | 269 | 8 565 | 6 609 | 135 | Nombre d'unités |
| Value added | ... | ... | 240.8 | ... | 25.3 | Valeur ajoutée |
| Number of engaged | 244.7 | 6.1 | 168.8 | 61.2 | 8.6 | Nombre de personnes occupées |
| Employees: Number | 233.3 | 5.8 | 164.9 | 54.0 | 8.6 | Salariés: Nombre |
| Wages and salaries | ... | ... | 128.3 | ... | 7.3 | Traitements et salaires |
| Operatives: Number | ... | ... | 142.9 | ... | 5.7 | Ouvriers: Nombre |
| Wages and salaries | ... | ... | 103.6 | ... | 4.8 | Traitements et salaires |
| Capacity of installed power equipment | | ... | 785.2 | ... | 1 931.1 | Puissance installée |

### b. Structure

| Year and item of data / ISIC | All industrial activity / Toutes industries (1-4,511-512) | Mining / Industries extractives (1) | Manufacturing [2] / Industries manufacturières [2] (2-3) | Construction [3] / Bâtiment et travaux publics [3] (4) | Electricity and gas / Electricité et gaz (511-512) | Année et rubrique / CITI |
|---|---|---|---|---|---|---|
| 1.IV.1958 31.III.1959 | | | | | | 1.IV.1958 - 31.III.1959 |
| Distribution in percent of number of engaged | 100.0 | 2.5 | 69.0 | 25.0 | 3.5 | Distribution en pourcentage du nombre de personnes occupées |
| Per person engaged: Value added | 1.50 | ... | 1.43 | ... | 2.94 | Par personne occupée: Valeur ajoutée |
| Capacity of installed power equipment | | ... | 4.65 | ... | 224.5 | Puissance installée |
| Employees as a percent of engaged | 95.3 | 95.1 | 97.7 | 88.2 | 100.0 | Salariés en pourcentage des personnes occupées |
| Value added per unit of wages and salaries | ... | ... | 1.88 | ... | 3.46 | Valeur ajoutée par unité de traitements et salaires |
| Operatives as a percent of employees | ... | ... | 62.8 | ... | 66.3 | Ouvriers en pourcentage des salariés |
| Wages and salaries per employee | ... | ... | ... | ... | ... | Traitements et salaires par salarié |
| Per operative: Wages and salaries | ... | ... | 0.72 | ... | 0.84 | Par ouvrier: Traitements et salaires |
| Capacity of installed power equipment | | ... | 5.49 | ... | 338.7 | Puissance installée |

For footnotes see end of table.

Pour les notes, voir au bas du tableau.

## B. The Major Groups of Manufacturing — Les classes de la branche Industries manufacturières

| Year and item of data | Manufacturing[2]<br>Industries manufacturières[2] | Food, beverages and tobacco[2]<br>Industries alimentaires, boissons, tabac[2] | Textiles | Clothing, footwear and made-up textiles[2]<br>Articles d'habillement, chaussures et ouvrages en tissu[2] | Wood products and furniture<br>Bois et meubles | Paper and paper products<br>Papier et ouvrages en papier | Printing and publishing<br>Imprimerie et édition | Leather and leather products except wearing apparel<br>Cuir et articles en cuir, à l'exclusion des articles d'habillement | Rubber products<br>Ouvrages en caoutchouc | Chemicals and chemical, petroleum and coal products<br>Produits chimiques et dérivés du pétrole et du charbon | Non-metallic mineral products<br>Produits minéraux non métalliques | Basic metals[2]<br>Métallurgie de base[2] | Metal products[2]<br>Ouvrages en métaux[2] | Other manufacturing[1,2]<br>Autres industries manufacturières[1,2] | Année et rubrique |
|---|---|---|---|---|---|---|---|---|---|---|---|---|---|---|---|
| ISIC | 2–3 | 20–22 | 23 | 24 | 25–26 | 27 | 28 | 29 | 30 | 31–32 | 33 | 34 | 35–38 | 39 | CITI |
| *a. Absolute Figures — Chiffres absolus* | | | | | | | | | | | | | | | |
| 1.IV.1938–31.III.1939 | | | | | | | | | | | | | | | 1.IV.1938–31.III.1939 |
| Number of establishments. | 6 002 | 1 004 | 125 | 502 | 1 073 | 23 | 373 | 103 | [1] | 173 | 318 | 49 | 2 044 | 215 | Nombre d'établissements |
| Value added. | 36.8 | 10.3 | 1.3 | 2.8 | 5.1 | 0.2 | 3.4 | 0.4 | [1] | 1.8 | 1.9 | 0.4 | 7.6 | 1.6 | Valeur ajoutée |
| Number of engaged (Annual average). | 96.8 | 20.8 | 5.0 | 16.0 | 13.3 | 0.6 | 8.3 | 1.1 | [1] | 2.9 | 3.7 | 1.0 | 21.0 | 3.1 | Nombre de personnes occupées (moyenne annuelle) |
| Number of employees (Annual average). | 94.1 | 20.6 | 4.9 | 15.7 | 12.7 | 0.6 | 8.1 | 1.0 | [1] | 2.9 | 3.6 | 1.0 | 20.0 | 3.0 | Nombre de salariés (moyenne annuelle) |
| Wages and salaries paid. | 20.7 | 5.2 | 1.1 | 2.2 | 3.1 | 0.1 | 2.0 | 0.2 | [1] | 0.7 | 0.9 | 0.2 | 4.6 | 0.4 | Traitements et salaires payés |
| Capacity of installed power equipment. | 263.4 | 97.0 | 12.5 | 3.9 | 54.6 | 0.7 | 11.1 | 2.5 | [1] | 12.2 | 31.9 | 2.1 | 24.8 | 10.1 | Puissance installée |
| 1.IV.1947–31.III.1948 | | | | | | | | | | | | | | | 1.IV.1947–31.III.1948 |
| Number of establishments. | 7 823 | 1 058 | 158 | 814 | 1 476 | 40 | 358 | 149 | 88 | 267 | 479 | 2 658 | | 278 | Nombre d'établissements |
| Value added. | 86.9 | 21.8 | 3.8 | 8.6 | 11.1 | 0.8 | 5.5 | 1.3 | 1.0 | 4.3 | 4.5 | 20.0 | | 4.2 | Valeur ajoutée |
| Number of engaged (Annual average). | 134.1 | 26.2 | 6.4 | 22.4 | 17.1 | 1.1 | 8.2 | 2.3 | 1.5 | 4.9 | 5.8 | 32.5 | | 5.7 | Nombre de personnes occupées (moyenne annuelle) |
| Number of employees (Annual average). | 130.9 | 26.0 | 6.4 | 22.1 | 16.2 | 1.1 | 8.0 | 2.3 | 1.5 | 4.9 | 5.6 | 31.3 | | 5.5 | Nombre de salariés (moyenne annuelle) |
| Wages and salaries paid. | 49.5 | 11.1 | 2.1 | 6.1 | 6.8 | 0.4 | 3.1 | 0.9 | 0.6 | 1.8 | 2.3 | 12.2 | | 2.1 | Traitements et salaires payés |
| Number of operatives (Annual average). | 112.4 | 21.9 | 3.5 | 22.1 | 14.5 | 1.0 | 6.4 | 2.0 | 1.2 | 3.8 | 4.9 | 26.3 | | 4.8 | Nombre d'ouvriers (moyenne annuelle) |
| Capacity of installed power equipment. | 425.6 | 122.1 | 17.0 | 8.9 | 111.1 | 1.8 | 13.5 | 4.4 | 6.0 | 22.5 | 41.2 | 54.3 | | 22.8 | Puissance installée |
| 1.IV.1953–31.III.1954 | | | | | | | | | | | | | | | 1.IV.1953–31.III.1954 |
| Number of establishments. | 8 377 | 993 | 193 | 1 165 | 1 694 | 93 | 393 | 105 | 78 | 248 | 508 | 80 | 2 613 | 214 | Nombre d'établissements |
| Value added. | 162.5 | 41.6 | 8.0 | 15.0 | 19.0 | 4.9 | 10.1 | 1.5 | 3.7 | 8.0 | 8.7 | 1.0 | 38.7 | 2.3 | Valeur ajoutée |
| Number of engaged (Annual average). | 146.4 | 29.7 | 8.2 | 24.8 | 17.2 | 3.1 | 8.6 | 1.7 | 2.3 | 4.9 | 5.8 | 0.7 | 36.7 | 2.7 | Nombre de personnes occupées (moyenne annuelle) |
| Number of employees (Annual average). | 144.0 | 29.6 | 8.2 | 24.4 | 16.5 | 3.1 | 8.5 | 1.7 | 2.3 | 4.9 | 5.7 | 0.7 | 35.9 | 2.5 | Nombre de salariés (moyenne annuelle) |
| Wages and salaries paid. | 86.6 | 19.8 | 4.4 | 10.6 | 10.6 | 1.8 | 5.4 | 0.9 | 1.5 | 3.0 | 3.8 | 0.5 | 22.9 | 1.4 | Traitements et salaires payés |
| Operatives: Number (Annual average). | 125.1 | 25.4 | 7.5 | 22.3 | 14.5 | 2.8 | 6.9 | 1.4 | 1.9 | 4.0 | 5.0 | 0.6 | 30.6 | 2.2 | Ouvriers: Nombre (moyenne annuelle) |
| Wages and salaries. | 70.6 | 16.7 | 3.9 | 8.9 | 8.5 | 1.5 | 4.2 | 0.7 | 1.2 | 2.3 | 3.1 | 0.4 | 18.2 | 1.0 | Traitements et salaires |
| Capacity of installed power equipment. | 583.9 | 163.6 | 27.5 | 13.0 | 137.0 | 32.8 | 14.8 | 6.4 | 19.4 | 29.7 | 52.2 | 4.1 | 77.9 | 5.5 | Puissance installée |
| 1.IV.1958–31.III.1959 | | | | | | | | | | | | | | | 1.IV.1958–31.III.1959 |
| Number of establishments. | 8 565 | 848 | 184 | 1 069 | 1 624 | 100 | 409 | 94 | 89 | 260 | 539 | 80 | 3 038 | 231 | Nombre d'établissements |
| Value added. | 240.8 | 54.9 | 11.4 | 20.5 | 25.2 | 15.6 | 15.4 | 1.8 | 6.0 | 11.8 | 14.0 | 1.6 | 58.0 | 4.6 | Valeur ajoutée |
| Number of engaged (Annual average). | 168.8 | 34.3 | 9.6 | 26.0 | 17.8 | 5.2 | 10.4 | 1.6 | 2.9 | 5.7 | 6.8 | 0.9 | 44.2 | 3.4 | Nombre de personnes occupées (moyenne annuelle) |
| Employees: Number (Annual average). | 164.9 | 33.9 | 9.6 | 25.8 | 17.6 | 5.2 | 10.2 | 1.5 | 2.9 | 5.6 | 6.7 | 0.9 | 41.7 | 3.3 | Salariés: Nombre (moyenne annuelle) |
| Wages and salaries. | 128.3 | 29.6 | 6.2 | 14.1 | 14.0 | 4.4 | 8.3 | 1.1 | 2.7 | 4.6 | 5.5 | 0.8 | 34.6 | 2.4 | Traitements et salaires |
| Operatives: Number (Annual average). | 142.9 | 29.6 | 8.7 | 23.5 | 14.8 | 4.5 | 8.3 | 1.4 | 2.5 | 4.3 | 5.8 | 0.7 | 35.9 | 2.9 | Ouvriers: Nombre (moyenne annuelle) |
| Wages and salaries. | 103.6 | 25.2 | 5.4 | 11.7 | 11.2 | 3.6 | 6.4 | 0.9 | 2.2 | 3.2 | 4.5 | 0.6 | 26.8 | 1.9 | Traitements et salaires |
| Capacity of installed power equipment. | 785.2 | 200.5 | 31.4 | 15.9 | 156.3 | 100.3 | 19.2 | 6.6 | 23.2 | 41.8 | 75.8 | 5.7 | 100.4 | 8.1 | Puissance installée |
| *b. Structure* | | | | | | | | | | | | | | | |
| 1.IV.1938 — 31.III.1939 | | | | | | | | | | | | | | | 1.IV.1938 — 31.III.1939 |
| Distribution in percent of: | | | | | | | | | | | | | | | Distribution en pourcentage: |
| Value added. | 100.0 | 27.9 | 3.6 | 7.6 | 13.8 | 0.6 | 9.2 | 1.1 | ... | 4.9 | 5.2 | 1.1 | 20.6 | 4.4 | Valeur ajoutée |
| Number of engaged. | 100.0 | 21.4 | 5.2 | 16.5 | 13.8 | 0.6 | 8.6 | 1.1 | ... | 3.0 | 3.8 | 1.1 | 21.6 | 3.3 | Nombre de personnes occupées |
| Per person engaged: Value added. | 0.4 | 0.5 | 0.3 | 0.2 | 0.4 | 0.3 | 0.4 | 0.4 | ... | 0.6 | 0.5 | 0.4 | 0.4 | 0.5 | Par personne occupée: Valeur ajoutée |
| Capacity of installed power equipment. | 2.72 | 4.66 | 2.50 | 0.24 | 4.10 | 1.17 | 1.34 | 2.27 | ... | 4.21 | 8.62 | 2.10 | 1.18 | 3.26 | Puissance installée |
| Employees as a percent of engaged. | 97.2 | 99.0 | 98.0 | 98.1 | 95.5 | 100.0 | 97.6 | 90.9 | ... | 100.0 | 97.3 | 100.0 | 95.2 | 96.8 | Salariés en pourcentage des personnes occupées |
| Value added per unit of wages and salaries. | 1.78 | 1.98 | 1.18 | 1.27 | 1.64 | 2.00 | 1.70 | 2.00 | ... | 2.57 | 2.11 | 2.00 | 1.65 | 4.00 | Valeur ajoutée par unité de traitements et salaires |
| Wages and salaries per employee. | 0.22 | 0.25 | 0.22 | 0.14 | 0.24 | 0.17 | 0.25 | 0.20 | ... | 0.24 | 0.25 | 0.20 | 0.23 | 0.13 | Traitements et salaires par salarié |

For footnotes see end of table.

Pour les notes, voir au bas du tableau.

## B. The Major Groups of Manufacturing (continued) — Les classes de la branche Industries manufacturières (suite)

b. Structure (continued — suite)

| Year and item of data | Manufacturing[3] / Industries manufacturières[3] (2-3) | Food, beverages and tobacco[2] / Industries alimentaires, boissons, tabac[2] (20-22) | Textiles (23) | Clothing, footwear and made-up textiles[2] / Articles d'habillement, chaussures et ouvrages en tissu[2] (24) | Wood products and furniture / Bois et meubles (25-26) | Paper and paper products / Papier et ouvrages en papier (27) | Printing and publishing / Imprimerie et édition (28) | Leather and leather products except wearing apparel / Cuir et articles en cuir, à l'exclusion des articles d'habillement (29) | Rubber products / Ouvrages en caoutchouc (30) | Chemicals and chemical, petroleum and coal products / Produits chimiques et dérivés du pétrole et du charbon (31-32) | Non-metallic mineral products / Produits minéraux non métalliques (33) | Basic metals[2] / Métallurgie de base[2] (34) | Metal products[2] / Ouvrages en métaux[2] (35-38) | Other manufacturing[1,2] / Autres industries manufacturières[1,2] (39) | Année et rubrique |
|---|---|---|---|---|---|---|---|---|---|---|---|---|---|---|---|
| **1.IV.1947 — 31.III.1948** Distribution in percent of: | | | | | | | | | | | | | | | **1.IV.1947 — 31.III.1948** Distribution en pourcentage: |
| Value added | 100.0 | 25.0 | 4.4 | 9.9 | 12.8 | 0.9 | 6.3 | 1.5 | 1.2 | 4.9 | 5.2 | | 23.0 | 4.9 | Valeur ajoutée |
| Number of engaged | 100.0 | 19.5 | 4.8 | 16.7 | 12.7 | 0.8 | 6.2 | 1.7 | 1.1 | 3.6 | 4.4 | | 24.2 | 4.3 | Nombre de personnes occupées |
| Per person engaged: Value added | 0.6 | 0.8 | 0.6 | 0.4 | 0.6 | 0.7 | 0.7 | 0.6 | 0.7 | 0.9 | 0.8 | | 0.6 | 0.7 | Par personne occupée: Valeur ajoutée |
| Capacity of installed power equipment | 3.17 | 4.66 | 2.66 | 0.40 | 6.50 | 1.64 | 1.65 | 1.91 | 4.00 | 4.59 | 7.10 | | 1.67 | 4.00 | Puissance installée |
| Employees as a percent of engaged | 97.6 | 99.2 | 100.0 | 98.7 | 94.7 | 100.0 | 97.6 | 100.0 | 100.0 | 100.0 | 96.6 | | 96.3 | 96.5 | Salariés en pourcentage des personnes occupées |
| Value added per unit of wages and salaries | 1.76 | 1.96 | 1.81 | 1.41 | 1.63 | 2.00 | 1.77 | 1.44 | 1.67 | 2.39 | 1.96 | | 1.64 | 2.00 | Valeur ajoutée par unité de traitements et salaires |
| Wages and salaries per employee | 0.38 | 0.43 | 0.33 | 0.28 | 0.42 | 0.36 | 0.39 | 0.39 | 0.40 | 0.37 | 0.41 | | 0.39 | 0.38 | Traitements et salaires par salarié |
| Operatives as a percent of employees | 85.9 | 84.2 | 54.7 | 100.0 | 89.5 | 90.9 | 80.0 | 87.0 | 80.0 | 77.6 | 87.5 | | 84.0 | 87.3 | Ouvriers en pourcentage des salariés |
| Capacity of installed power equipment per operative | 3.79 | 5.58 | 4.86 | 0.40 | 7.66 | 1.80 | 2.11 | 2.20 | 5.00 | 59.2 | 8.41 | | 2.06 | 4.75 | Puissance installée par ouvrier |
| **1.IV.1953 — 31.III.1954** Distribution in percent of: | | | | | | | | | | | | | | | **1.IV.1953 — 31.III.1954** Distribution en pourcentage: |
| Value added | 100.0 | 25.6 | 4.9 | 9.2 | 11.7 | 3.0 | 6.2 | 1.0 | 2.2 | 5.0 | 5.3 | 0.6 | 23.8 | 1.5 | Valeur ajoutée |
| Number of engaged | 100.0 | 20.2 | 5.6 | 17.0 | 11.7 | 2.1 | 5.9 | 1.2 | 1.6 | 3.3 | 4.0 | 0.4 | 25.1 | 1.9 | Nombre de personnes occupées |
| Per person engaged: Value added | 1.1 | 1.4 | 1.0 | 0.6 | 1.1 | 1.6 | 1.2 | 0.9 | 1.6 | 1.6 | 1.5 | 1.4 | 1.0 | 0.8 | Par personne occupée: Valeur ajoutée |
| Capacity of installed power equipment | 3.99 | 5.51 | 3.35 | 0.52 | 7.96 | 10.58 | 1.72 | 3.76 | 8.43 | 6.06 | 9.00 | 5.86 | 2.12 | 2.04 | Puissance installée |
| Employees as a percent of engaged | 98.4 | 99.7 | 100.0 | 98.4 | 95.9 | 100.0 | 98.8 | 100.0 | 100.0 | 100.0 | 98.3 | 100.0 | 97.8 | 92.6 | Salariés en pourcentage des personnes occupées |
| Value added per unit of wages and salaries | 1.88 | 2.10 | 1.82 | 1.42 | 1.79 | 2.72 | 1.87 | 1.67 | 2.47 | 2.67 | 2.29 | 2.00 | 1.69 | 1.64 | Valeur ajoutée par unité de traitements et salaires |
| Wages and salaries per employee | 0.60 | 0.67 | 0.54 | 0.43 | 0.64 | 0.58 | 0.64 | 0.53 | 0.65 | 0.61 | 0.67 | 0.71 | 0.64 | 0.56 | Traitements et salaires par salarié |
| Operatives as a percent of employees | 86.9 | 85.8 | 91.5 | 91.4 | 87.9 | 90.3 | 81.2 | 82.4 | 82.6 | 81.6 | 87.7 | 85.7 | 85.2 | 88.0 | Ouvriers en pourcentage des salariés |
| Per operative: Wages and salaries | 0.56 | 0.66 | 0.52 | 0.40 | 0.59 | 0.54 | 0.61 | 0.50 | 0.63 | 0.58 | 0.62 | 0.67 | 0.59 | 0.45 | Par ouvrier: Traitements et salaires |
| Capacity of installed power equipment | 4.67 | 6.44 | 3.67 | 0.58 | 9.45 | 11.71 | 2.14 | 4.57 | 10.21 | 7.42 | 10.44 | 6.83 | 2.54 | 2.50 | Puissance installée |
| **1.IV.1958 — 31.III.1959** Distribution in percent of: | | | | | | | | | | | | | | | **1.IV.1958 — 31.III.1959** Distribution en pourcentage: |
| Value added | 100.0 | 22.7 | 4.8 | 8.5 | 10.5 | 6.4 | 6.4 | 0.8 | 2.5 | 4.9 | 5.8 | 0.7 | 24.0 | 2.0 | Valeur ajoutée |
| Number of engaged | 100.0 | 20.3 | 5.7 | 15.4 | 10.5 | 3.1 | 6.1 | 1.0 | 1.7 | 3.4 | 4.0 | 0.6 | 26.1 | 2.1 | Nombre de personnes occupées |
| Per person engaged: Value added | 1.4 | 1.6 | 1.2 | 0.8 | 1.4 | 3.0 | 1.5 | 1.1 | 2.1 | 2.1 | 2.0 | 1.8 | 1.3 | 1.4 | Par personne occupée: Valeur ajoutée |
| Capacity of installed power equipment | 4.65 | 5.84 | 3.27 | 0.61 | 8.78 | 19.29 | 1.85 | 4.12 | 8.00 | 7.33 | 11.15 | 6.33 | 2.27 | 2.38 | Puissance installée |
| Employees as a percent of engaged | 97.7 | 98.8 | 100.0 | 99.2 | 98.9 | 100.0 | 98.1 | 93.8 | 100.0 | 98.5 | 98.5 | 100.0 | 94.3 | 97.0 | Salariés en pourcentage des personnes occupées |
| Value added per unit of wages and salaries | 1.88 | 1.85 | 1.84 | 1.45 | 1.80 | 3.54 | 1.86 | 1.64 | 2.22 | 2.56 | 2.54 | 2.00 | 1.68 | 1.92 | Valeur ajoutée par unité de traitements et salaires |
| Wages and salaries per employee | 0.78 | 0.87 | 0.64 | 0.55 | 0.80 | 0.85 | 0.81 | 0.73 | 0.93 | 0.82 | 0.82 | 0.89 | 0.83 | 0.73 | Traitements et salaires par salarié |
| Operatives as a percent of employees | 86.6 | 87.3 | 90.6 | 91.1 | 84.1 | 86.5 | 81.4 | 93.3 | 86.2 | 76.8 | 86.6 | 77.8 | 86.1 | 87.9 | Ouvriers en pourcentage des salariés |
| Per operative: Wages and salaries | 0.72 | 0.85 | 0.62 | 0.50 | 0.76 | 0.80 | 0.77 | 0.64 | 0.88 | 0.74 | 0.78 | 0.86 | 0.75 | 0.66 | Par ouvrier: Traitements et salaires |
| Capacity of installed power equipment | 5.49 | 6.77 | 3.61 | 0.68 | 10.56 | 22.29 | 2.31 | 4.71 | 9.28 | 9.72 | 13.07 | 8.14 | 2.80 | 2.79 | Puissance installée |

[1] Includes, for 1938-39 and 1947-48, the following industries belonging to other ISIC major groups: sugar refining, paper milling, cigarette paper manufacturing, bituminized paper and products, coal carbonization and briquetting, glass manufacturing, ammunition, explosives and fireworks, starch manufacturing, sheep-dip manufacturing, match manufacturing, rope and twine making. Includes in addition, for 1938-39, the manufacturing of rubber products.

[2] Excludes abattoirs and bakeries (in ISIC major group 20) in all years; boot and shoe repairers and custom tailors, dressmakers and milliners (in ISIC major group 24) in 1953-54 and 1958-59; smithies (in ISIC major group 35) in all years; railway and tramway workshops and naval dockyard (in ISIC major group 38) and watch repairers (in ISIC major group 39) in 1953-54 and 1958-59.

[3] In the case of Construction (ISIC Division 4), the figures of number of persons engaged and number of employees relate to one period during the year.

[4] Units with one or more persons engaged in the case of Mining and Construction; all establishments in the case of Electricity and gas; and establishments in Manufacturing with two or more persons engaged and installed power equipment in the case of 1938-39 and 1947-48 and with two or more persons engaged in the case of 1953-54 and 1958-59.

[1] Y compris, pour 1938-39 et 1947-48, les industries suivantes qui font partie d'autres classes de la CITI: raffinage du sucre, fabrication du papier, fabrication du papier à cigarettes, du papier bitumé et des autres produits bitumés, carbonisation du charbon et fabrication des briquettes, fabrication du verre, munitions, explosifs industriels et d'artifices, fabrication des produits amylacés, des désinfectants liquides pour animaux, des allumettes, des cordes et des ficelles. Y compris en outre, pour 1938-39, la fabrication des ouvrages en caoutchouc.

[2] Non compris les abattoirs et les boulangeries (dans CITI classe 20) pour toutes les années; les cordonniers et les tailleurs, couturières et modistes travaillant à façon (dans CITI classe 24) en 1953-1954 et 1958-1959; les ateliers de forgerons (dans CITI classe 35) pour toutes les années; les ateliers de réparation des chemins de fer et tramways et les arsenaux (dans CITI classe 38), ainsi que les horlogers (dans CITI classe 39) en 1953-1954 et 1958-1959.

[3] Dans le cas du Bâtiment et des travaux publics (CITI branche 4) les chiffres relatifs au nombre de personnes occupées et au nombre de salariés se rapportent à une période de l'année.

[4] Pour les Industries extractives et pour le Bâtiment et les travaux publics, unités occupant une personne ou plus; pour l'Electricité et le gaz, tous les établissements; pour les Industries manufacturières, établissements occupant deux personnes ou plus et utilisant la force motrice dans le cas de 1938-1939 et 1947-1948, et établissements occupant deux personnes ou plus dans le cas de 1953-1954 et 1958-1959.

# NICARAGUA

## Index Numbers of Industrial Production

The index numbers of manufacturing activities shown in Table 1 are derived from *Indice de Producción Industrial de Nicaragua,* a paper presented by the Dirección General de Estadística y Censos of Nicaragua at a Seminar on Industrial Statistics held in October 1960 at Santiago, Chile.

The data utilized in computing the index are based upon returns from 318 establishments which covered 90 percent of the value added in the 1953 Industrial Census, which itself covered establishments with a gross value of production during 1953 exceeding 12 000 Córdobas or which had one employee or more. Indexes have been calculated for categories of industrial activity more detailed than groups by using relatives of the quantities of individual commodities produced. Then these series have been combined using as weights for series more detailed than groups, as well as groups and major groups, value added in 1953.

## Characteristics and Structure of Industrial Activity

The data shown in Table 2 are derived from the results of the 1953 Industrial Census published in the *Boletín de Estadística,* 111 Epoca, Numero 7, Junio de 1959, by the Dirección General de Estadística y Censos. The Census covered all establishments whose gross value of production during 1953 exceeding 12 000 Córdobas, or which had one employee or more.

The data on employment relate to the average number of persons engaged or persons employed during the fourth week of June and the third week of December 1953. The data on number of employees include homeworkers but wages and salaries relate only to payments made to persons working in the establishment during the year. Value added is based on the value of production at market prices. The capacity of installed power equipment is the sum of the horsepower of all prime movers and of electric motors that are run on purchased electricity.

## Indices de la production industrielle

Les indices relatifs aux activités manufacturières reproduits au tableau 1 sont tirés d'*Indice de Producción Industrial de Nicaragua,* étude présentée par la Dirección General de Estadística y Censos de Nicaragua à un séminaire portant sur les statistiques industrielles qui a eu lieu en octobre 1960 à Santiago du Chili.

Les données utilisées pour le calcul des indices sont tirées des réponses de 318 établissements, qui couvraient 90% de la valeur ajoutée du recensement industriel de 1953, lequel recensement couvrait les établissements justifiant d'une valeur de production dépassant 12 000 córdobas, ou occupant un salarié ou plus. Ces indices ont été calculés pour les catégories de l'activité industrielle plus détaillées que les groupes à partir des rapports quantitatifs relatifs à chaque marchandise produite. Puis ces séries ont été combinées en utilisant comme coefficients de pondération, pour les séries plus détailléés que les groupes aussi bien que pour les groupes et classes de l'activité industrielle, la valeur ajoutée en 1953.

## Caractéristiques et structure de l'activité industrielle

Les chiffres du tableau 2 sont tirés des résultats du recensement industriel de 1953 qui ont été publiés dans le *Boletín de Estadística,* 111 Epoca, Numero 7, Junio de 1959, par la Dirección General de Estadística y Censos. Ce recensement couvrait tous les établissements dont la valeur brute de la production avait dépassé 12 000 córdobas en 1953 ou qui occupaient un salarié ou plus.

Les chiffres de l'emploi correspondent à la moyenne du nombre des personnes occupées ou des salariés pendant la quatrième semaine de juin et la troisième semaine de décembre 1953. Les salariés comprennent les travailleurs à domicile, mais les traitements et salaires ne comprennent que la rémunération des personnes ayant travaillé dans l'établissement pendant l'année. La valeur ajoutée est fondée sur la valeur de la production aux prix du marché. La puissance installée est égale au nombre de chevaux-vapeur de tous les moteurs primaires et des moteurs électriques actionnés par de l'électricité achetée.

# NICARAGUA

## 1. INDEX NUMBERS OF INDUSTRIAL PRODUCTION, SELECTED MAJOR GROUPS OF MANUFACTURING
## INDICES DE LA PRODUCTION INDUSTRIELLE POUR QUELQUES CLASSES DE LA BRANCHE INDUSTRIES MANUFACTURIERES

| Period<br>Période | Manu-facturing [1]<br>Industries manufac-turières [1] | Food, beverages and tobacco<br>Industries alimen-taires, boissons, tabac | Textiles | Clothing, footwear and made-up textiles<br>Articles d'habil-lement, chaussures et ouvrages en tissu | Wood products and furniture<br>Bois et meubles | Leather and leather products except wearing apparel<br>Cuir et articles en cuir, à l'exclu-sion des articles d'habil-lement | Chemicals and chemical products<br>Produits chi-miques | Non-metallic mineral products<br>Produits minéraux non métal-liques |
|---|---|---|---|---|---|---|---|---|
| ISIC — CITI | 2–3 | 20–22 | 23 | 24 | 25–26 | 29 | 31 | 33 |
| *a.* Indexes — Indices (1958 = 100) | | | | | | | | |
| 1953............. | 64 | 61 | 62 | 72 | 66 | 64 | 81 | 67 |
| 1954............. | 73 | 67 | 98 | 84 | 88 | 65 | 95 | 72 |
| 1955............. | 81 | 75 | 105 | 102 | 95 | 76 | 98 | 82 |
| 1956............. | 81 | 78 | 79 | 96 | 86 | 70 | 97 | 104 |
| 1957............. | 90 | 89 | 88 | 96 | 87 | 88 | 90 | 107 |
| 1958............. | 100 | 100 | 100 | 100 | 100 | 100 | 100 | 100 |
| *b.* Average Annual Rate of Change — Taux annuel moyen de variation | | | | | | | | |
| 1954 – 1958....... | 8.2 | 10.5 | 0.5 | 4.4 | 3.2 | 11.4 | 1.3 | 8.6 |

[1] Excludes Printing and publishing (ISIC major group 28), Rubber products (ISIC major group 30), Metal products (ISIC major groups 35-38) and Other manufacturing (ISIC major group 39).

[1] Non compris Imprimerie et édition (CITI 28), Ouvrages en caoutchouc (CITI 30), Ouvrages en métaux (CITI 35-38) et Autres industries manufacturières (CITI 39).

## 2. CHARACTERISTICS OF MANUFACTURING ESTABLISHMENTS WITH ANNUAL PRODUCTION VALUED AT MORE THAN 12,000 CORDOBAS

### CARACTERISTIQUES DES ETABLISSEMENTS MANUFACTURIERS AYANT UNE PRODUCTION ANNUELLE EVALUEE A PLUS DE 12 000 CORDOBAS
#### 1953

Number of establishments in units; value added and wages and salaries in million Córdobas; number of engaged and employees in thousands; capacity of installed power equipment in thousand horsepower; value added per person engaged and wages and salaries per employee in thousand Córdobas; and capacity of installed power equipment per person engaged in horsepower.

Nombre d'établissements en unités; valeur ajoutée et traitements et salaires en millions de córdobas; nombre de personnes occupées et de salariés en milliers; puissance installée en milliers de chevaux-vapeur; valeur ajoutée par personne occupée et traitements et salaires par salarié en milliers de córdobas; puissance installée par personne occupée en chevaux-vapeur.

| Item of data | Manu-facturing Industries manufac-turières | Food beverages and tobacco Industries alimen-taires, boissons, tabac | Textiles | Clothing, footwear and made-up textiles Articles d'habil-lement, chaussures et ouvrages en tissu | Wood products and furniture Bois et meubles | Printing and publish-ing Im-primerie et édition | Leather and leather products except wearing apparel Cuir et articles en cuir, à l'exclu-sion des articles d'habil-lement | Rubber products Ouvrages en caout-chouc | Chemicals and chemical, petroleum and coal products Produits chi-miques et dérivés du pétrole et du charbon | Non-metallic mineral products Produits minéraux non métal-liques | Metal products Ouvrages en métaux | Other manu-factur-ing Autres in-dustries manufac-turières | Rubrique |
|---|---|---|---|---|---|---|---|---|---|---|---|---|---|
| **ISIC** | 2–3 | 20–22 | 23 | 24 | 25–26 | 28 | 29 | 30 | 31–32 | 33 | 35–38 | 39 | **CITI** |
| *a. Absolute Figures — Chiffres absolus* | | | | | | | | | | | | | |
| Number of establishments. | 1 575 | 852 | 8 | 288 | 90 | 25 | 80 | 6 | 43 | 53 | 61 | 69 | Nombre d'établissements |
| Value added......... | 142.3 | 92.0 | 4.4 | 8.7 | 11.2 | 2.7 | 5.1 | 0.3 | 4.8 | 7.8 | 1.8 | 3.5 | Valeur ajoutée |
| Number of engaged (Average of two periods during year).. | 18.9 | 11.4 | 0.7 | 2.3 | 1.5 | 0.4 | 0.5 | — | 0.6 | 0.6 | 0.4 | 0.5 | Nombre de personnes occupées (moyenne de deux périodes de l'année) |
| Number of employees: (Average of two periods during year).. | 16.5 | 10.0 | 0.7 | 1.9 | 1.4 | 0.3 | 0.4 | — | 0.5 | 0.5 | 0.4 | 0.4 | Nombre de salariés (moyenne de deux périodes de l'année) |
| Wages and salaries paid.............. | 51.4 | 30.4 | 2.2 | 4.5 | 5.7 | 1.5 | 0.8 | 0.1 | 1.8 | 2.2 | 1.0 | 1.2 | Traitements et salaires payés |
| Capacity of installed power equipment (31.XII.1953)........ | 17.8 | 9.4 | 2.3 | 0.1 | 3.2 | 0.1 | 0.2 | 0.1 | 0.5 | 0.8 | 0.2 | 0.9 | Puissance installée (31.XII.1953) |
| *b. Structure* | | | | | | | | | | | | | |
| Distribution in percent of: Value added........ | 100.0 | 64.6 | 3.1 | 6.1 | 7.9 | 1.9 | 3.6 | 0.2 | 3.3 | 5.5 | 1.3 | 2.5 | Distribution en pour-centage: Valeur ajoutée |
| Number of engaged... | 100.0 | 60.3 | 3.7 | 12.1 | 8.0 | 2.1 | 2.6 | — | 3.2 | 3.2 | 2.1 | 2.7 | Nombre de personnes occupées |
| Value added per person engaged............ | 7.5 | 8.1 | 6.3 | 3.8 | 7.5 | 6.8 | 10.2 | ... | 8.0 | 13.0 | 4.5 | 7.0 | Valeur ajoutée par personne occupée |
| Wages and salaries per employee........ | 3.1 | 3.0 | 3.1 | 2.4 | 4.1 | 5.0 | 2.0 | ... | 3.6 | 4.4 | 2.5 | 3.0 | Traitements et salaires par salarié |
| Employees as a percent of engaged........ | 87.3 | 87.7 | 100.0 | 82.6 | 93.3 | 75.0 | 80.0 | ... | 83.3 | 83.3 | 100.0 | 80.0 | Salariés en pourcentage des personnes occupées |
| Value added per unit of wages and salaries.............. | 2.77 | 3.03 | 2.00 | 1.93 | 1.96 | 1.80 | 6.38 | 3.00 | 2.67 | 3.54 | 1.80 | 2.92 | Valeur ajoutée par unité de traitements et salaires |
| Capacity of installed power equipment per person engaged.. | 0.94 | 0.82 | 3.28 | 0.04 | 2.13 | 0.25 | 0.40 | ... | 0.83 | 1.33 | 0.50 | 1.80 | Puissance installée par personne occupée |

# NIGERIA

## Gross Domestic Product and Gross Domestic Fixed Capital Formation

Estimates of the expenditure on and the origin of the gross domestic product and the origin of the expenditure on the gross domestic fixed capital formation are presented in Table 1. This table has been derived from data supplied by the Federal Office of Statistics, Lagos, in response to the United Nations national accounts questionnaire. Official estimates and a description of the sources and methods used can be found in the *National Income Report for Nigeria*.

## The Characteristics and Structure of Industrial Activity

The data presented in Table 2 have been extracted from *Nigerian National Accounts, 1950-1957* by Jackson and Okigbo (mimeographed paper). The data are for manufacturing establishments with 10 or more employees and include a certain number of estimates for about 30 delinquent establishments out of the 111 establishments covered in principle in 1957. These estimates amount to about seven percent of the total value added shown in 1957 and one percent in 1950. The definition of the value added shown coincides with the International Standards in Basic Industrial Statistics and is derived from the gross value of output valued at ex-factory prices (excluding excise duties).

## Produit intérieur brut et formation brute de capital fixe intérieur

Le tableau 1 contient les estimations suivantes : i) dépenses imputées au produit intérieur brut; ii) produit intérieur brut par secteur d'activité d'origine; iii) formation brute de capital fixe par secteur d'acquisition. Ce tableau a été établi à partir de données fournies par le Bureau fédéral de statistique, Lagos, en réponse au questionnaire de l'ONU sur la comptabilité nationale. Les estimations officielles, ainsi qu'un exposé des sources et méthodes utilisées, figurent dans *National Income Report for Nigeria*.

## Caractéristiques et structure de l'activité industrielle

Les données du tableau 2 sont tirées de *Nigerian National Accounts 1950-1957* par Jackson et Okigbo (document miméographié). Elles portent sur les établissements manufacturiers occupant 10 salariés ou plus et comprennent un certain nombre d'estimations faites pour les établissements qui n'ont pas répondu (une trentaine sur les 111 établissements recensés, en principe, en 1957). Ces estimations représentent près de 7 p. 100 de la valeur ajoutée indiquée pour 1957 et 1 p. 100 des chiffres correspondants de 1950. La valeur ajoutée est obtenue à partir de la valeur brute de la production aux prix départ usine (non compris les droits sur la consommation) et sa définition est conforme aux Normes internationales relatives aux statistiques industrielles de base.

## 1. THE GROSS DOMESTIC PRODUCT AND GROSS DOMESTIC FIXED CAPITAL FORMATION
## LE PRODUIT INTERIEUR BRUT ET LA FORMATION BRUTE DE CAPITAL FIXE INTERIEUR

Million Pounds            Milions de livres

### A. Expenditure on the Gross Domestic Product at Market Prices
### Dépenses relatives au produit intérieur brut aux prix du marché

| Item of data and year / Rubrique et année | Total | Consumption / Consommation | | Gross Domestic Capital Formation / Formation brute de capital intérieur | | Net exports of goods and services / Exportations nettes de biens et de services | |
| --- | --- | --- | --- | --- | --- | --- | --- |
| | | Total | Government [1] / Etat [1] | Total [2] | Fixed / Fixe | Exports less imports / Exportations moins importations | Exports / Exportations |
| *a. At Current Prices — Aux prix courants* | | | | | | | |
| Absolute figures — Chiffres absolus | | | | | | | |
| 1950 | 524.3 | 474.4 | 17.3 | 27.0 | 30.8 | 22.9 | 88.9 |
| 1951 | 587.0 | 534.2 | 19.3 | 42.1 | 37.8 | 10.7 | 114.2 |
| 1952 | 630.8 | 560.6 | 24.1 | 54.3 | 54.0 | 15.9 | 126.3 |
| 1953 | 682.9 | 607.5 | 27.2 | 58.6 | 58.8 | 16.8 | 128.6 |
| 1954 | 794.8 | 701.7 | 28.4 | 64.7 | 71.5 | 28.4 | 154.3 |
| 1955 | 851.2 | 784.5 | 41.4 | 90.8 | 85.7 | −24.1 | 128.2 |
| 1956 | 900.0 | 836.5 | 43.8 | 96.9 | 101.2 | −33.4 | 135.7 |
| 1957 | 938.7 | 863.1 | 47.6 | 122.1 | 113.0 | −46.5 | 129.1 |
| Percentage distribution of average annual expenditure — Distribution en pourcentage des dépenses annuelles moyennes | | | | | | | |
| 1950 – 1957 | 100.0 | 90.7 | 4.2 | 9.4 | 9.4 | −0.1 | 17.0 |
| 1950 | 100.0 | 90.5 | 3.3 | 5.1 | 5.9 | 4.4 | 17.0 |
| 1953 | 100.0 | 88.9 | 4.0 | 8.6 | 8.6 | 2.5 | 18.8 |
| 1954 | 100.0 | 88.3 | 3.6 | 8.1 | 9.0 | 3.6 | 19.4 |
| *b. At Prices of 1957 — Aux prix de 1957* | | | | | | | |
| Absolute figures — Chiffres absolus | | | | | | | |
| 1950 | 699.3 | 633.4 | 24.0 | 41.1 | 48.4 | 24.8 | 99.9 |
| 1951 | 754.0 | 677.0 | 26.8 | 66.0 | 59.7 | 11.0 | 93.6 |
| 1952 | 809.3 | 729.4 | 33.5 | 76.5 | 75.0 | 3.4 | 111.7 |
| 1953 | 827.7 | 747.2 | 29.9 | 79.8 | 79.9 | 0.7 | 114.8 |
| 1954 | 892.8 | 805.8 | 31.2 | 86.7 | 92.9 | 0.3 | 131.9 |
| 1955 | 921.8 | 851.0 | 45.5 | 107.2 | 102.6 | −36.4 | 126.9 |
| 1956 | 903.5 | 842.7 | 43.8 | 103.2 | 108.0 | −42.4 | 138.5 |
| 1957 | 938.7 | 863.1 | 47.6 | 122.1 | 113.0 | −46.5 | 129.1 |
| Percentage distribution of average annual expenditure — Distribution en pourcentage des dépenses annuelles moyennes | | | | | | | |
| 1950 – 1957 | 100.0 | 91.2 | 4.2 | 10.1 | 10.1 | −1.3 | 14.0 |
| 1950 | 100.0 | 90.6 | 3.4 | 5.9 | 6.9 | 3.5 | 14.3 |
| 1953 | 100.0 | 90.3 | 3.6 | 9.6 | 9.6 | 0.1 | 13.9 |
| 1954 | 100.0 | 90.3 | 3.5 | 9.7 | 10.4 | — | 14.8 |
| Average annual rate of Growth — Taux annuel moyen d'accroissement | | | | | | | |
| 1950 – 1957 | 4.3 | 4.5 | 10.3 | 16.8 | 12.9 | . | 3.7 |
| 1950 – 1953 | 5.8 | 5.7 | 7.6 | 24.8 | 18.2 | . | 4.7 |
| 1954 – 1957 | 1.7 | 2.3 | 15.1 | 12.1 | 6.7 | . | −0.7 |

[1] Excludes defence expenditure.
[2] Includes stocks held by Statutory Agricultural Produce Marketing Boards only.

[1] Non compris les dépenses relatives à la défense nationale.
[2] Il n'a été tenu compte que des stocks détenus par les organismes officiels de commercialisation des produits agricoles.

## B. The Gross Domestic Product at Factor Cost According to Origin
## Origine par secteur d'activité du produit intérieur brut au coût des facteurs

| Item of data and year<br>Rubrique et année | Total | Agricultural sector<br>Secteur agricole | Industrial Sector — Secteur industriel | | | | Transportation and communication<br>Transports et communications | Other sectors<br>Autres secteurs |
| | | | Total | Mining<br>Industries extractives | Manufacturing[1]<br>Industries manufacturières [1] | Construction<br>Bâtiment et travaux publics | | |
| ISIC — CITI | 0–9 | 0 | 1–5 | 1 | 2–3, 5 | 4 | 7 | 6, 8–9 |

*a. At Current Prices — Aux prix courants*

| | | | | | | | | |
|---|---|---|---|---|---|---|---|---|
| **Absolute figures — Chiffres absolus** | | | | | | | | |
| 1950............ | 512.1 | 376.4 | 32.7 | 5.5 | 19.1 | 8.1 | 24.7 | 78.3 |
| 1951............ | 573.2 | 408.6 | 42.3 | 10.7 | 19.4 | 12.2 | 28.9 | 93.4 |
| 1952............ | 614.5 | 422.7 | 49.1 | 11.4 | 20.9 | 16.8 | 31.5 | 111.2 |
| 1953............ | 665.0 | 466.0 | 51.3 | 11.2 | 22.5 | 17.6 | 42.9 | 104.8 |
| 1954............ | 774.2 | 551.2 | 62.3 | 11.0 | 23.3 | 28.0 | 48.2 | 112.5 |
| 1955............ | 827.5 | 552.5 | 66.4 | 10.2 | 24.8 | 31.4 | 56.3 | 152.3 |
| 1956............ | 870.6 | 582.7 | 73.4 | 8.2 | 28.7 | 36.5 | 68.1 | 146.4 |
| 1957............ | 910.0 | 576.9 | 82.2 | 9.4 | 29.8 | 43.0 | 77.7 | 173.2 |
| **Percentage distribution according to sector— Distribution en pourcentage par secteur** | | | | | | | | |
| 1950–1957..... | 100.0 | 68.5 | 8.0 | 1.3 | 3.3 | 3.4 | 6.6 | 16.9 |
| 1950............ | 100.0 | 73.5 | 6.4 | 1.1 | 3.7 | 1.6 | 4.8 | 15.3 |
| 1953............ | 100.0 | 70.1 | 7.7 | 1.7 | 3.4 | 2.6 | 6.4 | 15.8 |
| 1954............ | 100.0 | 71.2 | 8.0 | 1.4 | 3.0 | 3.6 | 6.2 | 14.6 |

*b. At Prices of 1957 — Aux prix de 1957*

| | | | | | | | | |
|---|---|---|---|---|---|---|---|---|
| **Absolute figures — Chiffres absolus** | | | | | | | | |
| 1950............ | 687.1 | 506.0 | 47.6 | 7.6 | 19.7 | 20.3 | 31.3 | 102.2 |
| 1951............ | 740.2 | 513.2 | 52.9 | 7.6 | 19.9 | 25.4 | 36.7 | 137.4 |
| 1952............ | 793.0 | 539.2 | 49.4 | 8.2 | 21.8 | 19.4 | 38.3 | 166.1 |
| 1953............ | 809.8 | 558.4 | 56.2 | 7.9 | 22.4 | 25.9 | 48.3 | 146.9 |
| 1954............ | 872.2 | 600.4 | 70.0 | 8.1 | 24.1 | 37.8 | 53.5 | 148.3 |
| 1955............ | 898.1 | 597.3 | 72.4 | 9.0 | 25.1 | 38.3 | 62.6 | 165.8 |
| 1956............ | 874.1 | 596.7 | 74.6 | 9.6 | 28.5 | 36.5 | 67.7 | 135.1 |
| 1957............ | 910.0 | 576.9 | 82.2 | 9.4 | 29.8 | 43.0 | 77.7 | 173.2 |
| **Percentage distribution according to sector— Distribution en pourcentage par secteur** | | | | | | | | |
| 1950–1957..... | 100.0 | 68.2 | 7.6 | 1.0 | 2.9 | 3.7 | 6.3 | 17.9 |
| 1950............ | 100.0 | 73.6 | 6.9 | 1.1 | 2.9 | 2.9 | 4.6 | 14.9 |
| 1953............ | 100.0 | 68.9 | 7.0 | 1.0 | 2.8 | 3.2 | 6.0 | 18.1 |
| 1954............ | 100.0 | 68.9 | 8.0 | 0.9 | 2.8 | 4.3 | 6.1 | 17.0 |
| **Average annual rate of growth—Taux annuel moyen d'accroissement** | | | | | | | | |
| 1950–1957..... | 4.1 | 1.9 | 8.1 | 3.1 | 6.1 | 11.3 | 13.9 | 7.8 |
| 1950–1953..... | 5.6 | 3.4 | 5.7 | 1.3 | 4.4 | 8.5 | 15.6 | 12.8 |
| 1954–1957..... | 1.4 | −1.3 | 5.5 | 5.1 | 7.3 | 4.4 | 13.2 | 5.3 |

[1] Includes Electricity, gas and water (ISIC division 5).      [1] Y compris Electricité, gaz et eau (CITI branche 5).

### C.  Gross Domestic Fixed Capital Formation According to Purchasing Sector
### La formation brute de capital fixe intérieur par secteur d'acquisition

| Item of data and year<br>Rubrique et année | Total [1] | Agricultural sector<br>Secteur agricole | Industrial Sector — Secteur industriel | | | | | Transportation and communication<br>Transports et communications | Other sectors [1]<br>Autres secteurs [1] |
|---|---|---|---|---|---|---|---|---|---|
| | | | Total | Mining<br>Industries extractives | Manufacturing<br>Industries manufacturières | Construction<br>Bâtiment et travaux publics | Electricity, gas and water<br>Electricité, gaz et eau | | |
| ISIC — CITI | 0–9 | 0 | 1–5 | 1 | 2–3 | 4 | 5 | 7 | 6, 8–9 |
| At Current Prices — Aux prix courants | | | | | | | | | |
| Absolute figures — Chiffres absolus | | | | | | | | | |
| 1958............ | 120.2 | 2.9 | 20.7 | 14.5 | 3.2 | 1.1 | 1.9 | 26.7 | 69.9 |
| 1959............ | 133.4 | 2.1 | 18.9 | 11.5 | 2.7 | 2.6 | 2.1 | 30.9 | 81.5 |
| 1960............ | 159.3 | 4.6 | 34.8 | 20.1 | 4.7 | 4.0 | 6.0 | 27.5 | 92.4 |
| Percentage distribution according to sector— Distribution en pourcentage par secteur | | | | | | | | | |
| 1958............ | 100.0 | 2.4 | 17.3 | 12.1 | 2.7 | 0.9 | 1.6 | 22.2 | 58.1 |
| 1960............ | 100.0 | 2.9 | 21.8 | 12.6 | 2.9 | 2.5 | 3.8 | 17.3 | 58.0 |

[1] Excludes Ownership of dwellings (ISIC division 9)      [1] Non compris Propriété de maisons d'habitation (CITI branche 9).

## 2.  VALUE ADDED OF MANUFACTURING ESTABLISHMENTS WITH 10 OR MORE EMPLOYEES
## VALEUR AJOUTEE PAR LES ETABLISSEMENTS MANUFACTURIERS AYANT 10 SALARIES OU PLUS
### 1950, 1953, 1957

Value added in Million Pounds                    Valeur ajoutée en millions de livres

| Year and item of data | Manufacturing<br>Industries manufacturières | Food, beverages and tobacco<br>Industries alimentaires, boissons, tabac | Textiles | Wood products and furniture<br>Bois et meubles | Leather and leather products except wearing apparel<br>Cuir et articles en cuir, à l'exclusion des articles d'habillement | Rubber products<br>Ouvrages en caoutchouc | Chemicals and chemical, petroleum and coal products<br>Produits chimiques et dérivés du pétrole et du charbon | Non-metallic mineral products<br>Produits minéraux non métalliques | Metal products<br>Ouvrages en métaux | Année et rubrique |
|---|---|---|---|---|---|---|---|---|---|---|
| ISIC | 2–3 | 20–22 | 23 | 25–26 | 29 | 30 | 31–32 | 33 | 35–38 | CITI |
| a. Absolute Figures — Chiffres absolus | | | | | | | | | | |
| Value added: | | | | | | | | | | Valeur ajoutée: |
| 1950.............. | 3.04 | 1.61 | 0.01 | 0.73 | 0.01 | 0.02 | 0.50 | — | 0.16 | 1950 |
| 1953.............. | 4.89 | 2.47 | 0.04 | 1.19 | 0.03 | 0.09 | 0.70 | — | 0.37 | 1953 |
| 1957.............. | 10.94 | 4.09 | 0.38 | 1.81 | 0.04 | 0.64 | 2.99 | 0.41 | 0.58 | 1957 |
| b. Structure | | | | | | | | | | |
| Distribution in percent of value added: | | | | | | | | | | Distribution en pourcentage de la valeur ajoutée: |
| 1950.............. | 100.0 | 52.9 | 0.3 | 24.1 | 0.3 | 0.6 | 16.5 | — | 5.3 | 1950 |
| 1953.............. | 100.0 | 50.5 | 0.8 | 24.3 | 0.6 | 1.9 | 14.3 | — | 7.6 | 1953 |
| 1957.............. | 100.0 | 37.3 | 3.5 | 16.6 | 0.3 | 5.9 | 27.3 | 3.7 | 5.4 | 1957 |

## Gross Domestic Product and Gross Fixed Capital Formation

The estimates of gross domestic product and gross fixed capital formation shown in Table 1 are from the reply to the United Nations national accounts questionnaire by the Central Bureau of Statistics, Oslo. Official estimates and descriptions are included in the annual report of the Bureau, *Økonomisk Utsyn* (Economic Survey). In replying to the United Nations questionnaire, the Central Bureau of Statistics has adjusted the official estimates, to the extent possible, to conform to the United Nations system of national accounts.

## Index Numbers of Industrial Production

The figures set out in Table 2 are derived from the two types of index numbers of industrial production that are calculated by the Central Bureau of Statistics. The data for the years, 1938-1960 were compiled from the annual index numbers constructed from the results of annual Industrial Censuses and published in *Statistisk Arsbok for Norge* and *Norges Industri*. The figures for 1961 are annual averages of the monthly index numbers calculated by the Central Bureau from a monthly survey of a sample of industrial units covered in the annual Industrial Censuses. The monthly indexes are published in *Statistiske Meldinger* and *Aktuell Statistikk*. The annual indexes are based on a larger number of returns and a greater number of indicators of output than the monthly indexes.

The annual and monthly index numbers are both base-weighted arithmetic averages based on relatives of quantities of output, in most instances, or of man-hours worked, in some cases. Weights for combining relatives for individual products into index numbers for each detailed category of industry are derived from the gross value of the output of the products during the base year; weights for aggregating the resulting indexes into index numbers for broader classes of industry are computed from value added at factor cost during the base year. The weight base years for the indexes shown in Table 2 are as follows: 1935 for 1938, 1949 for 1948-1954 and 1955 for 1955 and thereafter.

Further details on index numbers of industrial production may be found in the following publications of the Central Bureau of Statistics: *Statistiske Meddelelsen*, Nos. 11-12, 1937, indexes based on 1935, *Statistiske Meldinger*, Nos. 7 and 12, 1953, concerning the indexes based on 1949 and *Norges Industri, 1956* with regard to the indexes based on 1955.

## Index Numbers of Industrial Employment

The index numbers of employment shown in Table 3 were compiled by the Statistical Office of the United Na-

## Produit intérieur brut et la formation brute de capital fixe

Les estimations du produit intérieur brut et de la formation brute de capital fixe, reproduites au tableau 1 ont été calculées d'après la réponse du Bureau central de Statistique, Oslo au questionnaire de l'O.N.U. relatif aux comptes nationaux. Des estimations officielles ainsi que des explications figurent dans le rapport annuel du Bureau; *Økonomisk Utsyn* (Enquête économique). Pour remplir le questionnaire de l'O.N.U., le Bureau central de Statistique a ajusté les estimations officielles afin de les rendre aussi conformes que possible avec le système de comptabilité nationale de l'O.N.U.

## Indices de la production industrielle

Les chiffres du tableau 2 proviennent de deux types d'indices de la production industrielle, calculés par le Bureau central de Statistique à Oslo. Les données des années 1938-1960 ont été calculées à l'aide des indices annuels construits à partir des résultats des recensements annuels de l'industrie, et publiés dans *Statistisk Arsbok for Norge* et *Norges Industri*. Les chiffres de 1958 sont des moyennes annuelles des indices mensuels calculés par le Bureau central à partir d'une enquête mensuelle portant sur un échantillon des unités industrielles couvertes dans les recensements annuels de l'industrie. Les indices mensuels sont publiés dans *Statistiske Meldinger* et *Aktuell Statistikk*. Les indices annuels sont basés sur un plus grand nombre de réponses et un plus important nombre d'indicateurs de production que les indices mensuels.

Les indices annuels et mensuels sont les uns et les autres des moyennes arithmétiques à pondération fixe, dans la plupart des cas, de rapports quantitatifs de la production, mais aussi, parfois, des heures de travail effectuées. Les poids utilisés pour combiner les rapports concernant chaque marchandise en indices de catégorie sont tirés de la valeur brute de la production de ces marchandises pendant l'année de base; pour combiner ces indices de catégorie en indices plus larges, on a pondéré d'après la valeur ajoutée au coût des facteurs pendant l'année de base. Les années de pondération de base des indices du tableau 2 sont les suivantes: 1935 pour 1938, 1949 pour 1948-1954 et 1955 pour 1955 et les années suivantes.

Pour plus de détails sur les indices de la production industrielle, voir les publications ci-après du Bureau central de statistique: *Statistiske Meddelelsen*, Nos 11-12, 1937, pour les indices basés sur 1935, *Statistiske Meldinger*, Nos 7 et 12, 1953, pour les indices basés sur 1949 et *Norges Industri, 1956* pour ce qui concerne les indices basés sur 1955.

## Indices de l'emploi industriel

Les indices de l'emploi industriel reproduits au tableau 3 ont été élaborés par le Bureau de Statistique de l'O.N.U.

tions from absolute figures of employment resulting primarily from the annual Industrial Censuses of the Central Bureau of Statistics. The absolute figures are published in various issues of *Norges Industri* and the *Statistisk Arsbok for Norge*. The absolute figures of employment from which the indexes are computed, relate to the average number of employees during the year.

In order to compile comparable series of index numbers of employment for the period 1938-1960, the Statistical Office had to link differing series of absolute figures at 1948 and 1955, in the case of almost all kinds of industrial activity, and at 1951, in the case of a few industries. Effective with 1948, the Central Bureau of Statistics revised its scheme of industrial classification. The data for 1948 issued by the Bureau classified according to both the old and new industrial classification furnished the basis for linking. In 1955, changes were made in the field of manufacturing and other mining establishments covered in the annual Industrial Censuses; and alterations were introduced in the way in which the establishment was delineated where manufacturing and retailing were combined. These changes are described below. The issue by the Central Bureau of Statistics of data compiled on both the old and new bases again furnished the required links. In 1951, selected kinds of industrial activities (e.g. slaughtering or shoe repairing) were added to the field covered in the annual Industrial Census. It should be noted that comparable figures were available in the case of coal and metal mining and the electricity and gas industries for all the years shown in Table 3.

### The Characteristics and Structure of Industrial Activity

The data in Table 4 are derived from the results of the Censuses of Establishments of the Central Bureau of Statistics that were taken as of 9 October 1936 and 24 April 1953. The results have been published in *Bedriftstelling i Norge, 9 Oktober 1936* and *Statistisk Arsbok for Norge, 1955*. Although the size of units covered in both Censuses of Establishments are the same — all industrial units engaging two or more persons — the results of these Censuses are not comparable because of the differences between them in the statistical unit utilized and in the scheme applied in classifying according to kind of activity. The statistical and tabulation unit was the technical unit in the earlier Census, but the establishment in the 24 April 1953 Census. This would contribute a greater count of units as well as different classifications according to kind of activity in the earlier Census than in the later one. Also, the Central Bureau of Statistics revised its industrial classification in 1948 in the light of the ISIC, and although, in preparing Table 4, an effort was made to rearrange the data of the 9 October 1936 Census according to the revised classification, this was not entirely accomplished.

The figures of Tables 5 and 6 are based mainly on the results of annual Industrial Censuses taken by the Cen-

à partir des chiffres absolus de l'emploi résultant principalement des recensements industriels annuels effectués par le Bureau Central de Statistique. Ces chiffres absolus paraissent dans différentes publications du *Norge Industri* et du *Statistisk Arsbok for Norge*. Les chiffres absolus de l'emploi d'après lesquels les indices sont calculés concernent le nombre moyen de salariés pendant l'année.

Afin d'obtenir des séries comparables d'indices de l'emploi pour la période 1938-1960, le Bureau de Statistique a dû raccorder les séries différentes de chiffres absolus au niveau de 1948 et de 1955, dans le cas de la majeure partie de l'activité industrielle, et au niveau de 1951, dans le cas d'un nombre restreint d'industries. A partir de 1948 le Bureau central de Statistique a révisé son système de classification industrielle. Les données relatives à 1948 publiées par le Bureau, classifiées suivant l'ancien et le nouveau système de classification, fournissent la base de raccordement. En 1955, des changements ont été effectués dans le champ de couverture relatif aux établissements manufacturiers et à Autres industries extractives dans le recensement industriel annuel; des altérations ont été introduites dans les définitions relatives aux établissements dans lesquels l'activité commerciale de détail de l'activité manufacturière sont combinées. Ces changements sont décrits ci-dessous. La publication par le Bureau central de Statistique de données calculées d'après l'ancienne et d'après la nouvelle base permet aussi le raccordement recherché. En 1951, certaines activités industrielles (par exemple l'abattage de bétail ou la réparation de chaussures) ont été rajoutées au champ couvert par le recensement industriel. Il est bon de noter que des chiffres comparables relatifs aux industries extractives de minerais métalliques et de charbon et aux industries de l'électricité et du gaz sont disponibles pour toutes les années indiquées au tableau 3.

### Les caractéristiques et la structure de l'activité industrielle

Les chiffres du tableau 4 sont tirés des résultats des recensements des établissements exécutés par le Bureau central de Statistique les 9 octobre 1936 et 24 avril 1953. Ces résultats ont été publiés dans *Bedriftstelling i Norge, 9 Oktober 1936* et *Statistisk Arsbok for Norge, 1955*. Bien que la dimension des unités couvertes dans les deux recensements des établissements soit la même (toutes les unités industrielles occupant 2 personnes ou plus), les résultats des deux recensements ne sont pas comparables car l'unité statistique utilisée et la méthode suivie pour le classement selon le type d'activité étaient différentes. L'unité statistique (employée aussi pour le classement) était l'unité technique dans le premier recensement, mais l'établissement dans celui du 24 avril 1953, d'où plus d'unités dénombrées dans le premier recensement que dans le second, et différences dans le classement selon le type d'activité. Qui plus est, le Bureau central de Statistique a modifié sa nomenclature industrielle en 1948 pour l'aligner sur la CITI et, bien que l'on se soit efforcé, dans le tableau 4, de présenter les données du recensement au 9 octobre 1936 suivant la classification révisée, on n'y est pas parvenu complètement.

Les chiffres des tableaux 5 et 6 sont essentiellement fondés sur les résultats des recensements annuels de l'indus-

tral Bureau of Statistics. The data were compiled primarily from the following publications of the Central Bureau: *Norges Industri, 1938, 1939, 1948, 1953* or *1958; Norges Elektrisitetsverker, 1939-1941, 1949* or *1953;* and various issues of the *Statistisk Arsbok for Norge.* Some of the data were derived from correspondence with the Central Bureau.

The figures set out in Tables 5 and 6 relate to the activity of all coal and metal mining establishments and practically all electricity and gas producing and distributing units but the activities of only the larger manufacturing establishments. For the most part, in the case of the data for 1938, 1948 and 1953, manufacturing establishments which accounted for at least 12 000 man-hours of work annually or had five or more employees were covered. However, for certain classes of industry, the lower limit for the annual amount of man-hours worked was 3 000 to 6 000; and, in some classes of manufacturing, all establishments were covered in the annual Industrial Censuses. In the case of the data for 1958, generally, manufacturing units engaging at least 6 persons were included, though for selected classes of industrial activity, three persons engaged was the lower limit of coverage and in some instances, all establishments were covered. On the whole, the same classes of industrial activity were the subject of less selective criteria of coverage with regard to size in the case of the data for 1958 as in the case of the data for earlier years. However, the criteria with regard to size utilized to define the coverage of the 1958 Industrial Census resulted in the inclusion of a larger part of total manufacturing activity than those utilized in the 1938, 1948 and 1953 Industrial Censuses. Differences in the field of manufacturing covered also occur between the 1938 and 1948 Censuses on the one hand, and the 1953 and 1958 Censuses, on the other, because selected kinds of manufacturing (e.g. slaughtering, meat processing, or shoe repairing) were included in the latter Censuses but excluded in the former.

Additional incomparabilities exist between the data for 1938 and that for later years because of the revision by the Central Bureau of its scheme of industrial classification which was introduced beginning with the data for 1948. Changes beginning in 1955 in the delineation of manufacturing establishments where manufacturing and retailing were combined at the same location contributed, to some extent, to a lack of comparability between the data for 1958 and that for the earlier years shown in Tables 5 and 6. These changes consisted of covering the resources and activities involved in retailing as part of the manufacturing establishment. Before, if one or more persons were engaged in the retailing activities, these resources and activities were not included in the data for the manufacturing establishment.

trie exécutés par le Bureau central de Statistique. Les données ont été tirées principalement des publications ci-après du Bureau central: *Norges Industri, 1938, 1939, 1948, 1953* ou *1958; Norges Elektrisitetsverker, 1939-1941, 1949* ou *1953;* et différents numéros du *Statistisk Arsbok for Norge.* Certaines de ces données proviennent d'un échange de correspondance avec le Bureau central.

Les chiffres des tableaux 5 et 6 portent sur tous les établissements extractifs de charbon et de minerais métalliques et sur presque toutes les unités du groupe production et distribution d'électricité et de gaz, mais seulement sur les grands établissements manufacturiers. Dans la plupart des cas, pour les données relatives aux années 1938, 1948 et 1953, les établissements manufacturiers ayant à leur actif au moins 12 000 heures de travail par an ou comptant au moins 5 salariés ont été recensés. Toutefois, dans certains secteurs industriels, la limite inférieure pour le nombre d'heures de travail a été abaissée à un chiffre compris entre 3 000 et 6 000 et, dans quelques-unes des industries manufacturières, tous les établissements ont été recensés. Dans le cas des données relatives à 1958, d'une façon générale, les unités manufacturières occupant au moins six personnes ont été recensées, quoique pour certaines classes de l'activité industrielle, trois personnes occupées a été la limite la plus basse retenue, et dans certains cas même tous les établissements ont été recensés. Dans l'ensemble, les mêmes classes de l'activité industrielle ont été soumises à des critères se rapportant à la taille, moins sélectifs pour les unes que pour les autres, dans le cas des données relatives à 1958 aussi bien que dans le cas des données relatives aux années précédentes. Cependant, du critère taille adopté pour définir le champ couvert par le recensement industriel de 1958 a résulté la couverture d'une partie plus importante de la totalité de l'activité manufacturière qu'il n'est résulté des critères utilisés dans les recensements industriels de 1938, 1948 et 1953. Des différences, quant aux champs des industries manufacturières couverts existent d'une part entre le recensement de 1938 et celui de 1948, et d'autre part entre le recensement de 1953 et celui de 1958, vu que certains types d'industries manufacturières (telles qu'abattage de bétail, préparation de conserves de viande, réparation de chaussures) sont inclus dans les derniers recensements et exclus des premiers.

La révision par le Bureau central de son système de classification industrielle, lequel a été mis en vigueur à partir de 1948, a introduit des défauts de comparabilité entre les données relatives à 1938 et celles relatives aux années suivantes. Les changements en 1955 des délimitations adoptées pour les établissements manufacturiers où l'activité de commerce de détail et l'activité manufacturière sont combinées dans la même unité ont contribué, à un certain point, à un défaut de comparabilité entre les données relatives à 1958 et les données relatives aux années précédentes reproduites aux tableaux 5 et 6. Ces changements consistent à recouvrir les ressources des activités de commerce de détail considérées comme faisant partie de l'activité de l'établissement manufacturier. Auparavant, si une personne ou plus dans un établissement manufacturier était engagée dans le commerce de détail, les ressources et activités qui découlent sont exclues des données relatives à l'établissement manufacturier.

The same definitions seem to have been utilized for items of data that are identical for the various censuses for which data are presented in Tables 4, 5, and 6; and, where applicable, these definitions are consistent with the International Standards in Basic Industrial Statistics. Value added is priced at factor cost. The capacity of installed (in use and in reserve) power equipment is, in general, the sum of the rated horsepower of prime movers connected to machinery other than generators and of all electric motors. In the case of the electricity producing industry, the figures of horsepower were computed from data on the rated capacity, in kilowatts, of all prime movers, including those connected to electric generators. The figures of energy consumed relate to the quantity of various fuels consumed and electricity purchased. Coal, coke or other fuels consumed as raw materials are not included. Because, in Norway, establishments make considerable use of water power in generating electricity for their own use, the figures of energy consumed are understated, especially in the case of such industries as the manufacture of paper or textiles.

Les mêmes définitions semblent avoir été utilisées pour les rubriques qui sont identiques au cours des trois recensements pour lesquels on présente des chiffres dans les tableaux 4, 5 et 6; et où il a été possible de le faire, ces définitions sont compatibles avec les Normes internationales relatives aux statistiques industrielles de base. La valeur ajoutée est comptée au coût des facteurs. La puissance installée (en service ou en réserve) est en général égale à la puissance nominale des moteurs primaires entraînant des machines autres que des générateurs, plus celle de tous les moteurs électriques. Dans le cas du groupe production d'électricité, les chevaux-vapeur ont été calculés d'après la puissance nominale en kilowatts de tous les moteurs primaires, y compris ceux connectés aux générateurs électriques. Les chiffres relatifs à l'énergie consommé couvrent le volume de différents combustibles consommés et le volume de l'électricité achetée. Le charbon, coke et autres combustibles utilisés comme matière première sont exclus. Du fait qu'en Norvège les établissements utilisent beaucoup la puissance hydraulique pour fabriquer l'électricité nécessaire à l'autoconsommation, les chiffres relatifs à l'énergie consommé sont sous-estimés, spécialement dans des industries telles que la fabrication de papier ou de textiles.

# NORWAY

## 1. THE GROSS DOMESTIC PRODUCT AND GROSS DOMESTIC FIXED CAPITAL FORMATION
### PRODUIT INTERIEUR BRUT ET FORMATION BRUTE DE CAPITAL FIXE INTERIEUR

Million Kroner            Millions de couronnes

### A. Expenditure on the Gross Domestic Product at Market Prices
### Dépenses relatives au produit intérieur brut aux prix du marché

| Item of data and year / Rubrique et année | Total | Consumption / Consommation | | Gross Domestic Capital Formation / Formation brute de capital intérieur | | Net exports of goods and services / Exportations nettes de biens et de services | |
|---|---|---|---|---|---|---|---|
| | | Total | Government / Etat | Total | Fixed / Fixe | Exports less imports / Exportations moins importations | Exports / Exportations |
| _a. At Current Prices — Aux prix courants_ | | | | | | | |
| **Absolute figures — Chiffres absolus** | | | | | | | |
| 1950 | 15 028 | 11 495 | 1 688 | 4 381 | 4 104 | −848 | 5 771 |
| 1951 | 18 628 | 13 004 | 2 088 | 5 378 | 4 454 | 246 | 8 712 |
| 1952 | 20 540 | 14 657 | 2 561 | 5 910 | 5 354 | −27 | 8 715 |
| 1953 | 20 786 | 15 659 | 2 896 | 6 033 | 6 093 | −906 | 7 947 |
| 1954 | 22 440 | 16 767 | 3 089 | 6 823 | 6 599 | −1 150 | 8 548 |
| 1955 | 23 879 | 17 504 | 3 085 | 7 143 | 7 063 | −768 | 9 777 |
| 1956 | 26 998 | 18 842 | 3 458 | 7 929 | 7 305 | 227 | 11 903 |
| 1957 | 28 602 | 19 935 | 3 800 | 8 344 | 8 009 | 323 | 12 879 |
| 1958 | 28 434 | 20 745 | 4 030 | 8 570 | 8 847 | −881 | 11 639 |
| 1959 | 30 092 | 22 131 | 4 408 | 8 344 | 8 523 | −383 | 12 461 |
| 1960 | 32 200 | 23 623 | 4 637 | 9 255 | 8 759 | −678 | 13 346 |
| 1961 | 34 854 | 25 417 | 4 952 | 10 648 | 10 070 | −1 211 | 13 999 |
| **Percentage distribution of average annual expenditure — Distribution en pourcentage des dépenses annuelles moyennes** | | | | | | | |
| 1950−1960 | 100.0 | 72.6 | 13.4 | 29.2 | 28.1 | −1.8 | 41.7 |
| 1950 | 100.0 | 76.4 | 11.2 | 29.2 | 27.3 | −5.6 | 38.4 |
| 1953 | 100.0 | 75.3 | 13.9 | 29.0 | 29.3 | −4.3 | 38.2 |
| 1954 | 100.0 | 74.7 | 13.8 | 30.4 | 29.4 | −5.1 | 38.1 |
| 1958 | 100.0 | 72.9 | 14.2 | 30.1 | 31.1 | −3.0 | 40.9 |
| 1960 | 100.0 | 73.3 | 14.4 | 28.8 | 27.2 | −2.1 | 41.4 |
| _b. At Prices of 1958 — Aux prix de 1958_ | | | | | | | |
| **Absolute figures — Chiffres absolus** | | | | | | | |
| 1950 | 22 404 | 16 818 | 2 661 | 6 766 | 6 428 | −1 180 | 7 300 |
| 1951 | 23 134 | 16 854 | 2 971 | 7 215 | 6 260 | −935 | 8 060 |
| 1952 | 23 999 | 17 585 | 3 234 | 7 230 | 6 631 | −816 | 7 951 |
| 1953 | 24 962 | 18 499 | 3 594 | 7 332 | 7 401 | −869 | 8 488 |
| 1954 | 26 108 | 19 148 | 3 741 | 8 019 | 7 739 | −1 059 | 9 309 |
| 1955 | 26 682 | 19 589 | 3 640 | 8 261 | 8 171 | −1 168 | 9 910 |
| 1956 | 27 988 | 20 107 | 3 731 | 8 847 | 8 200 | −966 | 10 911 |
| 1957 | 28 560 | 20 536 | 3 871 | 8 765 | 8 456 | −741 | 11 335 |
| 1958 | 28 434 | 20 745 | 4 030 | 8 570 | 8 847 | −881 | 11 639 |
| 1959 | 29 498 | 21 687 | 4 289 | 8 235 | 8 407 | −424 | 12 735 |
| 1960 | 31 331 | 22 917 | 4 446 | 9 090 | 8 524 | −676 | 13 937 |
| 1961 | 33 351 | 24 307 | 4 664 | 10 228 | 9 594 | −1 184 | 14 861 |
| **Percentage distribution of average annual expenditure — Distribution en pourcentage des dépenses annuelles moyennes** | | | | | | | |
| 1950−1960 | 100.0 | 73.1 | 13.7 | 30.2 | 29.0 | −3.3 | 38.1 |
| 1950 | 100.0 | 75.0 | 11.9 | 30.2 | 28.7 | −5.2 | 32.6 |
| 1953 | 100.0 | 74.1 | 14.4 | 29.3 | 29.6 | −3.4 | 34.0 |
| 1954 | 100.0 | 73.3 | 14.3 | 30.7 | 29.6 | −4.0 | 35.6 |
| 1958 | 100.0 | 72.9 | 14.2 | 30.1 | 31.1 | −3.0 | 40.9 |
| 1960 | 100.0 | 73.1 | 14.2 | 29.0 | 27.2 | −2.1 | 44.5 |
| **Average annual rate of growth — Taux annuel moyen d'accroissement** | | | | | | | |
| 1950−1960 | 3.4 | 3.1 | 5.3 | 3.0 | 2.9 | . | 6.7 |
| 1950−1953 | 3.7 | 3.2 | 10.5 | 2.7 | 4.8 | . | 5.2 |
| 1954−1958 | 2.2 | 2.0 | 1.9 | 1.6 | 3.4 | . | 5.7 |
| 1958−1960 | 5.0 | 5.1 | 5.0 | 3.0 | −1.9 | . | 9.4 |

## B. The Gross Domestic Product at Factor Cost According to Origin
### Origine par secteur d'activité du produit intérieur brut au coût des facteurs

| Item of data and year / Rubrique et année | Total | Agricultural sector / Secteur agricole | Industrial Sector — Secteur Industriel | | | | | Transportation and communication / Transports et communications | Other sectors / Autres secteurs |
|---|---|---|---|---|---|---|---|---|---|
| | | | Total | Mining / Industries extractives | Manufacturing / Industries manufacturières | Construction / Bâtiment et travaux publics | Electricity, gas and water / Electricité, gaz et eau | | |
| ISIC — CITI | 0–9 | 0 | 1–5 | 1 | 2–3 | 4 | 5 | 7 | 6, 8–9 |
| *a. At Current Prices — Aux prix courants* | | | | | | | | | |
| **Absolute figures — Chiffres absolus** | | | | | | | | | |
| 1950 | 14 017 | 2 094 | 5 342 | 150 | 3 887 | 1 017 | 288 | 2 370 | 4 211 |
| 1951 | 16 960 | 2 416 | 6 349 | 198 | 4 726 | 1 116 | 309 | 3 378 | 4 817 |
| 1952 | 18 528 | 2 777 | 6 751 | 273 | 4 842 | 1 314 | 322 | 3 511 | 5 489 |
| 1953 | 18 855 | 2 621 | 7 213 | 302 | 5 086 | 1 470 | 355 | 3 188 | 5 833 |
| 1954 | 20 303 | 2 817 | 8 067 | 291 | 5 723 | 1 639 | 414 | 3 097 | 6 322 |
| 1955 | 21 592 | 2 899 | 8 385 | 298 | 5 954 | 1 670 | 463 | 3 735 | 6 573 |
| 1956 | 24 414 | 3 340 | 9 067 | 347 | 6 581 | 1 650 | 489 | 4 761 | 7 246 |
| 1957 | 25 897 | 3 267 | 9 474 | 325 | 6 796 | 1 772 | 581 | 5 160 | 7 996 |
| 1958 | 25 491 | 3 076 | 9 581 | 301 | 6 739 | 1 881 | 660 | 4 409 | 8 425 |
| 1959 | 26 888 | 3 199 | 10 100 | 275 | 7 088 | 1 999 | 738 | 4 483 | 9 106 |
| 1960 | 28 880 | 3 141 | 11 078 | 290 | 7 850 | 2 108 | 830 | 4 710 | 9 951 |
| 1961 | 31 152 | 3 412 | 12 040 | 294 | 8 519 | 2 331 | 896 | 5 034 | 10 666 |
| **Percentage distribution according to sector — Distribution en pourcentage par secteur** | | | | | | | | | |
| 1950–1960 | 100.0 | 13.0 | 37.8 | 1.3 | 27.0 | 7.3 | 2.2 | 17.7 | 31.5 |
| 1950 | 100.0 | 14.9 | 38.1 | 1.1 | 27.7 | 7.2 | 2.1 | 16.9 | 30.1 |
| 1953 | 100.0 | 13.9 | 38.2 | 1.6 | 26.9 | 7.8 | 1.9 | 16.9 | 31.0 |
| 1954 | 100.0 | 13.8 | 39.8 | 1.5 | 28.1 | 8.1 | 2.1 | 15.2 | 31.2 |
| 1958 | 100.0 | 12.0 | 37.6 | 1.2 | 26.4 | 7.4 | 2.6 | 17.3 | 33.1 |
| 1960 | 100.0 | 10.8 | 38.4 | 1.0 | 27.2 | 7.3 | 2.9 | 16.3 | 34.5 |
| *b. At Prices of 1958 — Aux prix de 1958* | | | | | | | | | |
| **Absolute figures — Chiffres absolus** | | | | | | | | | |
| 1950 | 19 988 | 3 091 | 7 523 | 221 | 5 206 | 1 727 | 369 | 2 874 | 6 500 |
| 1951 | 20 757 | 2 983 | 7 921 | 235 | 5 606 | 1 691 | 389 | 3 197 | 6 656 |
| 1952 | 21 514 | 3 314 | 7 940 | 258 | 5 503 | 1 780 | 399 | 3 274 | 6 986 |
| 1953 | 22 336 | 3 155 | 8 366 | 276 | 5 787 | 1 879 | 424 | 3 503 | 7 312 |
| 1954 | 23 286 | 3 159 | 8 906 | 274 | 6 166 | 1 993 | 473 | 3 537 | 7 684 |
| 1955 | 23 845 | 2 972 | 9 140 | 297 | 6 384 | 1 960 | 499 | 3 905 | 7 828 |
| 1956 | 25 060 | 3 401 | 9 391 | 326 | 6 777 | 1 768 | 520 | 4 153 | 8 115 |
| 1957 | 25 602 | 3 324 | 9 625 | 301 | 6 829 | 1 896 | 599 | 4 327 | 8 326 |
| 1958 | 25 491 | 3 076 | 9 581 | 301 | 6 739 | 1 881 | 660 | 4 409 | 8 425 |
| 1959 | 26 542 | 3 127 | 10 043 | 309 | 7 084 | 1 991 | 659 | 4 646 | 8 726 |
| 1960 | 28 160 | 3 076 | 10 688 | 329 | 7 642 | 2 003 | 714 | 5 092 | 9 304 |
| 1961 | 29 826 | 3 183 | 11 304 | 332 | 8 137 | 2 065 | 770 | 5 517 | 9 822 |
| **Percentage distribution according to sector — Distribution en pourcentage par secteur** | | | | | | | | | |
| 1950–1960 | 100.0 | 13.2 | 37.7 | 1.1 | 26.6 | 7.8 | 2.2 | 16.4 | 32.7 |
| 1950 | 100.0 | 15.4 | 37.7 | 1.1 | 26.1 | 8.6 | 1.9 | 14.3 | 32.6 |
| 1953 | 100.0 | 14.1 | 37.4 | 1.2 | 25.9 | 8.4 | 1.9 | 15.7 | 32.8 |
| 1954 | 100.0 | 13.5 | 38.3 | 1.2 | 26.5 | 8.5 | 2.1 | 15.2 | 33.0 |
| 1958 | 100.0 | 12.0 | 37.6 | 1.2 | 26.4 | 7.4 | 2.6 | 17.3 | 33.1 |
| 1960 | 100.0 | 10.9 | 37.9 | 1.1 | 27.2 | 7.1 | 2.5 | 18.1 | 33.1 |
| **Average annual rate of growth — Taux annuel moyen d'accroissement** | | | | | | | | | |
| 1950–1960 | 3.5 | −0.1 | 3.6 | 4.1 | 3.9 | 1.5 | 6.8 | 5.9 | 3.6 |
| 1950–1953 | 3.8 | 0.7 | 3.6 | 7.7 | 3.6 | 2.9 | 4.7 | 6.8 | 4.0 |
| 1954–1958 | 2.3 | −0.7 | 1.8 | 2.4 | 2.2 | −1.4 | 8.7 | 5.7 | 2.3 |
| 1958–1960 | 5.1 | — | 5.6 | 4.5 | 6.5 | 3.2 | 4.0 | 7.5 | 5.1 |

# NORWAY

## C. Gross Domestic Fixed Capital Formation According to Purchasing Sector
## Formation brute de capital fixe intérieur par secteur d'acquisition

| Item of data and year / Rubrique et année | Total | Agricultural sector / Secteur agricole | Industrial Sector — Secteur Industriel | | | | | Transportation and communication / Transports et communications | Other sectors / Autres secteurs |
| --- | --- | --- | --- | --- | --- | --- | --- | --- | --- |
| | | | Total | Mining / Industries extractives | Manufacturing / Industries manufacturières | Construction / Bâtiment et travaux publics | Electricity, gas and water / Electricité, gaz et eau | | |
| ISIC — CITI | 0–9 | 0 | 1–5 | 1 | 2–3 | 4 | 5 | 7 | 6, 8–9 |
| *a. At Current Prices — Aux prix courants* | | | | | | | | | |
| **Absolute figures — Chiffres absolus** | | | | | | | | | |
| 1950 | 4 104 | 400 | 1 184 | 51 | 758 | 36 | 339 | 1 264 | 1 256 |
| 1951 | 4 454 | 505 | 1 308 | 65 | 796 | 48 | 399 | 1 142 | 1 499 |
| 1952 | 5 354 | 577 | 1 715 | 67 | 1 072 | 84 | 492 | 1 226 | 1 836 |
| 1953 | 6 093 | 591 | 1 765 | 55 | 1 118 | 84 | 508 | 1 591 | 2 146 |
| 1954 | 6 599 | 642 | 1 894 | 54 | 1 250 | 98 | 492 | 1 765 | 2 298 |
| 1955 | 7 063 | 674 | 1 749 | 62 | 1 056 | 107 | 524 | 2 132 | 2 508 |
| 1956 | 7 305 | 716 | 1 946 | 48 | 1 171 | 140 | 587 | 2 249 | 2 394 |
| 1957 | 8 009 | 765 | 2 251 | 69 | 1 323 | 155 | 704 | 2 306 | 2 687 |
| 1958 | 8 847 | 783 | 2 183 | 59 | 1 287 | 147 | 690 | 3 141 | 2 740 |
| 1959 | 8 523 | 737 | 2 147 | 101 | 1 172 | 173 | 701 | 2 716 | 2 923 |
| 1960 | 8 759 | 784 | 2 615 | 120 | 1 521 | 223 | 751 | 2 217 | 3 143 |
| 1961 | 10 070 | 846 | 2 970 | 131 | 1 786 | | 797 | 2 796 | 3 458 |
| **Percentage distribution according to sector — Distribution en pourcentage par secteur** | | | | | | | | | |
| 1950–1960 | 100.0 | 9.5 | 27.6 | 1.0 | 16.7 | 1.7 | 8.2 | 29.0 | 33.9 |
| 1950 | 100.0 | 9.7 | 28.8 | 1.2 | 18.5 | 0.9 | 8.2 | 30.8 | 30.7 |
| 1953 | 100.0 | 9.6 | 29.0 | 1.0 | 18.3 | 1.4 | 8.3 | 26.1 | 35.3 |
| 1954 | 100.0 | 9.7 | 28.7 | 0.8 | 18.9 | 1.5 | 7.5 | 26.7 | 34.9 |
| 1958 | 100.0 | 8.8 | 24.7 | 0.7 | 14.5 | 1.7 | 7.8 | 35.5 | 31.0 |
| 1960 | 100.0 | 8.9 | 29.9 | 1.4 | 17.3 | 2.6 | 8.6 | 25.3 | 35.9 |
| *b. At Prices of 1958 — Aux prix de 1958* | | | | | | | | | |
| **Absolute figures — Chiffres absolus** | | | | | | | | | |
| 1950 | 6 428 | 611 | 1 708 | 65 | 1 057 | 45 | 541 | 2 179 | 1 930 |
| 1951 | 6 260 | 645 | 1 658 | 78 | 969 | 51 | 560 | 1 957 | 2 000 |
| 1952 | 6 631 | 696 | 2 037 | 76 | 1 248 | 90 | 623 | 1 683 | 2 215 |
| 1953 | 7 401 | 706 | 2 135 | 64 | 1 326 | 95 | 650 | 2 012 | 2 54[a] |
| 1954 | 7 739 | 749 | 2 261 | 62 | 1 468 | 109 | 622 | 2 030 | 2 6⁹ |
| 1955 | 8 171 | 771 | 2 038 | 70 | 1 216 | 115 | 637 | 2 527 | 2 835 |
| 1956 | 8 200 | 776 | 2 106 | 53 | 1 251 | 145 | 657 | 2 788 | 2 530 |
| 1957 | 8 456 | 789 | 2 304 | 72 | 1 350 | 160 | 722 | 2 644 | 2 719 |
| 1958 | 8 847 | 783 | 2 183 | 59 | 1 287 | 147 | 690 | 3 141 | 2 740 |
| 1959 | 8 407 | 775 | 2 163 | 100 | 1 176 | 179 | 708 | 2 593 | 2 876 |
| 1960 | 8 524 | 776 | 2 633 | 112 | 1 569 | 211 | 741 | 2 110 | 3 005 |
| 1961 | 9 594 | 848 | 2 852 | 123 | 1 711 | 242 | 776 | 2 706 | 3 188 |
| **Percentage distribution according to sector — Distribution en pourcentage par secteur** | | | | | | | | | |
| 1950–1960 | 100.0 | 9.4 | 27.3 | 1.0 | 16.4 | 1.5 | 8.4 | 30.2 | 33.1 |
| 1950 | 100.0 | 9.5 | 26.5 | 1.0 | 16.4 | 0.7 | 8.4 | 33.9 | 30.1 |
| 1953 | 100.0 | 9.5 | 28.8 | 0.9 | 17.9 | 1.3 | 8.7 | 27.2 | 34.5 |
| 1954 | 100.0 | 9.6 | 29.2 | 0.8 | 19.0 | 1.4 | 8.0 | 26.3 | 34.9 |
| 1958 | 100.0 | 8.8 | 24.7 | 0.7 | 14.5 | 1.7 | 7.8 | 35.5 | 31.0 |
| 1960 | 100.0 | 9.1 | 30.8 | 1.3 | 18.4 | 2.4 | 8.7 | 24.8 | 35.3 |
| **Average annual rate of growth — Taux annuel moyen d'accroissement** | | | | | | | | | |
| 1950–1960 | 2.9 | 2.4 | 4.4 | 5.6 | 4.0 | 16.7 | 3.2 | −0.3 | 4.5 |
| 1950–1953 | 4.8 | 4.9 | 7.7 | −0.5 | 7.8 | 28.3 | 6.3 | −2.6 | 9.7 |
| 1954–1958 | 3.4 | 1.1 | −0.9 | −1.2 | −3.2 | 7.8 | 2.6 | 11.5 | 0.4 |
| 1958–1960 | −1.9 | −0.5 | 9.8 | 37.8 | 10.4 | 19.8 | 3.6 | −18.0 | 4.7 |

## 2. INDEX NUMBERS OF INDUSTRIAL PRODUCTION
### INDICES DE LA PRODUCTION INDUSTRIELLE

### A. Selected Divisions of Industrial Activity
### Quelques branches de l'activité industrielle

| Period Période | Total | Mining Industries extractives | Manufacturing [1] Industries manufacturières [1] | Electricity and gas Electricité et gaz |
|---|---|---|---|---|
| ISIC — CITI | 1-3, 511-512 | 1 | 2-3 | 511-512 |

a. Indexes — Indices (1958 = 100)

| | | | | |
|---|---|---|---|---|
| 1938.......... | 46 | 113 [2] | 42 [2] | 38 |
| 1948.......... | 57 | 47 [2] | 58 [2] | 47 |
| 1949.......... | − 63 − | − 56 − | − 63 − | − 57 − |
| 1950.......... | 68 | 56 | 70 | 64 |
| 1951.......... | 74 | 61 | 75 | 64 |
| 1952.......... | 74 | 71 | 74 | 68 |
| 1953.......... | 78 | 80 | 78 | 71 |
| 1954.......... | 84 | 80 | 85 | 79 |
| 1955.......... | − 91 − | − 88 − | − 92 − | − 83 − |
| 1956.......... | 95 | 98 | 96 | 87 |
| 1957.......... | 100 | 100 | 100 | 94 |
| 1958.......... | 100 | 100 | 100 | 100 |
| 1959.......... | 106 | 98 | 106 | 104 |
| 1960.......... | 117 | 111 | 117 | 114 |
| 1961.......... | 123 | 102 | 127 | 124 |

b. Average Annual Rate of Change — Taux annuel moyen de variation

| | | | | |
|---|---|---|---|---|
| 1938 − 1960.... | 4.3 | −0.1 | 4.8 | 5.1 |
| 1938 − 1948.... | 2.2 | −8.4 | 3.3 | 2.1 |
| 1950 − 1960.... | 5.6 | 7.1 | 5.3 | 5.9 |
| 1948 − 1953.... | 6.5 | 11.2 | 6.1 | 8.6 |
| 1954 − 1958.... | 4.4 | 5.7 | 4.1 | 6.1 |
| 1958 − 1960.... | 8.2 | 5.4 | 8.2 | 6.8 |

For footnotes see end of table.

### B. The Major Groups of Mining
### Les classes de la branche Industries extractives

| Period Période | All mining Toutes industries extractives | Coal mining Extraction du charbon | Metal mining Extraction des minerais métalliques | Other mining Autres industries extractives |
|---|---|---|---|---|
| ISIC — CITI | 1 | 11 | 12 | 14-19 |

a. Indexes — Indices (1958 = 100)

| | | | | |
|---|---|---|---|---|
| 1938.......... | 113 [2] | 104 | 110 | ... |
| 1948.......... | 47 [2] | 154 | 46 | ... |
| 1949.......... | − 56 − | − 160 − | − 49 − | 53 |
| 1950.......... | 56 | 128. | 50 | 53 |
| 1951.......... | 61 | 165 | 50 | 67 |
| 1952.......... | 71 | − 158 − | − 63 − | 66 |
| 1953.......... | 80 | 149 | 76 | 69 |
| 1954.......... | 80 | 119 | 79 | 71 |
| 1955.......... | − 88 − | 112 | 88 | − 81 − |
| 1956.......... | 98 | 136 | 97 | 89 |
| 1957.......... | 100 | 134 | 98 | 98 |
| 1958.......... | 100 | 100 | 100 | 100 |
| 1959.......... | 98 | 88 | 97 | 111 |
| 1960.......... | 111 | 141 | 105 | 128 |
| 1961.......... | 102 | 128 | 104 | ... |

b. Average Annual Rate of Change — Taux annuel moyen de variation

| | | | | |
|---|---|---|---|---|
| 1938 − 1960.... | −0.1 | 1.4 | −0.2 | ... |
| 1938 − 1948.... | −8.4 | 4.0 | −8.4 | ... |
| 1950 − 1960.... | 7.1 | 1.0 | 7.7 | 9.2 |
| 1948 − 1953.... | 11.2 | −0.6 | 10.6 | ... |
| 1954 − 1958.... | 5.7 | −4.3 | 6.1 | 8.9 |
| 1958 − 1960.... | 5.4 | 18.7 | 2.5 | 13.1 |

Pour les notes, voir au bas du tableau.

## C.   The Major Groups of Manufacturing — Les classes de la branche Industries manufacturières

| Period / Période | Manufacturing [1] — Industries manufacturières [1] | Food, beverages and tobacco — Industries alimentaires, boissons, tabac | Textiles | Clothing, footwear and made-up textiles — Articles d'habillement, chaussures et ouvrages en tissu | Wood products and furniture — Bois et meubles | Paper and paper products — Papier et ouvrages en papier | Printing [1] — Imprimerie [1] | Leather and leather products except wearing apparel — Cuir et articles en cuir, à l'exclusion des articles d'habillement | Rubber products — Ouvrages en caoutchouc | Chemicals and chemical, petroleum and coal products — Produits chimiques et dérivés du pétrole et du charbon | Non-metallic mineral products — Produits minéraux non métalliques | Basic metals — Métallurgie de base | Metal products — Ouvrages en métaux | Other manufacturing — Autres industries manufacturières |
|---|---|---|---|---|---|---|---|---|---|---|---|---|---|---|
| ISIC — CITI | 2–3 | 20–22 | 23 | 24 | 25–26 | 27 | 28 | 29 | 30 | 31–32 | 33 | 34 | 35–38 | 39 |

### a. Indexes — Indices (1958 = 100)

| Period | | | | | | | | | | | | | | |
|---|---|---|---|---|---|---|---|---|---|---|---|---|---|---|
| 1938.............. | 42[2] | 55 | 56 | 44 | 49 | 46 | 73 | 96 | 36 | 31 | 31[2] | 38 | 33 | ... |
| 1948.............. | 58[2] | 75 | 81 | 61 | 72 | 62 | 80 | 139 | 86 | 40 | 48[2] | 38 | 49 | ... |
| 1949.............. | – 63 – | – 79 – | – 95 – | – 67 – | – 76 – | – 64 – | – 82 – | – 158 – | – 83 – | – 50 – | – 53 – | – 44 – | – 53 – | 38 |
| 1950.............. | 70 | 81 | 110 | 76 | 76 | 73 | 85 | 161 | 82 | 66 | 62 | 50 | 59 | 49 |
| 1951.............. | 75 | 84 | 116 | 75 | 76 | 78 | 89 | 139 | 95 | 79 | 69 | 55 | 64 | 50 |
| 1952.............. | 74 | 84 | 98 | 81 | 82 | 73 | 90 | 88 | 86 | 77 | 75 | 58 | 66 | 53 |
| 1953.............. | 78 | 84 | 106 | 91 | 90 | 80 | 91 | 93 | 93 | 77 | 76 | 60 | 72 | 58 |
| 1954.............. | 85 | 87 | 106 | 93 | 98 | 89 | 95 | 106 | 101 | 96 | 84 | 62 | 78 | 73 |
| 1955.............. | – 92 – | – 95 – | – 104 – | – 98 – | – 100 – | – 95 – | – 96 – | – 104 – | – 106 – | – 96 – | 88 | – 74 – | – 88 – | – 81 – |
| 1956.............. | 96 | 101 | 114 | 104 | 102 | 95 | 99 | 111 | 96 | 100 | 90 | 90 | 91 | 93 |
| 1957.............. | 100 | 101 | 114 | 109 | 104 | 101 | 100 | 105 | 98 | 102 | 96 | 98 | 96 | 104 |
| 1958.............. | 100 | 100 | 100 | 100 | 100 | 100 | 100 | 100 | 100 | 100 | 100 | 100 | 100 | 100 |
| 1959.............. | 106 | 107 | 119 | 113 | 107 | 108 | 95 | 107 | 105 | 109 | 111 | 112 | 99 | 111 |
| 1960.............. | 117 | 113 | 124 | 122 | 119 | 121 | 97 | 98 | 127 | 118 | 120 | 128 | 114 | 127 |
| 1961.............. | 127 | 115 | 125 | 122 | 124 | 125 | 97 | 87 | 116 | 152 | 129 | 134 | 124 | 151 |

### b. Average Annual Rate of Change — Taux annuel moyen de variation

| Period | | | | | | | | | | | | | | |
|---|---|---|---|---|---|---|---|---|---|---|---|---|---|---|
| 1938 – 1960....... | 4.8 | 3.3 | 3.7 | 4.7 | 4.1 | 4.6 | 1.3 | 0.1 | 5.9 | 6.3 | 6.4 | 5.7 | 5.8 | ... |
| 1938 – 1948....... | 3.3 | 3.2 | 3.8 | 3.3 | 3.9 | 3.0 | 0.9 | 3.8 | 9.1 | 10.9 | 4.5 | — | 4.0 | ... |
| 1950 – 1960....... | 5.3 | 3.4 | 1.2 | 4.8 | 4.6 | 5.2 | 1.3 | −4.8 | 4.5 | 6.0 | 6.8 | 9.9 | 6.8 | 10.0 |
| 1948 – 1953....... | 6.1 | 2.3 | 5.5 | 8.3 | 4.6 | 5.2 | 2.6 | −7.7 | 1.6 | 14.0 | 9.6 | 9.6 | 8.0 | ... |
| 1954 – 1958....... | 4.1 | 3.5 | −1.4 | 1.8 | 0.5 | 3.0 | 1.3 | −1.4 | −0.2 | 1.0 | 4.4 | 12.7 | 6.4 | 8.2 |
| 1958 – 1960....... | 8.2 | 6.3 | 11.4 | 10.5 | 9.1 | 10.0 | −1.5 | −1.0 | 9.5 | 8.6 | 9.5 | 13.1 | 6.8 | 12.7 |

[1] Publishing (part of ISIC 28) is not included.
[2] For 1938 and 1948, Stone, clay and sand quarrying (ISIC major group 14) is included in Manufacturing under Non-metallic mineral products (ISIC major group 33) instead of in Mining.

[1] Non compris l'édition (dans CITI 28).
[2] En 1938 et 1948, l'Extraction de la pierre à bâtir, de l'argile et du sable (CITI 14) est incluse dans les Industries manufacturières sous Produits minéraux non métalliques (CITI 33) et non dans les Industries extractives.

# 3. INDEX NUMBERS OF INDUSTRIAL EMPLOYMENT
## INDICES DE L'EMPLOI DANS L'INDUSTRIE

## A. Selected Divisions of Industrial Activity
### Quelques branches de l'activité industrielle

| Period<br>Période | Total [2] | Mining<br>Industries<br>extractives | Manu-<br>facturing [2]<br>Industries<br>manu-<br>facturières [2] | Electricity<br>and gas<br>Electricité<br>et gaz |
|---|---|---|---|---|
| ISIC — CITI | 1–3, 511–512 | 1 | 2–3 | 511–512 |

### a. Indexes — Indices (1958 = 100)

| | | | | |
|---|---|---|---|---|
| 1938.......... | ... | ... | 58 [1] | 70 |
| 1948.......... | ... | ... | – 84 – | 89 |
| 1949.......... | ... | ... | 88 | 90 |
| 1950.......... | 91 | 80 | 91 | 93 |
| 1951.......... | – 94 – | 84 | – 95 – | 95 |
| 1952.......... | 94 | 95 | 94 | 98 |
| 1953.......... | 95 | 96 | 95 | 99 |
| 1954.......... | 98 | 99 | 98 | 100 |
| 1955.......... | – 101 – | – 102 – | – 101 – | 102 |
| 1956.......... | 101 | 108 | 101 | 103 |
| 1957.......... | 102 | 107 | 102 | 101 |
| 1958.......... | 100 | 100 | – 100 – | 100 |
| 1959.......... | 100 | 95 | 101 | 101 |
| 1960.......... | 106 | 95 | 107 | 101 |
| 1961.......... | 109 | 95 | 110 | 102 |

### b. Average Annual Rate of Change — Taux annuel moyen de variation

| | | | | |
|---|---|---|---|---|
| 1938 – 1960.... | ... | ... | 2.8 | 1.7 |
| 1938 – 1948.... | ... | ... | 3.8 | 2.4 |
| 1950 – 1960.... | 1.5 | 1.7 | 1.6 | 0.8 |
| 1948 – 1953.... | ... | ... | 2.5 | 2.1 |
| 1954 – 1958.... | 0.5 | 0.2 | 0.5 | — |
| 1958 – 1960.... | 3.0 | –2.5 | 3.4 | 0.5 |

For footnotes see end of table.
Pour les notes, voir au bas du tableau.

## B. The Major Groups of Mining
### Les classes de la branche Industries extractives

| Period<br>Période | All mining<br>Toutes<br>industries<br>extractives | Coal<br>mining<br>Extraction<br>du charbon | Metal mining<br>Extraction<br>des minerais<br>métalliques | Other mining<br>Autres<br>industries<br>extractives |
|---|---|---|---|---|
| ISIC — CITI | 1 | 11 | 12 | 14–19 |

### a. Indexes — Indices (1958 = 100)

| | | | | |
|---|---|---|---|---|
| 1950.......... | 80 | 105 | 68 | 100 |
| 1951.......... | 84 | 109 | 72 | 102 |
| 1952.......... | 95 | 108 | 92 | 96 |
| 1953.......... | 96 | 90 | 98 | 91 |
| 1954.......... | 99 | 90 | 103 | 91 |
| 1955.......... | – 102 – | 97 | 104 | – 97 – |
| 1956.......... | 108 | 116 | 108 | 104 |
| 1957.......... | 107 | 131 | 104 | 106 |
| 1958.......... | 100 | 100 | 100 | 100 |
| 1959.......... | 95 | 82 | 95 | 101 |
| 1960.......... | 95 | 73 | 95 | 104 |
| 1961.......... | 95 | 72 | 93 | 107 |

### b. Average Annual Rate of Change — Taux annuel moyen de variation

| | | | | |
|---|---|---|---|---|
| 1950 – 1960.... | 1.7 | –3.6 | 3.4 | 0.4 |
| 1954 – 1958.... | 0.2 | 2.7 | –0.7 | 2.4 |
| 1958 – 1960.... | –2.5 | –14.6 | –2.5 | 2.0 |

# NORWAY

## C. The Major Groups of Manufacturing — Les classes de la branche Industries manufacturières

| Period / Période | Manu-facturing [2] / Industries manufac-turières [2] | Food, beverages and tobacco [2] / Industries alimen-taires, boissons, tabac [2] | Textiles | Clothing, footwear and made-up textiles [2] / Articles d'habil-lement, chaussures et ouvrages en tissu [2] | Wood products and furniture / Bois et meubles | Paper and paper products / Papier et ouvrages en papier | Printing [2] / Im-primerie [2] | Leather and leather products except wearing apparel / Cuir et articles en cuir, à l'exclu-sion des articles d'habil-element | Rubber products / Ouvrages en caout-chouc | Chemicals and chemical, petroleum and coal products / Produits chi-miques et dérivés du pétrole et du charbon | Non-metallic mineral products / Produits minéraux non métal-liques | Basic metals / Métal-lurgie de base | Metal products / Ouvrages en métaux | Other manu-facturing / Autres industries manufac-turières |
|---|---|---|---|---|---|---|---|---|---|---|---|---|---|---|
| ISIC — CITI | 2–3 | 20–22 | 23 | 24 | 25–26 | 27 | 28 | 29 | 30 | 31–32 | 33 | 34 | 35–38 | 39 |

### a. Indexes — Indices (1958 = 100)

| Period | 2–3 | 20–22 | 23 | 24 | 25–26 | 27 | 28 | 29 | 30 | 31–32 | 33 | 34 | 35–38 | 39 |
|---|---|---|---|---|---|---|---|---|---|---|---|---|---|---|
| 1938 | 58[1] | 71 | 84 | 70 | 62 | 66 | 60 | 87 | 60 | 42 | 64[1] | 49 | 47 | 52 |
| 1948 | –84– | –80– | –110– | –91– | –103– | –83– | –81– | –133– | –122– | –71– | –90– | –56– | –83– | –87– |
| 1949 | 88 | 83 | 119 | 99 | 110 | 84 | 82 | 155 | 121 | 72 | 92 | 66 | 85 | 97 |
| 1950 | 91 | 83 | 130 | 105 | 109 | 87 | 83 | 148 | 119 | 76 | 98 | 70 | 87 | 102 |
| 1951 | –95– | –84– | –138– | –108– | 105 | –92– | 88 | 136 | 126 | –85– | –102– | 73 | 90 | 102 |
| 1952 | 94 | 81 | 126 | 109 | 106 | 93 | 91 | 108 | 118 | 89 | 101 | 75 | 91 | 95 |
| 1953 | 95 | 81 | 125 | 115 | 108 | 94 | 92 | 105 | 121 | 92 | 103 | 75 | 90 | 93 |
| 1954 | 98 | 85 | 122 | 114 | 111 | 98 | 94 | 108 | 113 | 98 | 106 | 76 | 95 | 102 |
| 1955 | –101– | –87– | –117– | –119– | –116– | –102– | –96– | –109– | –114– | –99– | –107– | –88– | –98– | –112– |
| 1956 | 101 | 87 | 117 | 114 | 108 | 101 | 98 | 110 | 104 | 103 | 100 | 95 | 100 | 108 |
| 1957 | 102 | 87 | 115 | 112 | 106 | 102 | 100 | 109 | 104 | 103 | 100 | 98 | 102 | 112 |
| 1958 | 100 | 100 | 100 | 100 | 100 | 100 | 100 | 100 | 100 | 100 | 100 | 100 | 100 | 100 |
| 1959 | 101 | 104 | 106 | 101 | 96 | 102 | 97 | 99 | 102 | 100 | 99 | 102 | 100 | 103 |
| 1960 | 107 | 114 | 108 | 105 | 102 | 107 | 100 | 89 | 109 | 103 | 103 | 106 | 106 | 114 |
| 1961 | 110 | 119 | 109 | 105 | 102 | 107 | 105 | 86 | 110 | 104 | 102 | 108 | 111 | 129 |

### b. Average Annual Rate of Change — Taux annuel moyen de variation

| Period | 2–3 | 20–22 | 23 | 24 | 25–26 | 27 | 28 | 29 | 30 | 31–32 | 33 | 34 | 35–38 | 39 |
|---|---|---|---|---|---|---|---|---|---|---|---|---|---|---|
| 1938 – 1960 | 2.8 | 2.2 | 1.2 | 1.9 | 2.3 | 2.2 | 2.4 | 0.1 | 2.8 | 4.2 | 2.2 | 3.6 | 3.8 | 3.6 |
| 1938 – 1948 | 3.8 | 1.2 | 2.7 | 2.7 | 5.2 | 2.3 | 3.0 | 4.3 | 7.4 | 5.4 | 3.5 | 1.3 | 5.9 | 5.3 |
| 1950 – 1960 | 1.6 | 3.2 | –1.8 | — | –0.7 | 2.1 | 1.9 | –5.0 | –0.9 | 3.1 | 0.5 | 4.2 | 2.0 | 1.1 |
| 1948 – 1953 | 2.5 | 0.2 | 2.6 | 4.8 | 0.9 | 2.5 | 2.6 | –4.6 | –0.2 | 5.3 | 2.7 | 6.0 | 1.6 | 1.3 |
| 1954 – 1958 | 0.5 | 4.1 | –4.8 | –3.2 | –2.6 | 0.5 | 1.6 | –1.9 | –3.0 | 0.5 | –1.4 | 7.1 | 1.3 | –0.5 |
| 1958 – 1960 | 3.4 | 6.8 | 3.9 | 2.5 | 1.0 | 3.4 | — | –5.7 | 4.4 | 1.5 | 1.5 | 3.0 | 3.0 | 6.8 |

[1] Includes Stone, sand and clay quarrying (ISIC major group 14).
[2] Dairies and fish salting and smoking (part of ISIC major group 20) and publishing (part of ISIC major group 28) are not covered. In addition, slaughtering and meat processing (part of ISIC major group 20) and shoe repairing (part of ISIC major group 24) were not included in the data before 1951.

[1] Y compris l'Extraction de la pierre à bâtir, du sable et de l'argile (CITI 14).
[2] Non compris les laiteries et le saurissage de poissons (dans CITI 20) et l'édition (dans CITI 28). En outre, l'abattage du bétail et la fabrication de préparations et conserves de viande (dans CITI 20), ainsi que la réparation des chaussures (dans CITI 24), ne sont compris dans les données qu'à partir de 1951.

## 4. CHARACTERISTICS OF INDUSTRIAL UNITS ENGAGING TWO OR MORE PERSONS
### 9 October 1936 and 24 April 1953

## CARACTERISTIQUES DES UNITES INDUSTRIELLES OCCUPANT DEUX PERSONNES OU PLUS
### 9 octobre 1936 et 24 avril 1953

Number of technical units or establishments in units; number of engaged and employees in thousands; and wages and salaries in million Kroner; wages and salaries per employee in thousand Kroner.

Nombre d'unités techniques ou d'établissements en unités; nombre de personnes occupées et de salariés en milliers; traitements et salaires en millions de couronnes norvégiennes; traitements et salaires par salarié en milliers de couronnes.

### A. The Divisions of Industrial Activity — Les branches de l'activité industrielle

| Item of data | All industrial activity Toutes industries | | Mining Industries extractives | | Manufacturing Industries manufacturières | | Construction Bâtiment et travaux publics | | Electricity and gas Electricité et gaz | | Rubrique |
|---|---|---|---|---|---|---|---|---|---|---|---|
| | 9.X.1936 | 24.IV.1953 | 9.X.1936 | 24.IV.1953 | 9.X.1936 | 24.IV.1953 | 9.X.1936 | 24.IV.1953 | 9.X.1936 | 24.IV.1953 | |
| ISIC | 1–4, 511–512 | | 1 | | 2–3 | | 4 | | 511–512 | | CITI |
| Number of units [1] | 29 512 | 35 499 | 738 | 597 | 21 920 | 26 731 | 6 064 | 7 141 | 790 | 1 030 | Nombre d'unités [1] |
| Number of engaged (As of census date) | 300.3 | 438.7 | 10.9 | 9.8 | 212.4 | 350.7 | 69.6 | 68.0 | 7.4 | 10.2 | Nombre de personnes occupées (à la date du recensement) |
| Number of employees (As of census date) | 295.3 | 407.3 | 10.9 | 9.4 | 208.8 | 327.1 | 68.2 | 60.6 | 7.4 | 10.2 | Nombre de salariés (à la date du recensement) |
| Wages and salaries paid (Calendar year preceding census date) | 597.5 | 3 375.3 | 22.1 | 95.1 | 427.8 | 2 616.3 | 123.7 | 572.1 | 23.9 | 91.8 | Traitements et salaires payés (année civile précédant le recensement) |
| Distribution in per cent of number of engaged | 100.0 | 100.0 | 3.6 | 2.2 | 70.7 | 79.9 | 23.2 | 15.5 | 2.5 | 2.4 | Distribution en pourcentage du nombre de personnes occupées |
| Wages and salaries per employee | 2.0 | 8.3 | 2.0 | 10.1 | 2.0 | 8.0 | 1.8 | 9.4 | 3.2 | 9.0 | Traitements et salaires par salarié |
| Employees as a per cent of engaged | 98.3 | 92.8 | 100.0 | 95.9 | 98.3 | 93.3 | 98.0 | 89.1 | 100.0 | 100.0 | Salariés en pourcentage des personnes occupées |

[1] Technical units as of 9.X.1936, but establishments as of 24.IV.1953.

[1] Unités techniques au 9.X.1936, mais établissements au 24.IV.1953.

### B. The Major Groups of Mining — Les classes de la branche Industries extractives

| Item of data | 9.X.1936 | | | | 24.IV.1953 | | | | Rubrique |
|---|---|---|---|---|---|---|---|---|---|
| | All mining Toutes industries extractives | Coal mining Extraction du charbon | Metal mining Extraction des minerais métalliques | Other mining Divers | All mining Toutes industries extractives | Coal mining Extraction du charbon | Metal mining Extraction des minerais métalliques | Other mining Divers | |
| ISIC | 1 | 11 | 12 | 14–19 | 1 | 11 | 12 | 14–19 | CITI |
| Number of units [1] | 738 | — | 50 | 688 | 597 | 2 | 30 | 565 | Nombre d'unités [1] |
| Number of engaged (As of census date) | 10.9 | — | 6.0 | 4.9 | 9.8 | 0.9 | 5.4 | 3.5 | Nombre de personnes occupées (à la date du recensement) |
| Number of employees (As of census date) | 10.9 | — | 6.0 | 4.9 | 9.4 | 0.9 | 5.4 | 3.1 | Nombre de salariés (à la date du recensement) |
| Wages and salaries paid (Calendar year preceding census date) | 22.1 | — | 14.0 | 8.1 | 95.1 | 17.4 | 53.7 | 24.0 | Traitements et salaires payés (année civile précédant le recensement) |
| Distribution in per cent of number of engaged | 100.0 | — | 55.0 | 45.0 | 100.0 | 9.2 | 55.1 | 35.7 | Distribution en pourcentage du nombre de personnes occupées |
| Wages and salaries per employee | 2.0 | — | 2.3 | 1.6 | 10.1 | 19.3 | 9.9 | 7.7 | Traitements et salaires par salarié |
| Employees as a per cent of engaged | 100.0 | — | 100.0 | 100.0 | 95.9 | 100.0 | 100.0 | 88.6 | Salariés en pourcentage des personnes occupées |

[1] Technical units as of 9.X.1936, but establishments as of 24.IV.1953.

[1] Unités techniques au 9.X.1936, mais établissements au 24.IV.1953.

## C. The Major Groups of Manufacturing — Les classes de la branche Industries manufacturières

| Year and item of data | Manufacturing / Industries manufacturières | Food, beverages and tobacco / Industries alimentaires, boissons, tabac | Textiles | Clothing, footwear and made-up textiles / Articles d'habillement, chaussures et ouvrages en tissu | Wood products and furniture / Bois et meubles | Paper and paper products / Papier et ouvrages en papier | Printing and publishing / Imprimerie et édition | Leather and leather products except wearing apparel / Cuir et articles en cuir, à l'exclusion des articles d'habillement | Rubber products / Ouvrages en caoutchouc | Chemicals and chemical, petroleum and coal products / Produits chimiques et dérivés du pétrole et du charbon | Non-metallic mineral products / Produits minéraux non métalliques | Basic metals / Métallurgie de base | Metal products / Ouvrages en métaux | Other manufacturing / Autres industries manufacturières | Année et rubrique |
|---|---|---|---|---|---|---|---|---|---|---|---|---|---|---|---|
| ISIC | 2–3 | 20–22 | 23 | 24 | 25–26 | 27 | 28 | 29 | 30 | 31–32 | 33 | 34 | 35–38 | 39 | CITI |
| **9.X.1936** | | | | | | | | | | | | | | | **9.X.1936** |
| Number of technical units.............. | 21 920 | 5 817 | 539 | 3 152 | 5 457 | 251 | 908 | 401 | 106 | 638 | 636 | 729 | 2 552 | 734 | Nombre d'unités techniques |
| Number of engaged.... | 212.4 | 37.6 | 16.0 | 26.5 | 24.4 | 18.5 | 9.3 | 2.6 | 2.3 | 10.2 | 9.2 | 11.7 | 40.8 | 3.3 | Nombre de personnes occupées |
| Number of employees... | 208.8 | 36.8 | 15.9 | 25.8 | 23.6 | 18.5 | 9.1 | 2.5 | 2.3 | 10.1 | 9.2 | 11.5 | 40.3 | 3.2 | Nombre de salariés |
| Wages and salaries paid (Calendar year preceding census date). | 427.8 | 71.0 | 28.3 | 35.9 | 31.9 | 48.5 | 25.5 | 5.1 | 3.9 | 32.2 | 18.9 | 30.7 | 88.8 | 7.1 | Traitements et salaires payés (année civile précédant le recensement) |
| Distribution in percent of number of engaged... | 100.0 | 17.7 | 7.5 | 12.5 | 11.4 | 8.8 | 4.3 | 1.3 | 1.0 | 4.8 | 4.4 | 5.5 | 19.2 | 1.6 | Distribution en pourcentage du nombre de personnes occupées |
| Wages and salaries per employee........ | 2.0 | 1.9 | 1.8 | 1.4 | 1.4 | 2.6 | 2.8 | 2.0 | 1.7 | 3.2 | 2.0 | 2.7 | 2.2 | 2.2 | Traitements et salaires par salarié |
| Employees as a percent of engaged ......... | 98.3 | 97.9 | 99.4 | 97.4 | 96.7 | 100.0 | 97.8 | 96.2 | 100.0 | 99.0 | 100.0 | 98.3 | 98.8 | 97.0 | Salariés en pourcentage des personnes occupées |
| **24.IV.1953** | | | | | | | | | | | | | | | **24.IV.1953** |
| Number of establishments. | 26 731 | 5 723 | 622 | 2 836 | 7 336 | 303 | 1 276 | 254 | 155 | 658 | 880 | 169 | 5 310 | 1 209 | Nombre d'établissements |
| Number of engaged.... | 350.7 | 51.2 | 22.3 | 36.4 | 47.0 | 22.9 | 19.3 | 2.5 | 3.9 | 19.7 | 12.9 | 16.2 | 89.2 | 7.2 | Nombre de personnes occupées |
| Number of employees... | 327.1 | 46.8 | 21.8 | 33.6 | 39.5 | 22.8 | 18.6 | 2.3 | 3.8 | 19.5 | 12.1 | 16.1 | 84.2 | 6.0 | Nombre de salariés |
| Wages and salaries paid (Calendar year preceding census date). | 2 616.3 | 325.6 | 151.5 | 208.4 | 253.0 | 219.2 | 145.3 | 18.0 | 32.0 | 191.0 | 105.6 | 168.8 | 749.2 | 48.7 | Traitements et salaires payés (année civile précédant le recensement) |
| Distribution in percent of number of engaged... | 100.0 | 14.5 | 6.4 | 10.4 | 13.4 | 6.5 | 5.5 | 0.7 | 1.1 | 5.7 | 3.6 | 4.7 | 25.4 | 2.1 | Distribution en pourcentage du nombre de personnes occupées |
| Wages and salaries per employee.......... | 8.0 | 7.0 | 6.9 | 6.2 | 6.4 | 9.6 | 7.8 | 7.8 | 8.4 | 9.8 | 8.7 | 10.5 | 8.9 | 8.1 | Traitements et salaires par salarié |
| Employees as a percent of engaged........ | 93.3 | 91.4 | 97.8 | 92.3 | 84.0 | 99.6 | 96.4 | 92.0 | 97.4 | 99.0 | 93.8 | 99.4 | 94.4 | 83.3 | Salariés en pourcentage des personnes occupées |

## 5. CHARACTERISTICS OF LARGER INDUSTRIAL ESTABLISHMENTS[1]
## CARACTERISTIQUES DES ETABLISSEMENTS INDUSTRIELS DEPASSANT UNE CERTAINE DIMENSION[1]
### 1938, 1948, 1953, 1958

Number of establishments in units; value added and wages and salaries in million Kroner; number of engaged, employees and operatives in thousands; man-hours worked in millions; energy consumed in thousand metric tons of coal equivalents, electricity consumed in million KWH; capacity of installed power equipment in thousand horsepower; value added per engaged or per employee and wages and salaries per employee and per thousand operative man-hours in thousand Kroner; average annual man-hours per operative in thousands; energy consumed per engaged or per employee and per thousand operative man-hours in metric tons of coal equivalents; electricity consumed per engaged or per employee and per thousand operative man-hours in thousand KWH; capacity of installed power equipment per engaged or per employee and per thousand operative man-hours in horsepower.

Nombre d'établissements en unités; valeur ajoutée et traitements et salaires en millions de couronnes; nombre de personnes occupées, de salariés et d'ouvriers en milliers; heures de travail effectuées en millions; énergie consommée en milliers de tonnes métriques d'équivalent charbon; électricité consommée en millions de kWh; puissance installée en milliers de chevaux-vapeur; valeur ajoutée par personne occupée ou par salarié et traitements et salaires par salarié et par millier d'heures-ouvrier en milliers de couronnes; moyenne annuelle des heures de travail par ouvrier en milliers; énergie consommée par personne occupée ou par salarié et par millier d'heures-ouvrier en tonnes métriques d'équivalent charbon; électricité consommée par personne occupée ou par salarié et par millier d'heures-ouvrier en milliers de kWh; puissance installée par personne occupée ou par salarié et par millier d'heures-ouvrier en chevaux-vapeur.

### A. Selected Divisions of Industrial Activity — Quelques branches de l'activité industrielle

| Year and item of data | Total [2] | Mining Industries ex-tractives | Manu-facturing [2] Industries manu-facturières[2] | Electricity and gas Electricité et gaz | Année et rubrique |
|---|---|---|---|---|---|
| ISIC | 1-3,511-512 | 1 | 2-3 | 511-512 | CITI |
| | **a. Absolute Figures — Chiffres absolus** | | | | |
| **1953** | | | | | **1953** |
| Number of establishments | 7 066 | 175 | 6 087 | 804 | Nombre d'établissements |
| Value added | 5 950.0 | 265.2 | 5 304.7 | 380.1 | Valeur ajoutée |
| Employees: | | | | | Salariés: |
| Number (Average during year) | 281.7 | 8.2 | 261.9 | 11.6 | Nombre (moyenne pour l'année) |
| Wages and salaries | 2 647.8 | 92.9 | 2 445.5 | 109.4 | Traitements et salaires |
| Operatives: | | | | | Ouvriers: |
| Number (Average during year) | 235.2 | 7.4 | 220.1 | 7.7 | Nombre (moyenne pour l'année) |
| Man-hours worked | 496.6 | 15.2 | 465.2 | 16.2 | Heures de travail effectuées |
| Wages and salaries | 2 079.1 | 80.6 | 1 927.9 | 70.6 | Traitements et salaires |
| Energy consumed | ... | 47.6 | 2 026.2 | ... | Energie consommée |
| Electricity consumed | ... | 184.6 | 9 760.9 | ... | Electricité consommée |
| Capacity of installed power equipment | ... | 118 | 1 658 | ... | Puissance installée |
| **1958** | | | | | **1958** |
| Number of establishments | 876.4 | 217 | 7 722 | 825 | Nombre d'établissements |
| Value added | 8 079.2 | 293.0 | 7 061.7 | 724.5 | Valeur ajoutée |
| Number of engaged (Average during year) | 306.2 | 8.8 | 285.9 | 11.5 | Nombre de personnes occupées (moyenne pour l'année) |
| Employees: | | | | | Salariés: |
| Number (Average during year) | 301.8 | 8.7 | 281.6 | 11.5 | Nombre (moyenne pour l'année) |
| Wages and salaries | 3 784.2 | 129.7 | 3 504.2 | 150.3 | Traitements et salaires |
| Operatives: | | | | | Ouvriers: |
| Number (Average during year) | 245.5 | 7.5 | 230.6 | 7.4 | Nombre (moyenne pour l'année) |
| Man-hours worked | ... | 15.5 | 478.8 | ... | Heures de travail effectuées |
| Wages and salaries | 2 862.0 | 107.5 | 2 663.8 | 90.7 | Traitements et salaires |
| Energy consumed | ... | 63.3 | 2 838.5 | ... | Energie consommée |
| Electricity consumed | ... | 264.9 | 14 325.1 | ... | Electricité consommée |
| Capacity of installed power equipment | ... | 147.9 | 2 295.7 | ... | Puissance installée |

| Year and item of data | Total | Mining Industries ex-tractives | Manu-facturing Industries manu-facturières | Electricity and gas Electricité et gaz | Année et rubrique |
|---|---|---|---|---|---|
| ISIC | -3,511-512 | 1 | 2-3 | 511-512 | CITI |
| | **b. Structure** | | | | |
| **1953** | | | | | **1953** |
| Distribution in percent of: | | | | | Distribution en pourcentage: |
| Value added | 100.0 | 4.4 | 89.2 | 6.4 | Valeur ajoutée |
| Number of employees | 100.0 | 2.9 | 93.0 | 4.1 | Nombre de salariés |
| Per employee: | | | | | Par salarié: |
| Value added | 21.1 | 32.3 | 20.2 | 32.8 | Valeur ajoutée |
| Wages and salaries | 9.4 | 11.3 | 9.3 | 9.4 | Traitements et salaires |
| Energy consumed | ... | 5.80 | 7.74 | ... | Energie consommée |
| Electricity consumed | ... | 22.5 | 37.3 | ... | Electricité consommée |
| Capacity of installed power equipment | ... | 14.39 | 6.33 | ... | Puissance installée |
| Value added per unit of wages and salaries | 2.25 | 2.85 | 2.17 | 3.47 | Valeur ajoutée par unité de traitements et salaires |
| Operatives as a percent of employees | 83.5 | 90.2 | 84.0 | 66.4 | Ouvriers en pourcentage des salariés |
| Average man-hours per operative | 2.11 | 2.05 | 2.11 | 2.10 | Heures de travail: moyenne par ouvrier |
| Per thousand operative man-hours: | | | | | Par millier d'heures-ouvrier: |
| Wages and salaries | 4.19 | 5.30 | 4.14 | 4.36 | Traitements et salaires |
| Energy consumed | ... | 3.13 | 4.36 | ... | Energie consommée |
| Electricity consumed | ... | 12.14 | 20.98 | ... | Electricité consommée |
| Capacity of installed power equipment | ... | 7.76 | 3.56 | ... | Puissance installée |
| **1958** | | | | | **1958** |
| Distribution in percent of: | | | | | Distribution en pourcentage: |
| Value added | 100.0 | 3.6 | 87.4 | 9.0 | Valeur ajoutée |
| Number of engaged | 100.0 | 2.9 | 93.4 | 3.7 | Nombre de personnes occupées |
| Per person engaged: | | | | | Par personne occupée: |
| Value added | 26.4 | 33.3 | 24.7 | 63.0 | Valeur ajoutée |
| Energy consumed | ... | 7.19 | 9.93 | ... | Energie consommée |
| Electricity consumed | ... | 30.1 | 50.1 | ... | Electricité consommée |
| Capacity of installed power equipment | ... | 16.81 | 8.03 | ... | Puissance installée |
| Employees as a percent of engaged | 98.6 | 98.9 | 98.5 | 100.0 | Salariés en pourcentage des personnes occupées |
| Value added per unit of wages and salaries | 2.13 | 2.26 | 2.02 | 4.82 | Valeur ajoutée par unité de traitements et salaires |
| Wages and salaries per employee | 12.5 | 14.9 | 12.4 | 13.1 | Traitements et salaires par salarié |
| Operatives as a percent of employees | 81.3 | 86.2 | 81.9 | 64.3 | Ouvriers en pourcentage des salariés |
| Average man-hours per operative | ... | 2.07 | 2.08 | ... | Heures de travail: moyenne par ouvrier |
| Per thousand operative man-hours: | | | | | Par millier d'heures-ouvrier: |
| Wages and salaries | ... | 6.94 | 5.56 | ... | Traitements et salaires |
| Energy consumed | ... | 4.06 | 5.93 | ... | Energie consommée |
| Electricity consumed | ... | 17.09 | 29.92 | ... | Electricité consommée |
| Capacity of installed power equipment | ... | 9.54 | 4.79 | ... | Puissance installée |

For footnotes see end of table.     Pour les notes, voir au bas du tableau.

# NORWAY

## C. The Major Groups of Mining — Les classes de la branche Industries extractives

### a. Absolute Figures — Chiffres absolus

| Year and item of data | All mining — Toutes industries extractives | Coal mining — Extraction du charbon | Metal mining — Extraction des minerais métalliques | Other mining — Divers | Année et rubrique |
|---|---|---|---|---|---|
| ISIC | 1 | 11 | 12 | 14-19 | CITI |
| **1953** | | | | | **1953** |
| Number of establishments | 175 | 2 | 28 | 145 | Nombre d'établissements |
| Value added | 265.2 | 28.7 | 201.1 | 35.4 | Valeur ajoutée |
| Employees: | | | | | Salariés: |
| Number (Average during year) | 8.2 | 0.8 | 5.5 | 1.9 | Nombre (moyenne pour l'année) |
| Wages and salaries | 92.9 | 17.6 | 57.2 | 18.1 | Traitements et salaires |
| Operatives: | | | | | Ouvriers: |
| Number (Average during year) | 7.4 | 0.8 | 4.9 | 1.7 | Nombre (moyenne pour l'année) |
| Man-hours worked | 15.2 | 1.9 | 10.0 | 3.3 | Heures de travail effectuées |
| Wages and salaries | 80.6 | 15.8 | 48.5 | 16.3 | Traitements et salaires |
| Energy consumed | 47.6 | 21.8 | 20.6 | 5.2 | Energie consommée |
| Electricity consumed | 184.6 | 15.3 | 151.9 | 17.4 | Electricité consommée |
| Capacity of installed power equipment | 118 | 9 | 86 | 23 | Puissance installée |
| **1958** | | | | | **1958** |
| Number of establishments | 217 | 2 | 26 | 189 | Nombre d'établissements |
| Value added | 293.0 | 17.9 | 215.7 | 59.4 | Valeur ajoutée |
| Number of engaged (Average during year) | 8.8 | 0.9 | 5.6 | 2.3 | Nombre de personnes occupées (moyenne pour l'année) |
| Employees: | | | | | Salariés: |
| Number (Average during year) | 8.7 | 0.9 | 5.6 | 2.2 | Nombre (moyenne pour l'année) |
| Wages and salaries | 129.7 | 22.0 | 78.4 | 29.3 | Traitements et salaires |
| Operatives: | | | | | Ouvriers: |
| Number (Average during year) | 7.5 | 0.8 | 4.7 | 2.0 | Nombre (moyenne pour l'année) |
| Man-hours worked | 15.5 | 2.1 | 9.3 | 4.1 | Heures de travail effectuées |
| Wages and salaries | 107.5 | 18.5 | 62.9 | 26.1 | Traitements et salaires |
| Energy consumed | 63.3 | 21.9 | 33.5 | 7.9 | Energie consommée |
| Electricity consumed | 264.9 | 16.0 | 214.9 | 34.0 | Electricité consommée |
| Capacity of installed power equipment | 147.9 | 10.2 | 103.9 | 33.8 | Puissance installée |

### b. Structure

| Year and item of data | All mining — Toutes industries extractives | Coal mining — Extraction du charbon | Metal mining — Extraction des minerais métalliques | Other mining — Divers | Année et rubrique |
|---|---|---|---|---|---|
| ISIC | 1 | 11 | 12 | 14-19 | CITI |
| **1953** | | | | | **1953** |
| Distribution in percent of: | | | | | Distribution en pourcentage: |
| Value added | 100.0 | 10.8 | 75.8 | 13.4 | Valeur ajoutée |
| Number of employees | 100.0 | 9.7 | 67.1 | 23.2 | Nombre de salariés |
| Per employee: | | | | | Par salarié: |
| Value added | 32.3 | 35.9 | 36.6 | 18.6 | Valeur ajoutée |
| Wages and salaries | 11.3 | 22.0 | 10.4 | 9.5 | Traitements et salaires |
| Energy consumed | 5.80 | 27.25 | 3.74 | 2.74 | Energie consommée |
| Electricity consumed | 22.5 | 19.1 | 27.6 | 9.2 | Electricité consommée |
| Capacity of installed power equipment | 14.39 | 11.25 | 15.64 | 12.10 | Puissance installée |
| Value added per unit of wages and salaries | 2.85 | 1.63 | 3.52 | 1.96 | Valeur ajoutée par unité de traitements et salaires |
| Operatives as a percent of employees | 90.2 | 100.0 | 89.1 | 89.5 | Ouvriers en pourcentage des salariés |
| Average man-hours per operative | 2.05 | 2.38 | 2.04 | 1.94 | Heures de travail: moyenne par ouvrier |
| Per thousand operative man-hours: | | | | | Par millier d'heures-ouvrier: |
| Wages and salaries | 5.30 | 8.32 | 4.85 | 4.94 | Traitements et salaires |
| Energy consumed | 3.13 | 11.47 | 2.06 | 1.58 | Energie consommée |
| Electricity consumed | 12.14 | 8.05 | 15.19 | 5.27 | Electricité consommée |
| Capacity of installed power equipment | 7.76 | 4.74 | 8.60 | 6.97 | Puissance installée |
| **1958** | | | | | **1958** |
| Distribution in percent of: | | | | | Distribution en pourcentage: |
| Value added | 100.0 | 6.1 | 73.6 | 20.3 | Valeur ajoutée |
| Number of engaged | 100.0 | 10.2 | 63.6 | 26.2 | Nombre de personnes occupées |
| Per person engaged: | | | | | Par personne occupée: |
| Value added | 33.3 | 19.9 | 38.5 | 25.8 | Valeur ajoutée |
| Energy consumed | 7.19 | 24.33 | 5.98 | 3.43 | Energie consommée |
| Electricity consumed | 30.1 | 17.8 | 38.4 | 14.8 | Electricité consommée |
| Capacity of installed power equipment | 16.81 | 11.33 | 18.55 | 14.70 | Puissance installée |
| Employees as a percent of engaged | 98.9 | 100.0 | 100.0 | 95.6 | Salariés en pourcentage des personnes occupées |
| Value added per unit of wages and salaries | 2.26 | 0.81 | 2.75 | 2.03 | Valeur ajoutée par unité de traitements et salaires |
| Wages and salaries per employee | 14.9 | 24.4 | 14.0 | 13.3 | Traitements et salaires par salarié |
| Operatives as a percent of employees | 86.2 | 88.9 | 83.9 | 90.9 | Ouvriers en pourcentage des salariés |
| Average man-hours per operative | 2.07 | 2.62 | 1.98 | 2.05 | Heures de travail: moyenne par ouvrier |
| Per thousand operative man-hours: | | | | | Par millier d'heures-ouvrier: |
| Wages and salaries | 6.94 | 8.81 | 6.76 | 6.36 | Traitements et salaires |
| Energy consumed | 4.08 | 10.43 | 3.60 | 1.93 | Energie consommée |
| Electricity consumed | 17.09 | 7.62 | 23.11 | 8.29 | Electricité consommée |
| Capacity of installed power equipment | 9.54 | 4.86 | 11.17 | 8.24 | Puissance installée |

## C. The Major Groups of Manufacturing — Les classes de la branche Industries manufacturières

| Year and Item of data | Manufacturing [2] — Industries manufacturières [2] (2-3) | Food, beverages and tobacco [2] — Industries alimentaires, boissons, tabac [2] (20-22) | Textiles (23) | Clothing, footwear and made-up textiles [2] — Articles d'habillement, chaussures et ouvrages en tissu [2] (24) | Wood products and furniture — Bois et meubles (25-26) | Paper and paper products — Papier et ouvrages en papier (27) | Printing and publishing [2] — Imprimerie et édition [2] (28) | Leather and leather products except wearing apparel — Cuir et articles en cuir, à l'exclusion des articles d'habillement (29) | Rubber products — Ouvrages en caoutchouc (30) | Chemicals and chemical, petroleum and coal products — Produits chimiques et dérivés du pétrole et du charbon (31-32) | Non-metallic mineral products [2] — Produits minéraux non métalliques [2] (33) | Basic metals — Métallurgie de base (34) | Metal products — Ouvrages en métaux (35-38) | Other manufacturing — Autres industries manufacturières (39) | Année et rubrique |
|---|---|---|---|---|---|---|---|---|---|---|---|---|---|---|---|
| **ISIC** | 2-3 | 20-22 | 23 | 24 | 25-26 | 27 | 28 | 29 | 30 | 31-32 | 33 | 34 | 35-38 | 39 | **CITI** |
| | | | | | | *a.* Absolute Figures — Chiffres absolus | | | | | | | | | |
| **1938** | | | | | | | | | | | | | | | **1938** |
| Number of establishments | 4 445.7 | 760 | 218 | 372 | 874 | 194 | 290 | 68 | 20 | 324 | 417 | 29 | 851 | 40 | Nombre d'établissements |
| Value added | 982.6 | 225.2 | 55.7 | 54.9 | 48.1 | 95.3 | 41.4 | 9.1 | 12.3 | 107.0 | 32.3 | 69.5 | 223.5 | 8.3 | Valeur ajoutée |
| Employees: | | | | | | | | | | | | | | | Salariés: |
| Number (Average during year) | 155.2 | 18.9 | 14.0 | 15.2 | 13.6 | 16.5 | 6.6 | 1.8 | 1.8 | 8.7 | 7.9 | 6.7 | 42.3 | 1.2 | Nombre (moyenne pour l'année) |
| Wages and salaries | 492.6 | 53.7 | 33.2 | 35.2 | 35.4 | 55.8 | 26.1 | 5.8 | 5.0 | 34.9 | 24.3 | 28.9 | 150.3 | 4.0 | Traitements et salaires |
| Operatives: | | | | | | | | | | | | | | | Ouvriers: |
| Number (Average during year) | 137.0 | 16.0 | 12.7 | 13.8 | 12.5 | 15.0 | 6.0 | 1.5 | 1.6 | 7.0 | 7.2 | 6.0 | 36.6 | 1.1 | Nombre (moyenne pour l'année) |
| Man-hours worked | 296.7 | 31.3 | 26.5 | 28.7 | 27.0 | 33.5 | 14.0 | 3.3 | 3.2 | 16.0 | 14.9 | 14.0 | 82.1 | 2.2 | Heures de travail effectuées |
| Wages and salaries | 398.7 | 38.6 | 26.3 | 29.4 | 31.3 | 46.7 | 23.0 | 4.4 | 4.0 | 25.3 | 20.8 | 23.9 | 121.7 | 3.3 | Traitements et salaires |
| Capacity of installed power equipment | 991 | 106 | 32 | 5 | 122 | 374 | 10 | 6 | 8 | 104 | 35 | 55 | 132 | 2 | Puissance installée |
| **1948** | | | | | | | | | | | | | | | **1948** |
| Number of establishments | 5 842 | 774 | 244 | 633 | 1 247 | 217 | 329 | 84 | 32 | 336 | 408 | 103 | 1 274 | 161 | Nombre d'établissements |
| Value added | 3 305.8 | 804.2 | 170.7 | 171.6 | 211.1 | 454.0 | 100.0 | 25.1 | 51.8 | 273.1 | 99.8 | 181.2 | 720.8 | 42.4 | Valeur ajoutée |
| Employees: | | | | | | | | | | | | | | | Salariés: |
| Number (Average during year) | 226.6 | 21.9 | 17.5 | 20.1 | 22.6 | 20.3 | 9.0 | 2.3 | 3.6 | 14.6 | 9.9 | 11.7 | 69.5 | 3.6 | Nombre (moyenne pour l'année) |
| Wages and salaries | 1 399.4 | 121.0 | 85.3 | 99.4 | 134.2 | 137.9 | 59.1 | 14.8 | 22.6 | 101.5 | 63.3 | 83.8 | 454.1 | 22.4 | Traitements et salaires |
| Operatives: | | | | | | | | | | | | | | | Ouvriers: |
| Number (Average during year) | 193.6 | 18.0 | 15.5 | 17.5 | 20.2 | 17.8 | 7.8 | 2.0 | 3.1 | 11.3 | 8.7 | 10.1 | 58.6 | 3.0 | Nombre (moyenne pour l'année) |
| Man-hours worked | 410.2 | 37.9 | 31.1 | 36.1 | 42.6 | 41.0 | 17.3 | 4.1 | 6.4 | 24.5 | 18.0 | 21.7 | 123.1 | 6.4 | Heures de travail effectuées |
| Wages and salaries | 1 129.7 | 89.2 | 69.2 | 78.8 | 118.3 | 113.7 | 50.7 | 12.0 | 18.3 | 72.2 | 53.6 | 70.0 | 365.4 | 18.3 | Traitements et salaires |
| Capacity of installed power equipment | 1 336 | 134 | 47 | 11 | 210 | 392 | 15 | 10 | 13 | 163 | 52 | 70 | 214 | 5 | Puissance installée |
| **1953** | | | | | | | | | | | | | | | **1953** |
| Number of establishments | 6 087 | 902 | 281 | 656 | 1 248 | 220 | 381 | 58 | 23 | 284 | 380 | 106 | 1 389 | 159 | Nombre d'établissements |
| Value added | 5 304.7 | 1 133.2 | 279.0 | 310.3 | 267.8 | 547.3 | 164.9 | 29.0 | 65.9 | 485.4 | 201.7 | 468.7 | 1 274.0 | 77.5 | Valeur ajoutée |
| Employees: | | | | | | | | | | | | | | | Salariés: |
| Number (Average during year) | 261.9 | 28.6 | 20.0 | 25.7 | 23.6 | 22.5 | 10.3 | 1.8 | 3.6 | 19.5 | 11.6 | 15.6 | 75.2 | 3.9 | Nombre (moyenne pour l'année) |
| Wages and salaries | 2 445.5 | 238.6 | 149.6 | 187.7 | 213.2 | 232.1 | 102.0 | 16.6 | 32.2 | 204.6 | 111.9 | 172.9 | 747.0 | 37.1 | Traitements et salaires |
| Operatives: | | | | | | | | | | | | | | | Ouvriers: |
| Number (Average during year) | 220.1 | 22.9 | 17.5 | 22.5 | 21.2 | 19.6 | 8.8 | 1.5 | 3.0 | 14.9 | 10.1 | 13.2 | 61.7 | 3.2 | Nombre (moyenne pour l'année) |
| Man-hours worked | 465.2 | 47.8 | 35.6 | 45.6 | 44.8 | 44.0 | 19.1 | 3.2 | 6.3 | 32.1 | 21.0 | 28.1 | 130.7 | 6.9 | Heures de travail effectuées |
| Wages and salaries | 1 927.9 | 175.5 | 119.4 | 151.1 | 186.6 | 190.7 | 85.3 | 13.2 | 25.2 | 143.6 | 93.5 | 139.7 | 574.6 | 29.5 | Traitements et salaires |
| Energy consumed | 2 026.2 | 128.0 | 60.3 | 16.3 | 27.8 | 582.3 | 10.7 | 6.6 | 14.3 | 472.9 | 284.8 | 278.3 | 140.1 | 3.8 | Energie consommée |
| Electricity consumed | 9 760.9 | 203.7 | 141.5 | 37.6 | 108.7 | 1 436.0 | 31.9 | 8.4 | 21.8 | 3 771.0 | 234.0 | 3 397.4 | 356.7 | 12.2 | Electricité consommée |
| Capacity of installed power equipment | 1 658 | 110 | 56 | 14 | 148 | 539 | 17 | 11 | 17 | 304 | 75 | 116 | 243 | 8 | Puissance installée |
| **1958** | | | | | | | | | | | | | | | **1958** |
| Number of establishments | 7 722 | 1 548 | 274 | 704 | 1 527 | 234 | 466 | 70 | 35 | 321 | 439 | 128 | 1 775 | 201 | Nombre d'établissements |
| Value added | 7 061.7 | 1 101.2 | 302.6 | 352.8 | 427.5 | 692.7 | 252.0 | 33.6 | 68.1 | 746.0 | 283.2 | 718.5 | 1 978.0 | 105.5 | Valeur ajoutée |
| Number of engaged (Average during year) | 285.9 | 37.5 | 16.3 | 23.2 | 23.9 | 24.1 | 11.6 | 1.9 | 3.0 | 21.4 | 11.7 | 20.9 | 85.9 | 4.5 | Nombre de personnes occupées (moyenne pour l'année) |
| Employees: | | | | | | | | | | | | | | | Salariés: |
| Number (Average during year) | 281.6 | 37.0 | 16.2 | 22.8 | 22.8 | 24.0 | 11.4 | 1.8 | 2.8 | 21.3 | 11.4 | 20.8 | 84.9 | 4.4 | Nombre (moyenne pour l'année) |
| Wages and salaries | 3 504.2 | 400.0 | 157.5 | 212.6 | 266.0 | 312.8 | 151.0 | 20.7 | 37.1 | 294.6 | 145.2 | 303.6 | 1 149.6 | 53.5 | Traitements et salaires |
| Operatives: | | | | | | | | | | | | | | | Ouvriers: |
| Number (Average during year) | 230.6 | 29.0 | 13.7 | 19.4 | 20.3 | 20.5 | 9.9 | 1.5 | 2.4 | 15.3 | 9.7 | 17.1 | 68.1 | 3.7 | Nombre (moyenne pour l'année) |
| Man-hours worked | 478.8 | 60.3 | 27.0 | 38.0 | 42.6 | 44.4 | 21.2 | 3.1 | 5.0 | 32.2 | 19.9 | 35.8 | 141.6 | 7.7 | Heures de travail effectuées |
| Wages and salaries | 2 663.8 | 288.7 | 119.5 | 162.5 | 230.4 | 251.2 | 127.3 | 16.1 | 27.2 | 187.7 | 114.8 | 234.1 | 862.5 | 41.8 | Traitements et salaires |
| Energy consumed | 2 838.5 | 245.4 | 63.4 | 20.3 | 44.8 | 711.8 | 18.2 | 6.9 | 16.0 | 562.6 | 331.6 | 612.7 | 197.7 | 7.1 | Energie consommée |
| Electricity consumed | 14 325.1 | 435.4 | 143.0 | 66.4 | 193.0 | 2 010.1 | 65.0 | 12.1 | 26.0 | 4 299.0 | 313.5 | 6 190.0 | 542.0 | 29.6 | Electricité consommée |
| Capacity of installed power equipment | 2 295.7 | 196.6 | 61.3 | 16.5 | 190.0 | 710.5 | 22.4 | 9.2 | 20.5 | 384.9 | 85.8 | 266.3 | 320.6 | 11.1 | Puissance installée |

For footnotes see end of table.     Pour les notes, voir le bas du tableau.

## C. The Major Groups of Manufacturing (continued) — Les classes de la branche Industries manufacturières (suite)

b. Structure

| Year and item of data | Manufacturing² Industries manufacturières² | Food, beverages and tobacco² Industries alimentaires, boissons, tabac² | Textiles | Clothing, footwear and made-up textiles² Articles d'habillement, chaussures et ouvrages en tissu² | Wood products and furniture Bois et meubles | Paper and paper products Papier et ouvrages en papier | Printing and publishing² Imprimerie et édition² | Leather and leather products except wearing apparel Cuir et articles en cuir, à l'exclusion des articles d'habillement | Rubber products Ouvrages en caoutchouc | Chemicals and chemical, petroleum and coal products Produits chimiques et dérivés du pétrole et du charbon | Non-metallic mineral products² Produits minéraux non métalliques² | Basic metals Métallurgie de base | Metal products Ouvrages en métaux | Other manufacturing Autres industries manufacturières | Année et rubrique |
|---|---|---|---|---|---|---|---|---|---|---|---|---|---|---|---|
| ISIC | 2-3 | 20-22 | 23 | 24 | 25-26 | 27 | 28 | 29 | 30 | 31-32 | 33 | 34 | 35-38 | 39 | CITI |
| **1938** | | | | | | | | | | | | | | | **1938** |
| Distribution in percent of: | | | | | | | | | | | | | | | Distribution en pourcentage: |
| Value added | 100.0 | 22.9 | 5.7 | 5.6 | 4.9 | 9.7 | 4.2 | 0.9 | 1.3 | 10.9 | 3.3 | 7.1 | 22.7 | 0.8 | Valeur ajoutée |
| Number of employees | 100.0 | 12.2 | 9.0 | 9.8 | 8.8 | 10.6 | 4.3 | 1.1 | 1.1 | 5.6 | 5.1 | 4.3 | 27.3 | 0.8 | Nombre de salariés |
| Per employee: | | | | | | | | | | | | | | | Par salarié: |
| Value added | 6.3 | 11.9 | 4.0 | 3.6 | 3.5 | 5.8 | 6.3 | 5.0 | 6.8 | 12.3 | 4.1 | 10.4 | 5.3 | 6.9 | Valeur ajoutée |
| Wages and salaries | 3.2 | 2.8 | 2.4 | 2.3 | 2.6 | 3.4 | 4.0 | 3.2 | 2.8 | 4.0 | 3.1 | 4.3 | 3.6 | 3.3 | Traitements et salaires |
| Capacity of installed power equipment | 6.38 | 5.61 | 2.28 | 0.33 | 8.97 | 22.67 | 1.52 | 3.33 | 4.44 | 11.95 | 4.43 | 8.21 | 3.12 | 1.67 | Puissance installée |
| Value added per unit of wages and salaries | 1.99 | 4.19 | 1.68 | 1.56 | 1.36 | 1.71 | 1.59 | 1.57 | 2.46 | 3.06 | 1.33 | 2.40 | 1.49 | 2.08 | Valeur ajoutée par unit de traitements et salaires |
| Operatives as a percent of employees | 88.3 | 84.6 | 90.7 | 90.8 | 91.9 | 90.9 | 90.9 | 83.3 | 88.9 | 80.4 | 91.1 | 89.6 | 86.5 | 91.7 | Ouvriers en pourcentag des salariés |
| Average man-hours per operative | 2.16 | 1.96 | 2.09 | 2.08 | 2.16 | 2.23 | 2.33 | 2.20 | 2.00 | 2.28 | 2.07 | 2.33 | 2.24 | 2.00 | Heures de travail: moyenne par ouvrier |
| Per thousand operative man-hours: | | | | | | | | | | | | | | | Par millier d'heures-ouvrier: |
| Wages and salaries | 1.34 | 1.23 | 0.99 | 1.02 | 1.16 | 1.39 | 1.64 | 1.33 | 1.25 | 1.58 | 1.40 | 1.71 | 1.48 | 1.50 | Traitements et salaires |
| Capacity of installed power equipment | 3.34 | 3.39 | 1.21 | 0.17 | 4.52 | 11.16 | 0.71 | 1.82 | 2.50 | 6.50 | 2.35 | 3.93 | 1.61 | 0.91 | Puissance installée |
| **1948** | | | | | | | | | | | | | | | **1948** |
| Distribution in percent of: | | | | | | | | | | | | | | | Distribution en pourcentage: |
| Value added | 100.0 | 24.3 | 5.2 | 5.2 | 6.4 | 13.7 | 3.0 | 0.7 | 1.6 | 8.3 | 3.0 | 5.5 | 21.8 | 1.3 | Valeur ajoutée |
| Number of employees | 100.0 | 9.6 | 7.7 | 8.9 | 10.0 | 8.9 | 4.0 | 1.0 | 1.6 | 6.4 | 4.4 | 5.2 | 30.7 | 1.6 | Nombre de salariés |
| Per employee: | | | | | | | | | | | | | | | Par salarié: |
| Value added | 14.6 | 36.7 | 9.8 | 8.5 | 9.3 | 22.4 | 11.1 | 10.9 | 14.4 | 18.7 | 10.1 | 15.5 | 10.4 | 11.8 | Valeur ajoutée |
| Wages and salaries | 6.2 | 5.5 | 4.9 | 4.9 | 5.9 | 6.8 | 6.6 | 6.4 | 6.3 | 7.0 | 6.4 | 7.2 | 6.5 | 6.2 | Traitements et salaires |
| Capacity of installed power equipment | 5.90 | 6.12 | 2.68 | 0.55 | 9.29 | 19.31 | 1.67 | 4.35 | 3.61 | 11.16 | 5.25 | 5.98 | 3.08 | 1.39 | Puissance installée |
| Value added per unit of wages and salaries | 2.36 | 6.65 | 2.00 | 1.73 | 1.57 | 3.29 | 1.69 | 1.70 | 2.29 | 2.69 | 1.58 | 2.16 | 1.59 | 1.89 | Valeur ajoutée par unit de traitements et salaires |
| Operatives as a percent of employees | 85.4 | 82.2 | 88.6 | 87.1 | 89.4 | 87.7 | 86.7 | 87.0 | 86.1 | 77.4 | 87.9 | 86.3 | 84.3 | 83.3 | Ouvriers en pourcentag des salariés |
| Average man-hours per operative | 2.12 | 2.10 | 2.01 | 2.06 | 2.11 | 2.30 | 2.22 | 2.05 | 2.06 | 2.17 | 2.07 | 2.15 | 2.10 | 2.13 | Heures de travail: moyenne par ouvrier |
| Per thousand operative man-hours: | | | | | | | | | | | | | | | Par millier d'heures-ouvrier: |
| Wages and salaries | 2.75 | 2.35 | 2.22 | 2.18 | 2.78 | 2.77 | 2.93 | 2.93 | 2.86 | 2.95 | 2.98 | 3.22 | 2.97 | 2.86 | Traitements et salaires |
| Capacity of installed power equipment | 3.26 | 3.54 | 1.51 | 0.30 | 4.93 | 9.56 | 0.87 | 2.44 | 2.03 | 6.65 | 2.89 | 3.22 | 1.74 | 0.78 | Puissance installée |
| **1953** | | | | | | | | | | | | | | | **1953** |
| Distribution in percent of: | | | | | | | | | | | | | | | Distribution en pourcentage: |
| Value added | 100.0 | 21.4 | 5.3 | 5.8 | 5.1 | 10.3 | 3.1 | 0.5 | 1.2 | 9.2 | 3.8 | 8.8 | 24.0 | 1.5 | Valeur ajoutée |
| Number of employees | 100.0 | 10.9 | 7.6 | 9.8 | 9.0 | 8.6 | 3.9 | 0.7 | 1.4 | 7.5 | 4.4 | 6.0 | 28.7 | 1.5 | Nombre de salariés |
| Per employee: | | | | | | | | | | | | | | | Par salarié: |
| Value added | 20.2 | 39.6 | 14.0 | 12.1 | 11.3 | 24.3 | 16.0 | 16.1 | 18.3 | 24.9 | 17.4 | 30.0 | 16.9 | 19.9 | Valeur ajoutée |
| Wages and salaries | 9.3 | 8.3 | 7.5 | 7.3 | 9.0 | 10.3 | 9.9 | 9.2 | 8.9 | 10.5 | 9.6 | 11.1 | 9.9 | 9.5 | Traitements et salaires |
| Energy consumed | 7.74 | 4.48 | 3.02 | 0.63 | 1.18 | 25.88 | 1.04 | 3.67 | 3.97 | 24.25 | 24.55 | 17.84 | 1.86 | 0.97 | Energie consommée |
| Electricity consumed | 37.3 | 7.1 | 7.1 | 1.5 | 4.6 | 63.8 | 3.1 | 4.7 | 6.0 | 193.4 | 20.2 | 217.8 | 4.7 | 3.1 | Electricité consommée |
| Capacity of installed power equipment | 6.33 | 3.85 | 2.80 | 0.54 | 6.27 | 23.96 | 1.65 | 6.11 | 4.72 | 15.59 | 6.46 | 7.44 | 3.23 | 2.05 | Puissance installée |
| Value added per unit of wages and salaries | 2.17 | 4.75 | 1.86 | 1.65 | 1.26 | 2.36 | 1.62 | 1.75 | 2.05 | 2.37 | 1.80 | 2.71 | 1.70 | 2.09 | Valeur ajoutée par unit de traitements et salaires |
| Operatives as a percent of employees | 84.0 | 80.1 | 87.5 | 87.5 | 89.8 | 87.1 | 85.4 | 83.3 | 83.3 | 76.4 | 87.1 | 84.6 | 82.0 | 82.0 | Ouvriers en pourcentage des salariés |
| Average man-hours per operative | 2.11 | 2.09 | 2.03 | 2.03 | 2.11 | 2.24 | 2.17 | 2.13 | 2.10 | 2.15 | 2.08 | 2.13 | 2.12 | 2.16 | Heures de travail: moyenne par ouvrier |
| Per thousand operative man-hours: | | | | | | | | | | | | | | | Par millier d'heures-ouvrier: |
| Wages and salaries | 4.14 | 3.67 | 3.35 | 3.31 | 4.16 | 4.33 | 4.46 | 4.12 | 4.00 | 4.47 | 4.45 | 4.97 | 4.40 | 4.28 | Traitements et salaires |
| Energy consumed | 4.36 | 2.68 | 1.69 | 0.36 | 0.62 | 13.23 | 0.56 | 2.06 | 2.27 | 14.73 | 13.56 | 9.90 | 1.07 | 0.55 | Energie consommée |
| Electricity consumed | 20.98 | 4.26 | 3.97 | 0.82 | 2.43 | 32.64 | 1.67 | 2.62 | 3.46 | 117.48 | 11.14 | 120.90 | 2.73 | 1.77 | Electricité consommée |
| Capacity of installed power equipment | 3.56 | 2.30 | 1.57 | 0.31 | 3.30 | 12.25 | 0.89 | 3.44 | 2.70 | 9.47 | 3.57 | 4.13 | 1.86 | 1.16 | Puissance installée |

For footnotes see end of table.　　　　　Pour les notes, voir au bas fin du tableau.

## C. The Major Groups of Manufacturing (continued) — Les classes de la branche Industries manufacturières (suite)

| Year and item of data | Manufacturing [2] Industries manufacturières [2] | Food, beverages and tobacco Industries alimentaires, boissons, tabac | Textiles | Clothing, footwear and made-up textiles [2] Articles d'habillement, chaussures et ouvrages en tissu [2] | Wood products and furniture Bois et meubles | Paper and paper products Papier et ouvrages en papier | Printing and publishing [2] Imprimerie et édition [2] | Leather and leather products except wearing apparel Cuir et articles en cuir, à l'exclusion des articles d'habillement | Rubber products Ouvrages en caoutchouc | Chemicals and chemical, petroleum and coal products Produits chimiques et dérivés du pétrole et du charbon | Non-metallic mineral products [2] Produits minéraux non métalliques [2] | Basic metals Métallurgie de base | Metal products Ouvrages en métaux | Other manufacturing Autres industries manufacturières | Année et rubrique |
|---|---|---|---|---|---|---|---|---|---|---|---|---|---|---|---|
| ISIC | 2-3 | 20-22 | 23 | 24 | 25-26 | 27 | 28 | 29 | 30 | 31-32 | 33 | 34 | 35-38 | 39 | CITI |
| | | | | | | | b. Structure | | | | | | | | | |
| **1958** Distribution in percent of: | | | | | | | | | | | | | | | **1958** Distribution en pourcentage: |
| Value added........ | 100.0 | 15.6 | 4.3 | 5.0 | 6.0 | 9.8 | 3.6 | 0.4 | 1.0 | 10.6 | 4.0 | 10.2 | 28.0 | 1.5 | Valeur ajoutée |
| Number of engaged... | 100.0 | 13.1 | 5.7 | 8.1 | 8.4 | 8.4 | 4.1 | 0.7 | 1.0 | 7.5 | 4.1 | 7.3 | 30.0 | 1.6 | Nombre de personnes occupées |
| Per person engaged: | | | | | | | | | | | | | | | Par personne occupée: |
| Value added........ | 24.7 | 29.4 | 18.6 | 15.2 | 17.9 | 28.7 | 21.7 | 17.7 | 22.7 | 34.8 | 24.2 | 34.4 | 23.0 | 23.4 | Valeur ajoutée |
| Energy consumed..... | 9.93 | 6.54 | 3.89 | 0.88 | 1.87 | 29.54 | 1.57 | 3.63 | 5.33 | 26.29 | 28.34 | 29.32 | 2.30 | 1.58 | Energie consommée |
| Electricity consumed... | 50.1 | 11.6 | 8.8 | 2.9 | 8.1 | 83.4 | 5.6 | 6.4 | 8.7 | 200.9 | 26.8 | 296.2 | 6.3 | 6.6 | Electricité consommée |
| Capacity of installed power equipment..... | 8.03 | 5.24 | 3.76 | 0.71 | 7.95 | 29.48 | 1.93 | 4.84 | 6.83 | 17.98 | 7.33 | 12.74 | 3.73 | 2.47 | Puissance installée |
| Employees as a percent of engaged......... | 98.5 | 98.7 | 99.4 | 98.3 | 95.4 | 99.6 | 98.3 | 94.7 | 93.3 | 99.5 | 97.4 | 99.5 | 98.8 | 97.8 | Salariés en pourcentage des personnes occupées |
| Value added per unit of wages and salaries............. | 2.02 | 2.75 | 1.92 | 1.66 | 1.61 | 2.21 | 1.67 | 1.62 | 1.84 | 2.53 | 1.95 | 2.37 | 1.72 | 1.97 | Valeur ajoutée par unité de traitements et salaires |
| Wages and salaries per employee........ | 12.4 | 10.8 | 9.7 | 9.3 | 11.7 | 13.0 | 13.2 | 11.5 | 13.2 | 13.8 | 12.7 | 14.6 | 13.5 | 12.2 | Traitements et salaires par salarié |
| Operatives as a percent of employees......... | 81.9 | 78.4 | 84.6 | 85.1 | 89.0 | 85.4 | 86.8 | 83.3 | 85.7 | 71.8 | 85.1 | 82.2 | 80.2 | 84.1 | Ouvriers en pourcentage des salariés |
| Average man-hours per operative........ | 2.08 | 2.08 | 1.97 | 1.96 | 2.10 | 2.16 | 2.14 | 2.07 | 2.08 | 2.10 | 2.05 | 2.09 | 2.08 | 2.08 | Heures de travail: moyenne par ouvrier |
| Per thousand operative man-hours: | | | | | | | | | | | | | | | Par millier d'heures-ouvrier: |
| Wages and salaries... | 5.56 | 4.79 | 4.42 | 4.28 | 5.41 | 5.66 | 6.00 | 5.19 | 5.44 | 5.83 | 5.77 | 6.54 | 6.09 | 5.43 | Traitements et salaires |
| Energy consumed..... | 5.93 | 4.07 | 2.35 | 0.53 | 1.05 | 16.03 | 0.86 | 2.22 | 3.20 | 17.47 | 16.66 | 17.11 | 1.40 | 0.92 | Energie consommée |
| Electricity consumed... | 29.92 | 7.22 | 5.30 | 1.75 | 4.53 | 45.27 | 3.07 | 3.90 | 5.20 | 133.51 | 15.75 | 172.90 | 3.83 | 3.84 | Electricité consommée |
| Capacity of installed power equipment..... | 4.79 | 3.26 | 2.27 | 0.43 | 4.46 | 16.00 | 1.06 | 2.97 | 4.10 | 11.95 | 4.31 | 7.44 | 2.26 | 1.44 | Puissance installée |

[1] Establishments irrespective of size principally engaged in Coal and Metal mining (ISIC major groups 11 and 12) in all years. Establishments primarily engaged in Manufacturing (ISIC Division 2-3) and Other mining (ISIC major groups 14-19): Generally in which operatives worked an annual total of 12,000 or more man-hours or there were five or more employees in the case of the data for 1938, 1948 and 1953 and in which there were five or more persons engaged for 1958. For selected classes of manufacturing, 3,000 to 6,000 operative man-hours or three persons engaged were the lower limits for coverage in the case of the earlier three years and 1958, respectively. In a few classes of manufacturing, establishments irrespective of size were covered.

[2] Activities included in 1953 and 1958 but not 1938 and 1948 were: Slaughtering and meat-packing, food freezing and fish food manufacturing and bakeries (all part of ISIC major group 20), dyeing and finishing of textiles (part of ISIC major group 23) and mirror polishing (part of ISIC major group 33). Activities excluded in all years were dairies and fish curing (part of ISIC major group 20) and publishing (part of ISIC major group 28).

[1] Etablissements, quelle que soit leur dimension, dont l'activité principale relève des Industries extractives de charbon et de minerais métalliques (CITI 11 et 12) pour toutes les années. Etablissements dont l'activité principale relève des Industries manufacturières (CITI 2-3) et Autres industries extractives (CITI 14-19) et dans lesquels les ouvriers ont effectué un total annuel de 12 000 heures de travail au moins ou qui ont occupé cinq salariés ou plus en 1938, 1948 et 1953 et cinq personnes ou plus en 1958. Pour certaines classes des industries manufacturières, il fallait au moins 3 000 à 6 000 heures-ouvrier pendant les trois premières années et 3 personnes occupées en 1958. Dans quelques classes, tous les établissements, quelle que soit leur taille, sont compris.

[2] Compris en 1953 et 1958, mais exclu en 1938 et 1948: abattage du bétail, fabrication des préparations et conserves de viande et de poissons, congélation des produits alimentaires, boulangerie et patisserie (tous dans CITI 20), teinture et finissage des textiles (dans CITI 23), miroiterie (dans CITI 33). Non compris, pour toutes les années: industrie du lait et saurissage du poisson (dans CITI 20) et édition (dans CITI 28).

## 6. FUELS AND ELECTRICITY CONSUMED, LARGER INDUSTRIAL ESTABLISHMENTS[1]
## CONSOMMATION DE COMBUSTIBLES ET D'ELECTRICITE DES GRANDS ETABLISSEMENTS INDUSTRIELS[1]
### 1938, 1948, 1953, 1958

### A. Percentage Distribution of Energy Consumed According to Source
### Répartition en pourcentage de l'énergie consommée suivant la source

Quantities in thousand metric tons of coal equivalents　　　　　　Quantités en milliers de tonnes métriques d'équivalent charbon

### a. The Major Groups of Mining
### Les classes de la branche Industries extractives

| Year and item of data | Total | Coal mining Extraction du charbon | Metal mining Extraction des minerais métalliques | Other mining Divers | Année et rubrique |
|---|---|---|---|---|---|
| ISIC | 1 | 11 | 12 | 14–19 | CITI |
| **1953** | | | | | **1953** |
| Total energy consumed.. | 47.6 | 21.8 | 20.6 | 5.2 | Energie totale consommée |
| Percent consumed as: | | | | | Pourcentage consommé sous forme de: |
| Coal.............. | 54.2 | 98.6 | 17.0 | 15.4 | Charbon |
| Wood............. | 1.7 | — | 3.4 | 1.9 | Bois |
| Coke............. | 1.7 | — | 3.9 | — | Coke |
| Refined oil fuels...... | 26.9 | 1.4 | 46.1 | 57.7 | Pétrole raffiné |
| Electricity purchased... | 15.5 | — | 29.6 | 25.0 | Electricité achetée |
| Other fuels[3]........ | — | — | — | — | Autres combustibles[3] |
| **1958** | | | | | **1958** |
| Total energy consumed.. | 63.3 | 21.9 | 33.5 | 7.9 | Energie totale consommée |
| Percent consumed as: | | | | | Pourcentage consommé sous forme de: |
| Coal.............. | 38.7 | 96.8 | 9.8 | — | Charbon |
| Wood............. | 1.0 | — | 1.2 | 2.5 | Bois |
| Coke............. | 1.4 | — | 2.7 | — | Coke |
| Refined oil fuels...... | 29.2 | 3.2 | 39.7 | 57.0 | Pétrole raffiné |
| Electricity purchased... | 29.7 | — | 46.6 | 40.5 | Electricité achetée |
| Other fuels[3]........ | — | — | — | — | Autres combustibles[3] |

### b. The Major Groups of Manufacturing — Les classes de la branche Industries manufacturières

| Year and item of data | Manufacturing[2] Industries manufacturières[2] | Food, beverages and tobacco[2] Industries alimentaires, boissons, tabac[2] | Textiles[2] | Clothing, footwear and made-up textiles[2] Articles d'habillement, chaussures et ouvrages en tissu[2] | Wood products and furniture Bois et meubles | Paper and paper products Papier et ouvrages en papier | Printing and publishing[2] Imprimerie et édition[2] | Leather and leather products except wearing apparel Cuir et articles en cuir, à l'exclusion des articles d'habillement | Rubber products Ouvrages en caoutchouc | Chemicals and chemical, petroleum and coal products Produits chimiques et dérivés du pétrole et du charbon | Non-metallic mineral products[2] Produits minéraux non métalliques[2] | Basic metals Métallurgie de base | Metal products Ouvrages en métaux | Other manufacturing Autres industries manufacturières | Année et rubrique |
|---|---|---|---|---|---|---|---|---|---|---|---|---|---|---|---|
| ISIC | 2–3 | 20–22 | 23 | 24 | 25–26 | 27 | 28 | 29 | 30 | 31–32 | 33 | 34 | 35–38 | 39 | CITI |
| **1953** | | | | | | | | | | | | | | | **1953** |
| Total energy consumed: Quantity.......... | 2 026.2 | 128.0 | 60.3 | 16.3 | 27.8 | 582.3 | 10.7 | 6.6 | 14.3 | 472.9 | 284.8 | 278.3 | 140.1 | 3.8 | Energie totale consommée: Quantité |
| Percent of total in specified industry..... | 100.0 | 6.3 | 3.0 | 0.8 | 1.4 | 28.8 | 0.5 | 0.3 | 0.7 | 23.3 | 14.1 | 13.7 | 6.9 | 0.2 | Pourcentage du total par industrie indiquée |
| Percent consumed as: | | | | | | | | | | | | | | | Pourcentage consommée sous forme de: |
| Coal.............. | 11.7 | 17.7 | 14.9 | 4.3 | 6.1 | 11.2 | 7.5 | 10.6 | 1.4 | 3.6 | 26.6 | 7.4 | 15.2 | 15.8 | Charbon |
| Wood............. | 1.7 | 9.8 | 1.3 | 6.7 | 13.0 | 1.4 | 5.6 | — | — | 0.2 | 1.1 | 0.4 | 2.0 | 5.3 | Bois |
| Coke............. | 2.2 | 1.7 | 0.8 | 5.5 | 1.4 | 0.1 | 9.3 | 1.5 | 0.7 | 0.5 | 3.1 | 4.6 | 9.7 | 7.9 | Coke |
| Refined oil fuels...... | 51.6 | 49.1 | 59.1 | 52.2 | 34.9 | 66.9 | 35.5 | 68.2 | 77.6 | 53.0 | 58.2 | 15.6 | 42.0 | 28.9 | Pétrole raffiné |
| Electricity purchased... | 31.3 | 18.8 | 22.4 | 28.8 | 43.9 | 17.4 | 37.4 | 15.2 | 18.9 | 42.4 | 9.7 | 71.9 | 30.1 | 39.5 | Electricité achetée |
| Other fuels[3]........ | 1.5 | 2.9 | 1.5 | 2.5 | 0.7 | 3.0 | 4.7 | 4.5 | 1.4 | 0.3 | 1.3 | 0.1 | 1.0 | 2.6 | Autres combustibles[3] |
| **1958** | | | | | | | | | | | | | | | **1958** |
| Total energy consumed: Quantity.......... | 2 838.5 | 245.4 | 63.4 | 20.3 | 44.8 | 711.8 | 18.2 | 6.9 | 16.0 | 562.6 | 331.6 | 612.7 | 197.7 | 7.1 | Energie totale consommée: Quantité |
| Percent of total in specified industry..... | 100.0 | 8.7 | 2.2 | 0.7 | 1.4 | 25.1 | 0.6 | 0.3 | 0.6 | 19.9 | 11.7 | 21.6 | 6.9 | 0.3 | Pourcentage du total par industrie indiquée |
| Percent consumed as: | | | | | | | | | | | | | | | Pourcentage consommée sous forme de: |
| Coal.............. | 3.8 | 4.5 | 3.2 | 1.0 | 2.0 | 4.6 | 2.7 | — | 1.2 | 2.2 | 11.6 | 0.6 | 2.5 | 1.4 | Charbon |
| Wood............. | 1.0 | 6.9 | 0.6 | 2.9 | 7.2 | 0.1 | 1.1 | — | — | 0.1 | 0.8 | 0.1 | 0.8 | 2.8 | Bois |
| Coke............. | 0.8 | 0.6 | 0.3 | 2.0 | 1.1 | 0.1 | 5.0 | — | 0.6 | 0.2 | 3.8 | 0.2 | 2.3 | 2.8 | Coke |
| Refined oil fuels...... | 52.0 | 63.7 | 72.7 | 51.7 | 39.3 | 68.6 | 44.5 | 76.8 | 76.9 | 52.9 | 71.2 | 12.6 | 59.8 | 36.6 | Pétrole raffiné |
| Electricity purchased... | 39.8 | 2.8 | 21.8 | 40.9 | 50.2 | 20.7 | 44.5 | 21.7 | 20.0 | 42.3 | 1.4 | 86.4 | 33.1 | 52.2 | Electricité achetée |
| Other fuels[3]........ | 2.6 | 21.5 | 1.4 | 1.5 | 0.2 | 5.9 | 2.2 | 1.5 | 1.3 | 2.3 | 11.2 | 0.1 | 1.5 | 4.2 | Autres combustibles[3] |

For footnotes see end of table.　　　　　　Pour les notes, voir le bas du tableau.

## B. Quantity and Value of Fuels Consumed and Electricity Purchased and Produced
### Consommation de combustibles et électricité achetée et produite: quantités et valeur

Coal, coke and refined oil fuels in thousand metric tons; gas in million cubic metres; electricity in million KWH; wood in thousand cubic metres; other fuels in thousand metric tons of coal equivalents; values in million Kroner.

Charbon, lignite, coke et pétrole raffiné en milliers de tonnes métriques; gaz en millions de mètres cubes; électricité en millions de kWh; bois en milliers de mètres cubes; autres combustibles en milliers de tonnes métriques d'équivalent charbon; valeur en milliers de couronnes.

### a. The Major Groups of Mining
### Les classes de la branche Industries extractives

| Year and source of energy | Total | Coal mining Extraction du charbon | Metal mining Extraction des minerais métalliques | Other mining Divers | Année et source d'énergie |
|---|---|---|---|---|---|
| ISIC | 1 | 11 | 12 | 14–19 | CITI |
| **1953** | | | | | **1953** |
| Coal: | | | | | Charbon: |
| Quantity | 25.8 | 21.5 | 3.5 | 0.8 | Quantité |
| Value | 1.9 | 1.3 | 0.5 | 0.1 | Valeur |
| Coke: | | | | | Coke: |
| Quantity | 0.9 | — | 0.9 | — | Quantité |
| Value | 0.2 | — | 0.2 | — | Valeur |
| Refined oil fuels: | | | | | Pétrole raffiné: |
| Quantity | 8.5 | 0.2 | 6.3 | 2.0 | Quantité |
| Value | 2.7 | 0.1 | 1.9 | 0.7 | Valeur |
| Electricity: | | | | | Electricité: |
| Purchased: | | | | | Achetée: |
| Quantity | 59.5 | — | 48.9 | 10.6 | Quantité |
| Value | 1.8 | — | 1.2 | 0.6 | Valeur |
| | | | | | Produite pour l'auto-consommation: |
| Produced for own use: | | | | | |
| Quantity | 125.2 | 15.3 | 103.0 | 6.9 | Quantité |
| Value | 6.5 | — | 6.5 | — | Valeur |
| Wood: | | | | | Bois: |
| Quantity | 4.8 | — | 4.4 | 0.4 | Quantité |
| Value | 0.1 | — | 0.1 | — | Valeur |
| Other fuels [3]: | | | | | Autres combustibles [3]: |
| Quantity | — | — | — | — | Quantité |
| Value | — | — | — | — | Valeur |
| **1958** | | | | | **1958** |
| Coal: | | | | | Charbon: |
| Quantity | 24.5 | 21.2 | 3.3 | — | Quantité |
| Value | 1.6 | 1.0 | 0.6 | — | Valeur |
| Coke: | | | | | Coke: |
| Quantity | 1.0 | — | 1.0 | — | Quantité |
| Value | 0.2 | — | 0.2 | — | Valeur |
| Refined oil fuels: | | | | | Pétrole raffiné: |
| Quantity | 12.3 | 0.4 | 8.9 | 3.0 | Quantité |
| Value | 3.8 | 0.2 | 2.3 | 1.3 | Valeur |
| Electricity: | | | | | Electricité: |
| Purchased: | | | | | Achetée: |
| Quantity | 150.2 | — | 124.7 | 25.5 | Quantité |
| Value | 5.4 | — | 4.0 | 1.4 | Valeur |
| | | | | | Produite pour l'auto-consommation: |
| Produced for own use: | | | | | |
| Quantity | 114.7 | 16.0 | 90.2 | 8.5 | Quantité |
| Value | 7.7 | — | 7.6 | 0.1 | Valeur |
| Wood: | | | | | Bois: |
| Quantity | 3.0 | — | 2.1 | 0.9 | Quantité |
| Value | 0.1 | — | 0.1 | — | Valeur |
| Other fuels: [3] | | | | | Autres combustibles [3]: |
| Quantity | — | — | — | — | Quantité |
| Value | — | — | — | — | Valeur |

For footnotes see end of table.

Pour les notes, voir au bas du tableau.

## b. The Major Groups of Manufacturing — Les classes de la branche Industries manufacturières

| Year and source of energy / ISIC | Manufacturing / Industries manufacturières 2-3 | Food, beverages and tobacco / Industries alimentaires, boissons, tabac 20-22 | Textiles 23 | Clothing, footwear and made-up textiles / Articles d'habillement, chaussures et ouvrages en tissu 24 | Wood products and furniture / Bois et meubles 25-26 | Paper and paper products / Papier et ouvrages en papier 27 | Printing and publishing / Imprimerie et édition 28 | Leather and leather products except wearing apparel / Cuir et articles en cuir, à l'exclusion des articles d'habillement 29 | Rubber products / Ouvrages en caoutchouc 30 | Chemicals and chemical, petroleum and coal products / Produits chimiques et dérivés du pétrole et du charbon 31-32 | Non-metallic mineral products / Produits minéraux non métalliques 33 | Basic metals / Métallurgie de base 34 | Metal products / Ouvrages en métaux 35-38 | Other manufacturing / Autres industries manufacturières 39 | Année et source d'énergie / CITI |
|---|---|---|---|---|---|---|---|---|---|---|---|---|---|---|---|
| **1938** [4] | | | | | | | | | | | | | | | **1938** [4] |
| Coal: | | | | | | | | | | | | | | | Charbon: |
| Quantity | 790.1 | 44.9 | 33.8 | 2.0 | 1.3 | 399.7 | 0.7 | 4.2 | 5.2 | 109.5 | 138.0 | 11.2 | 39.5 | 0.1 | Quantité |
| Value | 20.8 | 1.6 | 1.0 | 0.1 | — | 9.8 | — | 0.1 | 0.2 | 3.0 | 3.4 | 0.3 | 1.3 | — | Valeur |
| Coke: | | | | | | | | | | | | | | | Coke: |
| Quantity | 58.6 | 3.1 | 1.6 | 2.7 | 0.5 | 1.2 | 4.1 | 0.5 | — | 11.9 | 4.1 | 3.5 | 25.3 | 0.1 | Quantité |
| Value | 2.7 | 0.2 | — | 0.1 | — | | 0.2 | | | 0.5 | 0.1 | 0.2 | 1.4 | — | Valeur |
| Refined oil fuels: | | | | | | | | | | | | | | | Pétrole raffiné: |
| Quantity | 37.1 | 5.4 | 0.4 | 0.4 | 1.1 | 0.5 | 0.6 | 0.2 | — | 9.4 | 2.5 | 8.2 | 8.4 | — | Quantité |
| Value | 4.2 | 1.0 | 0.1 | — | 0.2 | 0.1 | 0.1 | | | 0.7 | 0.4 | 0.6 | 1.0 | — | Valeur |
| Manufactured gas: | | | | | | | | | | | | | | | Gaz manufacturé: |
| Quantity | 3 405 | 1 250 | 48 | 218 | — | 71 | 640 | 28 | 126 | 76 | — | — | 698 | 250 | Quantité |
| Value | 0.3 | 0.1 | | | | | 0.1 | | | | — | — | 0.1 | — | Valeur |
| Wood: | | | | | | | | | | | | | | | Bois: |
| Quantity | 155.6 | 71.3 | 5.0 | 1.6 | 9.8 | 28.0 | 1.8 | 2.6 | 0.2 | 3.5 | 14.0 | 4.3 | 13.5 | — | Quantité |
| Value | 1.0 | 0.6 | | | 0.1 | 0.2 | | | | | | | 0.1 | — | Valeur |
| **1948** [4] | | | | | | | | | | | | | | | **1948** [4] |
| Coal: | | | | | | | | | | | | | | | Charbon: |
| Quantity | 401.4 | 42.0 | 15.3 | 1.2 | 1.0 | 121.8 | 1.3 | 3.3 | 1.6 | 39.0 | 126.8 | 14.0 | 34.0 | 0.1 | Quantité |
| Value | 36.7 | 3.2 | 1.8 | 0.1 | 0.1 | 11.3 | 0.1 | 0.4 | 0.2 | 4.0 | 10.4 | 1.4 | 3.7 | — | Valeur |
| Coke: | | | | | | | | | | | | | | | Coke: |
| Quantity | 60.5 | 2.0 | 1.0 | 2.7 | 0.7 | 1.0 | 1.9 | 0.4 | 0.2 | 9.8 | 5.5 | 4.3 | 30.9 | 0.1 | Quantité |
| Value | 8.4 | | 0.1 | 0.3 | 0.1 | 0.2 | 0.2 | 0.1 | | 1.3 | 0.6 | 0.6 | 4.6 | — | Valeur |
| Refined oil fuels: | | | | | | | | | | | | | | | Pétrole raffiné: |
| Quantity | 374.7 | 30.2 | 13.8 | 2.5 | 3.2 | 175.6 | 1.0 | 2.6 | 4.9 | 55.1 | 44.8 | 14.1 | 26.8 | 0.1 | Quantité |
| Value | 60.2 | 5.7 | 2.6 | 0.6 | 1.4 | 24.3 | 0.3 | 0.5 | 1.4 | 9.3 | 5.6 | 2.1 | 6.4 | — | Valeur |
| Manufactured gas: | | | | | | | | | | | | | | | Gaz manufacturé: |
| Quantity | 3 641.9 | 1 233.2 | 131.9 | 138.1 | — | 54.1 | 595.5 | — | — | 93.1 | — | — | 1 039.0 | 357.0 | Quantité |
| Value | 0.4 | 0.2 | | | | | 0.1 | — | — | | — | — | 0.1 | — | Valeur |
| Wood: | | | | | | | | | | | | | | | Bois: |
| Quantity | 279.4 | 86.0 | 9.3 | 14.2 | 42.3 | 28.8 | 5.2 | 2.3 | 0.5 | 8.4 | 25.2 | 4.1 | 52.5 | 0.6 | Quantité |
| Value | 4.3 | 1.8 | 0.1 | 0.3 | 0.3 | 0.3 | 0.1 | | | 0.1 | 0.3 | 0.1 | 0.9 | — | Valeur |
| **1953** | | | | | | | | | | | | | | | **1953** |
| Coal: | | | | | | | | | | | | | | | Charbon: |
| Quantity | 236.3 | 22.7 | 9.0 | 0.7 | 1.7 | 65.0 | 0.8 | 0.7 | 0.2 | 17.2 | 75.7 | 20.7 | 21.3 | 0.6 | Quantité |
| Value | 29.7 | 3.1 | 1.3 | 0.1 | 0.2 | 8.0 | 0.1 | 0.1 | | 2.1 | 8.4 | 3.2 | 3.0 | 0.1 | Valeur |
| Coke: | | | | | | | | | | | | | | | Coke: |
| Quantity | 48.4 | 2.4 | 0.5 | 1.0 | 0.4 | 0.5 | 1.2 | 0.1 | 0.1 | 2.8 | 9.7 | 14.1 | 15.2 | 0.4 | Quantité |
| Value | 9.1 | 0.4 | 0.1 | 0.2 | 0.1 | 0.1 | 0.2 | — | | 0.5 | 1.6 | 2.8 | 3.0 | 0.1 | Valeur |
| Refined oil fuels | | | | | | | | | | | | | | | Pétrole raffiné: |
| Quantity | 696.6 | 41.8 | 23.7 | 5.6 | 6.5 | 259.8 | 2.6 | 3.0 | 7.4 | 166.9 | 110.4 | 29.0 | 39.2 | 0.7 | Quantité |
| Value | 133.1 | 13.4 | 5.4 | 1.7 | 3.9 | 41.4 | 1.1 | 0.7 | 1.4 | 28.5 | 16.3 | 6.3 | 12.6 | 0.4 | Valeur |
| Electricity: | | | | | | | | | | | | | | | Electricité: |
| Purchased: | | | | | | | | | | | | | | | Achetée: |
| Quantity | 5 082.9 | 192.2 | 108.1 | 37.5 | 98.0 | 810.5 | 31.9 | 8.4 | 21.8 | 1 603.6 | 221.4 | 1 600.0 | 337.3 | 12.2 | Quantité |
| Value | 99.2 | 8.6 | 3.0 | 2.1 | 5.5 | 15.6 | 1.7 | 0.4 | 0.8 | 21.1 | 5.5 | 21.2 | 13.0 | 0.7 | Valeur |
| Produced for own use: | | | | | | | | | | | | | | | Produite pour l'auto-consommation: |
| Quantity | 4 677.8 | 11.5 | 33.4 | — | 10.6 | 625.5 | — | — | — | 2 167.4 | 12.6 | 1 797.4 | 19.4 | — | Quantité |
| Value | 36.2 | 0.7 | 0.9 | | 0.7 | 8.6 | — | | | 11.1 | 0.5 | 13.2 | 0.5 | — | Valeur |
| Wood: | | | | | | | | | | | | | | | Bois: |
| Quantity | 207.4 | 74.0 | 4.7 | 6.6 | 21.0 | 49.5 | 3.3 | 0.3 | 0.1 | 4.5 | 19.0 | 7.0 | 16.2 | 1.2 | Quantité |
| Value | 3.7 | 1.7 | 0.1 | 0.1 | 0.4 | 0.7 | 0.1 | | | 0.1 | 0.3 | 0.2 | 0.3 | — | Valeur |
| Other fuels [3] | | | | | | | | | | | | | | | Autres combustibles [3] |
| Quantity | 30.7 | 3.7 | 0.9 | 0.4 | 0.2 | 17.4 | 0.5 | 0.3 | 0.2 | 1.6 | 3.8 | 0.2 | 1.4 | 0.1 | Quantité |
| Value | 3.9 | 0.7 | 0.1 | 0.1 | 0.1 | 1.9 | 0.1 | | | 0.2 | 0.4 | | 0.3 | — | Valeur |
| **1958** | | | | | | | | | | | | | | | **1958** |
| Coal: | | | | | | | | | | | | | | | Charbon: |
| Quantity | 106.9 | 11.2 | 2.0 | 0.2 | 0.9 | 32.4 | 0.5 | | | 12.3 | 38.4 | 3.8 | 4.9 | 0.1 | Quantité |
| Value | 13.3 | 1.9 | 0.3 | — | 0.2 | 2.9 | 0.1 | | | 1.0 | 5.4 | 0.6 | 0.9 | — | Valeur |
| Coke: | | | | | | | | | | | | | | | Coke: |
| Quantity | 26.2 | 1.5 | 0.2 | 0.4 | 0.6 | 0.9 | 1.0 | | 0.1 | 1.1 | 13.8 | 1.3 | 5.1 | 0.2 | Quantité |
| Value | 4.9 | | — | 0.1 | 0.1 | 0.2 | 0.2 | | | 0.3 | 2.1 | 0.2 | 1.3 | — | Valeur |
| Refined oil fuels: | | | | | | | | | | | | | | | Pétrole raffiné: |
| Quantity | 984.3 | 104.3 | 30.7 | 7.0 | 11.8 | 325.5 | 5.4 | 3.5 | 8.2 | 198.6 | 157.4 | 51.4 | 78.8 | 1.7 | Quantité |
| Value | 200.4 | 32.1 | 7.0 | 3.0 | 6.4 | 47.4 | 2.3 | 1.0 | 1.7 | 36.4 | 24.6 | 12.1 | 25.5 | 0.9 | Valeur |
| Electricity: | | | | | | | | | | | | | | | Electricité: |
| Purchased: | | | | | | | | | | | | | | | Achetée: |
| Quantity | 9 045.9 | 421.4 | 110.2 | 66.4 | 179.8 | 1 179.0 | 65.0 | 11.8 | 26.0 | 1 902.2 | 296.5 | 4 235.0 | 523.0 | 29.6 | Quantité |
| Value | 209.8 | 20.2 | 4.1 | 3.2 | 8.7 | 31.6 | 3.0 | 0.6 | 1.2 | 31.6 | 10.6 | 68.5 | 25.1 | 1.4 | Valeur |
| Produced for own use: | | | | | | | | | | | | | | | Produite pour l'auto-consommation: |
| Quantity | 5 279.2 | 14.0 | 32.8 | — | 13.2 | 831.1 | — | 0.3 | — | 2 396.8 | 17.0 | 1 955.0 | 19.0 | — | Quantité |
| Value | 64.9 | 0.7 | 0.9 | | 0.8 | 16.7 | — | | | 23.5 | 0.8 | 21.2 | 0.3 | — | Valeur |
| Wood: | | | | | | | | | | | | | | | Bois: |
| Quantity | 162.8 | 99.2 | 2.2 | 3.6 | 18.6 | 4.7 | 1.4 | 0.1 | — | 2.5 | 15.7 | 4.8 | 9.0 | 1.0 | Quantité |
| Value | 3.5 | 2.6 | — | 0.1 | 0.2 | 0.1 | | | | — | 0.1 | 0.1 | 0.2 | — | Valeur |
| Other fuels [3] | | | | | | | | | | | | | | | Autres combustibles [3] |
| Quantity | 72.8 | 6.8 | 0.9 | 0.3 | 0.1 | 42.2 | 0.4 | 0.1 | 0.2 | 13.3 | 4.8 | 0.4 | 3.0 | 0.3 | Quantité |
| Value | 8.6 | 1.3 | 0.1 | 0.1 | 0.2 | 4.1 | 0.1 | | | 1.6 | 0.5 | 0.1 | 0.6 | — | Valeur |

[1] Establishments irrespective of size principally engaged in Coal and Metal mining (ISIC major groups 11 and 12) in all years. Establishments primarily engaged in Manufacturing (ISIC Division 2-3) and Other mining (ISIC major groups 14-19): Generally in which operatives worked an annual total of 12,000 or more man-hours or there were five or more employees in the case of the data for 1938, 1948 and 1953 and in which there were five or more persons engaged for 1958. For selected classes of manufacturing, 3,000 to 6,000 operative man-hours or three persons engaged were the lower limits for coverage in the case of the earlier three years and 1958, respectively. In a few classes of manufacturing, establishments irrespective of size were covered.

[2] Activities included in 1953 and 1958 but not 1938 and 1948 were: Slaughtering and meat-packing, food freezing and fish food manufacturing and bakeries (all part of ISIC major group 20), dyeing and finishing of textiles (part of ISIC major group 23) and mirror polishing (part of ISIC major group 33). Activities excluded in all years were dairies and fish curing (part of ISIC major group 20) and publishing (part of ISIC major group 28).

[3] Manufactured gas is included in Other fuels in the case of the data for 1953 and 1958.

[4] For 1938 and 1948, data are not available on electricity purchased or produced for own use or on Other fuels.

[1] Etablissements, quelle que soit leur dimension, dont l'activité principale relève des Industries extractives de charbon et de minerais métalliques (CITI 11 et 12) pour toutes les années. Etablissements dont l'activité principale relève des Industries manufacturières (CITI 2-3) et Autres industries extractives (CITI 14-19) et généralement dans lesquels les ouvriers ont effectué un total annuel de 12 000 heures de travail au moins ou qui comptaient cinq salariés ou plus en 1938, 1948 et 1953 et qui ont occupé cinq personnes ou plus en 1958. Pour certaines classes des industries manufacturières, les critères adoptés ont été les suivants: de 3 000 à 6 000 heures-ouvrier pour les trois premières années et 3 personnes occupées ou plus en 1958. Dans quelques classes, tous les établissements sont compris, quelle que soit leur dimension.

[2] Compris en 1953 et 1958, mais exclu en 1938 et 1948: abattage du bétail, fabrication des préparations et conserves de viande et de poisson, congélation des produits alimentaires, boulangerie et pâtisserie (tous dans CITI 20), teinture et finissage des textiles (dans CITI 23), miroiterie (dans CITI 33). Non compris pour toutes les années: industrie du lait et saurissage du poisson (dans CITI 20) et édition (dans CITI 28).

[3] En 1953 et 1958, la production de gaz est comprise dans Autres combustibles.

[4] Pour 1938 et 1948, on ne dispose d'aucune donnée sur l'électricité achetée, ou produite pour l'auto-consommation, non plus que sur les Autres combustibles.

# PAKISTAN

## Net Domestic Product

Estimates of the origin of the net domestic product are presented in Table 1. The data are derived from information contained in correspondence from the Central Statistical Office, Karachi. Details of the methods and sources used have been published in "National Income Estimation in Pakistan," *Statistical Bulletin, Vol. 3, No. 2* issued by the same Office.

## Index of Industrial Production

The index numbers of mining and manufacturing production presented in Table 2 are derived from indexes compiled by the Central Statistical Office, Karachi and published in the *Pakistan Statistical Bulletin*. The annual indexes are built up from indexes based on the quantity produced for 25 individual items. The index numbers for these items are combined into index numbers for mining as a whole, manufacturing as a whole, and mining and manufacturing combined, using as weights values added derived from the results of the 1954 Census of Industrial Production, which covered in principle all establishments with 20 or more employees and using power. Further details concerning the compilation of this index can be found in the *Pakistan Statistical Bulletin, No. 10-12* for October-December 1957.

## Index of Industrial Employment

The index numbers of industrial employment presented in Table 3 are compiled by the Statistical Office of the United Nations based on data of the absolute number of employees.

The annual absolute figures of employees in mining are the daily averages during the year and are collected by the Chief Inspector of Mines under the Mines Act, 1923. All mines, coke-oven plants and mineral dressing plants are included in the coverage. These data have been published in the *Pakistan Statistical Yearbook* by the Central Statistical Office, Karachi. The annual absolute figures of employees in manufacturing are derived from the results of the annual Censuses of Manufacturing Industries and are the daily averages during the year. The Censuses, which are described below under Table 4, cover all establishments with 20 or more employees and using power. The Census results have been published in various editions of *Census of Manufacturing Industries* by the Central Statistical Office, Karachi.

## Produit intérieur net

Le tableau 1 contient des estimations du produit intérieur net par branche d'activité d'origine. Ces données sont tirées de renseignements que l'Office central de statistique, Karachi, a communiqués par correspondance au Bureau de statistique de l'ONU. Un exposé détaillé des sources et méthodes adoptées figure dans "National Income Estimation in Pakistan", *Statistical Bulletin, Vol. 3, No. 2,* publié par le même Office.

## Indices de la production industrielle

Les indices du tableau 2 relatifs à la production des industries extractives et manufacturières sont tirés d'indices établis par l'Office central de statistique, Karachi, et publiés dans *Pakistan Statistical Bulletin*. Les indices annuels ont été construits à partir d'indices fondés sur les quantités produites de 25 marchandises différentes. Les indices relatifs à ces marchandises ont été combinés en indices concernant l'ensemble des industries extractives, l'ensemble des industries manufacturières et l'ensemble des industries extractives et manufacturières combinées; la base de pondération utilisée à cette fin est la valeur ajoutée calculée d'après les résultats du recensement de la production industrielle de 1954, qui portait en principe sur tous les établissements occupant 20 salariés ou plus et utilisant la force motrice. Pour plus de détails sur le calcul de cet indice, voir *Pakistan Statistical Bulletin, No. 10-12,* octobre-décembre 1957.

## Indices de l'emploi dans l'industrie

Les indices de l'emploi dans l'industrie présentés au tableau 3 ont été établis par le Bureau de statistique de l'ONU à partir de données relatives au nombre absolu de salariés.

Les chiffres absolus annuels indiquant le nombre de salariés dans les industries extractives sont les moyennes journalières pendant l'année et sont recueillis par l'inspecteur en chef des mines en application du *Mines Act, 1923*. Toutes les mines, cokeries et usines de lavage des minerais sont recensées. Ces données ont été publiées dans le *Pakistan Statistical Yearbook* par l'Office central de statistique, Karachi. Les chiffres absolus annuels concernant le nombre de salariés dans les industries manufacturières sont tirés des résultats des recensements annuels des industries manufacturières et représentent les moyennes journalières pendant l'année. Les recensements, qui sont décrits ci-dessous dans le commentaire du tableau 4, portent sur tous les établissements occupant 20 salariés ou plus et utilisant la force motrice. Les résultats des recensements ont été publiés dans différents numéros de *Census of Manufacturing Industries* par l'Office central de statistique, Karachi.

587

# PAKISTAN

### The Characteristics and Structure of Industrial Activity

The data presented in Table 4 have been derived from the results of the annual Censuses of Manufacturing Industries conducted and published in *Census of Manufacturing Industries, 1955* and *1958,* by the Central Statistical Office, Karachi.

The Censuses, in principle, cover all establishments with 20 employees or more and utilizing power. However, all establishments operated by the Ministry of Defence and the Ministry of Railways or attached to training institutions have been excluded.

In general the definitions of the items of data shown are consistent with the International Standards in Basic Industrial Statistics. However, although payments of wages and salaries include payments to labour contractors for contract labour, the number of workers involved in this arrangement is not included with the number of employees. In 1955 payments of wages and salaries to the establishments' own employees and payments to labour contractors are available separately and are shown separately in the table. In 1958 these two elements of labour costs are not available separately. The wages and salaries paid in both Censuses include payments in kind.

### Caractéristiques et structure de l'activité industrielle

Les données du tableau 4 sont tirées des résultats des recensements annuels des industries manufacturières effectués par l'Office central de statistique, Karachi; ces résultats ont été publiés par le même Office dans *Census of Manufacturing Industries,* 1955 et 1958.

Les recensements portent, en principe, sur les établissements manufacturiers comptant 20 salariés ou plus et utilisant la force motrice. Cependant, tous les établissements gérés par le Ministère de la défense et le Ministère des chemins de fer ou faisant partie d'instituts de formation ont été exclus.

En général, les définitions des rubriques utilisées sont conformes aux Normes internationales relatives aux statistiques industrielles de base. Cependant, bien que les traitements et salaires comprennent les sommes versées directement aux entrepreneurs fournissant de la main-d'œuvre, les travailleurs fournis par ces entrepreneurs ne sont pas compris dans les chiffres relatifs au nombre de salariés. Pour 1955, les traitements et salaires payés par les établissements à leurs propres salariés et les sommes versées aux entrepreneurs fournissant de la main-d'œuvre sont reproduits séparément dans le tableau. Pour 1958, on ne disposait pas de données distinctes sur ces deux éléments constitutifs du coût de la main-d'œuvre. Dans le cas des deux recensements, les traitements et salaires versés comprennent les paiements en nature.

## 1. THE NET DOMESTIC PRODUCT AT FACTOR COST ACCORDING TO ORIGIN
## ORIGINE PAR SECTEUR D'ACTIVITE DU PRODUIT INTERIEUR NET AU COUT DES FACTEURS

Million Rupees — Millions de roupies

| Item of data and year [1] / Rubrique et année [1] | Total | Agricultural sector / Secteur agricole | Mining / Industries extractives | Manufacturing [2] / Industries manufacturières [2] | Transportation and communication / Transports et communications | Other sectors [3] / Autres secteurs [3] |
|---|---|---|---|---|---|---|
| ISIC — CITI | 0–9 | 0 | 1 | 2–3 | 7 | 6, 8–9 |
| *At Prices of 1949–1952 — Aux prix de 1949–1952* | | | | | | |
| Absolute figures — Chiffres absolus | | | | | | |
| 1954 | 20 116 | 11 858 | 35 | 1 958 | 538 | 5 727 |
| 1955 | 19 962 | 11 335 | 37 | 2 219 | 565 | 5 806 |
| 1956 | 21 286 | 12 224 | 44 | 2 392 | 584 | 6 042 |
| 1957 | 21 369 | 12 099 | 47 | 2 491 | 611 | 6 121 |
| 1958 | 21 379 | 11 819 | 52 | 2 603 | 646 | 6 259 |
| 1959 | 22 492 | 12 578 | 56 | 2 801 | 685 | 6 372 |
| 1960 | 23 334 | 13 051 | 65 | 2 918 | 701 | 6 599 |
| 1961 | 24 069 | 13 357 | 70 | 3 131 | 712 | 6 799 |
| Percentage distribution according to sector— Distribution en pourcentage par secteur | | | | | | |
| 1954–1960 | 100.0 | 56.7 | 0.2 | 11.6 | 2.9 | 28.6 |
| 1954 | 100.0 | 58.9 | 0.2 | 9.7 | 2.7 | 28.5 |
| 1958 | 100.0 | 55.3 | 0.2 | 12.2 | 3.0 | 29.3 |
| 1960 | 100.0 | 55.9 | 0.3 | 12.5 | 3.0 | 28.3 |
| Average annual rate of growth—Taux annuel moyen d'accroissement | | | | | | |
| 1954–1960 | 2.5 | 1.6 | 10.9 | 6.9 | 4.5 | 2.4 |
| 1954–1958 | 1.5 | −0.1 | 10.4 | 7.4 | 4.7 | 2.2 |
| 1958–1960 | 4.5 | 5.1 | 11.8 | 5.9 | 4.2 | 2.7 |

[1] Fiscal year beginning 1st April.
[2] Includes Electricity, gas and water (ISIC division 5).
[3] Includes Construction (ISIC division 4).

[1] Exercice financier commençant le 1er avril.
[2] Y compris Electricité, gaz et eau (CITI branche 5).
[3] Y compris Bâtiment et travaux publics (CITI branche 4).

## 2. INDEX NUMBERS OF INDUSTRIAL PRODUCTION — INDICES DE LA PRODUCTION INDUSTRIELLE

| Period<br>Période | Total | Mining<br>Industries<br>extractives | Manu-<br>facturing [1]<br>Industries<br>manu-<br>facturières[1] |
|---|---|---|---|
| ISIC — CITI | 1–3, 511–512 | 1 | 2–3 |

### a. Indexes — Indices (1958 = 100)

| | | | |
|---|---|---|---|
| 1950............. | 24 | 46 | 23 |
| 1951............. | 30 | 49 | 29 |
| 1952............. | 37 | 61 | 36 |
| 1953............. | 48 | 67 | 47 |
| 1954............. | 62 | 68 | 62 |
| 1955............. | 78 | 72 | 78 |
| 1956............. | 88 | 84 | 89 |
| 1957............. | 93 | 88 | 94 |
| 1958............. | 100 | 100 | 100 |
| 1959............. | 112 | 104 | 112 |
| 1960............. | 119 | 122 | 118 |
| 1961............. | 126 | 136 | 125 |

### b. Average Annual Rate of Change — Taux annuel moyen de variation

| | | | |
|---|---|---|---|
| 1950 – 1960...... | 17.4 | 10.2 | 17.8 |
| 1954 – 1958...... | 12.7 | 10.1 | 12.7 |
| 1958 – 1960...... | 9.1 | 10.5 | 8.6 |

[1] Does not cover production in much of food manufacturing (e.g., in ISIC groups 201–206 and 208), Clothing, footwear and made-up textiles (ISIC major group 24), Wood and furniture (ISIC major groups 25–26), Printing (ISIC major group 28), much of Chemicals (e.g., ISIC groups 311 and 313), most of Non-metallic mineral products (e.g., ISIC groups 331–333), and in Metal products (ISIC major groups 35–38) and Miscellaneous manufacturing (ISIC major group 39).

[1] Non compris la production dans les industries suivantes: industries alimentaires, en grande partie (par exemple, groupes 201–206 et 208 de la CITI); Articles d'habillement, chaussures et ouvrages en tissu (CITI classe 24); Bois et meubles (CITI classes 25–26); Imprimerie (CITI classe 28); Industrie chimique, en grande partie (par exemple, groupes 311 et 313 de la CITI); Produits minéraux non métalliques, en majeure partie (par exemple, groupes 331–333 de la CITI); Ouvrages en métaux (CITI classes 35–38) et Industries manufacturières diverses (CITI classe 39).

## 3. INDEX NUMBERS OF INDUSTRIAL EMPLOYMENT — INDICES DE L'EMPLOI DANS L'INDUSTRIE

### A.   The Major Groups of Mining
### Les classes de la branche Industries extractives

| Period<br>Période | All mining [1]<br>Toutes<br>industries<br>extractives [1] | Coal<br>mining<br>Extraction<br>du charbon | Metal mining<br>Extraction<br>des minerais<br>métalliques | Crude petro-<br>leum and<br>natural gas<br>Pétrole brut<br>et gaz naturel | Other mining<br>Autres<br>industries<br>extractives |
|---|---|---|---|---|---|
| ISIC — CITI | 1 | 11 | 12 | 13 | 14–19 |

### a. Indexes — Indices (1958 = 100)

| | | | | | |
|---|---|---|---|---|---|
| 1949....... | 39 | 30 | 37 | ... | 53 |
| 1950....... | 48 | 43 | 39 | ... | 50 |
| 1951....... | – 48 – | 40 | 37 | 69 | 55 |
| 1952....... | 58 | 50 | 48 | 76 | 68 |
| 1953....... | 59 | 46 | 72 | 83 | 78 |
| 1954....... | 69 | 65 | 92 | 80 | 69 |
| 1955....... | 73 | 56 | 96 | 101 | 100 |
| 1956....... | 80 | 69 | 127 | 96 | 94 |
| 1957....... | 85 | 74 | 135 | 124 | 84 |
| 1958....... | 100 | 100 | 100 | 100 | 100 |

### b. Average Annual Rate of Change — Taux annuel moyen de variation

| | | | | | |
|---|---|---|---|---|---|
| 1954 – 1958. | 9.7 | 11.4 | 2.1 | 5.7 | 9.7 |

For footnotes see end of table.

Pour les notes, voir au bas du tableau.

## B.  The Major Groups of Manufacturing — Les classes de la branche Industries manufacturières

| Period<br>Période | Manu-facturing [2]<br>Industries manufac-turières[2] | Food, beverages and tobacco<br>Industries alimen-taires, boissons, tabac | Textiles | Clothing, footwear and made-up textiles<br>Articles d'habil-lement, chaussures et ouvrages en tissu | Wood products and furniture<br>Bois et meubles | Paper and paper products<br>Papier et ouvrages en papier | Printing and publishing<br>Im-primerie et édition | Leather and leather products except wearing apparel<br>Cuir et articles en cuir, à l'exclu-sion des articles d'habil-lement | Rubber products<br>Ouvrages en caout-chouc | Chemicals and chemical products<br>Produits chi-miques | Non-metallic mineral products<br>Produits minéraux non métal-liques | Basic metals<br>Métal-lurgie de base | Metal products<br>Ouvrages en métaux | Other manu-facturing<br>Autres industries manufac-turières |
|---|---|---|---|---|---|---|---|---|---|---|---|---|---|---|
| ISIC — CITI | 2–3 | 20–22 | 23 | 24 | 25–26 | 27 | 28 | 29 | 30 | 31 | 33 | 34 | 35–38 | 39 |
| *a.* Indexes — Indices (1958 = 100) | | | | | | | | | | | | | | |
| 1955............. | 73 | 85 | 72 | 94 | 79 | 54 | 87 | 81 | 80 | 73 | 79 | 53 | 58 | 133 |
| 1957............. | 86 | 92 | 84 | 106 | 104 | 77 | 97 | 86 | 95 | 88 | 103 | 74 | 88 | 86 |
| 1958............. | 100 | 100 | 100 | 100 | 100 | 100 | 100 | 100 | 100 | 100 | 100 | 100 | 100 | 100 |
| 1959............. | 113 | 138 | 110 | 108 | 111 | 87 | 102 | 105 | 106 | 108 | 133 | 105 | 118 | 128 |
| *b.* Average Annual Rate of Change — Taux annuel moyen de variation | | | | | | | | | | | | | | |
| 1955 – 1959....... | 11.5 | 12.9 | 11.2 | 3.5 | 8.9 | 12.7 | 4.0 | 6.7 | 7.3 | 10.3 | 13.6 | 18.6 | 19.4 | −1.0 |

[1] Excludes Crude petroleum and natural gas (ISIC major group 13) in 1949 and 1950.
[2] Excludes Products of petroleum and coal (ISIC major group 32).

[1] Non compris Pétrole brut et gaz naturel (CITI classe 13) en 1949 et 1950.
[2] Non compris Dérivés du pétrole et du charbon (CITI classe 32).

## 4. CHARACTERISTICS OF MANUFACTURING ESTABLISHMENTS EMPLOYING 20 OR MORE PERSONS AND USING POWER

## CARACTERISTIQUES DES ETABLISSEMENTS MANUFACTURIERS EMPLOYANT 20 PERSONNES OU PLUS ET UTILISANT LA FORCE MOTRICE

### 1955, 1958

Number of establishments in units; value added and wages and salaries in million Rupees; number of employees and operatives in thousands; value added per employee and wages and salaries per employee in thousand Rupees.

Nombre d'établissements en unités; valeur ajoutée et traitements et salaires en millions de roupies; nombre de salariés et d'ouvriers en milliers; valeur ajoutée par salarié et traitements et salaires par salarié en milliers de roupies.

| Year and item of data | Manu-facturing Industries manufac-turières | Food, beverages and tobacco Industries alimen-taires, boissons, tabac | Textiles | Clothing, footwear and made-up textiles Articles d'habil-lement, chaussures et ouvrages en tissu | Wood products and furniture Bois et meubles | Paper and paper products Papier et ouvrages en papier | Printing and publish-ing Im-primerie et édition | Leather and leather products except wearing apparel Cuir et articles en cuir, à l'exclu-sion des articles d'habil-lement | Rubber products Ouvrages en caout-chouc | Chemicals and chemical, petroleum and coal products Produits chi-miques et dérivés du pétrole et du charbon | Non-metallic mineral products Produits minéraux non métal-liques | Basic metals Métal-lurgie de base | Metal products Ouvrages en métaux | Other manu-factur-ing Autres in-dustries manufac-turières | Année et rubrique |
|---|---|---|---|---|---|---|---|---|---|---|---|---|---|---|---|
| ISIC | 2–3 | 20–22 | 23 | 24 | 25–26 | 27 | 28 | 29 | 30 | 31–32 | 33 | 34 | 35–38 | 39 | CITI |
| a. Absolute Figures — Chiffres absolus | | | | | | | | | | | | | | | |
| **1955** | | | | | | | | | | | | | | | **1955** |
| Number of establishments. | 2 458 | 283 | 793 | 100 | 26 | 9 | 125 | 74 | 28 | 287 | 54 | 43 | 487 | 149 | Nombre d'établissements |
| Value added.......... | 812.6 | 95.3 | 444.0 | 20.9 | 1.8 | 15.6 | 21.4 | 8.4 | 3.2 | 98.0 | 28.8 | 16.8 | 45.8 | 12.6 | Valeur ajoutée |
| Number of employees (Average during the year)........... | 290.3 | 21.4 | 172.8 | 5.8 | 1.6 | 3.6 | 10.3 | 3.6 | 1.4 | 20.9 | 9.2 | 5.4 | 27.0 | 7.3 | Nombre de salariés (moyenne pendant l'année) |
| Wages and salaries..... | 300.6 | 22.9 | 171.6 | 7.2 | 1.5 | 6.1 | 12.4 | 3.3 | 1.2 | 23.4 | 12.7 | 6.6 | 25.9 | 5.8 | Traitements et salaires: |
| Paid to employees.... | 280.2 | 20.7 | 158.9 | 7.1 | 1.4 | 5.6 | 12.0 | 3.3 | 1.2 | 22.5 | 10.9 | 6.2 | 24.8 | 5.6 | Payés aux salariés |
| Paid to labour contractors......... | 20.4 | 2.2 | 12.7 | 0.1 | 0.1 | 0.5 | 0.4 | — | — | 0.9 | 1.8 | 0.4 | 1.1 | 0.2 | Payés aux entre-preneurs fournissant de la main-d'œuvre |
| Operatives: Number (Average during the year)...... | 263.8 | 18.4 | 160.5 | 5.2 | 1.5 | 3.1 | 8.7 | 3.2 | 1.2 | 17.6 | 8.2 | 5.1 | 24.4 | 6.7 | Ouvriers: Nombre (moyenne pendant l'année) |
| Wages and salaries... | 223.4 | 15.7 | 134.9 | 4.6 | 1.1 | 4.3 | 9.2 | 2.4 | 0.8 | 13.8 | 8.1 | 5.1 | 19.3 | 4.1 | Traitements et salaires |
| **1958** | | | | | | | | | | | | | | | **1958** |
| Number of establishments. | 3 170 | 293 | 895 | 98 | 54 | 21 | 179 | 95 | 31 | 384 | 62 | 94 | 809 | 155 | Nombre d'établissements |
| Value added.......... | 1 338.9 | 187.0 | 638.5 | 24.6 | 5.2 | 32.0 | 36.6 | 15.9 | 7.0 | 178.0 | 43.9 | 41.5 | 114.6 | 14.1 | Valeur ajoutée |
| Number of employees (Average during the year)........... | 397.9 | 25.1 | 238.2 | 6.2 | 2.2 | 6.7 | 11.8 | 4.4 | 1.7 | 28.3 | 11.6 | 10.1 | 46.1 | 5.5 | Nombre de salariés (moyenne pendant l'année) |
| Wages and salaries (including payments for contract labour)... | 461.8 | 36.5 | 246.5 | 10.8 | 2.4 | 10.5 | 16.9 | 4.6 | 2.2 | 44.1 | 15.3 | 12.5 | 53.5 | 6.0 | Traitements et salaires (y compris les sommes versées aux entre-preneurs fournissant de la main-d'œuvre) |
| b. Structure | | | | | | | | | | | | | | | |
| **1955** | | | | | | | | | | | | | | | **1955** |
| Distribution in percent of: | | | | | | | | | | | | | | | Distribution en pour-centage: |
| Value added....... | 100.0 | 11.7 | 54.6 | 2.6 | 0.2 | 1.9 | 2.7 | 1.0 | 0.4 | 12.1 | 3.5 | 2.1 | 5.6 | 1.6 | Valeur ajoutée |
| Number of employees. | 100.0 | 7.3 | 59.5 | 2.0 | 0.6 | 1.2 | 3.6 | 1.2 | 0.5 | 7.2 | 3.2 | 1.8 | 9.3 | 2.6 | Nombre de salariés |
| Per employee: | | | | | | | | | | | | | | | Par salarié: |
| Value added....... | 2.8 | 4.4 | 2.6 | 3.6 | 1.1 | 4.3 | 2.1 | 2.3 | 2.3 | 4.7 | 3.1 | 3.1 | 1.7 | 1.7 | Valeur ajoutée |
| Wages and salaries[1].. | 1.0 | 1.0 | 0.9 | 1.2 | 0.9 | 1.6 | 1.2 | 0.9 | 0.8 | 1.1 | 1.2 | 1.1 | 0.9 | 0.8 | Traitements et salaires[1] |
| Value added per unit of wages and salaries[2]........... | 2.70 | 4.16 | 2.59 | 2.90 | 1.20 | 2.56 | 1.72 | 2.54 | 2.67 | 4.19 | 2.27 | 2.54 | 1.77 | 2.17 | Valeur ajoutée par unité de traitements et salaires[2] |
| Operatives as a percent of employees........ | 90.9 | 86.0 | 92.9 | 89.6 | 93.8 | 86.1 | 84.5 | 88.9 | 85.7 | 84.2 | 89.1 | 94.4 | 90.4 | 91.8 | Ouvriers en pourcentage des salariés |
| **1958** | | | | | | | | | | | | | | | **1958** |
| Distribution in percent of: | | | | | | | | | | | | | | | Distribution en pour-centage: |
| Value added....... | 100.0 | 13.9 | 47.7 | 1.8 | 0.4 | 2.4 | 2.8 | 1.1 | 0.6 | 13.3 | 3.2 | 3.1 | 8.6 | 1.1 | Valeur ajoutée |
| Number of employees. | 100.0 | 6.3 | 59.8 | 1.6 | 0.5 | 1.7 | 3.0 | 1.1 | 0.4 | 7.1 | 2.9 | 2.6 | 11.6 | 1.4 | Nombre de salariés |
| Value added per employee........... | 3.4 | 7.4 | 2.7 | 4.0 | 2.4 | 4.8 | 3.1 | 3.6 | 4.1 | 6.3 | 3.8 | 4.1 | 2.5 | 2.6 | Valeur ajoutée par salarié |
| Value added per unit of wages and salaries[2]........... | 2.90 | 5.12 | 2.59 | 2.28 | 2.17 | 3.05 | 2.16 | 3.46 | 3.18 | 4.04 | 2.87 | 3.32 | 2.14 | 2.35 | Valeur ajoutée par unité de traitements et salaires[2] |

[1] "Wages and salaries per employee" excludes the amounts paid to labour contractor for contract labour.
[2] Wages and salaries includes the amounts paid to labour contractors for contract labour.

[1] Les "Traitements et salaires par salarié" ne comprennent pas les sommes versées aux entre-preneurs fournissant de la main-d'œuvre.
[2] Les traitements et salaires comprennent les sommes versées aux entrepreneurs fournissant de la main-d'œuvre.

# PANAMA

## Gross Domestic Product

Estimates of the expenditure on and the industrial origin of the gross domestic product are presented in Table 1. This table has been compiled from data supplied by the Dirección de Estadística y Censos, Panama, in response to the United Nations national accounts questionnaire.

## The Characteristics and Structure of Industrial Activity

The data shown in Table 2 are derived from the results of Panama's fourth industrial inquiry, la Cuarta Encuesta Industrial published by the Dirección de Estadística y Censos in *Estadística Panameña, Industrias: Encuesta de 1959, Año 1958* (Serie F.1, No. 1.) Febrero de 1960. The inquiry was conducted in April 1959 and referred to operations during 1958.

The inquiry covered 185 selected establishments with a declared capital of 5,000 Balboas or more. Data for 12 of the 185 establishments are partly estimated, based on the results for those establishments in the 1957 inquiry.

The definitions of the items of data conform to the International Standards in Basic Industrial Statistics. Value added is valued at market price. The data on engaged and operatives relate to the average of the number as of the 15th of February, 15th May, 15th August and 15th November.

## Produit intérieur brut

Les estimations des dépenses imputées au produit intérieur brut et des composantes du produit intérieur brut ventilées suivant le secteur d'activité industrielle sont reproduites au tableau 1. Ce tableau a été construit à partir de données fournies par la Dirección de Estadística y Censos Panama, en réponse au questionnaire de l'O.N.U. relatif aux comptes nationaux.

## Caractéristiques et structures de l'activité industrielle

Les données reproduites au tableau 2 ont été tirées des résultats de la quatrième enquête industrielle effectuée en Panama, la Cuarta Encuesta Industrial, publié par la Dirección de Estadística y Censos dans *Estadística Panemeña, Industrias: Encuesta de 1959, Año 1958* (Serie F. 1, No. 1) Febrero de 1960. L'enquête a été exécutée en avril 1959 et se rapporte aux activités durant 1958.

L'enquête a couvert 185 établissements d'un capital déclaré de 5 000 Balboas ou plus. Les données relatives à 12 des 185 établissements sont en partie estimées, estimations basées sur les résultats relatifs à ces établissements de l'enquête de 1957.

Les définitions des rubriques sont conformes aux Normes internationales relatives aux statistiques industrielles de base. La valeur ajoutée est évaluée aux prix du marché. Les données concernant les personnes occupées et les ouvriers sont les nombres moyens au 15 février, 15 mai, 15 août et 15 novembre.

# 1. THE GROSS DOMESTIC PRODUCT
## LE PRODUIT INTERIEUR BRUT

Million Balboas          Millions de balboas

## A. Expenditure on the Gross Domestic Product at Market Prices
## Dépenses relatives au produit intérieur brut aux prix du marché

| Item of data and year<br>Rubrique et année | Total | Consumption [1]<br>Consommation [1] | | Gross Domestic Capital Formation [1]<br>Formation brute de capital intérieur [1] | | Net exports of goods and services [2]<br>Exportations nettes de biens et de services [2] | |
|---|---|---|---|---|---|---|---|
| | | Total | Government<br>Etat | Total | Fixed<br>Fixe | Exports<br>less imports<br>Exportations<br>moins<br>importations | Exports<br>Exportations |
| | | | | a. At Current Prices — Aux prix courants | | | |
| Absolute figures — Chiffres absolus | | | | | | | |
| 1954 | 318.0 | 283.0 | 36.2 | ... | 34.4 | 0.6 | 110.1 |
| 1955 | 339.9 | 302.0 | 37.9 | ... | 37.1 | 0.8 | 117.2 |
| 1956 | 351.4 | 314.0 | 43.0 | ... | 48.1 | −10.7 | 119.4 |
| 1957 | 384.8 | 346.3 | 42.4 | ... | 54.6 | −16.1 | 124.2 |
| 1958 | 387.1 | 353.1 | 46.7 | ... | 55.1 | −21.1 | 114.6 |
| 1959 | 414.2 | 378.7 | 48.7 | ... | 60.1 | −24.6 | 117.0 |
| 1960 | 437.0 | 408.2 | 52.5 | ... | 71.9 | −43.1 | 113.0 |
| Percentage distribution of average annual expenditure — Distribution en pourcentage des dépenses annuelles moyennes | | | | | | | |
| 1954 | 100.0 | 89.0 | 11.4 | — | 10.8 | 0.2 | 34.6 |
| 1958 | 100.0 | 91.2 | 12.1 | — | 14.2 | −5.4 | 29.6 |
| 1960 | 100.0 | 93.4 | 12.0 | — | 16.5 | −9.9 | 25.9 |

For footnotes see end of table.      Pour les notes, voir au bas du tableau.

## B. The Gross Domestic Product at Factor Cost According to Origin
## Origine par secteur d'activité du produit intérieur brut au coût des facteurs

| Item of data and year<br>Rubrique et année | Total | Agricultural sector<br>Secteur agricole | Industrial Sector — Secteur Industriel | | | | Transportation and communication<br>Transport et communication | Other sectors [2]<br>Autres secteurs [2] |
|---|---|---|---|---|---|---|---|---|
| | | | Total | Manufacturing<br>Industries manufacturières | Construction [3]<br>Bâtiments et travaux publics [3] | Electricity, gas and water<br>Electricité, gaz et eau | | |
| ISIC — CITI | 0–9 | 0 | 1–5 | 2–3 | 4 | 5 | 7 | 6, 8–9 |
| | | | a. At Current Prices — Aux prix courants | | | | | |
| Absolute figures<br>— Chiffres absolus | | | | | | | | |
| 1954 | 294.3 | 85.5 | 46.5 | 28.9 | 12.5 | 5.1 | 14.0 | 148.3 |
| 1955 | 315.8 | 93.3 | 48.3 | 29.5 | 13.5 | 5.3 | 14.5 | 159.7 |
| 1956 | 325.2 | 87.1 | 52.4 | 30.0 | 17.0 | 5.4 | 16.9 | 168.8 |
| 1957 | 355.4 | 98.9 | 58.4 | 33.3 | 19.2 | 5.9 | 16.3 | 181.8 |
| 1958 | 360.3 | 97.1 | 59.2 | 34.0 | 19.0 | 6.2 | 16.4 | 187.6 |
| 1959 | 385.5 | 103.2 | 62.5 | 35.7 | 20.3 | 6.5 | 18.4 | 201.4 |
| 1960 | 404.7 | 98.3 | 71.2 | 38.9 | 25.6 | 6.7 | 20.9 | 214.3 |
| Percentage distribution according to sector— Distribution en pourcentage par secteur | | | | | | | | |
| 1954 | 100.0 | 29.0 | 15.8 | 9.8 | 4.3 | 1.7 | 4.8 | 50.4 |
| 1958 | 100.0 | 26.9 | 16.4 | 9.4 | 5.3 | 1.7 | 4.6 | 52.1 |
| 1960 | 100.0 | 24.3 | 17.6 | 9.6 | 6.3 | 1.7 | 5.2 | 52.9 |

[1] Consumption expenditure includes Increases in Stocks which should be part of Gross domestic capital formation.
[2] Factor and non-factor services rendered by residents of Panama to the Canal Zone and to the Colon Free Zone are treated uniformly as non-factor services to the rest of the world. These services are included in exports of goods and services in Table A and in the "Other sectors" component of Table B.
[3] Includes Mining.

[1] Dépense de consommation privée comprend l'accroissement des stocks qui devrait appartenir à la formation brute de capital intérieur.
[2] Les services facteurs et non facteurs rendus par des résidents du Panama à la zone du Canal et à la zone franche de Colon sont uniformément traités comme des services non facteurs rendus au reste du monde. Ces services sont compris dans les exportations de biens et de services au tableau A et dans l'élément "Autres secteurs" au tableau B.
[3] Y compris industries extractives.

## 2. SELECTED INDUSTRIAL ESTABLISHMENTS WITH A DECLARED CAPITAL OF 5000 BALBOAS OR MORE
## QUELQUES ETABLISSEMENTS INDUSTRIELS AVEC UN CAPITAL DECLARE DE 5000 BALBOAS OU PLUS
### 1958

Number of establishments in units; value added and wages and salaries in million Balboas; number of engaged and operatives in thousands; man-hours worked in millions; value added per person engaged and wages and salaries per thousand operative man-hours in thousand Balboas; average annual man-hours per operative in thousands.

Nombre d'établissements en unités; valeur ajoutée et traitements et salaires en millions de Balboas; nombre de personnes occupées et d'ouvriers en milliers; heures de travail en millions; valeur ajoutée par personne occupée et traitements et salaires par millier d'heures-ouvrier en milliers de Balboas; moyenne annuelle des heures de travail par ouvrier en milliers.

### A. Selected Divisions of Industrial Activity — Quelques branches de l'activité industrielle

| Item of data | Total | Manufacturing Industries manufacturières | Electricity Electricité | Rubrique | Item of data | Total | Manufacturing Industries manufacturières | Electricity Electricité | Rubrique |
|---|---|---|---|---|---|---|---|---|---|
| ISIC | 2-3, 511 | 2-3 | 511 | CITI | ISIC | 2-3, 511 | 2-3 | 511 | CITI |
| | a. Absolute Figures — Chiffres absolus | | | | | b. Structure | | | |
| Number of establishments...... | 185 | 178 | 7 | Nombre d'établissements | Distribution in percent of: | | | | Distribution en pourcentage: |
| Value added.............. | 24.9 | 19.0 | 5.9 | Valeur ajoutée | Value added............... | 100.0 | 76.3 | 23.7 | Valeur ajoutée |
| Number of engaged (Average | | | | Nombre de personnes occupées | Number of engaged.......... | 100.0 | 88.7 | 11.3 | Nombre de personnes occupées |
| during the year)........... | 9.7 | 8.6 | 1.1 | (Moyenne pendant l'année) | Value added per person | | | | Valeur ajoutée par personne |
| Wages and salaries............ | 11.2 | 9.1 | 2.1 | Traitements et salaires | engaged................. | 2.6 | 2.2 | 5.4 | occupée |
| Operatives: | | | | Ouvriers: | Value added per unit of | | | | Valeur ajoutée par traitements |
| Number (Average during | | | | Nombre (Moyenne pendant | wages and salaries.......... | 2.22 | 2.09 | 2.81 | et salaires unitaire |
| the year)................ | 8.0 | 7.2 | 0.8 | l'année) | Operatives as a percent of | | | | Ouvriers en pourcentage des |
| Man-hours worked........... | 17.5 | 15.4 | 2.1 | Heures de travail | engaged................. | | | | personnes occupées |
| Wages and salaries.......... | 7.1 | 5.6 | 1.5 | Traitements et salaires | Average man-hours per | | | | Heures de travail: moyenne par |
| | | | | | operative................. | 2.19 | 2.14 | 2.62 | ouvrier |
| | | | | | Wages and salaries per | | | | Traitements et salaires par |
| | | | | | thousand operative man-hours | 0.40 | 0.36 | 0.71 | millier d'heures de travail d'ouvrier |

## B. The Major Groups of Manufacturing

## Les classes de la branche Industries manufacturières

| Item of data | Manu-facturing<br><br>Industries manufac-turières | Food beverages and tobacco<br><br>Industries alimen-taires, boissons, tabac | Clothing, footwear and made-up textiles<br><br>Articles d'habil-lement, chaussures et ouvrages en tissu | Wood products and furniture<br><br>Bois et meubles | Paper and paper products<br><br>Papier et ouvrages en papier | Leather and leather products except wearing apparel<br><br>Cuir et articles en cuir, à l'exclu-sion des articles d'habil-lement | Chemicals and chemical, petroleum and coal products<br><br>Produits chi-miques et dérivés du pétrole et du charbon | Non-metallic mineral products<br><br>Produits minéraux non métal-liques | Metal products<br><br>Ouvrages en métaux | Rubrique |
|---|---|---|---|---|---|---|---|---|---|---|
| ISIC | 2–3 | 20–22 | 24 | 25–26 | 27 | 29 | 31–32 | 33 | 35–38 | CITI |
| | | | | *a.* Absolute Figures — Chiffres absolus | | | | | | |
| Number of establishments. | 178 | 79 | 36 | 18 | 6 | 6 | 14 | 16 | 3 | Nombre d'établissements |
| Value added......... | 19.0 | 11.8 | 2.1 | 1.4 | 0.3 | 0.4 | 0.4 | 2.3 | 0.3 | Valeur ajoutée |
| Number of engaged (Average during the year)........... | 8.6 | 5.2 | 1.4 | 0.7 | 0.1 | 0.2 | 0.2 | 0.7 | 0.1 | Nombre de personnes occupées (moyenne pendant l'année) |
| Wages and salaries paid............ | 9.1 | 5.5 | 1.1 | 0.8 | 0.2 | 0.2 | 0.2 | 1.0 | 0.1 | Traitements et salaires payés |
| Operatives: Number (Average during the year).... | 7.2 | 4.4 | 1.3 | 0.6 | 0.1 | 0.1 | 0.1 | 0.6 | — | Ouvriers: Nombre (moyenne pendant l'année) |
| Man-hours worked.... | 15.4 | 8.6 | 2.9 | 1.6 | 0.2 | 0.3 | 0.2 | 1.5 | 0.1 | Heures de travail effectuées |
| Wages and salaries... | 5.6 | 3.0 | 0.9 | 0.6 | 0.1 | 0.1 | 0.1 | 0.7 | 0.1 | Traitements et salaires |
| | | | | *b.* Structure | | | | | | |
| Distribution in percent of: Value added........ | 100.0 | 62.1 | 11.0 | 7.4 | 1.6 | 2.1 | 2.1 | 12.1 | 1.6 | Distribution en pour-centage: Valeur ajoutée |
| Number of engaged.. | 100.0 | 60.4 | 16.3 | 8.1 | 1.2 | 2.3 | 2.3 | 8.2 | 1.2 | Nombre de personnes occupées |
| Value added per person engaged.......... | 2.2 | 2.3 | 1.5 | 2.0 | 3.0 | 2.0 | 2.0 | 3.3 | 3.0 | Valeur ajoutée par personne occupée |
| Value added per unit of wages and salaries. | 2.09 | 2.14 | 1.91 | 1.75 | 1.50 | 2.00 | 2.00 | 2.30 | 3.00 | Valeur ajoutée par traitements et salaires unitaire |
| Operatives as a percent of engaged......... | 83.7 | 84.6 | 92.8 | 85.7 | 100.0 | 50.0 | 50.0 | 85.7 | ... | Ouvriers en pourcentage des personnes occupées |
| Average man-hours per operative........ | 2.14 | 1.95 | 2.23 | 2.67 | 2.00 | 3.00 | 2.00 | 2.50 | ... | Heures de travail: moyenne par ouvrier |
| Wages and salaries per thousand operative man-hours.. | 0.36 | 0.35 | 0.31 | 0.38 | 0.50 | 0.33 | 0.50 | 0.47 | 1.00 | Traitements et salaires par millier d'heures de travail d'ouvrier |

# PARAGUAY

## Gross Domestic Product

Estimates of the expenditure on and the industrial origin of the gross domestic product are presented in Table 1. This table has been compiled from data supplied by the Departamento de Estudios Económicos, Banco Central del Paraguay in response to the United Nations national accounts questionnaire.

Further information concerning concepts, definitions and primary sources is published by the Banco in *Cuentas Nacionales del Paraguay 1956 y 1957*, (Asunción 1959).

## Characteristics and Structure of Industrial Activity

The data shown in Tables 2 and 3 are derived from the results of Paraguay's First Industrial Census carried out and published by the Ministerio de Industria y Comercio in *Premier Censo Industrial*, Asunción, 1958. The data shown in Tables 4 and 5 are derived from the results of Paraguay's Second Industrial Census—Encuesta Industrial, 1958—carried out by the Ministerio de Industria y Comercio and published in summary form by the Dirección General de Estadística y Censos on pages 57 to 80 of the *Boletín Estadístico del Paraguay, abril 1960*.

Although in principle, for the First Industrial Census in 1955, all establishments, regardless of size, which were engaged in industrial activity during 1955 were to be included in the census; the coverage is in fact incomplete, particularly for the smaller establishments, because of non-response. In the case of manufacturing about 88% of the questionnaires sent out were completed and returned.

Again in 1958, in principle, all industrial establishments which were operating during 1958, regardless of size, were to be included in the Second Industrial Census. In fact, however, coverage was incomplete because of non-response; and the data published in Tables 4 and 5 are selected results of the census edited for publication by the Dirección General de Estadística y Censos.

The definitions of the items of data collected in the censuses are consistent with the International Standards in Basic Industrial Statistics. Value added is valued at market prices. In 1955 the capacity of installed power equipment is the sum of the horsepower of all prime movers connected directly to machinery other than generators and the horsepower of all electric motors.

## Produit intérieur brut

Les estimations des dépenses imputées au produit intérieur brut et des composantes du produit intérieur brut ventilées suivant le secteur d'activité industrielle sont reproduites au tableau 1. Ce tableau a été construit à partir de données fournies par le Departamento de Estudios Económicos, Banco Central del Paraguay, dans sa réponse au questionnaire de l'O.N.U. relatif aux comptes nationaux.

Plus amples détails concernant les concepts, définitions et sources principales sont fournis par la Banco dans *Cuentas Nacionales del Paraguay 1956 y 1957*, (Asunción 1959).

## Caractéristiques et structure de l'activité industrielle

Les données reproduites au tableau 3 et 4 sont tirées des résultats du premier recensement industriel du Paraguay exécuté et publiés par le Ministerio de Industria y Comercio dans *Premier Censo Industrial*, Asunción, 1958. Les données des tableaux 5 et 6 sont tirées des résultats du second recensement industriel du Paraguay — Encuesta Industrial, 1958 — exécuté par le Ministerio de Industria y Comercio et publiés sous une forme sommaire par la Dirección General de Estadística y Censos aux pages 57 à 80 du *Boletín Estadístico del Paraguay — abril 1960*.

Quoique, en principe, pour le premier recensement en 1955, tous les établissements, quelle que soit leur dimension, qui exerçaient une activité industrielle durant 1955 devaient être recensés, le champ de couverture est en fait incomplet, en particulier en ce qui concerne les petits établissements, à cause des non-réponses. Dans le cas des industries manufacturières, 88% à peu près des questionnaires distribués ont été remplis et renvoyés.

De même en 1958, en principe, tous les établissements industriels, quelle que soit leur taille, devaient être inclus dans le second recensement industriel. En fait, cependant, le champ couvert était incomplet, à cause des non-réponses; et les données publiées aux tableaux 5 et 6 sont des résultats sélectionnés du recensement en vue d'être publiés par la Dirección General de Estadística y Censos.

Les définitions des rubriques figurant sur les questionnaires sont conformes aux Normes internationales relatives aux statistiques industrielles de base. La valeur ajoutée est comptée aux prix du marché. En 1955 la puissance installée est égale au nombre de chevaux-vapeur de tous les moteurs primaires entraînant directement des machines autres que des générateurs et de tous les moteurs électriques.

# 1. THE GROSS DOMESTIC PRODUCT
## LE PRODUIT INTERIEUR BRUT

Million Guaraníes                                    Millions de guaraníes

## A. Expenditure on the Gross Domestic Product at Market Prices
### Dépenses relatives au produit intérieur brut aux prix du marché

| Item of data and year<br>Rubrique et année | Total | Consumption<br>Consommation | | Gross Domestic Capital Formation<br>Formation brute de capital intérieur | | Net exports of goods and services<br>Exportations nettes de biens et de services | |
| --- | --- | --- | --- | --- | --- | --- | --- |
| | | Total | Government<br>Etat | Total | Fixed<br>Fixe | Exports<br>less imports<br>Exportations<br>moins<br>importations | Exports<br>Exportations |
| *a.* At Current Prices — Aux prix courants | | | | | | | |
| Absolute figures — Chiffres absolus | | | | | | | |
| 1951 | 2 384 | 2 115 | 110 | ... | 208 | 61 | ... |
| 1952 | 4 823 | 4 476 | 302 | ... | 538 | −191 | ... |
| 1953 | 7 511 | 7 331 | 408 | ... | 796 | −616 | ... |
| 1954 | 9 900 | 9 109 | 630 | ... | 1 128 | −337 | ... |
| 1955 | 12 311 | 10 913 | 837 | ... | 1 196 | 202 | ... |
| 1956 | 15 762 | 14 029 | 1 242 | ... | 1 266 | 467 | ... |
| 1957 | 19 146 | 18 722 | 1 790 | ... | 1 715 | −1 291 | ... |
| 1958 | 21 220 | 20 101 | 2 154 | ... | 2 749 | −1 630 | ... |
| 1959 | 23 460 | 22 367 | 2 632 | ... | 1 847 | −754 | ... |
| 1960 | 25 222 | 24 396 | 2 905 | ... | 2 413 | −1 587 | ... |
| 1961 | 28 746 | 28 225 | 3 262 | ... | 2 340 | −1 819 | ... |
| Percentage distribution of average annual expenditure — Distribution en pourcentage des dépenses annuelles moyennes | | | | | | | |
| 1953 | 100.0 | 97.6 | 5.4 | ... | 10.6 | −8.2 | ... |
| 1954 | 100.0 | 92.0 | 6.4 | ... | 11.4 | −3.4 | ... |
| 1958 | 100.0 | 94.7 | 10.2 | ... | 13.0 | −7.7 | ... |
| 1960 | 100.0 | 96.7 | 11.5 | ... | 9.6 | −6.3 | ... |
| *b.* At Prices of 1956 — Aux prix de 1956 | | | | | | | |
| Absolute figures — Chiffres absolus | | | | | | | |
| 1951 | 14 900 | 13 220 | 687 | ... | 1 297 | 383 | ... |
| 1952 | 11 849 | 10 996 | 741 | ... | 1 322 | −469 | ... |
| 1953 | 14 330 | 13 986 | 779 | ... | 1 519 | −1 175 | ... |
| 1954 | 15 454 | 14 219 | 982 | ... | 1 760 | −525 | ... |
| 1955 | 16 704 | 14 808 | 1 136 | ... | 1 623 | 273 | ... |
| 1956 | 15 762 | 14 029 | 1 242 | ... | 1 266 | 467 | ... |
| 1957 | 16 434 | 16 070 | 1 536 | ... | 1 472 | −1 108 | ... |
| 1958 | 16 921 | 16 028 | 1 717 | ... | 2 192 | −1 299 | ... |
| 1959 | 15 116 | 14 412 | 1 696 | ... | 1 190 | −486 | ... |
| 1960 | 15 231 | 14 732 | 1 754 | ... | 1 457 | −958 | ... |
| 1961 | 15 263 | 15 340 | 1 773 | ... | 1 272 | −989 | ... |
| Percentage distribution of average annual expenditure — Distribution en pourcentage des dépenses annuelles moyennes | | | | | | | |
| 1953 | 100.0 | 97.6 | 5.4 | ... | 10.6 | −8.2 | ... |
| 1954 | 100.0 | 92.0 | 6.4 | ... | 11.4 | −3.4 | ... |
| 1958 | 100.0 | 94.7 | 10.1 | ... | 13.0 | −7.7 | .. |
| 1960 | 100.0 | 96.7 | 11.5 | ... | 9.6 | −6.3 | ... |
| Average annual rate of growth — Taux annuel moyen d'accroissement | | | | | | | |
| 1954−1958 | 2.3 | 3.0 | 15.0 | ... | 5.6 | 25.4 | ... |
| 1958−1960 | −4.9 | −4.1 | 1.1 | ... | −18.4 | 14.2 | ... |

## B. The Gross Domestic Product at Market Prices According to Origin
### Origine par secteur d'activité du produit intérieur brut aux prix du marché

| Item of data and year<br>Rubrique et année | Total | Agricultural sector<br>Secteur agricole | Industrial Sector — Secteur Industriel | | | | Transportation and communication<br>Transport et communication | Other sectors<br>Autres secteurs |
|---|---|---|---|---|---|---|---|---|
| | | | Total | Mining and Manufacturing<br>Industries extractives et manufacturières | Construction<br>Bâtiment et travaux publics | Electricity<br>Electricité | | |
| ISIC — CITI | 0–9 | 0 | 1–4, 511 | 1–3 | 4 | 511 | 7 | 512–522, 6, 8–9 |
| | | | | a. At Current Prices — Aux prix courants | | | | |
| **Absolute figures — Chiffres absolus** | | | | | | | | |
| 1954 | 9 901 | 4 380 | 1 374 | 1 237 | 103 | 34 | 173 | 3 974 |
| 1955 | 12 311 | 5 679 | 1 552 | 1 392 | 106 | 54 | 218 | 4 862 |
| 1956 | 15 762 | 7 096 | 2 213 | 2 006 | 126 | 81 | 278 | 6 175 |
| 1957 | 19 146 | 8 177 | 2 950 | 2 698 | 151 | 101 | 314 | 7 705 |
| 1958 | 21 219 | 8 885 | 3 337 | 3 011 | 192 | 134 | 357 | 8 640 |
| 1959 | 23 461 | 9 271 | 3 667 | 3 313 | 181 | 173 | 380 | 10 143 |
| 1960 | 25 223 | 10 084 | 3 983 | 3 505 | 188 | 290 | 414 | 10 742 |
| 1961 | 28 746 | 11 028 | 4 566 | 4 022 | 235 | 309 | 519 | 12 633 |
| **Percentage distribution according to sector— Distribution en pourcentage par secteur** | | | | | | | | |
| 1954 | 100.0 | 44.2 | 13.9 | 12.5 | 1.0 | 0.4 | 1.7 | 40.2 |
| 1958 | 100.0 | 41.8 | 15.7 | 14.2 | 0.9 | 0.6 | 1.7 | 40.8 |
| 1960 | 100.0 | 39.9 | 15.8 | 13.9 | 0.8 | 1.1 | 1.7 | 42.6 |
| | | | | b. At Prices of 1956 — Aux prix de 1956 | | | | |
| **Absolute figures — Chiffres absolus** | | | | | | | | |
| 1954 | 15 455 | 6 843 | 2 143 | 1 930 | 161 | 52 | 270 | 6 199 |
| 1955 | 16 734 | 7 706 | 2 106 | 1 889 | 144 | 73 | 296 | 6 626 |
| 1956 | 15 762 | 7 096 | 2 213 | 2 006 | 126 | 81 | 278 | 6 175 |
| 1957 | 16 434 | 7 019 | 2 532 | 2 316 | 130 | 86 | 270 | 6 613 |
| 1958 | 16 921 | 7 086 | 2 661 | 2 401 | 153 | 107 | 284 | 6 890 |
| 1959 | 15 116 | 5 973 | 2 363 | 2 135 | 117 | 111 | 245 | 6 535 |
| 1960 | 15 231 | 6 089 | 2 406 | 2 117 | 114 | 175 | 250 | 6 486 |
| 1961 | 15 623 | 5 984 | 2 481 | 2 186 | 127 | 168 | 282 | 6 876 |
| **Percentage distribution according to sector— Distribution en pourcentage par secteur** | | | | | | | | |
| 1954 | 100.0 | 44.2 | 13.9 | 12.5 | 1.1 | 0.3 | 1.7 | 40.2 |
| 1958 | 100.0 | 41.9 | 15.7 | 14.2 | 0.9 | 0.6 | 1.7 | 40.7 |
| 1960 | 100.0 | 39.9 | 15.8 | 13.9 | 0.8 | 1.1 | 1.7 | 42.6 |
| **Average annual rate of growth—Taux annuel moyen d'accroissement** | | | | | | | | |
| 1954–1958 | 2.3 | 0.9 | 5.6 | 5.6 | −1.3 | 19.8 | 1.3 | 2.7 |
| 1958–1960 | −5.1 | −7.3 | −4.9 | −6.1 | −13.7 | 27.9 | −6.2 | −3.0 |

## 2. CHARACTERISTICS OF ESTABLISHMENTS ENGAGED IN MANUFACTURING ACTIVITY
## CARACTERISTIQUES DES ETABLISSEMENTS EXERÇANT UNE ACTIVITE MANUFACTURIERE
### 1955

Number of establishments in units; value added and wages and salaries in million Guaraníes; number of engaged, employees and operatives in thousands; energy consumed in thousand metric tons of coal equivalents; electricity consumed in million KWH; capacity of installed power equipment in thousand horsepower; value added per engaged and wages and salaries per employee and per operative in thousand Guaraníes; energy consumed per engaged and per operative in metric tons of coal equivalents; electricity consumed per engaged and per operative in thousand KWH; capacity of installed power equipment per engaged and per operative in horsepower.

Nombre d'établissements en unités; valeur ajoutée et traitements et salaires en millions de Guaraníes; nombre de personnes occupées, de salariés et d'ouvriers en milliers; énergie consommée en milliers de tonnes métriques d'équivalent charbon; électricité consommée en millions de kWh; puissance installée en milliers de chevaux-vapeur; valeur ajoutée par personne occupée et traitements et salaires par salarié et par ouvrier en milliers de Guaraníes; énergie consommée par personne occupée et par ouvrier en tonnes métriques d'équivalent charbon; électricité consommée par personne occupée et par ouvrier en milliers de kWh; puissance installée par personne occupée et par ouvrier en chevaux-vapeur.

| Item of data | Manufacturing[3] Industries manufacturières[3] | Food beverages and tobacco[1] Industries alimentaires, boissons. tabac[1] | Textiles | Clothing, footwear and made-up textiles Articles d'habillement, chaussures et ouvrages en tissu | Wood products and furniture Bois et meubles | Paper and paper products Papier et ouvrages en papier | Printing and publishing Imprimerie et édition | Leather and leather products except wearing apparel Cuir et articles en cuir, à l'exclusion des articles d'habillement | Rubber products Ouvrages en caoutchouc | Chemicals and chemical, petroleum and coal products[2] Produits chimiques et dérivés du pétrole et du charbon[2] | Non-metallic mineral products Produits minéraux non métalliques | Metal products Ouvrages en métaux | Other manufacturing Autres industries manufacturières | Rubrique |
|---|---|---|---|---|---|---|---|---|---|---|---|---|---|---|
| ISIC | 2–3 | 20–22 | 23 | 24 | 25–26 | 27 | 28 | 29 | 30 | 31–32 | 33 | 35–38 | 39 | CITI |
| _a. Absolute Figures — Chiffres absolus_ | | | | | | | | | | | | | | |
| Number of establishments | 2 723 | 950 | 28 | 431 | 352 | 3 | 37 | 108 | 15 | 118 | 367 | 261 | 53 | Nombre d'établissements |
| Value added | 1 594.8 | 568.0 | 256.5 | 106.6 | 106.6 | 2.4 | 56.3 | 53.8 | 4.3 | 298.8 | 73.3 | 59.6 | 8.6 | Valeur ajoutée |
| Number of engaged (During second half of June) | 34.3 | 11.4 | 2.9 | 3.0 | 2.9 | 0.1 | 0.7 | 0.7 | 0.1 | 8.1 | 2.4 | 1.8 | 0.2 | Nombre de personnes occupées (pendant la deuxième quinzaine de juin) |
| Number of employees (During second half of June) | 29.9 | 9.4 | 2.9 | 2.4 | 2.4 | 0.1 | 0.6 | 0.6 | 0.1 | 7.9 | 1.9 | 1.5 | 0.1 | Nombre de salariés (pendant la deuxième quinzaine de juin) |
| Wages and salaries paid | 560.5 | 158.7 | 70.1 | 29.0 | 40.1 | 1.7 | 17.0 | 12.3 | 0.9 | 168.1 | 25.2 | 35.4 | 2.0 | Traitements et salaires payés |
| Number of operatives (During second half of June) | 26.3 | 8.3 | 2.5 | 2.2 | 2.2 | — | 0.4 | 0.5 | — | 7.0 | 1.8 | 1.3 | 0.1 | Nombre d'ouvriers (pendant la deuxième quinzaine de juin) |
| Wages and salaries paid to operatives | 446.9 | 116.7 | 51.6 | 26.1 | 34.6 | 1.7 | 12.4 | 9.9 | 0.8 | 140.1 | 22.7 | 28.7 | 1.6 | Traitements et salaires payés aux ouvriers |
| Energy consumed | 168.2 | 94.1 | 5.6 | — | 8.8 | — | 0.2 | 2.0 | 0.1 | 10.0 | 41.9 | 5.5 | — | Energie consommée |
| Electricity consumed | 29.9 | 11.0 | 6.6 | 0.1 | 0.6 | — | 0.2 | 0.1 | 0.1 | 8.5 | 2.3 | 0.4 | — | Electricité consommée |
| Capacity of installed power equipment (31.XII.1955) | 43.9 | 16.6 | 5.2 | 0.3 | 5.9 | 0.3 | 0.3 | 0.6 | 0.1 | 9.0 | 4.2 | 1.4 | — | Puissance installée (31.XII.1955) |
| _b. Structure_ | | | | | | | | | | | | | | |
| Distribution in percent of: Value added | 100.0 | 35.6 | 16.1 | 6.7 | 6.7 | 0.1 | 3.6 | 3.3 | 0.3 | 18.7 | 4.6 | 3.7 | 0.6 | Répartition en pourcentage: De la valeur ajoutée |
| Number of engaged | 100.0 | 33.2 | 8.4 | 8.8 | 8.4 | 0.3 | 2.1 | 2.0 | 0.3 | 23.6 | 7.0 | 5.3 | 0.6 | Du nombre de personnes occupées |
| Per person engaged: Value added | 46.5 | 49.8 | 88.4 | 35.5 | 36.8 | 24.0 | 80.4 | 76.8 | 43.0 | 36.9 | 30.5 | 33.1 | 43.0 | Par personne occupée: Valeur ajoutée |
| Energy consumed | 4.90 | 8.25 | 1.93 | — | 3.03 | — | 0.28 | 2.86 | 1.00 | 1.23 | 17.46 | 3.06 | — | Energie consommée |
| Electricity consumed | 0.9 | 1.0 | 2.3 | — | 0.2 | — | 0.3 | 0.1 | 1.0 | 1.0 | 1.0 | 0.2 | — | Electricité consommée |
| Capacity of installed power equipment | 1.28 | 1.46 | 1.79 | 0.10 | 2.03 | 3.00 | 0.43 | 0.86 | 1.00 | 1.11 | 1.75 | 0.78 | — | Puissance installée |
| Employees as a percent of engaged | 87.2 | 82.4 | 100.0 | 80.0 | 82.8 | 100.0 | 85.7 | 85.7 | 100.0 | 97.5 | 79.2 | 83.3 | 50.0 | Salariés en pourcentage des personnes occupées |
| Value added per unit of wages and salaries | 2.84 | 3.58 | 3.66 | 3.68 | 2.66 | 1.41 | 3.31 | 4.37 | 4.78 | 1.78 | 2.91 | 1.68 | 4.30 | Valeur ajoutée par traitements et salaires unitaire |
| Operatives as a percent of employees | 88.0 | 88.3 | 86.2 | 91.7 | 91.7 | — | 66.7 | 83.3 | — | 88.6 | 94.7 | 86.7 | 100.0 | Ouvriers en pourcentage des salariés |
| Wages and salaries per employee | 18.7 | 16.9 | 24.2 | 12.1 | 16.7 | 17.0 | 28.3 | 20.5 | 9.0 | 21.3 | 13.3 | 23.6 | 20.0 | Traitements et salaires par salarié |
| Per operative: Wages and salaries | 16.99 | 14.06 | 20.64 | 11.86 | 15.73 | — | 31.00 | 19.80 | — | 20.01 | 12.61 | 22.08 | 16.00 | Par ouvrier: Traitements et salaires |
| Energy consumed | 6.40 | 11.34 | 2.24 | — | 4.00 | — | 0.50 | 4.00 | — | 1.43 | 23.28 | 4.23 | — | Energie consommée |
| Electricity consumed | 1.14 | 1.32 | 2.64 | 0.04 | 0.27 | — | 0.50 | 0.20 | — | 1.21 | 1.28 | 0.31 | — | Electricité consommée |
| Capacity of installed power equipment | 1.67 | 2.00 | 2.08 | 0.14 | 2.68 | — | 0.75 | 1.20 | — | 1.28 | 2.33 | 1.08 | — | Puissance installée |

[1] Excludes abattoirs.
[2] Production of essential oils is mainly excluded.
[3] Excludes Basic metals (ISIC major group 34).

[1] Non compris les abattoirs.
[2] Non compris la majeure partie de la production des huiles essentielles.
[3] Non compris Métallurgie de base (CITI 34).

## 3. FUELS AND ELECTRICITY CONSUMED BY ESTABLISHMENTS ENGAGED IN MANUFACTURING ACTIVITY
### CONSOMMATION DE COMBUSTIBLES ET D'ELECTRICITE PAR LES ETABLISSEMENTS EXERÇANT UNE ACTIVITE MANUFACTURIERE
#### 1955

### A. Percentage Distribution of Purchased Energy Consumed According to Source
### Distribution en pourcentage, de l'énergie achetée et consommée suivant la source

Quantities in thousand metric tons of coal equivalents.   Quantités en milliers de tonnes métriques d'équivalent charbon.

| Item of data | Manufacturing / Industries manufacturières | Food, beverages and tobacco [1] / Industries alimentaires, boissons, tabac [1] | Textiles | Clothing, footwear and made-up textiles / Articles d'habillement, chaussures et ouvrages en tissu | Wood products and furniture / Bois et meubles | Paper and paper products / Papier et ouvrages en papier | Printing and publishing / Imprimerie et édition | Leather and leather products except wearing apparel / Cuir et articles en cuir, à l'exclusion des articles d'habillement | Rubber products / Ouvrages en caoutchouc | Chemicals and chemical, petroleum and coal products [2] / Produits chimiques et dérivés du pétrole et du charbon [2] | Non-metallic mineral products / Produits minéraux non métalliques | Basic metals / Métallurgie de base | Metal products / Ouvrages en métaux | Other manufacturing / Autres industries manufacturières | Rubrique |
|---|---|---|---|---|---|---|---|---|---|---|---|---|---|---|---|
| ISIC | 2–3 | 20–22 | 23 | 24 | 25–26 | 27 | 28 | 29 | 30 | 31–32 | 33 | 34 | 35–38 | 39 | CITI |
| **Total energy consumed:** | | | | | | | | | | | | | | | Energie totale consommée: |
| Quantity | 168.4 | 94.1 | 5.6 | — | 8.8 | — | 0.2 | 2.0 | 0.1 | 10.0 | 41.9 | 0.2 | 5.5 | — | Quantité |
| Percent of total in specified industry | 100.0 | 55.7 | 3.4 | — | 5.2 | — | 0.2 | 1.2 | 0.1 | 5.9 | 24.9 | 0.1 | 3.3 | — | Pourcentage du total par industrie indiquée |
| **Percent consumed as:** | | | | | | | | | | | | | | | Pourcentage consommé comme: |
| Coal [3] | 1.5 | 0.2 | 0.2 | — | 0.3 | — | 1.1 | 0.3 | 3.0 | 4.0 | 3.2 | 63.1 | 10.4 | — | Charbon [3] |
| Wood | 91.4 | 95.9 | 69.2 | — | 95.0 | — | 77.2 | 90.4 | 61.1 | 75.6 | 88.3 | 33.0 | 81.6 | — | Bois |
| Refined oil fuels | 6.2 | 3.0 | 24.2 | — | 4.1 | — | 10.1 | 8.4 | 29.0 | 17.8 | 8.5 | 3.3 | 7.1 | — | Pétrole raffiné |
| Electricity purchased | 0.9 | 0.9 | 6.4 | — | 0.6 | — | 11.6 | 0.9 | 6.9 | 2.6 | — | 0.6 | 0.9 | — | Electricité achetée |

For footnotes see end of table.   Pour les notes, voir au bas du tableau.

### B. Quantity and Value of Purchased Fuels Consumed and Electricity Purchased, Produced and Sold
### Volume et valeur des combustibles achetés et consommés, de l'électricité achetée produite et vendue

Coal, and refined oil fuels in thousand metric tons; electricity in million KWH; wood in thousand cubic metres; value in million guaraníes.   Charbon, et pétrole raffiné en milliers de tonnes métriques; électricité en millions de kWh; bois en milliers de mètres cubes; valeur en millions de guaraníes.

| Source of energy | Manufacturing / Industries manufacturières | Food beverages and tobacco / Industries alimentaires, boissons, tabac | Textiles | Clothing, footwear and made-up textiles / Articles d'habillement, chaussures et ouvrages en tissu | Wood products and furniture / Bois et meubles | Paper and paper products / Papier et ouvrages en papier | Printing and publishing / Imprimerie et édition | Leather and leather products except wearing apparel / Cuir et articles en cuir, à l'exclusion des articles d'habillement | Rubber products / Ouvrages en caoutchouc | Chemicals and chemical, petroleum and coal products / Produits chimiques et dérivés du pétrole et du charbon | Non-metallic mineral products / Produits minéraux non métalliques | Basic metals / Métallurgie de base | Metal products / Ouvrages en métaux | Other manufacturing / Autres industries manufacturières | Source d'énergie |
|---|---|---|---|---|---|---|---|---|---|---|---|---|---|---|---|
| ISIC | 2–3 | 20–22 | 23 | 24 | 25–26 | 27 | 28 | 29 | 30 | 31–32 | 33 | 34 | 35–38 | 39 | CITI |
| **Coal: [3]** | | | | | | | | | | | | | | | Charbon: [3] |
| Quantity | 2.6 | 0.2 | — | — | — | — | — | — | — | 0.4 | 1.3 | 0.1 | 0.6 | — | Quantité |
| Value | 4.1 | 0.3 | — | — | — | — | — | — | — | 0.7 | 1.6 | 0.5 | 1.0 | — | Valeur |
| **Refined oil fuels:** | | | | | | | | | | | | | | | Pétrole raffiné: |
| Quantity | 7.3 | 2.0 | 0.9 | — | 0.3 | — | — | 0.1 | — | 1.3 | 2.4 | — | 0.3 | — | Quantité |
| Value | 46.5 | 12.8 | 4.8 | 0.1 | 2.0 | 0.2 | 0.2 | 0.5 | 0.1 | 8.4 | 15.5 | — | 1.8 | 0.1 | Valeur |
| **Electricity** | | | | | | | | | | | | | | | Electricité |
| **Purchased:** | | | | | | | | | | | | | | | Achetée: |
| Quantity | 12.5 | 6.2 | 2.9 | 0.1 | 0.4 | — | 0.2 | 0.1 | 0.1 | 2.0 | 0.1 | — | 0.4 | — | Quantité |
| Value | 25.6 | 12.6 | 5.5 | 0.2 | 1.0 | — | 0.6 | 0.3 | 0.2 | 4.1 | 0.3 | — | 0.7 | 0.1 | Valeur |
| **Produced:** | | | | | | | | | | | | | | | Produite: |
| Quantity | 17.7 | 5.0 | 3.9 | — | 0.2 | — | — | — | — | 6.4 | 2.2 | — | — | — | Quantité |
| **Sold:** | | | | | | | | | | | | | | | Vendue: |
| Quantity | 0.3 | 0.1 | 0.2 | — | | | | | | | | | | | Quantité |
| **Wood:** | | | | | | | | | | | | | | | Bois: |
| Quantity | 752 | 442 | 19 | — | 41 | — | 1 | 9 | — | 37 | 181 | — | 22 | — | Quantité |
| Value | 64.1 | 40.7 | 4.4 | — | 1.7 | — | 0.2 | 1.1 | 0.1 | 3.0 | 10.9 | 0.1 | 1.9 | — | Valeur |

[1] Excludes abattoirs.
[2] Production of essential oils is mainly excluded.
[3] Includes some other solid fuels.

[1] Non compris les abattoirs.
[2] Non compris la majeure partie de la production des huiles essentielles.
[3] Y compris d'autres combustibles solides.

# 4. CHARACTERISTICS OF SELECTED MANUFACTURING ESTABLISHMENTS
## CARACTERISTIQUES DE QUELQUES ETABLISSEMENTS MANUFACTURIERS
### 1958

Number of establishments in units; value added and wages and salaries in million Guaraníes; number of engaged, employees and operatives in thousands; energy consumed in thousand metric tons of coal equivalents; value added per engaged and wages and salaries per employee and per operative in thousand Guaraníes; energy consumed per engaged and per operative in metric tons of coal equivalents.

Nombre d'établissements en unités; valeur ajoutée et traitements et salaires en millions de guaranies; nombre de personnes occupées, de salariés et d'ouvriers en milliers; énergie consommée en milliers de tonnes métriques d'équivalent charbon; valeur ajoutée par personne occupée et traitements et salaires par salarié et par ouvrier en milliers de guaranies; énergie consommée par personne occupée et par ouvrier en tonnes métriques d'équivalent charbon.

| Item of data | Manu-facturing [1] / Industries manufac-turières [1] | Food beverages and tobacco / Industries alimen-taires, boissons, tabac | Textiles | Wood products and furniture / Bois et meubles | Paper and paper products / Papier et ouvrages en papier | Printing and publish-ing / Im-primerie et édition | Leather and leather products except wearing apparel / Cuir et articles en cuir, à l'exclu-sion des articles d'habil-lement | Chemicals and chemical, petroleum and coal products / Produits chi-miques et dérivés du pétrole et du charbon | Non-metallic mineral products / Produits minéraux non métal-liques | Metal products / Ouvrages en métaux | Rubrique |
|---|---|---|---|---|---|---|---|---|---|---|---|
| ISIC | 2–3 | 20–22 | 23 | 25–26 | 27 | 28 | 29 | 31–32 | 33 | 35–38 | CITI |
| | | | | | *a. Absolute Figures — Chiffres absolus* | | | | | | |
| Number of establishments. | 720 | 296 | 25 | 179 | 1 | 35 | 77 | 82 | 9 | 16 | Nombre d'établissements |
| Value added.......... | 1 998.0 | 1 057.5 | 418.4 | 57.3 | 4.9 | 66.0 | 30.9 | 316.8 | 26.8 | 19.4 | Valeur ajoutée |
| Number of engaged.... | 19.4 | 6.7 | 2.3 | 1.8 | 0.1 | 0.7 | 0.6 | 6.1 | 0.7 | 0.4 | Nombre de personnes occupées |
| Employees: | | | | | | | | | | | Salariés: |
| Number............ | 18.6 | 6.4 | 2.3 | 1.7 | 0.1 | 0.6 | 0.5 | 5.9 | 0.7 | 0.4 | Nombre |
| Wages and salaries... | 910.8 | 352.0 | 132.2 | 69.8 | 2.5 | 30.5 | 22.7 | 258.6 | 26.7 | 15.8 | Traitements et salaires |
| Operatives: | | | | | | | | | | | Ouvriers: |
| Number............ | 15.6 | 5.5 | 2.0 | 1.4 | 0.1 | 0.4 | 0.4 | 5.0 | 0.6 | 0.2 | Nombre |
| Wages and salaries... | 669.5 | 264.5 | 88.6 | 56.7 | 2.1 | 16.9 | 15.4 | 196.3 | 18.4 | 10.6 | Traitements et salaires |
| Energy consumed...... | 79.3 | 56.5 | 2.4 | 0.7 | 1.0 | — | 1.2 | 3.4 | 14.0 | 0.1 | Energie consommée |
| | | | | | *b. Structure* | | | | | | |
| Distribution in percent of: | | | | | | | | | | | Distribution en pour-centage: |
| Value added........ | 100.0 | 52.9 | 20.9 | 2.9 | 0.2 | 3.3 | 1.6 | 15.8 | 1.4 | 1.0 | Valeur ajoutée |
| Number of engaged.. | 100.0 | 34.5 | 11.8 | 9.3 | 0.5 | 3.6 | 3.1 | 31.5 | 3.6 | 2.1 | Nombre de personnes occupées |
| Per person engaged: | | | | | | | | | | | Par personne occupée: |
| Value added........ | 103.0 | 157.8 | 181.9 | 31.8 | 49.0 | 94.3 | 51.5 | 51.9 | 38.3 | 48.5 | Valeur ajoutée |
| Energy consumed..... | 4.09 | 8.43 | 1.04 | 0.39 | 10.00 | — | 2.00 | 0.56 | 20.00 | 0.25 | Energie consommée |
| Employees as a percent of engaged......... | 95.9 | 95.5 | 100.0 | 94.4 | 100.0 | 85.7 | 83.3 | 96.7 | 100.0 | 100.0 | Salariés en pourcentage des personnes occupées |
| Value added per unit of wages and salaries. | 2.19 | 3.00 | 3.16 | 0.82 | 1.96 | 2.16 | 1.36 | 1.22 | 1.00 | 1.23 | Valeur ajoutée par traitements et salaires unitaires |
| Operatives as a percent of employees....... | 83.9 | 85.9 | 87.0 | 82.4 | 100.0 | 66.7 | 80.0 | 84.7 | 85.7 | 50.0 | Ouvriers en pourcentage des salariés |
| Wages and salaries per employee........ | 49.0 | 55.0 | 57.5 | 41.0 | 25.0 | 50.8 | 45.4 | 43.8 | 38.1 | 39.5 | Traitements et salaires par salarié |
| Per operative: | | | | | | | | | | | Par ouvrier: |
| Wages and salaries... | 42.92 | 48.09 | 44.30 | 40.50 | 21.00 | 42.25 | 38.50 | 39.26 | 30.67 | 53.00 | Traitements et salaires |
| Energy consumed..... | 5.08 | 10.27 | 1.20 | 0.50 | 10.00 | — | 3.00 | 0.68 | 23.33 | 0.50 | Energie consommée |

[1] Excluding Clothing, footwear and made-up textiles (ISIC Major group 24), Rubber products (ISIC Major group 30), Basic metals (ISIC Major group 34) and Other manufacturing (ISIC Major group 39).

[1] Non compris Articles d'habillement, chaussures et ouvrages en tissus (CITI classe 24), Ouvrages en caoutchouc (CITI classe 30), Métallurgie de base (CITI classe 34) et Autres industries manufacturières (CITI classe 39).

## 5. PURCHASED FUELS AND ELECTRICITY CONSUMED, SELECTED ESTABLISHMENTS ENGAGED IN MANUFACTURING ACTIVITY

### CONSOMMATION DE COMBUSTIBLES ET D'ELECTRICITE ACHETES, QUELQUES ETABLISSEMENTS EXERÇANT UNE ACTIVITE MANUFACTURIERE

### 1958

### A. Percentage Distribution of Purchased Energy Consumed According to Source

### Distribution en pourcentage de l'énergie achetée et consommée suivant la source

Quantities in thousand metric tons of coal equivalents.     Quantités en milliers de tonnes métriques d'équivalent charbon

| Item of data | Manufacturing<br>Industries manufacturières | Food beverages and tobacco<br>Industries alimentaires, boissons, tabac | Textiles | Wood products and furniture<br>Bois et meubles | Paper and paper products<br>Papier et ouvrages en papier | Printing and publishing<br>Imprimerie et édition | Leather and leather products except wearing apparel<br>Cuir et articles en cuir, à l'exclusion des articles d'habillement | Chemicals and chemical, petroleum and coal products<br>Produits chimiques et dérivés du pétrole et du charbon | Non-metallic mineral products<br>Produits minéraux non métalliques | Metal products<br>Ouvrages en métaux | Rubrique |
|---|---|---|---|---|---|---|---|---|---|---|---|
| ISIC | 2–3 | 20–22 | 23 | 25–26 | 27 | 28 | 29 | 31–32 | 33 | 35–38 | CITI |
| Total energy consumed:<br>Quantity | 79.3 | 56.5 | 2.4 | 0.7 | 1.0 | — | 1.2 | 3.4 | 14.0 | 0.1 | Energie totale consommée:<br>Quantité |
| Percent of total in specified industry | 100.0 | 71.2 | 3.1 | 0.9 | 1.2 | — | 1.5 | 4.3 | 17.6 | 0.2 | Pourcentage du total par industrie indiquée |
| Percent consumed as:<br>Coal | 0.1 | 0.1 | — | — | — | — | — | — | — | 24.1 | Pourcentage consommé comme:<br>Charbon |
| Wood | 85.8 | 93.2 | 62.5 | — | 48.1 | — | 84.7 | 45.7 | 76.8 | 31.0 | Bois |
| Refined oil fuels | 7.4 | 3.3 | 14.8 | 56.5 | — | — | 14.2 | 1.6 | 21.6 | 39.1 | Pétrole raffiné |
| Electricity | 3.6 | 2.2 | 18.0 | 12.1 | — | — | 1.1 | 25.2 | 1.6 | 5.8 | Electricité |
| Other fuels | 3.1 | 1.2 | 4.7 | 31.4 | 51.9 | — | — | 27.5 | — | — | Autres combustibles |

For footnotes see end of table.                              Pour les notes, voir au bas du tableau.

### B. Quantity and Value of Purchased Fuels Consumed and Electricity Purchased

### Volume et valeur des combustibles achetés et consommés, et de l'électricité achetée

Coal and refined oil fuels in thousand metric tons; electricity in million KWH; wood in thousand cubic metres; other fuels in thousand metric tons of coal equivalents; value in million Guaraníes.

Charbon et pétrole raffiné en milliers de tonnes métriques; électricité en millions de kWh; bois en milliers de mètres cubes; autres combustibles en milliers de tonnes métriques d'équivalent houille; valeur en millions de guaraníes.

| Source of energy | Manufacturing<br>Industries manufacturières | Food beverages and tobacco<br>Industries alimentaires, boissons, tabac | Textiles | Wood products and furniture<br>Bois et meubles | Paper and paper products<br>Papier et ouvrages en papier | Printing and publishing<br>Imprimerie et édition | Leather and leather products except wearing apparel<br>Cuir et articles en cuir, à l'exclusion des articles d'habillement | Chemicals and chemical, petroleum and coal products<br>Produits chimiques et dérivés du pétrole et du charbon | Non-metallic mineral products<br>Produits minéraux non métalliques | Metal products<br>Ouvrages en métaux | Source d'énergie |
|---|---|---|---|---|---|---|---|---|---|---|---|
| ISIC | 1–2 | 20–22 | 23 | 25–26 | 27 | 28 | 29 | 31–32 | 33 | 35–38 | CITI |
| Coal:<br>Quantity | 0.1 | 0.1 | — | — | — | — | — | — | — | — | Charbon:<br>Quantité |
| Value | 0.3 | 0.2 | — | — | — | — | — | — | — | 0.1 | Valeur |
| Refined oil fuels:<br>Quantity | 3.8 | 1.2 | 0.2 | 0.3 | — | — | 0.1 | — | 2.0 | — | Pétrole raffiné:<br>Quantité |
| Value | 32.3 | 11.1 | 1.7 | 0.9 | — | — | 0.3 | 0.2 | 18.1 | — | Valeur |
| Electricity:<br>Quantity | 22.7 | 9.7 | 3.5 | 0.7 | — | 0.2 | 0.1 | 6.8 | 1.7 | — | Electricité:<br>Quantité |
| Value | 83.4 | 32.6 | 11.8 | 2.6 | — | 0.7 | 0.1 | 27.9 | 7.5 | 0.2 | Valeur |
| Wood:<br>Quantity | 333.2 | 258.0 | 7.5 | — | 2.2 | — | 5.0 | 7.6 | 52.8 | 0.1 | Bois:<br>Quantité |
| Value | 57.5 | 43.4 | 1.6 | — | 0.4 | — | 1.2 | 5.3 | 5.6 | — | Valeur |
| Other fuels:<br>Quantity | 2.4 | 0.7 | 0.1 | 0.2 | 0.5 | — | — | 0.9 | — | — | Autres combustibles:<br>Quantité |
| Value | 16.0 | 1.1 | 0.3 | 1.6 | 0.4 | — | — | 12.6 | — | — | Valeur |

[1] Excluding Clothing, footwear and made-up textiles (ISIC Major group 24), Rubber products (ISIC Major group 30), Basic metals (ISIC Major group 34) and Other manufacturing (ISIC Major group 39).

[1] Non compris Articles d'habillement, chaussures et ouvrages en tissus (CITI classe 24), Ouvrages en caoutchouc (CITI classe 30), Métallurgie de base (CITI classe 34) et Autres industries manufacturières (CITI classe 39).

## Gross Domestic Product and the Gross Domestic Fixed Capital Formation

Estimates of the expenditure on and the industrial origin of the gross domestic product, and of the industrial composition of the gross fixed capital formation, are presented in Table 1. This table has been computed from data supplied by the Dirección Nacional de Estadística y Censos, Ministerio de Hacienda y Comercio of Peru in response to the United Nations national accounts questionnaire. The official estimates are issued in *Renta Nacional del Perú, 1942-1958*, published by the Banco Central de Reserva del Perú 1960; and in *Boletín de Estadística Peruana*, published by the Dirección Nacional de Estadística, No. 4, 1960, Lima.

## Index Numbers of Industrial Production

The index numbers of production shown in Table 2 are compiled on an ISIC basis by the Dirección Nacional de Estadística y Censos. The index numbers presented for the individual major groups and the total manufacturing activity for the years, 1948 to 1954, are taken from the *Annuario Estadístico del Perú, 1955,* published by the Ministerio de Haciendo y Comercio. The indexes for 1955 to 1959 in the same series are taken from *Estimaciones del Indice de Quantum de la Producción Industrial del Perú,* a paper presented by the Dirección Nacional de Estadística y Censos of Peru at a Seminar on Industrial Statistics held at Santiago Chile in October 1960. The indexes for the individual major groups and the total of mining activity for the years 1948, 1949 and 1960 have been obtained by correspondence with the Dirección Nacional de Estadística y Censos. The same series for the years, 1950-1959 are derived from the above-mentioned paper, *Estimaciones del Indice de Quantum de la Producción Industrial del Perú.*

The indexes are computed as base-weighted arithmetic averages of elementary series which relate either to quantities produced or to the imports of raw materials consumed. The elementary series are combined into index numbers for detailed categories of manufacturing by using as weights gross value of producción of the commodities for which they serve as indicators. These indexes are combined into index numbers for broader classes of industrial activity by the use of weights proportional to value added at market prices. In both cases the weights are derived from the results of the annual Census of Manufacturing for 1954.

The total index for mining and manufacturing activity combined is computed by the Statistical Office of the United Nations. The weights utilized are proportional to estimates of value added at market prices during 1953

## Produit intérieur brut et la formation brute de capital fixe intérieur

Des estimations du produit intérieur brut, de ses composantes par secteur d'activité industrielle et des éléments de la formation brute de capital fixe, sont reproduites au tableau 1. Ce tableau a été construit à partir de données fournies par la Dirección Nacional de Estadística y Censos, Ministerio de Hacienda y Comercio du Pérou en réponse au questionnaire de l'O.N.U. relatif aux comptes nationaux. Les estimations officielles paraissent dans *Renta Nacional del Perú, 1942-1958,* publié par la Banco Central de Reserva del Perú 1960; et dans *Boletín de Estadística Peruana,* publié par la Dirección Nacional de Estadística, No. 4, 1960, Lima.

## Indices de la production industrielle

Les indices de la production des industries manufacturières qui sont reproduits au tableau 2 sont établis sur la base de la CITI par la Dirección Nacional de Estadística y Censos. Les indices relatifs aux différentes classes et à l'ensemble de la branche industries manufacturières pour les années, 1948 à 1954, sont tirés de l'*Annuario Estadístico del Perú, 1955,* publié par le Ministerio de Hacienda y Comercio. Les indices pour 1955 à 1959 relatives aux mêmes séries sont tirés de *Estimaciones del Indice de Quantum de la Producción Industrial del Perú,* étude présentée par la Dirección Nacional de Estadística y Censos du Pérou lors d'un séminaire portant sur les statistiques industrielles organise à Santiago du Chili en octobre 1960. Les indices des diverses classes et de l'ensemble de la branche industries extractives pour les années 1948, 1949 et 1960 ont été obtenus par un échange de lettres avec la Dirección Nacional de Estadística y Censos. Les mêmes séries pour les années 1950-1959 ont été tirées de l'étude ci-dessus mentionnée, *Estimaciones del Indice de Quantum de la Producción Industrial del Perú.*

Les indices sont des moyennes arithmétiques pondérées (coefficients constants) de séries élémentaires correspondant soit aux quantités produites, soit au volume des importations des matières premières consommées. Ces séries élémentaires sont combinées en indices pour les diverses catégories d'industries manufacturières, la pondération se faisant au moyen de la valeur brute de la production des marchandises pour lesquelles elles servent d'indicateurs. On passe ensuite de ces indices de catégorie à des indices de subdivisions plus larges de l'activité économique en pondérant proportionnellement à la valeur ajoutée, aux prix du marché. Dans les deux cas, les poids sont tirés des résultats du recensement annuel des industries manufacturières pour 1954.

Les indices relatifs à l'ensemble des industries extractives et manufacturières combinées sont calculés par le Bureau de statistique de l'O.N.U. Les coefficients de pondération utilisés à cette fin sont proportionnels aux esti-

adjusted to 1954 by the use of the national index of industrial production for mining and manufacturing respectively.

### Index Numbers of Industrial Employment

The index numbers of industrial employment given in Table 3 have been based on data derived from a number of sources.

The index numbers for mining were computed by the Statistical Office of the United Nations from absolute figures of the monthly average of the number of employees obtained by correspondence with the Dirección Nacional de Estadística y Censos, Instituto Nacional de Planificación.

The index numbers for manufacturing are also calculated by the Statistical Office of the United Nations from absolute figures of the number of employees in registered industrial establishments, published in various editions of *Renta Nacional del Perú* by the Banco Central de Reserva del Perú. In principle, all manufacturing units except handicrafts are required to be registered but it is thought likely that many small establishemnts are not registered.

The index numbers of employment for mining and manufacturing combined were calculated by the United Nations Statistical Office. The weights utilized are proportional to estimates of the total number of engaged during 1953, in the case of indexes for the years 1939-1954, and during 1958 in the case of the indexes for 1955 and thereafter.

### Characteristics and Structure of Manufacturing Establishments

The data shown in Table 4 are derived from the results of the 1954 annual survey of manufacturing as published by the Subdirección de Industrias, Ministerio de Fomento y Obras Públicas, in *Estadística Industrial Año 1954 y Padrón de Industrias Manufactureras*. These annual surveys are intended to cover all units, regardless of size, which are inscribed in the register of manufacturing establishments. However, the coverage in 1954 was notably incomplete, especially among smaller establishments, either because of failure to register or because of nonresponse.

The data on number of establishments relate to those respondent units that were engaged in manufacturing during 1954. The data on number of engaged relate to persons engaged during the last pay period in November. The data on value added relate to the gross value, at market prices, of production during the year less the cost of raw materials consumed but are gross of the cost of the electricity and fuels consumed in this production.

mations de la valeur ajoutée aux prix du marché en 1953, ajustées à 1954 par le biais des indices nationaux de la production industrielle relatifs aux industries extractives et manufacturières respectivement.

### Indices de l'emploi industriel

Les indices de l'emploi industriel reproduits au tableau 3 ont été calculés d'après des sources variées.

Les indices relatifs aux industries extractives sont calculés par le Bureau de statistique de l'O.N.U. à partir des chiffres absolus relatifs à la moyenne mensuelle du nombre de salariés, obtenus par échange de correspondance avec la Dirección Nacional de Estadística y Censos, Instituto Nacional de Planificación.

Les indices relatifs à la branche "industries manufacturières" sont calculés également par le Bureau de statistique de l'O.N.U. à partir des chiffres absolus donnant le nombre de salariés appartenant aux établissements industriels enregistrés, publiés dans différents numéros de *Renta Nacional del Perú*, par la Banco Central de Reserva del Perú. En principe, toutes les unités manufacturières, à l'exclusion des unités artisanales sont tenues de se faire enregistrer, mais on est porté à croire que nombre de petits établissements ne l'ont pas été.

Les indices de l'emploi pour l'ensemble des industries extractives et manufacturières combinées sont calculés par le Bureau de statistique de l'O.N.U. Les coefficients de pondération utilisés sont proportionnels aux estimations relatives au total des personnes occupées en 1953, dans le cas des indices relatifs aux années 1939-1954, et en 1958 pour les indices relatifs à 1955 et aux années suivantes.

### Caractéristiques et structure des établissements manufacturiers

Les données du tableau 4 sont tirées des résultats de l'enquête annuelle de 1954 sur les industries manufacturières, publiés par la Subdirección de Industrias, Ministerio de Fomento y Obras Públicas, dans *Estadística Industrial Año 1954 y Padrón de Industrias Manufactureras*. Les enquêtes annuelles de ce genre portent en principe sur toutes les unités, quelle que soit leur dimension, qui figurent dans le répertoire des établissements manufacturiers. Cependant, l'enquête de 1954 était très incomplète, notamment en ce qui concerne les petits établissements, parce que ceux-ci ont omis de se faire enregistrer ou de répondre au questionnaire.

Le nombre d'établissements est celui des unités manufacturières qui étaient en activité en 1954 et qui ont répondu au questionnaire. Le nombre des personnes occupées est celui des personnes occupées pendant la dernière période de paie de novembre. Les chiffres de la valeur ajoutée représentent la valeur brute, aux prix du marché, de la production de l'année, déduction faite du coût des matières premières consommées, mais non du coût de l'électricité et des combustibles consommés pour cette production.

The data shown in Table 5 are derived from the 1958 industrial survey as published by the Subdirección de Industrias, Departamento de Estadística Industrial of the Ministerio de Fomento y Obras Publicas in *Informativo No. 1*. The survey, in principle, covered registered establishments with 5 or more employees or with a value of production of 100 000 Soles or more. The definitions of the items of data shown in Table 5 are identical with those for the same items in Table 4, and again the data relate to respondent units engaged in manufacturing.

Les données du tableau 5 sont tirées de l'enquête industrielle de 1958 publiée par la Subdirección de Industrias, Departamento de Estadística Industrial du Ministerio de Fomento y Obras Públicas dans *Informativo No 1*. L'enquête couvre en principe les établissements enregistrés, de 5 salariés ou plus ou justifiant d'une valeur de production de 100 000 sols ou plus. Les définitions des rubriques du tableau 5 sont identiques à celles des mêmes articles du tableau 4, et une fois de plus, les données concernent seulement les unités répondantes exerçant une activité manufacturière.

## 1. THE GROSS DOMESTIC PRODUCT AND THE GROSS DOMESTIC FIXED CAPITAL FORMATION
### PRODUIT INTERIEUR BRUT ET FORMATION BRUTE DE CAPITAL FIXE INTERIEUR

Million Soles          Millions de sols

### A. Expenditure on the Gross Domestic Product at Market Prices
### Dépenses relatives au produit intérieur brut aux prix du marché

| Item of data and year<br>Rubrique et année | Total | Consumption<br>Consommation | | Gross Domestic Capital Formation<br>Formation brute de capital intérieur | | Net exports of goods and services<br>Exportations nettes de biens et de services | |
|---|---|---|---|---|---|---|---|
| | | Total | Government<br>Etat | Total | Fixed<br>Fixe | Exports less imports [1]<br>Exportations moins importations [1] | Exports [1]<br>Exportations [1] |
| | | | | *a.* At Current Prices — Aux prix courants | | | |
| **Absolute figures — Chiffres absolus** | | | | | | | |
| 1950............... | 15 297 | 12 108 | 1 293 | 3 095 | 2 700 | 94 | 3 307 |
| 1951............... | 19 034 | 14 145 | 1 356 | 5 080 | 4 373 | −191 | 4 222 |
| 1952............... | 21 283 | 16 147 | 1 659 | 5 550 | 5 044 | −414 | 4 550 |
| 1953............... | 22 992 | 18 107 | 1 937 | 5 631 | 5 223 | −746 | 4 641 |
| 1954............... | 25 515 | 19 439 | 2 237 | 5 874 | 5 351 | 202 | 5 821 |
| 1955............... | 28 982 | 21 633 | 2 306 | 7 632 | 6 968 | −283 | 6 231 |
| 1956............... | 32 244 | 24 685 | 3 456 | 8 725 | 8 170 | −1 166 | 7 088 |
| 1957............... | 34 342 | 26 448 | 3 547 | 9 971 | 9 149 | −2 077 | 7 423 |
| 1958............... | 37 691 | 29 831 | 4 302 | 9 588 | 8 643 | −1 728 | 8 264 |
| 1959............... | 43 610 | 35 262 | 5 021 | 7 769 | 6 673 | 579 | 10 635 |
| **Percentage distribution of average annual expenditure — Distribution en pourcentage des dépenses annuelles moyennes** | | | | | | | |
| 1950–1959......... | 100.0 | 80.4 | 10.4 | 18.4 | 15.9 | 1.1 | 23.7 |
| 1950............... | 100.0 | 79.2 | 8.4 | 20.2 | 17.6 | 0.6 | 21.6 |
| 1953............... | 100.0 | 78.8 | 8.4 | 24.5 | 22.7 | −3.3 | 20.2 |
| 1954............... | 100.0 | 76.2 | 8.8 | 23.0 | 21.0 | 0.8 | 22.8 |
| 1958............... | 100.0 | 79.2 | 11.4 | 25.4 | 22.9 | −4.6 | 21.9 |

[1] Includes current transfers.      [1] Y compris les transferts courants.

## B. The Gross Domestic Product at Factor Cost According to Origin
### Origine par secteur d'activité du produit intérieur brut au coût des facteurs

| Item of data and year<br>Rubrique et année | Total | Agricultural sector<br>Secteur agricole | Mining<br>Industries extractives | Manufacturing and construction<br>Industries manufacturières; bâtiment et travaux publics | Transportation, communication, electricity, gas and water<br>Transports, communications, électricité, gaz et eau | Other sectors<br>Autres secteurs |
|---|---|---|---|---|---|---|
| ISIC — CITI | 0–9 | 0 | 1 | 2–4 | 5, 7 | 6, 8–9 |
| *a. At Current Prices — Aux prix courants* | | | | | | |
| **Absolute figures — Chiffres absolus** | | | | | | |
| 1950............ | 14 854 | 5 531 | 1 635 | 2 148 | 816 | 4 724 |
| 1951............ | 18 166 | 6 734 | 2 234 | 2 398 | 7 000 | 5 800 |
| 1952............ | 20 201 | 6 871 | 2 366 | 2 749 | 1 130 | 7 085 |
| 1953............ | 21 765 | 7 074 | 2 491 | 3 129 | 1 181 | 7 890 |
| 1954............ | 24 158 | 7 539 | 3 145 | 3 849 | 1 281 | 8 344 |
| 1955............ | 27 230 | 7 762 | 3 760 | 4 059 | 1 425 | 10 224 |
| 1956............ | 30 215 | 7 348 | 4 234 | 4 746 | 1 714 | 12 173 |
| 1957............ | 32 177 | 7 328 | 4 143 | 5 600 | 2 008 | 13 098 |
| 1958............ | 35 717 | 8 545 | 4 228 | 5 868 | 2 246 | 14 830 |
| 1959............ | 41 351 | 9 978 | 4 940 | 6 840 | 2 672 | 16 921 |
| **Percentage distribution according to sector— Distribution en pourcentage par secteur** | | | | | | |
| 1950 – 1959..... | 100.0 | 27.6 | 11.7 | 16.0 | 6.2 | 38.5 |
| 1950............ | 100.0 | 37.2 | 11.0 | 14.5 | 5.4 | 31.9 |
| 1953............ | 100.0 | 32.5 | 11.4 | 14.4 | 5.4 | 36.3 |
| 1954............ | 100.0 | 31.2 | 13.0 | 15.9 | 5.3 | 34.6 |
| 1958............ | 100.0 | 23.9 | 11.8 | 16.4 | 6.3 | 41.6 |

## C. Gross Domestic Fixed Capital Formation at Market Prices According to Purchasing Industry
### Formation brute de capital fixe intérieur aux prix du marché par secteur d'acquisition

| Item of data and year<br>Rubrique et année | Total | Agricultural sector<br>Secteur agricole | Mining<br>Industries extractives | Manufacturing<br>Industries manufacturières | Construction and commerce<br>Bâtiment et travaux publics; commerce | Electricity, gas and water<br>Electricité, gaz et eau | Transportation and communication<br>Transports et communications | Services |
|---|---|---|---|---|---|---|---|---|
| ISIC — CITI | 0–9 | 0 | 1 | 2–3 | 4, 6, 9 | 5 | 7 | 8 |
| *a. At Current Prices — Aux prix courants* | | | | | | | | |
| **Absolute figures — Chiffres absolus** | | | | | | | | |
| 1950............ | 2 700 | 40 | 61 | 1 078 | 1 290 | 20 | 79 | 132 |
| 1951............ | 4 373 | 127 | 92 | 2 196 | 1 474 | 9 | 164 | 311 |
| 1952............ | 5 044 | 184 | 108 | 2 158 | 1 933 | 9 | 321 | 331 |
| 1953............ | 5 223 | 157 | 87 | 1 781 | 2 361 | 27 | 305 | 505 |
| 1954............ | 5 351 | 119 | 104 | 1 824 | 2 646 | 17 | 217 | 424 |
| 1955............ | 6 968 | 258 | 143 | 2 304 | 2 900 | 59 | 419 | 885 |
| 1956............ | 8 170 | 351 | 164 | 3 433 | 3 115 | 37 | 303 | 767 |
| 1957............ | 9 149 | 231 | 196 | 3 915 | 3 496 | 88 | 371 | 852 |
| 1958............ | 8 643 | 400 | 187 | 3 724 | 3 458 | 95 | 185 | 594 |
| 1959............ | 6 673 | 142 | 37 | 2 950 | 2 777 | 85 | 221 | 461 |
| **Percentage distribution according to sector— Distribution en pourcentage par secteur** | | | | | | | | |
| 1950 – 1959..... | 100.0 | 1.9 | 1.0 | 43.0 | 43.4 | 1.1 | 3.2 | 6.3 |
| 1950............ | 100.0 | 1.4 | 2.3 | 39.9 | 47.8 | 0.7 | 3.0 | 4.9 |
| 1953............ | 100.0 | 3.0 | 1.6 | 34.1 | 45.2 | 0.5 | 5.9 | 9.7 |
| 1954............ | 100.0 | 2.2 | 1.9 | 34.1 | 49.5 | 0.3 | 4.0 | 8.0 |
| 1958............ | 100.0 | 4.6 | 2.1 | 43.1 | 40.0 | 1.1 | 2.2 | 6.9 |

## 2. INDEX NUMBERS OF INDUSTRIAL PRODUCTION
### INDICES DE LA PRODUCTION INDUSTRIELLE

### A. Selected Divisions of Industrial Activity
### Quelques branches de l'activité industrielle

| Period / Période | Total | Mining — Industries extractives | Manufacturing[1] — Industries manufacturières[1] |
|---|---|---|---|
| ISIC — CITI | 1-3 | 1 | 2-3 |
| *a. Indexes — Indices (1958 = 100)* | | | |
| 1938 | ... | 21 | ... |
| 1948 | 35 | 20 | 50 |
| 1949 | 40 | 22 | 57 |
| 1950 | 48 | 38 | 58 |
| 1951 | 54 | 42 | 65 |
| 1952 | 58 | 47 | 68 |
| 1953 | 69 | 62 | 76 |
| 1954 | 78 | 73 | 82 |
| 1955 | 77 | 66 | 87 |
| 1956 | 92 | 92 | 92 |
| 1957 | 103 | 106 | 101 |
| 1958 | 100 | 100 | 100 |
| 1959 | 100 | 96 | 103 |
| *b. Average Annual Rate of Change — Taux annuel moyen de variation* | | | |
| 1950-1959 | 8.5 | 10.8 | 6.6 |
| 1948-1953 | 14.5 | 25.4 | 8.7 |
| 1954-1958 | 6.4 | 8.2 | 5.1 |

For footnotes see end of table.

Pour les notes, voir au bas du tableau.

### B. The Major Groups of Mining
### Les classes de la branche Industries extractives

| Period / Période | All mining — Toutes industries extractives | Coal mining — Extraction du charbon | Metal mining — Extraction des minerais métalliques | Crude petroleum and natural gas — Pétrole brut et gaz naturel | Other mining — Autres industries extractives |
|---|---|---|---|---|---|
| ISIC — CITI | 1 | 11 | 12 | 13 | 14-19 |
| *a. Indexes — Indices (1958 = 100)* | | | | | |
| 1938 | 21 | 27 | 4 | 85 | 58 |
| 1948 | 20 | 68 | 4 | 76 | 80 |
| 1949 | 22 | 56 | 5 | 80 | 80 |
| 1950 | 38 | 63 | 28 | 81 | 57 |
| 1951 | 42 | 74 | 32 | 86 | 69 |
| 1952 | 47 | 90 | 36 | 88 | 89 |
| 1953 | 62 | 82 | 55 | 86 | 97 |
| 1954 | 73 | 84 | 68 | 92 | 103 |
| 1955 | 66 | 43 | 59 | 92 | 106 |
| 1956 | 92 | 45 | 90 | 98 | 107 |
| 1957 | 106 | 44 | 107 | 103 | 123 |
| 1958 | 100 | 100 | 100 | 100 | 100 |
| 1959 | 96 | 69 | 96 | 95 | 117 |
| 1960 | 132 | 56 | 141 | 101 | 108 |
| 1961 | 140 | 53 | 152 | 96 | 107 |
| *b. Average Annual Rate of Change — Taux annuel moyen de variation* | | | | | |
| 1938-1960 | 8.7 | 3.4 | 17.6 | 0.8 | 2.9 |
| 1938-1948 | —0.5 | 9.7 | — | —1.1 | 3.3 |
| 1950-1960 | 13.3 | —1.2 | 17.6 | 2.2 | 6.6 |
| 1948-1953 | 25.4 | 4.1 | 68.9 | 2.5 | 3.9 |
| 1954-1958 | 8.2 | 4.4 | 10.1 | 2.1 | —0.7 |
| 1958-1960 | 14.9 | —25.3 | 18.7 | 0.5 | 3.9 |

### C. The Major Groups of Manufacturing — Les classes de la branche Industries manufacturières

| Period / Période | Manufacturing[1] — Industries manufacturières[1] | Food, beverages and tobacco — Industries alimentaires, boissons, tabac | Textiles | Clothing, footwear and made-up textiles — Articles d'habillement, chaussures et ouvrages en tissu | Wood products — Bois | Paper and paper products — Papier et ouvrages en papier | Printing and publishing — Imprimerie et édition | Leather and leather products except wearing apparel — Cuir et articles en cuir, à l'exclusion des articles d'habillement | Rubber products — Ouvrages en caoutchouc | Chemicals and chemical, petroleum and coal products — Produits chimiques et dérivés du pétrole et du charbon | Non-metallic mineral products — Produits minéraux non métalliques | Basic metals and metal products — Métallurgie de base et ouvrages en métaux | Other manufacturing — Autres industries manufacturières |
|---|---|---|---|---|---|---|---|---|---|---|---|---|---|
| ISIC — CITI | 2-3 | 20-22 | 23 | 24 | 25 | 27 | 28 | 29 | 30 | 31-32 | 33 | 34, 36-38 | 39 |
| *a. Indexes — Indices (1958 = 100)* | | | | | | | | | | | | | |
| 1948 | 50 | 57 | 69 | 36 | 38 | 27 | 42 | 64 | 42 | 51 | 57 | 25 | ... |
| 1949 | 57 | 62 | 75 | 39 | 37 | 31 | 74 | 67 | 41 | 58 | 55 | 33 | ... |
| 1950 | 58 | 67 | 66 | 45 | 62 | 27 | 63 | 81 | 40 | 55 | 55 | 34 | ... |
| 1951 | 65 | 70 | 73 | 54 | 97 | 44 | 82 | 91 | 62 | 65 | 57 | 41 | ... |
| 1952 | 68 | 77 | 75 | 61 | 98 | 38 | 79 | 93 | 54 | 68 | 55 | 42 | ... |
| 1953 | 76 | 88 | 76 | 71 | 98 | 53 | 83 | 92 | 83 | 69 | 64 | 48 | ... |
| 1954 | 82 | 89 | 94 | 82 | 104 | 71 | 103 | 91 | 78 | 76 | 77 | 50 | 72 |
| 1955 | 87 | 94 | 93 | 96 | 169 | 70 | 120 | 104 | 79 | 78 | 86 | 42 | 93 |
| 1956 | 92 | 95 | 98 | 107 | 121 | 90 | 136 | 122 | 74 | 89 | 82 | 64 | 92 |
| 1957 | 101 | 102 | 114 | 122 | 129 | 95 | 145 | 99 | 81 | 95 | 91 | 70 | 100 |
| 1958 | 100 | 100 | 100 | 100 | 100 | 100 | 100 | 100 | 100 | 100 | 100 | 100 | 100 |
| 1959 | 103 | 105 | 100 | 108 | 100 | 121 | 111 | 101 | 90 | 103 | 98 | 89 | 100 |
| *b. Average Annual Rate of Change — Taux annuel moyen de variation* | | | | | | | | | | | | | |
| 1950-1959 | 6.6 | 5.1 | 4.7 | 10.2 | 5.5 | 18.1 | 6.5 | 2.5 | 9.4 | 7.2 | 6.6 | 11.3 | ... |
| 1948-1953 | 8.7 | 9.1 | 1.9 | 14.5 | 20.9 | 14.4 | 14.6 | 7.5 | 14.6 | 6.2 | 2.3 | 13.9 | ... |
| 1954-1958 | 5.1 | 3.0 | 1.6 | 5.1 | —1.0 | 8.9 | —0.7 | 2.4 | 6.4 | 7.1 | 6.8 | 18.9 | 8.6 |

[1] Excludes Manufacture of Furniture and Fixtures (ISIC major group 26).

[1] Non compris l'Industrie du meuble (CITI 26).

## 3. INDEX NUMBERS OF INDUSTRIAL EMPLOYMENT
### INDICES DE L'EMPLOI DANS L'INDUSTRIE

### A. Selected Divisions of Industrial Activity
#### Quelques branches de l'activité industrielle

| Period<br>Période | Total [2] | Mining [1]<br>Industries extractives [1] | Manu-facturing [1,2]<br>Industries manu-facturières [1,2] |
|---|---|---|---|
| ISIC — CITI | 1-3 | 1 | 2-3 |

*a. Indexes — Indices (1958 = 100)*

| | | | |
|---|---|---|---|
| 1948............ | 74 | 84 | 74 |
| 1949............ | 78 | 88 | 78 |
| 1950............ | 77 | 89 | 77 |
| 1951............ | 80 | 97 | 80 |
| 1952............ | 84 | 99 | 84 |
| 1953............ | 91 | 103 | 91 |
| 1954............ | 92 | 104 | 92 |
| 1955............ | − 89 − | − 110 − | 88 |
| 1956............ | 95 | 110 | 94 |
| 1957............ | 112 | 104 | 113 |
| 1958............ | 100 | 100 | 100 |
| 1959............ | 107 | 100 | 108 |
| 1960............ | 117 | 108 | 118 |

*b. Average Annual Rate of Change — Taux annuel moyen de variation*

| | | | |
|---|---|---|---|
| 1950 − 1960...... | 4.3 | 1.9 | 4.4 |
| 1948 − 1953...... | 4.2 | 4.2 | 4.2 |
| 1954 − 1958...... | 2.1 | −1.0 | 2.1 |
| 1958 − 1960...... | 8.2 | 3.9 | 8.6 |

For footnotes see end of table.

Pour les notes, voir au bas du tableau.

### B. The Major Groups of Mining
#### Les classes de la branche Industries extractives

| Period<br>Période | All mining [1]<br>Toutes industries extractives [1] | Coal mining<br>Extraction du charbon | Metal mining<br>Extraction des minerais métalliques | Crude petro-leum and natural gas [1]<br>Pétrole brut et gaz naturel [1] | Other mining<br>Autres industries extractives |
|---|---|---|---|---|---|
| ISIC — CITI | 1 | 11 | 12 | 13, 32 | 14-19 |

*a. Indexes — Indices (1958 = 100)*

| | | | | | |
|---|---|---|---|---|---|
| 1939....... | 77 | 53 | 81 | 73 | 86 |
| 1948....... | 84 | 91 | 79 | 88 | 96 |
| 1949....... | 88 | 82 | 91 | 86 | 91 |
| 1950....... | 89 | 91 | 88 | 88 | 106 |
| 1951....... | 97 | 75 | 96 | 97 | 119 |
| 1952....... | 99 | 120 | 96 | 98 | 113 |
| 1953....... | 103 | 99 | 100 | 99 | 137 |
| 1954....... | 104 | 121 | 103 | 103 | 108 |
| 1955....... | − 110 − | 77 | 107 | 103 | 164 |
| 1956....... | 110 | 78 | 111 | 98 | 158 |
| 1957....... | 104 | 70 | 116 | 85 | 113 |
| 1958....... | 100 | 100 | 100 | 100 | 100 |
| 1959....... | 100 | 95 | 111 | 87 | 81 |
| 1960....... | 108 | 64 | 130 | 81 | 89 |

*b. Average Annual Rate of Change — Taux annuel moyen de variation*

| | | | | | |
|---|---|---|---|---|---|
| 1939 − 1960. | 1.6 | 0.9 | 2.3 | 0.5 | 0.2 |
| 1939 − 1948. | 1.0 | 5.6 | −0.3 | 2.0 | 1.1 |
| 1950 − 1960. | 1.9 | −3.5 | 4.0 | −0.8 | −1.7 |
| 1948 − 1953. | 4.2 | 1.7 | 4.8 | 2.4 | 7.4 |
| 1954 − 1958. | −1.0 | −4.7 | −0.7 | −0.7 | −1.9 |
| 1958 − 1960. | 3.9 | −20.0 | 14.0 | −5.1 | −5.7 |

For footnotes see end of table.

Pour les notes, voir au bas du tableau.

## C. The Major Groups of Manufacturing — Les classes de la branche Industries manufacturières

| Period / Période | Manufacturing [1,2] / Industries manufacturières [1,2] | Food and beverages / Industries alimentaires et boissons | Textiles | Clothing, footwear and made-up textiles / Articles d'habillement, chaussures et ouvrages en tissu | Wood products and furniture / Bois et meubles | Paper and paper products / Papier et ouvrages en papier | Printing and publishing / Imprimerie et édition | Leather and leather products except wearing apparel / Cuir et articles en cuir, à l'exclusion des articles d'habillement | Rubber products / Ouvrages en caoutchouc | Chemicals and chemical products [1] / Produits chimiques [1] | Non-metallic mineral products / Produits minéraux non métalliques | Basic metal and metal products / Métallurgie de base et ouvrages en métaux | Other manufacturing / Autres industries manufacturières |
|---|---|---|---|---|---|---|---|---|---|---|---|---|---|
| ISIC — CITI | 2–3 | 20–21 | 23 | 24 | 25–26 | 27 | 28 | 29 | 30 | 31 | 33 | 34–38 | 39 |

### a. Indexes — Indices (1958 = 100)

| Period | 2–3 | 20–21 | 23 | 24 | 25–26 | 27 | 28 | 29 | 30 | 31 | 33 | 34–38 | 39 |
|---|---|---|---|---|---|---|---|---|---|---|---|---|---|
| 1948 | 74 | 61 | 83 | 77 | 93 | 134 | 82 | 121 | 62 | 58 | 72 | 61 | 162 |
| 1949 | 78 | 72 | 80 | 92 | 101 | 70 | 84 | 120 | 82 | 62 | 74 | 66 | 247 |
| 1950 | 77 | 71 | 71 | 96 | 97 | 71 | 120 | 130 | 62 | 67 | 64 | 73 | 95 |
| 1951 | 80 | 71 | 74 | 101 | 89 | 74 | 124 | 115 | 69 | 84 | 71 | 70 | 188 |
| 1952 | 84 | 77 | 77 | 101 | 105 | 74 | 121 | 127 | 71 | 88 | 68 | 77 | 118 |
| 1953 | 91 | 84 | 88 | 102 | 118 | 97 | 98 | 118 | 80 | 94 | 82 | 83 | 123 |
| 1954 | 92 | 83 | 91 | 109 | 106 | 92 | 90 | 121 | 77 | 99 | 84 | 82 | 141 |
| 1955 | 88 | 80 | 92 | 94 | 107 | 90 | 84 | 107 | 74 | 82 | 84 | 87 | 106 |
| 1956 | 94 | 80 | 96 | 96 | 112 | 101 | 103 | 119 | 91 | 105 | 90 | 99 | 91 |
| 1957 | 113 | 93 | 130 | 110 | 128 | 123 | 106 | 103 | 104 | 110 | 109 | 116 | 104 |
| 1958 | 100 | 100 | 100 | 100 | 100 | 100 | 100 | 100 | 100 | 100 | 100 | 100 | 100 |
| 1959 | 108 | 110 | 106 | 113 | 101 | 104 | 95 | 97 | 106 | 117 | 113 | 102 | 111 |
| 1960 | 118 | 137 | 98 | 122 | 135 | 98 | 122 | 138 | 125 | 130 | 110 | 105 | ... |

### b. Average Annual Rate of Change — Taux annuel moyen variation

| Period | 2–3 | 20–21 | 23 | 24 | 25–26 | 27 | 28 | 29 | 30 | 31 | 33 | 34–38 | 39 |
|---|---|---|---|---|---|---|---|---|---|---|---|---|---|
| 1950 – 1960 | 4.4 | 6.8 | 3.3 | 2.4 | 3.4 | 3.3 | 0.2 | 0.6 | 7.3 | 6.9 | 5.6 | 3.7 | ... |
| 1948 – 1953 | 4.2 | 6.6 | 1.2 | 5.8 | 4.9 | −6.2 | 3.6 | −0.5 | 5.2 | 10.1 | 2.6 | 6.4 | −5.4 |
| 1954 – 1958 | 2.1 | 4.8 | 2.4 | −2.1 | −1.4 | 2.1 | 2.7 | −4.7 | 6.8 | 0.2 | 4.4 | 5.1 | −8.2 |
| 1958 – 1960 | 8.6 | 17.0 | −1.0 | 10.5 | 16.2 | −1.0 | 10.5 | 17.5 | 11.8 | 14.0 | 4.9 | 2.5 | ... |

[1] Petroleum refining (ISIC major group 32) is included in mining under Crude petroleum and natural gas (ISIC major group 13).
[2] Excludes Tobacco manufactures (ISIC major group 22) in all years and Other manufacturing (ISIC 39) in 1960.

[1] Le Raffinage du pétrole (CITI 32) est compris dans les industries extractives sous Pétrole brut et gaz naturel (CITI 13).
[2] Non compris, pour toutes les années, Industrie du tabac (CITI 22) et, en 1960, Autres industries manufacturières (CITI 39).

# 4. THE CHARACTERISTICS OF MANUFACTURING ESTABLISHMENTS
## CARACTERISTIQUES DES ETABLISSEMENTS MANUFACTURIERS
### 1954

Number of establishments in units; value added and wages and salaries in million Soles; numbers of engaged in thousands; value added per person engaged in thousand Soles

Nombre d'établissements en unités; valeur ajoutée et traitements et salaires en millions de sols; nombre de personnes occupées en milliers; valeur ajoutée par personne occupée en milliers de sols

| Item of data | Manufacturing 1,2 / Industries manufacturières 1,2 | Food and beverages / Industries alimentaires et boissons | Textiles | Clothing, footwear and made-up textiles / Articles d'habillement, chaussures et ouvrages en tissu | Wood products and furniture / Bois et meubles | Paper and paper products / Papier et ouvrages en papier | Printing and publishing / Imprimerie et édition | Leather and leather products except wearing apparel / Cuir et articles en cuir, à l'exclusion des articles d'habillement | Rubber products / Ouvrages en caoutchouc | Chemicals and chemical, petroleum and coal products 2 / Produits chimiques et dérivés du pétrole et du charbon 2 | Non-metallic mineral products / Produits minéraux non métalliques | Basic metals / Métallurgie de base | Metal products / Ouvrages en métaux | Other manufacturing / Autres industries manufacturières | Rubrique |
|---|---|---|---|---|---|---|---|---|---|---|---|---|---|---|---|
| ISIC | 2–3 | 20–21 | 23 | 24 | 25–26 | 27 | 28 | 29 | 30 | 31–32 | 33 | 34 | 35–38 | 39 | CITI |
| *a. Absolute Figures — Chiffres absolus* | | | | | | | | | | | | | | | |
| Number of establishments | 2 606 | 758 | 205 | 296 | 226 | 33 | 143 | 65 | 23 | 197 | 118 | 25 | 358 | 159 | Nombre d'établissements |
| Value added | 2 548.2 | 896.5 | 561.4 | 123.1 | 48.6 | 42.7 | 88.8 | 48.8 | 28.3 | 206.2 | 246.2 | 61.0 | 145.3 | 51.3 | Valeur ajoutée |
| Number of engaged | 117.0 | 43.8 | 24.7 | 8.7 | 3.7 | 1.5 | 3.6 | 2.2 | 1.0 | 6.6 | 8.2 | 3.7 | 6.8 | 2.5 | Nombre de personnes occupées |
| Wages and salaries paid | 983.4 | 270.4 | 260.2 | 61.9 | 31.2 | 13.1 | 41.6 | 17.0 | 12.8 | 76.9 | 78.1 | 36.6 | 62.9 | 20.7 | Traitements et salaires payés |
| *b. Structure* | | | | | | | | | | | | | | | |
| Distribution in percent of: Value added | 100.0 | 35.1 | 22.1 | 4.8 | 1.9 | 1.7 | 3.5 | 1.9 | 1.1 | 8.1 | 9.6 | 2.4 | 5.7 | 2.1 | Distribution en pourcentage: De la valeur ajoutée |
| Number of engaged | 100.0 | 37.4 | 21.1 | 7.4 | 3.2 | 1.3 | 3.1 | 1.8 | 0.9 | 5.6 | 7.0 | 3.2 | 5.8 | 2.2 | Du nombre de personnes occupées |
| Value added per person engaged | 21.8 | 20.5 | 22.7 | 14.1 | 13.1 | 28.5 | 24.7 | 22.2 | 28.3 | 31.2 | 30.0 | 16.5 | 21.4 | 20.5 | Valeur ajoutée par personne occupée |
| Value added per unit of wages and salaries | 2.59 | 3.32 | 2.16 | 1.99 | 1.56 | 3.26 | 2.13 | 2.87 | 2.21 | 2.68 | 3.15 | 1.67 | 2.31 | 2.48 | Valeur ajoutée par unité de traitements et salaires |

[1] Excludes tobacco manufactures.
[2] Excludes Petroleum refining (ISIC group 321).

[1] Non compris l'industrie du tabac.
[2] Non compris les raffineries de pétrole (CITI 321).

# 5. THE CHARACTERISTICS OF MANUFACTURING ESTABLISHMENTS EMPLOYING 5 OR MORE PERSONS OR HAVING A VALUE OF PRODUCTION OF 100,000 SOLES OR MORE DURING THE YEAR
## CARACTERISTIQUES DES ETABLISSEMENTS MANUFACTURIERS COMPTANT AU MOINS 5 SALARIES OU AYANT EU UNE PRODUCTION ANNUELLE A 100 000 SOLS OU PLUS
### 1958

Number of establishments in units; value added and wages and salaries in million Soles; number of engaged in thousands; value added per person engaged in thousand Soles.

Nombre d'établissements en unités; valeur ajoutée et traitements et salaires en millions de sols; nombre de personnes occupées en milliers; valeur ajoutée par personne occupée en milliers de sols.

| Item of data | Manufacturing 1 / Industries manufacturières 1 | Food and beverages / Industries alimentaires et boissons | Textiles | Clothing, footwear and made-up textiles / Articles d'habillement, chaussures et ouvrages en tissu | Wood products and furniture / Bois et meubles | Paper and paper products / Papier et ouvrages en papier | Printing and publishing / Imprimerie et édition | Leather and leather products except wearing apparel / Cuir et articles en cuir, à l'exclusion des articles d'habillement | Rubber products / Ouvrages en caoutchouc | Chemicals and chemical products / Produits chimiques | Non-metallic mineral products / Produits minéraux non métalliques | Basic metals / Métallurgie de base | Metal products / Ouvrages en métaux | Other manufacturing / Autres industries manufacturières | Rubrique |
|---|---|---|---|---|---|---|---|---|---|---|---|---|---|---|---|
| ISIC | 2–3 | 20–21 | 23 | 24 | 25–26 | 27 | 28 | 29 | 30 | 31 | 33 | 34 | 35–38 | 39 | CITI |
| *a. Absolute Figures — Chiffres absolus* | | | | | | | | | | | | | | | |
| Number of establishments | 2 263 | 723 | 229 | 227 | 177 | 22 | 114 | 55 | 8 | 165 | 98 | 29 | 305 | 111 | Nombre d'établissements |
| Value added | 4 602.0 | 1 630.1 | 844.4 | 196.2 | 93.3 | 115.2 | 145.3 | 69.5 | 75.3 | 476.6 | 187.2 | 368.4 | 278.6 | 121.9 | Valeur ajoutée |
| Number of engaged (XI.1958) | 116.3 | 42.5 | 23.5 | 8.7 | 3.9 | 2.1 | 3.6 | 2.1 | 0.9 | 7.7 | 5.8 | 3.4 | 9.0 | 3.1 | Nombre de personnes occupées (XI.1958) |
| Wages and salaries | 1 531.0 | 459.0 | 363.0 | 91.7 | 47.4 | 30.8 | 66.6 | 26.0 | 22.2 | 131.9 | 82.2 | 50.3 | 121.7 | 38.2 | Traitements et salaires |
| *b. Structure* | | | | | | | | | | | | | | | |
| Distribution in percent of: Value added | 100.0 | 35.4 | 18.3 | 4.3 | 2.0 | 2.5 | 3.2 | 1.5 | 1.6 | 10.4 | 4.0 | 8.0 | 6.1 | 2.7 | Distribution en pourcentage: Valeur ajoutée |
| Number of engaged | 100.0 | 36.5 | 20.2 | 7.5 | 3.3 | 1.8 | 3.1 | 1.8 | 0.8 | 6.6 | 5.0 | 2.9 | 7.8 | 2.7 | Nombre de personnes occupées |
| Value added per person engaged | 39.6 | 38.4 | 35.9 | 22.6 | 23.9 | 54.8 | 40.4 | 33.1 | 83.7 | 61.9 | 32.3 | 108.4 | 31.0 | 39.3 | Valeur ajoutée par personne occupée |
| Value added per unit of wages and salaries | 3.00 | 3.55 | 2.33 | 2.14 | 1.97 | 3.74 | 2.18 | 2.67 | 3.39 | 3.61 | 2.28 | 7.32 | 2.29 | 3.19 | Valeur ajoutée par unité de traitements et salaires |

[1] Excludes tobacco manufactures and petroleum refining.

[1] Non compris l'industrie du tabac et le raffinage du pétrole.

# PHILIPPINES

## Domestic and National Product and Gross Domestic Fixed Capital Formation

Estimates of the expenditure of the gross domestic and national product, the origin of the net national product and the origin of the gross domestic capital formation are presented in Table 1. This table has been derived from data supplied by the National Economic Council, Manila, in response to the United Nations national accounts questionnaire. Official estimates and descriptions of the sources and methods used have been published annually by the Council in the April issue of the *Statistical Reporter*.

## Index Numbers of Industrial Production

The index numbers of production for manufacturing industries and metal mining presented in Table 2 have been derived from index numbers compiled quarterly by the Central Bank of the Philippines and made available to the Statistical Office of the United Nations through correspondence. Some of these index numbers have also been published by the Bank in its *Statistical Bulletin*.

These index numbers are based on monthly data provided by about 800 firms and covering the quantities of production of 577 individual commodities. The series derived from these detailed items are combined into indexes for major groups, and these major group indexes are, in turn, combined into indexes for manufacturing as a whole, using as weights at both stages the gross value of production in the base year. For the years up to 1954, the index numbers have been calculated with 1952 as the base year and for later years, 1955 has been used as the base year. The two series of index numbers have been linked at 1955.

The remaining index numbers shown in Table 2 for coal mining, other mining, total mining, electricity, and mining, manufacturing and electricity, combined, have been compiled by the Statistical Office of the United Nations, based on quantities produced. In the case of coal mining and other mining, the basic quantity data has been provided by the Central Bank of the Philippines by means of correspondence. Where necessary, the series derived from the quantity data have been combined into major group indexes using the gross value of production in 1953-54 as weights. The basic quantity data on which the electricity index is based has been published by the Bank in its *Statistical Bulletin*. The index numbers for total mining and for mining, manufacturing and electricity, combined, have been calculated using as weights,

## Produit intérieur et national et formation brute de capital fixe

Le tableau 1 contient des estimations des dépenses imputées au produit intérieur et au produit national, du produit national net par secteur d'activité d'origine et de la formation brute de capital fixe intérieur par secteur d'acquisition. Ce tableau a été établi à partir de données fournies par le *National Economic Council*, Manille, en réponse au questionnaire de l'ONU sur la comptabilité nationale. Les estimations officielles, ainsi qu'une description des sources et méthodes adoptées, ont été publiées annuellement par ce conseil dans le numéro d'avril du *Statistical Reporter*.

## Indices de la production industrielle

Les indices de la production dans les industries manufacturières et les industries extractives de minerais métalliques, reproduits au tableau 2, sont tirés d'indices calculés trimestriellement par la Banque centrale des Philippines et communiqués au Bureau de statistique de l'ONU par correspondance. La Banque a publié également certains de ces indices dans son *Statistical Bulletin*.

Ces indices sont fondés sur des données mensuelles fournies par quelque 800 entreprises et portent sur les quantités produites de 577 marchandises différentes. Les séries tirées de ces données détaillées sont combinées en indices de classes, qui sont à leur tour combinés en indices pour l'ensemble des industries manufacturières, les coefficients de pondération utilisés aux deux stades du calcul étant la valeur brute de la production pendant l'année de base. Les indices sont basés sur 1952 pour les années antérieures à 1955 et sur 1955 pour les années suivantes. Les deux séries d'indices ont été raccordées au niveau de 1955.

Les autres séries d'indices du tableau 2 relatives aux industries extractives de charbon, aux autres industries extractives, à l'ensemble des industries extractives, à la production d'électricité, et à l'ensemble des industries extractives, manufacturières et productrices d'électricité ont été calculées par le Bureau de statistique de l'ONU en fonction des quantités produites. Pour les industries extractives de charbon et les autres industries extractives, les données quantitatives de base ont été communiquées, par correspondance, par la Banque centrale des Philippines. Le cas échéant, les séries calculées à partir des données sur les quantités produites ont été combinées en indices de classes; on a alors utilisé la valeur brute de la production en 1953-1954 comme base de pondération. Les données quantitatives de base qui ont servi au calcul

estimates of value added in 1953 for the years up to 1955, and in 1958 for later years, a link being made at 1955.

### Index of Industrial Employment

The index numbers of industrial employment presented in Table 3 are derived from index numbers compiled and published by the Central Bank of the Philippines in the *Statistical Bulletin*.

The Bank is provided monthly with employment data by 1,289 establishments (643 being industrial establishments) and publishes the index under the title of "Employment Index of Reporting Non-Agricultural Establishments." It is thought that reservations should be attached to the index numbers published as it seems likely that there are some fluctuations in the number of reporting establishments.

### The Characteristics and Structure of Industrial Activity

The data set out in Table 4 are derived from the results of Censuses of Mining and Manufacturing taken for 1938 and 1948 by the Bureau of Census and Statistics, Manila, that were published in the *Statistical Abstracts of the Philippines (A Reprint)*, 1950 and *Economic Census Report, Census of the Philippines: 1948*, Vol. IV, 1953, respectively. The earlier Census covered all establishments, irrespective of size or location, whereas the latter Census related only to establishments with a proper Internal Revenue license—generally the larger units located in business premises. The two censuses are therefore not comparable in coverage, especially with respect to industries such as textiles, clothing and wood products. It should be noted that although the 1948 Census of Manufactures did not cover sawmills, data for sawmills during 1948 are included in Table 4 and were derived from the results of the Census of Forestry, which also appear in the publication listed above.

In addition to differences in coverage between the 1938 and 1948 Censuses, there is an important difference in the item of data on the gross value of output. The figures of gross receipts, in the case of the 1938 Census, relate to the moneys received for the sale of goods and services whereas the figures of gross value of production, in the case of the 1948 Census, measure the value, during the year, of commodities produced on own account, including goods for stock, and of industrial services rendered. Both items of data are valued at market prices. The definitions utilized in the two censuses for the other items of data on the same subject seem to be similar.

des indices de la production d'électricité ont été publiées par la Banque dans son *Statistical Bulletin*. Pour calculer les indices relatifs à l'ensemble des industries extractives et à l'ensemble des industries extractives, manufacturières et productrices d'électricité, on a utilisé comme coefficients de pondération des estimations de la valeur ajoutée en 1953 pour 1955 et les années antérieures, et en 1958 pour les années suivantes; un raccordement a été fait au niveau de 1955.

### Indices de l'emploi dans l'industrie

Les indices de l'emploi dans l'industrie présentés au tableau 3 sont tirés d'indices calculés par la Banque centrale des Philippines et publiés dans son *Statistical Bulletin*.

La Banque recueille des données mensuelles sur l'emploi auprès de 1 289 établissements (dont 643 établissements industriels) et publie l'indice sous le titre de *"Employment Index of Reporting Non-Agricultural Establishments"*. Les indices publiés semblent être sujet à caution car il existe probablement certaines fluctuations dans le nombre des établissements qui fournissent les données.

### Caractéristiques et structure de l'activité industrielle

Les données du tableau 4 sont tirées des résultats des recensements des industries extractives et manufacturières exécutés en 1938 et 1948 par le Bureau des recensements et de la statistique, Manille; ces résultats ont été publiés dans *Statistical Abstracts of the Philippines (A Reprint)*, *1950* et dans *Economic Census Report, Census of the Philippines : 1948*, Vol. IV, 1953, respectivement. Le premier de ces recensements portait sur tous les établissements, quels que fussent leur emplacement et leur dimension, tandis que le second ne couvrait que les établissements dûment patentés par le fisc — généralement les unités relativement importantes occupant des locaux industriels ou commerciaux. Ces deux recensements ne sont donc pas comparables du point de vue de la couverture, surtout en ce qui concerne des industries telles que les textiles, les articles d'habillement et l'industrie du bois. On notera que, si les scieries n'ont pas été dénombrées lors du recensement des industries manufacturières de 1948, des données sont cependant fournies à leur sujet, dans le tableau 4, pour 1948; elles ont été tirées des résultats du recensement de l'industrie forestière, parus également dans la dernière publication précitée.

En plus des différences de couverture entre le recensement de 1938 et celui de 1948, on note une divergence importante en ce qui concerne la valeur brute de la production. Le chiffre des recettes brutes, dans le cas du recensement, de 1938, représente les sommes reçues pour vente de biens et services, tandis que le chiffre de la valeur brute de la production, dans le cas du recensement de 1948, représente la valeur, pendant l'année, des marchandises produites pour compte propre, y compris les marchandises destinées au stockage, et des services industriels fournis à des tiers. Dans les deux cas, il s'agit de la valeur aux prix du marché. Les définitions utilisées

The capacity of installed power equipment is the sum of the rated horsepower of all prime movers and of electric motors driven by purchased electricity that are in use and in reserve.

The figures presented in Table 5 result from the first and third Annual Surveys of Manufactures which have been issued in *1956 Annual Survey of Manufactures,* Vol. I, Series 2, published jointly by the National Economic Council and the Bureau of the Census and Statistics, Manila, 1958, and in *Annual Survey of Manufactures, 1958,* Vol. III, published by the Bureau of Census and Statistics. These Annual Surveys related to all establishments engaging five or more persons which were operating during the year and involved the collection of data from all establishments engaging 20 or more persons and a sample of the rest, stratified according to size and location primarily.

The definitions of the items of data shown in Table 5 conform, on the whole, to the International Standards in Basic Industrial Statistics. Homeworkers have been excluded from the number of engaged and payments to homeworkers have been treated as payments for work done by others. The number of persons employed is the average of the number during the pay period ending nearest the 15th of February, May, August and November. Wages and salaries paid include payments in kind, valued at cost to the establishment. Value added is valued at market prices ex-factory.

dans les deux recensements pour les autres rubriques du même ordre semblent être analogues. La puissance installée est la puissance nominale de tous les moteurs primaires et des moteurs électriques actionnés par de l'électricité achetée, en service et en réserve.

Les chiffres du tableau 5 proviennent des première et troisième enquêtes annuelles sur les industries manufacturières, dont les résultats ont paru dans *1956 Annual Survey of Manufactures,* Vol. I, série 2, publié conjointement par le Conseil économique national et le Bureau des recensements et de la statistique, Manille, 1958 et dans *Annual Survey of Manufactures, 1958,* Vol. III, publié par le Bureau des recensements et de la statistique. Ces enquêtes annuelles portaient sur tous les établissements occupant cinq personnes ou plus qui étaient en activité pendant l'année; des données ont été recueillies sur tous les établissements occupant 20 personnes ou plus et sur un échantillon du reste, stratifié essentiellement selon la dimension et l'emplacement.

Les définitions des rubriques du tableau 5 sont conformes, dans l'ensemble, aux Normes internationales relatives aux statistiques industrielles de base. Le nombre de personnes occupées ne comprend pas les travailleurs à domicile et les sommes versées à ces travailleurs ont été considérées comme des paiements pour des travaux confiés à des tiers. Le nombre de salariés est la moyenne pendant la période de paie la plus rapprochée du 15 février, mai, août et novembre. Les traitements et salaires payés comprennent les paiements en nature, évalués au coût pour l'établissement. La valeur ajoutée est comptée aux prix du marché, départ usine.

## 1. THE GROSS PRODUCT, THE NET NATIONAL PRODUCT, AND GROSS DOMESTIC FIXED CAPITAL FORMATION
## LE PRODUIT BRUT, LE PRODUIT NATIONAL NET ET LA FORMATION BRUTE DE CAPITAL FIXE INTERIEUR

Million Pesos — Millions de pesos

### A. Expenditure on the Gross Product at Market Prices — Dépenses relatives au produit brut aux prix du marché

| Item of data and year / Rubrique et année | Total | Consumption / Consommation | | Gross Domestic Capital Formation / Formation brute de capital intérieur | | Net exports of goods and services / Exportations nettes de biens et de services | |
|---|---|---|---|---|---|---|---|
| | | Total | Government / Etat | Total | Fixed / Fixe | Exports less imports / Exportations moins importations | Exports / Exportations |

*a. Gross Domestic Product at Current Prices — Produit intérieur brut aux prix courants*

| Absolute figures — Chiffres absolus | | | | | | | |
|---|---|---|---|---|---|---|---|
| 1948 | 6 222 | 5 597 | 403 | 768 | 645 | −143 | ... |
| 1950 | 6 655 | 6 009 | 476 | 569 | 485 | 77 | 946 |
| 1951 | 7 415 | 6 911 | 540 | 559 | 491 | −55 | 1 087 |
| 1952 | 7 576 | 7 079 | 600 | 552 | 486 | −55 | 1 001 |
| 1953 | 8 111 | 7 447 | 631 | 659 | 559 | 5 | 1 141 |
| 1954 | 8 283 | 7 614 | 654 | 719 | 563 | −50 | 1 118 |
| 1955 | 8 820 | 8 219 | 718 | 789 | 624 | −188 | 1 130 |
| 1956 | 9 537 | 8 673 | 800 | 872 | 777 | −8 | 1 226 |
| 1957 | 10 119 | 9 376 | 853 | 1 036 | 890 | −293 | 1 204 |
| 1958 | 10 779 | 9 893 | 911 | 960 | 871 | −74 | 1 274 |
| 1959 | 11 499 | 10 378 | 986 | 1 013 | 945 | 108 | 1 344 |
| 1960 | 12 447 | 11 214 | 1 079 | 1 251 | 1 184 | −18 | 1 394 |
| 1961 | 13 213 | 12 289 | 1 184 | 1 073 | 1 067 | −149 | 1 310 |
| **Percentage distribution of average annual expenditure — Distribution en pourcentage des dépenses annuelles moyennes** | | | | | | | |
| 1948 | 100.0 | 90.0 | 6.5 | 12.3 | 10.4 | −2.3 | ... |
| 1950 − 1960 | 100.0 | 91.7 | 8.1 | 8.8 | 7.8 | −0.5 | 12.7 |
| 1950 | 100.0 | 90.3 | 7.2 | 8.5 | 7.3 | 1.2 | 14.2 |
| 1953 | 100.0 | 91.8 | 7.8 | 8.1 | 6.9 | 0.1 | 14.1 |
| 1954 | 100.0 | 91.9 | 7.9 | 8.7 | 6.8 | −0.6 | 13.5 |
| 1958 | 100.0 | 91.8 | 8.5 | 8.9 | 8.1 | −0.7 | 11.8 |
| 1960 | 100.0 | 90.1 | 8.7 | 10.0 | 9·5 | −0.1 | 11.2 |

*b. Gross National Product at Prices of 1955 — Produit national brut aux prix de 1955*

| Absolute figures — Chiffres absolus | | | | | | [1] | |
|---|---|---|---|---|---|---|---|
| 1948 | 5 373 | 4 889 | 368 | 665 | 548 | −181 | ... |
| 1950 | 6 228 | 5 591 | 454 | 591 | 506 | 46 | ... |
| 1951 | 6 523 | 6 148 | 471 | 455 | 390 | −80 | ... |
| 1952 | 7 093 | 6 757 | 562 | 434 | 368 | −98 | ... |
| 1953 | 7 646 | 7 180 | 611 | 562 | 462 | −96 | ... |
| 1954 | 8 058 | 7 530 | 646 | 683 | 533 | −155 | ... |
| 1955 | 8 687 | 8 219 | 718 | 789 | 624 | −321 | ... |
| 1956 | 9 132 | 8 444 | 778 | 818 | 725 | −130 | ... |
| 1957 | 9 532 | 8 967 | 811 | 940 | 804 | −375 | ... |
| 1958 | 9 929 | 9 237 | 920 | 862 | 779 | −170 | ... |
| 1959 | 10 514 | 9 773 | 995 | 838 | 777 | −97 | ... |
| 1960 | 10 936 | 10 141 | 1 051 | 925 | 866 | −130 | ... |
| 1961 | 11 606 | 10 966 | 1 095 | 792 | 783 | −152 | ... |
| **Percentage distribution of average annual expenditure — Distribution en pourcentage des dépenses annuelles moyennes** | | | | | | | |
| 1948 | 100.0 | 91.0 | 6.8 | 12.4 | 10.2 | −3.4 | ... |
| 1950 − 1960 | 100.0 | 93.3 | 8.5 | 8.4 | 7.2 | −1.7 | ... |
| 1950 | 100.0 | 89.8 | 7.3 | 9.5 | 8.1 | 0.7 | ... |
| 1953 | 100.0 | 93.9 | 8.0 | 7.4 | 6.0 | −1.3 | ... |
| 1954 | 100.0 | 93.4 | 8.0 | 8.5 | 6.6 | −1.9 | ... |
| 1958 | 100.0 | 93.0 | 9.3 | 8.7 | 7.8 | −1.7 | ... |
| 1960 | 100.0 | 92.7 | 9.6 | 8.5 | 7.9 | −1.2 | ... |
| **Average annual rate of growth — Taux annuel moyen d'accroissement** | | | | | | | |
| 1948 − 1953 | 7.3 | 8.0 | 10.7 | −3.3 | −3.4 | . | . |
| 1950 − 1960 | 5.8 | 6.1 | 8.8 | 4.6 | 5.5 | . | . |
| 1950 − 1953 | 7.1 | 8.7 | 10.4 | −1.7 | −3.0 | . | . |
| 1954 − 1958 | 5.4 | 5.2 | 9.2 | 6.0 | 10.0 | . | . |
| 1958 − 1960 | 4.9 | 4.8 | 6.9 | 3.6 | 5.5 | . | . |

[1] Includes net factor income from abroad.

[1] Y compris le revenu net de facteurs reçu de l'étranger.

## B. The Net National Product at Factor Cost According to Origin
### Origine par secteur d'activité du produit national net au coût des facteurs

| Item of data and year<br>Rubrique et année | Total | Agricultural sector<br>Secteur agricole | Mining<br>Industries extractives | Manufacturing<br>Industries manufacturières | Construction<br>Bâtiment et travaux publics | Electricity, gas and water, and transportation and communication<br>Electricité, gaz et eau, et transports et communications | Other sectors<br>Autres secteurs |
|---|---|---|---|---|---|---|---|
| ISIC — CITI | 0–9 | 0 | 1 | 2–3 | 4 | 5, 7 | 6, 8–9 |
| | | | *a.* At Current Prices — Aux prix courants | | | | |
| **Absolute figures — Chiffres absolus** | | | | | | | |
| 1948............ | 5 511 | 2 386 | 25 | 440 | 307 | 195 | 2 158 |
| 1950............ | 5 922 | 2 505 | 55 | 502 | 239 | 205 | 2 416 |
| 1951............ | 6 487 | 2 787 | 79 | 630 | 237 | 228 | 2 526 |
| 1952............ | 6 554 | 2 806 | 98 | 639 | 221 | 242 | 2 548 |
| 1953............ | 7 015 | 3 009 | 107 | 834 | 236 | 242 | 2 587 |
| 1954............ | 7 145 | 3 118 | 105 | 850 | 205 | 235 | 2 632 |
| 1955............ | 7 624 | 3 161 | 121 | 1 001 | 230 | 250 | 2 861 |
| 1956............ | 8 288 | 3 049 | 122 | 1 195 | 296 | 286 | 3 340 |
| 1957............ | 8 764 | 3 050 | 142 | 1 418 | 329 | 321 | 3 504 |
| 1958............ | 9 436 | 3 149 | 142 | 1 677 | 297 | 351 | 3 820 |
| 1959............ | 10 008 | 3 384 | 171 | 1 701 | 326 | 361 | 4 065 |
| 1960............ | 10 785 | 3 709 | 177 | 1 815 | 315 | 385 | 4 384 |
| 1961............ | 11 518 | 3 909 | 210 | 2 015 | 372 | 416 | 4 596 |
| **Percentage distribution according to sector— Distribution en pourcentage par secteur** | | | | | | | |
| 1948............ | 100.0 | 43.3 | 0.4 | 8.0 | 5.6 | 3.5 | 39.2 |
| 1950 – 1960..... | 100.0 | 38.3 | 1.5 | 14.0 | 3.3 | 3.5 | 39.4 |
| 1950............ | 100.0 | 42.3 | 0.9 | 8.5 | 4.0 | 3.5 | 40.8 |
| 1953............ | 100.0 | 42.9 | 1.5 | 11.9 | 3.4 | 3.4 | 36.9 |
| 1954............ | 100.0 | 43.6 | 1.5 | 11.9 | 2.9 | 3.3 | 36.8 |
| 1958............ | 100.0 | 33.4 | 1.5 | 17.8 | 3.1 | 3.7 | 40.5 |
| 1960............ | 100.0 | 34.4 | 1.6 | 16.8 | 2.9 | 3.6 | 40.7 |
| | | | *b.* At Prices of 1955 — Aux prix de 1955 | | | | |
| **Absolute figures — Chiffres absolus** | | | | | | | |
| 1948............ | 4 806 | 1 937 | 42 | 443 | 265 | 168 | 1 951 |
| 1950............ | 5 567 | 2 214 | 74 | 567 | 224 | 192 | 2 296 |
| 1951............ | 5 788 | 2 453 | 92 | 665 | 198 | 191 | 2 189 |
| 1952............ | 6 211 | 2 597 | 113 | 700 | 202 | 221 | 2 378 |
| 1953............ | 6 734 | 2 900 | 119 | 791 | 218 | 223 | 2 483 |
| 1954............ | 7 060 | 3 039 | 111 | 889 | 200 | 229 | 2 592 |
| 1955............ | 7 624 | 3 161 | 121 | 1 001 | 230 | 250 | 2 861 |
| 1956............ | 8 293 | 3 190 | 134 | 1 158 | 281 | 278 | 3 252 |
| 1957............ | 8 550 | 3 186 | 150 | 1 251 | 303 | 307 | 3 353 |
| 1958............ | 8 766 | 2 936 | 148 | 1 347 | 275 | 325 | 3 735 |
| 1959............ | 9 438 | 3 235 | 160 | 1 459 | 287 | 337 | 3 960 |
| 1960............ | 9 729 | 3 342 | 153 | 1 503 | 260 | 345 | 4 126 |
| 1961............ | 10 186 | 3 443 | 168 | 1 604 | 310 | 370 | 4 291 |
| **Percentage distribution according to sector— Distribution en pourcentage par secteur** | | | | | | | |
| 1948............ | 100.0 | 40.3 | 0.9 | 9.2 | 5.5 | 3.5 | 40.6 |
| 1950 – 1960..... | 100.0 | 38.5 | 1.6 | 13.5 | 3.2 | 3.5 | 39.7 |
| 1950............ | 100.0 | 39.8 | 1.3 | 10.2 | 4.0 | 3.5 | 41.2 |
| 1953............ | 100.0 | 43.1 | 1.8 | 11.7 | 3.2 | 3.3 | 36.9 |
| 1954............ | 100.0 | 43.0 | 1.6 | 12.6 | 2.8 | 3.3 | 36.7 |
| 1958............ | 100.0 | 33.5 | 1.7 | 15.4 | 3.1 | 3.7 | 42.6 |
| 1960............ | 100.0 | 34.4 | 1.6 | 15.4 | 2.7 | 3.5 | 42.4 |
| **Average annual rate of growth—Taux annuel moyen d'accroissement** | | | | | | | |
| 1948 – 1953..... | 7.0 | 8.4 | 23.2 | 12.3 | —3.8 | 5.8 | 5.0 |
| 1950 – 1960..... | 5.7 | 4.2 | 7.5 | 10.2 | 1.5 | 6.0 | 6.0 |
| 1950 – 1953..... | 6.6 | 9.4 | 17.2 | 11.7 | —0.9 | 5.1 | 2.6 |
| 1954 – 1958..... | 5.6 | —0.9 | 7.5 | 10.9 | 8.3 | 9.1 | 9.6 |
| 1958 – 1960..... | 5.4 | 6.7 | 1.7 | 5.6 | 2.8 | 3.1 | 5.1 |

## C. Gross Domestic Fixed Capital Formation According to Purchasing Sector
### La formation brute de capital fixe intérieur par secteur d'acquisition

| Item of data and year<br>Rubrique et année | Total | Agricultural sector<br>Secteur agricole | Mining<br>Industries extractives | Manufacturing<br>Industries manufacturières | Construction<br>Bâtiment et travaux publics | Electricity, gas and water, and transportation and communication<br>Electricité, gaz et eau, et transports et communications | Other sectors<br>Autres secteurs |
|---|---|---|---|---|---|---|---|
| ISIC — CITI | 0–9 | 0 | 1 | 2–3 | 4 | 5, 7 | 6, 8–9 |
| | | | | a. At Current Prices — Aux prix courants | | | |
| Absolute figures<br>— Chiffres absolus | | | | | | | |
| 1956............ | 777 | 51 | 36 | 160 | 18 | 76 | 436 |
| 1957............ | 890 | 54 | 32 | 193 | 28 | 120 | 463 |
| 1958............ | 871 | 40 | 19 | 239 | 29 | 106 | 438 |
| 1959............ | 945 | 32 | 26 | 234 | 18 | 146 | 489 |
| 1960............ | 1 184 | 60 | 19 | 257 | 17 | 361 | 470 |
| 1961............ | 1 067 | 44 | 14 | 244 | 18 | 187 | 560 |
| Percentage distribution according to sector—<br>Distribution en pourcentage par secteur | | | | | | | |
| 1958............ | 100.0 | 4.6 | 2.2 | 27.4 | 3.3 | 12.2 | 50.3 |
| 1960............ | 100.0 | 5.1 | 1.6 | 21.7 | 1.4 | 30.5 | 39.7 |

## 2. INDEX NUMBERS OF INDUSTRIAL PRODUCTION — INDICES DE LA PRODUCTION INDUSTRIELLE

### A. Selected Divisions of Industrial Activity
### Quelques branches de l'activité industrielle

| Period Période | Total | Mining Industries extractives | Manu-facturing [1] Industries manu-facturières [1] | Electricity [2] Electricité [2] |
|---|---|---|---|---|
| ISIC — CITI | 1–3, 511 | 1 | 2–3 | 511 |

a. Indexes — Indices (1958 = 100)

| | | | | |
|---|---|---|---|---|
| 1949.......... | 37 | 54 | 35 | 29 |
| 1950.......... | 44 | 64 | 42 | 31 |
| 1951.......... | 50 | 68 | 49 | 34 |
| 1952.......... | −54− | 80 | 52 | −38− |
| 1953.......... | 61 | 81 | 59 | 45 |
| 1954.......... | 67 | 82 | 66 | 55 |
| 1955.......... | −75− | −89− | −74− | 62 |
| 1956.......... | 86 | 89 | 86 | 73 |
| 1957.......... | 94 | 108 | 93 | 85 |
| 1958.......... | 100 | 100 | 100 | 100 |
| 1959.......... | 109 | 116 | 108 | 116 |
| 1960.......... | 113 | 117 | 112 | 129 |
| 1961.......... | 119 | 110 | 119 | 145 |

b. Average Annual Rate of Change — Taux annuel moyen de variation

| | | | | |
|---|---|---|---|---|
| 1950 – 1960.... | 9.9 | 6.2 | 10.3 | 15.3 |
| 1949 – 1953.... | 13.3 | 10.7 | 14.0 | 11.6 |
| 1954 – 1958.... | 10.5 | 5.1 | 10.9 | 16.1 |
| 1958 – 1960.... | 6.3 | 8.2 | 5.8 | 13.6 |

### B. The Major Groups of Mining
### Les classes de la branche Industries extractives

| Period Période | All mining Toutes industries extractives | Coal mining Extraction du charbon | Metal mining Extraction des minerais métalliques | Other mining Autres industries extractives |
|---|---|---|---|---|
| ISIC — CITI | 1 | 11 | 12 | 14–19 |

a. Indexes — Indices (1958 = 100)

| | | | | |
|---|---|---|---|---|
| 1949.......... | 54 | 114 | 39 | 150 |
| 1950.......... | 64 | 147 | 50 | 146 |
| 1951.......... | 68 | 140 | 62 | 99 |
| 1952.......... | 80 | 129 | 76 | 97 |
| 1953.......... | 81 | 144 | 80 | 77 |
| 1954.......... | 82 | 111 | 75 | 128 |
| 1955.......... | −89− | 121 | 82 | 138 |
| 1956.......... | 89 | 141 | 91 | 66 |
| 1957.......... | 108 | 177 | 101 | 153 |
| 1958.......... | 100 | 100 | 100 | 100 |
| 1959.......... | 116 | 130 | 108 | 169 |
| 1960.......... | 117 | 137 | 104 | 207 |
| 1961.......... | 110 | 141 | 114 | 78 |

b. Average Annual Rate of Change — Taux annuel moyen de variation

| | | | | |
|---|---|---|---|---|
| 1950 – 1960.... | 6.2 | −0.7 | 7.6 | 3.6 |
| 1949 – 1953.... | 10.7 | 6.0 | 19.7 | −15.4 |
| 1954 – 1958.... | 5.1 | −2.6 | 7.5 | −6.0 |
| 1958 – 1960.... | 8.2 | 17.0 | 2.0 | 43.9 |

### C. Selected Major Groups of Manufacturing — Quelques classes de la branche Industries manufacturières

| Period Période | Manu-facturing [1] Industries manu-facturières [1] | Food, beverages and tobacco Industries alimen-taires, boissons, tabac | Textiles | Clothing, footwear and made-up textiles Articles d'habil-lement, chaussures et ouvrages en tissu | Wood products and furniture Bois et meubles | Paper and paper products Papier et ouvrages en papier | Printing and publishing Im-primerie et édition | Leather and leather products except wearing apparel Cuir et articles en cuir, à l'exclu-sion des articles d'habil-lement | Rubber products Ouvrages en caout-chouc | Chemicals and chemical, petroleum and coal products Produits chi-miques et dérivés du pétrole et du charbon | Non-metallic mineral products Produits minéraux non métal-liques | Metal products Ouvrages en métaux | Other manu-facturing Autres industries manufac-turières |
|---|---|---|---|---|---|---|---|---|---|---|---|---|---|
| ISIC — CITI | 2–3 | 20–22 | 23 | 24 | 25–26 | 27 | 28 | 29 | 30 | 31–32 | 33 | 35–38 | 39 |

a. Indexes — Indices (1958 = 100)

| | | | | | | | | | | | | | |
|---|---|---|---|---|---|---|---|---|---|---|---|---|---|
| 1952.......... | 52 | 62 | 64 | 116 | 45 | 43 | ... | 18 | 58 | 49 | 59 | 36 | ... |
| 1953.......... | 59 | 65 | 61 | 135 | 52 | 72 | ... | 25 | 57 | 55 | 64 | 48 | ... |
| 1954.......... | 66 | 71 | 59 | 142 | 70 | 73 | ... | 42 | 54 | 58 | 63 | 54 | ... |
| 1955.......... | −74− | −83− | −48− | −148− | −77− | −73− | −82− | −56− | −60− | −68− | −64− | −75− | −76− |
| 1956.......... | 86 | 90 | 64 | 102 | 91 | 86 | 89 | 80 | 66 | 86 | 72 | 98 | 80 |
| 1957.......... | 93 | 96 | 80 | 96 | 109 | 89 | 90 | 126 | 97 | 89 | 84 | 104 | 92 |
| 1958.......... | 100 | 100 | 100 | 100 | 100 | 100 | 100 | 100 | 100 | 100 | 100 | 100 | 100 |
| 1959.......... | 108 | 109 | 122 | 86 | 118 | 112 | 107 | 139 | 148 | 101 | 108 | 109 | 82 |
| 1960.......... | 112 | 116 | 133 | 77 | 93 | 122 | 105 | 88 | 148 | 103 | 111 | 102 | 90 |
| 1961.......... | 119 | 119 | 136 | 70 | 89 | 134 | 96 | 90 | 153 | 108 | 129 | 135 | 96 |

b. Average Annual Rate of Change — Taux annuel moyen de variation

| | | | | | | | | | | | | | |
|---|---|---|---|---|---|---|---|---|---|---|---|---|---|
| 1954 – 1958...... | 10.9 | 8.9 | 14.1 | −8.4 | 9.3 | 8.2 | ... | 24.2 | 16.7 | 14.6 | 12.2 | 16.7 | ... |
| 1958 – 1960...... | 5.8 | 7.7 | 15.3 | −12.2 | −3.6 | 10.5 | 2.5 | −6.2 | 21.7 | 1.5 | 5.4 | 1.0 | −5.1 |

[1] Excludes Basic metals (ISIC major group 34) in all years; Printing and publishing (ISIC major group 28); Petroleum and coal products (ISIC major group 32); Transport equipment (ISIC major group 38) and Other manufacturing (ISIC major group 39) in the years before 1955.
[2] Covers Manila only up to 1951.

[1] Non compris Métallurgie de base (CITI classe 34) pour toutes les années; Imprimerie et édition (CITI classe 28), Dérivés du pétrole et du charbon (CITI classe 32), Construction de matériel de transport (CITI classe 38) et Autres industries manufacturières (CITI classe 39) pour les années antérieures à 1955.
[2] Jusqu'en 1951, les données ne concernent que Manille.

## 3. INDEX NUMBERS OF INDUSTRIAL EMPLOYMENT — INDICES DE L'EMPLOI DANS L'INDUSTRIE

### A. The Divisions of Industrial Activity
### Les branches de l'activité industrielle

| Period<br>Période | Total | Mining<br>Industries<br>extractives | Manu-<br>facturing<br>Industries<br>manu-<br>facturières | Construction<br>Bâtiment<br>et travaux<br>publics | Electricity<br>and gas<br>Electricité<br>et gaz |
|---|---|---|---|---|---|
| ISIC — CITI | 1–3, 511–512 | 1 | 2–3 | 4 | 511–512 |

a. Indexes — Indices (1958 = 100)

| Period | Total | Mining | Manufacturing | Construction | Electricity and gas |
|---|---|---|---|---|---|
| 1949....... | 71 | 101 | 81 | 166 | 68 |
| 1950....... | 81 | 122 | 79 | 116 | 71 |
| 1951....... | 83 | 145 | 80 | 73 | 67 |
| 1952....... | 83 | 152 | 80 | 85 | 64 |
| 1953....... | 90 | 140 | 88 | 77 | 65 |
| 1954....... | 94 | 108 | 94 | 92 | 64 |
| 1955....... | 95 | 114 | 94 | 66 | 75 |
| 1956....... | 95 | 113 | 94 | 76 | 90 |
| 1957....... | 100 | 108 | 100 | 90 | 94 |
| 1958....... | 100 | 100 | 100 | 100 | 100 |
| 1959....... | 104 | 96 | 105 | 104 | 102 |
| 1960....... | 107 | 95 | 108 | 111 | 105 |
| 1961....... | 109 | 92 | 110 | 117 | 104 |

b. Average Annual Rate of Change — Taux annuel moyen de variation

| Period | Total | Mining | Manufacturing | Construction | Electricity and gas |
|---|---|---|---|---|---|
| 1950–1960. | 2.8 | −2.5 | 3.2 | −0.4 | 4.0 |
| 1949–1953. | 6.1 | 8.5 | 2.1 | −17.5 | −1.1 |
| 1954–1958. | 1.6 | −1.9 | 1.6 | 2.1 | 11.8 |
| 1958–1960. | 3.4 | −2.5 | 3.9 | 5.4 | 2.5 |

### B. The Major Groups of Manufacturing — Les classes de la branche Industries manufacturières

| Period<br>Période | Manu-<br>facturing<br>Industries<br>manufac-<br>turières | Food,<br>beverages<br>and<br>tobacco<br>Industries<br>alimen-<br>taires,<br>boissons,<br>tabac | Textiles | Clothing,<br>footwear<br>and<br>made-up<br>textiles<br>Articles<br>d'habil-<br>lement,<br>chaussures<br>et<br>ouvrages<br>en tissu | Wood<br>products<br>and<br>furniture<br>Bois et<br>meubles | Paper<br>and<br>paper<br>products<br>Papier<br>et<br>ouvrages<br>en<br>papier | Printing<br>and<br>publishing<br>Im-<br>primerie<br>et<br>édition | Leather<br>and<br>leather<br>products<br>except<br>wearing<br>apparel<br>Cuir et<br>articles<br>en cuir,<br>à l'exclu-<br>sion<br>des<br>articles<br>d'habil-<br>lement | Rubber<br>products<br>Ouvrages<br>en<br>caout-<br>chouc | Chemicals<br>and<br>chemical,<br>petroleum<br>and<br>coal<br>products<br>Produits<br>chi-<br>miques<br>et<br>dérivés<br>du<br>pétrole<br>et du<br>charbon | Non-<br>metallic<br>mineral<br>products<br>Produits<br>minéraux<br>non<br>métal-<br>liques | Metal<br>products<br>Ouvrages<br>en<br>métaux | Other<br>manu-<br>facturing<br>Autres<br>industries<br>manufac-<br>turières |
|---|---|---|---|---|---|---|---|---|---|---|---|---|---|
| ISIC — CITI | 2–3 | 20–22 | 23 | 24 | 25–26 | 27 | 28 | 29 | 30 | 31–32 | 33 | 35–38 | 39 |

a. Indexes — Indices (1958 = 100)

| Period | Manufacturing | Food, beverages and tobacco | Textiles | Clothing, footwear | Wood products | Paper | Printing | Leather | Rubber | Chemicals | Non-metallic mineral | Metal products | Other |
|---|---|---|---|---|---|---|---|---|---|---|---|---|---|
| 1949............. | 81 | 84 | 73 | 112 | 106 | 70 | 71 | — | 68 | 62 | 87 | 68 | 62 |
| 1950............. | 79 | 80 | 76 | 81 | 108 | 78 | 70 | — | 76 | 68 | 91 | 77 | 66 |
| 1951............. | 80 | 81 | 79 | 78 | 105 | 88 | 68 | — | 75 | 75 | 93 | 77 | 72 |
| 1952............. | 80 | 84 | 79 | 71 | 97 | 94 | 70 | — | 67 | 71 | 95 | 73 | 72 |
| 1953............. | 88 | 96 | 73 | 78 | 101 | 93 | 73 | — | 75 | 82 | 102 | 77 | 70 |
| 1954............. | 94 | 100 | 72 | 107 | 106 | 98 | 78 | — | 69 | 93 | 113 | 73 | 80 |
| 1955............. | 94 | 102 | 73 | 105 | 93 | 97 | 84 | 92 | 70 | 97 | 122 | 76 | 82 |
| 1956............. | 94 | 96 | 81 | 108 | 95 | 87 | 92 | 88 | 67 | 98 | 129 | 76 | 83 |
| 1957............. | 100 | 102 | 88 | 102 | 100 | 94 | 95 | 98 | 85 | 107 | 134 | 91 | 88 |
| 1958............. | 100 | 100 | 100 | 100 | 100 | 100 | 100 | 100 | 100 | 100 | 100 | 100 | 100 |
| 1959............. | 105 | 104 | 119 | 101 | 96 | 99 | 102 | 124 | 107 | 105 | 109 | 101 | 126 |
| 1960............. | 108 | 108 | 128 | 108 | 88 | 97 | 108 | 122 | 104 | 106 | 109 | 107 | 131 |
| 1961............. | 110 | 110 | 136 | 105 | 88 | 105 | 112 | 127 | 103 | 111 | 129 | 113 | 118 |

b. Average Annual Rate of Change — Taux annuel moyen de variation

| Period | Manufacturing | Food, beverages and tobacco | Textiles | Clothing, footwear | Wood products | Paper | Printing | Leather | Rubber | Chemicals | Non-metallic mineral | Metal products | Other |
|---|---|---|---|---|---|---|---|---|---|---|---|---|---|
| 1950–1960...... | 3.2 | 3.0 | 5.4 | 2.9 | −2.0 | 2.2 | 4.4 | ... | 3.2 | 4.5 | 1.8 | 3.3 | 7.1 |
| 1949–1953...... | 2.1 | 3.4 | — | −8.7 | −1.2 | 7.3 | 0.7 | ... | 2.5 | 7.2 | 4.0 | 3.1 | 3.1 |
| 1954–1958...... | 1.6 | — | 8.6 | −1.7 | −1.5 | 0.5 | 6.4 | ... | 9.7 | 1.8 | −3.0 | 8.2 | 5.7 |
| 1958–1960...... | 3.9 | 3.9 | 13.1 | 3.9 | −6.2 | −1.5 | 3.9 | 10.5 | 2.0 | 3.0 | 4.4 | 3.4 | 14.5 |

618

# 4. CHARACTERISTICS OF ESTABLISHMENTS ENGAGED IN MINING AND MANUFACTURING
## CARACTERISTIQUES DES ETABLISSEMENTS MINIERS ET MANUFACTURIERS

**ALL ESTABLISHMENTS IN 1938 AND LICENSED ESTABLISHMENTS IN 1948**
Number of establishments in units; gross receipts, value of production and wages and salaries in million Pesos; number of engaged and employees in thousands; capacity of installed power equipment in thousand horsepower; and capacity of installed power equipment per employee in horsepower.

**TOUS ETABLISSEMENTS EN 1938 ET ETABLISSEMENTS PATENTES EN 1948**
Nombre d'établissements en unités; recettes brutes, valeur de la production et traitements et salaires en millions de pesos; nombre de personnes occupées et de salariés en milliers; puissance installée en milliers de chevaux-vapeur; puissance installée par salarié en chevaux-vapeur.

## A. The Major Groups of Mining — Les classes de la branche Industries extractives

| Item of data | All mining<br>Toutes industries extractives | Coal mining [1]<br>Extraction du charbon [1] | Metal mining<br>Extraction des minerais métalliques | Crude petroleum and natural gas<br>Pétrole brut et gaz naturel | Other mining<br>Divers | Rubrique | Item of data | All mining<br>Toutes industries extractives | Coal mining [1]<br>Extraction du charbon [1] | Metal mining<br>Extraction des minerais métalliques | Crude petroleum and natural gas<br>Pétrole brut et gaz naturel | Other mining<br>Divers | Rubrique |
|---|---|---|---|---|---|---|---|---|---|---|---|---|---|
| ISIC | 1 | 11 | 12 | 13 | 14-19 | CITI | ISIC | 1 | 11 | 12 | 13 | 14-19 | CITI |
| | **a. Absolute Figures — Chiffres absolus** | | | | | | | **b. Structure** | | | | | |
| Number of establishments... | 67 | 6 | 54 | 2 | 5 | Nombre d'établissements | Distribution in percent of number of employees.... | | | | | | Distribution en pourcentage du nombre de salariés |
| Gross value of production...... | | 1.0 | 27.3 | ... | 0.6 | Valeur brute de la production | Per employee: | 100.0 | 7.0 | 90.4 | 0.9 | 1.7 | Par salarié: |
| Number of employees (Average for the year).... | 11.5 | 0.8 | 10.4 | 0.1 | 0.2 | Nombre de salariés (moyenne pour l'année) | Wages and salaries......... | 0.8 | 0.8 | 0.8 | 2.0 | 1.0 | Traitements et salaires |
| Wages and salaries paid.......... | 9.6 | 0.6 | 8.6 | 0.2 | 0.2 | Traitements et salaires payés | Capacity of installed power equipment....... | 2.2 | 1.0 | 2.3 | 1.0 | 4.5 | Puissance installée |
| Capacity of installed power equipment....... | 25.3 | 0.8 | 23.5 | 0.1 | 0.9 | Puissance installée | | | | | | | |

[1] Includes asbestos.

[1] Y compris l'amiante.

## B. The Major Groups of Manufacturing — Les classes de la branche Industries manufacturières

| Year and item of data | Manu-facturing<br>Industries manufacturières | Food beverages and tobacco<br>Industries alimentaires, boissons, tabac | Textiles | Clothing, footwear and made-up textiles [1]<br>Articles d'habillement, chaussures et ouvrages en tissu [1] | Wood products and furniture<br>Bois et meubles | Paper and paper products<br>Papier et ouvrages en papier | Printing and publishing<br>Imprimerie et édition | Leather and leather products except wearing apparel<br>Cuir et articles en cuir, à l'exclusion des articles d'habillement | Chemicals and chemical, petroleum and coal products<br>Produits chimiques et dérivés du pétrole et du charbon | Non-metallic mineral products<br>Produits minéraux non métalliques | Metal products<br>Ouvrages en métaux | Other manu-facturing<br>Autres industries manufacturières | Année et rubrique |
|---|---|---|---|---|---|---|---|---|---|---|---|---|---|
| ISIC | 2-3 | 20-22 | 23 | 24, 30 | 25-26 | 27 | 28 | 29 | 31-32 | 33 | 35-38 | 39 | CITI |
| | **a. Absolute Figures — Chiffres absolus** | | | | | | | | | | | | |
| **1938** | | | | | | | | | | | | | **1938** |
| Gross receipts......... | 380.7 | 273.0 | 7.9 | 28.3 | 32.2 | 1.0 | 10.9 | 0.8 | 7.8 | 2.0 | 5.2 | 11.6 | Recettes brutes |
| Number of employees (Average for the year)........... | 424.6 | ... | ... | ... | ... | ... | ... | ... | ... | ... | ... | ... | Nombre de salariés (moyenne pour l'année) |
| Wages and salaries paid.............. | 50.9 | ... | ... | ... | ... | ... | ... | ... | ... | ... | ... | ... | Traitements et salaires payés |
| Capacity of installed power equipment..... | 295.8 | ... | ... | ... | ... | ... | ... | ... | ... | ... | ... | ... | Puissance installée |
| **1948** | | | | | | | | | | | | | **1948** |
| Number of establishments. | 28 889 | 12 804 | 1 323 | 6 808 | 2 107 | 32 | 231 | 83 | 199 | 1 628 | 2 018 | 1 656 | Nombre d'établissements |
| Gross value of production............. | 1 039.7 | 707.8 | 35.6 | 61.1 | 137.9 [2] | 0.8 | 20.6 | 0.9 | 16.0 | 14.8 | 29.5 | 14.7 | Valeur brute de la production |
| Number of engaged (Average for the year)........... | 269.6 | ... | ... | ... | ... | ... | ... | ... | ... | ... | ... | ... | Nombre de personnes occupées (moyenne pour l'année) |
| Number of employees (Average for the year)........... | 185.1 | 87.3 | 5.9 | 31.2 | 27.3 | 0.3 | 3.4 | 0.5 | 1.6 | 9.1 | 11.7 | 6.8 | Nombre de salariés (moyenne pour l'année) |
| Wages and salaries paid.............. | 99.2 | 43.6 | 2.3 | 8.9 | 23.1 | 0.1 | 3.7 | 0.2 | 1.0 | 4.8 | 9.1 | 2.4 | Traitements et salaires payés |
| Capacity of installed power equipment..... | 3 002.7 | ... | ... | ... | ... | ... | ... | ... | ... | ... | ... | ... | Puissance installée |
| | **b. Structure** | | | | | | | | | | | | |
| **1948** | | | | | | | | | | | | | **1948** |
| Distribution in percent of number of employees..... | 100.0 | 47.2 | 3.2 | 16.8 | 14.7 | 0.2 | 1.8 | 0.3 | 0.9 | 4.9 | 6.3 | 3.7 | Distribution en pourcentage du nombre de salariés |
| Wages and salaries per employee....... | 0.5 | 0.5 | 0.4 | 0.3 | 0.8 | 0.3 | 1.1 | 0.4 | 0.6 | 0.5 | 0.8 | 0.4 | Traitements et salaires par salarié |

[1] Includes the manufacture of Rubber products (ISIC major group 30).
[2] Gross receipts.

[1] Y compris la fabrication d'Ouvrages en caoutchouc (CITI classe 30).
[2] Recettes brutes.

## 5. CHARACTERISTICS OF MANUFACTURING ESTABLISHMENTS ENGAGING FIVE OR MORE PERSONS
### CARACTERISTIQUES DES ETABLISSEMENTS MANUFACTURIERS OCCUPANT CINQ PERSONNES OU PLUS
#### 1956, 1958

Number of establishments in units; value added and wages and salaries in million Pesos; and value added per person engaged in thousand Pesos.

Nombre d'établissements en unités; valeur ajoutée et traitements et salaires en millions de pesos; valeur ajoutée par personne occupée en milliers de pesos.

| Year and item of data | Manufacturing / Industries manufacturières | Food: beverages and tobacco / Industries alimentaires, boissons, tabac | Textiles | Clothing, footwear and made-up textiles / Articles d'habillement, chaussures et ouvrages en tissu | Wood products and furniture / Bois et meubles | Paper and paper products / Papier et ouvrages en papier | Printing and publishing / Imprimerie et édition | Leather and leather products except wearing apparel / Cuir et articles en cuir, à l'exclusion des articles d'habillement | Rubber products / Ouvrages en caoutchouc | Chemicals and chemical products[1] / Produits chimiques[1] | Non-metallic mineral products / Produits minéraux non métalliques | Basic metals / Métallurgie de base | Metal products / Ouvrages en métaux | Other manufacturing[1] / Autres industries manufacturières[1] |
|---|---|---|---|---|---|---|---|---|---|---|---|---|---|---|
| ISIC | 2–3 | 20–22 | 23 | 24 | 25–26 | 27 | 28 | 29 | 30 | 31 | 33 | 34 | 35–38 | 32, 39 |
| **a. Absolute Figures — Chiffres absolus** | | | | | | | | | | | | | | |
| **1956** | | | | | | | | | | | | | | |
| Number of establishments | 7 208 | 2 884 | 186 | 1 725 | 684 | 75 | 299 | 29 | 20 | 252 | 168 | 36 | 539 | 311 |
| Value added | 978.9 | 425.5 | 43.2 | 60.7 | 62.3 | 18.8 | 33.8 | 2.9 | 8.5 | 91.5 | 42.7 | 8.5 | 78.6 | 101.9 |
| Number of engaged (Average for the year) | 205.8 | 76.7 | 10.1 | 33.9 | 26.1 | 3.2 | 9.8 | 0.7 | 2.6 | 9.6 | 6.0 | 1.3 | 19.4 | 6.4 |
| Employees: Number (Average for the year) | 196.1 | 72.2 | 10.0 | 31.1 | 25.5 | 3.0 | 9.6 | 0.7 | 2.6 | 9.4 | 5.8 | 1.3 | 18.8 | 6.1 |
| Wages and salaries | 340.2 | 119.8 | 17.7 | 31.2 | 40.7 | 5.7 | 23.6 | 0.9 | 3.9 | 25.5 | 12.1 | 2.8 | 41.7 | 14.6 |
| Operatives: Number (Average for the year) | 159.0 | 56.5 | 8.6 | 28.5 | 21.5 | 2.5 | 6.9 | 0.6 | 2.3 | 6.1 | 4.7 | 1.1 | 15.1 | 4.6 |
| Wages and salaries | 219.3 | 74.5 | 13.3 | 25.1 | 26.6 | 3.7 | 14.4 | 0.6 | 2.9 | 11.5 | 9.2 | 2.3 | 26.2 | 9.0 |
| **1958** | | | | | | | | | | | | | | |
| Number of establishments | 7 411 | 2 599 | 102 | 1 930 | 825 | 53 | 336 | 40 | 36 | 281 | 193 | 33 | 679 | 304 |
| Value added | 1 404.3 | 580.8 | 81.0 | 60.2 | 84.8 | 29.2 | 55.0 | 3.6 | 46.6 | 113.0 | 59.7 | 16.6 | 149.8 | 124.0 |
| Number of engaged (Average for the year) | 228.4 | 76.1 | 17.2 | 31.2 | 30.6 | 3.0 | 10.6 | 1.0 | 4.8 | 11.6 | 7.7 | 2.6 | 25.6 | 6.4 |
| Employees: Number (Average for the year) | 218.4 | 72.3 | 17.1 | 27.8 | 29.9 | 2.9 | 10.2 | 1.0 | 4.8 | 11.4 | 7.4 | 2.6 | 24.9 | 6.1 |
| Wages and salaries | 409.7 | 130.6 | 30.2 | 29.0 | 46.5 | 7.2 | 26.6 | 1.3 | 10.6 | 34.0 | 15.7 | 5.3 | 58.6 | 14.1 |
| Operatives: Number (Average for the year) | 172.8 | 55.1 | 14.9 | 25.2 | 24.7 | 2.3 | 7.9 | 0.8 | 3.9 | 6.8 | 5.8 | 2.1 | 19.4 | 3.9 |
| Wages and salaries | 259.4 | 79.2 | 21.7 | 22.9 | 33.5 | 4.4 | 18.1 | 0.9 | 6.5 | 14.6 | 10.5 | 4.1 | 34.6 | 8.4 |
| **b. Structure** | | | | | | | | | | | | | | |
| **1956 — Distribution in percent of:** | | | | | | | | | | | | | | |
| Value added | 100.0 | 43.5 | 4.4 | 6.2 | 6.4 | 1.9 | 3.4 | 0.3 | 0.9 | 9.3 | 4.4 | 0.9 | 8.0 | 10.4 |
| Number of engaged | 100.0 | 37.3 | 4.9 | 16.5 | 12.7 | 1.5 | 4.8 | 0.3 | 1.3 | 4.7 | 2.9 | 0.6 | 9.4 | 3.1 |
| Value added per person engaged | 4.8 | 5.5 | 4.3 | 1.8 | 2.4 | 5.9 | 3.4 | 4.1 | 3.3 | 9.5 | 7.1 | 6.5 | 4.0 | 15.9 |
| Employees as a percent of engaged | 95.3 | 94.1 | 99.0 | 91.7 | 97.7 | 93.8 | 98.0 | 100.0 | 100.0 | 97.9 | 96.7 | 100.0 | 96.9 | 95.3 |
| Value added per unit of wages and salaries | 2.88 | 3.55 | 2.44 | 1.94 | 1.53 | 3.30 | 1.43 | 3.22 | 2.18 | 3.59 | 3.53 | 3.04 | 1.88 | 6.98 |
| Operatives as a percent of employees | 81.1 | 78.2 | 86.0 | 91.6 | 84.3 | 83.3 | 71.9 | 85.7 | 88.5 | 64.9 | 81.0 | 84.6 | 80.3 | 75.4 |
| Wages and salaries per employee | 1.7 | 1.6 | 1.8 | 1.0 | 1.6 | 1.9 | 2.4 | 1.3 | 1.5 | 2.7 | 2.1 | 2.2 | 2.2 | 2.4 |
| Wages and salaries per operative | 1.4 | 1.3 | 1.5 | 0.9 | 1.2 | 1.5 | 2.1 | 1.0 | 1.3 | 1.9 | 2.0 | 2.1 | 1.7 | 2.0 |
| **1958 — Distribution in percent of:** | | | | | | | | | | | | | | |
| Value added | 100.0 | 41.4 | 5.8 | 4.3 | 6.0 | 2.1 | 3.9 | 0.3 | 3.3 | 8.0 | 4.2 | 1.2 | 10.7 | 8.8 |
| Number of engaged | 100.0 | 33.3 | 7.5 | 13.7 | 13.4 | 1.3 | 4.6 | 0.4 | 2.1 | 5.1 | 3.4 | 1.1 | 11.2 | 2.9 |
| Value added per person engaged | 6.1 | 7.6 | 4.7 | 1.9 | 2.8 | 9.7 | 5.2 | 3.6 | 9.7 | 9.7 | 7.8 | 6.4 | 5.8 | 19.4 |
| Employees as a percent of engaged | 95.6 | 95.0 | 99.4 | 89.1 | 97.7 | 96.7 | 96.2 | 100.0 | 100.0 | 98.3 | 96.1 | 100.0 | 97.3 | 95.3 |
| Value added per unit of wages and salaries | 3.43 | 4.45 | 2.68 | 2.08 | 1.82 | 4.06 | 2.07 | 2.77 | 4.40 | 3.32 | 3.80 | 3.13 | 2.56 | 8.79 |
| Operatives as a percent of employees | 79.1 | 76.2 | 87.1 | 90.6 | 82.6 | 79.3 | 77.4 | 80.0 | 81.2 | 59.6 | 78.4 | 80.8 | 77.9 | 63.9 |
| Wages and salaries per employee | 1.9 | 1.8 | 1.8 | 1.0 | 1.6 | 2.5 | 2.6 | 1.3 | 2.2 | 3.0 | 2.1 | 2.0 | 2.4 | 2.3 |
| Wages and salaries per operative | 1.5 | 1.4 | 1.5 | 0.9 | 1.4 | 1.9 | 2.3 | 1.1 | 1.7 | 2.1 | 1.8 | 2.0 | 1.8 | 2.2 |

[1] The manufacture of petroleum and coal products is included with Other manufacturing (ISIC major group 39) instead of with Chemicals and chemical products (ISIC major group 31).

[1] La fabrication des dérivés du pétrole et du charbon est comprise dans Autres industries manufacturières (CITI classe 39) et non dans Produits chimiques (CITI classe 31).

# POLAND — POLOGNE

## Net Material Product and the Available Goods and Services

The figures in Table 1 on the net material products and the goods and production services available for distribution are derived from figures furnished to the Statistical Office of the United Nations by the Central Statistical Office of Poland, Warsaw. The official estimates are published annually by that office in *Rocznik Statystyczny*. The concepts and methods utilized in making these estimates are described in *Rocznik Statystyczny, 1962, Concise Statistical Yearbook of Poland, 1962* and *Dochód Narodowy Polski 1957 i 1958 oraz wstepny szacunek 1959.*

The concepts governing the official estimates of Poland, as well as those shown in Table 1, are those of the system of material product accounts which is briefly described in the introduction to this publication. This system of accounts differs from the United Nations system of national accounts with regard to the boundaries of production, as well as in other respects. It should be noted that the data on goods and productive services available for distribution and the net material product shown in Table 1A differ in concept for one another in that net exports of goods and productive services are not included in the former. The data set out in Table 1B on the domestic (home produced) net material product also differ in concept from that in Table 1A on the net material product. Imports of goods and productive services consumed in economic sectors other than those covered in material production and gains or losses in foreign exchange transactions, measured in domestic prices, are excluded from the former estimates but included in the latter figures.

## Index Numbers of Industrial Production

The indexes of industrial production set out in Table 2 are compiled by the Central Statistical Office of Poland and published in *Rocznik Statystyczny* or furnished by that Office in correspondance with the Statistical Office of the United Nations. The distinctions drawn between mining and manufacturing in the case of the index numbers shown in Table 2A are like the distinctions made in the International Standard Industrial Classification of all Economic Activities. Such distinctions are not made in the case of the index numbers in Table 2B, where the scheme of industrial classification utilized is based on the branches of industrial activity shown in the National Economy Classification of Poland.

The series of index numbers shown in Table 1, excepting those for construction, relate to all enterprises (establishments) which are publicly-owned, co-operatives

## Produit matériel net et biens et services disponibles

Les chiffres du tableau 1 relatifs au produit matériel net et aux biens et services disponibles pour la distribution ont été calculés à partir de chiffres fournis au Bureau de statistique de l'ONU par l'Office central de statistique de Pologne, Varsovie. Les estimations officielles sont publiées annuellement par cet Office dans *Rocznik Statystyczny*. Les concepts et méthodes adoptés pour établir ces estimations sont exposés dans *Rocznik Statystyczny, 1962, Concise Statistical Yearbook of Poland 1962* et *Dochód Narodowy Polski 1957 i 1958 oraz wstepny szacunek 1959.*

Les concepts sur lesquels reposent les estimations officielles de la Pologne, ainsi que les chiffres du tableau 1, sont ceux du système de comptabilité relatif au produit matériel, qui est décrit brièvement dans l'introduction de cette publication. Ce système de comptabilité diffère de celui des Nations Unies quant aux limites du secteur de la production, ainsi qu'à d'autres égards. Il y a lieu de noter que, dans le tableau 1 A, les données relatives aux biens et aux services productifs disponibles pour la distribution et les chiffres concernant le produit matériel net ne reposent pas sur les mêmes concepts en ce sens que les exportations nettes de biens et de services productifs ne sont pas comprises dans le premier agrégat. De même, les données du tableau 1 B relatives au produit matériel intérieur net ne reposent pas sur les mêmes concepts que les chiffres du tableau 1 A concernant le produit matériel net. Les importations de biens et de services productifs consommés par les secteurs économiques autres que ceux qui contribuent à la production matérielle, ainsi que les profits et pertes résultant des transactions avec l'étranger, évalués aux prix intérieurs, sont exclus dans le premier cas mais compris dans le second.

## Indices de la production industrielle

Les indices de la production industrielle reproduits au tableau 2 sont calculés par l'Office central de statistique de Pologne et publiés dans *Rocznik Statystyczny* ou fournis par correspondance au Bureau de statistique de l'ONU. Dans le cas des indices du tableau 2 A, les distinctions faites entre les industries extractives et les industries manufacturières sont analogues aux distinctions observées dans la classification internationale type, par industrie, de toutes les branches d'activité économique. De telles distinctions n'ont pas été faites dans le cas des indices du tableau 2 B, pour lesquelles le système de classification adopté est fondé sur les branches de l'activité industrielle de la Classification économique nationale de Pologne.

Les séries d'indices du tableau 1, à l'exception de celles qui concernent le bâtiment et les travaux publics, se rapportent à toutes les entreprises (établissements) qui

or privately-owned and registered members of national associations of private industry, and which are mainly engaged in mining, manufacturing and the production of electricity, gas or steam. The index numbers for construction cover publicly-owned or co-operative enterprises classified to the construction industry.

In both cases, the index numbers are compiled from figures of the value, in constant enterprise prices (i.e., excluding turnover and other indirect taxes) of the total gross output of the enterprises covered. In the case of the mining, manufacturing and public utility establishments, the value of gross output is the sum of the value of products made and ready for sale, the value of fabricating and other industrial services rendered to others, plus the value of any raw materials owned by others that are processed, and the value of the net change during the period in work-in-progress. The constant prices utilized in valuing the gross output are prices established as of 1 January 1950, on the basis of average prices during 1937, in the case of the indexes for 1938-1954; and prices set as of 1 January 1956, in the light of actual costs of production during 1954 adjusted for anticipated changes, in the case of the indexes for 1955-1961. For construction enterprises, the index numbers are based on all the work put in place during the year valued at estimated average transaction prices during 1961.

The series of index numbers shown in Table 1 are equivalent to indexes computed as base-weighted arithmetic averages of series of elementary relatives, where the data utilized in the computations relate to all of the output covered in the indexes. The bases of comparison for the elementary relatives utilized in the index numbers shown in Table 1, except those for the construction industry, are quantities of individual commodities produced during 1950 in the case of the indexes for 1938-1954 and during 1955 for the indexes for 1955-1961. The weights for combining these relatives into index numbers may be considered to be each of the quantities multiplied by the corresponding price as of 1 January 1950 or 1 January 1956, respectively. In the case of construction, the basis of comparison for the elementary relatives are quanta of production during 1956 and the weights are these quanta multiplied by the corresponding prices set as of 1 January 1961.

Further details concerning the series of index numbers may be found in *Rocznik Statystyczny, 1961* or *1962* and *Concise Statistical Yearbook of Poland, 1961* or *1962*.

### Index Numbers of Industrial Employment

The index numbers appearing in Table 3 were derived from indexes (1958 = 100) or absolute figures of employment compiled by the Central Statistical Office of Poland and published in various issues of *Rocznik Statystyczny*. The index numbers or absolute figures utilized for pur-

sont publiques, coopératives ou privées et affiliées à des associations nationales de l'industrie privée et dont l'activité principale relève des industries extractives, manufacturières ou productrices d'électricité, de gaz ou de vapeur. Les indices relatifs au bâtiment et aux travaux publics portent sur les entreprises publiques et coopératives classées dans les industries du bâtiment et des travaux publics.

Dans les deux cas, les indices sont construits à partir des chiffres indiquant la valeur, en prix constants des entreprises (c'est-à-dire non compris les impôts sur le chiffre d'affaires et autres impôts indirects) de la production brute totale des entreprises intéressées. Pour les établissements des industries extractives, des industries manufacturières et des services d'utilité publique, la valeur de la production brute représente la somme des éléments suivants : valeur des produits fabriqués et prêts à la vente; valeur des travaux à façon et autres services rendus à des tiers; valeur de toutes les matières premières traitées appartenant à des tiers; variations nettes, pendant la période considérée, de la valeur des travaux en cours. Les prix constants adoptés pour évaluer la production brute pour les indices de 1938-1954 sont les prix établis au 1er janvier 1950 sur la base des prix moyens en 1937 et pour les indices de 1955-1961 les prix établis au 1er janvier 1956 en fonction des coûts réels de production pendant 1954 et compte tenu des variations probables. Dans le cas des entreprises du bâtiment et des travaux publics, les indices sont fondés sur tous les travaux achevés pendant l'année, évalués aux prix estimatifs moyens des transactions pendant 1961.

Les séries d'indices du tableau 1 équivalent à des moyennes arithmétiques à pondération fixe de séries élémentaires de rapports, calculées au moyen de données se rapportant à la totalité de la production sur laquelle portent les indices. Les bases de comparaison des rapports élémentaires ayant servi à calculer les indices du tableau 1 sont, sauf pour les industries du bâtiment et des travaux publics, les quantités de chaque marchandise produite en 1950 dans le cas des indices de 1938-1954, et en 1955 dans le cas des indices de 1955-1961. Les coefficients de pondération utilisés pour combiner ces rapports en indices peuvent être considérés comme étant les valeurs de chacune des quantités en fonction des prix établis aux 1er janvier 1950 et 1er janvier 1956 respectivement. Dans le cas des entreprises du bâtiment et des travaux publics, la base de comparaison des séries élémentaires de rapports est constituée par les quanta de production pendant 1956 et les coefficients de pondération sont les valeurs de ces quanta en fonction des prix établis au 1er janvier 1956.

Pour plus de détails sur les séries d'indices, voir *Rocznik Statystyczny, 1961* ou *1962* et *Concise Statistical Yearbook of Poland, 1961* ou *1962*.

### Indices de l'emploi dans l'industrie

Les indices du tableau 3 ont été obtenus à partir d'indices (1958 = 100) ou de chiffres absolus de l'emploi calculés par l'Office central de statistique de Pologne et publiés dans différents numéros de *Rocznik Statystyczny*. Les indices ou chiffres absolus utilisés pour établir le

poses of Table 3 relate to the average during the year of the monthly number of all persons engaged in the same field of enterprises (establishments) as are covered by the index numbers of industrial production for the corresponding kind of economic activity. The definition of the figures of persons engaged is like that in the International Standards in Basic Industrial Statistics, i.e., employees, homeworkers, working proprietors, unpaid family workers are all included.

### The Characteristics and Structure of Industrial Activity

The data set out in Tables 4 and 5 have been compiled from *Rocznik Statystyczny, 1960* or *1961*. The figures shown in Table 4, except those for the construction industry, relate to all industrial establishments which are publicly-owned, co-operatives, or privately-owned and registered members of national associations of private industry. The figures in Table 4 for the construction industry refer to publicly-owned and co-operative contract enterprises only. The data appearing in Table 5 cover publicly-owned and co-operative establishments only. The scheme utilized in classifying the data shown in Tables 4 and 5 is essentially that of the National Economy Classification of Poland.

The items of data which are common to Tables 4 and 5, except for value of gross output, are defined in identical fashion. In the case of Table 4, the value of gross output is expressed in the constant enterprise prices (i.e., excluding turnover and other indirect taxes) as of 1 January 1956 mentioned above in describing the index numbers of industrial production. In the case of Table 5, however, gross output is valued in actual current industrial prices (i.e., including turnover and other indirect taxes). In both tables, the scope of gross output is the same as that described in connection with the index numbers of industrial production. The definition, but not the field covered, of the data on the contribution to the net material product shown in Table 5 is the same as that on the contribution to the net domestic material product shown in Table 1B. The data on the number of establishments and on the number of persons engaged appearing in Tables 4 and 5 are defined in the same way as is recommended in the International Standards in Basic Industrial Statistics. However, the figures of the number of operative and man-hours worked by operatives are restricted to manual workers engaged in the industrial activities of establishments. This is also the case for the data in electricity consumed and capacity of installed power equipment. The capacity of installed power equipment is the sum of the capacity of prime movers connected directly to machinery other than generators and the capacity of all installed electric motors.

tableau 3 portent sur la moyenne, pendant l'année, du nombre mensuel de personnes occupées dans le même ensemble d'entreprises (établissements) que celles sur lesquelles portent les indices de la production industrielle pour les types correspondants d'activité économique. Les personnes occupées sont définies conformément aux Normes internationales relatives aux statistiques industrielles de base; elles comprennent donc les salariés, les travailleurs à domicile, les propriétaires qui travaillent et les travailleurs familiaux non rémunérés.

### Caractéristiques et structure de l'activité industrielle

Les données des tableaux 4 et 5 sont tirées du *Rocznik Statystyczny, 1960* ou *1961*. Les chiffres du tableau 4, à l'exception de ceux qui concernent les industries du bâtiment et des travaux publics, se rapportent à tous les établissements industriels publics, coopératifs, ou privés et affiliés à des associations nationales de l'industrie privée. Les chiffres du tableau 4 concernant l'industrie du bâtiment et des travaux publics ne portent que sur les entreprises contractuelles des secteurs publics et privés. Les données du tableau 5 concernent les établissements publics et coopératifs seulement. Le système adopté pour classer les données des tableaux 4 et 5 est essentiellement celui de la Classification économique nationale de Pologne.

Les rubriques communes aux tableaux 4 et 5 sont définies de façon identique, à l'exception de la valeur de la production brute. Dans le cas du tableau 4, la valeur de la production brute est exprimée en prix constants de l'entreprise (c'est-à-dire non compris les impôts sur le chiffre d'affaires et autres impôts indirects) au 1er janvier 1956, comme on l'a indiqué plus haut lors de la description des indices de la production industrielle. Dans le cas du tableau 5, en revanche, la production brute est évaluée aux prix courants effectifs des industries (c'est-à-dire y compris les impôts sur le chiffre d'affaires et autres impôts indirects). Dans les deux tableaux, la production brute englobe les mêmes éléments que dans le cas des indices de la production industrielle. La définition, mais non la portée, des données sur la contribution au produit matériel net intérieur reproduites au tableau 5 est la même que celle des données sur la contribution au produit matériel net intérieur reproduites au tableau 1B. Les données des tableaux 4 et 5 relatives au nombre d'établissements et au nombre de personnes occupées sont définies conformément aux Normes internationales relatives aux statistiques industrielles de base. Cependant, les chiffres indiquant le nombre d'ouvriers et d'heures-ouvrier ne concernent que les travailleurs manuels affectés aux activités industrielles des établissements. C'est également le cas pour les données relatives à l'électricité consommée et à la puissance installée. La puissance installée est la puissance nominale des moteurs primaires reliés directement à des machines autres que des générateurs d'électricité et celle de tous les moteurs électriques.

# POLAND

## 1. THE NET MATERIAL PRODUCT AND THE AVAILABLE GOODS AND PRODUCTIVE SERVICES
## LE PRODUIT MATERIEL NET ET LES BIENS ET SERVICES PRODUCTIFS DISPONIBLES

Thousand million Zlotys — Milliards de zlotys

### A. Expenditure on the Net Material Product and the Available Goods and Productive Services
### Dépenses imputées au produit matériel net et aux biens et services productifs disponibles

| Item of data and year [1]<br>Rubrique et année [1] | Total | Consumption<br>Consommation<br>Total | Collective consumption [2]<br>Consommation collective [2] | Net Domestic Capital Formation<br>Formation nette de capital intérieur<br>Total | Fixed<br>Fixe | Net exports of goods and productive services [3]<br>Exportations nettes de biens et de services productifs [3] |
|---|---|---|---|---|---|---|
| *a. Net Material Product in Current Prices — Produit matériel net aux prix courants* | | | | | | |
| Absolute figures — Chiffres absolus | | | | | | |
| 1955.................... | 222.6 | 184.9 | 17.3 | 44.7 | 28.6 | —7.0 |
| 1956.................... | 252.1 | 206.9 | 19.0 | 50.8 | 35.9 | —5.6 |
| 1957.................... | 301.4 | 240.0 | 21.8 | 74.2 | 48.5 | —12.8 |
| 1958.................... | 321.3 | 255.3 | 24.7 | 77.5 | 53.8 | —11.5 |
| 1959.................... | 345.4 | 274.7 | 28.6 | 87.4 | 65.8 | —16.7 |
| 1960.................... | 371.5 | 284.2 | 31.7 | 99.4 | 73.2 | —12.1 |
| 1960.................... | 377.4 | 283.9 | 27.9 | 96.3 | 71.2 | —2.8 |
| 1961.................... | 415.8 | 305.4 | 31.9 | 113.9 | 82.6 | —3.5 |
| Percentage distribution of average annual expenditure — Distribution en pourcentage des dépenses annuelles moyennes | | | | | | |
| 1955 – 1960......................... | 100.0 | 79.7 | 7.8 | 24.0 | 16.8 | —3.7 |
| 1955.................... | 100.0 | 83.1 | 7.8 | 20.1 | 12.8 | —3.2 |
| 1958.................... | 100.0 | 79.5 | 7.7 | 24.1 | 16.7 | —3.6 |
| 1960.................... | 100.0 | 76.5 | 8.5 | 26.8 | 19.7 | —3.3 |
| *b. Available Goods and Productive Services in Constant Prices [4] — Biens et services productifs disponibles en prix constants [4]* | | | | | | |
| Absolute figures — Chiffres absolus | | | | | | |
| 1950.................... | 157.4 | 126.0 | 7.6 | 31.4 | 19.3 | . |
| 1951.................... | 169.3 | 136.1 | 8.9 | 33.2 | 21.9 | . |
| 1952.................... | 179.8 | 140.2 | 12.0 | 39.6 | 26.3 | . |
| 1953.................... | 198.3 | 144.6 | 12.0 | 53.7 | 31.7 | . |
| 1954.................... | 219.4 | 170.2 | 14.4 | 49.2 | 33.8 | . |
| 1955.................... | 239.1 | 187.4 | 17.7 | 51.7 | 34.9 | . |
| 1956.................... | 257.7 | 206.9 | 19.0 | 50.8 | 35.9 | . |
| 1957.................... | 292.9 | 229.9 | 20.7 | 63.0 | 39.8 | . |
| 1958.................... | 302.2 | 237.2 | 22.5 | 65.0 | 43.6 | . |
| 1959.................... | 323.4 | 252.1 | 24.9 | 71.3 | 51.6 | . |
| 1960.................... | 333.1 | 256.5 | 26.6 | 76.6 | 53.9 | . |
| 1960.................... | 390.2 | 286.8 | 28.7 | 103.4 | 77.0 | . |
| 1961.................... | 419.3 | 305.4 | 31.9 | 113.9 | 82.6 | . |
| Percentage distribution of average annual expenditure — Distribution en pourcentage des dépenses annuelles moyennes | | | | | | |
| 1950 – 1960......................... | 100.0 | 78.0 | 7.0 | 22.0 | 14.7 | . |
| 1950.................... | 100.0 | 80.0 | 4.8 | 20.0 | 12.2 | . |
| 1953.................... | 100.0 | 72.9 | 6.1 | 27.1 | 16.0 | . |
| 1954.................... | 100.0 | 77.6 | 6.6 | 22.4 | 15.4 | . |
| 1958.................... | 100.0 | 78.5 | 7.4 | 21.5 | 14.4 | . |
| 1960.................... | 100.0 | 77.0 | 8.0 | 23.0 | 16.2 | . |
| Average annual rate of growth — Taux annuel moyen d'accroissement | | | | | | |
| 1950 – 1960......................... | 7.8 | 7.4 | 13.3 | 9.3 | 10.8 | . |
| 1950 – 1953......................... | 8.0 | 4.7 | 16.4 | 19.6 | 18.0 | . |
| 1954 – 1958......................... | 8.3 | 8.7 | 11.8 | 7.2 | 6.6 | . |
| 1958 – 1960......................... | 5.0 | 4.0 | 8.7 | 8.5 | 11.2 | . |

For footnotes see end of table.          Pour les notes, voir au bas du tableau.

## B. The Domestic Net Material Product According to Origin
## Origine par secteur d'activité du produit matériel net intérieur

| Item of data and year [1]<br>Rubrique et année [1] | Total | Agricultural sector<br><br>Secteur agricole | Mining, manufacturing, electricity, and gas<br><br>Industries extractives et manufacturières, et électricité, et gaz | Construction<br><br>Bâtiment et travaux publics | Transportation and communication [1]<br><br>Transports et communications [1] | Other sectors<br><br>Autres secteurs |
|---|---|---|---|---|---|---|
| ISIC — CITI | 0-521, 61, 7, 841, 852 | 0 | 1-3, 51 | 4 | 7 | 521, 61, 841, 852 |
| *a. At Current Prices — Aux prix courants* | | | | | | |
| Absolute figures<br>— Chiffres absolus | | | | | | |
| 1955 | 228.7 | 56.8 | 119.9 | 17.0 | 6.7 | 28.3 |
| 1956 | 251.0 | 70.0 | 125.0 | 22.3 | 7.3 | 26.4 |
| 1957 | 296.5 | 85.8 | 143.1 | 24.8 | 8.3 | 34.5 |
| 1958 | 318.4 | 89.6 | 156.0 | 27.6 | 8.5 | 36.7 |
| 1959 | 339.8 | 89.7 | 170.3 | 35.4 | 7.9 | 36.5 |
| 1960 | 374.9 | 96.7 | 186.5 | 35.6 | 12.8 | 43.3 |
| 1960 | 376.5 | 96.0 | 179.5 | 35.2 | 21.9 | 43.9 |
| Percentage distribution according to sector—<br>Distribution en pourcentage par secteur | | | | | | |
| 1955 - 1960 | 100.0 | 27.0 | 49.7 | 9.0 | 2.9 | 11.4 |
| 1955 | 100.0 | 24.8 | 52.4 | 7.4 | 3.0 | 12.4 |
| 1958 | 100.0 | 28.1 | 49.0 | 8.7 | 2.6 | 11.6 |
| 1960 | 100.0 | 25.7 | 49.8 | 9.5 | 3.4 | 11.6 |
| *b. In Constant Prices [5] — En prix constants [5]* | | | | | | |
| Absolute figures<br>— Chiffres absolus | | | | | | |
| 1957 | 298.6 | 86.9 | 144.1 | 24.9 | 8.3 | 34.4 |
| 1958 | 318.4 | 89.6 | 156.0 | 27.6 | 8.5 | 36.7 |
| 1959 | 334.7 | 85.4 | 168.1 | 35.4 | 9.5 | 36.3 |
| 1960 | 356.0 | 89.5 | 182.0 | 35.2 | 10.3 | 39.0 |
| 1960 | 382.4 | 97.2 | 184.0 | 35.1 | 26.1 | 40.0 |
| 1961 | 416.9 | 108.9 | 202.0 | 35.1 | 27.8 | 43.1 |
| Percentage distribution according to sector—<br>Distribution en pourcentage par secteur | | | | | | |
| 1958 | 100.0 | 28.1 | 49.0 | 8.7 | 2.6 | 11.6 |
| 1960 | 100.0 | 25.1 | 51.1 | 9.9 | 2.9 | 11.0 |
| Average annual rate of growth—Taux annuel moyen d'accroissement | | | | | | |
| 1958 - 1960 | 5.7 | —0.5 | 8.0 | 12.9 | 10.1 | 3.1 |

[1] The second set of figures for 1960 and the figures for 1961 are not comparable to the first set of figures for 1960 and the data for earlier years because of changes in the definition of material production (for example, the inclusion of passenger transport and all communication services in addition to transport of goods and communication services for productive enterprises only) and in other methods of estimation beginning with the second sets of figures for 1960. The figures of distributions in percent and of average annual rates of growth presented in the table are computed using the first set of data for 1960.
[2] Material consumption by "non-production" institutions.
[3] Includes statitiscal discrepancy and losses in national income.
[4] The data for the years, 1950-1960, are valued at prices of 1956 whereas the data for the years, 1960-1961, are valued at prices of 1961.
[5] The data for the years, 1957-1960, are valued at prices of 1958 whereas the data for the years, 1960-1961, are valued at prices of 1961.

[1] Le second ensemble de chiffres de 1960 et les chiffres de 1961 ne sont pas comparables au premier ensemble de chiffres de 1960 et aux données concernant les années précédentes en raison des changements apportés, à partir du second ensemble de chiffres de 1960, à la définition du produit matériel (par exemple, l'inclusion des transports de passagers et de tous les services de communications en plus des transports de marchandises et des services de communications pour les seules entreprises qui concourent à la formation du produit matériel) et aux autres méthodes d'estimation. Les répartitions en pourcentage et les taux annuels moyens d'accroissement ont été calculés à partir du premier ensemble de données de 1960.
[2] Produit matériel consommé par les organismes qui ne concourent pas à sa formation.
[3] Y compris les écarts statistiques et les pertes de revenu national.
[4] Les données de 1950-1960 sont évaluées aux prix de 1956, tandis que celles de 1960-1961 le sont aux prix de 1961.
[5] Les données de 1957-1960 sont évaluées aux prix de 1958, tandis que celles de 1960-1961 le sont aux prix de 1961.

## 2. INDEX NUMBERS OF INDUSTRIAL PRODUCTION — INDICES DE LA PRODUCTION INDUSTRIELLE

### A. The Divisions of Industrial Activity
### Les branches de l'activité industrielle

| Period<br>Période | Total excluding construction<br>—<br>Total, à l'exclusion du bâtiment et des travaux publics | Mining<br>Industries extractives | Manu-facturing [1]<br>Industries manu-facturières [1] | Construction<br>Bâtiment et travaux publics | Electricity and steam<br>Electricité et vapeur |
|---|---|---|---|---|---|
| ISIC — CITI | 1-3, 511-521 | 1 | 2-3, 512, 521 | 4 | 511, 513 |

#### a. Indexes — Indices (1958 = 100)

| | | | | | |
|---|---|---|---|---|---|
| 1938....... | 16 | ... | ... | ... | ... |
| 1948....... | 24 | ... | ... | ... | ... |
| 1949....... | 28 | 61 | 26 | ... | 31 |
| 1950....... | 36 | 65 | 34 | 37 | 35 |
| 1951....... | 44 | 69 | 43 | 50 | 38 |
| 1952....... | 52 | 76 | 51 | 61 | 39 |
| 1953....... | 61 | 84 | 60 | 74 | 49 |
| 1954....... | 68 | 90 | 67 | 77 | 57 |
| 1955....... | —76— | —95— | —75— | 82 | —69— |
| 1956....... | 83 | 99 | 82 | 86 | 81 |
| 1957....... | 91 | 98 | 91 | 92 | 88 |
| 1958....... | 100 | 100 | 100 | 100 | 100 |
| 1959....... | 109 | 106 | 109 | 114 | 110 |
| 1960....... | 121 | 113 | 121 | 122 | 124 |
| 1961....... | 134 | ... | ... | 127 | 141 |

#### b. Average Annual Rate of Change — Taux annuel moyen de variation

| | | | | | |
|---|---|---|---|---|---|
| 1950 − 1960. | 12.9 | 5.7 | 13.5 | 12.7 | 13.5 |
| 1950 − 1953. | 19.2 | 8.9 | 20.9 | 26.0 | 11.9 |
| 1954 − 1958. | 10.1 | 2.7 | 10.5 | 6.8 | 15.1 |
| 1958 − 1960. | 10.0 | 6.3 | 10.0 | 10.5 | 11.4 |

For footnotes, see end of table.
Pour les notes, voir au bas du tableau.

## B. The Major Sub-divisions of Mining and Manufacturing

## Les principales subdivisions des Industries extractives et manufacturières

| Period / Période | Mining and manufacturing [1] / Industries extractives et manufacturieres [1] | Food, beverages and tobacco [1,2] / Industries alimentaires, boissons, tabac [1,2] | Textiles | Clothing and made-up textiles / Articles d'habillement et ouvrages en tissu | Wood products and furniture [3] / Bois et meubles [3] | Paper and paper products / Papier et ouvrages en papier | Printing [1,5] / Imprimerie [1,5] | Leather and leather products / Cuir et articles en cuir | Rubber products [6] / Ouvrages en caoutchouc [6] | Chemicals, coal, crude petroleum and products [2] / Produits chimiques, charbon, pétrole brut et produits dérivés [2] | Non-metallic minerals and products [6] / Minéraux non métalliques et produits dérivés [6] | Metal mining and basic metals / Minerais métalliques et métallurgie de base | Metal products [3,4] / Ouvrages en métaux [3,4] | Other manufacturing [1,2] / Autres industries manufacturieres [1,2] |
|---|---|---|---|---|---|---|---|---|---|---|---|---|---|---|
| ISIC — CITI | 1-3, 512, 521 | 191, 20-22 | 23 | 243-244 | 25-26 | 27 | 28 | 241, 29 | 30 | 11,13,192, 31-32, 512 | 14, 199, 33 | 12, 34 | 35-38, 391-393 | 399, 521 |

### a. Indexes — Indices (1958 = 100)

| | | | | | | | | | | | | | | |
|---|---|---|---|---|---|---|---|---|---|---|---|---|---|---|
| 1949 | 28 | 34 | 38 | 16 | 24 | 34 | 29 | 20 | 23 | 43 | 27 | 38 | 14 | 15 |
| 1950 | 36 | 50 | 40 | 33 | 36 | 39 | 41 | 38 | 33 | 48 | 32 | 44 | 18 | 24 |
| 1951 | 44 | 57 | 48 | 48 | 45 | 49 | 46 | 53 | 41 | 53 | 40 | 48 | 28 | 35 |
| 1952 | 52 | 62 | 58 | 53 | 56 | 57 | 46 | 52 | 53 | 61 | 51 | 54 | 39 | 48 |
| 1953 | 61 | 68 | 65 | 54 | 73 | 63 | 53 | 55 | 57 | 66 | 61 | 68 | 52 | 51 |
| 1954 | 68 | 73 | 67 | 55 | 79 | 76 | 60 | 66 | 68 | 74 | 67 | 75 | 61 | 59 |
| 1955 | 76 — | 78 — | 77 — | 64 — | 89 — | 84 — | 71 — | 72 — | 74 — | 83 — | 75 — | 82 — | 67 — | 73 — |
| 1956 | 83 | 84 | 84 | 71 | 90 | 88 | 78 | 81 | 78 | 87 | 81 | 88 | 76 | 80 |
| 1957 | 91 | 92 | 91 | 89 | 97 | 93 | 89 | 90 | 93 | 92 | 88 | 95 | 87 | 90 |
| 1958 | 100 | 100 | 100 | 100 | 100 | 100 | 100 | 100 | 100 | 100 | 100 | 100 | 100 | 100 |
| 1959 | 109 | 103 | 109 | 92 | 107 | 114 | 108 | 107 | 110 | 111 | 122 | 108 | 120 | 112 |
| 1960 | 121 | 113 | 114 | 97 | 116 | 124 | 117 | 111 | 128 | 126 | 124 | 120 | 142 | 132 |
| 1961 | 134 | 120 | 121 | 108 | 126 | 136 | 127 | 111 | 153 | 141 | 136 | 133 | 167 | ... |

### b. Average Annual Rate of Change — Taux annuel moyen de variation

| | | | | | | | | | | | | | | |
|---|---|---|---|---|---|---|---|---|---|---|---|---|---|---|
| 1950–1960 | 12.9 | 8.5 | 11.0 | 11.4 | 12.4 | 12.3 | 11.1 | 11.3 | 14.5 | 10.1 | 14.5 | 10.6 | 22.9 | 18.6 |
| 1950–1953 | 19.2 | 10.8 | 17.6 | 17.8 | 26.6 | 17.3 | 8.9 | 13.1 | 20.0 | 11.2 | 24.0 | 15.6 | 42.4 | 28.6 |
| 1954–1958 | 10.1 | 8.2 | 10.5 | 16.1 | 6.1 | 7.1 | 13.6 | 10.9 | 10.1 | 7.8 | 10.5 | 7.5 | 13.1 | 14.1 |
| 1958–1960 | 10.0 | 6.3 | 6.8 | -1.5 | 7.7 | 11.4 | 8.2 | 5.4 | 13.1 | 12.2 | 11.4 | 9.5 | 19.2 | 14.9 |

[1] Includes open sea fishing (part of ISIC major group 04), Extraction of salt (ISIC group 191) and cold storage (part of ISIC major group 72) under Food, beverages and tobacco (ISIC major group 20-22); dry cleaning (part of ISIC group 854) and Water supply (ISIC group 521) under Other manufacturing (ISIC major group 39); and the developing and printing of photographic film (part of ISIC group 856) under Printing (ISIC major group 28); but excludes publishing (part of ISIC major group 28).
[2] Includes the manufacturing of artificial ice (part of ISIC major group 31); excludes the preparation of animal fodder, which is covered in Other manufacturing (ISIC major group 39).
[3] Metal furniture is excluded from Furniture (ISIC major group 26) and included in Metal products (ISIC major group 35-38).
[4] Includes the following kinds of manufacturing: Professional and scientific equipment, Photographic and optical goods, and Watches and clocks (ISIC groups 391-393, respectively).
[5] The manufacturing of musical instruments, toys and art work other than wooden (all part of ISIC major group 39) is included under Printing (ISIC major group 28).
[6] The manufacture of asbestos products (part of ISIC major group 33) is included under Rubber products (ISIC major group 30).

[1] Y compris la pêche en mer (dans CITI classe 04), l'Extraction du sel (CITI groupe 191) et les entrepôts frigorifiques (dans CITI classe 72) sous Industries alimentaires, boissons et tabac (CITI classes 20-22), le nettoyage à sec (dans CITI groupe 854) et la Distribution d'eau (CITI groupe 521) sous Autres industries manufacturières (CITI classe 39), ainsi que le développement et le tirage des pellicules photographiques (dans CITI groupe 856) sous Imprimerie (CITI classe 28); mais non compris l'édition (dans CITI classe 28).
[2] Y compris la fabrication de la glace carbonique (dans CITI classe 31); non compris la préparation des fourrages, qui est incluse dans Autres industries manufacturières (CITI classe 39).
[3] Les meubles métalliques ne sont pas compris dans Industrie du meuble (CITI classe 26); ils sont inclus dans Ouvrages en métaux (CITI classes 35-38).
[4] Y compris les types suivants d'industries manufacturières: Matériel médico-chirurgical et instruments de précision, Matériel photographique et instruments d'optiques, Montres et horloges (CITI groupes 391-393 respectivement).
[5] La fabrication des instruments de musique, jouets et objets d'art autres qu'en bois (tous dans CITI classe 39) est comprise dans Imprimerie (CITI classe 28).
[6] La fabrication des ouvrages en amiante (dans CITI classe 33) est comprise dans Ouvrages en caoutchouc (ITI classe 30).

## A. The Divisions of Industrial Activity
### Les branches de l'activité industrielle

| Period<br>Période | Total excluding construction<br>Total, à l'exclusion du bâtiment et des travaux publics | Mining and manufacturing [1]<br>Industries extractives et manufacturières [1] | Construction<br>Bâtiment et travaux publics | Electricity and steam<br>Electricité et vapeur |
|---|---|---|---|---|
| ISIC — CITI | 1–3, 511–521 | 2–3, 512, 521 | 4 | 511, 513 |

### a. Indexes — Indices (1958 = 100)

| | | | | |
|---|---|---|---|---|
| 1949 | 59 | 59 | ... | 77 |
| 1950 | 69 | 69 | 85 | 86 |
| 1951 | 75 | 75 | 95 | 86 |
| 1952 | 79 | 79 | 102 | 83 |
| 1953 | 84 | 84 | 110 | 85 |
| 1954 | 87 | 87 | 103 | 88 |
| 1955 | 91 | 91 | 100 | 88 |
| 1956 | 95 | 95 | 102 | 98 |
| 1957 | 99 | 99 | 100 | 99 |
| 1958 | 100 | 100 | 100 | 100 |
| 1959 | 101 | 101 | 111 | 100 |
| 1960 | 102 | 102 | 108 | 97 |
| 1961 | 105 | 106 | 109 | 99 |

### b. Average Annual Rate of Change — Taux annuel moyen de variation

| | | | | |
|---|---|---|---|---|
| 1950 – 1960 | 4.0 | 4.0 | 2.4 | 1.2 |
| 1950 – 1953 | 6.8 | 6.8 | 9.0 | −0.4 |
| 1954 – 1958 | 3.5 | 3.5 | −0.7 | 3.2 |
| 1958 – 1960 | 1.0 | 1.0 | 3.9 | −1.5 |

For footnotes see end of table.

Pour les notes, voir au bas du tableau.

## B.   The Major Sub-divisions of Mining and Manufacturing

## Les principales subdivisions des industries extractives et manufacturières

| Period / Période | Mining and manufacturing [1] / Industries extractives et manufacturières [1] | Food, beverages and tobacco [1,2] / Industries alimentaires, boissons, tabac [1,2] | Textiles | Clothing and made-up textiles / Articles d'habillement et ouvrages en tissu | Wood products and furniture [3] / Bois et meubles [3] | Paper and paper products / Papier et ouvrages en papier | Printing [1,5] / Imprimerie [1,5] | Leather and leather products / Cuir et articles en cuir | Rubber products [6] / Ouvrages en caoutchouc [6] | Chemicals, coal, crude petroleum and products [2] / Produits chimiques, charbon, pétrole brut et produits dérivés [2] | Non-metallic minerals and products [6] / Minéraux non métalliques et produits dérivés [6] | Metal mining and basic metals / Minerais métalliques et métallurgie de base | Metal products [3,4] / Ouvrages en métaux [3,4] | Other manufacturing [1,2] / Autres industries manufacturières [1,2] |
|---|---|---|---|---|---|---|---|---|---|---|---|---|---|---|
| ISIC — CITI | 1-3, 512, 521 | 191, 20-22 | 23 | 243-244 | 25-26 | 27 | 28 | 241, 29 | 30 | 11, 13, 192, 31-32, 512 | 14, 199, 33 | 12, 34 | 35-38, 391-393 | 399, 521 |

### a. Indexes — Indices (1958 = 100)

| Period | | | | | | | | | | | | | | |
|---|---|---|---|---|---|---|---|---|---|---|---|---|---|---|
| 1949............. | 59 | 51 | 90 | 47 | 62 | 90 | 71 | 34 | 46 | 68 | 53 | 71 | 44 | 23 |
| 1950............. | 69 | 63 | 94 | 88 | 81 | 97 | 82 | 64 | 50 | 72 | 60 | 78 | 52 | 38 |
| 1951............. | 75 | 70 | 94 | 97 | 82 | 107 | 87 | 77 | 54 | 72 | 66 | 81 | 63 | 58 |
| 1952............. | 79 | 76 | 89 | 87 | 91 | 107 | 73 | 78 | 71 | 74 | 72 | 85 | 74 | 79 |
| 1953............. | 84 | 83 | 90 | 86 | 94 | 94 | 74 | 75 | 77 | 78 | 78 | 90 | 85 | 82 |
| 1954............. | 87 | 87 | 85 | 80 | 92 | 100 | 80 | 86 | 83 | 86 | 83 | 95 | 90 | 89 |
| 1955............. | 91 | 90 | 92 | 85 | 98 | 98 | 93 | 93 | 85 | 92 | 88 | 99 | 90 | 94 |
| 1956............. | 95 | 94 | 93 | 88 | 99 | 102 | 99 | 95 | 92 | 96 | 92 | 100 | 95 | 96 |
| 1957............. | 99 | 97 | 97 | 94 | 99 | 101 | 100 | 96 | 97 | 101 | 97 | 101 | 100 | 101 |
| 1958............. | 100 | 100 | 100 | 100 | 100 | 100 | 100 | 100 | 100 | 100 | 100 | 100 | 100 | 100 |
| 1959............. | 101 | 102 | 104 | 95 | 99 | 108 | 100 | 100 | 103 | 101 | 101 | 98 | 103 | 96 |
| 1960............. | 102 | 103 | 101 | 92 | 100 | 108 | 102 | 96 | 105 | 102 | 100 | 99 | 106 | 102 |
| 1961............. | 106 | 107 | 104 | 92 | 102 | 110 | 105 | 94 | 113 | 104 | 101 | 102 | 113 | 120 |

### b. Average Annual Rate of Change — Taux annuel moyen de variation

| Period | | | | | | | | | | | | | | |
|---|---|---|---|---|---|---|---|---|---|---|---|---|---|---|
| 1950-1960....... | 4.0 | 5.0 | 0.7 | 0.4 | 2.1 | 1.1 | 2.2 | 4.1 | 7.7 | 3.5 | 5.2 | 2.4 | 7.4 | 10.4 |
| 1950-1953....... | 6.8 | 9.6 | −1.5 | −0.8 | 5.1 | −1.0 | −3.4 | 5.4 | 15.5 | 2.7 | 9.1 | 4.9 | 17.8 | 25.9 |
| 1954-1958....... | 3.5 | 3.5 | 4.1 | 5.7 | 2.1 | — | 5.7 | 3.8 | 4.8 | 3.8 | 4.8 | 1.3 | 2.7 | 3.0 |
| 1958-1960....... | 1.0 | 1.5 | 0.5 | −4.1 | — | 3.9 | 1.0 | −2.0 | 2.5 | 1.0 | — | −0.5 | 3.0 | 1.0 |

[1] Includes open sea fishing (part of ISIC major group 04), Extraction of salt (ISIC group 191) and cold storage (part of ISIC major group 72) under Food, beverages and tobacco (ISIC major group 20-22); dry cleaning (part of ISIC group 854) and Water supply (ISIC group 521) under Other manufacturing (ISIC major group 39); and the developing and printing of photographic film (part of ISIC group 856) under Printing (ISIC major group 28); but excludes publishing (part of major group 28).
[2] Includes the manufacturing of artificial ice (part of ISIC major group 31); excludes the preparation of animal fodder, which is covered in Other manufacturing (ISIC major group 39).
[3] Metal furniture is excluded from Furniture (ISIC major group 26) and included in Metal products (ISIC major groups 35-38).
[4] Includes the following kinds of manufacturing: Professional and scientific equipment, Photographic and optical goods, and Watches and clocks (ISIC groups 391-393, respectively).
[5] The manufacturing of musical instruments, toys and artwork other than wooden (all part of ISIC major group 39) is included under Printing (ISIC major group 28).
[6] The manufacture of asbestos products (part of ISIC major group 33) is included under Rubber products (ISIC major group 30).

[1] Y compris la pêche en mer (dans CITI classe 04), l'Extraction du sel (CITI groupe 191) et les entrepôts frigorifiques (dans CITI classe 72) sous Industries alimentaires, boissons et tabac (CITI classes 20-22), le nettoyage à sec (dans CITI groupe 854) et la Distribution d'eau (CITI groupe 521) sous Autres industries manufacturières (CITI classe 39), ainsi que le développement et le tirage des pellicules photographiques (dans CITI groupe 856) sous Imprimerie (CITI classe 28); mais non compris l'édition (dans CITI classe 28).
[2] Y compris la fabrication de la glace carbonique (dans CITI classe 31); non compris la préparation des fourrages, qui est incluse dans Autres industries manufacturières (CITI classe 39).
[3] Les meubles métalliques ne sont pas compris dans Industrie du meuble (CITI classe 26); ils sont inclus dans Ouvrages en métaux (CITI classes 35-38).
[4] Y compris les types suivants d'industries manufacturières: Matériel médico-chirurgical et instruments de précision, Matériel photographique et instruments d'optique, Montres et horloges (CITI groupes 391-393 respectivement).
[5] La fabrication des instruments de musique, jouets et objets d'art autres qu'en bois (tous dans CITI classe 39) est comprise dans Imprimerie (CITI classe 28).
[6] La fabrication des ouvrages en amiante (dans CITI classe 33) est comprise dans Ouvrages en caoutchouc (CITI classe 30).

## 4. THE CHARACTERISTICS OF INDUSTRIAL ESTABLISHMENTS
## CARACTERISTIQUES DES ETABLISSEMENTS INDUSTRIELS
### 1955, 1958

Number of establishments in units; value of gross output in million Zlotys (prices as of 1 January 1956); and number of engaged and operatives in thousands; and man-hours worked in millions

Nombre d'établissements en unités; valeur de la production brute en millions de zlotys (prix au 1er janvier 1956); nombre de personnes occupées et d'ouvriers en milliers et heures de travail effectuées en millions

### A. The Divisions of Industrial Activity — Les branches de l'activité industrielle

| Year and item of data | Mining and manufacturing [1] Industries extractives et manufacturières [1] | | | | Construction Bâtiment et travaux publics | Electricity and steam Electricité et vapeur | | Année et rubrique |
|---|---|---|---|---|---|---|---|---|
| | All Tous éta-blissements | Publicly owned establishments Etablissements du secteur public | Co-operatives Coopératives | Privately owned establishments Etablissements privés | Publicly owned enterprises and co-operatives Entreprises publiques et coopératives | All Tous éta-blissements | Publicly owned establishments Etablissements du secteur public | |
| ISIC | 1–3, 512, 521 | | | | 4 | 511, 513 | | CITI |
| 1955 | | | | | | | | 1955 |
| Gross output.............. | 236 102.2 | 211 449.5 | 23 266.8 | 1 385.9 | ... | 5 003.5 | 5 003.5 | Production brute |
| Number of engaged | | | | | | | | Nombre de personnes occupées |
| (Average during the year)... | 2 642.4 | 2 310.8 | 320.5 | 11.1 | 647.0 | 59.2 | 59.2 | (Moyenne pendant l'année) |
| 1958 | | | | | | | | 1958 |
| Number of establishments...... | 47 075 | 14 743 | 22 576 | 9 756 | 1 180 | 419 | 419 | Nombre d'établissements |
| Gross output.............. | 310 112.4 | 265 220.4 | 41 867.0 | 3 025.0 | 40 476.0 | 7 291.7 | 7 291.7 | Production brute |
| Number of engaged | | | | | | | | Nombre de personnes occupées |
| (Average during the year)... | 2 891.2 | 2 486.2 | 375.1 | 29.9 | 646.1 | 67.5 | 67.5 | (Moyenne pendant l'année) |

For footnotes see end of table.                                          Pour les notes, voir au bas du tableau.

## B. The Major Sub-divisions of Mining and Manufacturing
## Les principales subdivisions des Industries extractives et manufacturières

| Year and item of data | Mining and manufacturing [1] — Industries extractives et manufacturières [1] | Food, beverages and tobacco [1,2] — Industries alimentaires, boissons, tabac [1,2] | Textiles | Clothing, and made-up textiles — Articles d'habillement et ouvrages en tissu | Wood products and furniture [3] — Bois et meubles [3] | Paper and paper products — Papier et ouvrages en papier | Printing [1,5] — Imprimerie [1,5] | Leather and leather products — Cuir et articles en cuir | Rubber products [6] — Ouvrages en caoutchouc [6] | Chemicals coal, crude petroleum and products [2] — Produits chimiques charbon pétrole brut et produits dérivés [2] | Non-metallic minerals and products [6] — Minéraux non métalliques et produits dérivés [6] | Metal mining and basic metals — Minerais métalliques et métallurgie de base | Metal products [3,4] — Ouvrages en métaux [3,4] | Other manufacturing [1,2] — Autres industries manufacturières [1,2] | Année et rubrique |
|---|---|---|---|---|---|---|---|---|---|---|---|---|---|---|---|
| ISIC | 1-3, 512, 521 | 191, 20–22 | 23 | 243-244 | 25–26 | 27 | 28 | 241, 29 | 30 | 11,13,192 31–32 512 | 14, 199, 33 | 12, 34 | 35–38 391–393 | 399, 521 | CITI |
| *a. All types of Establishments — Tous établissements* | | | | | | | | | | | | | | | |
| **1955** | | | | | | | | | | | | | | | **1955** |
| Gross output | 236 102.2 | 74 621.8 | 31 837.4 | 6 292.6 | 8 796.7 | 2 956.7 | 1 422.5 | 6 384.3 | 2 251.8 | 30 076.3 | 7 642.6 | 21 276.4 | 41 055.7 | 1 487.4 | Production brute |
| Number of engaged (Average during the year) | 2 642.0 | 327.8 | 339.5 | 113.0 | 156.8 | 40.5 | 32.7 | 104.5 | 21.1 | 469.7 | 208.0 | 167.0 | 635.0 | 26.4 | Nombre de personnes occupées (moyenne pendant l'année) |
| Operatives: Number (Average during the year) | 2 018.9 | 211.7 | 278.3 | 96.0 | 123.5 | 32.4 | 25.9 | 84.9 | 17.4 | 372.8 | 167.2 | 125.4 | 463.3 | 20.1 | Ouvriers: Nombre (moyenne pendant l'année) |
| Man-hours worked | 4 460.7 | 482.8 | 579.5 | 205.2 | 267.4 | 73.3 | 54.6 | 182.3 | 37.2 | 876.0 | 369.8 | 286.8 | 1 001.4 | 44.4 | Heures de travail effectuées |
| Distribution in percent of: | | | | | | | | | | | | | | | Distribution en pourcentage: |
| Number of engaged | 100.0 | 12.4 | 12.8 | 4.3 | 5.9 | 1.6 | 1.2 | 3.9 | 0.8 | 17.8 | 7.9 | 6.3 | 24.1 | 1.0 | Nombre de personnes occupées |
| Number of operatives | 100.0 | 10.4 | 13.8 | 4.8 | 6.1 | 1.6 | 1.3 | 4.2 | 0.8 | 18.5 | 8.3 | 6.2 | 23.0 | 1.0 | Nombre d'ouvriers |
| **1958** | | | | | | | | | | | | | | | **1958** |
| Number of establishments | 47 075 | 20 360 | 1 614 | 2 341 | 4 081 | 317 | 610 | 4 746 | 281 | 1 959 | 5 190 | 84 | 4 587 | 905 | Nombre d'établissements |
| Gross output | 310 112.4 | 96 022.9 | 41 476.0 | 9 853.7 | 9 917.9 | 3 523.7 | 2 014.6 | 8 910.9 | 3 033.2 | 36 394.5 | 10 148.9 | 25 956.9 | 60 812.2 | 2 047.0 | Production brute |
| Number of engaged (Average during the year) | 2 891.3 | 364.8 | 368.3 | 133.5 | 160.9 | 41.4 | 35.4 | 112.0 | 24.8 | 508.9 | 236.9 | 168.9 | 707.5 | 28.0 | Nombre de personnes occupées (moyenne pendant l'année) |
| Operatives: Number (Average during the year) | 2 257.6 | 248.2 | 306.3 | 115.5 | 128.4 | 33.7 | 29.0 | 93.1 | 20.3 | 407.1 | 190.9 | 132.3 | 530.3 | 22.5 | Ouvriers: Nombre (moyenne pendant l'année) |
| Man-hours worked | 4 837.1 | 567.7 | 630.8 | 239.1 | 271.7 | 72.6 | 59.6 | 196.3 | 41.2 | 888.0 | 412.6 | 295.6 | 1 115.0 | 46.7 | Heures de travail effectuées |
| Distribution in percent of: | | | | | | | | | | | | | | | Distribution en pourcentage: |
| Number of engaged | 100.0 | 12.6 | 12.7 | 4.6 | 5.6 | 1.4 | 1.2 | 3.9 | 0.9 | 17.6 | 8.2 | 5.8 | 24.5 | 1.0 | Nombre de personnes occupées |
| Number of operatives | 100.0 | 10.9 | 13.6 | 5.1 | 5.7 | 1.5 | 1.3 | 4.1 | 0.9 | 18.0 | 8.5 | 5.9 | 23.5 | 1.0 | Nombre d'ouvriers |
| *b. Publicly Owned Establishments — Etablissements du secteur public* | | | | | | | | | | | | | | | |
| **1955** | | | | | | | | | | | | | | | **1955** |
| Gross output | 211 449.5 | 63 161.5 | 30 767.6 | 4 158.5 | 6 870.0 | 2 703.6 | 986.8 | 5 371.0 | 1 908.7 | 28 966.7 | 6 956.8 | 21 276.4 | 37 446.1 | 875.8 | Production brute |
| Number of engaged (Average during the year) | 2 310.6 | 264.4 | 320.8 | 59.2 | 123.5 | 35.3 | 24.4 | 50.1 | 19.0 | 457.4 | 189.6 | 167.0 | 583.7 | 16.2 | Nombre de personnes occupées (moyenne pendant l'année) |
| Distribution in percent of number of engaged | 100.0 | 11.4 | 13.9 | 2.5 | 5.4 | 1.5 | 1.1 | 2.1 | 0.9 | 19.8 | 8.2 | 7.2 | 25.2 | 0.8 | Distribution en pourcentage du nombre de personnes occupées |
| **1958** | | | | | | | | | | | | | | | **1958** |
| Number of establishments | 14 743 | 5 869 | 636 | 306 | 1 656 | 144 | 301 | 246 | 57 | 872 | 2 505 | 84 | 1 894 | 173 | Nombre d'établissements |
| Gross output | 265 220.4 | 69 575.1 | 39 541.0 | 5 774.2 | 8 274.0 | 3 202.8 | 1 449.2 | 6 547.1 | 2 793.3 | 34 597.9 | 8 974.9 | 25 956.9 | 57 205.9 | 1 328.1 | Production brute |
| Number of engaged (Average during the year) | 2 486.2 | 251.2 | 347.0 | 71.4 | 127.0 | 36.8 | 26.9 | 61.0 | 22.4 | 494.5 | 205.9 | 168.9 | 656.7 | 16.5 | Nombre de personnes occupées (moyenne pendant l'année) |
| Distribution in percent of number of engaged | 100.0 | 10.1 | 14.0 | 2.9 | 5.1 | 1.5 | 1.1 | 2.4 | 0.9 | 19.9 | 8.3 | 6.8 | 26.4 | 0.6 | Distribution en pourcentage du nombre de personnes occupées |

For footnotes see end of table.          Pour les notes, voir au bas du tableau.

# POLAND

## B. The Major Sub-divisions of Mining and Manufacturing (continued)
## Les principales subdivisions des Industries extractives et manufacturières (suite)

| Year and item of data | Mining and manufacturing [1] / Industries extractives et manufacturières [1] | Food, beverages and tobacco [1,2] / Industries alimentaires, boissons, tabac [1,2] | Textiles | Clothing, footwear and made-up textiles / Articles d'habillement et ouvrages en tissu | Wood products and furniture [3] / Bois et meubles [3] | Paper and paper products / Papier et ouvrages en papier | Printing [1,5] / Imprimerie [1,5] | Leather and leather products / Cuir et articles en cuir | Rubber products [6] / Ouvrages en caoutchouc [6] | Chemicals coal, crude petroleum and products [2] / Produits chimiques charbon, pétrole brut et produits dérivés [2] | Non-metallic minerals and products [6] / Minéraux non métalliques et produits dérivés [6] | Metal mining and basic metals / Minerais métalliques et métallurgie de base | Metal products [3,4] / Ouvrages en métaux [3,4] | Other manufacturing [1,2] / Autres industries manufacturières [1,2] | Année et rubrique |
|---|---|---|---|---|---|---|---|---|---|---|---|---|---|---|---|
| ISIC | 1-3, 512, 521 | 191, 20-22 | 23 | 243-244 | 25-26 | 27 | 28 | 241, 29 | 30 | 11, 13, 192, 31-32, 512 | 14, 199, 33 | 12, 34 | 35-38 391-393 | 399, 521 | CITI |
| **c. Co-operatives — Coopératives** | | | | | | | | | | | | | | | |
| 1955 | | | | | | | | | | | | | | | 1955 |
| Gross output | 23 266.8 | 10 488.7 | 1 069.1 | 2 128.5 | 1 807.8 | 251.8 | 435.5 | 1 006.6 | 342.0 | 1 002.9 | 653.8 | — | 3 551.3 | 528.8 | Production brute |
| Number of engaged (Average during the year) | 320.4 | 57.7 | 18.6 | 53.7 | 32.0 | 5.2 | 8.3 | 54.2 | 2.1 | 11.3 | 17.8 | — | 50.3 | 9.2 | Nombre de personnes occupées (moyenne pendant l'année) |
| Distribution in percent of number of engaged | 100.0 | 18.0 | 5.8 | 16.7 | 10.0 | 1.6 | 2.6 | 16.9 | 0.7 | 3.5 | 5.6 | — | 15.7 | 2.9 | Distribution en pourcentage du nombre de personnes occupées |
| 1958 | | | | | | | | | | | | | | | 1958 |
| Number of establishments | 22 576 | 9 415 | 631 | 1 948 | 1 453 | 147 | 280 | 4 421 | 170 | 587 | 931 | — | 2 162 | 431 | Nombre d'établissements |
| Gross output | 41 867.0 | 24 696.1 | 1 921.2 | 4 073.5 | 1 384.9 | 317.0 | 558.0 | 2 356.6 | 222.6 | 1 498.8 | 826.7 | — | 3 451.1 | 560.5 | Production brute |
| Number of engaged (Average during the year) | 375.1 | 102.9 | 20.8 | 61.9 | 31.2 | 4.5 | 8.4 | 50.8 | 2.2 | 12.0 | 22.0 | — | 48.8 | 9.6 | Nombre de personnes occupées (moyenne pendant l'année) |
| Distribution in percent of number of engaged | 100.0 | 27.4 | 5.6 | 16.5 | 8.3 | 1.2 | 2.2 | 13.6 | 0.6 | 3.2 | 5.9 | — | 13.0 | 2.5 | Distribution en pourcentage du nombre de personnes occupées |
| **d. Privately Owned Establishments — Etablissements du secteur privé** | | | | | | | | | | | | | | | |
| 1955 | | | | | | | | | | | | | | | 1955 |
| Gross output | 1 385.9 | 971.6 | 0.7 | 5.6 | 118.9 | 1.3 | 0.2 | 6.7 | 1.1 | 106.7 | 32.0 | — | 58.3 | 82.8 | Production brute |
| Number of engaged (Average during the year) | 11.0 | 5.7 | 0.1 | 0.1 | 1.3 | — | — | 0.2 | — | 1.0 | 0.6 | — | 1.0 | 1.0 | Nombre de personnes occupées (moyenne pendant l'année) |
| Distribution in percent of number of engaged | 100.0 | 51.8 | 0.9 | 0.9 | 11.8 | — | — | 1.8 | — | 9.1 | 5.5 | — | 9.1 | 9.1 | Distribution en pourcentage du nombre de personnes occupées |
| 1958 | | | | | | | | | | | | | | | 1958 |
| Number of establishments | 9 756 | 5 076 | 347 | 87 | 972 | 26 | 29 | 79 | 54 | 500 | 1 754 | — | 531 | 301 | Nombre d'établissements |
| Gross output | 3 025.0 | 1 751.7 | 13.8 | 6.0 | 259.0 | 3.9 | 7.4 | 7.2 | 17.3 | 297.8 | 347.3 | — | 155.2 | 158.4 | Production brute |
| Number of engaged (Average during the year) | 30.0 | 10.7 | 0.5 | 0.2 | 2.7 | 0.1 | 0.1 | 0.2 | 0.2 | 2.4 | 9.0 | — | 2.0 | 1.9 | Nombre de personnes occupées (moyenne pendant l'année) |
| Distribution in percent of number of engaged | 100.0 | 35.7 | 1.7 | 0.7 | 9.0 | 0.3 | 0.3 | 0.7 | 0.7 | 8.0 | 30.0 | — | 6.7 | 6.2 | Distribution en pourcentage du nombre de personnes occupées |

[1] Includes open sea fishing (part of ISIC major group 04), Extraction of salt (ISIC group 191) and cold storage (part of ISIC major group 72) under Food, beverages and tobacco (ISIC major group 20-22); dry cleaning (part of ISIC group 854) and Water supply (ISIC group 521) under Other manufacturing (ISIC major group 39); and the developing and printing of photographic film (part of ISIC group 856 under Printing (ISIC major group 28); but excludes publishing (part of ISIC major group 28).

[2] Includes the manufacturing of artificial ice (part of ISIC major group 31); excludes the preparation of animal fodder, which is covered in Other manufacturing (ISIC major group 39).

[3] Metal furniture is excluded from Furniture (ISIC major group 26) and included in Metal products (ISIC major groups 35-38).

[4] Includes the following kinds of manufacturing: Professional and scientific equipment, Photographic and optical goods, and Watches and clocks (ISIC groups 391-393, respectively).

[5] The manufacturing of musical instruments, toys and artwork other than wooden (all part of ISIC major group 39) is included under Printing (ISIC major group 28).

[6] The manufacture of asbestos products (part of ISIC major group 33) is included under Rubber products (ISIC major group 30).

[1] Y compris la pêche en mer (dans CITI classe 04), l'Extraction du sel (CITI groupe 191) et les entrepôts frigorifiques (dans CITI classe 72) sous Industries alimentaires, boissons et tabac (CITI classes 20-22), le nettoyage à sec (dans CITI groupe 854) et la Distribution d'eau (CITI groupe 521) sous Autres industries manufacturières (CITI classe 39), ainsi que le développement et le tirage des pellicules photographiques (dans CITI groupe 856) sous Imprimerie (CITI classe 28); mais non compris l'édition (dans CITI classe 28).

[2] Y compris la fabrication de la glace carbonique (dans CITI classe 31); non compris la préparation des fourrages, qui est incluse dans Autres industries manufacturières (CITI classe 39).

[3] Les meubles métalliques ne sont pas compris dans Industrie du meuble (CITI classe 26); ils sont inclus dans Ouvrages en métaux (CITI classes 35-38).

[4] Y compris les types suivants d'industries manufacturières: Matériel médico-chirurgical et instruments de précision, Matériel photographique et instruments d'optique, Montres et horloges (CITI groupes 391-393 respectivement).

[5] La fabrication des instruments de musique, jouets et objets d'art autres qu'en bois (tous dans CITI classe 39) est comprise dans Imprimerie (CITI classe 28).

[6] La fabrication des ouvrages en amiante (dans CITI classe 33) est comprise dans Ouvrages en caoutchouc (CITI classe 30).

# 5. THE CHARACTERISTICS OF THE PUBLICLY OWNED AND CO-OPERATIVE INDUSTRIAL ESTABLISHMENTS
## CARACTERISTIQUES DES ETABLISSEMENTS INDUSTRIELS PUBLICS ET COOPERATIFS
### 1957, 1958

Number of establishments in units; value of gross output and net material product in million Zlotys; number of persons engaged and operatives in thousands; man-hours worked in millions; electricity consumed in million KWH; capacity of installed power equipment in thousand horsepower; contribution to net material product per person engaged in thousand Zlotys; average annual man-hours worked per operative in thousands; electricity consumed per person engaged and per operative in thousand KWH; capacity of installed power equipment per person engaged and per operative in horsepower.

Nombre d'établissements en unités; production brute et produit matériel net en millions de zlotys; nombre de personnes occupées et d'ouvriers en milliers; heures de travail effectuées en millions; électricité consommée en millions de kWh; puissance installée en milliers de chevaux-vapeur; produit matériel net par personne occupée en milliers de zlotys; moyenne annuelle des heures de travail effectuées par ouvrier en milliers; électricité consommée par ouvrier en milliers de kWh; puissance installée par ouvrier en chevaux-vapeur.

| Item of data | Mining and manufacturing [1] — Industries extractives et manufacturières [1] | Food, beverages and tobacco [1,2] — Industries alimentaires, boissons, tabac [1,2] | Textiles | Clothing and made-up textiles — Articles d'habillement et ouvrages en tissu | Wood products and furniture [3] — Bois et meubles [3] | Paper and paper products — Papier et ouvrages en papier | Printing [1,5] — Imprimerie [1,5] | Leather and leather products — Cuir et articles en cuir | Rubber products [6] — Ouvrages en caoutchouc [6] | Chemicals, coal, crude petroleum and products [2] — Produits chimiques, charbon, pétrole brut et produits dérivés [2] | Non-metallic minerals and products [6] — Minéraux non métalliques et produits dérivés [6] | Metal mining and basic metals — Minerais métalliques et métallurgie de base | Metal products [3,4] — Ouvrages en métaux [3,4] | Other manufacturing [1,2] — Autres industries manufacturières [1,2] | Electricity and steam — Electricité et vapeur | Rubrique |
|---|---|---|---|---|---|---|---|---|---|---|---|---|---|---|---|---|
| ISIC | 1-3, 512, 521 | 191, 20-22 | 23 | 243-244 | 25-26 | 27 | 28 | 241, 29 | 30 | 11, 13, 192, 31-32, 512 | 14, 199, 33 | 12, 34 | 35-38, 391-393 | 399, 521 | 511, 513 | CITI |
| *a. Absolute Figures — Chiffres absolus* | | | | | | | | | | | | | | | | |
| **1957** Number of engaged (Average during the year) | 2 833.1 | 344.0 | 364.1 | 124.5 | 157.9 | 37.9 | 52.3 | 103.2 | 24.0 | 516.1 | 223.0 | 171.2 | 701.6 | 13.3 | 67.0 | **1957** Nombre de personnes occupées (moyenne pendant l'année) |
| Operatives: Number (Average during the year) | 2 204.4 | 232.5 | 303.1 | 106.4 | 126.4 | 30.2 | 42.2 | 85.1 | 19.5 | 412.6 | 181.6 | 132.7 | 521.2 | 10.9 | 45.9 | Ouvriers: Nombre (moyenne pendant l'année) |
| Man-hours worked | 4 672.1 | 520.4 | 615.3 | 217.0 | 265.8 | 64.5 | 87.1 | 179.1 | 39.2 | 902.2 | 388.3 | 293.9 | 1 077.3 | 22.0 | 105.4 | Heures de travail effectuées |
| Electricity consumed | 13 370.8 | 708.8 | 762.3 | 25.5 | 149.7 | 626.4 | 42.8 | 43.9 | 86.2 | 5 681.6 | 769.8 | 3 181.1 | 1 273.8 | 18.9 | 1 274.3 | Electricité consommée |
| Capacity of installed power equipment (as of 31.XII) | 12 488.1 | 1 239.2 | 579.3 | 19.4 | 284.4 | 433.5 | 50.7 | 66.2 | 66.2 | 5 074.0 | 768.5 | 2 006.2 | 1 870.8 | 29.7 | 5 116.5 | Puissance installée (au 31.XII) |
| **1958** Number of establishments | 37 319 | 15 284 | 1 267 | 2 254 | 3 109 | 291 | 581 | 4 667 | 227 | 1 459 | 3 436 | 84 | 4 056 | 604 | 419 | **1958** Nombre d'établissements |
| Gross output | 406 616.7 | 138 113.1 | 55 674.6 | 14 186.6 | 19 473.2 | 8 062.9 | 2 505.4 | 14 663.4 | 3 803.0 | 41 422.0 | 13 286.8 | 30 647.5 | 62 238.2 | 2 540.0 | 5 352.2 | Production brute |
| Net material product | 142 768.9 | 41 731.1 | 23 450.7 | 3 548.6 | 5 286.8 | 2 515.4 | 1 050.0 | 6 782.8 | 1 612.2 | 13 293.8 | 7 410.2 | 6 847.0 | 28 181.0 | 1 059.3 | 1 925.3 | Produit matériel net |
| Number of engaged (Average during the year) | 2 861.3 | 354.1 | 367.8 | 133.3 | 158.2 | 41.3 | 35.3 | 111.8 | 24.6 | 506.5 | 227.9 | 168.9 | 705.5 | 26.1 | 67.5 | Nombre de personnes occupées (moyenne pendant l'année) |
| Operatives: Number (Average during the year) | 2 245.2 | 245.8 | 306.2 | 115.4 | 127.5 | 33.7 | 28.9 | 93.0 | 20.2 | 405.8 | 185.9 | 132.4 | 529.2 | 21.2 | 45.9 | Ouvriers: Nombre (moyenne pendant l'année) |
| Man-hours worked | 4 810.5 | 562.4 | 630.6 | 239.1 | 269.7 | 72.6 | 59.5 | 196.2 | 40.9 | 885.4 | 402.0 | 295.6 | 1 112.6 | 43.9 | 106.1 | Heures de travail effectuées |

For footnotes see end of table.

Pour les notes, voir au bas du tableau.

# POLAND

## 5. THE CHARACTERISTICS OF THE PUBLICLY OWNED AND CO-OPERATIVE INDUSTRIAL ESTABLISHMENTS (continued)
### CARACTERISTIQUES DES ETABLISSEMENTS INDUSTRIELS PUBLICS ET COOPERATIFS (suite)

### 1957, 1958

| Item of data | Mining and manufacturing [1] — Industries extractives et manufacturières [1] | Food, beverages and tobacco [1,2] — Industries alimentaires, boissons, tabac [1,2] | Textiles | Clothing and made-up textiles — Articles d'habillement et ouvrages en tissu | Wood products and furniture [3] — Bois et meubles [3] | Paper and paper products — Papier et ouvrages en papier | Printing [1,5] — Imprimerie [1,5] | Leather and leather products — Cuir et articles en cuir | Rubber products [6] — Ouvrages en caoutchouc [6] | Chemicals, coal, crude petroleum and products [2] — Produits chimiques, charbon, pétrole brut et produits dérivés [2] | Non-metallic minerals and products [6] — Minéraux non métalliques et produits dérivés [6] | Metal mining and basic metals — Minerais métalliques et métallurgie de base | Metal products [3,4] — Ouvrages en métaux [3,4] | Other manufacturing [1,2] — Autres industries manufacturières [1,2] | Electricity and steam — Electricité et vapeur | Rubrique |
|---|---|---|---|---|---|---|---|---|---|---|---|---|---|---|---|---|
| ISIC | 1-3, 512, 521 | 191, 20-22 | 23 | 243-244 | 25-26 | 27 | 28 | 241, 29 | 30 | 11, 13, 192, 31-32, 512 | 14, 199, 33 | 12, 34 | 35-38, 391-393 | 399, 521 | 511, 513 | CITI |
| *b. Structure* | | | | | | | | | | | | | | | | |
| **1957** | | | | | | | | | | | | | | | | **1957** |
| Distribution in percent of number of engaged | 100.0 | 12.1 | 12.8 | 4.4 | 5.6 | 1.3 | 1.9 | 3.6 | 0.9 | 18.2 | 7.9 | 6.0 | 24.8 | 0.5 | . | Distribution en pourcentage du nombre de personnes occupées |
| Per person engaged: Electricity consumed | 4.72 | 2.06 | 2.09 | 0.20 | 0.95 | 16.53 | 0.82 | 0.42 | 3.59 | 11.01 | 3.45 | 18.58 | 1.82 | 1.42 | 19.02 | Par personne occupée: Electricité consommée |
| Capacity of installed power equipment | 4.41 | 3.60 | 1.59 | 0.16 | 1.80 | 11.44 | 0.97 | 0.64 | 2.76 | 9.83 | 3.45 | 11.72 | 2.67 | 2.23 | 76.36 | Puissance installée |
| Operatives as a percent of engaged | 77.8 | 67.6 | 83.2 | 85.5 | 80.0 | 79.7 | 80.7 | 82.5 | 81.2 | 79.9 | 81.4 | 77.5 | 74.3 | 82.0 | 68.5 | Ouvriers en pourcentage des personnes occupées |
| Per operative: Man-hours worked | 2.12 | 2.24 | 2.03 | 2.04 | 2.10 | 2.14 | 2.06 | 2.10 | 2.01 | 2.19 | 2.14 | 2.21 | 2.07 | 2.02 | 2.30 | Par ouvrier: Heures de travail effectuées |
| Electricity consumed | 6.06 | 3.05 | 2.52 | 0.24 | 1.18 | 20.74 | 1.01 | 0.52 | 4.42 | 13.77 | 4.24 | 23.97 | 2.44 | 1.73 | 27.76 | Electricité consommée |
| Capacity of installed power equipment | 5.66 | 5.33 | 1.91 | 0.18 | 2.25 | 14.35 | 1.20 | 0.78 | 3.39 | 12.30 | 4.23 | 15.12 | 3.59 | 2.72 | 111.47 | Puissance installée |
| **1958** Distribution in percent of: Net material product | 100.0 | 29.2 | 16.4 | 2.5 | 3.7 | 1.8 | 0.7 | 4.7 | 1.2 | 9.3 | 5.2 | 4.8 | 19.7 | 0.8 | . | **1958** Distribution en pourcentage: Produit matériel net |
| Number of engaged | 100.0 | 12.3 | 12.9 | 4.6 | 5.6 | 1.4 | 1.2 | 4.0 | 0.8 | 17.7 | 8.0 | 5.9 | 24.6 | 1.0 | . | Nombre de personnes occupées |
| Net material product per person engaged | 49.90 | 117.85 | 63.76 | 26.62 | 33.42 | 60.90 | 29.74 | 60.67 | 65.54 | 26.25 | 32.52 | 40.54 | 39.94 | 40.59 | 28.52 | Produit matériel net par personne occupée |
| Operatives as a percent of engaged | 78.5 | 69.4 | 83.2 | 86.6 | 80.6 | 81.6 | 81.9 | 83.2 | 82.1 | 80.1 | 81.6 | 78.4 | 75.0 | 81.2 | 68.0 | Ouvriers en pourcentage des personnes occupées |
| Man-hours worked per operative | 2.14 | 2.29 | 2.06 | 2.07 | 2.30 | 2.15 | 2.06 | 2.11 | 2.02 | 2.18 | 2.16 | 2.23 | 2.10 | 2.07 | 2.31 | Heures de travail effectuées par ouvrier |

[1] Includes open sea fishing (part of ISIC major group 04), Extraction of salt (ISIC group 191) and cold storage (part of ISIC major group 72) under Food, beverages and tobacco (ISIC major group 20-22); dry cleaning (part of ISIC group 854) and Water supply (ISIC group 521) under Other manufacturing (ISIC major group 39); and the developing and printing of photographic film (part of ISIC group 856) under Printing (ISIC major group 28); but excludes publishing (part of ISIC major group 28).

[2] Includes the manufacturing of artificial ice (part of ISIC major group 31); excludes the preparation of animal fodder, which is covered in Other manufacturing (ISIC major group 39).

[3] Metal furniture is excluded from Furniture (ISIC major group 26) and included in Metal products (ISIC major groups 35-38).

[4] Includes the following kinds of manufacturing: Professional and scientific equipment, Photographic and optical goods, and Watches and clocks (ISIC groups 391-393, respectively).

[5] The manufacturing of musical instruments, toys and artwork other than wooden (all part of ISIC major group 39) is included under Printing (ISIC major group 28).

[6] The manufacture of asbestos products (part of ISIC major group 33) is included under Rubber products (ISIC major group 30).

[1] Y compris la pêche en mer (dans CITI classe 04), l'Extraction du sel (CITI groupe 191) et les entrepôts frigorifiques (dans CITI classe 72) sous Industries alimentaires, boissons et tabac (CITI classes 20-22), le nettoyage à sec (dans CITI groupe 854) et la Distribution d'eau (CITI groupe 521 sous Autres industries manufacturières (CITI classe 39), ainsi que le développement et le tirage des pellicules photographiques (dans CITI groupe 856) sous Imprimerie (CITI classe 28); mais non compris l'édition (dans CITI classe 28).

[2] Y compris la fabrication de la glace carbonique (dans CITI classe 31); non compris la préparation des fourrages, qui est incluse dans Autres industries manufacturières (CITI classe 39).

[3] Les meubles métalliques ne sont pas compris dans Industrie du meuble (CITI classe 26); ils sont inclus dans Ouvrages en métaux (CITI classes 35-38).

[4] Y compris les types suivants d'industries manufacturières: Matériel médico-chirurgical, et instruments de précision, Matériel photographique et instruments d'optique, Montres et horloges (CITI groupes 391-393 respectivement).

[5] La fabrication des instruments de musique, jouets et objets d'art autres qu'en bois (tous dans CITI classe 39) est comprise dans Imprimerie (CITI classe 28).

[6] La fabrication des ouvrages en amiante (dans CITI classe 33) est comprise dans Ouvrages en caoutchouc (CITI classe 30).

# PORTUGAL

## Gross Domestic Product and Gross Fixed Capital Formation

The figures of the gross domestic product and gross domestic fixed capital formation set out in Table 1 are from the reply by the Instituto Nacional de Estatística, Lisbon to the United Nations national accounts questionnaire. The sources and methods utilized in estimating these data are described in *O Rendimento Nacional Português* of *Estudos,* No. 34, of the Instituto.

## Index Numbers of Industrial Production

The index numbers of industrial production shown in Table 2 are supplied to the Statistical Office of the United Nations by the Associação Industrial Portuguesa, Lisbon, and are the indexes which the Associação compiles annually.

This series of index numbers cover, in principle, establishments irrespective of size located in the European territory of Portugal, excepting Madeira and the Azores. The index numbers are computed as base-weighted arithmetic means, in successive stages. First, elementary series of relatives, based on quantities of industrial commodities produced, are combined into index numbers for detailed categories of industrial activity. Then, the resulting indexes are combined into index numbers for major groups of industrial activity; and the indexes for the major groups furnish the basis for compiling index numbers for the divisions of industrial activity. The weights for the first two stages of compilation are derived from value added, at factor cost, during 1958. The weights for the final stage of combination are based on value added, at factor cost, during 1953.

Further details concerning the series of index numbers of industrial production are available in *Indices Mensais da Produção Industrial, Estudos de Economia Aplicada,* No. 5 of the Associaçao Industrial Portuguesa. An additional publication, No. 15 of the above series, concerning the series of index numbers is to be issued.

## The Characteristics and Structure of Industrial Activity

The data shown in Tables 3 and 4 were compiled from *Estatística Industrial, 1953, 1958* and *1959,* published by the Instituto Nacional de Estatística, Lisbon. These series of publications give the results of the annual Censuses of Industry taken by the Instituto.

Establishments, irrespective of size, in selected kinds of industrial activity are covered in the annual Censuses of Industry. Because of the differences between the Censuses of 1953 and 1958 in the selected kinds of industrial activity covered, described in the footnotes to Tables 4

## Produit intérieur brut et formation brute de capital fixe

Les chiffres relatifs au produit intérieur brut et à la formation brute de capital fixe, reproduits au tableau 1 proviennent de la réponse de l'Instituto Nacional de Estatística, Lisbonne au questionnaire de l'O.N.U. relatif aux comptes nationaux. Les sources et méthodes utilisées pour estimer ces données sont décrites dans *O Rendimento Nacional Português* de *Estudos,* No. 34 de l'Instituto.

## Indices de la production industrielle

Les indices de la production industrielle reproduits au tableau 2 sont fournis au Bureau de statistique de l'O.N.U. par l'Associação Industrial Portuguesa, Lisbonne; ce sont les indices que l'Associação calcule annuellement.

Ces séries d'indices couvrent, en principe, les établissements, quelle que soit leur taille, situés dans le territoire européen du Portugal, à l'exclusion de Madeira et des Açores. Ces indices sont des moyennes arithmétiques à pondération fixe, calculées en plusieurs étapes. Au premier stade, des séries élémentaires de rapports construits à partir du volume de chaque marchandise produite, sont combinés en indices relatifs à des catégories détaillées de l'activité industrielle; au second stade, les indices obtenus sont combinés en indices pour les classes de l'activité industrielle, lesquelles permettent de construire des indices pour les branches de l'activité industrielle. Les coefficients de pondération adoptés à ces deux stades du calcul, sont basés sur la valeur ajoutée, au coût des facteurs, durant 1953.

Plus amples détails concernant les séries d'indices de la production industrielle peuvent être trouvés dans *Indices Mensais da Produção Industrial, Estudos de Economia Aplicada,* No. 5 de l'Associação Industrial Portuguesa. Un numéro supplémentaire, No. 15, concernant les séries d'indices est sur le point de paraître.

## Caractéristiques et structure de l'activité industrielle

Les données reproduites aux tableaux 3 et 4 sont tirées de *Estatística Industrial, 1953, 1958* et *1959,* publié par l'Instituto Nacional de Estatística, Lisbonne. Dans ces séries de publications paraissent les résultats des recensements annuels de l'industrie effectués par l'Instituto.

Les établissements, quelle que soit leur taille, engagés dans certains types d'activité industrielle, sont couverts par le recensement annuel de l'industrie. Des différences entre le recensement de 1953 et celui de 1958 dans le choix des activités industrielles à couvrir, différences décrites en

and 5, there is a lack of comparability between the data shown in the table for 1953 and 1958. Additional incomparabilities may occur as a result of probable differences between the two Censuses in the rate of response to questionnaires. In this connection, it should be emphasized that the figures of number of establishments shown in Table 4 relate to the number of units operating and not the number of units responding to questionnaires.

The figures of value added set out in Table 4 were computed by the Statistical Office of the United Nations from data shown in *Estatística Industrial* on the gross value of production and the costs of the raw materials, fuels and electricity consumed in this production. Gross value of production was priced at factor cost ex-establishment. The definitions of the items of data on labour are consistent with those of the International Standards in Basĭc Industrial Statistics. Homeworkers may not be included in the count of persons engaged. The data on purchased fuels consumed, and therefore energy consumed, may include coal, coke or other fuels utilized as raw materials as well as for heat and power.

notes aux tableaux 4 et 5, découle un défaut de comparabilité entre les données du tableau relatives à 1953 et 1958. D'autres défauts de comparabilité peuvent résulter de différences possibles entre les deux recensements, quant au taux de réponse aux questionnaires. De ce fait, il est utile de souligner que les chiffres relatifs au nombre d'établissements, reproduits au tableau 4 concernent les unités en activité et non pas les unités ayant répondu aux questionnaires.

Les chiffres relatifs à la valeur ajoutée reproduite au tableau 4 ont été élaborés par le Bureau de statistique de l'O.N.U. à partir des données publiées dans *Estatística Industrial,* relatives à la valeur brute de la production et aux coûts des matières premières des combustibles et de l'électricité consommés pour cette production. La valeur brute de la production est évaluée au coût des facteurs, départ-usine. Les définitions des rubriques relatives à la main-d'œuvre sont cohérentes avec celles des Normes internationales relatives aux statistiques industrielles de base. Les travailleurs à domicile peuvent n'avoir pas été inclus dans le nombre de personnes engagées. Les données relatives aux combustibles achetés et consommés, et par conséquent à l'énergie consommée, peuvent comprendre le charbon, le coke ou d'autres combustibles utilisés comme matières premières aussi bien que comme sources de chaleur ou de puissance.

## 1. THE GROSS DOMESTIC PRODUCT AND GROSS DOMESTIC FIXED CAPITAL FORMATION
## LE PRODUIT INTERIEUR BRUT ET LA FORMATION BRUTE DE CAPITAL FIXE INTERIEUR

Million escudos — Millions d'escudos

### A. Expenditure on the Gross Domestic Product at Market Prices —
### Sources des dépenses relatives au produit intérieur brut aux prix du marché

| Item of data and year / Rubrique et année | Total | Consumption / Consommation | | Gross Domestic Capital Formation / Formation brute de capital intérieur | | Net exports of goods and services / Exportations nettes de biens et de services | |
|---|---|---|---|---|---|---|---|
| | | Total | Government / Etat | Total | Fixed / Fixe | Exports less imports / Exportations moins importations | Exports / Exportations |
| **a. At Current Prices — Aux prix courants** | | | | | | | |
| **Absolute figures — Chiffres absolus** | | | | | | | |
| 1948 | 36 327 | ... | 4 040 | ... | ... | −5 312 | 4 869 |
| 1950 | 40 057 | ... | 4 417 | ... | ... | −1 872 | 6 065 |
| 1951 | 43 406 | ... | 4 513 | ... | ... | −1 191 | 8 631 |
| 1952 | 44 470 | 39 742 | 4 501 | 7 028 | 8 489 | −2 300 | 8 103 |
| 1953 | 46 544 | 41 002 | 5 084 | 7 910 | 6 823 | −2 368 | 7 564 |
| 1954 | 48 066 | 42 464 | 5 766 | 7 537 | 6 918 | −1 935 | 8 750 |
| 1955 | 50 886 | 46 015 | 5 951 | 7 237 | 7 228 | −2 366 | 9 752 |
| 1956 | 54 859 | 49 488 | 5 971 | 7 881 | 7 938 | −2 510 | 10 748 |
| 1957 | 57 708 | 52 092 | 6 427 | 9 861 | 8 697 | −4 245 | 10 759 |
| 1958 | 59 019 | 52 886 | 6 633 | 9 550 | 9 746 | −3 417 | 11 103 |
| 1959 | 62 864 | 56 361 | 7 657 | 10 230 | 10 713 | −3 727 | 10 669 |
| 1960 | 69 046 | 61 214 | 8 231 | 12 350 | 12 593 | −4 518 | 12 033 |
| 1961 | 74 689 | 67 708 | 10 412 | 15 718 | 13 723 | −8 737 | 12 125 |
| **Percentage distribution of average annual expenditure — Distribution en pourcentage des dépenses annuelles moyennes** | | | | | | | |
| 1948 | 100.0 | ... | 11.1 | ... | ... | −14.6 | 13.4 |
| 1950−1960 | 100.0 | ... | 11.3 | ... | ... | −5.3 | 18.0 |
| 1950 | 100.0 | ... | 11.0 | ... | ... | −4.7 | 15.1 |
| 1953 | 100.0 | 88.1 | 10.9 | 17.0 | 14.7 | −5.1 | 16.3 |
| 1954 | 100.0 | 88.3 | 12.0 | 15.7 | 14.4 | −4.0 | 18.2 |
| 1958 | 100.0 | 89.6 | 11.2 | 16.2 | 16.5 | −5.8 | 18.8 |
| 1960 | 100.0 | 88.6 | 11.9 | 17.9 | 18.2 | −6.5 | 17.4 |
| **b. At Prices of 1954 — Aux prix de 1954** | | | | | | | |
| **Absolute figures — Chiffres absolus** | | | | | | | |
| 1948 | 38 254 | ... | 4 174 | ... | ... | ... | ... |
| 1950 | 40 964 | ... | 4 404 | ... | ... | −3 069 | 6 947 |
| 1951 | 42 669 | ... | 4 531 | ... | ... | −1 654 | 7 990 |
| 1952 | 42 941 | 39 122 | 4 515 | 6 774 | 6 252 | −2 955 | 7 078 |
| 1953 | 45 819 | 40 896 | 5 049 | 7 854 | 6 689 | −2 931 | 7 190 |
| 1954 | 48 066 | 42 464 | 5 766 | 7 537 | 6 918 | −1 935 | 8 750 |
| 1955 | 50 272 | 45 879 | 5 957 | 7 129 | 7 155 | −2 736 | 9 301 |
| 1956 | 52 407 | 48 503 | 5 791 | 7 739 | 7 719 | −3 835 | 9 223 |
| 1957 | 54 683 | 50 577 | 6 148 | 9 431 | 8 395 | −5 325 | 9 255 |
| 1958 | 55 483 | 50 787 | 6 246 | 9 357 | 9 496 | −4 661 | 9 748 |
| 1959 | 58 730 | 52 426 | 7 136 | 9 919 | 10 374 | −3 615 | 10 287 |
| 1960 | 63 476 | 55 627 | 7 517 | 11 739 | 11 997 | −3 890 | 11 021 |
| 1961 | 68 494 | 60 674 | 9 457 | 14 615 | 12 909 | −6 795 | 11 128 |
| **Percentage distribution of average annual expenditure — Distribution en pourcentage des dépenses annuelles moyennes** | | | | | | | |
| 1948 | 100.0 | ... | 10.9 | ... | ... | ... | ... |
| 1950−1960 | 100.0 | ... | 11.4 | ... | ... | −6.6 | 17.4 |
| 1950 | 100.0 | ... | 10.8 | ... | ... | −7.5 | 17.0 |
| 1953 | 100.0 | 89.3 | 11.0 | 17.1 | 14.6 | −6.4 | 15.7 |
| 1954 | 100.0 | 88.3 | 12.0 | 15.7 | 14.4 | −4.0 | 18.2 |
| 1958 | 100.0 | 91.5 | 11.3 | 16.9 | 17.1 | −8.4 | 17.6 |
| 1960 | 100.0 | 87.6 | 11.8 | 18.5 | 18.9 | −6.1 | 17.4 |
| **Average annual rate of growth — Taux annuel moyen d'accroissement** | | | | | | | |
| 1948−1953 | 3.7 | ... | 3.9 | ... | ... | . | ... |
| 1950−1960 | 4.5 | ... | 5.5 | ... | ... | . | 4.7 |
| 1950−1953 | 3.8 | ... | 4.6 | ... | ... | . | 1.2 |
| 1954−1958 | 3.6 | 4.6 | 2.0 | 5.5 | 8.2 | . | 2.7 |
| 1958−1960 | 7.0 | 4.6 | 9.7 | 12.0 | 12.4 | . | 6.3 |

# PORTUGAL

## B. The Gross Domestic Product at Factor Cost According to Origin
### Origine par secteur d'activité du produit intérieur brut au coût des facteurs

| Item of data and year / Rubrique et année | Total | Agricultural sector / Secteur agricole | Industrial sector — Secteur industriel | | | | Transportation and communication / Transport et communication | Other sectors / Autres secteurs |
| | | | Total | Mining / Industries extractives | Manufacturing and construction / Industries manufacturières et bâtiment et travaux publics | Electricity, gas and water / Electricité, gaz et eau | | |
| ISIC — CITI | 0–9 | 0 | 1–5 | 1 | 2–4 | 5 | 7 | 6, 8–9 |
| **a. At Current Prices — Aux prix courants** | | | | | | | | |
| Absolute figures — Chiffres absolus | | | | | | | | |
| 1948............ | 33 851 | 10 860 | 12 467 | 299 | 11 809 | 359 | 1 707 | 8 817 |
| 1950............ | 37 138 | 12 398 | 13 071 | 338 | 12 261 | 472 | 1 869 | 9 800 |
| 1951............ | 40 413 | 13 966 | 14 179 | 675 | 13 049 | 455 | 2 020 | 10 248 |
| 1952............ | 41 412 | 12 949 | 15 434 | 691 | 14 058 | 685 | 2 041 | 10 988 |
| 1953............ | 43 327 | 13 726 | 15 814 | 567 | 14 569 | 678 | 2 123 | 11 664 |
| 1954............ | 44 641 | 13 831 | 16 331 | 483 | 14 981 | 867 | 2 328 | 12 151 |
| 1955............ | 47 144 | 14 178 | 17 631 | 577 | 16 132 | 922 | 2 597 | 12 738 |
| 1956............ | 50 925 | 14 991 | 19 671 | 627 | 18 025 | 1 019 | 2 722 | 13 541 |
| 1957............ | 53 567 | 15 349 | 20 940 | 487 | 19 416 | 1 037 | 2 908 | 14 370 |
| 1958............ | 54 697 | 14 733 | 22 023 | 390 | 20 334 | 1 299 | 3 032 | 14 909 |
| 1959............ | 58 214 | 15 542 | 22 949 | 409 | 21 123 | 1 417 | 3 178 | 16 545 |
| 1960............ | 63 866 | 16 171 | 25 987 | 422 | 23 970 | 1 595 | 3 563 | 18 145 |
| 1961............ | 68 474 | 16 665 | 28 261 | 405 | 26 014 | 1 842 | 3 853 | 19 695 |
| Percentage distribution according to sector— Distribution en pourcentage par secteur | | | | | | | | |
| 1948............ | 100.0 | 32.1 | 36.9 | 0.9 | 34.9 | 1.1 | 5.0 | 26.0 |
| 1950 – 1960..... | 100.0 | 29.5 | 38.1 | 1.0 | 35.1 | 2.0 | 5.3 | 27.1 |
| 1950............ | 100.0 | 33.4 | 35.2 | 0.9 | 33.0 | 1.3 | 5.0 | 26.4 |
| 1953............ | 100.0 | 31.7 | 36.5 | 1.3 | 33.6 | 1.6 | 4.9 | 26.9 |
| 1954............ | 100.0 | 31.0 | 36.6 | 1.1 | 33.6 | 1.9 | 5.2 | 27.2 |
| 1958............ | 100.0 | 26.9 | 40.3 | 0.7 | 37.2 | 2.4 | 5.5 | 27.3 |
| 1960............ | 100.0 | 25.3 | 40.7 | 0.7 | 37.5 | 2.5 | 5.6 | 28.4 |
| **b. At Prices of 1954 — Aux prix de 1954** | | | | | | | | |
| Absolute figures — Chiffres absolus | | | | | | | | |
| 1948............ | 35 696 | 10 748 | 13 872 | 370 | 13 048 | 454 | 1 689 | 9 387 |
| 1950............ | 38 054 | 12 707 | 13 614 | 386 | 12 719 | 509 | 1 738 | 9 995 |
| 1951............ | 39 664 | 13 703 | 13 794 | 518 | 12 719 | 557 | 1 786 | 10 381 |
| 1952............ | 39 873 | 12 187 | 14 680 | 521 | 13 453 | 706 | 1 996 | 11 010 |
| 1953............ | 42 624 | 13 786 | 15 163 | 536 | 13 902 | 725 | 2 164 | 11 511 |
| 1954............ | 44 641 | 13 831 | 16 331 | 483 | 14 981 | 867 | 2 328 | 12 151 |
| 1955............ | 46 526 | 13 603 | 17 665 | 511 | 16 164 | 990 | 2 567 | 12 691 |
| 1956............ | 48 591 | 13 688 | 19 131 | 521 | 17 483 | 1 127 | 2 725 | 13 047 |
| 1957............ | 50 720 | 14 184 | 20 103 | 523 | 18 456 | 1 124 | 2 804 | 13 629 |
| 1958............ | 51 413 | 13 416 | 21 096 | 442 | 19 310 | 1 344 | 2 972 | 13 929 |
| 1959............ | 54 397 | 13 896 | 22 156 | 443 | 20 194 | 1 519 | 3 143 | 15 202 |
| 1960............ | 58 745 | 14 277 | 24 692 | 430 | 22 381 | 1 881 | 3 362 | 16 414 |
| 1961............ | 62 849 | 14 760 | 26 946 | 440 | 24 404 | 2 102 | 3 479 | 17 664 |
| Percentage distribution according to sector— Distribution en pourcentage par secteur | | | | | | | | |
| 1948............ | 100.0 | 30.1 | 38.9 | 1.0 | 36.6 | 1.3 | 4.7 | 26.3 |
| 1950 – 1960..... | 100.0 | 29.0 | 38.5 | 1.0 | 35.3 | 2.2 | 5.4 | 27.1 |
| 1950............ | 100.0 | 33.4 | 35.7 | 1.0 | 33.4 | 1.3 | 4.6 | 26.3 |
| 1953............ | 100.0 | 32.3 | 35.6 | 1.3 | 32.6 | 1.7 | 5.1 | 27.0 |
| 1954............ | 100.0 | 31.0 | 36.6 | 1.1 | 33.6 | 1.9 | 5.2 | 27.2 |
| 1958............ | 100.0 | 26.1 | 41.0 | 0.9 | 37.5 | 2.6 | 5.8 | 27.1 |
| 1960............ | 100.0 | 24.3 | 42.0 | 0.7 | 38.1 | 3.2 | 5.7 | 28.0 |
| Average annual rate of growth—Taux annuel moyen d'accroissement | | | | | | | | |
| 1948 – 1953..... | 3.6 | 5.1 | 1.8 | 7.7 | 1.3 | 9.8 | 5.1 | 4.2 |
| 1950 – 1960..... | 4.4 | 1.2 | 6.1 | 1.1 | 5.8 | −9.5 | 6.8 | 5.1 |
| 1950 – 1953..... | 3.8 | 2.8 | 3.7 | 11.6 | 3.0 | 12.5 | 7.6 | 4.8 |
| 1954 – 1958..... | 3.6 | −0.8 | 6.6 | −4.6 | 6.6 | 11.6 | 6.3 | 3.5 |
| 1958 – 1960..... | 6.9 | 3.2 | 8.2 | −1.4 | 7.7 | 18.3 | 6.3 | 8.5 |

## C. Gross Domestic Fixed Capital Formation According to Purchasing Sector
### La formation brute de capital fixe intérieur par secteur d'acquisition

| Item of data and year<br>Rubrique et année | Total | Agricultural sector<br>Secteur agricole | Industrial sector — Secteur industriel | | | | Transportation and communication<br>Transport et communication | Other sectors<br>Autres secteurs |
| | | | Total | Mining<br>Industries extractives | Manufacturing and construction<br>Industries manufacturières et bâtiment et travaux publics | Electricity, gas and water<br>Electricité, gaz et eau | | |
| ISIC — CITI | 0–9 | 0 | 1–5 | 1 | 2–4 | 5 | 7 | 6, 8–9 |
| | a. At Current Prices — Aux prix courants | | | | | | | |
| **Absolute figures — Chiffres absolus** | | | | | | | | |
| 1952 | 6 489 | 888 | 2 196 | 164 | 1 486 | 546 | 1 207 | 2 198 |
| 1953 | 6 823 | 812 | 2 382 | 163 | 1 469 | 750 | 1 060 | 2 569 |
| 1954 | 6 918 | 941 | 2 433 | 117 | 1 480 | 836 | 1 122 | 2 422 |
| 1955 | 7 228 | 920 | 2 292 | 190 | 1 356 | 746 | 1 387 | 2 629 |
| 1956 | 7 938 | 905 | 2 849 | 158 | 1 685 | 1 006 | 1 171 | 3 013 |
| 1957 | 8 697 | 1 013 | 3 038 | 146 | 1 817 | 1 075 | 1 458 | 3 188 |
| 1958 | 9 746 | 1 229 | 3 374 | 167 | 2 175 | 1 032 | 1 683 | 3 460 |
| 1959 | 10 713 | 1 061 | 4 026 | 156 | 2 705 | 1 165 | 1 933 | 3 693 |
| 1960 | 12 593 | 1 030 | 5 544 | 125 | 4 324 | 1 095 | 2 110 | 3 909 |
| 1961 | 13 723 | 1 087 | 6 207 | 146 | 4 790 | 1 271 | 2 121 | 4 308 |
| **Percentage distribution according to sector— Distribution en pourcentage par secteur** | | | | | | | | |
| 1952 – 1960 | 100.0 | 11.4 | 36.5 | 1.8 | 24.0 | 10.7 | 17.0 | 35.1 |
| 1953 | 100.0 | 11.9 | 34.9 | 2.4 | 21.5 | 11.0 | 15.5 | 37.7 |
| 1954 | 100.0 | 13.6 | 35.2 | 1.7 | 21.4 | 12.1 | 16.2 | 35.0 |
| 1958 | 100.0 | 12.6 | 34.6 | 1.7 | 22.3 | 10.6 | 17.3 | 35.5 |
| 1960 | 100.0 | 8.2 | 44.0 | 1.0 | 34.3 | 8.7 | 16.8 | 31.0 |
| | b. At Prices of 1954 — Aux prix de 1954 | | | | | | | |
| **Absolute figures — Chiffres absolus** | | | | | | | | |
| 1952 | 6 252 | 873 | 2 119 | 159 | 1 429 | 531 | 1 165 | 2 095 |
| 1953 | 6 689 | 790 | 2 333 | 159 | 1 427 | 747 | 1 032 | 2 534 |
| 1954 | 6 918 | 941 | 2 433 | 117 | 1 480 | 836 | 1 122 | 2 422 |
| 1955 | 7 155 | 922 | 2 279 | 189 | 1 354 | 736 | 1 372 | 2 582 |
| 1956 | 7 719 | 871 | 2 773 | 154 | 1 637 | 982 | 1 145 | 2 930 |
| 1957 | 8 395 | 967 | 2 929 | 141 | 1 741 | 1 047 | 1 412 | 3 087 |
| 1958 | 9 496 | 1 173 | 3 249 | 162 | 2 081 | 1 006 | 1 627 | 3 447 |
| 1959 | 10 374 | 992 | 3 879 | 150 | 2 594 | 1 135 | 1 866 | 3 637 |
| 1960 | 11 997 | 947 | 5 251 | 119 | 4 062 | 1 070 | 2 009 | 3 790 |
| 1961 | 12 909 | 971 | 5 861 | 139 | 4 507 | 1 215 | 2 012 | 4 065 |
| **Percentage distribution according to sector— Distribution en pourcentage par secteur** | | | | | | | | |
| 1952 – 1960 | 100.0 | 11.3 | 36.3 | 1.8 | 23.7 | 10.8 | 17.0 | 35.4 |
| 1953 | 100.0 | 11.8 | 34.9 | 2.4 | 21.3 | 11.2 | 15.4 | 37.9 |
| 1954 | 100.0 | 13.6 | 35.2 | 1.7 | 21.4 | 12.1 | 16.2 | 35.0 |
| 1958 | 100.0 | 12.4 | 34.2 | 1.7 | 21.9 | 10.6 | 17.1 | 36.3 |
| 1960 | 100.0 | 7.9 | 43.8 | 1.0 | 33.9 | 8.9 | 16.7 | 31.6 |
| **Average annual rate of growth—Taux annuel moyen d'accroissement** | | | | | | | | |
| 1952 – 1960 | 8.5 | 1.0 | 12.0 | −3.6 | 13.9 | 9.2 | 7.0 | 7.7 |
| 1954 – 1958 | 8.2 | 5.7 | 7.5 | 8.5 | 8.9 | 4.7 | 9.7 | 9.2 |
| 1958 – 1960 | 12.4 | −10.2 | 27.1 | −14.3 | 39.7 | 3.2 | 11.1 | 4.9 |

## 2. INDEX NUMBERS OF INDUSTRIAL PRODUCTION
### INDICES DE LA PRODUCTION INDUSTRIELLE

### A. Selected Divisions of Industrial Activity
### Quelques branches de l'activité industrielle

| Period<br>Période | Total [1] | Mining<br>Industries<br>extractives | Manu-<br>facturing [1]<br>Industries<br>manu-<br>facturières [1] | Electricity<br>Electricité |
|---|---|---|---|---|
| ISIC — CITI | 1–3, 511 | 1 | 2–3 | 511 |

#### a. Indexes — Indices (1958 = 100)

| | | | | |
|---|---|---|---|---|
| 1953........... | 68 | 128 | 68 | 52 |
| 1954........... | 76 | 112 | 76 | 62 |
| 1955........... | 81 | 102 | 81 | 71 |
| 1956........... | 88 | 104 | 88 | 82 |
| 1957........... | 93 | 117 | 94 | 81 |
| 1958........... | 100 | 100 | 100 | 100 |
| 1959........... | 105 | 100 | 105 | 112 |
| 1960........... | 117 | 101 | 116 | 122 |
| 1961........... | 129 | 119 | 128 | 136 |

#### b. Average Annual Rate of Change — Taux annuel moyen de variation

| | | | | |
|---|---|---|---|---|
| 1954–1958.... | 7.1 | −2.8 | 7.1 | 12.7 |
| 1958–1960.... | 8.2 | 0.5 | 7.7 | 10.5 |

For footnotes see end of table.

Pour les notes, voir au bas du tableau.

### B. The Major Groups of Mining
### Les classes de la branche Industries extractives

| Period<br>Période | All mining<br>Toutes<br>industries<br>extractives | Coal<br>mining<br>Extraction<br>du charbon | Metal mining<br>Extraction<br>des minerais<br>métalliques | Other mining<br>Autres<br>industries<br>extractives |
|---|---|---|---|---|
| ISIC — CITI | 1 | 11 | 12 | 14–19 |

#### a. Indexes — Indices (1958 = 100)

| | | | | |
|---|---|---|---|---|
| 1953........... | 128 | 76 | 149 | 128 |
| 1954........... | 112 | 68 | 128 | 113 |
| 1955........... | 102 | 68 | 115 | 100 |
| 1956........... | 104 | 77 | 115 | 102 |
| 1957........... | 117 | 94 | 125 | 118 |
| 1958........... | 100 | 100 | 100 | 100 |
| 1959........... | 100 | 95 | 103 | 97 |
| 1960........... | 101 | 81 | 110 | 99 |
| 1961........... | 119 | 86 | 133 | 118 |

#### b. Average Annual Rate of Change — Taux annuel moyen de variation

| | | | | |
|---|---|---|---|---|
| 1954–1958.... | −2.8 | 10.1 | −6.0 | −3.0 |
| 1958–1960.... | 0.5 | −10.0 | 4.9 | −0.5 |

### C. The Major Groups of Manufacturing — Les classes de la branche Industries manufacturières

| Period<br>Période | Manu-<br>facturing [1]<br>Industries<br>manufac-<br>turières [1] | Food,<br>beverages<br>and<br>tobacco<br>Industries<br>alimen-<br>taires,<br>boissons,<br>tabac | Textiles,<br>clothing,<br>footwear<br>and<br>made-up<br>textiles<br>Textiles,<br>articles<br>d'habil-<br>lement,<br>chaussures<br>et<br>ouvrages<br>en tissu | Wood<br>products<br>and<br>furniture<br>Bois et<br>meubles | Paper<br>and<br>paper<br>products<br>Papier<br>et<br>ouvrages<br>en<br>papier | Leather<br>and<br>leather<br>products<br>except<br>wearing<br>apparel<br>Cuir et<br>articles<br>en cuir,<br>à l'exclu-<br>sion<br>des<br>articles<br>d'habil-<br>lement | Rubber<br>products<br>Ouvrages<br>en<br>caout-<br>chouc | Chemicals<br>and<br>chemical,<br>petroleum<br>and<br>coal<br>products<br>Produits<br>chi-<br>miques<br>et<br>dérivés<br>du<br>pétrole<br>et du<br>charbon | Non-<br>metallic<br>mineral<br>products<br>Produits<br>minéraux<br>non<br>métal-<br>liques | Basic<br>metals<br>Métal-<br>lurgie<br>de base | Metal<br>products<br>Ouvrages<br>en<br>métaux |
|---|---|---|---|---|---|---|---|---|---|---|---|
| ISIC — CITI | 2–3 | 20–22 | 23–24 | 25–26 | 27 | 29 | 30 | 31–32 | 33 | 34 | 35–38 |

#### a. Indexes — Indices (1958 = 100)

| | | | | | | | | | | | |
|---|---|---|---|---|---|---|---|---|---|---|---|
| 1953............. | 68 | 76 | 75 | 79 | 35 | 64 | 85 | 70 | 74 | 56 | 55 |
| 1954............. | 76 | 83 | 81 | 77 | 63 | 72 | 102 | 77 | 73 | 62 | 64 |
| 1955............. | 81 | 81 | 90 | 90 | 79 | 81 | 97 | 83 | 81 | 73 | 67 |
| 1956............. | 88 | 92 | 91 | 93 | 91 | 84 | 101 | 89 | 95 | 81 | 78 |
| 1957............. | 94 | 93 | 95 | 98 | 99 | 89 | 126 | 92 | 92 | 85 | 92 |
| 1958............. | 100 | 100 | 100 | 100 | 100 | 100 | 100 | 100 | 100 | 100 | 100 |
| 1959............. | 105 | 106 | 99 | 107 | 106 | 108 | 141 | 106 | 106 | 94 | 109 |
| 1960............. | 116 | 116 | 108 | 128 | 130 | 110 | 179 | 119 | 113 | 93 | 118 |
| 1961............. | 128 | 120 | 115 | 146 | 138 | 100 | 219 | 122 | 127 | 127 | 137 |

#### b. Average Annual Rate of Change — Taux annuel moyen de variation

| | | | | | | | | | | | |
|---|---|---|---|---|---|---|---|---|---|---|---|
| 1954–1958........ | 7.1 | 4.8 | 5.4 | 6.8 | 12.2 | 8.6 | −0.5 | 6.8 | 8.2 | 12.7 | 11.8 |
| 1958–1960........ | 7.7 | 7.7 | 3.9 | 13.1 | 14.0 | 4.9 | 33.8 | 9.1 | 6.3 | −3.6 | 8.6 |

[1] Excludes Printing and publishing (ISIC major group 28), Other manufacturing (ISIC major group 39) and most of Clothing, footwear and made-up textiles (ISIC major group 24).

[1] Non compris Imprimerie et édition (CITI classe 28), Autres industries manufacturières (CITI classe 39) et la plupart des Industries du vêtement, de la chaussure et des ouvrages en tissu (CITI classe 24).

# 3. CHARACTERISTICS OF ALL ESTABLISHMENTS ENGAGED IN SELECTED CLASSES OF INDUSTRIAL ACTIVITY

## CARACTERISTIQUES DE TOUS LES ETABLISSEMENTS DE QUELQUES CLASSES DE L'ACTIVITE INDUSTRIELLE

### 1953, 1958

Number of establishments in units; value added and wages and salaries in million Escudos; number of engaged, employees and operatives in thousands; energy consumed in thousand metric tons of coal equivalents, electricity consumed in million KWH; value added per engaged and wages and salaries per employee in thousand Escudos; energy consumed per engaged and per operative in metric tons of coal equivalents; electricity consumed per engaged and per operative in thousand KWH.

Nombre d'établissements en unités; valeur ajoutée et traitements et salaires en millions d'escudos; nombre de personnes occupées, de salariés et d'ouvriers en milliers; énergie consommée en milliers de tonnes métriques d'équivalent charbon; électricité consommée en millions de kWh; valeur ajoutée par personne occupée et traitements et salaires par salarié en milliers d'escudos; énergie consommée par personne occupée et par ouvrier en tonnes métriques d'équivalent charbon; électricité consommée par personne occupée et par ouvrier en milliers de kWh.

## A. Selected Major Groups of Mining — Quelques classes de la branche Industries extractives

### a. Absolute Figures — Chiffres absolus

| Year and item of data | Total[1] | Coal mining[1] Extraction du charbon[1] | Other mining Divers | Année et rubrique |
|---|---|---|---|---|
| ISIC | 11, 14-19 | 11 | 14-19 | CITI |
| **1953** | | | | **1953** |
| Number of establishments (Operating during year) | 551 | 11 | 540 | Nombre d'établissements (en exercice pendant l'année) |
| Value added | 299 | 55 | 244 | Valeur ajoutée |
| Number of engaged (Average during year) | 15.8 | 5.9 | 9.9 | Nombre de personnes occupées (moyenne pour l'année) |
| Employees: | | | | Salariés: |
| Number (Average during year) | 15.8 | 5.9 | 9.9 | Nombre (moyenne pour l'année) |
| Wages and salaries | 118.7 | 45.2 | 73.5 | Traitements et salaires |
| Operatives: | | | | Ouvriers: |
| Number (Average during year) | 15.3 | 5.6 | 9.7 | Nombre (moyenne pour l'année) |
| Wages and salaries | 106.0 | 38.0 | 68.0 | Traitements et salaires |
| Energy consumed | 21.6 | 2.8 | 18.8 | Energie consommée |
| Electricity consumed | 15.0 | 6.5 | 8.5 | Electricité consommée |
| **1958** | | | | **1958** |
| Number of establishments (Operating during year) | 737 | 33 | 704 | Nombre d'établissements (en exercice pendant l'année) |
| Value added | 236.5 | 78.7 | 157.8 | Valeur ajoutée |
| Number of engaged (Average during year) | 15.8 | 5.6 | 10.2 | Nombre de personnes occupées (moyenne pour l'année) |
| Employees: | | | | Salariés: |
| Number (Average during year) | 15.8 | 5.6 | 10.2 | Nombre (moyenne pour l'année) |
| Wages and salaries | 142.5 | 54.5 | 88.0 | Traitements et salaires |
| Operatives: | | | | Ouvriers: |
| Number (Average during year) | 15.1 | 5.3 | 9.8 | Nombre (moyenne pour l'année) |
| Wages and salaries | 124.8 | 46.1 | 78.7 | Traitements et salaires |
| Electricity consumed | 26.6 | 11.2 | 15.4 | Electricité consommée |

### b. Structure

| Year and item of data | All mining[1] Toutes industries extractives[1] | Coal mining[1] Extraction du charbon[1] | Other mining Divers | Année et rubrique |
|---|---|---|---|---|
| ISIC | 11, 14-19 | 11 | 14-19 | CITI |
| **1953** | | | | **1953** |
| Distribution in percent of: | | | | Distribution en pourcentage: |
| Value added | 100.0 | 18.4 | 81.6 | Valeur ajoutée |
| Number of engaged | 100.0 | 37.3 | 62.7 | Nombre de personnes occupées |
| Per person engaged: | | | | Par personne occupée: |
| Value added | 18.9 | 9.3 | 24.6 | Valeur ajoutée |
| Energy consumed | 1.37 | 0.47 | 1.90 | Energie consommée |
| Electricity consumed | 0.9 | 1.1 | 0.8 | Electricité consommée |
| Employees as a percent of engaged | 100.0 | 100.0 | 100.0 | Salariés en pourcentage des personnes occupées |
| Value added per unit of wages and salaries | 2.52 | 1.22 | 3.32 | Valeur ajoutée par unité de traitements et salaires |
| Operatives as a percent of employees | 96.8 | 94.9 | 98.0 | Ouvriers en pourcentage de salariés |
| Wages and salaries per employee | 7.5 | 7.7 | 7.4 | Traitements et salaires par salarié |
| Per operative: | | | | Par ouvrier: |
| Wages and salaries | 6.93 | 6.78 | 7.01 | Traitements et salaires |
| Energy consumed | 1.41 | 0.50 | 1.94 | Energie consommée |
| Electricity consumed | 0.98 | 1.16 | 0.88 | Electricité consommée |
| **1958** | | | | **1958** |
| Distribution in percent of: | | | | Distribution en pourcentage: |
| Value added | 100.0 | 33.3 | 66.7 | Valeur ajoutée |
| Number of engaged | 100.0 | 35.4 | 64.6 | Nombre de personnes occupées |
| Per person engaged: | | | | Par personne occupée: |
| Value added | 15.0 | 14.0 | 15.5 | Valeur ajoutée |
| Electricity consumed | 1.7 | 2.0 | 1.5 | Electricité consommée |
| Employees as a percent of engaged | 100.0 | 100.0 | 100.0 | Salariés en pourcentage des personnes occupées |
| Value added per unit of wages and salaries | 1.66 | 1.44 | 1.79 | Valeur ajoutée par unité de traitements et salaires |
| Operatives as a percent of employees | 95.6 | 94.6 | 96.1 | Ouvriers en pourcentage des salariés |
| Wages and salaries per employee | 9.0 | 9.7 | 8.6 | Traitements et salaires par salarié |
| Per operative: | | | | Par ouvrier: |
| Wages and salaries | 8.26 | 8.70 | 8.03 | Traitements et salaires |
| Electricity consumed | 1.76 | 2.11 | 1.57 | Electricité consommée |

For footnotes see end of table.

Pour les notes, voir au bas du tableau.

# PORTUGAL

## B. The Major Groups of Manufacturing — Les classes de la branche Industries manufacturières

| Year and item of data | Manufacturing[1,2] Industries manufacturières[1,2] | Food beverages and tobacco[2] Industries alimentaires, boissons, tabac[2] | Textiles | Clothing[2] Articles d'habillement[2] | Wood products[2] Bois[2] | Paper and paper products[2] Papier et ouvrages en papier[2] | Leather Cuir | Rubber products Ouvrages en caoutchouc | Chemical products[2] Produits chimiques[2] | Non-metallic mineral products[2] Produits minéraux non métalliques[2] | Basic metals[1] Métallurgie de base[1] | Metal products[2] Ouvrages en métaux[2] | Other manufacturing[2] Autres industries manufacturières[2] | Année et rubrique |
|---|---|---|---|---|---|---|---|---|---|---|---|---|---|---|
| ISIC | 2–3 | 20–22 | 23 | 243 | 25 | 27 | 291 | 30 | 31 | 33 | 34 | 35,37–38 | 399 | CITI |

a. Absolute Figures — Chiffres absolus

| Year and item of data | 2–3 | 20–22 | 23 | 243 | 25 | 27 | 291 | 30 | 31 | 33 | 34 | 35,37–38 | 399 | Année et rubrique |
|---|---|---|---|---|---|---|---|---|---|---|---|---|---|---|
| **1953** | | | | | | | | | | | | | | **1953** |
| Number of establishments (Operating during year) | 6 443 | 2 217 | 1 455 | 20 | 617 | 103 | 375 | 30 | 604 | 290 | 525 | 156 | 51 | Nombre d'établissements (En exercice pendant l'année) |
| Value added | ... | 1 047 | 2 232 | ... | ... | 110 | 87 | 88 | 504 | 611 | 438 | 112 | 8 | Valeur ajoutée |
| Number of engaged (Average during year) | 259.9 | 39.9 | 105.6 | 1.3 | 20.5 | 4.5 | 3.7 | 2.7 | 9.7 | 31.1 | 32.4 | 6.8 | 1.7 | Nombre de personnes occupées (moyenne pour l'année) |
| Employees: Number (Average during year) | 257.9 | 39.1 | 105.0 | 1.3 | 20.5 | 4.5 | 3.6 | 2.7 | 9.6 | 30.9 | 32.3 | 6.7 | 1.7 | Salariés: Nombre (moyenne pour l'année) |
| Wages and salaries | 1 601.5 | 220.9 | 637.1 | 9.4 | 122.6 | 29.6 | 25.0 | 27.0 | 86.2 | 222.5 | 169.7 | 46.5 | 5.0 | Traitements et salaires |
| Operatives: Number (Average during year) | 245.3 | 35.8 | 101.9 | 1.2 | 20.0 | 4.2 | 3.4 | 2.4 | 8.3 | 29.2 | 31.0 | 6.3 | 1.6 | Ouvriers: Nombre (moyenne pour l'année) |
| Wages and salaries | 1 337.3 | 157.6 | 570.9 | 7.4 | 112.7 | 23.4 | 21.3 | 16.2 | 59.9 | 179.5 | 146.9 | 36.8 | 4.7 | Traitements et salaires |
| Energy consumed | 831.3 | 69.7 | 177.8 | 4.7 | 30.0 | 25.9 | 3.7 | 10.4 | 37.2 | 437.9 | 24.8 | 9.0 | 0.2 | Energie consommée |
| Electricity consumed | 436.1 | 38.2 | 137.5 | 0.6 | 10.8 | 16.8 | 3.2 | 6.2 | 67.7 | 105.0 | 43.8 | 5.6 | 0.7 | Electricité consommée |
| **1958** | | | | | | | | | | | | | | **1958** |
| Number of establishments (Operating during year) | 677.5 | 2 175 | 1 498 | 20 | 682 | 233 | 378 | 34 | 536 | 380 | 512 | 191 | 136 | Nombre d'établissements (En exercice pendant l'année) |
| Value added | 8 510.3 | 1 708.9 | 3 034.6 | 15.7 | 498.8 | 411.3 | 107.4 | 116.9 | 675.1 | 848.3 | 182.7 | 820.8 | 89.8 | Valeur ajoutée |
| Number of engaged (Average during year) | 254.9 | 46.7 | 98.5 | 1.2 | 19.6 | 8.6 | 3.4 | 3.2 | 9.9 | 30.1 | 9.7 | 20.4 | 3.6 | Nombre de personnes occupées (moyenne pour l'année) |
| Employees: Number (Average during year) | 253.0 | 46.4 | 97.6 | 1.2 | 19.5 | 8.5 | 3.3 | 3.2 | 9.7 | 30.0 | 9.7 | 20.3 | 3.6 | Salariés: Nombre (moyenne pour l'année) |
| Wages and salaries | 2 191.4 | 364.0 | 727.4 | 9.3 | 152.4 | 75.2 | 29.1 | 38.5 | 128.1 | 302.2 | 88.3 | 254.3 | 22.6 | Traitements et salaires |
| Operatives: Number (Average during year) | 235.5 | 41.6 | 93.8 | 1.1 | 18.9 | 7.9 | 3.0 | 2.8 | 7.8 | 27.8 | 9.1 | 18.4 | 3.3 | Ouvriers: Nombre (moyenne pour l'année) |
| Wages and salaries | 1 739.3 | 258.7 | 631.8 | 7.0 | 139.8 | 53.2 | 24.4 | 23.3 | 78.0 | 240.4 | 66.7 | 197.1 | 18.9 | Traitements et salaires |
| Electricity consumed | 690.2 | 73.2 | 240.9 | 0.6 | 14.1 | 64.4 | 3.9 | 10.2 | 53.5 | 161.7 | 38.4 | 23.5 | 5.8 | Electricité consommée |

For footnotes, see end of table.

Pour les notes, voir au bas du tableau.

## B. The Major Groups of Manufacturing (continued) — Les classes de la branche industries manufacturières (suite)

| Year and item of data | Manufacturing[1,2] Industries manufacturières[1,2] | Food beverages and tobacco[2] Industries alimentaires, boissons, tabac[2] | Textiles | Clothing,[2] Articles d'habillement,[2] | Wood products[2] Bois | Paper and paper products[2] Papier et ouvrages en papier[2] | Leather Cuir | Rubber products Ouvrages en caoutchouc | Chemical products[2] Produits chimiques[2] | Non-metallic mineral products[2] Produits minéraux non métalliques[2] | Basic metals[1] Métallurgie de base[1] | Metal products[2] Ouvrages en métaux[2] | Other manufacturing[2] Autres industries manufacturières[2] | Année et rubrique |
|---|---|---|---|---|---|---|---|---|---|---|---|---|---|---|
| ISIC | 2–3 | 20–22 | 23 | 243 | 25 | 27 | 291 | 30 | 31 | 33 | 34 | 35,37–38 | 399 | CITI |

### b. Structure

| | | | | | | | | | | | | | | |
|---|---|---|---|---|---|---|---|---|---|---|---|---|---|---|
| **1953** | | | | | | | | | | | | | | **1953** |
| Distribution in percent of: Number of engaged | 100.0 | 15.4 | 40.6 | 0.5 | 7.9 | 1.7 | 1.4 | 1.0 | 3.7 | 12.0 | 12.5 | 2.6 | 0.7 | Distribution en pourcentage: Nombre de personnes occupées |
| Per person engaged: Value added | ... | 26.2 | 21.1 | ... | ... | 24.4 | 23.5 | 32.6 | 52.0 | 19.6 | 13.5 | 16.5 | 4.7 | Par personne occupée: Valeur ajoutée |
| Energy consumed | 3.20 | 1.75 | 1.68 | 3.62 | 1.46 | 5.76 | 1.00 | 3.85 | 3.84 | 14.08 | 0.76 | 1.32 | 0.12 | Energie consommée |
| Electricity consumed | 1.7 | 1.0 | 1.3 | 0.5 | 0.5 | 3.7 | 0.9 | 2.3 | 7.0 | 3.4 | 1.4 | 0.8 | 0.4 | Electricité consommée |
| Employees as a percent of engaged | 99.2 | 98.0 | 99.4 | 100.0 | 100.0 | 100.0 | 97.3 | 100.0 | 99.0 | 99.4 | 99.7 | 98.5 | 100.0 | Salariés en pourcentage des personnes occupées |
| Value added per unit of wages and salaries | ... | 4.74 | 3.50 | ... | ... | 3.72 | 3.48 | 3.26 | 5.85 | 2.75 | 2.58 | 2.41 | 1.60 | Valeur ajoutée par unité de traitements et salaires |
| Wages and salaries per employee | 6.2 | 5.6 | 6.1 | 7.2 | 6.0 | 6.6 | 6.9 | 10.0 | 9.0 | 7.2 | 5.2 | 6.9 | 2.9 | Traitements et salaires par salarié |
| Operatives as a percent of employees | 95.1 | 91.6 | 97.0 | 92.3 | 97.6 | 93.3 | 94.4 | 88.9 | 86.4 | 94.5 | 96.0 | 94.0 | 94.1 | Ouvriers en pourcentage des salariés |
| Per operative: Wages and salaries | 5.45 | 4.40 | 5.60 | 6.17 | 5.64 | 5.57 | 6.26 | 6.75 | 7.22 | 6.15 | 4.74 | 5.84 | 2.94 | Par ouvrier: Traitements et salaires |
| Energy consumed | 3.39 | 1.95 | 1.74 | 3.92 | 1.50 | 6.17 | 1.09 | 4.33 | 4.48 | 15.00 | 0.80 | 1.43 | 0.12 | Energie consommée |
| Electricity consumed | 1.78 | 1.07 | 1.35 | 0.50 | 0.54 | 4.00 | 0.94 | 2.58 | 8.16 | 3.60 | 1.41 | 0.89 | 0.44 | Electricité consommée |
| **1958** | | | | | | | | | | | | | | **1958** |
| Distribution in percent of: Value added | 100.0 | 20.1 | 35.7 | 0.2 | 5.9 | 4.8 | 1.3 | 1.4 | 7.9 | 10.0 | 2.1 | 9.6 | 1.0 | Distribution en pourcentage: Valeur ajoutée Nombre de personnes occupées |
| Number of engaged | 100.0 | 18.3 | 38.6 | 0.5 | 7.7 | 3.4 | 1.3 | 1.3 | 3.9 | 11.8 | 3.8 | 8.0 | 1.4 | |
| Per person engaged: Value added | 33.39 | 36.6 | 30.8 | 13.1 | 25.4 | 47.8 | 31.6 | 36.5 | 68.2 | 28.2 | 18.8 | 40.2 | 24.9 | Par personne occupée: Valeur ajoutée |
| Electricity consumed | 2.7 | 1.6 | 2.4 | 0.5 | 0.7 | 7.5 | 1.1 | 3.2 | 5.4 | 5.4 | 4.0 | 1.2 | 1.6 | Electricité consommée |
| Employees as a percent of engaged | 99.2 | 99.4 | 99.1 | 100.0 | 99.5 | 98.8 | 97.0 | 100.0 | 98.0 | 99.7 | 100.0 | 99.5 | 100.0 | Salariés en pourcentage des personnes occupées |
| Value added per unit of wages and salaries | 3.88 | 4.69 | 4.17 | 1.69 | 3.27 | 5.47 | 3.69 | 3.04 | 5.27 | 2.81 | 2.07 | 3.23 | 3.97 | Valeur ajoutée par unité de traitements et salaires |
| Wages and salaries per employee | 8.7 | 7.8 | 7.4 | 7.8 | 7.8 | 8.8 | 8.8 | 12.0 | 13.2 | 10.1 | 9.1 | 12.5 | 6.3 | Traitements et salaires par salarié |
| Operatives as a percent of employees | 93.1 | 89.6 | 96.1 | 91.7 | 96.9 | 92.9 | 90.9 | 87.5 | 80.4 | 92.7 | 93.8 | 90.6 | 91.7 | Ouvriers en pourcentage des salariés |
| Per operative: Wages and salaries | 7.39 | 6.22 | 6.74 | 6.36 | 7.40 | 6.73 | 8.13 | 8.32 | 10.0 | 8.65 | 7.33 | 10.71 | 5.73 | Par ouvrier: Traitements et salaires |
| Electricity consumed | 2.93 | 1.76 | 2.57 | 0.54 | 0.75 | 8.15 | 1.30 | 3.64 | 6.86 | 5.82 | 4.22 | 1.28 | 1.76 | Electricité consommée |

[1] Metal mining (ISIC major group 12) is included in Manufacturing under Basic metals (ISIC major group 34) and coal briquetting and coking (part of ISIC major group 32) is included in Mining under Coal mining (ISIC major group 12).

[2] The following significant activities are not covered under Manufacturing in 1953 or 1958: Selected kinds of bakeries, salt refining and wine manufacture (all part of ISIC major groups 20–21); Clothing, footwear and other wearing apparel (ISIC major group 24) except hats and fur apparel; Wood products and furniture (ISIC major groups 25–26) except cork products and wood veneers; Printing and publishing (ISIC major group 28); Leather and fur products (ISIC groups 292–293); basic chemicals such as acids and bases (part of ISIC major group 31); Petroleum and coal products (ISIC group 32); Machinery except electrical machinery (ISIC major group 36); Electric machinery, apparatus and supplies (ISIC major group 37) except cables, conductors and condensers; Transport equipment (ISIC major group 38) except ship wrights; and Miscellaneous manufacturing (ISIC major group 39) except buttons, plastic products and related articles. In addition, the following manufacturing activities are excluded in 1953 but included in 1958: Additional kinds of bakeries, the manufacture of macaroni products, olive oil, margarine and animal feeds (all part of ISIC major group 20); Articles of paper and paperboard (ISIC group 272); cosmetics (part of ISIC group 319); cement products (part of ISIC group 339); the manufacture of cables, conductors and condensers (part of ISIC major group 37); and ship wrights (part of ISIC major group 38).

[1] Les industries extractives de minerais métalliques (CITI classe 12) sont incluses dans les Industries manufacturières sous la rubrique Métallurgie de base (CITI classe 34); la fabrication de briquettes en charbon et les cokeries (dans CITI classe 32) sont incluses dans la classe Industries extractives sous Industries extractives de charbon (CITI classe 12).

[2] Les activités majeures qui suivent ne sont pas couvertes par la rubrique Industries manufacturières en 1953 ou 1958; certaines boulangeries et pâtisseries, Industries de sel raffiné et de vin (tous dans CITI classes 20–21), Vêtements, chaussures et autres articles d'habillement (CITI classe 26) à l'exclusion des chapeaux et des articles d'habillement en fourrure. Ouvrages en bois et meubles (CITI classes 25–26) à l'exclusion des ouvrages en liège et du placage; Imprimeries et édition (CITI classe 28). Cuir et articles en fourrure (CITI classe 31); Produits dérivés du charbon et du pétrole (CITI groupe 32); Machines à l'exclusion des machines électriques (CITI classe 36). Machines électriques; Appareils et fournitures (CITI classe 37) à l'exclusion des câbles, conducteurs et condenseurs; équipements de transport (CITI classe 38) à l'exclusion de la construction navale; et Industries manufacturières diverses (CITI classe 39) à l'exclusion des boutons, des ouvrages en plastique et des articles s'y rapportant. De plus, les activités suivantes sont exclues pour 1953 mais incluses pour 1958: des catégories additionnelles de boulangeries et de pâtisseries, la fabrication de pâtes alimentaires, d'huile d'olive, de margarine, des produits pour l'alimentation des animaux (tous dans CITI classe 20); Articles en papier et en carton (CITI groupe 272); produits de beauté (dans CITI groupe 319); produits en ciment (dans CITI groupe 339); la fabrication de câbles, conducteurs et condenseurs (dans CITI classe 37) et la construction navale (dans CITI classe 38).

## 4. PURCHASED FUELS AND ELECTRICITY CONSUMED, ALL ESTABLISHMENTS IN SELECTED CLASSES OF INDUSTRIAL ACTIVITY

### COMBUSTIBLES ACHETES ET CONSOMMES ET ELECTRICITE CONSOMMEE, TOUS LES ETABLISSEMENTS DANS QUELQUES CLASSES DE L'ACTIVITE INDUSTRIELLE

### 1953, 1958

### A. Percentage Distribution of Purchased Energy Consumed According to Source

### Distribution en pourcentage de l'énergie achetée et consommée suivant la source

Quantities in thousand metric tons of coal equivalents.

Quantités en milliers de tonnes métriques d'équivalent houille.

### a. Selected Major Groups of Mining

### Quelques classes des industries extractives

| Year and item of data | Total [1] | Coal mining [1] Extraction du charbon[1] | Other mining Divers | Année et rubrique |
|---|---|---|---|---|
| ISIC | 1 | 11 | 14–19 | CITI |
| **1953** | | | | **1953** |
| Total energy consumed.. | 21.6 | 2.8 | 18.8 | Energie totale consommée |
| Percent initially consumed as: | | | | Pourcentage consommé à l'origine comme: |
| Coal [3] | 24.1 | 60.7 | 18.6 | Charbon [3] |
| Lignite [3] | — | — | — | Lignite [3] |
| Coke | 30.6 | — | 35.1 | Coke |
| Refined oil fuels | 26.8 | 14.3 | 28.7 | Pétrole raffiné |
| Wood | 13.4 | — | 15.4 | Bois |
| Electricity purchased... | 5.1 | 25.0 | 2.2 | Electricité achetée |

For footnotes see end of table.

Pour les notes, voir au bas du tableau.

### b. The Major Groups of Manufacturing — Les classes de la branche Industries manufacturières

| Year and item of data | Manufacturing [1,2] Industries manufacturières[1,2] | Food, beverages and tobacco [2] Industries alimentaires, boissons, tabac [2] | Textiles | Clothing [2] Articles d'habillement [2] | Wood products[2] Bois [2] | Paper and paper products [2] Papier et ouvrages en papier [2] | Leather Cuir | Rubber products Ouvrages en caoutchouc | Chemical products[2] Produits chimiques [2] | Non-metallic mineral products [2] Produits minéraux non métalliques [2] | Basic metals [1] Métallurgie de base [1] | Metal products [2] Ouvrages en métaux [2] | Other manufacturing [2] Autres industries manufacturières [2] | Année et rubrique |
|---|---|---|---|---|---|---|---|---|---|---|---|---|---|---|
| ISIC | 2–3 | 20–22 | 23 | 243 | 25 | 27 | 291 | 30 | 31 | 33 | 34 | 35,37–38 | 399 | CITI |
| **1953** | | | | | | | | | | | | | | **1953** |
| Total energy consumed: | | | | | | | | | | | | | | Energie totale consommée: |
| Quantity | 831.3 | 69.9 | 177.7 | 4.7 | 30.0 | 26.0 | 3.7 | 10.4 | 37.3 | 437.8 | 24.8 | 8.9 | 0.1 | Quantité |
| Percent of total in specified industry | 100.0 | 8.4 | 21.4 | 0.6 | 3.6 | 3.1 | 0.4 | 1.2 | 4.5 | 52.7 | 3.0 | 1.1 | — | Pourcentage du total par industrie indiquée |
| Percent consumed as: | | | | | | | | | | | | | | Pourcentage consommé comme: |
| Coal [3] | 43.4 | 23.6 | 42.9 | — | 5.7 | 12.3 | 21.6 | 60.6 | 8.3 | 56.8 | 4.8 | 34.8 | — | Charbon [3] |
| Lignite [3] | 0.3 | 1.6 | 0.3 | — | — | 0.4 | — | — | 0.8 | — | 0.8 | — | — | Lignite [3] |
| Coke | 1.6 | 1.6 | — | — | — | — | — | — | 0.5 | 0.9 | 31.1 | 9.0 | — | Coke |
| Refined oil fuels | 18.8 | 35.9 | 26.4 | — | 20.3 | 40.4 | 13.5 | 26.9 | 23.3 | 10.4 | 29.4 | 30.3 | — | Pétrole raffiné |
| Wood | 29.4 | 31.0 | 21.8 | 97.9 | 55.7 | 41.9 | 54.1 | 4.8 | 44.8 | 29.1 | 15.3 | 18.0 | — | Bois |
| Electricity purchased.. | 5.9 | 5.9 | 8.6 | 2.1 | 4.0 | 5.0 | 10.8 | 7.7 | 22.3 | 2.7 | 18.6 | 7.9 | 100.0 | Electricité achetée |
| Other fuels | 0.6 | 0.4 | — | — | 14.3 | — | — | — | — | 0.1 | — | — | — | Autres combustibles |

For footnotes, see end of table.

Pour les notes, voir au bas du tableau.

**B.   Quantity and Value of Purchased Fuels Consumed and Electricity Purchased and Produced for Own Use**

**Volume et valeur de combustibles achetés et consommés, de l'électricité achetée et produite pour l'auto-consommation**

Coal, lignite, coke, refined oil fuels and wood in thousand metric tons; gas in million cubic metres; electricity in million KWH; other fuels in thousand metric tons of coal equivalents.

Charbon, lignite, coke, pétrole raffiné et bois en milliers de tonnes métriques; gaz en millions de mètres cubes; électricité en millions de kWh; autres fuels en milliers de tonnes métriques d'équivalent houille.

### a.   Selected Major Groups of Mining
### Quelques classes des Industries extractives

| Year and source of energy | Total [1] | Coal mining [1] Extraction du charbon[1] | Other mining Divers | Année et source d'énergie |
|---|---|---|---|---|
| ISIC | 1 | 11 | 14–19 | CITI |
| **1953** | | | | **1953** |
| Coal [3] | | | | Charbon [3] |
| Quantity | 5.2 | 1.7 | 3.5 | Quantité |
| Value | 2.6 | 0.2 | 2.4 | Valeur |
| Lignite [3] | | | | Lignite [3] |
| Quantity | — | — | — | Quantité |
| Value | — | — | — | Valeur |
| Coke | | | | Coke |
| Quantity | 7.4 | — | 7.4 | Quantité |
| Value | 5.6 | — | 5.6 | Valeur |
| Refined oil fuels | | | | Pétrole raffiné |
| Quantity | 3.8 | 0.2 | 3.6 | Quantité |
| Value | 7.5 | 0.5 | 7.0 | Valeur |
| Electricity | | | | Electricité |
| Purchased: | | | | Achetée: |
| Quantity | 8.8 | 6.0 | 2.8 | Quantité |
| Value | 6.3 | 3.8 | 2.5 | Valeur |
| | | | | Produite pour l'auto-consommation: |
| Produced for own use: | | | | |
| Quantity | 6.3 | 0.6 | 5.7 | Quantité |
| Wood | | | | Bois |
| Quantity | 5.9 | 0.1 | 5.8 | Quantité |
| Value | 1.0 | — | 1.0 | Valeur |
| **1958** | | | | **1958** |
| Electricity | | | | Electricité |
| Purchased: | | | | Achetée: |
| Quantity | 15.6 | 9.2 | 6.4 | Quantité |
| Value | 8.8 | 4.9 | 3.9 | Valeur |
| | | | | Produite pour l'auto-consommation: |
| Produced for own use: | | | | |
| Quantity | 10.9 | 1.9 | 9.0 | Quantité |

For footnotes, see end of table.

Pour les notes, voir au bas du tableau.

# PORTUGAL

## b. The Major Groups of Manufacturing — Les classes de la branche Industries manufacturières

| Year and source of energy | Manufacturing [1,2] Industries manufacturières [1,2] | Food, beverages and tobacco [2] Industries alimentaires, boissons, tabac [2] | Textiles | Clothing [2] Articles d'habillement [2] | Wood products [2] Bois [2] | Paper and paper products [2] Papier et ouvrages en papier [2] | Leather Cuir | Rubber products Ouvrages en caoutchouc | Chemical products [2] Produits chimiques [2] | Non-metallic mineral products [2] Produits minéraux non métalliques [2] | Basic metals [1] Métallurgie de base [1] | Metal products [2] Ouvrages en métaux [2] | Other manufacturing [2] Autres industries manufacturières [2] | Année et source d'énergie |
|---|---|---|---|---|---|---|---|---|---|---|---|---|---|---|
| ISIC | 2–3 | 20–22 | 23 | 243 | 25 | 27 | 291 | 30 | 31 | 33 | 34 | 35,37–38 | 399 | CITI |
| **1953** | | | | | | | | | | | | | | **1953** |
| Coal [3] | | | | | | | | | | | | | | Charbon [3] |
| Quantity | 360.7 | 16.5 | 76.2 | — | 1.7 | 3.2 | 0.8 | 6.3 | 3.1 | 248.6 | 1.2 | 3.1 | — | Quantité |
| Value | 122.8 | 11.7 | 24.8 | — | 1.2 | 1.4 | 0.6 | 2.0 | 2.2 | 75.6 | 1.0 | 2.3 | — | Valeur |
| Lignite [3] | | | | | | | | | | | | | | Lignite [3] |
| Quantity | 5.2 | 2.2 | 1.2 | — | 0.1 | 0.2 | — | — | 0.6 | 0.4 | 0.4 | 0.1 | — | Quantité |
| Value | 4.8 | 2.1 | 0.9 | — | — | 0.2 | — | — | 0.7 | 0.4 | 0.4 | 0.1 | — | Valeur |
| Coke | | | | | | | | | | | | | | Coke |
| Quantity | 15.4 | 1.2 | 0.1 | — | — | — | — | — | 0.2 | 4.4 | 8.6 | 0.9 | — | Quantité |
| Value | 11.5 | 0.9 | 0.1 | — | — | — | — | — | 0.2 | 1.1 | 8.4 | 0.8 | — | Valeur |
| Refined oil fuels | | | | | | | | | | | | | | Pétrole raffiné |
| Quantity | 104.3 | 16.7 | 31.3 | — | 4.1 | 7.0 | 0.4 | 1.8 | 5.8 | 30.5 | 4.9 | 1.8 | — | Quantité |
| Value | 121.3 | 18.9 | 33.6 | — | 6.0 | 7.9 | 0.6 | 2.3 | 4.7 | 34.5 | 10.1 | 2.7 | — | Valeur |
| Manufactured gas | | | | | | | | | | | | | | Gaz manufacturé |
| Quantity | 0.4 | 0.4 | — | — | — | — | — | — | — | — | — | — | — | Quantité |
| Value | 0.7 | 0.7 | — | — | — | — | — | — | — | — | — | — | — | Valeur |
| Electricity Purchased: | | | | | | | | | | | | | | Electricité Achetée: |
| Quantity | 389.6 | 32.5 | 121.8 | 0.6 | 9.5 | 10.3 | 3.2 | 6.2 | 66.2 | 96.3 | 36.7 | 5.6 | 0.7 | Quantité |
| Value | 214.1 | 24.9 | 75.0 | 0.4 | 8.7 | 6.5 | 2.5 | 3.9 | 16.8 | 52.9 | 17.6 | 4.4 | 0.5 | Valeur |
| Produced for own use: | | | | | | | | | | | | | | Produite pour l'auto-consommation: |
| Quantity | 46.4 | 5.7 | 15.6 | — | 1.4 | 6.5 | — | — | 1.6 | 8.6 | 7.0 | — | | Quantité |
| Wood | | | | | | | | | | | | | | Bois |
| Quantity | 489.0 | 43.3 | 77.5 | 9.2 | 33.3 | 21.7 | 3.9 | 1.1 | 33.5 | 254.5 | 7.6 | 3.3 | 0.1 | Quantité |
| Value | 99.8 | 10.4 | 14.0 | 1.4 | 6.2 | 4.4 | 0.6 | 0.2 | 6.8 | 53.4 | 1.6 | 0.8 | — | Valeur |
| Other fuels | | | | | | | | | | | | | | Autres combustibles |
| Quantity | 4.5 | — | — | — | 4.3 | — | — | — | — | 0.2 | — | — | — | Quantité |
| Value | 2.5 | — | — | — | 2.4 | — | — | — | — | 0.1 | — | — | — | Valeur |
| **1958** | | | | | | | | | | | | | | **1958** |
| Electricity Purchased: | | | | | | | | | | | | | | Electricité Achetée: |
| Quantity | 606.7 | 66.2 | 218.1 | 0.6 | 12.8 | 32.9 | 3.9 | 10.2 | 51.7 | 149.6 | 31.7 | 23.2 | 5.8 | Quantité |
| Value | 331.6 | 44.4 | 120.3 | 0.4 | 10.4 | 17.1 | 2.8 | 6.2 | 17.8 | 76.8 | 15.0 | 16.3 | 4.1 | Valeur |
| Produced for own use: | | | | | | | | | | | | | | Produite pour l'auto-consommation: |
| Quantity | 83.6 | 7.0 | 22.8 | — | 1.3 | 31.5 | — | — | 1.8 | 12.2 | 6.7 | 0.3 | | Quantité |

[1] Metal mining (ISIC major group 12) is included in Manufacturing under Basic metals (ISIC major group 34) and coal briquetting and coking (part of ISIC major group 32) is included in Mining under Coal mining (ISIC major group 12).

[2] The following significant activities are not covered under Manufacturing in 1953 or 1958: Selected kinds of bakeries, salt refining and wine manufacture (all part of ISIC major groups 20–21); Clothing, footwear and other wearing apparel (ISIC major group 24) except hats and fur apparel; Wood products and furniture (ISIC major groups 25–26) except cork products and wood veneers; Printing and publishing (ISIC major group 28); Leather and fur products (ISIC groups 292–293); basic chemicals such as acids and bases (part of ISIC major group 31); Petroleum and coal products (ISIC group 32); Machinery except electrical machinery (ISIC major group 36); Electric machinery, apparatus and supplies (ISIC major group 37) except cables, conductors and condensers; Transport equipment (ISIC major group 38) except ship wrights; and Miscellaneous manufacturing (ISIC major group 39) except buttons, plastic products and related articles. In addition, the following manufacturing activities are excluded in 1953 but included in 1958: Additional kinds of bakeries, the manufacture of macaroni products, olive oil, margarine and animal feeds (all part of ISIC major group 20); Articles of paper and paperboard (ISIC group 272); cosmetics (part of ISIC group 319); cement products (part of ISIC group 339); the manufacture of cables, conductors and condensers (part of ISIC major group 37); and ship wrights (part of ISIC major group 38).

[3] Includes briquettes.

[1] Les industries extractives de minerais métalliques (CITI classe 12) sont incluses dans les Industries manufacturières sous la rubrique Metallurgie de base (CITI classe 34); la fabrication de briquettes en charbon et les cokeries (dans CITI classe 32) sont incluses dans la classe Industries extractives sous Industries extractives de charbon (CITI classe 12).

[2] Les activités majeures qui suivent ne sont pas couvertes par la rubrique Industries manufacturières en 1953 ou 1958; certaines boulangeries et pâtisseries, Industries de sel raffiné et de vin (tous dans CITI classes 20–21), Vêtements, chaussures et autres articles d'habillement (CITI classe 26) à l'exclusion des chapeaux et des articles d'habillement en fourrure. Ouvrages en bois et meubles (CITI classes 25–26) à l'exclusion des ouvrages en liège et du placage; Imprimeries et édition (CITI classe 28). Cuir et articles en fourrure (CITI classe 31); Produits dérivés du charbon et du pétrole (CITI groupe 32); Machines à l'exclusion des machines électriques (CITI classe 36). Machines électriques; Appareils et fournitures (CITI classe 37) à l'exclusion des câbles, conducteurs et condenseurs; équipements de transport (CITI classe 38) à l'exclusion de la construction navale; et Industries manufacturières diverses (CITI classe 39) à l'exclusion des boutons, des ouvrages en plastique et des articles s'y rapportant. De plus, les activités manufacturières suivantes sont exclues pour 1953 mais incluses pour 1958: des catégories additionnelles de boulangeries et de pâtisseries, la fabrication de pâtes alimentaires, d'huile d'olive, de margarine, des produits pour l'alimentation des animaux (tous dans CITI classe 20); Articles en papier et en carton (CITI groupe 272); produits de beauté (dans CITI groupe 319); produits en ciment (dans CITI groupe 339); la fabrication de câbles, conducteurs et condenseurs (dans CITI classe 37) et la construction navale (dans CITI classe 38).

[3] Y compris les briquettes.

# PUERTO RICO — PORTO RICO

## The Gross Domestic Product

Estimates of the expenditure on and the industrial origin of the gross domestic product are presented in Table 1. This table has been compiled from data supplied by the Puerto Rican Planning Board, Bureau of Economics and Statistics, San Juan, in response to the United Nations national accounts questionnaire. The official estimates and descriptions of sources and methods can be found in *Net Income and Gross Product, Puerto Rico: 1940 and 1947-1955;* and in *Income and Product, 1961,* published by the Planning Board.

## Le produit intérieur brut

Les estimations des dépenses imputées au produit intérieur brut et des composantes du produit intérieur brut ventilées suivant la branche d'activité d'origine sont reproduites au tableau 1. Ce tableau a été construit à partir des données fournies par le Puerto Rican Planning Board, Bureau of Economics and Statistics, San Juan, en réponse au questionnaire de l'O.N.U. relatif aux comptes nationaux. Les estimations officielles et les indications sur les sources et méthodes figurent dans *Net Income and Gross Product, Puerto Rico: 1940 and 1947-1955;* et dans *Income and Product, 1961,* publiés par le Planning Board.

## Index Numbers of Industrial Employment

The index numbers of industrial employment for manufacturing industries presented in Table 2 are based on absolute figures of total employment published monthly in *Employment, Hours and Earnings in the Manufacturing Industries in Puerto Rico,* by the Puerto Rico Bureau of Labour Statistics. The data are based on a probability sample drawn from a population covering all establishments irrespective of size. In 1956 the sample consisted of about 1 000 establishments employing approximately 94 percent of all persons engaged in the industries covered as shown in the October 1956 Census of Employment in the Manufacturing Industries. The data refer to the number of employees who worked during, or received pay for, all or any part of the pay period ending nearest the 15th of each month. This excludes persons who were on unpaid leave or on strike for the whole pay period. The annual absolute figures used to calculate the index are the arithmetic averages of the monthly figures.

The index numbers of employment for the construction industry, also in Table 2, are based on absolute figures of total employment derived from a quarterly survey conducted by the Puerto Rico Bureau of Labour Statistics. The results are published quarterly in *Employment and Unemployment in Puerto Rico* by the Bureau of Labour Statistics, and annually in the *Statistical Yearbook, Puerto Rico* by the Bureau of Economics and Statistics of the Puerto Rican Planning Board. The quarterly survey covers a probability sample of dwellings and is taken during January, April, July and October of each year. The absolute figures of employed persons basically cover all persons over 14 years of age who worked for pay or profit during the week surveyed, including unpaid family workers who worked for 15 hours or more and persons on strike, sick leave, vacation, or temporarily laid off. The annual absolute figures are arithmetic averages of the quarterly figures.

## Indices de l'emploi industriel

Les indices de l'emploi industriel relatifs aux industries manufacturières reproduits au tableau 2 sont fondés sur les chiffres absolus de l'emploi publiés mensuellement dans *Employment, Hours and Earnings in the Manufacturing Industries in Puerto Rico,* par le Puerto Rico Bureau of Labour Statistics. Les données sont basées sur un échantillon probabiliste tiré d'un univers couvrant tous les établissements, quelle que soit leur taille. En 1956 l'échantillon comprenait 1 000 établissements à peu près occupant approximativement 94% des personnes occupées dans les industries couvertes par le recensement de l'emploi d'octobre 1956 dans les industries manufacturières. Les données couvrent le nombre de salariés ayant travaillé ou reçu une paie, soit pendant la totalité, soit pendant une partie de la période de paie la plus rapprochée du 15 de chaque mois. Ceci exclut les personnes en congé sans solde ou en grève pendant toute la période de la paie. Les chiffres absolus annuels utilisés pour calculer les indices sont les moyennes arithmétiques des chiffres mensuels.

Les indices de l'emploi relatifs au bâtiment et travaux publics également au tableau 2 sont calculés à partir de chiffres absolus de l'emploi provenant des résultats d'une enquête trimestrielle exécutée par le Puerto Rico Bureau of Labour Statistics. Les résultats sont publiés trimestriellement dans *Employment and Unemployment in Puerto Rico* par le Bureau of Labour Statistics, et annuellement dans le *Statistical Yearbook, Puerto Rico* par le Bureau of Economics and Statistics of the Puerto Rican Planning Board. L'enquête couvre un échantillon probabiliste de logements et est exécutée aux mois de janvier, avril, juillet et octobre de chaque année. Les chiffres absolus de personnes occupées couvrent toute personne âgée de plus de 14 ans qui a travaillé moyennant une paie ou un autre profit durant la semaine de l'enquête, y compris les travailleurs familiaux ayant travaillé 15 heures ou plus, les personnes en grève, en congé de maladie, en congé annuel ou temporairement renvoyées. Les chiffres absolus annuels sont les moyennes arithmétiques des chiffres trimestriels.

# PUERTO RICO

The index numbers for manufacturing and construction activity combined were calculated by the Statistical Office of the United Nations. The weights utilized are proportional to the number of persons employed as shown by the quarterly labour force survey mentioned above from which the construction index was derived. In the case of the index numbers for 1953 and 1954, the weights utilized were derived from the results of the survey for the financial year, 1952-1953, while for the indexes for 1955 and thereafter, the weights used were from the survey results for the financial year, 1957-1958.

## Characteristics and Structure of Manufacturing Activity

The information shown in Table 3 is derived from the Censuses of Manufacturing for the years 1939, 1949, 1954 and 1958. The data were collected and published jointly by the United States Bureau of the Census and the Puerto Rico Bureau of Economics and Statistics, in *Puerto Rico, Census of Manufactures, 1949* (which also includes comparative figures for 1939), in *Puerto Rico, Census of Manufactures, 1954,* and in *Puerto Rico Census of Manufactures, 1958.*

The 1939 Census covered manufacturing establishments whose value of production during the year amounted to $2,000 or more except those engaged in coffee roasting and grinding and in tobacco stemming and redrying. The 1949 Census covered establishments irrespective of size, and the 1954 and 1958 Censuses dealt with establishments with one or more employees. All four censuses excluded establishments which sold most' of their products at retail on the premises (e.g., single-shop retail bakeries), did custom work to the individual order of domestic consumers, such as custom tailoring or wood-working, or performed repair and other service activities at retail.

Data on employment in 1939 are not comparable to those for the later years since they relate to operatives only. For all the censuses, data on homeworkers are excluded from the figures on persons engaged and on wages and salaries paid. For 1939, 1949 and 1954, value added is based on the value of products sold (value of shipments in 1954), ex-plant, at factor cost. In 1958, value added at factor cost was based on the value of production (i.e., the value of shipments with an adjustment for stock changes) and thus conforms with the International Standards in Basic Industrial Statistics.

Les indices relatifs aux activités des industries manufacturières et au bâtiment et travaux publics combinés ont été calculés par le Bureau de statistique de l'O.N.U. Les coefficients de pondération utilisés sont proportionnels au nombre de personnes occupées comme indiqué dans l'enquête trimestrielle portant sur la main-d'œuvre mentionnée ci-dessus de laquelle sont tirés les indices relatifs au bâtiment et travaux publics. Dans le cas des indices de 1953 et 1954, les coefficients de pondération utilisés ont été tirés des résultats de l'enquête relative à l'année financière 1952-1953, tandis que pour les indices pour 1955 et les années suivantes les coefficients de pondération ont été tirés des résultats de l'enquête relative à l'année financière 1957-1958.

## Caractéristiques et structure des activités manufacturières

Les renseignements du tableau 3 sont tirés des recensements des industries manufacturières pour les années 1939, 1949, 1954 et 1956. Les données ont été recueillies et publiées conjointement par le Bureau of the Census des Etats-Unis et le Puerto Rico Bureau of Economics and Statistics, dans *Puerto Rico, Census of Manufactures, 1949* (où figurent aussi des chiffres comparatifs pour 1939) dans *Puerto Rico, Census of Manufactures, 1954,* et dans *Puerto Rico Census of Manufactures, 1958.*

Le recensement de 1939 couvrait tous les établissements dont la production pendant l'année avait une valeur de 2 000 dollars ou plus, à l'exclusion cependant des établissements se livrant à la torréfaction et au moulage du café, ainsi qu'à l'écotage et à la dessiccation du tabac. Le recensement de 1949 couvrait tous les établissements, quelle que soit leur dimension, ceux de 1954 et 1958 couvraient seulement les établissements occupant 1 salarié ou plus. Dans aucun de ces quatre recensements on n'a tenu compte de certains établissements qui vendent la majeure partie de leurs produits sur place, au détail (par exemple, les boulangeries sans succursale), des travaux à façon exécutés sur commande pour des particuliers (comme par exemple la confection de vêtements sur mesure ou les travaux de menuiserie), des travaux de réparation et autres services analogues, au stade du détail.

Les chiffres de l'emploi en 1939 ne sont pas comparables à ceux des années suivantes parce qu'ils ne portent que sur les ouvriers. Dans tous les recensements les travailleurs à domicile ne sont pas compris dans le nombre de personnes occupées et il n'en est pas tenu compte non plus dans les traitements et salaires pour 1939, 1949 et 1954. La valeur ajoutée est calculée d'après la valeur des produits vendus (valeur des expéditions en 1954), départ usine, au coût des facteurs. En 1958 le calcul de la valeur ajoutée est fondé sur la valeur de la production (c'est à dire, la valeur des expéditions corrigée des variations de stocks), au coût des facteurs, ce qui est conforme aux Normes internationales relatives aux statistiques industrielles de base.

# 1. THE GROSS DOMESTIC PRODUCT — PRODUIT INTERIEUR BRUT

Million U. S. dollars                    Millions de dollars des Etats-Unis

## A. Expenditure on the Gross Domestic Product at Market Prices
## Dépenses relatives au produit intérieur brut aux prix du marché

| Item of data and year[1] Rubrique et année[1] | Total | Consumption Consommation | | Gross Domestic Capital Formation Formation brute de capital intérieur | | Net exports of goods and services Exportations nettes de biens et de services | |
|---|---|---|---|---|---|---|---|
| | | Total | Government Etat | Total[2] | Fixed Fixe | Exports less imports Exportations moins importations | Exports Exportations |
| **a. At Current Prices — Aux prix courants** | | | | | | | |
| **Absolute figures — Chiffres absolus** | | | | | | | |
| 1948 | 681.1 | 728.7 | 93.3 | 121.7 | 116.0 | −169.3 | 255.8 |
| 1950 | 767.9 | 820.7 | 98.7 | 144.9 | 125.2 | −197.7 | 330.8 |
| 1951 | 877.5 | 907.4 | 111.4 | 192.7 | 150.5 | −222.6 | 338.5 |
| 1952 | 933.7 | 982.1 | 119.4 | 157.5 | 159.0 | −205.9 | 415.7 |
| 1953 | 1 006.5 | 1 041.5 | 129.7 | 185.9 | 172.7 | −220.9 | 440.4 |
| 1954 | 1 062.3 | 1 103.9 | 139.5 | 217.1 | 202.6 | −258.7 | 460.8 |
| 1955 | 1 149.0 | 1 170.2 | 148.2 | 229.7 | 217.3 | −250.9 | 531.3 |
| 1956 | 1 240.8 | 1 247.0 | 180.8 | 274.8 | 259.9 | −281.0 | 590.8 |
| 1957 | 1 351.0 | 1 344.3 | 190.2 | 302.1 | 279.5 | −295.4 | 610.2 |
| 1958 | 1 463.4 | 1 445.5 | 207.0 | 331.6 | 294.5 | −313.7 | 680.3 |
| 1959 | 1 649.7 | 1 571.1 | 217.8 | 392.3 | 347.8 | −313.7 | 800.0 |
| 1960 | 1 807.1 | 1 698.4 | 249.5 | 387.2 | 363.6 | −278.5 | 866.2 |
| 1961 | 2 015.2 | 1 890.4 | 281.4 | 504.1 | 442.9 | −379.3 | 959.9 |
| **Percentage distribution of average annual expenditure — Distribution en pourcentage des dépenses annuelles moyennes** | | | | | | | |
| 1948 | 100.0 | 107.0 | 13.7 | 17.9 | 17.0 | −24.9 | 37.6 |
| 1950 − 1960 | 100.0 | 100.2 | 13.5 | 21.1 | 19.3 | −21.3 | 45.6 |
| 1950 | 100.0 | 106.9 | 12.8 | 18.9 | 16.3 | −25.8 | 43.1 |
| 1953 | 100.0 | 103.5 | 12.9 | 18.5 | 17.2 | −22.0 | 43.8 |
| 1954 | 100.0 | 103.9 | 13.1 | 20.4 | 19.1 | −24.3 | 43.4 |
| 1958 | 100.0 | 98.8 | 14.1 | 22.7 | 20.1 | −21.5 | 46.5 |
| 1960 | 100.0 | 94.0 | 13.8 | 21.4 | 20.1 | −15.4 | 47.9 |
| **b. At Prices of 1958 — Aux prix de 1958** | | | | | | | |
| **Absolute figures — Chiffres absolus** | | | | | | | |
| 1948 | 845.3 | 882.2 | 113.2 | 151.8 | 145.6 | −188.7 | 285.2 |
| 1950 | 948.6 | 996.7 | 118.9 | 173.5 | 151.2 | −221.6 | 370.9 |
| 1951 | 1 000.8 | 1 025.7 | 125.5 | 213.7 | 171.0 | −238.6 | 362.8 |
| 1952 | 1 048.8 | 1 091.6 | 133.7 | 179.6 | 179.6 | −222.4 | 448.9 |
| 1953 | 1 092.3 | 1 123.7 | 140.7 | 206.6 | 193.1 | −238.0 | 474.6 |
| 1954 | 1 153.9 | 1 188.8 | 151.5 | 240.0 | 225.4 | −274.9 | 489.7 |
| 1955 | 1 228.1 | 1 248.9 | 156.5 | 243.9 | 231.6 | −264.7 | 560.4 |
| 1956 | 1 296.3 | 1 305.3 | 188.1 | 281.6 | 266.3 | −290.6 | 611.0 |
| 1957 | 1 381.6 | 1 378.1 | 193.7 | 302.2 | 279.6 | −298.7 | 617.0 |
| 1958 | 1 463.4 | 1 445.5 | 207.0 | 331.6 | 294.5 | −313.7 | 680.3 |
| 1959 | 1 608.4 | 1 530.8 | 209.2 | 386.6 | 344.0 | −309.0 | 788.2 |
| 1960 | 1 709.9 | 1 619.5 | 236.9 | 375.7 | 354.5 | −285.3 | 960.0 |
| 1961 | 1 871.2 | 1 784.4 | 262.3 | 482.3 | 427.3 | −395.5 | 1 039.7 |
| **Percentage distribution of average annual expenditure — Distribution en pourcentage des dépenses annuelles moyennes** | | | | | | | |
| 1948 | 100.0 | 104.4 | 13.4 | 17.9 | 17.2 | −22.3 | 33.7 |
| 1950 − 1960 | 100.0 | 100.1 | 13.4 | 21.1 | 19.3 | −21.2 | 45.7 |
| 1950 | 100.0 | 105.1 | 12.5 | 18.3 | 15.9 | −23.4 | 39.1 |
| 1953 | 100.0 | 102.9 | 12.9 | 18.9 | 17.7 | −21.8 | 43.4 |
| 1954 | 100.0 | 103.0 | 13.1 | 20.8 | 19.5 | −23.8 | 42.4 |
| 1958 | 100.0 | 98.8 | 14.1 | 22.6 | 20.1 | −21.4 | 46.5 |
| 1960 | 100.0 | 94.7 | 13.8 | 22.0 | 20.7 | −16.7 | 56.1 |
| **Average annual rate of growth — Taux annuel moyen d'accroissement** | | | | | | | |
| 1948 − 1953 | 5.3 | 5.0 | 4.4 | 6.4 | 5.8 | . | 10.7 |
| 1950 − 1960 | 6.1 | 5.0 | 7.2 | 8.0 | 8.9 | . | 10.0 |
| 1950 − 1953 | 4.8 | 4.1 | 5.8 | 6.0 | 8.5 | . | 8.6 |
| 1954 − 1958 | 6.1 | 5.0 | 8.1 | 8.4 | 6.9 | . | 8.6 |
| 1958 − 1960 | 8.1 | 5.8 | 2.4 | 6.4 | 9.7 | . | 18.8 |

For footnotes see end of table.            Pour les notes, voir au bas du tableau.

## B. The Gross Domestic Product at Factor Cost According to Origin
### Origine par secteur d'activité du produit intérieur brut au coût des facteurs

| Item of data and year [1]<br>Rubrique et année [1] | Total [2] | Agricultural sector<br>Secteur agricole | Industrial Sector — Secteur Industriel | | | | | Transportation and communication<br>Transports et communications | Other sectors [4]<br>Autres secteurs [4] |
| | | | Total | Mining<br>Industries extractives | Manufacturing<br>Industries manufacturières | Construction [3]<br>Bâtiment et travaux publics [3] | Electricity, gas and water<br>Electricité, gaz et eau | | |
| ISIC — CITI | 0–9 | 0 | 1–5 | 1 | 2–3 | 4 | 5 | 7 | 6, 8–9 |
| a. At Current Prices — Aux prix courants | | | | | | | | | |
| **Absolute figures — Chiffres absolus** | | | | | | | | | |
| 1948 | 590.9 | 153.1 | 136.1 | 1.3 | 87.4 | 32.7 | 14.7 | 40.2 | 261.5 |
| 1950 | 699.3 | 159.5 | 171.8 | 1.8 | 114.0 | 36.4 | 19.6 | 42.7 | 325.3 |
| 1951 | 786.6 | 196.6 | 193.0 | 2.3 | 123.9 | 46.1 | 20.7 | 46.7 | 350.3 |
| 1952 | 822.2 | 174.4 | 213.6 | 2.1 | 147.1 | 42.4 | 22.0 | 51.2 | 383.0 |
| 1953 | 892.4 | 171.6 | 239.0 | 2.0 | 166.7 | 44.7 | 25.6 | 57.5 | 424.3 |
| 1954 | 946.0 | 170.7 | 260.4 | 1.9 | 181.6 | 49.3 | 27.6 | 62.9 | 452.0 |
| 1955 | 1 029.1 | 177.1 | 296.9 | 2.2 | 212.5 | 50.5 | 31.7 | 68.9 | 486.2 |
| 1956 | 1 109.7 | 162.7 | 332.0 | 2.5 | 231.6 | 60.7 | 37.2 | 74.2 | 540.8 |
| 1957 | 1 199.4 | 164.7 | 354.7 | 2.0 | 239.9 | 71.3 | 41.5 | 79.8 | 600.2 |
| 1958 | 1 334.6 | 177.9 | 406.9 | 2.3 | 267.8 | 91.6 | 45.2 | 83.4 | 666.4 |
| 1959 | 1 488.6 | 191.3 | 470.0 | 2.5 | 314.0 | 103.1 | 50.4 | 95.1 | 732.2 |
| 1960 | 1 637.2 | 202.5 | 527.1 | 2.8 | 358.8 | 110.3 | 55.2 | 102.2 | 805.4 |
| 1961 | 1 832.5 | 212.3 | 600.5 | 2.8 | 410.3 | 126.0 | 61.4 | 115.6 | 904.1 |
| **Percentage distribution according to sector — Distribution en pourcentage par secteur** | | | | | | | | | |
| 1948 | 100.0 | 25.9 | 23.0 | 0.2 | 14.8 | 5.5 | 2.5 | 6.8 | 44.3 |
| 1950 – 1960 | 100.0 | 16.3 | 29.0 | 0.2 | 19.7 | 5.9 | 3.2 | 6.4 | 48.3 |
| 1950 | 100.0 | 22.8 | 24.6 | 0.3 | 16.3 | 5.2 | 2.8 | 6.1 | 46.5 |
| 1953 | 100.0 | 19.2 | 26.8 | 0.2 | 18.7 | 5.0 | 2.9 | 6.4 | 47.6 |
| 1954 | 100.0 | 18.0 | 27.5 | 0.2 | 19.2 | 5.2 | 2.9 | 6.7 | 47.8 |
| 1958 | 100.0 | 13.3 | 30.5 | 0.2 | 20.0 | 6.9 | 3.4 | 6.3 | 49.9 |
| 1960 | 100.0 | 12.3 | 32.2 | 0.2 | 21.9 | 6.7 | 3.4 | 6.3 | 49.2 |

[1] All figures are for the fiscal year beginning 1 July.
[2] The estimates do not include adjustments for changes in the valuation of stocks.
[3] Contract construction only.
[4] Includes all activities of general government.

[1] Tous les chiffres sont relatifs à l'année fiscale commençant le 1er juillet.
[2] Les évaluations ne comprennent pas les variations de la valeur des stocks.
[3] Travaux de construction contractuels seulement.
[4] Y compris toutes les activités de l'Etat.

## 2. INDEX NUMBERS OF INDUSTRIAL EMPLOYMENT
## INDICES DE L'EMPLOI DANS L'INDUSTRIE

### A. Selected Divisions of Industrial Activity
### Quelques branches de l'activité industrielle

| Period<br>Période | Total | Manu-<br>facturing<br>Industries<br>manu-<br>facturières | Construction<br>Bâtiment<br>et travaux<br>publics |
|---|---|---|---|
| ISIC — CITI | 2–4 | 2–3 | 4 |

*a. Indexes — Indices (1958 = 100)*

| | | | |
|---|---|---|---|
| 1948............ | ... | ... | 97 |
| 1949............ | ... | ... | 86 |
| 1950............ | ... | ... | 76 |
| 1951............ | ... | ... | 81 |
| 1952............ | ... | ... | 97 |
| 1953............ | 92 | 90 | 97 |
| 1954............ | 93 | 95 | 89 |
| 1955............ | – 98 – | 98 | 97 |
| 1956............ | 104 | 104 | 105 |
| 1957............ | 102 | 102 | 103 |
| 1958............ | 100 | 100 | 100 |
| 1959............ | 110 | 111 | 108 |
| 1960............ | 120 | 116 | 130 |
| 1961............ | 124 | 123 | 127 |

*b. Average Annual Rate of Change — Taux annuel moyen de variation*

| | | | |
|---|---|---|---|
| 1950 – 1960...... | ... | ... | 5.5 |
| 1948 – 1953...... | ... | ... | — |
| 1954 – 1958...... | 1.8 | 1.3 | 3.0 |
| 1958 – 1960...... | 10.0 | 7.7 | 14.0 |

### B. The Major Groups of Manufacturing — Les classes de la branche Industries manufacturières

| Period<br>Période | Manu-<br>facturing<br>Industries<br>manufac-<br>turières | Food,<br>beverages<br>and<br>tobacco<br>Industries<br>alimen-<br>taires,<br>boissons,<br>tabac | Textiles | Clothing,<br>footwear<br>and<br>made-up<br>textiles<br>Articles<br>d'habil-<br>lement,<br>chaussures<br>et<br>ouvrages<br>en tissu | Wood<br>products<br>and<br>furniture<br>Bois et<br>meubles | Paper<br>and paper<br>products,<br>printing<br>and<br>publishing<br>Papier et<br>ouvrages<br>en<br>papier,<br>imprimerie<br>et<br>édition | Leather<br>and<br>leather<br>products<br>except<br>wearing<br>apparel<br>Cuir et<br>articles<br>en cuir,<br>à l'exclu-<br>sion<br>des<br>articles<br>d'habil-<br>lement | Rubber<br>products,<br>chemicals<br>and<br>chemical<br>petroleum<br>and coal<br>products<br>Ouvrages<br>en<br>caoutchouc,<br>produits<br>chimiques<br>et dérivés<br>du pétrole<br>et du<br>charbon | Non-<br>metallic<br>mineral<br>products<br>Produits<br>minéraux<br>non<br>métal-<br>liques | Metal<br>products<br>Ouvrages<br>en<br>métaux | Other<br>manu-<br>facturing<br>Autres<br>industries<br>manufac-<br>turières |
|---|---|---|---|---|---|---|---|---|---|---|---|
| ISIC — CITI | 2–3 | 20–22 | 23 | 24 | 25–26 | 27–28 | 29 | 30–32 | 33 | 35–38 | 39 |

*a. Indexes — Indices (1958 = 100)*

| | | | | | | | | | | | |
|---|---|---|---|---|---|---|---|---|---|---|---|
| 1953............. | 90 | 112 | 76 | 94 | 97 | 85 | 78 | 37 | 79 | 53 | 90 |
| 1954............. | 95 | 122 | 73 | 98 | 90 | 90 | 63 | 40 | 74 | 65 | 100 |
| 1955............. | 98 | 116 | 82 | 101 | 97 | 95 | 78 | 46 | 90 | 75 | 108 |
| 1956............. | 104 | 113 | 100 | 110 | 100 | 100 | 89 | 60 | 102 | 87 | 116 |
| 1957............. | 102 | 97 | 109 | 107 | 103 | 100 | 89 | 77 | 108 | 100 | 120 |
| 1958............. | 100 | 100 | 100 | 100 | 100 | 100 | 100 | 100 | 100 | 100 | 100 |
| 1959............. | 111 | 109 | 116 | 113 | 110 | 125 | 122 | 106 | 105 | 113 | 106 |
| 1960............. | 116 | 107 | 111 | 124 | 110 | 130 | 137 | 117 | 113 | 127 | 112 |
| 1961............. | 123 | 116 | 107 | 129 | 113 | 140 | 156 | 120 | 118 | 137 | 118 |

*b. Average Annual Rate of Change — Taux annuel moyen de variation*

| | | | | | | | | | | | |
|---|---|---|---|---|---|---|---|---|---|---|---|
| 1954 – 1958........ | 1.3 | –4.8 | 8.2 | 0.5 | 2.7 | 2.7 | 12.2 | 25.7 | 7.8 | 11.4 | — |
| 1958 – 1960........ | 7.7 | 3.4 | 5.4 | 11.4 | 4.9 | 14.0 | 17.0 | 8.2 | 6.3 | 12.7 | 5.8 |

651

## 3. THE CHARACTERISTICS OF MANUFACTURING ESTABLISHMENTS
## CARACTERISTIQUES DES ETABLISSEMENTS MANUFACTURIERS
### 1939, 1949, 1954, 1958

Number of establishments in units; value added and wages and salaries in million Dollars; number of engaged, employees, and operatives in thousands; value added per engaged and wages and salaries per employee in thousand Dollars.

Nombre d'établissements en unités; valeur ajoutée et traitements et salaires en millions de dollars; nombre de personnes occupées, de salariés et d'ouvriers en milliers; valeur ajoutée par personne occupée et traitements et salaires par salarié en milliers de dollars.

| Year and item of data | Manufacturing [1,2] / Industries manufacturières [1,2] | Food, beverages and tobacco [1] / Industries alimentaires, boissons, tabac [1] | Textiles | Clothing, footwear and made-up textiles [3] / Articles d'habillement, chaussures et ouvrages en tissu [3] | Wood products and furniture / Bois et meubles | Paper and paper products / Papier et ouvrages en papier | Printing and publishing / Imprimerie et édition | Leather and leather products except wearing apparel / Cuir et articles en cuir, à l'exclusion des articles d'habillement | Rubber products / Ouvrages en caoutchouc | Chemicals and chemical, petroleum and coal products / Produits chimiques et dérivés du pétrole et du charbon | Non-metallic mineral products [4] / Produits minéraux non métalliques [4] | Basic metals / Métallurgie de base | Metal products / Ouvrages en métaux | Other manufacturing / Autres industries manufacturières | Année et rubrique |
|---|---|---|---|---|---|---|---|---|---|---|---|---|---|---|---|
| ISIC | 2–3 | 20–22 | 23 | 24 | 25–26 | 27 | 28 | 29 | 30 | 31–32 | 33 | 34 | 35–38 | 39 | CITI |

*a. Absolute Figures — Chiffres absolus*

| Year and item of data | 2–3 | 20–22 | 23 | 24 | 25–26 | 27 | 28 | 29 | 30 | 31–32 | 33 | 34 | 35–38 | 39 | Année et rubrique |
|---|---|---|---|---|---|---|---|---|---|---|---|---|---|---|---|
| **1939** | | | | | | | | | | | | | | | **1939** |
| Number of establishments | 798 | 426 | 3 | 135 | 65 | 1 | 59 | 15 | 1 | 39 | 23 | — | 18 | 13 | Nombre d'établissements |
| Value added | 35.2 | 23.4 | 0.1 | 7.3 | 0.7 | 0.1 | 1.0 | 0.1 | ... | 1.0 | 0.2 | — | 0.7[2] | 0.6[2] | Valeur ajoutée |
| Number of operatives (Average for the year) | 23.5 | 13.4 | 0.1 | 6.3 | 1.0 | 0.1 | 0.7 | 0.1 | ... | 0.4 | 0.3 | — | 0.5[2] | 0.6[2] | Nombre d'ouvriers (moyenne pour l'année) |
| **1949** | | | | | | | | | | | | | | | **1949** |
| Number of establishments | 1 998 | 1 152 | 10 | 263 | 237 | 5 | 77 | 22 | 1 | 49 | 87 | 1 | 48 | 46 | Nombre d'établissements |
| Value added | 93.4 | 59.1 | 0.6 | 9.3 | 2.9 | 0.8 | 3.7 | 0.9 | ... | 4.4 | 6.4 | ... | ... | 2.5 | Valeur ajoutée |
| Number of engaged (Average for the year) | 56.9 | 31.4 | 1.4 | 11.0 | 2.5 | 0.3 | 1.5 | 0.9 | ... | 1.3 | 2.6 | ... | ... | 2.5 | Nombre de personnes occupées (moyenne pour l'année) |
| Number of employees (Average for the year) | 55.1 | 30.3 | 1.4 | 10.8 | 2.2 | 0.3 | 1.5 | 0.9 | ... | 1.3 | 2.6 | ... | ... | 2.4 | Nombre de salariés (moyenne pour l'année) |
| Wages and salaries paid | 49.2 | 28.9 | 0.6 | 6.5 | 1.8 | 0.4 | 2.2 | 0.6 | ... | 1.5 | 3.1 | ... | ... | 1.6 | Traitements et salaires payés |
| Operatives: Number (Average for the year) | 47.7 | 26.3 | 1.3 | 9.8 | 2.0 | 0.3 | 1.0 | 0.4 | ... | 1.0 | 2.2 | ... | ... | 2.2 | Ouvriers: Nombre (moyenne pour l'année) |
| Wages and salaries | 35.7 | 21.2 | 0.5 | 4.9 | 1.5 | 0.3 | 1.3 | 0.4 | ... | 0.9 | 2.2 | ... | ... | 1.3 | Traitements et salaires |
| **1954** | | | | | | | | | | | | | | | **1954** |
| Number of establishments | 1 938 | 756 | 36 | 353 | 240 | 9 | 93 | 16 | 6 | 74 | 132 | 10 | 115 | 98 | Nombre d'établissements |
| Value added | 188.3 | 83.0 | 8.6 | 33.1 | 7.1 | 3.1 | 4.4 | 1.2 | ... | 7.6[2] | 9.4 | 0.4 | 14.3 | 15.3 | Valeur ajoutée |
| Number of engaged (Average for the year) | 70.3 | 29.2 | 2.8 | 18.8 | 3.3 | 0.5 | 1.4 | 0.7 | ... | 1.5[2] | 3.2 | 0.1 | 3.5 | 5.2 | Nombre de personnes occupées (moyenne pour l'année) |
| Number of employees (Average for the year) | 69.0 | 28.6 | 2.8 | 18.6 | 3.1 | 0.5 | 1.3 | 0.7 | ... | 1.4[2] | 3.1 | 0.1 | 3.4 | 5.2 | Nombre de salariés (moyenne pour l'année) |
| Wages and salaries paid | 83.3 | 36.9 | 3.3 | 15.4 | 3.5 | 0.9 | 2.2 | 0.6 | ... | 2.7[2] | 5.0 | 0.1 | 6.1 | 6.3 | Traitements et salaires payés |
| Operatives: Number (Average for the year) | 60.4 | 24.5 | 2.5 | 17.0 | 2.8 | 0.4 | 0.9 | 0.6 | ... | 1.1[2] | 2.7 | 0.1 | 2.9 | 4.8 | Ouvriers: Nombre (moyenne pour l'année) |
| Wages and salaries | 59.3 | 25.3 | 2.7 | 12.6 | 2.8 | 0.6 | 1.3 | 0.4 | ... | 1.2[2] | 3.5 | 0.1 | 3.9 | 4.8 | Traitements et salaires |
| **1958** | | | | | | | | | | | | | | | **1958** |
| Number of establishments | 2 042 | 652 | 53 | 367 | 253 | 10 | 109 | 18 | 5 | 76 | 171 | 14 | 194 | 120 | Nombre d'établissements |
| Value added | 292.1 | 105.7 | 15.5 | 49.3 | 10.1 | 3.9 | 6.1 | 2.3 | 1.3 | 9.3[2] | 19.2 | 1.8 | 36.2[2] | 18.0 | Valeur ajoutée |
| Number of engaged (Average for the year) | 72.3 | 22.1 | 4.6 | 19.9 | 3.6 | 0.6 | 1.6 | 1.0 | 0.2 | 1.5[2] | 4.2 | 0.4 | 5.8[2] | 5.8 | Nombre de personnes occupées (moyenne pour l'année) |
| Employees: Number (Average for the year) | 71.2 | 21.6 | 4.6 | 19.7 | 3.4 | 0.6 | 1.5 | 1.0 | 0.2 | 1.5[2] | 4.1 | 0.4 | 5.7[2] | 5.7 | Salariés: Nombre (moyenne pour l'année) |
| Wages and salaries | 132.2 | 41.7 | 8.3 | 27.1 | 5.1 | 1.9 | 3.6 | 1.4 | 0.5 | 4.2[2] | 9.0 | 1.2 | 13.9[2] | 9.6 | Traitements et salaires |
| Operatives: Number (Average for the year) | 60.0 | 16.6 | 4.2 | 18.3 | 3.0 | 0.5 | 0.9 | 0.9 | 0.1 | 1.0[2] | 3.4 | 0.3 | 4.8[2] | 5.1 | Ouvriers: Nombre (moyenne pour l'année) |
| Wages and salaries | 93.2 | 25.8 | 6.8 | 23.1 | 3.9 | 1.2 | 2.0 | 1.1 | 0.3 | 2.0[2] | 6.2 | 0.7 | 9.8[2] | 7.7 | Traitements et salaires |

For footnotes see end of table.

Pour les notes, voir au bas du tableau.

# 3. THE CHARACTERISTICS OF MANUFACTURING ESTABLISHMENTS (continued)
## CARACTERISTIQUES DES ETABLISSEMENTS MANUFACTURIERS (suite)
### 1939, 1949, 1954, 1958

| Year and item of data | Manufacturing [1,2]  Industries manufacturières [1,2] | Food, beverages and tobacco [1]  Industries alimentaires, boissons, tabac [1] | Textiles | Clothing, footwear and made-up textiles [3]  Articles d'habillement, chaussures et ouvrages en tissu [3] | Wood products and furniture  Bois et meubles | Paper and paper products  Papier et ouvrages en papier | Printing and publishing  Imprimerie et édition | Leather and leather products except wearing apparel  Cuir et articles en cuir, à l'exclusion des articles d'habillement | Rubber products  Ouvrages en caoutchouc | Chemicals and chemical, petroleum and coal products  Produits chimiques et dérivés du pétrole et du charbon | Non-metallic mineral products [4]  Produits minéraux non métalliques [4] | Basic metals  Métallurgie de base | Metal products  Ouvrages en métaux | Other manufacturing  Autres industries manufacturières | Année et rubrique |
|---|---|---|---|---|---|---|---|---|---|---|---|---|---|---|---|
| ISIC | 2–3 | 20–22 | 23 | 24 | 25–26 | 27 | 28 | 29 | 30 | 31–32 | 33 | 34 | 35–38 | 39 | CITI |
| b. Structure | | | | | | | | | | | | | | | |
| **1939** Distribution in percent of: | | | | | | | | | | | | | | | **1939** Distribution en pourcentage: |
| Value added | 100.0 | 66.4 | 0.3 | 20.8 | 1.9 | 0.3 | 2.9 | 0.3 | — | 2.9 | 0.6 | — | 1.9 | 1.8 | Valeur ajoutée |
| Number of operatives | 100.0 | 57.0 | 0.4 | 26.8 | 4.3 | 0.4 | 3.0 | 0.4 | — | 1.7 | 1.3 | — | 2.1 | 2.6 | Nombre d'ouvriers |
| Value added per operative | 1.5 | 1.7 | 1.0 | 1.2 | 0.7 | 1.0 | 1.4 | 1.0 | ... | 2.5 | 0.7 | ... | 1.4 | 1.0 | Valeur ajoutée par ouvrier |
| **1949** Distribution in percent of: | | | | | | | | | | | | | | | **1949** Distribution en pourcentage: |
| Value added | 100.0 | 63.3 | 0.6 | 10.0 | 3.1 | 0.8 | 4.0 | 1.0 | ... | 4.7 | 6.8 | ... | ... | 2.7 | Valeur ajoutée |
| Number of engaged | 100.0 | 55.2 | 2.5 | 19.3 | 4.4 | 0.5 | 2.6 | 1.6 | ... | 2.3 | 4.6 | ... | ... | 4.4 | Nombre de personnes occupées |
| Value added per person engaged | 1.6 | 1.9 | 0.4 | 0.8 | 1.2 | 2.7 | 2.5 | 1.0 | ... | 3.4 | 2.5 | ... | ... | *1.0 | Valeur ajoutée par personne occupée |
| Wages and salaries per employee | 0.9 | 1.0 | 0.4 | 0.6 | 0.8 | 1.3 | 1.5 | 0.7 | ... | 1.2 | 1.2 | ... | ... | 0.7 | Traitements et salaires par salarié |
| Employees as a percent of engaged | 96.8 | 96.5 | 100.0 | 98.2 | 88.0 | 100.0 | 100.0 | 100.0 | ... | 100.0 | 100.0 | ... | ... | 96.0 | Salariés en pourcentage des personnes occupées |
| Value added per unit of wages and salaries | 1.90 | 2.04 | 1.00 | 1.43 | 1.61 | 2.00 | 1.68 | 1.50 | ... | 2.93 | 2.06 | ... | ... | 1.56 | Valeur ajoutée par unité de traitements et salaires |
| Operatives as a percent of employees | 86.6 | 86.8 | 92.8 | 90.7 | 90.9 | 100.0 | 66.7 | 44.4 | ... | 76.9 | 84.6 | ... | ... | 91.7 | Ouvriers en pourcentage des salariés |
| **1954** Distribution in percent of: | | | | | | | | | | | | | | | **1954** Distribution en pourcentage: |
| Value added | 100.0 | 44.0 | 4.6 | 17.6 | 3.7 | 1.7 | 2.3 | 0.7 | ... | 4.0 | 5.0 | 0.2 | 7.6 | 8.2 | Valeur ajoutée |
| Number of engaged | 100.0 | 41.5 | 4.0 | 26.7 | 4.7 | 0.7 | 2.0 | 1.0 | ... | 2.1 | 4.5 | 0.2 | 5.0 | 7.4 | Nombre de personnes occupées |
| Value added per person engaged | 2.7 | 2.8 | 3.1 | 1.8 | 2.2 | 6.2 | 3.1 | 1.7 | ... | 5.1 | 2.9 | 4.0 | 4.1 | 2.9 | Valeur ajoutée par personne occupée |
| Wages and salaries per employee | 1.2 | 1.3 | 1.2 | 0.8 | 1.1 | 1.8 | 1.7 | 0.8 | ... | 1.9 | 1.6 | 1.0 | 1.8 | 1.2 | Traitements et salaires par salarié |
| Employees as a percent of engaged | 98.2 | 97.9 | 100.0 | 98.9 | 93.9 | 100.0 | 92.8 | 100.0 | ... | 93.3 | 96.9 | (100.0) | 97.1 | 100.0 | Salariés en pourcentage des personnes occupées |
| Value added per unit of wages and salaries | 2.26 | 2.25 | 2.61 | 2.15 | 2.03 | 3.44 | 2.00 | 2.00 | ... | 2.81 | 1.88 | 4.00 | 2.34 | 2.43 | Valeur ajoutée par unité de traitements et salaires |
| Operatives as a percent of employees | 87.5 | 85.7 | 89.3 | 91.4 | 90.3 | 80.0 | 69.2 | 85.7 | ... | 78.6 | 87.1 | 100.0 | 85.3 | 92.3 | Ouvriers en pourcentage des salariés |
| **1958** Distribution in percent of: | | | | | | | | | | | | | | | **1958** Distribution en pourcentage: |
| Value added | 100.0 | 36.2 | 5.3 | 16.9 | 3.4 | 1.3 | 2.1 | 0.8 | 0.4 | 3.2 | 6.6 | 0.6 | 12.4 | 6.2 | Valeur ajoutée |
| Number of engaged | 100.0 | 30.6 | 6.4 | 27.5 | 5.0 | 0.8 | 2.2 | 1.4 | 0.3 | 2.1 | 5.8 | 0.6 | 8.0 | 8.0 | Nombre de personnes occupées |
| Value added per person engaged | 4.0 | 4.8 | 3.4 | 2.5 | 2.8 | 6.5 | 3.8 | 2.3 | 6.5 | 6.2 | 4.6 | 4.5 | 6.2 | 3.1 | Valeur ajoutée par personne occupée |
| Wages and salaries per employee | 1.8 | 1.9 | 1.8 | 1.4 | 1.5 | 3.2 | 2.4 | 1.4 | 2.5 | 2.8 | 2.2 | 3.0 | 2.4 | 1.7 | Traitements et salaires par salarié |
| Employees as a percent of engaged | 98.5 | 97.7 | 100.0 | 99.0 | 94.4 | 100.0 | 93.8 | 100.0 | 100.0 | 100.0 | 97.6 | 100.0 | 98.3 | 98.3 | Salariés en pourcentage des personnes occupées |
| Value added per unit of wages and salaries | 2.21 | 2.53 | 1.87 | 1.82 | 1.98 | 2.05 | 1.69 | 1.64 | 2.60 | 2.21 | 2.13 | 1.50 | 2.60 | 1.88 | Valeur ajoutée par unité de traitements et salaires |
| Operatives as a percent of employees | 84.3 | 76.8 | 91.3 | 92.9 | 88.2 | 83.3 | 60.0 | 90.0 | 50.0 | 66.7 | 82.9 | 75.0 | 84.2 | 89.5 | Ouvriers en pourcentage des salariés |

[1] Excluding coffee roasting and grinding, tobacco stemming and redrying in 1939, small cigar manufacturing establishments with no paid employees in 1939 and 1954; and the pasteurization and bottling of milk in 1939 and 1949.

[2] The manufacturing total includes the following items which are not available separately except for the number of establishments: In 1939, Rubber products (ISIC major group 30), Transportation equipment (ISIC major group 38) and Watches and clocks (ISIC group 393). In 1949, Rubber products (ISIC major group 30), Basic metals (ISIC major group 34), Electrical machinery (ISIC major group 37), Transportation equipment (ISIC major group 38), Surgical appliances and optical goods (part of ISIC major group 39). In 1954, Petroleum products (ISIC group 329) and Transportation equipment (ISIC major group 38). In 1958, Petroleum refining (ISIC group 321) and Transportation equipment (ISIC major group 38).

[3] In 1939 and 1949, Manufacture of footwear (ISIC group 241) is included under Leather and leather products except wearing apparel (ISIC major group 29).

[4] Ready mixed concrete manufacturing included for the first time in 1958.

[1] Non compris la torréfaction et le moulage du café, l'écotage et la dessiccation du tabac en 1939; la fabrication des cigares par de petits établissements n'ayant pas de salariés en 1939 et 1954; et la pasteurisation et la mise en bouteilles du lait en 1939 et 1949.

[2] Sont comprises les industries manufacturières ci-après, pour lesquelles on ne dispose pas de données distinctes, à l'exception du nombre d'établissements: En 1939, Ouvrages en caoutchouc (CITI 30), Matériel de transport (CITI 38) et Fabrication des montres et horloges (CITI 393). En 1949, Ouvrages en caoutchouc (CITI 30), Industrie métallurgique de base (CITI 34), Construction de machines, appareils et fournitures électriques (CITI 37), Matériel de transport (CITI 38), Fabrication du matériel médico-chirurgical et des instruments d'optique (dans CITI 39). En 1954, Fabrication des dérivés du pétrole (CITI 329) et Matériel de transport (CITI 38). En 1958, Raffinage du pétrole (CITI 321) et Matériel de transport (CITI 38).

[3] En 1939 et 1949, la Fabrication de chaussures (CITI 241) est comprise dans Cuir et articles en cuir, à l'exclusion des articles d'habillement (CITI 29).

[4] Y compris, pour la première fois en 1958, la fabrication de béton préparé.

# ROMANIA — ROUMANIE

## Net Material Product

The data on the net material product shown in Table 1 are from the *Anuarul Statistic Al R.P.R., 1962,* published by the Central Statistical Office, Bucharest. The concepts and definitions governing these data are briefly described in that publication. These concepts are those of the system of material product accounts, which is briefly described in the introduction to this publication and differs, in a number of respects, from the principles and definitions of the United Nations system of national accounts.

## Index Numbers of Industrial Production

The index numbers set out in Table 2 were compiled from *Anuarul Statistic Al R.P.R., 1962* or communications from the Central Statistical Office, Bucharest. In particular, the index numbers for the divisions of industrial activity shown in Table 2 were derived from correspondence with that Office.

The index numbers of industrial production relate to the value of gross output, in constant enterprise prices (i.e., excluding turnover and other indirect taxes), of all statistical units mainly engaged in mining, manufacturing and the production of electricity, gas and steam. The statistical unit is the enterprise in the case of publicly-owned, republican-scale industry but appears to be the plant or work shop (i.e., establishment) in the case of publicly-owned, local-scale industry and co-operative or privately-owned enterprises. The index numbers cover only the gross industrial output of these units. The constant prices utilized in valuing gross output are prices set as of 1 January 1948 in the case of the indexes for the years, 1938-1954, and prices set as of 1 January 1955 in the case of the indexes for 1955 and later years. The original bases of comparison for the indexes shown in Table 2 are gross industrial output during 1938 valued at prices as of 1 January 1948 in the case of the indexes for 1938-1954 and the gross industrial output during 1955 valued at prices as of 1 January 1955 in the case of the indexes for 1955-1961.

The indexes of industrial production shown in Table 2 are equivalent to index numbers computed as base-weighted arithmetic averages of series of relatives covering the totality of the gross industrial output of industrial units. In the case of the indexes for 1938-1954, the bases of comparison for the relatives are, in effect, quantities of output during 1938 and the weights for combining these relatives into indexes may be considered to be the gross value of these outputs expressed in prices as of 1 January 1948. In the case of the indexes for 1955-1961, the equivalent items of data are, in effect, quantities

## Produit matériel net

Les données du tableau 1 relatives au produit matériel net sont tirées de l'*Anuarul Statistic Al R.P.R., 1962,* publié par l'Office central de statistique, Bucarest. Les concepts et définitions sur lesquels reposent les données sont exposés brièvement dans cette publication. Ces concepts sont ceux du système de comptabilité du produit matériel, qui est décrit brièvement dans l'introduction de cette publication et qui, à plus d'un égard, diffère du système de comptabilité nationale de l'ONU quant aux principes et définitions adoptés.

## Indices de la production industrielle

Les indices du tableau 2 ont été tirés de l'*Anuarul Statistic Al R.P.R., 1962* ou communiqués par l'Office central de statistique, Bucarest. En particulier, les indices relatifs aux branches de l'activité industrielle ont été fournis par cet Office par voie de correspondance.

Les indices de la production industrielle ont trait à la valeur de la production brute, en prix constants des entreprises (c'est-à-dire, non compris l'impôt sur le chiffre d'affaires et autres impôts indirects), de toutes les unités statistiques dont l'activité principale relève des industries extractives, manufacturières et productrices d'électricité, de gaz et de vapeur. L'unité statistique est l'entreprise dans le cas des industries publiques gérées à l'échelle nationale, mais semble être l'usine ou l'atelier (c'est-à-dire l'établissement) dans le cas des industries publiques gérées à l'échelle locale et des entreprises coopératives ou privées. Les indices portent seulement sur la production industrielle brute de ces unités. Les prix constants adoptés pour évaluer la production brute sont ceux qui ont été établis au 1er janvier 1948 dans le cas des indices de 1938-1954, et les prix établis au 1er janvier 1955 dans le cas des indices de 1955 et des années suivantes. Les bases de comparaison adoptées initialement pour les indices du tableau 2 sont la production industrielle brute pendant 1938 évaluée aux prix établis au 1er janvier 1948 dans le cas des indices de 1938-1954 et la production industrielle brute pendant 1955 évaluée aux prix établis au 1er janvier 1955 dans le cas des indices de 1955-1961.

Les indices de la production industrielle reproduits au tableau 2 équivalent à des moyennes arithmétiques à pondération fixe de séries de rapports portant sur la totalité de la production industrielle des unités industrielles. Dans le cas des indices de 1938-1954, les bases de comparaison adoptées pour les rapports sont, en fait, les quantités produites en 1938 et les coefficients de pondération utilisés pour combiner ces rapports en indices peuvent être considérés comme étant les valeurs brutes de ces productions, calculées aux prix établis au 1er janvier 1948. Pour les indices de 1955-1961, les rubriques

of output during 1955 and the corresponding gross value expressed in prices as of 1 January 1955.

équivalentes sont effectivement les quantités produites en 1955 et la valeur brute correspondante aux prix établis au 1er janvier 1955.

### Index Numbers of Industrial Employment

The index numbers shown in Table 3 were compiled from absolute figures or index numbers of the employment of operatives appearing in *Anuarul Statistic Al R.P.R., 1962*. In the case of mining, manufacturing and electricity, gas and steam, these data relate to the average number of operatives (manual workers) during each month of the year employed in the industrial activities of publicly-owned and co-operative units classified to these industries. The type of statistical units employed in gathering and classifying these data for these various forms of ownership are those indicated above in describing the index numbers of industrial production. In the case of co-operatives, persons engaged in manual work, whether or not they are employees, seem to be included among operatives. The absolute figures utilized in compiling the index numbers for the construction industry relate to the average number of operatives (manual workers) during each month of the year employed by all contract construction enterprises.

### Indices de l'emploi dans l'industrie

Les indices du tableau 3 ont été calculés à partir de chiffres absolus ou d'indices de l'emploi relatifs aux ouvriers qui ont paru dans *Anuarul Statistic Al R.P.R. 1962*. Pour les industries extractives, manufacturières et productrices d'électricité, de gaz et de vapeur, ces données portent sur le nombre moyen, pendant chaque mois de l'année, des ouvriers (travailleurs manuels) affectés aux activités industrielles des unités publiques coopératives de ces industries. Les types d'unités statistiques adoptés pour rassembler et classer les données correspondant à ces diverses formes juridiques sont les mêmes que pour les indices de la production industrielle (voir plus haut). Dans le cas des coopératives, les personnes chargées des travaux manuels, qu'elles soient salariées ou non, semblent être comprises dans le nombre des ouvriers. Les chiffres absolus utilisés pour calculer les indices relatifs aux industries du bâtiment et des travaux publics représentent le nombre moyen, pendant chaque mois de l'année, des ouvriers (travailleurs manuels) employés par toutes les entreprises de construction effectuant des travaux contractuels.

### The Characteristics and Structure of Industrial Activity

The data shown in Table 4 were abstracted from *Anuarul Statistic Al R.P.R., 1962* and *1960*. These data relate to all statistical units mainly engaged in mining, manufacturing and the production of electricity, gas and steam. As for the indexes of industrial production, the statistical unit is the enterprise in the case of publicly-owned republican-scale industry but apparently the plant or workshop in the case of other types of organizations. Republican-scale enterprises are those which are under the management of central governmental authorities.

The figures of gross output for which distributions in percent are given in Table 4 are valued at enterprise prices as of 1 January 1948 in the case of 1938 and as of 1 January 1955 in the case of 1955 and 1959. The scope of the gross output covered in these data is the same as that in the case of the indexes of industrial production. The figures of all other items of data shown in Table 4, except those of the number of persons engaged are also restricted in scope to the industrial activities of the units covered. The data on number of persons engaged refer to employees, working proprietors and family members engaged in any of the activities of the units covered. The capacity of installed power equipment measured by the data in Table 4 is that of prime movers connected directly to machinery other than electric generators plus that of all installed electric motors.

### Caractéristiques et structure de l'activité industrielle

Les données du tableau 4 sont tirées de l'*Anuarul Statistic Al R.P.R., 1962* et *1960*. Elles concernent toutes les unités statistiques dont l'activité principale relève des industries extractives, manufacturières et productrices d'électricité, de gaz et de vapeur. Comme pour les indices de la production industrielle, l'unité statistique est l'entreprise dans le cas des industries publiques gérées à l'échelle nationale, mais apparemment l'usine ou l'atelier dans le cas des autres types d'organisations. Les entreprises gérées à l'échelle nationale sont celles qui sont administrées par le gouvernement central.

Les chiffres de la production brute pour lesquels une répartition en pourcentage est indiquée dans le tableau 4 sont calculés aux prix des entreprises établis au 1er janvier 1948 dans le cas des chiffres de 1938 et aux prix établis au 1er janvier 1955 dans le cas de 1955 et 1959. Ces données concernent la production brute telle qu'elle est définie dans le cas des indices de la production industrielle. Les chiffres de toutes les autres rubriques du tableau 4, à l'exclusion du nombre de personnes occupées, n'ont trait qu'aux activités industrielles des unités étudiées. Le nombre de personnes occupées comprend les salariés, les propriétaires qui travaillent et les travailleurs familiaux affectés à l'une quelconque des activités des unités recensées. La puissance installée indiquée au tableau 4 est celle des moteurs primaires reliés directement à des machines autres que des générateurs d'électricité, plus celle de tous les moteurs électriques installés.

## 1. THE NET MATERIAL PRODUCT ACCORDING TO ORIGIN

## ORIGINE PAR SECTEUR D'ACTIVITE DU PRODUIT MATERIEL NET

| Item of data and year<br>Rubrique et année | Total | Agricultural sector<br>Secteur agricole | Mining, manufacturing, electricity, gas and water<br>Industries extractives et manufacturières, et électricité, gaz et eau | Construction<br>Bâtiment et travaux publics | Transportation and communication [1]<br>Transports et communications [1] | Other sectors [2]<br>Autres secteurs [2] |
|---|---|---|---|---|---|---|
| ISIC — CITI | 0-521, 61, 7, 841, 852 | 0 | 1-3, 511-521 | 4 | 7 | 61, 841, 852 |
| **a. At Current Prices — Aux prix courants** | | | | | | |
| Percentage distribution according to sector— Distribution en pourcentage par secteur | | | | | | |
| 1938............ | 100.0 | 38.5 | 30.8 | 4.4 | 6.5 | 19.8 |
| 1950............ | 100.0 | 28.0 | 44.0 | 6.0 | 4.3 | 17.7 |
| 1953............ | 100.0 | 33.9 | 42.2 | 6.8 | 3.9 | 13.2 |
| 1954............ | 100.0 | 36.7 | 39.7 | 5.0 | 4.0 | 14.6 |
| 1958............ | 100.0 | 34.8 | 42.7 | 7.7 | 4.1 | 10.7 |
| 1960............ | 100.0 | 33.1 | 44.1 | 9.0 | 3.8 | 10.0 |
| 1961............ | 100.0 | 33.0 | 45.0 | 8.7 | 3.7 | 9.6 |
| **b. At Constant Prices [3] — En prix constants [3]** | | | | | | |
| Index Numbers—Indices (1958 = 100) | | | | | | |
| 1938............ | 47 | 114 | 21 | 14 | 46 | 115 |
| 1948............ | 32 | 68 | 20 | 11 | 28 | 60 |
| 1950............ | — 47 — | — 80 — | — 35 — | — 33 — | — 37 — | — 77 — |
| 1951............ | 61 | 107 | 45 | 45 | 45 | 100 |
| 1952............ | 64 | 93 | 52 | 56 | 59 | 89 |
| 1953............ | 74 | 112 | 60 | 70 | 70 | 98 |
| 1954............ | 74 | 100 | 64 | 52 | 76 | 103 |
| 1955............ | — 90 — | — 135 — | — 76 — | — 72 — | — 87 — | — 114 — |
| 1956............ | 84 | 84 | 78 | 86 | 96 | 102 |
| 1957............ | 97 | 126 | 88 | 92 | 102 | 103 |
| 1958............ | 100 | 100 | 100 | 100 | 100 | 100 |
| 1959............ | 114 | 134 | 111 | 117 | 103 | 95 |
| 1960............ | 125 | 134 | 130 | 141 | 122 | 102 |
| 1961............ | 138 | 138 | 147 | 154 | 143 | 110 |
| Average annual rate of growth—Taux annuel moyen d'accroissement | | | | | | |
| 1938 – 1960..... | 4.5 | 0.7 | 8.6 | 11.1 | 4.5 | — 0.5 |
| 1938 – 1948..... | — 3.8 | — 5.0 | — 0.5 | — 2.4 | — 4.8 | — 6.3 |
| 1948 – 1953..... | 18.2 | 10.5 | 24.6 | 44.8 | 20.1 | 10.3 |
| 1950 – 1960..... | 10.3 | 5.3 | 14.0 | 15.6 | 12.7 | 2.9 |
| 1950 – 1953..... | 16.3 | 11.9 | 19.7 | 28.5 | 23.7 | 8.4 |
| 1954 – 1958..... | 7.8 | — | 11.8 | 17.8 | 7.1 | — 0.7 |
| 1958 – 1960..... | 11.8 | 15.8 | 14.0 | 18.7 | 10.5 | 1.0 |

[1] Transportation of goods and communication services for "productive" enterprises only.
[2] Also includes home and craft production of goods.
[3] In constant prices of 1948 for 1938 and 1948, of 1950 for 1950-1954 and of 1955 for 1955-1961. The series of index numbers were linked to one another at 1950 and 1955.

[1] Transports de marchandises et services de communications desservant les entreprises qui concourent à la formation du produit matériel seulement.
[2] Comprend également la production de marchandises à l'échelle familiale ou artisanale.
[3] En prix constants de 1948 dans le cas de 1938 et 1948, de 1950 dans le cas de 1950-1954 et de 1955 dans le cas de 1955-1961. Les séries d'indices ont été raccordées l'une à l'autre au niveau de 1950 et 1955.

## 2. INDEX NUMBERS OF INDUSTRIAL PRODUCTION — INDICES DE LA PRODUCTION INDUSTRIELLE

### A. Selected Divisions of Industrial Activity
### Quelques branches de l'activité industrielle

| Period<br>Période | Total [1] | Mining [2]<br>Industries extractives [2] | Manu-facturing [1, 2]<br>Industries manu-facturières [1, 2] | Electricity and steam<br>Electricité et vapeur |
|---|---|---|---|---|
| ISIC — CITI | 1–3, 511–513 | 11–13, 199 | 2–3, 512 | 511, 513 |

#### a. Indexes — Indices (1958 = 100)

| | | | | |
|---|---|---|---|---|
| 1938.......... | 25 | 39 | 24 | 12 |
| 1948.......... | 22 | 29 | 20 | – 19 – |
| 1950.......... | 38 | 40 | 37 | 29 |
| 1951.......... | 46 | 48 | 47 | 35 |
| 1952.......... | 55 | 57 | 54 | 43 |
| 1953.......... | 63 | 72 | 62 | 53 |
| 1954.......... | 67 | 77 | 66 | 58 |
| 1955.......... | – 76 – | – 83 – | – 76 – | – 68 – |
| 1956.......... | 84 | 89 | 84 | 77 |
| 1957.......... | 91 | 94 | 91 | 87 |
| 1958.......... | 100 | 100 | 100 | 100 |
| 1959.......... | 110 | 107 | 111 | 110 |
| 1960.......... | 128 | 114 | 129 | 124 |
| 1961.......... | 148 | 124 | 150 | 143 |

#### b. Average Annual Rate of Change — Taux annuel moyen de variation

| | | | | |
|---|---|---|---|---|
| 1938 – 1960.... | 7.7 | 5.0 | 7.9 | 11.2 |
| 1938 – 1948.... | –1.3 | –2.9 | –1.8 | 4.7 |
| 1950 – 1960.... | 12.9 | 11.0 | 13.3 | 15.6 |
| 1948 – 1953.... | 23.4 | 19.9 | 25.4 | 22.8 |
| 1954 – 1958.... | 10.5 | 6.8 | 10.9 | 14.6 |
| 1958 – 1960.... | 13.1 | 6.8 | 13.6 | 11.4 |

For footnotes see end of table.

### B. The Major Groups of Mining
### Les classes de la branche Industries extractives

| Period<br>Période | All mining [3]<br>Toutes industries extractives [2] | Coal mining<br>Extraction du charbon | Metal mining<br>Extraction des minerais métalliques | Crude petro-leum and natural gas<br>Pétrole brut et gaz naturel | Other mining [2]<br>Autres industries extractives [2] |
|---|---|---|---|---|---|
| ISIC — CITI | 11–13, 199 | 11 | 12 | 13 | 199 |

#### a. Indexes — Indices (1958 = 100)

| | | | | | |
|---|---|---|---|---|---|
| 1938....... | 39 | 40 | 19 | 47 | 12 |
| 1948....... | 29 | 35 | 14 | 32 | 16 |
| 1950....... | 40 | 56 | 17 | 41 | 13 |
| 1951....... | 48 | 65 | 18 | 51 | 18 |
| 1952....... | 57 | 71 | 23 | 63 | 29 |
| 1953....... | 72 | 74 | 73 | 74 | 37 |
| 1954....... | 77 | 76 | 75 | 81 | 39 |
| 1955....... | – 83 – | – 84 – | – 78 – | – 87 – | – 48 – |
| 1956....... | 89 | 87 | 84 | 92 | 65 |
| 1957....... | 94 | 92 | 91 | 97 | 83 |
| 1958....... | 100 | 100 | 100 | 100 | 100 |
| 1959....... | 107 | 108 | 111 | 103 | 107 |
| 1960....... | 114 | 115 | 123 | 106 | 105 |
| 1961....... | 124 | 124 | ... | 111 | 123 |

#### b. Average Annual Rate of Change — Taux annuel moyen de variation

| | | | | | |
|---|---|---|---|---|---|
| 1938 – 1960. | 5.0 | 4.9 | 8.9 | 3.8 | 10.4 |
| 1938 – 1948. | –2.9 | –1.3 | –3.0 | –3.8 | 2.9 |
| 1950 – 1960. | 11.0 | 7.5 | 21.9 | 10.0 | 23.2 |
| 1948 – 1953. | 19.9 | 16.2 | 39.1 | 18.2 | 18.2 |
| 1954 – 1958. | 6.8 | 7.1 | 7.5 | 5.4 | 26.5 |
| 1958 – 1960. | 6.8 | 7.2 | 10.9 | 3.0 | 2.5 |

Pour les notes, voir au bas du tableau.

# ROMANIA

## C. The Major Groups of Manufacturing — Les classes de la branche Industries manufacturières

| Period / Période | Manufacturing[1,2] / Industries manufacturières[1,2] | Food, beverages and tobacco[1,2] / Industries alimentaires, boissons, tabac[1,2] | Textiles | Clothing, and made-up textiles[3] / Articles d'habillement, et ouvrages en tissu[3] | Wood products and furniture[1] / Bois et meubles[1] | Paper and paper products / Papier et ouvrages en papier | Printing[1,4] / Imprimerie[1,4] | Leather and leather products[3] / Cuir et articles en cuir[3] | Chemicals and chemical, rubber, petroleum and coal products[2] / Produits chimiques, ouvrages en caoutchouc et dérivés du pétrole et du charbon[2] | Non-metallic mineral products[2] / Produits minéraux non métalliques[2] | Basic metals / Métallurgie de base | Metal products / Ouvrages en métaux | Other manufacturing[4] / Autres industries manufacturières[4] |
|---|---|---|---|---|---|---|---|---|---|---|---|---|---|
| ISIC — CITI | 14, 191-192, 2-3, 512 | 191, 20-22 | 23 | 243, 244 | 25-26 | 27 | 28 | 241, 29 | 192, 30-32, 521 | 14, 33 | 34 | 35-38 | 39 |

### a. Indexes — Indices (1958 = 100)

| Period | | | | | | | | | | | | | |
|---|---|---|---|---|---|---|---|---|---|---|---|---|---|
| 1938 | 24 | 46 | 29 | 18 | 28 | 35 | 22 | 28 | 25 | 10 | 26 | 13 | 10 |
| 1948 | 20 | 28 | 27 | 22 | 26 | 42 | 29 | 29 | 21 | 13 | 28 | 12 | 12 |
| 1950 | 37 | 49 | 51 | 57 | 40 | 58 | 33 | 50 | 29 | 28 | 48 | 24 | 23 |
| 1951 | 47 | 60 | 62 | 65 | 45 | 62 | 44 | 57 | 36 | 34 | 54 | 33 | 32 |
| 1952 | 54 | 67 | 69 | 66 | 49 | 70 | 50 | 60 | 47 | 43 | 65 | 42 | 57 |
| 1953 | 62 | 68 | 72 | 74 | 58 | 73 | 58 | 62 | 54 | 58 | 73 | 52 | 57 |
| 1954 | 66 | 85 | 78 | 81 | 67 | 75 | 64 | 65 | 56 | 57 | 64 | 55 | 49 |
| 1955 | −76− | −83− | −88− | −85− | −72− | −79− | −69− | −85− | −65− | −69− | −72− | −66− | −53− |
| 1956 | 84 | 90 | 88 | 90 | 78 | 84 | 79 | 91 | 73 | 87 | 78 | 79 | 63 |
| 1957 | 91 | 92 | 92 | 98 | 89 | 90 | 91 | 95 | 86 | 92 | 86 | 91 | 77 |
| 1958 | 100 | 100 | 100 | 100 | 100 | 100 | 100 | 100 | 100 | 100 | 100 | 100 | 100 |
| 1959 | 111 | 104 | 101 | 102 | 106 | 112 | 107 | 106 | 116 | 108 | 136 | 116 | 104 |
| 1960 | 129 | 116 | 118 | 136 | 126 | 132 | 116 | 124 | 136 | 113 | 174 | 140 | 144 |
| 1961 | 150 | 125 | 143 | 159 | 142 | 157 | 142 | 132 | 165 | 133 | 205 | 167 | 150 |

### b. Average Annual Rate of Change — Taux annuel moyen de variation

| Period | | | | | | | | | | | | | |
|---|---|---|---|---|---|---|---|---|---|---|---|---|---|
| 1938−1960 | 7.9 | 4.3 | 6.6 | 9.6 | 7.1 | 6.2 | 7.8 | 7.0 | 8.0 | 11.7 | 9.0 | 11.4 | 12.9 |
| 1938−1948 | −1.8 | −4.8 | −0.7 | 2.0 | −0.7 | 1.8 | 2.8 | 0.4 | −1.7 | 2.7 | 0.7 | −0.8 | 1.8 |
| 1950−1960 | 13.3 | 9.0 | 8.8 | 9.1 | 12.2 | 8.6 | 13.4 | 9.5 | 16.7 | 15.0 | 13.7 | 19.3 | 20.1 |
| 1948−1953 | 25.4 | 19.4 | 21.7 | 27.5 | 17.4 | 11.7 | 14.9 | 16.4 | 20.8 | 34.9 | 21.1 | 34.1 | 36.6 |
| 1954−1958 | 10.9 | 4.1 | 6.4 | 5.4 | 10.5 | 7.5 | 11.8 | 11.4 | 15.6 | 15.1 | 11.8 | 16.1 | 19.5 |
| 1958−1960 | 13.6 | 7.7 | 8.6 | 16.6 | 12.2 | 14.9 | 7.7 | 11.4 | 16.6 | 6.3 | 31.9 | 18.3 | 20.0 |

[1] Fishing (ISIC major group 04) and Logging (ISIC group 022) are included under Manufacturing in Food, beverages and tobacco (ISIC major group 20-22) and Wood products (ISIC major group 25), respectively; but publishing (part of ISIC major group 28) is excluded from Manufacturing.

[2] Sand, stone and clay quarrying (ISIC major group 14), Salt extraction (ISIC group 191) and Extraction of chemical minerals (ISIC group 192) are included under Manufacturing in Non-Metallic mineral products (ISIC major group 33), Food, beverages and tobacco (ISIC major group 20-22) and Chemicals and chemical products (ISIC major group 31), respectively; whereas products made of abrasive substances and graphite (part of ISIC group 339) are included under Mining in Other mining (ISIC group 199).

[3] Footwear and leather apparel (part of ISIC major group 24) are included under Leather and leather products (ISIC major group 29).

[4] The following kinds of manufacturing are included under Printing (ISIC major group 28): Jewellery (ISIC group 394), Musical instruments (ISIC group 395) and toys (part of ISIC group 399).

[1] Pêche (CITI classe 04) et Exploitation forestière (CITI groupe 022) sont compris dans Industries manufacturières sous Industries alimentaires, boissons et tabac (CITI classes 20-22) et Ouvrages en bois (CITI classe 25) respectivement; mais l'édition (dans CITI classe 28) est exclue.

[2] Extraction de pierre à bâtir et d'argile (CITI classe 14), Extraction du sel (CITI groupe 191) et Extraction de minéraux pour l'industrie chimique (CITI groupe 192) sont compris dans les industries manufacturières sous Produits minéraux non métalliques (CITI classe 33), Industries alimentaires, boissons et tabac (CITI classes 20-22) et Industrie chimique, (CITI classe 31) respectivement; mais les produits fabriqués à partir des substances abrasives et du graphite (dans CITI groupe 339) sont compris dans les Industries extractives sous Autres industries extractives (CITI groupe 199).

[3] Chaussures et articles d'habillement en cuir (dans CITI classe 24) sont compris dans Cuir et articles en cuir (CITI classe 29).

[4] Les types d'industries manufacturières suivants sont compris sous Imprimerie (CITI classe 28); Bijouteries et orfèvreries (CITI groupe 394), Instruments de musique (CITI groupe 395) et jouets (dans CITI groupe 399).

## 3. INDEX NUMBERS OF INDUSTRIAL EMPLOYMENT — INDICES DE L'EMPLOI DANS L'INDUSTRIE

### A. The Divisions of Industrial Activity
### Branches de l'activité industrielle

| Period<br>Période | Mining, manufacturing, electricity, gas and steam [1]<br>Industries extractives et manufacturières et électricité, gaz et vapeur [1] | Construction<br>Bâtiment et travaux publics |
|---|---|---|
| ISIC — CITI | 1–3, 51 | 4 |

#### a. Indexes — Indices (1958 = 100)

| | | |
|---|---|---|
| 1950 | 65 | 67 |
| 1951 | 74 | 96 |
| 1952 | 83 | 126 |
| 1953 | 88 | 140 |
| 1954 | 91 | 120 |
| 1955 | 94 | 123 |
| 1956 | 96 | 122 |
| 1957 | 96 | 99 |
| 1958 | 100 | 100 |
| 1959 | 104 | 102 |
| 1960 | 109 | 126 |
| 1961 | 119 | 142 |

#### b. Average Annual Rate of Change — Taux annuel moyen de variation

| | | |
|---|---|---|
| 1950 – 1960 | 5.3 | 6.5 |
| 1950 – 1953 | 10.6 | 27.8 |
| 1954 – 1958 | 2.4 | −4.5 |
| 1958 – 1960 | 4.4 | 12.2 |

### B. Selected Sub-divisions of Mining and Manufacturing
### Quelques subdivisions des Industries extractives et manufacturières

| Period<br>Période | Mining, manufacturing electricity, gas and steam [1]<br>Industries extractives et manufacturières et électricité, gaz et vapeur [1] | Food, beverages and tobacco [1]<br>Industries alimentaires, boissons, tabac [1] | Textiles | Wood products and furniture [1]<br>Bois et meubles [1] | Leather and leather products [2]<br>Cuir et articles en cuir [2] | Chemicals coal, crude petroleum and products<br>Produits chimiques, charbon, pétrole brut et produits dérivés | Non-metallic minerals and products<br>Minéraux non métalliques et produits dérivés | Ferrous ores and metals<br>Minerais et métaux ferreux | Metal products [3]<br>Ouvrages en metaux [3] |
|---|---|---|---|---|---|---|---|---|---|
| ISIC — CITI | 1–3, 51 | 191, 20–22 | 23 | 25–26 | 241, 29 | 11, 13, 192 30–32, 512 | 14, 199, 33 | 121, 341 | 35–38 391, 393 |

#### a. Indexes — Indices (1958 = 100)

| | | | | | | | | | |
|---|---|---|---|---|---|---|---|---|---|
| 1950 | 65 | 75 | 75 | 64 | 82 | 60 | 58 | 66 | 64 |
| 1955 | 94 | 99 | 99 | 93 | 94 | 93 | 89 | 88 | 94 |
| 1956 | 96 | 100 | 96 | 102 | 97 | 93 | 96 | 93 | 95 |
| 1957 | 96 | 97 | 95 | 98 | 97 | 98 | 98 | 96 | 96 |
| 1958 | 100 | 100 | 100 | 100 | 100 | 100 | 100 | 100 | 100 |
| 1959 | 104 | 98 | 105 | 101 | 106 | 103 | 102 | 108 | 111 |
| 1960 | 109 | 104 | 114 | 98 | 118 | 106 | 99 | 118 | 116 |
| 1961 | 119 | 112 | 131 | 104 | 124 | 114 | 107 | 125 | 126 |

#### b. Average Annual Rate of Change — Taux annuel moyen de variation

| | | | | | | | | | |
|---|---|---|---|---|---|---|---|---|---|
| 1950 – 1960 | 5.3 | 3.3 | 4.3 | 4.4 | 3.6 | 5.9 | 5.5 | 6.0 | 6.1 |
| 1950 – 1955 | 7.6 | 5.7 | 5.7 | 7.8 | 2.8 | 9.2 | 8.9 | 5.9 | 8.0 |
| 1955 – 1960 | 3.0 | 1.0 | 2.9 | 1.1 | 4.6 | 2.7 | 2.1 | 6.0 | 4.3 |

[1] Fishing (ISIC major group 04) and Logging (ISIC group 022) is included under Manufacturing in Food, beverages and tobacco (ISIC major group 20–22) and Wood products (ISIC major group 25), respectively; but publishing (part of ISIC major group 28) is excluded. Although index numbers for selected sub-divisions only are shown in Table 3B, the indexes shown for Mining, manufacturing and electricity, gas and steam as a whole relate to this entire field.
[2] Footwear and leather apparel (part of ISIC major group 24) are included in Leather and leather products (ISIC major group 29).
[3] Includes the following kinds of manufacturing: Professional and scientific equipment and Watches and clocks (ISIC groups 391 393, respectively).

[1] Pêche (CITI classe 04) et Exploitation forestière (CITI groupe 022) sont compris dans Industries manufacturières sous Industries alimentaires, boissons et tabac (CITI classes 20–22) et Ouvrages en bois (CITI classe 25), respectivement; mais l'édition (dans CITI classe 28) est exclue. Quoique les indices du tableau 3B concernent quelques subdivisions seulement, les indices relatifs à l'ensemble des Industries extractives et manufacturières et des Industries de l'électricité, du gaz et de la vapeur portent sur la totalité de ces branches d'activité.
[2] Chaussures et articles d'habillement en cuir (dans CITI classe 24) sont compris dans Cuir et articles en cuir (CITI classe 29).
[3] Y compris les types suivants d'industries manufacturières: Matériel médico-chirurgical et instruments de précision, Montres et horloges (CITI groupes 391 et 393 respectivement).

## ROMANIA

### 4. CHARACTERISTICS OF INDUSTRIAL ENTERPRISES — CARACTERISTIQUES DES ENTREPRISES INDUSTRIELLES

Number of enterprises and units in units; number of engaged and operatives in thousands; electricity consumed in million KWH; capacity of installed power equipment in thousand horsepower; electricity consumed per operative in thousand KWH; capacity of installed power equipment per operative in horsepower.

Nombre d'entreprises et d'unités en unités; nombre de personnes occupées et d'ouvriers en milliers; électricité consommée en millions de kWh; puissance installée en milliers de chevaux-vapeur; électricité consommée par ouvrier en milliers de kWh; puissance installée par ouvrier en chevaux-vapeur.

#### A. Industrial Entreprises According to Form of Ownership [1]
#### Entreprises industrielles suivant la forme juridique [1]

| Item of data and year | All enterprises Toutes les entreprises | Publicly-owned enterprises Entreprises publiques | | | Co-operatives enterprises Entreprises coopératives | Privately-owned enterprises Entreprises privées | Rubrique et année |
| | | Total | Republican-scale A l'échelle nationale | Local-scale A l'échelle locale | | | |
|---|---|---|---|---|---|---|---|
| ISIC | 1–3, 51 | 1–3, 51 | 1–3, 51 | 1–3, 51 | 1–3, 51 | 1–3, 51 | CITI |
| Number of units (As of end of year): | | | | | | | Nombre d'unités (à la fin de l'année): |
| 1955..................... | . | 1 598 | 1 306 | 292 | 625 | 124 501 | 1955 |
| 1959..................... | . | 1 468 | 1 049 | 419 | 341 | 100 755 | 1959 |
| Distribution in percent of value of gross output: | | | | | | | Répartition en pourcentage de la valeur de la production brute: |
| 1950..................... | 100.0 | 88.6 | 82.6 | 6.0 | 3.8 | 7.6 | 1950 |
| 1955..................... | 100.0 | 90.2 | 83.4 | 6.8 | 6.8 | 3.0 | 1955 |
| 1959..................... | 100.0 | 94.9 | 85.3 | 9.6 | 3.4 | 1.7 | 1959 |
| Persons engaged (Average during year) Number: | | | | | | | Personnes occupées (moyenne pendant l'année) Nombre: |
| 1950..................... | 1 002.4 | 747.6 | ... | ... | 65.9 | 188.9 | 1950 |
| 1955..................... | 1 213.3 | 955.6 | 780.9 | 174.7 | 128.7 | 129.0 | 1955 |
| 1959..................... | 1 306.4 | 1 112.6 | 960.5 | 152.1 | 85.0 | 108.8 | 1959 |
| Number of operatives (Average during year): | | | | | | | Nombre d'ouvriers (moyenne pendant l'année): |
| 1950..................... | ... | 582.8 | 548.5 | 34.3 | 57.6 | ... | 1950 |
| 1955..................... | ... | 804.0 | 700.5 | 103.5 | 112.4 | ... | 1955 |
| 1959..................... | ... | 937.9 | 804.4 | 133.5 | 76.1 | ... | 1959 |

For footnotes see end of table.

Pour les notes, voir au bas du tableau.

## B. The Major Sub-divisions of Mining and Manufacturing and Electricity and Steam
## Les principales subdivisions des Industries extractives et manufacturières et Electricité et vapeur

| Year and item of data | Mining, manufacturing, gas and steam [1] / Industries extractives et manufacturières et électricité, gaz et vapeur [1] | Food beverages and tobacco [1] / Industries alimentaires, boissons, tabac [1] | Textiles | Clothing, and made-up textiles [2] / Articles d'habillement, et ouvrages en tissu [2] | Wood products and furniture [1] / Bois et meubles [1] | Paper and paper products / Papier et ouvrages en papier | Printing [1] / Imprimerie [1] | Leather and leather products [2] / Cuir et articles en cuir [2] | Chemicals, coal, crude petroleum and products / Produits chimiques charbon, pétrole brut et produits dérivés | Non-métallic minerals and products / Minéraux non métalliques et produits dérivés | Metal mining and basic metals / Minerais métalliques et métallurgie de base | Metal products [4] / Ouvrages en métaux [4] | Other manufacturing / Autres industries manufacturières | Electricity and steam / Electricité et vapeur | Année et rubrique |
|---|---|---|---|---|---|---|---|---|---|---|---|---|---|---|---|
| ISIC | 1-3, 51 | 191, 20-22 | 23 | 243-244 | 25-26 | 27 | 28, 394-395 | 241, 29 | 11, 13, 192, 30-32, 512 | 14, 199, 33 | 12, 34 | 35-38, 391-393 | 399 | 511, 513 | CITI |
| **All Units — Toutes les unités** | | | | | | | | | | | | | | | |
| Distribution in percent of value of gross output: | | | | | | | | | | | | | | | Répartition en pourcentage de la valeur de la production brute: |
| 1938 | 100.0 | 32.4 | 9.4 | 3.4 | 9.5 | 1.2 | 0.8 | 3.3 | 20.0 | 1.7 | 6.7 | 10.2 | 0.3 | 1.1 | 1938 |
| 1950 | 100.0 | 24.2 | 11.1 | 7.5 | 9.9 | 1.3 | 0.8 | 4.0 | 14.8 | 3.2 | 7.5 | 13.3 | 0.5 | 1.9 | 1950 |
| 1955 | 100.0 | 21.7 | 10.0 | 5.9 | 8.9 | 0.9 | 0.9 | 3.5 | 16.1 | 4.1 | 6.5 | 18.8 | 0.5 | 2.2 | 1955 |
| 1959 | 100.0 | 19.2 | 7.8 | 4.9 | 8.2 | 0.9 | 1.0 | 2.9 | 16.4 | 4.4 | 8.2 | 22.9 | 0.7 | 2.5 | 1959 |
| Persons engaged — 1959: | | | | | | | | | | | | | | | Personnes occupées — 1959: |
| Number (Average during year) | 1 306.3 | 127.9 | 134.4 | 82.4 | 231.1 | 11.9 | 17.8 | 62.1 | 137.1 | 92.5 | 101.7 | 275.3 | 16.4 | 15.7 | Nombre (moyenne pendant l'année) |
| Distribution in percent | 100.0 | 9.7 | 10.3 | 6.3 | 17.7 | 0.9 | 1.4 | 4.8 | 10.5 | 7.0 | 7.8 | 21.1 | 1.2 | 1.3 | Répartition en pourcentage |
| **Publicly-owned and Co-operative Units — Unités publiques et coopératives** | | | | | | | | | | | | | | | |
| Persons engaged — 1959: | | | | | | | | | | | | | | | Personnes occupées — 1959: |
| Number (Average during year) | 1 197.6 | 112.1 | 132.6 | 48.9 | 210.4 | 11.9 | 17.8 | 51.5 | 135.9 | 92.5 | 82.0 | 275.3 | 11.0 | 15.7 | Nombre (moyenne pendant l'année) |
| Distribution in percent | 100.0 | 9.3 | 11.1 | 4.1 | 17.5 | 1.0 | 1.5 | 4.3 | 11.4 | 7.7 | 6.8 | 23.0 | 0.9 | 1.4 | Répartition en pourcentage: |
| Operatives: Number (Average during year): | | | | | | | | | | | | | | | Ouvriers: Nombre (moyenne pendant l'année): |
| 1950 [5] | 640.4 | 67.7 | 85.0 | ... | 118.1 | ... | ... | 35.4 | 63.0 | 44.6 | 23.7 | 131.1 | ... | ... | 1950 [5] |
| 1955 [5] | 916.4 | 89.7 | 111.9 | ... | 172.1 | ... | ... | 40.1 | 97.8 | 68.4 | 31.7 | 192.4 | ... | ... | 1955 [5] |
| 1959 [5] | 1 014.0 | 88.3 | 118.9 | ... | 186.5 | ... | ... | 45.7 | 108.0 | 78.2 | 38.7 | 222.8 | ... | ... | 1959 [5] |
| 1959 [6] | 1 014.0 | 88.3 | 118.9 | 44.3 | 186.5 | 10.1 | 15.3 | 45.7 | 112.3 | 82.8 | 69.8 | 222.8 | 5.9 | 11.3 | 1959 [6] |
| Distribution in percent: | | | | | | | | | | | | | | | Répartition en pourcentage: |
| 1950 | 100.0 | 10.6 | 13.3 | ... | 18.4 | ... | ... | 5.5 | 9.8 | 7.0 | 3.7 | 20.5 | ... | ... | 1950 |
| 1955 | 100.0 | 9.8 | 12.2 | ... | 18.8 | ... | ... | 4.4 | 10.7 | 7.5 | 3.5 | 21.0 | ... | ... | 1955 |
| 1959 | 100.0 | 8.7 | 11.7 | ... | 18.4 | ... | ... | 4.5 | 10.6 | 7.7 | 3.8 | 22.0 | ... | ... | 1959 |
| 1959 | 100.0 | 8.7 | 11.7 | 4.4 | 18.4 | 1.0 | 1.5 | 4.5 | 11.0 | 8.2 | 6.9 | 22.0 | 0.5 | 1.2 | 1959 |
| **Publicly owned, Republican-scale Enterprises — Entreprises publiques à l'échelle nationale** | | | | | | | | | | | | | | | |
| 1959 [5] | | | | | | | | | | | | | | | 1959 [5] |
| Number of enterprises (As of 31.XII) | 1 049 | 209 | 136 | ... | 135 | 17 | 17 | 40 | 81 | 88 | 35 | 220 | ... | ... | Nombre d'entreprises (au 31.XII) |
| Number of operatives (Average during the year) | 804.4 | 54.6 | 106.8 | ... | 147.4 | 10.4 | 10.4 | 26.9 | 103.0 | 45.5 | 79.7 | 179.3 | ... | ... | Nombre d'ouvriers (moyenne pendant l'année) |
| Electricity consumed | 4 502.4 | 160.1 | 268.7 | ... | 98.0 | 214.2 | 11.7 | 25.0 | 1 311.9 | 337.0 | 791.4 | 565.0 | ... | ... | Electricité consommée |
| Capacity of installed power equipment (As of 31.XII) | 3 550 | 186 | 151 | ... | 123 | 111 | 16 | 35 | 961 | 237 | 758 | 685 | ... | ... | Puissance installée (au 31.XII) |
| Electricity consumed per operative | 5.60 | 2.93 | 2.52 | ... | 0.66 | 20.60 | 1.12 | 0.93 | 12.74 | 7.41 | 9.97 | 3.15 | ... | ... | Electricité consommée par ouvrier |
| Capacity of installed power equipment per operative | 4.41 | 3.41 | 1.41 | ... | 0.83 | 10.67 | 1.54 | 1.30 | 9.33 | 5.21 | 9.51 | 3.82 | ... | ... | Puissance installée par ouvrier |

For footnotes see end of table.  Pour les notes, voir au bas du tableau.

# ROMANIA

## B. The Major Sub-division of Mining and Manufacturing and Electricity and Steam (continued)
## Les principales subdivisions des Industries extractives et manufacturières et Electricité et vapeur (suite)

| Year and item of data | Mining, manufacturing, gas and steam [1] / Industries extractives et manufacturières et électricité, gaz et vapeur [1] | Food beverages and tobacco[1] / Industries alimentaires, boissons, tabac [1] | Textiles | Clothing, and made-up textiles [2] / Articles d'habillement et ouvrages en tissu [2] | Wood products and furniture[1] / Bois et meubles[1] | Paper and paper products / Papier et ouvrages en papier | Printing[1] / Imprimerie[1] | Leather and leather products[2] / Cuir et articles en cuir [2] | Chemicals, coal, crude petroleum and products / Produits chimiques charbon, pétrole brut et produits dérivés | Non-metallic minerals and products / Minéraux non métalliques et produits dérivés | Metal mining and basic metals / Minerais métalliques et métallurgie de base | Metal products[4] / Ouvrages en métaux[4] | Other manufacturing / Autres industries manufacturières | Electricity and steam / Electricité et vapeur | Année et rubrique |
|---|---|---|---|---|---|---|---|---|---|---|---|---|---|---|---|
| ISIC | 1-3, 51 | 191, 20–22 | 23 | 243-244 | 25–26 | 27 | 28, 394-395 | 241, 29 | 11, 13, 192, 30-32, 512 | 14, 199, 33 | 12, 34 | 35-38, 391-393 | 399 | 511 | CITI |
| | | | | | Privately-owned Units — Unités privées | | | | | | | | | | |
| Number of units (As of 31.XII): | | | | | | | | | | | | | | | Nombre d'unités (au 31.XII): |
| 1955 | 124 501 | 13 614 | 3 470 | 32 164 | 24 200 | — | — | 14 666 | 1 602 | — | 28 995 | — | 5 790 | — | 1955 |
| 1959 | 100 755 | 14 585 | 1 685 | 31 742 | 18 473 | — | — | 10 319 | 889 | — | 18 412 | — | 4 650 | — | 1959 |
| Persons engaged: Number (Average during the year): | | | | | | | | | | | | | | | Personnes occupées: Nombre (moyenne pendant l'année): |
| 1955 | 129.1 | 14.0 | 3.8 | 33.0 | 25.4 | — | — | 15.0 | 1.9 | — | 30.0 | — | 6.0 | — | 1955 |
| 1959 | 108.7 | 15.8 | 1.8 | 33.5 | 20.7 | — | — | 10.6 | 1.2 | — | 19.7 | — | 5.4 | — | 1959 |
| Distribution in percent: | | | | | | | | | | | | | | | Répartition en pourcentage: |
| 1955 | 100.0 | 10.8 | 2.9 | 25.6 | 19.7 | — | — | 11.6 | 1.5 | — | 23.2 | — | 4.7 | — | 1955 |
| 1959 | 100.0 | 14.5 | 1.6 | 30.9 | 19.0 | — | — | 9.8 | 1.1 | — | 18.1 | — | 5.0 | — | 1959 |

[1] Fishing (ISIC major group 04) and Logging (ISIC group 022) are included under Food, beverages and tobacco (ISIC major groups 20-22) and Wood products (ISIC major group 25), respectively but publishing (part of ISIC major group 28) is excluded.
[2] Footwear and leather apparel (part of ISIC major group 24) are included under Leather and leather products (ISIC major group 29).
[3] The following kinds of manufacturing are included under Printing (ISIC major group 28): Jewellery (ISIC group 394), musical instruments (ISIC group 395) and toys (part of ISIC group 399).
[4] Includes the following kinds of manufacturing: Professional and scientific equipment, Photographic and optical equipment and Watches and clocks (ISIC groups 391, 392 and 393, respectively).
[5] Excludes the following in the case of the kinds of activities for which data are shown: Soap and cosmetic manufacturing under Chemical products (ISIC major group 31), mining of certain non-metallic ores and products of abrasive substances under Non-metallic mineral and products (ISIC major groups 14, 199 and 33) and Non-ferrous ore mining and refining (ISIC groups 122 and 342, respectively), under Metal mining and basic metals (ISIC major groups 12 and 34).
[6] The industrial classification of certain enterprises in the two sets of data on number of operatives for 1959 differ from one another. The industrial classification of the enterprises in the second set of the data is the same as that for the figures of persons engaged during 1959.

[1] Pêche (CITI classe 04) et Exploitation forestière (CITI groupe 022) sont compris dans Industries manufacturières sous Industries alimentaires, boissons et tabac (CITI classes 20-22) et Ouvrages en bois (CITI classe 25) respectivement; mais l'édition (dans CITI classe 28) est exclue.
[2] Chaussures et articles d'habillement en cuir (dans CITI classe 24) sont compris dans Cuir et articles en cuir (CITI classe 29).
[3] Les types d'industries manufacturières suivants sont compris dans Imprimerie (CITI classe 38): Bijouteries et orfèvreries (CITI groupe 394), Instruments de musique (CITI groupe 395) et jouets (dans CITI groupe 399).
[4] Y compris les types suivants d'industries manufacturières: Matériel médico-chirurgical et instruments de précision et matériel photographique et instruments d'optique, Montres et horloges (CITI groupes 391, 392 et 393 respectivement).
[5] Non compris les industries ci-après dans le cas des types d'activités pour lesquels des données sont fournies: Industries du savon et des produits de beauté dans Produits chimiques (CITI classe 31), Industries extractives de certains minerais nonmétalliques et produits en substances abrasives dans Produits et minéraux non métalliques (CITI classes 14 et 33, et groupe 199) et Extraction et affinage de minerais non ferreux (CITI groupes 122 et 342 respectivement), dans Extraction de minerais métalliques et métallurgie de base (CITI classes 12 et 34).
[6] La classification industrielle de certaines entreprises dans les deux séries de données sur le nombre d'ouvriers pour 1959 diffère. La classification industrielle des entreprises dans la seconde série de données est la même que celle utilisée pour le nombre de personnes occupées en 1959.

## Gross Domestic Product

The data shown in Table 1 are abstracted from *Comptes économiques et modèles,* published by the Ministère de la Coopération, France, in April 1962, and from *Comptes économiques du Sénégal, Année 1959, supplément au Bulletin statistique et économique mensuel, No. 8,* issued by the Commissariat général au plan — Service de la statistique et de la mécanographie, Sénégal. The figures shown in the former publication were derived from estimates made by the statistical authorities of Senegal. The figures for gross domestic product at factor cost, which is termed "Gross Domestic Production" in that publication, differs in certain respects from that for the gross domestic product at factor cost in the United Nations system of national accounts, mainly in that wages and salaries paid by government and private non-profit organizations are excluded.

## Produit intérieur brut

Les données du tableau 1 sont tirées de *Comptes économiques et modèles,* publié par le Ministère de la Coopération, France, en avril 1962, et de *Comptes économiques du Sénégal, Année 1959, supplément au Bulletin statistique et économique mensuel No. 8,* publié par le Commissariat général au plan — Service de la statistique et de la mécanographie, Sénégal. Les chiffres reproduits dans la première publication ont été tirés d'estimations faites par les services de statistique du Sénégal. Les chiffres relatifs au produit intérieur brut au coût des facteurs appelé "Production intérieure brute" dans cette publication, différent à certains égards de ceux donnant le produit intérieur brut au coût des facteurs tel qu'il est défini dans le système de comptabilité nationale de l'ONU; notamment les traitements et salaires payés par les organismes d'Etat et les organisations privées à but non lucratif en sont exclus.

## Characteristics of Industrial Activity

The figures shown in Table 2 are obtained from *La structure de l'industrie sénégalaise d'après la comptabilité économique, 1959-1960, supplément au Bulletin mensuel de statistique, No. 9.* The data relate to industrial enterprises excluding handicrafts. Value added relates to the contribution to the gross domestic product and is valued at market prices.

## Caractéristiques des activités industrielles

Les chiffres reproduits dans le tableau 2 ont été tirés de *La structure de l'industrie sénégalaise d'après la comptabilité économique 1959-1960, supplément au Bulletin mensuel de statistique No. 9.* Les données concernent les entreprises industrielles à l'exclusion des entreprises artisanales. La valeur ajoutée est définie comme étant la contribution à la formation du produit intérieur brut.

## 1. THE GROSS DOMESTIC PRODUCT — LE PRODUIT INTERIEUR BRUT

Billion Francs C.F.A.                                        Milliards de francs C.F.A.

### A. Expenditure on the Gross Domestic Product at Market Prices
### Dépenses relatives au produit intérieur brut aux prix du marché

| Item of data and year<br>Rubrique et année | Total | Consumption<br>Consommation | | Gross Capital Formation<br>Formation brute de capital intérieur | Net exports of goods and services<br>Exportations nettes de biens et de services | |
| --- | --- | --- | --- | --- | --- | --- |
| | | Total | Government [1]<br>Etat [1] | | Exports<br>less imports<br>Exportations<br>moins<br>importations | Exports<br>Exportations |
| **Absolute figures — Chiffres absolus** | | | | | | |
| 1956 | 112.3 | 105.7 | 24.7 | 10.2 | —3.6 | 40.6 |
| 1959 | 140.7 | 125.2 | 31.1 | 17.0 | —1.5 | 55.5 |
| **Percentage distribution — Distribution en pourcentage** | | | | | | |
| 1956 | 100.0 | 94.1 | 22.0 | 9.1 | —3.2 | 36.2 |
| 1959 | 100.0 | 88.9 | 22.1 | 12.1 | —1.0 | 39.4 |

For footnotes see end of table.                              Pour les notes, voir au bas du tableau.

663

## B.  The Gross Domestic Product According to Origin
### Origine par secteur d'activité du produit intérieur brut

| Item of data and year | Total | Agricultural sector<br><br>Secteur agricole | Mining, manufacturing, electricity, gas and water, and construction<br><br>Industries extractives, manufacturières, électricité, gaz et eau, et bâtiment et travaux publics | Commerce, transportation and communication, and other services<br><br>Commerce, transports et communications, et autres services | Government [1]<br><br>Etat [1] | Rubrique et année |
|---|---|---|---|---|---|---|
| ISIC | 0-9 | 0 | 1-5 | 61-64, 71-73, 83-9 | 81-82 | CITI |
| At market prices | | | | | | Aux prix du marché |
| Absolute figures | | | | | | Chiffres absolus |
| 1956 | 112.3 | 39.2 | 13.2 | 39.1 | 20.8 | 1956 |
| 1959 | 140.7 | 37.7 | 23.2 | 49.8 | 30.0 | 1959 |
| Percentage distribution | | | | | | Distribution en pourcentage |
| 1956 | 100.0 | 34.9 | 11.7 | 34.9 | 18.5 | 1956 |
| 1959 | 100.0 | 26.8 | 16.5 | 35.4 | 21.3 | 1959 |
| At factor cost | | | | | | Au coût des facteurs |
| Absolute figures | | | | | | Chiffres absolus |
| 1956 | 77.3 | 39.2 | 10.5 | 27.6 | . | 1956 |
| 1959 | 89.0 | 37.7 | 17.3 | 34.0 | . | 1959 |
| Percentage distribution | | | | | | Distribution en pourcentage |
| 1956 | 100.0 | 50.7 | 13.6 | 35.7 | . | 1956 |
| 1959 | 100.0 | 42.4 | 19.4 | 38.2 | . | 1959 |

[1] Includes public administration and defense, government agencies and organizations furnishing educational, health and similar services, and private non-profit organizations furnishing services to households except private schools and hospitals. Excludes government enterprises.

[1] Y compris les administrations publiques et la défense nationale, et les services de l'Etat et organisations tels que l'enseignement, la santé et les autres services similaires, et les institutions pirvées à but non lucratif fournissant des services aux ménages à l'exclusion des écoles et hopitaux privés. Non compris les entreprises de l'Etat.

## 2.  CHARACTERISTICS OF INDUSTRIAL ENTERPRISES, EXCEPT HANDICRAFTS
### CARACTERISTIQUES DES ENTREPRISES INDUSTRIELLES, A L'EXCLUSION DE L'ARTISANAT
### 1959

Number of enterprises in units; value added in million Francs C.F.A.　　　　Nombre d'entreprises en unités; valeur ajoutée en millions de francs C.F.A.

| Item of data | Total | Mining, coal and petroleum products, and electricity, gas and water<br><br>Industries extractives, dérivés du charbon et du pétrole, et électricité, gaz et eau | Total [1] | Food, beverages and tobacco<br><br>Industries alimentaires, boissons, tabac | Textiles, clothing, footwear and made-up textiles and leather products<br><br>Textiles, articles d'habillement, chaussures et ouvrages en tissu et cuir et articles en cuir | Wood products and furniture<br><br>Bois et meubles | Printing and publishing<br><br>Imprimerie et édition | Chemicals and chemical products<br><br>Produits chimiques | Basic metals and metal products<br><br>Métallurgie de base et ouvrages en métaux | Non-metallic mineral products and construction<br><br>Produits minéraux non métalliques et bâtiment et travaux publics | Rubrique |
|---|---|---|---|---|---|---|---|---|---|---|---|
| ISIC | 1-521 | 1, 32, 511-521 | 2-3 | 20-22 | 23, 24, 29 | 25-26 | 28 | 31 | 34-38 | 33, 40 | CITI |
| Number of enterprises | 320 | 14 | 181 | 66 | 26 | 20 | 15 | 9 | 45 | 125 | Nombre d'entreprises |
| Value added | 17 614 | 2 155 | 11 726 | 9 294 | 1 118 | 293 | 336 | 249 | 436 | 3 733 | Valeur ajoutée |
| Distribution in percent of value added | 100.0 | 12.2 | 66.6 | 52.8 | 6.3 | 1.7 | 1.9 | 1.4 | 2.5 | 21.2 | Distribution en pourcentage de la valeur ajoutée |

Selected Major Groups of Manufacturing — Quelques classes de la branche Industries manufacturières

[1] Excludes Non-metallic mineral products (ISIC major group 33) and Petroleum and coal products (ISIC major group 32).

[1] Non compris produits minéraux non métalliques (CITI classe 33) et dérivés du pétrole et du charbon (CITI classe 32).

# SINGAPORE — SINGAPOUR

## Index Numbers of Industrial Employment

The index numbers of industrial employment presented in Table 1 have been compiled by the Statistical Office of the United Nations based on absolute figures of the number of operatives employed. These figures have been collected by the Labour Department for the 29th March and the 30th September of each year and published in the *Annual Report of the Labour Department 1957 and 1958*. The figures can also be found in *Digest of Economic and Social Statistics (State of Singapore and Federation of Malaya)* which was published monthly up to December 1962 and in its successor publication for Singapore only, the *Monthly Digest of Statistics* published by the Department of Statistics, Singapore.

The absolute figures of the number of operatives are, in principle, for all industrial establishments. The annual absolute figures of the number of operatives used as the basis for the index are the arithmetic averages of the number as on the 29th March and the 30th September of each year in all establishments in Singapore. However in 1952, only the figures as on the 30th September are available. These figures have been linked to the series at 1953 by means of the figures as at the 30th September 1953.

The indexes for mining as a whole, for manufacturing as a whole and for mining, manufacturing and electricity combined are based on the unweighted aggregated absolute figures of their constituent major groups.

## The Characteristics and Structure of Industrial Activity

The data presented in Table 2 are derived from the results of the Census of Industrial Production 1959. The Statistical Office of the United Nations has received these results by letter from the Department of Statistics, Singapore.

The Census covered private industrial establishments employing 10 persons or more. It excluded all government industrial activity including statutory boards and establishments of the armed services.

## Indices de l'emploi dans l'industrie

Les indices de l'emploi dans l'industrie, présentés au tableau 1, ont été calculés par le Bureau de statistique de l'ONU à partir de chiffres absolus indiquant l'effectif des ouvriers. Ces chiffres ont été recueillis par le Département du travail aux 29 mars et 30 septembre de chaque année, et publiés dans *Annual Report of the Labour Department 1957 and 1958*. Ces chiffres figurent également dans *Digest of Economic and Social Statistics (State of Singapore and Federation of Malaya)*, qui a été publié tous les mois jusqu'en décembre 1962, et dans la publication qui lui a succédé concernant Singapour seulement, le *Monthly Digest of Statistics*, publié par le Département de la statistique, Singapour.

Les chiffres absolus indiquant le nombre d'ouvriers concernent, en principe, tous les établissements industriels. Les chiffres absolus annuels relatifs au nombre d'ouvriers que l'on a utilisés pour le calcul des indices sont les moyennes arithmétiques du nombre d'ouvriers aux 29 mars et 30 septembre de chaque année dans tous les établissements de Singapour. Pour 1952, cependant, on ne disposait que des chiffres relevés au 30 septembre. Ces chiffres ont été raccordés aux séries, au niveau de 1953, au moyen des chiffres relatifs au 30 septembre 1953.

Les indices relatifs à l'ensemble des industries extractives, à l'ensemble des industries manufacturières, et à l'ensemble des industries extractives, manufacturières et productrices d'électricité sont fondés sur les totaux non pondérés des chiffres absolus concernant les classes de ces branches d'activité.

## Caractéristiques et structure de l'activité industrielle

Les données du tableau 2 sont tirées des résultats du recensement de la production industrielle de 1959. Le Département de la statistique, Singapour, a communiqué ces résultats au Bureau de statistique de l'ONU par voie de correspondance.

Le recensement portait sur les établissements industriels du secteur privé occupant 10 salariés ou plus. En étaient exclues toutes les activités industrielles du secteur public, y compris les organismes créés en vertu d'une loi et les établissements relevant des services armés.

## 1. INDEX NUMBERS OF INDUSTRIAL EMPLOYMENT — INDICES DE L'EMPLOI DANS L'INDUSTRIE

### A. The Divisions of Industrial Activity
### Les branches de l'activité industrielle

| Period<br>Période | Total [1] | Mining [2]<br>Industries<br>extractives [2] | Manu-<br>facturing<br>Industries<br>manu-<br>facturières | Construction<br>Bâtiment<br>et travaux<br>publics | Electricity<br>and gas<br>Electricité<br>et gaz |
|---|---|---|---|---|---|
| ISIC — CITI | 1-3, 511-512 | 1 | 2-3 | 4 | 511–512 |

#### a. Indexes — Indices (1958 = 100)

| | | | | | |
|---|---|---|---|---|---|
| 1952....... | 103 | 89 | 103 | 134 | 72 |
| 1953....... | 107 | 82 | 107 | 122 | 91 |
| 1954....... | 112 | 87 | 112 | 133 | 102 |
| 1955....... | 107 | 82 | 106 | 126 | 97 |
| 1956....... | 111 | 101 | 110 | 112 | 99 |
| 1957....... | 108 | 105 | 106 | 112 | 104 |
| 1958....... | 100 | 100 | 100 | 100 | 100 |
| 1959....... | 92 | 78 | 92 | 82 | 103 |
| 1960....... | 86 | 79 | 86 | 66 | 98 |
| 1961....... | 88 | 64 | 88 | 82 | 97 |

#### b. Average Annual Rate of Change — Taux annuel moyen de variation

| | | | | | |
|---|---|---|---|---|---|
| 1954 – 1958. | −2.8 | 3.5 | −2.8 | −6.9 | −0.5 |
| 1958 – 1960. | −7.3 | −11.1 | −7.3 | −18.8 | −1.0 |

### B. The Major Groups of Manufacturing — Les classes de la branche Industries manufacturières

| Period<br>Période | Manu-<br>facturing<br>Industries<br>manufac-<br>turières | Food,<br>beverages<br>and<br>tobacco<br>Industries<br>alimen-<br>taires,<br>boissons,<br>tabac | Textiles<br>Textiles | Clothing,<br>footwear<br>and<br>made-up<br>textiles<br>Articles<br>d'habil-<br>lement,<br>chaussures<br>et<br>ouvrages<br>en tissu | Wood<br>products<br>and<br>furniture<br>Bois et<br>meubles | Paper<br>and<br>paper<br>products<br>Papier<br>et<br>ouvrages<br>en<br>papier | Printing<br>and<br>publishing<br>Im-<br>primerie<br>et<br>édition | Leather<br>and<br>leather<br>products<br>except<br>wearing<br>apparel<br>Cuir et<br>articles<br>en cuir,<br>à l'exclu-<br>sion<br>des<br>articles<br>d'habil-<br>lement | Rubber<br>products<br>Ouvrages<br>en<br>caout-<br>chouc | Chemicals<br>and<br>chemical,<br>petroleum<br>and<br>coal<br>products<br>Produits<br>chi-<br>miques<br>et<br>dérivés<br>du<br>pétrole<br>et du<br>charbon | Non-<br>metallic<br>mineral<br>products<br>Produits<br>minéraux<br>non<br>métal-<br>liques | Basic<br>metals<br>Métal-<br>lurgie<br>de base | Metal<br>products<br>Ouvrages<br>en<br>métaux | Other<br>manu-<br>facturing<br>Autres<br>industries<br>manufac-<br>turières |
|---|---|---|---|---|---|---|---|---|---|---|---|---|---|---|
| ISIC — CITI | 2-3 | 20–22 | 23 | 24 | 25–26 | 27 | 28 | 29 | 30 | 31–32 | 33 | 34 | 35–38 | 39 |

#### a. Indexes — Indices (1958 = 100)

| | | | | | | | | | | | | | | |
|---|---|---|---|---|---|---|---|---|---|---|---|---|---|---|
| 1952............. | 103 | 97 | 44 | 70 | 102 | 60 | 82 | 76 | 158 | 154 | 94 | 137 | 96 | 93 |
| 1953............. | 107 | 103 | 102 | 76 | 113 | 73 | 85 | 113 | 143 | 136 | 84 | 132 | 104 | 110 |
| 1954............. | 112 | 109 | 92 | 80 | 112 | 95 | 91 | 123 | 147 | 112 | 103 | 117 | 110 | 107 |
| 1955............. | 106 | 103 | 136 | 85 | 105 | 103 | 94 | 110 | 135 | 113 | 117 | 116 | 102 | 96 |
| 1956............. | 110 | 101 | 116 | 111 | 112 | 112 | 103 | 126 | 130 | 111 | 122 | 132 | 105 | 104 |
| 1957............. | 106 | 103 | 111 | 108 | 103 | 102 | 104 | 102 | 120 | 106 | 109 | 121 | 104 | 105 |
| 1958............. | 100 | 100 | 100 | 100 | 100 | 100 | 100 | 100 | 100 | 100 | 100 | 100 | 100 | 100 |
| 1959............. | 92 | 98 | 98 | 86 | 84 | 87 | 97 | 92 | 87 | 93 | 95 | 81 | 93 | 79 |
| 1960............. | 86 | 94 | 82 | 71 | 71 | 94 | 96 | 89 | 77 | 96 | 77 | 83 | 91 | 47 |
| 1961............. | 88 | 100 | 92 | 72 | 73 | 109 | 99 | 128 | 78 | 85 | 90 | 77 | 91 | 45 |

#### b. Average Annual Rate of Change — Taux annuel moyen de variation

| | | | | | | | | | | | | | | |
|---|---|---|---|---|---|---|---|---|---|---|---|---|---|---|
| 1954 – 1958....... | −2.8 | −2.1 | 2.1 | 5.7 | −2.8 | 1.3 | 2.4 | −5.0 | −9.2 | −2.8 | −0.7 | −3.8 | −2.4 | −1.7 |
| 1958 – 1960....... | −7.3 | −3.0 | −9.4 | −15.7 | −15.7 | −3.0 | −2.0 | −5.7 | −12.2 | −2.0 | −12.2 | −8.9 | −4.6 | −31.4 |

[1] Excludes construction (ISIC division 4).
[2] Includes Other mining (ISIC major groups 14-19) only.

[1] Non compris Bâtiment et travaux publics (CITI branche 4).
[2] Il s'agit exclusivement de Autres industries extractives (CITI classes 14-19).

## 2. CHARACTERISTICS OF PRIVATE INDUSTRIAL ESTABLISHMENTS WITH 10 EMPLOYEES OR MORE

## CARACTERISTIQUES DES ETABLISSEMENTS INDUSTRIELS PRIVES AYANT 10 SALARIES OU PLUS

### 1959

Number of establishments in units; value added and wages and salaries in million Malay Dollars; number of employees in thousands; value added per employee and wages and salaries per employee in thousand Malay Dollars.

Nombre d'établissements en unités; valeur ajoutée et traitements et salaires en millions de dollars malais; nombre de salariés en milliers; valeur ajoutée par salarié et traitements et salaires par salarié en milliers de dollars malais.

### A. The Divisions of Industrial Activitiy — Les branches de l'activité industrielle

| Item of data | Total | Mining [1] Industries ex-tractives [1] | Manu-facturing Industries manu-facturières | Rubrique | Item of data | Total | Mining [1] Industries ex-tractives [1] | Manu-facturing Industries manu-facturières | Rubrique |
|---|---|---|---|---|---|---|---|---|---|
| ISIC | 1-3 | 1 | 2-3 | CITI | ISIC | 1-3 | 1 | 2-3 | CITI |
| | a. Absolute Figures Chiffres absolus | | | | | b. Structure | | | |
| Number of establishments...... | 564 | 10 | 554 | Nombre d'établissements | Distribution in percent of: | | | | Distribution en pourcentage: |
| Value added................ | 159.2 | 2.4 | 156.8 | Valeur ajoutée | Value added................ | 100.0 | 1.5 | 98.5 | Valeur ajoutée |
| Employees: | | | | Salariés: | Number of employees........ | 100.0 | 1.9 | 98.1 | Nombre de salariés |
| Number.................. | 31.6 | 0.6 | 31.0 | Nombre | Per employee: | | | | Par salarié: |
| Wages and salaries.......... | 70.5 | 1.5 | 69.0 | Traitements et salaires | Value added................ | 5.0 | 4.0 | 5.0 | Valeur ajoutée |
| | | | | | Wages and salaries.......... | 2.2 | 2.5 | 2.2 | Traitements et salaires |
| | | | | | Value added per unit of wages and salaries.......... | 2.26 | 1.60 | 2.27 | Valeur ajoutée par unité de traitements et salaires |

For footnotes see end of table.

Pour les notes, voir au bas du tableau.

### B. The Major Groups of Manufacturing — Les classes de la branche Industries manufacturières

| Item of data | Manu-facturing Industries manufac-turières | Food beverages and tobacco Industries alimen-taires, boissons, tabac | Textiles, clothing, footwear and made-up textiles [2] Textiles, articles d'habil-lement, chaus-sures et ouvrages en tissu [2] | Wood products and furniture Bois et meubles | Paper and paper products Papier et ouvrages en papier | Printing and publish-ing Im-primerie et édition | Rubber products Ouvrages en caout-chouc | Chemicals and chemical, petroleum and coal products Produits chi-miques et dérivés du pétrole et du charbon | Non-metallic mineral products Produits minéraux non métal-liques | Basic metals Métal-lurgie de base | Metal products Ouvrages en métaux | Other manu-factur-ing Autres in-dustries manufac-turières | Rubrique |
|---|---|---|---|---|---|---|---|---|---|---|---|---|---|
| ISIC | 2-3 | 20-22 | 23-24,29 | 25-26 | 27 | 28 | 30 | 31-32 | 33 | 34 | 35-38 | 39 | CITI |
| | a. Absolute Figures — Chiffres absolus | | | | | | | | | | | | |
| Number of establishments | 554 | 129 | 31 | 48 | 10 | 87 | 36 | 32 | 23 | 11 | 129 | 18 | Nombre d'établissements |
| Value added.......... | 156.8 | 41.0 | 3.7 | 10.8 | 1.5 | 22.4 | 16.7 | 9.4 | 9.5 | 1.9 | 38.3 | 1.6 | Valeur ajoutée |
| Employees: | | | | | | | | | | | | | Salariés: |
| Number............. | 31.0 | 6.1 | 1.2 | 2.8 | 0.3 | 3.5 | 6.3 | 1.4 | 2.3 | 0.6 | 6.1 | 0.4 | Nombre |
| Wages and salaries... | 69.0 | 12.6 | 2.3 | 6.8 | 0.5 | 8.7 | 11.5 | 2.8 | 5.4 | 1.2 | 16.5 | 0.7 | Traitements et salaires |
| | b. Structure | | | | | | | | | | | | |
| Distribution in percent of: | | | | | | | | | | | | | Distribution en pour-centage: |
| Value added........ | 100.0 | 26.1 | 2.4 | 6.9 | 1.0 | 14.3 | 10.6 | 6.0 | 6.1 | 1.2 | 24.4 | 1.0 | Valeur ajoutée |
| Number of employees. | 100.0 | 19.7 | 3.9 | 9.0 | 1.0 | 11.3 | 20.3 | 4.5 | 7.4 | 1.9 | 19.7 | 1.3 | Nombre de salariés |
| Per employee: | | | | | | | | | | | | | Par salarié: |
| Value added........ | 5.0 | 6.7 | 3.1 | 3.8 | 5.0 | 6.4 | 2.6 | 6.7 | 4.1 | 3.2 | 6.3 | 4.0 | Valeur ajoutée |
| Wages and salaries... | 2.2 | 2.1 | 1.9 | 2.4 | 1.7 | 2.5 | 1.8 | 2.0 | 2.3 | 2.0 | 2.7 | 1.8 | Traitements et salaires |
| Value added per unit of wages and salaries............ | 2.27 | 3.25 | 1.61 | 1.59 | 3.00 | 2.57 | 1.45 | 3.36 | 1.76 | 1.58 | 2.32 | 2.28 | Valeur ajoutée par unité de traitements et salaires |

[1] Consists of granite quarrying (part of ISIC major group 14) only.
[2] Includes Leather and leather products except wearing apparel (ISIC major group 29).

[1] Extraction du granit (dans CITI classe 14) seulement.
[2] Y compris Cuir et articles en cuir, à l'exclusion des articles d'habillement (CITI classe 29).

## SOUTH AFRICA — AFRIQUE DU SUD

### Domestic Product

Estimates of the expenditure on the gross domestic product and the origin of the net domestic product are presented in Table 1. The table is derived from data supplied by the South African Reserve Bank, Pretoria, and the Bureau of Census and Statistics in response to the United Nations national accounts questionnaire. The basic data for the first part of the table concerning the expenditure on the gross domestic product have been compiled by the South African Reserve Bank and is published in its *Quarterly Bulletin of Statistics*. These figures refer to the Republic of South Africa, South West Africa, Swaziland, Basutoland and Bechuanaland. The basic data for the second part of the table concerning the origin of the net domestic product have been compiled by Bureau of Census and Statistics and is published annually in its *Quarterly Bulletin of Statistics*. *National Accounts Memorandum No. 13* contains descriptions of the sources and methods which have been utilized. The figures in this case refer to the Republic of South Africa only.

It should be noted that the data in Table 1 are given in Rands whilst the values in Tables 4 and 5 are given in Pounds. One Pound equals 2 Rands. The Republic of South Africa made this currency change on 14 February 1961.

### Index Numbers of Industrial Production

The index numbers of industrial production presented in Table 2 have been derived from various sources.

The index numbers for manufacturing have been derived from three series of index numbers which have been linked together to make up the series presented here. In the case of the years, 1948 to 1953, and 1957 onwards the indexes are based on index numbers of manufacturing production compiled by the South African Bureau of Census and Statistics. The indexes used for the years, 1948 to 1953, have originally been published on a base 1952 = 100 by the Bureau in *Union Statistics for Fifty Years—Jubilee Issue 1910-1960*. These indexes have been based on the results of the Annual Industrial Censuses. Indexes derived from the quantities of production of the individual products have been combined into index numbers for major groups and these major group indexes into indexes for manufacturing as a whole using as weights the value added (valued less subsidies and less excise duties) derived from the Annual Industrial Censuses. The indexes have been computed initially as moving weight and comparison base arithmetic averages which have then been chained to one another. The weight and preliminary comparison base for the index in each year is the preceding year.

### Produit intérieur

Le tableau 1 contient des estimations des dépenses imputées au produit intérieur brut et des estimations du produit intérieur net par secteur d'activité d'origine. Ce tableau est établi à partir de données fournies par la South African Reserve Bank, Pretoria, et le Bureau of Census and Statistics en réponse au questionnaire de l'ONU sur la comptabilité nationale. Les données de base utilisées pour la première partie du tableau concernant les dépenses imputées au produit intérieur brut ont été élaborées par la South African Reserve Bank et sont publiées dans son *Quarterly Bulletin of Statistics*. Ces chiffres concernent la République sud-africaine, le Sud-Ouest africain, la Souaziland, le Bassoutoland et le Betchouanaland. Les données de base utilisées pour la seconde partie du tableau concernant le produit intérieur brut par secteur d'activité d'origine ont été établies par le Bureau of Census and Statistics et sont publiées annuellement dans son *Quarterly Bulletin of Statistics*. Le *National Accounts Memorandum No. 13* contient une description des sources et méthodes adoptées. Les chiffres qui y sont indiqués ne concernent que la République sud-africaine.

Il y a lieu de noter que les chiffres du tableau 1 sont exprimés en rands, tandis que, dans les tableaux 4 et 5 les valeurs sont exprimées en livres. Une livre équivaut à 2 rands. La République sud-africaine a opéré ce changement de monnaie le 14 février 1961.

### Indices de la production industrielle

Les indices de la production industrielle présentés au tableau 2 sont tirés de sources diverses.

Les indices relatifs aux industries manufacturières ont été tirés de trois séries d'indices qui, raccordées les unes aux autres, ont fourni les séries présentées ici. Pour les années 1948 à 1953 et pour 1957 et les années suivantes, les indices sont fondés sur des indices de la production manufacturière calculés par le South African Bureau of Census and Statistics. Les indices des années 1948 à 1953 avaient été publiés initialement par le Bureau, sur la base 1952 = 100, dans *Union Statistics for Fifty years — Jubilee Issue 1910-1960*. Ces indices étaient fondés sur les résultats des recensements industriels annuels. Les indices construits à partir des quantités produites de chaque marchandise ont été combinés en indices de classe et ceux-ci en indices relatifs à l'ensemble des industries manufacturières, les coefficients de pondération utilisés étant les valeurs ajoutées (non compris les subventions et les impôts indirects) fournies par les recensements industriels annuels. Les indices étaient initialement des moyennes arithmétiques à bases de pondération et de comparaison variables, que l'on a ensuite raccordées les unes aux autres. La base de pondération et la base initiale de comparaison étaient, pour les indices de chaque année, l'année précédente.

The indexes used for 1957 and later years have been shown annually since 1956-57 and monthly since January 1961 on a base of 1956-57 = 100 and have been published periodically in *Statistical News Release* by the Bureau. These indexes have also been computed initially as moving weight and comparison base arithmetic averages which have then been chained to one another. The major group indexes have been combined into indexes for total manufacturing using as weights the value added in the base period derived from the results of the Annual Industrial Censuses.

In order to complete the indexes published here for the missing years 1938, and 1954 to 1957, the Statistical Office of the United Nations has compiled and linked to the abovementioned indexes at 1948, 1953 and 1957 indexes of manufacturing production based on data of the quantity of production of individual items derived from the results of the Annual Industrial Censuses.

The basic data on which these manufacturing indexes have been based refers to private manufacturing establishments and public corporations.

The index numbers for mining have been compiled by the Statistical Office of the United Nations based on the quantities of production for individual minerals. This production data has been published by the Bureau of Census and Statistics in *Union Statistics for Fifty Years* and the most recent figures in *Monthly Bulletin of Statistics*. The indexes based on the individual product data have been combined where necessary into indexes for major groups and these major group indexes into index numbers for mining as a whole using as weights, the gross value of sales in 1953 for the years up to 1955 and in 1958 for the years after 1955. The two series were then linked at 1955.

### Index Numbers of Industrial Employment

The index numbers of industrial employment presented in Table 3 have been compiled by the Statistical Office of the United Nations based on absolute figures of the number of employees and persons engaged.

In the case of mining the absolute figures of the daily average number of employees for all mines have been compiled by the Department of Mines and published in its *Annual Report;* since 1955 the data have also been published by the Bureau of Census and Statistics in the *Monthly Bulletin of Statistics*.

In the case of the manufacturing, construction and electricity indexes up to 1959, the absolute figures of the annual average number of persons engaged have been derived from the results of the Annual Industrial Censuses described under Table 4. For 1956 and the following years the Censuses confined their coverage to private industrial establishments only, and the indexes based on

Les indices utilisés pour 1957 et les années suivantes ont été reproduits annuellement à partir de 1956-1957 et mensuellement à partir de janvier 1961 sur la base de 1956-1957 = 100; ils ont été publiés périodiquement par le Bureau dans *Statistical News Release*. Ces indices étaient aussi, initialement, des moyennes arithmétiques à bases de pondération et de comparaison variables, que l'on a ensuite raccordées les unes aux autres. Les indices de classe ont été combinés en indices relatifs à l'ensemble des industries manufacturières, les coefficients de pondération utilisés étant les valeurs ajoutées pendant la période de base fournies par les recensements industriels annuels.

Afin de compléter, pour les années manquantes 1938 et 1954 à 1957, les séries d'indices publiés ici, le Bureau de statistique de l'ONU a calculé des indices de la production manufacturière d'après les données sur les quantités produites de chaque marchandise fournies par les résultats des recensements industriels annuels, puis il a raccordé ces indices aux indices ci-dessus mentionnés au niveau de 1948, 1953 et 1957.

Les données de base sur lesquelles sont fondés ces indices relatifs aux industries manufacturières se rapportent aux établissements manufacturiers privés et aux sociétés publiques.

Les indices relatifs aux industries extractives ont été calculés par le Bureau de statistique de l'ONU d'après les quantités produites de chaque substance minérale. Ces données sur la production ont été publiées par le Bureau of Census and Statistics dans *Union Statistics for Fifty Years* et les chiffres les plus récents dans le *Monthly Bulletin of Statistics*. Les indices fondés sur les données concernant chaque produit ont été combinés, le cas échéant, en indices de classe et ceux-ci en indices relatifs à l'ensemble des industries extractives, les coefficients de pondération utilisés étant les valeurs brutes des ventes en 1953 pour 1955 et les années antérieures, et en 1958 pour les années postérieures à 1955. Les deux séries d'indices ont été raccordées au niveau de 1955.

### Indices de l'emploi dans l'industrie

Les indices de l'emploi dans l'industrie présentés au tableau 3 ont été calculés par le Bureau de statistique de l'ONU et sont fondés sur des chiffres absolus concernant le nombre de salariés et de personnes occupées.

Dans le cas des industries extractives, les chiffres absolus concernant le nombre journalier moyen de salariés dans toutes les mines ont été calculés par le Département des mines et publiés dans son *Annual Report;* depuis 1955, ces données sont également publiées par le Bureau of Census and Statistics dans le *Monthly Bulletin of Statistics*.

Dans le cas des indices concernant les industries manufacturières, le bâtiment et les travaux publics et l'électricité jusqu'en 1959, les chiffres absolus indiquant le nombre annuel moyen de personnes occupées ont été tirés des résultats des recensements industriels annuels décrits dans le commentaire du tableau 4. Pour 1956 et les années suivantes, les recensements portaient sur les

the results of these Censuses have been linked where necessary, to the earlier indexes at 1956.

For the years 1959 and later—1955 and later in the case of Rubber products (ISIC major group 30) and Metal products (ISIC major group 35-38)—the indexes have been based on the absolute figures of the monthly average of the number of employees in private industry. These absolute figures have been derived from monthly figures resulting from a sample survey conducted by the Bureau and published in the *Monthly Bulletin of Statistics*. The sample, consisting of about 1700 establishments, has been drawn from a field stratified according to major group of industrial activity and size, determined by the average annual number of employees. The establishments selected from each strata to make up the sample covered in almost every case at least 60 percent of the total employees in each strata, based on the 1953-1954 Annual Industrial Census. The sample used has been revised every two years.

The indexes for total mining, total manufacturing and mining, manufacturing construction and electricity combined are derived from the aggregated unweighted absolute figures of their constituent major groups and divisions.

### The Characteristics and Structure of Industrial Activity

The data set out in Tables 4 and 5 are derived from the results of the annual Censuses taken by the Bureau of Census and Statistics, Pretoria, that have been published in *Census of Industrial Establishments, 1937-1938* or *1947-1948, Thirty-sixth Industrial Census, 1952-1953 (Preliminary Report)* and in *Industrial Censuses, 1956-1957 and 1957-1958, Special Report No. 229.* Certain details have been provided to the Statistical Office of the United Nations in correspondence.

The data presented in Table 4 relates to both public corporations and private industrial establishments, whilst the data presented in Table 5 relates to private industrial establishments only, except in the case of electricity (ISIC group 511) in which case public establishments have also been covered. In all cases the establishments covered are restricted to those engaging three or more persons or utilizing power equipment.

In the case of all Censuses, particularly for the major groups of manufacturing, there are some minor differences leading to incomparability resulting from differences between the schemes of industrial classification utilized in tabulating the results of the Censuses. In addition, in the case of the 1957-1958 Census, a number of activities previously included in the Censuses were omitted entirely. The most important of these were all activities connected with the motor industry, the assembling and repair of motor vehicles (part of ISIC major group 38), and the manufacture of motor-vehicle tires part of ISIC major group 30). In addition a number of minor

établissements industriels privés seulement, et les indices fondés sur les résultats de ces recensement ont été raccordés, le cas échéant, aux indices des années antérieures au niveau de 1956.

Pour 1959 et les années suivantes – 1955 et les années suivantes dans le cas des Ouvrages en caoutchouc (CITI classe 30) et des Ouvrages en métaux (CITI classes 35-38) – les indices ont été calculés d'après les chiffres absolus concernant la moyenne mensuelle du nombre de salariés dans l'industrie privée. Ces chiffres absolus ont été tirés de chiffres mensuels fournis par une enquête par sondage qui a été exécutée par le Bureau et dont les résultats ont été publiés dans le *Monthly Bulletin of Statistics*. L'échantillon, qui comprend 1 700 établissements, a été tiré d'une population stratifiée selon les classes de l'activité industrielle et la taille de l'établissement, c'est-à-dire le nombre annuel moyen de salariés. Les salariés des établissements choisis dans chaque strate pour constituer l'échantillon représentaient, dans presque tous les cas 60 p. 100 au moins du total des salariés de chaque strate indiqué par le recensement industriel annuel de 1953-1954. L'échantillon utilisé a été revisé tous les deux ans.

Les indices relatifs à l'ensemble des industries extractives, à l'ensemble des industries extractives et manufacturières et à l'ensemble constitué par les industries manufacturières, le bâtiment et les travaux publics et l'électricité sont fondés sur les totaux non pondérés des chiffres absolus concernant les classes ou les branches qui composent ces ensembles.

### Caractéristiques et structure de l'activité industrielle

Les chiffres des tableaux 4 et 5 sont tirés des résultats des recensements annuels effectués par le Bureau of Census and Statistics, Pretoria; ces résultats ont été publiés dans *Census of Industrial Establishments, 1937-1938* ou *1947-1948, Thirty-sixth Industrial Census, 1952-1953 (Preliminary Report)* et *Industrial Censuses, 1956-1957 and 1957-1958, Special Report No. 229.* Certains détails ont été communiqués par correspondance au Bureau de statistique de l'ONU.

Les données du tableau 4 portent sur les sociétés publiques et les établissements industriels privés, tandis que les données du tableau 5 se rapportent aux établissements industriels privés seulement, sauf dans le cas de l'électricité (CITI groupe 511), où les établissements publics sont également compris. Dans tous les cas, les données ne concernent que les établissements occupant au moins trois personnes ou utilisant la force motrice.

Dans tous les recensements, notamment pour les classes des industries manufacturières, on constate un défaut de comparabilité dû à de légères différences provenant des écarts existant entre les nomenclatures industrielles utilisées pour l'exploitation des résultats des recensements. De plus, dans le cas du recensement de 1957-1958, un certain nombre d'activités incluses dans les recensements précédents ont été entièrement omises, notamment toutes celles qui concernent l'industrie des moteurs, l'assemblage et la réparation des véhicules automobiles (dans CITI classe 38) et la fabrication des pneumatiques pour véhicules automobiles (dans CITI classe 30). En outre,

activities as follows were also excluded; manufacturing mainly for consumption on the premises (e.g. ice cream made in cafes), custom grain milling and sawmilling carried out by individual farms or retail stores for their own convenience; repair and service work carried out by commercial establishments such as bicycle shops; jewellers and outfitters, and finally cold storage used for storage only and not in connection with manufacture.

The footnotes to Tables 4 and 5 indicate the main inconsistencies of classification and scope and a comparison of data between years should only be undertaken with care. It should also be noted that in the case of the Censuses for 1937-1938, 1947-1948 and 1952-1953 the data relates to financial years of the establishments ending in 1938, 1948 and 1953. However, in the case of the 1957-1958 Census the data relate to the financial years ending between 1st July 1957 and 30th June 1958.

The definitions of the items of data shown in both tables were the same in the four Censuses and, except for the exclusion of the merchandising activities of industrial establishments from the figures of value added, are consistent with the International Standards in Basic Industrial Statistics. The statistical unit was the establishment in the case of manufacturing but the firm in the case of the construction and electricity and gas industries. The figures of value added exclude excise duties and subsidies. The capacity of installed (in use and in reserve) power equipment is the sum of the rated horsepower of all prime movers and electric motors driven by purchased electricity. In the case of the electricity industry, only prime movers are included.

un certain nombre d'activités peu importantes ont été exclues : les industries manufacturières de produits destinés essentiellement à être consommés sur place (par exemple les glaces préparées dans les cafés); les travaux de minoterie ou de scierie effectués par des fermes ou des magasins de détail pour satisfaire leurs propres besoins; les réparations et les travaux d'entretien effectués par des établissements commerciaux tels que les ateliers de réparation de cycles; les bijouteries, les magasins de vêtement et, enfin, les entrepôts frigorifiques utilisés pour l'emmagasinage seulement et non dans le cadre de la production.

Les notes des tableaux 4 et 5 indiquent les principales incohérences concernant la classification et le champ et il faut procéder avec prudence si l'on veut comparer les données d'une année à l'autre. Il y a lieu de noter également que, dans le cas des recensements de 1937-1938, 1947-1948 et 1952-1953, les données se rapportent aux exercices financiers des établissements se terminant en 1938, 1948 et 1953 respectivement. Cependant, pour le recensement de 1957-1958, les données se rapportent aux exercices financiers se terminant entre le 1er juillet 1957 et le 30 juin 1958.

Les définitions des rubriques figurant dans les deux tableaux ont été les mêmes au cours des quatre recensements et elles sont compatibles avec les Normes internationales relatives aux statistiques industrielles de base, si ce n'est que les recettes tirées de la revente de marchandises en l'état par les établissements industriels ne sont pas comprises dans la valeur ajoutée. L'unité statistique était l'établissement dans le cas des industries manufacturières, mais la société dans le cas du bâtiment et des travaux publics et des industries de l'électricité et du gaz. Les chiffres de la valeur ajoutée ne comprennent ni les droits et impôts indirects, ni les subventions. La puissance installée (en service et en réserve) correspond à la puissance nominale de tous les moteurs primaires et des moteurs électriques actionnés par de l'électricité achetée. Dans le cas de l'industrie de l'électricité, seuls les moteurs primaires sont inclus.

# SOUTH AFRICA

## 1. THE DOMESTIC PRODUCT — PRODUIT INTERIEUR

Million Rands                                                                Millions de rands

### A. Expenditure on the Gross Domestic Product at Market Prices
### Dépenses relatives au produit intérieur brut aux prix du marché

In addition to the Republic of South Africa this table includes South West Africa and the three British Protectorates: Swaziland, Basutoland and Bechuanaland.

En plus de la République Sud-africaine, ce tableau se rapporte au Sud-Ouest africain et aux trois protectorats britanniques: le Souaziland, le Bassoutoland et le Betchouanaland.

| Item of data and year / Rubrique et année | Total | Consumption / Consommation | | Gross Domestic Capital Formation / Formation brute de capital intérieur | | Net exports of goods and services / Exportations nettes de biens et de services | |
|---|---|---|---|---|---|---|---|
| | | Total | Government / Etat | Total | Fixed / Fixe | Exports less imports / Exportations moins importations | Exports / Exportations |
| | | | | At Current Prices — Aux prix courants | | | |
| **Absolute figures — Chiffres absolus** | | | | | | | |
| 1948.................................... | 2 034 | 1 754 | 233 | 559 | 470 | —279 | 550 |
| 1950.................................... | 2 581 | 1 956 | 270 | 546 | 541 | 79 | 801 |
| 1951.................................... | 2 849 | 2 180 | 315 | 800 | 635 | —131 | 959 |
| 1952.................................... | 3 128 | 2 483 | 358 | 676 | 787 | —31 | 972 |
| 1953.................................... | 3 567 | 2 731 | 387 | 864 | 874 | —28 | 992 |
| 1954.................................... | 3 860 | 2 870 | 394 | 951 | 891 | 39 | 1 089 |
| 1955.................................... | 4 127 | 3 088 | 421 | 979 | 862 | 60 | 1 210 |
| 1956.................................... | 4 510 | 3 351 | 474 | 990 | 882 | 169 | 1 341 |
| 1957.................................... | 4 756 | 3 533 | 495 | 1 066 | 956 | 157 | 1 464 |
| 1958.................................... | 4 915 | 3 807 | 529 | 1 094 | 1 069 | 14 | 1 332 |
| 1959.................................... | 5 197 | 3 924 | 557 | 939 | 1 038 | 334 | 1 501 |
| 1960.................................... | 5 520 | 4 160 | 601 | 1 140 | 1 101 | 220 | 1 532 |
| 1961.................................... | 5 703 | 4 190 | 664 | 1 092 | 1 113 | 421 | 1 627 |
| **Percentage distribution of average annual expenditure — Distribution en pourcentage des dépenses annuelles moyennes** | | | | | | | |
| 1948.................................... | 100.0 | 86.2 | 11.5 | 27.5 | 23.1 | —13.7 | 27.0 |
| 1950 – 1960............................. | 100.0 | 75.7 | 10.7 | 22.3 | 21.4 | 2.0 | 29.3 |
| 1950.................................... | 100.0 | 75.8 | 10.5 | 21.1 | 21.0 | 3.1 | 31.0 |
| 1953.................................... | 100.0 | 76.6 | 10.9 | 24.2 | 24.5 | —0.8 | 27.8 |
| 1954.................................... | 100.0 | 74.4 | 10.2 | 24.6 | 23.1 | 1.0 | 28.2 |
| 1958.................................... | 100.0 | 77.5 | 10.8 | 22.2 | 21.7 | 0.3 | 27.1 |
| 1960.................................... | 100.0 | 75.4 | 10.9 | 20.6 | 19.9 | 4.0 | 27.8 |

## B. The Net Domestic Product at Factor Cost According to Origin
## Origine par secteur d'activité du produit intérieur net au coût des facteurs

This table covers the Republic of South Africa only and excludes South West Africa and the three British Protectorates: Swaziland, Basutoland and Bechuanaland.

Ce tableau se rapporte à la République Sud-africaine et ne concerne ni le Sud-Ouest africain, ni les trois protectorats britanniques: le Souaziland, le Bassoutoland et le Betchouanaland.

| Item of data and year [1]<br>Rubrique et année [1] | Total | Agricultural sector<br>Secteur agricole | Mining<br>Industries extractives | Manufacturing and construction [2]<br>Industries manufacturières et bâtiment et travaux publics [2] | Transportation<br>Transports | Other sectors [3]<br>Autres secteurs [3] |
|---|---|---|---|---|---|---|
| ISIC — CITI | 0–9 | 0 | 1 | 2–4 | 71 | 5, 6, 72–9 |
| At Current Prices — Aux prix courants | | | | | | |
| Absolute figures<br>— Chiffres absolus | | | | | | |
| 1948............ | 1 800 | 244 | 186 | 391 | 171 | 808 |
| 1951............ | 2 609 | 352 | 339 | 618 | 228 | 1 072 |
| 1952............ | 2 893 | 443 | 336 | 687 | 234 | 1 193 |
| 1953............ | 3 144 | 493 | 342 | 740 | 265 | 1 304 |
| 1954............ | 3 377 | 461 | 393 | 797 | 308 | 1 418 |
| 1955............ | 3 620 | 476 | 454 | 864 | 307 | 1 519 |
| 1956............ | 3 959 | 557 | 501 | 928 | 327 | 1 646 |
| 1957............ | 4 044 | 464 | 519 | 966 | 342 | 1 753 |
| 1958............ | 4 178 | 447 | 557 | 993 | 347 | 1 834 |
| 1959............ | 4 526 | 509 | 621 | 1 060 | 378 | 1 958 |
| 1960............ | 4 791 | 531 | 658 | 1 137 | 388 | 2 077 |
| 1961............ | 5 004 | 537 | 673 | 1 206 | 398 | 2 190 |
| Percentage distribution according to sector—<br>Distribution en pourcentage par secteur | | | | | | |
| 1948............ | 100.0 | 13.6 | 10.3 | 21.7 | 9.5 | 44.9 |
| 1951–1960..... | 100.0 | 12.7 | 12.7 | 23.7 | 8.4 | 42.5 |
| 1953............ | 100.0 | 15.7 | 10.9 | 23.5 | 8.4 | 41.5 |
| 1954............ | 100.0 | 13.7 | 11.6 | 23.6 | 9.1 | 42.0 |
| 1958............ | 100.0 | 10.7 | 13.3 | 23.8 | 8.3 | 43.9 |
| 1960............ | 100.0 | 11.1 | 13.7 | 23.7 | 8.1 | 43.4 |

[1] Fiscal year beginning 1st July.
[2] Covers the private sector only; Government manufacturing and construction activity is included in "Other sectors".
[3] Includes Electricity, gas and water (ISIC division 5) and Storage, warehousing, and communication (ISIC major group 72-73).

[1] Exercice financier commençant le 1er juillet.
[2] Il s'agit exclusivement des industries du secteur privé; les activités de l'Etat relevant des industries manufacturières, ainsi que du bâtiment et des travaux publics, sont comprises dans "Autres secteurs".
[3] Y compris Electricité, gaz et eau (CITI branche 5) et Entrepôts magasins et communications (CITI classes 72-73).

## 2. INDEX NUMBERS OF INDUSTRIAL PRODUCTION — INDICES DE LA PRODUCTION INDUSTRIELLE

### A. The Major Groups of Mining
### Les classes de la branche Industries extractives

| Period Période | All mining Toutes industries extractives | Coal mining Extraction du charbon | Metal mining Extraction des minerais métalliques | Other mining Autres industries extractives |
|---|---|---|---|---|
| ISIC — CITI | 1 | 11 | 12 | 14–19 |

*a.* Indexes — Indices (1958 = 100)

| | | | | |
|---|---|---|---|---|
| 1938......... | 58 | 44 | 63 | 19 |
| 1948......... | 61 | 65 | 62 | 48 |
| 1949......... | 63 | 69 | 64 | 56 |
| 1950......... | 66 | 71 | 65 | 72 |
| 1951......... | 67 | 72 | 65 | 83 |
| 1952......... | 69 | 76 | 67 | 86 |
| 1953......... | 70 | 77 | 68 | 85 |
| 1954......... | 77 | 79 | 75 | 92 |
| 1955......... | – 83 – | 87 | – 82 – | – 88 – |
| 1956......... | 90 | 91 | 90 | 91 |
| 1957......... | 96 | 94 | 96 | 96 |
| 1958......... | 100 | 100 | 100 | 100 |
| 1959......... | 111 | 98 | 113 | 105 |
| 1960......... | 118 | 103 | 121 | 108 |
| 1961......... | 128 | 107 | 130 | 128 |

*b.* Average Annual Rate of Change — Taux annuel moyen de variation

| | | | | |
|---|---|---|---|---|
| 1938 – 1960.... | 3.3 | 3.9 | 3.0 | 8.2 |
| 1938 – 1948.... | 0.5 | 4.0 | –0.2 | 9.7 |
| 1950 – 1960.... | 6.0 | 3.8 | 6.4 | 4.1 |
| 1948 – 1953.... | 2.8 | 3.4 | 1.9 | 12.1 |
| 1954 – 1958.... | 6.8 | 6.1 | 7.5 | 2.1 |
| 1958 – 1960.... | 8.6 | 1.5 | 10.0 | 8.6 |

## B.  The Major Groups of Manufacturing — Les classes de la branche Industries manufacturières

| Period / Période | Manufacturing [1] / Industries manufacturières [1] | Food, beverages and tobacco / Industries alimentaires, boissons, tabac | Textiles | Clothing, footwear and made-up textiles / Articles d'habillement, chaussures et ouvrages en tissu | Furniture / Meubles | Paper and paper products / Papier et ouvrages en papier | Printing and publishing / Imprimerie et édition | Leather and leather products except wearing apparel / Cuir et articles en cuir, à l'exclusion des articles d'habillement | Chemicals and chemical, petroleum and coal products / Produits chimiques et dérivés du pétrole et du charbon | Non-metallic mineral products / Produits minéraux non métalliques | Basic metals / Métallurgie de base | Metal products [2] / Ouvrages en métaux [2] |
|---|---|---|---|---|---|---|---|---|---|---|---|---|
| ISIC — CITI | 2–3 | 20–22 | 23 | 24 | 26 | 27 | 28 | 29 | 31–32 | 33 | 34 | 35–38 |

### a. Indexes — Indices (1958 = 100)

| Period / Période | 2–3 | 20–22 | 23 | 24 | 26 | 27 | 28 | 29 | 31–32 | 33 | 34 | 35–38 |
|---|---|---|---|---|---|---|---|---|---|---|---|---|
| 1938 | 31 | 38 | 20 | 52 | ... | ... | ... | 40 | ... | 27 | 21 | 38 |
| 1948 | −53− | −63− | −32− | −62− | ... | ... | ... | −73− | ... | −48− | −46− | −55− |
| 1949 | 58 | 69 | 37 | 68 | ... | ... | ... | 78 | 54 | 53 | 50 | 58 |
| 1950 | 62 | 72 | 45 | 70 | ... | ... | ... | 83 | 60 | 58 | 50 | 64 |
| 1951 | 68 | 79 | 54 | 81 | ... | ... | ... | 88 | 68 | 66 | 53 | 76 |
| 1952 | 73 | 82 | 57 | 80 | ... | ... | ... | 87 | 67 | 73 | 66 | 85 |
| 1953 | 77 | 84 | 68 | 89 | ... | ... | ... | 93 | 71 | 77 | 74 | 85 |
| 1954 | −84− | −86− | −82− | −99− | ... | ... | ... | −105− | −82− | −79− | −79− | −94− |
| 1955 | 89 | 88 | 82 | 98 | ... | ... | ... | 101 | 90 | 91 | 86 | 98 |
| 1956 | 92 | 93 | 86 | 98 | ... | ... | ... | 91 | 96 | 98 | 89 | 95 |
| 1957 | −94− | −92− | −98− | −98− | 93 | 96 | 97 | −100− | −99− | −97− | −93− | −95− |
| 1958 | 100 | 100 | 100 | 100 | 100 | 100 | 100 | 100 | 100 | 100 | 100 | 100 |
| 1959 | 102 | 104 | 104 | 100 | 97 | 102 | 99 | 100 | 106 | 98 | 100 | 100 |
| 1960 | 108 | 108 | 136 | 103 | 99 | 113 | 107 | 90 | 115 | 101 | 118 | 96 |
| 1961 | 1·16 | 113 | 160 | 115 | 96 | 132 | 132 | 96 | 125 | 101 | 127 | 97 |

### b. Average Annual Rate of Change — Taux annuel moyen de variation

| Period / Période | 2–3 | 20–22 | 23 | 24 | 26 | 27 | 28 | 29 | 31–32 | 33 | 34 | 35–38 |
|---|---|---|---|---|---|---|---|---|---|---|---|---|
| 1938–1960 | 5.8 | 4.9 | 9.1 | 3.2 | ... | ... | ... | 3.8 | ... | 6.2 | 8.2 | 4.3 |
| 1938–1948 | 5.5 | 5.2 | 4.8 | 1.8 | ... | ... | ... | 6.2 | ... | 5.9 | 8.2 | 3.8 |
| 1950–1960 | 5.7 | 4.1 | 11.7 | 3.9 | ... | ... | ... | 0.8 | 6.7 | 5.7 | 9.0 | 4.1 |
| 1948–1953 | 7.8 | 5.9 | 16.3 | 7.5 | ... | ... | ... | 5.0 | ... | 9.9 | 10.0 | 9.1 |
| 1954–1958 | 4.4 | 3.8 | 5.1 | 0.2 | ... | ... | ... | −1.2 | 5.1 | 6.1 | 6.1 | 1.6 |
| 1958–1960 | 8.6 | 8.6 | 16.6 | 1.5 | −0.5 | 6.3 | 3.4 | −5.1 | 7.2 | 0.5 | 8.6 | −2.0 |

[1] Although a number of individual major groups are not shown for some or all years the total manufacturing index includes all major groups of the manufacturing division of the International Standard Industrial Classification except Manufactures of Wood and Cork (ISIC major group 25); the manufacture of automobile tires (part of ISIC major group 30) and all other activities connected with the automobile industry (mainly part of ISIC major group 38) for the years 1957 onwards.
[2] Excludes Manufacture of machinery (ISIC major group 36), Manufacture of electrical machinery (ISIC major group 37) and Manufacture of transport equipment (ISIC major group 38) up to 1957.

[1] Bien que les données relatives à quelques classes ne soient pas reproduites pour certaines des années, voire pour toutes, l'indice concernant l'ensemble des Industries manufacturières se rapporte à toutes les classes de la branche Industries manufacturières telle qu'elle est définie dans la Classification internationale type, par industrie de toutes les branches d'activité économique, à l'exclusion des industries du bois et du liège (CITI classe 25), de la fabrication des pneumatiques d'automobiles (dans CITI classe 30) et de toutes les autres activités relatives à l'industrie automobile (la plupart dans CITI classe 38) à partir de 1957.
[2] Non compris la Construction des machines (CITI classe 36), la Construction des machines électriques (CITI classe 37) et la Construction du matériel de transport (CITI classe 38) jusqu'en 1957.

# SOUTH AFRICA

## 3. INDEX NUMBERS OF INDUSTRIAL EMPLOYMENT — INDICES DE L'EMPLOI DANS L'INDUSTRIE

### A. The Divisions of Industrial Activity
### Les branches de l'activité industrielle

| Period / Période | Total | Mining [1,2] Industries extractives [1,2] | Manufacturing [10] Industries manufacturières [10] | Construction [11] Bâtiment et travaux publics [11] | Electricity, and gas [12] Electricité, et gaz [12] |
|---|---|---|---|---|---|
| ISIC — CITI | 1-3, 511-512 | 1 | 2-3 | 4 | 511-512 |

*a. Indexes — Indices (1958 = 100)*

| | | | | | |
|---|---|---|---|---|---|
| 1938....... | 56 | 83 | 35 | 47 | 74 |
| 1948....... | −71− | −79− | 63 | 73 | 95 |
| 1949....... | 76 | 84 | 69 | 83 | 100 |
| 1950....... | −80− | 89 | −72− | 79 | 103 |
| 1951....... | −83− | 89 | −76− | −83− | 96 |
| 1952....... | −86− | −91− | 81 | 90 | 100 |
| 1953....... | 87 | 90 | 83 | 89 | 104 |
| 1954....... | −91− | 94 | 88 | 92 | −106− |
| 1955....... | −94− | 96 | −92− | 96 | 111 |
| 1956....... | −97− | 98 | −95− | −99− | −115− |
| 1957....... | 99 | 100 | 98 | 96 | 98 |
| 1958....... | −100− | −100− | 100 | 100 | 100 |
| 1959....... | −104− | 107 | −101− | −104− | 103 |
| 1960....... | ... | 108 | 102 | 106 | ... |
| 1961....... | ... | 111 | 102 | 105 | ... |

*b. Average Annual Rate of Change — Taux annuel moyen de variation*

| | | | | | |
|---|---|---|---|---|---|
| 1938 – 1960. | 3.1 | 1.2 | 5.0 | 3.8 | ... |
| 1938 – 1948. | 2.6 | −0.5 | 6.1 | 4.5 | 2.5 |
| 1950 – 1960. | 2.8 | 1.9 | 3.5 | 3.0 | ... |
| 1948 – 1953. | 4.1 | 2.6 | 5.7 | 4.0 | 1.8 |
| 1954 – 1958. | 2.4 | 1.6 | 3.2 | 2.1 | −1.4 |
| 1958 – 1960. | 2.5 | 3.9 | 1.0 | 3.0 | ... |

For footnotes see end of table.

### B. The Major Groups of Mining
### Les classes de la branche Industries extractives

| Period / Période | All mining [1,2] Toutes industries extractives [1,2] | Coal mining Extraction du charbon | Metal mining [1] Extraction des minerais métalliques [1] | Other mining [2] Autres industries extractives [2] |
|---|---|---|---|---|
| ISIC — CITI | 1 | 11 | 12 | 14–19 |

*a. Indexes — Indices (1958 = 100)*

| | | | | |
|---|---|---|---|---|
| 1938.......... | 83 | 51 | 91 | 50 |
| 1948.......... | −79− | 76 | 82 | −56− |
| 1949.......... | 84 | 80 | 87 | 67 |
| 1950.......... | 89 | 83 | 91 | 74 |
| 1951.......... | 89 | 83 | 90 | 83 |
| 1952.......... | −91− | 87 | 92 | −93− |
| 1953.......... | 90 | 85 | 91 | 87 |
| 1954.......... | 94 | 86 | 96 | 86 |
| 1955.......... | 96 | 90 | 98 | 85 |
| 1956.......... | 98 | 91 | 101 | 88 |
| 1957.......... | 100 | 95 | 101 | 94 |
| 1958.......... | −100− | −100− | −100− | 100 |
| 1959.......... | 107 | 102 | 110 | 105 |
| 1960.......... | 108 | 101 | 112 | 98 |
| 1961.......... | 111 | 107 | 114 | 106 |

*b. Average Annual Rate of Change — Taux annuel moyen de variation*

| | | | | |
|---|---|---|---|---|
| 1938 – 1960.... | 1.2 | 3.1 | 0.9 | 3.1 |
| 1938 – 1948.... | −0.5 | 4.1 | −1.0 | 1.1 |
| 1950 – 1960.... | 1.9 | 2.0 | 2.1 | 2.8 |
| 1948 – 1953.... | 2.6 | 2.3 | 2.1 | 9.2 |
| 1954 – 1958.... | 1.6 | 3.8 | 1.0 | 3.8 |
| 1958 – 1960.... | 3.9 | 0.5 | 5.8 | −1.0 |

Pour les notes, voir au bas du tableau.

## C.  The Major Groups of Manufacturing — Les classes de la branche Industries manufacturières

| Period / Période | Manufacturing[10] / Industries manufacturières[10] | Food, beverages and tobacco[3] / Industries alimentaires, boissons, tabac[3] | Textiles | Clothing, footwear and made-up textiles[4] / Articles d'habillement, chaussures et ouvrages en tissu[4] | Wood products and furniture[5] / Bois et meubles[5] | Paper and paper products[6] / Papier et ouvrages en papier[6] | Printing and publishing[7] / Imprimerie et édition[7] | Leather and leather products except wearing apparel / Cuir et articles en cuir, à l'exclusion des articles d'habillement | Rubber products / Ouvrages en caoutchouc | Chemicals and chemical, petroleum and coal products[8] / Produits chimiques et dérivés du pétrole et du charbon[8] | Non-metallic mineral products / Produits minéraux non métalliques | Basic metals / Métallurgie de base | Metal products[9] / Ouvrages en métaux[9] | Other manufacturing / Autres industries manufacturières |
|---|---|---|---|---|---|---|---|---|---|---|---|---|---|---|
| ISIC — CITI | 2–3 | 20–22 | 23 | 24 | 25–26 | 27 | 28 | 29 | 30 | 31–32 | 33 | 34 | 35–38 | 39 |

### a.  Indexes — Indices (1958 = 100)

| Period / Période | 2–3 | 20–22 | 23 | 24 | 25–26 | 27 | 28 | 29 | 30 | 31–32 | 33 | 34 | 35–38 | 39 |
|---|---|---|---|---|---|---|---|---|---|---|---|---|---|---|
| 1938 | 35 | 38 | 12 | 42 | 35 | 7 | 46 | 57 | 17 | 30 | 51 | 32 | | 23 |
| 1948 | 63 | 64 | 27 | 72 | 76 | 46 | 71 | 96 | 47 | 65 | 71 | 60 | | 40 |
| 1949 | 69 | 68 | 38 | 79 | 78 | 53 | 75 | 104 | 56 | 69 | 76 | 55 | | 45 |
| 1950 | –72– | 71 | 46 | 84 | 80 | 57 | 75 | 109 | 61 | –71– | 76 | 69 | | 49 |
| 1951 | –76– | 75 | 59 | 91 | 89 | –58– | 79 | 110 | 66 | 72 | 85 | 62 | 70 | 60 |
| 1952 | 81 | 80 | 63 | 91 | 95 | 63 | 80 | 107 | 72 | 73 | 90 | 74 | 75 | 64 |
| 1953 | 83 | 82 | 73 | 94 | 96 | 64 | 83 | 107 | 79 | 75 | 90 | 75 | 77 | 71 |
| 1954 | 88 | 84 | 81 | 98 | 97 | 77 | 86 | 110 | 89 | 78 | 95 | 77 | 82 | 76 |
| 1955 | –92– | –89– | 89 | –97– | –102– | 81 | 87 | 111 | –97– | 86 | 100 | 79 | –85– | 81 |
| 1956 | –95– | –94– | 95 | –96– | –105– | 91 | –92– | –103– | 103 | –88– | –104– | –89– | 88 | –85– |
| 1957 | 98 | 98 | 106 | 99 | 99 | 98 | 99 | 102 | 102 | 97 | 100 | 98 | 96 | 91 |
| 1958 | 100 | 100 | 100 | 100 | 100 | 100 | 100 | 100 | 100 | 100 | 100 | 100 | 100 | 100 |
| 1959 | –101– | –101– | –99– | –99– | –101– | –104– | –100– | –97– | 95 | –100– | –100– | –104– | 96 | –100– |
| 1960 | 102 | 100 | 109 | 99 | 104 | 106 | 102 | 97 | 89 | 100 | 102 | 106 | 97 | 102 |
| 1961 | 102 | 101 | 114 | 95 | 102 | 110 | 106 | 89 | 86 | 102 | 97 | 107 | 98 | |

### b.  Average Annual Rate of Change — Taux annuel moyen de variation

| Period / Période | 2–3 | 20–22 | 23 | 24 | 25–26 | 27 | 28 | 29 | 30 | 31–32 | 33 | 34 | 35–38 | 39 |
|---|---|---|---|---|---|---|---|---|---|---|---|---|---|---|
| 1938 – 1960 | 5.0 | 4.5 | 10.5 | 4.0 | 5.1 | 13.1 | 3.7 | 2.4 | 7.8 | 5.6 | 3.2 | ... | ... | 6.9 |
| 1938 – 1948 | 6.1 | 5.4 | 8.4 | 5.5 | 8.1 | 20.7 | 4.4 | 5.4 | 10.7 | 8.0 | 3.4 | 6.5 | | 5.7 |
| 1950 – 1960 | 3.5 | 3.5 | 9.0 | 1.7 | 2.7 | 6.4 | 3.1 | –1.2 | 3.8 | 3.6 | 3.0 | ... | ... | 9.4 |
| 1948 – 1953 | 5.7 | 5.1 | 22.0 | 5.5 | 4.8 | 6.8 | 3.2 | 2.2 | 10.9 | 2.9 | 4.9 | ... | ... | 12.2 |
| 1954 – 1958 | 3.2 | 4.4 | 5.4 | 0.5 | 0.8 | 6.8 | 3.8 | –2.4 | 2.9 | 6.4 | 1.3 | 6.8 | 5.1 | 7.1 |
| 1958 – 1960 | 1.0 | — | 4.4 | –0.5 | 2.0 | 3.0 | 1.0 | –1.5 | –5.7 | — | 1.0 | 3.0 | –1.5 | — |

1 Excluding platinum mining 1958 onwards.
2 Excluding salt quarries up to 1952, and salt pans and salt refining in 1938 and 1948.
3 Excludes custom grain-milling and production for consumption on the premises 1955 onwards.
4 Excludes repairs done by commercial establishments 1955 onwards.
5 Excludes sawmilling done by farmers for their own convenience and by retail stores for their customers' convenience.
6 Covers only paper bags and cardboard boxes and mounts up to 1951, includes Printing and publishing (ISIC major group 28) for 1959 onwards.
7 Includes Paper and paper products (ISIC major group 27) for 1959 onwards.
8 Includes margarine (part of ISIC major group 20) up to 1950.
9 Includes electrical contracting up to 1950.
10 The above footnotes numbered 3, 4, 5, and 9 are applicable.
11 Excludes public civil engineering projects and electrical contracting up to 1951.
12 Excludes electricity distribution up to 1954, includes the generation of electricity by factories primarily for own use up to 1956.

1 Non compris les industries extractives de platine à partir de 1958.
2 Non compris les carrières de sel jusqu'en 1952, non plus que le lavage et le raffinage du sel en 1938 et 1948.
3 Non compris les travaux de meunerie à façon et la production pour l'auto-consommation à partir de 1955.
4 Non compris les travaux de réparation effectués par des établissements commerciaux à partir de 1955.
5 Non compris l'utilisation des scieries par les fermiers pour satisfaire leurs propres besoins et par les magasins de détail pour répondre aux besoins de leurs clients.
6 Sacs en papier et les caisses en carton seulement jusqu'en 1951; y compris Imprimerie et édition (CITI classe 28) à partir de 1959.
7 Y compris Papier et ouvrages en papier (CITI classe 27) à partir de 1959.
8 Y compris la margarine (dans CITI classe 20) jusqu'en 1950.
9 Y compris les travaux électriques effectués par des sous traitants jusqu'en 1950.
10 Les notes 3, 4, 5, et 9 s'appliquent également à cette rubrique.
11 Non compris les projets du génie civil public et les travaux électriques effectués par des sous traitants jusqu'en 1951.
12 Non compris la distribution d'électricité jusqu'en 1954; y compris la production d'électricité par les usines essentiellement pour l'auto-consommation jusqu'en 1956.

## 4. THE CHARACTERISTICS OF PUBLIC AND PRIVATE INDUSTRIAL ESTABLISHMENTS ENGAGING THREE OR MORE PERSONS OR UTILISING MOTIVE POWER

### CARACTERISTIQUES DES ETABLISSEMENTS INDUSTRIELS, PUBLICS ET PRIVES, OCCUPANT TROIS PERSONNES OU PLUS OU UTILISANT LA FORCE MOTRICE

#### 1937–1938, 1947–1948, 1952–1953

Number of establishments in units; value added and wages and salaries in million Pounds; number of engaged and employees in thousands; capacity of installed power equipment in thousand horsepower; value added per engaged and wages and salaries per employee in thousand Pounds; capacity of installed power equipment per engaged in horsepower.

Nombre d'établissements en unités; valeur ajoutée et traitements et salaires en millions de livres; nombre de personnes occupées et de salariés en milliers; puissance installée en milliers de chevaux-vapeur; valeur ajoutée par personne occupée et traitements et salaires par salarié en milliers de livres; puissance installée par personne occupée en chevaux-vapeur.

### A.   Selected Divisions of Industrial Activity — Quelques branches de l'activité industrielle

| Year and item of data | Manu-facturing / Industries manu-facturières | Con-struction [1] / Bâtiment et travaux publics [1] | Electricity, gas and steam [2] / Electricité gaz et vapeur [2] | Année et rubrique | Year and item of data | Manu-facturing / Industries manu-facturières | Con-struction[1] / Bâtiment et travaux publics [1] | Electricity, gas and steam [2] / Electricité gaz et vapeur [2] | Année et rubrique |
|---|---|---|---|---|---|---|---|---|---|
| ISIC | 2–3 | 4 | 511–513 | CITI | ISIC | 2–3 | 4 | 511–513 | CITI |
| | **a. Absolute Figures** / **Chiffres absolus** | | | | | **b. Structure** | | | |
| **1937–1938** | | | | **1937–1938** | **1937–1938** | | | | **1937–1938** |
| Number of establishments | 8 791 | 1 044 | 282 | Nombre d'établissements | Per person engaged: | | | | Par personne occupée: |
| Value added | 69.7 | 8.9 | 7.8 | Valeur ajoutée | Value added | 0.2 | 0.2 | 0.5 | Valeur ajoutée |
| Number of engaged | 276.9 | 52.6 | 15.1 | Nombre de personnes occupées | Capacity of installed power | | | | |
| Wages and salaries | 35.4 | 6.8 | 2.2 | Traitements et salaires | equipment | 1.86 | 0.37 | 131.5 | Puissance installée |
| Capacity of installed power | | | | | Value added per unit of | | | | Valeur ajoutée par unité de |
| equipment | 513.7 | 19.7 | 1 985.8 | Puissance installée | wages and salaries | 1.97 | 1.31 | 3.54 | traitements et salaires |
| **1947–1948** | | | | **1947–1948** | **1947–1948** | | | | **1947–1948** |
| Number of establishments | 11 444 | 1 572 | 297 | Nombre d'établissements | Per person engaged: | | | | Par personne occupée: |
| Value added | 214.0 | 22.9 | 13.8 | Valeur ajoutée | Value added | 0.4 | 0.3 | 0.6 | Valeur ajoutée |
| Number of engaged | 471.5 | 82.2 | 21.1 | Nombre de personnes occupées | Capacity of installed power | | | | |
| Employees: | | | | Salariés: | equipment | 2.18 | 0.35 | 1438.3 | Puissance installée |
| Number | 464.3 | 80.9 | 21.1 | Nombre | Employees as a percent of | | | | Salariés en pourcentage des |
| Wages and salaries | 111.4 | 17.0 | 5.2 | Traitements et salaires | engaged | 96.4 | 98.4 | 100.0 | personnes occupées |
| Capacity of installed power | | | | | Value added per unit of | | | | Valeur ajoutée par unité de |
| equipment | 1 029.1 | 29.0 | 3 034.9 | Puissance installée | wages and salaries | 1.92 | 1.35 | 2.65 | traitements et salaires |
| | | | | | Wages and salaries per | | | | Ouvriers en pourcentage des |
| | | | | | employee | 0.2 | 0.2 | 0.2 | salariés |
| **1952–1953** | | | | **1952–1953** | **1952–1953** | | | | **1952–1953** |
| Number of establishments | 12 567 | 2 086 | 297 | Nombre d'établissements | Per person engaged: | | | | Par personne occupée: |
| Value added | 399.6 | 59.6 | 19.2 | Valeur ajoutée | Value added | 0.6 | 0.4 | 0.8 | Valeur ajoutée |
| Number of engaged | 610.0 | 134.2 | 23.0 | Nombre de personnes occupées | Capacity of installed power | | | | |
| Employees: | | | | Salariés: | equipment | 3.06 | 0.45 | 126.67 | Puissance installée |
| Number | 603.6 | 132.7 | 23.0 | Nombre | Employees as a percent of | | | | Salariés en pourcentage des |
| Wages and salaries | 194.2 | 39.0 | 7.2 | Traitements et salaires | engaged | 99.0 | 98.9 | 100.0 | personnes occupées |
| Capacity of installed power | | | | | Value added per unit of | | | | Valeur ajoutée par unité de |
| equipment | 1 864.1 | 60.7 | 2 913.4 | Puissance installée | wages and salaries | 2.06 | 1.53 | 2.67 | traitements et salaires |
| | | | | | Wages and salaries per | | | | Ouvriers en pourcentage des |
| | | | | | employee | 0.3 | 0.3 | 0.3 | salariés |

[1] Excludes public civil engineering projects.
[2] Includes in all years ancillary units generating electricity for own use.

[1] Non compris les projets du génie civil public.
[2] Y compris, pour toutes les années, les unités auxiliaires produisant de l'électricité pour l'auto-consommation.

## B. The Major Groups of Manufacturing — Les classes de la branche Industries manufacturières

*a. Absolute Figures — Chiffres absolus*

| Year and item of data | Manufacturing[3] / Industries manufacturières[3] | Food, beverages and tobacco[1] / Industries alimentaires, boissons, tabac[1] | Textiles | Clothing, footwear and made-up textiles / Articles d'habillement, chaussures et ouvrages en tissu | Wood products and furniture / Bois et meubles | Paper and paper products[2] / Papier et ouvrages en papier[2] | Printing and publishing / Imprimerie et édition | Leather and leather products except wearing apparel / Cuir et articles en cuir, à l'exclusion des articles d'habillement | Rubber products / Ouvrages en caoutchouc | Chemicals and chemical, petroleum and coal products / Produits chimiques et dérivés du pétrole et du charbon | Non-metallic mineral products / Produits minéraux non métalliques | Basic metals / Métallurgie de base | Metal products / Ouvrages en métaux | Other manufacturing[3] / Autres industries manufacturières[3] | Année et rubrique |
|---|---|---|---|---|---|---|---|---|---|---|---|---|---|---|---|
| ISIC | 2-3 | 20-22 | 23 | 24 | 25-26 | 27 | 28 | 29 | 30 | 31-32 | 33 | 34 | 35-38 | 39 | CITI |
| **1937-1938** | | | | | | | | | | | | | | | **1937-1938** |
| Number of establishments | 8 791 | 2 252 | | 1 189 | 765 | | 478 | 99 | 48 | 229 | 575 | | 3 011 | 145 | Nombre d'établissements |
| Value added | 69.7 | 14.6 | | 6.6 | 4.3 | | 5.7 | 0.6 | 1.3 | 5.4 | 4.8 | | 25.6 | 0.8 | Valeur ajoutée |
| Number of engaged (Average during year) | 276.9 | 47.0 | | 37.8 | 19.9 | | 13.6 | 2.8 | 1.9 | 13.8 | 31.3 | | 106.0 | 2.8 | Nombre de personnes occupées (moyenne pendant l'année) |
| Wages and salaries paid | 35.4 | 4.2 | | 3.8 | 2.6 | | 3.0 | 0.3 | 0.3 | 1.5 | 2.0 | | 17.2 | 0.5 | Traitements et salaires payés |
| Capacity of installed power equipment | 513.7 | 135.9 | | 15.1 | 42.3 | | 15.6 | 4.1 | 7.5 | 34.3 | 52.5 | | 204.2 | 2.2 | Puissance installée |
| **1947-1948** | | | | | | | | | | | | | | | **1947-1948** |
| Number of establishments | 11 444 | 2 506 | | 1 446 | 1 149 | | 544 | 109 | 88 | 350 | 647 | | 4 344 | 261 | Nombre d'établissements |
| Value added | 214.0 | 38.5 | | 26.9 | 14.6 | | 17.0 | 1.9 | 4.5 | 17.9 | 12.3 | | 75.1 | 5.3 | Valeur ajoutée |
| Number of engaged (Average during year) | 471.5 | 80.0 | | 66.7 | 43.1 | | 24.2 | 4.7 | 5.3 | 29.9 | 43.7 | | 169.0 | 4.9 | Nombre de personnes occupées (moyenne pendant l'année) |
| Number of employees (Average during year) | 464.3 | 78.5 | | 65.7 | 42.4 | | 23.6 | 4.7 | 5.3 | 29.8 | 43.4 | | 166.2 | 4.7 | Nombre de salariés (moyenne pendant l'année) |
| Wages and salaries paid | 111.4 | 14.7 | | 15.1 | 8.4 | | 8.6 | 1.1 | 1.5 | 6.2 | 6.1 | | 47.7 | 2.0 | Traitements et salaires payés |
| Capacity of installed power equipment | 1 029.1 | 211.7 | | 32.1 | 106.0 | | 37.9 | 8.9 | 27.6 | 85.1 | 126.2 | | 388.9 | 4.7 | Puissance installée |
| **1952-1953** | | | | | | | | | | | | | | | **1952-1953** |
| Number of establishments | 12 567 | 2 333 | 146 | 1 620 | 1 216 | 106 | 478 | 98 | 111 | 353 | 736 | 113 | 4 771 | 486 | Nombre d'établissements |
| Value added | 399.6 | 67.8 | 13.1 | 39.9 | 24.7 | 9.6 | 17.8 | 2.8 | 10.3 | 35.8 | 24.5 | 32.3 | 113.8 | 7.2 | Valeur ajoutée |
| Number of engaged (Average during year) | 610.0 | 100.6 | 27.0 | 74.7 | 52.7 | 11.0 | 17.9 | 5.3 | 8.9 | 39.0 | 55.1 | 29.6 | 178.2 | 10.0 | Nombre de personnes occupées (moyenne pendant l'année) |
| Number of employees (Average during year) | 603.5 | 99.3 | 27.0 | 74.1 | 52.0 | 11.0 | 17.7 | 5.3 | 8.9 | 38.9 | 54.7 | 29.6 | 175.2 | 9.8 | Nombre de salariés (moyenne pendant l'année) |
| Wages and salaries paid | 194.2 | 23.9 | 6.3 | 23.0 | 13.4 | 4.3 | 10.1 | 1.7 | 3.5 | 12.0 | 11.0 | 12.4 | 68.7 | 3.9 | Traitements et salaires payés |
| Capacity of installed power equipment | 1 864.1 | 273.7 | 51.4 | 25.2 | 143.6 | 43.6 | 25.3 | 11.5 | 39.4 | 151.1 | 262.2 | 383.2 | 418.0 | 35.9 | Puissance installée |

## B. The Major Groups of Manufacturing (continued) — Les classes de la branche Industries manufacturières (suite)

| Year and item of data | Manufacturing [3] Industries manufacturières [3] | Food, beverages and tobacco [1] Industries alimentaires, boissons, tabac [1] | Textiles | Clothing, footwear and made-up textiles Articles d'habillement, chaussures et ouvrages en tissu | Wood products and furniture Bois et meubles | Paper and paper products [2] Papier et ouvrages en papier [2] | Printing and publishing Imprimerie et édition | Leather and leather products except wearing apparel Cuir et articles en cuir, à l'exclusion des articles d'habillement | Rubber products Ouvrages en caoutchouc | Chemicals and chemical, petroleum and coal products Produits chimiques et dérivés du pétrole et du charbon | Non-metallic mineral products Produits minéraux non métalliques | Basic metals Métallurgie de base | Metal products Ouvrages en métaux | Other manufacturing [3] Autres industries manufacturières [3] | Année et rubrique |
|---|---|---|---|---|---|---|---|---|---|---|---|---|---|---|---|
| ISIC | 2-3 | 20-22 | 23 | 24 | 25-26 | 27 | 28 | 29 | 30 | 31-32 | 33 | 34 | 35-38 | 39 | CITI |

*b. Structure*

| Year and item of data | 2-3 | 20-22 | 23 | 24 | 25-26 | 27 | 28 | 29 | 30 | 31-32 | 33 | 34 | 35-38 | 39 | Année et rubrique |
|---|---|---|---|---|---|---|---|---|---|---|---|---|---|---|---|
| *1937-1938* Distribution in percent of: Value added........ | 100.0 | 20.9 | 9.4 | 6.2 | 8.2 | 0.9 | 1.9 | 7.7 | 6.9 | 36.7 | | 1.2 | | | *1937-1938* Distribution en pourcentage: Valeur ajoutée |
| Number of engaged.. | 100.0 | 17.0 | 13.7 | 7.2 | 4.9 | 1.0 | 0.7 | 5.0 | 11.3 | 38.2 | | 1.0 | | | Nombre de personnes occupées |
| Value added per person engaged............ | 0.2 | 0.3 | 0.2 | 0.2 | 0.4 | 0.2 | 0.7 | 0.4 | 0.2 | 0.2 | | 0.3 | | | Valeur ajoutée par personne occupée |
| Value added per unit of wages and salaries........... | 1.97 | 3.48 | 1.74 | 1.65 | 1.90 | 2.00 | 4.33 | 3.60 | 2.40 | 1.49 | | 1.60 | | | Valeur ajoutée par unité de traitements et salaires |
| Capacity of installed power equipment per person engaged...... | 1.86 | 2.89 | 0.40 | 2.12 | 1.15 | 1.46 | 3.95 | 2.48 | 1.68 | 1.93 | | 0.78 | | | Puissance installée par personne occupée |
| *1947-1948* Distribution in percent of: Value added........ | 100.0 | 17.9 | 12.6 | 6.8 | 8.0 | 0.9 | 2.1 | 8.3 | 5.8 | 35.1 | | 2.5 | | | *1947-1948* Distribution en pourcentage: Valeur ajoutée |
| Number of engaged.. | 100.0 | 16.9 | 14.2 | 9.1 | 5.1 | 1.0 | 1.2 | 6.3 | 9.3 | 35.8 | | 1.1 | | | Nombre de personnes occupées |
| Value added per person engaged............ | 0.4 | 0.5 | 0.4 | 0.3 | 0.7 | 0.4 | 0.8 | 0.6 | 0.3 | 0.4 | | 1.1 | | | Valeur ajoutée par personne occupée |
| Value added per unit of wages and salaries........... | 1.92 | 2.62 | 1.78 | 1.74 | 1.98 | 1.73 | 3.00 | 2.89 | 2.02 | 1.57 | | 2.65 | | | Valeur ajoutée par unité de traitements et salaires |
| Capacity of installed power equipment per person engaged...... | 2.18 | 2.65 | 0.48 | 2.46 | 1.57 | 1.89 | 5.21 | 2.85 | 2.89 | 2.30 | | 0.96 | | | Puissance installée par personne occupée |
| Employees as a percent of engaged........ | 98.5 | 98.1 | 98.5 | 98.4 | 97.5 | | 100.0 | 100.0 | 99.7 | 99.3 | 98.3 | | 95.9 | | Salariés en pourcentage des personnes occupées |
| Wages and salaries per employee........ | 0.2 | 0.2 | 0.2 | 0.2 | 0.4 | | 0.2 | 0.3 | 0.2 | 0.1 | 0.3 | | 0.4 | | Traitements et salaires par salarié |
| *1952-1953* Distribution in percent of: Value added........ | 100.0 | 16.9 | 3.3 | 10.0 | 6.2 | 2.4 | 4.4 | 0.7 | 2.6 | 9.0 | 6.1 | 8.1 | 28.4 | 1.9 | *1952-1953* Distribution en pourcentage: Valeur ajoutée |
| Number of engaged.. | 100.0 | 16.4 | 4.5 | 12.2 | 8.7 | 1.8 | 2.9 | 0.9 | 1.4 | 6.4 | 9.0 | 4.9 | 29.2 | 1.7 | Nombre de personnes occupées |
| Value added per person engaged............ | 0.6 | 0.7 | 0.5 | 0.5 | 0.5 | 0.9 | 1.0 | 0.5 | 1.2 | 0.9 | 0.4 | 1.1 | 0.6 | 0.7 | Valeur ajoutée par personne occupée |
| Value added per unit of wages and salaries........ | 2.06 | 2.84 | 2.08 | 1.73 | 1.84 | 2.23 | 1.76 | 1.65 | 2.94 | 2.98 | 2.23 | 2.60 | 1.66 | 1.85 | Valeur ajoutée par unité de traitements et salaires |
| Capacity of installed power equipment per person engaged...... | 3.06 | 2.72 | 1.90 | 0.34 | 2.72 | 3.96 | 1.41 | 2.17 | 4.43 | 3.87 | 4.76 | 12.94 | 2.34 | 3.59 | Puissance installée par personne occupée |
| Employees as a percent of engaged........ | 97.9 | 98.7 | 100.0 | 99.2 | 98.7 | 100.0 | 98.9 | 100.0 | 100.0 | 99.7 | 99.3 | 100.0 | 98.3 | 98.0 | Salariés en pourcentage des personnes occupées |
| Wages and salaries per employee........ | 0.3 | 0.2 | 0.2 | 0.3 | 0.2 | 0.4 | 0.6 | 0.3 | 0.4 | 0.3 | 0.2 | 0.4 | 0.4 | 0.4 | Traitements et salaires par salarié |

[1] Cotton ginning, classified in Textiles (ISIC major group 23), is included in the figures for 1937-1938 and 1947-1948.

[2] The manufacturing of photographic and carbon paper, which is classified in Miscellaneous manufacturing (ISIC major group 39), is included in the figures for 1937-1938 and 1947-1948. Also in the case of 1937-1938, the manufacturing of rubber stamps, which also belongs in Miscellaneous manufacturing, is included.

[3] Whaling, classified in Fishing (ISIC major group 04), and cold storage, classified in Storage and warehousing (ISIC major group 72), are included in the figures for each period. In addition film producing, classified in Motion picture production (ISIC group 841), is included in the figures for 1952-1953.

[1] L'égrenage du coton, classé dans Textiles (CITI classe 23), est compris dans les chiffres de 1937-1938 et de 1947-1948.

[2] La fabrication du papier photographique et du papier carbone, classée dans Autres industries manufacturières (CITI classe 39), est comprise dans les chiffres de 1937-1938 et de 1947-1948. De même, la fabrication des tampons en caoutchouc, qui appartient aussi aux Autres industries manufacturières, est comprise dans les chiffres de 1937-1938.

[3] La chasse à la baleine, classée dans Pêche (CITI classe 04), et les entrepôts frigorifiques, classés dans Entrepôts et magasins (CITI classe 72), sont compris dans les chiffres de chaque période. De plus, la production de films cinématographiques, classée dans Production, distribution et projection de films cinématographiques (CITI groupe 841), est comprise dans les chiffres de 1952-1953.

## 5. CHARACTERISTICS OF PRIVATE INDUSTRIAL ESTABLISHMENTS ENGAGING THREE PERSONS OR MORE OR UTILISING MOTIVE POWER

## CARACTERISTIQUES DES ETABLISSEMENTS INDUSTRIELS PRIVES OCCUPANT TROIS PERSONNES OU PLUS OU UTILISANT LA FORCE MOTRICE

### 1952-1953, 1957-1958

Number of establishments in units; value added and wages and salaries in million Pounds; number of engaged and employees in thousands; value added per engaged and wages and salaries per employee in thousand Pounds.

Nombre d'établissements en unités; valeur ajoutée et traitements et salaires en millions de livres; nombre de personnes occupées et de salariés en milliers; valeur ajoutée par personne occupée et traitements et salaires par salarié en milliers de livres.

## A. Selected Divisions of Industrial Activity — Quelques branches de l'activité industrielle

| Year and item of data | Manufacturing — Industries manufacturières | Construction [1] — Bâtiment et travaux publics [1] | Electricity, gas and steam [2] — Electricité gaz et vapeur [2] | Année et rubrique | Year and item of data | Manufacturing — Industries manufacturières | Construction [1] — Bâtiment et travaux publics [1] | Electricity, gas and steam [2] — Electricité gaz et vapeur [2] | Année et rubrique |
|---|---|---|---|---|---|---|---|---|---|
| ISIC | 2–3 | 4 | 511–513 | CITI | ISIC | 2–3 | 4 | 511–513 | CITI |
| | a. Absolute Figures — Chiffres absolus | | | | | b. Structure | | | |
| **1952 – 1953** | | | | **1952 – 1953** | **1952 – 1953** | | | | **1952 – 1953** |
| Number of establishments | 12 337 | 2 591 | 127 | Nombre d'établissements | Per person engaged: | | | | Par personne occupée: |
| Value added | 376.0 | 48.4 | 10.6 | Valeur ajoutée | Value added | 0.6 | 0.4 | 0.8 | Valeur ajoutée |
| Number of engaged | 570.0 | 108.8 | 12.9 | Nombre de personnes occupées | Capacity of installed power equipment | 3.1 | 0.6 | 225.8 | Puissance installée |
| Employees: | | | | Salariés: | Employees as a percent of engaged | 98.8 | 98.5 | 100.0 | Salariés en pourcentage des personnes occupées |
| Number | 563.5 | 107.2 | 12.9 | Nombre de personnes occupées | Value added per unit of wages and salaries | 2.14 | 1.65 | 2.79 | Valeur ajoutée par unité de traitements et salaires |
| Wages and salaries | 175.4 | 29.3 | 3.8 | Traitements et salaires | Wages and salaries per employee | 0.3 | 0.3 | 0.3 | Traitements et salaires par salarié |
| Capacity of installed power equipment | 1 753.0 | 60.7 | 2 913.4 | Puissance installée | | | | | |
| **1957 – 1958** | | | | **1957 – 1958** | **1957 – 1958** | | | | **1957 – 1958** |
| Number of establishments | 8 912 | 3 249 | 256 | Nombre d'établissements | Value added per person engaged | 0.8 | 0.5 | 1.4 | Valeur ajoutée par personne occupée |
| Value added | 463.7 | 59.6 | 38.2 | Valeur ajoutée | Value added per unit of wages and salaries | 2.07 | 3.03 | 2.59 | Valeur ajoutée par unité de traitements et salaires |
| Number of engaged | 616.9 | 121.9 | 27.2 | Nombre de personnes occupées | | | | | |
| Wages and salaries | 224.1 | 40.2 | 10.5 | Traitements et salaires | | | | | |

[1] Excludes public civil engineering projects.
[2] Includes public electricity undertakings in 1957–1958 and ancillary units generating electricity for own use in 1952–1953.

[1] Non compris les projets du génie civil public.
[2] Y compris les entreprises publiques productrices d'électricité en 1957–1958 et les unités auxiliaires produisant de l'électricité pour l'auto-consommation en 1952–1953.

## B.  The Major Groups of Manufacturing — Les classes de la branche Industries manufacturières

| Year and item of data | Manufacturing [1,2] Industries manufacturières [1,2] | Food beverages and tobacco [3] Industries alimentaires, boissons, tabac [3] | Textiles | Clothing, footwear and made-up textiles Articles d'habillement, chaussures et ouvrages en tissu | Wood products and furniture Bois et meubles | Paper and paper products Papier et ouvrages en papier | Printing and publishing Imprimerie et édition | Leather and leather products except wearing apparel Cuir et articles en cuir, à l'exclusion des articles d'habillement | Rubber products [1] Ouvrages en caoutchouc [1] | Chemicals and chemical, petroleum and coal products Produits chimiques et dérivés du pétrole et du charbon | Non-metallic mineral products Produits minéraux non métalliques | Basic metals Métallurgie de base | Metal products [2] Ouvrages en métaux [2] | Other manufacturing Autres industries manufacturières | Année et rubrique |
|---|---|---|---|---|---|---|---|---|---|---|---|---|---|---|---|
| ISIC | 2–3 | 20–22 | 23 | 24 | 25–26 | 27 | 28 | 29 | 30 | 31–32 | 33 | 34 | 35–38 | 39 | CITI |
| | | | | | *a. Absolute Figures — Chiffres absolus* | | | | | | | | | | |
| **1952–1953** | | | | | | | | | | | | | | | **1952–1953** |
| Number of establishments. | 12 337 | 2 285 | 146 | 1 612 | 1 185 | 106 | 476 | 96 | 111 | 340 | 719 | 104 | 4 684 | 470 | Nombre d'établissements |
| Value added......... | 376.0 | 66.8 | 13.1 | 39.7 | 23.5 | 9.6 | 16.8 | 2.8 | 10.3 | 35.0 | 24.4 | 31.2 | 95.8 | 7.0 | Valeur ajoutée |
| Number of engaged.... | 570.0 | 100.1 | 27.0 | 74.3 | 48.4 | 11.0 | 16.5 | 5.3 | 8.9 | 37.6 | 54.6 | 27.9 | 148.7 | 9.7 | Nombre de personnes occupées |
| Employees: | | | | | | | | | | | | | | | Salariés: |
| Number............ | 563.5 | 98.7 | 27.0 | 73.7 | 47.7 | 11.0 | 16.3 | 5.3 | 8.9 | 37.6 | 54.3 | 27.8 | 145.7 | 9.5 | Nombre |
| Wages and salaries... | 175.4 | 23.9 | 6.3 | 22.8 | 12.4 | 4.3 | 9.3 | 1.7 | 3.5 | 11.5 | 11.0 | 11.6 | 53.3 | 3.8 | Traitements et salaires |
| Capacity of installed power equipment..... | 1 753.0 | 272.3 | 51.4 | 25.2 | 129.7 | 43.6 | 23.3 | 11.5 | 39.4 | 148.8 | 260.3 | 378.9 | 342.6 | 26.0 | Puissance installée |
| **1957–1958** | | | | | | | | | | | | | | | **1957–1958** |
| Number of establishments. | 8 912 | 1 704 [3] | 184 | 1 602 | 1 056 | 121 | 529 | 91 | 24 | 416 | 738 | 118 | 1 829 | 500 | Nombre d'établissements |
| Value added......... | 463.7 | 90.1 | 20.2 | 45.4 | 24.6 | 17.5 | 22.7 | 2.9 | 3.1 | 52.5 | 32.2 | 45.8 | 97.1 | 9.6 | Valeur ajoutée |
| Number of engaged.... | 616.9 | 120.7 | 36.9 | 78.7 | 51.1 | 17.3 | 20.1 | 4.9 | 4.1 | 49.6 | 60.7 | 37.3 | 123.8 | 11.7 | Nombre de personnes occupées |
| Wages and salaries..... | 224.1 | 34.5 | 10.0 | 25.7 | 14.2 | 7.5 | 13.2 | 1.8 | 1.4 | 21.5 | 15.5 | 19.2 | 54.6 | 5.0 | Traitements et salaires |
| | | | | | *b. Structure* | | | | | | | | | | |
| **1952–1953** | | | | | | | | | | | | | | | **1952–1953** |
| Distribution in percent of: | | | | | | | | | | | | | | | Distribution en pourcentage: |
| Value added........ | 100.0 | 17.8 | 3.5 | 10.6 | 6.2 | 2.5 | 4.5 | 0.7 | 2.7 | 9.3 | 6.5 | 8.3 | 25.5 | 1.9 | Valeur ajoutée |
| Number of engaged... | 100.0 | 17.6 | 4.7 | 13.0 | 8.5 | 1.9 | 2.9 | 0.9 | 1.6 | 6.6 | 9.6 | 4.9 | 26.1 | 1.7 | Nombre de personnes occupées |
| Per person engaged: | | | | | | | | | | | | | | | Par personne occupée: |
| Value added........ | 0.6 | 0.7 | 0.5 | 0.8 | 0.5 | 0.9 | 1.0 | 0.5 | 1.2 | 0.9 | 0.4 | 1.1 | 0.6 | 0.7 | Valeur ajoutée |
| Capacity of installed power equipment..... | 3.1 | 2.7 | 1.9 | 0.3 | 2.7 | 4.0 | 1.4 | 2.2 | 4.4 | 4.0 | 4.8 | 13.6 | 2.3 | 2.7 | Puissance installée |
| Employees as a percent of engaged........ | 98.8 | 98.6 | 100.0 | 99.2 | 98.6 | 100.0 | 98.8 | 100.0 | 100.0 | 100.0 | 99.4 | 99.6 | 98.0 | 97.9 | Salariés en pourcentage des personnes occupées |
| Value added per unit of wages and salaries.... | 2.14 | 2.79 | 2.08 | 1.74 | 1.90 | 2.23 | 1.81 | 1.65 | 2.94 | 3.04 | 2.22 | 2.69 | 1.80 | 1.84 | Valeur ajoutée par unité de traitements et salaires |
| Wages and salaries per employee........ | 0.3 | 0.2 | 0.2 | 0.3 | 0.2 | 0.4 | 0.6 | 0.3 | 0.4 | 0.3 | 0.2 | 0.4 | 0.4 | 0.4 | Ouvriers en pourcentage des salariés |
| **1957–1958** | | | | | | | | | | | | | | | **1957–1958** |
| Distribution in percent of: | | | | | | | | | | | | | | | Distribution en pourcentage: |
| Value added........ | 100.0 | 19.4 | 4.3 | 9.8 | 5.3 | 3.8 | 4.9 | 0.6 | 0.7 | 11.3 | 7.0 | 9.8 | 21.0 | 2.1 | Valeur ajoutée |
| Number of engaged... | 100.0 | 19.5 | 6.0 | 12.8 | 8.2 | 2.8 | 3.3 | 0.8 | 0.7 | 8.0 | 9.8 | 6.1 | 20.1 | 1.9 | Nombre de personnes occupées |
| Value added per person engaged...... | 0.8 | 0.7 | 0.5 | 0.6 | 0.5 | 1.0 | 1.1 | 0.6 | 0.8 | 1.0 | 0.5 | 1.2 | 0.8 | 0.8 | Valeur ajoutée par personne occupée |
| Value added per unit of wages and salaries............ | 2.07 | 2.61 | 2.02 | 1.77 | 1.73 | 2.33 | 1.72 | 1.61 | 2.21 | 2.44 | 2.08 | 2.38 | 1.78 | 1.92 | Valeur ajoutée par unité de traitements et salaires |

[1] Excludes Manufacture of automobile tires (part of ISIC major group 30) in 1957-1958.
[2] Excludes the Manufacture and repair of automobiles and parts (part of ISIC major group 38) in 1957-1958.
[3] The fall in the number of establishments seems due to a change in the definition of the establishment in the Manufacture of grain mill products (ISIC group 205)—No. of establishments 1952-1953, 947; 1957-1958, 342.

[1] Non compris la fabrication des pneumatiques pour automobiles (dans CITI classe 30) en 1957-1958.
[2] Non compris la fabrication et la réparation des automobiles et des pièces detachées (dans CITI classe 38) en 1957-1958.
[3] La diminution du nombre d'établissements semble être due à un changement intervenu dans la définition de l'établissement en ce qui concerne la fabrication des produits de minoterie (CITI groupe 205). – Nombre d'établissements en 1952-1953: 947; en 1957-1958: 342.

# SPAIN — ESPAGNE

## Gross Domestic Product

The estimates of the gross domestic product shown in Table 1 are from the reply by the Instituto Nacional de Estadística to the United Nations national accounts questionnaire.

## Index Numbers of Industrial Production

The index numbers of industrial production set out in Table 2 were compiled from various issues of the *Anuario Estadístico de España* and *Boletín de Estadística* published by the Instituto Nacional de Estadística, Madrid.

The series of index numbers relate to all establishments engaged in selected kinds of industrial activity. The indexes are computed as base-weighted arithmetic averages, starting from elementary series of relatives derived almost entirely from the quantity of individual commodities produced. The weights utilized in compiling the indexes are proportional to value added during 1929-1931 in all cases except Metal and Other mining (ISIC major groups 12 and 14-19). For these two industries, the weights are derived from gross value of output during 1929-1931.

Further information concerning the series of index numbers is available in *Indices Mensuales de la Producción Industrial Española*, 1952, and *Suplemento del Boletín de Estadística*, No. 4, 1951. Both publications have been issued by the Instituto Nacional de Estadística.

## The Characteristics and Structure of Industrial Activity

The figures shown in Table 3 were compiled from *Estadística Industrial, 1958* issued by the Instituto Nacional de Estadística. These data result from the annual Industrial Censuses of the Instituto.

The annual Industrial Censuses cover establishments irrespective of size principally engaged in any type of mining, most kinds of manufacturing activity and the production of gas. The definitions utilized for the items of data shown in Table 3 seem consistent with the recommendations of the Statistical Commission on basic industrial statistics. Gross value of production is priced at factor cost.

## Produit intérieur brut

Les estimations du Produit intérieur brut reproduites au tableau 1 sont tirées de la réponse de l'Instituto Nacional de Estadística au questionnaire de l'O.N.U. relatif aux comptes nationaux.

## Indices de la production industrielle

Les indices de la production industrielle reproduits au tableau 2 ont été tirés de différents numéros de l'*Anuario Estadístico de España* et *Boletín de Estadística* publiés par l'Instituto Nacional de Estadística, Madrid.

Les séries d'indices se rapportent à tous les établissements engagés dans certains types d'activité industrielle. Ces indices sont des moyennes arithmétiques à pondération fixe, calculées à partir de séries élémentaires de rapports construits pour la plupart à partir du volume de chaque marchandise produite. A l'exception de la classe Industries extractives de minerais métalliques et de la classe Autres Industries extractives (CITI classes 12 et 14-19) pour lesquelles la valeur brute de la production durant 1929-1931 a été utilisée comme base de pondération, pour toutes les autres classes on a utilisé des coefficients de pondération proportionnels à la valeur ajoutée durant 1929-1931.

Plus amples renseignements concernant les séries d'indices peuvent être trouvés dans *Indices Mensuales de la Producción Industrial Española,* 1952, et *Suplemento del Boletín de Estadística*, No. 4, 1951, deux publications de l'Instituto Nacional de Estadística.

## Caractéristiques et structures de l'activité industrielle

Les chiffres du tableau 3 sont tirés du *Estadística Industrial, 1958* publié par l'Instituto Nacional de Estadística. Les données résultent des recensements industriels annuels de l'Instituto.

Les recensements industriels annuels couvrent les établissements, quelle que soit leur dimension, engagés essentiellement dans tout type d'industrie extractive, et dans la plupart des activités manufacturières et de production de gaz. Les définitions des rubriques reproduites au tableau 3 semblent cohérentes avec celles des Recommandations de la Commission de Statistiques relatives aux statistiques industrielles de base. La valeur brute de la production est évaluée au prix du marché.

# 1. THE GROSS DOMESTIC PRODUCT
## LE PRODUIT INTERIEUR BRUT

Million Pesetas                                      Millions de pesetas

## A. Expenditure on the Gross Domestic Product at Market Prices —
## Dépenses relatives au produit intérieur brut aux prix du marché

| Item of data and year / Rubrique et année | Total | Consumption Consommation | | Gross Domestic Capital Formation Formation brute de capital intérieur | | Net exports of goods and services Exportations nettes de biens et de services | |
|---|---|---|---|---|---|---|---|
| | | Total | Government Etat | Total | Fixed Fixe | Exports less imports Exportations moins importations | Exports Exportations |
| a. At Current Prices — Aux prix courants | | | | | | | |
| Absolute figures — Chiffres absolus | | | | | | | |
| 1954 | 337 522.7 | 279 063.5 | 28 907.9 | ... | 58 801.9 | −342.7 | 22 904.3 |
| 1955 | 376 272.1 | 309 422.6 | 32 794.4 | ... | 66 670.0 | 179.5 | 20 881.4 |
| 1956 | 431 412.7 | 357 028.4 | 38 676.8 | ... | 80 399.5 | −6 015.2 | 21 667.6 |
| 1957 | 505 398.5 | 417 492.4 | 48 086.0 | ... | 97 557.0 | −9 650.9 | 32 129.9 |
| 1958 | 575 108.7 | 472 231.1 | 46 847.5 | ... | 111 433.4 | −8 555.8 | 33 403.3 |
| 1959 | 567 980.9 | 466 458.8 | 52 510.6 | ... | 103 069.7 | −1 547.6 | 43 578.4 |
| 1960 | 583 814.5 | 463 442.4 | 54 565.8 | ... | 99 595.3 | 20 776.8 | 71 893.3 |
| Percentage distribution of average annual expenditure — Distribution en pourcentage des dépenses annuelles moyennes | | | | | | | |
| 1954 | 100.0 | 82.6 | 8.6 | ... | 17.5 | −0.1 | 6.8 |
| 1958 | 100.0 | 82.1 | 8.1 | ... | 19.4 | −1.5 | 5.8 |
| 1960 | 100.0 | 79.4 | 9.3 | ... | 17.0 | 3.6 | 12.3 |

## B. The Gross Domestic Product at Factor Cost According to Origin
## Origine par secteur d'activité du produit intérieur brut au coût des facteurs

| Item of data and year / Rubrique et année | Total | Agricultural sector Secteur agricole | Industrial Sector — Secteur Industriel | | | | | Transportation and communication Transport et communication | Other sectors Autres secteurs |
|---|---|---|---|---|---|---|---|---|---|
| | | | Total | Mining Industries extractives | Manufacturing Industries manufacturières | Construction Bâtiments et travaux publics | Electricity, gas and water Electricité, gaz et eau | | |
| ISIC — CITI | 0–9 | 0 | 1–5 | 1 | 2–3 | 4 | 5 | 7 | 6, 8–9 |
| a. At Current Prices — Aux prix courants | | | | | | | | | |
| Absolute figures — Chiffres absolus | | | | | | | | | |
| 1954 | 316 119.5 | 81 004.7 | 102 725.7 | 7 166.9 | 72 200.2 | 15 797.6 | 7 561.0 | 20 381.5 | 112 007.6 |
| 1955 | 351 619.6 | 85 664.5 | 117 306.7 | 8 134.1 | 81 341.5 | 18 386.4 | 9 444.7 | 22 673.0 | 125 975.4 |
| 1956 | 400 299.0 | 99 137.7 | 135 485.2 | 9 127.7 | 94 042.1 | 21 726.9 | 10 588.5 | 26 144.1 | 139 532.0 |
| 1957 | 470 180.9 | 118 736.4 | 159 475.7 | 11 283.3 | 109 588.9 | 25 504.1 | 13 099.4 | 30 635.8 | 161 333.0 |
| 1958 | 537 986.9 | 136 352.1 | 183 285.1 | 11 655.6 | 128 433.6 | 26 787.9 | 16 408.0 | 35 457.2 | 182 892.5 |
| 1959 | 526 740.8 | 140 111.0 | 175 959.1 | 10 586.5 | 122 257.5 | 26 684.5 | 16 430.6 | 34 535.8 | 176 134.9 |
| 1960 | 539 666.9 | 142 796.5 | 178 122.9 | 11 106.3 | 124 424.9 | 25 072.6 | 17 519.1 | 36 822.4 | 181 925.1 |
| Percentage distribution according to sector — Distribution en pourcentage par secteur | | | | | | | | | |
| 1954 | 100.0 | 25.6 | 32.5 | 2.2 | 22.9 | 5.0 | 2.4 | 6.4 | 35.5 |
| 1958 | 100.0 | 25.3 | 34.1 | 2.2 | 23.8 | 5.0 | 3.1 | 6.6 | 34.0 |
| 1960 | 100.0 | 26.4 | 33.0 | 2.1 | 23.0 | 4.7 | 3.2 | 6.8 | 33.8 |

# 2. INDEX NUMBERS OF INDUSTRIAL PRODUCTION
## INDICES DE LA PRODUCTION INDUSTRIELLE

## A. Selected Divisions of Industrial Activity
### Quelques branches de l'activité industrielle

| Period<br>Période | Total [1] | Mining [1]<br>Industries<br>extractives [1] | Manu-<br>facturing [1]<br>Industries<br>manu-<br>facturières [1] | Electricity<br>and gas<br>Electricité<br>et gaz |
|---|---|---|---|---|
| ISIC — CITI | 1–3, 511–512 | 1 | 2–3 | 511–512 |
| *a.* Indexes — Indices (1958 = 100) | | | | |
| 1940 | 34 | 49 | 43 | 25 |
| 1948 | 46 | 61 | 49 | 40 |
| 1949 | 44 | 62 | 47 | 36 |
| 1950 | 50 | 65 | 52 | 44 |
| 1951 | 56 | 70 | 55 | 53 |
| 1952 | 64 | 75 | 67 | 60 |
| 1953 | 68 | 76 | 72 | 63 |
| 1954 | 70 | 78 | 75 | 66 |
| 1955 | 79 | 82 | 80 | 78 |
| 1956 | 87 | 90 | 83 | 88 |
| 1957 | 91 | 97 | 90 | 91 |
| 1958 | 100 | 100 | 100 | 100 |
| 1959 | 104 | 94 | 105 | 108 |
| 1960 | 111 | 95 | 110 | 116 |
| 1961 | 121 | 98 | 126 | 127 |
| *b.* Average Annual Rate of Change — Taux annuel moyen de variation | | | | |
| 1940 – 1960 | 6.1 | 3.4 | 4.8 | 8.0 |
| 1940 – 1948 | 3.8 | 2.8 | 1.7 | 6.0 |
| 1950 – 1960 | 8.3 | 3.9 | 7.8 | 10.2 |
| 1948 – 1953 | 8.1 | 4.5 | 8.0 | 9.5 |
| 1954 – 1958 | 9.3 | 6.4 | 7.5 | 10.9 |
| 1958 – 1960 | 5.4 | −2.5 | 4.9 | 7.7 |

[1] For footnotes see end of table.
[1] Pour les notes, voir au bas du tableau.

## B. The Major Groups of Mining
### Les classes de la branche Industries extractives

| Period<br>Période | All mining [1]<br>Toutes<br>industries<br>extractives [1] | Coal<br>mining<br>Extraction<br>du charbon | Metal mining<br>Extraction<br>des minerais<br>métalliques | Other mining<br>Autres<br>industries<br>extractives |
|---|---|---|---|---|
| ISIC — CITI | 12, 14–19 | 11 | 12 | 14–19 |
| *a.* Indexes — Indices (1958 = 100) | | | | |
| 1940 | 49 | 55 | 49 | 27 |
| 1948 | 61 | 69 | 45 | 49 |
| 1949 | 62 | 70 | 49 | 44 |
| 1950 | 65 | 73 | 54 | 51 |
| 1951 | 70 | 75 | 66 | 56 |
| 1952 | 75 | 80 | 70 | 60 |
| 1953 | 76 | 82 | 78 | 55 |
| 1954 | 78 | 83 | 82 | 61 |
| 1955 | 82 | 84 | 92 | 70 |
| 1956 | 90 | 86 | 90 | 105 |
| 1957 | 97 | 97 | 99 | 103 |
| 1958 | 100 | 100 | 100 | 100 |
| 1959 | 94 | 92 | 96 | 98 |
| 1960 | 95 | 91 | 106 | 98 |
| 1961 | 98 | 85 | 119 | 103 |
| *b.* Average Annual Rate of Change — Taux annuel moyen de variation | | | | |
| 1940 – 1960 | 3.4 | 2.5 | 3.9 | 6.7 |
| 1940 – 1948 | 2.8 | 2.9 | −1.1 | 7.7 |
| 1950 – 1960 | 3.9 | 2.2 | 7.0 | 6.8 |
| 1948 – 1953 | 4.5 | 3.5 | 11.6 | 2.3 |
| 1954 – 1958 | 6.4 | 4.8 | 5.1 | 13.1 |
| 1958 – 1960 | −2.5 | −4.6 | 3.0 | −1.0 |

[1] For footnotes see end of table.
[1] Pour les notes, voir au bas du tableau.

## C. The Major Groups of Manufacturing
### Les classes de la branche Industries manufacturières

| Period<br>Période | Manu-facturing[1]<br>Industries manufac-turières[1] | Textiles | Chemicals and chemical and coal products<br>Produits chi-miques et dérivés du charbon | Cement<br>Fabrication des ciments | Basic metals<br>Métal-lurgie de base |
|---|---|---|---|---|---|
| ISIC — CITI | 2–3 | 23 | 31–32 | 334 | 34 |

### a. Indexes — Indices (1958 = 100)

| | | | | | |
|---|---|---|---|---|---|
| 1940 | 43 | 67 | 41 | 25 | 46 |
| 1948 | 49 | 76 | 41 | 34 | 41 |
| 1949 | 47 | 62 | 55 | 35 | 45 |
| 1950 | 52 | 66 | 48 | 40 | 52 |
| 1951 | 55 | 63 | 75 | 44 | 53 |
| 1952 | 67 | 77 | 75 | 47 | 59 |
| 1953 | 72 | 82 | 81 | 53 | 59 |
| 1954 | 75 | 75 | 83 | 64 | 69 |
| 1955 | 80 | 79 | 83 | 78 | 78 |
| 1956 | 83 | 83 | 90 | 83 | 81 |
| 1957 | 90 | 88 | 92 | 93 | 86 |
| 1958 | 100 | 100 | 100 | 100 | 100 |
| 1959 | 105 | 90 | 113 | 108 | 119 |
| 1960 | 110 | 95 | 119 | 108 | 126 |
| 1961 | 126 | 103 | 137 | 122 | 141 |

### b. Average Annual Rate of Change — Taux annuel moyen de variation

| | | | | | |
|---|---|---|---|---|---|
| 1940–1960 | 4.8 | 1.8 | 5.5 | 7.6 | 5.2 |
| 1940–1948 | 1.7 | 1.6 | — | 3.9 | −1.4 |
| 1950–1960 | 7.8 | 3.7 | 9.5 | 10.4 | 9.3 |
| 1948–1953 | 8.0 | 1.5 | 14.6 | 9.3 | 7.6 |
| 1954–1958 | 7.5 | 7.5 | 4.8 | 11.8 | 9.7 |
| 1958–1960 | 4.9 | −2.5 | 9.1 | 3.9 | 12.2 |

[1] Manufacturing covers Textiles (ISIC major group 23), Chemicals and coal products (ISIC major groups 31–32), cement products (ISIC group 334) and Basic metals (ISIC major group 34) only.

[1] Les Industries manufacturières comprennent les Industries textiles (CITI classe 23) les Industries chimiques et les Produits dérivés du charbon (CITI classes 31-32), les produits en ciment (CITI Branche 334) et les Métaux de base (CITI classe 34) seulement.

## 3. CHARACTERISTICS OF INDUSTRIAL ESTABLISHMENTS
## CARACTERISTIQUES D'ETABLISSEMENTS INDUSTRIELS
### 1958

Number of establishments in units; gross value of production and wages and salaries in million Pesetas; number of engaged, employees and operatives in thousands; man-hours worked in millions; electricity consumed in million KWH; wages and salaries per employee in thousand Pesetas; average annual man-hours per operative in thousands; electricity consumed per employee and per thousand operative man-hours in thousand KWH.

Nombre d'établissements en unités; valeur brute de la production et traitements et salaires en millions de pesetas; nombre de personnes occupées, de salariés et d'ouvriers en milliers; heures de travail en millions; électricité consommée en millions de kWh; traitements et salaires par salarié en milliers de pesetas; moyenne annuelle des heures de travail par ouvrier en milliers; électricité consommée par salarié et par millier d'heures-ouvrier en milliers de kWh.

### A. Selected Divisions of Industrial Activity — Quelques branches de l'activité industrielle

| Item of data | All industrial activity<br>Toutes industries | Mining<br>Industries ex-tractives | Manu-facturing[1]<br>Industries manu-facturières[1] | Gas<br>Gaz | Rubrique | Item of data | All industrial activity<br>Toutes industries | Mining<br>Industries ex-tractives | Manu-facturing<br>Industries manu-facturières | Gas<br>Gaz | Rubrique |
|---|---|---|---|---|---|---|---|---|---|---|---|
| ISIC | 1-3, 512 | 1 | 2–3 | 512 | CITI | ISIC | 1-3, 512 | 1 | 2–3 | 512 | CITI |
| | a. Absolute Figures — Chiffres absolus | | | | | | b. Structure | | | | |
| Number of establishments. | 96 439 [2] | 4 651 | 91 747 [2] | 41 | Nombre d'établissements | Distribution in percent of number of employees.... | | | | | Distribution en pourcentage du nombre de salariés |
| Employees: | | | | | Salariés: | Per employee: | 100.0 | 13.0 | 86.6 | 0.4 | Par salarié: |
| Number (As of end of year) | 1 512.5 | 198.1 | 1 308.7 | 5.7 | Nombre (en fin d'année) | Wages and salaries | 27.2 | 30.5 | 26.6 | 40.1 | Traitements et salaires |
| Wages and salaries | 41 081.4 | 6 049.2 | 34 803.4 | 228.8 | Traitements et salaires | Electricity consumed.... | ... | ... | 190.1 | 2.5 | Electricité consommée |
| Number of operatives (As of end of year) | ... | ... | 1 142.0 | 4.0 | Nombre d'ouvriers (en fin d'année) | Operatives as a percent of employees | ... | ... | 87.3 | 70.2 | Ouvriers en pourcentage des salariés |
| Electricity consumed | ... | ... | 248 812.2 | 14.4 | Electricité consommée | | | | | | |

For footnotes see end of table.

Pour les notes, voir au bas du tableau.

## B. The Major Groups of Mining — Les classes de la branche Industries extractives

| Item of data | All mining Toutes industries extractives | Coal mining Extraction du charbon | Metal mining Extraction des minerais métalliques | Crude petroleum and natural gas Pétrole brut et gaz naturel | Other mining Divers | Rubrique | Item of data | All mining Toutes industries extractives | Coal mining Extraction du charbon | Metal mining Extraction des minerais métalliques | Crude petroleum and natural gas Pétrole brut et gaz naturel | Other mining Divers | Rubrique |
|---|---|---|---|---|---|---|---|---|---|---|---|---|---|
| ISIC | 1 | 11 | 12 | 13 | 14-19 | CITI | ISIC | 1 | 11 | 12 | 13 | 14-19 | CITI |
| | **a. Absolute Figures — Chiffres absolus** | | | | | | | **b. Structure** | | | | | |
| Number of establishments... | 4 651 | 579 | 979 | 3 | 3 090 | Nombre d'établissements | Distribution in percent of number of employees...... | 100.0 | 54.0 | 25.9 | 0.5 | 19.6 | Distribution en pourcentage du nombre de salariés |
| Employees: Number (As of end of year)..... | 198.1 | 107.0 | 51.4 | 1.0 | 38.7 | Salariés: Nombre (en fin d'année) | Wages and salaries per employee.... | 30.5 | 36.0 | 27.1 | 30.7 | 20.0 | Traitements et salaires par salarié |
| Wages and salaries........ | 6 049.2 | 3 853.0 | 1 391.2 | 30.7 | 774.3 | Traitements et salaires | Operatives as a percent of employees...... | ... | 94.8 | 94.2 | 100.0 | ... | Ouvriers en pourcentage des salariés |
| Operatives: Number (As of end of year)..... | ... | 101.5 | 48.4 | 1.0 | ... | Ouvriers: Nombre (en fin d'année) | Average man-hours per operative.... | ... | 2.11 | 2.04 | 2.20 | ... | Heures de travail: moyenne par ouvrier |
| Man-hours worked.......... | 388.9 | 214.1 | 98.6 | 2.2 | 74.0 | Heures de travail effectuées | | | | | | | |

## C. The Major Groups of Manufacturing — Les classes de la branche Industries manufacturières

| Item of data | Manufacturing[1] Industries manufacturières[1] | Food beverages and tobacco Industries alimentaires, boissons, tabac | Textiles | Clothing, footwear and made-up textiles Articles d'habillement, chaussures et ouvrages en tissu | Wood products and furniture Bois et meubles | Paper and paper products Papier et ouvrages en papier | Printing and publishing Imprimerie et édition | Leather and leather products except wearing apparel Cuir et articles en cuir, à l'exclusion des articles d'habillement | Chemicals and chemical, petroleum and coal products Produits chimiques et dérivés du pétrole et du charbon | Non-metallic mineral products Produits minéraux non métalliques | Basic metals Métallurgie de base | Metal products Ouvrages en métaux | Other manufacturing[1] Autres industries manufacturières[1] | Rubrique |
|---|---|---|---|---|---|---|---|---|---|---|---|---|---|---|
| ISIC | 2-3 | 20-22 | 23 | 24 | 25-26 | 27 | 28 | 29 | 31-32 | 33 | 34 | 35-38 | 39 | CITI |
| | **a. Absolute Figures — Chiffres absolus** | | | | | | | | | | | | | |
| Number of establishments | 91 747[2] | 33 322 | 3 781 | 4 922 | 21 593[2] | 1 268 | 4 052 | 4 021 | 5 027 | 9 845 | 311 | 3 556 | 49 | Nombre d'établissements |
| Gross value of production............... | ... | 59 902.8 | ... | 9 091.9 | 15 970.5 | 7 687.8 | 5 773.1 | 4 503.0 | ... | ... | 31 135.3 | 36 383.6 | 119.7 | Valeur brute de la production |
| Number of engaged (As of end of year): | ... | ... | 252.8 | 78.8 | 156.6 | 37.9 | 51.7 | 21.7 | 139.5 | 131.4 | 89.5 | ... | 1.6 | Nombre de personnes occupées (en fin d'année) |
| Employees: Number (As of end of year)........ | 1 308.7 | 161.6 | 251.9 | 70.9 | 119.5 | 36.5 | 46.0 | 16.8 | 133.9 | 120.2 | 89.4 | 260.5 | 1.5 | Salariés: Nombre (en fin d'année): |
| Wages and salaries.... | 34 803.4 | 3 024.5 | 5 356.7 | 1 438.2 | 2 824.4 | 912.7 | 1 288.1 | 408.5 | 4 441.4 | 3 010.2 | 3 403.7 | 8 651.4 | 43.6 | Traitements et salaires |
| Operatives: Number (As of end of year)........... | 1 142.0 | 143.0 | 230.6 | 64.5 | 113.3 | 33.1 | 39.6 | 15.4 | 100.0 | 111.7 | 72.4 | 217.1 | 1.3 | Ouvriers: Nombre (en fin d'année) |
| Man-hours worked.... | 2 642.3 | 262.5 | 492.6 | 148.8 | 276.0 | 79.2 | 112.4 | 42.5 | 254.9 | 267.1 | 183.8 | 519.2 | 3.3 | Heures de travail effectuées |
| Electricity consumed..... | 248 812.2 | 31 733.0 | 432.8 | 24.3 | 127 803.2 | 422.6 | 29.7 | 24.6 | 1 850.1 | 738.4 | 1 605.5 | 84 146.7 | 1.3 | Electricité consommée |
| | **b. Structure** | | | | | | | | | | | | | |
| Distribution in percent of number of employees.......... | 100.0 | 12.3 | 19.2 | 5.5 | 9.1 | 2.8 | 3.5 | 1.3 | 10.2 | 9.2 | 6.8 | 19.9 | 0.2 | Distribution en pourcentage du nombre de salariés |
| Per employee: Wages and salaries... | 26.6 | 18.7 | 21.3 | 20.3 | 23.6 | 25.0 | 28.0 | 24.3 | 33.2 | 25.0 | 38.1 | 33.2 | 29.1 | Par salarié: Traitements et salaires |
| Electricity consumed... | 190.1 | 196.4 | 1.7 | 0.3 | 1 069.5 | 11.6 | 0.6 | 1.5 | 13.8 | 6.1 | 18.0 | 323.0 | 0.9 | Electricité consommée |
| Employees as a percent of engaged... | ... | ... | 99.6 | 90.0 | 76.3 | 96.3 | 89.0 | 77.4 | 96.0 | 91.5 | 99.9 | ... | 93.8 | Salariés en pourcentage des personnes occupées |
| Operatives as a percent of employees... | 87.3 | 88.5 | 91.5 | 91.0 | 94.8 | 90.7 | 86.1 | 91.7 | 74.7 | 92.9 | 81.0 | 83.3 | 86.7 | Ouvriers en pourcentage des salariés |
| Average man-hours per operative... | 2.31 | 1.84 | 2.14 | 2.31 | 2.44 | 2.39 | 2.84 | 2.76 | 2.55 | 2.39 | 2.54 | 2.39 | 2.54 | Heures de travail: moyenne par ouvrier |
| Electricity consumed per thousand operative man-hours.......... | 94.16 | 120.89 | 0.88 | 0.16 | 463.06 | 5.34 | 0.26 | 0.58 | 7.26 | 2.76 | 8.74 | 162.07 | 0.39 | Electricité consommée par millier d'heures-ouvrier |

[1] Excluded are Rubber products (ISIC major group 30); a number of classes of Manufacturing included in Other manufacturing (ISIC major group 39) and perhaps some other types of manufacturing activity.

[2] Sawmills are not covered in the count of establishments but are included in the data on other items.

[1] Non compris Ouvrages en caoutchouc (CITI classe 30); certaines classes des Industries manufacturières dans les Autres industries manufacturières (CITI classe 39) et peut-être quelques autres types d'activités manufacturières.

[2] Le nombre d'établissements ne comprend pas les scieries, elles sont comprises dans les données relatives à d'autres articles.

### Gross Domestic Product and Gross Domestic Fixed Capital Formation

Estimates of expenditures on, and industrial origin of, the gross domestic product and of the industrial composition of the gross fixed capital formation are shown in Table 1. These data were supplied by the Department of Statistics, Khartoum, in response to the United Nations questionnaire on national accounts. Official estimates are published annually by this Department in a publication entitled *National Income of Sudan*.

### The Characteristics and Structure of Industrial Activity

The figures set out in Tables 2 and 3 were taken from the publications: *The National Income of Sudan, 1955/56* prepared by Messrs. C. H. Harvie and J. G. Kleve and published by the Department of Statistics, Khartoum; and *National Income of Sudan, 1955/56-1959/60* prepared and published by the said Department. Dr. Kleve acted as adviser in the preparation of the second report.

Establishments engaged in manufacturing activities were regarded in these studies as falling into two broad categories, depending on whether or not the establishments used modern capital equipment. In this latter case, they were considered handicrafts. Table 2 gives data relating to all establishments while the data shown in Table 3 are confined only to establishments using modern capital equipment. The field of coverage of the information set out in these two tables excluded garages, newspapers, slaughter houses belonging to local councils, repair workshops of Sudan Railways, workshops of Stores and Equipment and other Government workshops which had no separate accounts.

The data in Table 3 on the number of employees refer to the number as of the end of the accounting year of the individual establishments. The figures of value added relate, generally speaking, to the financial year beginning 1st July and are, in fact, the contribution to the gross domestic product, i.e., they exclude all goods and both industrial and non-industrial services obtained from other establishments.

### Produit intérieur brut et formation brute de capital fixe intérieur

Le tableau 1 contient des estimations des dépenses imputées au produit intérieur brut, du produit intérieur brut par secteur d'activité et de la formation brute de capital fixe intérieur par secteur d'acquisition. Ces données ont été fournies par le Département de la statistique, Khartoum, en réponse au questionnaire de l'ONU sur la comptabilité nationale. Les estimations officielles sont publiées annuellement par ce Département dans une publication intitulé *National Income of Sudan*.

### Caractéristiques et structure de l'activité industrielle

Les chiffres des tableaux 2 et 3 sont tirés des publications suivantes : *The National Income of Sudan, 1955/56*, préparée par MM. C.H. Harvie et J. G. Kleve et publiée par le Département de la statistique; et *National Income of Sudan, 1955/56-1959/60*, préparée et publiée par ce même Département. M. Kleve a fait fonction de conseiller lors de la préparation du second rapport.

Dans ces études, les établissements exerçant des activités manufacturières ont été répartis en deux grandes catégories suivant qu'ils possédaient un équipement moderne ou non. Dans le second cas, ils étaient considérés comme unités artisanales. Les données du tableau 2 concernent tous les établissements, tandis que celles du tableau 3 portent seulement sur les établissements utilisant un équipement moderne. Les chiffres de ces deux tableaux ne portent pas sur les unités suivantes : garages, journaux, abattoirs appartenant aux municipalités, ateliers de réparation de la Sudan Railways, ateliers des Stores and Equipment et autres ateliers de l'Etat n'ayant pas de comptes à part.

Les données du tableau 3 relatives au nombre de salariés concernent le nombre de ces salariés à la fin de l'année comptable de chaque établissement. Les chiffres de la valeur ajoutée se rapportent, généralement, à l'exercice financier commençant le 1er juillet et représentent, en fait, les contributions au produit intérieur brut; ils ne portent donc pas sur les biens et les services, industriels ou non, fournis par d'autres établissements.

# 1. THE GROSS DOMESTIC PRODUCT AND GROSS DOMESTIC FIXED CAPITAL FORMATION
## LE PRODUIT INTERIEUR BRUT ET LA FORMATION BRUTE DE CAPITAL FIXE INTERIEUR

Thousand Sudanese pounds         Milliers de livres soudanaises

## A. Expenditure on the Gross Domestic Product at Market Prices
### Dépenses relatives au produit intérieur brut aux prix du marché

| Item of data and year [1]<br>Rubrique et année [1] | Total | Consumption<br>Consommation | | Gross Domestic Capital Formation<br>Formation brute de capital intérieur | | Net exports of goods and services<br>Exportations nettes de biens et de services |
|---|---|---|---|---|---|---|
| | | Total | Government<br>Etat | Total | Fixed<br>Fixe | |
| | | At Current Prices — Aux prix courants | | | | |
| Absolute figures — Chiffres absolus | | | | | | |
| 1955 | 300 243 | 271 499 | 21 229 | 15 768 | 21 233 | 12 976 |
| 1956 | 329 776 | 293 515 | 22 916 | 43 061 | 24 861 | −6 800 |
| 1957 | 328 365 | 308 782 | 27 788 | 34 083 | 39 483 | −14 500 |
| 1958 | 339 183 | 307 931 | 27 886 | 30 352 | 35 952 | 900 |
| 1959 | 380 689 | 332 902 | 30 793 | 42 387 | 38 287 | 5 400 |
| 1960 | 388 369 | 345 935 | 33 398 | 50 034 | 46 234 | −7 600 |
| 1961 | 435 987 | 377 232 | 38 324 | 81 555 | 59 201 | −22 800 |
| Percentage distribution of average annual expenditure — Distribution en pourcentage des dépenses annuelles moyennes | | | | | | |
| 1955−1960 | 100.0 | 90.0 | 7.9 | 10.4 | 10.0 | −0.4 |
| 1955 | 100.0 | 90.4 | 7.1 | 5.2 | 7.1 | 4.4 |
| 1958 | 100.0 | 90.7 | 8.2 | 9.0 | 10.6 | 0.3 |
| 1960 | 100.0 | 89.0 | 8.6 | 12.9 | 11.9 | −1.9 |

For footnotes see end of table.      Pour les notes, voir au bas du tableau.

## B. The Gross Domestic Product at Factor Cost According to Origin
### Origine par secteur d'activité du produit intérieur brut au coût des facteurs

| Item of data and year [1]<br>Rubrique et année[1] | Total | Agricultural sector<br>Secteur agricole | Industrial Sector — Secteur industriel | | | | | Transportation and communication<br>Transports et communications | Other sectors<br>Autres secteurs |
|---|---|---|---|---|---|---|---|---|---|
| | | | Total | Mining<br>Industries extractives | Manufacturing<br>Industries manufacturières | Construction<br>Bâtiment et travaux publics | Electricity, gas and water<br>Electricité, gaz et eau | | |
| ISIC — CITI | 0–9 | 0 | 1–5 | 1 | 2–3 | 4 | 5 | 7 | 6, 8–9 |
| | | | a. At Current Prices — Aux prix courants | | | | | | |
| Absolute figures — Chiffres absolus | | | | | | | | | |
| 1955 | 284 205 | 172 608 | 30 023 | 225 | 12 528 | 16 235 | 1 035 | 37 580 | 43 994 |
| 1956 | 312 666 | 196 206 | 32 401 | 234 | 13 260 | 17 747 | 1 160 | 37 359 | 46 700 |
| 1957 | 307 885 | 166 703 | 37 673 | 250 | 14 060 | 22 078 | 1 285 | 49 874 | 53 635 |
| 1958 | 318 465 | 188 219 | 38 026 | 254 | 14 970 | 21 392 | 1 410 | 38 087 | 54 133 |
| 1959 | 346 079 | 200 271 | 38 892 | 256 | 15 967 | 21 095 | 1 574 | 48 827 | 58 089 |
| 1960 | 354 549 | 202 226 | 42 664 | 261 | 17 752 | 22 933 | 1 718 | 47 984 | 61 675 |
| 1961 | 396 457 | 232 464 | 45 448 | 270 | 19 200 | 24 128 | 1 850 | 53 682 | 64 863 |
| Percentage distribution according to sector— Distribution en pourcentage par secteur | | | | | | | | | |
| 1955−1960 | 100.0 | 58.5 | 11.4 | 0.1 | 4.6 | 6.3 | 0.4 | 13.5 | 16.6 |
| 1955 | 100.0 | 60.7 | 10.5 | 0.1 | 4.4 | 5.7 | 0.3 | 13.3 | 15.5 |
| 1958 | 100.0 | 59.1 | 11.9 | 0.1 | 4.6 | 6.7 | 0.5 | 12.0 | 17.0 |
| 1960 | 100.0 | 57.0 | 12.0 | 0.1 | 5.0 | 6.4 | 0.5 | 13.6 | 17.4 |

For footnotes see end of table.      Pour les notes, voir au bas du tableau.

# SUDAN

## C. Gross Domestic Fixed Capital Formation According to Purchasing Sector
### La formation brute de capital fixe intérieur par secteur d'acquisition

| Item of data and year [1]<br>Rubrique et année [1] | Total | Agricultural sector<br>Secteur agricole | Industrial Sector — Secteur Industriel | | | | | Transportation and communication<br>Transports et communications | Other sectors<br>Autres secteurs |
|---|---|---|---|---|---|---|---|---|---|
| | | | Total | Mining<br>Industries extractives | Manufacturing<br>Industries manufacturières | Construction<br>Bâtiment et travaux publics | Electricity, gas and water<br>Electricité, gaz et eau | | |
| ISIC — CITI | 0–9 | 0 | 1–5 | 1 | 2–3 | 4 | 5 | 7 | 6, 8–9 |
| | At Current Prices — Aux prix courants | | | | | | | | |
| **Absolute figures — Chiffres absolus** | | | | | | | | | |
| 1955............ | 21 233 | 1 824 | 1 799 | — | 536 | 92 | 1 171 | 4 175 | 13 435 |
| 1956............ | 24 861 | 5 598 | 3 349 | 467 | 534 | 839 | 1 509 | 3 479 | 12 435 |
| 1957............ | 39 483 | 12 167 | 6 949 | 918 | 1 393 | 3 096 | 1 542 | 6 472 | 13 895 |
| 1958............ | 35 952 | 10 667 | 4 704 | 6 | 2 667 | 988 | 1 043 | 8 938 | 11 643 |
| 1959............ | 38 287 | 6 406 | 6 792 | 8 | 3 154 | 693 | 2 937 | 8 908 | 16 181 |
| 1960............ | 46 234 | 11 314 | 11 415 | 76 | 8 230 | 1 054 | 2 055 | 7 155 | 16 350 |
| 1961............ | 59 201 | 15 742 | 16 632 | 510 | 11 292 | 3 150 | 1 680 | 8 855 | 17 972 |
| **Percentage distribution according to sector— Distribution en pourcentage par secteur** | | | | | | | | | |
| 1955 – 1960..... | 100.0 | 23.2 | 17.0 | 0.7 | 8.1 | 3.2 | 5.0 | 19.0 | 40.8 |
| 1955............ | 100.0 | 8.5 | 8.5 | — | 2.6 | 0.4 | 5.5 | 19.7 | 63.3 |
| 1958............ | 100.0 | 29.6 | 13.1 | — | 7.5 | 2.7 | 2.9 | 24.9 | 32.4 |
| 1960............ | 100.0 | 24.4 | 24.7 | 0.2 | 17.8 | 2.3 | 4.4 | 15.5 | 35.4 |

[1] Fiscal year beginning 1 July.  [1] Exercice financier commençant le 1er juillet.

## 2. VALUE ADDED BY ALL INDUSTRIAL ESTABLISHMENTS
## VALEUR AJOUTEE PAR TOUS LES ETABLISSEMENTS INDUSTRIELS
### 1955-1956

Value added in thousand Sudanese pounds.          Valeur ajoutée en milliers de livres soudanaises.

### A. The Divisions of Industrial Activity
### Les branches de l'activité industrielle

| Item of data | All industrial activity<br>Toutes industries | Mining<br>Industries extractives | Manufacturing<br>Industries manufacturières | Construction<br>Bâtiment et travaux publics | Electricity gas and water<br>Electricité gaz et eau | Rubrique |
|---|---|---|---|---|---|---|
| ISIC | 1-5 | 1 | 2-3 | 4 | 5 | CITI |
| Value added...... | 30 023 | 225 | 12 528 | 16 235 | 1 035 | Valeur ajoutée |
| Distribution in percent of value added..... | 100.0 | 0.7 | 41.7 | 54.1 | 3.5 | Répartition en pourcentage de la valeur ajoutée |

### B. The Major Groups of Mining
### Les classes de la branche Industries extractives

| Item of data | All mining<br>Toutes industries extractives | Metal mining<br>Extraction des minerais métalliques | Other mining<br>Divers | Rubrique |
|---|---|---|---|---|
| ISIC | 1 | 12 | 14-19 | CITI |
| Value added................ | 225 | 111 | 114 | Valeur ajoutée |
| Distribution in percent of value added................ | 100.0 | 49.3 | 50.7 | Répartition en pourcentage de la valeur ajoutée |

690

## C. The Major Groups of Manufacturing — Les classes de la branche Industries manufacturières

| Item of data | Manu-facturing<br>Industries manufac-turières | Food beverages and tobacco<br>Industries alimen-taires, boissons, tabac | Textiles | Clothing, footwear and made-up textiles<br>Articles d'habil-lement, chaussures et ouvrages en tissu | Wood products and furniture<br>Bois et meubles | Printing and publish-ing<br>Im-primerie et édition | Leather and leather products except wearing apparel<br>Cuir et articles en cuir, à l'exclu-sion des articles d'habil-lement | Chemicals and chemical, petroleum and coal products<br>Produits chi-miques et dérivés du pétrole et du charbon | Non-metallic mineral products<br>Produits minéraux non métal-liques | Metal products<br>Ouvrages en métaux | Other manu-factur-ing<br>Autres in-dustries manufac-turières | Rubrique |
|---|---|---|---|---|---|---|---|---|---|---|---|---|
| ISIC | 2–3 | 20–22 | 23 | 24 | 25–26 | 28 | 29 | 31–32 | 33 | 35–38 | 39 | CITI |
| Value added.......... | 12 528 | 4 214 | 1 077 | 3 192 | 752 | 77 | 127 | 1 144 | 1 694 | 190 | 61 | Valeur ajoutée |
| Distribution in percent of value added...... | 100.0 | 33.6 | 8.6 | 25.5 | 6.0 | 0.6 | 1.0 | 9.1 | 13.5 | 1.6 | 0.5 | Répartition en pour-centage de la valeur ajoutée |

## 3. CHARACTERISTICS OF MANUFACTURING ESTABLISHMENTS EXCLUDING HANDICRAFT UNITS

## CARACTERISTIQUES DES ETABLISSEMENTS MANUFACTURIERS A L'EXCLUSION DES UNITES ARTISANALES

### 1955-1956, 1959-1960

Number of establishments in units; value added in thousand Sudanese pounds; number of employees in units; and value added per employee in Sudanese pounds.

Nombre d'établissements en unités; valeur ajoutée et traitements et salaires en milliers de livres soudanaises; nombre de salariés en unités; valeur ajoutée par salarié en livres soudanaises.

| Year and item of data | Manu-factur-ing [1]<br>Industries manufac-turières [1] | Food, beverages and tobacco<br>Industries alimen-taires, boissons, tabac | Textiles, clothing, footwear and made-up textiles<br>Textiles, articles d'habil-lement, chaussures et ouvrages en tissu | Furniture<br>Meubles | Paper, paper products and printing and publishing<br>Papier, ouvrages en papier, im-primerie et édition | Rubber and chemical products<br>Produits chi-miques et ouvrages en caout-chouc | Non-metallic mineral products<br>Produits minéraux non métal-liques | Metal products and other manu-facturing<br>Ouvrages en métaux et autres industries manufac-turières | Année et rubrique |
|---|---|---|---|---|---|---|---|---|---|
| ISIC | 2–3 | 20–22 | 23–24 | 26 | 27–28 | 30–31 | 33 | 35–39 | CITI |
| | | | *a.* Absolute Figures — Chiffres absolus | | | | | | |
| 1955–1956<br>Value added.......... | 2 762 | 989 | 25 | 67 | 77 | 1 157 | 249 | 198 | 1955–1956<br>Valeur ajoutée |
| Number of employees (As at end of accounting year)...... | 12 391 | 6 482 | 621 | 256 | 369 | 3 310 | 361 | 992 | Nombre de salariés (à la fin de l'année comptable) |
| 1959–1960<br>Value added.......... | 5 184 | 1 560 | 231 | 122 | 270 | 2 165 | 517 | 319 | 1959–1960<br>Valeur ajoutée |
| Number of employees (As at end of accounting year)...... | 18 462 | 7 415 | 1 732 | 517 | 699 | 5 966 | 564 | 1 569 | Nombre de salariés (à la fin de l'année comptable) |
| | | | *b.* Structure | | | | | | |
| 1955–1956<br>Distribution in percent of: | | | | | | | | | 1955–1956<br>Distribution en pour-centage: |
| Value added........ | 100.0 | 35.8 | 0.9 | 2.4 | 2.8 | 41.9 | 9.0 | 7.2 | Valeur ajoutée |
| Number of employees. | 100.0 | 52.3 | 5.0 | 2.0 | 3.0 | 26.7 | 2.9 | 8.1 | Nombre de salariés |
| Value added per employee...... | 222.9 | 152.6 | 40.2 | 261.7 | 208.7 | 349.5 | 689.8 | 199.6 | Valeur ajoutée par salarié |
| 1959–1960<br>Distribution in percent of: | | | | | | | | | 1959–1960<br>Distribution en pour-centage: |
| Value added........ | 100.0 | 30.0 | 4.5 | 2.4 | 5.2 | 41.7 | 10.0 | 6.2 | Valeur ajoutée |
| Number of employees. | 100.0 | 40.1 | 9.4 | 2.8 | 3.8 | 32.3 | 3.1 | 8.5 | Nombre de salariés |
| Value added per employee.......... | 280.8 | 210.4 | 133.4 | 236.0 | 386.3 | 362.9 | 916.7 | 203.3 | Valeur ajoutée par salarié |

[1] The manufacturing units to which this table relates are those which use modern capital equipment. Establishments which do not use such equipment are classified as handicrafts. However the statistics of this table exclude garages, newspapers, slaughter houses belonging to local councils, repair workshops of Sudan Railways, workshops of Stores and Equipment and other Government workshops which have no separate accounts.

[1] Les unités manufacturières auxquelles se rapporte ce tableau sont celles qui utilisent un équipement moderne. Les établisse-ments n'utilisant pas d'équipement de ce genre sont considérés comme unités artisanales. Cependant, les données du tableau ne portent pas sur les unités suivantes: garages, journaux, abattoirs appartenant aux municipalités, ateliers de répara-tion du Sudan Railways, ateliers des Stores and Equipment et autres ateliers de l'Etat n'ayant pas de comptes à part.

## SWEDEN — SUEDE

### Gross Domestic Product and Gross Fixed Capital Formation

The estimates of the gross domestic product according to source of expenditure and of the gross domestic fixed capital formation according to sector of purchase shown in Table 1 are from the reply of the Central Bureau of Statistics, Stockholm to the United Nations national accounts questionnaire. Official estimates are issued annually in *Nationalbokförung för Sverige* by the Konjunkturinstitutet, Stockholm. The official estimates have been adjusted by the Konjunkturinstitutet to the extent that available data would permit, to conform to the United Nations system of national accounts.

### Index Numbers of Industrial Production

The index numbers set out in Table 2 are derived from series of interlocking annual and monthly index numbers of industrial production. The indexes of the period 1938-58 are based on the final series of annual index numbers; and those for the years, 1959-1961, come from the preliminary series of monthly indexes. Part of the annual series has been published in *Kommersiella Meddelanden*, Nos. 11-12 of each year, and the remainder of this series has been supplied to the Statistical Office of the United Nations in correspondence. A portion of the monthly series has been issued in the above publication and *Sveriges Industriförbund;* and the rest of the monthly series has been obtained through correspondence.

The annual series of index numbers relate, in general, to the activity of industrial establishments with five or more employees and are derived from the results of the annual Industrial Census described below. The indexes are computed as base-weighted arithmetic averages; the base year is 1935. The indicators utilized in computing the indexes consist of series of relatives on the quantity of individual commodities produced, for the most part, or the value of production adjusted for price changes, in some cases. The relatives are combined into index numbers for detailed categories of industrial activity according to the gross value of production, in 1935, of the individual commodities to which they relate. These index numbers are weighted by estimated value added, at factor cost, during 1935 when aggregated into indexes for broader classes (e.g., sub-groups, groups and major groups) of industrial activity.

The field of coverage and the formulae utilized in compilation for the monthly series of index numbers of industrial production are the same as in the case of the annual series. However, the base period is 1947 and the weights utilized at each stage of computing the monthly indexes are proportional to value added at factor cost

### Produit intérieur brut et formation brute de capital fixe

Les estimations des composantes du produit intérieur brut ventilées suivant l'origine des dépenses et des composantes du capital brut fixe formé, ventilées suivant le secteur d'acquisition, reproduites au tableau 1, sont tirées de la réponse du Bureau central de statistique, Stockholm, au questionnaire de l'O.N.U. relatif aux comptes nationaux. Les estimations officielles paraissent annuellement dans *Nationalbokföring för Sverige* publié par le Konjunkturinstitutet, Stockholm. Ces estimations officielles ont été ajustées par le Konjunkturinstitutet, autant que les données disponibles le permettaient, afin qu'elles coïncident avec le système de comptabilité nationale de l'O.N.U.

### Indices de la production industrielle

Les indices reproduits au tableau 2 proviennent de séries emboîtées d'indices annuels et mensuels de la production industrielle. Les indices de la période 1938-58 sont fondés sur les séries définitives d'indices annuels, et ceux relatifs aux années 1959-61 ont été tirés des séries provisoires d'indices mensuels. Une partie des séries annuelles a été publiée dans *Kommersiella Meddelanden* dans les Nos. 11-12 de chaque année, et les séries restantes ont été fournies au Bureau de Statistique de l'O.N.U. par échange de lettres. Une partie des séries mensuelles a été tirée des numéros ci-dessus mentionnés et de *Sveriges Industriförbund*, et le reste a été obtenu par correspondance.

Les séries annuelles d'indices portent en général sur l'activité des établissements industriels employant 5 salariés ou plus et sont tirés des résultats du recensement industriel annuel décrit ci-dessous. Il s'agit de moyennes arithmétiques à pondération fixe, année de base 1935. Les indicateurs utilisés pour calculer les indices sont des séries de rapports concernant en général le volume de la production de chaque marchandise, mais parfois la valeur de la production corrigée des variations de prix. Les rapports sont combinés en indices de catégorie détaillée d'après la valeur brute de la production en 1935 de chacune des marchandises auxquelles ils correspondent. Pour combiner ces indices en indices plus larges (par exemple de sous-groupes, de groupes et de classes de l'activité industrielle), on pondère d'après la valeur ajoutée estimative, au coût de facteurs, en 1935.

Le champ de couverture et les formules utilisées pour élaborer les séries mensuelles d'indices de la production industrielle sont les mêmes que dans le cas des séries annuelles d'indices. Cependant, la période de base est 1947 et les coefficients de pondération utilisés à chaque stade du calcul des indices mensuels sont proportionnels à la

during 1947. Data for the elementary series of relatives are gathered from a sample of the establishments covered in the annual Industrial Censuses. Much greater use is made in the monthly series of indexes than in the annual series of indicators other than the quantity of individual commodities produced—for example, of man-hours worked and numbers employed. The monthly series of index numbers are adjusted to the corresponding available annual index numbers. The monthly indexes for years for which annual indexes are not yet available are linked to the last annual set of adjusted monthly indexes.

It should be noted that the Statistical Office of the United Nations calculated the index numbers shown in Table 2 for divisions of industrial activity from the indexes for the constituent major groups. The weights utilized for this purpose were proportional to value added, at factor cost, during 1953 in each major group.

For further information on the annual and monthly index numbers of the volume of industrial production see: *Kommersiella Meddelanden,* No. 6, 1938 and *Industriförbundets Reviderade Produktionsindex,* reprint from *Ekonomisk Tidskrift,* No. 2, 1950, by Industriens Utredningsinstitut, Stockholm, 1950, respectively.

### Index Numbers of Industrial Employment

The index numbers set out in Table 3 were compiled by the Statistical Office of the United Nations from absolute figures of employment resulting from the annual Industrial Censuses described below. The absolute figures have been published in the annual issue of *Industri* and in selected issues of *Kommersiella Meddelanden,* usually, No. 3 of each year. The figures appearing in the latter publication are preliminary. The absolute figures relate to the average number of employees during the year, in establishments covered in the Industrial Censuses. In general, since 1946, establishments having five or more employees have been included in these Censuses. Because of the change in the field of coverage in these Censuses that is described below, in order to compile index numbers for 1938 comparable to those for later years, it was necessary to link two series of absolute figures of employment at 1946. Linkage of differing series of these figures was also required because of the addition in 1954 of establishments which should have been covered in the Industrial Censuses for previous years as well.

### The Characteristics and Structure of Industrial Activity

The data shown in Table 4 are based on the results of Censuses of Establishments taken as of 25 September 1931 and 7 September 1951 that were issued by the Kommerskollegium in *1931 Ars Företagsräkning* and *1951 Ars Företagsräkning,* respectively. These censuses related to all establishments, irrespective of size, engaged in all kinds of non-agricultural activities.

valeur ajoutée au coût des facteurs en 1947. Les données relatives aux séries élémentaires de rapports sont recueillies auprès d'un échantillon d'établissements couverts par les recensements industriels annuels. On se sert bien plus souvent, dans les séries mensuelles d'indices que dans les séries annuelles d'indices, d'indicateurs autres que le volume de la production de chaque marchandise, — par exemple, le nombre d'heures de travail effectuées et l'emploi. Les séries mensuelles d'indices sont ajustées aux indices annuels disponibles correspondants. Les indices mensuels correspondants aux années pour lesquelles les indices annuels ne sont pas disponibles sont raccordés au dernier ensemble annuel d'indices mensuels ajustés.

Il est bon de noter que le Bureau de Statistique de l'O.N.U. a calculé les indices relatifs aux branches de l'activité industrielle reproduits au tableau 2, à partir des indices des classes composantes. A cette fin, on a utilisé des coefficients de pondération proportionnels à la valeur ajoutée au coût des facteurs durant 1953 pour chaque classe.

Pour plus amples renseignements sur les indices annuels et mensuels du volume de la production industrielle, voir respectivement: *Kommersiella Meddelanden,* No. 6, 1938, et *Industriförbundets Reviderade Produktionsindex,* reproduisant un article paru dans *Ekonomisk Tidskrift,* No. 2, 1950, par Industriens Utredningsinstitut, Stockholm, 1950.

### Indices de l'emploi industriel

Les indices reproduits au tableau 3 ont été élaborés par le Bureau de Statistique de l'O.N.U. à partir de chiffres absolus de l'emploi, provenant des résultats des recensements industriels décrits ci-dessous. Ces chiffres absolus ont paru dans la publication annuelle *Industri* et dans quelques numéros de *Kommersiella Meddelanden,* généralement le no. 3 de chaque année. Les chiffres parus dans le dernier numéro sont provisoires. Les chiffres absolus sont relatifs au nombre moyen de salariés durant l'année, dans les établissements couverts par les recensements industriels. En général, à partir de 1946, les établissements de cinq salariés ou plus ont été couverts par ces recensements. Vu les changements décrits ci-dessous affectant les champs couverts par les recensements, il était nécessaire de raccorder deux séries de chiffres absolus pour obtenir des indices pour 1938, comparables à ceux des années suivantes. Le raccordement des séries de chiffres ne couvrant pas le même champ était également nécessaire vu l'addition en 1954 d'établissements qui auraient dû aussi être couverts par les recensements industriels relatifs aux années précédentes.

### Les caractéristiques et la structure de l'activité industrielle

Les données du tableau 4 sont fondées sur les résultats des recensements des établissements, exécutés les 25 septembre 1931 et 7 septembre 1951. Ces résultats ont été publiés par le Kommerskollegium dans *1931 Ars Företagsräkning* et *1951 Ars Företagsräkning.* Les renseignements portaient sur tous les établissements, quelle que fût leur dimension, qui exerçaient une activité non agricole.

The data set out in Tables 5 and 6 are derived from the results of the Industrial Censuses taken annually by the Kommerskollegium that were published in *Industri, Berättelse för år 1938, 1948, 1953* or *1958*. Except for the 1938 Industrial Census, these inquiries were restricted in general to industrial establishments, excepting publishing and construction, with an average of five or more employees during the year. In the 1938 Census, the usual lower limit of coverage was ten operatives, gross value of annual production of 15 000 Kronor, or annual value of 4 000 Kronor. However, in all of these Industrial Censuses, establishments principally engaged in selected kinds of activity (e.g., coal and metal mining, breweries, distilleries, smelting, refining and casting of metal) were covered irrespective of size.

The difference between the 1938 Industrial Census and the 1948, 1953, and 1958 Censuses in the field of coverage results in incomparabilities in the data shown in Tables 5 and 6. The figures for 1948 and 1953 are also not exactly comparable with those for 1958 because of the amplification in 1954 of the lists of respondents for the annual Industrial Censuses. Further, as indicated in the footnotes of Table 5, in the case of some kinds of manufacturing activity, the figures of the various items of data for the same year are not precisely comparable. This is due to the differences in the extent of adjustments of the published data to the International Standard Industrial Classification that was feasible.

The definitions utilized for the same items of data in inquiries set out in Tables 4 and 5 are, on the whole, consistent with one another and with the International Standards in Basic Industrial Statistics, where applicable. The data in Table 5 on gross value of production and value added relate to goods produced on own account and receipts from industrial services rendered to others and are valued at factor cost. Receipts from goods sold without transformation by establishments are excluded from these items of data. The data on wages and salaries in Table 4, but not in Table 5, encompass payments to homeworkers. The figures of capacity of installed (in use and in reserve) power equipment, excepting the electricity producing industry, relate to prime movers connected directly to machinery other than electric generators and all electric motors. For the electricity producing industry, the rated horsepower of all prime movers is included.

In the case of mining and manufacturing, the figures of energy consumed cover coal, coke and other fuels utilized as sources of heat and power only. Though in the case of mining and manufacturing, these figures cover the consumption of fuels and electricity, whether or not purchased, significant duplication is not present in the data between the consumption of fuels to produce electricity and the use of this electricity. This is the case because, in most instances, electric power plants ancillary to mining and manufacturing establishments have been treated as separate statistical units and considered part of the

Les chiffres des tableaux 5 et 6 sont tirés des résultats des recensements industriels exécutés chaque année par le Kommerskollegium; ces résultats ont été publiés dans *Industri, Berättelse för år 1938, 1948, 1953* et *1958*. Ces recensements annuels ne couvrent que les établissements industriels, à l'exclusion de l'édition et du bâtiment et travaux publics, qui emploient en moyenne 5 salariés ou plus pendant l'année. Au recensement de 1938, la limite la plus basse du critère taille adoptée généralement était dix ouvriers, une valeur brute annuelle de la production de 15.000 couronnes ou une valeur ajoutée de 4.000 couronnes. Cependant, lors de tous ces recensements, les établissements engagés dans certains types d'activité (par exemple, extraction de charbon ou de minerais métallique, brasseries, distilleries, fonderies de minerais et affinage de métaux) ont été couverts, quelle que fût leur taille.

Les différences entre le recensement industriel de 1938 et ceux de 1948, 1953 et 1958, quant au champ de couverture, découlent des défauts de comparabilité entre les données reproduites aux tableaux 5 et 6. Les chiffres relatifs à 1948 et 1953 ne sont pas tout à fait comparables à ceux relatifs à 1958 vu l'ampleur en 1954 que prit la liste des répondants aux recensements industriels annuels. De plus, comme indiqué en note au tableau 5, dans le cas de certains types d'activités manufacturières, les chiffres des différentes rubriques relatifs à la même année, ne sont pas tout à fait comparables. Cela est dû aux différences de degrés d'ajustement possibles, des données publiées, aux Normes internationales de classification industrielle.

Les définitions utilisées pour les mêmes rubriques dans les enquêtes dont il est question aux tableaux 4 et 5 sont dans l'ensemble compatibles les unes avec les autres, ainsi qu'avec les Normes internationales relatives aux statistiques industrielles de base, quand elles correspondent. Les chiffres du tableau 5 concernant la valeur brute de la production et la valeur ajoutée correspondent aux marchandises produites pour compte propre et aux recettes pour services industriels fournis à des tiers; ils sont calculés au coût des facteurs. Les recettes tirées des marchandises revendues en l'état par les établissements ne sont pas comprises dans ces rubriques. Les chiffres des traitements et salaires du tableau 4, mais non ceux du tableau 5, comprennent les sommes versées aux travailleurs à domicile. La puissance installée (en service et en réserve), non compris l'industrie productrice d'électricité, est celle des moteurs primaires entraînant directement des machines autres que des générateurs électriques, plus celle de tous les moteurs électriques. Dans le cas de l'industrie productrice d'électricité, on a compté la puissance nominale de tous les moteurs primaires.

Dans le cas des industries extractives et manufacturières, les chiffres relatifs à l'énergie consommée couvrent le charbon, le coke et tout autre combustible utilisé comme source de chaleur ou de puissance seulement. Quoique en ce qui concerne les industries extractives et manufacturières, ces chiffres couvrent la consommation de combustible et d'électricité achetée ou non, il n'existe pas de double comptes significatifs entre les données relatives à la consommation de combustible en vue de produire de l'électricité et l'utilisation de cette électricité. C'est ainsi, vu que dans la plupart des cas, les unités productrices

electricity industry (ISIC group 511). There may, however, be duplication in the figures of energy consumed for mining and manufacturing between the consumption of coal or coke to make gas and the use of this gas. In the case of the electricity and gas industries combined (ISIC groups 511-512), the figures of energy consumed relate to the use of fuels other than gas to produce electricity or gas or as a source of heat. However, where data are shown separately on energy consumption in each of these industries, the consumption of gas is included in the case of electricity power and distribution stations and the consumption of electricity is included in the case of gasworks.

d'électricité rattachées aux établissements miniers et manufacturiers ont été traitées comme unités statistiques indépendantes et ont été rattachées aux industries productrices d'électricité (CITI groupe 511). Il peut, néanmoins, exister des doubles comptes dans les chiffres relatifs à l'énergie consommée par les industries extractives et les industries manufacturières, entre la consommation de charbon ou de coke en vue de produire du gaz et l'utilisation de ce gaz. Dans le cas des industries productrices de gaz et d'électricité (CITI groupes 511-512) les chiffres relatifs à l'énergie consommée concernent l'utilisation de combustibles autres que le gaz nécessaire à la production d'électricité ou de gaz, ou utilisé comme source de chaleur. Cependant, chaque fois que les données relatives à la consommation d'énergie sont, pour ces types d'industries, reproduites séparément, la consommation de gaz est comprise dans les données relatives aux unités productrices et distributrices d'électricité, et la consommation d'électricité est incluse dans les données relatives aux industries productrices de gaz.

## 1. THE GROSS DOMESTIC PRODUCT AND GROSS DOMESTIC íc FIXED CAPITAL FORMATION
## LE PRODUIT INTERIEUR BRUT ET LA FORMATION BRUTE DE CAPITAL FIXE INTERIEUR

Million Kronor                                                     Millions de couronnes

### A. Expenditure on the Gross Domestic Product at Market Prices
### Dépenses relatives au produit intérieur brut aux prix du marché

| Item of data and year / Rubrique et année | Total | Consumption / Consommation | | Gross Domestic Capital Formation / Formation brute de capital intérieur | | Net exports of goods and services / Exportations nettes de biens et de services | |
|---|---|---|---|---|---|---|---|
| | | Total [1] | Government / Etat | Total | Fixed [2] / Fixe [2] | Exports less imports [3] / Exportations moins importations [3] | Exports [3] / Exportations [3] |
| | | | | *a.* At Current Prices — Aux prix courants | | | |
| **Absolute figures — Chiffres absolus** | | | | | | | |
| 1948 | 25 701 | 21 213 | 3 465 | 4 911 | 4 662 | −423 | 5 417 |
| 1950 | 28 788 | 23 387 | 4 015 | 5 254 | 5 435 | 147 | 7 332 |
| 1951 | 35 253 | 26 790 | 4 963 | 7 590 | 6 475 | 873 | 11 677 |
| 1952 | 38 612 | 30 097 | 6 022 | 8 400 | 7 320 | 115 | 10 807 |
| 1953 | 39 468 | 31 619 | 6 651 | 7 534 | 8 164 | 315 | 10 290 |
| 1954 | 41 960 | 33 339 | 6 989 | 8 840 | 8 788 | −219 | 11 026 |
| 1955 | 45 273 | 35 698 | 7 627 | 10 058 | 9 035 | −483 | 12 046 |
| 1956 | 48 885 | 38 593 | 8 377 | 10 539 | 9 889 | −247 | 13 672 |
| 1957 | 52 600 | 41 098 | 9 266 | 11 733 | 10 500 | −231 | 15 494 |
| 1958 | 54 890 | 43 845 | 9 869 | 11 454 | 11 494 | −409 | 14 961 |
| 1959 | 58 104 | 45 911 | 10 537 | 12 357 | 12 660 [4] | −164 | 14 905 |
| 1960 | 63 350 | 48 559 | 11 222 | 15 488 | 13 937 [4] | −697 | 17 109 |
| 1961 | 69 124 | 52 471 | 12 197 | 16 684 | 15 375 | −31 | 17 930 |
| **Percentage distribution of average annual expenditure — Distribution en pourcentage des dépenses annuelles moyennes** | | | | | | | |
| 1948 | 100.0 | 82.5 | 13.5 | 19.1 | 18.1 | −1.6 | 21.1 |
| 1950–1960 | 100.0 | 78.6 | 16.9 | 21.5 | 24.4 | −0.1 | 27.5 |
| 1950 | 100.0 | 81.2 | 13.9 | 18.2 | 18.9 | 0.6 | 25.5 |
| 1953 | 100.0 | 80.1 | 16.8 | 19.1 | 20.7 | 0.8 | 26.1 |
| 1954 | 100.0 | 79.4 | 16.6 | 21.1 | 20.9 | −0.5 | 26.3 |
| 1958 | 100.0 | 79.8 | 18.0 | 20.9 | 20.9 | −0.7 | 27.2 |
| 1960 | 100.0 | 76.6 | 17.7 | 24.5 | 22.0 | −1.1 | 27.0 |
| | | | | *b.* At Prices of 1954 — Aux prix de 1954 | | | |
| **Absolute figures — Chiffres absolus** | | | | | | | |
| 1948 | 33 276 | 27 771 | 4 867 | 6 692 | 6 479 | −1 187 | 6 947 |
| 1950 | 37 227 | 29 603 | 5 490 | 6 798 | 7 088 | 826 | 9 456 |
| 1951 | 37 049 | 29 372 | 5 750 | 7 958 | 6 912 | −281 | 9 832 |
| 1952 | 38 058 | 30 496 | 6 100 | 7 967 | 7 026 | −405 | 9 227 |
| 1953 | 39 409 | 31 860 | 6 645 | 7 317 | 7 989 | 232 | 10 044 |
| 1954 | 41 960 | 33 339 | 6 989 | 8 840 | 8 788 | −219 | 11 026 |
| 1955 | 43 475 | 34 546 | 7 177 | 9 635 | 8 697 | −706 | 11 610 |
| 1956 | 44 831 | 35 661 | 7 495 | 9 570 | 8 952 | −400 | 12 731 |
| 1957 | 46 500 | 36 419 | 7 705 | 10 272 | 9 239 | −191 | 14 247 |
| 1958 | 47 009 | 37 576 | 7 943 | 10 013 | 10 044 [3] | −580 | 14 265 |
| 1959 | 49 327 | 39 118 | 8 336 | 10 695 | 11 048 [3] | −486 | 14 544 |
| 1960 | 51 317 | 39 782 | 8 424 | 12 803 | 11 442 | −1 268 | 16 199 |
| 1961 | 54 556 | 41 951 | 8 800 | 13 419 | 12 226 | −814 | 16 828 |
| **Percentage distribution of average annual expenditure — Distribution en pourcentage des dépenses annuelles moyennes** | | | | | | | |
| 1948 | 100.0 | 83.4 | 14.6 | 20.1 | 19.5 | −3.5 | 20.9 |
| 1950–1960 | 100.0 | 79.3 | 16.4 | 21.4 | 20.4 | −0.7 | 28.0 |
| 1950 | 100.0 | 79.5 | 14.7 | 18.2 | 19.0 | 2.3 | 25.4 |
| 1953 | 100.0 | 80.8 | 16.9 | 18.6 | 20.3 | 0.6 | 25.5 |
| 1954 | 100.0 | 79.4 | 16.6 | 21.1 | 20.9 | −0.5 | 26.3 |
| 1958 | 100.0 | 79.9 | 16.9 | 21.3 | 21.4 | −1.2 | 30.3 |
| 1960 | 100.0 | 77.5 | 16.4 | 24.9 | 22.3 | −2.4 | 31.6 |
| **Average annual rate of growth — Taux annuel moyen d'accroissement** | | | | | | | |
| 1948–1953 | 3.4 | 2.8 | 6.4 | 1.8 | 4.3 | . | 7.7 |
| 1950–1960 | 3.3 | 3.0 | 4.4 | 6.5 | 4.9 | . | 5.5 |
| 1950–1953 | 1.9 | 2.5 | 6.6 | 2.5 | 4.1 | . | 2.0 |
| 1954–1958 | 2.9 | 3.0 | 3.2 | 3.2 | 3.4 | . | 6.7 |
| 1958–1960 | 4.5 | 2.9 | 3.0 | 13.1 | 6.7 | . | 6.6 |

[1] Excludes all fees paid by households to general government and the net value of gifts from abroad.
[2] Includes major repair and maintenance expenditures.
[3] Wages and salaries and profits or losses of nationals from business activity abroad and of foreigners from business activity in Sweden are covered in exports and imports respectively and not in factor incomes received or paid. Receipts from copyrights, royalties and rents are treated in a similar fashion.
[4] A total of 100 million kronor was transferred from 1959 to 1960 in an attempt to correct the distortion caused by the imposition of a sales tax at the beginning of 1960.

[1] Non compris les redevances payées à l'Etat par les ménages, ni la valeur nette des dons provenant de l'étranger.
[2] Y compris les réparations importantes et les frais d'entretien.
[3] Traitements et salaires et bénéfices ou pertes de nationaux exerçant une activité industrielle et commerciale à l'étranger et des étrangers exerçant une activité industrielle et commerciale en Suède sont couverts par importations et exportations, respectivement et non par revenus des facteurs reçus ou payés. Recettes de droits d'auteur, redevances et loyers sont classés de la même façon.
[4] Un montant total de 100 millions de couronnes a été transféré de 1959 à 1960 pour corriger l'erreur résultant de l'introduction d'un impôt sur les ventes au début de 1960.

## B. Gross Domestic Fixed Capital Formation According to Purchasing Sector [1]
## La formation brute de capital fixe intérieur par secteur d'acquisition [1]

| Item of data and year / Rubrique et année | Total | Agricultural sector / Secteur agricole | Industrial sector — Secteur industriel | | | | Transportation and communication / Transport et communication | Other sectors / Autres secteurs |
| --- | --- | --- | --- | --- | --- | --- | --- | --- |
| | | | Total | Mining / Industries extractives | Manufacturing and construction / Industries manufacturières, bâtiment et travaux publics | Electricity, gas and water / Electricité, gaz et eau | | |
| ISIC — CITI | 0–9 | 0 | 1–5 | 1 | 2–3, 4 | 5 | 7 | 6, 8–9 |
| *a.* At Current Prices — Aux prix courants | | | | | | | | |
| **Absolute figures — Chiffres absolus** | | | | | | | | |
| 1948 | 4 662 | 355 | 1 710 | ... | 1 268 [2] | 442 | 997 | 1 600 |
| 1950 | 5 435 | 412 | 2 055 | ... | 1 514 [2] | 541 | 1 074 | 1 894 |
| 1951 | 6 475 | 468 | 2 366 | ... | 1 792 [2] | 574 | 1 476 | 2 165 |
| 1952 | 7 320 | 503 | 2 601 | 77 | 1 666 | 858 | 1 737 | 2 479 |
| 1953 | 8 164 | 497 | 2 537 | 102 | 1 436 | 999 | 2 184 | 2 946 |
| 1954 | 8 788 | 521 | 2 935 | 114 | 1 772 | 1 049 | 1 973 | 3 359 |
| 1955 | 9 035 | 431 | 2 979 | 116 | 1 848 | 1 015 | 2 086 | 3 539 |
| 1956 | 9 789 | 427 | 3 215 | 136 | 1 977 | 1 102 | 2 271 | 3 876 |
| 1957 | 10 500 | 448 | 3 376 | 142 | 2 017 | 1 217 | 2 503 | 4 173 |
| 1958 | 11 494 [3] | 448 | 3 961 | 163 | 2 390 | 1 408 | 2 608 | 4 477 |
| 1959 | 12 660 [3] | 475 | 4 308 | 166 | 2 605 | 1 537 | 2 992 | 4 885 |
| 1960 | 13 937 | 532 | 4 847 | 132 | 3 135 | 1 580 | 3 350 | 5 208 |
| 1961 | 15 375 | 607 | 5 834 | 118 | 4 026 | 1 690 | 3 079 | 5 855 |
| **Percentage distribution according to sector— Distribution en pourcentage par secteur** | | | | | | | | |
| 1948 | 100.0 | 7.6 | 36.6 | ... | 27.2 [2] | 9.4 | 21.4 | 34.4 |
| 1950–1960 | 100.0 | 4.9 | 34.0 | ... | 22.5 [2] | 11.5 | 23.4 | 37.7 |
| 1950 | 100.0 | 7.5 | 37.8 | ... | 27.9 [2] | 9.9 | 19.8 | 34.9 |
| 1953 | 100.0 | 6.0 | 31.1 | 1.3 | 17.6 | 12.2 | 26.8 | 36.1 |
| 1954 | 100.0 | 5.9 | 33.4 | 1.3 | 20.1 | 12.0 | 22.4 | 38.3 |
| 1958 | 100.0 | 3.8 | 34.5 | 1.5 | 20.8 | 12.2 | 22.7 | 39.0 |
| 1960 | 100.0 | 3.8 | 34.7 | 0.9 | 22.5 | 11.3 | 24.1 | 37.4 |
| *b.* At Prices of 1954 — Aux prix de 1954 | | | | | | | | |
| **Absolute figures — Chiffres absolus** | | | | | | | | |
| 1948 | 6 479 | 472 | 2 407 | ... | 1 767 [2] | 640 | 1 414 | 2 186 |
| 1950 | 7 088 | 514 | 2 719 | ... | 1 992 [2] | 727 | 1 370 | 2 485 |
| 1951 | 6 912 | 503 | 2 531 | ... | 1 904 [2] | 627 | 1 639 | 2 239 |
| 1952 | 7 026 | 498 | 2 469 | 74 | 1 567 | 828 | 1 669 | 2 390 |
| 1953 | 7 989 | 492 | 2 489 | 101 | 1 393 | 995 | 2 087 | 2 921 |
| 1954 | 8 788 | 521 | 2 936 | 114 | 1 772 | 1 050 | 1 972 | 3 359 |
| 1955 | 8 697 | 425 | 2 813 | 110 | 1 751 | 952 | 2 037 | 3 422 |
| 1956 | 8 952 | 400 | 2 885 | 122 | 1 768 | 995 | 2 080 | 3 587 |
| 1957 | 9 239 | 405 | 2 949 | 123 | 1 751 | 1 075 | 2 144 | 3 741 |
| 1958 | 10 044 | 393 | 3 457 | 142 | 2 081 | 1 234 | 2 180 | 4 014 |
| 1959 | 11 048 | 412 | 3 731 | 143 | 2 254 | 1 334 | 2 550 | 4 355 |
| 1960 | 11 442 | 433 | 3 910 | 106 | 2 504 | 1 300 | 2 770 | 4 329 |
| 1961 | 12 226 | 482 | 4 535 | 91 | 3 104 | 1 340 | 2 492 | 4 717 |
| **Percentage distribution according to sector— Distribution en pourcentage par secteur** | | | | | | | | |
| 1948 | 100.0 | 7.2 | 37.2 | ... | 27.3 [2] | 9.9 | 21.8 | 33.8 |
| 1950–1960 | 100.0 | 5.1 | 33.8 | ... | 22.4 [2] | 11.4 | 23.2 | 37.9 |
| 1950 | 100.0 | 7.2 | 38.4 | ... | 28.1 [2] | 10.3 | 19.3 | 35.1 |
| 1953 | 100.0 | 6.1 | 31.2 | 1.3 | 17.4 | 12.5 | 26.1 | 36.6 |
| 1954 | 100.0 | 5.9 | 33.4 | 1.3 | 20.1 | 12.0 | 22.4 | 38.3 |
| 1958 | 100.0 | 3.9 | 34.4 | 1.4 | 20.7 | 12.3 | 21.7 | 40.0 |
| 1960 | 100.0 | 3.7 | 34.2 | 1.0 | 21.8 | 11.4 | 24.2 | 37.9 |
| **Average annual rate of growth—Taux annuel moyen d'accroissement** | | | | | | | | |
| 1948–1953 | 4.3 | 0.8 | 0.7 | ... | −3.3 [2] | 9.2 | 8.1 | 6.0 |
| 1950–1960 | 4.9 | −1.7 | 3.7 | ... | 2.7 [2] | 6.0 | 7.3 | 5.7 |
| 1950–1953 | 4.1 | −1.5 | −2.9 | ... | −9.1 [2] | 11.0 | 15.1 | 5.5 |
| 1954–1958 | 3.4 | −6.8 | 4.2 | 5.7 | 4.1 | 4.1 | 2.5 | 4.6 |
| 1958–1960 | 6.7 | 5.0 | 6.3 | −13.6 | 9.7 | 2.6 | 12.7 | 3.8 |

[1] Includes major repair and maintenance expenditures.
[2] Includes mining.
[3] The data do not include the transfer of 150 million Kronor from 1959 to 1960 reflected in Table 1A because of inability to allocate the adjustment among sectors.

[1] Y compris les réparations importantes et les frais d'entretien.
[2] Y compris les industries extractives.
[3] Les données ne comprennent pas le transfert de 150 millions de Couronnes de 1959 à 1960, qui apparaît au tableau 1A vu l'impossibilité de répartir l'ajustement entre les secteurs de l'activité.

## 2. INDEX NUMBERS OF INDUSTRIAL PRODUCTION — INDICES DE LA PRODUCTION INDUSTRIELLE

### A. Selected Divisions of Industrial Activity
### Quelques branches de l'activité industrielle

| Period Période | Total [1] | Mining Industries extractives | Manu-facturing [1] Industries manu-facturières[1] | Electricity Electricité |
|---|---|---|---|---|
| ISIC — CITI | 1–3 | 1 | 2–3 | 511 |

*a. Indexes — Indices (1958 = 100)*

| | | | | |
|---|---|---|---|---|
| 1938.......... | 52 | 72 | 50 | 27 |
| 1948.......... | 74 | 74 | 74 | 46 |
| 1949.......... | 77 | 74 | 77 | 53 |
| 1950.......... | 79 | 73 | 80 | 60 |
| 1951.......... | 82 | 78 | 83 | 64 |
| 1952.......... | 81 | 85 | 81 | 68 |
| 1953.......... | 83 | 86 | 83 | 74 |
| 1954.......... | 86 | 81 | 87 | 79 |
| 1955.......... | 92 | 91 | 92 | 81 |
| 1956.......... | 95 | 99 | 95 | 88 |
| 1957.......... | 98 | 102 | 98 | 95 |
| 1958.......... | 100 | 100 | 100 | 100 |
| 1959.......... | 102 [2] | 96 [2] | 102 | 106 |
| 1960.......... | 108 [2] | 112 [2] | 108 | 114 |
| 1961.......... | 113 [2] | 121 [2] | 112 | 126 |

*b. Average Annual Rate of Change — Taux annuel moyen de variation*

| | | | | |
|---|---|---|---|---|
| 1938 – 1960.... | 3.4 | 2.0 | 3.6 | 6.8 |
| 1938 – 1948.... | 3.6 | 0.3 | 4.0 | 5.5 |
| 1950 – 1960.... | 3.2 | 4.4 | 3.0 | 6.6 |
| 1948 – 1953.... | 2.3 | 3.0 | 2.3 | 10.0 |
| 1954 – 1958.... | 3.8 | 5.4 | 3.5 | 6.1 |
| 1958 – 1960.... | 3.9 | 5.8 | 3.9 | 6.8 |

[1] Publishing is not covered.

[2] Excludes peat mining.

### B. The Major Groups of Mining
### Les classes de la branche Industries extractives

| Period Période | All mining Toutes industries extractives | Coal mining Extraction du charbon | Metal mining Extraction des minerais métalliques | Other mining Autres industries extractives |
|---|---|---|---|---|
| ISIC — CITI | 1 | 11 | 12 | 14–19 |

*a. Indexes — Indices (1958 = 100)*

| | | | | |
|---|---|---|---|---|
| 1938.......... | 72 | 120 | 72 | 77 |
| 1948.......... | 74 | 109 | 70 | 118 |
| 1949.......... | 74 | 102 | 73 | 92 |
| 1950.......... | 73 | 106 | 72 | 91 |
| 1951.......... | 78 | 99 | 76 | 98 |
| 1952.......... | 85 | 116 | 84 | 101 |
| 1953.......... | 86 | 92 | 85 | 95 |
| 1954.......... | 81 | 92 | 79 | 94 |
| 1955.......... | 91 | 90 | 90 | 103 |
| 1956.......... | 99 | 92 | 98 | 107 |
| 1957.......... | 102 | 101 | 102 | 108 |
| 1958.......... | 100 | 100 | 100 | 100 |
| 1959.......... | 96 [2] | 90 | 98 | 84 [2] |
| 1960.......... | 112 [2] | 82 | 114 | 84 [2] |
| 1961.......... | 121 [2] | 68 | 124 | 83 [2] |

*b. Average Annual Rate of Change — Taux annuel moyen de variation*

| | | | | |
|---|---|---|---|---|
| 1938 – 1960.... | 2.0 | −1.7 | 2.1 | 0.4 |
| 1938 – 1948.... | 0.3 | −1.0 | −0.3 | 4.4 |
| 1950 – 1960.... | 4.4 | −2.5 | 4.7 | −0.8 |
| 1948 – 1953.... | 3.0 | −3.3 | 4.0 | −4.2 |
| 1954 – 1958.... | 5.4 | 2.1 | 6.1 | 1.6 |
| 1958 – 1960.... | 5.8 | −9.4 | 6.8 | −8.3 |

[1] Non compris l'édition.

[2] Non compris l'extraction de la tourbe.

## C. The Major Groups of Manufacturing — Les classes de la branche Industries manufacturières

| Period<br>Période | Manu-facturing [1]<br>Industries manufac-turières [1] | Food, beverages and tobacco<br>Industries alimen-taires, boissons, tabac | Textiles | Clothing, footwear and made-up textiles<br>Articles d'habil-lement, chaussures et ouvrages en tissu | Wood products and furniture<br>Bois et meubles | Paper and paper products<br>Papier et ouvrages en papier | Printing [1]<br>Im-primerie [1] | Leather and leather products except wearing apparel<br>Cuir et articles en cuir, à l'exclu-sion des articles d'habil-lement | Rubber products<br>Ouvrages en caout-chouc | Chemicals and chemical, petroleum and coal products<br>Produits chi-miques et dérivés du pétrole et du charbon | Non-metallic mineral products<br>Produits minéraux non métal-liques | Basic metals<br>Métal-lurgie de base | Metal products<br>Ouvrages en métaux | Other manu-facturing<br>Autres industries manufac-turières |
|---|---|---|---|---|---|---|---|---|---|---|---|---|---|---|
| ISIC — CITI | 2–3 | 20–22 | 23 | 24 | 25–26 | 27 | 28 | 29 | 30 | 31–32 | 33 | 34 | 35–38 | 39 |

### a. Indexes — Indices (1958 = 100)

| Period | | | | | | | | | | | | | | |
|---|---|---|---|---|---|---|---|---|---|---|---|---|---|---|
| 1938 | 50 | 61 | 74 | 72 | 63 | 54 | 51 | 60 | 20 | 31 | 54 | 50 | 42 | 39 |
| 1948 | 74 | 82 | 101 | 105 | 84 | 69 | 77 | 135 | 46 | 58 | 80 | 55 | 68 | 89 |
| 1949 | 77 | 86 | 102 | 106 | 86 | 65 | 83 | 115 | 49 | 62 | 81 | 60 | 74 | 88 |
| 1950 | 80 | 86 | 106 | 105 | 89 | 72 | 83 | 107 | 61 | 69 | 84 | 61 | 78 | 85 |
| 1951 | 83 | 86 | 107 | 108 | 89 | 78 | 83 | 105 | 66 | 73 | 88 | 68 | 83 | 89 |
| 1952 | 81 | 88 | 89 | 92 | 76 | 68 | 80 | 98 | 64 | 72 | 90 | 77 | 85 | 88 |
| 1953 | 83 | 88 | 103 | 102 | 79 | 74 | 83 | 102 | 66 | 75 | 88 | 75 | 83 | 81 |
| 1954 | 87 | 90 | 103 | 100 | 88 | 85 | 85 | 101 | 85 | 79 | 96 | 82 | 84 | 88 |
| 1955 | 92 | 96 | 98 | 103 | 92 | 91 | 91 | 93 | 83 | 83 | 103 | 93 | 91 | 95 |
| 1956 | 95 | 99 | 101 | 105 | 91 | 96 | 93 | 95 | 86 | 92 | 100 | 103 | 92 | 93 |
| 1957 | 98 | 98 | 108 | 104 | 99 | 101 | 96 | 101 | 91 | 96 | 96 | 105 | 93 | 99 |
| 1958 | 100 | 100 | 100 | 100 | 100 | 100 | 100 | 100 | 100 | 100 | 100 | 100 | 100 | 100 |
| 1959 | 102 | 101 | 103 | ... | 94 | 109 | ... | ... | 106 | 116 | ... | 114 | ... | ... |
| 1960 | 108 | 104 | 110 | ... | 106 | 126 | ... | ... | 102 | 126 | ... | 125 | ... | ... |
| 1961 | 112 | 103 | 111 | ... | 103 | 131 | ... | ... | 101 | 131 | ... | 135 | ... | ... |

### b. Average Annual Rate of Change — Taux annuel moyen de variation

| Period | | | | | | | | | | | | | | |
|---|---|---|---|---|---|---|---|---|---|---|---|---|---|---|
| 1938–1960 | 3.6 | 2.5 | 1.8 | ... | 2.4 | 3.9 | ... | ... | 7.7 | 6.6 | ... | 4.3 | ... | ... |
| 1938–1948 | 4.0 | 3.0 | 3.2 | 3.8 | 2.9 | 2.5 | 4.2 | 8.4 | 8.7 | 6.5 | 4.0 | 1.0 | 4.9 | 8.6 |
| 1950–1960 | 3.0 | 1.9 | 0.4 | ... | 1.8 | 5.8 | ... | ... | 3.3 | 6.2 | ... | 7.4 | ... | ... |
| 1948–1953 | 2.3 | 1.4 | 0.4 | −0.6 | −1.2 | 1.4 | 1.5 | −5.4 | 7.5 | 5.3 | 1.9 | 6.4 | 4.1 | −1.9 |
| 1954–1958 | 3.5 | 2.7 | −0.7 | — | 3.2 | 4.1 | 4.1 | −0.3 | 4.1 | 6.1 | 1.0 | 5.1 | 4.4 | 3.2 |
| 1958–1960 | 3.9 | 2.0 | 4.9 | ... | 3.0 | 12.2 | ... | ... | 1.0 | 12.2 | ... | 11.8 | ... | ... |

[1] Publishing is not covered.       [1] Non compris l'édition.

## 3. INDEX NUMBERS OF INDUSTRIAL EMPLOYMENT
## INDICES DE L'EMPLOI DANS L'INDUSTRIE

### A. Selected Divisions of Industrial Activity
### Quelques branches de l'activité industrielle

| Period<br>Période | Total [1] | Mining<br>Industries<br>extractives | Manu-<br>facturing [1]<br>Industries<br>manu-<br>facturières [1] | Electricity<br>Electricité |
|---|---|---|---|---|
| ISIC — CITI | 1–3, 511 | 1 | 2–3 | 511 |

#### a. Indexes — Indices (1958 = 100)

| | | | | |
|---|---|---|---|---|
| 1938 [2].......... | 73 | 119 | 71 | 49 |
| 1948........... | 96 | 108 | 96 | 81 |
| 1949........... | 96 | 91 | 96 | 85 |
| 1950........... | 96 | 91 | 97 | 82 |
| 1951........... | 99 | 93 | 99 | 82 |
| 1952........... | 97 | 97 | 98 | 86 |
| 1953........... | 96 | 97 | 96 | 88 |
| 1954........... | −97− | −96− | −97− | −88− |
| 1955........... | 100 | 98 | 100 | 89 |
| 1956........... | 101 | 100 | 101 | 94 |
| 1957........... | 101 | 102 | 101 | 98 |
| 1958........... | 100 | 100 | 100 | 100 |
| 1959........... | 101 | 95 | 101 | 97 |
| 1960........... | 109 | 97 | 110 | ... |

#### b. Average Annual Rate of Change — Taux annuel moyen de variation

| | | | | |
|---|---|---|---|---|
| 1938 – 1960.... | 1.8 | −0.9 | 2.0 | ... |
| 1938 – 1948.... | 2.8 | −1.0 | 3.1 | 5.2 |
| 1950 – 1960.... | 1.3 | 0.6 | 1.3 | ... |
| 1948 – 1953.... | — | −2.1 | — | 1.7 |
| 1954 – 1958.... | 0.8 | 1.0 | 0.8 | 3.2 |
| 1958 – 1960.... | 4.4 | −1.5 | 4.9 | ... |

For footnotes see end of table.

### B. The Major Groups of Mining
### Les classes de la branche Industries extractives

| Period<br>Période | All mining<br>Toutes<br>industries<br>extractives | Coal<br>mining<br>Extraction<br>du charbon | Metal mining<br>Extraction<br>des minerais<br>métalliques | Other mining<br>Autres<br>industries<br>extractives |
|---|---|---|---|---|
| ISIC — CITI | 1 | 11 | 12 | 14–19 |

#### a. Indexes — Indices (1958 = 100)

| | | | | |
|---|---|---|---|---|
| 1938 [2].......... | 119 | 124 | 80 | 200 |
| 1948........... | 108 | 126 | 68 | 194 |
| 1949........... | 91 | 104 | 72 | 139 |
| 1950........... | 91 | 103 | 74 | 132 |
| 1951........... | 93 | 100 | 77 | 133 |
| 1952........... | 97 | 116 | 81 | 136 |
| 1953........... | 97 | 100 | 86 | 126 |
| 1954........... | −96− | −91− | −88− | −119− |
| 1955........... | 98 | 94 | 90 | 119 |
| 1956........... | 100 | 97 | 95 | 114 |
| 1957........... | 102 | 101 | 98 | 109 |
| 1958........... | 100 | 100 | 100 | 100 |
| 1959........... | 95 | 79 | 94 | 100 |
| 1960........... | 97 | 71 | 98 | 99 |

#### b. Average Annual Rate of Change — Taux annuel moyen de variation

| | | | | |
|---|---|---|---|---|
| 1938 – 1960.... | −0.9 | −2.5 | 0.9 | −3.1 |
| 1938 – 1948.... | −1.0 | 0.2 | −1.6 | −0.3 |
| 1950 – 1960.... | 0.6 | −3.7 | 2.8 | −2.8 |
| 1948 – 1953.... | −2.1 | −4.5 | 4.8 | −8.3 |
| 1954 – 1958.... | 1.0 | 2.4 | 3.2 | −4.3 |
| 1958 – 1960.... | −1.5 | −15.7 | −1.0 | −0.5 |

Pour les notes, voir au bas du tableau.

## C. The Major Groups of Manufacturing — Les classes de la branche Industries manufacturières

| Period / Période | Manufacturing [1] / Industries manufacturières [1] | Food, beverages and tobacco / Industries alimentaires, boissons, tabac | Textiles | Clothing, footwear and made-up textiles / Articles d'habillement, chaussures et ouvrages en tissu | Wood products and furniture / Bois et meubles | Paper and paper products / Papier et ouvrages en papier | Printing [1] / Imprimerie [1] | Leather and leather products except wearing apparel / Cuir et articles en cuir, à l'exclusion des articles d'habillement | Rubber products / Ouvrages en caoutchouc | Chemicals and chemical, petroleum and coal products / Produits chimiques et dérivés du pétrole et du charbon | Non-metallic mineral products / Produits minéraux non métalliques | Basic metals / Métallurgie de base | Metal products / Ouvrages en métaux | Other manufacturing / Autres industries manufacturières |
|---|---|---|---|---|---|---|---|---|---|---|---|---|---|---|
| ISIC — CITI | 2–3 | 20–22 | 23 | 24 | 25–26 | 27 | 28 | 29 | 30 | 31–32 | 33 | 34 | 35–38 | 39 |

### a. Indexes — Indices (1958 = 100)

| Period | 2–3 | 20–22 | 23 | 24 | 25–26 | 27 | 28 | 29 | 30 | 31–32 | 33 | 34 | 35–38 | 39 |
|---|---|---|---|---|---|---|---|---|---|---|---|---|---|---|
| 1938 [2] | 71 | 85 | 129 | 84 | 104 | 81 | 51 | 98 | 63 | 57 | 96 | 67 | 53 | 47 |
| 1948 | 96 | 101 | 137 | 116 | 115 | 84 | 82 | 129 | 86 | 99 | 113 | 88 | 85 | 80 |
| 1949 | 96 | 104 | 140 | 115 | 113 | 83 | 84 | 130 | 84 | 100 | 110 | 90 | 86 | 76 |
| 1950 | 97 | 103 | 141 | 114 | 113 | 83 | 87 | 123 | 84 | 104 | 109 | 91 | 87 | 73 |
| 1951 | 99 | 101 | 141 | 116 | 114 | 87 | 89 | 121 | 86 | 110 | 109 | 94 | 91 | 73 |
| 1952 | 98 | 100 | 134 | 108 | 103 | 91 | 91 | 116 | 81 | 95 | 104 | 100 | 91 | 90 |
| 1953 | 96 | 99 | 134 | 110 | 102 | 89 | 90 | 112 | 85 | 93 | 102 | 96 | 88 | 83 |
| 1954 | -97- | -99- | -128- | -107- | -107- | -93- | -93- | -106- | -93- | -94- | -105- | -96- | -89- | -88- |
| 1955 | 100 | 101 | 119 | 108 | 109 | 96 | 97 | 105 | 97 | 96 | 107 | 102 | 95 | 93 |
| 1956 | 101 | 102 | 114 | 108 | 103 | 99 | 98 | 104 | 96 | 99 | 105 | 104 | 97 | 96 |
| 1957 | 101 | 100 | 107 | 105 | 101 | 100 | 98 | 105 | 99 | 101 | 102 | 104 | 99 | 100 |
| 1958 | 100 | 100 | 100 | 100 | 100 | 100 | 100 | 100 | 100 | 100 | 100 | 100 | 100 | 100 |
| 1959 | 101 | 101 | 101 | 99 | 99 | 103 | 99 | 99 | 118 | 104 | 102 | 112 | 103 | 104 |
| 1960 | 110 | 103 | 103 | 100 | 104 | 107 | 102 | 99 | 116 | 104 | 107 | 112 | 109 | 115 |

### b. Average Annual Rate of Change — Taux annuel moyen de variation

| Period | 2–3 | 20–22 | 23 | 24 | 25–26 | 27 | 28 | 29 | 30 | 31–32 | 33 | 34 | 35–38 | 39 |
|---|---|---|---|---|---|---|---|---|---|---|---|---|---|---|
| 1938–1960 | 2.0 | 0.9 | −1.0 | 0.8 | — | 1.3 | 3.2 | — | 2.8 | 2.8 | 0.5 | 2.4 | 3.3 | 4.2 |
| 1938–1948 | 3.1 | 1.7 | 0.6 | 3.3 | 1.0 | 0.4 | 4.9 | 2.8 | 3.2 | 5.7 | 1.6 | 2.8 | 4.8 | 5.5 |
| 1950–1960 | 1.3 | — | −3.1 | −1.3 | −0.8 | 2.6 | 1.6 | −2.1 | 3.3 | — | −0.2 | 2.1 | 2.3 | 4.6 |
| 1948–1953 | — | −0.4 | −0.4 | −1.1 | −2.4 | 1.2 | 1.9 | −2.8 | −0.2 | −1.3 | −2.0 | 1.8 | 0.7 | 0.7 |
| 1954–1958 | 0.8 | 0.2 | −6.0 | −1.7 | −1.7 | 1.8 | 1.8 | −1.5 | 1.8 | 1.6 | −1.2 | 1.0 | 3.0 | 3.2 |
| 1958–1960 | 4.9 | 1.5 | 1.5 | — | 2.0 | 3.4 | 1.0 | −0.5 | 7.7 | 2.0 | 3.4 | 5.8 | 4.4 | 7.2 |

[1] Publishing is not covered.
[2] The data for 1938 are linked to the series for succeeding years at 1946.

[1] Non compris l'édition.
[2] Les données relatives à 1938 sont raccordées aux séries relatives aux années ultérieures au niveau de 1946.

## 4. THE CHARACTERISTICS OF ALL INDUSTRIAL ESTABLISHMENTS
### 25 September 1931 and 7 September 1951

## CARACTERISTIQUES DE TOUS LES ETABLISSEMENTS INDUSTRIELS
### 25 septembre 1931 et 7 septembre 1951

Number of establishments in units; number of engaged and employees in thousands; wages and salaries in million Kronor; and capacity of installed power equipment in thousand horsepower

Nombre d'établissements en unités; nombre de personnes occupées et de salariés en milliers; traitements et salaires en millions de couronnes suédoises; puissance installée en milliers de chevaux-vapeur

### A. The Divisions of Industrial Activity — Les branches de l'activité industrielle

| Item of data | All industrial activity / Toutes industries | | Mining / Industries extractives | | Manufacturing / Industries manufacturières | | Construction / Bâtiment et travaux publics | | Electricity and gas / Electricité et gaz | | Rubrique |
|---|---|---|---|---|---|---|---|---|---|---|---|
| | 25.IX.1931 | 7.IX.1951 | 25.IX.1931 | 7.IX.1951 | 25.IX.1931 | 7.IX.1951 | 25.IX.1931 | 7.IX.1951 | 25.IX.1931 | 7.IX.1951 | |
| ISIC | 1–4, 511–512 | | 1 | | 2–3 | | 4 | | 511–512 | | CITI |
| *a. Absolute Figures — Chiffres absolus* | | | | | | | | | | | |
| Number of establishments..... | 105 342 | 102 533 | 1 135 | 1 316 | 83 903 | 72 023 | 18 139 | 27 440 | 2 165 | 1 754 | Nombre d'établissements |
| Number of engaged......... | 842.2 | 1 278.9 | 24.0 | 23.5 | 655.5 | 990.6 | 151.2 | 243.0 | 11.5 | 21.8 | Nombre de personnes occupées |
| Number of employees........ | 752.1 | 1 144.3 | 23.7 | 22.7 | 582.6 | 885.2 | 134.4 | 214.7 | 11.4 | 21.7 | Nombre de salariés |
| Wages and salaries paid (During calendar year preceding census date)........ | . | 6 881.0 | . | 135.6 | . | 5 176.4 | . | 1 429.1 | . | 139.9 | Traitements et salaires payés (pendant l'année civile précédant le recensement) |
| Capacity of installed power equipment.............. | . | . | 116 | . | 2 120 | . | 40 | . | ... | . | Puissance installée |
| *b. Structure* | | | | | | | | | | | |
| Distribution in percent of number of engaged....... | 100.0 | 100.0 | 2.8 | 1.8 | 77.8 | 77.5 | 18.0 | 19.0 | 1.4 | 1.7 | Répartition en pourcentage du nombre de personnes occupées |
| Capacity of installed power equipment per person engaged............... | . | . | 4.83 | . | 3.24 | . | 0.26 | . | ... | . | Puissance installé par personne occupée |

### B. The Major Groups of Mining — Les classes de la branche Industries extractives

| Item of data | 25.IX.1931 | | | | 7.IX.1951 | | | | Rubrique |
|---|---|---|---|---|---|---|---|---|---|
| | All mining / Toutes industries extractives | Coal mining / Extraction du charbon | Metal mining / Extraction des minerais métalliques | Other mining / Divers | All mining / Toutes industries extractives | Coal mining / Extraction du charbon | Metal mining / Extraction des minerais métalliques | Other mining / Divers | |
| ISIC | 1 | 11 | 12 | 14–19 | 1 | 11 | 12 | 14–19 | CITI |
| *a. Absolute Figures — Chiffres absolus* | | | | | | | | | |
| Number of establishments........ | 1 135 | 6 | 107 | 1 022 | 1 316 | 17 | 114 | 1 185 | Nombre d'établissements |
| Number of engaged............ | 24.0 | 1.3 | 10.8 | 11.9 | 23.5 | 1.0 | 13.6 | 8.9 | Nombre de personnes occupées |
| Number of employees.......... | 23.7 | 1.3 | 10.8 | 11.6 | 22.7 | 1.0 | 13.6 | 8.1 | Nombre de salariés |
| Wages and salaries paid (During calendar year preceding census date)........ | . | . | . | . | 135.6 | 4.4 | 93.1 | 38.1 | Traitements et salaires payés (pendant l'année civile précédant le recensement) |
| Capacity of installed power equipment................. | 116 | 5 | 83 | 28 | . | . | . | . | Puissance installée |
| *b. Structure* | | | | | | | | | |
| Distribution in percent of number of engaged............... | 100.0 | 5.4 | 45.0 | 49.6 | 100.0 | 4.2 | 57.9 | 37.9 | Répartition en pourcentage du nombre de personnes occupées |
| Capacity of installed power equipment per person engaged..... | 4.83 | 3.85 | 7.69 | 2.35 | . | . | . | . | Puissance installée par personne occupée |

## C. The Major Groups of Manufacturing — Les classes de la branche Industries manufacturières

| Day and item of data | Manu-facturing / Industries manufac-turières | Food, beverages and tobacco / Industries alimen-taires, boissons, tabac | Textiles | Clothing, footwear and made-up textiles / Articles d'habil-lement, chaussures et ouvrages en tissu | Wood products and furniture / Bois et meubles | Paper and paper products / Papier et ouvrages en papier | Printing and publish-ing / Im-primerie et édition | Leather and leather products except wearing apparel / Cuir et articles en cuir, à l'exclu-sion des articles d'habil-lement | Rubber products / Ouvrages en caout-chouc | Chemicals and chemical, petroleum and coal products / Produits chi-miques et dérivés du pétrole et du charbon | Non-metallic mineral products / Produits minéraux non métal-liques | Basic metals / Métal-lurgie de base | Metal products / Ouvrages en métaux | Other manu-factur-ing / Autres in-dustries manufac-turières | Date et rubrique |
|---|---|---|---|---|---|---|---|---|---|---|---|---|---|---|---|
| ISIC | 2–3 | 20–22 | 23 | 24 | 25–26 | 27 | 28 | 29 | 30 | 31–32 | 33 | 34 | 35–38 | 39 | CITI |
| *a. Absolute Figures — Chiffres absolus* | | | | | | | | | | | | | | | |
| 25.IX.1931 Number of establishments | 83 903 | 17 041 | 2 012 | 27 855 | 13 333 | 296 | 1 674 | 1 738 | 399 | 741 | 2 318 | 150 | 13 785 | 2 561 | 25.IX.1931 Nombre d'établissements |
| Number of engaged | 655.5 | 89.6 | 54.1 | 104.9 | 87.4 | 42.2 | 29.9 | 7.1 | 6.9 | 17.1 | 31.5 | 33.8 | 140.5 | 10.5 | Nombre de personnes occupées |
| Number of employees | 582.6 | 75.8 | 52.4 | 77.9 | 77.1 | 42.1 | 28.6 | 5.5 | 6.5 | 16.8 | 29.8 | 33.7 | 128.2 | 8.2 | Nombre de salariés |
| Capacity of installed power equipment | 2 120 | 250 | 100 | 12 | 369 | 650 | 22 | 10 | 13 | 48 | 84 | 273 | 284 | 5 | Puissance installée |
| 7.IX.1951 Number of establishments | 72 023 | 11 244 | 1 692 | 18 109 | 13 282 | 565 | 2 283 | 966 | 560 | 1 095 | 3 407 | 520 | 16 535 | 1 765 | 7.IX.1951 Nombre d'établissements |
| Number of engaged | 990.6 | 103.3 | 73.8 | 114.1 | 101.0 | 59.9 | 46.6 | 11.1 | 11.2 | 37.0 | 45.3 | 57.6 | 313.2 | 16.5 | Nombre de personnes occupées |
| Number of employees | 885.2 | 90.3 | 63.5 | 81.0 | 85.7 | 59.0 | 44.2 | 8.9 | 10.3 | 36.2 | 41.8 | 57.0 | 293.9 | 13.4 | Nombre de salariés |
| Wages and salaries paid (During calendar year preceding census date) | 5 176.4 | 495.3 | 332.7 | 386.2 | 451.3 | 342.7 | 302.5 | 52.1 | 60.6 | 234.7 | 231.5 | 355.4 | 1 852.4 | 79.0 | Traitements et salaires payés (pendant l'année civile précédant le re-censement) |
| *b. Structure* | | | | | | | | | | | | | | | |
| 25.IX.1931 Distribution in percent of number of engaged | 100.0 | 13.6 | 8.3 | 16.0 | 13.3 | 6.4 | 4.6 | 1.1 | 1.0 | 2.7 | 4.8 | 5.1 | 21.4 | 1.7 | 25.IX.1931 Répartition en pourcen-tage du nombre de personnes occupées |
| Capacity of installed power equipment per person engaged | 3.23 | 2.79 | 1.85 | 0.11 | 4.22 | 15.40 | 0.74 | 1.41 | 1.88 | 2.81 | 2.67 | 8.08 | 2.02 | 0.48 | Puissance installée par personne occupée |
| 7.IX.1951 Distribution in percent of number of engaged | 100.0 | 10.4 | 7.4 | 11.5 | 10.2 | 6.1 | 4.7 | 1.1 | 1.1 | 3.8 | 4.6 | 5.8 | 31.6 | 1.7 | 7.IX.1951 Répartition en pourcen-tage du nombre de personnes occupées |

## 5. CHARACTERISTICS OF INDUSTRIAL ESTABLISHMENTS WITH FIVE OR MORE EMPLOYEES [1]
## CARACTERISTIQUES DES ETABLISSEMENTS INDUSTRIELS COMPTANT CINQ SALARIES OU PLUS [1]
### 1938, 1948, 1953, 1958

Number of establishments in units; value added, gross value of production, and wages and salaries in million Kronor; number of employees, engaged, and operatives in thousands; man-hours worked in millions; energy consumed in thousand metric tons of coal equivalents, electricity consumed in million KWH; capacity of installed power equipment in thousand horsepower; value added per employee and wages and salaries per employee and per thousand operative man-hours in thousand Kronor; average annual man-hours per operative in thousands; energy consumed per employee and per thousand operative man-hours in metric tons of coal equiva-lents; electricity consumed per employee and per thousand operative man-hours in thousand KWH; capacity of installed power equipment per employee and per thousand operative man-hours in horsepower.

Nombre d'établissements en unités; valeur ajoutée, valeur brute de la production et traitements et salaires en millions de couronnes suédoises; nombre de salariés, de personnes occupées et d'ouvriers en milliers; heures de travail en millions; énergie consommée en milliers de tonnes métriques d'équivalent charbon; électricité con-sommée en millions de kWh; puissance installée en milliers de chevaux-vapeur; valeur ajoutée par salarié et traitements et salaires par salarié et par millier d'heures-ouvrier en milliers de couronnes suédoises; moyenne annuelle des heures de travail par ouvrier en milliers; énergie consommée par salarié et par millier d'heures-ouvrier en tonnes métriques d'équivalent charbon; électricité consommée par salarié et par millier d'heures-ouvrier en milliers de kWh; puissance installée par salarié et par millier d'heures-ouvrier en chevaux-vapeur.

### A. Selected Divisions of Industrial Activity — Quelques branches de l'activité industrielle

| Year and item of data | Total | Mining / Industries ex-tractives | Manu-facturing[1,4] / Industries manufac-turières[1,4] | Electricity and gas[1] / Électricité et gaz[1] | Année et rubrique | Year and item of data | Total | Mining / Industries ex-tractives | Manu-facturing[1,4] / Industries manufac-turières[1,4] | Electricity and gas[1] / Électricité et gaz[1] | Année et rubrique |
|---|---|---|---|---|---|---|---|---|---|---|---|
| ISIC | 1-3, 511-512 | 1 | 2-3 | 511-512 | CITI | ISIC | 1-3, 511-512 | 1 | 2-3 | 511-512 | CITI |
| *a. Absolute Figures — Chiffres absolus* | | | | | | *b. Structure* | | | | | |
| 1938 Number of establishments | 17 691 | 654 | 16 331 | 706 | 1938 Nombre d'établissements | 1938 Distribution in percent of the number of employees | 100.0 | 4.4 | 93.9 | 1.7 | 1938 Distribution en pourcentage du nombre de salariés |
| Gross value of production | 7 225.2 | 303.2 | 6 675.7 | 246.3 | Valeur brute de la production | Per employee: | | | | | Par salarié: |
| Number of employees (Average during year) | 604.9 | 27.1 | 568.0 | 9.8 | Nombre de salariés (moyenne pour l'année) | Energy consumed | | 4.48 | 10.74 | 107.21 | Energie consommée |
| Number of operatives (Average during year) | 530.8 | 25.5 | 498.5 | 6.8 | Nombre d'ouvriers (moyenne pour l'année) | Electricity consumed | 9.3 | 9.6 | 9.3 | 9.8 | Electricité consommée |
| Energy consumed | . | 121.5 | 6 101.9 | 1 050.7 | Energie consommée | Capacity of installed power equipment | . | 6.12 | 4.52 | 207.96 | Puissance installée |
| Electricity consumed | 5 619.2 | 260.5 | 5 262.4 | 96.3 | Electricité consommée | Operatives as a percent of employees | 87.8 | 94.1 | 87.8 | 69.4 | Ouvriers en pourcentage des salariés |
| Capacity of installed power equipment (As of end of year) | . | 166 | 2 567 | 2 038 | Puissance installée (à la fin de l'année) | Per operative: | | | | | Par ouvrier : |
| | | | | | | Energy consumed | | 4.76 | 12.24 | 154.51 | Energie consommée |
| | | | | | | Electricity consumed | 10.59 | 10.22 | 10.56 | 14.16 | Electricité consommée |
| | | | | | | Capacity of installed power equipment | . | 6.51 | 5.15 | 299.70 | Puissance installée |

## A. Selected Divisions of Industrial Activity (continued) — Quelques branches de l'activité industrielle (suite)

| Year and item of data | Total | Mining — Industries extractives | Manufacturing[1,4] — Industries manufacturières[1,4] | Electricity and gas[1] — Électricité et gaz[1] | Année et rubrique | Year and item of data | Total | Mining — Industries extractives | Manufacturing[1,4] — Industries manufacturières[1,4] | Electricity and gas[1] — Électricité et gaz[1] | Année et rubrique |
|---|---|---|---|---|---|---|---|---|---|---|---|
| ISIC | 1-3, 511-512 | 1 | 2-3 | 511-512 | CITI | ISIC | 1-3, 511-512 | 1 | 2-3 | 511-512 | CITI |
| | **a Absolute Figures — Chiffres absolus** | | | | | | **b. Structure** | | | | |

**Left half (a. Absolute Figures):**

| Year and item of data | Total | Mining | Manufacturing[1,4] | Electricity and gas[1] | Année et rubrique |
|---|---|---|---|---|---|
| **1948** | | | | | **1948** |
| Number of establishments | 16 630 | 686 | 15 284 | 660 | Nombre d'établissements |
| Gross value of production | 20 326.5 | 442.3 | 19 223.3 | 660.9 | Valeur brute de la production |
| Number of employees (Average during year) | 789.9 | 24.6 | 749.0 | 16.3 | Nombre de salariés (moyenne pour l'année) |
| Operatives: Number (Average during year) | 655.6 | 23.1 | 619.6 | 12.9 | Ouvriers: Nombre (moyenne pour l'année) |
| Man-hours worked | 1 409.3 | 42.8 | 1 338.4 | 28.1 | Heures de travail effectuées |
| Energy consumed | . | 169.8 | 6 631.5 | 1 442.5 | Énergie consommée |
| Electricity consumed | 8 162.4 | 336.2 | 7 691.8 | 134.4 | Électricité consommée |
| Capacity of installed power equipment (As of end of year) | . | 290 | 3 784 | 4 215 | Puissance installée (à la fin de l'année) |
| **1953** | | | | | **1953** |
| Number of establishments | 15 044 | 534 | 14 029 | 481 | Nombre d'établissements |
| Value added | 13 097.5 | 983.2 | 11 345.2 | 769.1 | Valeur ajoutée |
| Gross value of production | 31 763.9 | 1 160.4 | 29 514.9 | 1 088.6 | Valeur brute de la production |
| Employees: Number (Average during year) | 789.5 | 23.2 | 748.6 | 17.7 | Salariés: Nombre (moyenne pour l'année) |
| Wages and salaries | 6 969.7 | 212.0 | 6 582.7 | 175.0 | Traitements et salaires |
| Operatives: Number (Average during year) | 633.7 | 20.5 | 601.0 | 12.2 | Ouvriers: Nombre (moyenne pour l'année) |
| Man-hours worked | 1 337.4 | 40.0 | 1 271.5 | 25.9 | Heures de travail effectuées |
| Wages and salaries | 5 082.0 | 179.9 | 4 791.3 | 110.8 | Traitements et salaires |
| Energy consumed | . | 189.1 | 7 445.8 | 1 395.7 | Énergie consommée |
| Electricity consumed | 12 380.9 | 522.8 | 11 642.7 | 215.4 | Électricité consommée |
| Capacity of installed power equipment (As of end of year) | . | 360 | 5 205 | 6 448 | Puissance installée (à la fin de l'année) |
| **1958** | | | | | **1958** |
| Number of establishments | 15 677 | 460 | 14 336 | 881 | Nombre d'établissements |
| Value added | 19 236.2 | 1 080.6 | 16 749.9 | 1 405.7 | Valeur ajoutée |
| Number of engaged (Average during year) | 854.5 | 24.2 | 810.1 | 20.2 | Nombre de personnes occupées (moyenne pour l'année) |
| Employees: Number (Average during year) | 847.4 | 24.0 | 803.2 | 20.2 | Salariés: Nombre (moyenne pour l'année) |
| Wages and salaries | 10 045.1 | 302.2 | 9 481.3 | 261.6 | Traitements et salaires |
| Operatives: Number (Average during year) | 663.7 | 20.5 | 629.5 | 13.7 | Ouvriers: Nombre (moyenne pour l'année) |
| Man-hours worked | 1 361.9 | 38.8 | 1 294.8 | 28.3 | Heures de travail effectuées |
| Wages and salaries | 7 085.3 | 242.4 | 6 681.6 | 161.3 | Traitements et salaires |
| Energy consumed | . | 251.9 | 8 773.8 | 1 432.3 | Énergie consommée |
| Electricity consumed | 16 498.3 | 773.6 | 15 225.5 | 499.2 | Électricité consommée |
| Capacity of installed power equipment (As of end of year) | . | 478.2 | 6 644.1 | 10 493.2 | Puissance installée (à la fin de l'année) |

**Right half (b. Structure):**

| Year and item of data | Total | Mining | Manufacturing[1,4] | Electricity and gas[1] | Année et rubrique |
|---|---|---|---|---|---|
| **1948** Distribution in percent of the number of employees | 100.0 | 3.1 | 94.8 | 2.1 | **1948** Distribution en pourcentage du nombre de salariés |
| Per employee: Energy consumed | . | 6.90 | 8.85 | 88.50 | Par salarié: Énergie consommée |
| Electricity consumed | 10.3 | 13.7 | 10.3 | 8.2 | Électricité consommée |
| Capacity of installed power equipment | . | 11.79 | 5.05 | 258.59 | Puissance installée |
| Operatives as a percent of employees | 83.0 | 93.9 | 82.7 | 79.1 | Ouvriers en pourcentage des salariés |
| Average man-hours per operative | 2.15 | 1.85 | 2.16 | 2.18 | Heures de travail: moyenne par ouvrier |
| Per thousand operative man-hour: Energy consumed | . | 3.97 | 4.95 | 51.33 | Par millier d'heures-ouvrier: Énergie consommée |
| Electricity consumed | 5.79 | 7.86 | 5.75 | 4.78 | Électricité consommée |
| Capacity of installed power equipment | . | 6.78 | 2.83 | 150.00 | Puissance installée |
| **1953** Distribution in percent of: Value added | 100.0 | 7.5 | 86.6 | 5.9 | **1953** Distribution en pourcentage: Valeur ajoutée |
| Number of employees | 100.0 | 2.9 | 94.8 | 2.3 | Nombre de salariés |
| Per employee: Value added | 16.6 | 42.4 | 15.2 | 43.4 | Par salarié: Valeur ajoutée |
| Wages and salaries | 8.8 | 9.1 | 8.8 | 9.9 | Traitements et salaires |
| Energy consumed | . | 8.15 | 9.95 | 78.85 | Énergie consommée |
| Electricity consumed | 15.7 | 22.5 | 15.6 | 12.2 | Électricité consommée |
| Capacity of installed power equipment | . | 15.52 | 6.95 | 364.29 | Puissance installée |
| Value added per unit of wages and salaries | 1.88 | 4.64 | 1.72 | 4.39 | Valeur ajoutée par unité de traitements et salaires |
| Operatives as a percent of employees | 80.3 | 88.4 | 80.3 | 68.9 | Ouvriers en pourcentage des salariés |
| Average man-hours per operative | 2.11 | 1.95 | 2.12 | 2.12 | Heures de travail: moyenne par ouvrier |
| Per thousand operative man-hour: Wages and salaries | 3.80 | 4.50 | 3.77 | 4.28 | Par millier d'heures-ouvrier: Traitements et salaires |
| Energy consumed | . | 4.73 | 5.86 | 53.89 | Énergie consommée |
| Electricity consumed | 9.26 | 13.07 | 9.16 | 8.32 | Électricité consommée |
| Capacity of installed power equipment | . | 9.00 | 4.09 | 248.96 | Puissance installée |
| **1958** Distribution in percent of: Value added | 100.0 | 5.6 | 87.0 | 7.4 | **1958** Distribution en pourcentage: Valeur ajoutée |
| Number of employees | 100.0 | 2.8 | 94.8 | 2.4 | Nombre de salariés |
| Per employee: Value added | 22.7 | 45.0 | 20.8 | 69.6 | Par salarié: Valeur ajoutée |
| Wages and salaries | 11.8 | 12.6 | 11.8 | 13.0 | Traitements et salaires |
| Energy consumed | . | 10.50 | 10.92 | 70.90 | Énergie consommée |
| Electricity consumed | 19.5 | 32.2 | 18.96 | 24.7 | Électricité consommée |
| Capacity of installed power equipment | . | 19.92 | 8.27 | 519.46 | Puissance installée |
| Employees as a percent of engaged | 99.2 | 99.2 | 99.1 | 100.0 | Salariés en pourcentage des personnes occupées |
| Value added per unit of wages and salaries | 1.91 | 3.58 | 1.77 | 5.37 | Valeur ajoutée par unité de traitements et salaires |
| Operatives as a percent of employees | 78.3 | 85.4 | 78.4 | 67.8 | Ouvriers en pourcentage des salariés |
| Average man-hours per operative | 2.05 | 1.89 | 2.06 | 2.06 | Heures de travail: moyenne par ouvrier |
| Per thousand operative man-hour: Wages and salaries | 5.20 | 6.25 | 5.16 | 5.70 | Par millier d'heures-ouvrier: Traitements et salaires |
| Energy consumed | . | 6.49 | 6.78 | 50.61 | Énergie consommée |
| Electricity consumed | 12.11 | 19.94 | 11.76 | 17.64 | Électricité consommée |
| Capacity of installed power equipment | . | 12.32 | 5.13 | 370.78 | Puissance installée |

For footnotes see end of table.　　Pour les notes, voir au bas du tableau.

## B. The Major Groups of Mining — Les classes de la branche Industries extractives

### a. Absolute Figures — Chiffres absolus

| Year and item of data | Total | Coal mining / Extraction du charbon | Metal mining / Extraction des minerais métalliques | Other mining / Divers | Année et rubrique |
|---|---|---|---|---|---|
| ISIC | 1 | 11 | 12 | 14-19 | CITI |
| **1938** | | | | | **1938** |
| Number of establishments | 654 | 6 | 123 | 525 | Nombre d'établissements |
| Gross value of production | 303.2 | 5.3 | 256.5 | 41.4 | Valeur brute de la production |
| Number of employees (Average during year) | 27.1 | 1.1 | 13.4 | 12.6 | Nombre de salariés (moyenne pour l'année) |
| Number of operatives (Average during year) | 25.5 | 1.0 | 12.5 | 12.0 | Nombre d'ouvriers (moyenne pour l'année) |
| Energy consumed | 121.5 | 4.1 | 106.4 | 11.0 | Energie consommée |
| Electricity consumed | 260.5 | 9.4 | 234.8 | 16.3 | Electricité consommée |
| Capacity of installed power equipment (As of end of year) | 166 | 6 | 136 | 24 | Puissance installée (à la fin de l'année) |
| **1948** | | | | | **1948** |
| Number of establishments | 686 | 21 | 100 | 565 | Nombre d'établissements |
| Gross value of production | 442.3 | 9.7 | 342.7 | 89.9 | Valeur brute de la production |
| Number of employees (Average during year) | 24.6 | 1.1 | 11.2 | 12.3 | Nombre de salariés (moyenne pour l'année) |
| Operatives: Number (Average during year) | 23.1 | 1.0 | 10.0 | 12.1 | Ouvriers: Nombre (moyenne pour l'année) |
| Man-hours worked | 42.8 | 1.8 | 20.6 | 20.4 | Heures de travail effectuées |
| Energy consumed | 169.8 | 9.1 | 147.9 | 12.8 | Energie consommée |
| Electricity consumed | 336.2 | 11.8 | 291.3 | 33.1 | Electricité consommée |
| Capacity of installed power equipment (As of end of year) | 290 | 9 | 219 | 62 | Puissance installée (à la fin de l'année) |
| **1953** | | | | | **1953** |
| Number of establishments | 534 | 16 | 103 | 415 | Nombre d'établissements |
| Value added | 983.2 | 7.1 | 887.1 | 89.0 | Valeur ajoutée |
| Gross value of production | 1 160.4 | 9.0 | 1 037.1 | 114.3 | Valeur brute de la production |
| Employees: Number (Average during year) | 23.2 | 0.9 | 14.3 | 8.0 | Salariés: Nombre (moyenne pour l'année) |
| Wages and salaries | 212.0 | 6.4 | 148.9 | 56.7 | Traitements et salaires |
| Operatives: Number (Average during year) | 20.5 | 0.8 | 12.6 | 7.1 | Ouvriers: Nombre (moyenne pour l'année) |
| Man-hours worked | 40.0 | 1.4 | 24.9 | 13.7 | Heures de travail effectuées |
| Wages and salaries | 179.9 | 5.8 | 125.8 | 48.3 | Traitements et salaires |
| Energy consumed | 189.1 | 3.4 | 169.6 | 16.1 | Energie consommée |
| Electricity consumed | 522.8 | 13.2 | 461.6 | 48.0 | Electricité consommée |
| Capacity of installed power equipment (As of end of year) | 360 | 10 | 286 | 64 | Puissance installée (à la fin de l'année) |
| **1958** | | | | | **1958** |
| Number of establishments | 460 | 10 | 94 | 356 | Nombre d'établissements |
| Value added | 1 080.6 | 8.7 | 968.6 | 103.3 | Valeur ajoutée |
| Number of engaged (Average during year) | 24.2 | 0.9 | 16.6 | 6.7 | Nombre de personnes occupées (moyenne pour l'année) |
| Employees: Number (Average during year) | 24.0 | 0.9 | 16.6 | 6.5 | Salariés: Nombre (moyenne pour l'année) |
| Wages and salaries | 302.2 | 8.8 | 229.3 | 64.1 | Traitements et salaires |
| Operatives: Number (Average during year) | 20.5 | 0.8 | 14.0 | 5.7 | Ouvriers: Nombre (moyenne pour l'année) |
| Man-hours worked | 38.8 | 1.4 | 26.9 | 10.5 | Heures de travail effectuées |
| Wages and salaries | 242.4 | 8.0 | 181.0 | 53.4 | Traitements et salaires |
| Energy consumed | 251.9 | 3.4 | 219.5 | 29.0 | Energie consommée |
| Electricity consumed | 773.6 | 12.5 | 705.0 | 56.1 | Electricité consommée |
| Capacity of installed power equipment (As of end of year) | 478.2 | 10.2 | 394.8 | 73.2 | Puissance installée (à la fin de l'année) |

### b. Structure

| Year and item of data | Total | Coal mining / Extraction du charbon | Metal mining / Extraction des minerais métalliques | Other mining / Divers | Année et rubrique |
|---|---|---|---|---|---|
| ISIC | 1 | 11 | 12 | 14-19 | CITI |
| **1938** Distribution in percent of the number of employees | 100.0 | 4.0 | 49.5 | 46.5 | **1938** Distribution en pourcentage du nombre de salariés |
| Per employee: Energy consumed | 4.48 | 3.73 | 7.94 | 0.87 | Par salarié: Energie consommée |
| Electricity consumed | 9.6 | 8.5 | 17.5 | 1.3 | Electricité consommée |
| Capacity of installed power equipment | 6.12 | 5.45 | 10.15 | 1.90 | Puissance installée |
| Operatives as a percent of employees | 94.1 | 90.9 | 93.3 | 95.2 | Ouvriers en pourcentage des salariés |
| Per operative: Energy consumed | 4.76 | 4.10 | 8.51 | 0.92 | Par ouvrier: Energie consommée |
| Electricity consumed | 10.22 | 9.40 | 18.78 | 1.36 | Electricité consommée |
| Capacity of installed power equipment | 6.51 | 6.00 | 10.88 | 2.00 | Puissance installée |
| **1948** Distribution in percent of the number of employees | 100.0 | 4.4 | 45.6 | 50.0 | **1948** Distribution en pourcentage du nombre de salariés |
| Per employee: Energy consumed | 6.90 | 8.27 | 13.20 | 1.04 | Par salarié: Energie consommée |
| Electricity consumed | 13.7 | 10.7 | 26.0 | 2.7 | Electricité consommée |
| Capacity of installed power equipment | 11.79 | 8.18 | 19.55 | 5.04 | Puissance installée |
| Operatives as a percent of employees | 93.9 | 90.9 | 89.3 | 98.4 | Ouvriers en pourcentage des salariés |
| Average man-hours per operative | 1.85 | 1.80 | 2.06 | 1.68 | Heures de travail: moyenne par ouvrier |
| Per thousand operative man-hour: Energy consumed | 3.97 | 5.06 | 7.18 | 0.63 | Par millier d'heures-ouvrier: Energie consommée |
| Electricity consumed | 7.86 | 6.56 | 14.14 | 1.62 | Electricité consommée |
| Capacity of installed power equipment | 6.78 | 5.00 | 10.63 | 3.04 | Puissance installée |
| **1953** Distribution in percent of: Value added | 100.0 | 0.7 | 90.2 | 9.1 | **1953** Distribution en pourcentage: Valeur ajoutée |
| Number of employees | 100.0 | 3.8 | 61.7 | 34.5 | Nombre de salariés |
| Per employee: Value added | 42.4 | 7.9 | 62.0 | 11.1 | Par salarié: Valeur ajoutée |
| Wages and salaries | 9.1 | 7.1 | 10.4 | 7.1 | Traitements et salaires |
| Energy consumed | 8.15 | 3.78 | 11.86 | 2.01 | Energie consommée |
| Electricity consumed | 22.5 | 14.7 | 32.3 | 6.0 | Electricité consommée |
| Capacity of installed power equipment | 15.52 | 11.11 | 20.00 | 8.00 | Puissance installée |
| Value added per unit of wages and salaries | 4.64 | 1.11 | 5.96 | 1.57 | Valeur ajoutée par unité de traitements et salaires |
| Operatives as a percent of employees | 88.4 | 88.9 | 88.1 | 88.8 | Ouvriers en pourcentage des salariés |
| Average man-hours per operative | 1.95 | 1.75 | 1.98 | 1.93 | Heures de travail: moyenne par ouvrier |
| Per thousand operative man-hour: Wages and salaries | 4.50 | 4.14 | 5.05 | 3.52 | Par millier d'heures-ouvrier: Traitements et salaires |
| Energy consumed | 4.73 | 2.43 | 6.81 | 1.18 | Energie consommée |
| Electricity consumed | 13.07 | 9.43 | 18.54 | 3.50 | Electricité consommée |
| Capacity of installed power equipment | 9.00 | 7.14 | 11.48 | 4.67 | Puissance installée |
| **1958** Distribution in percent of: Value added | 100.0 | 0.8 | 89.6 | 9.6 | **1958** Distribution en pourcentage: Valeur ajoutée |
| Number of employees | 100.0 | 3.7 | 68.6 | 27.7 | Nombre de salariés |
| Per employee: Value added | 45.0 | 9.7 | 58.3 | 15.9 | Par salarié: Valeur ajoutée |
| Wages and salaries | 12.6 | 9.8 | 13.8 | 9.9 | Traitements et salaires |
| Energy consumed | 10.50 | 3.78 | 13.22 | 4.46 | Energie consommée |
| Electricity consumed | 32.2 | 13.9 | 42.5 | 8.6 | Electricité consommée |
| Capacity of installed power equipment | 19.92 | 11.33 | 23.78 | 11.26 | Puissance installée |
| Employees as a percent of engaged | 99.2 | 100.0 | 100.0 | 97.0 | Salariés en pourcentage des personnes occupées |
| Value added per unit of wages and salaries | 3.58 | 0.99 | 4.22 | 1.61 | Valeur ajoutée par unité de traitements et salaires |
| Operatives as a percent of employees | 85.4 | 88.9 | 84.3 | 87.7 | Ouvriers en pourcentage des salariés |
| Average man-hours per operative | 1.89 | 1.75 | 1.92 | 1.84 | Heures de travail: moyenne par ouvrier |
| Per thousand operative man-hour: Wages and salaries | 6.25 | 5.71 | 6.73 | 5.08 | Par millier d'heures-ouvrier: Traitements et salaires |
| Energy consumed | 6.49 | 2.43 | 8.16 | 2.76 | Energie consommée |
| Electricity consumed | 19.94 | 8.93 | 26.21 | 5.34 | Electricité consommée |
| Capacity of installed power equipment | 12.32 | 7.28 | 14.68 | 6.97 | Puissance installée |

## C.  The Major Groups of Manufacturing — Les classes de la branche Industries manufacturières

*a. Absolute Figures — Chiffres absolus*

| Year and item of data | Manufacturing [1,4] / Industries manufacturières [1,4] | Food, beverages and tobacco / Industries alimentaires, boissons, tabac | Textiles [3] | Clothing, footwear and made-up textiles [2] / Articles d'habillement, chaussures et ouvrages en tissu [2] | Wood products and furniture [2] / Bois et meubles [2] | Paper and paper products / Papier et ouvrages en papier | Printing [1] / Imprimerie [1] | Leather and leather products except wearing apparel / Cuir et articles en cuir, à l'exclusion des articles d'habillement | Rubber products / Ouvrages en caoutchouc | Chemicals and chemical, petroleum and coal products [3] / Produits chimiques et dérivés du pétrole et du charbon [3] | Non-metallic mineral products / Produits minéraux non métalliques | Basic metals [4] / Métallurgie de base [4] | Metal products [4] / Ouvrages en métaux [4] | Other manufacturing [2,3] / Autres industries manufacturières [2,3] | Année et rubrique |
|---|---|---|---|---|---|---|---|---|---|---|---|---|---|---|---|
| ISIC / CITI | 2–3 | 20–22 | 23 | 24 | 25–26 | 27 | 28 | 29 | 30 | 31–32 | 33 | 34 | 35–38 | 39 | |
| **1938** | | | | | | | | | | | | | | | **1938** |
| Number of establishments | 16 331 | 4 543 | 548 | 931 | 3 647 | 458 | 778 | 155 | 70 | 506 | 958 | 155 | 3 417 | 165 | Nombre d'établissements |
| Gross value of production | 6 675.7 | 1 612.4 | 418.0 | 389.9 | 526.1 | 703.6 | 203.1 | 70.9 | 52.2 | 329.1 | 193.1 | 410.7 | 1 720.6 | 46.0 | Valeur brute de la production |
| Number of employees (Average during year) | 568.0 | 57.5 | 53.3 | 50.2 | 69.2 | 48.1 | 20.4 | 5.5 | 6.9 | 19.0 | 29.9 | 37.7 | 164.7 | 5.6 | Nombre de salariés (moyenne pour l'année) |
| Number of operatives (Average during year) | 498.5 | 49.2 | 48.0 | 44.9 | 64.6 | 43.6 | 16.3 | 4.8 | 6.0 | 15.2 | 27.5 | 173.7 | | 4.7 | Nombre d'ouvriers (moyenne pour l'année) |
| Energy consumed | 6 101.9 | 620.0 | 238.7 | 22.0 | 374.6 | 1 848.6 | 13.1 | 24.8 | 28.4 | 277.4 | 911.7 | 1 738.9 | | 3.7 | Énergie consommée |
| Electricity consumed | 5 262.4 | 231.4 | 158.6 | 21.4 | 235.8 | 2 209.2 | 22.6 | 9.4 | 21.4 | 509.4 | 150.9 | 1 688.3 | | 4.0 | Électricité consommée |
| Capacity of installed power equipment (As of end of year) | 2 567 | 260 | 124 | 13 | 330 | 853 | 25 | 13 | 16 | 73 | 114 | 740 | | 6 | Puissance installée (à la fin de l'année) |
| **1948** | | | | | | | | | | | | | | | **1948** |
| Number of establishments | 15 284 | 2 590 | 600 | 1 361 | 3 344 | 331 | 817 | 157 | 97 | 538 | 889 | 194 | 4 122 | 244 | Nombre d'établissements |
| Gross value of production | 19 223.3 | 4 245.1 | 1 247.6 | 1 299.4 | 1 342.8 | 2 128.1 | 519.6 | 199.8 | 188.3 | 1 229.5 | 529.8 | 1 325.5 | 4 790.1 | 177.7 | Valeur brute de la production |
| Number of employees (Average during year) | 749.0 | 64.8 | 57.6 | 68.3 | 73.0 | 50.0 | 32.7 | 6.9 | 9.3 | 30.7 | 34.6 | 49.2 | 260.7 | 11.2 | Nombre de salariés (moyenne pour l'année) |
| Operatives Number (Average during year) | 619.6 | 55.7 | 49.7 | 59.9 | 65.5 | 43.1 | 24.1 | 6.1 | 7.4 | 24.0 | 30.2 | 247.1 | | 6.8 | Ouvriers Nombre (moyenne pour l'année) |
| Man-hours worked | 1 338.4 | 119.0 | 107.6 | 123.0 | 134.3 | 98.0 | 54.6 | 13.4 | 16.1 | 52.6 | 64.9 | 540.5 | | 14.4 | Heures de travail effectuées |
| Energy consumed | 6 631.5 | 636.9 | 238.7 | 48.0 | 409.2 | 1 885.8 | 24.0 | 28.2 | 38.6 | 447.6 | 864.3 | 2 003.4 | | 6.8 | Énergie consommée |
| Electricity consumed | 7 691.8 | 387.3 | 199.8 | 34.9 | 370.6 | 2 528.6 | 36.8 | 16.1 | 46.6 | 1 112.2 | 343.4 | 2 607.8 | | 7.7 | Électricité consommée |
| Capacity of installed power equipment (At end of year) | 3 784 | 286 | 168 | 38 | 446 | 967 | 34 | 22 | 41 | 182 | 193 | 1 388 | | 19 | Puissance installée (à la fin de l'année) |
| **1953** | | | | | | | | | | | | | | | **1953** |
| Number of establishments | 14 029 | 2 309 | 595 | 1 250 | 2 879 | 327 | 789 | 137 | 82 | 443 | 776 | 260 | 3 924 | 258 | Nombre d'établissements |
| Value added | 11 345.2 | 1 192.0 | 630.7 | 666.4 | 769.6 | 1 006.9 | 584.3 | 70.9 | 155.3 | 708.8 | 473.6 | 857.5 | 4 103.0 | 126.2 | Valeur ajoutée |
| Gross value of production | 29 514.9 | 6 666.7 | 1 544.0 | 1 584.4 | 2 099.9 | 2 758.8 | 862.9 | 230.2 | 301.7 | 1 936.8 | 789.1 | 2 352.3 | 8 147.5 | 240.6 | Valeur brute de la production |
| Employees Number (Average during year) | 748.6 | 63.2 | 55.3 | 65.0 | 65.1 | 52.9 | 35.9 | 6.1 | 9.2 | 30.8 | 31.4 | 53.9 | 269.8 | 10.0 | Salariés Nombre (moyenne pour l'année) |
| Wages and salaries | 6 582.7 | 531.0 | 405.1 | 440.7 | 481.1 | 483.8 | 359.1 | 50.5 | 81.8 | 315.8 | 256.0 | 436.9 | 2 681.6 | 59.3 | Traitements et salaires |
| Operatives Number (Average during year) | 601.0 | 51.3 | 47.2 | 55.8 | 57.0 | 45.9 | 25.0 | 5.0 | 7.2 | 21.8 | 27.2 | 250.4 | | 7.2 | Ouvriers Nombre (moyenne pour l'année) |
| Man-hours worked | 1 271.5 | 109.8 | 97.3 | 110.4 | 117.2 | 101.6 | 55.4 | 10.6 | 15.2 | 46.6 | 57.3 | 535.1 | | 15.0 | Heures de travail effectuées |
| Wages and salaries | 4 791.3 | 391.3 | 301.7 | 320.9 | 400.0 | 391.0 | 227.7 | 37.6 | 56.2 | 181.2 | 206.0 | 2 221.4 | | 56.3 | Traitements et salaires |
| Energy consumed | 7 445.8 | 653.3 | 261.3 | 51.8 | 252.6 | 2 010.9 | 29.0 | 30.9 | 49.3 | 544.4 | 1 069.1 | 2 473.2 | | 20.0 | Énergie consommée |
| Electricity consumed | 11 642.7 | 505.5 | 258.8 | 45.3 | 301.8 | 4 043.5 | 60.4 | 19.4 | 64.4 | 1 639.3 | 495.0 | 4 183.7 | | 25.6 | Électricité consommée |
| Capacity of installed power equipment (At end of year) | 5 205 | 355 | 215 | 42 | 456 | 1 334 | 49 | 24 | 62 | 278 | 236 | 2 136 | | 18 | Puissance installée (à la fin de l'année) |
| **1958** | | | | | | | | | | | | | | | **1958** |
| Number of establishments | 14 336 | 2 231 | 469 | 1 254 | 2 808 | 331 | 822 | 117 | 95 | 454 | 776 | 241 | 4 422 | 316 | Nombre d'établissements |
| Value added | 16 749.9 | 1 855.5 | 626.3 | 819.1 | 1 070.6 | 1 572.9 | 857.4 | 85.2 | 238.8 | 1 070.2 | 663.6 | 1 317.5 | 6 347.5 | 225.3 | Valeur ajoutée |
| Number of engaged (Average during year) | 810.1 | 67.4 | 41.5 | 63.2 | 68.6 | 59.3 | 41.0 | 5.5 | 10.9 | 33.6 | 31.8 | 374.8 | | 12.5 | Nombre de personnes occupées (moyenne pour l'année) |
| Employees Number (Average during year) | 803.2 | 66.4 | 41.4 | 62.7 | 66.6 | 59.3 | 40.6 | 5.5 | 10.9 | 33.5 | 31.4 | 56.0 | 316.5 | 12.4 | Salariés Nombre (moyenne pour l'année) |
| Wages and salaries | 9 481.3 | 739.3 | 416.9 | 539.4 | 673.1 | 718.1 | 528.2 | 57.8 | 128.2 | 429.3 | 343.8 | 4 771.5 | | 135.7 | Traitements et salaires |
| Operatives Number (Average during year) | 629.5 | 53.3 | 35.4 | 52.8 | 58.3 | 50.9 | 27.7 | 4.6 | 8.3 | 22.2 | 26.5 | 280.3 | | 9.2 | Ouvriers Nombre (moyenne pour l'année) |
| Man-hours worked | 1 294.8 | 112.1 | 72.2 | 99.8 | 117.2 | 108.4 | 58.0 | 9.3 | 17.3 | 46.0 | 53.8 | 582.2 | | 18.5 | Heures de travail effectuées |
| Wages and salaries | 6 681.6 | 541.5 | 306.6 | 389.8 | 552.9 | 574.8 | 325.2 | 41.8 | 86.5 | 242.1 | 267.6 | 3 260.6 | | 92.2 | Traitements et salaires |
| Energy consumed | 8 773.8 | 647.3 | 232.9 | 56.4 | 287.7 | 2 575.5 | 38.8 | 28.3 | 62.3 | 776.7 | 1 048.6 | 2 976.1 | | 43.2 | Énergie consommée |
| Electricity consumed | 15 225.5 | 606.1 | 252.7 | 50.2 | 399.5 | 5 286.8 | 80.3 | 21.5 | 93.4 | 2 292.2 | 621.1 | 5 473.7 | | 48.0 | Électricité consommée |
| Capacity of installed power equipment (At end of year) | 6 644.1 | 381.6 | 197.5 | 46.3 | 553.4 | 1 894.3 | 54.5 | 26.6 | 82.1 | 359.8 | 305.6 | 2 701.7 | | 40.7 | Puissance installée (à la fin de l'année) |

## C. The Major Groups of Manufacturing (continued) — Les classes de la branche Industries manufacturières (suite)

b. Structure

| Year and item of data | Manufacturing 1,4 (2-3) | Food, beverages and tobacco (20-22) | Textiles 3 (23) | Clothing, footwear and made-up textiles 2 (24) | Wood products and furniture 2 (25-26) | Paper and paper products (27) | Printing 1 (28) | Leather and leather products except wearing apparel (29) | Rubber products (30) | Chemicals and chemical, petroleum and coal products 3 (31-32) | Non-metallic mineral products (33) | Basic metals 4 (34) | Metal products 4 (35-38) | Other manufacturing 2,3 (39) | Année et rubrique |
|---|---|---|---|---|---|---|---|---|---|---|---|---|---|---|---|
| **1938** | | | | | | | | | | | | | | | **1938** |
| Distribution in percent of the number of employees | 100.0 | 10.1 | 9.4 | 8.8 | 12.2 | 8.4 | 3.6 | 1.0 | 1.2 | 3.4 | 5.2 | 6.7 | 29.0 | 1.0 | Distribution en pourcentage du nombre de salariés |
| Per employee: | | | | | | | | | | | | | | | Par salarié: |
| Energy consumed | 10.74 | 10.78 | 4.48 | 0.44 | 5.41 | 38.43 | 0.64 | 4.51 | 4.12 | 14.60 | 30.49 | 8.59 | | 0.66 | Energie consommée |
| Electricity consumed | 9.3 | 4.0 | 3.0 | 0.4 | 3.4 | 45.9 | 1.1 | 1.7 | 3.1 | 26.8 | 5.0 | 8.3 | | 0.7 | Electricité consommée |
| Capacity of installed power equipment | 4.52 | 4.52 | 2.33 | 0.26 | 4.77 | 17.73 | 1.22 | 2.36 | 2.32 | 3.84 | 3.81 | 3.66 | | 1.07 | Puissance installée |
| Operatives as a percent of employees | 87.8 | 85.6 | 90.0 | 89.4 | 93.4 | 90.6 | 79.9 | 87.3 | 87.0 | 80.0 | 92.0 | 85.8 | | 83.9 | Ouvriers en pourcentage des salariés |
| Per operative: | | | | | | | | | | | | | | | Par ouvrier: |
| Energy consumed | 12.24 | 12.60 | 4.97 | 0.49 | 5.80 | 42.40 | 0.80 | 5.17 | 4.73 | 18.25 | 33.15 | 10.01 | | 0.79 | Energie consommée |
| Electricity consumed | 10.56 | 4.70 | 3.30 | 0.48 | 3.65 | 50.67 | 1.39 | 1.96 | 3.57 | 33.51 | 5.49 | 9.72 | | 0.85 | Electricité consommée |
| Capacity of installed power equipment | 5.15 | 5.28 | 2.58 | 0.29 | 5.11 | 19.56 | 1.53 | 2.71 | 2.67 | 4.80 | 4.14 | 4.26 | | 1.28 | Puissance installée |
| **1948** | | | | | | | | | | | | | | | **1948** |
| Distribution in percent of the number of employees | 100.0 | 8.6 | 7.7 | 9.1 | 9.8 | 6.6 | 4.4 | 0.9 | 1.3 | 4.1 | 4.6 | 6.5 | 34.9 | 1.5 | Distribution en pourcentage du nombre de salariés |
| Per employee: | | | | | | | | | | | | | | | Par salarié: |
| Energy consumed | 8.85 | 9.83 | 4.14 | 0.70 | 5.60 | 37.72 | 0.73 | 4.09 | 4.15 | 14.58 | 24.98 | 6.46 | | 0.61 | Energie consommée |
| Electricity consumed | 10.3 | 6.0 | 3.5 | 0.5 | 5.1 | 50.6 | 1.1 | 2.3 | 5.0 | 36.2 | 9.9 | 8.4 | | 0.7 | Electricité consommée |
| Capacity of installed power equipment | 5.05 | 4.41 | 2.92 | 0.56 | 6.11 | 19.34 | 1.04 | 3.19 | 4.41 | 5.93 | 5.58 | 4.48 | | 1.70 | Puissance installée |
| Operatives as a percent of employees | 82.7 | 86.0 | 86.3 | 87.7 | 89.7 | 86.2 | 73.7 | 88.4 | 79.6 | 78.2 | 87.3 | 79.7 | | 60.7 | Ouvriers en pourcentage des salariés |
| Average man-hours per operative | 2.16 | 2.14 | 2.16 | 2.05 | 2.05 | 2.27 | 2.26 | 2.20 | 2.18 | 2.19 | 2.15 | 2.19 | | 2.12 | Heures de travail: moyenne par ouvrier |
| Per thousand operative man-hour: | | | | | | | | | | | | | | | Par millier d'heures-ouvrier |
| Energy consumed | 4.95 | 5.35 | 2.22 | 0.39 | 3.05 | 19.24 | 0.44 | 2.10 | 2.40 | 8.51 | 13.32 | 3.71 | | 0.47 | Energie consommée |
| Electricity consumed | 5.75 | 3.25 | 1.86 | 0.28 | 2.76 | 25.80 | 0.67 | 1.20 | 2.89 | 21.14 | 5.29 | 4.82 | | 0.53 | Electricité consommée |
| Capacity of installed power equipment | 2.83 | 2.40 | 1.56 | 0.31 | 3.32 | 9.87 | 0.62 | 1.64 | 2.55 | 3.46 | 2.97 | 2.57 | | 1.32 | Puissance installée |
| **1953** | | | | | | | | | | | | | | | **1953** |
| Distribution in percent of: | | | | | | | | | | | | | | | Distribution en pourcentage: |
| Value added | 100.0 | 10.5 | 5.5 | 5.9 | 6.8 | 8.8 | 5.2 | 0.6 | 1.4 | 6.2 | 4.2 | 7.6 | 36.1 | 1.2 | Valeur ajoutée |
| Number of employees | 100.0 | 8.4 | 7.4 | 8.7 | 8.7 | 7.0 | 4.8 | 0.8 | 1.3 | 4.1 | 4.2 | 7.2 | 36.0 | 1.4 | Nombre de salariés |
| Per employee: | | | | | | | | | | | | | | | Par salarié: |
| Value added | 15.2 | 18.9 | 11.4 | 10.2 | 11.8 | 19.0 | 16.3 | 11.6 | 16.9 | 23.0 | 15.1 | 15.9 | 15.2 | 12.6 | Valeur ajoutée |
| Wages and salaries | 8.8 | 8.4 | 7.3 | 6.8 | 7.4 | 9.1 | 10.0 | 8.3 | 8.9 | 10.2 | 8.2 | 8.1 | 9.9 | 5.9 | Traitements et salaires |
| Energy consumed | 9.95 | 10.34 | 4.72 | 0.80 | 3.88 | 38.01 | 0.81 | 5.06 | 5.36 | 17.68 | 34.05 | 7.64 | | 2.00 | Energie consommée |
| Electricity consumed | 15.6 | 8.0 | 4.7 | 0.7 | 4.6 | 76.4 | 1.7 | 3.2 | 7.0 | 53.2 | 15.8 | 12.92 | | 2.6 | Electricité consommée |
| Capacity of installed power equipment | 6.95 | 5.62 | 3.89 | 0.65 | 7.00 | 25.22 | 1.36 | 3.93 | 6.74 | 9.02 | 7.52 | 6.60 | | 1.80 | Puissance installée |
| Value added per unit of wages and salaries | 1.72 | 2.24 | 1.56 | 1.51 | 1.60 | 2.08 | 1.63 | 1.40 | 1.90 | 2.24 | 1.85 | 1.96 | 1.53 | 2.13 | Valeur ajoutée par unité de traitements et salaires |
| Operatives as a percent of employees | 80.3 | 81.2 | 85.4 | 85.8 | 87.6 | 86.8 | 69.6 | 82.0 | 78.3 | 70.8 | 86.6 | 77.4 | | 72.0 | Ouvriers en pourcentage des salariés |
| Average man-hours per operative | 2.12 | 2.14 | 2.06 | 1.98 | 2.06 | 2.21 | 2.22 | 2.12 | 2.11 | 2.14 | 2.11 | 2.14 | | 2.08 | Heures de travail: moyenne par ouvrier |
| Per thousand operative man-hour: | | | | | | | | | | | | | | | Par millier d'heures-ouvrier: |
| Wages and salaries | 3.77 | 3.56 | 3.10 | 2.91 | 3.41 | 3.85 | 4.11 | 3.55 | 3.70 | 3.89 | 3.60 | 4.15 | | 3.75 | Traitements et salaires |
| Energy consumed | 5.86 | 5.95 | 2.68 | 0.47 | 2.16 | 19.79 | 0.52 | 2.92 | 3.24 | 11.68 | 18.66 | 4.62 | | 1.33 | Energie consommée |
| Electricity consumed | 9.16 | 4.60 | 2.66 | 0.41 | 2.58 | 39.80 | 1.09 | 1.83 | 4.24 | 35.18 | 8.64 | 7.82 | | 1.71 | Electricité consommée |
| Capacity of installed power equipment | 4.09 | 3.23 | 2.21 | 0.38 | 3.89 | 13.13 | 0.88 | 2.26 | 4.08 | 5.96 | 4.12 | 3.99 | | 1.20 | Puissance installée |

### C. The Major Groups of Manufacturing (continued) — Les classes de la branche Industries manufacturières (suite)

| Year and item of data | Manufacturing[1,4] Industries manufacturières[1,4] | Food, beverages and tobacco Industries alimentaires, boissons, tabac | Textiles[3] | Clothing, footwear and made-up textiles[2] Articles d'habillement, chaussures et ouvrages en tissu[2] | Wood products and furniture[2] Bois et meubles[2] | Paper and paper products Papier et ouvrages en papier | Printing[1] Imprimerie[1] | Leather and leather products except wearing apparel Cuir et articles en cuir, à l'exclusion des articles d'habillement | Rubber products Ouvrages en caoutchouc | Chemicals and chemical, petroleum and coal products[3] Produits chimiques et dérivés du pétrole et du charbon[3] | Non-metallic mineral products Produits minéraux non métalliques | Basic metals[4] Métallurgie de base[4] | Metal products[4] Ouvrages en métaux[4] | Other manufacturing[2,3] Autres industries manufacturières[2,3] | Année et rubrique |
|---|---|---|---|---|---|---|---|---|---|---|---|---|---|---|---|
| ISIC | 2–3 | 20–22 | 23 | 24 | 25–26 | 27 | 28 | 29 | 30 | 31–32 | 33 | 34 | 35–38 | 39 | CITI |
| **1958** | | | | | | | | | | | | | | | **1958** |
| Distribution in percent of: | | | | | | | | | | | | | | | Distribution en pourcentage: |
| Value added | 100.0 | 11.0 | 3.8 | 4.9 | 6.3 | 9.4 | 5.2 | 0.5 | 1.4 | 6.4 | 3.9 | 7.9 | 37.9 | 1.4 | Valeur ajoutée |
| Number of employees | 100.0 | 8.2 | 5.2 | 7.8 | 8.3 | 7.4 | 5.0 | 0.7 | 1.3 | 4.2 | 3.9 | 7.0 | 39.4 | 1.6 | Nombre de personnes occupées |
| Per employee: | | | | | | | | | | | | | | | Par salarié: |
| Value added | 20.8 | 27.9 | 15.1 | 13.1 | 16.1 | 26.5 | 21.1 | 15.5 | 21.9 | 31.9 | 21.1 | 23.5 | 20.0 | 18.2 | Valeur ajoutée |
| Wages and salaries | 11.8 | 11.1 | 10.1 | 8.6 | 10.1 | 12.1 | 13.0 | 10.5 | 11.8 | 12.8 | 10.9 | | 12.8 | 10.9 | Traitements et salaires |
| Energy consumed | 10.92 | 9.75 | 5.62 | 0.90 | 4.32 | 43.43 | 0.96 | 5.14 | 5.72 | 23.18 | 33.39 | | 7.99 | 3.5 | Energie consommée |
| Electricity consumed | 19.0 | 9.1 | 6.1 | 0.8 | 6.0 | 89.2 | 2.0 | 3.9 | 8.6 | 68.4 | 19.8 | | 14.7 | 3.9 | Electricité consommée |
| Capacity of installed power equipment | 8.27 | 5.75 | 4.77 | 0.74 | 8.31 | 31.94 | 1.34 | 4.84 | 7.53 | 10.74 | 9.73 | | 7.25 | 3.26 | Puissance installée |
| Employees as a percent of engaged | 99.1 | 98.5 | 99.8 | 99.2 | 97.1 | 100.0 | 99.0 | 100.0 | 100.0 | 99.7 | 98.7 | | 99.4 | 99.2 | Salariés en pourcentage des personnes occupées |
| Value added per unit of wages and salaries | 1.77 | 2.51 | 1.50 | 1.52 | 1.59 | 2.19 | 1.62 | 1.47 | 1.86 | 2.49 | 1.93 | | 1.61 | 1.66 | Valeur ajoutée par unité de traitements et salaires |
| Operatives as a percent of employees | 78.4 | 80.3 | 85.5 | 84.2 | 87.5 | 85.8 | 68.2 | 83.6 | 76.1 | 66.3 | 84.4 | | 75.2 | 74.2 | Ouvriers en pourcentage des salariés |
| Average man-hours per operative | 2.06 | 2.10 | 2.04 | 1.89 | 2.01 | 2.13 | 2.09 | 2.02 | 2.08 | 2.07 | 2.03 | | 2.08 | 2.01 | Heures de travail: moyenne par ouvrier |
| Per thousand operative man-hour: | | | | | | | | | | | | | | | Par millier d'heures-ouvrier: |
| Wages and salaries | 5.16 | 4.83 | 4.25 | 3.90 | 4.72 | 5.30 | 5.61 | 4.49 | 5.00 | 5.26 | 4.97 | | 5.60 | 4.98 | Traitements et salaires |
| Energy consumed | 6.78 | 5.77 | 3.22 | 0.56 | 2.45 | 23.76 | 0.67 | 3.04 | 3.60 | 16.88 | 19.49 | | 5.11 | 2.34 | Energie consommée |
| Electricity consumed | 11.76 | 5.41 | 3.50 | 0.50 | 3.41 | 48.77 | 1.38 | 2.31 | 5.40 | 49.83 | 11.54 | | 9.40 | 2.59 | Electricité consommée |
| Capacity of installed power equipment | 5.13 | 3.40 | 2.74 | 0.46 | 4.72 | 17.48 | 0.94 | 2.86 | 4.74 | 7.82 | 5.68 | | 4.64 | 2.20 | Puissance installée |

[1] In the case of the data for 1938, in general, establishments principally engaged in Manufacturing and Other mining (ISIC major groups 14–19) were covered which had ten or more operatives, annual gross production of 15 000 Kronor or more, or annual value added of 4 000 Kronor or more. In the case of a few kinds of industrial activity (e.g., coal mining, metal mining, distilleries and breweries and metal refining and smelting), establishments irrespective of size were covered. In the 1948, 1953 and 1958 Industrial Censuses, the general lower limit of coverage with regard to size was five employees. In a few kinds of activity, the same as in 1938, all establishments were included in the data for these years. Establishments primarily engaged in publishing were not covered in any of the years. The mining and manufacturing establishments were delineated so that excluded were significant ancillary electric power plants. These ancillary power plants were classified to the Electricity industry (ISIC group 511). Included in addition in this ISIC group are data on public service electricity power plants and distribution stations. Electricity plants with installed prime movers of 50 or more HP are covered in the data for 1938, 1948, 1953 and 1958.

[2] The data on wages and salaries paid to employees, on number of, wages and salaries paid to, and man-hours worked by operatives, on energy and electricity consumed in the case of all years that are shown for Clothing (ISIC major group 24) cover such activities as the manufacture of sun blinds, which should be classified in wood products (ISIC major group 25), and of artificial flowers and related articles, which should be in Other manufacturing (ISIC major group 39). Since this is not the case for the other items of data shown, ratios between the afore-listed items and other items of data may be slightly distorted.

[3] The data on number of, and man-hours worked by operatives and on energy and electricity consumed in 1948 that are shown for chemicals and petroleum and coal products (ISIC major groups 31–32) include the manufacturing of linoleum, which should be classified under Textiles (ISIC major group 23). This is the case in 1953, as well, for those items of data and wages and salaries paid, for the manufacture of plastic products, which belong in Other manufacturing (ISIC major group 39). As these deviations from the ISIC do not occur for the other items of data shown in the table, ratios between the items of data mentioned above and the other items may be somewhat distorted.

[4] For all years, the data on wages and salaries paid to employees, on number of, wages and salaries paid to and man-hours worked by operatives, and on energy and electricity consumed but not on other items for Basic metals and Metal products (ISIC major groups 34 and 35–38) cover plumbing, which should be classified under Construction (ISIC Division 4).

[1] Dans le cas des données relatives à 1938, généralement, parmi les établissements engagés principalement dans Industries manufacturières et Autres industries extractives (CITI classes 14–19) sont couverts: ceux employant dix ouvriers ou plus, ceux ayant une production brute annuelle d'une valeur de 15 000 Couronnes ou plus ou une valeur ajoutée annuelle de 4 000 Couronnes ou plus. Dans le cas de quelques types d'industries (par exemple, extraction de charbon, de minerais métalliques, distillerie et brasserie, fonderie de minerais et affinage des métaux) les établissements, quelle que soit leur dimension, sont couverts. Dans les recensements industriels de 1948, 1953 et 1958, cinq salariés a été la limite générale la plus basse adoptée. Dans un nombre restreint de types d'activités, les mêmes qu'en 1938, tous les établissements ont été couverts par les données relatives à ces années. Les établissements principalement engagés dans éditions ne sont couverts dans aucune de ces années. Les établissements miniers et manufacturiers ont été délimités de façon telle que des installations électriques secondaires d'une certaine importance ont été exclues. Ces installations secondaires ont été rattachées aux industries productrices de l'électricité (CITI groupe 511). Y compris en additif, à ce groupe de la CITI, les données relatives au service public d'installations électriques et aux stations de distribution. Les installations électriques activées par un moteur primaire de 50 CV ou plus sont couvertes par les données relatives à 1938, 1948, 1953 et 1958.

[2] Les données relatives aux traitements et salaires payés aux salariés, au nombre de salariés et salaires payés, d'heures de travail effectuées par des ouvriers, à l'énergie et à l'électricité consommées pour toutes les années qui sont reproduites pour articles d'habillement (CITI classe 24) couvrent des activités telles que la fabrication de stores qui devrait être classée dans Ouvrages en bois (CITI classe 25) et les fleurs artificielles et articles similaires, qui devraient être dans Autres industries manufacturières (CITI classe 39). Vu qu'il n'en a pas été ainsi dans le cas des autres rubriques reproduites, les ratios entre les articles susnommés et les autres rubriques peuvent être légèrement distordus.

[3] Les données relatives au nombre d'heures de travail effectuées par ouvrier, à la totalité du nombre d'heures de travail effectuées et à l'énergie et à l'électricité consommées en 1948 reproduites pour les industries chimiques et les produits dérivés du pétrole et du charbon (CITI classes 31–32) comprennent la fabrication de linoléum, qui devrait être classée sous Industries textiles (CITI classe 23). C'est le cas en 1953 aussi bien pour ces rubriques que pour traitements et salaires payés dans les industries des Ouvrages en plastique, qui appartiennent à Autres industries manufacturières (CITI classe 39). Comme ces écarts à la CITI ne se produisent pas dans le cas des autres rubriques reproduites au tableau, les ratios des rubriques mentionnées ci-dessus et des autres rubriques peuvent être quelque peu distordus.

[4] Pour toutes les années les données relatives aux traitements et salaires payés aux salariés, au nombre de traitements et salaires payés aux ouvriers, au nombre d'heures de travail effectuées par les ouvriers et à l'énergie et l'électricité consommées couvrent les plomberies, lesquelles ne sont pas couvertes par les autres rubriques relatives aux industries métallurgiques de base et Ouvrages en métaux (CITI classes 34 et 35–38). Les plomberies devraient être classées sous Construction (CITI branche 4).

## 6. FUELS AND ELECTRICITY CONSUMED, INDUSTRIAL ESTABLISHMENTS WITH FIVE OR MORE EMPLOYEES[1]
## COMBUSTIBLES ET ELECTRICITE CONSOMMES, ETABLISSEMENTS INDUSTRIELS COMPTANT CINQ SALARIES OU PLUS[1]

### A. Percentage Distribution of Energy Consumed According to Source
### Distribution en pourcentage de l'énergie consommée suivant la source

Quantities in thousand metric tons of coal equivalents.　　　　　Quantités en milliers de tonnes métriques d'équivalent houille.

### a. The Major Groups of Mining and Electricity and Gas
### Les classes des industries extractives et électricité et gaz

| Year and item of data | Mining — Industries extractives | | | | Electricity and gas Electricité et gaz | | | Année et rubrique |
| --- | --- | --- | --- | --- | --- | --- | --- | --- |
| | Total | Coal mining Extraction du charbon | Metal mining Extraction des minerais métalliques | Other mining Divers | Total [1] | Electricity [1] Electricité [1] | Gas Gaz | |
| ISIC | 1 | 11 | 12 | 14–19 | 511-512 | 511 | 512 | CITI |
| **1938** | | | | | | | | **1938** Energie totale consommée |
| Total energy consumed.. | 121.5 | 4.1 | 106.4 | 11.0 | 1 050.7 | 298.0 | 753.4 | |
| Percent consumed as: | | | | | | | | Pourcentage consommé comme: |
| Coal.............. | 16.9 | 70.5 | 13.0 | 33.6 | 89.8 | 93.6 | 88.2 | Charbon |
| Wood............. | 4.8 | — | 3.8 | 15.1 | 0.3 | 1.0 | — | Bois |
| Coke.............. | 37.4 | — | 42.6 | 3.0 | 8.3 | — | 11.6 | Coke |
| Refined oil fuels....... | 3.4 | 0.9 | 1.7 | 20.4 | 1.6 | 5.4 | 0.1 | Pétrole raffiné |
| Gas.............. | — | — | — | — | — | — | — | Gaz |
| Electricity.......... | 26.8 | 28.6 | 27.6 | 18.5 | — | — | 0.1 | Electricité |
| Peat and charcoal.... | 10.7 | — | 11.3 | 9.4 | — | — | — | Tourbière et charbon de bois |
| **1948** | | | | | | | | **1948** Energie totale consommée |
| Total energy consumed.. | 169.8 | 9.1 | 147.9 | 12.8 | 1 442.5 | 513.7 | 930.4 | |
| Percent consumed as: | | | | | | | | Pourcentage consommé comme: |
| Coal.............. | 11.4 | 49.8 | 8.7 | 16.0 | 77.0 | 64.1 | 84.0 | Charbon |
| Wood............. | 11.1 | 30.4 | 9.4 | 15.8 | 0.8 | 2.3 | — | Bois |
| Coke.............. | 34.0 | — | 38.8 | 2.3 | 10.2 | 0.1 | 15.7 | Coke |
| Refined oil fuels....... | 8.3 | 3.5 | 7.2 | 25.6 | 12.0 | 33.5 | 0.1 | Pétrole raffiné |
| Gas.............. | — | — | — | — | — | — | — | Gaz |
| Electricity.......... | 24.8 | 16.3 | 24.7 | 32.3 | — | — | 0.2 | Electricité |
| Peat and charcoal.... | 10.4 | — | 11.2 | 8.0 | — | — | — | Tourbière et charbon de bois |
| **1953** | | | | | | | | **1953** Energie totale consommée |
| Total energy consumed.. | 189.1 | 3.4 | 169.6 | 16.1 | 1 395.7 | 328.4 | 1 070.1 | |
| Percent consumed as: | | | | | | | | Pourcentage consommé comme: |
| Coal.............. | 4.4 | 48.0 | 3.1 | 8.9 | 82.4 | 67.4 | 86.8 | Charbon |
| Wood............. | 5.2 | — | 5.1 | 7.6 | 0.5 | 2.2 | — | Bois |
| Coke.............. | 38.4 | — | 42.6 | 2.2 | 10.0 | 0.1 | 12.9 | Coke |
| Refined oil fuels....... | 12.5 | 4.2 | 9.7 | 43.7 | 7.1 | 30.1 | 0.1 | Pétrole raffiné |
| Gas.............. | — | — | — | — | — | 0.2 | — | Gaz |
| Electricity.......... | 34.6 | 47.8 | 34.0 | 37.2 | — | — | 0.2 | Electricité |
| Peat and charcoal.... | 4.9 | — | 5.5 | 0.4 | — | — | — | Tourbière et charbon de bois |
| **1958** | | | | | | | | **1958** Energie totale consommée |
| Total energy consumed.. | 251.9 | 3.4 | 219.5 | 29.0 | 1 432.3 | 393.4 | 1 042.8 | |
| Percent consumed as: | | | | | | | | Pourcentage consommé comme: |
| Coal.............. | 1.8 | 49.7 | 0.9 | 3.2 | 67.9 | 16.2 | 87.1 | Charbon |
| Wood............. | 1.8 | — | 1.7 | 3.4 | 0.9 | 3.1 | — | Bois |
| Coke.............. | 31.6 | — | 36.0 | 1.1 | 8.3 | 0.2 | 11.4 | Coke |
| Refined oil fuels....... | 24.8 | 4.0 | 19.4 | 67.9 | 22.9 | 80.2 | 1.2 | Pétrole raffiné |
| Gas.............. | — | — | — | — | — | 0.2 | — | Gaz |
| Electricity.......... | 38.4 | 46.3 | 40.2 | 24.2 | — | — | 0.3 | Electricité |
| Peat and charcoal.... | 1.6 | — | 1.8 | 0.2 | — | 0.1 | — | Tourbière et charbon de bois |

For footnotes see end of table.　　　　　Pour les notes, voir au bas du tableau.

## B. The Major Groups of Manufacturing — Les classes de la branche Industries manufacturières

| Year and item of data | Manufacturing [1,4]<br>Industries manufacturières [1,4] | Food, beverages and tobacco<br>Industries alimentaires, boissons, tabac | Textiles [3] | Clothing, footwear and made-up textiles [2]<br>Articles d'habillement, chaussures et ouvrages en tissu [2] | Wood products and furniture [2]<br>Bois et meubles [2] | Paper and paper products<br>Papier et ouvrages en papier | Printing [1]<br>Imprimerie [1] | Leather and leather products except wearing apparel<br>Cuir et articles en cuir, à l'exclusion des articles d'habillement | Rubber products<br>Ouvrages en caoutchouc | Chemicals and chemical, petroleum and coal products [3]<br>Produits chimiques et dérivés du pétrole et du charbon [3] | Non-metallic mineral products<br>Produits minéraux non métalliques | Basic metals and metal products [4]<br>Métallurgie de base et ouvrages en métaux [4] | Other manufacturing [2,3]<br>Autres industries manufacturières [2,3] | Année et rubrique |
|---|---|---|---|---|---|---|---|---|---|---|---|---|---|---|
| ISIC | 2–3 | 20–22 | 23 | 24 | 25–26 | 27 | 28 | 29 | 30 | 31–32 | 33 | 34–38 | 39 | CITI |
| **1938** | | | | | | | | | | | | | | **1938** |
| Total energy consumed: | | | | | | | | | | | | | | Energie totale consommée: |
|   Quantity | 6 101.9 | 620.0 | 238.7 | 22.0 | 374.6 | 1 848.6 | 13.1 | 24.8 | 28.4 | 277.4 | 911.7 | 1 738.9 | 3.7 | Quantité |
| Percent of total in specified industry | 100.0 | 10.1 | 3.9 | 0.4 | 6.1 | 30.3 | 0.2 | 0.4 | 0.5 | 4.6 | 14.9 | 28.5 | 0.1 | Pourcentage du total par industrie indiquée |
| Percent consumed as: | | | | | | | | | | | | | | Pourcentage consommé comme: |
|   Coal | 57.2 | 67.3 | 82.7 | 31.8 | 12.3 | 67.3 | 7.6 | 82.9 | 86.7 | 56.9 | 82.1 | 35.8 | 19.4 | Charbon |
|   Wood | 15.4 | 18.2 | 4.8 | 18.2 | 77.4 | 17.1 | 5.7 | 8.9 | 0.1 | 11.7 | 10.6 | 4.0 | 14.2 | Bois |
|   Coke | 7.8 | 4.0 | 2.6 | 23.5 | 0.5 | 0.1 | 41.4 | 1.7 | 1.5 | 2.7 | 3.4 | 22.8 | 22.8 | Coke |
|   Refined oil fuels | 2.6 | 4.9 | 1.2 | 13.3 | 1.8 | 0.3 | 15.4 | 1.7 | 2.1 | 5.5 | 1.6 | 4.4 | 24.2 | Pétrole raffiné |
|   Gas | 0.2 | 0.8 | — | 0.8 | 0.1 | — | 8.1 | — | 0.2 | 0.1 | 0.1 | 0.3 | 5.7 | Gaz |
|   Electricity | 10.8 | 4.6 | 8.3 | 12.2 | 7.8 | 14.9 | 21.6 | 4.8 | 9.4 | 23.0 | 2.0 | 12.2 | 13.2 | Electricité |
|   Peat and charcoal | 6.0 | 0.2 | 0.4 | 0.2 | 0.1 | 0.3 | 0.2 | — | | 0.1 | 0.2 | 20.5 | 0.5 | Tourbière et charbon de bois |
| **1948** | | | | | | | | | | | | | | **1948** |
| Total energy consumed: | | | | | | | | | | | | | | Energie totale consommée: |
|   Quantity | 6 631.5 | 636.9 | 238.7 | 48.0 | 409.2 | 1 885.8 | 24.0 | 28.2 | 38.6 | 447.6 | 864.3 | 2 003.4 | 6.8 | Quantité |
| Percent of total in specified industry | 100.0 | 9.6 | 3.6 | 0.7 | 6.1 | 28.5 | 0.3 | 0.5 | 0.6 | 6.7 | 13.0 | 30.2 | 0.2 | Pourcentage du total par industrie indiquée |
| Percent consumed as: | | | | | | | | | | | | | | Pourcentage consommé comme: |
|   Coal | 33.0 | 28.2 | 34.7 | 14.3 | 9.9 | 42.4 | 10.5 | 37.8 | 41.5 | 25.2 | 59.4 | 21.0 | 15.3 | Charbon |
|   Wood | 17.4 | 27.5 | 8.7 | 29.5 | 70.8 | 16.0 | 21.9 | 10.6 | 5.9 | 11.3 | 14.2 | 8.3 | 21.4 | Bois |
|   Coke | 7.8 | 1.8 | 1.3 | 5.9 | 0.2 | 0.1 | 7.0 | 1.1 | 0.4 | 0.5 | 3.5 | 23.0 | 4.8 | Coke |
|   Refined oil fuels | 22.5 | 32.9 | 42.2 | 37.3 | 7.7 | 23.6 | 35.8 | 42.9 | 32.4 | 31.6 | 17.2 | 18.4 | 36.7 | Pétrole raffiné |
|   Gas | 0.3 | 0.9 | 0.1 | 1.9 | — | — | 4.4 | 7.2 | 0.3 | 0.1 | — | 0.4 | 4.7 | Gaz |
|   Electricity | 14.5 | 7.6 | 10.5 | 9.1 | 11.3 | 16.7 | 19.2 | 0.4 | 15.1 | 31.1 | 5.0 | 16.3 | 14.1 | Electricité |
|   Peat and charcoal | 4.5 | 1.1 | 2.5 | 2.0 | 0.1 | 1.2 | 1.2 | — | 4.4 | 0.2 | 0.7 | 12.6 | 3.0 | Tourbière et charbon de bois |
| **1953** | | | | | | | | | | | | | | **1953** |
| Total energy consumed: | | | | | | | | | | | | | | Energie totale consommée: |
|   Quantity | 7 445.9 | 653.3 | 261.3 | 51.8 | 252.6 | 2 010.9 | 29.0 | 30.9 | 49.3 | 544.4 | 1 069.1 | 2 473.2 | 20.1 | Quantité |
| Percent of total in specified industry | 100.0 | 8.7 | 3.5 | 0.7 | 3.4 | 27.0 | 0.4 | 0.4 | 0.7 | 7.3 | 14.4 | 33.2 | 0.3 | Pourcentage du total par industrie indiquée |
| Percent consumed as: | | | | | | | | | | | | | | Pourcentage consommé comme: |
|   Coal | 20.7 | 14.8 | 19.2 | 13.9 | 2.7 | 19.5 | 7.1 | 48.8 | 26.9 | 11.7 | 56.0 | 11.6 | 43.6 | Charbon |
|   Wood | 10.6 | 14.0 | 5.5 | 9.1 | 72.3 | 15.1 | 2.6 | 6.6 | 1.9 | 4.5 | 8.0 | 2.9 | 5.4 | Bois |
|   Coke | 10.0 | 1.8 | 0.6 | 4.3 | 0.3 | — | 5.1 | 1.7 | 0.2 | 0.5 | 3.5 | 27.9 | 2.6 | Coke |
|   Refined oil fuels | 37.0 | 58.4 | 61.9 | 60.5 | 9.7 | 39.5 | 57.5 | 34.9 | 54.2 | 45.5 | 26.5 | 31.1 | 29.0 | Pétrole raffiné |
|   Gas | 0.2 | 1.0 | — | 0.9 | — | — | 1.6 | — | 0.4 | 0.1 | 0.2 | 0.4 | 1.1 | Gaz |
|   Electricity | 19.6 | 9.6 | 12.4 | 10.9 | 14.9 | 25.1 | 26.0 | 7.8 | 16.3 | 37.6 | 5.7 | 21.1 | 16.0 | Electricité |
|   Peat and charcoal | 1.9 | 0.4 | 0.4 | 0.4 | 0.1 | 0.8 | 0.1 | 0.2 | 0.1 | 0.1 | 0.1 | 5.0 | 2.3 | Tourbière et charbon de bois |
| **1958** | | | | | | | | | | | | | | **1958** |
| Total energy consumed: | | | | | | | | | | | | | | Energie totale consommée: |
|   Quantity | 8 773.8 | 647.3 | 232.9 | 56.4 | 287.7 | 2 575.5 | 38.8 | 28.3 | 62.3 | 776.7 | 1 048.6 | 2 976.1 | 43.2 | Quantité |
| Percent of total in specified industry | 100.0 | 7.3 | 2.7 | 0.6 | 3.3 | 29.4 | 0.4 | 0.3 | 0.7 | 8.9 | 11.9 | 34.0 | 0.5 | Pourcentage du total par industrie indiquée |
| Percent consumed as: | | | | | | | | | | | | | | Pourcentage consommé comme: |
|   Coal | 7.1 | 3.8 | 7.1 | 4.4 | 0.8 | 5.2 | 1.2 | 14.7 | 2.6 | 2.1 | 29.8 | 2.9 | 45.6 | Charbon |
|   Wood | 8.5 | 12.2 | 4.3 | 8.0 | 63.3 | 12.3 | 0.6 | 7.8 | 0.9 | 3.1 | 7.1 | 1.7 | 5.6 | Bois |
|   Coke | 10.1 | 1.3 | 0.4 | 2.2 | 0.1 | — | 2.1 | 0.1 | 0.2 | 0.2 | 3.0 | 28.4 | 1.2 | Coke |
|   Refined oil fuels | 51.6 | 69.8 | 74.3 | 73.6 | 18.4 | 56.5 | 68.5 | 67.8 | 77.4 | 57.6 | 52.5 | 41.8 | 33.1 | Pétrole raffiné |
|   Gas | 0.3 | 1.1 | — | 0.6 | — | — | 1.7 | 0.1 | 0.1 | 0.1 | 0.1 | 0.4 | 0.5 | Gaz |
|   Electricity | 21.7 | 11.7 | 13.6 | 11.1 | 17.3 | 25.7 | 25.8 | 9.5 | 18.8 | 36.8 | 7.4 | 23.0 | 13.9 | Electricité |
|   Peat and charcoal | 0.7 | 0.1 | 0.3 | 0.1 | 0.1 | 0.3 | 0.1 | — | — | 0.1 | 0.1 | 1.8 | 0.1 | Tourbière et charbon de bois |

For footnotes see end of table.      Pour les notes, voir au bas du tableau.

## B. Quantity of Fuels and Electricity Consumed
### Volume de combustibles et d'électricité consommés

Coal, peat, coke and refined oil fuels in thousand metric tons; gas in million cubic metres; wood in thousand cubic metres; charcoal in hundred thousand litres; and electricity in million KWH.

Charbon, tourbière, coke et pétrole raffiné en milliers de tonnes métriques; gaz en millions de mètres cubes; bois en milliers de mètres cubes; charbon de bois en centaines de milliers de litres; et électricité en millions de kWh.

### a. The Major Groups of Mining and Electricity and Gas
### Les classes des industries extractives et électricité et gaz

| Year and source of energy | Mining — Industries extractives | | | | Electricity and gas Electricité et gaz | | | Année et source d'énergie |
| | Total | Coal mining Extraction du charbon | Metal mining Extraction des minerais métalliques | Other mining Divers | Total [1] | Electricity [1] Electricité [1] | Gas Gaz | |
| ISIC | 1 | 11 | 12 | 14–19 | 511-512 | 511 | 512 | CITI |
| **1938** | | | | | | | | **1938** |
| Coal | 20.5 | 2.9 | 13.9 | 3.7 | 943.8 | 279.1 | 664.7 | Charbon |
| Peat | 2.1 | — | — | 2.1 | — | — | — | Tourbière |
| Coke | 50.7 | — | 50.3 | 0.4 | 97.5 | 0.1 | 97.4 | Coke |
| Refined oil fuels | 2.7 | — | 1.2 | 1.5 | 10.8 | 10.6 | 0.2 | Pétrole raffiné |
| Manufactured gas | — | — | — | — | 19.4 | — | 19.4 | Gaz manufacturé |
| Electricity consumed | 260.5 | 9.4 | 234.8 | 16.3 | 96.3 | 89.8 | 6.5 | Electricité consommée |
| Wood | 43.4 | — | 32.2 | 11.2 | 24.5 | 24.5 | — | Bois |
| Charcoal | 704.0 | — | 703.9 | 0.1 | 0.4 | 0.4 | — | Charbon de bois |
| **1948** | | | | | | | | **1948** |
| Coal | 19.4 | 4.5 | 12.9 | 2.0 | 1 111.4 | 329.4 | 782.0 | Charbon |
| Peat | 2.0 | — | — | 2.0 | — | — | — | Tourbière |
| Coke | 64.1 | — | 63.8 | 0.3 | 162.7 | 0.3 | 162.4 | Coke |
| Refined oil fuels | 9.5 | 0.2 | 7.1 | 2.2 | 115.1 | 114.7 | 0.4 | Pétrole raffiné |
| Manufactured gas | — | — | — | — | 3.5 | 0.1 | 3.4 | Gaz manufacturé |
| Electricity consumed | 336.2 | 11.8 | 291.3 | 33.1 | 134.3 | 121.6 | 12.7 | Electricité consommée |
| Wood | 119.3 | 16.3 | 89.6 | 13.4 | 115.5 | 115.4 | 0.1 | Bois |
| Charcoal | 975.2 | — | 974.4 | 0.8 | 4.3 | 4.1 | 0.2 | Charbon de bois |
| **1953** | | | | | | | | **1953** |
| Coal | 8.4 | 1.7 | 5.3 | 1.4 | 1149.9 | 221.5 | 928.4 | Charbon |
| Peat | 5.0 | — | 4.9 | 0.1 | — | — | — | Tourbière |
| Coke | 80.8 | — | 80.4 | 0.4 | 154.6 | 0.5 | 154.1 | Coke |
| Refined oil fuels | 15.8 | 0.1 | 11.0 | 4.7 | 66.3 | 65.9 | 0.4 | Pétrole raffiné |
| Manufactured gas | — | — | — | — | 4.0 | 0.8 | 3.2 | Gaz manufacturé |
| Electricity consumed | 522.8 | 13.2 | 461.6 | 48.0 | 215.4 | 196.9 | 18.5 | Electricité consommée |
| Wood | 63.9 | — | 55.6 | 8.3 | 57.9 | 57.9 | — | Bois |
| Charcoal | 398.6 | — | 397.9 | 0.7 | 4.4 | 4.4 | — | Charbon de bois |
| **1958** | | | | | | | | **1958** |
| Coal | 4.7 | 1.7 | 2.1 | 0.9 | 972.6 | 64.1 | 908.5 | Charbon |
| Peat | 0.1 | — | — | 0.1 | — | — | — | Tourbière |
| Coke | 88.3 | — | 87.9 | 0.4 | 132.3 | 0.5 | 131.8 | Coke |
| Refined oil fuels | 41.6 | 0.1 | 28.4 | 13.1 | 218.6 | 210.3 | 8.3 | Pétrole raffiné |
| Manufactured gas | — | — | — | — | 3.8 | 1.2 | 2.6 | Gaz manufacturé |
| Electricity consumed | 773.6 | 12.5 | 705.0 | 56.1 | 499.2 | 473.8 | 25.4 | Electricité consommée |
| Wood | 34.1 | — | 26.4 | 7.7 | 122.5 | 122.5 | — | Bois |
| Charcoal | 229.3 | — | 229.1 | 0.2 | 10.3 | 8.3 | 2.0 | Charbon de bois |

For footnotes see end of table.

Pour les notes, voir au bas du tableau.

## B.  The Major Groups of Manufacturing — Les classes de la branche Industries manufacturières

| Year and source of energy | Manufacturing [1,4] Industries manufacturières [1,4] | Food, beverages and tobacco Industries alimentaires, boissons, tabac | Textiles [3] | Clothing, footwear and made-up textiles [2] Articles d'habillement, chaussures et ouvrages en tissu [2] | Wood products and furniture [2] Bois et meubles [2] | Paper and paper products Papier et ouvrages en papier | Printing [1] Imprimerie [1] | Leather and leather products except wearing apparel Cuir et articles en cuir, à l'exclusion des articles d'habillement | Rubber products Ouvrages en caoutchouc | Chemicals and chemical, petroleum and coal products [3] Produits chimiques et dérivés du pétrole et du charbon [3] | Non-metallic mineral products Produits minéraux non métalliques | Basic metals and metal products [4] Métallurgie de base et ouvrages en métaux [4] | Other manufacturing [2,3] Autres industries manufacturières [2,3] | Année et source d'énergie |
|---|---|---|---|---|---|---|---|---|---|---|---|---|---|---|
| ISIC | 2–3 | 20–22 | 23 | 24 | 25–26 | 27 | 28 | 29 | 30 | 31–32 | 33 | 34–38 | 39 | CITI |
| **1938** | | | | | | | | | | | | | | **1938** |
| Coal | 3 490.5 | 417.3 | 197.4 | 7.0 | 46.2 | 1 245.0 | 1.0 | 20.6 | 24.6 | 157.9 | 748.9 | 623.9 | 0.7 | Charbon |
| Peat | 14.2 | 1.2 | 1.5 | 0.1 | — | 8.3 | — | — | — | 0.2 | 1.8 | 1.1 | — | Tourbière |
| Coke | 534.1 | 27.6 | 7.0 | 5.8 | 2.1 | 2.1 | 6.0 | 0.5 | 0.4 | 8.4 | 34.1 | 439.2 | 0.9 | Coke |
| Refined oil fuels | 105.2 | 20.2 | 1.9 | 1.9 | 4.5 | 2.8 | 1.3 | 0.3 | 0.4 | 10.0 | 10.1 | 51.2 | 0.6 | Pétrole raffiné |
| Manufactured gas | 21.1 | 7.7 | 0.1 | 0.3 | — | 0.2 | 1.8 | — | 0.1 | 0.6 | 0.2 | 9.7 | 0.4 | Gaz manufacturé |
| Electricity consumed | 5 262.3 | 231.4 | 158.6 | 21.4 | 235.8 | 2 209.2 | 22.6 | 9.4 | 21.4 | 509.4 | 150.9 | 1 688.2 | 4.0 | Électricité consommée |
| Wood | 8 351.8 | 784.7 | 99.4 | 33.8 | 2 830.6 | 2 979.7 | 4.6 | 19.0 | 0.4 | 300.6 | 708.6 | 585.3 | 5.1 | Bois |
| Charcoal | 20 942.7 | 3.5 | 0.1 | 0.2 | 6.0 | 7.1 | — | — | — | 10.0 | 7.8 | 20 907.1 | 0.9 | Charbon de bois |
| **1948** | | | | | | | | | | | | | | **1948** |
| Coal | 2 191.0 | 179.7 | 83.0 | 6.9 | 40.5 | 801.4 | 2.5 | 10.6 | 16.0 | 113.2 | 513.8 | 422.4 | 1.0 | Charbon |
| Peat | 113.6 | 12.7 | 11.9 | 1.9 | 0.1 | 41.2 | 0.6 | 0.2 | 3.4 | 1.2 | 11.4 | 28.6 | 0.4 | Tourbière |
| Coke | 572.8 | 13.2 | 3.3 | 3.1 | 0.9 | 1.6 | 1.9 | 0.4 | 0.2 | 2.4 | 34.0 | 511.4 | 0.4 | Coke |
| Refined oil fuels | 998.6 | 139.7 | 67.2 | 11.9 | 20.9 | 296.1 | 5.7 | 8.1 | 8.3 | 94.3 | 98.8 | 245.9 | 1.7 | Pétrole raffiné |
| Manufactured gas | 29.1 | 9.8 | 0.4 | 1.5 | — | 0.4 | 1.8 | — | 0.2 | 0.9 | 0.6 | 13.0 | 0.5 | Gaz manufacturé |
| Electricity consumed | 7 691.8 | 387.3 | 199.8 | 34.9 | 370.6 | 2 528.6 | 36.8 | 16.1 | 46.6 | 1 112.2 | 343.4 | 2 607.8 | 7.7 | Électricité consommée |
| Wood | 9 959.9 | 1 414.6 | 161.3 | 104.0 | 2 784.7 | 2 715.6 | 42.6 | 27.0 | 20.9 | 460.1 | 934.9 | 1 282.9 | 11.3 | Bois |
| Charcoal | 13 981.9 | 2.4 | 0.8 | 0.2 | 4.8 | 13.4 | — | — | 0.4 | 2.6 | 3.9 | 13 952.6 | 0.8 | Charbon de bois |
| **1953** | | | | | | | | | | | | | | **1953** |
| Coal | 1 542.5 | 96.9 | 50.2 | 7.2 | 7.0 | 392.4 | 2.1 | 15.1 | 13.3 | 63.9 | 599.3 | 286.3 | 8.8 | Charbon |
| Peat | 41.8 | 4.1 | 1.8 | 0.3 | 0.1 | 29.1 | — | — | — | — | 0.2 | 5.3 | 0.9 | Tourbière |
| Coke | 833.0 | 12.9 | 1.7 | 2.5 | 0.6 | 1.0 | 1.6 | 0.6 | 0.1 | 3.1 | 41.5 | 766.8 | 0.6 | Coke |
| Refined oil fuels | 1 835.5 | 254.5 | 107.7 | 20.9 | 16.4 | 529.1 | 11.1 | 7.2 | 17.8 | 165.2 | 188.9 | 512.8 | 3.9 | Pétrole raffiné |
| Manufactured gas | 33.3 | 10.2 | 0.1 | 0.7 | 0.1 | 0.1 | 0.8 | — | 0.3 | 0.9 | 2.2 | 17.5 | 0.4 | Gaz manufacturé |
| Electricity consumed | 11 642.7 | 505.5 | 258.8 | 45.3 | 301.8 | 4 043.5 | 60.4 | 19.4 | 64.4 | 1 639.3 | 495.0 | 4 183.7 | 25.6 | Électricité consommée |
| Wood | 7 128.9 | 754.1 | 127.4 | 35.1 | 1 795.8 | 2 859.8 | 5.3 | 18.0 | 8.8 | 227.6 | 686.3 | 602.2 | 8.5 | Bois |
| Charcoal | 6 990.1 | 0.3 | — | — | 2.3 | 4.2 | — | 1.8 | 0.2 | 1.7 | 0.7 | 6 977.7 | 1.2 | Charbon de bois |
| **1958** | | | | | | | | | | | | | | **1958** |
| Coal | 625.5 | 24.6 | 16.7 | 2.5 | 2.4 | 136.0 | 0.5 | 4.2 | 1.7 | 17.0 | 313.4 | 86.8 | 19.7 | Charbon |
| Peat | 22.8 | 0.6 | 1.2 | — | — | 14.5 | — | — | — | — | 0.1 | 6.4 | — | Tourbière |
| Coke | 989.3 | 9.7 | 0.9 | 1.3 | 0.5 | 0.2 | 0.9 | — | 0.1 | 1.4 | 34.9 | 938.8 | 0.6 | Coke |
| Refined oil fuels | 3 017.2 | 301.3 | 115.3 | 27.7 | 35.2 | 970.1 | 17.7 | 12.8 | 32.1 | 298.2 | 367.4 | 829.9 | 9.5 | Pétrole raffiné |
| Manufactured gas | 36.8 | 11.3 | 0.2 | 0.5 | — | 0.2 | 1.1 | — | 0.2 | 1.2 | 2.1 | 19.6 | 0.4 | Gaz manufacturé |
| Electricity consumed | 15 225.5 | 606.1 | 252.7 | 50.2 | 399.5 | 5 286.8 | 80.3 | 21.5 | 93.4 | 2 292.2 | 621.1 | 5 473.7 | 48.0 | Électricité consommée |
| Wood | 6 830.3 | 653.7 | 91.1 | 32.1 | 1 759.4 | 2 995.6 | 1.9 | 18.5 | 5.0 | 226.8 | 583.4 | 440.3 | 22.5 | Bois |
| Charcoal | 2 931.1 | 0.1 | — | — | 1.1 | 1.7 | — | — | — | 0.6 | 1.9 | 2 924.9 | 0.8 | Charbon de bois |

[1] In the case of the data for 1938, in general, establishments principally engaged in Manufacturing and Other mining (ISIC major group 14–19) were covered which had ten or more operatives, annual gross production of 15 000 Kronor or more, or annual value added of 4 000 Kronor or more. In the case of a few kinds of industrial activity (e.g., coal mining, metal mining, distilleries and breweries and metal refining and smelting), establishments irrespective of size were covered. In the 1948, 1953 and 1958 Industrial Censuses, the general lower limit of coverage with regard to size was five employees. In a few kinds of activity, the same as in 1938, all establishments were included in the data for these years. Establishments primarily engaged in publishing were not covered in any of the years. The mining and manufacturing establishments were delineated so that excluded were significant ancillary electric power plants. These ancillary power plants were classified to the Electricity industry (ISIC group 511). Included, in addition, in this ISIC group are data on public service electricity power plants and distribution stations. Electricity plants with installed prime movers of 50 or more HP are covered in the data for 1938, 1948, 1953 and 1958.

[2] Included in Clothing (ISIC 24) are such activities as the manufacture of sun blinds, which belongs under Wood products (ISIC major group 25), and of artificial flowers and related items, which should be in Other manufacturing (ISIC major group 39).

[3] The 1948 data for chemicals and petroleum and coal products (ISIC major groups 31–32) include the manufacture of linoleum, which should be classified under Textiles (ISIC major group 23). The 1953 data for the former industry cover plastic products which belongs in Other manufacturing (ISIC major group 39).

[4] Included in Basic metals and metal products (ISIC major groups 34–38) is plumbing which should be classified in Construction (ISIC Division 4).

[1] Dans le cas des données relatives à 1938, généralement, parmi les établissements engagés principalement dans Industries manufacturières et Autres industries extractives (CITI classes 14–19) sont couverts: ceux employant dix ouvriers ou plus, ceux ayant une production brute annuelle d'une valeur de 15 000 Couronnes ou plus ou une valeur ajoutée annuelle de 4 000 Couronnes ou plus. Dans le cas de quelques types d'industries (par exemple, extraction de charbon, de minerais métalliques, distillerie et brasserie, fonderie de minerais et affinage des métaux) les établissements, quelle que soit leur dimension, sont couverts. Dans les recensements industriels de 1948, 1953 et 1958, cinq salariés a été la limite générale la plus basse adoptée. Dans un nombre restreint de types d'activités, les mêmes qu'en 1938, tous les établissements ont été couverts par les données relatives à ces années. Les établissements principalement engagés dans éditions ne sont couverts dans aucune de ces années. Les établissements miniers et manufacturiers ont été délimités de façon telle que des installations électriques secondaires d'une certaine importance ont été exclues. Ces installations secondaires ont été rattachées aux industries productrices de l'électricité (CITI groupe 511). Y compris en additif, à ce groupe de la CITI, les données relatives au service public d'installations électriques et aux stations de distribution. Les installations électriques activées par un moteur primaire de 50 CV ou plus sont couvertes par les données relatives à 1938, 1948, 1953 et 1958.

[2] Sont compris dans Articles d'habillement (CITI 24) des activités telles que la fabrication de stores qui appartient à la rubrique Ouvrages en bois (CITI classe 25), et fleurs artificielles et produits similaires qui devraient être dans Autres industries manufacturières (CITI classe 39).

[3] Les données de 1948 relatives aux Industries chimiques et Produits dérivés du pétrole et du charbon (CITI classes 31–32) comprennent la fabrication de linoléum, qui devrait être dans Industries textiles (CITI classe 23). Les données de 1953 relatives aux Industries textiles couvrent les produits en plastique qui appartiennent à Autres industries manufacturières (CITI classe 39).

[4] Y compris dans Industries métallurgiques de base et Ouvrages en métaux (CITI classes 34–38) les activités de plomberie qui appartiennent à Construction (CITI branche 4).

## Gross Domestic Product

The estimates of expenditure on gross domestic product shown in Table 1 are from the reply to the United Nations national accounts questionnaire by the Bureau fédéral de statistique, Bern. The official estimates are published each year in *La Situation Economique, Supplément de La Vie Economique*, November and in the *Annuaire statistique de la Suisse*.

## Index Numbers of Industrial Employment

The index numbers of industrial employment set out in Table 2 are based on indexes published in the *Annuaire statistique de la Suisse*, Bureau fédéral de statistique, and *Supplément trimestriel de La Vie Economique, La Situation Economique*, Commission de recherches économiques, Bern. This series of annual indexes refers to the average number of operatives employed by larger industrial establishments during the last pay-day of each quarter. In general, establishments with 10 or more employees are covered. The index numbers are compiled from the results of a quarterly survey of establishments taken by the Office Fédéral de l'industrie, des arts et métiers et du travail, Bern.

## Characteristics and Structure of Industrial Activity

Censuses of Establishments taken as of 24 August 1939 and 25 August 1955 provide the figures set out in Table 3. These censuses covered industrial and commercial establishments, irrespective of size. The Bureau Fédéral de statistique, Bern, published the results of the earlier census in *Recensement fédéral des entreprises, 24 août 1939*, Vols I-IV and of the last census, in summary fashion in *Annuaire statistique de la Suisse, 1957* and later years.

The statistical unit in both Censuses of Establishments was the establishment except for construction, for which enterprise was most commonly used. Business units which were temporarily closed on the census days were covered. The figures of numbers of persons engaged set out below include all persons who were working in or for the covered establishments on the census days except those who did so only occasionally and unpaid family workers on a part-time basis only. The data on the capacity installed (in use or in reserve) power equipment as of 24 August 1939 relate to the sum of the horsepowers of prime movers connected directly to machinery excepting electric generators and of all electric motors. Although similar data were gathered in the 25 August 1955 Census, the data are not available in the form needed in order to compile comparable figures of capacity of installed power equipment. It should be noted that in the case of the

## Produit intérieur brut

Les estimations des dépenses imputées au produit intérieur brut reproduites au tableau 1 sont tirées de la réponse du Bureau fédéral de statistique, Berne, au questionnaire de l'O.N.U. relatif aux comptes nationaux. Les estimations officielles sont publiées chaque année dans *La Situation Economique, Supplément de La Vie Economique*, novembre, et dans l'*Annuaire statistique de la Suisse*.

## Indices de l'emploi industriel

Les indices de l'emploi industriel reproduits au tableau 2 sont basés sur les indices publiés dans l'*Annuaire statistique de la Suisse*, Bureau fédéral de statistique, et *Supplément trimestriel de La Vie Economique, La Situation Economique*, Commission de recherches économiques, Berne. Les séries d'indices portent sur le nombre moyen d'ouvriers occupés dans les établissements industriels dépassant une certaine taille, durant le dernier jour de paye de chaque trimestre. En général, les établissements de 10 salariés ou plus sont couverts. Les indices sont calculés à partir des résultats d'une enquête trimestrielle auprès des établissements, exécutée par l'Office Fédéral de l'industrie, des arts et métiers et du travail, Berne.

## Caractéristiques et structure de l'activité industrielle

Les chiffres du tableau 3 sont tirés de recensements des établissements au 24 août 1939 et au 25 août 1955. Ces recensements portaient sur tous les établissements industriels et commerciaux, quelle que fût leur dimension. Le Bureau fédéral de statistique, Berne, a publié les résultats du premier de ces recensements dans *Recensement fédéral des entreprises, 24 août 1939*, vol. I-IV, et ceux du second, sous une forme résumée, dans l'*Annuaire statistique de la Suisse, 1957* et des années suivantes.

Dans ces deux recensements, l'unité statistique était l'établissement, sauf en ce qui concerne le bâtiment et les travaux publics, pour lesquels c'est l'entreprise qui a le plus souvent servi de base. Les unités qui étaient temporairement fermées le jour du recensement ont été recensées. Dans les tableaux qui suivent, le nombre de personnes occupées comprend toutes les personnes qui travaillaient dans les établissements recensés, ou pour ces établissements, au jour du recensement, à l'exclusion de celles qui ne travaillaient que de façon intermittente et des travailleurs familiaux non rémunérés ne travaillant qu'à temps partiel. Les chiffres de la puissance installée (en service normal ou en réserve) au 24 août 1939 représentent la puissance de tous les moteurs primaires actionnant directement des machines, exception faite des générateurs électriques, plus celle de tous les moteurs électriques. Des renseignements analogues ont été recueil-

electricity producing industry, the data on capacity of power equipment shown in Table 3 relate to the horse-power of all installed prime movers.

The data of Table 4 on number of establishments and employees result from the annual Censuses of Factories subject to the Factory Act, taken by the Office fédéral de l'industrie, des arts et métiers et du travail. In general, establishments with ten or more employees are covered in the annual Censuses.

lis lors du recensement du 25 août 1955, mais les données publiées jusqu'ici ne sont pas présentées sous la forme requise, qui permettrait d'obtenir des chiffres de puissance installée comparables. On notera que, dans le cas de la production d'électricité, les chiffres de la puissance installée reproduits au tableau 3 représentent la puissance de tous les moteurs primaires installés.

Les données du tableau 4 relatives au nombre d'établissements et de salariés proviennent des recensements annuels des fabriques assujetties à la loi sur les fabriques, exécutés par l'Office fédéral de l'industrie, des arts et métiers et du travail. En général les établissements de 10 salariés ou plus sont couverts par les recensements annuels.

## 1. EXPENDITURE ON THE GROSS DOMESTIC PRODUCT AT MARKET PRICES
## DEPENSES RELATIVES AU PRODUIT INTERIEUR BRUT AU PRIX DU MARCHE

Million francs      Millions de francs

| Item of data and year / Rubrique et année | Total | Consumption / Consommation | | Gross Domestic Capital Formation / Formation brute de capital intérieur | Net exports of goods and services / Exportations nettes de biens et de services | |
|---|---|---|---|---|---|---|
| | | Total | Government / Etat | | Exports less imports / Exportations moins importations | Exports / Exportations |
| *a. At Current Prices — Aux prix courants* | | | | | | |
| Absolute figures — Chiffres absolus | | | | | | |
| 1954.................... | 25 220 | 19 290 | 3 100 | 5 380 | 550 | 7 410 |
| 1955.................... | 27 030 | 20 760 | 3 300 | 6 120 | 150 | 7 980 |
| 1956.................... | 28 830 | 22 280 | 3 600 | 7 000 | −450 | 8 770 |
| 1957.................... | 30 670 | 23 750 | 3 800 | 7 700 | −780 | 9 440 |
| 1958.................... | 31 930 | 24 250 | 3 900 | 7 280 | 400 | 9 590 |
| 1959.................... | 33 520 | 25 380 | 4 050 | 7 990 | 150 | 10 470 |
| 1960.................... | 36 170 | ... | ... | ... | −270 | 11 720 |
| 1961.................... | 40 110 | ... | ... | ... | −1 620 | 12 920 |
| Percentage distribution of average annual expenditure — Distribution en pourcentage des dépenses annuelles moyennes | | | | | | |
| 1954.................... | 100.0 | 76.5 | 12.3 | 21.3 | 2.2 | 29.4 |
| 1958.................... | 100.0 | 75.9 | 12.2 | 22.8 | 1.3 | 30.0 |
| 1960.................... | 100.0 | ... | ... | ... | −0.7 | 32.4 |
| *b. At Prices of 1958 — Aux prix de 1958* | | | | | | |
| Absolute figures — Chiffres absolus | | | | | | |
| 1954.................... | 27 020 | 20 520 | 3 300 | 6 020 | 480 | 7 410 |
| 1955.................... | 28 620 | 21 880 | 3 480 | 6 570 | 170 | 8 150 |
| 1956.................... | 30 400 | 23 140 | 3 740 | 7 340 | −80 | 9 050 |
| 1957.................... | 31 700 | 24 190 | 3 870 | 7 810 | −300 | 9 540 |
| 1958.................... | 31 930 | 24 250 | 3 900 | 7 280 | 400 | 9 590 |
| 1959.................... | 33 550 | 25 560 | 4 080 | 7 920 | 70 | 10 810 |
| Percentage distribution of average annual expenditure — Distribution en pourcentage des dépenses annuelles moyennes | | | | | | |
| 1954.................... | 100.0 | 75.9 | 12.2 | 22.3 | 1.8 | 27.4 |
| 1958.................... | 100.0 | 75.9 | 12.2 | 22.8 | 1.3 | 30.0 |
| Average annual rate of growth — Taux annuel moyen d'accroissement | | | | | | |
| 1954 – 1958.................... | 4.3 | 4.3 | 4.3 | 4.9 | . | 6.7 |

## 2. INDEX NUMBERS OF INDUSTRIAL EMPLOYMENT, CONSTRUCTION AND MANUFACTURING
## INDICES DE L'EMPLOI DANS L'INDUSTRIE, BATIMENT ET INDUSTRIES MANUFACTURIERES

| Period<br>Période | Construction<br>Bâtiment et travaux publics | Manu-facturing<br>Industries manufac-turières | Food, beverages and tobacco<br>Industries alimen-taires, boissons, tabac | Textiles | Clothing, footwear and made-up textiles<br>Articles d'habil-lement, chaussures et ouvrages en tissu | Wood products and furniture<br>Bois et meubles | Paper and paper products<br>Papier et ouvrages en papier | Printing and publishing<br>Imprimerie et édition | Leather and leather and rubber products<br>Cuir et articles en cuir et caoutchouc | Chemicals and chemical, petroleum and coal products<br>Produits chi-miques et dérivés du pétrole et du charbon | Non-metallic mineral products<br>Produits minéraux non métal-liques | Basic metals and metal products<br>Métallurgie de base et ouvrages en métaux | Other manu-facturing<br>Autres industries manufac-turières |
|---|---|---|---|---|---|---|---|---|---|---|---|---|---|
| ISIC — CITI | 4 | 2–3 | 20–22 | 23 | 24 | 25–26 | 27 | 28 | 29–30 | 31–32 | 33 | 34, 35–38 | 39 |
| *a.* Indexes — Indices (1958 = 100) | | | | | | | | | | | | | |
| 1948............. | 91 | 84 | 86 | 104 | 96 | 105 | 82 | 76 | 83 | 86 | 93 | 77 | 86 |
| 1949............. | 85 | 80 | 83 | 94 | 86 | 90 | 75 | 75 | 82 | 80 | 83 | 72 | 85 |
| 1950............. | 85 | 78 | 85 | 96 | 86 | 89 | 77 | 74 | 83 | 77 | 82 | 69 | 80 |
| 1951............. | 98 | 86 | 85 | 105 | 92 | 97 | 83 | 77 | 90 | 85 | 89 | 78 | 90 |
| 1952............. | 94 | 88 | 88 | 99 | 87 | 96 | 83 | 80 | 87 | 84 | 89 | 82 | 98 |
| 1953............. | 97 | 88 | 88 | 101 | 92 | 94 | 82 | 81 | 87 | 84 | 88 | 81 | 97 |
| 1954............. | 102 | 90 | 89 | 104 | 94 | 97 | 85 | 85 | 92 | 86 | 92 | 83 | 93 |
| 1955............. | 105 | 93 | 92 | 104 | 94 | 102 | 91 | 89 | 97 | 90 | 98 | 89 | 95 |
| 1956............. | 112 | 97 | 95 | 104 | 98 | 104 | 94 | 92 | 102 | 93 | 102 | 95 | 102 |
| 1957............. | 115 | 102 | 99 | 107 | 103 | 105 | 99 | 96 | 105 | 98 | 104 | 101 | 107 |
| 1958............. | 100 | 100 | 100 | 100 | 100 | 100 | 100 | 100 | 100 | 100 | 100 | 100 | 100 |
| 1959............. | 105 | 99 | 99 | 96 | 99 | 99 | 99 | 104 | 101 | 103 | 103 | 99 | 93 |
| 1960............. | 112 | 105 | 103 | 102 | 104 | 107 | 102 | 108 | 100 | 109 | 111 | 106 | 100 |
| 1961............. | 123 | 113 | 109 | 104 | 109 | 116 | 107 | 114 | 108 | 115 | 119 | 116 | 109 |
| *b.* Average Annual Rate of Change — Taux annuel moyen de variation | | | | | | | | | | | | | |
| 1950–1960........ | 2.8 | 3.0 | 1.9 | 0.6 | 1.9 | 1.9 | 2.9 | 3.8 | 1.9 | 3.5 | 3.1 | 4.4 | 2.3 |
| 1948–1953........ | 1.3 | 0.9 | 0.5 | −0.6 | −0.9 | −2.2 | — | 1.3 | 0.9 | −0.5 | −1.1 | 1.0 | 2.4 |
| 1954–1958........ | −0.5 | 2.7 | 3.0 | −1.0 | 1.6 | 0.8 | 4.1 | 4.1 | 2.1 | 3.8 | 2.1 | 4.8 | 1.8 |
| 1958–1960........ | 5.8 | 2.5 | 1.5 | 1.0 | 2.0 | 3.4 | 1.0 | 3.9 | — | 4.4 | 5.4 | 3.0 | — |

## 3. CHARACTERISTICS OF ALL INDUSTRIAL ESTABLISHMENTS
### 24 August 1939 and 25 August 1955

## CARACTERISTIQUES DE TOUS LES ETABLISSEMENTS INDUSTRIELS
### 24 août 1939 et 25 août 1955

Number of establishments in units; number of engaged and employees in thousands; capacity of installed power equipment in thousand horsepower; capacity of installed power equipment per person engaged in horsepower

Nombre d'établissements en unités; nombre de personnes occupées et de salariés en milliers; puissance installée en milliers de chevaux-vapeur; puissance installée par personne occupée en chevaux-vapeur

## A. The Divisions of Industrial Activity — Les branches de l'activité industrielle

| Item of data | All industrial activity Toutes industries | | Mining [1] Industries extractives [1] | | Manufacturing [2] Industries manufacturières [2] | | Construction Bâtiment et travaux publics | | Electricity and gas Electricité et gaz | | Rubrique |
|---|---|---|---|---|---|---|---|---|---|---|---|
| | 24.VIII.1939 | 25.VIII.1955 | 24.VIII.1939 | 25.VIII.1955 | 24.VIII.1939 | 25.VIII.1955 | 24.VIII.1939 | 25.VIII.1955 | 24.VIII.1939 | 25.VIII.1955 | |
| ISIC | 1–4, 511–512 | | 1 | | 2–3 | | 4 | | 511–512 | | CITI |
| a. Absolute Figures — Chiffres absolus | | | | | | | | | | | |
| Number of establishments. | 115 986 | 117 031 | 1 714 | 1 025 | 97 628 | 97 146 | 15 971 | 17 877 | 673 | 983 | Nombre d'établissements |
| Number of engaged (As of census date).... | 788.5 | 1 148.8 | 9.6 | 8.2 | 651.7 | 923.4 | 116.2 | 200.2 | 11.0 | 17.0 | Nombre de personnes occupées (à la date du recensement) |
| Number of employees (As of census date).... | 631.2 | 1 041.6 | 7.9 | 7.6 | 514.0 | 835.6 | 98.3 | 181.4 | 11.0 | 17.0 | Nombre de salariés (à la date du recensement) |
| Capacity of installed power equipment (As of census date).... | . | ... | 37 | ... | 1 231 | ... | 80 | ... | 1 259 | ... | Puissance installée (à la date du recensement) |
| b. Structure | | | | | | | | | | | |
| Distribution in percent of number of engaged........... | 100.0 | 100.0 | 1.2 | 0.7 | 82.6 | 80.3 | 14.8 | 17.5 | 1.4 | 1.5 | Répartition en pourcentage du nombre de personnes occupées |
| Capacity of installed power equipment per person engaged...... | . | ... | 3.85 | ... | 1.89 | ... | 0.69 | ... | 114.45 | ... | Puissance installée par personne occupée |

[1] Almost entirely Other mining (ISIC major groups 14–19).
[2] Includes photography and photostating, which should be classified in ISIC division 8.

[1] Il s'agit presque exclusivement des Autres industries extractives (CITI 14–19).
[2] Y compris la photographie et la préparation des photostats, qui devraient être classées dans la branche 8 de la CITI.

## B. The Major Groups of Manufacturing — Les classes de la branche Industries manufacturières

| Day and item of data | Manufacturing[1] / Industries manufacturières[1] | Food, beverages and tobacco / Industries alimentaires, boissons, tabac | Textiles | Clothing, footwear and made-up textiles[3] / Articles d'habillement, chaussures et ouvrages en tissu | Wood products and furniture[3] / Bois et meubles[3] | Paper and paper products / Papier et ouvrages en papier | Printing and publishing[1] / Imprimerie et édition[1] | Leather and leather products except wearing apparel / Cuir et articles en cuir, à l'exclusion des articles d'habillement | Rubber products / Ouvrages en caoutchouc | Chemicals and chemical, petroleum and coal products / Produits chimiques et dérivés du pétrole et du charbon | Non-metallic mineral products / Produits minéraux non métalliques | Basic metals / Métallurgie de base | Metal products[3] / Ouvrages en métaux[3] | Other manufacturing / Autres industries manufacturières | Date et rubrique |
|---|---|---|---|---|---|---|---|---|---|---|---|---|---|---|---|
| ISIC | 2–3 | 20–22 | 23 | 24 | 25–26 | 27 | 28 | 29 | 30 | 31–32 | 33 | 34 | 35–38 | 39 | CITI |
| **a. Absolute Figures — Chiffres absolus** | | | | | | | | | | | | | | | |
| **24.VIII.1939** Number of establishments. | 97 628 | 19 828 | 2 339 | 28 069 | 16 394 | 287 | 3 851 | 2 839 | 78 | 1 238 | 1 353 | 316 | 16 903 | 4 133 | **24.VIII.1939** Nombre d'établissements |
| Number of engaged.... | 651.7 | 91.6 | 80.0 | 99.5 | 60.1 | 12.9 | 30.7 | 8.2 | 1.7 | 25.1 | 11.4 | 22.9 | 151.1 | 56.5 | Nombre de personnes occupées |
| Number of employees... | 514.0 | 65.8 | 71.5 | 54.8 | 41.2 | 11.9 | 26.2 | 4.8 | 1.6 | 24.0 | 10.0 | 22.4 | 132.3 | 47.5 | Nombre de salariés |
| Capacity of installed power equipment..... | 1 231 | 174 | 161 | 17 | 176 | 78 | 26 | 8 | 12 | 111 | 67 | 95 | 231 | 25 | Puissance installée |
| **25.VIII.1955** Number of establishments. | 97 146 | 19 908 | 2 512 | 19 421 | 16 163 | 359 | 4 877 | 2 578 | 404 | 1 296 | 1 834 | 1 920[2] | 19 988[2,4] | 5 886[4] | **25.VIII.1955** Nombre d'établissements |
| Number of engaged.... | 923.4 | 112.6 | 84.8 | 88.8 | 72.7 | 18.8 | 47.5 | 8.8 | 6.9 | 40.9 | 27.7 | 64.8[2] | 257.4[2,4] | 91.7[4] | Nombre de personnes occupées |
| Number of employees... | 835.6 | 95.9 | 82.9 | 70.0 | 57.3 | 18.6 | 43.0 | 6.3 | 6.7 | 40.2 | 26.2 | 63.1[2] | 238.9[2,4] | 86.5[4] | Nombre de salariés |
| **b. Structure** | | | | | | | | | | | | | | | |
| **24.VIII.1939** Distribution in percent of number of engaged............ | 100.0 | 14.0 | 12.3 | 15.2 | 9.3 | 2.0 | 4.7 | 1.2 | 0.3 | 3.8 | 1.8 | 3.5 | 23.2 | 8.7 | **24.VIII.1939** Répartition en pourcentage du nombre de personnes occupées |
| Capacity of installed power equipment per person engaged...... | 1.89 | 1.90 | 2.01 | 0.17 | 2.93 | 6.05 | 0.85 | 0.98 | 7.06 | 4.42 | 5.88 | 4.15 | 1.86 | 0.44 | Puissance installée par personne occupée |
| Employees as a percent of engaged......... | 78.9 | 71.8 | 89.4 | 55.1 | 68.6 | 92.2 | 85.3 | 58.5 | 94.1 | 95.6 | 87.7 | 97.8 | 87.6 | 84.1 | Salariés en pourcentage des personnes occupées |
| **25.VIII.1955** Distribution in percent of number of engaged............ | 100.0 | 12.1 | 9.2 | 9.6 | 7.9 | 2.1 | 5.1 | 1.0 | 0.7 | 4.4 | 3.0 | 7.0 | 27.9 | 10.0 | **25.VIII.1955** Répartition en pourcentage du nombre de personnes occupées |
| Employees as a percent of engaged......... | 90.5 | 85.2 | 97.8 | 78.8 | 78.8 | 98.9 | 90.5 | 71.6 | 97.1 | 98.3 | 94.6 | 97.4 | 92.8 | 94.3 | Salariés en pourcentage des personnes occupées |

[1] Includes photography and photostating, which are classified in ISIC division 8.
[2] For 25.VIII.1955 Census, Basic metals (ISIC major group 34) includes the manufacture of cutlery, machine tools, sheet metal and enamel ware, and cables and electric light bulbs and lamps, which should be classified in Metal products (ISIC major groups 35–38), and the making of insulation materials for electro-technical purposes, which should be in ISIC major groups 30, 33 or 37.
[3] The manufacture of metal furniture is covered in Metal products (ISIC major groups 35–38) instead of in Furniture (ISIC major group 26).
[4] For 25.VIII.1955 Census, Other manufacturing (ISIC major group 39) covers the manufacture of phonographs, television, radio, and dictating machines, which should be included in Metal products (ISIC major groups 35–38).

[1] Y compris la photographie et la préparation des photostats, qui sont classées dans la branche 8 de la CITI.
[2] Dans le recensement du 25.VIII.1955, la classe Métallurgie de base (CITI 34) comprend la coutellerie, la fabrication de machines-outils, d'ouvrages en tôle et en tôle émaillée, de câbles et d'ampoules et lampes électriques, qui devraient rentrer dans Ouvrages en métaux (CITI 35–38), ainsi que la fabrication de matières isolantes pour l'électrotechnique, qui devrait rentrer dans l'une des classes 30, 33 ou 37 de la CITI.
[3] La fabrication des meubles en métal est classée dans Ouvrages en métaux (CITI 35–38) et non dans Industrie du meuble (CITI 26).
[4] Dans le recensement du 25.VIII.1955, la classe Autres industries manufacturières (CITI 39) comprend la fabrication des phonographes, des postes de télévision et de T.S.F. et des appareils d'enregistrement du son, qui devrait rentrer dans Ouvrages en métaux (CITI 35–38).

## 4. NUMBER AND EMPLOYMENT OF LARGER INDUSTRIAL UNITS
### NOMBRE D'UNITES INDUSTRIELLES DEPASSANT UNE CERTAINE DIMENSION ET EMPLOI DANS CES UNITES

Number of establishments in units; number of employees in thousands.　　　　Nombre d'établissements en unités; nombre de salariés en milliers.

### A. Selected Divisions of Industrial Activity
### Quelques branches de l'activité industrielle

| Year and item of data | Total | Manufacturing Industries manufacturières | Electricity and gas Electricité et gaz | Année et rubrique |
|---|---|---|---|---|
| ISIC | 2-3, 511 | 2-3 | 511-512 | CITI |
| | a. Absolute Figures — Chiffres absolus | | | |
| 1937 | | | | 1937 |
| Number of establishments...... | 8 214 | 7 933 | 281 | Nombre d'établissements |
| Number of employees.......... | 357.3 | 352.9 | 4.4 | Nombre de salariés |
| 1948 | | | | 1948 |
| Number of establishments...... | 11 352 | 11 051 | 301 | Nombre d'établissements |
| Number of employees.......... | 527.4 | 522.4 | 5.0 | Nombre de salariés |
| 1953 | | | | 1953 |
| Number of establishments...... | 11 576 | 11 259 | 317 | Nombre d'établissements |
| Number of employees.......... | 547.7 | 542.6 | 5.1 | Nombre de salariés |
| 1958 | | | | 1958 |
| Number of establishments...... | 12 395 | 12 096 | 299 | Nombre d'établissements |
| Number of employees.......... | 617.8 | 612.8 | 5.0 | Nombre de salariés |

### B. The Major Groups of Manufacturing — Les classes de la branche Industries manufacturières

| Year and item of data | Manufacturing Industries manufacturières | Food beverages and tobacco Industries alimentaires, boissons, tabac | Textiles | Clothing, footwear and made-up textiles Articles d'habillement, chaussures et ouvrages en tissu | Wood products and furniture Bois et meubles | Paper and paper products Papier et ouvrages en papier | Printing and publishing Imprimerie et édition | Leather and leather products except wearing apparel Cuir et articles en cuir, à l'exclusion des articles d'habillement | Rubber products Ouvrages en caoutchouc | Chemicals and chemical, petroleum and coal products Produits chimiques et dérivés du pétrole et du charbon | Non-metallic mineral products Produits minéraux non métalliques | Basic metals Métallurgie de base | Metal products Ouvrages en métaux | Other manufacturing Autres industries manufacturières | Année et rubrique |
|---|---|---|---|---|---|---|---|---|---|---|---|---|---|---|---|
| ISIC | 2–3 | 20–22 | 23 | 24 | 25–26 | 27 | 28 | 29 | 30 | 31–32 | 33 | 34 | 35–38 | 39 | CITI |
| | a. Absolute Figures — Chiffres absolus | | | | | | | | | | | | | | |
| 1937 | | | | | | | | | | | | | | | 1937 |
| Number of establishments. | 7 933 | 644 | 905 | 1 054 | 1 247 | 163 | 611 | 95 | 16 | 277 | 376 | 108 | 1 508 | 929 | Nombre d'établissements |
| Number of employees... | 352.9 | 26.0 | 66.4 | 34.9 | 20.9 | 9.9 | 15.4 | 2.7 | 0.9 | 15.0 | 12.9 | 16.4 | 90.0 | 41.5 | Nombre de salariés |
| 1948 | | | | | | | | | | | | | | | 1948 |
| Number of establishments. | 11 051 | 806 | 1 066 | 1 369 | 1 821 | 219 | 684 | 181 | 25 | 399 | 468 | 147 | 2 478 | 1 388 | Nombre d'établissements |
| Number of employees... | 522.4 | 33.3 | 71.6 | 43.4 | 38.3 | 14.7 | 22.6 | 4.6 | 1.9 | 29.1 | 21.5 | 21.5 | 161.3 | 58.6 | Nombre de salariés |
| 1953 | | | | | | | | | | | | | | | 1953 |
| Number of establishments. | 11 259 | 778 | 1 035 | 1 294 | 1 817 | 216 | 765 | 168 | 29 | 393 | 445 | 148 | 2 697 | 1 474 | Nombre d'établissements |
| Number of employees... | 542.6 | 35.8 | 71.6 | 44.6 | 35.7 | 14.2 | 24.5 | 4.3 | 2.0 | 29.3 | 20.3 | 20.4 | 171.7 | 68.2 | Nombre de salariés |
| 1958 | | | | | | | | | | | | | | | 1958 |
| Number of establishments. | 12 096 | 786 | 1 002 | 1 372 | 1 899 | 220 | 786 | 162 | 47 | 419 | 485 | 152 | 3 147 | 1 619 | Nombre d'établissements |
| Number of employees... | 612.8 | 40.1 | 68.4 | 47.9 | 38.0 | 17.4 | 29.3 | 4.0 | 3.2 | 34.8 | 23.3 | 24.2 | 210.6 | 71.6 | Nombre de salariés |
| | b. Structure | | | | | | | | | | | | | | |
| 1937 | | | | | | | | | | | | | | | 1937 |
| Distribution in percent of the number of employees......... | 100.0 | 7.3 | 18.8 | 9.9 | 5.9 | 2.9 | 4.3 | 0.8 | 0.2 | 4.3 | 3.6 | 4.7 | 25.5 | 11.8 | Distribution en pourcentage du nombre de salariés |
| 1948 | | | | | | | | | | | | | | | 1948 |
| Distribution in percent of the number of employees......... | 100.0 | 6.3 | 13.7 | 8.3 | 7.4 | 2.8 | 4.3 | 0.9 | 0.4 | 5.5 | 4.1 | 4.1 | 30.9 | 11.3 | Distribution en pourcentage du nombre de salariés |
| 1953 | | | | | | | | | | | | | | | 1953 |
| Distribution in percent of the number of employees......... | 100.0 | 6.5 | 13.2 | 8.3 | 6.5 | 2.7 | 4.5 | 0.8 | 0.3 | 5.4 | 3.7 | 3.8 | 31.7 | 12.6 | Distribution en pourcentage du nombre de salariés |
| 1958 | | | | | | | | | | | | | | | 1958 |
| Distribution in percent of the number of employees......... | 100.0 | 6.5 | 11.2 | 7.8 | 6.2 | 2.8 | 4.8 | 0.6 | 0.6 | 5.6 | 3.9 | 3.9 | 34.4 | 11.7 | Distribution en pourcentage du nombre de salariés |

# SYRIA — SYRIE

## Net Domestic Product

Estimates of net domestic product according to origin shown in Table 1 were obtained from the *Statistical Abstract, 1961* issued by the Directorate of Statistics, Ministry of Planning, Damascus. The Directorate computes official estimates on this subject annually and publishes the estimates in the said publication.

## Index Numbers of Industrial Production

The index numbers of industrial production shown in Table 2 are obtained from indexes computed by the Directorate of Statistics, Ministry of Planning, Damascus and published in its *Statistical Abstract* starting with the 1960 issue.

The index numbers cover all establishments in selected industries of mining, manufacturing and electricity and are computed annually as base-weighted arithmetic averages of 31 quantity relatives for detailed kinds of industrial activity. The relatives are derived from quantities of output for individual products and are based on the year 1956. The weights utilized in combining the relatives into indexes for broader categories of industrial activities are the value added during 1956 by the respective industries covered in the indexes. The earliest year for which an index is available is 1954.

For further details regarding these index numbers, reference may be made to the aforementioned issues of the *Statistical Abstract* and to the publication issued by the Directorate entitled *Index Numbers of Industrial Production, 1954-1958*.

## Produit intérieur net

Les estimations du tableau 1 concernant le produit intérieur net par branche d'activité d'origine sont tirées de *Statistical Abstract, 1961*, publié par la Direction des statistiques, Ministère de la planification, Damas. Ce service établit annuellement des estimations officielles à cet égard et les fait paraître dans la publication précitée.

## Indices de la production industrielle

Les indices de la production industrielle présentés au tableau 2 ont été calculés à partir d'indices construits par la Direction des statistiques, Ministère de la planification, Damas, et publiés dans son *Statistical Abstract* à partir du numéro de 1960.

Les indices sont établis chaque année et concernent tous les établissements de certaines industries extractives, manufacturières et productrices d'électricité; ce sont des moyennes arithmétiques à pondération fixe de 31 rapports quantitatifs relatifs aux catégories détaillées de l'activité industrielle. Ces rapports sont fondés sur les quantités produites de chaque marchandise et ont 1956 pour année de base. Pour combiner les rapports quantitatifs en indices relatifs aux catégories plus larges de l'activité industrielle, on a utilisé comme coefficients de pondération la valeur ajoutée en 1956 par les industries respectives comprises dans les indices. L'année la plus reculée pour laquelle on dispose d'indices est 1954.

Pour plus de détails sur ces indices, voir les numéros déjà mentionnés du *Statistical Abstract* et la publication de la Direction des statistiques intitulée *Index Numbers of Industrial Production, 1954-1958*.

# SYRIA

## 1. THE NET DOMESTIC PRODUCT AT FACTOR COST ACCORDING TO ORIGIN
## ORIGINE PAR SECTEUR D'ACTIVITE DU PRODUIT INTERIEUR NET AU COUT DES FACTEURS

Million Syrian Pounds — Millions de livres syriennes

| Item of data and year / Rubrique et année | Total | Agricultural sector / Secteur agricole | Industrial Sector — Secteur industriel | | | Transportation and communication / Transports et communications | Other sectors / Autres secteurs |
|---|---|---|---|---|---|---|---|
| | | | Total | Mining, manufacturing, electricity, gas and water / Industries extractives et manufacturières, et électricité, gaz et eau | Construction / Bâtiment et travaux publics | | |
| ISIC — CITI | 0–9 | 0 | 1–5 | 1–3, 5 | 4 | 7 | 6, 8–9 |
| At Prices of 1956 — Au prix de 1956 | | | | | | | |
| Absolute figures — Chiffres absolus | | | | | | | |
| 1953 | 1 892 | 824 | 287 | 227 | 60 | 129 | 652 |
| 1954 | 2 176 | 927 | 326 | 246 | 80 | 142 | 781 |
| 1955 | 1 920 | 636 | 359 | 264 | 95 | 139 | 786 |
| 1956 | 2 303 | 936 | 365 | 267 | 98 | 137 | 865 |
| 1957 | 2 451 | 1 067 | 363 | 288 | 75 | 124 | 897 |
| 1958 | 2 102 | 702 | 394 | 304 | 90 | 130 | 876 |
| 1959 | 2 133 | 721 | 394 | 315 | 79 | 136 | 882 |
| 1960 | 2 123 | 636 | 458 | 341 | 117 | 140 | 889 |
| 1961 | 2 357 | 805 | 472 | 352 | 120 | 131 | 949 |
| Percentage distribution according to sector— Distribution en pourcentage par secteur | | | | | | | |
| 1953 – 1960 | 100.0 | 37.7 | 17.2 | 13.2 | 4.0 | 6.3 | 38.8 |
| 1953 | 100.0 | 43.5 | 15.2 | 12.0 | 3.2 | 6.8 | 34.5 |
| 1954 | 100.0 | 42.6 | 15.0 | 11.3 | 3.7 | 6.5 | 35.9 |
| 1958 | 100.0 | 33.4 | 18.7 | 14.4 | 4.3 | 6.2 | 41.7 |
| Average annual rate of growth—Taux annuel moyen d'accroissement | | | | | | | |
| 1953 – 1960 | 1.7 | −3.6 | 6.9 | 6.0 | 10.0 | 1.2 | 4.5 |
| 1954 – 1958 | −0.9 | −6.7 | 4.9 | 5.4 | 3.0 | −2.2 | 2.9 |
| 1958 – 1960 | 0.5 | −4.8 | 7.8 | 5.9 | 14.0 | 3.8 | 0.7 |

## 2. INDEX NUMBERS OF INDUSTRIAL PRODUCTION — INDICES DE LA PRODUCTION INDUSTRIELLE

### A. Selected Divisions of Industrial Activity
### Quelques branches de l'activité industrielle

| Period / Période | Total | Mining [1] / Industries extractives [1] | Manu-facturing / Industries manu-facturières | Electricity / Electricité |
|---|---|---|---|---|
| ISIC — CITI | 1–3, 511 | 1 | 2–3 | 511 |

#### a. Indexes — Indices (1958 = 100)

| | | | | |
|---|---|---|---|---|
| 1954.......... | 73 | 100 | 75 | 44 |
| 1955.......... | 81 | 79 | 84 | 50 |
| 1956.......... | 81 | 147 | 82 | 56 |
| 1957.......... | 89 | 113 | 88 | 89 |
| 1958.......... | 100 | 100 | 100 | 100 |
| 1959.......... | 100 | 110 | 98 | 114 |
| 1960.......... | 114 | 112 | 114 | 118 |
| 1961.......... | 121 | 68 | 121 | 125 |

#### b. Average Annual Rate of Change — Taux annuel moyen de variation

| | | | | |
|---|---|---|---|---|
| 1954 – 1958.... | 8.2 | — | 7.5 | 22.8 |
| 1958 – 1960.... | 6.8 | 5.8 | 6.8 | 8.6 |

For footnotes see end of table.

Pour les notes, voir au bas du tableau.

### B. Selected Major Groups of Manufacturing
### Quelques classes de la branche Industries manufacturières

| Period / Période | Manu-facturing / Industries manu-facturières | Food, beverages and tobacco / Industries alimen-taires, boissons, tabac | Textiles, clothing, footwear and made-up textiles / Textiles, articles d'habil-lement, chaussures et ouvrages en tissu | Paper and paper products / Papier et ouvrages en papier | Rubber products / Ouvrages en caout-chouc | Chemicals and chemical products / Produits chi-miques | Non-metallic mineral products / Produits minéraux non métal-liques |
|---|---|---|---|---|---|---|---|
| ISIC — CITI | 2–3 | 20–22 | 23–24 | 27 | 30 | 31 | 33 |

#### a. Indexes — Indices (1958 = 100)

| | | | | | | | |
|---|---|---|---|---|---|---|---|
| 1954............. | 75 | 69 | 84 | 87 | 62 | 55 | 64 |
| 1955............. | 84 | 83 | 93 | 88 | 79 | 65 | 60 |
| 1956............. | 82 | 88 | 81 | 101 | 66 | 67 | 81 |
| 1957............. | 88 | 88 | 93 | 106 | 94 | 93 | 72 |
| 1958............. | 100 | 100 | 100 | 100 | 100 | 100 | 100 |
| 1959............. | 98 | 82 | 101 | 101 | 139 | 127 | 105 |
| 1960............. | 114 | 117 | 109 | 101 | 141 | 126 | 120 |
| 1961............. | 121 | 128 | 113 | 101 | 215 | 128 | 122 |

#### b. Average Annual Rate of Change — Taux annuel moyen de variation

| | | | | | | | |
|---|---|---|---|---|---|---|---|
| 1954 – 1958....... | 7.5 | 9.7 | 4.4 | 3.5 | 12.7 | 16.1 | 11.8 |
| 1958 – 1960....... | 6.8 | 8.2 | 4.4 | 0.5 | 18.7 | 12.2 | 9.5 |

[1] Covers activities in Other mining (ISIC major groups 14–19) only.

[1] Il s'agit exclusivement des activités comprises dans Autres industries extractives (CITI classes 14–19).

# TANGANYIKA

## The Gross Domestic Product and the Gross Domestic Fixed Capital Formation

Estimates of the expenditure on and the origin of the gross domestic product and the origin of the gross domestic fixed capital formation are presented in Table 1. The table is derived from data supplied by the Economic and Statistics Division of the Treasury, Dar es Salaam, in response to the United Nations national accounts questionnaire. Official estimates and a description of the sources and methods used have been published in *The Gross Domestic Product of Tanganyika 1954-1957* prepared by the Tanganyika Unit of the East African Statistical Department. The estimates are also published in the *Statistical Abstract, 1962*. A description of the sources and methods which have been utilized can also be found in *The National Income of Tanganyika 1952-1954* by Alan T. Peacock and Douglas G. M. Dosser, Colonial Research Study, No. 26, Colonial Office, London, 1958.

## Index Numbers of Industrial Employment

The index numbers of industrial employment presented in Table 2 have been derived from absolute figures of the number of employees. In the case of mining up to 1959, the indexes are based on the annual average absolute number of employees derived from the *Annual Report of the Mines Division (Ministry of Commerce and Industry)*. This data covers all employees, African, European, Asian and other. The indexes for 1959 and 1960 are derived from data of the number of African employees as at the 30th June of each year obtained from the results of an annual enumeration of employees published in the *Annual Report of the Labour Division (Ministry of Health and Labour)*. The index for mining as a whole is derived from the aggregated absolute figures for the individual major groups. These two sets of index numbers are linked at 1959.

In the case of manufacturing and electricity the figures of the absolute number of employees are derived from the results of the annual registration of all factory premises conducted at the end of each year by the Ministry of Health and Labour and published in the *Annual Report of the Labour Division*. The index numbers for manufacturing as a whole are obtained from the aggregated absolute figures for the constituent major groups.

In the case of construction for all years, the index numbers are based on the number of employees as at the 30th June of each year derived from the results of an annual enumeration of employees published in the *Annual Report of the Labour Division (Ministry of Health and Labour)*. For all years the data relates to private

## Produit intérieur brut et la formation brute de capital fixe intérieur

Le tableau 1 contient des estimations des dépenses imputées au produit intérieur brut, du produit intérieur brut par secteur d'activité d'origine et de la formation brute de capital fixe intérieur par secteur d'acquisition. Ce tableau a été établi à partir de données fournies par l'Economic and Statistics Division of the Treasury, Dar es-Salam, en réponse au questionnaire de l'ONU sur la comptabilité nationale. Les estimations officielles et les renseignements concernant les sources et méthodes utilisées ont été publiés dans *The Gross Domestic Product of Tanganyika 1954-1957*, préparé par le Service du Tanganyika de l'East African Statistical Department. Les estimations ont aussi été publiées dans *Statistical Abstract, 1962*. Les sources et méthodes utilisées sont également indiquées dans *The National Income of Tanganyika 1952-1954*, par Alan T. Peacock et Douglas G. M. Dosser, Colonial Research Study, No 26, Colonial Office, London, 1958.

## Indices de l'emploi dans l'industrie

Les indices de l'emploi dans l'industrie présentés au tableau 2 ont été établis à partir de chiffres absolus concernant le nombre de salariés. Pour les industries extractives, les indices sont fondés, jusqu'en 1959, sur le nombre annuel moyen de salariés tiré de *Annual Report of the Mines Division (Ministry of Commerce and Industry)*. Ces données portent sur tous les salariés, africains, européens, asiatiques et autres. Les indices de 1959 et 1960 sont établis à partir de données sur le nombre de salariés africains au 30 juin de chaque année; ces données sont tirées des résultats d'un dénombrement annuel des salariés, qui sont publiés dans *Annual Report of the Labour Division (Ministry of Health and Labour)*. L'indice relatif à l'ensemble des industries extractives est construit à partir de la somme des chiffres absolus concernant les différentes classes. Ces deux séries d'indices ont été raccordées au niveau de 1959.

Pour les industries manufacturières et productrices d'électricité, les chiffres absolus concernant le nombre de salariés sont tirés des résultats du dénombrement annuel de toutes les usines effectué en fin d'année par le Ministère de la santé et du travail; ces résultats sont publiés dans *Annual Report of the Labour Division*. Les indices relatifs à l'ensemble des industries manufacturières sont construits à partir de la somme des chiffres absolus concernant les différentes classes.

Pour le bâtiment et les travaux publics, tous les indices sont fondés sur le nombre de salariés au 30 juin de chaque année, qui est tiré des résultats d'un dénombrement annuel des salariés; ces résultats sont publiés dans *Annual Report of the Labour Division (Ministry of Health and Labour)*. Pour toutes les années, les données se rappor-

construction establishments only and up to 1958 are restricted to African employees only. After 1958 the basic data refer to all employees.

The indexes for mining, manufacturing and electricity combined have been computed by combining the index numbers for the individual divisions of industrial activity using as weights, the number of employees in 1953 for the years up to 1955 and in 1958 for the later years.

## The Characteristics and Structure of Industrial Activity

The data presented in Table 3 are derived from the results of the first Survey of Industrial Production for the whole country. The results of the survey have been published in *Survey of Industrial Production, 1958,* by the East African Statistical Department, Tanganyika Unit, October 1960.

The survey covered, in principle, all establishments engaging five or more persons. However only 27 percent of all establishments in the field covered responded to the questionnaire, and estimates have not been made for the establishments which did not return questionnaires. In addition, although, in principle, central and local government industrial activity were to be covered in the survey, because of non-response, all local government construction activity and all of the Post and Telecommunications industrial activity are excluded from the data shown in Table 3. It is thought that these omissions, although large in terms of the number of establishments are considerably less in terms of the number of persons engaged and valued added, as the non-respondents would tend to be the smaller establishments.

A number of reservations also need to be made concerning particular industries. In the first place, the restriction of the coverage of the survey to establishments engaging five or more persons would lead to the exclusion of a large part of the tailoring, footwear and jewellery industries. As for the data gathered from covered establishments, the value added in the manufacture of food is probably inflated owing to the fact that a number of tea manufacturing establishments on tea estates did not include the raw tea utilized as a raw material in the costs reported by them.

The definitions of the items of data shown are generally consistent with the International Standards in Basic Industrial Statistics. The value added shown has been computed by the Statistical Office of the United Nations by deducting from the value of gross production at ex-factory prices, excluding excise duties, the value of raw materials and fuels used and the value of work done by others. The wages and salaries data, although, in principle, including payments in kind, exclude this item to some extent, especially as far as oil milling (part of ISIC major group 31) is concerned. The number engaged is the average of the number as at 31st December 1957 and 31st December 1958.

tent aux établissements de construction privés seulement et, jusqu'en 1958, ne portent que sur les salariés africains. A partir de 1958, les données de base portent sur tous les salariés.

Pour établir les indices relatifs à l'ensemble des industries extractives, manufacturières et productrices d'électricité, on a combiné les indices concernant les diverses branches de l'activité industrielle en pondérant par le nombre de salariés en 1953 pour 1955 et les années antérieures, et en 1958 pour les années suivantes.

## Caractéristiques et structures de l'activité industrielle

Les données du tableau 3 sont tirées des résultats de la première enquête sur la production industrielle dans l'ensemble du pays. Les résultats de l'enquête ont été publiées dans *Survey of Industrial Production, 1958* par le Service du Tanganyika de l'East African Statistical Department, octobre 1960.

L'enquête portait, en principe, sur tous les établissements occupant cinq personnes ou plus. Cependant, 27 p. 100 seulement des établissements appartenant au champ de l'enquête ont répondu au questionnaire et l'on n'a pas fait d'estimations pour tenir compte des non-réponses. De plus, bien qu'en principe l'enquête dût porter notamment sur l'activité industrielle de l'Etat et des collectivités locales, toutes les activités de construction des collectivités locales et toutes les activités industrielles des Postes et télécommunications sont exclues des données du tableau 3 en raison des non-réponses. On estime que ces omissions, importantes par le nombre d'établissements, le sont beaucoup moins en ce qui concerne le nombre de personnes occupées et la valeur ajoutée, car les non-réponses doivent provenir surtout des petits établissements.

Il y a lieu également de faire quelques réserves au sujet de certaines industries particulières. Tout d'abord, comme le champ de l'enquête était limité aux établissements employant cinq personnes ou plus, une grande partie des industries s'occupant de la confection d'articles d'habillement, de la fabrication de chaussures et de la bijouterie s'en trouvait exclue. Quant aux données recueillies auprès des établissements enquêtés, la valeur ajoutée dans les industries alimentaires est probablement exagérée, car un certain nombre d'établissements manufacturiers de thé situés dans les plantations mêmes n'ont pas tenu compte du thé brut utilisé comme matière première dans les coûts qu'ils ont déclarés.

Les définitions des rubriques utilisées sont, en général, conformes aux Normes internationales relatives aux statistiques industrielles de base. La valeur ajoutée indiquée a été calculée par le Bureau de statistique de l'ONU, qui a déduit de la valeur de la production brute aux prix départ usine — non compris les impôts indirects — la valeur des matières premières et des combustibles utilisés, ainsi que la valeur des travaux confiés à des tiers. Les traitements et salaires comprennent en principe les paiements en nature, mais ceux-ci sont parfois exclus, notamment dans le cas des huileries (dans CITI classe 31). Le nombre de personnes occupées est la moyenne au 31 décembre 1957 et au 31 décembre 1958.

# TANGANYIKA

## 1. THE GROSS DOMESTIC PRODUCT AND GROSS DOMESTIC FIXED CAPITAL FORMATION
## LE PRODUIT INTERIEUR BRUT ET LA FORMATION BRUTE DE CAPITAL FIXE INTERIEUR

Million Pounds                                                                 Millions de livres

### A. Expenditure on the Gross Domestic Product at Market Prices
### Dépenses relatives au produit intérieur brut aux prix du marché

| Item of data and year / Rubrique et année | Total¹ | Consumption / Consommation | | Gross Domestic Capital Formation / Formation brute de capital intérieur | | Net exports of goods and services / Exportations nettes de biens et de services | |
|---|---|---|---|---|---|---|---|
| | | Total | Government / Etat | Total | Fixed / Fixe | Exports less imports / Exportations moins importations | Exports / Exportations |
| | | | | At Current Prices — Aux prix courants | | | |
| **Absolute figures — Chiffres absolus** | | | | | | | |
| 1954 | 147.9 | 119.9 | 12.2 | ... | 26.0 | 2.0 | 38.8 |
| 1955 | 154.9 | 134.8 | 13.7 | ... | 28.9 | −8.7 | 39.1 |
| 1956 | 160.0 | 124.7 | 14.9 | ... | 27.6 | 7.7 | 48.4 |
| 1957 | 170.9 | 143.6 | 16.3 | ... | 29.5 | −2.2 | 43.1 |
| 1958 | 176.1 | 143.0 | 17.6 | ... | 27.4 | 5.7 | 46.4 |
| 1959 | 187.6 | 153.8 | 18.2 | ... | 26.6 | 7.2 | 49.8 |
| 1960 | 197.3 | 155.6 | 20.2 | ... | 29.8 | 11.9 | 58.9 |
| 1961 | 198.5 | 166.2 | 23.4 | ... | 29.8 | 2.5 | 52.8 |
| **Percentage distribution of average annual expenditure — Distribution en pourcentage des dépenses annuelles moyennes** | | | | | | | |
| 1954 – 1960 | 100.0 | 81.6 | 9.5 | — | 16.4 | 2.0 | 27.2 |
| 1954 | 100.0 | 81.1 | 8.2 | — | 17.6 | 1.3 | 26.2 |
| 1958 | 100.0 | 81.2 | 10.0 | — | 15.6 | 3.2 | 26.3 |
| 1960 | 100.0 | 78.9 | 10.2 | — | 15.1 | 6.0 | 29.8 |

¹ Excludes stock changes.                    ¹ Non compris les variations de stocks.

### B. The Gross Domestic Product at Factor Cost According to Origin
### Origine par secteur d'activité du produit intérieur brut au coût des facteurs

| Item of data and year / Rubrique et année | Total | Agricultural sector / Secteur agricole | Industrial Sector — Secteur industriel | | | | | Transportation and communication / Transports et communications | Other sectors / Autres secteurs |
|---|---|---|---|---|---|---|---|---|---|
| | | | Total | Mining / Industries extractives | Manufacturing / Industries manufacturières | Construction / Bâtiment et travaux publics | Electricity, gas and water / Electricité, gaz et eau | | |
| ISIC — CITI | 0–9 | 0 | 1–5 | 1 | 2–3 | 4 | 5 | 7 | 6, 8–9 |
| | | | | At Current Prices — Aux prix courants | | | | | |
| **Absolute figures — Chiffres absolus** | | | | | | | | | |
| 1954 | 141.6 | 88.2 | 24.7 | 4.6 | 8.9 | 10.5 | 0.7 | 8.0 | 20.9 |
| 1955 | 146.7 | 91.9 | 23.4 | 5.1 | 9.4 | 8.1 | 0.8 | 8.5 | 23.0 |
| 1956 | 152.4 | 94.7 | 24.5 | 5.0 | 9.3 | 9.3 | 0.9 | 9.0 | 24.1 |
| 1957 | 162.4 | 99.2 | 27.2 | 5.0 | 11.3 | 10.3 | 0.6 | 10.2 | 25.7 |
| 1958 | 167.1 | 98.3 | 30.1 | 6.2 | 12.4 | 10.5 | 1.0 | 11.4 | 27.2 |
| 1959 | 177.1 | 105.2 | 30.6 | 6.6 | 12.9 | 10.0 | 1.1 | 12.3 | 29.0 |
| 1960 | 186.2 | 109.5 | 32.5 | 7.0 | 13.5 | 10.9 | 1.1 | 13.3 | 31.0 |
| 1961 | 186.9 | 105.7 | 33.8 | 7.3 | 13.5 | 11.8 | 1.2 | 13.3 | 34.1 |
| **Percentage distribution according to sector — Distribution en pourcentage par secteur** | | | | | | | | | |
| 1954 – 1960 | 100.0 | 60.6 | 17.0 | 3.5 | 6.9 | 6.1 | 0.5 | 6.4 | 16.0 |
| 1954 | 100.0 | 62.2 | 17.4 | 3.2 | 6.3 | 7.4 | 0.5 | 5.7 | 14.7 |
| 1958 | 100.0 | 58.9 | 18.0 | 3.7 | 7.4 | 6.3 | 0.6 | 6.8 | 16.3 |
| 1960 | 100.0 | 58.8 | 17.5 | 3.8 | 7.2 | 5.9 | 0.6 | 7.1 | 16.6 |

## C. The Gross Domestic Fixed Capital Formation According to Purchasing Industry
### La formation brute de capital fixe intérieur par secteur d'acquisition

| Item of data and year / Rubrique et année | Total | Agricultural sector / Secteur agricole | Industrial Sector — Secteur industriel | | | | | Transportation and communication / Transports et communication | Other sectors / Autres secteurs |
|---|---|---|---|---|---|---|---|---|---|
| | | | Total | Mining / Industries extractives | Manufacturing / Industries manufacturières | Construction / Bâtiment et travaux publics | Electricity, gas and water / Electricité, gaz et eau | | |
| ISIC — CITI | 0–9 | 0 | 1–5 | 1 | 2–3 | 4 | 5 | 7 | 6, 8–9 |
| | At Current Prices — Aux prix courants | | | | | | | | |
| Absolute figures — Chiffres absolus | | | | | | | | | |
| 1954 | 26.0 | 2.1 | 3.9 | 1.1 | 1.0 | 1.2 | 0.6 | 5.6 | 14.3 |
| 1955 | 28.9 | 2.2 | 4.9 | 0.9 | 2.0 | 1.8 | 0.2 | 6.5 | 15.3 |
| 1956 | 27.6 | 2.4 | 4.9 | 1.1 | 1.9 | 1.5 | 0.4 | 4.0 | 16.5 |
| 1957 | 29.5 | 2.5 | 5.1 | 1.2 | 1.7 | 1.5 | 0.7 | 3.8 | 18.0 |
| 1958 | 27.4 | 2.4 | 5.0 | 1.3 | 2.0 | 1.5 | 0.2 | 2.7 | 17.4 |
| 1959 | 26.6 | 2.4 | 4.1 | 0.5 | 1.9 | 1.3 | 0.4 | 4.2 | 15.9 |
| 1960 | 29.8 | 3.0 | 4.9 | 0.6 | 2.4 | 1.7 | 0.2 | 5.6 | 16.2 |
| 1961 | 29.8 | 3.4 | 4.6 | 0.9 | 1.8 | 1.3 | 0.6 | 5.7 | 16.2 |
| Percentage distribution according to sector— Distribution en pourcentage par secteur | | | | | | | | | |
| 1954–1960 | 100.0 | 8.7 | 16.8 | 3.4 | 6.6 | 5.4 | 1.4 | 16.5 | 58.0 |
| 1954 | 100.0 | 8.1 | 15.1 | 4.3 | 3.9 | 4.6 | 2.3 | 21.6 | 55.2 |
| 1958 | 100.0 | 8.7 | 18.2 | 4.7 | 7.3 | 5.5 | 0.7 | 9.8 | 63.3 |
| 1960 | 100.0 | 10.1 | 16.5 | 2.0 | 8.1 | 5.7 | 0.7 | 18.9 | 54.5 |

## 2. INDEX NUMBERS OF INDUSTRIAL EMPLOYMENT — INDICES DE L'EMPLOI DANS L'INDUSTRIE

### A. The Divisions of Industrial Activity
### Les branches de l'activité industrielle

| Period / Période | Total | Mining / Industries extractives | Manufacturing / Industries manufacturières | Construction [2] / Bâtiment et travaux publics [2] | Electricity [1] / Electricité [1] |
|---|---|---|---|---|---|
| ISIC — CITI | 1–3, 511 | 1 | 2–3 | 4 | 511 |
| a. Indexes — Indices (1958 = 100) | | | | | |
| 1953 | 84 | 119 | 76 | 137 | 107 |
| 1954 | 84 | 106 | 79 | 157 | 107 |
| 1955 | — 87 — | 105 | 83 | 116 | 117 |
| 1956 | 89 | 108 | 84 | 124 | 119 |
| 1957 | 96 | 105 | 94 | 109 | 138 |
| 1958 | 100 | 100 | 100 | — 100 — | 100 |
| 1959 | — 100 — | — 88 — | 103 | 106 | 99 |
| 1960 | 111 | 102 | 113 | 88 | 82 |
| 1961 | ... | ... | 120 | ... | 82 |
| b. Average Annual Rate of Change — Taux annuel moyen de variation | | | | | |
| 1954–1958 | 4.4 | —1.4 | 6.1 | —10.7 | —1.7 |
| 1958–1960 | 5.4 | 1.0 | 6.3 | —6.2 | —9.4 |

For footnotes see end of table.

Pour les notes, voir au bas du tableau.

### B. The Major Groups of Mining
### Les classes de la branche Industries extractives

| Period / Période | All mining / Toutes industries extractives | Metal mining / Extraction des minerais métalliques | Crude petroleum and natural gas / Pétrole brut et gaz naturel | Other mining / Autres industries extractives |
|---|---|---|---|---|
| ISIC — CITI | 1 | 12 | 13 | 14–19 |
| a. Indexes — Indices (1958 = 100) | | | | |
| 1948 | 112 | ... | — | ... |
| 1949 | 122 | 192 | — | 88 |
| 1950 | 120 | 172 | — | 98 |
| 1951 | 113 | 150 | — | 98 |
| 1953 | 119 | 149 | — | 108 |
| 1954 | 106 | 129 | — | 100 |
| 1955 | 105 | 121 | — | 102 |
| 1956 | 108 | 110 | — | 113 |
| 1957 | 105 | 98 | 80 | 111 |
| 1958 | 100 | 100 | 100 | 100 |
| 1959 | — 88 — | — 89 — | 41 | — 90 — |
| 1960 | 102 | 86 | ... | 124 |
| b. Average Annual Rate of Change — Taux annuel moyen de variation | | | | |
| 1950–1960 | —1.6 | —6.7 | ... | 2.4 |
| 1948–1953 | 1.2 | —3.3 | ... | 8.4 |
| 1954–1958 | —1.4 | —6.2 | ... | —1.4 |
| 1958–1960 | 1.0 | —7.3 | ... | 11.4 |

# TANGANYIKA

## C. The Major Groups of Manufacturing — Les classes de la branche Industries manufacturières

| Period / Période | Manufacturing / Industries manufacturières | Food, beverages and tobacco / Industries alimentaires, boissons, tabac | Textiles | Clothing, footwear and made-up textiles / Articles d'habillement, chaussures et ouvrages en tissu | Wood products and furniture / Bois et meubles | Printing and publishing / Imprimerie et édition | Leather and leather products except wearing apparel / Cuir et articles en cuir, à l'exclusion des articles d'habillement | Rubber products / Ouvrages en caoutchouc | Chemicals and chemical, petroleum and coal products / Produits chimiques et dérivés du pétrole et du charbon | Non-metallic mineral products / Produits minéraux non métalliques | Basic metals / Métallurgie de base | Metal products / Ouvrages en métaux | Other manufacturing / Autres industries manufacturières |
|---|---|---|---|---|---|---|---|---|---|---|---|---|---|
| ISIC — CITI | 2–3 | 20–22 | 23 | 24 | 25–26 | 28 | 29 | 30 | 31–32 | 33 | 34 | 35–38 | 39 |

### a. Indexes — Indices (1958 = 100)

| | | | | | | | | | | | | | |
|---|---|---|---|---|---|---|---|---|---|---|---|---|---|
| 1953 | 76 | 60 | 72 | 80 | 87 | 80 | 97 | 54 | 95 | 62 | 206 | 94 | 88 |
| 1954 | 79 | 65 | 75 | 89 | 86 | 85 | 97 | 62 | 98 | 62 | 271 | 98 | 89 |
| 1955 | 83 | 70 | 80 | 93 | 93 | 76 | 100 | 78 | 88 | 46 | 229 | 101 | 90 |
| 1956 | 84 | 78 | 84 | 100 | 87 | 73 | 91 | 94 | 85 | 46 | 203 | 90 | 92 |
| 1957 | 94 | 90 | 96 | 100 | 94 | 86 | 93 | 70 | 93 | 108 | 81 | 94 | 92 |
| 1958 | 100 | 100 | 100 | 100 | 100 | 100 | 100 | 100 | 100 | 100 | 100 | 100 | 100 |
| 1959 | 103 | 103 | 108 | 100 | 89 | 109 | 108 | 102 | 101 | 103 | 113 | 100 | 100 |
| 1960 | 113 | 139 | 111 | 103 | 90 | 104 | 108 | 97 | 108 | 98 | 116 | 109 | 100 |
| 1961 | 120 | 156 | 117 | 116 | 86 | 108 | 110 | 122 | 114 | 99 | 158 | 112 | 98 |

### b. Average Annual Rate of Change — Taux annuel moyen de variation

| | | | | | | | | | | | | | |
|---|---|---|---|---|---|---|---|---|---|---|---|---|---|
| 1954–1958 | 6.1 | 11.4 | 7.6 | 3.0 | 3.8 | 4.1 | 0.7 | 12.7 | 0.5 | 12.7 | −32.0 | 0.5 | 3.0 |
| 1958–1960 | 6.3 | 17.9 | 5.4 | 1.5 | −5.1 | 2.0 | 3.9 | −1.5 | 3.9 | −1.0 | 7.7 | 4.4 | — |

[1] Private electricity generation establishments only.
[2] Private construction establishments only.

[1] Production d'électricité par les établissements privés seulement.
[2] Il s'agit uniquement des établissements privés relevant du bâtiment et des travaux publics.

## 3. CHARACTERISTICS OF ALL INDUSTRIAL ESTABLISHMENTS WITH FIVE OR MORE PERSONS ENGAGED

## CARACTERISTIQUES DES TOUS LES ETABLISSEMENTS INDUSTRIELS AYANT CINQ PERSONNES OCCUPEES OU PLUS

### 1958

Number of establishments in units; value added and wages and salaries in thousand Pounds; number of engaged in thousands; value added per engaged in Pounds.

Nombre d'établissements en unités; valeur ajoutée et traitements et salaires en milliers de livres; nombre de personnes occupées en milliers; valeur ajoutée par personne occupée en livres.

### A. The Divisions of Industrial Activity — Les branches de l'activité industrielle

| Item of data | All industrial activity / Toutes industries | Mining / Industries extractives | Manufacturing / Industries manufacturières | Construction / Bâtiment et travaux publics | Electricity and gas / Electricité et gaz | Rubrique | Item of data | All industrial activity / Toutes industries | Mining / Industries extractives | Manufacturing / Industries manufacturières | Construction / Bâtiment et travaux publics | Electricity and gas / Electricité et gaz | Rubrique |
|---|---|---|---|---|---|---|---|---|---|---|---|---|---|
| ISIC | 1-4,511-512 | 1 | 2-3 | 4 | 511-512 | CITI | ISIC | 1-4,511-512 | 1 | 2-3 | 4 | 511-512 | CITI |

| | a. Absolute Figures — Chiffres absolus | | | | | | | b. Structure | | | | | |
|---|---|---|---|---|---|---|---|---|---|---|---|---|---|
| Number of establishments | 343 | 27 | 272 | 30 | 14 | Nombre d'établissements | Distribution in percent of: | | | | | | Distribution en pourcentage: |
| Value added | 9 490 | 2 957 | 4 898 | 1 065 | 570 | Valeur ajoutée | Value added | 100.0 | 31.1 | 51.6 | 11.2 | 6.1 | Valeur ajoutée |
| Number of engaged | 57.0 | 9.6 | 25.0 | 20.8 | 1.6 | Nombre de personnes occupées | Number of engaged | 100.0 | 16.8 | 43.9 | 36.4 | 2.9 | Nombre de personnes occupées |
| Wages and salaries | 4 949 | 1 419 | 2 015 | 1 211 | 304 | Traitements et salaires | Value added per person engaged | 166 | 308 | 196 | 51 | 356 | Valeur ajoutée par personne occupée |
| | | | | | | | Value added per unit of wages and salaries | 1.92 | 2.08 | 2.43 | 0.88 | 1.88 | Valeur ajoutée par unité de traitements et salaires |

**B.   The Major Groups of Mining — Les classes de la branche Industries extractives**

| Item of data | All mining<br>Toutes industries extractives | Metal mining<br>Extraction des minerais métalliques | Other mining<br>Divers | Rubrique | Item of data | All mining<br>Toutes industries extractives | Metal mining<br>Extraction des minerais métalliques | Other mining<br>Divers | Rubrique |
|---|---|---|---|---|---|---|---|---|---|
| ISIC | 1 | 12 | 14-19 | CITI | ISIC | 1 | 12 | 14-19 | CITI |
| | *a.* Absolute Figures<br>Chiffres absolus | | | | | *b.* Structure | | | |
| Number of establishments...... | 27 | 10 | 17 | Nombre d'établissements | Distribution in percent of: | | | | Distribution en pourcentage: |
| Value added................. | 4 406 | 896 | 3 510 | Valeur ajoutée | Value added............... | 100.0 | 20.3 | 79.7 | Valeur ajoutée |
| Number of engaged........... | 9.6 | 5.0 | 4.6 | Nombre de personnes occupées | Number of engaged......... | 100.0 | 52.1 | 47.9 | Nombre de personnes occupées |
| Wages and salaries........... | 1 419 | 732 | 687 | Traitements et salaires | Value added per person engaged.................. | 459 | 179 | 763 | Valeur ajoutée par personne occupée |
| | | | | | Value added per unit of wages and salaries........... | 3.10 | 1.22 | 5.11 | Valeur ajoutée par unité de traitements et salaires |

**C.   The Major Groups of Manufacturing — Les classes de la branche Industries manufacturières**

| Item of data | Manufacturing<br>Industries manufacturières | Food beverages and tobacco<br>Industries alimentaires, boissons, tabac | Textiles | Clothing, footwear and made-up textiles<br>Articles d'habillement, chaussures et ouvrages en tissu | Wood products and furniture<br>Bois et meubles | Printing and publishing<br>Imprimerie et édition | Rubber products<br>Ouvrages en caoutchouc | Chemicals and chemical, petroleum and coal products<br>Produits chimiques et dérivés du pétrole et du charbon | Non-metallic mineral products<br>Produits minéraux non métalliques | Metal products<br>Ouvrages en métaux | Other manufacturing<br>Autres industries manufacturières | Rubrique |
|---|---|---|---|---|---|---|---|---|---|---|---|---|
| ISIC | 2–3 | 20–22 | 23 | 24 | 25–26 | 28 | 30 | 31–32 | 33 | 35–38 | 39 | CITI |
| | *a.* Absolute Figures — Chiffres absolus | | | | | | | | | | | |
| Number of establishments | 272 | 110 | 10 | 14 | 50 | 14 | 4 | 3 | 6 | 56 | 5 | Nombre d'établissements |
| Value added.......... | 4 898 | 2 957 | 351 | 30 | 611 | 306 | 30 | 55 | 41 | 438 | 79 | Valeur ajoutée |
| Number of engaged.... | 25.0 | 14.6 | 1.8 | 0.1 | 5.5 | 0.7 | 0.1 | 0.1 | 0.2 | 1.7 | 0.2 | Nombre de personnes occupées |
| Wages and salaries..... | 2 015 | 991 | 113 | 10 | 370 | 161 | 8 | 14 | 24 | 301 | 23 | Traitements et salaires |
| | *b.* Structure | | | | | | | | | | | |
| Distribution in percent of: | | | | | | | | | | | | Distribution en pourcentage: |
| Value added........ | 100.0 | 60.3 | 7.2 | 0.6 | 12.5 | 6.2 | 0.6 | 1.2 | 0.8 | 8.9 | 1.7 | Valeur ajoutée |
| Number of engaged... | 100.0 | 58.4 | 7.2 | 0.4 | 22.0 | 2.8 | 0.4 | 0.4 | 0.8 | 6.8 | 0.8 | Nombre de personnes occupées |
| Value added per person engaged...... | 196 | 202 | 195 | 300 | 111 | 437 | 300 | 550 | 205 | 257 | 395 | Valeur ajoutée par personne occupée |
| Value added per unit of wages and salaries............ | 2.43 | 2.98 | 3.11 | 3.00 | 1.65 | 1.90 | 3.75 | 3.93 | 1.71 | 1.46 | 3.43 | Valeur ajoutée par unité de traitements et salaires |

## Gross Domestic Product and Gross Domestic Fixed Capital Formation

The data given in Table 1 on gross domestic product and fixed capital formation were obtained from the replies of the Central Statistical Office of the National Economic Development Board, Bangkok, to the United Nations national accounts questionnaire. Official estimates are issued and published annually by the Office in *Thailand Statistical Yearbook*. Sources and methods of estimation are described in the *Economy and National Income of Thailand*, by Bundhit Kantabutra, Office of the National Economic Development Board, Bangkok.

## The Characteristics and Structure of Industrial Activity

The data set out in Table 2 are derived from the results of the 1954 Demographic and Economic Survey of Thailand that was taken by the Central Statistical Office, Bangkok. Most of the data in Table 2 have not yet been published; the figures were made available to the Statistical Office of the United Nations through correspondence.

The 1954 Demographic and Economic Survey related to the activities and employment of all kinds of non-agricultural business units, irrespective of size or location, that, in the case of small establishments (fewer than ten persons engaged), were in existence during the week preceding the listing and, in the case of large establishments (with ten or more persons engaged), were in business during the period, January 1954—June 1954. It should be noted that the dates of listing varied from province to province and were spread over a considerable period of time. Data were gathered from all large units and an area sample of the small establishments that was designed to include 1 in 20 of these units in the two provinces (Bangkok and Thomburi) and 1 in 50 of these units in other provinces.

The definitions for the items of data sought from business establishments in the 1954 Survey conformed to the International Standards in Basic Industrial Statistics, and the scheme of classification utilized in compiling the results of the Survey was consistent with the ISIC.

## Produit intérieur brut et la formation brute de capital fixe intérieur

Les données du tableau 1, relatives au produit intérieur brut et à la formation de capital fixe, ont été fournies par l'Office central de statistique du National Economic Development Board, Bangkok, en réponse au questionnaire de l'ONU sur la comptabilité nationale. Des estimations officielles sont publiées annuellement par l'Office de statistique dans *Thailand Statistical Yearbook*. Les sources et méthodes utilisées sont indiquées dans *Economy and National Income of Thailand*, par Bundhit Kantabutra, Office of the National Economic Development Board, Bangkok.

## Caractéristiques et structure de l'activité industrielle

Les données du tableau 2 sont tirées des résultats de l'enquête démographique et économique de 1954 effectuée par l'Office central de statistique, Bangkok. La plupart des données du tableau 2 n'ont pas encore été publiées; les chiffres ont été communiqués par correspondance au Bureau de statistique de l'Organisation des Nations Unies.

L'enquête démographique et économique de 1954 portait sur les activités des unités non agricoles de tous types —quelles que fussent leur dimension ou leur situation— et l'emploi dans ces unités. Les unités recensées étaient les suivantes: petits établissements (moins de 10 personnes occupées) qui existaient pendant la semaine précédant la préparation du répertoire et grands établissements (10 personnes occupées ou plus) qui étaient en activité pendant la période janvier 1954-juin 1954. Il convient de noter que le répertoire a été établi à des dates variant d'une province à l'autre et que le travail s'est étalé sur une très longue période. Des renseignements ont été recueillis auprès de toutes les unités importantes et d'échantillons régionaux de petits établissements (1 unité sur 20 dans les deux provinces de Bangkok et Thomburi, et 1 sur 50 dans les autres provinces).

Les définitions des rubriques utilisées pour les établissements non agricoles dans l'enquête de 1954 étaient conformes aux Normes internationales relatives aux statistiques industrielles de base, et le système de classement utilisé pour l'exploitation des résultats de l'enquête était compatible avec la CITI.

## 1. THE GROSS DOMESTIC PRODUCT AND GROSS DOMESTIC FIXED CAPITAL FORMATION
## LE PRODUIT INTERIEUR BRUT ET LA FORMATION BRUTE DE CAPITAL FIXE INTERIEUR

Million Baht                                           Millions de bahts

### A. The Gross Domestic Product at Market Prices According to Origin
### Origine par secteur d'activité du produit intérieur brut aux prix du marché

| Item of data and year / Rubrique et année | Total | Agricultural sector / Secteur agricole | Industrial Sector — Secteur industriel Total | Mining / Industries extractives | Manufacturing / Industries manufacturières | Construction / Bâtiment et travaux publics | Electricity, gas and water / Electricité, gaz et eau | Transportation and communication / Transports et communications | Other sectors / Autres secteurs |
|---|---|---|---|---|---|---|---|---|---|
| ISIC — CITI | 0–9 | 0 | 1–5 | 1 | 2–3 | 4 | 5 | 7 | 6, 8–9 |
| *a. At Current Prices — Aux prix courants* | | | | | | | | | |
| **Absolute figures — Chiffres absolus** | | | | | | | | | |
| 1951 | 28 209.9 | 14 139.1 | 4 279.6 | 537.4 | 2 900.6 | 810.4 | 31.2 | 883.4 | 8 907.8 |
| 1952 | 29 520.6 | 12 944.0 | 5 060.4 | 562.7 | 3 287.8 | 1 174.6 | 35.3 | 1 164.5 | 10 351.7 |
| 1953 | 32 228.5 | 14 017.6 | 5 613.0 | 527.6 | 3 714.2 | 1 328.2 | 43.0 | 1 614.7 | 10 983.2 |
| 1954 | 32 043.9 | 12 829.6 | 5 730.1 | 547.2 | 3 777.8 | 1 344.8 | 60.3 | 1 763.4 | 11 720.8 |
| 1955 | 39 447.7 | 16 568.1 | 6 933.1 | 615.5 | 4 647.4 | 1 586.0 | 84.2 | 2 014.0 | 13 932.5 |
| 1956 | 41 088.6 | 16 586.1 | 7 498.6 | 697.6 | 4 969.7 | 1 731.5 | 99.8 | 2 209.9 | 14 794.0 |
| 1957 | 41 766.8 | 16 485.8 | 7 486.4 | 698.5 | 4 810.3 | 1 874.3 | 103.3 | 2 497.1 | 15 297.5 |
| 1958 | 42 360.3 | 16 835.6 | 7 256.3 | 525.0 | 5 207.4 | 1 392.6 | 131.3 | 2 529.9 | 15 738.5 |
| 1959 | 46 810.4 | 17 968.1 | 8 643.3 | 642.9 | 5 859.5 | 1 990.8 | 150.1 | 3 233.2 | 16 965.8 |
| 1960 | 53 113.7 | 20 703.1 | 9 619.5 | 768.3 | 6 102.9 | 2 567.6 | 180.7 | 4 114.7 | 18 676.4 |
| 1961 | 57 222.5 | 21 716.1 | 11 036.3 | 853.8 | 6 739.1 | 3 246.9 | 196.5 | 4 730.4 | 19 739.7 |
| **Percentage distribution according to sector— Distribution en pourcentage par secteur** | | | | | | | | | |
| 1951 – 1960 | 100.0 | 41.2 | 17.6 | 1.6 | 11.7 | 4.1 | 0.2 | 5.7 | 35.5 |
| 1953 | 100.0 | 43.5 | 17.4 | 1.7 | 11.5 | 4.1 | 0.1 | 5.0 | 34.1 |
| 1954 | 100.0 | 40.0 | 17.9 | 1.7 | 11.8 | 4.2 | 0.2 | 5.5 | 36.6 |
| 1958 | 100.0 | 39.7 | 17.1 | 1.2 | 12.3 | 3.3 | 0.3 | 6.0 | 37.2 |
| 1960 | 100.0 | 39.0 | 18.1 | 1.5 | 11.5 | 4.8 | 0.3 | 7.7 | 35.2 |
| *b. At Prices of 1956 — Aux prix de 1956* | | | | | | | | | |
| **Absolute figures — Chiffres absolus** | | | | | | | | | |
| 1951 | 31 199.1 | 13 731.0 | 5 472.6 | 557.4 | 3 948.6 | 924.1 | 42.5 | 1 202.5 | 10 793.0 |
| 1952 | 32 814.0 | 13 375.6 | 5 887.7 | 579.8 | 4 022.8 | 1 241.9 | 43.2 | 1 424.9 | 12 125.8 |
| 1953 | 35 557.6 | 15 429.2 | 6 180.1 | 637.0 | 4 127.8 | 1 367.5 | 47.8 | 1 794.5 | 12 153.8 |
| 1954 | 35 440.3 | 14 297.2 | 6 248.2 | 643.9 | 4 189.2 | 1 348.3 | 66.8 | 1 955.5 | 12 939.4 |
| 1955 | 40 227.1 | 16 288.8 | 7 244.2 | 664.6 | 4 926.2 | 1 564.1 | 89.3 | 2 134.8 | 14 559.3 |
| 1956 | 41 088.6 | 16 586.1 | 7 498.6 | 697.6 | 4 969.7 | 1 731.5 | 99.8 | 2 209.9 | 14 794.0 |
| 1957 | 40 446.3 | 16 276.9 | 7 212.5 | 731.2 | 4 539.8 | 1 844.1 | 97.4 | 2 356.7 | 14 600.2 |
| 1958 | 40 530.0 | 17 078.9 | 6 695.9 | 537.3 | 4 644.1 | 1 397.4 | 117.1 | 2 256.2 | 14 499.0 |
| 1959 | 45 238.0 | 17 829.7 | 8 275.2 | 645.2 | 5 489.0 | 2 000.4 | 140.6 | 3 028.8 | 16 104.3 |
| 1960 | 50 880.5 | 20 099.3 | 9 222.6 | 764.1 | 5 720.8 | 2 568.3 | 169.4 | 3 857.1 | 17 701.5 |
| 1961 | 53 037.4 | 20 889.2 | 10 187.9 | 850.0 | 5 929.7 | 3 235.3 | 172.9 | 4 162.2 | 17 798.1 |
| **Percentage distribution according to sector— Distribution en pourcentage par secteur** | | | | | | | | | |
| 1951 – 1960 | 100.0 | 40.9 | 17.8 | 1.7 | 11.8 | 4.1 | 0.2 | 5.6 | 35.7 |
| 1953 | 100.0 | 43.4 | 17.4 | 1.8 | 11.6 | 3.9 | 0.1 | 5.0 | 34.2 |
| 1954 | 100.0 | 40.4 | 17.6 | 1.8 | 11.8 | 3.8 | 0.2 | 5.5 | 36.5 |
| 1958 | 100.0 | 42.1 | 16.5 | 1.3 | 11.5 | 3.4 | 0.3 | 5.6 | 35.8 |
| 1960 | 100.0 | 39.5 | 18.1 | 1.5 | 11.2 | 5.1 | 0.3 | 7.6 | 34.8 |
| **Average annual rate of growth—Taux annuel moyen d'accroissement** | | | | | | | | | |
| 1951 – 1960 | 5.6 | 4.3 | 6.0 | 3.6 | 4.2 | 12.0 | 16.6 | 13.8 | 5.7 |
| 1951 – 1953 | 6.8 | 6.0 | 6.3 | 6.9 | 2.2 | 21.6 | 6.1 | 22.2 | 6.1 |
| 1954 – 1958 | 3.4 | 4.6 | 1.8 | −4.4 | 2.6 | 0.9 | 15.1 | 3.6 | 2.9 |
| 1958 – 1960 | 12.0 | 8.5 | 17.3 | 19.3 | 11.0 | 35.6 | 20.4 | 30.8 | 10.5 |

# THAILAND

## B. Gross Domestic Fixed Capital Formation According to Purchasing Sector
### La formation brute de capital fixe intérieur par secteur d'acquisition

| Item of data and year — Rubrique et année | Total | Agricultural sector — Secteur agricole | Industrial Sector — Secteur industriel | | | | | Transportation and communication — Transports et communications | Other sectors — Autres secteurs |
|---|---|---|---|---|---|---|---|---|---|
| | | | Total | Mining — Industries extractives | Manufacturing — Industries manufacturières | Construction — Bâtiment et travaux publics | Electricity, gas and water — Electricité, gaz et eau | | |
| ISIC — CITI | 0–9 | 0 | 1–5 | 1 | 2–3 | 4 | 5 | 7 | 6, 8–9 |

### a. At Current Prices — Aux prix courants

| Absolute figures — Chiffres absolus | | | | | | | | | |
|---|---|---|---|---|---|---|---|---|---|
| 1952 | 3 712.7 | 698.8 | 1 539.7 | 251.9 | 942.1 | 168.0 | 177.7 | 1 125.9 | 348.3 |
| 1953 | 4 590.2 | 835.2 | 1 892.9 | 304.7 | 1 133.4 | 229.5 | 225.3 | 1 435.0 | 427.1 |
| 1954 | 4 725.8 | 839.9 | 1 994.7 | 316.9 | 1 179.4 | 234.9 | 263.5 | 1 362.2 | 529.0 |
| 1955 | 4 700.6 | 894.8 | 1 884.0 | 295.3 | 1 093.7 | 241.5 | 253.5 | 1 304.5 | 617.3 |
| 1956 | 5 056.5 | 931.7 | 2 198.0 | 341.6 | 1 281.3 | 307.4 | 267.7 | 1 227.7 | 699.1 |
| 1957 | 6 906.0 | 1 132.5 | 3 451.0 | 445.7 | 1 836.4 | 868.8 | 300.1 | 1 444.2 | 878.3 |
| 1958 | 6 930.8 | 1 293.2 | 3 219.9 | 453.0 | 1 858.9 | 647.2 | 260.8 | 1 376.2 | 1 041.5 |
| 1959 | 8 158.7 | 1 545.9 | 3 998.5 | 629.0 | 2 406.4 | 611.5 | 351.6 | 1 404.0 | 1 210.3 |
| 1960 | 8 948.7 | 1 694.9 | 4 185.8 | 619.8 | 2 303.3 | 697.3 | 565.4 | 1 619.4 | 1 448.6 |
| **Percentage distribution according to sector— Distribution en pourcentage par secteur** | | | | | | | | | |
| 1952–1960 | 100.0 | 18.4 | 45.3 | 6.8 | 26.1 | 7.4 | 5.0 | 22.9 | 13.4 |
| 1953 | 100.0 | 18.2 | 41.2 | 6.6 | 24.7 | 5.0 | 4.9 | 31.3 | 9.3 |
| 1954 | 100.0 | 17.8 | 42.2 | 6.7 | 24.9 | 5.0 | 5.6 | 28.8 | 11.2 |
| 1958 | 100.0 | 18.7 | 46.4 | 6.5 | 26.8 | 9.3 | 3.8 | 19.9 | 15.0 |
| 1960 | 100.0 | 18.9 | 46.8 | 6.9 | 25.8 | 7.8 | 6.3 | 18.1 | 16.2 |

### b. At Prices of 1956 — Aux prix de 1956

| Absolute figures — Chiffres absolus | | | | | | | | | |
|---|---|---|---|---|---|---|---|---|---|
| 1952 | 4 327.6 | 827.7 | 1 790.6 | 290.9 | 1 095.4 | 201.0 | 203.3 | 1 324.9 | 384.4 |
| 1953 | 4 849.2 | 883.3 | 1 998.7 | 322.1 | 1 197.5 | 242.0 | 237.1 | 1 515.6 | 451.6 |
| 1954 | 4 958.7 | 881.3 | 2 093.1 | 332.7 | 1 237.5 | 246.2 | 276.7 | 1 428.3 | 556.0 |
| 1955 | 4 817.9 | 915.7 | 1 933.2 | 303.0 | 1 122.1 | 247.3 | 260.8 | 1 338.0 | 631.0 |
| 1956 | 5 056.5 | 931.7 | 2 198.0 | 341.6 | 1 281.3 | 307.4 | 267.7 | 1 229.7 | 697.1 |
| 1957 | 6 685.0 | 1 097.8 | 3 339.6 | 432.6 | 1 778.1 | 839.6 | 289.3 | 1 396.6 | 851.0 |
| 1958 | 6 805.0 | 1 268.2 | 3 162.2 | 444.9 | 1 824.4 | 636.8 | 256.1 | 1 352.3 | 1 022.3 |
| 1959 | 8 092.7 | 1 532.3 | 3 966.5 | 623.4 | 2 388.1 | 606.1 | 348.9 | 1 392.8 | 1 201.1 |
| 1960 | 8 684.8 | 1 641.5 | 4 068.3 | 602.8 | 2 241.2 | 675.5 | 548.8 | 1 567.8 | 1 407.2 |
| **Percentage distribution according to sector— Distribution en pourcentage par secteur** | | | | | | | | | |
| 1952–1960 | 100.0 | 18.4 | 45.2 | 6.8 | 26.1 | 7.4 | 4.9 | 23.1 | 13.3 |
| 1953 | 100.0 | 18.2 | 41.2 | 6.6 | 24.7 | 5.0 | 4.9 | 31.3 | 9.3 |
| 1954 | 100.0 | 17.8 | 42.2 | 6.7 | 24.9 | 5.0 | 5.6 | 28.8 | 11.2 |
| 1958 | 100.0 | 18.6 | 46.5 | 6.5 | 26.8 | 9.4 | 3.8 | 19.9 | 15.0 |
| 1960 | 100.0 | 18.9 | 46.8 | 6.9 | 25.8 | 7.8 | 6.3 | 18.1 | 16.2 |
| **Average annual rate of Growth—Taux annuel moyen d'accroissement** | | | | | | | | | |
| 1952–1960 | 9.1 | 8.9 | 10.8 | 9.5 | 9.4 | 16.4 | 13.2 | 2.1 | 17.6 |
| 1954–1958 | 7.8 | 9.5 | 10.9 | 7.5 | 10.2 | 26.8 | −0.5 | −1.4 | 16.4 |
| 1958–1960 | 13.0 | 13.8 | 13.4 | 16.4 | 10.8 | 3.0 | 46.4 | 7.7 | 17.3 |

## 2. CHARACTERISTICS OF ALL INDUSTRIAL ESTABLISHMENTS
### January 1954–June 1954

## CARACTERISTIQUES DE TOUS LES ETABLISSEMENTS INDUSTRIELS
### Janvier 1954–juin 1954

Number of establishments in units; gross receipts and wages and salaries in million Baht; and number of engaged and employees in thousands

Nombre d'établissements en unités; recettes brutes et traitements et salaires en millions de bahts; nombre de personnes occupées et de salariés en milliers

### A. The Divisions of Industrial Activity — Les branches de l'activité industrielle

| Item of data | All industrial activity<br>Toutes industries | Mining<br>Industries extractives | Manufacturing<br>Industries manufacturières | Construction<br>Bâtiment et travaux publics | Electricity and gas<br>Electricité et gaz | Rubrique |
|---|---|---|---|---|---|---|
| ISIC | 1–4; 511–512 | 1 | 2–3 | 4 | 511–512 | CITI |
| Number of establishments | 31 848 | 583 | 30 846 | 295 | 124 | Nombre d'établissements |
| Gross receipts | 50 548 | 301.8 | 3 455.7 | 223.4 | 1 073.9 | Recettes brutes |
| Number of engaged (As of week ending 30 June 1954) | 216.2 | 13.1 | 189.8 | 8.3 | 5.0 | Nombre de personnes occupées (semaine terminée le 30 juin 1954) |
| Number of employees (As of week ending 30 June 1954) | 146.7 | 12.5 | 121.1 | 8.1 | 5.0 | Nombre de salariés (semaine terminée le 30 juin 1954) |
| Wages and salaries paid | 481.2 | 45.1 | 398.0 | 18.1 | 20.0 | Traitements et salaires payés |
| Distribution in percent of number of engaged | 100.0 | 6.1 | 87.8 | 3.8 | 2.3 | Répartition en pourcentage du nombre de personnes occupées |

### B. The Major Groups of Mining — Les classes de la branche Industries extractives

| Item of data | All mining<br>Toutes industries extractives | Coal mining<br>Extraction du charbon | Metal mining<br>Extraction des minerais métalliques | Other mining<br>Divers | Rubrique |
|---|---|---|---|---|---|
| ISIC | 1 | 11 | 12 | 14–19 | CITI |
| Number of establishments | 583 | 20 | 142 | 421 | Nombre d'établissements |
| Gross receipts | 301.8 | 0.2 | 290.5 | 11.1 | Recettes brutes |
| Number of engaged (As of week ending 30 June 1954) | 13.1 | 0.1 | 10.7 | 2.3 | Nombre de personnes occupées (semaine terminée le 30 juin 1954) |
| Number of employees (As of week ending 30 June 1954) | 12.5 | 0.1 | 10.6 | 1.8 | Nombre de salariés (semaine terminée le 30 juin 1954) |
| Wages and salaries paid | 45.1 | 0.1 | 41.0 | 4.0 | Traitements et salaires payés |
| Distribution in percent of number of engaged | 100.0 | 0.7 | 81.7 | 17.6 | Répartition en pourcentage du nombre de personnes occupées |

### C. The Major Groups of Manufacturing — Les classes de la branche Industries manufacturières

| Item of data | Manufacturing<br>Industries manufacturières | Food, beverages and tobacco<br>Industries alimentaires, boissons, tabac | Textiles<br>Textiles | Clothing, footwear and made-up textiles<br>Articles d'habillement, chaussures et ouvrages en tissu | Wood products and furniture<br>Bois et meubles | Paper and paper products<br>Papier et ouvrages en papier | Printing and publishing<br>Imprimerie et édition | Leather and leather products except wearing apparel<br>Cuir et articles en cuir, à l'exclusion des articles d'habillement | Rubber products<br>Ouvrages en caoutchouc | Chemicals and chemical, petroleum and coal products<br>Produits chimiques et dérivés du pétrole et du charbon | Non-metallic mineral products<br>Produits minéraux non métalliques | Basic metals<br>Métallurgie de base | Metal products<br>Ouvrages en métaux | Other manufacturing<br>Autres industries manufacturières | Rubrique |
|---|---|---|---|---|---|---|---|---|---|---|---|---|---|---|---|
| ISIC | 2–3 | 20–22 | 23 | 24 | 25–26 | 27 | 28 | 29 | 30 | 31–32 | 33 | 34 | 35–38 | 39 | CITI |
| Number of establishments | 30 846 | 12 867 | 1 416 | 1 767 | 4 049 | 325 | 483 | 225 | 263 | 497 | 1 462 | 322 | 4 887 | 2 283 | Nombre d'établissements |
| Gross receipts | 3 455.7 | 2 317.3 | 90.0 | 20.4 | 347.6 | 6.2 | 59.6 | 13.1 | 97.8 | 147.4 | 133.3 | 16.2 | 129.4 | 77.4 | Recettes brutes |
| Number of engaged (As of week ending 30 June 1954) | 189.8 | 90.9 | 7.1 | 6.1 | 25.8 | 2.0 | 6.2 | 1.1 | 4.5 | 6.8 | 9.5 | 1.4 | 19.6 | 8.8 | Nombre de personnes occupées (semaine terminée le 30 juin 1954) |
| Number of employees (As of week ending 30 June 1954) | 121.1 | 59.3 | 3.9 | 1.6 | 18.2 | 1.2 | 5.4 | 0.7 | 4.1 | 5.4 | 6.5 | 0.8 | 9.7 | 4.3 | Nombre de salariés (semaine terminée le 30 juin 1954) |
| Wages and salaries paid | 398.0 | 193.1 | 9.5 | 2.3 | 60.0 | 0.8 | 19.3 | 1.6 | 7.4 | 21.5 | 33.3 | 2.3 | 32.8 | 14.1 | Traitements et salaires payés |
| Distribution in percent of number of engaged | 100.0 | 47.8 | 3.8 | 3.2 | 13.6 | 1.0 | 3.3 | 0.6 | 2.4 | 3.5 | 5.0 | 0.8 | 10.3 | 4.7 | Répartition en pourcentage du nombre de personnes occupées |

## The Gross Domestic Product

Estimates of expenditure on and the industrial origin of the gross domestic product are presented in Table 1. This table has been compiled from data supplied by the Central Statistical Office, Port-of-Spain, in response to the United Nations national accounts questionnaire. Official estimates and descriptions of sources and methods are published in *The National Income of Trinidad and Tobago, 1951 to 1959* by the Central Statistical Office. The same estimates are also published in summary form in the *Annual Statistical Digest*.

## Index Numbers of Industrial Employment

The index numbers of employment in industrial activities are presented in Table 2. The indexes are based on absolute figures of the total numbers employed by industrial establishments employing 10 persons or more, published in the *Annual Statistical Digest* by the Central Statistical Office. In 1956 and 1957 the annual figures of numbers employed are the arithmetic averages of the number employed during the last pay periods of February, May, August and November. In 1958 the annual number employed is the arithmetic average of the number of persons employed during the last pay periods of February and November. Whilst for 1959 and thereafter the annual figure of numbers employed is the arithmetic average of the number of persons employed during the last pay periods of May and November.

## The Characteristics and Structure of Industrial Activity

Table 3 contains data derived from Trinidad and Tobago's First and Second Surveys of Industrial Establishments for the years 1953 and 1957, respectively, covering industrial establishments which employed 5 or more persons. The results of the First Survey were published by the Central Statistical Office in *The Structure and Output of Industry — Report on a Census of Industrial Establishments, 1953,* Trinidad 1956; and the results of the Second Survey were issued in *Industry 1957 — Report on the 1957 Survey of Industrial Establishments,* (2 Volumes), Trinidad 1960.

The definitions of the items of data conform to the International Standards in Basic Industrial Statistics. Value added is valued at market prices. Number engaged in 1953 is the average of employment during the weeks including 31 March, 30 June, 30 September and 31 December; in 1957, it is the average of employment as at 28 February, 31 May, 31 August and 30 November.

## Le produit intérieur brut

Les estimations des dépenses imputées au produit intérieur brut, et des composantes du produit intérieur brut, ventilées suivant le secteur d'activité industrielle, sont reproduites au tableau 1. Les chiffres ont été tirés des données fournies par le Central Statistical Office, Port-of-Spain, en réponse au questionnaire de l'O.N.U. relatif aux comptes nationaux. Les estimations officielles et les détails concernant les sources et méthodes adoptées ont été publiés par le Central Statistical Office dans *The National Income of Trinidad and Tobago, 1951 to 1959*. Les mêmes estimations peuvent être trouvées dans *Annual Statistical Digest* sous une forme sommaire.

## Indices de l'emploi industriel

Les indices de l'emploi dans les activités industrielles sont reproduits au tableau 2. Ces indices sont élaborés d'après les chiffres absolus donnant le total des effectifs occupés dans les établissements employant 10 personnes ou plus, publiés dans l'*Annual Statistical Digest* par le Central Statistical Office. En 1956 et 1957 les chiffres annuels des effectifs occupés sont les moyennes arithmétiques du nombre de personnes occupées durant la dernière période de paie de février, mai, août et novembre. En 1958, le nombre annuel de personnes occupées est la moyenne arithmétique du nombre de personnes occupées durant la dernière période de paie de février et de novembre. Tandis que pour 1959 et les années ultérieures, le chiffre annuel relatif aux effectifs occupés est la moyenne arithmétique du nombre de personnes occupées durant la dernière période de paie de mai et de novembre.

## Caractéristiques et structure de l'activité industrielle

Le tableau 3 comporte des données tirées de la première et seconde enquêtes auprès des établissements industriels de Trinité et Tobago, relatives aux années 1953 et 1957 respectivement, couvrant les établissements industriels occupant 5 personnes ou plus. Les résultats de la première enquête ont été publiés par le Central Statistical Office dans *The Structure and Output of Industry — Report on a Census of Industrial Establishments, 1953,* Trinité 1956; et ceux de la seconde enquête dans *Industry 1957 — Report on the 1957 Survey of Industrial Establishments* (2 tomes), Trinité 1960.

Les définitions des rubriques sont conformes aux Normes internationales relatives aux statistiques industrielles de base. La valeur ajoutée est calculée aux prix du marché. Le nombre de personnes occupées en 1953 est la moyenne de l'emploi durant les semaines couvrant le 31 mars, le 30 septembre et le 31 décembre; en 1957 c'est la moyenne de l'emploi au 28 février, 31 mai, 31 août et 30 novembre.

## 1.  THE GROSS DOMESTIC PRODUCT — PRODUIT INTERIEUR BRUT

Million B.W.I. dollars                                                                 Millions de dollars des Antilles britanniques

### A.  Expenditure on the Gross Domestic Product at Market Prices
### Dépenses relatives au produit intérieur brut aux prix du marché

| Item of data and year<br>Rubrique et année | Total | Consumption<br>Consommation | | Gross Domestic Capital Formation<br>Formation brute de capital intérieur | | Net exports of goods and services<br>Exportations nettes de biens et de services | |
|---|---|---|---|---|---|---|---|
| | | Total | Government<br>Etat | Total | Fixed<br>Fixe | Exports<br>less imports<br>Exportations<br>moins<br>importations | Exports<br>Exportations |
| *a.  At Current Prices — Aux prix courants* | | | | | | | |
| Absolute figures — Chiffres absolus | | | | | | | |
| 1951................................... | 328.6 | 240.2 | 35.2 | 85.8 | 69.8 | 2.6 | 241.5 |
| 1952................................... | 358.9 | 273.0 | 42.4 | 94.5 | 74.8 | −8.6 | 257.7 |
| 1953................................... | 402.0 | 290.4 | 47.1 | 85.9 | 78.8 | 25.7 | 286.1 |
| 1954................................... | 430.6 | 322.9 | 54.2 | 91.7 | 84.4 | 16.0 | 292.7 |
| 1955................................... | 499.4 | 386.6 | 58.1 | 115.5 | 108.8 | −2.7 | 318.9 |
| 1956................................... | 581.8 | 417.9 | 64.0 | 125.5 | 120.8 | 38.4 | 370.6 |
| 1957................................... | 686.5 | 464.3 | 62.2 | 172.5 | 161.3 | 49.7 | 445.0 |
| 1958................................... | 752.8 | 531.0 | 72.0 | 196.0 | 184.6 | 25.8 | 479.9 |
| 1959................................... | 824.0 | 580.3 | 73.3 | 236.8 | 231.2 | 6.9 | 507.1 |
| Percentage distribution of average annual expenditure — Distribution en pourcentage des dépenses annuelles moyennes | | | | | | | |
| 1951 − 1959......................... | 100.0 | 71.2 | 9.4 | 28.0 | 26.1 | 0.8 | 64.9 |
| 1951................................... | 100.0 | 73.1 | 10.7 | 26.1 | 21.2 | 0.8 | 73.5 |
| 1953................................... | 100.0 | 72.2 | 11.7 | 21.4 | 19.6 | 6.4 | 71.2 |
| 1954................................... | 100.0 | 75.0 | 12.6 | 21.3 | 19.6 | 3.7 | 68.0 |
| 1958................................... | 100.0 | 70.6 | 9.6 | 26.0 | 24.5 | 3.4 | 63.7 |
| *b.  At Prices of 1951 — Aux prix de 1951* | | | | | | | |
| Absolute figures — Chiffres absolus | | | | | | | |
| 1951................................... | 328.6 | 240.2 | 35.2 | 85.8 | 69.8 | 2.6 | 241.5 |
| 1952................................... | 340.3 | 258.4 | 41.1 | 88.2 | 69.5 | −6.3 | 246.8 |
| 1953................................... | 349.0 | 269.4 | 43.9 | 75.4 | 68.8 | 4.2 | 265.4 |
| 1954................................... | 355.6 | 295.6 | 47.7 | 79.0 | 72.0 | −19.0 | 264.2 |
| 1955................................... | 405.6 | 336.0 | 46.6 | 99.9 | 93.6 | −30.3 | 286.0 |
| 1956................................... | 489.8 | 357.4 | 50.2 | 104.8 | 100.5 | 27.6 | 346.4 |
| 1957................................... | 533.4 | 380.3 | 46.3 | 144.0 | 133.4 | 9.1 | 375.8 |
| 1958.....:............................. | 576.3 | 430.4 | 51.4 | 154.8 | 144.7 | −8.9 | 427.3 |
| 1959................................... | 607.0 | 460.8 | 51.3 | 179.2 | 174.1 | −33.0 | 456.4 |
| Percentage distribution of average annual expenditure — Distribution en pourcentage des dépenses annuelles moyennes | | | | | | | |
| 1951 − 1959......................... | 100.0 | 74.9 | 9.2 | 28.3 | 26.1 | −3.2 | 74.6 |
| 1951................................... | 100.0 | 73.1 | 10.7 | 26.1 | 21.2 | 0.8 | 73.5 |
| 1953................................... | 100.0 | 77.2 | 12.6 | 21.6 | 19.7 | 1.2 | 70.7 |
| 1954................................... | 100.0 | 83.1 | 13.4 | 22.2 | 20.2 | −5.3 | 74.3 |
| 1958................................... | 100.0 | 74.7 | 8.9 | 26.8 | 25.1 | −1.5 | 74.1 |
| Average annual rate of growth — Taux annuel moyen d'accroissement | | | | | | | |
| 1951 − 1959......................... | 7.9 | 8.4 | 4.8 | 9.6 | 12.1 | . | 8.2 |
| 1951 − 1953......................... | 3.1 | 5.9 | 11.7 | −6.2 | −1.0 | . | 4.8 |
| 1954 − 1959......................... | 11.3 | 9.3 | 1.5 | 17.8 | 19.3 | . | 13.1 |

## B. The Gross Domestic Product at Factor Cost According to Origin
### Origine par secteur d'activité du produit intérieur brut au coût des facteurs

| Item of data and year<br>Rubrique et année | Total | Agricultural sector<br>Secteur agricole | Industrial Sector — Secteur Industriel | | | | | Transportation and communication<br>Transports et communications | Other sectors<br>Autres secteurs |
|---|---|---|---|---|---|---|---|---|---|
| | | | Total | Mining[1]<br>Industries extractives[1] | Manufacturing[2]<br>Industries manufacturières[2] | Construction[3]<br>Bâtiment et travaux publics[3] | Electricity and gas<br>Electricité et gaz | | |
| ISIC — CITI | 0–9 | 0 | 1–51 | 1 | 2–3 | 4 | 51 | 7 | 52, 6, 8–9 |

*a. At Current Prices — Aux prix courants*

| | | | | | | | | | |
|---|---|---|---|---|---|---|---|---|---|
| Absolute figures — Chiffres absolus | | | | | | | | | |
| 1951 | 308.3 | 53.5 | 148.9 | 95.6 | 43.4 | 8.4 | 1.5 | 17.8 | 88.1 |
| 1952 | 337.3 | 58.5 | 158.8 | 100.8 | 46.8 | 9.3 | 1.9 | 19.2 | 100.8 |
| 1953 | 379.6 | 67.0 | 185.1 | 123.5 | 50.8 | 8.1 | 2.7 | 19.6 | 107.9 |
| 1954 | 404.2 | 74.5 | 189.5 | 122.5 | 54.0 | 10.1 | 2.9 | 20.4 | 119.7 |
| 1955 | 469.0 | 81.0 | 216.3 | 141.5 | 57.1 | 14.1 | 3.6 | 24.4 | 147.3 |
| 1956 | 547.3 | 81.0 | 270.7 | 190.2 | 59.3 | 17.0 | 4.2 | 26.9 | 168.7 |
| 1957 | 649.5 | 90.0 | 343.7 | 240.7 | 77.0 | 20.7 | 5.3 | 29.9 | 185.9 |
| 1958 | 705.8 | 99.7 | 344.9 | 227.7 | 90.9 | 20.5 | 5.8 | 33.7 | 227.5 |
| 1959 | 775.4 | 96.6 | 405.4 | 259.4 | 102.8 | 36.3 | 6.9 | 35.8 | 237.6 |
| Percentage distribution according to sector — Distribution en pourcentage par secteur | | | | | | | | | |
| 1951 – 1959 | 100.0 | 15.3 | 49.5 | 32.8 | 12.7 | 3.2 | 0.8 | 5.0 | 30.2 |
| 1951 | 100.0 | 17.4 | 48.3 | 31.0 | 14.1 | 2.7 | 0.5 | 5.7 | 28.6 |
| 1953 | 100.0 | 17.6 | 48.8 | 32.6 | 13.4 | 2.1 | 0.7 | 5.2 | 28.4 |
| 1954 | 100.0 | 18.4 | 46.9 | 30.3 | 13.4 | 2.5 | 0.7 | 5.1 | 29.6 |
| 1958 | 100.0 | 14.1 | 48.9 | 32.3 | 12.9 | 2.9 | 0.8 | 4.8 | 32.2 |

[1] Includes petroleum refining.
[2] Excludes petroleum refining.
[3] Excludes own-account construction by general government.

[1] Y compris le raffinage du pétrole.
[2] Non compris le raffinage du pétrole.
[3] Non compris la construction pour compte propre par l'Etat.

## 2. INDEX NUMBERS OF INDUSTRIAL EMPLOYMENT
### INDICES DE L'EMPLOI DANS L'INDUSTRIE

### A. The Divisions of Industrial Activity
### Les branches de l'activité industrielle

| Period<br>Période | Total | Mining[1]<br>Industries extractives[1] | Manufacturing[2]<br>Industries manufacturières[2] | Construction<br>Bâtiment et travaux publics | Electricity<br>Electricité |
|---|---|---|---|---|---|
| ISIC — CITI | 1-3, 511 | 1,32 | 2-3 | 4 | 511 |

*a. Indexes — Indices (1958 = 100)*

| | | | | | |
|---|---|---|---|---|---|
| 1956 | 94 | 100 | 91 | 85 | 89 |
| 1957 | 99 | 100 | 95 | 112 | 88 |
| 1958 | 100 | 100 | 100 | 100 | 100 |
| 1959 | 103 | 95 | 104 | 130 | 116 |
| 1960 | 105 | 92 | 110 | 130 | 141 |
| 1961 | 97 | 86 | 104 | 98 | 167 |

*b. Average Annual Rate of Change — Taux annuel moyen de variation*

| | | | | | |
|---|---|---|---|---|---|
| 1956 – 1960 | 2.8 | −2.1 | 4.9 | 11.2 | 12.2 |
| 1958 – 1960 | 2.5 | −4.1 | 4.9 | 14.0 | 18.7 |

For footnotes see end of table.

### B. The Major Groups of Mining
### Les classes de la branche Industries extractives

| Period<br>Période | All mining[1]<br>Toutes industries extractives[1] | Crude petroleum and natural gas[1]<br>Pétrole brut et gaz naturel[1] | Other mining<br>Autres industries extractives |
|---|---|---|---|
| ISIC — CITI | 1, 32 | 13, 32 | 14-19 |

*a. Indexes — Indices (1958 = 100)*

| | | | |
|---|---|---|---|
| 1956 | 100 | 101 | 99 |
| 1957 | 100 | 102 | 71 |
| 1958 | 100 | 100 | 100 |
| 1959 | 95 | 96 | 90 |
| 1960 | 92 | 92 | 81 |
| 1961 | 86 | 88 | 70 |

*b. Average Annual Rate of Change — Taux annuel moyen de variation*

| | | | |
|---|---|---|---|
| 1956 – 1960 | −2.1 | −2.3 | −4.9 |
| 1958 – 1960 | −4.1 | −4.1 | −10.0 |

Pour les notes, voir au bas du tableau.

## C. Selected Major Groups of Manufacturing

## Quelques classes de la branche Industries manufacturières

| Period<br>Période | Manu-<br>facturing [2]<br>Industries<br>manufac-<br>turières [2] | Food,<br>beverages<br>and<br>tobacco<br>Industries<br>alimen-<br>taires,<br>boissons,<br>tabac | Clothing,<br>footwear,<br>made-up<br>textiles,<br>leather and<br>leather<br>products<br>Articles<br>d'habil-<br>lement,<br>chaussures,<br>ouvrages<br>en tissu,<br>cuir et<br>articles<br>en cuir | Wood<br>products<br>and<br>furniture<br>Bois et<br>meubles | Printing<br>and<br>publishing<br>Im-<br>primerie<br>et<br>édition | Chemicals<br>and<br>chemical<br>products<br>Produits<br>chimiques | Non-<br>metallic<br>mineral<br>products<br>Produits<br>minéraux<br>non<br>métal-<br>liques | Metal<br>products<br>Ouvrages<br>en<br>métaux | Other<br>manu-<br>facturing<br>Autres<br>industries<br>manufac-<br>turières |
|---|---|---|---|---|---|---|---|---|---|
| ISIC — CITI | 2–3 | 20–22 | 24, 29 | 25–26 | 28 | 31 | 33 | 36–38 | 39 |

### a. Indexes — Indices (1958 = 100)

| | | | | | | | | | |
|---|---|---|---|---|---|---|---|---|---|
| 1956.............. | 91 | 111 | 64 | 73 | 79 | 119 | 68 | 76 | 68 |
| 1957.............. | 95 | 99 | 98 | 83 | 85 | 130 | 89 | 97 | 85 |
| 1958.............. | 100 | 100 | 100 | 100 | 100 | 100 | 100 | 100 | 100 |
| 1959.............. | 104 | 104 | 102 | 94 | 100 | 142 | 111 | 114 | 116 |
| 1960.............. | 110 | 111 | 102 | 90 | 94 | 193 | 126 | 115 | 113 |
| 1961.............. | 104 | 106 | 106 | 78 | 84 | 183 | 103 | 115 | 80 |

### b. Average Annual Rate of Change — Taux annuel moyen de variation

| | | | | | | | | | |
|---|---|---|---|---|---|---|---|---|---|
| 1956 – 1960........ | 4.9 | — | 12.4 | 5.4 | 4.4 | 12.9 | 16.7 | 10.9 | 13.5 |
| 1958 – 1960........ | 4.9 | 5.4 | 1.0 | −5.1 | −3.0 | 38.9 | 12.2 | 7.2 | 6.3 |

[1] Refining of petroleum (Part of ISIC major group 32) is included under Crude petroleum and natural gas (ISIC major group 13).
[2] Excludes Paper and paper products (ISIC major group 27) and Rubber products (ISIC major group 30).

[1] Le raffinage du pétrole (dans CITI 32) est compris dans Pétrole brut et gaz naturel. (CITI 13).
[2] Non compris Papier et ouvrages en papier (CITI 27) et Ouvrages en caoutchouc (CITI 30).

## 3. CHARACTERISTICS OF ESTABLISHMENTS EMPLOYING 5 OR MORE PERSONS

## CARACTERISTIQUES DES ETABLISSEMENTS EMPLOYANT 5 PERSONNES OU PLUS
### 1953, 1957

Number of establishments in units; value added and wages and salaries in million B.W.I. Dollars; number of engaged in thousands; value added per engaged in thousand B.W.I. Dollars.

Nombre d'établissements en unités; valeur ajoutée et traitements et salaires en millions de dollars des Antilles britanniques; nombre de personnes occupées en milliers; valeur ajoutée par personne occupée en milliers de dollars des Antilles britanniques.

## A. The Divisions of Industrial Activity — Les branches de l'activité industrielle

| Year and<br>item of data | All<br>industrial<br>activity<br>Toutes<br>industries | Mining [1]<br>Industries<br>ex-<br>tractives [1] | Manu-<br>facturing [2]<br>Industries<br>manufac-<br>turières [2] | Con-<br>struction<br>Bâtiment<br>et travaux<br>publics | Electricity<br>and water<br>Electricité<br>et eau | Année et rubrique | Year and<br>item of data | All<br>industrial<br>activity<br>Toutes<br>industries | Mining [1]<br>Industries<br>ex-<br>tractives [1] | Manu-<br>facturing [2]<br>Industries<br>manufac-<br>turières [2] | Con-<br>struction<br>Bâtiment<br>et travaux<br>publics | Electricity<br>and water<br>Electricité<br>et eau | Année et rubrique |
|---|---|---|---|---|---|---|---|---|---|---|---|---|---|
| ISIC | 1-4, 511,521 | 1 | 2–3 | 4 | 511,521 | CITI | ISIC | 1-4, 511,521 | 1 | 2–3 | 4 | 511,521 | CITI |
| | a. Absolute Figures — Chiffres absolus | | | | | | | b. Structure | | | | | |
| **1953**<br>Number of establishments... | 537 | 60 | 384 | 83 | 10 | 1953<br>Nombre d'établissements | 1953<br>Distribution in percent of: | | | | | | 1953<br>Distribution en pourcentage: |
| Value added....... | 186.4 | 140.1 | 32.0 | 9.8 | 4.5 | Valeur ajoutée | Value added..... | 100.0 | 75.1 | 17.2 | 5.2 | 2.5 | Valeur ajoutée |
| Number of engaged (Average during the year)....... | 43.4 | 16.9 | 14.6 | 9.2 | 2.7 | Nombre de personnes occupées (moyenne pendant l'année) | Number of engaged........ | 100.0 | 38.9 | 33.6 | 21.2 | 6.3 | Nombre de personnes occupées |
| Wages and salaries. | 56.1 | 30.7 | 14.3 | 8.0 | 3.1 | Traitements et salaires | Value added per person engaged.. | 4.3 | 8.3 | 2.2 | 1.1 | 1.7 | Valeur ajoutée par personne occupée |
| | | | | | | | Value added per unit of wages and salaries..... | 3.32 | 4.56 | 2.24 | 1.22 | 1.45 | Valeur ajoutée par unité de traitements et salaires |
| **1957**<br>Number of establishments... | 575 | 54 | 419 | 92 | 10 | 1957<br>Nombre d'établissements | 1957<br>Distribution in percent of: | | | | | | 1957<br>Distribution en pourcentage: |
| Value added....... | 291.1 | 207.5 | 57.8 | 18.2 | 7.6 | Valeur ajoutée | Value added..... | 100.0 | 71.2 | 19.9 | 6.2 | 2.7 | Valeur ajoutée |
| Number of engaged (Average during the year)....... | 53.2 | 17.8 | 18.3 | 14.3 | 2.8 | Nombre de personnes occupées (moyenne pendant l'année) | Number of engaged........ | 100.0 | 33.4 | 34.4 | 26.9 | 5.3 | Nombre de personnes occupées |
| Wages and salaries. | 80.0 | 40.0 | 21.6 | 14.3 | 4.1 | Traitements et salaires | Value added per person engaged.. | 5.5 | 11.6 | 3.2 | 1.3 | 2.7 | Valeur ajoutée par personne occupée |
| | | | | | | | Value added per unit of wages and salaries..... | 3.64 | 5.19 | 2.68 | 1.27 | 1.85 | Valeur ajoutée par unité de traitements et salaires |

For footnotes see end of table.

Pour les notes, voir au bas du tableau.

## B. The Major Groups of Manufacturing
## Les classes de la branche Industries manufacturières

| Year and item of data | Manufacturing [2] Industries manufacturières [2] | Food beverages and tobacco Industries alimentaires, boissons, tabac | Textiles [3] | Clothing, footwear and made-up textiles [3] Articles d'habillement, chaussures et ouvrages en tissu [3] | Wood products and furniture Bois et meubles | Printing and publishing Imprimerie et édition | Chemicals and chemical products [4] Produits chimiques [4] | Non-metallic mineral products Produits minéraux non métalliques | Metal products Ouvrages en métaux | Année et rubrique |
|---|---|---|---|---|---|---|---|---|---|---|
| ISIC | 2–3 | 20–22 | 23 | 24 | 25–26 | 28 | 27, 29–31, 39 | 33 | 35–38 | CITI |
| *a. Absolute Figures — Chiffres absolus* | | | | | | | | | | |
| **1953** | | | | | | | | | | **1953** |
| Number of establishments | 384 | 116 | 6 | 32 | 84 | 20 | 42 | 6 | 78 | Nombre d'établissements |
| Value added | 32.0 | 18.4 | 0.9 | 1.4 | 1.6 | 1.9 | 2.3 | 0.7 | 4.8 | Valeur ajoutée |
| Number of engaged (Average during the year) | 14.6 | 6.7 | 0.4 | 1.0 | 1.5 | 1.1 | 1.0 | 0.3 | 2.6 | Nombre de personnes occupées (moyenne pendant l'année) |
| Wages and salaries | 14.3 | 6.9 | 0.3 | 0.6 | 1.1 | 1.2 | 1.0 | 0.4 | 2.8 | Traitements et salaires |
| **1957** | | | | | | | | | | **1957** |
| Number of establishments | 419 | 106 | 17 | 44 | 88 | 24 | 54 | 11 | 75 | Nombre d'établissements |
| Value added | 57.8 | 26.9 | 1.4 | 1.7 | 2.0 | 3.3 | 12.0 | 5.0 | 5.5 | Valeur ajoutée |
| Number of engaged (Average during the year) | 18.3 | 7.6 | 0.8 | 1.2 | 1.6 | 1.6 | 1.5 | 1.0 | 3.0 | Nombre de personnes occupées (moyenne pendant l'année) |
| Wages and salaries | 21.6 | 9.3 | 0.6 | 0.8 | 1.4 | 2.0 | 1.8 | 1.6 | 4.1 | Traitements et salaires |
| *b. Structure* | | | | | | | | | | |
| **1953** | | | | | | | | | | **1953** |
| Distribution in percent of: | | | | | | | | | | Distribution en pourcentage: |
| Value added | 100.0 | 57.5 | 2.8 | 4.3 | 5.0 | 6.0 | 7.2 | 2.2 | 15.0 | Valeur ajoutée |
| Number of engaged | 100.0 | 45.8 | 2.8 | 6.8 | 10.3 | 7.5 | 6.9 | 2.0 | 17.9 | Nombre de personnes occupées |
| Value added per person engaged | 2.2 | 2.7 | 2.2 | 1.4 | 1.1 | 1.7 | 2.3 | 2.3 | 1.8 | Valeur ajoutée par personne occupée |
| Value added per unit of wages and salaries | 2.24 | 2.67 | 3.00 | 2.33 | 1.45 | 1.58 | 2.30 | 1.75 | 1.71 | Valeur ajoutée par unité de traitements et salaires |
| **1957** | | | | | | | | | | **1957** |
| Distribution in percent of: | | | | | | | | | | Distribution en pourcentage: |
| Value added | 100.0 | 46.5 | 2.4 | 3.0 | 3.4 | 5.7 | 20.8 | 8.6 | 9.6 | Valeur ajoutée |
| Number of engaged | 100.0 | 41.5 | 4.4 | 6.5 | 8.8 | 8.7 | 8.2 | 5.5 | 16.4 | Nombre de personnes occupées |
| Value added per person engaged | 3.2 | 3.5 | 1.8 | 1.4 | 1.2 | 2.1 | 8.0 | 5.0 | 1.8 | Valeur ajoutée par personne occupée |
| Value added per unit of wages and salaries | 2.68 | 2.89 | 2.33 | 2.12 | 1.43 | 1.65 | 6.67 | 3.12 | 1.34 | Valeur ajoutée par unité de traitements et salaires |

[1] Includes petroleum refining.
[2] Excludes petroleum refining.
[3] Includes the manufacture of hats and shoes which under the ISIC is in major group 24.
[4] Includes Paper and paper products (ISIC major group 27), Leather and leather products (ISIC major group 29), Rubber and rubber products (ISIC major group 30) and Other manufacturing (ISIC major group 39).

[1] Y compris le raffinage du pétrole.
[2] Non compris le raffinage du pétrole.
[3] Y compris la fabrication des chapeaux et chaussures, qui appartient à la classe 24 de la CITI.
[4] Y compris Papier et ouvrages en papier (CITI 27), Cuir et articles et cuir (CITI 29), Caoutchouc et ouvrages en caoutchouc (CITI 30) et Autres industries manufacturières (CITI 39).

# TUNISIA — TUNISIE

## Gross Domestic Product

Estimates of expenditure on and industrial origin of the Gross domestic product are shown in Table 1. These data were abstracted from *Perspectives décennales de développement 1962-1971* and *l'Economie de la Tunisie en chiffres 1961,* published by the Secrétariat d'Etat au plan et aux finances, Tunis.

## Index Numbers of Industrial Production

The index numbers set out in Table 2 are derived from indexes of industrial production computed by the Service tunisien de statistique and published in *Indices de la production minière,* December 1961. The index numbers are computed as base weighted arithmetic averages from series of relatives based on quantities produced for the four principal minerals (phosphate rock, iron ore, lead ore and zinc ore). It should be noted that these minerals accounted for about 90 per cent of the gross value of mineral production in 1956. The relatives are combined into indexes for three principal groups of minerals and the resulting indexes are combined into index numbers for mining as a whole. In computing these indexes, the Service tunisien de statistique has utilized as weights the figures of value added during 1957, derived from the Census of Industrial Production for that year.

## Index Numbers of Industrial Employment

The index numbers set out in Table 3 were computed by the Statistical Office of the United Nations from absolute figures of employment. In the case of mining, these figures were abstracted from *Bulletin de Statistique et d'Etudes Economiques,* issued by the Service tunisien de statistique; and in the case of manufacturing and electricity, gas and water, the figures are from the annual industrial censuses published in *Recensement des Activités Industrielles,* étude No. 3, described below.

The annual absolute figures of the number of operatives for mining are the arithmetic averages of the number as on the last working day of each month. The absolute figures for manufacturing employment relate to the number of persons engaged as of 31 December of each year in establishments covered in the industrial censuses.

## The Characteristics and Structure of Industrial Activity

The figures shown in Table 4 are derived from 1958 Census of Industrial Activity. The census covered, in

## Produit intérieur brut

Le tableau 1 contient des estimations des dépenses imputées au produit intérieur brut et des estimations du produit intérieur brut par branche d'activité d'origine. Ces données ont été tirées de *Perspectives décennales de développement 1962-1971* et de l'*Economie de la Tunisie en chiffres 1961,* publiés par le Secrétariat d'Etat au plan et aux finances, Tunis.

## Indices de la production industrielle

Les indices du tableau 1 sont tirés d'indices de la production industrielle établis par le Service tunisien de statistique et publiés dans *Indices de la production minière,* décembre 1961. Ces indices sont des moyennes arithmétiques à pondération fixe de séries de rapports fondés sur le volume de la production des quatre principaux minéraux extraits en Tunisie (phosphate naturel et minerais de fer, de plomb et de zinc). Il y a lieu de noter que la production de ces minéraux représentait 90 p. 100 environ de la valeur brute des minéraux extraits en 1956. Les rapports sont combinés en indices relatifs à trois principaux groupes de minéraux et les indices ainsi obtenus en indices concernant l'ensemble des industries extractives. Pour calculer ces indices, le Service tunisien de statistique a utilisé comme coefficients de pondération les chiffres de la valeur ajoutée en 1957, qu'il a tirés des résultats du recensement de la production industrielle de 1957.

## Indices de l'emploi dans l'industrie

Les indices du tableau 3 ont été calculés par le Bureau de statistique de l'ONU à partir de chiffres absolus de l'emploi. Pour les industries extractives, ces chiffres ont été tirés du *Bulletin de statistique et d'études économiques,* publié par le Service tunisien de statistique. Pour les industries manufacturières et les industries de l'électricité, du gaz et de l'eau, les chiffres ont été tirés des résultats des recensements industriels annuels décrits ci-dessous; ces résultats ont été publiés dans *Recensement des activités industrielles,* étude No 3.

Les chiffres absolus annuels concernant le nombre d'ouvriers employés dans les industries extractives sont les moyennes arithmétiques des nombres relevés à la fin de chaque mois. Les chiffres absolus de l'emploi dans les industries manufacturières représentent le nombre de personnes occupées, au 31 décembre de chaque année, dans les établissements recensés.

## Caractéristiques et structure de l'activité industrielle

Les chiffres du tableau 4 sont tirés des résultats du recensement des activités industrielles de 1958. Le recense-

principle, all industrial establishments, irrespective of size. However, in the case of certain industries, such as stone and sand quarrying, olive oil extraction, textiles, clothing and made-up textile goods, footwear manufacturing, wood products and furniture, complete questionnaires were not received from all establishments, and therefore the Service tunisien de statistique did not publish figures for these kinds of industrial activity.

The data on the number of engaged and of employees are as of 31 December 1958; both sets of figures cover seasonal workers (computed by dividing the number of man-days worked by these workers by 300). The data on wages and salaries includes withdrawals by working proprietors, which are treated as wages and salaries. Receipts from goods sold without transformation by the covered establishments are excluded from the figures of gross value of production.

ment portait, en principe, sur tous les établissements industriels, quelle que fût leur dimension. Cependant, dans le cas de certaines industries — notamment les industries extractives de pierre à bâtir et de sable, les industries s'occupant de l'extraction de l'huile d'olive, l'industrie textile, les industries fabriquant des articles d'habillement et des ouvrages en tissu, l'industrie des chaussures et l'industrie du bois et du meuble — tous les établissements n'ont pas répondu au questionnaire; le Service tunisien de statistique n'a donc pas publié de chiffres pour ces types d'activité industrielle.

Les données relatives au nombre de personnes occupées et de salariés sont relevées au 31 décembre 1958; les deux ensembles de chiffres comprennent le nombre des travailleurs saisonniers (que l'on a obtenu en divisant par 300 le nombre de journées de travail de ces travailleurs). Les données relatives aux traitements et salaires comprennent les sommes versées aux propriétaires qui travaillent, lesquelles sont considérées comme des traitements et salaires. Les recettes provenant de la vente de marchandises en l'état ne sont pas comprises dans les chiffres concernant la valeur brute de la production.

## 1. THE GROSS DOMESTIC PRODUCT AND GROSS DOMESTIC FIXED CAPITAL FORMATION
## LE PRODUIT INTERIEUR BRUT ET LA FORMATION BRUTE DE CAPITAL FIXE INTERIEUR

Million Dinars          Millions de dinars

### A. Expenditure on the Gross Domestic Product at Market Prices
### Dépenses relatives au produit intérieur brut aux prix du marché

| Item of data and year / Rubrique et année | Total | Total consumption / Consommation totale | Fixed capital formation / Formation de capital fixe | Net exports of goods and services / Exportations nettes de biens et de services | |
|---|---|---|---|---|---|
| | | | | Exports less imports / Exportations moins importations | Exports / Exportations |
| At Prices of 1957 — Aux prix de 1957 | | | | | |
| **Absolute figures — Chiffres absolus** | | | | | |
| 1950 | 204.2 | 168.5 | 42.0 | −6.3 | 57.6 |
| 1951 | 206.3 | 184.4 | 44.3 | −22.4 | 43.5 |
| 1952 | 231.8 | 212.3 | 39.9 | −20.4 | 42.3 |
| 1953 | 240.5 | 220.2 | 40.3 | −20.0 | 43.9 |
| 1954 | 245.7 | 220.7 | 36.0 | −11.0 | 53.6 |
| 1955 | 233.2 | 225.0 | 35.3 | −27.1 | 42.6 |
| 1956 | 248.7 | 253.4 | 28.5 | −33.2 | 39.6 |
| 1957 | 238.5 | 230.6 | 23.3 | −15.2 | 53.2 |
| 1958 | 269.5 | 250.7 | 27.8 | −9.0 | 57.5 |
| 1959 | 258.2 | 237.4 | 31.6 | −10.8 | 62.0 |
| 1960 | 290.1 | 269.4 | 45.7 | −25.0 | 51.0 |
| 1961 | 279.5 | 278.5 | 53.0 | −52.1 | 41.0 |
| **Percentage distribution of average annual expenditure — Distribution en pourcentage des dépenses annuelles moyennes** | | | | | |
| 1950−1960 | 100.0 | 92.7 | 14.8 | −7.5 | 20.5 |
| 1950 | 100.0 | 82.5 | 20.6 | −3.1 | 28.2 |
| 1953 | 100.0 | 91.6 | 16.7 | −8.3 | 18.3 |
| 1954 | 100.0 | 89.8 | 14.7 | −4.5 | 21.8 |
| 1958 | 100.0 | 93.0 | 10.3 | −3.3 | 21.3 |
| 1960 | 100.0 | 92.9 | 15.7 | −8.6 | 17.6 |
| **Average annual rate of growth — Taux annuel moyen d'accroissement** | | | | | |
| 1950−1960 | 3.6 | 4.8 | 0.8 | . | −1.2 |
| 1950−1953 | 5.6 | 9.3 | −1.4 | . | −8.7 |
| 1954−1958 | 2.4 | 3.2 | −6.3 | . | 1.8 |
| 1958−1960 | 3.7 | 3.7 | 28.2 | . | −5.8 |

## B. The Gross Domestic Product at Factor Cost According to Origin
### Origine par secteur d'activité du produit intérieur brut au coût des facteurs

| Item of data and year<br>Rubrique et année | Total | Agricultural sector<br>Secteur agricole | Industrial Sector — Secteur industriel | | | | | Transportation and communication<br>Transports et communications | Other sectors<br>Autres secteurs |
|---|---|---|---|---|---|---|---|---|---|
| | | | Total | Mining<br>Industries extractives | Manufacturing<br>Industries manufacturières | Construction<br>Bâtiments et travaux publics | Electricity, gas and water<br>Electricité, gaz et eau | | |
| ISIC — CITI | 0–9 | 0 | 1–5 | 1 | 2–3 | 4 | 5 | 7 | 6, 8–9 |
| At Prices of 1957 — Aux prix de 1957 | | | | | | | | | |
| **Absolute figures — Chiffres absolus** | | | | | | | | | |
| 1950 | 174.9 | 60.2 | 40.6 | 6.8 | 19.2 | 12.3 | 2.3 | 13.8 | 60.3 |
| 1951 | 173.6 | 51.7 | 43.3 | 7.9 | 18.9 | 13.9 | 2.6 | 16.0 | 62.6 |
| 1952 | 195.9 | 68.9 | 44.1 | 9.7 | 19.3 | 12.4 | 2.7 | 14.6 | 68.3 |
| 1953 | 200.4 | 73.0 | 42.8 | 8.4 | 19.3 | 12.4 | 2.7 | 14.6 | 70.0 |
| 1954 | 204.3 | 69.9 | 45.2 | 8.6 | 21.2 | 12.0 | 3.4 | 16.0 | 73.2 |
| 1955 | 190.1 | 54.1 | 46.9 | 9.5 | 21.5 | 12.2 | 3.7 | 17.0 | 72.1 |
| 1956 | 227.1 | 75.4 | 59.8 | 9.2 | 23.4 | 23.4 | 3.8 | 17.1 | 74.8 |
| 1957 | 201.4 | 68.4 | 44.0 | 9.1 | 23.8 | 7.1 | 4.0 | 17.4 | 71.6 |
| 1958 | 233.1 | 90.6 | 49.0 | 9.3 | 26.5 | 9.3 | 3.9 | 17.7 | 75.8 |
| 1959 | 219.5 | 77.4 | 47.2 | 8.5 | 24.3 | 10.4 | 4.0 | 17.9 | 77.0 |
| 1960 | 250.7 | 84.6 | 57.3 | 8.7 | 30.4 | 13.8 | 4.4 | 19.6 | 89.2 |
| 1961 | 236.4 | 57.5 | 62.6 | 7.9 | 33.3 | 16.9 | 4.5 | 19.3 | 97.0 |
| **Percentage distribution according to sector— Distribution en pourcentage par secteur** | | | | | | | | | |
| 1950–1960 | 100.0 | 34.1 | 22.9 | 4.2 | 10.9 | 6.1 | 1.6 | 8.1 | 35.0 |
| 1950 | 100.0 | 34.4 | 23.2 | 3.9 | 11.0 | 7.0 | 1.3 | 7.9 | 34.5 |
| 1953 | 100.0 | 36.4 | 21.4 | 4.2 | 9.6 | 6.2 | 1.4 | 7.3 | 34.9 |
| 1954 | 100.0 | 34.2 | 22.1 | 4.2 | 10.4 | 5.9 | 1.6 | 7.9 | 35.8 |
| 1958 | 100·0 | 38.9 | 21.0 | 4.0 | 11.4 | 3.9 | 1.7 | 7.6 | 32.5 |
| 1960 | 100.0 | 33.7 | 22.9 | 3.5 | 12.1 | 5.5 | 1.8 | 7.8 | 35.6 |
| **Average annual rate of growth—Taux annuel moyen d'accroissement** | | | | | | | | | |
| 1950–1960 | 3.5 | 3.5 | 3.5 | 2.4 | 4.7 | 3.2 | 6.7 | 3.5 | 4.0 |
| 1950–1953 | 4.6 | 6.6 | 1.8 | 7.3 | 0.2 | 0.3 | 5.5 | 1.9 | 5.1 |
| 1954–1958 | 3.4 | 6.7 | 2.0 | 2.0 | 5.7 | −6.2 | 3.5 | 3.8 | 0.9 |
| 1958–1960 | 3.7 | −3.4 | 8.1 | −3.3 | 7.1 | 21.8 | 6.2 | 5.2 | 8.5 |

## 2. INDEX NUMBERS OF MINING PRODUCTION — INDICES DE LA PRODUCTION MINIERE

| Period<br>Période | All mining<br>Toutes industries extractives | Metal mining<br>Extraction des minerais métalliques | Other mining<br>Autres industries extractives |
|---|---|---|---|
| ISIC — CITI | 1 | 12 | 14–19 |
| a. Indexes — Indices (1958 – 100) | | | |
| 1955 | 104 | 112 | 97 |
| 1956 | 100 | 110 | 92 |
| 1957 | 98 | 106 | 91 |
| 1958 | 100 | 100 | 100 |
| 1959 | 91 | 87 | 96 |
| 1960 | 91 | 90 | 93 |
| 1961 | 82 | 78 | 87 |
| b. Average Annual Rate of Change — Taux annuel moyen de variation | | | |
| 1955–1958 | −1.3 | −3.7 | 1.0 |
| 1958–1960 | −4.6 | −5.1 | −3.6 |

## 3. INDEX NUMBERS OF INDUSTRIAL EMPLOYMENT — INDICES DE L'EMPLOI DANS L'INDUSTRIE

### A. The Major Groups of Mining

### Les classes de la branche Industries extractives

| Period<br>Période | All mining<br>Toutes industries extractives | Metal mining<br>Extraction des minerais métalliques | Other mining<br>Autres industries extractives |
|---|---|---|---|
| ISIC — CITI | 1 | 12 | 14–19 |

#### a. Indexes — Indices (1958 = 100)

| | | | |
|---|---|---|---|
| 1955............. | 106 | 124 | 97 |
| 1956............. | 108 | 120 | 102 |
| 1957............. | 106 | 112 | 102 |
| 1958............. | 100 | 100 | 100 |
| 1959............. | 95 | 88 | 98 |
| 1960............. | 90 | 82 | 94 |
| 1961............. | 86 | 82 | 89 |

#### b. Average Annual Rate of Change — Taux annuel moyen de variation

| | | | |
|---|---|---|---|
| 1955 – 1958...... | −2.0 | −6.9 | 1.0 |
| 1958 – 1960...... | −5.1 | −9.4 | −3.0 |

### B. Selected Major Groups of Manufacturing and Electricity, gas and water

### Quelques classes de la branche Industries manufacturières et electricité, gaz et eau

| Period<br>Période | Manufacturing [1]<br>Industries manufacturières [1] | Food, beverages and tobacco<br>Industries alimentaires, boissons, tabac | Wood products and furniture<br>Bois et meubles | Paper and paper products<br>Papier et ouvrages en papier | Printing and publishing<br>Imprimerie et édition | Leather and leather products except wearing apparel<br>Cuir et articles en cuir, à l'exclusion des articles d'habillement | Chemicals and chemical, petroleum and coal products<br>Produits chimiques et dérivés du pétrole et du charbon | Non-metallic mineral products<br>Produits minéraux non métalliques | Other manufacturing [2]<br>Autres industries manufacturières [2] | Electricity, gas and water<br>Electricité gaz et eau |
|---|---|---|---|---|---|---|---|---|---|---|
| ISIC — CITI | 2–3 | 20–22 | 25–26 | 27 | 28 | 29 | 31–32 | 33 | 30, 34–39 | 511–512, 521 |

#### a. Indexes — Indices (1958 = 100)

| | | | | | | | | | | |
|---|---|---|---|---|---|---|---|---|---|---|
| 1957............. | 109 | 98 | 102 | 87 | 97 | 84 | 95 | 105 | 109 | 104 |
| 1958............. | 100 | 100 | 100 | 100 | 100 | 100 | 100 | 100 | 100 | 100 |
| 1959............. | 102 | 105 | 106 | 102 | 100 | 169 | 103 | 106 | 102 | 105 |
| 1960............. | 130 | 111 | 103 | 108 | 109 | 203 | 111 | 147 | 130 | 113 |

#### b. Average Annual Rate of Change — Taux annuel moyen de variation

| | | | | | | | | | | |
|---|---|---|---|---|---|---|---|---|---|---|
| 1958 – 1960...... | 14.0 | 5.4 | 1.5 | 3.9 | 4.4 | 42.5 | 5.4 | 21.2 | 14.0 | 12.7 |

[1] Excludes Textiles (ISIC major group 23) and Clothing, footwear and made-up textiles (ISIC major group 24) and Furniture manufacturing (ISIC major group 26).
[2] Includes Rubber products (ISIC major group 30), Basic metals (ISIC major group 34) and Metal products (ISIC major groups 35–38).

[1] Non compris Industrie textile (CITI classe 23), Articles d'habillement, chaussures et ouvrages en tissu (CITI classe 24) et Industrie du meuble (CITI classe 26).
[2] Y compris Ouvrages en caoutchouc (CITI classe 30), Métallurgie de base (CITI classe 34) et Ouvrages en métaux (CITI classes 35–38).

# 4. CHARACTERISTICS OF ALL INDUSTRIAL ESTABLISHMENTS
## CARACTERISTIQUES DE TOUS LES ETABLISSEMENTS INDUSTRIELS
### 1958

Number of establishments, number of engaged and number of employees in units; gross value of production and wages and salaries in thousand Dinars.

Nombre d'établissements, nombre de personnes occupées et nombre de salariés en unités; valeur brute de la production et traitements et salaires en milliers de dinars

## A. Selected Divisions of Industrial Activity
### Quelques branches de l'activité industrielle

| Item of data | Total | Mining [1] Industries extrac- tives [1] | Manu- facturing [2] Industries manufac- turières [2] | Electricity, gas and water Electricité, gaz et eau | Rubrique |
|---|---|---|---|---|---|
| ISIC | 1-3,511-512 521 | 1 | 2-3 | 511-512 521 | CITI |
| 1958 Number of establishments. | 486 | 17 | 460 | 9 | 1958 Nombre d'établissements |
| Gross value of production.. | 65 609 | 11 897 | 47 726 | 5 986 | Valeur brute de la production |
| Number of engaged (as of 31.XII)............. | 28 283 | 13 463 | 12 865 | 1 955 | Nombre de personnes occupées (au 31.XII) |
| Employees: Number (as of 31.XII)... | 27 756 | 13 663 | 12 207 | 1 886 | Salariés: Nombre (au 31.XII) |
| Wages and salaries...... | 8 650 | 3 787 | 3 814 | 1 049 | Traitements et salaires |
| Distribution in percent of number of engaged....... | 100.0 | 47.6 | 45.5 | 6.9 | Distribution en pourcentage du nombre de personnes occupées |

For footnotes see end of the table.

Pour les notes, voir au bas du tableau.

## B. Selected Major Groups of Mining
### Quelques classes de la branche Industries extractives

| Item of data | All mining Toutes industries extrac- tives | Metal mining Extraction des minerais métal- liques | Other mining [3] Divers [3] | Rubrique |
|---|---|---|---|---|
| ISIC | 1 | 12 | 14-19 | CITI |
| Number of establishments...... | 17 | 14 | 3 | Nombre d'établissements |
| Gross value of production....... | 11 897 | 6 698 | 5 199 | Valeur brute de la production |
| Number of engaged (as of 31.XII)............... | 13 463 | 4 967 | 8 496 | Nombre de personnes occupées (au 31.XII) |
| Employees: Number (as of 31.XII)........ | 13 363 | 4 913 | 8 450 | Salariés: Nombre (au 31.XII) |
| Wages and salaries.......... | 3 787 | 1 417 | 2 370 | Traitements et salaires |
| Distribution in percent of number of engaged.......... | 100.0 | 36.9 | 63.1 | Distribution en pourcentage du nombre de personnes occupées |

For footnotes see end of the table.

Pour les notes, voir au bas du tableau.

## C. Selected Major Groups of Manufacturing
## Quelques classes de la branche Industries manufacturières

| Item of data | Manu-facturing [2] Industries manufac-turières [2] | Food, beverages and tobacco Industries alimen-taires, boissons, tabac | Wood products [5] Bois [5] | Paper and paper products Papier et ouvrages en papier | Printing and publish-ing Im-primerie et édition | Leather and leather products except wearing apparel Cuir et articles en cuir, à l'exclu-sion des articles d'habil-lement | Chemicals and chemical, petroleum and coal products Produits chi-miques et dérivés du pétrole et du charbon | Non-metallic mineral products Produits minéraux non métal-liques | Basic metals and metal products Métal-lurgie de base et ouvrages en métaux | Other manu-factur-ing [4] Autres in-dustries manufac-turières [4] | Rubrique |
|---|---|---|---|---|---|---|---|---|---|---|---|
| ISIC | 2–3 | 20–22 | 25 | 27 | 28 | 29 | 31–32 | 33 | 34–38 | 30, 39 | CITI |
| Number of establishments. | 460 | 164 | 8 | 11 | 60 | 5 | 80 | 98 | 18 | 16 | Nombre d'établissements |
| Gross value of production.......... | 47 726 | 30 554 | 542 | 730 | 879 | 129 | 7 673 | 3 939 | 3 143 | 137 | Valeur brute de la production |
| Number of engaged (as of 31.XII)........ | 12 865 | 5 686 | 320 | 298 | 719 | 107 | 2 711 | 1 954 | 966 | 104 | Nombre de personnes occupées (au 31.XII) |
| Employees: | | | | | | | | | | | Salariés: |
| Number (as of 31.XII). | 12 207 | 5 437 | 307 | 275 | 633 | 971 | 2 606 | 1 833 | 932 | 87 | Nombre (au 31.XII) |
| Wages and salaries... | 3 814 | 1 610 | 43 | 91 | 246 | 10 | 931 | 540 | 312 | 31 | Traitements et salaires |
| Distribution in percent of number of engaged. | 100.0 | 44.2 | 2.5 | 2.3 | 5.6 | 0.8 | 21.1 | 15.2 | 7.5 | 0.8 | Distribution en pour-centage du nombre de personnes occupées |

[1] Includes Metal mining (ISIC major group 12) and phosphate rock mining (part of ISIC group 192) only.
[2] Excludes Textiles (ISIC major group 23) Clothing, footwear and made-up textile (ISIC major group 24) and Furniture manufacturing (ISIC group 26)
[3] Includes phosphate rock mining (part of ISIC group 192) only.
[4] Includes Rubber products (ISIC major group 30).
[5] Includes wood and cork manufacturing only.

[1] Il s'agit exclusivement de l'Extraction des minerais métalliques (CITI classe 12) et de l'extraction du phosphate naturel (dans CITI groupe 192).
[2] Non compris Industrie textile (CITI classe 23), Articles d'habillement, chaussures et ouvrages en tissu (CITI classe 24) et Industrie du meuble (CITI groupe 26).
[3] Il s'agit exclusivement de l'extraction du phosphate naturel (dans CITI groupe 192).
[4] Y compris Ouvrages en caoutchouc (CITI classe 30).
[5] Il s'agit exclusivement de l'industrie du bois et du liège.

# TURKEY — TURQUIE

## Gross Domestic Product

The figures given in Table 1 on the expenditure on and industrial origin of the gross domestic product are from the reply of the Central Statistical Office, Ankara, to the United Nations national accounts questionnaire. The concepts, methods and primary sources utilized in making the estimates are described in *National Income of Turkey, 1938, 1948-1951,* issued by that Office.

## Index Numbers of Industrial Production

The index numbers of industrial production shown in Table 2 were compiled from various issues of *Conjoncture,* Direction de la Conjoncture et des Publications, Ministère du Commerce, Ankara. The index numbers relate to the production of privately and publicly owned establishments in selected classes of industrial activity.

The index numbers are computed as base-weighted arithmetic averages in two stages. Index numbers for detailed categories of industrial activity are compiled from elementary series of relatives based on quantities of output for individual products. Secondly, the resulting indexes are combined into index numbers for broader classes of industrial activity. The weights utilized in the second step are proportional to value of production during 1948 except in the case of the extraction of crude petroleum, where average annual value of production during the period, 1955-1959, was utilized. The exact nature of these data on value of production is not known.

## Index Numbers of Industrial Employment

The index numbers of industrial employment shown in Table 3 were compiled from absolute figures of the average number of persons engaged during the year resulting from the annual surveys of manufacturing described below. The absolute figures have been obtained from various issues of *Istatistik Bülteni,* Central Statistical Office, Ankara, and correspondence with this Office. The absolute figures of the number of persons engaged refer to the employment of manufacturing establishments located in urban areas which have 10 or more such persons engaged or installed power capacity of 10 or more horsepower.

## The Characteristics and Structure of Industrial Activity

The data set out in Table 4 were compiled from the results of a Census of Establishments issued by the Cen-

## Produit intérieur brut

Les chiffres reproduits au tableau 1 relatifs aux dépenses imputées au produit intérieur brut et aux composantes du produit intérieur brut ventilées suivant le secteur d'activité ont été tirés de la réponse du Bureau central de statistique, Ankara, au questionnaire de l'O.N.U. relatif aux comptes nationaux. Les concepts, méthodes et sources essentielles utilisés dans la confection des estimations sont exposés dans *National Income of Turkey, 1938, 1948-1951,* publié par ce Bureau.

## Indices de la production industrielle

Les indices de la production industrielle reproduits au tableau 2 ont été tirés de différents numéros de *Conjoncture,* Direction de la Conjoncture et des Publications, Ministère du Commerce, Ankara. Ces indices concernent la production des établissements privés et publics appartenant à certaines classes de l'activité industrielle.

Ces indices sont des moyennes arithmétiques à pondération fixe calculées en deux étapes. A un premier stade les indices de catégories détaillées de l'activité industrielle sont calculés à partir de séries élémentaires de rapports, rapports fondés sur le volume de la production de chaque produit. Au second stade du calcul, on combine les indices obtenus en indices relatifs aux classes plus étendues de l'activité industrielle. Les coefficients de pondération utilisés au second stade du calcul sont proportionnels à la valeur de la production durant 1948, à l'exclusion du cas de l'extraction du pétrole brut auquel cas on utilise la valeur annuelle moyenne de la production durant la période 1955-1959. La nature exacte des données portant sur la valeur de la production n'est pas connue.

## Indices de l'emploi industriel

Les indices de l'emploi dans l'industrie reproduits au tableau 3 ont été calculés à partir des chiffres absolus portant sur le nombre moyen de personnes occupées durant l'année, provenant de l'enquête annuelle effectuée auprès des établissements manufacturiers décrite ci-dessous. Les chiffres absolus sont tirés de différents numéros de *Istatistik Bülteni,* Bureau central de statistique, Ankara, et d'un échange de lettres avec le Bureau. Les chiffres absolus relatifs au nombre de personnes occupées concernent l'emploi dans les établissements manufacturiers exerçant dans les régions urbaines, occupant 10 personnes ou plus, ou ayant une puissance installée de 10 chevaux-vapeur ou plus.

## Caractéristiques et structure de l'activité industrielle

Les données du tableau 4 ont été tirées des résultats d'un recensement des établissements, résultats qui ont été

tral Statistical Office, Ankara, in *Istatistik Bülteni*, Nos. 22-23, December 1955-January 1956. Although in the Census, data were sought for all kinds of industrial (mining, manufacturing, construction, electricity and gas producing) units, irrespective of size, and gathered from all such establishments in urban areas of 2,000 or more population and from a sample of these units in localities with 500 to 2,000 inhabitants, complete results have been published for manufacturing establishments in the former type of areas only. It should also be noted that the Census did not cover manufacturing establishments of the Ministry of Defence, repair shops of local authorities, or household or itinerant manufacturing activities. The figures of the number of establishments from the Census may be understated as a result of the omission of smaller units. This would affect the figures of other items of data to a lesser extent.

The figures of Table 5 were derived from the results of annual inquiries into larger manufacturing establishments taken by the Central Statistical Office since 1950. These figures appeared in *Istatistik Bülteni*, Nos. 42-43, August-September 1957 and No. 73, March 1960. The annual inquiries relate to manufacturing units in urban areas employing 10 or more persons or having installed power of 10 or more horsepower.

The definitions utilized for identical items of data in the Census of Establishments for 1950 and the annual inquiries for 1950, 1953 and 1958 seem to be identical and consistent with the International Standards in Basic Industrial Statistics. It should be noted that the number of persons engaged for each of these years is the sum of the average of the number of employees during a month of each quarter of the year and the number of working proprietors and unpaid family workers in October of the year. Homeworkers may be omitted from the data on the number of persons engaged. The data on value added relate to all activities of the covered establishments. It is not known whether value added is valued at market prices or at factor cost.

publiés par l'Office central de statistique, Ankara, dans *Istatistik Bülteni*, Nos 22-23, décembre 1955-janvier 1956. Si, lors de ce recensement, des données ont été rassemblées pour les unités industrielles de tous types (industries extractives, industries manufacturières, bâtiment et travaux publics, production de gaz et d'électricité), quelle que fût leur dimension, et recueillies auprès de tous les établissements des centres urbains comptant au moins 2.000 habitants et d'un échantillon d'établissements dans les localités comptant entre 500 et 2.000 habitants, des résultats complets n'ont cependant été publiés que pour les établissements manufacturiers des centres urbains d'au moins 2.000 habitants. On notera aussi que le recensement ne portait pas sur les établissements manufacturiers du Ministère de la défense, ni sur les ateliers de réparation des autorités locales, ni sur les unités manufacturières familiales ou itinérantes. Le nombre des établissements, qui est tiré du recensement des établissements, est peut-être au dessous de la vérité par suite de l'omission des petites unités. Les données des autres rubriques peuvent s'en ressentir, mais dans une moindre mesure.

Les chiffres du tableau 5 sont tirés des résultats d'enquêtes annuelles sur les grands établissements manufacturiers, effectuées depuis 1950 par l'Office central de statistique. Ces chiffres ont paru dans *Istatistik Bülteni*, Nos 42-43, août-septembre 1957 et No 73, mars 1960. Les enquêtes annuelles portent sur les unités manufacturières des centres urbains qui emploient au moins 10 personnes ou qui ont une puissance installée d'au moins 10 chevaux-vapeur.

Les définitions utilisées pour des rubriques identiques dans le recensement des établissements de 1950 et dans les enquêtes annuelles de 1950, 1953 et 1958 semblent être identiques et compatibles avec les Normes internationales relatives aux statistiques industrielles de base. On notera que le nombre de personnes occupées, pour chacune de ces années, est le nombre de salariés (moyenne mensuelle, un mois par trimestre), augmenté du nombre de propriétaires qui travaillent et de travailleurs familiaux non rémunérés (moyenne d'octobre). Les travailleurs à domicile peuvent ne pas être compris dans le nombre de personnes occupées. Les chiffres de la valeur ajoutée ont trait à toutes les activités des établissements recensés et l'on ne sait pas si la valeur ajoutée est calculée aux prix du marché ou au coût des facteurs.

# 1. THE GROSS DOMESTIC PRODUCT
# LE PRODUIT INTERIEUR BRUT

Million Turkish liras                    Millions de livres turques

## A. Expenditure on the Gross Domestic Product at Market Prices —
## Dépenses relatives au produit intérieur brut aux prix du marché

| Item of data and year / Rubrique et année | Total | Consumption / Consommation | | Gross Domestic Capital Formation / Formation brute de capital intérieur | | Net exports of goods and services / Exportations nettes de biens et de services | |
| --- | --- | --- | --- | --- | --- | --- | --- |
| | | Total[1] | Government / Etat | Total | Fixed / Fixe | Exports less imports / Exportations moins importations | Exports / Exportations |
| *a. At Current Prices — Aux prix courants* | | | | | | | |
| Absolute figures — Chiffres absolus | | | | | | | |
| 1955 | 21 133.0 | 18 659.3 | 2 588.4 | ... | 2 975.7 | −575.5 | ... |
| 1956 | 24 431.0 | 21 323.0 | 3 256.0 | ... | 3 366.0 | −258.0 | ... |
| 1957 | 30 668.0 | 26 823.0 | 3 669.0 | ... | 3 965.0 | −120.0 | ... |
| 1958 | 38 652.0 | 33 937.0 | 4 466.0 | ... | 4 904.0 | −189.0 | ... |
| 1959 | 47 980.0 | 42 491.0 | 5 970.0 | ... | 6 691.0 | −1 202.0 | ... |
| 1960 | 51 283.0 | 44 876.0 | 6 507.0 | ... | 7 516.0 | −1 109.0 | ... |
| 1961 | 54 338.0 | 47 918.0 | 7 728.0 | ... | 7 742.0 | −1 322.0 | ... |
| Percentage distribution of average annual expenditure — Distribution en pourcentage des dépenses annuelles moyennes | | | | | | | |
| 1955 – 1960 | 100.0 | 87.7 | 12.6 | ... | 14.5 | −2.3 | ... |
| 1955 | 100.0 | 88.3 | 12.2 | ... | 14.1 | −2.7 | ... |
| 1958 | 100.0 | 87.8 | 11.6 | ... | 12.7 | −0.5 | ... |
| 1960 | 100.0 | 87.5 | 12.7 | ... | 14.6 | −2.2 | ... |

[1] Includes increases in stocks.

[1] Y compris l'accroissement des stocks.

## B.  The Gross Domestic Product at Factor Cost According to Origin
### Origine par secteur d'activité du produit intérieur brut au coût des facteurs

| Item of data and year / Rubrique et année | Total | Agricultural sector / Secteur agricole | Industrial Sector — Secteur Industriel | | | | | Transportation and communication / Transport et communication | Other sectors / Autres secteurs |
| | | | Total | Mining / Industries extractives | Manufacturing / Industries manufacturières | Construction / Bâtiment et travaux publics | Electricity, gas and water / Electricité, gaz et eau | | |
| ISIC — CITI | 0–9 | 0 | 1–5 | 1 | 2–3 | 4 | 5 | 7 | 6, 8–9 |
| *a.  At Current Prices — Aux prix courants* | | | | | | | | | |
| Absolute figures — Chiffres absolus | | | | | | | | | |
| 1955............ | 19 199.0 | 7 862.3 | 3 821.9 | 268.8 | 2 389.8 | 1 075.8 | 87.5 | 1 449.3 | 6 065.5 |
| 1956............ | 22 390.5 | 9 335.6 | 4 765.4 | 299.4 | 3 109.1 | 1 253.9 | 103.0 | 1 718.2 | 6 571.3 |
| 1957............ | 27 991.9 | 12 247.6 | 6 106.8 | 297.9 | 3 981.0 | 1 696.4 | 131.5 | 2 071.7 | 7 565.8 |
| 1958............ | 35 567.4 | 16 407.3 | 7 842.7 | 565.9 | 5 066.0 | 2 070.0 | 140.8 | 2 400.2 | 8 917.2 |
| 1959............ | 43 942.1 | 18 781.0 | 9 703.1 | 856.6 | 5 899.6 | 2 684.9 | 262.0 | 3 305.1 | 12 152.9 |
| 1960............ | 46 871.5 | 19 543.9 | 10 317.0 | 818.2 | 6 207.9 | 2 967.0 | 323.9 | 3 588.9 | 13 421.7 |
| 1961............ | 49 273.5 | 19 380.1 | 11 001.2 | 790.6 | 6 893.2 | 2 937.0 | 380.4 | 4 012.7 | 14 879.5 |
| Percentage distribution according to sector— Distribution en pourcentage par secteur | | | | | | | | | |
| 1955–1960..... | 100.0 | 43.0 | 21.7 | 1.6 | 13.6 | 6.0 | 0.5 | 7.4 | 27.9 |
| 1955............ | 100.0 | 41.0 | 19.9 | 1.4 | 12.4 | 5.6 | 0.5 | 7.5 | 31.6 |
| 1958............ | 100.0 | 46.1 | 22.0 | 1.6 | 14.2 | 5.8 | 0.4 | 6.8 | 25.1 |
| 1960............ | 100.0 | 41.7 | 22.0 | 1.8 | 13.2 | 6.3 | 0.7 | 7.7 | 28.6 |
| *b.  At Prices of 1948 — Aux prix de 1948* | | | | | | | | | |
| Absolute figures — Chiffres absolus | | | | | | | | | |
| 1955............ | 12 899.7 | 5 716.1 | 2 211.2 | 168.4 | 1 289.9 | 688.9 | 64.0 | 1 091.7 | 3 880.7 |
| 1956............ | 13 777.1 | 6 212.8 | 2 320.5 | 197.4 | 1 351.5 | 699.0 | 72.6 | 1 133.0 | 4 110.8 |
| 1957............ | 14 648.4 | 6 369.3 | 2 604.4 | 214.7 | 1 442.7 | 865.0 | 82.0 | 1 212.3 | 4 462.4 |
| 1958............ | 16 377.4 | 7 484.9 | 2 742.6 | 202.1 | 1 518.6 | 929.8 | 92.1 | 1 201.8 | 4 948.1 |
| 1959............ | 17 096.6 | 7 459.1 | 2 853.5 | 189.8 | 1 579.2 | 982.6 | 101.9 | 1 451.9 | 5 332.1 |
| 1960............ | 17 505.1 | 7 547.0 | 2 896.2 | 193.2 | 1 610.5 | 982.8 | 109.7 | 1 481.7 | 5 580.2 |
| 1961............ | 17 415.8 | 7 316.9 | 2 815.2 | 187.8 | 1 625.2 | 883.7 | 118.5 | 1 534.3 | 5 749.4 |
| Percentage distribution according to sector— Distribution en pourcentage par secteur | | | | | | | | | |
| 1955–1960..... | 100.0 | 43.6 | 16.8 | 1.2 | 9.5 | 5.5 | 0.6 | 8.5 | 31.1 |
| 1955............ | 100.0 | 44.3 | 17.1 | 1.3 | 10.0 | 5.3 | 0.5 | 8.5 | 30.1 |
| 1958............ | 100.0 | 45.7 | 16.8 | 1.2 | 9.3 | 5.7 | 0.6 | 7.3 | 30.2 |
| 1960............ | 100.0 | 43.1 | 16.5 | 1.1 | 9.2 | 5.6 | 0.6 | 8.5 | 31.9 |
| Average annual rate of growth—Taux annuel moyen d'accroissement | | | | | | | | | |
| 1955–1960..... | 6.3 | 5.7 | 5.5 | 2.8 | 4.5 | 7.4 | 11.4 | 6.3 | 7.5 |
| 1955–1958..... | 8.3 | 9.4 | 7.4 | 6.3 | 5.6 | 10.5 | 12.9 | 3.3 | 8.4 |
| 1958–1960..... | 3.4 | 0.4 | 2.8 | −2.0 | 3.0 | 2.8 | 9.1 | 11.0 | 6.2 |

# 2. INDEX NUMBERS OF INDUSTRIAL PRODUCTION
## INDICES DE LA PRODUCTION INDUSTRIELLE

## A. Selected Divisions of Industrial Activity
### Quelques branches de l'activité industrielle

| Period<br>Période | Total [1, 2] | Mining [1]<br>Industries extractives [1] | Manu-facturing [2]<br>Industries manu-facturières [2] | Electricity<br>Electricité |
|---|---|---|---|---|
| ISIC — CITI | 1–3, 511 | 1 | 2–3 | 511 |

### a. Indexes — Indices (1958 = 100)

| | | | | |
|---|---|---|---|---|
| 1948.......... | 42 | 50 | 39 | 29 |
| 1949.......... | 46 | 58 | 42 | 32 |
| 1950.......... | 46 | 60 | 40 | 34 |
| 1951.......... | 53 | 68 | 47 | 38 |
| 1952.......... | 61 | 77 | 56 | 44 |
| 1953.......... | 70 | 90 | 63 | 52 |
| 1954.......... | 73 | 83 | 70 | 61 |
| 1955.......... | 81 | 86 | 80 | 68 |
| 1956.......... | 88 | 99 | 84 | 79 |
| 1957.......... | 99 | 109 | 95 | 89 |
| 1958.......... | 100 | 100 | 100 | 100 |
| 1959.......... | 104 | 93 | 110 | 105 |
| 1960.......... | 109 | 96 | 116 | 115 |
| 1961.......... | 108 | 91 | 113 | 132 |

### b. Average Annual Rate of Change — Taux annuel moyen de variation

| | | | | |
|---|---|---|---|---|
| 1950 – 1960.... | 9.0 | 4.8 | 11.2 | 13.0 |
| 1948 – 1953.... | 10.8 | 12.5 | 10.1 | 12.4 |
| 1954 – 1958.... | 8.2 | 4.8 | 9.3 | 13.1 |
| 1958 – 1960.... | 4.4 | −2.0 | 7.7 | 7.2 |

For footnotes see end of table.

Pour les notes, voir au bas du tableau.

## B. The Major Groups of Mining
### Les classes de la branche Industries extractives

| Period<br>Période | All mining [1]<br>Toutes industries extractives [1] | Coal mining<br>Extraction du charbon | Metal mining<br>Extraction des minerais métalliques | Crude petro-leum and natural gas<br>Pétrole brut et gaz naturel | Other mining<br>Aütres industries extractives |
|---|---|---|---|---|---|
| ISIC — CITI | 1 | 11 | 12 | 13 | 14–19 |

### a. Indexes — Indices (1958 = 100)

| | | | | | |
|---|---|---|---|---|---|
| 1948....... | 50 | 52 | 46 | ... | 20 |
| 1949....... | 58 | 56 | 66 | ... | 24 |
| 1950....... | 60 | 59 | 64 | ... | 47 |
| 1951....... | 68 | 62 | 93 | ... | 58 |
| 1952....... | 77 | 63 | 126 | ... | 65 |
| 1953....... | 90 | 76 | 139 | ... | 76 |
| 1954....... | 83 | 81 | 94 | ... | 78 |
| 1955....... | 86 | 80 | 112 | 51 | 90 |
| 1956....... | 99 | 89 | 136 | 88 | 108 |
| 1957....... | 109 | 98 | 149 | 86 | 102 |
| 1958....... | 100 | 100 | 100 | 100 | 100 |
| 1959....... | 93 | 96 | 83 | 107 | 104 |
| 1960....... | 96 | 94 | 100 | 104 | 133 |
| 1961....... | 91 | 93 | 72 | 119 | 280 |

### b. Average Annual Rate of Change — Taux annuel moyen de variation

| | | | | | |
|---|---|---|---|---|---|
| 1950 – 1960. | 4.8 | 4.8 | 4.6 | ... | 11.0 |
| 1948 – 1953. | 12.5 | 7.9 | 24.8 | ... | 30.6 |
| 1954 – 1958. | 4.8 | 5.4 | 1.6 | ... | 6.4 |
| 1958 – 1960. | −2.0 | −3.0 | — | 2.0 | 15.3 |

For footnotes see end of table.

Pour les notes, voir au bas du tableau.

## C.  Selected Major Groups of Manufacturing
## Quelques classes de la branche Industries manufacturières

| Period / Période | Manu-facturing [2] / Industries manufac-turières [2] | Food, beverages and tobacco / Industries alimen-taires, boissons, tabac | Textiles | Paper and paper products / Papier et ouvrages en papier | Non-metallic mineral products / Produits minéraux non métal-liques | Basic metals / Métal-lurgie de base |
|---|---|---|---|---|---|---|
| ISIC — CITI | 2–3 | 20–22 | 23 | 27 | 33 | 34 |

### a.  Indexes — Indices (1958 = 100)

| | | | | | | |
|---|---|---|---|---|---|---|
| 1948............. | 39 | 43 | 34 | 30 | 37 | 55 |
| 1949............. | 42 | 50 | 34 | 31 | 35 | 58 |
| 1950............. | 40 | 46 | 35 | 31 | 34 | 54 |
| 1951............. | 47 | 56 | 37 | 40 | 33 | 76 |
| 1952............. | 56 | 56 | 54 | 47 | 36 | 91 |
| 1953............. | 63 | 60 | 61 | 49 | 48 | 97 |
| 1954............. | 70 | 65 | 70 | 66 | 57 | 96 |
| 1955............. | 80 | 78 | 78 | 81 | 72 | 104 |
| 1956............. | 84 | 83 | 83 | 79 | 72 | 108 |
| 1957............. | 95 | 94 | 96 | 94 | 86 | 103 |
| 1958............. | 100 | 100 | 100 | 100 | 100 | 100 |
| 1959............. | 110 | 117 | 101 | 100 | 132 | 120 |
| 1960............. | 116 | 133 | 102 | 97 | 108 | 140 |
| 1961............. | 113 | 128 | 101 | 110 | 93 | 136 |

### b.  Average Annual Rate of Change — Taux annuel moyen de variation

| | | | | | | |
|---|---|---|---|---|---|---|
| 1950–1960........ | 11.2 | 11.2 | 11.3 | 12.1 | 12.2 | 10.0 |
| 1948–1953........ | 10.1 | 6.9 | 12.4 | 10.3 | 5.3 | 12.0 |
| 1954–1958........ | 9.3 | 11.4 | 9.3 | 10.9 | 15.1 | 1.0 |
| 1958–1961........ | 7.7 | 15.3 | 1.0 | −1.5 | 3.9 | 18.3 |

[1] Crude petroleum and natural gas (ISIC major group 13) is excluded for the years 1948–1954.
[2] Covered under Manufacturing (Division 2-3) are Food, beverages and tobacco (ISIC major groups 20–22), Textiles (ISIC major group 23), Paper and paper products (ISIC major group 27), Non-metallic mineral products (ISIC major group 33) and Basic metals (ISIC major group 34) only.

[1] L'extraction de pétrole brut et de gaz naturel (CITI classe 13) est exclue pour les années 1948–1954.
[2] Sont couverts par les Industries manufacturières (branches 2–3), les Industries alimentaires, boissons et tabacs (CITI classes 20–22), les Industries textiles (CITI classe 23), Papier et articles en papier (CITI classe 27), Produits minéraux non métalliques (CITI classe 33) et Métallurgie de base (CITI classe 34) seulement.

## 3.  INDEX NUMBERS OF MANUFACTURING EMPLOYMENT
## INDICES DE L'EMPLOI DANS LES INDUSTRIES MANUFACTURIERES

| Period / Période | Manu-facturing / Industries manufac-turières | Food, beverages and tobacco / Industries alimen-taires, boissons, tabac | Textiles | Clothing, footwear and made-up textiles / Articles d'habil-lement, chaussures et ouvrages en tissu | Wood products and furniture / Bois et meubles | Paper and paper products / Papier et ouvrages en papier | Printing and publishing / Imprimerie et édition | Leather and leather products except wearing apparel / Cuir et articles en cuir, à l'exclusion des articles d'habil-lement | Rubber products / Ouvrages en caout-chouc | Chemicals and chemical, petroleum and coal products / Produits chi-miques et dérivés du pétrole et du charbon | Non-metallic mineral products / Produits minéraux non métal-liques | Basic metals / Métal-lurgie de base | Metal products / Ouvrages en métaux | Other manu-facturing / Autres industries manufac-turières |
|---|---|---|---|---|---|---|---|---|---|---|---|---|---|---|
| ISIC — CITI | 2–3 | 20–22 | 23 | 24 | 25–26 | 27 | 28 | 29 | 30 | 31–32 | 33 | 34 | 35–38 | 39 |

### a.  Indexes — Indices (1958 = 100)

| | | | | | | | | | | | | | | |
|---|---|---|---|---|---|---|---|---|---|---|---|---|---|---|
| 1950............. | 56 | 61 | 55 | 82 | 63 | 68 | 46 | 56 | 52 | 47 | 39 | 46 | 62 | 24 |
| 1951............. | 60 | 76 | 54 | 66 | 64 | 64 | 42 | 55 | 46 | 48 | 40 | 52 | 60 | 27 |
| 1952............. | 62 | 70 | 61 | 73 | 68 | 68 | 47 | 53 | 62 | 53 | 49 | 55 | 64 | 23 |
| 1953............. | 71 | 85 | 66 | 73 | 66 | 68 | 67 | 55 | 76 | 70 | 56 | 50 | 71 | 33 |
| 1954............. | 75 | 86 | 73 | 74 | 74 | 64 | 73 | 57 | 62 | 67 | 64 | 50 | 75 | 36 |
| 1955............. | 80 | 93 | 77 | 76 | 80 | 76 | 71 | 61 | 70 | 76 | 71 | 70 | 78 | 44 |
| 1956............. | 83 | 97 | 79 | 79 | 82 | 79 | 78 | 64 | 69 | 81 | 73 | 67 | 78 | 53 |
| 1957............. | 91 | 98 | 90 | 87 | 94 | 94 | 94 | 85 | 75 | 90 | 80 | 88 | 89 | 63 |
| 1958............. | 100 | 100 | 100 | 100 | 100 | 100 | 100 | 100 | 100 | 100 | 100 | 100 | 100 | 100 |
| 1959............. | 103 | 98 | 102 | 106 | 118 | 105 | 104 | 112 | 106 | 111 | 99 | 114 | 108 | 120 |
| 1960............. | 102 | 100 | 99 | 109 | 113 | 114 | 107 | 104 | 82 | 110 | 102 | 121 | 105 | 100 |

### b.  Average Annual Rate of Change — Taux annuel moyen de variation

| | | | | | | | | | | | | | | |
|---|---|---|---|---|---|---|---|---|---|---|---|---|---|---|
| 1950–1960........ | 6.2 | 5.1 | 6.1 | 2.9 | 6.0 | 5.3 | 8.8 | 6.4 | 4.7 | 8.9 | 10.1 | 10.2 | 5.4 | 15.3 |
| 1950–1953........ | 8.2 | 11.7 | 6.3 | −3.8 | 1.6 | — | 13.3 | −0.6 | 13.5 | 14.2 | 12.8 | 2.8 | 4.6 | 11.2 |
| 1954–1958........ | 7.5 | 3.8 | 8.2 | 7.8 | 7.8 | 11.8 | 8.2 | 15.1 | 12.7 | 10.5 | 11.8 | 18.9 | 7.5 | 29.1 |
| 1958–1960........ | 1.0 | — | −0.5 | 4.4 | 6.3 | 6.8 | 3.4 | 2.0 | −9.4 | 4.9 | 1.0 | 10.0 | 2.5 | — |

# 4. CHARACTERISTICS OF ALL MANUFACTURING ESTABLISHMENTS IN URBAN AREAS OF 2 000 INHABITANTS AND OVER

## CARACTERISTIQUES DE TOUS LES ETABLISSEMENTS MANUFACTURIERS DES CENTRES URBAINS COMPTANT AU MOINS 2 000 HABITANTS

### 1950

Number of establishments in units; value added and wages and salaries paid in million Turkish Pounds; number of engaged and employees in thousands; value added per person engaged and wages and salaries per employee in thousand Turkish Pounds.

Nombre d'établissements en unités; valeur ajoutée et traitements et salaires payés en millions de livres turques; nombre de personnes occupées et de salariés en milliers; valeur ajoutée par personne occupée et traitements et salaires par salarié en milliers de livres turques.

| Item of data | Manu-facturing / Industries manufac-turières | Food, beverages and tobacco / Industries alimen-taires, boissons, tabac | Textiles | Clothing, footwear and made-up textiles / Articles d'habil-lement, chaussures et ouvrages en tissu | Wood products and furniture / Bois et meubles | Paper and paper products / Papier et ouvrages en papier | Printing and publish-ing / Im-primerie et édition | Leather and leather products except wearing apparel / Cuir et articles en cuir, à l'exclu-sion des articles d'habil-lement | Rubber products / Ouvrages en caout-chouc | Chemicals and chemical, petroleum and coal products / Produits chi-miques et dérivés du pétrole et du charbon | Non-metallic mineral products / Produits minéraux non métal-liques | Basic metals / Métal-lurgie de base | Metal products / Ouvrages en métaux | Other manu-factur-ing / Autres in-dustries manufac-turières | Rubrique |
|---|---|---|---|---|---|---|---|---|---|---|---|---|---|---|---|
| **ISIC** | 2–3 | 20–22 | 23 | 24 | 25–26 | 27 | 28 | 29 | 30 | 31–32 | 33 | 34 | 35–38 | 39 | **CITI** |
| *a. Absolute Figures — Chiffres absolus* | | | | | | | | | | | | | | | |
| Number of establishments | 82 381 | 10 327 | 3 571 | 31 783 | 6 368 | 212 | 849 | 4 264 | 335 | 1 184 | 1 517 | 484 | 19 420 | 2 067 | Nombre d'établissements |
| Value added | 938.2 | 379.3 | 211.1 | 45.9 | 28.9 | 12.2 | 15.6 | 11.0 | 14.8 | 57.5 | 32.7 | 27.1 | 94.6 | 7.5 | Valeur ajoutée |
| Number of engaged (Average during the year) | 322.9 | 75.6 | 63.8 | 59.2 | 16.2 | 4.0 | 4.3 | 7.5 | 4.4 | 9.7 | 9.7 | 6.8 | 57.8 | 3.9 | Nombre de personnes occupées (moyenne pendant l'année) |
| Number of employees (Average during the year) | 218.1 | 61.9 | 59.5 | 19.9 | 8.2 | 3.8 | 3.3 | 2.3 | 4.0 | 8.5 | 8.4 | 6.3 | 30.5 | 1.5 | Nombre de salariés (moyenne pendant l'année) |
| Wages and salaries paid | 279.4 | 67.6 | 80.1 | 12.9 | 7.7 | 7.3 | 9.3 | 2.4 | 4.6 | 13.0 | 11.8 | 14.2 | 47.1 | 1.4 | Traitements et salaires payés |
| *b. Structure* | | | | | | | | | | | | | | | |
| Distribution in percent of: Value added | 100.0 | 40.4 | 22.5 | 4.9 | 3.1 | 1.3 | 1.6 | 1.2 | 1.6 | 6.1 | 3.5 | 2.9 | 10.1 | 0.8 | Répartition en pour-centage: De la valeur ajoutée |
| Number of engaged | 100.0 | 23.4 | 19.7 | 18.4 | 5.0 | 1.2 | 1.3 | 2.4 | 1.3 | 3.0 | 3.0 | 2.1 | 17.9 | 1.3 | Du nombre de person-nes occupées |
| Value added per person engaged | 2.9 | 5.0 | 3.3 | 0.8 | 1.8 | 3.0 | 3.6 | 1.5 | 3.4 | 5.9 | 3.4 | 4.0 | 1.6 | 1.9 | Valeur ajoutée par per-sonne occupée |
| Employees as a percent of engaged | 67.5 | 81.9 | 93.3 | 33.6 | 50.6 | 95.0 | 76.7 | 30.7 | 90.9 | 87.6 | 86.6 | 92.6 | 52.8 | 38.5 | Salariés en pourcentage des personnes occupées |
| Value added per unit of wages and salaries | 3.36 | 5.61 | 2.64 | 3.56 | 3.75 | 1.67 | 1.68 | 4.58 | 3.22 | 4.42 | 2.77 | 1.91 | 2.01 | 5.36 | Valeur ajoutée par unité de traitements et sa-laires |
| Wages and salaries per employee | 1.3 | 1.1 | 1.3 | 0.6 | 0.9 | 1.9 | 2.8 | 1.0 | 1.2 | 1.5 | 1.4 | 2.2 | 1.5 | 0.9 | Traitements et salaires par salarié |

## 5. CHARACTERISTICS OF MANUFACTURING ESTABLISHMENTS EMPLOYING 10 OR MORE PERSONS OR HAVING INSTALLED POWER EQUIPMENT OF 10 HORSEPOWER OR MORE

## CARACTERISTIQUES DES ETABLISSEMENTS MANUFACTURIERS EMPLOYANT AU MOINS 10 PERSONNES OU AYANT UNE PUISSANCE INSTALLEE D'AU MOINS 10 CHEVAUX-VAPEUR

### 1950, 1953, 1958

Number of establishments in units; value added and wages and salaries paid in million Turkish Pounds; number of engaged and employees in thousands; value added per person engaged and wages and salaries per employee in thousand Turkish Pounds.

Nombre d'établissements en unités; valeur ajoutée et traitements et salaires payés en millions de livres turques; nombre de personnes occupées et de salariés en milliers; valeur ajoutée par personne occupée et traitements et salaires par salarié en milliers de livres turques.

| Year and item of data | Manu-facturing / Industries manufac-turières | Food, beverages and tobacco / Industries alimen-taires, boissons, tabac | Textiles | Clothing, footwear and made-up textiles / Articles d'habil-lement, chaussures et ouvrages en tissu | Wood products and furniture / Bois et meubles | Paper and paper products / Papier et ouvrages en papier | Printing and publish-ing / Im-primerie et édition | Leather and leather products except wearing apparel / Cuir et articles en cuir, à l'exclu-sion des articles d'habil-lement | Rubber products / Ouvrages en caout-chouc | Chemicals and chemical, petroleum and coal products / Produits chi-miques et dérivés du pétrole et du charbon | Non-metallic mineral products / Produits minéraux non métal-liques | Basic metals / Métal-lurgie de base | Metal products / Ouvrages en métaux | Other manu-factur-ing / Autres in-dustries manufac-turières | Année et rubrique |
|---|---|---|---|---|---|---|---|---|---|---|---|---|---|---|---|
| ISIC | 2–3 | 20–22 | 23 | 24 | 25–26 | 27 | 28 | 29 | 30 | 31–32 | 33 | 34 | 35–38 | 39 | CITI |
| **a. Absolute Figures — Chiffres absolus** | | | | | | | | | | | | | | | |
| **1950** | | | | | | | | | | | | | | | **1950** |
| Number of establishments | 2 618 | 1 023 | 457 | 27 | 234 | 11 | 81 | 42 | 48 | 316 | 101 | 50 | 186 | 42 | Nombre d'établissements |
| Value added | 733.8 | 329.2 | 195.6 | 8.6 | 10.6 | 10.6 | 9.6 | 2.5 | 14.0 | 40.6 | 27.2 | 24.8 | 58.1 | 2.4 | Valeur ajoutée |
| Number of engaged (Average during the year) | 165.5 | 53.5 | 55.4 | 2.2 | 3.8 | 3.3 | 2.1 | 0.9 | 3.8 | 7.7 | 6.8 | 5.6 | 19.9 | 0.5 | Nombre de personnes occupées (moyenne pendant l'année) |
| Number of employees (Average during the year) | 162.7 | 52.3 | 55.0 | 2.1 | 3.5 | 3.3 | 2.0 | 0.9 | 3.8 | 7.5 | 6.7 | 5.5 | 19.7 | 0.4 | Nombre de salariés (moyenne pendant l'année) |
| Wages and salaries paid | 235.7 | 58.6 | 76.3 | 3.3 | 4.2 | 6.9 | 3.6 | 1.3 | 4.4 | 11.9 | 10.1 | 13.5 | 40.9 | 0.7 | Traitements et salaires payés |
| **1953** | | | | | | | | | | | | | | | **1953** |
| Number of establishments | 3 504 | 1 395 | 639 | 12 | 256 | 10 | 89 | 43 | 65 | 436 | 249 | 51 | 216 | 43 | Nombre d'établissements |
| Value added | 1 366.5 | 485.9 | 436.2 | 15.1 | 15.5 | 23.1 | 18.3 | 6.3 | 26.9 | 83.5 | 49.9 | 81.7 | 119.2 | 4.9 | Valeur ajoutée |
| Number of engaged (Average during the year) | 210.8 | 75.2 | 65.9 | 1.9 | 4.0 | 3.4 | 3.0 | 0.9 | 5.6 | 11.6 | 9.7 | 6.0 | 22.9 | 0.7 | Nombre de personnes occupées (moyenne pendant l'année) |
| Number of employees (Average during the year) | 206.4 | 73.7 | 65.3 | 1.9 | 3.7 | 3.4 | 3.0 | 0.9 | 4.6 | 11.1 | 9.5 | 6.0 | 22.7 | 0.6 | Nombre de salariés (moyenne pendant l'année) |
| Wages and salaries paid | 409.9 | 108.4 | 137.0 | 4.8 | 6.1 | 9.0 | 8.4 | 1.9 | 9.2 | 24.2 | 19.3 | 17.8 | 62.5 | 1.3 | Traitements et salaires payés |
| **1958** | | | | | | | | | | | | | | | **1958** |
| Number of establishments | 5 121 | 1 616 | 993 | 36 | 469 | 26 | 138 | 73 | 144 | 557 | 453 | 99 | 430 | 87 | Nombre d'établissements |
| Value added | 3 768.2 | 1 239.6 | 1 132.1 | 26.9 | 69.9 | 50.7 | 79.9 | 20.6 | 80.0 | 368.5 | 165.7 | 235.8 | 279.4 | 19.1 | Valeur ajoutée |
| Number of engaged (Average during the year) | 295.3 | 88.0 | 100.0 | 2.6 | 6.0 | 5.0 | 4.5 | 1.7 | 7.4 | 16.5 | 17.4 | 12.2 | 32.0 | 2.0 | Nombre de personnes occupées (moyenne pendant l'année) |
| Number of employees (Average during the year) | 290.5 | 86.2 | 99.3 | 2.6 | 5.6 | 4.9 | 4.4 | 1.6 | 7.3 | 16.0 | 17.0 | 12.1 | 31.6 | 1.9 | Nombre de salariés (moyenne pendant l'année) |
| Wages and salaries paid | 1 191.6 | 275.3 | 415.6 | 12.4 | 21.3 | 24.3 | 25.4 | 8.7 | 33.3 | 73.7 | 67.7 | 66.3 | 158.6 | 9.0 | Traitements et salaires payés |

# 5 CHARACTERISTICS OF MANUFACTURING ESTABLISHMENTS EMPLOYING 10 OR MORE PERSONS OR HAVING INSTALLED POWER EQUIPMENT OF 10 HORSEPOWER OR MORE (continued)

## CARACTERISTIQUES DES ETABLISSEMENTS MANUFACTURIERS EMPLOYANT AU MOINS 10 PERSONNES OU AYANT UNE PUISSANCE INSTALLEE D'AU MOINS 10 CHEVAUX-VAPEUR (suite)

### 1950, 1953, 1958

| Year and item of data | Manufacturing — Industries manufacturières | Food, beverages and tobacco — Industries alimentaires, boissons, tabac | Textiles | Clothing, footwear and made-up textiles — Articles d'habillement, chaussures et ouvrages en tissu | Wood products and furniture — Bois et meubles | Paper and paper products — Papier et ouvrages en papier | Printing and publishing — Imprimerie et édition | Leather and leather products except wearing apparel — Cuir et articles en cuir, à l'exclusion des articles d'habillement | Rubber products — Ouvrages en caoutchouc | Chemicals and chemical, petroleum and coal products — Produits chimiques et dérivés du pétrole et du charbon | Non-metallic mineral products — Produits minéraux non métalliques | Basic metals — Métallurgie de base | Metal products — Ouvrages en métaux | Other manufacturing — Autres industries manufacturières | Année et rubrique |
|---|---|---|---|---|---|---|---|---|---|---|---|---|---|---|---|
| ISIC | 2-3 | 20-22 | 23 | 24 | 25-26 | 27 | 28 | 29 | 30 | 31-32 | 33 | 34 | 35-38 | 39 | CITI |
| *b. Structure* | | | | | | | | | | | | | | | |
| **1950** Distribution in percent of: | | | | | | | | | | | | | | | **1950** Distribution en pourcentage : |
| Value added........ | 100.0 | 44.8 | 26.7 | 1.1 | 1.5 | 1.4 | 1.3 | 0.4 | 1.9 | 5.5 | 3.7 | 3.4 | 7.9 | 0.4 | Valeur ajoutée |
| Number of engaged.. | 100.0 | 32.3 | 33.5 | 1.3 | 2.3 | 2.0 | 1.2 | 0.6 | 2.3 | 4.6 | 4.1 | 3.4 | 12.0 | 0.4 | Nombre de personnes occupées |
| Value added per person engaged........... | 4.4 | 6.2 | 3.5 | 3.9 | 2.8 | 3.2 | 4.6 | 2.8 | 3.7 | 5.3 | 4.0 | 4.4 | 2.9 | 4.8 | Valeur ajoutée par personne occupée |
| Employees as a percent of engaged........ | 98.3 | 97.8 | 99.3 | 95.4 | 92.1 | 100.0 | 95.2 | 100.0 | 100.0 | 97.4 | 98.5 | 98.2 | 99.0 | 80.0 | Salariés en pourcentage des personnes occupées |
| Value added per unit of wages and salaries............ | 3.11 | 5.62 | 2.56 | 2.61 | 2.52 | 1.54 | 2.67 | 1.92 | 3.18 | 3.41 | 2.69 | 1.84 | 1.42 | 3.43 | Valeur ajoutée par unité de traitements et salaires |
| Wages and salaries per employee........ | 1.4 | 1.1 | 1.4 | 1.6 | 1.2 | 2.1 | 1.8 | 1.4 | 1.2 | 1.6 | 1.5 | 2.4 | 2.1 | 1.8 | Traitements et salaires par salarié |
| **1953** Distribution in percent of: | | | | | | | | | | | | | | | **1953** Distribution en pourcentage: |
| Value added........ | 100.0 | 35.5 | 31.9 | 1.1 | 1.2 | 1.7 | 1.3 | 0.5 | 1.9 | 6.1 | 3.7 | 6.0 | 8.7 | 0.4 | Valeur ajoutée |
| Number of engaged.. | 100.0 | 35.6 | 31.3 | 0.9 | 1.9 | 1.6 | 1.4 | 0.4 | 2.7 | 5.5 | 4.6 | 2.9 | 10.8 | 0.4 | Nombre de personnes occupées |
| Value added per person engaged........... | 6.5 | 6.5 | 6.6 | 7.9 | 3.9 | 6.8 | 6.1 | 7.0 | 4.8 | 7.2 | 5.1 | 13.6 | 5.2 | 7.0 | Valeur ajoutée par personne occupée |
| Employees as a percent of engaged........ | 97.9 | 98.0 | 99.1 | 100.0 | 92.5 | 100.0 | 100.0 | 100.0 | 82.1 | 95.7 | 97.9 | 100.0 | 99.1 | 85.7 | Salariés en pourcentage des personnes occupées |
| Value added per unit of wages and salaries............ | 3.33 | 4.48 | 3.18 | 3.14 | 2.54 | 2.57 | 2.18 | 3.32 | 2.92 | 3.45 | 2.58 | 4.59 | 1.91 | 3.77 | Valeur ajoutée par unité de traitements et salaires |
| Wages and salaries per employee........ | 2.0 | 1.5 | 2.1 | 2.5 | 1.6 | 2.6 | 2.8 | 2.1 | 2.0 | 2.2 | 2.0 | 3.0 | 2.8 | 2.2 | Traitements et salaires par salarié |
| **1958** Distribution in percent of: | | | | | | | | | | | | | | | **1958** Distribution en pourcentage: |
| Value added........ | 100.0 | 32.8 | 30.1 | 0.7 | 1.9 | 1.3 | 2.1 | 0.6 | 2.1 | 9.8 | 4.4 | 6.2 | 7.4 | 0.6 | Valeur ajoutée |
| Number of engaged.. | 100.0 | 29.8 | 33.8 | 0.9 | 2.0 | 1.7 | 1.5 | 0.6 | 2.5 | 5.6 | 5.9 | 4.1 | 10.9 | 0.7 | Nombre de personnes occupées |
| Value added per person engaged........... | 12.8 | 14.1 | 11.3 | 10.3 | 11.6 | 10.1 | 17.8 | 12.1 | 10.8 | 22.3 | 9.5 | 19.3 | 8.7 | 9.6 | Valeur ajoutée par personne occupée |
| Employees as a percent of engaged........ | 98.4 | 98.0 | 99.3 | 100.0 | 93.3 | 98.0 | 97.8 | 94.1 | 98.6 | 97.0 | 97.7 | 99.2 | 98.8 | 95.0 | Salariés en pourcentage des personnes occupées |
| Value added per unit of wages and salaries............ | 3.16 | 4.50 | 2.72 | 2.17 | 3.28 | 2.09 | 3.14 | 2.37 | 2.40 | 5.00 | 2.45 | 3.56 | 1.76 | 2.12 | Valeur ajoutée par unité de traitements et salaires |
| Wages and salaries per employee........ | 4.1 | 3.2 | 4.2 | 4.8 | 3.8 | 5.0 | 5.8 | 5.4 | 4.6 | 4.6 | 4.0 | 5.5 | 5.0 | 4.7 | Traitements et salaires par salarié |

## Gross Domestic Product

Estimates of gross domestic product according to origin were obtained from replies of the Statistics Branch, Ministry of Economic Development, Entebbe, to the United Nations national accounts questionnaires. Official estimates are issued and published annually by the Statistics Branch in the *Statistical Abstract of Uganda*. Definitions and methods of estimation are described in the *Gross Domestic Product of Uganda, 1954-1959*.

## Index of Industrial Employment

The index numbers of industrial employment shown in Table 1 were calculated from absolute figures of employment covering all sizes of establishments as published in the *Statistical Abstract of Uganda, 1959, 1960* or *1961*. The absolute figures used for the calculation of the index numbers were those relating to labour of all races, i.e. African, European, Asian and other, as of June of each year.

## The Characteristics and Structure of Industry

The information shown in Table 3 was obtained from the *Statistical Abstract of Uganda, 1957* and *1959*. The Statistics Branch carries out in June of each year an annual Enumeration of Employees which prior to 1958 covered establishments engaging 5 or more persons. Since 1958 the coverage of the annual enumeration was extended to establishments of all sizes. The 1953 figures relating to labour (persons engaged and wages and salaries) are confined to Africans. The corresponding figures for 1956 and 1958 relate to labour of all races. The figure for persons engaged relate to June of the year in question. Wages and salaries relate to annual estimates obtained by multiplying the cash wages and salaries for June by 12. They include fixed bonuses or allowances but exclude overtime payments and production bonuses. Non-cash emoluments such as free rations, housing, etc., are also excluded.

Establishments engaged in the curing of coffee were included in the 1953 and 1956 data with Food manufacturing. According to the ISIC classification coffee curing belongs to Agricultural Services (ISIC group 012). It is probable that electricity, water and sanitary services were included with manufacturing activities for all the years.

## Produit intérieur brut

Les estimations du produit intérieur brut par branche d'activité d'origine ont été fournies par la Division des statistiques, Ministère du développement économique, Entebbe, en réponse au questionnaire de l'ONU sur la comptabilité nationale. Les estimations officielles sont publiées annuellement par la Division des statistiques dans *Statistical Abstract of Uganda*. Les définitions et méthodes d'estimation sont exposées dans *Gross Domestic Product of Uganda, 1954-1959*.

## Indices de l'emploi dans l'industrie

Les indices de l'emploi dans l'industrie (tableau 1) ont été calculés à partir de chiffres absolus de l'emploi dans les établissements de toutes dimensions, publiés dans *Statistical Abstract of Uganda, 1959, 1960* ou *1961*. Les chiffres absolus utilisés pour le calcul des indices concernent le nombre des travailleurs de toutes races (Africains, Européens, Asiatiques et autres) pendant le mois de juin de chaque année.

## Caractéristiques et structure de l'industrie

Les données du tableau 3 sont tirées du *Statistical Abstract of Uganda, 1957* et *1959*. La division des statistiques effectue, au mois de juin de chaque année, un dénombrement annuel des salariés, qui, jusqu'en 1958, portait sur les établissements occupant cinq personnes ou plus. Depuis 1958, ce dénombrement porte sur les établissements de toutes dimensions. Les chiffres de l'emploi en 1953, (personnes occupées et traitements et salaires) ne concernent que les Africains. Les chiffres correspondants de 1956 et 1958 portent sur les travailleurs de toutes races. Les chiffres concernant le nombre de personnes occupées sont relatifs au mois de juin de l'année en question. Les traitements et salaires sont des estimations annuelles obtenues en multipliant par 12 les sommes versées à ce titre pendant le mois de juin. Ils comprennent les primes et indemnités fixes, mais non la rémunération des heures supplémentaires ni les primes de rendement. Les paiements en nature sous forme de nourriture, logement, etc. sont également exclus.

En 1953 et 1956, les établissements s'occupant de la préparation des grains de café étaient inclus dans Industries alimentaires. Selon la CITI, la préparation des grains de café relève des Activités annexes de l'agriculture (CITI groupe 012). Il est probable que l'électricité, l'eau et les services sanitaires sont inclus dans les activités manufacturières pour toutes les années.

752

## 1. THE GROSS DOMESTIC PRODUCT AT FACTOR COST ACCORDING TO ORIGIN
## ORIGINE PAR SECTEUR D'ACTIVITE DU PRODUIT INTERIEUR BRUT AU COUT DES FACTEURS

Thousand Pounds Sterling      Milliers de livres sterling

| Item of data and year / Rubrique et année | Total | Agricultural sector / Secteur agricole | industrial Sector — Secteur industriel | | | | | Transportation and communication / Transports et communications | Other sectors / Autres secteurs |
|---|---|---|---|---|---|---|---|---|---|
| | | | Total | Mining / Industries extractives | Manufacturing / Industries manufacturières | Construction / Bâtiment et travaux publics | Electricity, gas and water / Electricité, gaz et eau | | |
| ISIC — CITI | 0–9 | 0 | 1–5 | 1 | 2–3 | 4 | 5 | 7 | 6, 8–9 |
| | At Current Prices — Aux prix courants | | | | | | | | |
| Absolute figures — Chiffres absolus | | | | | | | | | |
| 1954............ | 128 728 | 88 726 | 14 653 | 858 | 9 132 | 3 926 | 737 | 3 671 | 21 678 |
| 1955............ | 140 182 | 93 324 | 17 356 | 1 071 | 11 026 | 4 343 | 916 | 4 334 | 25 168 |
| 1956............ | 141 581 | 90 569 | 19 246 | 1 140 | 11 694 | 5 356 | 1 056 | 4 189 | 27 577 |
| 1957............ | 146 718 | 93 867 | 17 731 | 1 463 | 11 050 | 3 912 | 1 306 | 4 628 | 30 492 |
| 1958............ | 146 809 | 93 414 | 17 568 | 1 580 | 10 261 | 4 191 | 1 556 | 5 255 | 30 555 |
| 1959............ | 150 116 | 93 328 | 18 206 | 2 183 | 10 309 | 3 937 | 1 777 | 5 627 | 32 955 |
| 1960............ | 152 201 | 93 811 | 17 591 | 2 186 | 9 801 | 3 835 | 1 769 | 6 059 | 34 740 |
| Percentage distribution according to sector— Distribution en pourcentage par secteur | | | | | | | | | |
| 1954............ | 100.0 | 68.9 | 11.4 | 0.7 | 7.1 | 3.0 | 0.6 | 2.9 | 16.8 |
| 1958............ | 100.0 | 63.6 | 12.0 | 1.1 | 7.0 | 2.8 | 1.1 | 3.6 | 20.8 |
| 1960............ | 100.0 | 61.6 | 11.6 | 1.4 | 6.5 | 2.5 | 1.2 | 4.0 | 22.8 |

## 2. INDEX NUMBERS OF INDUSTRIAL EMPLOYMENT — INDICES DE L'EMPLOI DANS L'INDUSTRIE

### A. The Divisions of Industrial Activity
### Les branches de l'activité industrielle

| Period / Période | Total | Mining / Industries extractives | Manufacturing, electricity and water / Industries manufacturières et électricité et eau | Construction / Bâtiment et travaux publics |
|---|---|---|---|---|
| SIC — CITI | 1-3, 511, 521-522 | 1 | 2-3, 511, 521-522 | 4 |
| a. Indexes — Indices (1958 = 100) | | | | |
| 1958.......... | 100 | 100 | 100 | 100 |
| 1959.......... | 101 | 129 | 98 | 87 |
| 1960.......... | 103 | 134 | 99 | 80 |
| b. Average Annual Rate of Change — Taux annuel moyen de variation | | | | |
| 1958 – 1960.... | 1.4 | 15.8 | —0.5 | —10.6 |

### B. The Major Groups of Manufacturing
### Les classes de la branche industries manufacturières

| Period / Période | Manufacturing, electricity, and water / Industries manufacturières et électricité et eau | Food, beverages and tobacco / Industries alimentaires, boissons, tabac | Cotton ginning / Egrenage du coton | Other / Divers |
|---|---|---|---|---|
| ISIC — CITI | 2-3, 511, 521-522 | 20-22 | Part 231 | Part 231, 232-239, 24-39 |
| a. Indexes — Indices (1958 = 100) | | | | |
| 1958.......... | 100 | 100 | 100 | 100 |
| 1959.......... | 98 | 102 | 101 | 95 |
| 1960.......... | 99 | 109 | 103 | 94 |
| b. Average Annual Rate of Change — Taux annuel moyen de variation | | | | |
| 1958 – 1960.... | —0.5 | 4.4 | 1.5 | —3.0 |

# UGANDA

## 3.  THE CHARACTERISTICS OF INDUSTRIAL ESTABLISHMENTS
## CARACTERISTIQUES DES ETABLISSEMENTS INDUSTRIELS
### 1953, 1956, 1958

Number of establishments in units; wages and salaries in thousand Pounds Sterling; number of engaged in units.

Nombre d'établissements en unités; traitements et salaires en milliers de livres sterlings; nombre de personnes occupées en unités.

### A.  The Divisions of Industrial Activity
### Les branches de l'activité industrielle

| Year and item of data | Total | Mining Industries ex-tractives | Manufacturing, electricity and water [1] Industries manufacturières et électricité et eau [1] | Construction Bâtiment et travaux publics | Année et rubrique |
|---|---|---|---|---|---|
| ISIC | 1–4, 511, 521–522 | 1 | 2–3, 511, 521–522 | 4 | CITI |
| **1953** | | | | | **1953** |
| Number of establishments | 742 | 38 | 539 | 165 | Nombre d'établissements |
| Number of engaged (as of June) | 85 764 | 7 037 | 30 291 | 48 436 | Nombre de personnes occupées (en juin) |
| Wages and salaries | 6 917 | 675 | 2 910 | 3 332 | Traitements et salaires |
| Distribution in percent of number of persons engaged | 100.0 | 8.2 | 35.3 | 56.5 | Distribution en pourcentage du nombre de personnes occupées |
| **1956** | | | | | **1956** |
| Number of establishments | 867 | 38 | 607 | 222 | Nombre d'établissements |
| Number of engaged (as of June) | 80 839 | 6 106 | 36 617 | 38 116 | Nombre de personnes occupées (en juin) |
| Wages and salaries | 7 017 | 436 | 3 293 | 3 288 | Traitements et salaires |
| Distribution in percent of number of persons engaged | 100.0 | 7.6 | 45.3 | 47.1 | Distribution en pourcentage du nombre de personnes occupées |
| **1958** | | | | | **1958** |
| Number of establishments | 1 097 | 43 | 819 | 235 | Nombre d'établissements |
| Number of engaged (as of June) | 75 265 | 4 244 | 32 510 | 38 511 | Nombre de personnes occupées (en juin) |
| Wages and salaries | 7 658 | 492 | 3 729 | 3 437 | Traitements et salaires |
| Distribution in percent of number of persons engaged | 100.0 | 5.6 | 43.2 | 51.2 | Distribution en pourcentage du nombre de personnes occupées |

[1] The 1953 and 1956 figures include the curing of coffee which belong to Agricultural Services (ISIC group 012).

### B.  The Major Groups of Manufacturing
### Les classes de la branche Industrie manufacturières

| Year and item of data | Manufacturing, electricity and water [1] Industries manufacturières et électricité et eau [1] | Food, beverages and tobacco [1] Industries alimen-taires, boissons, tabac [1] | Cotton ginning Egrenage du coton | Other Divers | Année et rubrique |
|---|---|---|---|---|---|
| ISIC | 2–3, 511, 521–522 | 20–22 | Part 231 | Part 231, 232–239, 24–39 | CITI |
| **1953** | | | | | **1953** |
| Number of establishments | 539 | 97 | 141 | 301 | Nombre d'établissements |
| Number of engaged (as of June) | 30 291 | 9 825 | 6 258 | 14 208 | Nombre de personnes occupées (en juin) |
| Wages and salaries | 2 910 | 910 | 639 | 1 361 | Traitements et salaires |
| Distribution in percent of number of persons engaged | 100.0 | 32.4 | 20.7 | 46.9 | Distribution en pourcentage du nombre de personnes occupées |
| **1956** | | | | | **1956** |
| Number of establishments | 607 | 125 | 146 | 336 | Nombre d'établissements |
| Number of engaged (as of June) | 36 617 | 11 906 | 9 281 | 15 430 | Nombre de personnes occupées (en juin) |
| Wages and salaries | 3 293 | 872 | 551 | 1 870 | Traitements et salaires |
| Distribution in percent of number of persons engaged | 100.0 | 32.5 | 25.4 | 42.1 | Distribution en pourcentage du nombre de personnes occupées |
| **1958** | | | | | **1958** |
| Number of establishments | 819 | 127 | 142 | 550 | Nombre d'établissements |
| Number of engaged (as of June) | 32 510 | 7 693 | 4 470 | 20 349 | Nombre de personnes occupées (en juin) |
| Wages and salaries | 3 729 | 684 | 438 | 2 607 | Traitements et salaires |
| Distribution in percent of number of persons engaged | 100.0 | 23.7 | 13.7 | 62.6 | Distribution en pourcentage du nombre de personnes occupées |

[1] Les chiffres de 1953 et 1956 comprennent la préparation des grains de café, qui relève des Activités annexes de l'agriculture (CITI groupe 012).

# UNION OF SOVIET SOCIALIST REPUBLICS
# UNION DES REPUBLIQUES SOCIALISTES SOVIETIQUES

## Net Material Product

The figures of the net material product shown in Table 1 were compiled from *Narodnoe Khozaistvo, 1961,* published by the Central Statistical Administration, Moscow. The concepts governing the data are those of the system of material product accounts which is briefly described in the introduction to this publication. These concepts differ, in a number of respects, from the principles and definitions of the United Nations system of national accounts.

## Index Numbers of Industrial Production

The index numbers set out in Table 2 are compiled by the Central Statistical Administration of the USSR and have been published in *Narodnoe Khozaistvo, 1961* and earlier issues. These index numbers are shown in Table 2 essentially classified according to the broad categories of the industrial classification of the USSR.

The series of index numbers relate to the value of the gross industrial output, expressed in constant enterprise prices (i.e., excluding turnover taxes) of all publicly owned and co-operative enterprises principally engaged in mining, manufacturing and the production of electricity, gas and steam. The gross industrial output of these enterprises covers products shipped during the period; changes, between the beginning and end of the period, in stocks of products ready for shipment, in stocks of tools, dies, containers and the like made by ancillary shops for use in the enterprise, and in work-in-progress; capital repairs on own account during the period on machinery and equipment; and contract services of an industrial nature rendered to others. The constant prices utilized to value the gross industrial output were prices as of 1926-1927 for years prior to 1951, as of 1 January 1952 for 1951-1955 and as of 1 July 1955 for 1956 and later years.

The series of indexes shown in Table 2 are the equivalent of index numbers computed as base-weighted arithmetic averages of series of relatives on quanta of production for all of the elements of gross industrial output. The weights utilized in combining these relatives into indexes may be considered to be the value of the gross industrial output during the comparison base year expressed in the constant enterprise prices utilized for that year.

Further information concerning the series of index numbers may be found in *Narodnoe Khozaistvo, 1961* and *Industrial Statistics* by Dr. A. I. Ezkov, Deputy Di-

## Produit matériel net

Les chiffres du tableau 1 concernant le produit matériel net sont tirés du *Narodnoe Khozaistvo, 1961,* publié par l'Office central de statistique, Moscou. Les concepts sur lesquels reposent les données sont ceux du système de comptabilité du produit matériel, qui est décrit brièvement dans l'introduction de cette publication. Ces concepts diffèrent, à plusieurs égards, des principes et définitions du système de comptabilité nationale de l'ONU.

## Indices de la production industrielle

Les indices du tableau 2, calculés par l'Office central de statistique de l'URSS, ont été publiés dans *Narodnoe Khozaistvo, 1961,* ainsi que dans des numéros précédents de cette publication. Ils sont classés essentiellement selon les grandes catégories de la classification industrielle de l'URSS.

Les séries d'indices se rapportent à la valeur de la production industrielle brute, exprimée en prix constants des entreprises (c'est-à-dire non compris les impôts sur le chiffre d'affaires), de toutes les entreprises publiques et coopératives dont l'activité principale relève des industries extractives, manufacturières ou productrices d'électricité, de gaz et de vapeur. La production industrielle brute de ces entreprises comprend : les produits expédiés pendant la période de référence; les variations enregistrées, entre le début et la fin de la période de référence, dans les stocks de produits sur le point d'être expédiés, dans les stocks d'outils, de moules, de récipients et autres articles analogues fabriqués par des entreprises auxiliaires et destinés à être utilisés par l'entreprise, et dans les travaux en cours; les réparations de machines et d'équipement pour compte propre effectuées pendant la période et constituant une formation de capital; les services contractuels de caractère industriel rendus à des tiers. Les prix constants adoptés pour évaluer la production industrielle brute sont les prix établis en 1926-1927 pour les années antérieures à 1951, les prix établis au 1er janvier 1952 pour 1951-1955 et les prix établis au 1er juillet 1955 pour 1956 et les années suivantes.

Les séries d'indices du tableau 2 équivalent à des moyennes arithmétiques à pondération fixe de séries de rapports fondés sur les quanta de la production relatifs à tous les éléments constitutifs de la production industrielle brute. Pour combiner ces rapports en indices, on a utilisé des coefficients de pondération que l'on peut considérer comme étant la valeur de la production industrielle brute pendant l'année de référence, exprimée en prix constants des entreprises établis pour cette année.

Pour plus de renseignements sur les séries d'indices, voir *Narodnoe Khozaistvo, 1961* et *Industrial Statistics* de M. A. I. Ezkov, directeur adjoint de l'Office central

rector, Central Statistical Administration of the USSR, translated at and published by the Indian Statistical Institute, Calcutta, 1958.

de statistique de l'URSS, traduit et publié par l'Institut indien de statistique, Calcutta, 1958.

### Index Numbers of Industrial Employment

The index numbers appearing in Table 3 were compiled from absolute figures of the employment of operatives (manual workers) published in *Narodnoe Khozaistvo, 1961* and earlier issues. The absolute figures relate to the average number of operatives during each month of the year who are employed in the industrial activities of publicly owned enterprises classified to the mining, manufacturing, or electricity, gas or steam industries.

### Indices de l'emploi dans l'industrie

Les indices du tableau 3 ont été calculés à partir de chiffres absolus de l'emploi indiquant le nombre d'ouvriers (travailleurs manuels), qui ont été publiés dans *Narodnoe Khozaistvo, 1961* et dans des numéros précédents. Les chiffres absolus représentent le nombre moyen, pendant chaque mois de l'année, des ouvriers affectés aux activités industrielles des entreprises publiques relevant des industries extractives, manufacturières, et productrices d'électricité, de gaz ou de vapeur.

### The Characteristics of Industrial Activity

The data shown in Table 4 were abstracted from *Promyshlennost USSR,* published by the Central Statistical Administration, 1957 and *Narodnoe Khozaistvo, 1961* and earlier years. The classifications shown for the data are categories of the scheme of industrial classification of the USSR. The figures cover publicly owned enterprises.

In the case of enterprises classified to the mining, manufacturing and public utility industries, the data shown in Table 4 on number of persons engaged (i.e., employees) is restricted to those employed in "productive" activities only; and the count of operatives is restricted to manual workers employed in the industrial activities. In the case of enterprises mainly engaged in contract construction, the number of persons engaged (i.e., employees) covers those employed in construction activities only. All of the figures refer to the average number employed during each month of the year.

The figures of the value of fixed assets shown in Table 4 represent the cost of replacing them, given the present condition of these capital goods, measured in prices as of 1 January 1960. These data result from a special census of fixed assets taken as of 31 December 1959. The data on the contribution of the various costs of production to the total cost are based on valuations in current prices. The index numbers (1958 = 100) of electricity consumed per operative refer to the use of electricity in only the industrial activities of the enterprises covered.

### Caractéristiques de l'activité industrielle

Les données du tableau 4 sont tirées de *Promyshlennost USSR,* publié par l'Office central de statistique en 1957 et *Narodnoe Khozaistvo, 1961* et années précédentes. Les données sont classées suivant les catégories de la classification industrielle de l'URSS. Les chiffres concernent les entreprises publiques.

Pour le entreprises des industries extractives et manufacturières et des industries d'utilité publique, les données du tableau 4 relatives au nombre de personnes occupées (c'est-à-dire de salariés) concernent uniquement les activités qui contribuent à la formation du produit matériel et le nombre d'ouvriers est celui des travailleurs manuels affectés aux activités industrielles. Pour les entreprises effectuant principalement des travaux de construction contractuels, le nombre de personnes occupées (c'est-à-dire de salariés) concerne exclusivement les personnes affectées aux activités de construction. Tous les chiffres représentent les moyennes pendant chaque mois de l'année.

Les chiffres du tableau 4 relatifs à la valeur des capitaux fixes représentent le coût du remplacement des biens de capital, dans leur état actuel, en fonction des prix établis au 1er janvier 1960. Ces données proviennent d'un recensement spécial des capitaux fixes effectué au 31 décembre 1959. Les données concernant les différentes composantes du coût total de la production sont fondées sur des évaluations aux prix courants. Les indices (1958 = 100) relatifs à l'électricité consommée par ouvrier ne concernent que les activités industrielles des entreprises.

## 1. THE NET MATERIAL PRODUCT — PRODUIT MATERIEL NET

Thousand million New Rubles                    Milliards de nouveaux roubles

### A. The Net Material Product in Constant Prices [1] — Produit matériel net en prix constants [1]

| Year<br>Année | Index numbers<br>Indices<br>(1958 = 100) | Year<br>Année | Index numbers<br>Indices<br>(1958 = 100) | Period<br>Période | Average annual rate of growth<br>Taux annuel moyen d'accroissement |
|---|---|---|---|---|---|
| 1940 | 27 | 1955 | 75 | 1940–1960 | 7.6 |
| 1950 | 44 | 1956 | – 83 – | 1950–1960 | 10.3 |
| 1951 | –46– | 1957 | 89 | 1950–1953 | 10.9 |
| 1952 | 54 | 1958 | 100 | 1954–1958 | 10.5 |
| 1953 | 60 | 1959 | –108– | 1958–1960 | 8.2 |
| 1954 | 67 | 1960 | 117 | | |
| | | 1961 | 125 | | |

For footnotes see end of table.                    Pour les notes, voir au bas du tableau.

### B. The Net Material Product According to Origin
### Origine par secteur d'activité du produit matériel net

| Item of data and year<br>Rubrique et année | Total | Agricultural sector<br>Secteur agricole | Mining, manufacturing, electricity, gas and steam<br>Industries extractives et manufacturières, et électricité, gaz et vapeur | Construction<br>Bâtiment et travaux publics | Transportation and communication [2]<br>Transports et communications [2] | Other sectors<br>Autres secteurs |
|---|---|---|---|---|---|---|
| ISIC — CITI | 0–521, 61, 7, 841, 852 | 0 | 1–51 | 4 | 7 | 521, 61 841, 852 |
| | | | *a.* At Current Prices — Aux prix courants | | | |
| Absolute figures — Chiffres absolus<br>1961 | 152.9 | 32.5 | 79.2 | 14.9 | 8.6 | 17.7 |
| Percentage distribution according to sector — Distribution en pourcentage par secteur<br>1958 | 100.0 | 24.1 | 50.2 | 9.5 | 4.4 | 11.8 |
| 1959 | 100.0 | 21.3 | 52.3 | 9.5 | 4.8 | 12.1 |
| 1960 | 100.0 | 20.5 | 52.2 | 10.0 | 5.3 | 12.0 |
| 1961 | 100.0 | 21.2 | 51.8 | 9.8 | 5.6 | 11.6 |
| | | | *b.* In Constant Prices [1] — En prix constants [1] | | | |
| Index Numbers—Indices (1953=100)<br>1961 | 209 | 153 | 227 | 226 | 306 | 201 |
| Average annual rate of growth — Taux annuel moyen d'accroissement<br>1953–1961 | 9.7 | 5.5 | 10.8 | 10.7 | 15.0 | 9.1 |

For footnotes see end of table.                    Pour les notes, voir au bas du tableau.

## C. Expenditure on the Net Material Product — Dépenses relatives au produit matériel net

| Item of data and year<br>Rubrique et année | Total[3] | Consumption<br>Consommation | | Net Domestic Capital Formation<br>Formation nette de capital intérieur | |
| | | Total | Collective consumption[4]<br>Consommation collective[4] | Total | Fixed<br>Fixe |
| --- | --- | --- | --- | --- | --- |
| | | *a.* At Current Prices — Aux prix courants | | | |
| Absolute figures — Chiffres absolus | | | | | |
| 1959.......................... | 132.9 | 97.3 | 9.3 | 35.6 | 22.8 |
| 1960.......................... | 142.7 | 104.5 | 10.6 | 38.2 | 25.3 |
| 1961.......................... | 151.2 | 108.5 | 11.6 | 42.7 | 25.4 |
| Percentage distribution of average annual expenditure — Distribution en pourcentage des dépenses annuelles moyennes | | | | | |
| 1959.......................... | 100.0 | 73.2 | 7.0 | 26.8 | 17.2 |
| 1960.......................... | 100.0 | 73.2 | 7.4 | 26.8 | 17.7 |
| 1961.......................... | 100.0 | 71.8 | 7.7 | 28.2 | 16.8 |

[1] The constant prices utilized in compiling the index numbers were taken as of 1926-1927 for 1950 and earlier years, as of 1951 for 1951-1955, as of 1956 for 1956-1958 and as of 1958 for 1959 and later years. The series of index numbers were linked to one another at 1951, 1956 and 1959.
[2] Transportation of goods and communication services to "productive" enterprises only.
[3] The figures shown for "Total" are the sum of the figures for the components of the net material product that are shown. The figures shown for "Total" are less than the net material product due primarily to losses in the net material product before its use.
[4] Material consumption by "non-productive" institutions and organizations.

[1] Les prix constants utilisés pour calculer les indices sont les prix établis en 1926-1927 pour 1950 et les années précédentes en 1951 pour 1951-1955, en 1956 pour 1956-1958, et en 1958 pour 1959 et les années suivantes. Les séries d'indices sont raccordées les unes aux autres au niveau de 1951, 1956 et 1959.
[2] Il s'agit uniquement des transports de marchandises et des services de communications relatifs aux entreprises qui concourent à la formation de produit matériel.
[3] Les chiffres présentés sous "Total" sont les sommes des composantes du produit matériel net indiquées. Ils sont inférieurs aux chiffres du produit matériel net en raison, principalement, des pertes subies par le produit matériel net avant son usage.
[4] Produit matériel consommé par les institutions et organisations qui ne concourent pas à sa formation.

## 2. INDEX NUMBERS OF INDUSTRIAL PRODUCTION — INDICES DE LA PRODUCTION INDUSTRIELLE

### A. Selected Major Sub-divisions of Mining and Manufacturing and Electricity and steam
### Quelques subdivisions principales des Industries extractives et manufacturières et électricité et vapeur

| Period / Période | Mining, manufacturing, electricity, gas and steam [1] / Industries extractives et manufacturières et électricité, gaz et vapeur [1] | Food, beverages and tobacco [1] / Industries alimentaires, boissons, tabac [1] | Textiles, clothing and leather products / Textiles, articles d'habillement et articles en cuir | Wood products and furniture [1] / Bois et meubles [1] | Paper and paper products / Papier et ouvrages en papier | Chemicals and chemical and rubber products [2] / Produits, chimiques et ouvrages en caoutchouc [2] | Coal, crude petroleum and products / Charbon, pétrole brut et produits dérivés | Construction material [2] / Matériaux de construction [2] | Glass and porcelain products / Produits en verre et en porcelaine | Ferrous ores and metals / Métaux et minerais ferreux | Non-ferrous ores and metals / Métaux et minerais non-ferreux | Metal products [3] / Ouvrages en métaux [3] | Electricity and steam / Electricité et vapeur |
|---|---|---|---|---|---|---|---|---|---|---|---|---|---|
| ISIC — CITI | 1-3, 51 | 191, 20-22 | 23, 24, 29 | 25-26 | 27 | 192, 30-31 | 11, 13, 32, 512 | 14, 331, 334, 339 | 332-333 | 121, 341 | 122, 342 | 35-38, 391-393 | 511, 513 |

#### a. Indexes — Indices (1958 = 100)

| Period | | | | | | | | | | | | | |
|---|---|---|---|---|---|---|---|---|---|---|---|---|---|
| 1940 | 23 | 50 | 41 | 42 | 24 | 16 | 33 | 12 | 18 | 25 | 19 | 15 | 19 |
| 1950 | 40 | 49 | 46 | 55 | 46 | 30 | 47 | 24 | 35 | 47 | 40 | 31 | 36 |
| 1951 | -47- | -55- | -55- | -62- | -53- | -37- | -52- | -31- | -40- | -54- | -46- | -37- | -41- |
| 1952 | 52 | 60 | 60 | 64 | 59 | 43 | 58 | 36 | 45 | 61 | 55 | 43 | 46 |
| 1953 | 59 | 67 | 66 | 66 | 67 | 48 | 62 | 41 | 51 | 68 | 61 | 49 | 53 |
| 1954 | 66 | 74 | 75 | 74 | 74 | 56 | 68 | 47 | 59 | 74 | 70 | 58 | 60 |
| 1955 | 74 | 78 | 82 | 80 | 80 | 69 | 77 | 60 | 69 | 79 | 78 | 68 | 70 |
| 1956 | -82- | -85- | -88- | -84- | -86- | -79- | -83- | -62- | -79- | -92- | -84- | -78- | -78- |
| 1957 | 91 | 93 | 93 | 90 | 94 | 88 | 90 | 76 | 89 | 99 | 90 | 88 | 87 |
| 1958 | 100 | 100 | 100 | 100 | 100 | 100 | 100 | 100 | 100 | 100 | 100 | 100 | 100 |
| 1959 | 111 | 110 | 108 | 110 | 106 | 111 | 107 | 120 | 114 | 110 | 108 | 115 | 115 |
| 1960 | 122 | 114 | 115 | 116 | 113 | 124 | 116 | 144 | 129 | 121 | ... | 132 | 129 |
| 1961 | 133 | 121 | 119 | 121 | 119 | 140 | 122 | 156 | 143 | 132 | ... | 146 | 145 |

#### b. Average Annual Rate of Change — Taux annuel moyen de variation

| Period | | | | | | | | | | | | | |
|---|---|---|---|---|---|---|---|---|---|---|---|---|---|
| 1940 – 1960 | 8.7 | 4.2 | 5.3 | 5.2 | 8.1 | 10.8 | 6.5 | 13.2 | 10.3 | 8.2 | ... | 11.5 | 10.0 |
| 1940 – 1950 | 5.7 | -0.2 | 1.2 | 2.7 | 6.7 | 6.5 | 3.6 | 7.2 | 6.9 | 6.5 | 7.7 | 7.5 | 6.6 |
| 1950 – 1960 | 11.8 | 8.8 | 9.6 | 7.7 | 9.4 | 15.2 | 9.5 | 19.6 | 13.9 | 9.9 | ... | 15.6 | 13.6 |
| 1950 – 1953 | 13.8 | 11.0 | 12.8 | 6.3 | 13.3 | 17.0 | 9.7 | 19.5 | 13.4 | 13.1 | 15.1 | 16.5 | 13.8 |
| 1954 – 1958 | 10.9 | 7.8 | 7.5 | 7.8 | 7.8 | 15.5 | 10.1 | 20.8 | 14.1 | 7.8 | 9.3 | 14.6 | 13.6 |
| 1958 – 1960 | 10.5 | 6.8 | 7.2 | 7.7 | 6.3 | 11.4 | 7.7 | 20.0 | 13.6 | 10.0 | ... | 14.9 | 13.6 |

[1] Covers all industries classified to Mining, Manufacturing and Electricity, gas and steam, excepting publishing (part of ISIC major group 28) whether or not individual indexes are shown for these industries. Also includes Fishing (ISIC major group 04) and cold storage (part of ISIC major group 72) under Food, beverages and tobacco (ISIC major groups 20-22) and Logging (ISIC group 022) under Wood products and furniture (ISIC major groups 25-26).
[2] The photo-chemical industry (part of ISIC group 392) and the manufacturing of asbestos products (part of ISIC group 339) are included under Chemicals and rubber products (ISIC major groups 30-31).
[3] Includes the following kinds of manufacturing: Professional and scientific equipment, Photographic and optical goods, and Watches and clocks (ISIC groups 391, 392 and 393, respectively).

[1] Il s'agit de toutes les industries classées dans Industries extractives, Industries manufacturières et Electricité, gaz et vapeur, à l'exclusion de l'édition (dans CITI classes 28), que des indices distincts soient présentés ou non pour ces industries. Y compris également: Pêche (CITI classe 04) et entrepôts frigorifiques (dans CITI classe 72) dans Industries alimentaires, boissons et tabac (CITI classes 20-22), et Exploitation forestière (CITI groupe 022) dans Ouvrages en bois et meubles (CITI classes 25-26).
[2] Les industries photo-chimiques (dans CITI 392) et la fabrication des produits en amiante (dans CITI groupe 339) sont comprises dans produits chimiques et Ouvrages en caoutchouc (CITI classes 30-31).
[3] Y compris la fabrication des articles suivants: matériel médico-chirurgical et instruments de précision; matériel photographique et instruments d'optique; montres et horloges (CITI groupes 391, 392 et 393 respectivement).

## B.  Sub-divisions of Textiles, Clothing and Leather Products
### Subdivision des Textiles, articles d'habillement et articles en cuir

| Period / Période | Textiles, clothing and leather products / Textiles, articles d'habillement et articles en cuir | Cotton textiles / Textiles, en coton | Woollen textiles / Textiles en laine | Silk textiles / Textiles en soie | Knitting mills / Bonneterie | Clothing excluding footwear / Articles d'habillement, à l'exclusion des chaussures | Leather and leather products / Cuir et articles en cuir |
|---|---|---|---|---|---|---|---|
| ISIC — CITI | 23, 24, 29 | 231 | 231 | 231 | 232 | 243-244 | 241, 29 |

### a. Indexes — Indices (1958 = 100)

| | | | | | | | |
|---|---|---|---|---|---|---|---|
| 1940 | 41 | 50 | 27 | 30 | 28 | 38 | 43 |
| 1950 | 46 | 52 | 39 | 48 | 34 | 44 | 46 |
| 1951 | −55− | −64− | −42− | −60− | −44− | −49− | −57− |
| 1952 | 60 | 68 | 46 | 72 | 48 | 56 | 61 |
| 1953 | 66 | 76 | 55 | 80 | 55 | 63 | 65 |
| 1954 | 75 | 84 | 70 | 87 | 65 | 74 | 70 |
| 1955 | 82 | 90 | 73 | 96 | 75 | 82 | 77 |
| 1956 | −88− | −91− | −83− | −102− | −81− | −90− | −82− |
| 1957 | 93 | 95 | 90 | 101 | 90 | 91 | 91 |
| 1958 | 100 | 100 | 100 | 100 | 100 | 100 | 100 |
| 1959 | 108 | 106 | 109 | 109 | 109 | 110 | 108 |
| 1960 | 115 | 108 | 119 | 107 | 118 | 119 | 117 |
| 1961 | 119 | 106 | 129 | 105 | 124 | 128 | 124 |

### b. Average Annual Rate of Change — Taux annuel moyen de variation

| | | | | | | | |
|---|---|---|---|---|---|---|---|
| 1940 − 1960 | 5.3 | 3.9 | 7.7 | 6.5 | 7.5 | 5.9 | 5.1 |
| 1940 − 1950 | 1.2 | 0.4 | 3.7 | 4.8 | 2.0 | 1.5 | 0.7 |
| 1950 − 1960 | 9.6 | 7.6 | 11.8 | 8.3 | 13.2 | 10.5 | 9.8 |
| 1950 − 1953 | 12.8 | 13.5 | 12.1 | 18.6 | 17.4 | 12.7 | 12.2 |
| 1954 − 1958 | 7.5 | 4.4 | 9.3 | 3.5 | 11.4 | 7.8 | 9.3 |
| 1958 − 1961 | 7.2 | 3.9 | 9.1 | 3.4 | 8.6 | 9.1 | 8.2 |

## 3. INDEX NUMBERS OF INDUSTRIAL EMPLOYMENT — INDICES DE L'EMPLOI DANS L'INDUSTRIE

| Period<br>Période | Mining,<br>manufacturing,<br>electricity<br>gas and<br>steam [1]<br><br>Industries<br>extractives<br>et<br>manufacturières<br>et<br>électricité<br>gaz et<br>vapeur [1] | Selected Kinds of Industrial Activity — Quelques types d'activité industrielle | | | | | | |
|---|---|---|---|---|---|---|---|---|
| | | Food,<br>beverages<br>and<br>tobacco [1]<br><br>Industries<br>alimen-<br>taires,<br>boissons,<br>tabac [1] | Textiles,<br>clothing<br>and<br>leather<br>products<br><br>Textiles,<br>articles<br>d'habillement<br>et articles<br>en cuir | Coal and<br>coal<br>products<br><br>Charbon et<br>produits<br>dérivés | Crude<br>petroleum,<br>natural gas,<br>and products<br><br>Pétrole brut,<br>gaz naturel<br>et produits<br>dérivés | Construction<br>material [2]<br><br>Matériaux<br>de<br>construction [2] | Ferrous<br>ores and<br>metals<br><br>Métaux et<br>minerais<br>ferreux | Metal<br>products [3]<br><br>Ouvrages<br>en<br>métaux [3] |
| ISIC — CITI | 1-3, 51 | 191, 20-22 | 23, 24, 29 | 11, 329, 512 | 13, 321 | 14, 331, 334, 339 | 121, 341 | 35-38, 391-393 |

### a. Indexes — Indices (1958 = 100)

| | | | | | | | | |
|---|---|---|---|---|---|---|---|---|
| 1940 | 51 | 63 | 59 | 41 | 33 | 24 | 50 | 49 |
| 1955 | 88 | 89 | 86 | 84 | 88 | 77 | 91 | 86 |
| 1956 | 94 | 94 | 95 | 90 | 91 | 84 | ... | 92 |
| 1957 | 97 | 98 | 98 | 95 | 93 | 92 | ... | 96 |
| 1958 | 100 | 100 | 100 | 100 | 100 | 100 | 100 | 100 |
| 1959 | 103 | 102 | 102 | 100 | 101 | 108 | 104 | 104 |
| 1960 | 114 | 105 | 134 | 96 | 105 | 122 | 109 | 115 |
| 1961 | 120 | 110 | 138 | 94 | 112 | 128 | 114 | 126 |

### b. Average Annual Rate of Change — Taux annuel moyen de variation

| | | | | | | | | |
|---|---|---|---|---|---|---|---|---|
| 1940 – 1960 | 4.1 | 2.6 | 4.2 | 4.3 | 6.0 | 8.5 | 4.0 | 4.4 |
| 1955 – 1960 | 5.3 | 3.4 | 9.3 | 2.7 | 3.6 | 9.6 | 3.7 | 6.0 |
| 1955 – 1958 | 4.3 | 4.0 | 5.2 | 6.0 | 7.7 | 9.1 | 3.2 | 5.2 |
| 1958 – 1960 | 6.8 | 2.5 | 15.8 | — 2.0 | 2.5 | 10.5 | 4.4 | 7.2 |

[1] Covers all industries classified to Mining, Manufacturing and Electricity, gas and steam, excepting publishing (part of ISIC major group 28). Also includes Fishing (ISIC major group 04) and cold storage (part of ISIC major group 72) under Food, beverages and tobacco (ISIC major groups 20-22) and Logging (ISIC group 022).
[2] Excludes the manufacture of asbestos products (part of ISIC group 339).
[3] Includes the following kinds of manufacturing: Professional and scientific equipment, Photographic and optical goods, and Watches and clocks (ISIC groups 391, 392 and 393, respectively).

[1] Il s'agit de toutes les industries classées dans Industries extractives, Industries manufacturières et Electricité, gaz et vapeur, à l'exclusion de l'édition (dans CITI classe 28). Y compris également: Pêche (CITI classe 04) et entrepôts frigorifiques (dans CITI classe 72) dans Industries alimentaires, boissons et tabac (CITI classes 20-22) et Exploitation forestière (CITI groupe 022).
[2] Non compris la fabrication des produits en amiante (dans CITI groupe 339).
[3] Y compris la fabrication des articles suivants: matériel médico-chirurgical et instruments de précision; matériel photographique et instruments d'optique; montres et horloges (CITI groupes 391, 392 et 393 respectivement).

## 4. CHARACTERISTICS OF PUBLICLY OWNED INDUSTRIAL ENTERPRISES
## CARACTERISTIQUES DES ENTREPRISES INDUSTRIELLES PUBLIQUES

Number of persons engaged and of operatives in thousands; and value of fixed assets in thousand million New Rubles

Nombre de personnes occupées et d'ouvriers en milliers; valeur des capitaux fixes en milliards de nouveaux roubles

### A. Number of Engaged and Number of Operatives
### Nombre de personnes occupées et nombre d'ouvriers
### 1937 – 1961

| Year<br>Année | Mining, manufacturing, electricity and gas [1]<br>Industries extractives et manufacturières, électricité et gaz [1] | | Number of engaged in construction<br><br>Nombre de personnes occupées dans le bâtiment et les travaux publics |
|---|---|---|---|
| | Number of engaged<br>Nombre de personnes occupées | Number of operatives<br>Nombre d'ouvriers | |
| 1937 | 10 112 | 7 924 | 1 576 |
| 1950 | 14 144 | 11 308 | 2 569 |
| 1953 | 16 261 | ... | 2 843 |
| 1955 | 17 367 | 14 281 | 3 190 |
| 1956 | 18 500 | 15 226 | 3 550 |
| 1957 | 19 144 | 15 760 | 4 000 |
| 1958 | 19 675 | 16 632 | 4 421 |
| 1959 | 20 207 | 16 793 | 4 800 |
| 1960 | 22 291 | 18 574 | 5 143 |
| 1961 | 23 475 | 19 548 | 5 270 |

For footnotes see end of table.     Pour les notes, voir au bas du tableau.

# UNION OF SOVIET SOCIALIST REPUBLICS

## B. Number of Operatives, Value of Fixed Assets, Consumption of Electricity and Structure of Cost of Production
### Nombre d'ouvriers, valeur des capitaux fixes, consommation d'électricité et structure du coût de la production

### Selected Kinds of Industrial Activity — Quelques types de l'activité industrielle

| Item of data and year | Mining, manufacturing, electricity, gas and steam [1] / Industries extractives et manufacturières et électricité, gaz et vapeur [1] | Food beverages and tobacco [1] / Industries alimentaires, boissons, tabac [1] | Textiles, clothing and leather products / Textiles, articles d'habillement et articles en cuir | Chemicals and chemical and rubber products [2] / Produits chimiques et ouvrages en caoutchouc [2] | Coal mining / Extraction du charbon | Crude petroleum and natural gas / Pétrole brut et gaz naturel | Petroleum products / Produits dérivés du pétrole | Construction materiels / Matériaux de construction | Ferrous ore and metals / Minerais et métaux ferreux | Metal products [5] / Produits métalliques [5] | Rubrique et année |
|---|---|---|---|---|---|---|---|---|---|---|---|
| ISIC | 1–3, 51 | 191, 20-22 | 23-24, 29 | 192, 30-31 | 11 | 13 | 21 | 14, 331, 334, 339 | 121, 341 | 35–38, 391-393 | CITI |
| **Number of operatives:** | | | | | | | | | | | **Nombre d'ouvriers:** |
| 1940 | 8 290 | 1 049 | 1 489 | ... | 436 | 45 | 3 | 252 | 405 | 2 395 | 1940 |
| 1955 | 14 281 | 1 478 | 2 158 | ... | 897 | 122 | 3 | 830 | 742 | 4 256 | 1955 |
| 1959 | 16 793 | 1 688 | 2 579 | ... | 1 074 | 140 | 3 | 1 162 | 841 | 5 149 | 1959 |
| **Distribution in percent:** | | | | | | | | | | | **Distribution en pourcentage:** |
| 1940 | 100.0 | 12.6 | 18.0 | ... | 5.2 | 0.5 | 3 | 3.0 | 4.9 | 28.9 | 1940 |
| 1955 | 100.0 | 10.3 | 15.1 | ... | 6.3 | 0.8 | 3 | 5.8 | 5.2 | 29.8 | 1955 |
| 1959 | 100.0 | 10.0 | 15.4 | ... | 6.4 | 0.8 | 3 | 6.9 | 5.0 | 30.7 | 1959 |
| **Value of fixed assets (As of 31.XII.1959):** | | | | | | | | | | | **Valeur des capitaux fixes (au 31.XII.1959):** |
| Amount | 78.9 | 7.2 | 3.6 | 3.9 | 6.9 | 3.7 | 1.5 | 4.2 | 7.6 | 16.0 | Montants |
| Distribution in percent | 100.0 | 9.1 | 4.6 | 4.9 | 8.7 | 4.7 | 1.9 | 5.3 | 9.6 | 20.3 | Distribution en pourcentage |
| **Index numbers of consumption of electricity per operative (1958=100)** | | | | | | | | | | | **Indices de la consommation d'électricité par ouvrier (1958=100):** |
| 1950 | 59.2 | ... | ... | 67.8 | 57.5 | 64.9 | 37.9 | 47.8 [4] | 57.1 | 71.9 | 1950 |
| 1959 | 108.3 | ... | ... | 102.6 | 104.0 | 106.5 | 112.5 | 106.7 [4] | 108.6 | 103.6 | 1959 |
| **Percent of total cost of production during 1955 due to:** | 100.0 | ... | ... | ... | 100.0 | 100.0 | ... | ... | 100.0 | 100.0 | **Pourcentage du coût total de la production dû en 1955:** |
| Raw materials, fuels and electricity | 72.3 | ... | ... | ... | 21.5 | 20.4 | ... | ... | 71.7 | 59.0 | Aux matières premières, combustibles et électricité |
| Wages and salaries | 21.2 | ... | ... | ... | 64.1 | 25.4 | ... | ... | 20.7 | 33.2 | Aux traitements et salaires |
| Depreciation | 3.4 | ... | ... | ... | 6.3 | 42.8 | ... | ... | 5.1 | 4.1 | A l'amortissement |
| Other | 3.1 | ... | ... | ... | 8.1 | 11.4 | ... | ... | 2.5 | 3.7 | A d'autres facteurs |
| **1961 due to:** | 100.0 | 100.0 | 100.0 | 100.0 | 100.0 | 100.0 | 100.0 | 100.0 | 100.0 | 100.0 | **en 1961:** |
| Raw materials, fuels and electricity | 74.2 | 90.5 | 90.8 | 76.8 | 21.1 | 18.1 | ... | 54.3 | 70.8 | 60.8 | Aux matières premières, combustibles et électricité |
| Wages and salaries | 18.9 | 6.3 | 7.6 | 16.1 | 62.5 | 23.0 | ... | 29.9 | 20.0 | 31.3 | Aux traitements et salaires |
| Depreciation | 3.6 | 1.4 | 0.9 | 4.2 | 7.7 | 46.8 | ... | 6.6 | 6.1 | 3.8 | A l'amortissement |
| Other | 3.3 | 1.8 | 0.7 | 2.9 | 8.7 | 12.1 | ... | 9.2 | 3.1 | 4.1 | A d'autres facteurs |

[1] Includes Fishing (ISIC major group 04) and cold storage (part of ISIC major group 72) under Food beverages and tobacco (ISIC major groups 20-22) and Logging (ISIC group 022) but excludes publishing (part of ISIC major group 28).
[2] Includes the Extraction of chemical minerals (ISIC group 192), the photo-chemical industry (part of ISIC group 392) and the manufacture of asbesto products (part of ISIC group 339).
[3] Included in the figures of number of operatives for the Extraction of crude petroleum and natural gas (ISIC major group 13).
[4] Refers to the Manufacture of cement (ISIC group 334) only.
[5] Includes the following kinds of manufacturing: Professional and scientific equipment, Photographic and optical goods and Watches and clocks (ISIC groups 391, 392 and 393, respectively).

[1] Y compris Pêche (CITI classe 04) et entrepôts frigorifiques (dans CITI classe 72) dans Industrie alimentaire, boissons et tabac (CITI classes 20-22) et Exploitation forestière (CITI groupe 022) mais non compris l'édition (dans CITI classe 28).
[2] Y compris l'Extraction des minéraux pour l'industrie chimique (CITI groupe 192), les industries photo-chimiques (dans CITI groupe 392) et la fabrication des produits en amiante (dans CITI groupe 339).
[3] Compris dans les chiffres relatifs au nombre d'ouvriers indiqués pour les Industries extractives de pétrole brut et de gaz naturel (CITI classe 13).
[4] Industries du ciment (CITI groupe 334) seulement.
[5] Y compris la fabrication des articles suivants: matériel médico-chirurgical et instruments de précision; matériel photographique et instruments d'optique; montres et horloges (CITI groupes 391, 392 et 393 respectivement).

# UNITED ARAB REPUBLIC, EGYPT — REPUBLIQUE ARABE UNIE, EGYPTE

## Net Domestic Product

Estimates for the net domestic product at factor cost according to industrial origin are given in Table 1. The data were extracted from information supplied by the Statistics Department, Cairo, to the Statistical Office of the United Nations.

## Index Numbers of Industrial Production

The index numbers set out in Table 2 are derived from the annual indexes of industrial production compiled by the Research Department of the National Bank of Egypt, Cairo, that are published in the Bank's *Economic Bulletin* and made available to the Statistical Office of the United Nations through correspondence. The indexes for 1960 and 1961 were estimated by the Statistical Office of the United Nations using essentially the same methods and series of data as were utilised by the Research Department in the case of the indexes for earlier years.

The annual index numbers are computed from indicators of the quantity of output of individual commodities as base weighted arithmetic averages. The weights are figures of value added at factor cost during 1954 in establishments engaging 10 or more persons that were derived from the 1954 Census described below. For further details on the annual indexes see: *Supplement to the Monthly Bulletin of Statistics, 1959,* Statistical Office of the United Nations.

## Characteristics and Structure of Industrial Activity

The figures shown in Table 3 are based on the results of Censuses of Establishments taken by the Statistical Department, Cairo, as of specified census periods in 1937, 1947, 1954 and 1957. These results were published in *Industrial and Commercial Census, 1937* or *1947* and in *Annuaire Statistique, 1959.* These Censuses included all kinds of industrial establishments, irrespective of size, and related to the establishments in business as of the census dates.

The data in Table 4 provide information on more items than the figures in Table 3 but relate to only part of the mining and manufacturing establishments in operation during the year of inquiry. Establishments owned or managed by governmental authorities, handicrafts, repair, maintenance or training shops were not covered. These data result from the triennial Censuses of Production taken by the Statistical Department, Ministry of Finance, and were compiled from *Census of Industrial Production, 1947* or *1950.* It should be noted that in both the 1947 and 1950 Censuses of Industrial Production, not all of the covered establishments returned usable questionnaires and that the non-response seems to have been

## Produit intérieur net

Le tableau 1 contient des estimations du produit intérieur net au coût des facteurs par secteur d'activité d'origine. Les données ont été tirées de renseignements fournis par le Département de statistique, Le Caire, au Bureau de statistique de l'ONU.

## Indices de la production industrielle

Les indices du tableau 2 sont tirés des indices annuels de la production industrielle établis par le Département de la recherche de la Banque nationale d'Egypte, Le Caire; ces indices annuels sont publiés dans l'*Economic Bulletin* de la Banque et communiqués par correspondance au Bureau de statistique de l'ONU. Les indices de 1960 et 1961 ont été établis par le Bureau de statistique de l'ONU, qui a utilisé les méthodes et séries de données adoptées par le Département de la recherche pour la calcul des indices relatifs aux années antérieures.

Les indices annuels sont des moyennes arithmétiques à pondération fixe, établies à partir d'indicateurs du volume de la production de chaque marchandise. La pondération se fait en fonction de la valeur ajoutée en 1954 au coût des facteurs dans les établissements occupant 10 personnes ou plus, d'après les résultats du recensement de 1954 décrit ci-dessous. Pour plus de détails sur les indices annuels, voir le *Supplément au Bulletin mensuel de statistique, 1959* du Bureau de statistique de l'ONU.

## Caractéristiques et structure de l'activité industrielle

Les chiffres du tableau 3 sont tirés des résultats des recensements des établissements exécutés par le Département de statistique, Le Caire, aux périodes de recensement spécifiées en 1937, 1947, 1954 et 1957. Ces résultats ont été publiés dans *Industrial and Commercial Census, 1937* ou *1947* et dans l'*Annuaire statistique, 1959.* Ces recensements portaient sur les établissements industriels de tout type et de toute dimension qui étaient en activité aux dates des recensements.

Les données du tableau 4 donnent des renseignements sur un plus grand nombre de rubriques que les chiffres du tableau 3, mais elles ne portent que sur une partie des établissements miniers et manufacturiers qui étaient en activité pendant l'année de l'enquête. Les établissements du secteur public, les unités artisanales, les ateliers de réparation, d'entretien ou d'apprentissage n'ont pas été recensés. Les données en question proviennent des recensements de la production effectués tous les trois ans par le Département de la statistique du Ministère des finances; elles ont été tirées de *Census of Industrial Production, 1947* ou *1950.* On notera que, lors des deux recensements de la production industrielle de 1947 et 1950,

greater in the second than in the first of the two Censuses.

Table 5 gives information about the Censuses of Industrial Production of 1954 and 1958. The coverage of these censuses is limited to establishments engaging 10 or more persons during the year of inquiry. They also exclude all units owned or managed by governmental authorities and repair, maintenance or training shops. The 1954 Census is one of the series of biennial Censuses of Industrial Production taken by the Statistical Department, Cairo, between 1952 and 1956, which starting with 1957 became annual Censuses. The 1958 Census is one of these annual Censuses. The results of the 1954 and 1958 Censuses from which the information in Table 5 were compiled, are published in the *Statistical Pocket Year-Book, 1956* and *1959* issued by the Statistical Department, Cairo.

The figures relating to value added for the triennial Censuses shown in Table 4 are gross of the cost of work given out by the reporting establishments. On the other hand, the figures for value added given in Table 5 in respect of the 1954 and 1958 Censuses of Industrial Production exclude this cost. Excise and other indirect taxes levied on sales or production were excluded from the value added in all censuses. In all the censuses, figures for wages and salaries included value of payments in kind for all employees. The definition of the statistical unit—the establishment in the case of mining and manufacturing—seems to have been the same in all censuses and is consistent with the International Standards in Basic Industrial Statistics.

les établissements recensés n'ont pas tous retourné des questionnaires utilisables, et qu'il semble y avoir eu un plus grand nombre de non-réponses au deuxième recensement qu'au premier.

Le tableau 3 fournit des renseignements sur les recensements de la production industrielle de 1954 et 1958. Ces recensements ne portaient que sur les établissements occupant 10 personnes ou plus pendant l'année de l'enquête. En étaient exclus les unités du secteur public, ainsi que les ateliers de réparation, d'entretien ou d'apprentissage. Le recensement de 1954 appartient à la série des recensements bisannuels de la production industrielle exécutés par le Département de statistique, Le Caire, entre 1952 et 1956; ces recensements sont devenus annuels à partir de 1957. Le recensement de 1958 appartient donc à la série des recensements annuels. Les résultats des recensements de 1954 et 1958, d'où sont tirés les renseignements figurant au tableau 5, ont paru dans le *Statistical Pocket Year-Book, 1956* et *1959,* publiés par le Département de statistique, Le Caire.

Les chiffres du tableau 4 relatifs à la valeur ajoutée, qui proviennent des rec~ ~ments trisannuels comprennent le coût des travaux confiés à des sous-traitants par les établissements recensés. En revanche, les chiffres de la valeur ajoutée présentés au tableau 5, qui proviennent des recensements de la production industrielle de 1954 et 1958, ne comprennent pas ce coût. Les droits de consommation et autres impôts indirects frappant les ventes ou la production ont été exclus de la valeur ajoutée dans tous les recensements. Dans tous les recensements également, les chiffres relatifs aux traitements et salaires comprenaient la valeur des paiements en nature pour tous les salariés. La définition de l'unité statistique (l'établissement dans le cas des industries extractives et manufacturières) semble être la même dans tous les recensements et paraît être conforme aux normes internationales relatives aux statistiques industrielles de base.

## 1. THE NET DOMESTIC PRODUCT AT FACTOR COST ACCORDING TO ORIGIN
## ORIGINE PAR SECTEUR D'ACTIVITE DU PRODUIT INTERIEUR NET AU COUT DES FACTEURS

Million Egyptian Pounds        Millions de livres égyptiennes

| Item of data and year / Rubrique et année | Total | Agricultural sector / Secteur agricole | Industrial Sector — Secteur industriel | | | | | Other sectors / Autres secteurs |
|---|---|---|---|---|---|---|---|---|
| | | | Total | Mining / Industries extractives | Manufacturing / Industries manufacturières | Construction / Bâtiment et travaux publics | Electricity, gas and water / Electricité, gaz et eau | |
| ISIC — CITI | 0–9 | 0 | 1–5 | 1 | 2–3 | 4 | 5 | 6–9 |
| *a. At Current Prices — Aux prix courants* | | | | | | | | |
| Absolute figures — Chiffres absolus | | | | | | | | |
| 1950............ | 899.9 | 368.5 | 96.0 | 2.4 | 66.5 | 25.1 | 2.0 | 435.4 |
| 1951............ | 983.1 | 352.4 | 101.3 | 2.5 | 71.5 | 25.1 | 2.2 | 529.4 |
| 1952............ | 851.3 | 272.4 | 95.4 | 2.9 | 65.1 | 25.0 | 2.4 | 483.5 |
| 1953............ | 869.2 | 277.5 | 94.5 | 2.9 | 68.7 | 20.3 | 2.6 | 497.2 |
| 1954............ | 882.5 | 312.0 | 130.7 | 7.2 | 93.4 | 25.4 | 4.7 | 439.8 |
| 1957............ | 1 084.3 | 369.1 | 209.8 | 11.9 | 150.0 | 45.7 | 2.2 | 505.4 |
| 1958............ | 1 185.0 | 371.2 | 226.4 | 10.2 | 162.0 | 51.4 | 2.8 | 587.4 |
| Percentage distribution according to sector— Distribution en pourcentage par secteur | | | | | | | | |
| 1950–1954..... | 100.0 | 35.2 | 11.6 | 0.4 | 8.2 | 2.7 | 0.3 | 53.2 |
| 1950............ | 100.0 | 40.9 | 10.7 | 0.3 | 7.4 | 2.7 | 0.3 | 48.4 |
| 1953............ | 100.0 | 31.9 | 10.8 | 0.3 | 7.9 | 2.3 | 0.3 | 57.3 |
| 1954............ | 100.0 | 35.3 | 14.8 | 0.8 | 10.6 | 2.9 | 0.5 | 49.9 |
| 1958............ | 100.0 | 31.3 | 19.1 | 0.8 | 13.7 | 4.3 | 0.3 | 49.6 |
| *b. At Prices of 1954 — Aux prix de 1954* | | | | | | | | |
| Absolute figures — Chiffres absolus | | | | | | | | |
| 1950............ | 750.4 | 302.9 | 96.0 | 2.4 | 66.5 | 25.1 | 2.0 | 351.5 |
| 1951............ | 829.7 | 303.9 | 101.3 | 2.5 | 71.5 | 25.1 | 2.2 | 424.5 |
| 1952............ | 825.6 | 334.4 | 95.5 | 2.9 | 65.1 | 25.1 | 2.4 | 395.7 |
| 1953............ | 830.1 | 314.7 | 103.3 | 3.3 | 76.8 | 20.3 | 2.9 | 412.1 |
| 1954............ | 882.5 | 312.0 | 130.7 | 7.2 | 93.4 | 25.4 | 4.7 | 439.8 |
| 1955............ | 928.0 | 321.4 | 148.1 | 7.5 | 102.5 | 32.8 | 5.3 | 458.5 |
| 1956............ | 952.4 | 333.2 | 147.0 | 7.2 | 104.4 | 28.9 | 6.5 | 472.2 |
| 1957............ | 978.8 | 342.2 | 182.5 | 10.7 | 132.5 | 37.3 | 2.0 | 454.1 |
| 1958............ | 1 100.4 | 366.9 | 187.2 | 9.7 | 131.7 | 43.2 | 2.6 | 546.3 |
| Percentage distribution according to sector— Distribution en pourcentage par secteur | | | | | | | | |
| 1950–1954..... | 100.0 | 38.0 | 12.8 | 0.5 | 9.0 | 3.0 | 0.3 | 49.2 |
| 1950–1958..... | 100.0 | 36.2 | 14.8 | 0.7 | 10.5 | 3.2 | 0.4 | 49.0 |
| 1950............ | 100.0 | 40.3 | 12.8 | 0.3 | 8.9 | 3.3 | 0.3 | 46.9 |
| 1953............ | 100.0 | 37.9 | 12.4 | 0.4 | 9.2 | 2.5 | 0.3 | 49.7 |
| 1954............ | 100.0 | 35.3 | 14.8 | 0.8 | 10.6 | 2.9 | 0.5 | 49 9 |
| 1958............ | 100.0 | 33.3 | 17.0 | 0.9 | 11.9 | 4.0 | 0.2 | 49.7 |
| Average annual rate of growth—Taux annuel moyen d'accroissement | | | | | | | | |
| 1950–1958..... | 4.9 | 2.4 | 8.7 | 19.1 | 8.9 | 7.0 | 3.3 | 5.7 |
| 1950–1953..... | 3.4 | 1.3 | 2.5 | 11.2 | 4.9 | −6.8 | 13.2 | 5.4 |
| 1954–1958..... | 5.7 | 4.1 | 9.4 | 7.7 | 9.0 | 14.2 | −13.8 | 5.6 |

## 2. INDEX NUMBERS OF INDUSTRIAL PRODUCTION — INDICES DE LA PRODUCTION INDUSTRIELLE

### A. Selected Divisions of Industrial Activity
### Quelques branches de l'activité industrielle

| Period Période | Total | Mining [1] Industries extractives [1] | Manu-facturing [2] Industries manu-facturières [2] | Electricity Electricité |
|---|---|---|---|---|
| ISIC — CITI | 1-3, 511 | 1 | 2-3 | 511 |

#### a. Indexes — Indices (1958 = 100)

| | | | | |
|---|---|---|---|---|
| 1951............ | 66 | 76 | 67 | 32 |
| 1952............ | 69 | 77 | 70 | 33 |
| 1953............ | 70 | 73 | 70 | 63 |
| 1954............ | 73 | 65 | 74 | 65 |
| 1955............ | 80 | 68 | 82 | 74 |
| 1956............ | 84 | 62 | 86 | 81 |
| 1957............ | 90 | 77 | 92 | 89 |
| 1958............ | 100 | 100 | 100 | 100 |
| 1959............ | 103 | 100 | 103 | 112 |

#### b. Average Annual Rate of Change — Taux annuel moyen de variation

| | | | | |
|---|---|---|---|---|
| 1951-1959.... | 5.7 | 3.5 | 5.5 | 16.9 |
| 1951-1953.... | 3.0 | -2.0 | 2.2 | 40.3 |
| 1954-1958.... | 8.2 | 11.4 | 7.8 | 11.4 |

For footnotes see end of table.

Pour les notes, voir au bas du tableau.

### B. Selected Major Groups of Mining
### Quelques classes de la branche Industries extractives

| Period Période | All mining [1] Toutes industries extractives [1] | Crude petroleum and natural gas Pétrole brut et gaz naturel | Other mining [1] Autres industries extractives [1] |
|---|---|---|---|
| ISIC — CITI | 1 | 13 | 19 |

#### a. Indexes — Indices (1958 = 100)

| | | | |
|---|---|---|---|
| 1951............ | 76 | 73 | 108 |
| 1952............ | 77 | 75 | 102 |
| 1953............ | 73 | 71 | 89 |
| 1954............ | 65 | 62 | 100 |
| 1955............ | 68 | 63 | 112 |
| 1956............ | 62 | 57 | 116 |
| 1957............ | 77 | 74 | 104 |
| 1958............ | 100 | 100 | 100 |
| 1959............ | 100 | 99 | 115 |
| 1960............ | 106 | 104 | 119 |
| 1961............ | 120 | 120 | 126 |

#### b. Average Annual Rate of Change — Taux annuel moyen de variation

| | | | |
|---|---|---|---|
| 1951-1960...... | 3.8 | 4.0 | 1.1 |
| 1951-1953...... | -2.0 | -1.4 | -9.2 |
| 1954-1958...... | 11.4 | 12.7 | — |
| 1958-1960...... | 3.0 | 2.0 | 9.1 |

For footnotes see end of table.

Pour les notes, voir au bas du tableau.

### C. Selected Major Groups of Manufacturing
### Quelques classes de la branche Industries manufacturières

| Period Période | Manu-facturing [2] Industries manufacturières [2] | Food, beverages and tobacco Industries alimen-taires, boissons, tabac | Textiles | Furniture Meubles | Paper and paper products Papier et ouvrages en papier | Printing and publishing Im-primerie et édition | Leather and leather products except wearing apparel Cuir et articles en cuir, à l'exclu-sion des articles d'habil-lement | Chemicals and chemical, petroleum and coal products Produits chi-miques et dérivés du pétrole et du charbon | Non-metallic mineral products Produits minéraux non métal-liques | Basic metals Métal-lurgie de base |
|---|---|---|---|---|---|---|---|---|---|---|
| ISIC — CITI | 2-3 | 20-22 | 23 | 26 | 27 | 28 | 29 | 31-32 | 33 | 34 |

#### a. Indexes — Indices (1958 = 100)

| | | | | | | | | | | |
|---|---|---|---|---|---|---|---|---|---|---|
| 1951............. | 67 | 78 | 62 | 80 | 48 | 68 | 93 | 65 | 70 | 32 |
| 1952............. | 70 | 74 | 66 | 78 | 46 | 67 | 103 | 70 | 66 | 50 |
| 1953............. | 70 | 72 | 68 | 65 | 49 | 76 | 101 | 70 | 76 | 58 |
| 1954............. | 74 | 73 | 74 | 79 | 56 | 89 | 109 | 73 | 77 | 76 |
| 1955............. | 82 | 81 | 79 | 86 | 69 | 93 | 125 | 81 | 96 | 86 |
| 1956............. | 86 | 87 | 86 | 103 | 75 | 95 | 122 | 83 | 105 | 92 |
| 1957............. | 92 | 93 | 91 | 91 | 84 | 92 | 107 | 87 | 108 | 90 |
| 1958............. | 100 | 100 | 100 | 100 | 100 | 100 | 100 | 100 | 100 | 100 |
| 1959............. | 103 | 105 | 103 | 103 | 103 | 122 | 116 | 102 | 110 | 111 |
| 1960............. | ... | 112 | 113 | 92 | 124 | 155 | 122 | 108 | 118 | 124 |
| 1961............. | ... | 106 | 122 | 86 | 130 | 200 | 122 | 112 | 116 | 126 |

#### b. Average Annual Rate of Change — Taux annuel moyen de variation

| | | | | | | | | | | |
|---|---|---|---|---|---|---|---|---|---|---|
| 1951-1960........ | ... | 3.9 | 6.9 | 1.6 | 11.1 | 9.5 | 3.1 | 5.8 | 6.0 | 16.2 |
| 1951-1953........ | 2.2 | -3.8 | 4.7 | -9.9 | 1.0 | 5.7 | 4.2 | 3.8 | 4.2 | 34.6 |
| 1954-1958........ | 7.8 | 8.2 | 7.8 | 6.1 | 15.6 | 3.0 | -2.1 | 8.2 | 6.8 | 7.1 |
| 1958-1960........ | ... | 5.8 | 6.3 | -4.1 | 11.4 | 24.5 | 10.5 | 3.9 | 8.6 | 11.4 |

[1] Excludes Metal mining (ISIC major group 12) and Stone quarrying (ISIC major group 14).
[2] Does not relate to the manufacturing of Clothing and made-up textiles (ISIC groups 243-244), Wood products (ISIC major group 25), Rubber products (ISIC major group 30), Metal products except motor car repairing (ISIC major groups 35-38) or Miscellaneous manufacturing (ISIC major group 39).

[1] Non compris l'extraction des minerais métalliques (CITI classe 12) et l'extraction de la pierre à bâtir (CITI classe 14).
[2] Non compris Articles d'habillement et ouvrages en tissu (CITI groupes 243-244), Industrie du bois (CITI classe 25), Ouvrages en caoutchouc (CITI classe 30), Ouvrages en métaux, à l'exclusion de la réparation des automobiles (CITI classes 35-38) et Industries manufacturières diverses (CITI classe 39).

## 3. NUMBER AND EMPLOYMENT OF ALL INDUSTRIAL ESTABLISHMENTS
## NOMBRE D'ETABLISSEMENTS INDUSTRIELS ET EMPLOI DANS CES ETABLISSEMENTS
### 1937, 1947, 1954, 1957

Number of establishments in units; and number of employees in thousands        Nombre d'établissements en unités; nombre de salariés en milliers

### A. The Divisions of Industrial Activity
### Les branches de l'activité industrielle

| Year and item of data | Total | Mining<br>Industries extractives | Manufac-turing [1]<br>Industries manufac-turières [1] | Construc-tion<br>Bâtiment et travaux publics | Electricity, gas, water and sanitary services<br>Electricité, gaz, eau et services sanitaires | Année et rubrique |
|---|---|---|---|---|---|---|
| ISIC | 1-4, 511-522 | 1 | 2-3 | 4 | 511-522 | CITI |
| **1.III.1937**<br>Number of establishments .. | 74 091 | 48 | 69 781 | 833 | 3 429 | **1.III.1937**<br>Nombre d'établissements |
| Number of employees ..... | 260.6 | 6.1 | 235.1 | 7.5 | 11.9 | Nombre de salariés |
| Distribution in percent of number of employees.... | 100.0 | 2.3 | 90.2 | 2.9 | 4.6 | Répartition en pourcentage du nombre de salariés |
| **1.III.1947**<br>Number of establishments .. | 97 612 | 63 | 93 879 | 691 | 2 979 | **1.III.1947**<br>Nombre d'établissements |
| Number of employees ..... | 319.8 | 5.5 | 298.5 | 4.1 | 11.7 | Nombre de salariés |
| Distribution in percent of number of employees.... | 100.0 | 1.7 | 93.3 | 1.3 | 3.7 | Répartition en pourcentage du nombre de salariés |
| **3.VII.1954 – 15.VIII.1954**<br>Number of establishments .. | 73 654 | 59 | 71 823 | 1 650 | 122 | **3.VII.1954 – 15.VIII.1954**<br>Nombre d'établissements |
| Number of engaged ....... | 414 010 | 3 315 | 396 842 | 9 592 | 4 261 | Nombre de personnes occupées |
| Distribution in percent of number of engaged...... | 100.0 | 0.8 | 95.9 | 2.3 | 1.0 | Répartition en pourcentage du nombre de personnes occupées |
| **1.II.1957 – 7.II.1957**<br>Number of establishments .. | 79 616 | 60 | 77 668 | 1 759 | 129 | **1.II.1957 – 7.II.1957**<br>Nombre d'établissements |
| Number of engaged ....... | 465 240 | 8 093 | 437 256 | 15 191 | 4 700 | Nombre de personnes occupées |
| Distribution in percent of number of engaged...... | 100.0 | 1.7 | 94.0 | 3.3 | 1.0 | Répartition en pourcentage du nombre de personnes occupées |

For footnotes see end of table.        Pour les notes, voir au bas du tableau.

### B. The Major Groups of Mining — Les classes de la branche Industries extractives

| Item of data | 1.III.1937 | | | 1.III.1947 | | | Rubrique |
|---|---|---|---|---|---|---|---|
| | All mining<br><br>Toutes industries extractives | Metal mining and crude petroleum<br><br>Extraction des minerais métalliques et pétrole brut | Other mining<br><br>Divers | All mining<br><br>Toutes industries extractives | Metal mining and crude petroleum<br><br>Extraction des minerais métalliques et pétrole brut | Other mining<br><br>Divers | |
| ISIC | 1 | 12–13 | 14–19 | 1 | 12–13 | 14–19 | CITI |
| Number of establishments.. | 48 | 7 | 41 | 63 | 9 | 54 | Nombre d'établissements |
| Number of employees.... | 6.1 | 1.0 | 5.1 | 5.5 | 3.5 | 2.0 | Nombre de salariés |
| Distribution in percent of number of employees... | 100.0 | 16.3 | 83.7 | 100.0 | 63.6 | 36.4 | Répartition en pourcentage du nombre de salariés |

### C. The Major Groups of Manufacturing — Les classes de la branche Industries manufacturières

| Year and item of data | Manufacturing[1]<br>Industries manufacturières[1] | Food, beverages and tobacco<br>Industries alimentaires, boissons, tabac | Textiles | Clothing and made-up textiles[2]<br>Articles d'habillement et ouvrages en tissu[2] | Wood products and furniture<br>Bois et meubles | Paper and paper products<br>Papier et ouvrages en papier | Printing and publishing[1]<br>Imprimerie et édition[1] | Leather and leather products[2]<br>Cuir et articles en cuir[2] | Rubber products<br>Ouvrages en caoutchouc | Chemicals and chemical, petroleum and coal products<br>Produits chimiques et dérivés du pétrole et du charbon | Non-metallic mineral products<br>Produits minéraux non métalliques | Basic metals<br>Métallurgie de base | Metal products<br>Ouvrages en métaux | Other manufacturing<br>Autres industries manufacturières | Année et rubrique |
|---|---|---|---|---|---|---|---|---|---|---|---|---|---|---|---|
| ISIC | 2–3 | 20–22 | 23 | 243–244 | 25–26 | 27 | 28 | 29 | 30 | 31–32 | 33 | 34 | 35–38 | 39 | CITI |
| 1.III.1937 | | | | | | | | | | | | | | | 1.III.1937 |
| Number of establishments. | 69 781 | 8 652 | 6 419 | 29 857 | 8 275 | 101 | 1 052 | 852 | 75 | 484 | 1 336 | 10 075 | | 2 603 | Nombre d'établissements |
| Number of employees... | 235.1 | 62.3 | 48.6 | 32.9 | 13.1 | 2.7 | 8.6 | 2.2 | 0.1 | 7.2 | 9.9 | 39.3 | | 8.2 | Nombre de salariés |
| Distribution in percent of number of employees............ | 100.0 | 26.4 | 20.7 | 14.0 | 5.6 | 1.1 | 3.7 | 0.9 | 0.1 | 3.0 | 4.2 | 16.8 | | 3.5 | Répartition en pourcentage du nombre de salariés |
| 1.III.1947 | | | | | | | | | | | | | | | 1.III.1947 |
| Number of establishments. | 93 879 | 9 001 | 15 672 | 34 841 | 10 215 | 214 | 1 277 | 1 112 | 300 | 678 | 1 614 | 4 123 | 12 013 | 2 819 | Nombre d'établissements |
| Number of employees... | 298.5 | 72.2 | 74.9 | 31.1 | 12.7 | 3.0 | 9.5 | 5.3 | 1.1 | 12.6 | 14.5 | 12.5 | 45.5 | 3.6 | Nombre de salariés |
| Distribution in percent of number of employees............ | 100.0 | 24.1 | 25.1 | 10.4 | 4.3 | 1.0 | 3.2 | 1.8 | 0.3 | 4.3 | 4.8 | 4.2 | 15.2 | 1.3 | Répartition en pourcentage du nombre de salariés |

[1] Includes photography.
[2] The manufacture of shoes and fur apparel is included in Leather and leather products (ISIC major group 29) instead of in Clothing, footwear and made-up textiles (ISIC major group 24).

[1] Y compris la photographie.
[2] La fabrication des chaussures et des vêtements en fourrure est comprise dans Cuir et articles en cuir (CITI classe 29) et non dans Articles d'habillement, chaussures et ouvrages en tissu (CITI classe 24).

## 4. CHARACTERISTICS OF PRIVATELY-OWNED INDUSTRIAL ESTABLISHMENTS ENGAGED IN THE PRODUCTION OF GOODS, EXCLUDING HANDICRAFT UNITS

## CARACTERISTIQUES DES ETABLISSEMENTS INDUSTRIELS PRIVES PRODUISANT DES MARCHANDISES, A L'EXCLUSION DES UNITES ARTISANALES

### 1947, 1950

Number of establishments in units; value added and wages and salaries in thousand Egyptian pounds; number of engaged, employees and operatives in thousands; value added per engaged and wages and salaries per employee in thousand Egyptian pounds.

Nombre d'établissements en unités; valeur ajoutée et traitements et salaires en milliers de livres égyptiennes; nombre de personnes occupées, de salariés et d'ouvriers en milliers; valeur ajoutée par personne occupée et traitements et salaires par salarié en milliers de livres égyptiennes.

### A. Selected Divisions of Industrial Activity — Quelques branches de l'activité industrielle

#### a. Absolute Figures — Chiffres absolus

| Year and item of data | Total | Mining Industries extractives | Manufacturing Industries manufacturières | Electricity and gas Electricité et gaz | Année et rubrique |
|---|---|---|---|---|---|
| ISIC | 1-3,511-512 | 1 | 2-3 | 511-512 | CITI |
| **1947** | | | | | **1947** |
| Number of establishments | 26 707 | 31 | 26 666 | 10 | Nombre d'établissements |
| Value added | 64 494 | 4 418 | 57 618 | 2 458 | Valeur ajoutée |
| Number of engaged (Average during year) | 362.4 | 6.3 | 353.9 | 2.2 | Nombre de personnes occupées (moyenne pendant l'année) |
| Employees: Number (Average during year) | 332.5 | 6.3 | 324.0 | 2.2 | Salariés: Nombre (moyenne pendant l'année) |
| Wages and salaries | 23 955 | 701 | 22 721 | 533 | Traitements et salaires |
| Number of operatives (Average during year) | 305.2 | 5.4 | 298.5 | 1.3 | Nombre d'ouvriers (moyenne pendant l'année) |
| **1950** | | | | | **1950** |
| Number of establishments | 19 516 | 32 | 19 475 | 9 | Nombre d'établissements |
| Value added | 71 516 | 1 804 | 68 675 | 1 037 | Valeur ajoutée |
| Number of engaged (Average during year) | 304.5 | 5.1 | 297.6 | 1.8 | Nombre de personnes occupées (moyenne pendant l'année) |
| Employees: Number (Average during year) | 286.2 | 5.1 | 279.8 | 1.8 | Salariés: Nombre (moyenne pendant l'année) |
| Wages and salaries | 25 674 | 636 | 24 760 | 278 | Traitements et salaires |
| Number of operatives (Average during year) | 260.4 | 4.9 | 254.2 | 1.3 | Nombre d'ouvriers (moyenne pendant l'année) |

#### b. Structure

| Year and item of data | Total | Mining Industries extractives | Manufacturing Industries manufacturières | Electricity and gas Electricité et gaz | Année et rubrique |
|---|---|---|---|---|---|
| ISIC | 1-3,511-512 | 1 | 2-3 | 511-512 | CITI |
| **1947** | | | | | **1947** |
| Distribution in percent of: | | | | | Distribution en pourcentage: |
| Value added | 100.0 | 6.9 | 89.3 | 3.8 | Valeur ajoutée |
| Number of engaged | 100.0 | 1.7 | 97.7 | 0.6 | Nombre de personnes occupées |
| Value added per person engaged | 0.18 | 0.70 | 0.16 | 1.12 | Valeur ajoutée par personne occupée |
| Employees as a percent of engaged | 91.7 | 100.0 | 91.6 | 100.0 | Salariés en pourcentage des personnes occupées |
| Value added per unit of wages and salaries | 2.69 | 6.30 | 2.54 | 4.61 | Valeur ajoutée par unité de traitements et salaires |
| Wages and salaries per employee | 0.07 | 0.11 | 0.07 | 0.24 | Traitements et salaires par salarié |
| Operatives as a percent of employees | 91.8 | 85.7 | 92.1 | 59.1 | Ouvriers en pourcentage des salariés |
| **1950** | | | | | **1950** |
| Distribution in percent of: | | | | | Distribution en pourcentage: |
| Value added | 100.0 | 2.5 | 96.0 | 1.5 | Valeur ajoutée |
| Number of engaged | 100.0 | 1.7 | 97.7 | 0.6 | Nombre de personnes occupées |
| Value added per person engaged | 0.23 | 0.35 | 0.23 | 0.58 | Valeur ajoutée par personne occupée |
| Employees as a percent of engaged | 94.0 | 100.0 | 93.8 | 100.0 | Salariés en pourcentage des personnes occupées |
| Value added per unit of wages and salaries | 2.78 | 2.84 | 2.77 | 3.73 | Valeur ajoutée par unité de traitements et salaires |
| Wages and salaries per employee | 0.09 | 0.12 | 0.09 | 0.15 | Traitements et salaires par salarié |
| Operatives as a percent of employees | 91.0 | 96.1 | 91.0 | 72.2 | Ouvriers en pourcentage des salariés |

# UNITED ARAB REPUBLIC, EGYPT

## B. The Major Groups of Mining — Les classes de la branche Industries extractives

### a. Absolute Figures — Chiffres absolus

| Year and item of data | All mining — Toutes industries extractives | Metal mining — Extraction des minerais métalliques | Crude petroleum and natural gas — Pétrole brut et gaz naturel | Other mining — Divers | Année et rubrique |
|---|---|---|---|---|---|
| ISIC | 1 | 12 | 13 | 14–19 | CITI |
| **1947** | | | | | **1947** |
| Number of establishments | 31 | 5 | 1 | 25 | Nombre d'établissements |
| Value added | 4 418 | 51 | 3 494 | 873 | Valeur ajoutée |
| Number of engaged (Average during year) | 6.3 | 0.9 | 1.9 | 3.5 | Nombre de personnes occupées (moyenne pendant l'année) |
| Employees: Number (Average during year) | 6.3 | 0.9 | 1.9 | 3.5 | Salariés: Nombre (moyenne pendant l'année) |
| Wages and salaries | 701 | 22 | 353 | 326 | Traitements et salaires |
| Number of operatives (Average during year) | 5.4 | 0.5 | 1.6 | 3.3 | Nombre d'ouvriers (moyenne pendant l'année) |
| **1950** | | | | | **1950** |
| Number of establishments | 32 | 4 | 1 | 27 | Nombre d'établissements |
| Value added | 1 804 | 366 | 556 | 882 | Valeur ajoutée |
| Number of engaged (Average during year) | 5.1 | 1.2 | 0.2 | 3.7 | Nombre de personnes occupées (moyenne pendant l'année) |
| Employees: Number (Average during year) | 5.1 | 1.2 | 0.2 | 3.7 | Salariés: Nombre (moyenne pendant l'année) |
| Wages and salaries | 636 | 139 | 86 | 411 | Traitements et salaires |
| Number of operatives (Average during year) | 4.9 | 1.2 | 0.2 | 3.5 | Nombre d'ouvriers (moyenne pendant l'année) |

### b. Structure

| Year and item of data | All mining — Toutes industries extractives | Metal mining — Extraction des minerais métalliques | Crude petroleum and natural gas — Pétrole brut et gaz naturel | Other mining — Divers | Année et rubrique |
|---|---|---|---|---|---|
| ISIC | 1 | 12 | 13 | 14–19 | CITI |
| **1947** | | | | | **1947** |
| Distribution in percent of: | | | | | Distribution en pourcentage: |
| Value added | 100.0 | 1.1 | 79.1 | 19.8 | Valeur ajoutée |
| Number of engaged | 100.0 | 14.3 | 30.2 | 55.5 | Nombre de personnes occupées |
| Value added per person engaged | 0.70 | 0.06 | 1.84 | 0.25 | Valeur ajoutée par personne occupée |
| Employees as a percent of engaged | 100.0 | 100.0 | 100.0 | 100.0 | Salariés en pourcentage des personnes occupées |
| Value added per unit of wages and salaries | 6.30 | 2.32 | 9.90 | 2.68 | Valeur ajoutée par unité de traitements et salaires |
| Wages and salaries per employee | 0.11 | 0.02 | 0.18 | 0.09 | Traitements et salaires par salarié |
| Operatives as a percent of employees | 85.7 | 55.6 | 84.2 | 94.3 | Ouvriers en pourcentage des salariés |
| **1950** | | | | | **1950** |
| Distribution in percent of: | | | | | Distribution en pourcentage: |
| Value added | 100.0 | 20.3 | 30.8 | 48.9 | Valeur ajoutée |
| Number of engaged | 100.0 | 23.5 | 3.9 | 72.6 | Nombre de personnes occupées |
| Value added per person engaged | 0.35 | 0.30 | 2.78 | 0.24 | Valeur ajoutée par personne occupée |
| Employees as a percent of engaged | 100.0 | 100.0 | 100.0 | 100.0 | Salariés en pourcentage des personnes occupées |
| Value added per unit of wages and salaries | 2.84 | 2.63 | 6.46 | 2.14 | Valeur ajoutée par unité de traitements et salaires |
| Wages and salaries per employee | 0.12 | 0.12 | 0.43 | 0.11 | Traitements et salaires par salarié |
| Operatives as a percent of employees | 96.1 | 100.0 | 100.0 | 94.6 | Ouvriers en pourcentage des salariés |

## C. The Major Groups of Manufacturing — Les classes de la branche Industries manufacturières

| Year and item of data | Manufacturing — Industries manufacturières | Food, beverages and tobacco — Industries alimentaires, boissons tabac | Textiles | Clothing, footwear and made-up textiles — Articles d'habillement, chaussures et ouvrages en tissu | Wood products and furniture — Bois et meubles | Paper and paper products — Papier et ouvrages en papier | Printing and publishing — Imprimerie et édition | Leather and leather products except wearing apparel — Cuir et articles en cuir, à l'exclusion des articles d'habillement | Rubber products — Ouvrages en caoutchouc | Chemicals and chemical, petroleum and coal products — Produits chimiques et dérivés du pétrole et du charbon | Non-metallic mineral products — Produits minéraux non métalliques | Basic metals — Métallurgie de base | Metal products — Ouvrages en métaux | Other manufacturing — Autres industries manufacturières | Année et rubrique |
|---|---|---|---|---|---|---|---|---|---|---|---|---|---|---|---|
| ISIC | 2–3 | 20–22 | 23 | 24 | 25–26 | 27 | 28 | 29 | 30 | 31–32 | 33 | 34 | 35–38 | 39 | CITI |
| *a. Absolute Figures — Chiffres absolus* | | | | | | | | | | | | | | | |
| **1947** | | | | | | | | | | | | | | | **1947** |
| Number of establishments | 26 666 | 6 321 | 12 481 | 1 998 | 1 713 | 161 | 382 | 408 | 7 | 381 | 894 | 76 | 1 491 | 353 | Nombre d'établissements |
| Value added | 57 618 | 20 004 | 24 621 | 1 143 | 973 | 568 | 1 346 | 593 | 210 | 4 007 | 1 417 | 182 | 2 239 | 315 | Valeur ajoutée |
| Number of engaged (Average during the year) | 353.9 | 98.0 | 164.4 | 8.7 | 8.5 | 4.9 | 6.4 | 3.8 | 0.9 | 22.1 | 13.8 | 1.3 | 19.1 | 2.0 | Nombre de personnes occupées (moyenne pendant l'année) |
| Employees: Number (Average during the year) | 324.0 | 90.9 | 151.1 | 6.4 | 6.4 | 4.7 | 6.0 | 3.3 | 0.9 | 21.8 | 12.6 | 1.2 | 17.1 | 1.6 | Salariés: Nombre (moyenne pendant l'année) |
| Wages and salaries | 22 721 | 6 419 | 10 288 | 718 | 568 | 314 | 475 | 272 | 92 | 1 661 | 808 | 97 | 849 | 160 | Traitements et salaires |
| Number of operatives (Average during the year) | 298.5 | 80.5 | 141.7 | 6.0 | 6.2 | 4.4 | 5.2 | 3.0 | 0.8 | 19.7 | 12.1 | 1.2 | 16.2 | 1.5 | Nombre d'ouvriers (moyenne pendant l'année) |
| **1950** | | | | | | | | | | | | | | | **1950** |
| Number of establishments | 19 475 | 5 989 | 5 278 | 2 563 | 1 816 | 144 | 346 | 331 | 3 | 379 | 926 | 134 | 1 279 | 287 | Nombre d'établissements |
| Value added | 68 675 | 25 209 | 22 659 | 1 782 | 1 578 | 732 | 2 214 | 716 | 129 | 6 189 | 3 066 | 1 306 | 2 719 | 376 | Valeur ajoutée |
| Number of engaged (Average during the year) | 297.6 | 92.6 | 108.6 | 12.6 | 10.8 | 5.4 | 10.1 | 3.9 | 0.4 | 13.5 | 15.6 | 4.7 | 17.2 | 2.2 | Nombre de personnes occupées (moyenne pendant l'année) |
| Employees: Number (Average during the year) | 279.3 | 87.2 | 103.7 | 10.2 | 9.0 | 5.3 | 9.8 | 3.5 | 0.4 | 13.3 | 14.5 | 4.6 | 15.9 | 1.9 | Salariés: Nombre (moyenne pendant l'année) |
| Wages and salaries | 24 760 | 7 274 | 8 832 | 1 012 | 845 | 392 | 1 210 | 314 | 53 | 1 206 | 1 265 | 565 | 1 618 | 174 | Traitements et salaires |
| Number of operatives (Average during the year) | 254.2 | 76.6 | 97.0 | 9.5 | 8.5 | 4.9 | 8.4 | 3.4 | 0.4 | 11.1 | 13.7 | 4.1 | 14.9 | 1.7 | Nombre d'ouvriers (moyenne pendant l'année) |
| *b. Structure* | | | | | | | | | | | | | | | |
| **1947** | | | | | | | | | | | | | | | **1947** |
| Distribution in percent of: Value added | 100.0 | 34.7 | 42.7 | 2.0 | 1.7 | 1.0 | 2.3 | 1.0 | 0.4 | 6.9 | 2.5 | 0.3 | 3.9 | 0.6 | Distribution en pourcentage: Valeur ajoutée |
| Number of engaged | 100.0 | 27.6 | 46.5 | 2.5 | 2.4 | 1.3 | 1.8 | 1.1 | 0.3 | 6.2 | 3.9 | 0.4 | 5.4 | 0.6 | Nombre de personnes occupées |
| Value added per person engaged | 0.16 | 0.20 | 0.15 | 0.13 | 0.11 | 0.12 | 0.21 | 0.16 | 0.23 | 0.18 | 0.10 | 0.14 | 0.12 | 0.16 | Valeur ajoutée par personne occupée |
| Employees as a percent of engaged | 91.6 | 92.8 | 91.9 | 73.6 | 75.3 | 95.9 | 93.8 | 86.8 | 100.0 | 98.6 | 91.3 | 92.3 | 89.5 | 80.0 | Salariés en pourcentage des personnes occupées |
| Value added per unit of wages and salaries | 2.54 | 3.12 | 2.39 | 1.59 | 1.71 | 1.81 | 2.83 | 2.18 | 2.28 | 2.41 | 1.75 | 1.88 | 2.64 | 1.97 | Valeur ajoutée par unité de traitements et salaires |
| Wages and salaries per employee | 0.07 | 0.07 | 0.07 | 0.11 | 0.09 | 0.07 | 0.08 | 0.08 | 0.10 | 0.08 | 0.06 | 0.08 | 0.05 | 0.10 | Traitements et salaires par salarié |
| Operatives as a percent of employees | 92.1 | 88.6 | 93.8 | 93.8 | 96.9 | 93.6 | 86.7 | 90.9 | 88.9 | 90.4 | 96.0 | 100.0 | 94.7 | 93.8 | Ouvriers en pourcentage des salariés |
| **1950** | | | | | | | | | | | | | | | **1950** |
| Distribution in percent of: Value added | 100.0 | 36.7 | 33.0 | 2.5 | 2.3 | 1.1 | 3.2 | 1.1 | 0.2 | 9.0 | 4.4 | 1.9 | 4.0 | 0.6 | Distribution en pourcentage: Valeur ajoutée |
| Number of engaged | 100.0 | 31.1 | 36.5 | 4.2 | 3.6 | 1.8 | 3.4 | 1.3 | 0.2 | 4.5 | 5.3 | 1.5 | 5.8 | 0.8 | Nombre de personnes occupées |
| Value added per person engaged | 0.23 | 0.27 | 0.21 | 0.14 | 0.15 | 0.14 | 0.22 | 0.18 | 0.32 | 0.46 | 0.20 | 0.28 | 0.16 | 0.17 | Valeur ajoutée par personne occupée |
| Employees as a percent of engaged | 93.8 | 94.2 | 95.5 | 81.0 | 83.3 | 98.1 | 97.0 | 89.7 | 100.0 | 98.5 | 92.9 | 97.9 | 92.4 | 86.4 | Salariés en pourcentage des personnes occupées |
| Value added per unit of wages and salaries | 2.77 | 3.46 | 2.56 | 1.76 | 1.87 | 1.87 | 1.83 | 2.28 | 2.43 | 5.13 | 2.42 | 2.31 | 1.68 | 2.16 | Valeur ajoutée par unité de traitements et salaires |
| Wages and salaries per employee | 0.09 | 0.08 | 0.08 | 0.10 | 0.09 | 0.07 | 0.12 | 0.09 | 0.13 | 0.09 | 0.09 | 0.12 | 0.10 | 0.09 | Traitements et salaires par salarié |
| Operatives as a percent of employees | 91.0 | 87.8 | 93.5 | 93.1 | 94.4 | 92.4 | 85.7 | 97.1 | 100.0 | 83.4 | 94.5 | 89.1 | 93.7 | 89.5 | Ouvriers en pourcentage des salariés |

## 5. THE CHARACTERISTICS OF INDUSTRIAL ESTABLISHMENTS ENGAGING 10 OR MORE PERSONS
## CARACTERISTIQUES DES ETABLISSEMENTS INDUSTRIELS OCCUPANT 10 PERSONNES OU PLUS
### 1954, 1958

Number of establishments in units; value added and wages and salaries in thousand Egyptian Pounds; number of engaged and employees in thousands; and value added per person engaged in thousand Egyptian Pounds.

Nombre d'établissements en unités; valeur ajoutée et traitements et salaires en milliers de livres égyptiennes; nombre de personnes occupées et de salariés en milliers; valeur ajoutée par personne occupée en milliers de livres égyptiennes

### A. Selected Divisions of Industrial Activity — Quelques branches de l'activité industrielle

| Year and item of data | Total | Mining Industries ex-tractives | Manu-facturing Industries manu-facturières | Electricity and gas Electricité et gaz | Année et rubrique | Year and item of data | Total | Mining Industries ex-tractives | Manu-facturing Industries manu-facturières | Electricity and gas Electricité et gaz | Année et rubrique |
|---|---|---|---|---|---|---|---|---|---|---|---|
| ISIC | 1-3, 511-512 | 1 | 2-3 | 511-512 | CITI | ISIC | 1-3, 511-512 | 1 | 2-3 | 511-512 | CITI |
| | a. Absolute Figures — Chiffres absolus | | | | | | b. Structure | | | | |
| **1954** | | | | | **1954** | **1954** | | | | | **1954** |
| Number of establishments.. | 3 781 | 29 | 3 746 | 6 | Nombre d'établissements | Distribution in percent of: | | | | | Distribution en pourcen-tage: |
| Value added............ | 92 012 | 7 539 | 81 626 | 2 847 | Valeur ajoutée | Value added........... | 100.0 | 8.2 | 88.7 | 3.1 | Valeur ajoutée |
| Number of engaged....... | 273.4 | 6.5 | 264.5 | 2.4 | Nombre de personnes occupées | Number of engaged..... | 100.0 | 2.4 | 96.7 | 0.9 | Nombre de personnes occupées |
| Wages and salaries........ | 35 155 | 1 284 | 33 313 | 558 | Traitements et salaires | Value added per person engaged.............. | 0.34 | 1.16 | 0.31 | 1.19 | Valeur ajoutée par personne occupée |
| | | | | | | Value added per unit of wages and salaries...... | 2.62 | 5.87 | 2.45 | 5.10 | Valeur ajoutée par unité de traitements et salaires |
| **1958** | | | | | **1958** | **1958** | | | | | **1958** |
| Number of establishments.. | 3 222 | 55 | 3 164 | 3 | Nombre d'établissements | Distribution in percent of: | | | | | Distribution en pourcen-tage: |
| Value added............ | 125 645 | 9 137 | 114 048 | 2 460 | Valeur ajoutée | Value added........... | 100.0 | 7.3 | 90.8 | 1.9 | Valeur ajoutée |
| Number of engaged....... | 269.9 | 6.7 | 260.8 | 2.4 | Nombre de personnes occupées | Number of engaged..... | 100.0 | 2.5 | 96.6 | 0.9 | Nombre de personnes occupées |
| Wages and salaries........ | 39 896 | 1 404 | 37 960 | 532 | Traitements et salaires | Value added per person engaged.............. | 0.47 | 1.36 | 0.44 | 1.03 | Valeur ajoutée par personne occupée |
| | | | | | | Value added per unit of wages and salaries...... | 3.15 | 6.51 | 3.00 | 4.62 | Valeur ajoutée par unité de traitements et salaires |

### B. The Major Groups of Mining — Les classes de la branche Industries extractives

| Year and item of data | All mining Toutes industries extrac-tives | Metal mining Extraction des minerais métal-liques | Crude petroleum and natural gas Pétrole brut et gaz naturel | Other mining Divers | Année et rubrique | Year and item of data | All mining Toutes industries extrac-tives | Metal mining Extraction des minerais métal-liques | Crude petroleum and natural gas Pétrole brut et gaz naturel | Other mining Divers | Année et rubrique |
|---|---|---|---|---|---|---|---|---|---|---|---|
| ISIC | 1 | 12 | 13 | 14-19 | CITI | ISIC | 1 | 12 | 13 | 14-19 | CITI |
| | a. Absolute Figures — Chiffres absolus | | | | | | b. Structure | | | | |
| **1954** | | | | | **1954** | **1954** | | | | | **1954** |
| Number of establishments.. | 29 | 5 | 3 | 21 | Nombre d'établissements | Distribution in percent of: | | | | | Distribution en pourcen-tage: |
| Value added............ | 7 539 | 153 | 6 302 | 1 084 | Valeur ajoutée | Value added........... | 100.0 | 2.0 | 83.6 | 14.4 | Valeur ajoutée |
| Number of engaged....... | 6.5 | 0.6 | 1.3 | 4.6 | Nombre de personnes occupée | Number of engaged..... | 100.0 | 9.2 | 20.0 | 70.8 | Nombre de personnes occupées |
| Wages and salaries........ | 1 284 | 59 | 639 | 586 | Traitements et salaires | Value added per person engaged.............. | 1.16 | 0.26 | 4.85 | 0.24 | Valeur ajoutée par personne occupée |
| | | | | | | Value added per unit of wages and salaries...... | 5.87 | 2.59 | 9.86 | 1.85 | Valeur ajoutée par unité de traitements et salaires |
| **1958** | | | | | **1958** | **1958** | | | | | **1958** |
| Number of establishments.. | 55 | 8 | 2 | 45 | Nombre d'établissements | Distribution in percent of: | | | | | Distribution en pourcentage: |
| Value added............ | 9 137 | 390 | 6 885 | 1 862 | Valeur ajoutée | Value added........... | 100.0 | 4.3 | 75.3 | 20.4 | Valeur ajoutée |
| Number of engaged....... | 6.7 | 1.2 | 1.5 | 4.0 | Nombre de personnes occupées | Number of engaged..... | 100.0 | 17.9 | 22.4 | 59.7 | Nombre de personnes occupées |
| Wages and salaries........ | 1 404 | 170 | 679 | 555 | Traitements et salaires | Value added per person engaged.............. | 1.36 | 0.32 | 4.59 | 0.46 | Valeur ajoutée par personne occupée |
| | | | | | | Value added per unit of wages and salaries...... | 6.51 | 2.29 | 10.14 | 3.35 | Valeur ajoutée par unité de traitements et salaires |

## C. The Major Groups of Manufacturing — Les classes de la branche Industries manufacturières

| Year and item of data | Manu-facturing — Industries manufac-turières | Food, beverages and tobacco — Industries alimen-taires, boissons, tabac | Textiles | Clothing, footwear and made-up textiles — Articles d'habil-lement, chaussures et ouvrages en tissu | Wood products and furniture — Bois et meubles | Paper and paper products — Papier et ouvrages en papier | Printing and publish-ing — Im-primerie et édition | Leather and leather products except wearing apparel — Cuir et articles en cuir, à l'exclu-sion des articles d'habil-lement | Rubber products — Ouvrages en caout-chouc | Chemicals and chemical, petroleum and coal products — Produits chi-miques et dérivés du pétrole et du charbon | Non-metallic mineral products — Produits minéraux non métal-liques | Basic metals — Métal-lurgie de base | Metal products — Ouvrages en métaux | Other manu-factur-ing — Autres in-dustries manufac-turières | Année et rubrique |
|---|---|---|---|---|---|---|---|---|---|---|---|---|---|---|---|
| ISIC | 1–2 | 20–22 | 23 | 24 | 25–26 | 27 | 28 | 29 | 30 | 31–32 | 33 | 34 | 35–38 | 39 | CITI |
| *a.* Absolute Figures — Chiffres absolus | | | | | | | | | | | | | | | |
| **1954** | | | | | | | | | | | | | | | **1954** |
| Number of establishments | 3 746 | 1 477 | 639 | 220 | 237 | 44 | 161 | 75 | 7 | 118 | 263 | 29 | 416 | 60 | Nombre d'établissements |
| Value added | 81 626 | 19 572 | 35 076 | 1 032 | 1 296 | 1 125 | 2 123 | 518 | 307 | 7 060 | 4 759 | 1 899 | 6 170 | 689 | Valeur ajoutée |
| Number of engaged | 264.5 | 63.4 | 113.7 | 6.1 | 6.9 | 4.5 | 7.7 | 2.7 | 0.9 | 11.4 | 16.9 | 2.8 | 25.6 | 1.9 | Nombre de personnes occupées |
| Wages and salaries | 33 313 | 7 265 | 14 112 | 753 | 687 | 422 | 1 112 | 304 | 131 | 2 263 | 1 940 | 536 | 3 589 | 199 | Traitements et salaires |
| **1958** | | | | | | | | | | | | | | | **1958** |
| Number of establishments | 3 164 | 1 284 | 634 | 118 | 190 | 56 | 141 | 42 | 11 | 101 | 192 | 21 | 313 | 61 | Nombre d'établissements |
| Value added | 114 048 | 32 451 | 41 645 | 1 709 | 1 664 | 2 323 | 2 157 | 647 | 1 885 | 13 985 | 4 785 | 2 733 | 6 813 | 1 251 | Valeur ajoutée |
| Number of engaged | 260.8 | 59.7 | 123.0 | 4.2 | 6.6 | 5.0 | 7.4 | 1.7 | 1.6 | 14.5 | 11.9 | 3.3 | 18.3 | 3.6 | Nombre de personnes occupées |
| Wages and salaries | 37 960 | 7 193 | 16 994 | 677 | 2 076 | 577 | 1 247 | 225 | 273 | 3 102 | 1 572 | 796 | 2 769 | 459 | Traitements et salaires |
| *b.* Structure | | | | | | | | | | | | | | | |
| **1954** Distribution in percent of: | | | | | | | | | | | | | | | **1954** Distribution en pour-centage: |
| Value added | 100.0 | 23.9 | 43.0 | 1.3 | 1.6 | 1.3 | 2.6 | 0.7 | 0.3 | 8.7 | 5.8 | 2.3 | 7.6 | 0.9 | Valeur ajoutée |
| Number of engaged | 100.0 | 23.9 | 43.0 | 2.3 | 2.6 | 1.7 | 2.9 | 1.1 | 0.3 | 4.3 | 6.4 | 1.1 | 9.6 | 0.8 | Nombre de personnes occupées |
| Value added per person engaged | 0.31 | 0.31 | 0.31 | 0.17 | 0.19 | 0.25 | 0.28 | 0.19 | 0.34 | 0.62 | 0.28 | 0.68 | 0.24 | 0.36 | Valeur ajoutée par personne occupée |
| Value added per unit of wages and salaries | 2.45 | 2.69 | 2.48 | 1.37 | 1.89 | 2.66 | 1.91 | 1.70 | 2.34 | 3.12 | 2.45 | 3.54 | 1.72 | 3.46 | Valeur ajoutée par unité de traitements et salaires |
| **1958** Distribution in percent of: | | | | | | | | | | | | | | | **1958** Distribution en pour-centage: |
| Value added | 100.0 | 28.4 | 36.5 | 1.5 | 1.5 | 2.0 | 1.9 | 0.6 | 1.6 | 12.3 | 4.2 | 2.4 | 6.0 | 1.1 | Valeur ajoutée |
| Number of engaged | 100.0 | 22.8 | 47.2 | 1.6 | 2.5 | 2.0 | 2.8 | 0.7 | 0.6 | 5.5 | 4.6 | 1.3 | 7.0 | 1.4 | Nombre de personnes occupées |
| Value added per person engaged | 0.44 | 0.54 | 0.34 | 0.41 | 0.25 | 0.46 | 0.29 | 0.38 | 1.18 | 0.96 | 0.40 | 0.83 | 0.37 | 0.35 | Valeur ajoutée par personne occupée |
| Value added per unit of wages and salaries | 3.00 | 4.51 | 2.45 | 2.52 | 0.80 | 4.02 | 1.73 | 2.88 | 6.90 | 4.51 | 3.04 | 3.43 | 2.46 | 2.72 | Valeur ajoutée par unité de traitements et salaires |

## Gross Domestic Product and Gross Domestic Fixed Capital Formation

The estimates of expenditure on and industrial origin of gross domestic product and of the industrial use of gross domestic fixed capital formation shown in Table 1 are based on the reply of the Central Statistical Office, London to the United Nations national accounts questionnaire. Official estimates are published in *National Income and Expenditure*, issued annually by the above office. A complete description of sources and methods is given in *National Income Statistics, Sources and Methods*, London, 1956.

## Index Numbers of Industrial Production

The index numbers shown in Table 2 for 1948 and subsequent years, are derived from the indexes of industrial production computed by the Central Statistical Office; and published in *The Index of Industrial Production*, Studies in Official Statistics, No. 7, September 1959, the *Monthly Digest of Statistics* and *Annual Abstract of Statistics* or obtained through correspondence. In the case of 1938, the indexes shown in Table 2 were derived by linking, at 1946, the pre-war index numbers of industrial production of the Board of Trade to the indexes of the Central Statistical Office. The sources utilized for data on these index numbers were *Board of Trade Journal*, 29 October 1949 and other issues, and No. 7 of *Studies in Official Statistics*, respectively.

The series of index numbers shown in Table 2 for 1948 and subsequent years relate, in principle, to establishments irrespective of size but do not cover selected kinds of activities which are included in manufacturing in the International Standard Industrial Classification. These activities consist of repair services and custom manufacturing, primarily for households, slaughtering or bottling by wholesalers and a few other activities, all of which are mentioned in the footnotes to Table 2. Though the series of index numbers for 1938 cover, in principle, repair services and custom manufacturing for households, this series refers to units engaging 10 or more persons. The weight base years for the series of index numbers shown in Table 2 are 1930 in the case of the indexes for 1938, 1954 for the indexes for 1948-1957, and 1958 in the case of the indexes for 1958 and subsequent years. The weights utilized are proportional to the contribution to the gross domestic products, at factor cost.

## Le produit intérieur brut et la formation brute de capital fixe intérieur

Les estimations des dépenses imputées au produit intérieur brut et des composantes du produit intérieur brut suivant le secteur industriel d'origine ainsi que des composantes du capital brut intérieur fixe formé ventilées suivant le secteur d'activité industrielle, reproduites au tableau 1, ont été faites à partir de la réponse du Central Statistical Office, Londres, au questionnaire de l'O.N.U. relatif aux comptes nationaux. Des estimations officielles peuvent être trouvées dans *National Income and Expenditure*, publié annuellement par l'office ci-dessus mentionné. Une description exhaustive des sources et méthodes adoptées est donnée dans *National Income Statistics, Sources and Methods*, Londres, 1956.

## Indices de la production industrielle

Les indices du tableau 2 pour 1948 et les années suivantes sont tirés des indices de la production industrielle calculés par l'Office central de statistique et publiés dans *The Index of Industrial Production*, Studies in Official Statistics, No. 7, septembre 1959, le *Monthly Digest of Statistics* et *Annual Abstract of Statistics* ou obtenus par correspondance. Dans le cas de 1938, les indices du tableau 2 ont été obtenus en raccordant les indices d'avant guerre de la production industrielle, publiés par le Board of Trade, aux indices de l'Office central de statistique au niveau de 1946. Les sources, en ce qui concerne ces indices, sont le *Board of Trade Journal*, du 29 octobre 1949 et autres numéros, et le No. 7 de *Studies in Official Statistics*, respectivement.

Les séries d'indices reproduites au tableau 2 pour 1948 et les années suivantes se rapportent, en principe, aux établissements quelle que soit leur dimension, mais ne couvrent pas certains types d'activité qui appartiennent à la branche des industries manufacturières d'après la classification industrielle type internationale. Ces activités consistent en services de réparations et travaux manufacturiers sur commande, essentiellement pour le compte des ménages, abattage de bétails ou mise en bouteilles par les grossistes, plus quelques autres activités, mentionnées toutes dans la note au bas du tableau 2. Quoique les séries d'indices relatifs à 1938 couvrent, en principe, les services de réparations et les travaux manufacturiers sur commande pour le compte des ménages, ces séries se rapportent aux unités occupant dix personnes ou plus. L'année de pondération de base pour les séries d'indices reproduites au tableau 2 est 1930 dans le cas des indices relatifs à 1938, 1954 dans le cas des indices relatifs aux années 1948-1957 et 1958 dans le cas des indices relatifs à 1958 et aux années suivantes. Les coefficients de pondération utilisés sont proportionnels à la contribution au produit intérieur brut, au coût des facteurs.

Each of the series of index numbers mentioned above have been computed as base-weighted arithmetic averages. The elementary series of relatives utilized in constructing each of the series of index numbers are based, in most instances, on quantity of individual commodities produced and, in some instances, on gross value of production of individual commodities adjusted for price changes, quantity of individual raw materials consumed in production or employment. A greater number of, as well as improved, elementary series of relatives are utilized in the series of indexes based on 1958 than in the indexes based on 1954. The indexes, of the Board of Trade, 1930=100, were based on a much smaller number of elementary series of relatives than those of the Central Statistical Office.

Further details on the series of index numbers may be found in the following publications: The index numbers of the Board of Trade, "Industrial Production in the United Kingdom, 1900-1953" by T. M. Ridley in *Economica*, February 1955; the indexes, 1954=100, *The Index of Industrial Production*, Studies in Official Statistics, No. 7; the indexes, 1958=100, *Economic Trends*, No. 101, March 1962. The last three are publications of the Central Statistical Office.

### Index Numbers of Industrial Employment

The index numbers of employment set out in Table 3 for the years, 1948-1958, have been compiled primarily from absolute figures of employment resulting from the annual and basic Censuses of Production taken by the Board of Trade, London and issued in the publications concerning these censuses. In the case of selected kinds of manufacturing for some of the years between basic censuses, absolute figures of employment resulting from the administration of the National Insurance Scheme were utilized in compiling the indexes for all these years on as comparable a basis nationally and internationally as possible.

The absolute figures for employment from National Insurance Scheme also provided the basis for compiling the index numbers of employment for the years, 1959-1961, since data on employment were not gathered in the annual industrial inquiries for these years. The two series of data on employment were linked at 1958 in compiling the indexes. The employment data from the National Insurance Scheme utilized in computing the index numbers of employment were abstracted from various issues of the *Ministry of Labour Gazette*, London.

Both the series of absolute figures utilized in compiling the indexes relate to the average monthly employment of establishments irrespective of size. The data from the Censuses of Production cover employees, working proprietors and unpaid family workers; those from the National Insurance Scheme refer to employees only except in the case of Construction, where working proprietors are also included. The counts of employees are defined in the same fashion in both series. However, as may be noted

Chacune de ces séries d'indices est une série de moyennes arithmétiques à pondération fixe. Les séries élémentaires de rapports utilisées sont dans la plupart des cas fondées sur le volume de la production de chaque marchandise et, parfois, la valeur brute de la production de chaque marchandise, corrigée des variations de prix, sur la quantité de chaque matière première consommée pour la production, ou encore sur l'emploi. Pour les séries d'indices basées sur 1958 on a utilisé des séries élémentaires plus nombreuses et plus perfectionnées que pour les séries d'indices basées sur 1954. Les indices du Board of Trade 1930 = 100 sont basés sur un nombre beaucoup plus restreint de séries élémentaires de rapports que les indices construits par l'Office central de statistique.

Pour plus de détails sur ces séries d'indices, voir les publications suivantes: en ce qui concerne les indices du Board of Trade, "Industrial Production in the United Kingdom, 1900-1953" par T. M. Ridley dans *Economica*, février 1955; en ce qui concerne les indices 1954 = 100, *The Index of Industrial Production*, Studies in Official Statistics, No. 7; en ce qui concerne les indices 1958 = 100, *Economic Trends*, No. 101, mars 1962. Les trois dernières publications sont éditées par l'Office central de statistique.

### Indices de l'emploi industriel

Les indices de l'emploi reproduits au tableau 3 pour les années 1948-1958, ont été calculés essentiellement à partir des chiffres absolus de l'emploi résultant des recensements annuels de base de la production, exécutés par le Board of Trade, Londres, et parus dans les publications traitant de ces recensements. Pour certains types d'industries manufacturières dans le cas de quelques unes des années appartenant à la période séparant les recensements de base, des chiffres absolus de l'emploi provenant des administrations des systèmes nationaux de l'Assurance sociale ont été utilisés dans le calcul des indices sur une base aussi comparable que possible tant nationalement qu'internationalement.

Les chiffres absolus de l'emploi provenant des services nationaux d'Assurance sociale fournissent également une base au calcul des indices de l'emploi pour les années 1959-1961, du fait que les données sur l'emploi n'ont pas été rassemblées dans les enquêtes industrielles annuelles relatives à ces années. Lors du calcul des indices, les deux séries de données sur l'emploi ont été raccordées au niveau de 1958. Les données sur l'emploi fournies par les systèmes nationaux d'Assurance sociale utilisées dans le calcul des indices ont été tirées de différents numéros du *Ministry of Labour Gazette*, Londres.

Les deux séries de chiffres absolus utilisées dans le calcul des indices concernent l'emploi moyen mensuel dans les établissements, quelle que soit leur taille. Les données découlant des recensements de la production, couvrent les salariés, les propriétaires qui travaillent et les travailleurs familiaux non rémunérés; celles provenant des services nationaux d'Assurance sociale concernent les salariés seulement, à l'exception du cas de la branche Bâtiment et travaux publics pour laquelle les propriétaires qui tra-

from the footnotes to Table 3, some differences occur in the kinds of activities covered between the index numbers for 1948-1957 and those for 1958-1961. This is the consequence of the revisions in the scheme of industrial classification introduced beginning with the 1958 Census of Production which are described below.

### The Characteristics and Structure of Industrial Activity

The data shown in Tables 4 through 7 result from the Censuses of Production taken by the Board of Trade. The publications from which these data were compiled are: *Report on the Census of Production for 1951, for 1954 or for 1958* and *Annual Abstract of Statistics, 1938-1950*. The first three publications were issued by the Board of Trade and the last publication was issued by the Central Statistical Office. Each of the post-war Censuses from which data have been derived for Tables 4 through 7 were full Censuses of Production in the cycle of the Board of Trade of full inquiries every third or fourth year and less complete inquiries in the intervening years. However, even in the full Censuses only a few items of data (on identifying characteristics and employment) were gathered with regard to smaller establishments. The larger establishments consist of those engaging 11 or more persons in the case of the Censuses for 1935, 1948, 1951 and 1954 and of those engaging 25 or more persons in the case of the Census for 1958. The data on value added for all establishments that are shown in Tables 4 and 5 are, therefore, estimates of the Board of Trade based on the few items of data sought for these small establishments and the complete range of items sought for the larger units. However, all of the figures set out in Tables 6 and 7 for establishments with 11 or more persons engaged result directly from the full Censuses.

Except for the differences between the Censuses in coverage with regard to territory and kind of industrial activity that are described in footnotes to the tables, the Censuses that are grouped together in Tables 4 through 7 are, on the whole, comparable to one another with regard to the scheme of industrial classification utilized and coverage. It should be noted that two different sets of figures for 1954 are shown in the Tables — data which are most comparable to the figures for earlier years in the case of Tables 4, 6 and 7 and data which are most comparable to the figures for 1958 in the case of Table 5. In the case of the 1958 Census of Production, the scheme of industrial classification utilized differed from that utilized in earlier Censuses. Further, the instructions for delineating the unit for which data were to be furnished, permitted combined returns for two or more establishments operated by the same firm to be made more freely in the case of the 1958 Census than in earlier Censuses; and resulted in the inclusion, in the items of data, of subsidiary or ancillary activities to a greater extent in the 1958 Census than in earlier Censuses. The gathering in the

vaillent sont inclus. Le calcul du nombre de salariés est défini de la même façon dans les deux séries. Cependant, comme il est dit dans la note au bas du tableau 3, quelques différences existent quant aux types d'activités couvertes par chacune des deux séries d'indices, celle de 1948-1957 et celle de 1958-1961. Ceci est dû aux revisions apportées au système de classification industrielle ayant pris effet avec le recensement de la production de 1958, lesquelles revisions sont décrites ci-dessous.

### Les caractéristiques et la structure de l'activité industrielle

Les chiffres des tableaux 4 jusqu'à 7 sont tirés des résultats des recensements de la production exécutés par le Board of Trade. Ces résultats ont été publiés dans *Report on the Census of Production for 1951*, et, *ibid., for 1954* ou *for 1958*, ainsi que dans *Annual Abstract of Statistics, 1938-1950*. Les trois premiers ouvrages ont été publiés par le Board of Trade et le dernier par l'Office central de statistique. Chacun des deux recensements d'après guerre, dont on a utilisé les résultats pour établir les tableaux 4 jusqu'à 7, était un recensement général de la production rentrant dans le cycle des recensements du Board of Trade, à savoir un recensement général tous les trois ou quatre ans et une enquête moins vaste les années intermédiaires. Cependant, même dans les recensements généraux, seules quelques questions (sur les caractéristiques et sur l'emploi) ont été posées au sujet des établissements les moins importants. Les établissements les plus importants sont les établissements occupant 11 personnes ou plus dans le cas des recensements de 1935, 1948, 1951 et 1954, et ceux occupant 25 personnes ou plus dans le cas du recensement de 1958. Les chiffres de la valeur ajoutée pour tous les établissements, qui sont reproduits aux tableaux 4 et 5, sont donc des estimations du Board of Trade fondées sur les réponses aux quelques questions posées à ces petits établissements et sur les renseignements complets demandés aux grandes unités. Néanmoins, tous les chiffres des tableaux 6 et 7 relatifs aux établissements occupant 11 personnes ou plus sont tirés directement des recensements généraux.

Exception faite des différences de couverture (territoire et type d'activité industrielle) décrites dans les notes des tableaux, les recensements qui sont groupés aux tableaux 4 à 7 sont comparables pour ce qui est du système de classification industrielle adopté et de la couverture. Il est bon de noter que deux ensembles de données sont reproduites dans les tableaux pour l'année 1954 — des données qui sont plus comparables aux chiffres relatifs aux années précédant 1954, dans le cas des tableaux 4, 6 et 7 et des données plus comparables aux chiffres de 1958 dans le cas du tableau 5. Dans le cas du recensement de la production de 1958, le système de classification industrielle adopté différait de celui adopté pour les recensements ultérieurs. De plus, les instructions délimitant les unités pour lesquelles des données doivent être fournies, ont permis aux firmes gérant deux établissements ou plus de renvoyer un questionnaire dans lequel les résultats concernant tous les établissements sont combinés, ces instructions permettant plus de liberté dans les combinaisons pour le recensement de 1958 que pour les recensements ultérieurs. Il en est découlé également l'inclusion, dans

1958 Census of separate data on goods sold in the same condition as purchased also permitted more precise distinctions to be made than in earlier Censuses between establishments primarily engaged in industrial activities and those primarily engaged in the distributive trades. The data for 1954 shown in Table 5 results from the tabulation of the returns received in the 1954 Census on as comparable a basis as possible to the 1958 Census.

The definitions utilized in the various Censuses for the same item of data are comparable, on the whole, to one another as well as to the definitions included in the International Recommendations in Basic Industrial Statistics. Value added is priced at factor cost. Homeworkers are not included in the number of engaged. It should also be noted that, among the engaged, the number of employees and operatives is measured in terms of an average during the year but the number of working proprietors and unpaid family workers is taken as of one period during the year. The capacity of installed (in use and in reserve) power equipment is the sum of the horsepowers of prime movers connected directly to machinery other than electric generators and of all electric motors. In the case of the mining and manufacturing industries, the data shown for 1954 on energy consumed cover fuels and electricity purchased or obtained from other establishments which are utilized as a source of power or heat only. In the case of the Electricity or Gas industries, purchases of electricity or gas, respectively, are not included in the figures of energy consumed. Thus, these figures represent the consumption of fuels in each of these industries to produce electricity or gas, respectively. In order to show the same kind of data for energy consumed for these two industries combined, purchases of both electricity and gas were excluded from these figures.

les rubriques, d'activités auxiliaires ou subordonnées à une plus grande échelle dans le recensement de 1958 que dans les recensements précédents. La collecte dans le recensement de 1958 de données séparées pour les biens revendus en l'état permit également de faire des distinctions plus précises que dans les recensements ultérieurs entre établissements exerçant essentiellement des activités industrielles et ceux exerçant une activité commerciale distributive. Les données pour 1954 reproduites au tableau 5 proviennent de la tabulation des réponses reçues au recensement de 1954, sur une base aussi comparable que possible au recensement de 1958.

Les définitions adoptées dans les différents recensements pour les mêmes rubriques sont dans l'ensemble comparables, aussi bien les unes aux autres qu'aux définitions indiquées dans les Recommandations relatives aux statistiques industrielles de base. La valeur ajoutée est comptée au coût des facteurs. Les travailleurs à domicile ne sont pas compris parmi les personnes occupées. On notera aussi que, parmi ces dernières, le nombre des salariés et d'ouvriers est une moyenne annuelle tandis que le nombre des propriétaires qui travaillent et des travailleurs familiaux non rémunérés est le nombre relevé pendant une période de l'année. La puissance installée (en service et en réserve) est égale au nombre de chevaux-vapeur des moteurs primaires entraînant directement des machines autres que des générateurs électriques et de tous les moteurs électriques. Dans le cas des industries extractives et manufacturières, les données reproduites pour 1954 relatives à l'énergie consommée couvrent les combustibles et l'électricité achetés ou fournis par d'autres établissements, et utilisés comme sources de puissance ou de chaleur seulement. Dans le cas des industries du gaz et de l'électricité, les achats de gaz ou d'électricité, respectivement, ne sont pas comprises dans les chiffres donnant l'énergie consommée. Par conséquent, ces chiffres sont ceux de la consommation de combustibles dans chacune de ces industries, nécessaires à la production d'électricité ou de gaz, respectivement. Afin de présenter les mêmes types de données pour l'énergie consommée par ces deux industries combinées, les achats d'électricité et de gaz sont exclus de ces chiffres.

## 1. THE GROSS DOMESTIC PRODUCT AND GROSS DOMESTIC FIXED CAPITAL FORMATION
## PRODUIT INTERIEUR BRUT ET FORMATION BRUTE DE CAPITAL FIXE INTERIEUR

Million Pounds                                            Millions de livres

### A. Expenditure on the Gross Domestic Product at Market Prices
### Dépenses relatives au produit intérieur brut aux prix du marché

| Item of data and year / Rubrique et année | Total | Consumption / Consommation | | Gross Domestic Capital Formation / Formation brute de capital intérieur | | Net exports of goods and services / Exportations nettes de biens et de services | |
|---|---|---|---|---|---|---|---|
| | | Total | Government / Etat | Total | Fixed / Fixe | Exports less imports / Exportations moins importations | Exports / Exportations |
| **a. At Current Prices — Aux prix courants** | | | | | | | |
| *Absolute figures — Chiffres absolus* | | | | | | | |
| 1948 | 11 720 | 10 371 | 1 775 | 1 587 | 1 412 | −238 | 2 196 |
| 1951 | 14 385 | 12 688 | 2 516 | 2 390 | 1 815 | −693 | 3 644 |
| 1952 | 15 606 | 13 735 | 3 011 | 2 052 | 2 002 | −181 | 3 760 |
| 1953 | 16 711 | 14 487 | 3 162 | 2 387 | 2 262 | −163 | 3 689 |
| 1954 | 17 672 | 15 267 | 3 211 | 2 541 | 2 485 | −136 | 3 841 |
| 1955 | 18 989 | 16 255 | 3 278 | 3 051 | 2 751 | −317 | 4 185 |
| 1956 | 20 612 | 17 277 | 3 569 | 3 306 | 3 045 | 29 | 4 604 |
| 1957 | 21 707 | 18 139 | 3 692 | 3 530 | 3 307 | 38 | 4 834 |
| 1958 | 22 633 | 18 996 | 3 797 | 3 535 | 3 436 | 102 | 4 687 |
| 1959 | 23 693 | 19 928 | 4 014 | 3 842 | 3 673 | −77 | 4 842 |
| 1960 | 25 073 | 20 854 | 4 251 | 4 666 | 4 083 | −447 | 5 149 |
| 1961 | 26 491 | 21 929 | 4 630 | 4 775 | 4 499 | −213 | 5 367 |
| *Percentage distribution of average annual expenditure — Distribution en pourcentage des dépenses annuelles moyennes* | | | | | | | |
| 1948 | 100.0 | 88.5 | 15.1 | 13.5 | 12.0 | −2.0 | 18.7 |
| 1951 − 1960 | 100.0 | 85.0 | 17.5 | 15.9 | 14.6 | −0.9 | 21.9 |
| 1951 | 100.0 | 88.2 | 17.5 | 16.6 | 12.6 | −4.8 | 25.3 |
| 1953 | 100.0 | 86.7 | 18.9 | 14.3 | 13.5 | −1.0 | 22.1 |
| 1954 | 100.0 | 86.4 | 18.2 | 14.4 | 14.1 | −0.8 | 21.7 |
| 1958 | 100.0 | 83.9 | 16.8 | 15.6 | 15.2 | 0.5 | 2.07 |
| 1960 | 100.0 | 83.2 | 17.0 | 18.6 | 16.3 | −1.8 | 2.05 |
| **b. At Prices of 1958 — Aux prix de 1958** | | | | | | | |
| *Absolute figures — Chiffres absolus* | | | | | | | |
| 1948 | 17 657 | 15 500 | 3 031 | 2 372 | 2 120 | −215 | 3 103 |
| 1951 | 19 476 | 16 468 | 3 604 | 2 986 | 2 371 | 22 | 3 899 |
| 1952 | 19 445 | 16 790 | 3 989 | 2 421 | 2 356 | 234 | 3 821 |
| 1953 | 20 240 | 17 376 | 4 103 | 2 769 | 2 634 | 95 | 3 983 |
| 1954 | 21 057 | 17 914 | 4 058 | 2 959 | 2 905 | 184 | 4 212 |
| 1955 | 21 754 | 18 339 | 3 943 | 3 377 | 3 064 | 38 | 4 474 |
| 1956 | 22 199 | 18 498 | 3 957 | 3 479 | 3 233 | 222 | 4 674 |
| 1957 | 22 576 | 18 699 | 3 853 | 3 631 | 3 395 | 246 | 4 791 |
| 1958 | 22 633 | 18 996 | 3 797 | 3 535 | 3 436 | 102 | 4 687 |
| 1959 | 23 484 | 19 686 | 3 845 | 3 879 | 3 706 | −81 | 4 848 |
| 1960 | 24 540 | 20 313 | 3 920 | 4 682 | 4 102 | −455 | 5 127 |
| 1961 | 25 114 | 20 739 | 4 121 | 4 670 | 4 407 | −295 | 5 290 |
| *Percentage distribution of average annual expenditure — Distribution en pourcentage des dépenses annuelles moyennes* | | | | | | | |
| 1948 | 100.0 | 87.7 | 17.2 | 13.5 | 12.0 | −1.2 | 17.6 |
| 1951 − 1960 | 100.0 | 84.2 | 18.0 | 15.5 | 14.5 | 0.3 | 20.5 |
| 1951 | 100.0 | 84.5 | 18.5 | 15.3 | 12.2 | 0.2 | 20.0 |
| 1953 | 100.0 | 85.8 | 20.3 | 13.7 | 13.0 | 0.5 | 19.7 |
| 1954 | 100.0 | 85.0 | 19.3 | 14.1 | 13.8 | 0.9 | 20.0 |
| 1958 | 100.0 | 83.9 | 16.8 | 15.6 | 15.2 | 0.5 | 20.7 |
| 1960 | 100.0 | 82.7 | 16.0 | 19.1 | 16.7 | −1.8 | 20.9 |
| *Average annual rate of growth — Taux annuel moyen d'accroissement* | | | | | | | |
| 1948 − 1953 | 2.8 | 2.3 | 6.2 | 3.1 | 4.4 | · | 5.1 |
| 1951 − 1960 | 2.6 | 2.4 | 0.9 | 5.1 | 6.3 | · | 3.1 |
| 1951 − 1953 | 1.9 | 2.7 | 6.7 | −3.7 | 5.4 | · | 1.1 |
| 1954 − 1958 | 1.8 | 1.5 | −1.6 | 4.6 | 4.3 | · | 2.7 |
| 1958 − 1960 | 4.1 | 3.4 | 1.6 | 15.1 | 9.3 | · | 4.6 |

## B. The Gross Domestic Product at Factor Cost According to Origin
## Origine par secteur d'activité du produit intérieur brut au coût des facteurs

| Item of data and year / Rubrique et année | Total | Agricultural sector / Secteur agricole | Industrial Sector — Secteur Industriel Total | Mining / Industries extractives | Manufacturing / Industries manufacturières | Construction / Bâtiment et travaux publics | Electricity, gas and water / Electricité, gaz et eau | Transportation and communication / Transports et communications | Other sectors [1] / Autres secteurs [1] |
|---|---|---|---|---|---|---|---|---|---|
| ISIC — CITI | 0–9 | 0 | 1–521 | 1 | 2–3 | 4 | 511–521 | 7 | 522, 6, 8–9 |
| *a. At Current Prices — Aux prix courants* | | | | | | | | | |
| **Absolute figures — Chiffres absolus** | | | | | | | | | |
| 1948 | 10 280 | 652 | 4 703 | 384 | 3 543 | 568 | 208 | 871 | 4 054 |
| 1951 | 12 584 | 726 | 6 147 | 449 | 4 725 | 699 | 274 | 1 140 | 4 571 |
| 1952 | 13 733 | 770 | 6 302 | 505 | 4 738 | 752 | 307 | 1 200 | 5 461 |
| 1953 | 14 710 | 786 | 6 825 | 544 | 5 116 | 830 | 335 | 1 195 | 5 904 |
| 1954 | 15 592 | 776 | 7 436 | 564 | 5 609 | 896 | 367 | 1 249 | 6 131 |
| 1955 | 16 683 | 800 | 8 115 | 585 | 6 150 | 979 | 401 | 1 393 | 6 375 |
| 1956 | 18 149 | 822 | 8 712 | 676 | 6 488 | 1 103 | 445 | 1 534 | 7 081 |
| 1957 | 19 153 | 863 | 9 179 | 707 | 6 869 | 1 130 | 473 | 1 620 | 7 491 |
| 1958 | 19 991 | 873 | 9 394 | 709 | 6 977 | 1 183 | 525 | 1 575 | 8 149 |
| 1959 | 20 877 | 880 | 9 941 | 674 | 7 438 | 1 258 | 571 | 1 669 | 8 387 |
| 1960 | 22 185 | 919 | 10 719 | 671 | 8 056 | 1 385 | 607 | 1 893 | 8 654 |
| 1961 | 23 449 | 966 | 11 128 | 694 | 8 256 | 1 514 | 664 | 1 929 | 9 426 |
| **Percentage distribution according to sector — Distribution en pourcentage par secteur** | | | | | | | | | |
| 1948 | 100.0 | 6.3 | 45.7 | 3.7 | 34.5 | 5.5 | 2.0 | 8.5 | 39.5 |
| 1951 – 1960 | 100.0 | 4.7 | 47.6 | 3.5 | 35.8 | 5.9 | 2.4 | 8.4 | 39.3 |
| 1951 | 100.0 | 5.7 | 48.9 | 3.6 | 37.5 | 5.6 | 2.2 | 9.0 | 36.4 |
| 1953 | 100.0 | 5.3 | 46.4 | 3.7 | 34.8 | 5.6 | 2.3 | 8.1 | 40.2 |
| 1954 | 100.0 | 4.9 | 47.7 | 3.6 | 36.0 | 5.8 | 2.3 | 8.0 | 39.4 |
| 1958 | 100.0 | 4.3 | 47.0 | 3.6 | 34.9 | 5.9 | 2.6 | 7.9 | 40.8 |
| 1960 | 100.0 | 4.1 | 48.3 | 3.0 | 36.3 | 6.3 | 2.7 | 8.5 | 39.1 |
| *b. At Constant Prices [2] — En prix constants [2]* | | | | | | | | | |
| **Index numbers — Indices (1958 = 100)** | | | | | | | | | |
| 1948 | 79 | 80 | 74 | 96 | 72 | 83 | 58 | 85 | 84 |
| 1951 | 87 | 90 | 86 | 104 | 86 | 83 | 72 | 93 | 88 |
| 1952 | 86 | 92 | 84 | 105 | 83 | 86 | 74 | 94 | 88 |
| 1953 | 90 | 94 | 89 | 105 | 88 | 92 | 77 | 96 | 91 |
| 1954 | 94 | 95 | 94 | 106 | 94 | 95 | 84 | 97 | 93 |
| 1955 | 97 | 95 | 99 | 105 | 100 | 96 | 88 | 99 | 96 |
| 1956 | 98 | 100 | 99 | 105 | 99 | 101 | 92 | 101 | 97 |
| 1957 | 100 | 102 | 101 | 104 | 101 | 101 | 96 | 101 | 99 |
| 1958 | – 100 – | – 100 – | – 100 – | – 100 – | – 100 – | – 100 – | – 100 – | – 100 – | – 100 – |
| 1959 | 105 | 104 | 105 | 97 | 106 | 106 | 103 | 104 | 103 |
| 1960 | 110 | 110 | 113 | 94 | 115 | 111 | 110 | 109 | 106 |
| 1961 | 112 | 114 | 114 | 93 | 115 | 120 | 116 | 112 | 109 |
| **Average annual rate of growth — Taux annuel moyen d'accroissement** | | | | | | | | | |
| 1948 – 1953 | 2.6 | 3.3 | 3.8 | 1.8 | 4.1 | 2.1 | 5.8 | 2.5 | 1.6 |
| 1951 – 1960 | 2.6 | 2.3 | 3.0 | – 1.1 | 3.3 | 3.3 | 5.0 | 1.8 | 2.1 |
| 1951 – 1953 | 1.7 | 2.2 | 1.7 | 0.5 | 1.1 | 5.3 | 3.4 | 1.6 | 1.7 |
| 1954 – 1958 | 1.6 | 1.3 | 1.6 | – 1.5 | 1.6 | 1.3 | 4.4 | 0.8 | 1.8 |
| 1958 – 1960 | 4.9 | 4.9 | 6.3 | – 3.0 | 7.2 | 5.4 | 4.9 | 4.4 | 3.0 |

[1] Includes adjustments for changes in stocks, which are not distributed among the various sectors and residual errors.
[2] The weight base years (in other words, the years of constant prices) are 1954 in the case of the indexes for the period, 1948-1957, and 1958 in the case of the indexes for 1958 and thereafter. The two series were linked to one another at 1958.

[1] Y compris l'ajustement pour variations de stocks qui n'est pas réparti entre les différents secteurs ainsi que les erreurs résiduelles.
[2] Les années de pondération de base (en d'autres termes, les années à prix constants) sont 1954 dans le cas des données relatives aux années 1948-1957, et 1958 dans le cas des indices relatifs à 1958 et aux années suivantes. Les deux séries sont raccordées l'une à l'autre au niveau de 1958.

## C. Gross Domestic Fixed Capital Formation According to Purchasing Sector
### Formation brute de capital fixe intérieur par secteur d'acquisition

| Item of data and year / Rubrique et année | Total[1] | Agricultural sector / Secteur agricole | Industrial Sector — Secteur Industriel | | | | | Transportation and communication[2] / Transports et communications[2] | Other sectors[2] / Autres secteurs[2] |
| | | | Total | Mining industries extractives | Manufacturing[3] / Industries manufacturières[3] | Construction[3] / Bâtiment et travaux publics[3] | Electricity, gas and water / Electricité, gaz et eau | | |
| ISIC — CITI | 0–9 | 0 | 1–521 | 1 | 2–3 | 4 | 511–521 | 7 | 522, 6, 8–9 |

### a. At Current Prices — Aux prix courants

| | | | | | | | | | |
|---|---|---|---|---|---|---|---|---|---|
| **Absolute figures — Chiffres absolus** | | | | | | | | | |
| 1948 | 1 422 | 94 | 515 | 28 | 328 | 21 | 138 | 210 | 603 |
| 1951 | 1 884 | 94 | 798 | 34 | 514 | 33 | 217 | 199 | 793 |
| 1952 | 2 102 | 97 | 870 | 46 | 549 | 36 | 239 | 205 | 930 |
| 1953 | 2 355 | 94 | 909 | 62 | 547 | 35 | 265 | 264 | 1 088 |
| 1954 | 2 542 | 100 | 1 008 | 79 | 581 | 44 | 304 | 275 | 1 159 |
| 1955 | 2 797 | 110 | 1 157 | 86 | 678 | 50 | 343 | 288 | 1 242 |
| 1956 | 3 101 | 102 | 1 329 | 91 | 845 | 53 | 340 | 363 | 1 307 |
| 1957 | 3 376 | 114 | 1 451 | 103 | 931 | 57 | 360 | 460 | 1 351 |
| 1958 | 3 493 | 134 | 1 478 | 105 | 922 | 62 | 389 | 467 | 1 414 |
| 1959 | 3 718 | 151 | 1 463 | 116 | 863 | 61 | 423 | 499 | 1 605 |
| 1960 | 4 115 | 153 | 1 622 | 95 | 1 028 | 70 | 429 | 542 | 1 798 |
| 1961 | 4 522 | 166 | 1 902 | 102 | 1 276 | 77 | 447 | 515 | 1 939 |
| **Percentage distribution according to sector — Distribution en pourcentage par secteur** | | | | | | | | | |
| 1948 | 100.0 | 6.6 | 36.2 | 1.9 | 23.1 | 1.5 | 9.7 | 14.7 | 42.5 |
| 1951 – 1960 | 100.0 | 3.8 | 41.0 | 2.8 | 25.3 | 1.7 | 11.2 | 12.1 | 43.1 |
| 1951 | 100.0 | 4.9 | 42.4 | 1.8 | 27.3 | 1.8 | 11.5 | 10.6 | 42.1 |
| 1953 | 100.0 | 3.9 | 38.6 | 2.7 | 23.2 | 1.5 | 11.2 | 11.3 | 46.2 |
| 1954 | 100.0 | 3.9 | 39.6 | 3.1 | 22.8 | 1.8 | 11.9 | 10.8 | 45.6 |
| 1958 | 100.0 | 3.8 | 42.3 | 3.0 | 26.4 | 1.8 | 11.1 | 13.4 | 40.5 |
| 1960 | 100.0 | 3.7 | 39.4 | 2.3 | 25.0 | 1.7 | 10.4 | 13.2 | 43.7 |

### b. At Prices of 1958 — Aux prix de 1958

| | | | | | | | | | |
|---|---|---|---|---|---|---|---|---|---|
| **Absolute figures — Chiffres absolus** | | | | | | | | | |
| 1948 | 2 135 | 136 | 805 | 45 | 520 | 34 | 206 | 333 | 861 |
| 1951 | 2 461 | 117 | 1 091 | 47 | 716 | 44 | 284 | 281 | 972 |
| 1952 | 2 474 | 109 | 1 069 | 58 | 684 | 43 | 284 | 257 | 1 039 |
| 1953 | 2 742 | 106 | 1 091 | 75 | 666 | 41 | 309 | 311 | 1 234 |
| 1954 | 2 972 | 113 | 1 207 | 96 | 703 | 52 | 356 | 325 | 1 327 |
| 1955 | 3 115 | 122 | 1 317 | 99 | 779 | 57 | 382 | 323 | 1 353 |
| 1956 | 3 292 | 108 | 1 428 | 99 | 914 | 57 | 358 | 396 | 1 360 |
| 1957 | 3 466 | 117 | 1 492 | 106 | 961 | 58 | 367 | 481 | 1 376 |
| 1958 | 3 493 | 134 | 1 478 | 105 | 922 | 62 | 389 | 467 | 1 414 |
| 1959 | 3 751 | 151 | 1 471 | 116 | 867 | 62 | 426 | 496 | 1 633 |
| 1960 | 4 134 | 154 | 1 622 | 95 | 1 024 | 72 | 431 | 535 | 1 823 |
| 1961 | 4 430 | 164 | 1 844 | 99 | 1 229 | 77 | 439 | 501 | 1 921 |
| **Percentage distribution according to sector — Distribution en pourcentage par secteur** | | | | | | | | | |
| 1948 | 100.0 | 6.3 | 37.7 | 2.1 | 24.4 | 1.6 | 9.6 | 15.6 | 40.4 |
| 1951 – 1960 | 100.0 | 3.8 | 41.6 | 2.8 | 25.8 | 1.8 | 11.2 | 12.1 | 42.5 |
| 1951 | 100.0 | 4.7 | 44.3 | 1.9 | 29.1 | 1.8 | 11.5 | 11.5 | 39.5 |
| 1953 | 100.0 | 3.8 | 39.8 | 2.8 | 24.2 | 1.5 | 11.3 | 11.3 | 45.1 |
| 1954 | 100.0 | 3.8 | 40.6 | 3.2 | 23.6 | 1.8 | 12.0 | 10.9 | 44.7 |
| 1958 | 100.0 | 3.8 | 42.3 | 3.0 | 26.4 | 1.8 | 11.1 | 13.4 | 40.5 |
| 1960 | 100.0 | 3.7 | 39.2 | 2.3 | 24.7 | 1.8 | 10.4 | 13.0 | 44.1 |
| **Average annual rate of growth — Taux annuel moyen d'accroissement** | | | | | | | | | |
| 1948 – 1953 | 5.1 | −4.9 | 6.3 | 10.8 | 5.1 | 3.8 | 8.4 | −1.4 | 7.5 |
| 1951 – 1960 | 5.9 | 3.1 | 4.5 | 8.1 | 4.1 | 5.6 | 4.7 | 7.4 | 7.2 |
| 1951 – 1953 | 5.5 | −4.8 | — | 26.3 | −3.6 | −3.5 | 4.3 | 5.2 | 12.7 |
| 1954 – 1958 | 4.1 | 4.4 | 5.2 | 2.3 | 7.0 | 4.5 | 2.2 | 9.5 | 1.6 |
| 1958 – 1960 | 8.8 | 7.2 | 4.7 | −4.8 | 5.4 | 7.7 | 5.3 | 7.1 | 13.5 |

[1] Includes fixed capital expenditure for military defense and therefore differs from figures of Table 1A.
[2] Fixed capital formation in taxis and private-hire cars, before 1960, and in road goods haulage, for all years, is included under Other sectors instead of under Transportation.
[3] The statistical unit is the establishment in the case of the figures before 1956 but the enterprise in the case of the data for 1956 and thereafter.

[1] Y compris les dépenses de capital fixe imputées à la défense nationale; les valeurs indiquées ici diffèrent donc de celles des rubriques correspondantes du tableau 1A.
[2] La formation brute de capital fixe en taxis et voitures de location avant 1960 et en services de transport routier de marchandises pour toutes les années est incluse dans Autres secteurs au lieu de figurer sous Transports et communications.
[3] L'unité statistique est l'établissement dans le cas des chiffres d'avant 1956 et l'entreprise dans le cas des données relatives à 1956 et aux années ultérieures.

## 2. INDEX NUMBERS OF INDUSTRIAL PRODUCTION
### INDICES DE LA PRODUCTION INDUSTRIELLE

### A. The Divisions of Industrial Activity
### Les branches de l'activité industrielle

| Period Période | Total [1] | Mining [2] Industries extractives [2] | Manu- facturing [1] Industries manu- facturières [1] | Construction [2] Bâtiment et travaux publics [2] | Electricity, gas and water Electricité, gaz et eau |
|---|---|---|---|---|---|
| ISIC — CITI | 1–4, 511–521 | 1 | 2–3 | 4 | 511–521 |
| *a.* Indexes — Indices (1958 = 100) | | | | | |
| 1938...... | 67 | 111 | 62 | 104 | 37 |
| 1948...... | 74 | 96 | 72 | 82 | 58 |
| 1949...... | 79 | 99 | 77 | 86 | 62 |
| 1950...... | 83 | 100 | 82 | 86 | 68 |
| 1951...... | 86 | 104 | 86 | 83 | 72 |
| 1952...... | 84 | 105 | 82 | 86 | 74 |
| 1953...... | 89 | 105 | 88 | 92 | 78 |
| 1954...... | 94 | 106 | 94 | 95 | 84 |
| 1955...... | 99 | 105 | 100 | 96 | 88 |
| 1956...... | 99 | 105 | 99 | 101 | 94 |
| 1957...... | 101 | 104 | 101 | 100 | 96 |
| 1958...... | – 100 – | – 100 – | – 100 – | – 100 – | – 100 – |
| 1959...... | 105 | 97 | 106 | 106 | 103 |
| 1960...... | 112 | 94 | 115 | 111 | 110 |
| 1961...... | 114 | 93 | 115 | 120 | 116 |
| *b.* Average Annual Rate of Change — Taux annuel moyen de variation | | | | | |
| 1938 – 1960. | 2.4 | −0.8 | 2.8 | 0.3 | 5.1 |
| 1938 – 1948. | 1.0 | −1.4 | 1.5 | −2.4 | 4.6 |
| 1950 – 1960. | 3.0 | −0.6 | 3.4 | 2.6 | 4.8 |
| 1948 – 1953. | 3.8 | 1.8 | 4.1 | 2.3 | 6.0 |
| 1954 – 1958. | 1.6 | −1.4 | 1.6 | 1.3 | 4.0 |
| 1958 – 1960. | 5.8 | −3.0 | 7.2 | 5.4 | 4.9 |

For footnotes see end of table.
Pour les notes, voir au bas du tableau.

### B. The Major Groups of Mining
### Les classes de la branche Industries extractives

| Period Période | All mining [2] Toutes industries extractives [2] | Coal mining [2] Extraction du charbon [2] | Metal mining Extraction des minerais métalliques | Other mining Autres industries extractives |
|---|---|---|---|---|
| ISIC — CITI | 1 | 11 | 12 | 14–19 |
| *a.* Indexes — Indices (1958 = 100) | | | | |
| 1938.......... | 111 | 112 | 114 | 94 |
| 1948.......... | 96 | 98 | 101 | 77 |
| 1949.......... | 99 | 101 | 102 | 88 |
| 1950.......... | 100 | 101 | 96 | 93 |
| 1951.......... | 104 | 105 | 106 | 93 |
| 1952.......... | 105 | 106 | 107 | 100 |
| 1953.......... | 105 | 105 | 109 | 100 |
| 1954.......... | 106 | 106 | 105 | 106 |
| 1955.......... | 105 | 104 | 110 | 111 |
| 1956.......... | 105 | 104 | 110 | 114 |
| 1957.......... | 104 | 104 | 115 | 105 |
| 1958.......... | – 100 – | – 100 – | – 100 – | – 100 – |
| 1959.......... | 97 | 97 | 105 | 101 |
| 1960.......... | 94 | 92 | 118 | 104 |
| 1961.......... | 93 | 90 | 115 | 111 |
| *b.* Average Annual Rate of Change — Taux annuel moyen de variation | | | | |
| 1938 – 1960..... | −0.8 | −0.9 | 0.2 | 0.5 |
| 1938 – 1948..... | −1.4 | −1.3 | −1.2 | −2.0 |
| 1950 – 1960..... | −0.6 | −0.9 | 2.1 | 1.1 |
| 1948 – 1953..... | 1.8 | 1.4 | 1.5 | 5.4 |
| 1954 – 1958..... | −1.4 | −1.4 | −1.2 | −1.4 |
| 1958 – 1960..... | −3.0 | −4.1 | 8.6 | 2.0 |

For footnotes see end of table.
Pour les notes, voir au bas du tableau.

## C. The Major Groups of Manufacturing — Les classes de la branche Industries manufacturières

| Period<br>Période | Manu-facturing [1]<br>Industries manufac-turières [1] | Food, beverages and tobacco [1]<br>Industries alimen-taires, boissons, tabac [1] | Textiles | Clothing, footwear and made-up textiles [1,3]<br>Articles d'habil-lement, chaussures et ouvrages en tissu [1,3] | Wood products and furniture<br>Bois et meubles | Paper, paper products, printing and publishing<br>Papier, ouvrages en papier, imprimerie et édition | Leather and leather products except wearing apparel [3]<br>Cuir et articles en cuir, à l'exclu-sion des articles d'habil-lement [3] | Rubber products<br>Ouvrages en caoutchouc | Chemicals and chemical, petroleum and coal products<br>Produits chi-miques et dérivés du pétrole et du charbon | Non-metallic mineral products<br>Produits minéraux non métal-liques | Basic metals<br>Métal-lurgie de base | Metal products [1]<br>Ouvrages en métaux [1] | Other manu-facturing [1]<br>Autres industries manufac-turières [1] |
|---|---|---|---|---|---|---|---|---|---|---|---|---|---|
| ISIC — CITI | 2–3 | 20–22 | 23 | 24 | 25–26 | 27–28 | 29 | 30 | 31–32 | 33 | 34 | 35–38 | 39 |

### a. Indexes — Indices (1958 = 100)

| | | | | | | | | | | | | | |
|---|---|---|---|---|---|---|---|---|---|---|---|---|---|
| 1938............. | 62 | 68 | 108 | 93 | 75 | 55 | 140 | 50 | 34 | 62 | 62 | 49 | 44 |
| 1948............. | 72 | 80 | 101 | 87 | 75 | 59 | 122 | 74 | 60 | 81 | 82 | 66 | 62 |
| 1949............. | 77 | 83 | 108 | 95 | 86 | 68 | 124 | 70 | 62 | 86 | 83 | 70 | 68 |
| 1950. ........... | 82 | 82 | 117 | 100 | 90 | 78 | 125 | 85 | 71 | 91 | 87 | 75 | 74 |
| 1951............. | 86 | 85 | 116 | 94 | 97 | 82 | 121 | 91 | 75 | 96 | 92 | 80 | 77 |
| 1952............. | 82 | 86 | 96 | 90 | 86 | 69 | 107 | 79 | 70 | 94 | 95 | 80 | 72 |
| 1953............. | 88 | 90 | 112 | 99 | 95 | 77 | 115 | 84 | 79 | 99 | 93 | 83 | 76 |
| 1954............. | 94 | 91 | 115 | 98 | 107 | 90 | 114 | 92 | 88 | 102 | 99 | 89 | 87 |
| 1955. ........... | 100 | 94 | 112 | 102 | 107 | 97 | 113 | 104 | 94 | 106 | 107 | 98 | 93 |
| 1956............. | 99 | 96 | 110 | 104 | 100 | 96 | 106 | 95 | 98 | 104 | 109 | 96 | 94 |
| 1957............. | 101 | 98 | 110 | 104 | 103 | 98 | 106 | 99 | 101 | 101 | 110 | 99 | 99 |
| 1958............. | – 100 – | – 100 – | – 100 – | – 100 – | – 100 – | – 100 – | – 100 – | – 100 – | – 100 – | – 100 – | – 100 – | – 100 – | – 100 – |
| 1959............. | 106 | 104 | 104 | 112 | 112 | 107 | 103 | 108 | 112 | 107 | 104 | 105 | 108 |
| 1960............. | 115 | 107 | 107 | 120 | 114 | 119 | 102 | 121 | 125 | 119 | 122 | 112 | 120 |
| 1961............. | 115 | 110 | 102 | 122 | 116 | 120 | 102 | 112 | 126 | 124 | 114 | 113 | 122 |

### b. Average Annual Rate of Change — Taux annuel moyen de variation

| | | | | | | | | | | | | | |
|---|---|---|---|---|---|---|---|---|---|---|---|---|---|
| 1938 – 1960........ | 2.8 | 2.1 | — | 1.2 | 1.9 | 3.6 | −1.4 | 4.1 | 6.1 | 2.9 | 3.1 | 3.8 | 4.7 |
| 1938 – 1948........ | 1.5 | 1.6 | −0.7 | −0.7 | — | 0.7 | −1.4 | 4.0 | 5.7 | 2.7 | 2.8 | 3.0 | 3.5 |
| 1950 – 1960........ | 3.4 | 2.7 | −0.9 | 1.8 | 2.4 | 4.3 | −2.0 | 3.6 | 5.8 | 2.5 | 3.4 | 4.1 | 4.8 |
| 1948 – 1953........ | 4.1 | 2.4 | 2.1 | 2.6 | 4.8 | 5.5 | −1.2 | 2.6 | 5.7 | 4.1 | 2.5 | 4.7 | 4.2 |
| 1954 – 1958........ | 1.6 | 2.4 | −3.4 | 0.5 | −1.7 | 2.7 | −3.2 | 2.1 | 3.2 | −0.5 | 0.2 | 3.0 | 3.5 |
| 1958 – 1960........ | 7.2 | 3.4 | 3.4 | 9.5 | 6.8 | 9.1 | 1.0 | 10.0 | 11.8 | 9.1 | 10.5 | 5.8 | 9.5 |

[1] The following manufacturing activities are not covered, in principle, in the indexes for all years: Slaughtering or bottling by wholesalers, tea blending and coffee roasting (all part of ISIC major group 20). In the case of the indexes for 1948 and thereafter, the following additional manufacturing activities are, in principle, excluded: Fish curing by wholesalers and milk pasteurizing and bottling (part of ISIC major group 20), custom tailoring and dress making (part of ISIC major group 24), repair of motor cars, motorcycles or bicycles (part of ISIC major group 38), repair of musical instruments or jewellery and plate (part of ISIC major group 39), and other repair work and manufacturing at retail.
[2] Open cast coal mining is covered under Construction (ISIC Division 4) instead of under Coal mining (ISIC major group 11).
[3] The manufacture of fur apparel is included under Leather and leather products (ISIC major group 29) instead of under Clothing (ISIC major group 24).

[1] En principe, les activités manufacturières ci-après sont exclues des indices pour toutes les années: abattage du bétail ou mise en bouteille par les grossistes, mélange du thé et torré-faction du café (dans CITI 20). A partir de 1948, sont également exclues, en principe, les activités manufacturières suivantes: Saurissage de poissons par les grossistes, pasteurisation et mise en bouteille du lait (dans CITI 20), fabrication de vêtements sur mesures (dans CITI 24), réparation des automobiles, motorcycles et bicyclettes (dans CITI 38), réparation des instru-ments de musique, bijoux et articles d'orfèvrerie (dans CITI 39) et autres travaux de répara-tions et activités manufacturières au détail.
[2] L'extraction du charbon à ciel ouvert est comprise dans Bâtiment et travaux publics (CITI 4) et non dans Extraction du charbon (CITI 11).
[3] La fabrication de vêtements en fourrure est comprise dans Cuir et articles en cuir (CITI 29) et non dans Articles d'habillement (CITI 24).

# 3. INDEX NUMBERS OF INDUSTRIAL EMPLOYMENT
## INDICES DE L'EMPLOI DANS L'INDUSTRIE

## A. The Divisions of Industrial Activity
### Les branches de l'activité industrielle

| Period Période | Total [1,2] | Mining [2] Industries extractives [2] | Manu-facturing [1] Industries manu-facturières [1] | Construction Bâtiment et travaux publics | Electricity and gas Electricité et gaz |
|---|---|---|---|---|---|
| ISIC — CITI | 1–4, 511–512 | 1 | 2–3 | 4 | 511–512 |

### a. Indexes — Indices (1958 = 100)

| Period Période | Total | Mining | Manufacturing | Construction | Electricity and gas |
|---|---|---|---|---|---|
| 1948....... | 92 | 100 | 90 | 100 | 85 |
| 1949....... | 91 | 100 | 92 | 80 | 90 |
| 1950....... | 92 | 97 | 92 | 90 | 94 |
| 1951....... | 97 | 97 | 96 | 99 | 97 |
| 1952....... | 98 | 101 | 96 | 100 | 98 |
| 1953....... | 98 | 100 | 97 | 100 | 98 |
| 1954....... | 99 | 100 | 99 | 100 | 99 |
| 1955....... | 101 | 99 | 101 | 101 | 100 |
| 1956....... | 101 | 100 | 101 | 103 | 100 |
| 1957....... | 102 | 101 | 101 | 102 | 100 |
| 1958....... | – 100 – | – 100 – | – 100 – | – 100 – | – 100 – |
| 1959....... | 100 | 96 | 100 | 100 | 99 |
| 1960....... | 102 | 89 | 104 | 102 | 99 |
| 1961....... | 104 | 86 | 105 | 108 | 100 |

### b. Average Annual Rate of Change — Taux annuel moyen de variation

| Period | Total | Mining | Manufacturing | Construction | Electricity and gas |
|---|---|---|---|---|---|
| 1950 – 1960. | 1.0 | −0.9 | 1.2 | 1.3 | 0.5 |
| 1948 – 1953. | 1.3 | — | 1.5 | — | 2.9 |
| 1954 – 1958. | 0.2 | — | 0.2 | — | 0.2 |
| 1958 – 1960. | 1.0 | −5.7 | 2.0 | 1.0 | −0.5 |

For footnotes see end of table.

Pour les notes, voir au bas du tableau.

## B. The Major Groups of Mining
### Les classes de la branche Industries extractives

| Period Période | All mining [2] Toutes industries extractives [2] | Coal mining Extraction du charbon | Other mining [3] Autres industries extractives [3] |
|---|---|---|---|
| ISIC — CITI | 1 | 11 | 14–19 |

### a. Indexes — Indices (1958 = 100)

| Period Période | All mining | Coal mining | Other mining |
|---|---|---|---|
| 1948............ | 100 | 99 | 117 |
| 1949............ | 100 | 98 | 125 |
| 1950............ | 97 | 95 | 120 |
| 1951............ | 97 | 96 | 116 |
| 1952............ | 101 | 100 | 117 |
| 1953............ | 100 | 99 | 115 |
| 1954............ | 100 | 99 | 110 |
| 1955............ | 99 | 99 | 110 |
| 1956............ | 100 | 100 | 105 |
| 1957............ | 101 | 101 | 107 |
| 1958............ | – 100 – | – 100 – | – 100 – |
| 1959............ | 96 | 96 | 96 |
| 1960............ | 89 | 89 | 96 |
| 1961............ | 86 | 84 | ... |

### b. Average Annual Rate of Change — Taux annuel moyen de variation

| Period | All mining | Coal mining | Other mining |
|---|---|---|---|
| 1950 – 1960...... | −0.9 | −0.6 | −2.2 |
| 1948 – 1953...... | — | — | −0.3 |
| 1954 – 1958...... | — | 0.2 | −2.4 |
| 1958 – 1960...... | −5.7 | −5.7 | −2.0 |

For footnotes see end of table.

Pour les notes, voir au bas du tableau.

# UNITED KINGDOM

## C. The Major Groups of Manufacturing — Les classes de la branche Industries manufacturières

| Period / Période | Manufacturing [1] / Industries manufacturières [1] | Food, beverages and tobacco [1,3] / Industries alimentaires, boissons, tabac [1,3] | Textiles | Clothing, footwear and made-up textiles [1,4] / Articles d'habillement, chaussures et ouvrages en tissu [1,4] | Wood products and furniture / Bois et meubles | Paper and paper products / Papier et ouvrages en papier | Printing and publishing / Imprimerie et édition | Leather and leather products except wearing apparel [4] / Cuir et articles en cuir, à l'exclusion des articles d'habillement [4] | Rubber products / Ouvrages en caoutchouc | Chemicals and chemical, petroleum and coal products / Produits chimiques et dérivés du pétrole et du charbon | Non-metallic mineral products / Produits minéraux non métalliques | Basic metals / Métallurgie de base | Metal products [1] / Ouvrages en métaux [1] | Other manufacturing [1] / Autres industries manufacturières [1] |
|---|---|---|---|---|---|---|---|---|---|---|---|---|---|---|
| ISIC — CITI | 2-3 | 20-22 | 23 | 24 | 25-26 | 27 | 28 | 29 | 30 | 31-32 | 33 | 34 | 35-38 | 39 |

### a. Indexes — Indices (1958 = 100)

| Period | | | | | | | | | | | | | | |
|---|---|---|---|---|---|---|---|---|---|---|---|---|---|---|
| 1948 | 90 | 82 | 109 | 101 | 107 | 76 | 83 | 128 | 83 | 82 | 99 | 96 | 84 | 93 |
| 1949 | 92 | 84 | 115 | 107 | 111 | 79 | 86 | 125 | 81 | 84 | 101 | 97 | 84 | 94 |
| 1950 | 92 | 81 | 119 | 109 | 112 | 84 | 90 | 127 | 87 | 87 | 103 | 98 | 84 | 95 |
| 1951 | 96 | 88 | 121 | 111 | 110 | 89 | 90 | 128 | 94 | 91 | 105 | 98 | 89 | 96 |
| 1952 | 96 | 90 | 109 | 110 | 108 | 84 | 89 | 125 | 94 | 90 | 104 | 100 | 92 | 95 |
| 1953 | 97 | 89 | 116 | 112 | 110 | 85 | 92 | 120 | 93 | 90 | 107 | 98 | 93 | 94 |
| 1954 | 99 | 91 | 116 | 109 | 109 | 91 | 92 | 122 | 100 | 93 | 104 | 97 | 95 | 96 |
| 1955 | 101 | 93 | 112 | 108 | 107 | 95 | 96 | 122 | 101 | 95 | 106 | 100 | 99 | 102 |
| 1956 | 101 | 93 | 110 | 106 | 104 | 97 | 96 | 114 | 102 | 97 | 104 | 102 | 100 | 101 |
| 1957 | 101 | 94 | 110 | 107 | 104 | 98 | 98 | 115 | 101 | 97 | 105 | 103 | 100 | 102 |
| 1958 | −100− | −100− | −100− | −100− | −100− | −100− | −100− | −100− | −100− | −100− | −100− | −100− | −100− | −100− |
| 1959 | 100 | 100 | 97 | 100 | 103 | 102 | 101 | 101 | 102 | 101 | 101 | 100 | 101 | 101 |
| 1960 | 104 | 102 | 97 | 102 | 105 | 108 | 105 | 101 | 108 | 104 | 104 | 106 | 106 | 109 |
| 1961 | 105 | 104 | 96 | 102 | 104 | 112 | 107 | 101 | 109 | 104 | 106 | 108 | 107 | 112 |

### b. Average Annual Rate of Change — Taux annuel moyen de variation

| Period | | | | | | | | | | | | | | |
|---|---|---|---|---|---|---|---|---|---|---|---|---|---|---|
| 1950 − 1960 | 1.2 | 2.3 | −2.0 | −0.7 | −0.6 | 2.5 | 1.6 | −2.3 | 2.2 | 1.8 | 0.1 | 0.8 | 2.4 | 1.4 |
| 1948 − 1953 | 1.5 | 1.6 | 1.2 | 2.1 | 0.6 | 2.3 | 2.1 | −1.3 | 2.3 | 1.9 | 1.6 | 0.4 | 2.1 | 0.2 |
| 1954 − 1958 | 0.2 | 2.4 | −3.6 | −2.1 | −2.1 | 2.4 | 2.1 | −4.8 | — | 1.8 | −1.0 | 0.8 | 1.3 | 1.0 |
| 1958 − 1960 | 2.0 | 1.0 | −1.5 | 1.0 | 2.5 | 3.9 | 2.5 | 0.5 | 3.9 | 2.0 | 2.0 | 3.0 | 3.0 | 4.4 |

[1] In the case of the indexes for all years, not covered are the following manufacturing activities: Slaughtering or bottling by wholesalers, tea blending and coffee roasting (all part of ISIC major group 20). In the case of the indexes for 1958 and thereafter, the following additional manufacturing activities are not covered: Fish curing by wholesalers and milk pasteurizing and bottling (part of ISIC major group 20), custom tailoring and dress making (part of ISIC major group 24), repair of motor cars, motorcycles or bicycles (part of ISIC major group 38), repair of musical instruments or jewellery and plate (part of ISIC major group 39), and other repair work and manufacturing at retail.

[2] Though indexes are not shown for Metal mining, (ISIC major group 12) employment in this industry is covered in the indexes for Mining (ISIC Division 1). However, mining employment in Northern Ireland is not covered in the indexes for Mining.

[3] Salt refining is included in Other mining (ISIC major group 19) instead of in Food (ISIC major group 20).

[4] Employment in the manufacture of fur apparel is covered under Leather and leather products (ISIC major group 29) rather than under Clothing (ISIC major group 24).

[1] Les activités manufacturières ci-après sont exclues des indices pour toutes les années: abattage du bétail ou mise en bouteille par les grossistes, mélange du thé et torréfaction du café (dans CITI 20). A partir de 1958, sont également exclues les activités manufacturières suivantes: Saurissage de poissons par les grossistes, pasteurisation et mise en bouteille du lait (dans CITI 20), fabrication de vêtements sur mesure (dans CITI 24), réparation des automobiles, motocycles et bicyclettes (dans CITI 38), réparation des instruments de musique, bijoux et articles d'orfèvrerie (dans CITI 39) et autres travaux de réparation et activités manufacturières au détail.

[2] Aucun indice n'est donné pour l'Extraction des métaux (CITI 12), mais l'emploi dans cette industrie est compris dans les indices relatifs aux Industries extractives (CITI 1). Cependant, l'emploi dans les industries extractives de l'Irlande du Nord n'est pas compris dans les indices relatifs aux Industries extractives.

[3] La raffinage du sel est compris dans Autres industries extractives (CITI 19) et non dans Industries alimentaires (CITI 20).

[4] L'emploi dans l'industrie des vêtements en fourrure est compris dans Cuir et articles en cuir (CITI 29) et non dans Articles d'habillement (CITI 24).

# 4. CHARACTERISTICS OF ALL INDUSTRIAL ESTABLISHMENTS
## CARACTERISTIQUES DE TOUS LES ETABLISSEMENTS INDUSTRIELS
### 1948, 1951, 1954

Value added in million Pounds; number of engaged in thousands; and value added per person engaged in thousand Pounds

Valeur ajoutée en millions de livres; nombre de personnes occupées en milliers; valeur ajoutée par personne occupée en milliers de livres

## A. The Divisions of Industrial Activity — Les branches de l'activité industrielle

| Item of data | All industrial activity [1,2] Toutes industries [1,2] | | | Mining [1,3] Industries extractives [1,3] | | | Manufacturing [2,3] Industries manufacturières [2,3] | | | Construction Bâtiment et travaux publics | | | Electricity and gas Electricité et gaz | | | Rubrique |
|---|---|---|---|---|---|---|---|---|---|---|---|---|---|---|---|---|
| | 1948 | 1951 | 1954 | 1948 | 1951 | 1954 | 1948 | 1951 | 1954 | 1948 | 1951 | 1954 | 1948 | 1951 | 1954 | |
| ISIC | 1–4; 511–512 | | | 1 | | | 2–3 | | | 4 | | | 511–512 | | | CITI |
| *a. Absolute Figures — Chiffres absolus* | | | | | | | | | | | | | | | | |
| Value added | 5 308.4 | 6 755.7 | 8 336.5 | 407.3 | 471.3 | 576.9 | 4 048.3 | 5 229.9 | 6 391.3 | 630.8 | 769.5 | 983.3 | 222.0 | 285.0 | 385.0 | Valeur ajoutée |
| Number of engaged (Average during year) | 10 081.2 | 10 598.0 | 10 820.8 | 833.5 | 810.3 | 833.1 | 7 278.3 | 7 797.3 | 7 981.6 | 1 679.4 | 1 659.4 | 1 668.1 | 290.0 | 331.0 | 338.0 | Nombre de personnes occupées (moyenne pendant l'année) |
| *b. Structure* | | | | | | | | | | | | | | | | |
| Distribution in percent of: | | | | | | | | | | | | | | | | Distribution en pourcentage: |
| Value added | 100.0 | 100.0 | 100.0 | 7.6 | 6.9 | 6.9 | 76.3 | 77.4 | 76.6 | 11.9 | 11.4 | 11.8 | 4.2 | 4.3 | 4.7 | De la valeur ajoutée |
| Number of engaged | 100.0 | 100.0 | 100.0 | 8.2 | 7.6 | 7.6 | 72.2 | 73.6 | 73.8 | 16.7 | 15.6 | 15.4 | 2.9 | 3.2 | 3.2 | Du nombre de personnes occupées |
| Value added per person engaged | 0.5 | 0.6 | 0.8 | 0.5 | 0.6 | 0.7 | 0.6 | 0.7 | 0.8 | 0.4 | 0.5 | 0.6 | 0.8 | 0.9 | 1.1 | Valeur ajoutée par personne occupée |

[1] Mining in Northern Ireland is not covered.
[2] Excluded are slaughtering carried on by units which are primarily wholesalers of meat and meat products, tea blending and coffee roasting and shoe repairing.
[3] Salt refining is covered in Mining (Division 1) instead of in Manufacturing (Division 2–3).

[1] Non compris les industries extractives en Irlande du Nord.
[2] Non compris l'abattage du bétail exécuté par des unités qui sont essentiellement des grossistes de la boucherie, le mélange du thé, la torréfaction du café et la réparation des chaussures.
[3] Le raffinage du sel est compris dans les Industries extractives (CITI branche 1) et non dans les Industries manufacturières (CITI branche 2–3).

## B. The Major Groups of Mining — Les classes de la branche Industries extractives

| Item of data | 1948 [1] | | | | 1951 [1] | | | | 1954 [1] | | | | Rubrique |
|---|---|---|---|---|---|---|---|---|---|---|---|---|---|
| | All mining Toutes industries extractives | Coal mining Extraction du charbon | Metal mining Extraction des minerais métalliques | Other mining [2] Divers [2] | All mining Toutes industries extractives | Coal mining Extraction du charbon | Metal mining Extraction des minerais métalliques | Other mining [2] Divers [2] | All mining Toutes industries extractives | Coal mining Extraction du charbon | Metal mining Extraction des minerais métalliques | Other mining [2] Divers [2] | |
| ISIC | 1 | 11 | 12 | 14–19 | 1 | 11 | 12 | 14–19 | 1 | 11 | 12 | 14–19 | CITI |
| *a. Absolute Figures — Chiffres absolus* | | | | | | | | | | | | | |
| Value added | 407.3 | 365.0 | 3.3 | 39.0 | 471.3 | 419.3 | 4.8 | 47.2 | 576.9 | 513.4 | 7.3 | 56.2 | Valeur ajoutée |
| Number of engaged (Average during the year) | 833.5 | 763.8 | 7.4 | 62.3 | 810.3 | 740.8 | 8.1 | 61.4 | 833.1 | 766.1 | 8.7 | 58.3 | Nombre de personnes occupées (moyenne pendant l'année) |
| *b. Structure* | | | | | | | | | | | | | |
| Distribution in percent of: | | | | | | | | | | | | | Distribution en pourcentage: |
| Value added | 100.0 | 89.6 | 0.8 | 9.6 | 100.0 | 88.9 | 1.0 | 10.1 | 100.0 | 88.9 | 1.3 | 9.8 | De la valeur ajoutée |
| Number of engaged | 100.0 | 91.6 | 0.9 | 7.5 | 100.0 | 91.4 | 1.0 | 7.6 | 100.0 | 91.9 | 1.1 | 7.0 | Du nombre de personnes occupées |
| Value added per person engaged | 0.5 | 0.5 | 0.4 | 0.6 | 0.6 | 0.6 | 0.6 | 0.8 | 0.7 | 0.7 | 0.8 | 1.0 | Valeur ajoutée par personne occupée |

[1] Mining in Northern Ireland is not included.
[2] Includes salt refining which should be classified in Food manufacturing (ISIC major group 20).

[1] Non compris les industries extractives en Irlande du Nord.
[2] Y compris le raffinage du sel qui devrait être classé dans les Industries alimentaires (CITI 20).

## C.   The Major Groups of Manufacturing — Les classes de la branche Industries manufacturières

| Year and item of data | Manufacturing<br>Industries manufacturières | Food, beverages and tobacco[1]<br>Industries alimentaires, boissons, tabac[1] | Textiles | Clothing, footwear and made-up textiles [2,3]<br>Articles d'habillement, chaussures et ouvrages en tissu [2,3] | Wood products and furniture<br>Bois et meubles | Paper and paper products<br>Papier et ouvrages en papier | Printing and publishing<br>Imprimerie et édition | Leather and leather products except wearing apparel[3]<br>Cuir et articles en cuir, à l'exclusion des articles d'habillement[3] | Rubber products<br>Ouvrages en caoutchouc | Chemicals and chemical, petroleum and coal products<br>Produits chimiques et dérivés du pétrole et du charbon | Non-metallic mineral products<br>Produits minéraux non métalliques | Basic metals<br>Métallurgie de base | Metal products<br>Ouvrages en métaux | Other manufacturing<br>Autres industries manufacturières | Année et rubrique |
|---|---|---|---|---|---|---|---|---|---|---|---|---|---|---|---|
| ISIC | 2–3 | 20–22 | 23 | 24 | 25–26 | 27 | 28 | 29 | 30 | 31–32 | 33 | 34 | 35–38 | 39 | CITI |

### a.   Absolute Figures — Chiffres absolus

| Year and item of data | 2–3 | 20–22 | 23 | 24 | 25–26 | 27 | 28 | 29 | 30 | 31–32 | 33 | 34 | 35–38 | 39 | Année et rubrique |
|---|---|---|---|---|---|---|---|---|---|---|---|---|---|---|---|
| **1948** Value added | 4 048.3 | 496.2 | 433.4 | 225.6 | 140.5 | 95.8 | 177.2 | 48.6 | 54.2 | 292.9 | 168.5 | 322.7 | 1 471.7 | 121.0 | **1948** Valeur ajoutée |
| Number of engaged (Average during the year) | 7 278.3 | 687.9 | 866.4 | 560.9 | 275.1 | 156.8 | 281.0 | 68.5 | 88.7 | 386.2 | 304.1 | 530.3 | 2 841.4 | 231.0 | Nombre de personnes occupées (moyenne pendant l'année) |
| **1951** Value added | 5 229.9 | 567.5 | 585.1 | 255.7 | 161.0 | 189.4 | 221.5 | 42.3 | 77.2 | 420.9 | 216.1 | 442.8 | 1 906.5 | 143.9 | **1951** Valeur ajoutée |
| Number of engaged (Average during the year) | 7 797.3 | 741.5 | 957.1 | 615.0 | 285.1 | 184.5 | 306.7 | 68.2 | 100.8 | 429.0 | 323.6 | 542.3 | 3 004.5 | 239.0 | Nombre de personnes occupées (moyenne pendant l'année) |
| **1954** Value added | 6 391.3 | 695.3 | 581.6 | 290.2 | 187.7 | 185.7 | 263.0 | 43.8 | 89.9 | 580.3 | 258.9 | 519.4 | 2 520.1 | 175.4 | **1954** Valeur ajoutée |
| Number of engaged (Average during the year) | 7 981.6 | 756.1 | 921.9 | 606.2 | 280.3 | 189.2 | 313.2 | 65.0 | 106.9 | 438.3 | 322.1 | 533.9 | 3 208.7 | 239.8 | Nombre de personnes occupées (moyenne pendant l'année) |

### b.   Structure

| Year and item of data | 2–3 | 20–22 | 23 | 24 | 25–26 | 27 | 28 | 29 | 30 | 31–32 | 33 | 34 | 35–38 | 39 | Année et rubrique |
|---|---|---|---|---|---|---|---|---|---|---|---|---|---|---|---|
| **1948** Distribution in percent of: Value added | 100.0 | 12.2 | 10.7 | 5.6 | 3.5 | 2.3 | 4.4 | 1.2 | 1.3 | 7.3 | 4.1 | 8.0 | 36.4 | 3.0 | **1948** Distribution en pourcentage: De la valeur ajoutée |
| Number of engaged | 100.0 | 9.4 | 11.9 | 7.7 | 3.8 | 2.1 | 3.9 | 0.9 | 1.3 | 5.3 | 4.2 | 7.2 | 39.1 | 3.2 | Du nombre de personnes occupées |
| Value added per person engaged | 0.6 | 0.7 | 0.5 | 0.4 | 0.5 | 0.6 | 0.6 | 0.7 | 0.6 | 0.8 | 0.6 | 0.6 | 0.5 | 0.5 | Valeur ajoutée par personne occupée |
| **1951** Distribution in percent of: Value added | 100.0 | 10.8 | 11.2 | 4.9 | 3.1 | 3.6 | 4.2 | 0.8 | 1.5 | 8.0 | 4.2 | 8.4 | 36.5 | 2.8 | **1951** Distribution en pourcentage: De la valeur ajoutée |
| Number of engaged | 100.0 | 9.5 | 12.2 | 7.9 | 3.7 | 2.3 | 4.0 | 0.9 | 1.2 | 5.5 | 4.2 | 7.0 | 38.5 | 3.1 | Du nombre de personnes occupées |
| Value added per person engaged | 0.7 | 0.8 | 0.6 | 0.4 | 0.6 | 1.0 | 0.7 | 0.6 | 0.8 | 1.0 | 0.7 | 0.8 | 0.6 | 0.6 | Valeur ajoutée par personne occupée |
| **1954** Distribution in percent of: Value added | 100.0 | 10.8 / 9.4 | 9.1 | 4.6 | 2.9 | 2.9 | 4.1 | 0.7 | 1.4 | 9.1 | 4.0 | 8.2 | 39.4 | 2.8 | **1954** Distribution en pourcentage: De la valeur ajoutée |
| Number of engaged | 100.0 | | 11.6 | 7.6 | 3.5 | 2.4 | 3.9 | 0.8 | 1.3 | 5.5 | 4.1 | 6.6 | 40.2 | 3.1 | Du nombre de personnes occupées |
| Value added per person engaged | 0.8 | 0.9 | 0.6 | 0.5 | 0.7 | 1.0 | 0.8 | 0.7 | 0.8 | 1.3 | 0.8 | 1.0 | 0.8 | 0.7 | Valeur ajoutée par personne occupée |

[1] Excluded are slaughtering and meat packing by units which are primarily wholesalers of meat and meat products, tea blending and coffee roasting and salt refining. Salt refining is included in Other mining (ISIC major groups 14–19).
[2] Excluded is shoe repairing.
[3] The manufacture of apparel of fur is included in Leather and leather products (ISIC major group 29) instead of Clothing (ISIC major group 24).

[1] Non compris l'abattage du bétail et la fabrication des préparations et conserves de viande par des unités qui sont essentiellement des grossistes de la boucherie, le mélange du thé, la torréfaction du café et le raffinage du sel. Le raffinage du sel est compris dans les Autres industries extractives (CITI 14–19).
[2] Non compris la réparation des chaussures.
[3] La fabrication des vêtements en fourrure est comprise dans l'Industrie du cuir et des articles en cuir (CITI 29) et non dans l'Habillement (CITI 24).

## 5. CHARACTERISTICS OF ALL INDUSTRIAL ESTABLISHMENTS
## CARACTERISTIQUES DE TOUS LES ETABLISSEMENTS INDUSTRIELS
### 1954, 1958

Number of establishments in units; value added and wages and salaries in million Pounds; number of engaged, employees and operatives in thousands; value added per engaged and wages and salaries per employee and per operative in thousand Pounds.

Nombre d'établissements en unités; valeur ajoutée et traitements et salaires en millions de livres; nombre de personnes occupées, de salariés et d'ouvriers en milliers; valeur ajoutée par personne occupée et traitements et salaires par salarié et par ouvrier en milliers de livres.

## A. The Divisions of Industrial Activity — Les branches de l'activité industrielle

| Year and item of data | All industrial activity[1,2] Toutes industries[1,2] | Mining[1,3] Industries extractives[1,3] | Manufacturing[2,3] Industries manufacturières[2,3] | Construction Bâtiment et travaux publics | Electricity and gas Electricité et gaz | Année et rubrique | Year and item of data | All industrial activity[1,2] Toutes industries[1,2] | Mining[1,3] Industries extractives[1,3] | Manufacturing[2,3] Industries manufacturières[2,3] | Construction Bâtiment et travaux publics | Electricity and gas Electricité et gaz | Année et rubrique |
|---|---|---|---|---|---|---|---|---|---|---|---|---|---|
| ISIC | 1-4,511-512 | 1 | 2-3 | 4 | 511-512 | CITI | ISIC | 1-4,511-512 | 1 | 2-3 | 4 | 511-512 | CITI |
| | a. Absolute Figures — Chiffres absolus | | | | | | | b. Structure | | | | | |
| **1954** | | | | | | **1954** | **1954** | | | | | | **1954** |
| Value added....... | 8 128.4 | 574.6 | 6 235.1 | 933.4 | 385.3 | Valeur ajoutée | Distribution in percent of: | | | | | | Distribution en pourcentage: |
| Number of engaged (Average during year)........... | 10 409.1 | 832.2 | 7 672.2 | 1 566.9 | 337.8 | Nombre de personnes occupées (moyenne pendant l'année) | Value added..... | 100.0 | 7.0 | 76.7 | 11.5 | 4.8 | Valeur ajoutée |
| Employees: Number (Average during year)..... | 10 272.0 | 831.7 | 7 649.7 | 1 452.8 | 337.8 | Salariés: Nombre (moyenne pendant l'année) | Number of engaged......... | 100.0 | 7.9 | 73.8 | 15.0 | 3.3 | Nombre de persones occupées |
| Wages and salaries........ | 4 730.1 | 461.3 | 3 428.7 | 673.9 | 166.2 | Traitements et salaires | Value added per person engaged.. | 0.78 | 0.69 | 0.81 | 0.60 | 1.14 | Valeur ajoutée par personne occupée |
| Operatives: Number (Average during year)..... | 8 536.8 | 781.6 | 6 232.8 | 1 283.0 | 239.4 | Ouvriers: Nombre (moyenne pendant l'année) | Employees as a percent of engaged......... | 98.7 | 99.9 | 99.7 | 92.7 | 100.0 | Salariés en pourcentage des personnes occupées |
| Wages and salaries........ | 3 698.2 | 431.6 | 2 574.6 | 581.7 | 110.3 | Traitements et salaires | Value added per unit of wages and salaries..... | 1.72 | 1.24 | 1.82 | 1.38 | 2.32 | Valeur ajoutée par unité de traitements et salaires |
| | | | | | | | Operatives as a percent of employees...... | 83.1 | 94.0 | 81.5 | 88.3 | 70.9 | Ouvriers en pourcentage des salariés |
| | | | | | | | Wages and salaries per employee.... | 0.46 | 0.55 | 0.45 | 0.46 | 0.49 | Traitements et salaires par salarié |
| | | | | | | | Wages and salaries per operative.... | 0.43 | 0.55 | 0.41 | 0.45 | 0.46 | Traitements et salaires par ouvrier |
| **1958** | | | | | | **1958** | **1958** | | | | | | **1958** |
| Number of establishments... | 192 709 | 3 372 | 92 785 | 95 629 | 923 | Nombre d'établissements | Distribution in percent of: | | | | | | Distribution en pourcentage: |
| Value added....... | 10 373.4 | 726.1 | 7 848.9 | 1 244.7 | 553.7 | Valeur ajoutée | Value added..... | 100.0 | 6.9 | 75.7 | 12.0 | 5.4 | Valeur ajoutée |
| Number of engaged (Average during year)........... | 10 526.0 | 832.0 | 7 781.2 | 1 572.5 | 340.3 | Nombre de personnes occupées (moyenne pendant l'année) | Number of engaged......... | 100.0 | 7.9 | 73.9 | 14.9 | 3.3 | Nombre de personnes occupées |
| Employees: Number (Average during year)..... | 10 394.0 | 831.3 | 7 747.7 | 1 474.7 | 340.3 | Salariés: Nombre (moyenne pendant l'année) | Value added per person engaged.. | 0.98 | 0.87 | 1.01 | 0.79 | 1.63 | Valeur ajoutée par personne occupée |
| Wages and salaries........ | 6 118.5 | 565.4 | 4 453.7 | 881.8 | 217.6 | Traitements et salaires | Employees as a percent of engaged......... | 98.7 | 99.9 | 99.6 | 93.8 | 100.0 | Salariés en pourcentage des personnes occupées |
| Operatives: Number (Average during year)..... | 8 380.1 | 769.5 | 6 095.5 | 1 279.6 | 235.5 | Ouvriers: Nombre (moyenne pendant l'année) | Value added per unit of wages and salaries..... | 1.70 | 1.28 | 1.76 | 1.41 | 2.54 | Valeur ajoutée par unité de traitements et salaires |
| Wages and salaries........ | 4 618.8 | 518.3 | 3 218.4 | 741.5 | 140.6 | Traitements et salaires | Operatives as a percent of employees...... | 80.6 | 92.6 | 78.7 | 86.8 | 69.2 | Ouvriers en pourcentage des salariés |
| | | | | | | | Wages and salaries per employee.... | 0.59 | 0.68 | 0.57 | 0.60 | 0.64 | Traitements et salaires par salarié |
| | | | | | | | Wages and salaries per operative.... | 0.55 | 0.67 | 0.53 | 0.58 | 0.60 | Traitements et salaires par ouvrier |

For footnote see end of table.

Pour les notes, voir au bas du tableau.

## B. The Major Groups of Mining — Les classes de la branche Industries extractives

| Year and item of data | All mining [1] Toutes industries extrac-tives [1] | Coal mining Extraction du charbon | Metal mining Extraction des minerais métal-liques | Other mining [3] Divers [3] | Année et rubrique | Year and item of data | All mining [1] Toutes industries extrac-tives [1] | Coal mining Extraction du charbon | Metal mining Extraction des -minerais métal-liques | Other mining [3] Divers [3] | Année et rubrique |
|---|---|---|---|---|---|---|---|---|---|---|---|
| ISIC | 1 | 11 | 12 | 14-19 | CITI | ISIC | 1 | 11 | 12 | 14-19 | CITI |
| | **a. Absolute Figures — Chiffres absolus** | | | | | | **b. Structure** | | | | |
| **1954** | | | | | 1954 | **1954** | | | | | 1954 |
| Value added.............. | 574.6 | 513.4 | 7.2 | 54.0 | Valeur ajoutée | Distribution in percent of: | | | | | Distribution en pourcentage: |
| Number of engaged (Average during year)... | 832.2 | 766.1 | 8.6 | 57.5 | Nombre de personnes occupées (moyenne pendant l'année) | Value added............. | 100.0 | 89.3 | 1.3 | 9.4 | Valeur ajoutée Nombre de personnes occupées |
| Employees | | | | | Salariés | Number of engaged..... | 100.0 | 92.1 | 1.0 | 6.9 | Valeur ajoutée par personne occupée |
| Number (Average during year)............ | 831.7 | 765.8 | 8.6 | 57.3 | Nombre (moyenne pendant l'année) | Value added per person engaged............. | 0.69 | 0.67 | 0.84 | 0.94 | Salariés en pourcentage des personnes occupées |
| Wages and salaries...... | 461.3 | 429.4 | 4.2 | 27.7 | Traitements et salaires | Employees as a percent of engaged......... | 99.9 | 100.0 | 100.0 | 99.6 | Valeur ajoutée par unité de traitements et salaires |
| Operatives | | | | | Ouvriers | Value added per unit of wages and salaries...... | 1.24 | 1.20 | 1.71 | 1.95 | Ouvriers en pourcentage des salariés |
| Number (Average during year)............ | 781.6 | 724.0 | 7.7 | 49.9 | Nombre (moyenne pendant l'année) | Operatives as a percent of employees.......... | 94.0 | 94.5 | 89.5 | 87.1 | Traitements et salaires par salarié |
| Wages and salaries...... | 431.6 | 404.8 | 3.6 | 23.2 | Traitements et salaires | Wages and salaries per employee............. | 0.55 | 0.56 | 0.49 | 0.48 | Traitements et salaires par ouvrier |
| | | | | | | Wages and salaries per operative............. | 0.55 | 0.56 | 0.47 | 0.46 | |
| **1958** | | | | | 1958 | **1958** | | | | | 1958 |
| Number of establishments. | 3 372 | 1 308 | 68 | 1 996 | Nombre d'établissements | Distribution in percent of: | | | | | Distribution en pourcentage: |
| Value added.............. | 726.1 | 645.1 | 8.9 | 72.1 | Valeur ajoutée | Value added............. | 100.0 | 88.8 | 1.2 | 10.0 | Valeur ajoutée Nombre de personnes occupées |
| Number of engaged (Average during year)... | 832.0 | 771.6 | 8.0 | 52.4 | Nombre de personnes occupées (moyenne pendant l'année) | Number of engaged..... | 100.0 | 92.7 | 1.0 | 6.3 | Valeur ajoutée par personne occupée |
| Employees | | | | | Salariés | Value added per person engaged............. | 0.87 | 0.84 | 1.11 | 1.38 | Salariés en pourcentage des personnes occupées |
| Number (Average during year)............ | 831.3 | 771.2 | 8.0 | 52.1 | Nombre (moyenne pendant l'année) | Employees as a percent of engaged......... | 99.9 | 99.9 | 100.0 | 99.4 | Valeur ajoutée par unité de traitements et salaires |
| Wages and salaries...... | 565.4 | 528.5 | 5.1 | 31.8 | Traitements et salaires | Value added per unit of wages and salaries...... | 1.28 | 1.22 | 1.68 | 2.27 | Ouvriers en pourcentage des salariés |
| Operatives | | | | | Ouvriers | Operatives as a percent of employees.......... | 92.6 | 93.1 | 87.5 | 85.0 | Traitements et salaires par salarié |
| Number (Average during year)............ | 769.5 | 718.2 | 7.0 | 44.3 | Nombre (moyenne pendant l'année) | Wages and salaries per employee............. | 0.68 | 0.68 | 0.64 | 0.61 | Traitements et salaires par ouvrier |
| Wages and salaries...... | 518.3 | 488.2 | 4.3 | 25.8 | Traitements et salaires | Wages and salaries per operative............. | 0.67 | 0.68 | 0.61 | 0.58 | |

For footnotes, see end of table.

Pour les notes, voir au bas du tableau.

## C. The Major Groups of Manufacturing — Les classes de la branche Industries manufacturières

| Year and item of data | Manufacturing [2,3] — Industries manufacturières [2,3] | Food, beverages and tobacco [2,3] — Industries alimentaires, boissons, tabac [2,3] | Textiles [2] | Clothing, footwear and made-up textiles [2,4] — Articles d'habillement, chaussures et ouvrages en tissu [2,4] | Wood products and furniture — Bois et meubles | Paper and paper products — Papier et ouvrages en papier | Printing and publishing — Imprimerie et édition | Leather and leather products except wearing apparel [4] — Cuir et articles en cuir, à l'exclusion des articles d'habillement [4] | Rubber products — Ouvrages en caoutchouc | Chemicals and chemical, petroleum and coal products — Produits chimiques et dérivés du pétrole et du charbon | Non-metallic mineral products — Produits minéraux non métalliques | Basic metals [5] — Métallurgie de base [5] | Metal products [2] — Ouvrages en métaux [2] | Other manufacturing [2,5] — Autres industries manufacturières [2,5] | Année et rubrique |
|---|---|---|---|---|---|---|---|---|---|---|---|---|---|---|---|
| ISIC | 2–3 | 20–22 | 23 | 24 | 25–26 | 27 | 28 | 29 | 30 | 31–32 | 33 | 34 | 35–38 | 39 | CITI |
| *a. Absolute Figures — Chiffres absolus* | | | | | | | | | | | | | | | |
| **1954** | | | | | | | | | | | | | | | **1954** |
| Value added | 6 235.1 | 644.9 | 578.5 | 287.8 | 184.9 | 185.7 | 259.8 | 44.8 | 90.0 | 590.3 | 267.6 | 532.5 | 2 380.1 | 188.2 | Valeur ajoutée |
| Number of engaged (Average during year) | 7 672.2 | 656.7 | 917.5 | 599.6 | 275.6 | 192.1 | 306.4 | 66.3 | 107.3 | 445.1 | 337.1 | 550.0 | 2 960.6 | 257.9 | Nombre de personnes occupées (moyenne pendant l'année) |
| Employees: Number (Average during year) | 7 649.7 | 654.1 | 915.7 | 596.0 | 273.2 | 191.8 | 304.8 | 65.8 | 107.2 | 444.5 | 336.0 | 549.2 | 2 954.8 | 256.6 | Salariés: Nombre (moyenne pendant l'année) |
| Wages and salaries | 3 428.7 | 259.8 | 330.1 | 183.6 | 122.0 | 82.7 | 156.9 | 27.1 | 49.2 | 231.7 | 155.7 | 288.7 | 1 436.3 | 104.9 | Traitements et salaires |
| Operatives: Number (Average during year) | 6 232.8 | 534.3 | 824.5 | 535.3 | 234.0 | 161.2 | 221.8 | 56.6 | 86.3 | 311.4 | 284.6 | 457.0 | 2 320.6 | 205.2 | Ouvriers: Nombre (moyenne pendant l'année) |
| Wages and salaries | 2 574.6 | 188.7 | 270.2 | 148.2 | 98.0 | 62.9 | 103.7 | 20.6 | 36.7 | 143.2 | 124.8 | 233.3 | 1 069.6 | 74.7 | Traitements et salaires |
| **1958** | | | | | | | | | | | | | | | **1958** |
| Number of establishments | 92 785 | 9 233 | 7 893 | 10 075 | 9 976 | 1 632 | 7 739 | 1 945 | 587 | 3 595 | 5 345 | 2 876 | 26 540 | 5 349 | Nombre d'établissements |
| Value added | 7 848.9 | 916.5 | 550.3 | 320.1 | 211.9 | 222.0 | 355.0 | 43.3 | 102.8 | 783.6 | 318.3 | 689.3 | 3 091.7 | 244.1 | Valeur ajoutée |
| Number of engaged (Average during year) | 7 781.2 | 725.9 | 788.7 | 550.8 | 253.7 | 210.3 | 331.4 | 54.4 | 107.7 | 480.1 | 323.1 | 568.4 | 3 119.7 | 267.0 | Nombre de personnes occupées (moyenne pendant l'année) |
| Employees: Number (Average during year) | 7 747.7 | 722.8 | 775.4 | 547.6 | 251.6 | 210.0 | 329.6 | 53.9 | 107.6 | 478.7 | 322.1 | 568.0 | 3 114.6 | 265.8 | Salariés: Nombre (moyenne pendant l'année) |
| Wages and salaries | 4 453.7 | 367.0 | 343.5 | 211.4 | 140.6 | 114.4 | 222.6 | 27.5 | 63.8 | 314.8 | 185.8 | 382.3 | 1 941.1 | 138.9 | Traitements et salaires |
| Operatives: Number (Average during year) | 6 095.5 | 582.6 | 683.0 | 485.4 | 210.5 | 171.7 | 235.0 | 45.8 | 83.2 | 320.2 | 264.1 | 461.8 | 2 349.6 | 202.6 | Ouvriers: Nombre (moyenne pendant l'année) |
| Wages and salaries | 3 218.4 | 265.1 | 274.3 | 169.2 | 110.4 | 85.9 | 148.0 | 20.8 | 46.3 | 185.0 | 142.9 | 302.6 | 1 373.9 | 94.0 | Traitements et salaires |
| *b. Structure* | | | | | | | | | | | | | | | |
| **1954** | | | | | | | | | | | | | | | **1954** |
| Distribution in percent of: Value added | 100.0 | 10.3 | 9.3 | 4.6 | 2.9 | 3.0 | 4.2 | 0.7 | 1.5 | 9.4 | 4.3 | 8.6 | 38.1 | 3.1 | Distribution en pourcentage: Valeur ajoutée |
| Number of engaged | 100.0 | 8.5 | 12.0 | 7.8 | 3.6 | 2.5 | 4.0 | 0.8 | 1.4 | 5.8 | 4.4 | 7.2 | 38.6 | 3.4 | Nombre de personnes occupées |
| Value added per person engaged | 0.81 | 0.98 | 0.63 | 0.48 | 0.67 | 0.97 | 0.85 | 0.68 | 0.84 | 1.33 | 0.79 | 0.97 | 0.80 | 0.73 | Valeur ajoutée par personne occupée |
| Employees as a percent of engaged | 99.7 | 99.6 | 99.8 | 99.4 | 99.1 | 99.8 | 99.5 | 99.2 | 99.9 | 99.9 | 99.7 | 99.8 | 99.8 | 99.5 | Salariés en pourcentage des personnes occupées |
| Value added per unit of wages and salaries | 1.82 | 2.48 | 1.75 | 1.57 | 1.52 | 2.24 | 1.66 | 1.65 | 1.83 | 2.55 | 1.72 | 1.84 | 1.66 | 1.79 | Valeur ajoutée par unité de traitements et salaires |
| Operatives as a percent of employees | 81.5 | 81.7 | 90.0 | 89.8 | 85.6 | 84.0 | 72.8 | 86.0 | 80.5 | 70.0 | 84.7 | 83.2 | 78.5 | 80.0 | Ouvriers en pourcentage des salariés |
| Wages and salaries per employee | 0.45 | 0.40 | 0.36 | 0.31 | 0.45 | 0.43 | 0.51 | 0.41 | 0.46 | 0.52 | 0.46 | 0.52 | 0.49 | 0.41 | Traitements et salaires par salarié |
| Wages and salaries per operative | 0.41 | 0.35 | 0.33 | 0.28 | 0.42 | 0.39 | 0.47 | 0.36 | 0.42 | 0.46 | 0.44 | 0.51 | 0.46 | 0.36 | Traitements et salaires par ouvrier |
| **1958** | | | | | | | | | | | | | | | **1958** |
| Distribution in percent of: Value added | 100.0 | 11.6 | 7.0 | 4.1 | 2.7 | 2.8 | 4.6 | 0.5 | 1.3 | 10.0 | 4.1 | 8.7 | 39.4 | 3.2 | Distribution en pourcentage: Valeur ajoutée |
| Number of engaged | 100.0 | 9.3 | 10.1 | 7.1 | 3.3 | 2.7 | 4.2 | 0.7 | 1.4 | 6.2 | 4.1 | 7.3 | 40.1 | 3.5 | Nombre de personnes occupées |
| Value added per person engaged | 1.01 | 1.26 | 0.70 | 0.58 | 0.84 | 1.06 | 1.07 | 0.80 | 0.95 | 1.63 | 0.98 | 1.21 | 0.99 | 0.91 | Valeur ajoutée par personne occupée |
| Employees as a percent of engaged | 99.6 | 99.6 | 98.3 | 99.4 | 99.2 | 99.8 | 99.4 | 99.1 | 99.9 | 99.7 | 99.7 | 99.9 | 99.8 | 99.6 | Salariés en pourcentage des personnes occupées |
| Value added per unit of wages and salaries | 1.76 | 2.50 | 1.60 | 1.51 | 1.51 | 1.94 | 1.59 | 1.57 | 1.61 | 2.49 | 1.71 | 1.80 | 1.59 | 1.76 | Valeur ajoutée par unité de traitements et salaires |
| Operatives as a percent of employees | 78.7 | 80.6 | 88.1 | 88.6 | 83.7 | 81.8 | 71.3 | 85.0 | 77.3 | 66.9 | 82.0 | 81.3 | 75.4 | 76.2 | Ouvriers en pourcentage des salariés |
| Wages and salaries per employee | 0.57 | 0.51 | 0.44 | 0.39 | 0.56 | 0.54 | 0.68 | 0.51 | 0.59 | 0.66 | 0.58 | 0.67 | 0.62 | 0.52 | Traitements et salaires par salarié |
| Wages and salaries per operative | 0.53 | 0.46 | 0.40 | 0.35 | 0.52 | 0.50 | 0.63 | 0.45 | 0.56 | 0.58 | 0.54 | 0.66 | 0.58 | 0.46 | Traitements et salaires par ouvrier |

[1] Mining in Northern Ireland is not covered.
[2] Excluded from Manufacturing (Division 2-3) are the following kinds of activities: Slaughtering or fish curing by units which are primarily wholesalers or retailers, milk pasteurizing and bottling, tea blending or coffee roasting, or bottling by wholesalers (all part of ISIC major groups 20-22), processing of flax or cotton and rayon waste (part of ISIC major group 23), custom tailoring or dress making or shoe repairing (part of ISIC major group 24), repair of motor cars, motorcycles or bicycles (part of ISIC major group 38), repair of musical instruments or jewellery and plate (part of ISIC major group 39), other repair work at retail and other custom manufacturing.
[3] Salt refining is included in Other mining (ISIC major group 19) rather than Food manufacturing (ISIC major group 20).
[4] The manufacture of fur apparel is included in Leather and leather products (ISIC major group 29) instead of Clothing (ISIC major group 24).
[5] The refining of precious metals is covered under Other manufacturing (ISIC major group 39) instead of Basic metals (ISIC major group 34).

[1] Non compris les industries extractives d'Irlande du Nord.
[2] Sont exclus des Industries manufacturières (CITI 2-3) les types suivants d'activité: abattage du bétail et saurissage du poisson exécutés par des unités pratiquant essentiellement le commerce de gros ou de détail, pasteurisation et mise en bouteille du lait, mélange du thé et torréfaction du café ou mise en bouteille par des grossistes (tous dans CITI 20-22), préparation du lin ou du coton et des déchets de rayonne (dans CITI 23), fabrication de vêtements sus mesure ou réparation des chaussures (dans CITI 24), réparation des automobiles, motocycles et bicyclettes (dans CITI 38), réparation des instruments de musique, des bijoux et des articles d'orfèvrerie (dans CITI 39), autres réparations au détail, et fabrication d'autres articles sur commande.
[3] Le raffinage du sel est compris dans Autres industries extractives (CITI 19) et non dans Industries alimentaires (CITI 20).
[4] La fabrication d'articles d'habillement en fourrure est comprise dans Cuir et articles en cuir (CITI 29) et non dans Articles d'habillement (CITI 24).
[5] L'affinage des métaux précieux est compris dans Autres industries manufacturières (CITI 39) et non dans Industries métallurgiques de base (CITI 34).

## 6. CHARACTERISTICS OF INDUSTRIAL ESTABLISHMENTS ENGAGING MORE THAN 10 PERSONS
## CARACTERISTIQUES DES ETABLISSEMENTS INDUSTRIELS OCCUPANT PLUS DE 10 PERSONNES
### 1935, 1948, 1951, 1954

Number of establishments in units; value added and wages and salaries in million Pounds; number of engaged, employees and operatives in thousands; energy consumed in thousand metric tons of coal equivalents, electricity consumed in million KWH; capacity of installed power equipment in thousand horsepower; value added per engaged and wages and salaries per employee in thousand Pounds; energy consumed per engaged and per operative in metric tons of coal equivalents; electricity consumed per engaged and per operative in thousand KWH; capacity of installed power equipment per engaged and per operative in horsepower.

Nombre d'établissements en unités; valeur ajoutée et traitements et salaires en millions de livres; nombre de personnes occupées, de salariés et d'ouvriers en milliers; énergie consommée en milliers de tonnes métriques d'équivalent charbon; électricité consommée en millions de kWh; puissance installée en milliers de chevaux-vapeur; valeur ajoutée par personne occupée et traitements et salaires par salarié en milliers de livres; énergie consommée par personne occupée et par ouvrier en tonnes métriques d'équivalent charbon; électricité consommée par personne occupée et par ouvrier en milliers de kWh; puissance installée par personne occupée et par ouvrier en chevaux-vapeur.

### A. The Divisions of Industrial Activity — Les branches de l'activité industrielle

| Year and item of data | All industrial activity [3] Toutes industries[3] | Mining [4] Industries extractives [4] | Manufacturing [3,4] Industries manufacturières[3,4] | Construction Bâtiment et travaux publics | Electricity and gas Electricité et gaz | Année et rubrique | Year and item of data | All industrial activity [3] Toutes industries[3] | Mining [4] Industries extractives [4] | Manufacturing[3,4] Industries manufacturières[3,4] | Construction Bâtiment et travaux publics | Electricity and gas Electricité et gaz | Année et rubrique |
|---|---|---|---|---|---|---|---|---|---|---|---|---|---|
| ISIC | 1-4,511-512 | 1 | 2-3 | 4 | 511-512 | CITI | ISIC | 1-4,511-512 | 1 | 2-3 | 4 | 511-512 | CITI |
| | a. Absolute Figures — Chiffres absolus | | | | | | | b. Structure | | | | | |
| **1935** Number of establishments... | ... | 2 987 | 49 444 | ... | 1 321 | **1935** Nombre d'établissements | **1935** Distribution in percent of: | | | | | | **1935** Distribution en pourcentage: |
| Value added....... | 1 600.2 | 136.4 | 1 210.4 | 150.0 | 103.4 | Valeur ajoutée | Value added..... | 100.0 | 8.5 | 75.6 | 9.4 | 6.5 | Valeur ajoutée |
| Number of engaged (Average during year).......... | 7 231.0 | 842.0 | 5 342.0 | 821.0 | 226.0 | Nombre de personnes occupées | Number of engaged........ | 100.0 | 11.6 | 73.9 | 11.3 | 3.2 | Nombre de personnes occupées Par personne occupée: |
| Number of operatives (Average during year).......... | 6 220.8 | 819.7 | 4 560.0 | 665.4 | 175.7 | Nombre d'ouvriers (moyenne pendant l'année) | Per person engaged: Value added..... Electricity consumed....... | 0.22 ... | 0.16 3.45 | 0.23 2.15 | 0.18 0.31 | 0.46 ... | Valeur ajoutée Electricité consommée |
| Electricity consumed...... | ... | 2 904.1 | 11 464.9 | 253.4 | ... | Electricité consommée | Operatives as a percent of engaged........ | 86.0 | 97.4 | 85.4 | 81.0 | 77.7 | Ouvriers en pourcentage des personnes occupées |
| | | | | | | | Electricity consumed per operative.... | ... | 3.54 | 2.51 | 0.38 | ... | Electricité consommée par ouvrier |
| **1948** [1] Number of establishments... | 74 863 | 2 357 | 54 072 | 17 379 | 1 055 | **1948** [1] Nombre d'établissements | **1948** [1] Distribution in percent of: | | | | | | **1948** [1] Distribution en pourcentage: |
| Value added....... | 4 874.6 | 402.9 | 3 739.4 | 515.6 | 216.7 | Valeur ajoutée | Value added..... | 100.0 | 8.2 | 76.7 | 10.6 | 4.5 | Valeur ajoutée |
| Number of engaged (Average during year).......... | 9 073.1 | 826.5 | 6 681.9 | 1 280.9 | 283.8 | Nombre de personnes occupées (moyenne pendant l'année) | Number of engaged........ | 100.0 | 9.1 | 73.6 | 14.1 | 3.2 | Nombre de personnes occupées Par personne occupée: |
| Employees: Number (Average during year)..... | 9 051.9 | 826.2 | 6 671.9 | 1 270.0 | 283.8 | Salariés: Nombre (moyenne pendant l'année) | Per person engaged: Value added..... Electricity consumed....... | 0.54 ... | 0.49 4.81 | 0.56 3.24 | 0.40 ... | 0.76 28.63 | Valeur ajoutée Electricité consommée |
| Wages and salaries......... | 2 904.8 | 320.7 | 2 081.8 | 404.2 | 98.1 | Traitements et salaires | Employees as a percent of engaged........ | 99.8 | 100.0 | 99.8 | 99.1 | 100.0 | Salariés en pourcentage des personnes occupées |
| Operatives: Number (Average during year)..... | 7 732.9 | 785.3 | 5 584.6 | 1 151.6 | 211.4 | Ouvriers: Nombre (moyenne pendant l'année) | Value added per unit of wages and salaries..... | 1.68 | 1.26 | 1.80 | 1.28 | 2.21 | Valeur ajoutée par unité de traitements et salaires |
| Wages and salaries......... | 2 324.1 | 302.0 | 1 595.9 | 357.6 | 68.6 | Traitements et salaires | Operatives as a percent of employees....... | 85.4 | 95.0 | 83.7 | 90.7 | 74.5 | Ouvriers en pourcentages des salariés |
| Electricity consumed...... | ... | 3 977.4 | 21 687.9 | ... | 8 124.4 | Electricité consommée | Wages and salaries per employee.... | 0.32 | 0.39 | 0.31 | 0.32 | 0.34 | Traitements et salaires par salarié |
| | | | | | | | Per operative: Wages and salaries........ Electricity consumed...... | 0.30 ... | 0.38 5.06 | 0.28 3.88 | 0.31 ... | 0.32 38.43 | Par ouvrier: Traitements et salaires Electricité consommée |

For footnotes see end of table.

Pour les notes, voir au bas du tableau.

## A. The Divisions of Industrial Activity (continued) — Les branches de l'activité industrielle (suite)

| Year and item of data | All industrial activity [3] Toutes industries[3] | Mining [4] Industries extractives [4] | Manu-facturing[3],[4] Industries manufac-turières[3],[4] | Con-struction Bâtiment et travaux publics | Electricity and gas Electricité et gaz | Année et rubrique |
|---|---|---|---|---|---|---|
| ISIC | 1-4,511-512 | 1 | 2-3 | 4 | 511-512 | CITI |

### a. Absolute Figures — Chiffres absolus

| | All industrial activity | Mining | Manu-facturing | Con-struction | Electricity and gas | Année et rubrique |
|---|---|---|---|---|---|---|
| **1951** [2] | | | | | | **1951** [2] |
| Number of establishments... | 81 590 | 2 210 | 57 823 | 20 188 | 1 369 | Nombre d'établissements |
| Value added...... | 6 415.1 | 466.2 | 5 006.0 | 657.7 | 285.2 | Valeur ajoutée |
| Number of engaged (Average during year).......... | 9 907.7 | 803.5 | 7 423.2 | 1 349.8 | 331.2 | Nombre de personnes occupées (moyenne pendant l'année) |
| Employees: Number (Average during year)..... | 9 882.6 | 803.2 | 7 412.1 | 1 336.1 | 331.2 | Salariés: Nombre (moyenne pendant l'année) |
| Wages and salaries........ | 3 739.8 | 368.2 | 2 726.8 | 510.6 | 134.2 | Traitements et salaires |
| Operatives: Number (Average during year)..... | 8 338.6 | 758.9 | 6 144.8 | 1 199.3 | 235.6 | Ouvriers: Nombre (moyenne pendant l'année) |
| Wages and salaries........ | 2 949.8 | 345.9 | 2 068.9 | 446.1 | 88.9 | Traitements et salaires |
| **1954** [2] | | | | | | **1954** [2] |
| Number of establishments... | 78 052 | 2 286 | 56 712 | 17 766 | 1 288 | Nombre d'établissements |
| Value added....... | 7 910.1 | 569.9 | 6 120.9 | 834.0 | 385.3 | Valeur ajoutée |
| Number of engaged (Average during year).......... | 10 113.9 | 825.4 | 7 602.0 | 1 348.7 | 337.8 | Nombre de personnes occupées (moyenne pendant l'année) |
| Employees: Number (Average during year)..... | 10 095.1 | 825.2 | 7 593.0 | 1 339.1 | 337.8 | Salariés: Nombre (moyenne pendant l'année) |
| Wages and salaries........ | 4 677.3 | 458.5 | 3 414.1 | 638.5 | 166.2 | Traitements et salaires |
| Operatives: Number (Average during year)..... | 8 398.3 | 775.7 | 6 193.4 | 1 189.8 | 239.4 | Ouvriers: Nombre (moyenne pendant l'année) |
| Wages and salaries........ | 3 663.0 | 429.0 | 2 570.0 | 553.7 | 110.3 | Traitements et salaires |
| Energy consumed... | ... | 13 522.7 | 80 356.9 | ... | 71 546.0 | Energie consommée |
| Electricity consumed...... | ... | 5 175.9 | 34 175.6 | ... | 12 764.1 | Electricité consommée |

### b. Structure

| Year and item of data | All industrial activity [3] Toutes industries [3] | Mining [4] Industries ex-tractives [4] | Manu-facturing[3],[4] Industries manufac-turières[3],[4] | Con-struction Bâtiment et travaux publics | Electricity and gas Electricité et gaz | Année et rubrique |
|---|---|---|---|---|---|---|
| ISIC | 1-4,511-512 | 1 | 2-3 | 4 | 511-512 | CITI |
| **1951** [2] | | | | | | **1951** [2] |
| Distribution in percent of: Value added..... | 100.0 | 7.2 | 78.1 | 10.2 | 4.5 | Distribution en pourcentage: Valeur ajoutée |
| Number of engaged........ | 100.0 | 8.1 | 74.9 | 13.6 | 3.4 | Nombre de personnes occupées |
| Value added per person engaged.. | 0.65 | 0.58 | 0.67 | 0.49 | 0.86 | Valeur ajoutée par personne occupée |
| Employees as a percent of engaged........ | 99.7 | 100.0 | 99.8 | 99.0 | 100.0 | Salariés en pourcentage des personnes occupées |
| Value added per unit of wages and salaries..... | 1.72 | 1.27 | 1.84 | 1.29 | 2.12 | Valeur ajoutée par unité de traitements et salaires |
| Operatives as a percent of employees....... | 84.4 | 94.5 | 82.9 | 89.8 | 71.1 | Ouvriers en pourcentage des salariés |
| Wages and salaries per employee.... | 0.38 | 0.46 | 0.37 | 0.38 | 0.40 | Traitements et salaires par salarié |
| Per operative: Wages and salaries........ | 0.35 | 0.46 | 0.34 | 0.37 | 0.38 | Par ouvrier: Traitements et salaires |
| Capacity of installed power equipment....... | ... | ... | 3.45 | ... | ... | Puissance installée |
| **1954** [2] | | | | | | **1954** [2] |
| Distribution in percent of: Value added..... | 100.0 | 7.2 | 77.3 | 10.6 | 4.9 | Distribution en pourcentage: Valeur ajoutée |
| Number of engaged........ | 100.0 | 8.1 | 75.2 | 13.3 | 3.4 | Nombre de personnes occupées |
| Per person engaged: Value added.. | 0.78 | 0.69 | 0.80 | 0.62 | 1.14 | Par personne occupée: Valeur ajoutée |
| Energy consumed........ | ... | 16.38 | 10.57 | ... | 211.80 | Energie consommée |
| Electricity consumed...... | ... | 6.27 | 4.50 | ... | 37.78 | Electricité consommée |
| Employees as a percent of engaged........ | 99.8 | 100.0 | 99.9 | 99.3 | 100.0 | Salariés en pourcentage des personnes occupées |
| Value added per unit of wages and salaries..... | 1.69 | 1.24 | 1.79 | 1.31 | 2.32 | Valeur ajoutée par unité de traitements et salaires |
| Operatives as a percent of employees....... | 83.2 | 94.0 | 81.6 | 88.8 | 70.9 | Ouvriers en pourcentage des salariés |
| Wages and salaries per employee.... | 0.46 | 0.56 | 0.45 | 0.48 | 0.49 | Traitements et salaires par salarié |
| Per operative: Wages and salaries........ | 0.44 | 0.55 | 0.41 | 0.46 | 0.46 | Par ouvrier: Traitements et salaires |
| Energy consumed. | ... | 17.43 | 12.97 | ... | 298.86 | Energie consommée |
| Electricity consumed...... | ... | 6.67 | 5.52 | ... | 53.32 | Electricité consommée |

[1] Industrial activity in Northern Ireland is not covered.
[2] Mining in Northern Ireland is not covered.
[3] Not included in manufacturing is slaughtering carried on by units which are primarily wholesalers of meat and meat products, tea blending and coffee roasting, and shoe repairing (ISIC group 242). In addition, for 1935, the following classes of manufacturing were not covered: The processing of flax, publishing, automobile repairing, cinematograph film manufacturing and perhaps the repair and rebuilding of locomotives and related equipment by railroad employees.
[4] Salt refining is covered in Mining (ISIC division 1) instead of in Manufacturing (ISIC division 2-3).

[1] Non compris l'activité industrielle en Irlande du Nord.
[2] Non compris les industries extractives en Irlande du Nord.
[3] Les industries manufacturières ne comprennent ni l'abattage du bétail exécuté par des unités qui sont essentiellement des grossistes de la boucherie, ni le mélange du thé, ni la torréfaction du café, ni la réparation des chaussures (CITI 242). De plus, les industries manufacturières ci-après sont exclues des chiffres de 1935: préparation du lin, édition, réparation des automobiles, fabrication de pellicules cinématographiques et, peut-être, réparation et reconstruction de locomotives et de matériel connexe par les agents des chemins de fer.
[4] Le raffinage du sel est compris dans les Industries extractives (CITI branche 1) et non dans les Industries manufacturières (CITI branche 2-3).

## B. The Major Groups of Mining — Les classes de la branche Industries extractives

### a. Absolute Figures — Chiffres absolus

| Year and item of data (ISIC) | All mining Toutes industries extractives (1) | Coal mining Extraction du charbon (11) | Metal mining Extraction des minerais métalliques (12) | Other mining² Divers² (14-19) | Année et rubrique (CITI) |
|---|---|---|---|---|---|
| **1935[1]** | | | | | **1935[1]** |
| Number of establishments | 2 987 | 1 334 | 85 | 1 568 | Nombre d'établissements |
| Value added | 136.4 | 121.3 | 2.3 | 12.8 | Valeur ajoutée |
| Number of engaged (Average during year) | 842.0 | 764.0 | 11.0 | 67.0 | Nombre de personnes occupées (moyenne pendant l'année) |
| Number of operatives (Average during year) | 819.7 | 746.8 | 10.3 | 62.6 | Nombre d'ouvriers (moyenne pendant l'année) |
| Electricity consumed | 2 904.1 | 2 724.9 | 50.2 | 129.0 | Electricité consommée |
| **1948[1]** | | | | | **1948[1]** |
| Number of establishments | 2 357 | 1 181 | 57 | 1 119 | Nombre d'établissements |
| Value added | 402.9 | 364.6 | 3.3 | 35.0 | Valeur ajoutée |
| Number of engaged | 826.5 | 763.0 | 7.3 | 56.2 | Nombre de personnes occupées (moyenne pendant l'année) |
| Employees: Number (Average during year) | 826.2 | 762.9 | 7.3 | 56.0 | Salariés: Nombre (moyenne pendant l'année) |
| Wages and salaries | 320.7 | 299.6 | 2.4 | 18.7 | Traitements et salaires |
| Operatives: Number (Average during year) | 785.3 | 729.0 | 6.6 | 49.7 | Ouvriers: Nombre (moyenne pendant l'année) |
| Wages and salaries | 302.0 | 284.0 | 2.1 | 15.9 | Traitements et salaires |
| Electricity consumed | 3 977.4 | 3 582.9 | 52.8 | 341.7 | Electricité consommée |
| **1951[1]** | | | | | **1951[1]** |
| Number of establishments | 2 210 | 1 062 | 64 | 1 084 | Nombre d'établissements |
| Value added | 466.2 | 418.9 | 4.8 | 42.5 | Valeur ajoutée |
| Number of engaged (Average during year) | 803.5 | 740.0 | 8.0 | 55.5 | Nombre de personnes occupées (moyenne pendant l'année) |
| Employees: Number (Average during year) | 803.2 | 739.8 | 8.0 | 55.4 | Salariés: Nombre (moyenne pendant l'année) |
| Wages and salaries | 368.2 | 342.6 | 3.3 | 22.3 | Traitements et salaires |
| Operatives: Number (Average during year) | 758.9 | 703.0 | 7.2 | 48.7 | Ouvriers: Nombre (moyenne pendant l'année) |
| Wages and salaries | 345.9 | 324.2 | 2.9 | 18.8 | Traitements et salaires |
| Capacity of installed power equipment | ... | ... | 105 | 472 | Puissance installée |
| **1954[1]** | | | | | **1954[1]** |
| Number of establishments | 2 286 | 1 091 | 68 | 1 127 | Nombre d'établissements |
| Value added | 569.9 | 512.8 | 7.3 | 49.8 | Valeur ajoutée |
| Number of engaged | 825.4 | 765.1 | 8.6 | 51.7 | Nombre de personnes occupées (moyenne pendant l'année) |
| Employees: Number (Average during year) | 825.2 | 765.0 | 8.6 | 51.6 | Salariés: Nombre (moyenne pendant l'année) |
| Wages and salaries | 458.5 | 429.0 | 4.2 | 25.3 | Traitements et salaires |
| Operatives: Number (Average during year) | 775.7 | 723.3 | 7.7 | 44.7 | Ouvriers: Nombre (moyenne pendant l'année) |
| Wages and salaries | 429.0 | 404.4 | 3.6 | 21.0 | Traitements et salaires |
| Energy consumed | 13 522.7 | 12 263.4 | 163.6 | 1 095.7 | Energie consommée |
| Electricity consumed | 5 175.9 | 4 619.3 | 87.4 | 469.2 | Electricité consommée |

### b. Structure

| Year and item of data (ISIC) | All mining Toutes industries extractives (1) | Coal mining Extraction du charbon (11) | Metal mining Extraction des minerais métalliques (12) | Other mining² Divers² (14-19) | Année et rubrique (CITI) |
|---|---|---|---|---|---|
| **1935[1]** Distribution in percent of: | | | | | **1935[1]** Distribution en pourcentage: |
| Value added | 100.0 | 88.9 | 1.7 | 9.4 | Valeur ajoutée |
| Number of engaged | 100.0 | 90.7 | 1.3 | 8.0 | Nombre de personnes occupées |
| Per person engaged: Value added | 0.16 | 0.16 | 0.21 | 0.19 | Par personne occupée: Valeur ajoutée |
| Electricity consumed | 3.45 | 3.57 | 4.56 | 1.92 | Electricité consommée |
| Operatives as a percent of engaged | 97.4 | 97.7 | 93.6 | 93.4 | Ouvriers en pourcentage des personnes occupées |
| Electricity consumed per operative | 3.54 | 3.65 | 4.87 | 2.06 | Electricité consommée par ouvrier |
| **1948[1]** Distribution in percent of: | | | | | **1948[1]** Distribution en pourcentage: |
| Value added | 100.0 | 90.5 | 0.8 | 8.7 | Valeur ajoutée |
| Number of engaged | 100.0 | 92.3 | 0.9 | 6.8 | Nombre de personnes occupées |
| Per person engaged: Value added | 0.49 | 0.48 | 0.45 | 0.62 | Par personne occupée: Valeur ajoutée |
| Electricity consumed | 4.81 | 4.70 | 7.23 | 6.08 | Electricité consommée |
| Employees as a percent of engaged | 100.0 | 100.0 | 100.0 | 99.6 | Salariés en pourcentage des personnes occupées |
| Value added per unit of wages and salaries | 1.26 | 1.22 | 1.38 | 1.87 | Valeur ajoutée par unité de traitements et salaires |
| Operatives as a percent of employees | 95.0 | 95.6 | 90.4 | 88.8 | Ouvriers en pourcentage des salariés |
| Wages and salaries per employee | 0.39 | 0.39 | 0.33 | 0.33 | Traitements et salaires par salariés |
| Per operative: Wages and salaries | 0.38 | 0.39 | 0.32 | 0.32 | Par ouvrier: Traitements et salaires |
| Electricity consumed | 5.06 | 4.91 | 8.00 | 6.88 | Electricité consommée |
| **1951[1]** Distribution in percent of: | | | | | **1951[1]** Distribution en pourcentage: |
| Value added | 100.0 | 89.8 | 1.0 | 9.2 | Valeur ajoutée |
| Number of engaged | 100.0 | 92.1 | 1.0 | 6.9 | Nombre de personnes occupées |
| Per person engaged: Value added | 0.58 | 0.57 | 0.60 | 0.76 | Par personne occupée: Valeur ajoutée |
| Capacity of installed power equipment | ... | ... | 13.12 | 8.50 | Puissance installée |
| Employees as a percent of engaged | 100.0 | 100.0 | 100.0 | 99.8 | Salariés en pourcentage des personnes occupées |
| Value added per unit of wages and salaries | 1.27 | 1.22 | 1.45 | 1.90 | Valeur ajoutée par unité de traitements et salaires |
| Operatives as a percent of employees | 94.5 | 95.0 | 90.0 | 87.9 | Ouvriers en pourcentage des salariés |
| Wages and salaries per employee | 0.46 | 0.46 | 0.41 | 0.40 | Traitement et salaires par salarié |
| Per operative: Wages and salaries | 0.46 | 0.46 | 0.40 | 0.39 | Par ouvrier: Traitements et salaires |
| Capacity of installed power equipment | ... | ... | 14.58 | 9.69 | Puissance installée |
| **1954[1]** Distribution in percent of: | | | | | **1954[1]** Distribution en pourcentage: |
| Value added | 100.0 | 90.0 | 1.3 | 8.7 | Valeur ajoutée |
| Number of engaged | 100.0 | 92.7 | 1.0 | 6.3 | Nombre de personnes occupées |
| Per person engaged: Value added | 0.69 | 0.67 | 0.85 | 0.96 | Par personne occupée: Valeur ajoutée |
| Energy consumed | 16.38 | 16.03 | 19.02 | 21.19 | Energie consommée |
| Electricity consumed | 6.27 | 6.04 | 10.16 | 9.08 | Electricité consommée |
| Employees as a percent of engaged | 100.0 | 100.0 | 100.0 | 99.8 | Salariés en pourcentage des personnes occupées |
| Value added per unit of wages and salaries | 1.24 | 1.20 | 1.74 | 1.97 | Valeur ajoutée par unité de traitements et salaires |
| Operatives as a percent of employees | 94.0 | 94.5 | 89.5 | 86.6 | Ouvriers en pourcentage des salariés |
| Wages and salaries per employee | 0.56 | 0.56 | 0.49 | 0.49 | Traitements et salaires par salarié |
| Per operative: Wages and salaries | 0.55 | 0.56 | 0.47 | 0.47 | Par ouvrier: Traitements et salaires |
| Energy consumed | 17.43 | 16.95 | 21.25 | 24.51 | Energie consommée |
| Electricity consumed | 6.67 | 6.39 | 11.35 | 10.50 | Electricité consommée |

[1] Mining in Northern Ireland is covered for 1935 only.
[2] Includes salt refining.

[1] Les industries extractives en Irlande du Nord ne sont comprises que dans les chiffres de 1935.
[2] Y compris le raffinage du sel.

## C. The Major Groups of Manufacturing — Les classes de la branche Industries manufacturières

| Year and Item of data | Manu-facturing / Industries manufac-turières | Food, beverages and tobacco[5] / Industries alimen-taires, boissons, tabac[5] | Textiles | Clothing, footwear and made-up textiles[6] / Articles d'habil-lement, chaussures et ouvrages en tissu[6] | Wood products and furniture / Bois et meubles | Paper and paper products / Papier et ouvrages en papier | Printing and publish-ing / Im-primerie et édition | Leather and leather products except wearing apparel[6] / Cuir et articles en cuir, à l'exclu-sion des articles d'habil-lement[6] | Rubber products / Ouvrages en caout-chouc | Chemicals and chemical, petroleum and coal products / Produits chi-miques et dérivés du pétrole et du charbon | Non-metallic mineral products / Produits minéraux non métal-liques | Basic metals / Métal-lurgie de base | Metal products / Ouvrages en métaux | Other manu-factur-ing / Autres in-dustries manufac-turières | Année et rubrique |
|---|---|---|---|---|---|---|---|---|---|---|---|---|---|---|---|
| ISIC | 2–3 | 20–22 | 23 | 24 | 25–26 | 27 | 28 | 29 | 30 | 31–32 | 33 | 34 | 35–38 | 39 | CITI |

**a. Absolute Figures — Chiffres absolus**

| Year and Item of data | 2–3 | 20–22 | 23 | 24 | 25–26 | 27 | 28 | 29 | 30 | 31–32 | 33 | 34 | 35–38 | 39 | Année et rubrique |
|---|---|---|---|---|---|---|---|---|---|---|---|---|---|---|---|
| **1935[1]** | | | | | | | | | | | | | | | **1935[1]** |
| Number of establishments | 49 444 | 6 324 | 6 911 | 6 716 | 3 829 | 1 217 | 3 211 | 1 072 | 185 | 1 957 | 3 106 | 1 752 | 11 277 | 1 887 | Nombre d'établissements |
| Value added | 1 210.4 | 189.6 | 151.4 | 78.8 | 40.1 | 32.6 | 78.1 | 13.0 | 14.0 | 97.6 | 59.2 | 88.4 | 342.1 | 25.5 | Valeur ajoutée |
| Number of engaged (Average during year) | 5 342 | 500 | 1 012 | 528 | 206 | 143 | 260 | 59 | 54 | 245 | 264 | 362 | 1 580 | 129 | Nombre de personnes occupées (moyenne pendant l'année) |
| Number of operatives (Average during year) | 4 560.0 | 396.7 | 951.7 | 477.0 | 182.9 | 127.4 | 203.6 | 52.4 | 44.6 | 189.0 | 239.3 | 326.5 | 1 260.2 | 108.7 | Nombre d'ouvriers (moyenne pendant l'année) |
| Electricity consumed | 11 464.9 | 856.3 | 1 175.6 | 136.9 | 158.6 | 1 239.9 | 166.4 | 54.0 | 235.4 | 2 082.2 | 1 025.6 | 2 232.1 | 2 017.7 | 84.2 | Électricité consommée |
| **1948[2,3]** | | | | | | | | | | | | | | | **1948[2,3]** |
| Number of establishments | 54 072 | 6 231 | 6 359 | 6 679 | 4 045 | 1 105 | 3 060 | 1 045 | 326 | 2 356 | 2 757 | 1 998 | 15 617 | 2 494 | Nombre d'établissements |
| Value added | 3 739.4 | 412.1 | 401.3 | 194.9 | 112.0 | 93.2 | 163.6 | 43.0 | 53.2 | 282.5 | 157.4 | 319.5 | 1 397.3 | 109.4 | Valeur ajoutée |
| Number of engaged (Average during year) | 6 681.9 | 552.4 | 791.2 | 482.0 | 219.3 | 152.2 | 252.9 | 58.3 | 87.1 | 372.9 | 285.1 | 525.0 | 2 695.4 | 208.1 | Nombre de personnes occupées (moyenne pendant l'année) |
| Number of employees (Average during year) | 6 671.9 | 551.3 | 790.2 | 479.8 | 218.2 | 152.0 | 252.3 | 58.0 | 87.1 | 372.7 | 284.7 | 524.8 | 2 693.3 | 207.5 | Nombre de salariés (moyenne pendant l'année) |
| Wages and salaries paid | 2 081.8 | 160.1 | 197.1 | 113.9 | 67.2 | 44.1 | 87.1 | 18.1 | 27.9 | 128.6 | 89.2 | 192.7 | 891.4 | 64.4 | Traitements et salaires payés |
| Operatives: Number (Average during year) | 5 584.6 | 453.8 | 721.3 | 432.3 | 190.4 | 129.9 | 188.0 | 50.5 | 72.0 | 273.0 | 248.7 | 448.7 | 2 207.4 | 168.6 | Ouvriers: Nombre (moyenne pendant l'année) |
| Wages and salaries | 1 595.9 | 115.8 | 161.9 | 91.1 | 54.5 | 33.1 | 56.7 | 13.6 | 21.5 | 81.5 | 73.2 | 159.4 | 689.8 | 43.8 | Traitements et salaires |
| Electricity consumed | 21 687.9 | 1 257.7 | 1 488.4 | 176.9 | 242.5 | 1 500.0 | 232.7 | 89.7 | 524.9 | 4 274.4 | 1 585.5 | 5 459.3 | 4 622.7 | 233.2 | Électricité consommée |
| **1951[2]** | | | | | | | | | | | | | | | **1951[2]** |
| Number of establishments | 57 823 | 6 436 | 7 080 | 7 764 | 4 384 | 1 181 | 3 499 | 1 039 | 328 | 2 361 | 2 894 | 2 070 | 16 263 | 2 524 | Nombre d'établissements |
| Value added | 5 006.0 | 504.6 | 575.3 | 236.2 | 138.8 | 187.1 | 210.0 | 37.7 | 76.3 | 410.5 | 205.8 | 439.2 | 1 851.7 | 132.8 | Valeur ajoutée |
| Number of engaged (Average during year) | 7 423.2 | 636.8 | 942.0 | 569.9 | 245.8 | 181.6 | 284.5 | 59.9 | 99.6 | 418.4 | 308.8 | 537.8 | 2 918.4 | 219.7 | Nombre de personnes occupées (moyenne pendant l'année) |
| Number of employees (Average during year) | 7 412.1 | 635.5 | 940.7 | 567.0 | 244.7 | 181.4 | 283.8 | 59.6 | 99.6 | 418.3 | 308.4 | 537.6 | 2 916.3 | 219.2 | Nombre de salariés (moyenne pendant l'année) |
| Wages and salaries paid | 2 726.8 | 210.8 | 287.1 | 150.5 | 89.9 | 64.9 | 117.3 | 21.1 | 38.0 | 175.5 | 116.3 | 234.4 | 1 144.5 | 76.5 | Traitements et salaires payés |
| Operatives: Number (Average during year) | 6 144.8 | 526.0 | 855.3 | 510.9 | 211.8 | 154.0 | 210.2 | 51.5 | 81.1 | 301.3 | 266.6 | 453.0 | 2 345.9 | 177.2 | Ouvriers: Nombre (moyenne pendant l'année) |
| Wages and salaries | 2 068.9 | 155.2 | 235.7 | 120.5 | 72.8 | 48.4 | 76.8 | 15.9 | 28.5 | 110.1 | 94.4 | 190.9 | 866.6 | 53.1 | Traitements et salaires |
| Capacity of installed power equipment [4] (As of 22 September) | 21 288 | 1 358 | 2 392 | 190 | 676 | 991 | 297 | 145 | 422 | 2 164 | 1 103 | 4 334 | 6 919 | 237 | Puissance installée [4] (au 22 septembre) |
| **1954[2]** | | | | | | | | | | | | | | | **1954[2]** |
| Number of establishments | 56 712 | 6 174 | 6 993 | 7 352 | 4 105 | 1 159 | 3 380 | 958 | 337 | 2 219 | 2 876 | 1 964 | 16 809 | 2 386 | Nombre d'établissements |
| Value added | 6 120.9 | 629.9 | 571.0 | 269.2 | 158.1 | 183.1 | 246.0 | 38.1 | 88.3 | 565.7 | 246.1 | 514.2 | 2 449.6 | 161.6 | Valeur ajoutée |
| Number of engaged (Average during year) | 7 602.0 | 668.5 | 905.5 | 558.9 | 235.9 | 186.2 | 287.2 | 56.2 | 105.1 | 427.1 | 306.9 | 528.0 | 3 116.9 | 219.6 | Nombre de personnes occupées (moyenne pendant l'année) |
| Number of employees (Average during year) | 7 593.0 | 667.4 | 904.3 | 556.7 | 235.0 | 186.0 | 286.6 | 56.0 | 105.1 | 427.0 | 306.5 | 527.9 | 3 115.3 | 219.2 | Nombre de salariés (moyenne pendant l'année) |
| Wages and salaries paid | 3 414.1 | 264.2 | 325.6 | 172.7 | 104.0 | 81.0 | 146.3 | 23.1 | 48.3 | 219.2 | 141.3 | 277.8 | 1 518.6 | 92.0 | Traitements et salaires payés |
| Operatives: Number (Average during year) | 6 193.4 | 549.7 | 813.2 | 500.0 | 201.6 | 156.1 | 207.3 | 48.1 | 84.7 | 300.8 | 261.0 | 439.2 | 2 457.3 | 174.4 | Ouvriers: Nombre (moyenne pendant l'année) |
| Wages and salaries | 2 570.0 | 195.5 | 266.1 | 139.9 | 83.7 | 61.6 | 96.1 | 17.6 | 36.1 | 135.6 | 114.2 | 224.6 | 1 135.2 | 63.8 | Traitements et salaires |
| Energy consumed | 80 356.9 | 5 373.8 | 6 323.7 | 393.8 | 380.6 | 4 597.0 | 278.1 | 322.8 | 841.2 | 12 286.9 | 11 159.1 | 28 932.0 | 9 096.0 | 371.9 | Énergie consommée |
| Electricity consumed | 34 175.6 | 2 081.3 | 2 463.4 | 276.0 | 492.9 | 2 616.2 | 331.5 | 106.5 | 727.6 | 7 682.9 | 2 609.4 | 6 924.9 | 7 496.0 | 367.0 | Électricité consommée |

**b. Structure**

| Year and Item of data | 2–3 | 20–22 | 23 | 24 | 25–26 | 27 | 28 | 29 | 30 | 31–32 | 33 | 34 | 35–38 | 39 | Année et rubrique |
|---|---|---|---|---|---|---|---|---|---|---|---|---|---|---|---|
| **1935[1]** | | | | | | | | | | | | | | | **1935[1]** |
| Distribution in percent of: Value added | 100.0 | 15.6 | 12.5 | 6.5 | 3.3 | 2.7 | 6.5 | 1.1 | 1.1 | 8.1 | 4.9 | 7.3 | 28.2 | 2.2 | Distribution en pour-centage: Valeur ajoutée |
| Number of engaged | 100.0 | 9.3 | 19.0 | 9.8 | 3.9 | 2.7 | 4.8 | 1.1 | 1.1 | 4.5 | 5.0 | 6.8 | 29.5 | 2.5 | Nombre de personnes occupées |
| Per person engaged: Value added | 0.23 | 0.38 | 0.15 | 0.15 | 0.19 | 0.23 | 0.30 | 0.22 | 0.26 | 0.40 | 0.22 | 0.24 | 0.22 | 0.20 | Par personne occupée: Valeur ajoutée |
| Electricity consumed | 2.15 | 1.71 | 1.16 | 0.26 | 0.77 | 8.67 | 0.64 | 0.92 | 4.36 | 8.50 | 3.88 | 6.17 | 1.28 | 0.65 | Électricité consommée |
| Operatives as a percent of engaged | 85.4 | 79.3 | 94.0 | 90.3 | 88.8 | 89.1 | 78.3 | 88.8 | 82.6 | 77.1 | 90.6 | 90.2 | 79.8 | 84.3 | Ouvriers en pourcentage des personnes occupées |
| Electricity consumed per operative | 2.51 | 2.16 | 1.24 | 0.29 | 0.87 | 9.73 | 0.82 | 1.03 | 5.28 | 11.02 | 4.28 | 6.84 | 1.60 | 0.77 | Électricité con sommée par ouvrier |

For footnotes see end of table.　　　　　　　　　Pour les notes, voir au bas du tableau.

### C. The Major Groups of Manufacturing (continued) — Les classes de la branche Industries manufacturières (suite)

| Year and item of data | Manufacturing — Industries manufacturières | Food, beverages and tobacco[5] — Industries alimentaires, boissons, tabac[5] | Textiles | Clothing, footwear and made-up textiles[6] — Articles d'habillement, chaussures et ouvrages en tissu[6] | Wood products and furniture — Bois et meubles | Paper and paper products — Papier et ouvrages en papier | Printing and publishing — Imprimerie et édition | Leather and leather products except wearing apparel[6] — Cuir et articles en cuir, à l'exclusion des articles d'habillement[6] | Rubber products — Ouvrages en caoutchouc | Chemicals and chemical, petroleum and coal products — Produits chimiques et dérivés du pétrole et du charbon | Non-metallic mineral products — Produits minéraux non métalliques | Basic metals — Métallurgie de base | Metal products — Ouvrages en métaux | Other manufacturing — Autres industries manufacturières | Année et rubrique |
|---|---|---|---|---|---|---|---|---|---|---|---|---|---|---|---|
| ISIC | 2–3 | 20–22 | 23 | 24 | 25–26 | 27 | 28 | 29 | 30 | 31–32 | 33 | 34 | 35–38 | 39 | CITI |

**b. Structure**

| Year and item of data | 2–3 | 20–22 | 23 | 24 | 25–26 | 27 | 28 | 29 | 30 | 31–32 | 33 | 34 | 35–38 | 39 | Année et rubrique |
|---|---|---|---|---|---|---|---|---|---|---|---|---|---|---|---|
| **1948 [2,3]** | | | | | | | | | | | | | | | **1948 [2,3]** |
| Distribution in percent of: | | | | | | | | | | | | | | | Distribution en pourcentage: |
| Value added | 100.0 | 11.0 | 10.7 | 5.2 | 3.0 | 2.5 | 4.4 | 1.1 | 1.4 | 7.6 | 4.2 | 8.6 | 37.3 | 3.0 | Valeur ajoutée |
| Number of engaged | 100.0 | 8.2 | 11.9 | 7.2 | 3.3 | 2.2 | 3.8 | 0.9 | 1.3 | 5.6 | 4.2 | 7.9 | 40.3 | 3.2 | Nombre de personnes occupées |
| Per person engaged: | | | | | | | | | | | | | | | Par personne occupée: |
| Value added | 0.56 | 0.75 | 0.51 | 0.40 | 0.51 | 0.61 | 0.65 | 0.74 | 0.61 | 0.76 | 0.55 | 0.61 | 0.52 | 0.52 | Valeur ajoutée |
| Electricity consumed | 3.24 | 2.28 | 1.88 | 0.37 | 1.10 | 9.86 | 0.92 | 1.54 | 6.03 | 11.46 | 5.56 | 10.40 | 1.72 | 1.12 | Electricité consommée |
| Employees as a percent of engaged | 99.8 | 99.8 | 99.9 | 99.5 | 99.5 | 99.9 | 99.8 | 99.5 | 100.0 | 99.9 | 99.8 | 100.0 | 99.9 | 99.7 | Salariés en pourcentage des personnes occupées |
| Value added per unit of wages and salaries | 1.80 | 2.57 | 2.04 | 1.71 | 1.67 | 2.11 | 1.88 | 2.38 | 1.91 | 2.20 | 1.76 | 1.66 | 1.57 | 1.70 | Valeur ajoutée par unité de traitements et salaires |
| Operatives as a percent of employees | 83.7 | 82.3 | 91.3 | 90.1 | 87.2 | 85.5 | 74.5 | 87.1 | 82.7 | 73.2 | 87.4 | 85.5 | 82.0 | 81.2 | Ouvriers en pourcentage des salariés |
| Wages and salaries per employee | 0.31 | 0.29 | 0.25 | 0.24 | 0.31 | 0.29 | 0.34 | 0.31 | 0.32 | 0.34 | 0.31 | 0.37 | 0.33 | 0.31 | Traitements et salaires par salarié |
| Per operative: | | | | | | | | | | | | | | | Par ouvrier: |
| Wages and salaries | 0.28 | 0.26 | 0.22 | 0.21 | 0.29 | 0.25 | 0.30 | 0.27 | 0.30 | 0.30 | 0.29 | 0.36 | 0.31 | 0.26 | Traitements et salaires |
| Electricity consumed | 3.88 | 2.77 | 2.06 | 0.41 | 1.27 | 11.55 | 1.24 | 1.78 | 7.29 | 15.66 | 6.38 | 12.17 | 2.09 | 1.38 | Electricité consommée |
| **1951 [2]** | | | | | | | | | | | | | | | **1951 [2]** |
| Distribution in percent of: | | | | | | | | | | | | | | | Distribution en pourcentage: |
| Value added | 100.0 | 10.0 | 11.5 | 4.7 | 2.8 | 3.8 | 4.1 | 0.8 | 1.5 | 8.2 | 4.1 | 8.8 | 37.0 | 2.7 | Valeur ajoutée |
| Number of engaged | 100.0 | 8.5 | 12.7 | 7.7 | 3.3 | 2.5 | 3.8 | 0.8 | 1.3 | 5.7 | 4.1 | 7.3 | 39.3 | 3.0 | Nombre de personnes occupées |
| Per person engaged: | | | | | | | | | | | | | | | Par personne occupée: |
| Value added | 0.67 | 0.79 | 0.61 | 0.41 | 0.56 | 1.03 | 0.74 | 0.63 | 0.77 | 0.98 | 0.67 | 0.82 | 0.63 | 0.60 | Valeur ajoutée |
| Capacity of installed power equipment | 2.86 | 2.13 | 2.54 | 0.33 | 2.75 | 5.46 | 1.04 | 2.42 | 4.24 | 5.17 | 3.57 | 8.06 | 2.37 | 1.08 | Puissance installée |
| Employees as a percent of engaged | 99.8 | 99.8 | 99.9 | 99.5 | 99.6 | 99.9 | 99.8 | 99.5 | 100.0 | 100.0 | 99.9 | 100.0 | 99.9 | 99.8 | Salariés en pourcentage des personnes occupées |
| Value added per unit of wages and salaries | 1.84 | 2.39 | 2.00 | 1.57 | 1.54 | 2.88 | 1.79 | 1.79 | 2.01 | 2.34 | 1.77 | 1.87 | 1.62 | 1.74 | Valeur ajoutée par unité de traitements et salaires |
| Operatives as a percent of employees | 82.9 | 82.8 | 90.9 | 90.1 | 86.6 | 84.9 | 74.1 | 86.4 | 81.4 | 72.0 | 86.4 | 84.3 | 80.4 | 80.8 | Ouvriers en pourcentage des salariés |
| Wages and salaries per employee | 0.37 | 0.33 | 0.30 | 0.26 | 0.37 | 0.36 | 0.41 | 0.35 | 0.38 | 0.42 | 0.38 | 0.44 | 0.39 | 0.35 | Traitements et salaires par salarié |
| Per operative: | | | | | | | | | | | | | | | Par ouvrier: |
| Wages and salaries | 0.34 | 0.30 | 0.28 | 0.24 | 0.34 | 0.31 | 0.36 | 0.31 | 0.35 | 0.36 | 0.35 | 0.42 | 0.37 | 0.30 | Traitements et salaires |
| Capacity of installed power equipment | 3.45 | 2.58 | 2.80 | 0.37 | 3.19 | 6.44 | 1.41 | 2.82 | 5.20 | 7.18 | 4.14 | 9.57 | 2.95 | 1.34 | Puissance installée |
| **1954 [2]** | | | | | | | | | | | | | | | **1954 [2]** |
| Distribution in percent of: | | | | | | | | | | | | | | | Distribution en pourcentage: |
| Value added | 100.0 | 10.2 | 9.4 | 4.4 | 2.6 | 2.9 | 4.1 | 0.6 | 1.4 | 9.3 | 4.0 | 8.4 | 40.0 | 2.7 | Valeur ajoutée |
| Number of engaged | 100.0 | 8.7 | 12.0 | 7.3 | 3.1 | 2.5 | 3.7 | 0.8 | 1.4 | 5.6 | 4.0 | 7.0 | 41.0 | 2.9 | Nombre de personnes occupées |
| Per person engaged: | | | | | | | | | | | | | | | Par personne occupée: |
| Value added | 0.80 | 0.94 | 0.63 | 0.48 | 0.67 | 0.98 | 0.86 | 0.68 | 0.84 | 1.32 | 0.80 | 0.97 | 0.78 | 0.74 | Valeur ajoutée |
| Energy consumed | 10.57 | 8.04 | 6.98 | 0.70 | 1.61 | 24.69 | 0.97 | 5.74 | 8.00 | 28.77 | 36.36 | 54.80 | 2.92 | 1.69 | Energie consommée |
| Electricity consumed | 4.50 | 3.11 | 2.72 | 0.49 | 2.09 | 14.05 | 1.15 | 1.90 | 6.92 | 17.99 | 8.50 | 13.12 | 2.40 | 1.67 | Electricité consommée |
| Employees as a percent of engaged | 99.9 | 99.8 | 99.9 | 99.6 | 99.6 | 99.9 | 99.8 | 99.6 | 100.0 | 100.0 | 99.9 | 100.0 | 99.9 | 99.8 | Salariés en pourcentage des personnes occupées |
| Value added per unit of wages and salaries | 1.79 | 2.38 | 1.75 | 1.56 | 1.52 | 2.26 | 1.68 | 1.65 | 1.83 | 2.58 | 1.74 | 1.85 | 1.61 | 1.76 | Valeur ajoutée par unité de traitements et salaires |
| Operatives as a percent of employees | 81.6 | 82.4 | 89.9 | 89.8 | 85.8 | 83.9 | 72.3 | 85.9 | 80.6 | 70.4 | 85.2 | 83.2 | 78.9 | 79.6 | Ouvriers en pourcentage des salariés |
| Wages and salaries per employee | 0.45 | 0.40 | 0.36 | 0.31 | 0.44 | 0.44 | 0.51 | 0.41 | 0.46 | 0.51 | 0.46 | 0.53 | 0.49 | 0.42 | Traitements et salaires par salarié |
| Per operative: | | | | | | | | | | | | | | | Par ouvrier: |
| Wages and salaries | 0.41 | 0.36 | 0.33 | 0.28 | 0.42 | 0.39 | 0.46 | 0.36 | 0.43 | 0.45 | 0.44 | 0.51 | 0.46 | 0.36 | Traitements et salaires |
| Energy consumed | 12.97 | 9.78 | 7.78 | 0.79 | 1.89 | 29.45 | 1.34 | 6.71 | 9.93 | 40.85 | 42.76 | 65.87 | 3.70 | 2.13 | Energie consommée |
| Electricity consumed | 5.52 | 3.79 | 3.03 | 0.55 | 2.44 | 16.76 | 1.60 | 2.21 | 8.59 | 25.54 | 10.00 | 15.77 | 3.05 | 2.10 | Electricité consommée |

[1] The following types of manufacturing are not covered: slaughtering by units which are primarily wholesalers of meat and meat products, the processing of flax, shoe repairing, publishing, automobile repairing, the manufacture of cinematographic film and perhaps the repair and rebuilding of locomotives and similar equipment by employees of railways. The manufacture of metal furniture is included in Metal products (ISIC major groups 35–38) instead of in Wood products and furniture (ISIC major groups 25–26).

[2] Not covered are slaughtering carried on by establishments which are primarily wholesalers of meat and meat products, tea blending and coffee roasting, and shoe repairing.

[3] Manufacturing in Northern Ireland is excluded.

[4] Excludes capacity of power equipment installed in manufacturing establishments in Northern Ireland.

[5] Salt refining is not included.

[6] The manufacture of apparel of fur is covered in Leather and leather products (ISIC major group 29) instead of in Clothing (ISIC major group 24).

[1] Non compris les industries manufacturières ci-après: abattage du bétail exécuté par des unités qui sont essentiellement des grossistes de la boucherie, préparation du lin, réparation des chaussures, édition, réparation des automobiles, fabrication de pellicules cinématographiques et, peut-être, réparation et reconstruction de locomotives et matériel connexe par les agents des chemins de fer. La fabrication des meubles en métal est comprise dans les Ouvrages en métaux (CITI 35–38) et non dans l'Industrie du bois et du meuble (CITI 25–26).

[2] Non compris l'abattage du bétail par des établissements qui sont essentiellement des grossistes de la boucherie, le mélange du thé, la torréfaction du café, et la réparation des chaussures.

[3] Non compris les industries manufacturières en Irlande du Nord.

[4] Non compris la puissance installée dans les établissements manufacturiers d'Irlande du Nord.

[5] Non compris le raffinage du sel.

[6] La fabrication des vêtements en fourrure est comprise dans l'Industrie du cuir et des articles en cuir (CITI 29) et non dans l'Habillement (CITI 24).

## 7. FUELS PURCHASED AND ELECTRICITY CONSUMED, INDUSTRIAL ESTABLISHMENTS ENGAGING MORE THAN 10 PERSONS

### COMBUSTIBLES ACHETES ET ELECTRICITE CONSOMMEE PAR LES ETABLISSEMENTS INDUSTRIELS OCCUPANT PLUS DE 10 PERSONNES

### A. Percentage Distribution of Purchased Energy According to Source
### Répartition en pourcentage de l'énergie achetée suivant la source

#### 1954

Quantities in thousand metric tons of coal equivalents.　　　　　　　Quantités en milliers de tonnes métriques d'équivalent charbon.

#### a. The Major Groups of Mining and Electricity and Gas
#### Les classes des Industries extractives et Electricité et gaz

| Year and item of data | Mining [1] Industries extractives [1] | | | | Electricity and gas [4] Electricité et gaz [4] | | | Année et rubrique |
|---|---|---|---|---|---|---|---|---|
| | Total [2] | Coal mining [3] Extraction du charbon [3] | Metal mining Extraction des minerais métalliques | Other mining [2] Divers [2] | Total | Electricity Electricité | Gas Gaz | |
| ISIC | 1 | 11 | 12 | 14–19 | 511-512 | 511 | 512 | CITI |
| 1954 | | | | | | | | 1954 |
| Total energy consumed.. | 13 522.7 | 12 263.4 | 163.6 | 1 095.7 | 71 546.0 | 42 426.3 | 29 176.3 | Energie totale consommée |
| Percent initially consumed as: | | | | | | | | Pourcentage consommé sous forme de: |
| Coal.............. | 94.0 | 95.6 | 86.0 | 77.0 | 96.6 | 96.4 | 96.5 | Charbon |
| Coke.............. | 0.9 | 0.3 | 3.3 | 6.6 | 1.6 | 2.5 | 0.2 | Coke |
| Refined oil fuels...... | 1.2 | 0.3 | 4.2 | 12.1 | 1.8 | 1.0 | 3.1 | Pétrole raffiné |
| Gas............... | 0.4 | 0.4 | — | — | — | 0.1 | — | Gaz |
| Electricity.......... | 3.5 | 3.4 | 6.5 | 4.3 | — | — | 0.2 | Electricité |

For footnotes see end of table.　　　　　　　Pour les notes, voir au bas du tableau.

#### b. The Major Groups of Manufacturing — Les classes de la branche Industries manufacturières

| Year and item of data | Manufacturing [6] Industries manufacturières [6] | Food, beverages and tobacco [2, 6] Industries alimentaires, boissons, tabac [2, 6] | Textiles [6] | Clothing, footwear and made-up textiles [6, 7] Articles d'habillement, chaussures et ouvrages en tissu [6, 7] | Wood products and furniture Bois et meubles | Paper and paper products Papier et ouvrages en papier | Printing and publishing Imprimerie et édition | Leather and leather products except wearing apparel [7] Cuir et articles en cuir, à l'exclusion des articles d'habillement [7] | Rubber products Ouvrages en caoutchouc | Chemicals and chemical, petroleum and coal products Produits chimiques et dérivés du pétrole et du charbon | Non-metallic mineral products Produits minéraux non métalliques | Basic metals Métallurgie de base | Metal products [6] Ouvrages en métaux [6] | Other manufacturing [6] Autres industries manufacturières [6] | Année et rubrique |
|---|---|---|---|---|---|---|---|---|---|---|---|---|---|---|---|
| ISIC | 2–3 | 20–22 | 23 | 24 | 25–26 | 27 | 28 | 29 | 30 | 31–32 | 33 | 34 | 35–38 | 39 | CITI |
| 1954 | | | | | | | | | | | | | | | 1954 |
| Total energy consumed | | | | | | | | | | | | | | | Energie totale consommée |
| Quantity........... | 80 356.9 | 5 373.8 | 6 323.7 | 393.8 | 380.6 | 4 597.0 | 278.1 | 322.8 | 841.2 | 12 286.9 | 11 159.1 | 28 932.0 | 9 096.0 | 371.9 | Quantité |
| Percent of total in specified industry..... | 100.0 | 6.6 | 7.9 | 0.5 | 0.5 | 5.7 | 0.3 | 0.4 | 1.1 | 15.3 | 13.9 | 36.0 | 11.3 | 0.5 | Pourcentage du total par industrie indiquée |
| Percent consumed as: | | | | | | | | | | | | | | | Pourcentage consommé sous forme de: |
| Coal.............. | 54.0 | 70.5 | 89.2 | 51.2 | 41.6 | 91.8 | 27.4 | 82.8 | 78.5 | 65.6 | 84.2 | 22.9 | 45.8 | 42.5 | Charbon |
| Coke.............. | 20.0 | 6.1 | 1.4 | 17.0 | 12.9 | 1.9 | 17.6 | 6.6 | 1.6 | 4.2 | 5.1 | 44.9 | 13.7 | 12.0 | Coke |
| Refined oil fuels...... | 9.4 | 14.7 | 4.8 | 12.4 | 24.7 | 4.3 | 23.2 | 6.0 | 7.7 | 7.0 | 5.1 | 9.3 | 19.3 | 20.8 | Pétrole raffiné |
| Gas............... | 12.3 | 4.6 | 0.5 | 10.7 | 5.3 | 0.2 | 17.1 | 1.1 | 1.5 | 17.3 | 2.9 | 20.4 | 11.6 | 13.1 | Gaz |
| Electricity.......... | 4.3 | 4.1 | 4.1 | 8.7 | 15.5 | 1.8 | 14.7 | 3.5 | 10.7 | 5.9 | 2.7 | 2.5 | 9.6 | 11.6 | Electricité |

For footnotes see end of table.　　　　　　　Pour les notes, voir au bas du tableau.

# UNITED KINGDOM

## B. Quantity of Purchased Fuels and Electricity Purchased, Produced and Sold

### Quantités de combustibles achetés et d'électricité achetée, produite et vendue
### 1935, 1948, 1951, 1954

Coal, coke and refined oil fuels in thousand metric tons; gas in million cubic metres; electricity in million KWH.    Charbon, coke et pétrole raffiné en milliers de tonnes métriques; gaz en millions de métres cubes; électricité en millions de kWh.

### a. The Major Groups of Mining and Electricity and Gas
### Les classes des Industries extractives et Electricité et gaz

| Year and source of energy | Mining [1] Industries extractives [1] | | | | Electricity and gas Electricité et gaz | | | Année et source d'énergie |
| | Total [2] | Coal mining [3] Extraction du charbon[3] | Metal mining Extraction des minerais métalliques | Other mining [2] Divers [2] | Total | Electricity Electricité | Gas Gaz | |
| ISIC | 1 | 11 | 12 | 14–19 | 511-512 | 511 | 512 | CITI |
| **1935** [8] | | | | | | | | **1935** [8] |
| Coal................ | 13 305.3 | 12 161.0 | 189.4 | 954.9 | 30 921.9 | 12 743.5 | 18 178.4 | Charbon |
| Coke................ | 206.7 | 128.5 | 6.8 | 71.4 | 327.8 | 191.7 | 136.1 | Coke |
| Electricity: | | | | | | | | Electricité: |
| Purchased.......... | 1 422.3 | 1 286.7 | 46.9 | 88.7 | 220.6 | 205.0 | 15.6 | Achetée |
| Produced.......... | 2 139.5 | 2 076.2 | 3.3 | 60.0 | 69.6 | ... | 69.6 | Produite |
| Sold.............. | 657.7 | 638.0 | — | 19.7 | ... | ... | ... | Vendue |
| **1948** [5, 8] | | | | | | | | **1948** [5, 8] |
| Coal................ | 12 402.1 | 11 422.3 | 125.0 | 854.8 | 54 243.4 | 29 555.7 | 24 687.7 | Charbon |
| Coke................ | 342.6 | 95.8 | 9.2 | 237.6 | 833.5 | 456.3 | 377.2 | Coke |
| Electricity: | | | | | | | | Electricité: |
| Purchased.......... | 2 701.8 | 2 421.0 | 51.7 | 229.1 | 878.9 | 778.0 | 100.9 | Achetée |
| Produced.......... | *2 224.5 | 2 079.6 | 1.1 | 143.8 | 48 324.8 | 48 234.0 | 90.8 | Produite |
| Sold.............. | 948.9 | 917.7 | — | 31.2 | 41 079.3 | 41 077.0 | 2.3 | Vendue |
| **1951** [8] | | | | | | | | **1951** [8] |
| Coal and coke........ | 12 063.2 | 10 834.3 | 140.5 | 1 088.4 | ... | 37 317.6 | ... | Charbon et coke |
| Refined oil fuels........ | 115.6 | 15.7 | 3.8 | 96.1 | 176.6 | 141.8 | 34.8 | Pétrole raffiné |
| Electricity: | | | | | | | | Electricité: |
| Purchased.......... | 2 811.5 | 2 462.9 | 64.3 | 284.3 | ... | ... | 182.7 | Achetée |
| Produced.......... | 2 086.0 | 1 951.3 | 1.2 | 133.5 | ... | ... | 94.5 | Produite |
| **1954** | | | | | | | | **1954** |
| Coal................ | 12 718.4 | 11 733.3 | 140.7 | 844.4 | 69 097.3 | 40 939.6 | 28 157.7 | Charbon |
| Coke................ | 127.6 | 41.7 | 6.1 | 79.8 | 1 261.0 | 1 168.5 | 92.5 | Coke |
| Refined oil fuels........ | 111.1 | 18.2 | 4.6 | 88.3 | 875.9 | 274.8 | 601.1 | Pétrole raffiné |
| Manufactured gas purchased........... | 101.1 | 100.5 | — | 0.6 | 1 238.0 | 38.1 | 1 199.9 | Gaz manufacturé acheté |
| Gas produced and consumed in the same establishment.... | 21.8 | 21.8 | — | — | ... | — | ... | Gaz produit et consommé dans le même établissement |
| Electricity: | | | | | | | | Electricité: |
| Purchased.......... | 3 698.2 | 3 241.0 | 83.7 | 373.5 | 1 548.8 | 1 278.0 | 270.8 | Achetée |
| Produced.......... | 1 772.1 | 1 664.2 | 3.7 | 104.2 | 75 852.4 | 75 744.0 | 108.4 | Produite |
| Sold.............. | 294.4 | 285.9 | — | 8.5 | 64 637.1 | 64 633.0 | 4.1 | Vendue |

For footnotes see end of table.    Pour les notes, voir au bas du tableau.

## b. The Major Groups of Manufacturing — Les classes de la branche Industries manufacturières

| Year and source of energy | Manufacturing Industries manufacturières [6] | Food, beverages and tobacco [2,6] Industries alimentaires, boissons, tabac [2,6] | Textiles | Clothing, footwear and made-up textiles [7] Articles d'habillement, chaussures et ouvrages en tissu [7] | Wood products and furniture Bois et meubles | Paper and paper products Papier et ouvrages en papier | Printing and publishing Imprimerie et édition | Leather and leather products except wearing apparel [7] Cuir et articles en cuir, à l'exclusion des articles d'habillement [7] | Rubber products Ouvrages en caoutchouc | Chemicals and chemical, petroleum and coal products Produits chimiques et dérivés du pétrole et du charbon | Non-metallic mineral products Produits minéraux non métalliques | Basic metals Métallurgie de base | Metal products Ouvrages en métaux | Other manufacturing Autres industries manufacturières | Année et source d'énergie |
|---|---|---|---|---|---|---|---|---|---|---|---|---|---|---|---|
| ISIC | 2–3 | 20–22 | 23 | 24 | 25–26 | 27 | 28 | 29 | 30 | 31–32 | 33 | 34 | 35–38 | 39 | CITI |
| **1935** [8] | | | | | | | | | | | | | | | **1935** [8] |
| Coal | 41 212.8 | 3 576.5 | 7 319.0 | 182.5 | 131.0 | 3 141.8 | 71.3 | 250.1 | 404.3 | 5 050.8 | 9 213.7 | 9 160.3 | 2 617.2 | 94.3 | Charbon |
| Coke | 10 474.1 | 452.9 | 87.3 | 77.8 | 27.5 | 19.7 | 55.3 | 31.3 | 6.1 | 324.6 | 346.5 | 8 054.9 | 953.7 | 36.5 | Coke |
| Electricity | | | | | | | | | | | | | | | Electricité |
| Purchased | 7 199.1 | 617.2 | 778.2 | 126.3 | 134.3 | 156.3 | 159.0 | 38.2 | 220.3 | 968.2 | 771.9 | 1 455.8 | 1 699.3 | 74.1 | Achetée |
| Produced | 5 348.1 | 243.6 | 416.0 | 11.2 | 24.6 | 1 096.2 | 8.4 | 16.8 | 15.1 | 1 425.2 | 320.0 | 1 403.1 | 357.8 | 10.1 | Produite |
| Sold | 1 082.3 | 4.5 | 18.6 | 0.6 | 0.3 | 12.6 | 1.0 | 1.0 | — | 311.2 | 66.3 | 626.8 | 39.4 | — | Vendue |
| **1948** [5,8] | | | | | | | | | | | | | | | **1948** [5,8] |
| Coal | 39 611.4 | 3 585.1 | 5 562.4 | 180.4 | 145.7 | 3 063.3 | 54.4 | 282.4 | 519.9 | 6 228.6 | 7 982.2 | 8 505.5 | 3 374.0 | 127.5 | Charbon |
| Coke | 15 047.2 | 515.9 | 94.8 | 71.7 | 46.1 | 87.9 | 56.9 | 29.3 | 24.7 | 512.3 | 401.7 | 11 712.2 | 1 440.1 | 53.6 | Coke |
| Electricity | | | | | | | | | | | | | | | Electricité |
| Purchased | 17 242.2 | 1 014.2 | 1 144.0 | 163.7 | 213.5 | 391.0 | 224.5 | 67.8 | 508.4 | 2 958.9 | 1 381.0 | 4 767.5 | 4 200.3 | 207.4 | Achetée |
| Produced | 6 068.6 | 245.4 | 355.0 | 13.7 | 29.0 | 1 250.2 | 10.3 | 22.4 | 16.5 | 1 734.1 | 206.3 | 1 658.7 | 500.8 | 26.2 | Produite |
| Sold | 1 622.9 | 1.9 | 10.6 | 0.5 | — | 141.2 | 2.1 | 0.5 | — | 418.6 | 1.8 | 966.9 | 78.4 | 0.4 | Vendue |
| **1951** [8] | | | | | | | | | | | | | | | **1951** [8] |
| Coal and coke | 61 733.1 | 4 186.3 | 5 792.3 | 302.1 | 281.7 | 3 834.2 | 138.1 | 323.3 | 627.9 | 10 863.9 | 9 270.8 | 20 319.2 | 5 573.8 | 219.5 | Charbon et coke |
| Refined oil fuels | 4 011.3 | 470.0 | 200.6 | 31.9 | 74.6 | 107.3 | 36.3 | 12.0 | 35.6 | 502.0 | 344.9 | 1 287.9 | 853.9 | 54.3 | Pétrole raffiné |
| Electricity | | | | | | | | | | | | | | | Electricité |
| Purchased | 21 813.1 | 1 296.4 | 1 429.2 | 210.5 | 280.9 | 652.0 | 243.8 | 76.5 | 610.3 | 4 549.2 | 1 822.1 | 5 199.0 | 5 155.3 | 287.9 | Achetée |
| Produced | 7 623.5 | 337.3 | 493.2 | 20.4 | 32.3 | 1 825.5 | 15.3 | 19.9 | 18.1 | 2 042.2 | 273.4 | 1 877.0 | 640.5 | 28.4 | Produite |
| **1954** | | | | | | | | | | | | | | | **1954** |
| Coal | 43 444.5 | 3 791.7 | 5 643.5 | 201.9 | 158.4 | 4 221.0 | 76.4 | 267.5 | 660.9 | 8 067.7 | 9 398.6 | 6 629.4 | 4 169.3 | 158.2 | Charbon |
| Coke | 17 860.9 | 361.1 | 95.9 | 74.1 | 54.5 | 100.9 | 54.2 | 23.6 | 14.8 | 566.7 | 635.6 | 14 448.7 | 1 381.3 | 49.5 | Coke |
| Refined oil fuels | 5 033.2 | 527.3 | 202.6 | 32.7 | 62.7 | 130.2 | 43.1 | 12.9 | 43.3 | 577.9 | 375.9 | 1 797.9 | 1 175.1 | 51.6 | Pétrole raffiné |
| Manufactured gas purchased | 16 435.3 | 413.5 | 61.7 | 70.5 | 33.8 | 18.8 | 79.3 | 6.0 | 20.1 | 3 531.7 | 543.0 | 9 827.0 | 1 748.8 | 81.1 | Gaz manufacturé acheté |
| Gas produced and consumed in the same establishment | 15 271.0 | — | — | — | — | — | — | — | — | 3 304.1 | 689.3 | 10 907.1 | 370.5 | — | Gaz produit et consommé dans le même établissement |
| Electricity | | | | | | | | | | | | | | | Electricité |
| Purchased | 27 413.6 | 1 743.7 | 2 024.4 | 270.9 | 470.1 | 628.9 | 325.9 | 88.2 | 720.4 | 5 786.6 | 2 391.4 | 5 646.3 | 6 973.0 | 343.8 | Achetée |
| Produced | 8 557.9 | 340.9 | 450.7 | 5.5 | 23.1 | 2 029.6 | 6.5 | 19.3 | 7.2 | 2 423.9 | 278.1 | 2 326.6 | 622.3 | 24.2 | Produite |
| Sold | 1 795.9 | 3.3 | 11.7 | 0.4 | 0.3 | 42.3 | 0.9 | 1.0 | — | 527.6 | 60.1 | 1 048.0 | 99.3 | 1.0 | Vendue |

[1] Mining in Northern Ireland is excluded during all years.
[2] Salt refining is included in Other manufacturing (ISIC major group 19) instead of Food manufacturing (ISIC major group 20).
[3] In the case of Coal mining (ISIC major group 11) coal extracted for own consumption is included in addition to fuels purchased.
[4] In the case of the Electricity and Gas industries, purchases of the forms of energy which are the main products of the industry are excluded. Thus, for example, purchases of electricity or gas are excluded from the figures for the Electricity and gas industries (ISIC major group 51) combined; and, duplications do not occur in the figures of fuels purchased, primarily to produce electricity or gas.
[5] Manufacturing in Northern Ireland is excluded from the data for 1948.
[6] Not covered in the case of the data for all years is slaughtering by wholesale or retail dealers in meat and meat products and tea blending and coffee roasting (part of ISIC major group 20) and shoe repairing (part of ISIC major group 24). In the case of the data for 1935, the following additional types of manufacturing activities are not covered: Processing of flax (part of ISIC major group 23), publishing (part of ISIC major group 28); automobile repairing and perhaps locomotive repairing and rebuilding by railway employees (part of ISIC major group 38), and the manufacture of cinematographic film (part of ISIC major group 39).
[7] In the case of the data for all years, the manufacture of fur apparel is covered under Leather and leather products (ISIC major group 29) instead of Clothing (ISIC major group 24). In the case of the data for 1935, the manufacture of metal furniture is included in Metal products (ISIC major group 35) instead of Furniture (ISIC major group 26).
[8] Complete data on selected fuels only are available for 1935, 1948 and 1951.

[1] Non compris, pour toutes les années, les Industries extractives d'Irlande du Nord.
[2] Le raffinage du sel est compris dans Autres industries extractives (CITI 19) et non dans Industries alimentaires (CITI 20).
[3] Dans le cas de l'Extraction du charbon (CITI 11), le charbon extrait pour l'auto-consommation est compris en plus des combustibles achetés.
[4] Dans le cas des industries de l'électricité et du gaz, les achats des formes d'énergie qui sont les produits principaux de ces industries sont exclus. Ainsi, par exemple, les achats d'électricité ou de gaz sont exclus des données concernant l'ensemble des Industries de l'électricité et du gaz (CITI 51); il n'y a donc pas de doubles emplois dans les chiffres relatifs aux combustibles achetés, principalement en vue de la production d'électricité ou de gaz.
[5] Les Industries manufacturières d'Irlande du Nord sont exclues des données relatives à 1948.
[6] Non compris, pour toutes les années, les activités suivantes: abattage du bétail par des grossistes ou des détaillants de la boucherie, mélange du thé et torréfaction du café (dans CITI 20) et réparation des chaussures (dans CITI 24). En 1935, les types ci-après d'activités manufacturières sont également exclus: préparation du lin (dans CITI 23), édition (dans CITI 28); réparation des automobiles et, éventuellement, réparation et reconstruction de locomotives par du personnel des chemins de fer (dans CITI 38) et fabrication de pellicules cinématographiques (dans CITI 39).
[7] Pour toutes les années, la confection des vêtements en fourrure est comprise dans Cuir et articles en cuir (CITI 29) et non dans Articles d'habillement (CITI 24). En 1935, la fabrication de mobilier métallique est comprise dans Ouvrages en métaux (CITI 35) et non dans Industrie du meuble (CITI 26).
[8] On dispose de données complètes sur certains combustibles seulement pour 1935, 1948 et 1951.

### Gross Domestic Product and Gross Domestic Fixed Capital Formation

The data shown in Table 1 on the gross domestic product distributed according to source of expenditure, the net domestic product classified by industrial origin and gross domestic fixed capital formation distributed according to sector of acquisition are from the reply of the Office of Business Economics, Department of Commerce, Washington, D.C., to the United Nations national accounts questionnaire. Official estimates are published in *United States Income and Output,* an annual supplement to the *Survey of Current Business,* Department of Commerce, and the July issue of the *Survey.* Descriptions of the concepts and definitions and sources and methods utilized in the estimates are given in *National Income, 1954 Edition,* a special supplement to the *Survey of Current Business.* For purposes of the United Nations national accounts questionnaire, the official estimates have been adjusted to the United Nations system of national accounts in-so-far as existing data would permit.

### Index Numbers of Industrial Production

The index numbers set out in Table 2 are derived from indexes of industrial production compiled by the Division of Research and Statistics, Board of Governors of the Federal Reserve System and published in the *Federal Reserve Bulletin.*

The series of index numbers are computed as base-weighted arithmetic averages, starting from monthy series of relatives on indicators of output. The indicators of output utilized for mining and manufacturing are production for individual commodities, in most cases, and, where such figures are not available, quantity of individual raw materials consumed, value of shipments of individual products adjusted for price changes or man-hours worked by operatives adjusted by changes in productivity. The indicators of output utilized for electricity and gas industries consist entirely of quantities produced.

In a number of instances the monthly series of relatives are adjusted each year to the levels of output indicated by more complete or appropriate annual series of relatives, as the required annual data becomes available. This practice is followed, in particular, where figures of man-hours worked furnish the basis for the monthly series of relatives or where relatively rapid changes commonly occur in the characteristics or mix of products made. All series of relatives are reviewed, revised and supplemented

### Produit intérieur brut et formation brute de capital fixe intérieur

Les données du tableau 1 relatives au produit intérieur brut ventilé suivant la source de dépense, au produit intérieur net ventilé suivant la branche d'activité et au capital brut fixe intérieur formé distribué suivant le secteur d'acquisition sont tirées de la réponse de l'Office of Business Economics, Department of Commerce, Washington, D.C., au questionnaire de l'O.N.U. relatif aux comptes nationaux. Les estimations officielles sont publiées dans *United States Income and Output,* supplément annuel au *Survey of Current Business,* Department of Commerce, et dans le numéro de juillet du *Survey.* Des descriptions des concepts et définitions et des sources et méthodes adoptées lors des estimations sont fournies dans *National Income, 1954 Edition,* supplément spécial au *Survey of Current Business.* Pour remplir le questionnaire de l'O.N.U. relatix aux comptes nationaux, dans la mesure où les données s'y prêtaient, les estimations officielles ont été alignées sur le système de comptabilité nationale de l'O.N.U.

### Indices de la production industrielle

Les indices du tableau 2 sont tirés des indices de la production industrielle établis par la Division of Research and Statistics, Board of Governors of the Federal Reserve System, et publiés dans le *Federal Reserve Bulletin.*

Les séries d'indices sont des moyennes arithmétiques à pondération fixe, construites à partir de séries mensuelles de rapports concernant les indicateurs de la production. L'indicateur de la production utilisé pour les industries extractives et manufacturières est, dans la plupart des cas, le volume de la production de chaque marchandise; lorsqu'on n'avait pas de chiffres sur cette production, on a pris le volume de la consommation de chaque matière première, la valeur des expéditions de chaque produit, ajustée pour tenir compte des fluctuations de prix, ou encore les heures de travail effectuées par les ouvriers, ajustées pour tenir compte des variations de la productivité. Dans le cas des industries de l'électricité et du gaz, les indicateurs de la production sont exclusivement les quantités produites.

Dans un grand nombre de cas, les séries mensuelles de rapports sont ajustées chaque année aux niveaux de la production indiqués par des séries annuelles de rapports plus complètes ou plus appropriées au fur et à mesure que ces données annuelles sont disponibles. Cette pratique est suivie, en particulier, quand des chiffres relatifs aux heures de travail effectuées fournissent une base de construction aux séries mensuelles de rapports, ou lorsque des variations relativement rapides affectent les caractéristi-

---

[1] Unless specifically noted otherwise, the data presented in this chapter relate to the United States, excluding Alaska, Hawaii, territories. Puerto Rico or other possessions of the United States.

[1] Sauf contre-indication, les données présentées sous ce chapitre concernent les Etats-Unis, non compris l'Alaska, Hawaii, les territoires, Porto-Rico et autres possessions des Etats-Unis.

periodically as comprehensive data becomes available from the quinquennial Censuses of Mineral Industries and Manufacturing, on quantities and values for individual products. The last such review and revision was based on the 1954 Census. The index numbers through the year 1961 also reflect revisions resulting from a preliminary review in the light of the 1958 Census and the 1959 and 1960 Annual Surveys of Manufactures of the Bureau of the Census.

The weights utilized to combine series of relatives into indexes for detailed categories of industrial activity and these indexes for broader classes are proportional to value added, at factor cost, during the weighting year in the production activity measured by the relative or index except in the case of the indexes for mining for 1938. For this series, the weights utilized were proportional to gross value of production during the weighting year. In the case of mining and manufacturing, the field covered by the weights, and therefore by the indexes, is identical with that covered by the Censuses described below. In the case of the electricity and gas industries, the weights and the indexes relate to all establishments primarily engaged in the production and distribution of electricity and gas, whether publicly or privately owned.

The weighting years utilized in the series of indexes are 1937 for the indexes covering 1938, 1947 for the series of index numbers for the years, 1948-1952, and 1957 for the indexes for 1953 and thereafter. The corresponding original comparison base periods are 1935-1939, 1947-1949 and 1957-1959, respectively. The Division of Research and Statistics, Board of Governors of the Federal Reserve System has utilized the same scheme of industrial classification — namely, the 1957 version of the Standard Industrial Classification of the United States — in compiling the series of index numbers for 1947 and later years.

For further details concerning the index numbers of industrial production see the following publications: *Federal Reserve Index of Industrial Production, October 1943, Federal Reserve Monthly Index of Industrial Production, 1953 Revision*, and *Index of Electricity and Gas Output*, reprints from the *Federal Reserve Bulletin; Industrial Production, 1959 Revision* and *Industrial Production, 1957-1959 Base*, Board of Governors of the Federal Reserve System; and *Indexes of Production, Census of Manufactures: 1947* and *1954 Census of Manufactures*, U.S. Department of Commerce and Board of Governors of the Federal Reserve System.

### Index Numbers of Industrial Employment

The index numbers of industrial employment shown in Table 3 were computed from absolute figures of pay roll employment compiled by the Bureau of Labor Statistics,

ques ou la composition des produits fabriqués. Toutes les séries sont revues, corrigées et complétées périodiquement à mesure que les données plus complètes relatives aux quantités et valeur de chaque produit fournies par les recensements quinquennaux des industries minérales et manufacturières deviennent disponibles. Les dernières revision et correction ont été effectuées sur la base du recensement de 1954. Les indices relatifs à toutes les années et jusqu'à ceux de 1961 reflètent également des corrections découlant d'une revision préliminaire à la lumière du recensement de 1958 et des enquêtes annuelles auprès des industries manufacturières de 1959 et 1960 du Bureau of the Census.

Les poids utilisés pour combiner les séries de rapports en indices de catégories détaillées de l'activité industrielle, puis pour passer aux indices plus larges, sont proportionnels à la valeur ajoutée, au coût des facteurs, pendant l'année de pondération de base pour la production mesurée par le rapport ou l'indice dont il s'agit, à l'exception du cas des indices relatifs à 1938 pour les industries extractives. Pour ces séries les coefficients de pondération utilisés sont proportionnels à la valeur brute de la production durant l'année de pondération de base. Dans le cas des industries minières et manufacturières, les poids — et par conséquent les indices — portent sur les mêmes éléments que les recensements décrits ci-après. Pour ce qui est des industries de l'électricité et du gaz, les poids et les indices concernent tous les établissements, publics ou privés, dont l'activité principale est la production et la distribution d'électricité et de gaz.

Les années de pondération de base utilisées dans les séries d'indices sont 1937 pour les séries couvrant 1938, 1947 pour les séries d'indices relatives aux années 1948-1952, et 1957 pour les indices pour 1953 et les années suivantes. Les années de comparaison de base, correspondantes, utilisées initialement sont celles relatives aux périodes 1935-1939, 1947-1949 et 1957-1959 respectivement. La Division of Research and Statistics, Board of Governors of the Federal Reserve System a utilisé le même système de classification industrielle, plus précisément, la version de 1957 de la Classification industrielle internationale des Etats-Unis — dans le calcul des séries d'indices relatifs à 1947 et aux années suivantes.

On trouvera plus de détails sur les indices de la production industrielle dans les publications suivantes: *Federal Reserve Index of Industrial Production, October 1943, Federal Reserve Monthly Index of Industrial Production, 1953 Revision*, et *Index of Electricity and Gas Output*, des réimpressions tirées du *Federal Reserve Bulletin; Industrial Production, 1959 Revision* et *Industrial Production, 1957-1959 Base*, Board of Governors of the Federal Reserve System; et *Indexes of Production, Census of Manufactures: 1947* et *1954 Census of Manufactures*, U.S. Department of Commerce and Board of Governors of the Federal Reserve System.

### Indices de l'emploi industriel

Les indices de l'emploi industriel reproduits au tableau 3 ont été construits à partir de chiffres absolus relevés sur des feuilles de paye, relatifs à l'emploi, calculés par le

United States Department of Labor and issued monthly by the Bureau in *Employment and Earnings*. The absolute figures which furnished the basis of the indexes shown in the table through 1960 were abstracted from *Employment and Earnings Statistics for the United States, 1909-60,* Bulletin No. 1312, Bureau of Labor Statistics. All of the absolute figures on which the indexes are based were classified by the Bureau of Labor Statistics according to the 1957 version of the Standard Industrial Classification of the United States.

The absolute figures utilized in compiling index numbers relate to the average of the number of employees who received pay for any part of the pay period ending nearest the 15th of each month of all establishments in the various kinds of industrial activity. The definition of the count of employees corresponds to that in the International Standards in Basic Industrial Statistics. The absolute figures are estimated from a monthly survey of a probability sample of the establishments covered. These estimates are revised periodically in the light of basic data on the employment of all of the establishments covered. The basic data are derived from figures resulting from the administration of social security laws and regulations and some other supplementary sources. The basic data utilized in the last revision of the figures related to March 1959.

For further details concerning the absolute figures of employment see any of the publications referred to above.

### Characteristics and Structure of Industrial Activity

The data shown in Table 4 through 6 result from the quinquennial Censuses of Mineral Industries and Manufactures taken by the Bureau of the Census. The figures relating to mining have been derived from *Census of Mineral Industries, 1954* and *1958*. The data for 1939 concerning manufacturing have been compiled from a number of publications: *Census of Manufactures: 1947,* Volume I for figures of number of establishments and value added; *Census of Manufactures: 1947, Indexes of Production* for figures of number of employees; *Sixteenth Census of the United States: 1940; Manufactures, 1939,* Vol. I, for data on wages and salaries; and *Census of Manufactures, 1954,* for figures of capacity of installed power equipment. The figures for 1947, 1954 and 1958 relating to manufacturing were derived from *Census of Manufactures, 1947, 1954* and *1958.*

Differences occur in the field covered between the 1939 Census of Mineral Industries, on the one hand, and the 1954 and 1958 Censuses, on the other. Though the same type of criteria (i.e. gross value of production, value of principal current expenses and value of capital expenditures) were utilized in defining the size of operations to be covered, the lower limit set for inclusion in the 1939 Census for each of these criteria was $2,500 in contrast to $500 in the 1954 and 1958 Censuses. In addition, in the case of the 1939 Census, higher lower limits were set for the mining of bituminous coal and lignite and the quarrying of sand and gravel. Though an added criterion in

Bureau of Labor Statistics, United States Department of Labor et publiés mensuellement par le Bureau dans *Employment and Earnings*. Les chiffres absolus qui ont fourni la base de calcul des indices reproduits au tableau, indices jusqu'en 1960, ont été tirés de *Employment and Earnings Statistics for the United States, 1909-60,* Bulletin No. 1312, Bureau of Labor Statistics. Tous les chiffres absolus sur lesquels les indices sont basés ont été classifiés par le *Bureau of Labor Statistics* suivant la version de 1957 de la Classification industrielle internationale des Etats-Unis.

Les chiffres absolus utilisés dans le calcul des indices couvrent la moyenne du nombre de salariés qui reçoivent une rétribution pour une partie quelconque de la période de paye expirant le plus près du 15 de chaque mois, cela pour tous les établissements appartenant aux différents types d'activités industrielles. La définition du dénombrement des salariés correspond à celle des définitions types relatives aux statistiques industrielles de base. Les chiffres absolus sont estimés à partir d'enquêtes mensuelles sur échantillons probabilistes des établissements couverts. Ces estimations sont revisées périodiquement à la lumière des données de base sur l'emploi dans tous les établissements couverts. Ces données de base sont tirées de résultats de des lois et reglements de l'administration de la securité sociale et de quelques autres sources supplémentaires. Les données de base utilisées dans la dernière revision des chiffres se rapportent à mars 1959.

Pour plus amples détails concernant les chiffres absolus de l'emploi, voir l'une des publications mentionnées ci-dessus.

### Caractéristiques et structure de l'activité industrielle

Les données des tableaux 4 à 6 proviennent des recensements quinquennaux des industries minières et manufacturières effectués par le Bureau of the Census. Les chiffres relatifs aux industries extractives ont été tirés de *Census of Mineral Industries, 1954* et *1958*. Les données de 1939 concernant les industries manufacturières ont été extraites d'un certain nombre de publications: *Census of Manufactures: 1947,* Volume I, pour le nombre des établissements et la valeur ajoutée; *Census of Manufactures: 1947; Indexes of Production,* pour le nombre de salariés; *Sixteenth Census of the United States: 1940; Manufactures, 1939,* vol. I, pour les traitements et salaires; *Census of Manufactures, 1954,* pour la puissance installée. Les chiffres de 1947, 1954 et de 1958 pour les industries manufacturières ont été tirés de *Census of Manufactures, 1947, 1954* et *1958.*

Il existe des différences de couverture entre le recensement de 1939 des industries minérales d'une part et les recensements de 1954 et 1958 d'autre part. Bien que le même type de critères (valeur brute de la production, dépenses directes de production et dépenses d'équipement) ait été utilisé pour définir l'importance des opérations à recenser, la limite minimum fixée à cette fin pour chacun des critères a été de 2.500 dollars pour le recensement de 1939 par opposition à 500 dollars pour les recensements de 1954 et 1958. De plus, dans le cas du premier recensement, des limites minimums plus élevées ont été fixées pour l'extraction des charbons bitumineux et du lignite,

case of the 1958 Census, was having at least one employee sometime during the year, the Bureau of the Census considers that the field of coverage in the 1954 and 1958 Censuses was essentially the same. None of the mining censuses covered the extraction of minerals, particularly sand, gravel and stone, by governmental authorities, highway contractors or similar operators who produce exclusively for their own use. Also, the data shown in Table 4 for the three censuses relate to certain mining operations of establishments classified in manufacturing (e.g., the quarrying of dimension and broken stone, clay, ceramic and refractory minerals or of gypsum) and exclude the activities of mining units which were not operating during the years of inquiry. It should be noted that the mining operations of manufacturing establishments are also included in the statistics shown in Table 4 for Manufacturing.

Although the field of manufacturing covered in the data of Table 4 for 1939, on the one hand, and 1947, 1954 and 1958, on the other, also are not identical, these differences do not appreciably affect the comparability of the data, excepting figures of number of establishments, for the two sets of years. The inclusion of establishments with gross value of production of $5,000 or more but less than one employee in the 1939 Census is, according to the Bureau of the Census, counterbalanced by the inclusion in the 1947 and later Censuses of all establishments with one or more employees. Although differences in the type of activity covered also occurred between the four Censuses, the resulting incomparabilities have been eliminated from the data set out in Table 4 and 5, excepting those noted in the footnotes to the table. It should be noted that in the data shown in Tables 4 through 6, for all of the Censuses, only manufacturing establishments operating during the year of inquiry were covered, and large central and similar offices of the parent enterprises of the covered manufacturing units located at a considerable distance from these units were not covered. The manufacturing activities of establishments owned and operated by the Federal Government and of Federal and State prisons are also excluded from the data for all years.

Incomparabilities occur, however, in the classification of the data shown in Tables 4 and 6 according to kind of manufacturing activity, in particular, between 1954, 1947 and 1939, in the one hand, and the data for 1958, on the other. These incomparabilities are primarily the results of the differences between the schemes of industrial classification utilized in the 1958 Census of Manufactures and the 1954 and earlier Censuses. The 1957 version of the Standard Industrial Classification of the United States furnished the basis for coding returns in the case of 1958 Census whereas the 1945 version of the Classification was utilized for this purpose in the case of the 1954 and 1947

ainsi que pour l'extraction du sable et du gravier. Quoiqu'un critère supplémentaire ait été ajouté dans le cas de 1958, celui d'avoir au moins un salarié à un moment de l'année, le Bureau of the Census considère que le champ de couverture dans les recensements de 1954 et 1958 est fondamentalement le même. D'un autre côté, ni l'un ni l'autre de ces deux recensements n'a couvert l'extraction des minéraux, en particulier du sable, du gravier et de la pierre, par les pouvoirs publics, les entrepreneurs travaillant pour les ponts et chaussées et autre entrepreneurs qui produisent exclusivement pour compte propre. De même, les données qui ont été publiées au tableau 4 en ce qui concerne les trois recensements, portent sur certaines opérations minières (par exemple l'extraction de la pierre de taille, de la pierre de construction, de l'argile, du kaolin, des terres réfractaires et du gypse) d'établissements classés dans les industries manufacturières, et excluent l'activité des mines et carrières qui n'étaient pas exploitées pendant les années de recensement. On notera que les opérations minières des établissements manufacturiers sont aussi comprises dans les statistiques données au tableau 4 pour les Industries manufacturières.

Bien que les industries manufacturières couvertes par les chiffres du tableau 4 pour 1939, d'une part, et pour 1947, 1954 et 1958, d'autre part, ne soient pas, elles non plus, identiques, les différences n'ont guère d'effets sur la comparabilité des données, sauf en ce qui concerne le nombre des établissements. Le fait que, pour être recensés en 1939, les établissements devaient avoir une production dont la valeur brute atteignait au moins 5.000 dollars, mais n'étaient même pas tenus d'employer 1 salarié, est compensé, selon le Bureau of the Census, par le fait que le recensement de 1947 et les années suivantes exigeait au moins 1 salarié, mais n'imposait pas un minimum pour la valeur brute de la production. Bien qu'il existe aussi quelques différences en ce qui concerne le type d'activité couvert, entre les quatres recensements, les défauts de comparabilité qui en résultent pour les données du tableau 4 et 5 ont été éliminés — sauf exceptions spécifiées dans les notes du tableau. On notera que, dans les données relatives aux recensements reproduites aux tableaux 4 à 6, seuls les établissements manufacturiers ayant fonctionné pendant l'année de l'enquête ont été recensés, et que les grands bureaux centraux et services analogues des entreprises mères des unités manufacturières recensées, mais qui se trouvaient assez éloignés desdites unités, n'ont pas été recensés. Les activités manufacturières des établissements appartenant au gouvernement fédéral et dirigé par lui et des prisons fédérales étatiques sont également exclues des données relatives à toutes les années.

Des incomparabilités existent, cependant, dans la classification des données dans les tableaux 4 et 6 suivant le type d'activité manufacturière, en particulier, entre les données relatives à 1954, 1947 et 1939, d'une part, et les données relatives à 1958, d'autre part. Ces incomparabilités sont essentiellement dues aux différences entre les systèmes de classification industrielle adoptés au recensement de 1958 et aux recensements de 1954, 1947 et 1949. La classification industrielle type des Etats-Unis, version 1957, fournissait un code de base dans le cas du recensement de 1958 tandis que la classification, version 1945, a été utilisée à cette fin dans le cas des recensements de 1954 et de

Censuses. The dimensions of the resulting incomparabilities in classification of the data according to the major groups of manufacturing is suggested by the differences between the two sets of data shown in Table 4 for 1954, in particular, the figures of number of establishments and number of persons engaged. As may be noted from the footnotes to Table 4, the second set of data for 1954 is most comparable to the figures for 1958, whereas the first set of figures for 1954 is most comparable with the data for 1947 and 1939.

It should also be noted that the figures shown for some classes of manufacturing in 1939 for different items of data are not exactly comparable to one another because of differences in the methods utilized in adjusting the 1939 data for different items of data to the scheme of industrial classification of the 1947 and 1954 data. Essentially these differences result from the use of estimates in reclassifying some of the 1939 data on number of employees, wages and salaries or capacity of installed power equipment, but not in retabulating any of the 1939 figures of number of establishments or value added. It is believed, however, that this difference in method of retabulation has resulted, at most, in minor incomparabilities in the 1939 data on different items and that the ratios for the broad categories of manufacturing shown in Table 4, such as value added per person engaged or value added per unit of wages and salaries, have not been distorted.

The definitions of the items of data, excepting value added, for which figures are shown in Table 4 were similar for the three Censuses of Mineral Industries as well as for the four Censuses of Manufactures. The number of engaged in both types of Censuses relates to working proprietors and employees. In the case of the Censuses of Mineral Industries, the number of operatives is an average for the year and the number of other employees and working proprietors is taken as of one period. In the case of Censuses of Manufactures, the number of all employees is an average for the year and only the number of working proprietors is taken as of one period. The computation of value added, excluding excise and other indirect taxes, is based on value of production in case of the 1939 Censuses but on value of shipments, without adjustments for changes in inventories of finished and semifinished goods, plus receipts for work done for others in case of the 1954 and 1958 Censuses of Mineral Industries and the 1947 and 1954 Censuses of Manufactures. The value added in the merchandising of goods by mining and manufacturing establishments is not included in any of these figures of value added. However, in computing value added in the 1958 Census of Manufactures, account was taken of the changes in inventories of finished and semi-finished goods and of the value added in the merchandising of goods. The second set of figures of value added for 1954 in Table 4 were compiled on the same basis as the 1958 figures of value added.

The concept of value added utilized in the 1958 Census of Manufactures and the definitions of the numbers of employees and operatives, of wages and salaries paid to them, man-hours worked by operatives, and of capacity

1947 seulement. L'importance des défauts de comparabilité due à la classification des données suivant les classes des industries manufacturières est montrée par les différences entre les deux ensembles de données reproduites au tableau 4 pour 1954, en particulier, les chiffres relatifs au nombre d'établissements et de personnes occupées. Comme indiqué en note au tableau 4 le second ensemble de données relatives à 1954 est plus comparable aux données relatives à 1947 et 1939 qu'aux autres.

Il y a lieu de noter aussi que les chiffres donnés pour certaines classes des industries manufacturières en 1939, au sujet des diverses rubriques, ne sont pas exactement comparables les uns avec les autres en raison des différences existant entre les méthodes utilisées pour aligner les chiffres de 1939 touchant les diverses rubriques sur la nomenclature industrielle adoptée pour les recensements de 1947 et de 1954. Ces différences tiennent essentiellement à ce que l'on a employé des estimations pour reclasser certaines des données de 1939 concernant le nombre de salariés, les traitements et salaires ou la puissance installée, mais non pour reclasser le nombre d'établissements ou la valeur ajoutée. On pense cependant que cette différence de méthode dans le reclassement a provoqué, tout au plus, de très légers défauts de comparabilité entre les diverses rubriques, pour 1939, et que les rapports donnés au tableau 4 pour les diverses classes des industries manufacturières — par exemple, la valeur ajoutée par personne occupée ou la valeur ajoutée par unité de traitements et salaires — ne s'en trouvent pas faussés.

Les définitions des rubriques (à l'exception de la valeur ajoutée) au sujet desquelles des chiffres sont donnés au tableau 4 ont été semblables pour les trois recensements des industries minérales et pour les quatre recensements des industries manufacturières. Dans les deux types de recensements, le nombre des personnes occupées comprend les propriétaires qui travaillent et les salariés. Dans le cas des recensements des industries minérales, le nombre des ouvriers est la moyenne de l'année, tandis que le nombre des autres salariés, des propriétaires qui travaillent et des associés est le nombre relevé pendant une période donnée. Dans les recensements des industries manufacturières, le nombre de tous les salariés est la moyenne de l'année, tandis que seul le nombre des propriétaires qui travaillent est le nombre relevé pendant une période donnée. Le calcul de la valeur ajoutée, non compris les droits et impôts indirects, est fondé sur la valeur de la production dans le cas des recensements effectués en 1939, mais sur la valeur des expéditions, non corrigée pour tenir compte des mouvements de stocks de produits finis et semi-finis, plus les recettes pour travaux à façon dans le cas des recensements des industries minérales de 1954 et 1958 dans le cas des recensements des industries manufacturières effectués en 1947 et en 1954. La valeur ajoutée correspondant à la revente de marchandises en l'état par les établissements miniers et manufacturiers n'est comprise dans aucun des chiffres de valeur ajoutée.

Cependant lors du calcul de la valeur ajoutée au recensement des industries manufacturières de 1958 il est tenu compte des variations des inventaires de biens finis et semi-finis et de la valeur ajoutée correspondant à la

of installed power equipment utilized in all Censuses are consistent with the recommendations in the International Standards in Basic Industrial Statistics. The capacity of installed (in use or available for use) power equipment is the sum of the rated horsepower of all prime movers and electric motors driven by purchased electricity. The figures of energy and fuels consumed shown in Tables 4 and 5 relate only to fuels and electricity purchased or acquired from others, excepting the instances mentioned in the footnotes to Table 5, and utilized as a source of heat or power.

vente de marchandises en l'état. Le second ensemble de chiffres de valeur ajoutée relatifs à 1954 du tableau 4 ont été construits sur la même base que les chiffres de 1958 relatifs à la valeur ajoutée.

Le concept de valeur ajoutée utilisé au recensement des manufactures de 1958 et les définitions relatives aux nombres de salariés et d'ouvriers, et aux traitements et salaires qui leur sont versés, les heures de travail effectuées, et la puissance installée adoptées dans tous les recensements sont conformes aux Normes internationales relatives aux statistiques industrielles de base. La puissance installée (en service ou en réserve) représente la puissance nominale de tous les moteurs primaires et de tous les moteurs électriques actionnés par de l'électricité achetée. Les chiffres relatifs à l'énergie consommée reproduits aux tableaux 4 et 5 concernent seulement les combustibles et l'électricité achetés ou fournis par l'extérieur, à l'exception des cas indiqués en note au tableau 5, et utilisés comme source de chaleur ou de puissance.

# UNITED STATES

## 1. THE DOMESTIC PRODUCT AND GROSS DOMESTIC FIXED CAPITAL FORMATION
## PRODUIT INTERIEUR ET FORMATION BRUTE DE CAPITAL FIXE INTERIEUR

Million dollars — Millions de dollars

### A. Expenditure on the Gross Domestic Product at Market Prices
### Dépenses relatives au produit intérieur brut aux prix du marché

| Item of data and year — Rubrique et année | Total | Consumption — Consommation | | Gross Domestic Capital Formation — Formation brute de capital intérieur | | Net exports of goods and services — Exportations nettes de biens et de services | |
|---|---|---|---|---|---|---|---|
| | | Total | Government [1] Etat [1] | Total [1] | Fixed [1] Fixe [1] | Exports less imports Exportations moins importations | Exports Exportations |
| | | | | | *a. At Current Prices — Aux prix courants* | | |
| **Absolute figures — Chiffres absolus** | | | | | | | |
| 1948 | 259 137 | 205 003 | 28 266 | 48 770 | 42 852 | 5 364 | 15 433 |
| 1950 | 284 776 | 228 047 | 34 998 | 56 192 | 49 759 | 537 | 12 290 |
| 1951 | 329 822 | 261 861 | 54 136 | 65 787 | 53 998 | 2 174 | 16 961 |
| 1952 | 348 214 | 287 820 | 70 468 | 59 512 | 55 124 | 882 | 16 252 |
| 1953 | 365 874 | 303 953 | 74 418 | 62 977 | 58 616 | −1 056 | 15 138 |
| 1954 | 363 155 | 303 083 | 68 358 | 60 440 | 60 090 | −368 | 15 687 |
| 1955 | 397 152 | 322 240 | 69 036 | 75 481 | 68 127 | −569 | 17 448 |
| 1956 | 418 284 | 338 531 | 72 979 | 78 080 | 73 763 | 1 673 | 21 073 |
| 1957 | 441 764 | 360 514 | 80 193 | 77 792 | 76 981 | 3 458 | 23 831 |
| 1958 | 444 188 | 372 292 | 84 015 | 71 900 | 72 367 | −4 | 20 382 |
| 1959 | 482 026 | 396 596 | 88 359 | 87 533 | 80 550 | −2 103 | 20 412 |
| 1960 | 502 117 | 413 978 | 91 474 | 86 619 | 82 513 | 1 520 | 23 770 |
| 1961 | 517 334 | 430 790 | 99 050 | 84 223 | 82 396 | 2 321 | 24 363 |
| **Percentage distribution of average annual expenditure — Distribution en pourcentage des dépenses annuelles moyennes** | | | | | | | |
| 1948 | 100.0 | 79.1 | 10.9 | 18.8 | 16.5 | 2.1 | 6.0 |
| 1950 – 1960 | 100.0 | 82.0 | 18.1 | 17.9 | 16.8 | 0.1 | 4.7 |
| 1950 | 100.0 | 80.1 | 12.3 | 19.7 | 17.5 | 0.2 | 4.3 |
| 1953 | 100.0 | 83.1 | 20.3 | 17.2 | 16.0 | −0.3 | 4.1 |
| 1954 | 100.0 | 83.5 | 18.8 | 16.6 | 16.5 | −0.1 | 4.3 |
| 1958 | 100.0 | 83.8 | 18.9 | 16.2 | 16.3 | — | 4.6 |
| 1960 | 100.0 | 82.4 | 18.2 | 17.3 | 16.4 | 0.3 | 4.7 |
| | | | | | *b. At Prices of 1958 — Aux prix de 1958* | | |
| **Absolute figures — Chiffres absolus** | | | | | | | |
| 1948 | 321 600 | 252 300 | 40 600 | 64 200 | 58 800 | 5 000 | 16 600 |
| 1950 | 351 800 | 277 800 | 47 800 | 72 900 | 65 100 | 1 100 | 14 400 |
| 1951 | 377 500 | 298 900 | 66 900 | 75 500 | 65 500 | 3 100 | 17 400 |
| 1952 | 393 900 | 322 800 | 85 000 | 69 200 | 65 100 | 1 900 | 16 700 |
| 1953 | 409 800 | 338 000 | 89 300 | 72 300 | 68 100 | −500 | 15 900 |
| 1954 | 402 300 | 332 300 | 80 600 | 69 200 | 69 600 | 700 | 16 600 |
| 1955 | 434 300 | 349 200 | 78 800 | 84 600 | 76 800 | 400 | 18 300 |
| 1956 | 443 000 | 357 600 | 78 800 | 82 700 | 78 200 | 2 700 | 21 600 |
| 1957 | 451 800 | 368 500 | 82 500 | 79 300 | 78 100 | 3 900 | 23 500 |
| 1958 | 444 200 | 372 300 | 84 000 | 71 900 | 72 400 | — | 20 400 |
| 1959 | 474 400 | 390 500 | 85 800 | 85 900 | 78 900 | −2 000 | 20 700 |
| 1960 | 486 300 | 400 400 | 86 300 | 84 100 | 80 000 | 1 800 | 23 800 |
| 1961 | 495 000 | 411 700 | 91 300 | 81 400 | 79 500 | 1 900 | 24 000 |
| **Percentage distribution of average annual expenditure — Distribution en pourcentage des dépenses annuelles moyennes** | | | | | | | |
| 1948 | 100.0 | 78.4 | 12.6 | 20.0 | 18.3 | 1.6 | 5.2 |
| 1950 – 1960 | 100.0 | 81.6 | 18.5 | 18.1 | 17.1 | 0.3 | 4.5 |
| 1950 | 100.0 | 79.0 | 13.6 | 20.7 | 18.5 | 0.3 | 4.1 |
| 1953 | 100.0 | 82.5 | 21.8 | 17.6 | 16.6 | −0.1 | 3.9 |
| 1954 | 100.0 | 82.6 | 20.0 | 17.2 | 17.3 | 0.2 | 4.1 |
| 1958 | 100.0 | 83.8 | 18.9 | 16.2 | 16.3 | — | 4.6 |
| 1960 | 100.0 | 82.3 | 17.7 | 17.3 | 16.4 | 0.4 | 4.9 |
| **Average annual rate of growth — Taux annuel moyen d'accroissement** | | | | | | | |
| 1948 – 1953 | 5.0 | 6.0 | 17.1 | 2.4 | 3.0 | . | −0.9 |
| 1950 – 1960 | 3.3 | 3.7 | 6.1 | 1.4 | 2.1 | . | 5.2 |
| 1950 – 1953 | 5.2 | 6.8 | 23.2 | −0.3 | 1.5 | . | 3.4 |
| 1954 – 1958 | 2.5 | 2.9 | 1.0 | 1.0 | 1.0 | . | 5.3 |
| 1958 – 1960 | 4.6 | 3.7 | 1.3 | 8.2 | 5.1 | . | 8.0 |

For footnotes see end of table.  —  Pour les notes, voir au bas du tableau.

## B. The Net Domestic Product at Factor Cost According to Origin
### Origine par secteur d'activité du produit intérieur net au coût des facteurs

| Item of data and year / Rubrique et année | Total | Agricultural sector / Secteur agricole | Industrial Sector — Secteur industriel | | | | | Transportation and communication / Transports et communications | Other sectors[2] / Autres secteurs[2] |
|---|---|---|---|---|---|---|---|---|---|
| | | | Total | Mining / Industries extractives | Manufacturing / Industries manufacturières | Construction / Bâtiment et travaux publics | Electricity, gas and water / Electricité, gaz et eau | | |
| ISIC — CITI | 0–9 | 0 | 1–5 | 1 | 2–3 | 4 | 5 | 7 | 6, 8–9 |
| a. At Current Prices — Aux prix courants | | | | | | | | | |
| Absolute figures — Chiffres absolus | | | | | | | | | |
| 1948 | 222 234 | 21 431 | 85 781 | 5 247 | 66 777 | 10 576 | 3 181 | 15 395 | 99 627 |
| 1950 | 239 834 | 17 439 | 95 134 | 5 010 | 74 371 | 11 833 | 3 920 | 16 556 | 110 705 |
| 1951 | 277 070 | 19 956 | 112 783 | 5 499 | 88 495 | 14 213 | 4 576 | 18 595 | 125 736 |
| 1952 | 290 271 | 18 939 | 115 869 | 5 237 | 90 172 | 15 383 | 5 077 | 19 513 | 135 950 |
| 1953 | 303 185 | 16 891 | 124 534 | 5 208 | 97 953 | 15 881 | 5 492 | 20 389 | 141 371 |
| 1954 | 298 676 | 16 351 | 117 884 | 4 923 | 91 057 | 16 043 | 5 861 | 19 340 | 145 101 |
| 1955 | 326 609 | 15 497 | 133 667 | 5 609 | 104 490 | 17 358 | 6 210 | 21 248 | 156 197 |
| 1956 | 346 555 | 15 579 | 141 673 | 6 243 | 109 268 | 19 515 | 6 647 | 22 852 | 166 451 |
| 1957 | 362 113 | 15 838 | 145 966 | 6 238 | 112 476 | 20 247 | 7 005 | 23 608 | 176 701 |
| 1958 | 362 650 | 17 751 | 136 503 | 5 435 | 103 817 | 19 870 | 7 381 | 23 227 | 185 169 |
| 1959 | 395 601 | 15 704 | 154 898 | 5 283 | 119 929 | 21 558 | 8 128 | 25 160 | 199 839 |
| 1960 | 409 927 | 16 656 | 157 825 | 5 207 | 121 987 | 21 884 | 8 747 | 25 926 | 209 520 |
| 1961 | 421 758 | 17 862 | 157 929 | 4 977 | 121 704 | 22 141 | 9 107 | 26 258 | 219 709 |
| Percentage distribution according to sector — Distribution en pourcentage par secteur | | | | | | | | | |
| 1948 | 100.0 | 9.6 | 38.6 | 2.4 | 30.0 | 4.8 | 1.4 | 6.9 | 44.9 |
| 1950–1960 | 100.0 | 5.1 | 39.8 | 1.7 | 30.8 | 5.4 | 1.9 | 6.5 | 48.6 |
| 1950 | 100.0 | 7.2 | 39.7 | 2.1 | 31.0 | 5.0 | 1.6 | 6.9 | 46.2 |
| 1953 | 100.0 | 5.5 | 41.1 | 1.7 | 32.3 | 5.3 | 1.8 | 6.7 | 46.7 |
| 1954 | 100.0 | 5.4 | 39.5 | 1.7 | 30.5 | 5.3 | 2.0 | 6.5 | 48.6 |
| 1958 | 100.0 | 4.8 | 37.7 | 1.5 | 28.7 | 5.4 | 2.1 | 6.4 | 51.1 |
| 1960 | 100.0 | 4.0 | 38.5 | 1.3 | 29.7 | 5.4 | 2.1 | 6.3 | 51.2 |

For footnotes see end of table.          Pour les notes, voir au bas du tableau.

## C. Gross Domestic Fixed Capital Formation According to Purchasing Sector
## Formation brute de capital fixe intérieur par secteur d'acquisition

| Item of data and year / Rubrique et année | Total [3] | Agricultural sector / Secteur agricole | Industrial Sector — Secteur industriel | | | | Transportation and communication / Transports et communications | Other sectors / Autres secteurs |
| --- | --- | --- | --- | --- | --- | --- | --- | --- |
| | | | Total | Mining / Industries extractives | Manufacturing / Industries manufacturières | Electricity, gas and water / Electricité, gaz et eau | | |
| ISIC — CITI | 0–9 | 0 | 1–3, 5 | 1 | 2–3 | 5 | 7 | 4, 6, 8–9 |
| a. At Current Prices — Aux prix courants | | | | | | | | |
| **Absolute figures — Chiffres absolus** | | | | | | | | |
| 1948 | 40 758 | 3 366 | 12 559 | 882 | 9 134 | 2 543 | 4 346 | 20 487 |
| 1950 | 45 690 | 3 618 | 11 507 | 707 | 7 491 | 3 309 | 3 427 | 27 138 |
| 1951 | 50 851 | 3 918 | 15 445 | 929 | 10 852 | 3 664 | 4 283 | 27 205 |
| 1952 | 52 276 | 3 722 | 16 504 | 985 | 11 632 | 3 887 | 4 433 | 27 617 |
| 1953 | 55 351 | 3 720 | 17 446 | 986 | 11 908 | 4 552 | 4 566 | 29 619 |
| 1954 | 55 738 | 3 183 | 16 232 | 975 | 11 038 | 4 219 | 4 083 | 32 240 |
| 1955 | 61 566 | 3 343 | 16 705 | 957 | 11 439 | 4 309 | 4 508 | 37 010 |
| 1956 | 67 579 | 3 034 | 21 090 | 1 241 | 14 954 | 4 895 | 5 627 | 37 828 |
| 1957 | 70 267 | 3 123 | 23 397 | 1 243 | 15 959 | 6 195 | 6 199 | 37 548 |
| 1958 | 66 690 | 3 643 | 18 462 | 941 | 11 433 | 6 088 | 4 869 | 39 716 |
| 1959 | 73 796 | 3 761 | 18 730 | 990 | 12 070 | 5 670 | 5 610 | 45 695 |
| 1960 | 75 059 | 3 295 | 21 150 | 990 | 14 480 | 5 680 | 6 100 | 44 514 |
| 1961 | 75 116 | 3 445 | 20 180 | 980 | 13 680 | 5 520 | 5 740 | 45 751 |
| **Percentage distribution according to sector— Distribution en pourcentage par secteur** | | | | | | | | |
| 1948 | 100.0 | 8.2 | 30.8 | 2.2 | 22.4 | 6.2 | 10.7 | 50.3 |
| 1950–1960 | 100.0 | 5.6 | 29.2 | 1.7 | 19.7 | 7.8 | 7.9 | 57.3 |
| 1950 | 100.0 | 7.9 | 25.2 | 1.5 | 16.4 | 7.3 | 7.5 | 59.4 |
| 1953 | 100.0 | 6.7 | 31.5 | 1.8 | 21.5 | 8.2 | 8.2 | 53.6 |
| 1954 | 100.0 | 5.7 | 29.1 | 1.7 | 19.8 | 7.6 | 7.3 | 57.9 |
| 1958 | 100.0 | 5.4 | 27.7 | 1.4 | 17.2 | 9.1 | 7.3 | 59.6 |
| 1960 | 100.0 | 4.3 | 28.2 | 1.4 | 19.3 | 7.5 | 8.1 | 59.4 |

[1] Changes in stocks of Governmental agencies, other than those of Federal Government enterprises and those in strategic and critical materials, and Government expenditures on equipment are reflected in the consumption expenditures of Governments instead of in gross capital formation.
[2] Business transfer payments, which could not be allocated according to kind of economic activity, are included under other sectors.
[3] The estimates of gross fixed capital formation shown in Table 1 C are not comparable to those set out in Table 1 A because of the exclusion in the figures of Table 1 C of certain types of capital outlays which are charged to current expenditures by enterprises and other statistical units and of certain capital outlays of institutions, banks, insurance and real estate firms and professional persons. In the case of General Government capital expenditures for non-defense construction only are included under Other sectors. Capital expenditures of Government units which should be classified under Agriculture, Mining, Manufacturing, Electricity and Gas and Transportation are not included in the estimates shown for these sectors.

[1] Les variations des stocks des organismes gouvernementaux, autres que ceux des entreprises fédérales et que les stocks de matières stratégiques et assimilées, ainsi que les dépenses publiques en équipement, sont comprises dans les dépenses de consommation des pouvoirs publics au lieu de l'être dans la formation brute de capital.
[2] Les paiements de transferts industriels et commerciaux qui ne peuvent être répartis entre les types d'activité industrielle sont inclus dans "Autres secteurs".
[3] Les estimations de la formation brute de capital fixe indiquées au tableau 1 C ne sont pas comparables à celles du tableau 1 A, vu que les estimations du tableau 1 C ne comprennent pas certaines dépenses en capital imputées sur le compte des dépenses courantes par les entreprises et autres unités statistiques ni certaines dépenses en capital des institutions, banques, compagnies d'assurances et agences immobilières et de professionnels. Dans le cas de l'Etat, les dépenses en capital pour la construction à des fins autres que la défense nationale sont incluses dans "Autres secteurs." Les dépenses en capital des services gouvernementaux qui devraient être classées dans Agriculture, Industries extractives, Industries manufacturières, Electricité et gaz et Transports ne sont pas comprises dans les estimations relatives à ces secteurs.

## 2. INDEX NUMBERS OF INDUSTRIAL PRODUCTION
### INDICES DE LA PRODUCTION INDUSTRIELLE

### A. Selected Divisions of Industrial Activity
### Quelques branches de l'activité industrielle

| Period<br>Période | Total [1] | Mining<br>Industries<br>extractives | Manu-<br>facturing [1]<br>Industries<br>manu-<br>facturières [1] | Electricity<br>and gas<br>Electricité<br>et gaz |
|---|---|---|---|---|
| ISIC — CITI | 1–3, 511–512 | 1 | 2–3 | 511–512 |

#### a. Indexes — Indices (1958 = 100)

| | | | | |
|---|---|---|---|---|
| 1938........... | 33 | 52 | 34 | 17 |
| 1948........... | –73– | –88– | –74– | –42– |
| 1949........... | 69 | 78 | 70 | 44 |
| 1950........... | 80 | 87 | 82 | 50 |
| 1951........... | 87 | 96 | 88 | 58 |
| 1952........... | 90 | 95 | 92 | 62 |
| 1953........... | –97– | –97– | –99– | –68– |
| 1954........... | 92 | 94 | 92 | 73 |
| 1955........... | 103 | 104 | 104 | 82 |
| 1956........... | 107 | 110 | 108 | 90 |
| 1957........... | 107 | 109 | 108 | 96 |
| 1958........... | 100 | 100 | 100 | 100 |
| 1959........... | 113 | 104 | 114 | 110 |
| 1960........... | 116 | 106 | 117 | 118 |
| 1961........... | 117 | 107 | 118 | 125 |

#### b. Average Annual Rate of Change — Taux annuel moyen de variation

| | | | | |
|---|---|---|---|---|
| 1938 – 1960.... | 5.9 | 3.3 | 5.8 | 9.2 |
| 1938 – 1948.... | 8.3 | 5.4 | 8.1 | 9.5 |
| 1950 – 1960.... | 3.8 | 2.0 | 3.6 | 9.0 |
| 1948 – 1953.... | 5.8 | 2.0 | 6.0 | 10.1 |
| 1954 – 1958.... | 2.1 | 1.6 | 2.1 | 8.2 |
| 1958 – 1960.... | 7.7 | 3.0 | 8.2 | 8.6 |

For footnotes see end of table.

### B. The Major Groups of Mining
### Les classes de la branche Industries extractives

| Period<br>Période | All mining<br>Toutes<br>industries<br>extractives | Coal<br>mining<br>Extraction<br>du charbon | Metal mining<br>Extraction<br>des minerais<br>métalliques | Crude petro-<br>leum and<br>natural gas<br>Pétrole brut<br>et gaz naturel | Other mining<br>Autres<br>industries<br>extractives |
|---|---|---|---|---|---|
| ISIC — CITI | 1 | 11 | 12 | 13 | 14–19 |

#### a. Indexes — Indices (1958 = 100)

| | | | | | |
|---|---|---|---|---|---|
| 1938....... | 52 | 100 | 66 | 46 | 32 |
| 1948....... | –88– | –159– | –92– | –75– | 61 |
| 1949....... | 78 | 117 | 82 | 71 | 59 |
| 1950....... | 87 | 135 | 95 | 78 | 67 |
| 1951....... | 96 | 138 | 102 | 88 | 73 |
| 1952....... | 95 | 122 | 94 | 91 | 77 |
| 1953....... | –97– | –115– | –105– | –95– | –79– |
| 1954....... | 94 | 99 | 86 | 95 | 87 |
| 1955....... | 104 | 117 | 109 | 102 | 94 |
| 1956....... | 110 | 125 | 115 | 107 | 102 |
| 1957....... | 109 | 121 | 121 | 107 | 102 |
| 1958....... | 100 | 100 | 100 | 100 | 100 |
| 1959....... | 104 | 100 | 93 | 105 | 110 |
| 1960....... | 106 | 100 | 117 | 105 | 114 |
| 1961....... | 107 | 96 | 117 | 107 | 113 |

#### b. Average Annual Rate of Change — Taux annuel moyen de variation

| | | | | | |
|---|---|---|---|---|---|
| 1938 – 1960. | 3.3 | — | 2.6 | 3.8 | 5.9 |
| 1938 – 1948. | 5.4 | 4.7 | 3.4 | 5.0 | 6.7 |
| 1950 – 1960. | 2.0 | –3.0 | 2.1 | 3.0 | 5.5 |
| 1948 – 1953. | 2.0 | –6.3 | 2.7 | 4.8 | 5.3 |
| 1954 – 1958. | 1.6 | 0.2 | 3.8 | 1.3 | 3.5 |
| 1958 – 1960. | 3.0 | — | 8.2 | 2.5 | 6.8 |

Pour les notes, voir au bas du tableau

## C. The Major Groups of Manufacturing — Les classes de la branche Industries manufacturières

| Period / Période | Manufacturing[1] / Industries manufacturières[1] | Food, beverages and tobacco[1,2] / Industries aiimentaires, boissons, tabac[1,2] | Textiles[1] | Clothing, footwear and made-up textiles[1,3] / Articles d'habillement, chaussures et ouvrages en tissu[1,3] | Wood products and furniture[1,4] / Bois et meubles[1,4] | Paper and paper products / Papier et ouvrages en papier | Printing and publishing / Imprimerie et édition | Leather and leather products except wearing apparel[3,4] / Cuir et articles en cuir, à l'exclusion des articles d'habillement[3,4] | Rubber products / Ouvrages en caoutchouc | Chemicals and chemical, petroleum and coal products[2,4] / Produits chimiques et dérivés du pétrole et du charbon[2,4] | Non-metallic mineral products / Produits minéraux non métalliques | Basic metals / Métallurgie de base | Metal products[1,4] / Ouvrages en métaux[1,4] | Other manufacturing[1,3,4] / Autres industries manufacturières[1,3,4] |
|---|---|---|---|---|---|---|---|---|---|---|---|---|---|---|
| ISIC — CITI | 2–3 | 20–22 | 23 | 24 | 25–26 | 27 | 28 | 29 | 30 | 31–32 | 33 | 34 | 35–38 | 39 |

### a. Indexes — Indices (1958 = 100)

| | | | | | | | | | | | | | | |
|---|---|---|---|---|---|---|---|---|---|---|---|---|---|---|
| 1938 | 34 | 50 | 48 | 79 | 54 | 38 | 47 | 84 | 30 | 20 | 34 | 36 | 20 | 35 |
| 1948 | −74− | −80− | −96− | −82− | −88− | −66− | −76− | −101− | −75− | −52− | −76− | −108− | −66− | −68− |
| 1949 | 70 | 81 | 89 | 81 | 79 | 63 | 77 | 93 | 69 | 51 | 71 | 91 | 61 | 63 |
| 1950 | 82 | 84 | 101 | 87 | 96 | 76 | 81 | 98 | 83 | 61 | 86 | 114 | 75 | 75 |
| 1951 | 88 | 86 | 100 | 85 | 93 | 80 | 83 | 93 | 88 | 69 | 95 | 124 | 88 | 77 |
| 1952 | 92 | 88 | 100 | 90 | 94 | 77 | 82 | 95 | 89 | 72 | 91 | 113 | 97 | 84 |
| 1953 | −99− | −89− | −101− | −91− | −98− | −83− | −86− | −97− | −95− | −78− | −93− | −128− | −111− | −93− |
| 1954 | 92 | 90 | 95 | 89 | 98 | 84 | 90 | 94 | 89 | 77 | 90 | 104 | 98 | 89 |
| 1955 | 104 | 94 | 105 | 97 | 109 | 95 | 95 | 102 | 111 | 88 | 102 | 135 | 111 | 98 |
| 1956 | 108 | 97 | 106 | 101 | 108 | 100 | 100 | 104 | 104 | 94 | 107 | 133 | 114 | 105 |
| 1957 | 108 | 97 | 102 | 102 | 102 | 99 | 102 | 102 | 107 | 99 | 106 | 128 | 116 | 105 |
| 1958 | 100 | 100 | 100 | 100 | 100 | 100 | 100 | 100 | 100 | 100 | 100 | 100 | 100 | 100 |
| 1959 | 114 | 104 | 116 | 113 | 116 | 110 | 108 | 111 | 117 | 113 | 116 | 115 | 118 | 118 |
| 1960 | 117 | 107 | 111 | 115 | 114 | 111 | 114 | 109 | 115 | 119 | 116 | 116 | 122 | 124 |
| 1961 | 118 | 111 | 113 | 115 | 113 | 117 | 115 | 111 | 112 | 125 | 114 | 113 | 120 | 126 |

### b. Average Annual Rate of Change — Taux annuel moyen de variation

| | | | | | | | | | | | | | | |
|---|---|---|---|---|---|---|---|---|---|---|---|---|---|---|
| 1938–1960 | 5.8 | 3.5 | 3.9 | 1.7 | 3.5 | 5.0 | 4.1 | 1.2 | 6.3 | 8.4 | 5.7 | 5.5 | 8.6 | 5.9 |
| 1938–1948 | 8.1 | 4.8 | 7.2 | 0.4 | 5.0 | 5.7 | 4.9 | 1.9 | 9.6 | 10.0 | 8.4 | 11.6 | 12.7 | 6.9 |
| 1950–1960 | 3.6 | 2.5 | 0.9 | 2.8 | 1.7 | 3.9 | 3.5 | 1.1 | 3.3 | 6.9 | 3.0 | 0.2 | 5.0 | 5.2 |
| 1948–1953 | 6.0 | 2.1 | 1.0 | 2.1 | 2.2 | 4.7 | 2.5 | −0.8 | 4.8 | 8.4 | 4.1 | 3.5 | 11.0 | 6.5 |
| 1954–1958 | 2.1 | 2.7 | 1.3 | 3.0 | 0.5 | 4.4 | 2.7 | 1.6 | 3.0 | 6.8 | 2.7 | −1.0 | 0.5 | 3.0 |
| 1958–1960 | 8.2 | 3.4 | 5.4 | 7.2 | 6.8 | 5.4 | 6.8 | 4.4 | 7.2 | 9.1 | 7.7 | 7.7 | 10.5 | 11.4 |

[1] In the case of all years, not covered are establishments primarily engaged in manufacturing which sell most of their products on the premises at retail, which do custom work to the order of households or which primarily perform repair and related services, excepting a few such specified services "for the trade". In the case of 1938, excluded is the pasteurizing and related processing of fluid milk (part of ISIC major group 25). Included, in the case of all years, are jobbers of textiles, apparel and leather products who contract out all manufacturing activity and are therefore classified outside of manufacturing in the ISIC.
[2] Beginning with 1948 the manufacture of non-edible animal fats and the extracting and processing of vegetables and fish oils are included in Food manufacturing (ISIC major group 20) instead of in Chemicals and chemical products (ISIC major group 31).
[3] The manufacturing of leather gloves and of umbrellas and similar items (all part of ISIC major group 24) are included in Leather products (ISIC major group 29) and Miscellaneous manufacturing (ISIC major group 39), respectively.
[4] Included in Miscellaneous manufacturing (ISIC major group 39) are manufacture of morticians' goods (part of ISIC major group 25), the dressing and dyeing of furs (part of ISIC major group 29), the manufacture of matches and candles (part of ISIC major group 31), and the manufacture of mechanical measuring instruments (part of ISIC major group 36). On the other hand, the manufacture of electrical measuring instruments (part of ISIC major group 39) is covered under Metal products (ISIC major groups 35-83) instead of Miscellaneous manufacturing.

[1] Pour toutes les années, non compris les établissements dont l'activité principale relève des industries manufacturières, et qui vendent la majeure partie de leurs produits au détail dans leurs propres locaux, qui travaillent à façon pour les ménages, ou encore qui effectuent principalement des réparations ou fournissent des services connexes, à l'exclusion des services expressément "réservés aux professionnels". En 1938, sont exclues la pasteurisation du lait et les opérations connexes (dans CITI 20). Pour toutes les années, sont compris, dans le cas des textiles, du vêtement et des articles en cuir, les "jobbers" qui confient à des sous-traitants la totalité des travaux de fabrication et qui ne sont donc pas classés, dans la CITI, avec les industries manufacturières.
[2] A partir de 1948, la préparation des graisses animales non comestibles, ainsi que l'extraction et la préparation des huiles végétales et des huiles de poissons sont comprises dans les Industries alimentaires (CITI 20) et non dans Produits chimiques (CITI 31).
[3] La fabrication des gants en cuir et la fabrication des parapluies et articles analogues (tous dans CITI 24) sont comprises respectivement dans Cuir et articles en cuir (CITI 29) et Industries manufacturières diverses (CITI 39).
[4] Sont comprises dans les Industries manufacturières diverses (CITI 39): fabrication des articles mortuaires (dans CITI 25), préparation et teinture des fourrures (dans CITI 29), fabrication des allumettes et des bougies (dans CITI 31) et fabrication des instruments de mesure mécaniques (dans CITI 36). En revanche, la fabrication des instruments de mesure électriques (dans CITI 39) est comprise dans Ouvrages en métaux (CITI 35-38) et non dans Industries manufacturières diverses.

## 3. INDEX NUMBERS OF INDUSTRIAL EMPLOYMENT[1]
### INDICES DE L'EMPLOI DANS L'INDUSTRIE[1]

### A. The Divisions of Industrial Activity
### Les branches de l'activité industrielle

| Period<br>Période | Total [2] | Mining<br>Industries extractives | Manu-facturing [2]<br>Industries manu-facturières [2] | Construction<br>Bâtiment et travaux publics | Electricity and gas<br>Electricité et gaz |
|---|---|---|---|---|---|
| ISIC — CITI | 1–4, 511–512 | 1 | 2–3 | 4 | 511–512 |
| *a.* Indexes — Indices (1958 = 100) | | | | | |
| 1948....... | 96 | 132 | 98 | 78 | 86 |
| 1949....... | 90 | 124 | 90 | 78 | 88 |
| 1950....... | 95 | 120 | 96 | 84 | 90 |
| 1951....... | 102 | 110 | 103 | 94 | 92 |
| 1952....... | 103 | 120 | 104 | 95 | 93 |
| 1953....... | 108 | 115 | 110 | 94 | 95 |
| 1954....... | 101 | 105 | 102 | 94 | 96 |
| 1955....... | 105 | 105 | 106 | 101 | 97 |
| 1956....... | 108 | 109 | 108 | 108 | 98 |
| 1957....... | 107 | 110 | 108 | 105 | 100 |
| 1958....... | 100 | 100 | 100 | 100 | 100 |
| 1959....... | 104 | 97 | 104 | 106 | 100 |
| 1960....... | 105 | 94 | 106 | 104 | 100 |
| 1961....... | 101 | 89 | 102 | 99 | 100 |
| *b.* Average Annual Rate of Change — Taux annuel moyen de variation | | | | | |
| 1950–1960. | 1.0 | −2.4 | 1.0 | 2.2 | 1.1 |
| 1948–1953. | 2.4 | −2.7 | 2.3 | 3.8 | 2.0 |
| 1954–1958. | −0.3 | −1.2 | −0.5 | 1.6 | 1.0 |
| 1958–1960. | 2.5 | −3.0 | 3.0 | 2.0 | — |

### B. The Major Groups of Mining
### Les classes de la branche Industries extractives

| Period<br>Période | All mining<br>Toutes industries extractives | Coal mining<br>Extraction du charbon | Metal mining<br>Extraction des minerais métalliques | Crude petro-leum and natural gas<br>Pétrole brut et gaz naturel | Other mining<br>Autres industries extractives |
|---|---|---|---|---|---|
| ISIC — CITI | 1 | 11 | 12 | 13 | 14–19 |
| *a.* Indexes — Indices (1958 = 100) | | | | | |
| 1948....... | 132 | 240 | 112 | 84 | 87 |
| 1949....... | 124 | 219 | 105 | 81 | 83 |
| 1950....... | 120 | 206 | 104 | 81 | 83 |
| 1951....... | 110 | 205 | 108 | 87 | 89 |
| 1952....... | 120 | 182 | 107 | 93 | 90 |
| 1953....... | 115 | 159 | 114 | 95 | 92 |
| 1954....... | 105 | 125 | 106 | 97 | 91 |
| 1955....... | 105 | 116 | 109 | 101 | 94 |
| 1956....... | 109 | 120 | 117 | 104 | 100 |
| 1957....... | 110 | 120 | 120 | 105 | 99 |
| 1958....... | 100 | 100 | 100 | 100 | 100 |
| 1959....... | 97 | 91 | 90 | 101 | 104 |
| 1960....... | 94 | 85 | 100 | 96 | 104 |
| 1961....... | 89 | 72 | 94 | 94 | 100 |
| *b.* Average Annual Rate of Change — Taux annuel moyen de variation | | | | | |
| 1950–1960. | −2.4 | −8.5 | −0.4 | 1.7 | 2.3 |
| 1948–1953. | −2.7 | −7.9 | 0.4 | 2.5 | 1.1 |
| 1954–1958. | −1.2 | −5.4 | −1.5 | 0.8 | 2.4 |
| 1958–1960. | −3.0 | −7.8 | — | −2.0 | 2.0 |

For footnotes, see end of table.

Pour les notes, voir au bas du tableau.

## C. The Major Groups of Manufacturing — Les classes de la branche Industries manufacturières

| Period / Période | Manufacturing [2] / Industries manufacturières [2] | Food, beverages and tobacco [2,3] / Industries alimentaires, boissons, tabac [2,3] | Textiles [2] | Clothing, footwear and made-up textiles [2,4] / Articles d'habillement, chaussures et ouvrages en tissu [2,4] | Wood products and furniture [2,5] / Bois et meubles [2,5] | Paper and paper products / Papier et ouvrages en papier | Printing and publishing / Imprimerie et édition | Leather and leather products except wearing apparel [4,5] / Cuir et articles en cuir, à l'exclusion des articles d'habillement [4,5] | Rubber products / Ouvrages en caoutchouc | Chemicals and chemical, petroleum and coal products [3,5] / Produits chimiques et dérivés du pétrole et du charbon [3,5] | Non-metallic mineral products / Produits minéraux non métalliques | Basic metals / Métallurgie de base | Metal products [2,5] / Ouvrages en métaux [2,5] | Other manufacturing [2,4,5] / Autres industries manufacturières [2,4,5] |
|---|---|---|---|---|---|---|---|---|---|---|---|---|---|---|
| ISIC — CITI | 2-3 | 20-22 | 23 | 24 | 25-26 | 27 | 28 | 29 | 30 | 31-32 | 33 | 34 | 35-38 | 39 |

### a. Indexes — Indices (1958 = 100)

| | | | | | | | | | | | | | | |
|---|---|---|---|---|---|---|---|---|---|---|---|---|---|---|
| 1948 | 98 | 102 | 145 | 103 | 121 | 84 | 85 | 125 | 128 | 87 | 98 | 112 | 85 | 86 |
| 1949 | 90 | 101 | 129 | 101 | 110 | 81 | 85 | 113 | 116 | 82 | 91 | 98 | 76 | 78 |
| 1950 | 96 | 101 | 137 | 103 | 122 | 86 | 86 | 117 | 128 | 84 | 97 | 108 | 82 | 81 |
| 1951 | 103 | 103 | 135 | 103 | 123 | 91 | 88 | 114 | 109 | 92 | 104 | 118 | 96 | 96 |
| 1952 | 104 | 104 | 127 | 104 | 118 | 89 | 89 | 113 | 110 | 95 | 100 | 111 | 104 | 97 |
| 1953 | 110 | 104 | 126 | 106 | 117 | 94 | 92 | 114 | 114 | 99 | 103 | 120 | 115 | 105 |
| 1954 | 102 | 103 | 113 | 101 | 108 | 94 | 93 | 106 | 102 | 97 | 98 | 106 | 103 | 99 |
| 1955 | 106 | 103 | 114 | 104 | 114 | 98 | 96 | 113 | 112 | 99 | 105 | 115 | 107 | 102 |
| 1956 | 108 | 104 | 112 | 104 | 113 | 101 | 99 | 112 | 111 | 101 | 108 | 117 | 111 | 105 |
| 1957 | 108 | 102 | 107 | 103 | 106 | 101 | 100 | 106 | 109 | 102 | 106 | 117 | 113 | 105 |
| 1958 | 100 | 100 | 100 | 100 | 100 | 100 | 100 | 100 | 100 | 100 | 100 | 100 | 100 | 100 |
| 1959 | 104 | 101 | 103 | 104 | 107 | 104 | 102 | 104 | 106 | 101 | 107 | 102 | 107 | 106 |
| 1960 | 106 | 101 | 100 | 104 | 104 | 105 | 105 | 101 | 107 | 102 | 106 | 106 | 108 | 108 |
| 1961 | 102 | 100 | 96 | 102 | 99 | 104 | 106 | 100 | 103 | 102 | 101 | 99 | 104 | 106 |

### b. Average Annual Rate of Change — Taux annuel moyen de variation

| | | | | | | | | | | | | | | |
|---|---|---|---|---|---|---|---|---|---|---|---|---|---|---|
| 1950-1960 | 1.0 | — | -3.1 | 0.1 | -1.6 | 2.0 | 2.0 | -1.5 | -1.8 | 2.0 | 0.9 | -0.2 | 2.8 | 2.9 |
| 1948-1953 | 2.3 | 0.4 | -2.8 | 0.6 | -0.7 | 2.3 | 1.6 | -1.8 | -2.3 | 2.6 | 1.0 | 1.4 | 6.2 | 4.1 |
| 1954-1958 | -0.5 | -0.7 | -3.0 | -0.3 | -1.9 | 1.6 | 1.8 | -1.5 | -0.5 | 0.8 | 0.5 | -1.5 | -0.7 | 0.2 |
| 1958-1960 | 3.0 | 0.5 | — | 2.0 | 2.0 | 2.5 | 2.5 | 0.5 | 3.4 | 1.0 | 3.0 | 3.0 | 3.9 | 3.9 |

[1] Alaska and Hawaii are covered in the indexes for 1959 and later years.
[2] Excluded are establishments primarily engaged in manufacturing which sell most of their products on the premises at retail, which do custom work for households or which primarily perform repair and related services, excepting a few such specified services "for the trade". Included are jobbers of textiles, apparel and leather products who contract out all manufacturing activity and are therefore classified out of manufacturing in the ISIC.
[3] The manufacture of non-edible animal fats and the extracting and processing of vegetable and fish oils are included in Food manufacturing (ISIC major group 20) instead of in Chemicals and chemical products (ISIC major group 31).
[4] The manufacture of leather gloves and of umbrellas and similar items (part of ISIC major group 24) are included in Leather products (ISIC major group 29) and Miscellaneous manufacturing (ISIC major group 39), respectively.
[5] Included in Miscellaneous manufacturing (ISIC major group 39) are the manufacture of morticians goods (part of ISIC major group 25), the dressing and dyeing of furs (part of ISIC major group 29), the manufacture of matches and candles (part of ISIC major group 31) and the manufacture of mechanical measuring instruments (part of ISIC major group 36). On the other hand, the manufacture of electrical measuring instruments (part of ISIC major group 39) is covered under Metal products (ISIC major group 35-38) instead of Miscellaneous manufacturing.

[1] L'Alaska et les îles Hawaii sont compris dans les indices à partir de 1959.
[2] Non compris les établissements dont l'activité principale relève des industries manufacturières, et qui vendent la majeure partie de leurs produits au détail dans leurs propres locaux, qui travaillent à façon pour les ménages ou encore qui effectuent principalement des réparations ou fournissent des services connexes, à l'exclusion des services expressément "réservés aux professionnels". Sont compris, dans le cas des textiles, du vêtement et des articles en cuir, les "jobbers" qui confient à des sous traitants la totalité des travaux de fabrication et qui ne sont donc pas classés, dans la CITI, avec les industries manufacturières.
[3] La préparation des graisses animales non comestibles, ainsi que l'extraction et la préparation des huiles végétales et des huiles de poissons sont comprises dans les Industries alimentaires (CITI 20) et non dans Produits chimiques (CITI 31).
[4] La fabrication des gants en cuir, et la fabrication des parapluies et articles analogues (dans CITI 24) sont comprises respectivement dans Cuir et articles en cuir (CITI 29) et Industries manufacturières diverses (CITI 39).
[5] Sont comprises dans les Industries manufacturières diverses (CITI 39): fabrication des articles mortuaires (dans CITI 25), préparation et teinture des fourrures (dans CITI 29), fabrication des allumettes et des bougies (dans CITI 31) et fabrication des instruments de mesure mécaniques (dans CITI 36). En revanche, la fabrication des instruments de mesure électriques (dans CITI 39) est comprise dans Ouvrages en métaux (CITI 35-38) et non dans Industries manufacturières diverses.

# 4. THE CHARACTERISTICS OF MINING AND MANUFACTURING ESTABLISHMENTS
## CARACTERISTIQUES DES ETABLISSEMENTS MINIERS ET MANUFACTURIERS

Number of mines, quarries and wells and of establishments in units; value added and wages and salaries in million dollars; number of engaged, employees and operatives in thousands; man-hours worked in millions; energy consumed in thousand metric tons of coal equivalents; electricity consumed in million KWH; capacity of installed power equipment in thousand horsepower; value added per engaged and wages and salaries per employee and per thousand operative man-hours in thousand dollars; average annual man-hours per operative in thousands; energy consumed per engaged and per thousand operative man-hours in metric tons of coal equivalents; electricity consumed per engaged and per thousand operative man-hours in thousand KWH; capacity of installed power equipment per engaged and per thousand operative man-hours in horsepower.

Nombre de mines, carrières et puits ou d'établissements en unités; valeur ajoutée et traitements et salaires en millions de dollars; nombre de personnes occupées, de salariés et d'ouvriers en milliers; heures de travail effectuées en millions; énergie consommée en milliers de tonnes métriques d'équivalent charbon; électricité consommée en millions de kWh; puissance installée en milliers de chevaux-vapeur; valeur ajoutée par personne occupée et traitements et salaires par salarié et par millier d'heures-ouvrier en milliers de dollars; moyenne annuelle des heures de travail par ouvrier en milliers; énergie consommée par personne occupée et par millier d'heures-ouvrier en tonnes métriques d'équivalent charbon; électricité consommée par personne occupée et par millier d'heures-ouvrier en milliers de kWh; puissance installée par personne occupée et par millier d'heures-ouvrier en chevaux-vapeur.

## A. The Major Groups of Mining — Les classes de la branche Industries extractives

### 1939, 1954, 1958

Establishments for which the Gross Value of Production, Principal Expenses and Capital Expenditures each equal $2,500 or more in the case of 1939 [1] or $500 or more in the case of 1954 and 1958 [2].

Etablissements pour lesquels le chiffre de la valeur brute de la production, celui des dépenses directes de production et celui des dépenses d'équipement atteignaient chacun 2,500 dollars ou plus en 1939 [1] ou 500 dollars ou plus en 1954 et 1958 [2].

### a. Absolute Figures — Chiffres absolus

| Year and item of data | All mining — Toutes industries extractives | Coal mining — Extraction du charbon | Metal mining — Extraction des minerais métalliques | Crude petroleum and natural gas — Pétrole brut et gaz naturel | Other mining — Divers | Année et rubrique |
|---|---|---|---|---|---|---|
| ISIC | 1 | 11 | 12 | 13 | 14-19 | CITI |
| **1939** | | | | | | **1939** |
| Number of mines, quarries and wells | 361 202 | 6 365 | 2 095 | 347 645 | 5 097 | Nombre de mines, carrières et puits |
| Value added | 2 765.4 | 764.7 | 417.0 | 1 328.0 | 255.7 | Valeur ajoutée |
| Number of engaged (Average during year) | 872 | 484 | 101 | 194 | 93 | Nombre de personnes occupées (moyenne pendant l'année) |
| Employees: Number (Average during year) | 856 | 480 | 100 | 186 | 90 | Salariés: Nombre (moyenne pendant l'année) |
| Wages and salaries | 1 174.7 | 596.8 | 153.9 | 318.3 | 105.7 | Traitements et salaires |
| Operatives: Number (Average during year) | 774.1 | 454.0 | 89.8 | 149.0 | 81.3 | Ouvriers: Nombre (moyenne pendant l'année) |
| Man-hours worked | 1 287.8 | 670.2 | 190.8 | 265.0 | 161.8 | Heures de travail effectuées |
| Wages and salaries | 970.9 | 540.0 | 127.1 | 220.4 | 83.4 | Traitements et salaires |
| Energy consumed | 27 055.7 | 5 013.1 | 1 736.8 | 18 026.3 | 2 279.5 | Energie consommée |
| Electricity consumed | 8 399 | 3 539 | 2 922 | 838 | 1 100 | Electricité consommée |
| Capacity of installed power equipment (As of end of year) | 14 160 | 4 465 | 2 264 | 5 101 | 2 330 | Puissance installée (à la fin de l'année) |

### b. Structure

| Year and item of data | All mining — Toutes industries extractives | Coal mining — Extraction du charbon | Metal mining — Extraction des minerais métalliques | Crude petroleum and natural gas — Pétrole brut et gaz naturel | Other mining — Divers | Année et rubrique |
|---|---|---|---|---|---|---|
| ISIC | 1 | 11 | 12 | 13 | 14-19 | CITI |
| **1939** Distribution in percent of: | | | | | | **1939** Distribution en pourcentage: |
| Value added | 100.0 | 27.6 | 15.1 | 48.0 | 9.3 | Valeur ajoutée |
| Number of engaged | 100.0 | 55.5 | 11.5 | 22.3 | 10.7 | Nombre de personnes occupées |
| Per person engaged: Value added | 3.2 | 1.6 | 4.1 | 6.8 | 2.7 | Par personne occupée: Valeur ajoutée |
| Energy consumed | 31.03 | 10.36 | 17.20 | 92.92 | 24.51 | Energie consommée |
| Electricity consumed | 9.6 | 7.3 | 28.9 | 4.3 | 11.8 | Electricité consommée |
| Capacity of installed power equipment | 16.24 | 9.22 | 22.42 | 26.29 | 25.05 | Puissance installée |
| Employees as a percent of engaged | 98.2 | 99.2 | 99.0 | 95.9 | 96.8 | Salariés en pourcentage des personnes occupées |
| Value added per unit of wages and salaries | 2.35 | 1.28 | 2.71 | 4.17 | 2.42 | Valeur ajoutée par unité de traitements et salaires |
| Wages and salaries per employee | 1.4 | 1.2 | 1.5 | 1.7 | 1.2 | Traitements et salaires par salarié |
| Operatives as a percent of employees | 90.4 | 94.6 | 89.8 | 80.1 | 90.3 | Ouvriers en pourcentage des salariés |
| Average man-hours per operative | 1.66 | 1.48 | 2.12 | 1.78 | 1.99 | Heures de travail: moyenne par ouvrier |
| Per thousand operative man-hour: Wages and salaries | 0.75 | 0.80 | 0.67 | 0.83 | 0.52 | Par millier d'heures-ouvrier: Traitements et salaires |
| Energy consumed | 21.01 | 7.48 | 9.10 | 68.02 | 14.09 | Energie consommée |
| Electricity consumed | 6.52 | 5.28 | 15.31 | 3.16 | 6.80 | Electricité consommée |
| Capacity of installed power equipment | 11.00 | 6.66 | 11.86 | 19.25 | 14.40 | Puissance installée |

For footnotes, see end of table.

Pour les notes, voir au bas du tableau.

# UNITED STATES

## A. The Major Groups of Mining (continued) — Les classes de la branche Industries extractives (suite)

### a. Absolute Figures — Chiffres absolus

| Year and item of data | All mining — Toutes industries extractives | Coal mining — Extraction du charbon | Metal mining — Extraction des minerais métalliques | Crude petroleum and natural gas — Pétrole brut et gaz naturel | Other mining — Divers | Année et rubrique |
|---|---|---|---|---|---|---|
| ISIC / CITI | 1 | 11 | 12 | 13 | 14-19 | CITI |
| **1954 [3]** | | | | | | **1954 [3]** |
| Number of mines, quarries and wells | 514 347 | 8 107 | 3 356 | 493 611 | 9 273 | Nombre de mines, carrières et puits |
| Value added | 11 740.0 | 1 615.2 | 1 075.5 | 7 673.7 | 1 375.6 | Valeur ajoutée |
| Number of engaged (Average during year) | 846 | 266 | 104 | 336 | 140 | Nombre de personnes occupées (moyenne pendant l'année) |
| Employees: Number (Average during year) | 806 | 256 | 100 | 316 | 134 | Salariés: Nombre (moyenne pendant l'année) |
| Wages and salaries | 3 457.0 | 1 010.2 | 463.0 | 1 462.4 | 521.4 | Traitements et salaires |
| Operatives: Number (Average during year) | 666.7 | 232.7 | 81.9 | 235.5 | 116.6 | Ouvriers: Nombre (moyenne pendant l'année) |
| Man-hours worked | 1 288.4 | 374.0 | 168.3 | 491.7 | 254.4 | Heures de travail effectuées |
| Wages and salaries | 2 639.4 | 878.8 | 353.3 | 976.6 | 430.7 | Traitements et salaires |
| Energy consumed | 45 651.7 | 2 752.0 | 2 585.5 | 34 858.2 | 5 456.0 | Energie consommée |
| Electricity consumed | 16 852 | 4 600 | 4 711 | 4 062 | 3 479 | Electricité consommée |
| Capacity of installed power equipment (As of end of year) | 40 879 | 7 838 | 5 113 | 20 101 | 7 827 | Puissance installée (à la fin de l'année) |
| **1958 [3]** | | | | | | **1958 [3]** |
| Number of establishments | 37 784 | 8 178 | 2 233 | 18 501 | 8 872 | Nombre d'établissements |
| Value added | 13 680.9 | 1 774.4 | 1 187.3 | 9 035.3 | 1 683.9 | Valeur ajoutée |
| Number of engaged (Average during year) | 790.6 | 219.7 | 94.3 | 333.2 | 143.4 | Nombre de personnes occupées (moyenne pendant l'année) |
| Employees: Number (Average during year) | 753.5 | 210.5 | 92.5 | 312.8 | 137.7 | Salariés: Nombre (moyenne pendant l'année) |
| Wages and salaries | 3 826.7 | 1 006.2 | 487.8 | 1 699.4 | 633.3 | Traitements et salaires |
| Operatives: Number (Average during year) | 584.0 | 183.6 | 71.4 | 213.9 | 115.1 | Ouvriers: Nombre (moyenne pendant l'année) |
| Man-hours worked | 1 116.9 | 298.6 | 136.8 | 440.1 | 241.4 | Heures de travail effectuées |
| Wages and salaries | 2 695.6 | 839.8 | 356.2 | 1 010.7 | 488.9 | Traitements et salaires |
| Energy consumed | 49 148.4 | 2 273.4 | 3 316.1 | 37 802.3 | 5 756.6 | Energie consommée |
| Electricity consumed | 20 875 | 5 064 | 6 068 | 5 829 | 3 914 | Electricité consommée |

### b. Structure

| Year and item of data | All mining — Toutes industries extractives | Coal mining — Extraction du charbon | Metal mining — Extraction des minerais métalliques | Crude petroleum and natural gas — Pétrole brut et gaz naturel | Other mining — Divers | Année et rubrique |
|---|---|---|---|---|---|---|
| ISIC / CITI | 1 | 11 | 12 | 13 | 14-19 | CITI |
| **1954 [3]** | | | | | | **1954 [3]** |
| Distribution in percent of: | | | | | | Distribution en pourcentage: |
| Value added | 100.0 | 13.7 | 9.2 | 65.3 | 11.8 | Valeur ajoutée |
| Number of engaged | 100.0 | 31.4 | 12.3 | 39.7 | 16.6 | Nombre de personnes occupées |
| Per person engaged: | | | | | | Par personne occupée: |
| Value added | 13.9 | 6.1 | 10.3 | 22.8 | 9.8 | Valeur ajoutée |
| Energy consumed | 53.96 | 10.34 | 24.86 | 103.74 | 38.97 | Energie consommée |
| Electricity consumed | 19.9 | 17.3 | 45.3 | 12.1 | 24.8 | Electricité consommée |
| Capacity of installed power equipment | 48.32 | 29.47 | 49.16 | 59.82 | 55.91 | Puissance installée |
| Employees as a percent of engaged | 95.3 | 96.2 | 96.2 | 94.0 | 95.7 | Salariés en pourcentage des personnes occupées |
| Value added per unit of wages and salaries | 3.40 | 1.60 | 2.32 | 5.25 | 2.64 | Valeur ajoutée par unité de traitements et salaires |
| Wages and salaries per employee | 4.3 | 3.9 | 4.6 | 4.6 | 3.9 | Traitements et salaires par salarié |
| Operatives as a percent of employees | 82.7 | 90.9 | 81.9 | 74.5 | 87.0 | Ouvriers en pourcentage des salariés |
| Average man-hours per operative | 1.93 | 1.61 | 2.05 | 2.09 | 2.18 | Heures de travail: moyenne par ouvrier |
| Per thousand operative man-hour: | | | | | | Par millier d'heures-ouvrier: |
| Wages and salaries | 2.05 | 2.35 | 2.10 | 1.99 | 1.69 | Traitements et salaires |
| Energy consumed | 35.43 | 7.36 | 15.36 | 70.89 | 21.45 | Energie consommée |
| Electricity consumed | 13.08 | 12.30 | 27.99 | 8.26 | 13.68 | Electricité consommée |
| Capacity of installed power equipment | 31.73 | 20.96 | 30.38 | 40.88 | 30.77 | Puissance installée |
| **1958 [3]** | | | | | | **1958 [3]** |
| Distribution in percent of: | | | | | | Distribution en pourcentage: |
| Value added | 100.0 | 12.9 | 8.7 | 66.0 | 12.4 | Valeur ajoutée |
| Number of engaged | 100.0 | 27.7 | 12.0 | 42.1 | 18.2 | Nombre de personnes occupées |
| Per person engaged: | | | | | | Par personne occupée: |
| Value added | 17.3 | 8.1 | 12.6 | 27.1 | 11.7 | Valeur ajoutée |
| Energy consumed | 62.16 | 10.35 | 35.16 | 11 3.45 | 40.14 | Energie consommée |
| Electricity consumed | 26.4 | 23.0 | 64.3 | 17.5 | 27.3 | Electricité consommée |
| Employees as a percent of engaged | 95.3 | 95.8 | 98.1 | 93.9 | 96.0 | Salariés en pourcentage des personnes occupées |
| Value added per unit of wages and salaries | 3.58 | 1.76 | 2.43 | 5.32 | 2.66 | Valeur ajoutée par unité de traitements et salaires |
| Wages and salaries per employee | 5.1 | 4.8 | 5.3 | 5.4 | 4.6 | Traitements et salaires par salarié |
| Operatives as a percent of employees | 77.5 | 87.2 | 77.2 | 68.4 | 83.6 | Ouvriers en pourcentage des salariés |
| Average man-hours per operative | 1.91 | 1.63 | 1.92 | 2.06 | 2.10 | Heures de travail: moyenne par ouvrier |
| Per thousand operative man-hour: | | | | | | Par millier d'heures-ouvrier: |
| Wages and salaries | 2.41 | 2.81 | 2.60 | 2.30 | 2.02 | Traitements et salaires |
| Energy consumed | 44.00 | 7.61 | 24.24 | 85.89 | 23.85 | Energie consommée |
| Electricity consumed | 18.69 | 16.96 | 44.36 | 13.24 | 16.21 | Electricité consommée |

---

[1] In 1939, in the case of the mining of bituminous coal and lignite, 1,000 tons was substituted for $2,500 as the minimum for production and in the case of quarrying of sand and gravel, establishments extracting less than 15,000 tons and making capital expenditures of less than $15,000 during the year were not covered.

[2] In 1954 and 1958, gross value of products shipped and services rendered was utilized as a criterion in place of gross value of production. An additional criterion for coverage in the case of 1958 was having at least one employee at any time during the year.

[3] Included in the case of all items of data, except energy and electricity consumed, are certain mining operations of establishments classified in manufacturing, such as the quarrying of dimension, crushed or broken stone, clay, ceramic and refractory minerals or gypsum. The inclusion of these mining operations in the figures for 1954 and 1958 contributes to the comparability with the figures for 1939.

[1] En 1939, le minimum de production pris comme critère dans le cas de l'extraction du charbon bitumineux et du lignite était de 1.000 tonnes au lieu de 2.500 dollars; dans le cas de l'extraction du sable et du gravier, les établissements ayant extrait moins de 15.000 tonnes et effectué des dépenses d'équipement inférieures à 15.000 dollars pendant l'année n'ont pas été compris dans les chiffres.

[2] En 1954 et 1958, la valeur brute des produits expédiés et des services fournis a été prise comme critère au lieu de la valeur brute de la production. En outre, les établissements devaient avoir eu, en 1958, un salarié au moins à un moment quelconque de l'année.

[3] Y compris, dans le cas de toutes les rubriques, à l'exclusion de l'énergie et de l'électricité consommées, certaines opérations d'extraction effectuées par des établissements classés dans les industries manufacturières: par exemple, extraction de la pierre de taille et de la pierre de construction, de l'argile, du kaolin, des terres réfractaires et du gypse. Le fait que ces opérations sont comprises dans les chiffres de 1954 et 1958 renforce la comparabilité de ces chiffres avec ceux de 1939.

## B.  The Major Groups of Manufacturing — Les classes de la branche Industries manufacturières
### 1939, 1947, 1954, 1958

Establishments with Gross Value of Production of $5 000 or more in 1939, or with One or More Employees in 1947, 1954 and 1958.

Etablissements dont la production avait une valeur brute de 5.000 dollars ou plus en 1939, et établissements qui comptaient au moins un salarié en 1947, 1954 et 1958.

### a.  Absolute Figures — Chiffres absolus

| Year and item of data | Manufacturing[1] / Industries manufacturières[1] | Food, beverages and tobacco[2] / Industries alimentaires, boissons, tabac[2] | Textiles | Clothing, footwear and made-up textiles / Articles d'habillement, chaussures et ouvrages en tissu | Wood products and furniture / Bois et meubles | Paper and paper products / Papier et ouvrages en papier | Printing and publishing / Imprimerie et édition | Leather and leather products except wearing apparel / Cuir et articles en cuir, à l'exclusion des articles d'habillement | Rubber products / Ouvrages en caoutchouc | Chemicals and chemical, petroleum and coal products / Produits chimiques et dérivés du pétrole et du charbon | Non-metallic mineral products / Produits minéraux non métalliques | Basic metals / Métallurgie de base | Metal products[3] / Ouvrages en métaux[3] | Other manufacturing / Autres industries manufacturières |
|---|---|---|---|---|---|---|---|---|---|---|---|---|---|---|
| ISIC / CITI | 2–3 | 20–22 | 23 | 24 | 25–26 | 27 | 28 | 29 | 30 | 31–32 | 33 | 34 | 35–38 | 39 |
| **1939[4]** | | | | | | | | | | | | | | |
| Number of establishments | 173 802 | 44 472 | 6 388 | 21 801 | 19 020 | 3 328 | 24 878 | 2 205 | 595 | 10 141 | 6 678 | 3 512 | 22 395 | 8 389 |
| Value added | 24 487.3 | 3 852.8 | 1 818.0 | 1 766.3 | 1 196.8 | 888.4 | 1 765.3 | 224.3 | 406.2 | 2 515.5 | 856.3 | 2 168.9 | 6 176.2 | 852.3 |
| Number of engaged (Average during year) | 9 672 | 1 229 | 1 147 | 1 144 | 767 | 324 | 570 | 114 | 149 | 538 | 316 | 773 | 2 227 | 374 |
| Employees: Number (Average during year) | 9 561 | 1 199 | 1 145 | 1 127 | 753 | 323 | 552 | 112 | 149 | 534 | 312 | 772 | 2 215 | 368 |
| Wages and salaries | 12 706 | 1 530 | 1 093 | 1 111 | 734 | 444 | 977 | 134 | 227 | 859 | 414 | 1 206 | 3 495 | 482 |
| Operatives: Number (Average during year) | 7 808.0 | 893.4 | 1 081.7 | 988.2 | 627.7 | 270.2 | 324.4 | 99.6 | 120.7 | 387.0 | 267.1 | 672.4 | 1 788.0 | 287.6 |
| Wages and salaries | 8 997.5 | 968.6 | 906.5 | 858.4 | 559.2 | 316.5 | 493.3 | 103.3 | 161.4 | 522.8 | 309.6 | 978.4 | 2 524.7 | 294.8 |
| Electricity consumed | 70 868.8 | 6 568.2 | 6 804.6 | 522.0 | 1 879.4 | 9 393.5 | 859.2 | 244.1 | 1 584.4 | 13 221.0 | 4 851.6 | 18 191.6 | 6 366.6 | 382.6 |
| Capacity of installed power equipment (End of year) | 49 891 | 5 277 | 3 670 | 412 | 3 562 | 4 131 | 771 | 310 | 989 | 6 113 | 3 026 | 12 670 | 8 344 | 616 |
| **1947[8]** | | | | | | | | | | | | | | |
| Number of establishments | 240 807 | 41 054 | 8 157 | 33 144 | 34 467 | 4 100 | 28 978 | 3 467 | 872 | 11 548 | 11 643 | 5 364 | 42 291 | 15 722 |
| Value added | 74 290.5 | 9 689.6 | 5 322.9 | 5 315.9 | 3 970.8 | 2 913.2 | 4 248.8 | 715.4 | 1 299.5 | 7 331.5 | 2 298.5 | 5 733.0 | 22 463.7 | 2 987.7 |
| Number of engaged (Average during year) | 14 482 | 1 591 | 1 236 | 1 374 | 1 018 | 455 | 738 | 134 | 259 | 845 | 471 | 1 161 | 4 534 | 666 |
| Employees: Number (average during year) | 14 293 | 1 559 | 1 232 | 1 345 | 982 | 454 | 715 | 131 | 258 | 841 | 461 | 1 158 | 4 504 | 653 |
| Wages and salaries | 39 695.6 | 4 003.8 | 2 832.7 | 3 097.1 | 2 225.7 | 1 294.5 | 2 276.3 | 336.0 | 781.4 | 2 640.4 | 1 206.9 | 3 601.8 | 13 640.8 | 1 758.2 |
| Operatives: Number (Average during year) | 11 917.8 | 1 206.8 | 1 146.3 | 1 213.6 | 899.7 | 391.7 | 437.9 | 117.5 | 213.8 | 637.0 | 404.9 | 1 012.0 | 3 679.4 | 557.2 |
| Man-hours worked | 24 316.3 | 2 575.1 | 2 306.6 | 2 268.4 | 1 882.2 | 857.3 | 888.2 | 239.1 | 423.7 | 1 343.8 | 838.3 | 2 053.7 | 7 507.7 | 1 132.2 |
| Wages and salaries | 30 243.9 | 2 753.3 | 2 447.8 | 2 499.1 | 1 880.5 | 1 018.3 | 1 317.6 | 269.3 | 613.2 | 1 792.4 | 992.0 | 2 982.7 | 10 334.1 | 1 343.6 |
| Energy consumed | 323 530.1 | 23 619.2 | 9 803.3 | 1 283.3 | 6 290.3 | 20 058.3 | 1 119.7 | 1 092.0 | 3 538.8 | 55 363.3 | 29 242.8 | 145 223.7 | 25 062.7 | 1 832.7 |
| Electricity consumed | 140 947 | 10 485 | 10 041 | 1 093 | 3 244 | 15 386 | 1 280 | 352 | 3 445 | 26 057 | 7 898 | 40 645 | 19 513 | 1 508 |
| **1954[6]** | | | | | | | | | | | | | | |
| Number of establishments | 273 952 | 43 039 | 8 070 | 33 280 | 39 490 | 5 004 | 32 531 | 3 237 | 1 406 | 12 605 | 11 162 | 5 838 | 59 573 | 18 717 |
| Value added | 116 522.6 | 14 437.1 | 4 748.6 | 6 195.2 | 4 876.7 | 4 580.9 | 6 264.6 | 628.4 | 1 903.7 | 12 041.1 | 3 821.7 | 9 372.9 | 42 976.0 | 4 675.7 |
| Number of engaged (Average during year) | 15 760 | 1 777 | 1 040 | 1 458 | 966 | 532 | 829 | 121 | 247 | 967 | 500 | 1 119 | 5 483 | 721 |
| Employees: Number (Average during year) | 15 575 | 1 746 | 1 037 | 1 433 | 930 | 530 | 804 | 120 | 246 | 963 | 492 | 1 117 | 5 448 | 709 |
| Wages and salaries | 62 782.7 | 6 477.6 | 3 032.5 | 3 862.5 | 2 987.6 | 2 217.4 | 3 625.1 | 392.4 | 1 059.3 | 4 530.7 | 1 938.1 | 5 097.5 | 24 844.2 | 2 717.8 |
| Operatives: Number (Average during year) | 12 304.7 | 1 228.6 | 947.5 | 1 291.5 | 815.5 | 435.7 | 499.7 | 105.4 | 196.2 | 671.5 | 412.0 | 938.5 | 4 207.6 | 555.0 |
| Man-hours worked | 24 225.6 | 2 486.9 | 1 821.1 | 2 292.8 | 1 592.7 | 919.9 | 961.5 | 203.0 | 377.4 | 1 351.1 | 827.0 | 1 812.0 | 8 490.6 | 1 089.6 |
| Wages and salaries | 44 413.1 | 3 991.5 | 2 526.6 | 3 066.6 | 2 361.7 | 1 656.7 | 2 115.3 | 308.3 | 775.5 | 2 799.0 | 1 496.0 | 3 985.5 | 17 500.5 | 1 829.9 |
| Energy consumed | 374 073.7 | 29 125.7 | 9 323.7 | 1 093.0 | 5 091.8 | 25 695.7 | 1 424.1 | 815.7 | 3 346.6 | 76 085.5 | 32 442.4 | 157 413.5 | 29 699.4 | 2 516.6 |
| Electricity consumed | 247 623 | 14 478 | 12 322 | 1 209 | 5 511 | 23 539 | 1 685 | 433 | 3 749 | 71 602 | 11 573 | 65 932 | 32 757 | 2 833 |
| Capacity of installed power equipment (End of year) | 107 645[5] | 7 899 | 4 595 | ... | 5 616 | 8 256 | 975 | 338 | 1 848 | 21 689 | 4 811 | 24 482 | 25 109 | 2 027 |
| **1954[7]** | | | | | | | | | | | | | | |
| Number of establishments | 273 949 | 42 002 | 8 054 | 33 120 | 39 455 | 5 004 | 32 530 | 3 397 | 1 406 | 13 443 | 11 162 | 6 170 | 59 671 | 18 535 |
| Value added | 116 639.4 | 14 397.1 | 4 606.0 | 6 191.2 | 4 941.7 | 4 630.2 | 6 403.1 | 653.7 | 1 954.4 | 12 214.3 | 3 866.2 | 9 899.1 | 42 437.8 | 4 444.6 |
| Number of engaged (Average during year) | 15 753.9 | 1 734.2 | 1 030.9 | 1 454.2 | 963.6 | 529.1 | 827.8 | 124.9 | 247.1 | 968.7 | 499.6 | 1 171.8 | 5 502.7 | 699.3 |
| **1958** | | | | | | | | | | | | | | |
| Number of establishments | 285 377 | 41 039 | 7 675 | 30 878 | 35 736 | 5 271 | 35 368 | 3 213 | 1 240 | 14 110 | 15 022 | 6 446 | 69 588 | 19 791 |
| Value added | 140 883.1 | 18 549.2 | 4 857.6 | 7 192.4 | 5 267.6 | 5 707.5 | 7 923.0 | 749.7 | 2 347.7 | 15 245.1 | 5 529.0 | 11 671.3 | 49 487.5 | 6 355.5 |
| Number of engaged (Average during year) | 15 493.2 | 1 777.4 | 904.3 | 1 435.9 | 905.2 | 556.8 | 889.0 | 120.5 | 231.9 | 923.1 | 562.7 | 1 098.6 | 5 323.6 | 764.2 |
| Employees: Number (Average during year) | 15 322.4 | 1 750.2 | 901.7 | 1 416.5 | 874.8 | 555.4 | 864.1 | 118.7 | 231.5 | 919.2 | 554.0 | 1 096.4 | 5 286.9 | 753.0 |
| Wages and salaries | 73 522.9 | 7 694.4 | 2 938.1 | 4 311.2 | 3 221.8 | 2 779.9 | 4 479.7 | 446.4 | 1 212.1 | 5 247.7 | 2 595.0 | 6 303.4 | 28 826.7 | 3 466.5 |
| Operatives: Number (Average during year) | 11 581.9 | 1 189.2 | 810.5 | 1 244.4 | 744.4 | 448.5 | 529.5 | 102.3 | 178.5 | 614.9 | 445.9 | 886.6 | 3 817.6 | 569.6 |
| Man-hours worked | 22 523.9 | 2 374.6 | 1 568.0 | 2 217.2 | 1 444.4 | 934.4 | 995.9 | 194.0 | 347.7 | 1 231.5 | 883.8 | 1 676.9 | 7 544.2 | 1 111.3 |
| Wages and salaries | 49 309.1 | 4 269.2 | 2 408.3 | 3 361.3 | 2 502.7 | 2 039.0 | 2 115.3 | 342.0 | 862.5 | 1 933.9 | 1 127.5 | 1 933.9 | 18 547.0 | 2 233.1 |
| Energy consumed | 403 287.9 | 29 110.7 | 9 072.5 | 1 552.2 | 4 794.9 | 30 061.5 | 1 867.3 | 1 026.4 | 3 838.9 | 86 351.3 | 35 135.7 | 165 933.4 | 31 059.8 | 3 483.3 |
| Electricity consumed | 318 001 | 16 691 | 12 828 | 2 100 | 5 823 | 29 274 | 3 014 | 611 | 4 120 | 116 369 | 14 357 | 70 528 | 38 168 | 4 118 |

For foot notes see end of table.

## B.  The Major Groups of Manufacturing (continued) — Les classes de la branche Industries manufacturières (suite)

| Year and item of data | Manufacturing[1]<br>Industries manufacturières[1] | Food, beverages and tobacco[2]<br>Industries alimentaires, boissons, tabac[2] | Textiles | Clothing, footwear and made-up textiles<br>Articles d'habillement, chaussures et ouvrages en tissu | Wood products and furniture<br>Bois et meubles | Paper and paper products<br>Papier et ouvrages en papier | Printing and publishing<br>Imprimerie et édition | Leather and leather products except wearing apparel<br>Cuir et articles en cuir, à l'exclusion des articles d'habillement | Rubber products<br>Ouvrages en caoutchouc | Chemicals and chemical, petroleum and coal products<br>Produits chimiques et dérivés du pétrole et du charbon | Non-metallic mineral products<br>Produits minéraux non métalliques | Basic metals<br>Métallurgie de base | Metal products[3]<br>Ouvrages en métaux[3] | Other manufacturing<br>Autres industries manufacturières | Année et rubrique |
|---|---|---|---|---|---|---|---|---|---|---|---|---|---|---|---|
| ISIC | 2–3 | 20–22 | 23 | 24 | 25–26 | 27 | 28 | 29 | 30 | 31–32 | 33 | 34 | 35–38 | 39 | CITI |
| | | | | | | | | *b.  Structure* | | | | | | | |
| **1939 [4]** | | | | | | | | | | | | | | | **1939 [4]** |
| Distribution in percent of: | | | | | | | | | | | | | | | Distribution en pourcentage: |
| Value added | 100.0 | 15.7 | 7.4 | 7.2 | 4.9 | 3.6 | 7.2 | 1.0 | 1.6 | 10.3 | 3.5 | 8.8 | 25.3 | 3.5 | Valeur ajoutée |
| Number of engaged | 100.0 | 12.7 | 11.8 | 11.8 | 8.0 | 3.3 | 5.9 | 1.2 | 1.5 | 5.6 | 3.3 | 8.0 | 23.0 | 3.9 | Nombre de personnes occupées |
| Per person engaged: | | | | | | | | | | | | | | | Par personne occupée: |
| Value added | 2.5 | 3.1 | 1.6 | 1.5 | 1.6 | 2.7 | 3.1 | 2.0 | 2.7 | 4.7 | 2.7 | 2.8 | 2.8 | 2.3 | Valeur ajoutée |
| Electricity consumed | 7.3 | 5.3 | 5.9 | 0.4 | 2.4 | 29.0 | 1.5 | 2.1 | 10.6 | 24.6 | 15.4 | 23.5 | 2.8 | 1.0 | Électricité consommée |
| Capacity of installed power equipment | 5.16 | 4.29 | 3.20 | 0.36 | 4.64 | 12.75 | 1.35 | 2.72 | 6.64 | 11.36 | 9.58 | 16.39 | 3.75 | 1.65 | Puissance installée |
| Employees as a percent of engaged | 98.8 | 97.6 | 99.8 | 98.5 | 98.2 | 99.7 | 96.8 | 98.2 | 100.0 | 99.2 | 98.7 | 99.9 | 99.5 | 98.4 | Salariés en pourcentage des personnes occupées |
| Value added per unit of wages and salaries | 1.93 | 2.52 | 1.66 | 1.59 | 1.63 | 2.00 | 1.81 | 1.67 | 1.79 | 2.93 | 2.07 | 1.80 | 1.77 | 1.77 | Valeur ajoutée par unité de traitements et salaires |
| Wages and salaries per employee | 1.3 | 1.3 | 1.0 | 1.0 | 1.0 | 1.4 | 1.8 | 1.2 | 1.5 | 1.6 | 1.3 | 1.6 | 1.6 | 1.3 | Traitements et salaires par salarié |
| Operatives as a percent of employees | 81.7 | 74.5 | 94.5 | 87.7 | 83.4 | 83.6 | 58.8 | 88.9 | 81.0 | 72.5 | 85.6 | 87.1 | 80.7 | 78.2 | Ouvriers en pourcentage des salariés |
| **1947 [8]** | | | | | | | | | | | | | | | **1947 [8]** |
| Distribution in percent of: | | | | | | | | | | | | | | | Distribution en pourcentage: |
| Value added | 100.0 | 13.0 | 7.2 | 7.1 | 5.4 | 3.9 | 5.7 | 1.0 | 1.7 | 9.9 | 3.1 | 7.7 | 30.2 | 4.1 | Valeur ajoutée |
| Number of engaged | 100.0 | 10.9 | 8.6 | 9.5 | 7.0 | 3.1 | 5.1 | 1.0 | 1.7 | 5.9 | 3.2 | 8.0 | 31.4 | 4.6 | Nombre de personnes occupées |
| Per person engaged: | | | | | | | | | | | | | | | Par personne occupée: |
| Value added | 5.1 | 6.1 | 4.3 | 3.9 | 3.9 | 6.4 | 5.8 | 5.3 | 5.0 | 8.7 | 4.9 | 4.9 | 5.0 | 4.5 | Valeur ajoutée |
| Energy consumed | 22.34 | 14.84 | 7.93 | 0.93 | 6.18 | 44.08 | 1.52 | 8.15 | 13.66 | 65.52 | 62.09 | 125.08 | 5.53 | 2.75 | Énergie consommée |
| Electricity consumed | 9.7 | 6.6 | 8.1 | 0.8 | 3.2 | 33.8 | 1.7 | 2.6 | 13.3 | 30.8 | 16.8 | 35.0 | 4.3 | 2.3 | Électricité consommée |
| Employees as a percent of engaged | 98.7 | 98.0 | 99.7 | 97.9 | 96.5 | 99.8 | 96.9 | 97.8 | 99.6 | 99.5 | 97.9 | 99.7 | 99.3 | 98.0 | Salariés en pourcentage des personnes occupées |
| Value added per unit of wages and salaries | 1.87 | 2.42 | 1.88 | 1.72 | 1.78 | 2.25 | 1.87 | 2.13 | 1.66 | 2.78 | 1.90 | 1.59 | 1.65 | 1.70 | Valeur ajoutée par unité de traitements et salaires |
| Wages and salaries per employee | 2.8 | 2.6 | 2.3 | 2.3 | 2.3 | 2.8 | 3.2 | 2.6 | 3.0 | 3.1 | 2.6 | 3.1 | 3.0 | 2.7 | Traitements et salaires par salarié |
| Operatives as a percent of employees | 83.4 | 77.4 | 93.0 | 90.2 | 91.6 | 86.3 | 61.2 | 89.7 | 82.9 | 75.7 | 87.8 | 87.4 | 81.7 | 85.3 | Ouvriers en pourcentage des salariés |
| Average man-hours per operative | 2.04 | 2.13 | 2.01 | 1.87 | 2.09 | 2.19 | 2.03 | 2.03 | 1.98 | 2.11 | 2.07 | 2.03 | 2.04 | 2.03 | Heures de travail: moyenne par ouvrier |
| Per thousand operative man-hour: | | | | | | | | | | | | | | | Par millier d'heures-ouvrier: |
| Wages and salaries | 1.24 | 1.07 | 1.06 | 1.10 | 1.00 | 1.19 | 1.48 | 1.13 | 1.45 | 1.33 | 1.18 | 1.45 | 1.38 | 1.19 | Traitements et salaires |
| Energy consumed | 13.30 | 9.17 | 4.25 | 0.56 | 3.34 | 23.40 | 1.26 | 4.57 | 8.35 | 41.20 | 34.88 | 70.71 | 3.34 | 1.62 | Énergie consommée |
| Electricity consumed | 5.80 | 4.07 | 4.35 | 0.48 | 1.72 | 17.95 | 1.44 | 1.47 | 8.13 | 19.39 | 9.42 | 19.79 | 2.60 | 1.33 | Électricité consommée |
| **1954 [6]** | | | | | | | | | | | | | | | **1954 [6]** |
| Distribution in percent of: | | | | | | | | | | | | | | | Distribution en pourcentage: |
| Value added | 100.0 | 12.3 | 4.1 | 5.3 | 4.2 | 3.9 | 5.4 | 0.6 | 1.6 | 10.3 | 3.3 | 8.1 | 36.8 | 4.1 | Valeur ajoutée |
| Number of engaged | 100.0 | 11.2 | 6.6 | 9.3 | 6.1 | 3.4 | 5.2 | 0.8 | 1.6 | 6.1 | 3.2 | 7.1 | 34.8 | 4.6 | Nombre de personnes occupées |
| Per person engaged: | | | | | | | | | | | | | | | Par personne occupée: |
| Value added | 7.4 | 8.1 | 4.6 | 4.2 | 5.0 | 8.6 | 7.6 | 5.2 | 7.7 | 12.5 | 7.6 | 8.4 | 7.8 | 6.5 | Valeur ajoutée |
| Energy consumed | 23.74 | 16.39 | 8.96 | 0.75 | 5.27 | 48.30 | 1.72 | 6.74 | 13.55 | 78.68 | 64.88 | 140.67 | 5.42 | 2.75 | Énergie consommée |
| Electricity consumed | 15.7 | 8.1 | 11.8 | 0.8 | 5.7 | 44.2 | 2.0 | 3.6 | 15.2 | 74.0 | 23.1 | 58.9 | 6.0 | 3.49 | Électricité consommée |
| Capacity of installed power equipment | 7.53[5] | 4.44 | 4.42 | ... | 5.81 | 15.52 | 1.18 | 2.79 | 7.48 | 22.43 | 9.62 | 21.88 | 4.58 | 2.81 | Puissance installée |
| Employees as a percent of engaged | 98.8 | 98.2 | 99.7 | 98.3 | 96.3 | 99.6 | 97.0 | 99.2 | 99.6 | 99.6 | 98.4 | 99.8 | 99.4 | 98.3 | Salariés en pourcentage des personnes occupées |
| Value added per unit of wages and salaries | 1.86 | 2.23 | 1.57 | 1.60 | 1.63 | 2.07 | 1.73 | 1.60 | 1.80 | 2.66 | 1.97 | 1.84 | 1.73 | 1.72 | Valeur ajoutée par unité de traitements et salaires |
| Wages and salaries per employee | 4.0 | 3.7 | 2.9 | 2.7 | 3.2 | 4.2 | 4.5 | 3.3 | 4.3 | 4.7 | 3.9 | 4.6 | 4.6 | 3.8 | Traitements et salaires par salarié |
| Operatives as a percent of employees | 79.0 | 70.4 | 91.4 | 90.1 | 87.7 | 82.2 | 62.2 | 87.8 | 79.8 | 69.7 | 83.7 | 84.0 | 77.2 | 78.3 | Ouvriers en pourcentage des salariés |
| Average man-hours per operative | 1.97 | 2.02 | 1.92 | 1.78 | 1.95 | 2.11 | 1.92 | 1.92 | 1.92 | 2.01 | 2.01 | 1.93 | 2.02 | 1.96 | Heures de travail: moyenne par ouvrier |
| Per thousand operative man-hour: | | | | | | | | | | | | | | | Par millier d'heures-ouvrier: |
| Wages and salaries | 1.83 | 1.60 | 1.39 | 1.34 | 1.48 | 1.80 | 2.20 | 1.52 | 2.05 | 2.07 | 1.81 | 2.20 | 2.06 | 1.68 | Traitements et salaires |
| Energy consumed | 15.44 | 11.71 | 5.12 | 0.48 | 3.20 | 27.93 | 1.48 | 4.02 | 8.87 | 56.31 | 39.23 | 86.87 | 3.50 | 2.31 | Énergie consommée |
| Electricity consumed | 10.22 | 5.82 | 6.77 | 0.53 | 3.46 | 25.59 | 1.75 | 2.13 | 9.93 | 53.00 | 13.99 | 36.39 | 3.86 | 2.60 | Électricité consommée |
| Capacity of installed power equipment | 4.91[5] | 3.18 | 2.52 | ... | 3.53 | 8.97 | 1.01 | 1.66 | 4.90 | 16.05 | 5.82 | 13.51 | 2.96 | 1.86 | Puissance installée |

For footnotes see end of table.  Pour les notes, voir au bas du tableau.

## B. The Major Groups of Manufacturing (continued) — Les classes de la branche Industries manufacturières (suite)

| Year and item of data | Manu-facturing [1] / Industries manufac-turières [1] | Food beverages and tobacco [2] / Industries alimen-taires, boissons, tabac [2] | Textiles | Clothing, footwear and made-up textiles / Articles d'habil-lement, chaussures et ouvrages en tissu | Wood products and furniture / Bois et meubles | Paper and paper products / Papier et ouvrages en papier | Printing and publish-ing / Im-primerie et édition | Leather and leather products except wearing apparel / Cuir et articles en cuir, à l'exclu-sion des articles d'habil-lement | Rubber products / Ouvrages en caout-chouc | Chemicals and chemical, petroleum and coal products / Produits chi-miques et dérivés du pétrole et du charbon | Non-metallic mineral products / Produits minéraux non métal-liques | Basic metals / Métal-lurgie de base | Metal products [3] / Ouvrages en métaux [3] | Other manu-factur-ing / Autres in-dustries manufac-turières | Année et rubrique |
|---|---|---|---|---|---|---|---|---|---|---|---|---|---|---|---|
| ISIC | 2–3 | 20–22 | 23 | 24 | 25–26 | 27 | 28 | 29 | 30 | 31–32 | 33 | 34 | 35–38 | 39 | CITI |

b. Structure

| | | | | | | | | | | | | | | | |
|---|---|---|---|---|---|---|---|---|---|---|---|---|---|---|---|
| **1954 [7]** Distribution in percent of: | | | | | | | | | | | | | | | **1954 [7]** Distribution en pour-centage: |
| Value added........ | 100.0 | 12.3 | 3.9 | 5.4 | 4.2 | 4.0 | 5.4 | 0.6 | 1.7 | 10.5 | 3.3 | 8.5 | 36.3 | 3.9 | Valeur ajoutée |
| Number of engaged... | 100.0 | 11.0 | 6.5 | 9.2 | 6.1 | 3.4 | 5.3 | 0.8 | 1.5 | 6.2 | 3.1 | 7.5 | 34.9 | 4.5 | Nombre de personnes occupées |
| **1958** Distribution in percent of: | | | | | | | | | | | | | | | **1958** Distribution en pour-centage: |
| Value added........ | 100.0 | 13.1 | 3.5 | 5.1 | 3.7 | 4.1 | 5.6 | 0.5 | 1.7 | 10.8 | 3.9 | 8.3 | 35.1 | 4.6 | Valeur ajoutée |
| Number of engaged... | 100.0 | 11.4 | 5.9 | 9.2 | 5.9 | 3.6 | 5.7 | 0.8 | 1.5 | 5.9 | 3.7 | 7.1 | 34.3 | 5.0 | Nombre de personnes occupées |
| Per person engaged: | | | | | | | | | | | | | | | Par personne occupée: |
| Value added..... | 9.1 | 10.4 | 5.4 | 5.0 | 5.8 | 10.2 | 8.9 | 6.2 | 10.1 | 16.5 | 9.8 | 10.6 | 9.3 | 8.3 | Valeur ajoutée |
| Energy consumed..... | 26.03 | 16.38 | 10.03 | 1.08 | 5.30 | 53.99 | 2.10 | 8.52 | 16.55 | 93.54 | 62.44 | 151.05 | 5.83 | 4.56 | Energie consommée |
| Electricity consumed... | 20.5 | 9.4 | 14.2 | 1.5 | 6.4 | 52.6 | 3.4 | 5.1 | 17.8 | 126.1 | 25.5 | 64.2 | 7.2 | 5.4 | Electricité consommée |
| Employees as a percent of engaged... | 98.9 | 98.5 | 99.7 | 98.6 | 96.6 | 99.7 | 97.2 | 98.5 | 99.8 | 99.6 | 98.4 | 99.8 | 99.3 | 98.5 | Salariés en pourcentage des personnes occupées |
| Value added per unit of wages and salaries............ | 1.92 | 2.41 | 1.65 | 1.67 | 1.63 | 2.05 | 1.77 | 1.68 | 1.94 | 2.90 | 2.13 | 1.85 | 1.72 | 1.83 | Valeur ajoutée par unité de traitements et salaires |
| Wages and salaries per employee........ | 4.8 | 4.4 | 3.2 | 3.0 | 3.7 | 5.0 | 5.2 | 3.8 | 5.2 | 5.7 | 4.7 | 5.7 | 5.4 | 4.6 | Traitements et salaires par salarié |
| Operatives as a percent of employees........ | 75.6 | 67.9 | 89.9 | 87.8 | 85.1 | 80.8 | 61.3 | 86.2 | 77.1 | 66.9 | 80.5 | 80.9 | 72.2 | 75.6 | Ouvriers en pourcentage des salariés |
| Average man-hours per operative........ | 1.94 | 2.00 | 1.93 | 1.78 | 1.94 | 2.08 | 1.88 | 1.90 | 1.95 | 2.00 | 1.98 | 1.89 | 1.98 | 1.95 | Heures de travail: moyenne par ouvrier |
| Per thousand operative man-hour: | | | | | | | | | | | | | | | Par millier d'heures-ouvrier: |
| Wages and salaries... | 2.19 | 1.96 | 1.54 | 1.52 | 1.73 | 2.18 | 2.60 | 1.76 | 2.48 | 2.54 | 2.19 | 2.81 | 2.46 | 2.01 | Traitements et salaires |
| Energy consumed..... | 17.90 | 12.26 | 5.79 | 0.70 | 3.32 | 32.17 | 1.87 | 5.29 | 11.04 | 70.12 | 39.76 | 98.95 | 4.12 | 3.13 | Energie consommée |
| Electricity consumed... | 14.12 | 7.03 | 8.18 | 0.95 | 4.03 | 31.33 | 3.03 | 3.15 | 11.85 | 94.49 | 16.24 | 42.06 | 5.06 | 3.70 | Electricité consommée |

[1] Does not include establishments primarily engaged in manufacturing which sell most of their products on the premises at retail (e.g., single shop bakeries), which do custom work to the order of households (e.g., custom tailoring), or which primarily perform repair and related services (including machine shops engaged exclusively or almost so in these activities) except specified services "for the trade". On the other hand, jobbers of textiles, apparel and leather products who contracted out all manufacturing activities and therefore are considered to be wholesalers in the ISIC were included in manufacturing.

[2] The pasteurization and related processing of fluid milk is excluded from the figures for 1939 and 1947 but included in the figures for 1954 and 1958. Coffee and spice roasting and grinding, tobacco stemming and drying are excluded from the figures for 1939 but included in the figures for 1947, 1954 and 1958.

[3] The manufacture of ordnance is excluded from the data for 1939 and 1947 but included in the data for 1954 and 1958.

[4] The data for each major group of manufacturing on number of establishments and value added, employment and capacity of installed power equipment are not exactly comparable. However the incomparabilities between the figures for these different items of data are not significant.

[5] Excludes the capacity of installed power equipment in Clothing, footwear and made-up textiles (ISIC major group 24).

[6] Denotes data for 1954 most comparable with that for earlier years.

[7] Denotes data for 1954 most comparable with that for 1958.

[8] Due to the omission of very small establishments from the figures of energy and electricity consumed, these figures are not exactly comparable to those on other items of data for 1947 or to the figures of energy and electricity consumed for other years. For more details and the magnitude of omission, see the footnotes to Table 5 B.

[1] Non compris les établissements dont l'activité principale relève des industries manufacturières, et qui vendent la majeure partie de leur production au détail dans leurs propres locaux (par exemple, les boulangeries sans succursales), qui travaillent à façon pour les ménages (par exemple, les tailleurs sur mesures), ou encore qui font principalement des réparations ou fournissent des services connexes (y compris les ateliers de mécanique dont l'activité exclusive ou principale relève des mêmes domaines), à l'exclusion des services expressément "réservés aux professionnels". En revanche, dans le cas des textiles, du vêtement et des articles en cuir, les "jobbers" qui confiaient à des sous-traitants la totalité des travaux de fabrication, et qui sont donc considérés comme des grossistes dans la CITI, ont été recensés dans les industries manufacturières.

[2] La pasteurisation du lait et les opérations annexes ne sont pas comprises dans les chiffres de 1939 et de 1947, mais comprises dans ceux de 1954 et 1958. La torréfaction du café, la mouture des épices et l'écotage et la dessication du tabac ne sont pas compris dans les chiffres de 1939 mais compris dans ceux de 1947, de 1954 et de 1958.

[3] L'armurerie n'est pas comprise dans les chiffres de 1939 et de 1947, mais comprise dans ceux de 1954 et de 1958.

[4] Les chiffres indiqués pour les diverses classes des industries manufacturières en ce qui concerne le nombre d'établissements et la valeur ajoutée, l'emploi et la puissance installée ne sont pas exactement comparables. Cependant, les défauts de comparabilité qui existent n'ont guère d'importance.

[5] Non compris la puissance installée dans Articles d'habillement, chaussures et ouvrages en tissu (CITI 24).

[6] Données pour 1954 plus comparables avec celles des années précédentes.

[7] Données pour 1954 plus comparables avec celles de 1958.

[8] Etant donné que les très petits établissements ne sont pas compris dans les chiffres relatifs à l'énergie et à l'électricité consommées, ces chiffres ne sont pas tout à fait comparables aux chiffres de 1947 indiqués sous les autres rubriques ou aux chiffres de l'énergie et l'électricité consommées au cours des autres années. Des renseignements plus détaillés, ainsi que l'ordre de grandeur des chiffres omis, sont donnés dans les notes du tableau 5 B.

## 5. QUANTITY AND VALUE OF PURCHASED FUELS CONSUMED AND ELECTRICITY PURCHASED, PRODUCED AND SOLD; MINING AND MANUFACTURING ESTABLISHMENTS
## CONSOMMATION DE COMBUSTIBLES ACHETES ET ELECTRICITE ACHETEE; PRODUITE ET VENDUE; QUANTITES ET VALEUR; ETABLISSEMENTS MINIERS ET MANUFACTURIERS

Coal and refined oil fuels in thousand metric tons; gas in million cubic metres; electricity in million KWH; other fuels in thousand metric tons of coal equivalents; values in thousand Dollars

Charbon et pétrole raffiné en milliers de tonnes métriques; gaz en millions de mètres cubes; électricité en millions de kWh; autres combustibles en milliers de tonnes métriques d'équivalent charbon; valeur en milliers de dollars

### A. The Major Groups of Mining
### Les classes de la branche Industries extractives
### 1939, 1954, 1958

Establishments for which the Gross Value of Production, Principal Expenses and Capital Expenditures each equal $2,500 or more in the case of 1939 [1] or $500 or more in the case of 1954 or 1958 [2]

Etablissements pour lesquels le chiffre de la valeur brute de la production, celui des dépenses directes de production et celui des dépenses d'équipement atteignaient chacun 2.500 dollars ou plus en 1939 [1], ou 500 dollars ou plus en 1958 [2]

| Year and source of energy | Total | Coal mining [3] Extraction du charbon [3] | Metal mining Extraction des minerais métalliques | Crude petroleum and natural gas [3] Pétrole brut et gaz naturel [3] | Other mining [4] Divers [4] | Année et source d'énergie |
|---|---|---|---|---|---|---|
| ISIC | 1 | 11 | 12 | 13 | 14–19 | CITI |
| **1939** | | | | | | **1939** |
| Coal — quantity | 6 519.0 | 4 636.6 | 877.2 | 23.6 | 981.6 | Charbon — quantité |
| Refined oil fuels — quantity | 884.7 | 36.0 | 160.4 | 339.3 | 349.0 | Pétrole raffiné — quantité |
| Natural gas — quantity | 13 848.4 | 2.9 | 248.7 | 13 091.8 | 505.0 | Gaz naturel — quantité |
| Electricity: | | | | | | Electricité: |
| Purchased — quantity | 6 329 | 2 549 | 2 306 | 652 | 822 | Achetée — quantité |
| Produced — quantity | 2 195 | 1 072 | 649 | 190 | 284 | Produite — quantité |
| Sold — quantity | 125 | 82 | 33 | 4 | 6 | Vendue — quantité |
| **1954** | | | | | | **1954** |
| Coal: | | | | | | Charbon: |
| Quantity | 2 578.2 | 1 429.7 | 672.2 | 6.4 | 469.9 | Quantité |
| Value | ... | ... | 6 052 | 52 | 3 541 | Valeur |
| Refined oil fuels: | | | | | | Pétrole raffiné: |
| Quantity | 2 353.6 | 355.0 | 291.4 | 664.8 | 1 042.4 | Quantité |
| Value | ... | 12 267 | 10 641 | ... | 26 081 | Valeur |
| Natural gas: | | | | | | Gaz naturel: |
| Quantity | 26 383.1 | 14.4 | 704.8 | 23 854.9 | 1 809.0 | Quantité |
| Value | ... | 125 | 5 478 | ... | 9 903 | Valeur |
| Electricity: | | | | | | Electricité: |
| Purchased: | | | | | | Achetée: |
| Quantity | 13 250 | 4 359 | 3 184 | 2 748 | 2 959 | Quantité |
| Value | 160 855 | 56 589 | 32 662 | 35 017 | 36 587 | Valeur |
| Produced — quantity | 4 493 | 582 | 2 029 | 1 349 | 533 | Produite — quantité |
| Sold: | | | | | | Vendue: |
| Quantity | 891 | 341 | 502 | 35 | 13 | Quantité |
| Value | 8 652 | 4 020 | 4 095 | 357 | 180 | Valeur |
| Other and unspecified fuels [5]: | | | | | | Autres combustibles et combustibles non spécifiés [5]: |
| Quantity | 2 816.6 | 225.8 | 140.8 | 1 803.3 | 646.7 | Quantité |
| Value | 95 347 | 7 643 | 4 765 | 61 047 | 21 892 | Valeur |
| **1958** | | | | | | **1958** |
| Coal: | | | | | | Charbon: |
| Quantity | 2 149.1 | 773.8 | 954.4 | — | 420.9 | Quantité |
| Value | ... | ... | 9 358 | — | 3 473 | Valeur |
| Refined oil fuels: | | | | | | Pétrole raffiné: |
| Quantity | 2 158.9 | 308.0 | 374.1 | 822.7 | 654.1 | Quantité |
| Value | ... | 12 178 | 11 994 | ... | 18 405 | Valeur |
| Natural gas: | | | | | | Gaz naturel: |
| Quantity | 28 227.1 | 15.1 | 803.9 | 25 322.5 | 2 085.6 | Quantité |
| Value | ... | 212 | 7 829 | ... | 15 262 | Valeur |
| Electricity: | | | | | | Electricité: |
| Purchased: | | | | | | Achetée: |
| Quantity | 16 393 | 4 916 | 3 876 | 4 275 | 3 326 | Quantité |
| Value | 201 055 | 64 001 | 37 230 | 53 333 | 46 491 | Valeur |
| Produced — quantity | 5 139 | ... | 2 751 | 1 603 | ... | Produite — quantité |
| Sold — quantity | 810 | ... | 559 | 49 | ... | Vendue — quantité |
| Other and unspecified fuels [5]: | | | | | | Autres combustibles et combustibles non spécifiés [5]: |
| Quantity | 4 188.4 | 403.0 | 246.8 | 2 373.7 | 1 164.9 | Quantité |
| Value | 149 452 | 14 380 | 8 805 | 84 700 | 41 567 | Valeur |

[1] In 1939, in the case of the mining of bituminous coal and lignite, 1,000 tons was substituted for $2,500 as the minimum for production and in the case of quarrying of sand and gravel, establishments extracting less than 15,000 tons and making capital expenditures of less than $15,000 during the year were not covered.

[2] In 1954 and 1958, gross value of products shipped and services rendered was utilized as a criterion in place of gross value of production. An additional criterion for coverage in the case of 1958 was having at least one employee at anytime during the year.

[3] In the case of Coal mining (ISIC major group 11) and Crude petroleum and natural gas (ISIC major group 13), coal and crude petroleum and natural gas, respectively, extracted and used as a source of heat and power are included in the data.

[4] Included in the data for 1939 but not for 1954 or 1958 are dimension, crushed and broken stone, clay and gypsum mines operated as part of manufacturing establishments.

[5] Includes types of fuels other than those listed in the case of units required to report quantities and costs for individual fuels and all types of fuels in the case of the smaller units not required to report quantities and costs for individual fuels. In the 1954 census many more small units were required to furnish data on individual fuels than in the 1958 Census.

[1] En 1939, la production minimum prise comme critère pour l'extraction du charbon bitumineux et du lignite a été de 1.000 tonnes au lieu de 2.500 dollars; pour l'extraction du sable et du gravier, on a exclu les établissements ayant extrait moins de 15.000 tonnes et effectué des dépenses d'équipement inférieures à 15.000 dollars pendant l'année.

[2] En 1954 et 1958, on a pris comme critère la valeur brute des produits expédiés et des services fournis au lieu de la valeur brute de la production. En 1958, les établissements devaient en outre avoir occupé un salarié au moins à un moment quelconque de l'année.

[3] Dans le cas de l'extraction du charbon (CITI 11) ainsi que du pétrole brut et du gaz naturel (CITI 13), les données comprennent, d'une part, la charbon et, d'autre part, le pétrole brut et le gaz naturel extraits et utilisés comme source de chaleur et d'énergie.

[4] L'extraction de pierre de taille et de pierre à bâtir, d'argile et de gypse, effectuée per des établissements classés dans les industries manufacturières est comprise dans les données de 1939, mais non dans celles de 1954 et de 1958.

[5] Cette rubrique comprend, d'une part, les types de combustibles autres que ceux qui étaient indiqués dans le cas des unités tenues de préciser la quantité et le coût de chaque combustible séparément et, d'autre part, tous les types de combustibles dans le cas des unités plus petites qui n'étaient pas tenues de donner des renseignements distincts pour chaque combustible. Lors du recensement de 1954, on a demandé à un nombre beaucoup plus grand de petites unités de fournir des données distinctes sur chaque combustible que lors du recensement de 1958.

## B. The Major Groups of Manufacturing — Les classes de la branche Industries manufacturières
### 1939, 1947, 1954, 1958

Establishments with Gross Value of Production of $5,000 or More in 1939, or with One or More Employees in 1947, 1954 or 1958.

Etablissements dont la production avait une valeur brute de 5.000 dollars ou plus en 1939, et établissements qui comptaient au moins un salarié en 1947, 1954 ou 1958.

| Year and source of energy | Manufacturing / Industries manufacturières | Food, beverages and tobacco / Industries alimentaires, boissons, tabac | Textiles | Clothing, footwear and made-up textiles / Articles d'habillement, chaussures et ouvrages en tissu | Wood products and furniture / Bois et meubles | Paper and paper products / Papier et ouvrages en papier | Printing and publishing / Imprimerie et édition | Leather and leather products except wearing apparel / Cuir et articles en cuir, à l'exclusion des articles d'habillement | Rubber products / Ouvrages en caoutchouc | Chemicals and chemical, petroleum and coal products [4] / Produits chimiques et dérivés du pétrole et du charbon [4] | Non-metallic mineral products / Produits minéraux non métalliques | Basic metals [5] / Métallurgie de base [5] | Metal products / Ouvrages en métaux | Other manufacturing / Autres industries manufacturières | Année et source d'énergie |
|---|---|---|---|---|---|---|---|---|---|---|---|---|---|---|---|
| ISIC | 2–3 | 20–22 | 23 | 24 | 25–26 | 27 | 28 | 29 | 30 | 31–32 | 33 | 34 | 35–38 | 39 | CITI |
| **1947** [1] | | | | | | | | | | | | | | | **1947** [1] |
| Coal: | | | | | | | | | | | | | | | Charbon: |
| Quantity | 100 578.1 | 13 003.5 | 5 998.3 | 789.2 | 1 811.6 | 13 494.3 | 336.6 | 892.7 | 2 578.2 | 19 142.4 | 15 408.5 | 14 214.6 | 11 945.7 | 962.5 | Quantité |
| Value | 692 827 | 88 183 | 51 205 | 6 506 | 13 124 | 106 446 | 2 825 | 7 325 | 15 830 | 123 962 | 99 424 | 85 723 | 84 486 | 7 788 | Valeur |
| Coke: | | | | | | | | | | | | | | | Coke: |
| Quantity | 60 029.0 | 176.9 | 16.3 | 6.4 | 6.4 | 10.9 | 3.6 | 0.9 | 2.7 | 1 955.0 | 335.6 | 56 061.0 | 1 440.6 | 12.7 | Quantité |
| Value | 729 399 | 2 722 | 246 | 69 | 55 | 100 | 43 | 9 | 29 | 24 471 | 5 291 | 672 144 | 24 018 | 202 | Valeur |
| Refined oil fuels: | | | | | | | | | | | | | | | Pétrole raffiné: |
| Quantity | 24 153.8 | 2 236.0 | 1 637.8 | 130.1 | 563.8 | 1 722.8 | 107.8 | 89.3 | 211.2 | 2 940.0 | 2 123.8 | 9 313.3 | 2 757.3 | 320.6 | Quantité |
| Value | 474 945 | 44 057 | 29 865 | 3 047 | 13 285 | 27 664 | 2 371 | 1 827 | 3 619 | 53 095 | 38 844 | 191 157 | 59 600 | 6 514 | Valeur |
| Natural and manufactured gas: | | | | | | | | | | | | | | | Gaz naturel et manufacturé: |
| Quantity | 113 408.1 | 3 695.4 | 190.4 | 100.6 | 187.8 | 2 003.2 | 229.1 | 13.2 | 224.6 | 24 530.5 | 7 073.2 | 70 890.6 | 4 094.9 | 174.6 | Quantité |
| Value | 383 169 | 32 081 | 2 046 | 1 677 | 2 037 | 9 187 | 3 591 | 193 | 1 640 | 67 970 | 54 639 | 155 307 | 49 555 | 3 246 | Valeur |
| Electricity: | | | | | | | | | | | | | | | Électricité: |
| Purchased: | | | | | | | | | | | | | | | Achetée: |
| Quantity | 102 822 | 8 606 | 8 288 | 1 066 | 2 279 | 6 175 | 1 251 | 268 | 2 650 | 15 712 | 5 865 | 31 428 | 17 842 | 1 392 | Quantité |
| Value | 954 717 | 110 972 | 82 456 | 25 136 | 32 818 | 50 606 | 23 796 | 4 798 | 24 685 | 113 755 | 54 878 | 188 784 | 219 666 | 22 367 | Valeur |
| Produced—quantity | 43 936 | 1 982 | 1 959 | 33 | 1 141 | 9 626 | 39 | 102 | 810 | 11 268 | 2 155 | 11 851 | 2 840 | 130 | Produite—quantité |
| Sold: | | | | | | | | | | | | | | | Vendue: |
| Quantity | 5 811 | 103 | 206 | 6 | 176 | 415 | 10 | 18 | 15 | 923 | 122 | 2 634 | 1 169 | 14 | Quantité |
| Value | 40 815 | 1 190 | 2 122 | 57 | 1 555 | 3 430 | 140 | 288 | 104 | 4 877 | 788 | 16 599 | 9 464 | 201 | Valeur |
| Other and unspecified fuels [2]: | | | | | | | | | | | | | | | Autres combustibles et combustibles non spécifiés [2]: |
| Quantity | 11 534.9 | 1 411.3 | 70.4 | 52.6 | 3 112.7 | 557.8 | 217.8 | 16.4 | 16.5 | 1 352.7 | 656.2 | 3 010.2 | 1 018.9 | 41.4 | Quantité |
| Value | 96 457 | 11 149 | 674 | 542 | 30 660 | 4 273 | 2 579 | 147 | 109 | 7 007 | 4 672 | 24 021 | 10 169 | 455 | Valeur |
| **1954** [3] | | | | | | | | | | | | | | | **1954** [3] |
| Coal: | | | | | | | | | | | | | | | Charbon: |
| Quantity | 82 753.4 | 10 846.3 | 4 503.3 | ... | 1 338.1 | 11 405.1 | ... | 440.9 | 2 026.6 | 20 002.5 | 12 368.6 | 8 944.8 | 9 882.9 | 994.3 | Quantité |
| Value | 674 423 | 92 176 | 38 606 | ... | 13 309 | 104 088 | ... | 5 304 | 14 522 | 148 416 | 95 803 | 66 884 | 85 291 | 10 024 | Valeur |
| Coke: | | | | | | | | | | | | | | | Coke: |
| Quantity | 49 323.7 | 91.6 | 20.9 | ... | 10.0 | 10.9 | ... | 0.9 | 0.9 | 84.4 | 173.3 | 48 279.5 | 645.9 | 5.4 | Quantité |
| Value | 867 855 | 1 899 | 332 | ... | 200 | 223 | ... | 16 | 15 | 785 | 3 439 | 843 903 | 16 884 | 159 | Valeur |
| Refined oil fuels: | | | | | | | | | | | | | | | Pétrole raffiné: |
| Quantity | 26 669.3 | 3 003.0 | 1 622.0 | ... | 563.8 | 3 251.2 | ... | 144.2 | 283.1 | 3 174.7 | 2 270.0 | 8 138.7 | 3 710.6 | 508.0 | Quantité |
| Value | 573 273 | 68 594 | 31 022 | ... | 16 446 | 57 489 | ... | 3 029 | 5 372 | 61 474 | 51 194 | 175 527 | 91 352 | 11 774 | Valeur |
| Natural and manufactured gas: | | | | | | | | | | | | | | | Gaz naturel et manufacturé: |
| Quantity | 167 365.4 | 7 567.3 | 645.1 | ... | 673.1 | 3 301.9 | ... | 71.3 | 334.8 | 38 324.4 | 11 067.4 | 99 364.0 | 5 644.8 | 371.3 | Quantité |
| Value | 846 178 | 70 517 | 8 614 | ... | 6 898 | 24 839 | ... | 998 | 3 520 | 231 367 | 112 441 | 293 043 | 88 065 | 5 876 | Valeur |
| Electricity: | | | | | | | | | | | | | | | Électricité: |
| Purchased: | | | | | | | | | | | | | | | Achetée: |
| Quantity | 186 986 | 12 332 | 11 105 | 1 199 | 4 368 | 10 852 | 1 680 | 372 | 3 087 | 52 899 | 9 157 | 46 418 | 31 010 | 2 507 | Quantité |
| Value | 1 724 773 | 172 495 | 114 758 | 29 199 | 60 892 | 91 452 | 36 150 | 6 410 | 32 745 | 342 171 | 95 116 | 305 346 | 397 771 | 40 268 | Valeur |
| Produced—quantity | 69 681 | 2 253 | 1 454 | 10 | 1 369 | 14 183 | 5 | 64 | 732 | 20 672 | 2 510 | 23 271 | 2 797 | 361 | Produite—quantité |
| Sold: | | | | | | | | | | | | | | | Vendue: |
| Quantity | 9 044 | 107 | 237 | — | 226 | 1 496 | — | 3 | 70 | 1 969 | 94 | 3 757 | 1 050 | 35 | Quantité |
| Value | 85 830 | 1 041 | 2 154 | — | 1 369 | 13 836 | 47 | 81 | 549 | 18 205 | 628 | 34 375 | 13 004 | 541 | Valeur |
| Other and unspecified fuels [2]: | | | | | | | | | | | | | | | Autres combustibles et combustibles non spécifiés [2]: |
| Quantity | 21 807.3 | 2 699.6 | 210.8 | 943.1 | 1 530.3 | 3 694.4 | 1214.1 | 32.9 | 71.0 | 2 865.5 | 1 351.6 | 3 415.6 | 3 670.1 | 108.4 | Quantité |
| Value | 219 978 | 25 295 | 2 144 | 12 534 | 18 700 | 33 397 | 16 135 | 418 | 576 | 19 027 | 11 866 | 31 799 | 46 647 | 1 440 | Valeur |

For footnotes see end of table.

Pour les notes, voir au bas du tableau.

### B.   The Major Groups of Manufacturing (continued) — Les classes de la branche Industries manufacturières (suite)
### 1939, 1947, 1954, 1958

| Year and source of energy | Manufacturing Industries manufacturières | Food, beverages and tobacco Industries alimentaires, boissons, tabac | Textiles | Clothing, footwear and made-up textiles Articles d'habillement, chaussures et ouvrages en tissu | Wood products and furniture Bois et meubles | Paper and paper products Papier et ouvrages en papier | Printing and publishing Imprimerie et édition | Leather and leather products except wearing apparel Cuir et articles en cuir, à l'exclusion des articles d'habillement | Rubber products Ouvrages en caoutchouc | Chemicals and chemical, petroleum and coal products [4] Produits chimiques et dérivés du pétrole et du charbon [4] | Non-metallic mineral products Produits minéraux non métalliques | Basic metals [5] Métallurgie de base [5] | Metal products Ouvrages en métaux | Other manufacturing Autres industries manufacturières | Année et source d'énergie |
|---|---|---|---|---|---|---|---|---|---|---|---|---|---|---|---|
| ISIC | 2–3 | 20–22 | 23 | 24 | 25–26 | 27 | 28 | 29 | 30 | 31–32 | 33 | 34 | 35–38 | 39 | CITI |
| **1958** | | | | | | | | | | | | | | | **1958** |
| Coal: | | | | | | | | | | | | | | | Charbon: |
| Quantity | 74 121.1 | 7 475.2 | 2 781.4 | ... | 545.2 | 13 122.4 | ... | 423.6 | 2 080.2 | 19 328.4 | 10 692.0 | 10 273.8 | 6 776.6 | 622.3 | Quantité |
| Value | 637 446 | 63 974 | 27 250 | ... | 6 055 | 123 526 | ... | 3 649 | 15 510 | 150 824 | 94 382 | 83 536 | 62 587 | 6 153 | Valeur |
| Coke: | | | | | | | | | | | | | | | Coke: |
| Quantity | 12 323.2 | 59.0 | — | ... | — | — | ... | — | — | — | 150.6 | 11 792.5 | 321.1 | — | Quantité |
| Value | 271 007 | 1 617 | — | ... | — | — | ... | — | — | — | 3 547 | 254 707 | 11 136 | — | Valeur |
| Refined oil fuels: | | | | | | | | | | | | | | | Pétrole raffiné: |
| Quantity | 23 998.0 | 3 541.5 | 1 153.5 | ... | 278.4 | 3 658.2 | ... | 133.1 | 273.3 | 2 990.0 | 1 975.0 | 6 812.0 | 2 890.8 | 292.2 | Quantité |
| Value | 517 657 | 64 619 | 23 128 | ... | 10 280 | 69 870 | ... | 3 120 | 6 669 | 64 240 | 46 192 | 157 803 | 63 445 | 8 291 | Valeur |
| Natural and manufactured gas: | | | | | | | | | | | | | | | Gaz naturel et manufacturé: |
| Quantity | 88 106.2 | 6 454.0 | 912.3 | ... | 262.9 | 6 009.2 | ... | 54.6 | 471.6 | 38 805.8 | 12 632.5 | 17 972.3 | 4 335.1 | 195.9 | Quantité |
| Value | 900 396 | 83 151 | 11 696 | ... | 4 630 | 53 952 | ... | 929 | 5 053 | 284 728 | 155 243 | 220 694 | 76 735 | 3 585 | Valeur |
| Electricity: Purchased: | | | | | | | | | | | | | | | Electricité: Achetée: |
| Quantity | 251 545 | 14 556 | 11 925 | 2 081 | 4 784 | 12 438 | 3 004 | 455 | 3 484 | 96 503 | 12 089 | 49 611 | 36 882 | 3 733 | Quantité |
| Value | 2 226 584 | 209 771 | 117 137 | 42 378 | 73 505 | 116 262 | 51 592 | 8 310 | 38 930 | 522 985 | 130 791 | 369 776 | 485 320 | 59 827 | Valeur |
| Produced—quantity | 73 555 | 2 200 | 1 123 | 20 | 1 357 | 17 733 | 11 | 157 | 702 | 21 602 | 2 362 | 24 180 | 1 694 | 414 | Produite—quantité |
| Sold—quantity | 7 099 | 65 | 220 | 1 | 318 | 897 | 1 | 1 | 66 | 1 736 | 94 | 3 263 | 408 | 29 | Vendue—quantité |
| Other and unspecified fuels [2]: | | | | | | | | | | | | | | | Autres combustibles et combustibles non spécifiés [2]: |
| Quantity | 42 497.8 | 6 389.9 | 1 981.8 | 1 292.1 | 2 912.8 | 1 974.9 | 1 491.8 | 286.4 | 296.7 | 8 183.3 | 3 835.6 | 1 727.0 | 10 345.4 | 1 780.1 | Quantité |
| Value | 490 113 | 65 241 | 21 959 | 18 839 | 47 566 | 18 406 | 21 751 | 3 228 | 2 599 | 61 866 | 38 548 | 26 769 | 137 387 | 25 954 | Valeur |

[1] In the case of the 1947 Census, the data do not cover fuels and electricity utilized by very small establishments, which were requested to include the cost of purchased fuels and electricity consumed in the figures of the cost of purchased raw materials, supplies, etc., consumed. Though, in aggregate, the omitted small establishments accounted for only 1.5 per cent of the number of employees recorded in the 1947 Census and one percent of value added, the very small establishments accounted for larger proportions of employment in the case of selected kinds of manufacturing. For example, in the case of Clothing, footwear and made-up textiles (ISIC major group 24), Furniture (ISIC major group 26), and Miscellaneous manufacturing (ISIC major group 39), data on fuels and electricity are not included for very small establishments which contributed 3 to 6 percent of the employment in the industry.

[2] Includes fuels not specifically listed above—namely, gasoline, liquefied petroleum gas and wood—and data on fuels for the smaller establishments for which a single figure was gathered or estimated concerning the cost of all purchased fuels consumed. The kinds of smaller establishments for which this practice was followed varied from Census to Census. In the 1947 Census, a single figure was gathered on the cost of fuels for smaller establishments in Printing and publishing (ISIC major group 28). In the 1954 Census, a single figure on the cost of all fuels was, in effect, gathered for all establishments classified to Clothing and made-up textiles (ISIC major group 24) and Printing and publishing (ISIC major group 28) and single-unit establishments with less than six employees in the case of other kinds of industrial activities. In the 1958 Census, this practice was extended to additional kinds of industrial activity and to establishments which in 1958 expended less than $5,000 on fuels.

[3] The scheme of classification utilized in the case of the data shown for 1954 differs substantially from that utilized in the case of the data shown for 1958 but not for 1947.

[4] Excludes in the case of all years, fuel oils, coke or manufactured gas made from crude petroleum and coal or coke, respectively, which are considered raw materials and therefore not included in the data, and consumed in the same establishment as a source of heat and power. The pertinent figures in the case of 1958 are 9,564 thousand metric tons of fuel oil and 19,029 million cubic metres of gas.

[5] In the case of 1958, includes 32,859 thousand metric tons of coke and 137,012 cubic metres of manufactured gas made and consumed in the same establishments as a source of heat or power. This adjustment brings the data for 1958 into comparability with that for earlier years, when in contrast to 1958, coke ovens which were part of blast furnace and steel works were treated as independent establishments separate from blast furnaces and steel works and classified in the equivalent of ISIC major group 32. The coke and gas obtained by blast furnaces and steel works from such coke ovens were therefore considered purchases.

[1] Dans le cas du recensement de 1947, les données ne comprennent pas les combustibles et l'électricité utilisés par les très petits établissements, auxquels on avait demandé d'inclure le coût des achats de combustibles et d'électricité consommés dans le coût des achats de matières premières, fournitures, etc., consommées. Bien que les petits établissements ne représentent, au total, que 1,5 p. 100 du nombre de salariés recensés en 1947 et 1 p. 100 de la valeur ajoutée, les très petits établissements détiennent une proportion plus grande de l'emploi dans le cas de certains types d'industries manufacturières. Ainsi, pour la Fabrication de vêtements, chaussures et ouvrages en tissu (CITI 24), l'Industrie du meuble (CITI 26) et les Industries manufacturières diverses (CITI 39), les données relatives aux combustibles et à l'électricité sont exclues pour les très petits établissements, qui détenaient de 3 à 6 p. 100 de l'emploi dans les industries.

[2] Y compris les combustibles non expressément indiqués ci-dessus—à savoir, gazoline, gaz liquéfié et bois—et les données sur les combustibles relatives aux petits établissements, pour lesquels on a relevé ou évalué uniquement le coût global de tous les combustibles achetés et consommés. Les types de petits établissements pour lesquels cette pratique est suivie varient d'un recensement à l'autre. Lors du recensement de 1947, on n'a recueilli que le coût global des combustibles consommés par les petits établissements appartenant à la classe imprimerie et édition (CITI 28). Lors du recensement de 1954, on n'a effectivement relevé que le coût global de l'ensemble des combustibles par les petits établissements des classes Industrie du vêtement et confection d'ouvrages en tissu (CITI 24) et Imprimerie et édition (CITI 28), ainsi que pour les établissements des autres classes qui ne représentaient qu'une seule unité et qui comptaient moins de 6 salariés. Pour le recensement de 1958, cette pratique a été étendue à d'autres types d'activité industrielle et aux établissements dont les dépenses de combustibles ont été inférieures à 5.000 dollars en 1958.

[3] Le système de classification adopté pour 1954 est analogue au système utilisé pour 1947, mais il diffère sensiblement de celui qui est appliqué aux données de 1958.

[4] Non compris, pour toutes les années, les fuel oils, le coke ou le gaz fabriqués à partir de pétrole brut, de charbon ou de coke respectivement, qui sont considérés comme matières premières et sont, par conséquent, exclus des données, et consommés dans le même établissement comme source de chaleur ou d'énergie. En 1958, les chiffres correspondants étaient les suivants: 9.564 milliers de tonnes métriques de fuel oils et 19.029 millions de mètres cubes de gaz.

[5] Y compris en 1958, 32.859 milliers de tonnes métriques de coke et 137.012 mètres cubes de gaz fabriqués et consommés dans le même établissement comme source de chaleur ou d'énergie. Cet ajustement assure la comparabilité des chiffres de 1958 et de ceux des années précédentes, pour lesquelles, à l'opposé de 1958, les cokeries qui faisaient partie des hauts fourneaux et des usines sidérurgiques ont été traitées comme des établissements indépendants distincts des hauts fourneaux et des usines sidérurgiques et classées dans l'équivalent de la classe 32 de la CITI. Le coke et le gaz produits par les cokeries desservant les hauts fourneaux et les usines sidérurgiques ont donc été considérés comme achetés.

## 6. CHARACTERISTICS OF MINING AND MANUFACTURING ESTABLISHMENTS; ALASKA AND HAWAII
## CARACTERISTIQUES DES ETABLISSEMENTS MINIERS ET MANUFACTURIERS; ALASKA ET HAWAII

Number of establishments in units; value added and wages and salaries in thousand Dollars; number of employees and operatives in units; man-hours worked in thousands; value added and wages and salaries per employee and per thousand operative man-hours in thousand Dollars; average annual man-hours per operative in thousands.

Nombre d'établissements en unités; valeur ajoutée et traitements et salaires en milliers de dollars; nombre de salariés et d'ouvriers en unités; heures de travail effectuées en milliers; valeur ajoutée par salarié et traitements et salaires par salarié et par millier d'heures-ouvrier en milliers de dollars; moyenne annuelle des heures de travail par ouvrier en milliers.

### A. The Major Groups of Mining — Les classes de la branche Industries extractives

Establishments for which the Gross Value of Production, Principal Expenses and Capital Expenditure each equal $500 or more in the case of 1954 and which in addition had one employee anytime during the year in the case of 1958.

Etablissements pour lesquels le chiffre de la valeur brute de la production, celui des dépenses directes de production et celui des dépenses d'équipement atteignaient chacun 500 dollars ou plus en 1954 et qui, en 1958, ont occupé un salarié à un moment quelconque de l'année.

#### a. Absolute Figures — Chiffres absolus — a. ALASKA

| Year and item of data | All mining — Toutes industries extractives | Coal mining — Extraction du charbon | Metal mining — Extraction des minerais métalliques | Crude petroleum and natural gas — Pétrole brut et gaz naturel | Other mining[1] — Divers[1] | Année et rubrique |
|---|---|---|---|---|---|---|
| ISIC | 1 | 11 | 12 | 13 | 14-19 | CITI |
| **1954** | | | | | | **1954** |
| Number of establishments | 194 | 10 | 172 | 6 | 6 | Nombre d'établissements |
| Value added | ... | 5 777 | 8 623 | ... | ... | Valeur ajoutée |
| Employees: Number | 1 436 | 373 | 960 | 73 | 30 | Salariés: Nombre |
| Wages and salaries | 9 529 | 3 110 | 5 710 | 409 | 300 | Traitements et salaires |
| Operatives: Number | 1 197 | 315 | 819 | 35 | 28 | Ouvriers: Nombre |
| Man-hours worked | 2 990 | 688 | 2 151 | 75 | 76 | Heures de travail effectuées |
| Wages and salaries | 7 663 | 2 484 | 4 699 | 190 | 290 | Traitements et salaires |
| **1958** | | | | | | **1958** |
| Number of establishments | 156 | 10 | 121 | 21 | 4 | Nombre d'établissements |
| Value added | ... | 5 780 | 5 448 | ... | 388 | Valeur ajoutée |
| Employees: Number | 976 | 257 | 548 | 116 | 55 | Salariés: Nombre |
| Wages and salaries | 7 549 | 2 282 | 3 776 | 1 263 | 228 | Traitements et salaires |
| Operatives: Number | 804 | 197 | 493 | 66 | 48 | Ouvriers: Nombre |
| Man-hours worked | 2 027 | 471 | 1 310 | 154 | 92 | Heures de travail effectuées |
| Wages and salaries | 5 632 | 1 736 | 3 141 | 559 | 196 | Traitements et salaires |

#### b. Structure — a. ALASKA

| Year and item of data | All mining — Toutes industries extractives | Coal mining — Extraction du charbon | Metal mining — Extraction des minerais métalliques | Crude petroleum and natural gas — Pétrole brut et gaz naturel | Other mining[1] — Divers[1] | Année et rubrique |
|---|---|---|---|---|---|---|
| ISIC | 1 | 11 | 12 | 13 | 14-19 | CITI |
| **1954** | | | | | | **1954** |
| Distribution in percent of number of employees | 100.0 | 25.9 | 66.9 | 5.1 | 2.1 | Distribution en pourcentage du nombre de salariés |
| Per employee: Value added | ... | 15.5 | 9.0 | ... | ... | Par salarié: Valeur ajoutée |
| Wages and salaries | 6.6 | 8.3 | 5.9 | 5.6 | 10.0 | Traitements et salaires |
| Value added per unit of wages and salaries | ... | 1.86 | 1.51 | ... | ... | Valeur ajoutée par unité de traitements et salaires |
| Operatives as a percent of employees | 83.4 | 84.4 | 85.3 | 47.9 | 93.3 | Ouvriers en pourcentage des salariés |
| Average man-hours per operative | 2.50 | 2.18 | 2.63 | 2.14 | 2.71 | Heures de travail: moyenne par ouvrier |
| Wages and salaries per thousand operative man-hour | 2.56 | 3.61 | 2.18 | 2.53 | 3.82 | Traitements et salaires par millier d'heures-ouvrier |
| **1958** | | | | | | **1958** |
| Distribution in percent of number of employees | 100.0 | 26.3 | 56.1 | 11.9 | 5.7 | Distribution en pourcentage du nombre de salariés |
| Per employee: Value added | ... | 22.5 | 9.9 | ... | 7.0 | Par salarié: Valeur ajoutée |
| Wages and salaries | 7.7 | 8.9 | 6.9 | 10.9 | 4.1 | Traitements et salaires |
| Value added per unit of wages and salaries | ... | 2.53 | 1.44 | ... | 1.70 | Valeur ajoutée par unité de traitements et salaires |
| Operatives as a percent of employees | 82.4 | 76.6 | 90.0 | 56.9 | 87.3 | Ouvriers en pourcentage des salariés |
| Average man-hours per operative | 2.52 | 2.39 | 2.66 | 2.33 | 1.92 | Heures de travail: moyenne par ouvrier |
| Wages and salaries per thousand operative man-hour | 2.78 | 3.68 | 2.40 | 3.63 | 2.13 | Traitements et salaires par d'heures-ouvrier |

For footnotes, see end of table.

Pour les notes, voir au bas du tableau.

## A. The Major Groups of Mining (continued) — Les classes de la branche Industries extractives (suite)

### a. Absolute Figures — Chiffres absolus — a. HAWAII

| Year and item of data | All mining Toutes industries extractives | Coal mining Extraction du charbon | Metal mining Extraction des minerais métalliques | Crude petroleum and natural gas Pétrole brut et gaz naturel | Other mining [1] Divers [1] | Année et rubrique |
|---|---|---|---|---|---|---|
| ISIC | 1 | 11 | 12 | 13 | 14-19 | CITI |
| **1954** | | | | | | **1954** |
| Number of establishments... | 13 | — | — | — | 13 | Nombre d'établissements |
| Value added....... | 1 266 | — | — | — | 1 266 | Valeur ajoutée |
| Employees: | | | | | | Salariés: |
| Number......... | 171 | — | — | — | 171 | Nombre |
| Wages and salaries......... | 598 | — | — | — | 598 | Traitements et salaires |
| Operatives: | | | | | | Ouvriers: |
| Number......... | 156 | — | — | — | 156 | Nombre |
| Man-hours worked......... | 320 | — | — | — | 320 | Heures de travail effectuées |
| Wages and salaries......... | 517 | — | — | — | 517 | Traitements et salaires |
| **1958** | | | | | | **1958** |
| Number of establishments... | 20 | — | — | — | 20 | Nombre d'établissements |
| Value added....... | 4 550 | — | — | — | 4 550 | Valeur ajoutée |
| Employees: | | | | | | Salariés: |
| Number......... | 421 | — | — | — | 421 | Nombre |
| Wages and salaries......... | 1 724 | — | — | — | 1 724 | Traitements et salaires |
| Operatives: | | | | | | Ouvriers: |
| Number......... | 367 | — | — | — | 367 | Nombre |
| Man-hours worked......... | 746 | — | — | — | 746 | Heures de travail effectuées |
| Wages and salaries......... | 1 426 | — | — | — | 1 426 | Traitements et salaires |

### b. Structure — b. HAWAII

| Year and item of data | All mining Toutes industries extractives | Coal mining Extraction du charbon | Metal mining Extraction des minerais métalliques | Crude petroleum and natural gas Pétrole brut et gaz naturel | Other mining [1] Divers [1] | Année et rubrique |
|---|---|---|---|---|---|---|
| ISIC | 1 | 11 | 12 | 13 | 14-19 | CITI |
| **1954** | | | | | | **1954** |
| Per employee: | | | | | | Par salarié: |
| Value added..... | 7.4 | — | — | — | 7.4 | Valeur ajoutée |
| Wages and salaries......... | 3.5 | — | — | — | 3.5 | Traitements et salaires |
| Value added per unit of wages and salaries..... | 2.12 | — | — | — | 2.12 | Valeur ajoutée par unité de traitements et salaires |
| Operatives as a percent of employees....... | 91.2 | — | — | — | 91.2 | Ouvriers en pourcentage des salariés |
| Average man-hours per operative.... | 2.05 | — | — | — | 2.05 | Heures de travail: moyenne par ouvrier |
| Wages and salaries per thousand operative man-hour....... | 162 | — | — | — | 162 | Traitements et salaires par millier d'heures-ouvrier |
| **1958** | | | | | | **1958** |
| Per employee: | | | | | | Par salarié |
| Value added..... | 10.8 | — | — | — | 10.8 | Valeur ajoutée |
| Wages and salaries......... | 4.1 | — | — | — | 4.1 | Traitements et salaires |
| Value added per unit of wages and salaries..... | 2.64 | — | — | — | 2.64 | Valeur ajoutée par unité de traitements et salaires |
| Operatives as a percent of employees....... | 87.2 | — | — | — | 87.2 | Ouvriers en pourcentage des salariés |
| Average man-hours per operative.... | 2.03 | — | — | — | 2.03 | Heures de travail: moyenne par ouvrier |
| Wages and salaries per thousand operative man-hour....... | 1.91 | — | — | — | 1.91 | Traitements et salaires par millier d'heures-ouvrier |

[1] Excludes quarrying of stone, clay, sand, gravel and gypsum by establishments classified in manufacturing.

[1] Non compris l'extraction de pierre à bâtir, d'argile, de sable, de gravier et de gypse par les établissements classés dans les industries manufacturières.

## B. The Major Groups of Manufacturing, Establishments with One or More Employees
## Les classes de la branche Industries manufacturières, établissements comptant au moins un salarié

| Year and item of data | Manu-facturing [1,2]<br>Industries manufac-turières [1,2] | Food, and bev-erages [3]<br>Industries alimen-taires et boissons [3] | Clothing, and made-up textiles [4]<br>Articles d'habil-lement et ouvrages en tissu [4] | Wood products<br>Industrie du bois | Furniture<br>Industrie du meuble | Printing and publish-ing<br>Im-primerie et édition | Leather and leather products except wearing apparel [4]<br>Cuir et articles en cuir, à l'exclu-sion des articles d'habil-lement [4] | Chemical prod-ucts [3]<br>Produits chimi-ques [3] | Non-metallic mineral products<br>Produits minéraux non métal-liques | Metal products<br>Ouvrages en métaux | Other manu-facturing [5]<br>Autres in-dustries manufac-turières [5] | Année et rubrique |
|---|---|---|---|---|---|---|---|---|---|---|---|---|
| ISIC | 2–3 | 20–21 | 243, 244 | 25 | 26 | 28 | 29 | 31 | 33 | 36–38 | 39 | CITI |
| | | | | | | *a.* ALASKA | | | | | | | |
| **1954** | | | | | | | | | | | | **1954** |
| Number of establishments. | 219 | 105 | 2 | 55 | 2 | 23 | 1 | 6 | 4 | 8 | 5 | Nombre d'établissements |
| Value added.......... | 40 235 | 29 940 | ... | 4 099 | ... | 2 650 | ... | 807 | 64 | 331 | 117 | Valeur ajoutée |
| Employees: | | | | | | | | | | | | Salariés: |
| Number............ | 4 092 | 2 596 | ... | 612 | ... | 295 | ... | 53 | 12 | 48 | 11 | Nombre |
| Wages and salaries... | 20 365 | 11 836 | ... | 2 903 | ... | 1 615 | ... | 439 | 36 | 235 | 56 | Traitements et salaires |
| Operatives: | | | | | | | | | | | | Ouvriers: |
| Number............ | 3 531 | 2 345 | ... | 572 | ... | 166 | ... | 35 | 10 | 44 | 9 | Nombre |
| Man-hours worked.... | 7 048 | 4 651 | ... | 985 | ... | 394 | ... | 124 | 14 | 83 | 16 | Heures de travail effectuées |
| Wages and salaries... | 16 546 | 10 127 | ... | 2 646 | ... | 943 | ... | 289 | 23 | 209 | 39 | Traitements et salaires |
| Distribution in percent of: | | | | | | | | | | | | Distribution en pour-centage: |
| Value added........ | 100.0 | 74.4 | ... | 10.2 | ... | 6.6 | ... | 2.0 | 0.2 | 0.8 | 0.3 | Valeur ajoutée |
| Number of employees. | 100.0 | 63.4 | ... | 15.0 | ... | 7.2 | ... | 1.3 | 0.3 | 1.2 | 0.3 | Nombre de salariés |
| Per employee: | | | | | | | | | | | | Par salarié |
| Value added........ | 9.8 | 11.5 | ... | 6.7 | ... | 9.0 | ... | 15.2 | 5.3 | 6.9 | 10.6 | Valeur ajoutée |
| Wages and salaries... | 5.0 | 4.6 | ... | 4.7 | ... | 5.5 | ... | 8.3 | 3.0 | 4.9 | 5.1 | Traitements et salaires |
| Value added per unit of wages and salaries............ | 1.98 | 2.53 | ... | 1.41 | ... | 1.64 | ... | 1.84 | 1.78 | 1.41 | 2.09 | Valeur ajoutée par unité de traitements et salaires |
| Operatives as a percent of employees........ | 86.3 | 90.3 | ... | 93.5 | ... | 56.3 | ... | 66.0 | 83.3 | 91.7 | 81.8 | Ouvriers en pourcentage des salariés |
| Average man-hours per operative........ | 2.00 | 1.98 | ... | 1.72 | ... | 2.37 | ... | 3.54 | 1.40 | 1.89 | 1.78 | Heures de travail: moyenne par ouvrier |
| Wages and salaries per thousand operative man-hour... | 2.35 | 2.18 | ... | 2.69 | ... | 2.39 | ... | 2.33 | 1.64 | 2.52 | 2.44 | Traitements et salaires par millier d'heures-ouvrier |
| **1958** | | | | | | | | | | | | **1958** |
| Number of establishments. | 245 | 112 | 3 | 57 | — | 27 | — | 2 | 12 | 14 | 7 | Nombre d'établissements |
| Value added.......... | 64 595 | 37 542 | ... | 4 233 | — | 3 589 | — | ... | 2 275 | 446 | 176 | Valeur ajoutée |
| Employees: | | | | | | | | | | | | Salariés: |
| Number............ | 4 802 | 3 046 | ... | 617 | — | 322 | — | ... | 174 | 47 | 24 | Nombre |
| Wages and salaries... | 25 670 | 15 113 | ... | 2 873 | — | 2 066 | — | ... | 1 102 | 269 | 72 | Traitements et salaires |
| Operatives: | | | | | | | | | | | | Ouvriers: |
| Number............ | 3 931 | 2 542 | ... | 538 | — | 197 | — | ... | 142 | 43 | 20 | Nombre |
| Man-hours worked.... | 7 258 | 4 687 | ... | 933 | — | 373 | — | ... | 215 | 69 | 40 | Heures de travail effectuées |
| Wages and salaries... | 19 850 | 11 946 | ... | 2 400 | — | 1 264 | — | ... | 852 | 234 | 61 | Traitements et salaires |
| Distribution in percent of: | | | | | | | | | | | | Distribution en pour-centage: |
| Value added........ | 100.0 | 58.1 | ... | 6.6 | — | 5.6 | — | ... | 3.5 | 0.7 | 0.3 | Valeur ajoutée |
| Number of employees. | 100.0 | 63.4 | ... | 12.8 | — | 6.7 | — | ... | 3.6 | 1.0 | 0.5 | Nombre de salariés |
| Per employee: | | | | | | | | | | | | Par salarié |
| Value added........ | 13.4 | 12.3 | ... | 6.9 | — | 11.1 | — | ... | 13.1 | 9.5 | 7.3 | Valeur ajoutée |
| Wages and salaries... | 5.3 | 5.0 | ... | 4.6 | — | 6.4 | — | ... | 6.3 | 5.7 | 3.0 | Traitements et salaires |
| Value added per unit of wages and salaries............ | 2.52 | 2.48 | ... | 1.47 | — | 1.74 | — | ... | 2.06 | 1.66 | 2.44 | Valeur ajoutée par unité de traitements et salaires |
| Operatives as a percent of employees........ | 81.9 | 83.4 | ... | 87.2 | — | 61.2 | — | ... | 81.6 | 91.5 | 83.3 | Ouvriers en pourcentage des salariés |
| Average man-hours per operative........ | 1.85 | 1.84 | ... | 1.73 | — | 1.89 | — | ... | 1.51 | 1.60 | 2.00 | Heures de travail: moyenne par ouvrier |
| Wages and salaries per thousand operative man-hour... | 2.73 | 2.55 | ... | 2.57 | — | 3.39 | — | ... | 3.96 | 3.39 | 1.52 | Traitements et salaires par millier d'heures-ouvrier |

For footnotes see end of table.　　　　Pour les notes, voir au bas du tableau.

## B. The Major Groups of Manufacturing, Establishments with One or More Employees (continued)
## Les classes de la branche Industries manufacturières, établissements comptant au moins un salarié (suite)

| Year and item of data | Manufacturing [1,2] Industries manufacturières [1,2] | Food and beverages [3] Industries alimentaires, et boissons [3] | Clothing, and made-up textiles [4] Articles d'habillement et ouvrages en tissu [4] | Wood products Industrie du bois | Furniture Industrie du meuble | Printing and publishing Imprimerie et édition | Leather and leather products except wearing apparel [4] Cuir et articles en cuir, à l'exclusion des articles d'habillement [4] | Chemical products [3] Produits chimiques [3] | Non-metallic mineral products Produits minéraux non métalliques | Metal products Ouvrages en métaux | Other manufacturing [5] Autres industries manufacturières [5] | Année et rubrique |
|---|---|---|---|---|---|---|---|---|---|---|---|---|
| ISIC | 2–3 | 20–21 | 243,244 | 25 | 26 | 28 | 29 | 31 | 33 | 36–38 | 39 | CITI |

b. HAWAII

| Year and item of data | 2–3 | 20–21 | 243,244 | 25 | 26 | 28 | 29 | 31 | 33 | 36–38 | 39 | Année et rubrique |
|---|---|---|---|---|---|---|---|---|---|---|---|---|
| **1954** | | | | | | | | | | | | **1954** |
| Number of establishments. | 516 | 250 | 56 | 24 | 30 | 53 | 10 | 22 | 9 | 20 | 19 | Nombre d'établissements |
| Value added......... | 140 275 | 105 655 | 3 518 | 1 226 | 1 648 | 9 734 | 387 | 1 900 | 578 | 1 832 | 348 | Valeur ajoutée |
| Employees: | | | | | | | | | | | | Salariés: |
| Number............ | 24 381 | 19 272 | 998 | 233 | 390 | 1 493 | 87 | 345 | 85 | 370 | 97 | Nombre |
| Wages and salaries... | 77 130 | 60 364 | 2 240 | 701 | 1 374 | 5 682 | 173 | 1 390 | 273 | 1 249 | 259 | Traitements et salaires |
| Operatives: | | | | | | | | | | | | Ouvriers: |
| Number............ | 19 524 | 15 806 | 896 | 175 | 305 | 790 | 80 | 221 | 75 | 299 | 81 | Nombre |
| Man-hours worked.... | 36 114 | 28 921 | 1 759 | 337 | 621 | 1 456 | 162 | 440 | 139 | 539 | 139 | Heures de travail effectuées |
| Wages and salaries... | 50 806 | 40 268 | 1 753 | 484 | 910 | 2 689 | 155 | 711 | 226 | 895 | 197 | Traitements et salaires |
| Distribution in percent of: | | | | | | | | | | | | Distribution en pourcentage: |
| Value added........ | 100.0 | 75.3 | 2.5 | 0.9 | 1.2 | 6.9 | 0.3 | 1.4 | 0.4 | 1.3 | 0.2 | Valeur ajoutée |
| Number of employees. | 100.0 | 79.0 | 4.1 | 1.0 | 1.6 | 6.1 | 0.4 | 1.4 | 0.3 | 1.5 | 0.4 | Nombre de salariés |
| Per employee: | | | | | | | | | | | | Par salarié: |
| Value added........ | 5.8 | 5.5 | 3.5 | 5.3 | 4.2 | 6.5 | 4.4 | 5.5 | 6.8 | 5.0 | 3.6 | Valeur ajoutée |
| Wages and salaries... | 3.2 | 3.1 | 2.2 | 3.0 | 3.5 | 3.8 | 2.0 | 4.0 | 3.2 | 3.4 | 2.7 | Traitements et salaires |
| Value added per unit of wages and salaries........... | 1.82 | 1.75 | 1.57 | 1.75 | 1.20 | 1.71 | 2.24 | 1.37 | 2.12 | 1.47 | 1.34 | Valeur ajoutée par unité de traitements et salaires |
| Operatives as a percent of employees........ | 80.1 | 82.0 | 89.8 | 75.1 | 78.2 | 52.9 | 92.0 | 64.0 | 88.2 | 80.8 | 83.5 | Ouvriers en pourcentage des salariés |
| Average man-hours per operative........ | 1.85 | 1.83 | 1.96 | 1.92 | 2.04 | 1.84 | 2.02 | 1.99 | 1.85 | 1.80 | 1.72 | Heures de travail: moyenne par ouvrier |
| Wages and salaries per thousand operative man-hour... | 1.41 | 1.39 | 1.00 | 1.44 | 1.46 | 1.85 | 0.96 | 1.62 | 1.62 | 1.66 | 1.42 | Traitements et salaires par millier d'heures-ouvrier |
| **1958** | | | | | | | | | | | | **1958** |
| Number of establishments. | 609 | 252 | 61 | 32 | 19 | 61 | 15 | 20 | 21 | 32 | 26 | Nombre d'établissements |
| Value added......... | 164 861 | 115 057 | 6 785 | 2 285 | 1 616 | 12 510 | 542 | ... | 3 332 | 2 330 | 854 | Valeur ajoutée |
| Employees: | | | | | | | | | | | | Salariés: |
| Number............ | 23 015 | 16 042 | 1 674 | 434 | 242 | 1 639 | 115 | ... | 295 | 329 | 162 | Nombre |
| Wages and salaries... | 78 806 | 52 560 | 4 337 | 1 615 | 826 | 7 300 | 282 | ... | 1 401 | 1 233 | 559 | Traitements et salaires |
| Operatives: | | | | | | | | | | | | Ouvriers: |
| Number............ | 17 823 | 12 714 | 1 372 | 370 | 196 | 864 | 97 | ... | 213 | 274 | 133 | Nombre |
| Man-hours worked.... | 31 930 | 22 487 | 2 427 | 650 | 376 | 1 525 | 159 | ... | 421 | 441 | 194 | Heures de travail effectuées |
| Wages and salaries... | 51 802 | 34 981 | 3 416 | 1 173 | 600 | 3 570 | 232 | ... | 936 | 919 | 437 | Traitements et salaires |
| Distribution in percent of: | | | | | | | | | | | | Distribution en pourcentage: |
| Value added........ | 100.0 | 69.8 | 4.1 | 1.4 | 1.0 | 7.6 | 0.3 | ... | 2.0 | 1.4 | 0.5 | Valeur ajoutée |
| Number of employees. | 100.0 | 69.7 | 7.3 | 1.9 | 1.0 | 7.1 | 0.5 | ... | 1.3 | 1.4 | 0.7 | Nombre de salariés |
| Per employee: | | | | | | | | | | | | Par salarié: |
| Value added........ | 7.2 | 7.2 | 4.0 | 5.3 | 6.7 | 7.6 | 4.7 | ... | 11.3 | 7.1 | 5.3 | Valeur ajoutée |
| Wages and salaries... | 3.4 | 3.3 | 2.6 | 3.7 | 3.4 | 4.4 | 2.4 | ... | 4.7 | 3.7 | 3.4 | Traitements et salaires |
| Value added per unit of wages and salaries........ | 2.09 | 2.19 | 1.56 | 1.41 | 1.96 | 1.71 | 1.92 | ... | 2.38 | 1.89 | 1.53 | Valeur ajoutée par unité de traitements et salaires |
| Operatives as a percent of employees........ | 77.4 | 79.2 | 82.0 | 85.2 | 81.0 | 52.7 | 84.3 | ... | 72.2 | 83.3 | 82.1 | Ouvriers en pourcentage des salariés |
| Average man-hours per operative........ | 1.79 | 1.77 | 1.77 | 1.76 | 1.92 | 1.76 | 1.64 | ... | 1.98 | 1.61 | 1.46 | Heures de travail: moyenne par ouvrier |
| Wages and salaries per thousand operative man-hour... | 1.62 | 1.56 | 1.41 | 1.80 | 1.60 | 2.34 | 1.46 | ... | 2.22 | 2.08 | 2.25 | Traitements et salaires par millier d'heures-ouvrier |

[1] The figures for manufacturing as a whole cover the data for the various major groups of manufacturing for which it is indicated in the table that specific figures are not available as well as for some major groups which are shown in the table. The major groups not shown in the table are Textiles (ISIC major group 23), in which there were 3 establishments in 1958 in Hawaii. Paper and paper products (ISIC major group 27) in which there were 1 establishment in both 1954 and 1958 in Alaska and 4 and 8 establishments in 1954 and 1958, respectively, in Hawaii; Rubber products (ISIC major group 30) in which there was 1 establishment in both 1954 and 1958 in Hawaii; Petroleum and coal products (ISIC major group 32) in which there were 3 establishments in both 1954 and 1958 in Hawaii; Basic metals (ISIC major group 34) in which there were 1 establishment in 1954 in Alaska and 1 establishment in both 1954 and 1958 in Hawaii; and Metal products, except machinery and transport equipment, and Electrical machinery (ISIC major groups 35 and 37) in which there were 5 and 9 establishments in 1954 and 1958, respectively, in Alaska and 11 and 23 establishments in 1954 and 1958, respectively, in Hawaii.
[2] Excluded are establishments primarily engaged in manufacturing which sell most of their products on the premises at retail, which do custom work for households or which perform repair and related services excepting a few such specified services "for the trade".
[3] The manufacture of non-edible animal fats and the extracting and processing of fish and vegetable oils (part of ISIC major group 31), is included in Chemical products (ISIC major group 31) in the case of 1954 but in Food manufacturing (ISIC major group 20) in the case of 1958.
[4] The manufacture of footwear and leather gloves (part of ISIC major group 24) is included in Leather and Leather products (ISIC major group 29).
[5] Included in Miscellaneous manufacturing (ISIC major group 39) are the manufacture of morticians' goods (part of ISIC major group 25), the dressing and dyeing of furs (ISIC major group 29) and the manufacture of matches and candles (part of ISIC major group 31).

[1] Les chiffres relatifs à l'ensemble des industries manufacturières comprennent les données concernant les diverses classes d'industries manufacturières pour lesquelles il est indiqué dans le tableau qu'on ne dispose pas de chiffres distincts, ainsi que les données relatives à certaines des classes figurant dans le tableau. Les classes omises sont les suivantes: Industrie textile (CITI 23), qui comprenait 3 établissements dans les îles Hawaii en 1958; Industrie du papier et des articles en papier (CITI 27), qui comprenait 1 établissement en Alaska en 1954 et 1958 et, aux îles Hawaii, 4 établissements en 1954 et 8 en 1958; Industries du caoutchouc (CITI 30), qui comprenait 1 établissement aux îles Hawaii en 1954 et 1958; Industrie des dérivés du pétrole et du charbon (CITI 32), qui comprenait 3 établissements aux îles Hawaii en 1954 et 1958; Industrie métallurgique de base (CITI 34), qui comprenait 1 établissement en Alaska en 1954 et 1 établissement aux îles Hawaii en 1954 et 1958; Industries des ouvrages en métaux, à l'exclusion des machines et du matériel de transport, et Construction de machines électriques (CITI 35 et 37), qui comprenaient, en Alaska, 5 établissements en 1954 et 9 en 1958 et, aux îles Hawaii, 11 établissements en 1954 et 23 en 1958.
[2] Sont exclus les établissements exerçant essentiellement une activité manufacturière qui vendent la majeure partie de leurs produits au détail dans leurs propres locaux, qui font des travaux à façon pour le compte des ménages ou qui effectuent des réparations ou fournissent des services connexes, à l'exception des services expressément réservés aux professionnels.
[3] La fabrication des graisses animales non comestibles, ainsi que l'extraction et la préparation des huiles végétales et des huiles de poissons (dans CITI 31) sont comprises dans Produits chimiques (CITI 31) en 1954 et dans Industries alimentaires (CITI 20) en 1958.
[4] La fabrication des chaussures et des gants en cuir (dans CITI 24) est comprise dans Cuir et ouvrages en cuir (CITI 29).
[5] Sont comprises dans Industries manufacturières diverses (CITI 39) la fabrication d'articles mortuaires (dans CITI 25), la fabrication et la teinture des fourrures (dans CITI 29) et la fabrication des allumettes et des bougies (dans CITI 31).

# URUGUAY

## Index Numbers of Industrial Employment

The index numbers of industrial employment which are presented in Table 1 are derived from the results of the annual survey of registered industrial establishments, also dealt with below, published by the Dirección General de Estadística y Censos of the Ministerio de Hacienda in *Estadísticas Retrospectivas del Uruguay*, Montevideo, July 1961.

The index numbers are calculated from absolute figures of the number of employees. The employees consist of operatives and other employees. The figures for operatives are the average of the number employed during the last two weeks of the four months — March, June, September and December. The figures for other employees are the average number employed during December.

## The Characteristics and Structure of Industrial Activity

The data set out in Table 2 are derived from annual surveys of registered industrial establishments. In principle, all industrial units are registered. The results are published by the Dirección General de Estadística y Censos in *Estadísticas Retrospectivas del Uruguay*, Montevideo, July 1961. The definitions of the items of data correspond with the International Standards in Basic Industrial Statistics. The gross value of production is at market prices and the number of employees are as described above.

## Indices de l'emploi industriel

Les indices de l'emploi industriel reproduits au tableau 1 sont tirés des résultats de l'enquête annuelle auprès des établissements industriels enregistrés, à laquelle on s'est référé également ci-dessous, publiée par la Dirección General de Estadística y Censos du Ministerio de Hacienda dans *Estadísticas Retrospectivas del Uruguay*, Montevideo, juillet 1961.

Ces indices sont calculés à partir des chiffres absolus relatifs au nombre de salariés. Les salariés comprennent les ouvriers et autres salariés. Les chiffres concernant les ouvriers portent sur la moyenne du nombre des personnes occupées durant les deux dernières semaines des quatre mois — mars, juin, septembre et décembre. Les chiffres relatifs aux autres salariés portent sur le nombre moyen de personnes occupées durant décembre.

## Caractéristiques et structure de l'activité industrielle

Les données du tableau 2 sont issues d'enquêtes annuelles auprès des établissements industriels enregistrés. En principe, toutes les unités industrielles sont enregistrées. Les résultats sont publiés par la Dirección General de Estadística y Censos dans *Estadísticas Retrospectivas del Uruguay*, Montevideo, juillet 1961. Les définitions des rubriques coincident avec les Normes internationales relatives aux statistiques industrielles de base. La valeur brute de la production est calculée aux prix du marché et le nombre de salariés est évalué comme exposé ci-dessus.

## 1. INDEX NUMBERS OF INDUSTRIAL EMPLOYMENT
## INDICES DE L'EMPLOI DANS L'INDUSTRIE

### A. The Divisions of Industrial Activity
### Les branches de l'activité industrielle

| Period / Période | Total | Mining [1] / Industries extractives [1] | Manufacturing / Industries manufacturières | Construction / Bâtiment et travaux publics | Electricity, gas and water / Electricité, gaz et eau |
|---|---|---|---|---|---|
| ISIC — CITI | 1-4, 511-521 | 1 | 2-3 | 4 | 511-521 |

*a.* Indexes — Indices (1958 = 100)

| | | | | | |
|---|---|---|---|---|---|
| 1954....... | 82 | 103 | 86 | 71 | 55 |
| 1955....... | 82 | 108 | 84 | 69 | 87 |
| 1956....... | 88 | 91 | 89 | 83 | 86 |
| 1957....... | 96 | 91 | 96 | 100 | 88 |
| 1958....... | 100 | 100 | 100 | 100 | 100 |
| 1959....... | 106 | 98 | 108 | 106 | 79 |

*b.* Average Annual Rate of Change — Taux annuel moyen de variation

| | | | | | |
|---|---|---|---|---|---|
| 1954 – 1958. | 5.1 | −0.7 | 3.8 | 8.9 | 16.1 |

[1] Consists of stone quarrying, clay and sand pits (ISIC major group 14) only.
[1] Extraction de la pierre à bâtir, de l'argile et du sable (CITI 14) seulement.

### B. The Major Groups of Manufacturing — Les classes de la branche Industries manufacturières

| Period / Période | Manufacturing / Industries manufacturières | Food, beverages and tobacco / Industries alimentaires, boissons, tabac | Textiles | Clothing, footwear and made-up textiles / Articles d'habillement, chaussures et ouvrages en tissu | Wood products and furniture / Bois et meubles | Paper and paper products / Papier et ouvrages en papier | Printing and publishing / Imprimerie et édition | Leather and leather products except wearing apparel / Cuir et articles en cuir, à l'exclusion des articles d'habillement | Rubber products / Ouvrages en caoutchouc | Chemicals and chemical, petroleum and coal products / Produits chimiques et dérivés du pétrole et du charbon | Non-metallic mineral products / Produits minéraux non métalliques | Basic metals / Métallurgie de base | Metal products / Ouvrages en métaux | Other manufacturing / Autres industries manufacturières |
|---|---|---|---|---|---|---|---|---|---|---|---|---|---|---|
| ISIC — CITI | 2-3 | 20–22 | 23 | 24 | 25–26 | 27 | 28 | 29 | 30 | 31–32 | 33 | 34 | 35–38 | 39 |

*a.* Indexes — Indices (1958 = 100)

| | | | | | | | | | | | | | | |
|---|---|---|---|---|---|---|---|---|---|---|---|---|---|---|
| 1954.............. | 86 | 92 | 97 | 70 | 90 | 109 | 83 | 82 | 94 | 90 | 90 | 76 | 77 | 76 |
| 1955.............. | 84 | 92 | 95 | 58 | 83 | 92 | 93 | 84 | 81 | 88 | 86 | 76 | 81 | 63 |
| 1956.............. | 89 | 94 | 93 | 76 | 89 | 85 | 93 | 86 | 143 | 90 | 92 | 93 | 78 | 100 |
| 1957.............. | 96 | 98 | 96 | 92 | 95 | 108 | 104 | 96 | 148 | 108 | 95 | 103 | 86 | 93 |
| 1958.............. | 100 | 100 | 100 | 100 | 100 | 100 | 100 | 100 | 100 | 100 | 100 | 100 | 100 | 100 |
| 1959.............. | 108 | 112 | 104 | 112 | 109 | 113 | 102 | 103 | 106 | 102 | 104 | 100 | 109 | 104 |

*b.* Average Annual Rate of Change — Taux annuel moyen de variation

| | | | | | | | | | | | | | | |
|---|---|---|---|---|---|---|---|---|---|---|---|---|---|---|
| 1954 – 1958........ | 3.8 | 2.1 | 0.8 | 9.3 | 2.7 | −2.1 | 4.8 | 5.1 | 1.6 | 2.7 | 2.7 | 7.1 | 6.8 | 7.1 |

## 2. CHARACTERISTICS OF REGISTERED INDUSTRIAL ESTABLISHMENTS
## CARACTERISTIQUES DES ETABLISSEMENTS INDUSTRIELS ENREGISTRES
### 1936, 1954, 1958

Number of establishments in units; gross value of production in million pesos; number of employees in thousands.

Nombre d'établissements en unités; valeur brute de la production en millions de pesos; nombre de salariés en milliers.

### A. The Divisions of Industrial Activity — Les branches de l'activité industrielle

| Year and item of data | All industrial activity — Toutes industries | Mining — Industries extractives | Manufacturing — Industries manufacturières | Construction — Bâtiment et travaux publics | Electricity, gas and water — Electricité, gaz et eau | Année et rubrique | Year and item of data | All industrial activity — Toutes industries | Mining — Industries extractives | Manufacturing — Industries manufacturières | Construction — Bâtiment et travaux publics | Electricity, gas and water — Electricité, gaz et eau | Année et rubrique |
|---|---|---|---|---|---|---|---|---|---|---|---|---|---|
| ISIC | 1-4,511-521 | 1 | 2-3 | 4 | 511-521 | CITI | ISIC | 1-4,511-521 | 1 | 2-3 | 4 | 511-521 | CITI |
| | a. Absolute Figures — Chiffres absolus | | | | | | | b. Structure | | | | | |
| 1936 Number of establishments... | 11 178 | 60 | 10 277 | 817 | 24 | 1936 Nombre d'établissements | 1936 Distribution in percent of number of employees....... | | | | | | 1936 Distribution en pourcentage du nombre de salariés |
| Gross value of production....... | 270.8 | 2.6 | 237.6 | 16.7 | 13.9 | Valeur brute de la production | | 100.0 | 2.6 | 75.6 | 18.1 | 3.7 | |
| Number of employees....... | 86.0 | 2.2 | 65.0 | 15.6 | 3.2 | Nombre de salariés | | | | | | | |
| 1954 Number of establishments... | 24 630 | 149 | 20 379 | 3 754 | 348 | 1954 Nombre d'établissements | 1954 Distribution in percent of number of employees....... | | | | | | 1954 Distribution en pourcentage du nombre de salariés |
| Gross value of production....... | 2 414.1 | 8.6 | 2 130.2 | 191.1 | 84.2 | Valeur brute de la production | | 100.0 | 0.7 | 81.8 | 13.8 | 3.6 | |
| Number of employees....... | 202.2 | 1.5 | 165.4 | 28.0 | 7.3 | Nombre de salariés | | | | | | | |
| 1958 Number of establishments... | 31 339 | 202 | 25 626 | 5 147 | 364 | 1958 Nombre d'établissements | 1958 Distribution in percent of number of employees....... | | | | | | 1958 Distribution en pourcentage du nombre de salariés |
| Gross value of production....... | 3 810.3 | 14.9 | 3 345.7 | 295.3 | 154.4 | Valeur brute de la production | | 100.0 | 0.6 | 78.0 | 16.0 | 5.4 | |
| Number of employees....... | 245.5 | 1.5 | 191.4 | 39.3 | 13.3 | Nombre de salariés | | | | | | | |

### B. The Major Groups of Manufacturing — Les classes de la branche Industries manufacturières

| Year and item of data | Manufacturing — Industries manufacturières | Food, beverages and tobacco — Industries alimentaires, boissons, tabac | Textiles | Clothing, footwear and made-up textiles — Articles d'habillement, chaussures et ouvrages en tissu | Wood products and furniture — Bois et meubles | Paper and paper products — Papier et ouvrages en papier | Printing and publishing — Imprimerie et édition | Leather and leather products except wearing apparel — Cuir et articles en cuir, à l'exclusion des articles d'habillement | Rubber products — Ouvrages en caoutchouc | Chemicals and chemical, petroleum and coal products — Produits chimiques et dérivés du pétrole et du charbon | Non-metallic mineral products — Produits minéraux non métalliques | Basic metals — Métallurgie de base | Metal products — Ouvrages en métaux | Other manufacturing — Autres industries manufacturières | Année et rubrique |
|---|---|---|---|---|---|---|---|---|---|---|---|---|---|---|---|
| ISIC | 2-3 | 20-22 | 23 | 24 | 25-26 | 27 | 28 | 29 | 30 | 31-32 | 33 | 34 | 35-38 | 39 | CITI |
| | a. Absolute Figures — Chiffres absolus | | | | | | | | | | | | | | |
| 1936 Number of establishments | 10 277 | 2 965 | 109 | 2 147 | 1 012 | 44 | 265 | 175 | 107 | 291 | 469 | 15 | 2 113 | 565 | 1936 Nombre d'établissements |
| Gross value of production.......... | 237.6 | 131.6 | 18.6 | 19.1 | 7.8 | 2.7 | 5.6 | 5.6 | 1.5 | 16.3 | 8.7 | 0.8 | 16.7 | 2.6 | Valeur brute de la production |
| Number of employees... | 65.0 | 25.6 | 6.6 | 7.2 | 3.9 | 0.9 | 2.9 | 1.2 | 0.8 | 2.1 | 3.6 | 0.4 | 8.3 | 1.5 | Nombre de salariés |
| 1954 Number of establishments. | 20 379 | 5 179 | 457 | 3 032 | 2 202 | 75 | 428 | 324 | 192 | 522 | 1 268 | 66 | 5 448 | 1 186 | 1954 Nombre d'établissements |
| Gross value of production.......... | 2 130.2 | 836.7 | 285.0 | 107.5 | 75.6 | 32.9 | 53.8 | 27.4 | 41.7 | 297.8 | 83.8 | 17.9 | 233.1 | 37.0 | Valeur brute de la production |
| Number of employees... | 165.4 | 48.5 | 25.1 | 13.5 | 9.5 | 3.3 | 5.2 | 2.2 | 3.2 | 11.2 | 9.2 | 1.3 | 27.9 | 5.3 | Nombre de salariés |
| 1958 Number of establishments. | 25 626 | 6 030 | 566 | 3 987 | 2 752 | 88 | 520 | 369 | 312 | 640 | 1 433 | 91 | 7 171 | 1 667 | 1958 Nombre d'établissements |
| Gross value of production.......... | 3 345.7 | 1 298.5 | 460.5 | 193.9 | 105.7 | 64.4 | 99.8 | 41.3 | 86.1 | 362.5 | 142.1 | 35.6 | 384.0 | 71.3 | Valeur brute de la production |
| Number of employees... | 191.4 | 52.9 | 25.8 | 19.1 | 10.6 | 3.0 | 6.3 | 2.7 | 3.4 | 12.4 | 10.3 | 1.8 | 36.1 | 7.0 | Nombre de salariés |
| | b. Structure | | | | | | | | | | | | | | |
| 1936 Distribution in percent of number of employees.......... | 100.0 | 39.4 | 10.2 | 11.1 | 6.0 | 1.4 | 4.5 | 1.8 | 1.2 | 3.2 | 5.5 | 0.6 | 12.8 | 2.3 | 1936 Distribution en pourcentage du nombre de salariés |
| 1954 Distribution in percent of number of employees.......... | 100.0 | 29.3 | 15.2 | 8.2 | 5.7 | 2.0 | 3.1 | 1.3 | 1.9 | 6.8 | 5.6 | 0.8 | 16.9 | 3.2 | 1954 Distribution en pourcentage du nombre de salariés |
| 1958 Distribution in percent of number of employees.......... | 100.0 | 27.6 | 13.5 | 10.0 | 5.5 | 1.6 | 3.3 | 1.4 | 1.8 | 6.5 | 5.4 | 0.9 | 18.9 | 3.6 | 1958 Distribution en pourcentage du nombre de salariés |

# VENEZUELA

## Gross Domestic Product and the Gross Domestic Fixed Capital Formation

Estimates of the expenditure on and industrial origin of the gross domestic product, and of the industrial composition of the gross domestic fixed capital formation, are presented in Table 1. This table has been compiled from data supplied by the Banco Central de Venezuela, Caracas in response to the United Nations national accounts questionnaire. Official estimates are published by the Banco in its annual report *Memoria*.

## Produit intérieur brut et formation brute de capital fixe intérieur

Les estimations des dépenses imputées au produit intérieur brut et des composantes du produit intérieur brut suivant le secteur industriel d'origine ainsi que des composantes du capital brut intérieur fixe formé ventilées suivant le secteur d'activité industrielle sont reproduites au tableau 1. Ce tableau a été construit à partir de données fournies par la Banco Central de Venezuela, Caracas en réponse au questionnaire de l'O.N.U. relatif aux comptes nationaux. Des estimations officielles sont publiées par la Banco dans son rapport annuel *Memoria*.

## Index Numbers of Industrial Production

The indexes presented in Table 2 are derived from index numbers of industrial production compiled by the Banco Central de Venezuela. The index numbers for mining for the years 1938-1960 have been extracted from a mimeographed paper, *Indices de Producción de las Industrias Extractivas* which also contains a description of the sources and methods used. The index numbers for the manufacturing sector for the years 1948 and 1949 have been extracted from a short mimeographed paper, *El Indice de Producción Industrial*, whilst those for the years 1950 and thereafter are published in *Memoria, 1959* and subsequent issues of the same publication. A description of the sources and methods used can be found in a mimeographed paper, *Indices de Producción de la Industria Manufacturera*. The index numbers for electricity are also published in various editions of *Memoria*. The Statistical Office of the United Nations also received much of the information by correspondence from the Banco Central.

The product series indicating manufacturing activity have been combined into indexes for major groups by using as weights value added at prices, ex-factory, for 1957 and quantities produced for 1953. The major group indexes were combined into an index of production for total manufacturing using as weights, value added in 1953 obtained from the Industrial Census described below. In the case of mining the weights used both for the purpose of combining the product series into major groups, and these major groups into mining as a whole were the value added at prices of 1957. In both manufacturing and mining, the original comparison base for the indexes was 1953.

The production index for mining, manufacturing and electricity combined has been calculated by the Statistical Office of the United Nations using as weights, value added

## Indices de la production industrielle

Les indices du tableau 2 ont été tirés d'indices de la production industrielle calculés par la Banco Central de Venezuela. Les indices relatifs aux Industries extractives pour les années 1938-1960 ont été tirés d'un document miméographié intitulé *Indices de Producción de las Industrias Extractivas* qui comporte également une description des sources et méthodes utilisées. Les indices relatifs au secteur manufacturier pour les années 1948 et 1949 ont été extraits du même type de document intitulé *El Indice de Producción Industrial* tandis que ceux relatifs à 1950 et aux années ultérieures sont publiés dans *Memoria 1959* et dans les numéros suivants de la même publication. Une description des sources et méthodes utilisées peut être trouvée dans un document miméographié intitulé *Indices de Producción de la Industria Manufacturera*. Les indices relatifs à l'électricité sont également publiés dans différents numéros de *Memoria*. Le Bureau de statistique de l'O.N.U. reçoit la plus grande partie des informations qu'il utilise, par l'intermédiaire de sa correspondance avec la Banco Central.

Les séries d'indices relatifs aux activités manufacturières ont été combinées en indices de classes; pour cela la valeur ajoutée aux prix — départ usine — pour 1957 et les quantités produites pour 1953 ont été utilisées comme coefficients de pondération. Les indices de classe ont été combinés en indices relatifs à l'ensemble des activités manufacturières, utilisant comme coefficient de pondération la valeur ajoutée en 1953 tirée du recensement industriel décrit ci-dessous. Dans le cas des Industries extractives on a utilisé la valeur ajoutée aux prix de 1957 comme base de pondération pour combiner les séries en indices relatifs aux classes et ceux-ci en indices relatifs à l'ensemble de l'Activité extractive. Pour les indices relatifs aux industries manufacturières et aux industries extractives, l'année de comparaison de base était 1953.

Les indices de la production relatifs à l'ensemble des industries extractives, industries manufacturières et électricité ont été calculés par le Bureau de statistique de

in 1957, estimates of which were provided by the Banco Central through correspondence.

### Index Numbers of Industrial Employment

The index numbers of industrial employment presented in Table 3 are derived from indexes compiled by the Banco Central de Venezuela. The data for the years 1950-1959 are published by the Banco in *Memoria, 1959*. The data for other years have been obtained through correspondence with the Banco.

These indexes are based on annual absolute figures of the number of persons engaged; these absolute figures are part of estimates of the number of economically active persons made by the Banco Central and based upon the 1950 census of population.

### The Characteristics and Structure of Industrial Activity

The data shown in Table 4 are derived from the final results of the 1936 Economic Census and the provisional results of the 1953 Economic Census. The former have been published by the Dirección General de Estadística in *Censos Industrial, Comercial y Empresas que Prestan Servicios, 1936*. The latter have been made available by the Dirección General de Estadística to the Statistical Office of the United Nations. Both Censuses cover all establishments, regardless of size, which were engaged in industrial activity during the census year.

The count of establishments relates to units that were in business during the census year as well as at the time the Censuses were taken. Value added during 1936 is based on the value of sales at market prices whereas value added during 1953 is derived from the value of production at market prices. The figures of number of engaged in 1936 do not cover homeworkers, and the data on wages and salaries paid during 1936 are somewhat incomplete because of the omission of salaries paid to employees other than wage earners (operatives) by establishments in the Federal District of Venezuela.

### Indices de l'emploi industriel

Les indices de l'emploi reproduits au tableau 3 ont été tirés d'indices calculés par la Banco Central de Venezuela. Les données relatives aux années 1950-1959 sont publiées par la Banco dans *Memoria 1959*. Les données relatives aux autres années ont été communiquées par correspondance avec la Banco.

Ces indices sont fondés sur les chiffres absolus annuels donnant le nombre de personnes engagées. Ces chiffres font partie des estimations du nombre de personnes économiquement actives, faites par la Banco Central d'après le recensement de la population de 1950.

### Caractéristiques et structure de l'activité industrielle

Les chiffres du tableau 4 sont tirés des résultats définitifs du recensement économique de 1936 et des résultats provisoires du recensement économique de 1953. Les premiers ont été publiés par la Dirección General de Estadística dans *Censos Industrial, Comercial y Empresas que Prestan Servicios, 1936*. Ceux de 1953 ont été communiqués au Bureau de statistique de l'O.N.U. par la Dirección General de Estadística. Les deux recensements couvrent tous les établissements, quelle que soit leur dimension, qui exerçaient une activité industrielle pendant l'année du recensement.

Le nombre des établissements est celui des unités qui étaient en activité pendant l'année du recensement et à la date du recensement. La valeur ajoutée en 1936 est fondée sur la valeur des ventes aux prix du marché, tandis que la valeur ajoutée en 1953 est tirée de la valeur de la production aux prix du marché. Les chiffres relatifs au nombre de personnes occupées en 1936 ne comprennent pas les travailleurs à domicile et les données sur les traitements et salaires versés aux salariés durant 1936 sont quelque peu incomplètes vu l'omission des salaires versés aux salariés autres que les ouvriers, par les établissements situés dans le District fédéral du Venezuela.

l'O.N.U., utilisant comme base de pondération, la valeur ajoutée en 1957, dont les estimations sont fournies par la Banco Central, par un échange de lettres.

# VENEZUELA

## 1. GROSS DOMESTIC PRODUCT AND GROSS DOMESTIC FIXED CAPITAL FORMATION
## PRODUIT INTERIEUR BRUT ET FORMATION BRUTE DE CAPITAL FIXE INTERIEUR

Million Bolivares                                                                    Millions de bolivars

### A. Expenditure on the Gross Domestic Product at Market Prices
### Dépenses relatives au produit intérieur brut aux prix du marché

| Item of data and year / Rubrique et année | Total | Consumption / Consommation | | Gross Domestic Capital Formation [1] / Formation brute de capital intérieur [1] | | Net exports of goods and services / Exportations nettes de biens et de services | |
|---|---|---|---|---|---|---|---|
| | | Total | Government / Etat | Total | Fixed / Fixe | Exports less imports / Exportations moins importations | Exports[2] / Exportations[2] |
| | | | | *a.* At Current Prices — Aux prix courants | | | |
| **Absolute figures — Chiffres absolus** | | | | | | | |
| 1950 | 11 826 | 7 972 | 1 602 | 2 874 | 2 756 | 980 | 3 619 |
| 1951 | 13 007 | 8 353 | 1 740 | 3 287 | 3 159 | 1 367 | 4 182 |
| 1952 | 13 981 | 8 404 | 1 830 | 4 407 | 4 012 | 1 170 | 4 512 |
| 1953 | 14 806 | 9 356 | 1 920 | 4 316 | 4 282 | 1 134 | 4 709 |
| 1954 | 16 377 | 9 935 | 2 123 | 5 043 | 4 993 | 1 399 | 5 197 |
| 1955 | 17 893 | 11 367 | 2 241 | 4 620 | 4 410 | 1 906 | 5 914 |
| 1956 | 20 400 | 13 145 | 2 284 | 5 327 | 5 098 | 1 928 | 6 906 |
| 1957 | 23 847 | 15 932 | 2 556 | 6 253 | 5 950 | 1 662 | 8 521 |
| 1958 | 24 585 | 17 184 | 3 573 | 6 314 | 5 964 | 1 087 | 7 834 |
| 1959 | 25 557 | 17 733 | 3 130 | 6 345 | 6 060 | 1 479 | 7 803 |
| 1960 | 24 837 | 17 290 | 3 094 | 4 373 | 4 774 | 3 174 | 7 992 |
| 1961 | 25 985 | 18 269 | 3 241 | 4 235 | 4 201 | 3 481 | 8 570 |
| **Percentage distribution of average annual expenditure — Distribution en pourcentage des dépenses annuelles moyennes** | | | | | | | |
| 1950 – 1960 | 100.0 | 66.0 | 12.6 | 25.7 | 24.8 | 8.3 | 32.4 |
| 1950 | 100.0 | 67.4 | 13.5 | 24.3 | 23.3 | 8.3 | 30.6 |
| 1953 | 100.0 | 63.2 | 13.0 | 29.2 | 28.9 | 7.6 | 31.8 |
| 1954 | 100.0 | 60.7 | 13.0 | 30.8 | 30.5 | 8.5 | 31.7 |
| 1958 | 100.0 | 69.9 | 14.5 | 25.7 | 24.2 | 4.4 | 31.9 |
| 1960 | 100.0 | 69.6 | 12.4 | 17.6 | 19.2 | 12.8 | 32.2 |

For footnotes see end of table.                                        Pour les notes, voir au bas du tableau.

## B. The Gross Domestic Product at Market Prices According to Origin
### Origine par secteur d'activité du produit intérieur brut aux prix du marché

| Item of data and year / Rubrique et année | Total | Agricultural sector / Secteur agricole | Industrial Sector — Secteur Industriel | | | | | Transportation and communication / Transports et communications | Other sectors / Autres secteurs |
| | | | Total | Mining / Industries extractives | Manufacturing / Industries manufacturières | Construction / Bâtiment et travaux publics | Electricity, gas and water / Electricité, gaz et eau | | |
| ISIC — CITI | 0–9 | 0 | 1–5 | 1 | 2–3 | 4 | 5 | 7 | 6, 8–9 |
| --- | --- | --- | --- | --- | --- | --- | --- | --- | --- |
| **a. At Current Prices — Aux prix courants** | | | | | | | | | |
| Absolute figures — Chiffres absolus | | | | | | | | | |
| 1959 | 23 887 | 1 637 | 10 578 | 6 383 | 2 709 | 1 166 | 320 | 803 | 10 869 |
| 1960 | 23 721 | 1 665 | 10 303 | 6 425 | 2 641 | 890 | 347 | 747 | 11 006 |
| Percentage distribution according to sector — Distribution en pourcentage par secteur | | | | | | | | | |
| 1959 | 100.0 | 6.8 | 44.3 | 26.7 | 11.4 | 4.8 | 1.4 | 3.3 | 45.6 |
| 1960 | 100.0 | 7.0 | 43.4 | 27.1 | 11.1 | 3.7 | 1.5 | 3.2 | 46.4 |
| **b. At Prices of 1957 — Aux prix de 1957** | | | | | | | | | |
| Absolute figures — Chiffres absolus | | | | | | | | | |
| 1950 | 12 727.5 | 1 014.4 | 5 987.3 | 3 940.8 | 1 150.5 | 827.1 | 68.9 | 698.8 | 5 027.0 |
| 1951 | 14 212.2 | 1 156.4 | 6 838.5 | 4 523.4 | 1 200.3 | 1 031.7 | 83.1 | 706.4 | 5 510.9 |
| 1952 | 15 247.9 | 1 238.6 | 7 488.9 | 4 843.1 | 1 404.5 | 1 144.5 | 96.8 | 674.7 | 5 845.7 |
| 1953 | 16 190.2 | 1 280.2 | 7 690.8 | 4 781.1 | 1 570.2 | 1 220.5 | 119.0 | 842.3 | 6 376.9 |
| 1954 | 17 749.4 | 1 284.3 | 8 527.3 | 5 208.3 | 1 807.7 | 1 376.2 | 135.1 | 876.1 | 7 061.7 |
| 1955 | 19 324.8 | 1 352.2 | 9 524.1 | 5 998.1 | 2 003.7 | 1 363.2 | 159.1 | 951.0 | 7 497.5 |
| 1956 | 21 366.3 | 1 445.6 | 10 856.0 | 6 879.4 | 2 183.9 | 1 605.2 | 187.5 | 945.3 | 8 119.4 |
| 1957 | 23 847.6 | 1 507.4 | 12 102.8 | 7 855.5 | 2 428.7 | 1 580.5 | 238.1 | 939.7 | 9 297.7 |
| 1958 | 24 164.1 | 1 576.4 | 11 958.0 | 7 452.7 | 2 607.0 | 1 617.8 | 280.5 | 1 001.8 | 9 627.9 |
| 1959 | 26 064.7 | 1 642.4 | 13 033.7 | 7 979.5 | 3 011.7 | 1 706.7 | 335.8 | 1 089.8 | 10 298.8 |
| 1960 | 26 432.6 | 1 806.6 | 12 974.1 | 8 265.3 | 2 898.5 | 1 443.5 | 366.8 | 1 040.7 | 10 611.2 |
| Percentage distribution according to sector — Distribution en pourcentage par secteur | | | | | | | | | |
| 1950 – 1960 | 100.0 | 7.0 | 49.2 | 31.2 | 10.2 | 6.9 | 0.9 | 4.5 | 39.3 |
| 1950 | 100.0 | 7.9 | 47.1 | 31.0 | 9.0 | 6.5 | 0.6 | 5.5 | 39.5 |
| 1953 | 100.0 | 7.9 | 47.5 | 29.5 | 9.7 | 7.5 | 0.8 | 5.2 | 39.4 |
| 1954 | 100.0 | 7.2 | 48.0 | 29.3 | 10.2 | 7.8 | 0.7 | 5.0 | 39.8 |
| 1958 | 100.0 | 6.5 | 49.5 | 30.8 | 10.8 | 6.7 | 1.2 | 4.1 | 39.9 |
| 1960 | 100.0 | 6.8 | 49.1 | 31.3 | 10.9 | 5.5 | 1.4 | 3.9 | 40.2 |
| Average annual rate of growth — Taux annuel moyen d'accroissement | | | | | | | | | |
| 1950 – 1960 | 7.6 | 5.9 | 8.0 | 7.7 | 9.7 | 5.7 | 18.2 | 4.1 | 7.8 |
| 1950 – 1953 | 8.4 | 8.1 | 8.7 | 6.6 | 10.9 | 13.9 | 20.0 | 6.4 | 8.2 |
| 1954 – 1958 | 8.0 | 5.2 | 8.8 | 9.4 | 9.6 | 4.1 | 20.0 | 3.4 | 8.1 |
| 1958 – 1960 | 4.6 | 7.1 | 4.2 | 5.3 | 5.5 | −5.6 | 14.4 | 1.9 | 5.0 |

**C.  Gross Domestic Fixed Capital Formation According to Purchasing Sector**

**Formation brute de capital fixe intérieur par secteur d'acquisition**

| Item of data and year<br>Rubrique et année | Total [1] | Agricultural sector [1]<br>Secteur agricole [1] | Industrial Sector — Secteur Industriel | | | | | Transportation and communication<br>Transports et communications | Other sectors<br>Autres secteurs |
|---|---|---|---|---|---|---|---|---|---|
| | | | Total | Mining [3]<br>Industries extractives [3] | Manufacturing [3]<br>Industries manufacturières [3] | Construction<br>Bâtiment et travaux publics | Electricity, gas and water<br>Electricité, gaz et eau | | |
| ISIC — CITI | 0–9 | 0 | 1–5 | 1 | 2–3 | 4 | 5 | 7 | 6, 8–9 |
| *a. At Current Prices — Aux prix courants* | | | | | | | | | |
| Absolute figures — Chiffres absolus | | | | | | | | | |
| 1959........................ | 6 059 | 654 | 2 625 | 1 495 | 852 | 48 | 230 | 1 019 | 1 761 |
| 1960........................ | 4 771 | 679 | 1 875 | 1 031 | 600 | 18 | 226 | 747 | 1 470 |
| 1961........................ | 4 163 | 736 | 1 599 | 686 | 557 | 18 | 338 | 709 | 1 119 |
| Percentage distribution according to sector — Distribution en pourcentage par secteur | | | | | | | | | |
| 1959........................ | 100.0 | 10.7 | 43.4 | 24.7 | 14.1 | 0.8 | 3.8 | 16.8 | 29.1 |
| 1960........................ | 100.0 | 14.2 | 39.3 | 21.6 | 12.6 | 0.3 | 4.8 | 15.6 | 30.9 |
| *b. At Prices of 1957 — Aux prix de 1957* | | | | | | | | | |
| Absolute figures — Chiffres absolus | | | | | | | | | |
| 1950........................ | 3 264 | 365 | 1 040 | 703 | 226 | 56 | 55 | 468 | 1 391 |
| 1951........................ | 3 471 | 322 | 1 124 | 784 | 253 | 39 | 48 | 506 | 1 520 |
| 1952........................ | 4 358 | 383 | 1 513 | 1 149 | 280 | 21 | 63 | 489 | 1 974 |
| 1953........................ | 4 784 | 417 | 1 378 | 1 026 | 287 | 27 | 38 | 556 | 2 434 |
| 1954........................ | 5 466 | 603 | 1 572 | 1 051 | 341 | 71 | 109 | 1 046 | 2 245 |
| 1955........................ | 5 161 | 570 | 1 613 | 1 161 | 318 | 59 | 75 | 944 | 2 034 |
| 1956........................ | 5 597 | 605 | 2 158 | 1 614 | 358 | 82 | 104 | 1 047 | 1 785 |
| 1957........................ | 5 950 | 608 | 2 740 | 1 775 | 493 | 292 | 180 | 398 | 2 201 |
| 1958........................ | 5 897 | 540 | 2 802 | 1 629 | 549 | 85 | 539 | 403 | 2 152 |
| 1959........................ | 6 066 | 655 | 2 628 | 1 497 | 853 | 48 | 230 | 1 020 | 1 763 |
| 1960........................ | 4 701 | 669 | 1 848 | 1 016 | 591 | 18 | 223 | 736 | 1 448 |
| 1961........................ | 3 969 | 702 | 1 524 | 654 | 531 | 17 | 322 | 676 | 1 067 |
| Percentage distribution according to sector — Distribution en pourcentage par secteur | | | | | | | | | |
| 1950 – 1960.............. | 100.0 | 10.4 | 37.4 | 24.5 | 8.4 | 1.4 | 3.1 | 13.9 | 38.3 |
| 1950..................... | 100.0 | 11.1 | 31.9 | 21.6 | 6.9 | 1.7 | 1.7 | 14.3 | 42.7 |
| 1953..................... | 100.0 | 8.7 | 28.8 | 21.4 | 6.0 | 0.6 | 0.8 | 11.6 | 50.9 |
| 1954..................... | 100.0 | 11.0 | 28.7 | 19.2 | 6.2 | 1.3 | 2.0 | 19.2 | 41.1 |
| 1958..................... | 100.0 | 9.1 | 47.5 | 27.6 | 9.3 | 1.5 | 9.1 | 6.9 | 36.5 |
| 1960..................... | 100.0 | 14.2 | 39.3 | 21.6 | 12.6 | 0.3 | 4.8 | 15.6 | 30.9 |
| Average annual rate of growth — Taux annuel moyen d'accroissement | | | | | | | | | |
| 1950 – 1960.............. | 3.7 | 6.2 | 5.9 | 3.7 | 10.1 | −10.7 | 15.0 | 4.6 | 0.4 |
| 1950 – 1953.............. | 13.6 | 4.5 | 9.8 | 13.4 | 8.3 | −21.6 | −11.6 | 5.9 | 20.5 |
| 1954 – 1958.............. | 1.9 | −2.7 | 15.5 | 11.6 | 12.6 | 4.6 | 49.1 | −21.2 | −1.1 |
| 1958 – 1960.............. | −10.7 | 11.3 | −18.8 | −21.0 | 3.7 | −54.0 | −35.6 | 35.1 | −18.0 |

[1] Includes changes in stocks of livestock on farms.
[2] Exports (f.o.b.) of goods only. Net exports of services are included under the item 'Exports less Imports'.
[3] Refining of petroleum is included under Mining.

[1] Y compris les variations du cheptel dans les exploitations agricoles.
[2] Exportations (f.o.b.) de marchandises seulement. Les exportations nettes de services figurent sous la rubrique "Exportations moins Importations".
[3] Le raffinage du pétrole est compris dans les Industries extractives.

## 2. INDEX NUMBERS OF INDUSTRIAL PRODUCTION
### INDICES DE LA PRODUCTION INDUSTRIELLE

### A. Selected Divisions of Industrial Activity
### Quelques branches de l'activité industrielle

| Period<br>Période | Total | Mining [1]<br>Industries<br>extractives [1] | Manu-<br>facturing [2]<br>Industries<br>manu-<br>facturières [2] | Electricity<br>Electricité |
|---|---|---|---|---|
| ISIC — CITI | 1–3, 511 | 1 | 2–3 | 511 |

*a.* Indexes — Indices (1958 = 100)

| | | | | |
|---|---|---|---|---|
| 1948........... | 38 | 44 | 25 | 17 |
| 1949........... | 39 | 43 | 29 | 20 |
| 1950........... | 45 | 49 | 34 | – 25 – |
| 1951........... | 51 | 57 | 39 | 30 |
| 1952........... | 57 | 61 | 47 | 34 |
| 1953........... | 58 | 60 | 55 | 42 |
| 1954........... | 67 | 67 | 65 | 48 |
| 1955........... | 78 | 79 | 75 | 57 |
| 1956........... | 88 | 91 | 81 | 67 |
| 1957........... | 102 | 106 | 92 | 85 |
| 1958........... | 100 | 100 | 100 | 100 |
| 1959........... | 110 | 107 | 117 | 121 |
| 1960........... | 113 | 112 | 115 | 132 |
| 1961........... | 113 | 109 | 121 | 151 |

*b.* Average Annual Rate of Change — Taux annuel moyen de variation

| | | | | |
|---|---|---|---|---|
| 1950 – 1960..... | 9.6 | 8.6 | 13.0 | 18.1 |
| 1948 – 1953..... | 8.8 | 6.4 | 17.1 | 19.8 |
| 1954 – 1958..... | 10.5 | 10.5 | 11.4 | 20.1 |
| 1958 – 1960..... | 6.3 | 5.8 | 7.2 | 14.9 |

For footnotes see end of table.
Pour les notes, voir au bas du tableau.

### B. The Major Groups of Mining
### Les classes de la branche Industries extractives

| Period<br>Période | Total [1] | Coal<br>mining<br>Extraction<br>du charbon | Metal mining<br>Extraction<br>des minerais<br>métalliques | Crude petro-<br>leum and<br>natural gas<br>Pétrole brut<br>et gaz naturel | Other mining [1]<br>Autres<br>industries<br>extractives [1] |
|---|---|---|---|---|---|
| ISIC — CITI | 1 | 11 | 12 | 13 | 19 |

*a.* Indexes — Indices (1958 = 100)

| | | | | | |
|---|---|---|---|---|---|
| 1938....... | 17 | 16 | 43 | 19 | 20 |
| 1948....... | 44 | 7 | 19 | 51 | 46 |
| 1949....... | 43 | 5 | 23 | 50 | 61 |
| 1950....... | 49 | 4 | 14 | 57 | 54 |
| 1951....... | 57 | 76 | 7 | 64 | 44 |
| 1952....... | 61 | 69 | 11 | 68 | 101 |
| 1953....... | 60 | 81 | 20 | 67 | 71 |
| 1954....... | 67 | 89 | 45 | 72 | 82 |
| 1955....... | 79 | 84 | 61 | 82 | 87 |
| 1956....... | 91 | 84 | 82 | 94 | 67 |
| 1957....... | 106 | 95 | 109 | 106 | 144 |
| 1958....... | 100 | 100 | 100 | 100 | 100 |
| 1959....... | 107 | 93 | 99 | 107 | 89 |
| 1960....... | 112 | 97 | 106 | 110 | 51 |
| 1961....... | 109 | 84 | 77 | 111 | 111 |

*b.* Average Annual Rate of Change — Taux annuel moyen de variation

| | | | | | |
|---|---|---|---|---|---|
| 1938 – 1960. | 8.9 | 8.5 | 4.2 | 8.3 | 4.3 |
| 1938 – 1948. | 10.0 | –7.9 | –7.8 | 10.4 | 8.7 |
| 1950 – 1960. | 8.6 | 37.6 | 22.2 | 6.8 | –0.6 |
| 1948 – 1953. | 6.4 | 63.2 | 1.0 | 5.6 | 9.1 |
| 1954 – 1958. | 10.5 | 3.0 | 22.1 | 8.6 | 5.1 |
| 1958 – 1960. | 5.8 | –1.5 | 3.0 | 4.9 | –28.6 |

For footnotes see end of table.
Pour les notes, voir au bas du tableau.

## C.  Selected Major Groups of Manufacturing — Quelques classes de la branche Industries manufacturières

| Period<br>Période | Manufac-turing [2]<br>Industries manufac-turières [2] | Food, beverages and tobacco [3]<br>Industries alimen-taires, boissons, tabac [3] | Textiles | Clothing, footwear and made-up textiles [4]<br>Articles d'habil-lement, chaussures et ouvrages en tissu [4] | Wood products and furniture [4]<br>Bois et meubles [4] | Paper and paper products [5]<br>Papier et ouvrages en papier [5] | Printing and publish-ing [5]<br>Im-primerie et édition [5] | Leather and leather products except wearing apparel<br>Cuir et articles en cuir, à l'exclu-sion des articles d'habil-lement | Rubber products<br>Ouvrages en caoutchouc | Chemicals and chemical, petroleum and coal products [3,5]<br>Produits chi-miques et dérivés du pétrole et du charbon [3,5] | Non-metallic mineral products<br>Produits minéraux non métal-liques | Metal products [5]<br>Ouvrages en métaux [5] | Other manu-facturing [5]<br>Autres industries manufac-turières [5] |
|---|---|---|---|---|---|---|---|---|---|---|---|---|---|
| ISIC — CITI | 2–3 | 20–22 | 23 | 24 | 25–26 | 27 | 28 | 29 | 30 | 31–32 | 33 | 35, 36, 38 | 39 |

### a. Indexes — Indices (1958 = 100)

| | | | | | | | | | | | | | |
|---|---|---|---|---|---|---|---|---|---|---|---|---|---|
| 1948............. | 25 | 36 | 33 | 14 | 50 | 13 | 17 | 25 | 9 | 16 | 21 | 12 | 8 |
| 1949............. | 29 | 40 | 30 | 16 | 46 | 13 | 24 | 28 | 9 | 20 | 30 | 15 | 12 |
| 1950............. | 34 | 44 | 28 | 22 | 53 | 12 | 28 | 31 | 21 | 29 | 41 | 21 | 11 |
| 1951............. | 39 | 48 | 40 | 26 | 57 | 21 | 32 | 35 | 23 | 36 | 45 | 23 | 14 |
| 1952............. | 47 | 57 | 47 | 41 | 66 | 25 | 41 | 44 | 29 | 43 | 56 | 26 | 21 |
| 1953............. | 55 | 62 | 52 | 60 | 79 | 32 | 49 | 49 | 39 | 53 | 65 | 34 | 30 |
| 1954. .......... | 65 | 70 | 62 | 79 | 96 | 80 | 55 | 56 | 61 | 58 | 78 | 48 | 43 |
| 1955............. | 75 | 81 | 64 | 91 | 105 | 66 | 81 | 63 | 65 | 71 | 82 | 55 | 52 |
| 1956............. | 81 | 84 | 73 | 110 | 104 | 73 | 78 | 86 | 75 | 78 | 88 | 63 | 67 |
| 1957............. | 92 | 90 | 91 | 103 | 109 | 99 | 83 | 92 | 88 | 92 | 111 | 79 | 92 |
| 1958............. | 100 | 100 | 100 | 100 | 100 | 100 | 100 | 100 | 100 | 100 | 100 | 100 | 100 |
| 1959............. | 117 | 116 | 123 | 127 | 106 | 176 | 110 | 121 | 120 | 112 | 112 | 124 | 111 |
| 1960............. | 115 | 129 | 139 | 109 | 71 | 196 | 108 | 105 | 126 | 111 | 93 | 126 | 145 |
| 1961............. | 121 | 132 | 147 | 118 | 69 | 216 | 101 | 148 | 126 | 120 | 94 | 132 | 192 |

### b. Average Annual Rate of Change — Taux annuel moyen de variation

| | | | | | | | | | | | | | |
|---|---|---|---|---|---|---|---|---|---|---|---|---|---|
| 1950 – 1960........ | 13.0 | 11.4 | 17.4 | 17.4 | 3.0 | 32.2 | 14.5 | 13.0 | 19.6 | 14.4 | 8.5 | 19.6 | 29.4 |
| 1948 – 1953........ | 17.1 | 11.5 | 9.5 | 33.8 | 9.6 | 19.7 | 23.6 | 14.0 | 34.1 | 27.1 | 25.4 | 23.2 | 30.3 |
| 1954 – 1958........ | 11.4 | 9.3 | 12.7 | 6.1 | 1.0 | 5.7 | 16.1 | 15.6 | 13.1 | 14.6 | 6.4 | 20.1 | 23.5 |
| 1958 – 1960........ | 7.2 | 13.6 | 17.9 | 4.4 | −15.7 | 40.0 | 3.9 | 2.5 | 12.2 | 5.4 | −3.6 | 12.2 | 20.4 |

[1] Excludes Stone Quarrying and Sand Pits (ISIC major group 14).
[2] Excludes Manufacture of footwear (ISIC group 241), Basic metals (ISIC major group 34), and Manufacture of electrical machinery (ISIC major group 37).
[3] Extraction of vegetable oils (part of ISIC group 312) is included under Food, beverages and tobacco (ISIC major groups 20-22).
[4] Excludes Manufacture of footwear (ISIC group 241); also manufacturing of mattresses (part of ISIC major group 26) is included under Clothing, footwear and made-up textiles (ISIC major group 24).
[5] Manufacture of paperboard (part of ISIC major group 27) and manufacture of batteries (part of ISIC major group 37) are included under Other manufacturing (ISIC major group 39). Manufacture of film (part of ISIC group 392) is included under Printing and publishing (ISIC major group 28) and the manufacture of jewelry (ISIC group 394) is included under Metal Products (ISIC major groups 35-38).

[1] Non compris l'Extraction de la pierre à bâtir et du sable (CITI 14).
[2] Non compris la Fabrication des chaussures (CITI 241), la Métallurgie de base (CITI 34) et la Fabrication de machines électriques (CITI 37).
[3] L'extraction des huiles végétales (dans CITI 312) est comprise dans Industries alimentaires, boissons et tabacs (CITI 20-22).
[4] Non compris la Fabrication des chaussures (CITI 241); la fabrication des matelas (dans CITI 26) est également comprise dans Articles d'habillement, chaussures et ouvrages en tissu (CITI 24).
[5] La fabrication du carton (dans CITI 27) et la fabrication des accumulateurs et des piles (dans CITI 37) sont comprises dans Autres industries manufacturières (CITI 39). La fabrication des pellicules (dans CITI 392) est comprise dans Imprimerie et édition (CITI 28), et la fabrication des bijoux (CITI 394) dans Ouvrages en métaux (CITI 35-38).

# 3. INDEX NUMBERS OF INDUSTRIAL EMPLOYMENT
## INDICES DE L'EMPLOI DANS L'INDUSTRIE

### A. The Divisions of Industrial Activity
### Les branches de l'activité industrielle

| Period / Période | Total | Mining / Industries extractives | Manu-facturing / Industries manu-facturières | Construction / Bâtiment et travaux publics | Electricity and gas / Electricité et gaz |
|---|---|---|---|---|---|
| ISIC — CITI | 1-4, 511-512 | 1 | 2-3 | 4 | 511-512 |

#### a. Indexes — Indices (1958 = 100)

| | | | | | |
|---|---|---|---|---|---|
| 1948....... | ... | 127 | 76 | ... | ... |
| 1949....... | ... | 97 | 78 | ... | ... |
| 1950....... | 70 | 87 | 81 | 51 | 47 |
| 1951....... | 71 | 87 | 81 | 52 | 52 |
| 1952....... | 78 | 95 | 87 | 63 | 57 |
| 1953....... | 80 | 91 | 88 | 65 | 62 |
| 1954....... | 84 | 94 | 92 | 71 | 69 |
| 1955....... | 84 | 94 | 95 | 65 | 75 |
| 1956....... | 93 | 96 | 96 | 88 | 83 |
| 1957....... | 100 | 102 | 99 | 102 | 91 |
| 1958....... | 100 | 100 | 100 | 100 | 100 |
| 1959....... | 103 | 98 | 102 | 104 | 113 |
| 1960....... | 94 | 94 | 100 | 85 | 119 |
| 1961....... | ... | 82 | ... | 72 | 131 |

#### b. Average Annual Rate of Change — Taux annuel moyen de variation

| | | | | | |
|---|---|---|---|---|---|
| 1950 - 1960. | 3.0 | 0.8 | 2.1 | 5.2 | 9.7 |
| 1948 - 1953. | ... | −6.5 | 3.0 | ... | ... |
| 1954 - 1958. | 4.4 | 1.6 | 2.1 | 8.9 | 9.7 |
| 1958 - 1960. | −3.0 | −3.0 | — | −7.8 | 9.1 |

For footnotes see end of table.
Pour les notes, voir au bas du tableau.

### B. The Major Groups of Mining
### Les classes de la branche Industries extractives

| Period / Période | All mining / Toutes industries extractives | Metal mining / Extraction des minerais métalliques | Crude petroleum and natural gas / Pétrole brut et gaz naturel | Other mining [1] / Autres industries extractives [1] |
|---|---|---|---|---|
| ISIC — CITI | 1 | 12 | 13 | 14-19 |

#### a. Indexes — Indices (1958 = 100)

| | | | | |
|---|---|---|---|---|
| 1938.......... | ... | — | ... | 33 |
| 1948.......... | 127 | — | 153 | 63 |
| 1949.......... | 97 | — | 111 | 75 |
| 1950.......... | 87 | 35 | 98 | 58 |
| 1951.......... | 87 | 35 | 103 | 36 |
| 1952.......... | 95 | 44 | 106 | 65 |
| 1953.......... | 91 | 47 | 103 | 56 |
| 1954.......... | 94 | 69 | 98 | 86 |
| 1955.......... | 94 | 72 | 97 | 90 |
| 1956.......... | 96 | 80 | 98 | 93 |
| 1957.......... | 102 | 99 | 103 | 96 |
| 1958.......... | 100 | 100 | 100 | 100 |
| 1959.......... | 98 | 100 | 97 | 104 |
| 1960.......... | 94 | 101 | 90 | 107 |
| 1961.......... | 82 | 97 | 82 | 72 |

#### b. Average Annual Rate of Change — Taux annuel moyen de variation

| | | | | |
|---|---|---|---|---|
| 1938 - 1960..... | ... | — | ... | 5.5 |
| 1938 - 1948..... | ... | — | ... | 6.7 |
| 1950 - 1960..... | 0.8 | 11.2 | −0.9 | 6.3 |
| 1948 - 1953..... | −6.5 | — | −7.6 | −2.3 |
| 1954 - 1958..... | 1.6 | 9.7 | 0.5 | 3.8 |
| 1958 - 1960..... | −3.0 | 0.5 | −5.1 | 3.4 |

For footnotes see end of table.
Pour les notes, voir au bas du tableau.

# VENEZUELA

## C. The Major Groups of Manufacturing — Les classes de la branche Industries manufacturières

| Period / Période | Manufacturing / Industries manufacturières | Food, beverages and tobacco / Industries alimentaires, boissons, tabac | Textiles | Clothing, footwear and made-up textiles / Articles d'habillement, chaussures et ouvrages en tissu | Wood products and furniture / Bois et meubles | Paper and paper products / Papier et ouvrages en papier | Printing and publishing / Imprimerie et édition | Leather and leather products except wearing apparel / Cuir et articles en cuir, à l'exclusion des articles d'habillement | Rubber products / Ouvrages en caoutchouc | Chemicals and chemical, petroleum and coal products / Produits chimiques et dérivés du pétrole et du charbon | Non-metallic mineral products / Produits minéraux non métalliques | Basic metal and metal products / Métallurgie de base et ouvrages en métaux | Other manufacturing / Autres industries manufacturières |
|---|---|---|---|---|---|---|---|---|---|---|---|---|---|
| ISIC — CITI | 2–3 | 20–22 | 23 | 24 | 25–26 | 27 | 28 | 29 | 30 | 31–32 | 33 | 34–38 | 39 |

### a. Indexes — Indices (1958 = 100)

| Period | | | | | | | | | | | | | |
|---|---|---|---|---|---|---|---|---|---|---|---|---|---|
| 1938 | ... | 64 | 93 | 90 | 30 | — | 17 | 49 | — | ... | 28 | 29 | 18 |
| 1948 | 76 | 70 | 70 | 103 | 58 | 62 | 53 | 72 | 15 | 40 | 63 | 64 | 19 |
| 1949 | 78 | 71 | 60 | 102 | 58 | 64 | 57 | 76 | 23 | 71 | 65 | 75 | 24 |
| 1950 | 81 | 73 | 59 | 103 | 60 | 62 | 59 | 80 | 31 | 87 | 68 | 85 | 24 |
| 1951 | 81 | 70 | 66 | 104 | 63 | 73 | 69 | 78 | 29 | 80 | 68 | 81 | 23 |
| 1952 | 87 | 77 | 74 | 109 | 70 | 74 | 71 | 88 | 37 | 86 | 68 | 86 | 30 |
| 1953 | 88 | 81 | 71 | 109 | 80 | 69 | 70 | 91 | 49 | 90 | 68 | 75 | 38 |
| 1954 | 92 | 81 | 80 | 108 | 94 | 67 | 71 | 94 | 76 | 92 | 80 | 83 | 47 |
| 1955 | 95 | 93 | 83 | 107 | 102 | 76 | 72 | 100 | 82 | 94 | 84 | 88 | 56 |
| 1956 | 96 | 90 | 90 | 105 | 102 | 83 | 78 | 96 | 82 | 94 | 89 | 89 | 69 |
| 1957 | 99 | 97 | 91 | 102 | 106 | 100 | 83 | 98 | 96 | 100 | 111 | 94 | 87 |
| 1958 | 100 | 100 | 100 | 100 | 100 | 100 | 100 | 100 | 100 | 100 | 100 | 100 | 100 |
| 1959 | 102 | 110 | 104 | 98 | 97 | 116 | 110 | 111 | 105 | 102 | 104 | 106 | 104 |
| 1960 | 100 | 116 | 116 | 92 | 75 | 119 | 114 | 108 | 102 | 101 | 103 | 116 | 114 |

### b. Average Annual Rate of Change — Taux annuel moyen de variation

| Period | | | | | | | | | | | | | |
|---|---|---|---|---|---|---|---|---|---|---|---|---|---|
| 1938–1960 | ... | 2.7 | 1.0 | 0.1 | 4.3 | — | 9.0 | 3.7 | — | ... | 6.1 | 6.5 | 8.8 |
| 1938–1948 | ... | 0.9 | −2.8 | 1.4 | 6.8 | — | 12.0 | 3.9 | — | ... | 8.4 | 8.2 | 0.5 |
| 1950–1960 | 2.1 | 4.7 | 7.0 | −1.1 | 2.3 | 6.7 | 6.8 | 3.0 | 12.6 | 1.5 | 4.2 | 3.2 | 16.9 |
| 1948–1953 | 3.0 | 3.0 | 0.3 | 1.1 | 6.6 | 2.2 | 5.7 | 4.8 | 26.7 | 17.6 | 1.5 | 3.2 | 14.9 |
| 1954–1958 | 2.1 | 5.4 | 5.7 | −1.9 | 1.6 | 10.5 | 8.9 | 1.6 | 7.1 | 2.1 | 5.7 | 4.8 | 20.8 |
| 1958–1960 | — | 7.7 | 7.7 | −4.1 | −13.4 | 9.1 | 6.8 | 3.9 | 1.0 | 0.5 | 1.5 | 7.7 | 6.8 |

[1] Includes Coal mining (ISIC major groups 11).        [1] Y compris l'Extraction du charbon (CITI 11).

## 4. CHARACTERISTICS OF ALL INDUSTRIAL ESTABLISHMENTS
## CARACTERISTIQUES DE TOUS LES ETABLISSEMENTS INDUSTRIELS
### 1936, 1953

Number of establishments in units; value added and wages and salaries in million Bolivares; number of engaged and employees in thousands; value added per person engaged and value added and wages and salaries per employee in thousand Bolivares.

Nombre d'établissements en unités; valeur ajoutée et traitements et salaires en millions de bolivars; nombre de personnes occupées et de salariés en milliers; valeur ajoutée par personne occupée et valeur ajoutée et traitements et salaires par salarié en milliers de bolivars.

### A. Selected Divisions of Industrial Activity — Quelques branches de l'activité industrielle

| Item of data | Manufacturing [1] / Industries manufacturières [1] | Construction / Bâtiment et travaux publics | Electricity and gas / Electricité et gaz | Rubrique |
|---|---|---|---|---|
| | 1953 | 1953 | 1953 | |
| ISIC | 2–3 | 4 | 511–512 | CITI |

#### a. Absolute Figures — Chiffres absolus

| | | | | |
|---|---|---|---|---|
| Number of units | 16 045 | 250 | 132 | Nombre d'unités |
| Value added | 1 229.5 | 372.8 | 101.2 | Valeur ajoutée |
| Number of engaged (As of 17.XI.1953) | 137.8 | 11.0 | 3.7 | Nombre de personnes occupées (au 17.XI.1953) |
| Number of employees (As of 17.XI.1953) | 95.5 | 10.8 | 3.6 | Nombre de salariés (au 17.XI.1953) |
| Wages and salaries paid | 462.3 | 100.9 | 29.4 | Traitements et salaires payés |

#### b. Structure

| | | | | |
|---|---|---|---|---|
| Value added per person engaged | 8.9 | 33.9 | 27.4 | Valeur ajoutée par personne occupée |
| Value added per unit of wages and salaries | 2.7 | 3.7 | 3.4 | Valeur ajoutée par unité de traitements et salaires |
| Wages and salaries per employee | 4.8 | 9.3 | 8.2 | Traitements et salaires par salarié |
| Employees as a percent of engaged | 69.3 | 98.2 | 97.3 | Salariés en pourcentage des personnes occupées |

[1] Excludes petroleum refineries.        [1] Non compris les raffineries de pétrole.

# VENEZUELA

## B. The Major Groups of Manufacturing — Les classes de la branche Industries manufacturières

| Year and item of data | Manufacturing[1] — Industries manufacturières[1] | Food, beverages and tobacco — Industries alimentaires, boissons, tabac | Textiles | Clothing, footwear and made-up textiles — Articles d'habillement, chaussures et ouvrages en tissu | Wood products and furniture — Bois et meubles | Paper and paper products — Papier et ouvrages en papier | Printing and publishing — Imprimerie et édition | Leather and leather products except wearing apparel — Cuir et articles en cuir, à l'exclusion des articles d'habillement | Rubber products — Ouvrages en caoutchouc | Chemicals and chemical, petroleum and coal products[1] — Produits chimiques et dérivés du pétrole et du charbon[1] | Non-metallic mineral products — Produits minéraux non métalliques | Basic metals — Métallurgie de base | Metal products — Ouvrages en métaux | Other manufacturing — Autres industries manufacturières | Année et rubrique |
|---|---|---|---|---|---|---|---|---|---|---|---|---|---|---|---|
| ISIC / CITI | 2–3 | 20–22 | 23 | 24 | 25–26 | 27 | 28 | 29 | 30 | 31–32 | 33 | 34 | 35–38 | 39 | |
| *a.  Absolute Figures — Chiffres absolus* | | | | | | | | | | | | | | | |
| **1936** | | | | | | | | | | | | | | | **1936** |
| Number of establishments. | 7 950[3] | 4 611 | 36 | 1 272[2] | 537 | 5 | 79 | 286 | 4 | 131 | 466 | 64 | 267 | 192[3] | Nombre d'établissements |
| Value added. . . . . . . . . | 157.0[3] | 82.1 | 7.0 | 17.2[2] | 7.0 | 0.1 | 7.0 | 4.9 | 0.5 | 7.0 | 5.9 | 0.5 | 3.8 | 14.0[3] | Valeur ajoutée |
| Number of employees... | 47.4[3] | 28.1 | 2.7 | 5.7[2] | 1.8 | 0.1 | 1.2 | 1.8 | 0.2 | 1.2 | 2.3 | 0.1 | 0.9 | 1.3[3] | Nombre de salariés |
| Wages and salaries paid [4]. . . . . . . . . . . | 56.2[3] | 23.7 | 4.2 | 8.6[3] | 2.8 | 0.1 | 4.2 | 2.0 | 0.3 | 2.1 | 3.0 | 0.2 | 1.6 | 3.4[3] | Traitements et salaires payés [4] |
| **1953** | | | | | | | | | | | | | | | **1953** |
| Number of establishments. | 16 045 | 6 262 | 296 | 3 860 | 1 648 | 37 | 358 | 148 | 104 | 174 | 674 | 6 | 2 002 | 476 | Nombre d'établissements |
| Value added. . . . . . . . . | 1 229.5 | 511.1 | 99.0 | 90.3 | 82.7 | 14.5 | 55.7 | 14.7 | 35.1 | 104.6 | 119.5 | 4.6 | 75.2 | 22.5 | Valeur ajoutée |
| Number of engaged (As of 17.XI.1953). . . . | 137.8 | 77.6 | 8.4 | 13.7 | 8.9 | 0.9 | 4.0 | 1.3 | 1.1 | 4.0 | 7.3 | 0.3 | 8.3 | 2.0 | Nombre de personnes occupées (au 17.XI.1953) |
| Number of employees (As of 17.XI.1953). . . . | 95.5 | 46.7 | 8.0 | 9.1 | 6.9 | 0.9 | 3.7 | 1.1 | 1.0 | 3.9 | 6.5 | 0.3 | 5.9 | 1.5 | Nombre de salariés (au 17.XI.1953) |
| Wages and salaries paid. . . . . . . . . . . . | 462.3 | 161.8 | 44.3 | 38.5 | 37.1 | 6.2 | 31.0 | 5.3 | 9.2 | 31.7 | 48.0 | 2.1 | 38.5 | 8.6 | Traitements et salaires payés |
| *b.  Structure* | | | | | | | | | | | | | | | |
| **1936** | | | | | | | | | | | | | | | **1936** |
| Distribution in percent of: | | | | | | | | | | | | | | | Distribution en pourcentage: |
| Value added. . . . . . . | 100.0 | 52.2 | 4.5 | 11.0 | 4.4 | 0.1 | 4.4 | 3.2 | 0.3 | 4.4 | 3.8 | 0.3 | 2.4 | 9.0 | De la valeur ajoutée |
| Number of employees. | 100.0 | 59.2 | 5.7 | 12.1 | 3.8 | 0.2 | 2.5 | 3.8 | 0.4 | 2.5 | 4.9 | 0.2 | 1.9 | 2.8 | Du nombre de salariés |
| Value added per employee | 3.3 | 2.9 | 2.6 | 3.0 | 3.9 | 1.0 | 5.8 | 2.7 | 2.5 | 5.8 | 2.6 | 5.0 | 4.2 | 10.8 | Valeur ajoutée par salarié |
| Value added per unit of wages and salaries [4]. . . . . . . . . . . | 2.79 | 3.46 | 1.67 | 2.00 | 2.50 | 1.00 | 1.67 | 2.45 | 1.67 | 3.33 | 1.97 | 2.50 | 2.38 | 4.12 | Valeur ajoutée par unité de traitements et salaires [4] |
| Wages and salaries per employee. . . . . . . | 1.2 | 0.8 | 1.6 | 1.5 | 1.6 | 1.0 | 3.5 | 1.1 | 1.5 | 1.8 | 1.3 | 2.0 | 1.8 | 2.6 | Traitements et salaires par salarié |
| **1953** | | | | | | | | | | | | | | | **1953** |
| Distribution in percent of: | | | | | | | | | | | | | | | Distribution en pourcentage: |
| Value added. . . . . . . | 100.0 | 41.5 | 8.1 | 7.3 | 6.7 | 1.2 | 4.6 | 1.1 | 2.9 | 8.5 | 9.7 | 0.4 | 6.1 | 1.9 | De la valeur ajoutée |
| Number of engaged. . | 100.0 | 56.3 | 6.1 | 9.9 | 6.5 | 0.6 | 2.9 | 1.0 | 0.8 | 2.9 | 5.3 | 0.2 | 6.0 | 1.5 | Du nombre de personnes occupées |
| Value added per person engaged. . . . . . . | 8.9 | 6.6 | 11.8 | 6.6 | 9.3 | 16.1 | 13.9 | 11.3 | 31.9 | 26.2 | 16.4 | 15.3 | 9.1 | 11.2 | Valeur ajoutée par personne occupée |
| Value added per employee | 12.9 | 10.9 | 12.4 | 9.9 | 12.0 | 16.1 | 15.1 | 13.4 | 35.1 | 26.8 | 18.4 | 15.3 | 12.7 | 15.0 | Valeur ajoutée par salarié |
| Value added per unit of wages and salaries. . . . . . . . . . . | 2.66 | 3.16 | 2.23 | 2.34 | 2.23 | 2.34 | 1.80 | 2.77 | 3.82 | 3.30 | 2.49 | 2.19 | 1.95 | 2.62 | Valeur ajoutée par unité de traitements et salaires |
| Wages and salaries per employee. . . . . . . | 4.8 | 3.5 | 5.5 | 4.2 | 5.4 | 6.9 | 8.4 | 4.8 | 9.2 | 8.1 | 7.4 | 7.0 | 6.5 | 5.7 | Traitements et salaires par salarié |
| Employees as a percent of engaged. . . . . . . . | 69.3 | 60.2 | 95.2 | 66.4 | 77.5 | 100.0 | 92.5 | 84.6 | 90.9 | 97.5 | 89.0 | 100.0 | 71.1 | 75.0 | Salariés en pourcentage des personnes occupées |

[1] Excludes petroleum refineries.
[2] Includes rope making.
[3] Includes some electric power plants and some other establishments belonging to industries in other major groups of manufacturing.
[4] Excludes salaries paid to employees other than wage earners (operatives) by establishments in the Federal District, which is the area of the capital of Venezuela.

[1] Non compris les raffineries de pétrole.
[2] Y compris la corderie.
[3] Y compris certaines centrales électriques et autres établissements appartenant à des industries qui relèvent d'autres classes de la branche Industries manufacturières.
[4] Non compris les traitements versés aux salariés autres que les ouvriers des établissements du District fédéral (district où est située la capitale du Venezuela).

# YUGOSLAVIA — YOUGOSLAVIE

## The Material Product and Gross Domestic Capital Formation

The data on the material product and on gross fixed capital formation set out in Table 1 are from the response of the Federal Statistical Institute, Belgrade, to the United Nations national accounts questionnaire. The official estimates and descriptions of the concepts, sources and methods utilized in compiling the figures are published annually in *Statistički Godišnjak FRNJ* (Statistical Yearbook of the Federal People's Republic of Yugoslavia) issued by that Office. It should be emphasized that the concepts and definitions employed in the estimates shown in Table 1 are, in a number of respects, not comparable to those of the United Nations system of national accounts. The estimates are those associated with the system of material product accounts, which is briefly described in the introduction to this publication.

## Index Numbers of Industrial Production

The indexes of industrial production shown in Table 2 are compiled by the Federal Statistical Institute, Belgrade, according to the International Standard Industrial Classification and supplied to the Statistical Office of the United Nations through correspondence. Similar series of index numbers are published in *Statistički Godišnjak FNRJ*.

The series of index numbers relate to the production of all publically-owned industrial enterprises, except the production of military equipment and goods and the output of some minor industrial units. The industrial production of handicraft enterprises or most manufacturing units in non-industrial enterprises is not covered in the series of indexes.

The series of index numbers of industrial production are computed as base-weighted arithmetic averages, starting from elementary series on the quantity of output of industrial finished products. In classifying these products according to industrial activity, the criterion utilized is the character of the product rather than the main industrial activity of the enterprise in which it was made. The weights utilized in combining the elementary series into indexes for categories of industrial activity and these indexes, in turn, into index numbers for broader classes are proportioned to the sum of the wages and salaries and payments into a central depreciation fund associated with each kind of production. The weights utilized relate to 1951 in the case of the indexes for the years 1939 and 1948-1952; 1953 for the index numbers for 1953-1957; and 1958 in the case of the indexes for 1958-1961.

## Le produit matériel et la formation brute de capital intérieur

Les données relatives au produit matériel et à la formation brute de capital fixe reproduites au tableau 1 ont été tirées de la réponse du Federal Statistical Institute, Belgrade, au questionnaire de l'O.N.U. relatif aux comptes nationaux. Les estimations officielles ainsi que les descriptions des sources et méthodes adoptées lors du calcul de ces estimations paraissent annuellement dans *Statistički Godišnjak FNRJ* (Annuaire statistique de la République Populaire Fédérative de Yougoslavie) publié par l'Institut. Il est bon de noter que les concepts et définitions adoptés en vue du calcul des estimations reproduites au tableau 1 sont, à plus d'un égard, peu comparables avec celles du système de comptabilité nationale des Nations Unies. Ces estimations sont celles associées au système de comptabilité de produit matériel décrit brièvement dans l'introduction à cette publication.

## Indices de la production industrielle

Les indices de la production industrielle reproduits au tableau 2 sont des indices calculés par l'Institut fédéral de statistique, Belgrade, suivant la classification internationale type industrielle et fournis au Bureau de statistique de l'O.N.U. par voie de correspondance. Des séries similaires d'indices sont publiées dans *Statistički Godišnjak FNRJ*.

Ces séries d'indices couvrent la production de toutes les entreprises industrielles publiques, à l'exception de la production d'équipements et de biens militaires, ainsi que la production de quelques unités industrielles secondaires. La production industrielle des entreprises artisanales ou de la plupart des unités manufacturières appartenant à des entreprises à caractère non industriel est exclue de ces séries d'indices.

Les séries d'indices de la production industrielle sont des moyennes arithmétiques à pondération fixe de séries élémentaires basées sur les quantités d'output de produits industriels finis (au stade de la firme). En classant ces produits suivant le secteur d'activité industrielle, le critère utilisé se rapporte au caractère du produit plutôt qu'à la principale activité industrielle de l'entreprise dans laquelle il est fabriqué. Pour combiner les séries élémentaires en indices relatifs aux catégories de l'activité industrielle et ces indices, à leur tour, en indices relatifs aux classes plus larges de l'activité industrielle, les coefficients de pondération adoptés sont proportionnels à la masse totale des traitements et salaires et des paiements à une caisse centrale d'amortissement pour chaque type de production. Les coefficients utilisés se rapportent à 1951 dans le cas des indices relatifs aux années 1939 et 1948-1952, à 1953 dans le cas des indices relatifs aux années 1953-1957, et à 1958 dans le cas des indices relatifs aux années 1958-1961.

Further details concerning the series of index numbers may be found in Indexes No. 9, 1954 and *Metodoloski Materijali,* Nos. 82 and 103, published by the Federal Statistical Institute, Belgrade.

Plus amples détails concernant les séries d'indices peuvent être trouvés dans Indices No. 9 et *Metodoloski Materijali,* Nos. 82 et 103, publiés par l'Institut fédéral de statistique, Belgrade.

### Index Numbers of Industrial Employment

The index numbers of industrial employment shown in Table 3 are compiled by the Federal Statistical Institute and published in *Statistički Godišnjak FRNJ.* These indexes, unlike those on industrial production are shown according to the industrial classification of Yugoslavia, which differs, in a number of respects, from the International Standard Industrial Classification. The series of index numbers are based on monthly figures of the number of employees, excluding apprentices, involved in industrial activities, gathered from practically all publically-owned industrial enterprises. These figures are gathered in the same monthly survey as the data on the output of individual products mentioned above. However, the data utilized to compile the index numbers of employment are classified according to the main industrial activity of each enterprise. For further details concerning the sources of data for the index numbers of employment, see *Metodoloski Materijali,* Nos. 82, 103 and 129.

### Indices de l'emploi industriel

Les indices de l'emploi reproduits au tableau 3 ont été construits par l'Institut fédéral de statistique et publiés dans *Statistički Godišnjak FNRJ.* Ces indices, à la différence de ceux relatifs à la production industrielle, sont présentés suivant la nomenclature industrielle yougoslave, laquelle diffère, à plus d'un égard, de la classification industrielle type internationale. Les séries d'indices sont basées sur des chiffres mensuels donnant le nombre de salariés, à l'exclusion des apprentis, exerçant une activité industrielle, fournis par la presque totalité des entreprises industrielles publiques. Ces chiffres sont rassemblés lors de la même enquête mensuelle que les données relatives à la production de chaque marchandise, enquête mentionnée ci-dessus. Cependant, les données qui ont servi au calcul des indices de l'emploi sont classées suivant l'activité industrielle principale de chaque entreprise. Pour plus amples détails concernant les sources des données relatives aux indices de l'emploi, voir *Metodoloski Materijali,* Nos. 82, 103 et 129.

### The Characteristics and Structure of Industrial Activity

The data shown in Tables 4 and 5 for publically-owned industrial enterprises were abstracted mainly from the *Statistički Godišnjak FNRJ, 1956, 1959* and *1960.* The figures set out in these tables are grouped essentially according to the industrial classification of Yugoslavia.

The data shown in Tables 4 and 5, with the exception of the figures on fuels and electricity, relate to all publically-owned enterprises principally engaged in mining, manufacturing, construction and production and distribution of electricity, which are not registered as handicrafts. Though the data on the quantity of selected fuels and electricity consumed, which result from the monthly surveys mentioned above, do not cover some minor publically-owned industrial enterprises, the comparability of these figures with the data on other items is not significantly impaired. The data set out in the two tables relate to all of the activities of the enterprise covered.

The figures of the gross material product in Table 4 are at market prices — i.e., including turnover taxes. The counts of employees which are equivalent to the number of engaged in the case of the publically-owned enterprises, do not include apprentices. Apprentices are also excluded from the figures on the number of operatives, who are defined as employees directly engaged in the production, shipment or transport of goods in work that is predominantly manual in character. Wages and salaries paid include, in addition to the payments to employees during the course of the year, payments to them for their share

### Les caractéristiques et la structure de l'activité industrielle

Les données des tableaux 4 et 5 relatives aux entreprises industrielles publiques ont été tirées principalement du *Statistički Godišnjak FNRJ, 1956, 1959* et *1960.* Les chiffres reproduits dans ce tableau sont groupés essentiellement suivant la nomenclature industrielle yougoslave.

Les données des tableaux 4 et 5, à l'exception des chiffres relatifs aux combustibles et à l'électricité, concernent toutes les entreprises publiques relevant des secteurs ci-après, principalement, industries extractives et manufacturières, bâtiment et travaux publics et production et distribution d'électricité, qui ne sont pas enregistrées comme unités artisanales. Quoique les données relatives aux quantités de certains combustibles et d'électricité consommés résultant des enquêtes mensuelles mentionnées ci-dessus ne couvrent pas la totalité des entreprises industrielles publiques, la comparabilité de ces chiffres avec ceux relatifs aux autres articles ne se trouve pas significativement perturbée. Les données reproduites aux deux tableaux concernent toutes les activités exercées par les entreprises couvertes.

Les chiffres du produit matériel brut du tableau 4 sont comptés aux prix du marché, c'est-à-dire comprennent les taxes sur le chiffre d'affaires. Le nombre de salariés, nombre équivalant à celui des personnes occupées dans le cas des entreprises publiques, ne comprend pas les apprentis. Les apprentis sont également exclus des chiffres donnant le nombre d'ouvriers, lesquels sont définis comme des salariés directement engagés dans la production, l'expédition et le transport des marchandises, ceci dans les travaux à caractère essentiellement manuel. Les traitements et salaires payés couvrent, outre les rémunérations versées

in the gains (profits) of the enterprises; and are defined in a manner consistent with the International Recommendations in Basic Industrial Statistics. The data on installed capacity of power equipment (converted from units expressed originally in kilowatts) are the sum of the capacity of all prime movers connected directly to machinery other than electric generators and the capacity of all electric motors. Power equipment both in use and reserve is covered. The figures of the quantity of selected fuels consumed cover the use of these fuels for all purposes — for example, as raw materials, in producing electricity and gas, and as a direct source of heat and power.

The data in Table 6 on handicraft establishments mainly engaged in mining, manufacturing and construction were compiled from the *Statistički Godišnjak* FNRJ, *1956* and *1962*. The data result from Censuses of Arts and Crafts taken as of 31 March 1951, 30 September 1954 and 15 December 1959. Due to differences between these three dates in the regulations in force governing the definition of arts and crafts, the results of the three censuses were not comparable with one another. In *Statistički Godišnjak, 1956,* the data resulting from the Censuses taken as of 31 March 1951 and 30 September 1954 are presented on as comparable a basis as was feasible. For this purpose, the definition of arts and crafts in force as of 31 March 1951, which was more restricted in scope than that in force as of 30 September 1954, was applied to the data gathered in the latter Census. In *Statistički Godišnjak, 1962,* the results of the Censuses taken as of 30 September 1954 and 15 December 1959 are shown on as comparable a basis as was feasible. In this case, the definition of arts and crafts in force as of 15 December 1959, which was broader in scope than that as of 31 March 1951 but more restricted than that as 30 September 1954, was utilized to retabulate the results of the Census taken as of 30 September 1954. This accounts for the fact that the second set of figures in Table 6 for 30 September 1954 are greater than the first set of figures shown for the same date.

The statistical unit employed in the Censuses of Arts and Crafts was the craft shop. This statistical unit is essentially of the same character as the establishment in the International Standards in Basic Industrial Statistics. The counts of the number of persons engaged shown in Table 6 do not include apprentices. The definition of the figures in Table 6 on the capacity of installed power equipment is the same as that for this data shown in Table 4.

aux salariés pendant l'année, les sommes qui leur sont versées et qui représentent leur part des gains (bénéfices) des entreprises, et sont en un sens conformes à la définition des traitements et salaires recommandés dans les Normes internationales relatives aux statistiques industrielles de base. Les données relatives à la puissance installée (exprimées à l'origine en kilowatts) sont celles de la puissance nominale de tous les moteurs primaires entraînant directement des machines autres que des générateurs, plus la puissance nominale de tous les moteurs électriques. La puissance installée tant en service qu'en réserve est couverte. Les chiffres relatifs aux quantités de certains combustibles consommés couvrent l'utilisation de ces combustibles à toutes les fins — par exemple, comme matière première, dans la production d'électricité ou de gaz, et comme source de chaleur ou de puissance.

Les données du tableau 6 relatives aux établissements artisanaux exerçant essentiellement une activité dans le secteur des industries extractives, des industries manufacturières, du bâtiment et travaux publics ont été tirées du *Statistički Godišnjak FNRJ, 1956* et *1962*. Les données résultent des recensements des Arts et métiers exécutés au 31 mars 1951, 30 septembre 1954 et 15 décembre 1959. Vu la différence à ces trois dates des réglementations en vigueur concernant la définition des Arts et métiers, les résultats des trois recensements ne sont pas comparables entre eux. Dans *Statistički Godišnjak, 1956,* les données résultant des recensements au 31 mars 1951 et au 30 septembre 1954 ont été présentées sur une base aussi comparable que possible. A cette fin, la définition des Arts et métiers en vigueur au 31 mars 1951, qui était moins étendue que celle qui était en vigueur au 30 septembre 1954, a été appliquée aux données du dernier recensement. Dan *Statistički Godišnjak, 1962,* les résultats des recensements exécutés au 30 septembre 1954 et au 15 décembre 1959 ont été reproduits sur une base aussi comparable que possible. Pour cela, la définition des Arts et métiers en vigueur au 30 décembre 1959, qui était plus large que celle au 31 mars 1951, mais plus restrictive que celle en vigueur au 30 septembre 1954, a été utilisée pour retabuler les résultats du recensement exécuté au 30 septembre 1954. Ceci explique le fait que la seconde série de chiffres du tableau 6 relative au 30 septembre 1954 est plus grande que la première série de chiffres reproduite pour la même date.

L'unité artisanale est l'unité statistique utilisée aux recensements des Arts et métiers. Cette unité statistique possède essentiellement les mêmes caractères que l'établissement en ce qui concerne la standardisation internationale des statistiques industrielles de base. Les chiffres des personnes occupées du tableau 6 ne comprennent pas les apprentis. La définition des chiffres du tableau 6 relatifs à la puissance installée est la même que pour les données reproduites au tableau 4.

## 1. THE MATERIAL PRODUCT AND GROSS DOMESTIC FIXED CAPITAL FORMATION
### PRODUIT MATERIEL ET FORMATION BRUTE DE CAPITAL FIXE INTERIEUR

Thousand million Dinars                                     Milliards de dinars

### A. Expenditure on the Gross Material Product — Dépenses relatives au produit matériel brut

| Item of data and year<br>Rubrique et année | Total | Consumption<br>Consommation | | Gross Domestic Capital Formation<br>Formation brute de capital intérieur | | Net exports of goods and productive services<br>Exportations nettes de biens et de services productifs |
| --- | --- | --- | --- | --- | --- | --- |
| | | Total | Collective consumption [1]<br>Consommation collective [1] | Total [2] | Fixed [3]<br>Fixe [3] | |
| | | | At Current Prices — Aux prix courants | | | |
| Absolute figures — Chiffres absolus | | | | | | |
| 1952 | 949 | 738 | 215 | 248 | 287 | —37 |
| 1953 | 1 134 | 812 | 214 | 388 | 363 | —66 |
| 1954 | 1 299 | 896 | 236 | 435 | 423 | —32 |
| 1955 | 1 552 | 1 049 | 237 | 553 | 449 | —50 |
| 1956 | 1 612 | 1 106 | 242 | 539 | 461 | —33 |
| 1957 | 1 991 | 1 286 | 258 | 764 | 550 | —59 |
| 1958 | 1 989 | 1 373 | 277 | 667 | 587 | —51 |
| 1959 | 2 446 | 1 588 | 319 | 905 | 750 | —47 |
| 1960 | 2 887 | 1 873 | 381 | 1 065 | 936 | —51 |
| 1961 | 3 380 | 2 206 | 441 | 1 244 | 1 166 | —70 |
| Percentage distribution of average annual expenditure — Distribution en pourcentage des dépenses annuelles moyennes | | | | | | |
| 1952—1960 | 100.0 | 67.6 | 15.0 | 35.0 | 30.3 | —2.6 |
| 1952 | 100.0 | 77.7 | 22.6 | 26.1 | 30.2 | —3.8 |
| 1954 | 100.0 | 69.0 | 18.2 | 33.5 | 32.6 | —2.5 |
| 1958 | 100.0 | 69.0 | 13.9 | 33.5 | 29.5 | —2.5 |
| 1960 | 100.0 | 64.8 | 13.2 | 36.9 | 32.4 | —1.7 |

For footnotes see end of table.                    Pour les notes, voir au bas du tableau.

## B. The Net Material Product According to Origin
### Origine par secteur d'activité du produit matériel net

| Item of data and year<br>Rubrique et année | Total | Agricultural sector<br>Secteur agricole | Industrial Sector — Secteur industriel | | | Transportation and communication<br>Transports et communications | Other sectors[4]<br>Autres secteurs[4] |
|---|---|---|---|---|---|---|---|
| | | | Total | Mining, manufacturing, and electricity and gas<br>Industries extractives et manufacturières; électricité et gaz | Construction<br>Bâtiment et travaux publics | | |
| ISIC — CITI | 0-512, 611-612, 841, 852 | 0 | 1-512 | 1-3, 511-512 | 4 | 7 | 611-612, 841, 852 |

### a. At Current Prices — Aux prix courants

| | | | | | | | |
|---|---|---|---|---|---|---|---|
| Absolute figures — Chiffres absolus | | | | | | | |
| 1952 | 854 | 221 | 467 | 403 | 64 | 43 | 123 |
| 1953 | 1 022 | 322 | 504 | 430 | 74 | 47 | 149 |
| 1954 | 1 162 | 327 | 584 | 497 | 87 | 52 | 199 |
| 1955 | 1 398 | 445 | 689 | 608 | 81 | 71 | 193 |
| 1956 | 1 444 | 450 | 694 | 629 | 65 | 86 | 214 |
| 1957 | 1 829 | 633 | 816 | 727 | 89 | 110 | 270 |
| 1958 | 1 835 | 537 | 912 | 805 | 107 | 93 | 293 |
| 1959 | 2 269 | 686 | 1 100 | 962 | 138 | 117 | 366 |
| 1960 | 2 687 | 708 | 1 348 | 1 171 | 177 | 170 | 461 |
| 1961 | 3 124 | 831 | 1 554 | 1 303 | 251 | 203 | 536 |
| Percentage distribution according to sector — Distribution en pourcentage par secteur | | | | | | | |
| 1952 – 1960 | 100.0 | 29.8 | 49.1 | 43.0 | 6.1 | 5.4 | 15.7 |
| 1952 | 100.0 | 25.8 | 54.7 | 47.2 | 7.5 | 5.0 | 14.5 |
| 1954 | 100.0 | 28.1 | 50.2 | 42.8 | 7.4 | 4.5 | 17.2 |
| 1958 | 100.0 | 29.2 | 49.7 | 43.9 | 5.8 | 5.1 | 16.0 |
| 1960 | 100.0 | 26.3 | 50.2 | 43.6 | 6.6 | 6.3 | 17.2 |

### b. At Prices of 1956 — Aux prix de 1956

| | | | | | | | |
|---|---|---|---|---|---|---|---|
| Absolute figures — Chiffres absolus | | | | | | | |
| 1952 | 1 050 | 372 | 451 | 392 | 59 | 60 | 168 |
| 1953 | 1 257 | 511 | 509 | 440 | 69 | 66 | 172 |
| 1954 | 1 292 | 453 | 580 | 507 | 73 | 71 | 189 |
| 1955 | 1 454 | 514 | 650 | 579 | 71 | 84 | 207 |
| 1956 | 1 444 | 450 | 694 | 629 | 65 | 86 | 214 |
| 1957 | 1 781 | 619 | 810 | 732 | 78 | 99 | 252 |
| 1958 | 1 811 | 530 | 900 | 817 | 83 | 109 | 272 |
| 1959 | 2 129 | 715 | 988 | 896 | 92 | 121 | 306 |
| 1960 | 2 247 | 633 | 1 128 | 1 029 | 99 | 142 | 344 |
| Percentage distribution according to sector — Distribution en pourcentage par secteur | | | | | | | |
| 1952 – 1960 | 100.0 | 33.1 | 46.4 | 41.6 | 4.8 | 5.8 | 14.7 |
| 1952 | 100.0 | 35.4 | 42.9 | 37.3 | 5.6 | 5.7 | 16.0 |
| 1954 | 100.0 | 35.0 | 44.9 | 39.2 | 5.7 | 5.5 | 14.6 |
| 1958 | 100.0 | 29.3 | 49.7 | 45.1 | 4.6 | 6.0 | 15.0 |
| 1960 | 100.0 | 28.2 | 50.2 | 45.8 | 4.4 | 6.3 | 15.3 |
| Average annual rate of growth — Taux annuel moyen d'accroissement | | | | | | | |
| 1952 – 1960 | 10.0 | 6.9 | 12.1 | 12.8 | 6.7 | 11.4 | 9.4 |
| 1954 – 1958 | 9.0 | 4.0 | 11.6 | 12.7 | 3.3 | 11.3 | 9.5 |
| 1958 – 1960 | 11.4 | 9.3 | 12.0 | 12.2 | 9.2 | 14.2 | 12.5 |

For footnotes, see end of table.        Pour les notes, voir au bas du tableau.

## C.  Gross Domestic Fixed Capital Formation According to Purchasing Sector
## Formation brute de capital fixe intérieur par secteur d'acquisition

| Item of data and year<br>Rubrique et année | Total [3] | Agricultural sector<br>Secteur agricole | Industrial Sector — Secteur industriel | | | Transportation and communication<br>Transports et communications | Other sectors [5]<br>Autres secteurs [5] |
| | | | Total | Mining, manufacturing and electricity and gas<br>Industries extractives et manufacturières; électricité et gaz | Construction<br>Bâtiment et travaux publics | | |
|---|---|---|---|---|---|---|---|
| ISIC — CITI | 0–9 | 0 | 1–512 | 1–3, 511–512 | 4 | 7 | 6, 8–9 |
| At Current Prices — Aux prix courants | | | | | | | |
| **Absolute figures — Chiffres absolus** | | | | | | | |
| 1952...................... | 287 | 15 | 187 | 179 | 8 | 48 | 37 |
| 1953...................... | 363 | 21 | 208 | 193 | 15 | 60 | 74 |
| 1954...................... | 423 | 21 | 213 | 195 | 18 | 70 | 119 |
| 1955...................... | 449 | 32 | 221 | 205 | 16 | 78 | 118 |
| 1956...................... | 461 | 44 | 195 | 185 | 10 | 95 | 127 |
| 1957...................... | 550 | 61 | 194 | 179 | 15 | 111 | 184 |
| 1958...................... | 587 | 79 | 193 | 177 | 16 | 108 | 207 |
| 1959...................... | 750 | 122 | 239 | 224 | 15 | 131 | 258 |
| 1960...................... | 936 | 118 | 331 | 311 | 20 | 155 | 332 |
| 1961...................... | 1 166 | 119 | 436 | 409 | 27 | 169 | 442 |
| **Percentage distribution according to sector — Distribution en pourcentage par secteur** | | | | | | | |
| 1952–1960................ | 100.0 | 10.6 | 41.2 | 38.5 | 2.7 | 17.9 | 30.3 |
| 1952...................... | 100.0 | 5.2 | 65.1 | 62.3 | 2.8 | 16.8 | 12.9 |
| 1954...................... | 100.0 | 4.9 | 50.4 | 46.1 | 4.3 | 16.5 | 28.2 |
| 1958...................... | 100.0 | 13.4 | 32.9 | 30.2 | 2.7 | 18.4 | 35.3 |
| 1960...................... | 100.0 | 12.6 | 35.3 | 33.2 | 2.1 | 16.6 | 35.5 |

[1] Expenditures on the material product to meet the requirements of those activities which are not included in the material product proper—eg., public administration and defence, education and other services.
[2] Includes a statistical discrepancy.
[3] Includes the value of major repairs in the case of the years, 1952-1957, but not 1958-1961.
[4] Includes in addition to the distributive trades and public catering, handicrafts and other branches of material production not classified under other headings.
[5] Includes craft and home industry in addition.

[1] Dépenses imputées au produit matériel pour les activités qui n'entrent pas dans le produit matériel proprement dit-c'est à dire besoins de l'administration publique et de la défense nationale, de l'enseignement et d'autres services.
[2] Y compris les écarts statistiques.
[3] Y compris la valeur des grosses réparations pour les années 1952-1957, mais non pour 1958-1961.
[4] Y compris, en plus de l'activité commerciale distributive et de l'approvisionnement des administrations publiques, la production artisanale et autres branches de la production matérielle non classées sous d'autres rubriques.
[5] Y compris les métiers artisanaux et les industries à domicile.

## 2. INDEX NUMBERS OF INDUSTRIAL PRODUCTION
### INDICES DE LA PRODUCTION INDUSTRIELLE

### A. Selected Divisions of Industrial Activity
### Quelques branches de l'activité industrielle

| Period / Période | Total | Mining / Industries extractives | Manu-facturing / Industries manu-facturières | Electricity and gas / Electricité et gaz |
|---|---|---|---|---|
| ISIC — CITI | 1-3, 511-512 | 1 | 2-3 | 511-512 |

a. Indexes — Indices (1958 = 100)

| Period | Total | Mining | Manufacturing | Electricity and gas |
|---|---|---|---|---|
| 1939 | 29 | 39 | 28 | 16 |
| 1948 | 43 | 50 | 44 | 28 |
| 1949 | 49 | 57 | 48 | 31 |
| 1950 | 50 | 60 | 49 | 33 |
| 1951 | 48 | 58 | 47 | 35 |
| 1952 | 48 | 60 | 45 | 37 |
| 1953 | -53- | -62- | -52- | -41- |
| 1954 | 60 | 71 | 59 | 47 |
| 1955 | 70 | 80 | 69 | 60 |
| 1956 | 77 | 89 | 76 | 70 |
| 1957 | 90 | 96 | 89 | 85 |
| 1958 | -100- | -100- | -100- | -100- |
| 1959 | 113 | 109 | 114 | 110 |
| 1960 | 130 | 121 | 133 | 120 |
| 1961 | 139 | 132 | 142 | 133 |

b. Average Annual Rate of Change — Taux annuel moyen de variation

| Period | Total | Mining | Manufacturing | Electricity and gas |
|---|---|---|---|---|
| 1939-1960 | 7.4 | 5.5 | 7.7 | 10.1 |
| 1939-1948 | 4.5 | 2.8 | 5.2 | 6.4 |
| 1950-1960 | 10.0 | 7.3 | 10.5 | 13.8 |
| 1948-1953 | 4.3 | 4.4 | 3.4 | 7.9 |
| 1954-1958 | 13.6 | 8.9 | 14.1 | 20.8 |
| 1958-1960 | 14.0 | 10.0 | 15.3 | 9.5 |

### B. The Major Groups of Mining
### Les classes de la branche Industries extractives

| Period / Période | All mining / Toutes industries extractives | Coal mining / Extraction du charbon | Metal mining / Extraction des minerais métalliques | Crude petroleum and natural gas / Pétrole brut et gaz naturel | Other mining / Autres industries extractives |
|---|---|---|---|---|---|
| ISIC — CITI | 1 | 11 | 12 | 13 | 14-19 |

a. Indexes — Indices (1958 = 100)

| Period | All mining | Coal mining | Metal mining | Crude petroleum and natural gas | Other mining |
|---|---|---|---|---|---|
| 1939 | 39 | 49 | 47 | — | 20 |
| 1948 | 50 | 62 | 49 | 8 | 40 |
| 1949 | 57 | 72 | 54 | 14 | 45 |
| 1950 | 60 | 75 | 54 | 24 | 47 |
| 1951 | 58 | 69 | 54 | 31 | 46 |
| 1952 | 60 | 69 | 58 | 32 | 49 |
| 1953 | -62- | -65- | -62- | -40- | -65- |
| 1954 | 71 | 76 | 70 | 50 | 69 |
| 1955 | 80 | 84 | 81 | 56 | 74 |
| 1956 | 89 | 94 | 91 | 65 | 80 |
| 1957 | 96 | 97 | 98 | 86 | 93 |
| 1958 | -100- | -100- | -100- | -100- | -100- |
| 1959 | 109 | 110 | 103 | 128 | 110 |
| 1960 | 121 | 117 | 109 | 201 | 127 |
| 1961 | 132 | 121 | 122 | 285 | 143 |

b. Average Annual Rate of Change — Taux annuel moyen de variation

| Period | All mining | Coal mining | Metal mining | Crude petroleum and natural gas | Other mining |
|---|---|---|---|---|---|
| 1939-1960 | 5.5 | 4.2 | 4.1 | . | 9.2 |
| 1939-1948 | 2.8 | 2.6 | 0.5 | | 8.0 |
| 1950-1960 | 7.3 | 4.6 | 7.3 | 23.7 | 10.5 |
| 1948-1953 | 4.4 | 0.9 | 4.8 | 38.0 | 10.2 |
| 1954-1958 | 8.9 | 7.1 | 9.3 | 18.9 | 9.7 |
| 1958-1960 | 10.0 | 8.2 | 4.4 | 41.8 | 12.7 |

## C. The Major Groups of Manufacturing — Les classes de la branche Industries manufacturières

| Period<br>Période | Manu-facturing<br>Industries manufac-turières | Food, beverages and tobacco<br>Industries alimen-taires, boissons, tabac | Textiles<br>Textiles | Clothing, footwear and made-up textiles<br>Articles d'habil-lement, chaussures et ouvrages en tissu | Wood products and furniture<br>Bois et meubles | Paper and paper products<br>Papier et ouvrages en papier | Printing and publishing<br>Im-primerie et édition | Leather and leather products except wearing apparel<br>Cuir et articles en cuir, à l'exclu-sion des articles d'habil-lement | Rubber products<br>Ouvrages en caout-chouc | Chemicals and chemical, petroleum and coal products<br>Produits chi-miques et dérivés du pétrole et du charbon | Non-metallic mineral products<br>Produits minéraux non métal-liques | Basic metals<br>Métal-lurgie de base | Metal products<br>Ouvrages en métaux | Other manu-facturing<br>Autres industries manufac-turières |
|---|---|---|---|---|---|---|---|---|---|---|---|---|---|---|
| ISIC — CITI | 2–3 | 20–22 | 23 | 24 | 25–26 | 27 | 28 | 29 | 30 | 31–32 | 33 | 34 | 35–38 | 39 |

### a. Indexes — Indices (1958 = 100)

| | | | | | | | | | | | | | | |
|---|---|---|---|---|---|---|---|---|---|---|---|---|---|---|
| 1939............. | 28 | 43 | 49 | 35 | 42 | 29 | ... | 51 | 31 | 19 | 34 | 17 | 9 | 38 |
| 1948............. | 44 | 67 | 70 | 99 | 67 | 38 | ... | 81 | 48 | 24 | 49 | 26 | 28 | 68 |
| 1949............. | 48 | 64 | 71 | 108 | 80 | 41 | ... | 98 | 59 | 29 | 54 | 28 | 33 | 59 |
| 1950............. | 49 | 60 | 68 | 99 | 88 | 42 | ... | 93 | 57 | 32 | 54 | 30 | 44 | 59 |
| 1951............. | 47 | 55 | 58 | 87 | 78 | 43 | ... | 80 | 56 | 31 | 47 | 32 | 38 | 65 |
| 1952.. ......... | 45 | 51 | 54 | 66 | 63 | 41 | ... | 65 | 52 | 30 | 52 | 35 | 44 | 68 |
| 1953............. | – 52 – | – 55 – | – 53 – | – 60 – | – 70 – | – 46 – | 50 | – 60 – | – 51 – | – 39 – | – 57 – | – 39 – | – 51 – | – 74 – |
| 1954............. | 59 | 63 | 66 | 70 | 71 | 50 | 52 | 68 | 60 | 46 | 63 | 47 | 57 | 70 |
| 1955............. | 69 | 67 | 77 | 75 | 78 | 60 | 60 | 81 | 64 | 62 | 72 | 64 | 68 | 82 |
| 1956............. | 76 | 75 | 80 | 73 | 80 | 84 | 74 | 90 | 76 | 72 | 76 | 71 | 74 | 91 |
| 1957............. | 89 | 91 | 92 | 87 | 94 | 94 | 88 | 96 | 94 | 85 | 89 | 89 | 88 | 87 |
| 1958............. | – 100 – | – 100 – | – 100 – | – 100 – | – 100 – | – 100 – | – 100 – | – 100 – | – 100 – | – 100 – | – 100 – | – 100 – | – 100 – | – 100 – |
| 1959............. | 114 | 105 | 108 | 115 | 121 | 111 | 110 | 110 | 113 | 122 | 112 | 114 | 120 | 122 |
| 1960............. | 133 | 120 | 123 | 138 | 138 | 132 | 127 | 128 | 142 | 136 | 128 | 131 | 147 | 154 |
| 1961............. | 142 | 124 | 126 | 147 | 154 | 163 | 145 | 131 | 152 | 147 | 138 | 138 | 155 | 164 |

### b. Average Annual Rate of Change — Taux annuel moyen de variation

| | | | | | | | | | | | | | | |
|---|---|---|---|---|---|---|---|---|---|---|---|---|---|---|
| 1939 – 1960........ | 7.7 | 5.0 | 4.5 | 6.8 | 5.8 | 7.5 | ... | 4.5 | 7.5 | 9.7 | 6.5 | 10.2 | 14.2 | 6.9 |
| 1939 – 1948........ | 5.2 | 5.1 | 4.0 | 12.2 | 5.3 | 3.0 | ... | 5.2 | 5.0 | 2.6 | 4.1 | 4.8 | 13.4 | 6.7 |
| 1950 – 1960........ | 10.4 | 7.2 | 6.1 | 3.4 | 4.6 | 12.1 | ... | 3.2 | 9.6 | 15.3 | 9.0 | 15.9 | 12.8 | 10.1 |
| 1948 – 1953........ | 3.4 | –3.9 | –5.4 | –9.5 | 0.9 | 3.9 | ... | –5.8 | 1.2 | 10.2 | 3.1 | 8.4 | 12.7 | 1.7 |
| 1954 – 1958........ | 14.1 | 12.2 | 10.9 | 9.3 | 8.9 | 18.9 | 17.8 | 10.1 | 13.6 | 21.4 | 12.2 | 20.8 | 15.1 | 9.3 |
| 1958 – 1960........ | 15.3 | 9.5 | 10.9 | 17.5 | 17.5 | 14.9 | 12.7 | 13.1 | 19.2 | 16.6 | 13.1 | 14.5 | 21.2 | 24.1 |

# 3. INDEX NUMBERS OF INDUSTRIAL EMPLOYMENT
## INDICES DE L'EMPLOI DANS L'INDUSTRIE

## A. The Divisions of Industrial Activity
### Les branches de l'activité industrielle

| Period<br>Période | Total | Mining and manufacturing [1]<br>Industries extractives et manufacturières [1] | Construction<br>Bâtiment et travaux publics | Electricity<br>Electricité |
|---|---|---|---|---|
| ISIC — CITI | 1–4, 511–512 | 1–3, 512 | 4 | 511 |

### a. Indexes — Indices (1958 = 100)

| | | | | |
|---|---|---|---|---|
| 1952........... | 60 | 59 | 64 | 64 |
| 1953........... | 66 | 62 | 82 | 67 |
| 1954........... | 77 | 70 | 102 | 77 |
| 1955........... | 84 | 79 | 104 | 85 |
| 1956........... | 84 | 84 | 83 | 94 |
| 1957........... | 92 | 91 | 96 | 100 |
| 1958........... | 100 | 100 | 100 | 100 |
| 1959........... | 108 | 108 | 108 | 105 |
| 1960........... | 117 | 117 | 121 | 101 |
| 1961........... | 121 | 121 | 122 | 104 |

### b. Average Annual Rate of Change — Taux annuel moyen de variation

| | | | | |
|---|---|---|---|---|
| 1952–1960.... | 8.7 | 8.9 | 8.3 | 5.9 |
| 1954–1958.... | 6.8 | 9.3 | −0.5 | 6.8 |
| 1958–1960.... | 8.2 | 8.2 | 10.0 | 0.5 |

For footnotes, see end of table.

Pour les notes, voir au bas du tableau.

## B. Major Sub-Divisions of Mining and Manufacturing
### Principales subdivisions des Industries extractives et manufacturières

| Period<br>Période | Mining and manu-facturing [1]<br>Industries extractives et manu-facturières [1] | Food, beverages and tobacco<br>Industries alimen-taires, boissons, tabac | Textiles and clothing [2]<br>Textiles et articles d'habil-lement [2] | Wood products and furniture [3]<br>Bois et meubles [3] | Paper and paper products [5]<br>Papier et ouvrages en papier [5] | Printing [1, 5]<br>Im-primerie [1, 5] | Leather and leather products [2]<br>Cuir et articles en cuir [2] | Rubber products<br>Ouvrages en caout-chouc | Chemicals and chemical products [4]<br>Produits chimiques [4] | Coal, crude petroleum and products [1]<br>Charbon, pétrole brut et produits dérivés [1] | Non-metallic minerals and products<br>Minéraux non métalliques et produits dérivés | Metal mining and basic metals<br>Minerais métalliques et métal-lurgie de base | Metal products [4]<br>Ouvrages en métaux [4] |
|---|---|---|---|---|---|---|---|---|---|---|---|---|---|
| ISIC — CITI | 1–3, 512 | 20–22 | 23, 243–244 | 25–26 | 27 | 28 | 241, 29 | 30 | 31 | 11, 13, 32 | 14–19, 33 | 12, 34 | 35–38 |

### a. Indexes — Indices (1958 = 100)

| | | | | | | | | | | | | | |
|---|---|---|---|---|---|---|---|---|---|---|---|---|---|
| 1952............. | 59 | 53 | 60 | 62 | 63 | 55 | 65 | 47 | 42 | 76 | 56 | 67 | 53 |
| 1953............. | 62 | 55 | 61 | 64 | 61 | 62 | 61 | 50 | 45 | 75 | 64 | 70 | 57 |
| 1954............. | 70 | 66 | 66 | 73 | 65 | 67 | 66 | 60 | 51 | 84 | 76 | 78 | 66 |
| 1955............. | 79 | 74 | 79 | 81 | 77 | 74 | 75 | 67 | 61 | 92 | 85 | 87 | 74 |
| 1956............. | 84 | 80 | 84 | 87 | 93 | 80 | 82 | 75 | 71 | 96 | 87 | 90 | 80 |
| 1957............. | 91 | 87 | 90 | 94 | 96 | 88 | 91 | 90 | 78 | 99 | 91 | 95 | 88 |
| 1958............. | 100 | 100 | 100 | 100 | 100 | 100 | 100 | 100 | 100 | 100 | 100 | 100 | 100 |
| 1959............. | 108 | 104 | 107 | 110 | 107 | 108 | 108 | 113 | 108 | 104 | 106 | 105 | 112 |
| 1960............. | 117 | 112 | 115 | 121 | 122 | 115 | 117 | 136 | 119 | 104 | 114 | 109 | 128 |
| 1961............. | 121 | 108 | 120 | 128 | 138 | 122 | 130 | 141 | 126 | 105 | 119 | 111 | 133 |

### b. Average Annual Rate of Change — Taux annuel moyen de variation

| | | | | | | | | | | | | | |
|---|---|---|---|---|---|---|---|---|---|---|---|---|---|
| 1952–1960........ | 8.9 | 9.8 | 8.5 | 8.7 | 8.6 | 9.7 | 7.6 | 14.2 | 13.9 | 4.0 | 9.3 | 6.3 | 11.7 |
| 1954–1958........ | 9.3 | 10.9 | 10.9 | 8.2 | 11.4 | 10.5 | 10.9 | 13.6 | 18.3 | 4.4 | 7.1 | 6.4 | 10.9 |
| 1958–1960........ | 8.2 | 5.8 | 7.2 | 10.0 | 10.5 | 7.2 | 8.2 | 16.6 | 9.1 | 2.0 | 6.8 | 4.4 | 13.1 |

[1] Includes the Gas industries (ISIC group 512) but excludes publishing (part of ISIC major group 28).
[2] Manufacturing of footwear, leather gloves and similar goods is included under Leather and leather products (ISIC major group 29) instead of under Clothing and wearing apparel (ISIC major group 24).
[3] Includes the manufacturing of wooden toys, musical instruments and cultural articles, pens, pencils, brooms, brushes and similar items (all part of ISIC group 399) but excludes the manufacture of metal furniture (part of ISIC major group 26).
[4] Included are the following kinds of manufacturing: Metal furniture (part of ISIC major group 26), Scientific and precision instruments and equipment (ISIC group 391) and Photographic and optical goods (ISIC group 392). The manufacture of film and similar photographic materials is, however, included under Chemical products (ISIC major group 31).
[5] Paper articles are covered under Printing (ISIC major group 28) instead of under Paper and paper products (ISIC major group 27).

[1] Y compris les Industries gazières (CITI 512), mais non compris l'édition (dans CITI 28).
[2] La fabrication des chaussures, gants en cuir et articles analogues est comprise dans Cuir et ouvrages en cuir (CITI 29) et non dans Vêtements et articles d'habillement (CITI 24).
[3] Y compris la fabrication des jouets en bois, des instruments de musique et d'articles culturels, crayons, porte-plumes, balais, brosses et articles analogues (tous dans CITI 399), mais non compris la fabrication des meubles métalliques (dans CITI 26).
[4] Sont comprises les industries manufacturières ci-après: fabrication des meubles métalliques (dans CITI 26), fabrication des instruments de précision et des appareils scientifiques (CITI 391) et fabrication des appareils photographiques et des instruments d'optique (CITI 392). La fabrication des pellicules et des articles photographiques analogues est cependant comprise dans Produits chimiques (CITI 31).
[5] Les articles en papier sont compris dans Imprimerie (CITI 28) et non dans Papier et ouvrages en papier (CITI 27).

# 4. THE CHARACTERISTICS OF ALL PUBLICALLY-OWNED INDUSTRIAL ENTERPRISES

## CARACTERISTIQUES DE TOUTES LES ENTREPRISES PUBLIQUES
### 1954, 1958

Number of enterprises in units; value added and wages and salaries in million Dinars; number of employees and operatives in thousands; electricity consumed in million KWH; capacity of installed power equipment in thousand horsepower; value added and wages and salaries per employee in thousand Dinars; electricity consumed per employee and per operative in thousand KWH; capacity of installed power equipment per employee and per operative in horsepower.

Nombre d'entreprises en unités; valeur ajoutée et traitements et salaires en millions de dinars; nombre de salariés et d'ouvriers en milliers; électricité consommée en millions de kWh; puissance installée en milliers de chevaux-vapeur; valeur ajoutée et traitements et salaires par salarié en milliers de dinars; électricité consommée par salarié et par ouvrier en milliers de kWh; puissance installée par salarié et par ouvrier en chevaux-vapeur.

## A. Divisions of Industrial Activity — Branches de l'activité industrielle

| Year and item of data | All industrial activity — Toutes industries | Mining and manufacturing [1] Industries extractives et manufacturières[1] | Construction Bâtiment et travaux publics | Electricity Electricité | Année et rubrique | Year and item of data | All industrial activity — Toutes industries | Mining and manufacturing [1] Industries extractives et manufacturières[1] | Construction Bâtiment et travaux publics | Electricity Electricité | Année et rubrique |
|---|---|---|---|---|---|---|---|---|---|---|---|
| ISIC | 1-4, 511-512 | 1-3, 512 | 4 | 511 | CITI | ISIC | 1-4, 511-512 | 1-3, 512 | 4 | 511 | CITI |
| | a. Absolute Figures — Chiffres absolus | | | | | | b. Structure | | | | |
| **1954** | | | | | **1954** | **1954** | | | | | **1954** |
| Number of enterprises..... | 2 851 | 2 330 | 379 | 142 | Nombre d'entreprises | | | | | | |
| Gross material product..... | 652 214 | 543 463 | 93 762 | 14 989 | Produit matériel brut | Distribution in percent of: | | | | | Distribution en pourcentage: |
| Employees: | | | | | Salariés: | Gross material product... | 100.0 | 83.3 | 14.4 | 2.3 | Produit matériel brut |
| Number (Average as of 31.III and 30.IX)........ | 981.9 | 699.6 | 266.2 | 16.1 | Nombre (moyenne au 31.III et 30.IX) | Number of employees... | 100.0 | 71.2 | 27.1 | 1.7 | Nombre de salariés |
| Wages and salaries...... | 117 082 | 77 993 | 37 146 | 1 943 | Traitements et salaires | Per employee: | | | | | Par salarié: |
| Number of operatives (Average as of 31.III and 30.IX)............... | ... | 61.5 | ... | 11.8 | Nombre d'ouvriers (moyenne au 31.III et 30.IX) | Gross material product... | 664.2 | 776.8 | 352.2 | 931.0 | Produit matériel brut |
| | | | | | | Wages and salaries... | 119.2 | 111.5 | 139.5 | 120.7 | Traitements et salaires |
| | | | | | | Gross material product per unit of wages and salaries........... | 5.57 | 6.97 | 2.52 | 7.71 | Produit matériel brut par unité de traitements et salaires |
| | | | | | | Operatives as a percent of employees........... | ... | 87.8 | ... | 73.3 | Ouvriers en pourcentage des salariés |
| **1958** | | | | | **1958** | **1958** | | | | | **1958** |
| Number of enterprises..... | 2 904 | 2 395 | 414 | 95 | Nombre d'entreprises | | | | | | |
| Gross material product..... | 995 838 | 840 603 | 114 523 | 40 712 | Produit matériel brut | Distribution in percent of: | | | | | Distribution en pourcentage: |
| Employees: | | | | | Salariés: | Gross material products.. | 100.0 | 84.4 | 11.5 | 4.1 | Produit matériel brut |
| Number (Average as of 31.III and 30.IX)........ | 1 232.8 | 943.3 | 266.0 | 23.5 | Nombre (moyenne au 31.III et 30.IX) | Number of employees... | 100.0 | 76.5 | 21.5 | 2.0 | Nombre de salariés |
| Wages and salaries...... | 223 451 | 162 992 | 55 078 | 5 381 | Traitements et salaires | Per employee: | | | | | Par salarié: |
| Number of operatives (Average as of 31.III and 30.IX) ............ | ... | 809.5 | ... | 16.1 | Nombre d'ouvriers (moyenne au 31.III et 30.IX) | Gross material product... | 807.8 | 891.1 | 430.5 | 1 732.4 | Produit matériel brut |
| | | | | | | Wages and salaries...... | 181.2 | 172.8 | 207.1 | 229.0 | Traitements et salaires |
| | | | | | | Electricity consumed..... | ... | 4.3 | ... | 10.1 | Electricité consommée |
| | | | | | | Capacity of installed power equipment....... | ... | 2.56 | ... | ... | Puissance installée |
| | | | | | | Gross material product per unit of wages and salaries........... | 4.46 | 5.16 | 2.08 | 7.56 | Produit matériel brut par unité de traitements et salaires |
| | | | | | | Operatives as a percent of employees........... | ... | 85.8 | ... | 68.5 | Ouvriers en pourcentage des salariés |

For footnotes, see end of table.

Pour les notes, voir au bas du tableau.

# YUGOSLAVIA

## B.   Major Sub-Divisions of Mining and Manufacturing
### Principales subdivisions des industries extractives et manufacturières

| Year and item of data | Mining and manufacturing [1] / Industries extractives et manufacturières [1] | Food, beverages and tobacco / Industries alimentaires, boissons, tabac | Textiles and clothing [2] / Textiles et articles d'habillement [2] | Wood products and furniture [3] / Bois et meubles [3] | Paper and paper products[5] / Papier et ouvrages en papier [5] | Printing [1,5] / Imprimerie [1,5] | Leather and leather products[2] / Cuir et articles en cuir [2] | Rubber products / Ouvrages en caoutchouc | Chemicals and chemical products[4] / Produits chimiques [4] | Coal, crude petroleum and products[1] / Charbon, pétrole brut et produits dérivés [1] | Non-metallic minerals and products / Minéraux non métalliques et produits dérivés | Metal mining and basic metals / Minerais métalliques et métallurgie de base | Metal products[4] / Ouvrages en métaux [4] | Année et rubrique |
|---|---|---|---|---|---|---|---|---|---|---|---|---|---|---|
| ISIC | 1-3, 512 | 20–22 | 23, 243-244 | 25–26 | 27 | 28 | 241, 29 | 30 | 31 | 11, 13, 32 | 149, 33 | 12, 34 | 35–38 | CITI |
| *a. Absolute Figures — Chiffres absolus* | | | | | | | | | | | | | | |
| **1954** | | | | | | | | | | | | | | **1954** |
| Number of enterprises... | 2 330 | 601 | 266 | 279 | 30 | 96 | 78 | 6 | 79 | 99 | 451 | 44 | 301 | Nombre d'entreprises |
| Gross material product.. | 543 463 | 72 597 | 84 721 | 42 920 | 14 335 | 5 536 | 11 037 | 5 436 | 26 498 | 59 303 | 39 361 | 66 085 | 115 634 | Produit matériel brut |
| Employees: | | | | | | | | | | | | | | Salariés: |
| Number (Average as of 31.III and 30.IX).... | 699.6 | 59.9 | 88.7 | 126.6 | 8.7 | 13.3 | 20.3 | 2.2 | 19.7 | 80.7 | 69.5 | 66.5 | 143.5 | Nombre (moyenne au 31.III et 30.IX) |
| Wages and salaries... | 77 993 | 6 649 | 9 565 | 9 802 | 1 058 | 1 709 | 1 921 | 538 | 2 419 | 10 768 | 7 076 | 8 523 | 17 965 | Traitements et salaires |
| Number of Operatives (Average as of 31.III and 30.IX)...... | 614.5 | 50.3 | 81.1 | 111.7 | 7.6 | 10.4 | 17.9 | 1.9 | 15.7 | 74.7 | 63.3 | 60.4 | 119.5 | Nombre d'ouvriers (moyenne au 31.III et 30.IX) |
| Electricity consumed..... | 1 988.0 | 108.9 | 163.2 | 55.9 | 78.7 | 6.6 | 24.6 | 6.0 | 314.6 | 253.8 | 166.2 | 630.3 | 179.2 | Electricité consommée |
| **1958** | | | | | | | | | | | | | | **1958** |
| Number of enterprises... | 2 395 | 583 | 277 | 263 | 29 | 98 | 87 | 6 | 101 | 108 | 472 | 49 | 322 | Nombre d'entreprises |
| Gross material product.. | 840 603 | 93 170 | 129 024 | 53 181 | 19 668 | 13 373 | 20 289 | 10 418 | 47 517 | 85 982 | 53 111 | 109 166 | 205 704 | Produit matériel brut |
| Employees: | | | | | | | | | | | | | | Salariés: |
| Number (Average as of 31.III and 30.IX)... | 943.3 | 91.9 | 130.3 | 132.4 | 9.4 | 20.8 | 29.1 | 4.1 | 33.8 | 99.2 | 91.1 | 86.0 | 215.2 | Nombre (moyenne au 31.III et 30.IX) |
| Wages and salaries... | 162 992 | 13 898 | 18 919 | 16 815 | 1 700 | 4 929 | 4 209 | 1 474 | 6 426 | 18 655 | 14 203 | 17 019 | 44 745 | Traitements et salaires |
| Number of Operatives (Average as of 31.III and 30.IX)...... | 809.5 | 76.8 | 117.5 | 116.8 | 8.0 | 16.9 | 25.7 | 3.5 | 26.5 | 90.2 | 80.9 | 76.3 | 170.4 | Nombre d'ouvriers (moyenne au 31.III et 30.IX) |
| Electricity consumed..... | 4 069.4 | 194.0 | 251.8 | 118.7 | 190.3 | 16.1 | 48.3 | 11.3 | 597.1 | 385.2 | 287.7 | 1 637.1 | 331.8 | Electricité consommée |
| Capacity of installed power equipment (As of end of 1957)... | 2 410.6 | 176.9 | 156.8 | 155.4 | 103.2 | 13.4 | 50.9 | 14.7 | 113.9 | 392.6 | 253.3 | 544.0 | 435.5 | Puissance installée (à la fin de 1957) |
| *b. Structure* | | | | | | | | | | | | | | |
| **1954** | | | | | | | | | | | | | | **1954** |
| Distribution in percent of: | | | | | | | | | | | | | | Distribution en pourcentage: |
| Gross material product. | 100.0 | 13.3 | 15.6 | 7.9 | 2.6 | 1.1 | 2.0 | 1.0 | 4.9 | 10.9 | 7.2 | 12.2 | 21.3 | Produit matériel brut |
| Number of employees. | 100.0 | 8.5 | 12.7 | 18.1 | 1.2 | 1.9 | 2.9 | 0.3 | 2.9 | 11.5 | 9.9 | 9.5 | 20.6 | Nombre de salariés |
| Per employee: | | | | | | | | | | | | | | Par salarié: |
| Gross material product. | 776.8 | 1 212.0 | 955.1 | 339.0 | 1 647.7 | 416.2 | 543.7 | 2 470.9 | 1 345.1 | 734.8 | 566.3 | 993.8 | 805.8 | Produit matériel brut |
| Wages and salaries... | 111.5 | 111.0 | 107.8 | 77.4 | 121.6 | 128.5 | 94.6 | 244.5 | 122.8 | 133.4 | 101.8 | 128.2 | 125.2 | Traitements et salaires |
| Electricity consumed... | 2.8 | 1.8 | 1.8 | 0.4 | 9.0 | 0.5 | 1.2 | 2.7 | 16.0 | 3.1 | 2.4 | 9.5 | 1.2 | Electricité consommée |
| Gross material product per unit of wages and salaries......... | 6.97 | 10.92 | 8.86 | 4.38 | 13.55 | 3.24 | 5.74 | 10.10 | 10.95 | 5.51 | 5.56 | 7.75 | 6.44 | Produit matériel brut par unité de traitements et salaires |
| Operatives as a percent of employees....... | 87.8 | 84.0 | 91.4 | 88.2 | 87.4 | 78.2 | 88.2 | 86.4 | 79.7 | 92.6 | 91.1 | 90.8 | 83.3 | Ouvriers en pourcentage des salariés |
| Electricity consumer per Operative....... | 3.2 | 2.2 | 2.0 | 0.5 | 10.4 | 0.6 | 1.4 | 3.2 | 20.0 | 3.4 | 2.6 | 10.4 | 1.5 | Electricité consommée par ouvrier |
| **1958** | | | | | | | | | | | | | | **1958** |
| Distribution in percent of: | | | | | | | | | | | | | | Distribution en pourcentage: |
| Gross material product. | 100.0 | 11.0 | 15.4 | 6.3 | 2.3 | 1.6 | 2.5 | 1.2 | 5.6 | 10.3 | 6.3 | 13.0 | 24.5 | Produit matériel brut |
| Number of employees. | 100.0 | 9.7 | 13.8 | 14.0 | 1.0 | 2.2 | 3.1 | 0.5 | 3.5 | 10.6 | 9.6 | 9.1 | 22.9 | Nombre de salariés |
| Per employee: | | | | | | | | | | | | | | Par salarié: |
| Gross material product. | 891.1 | 1 013.8 | 990.2 | 401.7 | 2 092.2 | 642.9 | 697.2 | 2 541.0 | 1 405.8 | 866.8 | 583.0 | 1 269.4 | 955.9 | Produit matériel brut |
| Wages and salaries... | 172.8 | 151.2 | 145.2 | 127.0 | 180.8 | 237.0 | 144.6 | 359.5 | 190.1 | 188.0 | 155.9 | 197.9 | 207.9 | Traitements et salaires |
| Electricity consumed... | 4.3 | 2.1 | 1.9 | 0.9 | 20.4 | 0.7 | 1.6 | 2.8 | 19.8 | 3.9 | 3.2 | 19.0 | 1.5 | Electricité consommée |
| Capacity of installed power equipment..... | 2.56 | 1.92 | 1.20 | 1.17 | 10.98 | 0.64 | 1.75 | 3.58 | 3.37 | 3.96 | 2.78 | 6.32 | 2.02 | Puissance installée |
| Gross material product per unit of wages and salaries......... | 5.16 | 6.70 | 6.82 | 3.16 | 11.57 | 2.71 | 4.82 | 7.07 | 7.39 | 4.61 | 3.74 | 6.41 | 4.60 | Produit matériel brut par unité de traitements et salaires |
| Operatives as a percent of employees....... | 85.8 | 83.6 | 90.2 | 88.2 | 85.1 | 81.2 | 88.3 | 85.4 | 78.4 | 90.9 | 88.8 | 88.7 | 79.2 | Ouvriers en pourcentage des salariés |
| Per operative: | | | | | | | | | | | | | | Par ouvrier: |
| Electricity consumed... | 5.0 | 2.5 | 2.1 | 1.0 | 23.8 | 1.0 | 1.9 | 3.2 | 22.5 | 4.3 | 3.6 | 21.4 | 1.9 | Electricité consommée |
| Capacity of installed power equipment (As of end of 1957)... | 2.98 | 2.30 | 1.33 | 1.33 | 12.90 | 0.79 | 1.98 | 4.20 | 4.30 | 4.35 | 3.13 | 7.13 | 2.56 | Puissance installée (à la fin de 1957) |

[1] Includes the Gas industries (ISIC group 512) but excludes publishing (part of ISIC major group 28).

[2] Manufacturing of footwear, leather gloves and similar goods is included under Leather and leather products (ISIC major group 29) instead of under clothing and wearing apparel (ISIC major group 24).

[3] Includes the manufacture of wooden toys, musical instruments and cultural articles, pens, pencils, brooms, brushes and similar articles (all part of ISIC group 399) but excludes the manufacture of metal furniture.

[4] Included are the following kinds of manufacturing: Metal furniture (part of ISIC major group 26), Scientific and precision instruments and equipment (ISIC group 391) and Photographic and optical goods (ISIC group 392). The manufacture of film and similar photographic materials is, however, included under chemical products (ISIC major group 31).

[5] Paper articles are covered under Printing (ISIC major group 28) instead of under Paper and paper products (ISIC major group 27).

[1] Y compris les Industries gazières (CITI 512), mais non compris l'édition (dans CITI 28).

[2] La fabrication de chaussures, de gants en cuir et de produits analogues est comprise dans Cuir et ouvrages en cuir (CITI 29) et non dans Vêtements et articles d'habillement (CITI 24)

[3] Y compris la fabrication de jouets en bois, d'instruments de musique et d'articles culturels, de crayons, porte-plumes, balais, brosses et articles analogues (tous dans CITI 399), mais non compris la fabrication de meubles métalliques.

[4] Sont inclus les types d'activité suivants: fabrication de meubles métalliques (dans CITI 26) d'Instruments de précision et d'appareils scientifiques (CITI 391) et fabrication de matériel photographique et d'instruments d'optique (CITI 392). La fabrication de pellicules et d'articles photographiques analogues est cependant comprise dans Produits chimiques (CITI 31).

[5] Les articles en papier sont compris dans Imprimerie (CITI 28) et non dans Papier et ouvrages en papier (CITI 27).

## 5. THE QUANTITY OF SELECTED FUELS AND OF ELECTRICITY CONSUMED BY PUBLICLY-OWNED INDUSTRIAL ENTERPRISES

## QUANTITES DE QUELQUES COMBUSTIBLES ET DE L'ELECTRICITE CONSOMMES PAR LES ENTREPRISES INDUSTRIELLES PUBLIQUES

### 1954, 1958

Coal, lignite, coke and refined fuel oils in thousand metric tons; wood in thousand cubic meters; electricity in million KWH.

Charbon, lignite, coke et pétrole raffiné en milliers de tonnes métriques; bois en milliers de mètres cubes; électricité en millions de kWh.

| Year and source of energy | Mining and manufacturing [1] — Industries extractives et manufacturières [1] | Food, beverages and tobacco — Industries alimentaires, boissons, tabac | Textiles and clothing [2] — Textiles et articles d'habillement [2] | Wood products and furniture [3] — Bois et meubles [3] | Paper and paper products [5] — Papier et ouvrages en papier [5] | Printing [1,5] — Imprimerie [1,5] | Leather and leather products [2] — Cuir et articles en cuir [2] | Rubber products — Ouvrages en caoutchouc | Chemicals and chemical products [4] — Produits chimiques [4] | Coal, crude petroleum and products [1] — Charbon, pétrole brut et produits dérivés [1] | Non-metallic minerals and products — Minéraux non métalliques et produits dérivés | Metal mining and basic metals — Minerais métalliques et métallurgie de base | Metal products [4] — Ouvrages en métaux [4] | Electricity [6] — Electricité [6] | Année et source d'énergie |
|---|---|---|---|---|---|---|---|---|---|---|---|---|---|---|---|
| ISIC | 1-3, 512 | 20-22 | 23, 243-244 | 25-26 | 27 | 28 | 241, 29 | 30 | 31 | 11,13,32 | 14-19,33 | 34 | 35-38 | 511 | CITI |
| **1954** | | | | | | | | | | | | | | | **1954** |
| Coal | 791.4 | 13.4 | 10.3 | 2.6 | 4.4 | — | 3.6 | — | 19.8 | 548.4 | 146.0 | 24.4 | 18.5 | 66.4 | Charbon |
| Lignite | 4 831.6 | 644.0 | 443.2 | 100.2 | 213.4 | 2.9 | 117.7 | 16.6 | 396.1 | 275.6 | 1 156.2 | 1 227.2 | 238.5 | 2 194.2 | Lignite |
| Coke | 630.5 | 5.3 | 0.2 | 0.1 | — | — | 0.1 | — | 21.5 | 11.6 | 24.4 | 527.1 | 40.2 | — | Coke |
| Refined oil fuels | 158.9 | 23.1 | 0.8 | 3.5 | — | 0.1 | 0.8 | — | 1.7 | 76.1 | 16.0 | 20.0 | 16.8 | 13.8 | Pétrole raffiné |
| Electricity | 1 988.0 | 108.9 | 163.2 | 55.9 | 78.7 | 6.6 | 24.6 | 6.0 | 314.6 | 253.8 | 166.2 | 630.3 | 179.2 | 109.2 | Electricité |
| Wood | 530.5 | 185.2 | 5.0 | 187.7 | 1.1 | 3.4 | 1.8 | — | 4.5 | 2.0 | 83.5 | 10.7 | 45.6 | 21.6 | Bois |
| **1958** | | | | | | | | | | | | | | | **1958** |
| Coal | 1 572.2 | 20.1 | 10.4 | 2.5 | 1.9 | 0.5 | 0.9 | — | 29.6 | 1 225.0 | 246.8 | 19.3 | 15.2 | 40.8 | Charbon |
| Lignite | 6 667.6 | 745.4 | 578.6 | 112.2 | 454.9 | 6.9 | 145.2 | 24.5 | 633.3 | 463.6 | 1 580.3 | 1 559.1 | 363.6 | 3 869.8 | Lignite |
| Coke | 1 121.3 | 7.3 | — | 0.9 | — | — | 0.2 | — | 35.8 | 11.9 | 21.6 | 993.4 | 50.2 | — | Coke |
| Refined oil fuels | 279.2 | 38.7 | 1.9 | 6.0 | 0.3 | 0.3 | 0.6 | 0.5 | 3.8 | 111.5 | 29.0 | 63.4 | 23.2 | 7.5 | Pétrole raffiné |
| Electricity | 4 069.4 | 194.0 | 251.8 | 118.7 | 190.3 | 16.1 | 48.3 | 11.3 | 597.1 | 385.2 | 2 87.7 | 1 637.1 | 331.8 | 237.4 | Electricité |
| Wood | 445.9 | 98.2 | 6.6 | 189.2 | 4.5 | 8.4 | 2.0 | — | 7.1 | 1.9 | 71.6 | 11.8 | 44.6 | 6.7 | Bois |

[1] Includes the Gas Industries (ISIC group 512) but excludes publishing (part of ISIC major group 28).

[2] Manufacturing of footwear, leather gloves and similar goods is included under Leather and leather products (ISIC major group 29) instead of under clothing and wearing apparel (ISIC major group 24).

[3] Includes the manufacturing of wooden toys, musical instruments and cultural articles, pens, pencils, brooms, brushes and similar items (all part of ISIC group 399) but excludes the manufacture of metal furniture (part of ISIC major group 26).

[4] Included are the following kinds of manufacturing: Metal furniture (part of ISIC major group 26), Scientific and precision instruments and equipment (ISIC group 391) and Photographic and optical goods (ISIC group 392). The manufacture of film and similar photographic materials is, however, included under chemical products (ISIC major group 31).

[5] Paper articles are covered under Printing (ISIC major group 28) instead of under Paper and paper products (ISIC major group 27).

[6] Covers only electricity power stations of enterprises classified to the Electricity industry.

[1] Y compris les Industries gazières (CITI 512), mais non compris l'édition (dans CITI 28).

[2] La fabrication de chaussures, de gants en cuir et d'articles analogues, est comprise dans Cuir et ouvrages en cuir (CITI 29) et non dans Vêtements et articles d'habillement (CITI 24).

[3] Y compris la fabrication de jouets en bois, d'instruments de musique et d'articles culturels, crayons, porte-plumes, balais, brosses et articles analogues (tous dans CITI 399), mais non compris la fabrication de meubles métalliques (dans CITI 26).

[4] Sont inclus les types d'activité manufacturière suivants: fabrication de meubles métalliques (dans CITI 26), d'instruments de précision et d'appareils scientifiques (CITI 391) et fabrication d'appareils photographiques et d'instruments d'optique (CITI 392). La fabrication de pellicules et d'articles photographiques analogues est cependant comprise dans Produits chimiques (CITI 31).

[5] Les articles en papier sont compris dans Imprimerie (CITI 28) et non dans Papier et ouvrages en papier (CITI 27).

[6] Ne sont comprises que les centrales électriques des entreprises classées dans l'Industrie de l'électricité.

## 6. CHARACTERISTICS OF ALL HANDICRAFT ENTERPRISES ENGAGED IN INDUSTRIAL ACTIVITY

### CARACTERISTIQUES DE TOUTES LES ENTREPRISES ARTISANALES EXERÇANT UNE ACTIVITE INDUSTRIELLE
### 31.III.1951, 30.IX.1954, 15.XII.1959

Number of establishments in units; number of persons engaged in thousands; capacity of installed power equipment in thousand horsepower; capacity of installed power equipment per person engaged in horsepower.

Nombre d'établissements en unités; nombre de personnes occupées en milliers; puissance installée en milliers de chevaux-vapeur; puissance installée par personne occupée en chevaux-vapeur.

| Year and item of data | Mining and manufacturing [4] / Industries extractives et manufacturières [4] | Food, beverages and tobacco / Industries alimentaires, boissons, tabac | Textiles and clothing / Textiles et articles d'habillement | Wood products and furniture [3] / Bois et meubles [3] | Paper and paper products / Papier et ouvrages en papier | Leather and leather products / Cuir et articles en cuir | Chemicals and chemical products [4] / Produits chimiques [4] | Non-metallic minerals and products / Minéraux non métalliques et produits dérivés | Basic metals and metal products [5] / Métallurgie de base et ouvrages en métaux [5] | Other manufacturing [6] / Autres industries manufacturières [6] | Construction / Bâtiment et travaux publics | Année et rubrique |
|---|---|---|---|---|---|---|---|---|---|---|---|---|
| ISIC | 14–19, 2–3 | 20–22 | 23, 243, 244 | 25–26 | 27 | 241, 29 | 31 | 14-19, 33 | 34–38 | 39 | 4 | CITI |
| *a. All enterprises — Toutes entreprises* | | | | | | | | | | | | |
| **31.III.1951** [1] Number of establishments | 103 028 | 10 989 | 24 752 | 20 710 | — | 15 332 | 701 | 2 752 | 24 335 | 3 457 | 5 642 | **31.III.1951** [1] Nombre d'établissements |
| Number of engaged | 204.2 | 20.0 | 47.8 | 39.0 | — | 36.3 | 1.8 | 7.3 | 44.1 | 7.9 | 12.0 | Nombre de personnes occupées |
| Capacity of installed power equipment | 115.3 | 43.7 | 4.8 | 40.7 | — | 1.8 | 0.9 | 3.4 | 17.9 | 2.1 | 1.1 | Puissance installée |
| Distribution in percent of the number of engaged | 100.0 | 9.7 | 23.5 | 19.1 | — | 17.7 | 0.9 | 3.6 | 21.6 | 3.9 | 100.0 | Distribution en pourcentage du nombre de personnes occupées |
| Capacity of installed power equipment per engaged | 0.56 | 2.18 | 0.10 | 1.04 | — | 0.05 | 0.50 | 0.46 | 0.40 | 0.26 | 0.09 | Puissance installée par personne occupée |
| **30.IX.1954** [1] Number of establishments | 133 522 | 17 821 | 29 730 | 27 096 | — | 18 154 | 1 211 | 4 893 | 29 964 | 4 653 | 14 315 | **30.IX.1954** [1] Nombre d'établissements |
| Number of engaged | 253.2 | 38.3 | 48.7 | 51.1 | — | 30.2 | 2.5 | 14.0 | 57.8 | 10.6 | 37.6 | Nombre de personnes occupées |
| Capacity of installed power equipment | 180.7 | 75.3 | 5.6 | 53.7 | — | 1.8 | 1.1 | 6.9 | 33.3 | 3.0 | 2.1 | Puissance installée |
| Distribution in percent of the number of engaged | 100.0 | 15.1 | 19.2 | 20.2 | — | 11.9 | 1.0 | 5.5 | 22.9 | 4.2 | 100.0 | Distribution en pourcentage du nombre de personnes occupées |
| Capacity of installed power equipment per engaged | 0.71 | 1.97 | 0.11 | 1.05 | — | 0.06 | 0.44 | 0.49 | 0.58 | 0.28 | 0.06 | Puissance installée par personne occupée |
| **30.IX.1954** [2] Number of establishments | 141 174 | 13 243 | 29 722 | 27 246 | 203 | 17 577 | 1 438 | 4 942 | 29 945 | 16 858 | 16 267 | **30.IX.1954** [2] Nombre d'établissements |
| Number of engaged | 280.4 | 36.0 | 50.9 | 54.2 | 0.5 | 30.8 | 3.3 | 15.2 | 61.9 | 27.6 | 39.9 | Nombre de personnes occupées |
| Capacity of installed power equipment | 214.0 | 20.1 | 5.2 | 46.6 | 0.1 | 1.6 | 1.4 | 6.3 | 27.1 | 105.6 | 1.7 | Puissance installée |
| Distribution in percent of the number of engaged | 100.0 | 12.8 | 18.1 | 19.4 | 0.1 | 11.0 | 1.2 | 5.4 | 22.1 | 9.9 | 100.0 | Distribution en pourcentage du nombre de personnes occupées |
| Capacity of installed power equipment per engaged | 0.76 | 0.56 | 0.10 | 0.86 | 0.20 | 0.05 | 0.42 | 0.41 | 0.44 | 3.83 | 0.04 | Puissance installée par personne occupée |
| **15.XII.1959** [2] Number of establishments | 103 987 | 12 324 | 20 858 | 17 158 | 211 | 12 107 | 1 750 | 3 759 | 22 787 | 13 033 | 10 879 | **15.XII.1959** [2] Nombre d'établissements |
| Number of engaged | 280.6 | 35.8 | 51.1 | 54.0 | 1.1 | 24.2 | 4.6 | 10.2 | 76.5 | 23.1 | 48.8 | Nombre de personnes occupées |
| Capacity of installed power equipment | 266.5 | 53.9 | 9.7 | 59.6 | 0.3 | 2.7 | 3.6 | 9.1 | 52.1 | 75.5 | 12.9 | Puissance installée |
| Distribution in percent of the number of engaged | 100.0 | 12.7 | 18.2 | 19.3 | 0.4 | 8.6 | 1.6 | 3.7 | 27.2 | 8.3 | 100.0 | Distribution en pourcentage du nombre de personnes occupées |
| Capacity of installed power equipment per engaged | 0.95 | 1.50 | 0.19 | 1.10 | 0.27 | 0.11 | 0.78 | 0.89 | 0.68 | 3.27 | 0.26 | Puissance installée par personne occupée |

For footnotes see end of table.

Pour les notes, voir au bas du tableau.

## 6. CHARACTERISTICS OF ALL HANDICRAFT ENTERPRISES ENGAGED IN INDUSTRIAL ACTIVITY (continued)
## CARACTERISTIQUES DE TOUTES LES ENTREPRISES ARTISANALES EXERÇANT UNE ACTIVITE INDUSTRIELLE (suite)
### 31.III.1951, 30.IX.1954, 15.XII.1959

| Year and item of data | Mining and manufacturing / Industries extractives et manufacturières [4] | Food, beverages and tobacco / Industries alimentaires, boissons, tabac | Textiles and clothing / Textiles et articles d'habillement | Wood products and furniture [3] / Bois et meubles [3] | Paper and paper products / Papier et ouvrages en papier | Leather and leather products / Cuir et articles en cuir | Chemicals and chemical products [4] / Produits chimiques [4] | Non-metallic minerals and products / Minéraux non métalliques et produits dérivés | Basic metals and metal products [5] / Métallurgie de base et ouvrages en métaux [5] | Other manufacturing [6] / Autres industries manufacturières [6] | Construction / Bâtiment et travaux publics | Année et rubrique |
|---|---|---|---|---|---|---|---|---|---|---|---|---|
| ISIC | 14–19, 2–3 | 20–22 | 23, 243, 244 | 25–26 | 27 | 241, 29 | 31 | 14-19, 33 | 34–38 | 39 | 4 | CITI |
| **b. Publicly-owned enterprises and co-operatives — Entreprises publiques et coopératives** | | | | | | | | | | | | |
| **30.IX.1954** [2] | | | | | | | | | | | | **30.IX.1954** [2] |
| Number of establishments. | 10 489 | 4 313 | 878 | 1 614 | 15 | 934 | 94 | 335 | 1 842 | 464 | 311 | Nombre d'établissements |
| Number of engaged.... | 111.7 | 22.4 | 16.2 | 21.3 | 0.3 | 10.6 | 1.1 | 7.6 | 24.9 | 7.3 | 15.9 | Nombre de personnes occupées |
| Capacity of installed power equipment..... | 52.1 | 6.7 | 1.6 | 20.7 | — | 0.7 | 0.5 | 3.1 | 14.4 | 4.4 | 0.9 | Puissance installée |
| Distribution in percent of the number of engaged........ | 100.0 | 20.0 | 14.5 | 19.1 | 0.2 | 9.5 | 1.0 | 6.8 | 22.3 | 6.6 | 100.0 | Distribution en pourcentage du nombre de personnes occupées |
| Capacity of installed power equipment per engaged........ | 0.47 | 0.30 | 0.10 | 0.97 | — | 0.07 | 0.45 | 0.41 | 0.58 | 0.60 | 0.06 | Puissance installée par personne occupée |
| **15.XII.1959** [2] | | | | | | | | | | | | **15.XII.1959** [2] |
| Number of establishments. | 6 635 | 2 243 | 791 | 920 | 32 | 588 | 106 | 173 | 1 333 | 449 | 607 | Nombre d'établissements |
| Number of engaged.... | 158.7 | 21.6 | 27.2 | 33.1 | 0.7 | 10.6 | 2.4 | 5.4 | 49.5 | 8.2 | 33.8 | Nombre de personnes occupées |
| Capacity of installed power equipment..... | 125.8 | 37.9 | 4.6 | 29.8 | 0.3 | 1.6 | 2.1 | 4.4 | 38.5 | 6.6 | 11.7 | Puissance installée |
| Distribution in percent of the number of engaged........ | 100.0 | 13.6 | 17.1 | 20.9 | 0.4 | 6.7 | 1.5 | 3.4 | 31.2 | 5.2 | 100.0 | Distribution en pourcentage du nombre de personnes occupées |
| Capacity of installed power equipment per engaged........ | 0.79 | 1.75 | 0.17 | 0.90 | 0.43 | 0.15 | 0.88 | 0.81 | 0.78 | 0.80 | 0.35 | Puissance installée par personne occupée |
| **c. Privately-owned enterprises — Entreprises privées** | | | | | | | | | | | | |
| **30.IX.1954** [2] | | | | | | | | | | | | **30.IX.1954** [2] |
| Number of establishments. | 130 685 | 8 930 | 28 844 | 25 632 | 188 | 16 643 | 1 344 | 4 607 | 28 103 | 16 394 | 15 956 | Nombre d'établissements |
| Number of engaged.... | 168.8 | 13.7 | 34.7 | 33.0 | 0.2 | 20.2 | 2.1 | 7.6 | 37.0 | 20.3 | 24.0 | Nombre de personnes occupées |
| Capacity of installed power equipment..... | 161.9 | 13.3 | 3.7 | 25.9 | — | 0.9 | 0.9 | 3.2 | 12.8 | 101.2 | 0.7 | Puissance installée |
| Distribution in percent of the number of engaged........ | 100.0 | 8.1 | 20.5 | 19.6 | 0.1 | 12.0 | 1.2 | 4.5 | 21.9 | 12.1 | 100.0 | Distribution en pourcentage du nombre de personnes occupées |
| Capacity of installed power equipment per engaged........ | 0.96 | 0.97 | 0.11 | 0.78 | — | 0.04 | 0.43 | 0.42 | 0.34 | 4.98 | 0.03 | Puissance installée par personne occupée |
| **15.XII.1959** [2] | | | | | | | | | | | | **15.XII.1959** [2] |
| Number of establishments. | 97 352 | 10 081 | 20 067 | 16 238 | 179 | 11 519 | 1 644 | 3 586 | 21 454 | 12 584 | 10 272 | Nombre d'établissements |
| Number of engaged.... | 122.0 | 14.2 | 23.9 | 20.9 | 0.4 | 13.6 | 2.2 | 4.8 | 27.0 | 15.0 | 15.0 | Nombre de personnes occupées |
| Capacity of installed power equipment..... | 140.5 | 16.0 | 5.1 | 29.8 | — | 1.1 | 1.4 | 4.7 | 13.6 | 68.8 | 1.2 | Puissance installée |
| Distribution in percent of the number of engaged........ | 100.0 | 11.6 | 19.6 | 17.1 | 0.3 | 11.2 | 1.8 | 3.9 | 22.2 | 12.3 | 100.0 | Distribution en pourcentage du nombre de personnes occupées |
| Capacity of installed power equipment per engaged........ | 1.15 | 1.13 | 0.21 | 1.42 | — | 0.08 | 0.64 | 0.98 | 0.50 | 4.59 | 0.08 | Puissance installée par personne occupée |

[1] Denotes comparable data for 31.III.1951 and 30.IX.1954.
[2] Denotes comparable data for 30.IX.1954 and 15.XII.1959.
[3] Includes the making of wooden toys and cultural articles (part of ISIC major group 39), cartwrights and the manufacture of wooden car-bodies and small craft (part of ISIC major group 38).
[4] Includes the manufacture of plastic goods (part of ISIC major group 39); and dyers and dry cleaners and sign painters, which are not classified in manufacturing in the ISIC.
[5] Includes jewelers, gold and silver smiths, and watch and precision instrument making and repairing (all part of ISIC major group 39).
[6] Includes manufacturing establishments which could not be classified to a specific subdivision of manufacturing.

[1] Indique que les données relevées au 31.III.1951 et au 30.IX.1954 sont comparables.
[2] Indique que les données relevées au 30.IX.1954 et au 15.XII.1959 sont comparables.
[3] Y compris la fabrication de jouets en bois et d'articles culturels (dans CITI 39) et la fabrication de charrettes, de carosseries de véhicules en bois et de petites embarcations (dans CITI 38).
[4] Y compris la fabrication d'articles en matière plastique (dans CITI 39), ainsi que la teinturerie, le nettoyage à sec et la peinture d'enseignes, qui, dans la CITI, ne sont pas classés dans les Industries manufacturières.
[5] Y compris la bijouterie, l'orfèvrerie en or et en argent, ainsi que la fabrication et la réparation des montres et des instruments de précision (tous dans CITI 39)
[6] Y compris les établissements manufacturiers qui n'ont pu être classés dans aucune des subdivisions des industries manufacturières.

# STATISTICAL YEARBOOK 1962

Fourteenth issue of a comprehensive collection of international statistics presented in 185 tables, generally covering the year 1948 and some nine most recent years. The *Yearbook* contains, *inter alia*, statistics relating to: population; structure of mining, manufacturing, construction and electricity and gas industries; production of commodities in agriculture, mining and manufacturing; textile and transport equipment; production, trade and consumption of energy; postal, telegraph and telephone services; civil aviation; tourist travel; external trade of virtually all trading countries; balance of payments; wages and prices; national income; finance; budget accounts and public debt; housing; medical personnel; educational institutions; newsprint and newspapers; books, films, cinemas and radio and television broadcasting receivers.

The tables are grouped under the following chapter headings:

- Population
- Manpower
- Production summary
- Agriculture
- Forestry
- Fishing
- Mining, quarrying
- Manufacturing
- Construction
- Energy
- Consumption
- Transport
- Communications
- Internal Trade
- External Trade
- Balance of payments
- Wages and prices
- National income
- Finance
- Public Finance
- Social Statistics
- Education, culture

The *Yearbook* includes also appendices showing conversion factors and alphabetical subject and country indexes.

Prepared by the Statistical Office of the United Nations
(U.N. publication, Sales No.: 63.XVII.1)
9 x 11½ in., 688 pages. Clothbound, $10.00; Paperbound, $8.00
(or equivalent in other currencies)
(See list of distributors at end of volume)

# ANNUAIRE STATISTIQUE 1962

Quatorzième édition d'un vaste recueil de statistiques internationales comportant 185 tableaux et se rapportant généralement à l'année 1948 et aux neuf dernières années. L'*Annuaire* contient notamment des séries sur les sujets suivants: population; structure des industries extractives et manufacturières, de la construction et des industries du gaz et de l'électricité; production de l'agriculture, des industries extractives et des industries manufacturières; équipement de l'industries textile et des transports; énergie: production, commerce et consommation; services postaux, télégraphiques et téléphoniques; aviation civile; tourisme; commerce extérieur de presque tous les pays participant à ce commerce balance des paiements; salaires et prix revenu national; finances; comptes budgétaires et dette publique; habitation; personnel médical; établissements d'enseignement; papier journal et journaux; livres, films, cinémas, radiodiffusion et télévision.

Ces tableaux sont groupés sous les titres suivants:

- Population
- Main-d'oeuvre
- Résumé de la production
- Agriculture
- Forêts
- Pêche
- Industries extractives
- Industries manufacturières
- Construction
- Energie
- Consommation
- Transports
- Communications
- Commerce intérieur
- Commerce extérieur
- Balance des paiements
- Salaires et prix
- Revenu national
- Finances
- Finances publiques
- Statistiques sociales
- Instruction, culture

L'*Annuaire* contient en annexe une table de conversion, un index alphabétique par sujets et un par pays.

Préparé par le Bureau de statistique de l'Organisation des Nations Unies
(Publication des Nations Unies, No de vente: 63.XVII.1)
23 x 29 cm, 688 pages. Relié toile: $10.00; Broché $8.00
(ou équivalent en monnaies nationales)
(Voir liste des dépositaires à la fin du volume)

# UNITED NATIONS      NATIONS UNIES

## PERIODICAL PUBLICATIONS
## STATISTICAL OFFICE OF THE UNITED NATIONS

**MONTHLY BULLETIN OF STATISTICS**
**(with SUPPLEMENT)**

*(E/F) Annual subscription: $10.00; $1.00 per copy.*

Provides monthly statistics on more than 60 subjects from over 170 countries and territories together with special tables illustrating important economic developments. Quarterly data for significant world and regional aggregates are also prepared regularly for the Bulletin.

**CURRENT ECONOMIC INDICATORS**

*(E/F) Annual subscription: $4.00; $1.00 per copy.*

This is a quarterly publication designed as a concise source of information on current trends and developments in the world economic situation. A system of 500 indicators is employed and quarterly changes in these indicators are presented in graphic as well as tabular form. A brief narrative draws attention to significant developments in the quarter under review.

**STATISTICAL YEARBOOK 1962**

*(E/F) Clothbound, $10.00; paperbound, $8.00*
*Sales No.: 63.XVII.1*

Fourteenth issue of a comprehensive and authoritative compilation of international statistics relating to: population; manpower; agricultural, mineral and manufacturing production; production, trade and consumption energy; transport; external trade; prices; national income; finance; social and cultural subjects. It contains 185 tables, most of which cover 1948, and some nine most recents years, alphabetical subject and country indexes, and an appendix containing conversion coefficients and factors.

**DEMOGRAPHIC YEARBOOK 1962**

*(E/F) Clothbound, $10.00; paperbound, $8.00*
*Sales No.: 63.XIII.1*

The fourteenth issue of this international compendium of demographic statistics, covering each of almost 250 countries and territories of the world, features selected results of population censuses held since 1955.

Characteristics of the enumerated population for which data are shown are sex and age, marital status, geographic distribution and distribution by type and size of household. Recent estimates of population by 5-year age groups and sex and of the population of cities are also shown.

Also included are the usual statistics of area, density, population growth rates, natality, mortality, expectation of life, nuptiality, and divorce, as well as estimates of the order of magnitude of world, continental and regional population aggregates and corresponding crude birth and death rates.

In addition to the Technical Notes, there is a special text on methods of estimating the reliability of population census results; a subject matter index covering each of the fourteen issues replaces the customary cumulative table of contents.

**YEARBOOK OF INTERNATIONAL TRADE STATISTICS, 1961**

*(E) $8.00. 710 pages. Sales No.: 62.XVII. 8*
Twelfth issue of a compilation of national tables showing annua figures. Among the data shown are: value of merchandise imports and exports in national currency and U.S. dollars; trade in gold; quantum and unit value indexes, currency conversion factors; trade in principal commodities (quantity and value) according to the SITC where possible, otherwise according to commodity classes based on the national classification; trade by principal countries of provenance and destination; duty receipts. Also provides regional summaries with grand totals relating to: value in U.S. dollars of imports and exports; provenance and destination of world exports (in matrix form) indexes of quantum, unit value and terms of trade. Also unit value indexes of exports of manufactured goods and price index of primary commodities, distinguishing principal components.

**POPULATION AND VITAL STATISTICS REPORTS**
**(Statistical Papers, Series A)**

*(E) Annual subscription: $1.00; $0.30 per copy.*

Quarterly publication containing, for each of some 250 geographic units comprising the world, the latest census returns, the latest official estimate of population, the estimate for 1961, and the latest birth, death and infant-mortality statistics. World and continental aggregates of population in 1961 are also included, together with a brief explanatory text. The quality of the statistics is indicated by means of codes.

**COMMODITY TRADE STATISTICS**
**(Statistical Papers, Series D)**

*(E) Annual subscription: $10,00; $0.50 per fascicle.*

Publication, issued in fascicle of about 150 pages as quarterly data become available, containing international commodity tables according to the United Nations Standard International Trade Classification (SITC) showing the imports and exports of countries reporting according to that classification (taken together, without duplication, the imports and exports of these countries cover about 90% of world trade). Tables are shown on the basis of the 625 commodity subgroups of the SITC and on the basis of SITC headings obtained by combining groups to form classes of major economic importance. In addition, data for the 1,312 items are available at cost on application to the Statistical Office. Within commodity headings trade is analysed by countries and regions of provenance and destination. Figures are in U.S. dollars and metric units of quantity.

**YEARBOOK OF NATIONAL ACCOUNTS STATISTICS, 1962**

*(E/F) $4.00 Sales No.: 63.XVII.2*

Sixth issue (319 pages). Contains detailed estimates of the following economic measurements of 76 countries: national product by type of expenditure and by industrial origin; national income by distributive shares; capital formation by type of capital good, industrial use and purchaser; sources for the financing of capital formation; sector accounts for households and government; private consumption expenditure by category of goods and services; external transactions of the nation. To facilitate country comparisons, the estimates for most countries are set out in standard tables and conform to the international standards and definitions in this field. The tables are supplemented by explanatory notes and source information. Includes also three international tables showing the principal aggregates and their interrelationships for 97 countries and territories for the years 1948–1961, rates of growth of total and per capita real gross domestic product for over 60 countries during the period 1951–1961, and estimates of total and per capita gross domestic product expressed in United States dollars for about 140 countries and territories in 1953, 1958 and 1961.

**WORLD ENERGY SUPPLIES, 1958–1961**
**(Statistical Papers, Series J, No. 6)**

*(E) $1.50 Sales No.: 63.XVII.4.*

This study is the sixth in a series on energy. Provides statistics on production, trade and consumption of solid and liquid fuels, gas and electricity for approximately 160 countries covering virtually all the world's population. Previous studies give data annually back to 1949 and for 1937 and 1929.

# WHERE TO BUY UNITED NATIONS PUBLICATIONS
# ADRESSES OÙ LES PUBLICATIONS DE L'ONU SONT EN VENTE

## AFRICA/AFRIQUE

**CAMEROON/CAMEROUN:**
LIBRAIRIE DU PEUPLE AFRICAIN
La Gérante, B. P. 1197, Yaoundé.
DIFFUSION INTERNATIONALE CAMEROUNAISE
DU LIVRE ET DE LA PRESSE, Sangmelima.
**CONGO (Léopoldville):** INSTITUT POLITIQUE
CONGOLAIS, B. P. 2307, Léopoldville.
**ETHIOPIA/ÉTHIOPIE:** INTERNATIONAL
PRESS AGENCY, P. O. Box 120, Addis Ababa.
**GHANA:** UNIVERSITY BOOKSHOP
University College of Ghana, Legon, Accra.
**KENYA:** THE E.S.A. BOOKSHOP
Box 30167, Nairobi.
**MOROCCO/MAROC:** CENTRE DE DIFFUSION
DOCUMENTAIRE DU B.E.P.I.
8, rue Michaux-Bellaire, Rabat.
**SOUTH AFRICA/AFRIQUE DU SUD:**
VAN SCHAIK'S BOOK STORE (PTY.), LTD.
Church Street, Box 724, Pretoria.
**SOUTHERN RHODESIA/RHODÉSIE DU SUD:**
THE BOOK CENTRE, First Street, Salisbury.
**UNITED ARAB REPUBLIC/RÉPUBLIQUE ARABE UNIE:**
LIBRAIRIE "LA RENAISSANCE D'ÉGYPTE"
9 Sh. Adly Pasha, Cairo.

## ASIA/ASIE

**BURMA/BIRMANIE:** CURATOR,
GOVT. BOOK DEPOT, Rangoon.
**CAMBODIA/CAMBODGE:** ENTREPRISE KHMÈRE
DE LIBRAIRIE
Imprimerie & Papeterie, S. à R. L., Phnom-Penh.
**CEYLON/CEYLAN:** LAKE HOUSE BOOKSHOP
Assoc. Newspapers of Ceylon, P. O. Box 244,
Colombo.
**CHINA/CHINE:**
THE WORLD BOOK COMPANY, LTD.
99 Chung King Road, 1st Section, Taipeh, Taiwan.
THE COMMERCIAL PRESS, LTD.
211 Honan Road, Shanghai.
**HONG KONG/HONG-KONG:**
THE SWINDON BOOK COMPANY
25 Nathan Road, Kowloon.
**INDIA/INDE:**
ORIENT LONGMANS
Bombay, Calcutta, Hyderabad, Madras & New Delhi.
OXFORD BOOK & STATIONERY COMPANY
Calcutta & New Delhi.
P. VARADACHARY & COMPANY, Madras.
**INDONESIA/INDONÉSIE:** PEMBANGUNAN, LTD.
Gunung Sahari 84, Djakarta.
**JAPAN/JAPON:** MARUZEN COMPANY, LTD.
6 Tori-Nichome, Nihonbashi, Tokyo.
**KOREA (REP. OF)/CORÉE (RÉP. DE):**
EUL-YOO PUBLISHING CO., LTD.
5, 2-KA, Chongno, Seoul.
**PAKISTAN:**
THE PAKISTAN CO-OPERATIVE BOOK SOCIETY
Dacca, East Pakistan.
PUBLISHERS UNITED, LTD., Lahore.
THOMAS & THOMAS, Karachi.
**PHILIPPINES:**
ALEMAR'S BOOK STORE, 769 Rizal Avenue, Manila.
POPULAR BOOKSTORE, 1573 Doroteo Jose, Manila.
**SINGAPORE/SINGAPOUR:** THE CITY BOOK
STORE, LTD., Collyer Quay.
**THAILAND/THAÏLANDE:**
PRAMUAN MIT, LTD.
55 Chakrawat Road, Wat Tuk, Bangkok.
NIBONDH & CO., LTD.
New Road, Sikak Phya Sri, Bangkok.
SUKSAPAN PANIT
Mansion 9, Rajadamnern Avenue, Bangkok.
**VIET-NAM (REP. OF/RÉP. DU):**
LIBRAIRIE-PAPETERIE XUÂN THU
185, rue Tu-do, B. P. 283, Saigon.

## EUROPE

**AUSTRIA/AUTRICHE:**
GEROLD & COMPANY, Graben 31, Wien, I.
B. WÜLLERSTORFF
Markus Sittikusstrasse 10, Salzburg.
GEORG FROMME & CO., Spengergasse 39, Wien, V.
**BELGIUM/BELGIQUE:** AGENCE
ET MESSAGERIES DE LA PRESSE, S. A.
14-22, rue du Persil, Bruxelles.
**BULGARIA/BULGARIE:** RAZNOÏZNOS
1, Tzar Assen, Sofia.

**CYPRUS/CHYPRE:** PAN PUBLISHING HOUSE
10 Alexander the Great Street, Strovolos.
**CZECHOSLOVAKIA/TCHÉCOSLOVAQUIE:**
ARTIA LTD., 30 ve Smečkách, Praha, 2.
ČESKOSLOVENSKÝ SPISOVATEL
Národní Třída 9, Praha, 1.
**DENMARK/DANEMARK:** EJNAR MUNKSGAARD, LTD.
Nørregade 6, København, K.
**FINLAND/FINLANDE:** AKATEEMINEN KIRJAKAUPPA
2 Keskuskatu, Helsinki.
**FRANCE:** ÉDITIONS A. PÉDONE
13, rue Soufflot, Paris (Vᵉ).
**GERMANY (FEDERAL REPUBLIC OF)/**
**ALLEMAGNE (RÉPUBLIQUE FÉDÉRALE D'):**
R. EISENSCHMIDT
Schwanthaler Str. 59, Frankfurt/Main.
ELWERT UND MEURER
Hauptstrasse 101, Berlin-Schöneberg.
ALEXANDER HORN
Spiegelgasse 9, Wiesbaden.
W. E. SAARBACH
Gertrudenstrasse 30, Köln (1).
**GREECE/GRÈCE:** LIBRAIRIE KAUFFMANN
28, rue du Stade, Athènes.
**HUNGARY/HONGRIE:** KULTURA
P. O. Box 149, Budapest 62.
**ICELAND/ISLANDE:** BÓKAVERZLUN SIGFÚSAR
EYMUNDSSONAR H. F.
Austurstraeti 18, Reykjavík.
**IRELAND/IRLANDE:**
STATIONERY OFFICE, Dublin.
**ITALY/ITALIE:**
LIBRERIA COMMISSIONARIA SANSONI
Via Gino Capponi 26, Firenze,
& Via Paolo Mercuri 19/B, Roma.
**LUXEMBOURG:**
LIBRAIRIE J. TRAUSCHSCHUMMER
Place du Théâtre, Luxembourg.
**NETHERLANDS/PAYS-BAS:**
N. V. MARTINUS NIJHOFF
Lange Voorhout 9, 's-Gravenhage.
**NORWAY/NORVÈGE:** JOHAN GRUNDT TANUM
Karl Johansgate, 41, Oslo.
**POLAND/POLOGNE:** PAN, Pałac Kultury i Nauki,
Warszawa.
**PORTUGAL:** LIVRARIA RODRIGUES & CIA.
186 Rua Aurea, Lisboa.
**ROMANIA/ROUMANIE:** CARTIMEX
Str. Aristide Briand 14-18,
P. O. Box 134-135, Bucureşti.
**SPAIN/ESPAGNE:**
LIBRERIA BOSCH
11 Ronda Universidad, Barcelona.
LIBRERIA MUNDI-PRENSA
Castelló 37, Madrid.
**SWEDEN/SUÈDE:** C. E. FRITZE'S
KUNGL. HOVBOKHANDEL A-B
Fredsgatan 2, Stockholm.
**SWITZERLAND/SUISSE:**
LIBRAIRIE PAYOT, S. A., Lausanne, Genève.
HANS RAUNHARDT, Kirchgasse 17, Zürich 1.
**TURKEY/TURQUIE:** LIBRAIRIE HACHETTE
469 Istiklal Caddesi, Beyoglu, Istanbul.
**UNION OF SOVIET SOCIALIST REPUBLICS/**
**UNION DES RÉPUBLIQUES SOCIALISTES**
**SOVIÉTIQUES:** MEZHDUNARODNAYA
KNYIGA, Smolenskaya Ploshchad, Moskva.
**UNITED KINGDOM/ROYAUME-UNI:**
H. M. STATIONERY OFFICE
P. O. Box 569, London, S.E. 1
(and HMSO branches in Belfast, Birmingham,
Bristol, Cardiff, Edinburgh, Manchester).
**YUGOSLAVIA/YOUGOSLAVIE:**
CANKARJEVA ZALOŽBA
Ljubljana, Slovenia.
DRŽAVNO PREDUZEĆE
Jugoslovenska Knjiga, Terazije 27/11, Beograd.
PROSVJETA
5, Trg Bratstva i Jedinstva, Zagreb.
PROSVETA PUBLISHING HOUSE
Import-Export Division, P. O. Box 559,
Terazije 16/1, Beograd.

## LATIN AMERICA/
## AMÉRIQUE LATINE

**ARGENTINA/ARGENTINE:** EDITORIAL
SUDAMERICANA, S. A., Alsina 500, Buenos Aires.
**BOLIVIA/BOLIVIE:** LIBRERIA SELECCIONES
Casilla 972, La Paz.

**BRAZIL/BRÉSIL:** LIVRARIA AGIR
Rua México 98-B, Caixa Postal 3291,
Rio de Janeiro.
**CHILE/CHILI:**
EDITORIAL DEL PACIFICO
Ahumada 57, Santiago.
LIBRERIA IVENS, Casilla 205, Santiago.
**COLOMBIA/COLOMBIE:** LIBRERIA BUCHHOLZ
Av. Jiménez de Quesada 8-40, Bogotá.
**COSTA RICA:** IMPRENTA Y LIBRERIA TREJOS
Apartado 1313, San José.
**CUBA:** LA CASA BELGA
O'Reilly 455, La Habana.
**DOMINICAN REPUBLIC/RÉPUBLIQUE**
**DOMINICAINE:** LIBRERIA DOMINICANA
Mercedes 49, Santo Domingo.
**ECUADOR/ÉQUATEUR:** LIBRERIA CIENTIFICA
Casilla 362, Guayaquil.
**EL SALVADOR/SALVADOR:** MANUEL NAVAS Y CIA.
1a. Avenida sur 37, San Salvador.
**GUATEMALA:**
SOCIEDAD ECONOMICA-FINANCIERA
6a. Av. 14-33, Ciudad de Guatemala.
**HAITI/HAÏTI:**
LIBRAIRIE "À LA CARAVELLE", Port-au-Prince.
**HONDURAS:**
LIBRERIA PANAMERICANA, Tegucigalpa.
**MEXICO/MEXIQUE:** EDITORIAL HERMES, S. A.
Ignacio Mariscal 41, México, D. F.
**PANAMA:** JOSE MENENDEZ
Agencia Internacional de Publicaciones,
Apartado 2052, Av. 8A, sur 21-58, Panamá.
**PARAGUAY:** AGENCIA DE LIBRERIAS
DE SALVADOR NIZZA
Calle Pte. Franco No. 39-43, Asunción.
**PERU/PÉROU:** LIBRERIA INTERNACIONAL
DEL PERU, S. A., Casilla 1417, Lima.
**URUGUAY:** REPRESENTACION DE EDITORIALES,
PROF. H. D'ELIA
Plaza Cagancha 1342, 1° piso, Montevideo.
**VENEZUELA:** LIBRERIA DEL ESTE
Av. Miranda, No. 52; Edf. Galipán, Caracas.

## MIDDLE EAST/MOYEN-ORIENT

**IRAQ/IRAK:**
MACKENZIE'S BOOKSHOP, Baghdad.
**ISRAEL/ISRAËL:** BLUMSTEIN'S BOOKSTORES
35 Allenby Rd. & 48 Nachlat Benjamin St.,
Tel Aviv.
**JORDAN/JORDANIE:** JOSEPH I. BAHOUS & CO.
Dar-ul-Kutub, Box 66, Amman.
**LEBANON/LIBAN:**
KHAYAT'S COLLEGE BOOK COOPERATIVE
92-94, rue Bliss, Beyrouth.

## NORTH AMERICA/
## AMÉRIQUE DU NORD

**CANADA:** THE QUEEN'S PRINTER
Ottawa, Ontario.
**UNITED STATES OF AMERICA/**
**ÉTATS-UNIS D'AMÉRIQUE:**
SALES SECTION, UNITED NATIONS, New York.

## OCEANIA/OCÉANIE

**AUSTRALIA/AUSTRALIE:**
WEA BOOKROOM, University, Adelaide, S.A.
UNIVERSITY BOOKSHOP, St. Lucia, Brisbane, Qld.
THE EDUCATIONAL AND TECHNICAL BOOK AGENCY
Parap Shopping Centre, Darwin, N.T.
COLLINS BOOK DEPOT PTY. LTD.
Monash University, Wellington Road, Clayton, Vic.
MELBOURNE CO-OPERATIVE BOOKSHOP LIMITED
10 Bowen Street, Melbourne C.1, Vic.
COLLINS BOOK DEPOT PTY. LTD.
363 Swanston Street, Melbourne, Vic.
THE UNIVERSITY BOOKSHOP, Nedlands, W.A.
UNIVERSITY BOOKROOM
University of Melbourne, Parkville N.2, Vic.
UNIVERSITY CO-OPERATIVE BOOKSHOP LIMITED
Manning Road, University of Sydney, N.S.W.
**NEW ZEALAND/NOUVELLE-ZÉLANDE:**
GOVERNMENT PRINTING OFFICE
Private Bag, Wellington
(and Government Bookshops in Auckland,
Christchurch and Dunedin).

[63B1]